Computer and Information Security Handbook

Computer and Information Security Handbook

Third Edition

Edited by

John R. Vacca

MORGAN KAUFMANN PUBLISHERS

AN IMPRINT OF ELSEVIER

Morgan Kaufmann is an imprint of Elsevier
50 Hampshire Street, 5th Floor, Cambridge, MA 02139, United States

Notices
Knowledge and best practice in this field are constantly changing. As new research and experience broaden our understanding, changes in research methods, professional practices, or medical treatment may become necessary.

Practitioners and researchers must always rely on their own experience and knowledge in evaluating and using any information, methods, compounds, or experiments described herein. In using such information or methods they should be mindful of their own safety and the safety of others, including parties for whom they have a professional responsibility.

To the fullest extent of the law, neither the Publisher nor the authors, contributors, or editors, assume any liability for any injury and/or damage to persons or property as a matter of products liability, negligence or otherwise, or from any use or operation of any methods, products, instructions, or ideas contained in the material herein.

Library of Congress Cataloging-in-Publication Data
A catalog record for this book is available from the Library of Congress

British Library Cataloguing-in-Publication Data
A catalogue record for this book is available from the British Library

ISBN: 978-0-12-803843-7

For information on all Morgan Kaufmann publications
visit our website at https://www.elsevier.com/books-and-journals

Working together
to grow libraries in
developing countries

www.elsevier.com • www.bookaid.org

Publisher: Todd Green
Acquisition Editor: Brian Romer
Editorial Project Manager: Charlie Kent
Production Project Manager: Priya Kumaraguruparan
Designer: Maria Inês Cruz

Typeset by TNQ Books and Journals

This book is dedicated to my wife, Bee.

Contents

Part VIII
Storage Security 875

Online Chapters and Appendices

Contributors

Edward G. Amoroso (Chapters 64, 67, 68), Senior Vice President, Chief Security Officer, TAG Cyber LLC

Jeffrey S. Bardin (Chapters 61, 89), Chief Intelligence Strategist, Treadstone 71 LLC, 515 Oakham Road, Barre, MA 01005

Cataldo Basile (Chapters 26, 55), Professor, Universita degli studi di Bergamo, Via Salvecchio 19, 24129 Bergamo Italy

Stefan Berthold (Chapter 53), Tek. Lic., Karlstad University, Universitetsgatan 2 S-65469, Karlstad/Sweden

Gerald Beuchelt (Chapters 10, 11), Principal Software Systems Engineer, Demandware, Inc., Burlington, MA

Rahul Bhaskar (Chapters 27, 82), Professor, Department of Information Systems and Decision Sciences, California State University, LH 564, Fullerton, California 92834

Chiara Braghin (Chapter 52), Professor, Dept. of Information Technology, University of Milan, via Bramante 65 − 26013, Crema, Italy

Albert Caballero (Chapters 24, 33), Chief Technology Officer - CTO, Digital Era Group, LLC, 9357 Abbot Ave., Surfside, Fl. 33154

Matteo Maria Casalino (Chapter 55), Professor, Universita degli studi di Bergamo, Via Salvecchio 19, 24129 Bergamo Italy

Erdal Cayirci (Chapters 17, 21), Professor, University of Stavanger, N-4036 Stavanger, Norway

Thomas M. Chen (Chapters 8, 18, 60), Professor, Swansea University, Singleton Park, SA2 8PP, Wales, United Kingdom

Hongbing Cheng (Chapters 17, 21), Professor, University of Stavanger, N-4036, Stavanger, Norway

Lauren Collins (Chapters 22, 36, 76, 77, 79, 81), Founder and Chief Strategy Officer, Managing Director, Winning Edge Communications, 8151 West Eagle Lake Road, Peotone, IL 60468

Marco Cremonini (Chapter 52), Professor, Dept. of Information Technology, University of Milan, via Bramante 65 − 26013, Crema, Italy

Samuel J.J. Curry (Chapter 51), Chief Technology and Security Officer, Arbor Networks, 76 Blanchard Road, Burlington MA 01803

Rozita Dara (Chapter 6), Professor, University of Guelph, School of Computer Science Guelph, ON, Canada

Christopher Day, CISSP, NSA:IEM (Chapter 72), Senior Vice President, Secure Information Systems, Terremark Worldwide, Inc., One Biscayne Tower 2 South Biscayne Blvd, Suite 2900, Miami, Florida 33131

Sabrina De Capitani di Vimercati (Chapter 57), Professor, Università degli Studi di Milano, DTI - Dipartimento di Tecnologie dell'Informazione, S207, Università degli Studi di Milano, Via Bramante 65, 26013 Crema − Italy

Tewfiq El Maliki (Chapter 71), Professor, University of Geneva, Switzerland, 2850 route nationale, 74120 Megève, France; Telecommunications labs, University of Applied Sciences of Geneva, Geneva, Switzerland

Scott R. Ellis (Chapters 3, 5, 23, 29, 30, 36, 40, 42, 75, 80), Manager, Infrastructure Engineering Team, kCura, 175 West Jackson Blvd., Suite 1000, Chicago, IL 60604

Michael Erbschloe (Foreword), Teaches Information Security courses at Webster University, St. Louis, Missouri 63119

Simone Fischer-Hbner (Chapter 53), Professor, Karlstad University, Department of Computer Science, Room no: 5A 435, Universitetsgatan 1, S 651 88, Karlstad/Sweden

Sara Foresti (Chapter 56), Professor, Università degli Studi di Milano, Information Technology Department, Università degli Studi di Milano, via Bramante, 6526013 Crema (CR) Italy

Errin W. Fulp (Chapter 74), Professor, Department of Computer Science, 239, Manchester Hall, P.O. Box 7311, Wake Forest University, Winston-Salem, North Carolina 27109

Angelo Genovese (Chapter 57), Professor, Università degli Studi di Milano, DTI - Dipartimento di Tecnologie dell'Informazione, S207, Università degli Studi di Milano, Via Bramante 65, 26013 Crema − Italy

Anna Granova (Chapter 83), Advocate of the High Court of South Africa, University of Pretoria, Computer Science Department, Information Technology Building, 49 Algernon Road, Norwood, Johannesburg, 2192, Republic of South Africa

William F. Gross (Chapters 35, 37), Private Investigator, Gross Security, LLC, 146 Main Street, Spencer, WV 25276

Yong Guan (Chapter 43), Litton Assistant Professor, Department of Electrical and Computer Engineering, Iowa State University, 3216 Coover Hall, Ames, Iowa 50011

Cem Gurkok (Chapters 41, 63), Threat Intelligence Development Manager, Terremark Worldwide, Inc., One Biscayne Tower, 2S. Biscayne Blvd., Suite 2800, Miami, Florida 33131

Feng Hao (Chapter 49), Professor, Newcastle University, School of Computing Science, Newcastle University, Newcastle Upon Tyne NE1 7RU

Tarfa Hamed (Chapter 6), Professor, University of Guelph, School of Computer Science Guelph, ON, Canada

James T. Harmening (Chapters 25, 58), President, Computer Bits, Inc., 123 W. Madison St. Suite 1005, Chicago, Illinois 60602

Rich Hoffman (Chapter 44), Assistant Vice President of Forensics and the Lead Examiner, UnitedLex, 6130 Sprint 5 Parkway, Suite 300, Overland Park, Kansas 66211

Emin Huseynov (Chapter 50), Professor, University of Geneva, Switzerland, CUI, Bureau, Battelle batiment A 7 route de Drize, c11-1227, 74120 Carouge, Switzerland

Markus Jakobsson (Chapter 59), Associate Professor of Informatics at IUB and Associate Director of CACR, Indiana University, 5631 E Kerr Creek Rd., Bloomington, IN 47408

Ravi Jhawar (Chapter 9), Professor, Universita' degli Studi di Milano, Department of Information Technology, Universita' degli Studi di Milano, via Bramante 65, 26013 Crema (CR) ITALY

Almantas Kakareka CISSP, GSNA, GSEC, CEH (Chapter 31), CTO, Demyo, Inc., 351 189th street, Sunny Isles Beach, FL 33160

Bhushan Kapoor (Chapters 27, 46, 82), Chair, Department of Information Systems and Decision Sciences, California State University, LH 564, Fullerton, California 92834

Sokratis K. Katsikas (Chapter 34), Department of Technology Education & Digital Systems, University of Piraeus, Piraeus 18532, Greece

Dalia Khader (Chapter 49), Collaborateur scientifique, University of Luxemburg, Campus Kirchberg, F 006, 6, rue Richard Coudenhove-Kalergi, L-1359 Luxembourg

John Benjamin Khan (Chapter 45), Former UNIX Operator, University of Massachusetts, Infragard Member 6 Stella Rd, Boston, MA 02131

Larry Korba (Chapter 54), Ottawa, Ontario, Canada K1G 5N7

Kameswari Kotapati (Chapter 20), Department of Computer Science and Engineering, The Pennsylvania State University, University Park, Pennsylvania 16802

Stefan C. Kremer (Chapter 6), Professor, University of Guelph, School of Computer Science, Guelph, ON, Canada

Thomas F. LaPorta (Chapter 20), Professor, Department of Computer Science and Engineering, The Pennsylvania State University, University Park, Pennsylvania 16802

Jean Lencrenon (Chapter 49), Professor, Interdisciplinary Centre for Security, Reliability and Trust, 6 rue Richard Coudenhove-Kalergi, L-1359 Luxembourg-Kirchberg, Luxembourg

Keith Lewis (Chapters 4, 38, 39, 65, 66, 78), IT Security Infrastructure Specialist, Keller Graduate School of Management, Naperville, Illinois

Peng Liu (Chapter 20), Director, Cyber Security Lab, College of Information Sciences and Technology, Pennsylvania State University, University Park, Pennsylvania 16802

Giovanni Livraga (Chapter 57), Professor, Università degli Studi di Milano, DTI - Dipartimento di Tecnologie dell'Informazione, S207, Università degli Studi di Milano, Via Bramante 65, 26013 Crema − Italy

John R. Mallery (Chapter 2), President, Mallery Technical Training and Consulting, Inc., 9393 West 110th St., Suite 500, Overland Park, Kansas, 66210

Bill Mansoor (Chapter 15), Information Security Analyst III, Information Security Office County of Riverside, 24711 Via Alvorado Mission Viejo, California 92692

Luther Martin (Chapter 70), Chief Security Architect, Voltage Security, 20400 Stevens Creek, Blvd STE 500 Cupertino, CA 95014

John McDonald (Chapter 61), EMC Corporation, Hopkinton, Massachusetts 01748

John McGowan (Chapter 61), EMC Corporation, Hopkinton, Massachusetts 01748

Nailah Mims (Chapters 14, 84), Information Systems Security Analyst, Bright Horizons, 2 Seven Springs Lane H, Burlington, MA 01803

Simone Mutti (Chapter 55), Professor, Universita degli studi di Bergamo, Via Salvecchio 19, 24129 Bergamo Italy

Peter F. Nicoletti (Chapter 87), Consultant, 110 Gumbo Limbo Lane Po Box 448Miami, Florida, Tavernier, FL 33070

Kevin Noble, CISSP GSEC (Chapter 85), Director, Secure Information Services, Terremark Worldwide Inc., 50 N.E. 9 Street, Miami, Florida 33132

Pramod Pandya (Chapters 16, 28, 46, 73, 91), Professor, Department of Information Systems and Decision Sciences, California State University, Fullerton, California 92834

Harsh Kupwade Patil (Chapters 18, 60), Professor, Southern Methodist University, Department of Computer Science and Engineering, Lyle School of Engineering, Caruth Hall 3145 Dyer Street, Suite 445 Dallas, Texas

Stefano Paraboschi (Chapters 26, 55), Professor, Universita degli studi di Bergamo, Via Salvecchio 19, 24129 Bergamo Italy

Thea Peacock (Chapter 90), Professor, University of Luxemburg, Faculte des Sciences, De la Technologie et de la Communication 6, Rue Richard Coudenhove-Kalergi L-1359 Luxembourg

Ken Perkins (Chapter 88), CIPP (Certified Information Privacy Professional), Sr. Systems Engineer, Blazent Incorporated, 3650 E. 1st Ave., Denver, Colorado 80206

Vincenzo Piuri (Chapters 9, 57), Professor, Universita' degli Studi di Milano, Department of Information Technology, Universita' degli Studi di Milano, via Bramante 65 26013 Crema (CR), ITALY

Henrik Plate (Chapter 26), Senior Researcher, CISSP, SAP Research Security & Trust, 805, avenue du docteur Maurice Donat 06250 Mougins, France

James Pooley (Chapter 1), Attorney, Orrick, Herrington & Sutcliffe LLP, 1000 Marsh Road, Menlo Park, CA 94025-1015

Chunming Rong (Chapters 17, 21), Professor, Ph.D., Chair of Computer Science Section, Faculty of Science and Technology, University of Stavanger, N-4036 Stavanger, Norway

Robert Rounsavall (Chapter 62), Co-founder, Trapezoid, Inc., 4931 SW 75th Ave., Miami, Florida 33155

Peter Y.A. Ryan (Chapters 49, 90), Professor of Information Security and Head of Applied Security and Information Assurance (APSIA) Group, GCWN, University of Luxemburg, Campus Kirchberg 6, rue Richard, Coudenhove-Kalergi, L-1359 Luxembourg

Pierangela Samarati (Chapter 56), Professor, Università degli Studi di Milano, Information Technology Department, Università degli Studi di Milano, via Bramante, 6526013 Crema (CR), Italy

Marco Santambrogio (Chapter 7), Professor, Politecnico di Milano, Milano, ITALY

Mario Santana (Chapter 12), Consultant, Terremark Worldwide, Inc., One Biscayne Tower, 2S., Biscayne Blvd., Suite 2800, Miami, Florida 33131

Steve Schneider (Chapter 90), Professor, University of Surrey, Department of Computing, Guildford, Surrey, GU2 7XH

Fabio Scotti (Chapter 57), Professor, Universita' degli Studi di Milano, Department of Information Technology, Universita' degli Studi di Milano, via Bramante 65, 26013 Crema (CR), ITALY

Jean-Marc Seigneur (Chapters 50, 71, 86), Professor, Advanced Systems Group, University of Geneva, Switzerland, Centre Universitaire d'Informatique, Office 234, Battelle batiment A 7 route de Drize, c11-1227, 74120 Carouge, Switzerland

Marco Slaviero (Chapter 83), Security Analyst, SensePost Pty Ltd, Lakeview 2, 138 Middel street, Nieuw Muckleneuk, Pretoria, South Africa

Daniel S. Soper (Chapter 47), Professor, Information and Decision Sciences Department, Mihaylo College of Business and Economics, California State University, Fullerton, California 92834-6848

Terence Spies (Chapter 48), Chief Technology Officer/Vice President of Engineering, Hewlett Packard Enterprise, 20400 Stevens Creek Blvd, Suite 500, Cupertino, CA 95014

William Stallings (Chapters 19, 69), Consultant and Writer, No affiliation, 845 Satucket Road P. O. Box 2405, Brewster, MA 02631

Alex Tsow (Chapter 59), Professor, Indiana University, 7514 Ambergate Pl., Mclean, Virginia 22102

Jesse Walker (Chapter 13), Principal Engineer, Intel Corporation, JF2-55 2111 N.E. 25th Avenue, Hillsboro, OR 97124

Michael A. West (Chapter 7), Senior Technical Writer, Truestone Maritime Operations Martinez, California 94553

Dan Wing (Chapter 60), Distinguished Engineer, Cisco Systems, Inc., 222 Coffeeberry Drive, San Jose, CA 95123

George O.M. Yee (Chapters 32, 54), Adjunct Research Professor, Carleton University, 17 Sai Crescent, Ottawa, ON, Canada K1G 5N7

Liang Yan (Chapters 17, 21), Professor, University of Stavanger, N-4036, Stavanger, Norway

Roman Zabicki (Chapter 75), Manager, Infrastructure Engineering Team, kCura, 175 West Jackson Blvd., Suite 1000, Chicago, IL 60604

Gansen Zhao (Chapters 17, 21), Professor, South China Normal University, Guangzhou 510631, P.R. China

Zhe Zias (Chapter 90), Professor, University of Surrey, Department of Computing Guildford, Surrey, GU2 7XH

About the Editor

John R. Vacca is an information technology consultant, researcher, professional writer, editor, reviewer, and internationally known, best-selling author based in Pomeroy, Ohio. Since 1982, John has authored or edited 79 books; some of his most recent books include:

- *Cloud Computing Security: Foundations and Challenges* (CRC Press, an imprint of Taylor & Francis Group, LLC, September 14, 2016).
- *Security in the Private Cloud* (CRC Press, an imprint of Taylor & Francis Group, LLC, August 26, 2016).
- *Handbook of Sensor Networking: Advanced Technologies and Applications* (CRC Press, an imprint of Taylor & Francis Group, LLC, January 14, 2015).
- *Network and System Security, Second Edition, 2E* (Syngress, an imprint of Elsevier Inc., September 23, 2013).
- *Cyber Security and IT Infrastructure Protection* (Syngress, an imprint of Elsevier Inc., September 23, 2013).
- *Managing Information Security, Second Edition, 2E* (Syngress, an imprint of Elsevier Inc., September 23, 2013).
- *Computer and Information Security Handbook, 2E* (Morgan Kaufmann, an imprint of Elsevier Inc., May 31, 2013).
- *Identity Theft (Cybersafety)* (Chelsea House Pub, April 1, 2012).
- *System Forensics, Investigation, and Response* (Jones & Bartlett Learning, September 24, 2010).
- *Managing Information Security* (Syngress, an imprint of Elsevier Inc., March 29, 2010).
- *Network and Systems Security* (Syngress, an imprint of Elsevier Inc., March 29, 2010).
- *Computer and Information Security Handbook, 1E* (Morgan Kaufmann, an imprint of Elsevier Inc., June 2, 2009).
- *Biometric Technologies and Verification Systems* (Elsevier Science & Technology Books, March 16, 2007).

- *Practical Internet Security* (Hardcover) (Springer, October 18, 2006).
- *Optical Networking Best Practices Handbook* (Hardcover) (Wiley-Interscience, November 28, 2006).
- *Guide to Wireless Network Security* (Springer, August 19, 2006).

He is also the author of more than 600 articles in the areas of advanced storage, computer security, and aerospace technology (copies of articles and books are available upon request).

John was also a configuration management specialist, computer specialist, and the computer security official (CSO) for NASA's space station program (Freedom) and the International Space Station Program, from 1988 until his retirement from NASA in 1995.

John is also an independent online book reviewer and one of the security consultants for the MGM movie *AntiTrust*, which was released on January 12, 2001. A detailed copy of his author bio can be viewed at http://www.johnvacca.com. John can be reached at john2164@windstream.net.

Foreword

We have all been there as an IT staffer. Suddenly, you have a new project which is not in your immediate area of expertise. You need to get moving and get moving quickly; and, of course, security issues must be addressed from inception through implementation. The third edition of the *Computer and Information Security Handbook* is a tool that will help you to hit the ground running.

With more than 30 new chapters, the newest edition of the *Computer and Information Security Handbook* covers security issues from A to Z. You will not need to mine the Internet and sort through a barrage of new material to determine what is valid, valuable, and usable. The vetting work has been done for you in this new edition of the handbook.

We all know that the new protocol is to effectively build security in from the start, so that you do not have to ineffectively add it on later. Many of the best minds in information technology and security have contributed their time, effort, and knowledge to this new edition so that you, as an IT professional, can save valuable time getting up to speed on a myriad of security topics.

The third edition of the *Computer and Information Security Handbook* provides you with a professional competitive advantage, thus enabling you to stay on top of current topics and to outperform your peers and your competitors. I highly recommend this new edition of the handbook.

Michael Erbschloe
Information Security Consultant
*Michael Erbschloe teaches information security
courses at Webster University in St. Louis, Missouri.*

Preface

This comprehensive third-edition handbook serves as a professional reference and as a practitioner's guide to today's most complete and concise view of computer and cyber-security and privacy available in two volumes. It offers in-depth coverage of computer and cyber-security theory, technology, and practice as they relate to established technologies as well as recent advancements. It explores practical solutions to a wide range of security issues. Individual chapters are authored by leading experts in the field and address the immediate and long-term challenges in the authors' respective areas of expertise.

The primary audience for this handbook consists of researchers and practitioners in industry and academia as well as security technologists, engineers, federal and state governments, and law enforcement, working with or interested in computer and cyber-security. This comprehensive reference and practitioner's guide will also be of value to students in upper-division undergraduate and graduate-level courses in computer and cyber-security.

1. ORGANIZATION OF THIS BOOK

The book is organized into 15 parts composed of 91 contributed chapters by leading experts in their fields, as well as 12 appendices, including an extensive glossary of cyber-security terms and acronyms.

Part 1: Overview of System and Network Security: A Comprehensive Introduction

Part 1 discusses how to build a secure organization; information security in the modern enterprise; how to generate cryptography; how to verify user and host identity; how to detect system intrusions; how to detect intrusions in contemporary environments, how to prevent system intrusions; how to guard against network intrusions, fault tolerance, and resilience in cloud computing environments; how to secure web applications, services, and servers; UNIX and Linux security; how to eliminate the security weakness of Linux and UNIX Operating systems; Internet and intranet security; the botnet problem; local area network (LAN) security; wireless network security;

wireless sensor network security of the Internet of Things (IoT); security for IoT; cellular network security, radio-frequency identification (RFID) security; optical network security; and, optical wireless security.

Chapter 1, "Information Security in the Modern Enterprise," provides a set of procedures and controls for conducting assessments of information security in the modern enterprise.

Chapter 2, "Building a Secure Organization," sets the stage for the rest of the book by presenting insight into where to start building a secure organization.

Chapter 3, "A Cryptography Primer," provides an overview of cryptography. It shows how communications may be encrypted and transmitted.

Chapter 4, "Verifying User and Host Identity," goes over general identity management concepts and how computer technology is used to validate a person's authenticity of gaining access to authorized systems.

Chapter 5, "Detecting System Intrusions," describes the characteristics of the intrusion detection system (IDS) technologies and provides recommendations for designing, implementing, configuring, securing, monitoring, and maintaining them.

Chapter 6, "Intrusion Detection in Contemporary Environments," discusses intrusion detection applications for two contemporary environments: mobile devices and cloud computing.

Chapter 7, "Preventing System Intrusions," discusses how to prevent system intrusions and where an unauthorized penetration of a computer in your enterprise or an address in your assigned domain can occur.

Chapter 8, "Guarding Against Network Intrusions," shows how to guard against network intrusions by understanding the variety of attacks, from exploits to malware and social engineering.

Chapter 9, "Fault Tolerance and Resilience in Cloud Computing Environments," focuses on characterizing the recurrent failures in a typical Cloud computing environment, analyzing the effects of failures on user's applications, and surveying fault tolerance solutions corresponding to each class of failures.

Chapter 10, "Securing Web Applications, Services, and Servers," provides a general overview of the breadth of web service security, an introduction to the subject area, and guides the reader to sources with deeper information.

Chapter 11, "UNIX and Linux Security," discusses how to scan for vulnerabilities; reduce denial-of-service (DoS) attacks; deploy firewalls to control network traffic; and build network firewalls.

Chapter 12, "Eliminating the Security Weakness of Linux and UNIX Operating Systems," presents an introduction to securing UNIX in general and Linux in particular, providing some historical context and describing some fundamental aspects of the secure operating system architecture.

Chapter 13, "Internet Security," shows you how cryptography can be used to address some of the security issues besetting communications protocols.

Chapter 14, "The Botnet Problem," describes the botnet threat and the countermeasures available to network security professionals.

Chapter 15, "Intranet Security," covers internal security strategies and tactics; external security strategies and tactics; network access security; and Kerberos.

Chapter 16, "Local Area Network Security," discusses network design and security deployment as well as ongoing management and auditing.

Chapter 17, "Wireless Network Security," presents an overview of wireless network security technology; how to design wireless network security and plan for wireless network security; how to install, deploy, and maintain wireless network security; information warfare countermeasures: the wireless network security solution; and wireless network security solutions and future directions.

Chapter 18, "Wireless Sensor Network Security: The Internet of Things," helps organizations design, implement, and evaluate wireless sensor intrusion detection systems, which aim at transferring the computational load of the operation from the sensors to the base station.

Chapter 19, "Security for the Internet of Things," is an overview of the IoT architecture developed by ITU-T, and defined in Y.2060.

Chapter 20, "Cellular Network Security," addresses the security of the cellular network; educates readers on the current state of security of the network and its vulnerabilities; outlines the cellular network specific attack taxonomy, also called three-dimensional attack taxonomy; discusses the vulnerability assessment tools for cellular networks; and provides insights into why the network is so vulnerable and why securing it can prevent communication outages during emergencies.

Chapter 21, "Radio Frequency Identification Security," describes the RFID tags and RFID reader and back-end database in detail.

Chapter 22, "Optical Network Security," presents an analysis of attack and protection problems in optical networks. It also proposes a conceptual framework for modeling attack problems and protection schemes for optical networks.

Chapter 23, "Optical Wireless Security," focuses on free space optics (FSO) and the security that has been developed to protect its transmissions, as well as an overview of the basic technology.

Part 2: Managing Information Security

Part 2 discusses how to protect mission-critical systems; deploying security management systems; policy-driven system management; IT security management; how intruders gain unlawful access to networks; social engineering deceptions and defenses; ethical hacking; how to conduct vulnerability assessments and security metrics; security education, training, and awareness; risk management; and insider threats.

Chapter 24, "Information Security Essentials for Information Technology Managers: Protecting Mission-Critical Systems," discusses how security goes beyond technical controls and encompasses people, technology, policy, and operations in a way that few other business objectives do.

Chapter 25, "Security Management Systems," examines documentation requirements and maintaining an effective security system as well as conducting assessments.

Chapter 26, "Policy-Driven System Management," focuses particularly on PBM's use for securing computing systems according to high-level security goals.

Chapter 27, "Information Technology Security Management," discusses the processes that are supported with enabling organizational structure and technology to protect an organization's information technology operations and IT assets against internal and external threats, intentional or otherwise.

Chapter 28, "The Enemy (The Intruder's Genesis)," discusses process of creating a formal set of governance to define cyber-security, and course of actions to be taken to defend against the cyber-attacks.

Chapter 29, "Social Engineering Deceptions and Defenses," illustrates a cross-section of socially engineered attacks.

Chapter 30, "Ethical Hacking," provides the foundation needed to become skilled at ethical hacking.

Chapter 31, "What Is Vulnerability Assessment?" covers the fundamentals: defining vulnerability, exploit, threat, and risk; analyzing vulnerabilities and exploits; and configuring scanners. It also shows you how to generate reports, assess risks in a changing environment, and manage vulnerabilities.

Chapter 32, "Security Metrics: An Introduction and Literature Review" describes the need for security metrics, followed by a discussion of the nature of security metrics, including what makes a good security metric, what security metrics have been used in the past, and how security metrics can be scientifically based.

Chapter 33, "Security Education, Training, and Awareness" is designed to facilitate the implementation of SETA program requirements and standards, within the full range of security disciplines that comprise physical- and cyber-security.

Chapter 34, "Risk Management," discusses physical security threats, environmental threats, and incident response.

Chapter 35, "Insider Threats," discusses how the insider threat is real; and, the damage done by insiders is increasing exponentially with more dependence on data and tele-communication systems.

Part 3: Disaster Recovery Security

Part 3 discusses disaster recovery and disaster recovery plans for small and medium business (SMB).

Chapter 36, "Disaster Recovery," provides insight to the job of Disaster Recovery (DR), and provides a framework of what is necessary to achieve a successful DR plan.

Chapter 37, "Disaster Recovery Plans for Small and Medium Business (SMBs)," looks at disaster recovery planning, business continuity, and business impact analysis in the scope of available resources to the average SMB.

Part 4: Security Standards and Policies

Part 4 discusses security certification and standards implementation and security policies and plans development.

Chapter 38, "Security Certification and Standards Implementation," covers the foundation frameworks for the latest Security Certification and Standards best practices for both commercial industry and government agencies.

Chapter 39, "Security Policies and Plans Development," covers the importance and structure of Security Policies.

Part 5: Cyber, Network, and Systems Forensics Security and Assurance

Part 5 discusses cyber forensics; cyber forensics and inci-dence response; how to secure e-discovery; network fo-rensics; Microsoft Office and metadata forensics; and hard drive imaging.

Chapter 40, "Cyber Forensics," is intended to provide an in-depth familiarization with computer forensics as a career, a job, and a science. It will help you avoid mistakes and find your way through the many aspects of this diverse and rewarding field.

Chapter 41, "Cyber Forensics and Incidence Response," discusses the steps and methods to respond to incidents and conduct cyber forensics investigations.

Chapter 42, "Securing e-Discovery," explains electronic discovery reference model (EDRM) from an industry insider perspective; collates issues of performance, urgency, accuracy, risk, and security to a zoned model that underpins the EDRM; explains the very real need for organizations to secure certain operations internally; provides examples through real-world experiences of flawed discovery, and what should have been done differently; and discusses how security from the information as well as security of it plays a critical role throughout much of the EDRM.

Chapter 43, "Network Forensics," helps you determine the path from a victimized network or system through any intermediate systems and communication pathways, back to the point of attack origination or the person who should be held accountable.

Chapter 44, "Microsoft Office and Metadata Forensics: A Deeper Dive," focuses on defining some of the specific issues encountered when analyzing Microsoft Office met-adata, the most common file types forensic investigators encounter.

Chapter 45, "Hard Drive Imaging," aims to jumpstart individuals interested in computer forensics and/or data recovery.

Part 6: Encryption Technology

Part 6 discusses how to implement data encryption, satellite encryption, public key infrastructure, password-based authenticated key establishment protocols, context-aware multifactor authentication and instant-messaging security.

Chapter 46, "Data Encryption," is about the role played by cryptographic technology in data security.

Chapter 47, "Satellite Encryption," proposes a method that enhances and complements satellite encryption's role in securing the information society. It also covers satellite encryption policy instruments; implementing satellite encryption; misuse of satellite encryption technology; and results and future directions.

Chapter 48, "Public Key Infrastructure," explains the cryptographic background that forms the foundation of Public Key Infrastructure (PKI) systems; the mechanics of the X.509 PKI system (as elaborated by the Internet Engineering Task Force); the practical issues surrounding the implementation of PKI systems; a number of alternative PKI standards; and alternative cryptographic strategies for solving the problem of secure public key distribution.

Chapter 49: "Password-Based Authenticated Key Estab-lishment Protocols," emphasizes that one of the main goals of cryptography is to provide secure communication channels between different parties and provides a short overview on a specific variant of authenticated key exchange protocols in which authentication between parties is established through knowledge of a simple, human-memorable password.

Chapter 50, "Context-Aware Multifactor Authentication Survey," reviews a wide variety of modern and classic multifactor authentication systems and methods.

Chapter 51, "Instant-Messaging Security," helps you develop an IM security plan, keep it current, and make sure it makes a difference.

Part 7: Privacy and Access Management

Part 7 discusses online privacy, privacy-enhancing technologies, personal privacy policies, detection of conflicts in security policies, detection of conflicts in security policies, supporting user privacy preferences in digital interactions, privacy and security in environmental monitoring systems: issues and solutions, virtual private networks, identity theft, and voice-over Internet protocol (VoIP) security.

Chapter 52, "Online Privacy," addresses the privacy issues in the digital society from various points of view, investigating the different aspects related to the notion of privacy and the debate that the intricate essence of privacy has stimulated; the most common privacy threats and the possible economic aspects that may influence the way privacy is (and especially is not currently) managed in most firms; the efforts in the computer science community to face privacy threats, especially in the context of mobile and database systems; and the network-based technologies available to date to provide anonymity when communicating over a private network.

Chapter 53, "Privacy-Enhancing Technologies," provides an overview to the area of Privacy-enhancing technologies (PETs), which help to protect privacy by technically enforcing legal privacy principles.

Chapter 54, "Personal Privacy Policies," begins with the derivation of policy content based on privacy legislation, followed by a description of how a personal privacy policy may be constructed semiautomatically. It then shows how to additionally specify policies so that negative unexpected outcomes can be avoided. Finally, it describes the author's Privacy Management Model, which explains how to use personal privacy policies to protect privacy, including what is meant by a "match" of consumer and service provider policies and how nonmatches can be resolved through negotiation.

Chapter 55, "Detection of Conflicts in Security Policies," identifies the common approaches to the identification of security conflicts considering three relevant scenarios: access control policies, policy execution, and network protection. The chapter focuses on the detection of the conflicts.

Chapter 56, "Supporting User Privacy Preferences in Digital Interactions," describes solutions supporting both client privacy preferences and server disclosure policies.

Chapter 57, "Privacy and Security in Environmental Monitoring Systems: Issues and Solutions," identifies the main security and privacy issues characterizing the environmental data as well as the environmental monitoring infrastructures.

Chapter 58, "Virtual Private Networks," covers VPN scenarios, VPN comparisons, and information assurance requirements. It also covers building VPN tunnels; applying cryptographic protection; implementing IP security; and deploying virtual private networks.

Chapter 59, "Identity Theft," describes the importance of understanding the human factor of ID theft security and details the findings from a study on deceit.

Chapter 60, "VoIP Security," deals with the attacks targeted toward a specific host and issues related to social engineering.

Part 8: Storage Security

Part eight covers storage area network (SAN) security and storage area networking devices security.

Chapter 61, "SAN Security," describes the following components: protection rings; security and protection; restricting access to storage; access control lists (ACLs) and policies; port blocks and port prohibits; and zoning and isolating resources.

Chapter 62, "Storage Area Networking Security Devices," covers all the issues and security concerns related to SAN security.

Part 9: Cloud Security

Part 9 discusses securing cloud computing systems, cloud security and private cloud security.

Chapter 63, "Securing Cloud Computing Systems," aims to discuss various cloud computing environments and methods to make them more secure for hosting companies and their customers.

Chapter 64, "Cloud Security," outlines trends in cloud security.

Chapter 65, "Private Cloud Security," covers the importance of private cloud security.

Chapter 66, "Virtual Private Cloud Security," covers the overall concepts of virtual private cloud security.

Part 10: Virtual Security

Part 10 discusses protecting the virtual infrastructure and software defined networking (SDN) and network function virtualization (NFV) security.

Chapter 67, "Protecting Virtual Infrastructure," outlines trends in security virtualization.

Chapter 68, "Software-Defined Networking and Network Function Virtualization Security," outlines software defined networking (SDN) and network function virtualization (NFV) technologies and gives attention to cascading threats as well as controller protections.

Part 11: Cyber Physical Security

Part 11 discusses physical security essentials and biometrics.

Chapter 69, "Physical Security Essentials," is concerned with physical security and some overlapping areas of premises security. It also looks at physical security threats and then considers physical security prevention measures.

Chapter 70, "Biometrics," discusses the different types of biometrics technology and verification systems and how the following work: biometrics eye analysis technology; biometrics facial recognition technology; facial thermal imaging; biometrics finger-scanning analysis technology; biometrics geometry analysis technology; biometrics verification technology; and privacy-enhanced, biometrics-based verification/authentication as well as biometrics solutions and future directions.

Part 12: Practical Security

Part 12 discusses online identity and user management services, Intrusion Prevention and Detection Systems, TCP/IP Packet Analysis, firewalls, penetration testing, system security, access controls, endpoint security, assessments and audits, and fundamentals of cryptography.

Chapter 71, "Online Identity and User Management Services," presents the evolution of identity management requirements. It also surveys how the most advanced identity management technologies fulfill present-day requirements. It discusses how mobility can be achieved in the field of identity management in an ambient intelligent/ubiquitous computing world.

Chapter 72, "Intrusion Prevention and Detection Systems," discusses the nature of computer system intrusions, the people who commit these attacks, and the various technologies that can be utilized to detect and prevent them.

Chapter 73, "Transmission Control Protocol/Internet Protocol Packet Analysis," discusses how TCP/IP packets are constructed and analyzed to interpret the applications that use the TCP/IP stack.

Chapter 74, "Firewalls," provides an overview of firewalls: policies, designs, features, and configurations. Of course, technology is always changing, and network firewalls are no exception. However, the intent of this chapter is to describe aspects of network firewalls that tend to endure over time.

Chapter 75, "Penetration Testing," describes how testing differs from an actual "hacker attack" as well as some of the

ways penetration tests are conducted, how they're controlled, and what organizations might look for when choosing a company to conduct a penetration test for them.

Chapter 76, "System Security," shows you how to protect your information from harm, and also ways to make your data readily available for access to an intended audience of users.

Chapter 77, "Access Controls," endeavors to inform the reader about the different types of access controls that are being used, and describes the pros and cons they might have.

Chapter 78, "Endpoint Security," covers the importance of endpoint security designing and the architectural functions and philosophy behind it.

Chapter 79, "Assessments and Audits," presents the basic technical aspects of conducting information security assessments and audits. It presents technical testing and examination methods and techniques that an organization might use as part of an assessment and audit, and offers insights to assessors on their execution and the potential impact they may have on systems and networks.

Chapter 80, "Fundamentals of Cryptography," discusses how information security is the discipline that provides protection of information from intrusion and accidental or incidental loss. It also provides a framework for the protection of information from unauthorized use, copying, distribution, or destruction of data.

Part 13: Critical Infrastructure Security

Part 13 discusses securing the infrastructure, homeland security, cyber warfare, and cyber-attack process.

Chapter 81, "Securing the Infrastructure," focuses on how security is presented to protect the infrastructure. Smart grid cyber-security in this chapter also addresses not only deliberate attacks, such as from disgruntled employees, industrial espionage, and terrorists, but also inadvertent compromises of the information infrastructure due to user errors, equipment failures, and natural disasters.

Chapter 82, "Homeland Security," describes some principle provisions of US homeland security-related laws and Presidential directives. It gives the organizational changes that were initiated to support homeland security in the United States. The chapter highlights the 9/11 Commission that Congress charted to provide a full account of the circumstances surrounding the 2001 terrorist attacks and to develop recommendations for corrective measures that could be taken to prevent future acts of terrorism. It also details the Intelligence Reform and Terrorism Prevention Act of 2004 and the Implementation of the 9/11 Commission Recommendations Act of 2007.

Chapter 83, "Cyber Warfare," defines cyber warfare (CW) and discusses its most common tactics, weapons, and tools as well as comparing CW terrorism with conventional warfare and addressing the issues of liability and the available legal remedies under international law.

Chapter 84, "Cyber-Attack Process," covers the cyber-attack process, to include the technical and nontechnical steps an attacker uses in order to exploit their targeted entity.

Part 14: Advanced Security

Part 14 discusses security through diversity, online reputation, content filtering, data loss protection, satellite cyber-attack search and destroy, verifiable voting systems and advanced data encryption. For instance:

Chapter 85, "Security Through Diversity," covers some of the industry trends in adopting diversity in hardware, software, and application deployments. This chapter also covers the risks of uniformity, conformity, and the ubiquitous impact of adopting standard organizational principals without the consideration of security.

Chapter 86, "e-Reputation and Online Reputation Management Survey," discusses the general understanding of the human notion of reputation. It explains how this concept of reputation fits into computer security. The chapter presents the state of the art of attack-resistant reputation computation. It also gives an overview of the current market of online reputation services. The chapter concludes by underlining the need to standardize online reputation for increased adoption and robustness.

Chapter 87, "Content Filtering," examines the many benefits and justifications of web-based content filtering such as legal liability risk reduction, productivity gains, and bandwidth usage. It also explores the downside and unintended consequences and risks that improperly deployed or misconfigured systems create. The chapter also looks into methods to subvert and bypass these systems and the reasons behind them.

Chapter 88, "Data Loss Protection," introduces the reader to a baseline understanding of how to investigate and evaluate DLP applications in the market today.

Chapter 89, "Satellite Cyber-Attack Search and Destroy," discusses satellite cyber-attacks with regards to hacking, interference, and jamming.

Chapter 90, "Verifiable Voting Systems," emphasizes the challenge to reconcile the secrecy of the ballot, with demonstrable correctness of the result.

Chapter 91, "Advanced Data Encryption," explores advanced data encryption algorithms.

2. SUPPLEMENTAL MATERIALS

Instructor materials, including appendices and glossary, lecture slides, figures from the text, exercise solutions, and sample syllabi are available at: store.elsevier.com/product.jsp?isbn59780123943972 (click the "Resources" tab at the bottom of the page).

John R. Vacca
Editor-in-Chief
john2164@windstream.net
www.johnvacca.com

Acknowledgments

There are many people who have contributed to this book's successful completion. I owe each a debt of gratitude and want to take this opportunity to offer my sincere thanks.

A very special thanks to my Senior Acquisitions Editor, Brian Romer, without whose continued interest and support would not have made this book possible. And, a very special thanks to Senior Editorial Project Manager, Charlie Kent, who provided staunch support and encouragement when it was most needed. Thanks to my Senior Project Managers Priya Kumaraguruparan and Udayakumar Raghavan; Copyeditors, whose fine editorial work has been invaluable. Thanks also to my Marketing Manager, whose efforts on this book have been greatly appreciated. Finally, thanks to all of the other people at Computer Networking and Computer and Information Systems Security, and Morgan Kaufmann Publishers/Elsevier Science & Technology Books, whose many talents and skills are essential to a finished book.

Thanks to my wife, Bee Vacca, for her love, her help, and her understanding of my long work hours. Also, special thanks to Michael Erbschloe for writing the foreword. Finally, I wish to thank all the following authors who contributed chapters that were necessary for the completion of this book: Edward Amoroso, Jeffrey S. Bardin, Cataldo Basile, Sanjay Bavisi, Stefan Berthold, Gerald Beuchelt, Rahul Bhaskar, Chiara Braghin, Albert Caballero, Matteo Maria Casalino, Erdal Cayirci, Tom Chen, Hongbing Cheng, Lauren Collins, Marco Cremonini, Sam Curry, Rozita Dara, Christopher Day, Sabrina De Capitani Di Vimercati, Scott R. Ellis, Tewfiq El Maliki, Michael Erbschloe, Simone Fischer-Hbner, Sara Foresti, Errin W. Fulp, Angelo Genovese, Anna Granova, William F. Gross, Yong Guan, Cem Gurkok, Feng Hao, Tarfa Hamed, James T. Harmening, Rich Hoffman, Emin Huseynov, Markus Jakobsson, Ravi Jhawar, Almantas Kakareka, Bhushan Kapoor, Sokratis K. Katsikas, Dalia Khader, John B. Khan, Larry Korba, Kameswari Kotapati, Stefan C. Kremer, Thomas F. LaPorta, Jean Lencrenon, Keith Lewis, Peng Liu, Giovanni Livraga, Tewfiq El Maliki, John R. Mallery, Bill Mansoor, Luther Martin, John McDonald, John McGowan, Nailah Mims, Simone Mutti, Peter Nicoletti, Kevin Noble, Pramod Pandya, Harsh Kupwade Patil, Stefano Paraboschi, Thea Peacock, Ken Perkins, Vincenzo Piuri, Henrik Plate, James Pooley, Daniel Ramsbrock, Chunming Rong, Robert Rounsavall, Peter Ryan, Pierangela Samarati, Marco Santambrogio, Mario Santana, Steve Schneider, Fabio Scotti, Jean-Marc Seigneur, Marco Slaviero, Daniel S. Soper, Terence Spies, William Stallings, Alex Tsow, Jesse Walker, Patrick J. Walsh, Michael A. West, Dan Wing, Zhe Xia, George O.M. Yee, Liang Yan, Roman Zabicki, and Gansen Zhao.

Part I

Overview of System and Network Security: A Comprehensive Introduction

Chapter 1

Information Security in the Modern Enterprise

James Pooley

A Professional Law Corporation, Orrick, Herrington & Sutcliffe LLP, Menlo Park, CA, United States

1. INTRODUCTION

We all can feel how the information age has changed our daily lives: how we communicate, how we find answers, how we find our way around the block, using tiny handheld computers that are much more powerful than the big machines available to businesses only a generation ago. The same kind of change has happened in information security, with increasingly complex threats directed at increasingly valuable assets.

In the 1970s data security consisted of not much more than guarding the photocopier and watching who went in and out of the front door. Now we confront an array of devices capable of grabbing gigabytes of data and moving them anywhere in the world in an instant. Our laptops, tablets, and smartphones, with direct connection to the company's data, have become "endpoints" in a sweeping global network, creating thousands or millions of "front doors." Never before has industrial data been so vulnerable to loss.

And never before has industrial data been so valuable and in need of secure protection. A generation ago the asset base of US public companies was more than 80% tangible property, like real estate, raw materials, and railroad cars. Today, as reflected in Fig. 1.1, it is intangibles that account for more than 80% of listed company value. In other words, in a single generation we have witnessed a fundamental shift in the nature of corporate assets on a scale not seen since the Industrial Revolution.

Management Matters as Much as Technology

This chapter is about the challenge of protecting those assets against loss or theft. As the title implies, computer systems play an important role in defining that challenge, for obvious reasons. But viewed more broadly, the security of a company's information assets depends only in part on technological tools. The best tools are useless unless applied intelligently to match a dynamic threat landscape. And human beings are ultimately at the controls of the majority of those tools, making judgments about risk and about deployment of efficient solutions. Indeed, one thing that hasn't changed much over the years is that humans remain the primary vector for loss. Therefore, the key message of this chapter is that management matters, not just technology. People and processes are equally important to achieving optimum security in the modern enterprise. And good management requires collaboration among multidisciplinary teams.

The information security function is more central to preserving corporate value than ever. In the past, we handled data *about* the business; increasingly, data *is* the business. This applies across the board, not just to information age companies like Google and Facebook. For example, manufacturers typically distinguish themselves on how well they can gather and manage data about customer needs and preferences, using sophisticated CRM software. IBM estimates that the world generates 2.5 quintillion bytes of data—every day. And the rapidly emerging Internet of Things will produce much more. General Electric is harnessing its engines with sensors that will gather detailed information about performance and wear, enabling more efficient servicing. If only 40,000 of these sensors were installed, each sending back 500 gigabytes a day, this would come to about 24 times the daily volume of the entire Internet in 2000.

Whether all of this data resides on a company's own servers, or as happens more frequently it is sent to the

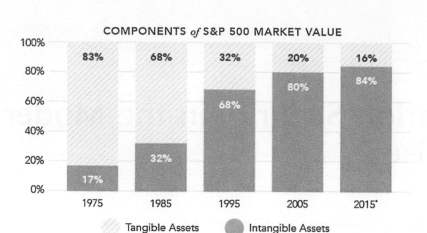

FIGURE 1.1 Change in public company assets from tangible to intangible.

Cloud, it needs careful attention, both at rest and in transit, to protect against loss. As we will see, the job has become more challenging, as the means for storage and communication of data have multiplied. Naturally, the specific risk profile of any operation varies, among other factors, according to the industry involved. The threats are different for financial versus manufacturing, hospitality versus healthcare, consumer-facing versus business-to-business. But for all modern industries, the information security function has become the primary guardian of corporate assets (in addition to customer information held in trust), and therefore the one that's often blamed for breaches or losses.

This chapter will give you a wealth of information about best practices in a number of specific areas. More generally, as we will see in this chapter, industry and government are coming up with standards for information security that should prove helpful to the professional tasked with providing a secure environment for the operation of any business.

This chapter provides context for understanding your responsibilities and how best to meet the expectations of your organization. We will consider the challenging nature of the modern environment, the risk management process as a framework for decision-making, a sampling of important policies and procedures and how to implement them, as well as the all-important area of training as a bulwark against loss. But first it will help to understand a bit about the legal implications of your work.

Trade Secrets and "Reasonable Efforts"

In the world of intellectual property, there are three areas that matter for data. The simplest is copyright, which protects only the specific expression of an idea, not the idea itself. For example, computer object code can be protected by copyright, and so it can be widely distributed to users without security measures. Patents protect novel inventions.

The underlying idea or architecture of a software program might be protectable by patents, which also apply to inventions in hundreds of other fields of technology. But whatever a business invents that is patentable, it begins life as a trade secret, until the patent application is published. This third legal category, trade secrets—which, unlike copyright and patent, does not require registration with the government—is enormously broader than the first two. Trade secrets protect any information that is not generally known and that provides some competitive advantage. They cover technical information like formulas and experimental research, but also a wide range of business information, such as "big data" analytics, unannounced products, business plans, and financial reports.

The vast majority of valuable corporate data today is protected by trade secret law. That law allows a company to get a court order to prevent a breach of confidentiality, or to recover damages if a breach has already happened. But in order to have access to these legal remedies, a company must have first complied with one basic requirement: it must be able to show that it exercised "reasonable efforts" to prevent the loss. And that is how the information security function helps meet the legal needs of modern business. Proper attention to data security will often prevent loss and mitigate consequences; but it also demonstrates that the company has met the "reasonable efforts" obligation, in case it has to go to court.

2. CHALLENGES FACING INFORMATION SECURITY

Minding a company's most valuable assets—its information—is not easy. A number of challenges confront security professionals in almost every organization.

First, everyone else has very high expectations for data security. Nothing will go wrong. You can rely on the system's availability 24/7 and from any place on the planet. Information will be available where and when it is supposed to be, but will never be accessed by those without a need to know. And all of these assumptions are wrapped up in a single comfortable feeling and tucked away. Information security will be noticed only when there is a problem.

Second, modern threats are ubiquitous and dynamic; you can never be sure what might happen next. Some important research universities have reported more than 100,000 penetration attempts daily. This happens because data thieves act like bank robbers do: they go to where the assets are. Their required investment—a laptop and Internet connection—is small, their tools are increasingly sophisticated, and their work can often be automated, allowing them to engage in thousands of attacks simultaneously.

Third, corporate systems were designed for performance, not security. Of course a certain amount of security functionality is installed or enabled in most systems, but it often seems like an afterthought. This should be no surprise; the customer who buys these systems is the same end user who tends to see security as an annoyance (see below). Whatever the cause, the security manager typically has to focus on reining in technology that was optimized only for performance.

Fourth, those same systems have been fractured, making them much harder to control. Back in the days when the main threat to corporate security was the photocopier, there were computers, but they normally were linked and controlled within a single facility. Even with the arrival of the Internet and email, the first corporate handheld devices tended to be Blackberries, which came with robust network controls that users could not compromise. Now, with Bring Your Own Device (BYOD) becoming an accepted feature of most workplaces, the IT department struggles to find platform-independent tools to provide essential functions such as remote wiping of a lost smartphone. Portable storage devices (USB drives) not only provide a simple and quick way to pull out information from the network, but also represent a vector for malware contamination: some hackers have left infected devices in parking lots where curious engineers pick them up. And the Internet provides a separate channel for information loss, as employees are tempted by convenience to email sensitive data to their private account, or send it to Dropbox, so that they can continue to work from home.

Fifth, the modern corporation is often ambivalent about secrecy. While information has never been more valuable or more vulnerable, companies also know that new products can't always be developed inside. "Open innovation"—collaborating with other companies sometimes located in distant countries—has become a new imperative of competition in global markets. Information must be shared with contractors, vendors, customers, and sometimes even competitors, in ways that multiply the system endpoints and compromise integrity of access controls. For the executives who manage these far-flung relationships, issues of investment, productivity, and profitability normally rank ahead of security concerns.

Sixth, and perhaps the most difficult challenge, is the general attitude about security within the organization. Users see security as mainly annoying, an irritating interference with an otherwise frictionless and convenient world of access and communication. They resist procedures like full disk encryption, two-factor authentication, or use of virtual private networks (VPNs) when traveling. Unconcerned about the risks of sloppy behavior, they download unauthorized apps and click on unknown email attachments. At the organizational level, security is too often viewed as a "cost center" and therefore less worthy of attention than other corporate functions that produce a profit.

Addressing these challenges effectively requires a thorough understanding of the enterprise, its mission and business strategies, its available resources, and all the competitive threats it faces, beyond those that apply to the integrity of its data. In other words, information security professionals need to appreciate the larger context of the business in order to advocate successfully for management support. Security cannot be delivered from a silo, but must emerge organically from the collaborative efforts of all the company's managers. This principle applies to every aspect of the function, including assessment, planning, establishment of policies and procedures, and training. When security managers present their issues in the right context to the entire management team, all of these obstacles can be overcome.

3. ASSESSMENT AND PLANNING

There is no such thing as perfect information security. Benjamin Franklin quipped that "three can keep a secret, if two of them are dead." In the globalized digital environment, companies can exploit their information advantage only if they are willing to take the risks that come with sharing it. That means that employees, customers, vendors, and business partners will all be given some level of access to an ever-changing soup of data. As one retired military security officer once said, "it's not a question of whether your secrets will become known, but when. The trick is to figure it out ahead of time and be prepared."

In other words, information security, like most other business processes, depends heavily on classical risk assessment: knowing what can go wrong, how likely it is to happen, and what you might be able to do about it. And risk management is closely related to business continuity: being prepared, when the worst happens, with contingency plans that will keep the company's most critical functions going while the situation is stabilized and repairs are made. This is why all serious data security programs include incident response plans. But let's go back to the beginning of the process and answer the question: who is in charge of this issue?

One of the biggest mistakes that organizations can make is assuming that security is an issue that can be "handled" by the CIO or the Director of IT, who as a specialist will simply know what needs to be done, find the cheapest way to do it, and make sure the systems are running. As we have already seen, the modern company is built on a foundation of information assets, and the intelligent management of those assets must be treated as a top priority. Otherwise, the company's competitive advantage will almost certainly degrade.

Because the question of information management is so important—indeed existential for companies in the most competitive industries—this function can't simply be delegated to a single department. Awareness and ownership have to happen at the board level, and all senior managers need to participate to some extent in the setting of strategies and policies for security. We will come back to this principle when we look at best practices and standards for creating and running programs. But at the outset it's critical to recognize that this is an issue of attitude and attention at the highest levels of leadership. It's part of the job of the information security professional to ensure that this message is delivered and repeated as necessary.

Know Where to Begin

Assuming that there is—or will be—acceptance of this reality at the top, the first operational step is to conduct an assessment of the organization's existing efforts to protect the integrity of its data. This should be done regardless of the company's level of sophistication and experience. After all, when your plan is finished and in operation, that necessarily leads you back to a review of how it's working so you can improve it.

There are literally hundreds of ways to take a reading on your company's existing security processes, but there is one aspect of this effort that bears special emphasis: you shouldn't do it yourself. That's not to say that you shouldn't gather whatever information you can from your team about perceived issues and problems; but you shouldn't rely only on internal assessments. The natural human tendencies toward justification and denial often lead us to overlook many of the most problematic areas of our operation. As a result, we need to look outside for independent advice.

A number of consulting firms are available to bring in a team of highly qualified professionals for this purpose. They come with the distinct advantage of having seen it all elsewhere. The diversity of their experience and their independence from your company's culture and politics will allow them to ask more and harder questions, and to avoid many of the assumptions that your own team may not even

be aware that they are making. The consultants can do their work by looking at your records, interviewing relevant actors, and even testing your systems and people for vulnerabilities, providing a specific roadmap for improvement.

But particularly for smaller companies it's not always necessary to spend what it takes for that kind of service, at least not at the beginning. For example, one very good, low-cost offering from CREATe.org, a not-for-profit organization, provides a basic approach in three parts. First, you participate in an online self-assessment that benchmarks your information security processes. Second, you get an interview from one of their experts, along with a review of relevant documents, leading to a report with recommendations. Third, the organization provides additional "guidance to help improve management systems and embed protections into business operations."[1]

Risk Management

As we've already noted, the ultimate exercise in planning for security is essentially about risk management. The basic notion is that any organization should be able to identify a set of things that might happen to imperil their business, and in the area of data security that would be threats to the integrity and control of the company's information assets. Having identified all the risks, the team then evaluates the likelihood that they will actually happen within a given time frame, and the relative impact on the company if they do. With this set of possibilities laid out in an organized fashion (often color-coded in a green-yellow-red range), managers can then take informed decisions about whether to ignore the risk (it seems truly remote), accept it as is, transfer it to some other entity (e.g., outsource the function), or mitigate the risk by some application of action or resources. In practice, most risks are treated with mitigation steps that will reduce their placement on the scale, with the objective of getting them moved out of the "red zone." The advantage of this process is that it clearly communicates to managers the consequences of their decisions among competing priorities, bringing a certain level of objectivity and accountability to management of the function.

Public Standards for Information Security

Perhaps the leading example of risk management applied to information security is the ISO/IEC 27001 standard, created in 2005 by an agreement between the International Organization for Standardization and the International Electrotechnical Commission, and most recently updated in 2013. It sets very specific requirements for security management systems and controls, allowing firms to apply to be audited

---

1. More information about the CREATe.org tool is available at https://create.org/services/create-leading-practices-for-trade-secret-protection/.

and certified as ISO/IEC 27001 compliant. The requirements for a qualifying system are comprehensive and detailed, beginning with identifying all of the company's assets, then placing them in an asset register that identifies location and ownership and classifies them according to level of needed protection, and finally creating a complete system for access control, including user registration, password management, applications controls, and network security.[2]

Another very useful construct for addressing data security is provided by the "NIST Framework," a document issued in February 2014 by the US National Institute of Standards and Technology (NIST). It was prepared in response to an Executive Order issued by President Obama a year before, calling for the development of a voluntary risk-based Cybersecurity Framework to protect the nation's "critical infrastructure," such as the banking system, the energy grid, and other strategic assets that are controlled through networks. The effort engaged not only staff and experts within the US Department of Commerce, but also many representatives of industry from a variety of sectors. The result was perhaps greater than had been requested, since the Framework addresses not just critical national infrastructure, but businesses of all types that depend on information assets. Its approach is easily adaptable to firms of all sizes and risk profiles, and can be very cost-effective.

The NIST Framework refers to and builds on many of the principles of the ISO/IEC 27001 standard and others, but treats issues well beyond the IT and physical security environment, including management and governance, staff policies and procedures, training, and supply chain management. It does this by organizing the security function into five main imperatives: identify, protect, detect, respond, and recover. Each of these functions is divided in turn by reference to several categories, which are displayed in Fig. 1.2. Organizations critically examine their capabilities according to these benchmarks, assigning to each an "implementation tier" that corresponds to their degree of sophistication, from "partial" to "adaptive," labels that the Framework identifies with a "progression from informal, reactive responses to approaches that are agile and risk-informed."[3]

Creating the Security Plan

Adapting these standards to create a security plan for any particular business requires a comprehensive focus on all the ways in which the company functions and internally

IDENTIFY	Asset Management Business Environment Governance Risk Assessment Risk Management Strategy
PROTECT	Access Control Awareness and Training Data Security Information Protection Processes and Procedures Maintenance Protective Technology
DETECT	Anomalies and Events Security Continuous Monitoring Detection Processes
RESPOND	Response Planning Communications Analysis Mitigation Improvements
RECOVER	Recovery Planning Improvements Communications

FIGURE 1.2 National Institute of Standards and Technology Framework functions and categories.

communicates. One helpful summary of the various processes that need to be addressed in security planning is shown in Fig. 1.3, courtesy of CREATe.org.

Among the major areas of concern, we have already addressed assessment, and we will deal below with two others (policies and procedures, and training). A few brief comments on the remaining categories follow:

- Information Protection Team. Information security affects every part of the modern firm's business and operations. The team that is assembled to address the issue must be multidisciplinary, and must come to the task with the active support of upper management. And its work is not finished when the plan is prepared, because this team is also responsible for implementation. Therefore, it should constitute itself as an ongoing cross-departmental structure, meeting periodically to check in and assess progress.
- Management of Third Parties. Information flows are not limited to the company's own staff, but increasingly reach outside to connect with customers, vendors, consultants, partners, and other third parties. Because they will all have some sort of access to the company's data, care must be taken not only to establish clear expectations for security, but also to actively manage how those third parties deal with their own systems. Recall that the infamous hack of Target, in which millions of customer records were compromised, came in through the less-secure system of a trusted air conditioning contractor.
- Security and Confidentiality Management. Security doesn't happen merely because we establish and

2. For official information from the ISO, see http://www.iso.org/iso/home/standards/management-standards/iso27001.htm.
3. More information on the NIST Framework, including ongoing efforts to update it with input from industry, can be found at http://csrc.nist.gov/groups/SMA/fisma/framework.html. And a very useful and accessible guide by PwC, titled *Why You Should Adopt the NIST Cybersecurity Framework*, is available for download at http://www.pwc.com/us/en/increasing-it-effectiveness/publications/adopt-the-nist.html.

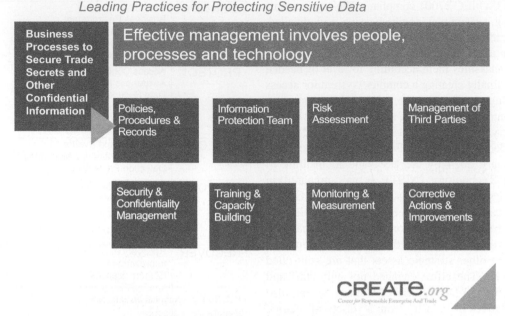

FIGURE 1.3 Leading practices for protecting sensitive data.

communicate rules. Without active management that demonstrates the critical nature of this function and the consequences of breach and data loss, staff, and others will tend to let down their guard. As we have seen, the vast majority of information loss happens through negligent behavior by well-meaning people. Managers in all areas of the company need to project and demonstrate their concern by carefully following procedures and insisting on the same from those whom they manage.

- Monitoring and Measurement. The effectiveness of any plan will diminish over time if it is not refreshed and adjusted in response to actual experience. Monitoring in this context is not about watching network traffic, although that can be very important; instead, it is about observing how well the overall security processes are actually working. Are you paying attention to how your staff actually behaves in regard to security hygiene? How frequently do you discover attempts to "work around" the system for the sake of convenience? Are you testing your staff on their retention of the security principles they have learned? How well has your plan performed against the specific expectations you had set? Close and constant review is a necessary predicate to the last step in the process.
- Corrective Actions and Improvements. As we all know from air or sea travel, a series of small course corrections can make all the difference in averting large disasters. Making those corrections requires at least two conditions. First, you must be aware of how you have been doing and to what extent you might be off course. Second,

you must be prepared to make changes to fix whatever is not working and return the system to optimum performance. Occasionally this will require difficult conversations in which you will request more resources or a shift in responsibility. But armed with the lessons of actual experience, coupled with the awareness of what is at stake, you should be able to take appropriate action.

4. POLICIES AND PROCEDURES

There is no "one size fits all" approach to establishing security policies and procedures, because every organization faces a unique set of threats to a unique set of information assets. This basic idea is embodied in the "reasonable efforts" requirement referred to earlier: if anything goes wrong and you need to invoke your legal rights, the courts will expect you to have taken steps that are reasonable for the risk environment that you face. In practice, this means that, once you have a basic understanding of the categories that apply to the company's valuable information, you can then apply the basic three-part test of value, risk, and cost. In other words, in deciding what policies or procedures might be appropriate to protect a certain kind of information (for example source code for a complex software product), you will consider how valuable the information is, the nature of the threat of loss that it faces, and whether reducing the risk is worth the cost (in money or inconvenience) of protective measures, such as restricted access (see checklist: "An Agenda for Action for Basic Protections that You Should Always Consider").

An Agenda for Action for Basic Protections that You Should Always Consider

There are certain basic protections that you should always consider that includes the following key activities (although their implementation might vary according to the threat landscape that confronts your company—check all tasks completed):

_____**1.** Premises security. Visitors should be required to sign in (preferably with a nondisclosure agreement) and be escorted inside the premises. You should keep particularly sensitive areas off limits to any tours, and ensure that white boards and computer screens are not visible. Be aware that smartphones have cameras that can be used to capture valuable information.

_____**2.** Classification of data. Sensitive information in documents, whether physical or electronic, should be classified and clearly marked as confidential. Paper documents should be controlled to limit copying and to provide for secure destruction.

_____**3.** Systems access. Partition access according to each person's (or position's) need to know. Passwords should be robust and required to be changed frequently. Better yet, convince management that passwords have become inherently insecure and that it is time to shift to two-factor authentication or biometrics. Deploy mobile device management tools to enable remote wiping. Encrypt where possible. Provide VPN resources for traveling staff.

_____**4.** Employee-owned devices. Create acceptable rules for registration of employee smartphones and other

mobile devices, with provisions that address privacy rights and the ability to access and remove company data.

_____**5.** Technological protections. Deploy appropriate technology to help prevent network breaches, but accept that perimeter defense is becoming more difficult all the time. Reserve sufficient attention and resources for monitoring and detection systems, so that you can know when a breach has occurred and initiate action.

_____**6.** Policies and rules. Taking into account staff and management input, publish clear policies and rules around information security hygiene. Monitor for compliance, and to the extent it falls short, reconsider either the rules, your training, or your enforcement.

_____**7.** Contracts. Employees and consultants should be required to sign legally binding confidentiality agreements. All outsiders who might come into contact with your information assets need to do the same.

_____**8.** Management. Establish clear points of authority and accountability. Be sure that all staff know where to go when they see a problem. Be sensitive to generational differences in staff attitudes about security.

_____**9.** Education. As described more fully below, proper training of the workforce is the most cost-effective step that can be taken to improve information security.

5. TRAINING

As we have noted early in this chapter, one aspect of information security that has remained constant over the decades is that humans (usually employees) are the biggest single source of loss. Moreover, this is not because all staff are spies or irresponsible. Rather, it is an issue of negligence. That means that behaviors can be changed, through effective education and training.

That is not to say that training is easy. In fact, it has become substantially more difficult in recent years, due in part to the proliferation of mobile devices, and in part to an attitude shift that has been enabled and encouraged by technology. In short, many of the workers that handle the company's most sensitive data are part of the "Facebook Generation," trained by the social media they use to engage in extensive disclosure of every aspect of their personal lives. In the evening, they expose their most intimate thoughts and actions (sometimes with photographic proof) to the online world and are rewarded by their network of friends. How then can we expect them to return the next morning and assume a completely different attitude about information, one in which disclosure is dangerous?

This kind of attitude shift is not impossible, but it requires a great deal of careful management and reinforcement. A robust training program is key to success. Watching a video as part of the onboarding process will not do. Training must be treated as part of the employee's continuing experience as a responsible member of the organizational team. Here are three imperatives for the process.

First, training should be inclusive. It should not be limited to new hires, or to the people who have access to the most sensitive information. Rather, everyone in the company must have a grounded understanding of the importance of data security. Even contractors, temporary staff, and interns should be included, in part because they are less likely to have a developed sense of loyalty to the institution. But the need for inclusiveness also goes in the other direction, up to managers. Their involvement in training programs, as participants or faculty, will help set the tone by adding credibility to the process, ultimately helping to establish a culture of awareness and compliance.

Second, the training has to be interesting and fresh. Where possible, use outside vendors or packaged programs that can be adapted to the company's needs. But keep changing how and where it's done, what people are presenting, what media are used, and what issues are addressed. Try to make it memorable.

Third, the effort must be a continuous program, not just an occasional class or webinar. It helps to follow up on classes with tips and stories sent to the participants to remind and refresh. And if the economics of your business take a turn for the worse, do not give in to the impulse to first cut the training budget, at least not for this area. The people that you train are the ones who every day are responsible for proper handling of the company's most valuable property.

6. SUMMARY

Information security has changed dramatically over recent decades. Rather than a commodity that helps business run, information is now the key asset of most companies. And this valuable information is more vulnerable than in the past, thanks to proliferating networks and endpoints that spread it around the globe. Nevertheless, human carelessness remains the single most common source of loss. Therefore, management is at least as important as technology in planning and implementing protection systems. The legal context for all this is trade secrets, and the law will enforce obligations of confidentiality owed by employees and outsiders. But it insists on self-help by the owner, who must show "reasonable efforts" to keep it safe. The information security function today faces many challenges, among them high expectations, a dynamic threat environment, systems optimized for performance rather than security, fractured systems with mobile devices challenging central control, corporate ambivalence over the value of the security function, and users who find security annoying and ignore basic hygiene. Information security is about risk management, which begins with an interdisciplinary assessment of what is at risk and how. Third-party tools and teams are available to help. Emerging standards from industry and government can be confusing, but some of them, notably the NIST Framework, provide helpful templates. Certain issues are common to all plans: team effort, close management of third parties, management of insiders, monitoring, and improvement. Security policies need to focus on multiple areas, including facilities, data classification, systems access, employee-owned devices, software tools, published rules, contracts, management, and training. And it is training where most benefit is realized. Well-run, professional programs will be continuous, varied, and based on specific risks and experiences of the company.

Finally, let's move on to the real interactive part of this chapter: review questions/exercises, hands-on projects, case projects, and optional team case project. The answers and/or solutions by chapter can be found in Appendix K.

CHAPTER REVIEW QUESTIONS/ EXERCISES

True/False

1. True or False? The information security function is more central to preserving corporate value than ever.
2. True or False? Corporate systems were not designed for performance, but for security.
3. True or False? Perhaps the least difficult challenge is the general attitude about security within the organization.
4. True or False? There is no such thing as perfect information security.
5. True or False? Information security, unlike most other business processes, depends heavily on classical risk assessment: knowing what can go wrong, how likely it is to happen, and what you might be able to do about it.

Multiple Choice

1. There are hundreds of ways to take a reading on your company's existing security processes, but there is one aspect of this effort that bears special emphasis:
   A. You should do it yourself
   B. You shouldn't gather whatever information you can from your team about perceived issues and problems
   C. You shouldn't rely only on internal assessments
   D. You shouldn't do it yourself
   E. All of the above
2. The ultimate exercise in planning for security is essentially about:
   A. Cross-site-request-forgery attacks
   B. Side-channel attacks (VM-to-VM)
   C. Token stealing
   D. Security Questionnaires
   E. Risk management
3. Perhaps the leading example of risk management applied to information security is the:
   A. ISO/IEC 27001 standard
   B. International Organization for Standardization
   C. International Electrotechnical Commission
   D. NIST Framework
   E. All of the above
4. Another very useful construct for addressing data security is provided by the:
   A. Cybersecurity Framework
   B. Critical infrastructure
   C. NIST Framework
   D. US Department of Commerce
   E. All of the above
5. The NIST Framework refers to and builds on many of the principles of the:
   A. Information Protection Team
   B. ISO/IEC 27001 standard

C. Management of Third Parties
D. Security and Confidentiality Management
E. All of the above

EXERCISE

Problem

How does an organization prepare for security and privacy control assessments?

Hands-On Projects

Project

How does an organization develop security and privacy assessment plans?

Case Projects

Problem

How does an organization go about conducting security and privacy control assessments?

Optional Team Case Project

Problem

How does an organization go about analyzing assessment report results?

Chapter 2

Building a Secure Organization

John R. Mallery

Mallery Technical Training and Consulting, Inc., Overland Park, KS, United States

It seems logical that any business, whether a commercial enterprise or a not-for-profit business, would understand that building a secure organization is important to long-term success. When a business implements and maintains a strong security posture, it can take advantage of numerous benefits. An organization that can demonstrate an infrastructure protected by robust security mechanisms can potentially see a reduction in insurance premiums. A secure organization can use its security program as a marketing tool, demonstrating to clients that it values their business so much that it takes a very aggressive stance on protecting their information. Most importantly, a secure organization will not have to spend time and money identifying security breaches and responding to the results of those breaches.

As of December 2011, according to the National Conference of State Legislatures, 46 states, the District of Columbia, Puerto Rico, and the Virgin Islands enacted legislation requiring notification of security breaches involving personal information. In 2011, 14 states expanded the scope of this legislation.[1] Security breaches can cost an organization significantly through a tarnished reputation, lost business, and legal fees. Numerous regulations such as the Health Insurance Portability and Accountability Act, the Gramm-Leach—Bliley Act, and the Sarbanes—Oxley Act require businesses to maintain the security of information. Despite the benefits of maintaining a secure organization and the potentially devastating consequences of not doing so, many organizations have poor security mechanisms, implementations, policies, and culture.

1. OBSTACLES TO SECURITY

In attempting to build a secure organization, we should take a close look at the obstacles that make it challenging to build a totally secure organization.

Security Is Inconvenient

By its very nature, security is inconvenient, and the more robust the security mechanisms are, the more inconvenient the process becomes. Employees in an organization have a job to do; they want to get to work right away. Most security mechanisms, from passwords to multifactor authentication, are seen as roadblocks to productivity. One of the current trends in security is to add whole-disk encryption to laptop computers. Although this is a highly recommended security process, it adds a second login step before a computer user can actually start working. Even if the step adds only 1 min to the login process, over the course of a year this results in 4 h of lost productivity. Some would argue that this lost productivity is balanced by the added level of security. Across a large organization, however, this lost productivity could prove significant.

To gain a full appreciation of the frustration caused by security measures, we have only to watch the Transportation Security Administration lines at any airport. Simply watch the frustration build as a particular item is run through the scanner for a third time while a passenger is running late to board his flight. Security implementations are based on a sliding scale; one end of the scale is total security and total inconvenience, and the other is total insecurity and complete ease of use. When we implement any security mechanism, it should be placed on the scale where the level of security and ease of use match the acceptable level of risk for the organization.

2. COMPUTERS ARE POWERFUL AND COMPLEX

Home computers have become storehouses of personal materials. Our computers now contain wedding videos, scanned family photos, music libraries, movie collections, and financial and medical records. Because computers

---

1. http://www.ncsl.org/issues-research/telecommunications-information-technology/security-breach-legislation-2011.aspx (February 2, 2012).

Computer and Information Security Handbook. http://dx.doi.org/10.1016/B978-0-12-803843-7.00002-8

contain such familiar objects, we have forgotten that computers are powerful and complex devices. It was not long ago that computers as powerful as our desktop and laptop computers would have filled one or more large rooms. In addition, today's computers present a "user-friendly" face to the world. Most people are unfamiliar with the way computers truly function and what goes on "behind the scenes." Things such as the Windows Registry, ports, and services are completely unknown to most users and are poorly understood by many computer industry professionals. For example, many individuals still believe that a Windows login password protects data on a computer. On the contrary: Someone can simply take the hard drive out of the computer, install it as a slave drive in another computer, or place it in a universal serial bus (USB) drive enclosure, and all of the data will be readily accessible.

Computer Users Are Unsophisticated

Many computer users believe that because they are skilled at generating spreadsheets, word processing documents, and presentations, they know everything about computers. These "power users" have moved beyond application basics, but many still do not understand even basic security concepts. Many users will indiscriminately install software and visit questionable websites even though these actions could violate company policies. The "bad guys" (people who want to steal information from or wreak havoc on computers systems) have also identified the average user as a weak link in the security chain. As companies began investing more money in perimeter defenses, attackers looked to the path of least resistance. They send malware as attachments to email, asking recipients to open the attachment. Despite being told not to open attachments from unknown senders or simply not to open attachments at all, employees consistently violate this policy, wreaking havoc on their networks. The "I Love You Virus" spread rapidly in this manner. More recently, phishing scams have been effective in convincing individuals to provide personal online banking and credit card information. Why would an attacker struggle to break through an organization's defenses when end users are more than willing to provide the keys to bank accounts? Addressing the threat caused by untrained and unwary end users is a significant part of any security program.

Computers Created Without a Thought to Security

During the development of personal computers (PCs), no thought was given to security. Early PCs were simple affairs that had limited computing power and no keyboards, and were programmed by flipping a series of switches.

They were developed almost as curiosities. Even as they became more advanced and complex, all effort was focused on developing greater sophistication and capabilities; no one thought they would have security issues. We only have to look at some of the early computers, such as the Berkeley Enterprises Geniac, the Heathkit EC-1, and the MITS Altair 8800, to understand why security was not an issue back then.[2] The development of computers was focused on what they could do, not how they could be attacked.

As computers began to be interconnected, the driving force was to provide the ability to share information, certainly not to protect it. Initially, the Internet was designed for military applications, but eventually it migrated to colleges and universities, the principal tenet of which is the sharing of knowledge.

3. CURRENT TREND IS TO SHARE, NOT PROTECT

Even now, despite the stories of compromised data, people still want to share their data with everyone. Web-based applications are making this easier to do than simply attaching a file to an email. Social networking sites such as Omemo provide the ability to share material: "Store your files online, share your stuff and browse what other users store in the world's largest multimedia library: The Omemo peer-to-peer virtual hard-drive."[3] In addition, many online data storage sites such as DropSend[4] and FilesAnywhere[5] provide the ability to share files. These sites can allow proprietary data to leave an organization by bypassing security mechanisms, exposing them to the possibility of unwanted review and distribution.

Data Accessible From Anywhere

As though employees' desire to share data is not enough of a threat to proprietary information, many business professionals want access to data from anywhere they work, on a variety of devices. To be productive, employees now request access to data and contact information on their laptops, desktops, home computers, and mobile devices. Therefore, information technology (IT) departments must now provide the ability to sync data with numerous systems. And if the IT department cannot or will not provide this capability, employees now have the power to take matters into their own hands by using online services.

In addition to the previously mentioned online file-sharing sites, numerous online file storage sites exist

2. Pop Quiz: What Was the First Personal Computer? www.blinkenlights.com/pc.shtml (February 2, 2012).

3. www.omemo.com (February 2, 2012).

4. www.dropsend.com (February 2, 2012).

5. www.filesanywhere.com (February 2, 2012).

(some sites offer both services). These storage sites are "springing up" everywhere, based on the desire to have access to data from absolutely everywhere. The latest operating systems from Microsoft and Apple supported this concept on a home network level when they created Homegroups[6] and AirDrop, respectively. Homegroups allow users to share specific volumes or folders across a network, whereas AirDrop allows users to share files between Macs without using an established network.

Looking for a fast way to share files with people nearby? With AirDrop, you can send files to anyone around you wirelessly—no Wi-Fi network required. And no complicated setup or special settings. Just click the AirDrop icon in the Finder sidebar, and your Mac automatically discovers other AirDrop users within about 30 feet of you. To share a file, simply drag it to someone's name. Once accepted, the fully encrypted file transfers directly to that person's Downloads folder.[7]

Employees always seem to want the same capabilities they have at home while in the workplace. This desire stems from the desire to work quickly and efficiently, with as few impediments in place as possible. Many computer users appreciate the simplicity with which they can access files while at home; they expect the same capabilities in the workplace.

Currently, the best-known file storage site is Dropbox.[8] To date, Dropbox provides 2 GB of free storage and software for Windows, Mac, Linux, and mobile devices, including iPhone, iPad, Blackberry, and Android. This matches their slogan, "Your files everywhere you are." However, you do not need to install the application on your computer; there is a Web interface that allows you to upload new files and access stored files. From an accessibility perspective, this is truly amazing. From a security perspective, it is a little unnerving. Some security professionals will not consider this an issue because they can simply "blacklist" the Dropbox website and prevent users from installing software. However, if one thinks about this, what is to stop someone from storing material on one of these sites while using a home or library computer? In addition, Dropbox is not the only "game in town." There are dozens of these sites; some are obscure, and new ones are created periodically. Table 2.1 identifies sites that have been identified as of this writing (and there are likely more in existence).

Some familiar tools also offer file storage capabilities. Google's free email service, Gmail, is a great tool that provides a robust service for free. What few people realize

---

6. http://windows.microsoft.com/en-US/windows7/Create-a-homegroup (February 23, 2012).
7. http://www.apple.com/macosx/whats-new/ (February 23, 2012).
8. http://www.dropbox.com.

TABLE 2.1 Current Sites

4Shared	www.4shared.com
Adrive	www.adrive.com
Amazon S3 (simple storage service)	www.amazon.com/s3
Box	www.box.net
Carbonite	www.carbonite.com
DocLocker	www.doclocker.com
Drive Headquarters	www.drivehq.com
DropBox	www.dropbox.com
Egnyte	www.egnyte.com
ElephantDrive	www.elephantdrive.com
fileden	www.fileden.com
Filegenie	www.filegenie.com
filesanywhere	www.filesanywhere.com
filocity.com	www.filocity.com
FirstBackup	www.firstbackup.com
FlipDrive	www.flipdrive.com
FreeDrive	www.freedrive.com
Google Docs	docs.google.com
iBackup	www.ibackup.com
iDrive	www.idrive.com
Justcloud	www.justcloud.com
KeepVault	www.keepvault.com
kineticD	www.kineticd.com
LiveDrive	www.livedrive.com
lockmydrive	lockmydrive.com
MediaFire	www.mediafire.com
Minus	www.minus.com
Mozy	www.mozy.com
MyDocsOnline	www.mydocsonline.com
MyOtherDrive	www.myotherdrive.com
MyPCBackup	www.mypcbackup.com
OffsiteBox	offsitebox.com
OLSEX	www.onilinestoragesolution.com
Omemo	www.omemo.com
online file folder	www.onlinefilefolder.com
OpenDrive	www.opendrive.com
orbitfiles.com	www.orbitfiles.com
ourdisk	www.ourdisk.com
SafeCopy	www.safecopybackup.com

Continued

TABLE 2.1 Current Sites—cont'd

SafeSync	www.safesync.com
SnapDrive.net	snapdrive.net
SPIDEROAK	www.spideroak.com
SugarSync	www.sugarsync.com
TrueShare	www.trueshare.com
Windows Live SkyDrive	skydrive.live.com
Wuala	www.wuala.com
zipcloud	www.zipcloud.com
zohodocs	www.zoho.com

is that Gmail provides more than 7 GB of storage that can also be used to store files, not just email. The shell extension, Gmail Drive,[9] provides access to your Gmail storage by means of a "drive" on your desktop. Fig. 2.1 shows the Gmail Drive login screen. This ability to transfer data easily outside the control of a company makes securing an organization's data that much more difficult. There is more to these sites than simply losing control of data. These are third-party sites and anything can happen. As an example,

```
▲ USBSTOR
  ▷ Disk&Ven_&Prod_Flash_Disk&Rev_8.00
  ▷ Disk&Ven_Generic&Prod_USB_CF_Reader&Rev_1.01
  ▷ Disk&Ven_Generic&Prod_USB_MS_Reader&Rev_1.03
  ▷ Disk&Ven_Generic&Prod_USB_SD_Reader&Rev_1.00
  ▷ Disk&Ven_Generic&Prod_USB_xD/SM_Reader&Rev_1.02
  ▷ Disk&Ven_HTC&Prod_Android_Phone&Rev_0100
  ▷ Disk&Ven_LaCie&Prod_d2_Quadra_v3&Rev_223X
  ▷ Disk&Ven_LG&Prod_USB_Drive&Rev_2.00
  ▷ Disk&Ven_Seagate&Prod_FreeAgent_GoFlex&Rev_0148
  ▷ Disk&Ven_ST310005&Prod_28AS&Rev_0041
  ▷ Disk&Ven_ST310005&Prod_28AS&Rev_CC3E
  ▷ Disk&Ven_ST320006&Prod_41AS&Rev_0041
  ▷ Disk&Ven_ST320006&Prod_41AS&Rev_CC13
  ▷ Disk&Ven_ST350041&Prod_8AS&Rev_0041
  ▷ Disk&Ven_ST500DM0&Prod_02-1BD142&Rev_0041
  ▷ Disk&Ven_TOSHIBA&Prod_MK2576GSX&Rev_
  ▷ Disk&Ven_TOSHIBA&Prod_TransMemory&Rev_PMAP
  ▷ Disk&Ven_USB&Prod_Flash_Disk&Rev_1100
  ▷ Disk&Ven_USB_TO_I&Prod_DE/SATA_Device&Rev_0041
  ▷ Disk&Ven_USB007&Prod_mini-USB2BU&Rev_0.00
  ▷ Disk&Ven_WIBU_-&Prod_CodeMeter-Stick&Rev_v1.0
```

FIGURE 2.1 Identifying connected universal serial bus devices in the USBStor Registry key.

in summer 2011, Dropbox had a security issue that allowed people to log into any account without using a password. Another issue is that the longevity of these sites is not guaranteed. For example, Xdrive, a popular online storage service created in 1999 and purchased by AOL in 2005 (allegedly for US$30 million), shut down on January 12, 2009. What happens to the data that are on systems that are no longer in service?

4. SECURITY IS NOT ABOUT HARDWARE AND SOFTWARE

Many businesses believe that if they purchase enough equipment, they can create a secure infrastructure. Firewalls, intrusion detection systems, antivirus programs, and two-factor authentication products are some of the tools available to assist in protecting a network and its data. It is important to keep in mind that no product or combination of products will create a secure organization by itself. Security is a process; there is no tool that you can "set and forget." All security products are only as secure as the people who configure and maintain them. The purchasing and implementation of security products should be only a percentage of the security budget. Employees tasked with maintaining the security devices should be provided with enough time, training, and equipment to support the products properly. Unfortunately, in many organizations security activities take a back seat to support activities. Highly skilled security professionals are often tasked with help-desk requests such as resetting forgotten passwords, fixing jammed printers, and setting up new employee workstations.

The Bad Guys Are Very Sophisticated

At one time the computer hacker was portrayed as a lone teenager with poor social skills who would break into systems, often for nothing more than bragging rights. As ecommerce has evolved, however, so has the profile of the hacker.

Now that vast collections of credit card numbers and intellectual property can be harvested, organized hacker groups such as Anonymous have been formed to operate as businesses. A document released in 2008 spells it out clearly: "Cybercrime companies that work much like real-world companies are starting to appear and are steadily growing, thanks to the profits they turn. Forget individual hackers or groups of hackers with common goals. Hierarchical cybercrime organizations where each cybercriminal has his or her own role and reward system is what you and your company should be worried about."[10]

9. http://www.viksoe.dk/gmail/ (February 22, 2012).

10. Report: Cybercrime Groups Starting to Operate Like the Mafia. http://arstechnica.com/business/news/2008/07/report-cybercrime-groups-starting-to-operate-like-the-mafia.ars (February 22, 2012).

State-sponsored hacking, which was discussed in security circles for years, received mainstream attention when a Chinese "how-to" hacking video was identified and discussed in the media.[11]

Now that organizations are being attacked by highly motivated and skilled groups of hackers, creating a secure infrastructure is mandatory.

Management Sees Security as a Drain on the Bottom Line

For most organizations, the cost of creating a strong security posture is seen as a necessary evil, similar to purchasing insurance. Organizations do not want to spend the money on it, but the risks of not making the purchase outweigh the costs. Because of this attitude, it is extremely challenging to create a secure organization. The attitude is enforced because requests for security tools are often supported by documents providing the average cost of a security incident instead of showing more concrete benefits of a strong security posture. The problem is exacerbated by the fact that IT professionals speak a language that is different from that of management. IT professionals are generally focused on technology, period. Management is focused on revenue. Concepts such as profitability, asset depreciation, return on investment, realization, and total cost of ownership are the mainstays of management. These are alien concepts to most IT professionals.

Realistically speaking, though, it would be helpful if management would take steps to learn some fundamentals of IT and if IT professionals took the initiative and learned some fundamental business concepts. Learning these concepts is beneficial to the organization because the technical infrastructure can then be implemented in a cost-effective manner, and they are beneficial from a career development perspective for IT professionals.

A Google search of "business skills for IT professionals" will identify numerous educational programs that might prove helpful. For those who do not have the time or inclination to attend a class, some useful materials can be found online. One such document, provided by the Government Chief Information Office of New South Wales, is *A Guide for Government Agencies Calculating Return on Security Investment*.[12] Although it is extremely technical, another often-cited document is *Cost-Benefit Analysis for Network Intrusion Detection Systems*, by Huaqiang Wei, Deb Frinke, Olivia Carter, and Chris Ritter.[13]

Regardless of the approach that is taken, it is important to remember that any tangible cost savings or revenue generation should be used when requesting new security products, tools, or policies. Security professionals often overlook the value of keeping Web portals open for employees. A database that is used by a sales staff to enter contracts or purchases or to check inventory will help generate more revenue if it has no downtime. A database that is not accessible or has been hacked is useless for generating revenue.

Strong security can be used to gain a competitive advantage in the marketplace. Having secured systems that are accessible 24 h/day, 7 days a week, means that an organization can reach and communicate with its clients and prospective clients more efficiently. An organization that becomes recognized as a good custodian of client records and information can incorporate its security record as part of its branding. This is no different from a car company being recognized for its safety record. In discussions of cars and safety, for example, Volvo is always the first manufacturer mentioned.[14]

What must be avoided is the "sky is falling" mentality. There are indeed numerous threats to a network, but we need to be realistic in allocating resources to protect against these threats. As of this writing, the National Vulnerability Database sponsored by the National Institute of Standards and Technology (NIST) lists 49,679 common vulnerabilities and exposures and publishes 14 new vulnerabilities per day.[15] In addition, the media are filled with stories of stolen laptops, credit card numbers, and identities. The volume of threats to a network can be mind numbing. It is important to approach management with "probable threats" as opposed to "describable threats." Probable threats are those that are most likely to have an impact on your business and the ones most likely to get the attention of management.

Perhaps the best approach is to recognize that management, including the board of directors, is required to exhibit a duty of care in protecting it assets that is comparable to that of other organizations in the industry. When a security breach or incident occurs, being able to demonstrate the high level of security within the organization can significantly reduce exposure to lawsuits, fines, and bad press.

The goal of any discussion with management is to convince it that in the highly technical and interconnected world in which we live, having a secure network and infrastructure is a "nonnegotiable requirement of doing business."[14] An excellent resource for both IT professionals and executives that can provide insight into these issues is computer emergency

11. http://www.pcworld.com/businesscenter/article/238655/china_ hacking_video_shows_glimpse_of_falun_gong_attack_tool.html (March 4, 2012).
12. http://services.nsw.gov.au/sites/default/files/ROSI%20Guideline% 20SGW%20%282.2%29%29%20Lockstep.pdf (February 22, 2012).
13. http://citeseerx.ist.psu.edu/viewdoc/summary?doi=10.1.1.20.5607 (February 22, 2012).

14. J. Allen, W. Pollak, Why Leaders Should Care about Security. Podcast, transcript, October 17, 2006. http://www.cert.org/podcast/transcripts/ 11eaders_care.pdf (February 22, 2012).
15. http://nvd.nist.gov/home.cfm (February 22, 2012).

response team's (CERT) technical report, *Governing for Enterprise Security.*[16]

5. TEN STEPS TO BUILDING A SECURE ORGANIZATION

Having identified some of the challenges to building a secure organization, let us now look at 10 ways to build a secure organization successfully. The following steps will put a business in a robust security posture.

Evaluate the Risks and Threats

In attempting to build a secure organization, where should you start? One commonly held belief is that you should initially identify your assets and allocate security resources based on the value of each asset. Although this approach might prove effective, it can lead to some significant vulnerabilities. An infrastructure asset might not hold a high value, for example, but it should be protected with the same effort as a high-value asset. If not, it could be an entry point into your network and provide access to valuable data.

Another approach is to begin by evaluating the threats posed to your organization and your data.

Threats Based on the Infrastructure Model

The first place to start is to identify risks based on an organization's infrastructure model. What infrastructure is in place that is necessary to support the operational needs of the business? A small business that operates out of one office has reduced risks, as opposed to an organization that operates out of numerous facilities, includes a mobile workforce using a variety of handheld devices, and offers products or services through a Web-based interface. An organization that has a large number of telecommuters must take steps to protect its proprietary information that could potentially reside on personally owned computers outside company control. An organization that has widely dispersed and disparate systems will have more risk potential than a centrally located one that uses uniform systems.

Threats Based on the Business Itself

Are there any specific threats for your particular business? Have high-level executives been accused of inappropriate activities whereby stockholders or employees would have incentive to attack the business? Are there any individuals who have a vendetta against the company for real or imagined slights or accidents? Does the community have a

history of antagonism against the organization? A risk management or security team should be asking these questions on a regular basis to evaluate the risks in real time. This part of the security process is often overlooked because of the focus on daily workload.

Threats Based on Industry

Businesses belonging to particular industries are targeted more frequently and more aggressively than are those in other industries. Financial institutions and online retailers are targeted because "that's where the money is." Pharmaceutical manufacturers could be targeted to steal intellectual property, but they also could be targeted by special interest groups, such as those that do not believe in testing drugs on live animals or that have spiritual beliefs opposing a particular product.

Identifying some of these threats requires active involvement in industry-specific trade groups in which businesses share information regarding recent attacks or threats they have identified.

Global Threats

Businesses are often so narrowly focused on their local sphere of influence that they forget that by having a network connected to the Internet, they are now connected to the rest of the world. If a piece of malware identified on the other side of the globe targets the identical software used in your organization, you can be sure that you will eventually be impacted by this malware. In addition, if extremist groups in other countries are targeting your specific industry, you will also be targeted.

Once threats and risks are identified, you can take one of four steps:

- *Ignore the risk.* This is never an acceptable response. This is simply burying your head in the sand and hoping the problem will go away, the business equivalent of not wearing a helmet when riding a motorcycle.
- *Accept the risk.* When the cost to remove the risk is greater than the risk itself, an organization will often decide simply to accept the risk. This is a viable option as long as the organization has spent the time required to evaluate the risk.
- *Transfer the risk.* Organizations with limited staff or other resources could decide to transfer the risk. One method of transferring the risk is to purchase specialized insurance targeted at a specific risk.
- *Mitigate the risk.* Most organizations mitigate risk by applying the appropriate resources to minimize the risks posed to their network and systems.

For organizations that would like to identify and quantify the risks to their network and information assets, CERT provides a free suite of tools to assist with the

---

16. www.cert.org/archive/pdf/05tn023.pdf.

project. Operationally, Critical Threat, Asset, and Vulnerability Evaluation (OCTAVE) provides risk-based assessment for security assessments and planning.[17] There are three versions of OCTAVE: the original OCTAVE, designed for large organizations (more than 300 employees); OCTAVE-S (100 people or fewer); and OCTAVE-Allegro, which is a streamlined version of the tools and focuses specifically on information assets.

Another risk assessment tool that might prove helpful is the Risk Management Framework (RMF) developed by Educause/Internet 2.[18] Targeted at institutions of higher learning, the approach could be applied to other industries. Another framework that might prove helpful was developed by the NIST. This is also referred to as the RMF and includes six steps as part of the process.[19]

Tracking specific threats to specific operating systems, products, and applications can be time-consuming. Visiting the National Vulnerability Database and manually searching for specific issues would not necessarily be an effective use of time. Fortunately, the Center for Education and Research in Information Assurance and Security at Purdue University has a tool called Cassandra that can be configured to notify you of specific threats to your particular products and applications.

Beware of Common Misconceptions

In addressing the security needs of an organization, professionals often succumb to some common misconceptions. Perhaps the most popular one is that the business is obscure, unsophisticated, or boring, simply not a target for malicious activity. Businesses must understand that any network that is connected to the Internet is a potential target regardless of the type of business.

Attackers will attempt to gain access to a network and its systems for several reasons. The first reason is to look around to see what they can find. Regardless of the type of business, personnel information will more than likely be stored on one of the systems. This includes Social Security numbers and other personal information. This type of information is a target—always.

Another possibility is that the attacker will modify the information he or she finds or simply reconfigure the systems to behave abnormally. This type of attacker is not interested in financial gain; he is simply the technology version of teenagers who soap windows, egg cars, and cover property with toilet paper. He attacks because he finds it entertaining to do so. In addition, these attackers could use the systems to store stolen "property" such as child pornography or credit card numbers. If a system is not secure, attackers can store these types of materials on your system and gain access to them at their leisure.

The final possibility is that an attacker will use the hacked systems to mount attacks on other unprotected networks and systems. Computers can be used to mount denial of service attacks, operate as "command and control systems" for a bot network, relay spam, or spread malicious software. Put simply, no computer or network is immune from attack.

Another common misconception is that an organization is immune from problems caused by employees, essentially saying, "We trust all our employees, so we don't have to focus our energies on protecting our assets from them." Although this is common for small businesses in which the owners know everyone, it also occurs in larger organizations in which companies believe they hire only "professionals." It is important to remember that no matter how well job candidates present themselves, a business can never know everything about an employee's past. For this reason it is important for businesses to conduct preemployment background checks on all employees. Furthermore, it is important to conduct these background checks properly and completely.

Many employers trust this task to an online solution that promises to conduct a complete background check on an individual for a minimal fee. Many of these sites play on individuals' lack of understanding of how some of these online databases are generated. These sites might not have access to the records of all jurisdictions, because many jurisdictions either do not make their records available online or do not provide them to these databases. In addition, many of the records are entered by minimum wage data-entry clerks whose accuracy is not always 100%.

Background checks should be conducted by organizations that have the resources at their disposal to obtain court records directly from the courthouses where the records are generated and stored. Some firms have a team of "runners" who visit the courthouses daily to pull records; others have a network of contacts who can visit the courts for them. Look for organizations that are active members of the National Association of Professional Background Screeners.[20] Members of this organization are committed to providing accurate and professional results. Perhaps more important, they can provide counseling regarding the proper approach to take and interpret the results of a background check.

If your organization does not conduct background checks, there are several firms that might be of assistance: Accurate Background, Inc., of Lake Forest, California[21];

---

17. OCTAVE, www.cert.org/octave/ (February 22, 2012).

18. Risk Management Framework, https://wiki.internet2.edu/confluence/display/itsg2/Risk+Management+Framework (February 22, 2012).

19. Risk Management Framework (RMF), http://csrc.nist.gov/groups/SMA/fisma/framework.html (March 4, 2012).

20. National Association of Professional Background Screeners, www.napbs.com.

21. www.accuratebackground.com.

Credential Check, Inc., of Troy, Michigan[22]; and Validity Screening Solutions in Overland Park, Kansas.[23] The websites of these companies provide informational resources to guide you in the process. (Note: For businesses outside the United States or for US businesses with locations overseas, the process might be more difficult because privacy laws could prevent a complete background check from being conducted. The firms we mention here should be able to provide guidance regarding international privacy laws.)

Another misconception is that a preemployment background check is all that is needed. Some erroneously believe that once a person is employed, he or she is "safe" and no longer can pose a threat. However, people's lives and fortunes can change during the course of employment. Financial pressures can cause otherwise law-abiding citizens to take risks they never would have thought possible. Drug and alcohol dependency can alter people's behavior as well. For these and other reasons, it is a good idea to perform an additional background check when an employee is promoted to a position of higher responsibility and trust. If this new position involves handling financial responsibilities, the background check should include a credit check.

Although these steps might sound intrusive, which is sometimes a reason cited not to conduct these types of checks, they can also be beneficial to the employee as well as the employer. If a problem is identified during the check, the employer can often offer assistance to help the employee get through a tough time. Financial counseling and substance abuse counseling often can turn a potentially problematic employee into a loyal and dedicated one.

Yet another common misconception involves IT professionals. Many businesses pay their IT staff fairly high salaries because they understand that having a properly functioning technical infrastructure is important for the continued success of the company. Because the staff is adept at setting up and maintaining systems and networks, there is a general assumption that they know "everything there is to know about computers." It is important to recognize that although an individual might be knowledgeable and technologically sophisticated, no one knows *everything* about computers. Because members of management do not understand technology, they are not in a good position to judge a person's depth of knowledge and experience in the field. Decisions are often based on the certifications a person has achieved during his or her career. Although certifications can be used to determine a person's level of competency, too much weight is given to them. Many certifications require nothing more than some time and dedication to study and pass a certification test. Some

training companies also offer boot camps that guarantee a person will pass the certification test. It is possible for people to become certified without having real-world experience with the operating systems, applications, or hardware addressed by the certification. When judging a person's competency, look at his or her experience level and background first, and if the person has achieved certifications in addition to having significant real-world experience, the certification probably reflects the employee's true capabilities.

The IT staff does a great deal to perpetuate the image that it knows everything about computers. One reason why people become involved in the IT field in the first place is because they have an opportunity to try new things and overcome new challenges. This is why when an IT professional is asked whether she knows how to do something, she will always respond "Yes." In reality, the real answer should be, "No, but I'll figure it out." Although they can frequently figure things out, when it comes to security we must keep in mind that it is a specialized area, and implementing a strong security posture requires significant training and experience.

Provide Security Training for Information Technology Staff: Now and Forever

Just as implementing a robust, secure environment is a dynamic process, creating a highly skilled staff of security professionals is a dynamic process. Even though an organization's technical infrastructure might not change frequently, new vulnerabilities are being discovered and new attacks are being launched on a regular basis. In addition, few organizations have a stagnant infrastructure; employees are constantly requesting new software and more technologies are added in an effort to improve efficiencies. Each new addition likely adds additional security vulnerabilities.

It is important for the IT staff to be prepared to identify and respond to new threats and vulnerabilities. It is recommended that those interested in gaining a deep security understanding start with a vendor-neutral program. A vendor-neutral program is one that focuses on concepts rather than specific products. The SysAdmin, Audit, Network, Security (SANS) Institute offers two introductory programs: Intro to Information Security (Security 301),[24] a 5-day class designed for people just starting out in the security field, and the SANS Security Essentials Bootcamp (Security 401),[25] a 6-day class designed for people with some security experience. Each class is also available as a

---

22. www.credentialcheck.com.
23. www.validityscreening.com.

24. https://www.sans.org/security-training/intro-information-security-106-mid.
25. https://www.sans.org/security-training/security-essentials-bootcamp-style-61-mid.

self-study program, and each can be used to prepare for a specific certification.

Another option is to start with a program that follows the CompTia Security + certification requirements, such as the Global Knowledge Essentials of Information Security.[26] Some colleges offer similar programs.

Once a person has a good fundamental background in security, he should undergo vendor-specific training to apply the concepts learned to specific applications and security devices employed in the work environment.

A great resource for keeping up with current trends in security is to become actively involved in a security-related trade organization. The key concept here is *actively involved*. Many professionals join organizations so that they can add an item to the "professional affiliations" section of their resume. Becoming actively involved means attending meetings on a regular basis and serving on a committee or in a position on the executive board. Although this seems like a daunting time commitment, the benefit is that the professional develops a network of resources that can be available to provide insight, serve as a sounding board, or provide assistance when a problem arises. Participating in these associations is a cost-effective way to get up to speed with current security trends and issues. Here are some organizations[27] that can prove helpful:

- ASIS International, the largest security-related organization in the world, focuses primarily on physical security but has started addressing computer security as well
- ISACA, formerly the Information Systems Audit and Control Association
- High Technology Crime Investigation Association (HTCIA)
- Information Systems Security Association (ISSA)
- InfraGard, a joint public and private organization sponsored by the Federal Bureau of Investigation (FBI)

In addition to monthly meetings, many local chapters of these organizations sponsor regional conferences that are usually reasonably priced and attract nationally recognized experts.

Arguably one of the best ways to determine whether an employee has a strong grasp of information security concepts is whether she can achieve the Certified Information Systems Security Professional (CISSP) certification. Candidates for this certification are tested on their understanding of the following 10 knowledge domains:

- access control
- application security

- business continuity and disaster recovery planning
- cryptography
- information security and risk management
- legal regulations, compliance, and investigations
- operations security
- physical (environmental) security
- security architecture and design
- telecommunications and network security

What makes this certification so valuable is that the candidate must have a minimum of 5 years of professional experience in the information security field or 4 years of experience and a college degree. To maintain certification, a certified individual is required to attend 120 h of continuing professional education during the 3-year certification cycle. This ensures that those holding the CISSP credential are staying up to date with current trends in security. CISSP certification is maintained by the Internet Systems Consortium.[28]

Think "Outside the Box"

For most businesses, the threat to their intellectual assets and technical infrastructure comes from the "bad guys" sitting outside their organizations, trying to break in. These organizations establish strong perimeter defenses, essentially "boxing in" their assets. However, internal employees have access to proprietary information to do their jobs, and they often disseminate this information to areas where it is no longer under the control of the employer. This dissemination of data is generally not performed with any malicious intent, but simply for employees to have access to data so that they can perform their job responsibilities more efficiently. However, this becomes a problem when an employee leaves and the organization takes no steps to collect or control their proprietary information in the possession of their now exemployee.

One of the most overlooked threats to intellectual property is the innocuous and now ubiquitous USB flash drive. These devices, which are the size of a tube of lipstick, are the modern-day floppy disk in terms of portable data storage. They are a convenient way to transfer data between computers. However, the difference between these devices and a floppy disk is that USB flash drives can store a large amount of data. A 16-GB USB flash drive has the same storage capacity as more than 10,000 floppy disks! As of this writing, a 16-GB USB flash drive can be purchased for less than $15. Businesses should keep in mind that as time goes by, the capacity of these devices will increase and the price will decrease, making them attractive to employees.

26. http://www.globalknowledge.com/training/course.asp? pageid=1&courseid=16259&catid=191&country=United+States.
27. ASIS International, www.asisonline.org; ISACA, www.isaca.org; HTCIA, www.htcia.org; ISSA, www.issa.org; InfraGard, www.infragard. net.
28. (ISC)², www.isc2.org.

These devices are not the only threat to data. Because other devices can be connected to the computer through the USB port, digital cameras, MP3 players, and external hard drives can be used to remove data from a computer and the network to which it is connected. Most people recognize that external hard drives pose a threat, but they may not recognize other devices as a threat. Cameras and music players are designed to store images and music, but to a computer they are simply additional mass storage devices. It is difficult for people to understand that an iPod can carry word-processing documents, databases, and spreadsheets as well as music. Fortunately, Microsoft Windows tracks the devices that are connected to a system in a Registry key, HKEY_Local_Machine\System\ControlSet00x\Enum\USBStor. It might prove interesting to look in this key on your own computer to see what types of devices have been connected. Fig. 2.2 shows a wide array of devices that have been connected to a system that includes USB flash drives, a digital camera, and several external hard drives.

Windows Vista has an additional key that tracks connected devices: HKEY_Local_Machine\Software\Microsoft\Windows Portable Devices\Devices.[29] (Note: Analyzing the Registry is a great way to investigate the activities of computer users. For many, however, the Registry is tough to navigate and interpret. If you are interested in understanding more about the Registry, you might want to download and play with Harlan Carvey's RegRipper.[30])

Another threat to information that carries data outside the walls of the organization is the plethora of handheld devices currently in use. Many of these devices have the ability to send and receive email as well as create, store, and transmit word-processing, spreadsheet, and PDF files. Although most employers will not purchase these devices

for their employees, they are more than happy to allow their employees to sync their personally owned devices with their corporate computers. Client contact information, business plans, and other materials can easily be copied from a system. Some businesses think that they have this threat under control because they provide their employees with corporate-owned devices and they can collect these devices when employees leave their employment. The only problem with this attitude is that employees can easily copy data from the devices to their home computers before the devices are returned.

Because of the threat of portable data storage devices and handheld devices, it is important for an organization to establish policies outlining the acceptable use of these devices as well as implement an enterprise-grade solution to control how, when, or if data can be copied to them. Filling all USB ports with epoxy is a cheap solution, but it is not really effective. Fortunately, several products can protect against this type of data leak. DeviceWall from Frontrange Solutions[31] and GFI Endpoint Security[32] are two popular ones.

DOXing

With the interest and ability to store data on third-party systems, it becomes increasingly necessary for security professionals to make "thinking outside the box" a part of their set of skills. Although it does not seem that security professionals should be concerned with data being stored on systems other than their own, the fact that materials critical and confidential to business are stored on third-party systems means that the success or profitability of a business requires that this information be secured.

In addition to data leaving an organization on thumb drives or to an external storage site, seemingly innocuous data can be collected from a variety of sources and can be used in a negative manner against an individual or organization. This process is called DOXing and is defined by the ProHackingTricks:

> DOXing is a way of tracing someone or getting information about an individual using sources on the internet and social engineering techniques. Its term was derived from—Documents—as a matter of fact it's the retrieval of Documents on a person or an organization.[33]

DOXing is essentially high-tech dumpster diving, in which information is gathered from the Internet as opposed to a waste bin. Initially developed by the hacker group

FIGURE 2.2   Gmail Drive login screen.

29. http://windowsir.blogspot.com/2008/06/portable-devices-on-vista.html (February 29, 2012).
30. RegRipper, www.regripper.net.

31. DeviceWall, http://www.frontrange.com/software/it-asset-management/endpoint-security.
32. http://www.gfi.com/usb-device-control.
33. http://prohackingtricks.blogspot.com/2011/06/doxing-way-of-tracing-anonymous-people.html (February 29, 2012).

Anonymous to harass law enforcement, the tactic was also employed by the Occupy Wall Street protesters. This technique is possible because individuals and organizations do not understand the significance of data posted on social networking sites, blogs, corporate websites, and other online repositories. A single piece of information posted on a website may not in and of itself have significance, but when combined with materials collected from a variety of sites, that small piece of information may help fill in a complete (and possibly uncomplimentary) picture of a person or business. Whereas this process has been targeted at law enforcement, it is just a matter of time before it will be used against executives and corporations. Being aware of this threat and educating others are now a part of the security process.

Train Employees: Develop a Culture of Security

One of the greatest security assets is a business's own employees, but only if they have been properly trained to comply with security policies and to identify potential security problems.

Many employees do not understand the significance of various security policies and implementations. As mentioned previously, they consider these policies to be nothing more than an inconvenience. Gaining the support and allegiance of employees takes time, but it is time well spent. Begin by carefully explaining the reasons behind any security implementation. One of the reasons could be ensuring employee productivity, but focus primarily on the security issues. File sharing using LimeWire and Shareazza might keep employees away from work, but they can also open up holes in a firewall. Downloading and installing unapproved software can install malicious software that can infect user systems, causing computers to function slowly or not at all. Although most employees understand that opening unknown or unexpected email attachments can lead to a malware infection, most are unaware of the advanced capabilities of recent malicious code. "Advanced Persistent Threat," or the ability for a system to remain infected despite the diligent use of antivirus programs, has become a major problem. Employees need to understand that indiscriminate Web surfing can result in "drive-by" installs of malware.

Perhaps the most direct way to gain employee support is to let employees know that the money needed to respond to attacks and fix problems initiated by users is money that is then not available for raises and promotions. Letting employees know that they now have some "skin in the game" is one way to get them involved in security efforts. If a budget is set aside to respond to security problems and employees help stay well within the budget, the difference between the money spent and the actual budget could be divided among employees as a bonus. Not only would employees be more likely to speak up if they noticed network or system slowdowns, they would probably be more likely to confront strangers wandering through the facility.

Another mechanism that can be used to gain security allies is to provide advice regarding the proper security mechanisms for securing home computers. Although some might not see this as directly benefiting the company, keep in mind that many employees have corporate data on their home computers. This advice can come from periodic live presentations (offer refreshments and attendance will be higher) or from a periodic newsletter that is either mailed or emailed to employees' personal addresses.

The goal of these activities is to encourage employees to approach management or the security team voluntarily. When this begins to happen on a regular basis, you will have expanded the capabilities of your security team and created a much more secure organization.

The security expert Roberta Bragg used to tell a story of one of her clients who took this concept to a high level. The client provided the company mail clerk with a Wi-Fi hotspot detector and promised him a free steak dinner for every unauthorized wireless access point he could find on the premises. The mail clerk was happy to have the opportunity to earn three free steak dinners.

Identify and Use Built-in Security Features of the Operating System and Applications

Many organizations and systems administrators state that they cannot create a secure organization because they have limited resources and simply do not have the funds to purchase robust security tools. This is a ridiculous approach to security because all operating systems and many applications include security mechanisms that require no organizational resources other than time to identify and configure these tools. For Microsoft Windows operating systems, a terrific resource is the online Microsoft TechNet Library.[34] Under the Solutions Accelerators link, you can find security resources for all recent Microsoft products. An example of the tools available is the Microsoft Security Compliance Manager. Fig. 2.3 shows the initial screen for this product.

TechNet is a great resource and can provide insight into managing numerous security issues, from Microsoft Office 2007 to security risk management. These documents can assist in implementing the built-in security features of Microsoft Windows products. Assistance is needed in identifying many of these capabilities because they are often hidden from view and are turned off by default.

---

34. Microsoft TechNet Library. http://technet.microsoft.com.

FIGURE 2.3 Microsoft security compliance manager.

One of the biggest current concerns in an organization is data leaks, which are ways in which confidential information can leave an organization despite robust perimeter security. As mentioned previously, USB flash drives are one cause of data leaks; another is the recovery of data found in the unallocated clusters of a computer's hard drive. Unallocated clusters, or *free space*, as it is commonly called, is the area of a hard drive where the operating system and applications dump their artifacts or residual data. Although these data are not viewable through the graphical user interface (GUI), the data can easily be identified (and sometimes recovered) using a hex editor such as WinHex[35] or one of several commercially available computer forensics programs. Fig. 2.4 shows the contents of unallocated clusters being displayed by EnCase Forensic.

If a computer is stolen or donated, it is possible that someone could access the data located in unallocated clusters. For this reason, many people struggle to find an appropriate "disk-scrubbing" utility. Many such commercial utilities exist, but one is built into Microsoft Windows operating systems. The command-line program cipher.exe is designed to display or alter the encryption of directories

(files) stored on new technology file system partitions. Few people know about this command; even fewer are familiar with the /w switch. Here is a description of the switch from the program's Help file:

Removes data from available unused disk space on the entire volume. If this option is chosen, all other options are ignored. The directory specified can be anywhere in a local volume. If it is a mount point or points to a directory in another volume, the data on that volume will be removed.

To use Cipher, click **Start** | and type **cmd** in the "**Search Programs and Files**" Bod. When the cmd.exe window opens, type **cipher/w:folder**, where *folder* is any folder in the volume that you want to clean, and then press **Enter**. Fig. 2.5 shows Cipher wiping a folder.

For more on secure file deletion issues, see the author's white paper in the SANS reading room, "Secure file deletion: Fact or fiction?"[36]

Another source of data leaks is the personal and editing information that can be associated with Microsoft Office files. In Microsoft Word 2003 you can configure the application to remove personal information on save and to

35. WinHex, www.x-ways.net/winhex/index-m.html.

36. Secure File Deletion: Fact or Fiction? www.sans.org/reading_room/whitepapers/incident/631.php (February 29, 2012).

FIGURE 2.4 View of unallocated clusters showing a Google query.

```
C:\Windows\system32\cmd.exe - cipher /W:C:\Secretstuff

C:\>cipher /W:C:\Secretstuff
To remove as much data as possible, please close all other applications while
running CIPHER /W.
Writing 0x00
```

FIGURE 2.5 Cipher wiping a folder called Secretstuff.

warn you when you are about to print, share, or send a document containing tracked changes or comments.

To access this feature, within Word click **Tools | Options** and then click the **Security** tab. Toward the bottom of the security window you will notice the two options described previously. Simply select the options you want to use. Fig. 2.9 shows these options. Microsoft Office 2007 made this tool more robust and accessible. A separate tool called Document Inspector can be accessed by clicking the **Microsoft Office** button, pointing to **Prepare Document**, and then clicking **Inspect Document**. Then select the items you want to remove.

In Microsoft Office 2010, click on **File, Info**, and **Check for Issues** to open the "Document Inspector" Window.

Implementing a strong security posture often begins by making the login process more robust. This includes increasing the complexity of the login password. All passwords can be cracked given enough time and resources, but the more difficult you make cracking a password, the greater the possibility the asset the password protects will stay protected.

All operating systems have some mechanism to increase the complexity of passwords. In Microsoft Windows 7, the preceding can be accomplished thus:

1. Open Local Security Policy by clicking the Start button, typing secpol.msc into the Search box, and then clicking secpol. If you are prompted for an administrator password or confirmation, type the password or provide confirmation.

2. In the Navigation pane, double-click Account Policies, and then click Password Policy.
3. Double-click the item in the Policy list that you want to change.[37]

In the right-hand panel you can enable password complexity. Once this is enabled, passwords must contain at least three of the four following password groups[35]:

- English uppercase characters (A through Z)
- English lowercase characters (a through z)
- Numerals (0–9)
- Nonalphabetic characters (such as !, $, #, and %)

It is important to recognize that all operating systems have embedded tools to assist with security. They often require a little research to find, but the time spent in identifying them is less than the money spent on purchasing additional security products or recovering from a security breach.

Although not yet used by many corporations, Mac OS X has some robust security features, including FileVault, which provides the ability to create an encrypted disk, including external drives. Fig. 2.6 shows the security options for Mac OS X Lion.

Monitor Systems

Even with the most robust security tools in place, it is important to monitor your systems. All security products

---

37. http://windows.microsoft.com/en-US/windows-vista/Change-password-policy-settings (February 29, 2012).

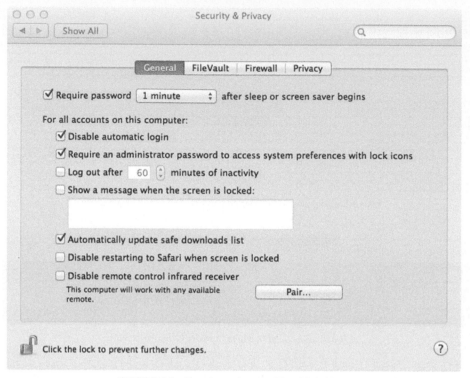

FIGURE 2.6 Security options for Mac OS X Lion.

are man-made and can fail or be compromised. As with any other aspect of technology, one should never rely on simply one product or tool. Enabling logging on your systems is one way to put your organization in a position to identify problem areas. The problem is determining what should be logged. There are some security standards that can help with this determination. One of these standards is the Payment Card Industry Data Security Standard (PCI DSS).[38] Requirement 10 of the PCI DSS states that organizations must "track and monitor access to network resources and cardholder data." If you simply substitute *confidential information* for the phrase *cardholder data*, this requirement is an excellent approach to a log management program. Requirement 10 is reproduced here:

Logging mechanisms and the ability to track user activities are critical. The presence of logs in all environments allows thorough tracking and analysis if something does go wrong. Determining the cause of a compromise is very difficult without system activity logs:

1. Establish a process for linking all access to system components (especially access done with administrative privileges such as root) to each individual user.
2. Implement automated audit trails for all system components to reconstruct the following events:
   - all individual user accesses to cardholder data

---

38. PCI DSS. www.pcisecuritystandards.org.

   - all actions taken by any individual with root or administrative privileges
   - access to all audit trails
   - invalid logical access attempts
   - use of identification and authentication mechanisms
   - initialization of the audit logs
   - creation and deletion of system-level objects
3. Record at least the following audit trail entries for all system components for each event:
   - user identification
   - type of event
   - date and time
   - success or failure indication
   - origination of event
   - identity or name of affected data, system component, or resource
4. Synchronize all critical system clocks and times.
5. Secure audit trails so that they cannot be altered:
   - Limit viewing of audit trails to those with a job-related need.
   - Protect audit trail files from unauthorized modifications.
   - Promptly back up audit trail files to a centralized log server or media that are difficult to alter.
   - Copy logs for wireless networks onto a log server on the internal local area network.
   - Use file integrity monitoring and change detection software on logs to ensure that existing log data

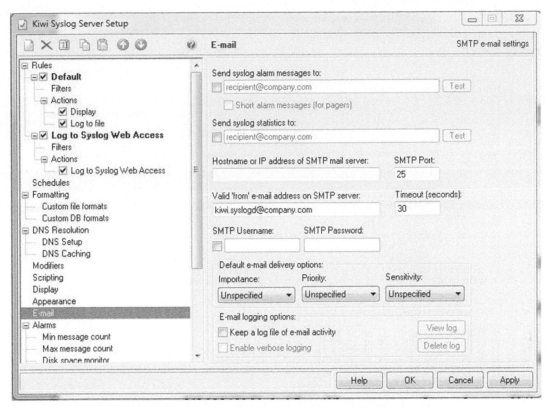

FIGURE 2.7 Kiwi Syslog Server Email Alert Configuration screen.

cannot be changed without generating alerts (although new data being added should not cause an alert).

6. Review logs for all system components at least daily. Log reviews must include servers that perform security functions such as intrusion detection system and authentication, authorization, and accounting protocol servers (for example, RADIUS). Note: Log harvesting, parsing, and alerting tools may be used to achieve compliance.

7. Retain audit trail history for at least 1 year, with a minimum of 3 months' online availability.

Item 6 looks overwhelming because few organizations have the time to review log files manually. Fortunately, there are tools that will collect and parse log files from a variety of sources. All of these tools have the ability to notify individuals of a particular event. One simple tool is the Kiwi Syslog Server[39] for Microsoft Windows. Fig. 2.7 shows the configuration screen for setting up email alerts in Kiwi.

Additional log parsing tools include Microsoft's Log Parser[40] and Swatch for Unix.[41] Commercial tools include

ArcSight Logger,[42] GFI EventsManager,[43] and LogRhythm.[44]

An even more detailed approach to monitoring your systems is to install a packet-capturing tool on your network so that you can analyze and capture traffic in real time. One tool that can be helpful is Wireshark, which is "an award-winning network protocol analyzer developed by an international team of networking experts."[45] Wireshark is based on the original packet capture tool, Ethereal. Analyzing network traffic is not a trivial task and requires some training, but it is perhaps the most accurate way to determine what is happening on your network. Fig. 2.8 shows Wireshark monitoring the traffic on a wireless interface.

Hire a Third Party to Audit Security

Regardless of how talented your staff is, there is always the possibility that they overlooked something or inadvertently misconfigured a device or setting. For this reason it is important to bring in an extra set of "eyes, ears, and hands" to review your organization's security posture.

---

39. Kiwi Syslog Server. www.kiwisyslog.com.
40. Log Parser 2.2. http://www.microsoft.com/download/en/details.aspx?id=24659.
41. Swatch, http://sourceforge.net/projects/swatch.
42. ArcSight Logger, http://www.arcsight.com/products/products-logger.
43. GFI EventsManager, www.gfi.com/eventsmanager.
44. LogRhythm, http://www.logrhythm.com.
45. Wireshark, www.wireshark.org.

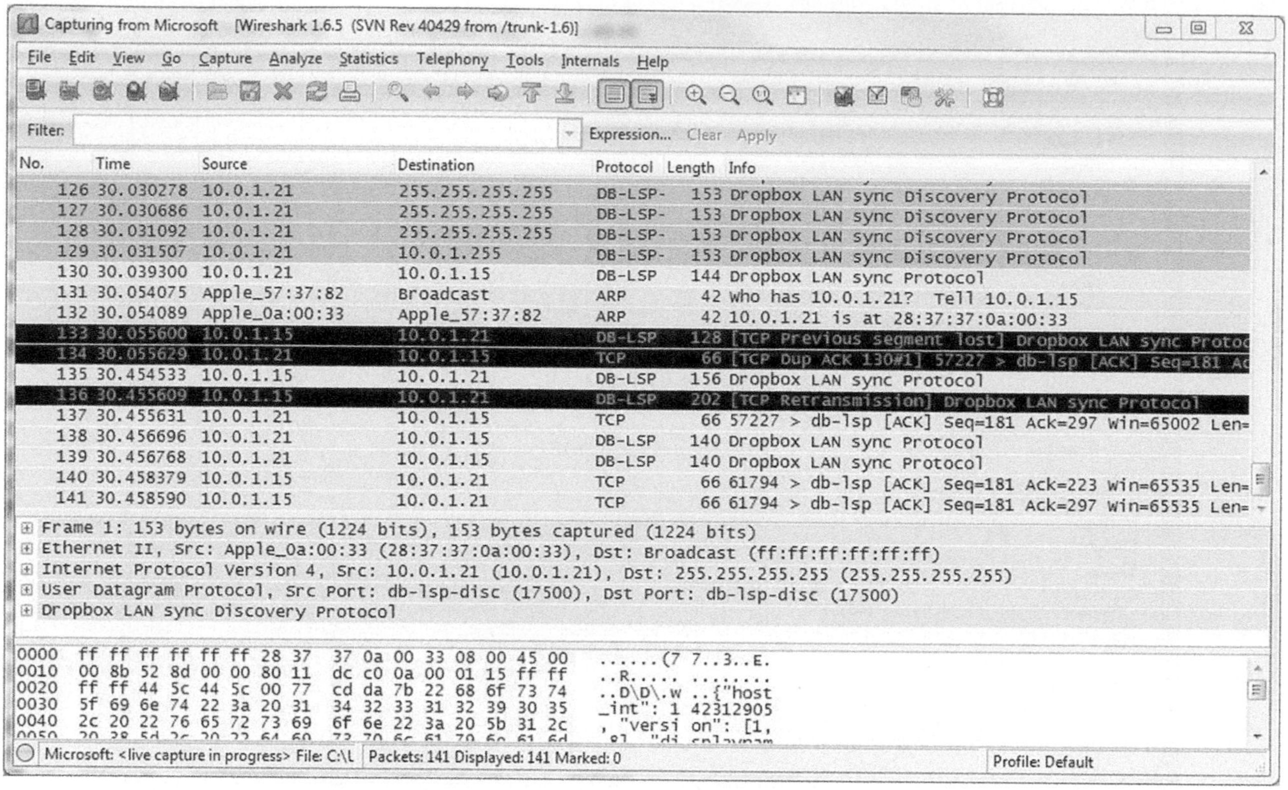

FIGURE 2.8   The protocol analyzer Wireshark monitoring a wireless interface.

Although some IT professionals will become paranoid about having a third party review their work, intelligent staff members will recognize that a security review by outsiders can be a great learning opportunity. The advantage of having a third party review your systems is that the outsiders have experience in reviewing a wide range of systems, applications, and devices in a variety of industries. They will know what works well and what might work but will cause problems in the future. They are also more likely to be up to speed on new vulnerabilities and the latest product updates. Why? Because this is all they do.

They are not encumbered by administrative duties, internal politics, and help desk requests. They will be more objective than in-house staff, and they will be in a position to make recommendations after their analysis.

The third-party analysis should involve a two-pronged approach: They should identify how the network appears to attackers and how secure the system is if attackers make it past the perimeter defenses. You do not want to have "Tootsie Pop security" (a hard crunchy shell with a soft center). The external review, often called a *penetration test*, can be accomplished in several ways; the first is a *no knowledge* approach, in which the consultants are provided with absolutely no information regarding the network and systems before their analysis. Although this is a realistic approach, it can be time-consuming and expensive. Using this approach, consultants must use publicly available information to start enumerating systems for testing. A *partial knowledge* analysis is more efficient and less expensive. If provided with a network topology diagram and a list of registered Internet Protocol addresses, third-party reviewers can complete the review more quickly and the results can be addressed in a much more timely fashion. Once the penetration test is complete, a review of the internal network can be initiated. The audit of the internal network will identify open shares, unpatched systems, open ports, weak passwords, rogue systems, and many other issues.

Do Not Forget the Basics

Many organizations spend a great deal of time and money addressing perimeter defenses and overlook some fundamental security mechanisms, as described here.

Change Default Account Passwords

Nearly all network devices come preconfigured with a password—username combination. This combination is included with the setup materials and is documented in numerous locations. Often these devices are the gateways to the Internet or other internal networks. If these default passwords are not changed upon configuration, it becomes a trivial matter for an attacker to get into these systems.

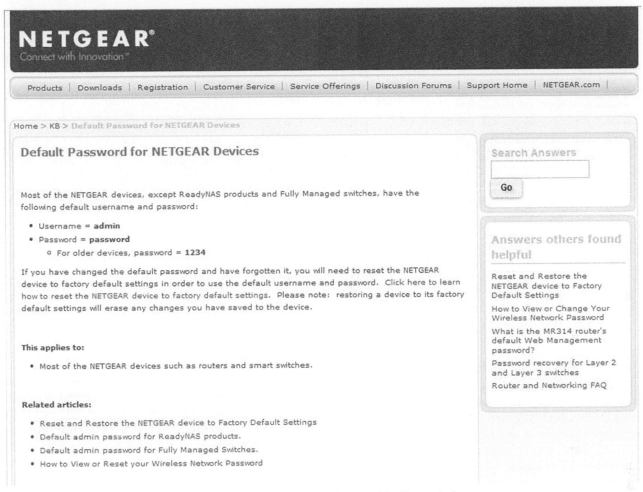

FIGURE 2.9 Default username and password for Netgear devices.

Hackers can find password lists on the Internet,[46] and vendors include default passwords in their online manuals. For example, Fig. 2.9 shows the default username and password for Netgear devices.

Use Robust Passwords

With the increased processing power of our computers and password-cracking software such as the Passware products[47] and AccessData's Password Recovery Toolkit,[48] cracking passwords is fairly simple and straightforward. For this reason it is extremely important to create robust passwords. Complex passwords are hard for users to remember, though, so it is a challenge to create passwords that can be remembered without writing them down. One solution is to use the first letter of each word in a phrase, such as "**I** **l**ike **t**o **e**at **i**mported **c**heese **f**rom **H**olland." This

becomes *IlteicfH*, which is an eight-character password using upper- and lowercase letters. This can be made even more complex by substituting an exclamation point for the letter *I* and substituting the number 3 for the letter "e," so that the password becomes *!lt3icfH*. This is a fairly robust password that can be remembered easily.

Close Unnecessary Ports

Ports on a computer are logical access points for communication over a network. Knowing what ports are open on your computers will allow you to understand the types of access points that exist. Well-known port numbers are 0–1023. Some easily recognized ports and what they are used for are:

- Port 21: File Transfer Protocol
- Port 23: Telnet
- Port 25: Simple Mail Transfer Protocol
- Port 53: Domain Name System
- Port 80: Hypertext Transfer Protocol
- Port 110: Post Office Protocol

---

46. http://cirt.net/passwords.

47. Passware. www.lostpassword.com.

48. Password Recovery Toolkit. http://accessdata.com/products/computer-forensics/decryption.

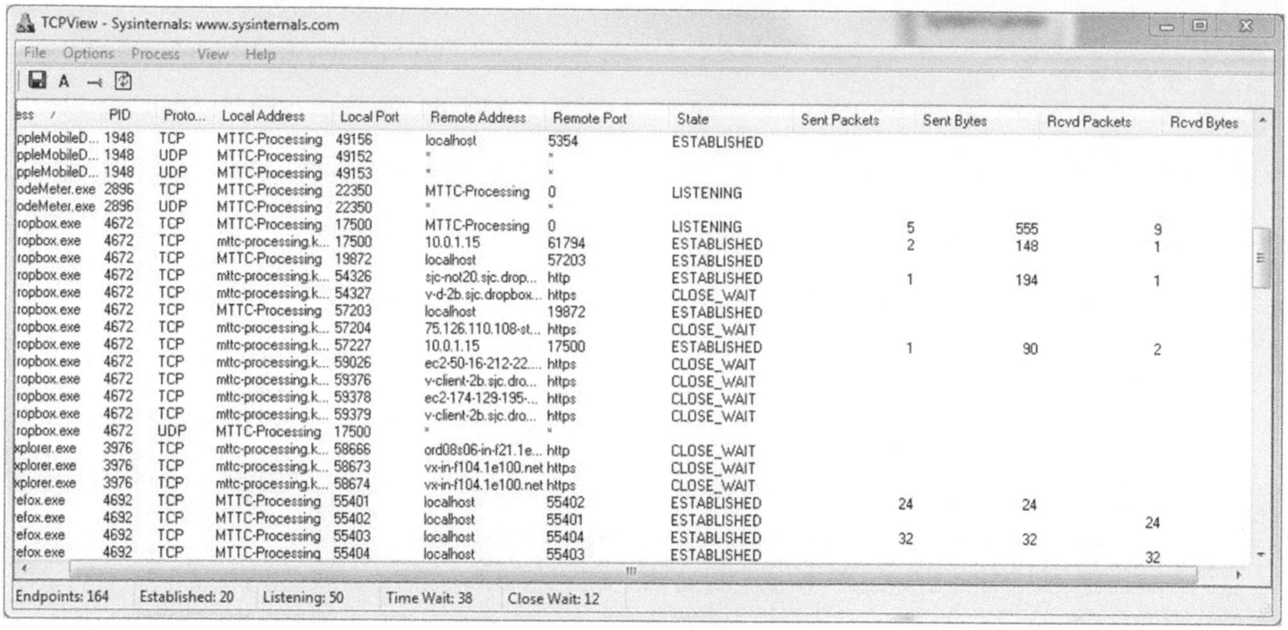

FIGURE 2.10   Sample output from Fport.

- Port 119: Network News Transfer Protocol

Because open ports that are not necessary can be an entrance into your systems, and open ports that are open unexpectedly could be a sign of malicious software, identifying open ports is an important security process. Several tools will allow you to identify open ports. The built-in command-line tool *netstat* will allow you to identify open ports and process IDs by using the following switches:

- *a* displays all connections and listening ports
- *n* displays addresses and port numbers in numerical form
- displays the owning process ID associated with each connection

(Note: In UNIX, netstat is also available but uses the following switches: *atvp*.)

Other tools that can prove helpful are CurrPorts,[49] a GUI tool that allows you to export the results in delimited format, and TCPView,[50] a tool provided by Microsoft. Sample results are shown in Fig. 2.10.

Patch, Patch, Patch

Nearly all operating systems have a mechanism for automatically checking for updates. This notification system should be turned on. Although there is some debate as to whether updates should be installed automatically, systems administrators should at least be notified of updates. They might not want to have them installed automatically, because patches and updates have been known to cause more problems than they solve. However, administrators should not wait too long before installing updates, because this can expose systems to attack unnecessarily. A simple tool that can help keep track of system updates is the Microsoft Baseline Security Analyzer,[51] which also will examine other fundamental security configurations.

Use Administrator Accounts for Administrative Tasks

A common security vulnerability is created when systems administrators conduct administrative or personal tasks while logged into their computers with administrator rights. Tasks such as checking email, surfing the Internet, and testing questionable software can expose the computer to malicious software. This means that the malicious software can run with administrator privileges, which can create serious problems. Administrators should log into their systems using a standard user account to prevent malicious software from gaining control of their computers.

Restrict Physical Access

With a focus on technology, it is often easy to overlook nontechnical security mechanisms. If an intruder can gain physical access to a server or other infrastructure asset, the intruder will own the organization. Critical systems should

---

49. CurrPorts, http://www.nirsoft.net/utils/cports.html.
50. TCPView, http://technet.microsoft.com/en-us/sysinternals/bb897437.

51. Microsoft Baseline Security Analyzer, http://technet.microsoft.com/en-us/security/cc184923.

be kept in secure areas. A secure area is one that provides the ability to control access only to those who need access to the systems as part of their job responsibilities. A room that is kept locked using a key that is provided only to the systems administrator, with the only duplicate stored in a safe in the office manager's office, is a good start. The room should have no windows that can open. In addition, the room should have no labels or signs identifying it as a server room or network operations center. The equipment should not be stored in a closet where other employees, custodians, or contractors can gain access. The validity of your security mechanisms should be reviewed during a third-party vulnerability assessment.

Do Not Forget Paper!

With the advent of advanced technology, people have forgotten how information was stolen in the past: on paper. Managing paper documents is fairly straightforward. Locking file cabinets should be used, and locked, consistently. Extra copies of proprietary documents, document drafts, and expired internal communications are some of the materials that should be shredded. A policy should be created to tell employees what they should and should not do with printed documents. The following example of the theft of trade secrets underscores the importance of protecting paper documents:

> A company surveillance camera caught Coca-Cola employee Joya Williams at her desk looking through files and "stuffing documents into bags," Nahmias and FBI officials said. Then in June, an undercover FBI agent met at the Atlanta airport with another of the defendants, handing him $30,000 in a yellow Girl Scout Cookie box in exchange for an Armani bag containing confidential Coca-Cola documents and a sample of a product the company was developing, officials said.[52]

The steps to achieving security mentioned in this chapter are only the beginning. They should provide some insight into where to start building a secure organization.

Finally, let us briefly look at the process of building and assessing the security controls in organizational information systems, including the activities carried out by organizations and assessors to prepare for security control assessments; the development of security assessment plans; the conduct of security control assessments and the analysis, documentation, and reporting of assessment results; and postassessment report analysis and follow-on activities carried out by organizations.

6. PREPARING FOR THE BUILDING OF SECURITY CONTROL ASSESSMENTS

Conducting security control assessments in today's complex environment of sophisticated IT infrastructures and high-visibility, mission-critical applications can be difficult, challenging, and resource-intensive. Success requires cooperation and collaboration among all parties with a vested interest in the organization's information security posture, including information system owners, common control providers, authorizing officials, chief information officers, senior information security officers, and chief executive officers/heads of departments. Establishing an appropriate set of expectations before, during, and after the assessment is paramount to achieving an acceptable outcome: that is, producing information necessary to help the authorizing official make a credible, risk-based decision regarding whether to place the information system into operation or continue its operation.

Thorough preparation by the organization and the assessors is an important aspect of conducting effective security control assessments. Preparatory activities address a range of issues relating to the cost, schedule, and performance of the assessment (see checklist: "An Agenda for Action for Preparatory Activities").

7. SUMMARY

In preparation for the assessment of security controls, this chapter covered how necessary background information is assembled and made available to the assessors or assessment team to build a secure organization. To the extent necessary to support the specific assessment, the organization identifies and arranges access to:

- elements of the organization responsible for developing, documenting, disseminating, reviewing, and updating all security policies and associated procedures for implementing policy-compliant controls;
- the security policies for the information system and any associated implementing procedures;
- individuals or groups responsible for the development, implementation, operation, and maintenance of security controls;
- any materials (security plans, records, schedules, assessment reports, after-action reports, agreements, and authorization packages) associated with the implementation and operation of security controls;
- the objects to be assessed.

The availability of essential documentation and access to key organizational personnel and the information system being assessed are paramount to a successful assessment of the security controls.

When building secure organizations, one must consider both the technical expertise and the level of independence required in selecting security control

52. Accused in Theft of Coke Secrets, The Washington Post (July 26, 2006). www.washingtonpost.com/wp-dyn/content/article/2006/07/05/AR2006070501717.html (February 29, 2012).

An Agenda for Action for Preparatory Activities

From the organizational perspective, preparing for the building of a security control assessment includes the following key activities (check all tasks completed):

_____**1.** Ensure that appropriate policies covering security control assessments are in place and understood by all affected organizational elements.

_____**2.** Ensure that all steps in the RMF before the security control assessment step have been completed successfully and received appropriate management oversight.

_____**3.** Ensure that security controls identified as common controls (and the common portion of hybrid controls) have been assigned to appropriate organizational entities (common control providers) for development and implementation.

_____**4.** Establish the objective and scope of the security control assessment (the purpose of the assessment and what is being assessed).

_____**5.** Notify key organizational officials of the impending security control assessment and allocate necessary resources to carry out the assessment.

_____**6.** Establish appropriate communication channels among organizational officials with an interest in the security control assessment.

_____**7.** Establish time frames for completing the security control assessment and key milestone decision points required by the organization to manage the assessment effectively.

_____**8.** Identify and select a competent assessor/assessment team that will be responsible for conducting the security control assessment, considering issues of assessor independence.

_____**9.** Collect artifacts to provide to the assessor/assessment team (policies, procedures, plans, specifications, designs, records, administrator/operator manuals, information system documentation, interconnection agreements, and previous assessment results).

_____**10.** Establish a mechanism between the organization and the assessor and/or assessment team to minimize ambiguities or misunderstandings about security control implementation or security control weaknesses/deficiencies identified during the assessment.

Security control assessors/assessment teams begin preparing for the assessment:

_____**11.** Obtain a general understanding of the organization's operations (including mission, functions, and business processes) and how the information system that is the subject of the security control assessment supports those organizational operations.

_____**12.** Obtain an understanding of the structure of the information system (system architecture).

_____**13.** Identify the organizational entities responsible for the development and implementation of the common controls (or the common portion of hybrid controls) supporting the information system.

_____**14.** Establish appropriate organizational points of contact needed to carry out the security control assessment.

_____**15.** Obtain artifacts needed for the security control assessment (policies, procedures, plans, specifications, designs, records, administrator/operator manuals, information system documentation, interconnection agreements, and previous assessment results).

_____**16.** Obtain previous assessment results that may be reused appropriately for the security control assessment [reports, audits, vulnerability scans, physical security inspections, prior assessments, developmental testing and evaluation, vendor flaw remediation activities, and International Organization for Standardization/International Electrotechnical Commission 15408 (Common Criteria) evaluations].

_____**17.** Meet with appropriate organizational officials to ensure common understanding for assessment objectives and the proposed rigor and scope of the assessment.

_____**18.** Develop a security assessment plan.

---

assessors. Organizations must ensure that security control assessors possess the required skills and technical expertise to carry out assessments of system-specific, hybrid, and common controls successfully. This includes knowledge of and experience with the specific hardware, software, and firmware components employed by the organization. An independent assessor is any individual or group capable of conducting an impartial assessment of security controls employed within or inherited by an information system.

Impartiality implies that assessors are free from any perceived or actual conflicts of interest with respect to the development, operation, and/or management of the information system or the determination of the effectiveness of security control. The authorizing official or designated representative determines the required level of independence for security control assessors based on the results of the security categorization process for the information system and the ultimate risk to organizational operations and assets, individuals, and other organizations. The authorizing official determines whether the level of assessor independence is sufficient to provide confidence that the assessment results produced are sound and can be used to make a risk-based decision regarding whether to place the information system into operation or continue its operation.

Independent security control assessment services can be obtained from other elements within the organization or can be contracted to a public or private sector entity outside the organization. In special situations (for example, when the organization that owns the information system is small or the organizational structure requires the security control assessment to be accomplished by individuals that are in the developmental, operational, and/or management chain of the system owner), independence in the assessment process can be achieved by ensuring that the assessment results are carefully reviewed and analyzed by an independent team of experts to validate the completeness, consistency, and veracity of the results.

Finally, let us move on to the real interactive part of this chapter: review questions/exercises, hands-on projects, case projects, and an optional team case project. The answers and/or solutions by chapter can be found in the Online Instructor's Solutions Manual.

CHAPTER REVIEW QUESTIONS/ EXERCISES

True/False

1. True or False? By its very nature, security is inconvenient, and the more robust the security mechanisms are, the more inconvenient the process becomes.
2. True or False? As though employees' desire to share data is not enough of a threat to proprietary information, many business professionals want access to data from anywhere they work, on a variety of devices.
3. True or False? Many businesses believe that if they purchase enough equipment, they can create a secure infrastructure.
4. True or False? For most organizations, the cost of creating a weak security posture is seen as a necessary evil, similar to purchasing insurance.
5. True or False? In addressing the security needs of an organization, it is common for professionals to succumb to some common misconceptions.

Multiple Choice

1. Many businesses believe that if they purchase enough equipment, they can create a secure:
   A. Firewall
   B. Workstation
   C. E-commerce
   D. Organization
   E. Infrastructure
2. Once threats and risks are identified, you can take one of four steps, except which of the following?
   A. Ignore the risk.

B. Accept the risk.
C. Transfer the risk.
D. Identify the risk.
E. Mitigate the risk.
3. Just as implementing a robust, secure environment is a dynamic process, creating a highly skilled staff of security professionals is a:
   A. Dynamic process
   B. Technical infrastructure
   C. Vendor-neutral program
   D. Work environment
   E. Professional affiliation
4. What is the largest security-related organization in the world that focuses primarily on physical security, but has more recently started addressing computer security as well?
   A. ISACA
   B. HTCIA
   C. ISSA
   D. ASIS
   E. InfraGard
5. Arguably one of the best ways to determine whether an employee has a strong grasp of information security concepts is if she or he can achieve Certified Information Systems Security Professional (CISSP) certification. Candidates for this certification are tested on their understanding of the following knowledge domains, except which one:
   A. Proprietary information
   B. Access control
   C. Cryptography
   D. Operations security
   E. Security architecture

EXERCISE

Problem

With regard to building a secure organization, the security assessment team (SAT) should determine organizational policies and procedures, the privileged commands for which dual authorization is to be enforced; and the information system, which enforces dual authorization based on organizational policies and procedures for organization-defined privileged commands. What should the SAT examine with regards to access enforcement of potential assessment methods and objects?

Hands-on Projects

Project

With regard to building a secure organization, the SAT should determine how the organization defines applicable policy for controlling the flow of information within the system and between interconnected systems; defines approved authorizations for controlling the flow of information within the system and between interconnected systems in accordance with applicable policy; and the information system enforces approved authorizations for controlling the flow of information within the system and between interconnected systems in accordance with applicable policy. What should the SAT examine with regards to the information flow enforcement potential of assessment methods and objects?

Case Projects

Problem

With regard to building a secure organization, what should the SAT examine with regard to security assessment and authorization?

Optional Team Case Project

Problem

With regard to building a secure organization, the SAT should determine how the organization develops a contingency plan for the information system that identifies essential missions and business functions and associated contingencies.

Requirements: provides recovery objectives, restoration priorities, and metrics; addresses contingency roles, responsibilities, assigned individuals with contact information; addresses maintaining essential missions and business functions despite an information system disruption, compromise, or failure; addresses eventual, full information system restoration without deterioration of security measures originally planned and implemented; and is reviewed and approved by designated officials within the organization. The SAT should also determine how the organization defines key contingency personnel (identified by name and/or by role) and organizational elements designated to receive copies of the contingency plan; and distributes copies of the contingency plan to organization-defined key contingency personnel and organizational elements. What should the SAT examine with regard to contingency planning?

Chapter 3

A Cryptography Primer

Scott R. Ellis

kCura Corporation, Chicago, IL, United States

"Cryptography," as a word, literally means the "study of hidden writing." It comes from the Greek κρυπτός, "hidden, secret"; and from γράφειν, *graphein*, "writing," or -λογία, *-logia*, "study."[1] In practice, it is so much more than that. The zeros and ones of compiled software binary, something that frequently requires encryption, can hardly be considered "writing." Were a new word for cryptography to be invented today, it would probably be "secret communications." It follows that, rather than point to the first altered writing as the origins of cryptography, we must look to the origins of communication and to the first known alterations of it in any form. Historically, then, you might say that cryptography is a built-in defense mechanism, as a property of language. As you will see in this chapter, ultimately this dependency is also the final, greatest weakness of any cryptographic system, even the perceivably unbreakable Advanced Encryption Standard (AES) system. From unique, cultural body language to language itself, to our every means of communication, it is in our nature to want to prevent others who would do us harm from intercepting private communications (which could be about them!). Perhaps nothing so perfectly illustrates this fact as the art of cryptography. It is, in its purpose, an art form entirely devoted to the methods whereby we can prevent information from falling into the hands of those who would use it against us: our enemies.

Since the beginning of sentient language, cryptography has been a part of communication. It is as old as language itself. In fact, one could make the argument that the desire and ability to encrypt communication, to alter a missive in such a way so that only the intended recipient may understand it, is an innate ability hard-wired into the human genome. Aside from the necessity to communicate, it could well be what led to the development of language itself. Over time, languages and dialects evolved, as we can see with Spanish, French, Portuguese, and Italian, all of which derived from Latin. People who speak French have a great deal of trouble understanding people who speak Spanish, and vice versa. The profusion of Latin cognates in these languages is undisputed, but generally speaking, the two languages are so far removed that they are not dialects but rather separate languages. But why is this? Certain abilities, such as walking, are built into our nervous systems; other abilities, such as language, are not. From Pig Latin to whispering circles to word jumbles, to languages so foreign that only the native speakers understand them, to diverse languages and finally modern cryptography, it is in our nature to keep our communications secret.

So why is language not hard-wired into our nervous system, as it is with bees, which are born knowing how to tell another bee how far away a flower is, as well as the quantity of pollen and whether there is danger present? Why do we humans not all speak the same language? The reason is undoubtedly because unlike bees, humans understand that knowledge is power, and knowledge is communicated via spoken and written words. Plus, we were not born with giant stingers with which to sting people we do not like. With the development of evolving languages innate in our genetic wiring, the inception of cryptography was inevitable.

In essence, computer-based cryptography is the art of creating a form of communication that embraces the following precepts:

- It can be readily understood by the intended recipients.
- It cannot be understood by unintended recipients.
- It can be adapted and changed easily with relatively small modifications, such as a changed passphrase or word.

---

1. H. Liddell, R. Scott, Greek-English Lexicon, Oxford University Press, 1984.

All artificially created lexicons, such as the Pig Latin of children, pictograph codes, gang-speak, and corporate lingo, and even the names of music albums, such as *Four Flicks*, are manners of cryptography in which real text, sometimes not so ciphered, is hidden in what appears to be plaintext. They are attempts at hidden communications.

1. WHAT IS CRYPTOGRAPHY? WHAT IS ENCRYPTION?

Ask any ancient Egyptian and he will undoubtedly define "cryptography" as the practice of burying the dead so that they cannot be found again. The Egyptians were good at it; thousands of years later, new crypts are still being discovered. The Greek root *krypt* literally means "a hidden place," and as such it is an appropriate base for any term involving cryptology. According to the *Online Etymology Dictionary*, *crypto-* as a prefix, meaning "concealed, secret," has been used since 1760, and from the Greek *graphikos*, "of or for writing, belonging to drawing, picturesque." Together, *crypto + graphy* would then mean "hiding place for ideas, sounds, pictures, or words." *Graph*, technically from its Greek root, is "the art of writing." "Encryption," in contrast, merely means the act of carrying out some aspect of cryptography. "Cryptology," with its *-ology* ending, is the study of cryptography. Encryption is subsumed by cryptography.

How Is Cryptography Done?

For most information technology (IT) occupations, knowledge of cryptography is a small part of a broader skill set and is generally limited to relevant applications. The argument could be made that this is why the Internet is so extraordinarily plagued with security breaches. The majority of IT administrators, software programmers, and hardware developers are barely cognizant of the power of true cryptography. Overburdened with battling the plague that they inherited, they cannot afford to devote the time or resources needed to implement a truly secure strategy. The reason, as we shall see, is that as good as cryptographers can be, for every cryptographer there is a decryptographer working just as diligently to decipher a new encryption algorithm.

Traditionally, cryptography has consisted of any means possible whereby communications may be encrypted and transmitted. This could be as simple as using a language with which the opposition is not familiar. Who has not been in a place where everyone around them was speaking a language they did not understand? There are thousands of languages in the world; nobody can know them all. As was shown in World War II, when the Allied forces used Navajo as a means of communicating freely, some languages are so obscure that an entire nation may not contain

one person who speaks it! All true cryptography is composed of three parts: a cipher, an original message, and the resultant encryption. The *cipher* is the method of encryption used. Original messages are referred to as *plaintext* or as *clear text*. A message that is transmitted without encryption is said to be sent "in the clear." The resultant message is called a *ciphertext* or *cryptogram*. This part of the chapter begins with a simple review of cryptography procedures and carries them through; each section builds on the next to illustrate the principles of cryptography.

2. FAMOUS CRYPTOGRAPHIC DEVICES

The past few hundred years of technical development and advances have brought greater and greater means to decrypt, encode, and transmit information. With the advent of the most modern warfare techniques and the increase in communication and ease of reception, the need for encryption has never been more urgent.

World War II publicized and popularized cryptography in modern culture. The Allied forces' ability to capture, decrypt, and intercept Axis communications is said to have hastened the end of the war by several years. Next, we take a quick look at some famous cryptographic devices from that era.

The Lorenz Cipher

The Lorenz cipher machine was an industrial-strength ciphering machine used in teleprinter circuits by the Germans during World War II. Not to be confused with its smaller cousin, the Enigma machine, the Lorenz cipher could possibly best be compared to a virtual private network tunnel for a telegraph line, only it was not sending Morse code, it was using a code like a sort of American Standard Code for Information Interchange (ASCII) format. A granddaddy of sorts, called the Baudot code, was used to send alphanumeric communications across telegraph lines. Each character was represented by a series of 5 bits.

The Lorenz cipher is often confused with the famous Enigma, but unlike the Enigma (which was a portable field unit), the Lorenz cipher could receive typed messages, encrypt them, and send them to another distant Lorenz cipher, which would then decrypt the signal. It used a pseudorandom cipher XOR'd (an encryption algorithm) with plaintext. The machine would be inserted inline as an attachment to a Lorenz teleprinter. Fig. 3.1 is a rendered drawing from a photograph of a Lorenz cipher machine.

Enigma

The Enigma machine was a field unit used in World War II by German field agents to encrypt and decrypt messages

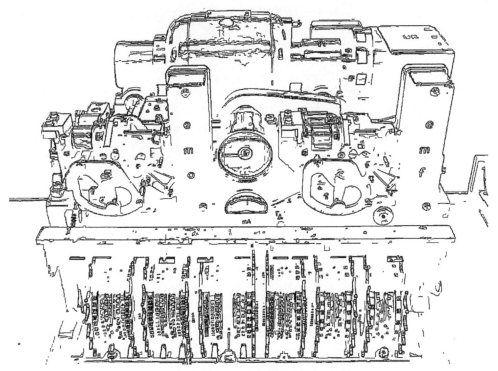

FIGURE 3.1 The Lorenz machine was set inline with a teletype to produce encrypted telegraphic signals.

and communications. Similar to the Feistel function of the 1970s, the Enigma machine was one of the first mechanized methods of encrypting text using an iterative cipher. It employed a series of rotors that, with some electricity, a light bulb, and a reflector, allowed the operator to either encrypt or decrypt a message. The original position of the rotors, set with each encryption and based on a prearranged pattern that in turn was based on the calendar, allowed the machine to be used even if it was compromised.

When the Enigma was in use, with each subsequent key press, the rotors would change in alignment from their set positions in such a way that a different letter was produced each time. With a message in hand, the operator would enter each character into the machine by pressing a typewriter-like key. The rotors would align and a letter would then illuminate, telling the operator what the letter *really* was. Likewise, when enciphering, the operator would press the key and the illuminated letter would be the cipher text. The continually changing internal flow of electricity that caused the rotors to change was not random, but it created a poly-alphabetic cipher that could be different each time it was used.

3. CIPHERS

Cryptography is built on one overarching premise: the need for a cipher that can be used reliably and portably to encrypt text so that through any means of cryptanalysis (differential, deductive, algebraic, or the like) the ciphertext cannot be undone with available technology. Throughout the

centuries, there have been many attempts to create simple ciphers that can achieve this goal. With the exception of the one-time pad, which is not particularly portable, success has been limited. Let us look at a few of these methods.

The Substitution Cipher

In this method, each letter of the message is replaced with a single character. Table 3.1 shows an example of a substitution cipher. Because some letters appear more often and certain words are used more than others, some ciphers are extremely easy to decrypt and can be deciphered at a glance by more practiced cryptologists.

Simply by understanding probability and employing some applied statistics, certain metadata about a language can be derived and used to decrypt any simple one-for-one substitution cipher. Decryption methods often rely on understanding the context of the *ciphertext*. What was encrypted: business communication? Spreadsheets? Technical data? Coordinates? For example, using a hex editor and an access database to conduct some statistics, we can use the information in Table 3.2 to gain highly specialized knowledge about the data in Chapter 40, "Cyber Forensics," by Scott R. Ellis, in this book. A long chapter at nearly 25,000 words, it provides a sufficiently large statistical pool to draw some meaningful analyses.

Table 3.3 gives additional data about the occurrence of specific words in Chapter 40. Note that because it is a technical text, words such as "computer," "files," "email,"

TABLE 3.1 Simple Substitution Cipher

A	B	C	D	E	F	G	H	I	J	K	L	M	N	O	P	Q	R	S	T	U	V	W	X	Y	Z
1	2	3	4	5	6	7	8	9	10	11	12	13	14	15	16	17	18	19	20	21	22	23	24	25	26
O	C	Q	W	B	X	Y	E	I	L	Z	A	D	R	J	S	P	F	G	K	H	N	T	U	M	V
15	3	17	23	2	24	25	5	9	12	26	1	4	18	10	19	16	6	7	11	8	14	20	21	13	22

Letters are numbered by their order in the alphabet, to provide a numeric reference key. To encrypt a message, the letters are replaced, or substituted, by the numbers. This is a particularly easy cipher to reverse.

TABLE 3.2 Statistical Data of Interest in Encryption

Character Analysis	Count
Number of distinct alphanumeric combinations	1958
Distinct characters	68
Number of four-letter words	984
Number of five-letter words	1375

An analysis of a selection of a manuscript (in this case, the preedited version of Chapter 40 of this book) can provide insight into the reasons why good ciphers need to be developed.

TABLE 3.3 Five-Letter Word Recurrences in Chapter 40

Words Field	Number of Recurrences
files	125
drive	75
there	67
email	46
these	43
other	42
about	41
where	36
would	33
every	31
court	30
their	30
first	28
using	28
which	24
could	22
table	22
after	21
image	21
don't	19
tools	19
being	18
entry	18

A glimpse of the leading five-letter words found in the preedited manuscript. Once unique letter groupings have been identified, substitution, often by trial and error, can result in a meaningful reconstruction that allows the entire cipher to be revealed.

and "drive" emerge as leaders. Analysis of these leaders can reveal individual and paired alpha frequencies. Being armed with knowledge about the type of communication can be beneficial in decrypting it.

Further information about types of data being encrypted includes word counts by the length of words. Table 3.4 contains such a list for Chapter 40. This information can be used to begin to piece together useful and meaningful short sentences, which can provide cues to longer and more

TABLE 3.4 Leaders by Word Length in the Preedited Manuscript for Chapter 40

Words Field	Number of Duplications	Word Length
XOriginalArrivalTime:	2	21
interpretations	2	15
XOriginatingIP:	2	15
electronically	4	14
investigations	5	14
interpretation	6	14
reconstructing	3	14
irreproducible	2	14
professionally	2	14
inexperienced	2	13
demonstrative	2	13
XAnalysisOut:	8	13
steganography	7	13
understanding	8	13
certification	2	13
circumstances	8	13
unrecoverable	4	13
investigation	15	13
automatically	2	13
admissibility	2	13
XProcessedBy:	2	13
administrator	4	13
determination	3	13
investigative	3	13
practitioners	2	13
preponderance	2	13
intentionally	2	13
consideration	2	13
interestingly	2	13

The context of the clear text can make the cipher less secure. After all, there are only a finite number of words. Few of them are long.

complex structures. It is exactly this sort of activity that good cryptography attempts to defeat.

If it was encrypted using a simple substitution cipher, a good start to deciphering Chapter 40 could be made using the information we have gathered. As a learning exercise, game, or logic puzzle, substitution ciphers are useful. Some substitution ciphers that are more elaborate can be just as difficult to crack. Ultimately, though, the weakness behind a substitution cipher is that the ciphertext remains a one-to-one, directly corresponding substitution; ultimately, anyone with a pen and paper and a large enough sample of the ciphertext can defeat it. Through use of a computer, deciphering a simple substitution cipher becomes child's play.

The Shift Cipher

Also known as the Caesar cipher, the shift cipher is one that anyone can readily understand and remember for decoding. It is a form of the substitution cipher. By shifting the alphabet a few positions in either direction, a simple sentence can become unreadable to casual inspection. Example 3.1 is an example of such a shift.[2]

Interestingly, for cryptogram word games, spaces are always included. Often puzzles use numbers instead of letters for the substitution. Removing the spaces in this particular example can make the ciphertext somewhat more secure. The possibility for multiple solutions becomes an issue; any number of words might fit the pattern.

Today many software tools are available to decode most cryptograms quickly and easily (at least, those not written in a dead language). You can have some fun with these tools; for example, the name Scott Ellis, when decrypted, turns into Still Books. The name of a friend of the author decrypts to "His Sinless." It is apparent, then, that smaller-sample simple substitution ciphers can have more than one solution.

Much has been written and stated about frequency analysis; it is considered the "end-all and be-all" with respect to cipher decryption. Frequency analysis is not to be confused with cipher breaking, which is a modern attack against the actual cryptographic algorithms themselves. However, to think simply plugging of in some numbers generated from a Google search is naïve. The frequency chart in Table 3.5 is commonplace on the Web.

It is beyond the scope of this chapter to delve into the accuracy of the table, but suffice it to say that our own analysis of Chapter 40's 118,000 characters, a technical

TABLE 3.5 "In a Random Sampling of 1000 Letters," This Pattern Emerges

Letter	Frequency
E	130
T	93
N	78
R	77
I	74
O	74
A	73
S	63
D	44
H	35
L	35
C	30
F	28
P	27
U	27
M	25
Y	19
G	16
W	16
V	13
B	9
X	5
K	3
Q	3
J	2
Z	1
Total	**1000**

text, yielded a much different result (Table 3.6). Perhaps the significantly larger sample and the fact that it is a technical text make the results different after the top two. In addition, where computers are concerned, an actual frequency analysis would take into consideration all ASCII characters, as shown in Table 3.6.

Frequency analysis is not difficult; once of all the letters of a text are pulled into a database program, it is straightforward to count all the duplicate values. The snippet of code in Example 3.2 demonstrates one way in which text can be transformed into a single column and imported into a database.

The cryptograms that use formatting (every word becomes the same length) are considerably more difficult

---

EXAMPLE 3.1 A Sample Cryptogram. Try This Out: Gv Vw, Dtwvg?

Hint: Caesar said it, and it is in Latin.

---

2. Et tu, Brute?

TABLE 3.6 Using MS Access to Perform Frequency Analysis of Chapter 40 in This Book

Chapter 40 Letters	Frequency
e	14,467
t	10,945
a	9,239
i	8,385
o	7,962
s	7,681
n	7,342
r	6,872
h	4,882
l	4,646
d	4,104
c	4,066
u	2,941
m	2,929
f	2,759
p	2,402
y	2,155
g	1,902
w	1,881
b	1,622
v	1,391
.	1,334
,	1,110
k	698
0	490
x	490
q	166
7	160
*	149
5	147
)	147
(	146
j	145
3	142
6	140
Æ	134
ò	134

Continued

TABLE 3.6 Using MS Access to Perform Frequency Analysis of Chapter 40 in This Book—cont'd

Chapter 40 Letters	Frequency
ô	129
ö	129
4	119
z	116
Total	**116,798**

Characters with fewer repetitions than z were excluded from the return. Character frequency analysis of different types of communications yields slightly different results.

EXAMPLE 3.2 How Text Can Be Transformed Into a Single Column and Imported Into a Database

```
1: Sub Letters2column ()
2: Dim bytText () As Byte
3: Dim bytNew() As Byte
4: Dim IngCount As Long
5: With ActiveDocument.Content
6: bytText = .Text
7: ReDim bytNew(((((UBound(bytText()) + 1) * 2) − 5))
8: For IngCount = 0 To (UBound(bytText()) − 2) Step two
9: bytNew((lngCount * 2)) = bytText(lngCount)
10: bytNew(((lngCount * 2) + 2)) = 13
11: Next IngCount
12: .Text = bytNew()
13: End With
14: End Sub
```

---

for basic online decryption programs to crack. They must take into consideration spacing and word lengths when considering whether a string matches a word. It stands to reason, then, that the formulation of the cipher (in which a substitution that is based partially on frequency similarities and with a whole lot of obfuscation, so that when messages are decrypted, they have ambiguous or multiple meanings) would be desirable for simple ciphers. However, this would be true only for very short and very obscure messages that could be code words to decrypt other messages or could simply be sent to misdirect the opponent. The amount of ciphertext needed to break a cipher successfully is called the *unicity distance*. Ciphers with small unicity distances are weaker than those with large ones.

Ultimately, substitution ciphers are vulnerable to either word-pattern analysis, letter-frequency analysis, or some combination of both. Where numerical information is encrypted, tools such as Benford's law can be used to elicit patterns of numbers that *should* be occurring. Forensic techniques incorporate such tools to uncover accounting fraud. Thus, although this particular cipher is a child's game, it is useful in that it is an underlying principle of cryptography and should be well understood before continuing. The primary purpose of discussing it here is as an introduction to ciphers.

Further topics of interest and places to find information involving substitution ciphers are the chi-square statistic, Edgar Allan Poe, Sherlock Holmes, Benford's law, Google, and Wikipedia. For example, an Internet search for Edgar Allan Poe + cryptography will lead you to articles detailing how Poe's interest in the subject and his use of it in stories such as "The Gold-Bug" served to popularize and raise awareness of cryptography in the general public.

The Polyalphabetic Cipher

The preceding clearly demonstrated that although the substitution cipher is fun and easy, it is also vulnerable and weak. It is especially susceptible to frequency analysis. Given a large enough sample, a cipher can easily be broken by mapping the frequency of the letters in the ciphertext to the frequency of letters in the language or dialect of the ciphertext (if it is known). To make ciphers more difficult to crack, Blaise de Vigenère, from the 16th-century court of Henry III of France, proposed a polyalphabetic substitution. In this cipher, instead of a one-to-one relationship, there is a one-to-many. A single letter can have multiple substitutes. The Vigenère solution was the first known cipher to use a keyword.

It works like this: First, a *tableau* is developed, as in Table 3.7. This tableau is a series of shift ciphers. In fact, because there can be only 26 additive shift ciphers, it is all of them.

In Table 3.7, a table combined with a keyword is used to create the cipher. For example, if we choose the keyword *rockerrooks*, overlay it over the plaintext, and cross-index it to Table 3.7, we can produce the ciphertext. In this example, the top row is used to look up the plaintext and the leftmost column is used to reference the keyword.

For example, we lay the word *rockerrooks* over the sentence "Ask not what your country can do for you." Line 1 is the keyword, line 2 is the plaintext, and line 3 is the ciphertext:

Keyword: ROC KER ROOK SROC KERROOK SRO CK ERR OOK
Plaintext: ASK NOT WHAT YOUR COUNTRY CAN DO FOR YOU
Ciphertext: RGM XSK NVOD QFIT MSLEHFI URB FY JFI MCE

The similarity of this tableau to a mathematical table like the one shown in Table 3.8 becomes apparent. Just think letters instead of numbers, and it becomes clear how

this works. The top row is used to "look up" a letter from the plaintext, the leftmost column is used to locate the overlaying keyword letter, and where the column and the row intersect is the ciphertext.

In fact, this similarity is the weakness of the cipher. Through some creative "factoring," the length of the keyword can be determined. Because the tableau is, in practice, a series of shift ciphers, the length of the keyword determines how many ciphers are used. With only six distinct letters the keyword *rockerrook* uses only six ciphers. Regardless, for nearly 300 years many people believed the cipher to be unbreakable.

The Kasiski–Kerckhoff Method

Now let us look at Kerckhoff's principle: "Only secrecy of the key provides security." (This principle is not to be confused with Kirchhoff's law, a totally different man and rule.) In the 19th century, Auguste Kerckhoff stated that essentially, a system should still be secure, even when everyone knows everything about the system (except the password). Basically, his thought was that if more than one person knows something, it is no longer a secret. Throughout modern cryptography, the inner workings of cryptographic techniques have been well-known and published. Creating a portable, secure, unbreakable code is easy if nobody knows how it works. The problem lies in the fact that we people just cannot keep a secret!

In 1863, Friedrich Kasiski, a Prussian major, proposed a method to crack the Vigenère cipher.[3] Briefly, his method required the cryptographer to deduce the length of the keyword used and then dissect the cryptogram into a corresponding number of ciphers. This is accomplished simply by examining the distance between repeated strings in the ciphertext. Each cipher would then be solved independently. The method required a suitable number of bigrams to be located. A *bigram* is a portion of the ciphertext two characters long, which repeats in a discernible pattern. In Example 3.3, a repetition has been deliberately made simple with a short keyword (*toto*) and engineered by crafting a harmonic between the keyword and the plaintext.

This might seem an oversimplification, but it effectively demonstrates the weakness of the polyalphabetic cipher. Similarly, the polyalphanumeric ciphers, such as the Gronsfeld cipher, are even weaker because they use 26 letters and 10 digits. This one also happens to decrypt to "On of when on of," but a larger sample with such a weak keyword would easily be cracked by even the least intelligent Web-based cryptogram solvers. The harmonic is created by the overlaying keyword with the underlying text; when the bigrams "line up" and repeat themselves,

3. D. Kahn, The Codebreakers—The Story of Secret Writing, Scribner, New York, NY, 1996. (ISBN:0,684,831,309)

TABLE 3.7 Vigenère's Tableau Arranging All Shift Ciphers Into a Single Table

Letter	A	B	C	D	E	F	G	H	I	J	K	L	M	N	O	P	Q	R	S	T	U	V	W	X	Y	Z
A	A	B	C	D	E	F	G	H	I	J	K	L	M	N	O	P	Q	R	S	T	U	V	W	X	Y	Z
B	B	C	D	E	F	G	H	I	J	K	L	M	N	O	P	Q	R	S	T	U	V	W	X	Y	Z	A
C	C	D	E	F	G	H	I	J	K	L	M	N	O	P	Q	R	S	T	U	V	W	X	Y	Z	A	B
D	D	E	F	G	H	I	J	K	L	M	N	O	P	Q	R	S	T	U	V	W	X	Y	Z	A	B	C
E	E	F	G	H	I	J	K	L	M	N	O	P	Q	R	S	T	U	V	W	X	Y	Z	A	B	C	D
F	F	G	H	I	J	K	L	M	N	O	P	Q	R	S	T	U	V	W	X	Y	Z	A	B	C	D	E
G	G	H	I	J	K	L	M	N	O	P	Q	R	S	T	U	V	W	X	Y	Z	A	B	C	D	E	F
H	H	I	J	K	L	M	N	O	P	Q	R	S	T	U	V	W	X	Y	Z	A	B	C	D	E	F	G
I	I	J	K	L	M	N	O	P	Q	R	S	T	U	V	W	X	Y	Z	A	B	C	D	E	F	G	H
J	J	K	L	M	N	O	P	Q	R	S	T	U	V	W	X	Y	Z	A	B	C	D	E	F	G	H	I
K	K	L	M	N	O	P	Q	R	S	T	U	V	W	X	Y	Z	A	B	C	D	E	F	G	H	I	J
L	L	M	N	O	P	Q	R	S	T	U	V	W	X	Y	Z	A	B	C	D	E	F	G	H	I	J	K
M	M	N	O	P	Q	R	S	T	U	V	W	X	Y	Z	A	B	C	D	E	F	G	H	I	J	K	L
N	N	O	P	Q	R	S	T	U	V	W	X	Y	Z	A	B	C	D	E	F	G	H	I	J	K	L	M
O	O	P	Q	R	S	T	U	V	W	X	Y	Z	A	B	C	D	E	F	G	H	I	J	K	L	M	N
P	P	Q	R	S	T	U	V	W	X	Y	Z	A	B	C	D	E	F	G	H	I	J	K	L	M	N	O
Q	Q	R	S	T	U	V	W	X	Y	Z	A	B	C	D	E	F	G	H	I	J	K	L	M	N	O	P
R	R	S	T	U	V	W	X	Y	Z	A	B	C	D	E	F	G	H	I	J	K	L	M	N	O	P	Q
S	S	T	U	V	W	X	Y	Z	A	B	C	D	E	F	G	H	I	J	K	L	M	N	O	P	Q	R
T	T	U	V	W	X	Y	Z	A	B	C	D	E	F	G	H	I	J	K	L	M	N	O	P	Q	R	S
U	U	V	W	X	Y	Z	A	B	C	D	E	F	G	H	I	J	K	L	M	N	O	P	Q	R	S	T
V	V	W	X	Y	Z	A	B	C	D	E	F	G	H	I	J	K	L	M	N	O	P	Q	R	S	T	U
W	W	X	Y	Z	A	B	C	D	E	F	G	H	I	J	K	L	M	N	O	P	Q	R	S	T	U	V
X	X	Y	Z	A	B	C	D	E	F	G	H	I	J	K	L	M	N	O	P	Q	R	S	T	U	V	W
Y	Y	Z	A	B	C	D	E	F	G	H	I	J	K	L	M	N	O	P	Q	R	S	T	U	V	W	X
Z	Z	A	B	C	D	E	F	G	H	I	J	K	L	M	N	O	P	Q	R	S	T	U	V	W	X	Y

Vigenère's tableau then implements a keyword to create a more complex cipher than the simple substitution or shift ciphers. The number of spurious keys, or bogus decryptions, that result from attempting to decrypt a polyalphabetic encryption, is greater than those created during the decryption of a single shift cipher.

TABLE 3.8 Multiplication Table Is the Inspiration for the Vigenère Tableau

Multiplier	1	2	3	4	5	6	7	8	9	10
1	1	2	3	4	5	6	7	8	9	10
2	2	4	6	8	10	12	14	16	18	20
3	3	6	9	12	15	18	21	24	27	30
4	4	8	12	16	20	24	28	32	36	40
5	5	10	15	20	25	30	35	40	45	50
6	6	12	18	24	30	36	42	48	54	60
7	7	14	21	28	35	42	49	56	63	70
8	8	16	24	32	40	48	56	64	72	80
9	9	18	27	36	45	54	63	72	81	90
10	10	20	30	40	50	60	70	80	90	100

EXAMPLE 3.3 A Repetitious, Weak Keyword Combines With Plaintext to Produce an Easily Deciphered Ciphertext

	to	to	toto	to	to	toto	to
Plaintext	it	is	what	it	is,	Isn't	it?
Ciphertext	BH	BG	PVTH	BH	BG	BGGH	BH

the highest frequency will be the length of the password. The distance between the two occurrences will be the length of the password. In Example 3.3, we see BH and BG repeating, and then we see BG repeating at a tight interval of 2, which tells us the password might be two characters long and based on two shift ciphers that, when decrypted side by side, will make a real word. Not all bigrams will be indicators of this, so some care must be taken. As can be seen, BH repeats with an interval of 8, but the password is not eight digits long (however, it is a factor of 8!). By locating the distance of all of the repeating bigrams and factoring them, we can deduce the length of the keyword.

4. MODERN CRYPTOGRAPHY

Some of cryptography's greatest stars emerged in World War II. For the first time during modern warfare, vast resources were devoted to enciphering and deciphering communications. Both sides made groundbreaking advances in cryptography. Understanding the need for massive calculations (for the time: more is probably happening in the random-access memory of this author's personal computer over a period of 5 min than happened in all of the war), both sides developed new machinery,

predecessors to modern solid-state computers, that could be coordinated to perform the calculations and procedures needed to crack enemy ciphers.

The Vernam Cipher (Stream Cipher)

Gilbert Sandford Vernam (1890—1960) invented the stream cipher in 1917; a patent was issued on July 22, 1919. Vernam worked for Bell Labs, and his patent described a cipher in which a prepared key, on a paper tape, combined with plaintext to produce a transmitted ciphertext message. He did not use the term "*d'art*" "XOR," but he implemented the same logic at the relay layer. The credit for automating cryptography goes to Vernam, who introduced the Baudot system, which is the Morse code of the teletype, to cryptography. In it, each character is represented by five units, or pulses. With the expectation that a set number of "pulses" would be transmitted over a given period of time, the pulse, or absence of it, creates a system of zeros and ones that flesh out a binary system. Vernam was the first to suggest that a prepunched tape (cipher) could *combine* with the plaintext and yield difficult to crack ciphertext. The same tape would then be used to decrypt the ciphertext. Through testing and development, it became apparent that two tapes could be used and offset against one another to produce many different ciphers. Later, methods were derived to employ a single stream of random numbers to create an unbreakable cipher. Physical problems barred this from gaining wide implementation; the logistics of managing or transmitting the random cipher, and then knowing which message to which it applied, were simply insurmountable in wartime, when messaging increased dramatically. Regardless, Vernam's accomplishment of employing a method of automation to encryption cannot be underestimated. He developed a way in which, using a series of magnets and relays, the cipher and plaintext pulses could be combined electrically.[4] Fig. 3.2 shows a page from the actual patent papers, Patent No. 1,310,719.[5]

In effect, the Vernam stream cipher and "one-time pad" ciphers are similar; in fact, Vernam later coinvented it. The primary difference is that the "one-time pad" cipher dictates that a truly random stream cipher be used for the encryption. The stream cipher had no such requirement and used a different method of relay logic to combine a pseudorandom stream of bits with the plaintext bits. (The XOR process is discussed in more detail in the section on XOR ciphering.) In practice today, the Vernam cipher is any stream cipher in which pseudorandom or random text is combined with plaintext to produce cipher text that is the same length as the cipher. RC4 is a modern example of a Vernam cipher.

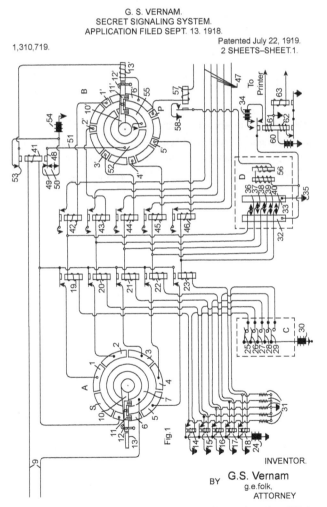

FIGURE 3.2 G. S. Vernam's Secret Signaling System introduced bit-by-bit enciphering using XOR technology to the world of cryptography for the first time.

4. D. Kahn, The Codebreakers—The Story of Secret Writing (394–403), (Scribner, 1996).
5. U.S. Patent 1,310,719.

The One-Time Pad

The "one-time pad" cipher, attributed to Joseph Mauborgne, is perhaps one of the most secure forms of cryptography. It is difficult to break if used properly, and if the key stream is perfectly random, the ciphertext gives away absolutely no details about the plaintext, which renders it unbreakable. As the name suggests, it uses a single random key that is the same length as the entire message, and it uses the key only once. The word "pad" is derived from the fact that the key is distributed on pads of paper, with each sheet torn off and destroyed as it is used.

There are several weaknesses to this cipher. We begin to see that the more secure the encryption is, the more it will rely on other means of key transmission. The more a key has to be moved around, the more likely it is that someone who should not have it will have it. The following weaknesses are apparent in this "bulletproof" style of cryptography:

- The key length has to equal plaintext length.
- It is susceptible to key interception; the key must be transmitted to the recipient, and the key is as long as the message.
- It is cumbersome, because it doubles the traffic on the line.
- The cipher must be perfectly random.
- One-time use is absolutely essential. As soon as two separate messages are available, the messages can be decrypted. Example 3.4 demonstrates this.

Since most people do not use binary, the author takes the liberty in Example 3.4 of using decimal numbers modulus 26 to represent the XOR that would take place in a bitstream encryption (see the section on the XOR cipher) that uses the method of the one-time pad.

A numeric value is assigned to each letter, as seen in Table 3.9. By assigning a numeric value to each letter, adding the plaintext value to the ciphertext value, modulus 26, yields a pseudo-XOR, or a wraparound Caesar shift that has a different shift for each letter in the entire message.

As this example demonstrates, by using the same cipher twice, a dimension is introduced that allows for the introduction of frequency analysis. By placing the two streams side by side, we can identify letters that are the same. In a large enough sample, in which the ciphertext is sufficiently randomized, frequency analysis of the aligned values will begin to crack the cipher wide open because we know that they are streaming in a logical order: the order in which they were written. One of the chief advantages of 21st-century cryptography is that the "eggs" are scrambled and descrambled during decryption based on the key, which in fact you do not want people to know. If the same cipher is used repeatedly, multiple inferences can be made, and eventually the entire key can be deconstructed. Because plaintext 1 and plaintext 2 are so similar, this sample yields

---

EXAMPLE 3.4 Using the Random Cipher, a Modulus Shift Instead of an XOR, and Plaintext to Produce Ciphertext

Plaintext 1

    t h i s w i l l b e s o e a s y t o b r e a k i t w i l l b e f u n n y
    20 8 9 19 23 9 12 12 2 5 19 15 5 1 19 25 20 15 2 18 5 1 11 9 20 23 9 12 12 2 5 6 21 14 14 25

Cipher 1

    q e r t y u i o p a s d f g h j k l z x c v b n m q a z w s x e r f v t
    17 5 18 20 25 21 9 15 16 1 19 4 6 7 8 10 11 12 26 24 3 22 2 14 13 17 1 26 23 19 24 5 18 6 22 20

Ciphertext 1

    11 13 1 13 22 4 21 1 18 6 12 19 11 8 1 9 5 1 2 16 8 23 13 23 7 14 10 12 9 21 3 11 13 20 10 19
    k m a m v d u a r f l s k h a i e a b p h w m w g n j l w u c k m t j s

Plaintext 2

    T h i s w i l l n o t b e e a s y t o b r e a k o r b e t o o f u n n y
    20 8 9 19 23 9 12 12 14 15 20 2 5 5 1 19 25 20 15 2 18 5 1 11 15 18 2 5 20 15 15 6 21 14 14 25

Ciphertext 2, also using Cipher 1

    11 13 1 13 22 4 21 1 4 16 13 6 11 12 9 3 10 6 15 0 21 1 3 25 2 9 3 5 17 8 13 11 13 20 10 19
    k m a m v d u a e p m f k l i f j f o z u a c y b i c e q h m k m t j s

---

Some Statistical Tests for Cryptographic Applications by Adrian Fleissig

In many applications, it is often important to determine whether a sequence is random. For example, a random sequence provides little or no information in cryptographic analysis. When estimating economic and financial models, it is important for the residuals from the estimated model to be random. Various statistical tests can be used to evaluate whether a sequence is actually random. For a truly random sequence, it is assumed that each element is generated independently of any prior and/or future elements. A statistical test is used to compute the probability that the observed sequence is random compared with a truly random sequence. The procedures have test statistics that are used to evaluate the null hypothesis, which typically assumes that the observed sequence is random. The alternative hypothesis is that the sequence is nonrandom. Thus, failing to accept the null hypothesis, at some critical level selected by the researcher, suggests that the sequence may be nonrandom.

There are many statistical tests to evaluate for randomness in a sequence, including frequency tests, runs tests, discrete Fourier transforms, and serial tests. The test statistics often have chi-square or standard normal distributions that are used to evaluate the hypothesis. Whereas no test is superior overall to the others, a frequency or runs test is a good starting point to examine for nonrandomness in a sequence. As an example, a frequency or runs test typically evaluates whether the number of zeros and ones in a sequence are about the same, as would be the case if the sequence were truly random.

It is important to examine the results carefully. For example, the researcher may incorrectly fail to accept the null hypothesis that the sequence is random, and therefore may make a type I error. Incorrectly accepting the null of randomness when the sequence is actually nonrandom results in committing a type II error. The reliability of the results depends on having a sufficiently large number of elements in a sequence. In addition, it is important to perform alternative tests to evaluate whether a sequence is random.

the following harmonics (in bold and boxed), as shown in Example 3.5.

Cracking Ciphers

One method of teasing out the frequency patterns is by applying some sort of mathematical formula to test a hypothesis against reality. The chi-square test is perhaps one of the most commonly used; it allows someone to use what is called *inferential statistics* to draw certain inferences about the data by testing them against known statistical distributions.

Using the chi-square test against an encrypted text would allow certain inferences to be made, but only where the contents, or the type of contents (random or of an expected distribution), of the text were known. For example, someone may use a program that encrypts files. By creating the null hypothesis that the text is completely random and by reversing the encryption steps, a block cipher may emerge as the null hypothesis is disproved through the chi-square test. This would be done by reversing the encryption method and XORing against the bytes with a block created from the known text. At the point where the nonencrypted text matches the positioning of the encrypted text, chi-square would reveal that the output is not random and the block cipher would be revealed.

Chi-squared $= \ldots (\text{observed-expected})2/(\text{expected})$

What would be observed would be the actual 0:1 ratio produced by XORing the data streams together, and what would be expected would be the randomness of zeros and ones (50:50) in a body of pseudorandom text.

Independent of having a portion of the text, a large body of encrypted text could be reverse-encrypted using a block size of all zeros. In this manner it may be possible to

TABLE 3.9 A Simple Key Is Created So That Random Characters and Regular Characters May Be Combined With a Modulus Function

Key																									
a	b	c	d	e	f	g	h	i	j	k	l	m	n	o	p	q	r	s	t	u	v	w	x	y	z
1	2	3	4	5	6	7	8	9	10	11	12	13	14	15	16	17	18	19	20	21	22	23	24	25	26

Without the original cipher, this key is meaningless intelligence. It is used here in a similar capacity as an XOR, which is also a function that everyone knows how to perform.

EXAMPLE 3.5 Where Plaintext 1 and Plaintext 2 Are so Similar, This Sample Yields the Following Harmonics (In Bold and Boxed)

Side by side, the two ciphertexts show a high level of harmonics. This indicates that two different ciphertexts actually have the same cipher. Where letters are different, because XOR is a known process and our encryption technique is also publicly known, it is a simple matter to say that $r = 18$, $e = 5$ (Table 3.9), and thus construct an algorithm that can tease apart the cipher and ciphertext to produce plaintext.

```
kmamvdua rflsk haieabphwmwgnjlwuck mtjs (ciphertext 1)
kmamvdua epmfk lifjfozuacybiceqhmk mtjs (ciphertext 2)
```

tease out a block cipher by searching for nonrandom block-sized strings. Modern encryption techniques generate many block cipher permutations that are layered against previous iterations $(n - 1)$ of permuted blocks. The feasibility of running such decryption techniques would require a heavy-duty programmer and a statistician, an incredible amount of processing power, and in-depth knowledge of the encryption algorithm used. An unpublished algorithm would render such testing worthless.

The methods and procedures employed in breaking encryption algorithms are used throughout society in many applications where a null hypothesis needs to be tested. Forensic consultants use pattern matching and similar decryption techniques to combat fraud on a daily basis. Adrian Fleissig, a seasoned economist, uses many statistical tests to examine corporate data (see the sidebar, "Some Statistical Tests for Cryptographic Applications").[6]

The XOR Cipher and Logical Operands

In practice, the XOR cipher is not so much a cipher as it is a mechanism whereby ciphertext is produced. "Random binary stream cipher" would be a better term. The terms "XOR," "logical disjunction," and "inclusive" may be used interchangeably. Most people are familiar with the logical functions of speech, which are words such as "and," "or," "nor," and "not." A girl can tell her brother, "Mother is either upstairs or at the neighbor's," which means she could be in either state, but you have no way of knowing which one it is. The mother could be in either place, and you cannot infer from the statement the greater likelihood of either. The outcome is undecided.

Alternatively, if a salesman offers a customer either a blue car or a red car, the customer knows that he can have red or he can have blue. Both statements are true. Blue cars and red cars exist simultaneously in the world. A person can own both a blue car and a red car. But Mother will never be in more than one place at a time. Purportedly, there is a widespread belief that no author has produced an example of an English *or* sentence that appears to be false because both of its inputs are true.[7] Quantum physics takes considerable exception to this statement (which explains quantum physicists) at the quantum-mechanical level. In the Schrödinger cat experiment, the sentence "The cat is alive or dead" or the statement "The photon is a particle and a wave until you look at it, then it is a particle or a wave, depending on how you observed it" both create a quandary for logical operations, and there are

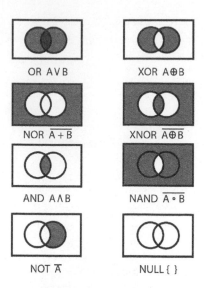

RELATIΦNSHIPS

FIGURE 3.3 In each Venn diagram, the possible outcome of two inputs is decided.

no Venn diagrams or words that depend on time or quantum properties of the physical universe. Regardless of this exception, when speaking of things in the world in a more rigorously descriptive fashion (in the macroscopically nonphenomenological sense), greater accuracy is needed.

To create a greater sense of accuracy in discussions of logic, the operands as listed in Fig. 3.3 were created. When attempting to understand this chart, the best thing to do is to assign a word to the A and B values and think of each Venn diagram as a universe of documents, perhaps in a document database or just on a computer being searched. If A stands for the word "tree" and B for "frog," each letter simply takes on a significant and distinct meaning.

In computing, it is traditional that a value of 0 is false and a value of 1 is true. Thus, an XOR operation is the determination of whether two possibilities can be combined to produce a value of true or false, based on whether both operations are true, both are false, or one of the values is true.

$$1 \text{ XOR } 1 = 0$$
$$0 \text{ XOR } 0 = 0$$
$$1 \text{ XOR } 0 = 1$$
$$0 \text{ XOR } 1 = 1$$

In an XOR operation, if the two inputs are different, the resultant is TRUE, or 1. If the two inputs are the same, the resultant value is FALSE, or 0.

In Example 3.6, the first string represents the plaintext and the second line represents the cipher. The third line represents the ciphertext. If, and only exactly if, just one of

---

6. Adrian Fleissig is the Senior Economist of Counsel for RGL Forensics, 2006–present. He is also a full professor, California State University Fullerton (CSUF) with a joint Ph.D. in Economics and Statistics from North Carolina State University in 1993.
7. Barrett, Stenner, The myth of the exclusive 'or,' Mind 80 (317) (1971) 116–121. [First names or initials needed for authors].

EXAMPLE 3.6 Lines 1 and 2 Are Combined With an XOR Operand to Produce Line 3
Line 1, plaintext: 1 0 0 1 1 1 0 1 0 1 1 0 1 1 1 1
Line 2, random cipher "": 1 0 0 0 1 1 0 1 0 1 0 0 1 0 0 1
Line 3, XOR ciphertext: 0 0 0 1 0 0 0 0 0 0 1 0 0 1 0 0

---

the items has a value of TRUE, the results of the XOR operation will be true.

Without the cipher, and if the cipher is truly random, decoding the string becomes impossible. However, as in the one-time pad, if the same cipher is used, then (1) the cryptography becomes vulnerable to a known text attack, and (2) it becomes vulnerable to statistical analysis. Example 3.7 demonstrates this by showing exactly where the statistical aberration can be culled in the stream. If we know they both used the same cipher, can anyone solve for Plaintext A and Plaintext B?

EXAMPLE 3.7 Where the Statistical Aberration Can Be Culled in the Stream
To reconstruct the cipher if the plaintext is known, PlaintextA can be XOR'd to ciphertextB to produce cipherA! Clearly, in a situation where plaintext may be captured, using the same cipher key twice could completely expose the message. By using statistical analysis, the unique possibilities for PlaintextA and PlaintextB will emerge; *unique possibilities* means that for ciphertext = x, where the cipher is truly random, this should be at about 50% of the sample. Additions of ciphertext $n + 1$ will increase the possibilities for unique combinations because, after all, these binary streams must be converted to text and the set of binary stream possibilities that will combine into ASCII characters is relatively small. Using basic programming skills, you can develop algorithms that will sort through these data quickly and easily to produce a deciphered result. An intelligent person with some time on her hands could sort it out on paper or on an Excel spreadsheet. When the choice is "The red house down the street from the green house is where we will meet" or a bunch of garbage, it begins to become apparent how to decode the cipher.

CipherA and PlaintextA are XOR'd to produce ciphertextA:
PlaintextA: 0 0 0 0 0 0 0 0 1 1 1 1 1 1 1 1
cipherA: 1 1 1 1 1 1 1 1 0 0 0 0 0 0 0 0
ciphertextA: 1 1 1 1 1 1 1 1 1 1 1 1 1 1 1 1
PlaintextB and cipherA are XOR'd to produce ciphertextB:
ciphertextB: 0 0 0 0 0 0 0 0 1 1 1 1 1 1 1 1
cipherA: 1 1 1 1 1 1 1 1 0 0 0 0 0 0 0 0
PlaintextB: 1 1 1 1 1 1 1 1 0 0 0 0 0 0 0 0
|<—— Column 1 ——>||<——Column 2 —— |
Note: Compare ciphertextA to ciphertextB!

Block Ciphers

Block ciphers work in a way similar to polyalphabetic ciphers, with the exception that a block cipher pairs together two algorithms for the creation of ciphertext and its decryption. It is also somewhat similar in that, whereas the polyalphabetic cipher uses a repeating key, the block cipher uses a permutating yet repeating cipher block. Each algorithm uses two inputs: a key and a "block" of bits, each of a set size. Each output block is the same size as the input block, the block being transformed by the key. The key, which is algorithm based, is able to select the permutation of its bijective mapping from $2n$, where n is equal to the number of bits in the *input* block. Often when 128-bit encryption is discussed, it is referring to the size of the *input* block. Typical encryption methods involve use of XOR chaining or some similar operation (Fig. 3.4).

Block ciphers have been widely used since 1976 in many encryption standards. As such, for a long time cracking these ciphers became the top priority of cipher crackers everywhere. Block ciphers provide the backbone algorithmic technology behind most modern-era ciphers.

5. THE COMPUTER AGE

Many people consider January 1, 1970, to be the dawn of the computer age. That is when Palo Alto Research Center (PARC) in California introduced modern computing; the graphical user interface (no more command line and punch cards), networking on an Ethernet, and object-oriented programming have all been attributed to PARC. The 1970s also featured the UNIX clock, Alan Shepard on the moon, the US Bicentennial, the civil rights movement, women's liberation, Robert Heinlein's sci-fi classic, *Stranger in a Strange Land*, the birth of my wife, and, most important to this chapter, modern cryptography. The late 1960s and early 1970s changed the face of the modern world at breakneck speed. Modern warfare reached tentative heights with radio-guided missiles, and warfare needed a new hero. And then there was the Data Encryption Standard (DES); in a sense, DES was the turning point for cryptography, in that for the first time it fully leveraged the power of modern computing in its algorithms. The sky appeared to be the limit, but, unfortunately for those who wanted to keep their information secure, decryption techniques were not far behind.

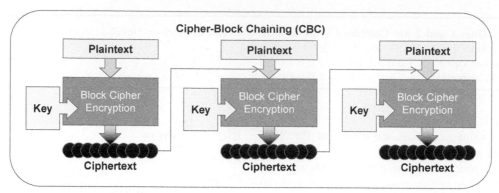

FIGURE 3.4 XOR chaining, or cipher-block chaining, is a method in which the next block of plaintext to be encrypted is XOR'd with the previous block of ciphertext before being encrypted.

Data Encryption Standard

In the mid-1970s, the US Government issued a public speci-fication, through its National Bureau of Standards (NBS), called the DES. This could perhaps be considered the dawn of modern cryptography because it was likely the first block ci-pher, or at least its first widespread implementation. However, the 1970s were a relatively untrusting time. "Big Brother" loomed right around the corner (as per George Orwell's *1984*), and most people did not understand or necessarily trust DES. Issued under the NBS, now called the National Institute of Standards and Technology (NIST), hand in hand with the National Security Agency (NSA), DES led to tremendous interest in the reliability of the standard among academia's ivory towers. A shortened key length and the implementation of substitution boxes, or "S-boxes," in the algorithm led many to think that the NSA had deliberately weakened the algo-rithms and left a security "back door" of sorts.

The use of S-boxes in the standard was not generally understood until the design was published in 1994 by Don Coppersmith. The S-boxes, it turned out, had been delib-erately designed to prevent a sort of cryptanalysis attack called *differential cryptanalysis*, as was discovered by IBM researchers in the early 1970s; the NSA had asked IBM to keep quiet about it. In 1990 the method was "re"-discovered independently, and when used against DES, the usefulness of the S-boxes became readily apparent.

Theory of Operation

DES used a 64-bit block cipher combined with a mode of operation based on cipher-block chaining (CBC) called the *Feistel function*. This consisted of an initial expansion permutation followed by 16 rounds of XOR key mixing via subkeys and a key schedule, substitution (S-boxes), and permutation.[8] In this strategy, a block is increased from 32

to 48 bits (expansion permutation). Then the 48-bit block is divided in half. The first half is XORs, with parts of the key according to a key schedule. These are called subkeys. Fig. 3.5 shows this concept in a simplified format.

The resulting cipher is then XOR'd with the half of the cipher that was not used in step 1. The two halves switch sides. Substitution boxes reduce the 48 bits down to 32 bits via a nonlinear function, and then a permutation, according to a permutation table, takes place. Then the entire process is repeated 16 times, except in the last step the two halves are not flipped. Finally, this diffusive strategy produced via substitution, permutation, and key schedules creates an effective ciphertext. Because a fixed-length cipher, a block cipher, is used, the permutations and the S-box introduce enough confusion that the cipher cannot be deduced through brute force methods without extensive computing power.

With the increase in size of hard drives and computer memory, the need for disk space and bandwidth still de-mands that a block-cipher algorithm be portable. DES, Triple DES, and the AES all provide or have provided solutions that are secure and practical.

Implementation

Despite the controversy at the time, DES was implemented. It became the encryption standard of choice until the late 1990s, when it was broken, when Deep Crack and distributed.net broke a DES key in 22 h 15 min. Later that year, a new form of DES called Triple DES, which encrypted the plaintext in three iterations, was published. It remained in effect until 2002, when it was superseded by AES.

Rivest, Shamir, and Adleman

The release of DES included the creation and release of Ron Rivest, Adi Shamir, and Leonard Adleman's encryp-tion algorithm [Rivest, Shamir, and Adleman (RSA)]. Rivest, Shamir, and Adleman, based at the Massachusetts Institute of Technology, publicly described the algorithm in

---

8. A. Sorkin, Lucifer: a cryptographic algorithm, Cryptologia 8 (1) (1984) 22−35.

Feistel Structure of DES (Simplified)

1. Plaintext	0	0	0	0	0	0	0	0	
2. Expanded plaintext A)*	0	0	0	0	0	0	>	>	
3. Cipher	1	0	1	0	0	1			
4. Ciphertext A	1	0	1	0	0	1			
5. Expanded Plaintext B)	0	0	1	1	1	1			
6. Cipher from Step 1:	1	0	1	0	0	0			
7. Ciphertext B	1	0	0	1	1	1			

Expanded Plaintext B:

>> | 0 | 0 | 1 | 1 | 1 | 1 |

Key Schedule
1. 101000
2. 100101
.
.
.
15. 010100
16. 101101

8. Cipher (B,A)   1 0 0 1 1 1   1 0 1 0 0 0
9. Substitution (S–box)   0 0 0 1   1 0 0 1
10. Permutation P–Box   0 1 0 0   0 1 1 0

Key (16 parts) : 101000 010101 101011 . . . 010100 100101 101010 101101

S – Box**	0011	0100
10	0101	1001
11	0001	1100

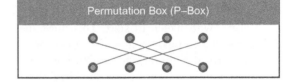

Permutation Box (P–Box)

*A bijective function is applied to expand from 32 bits (represented here by 8 bits) to 48 bits. A function is bijective if inverse relation f^{-1} (x) is also a function. Reduction is achieved through the S–box operation.

** This S–box is reduced to include only the four bits that are in our cipher. Typical S–boxes are as large as needed and may be based partially on the key.

FIGURE 3.5 The Feistel function with a smaller key size. *DES,* Data Encryption Standard.

1977. RSA is the first encryption standard to introduce (to public knowledge) the new concept of digital signing. In 1997 it was revealed through declassification of papers that Clifford Cocks, a British mathematician working for the UK Government Communications Headquarters, had written a paper in 1973 describing this process. Assigned top secret status, the work had never previously seen the light of day. Because it was submitted in 1973, the method had been considered unattainable, because computing power at the time could not handle its methods.

Advanced Encryption Standard (or Rijndael)

AES represents one of the latest chapters in the history of cryptography. Once it became clear that neither DES nor its answer to its weaknesses, "Triple-DES," could carry encryption through to the 21st century, a decree went out from the NIST so that a new standard might be achieved. AES won out over the other standards for several reasons, and it is currently one of the most popular encryption standards.

For people involved in any security work, its occurrence on the desktop is frequent. It also enjoys the free marketing and acceptance that it received when it was awarded the title of official cryptography standard in 2001.[9] This designation went into effect in May of the following year.

To a large degree, this part of the chapter is merely a rehashing/book report on the Federal Information Processing Standards (FIPS) 197 standard, because this appears to be one of the more authoritative guides available, short of the authors themselves. It provides a few original examples and some observations made by the author during his examination of the standard.

Similar to DES, AES encrypts plaintext in a series of rounds, involves the use of a key and block sizes, and leverages substitution and permutation boxes. It differs from DES in the following respects:

- It supports 128-bit block sizes.
- The key schedule is based on the S-box.

9. U.S. FIPS PUB 197 (FIPS 197), November 26, 2001.

- It expands the key, not the plaintext.
- It is not based on a Feistel cipher.
- It is extremely complex.

The AES algorithms are to symmetric ciphers what a bowl of spaghetti is to the shortest distance between two points. Through a series of networked XOR operations, key substitutions, temporary variable transformations, increments, iterations, expansions, value swapping, S-boxing, and the like, a strong encryption is created that, with modern computing, creates a cipher that in itself is impossible to break. Like all ciphers, though, AES is only as strong as its weakest link, which is the password routine. This weakness will be explored toward the end of this part of the chapter.

Overview

Simply put, it works like this: First, the idea is to confuse the real message and the encrypted message. Like other encryption methods, it uses the XOR to do this. AES requires 128, 192, or 256 bits to work; however, one must have a "key" with which to start. This might be a password or a string of random numbers stored on a card, or any input derived from an unchanging but unique thing, such as your retina. From there, the "key" needs to be both obfuscated and expanded to match the correct block size, and to be parceled up into the little packages, or blocks, that will be used in later operations of the encryption sequence. To accomplish this, a procedure called Password-Based Key Derivation Function (PBKDF2) is used.[10] Enciphering is then achieved by using an XOR and hashing the bits together repeatedly through a shift row offset. This effectively "shuffles the deck."

Next, introduce diffusion using a simple column transposition to rearrange the bits until they are no longer sensible as letters, and then hashing the bits using substitution (XOR). Furthermore, AES employs a key expansion and multiple rounds. For example, if you XOR a string and produce ciphertext, you have successfully obfuscated the message. If you want anyone to read it, just give them the key and they can reverse the XOR to get the correct text. The problem arises in portability: We want people to be able to decrypt our messages, but only if they have the pass key. This is where things get tricky, because we have to have a key that is long (128 or 256 bits), but that can be generated from a password that is reasonably short, so that we can remember it. Ultimately, this is the weakness of AES or actually the gateway into it: that is, the weak link.

The FIPS 197 standard canonicalizes the Rijndael algorithm (Fig. 3.6) [3,4], which is a symmetric block cipher with the capability of processing blocks of 128 bits. To do this, it employs a multistep operation, enciphering the plaintext blocks using cipher keys with lengths of 128, 192, and 256 bits. The Rijndael algorithm possesses the ability to handle additional block sizes and key lengths, so although the capability exists, it is not part of the published FIPS 197 standard. This part of the chapter will cover the following topics:

1. some definitions that have not yet been covered
2. a brief discussion of the notation and conventions used
3. some mathematical properties of the algorithm
4. a brief discussion of how a password becomes a 128 (or longer) cipher key
5. a summary of the algorithm specification, including the key expansion, encryption, and decryption routines
6. implementation issues
7. a step-by-step example from FIPS 197

The Basics of Advanced Encryption Standard

The basic unit of encryption is the byte. If you read the beginning of this part of the chapter, you already know that the cipher key must be in the form of 128, 192, or 256 bits, which is 16, 24, or 32 bytes, respectively. All bit values are 0 or 1; NULL values are disallowed. This of course may spark the question, "How, then, do NULL values get encrypted in BIT columns in a database?" In Microsoft SQL Server, an additional "hidden" column called a NULLmap exists; if a value is NULL, it will be set to 1 otherwise, 0.[11]

AES encryption operates at the byte level, with each 4 bits represented (for convenience here) hexidecimally so that the following is true:

Binary value.hexidecimal value

For example, the value 1100 1101 would be represented as/xCD. XOR'd, with 0111 0110/x76, would result in 1011 1011, or/xBB. (Note how obfuscating it is that two completely different pairs can XOR to the same value.)

6. HOW ADVANCED ENCRYPTION STANDARD WORKS

The following describes each step of the cipher. It is a simplification, intended to provide a solid foundation for future study of the standard.

---

10. RSA Laboratories Public-Key Cryptography Standards (PKCS) #5: Password-Based Cryptography Specification, Version 2.0. Network Working Group, B. Kaliski.

11. P.S. Randall, Misconceptions around Null Bitmap Size, 2012. http://www.sqlskills.com/BLOGS/PAUL/post/Misconceptions-around-null-bitmap-size.aspx.

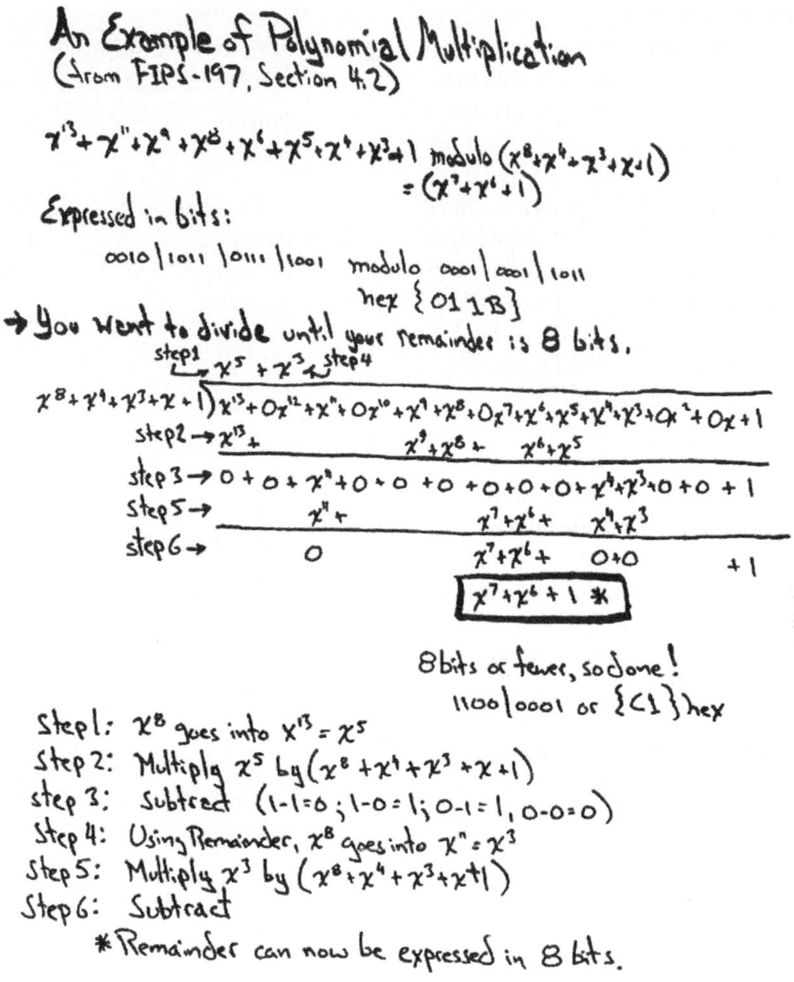

FIGURE 3.6   Handwritten example of polynomial expansion using the Rijndael/Advanced Encryption Standard encryption algorithm.

Bytes

Programmatically, to encipher the plaintext bits, the AES procedure requires all of the bits to be loaded and arranged into a two-dimensional array called the State. The State has four rows in it, and each row contains 4 bytes. This is a total of 16 bytes, or 128 bits.

Note: You might ask, "128 bits is great, but how did we go from a 32-bit password typed by a user to a 128-bit cipher key?" This can be done in a number of ways, and an industrious engineer may certainly write his own method for it, but for the readers of this book, check out the PBKDF2. This is a key derivation function that is part of RSA Laboratories Public Key Cryptography Standards. It replaces an earlier standard, PBKDF1, which could only produce derived keys up to 160 bits long.

The bytes are arranged in columns, so that the first column, first row (let us call it A1) has, right "beneath" it, A2, which would b the second byte of the string to be encrypted. The actual FIPS standard has more dramatic notations for this, but essentially what is happening is that in the State, bytes are referred to by row and by column, and they are loaded top to bottom, left to right. Each column of 4 bytes in the State is referred to as Word. Then it starts to do some math.

Math

The AES standard employs the mathematical operations of both addition and multiplication. Addition using the XOR has already been covered heavily in this chapter. For examples see Table 3.6. This standard also relies heavily on prime, or irreducible, polynomials to allow for enciphering of the bits and to keep things nice and tidy in 128-bit buckets. It is important that for reversibility, all of the multiplication operations, where strings of bits are represented as polynomials which can then be manipulated, allowing for the shifting of bits, remain irreducible.

For example, multiply together the primes 3, 7, and 17, and the resulting number is easily calculated as 357. By factoring it, you can easily derive the exact three numbers used in the original equation. Now multiply together 2, 8, and 16, and you get 256. Unfortunately, if you try to invert the operation, with the requirement that you want only three factors, you can arrive at 4, 4, and 16. Perhaps this is fine if you are writing a data-scrambling application, but an encryption utility is only as good as its ability to invert the cipher and decrypt the string. The AES standard outlines the mathematical polynomials used in the multiplication operations, and it defines them as being irreducible. For example, the purpose of one of the polynomial expressions in AES is simply to rotate the word, so that [b0, b1, b2, b3] is transformed into [b1, b2, b3, b0]. An irreducible polynomial is used so that no matter what the input produces, the inverse operation performed against the output cipher-text yields the correct input. The cipher key becomes the *solution* for an extremely long equation, a solution that has such great uniqueness that it cannot be guessed easily or quickly.

Fig. 3.5 provides an example of the actual mathematics behind the first expansion of the FIPS 197 standard. In it, each power of x takes a bit position, numbered as follows: 7654 3210. So, x^7 turns on the bit in position 7, x^6 in position 6, and x^0 (i.e., 1) takes the zeroth position. Hence, $x^7 + x^6 + 1 = 1100\ 0001$. This is why the remainder has to have x to the power of 7 or less, so it can be expressed in 8 bits. According to the standard, "these bytes are interpreted as finite field elements using a polynomial representation." Frequently, to conserve space or just to make things look less ridiculously *binary*, a hexadecimal value may be used. Table 3.10 demonstrates the conversion of binary to base 16, aka "hexidecimal."

In the Beginning

In the beginning, there are bits, and the bits have a physicality that is linear. That is, they are all lined up in one continuous string on the disk, unless the disk is fragmented, but that is another story. You should always keep your disks defragmented. Fragmentation is bad and will affect the performance of processing data for encryption. If, for example, you are encrypting thousands of files in a particular folder on the disk, and the files are all over the place, it will perform poorly. I digress. When a program that executes AES encryption gets its byte on your bits, the first thing it does is load them into a series of arrays called the State. This particular state is good because it will not take all of your money or tell you that you did not pay enough taxes last year. What it will do is provide a place where many different operations can be executed to encrypt your data better using a 128-bit cipher key. For the purpose of convenience, although AES can handle 192- and 256-bit encryption as well, the author simply refers to the 128-bit model. All operations are performed against this two-dimensional array of bytes

TABLE 3.10 Binary and Its Hexadecimal Equivalents

Binary	Hex
0000	0
0001	1
0010	2
0011	3
0100	4
0101	5
0110	6
0111	7
1000	8
1001	9
1010	a
1011	b
1100	c
1101	d
1110	e
1111	f

called the State, which contains four rows of bytes; each row holds Nb bytes, where Nb is the block length (128, 192, 256) divided by 32.

The State array, s, has two indices. Denoted by the symbol s, each individual byte has two indices, with its row number r in the range $0 \leq r < 4$ and its column number c in the range $0 \leq c < Nb$. This allows an individual byte of the State to be referred to as either sr,c or s[r,c]. AES requires Nb = 4, so that $0 \leq c < 4$. In other words, if you think of an input, a state, and an output array as being the program product line, each array will be the same size. AES explodes the size of the output file.

Rounds

The number of rounds to be executed by the algorithm depends on the key size. Nr = 10 when Nk = 4, Nr = 12 when Nk = 6, and Nr = 14 when Nk = 8. AES, for encipherment, uses a "round" methodology, where each round consists of four steps:

1. byte substitution driven by a substitution table (S-box)
2. the shifting of rows in the State array by an offset
3. bit and byte shuffling within each column of the State
4. adding a round key to the State

These transformations (and their inverses) are explained in detail in Sections 5.1.1–5.1.4 and 5.3.1–5.3.4 of FIPS

197. Details and code samples can be found in the standard. This example is drawn directly from the standard and details the operations of the cipher itself. Essentially, the following functions are described in the standard and can be understood to be the steps taken in each encryption round. The number of rounds depends on the size of the encryption key:

1. SubBytes(state)
2. ShiftRows(state)
3. MixColumns(state)
4. AddRoundKey(state, w[round*Nb, (round + 1)*Nb-1])

By now, the reader of this text should realize that public standards such as FIPS 197 contain a wealth of information and that the chapters in this book can merely provide (it is hoped) the background needed to lend clarity to the material. This part of the chapter is, of course, no substitution for actually reading and adhering to the standard as published.

Finally, it is conceivable that with so complex a series of operations, a computer file and block could be combined in such a way as to produce all zeros. Theoretically, the AES cipher could be broken by solving massive quadratic equations that take into consideration every possible vector and solve 8000 quadratic equations with 1600 binary unknowns. This sort of an attack is called an *algebraic attack*, and, where traditional methods such as differential or differential cryptanalysis fail, it is suggested that the strength in AES lies in the current inability to solve supermultivariate quadratic equations with any sort of efficiency.

Reports that AES is not as strong as it should be are currently likely to be overstated and inaccurate, because anyone can present a paper that is dense and difficult to understand and claims to achieve the incredible. It is unlikely that at any time in the near or maybe not so near future (this author hedges his bets), AES will be broken using multivariate quadratic polynomials in thousands of dimensions. Mathematica is very likely one of the most powerful tools that can solve quadratic equations, and it is still many years away from being able to perform this feat.

Ultimately, AES's biggest drawback is that a user can trigger an encryption using a password of his or her choice. Unfortunately, most people choose passwords that are not strong; they want something they will *remember*. There are many IT techs who lost their passwords and rendered systems inalterable. There have also been many sinister communications that may pass from an employee to a future employer, or a competitor with whom he has become friendly, and has decided to pass secrets. Intellectual property tort is a real facet of litigation, and to this end, large consultancies that deal in computer forensics and e-discovery host rack upon rack of devices that are designed specifically to decrypt files that have been encrypted using AES encryption. They do this not by attacking the algorithm, but by attacking using brute force. *Hash tables*, or rainbow tables, are basically a list of all the known hash values of common (and not so common) passwords. For example, one might take every known phone number in the United States and create a table of all of their known hashes. One might also create one of every known child's name and parse that into the hash tables. For example, a phone number of 847-555-5555 might be combined with the name "Ethan" (who is known to live at a certain address, 233 TreeView), into a password of 233Ethan5555tree! (I added the exclamation point to be even more "secure"…). In fact, some of the largest consultancy firms that manage large litigations have constructed exactly this sort of database of rainbow tables, and they are generating more and more hashes each day. Programs that provide entire disk encryption are the bane of both law enforcement and litigation.

Brute force attacks are the only way to crack in when no key can (or will) be produced. Why do rainbow tables work? The spectrum of possible passwords that people may choose to use *because they can remember* them is much smaller than the total number of possible passwords that exist. By leveraging as much as 7 terabytes of rainbow tables against an encrypted body, the estimated success rate of cracking files, speculatively, could be as high as 60% to 70%. This is a horrible statistic for an encryption algorithm that is supposedly "unbreakable." So perhaps the one take-away from this writing is that there is still room for improvement; a truly unbreakable system still does not exist, and although the algorithm of AES cannot be successfully attacked through decomposition of the ciphertext, any system that fails to take into account *every* attack vector ultimately will be no stronger than its weakest link.

Finally, let us briefly look at the process used to select cryptographic mechanisms. This is similar to the process used to select any IT mechanism.

7. SELECTING CRYPTOGRAPHY: THE PROCESS

The cryptography selection process is documented in the system development life cycle (SDLC) model. An organization can use many SDLC models to develop an information system effectively. A traditional SDLC is a linear sequential model. This model assumes that the system will be delivered near the end of its development life cycle. Another SDLC model employs prototyping, which is often used to develop an understanding of system requirements without developing a final operational system. More complex models have been developed to address the evolving complexity of advanced and large information system designs. The SDLC model is embedded in any of the major system developmental approaches:

- waterfall: The phases are executed sequentially.
- spiral: The phases are executed sequentially, with feedback loops to previous phases.
- incremental development: Several partial deliverables are constructed, and each deliverable has incrementally more functionality. Builds are constructed in parallel, using available information from previous builds. The product is designed, implemented, integrated, and tested as a series of incremental builds.
- evolutionary: There is replanning at each phase in the life cycle, based on feedback. Each phase is divided into multiple project cycles with deliverable measurable results at the completion of each cycle.

An Agenda for Action for Selecting the Cryptographic Process Activities

The following high-level checklist questions should be addressed in determining the appropriate cryptographic mechanisms, policies, and procedures for a system (check all tasks completed):

_____1. How critical is the system to the organization's mission, and what is the impact level?

_____2. What are the performance requirements for cryptographic mechanisms (communications throughput and processing latency)?

_____3. What intersystem and intrasystem compatibility and interoperability requirements need to be met by the system (algorithm, key establishment, and cryptographic and communications protocols)?

_____4. What are the security/cryptographic objectives required by the system (content integrity protection, source authentication required, confidentiality, and availability)?

_____5. For what period of time will the information need to be protected?

_____6. What regulations and policies are applicable in determining what is to be protected?

_____7. Who selects the protection mechanisms that are to be implemented in the system?

_____8. Are the users knowledgeable about cryptography, and how much training will they receive?

_____9. What is the nature of the physical and procedural infrastructure for the protection of cryptographic material and information (storage, accounting and audit, and logistics support)?

_____10. What is the nature of the physical and procedural infrastructure for the protection of cryptographic material and information at the facilities of outside organizations with which cryptographically protected communications are required (facilities and procedures for protection of physical keying material)?

Security should be incorporated into all phases, from initiation to disposition, of an SDLC model. The goal of the selection process is to specify and implement cryptographic methods that address specific agency/organization needs.

Before selecting a cryptographic method, an organization should consider the operational environment, application requirements, types of services that can be provided by each type of cryptography, and cryptographic objectives that must be met when selecting applicable products. Based on the requirements, several cryptographic methods may be required. For example, both symmetric and asymmetric cryptography may be needed in one system, each performing different functions (symmetric encryption, and asymmetric digital signature and key establishment). In addition, high-level checklist questions should be addressed in determining the appropriate cryptographic mechanisms, policies, and procedures for a system (see checklist: An Agenda for Action for Selecting the Cryptographic Process Activities).

8. SUMMARY

Today's IT security environment consists of highly interactive and powerful computing devices and interconnected systems of systems across global networks in which organizations routinely interact with industry, private citizens, state and local governments, and the governments of other nations. Consequently, both private and public sectors depend on information systems to perform essential and mission-critical functions. In this environment of increasingly open and interconnected systems and networks, network and data security are essential for the optimum use of this IT. For example, systems that carry out electronic financial transactions and electronic commerce must protect against unauthorized access to confidential records and the unauthorized modification of data.

Thus, in keeping with the preceding, this chapter provided guidance to organizations regarding how to select cryptographic controls for protecting sensitive information. However, to provide additional information, products of other standards organizations (the American National Standards Institute and International Organization for Standardization) were briefly discussed.

This chapter was also intended for security individuals responsible for designing systems and for procuring, installing, and operating security products to meet identified security requirements. This chapter may be used by:

- a manager responsible for evaluating an existing system and determining whether cryptographic methods are necessary;
- program managers responsible for selecting and integrating cryptographic mechanisms into a system;
- a technical specialist requested to select one or more cryptographic methods/techniques to meet a specified requirement;

- a procurement specialist developing a solicitation for a system or network that will require cryptographic methods to perform security functionality.

In other words, this chapter provided those individuals with sufficient information that allowed them to make informed decisions about the cryptographic methods that met their specific needs to protect the confidentiality, authentication, and integrity of data that are transmitted and/or stored in a system or network. In addition, this primer also provided information about selecting cryptographic controls and implementing the controls in new or existing systems.

Finally, let us move on to the real interactive part of this chapter: review questions/exercises, hands-on projects, case projects, and the optional team case project. The answers and/or solutions by chapter can be found in the Online Instructor's Solutions Manual.

CHAPTER REVIEW QUESTIONS/ EXERCISES

True/False

1. True or False? For most information technology occupations, knowledge of cryptography is a large part of a broader skill set and is generally limited to relevant applications.
2. True or False? Cryptography is built on one overarching premise: the need for a cipher that can be used reliably and portably to encrypt text so that through any means of cryptanalysis (differential, deductive, algebraic, or the like) the ciphertext can be undone with any available technology.
3. True or False? In effect, the Vernam stream cipher and "one-time pad" ciphers are different; in fact, Vernam later coinvented it.
4. True or False? DES used a 64-bit block cipher combined with a mode of operation based on cipher-block chaining (CBC) called the *Feistel function.*
5. True or False? The cryptography selection process is documented in the system development life cycle (SDLC) model.

Multiple Choice

1. In essence, computer-based cryptography is the art of creating a form of communication that embraces the following precepts, except which two?
   A. Can be readily misunderstood by the intended recipients
   B. Cannot be understood by the unintended recipients
   C. Can be understood by the unintended recipients
   D. Can be readily understood by the intended recipients

   E. Can be adapted and changed easily with relatively small modifications, such as a changed pass phrase or word
2. What is known as the method of encryption?
   A. Plaintext
   B. Clear text
   C. Ciphertext
   D. Cryptogram
   E. Cipher
3. Decryption methods often rely on understanding the context of the:
   A. Cipher
   B. Ciphertext
   C. Shift cipher
   D. Cryptogram
   E. Cryptographic algorithms
4. The amount of ciphertext needed to break a cipher successfully is known as:
   A. Benford's law
   B. Chi-square statistic
   C. Polyalphabetic cipher
   D. Kerckhoff's principle
   E. Unicity distance
5. One method of teasing out the frequency patterns is through the application of some sort of mathematical formula to test a hypothesis against reality. What test is perhaps one of the most commonly used?
   A. Inferential statistics test
   B. Chi-square test
   C. Statistical test
   D. Random binary stream cipher test
   E. Block cipher test

EXERCISE

Problem

OpenSSL has a trick in it that mixes uninitialized memory with the randomness generated by the operating system's formal generator. The standard idea here is that it is good practice to mix different sources of randomness into your own source. Modern operating systems take several random things such as disk drive activity and net activity and mix the measurements into one pool, and then run it through a fast hash to filter it. Cryptoplumbing, on the other hand, of necessity involves lots of errors and fixes and patches. Bug-reporting channels are important, and apparently this was used. A security team found the bug with an analysis tool. It was duly reported up to OpenSSL, but the handover was muffed. The reason it was muffed was that it was not obvious what was going on. The reason it was not obvious is that code was too clever for its own good. It tripped up the analysis tool and the programmers, and the fix did not alert the OpenSSL programmers.

Complexity is always the enemy in security code. So, with the preceding in mind, as a risk manager, what would you do to fix the problem?

Hands-On Projects

Project

What is the basic method for using the output of a random bit generator?

Case Projects

Problem

How would an organization go about generating key pairs for asymmetric key algorithms?

Optional Team Case Project

Problem

How would an organization go about generating keys for symmetric key algorithms?

Chapter 4

Verifying User and Host Identity

Keith Lewis

Keller Graduate School of Management, Naperville, IL, United States

1. INTRODUCTION: VERIFYING THE USER

With access granted and implemented to people who have authorized approval to secure data because of the increasing use of mobile devices and cloud-based solutions, criminals have become better at using advanced hacking techniques that continue to grow in complexity and design every year. Verifying user or host identity authenticity requires validation controls to stay ahead of these challenges. This is where identity access management design is important and user access management controls need to be fortified.

2. IDENTITY ACCESS MANAGEMENT: AUTHENTICATION AND AUTHORIZATION

Identity access management begins with the core security entry points a person or process must go through using authentication, authorization, and account provisioning. For user verification purposes, in this chapter we will review authentication and authorization (Fig. 4.1) in more detail.

Authentication

To verify that you are you in the digital computer landscape, the beginning process of authentication is required (your personal key in the door). Your first-level key of authentication usually consists of a username [your identifier (ID)] and password (the secret information you and the computer system agreed would validate that your digital identity is genuine).

Unfortunately it is no longer as simple as employing a username and password because hackers are getting better each year. Other important validations are now required to ensure a secure authentication experience. These validations can vary based on the types of systems you are accessing. Additional authentication techniques that commonly accompany username and password verifications are [1]:

- *Security questionnaires*: personal question information you were either required or volunteered to enter into the system while creating the account or during security validations;
- *Two- or multiple-factor authentication* (Fig. 4.2): a device, an interface, biometric security, location

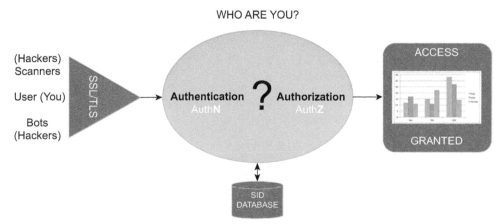

FIGURE 4.1 Authorization and authentication. *SSL*, Secure socket layer; *TLS*, transport layer security.

Computer and Information Security Handbook. http://dx.doi.org/10.1016/B978-0-12-803843-7.00004-1

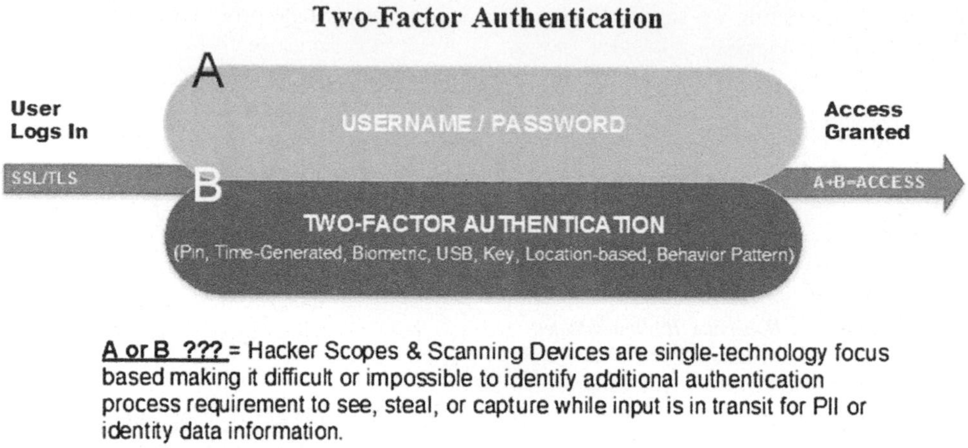

Two-Factor Authentication

A or B **???** = Hacker Scopes & Scanning Devices are single-technology focus based making it difficult or impossible to identify additional authentication process requirement to see, steal, or capture while input is in transit for PII or identity data information.

FIGURE 4.2   Two-factor authentication. *PII*, Personally identifiable information; *SSL*, secure socket layer; *TLS*, transport layer security; *USB*, universal serial bus.

information, or past behavioral responses that give additional security validation to the process;

- *Secure encryption:* when you enter your username, password, or other validation data during authentication, you want to make sure no one is spying on your information transmitted to the system by encrypting or hashing the data entered into data fields.

Password Rule Hardening: Practices

It is important to have a strong password policy rule set to prevent brute force attacks into your login pages. These kinds of policies prevent continuous hacking script-bots from attempting multiple key or password combinations into the login portal before a successful one is used and finally found by trial and error (see checklist: "An Agenda for Action for Password Rule Hardening Best Practices") [1].

An Agenda for Action for Password Rule Hardening Best Practices

Complex password requirements include the following key activities (check all tasks completed):

____1. 8−25 characters that require at least one capital letter, one unique character, (!, $, etc.), and one numeric character (0−9);

____2. 30-, 60-, or 90-day password change requirement;

____3. unique password history requirement (the last 10 passwords);

____4. common word restriction policy (such as that your name, user ID, the word "password," etc., cannot be used or be any part of your password);

____5. Limited password attempts (on many stronger systems, three failed attempts will lock out your account, requiring you to reset your password through controlled validations or requiring you to call or contact technical support to unlock your account once your identity has been thoroughly validated).

The Importance of Secure Socket Layer/Transport Layer Security

The bad guys (hackers) are almost everywhere on the Internet nowadays. They not only attempt to look for holes in security systems but also continuously monitor Internet traffic through scanner devices to pick up clear text transmissions of usernames, passwords, credit card numbers, or anything they can find to get them through the door of your data and financial systems. Secure socket layer protocol (SSL) and transport layer security (TLS) are the first line of defense when sending this kind of information over the Internet. This process encrypts the information you send into nonsense binary information that is understood and translated correctly only by the host computer after it is decrypted at its target security source location (e.g. the website and web services you are attempting to access). URL designations on your browser such as https:// (it is important to note the "s") identify that the site to which you are going is currently a trusted channel of communication. Once initial trust information validation is completed, your session stays encrypted over SSL throughout the session. Using this secure process provides protection against hackers eavesdropping, intercepting, capturing, or changing your secure data during communication transport. Encryption processing can also work on instant messaging (chat communication), faxing, email communication, and applications, and even through phone communication over voice-over-Internet protocol (IP) transmissions. For more detail on how SSL and TLS works, see Chapter 38 for more information.

Authorization

Now that your digital identity is authenticated and confirmed, your preconfigured authorized security access will allow you access to the resources for which you are preapproved. Types of authorization structures can be based their role or security group configuration. For internal network company-based operating systems such as Microsoft Windows PC operating systems, Active Directory domains are used with the security database and are managed by system support engineers for company network access to an organization's shared services (file shares, databases, printers, applications, etc.).

The Importance of Directory Services

Once a session is successfully authenticated, controlled authorization is required to identify the preapproved level of authority of permission of access for this user or process. This control process can use two security type techniques; role-based or security group–based:

1. *Role-based security access*: This methodology process focuses on granting appropriate system and data access to users based on their predefined business or organizational role in the system.
2. *Security group–based access*: This can be a unique approach of group designations that normally does not focus on role-based functions but still must adhere to a structured and validated approach to access based on the security control audit requirement. A user or computer process would use this type of security setting.

Directory services (Fig. 4.3) define the naming management tree configurations of access by using resources known as objects; these can be devices ranging from networking systems to printing systems, server systems, file shares, user accounts, security groups, phone devices, and many more physical or configured systems that reside on the computer's network. This layer of settings is needed to ensure the security structure for the entire infrastructure's framework that surrounds and binds together a computer

workgroup or enterprise. One of the leading and most used directory services in the industry is the Microsoft Active Directory Services systems. This solution uses domain architecture to manage all of its computer namespaces, users, and system entitlement needs. The X.500 Directory Service standard [3] is the foundation for almost all directory service–based solutions used in the industry today. Lightweight Directory Access Protocol (LDAP) is an industry open-standard process that Directory Services uses heavily to manage distribution management control over Directory Service object database structures.

3. SYNTHETIC OR REAL USER LOGGING

It is a growing challenge to verify that a user on a computer is a "real person" during the login session and it requires checks, validations, and security techniques beyond using just SSL encryption. In addition to complex passwords and security questionnaires, devices such as a mobile phone will use two-factor technologies to provide additional authenticity to the verification process. Leveraging the advantages of two- or multiple-factor authentication methodologies provides a much stronger identification process during the user's computer session by remote isolation through a completely different technology approach. This makes it much more difficult for hackers to find and break into because the activity is separate from the main channel session of attack. These additional solutions might come in the form of:

- mobile phone applications or text response notifications
- universal serial bus sticks, bank cards, or time-based generated key display devices
- pin-required login application program interfaces
- image verification through Completely Automated Public Turing Test to Tell Computers and Humans Apart (CAPTCHA)
- biometric technology such as:
  - voice recognition
  - fingerprint scanning
  - eye iris scanning
  - facial recognition
  - typing pattern matching

Completely Automated Public Turing Test to Tell Computers and Humans Apart

You may have seen CAPTCHA during a password or account creation process in which a randomly distorted image appears with numbers or letters, and the information page will ask you to identify the characters or numbers you see in the image. This process helps validate your identity with human observation and interaction. Most hackers deal with volume hacks and do not have time to perform physical image recognition required for the user account that uses

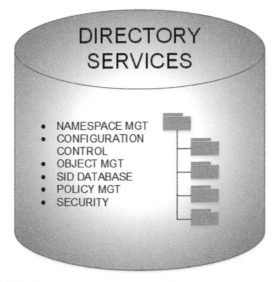

FIGURE 4.3 Directory services functionality. *MGT*, management; *SID*.

and stores private or personal information such as your Social Security card, your mother's maiden name, or any unique and private-centric information [4].

4. VERIFYING A USER IN CLOUD ENVIRONMENTS

Internet solutions now rely on cloud-based infrastructure solutions to manage business and organizations (Fig. 4.4). For security purposes, identity access management solutions have become extremely important because multiple system locations must manage digital user identities over vast landscapes of data centers and network end points to manage a user's security account information successfully.

Working in the cloud for identity management requires federated structures to work with identity service providers. When working with multiple service providers, the federated identity management model must be used so that it is reliable and can scale well with the current business or organization's growth capacity and still be secure. Systems for such large designs working over multiple data points across the Internet can leverage solutions such as Oracle Identity Management using the Oracle Internet Directory Services platform. Common conceptual, technical representations for user cloud security design are [2]:

- *The principal (known as the "subject")*: who requires this access?
- *The entitlement (the access framework)*: the definition of rules and permissions granted to the principal subject (aka the user ID) to route an object request to restricted systems

- *The data source (known as the "objects")*: an object can be a database, data source, or other access targets granted to the principal subject to use.

When verifying a user account in cloud environments, it is important to have a framework in place that immediately transports encrypted digital user identity information to approved and predefined entitlement definitions that will route users to their data information systems no matter which cloud-based data center they enter over the Internet. Cloud frameworks can have multiple data centers all over the globe and must have the identity access management highway roadmap in place so that secure access can be granted efficiently and safely throughout the Internet where these solutions are provided. By using a centralized cloud identity service provider model, you effectively create identity management as a service [3]. Protocol standards such as Security Assertion Markup Language (SAML) and Open Standard of Authorization are the digital identity transport coding streams needed to deliver these authentication validations safely [5].

Strong security model architectures using SAML rely on directory services such as LDAP and Microsoft Active Directory. For digital user accounts (principal subjects) to work seamlessly across multiple cloud providers over the Internet, a user management security model must be implemented using strong and reliable design concepts that follow [2]:

- user account life cycle provisioning and deprovisioning work flows
- rules-based access controls

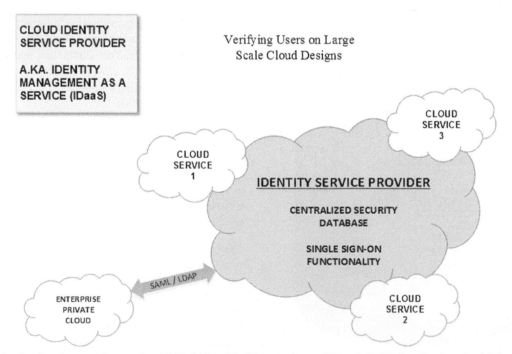

FIGURE 4.4 Cloud environment frameworks. *LDAP*, Lightweight Directory Access Protocol; *SAML*, Security Assertion Markup Language.

- resource-based controls
- single sign-on architecture
- encrypted authentication routing
- trusted cloud–host providers
- identity proxy mediation systems

5. VERIFYING HOSTS

To verify a host, we must define what a host is. When planning and designing security infrastructures, a computer host is the system server that delivers services, which can range from databases to web services, printer queues, file shares, authentication security services, and other multiple-user computer functions required to manage a business or organization's data information management needs.

Thus, if you are logging into a workstation or website, you are logging into a host server that is distributing and managing user account access to appropriate server resources. How can we be sure the host you are accessing is real and authentic? Unless you have a controlled application as your access portal tool set, you will most likely be using web services over the Internet through your browser to access your computer systems. If you are logging into a system through your web browser, it is important to note whether SSL encryption is engaged while you are entering your private security username and password. Fortunately, all of the leading industry browsers such as Chrome, Safari, and Microsoft Internet Explorer display an indicator that you are on a trusted and secured hosting site. Examples of these indicators on your browser can be [4]:

- a golden or displayed lock key icon
- the URL link starting with "https://"
- an eye icon indicating an open session
- your username or identity fields showing up as asterisk characters, representing that their content data fields are being hashed. (Important: Verify the first three points noted here before submitting trusted passwords. Hashed fields can be mimicked on fraudulent sites. Caution should always be taken before submitting your login request.)

6. VERIFYING HOST DOMAIN NAME SYSTEM AND INTERNET PROTOCOL INFORMATION

To ensure that a host identity is valid and registered accurately on the Internet (Fig. 4.5), you can go to an

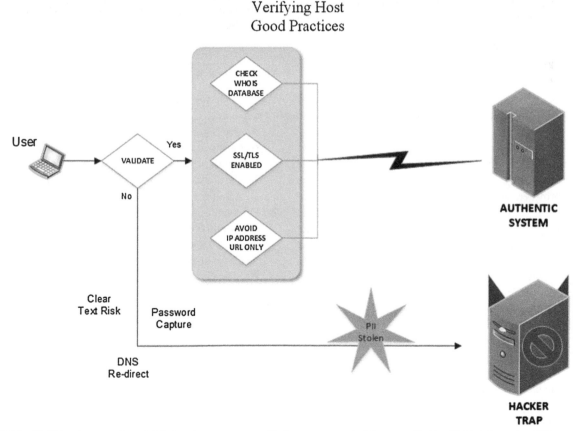

FIGURE 4.5 Verifying host practices. *DNS*, domain name system; *IP*, Internet protocol; *PII*, personally identifiable information; *SSL*, secure socket layer; *TLS*, transport layer security.

Internet database authority site such as https://www.internic.net/whois.html. The Whois database will display the administration account information, web administrator account information, and last creation and modification registration information. This will allow a security manager, system administrator, or tech-savvy user to verify the authenticity of the site by domain name (yahoo.com, etc.), IP address, or name server information [3].

7. SUMMARY

Let us look at the security actions and best practices that users should always take to ensure host validity:

1. *Email links*: Avoid clicking on links from untrustworthy or spammed email content sent to your email account. These links can lead you to a fraudulent or bogus site used to capture your username, password, or personally identifiable information that can be immediately exploited by a hacker to gain access to your systems.
2. *Password laziness*: The problem with having access to multiple web services and applications is that unless they reside on a company's internal single sign-on system, multiple usernames and passwords are required for management. People will tend to employ the same username and password over many systems. Hackers know and promote this, so it is easier for them just to grab a single username and password you most frequently use, and gain access to all of your finances and personal information over valid Internet host services you use every day, such as email, banks, social media sites, and more. Change your passwords frequently and avoid using the same username and password over multiple website services.
3. *Malware toolbar redirects*: Ensure that your computer has the latest antivirus and malware protection, so that you are not fooled into going to a fake website on your browser. A common practice for hackers is to entice you into innocently installing a toolbar plugin containing malware into your browser that can not only capture and send personal data to the hacker but also can also secretly redirect your URL link inquiries in the browser to malicious bogus websites. These fake sites will capture your data without your knowing it until it is too late. For example, avoid IP address links like: http://197.1.5.253/login.html.
4. *Always update operating systems and virus protection*: Make sure your operating system has the latest security patches and antivirus application and data feeds to cover all of the bases needed to avoid hacker system overrides to your system. Setting these local protection solutions to automated updating is essential to ensure you are not intentionally redirected to a hacker's fraudulent environment.

Finally, let us move on to the real interactive part of this chapter: review questions/exercises, hands-on projects, case projects, and an optional team case project. Answers and/or solutions by chapter can be found in Appendix K.

CHAPTER REVIEW QUESTIONS/ EXERCISES

True/False

1. True or False? Verifying a user or host identity authenticity requires validation controls to stay ahead of challenges.
2. True or False? Identity theft management begins with the core security entry points a person or process must go through using authentication, authorization, and account provisioning.
3. True or False? To begin verifying you are you in the digital computer landscape, the beginning process of authentication is required.
4. True or False? It is important to have a strong password policy rule set to prevent brute force attacks into your login pages.
5. True or False? URL designations on your browser such as https:// (it is important to note the "s") identify that the site to which you are going is currently a trusted channel of communication.

Multiple Choice

1. Your first-level key of authentication usually consists of:
   A. Username
   B. Password
   C. Validations
   D. Verifications
   E. All of the above
2. Personal question information you were either required or volunteered to enter into the system while creating the account or during security validations are:
   A. Cross-site−request−forgery attacks
   B. Side-channel attacks (VM-to-VM)
   C. Token stealing
   D. Security questionnaires
   E. All of the above
3. A device, an interface, biometric security, location information, are past behavioral responses that give additional security validation to the process are known as:
   A. Two- or multiple-factor authentication
   B. Low RTO, high cost
   C. Low RTO, low cost, all data
   D. Backup critical data with a low RTO and cost
   E. All of the above

4. When you are entering your username, password, or other validation data during authentication, you want to make sure no one is spying on your information transmitted to the system by encrypting or hashing the data entered into data fields. This is called:

  A. Hybrid
  B. Private
  C. Secure encryption
  D. Virtual private
  E. All of the above

5. What methodology process focuses on granting appropriate system and data access to users based on their predefined business or organizational role in the system?

  A. Role-based security access
  B. Security
  C. Governance
  D. Compliance
  E. All of the above

EXERCISE

Problem

Can social media such as Facebook be used to steal financial information from users?

Hands-On Projects

Project

How can you defend against social media fraud?

Case Projects

Problem

Website applications continue to bear the brunt of attempted fraud. This can result from a number of factors. What are those factors?

Optional Team Case Project

Problem

What is identity verification?

REFERENCES

[1] R. Lemnos, Are Your "Secret Questions" Too Easily Answered?, MIT Technology Review, May 18, 2009.
[2] R. Kanneganti, P. Chodavarapu, SOA Security, Manning Publications Company, 2008.
[3] J.M. Johansson, Microsoft Server 2008 Security Resource Kit, Microsoft Press, 2008.
[4] SANS. http://sans.org.
[5] Gartner. http://www.gartner.com/it-glossary/identity-and-access-management-iam/.

Chapter 5

Detecting System Intrusions

Scott R. Ellis

kCura Corporation, Chicago, IL, United States

1. INTRODUCTION

The data with the greatest usefulness to network security monitoring (NSM) are packet data, preferably full packet capture (FPC) data. Any effort to begin to detect system intrusions requires an unprecedented capability to observe: You must capture any and all FPC data that move through your network. FPC also serves the purpose of being as forensically viable as possible. Regardless of origin, if a hacker moves through your network, FPC is the virtual equivalent of a camera that follows him around, recording his every move. Just like a camera system, though, NSM will not do any good if nobody is watching it.

For this chapter, I will use the term "system" to denote a grouping of similar computing devices. Primarily, the system examined here will be my lab network, called "Lake Bluff Roasting Company," which is a simplistic setup of a handful of PCs, a printer, and assorted mobile devices. Starting with the premise that you cannot observe a stand-alone system from *within* that system, I introduce the concept of taps, and then tap my network. I explain in depth how to maintain and manage your sensor network. This is the heart and soul of NSM: competent administration of the system. To engage in the practice of intrusion detection, you have to be able to build your own tools and understand how they work from the inside out. You need command line, sql, sed, and grep commands, and encryption skills. This chapter endeavors to impart all of the skills needed to engage in *practical NSM*.

Ideally your tap network, the network within which your sensors reside, is isolated and not connected to the business network. If your tap network overlaps with your business network, any intruder can see your instrumentation. Fig. 5.1 shows you can how an intrusion detection system (IDS) can be inserted into the network. Sensors leverage a set of taps, physical devices that do not require a configuration from the perspective of the business network.

In Fig. 5.1, consider that a switch may contain as many as 48, 1-gigabyte/s (Gbps) ports. If it also has 10-Gbps

ports, a switched port analyzer (SPAN) of all traffic crossing the switch *may* not flood it, but depending on your network, you may see frequent spikes that will, and when flooding occurs, the SPAN is the first victim. This diagram may be representative of thousands of computers and switches. At scale, the points at which you tap remain unchanged.

Why Taps?

Without taps, observing the behavior of a hacker on your network cannot be undertaken: that is, not without extreme difficulty and not without the highly probable eventuality that if a hacker has taken control of the subsystem, your attempts to observe the intrusion will be detected, which may eventually trip off automated obfuscation tactics on the part of the attacker, or may just cause him to roll up and vanish without a trace. Worse, you may only see what he shows you. SPANs or mirrors are only ever a compromise. Given a choice, taps are always the best, for several reasons and for certain applications:

1. They are typically mechanical in nature and cannot be compromised without physical modification.
2. Taps are not subject to bandwidth restrictions; interport traffic on a single switch may be more difficult to obtain using a port SPAN or mirror, because the internal CPU of the switch may not be able to bear the load.
3. They are invisible. A hacker in the system who has achieved a privileged position (he is inside your switches) can read the configurations of a managed switch all day long, and he will never know that a tap has been installed between the switch and its access layer. However, you will have been able to watch him as he logged into it.

Practically speaking, SPANs and mirrors are the least desirable way to achieve lateral traffic between computers. They are an alternative when no other option is available. As you see in Fig. 5.1, the tap can intercept traffic at single points,

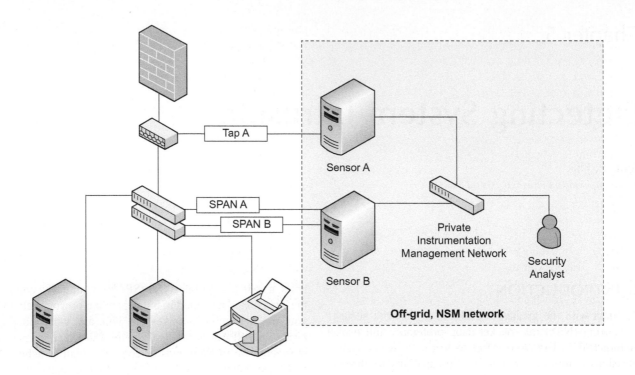

Hybrid Span/Tap Network

FIGURE 5.1 Isolate instrumentation from the business network. *NSM*, network security monitoring.

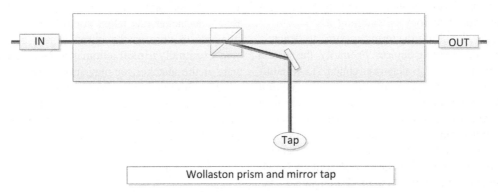

FIGURE 5.2 An optical tap is chiefly mechanical (not electronic) in nature. This simplified rendering demonstrates how an optical tap may be built using a Wollaston prism to split the signal, and a mirror to split it further, from where it passed through in the upper beam.

or bottlenecks, easily and at a low cost. For example, in a large enterprise of 5000 employees, you may have as many as 20 gateways to the Internet, and so you place a fiber tap at each location. But what of the 200 or so network switches that pass traffic from one computer to perhaps its neighbor?

Fig. 5.2 demonstrates functionally how a tap differs from a port mirror. A network designed from the ground up to accommodate a tapped infrastructure is essential for any new network being constructed. The gut reaction of most network infrastructure engineers will be, "I can implement a SPAN with just one command to my managed switch. Why should we spend the money on more hardware?" The

argument is one of demonstration, operating under the simple premise of "They are already inside."

Optical taps are similar to the vampire taps of yesteryear that were used to tap into old coaxial wires, and share the same paradigm. Using optical mirror and prism technology, they allow a copy of traffic to be made and sent to another device.

Network taps, such as those produced by Dualcomm, are electronic devices that offer aggregate and nonaggregate data ports, with internal circuitry responsible for copying and redirecting traffic. Ostensibly, the device is unmanaged and has no interface through which the internal programming could be attacked. Such a device may have vulnerabilities to traffic floods, and traffic can be dropped if an aggregate port is used and the load exceeds the aggregate capabilities.

The crude fact is that because the SPAN exists on the network and as part of it, it is vulnerable. It is not only vulnerable, *it is a target*. Accessing a switch and shutting off a SPAN may not be the number one action of a hacker, but as NSM solutions increase in prevalence, the adroit attacker will examine networks for evidence of monitoring solution implementations. Furthermore, she will disable them if she can.

Why the Secrecy?

The literal definition of the word "forensic" refers to the suitability of something to be presented in a public forum, such as a court. The first rule of a forensic investigation is: Change nothing. In today's computing environment, this rule can be difficult and expensive to follow. Ultimately, preservation is the cornerstone of a good case. Accessing the actual desktop of a suspect computer is tantamount to (1) announcing that you are aware of the intrusion, and (2) spoilage.

Once an intruder is aware he is being watched, he may begin to deploy forensic countermeasures, or worse, begin to take hostages: that is, he may decide to deploy ransomware across your network. This is an outcome that might have been avoided if you had been able to identify the intruder's scope of penetration fully and then successfully blocked all of his access simultaneously. Whereas a bit-by-bit copy of the entire surface of a disk is the de facto forensic standard, so, too, is a tapped network that collects and retains the last 6 months of data from the network. Anything less creates an opportunity not just for missed data but also for engendering misunderstanding of what occurred and what transactions transpired. SPANned networks are subject and vulnerable to compromise and forgery: The intruder can see you watching.

What, then, does this mean for the die-hard desktop support technician who has fallen back on traditional tools to "clean" infected computers? For many of the typical types of intrusions leveraged by the vast majority of unsophisticated intruders, it means that his tools are just fine. The sole purpose of many of these intruders is to create a slave computer for the purpose of hijacking the ads users of the network see on the Internet and thus boost the hacker's bottom line. There are other motives, many of which we will never understand or know.

Your typical hacker may be trying to build a large botnet and sell it on the darknet as a sort of time share. Likely, he does not even know he has infected your network. To him, you are just a number on a report. Many of the bad actors who do these things are purchasing or downloading well-known exploits to which a well-insulated system (one that is well-patched and firewalled) is immune. There are always users on any system who will make a mistake and get phished. These users inadvertently *grant permission* to the hacker to do as he wishes. This occurs mostly because you, as an admin, have had your arms twisted into such a position that you must grant administrative rights to all or most users.

For this threat model, the system administrator is well-equipped. Your everyday tool set, which is composed of antimalicious software (antimalware), antivirus, firewalls, antispam, and other assorted cleaner technologies, will work fine.

There is, however, an alternative threat model. In it, a sophisticated actor, possibly a state-level or organized crime actor, has gained access to your system for the sole purpose of exfiltrating data or placing spyware in key locations. Perhaps you possess sensitive information of great interest. Data such as trading transaction information, banking information, widely used software source code, and personally identifiable information are all high-value targets. In this model, eliminating access to the machine is not enough. Your discovery of a compromised machine, in which that machine has access to sensitive information that is of interest to the actors in your threat model, demands that you investigate. Furthermore, the very existence of such information on your network requires you to be prepared to conduct such an investigation. Secrecy, your invisibility on the corporate networking you are protecting, must be maintained. If the hacker can see you, if your security software is running on a port he can see, then that is a problem. Ideally your access to your sensor network is hard-wired to the security department, and access to the ports is locked down tight. Your computer should be the only one that can talk to your network port.

This chapter relies on examples and procedures that revolve around an open source security monitoring tool set called "Security Onion" (SO). Other tool sets exist that are equally capable, but this tool set is free for download and installation, and installation is easy and driven by graphical user interface (GUI)-style wizards. Integration of the tool set is on Ubuntu (also free), and Doug Burks does a great job of maintaining the suite; he also actively engages with its users on a Google group.

Maintenance of SO servers and sensors, and deep dives into its data require a higher level of command line—style interaction. SO relates well to the study of intrusion detection because this is the underlying principle of NSM: detecting and tracking intrusions.

2. DEVELOPING THREAT MODELS

Getting started: Is your corporation a "secure" organization? Rate the maturity of your systems by reviewing this roadmap (see checklist: "An Agenda for Action for Developing and Deploying a Security Roadmap"): How do you stack up? Has your organization advanced through a similar process? A conversation about security begins with understanding what it takes to become secure and the systems that need to

---

An Agenda for Action for Developing and Deploying a Security Roadmap

Consider spreading each step of this roadmap across a timeline of 6 months to a year or more. The following sample security roadmap outlines how you might approach becoming secure (check all tasks completed):

_____ **1.** Assess:
    _____ **a.** Define and identify security policy functions
    _____ **b.** Develop/adopt an information governance model
_____ **2.** Improve:
    _____ **a.** Evaluate effectiveness of security
    _____ **b.** Evolve policy strategy
    _____ **c.** Implement policy strategy
    _____ **d.** Identify the full policy stack
    _____ **e.** Refine policies and assign controls
    _____ **f.** Stage in the deployment of the full policy stack
_____ **3.** Respond:
    _____ **a.** Establish boundaries; identify and interview stakeholders

    _____ **b.** Configure/develop policies to detect responsive incidents
    _____ **c.** Deploy a supportable incident response standard operating procedure
_____ **4.** Privacy:
    _____ **a.** Identify protected information
    _____ **b.** Define security risk levels for the protected information
    _____ **c.** Messaging: let people know how information should be protected and its acceptable use
_____ **5.** Measure:
    _____ **a.** Monitor progress of plan implementation
    _____ **b.** Develop and refine success metrics on all controls
_____ **6.** Recovery:
    _____ **a.** Identify business-critical systems recovery time and point objectives (RTO/RPO)
    _____ **b.** Evaluate recovery model effectiveness
    _____ **c.** Remediate and deploy compliant RTO/RPO supporting systems

---

be in place that will allow you to assess, at any given time, whether you are secure.

3. SECURING COMMUNICATIONS

The world of security is characterized by skeptical, hyper-paranoid, critical, reality-seeking, hands-on professionals. The learning curve is a steep slope and it is slippery. It is a universe populated by people who read and understand network packets, program in languages such as Assembly and Lisp, and do everything from the command line.

The following sections highlight and give an overview of the tool set you will need to learn to become proficient at this work. The consummate security professional is characterized by his or her mastery of these tools.

The Favored Operating System: Linux

The general preference in the security community is to conduct business from Linux. It is a powerful tool and is believed to be far superior in terms of security compared with any other. Detecting intrusions, that is, the process of monitoring for, tracking down, and investigating a breach, will require the investigator to be more secure than the intruder.

There are many flavors of Linux. SO is built on Ubuntu. If you wanted to, you could build out a deployment of SO "from scratch." Doing so is a more advanced task and will not be covered in this chapter.

Step 1: Let Us Get Secure: Encrypting Files and Using Secure Shell

Let us begin with communications: how security professionals communicate among themselves about the things they learn and see on their network. Security professionals whose responsibility is intrusion detection will be seeing a lot of extremely sensitive data, and passwords and usernames that users foolishly send in clear text. You may need to send this file to an associate. If you attach it to an email, you become just as bad as the user who used an insecure File Transfer Protocol account to send sensitive corporate data to a consultant.

Note: Throughout this chapter, I will use a greater-than sign (">") to denote my command prompt. In other words, you do not need to type the greater-than sign. It is just a marker to tell you, "Hey, we are doing command line stuff now." Sometimes I will put comments after my > command line instructions, preceding each comment with a hashtag ("#"). You should take care not to type in the hashtag sign accidentally. If something is in _italics_, it means you need to replace it with something. In addition, not all prompts will be represented by a greater-than sign; some will denote that a change in permissions to the prompt has occurred, in which case the prompt will be "root@machinename:".

Often in security work, you will need to transfer files. Perhaps you have created a report that contains sensitive information, and you need to send it to your chief information security officer (CISO) to answer a request. The subject line of your email to the requester will be "Information as requested" and your attachment will be entitled "Information_yyyyy-mm-dd_hhmm". You have included the date in a chronologically sortable format because you know recipients may have, or will have, many such reports and revisions of same from you.

You encrypt this report because you have to operate under the presumption that someone is looking over your shoulder, that he has access to your email systems, and that all of your network routers and switches are compromised. Once you leave the relative safety of your secure shell (SSH) connection to your sensors and server and begin to interact with corporate systems, you must assume an increase in risk.

For most of your encryption needs, at least where attachments are concerned, many security professionals choose

Note: If you own a piece of equipment that has a default username and password, and if the device does not force you to change it the first time you login, and you have not checked to make certain its credentials were changed, you must assume that your network is or has been compromised. Act at all times as though someone is watching.

GNU Privacy Guard (GnuPG or GPG). It is open source and regularly maintained. The following steps explain how, at the time of this writing, to install and use GnuPG.

This is going to be all command line, all the time. Security is complex, and complexity and control over granular details is best achieved on the command line. Learning to work on the command line, all of the time, is a massive commitment and a huge change to how most people work. Much of the documentation is obscure at best, and assumes a high level of preexisting competency. It seems as if no author of a manual page (man page) assumes his or her man page will be the first you read. This chapter, and others like it, hopes to begin to bridge that gap and explain the necessity for it as well as the "how" of it.

Gnu Privacy Guard

GnuPG is an encryption suite that you can install at the command line (see Sidebar: "Installing Gnu Privacy Guard"). You can also use GnuPG to begin encrypting documents.

Notice that in the preceding, the key fingerprint is a hash of your key that is unique to your key. You will use this to verify keys. For example, in an Adium conversation

Tip: Typing the following command at the command line will spool out a list of all of the features inherent in the command. > man *command*

Installing GNU Privacy Guard

To install it, at the command line, type:
> sudo apt-get install gnupg
#installs the encryption suite.
Now, generate a key.
> gpg –gen-key
Please select what kind of key you want:
1. RSA and RSA (default)
2. DSA and Elgamal
3. DSA (sign only)
4. RSA (sign only)
   Your selection? 1
   RSA keys may be between 1024 and 4096 bits long.
   What keysize do you want? (2048) 2048
   Key is valid for? (0) 2y
   You need a user ID to identify your key; the software constructs the user ID from the Real Name, Comment and Email Address in this form:
   "Heinrich Heine (Der Dichter) <heinrichh@duessel dorf.de>"
   Real name: Scott R. Ellis
   Email address: scorellis@lakebluffroasting.com
   Comment: In the Shade of the Coffee Tree *
   *This is just an example. Your comment should be about you. Anyone who uses your key can see this.

We need to generate a lot of random bytes. It is a good idea to perform some other action (type on the keyboard, move the mouse, utilize the disks) during the prime generation; this gives the random number generator a better chance to gain enough entropy.
...+++++
gpg: key EB11566D marked as ultimately trusted
public and secret key created and signed.

Final key creation output:
gpg: checking the trustdb
gpg: 3 marginal(s) needed, 1 complete(s) needed, PGP trust model
gpg: depth: 0 valid: 2 signed: 0 trust: 0-, 0q, 0n, 0m, 0f, 2u
gpg: next trustdb check due at 2017-09-15
pub 2048R/EB11544D 2015-09-16 [expires: 2017-09-15]
   Key fingerprint = 1D73 C6A3 9FD2 4025 D6BE LBBC 204A 490D EB11 533D
uid   Scott R. Ellis (In the Shade of the Mesquite Tree) <sellis@lakebluffroasting.com>
sub 2048R/75LAKEBLUFFROASTING 2015-09-16 [expires: 2017-09-15]

Encrypting a File

When someone sends you a key, you save it and then you compact disk (CD) to the directory where you saved it. Then you TRUST the key. You do this by looking at the fingerprint, as I mentioned.

To get your fingerprint easily, just type:

> gpg –fingerprint sellis

My CSO, Kevin Davidson, has sent me his key in a file with the name" -public.asc."

Import it first:

> gpg –import kdavidson-public.asc

gpg: key F9AB6660: public key "Kevin David (Security Kev) <kdavidson@lakebluffroasting.com>" imported

gpg: Total number processed: 1

gpg: imported: 1 (RSA: 1)

Now check its fingerprint:

> gpg –fingerprint lbbrewco.com

pub 2048R/F9AB6660 2014-11-21 [expires: 2016-11-20]
   Key fingerprint = 7F27 133C 0C50 50EB 9F9C C0C9 087F 3E13 F9AB 6660

uid Kevin Davidson (Security Kev) <kdavidson@lakebluff roasting.com>

   sub 2048R/27E927B6 2014-11-21 [expires: 2018-11-20]

If the fingerprint matches, then you can trust it by signing it. If it does not, something went wrong; maybe he sent you the wrong fingerprint. The alternative is that there is a man in the middle executing a really deep and heinous attack and you should go lock and barricade your door:

   gpg –edit-key kdavidson notice that I only need to use enough of some part of his keynote that is unique in order for it to "get it" and open the key for editing.

gpg> **sign**

It will ask you if you are sure; say yes. Then you will be asked for your passphrase. Once you have entered it, the key is signed. Now you can encrypt and send Kevin messages that are truly as secure as open communication on the Internet can get. You may see a message such as "gpg-agent is not available in this session." Fear not, the key is signed. You can verify it signed by again typing:

   gpg> sign

   then

   gpg> q

to quit and **Save Changes (y/N)? y** to save changes.

Encrypting:

to encrypt a document, navigate (or alternately you can type in the path here) to its directory and enter the following command.

> gpg -a -o file.out.gpg -r username -e file.in.ext

where

-a = armor, which uuencodes the attachment so, technically, you could copy and paste the binary into the body of an email and it should survive.

-o = output (makes sense, right?)

file.out.gpg = this will be the final, encrypted file that you send, so give it whatever name you like.

file.in.ext = the name of the file you are getting. Here, you can include a path to the file if you like.

Now, if you want other people to be able to encrypt and send you files, they will need your public key:

> gpg –armor –export scorellis@lakebluffroasting.com > myPublicKey.txt

---

with my chief information officer (CIO), I had just generated a key that I would then email to him. I sent him the fingerprint via our secure Adium chat:

> gpg -a -o scott-key –export sellis@lakebluff roasting.com

Now your key has been exported to your directory as a file called "scott-key" you can send it to anyone you wish to be able to decrypt messages you send to them. However, there is a secret to the whole thing: So that you do not have to send a password to them every time you encrypt something, you use THEIR key AND your key to encrypt the file. Here is how it works (see sidebar: "Encrypting a File"):

Encrypting and Decrypting Using GNU Privacy Guard

The longer the key is, the more secure it is against brute-force attacks, but for almost all purposes the default key size is adequate because it would be cheaper to circumvent the encryption than to try to break it. "It would be cheaper

to attack on Vector A than Vector B, so Vector B security is good enough".[1]

Much of what is done in security relies more on raising the costs and increasing the complexity of attacks rather than on stopping them cold in their tracks. This is effective.

You may have the need to send encrypted files consistently to a group of people (see sidebar: "Sending Files to Multiple People"). GNU Privacy Guard supports this.

Secure Shell Access to Servers

Through the creation of a public key, an SSH-capable account is one of the first priorities when computing securely. You must be able to SSH into every machine on your sensor network. Use of SSH and X Windows is critical.

Above all, the work of an intrusion detection analyst must include 100% secure communications. To achieve

---

1. GnuPG online manual. Chapter 1. https://www.gnupg.org/gph/en/manual/c14.html.

Sending Files to Multiple People

On your computer, edit the gpg.conf file like so:
> vi ~user/.gnupg/gpg.conf

Add the following line:
> group secteam=user1 user2 user3 you

In that line, "user1 user2 user3" are the unique parts of the keys of people who you want to have in the group that you send to, and "you" is some unique part of *your* key. This will allow you to decrypt what you send. If you do not add yourself, you will not be able to see what you encrypted in the event that you fat-fingered something or reused an old command and have one of those sudden "What the heck did I just send?" moments (and not be able to find out).

Next, to encrypt to the secteam (or group name of your choice), you would enter:
> gpg -e <filename to encrypt>

Then, when prompted, enter the name of the group to which you want to send the file. You can also use the longer form:
> gpg -a -o file.out.gpg -r groupname -e file.in.ext

If someone sends you a file that is encrypted, here is how to decrypt it:
> gpg –output decrypted_filename.out –decrypt encrypted file.gpg

---

this, one must become extraordinarily familiar with command line. Doing everything at the command line is not always necessary, but learning *how* to do everything at the command line will facilitate your ability to do anything at the command line when the time comes. For this, we turn to SSH tunneling and opening an SSH to remote servers.

Do not become confused: SSH tunneling has nothing to do with GNU Privacy Guard file encryption and uses altogether different keys. An SSH tunnel is a secure channel of communication that you open between your local computer and a remote system. You will not be using some remote desktop utility to access your sensors. You will use an SSH Bourne Again shell (bash). Often you will be moving quickly between machines and may have a dozen or more open shells.

To facilitate making quick connections so that you do not have to type your password every time, we add our public key to the server (see sidebar: "Making Quick Connections

Without Having to Enter a Password"). Now only someone who has your private key on his machine can access the account.

Moving Files Securely

Now that you are SSH capable, using commands such as remote synchronization (rsync) will allow you easily to transfer files securely between machines. For example:

> rsync -avu serverTwelve:/home/sellis/interestingFile WithMyPublicKeyInIt.asc.

The -avu is just a concatenation of several "switches." Each has a function:

- -a archive
- -v increase verbosity

Making Quick Connections Without Having to Enter a Password

On your local machine, run:
> SSH-keygen -t ed25519

Hit enter when asked for a password. This will generate both a private and a public key. With older SSH versions, they will be stored in ~/.SSH/identity and ~/.SSH/identity.pub; with newer ones, they will be stored in ~/.SSH/id_rsa and ~/.SSH/id_rsa.pub.

Now, access the remote machine:
> SSH remote_machine_name
> SSH-keygen -t ed25519

Running the keygen on the remote system is not a required step. It accomplishes two things for you, though:
1. ensures the encryption level (ed25519) you intend to use is compatible with the remote machine's encryption capabilities;
2. creates needed directories and files for you.

Next, add the contents of your *local machine* public key file into ~/.SSH/authorized_keys on the *remote* machine:

> cat line-of-text.txt | SSH sellis@server "cat >> scotts-remote-file.txt"

Now, when you type:
> SSH machine name/IP

you should be able to connect and see something such as this
your-machine: ~ sellis$ SSH SensorOne
Welcome to Ubuntu 14.04.4 LTS (GNU/Linux 3.19.0-58-generic x86_64)
* Documentation: https://help.ubuntu.com/
0 packages can be updated.
0 updates are security updates.
Last login: Fri Apr 29 18:40:41 2016 from 192.0.102.168
scorellis@SensorOne:

You are connected now and can execute commands against the remote machine. Your first order of business may be to perform certain duties in your role as an administrator of the security systems.

- -u skip files that are newer on the receiver; means Do Not Overwrite the Modified Files at the Destination
- '.' the dot means "put the files here, in my current working directory"

Choose the file that you wish to transfer to machine.-transfer.remote. If you are wishing others on the remote system to view the file you are uploading, change the permissions before you send it. Gaining a deep knowledge of Linux permissions is essential to the duties of an intrusion detection analyst.

Exercise for the Reader

What would the advantages be of giving users remote access to the system from their computers without knowing their password, and allowing access based only on their machine's key? How would this increase (or decrease) security? As an exercise, list the pros and cons of each. Can you prevent a user who is in the sudo group from changing his password?

4. NETWORK SECURITY MONITORING AND INTRUSION DETECTION SYSTEMS

After convincing c-level that NSM is the only practical way to monitor your network IDS properly, and once you have servers and switches installed on an instrumentation network, you need to install software that will collect and examine the traffic. A simple Internet search for "Security Onion Download" should get you to the most recent version of SO. Download it, verify the checksum, and follow its prompts for installation. SO is built on an IDS called Snort (or Suricata) as the alerting center, with emphasis on follow-through hunting and forensic work via Bro and other logs. This is the system that you will build to capture, analyze, and categorize traffic.

There are two types of deployment capabilities within an IDS: passive monitoring and active response. An active response system deploys the IDS in line with the traffic and will drop packets and reset connections when bad behavior is located. Mature, stable, known, and highly purposed network, such as some sort of automated system in which all protocols and communications are standard and known, is suitable to this sort of intervention. Your typical office culture, with thousands of employees just trying to work, is more suited for passive monitoring.

Installing Security Onion in a Distributed Environment

SO is capable of operating in a number of different server/sensor configurations, in which one server serves as the "master" server and then additional servers are deployed to serve as sensors. One such configuration is a server/sensor–sensor paradigm, in which the central or "master" server also

serves as a sensor, and communicates with a larger array of sensors. The vast majority of data are stored locally on the sensors, with only enough data for reporting and alerting being sent up to the master server, often called just the "server." Ideally, first you will build out a test environment. To install, if you are following along with these directions, create a new virtual machine (VM) using the installation disk image (ISO) of the SO. Later, we will go through a physical (bare metal) installation. Choose a secure username/password and computer name. Because VMWare is freely available and one of the more popular virtualization platforms, it is the only method covered here. VirtualBox and other virtualization methods may also be compatible.

Complete the installation and reboot. Install VMWare tools:

- Installing VMWare tools (workstation)
- Highlight the target machine
- Click on Inventory|Virtual Machine|Guest | Install VMWare Tools
- A dialogue will open on the desktop of the guest machine. Essentially, Step 1 has caused an ISO to be mounted that contains the VMWare tools package.
- Drag and drop the VMWareTools-9.9.3-...tar.gz file to the desktop. Two-finger click or right-click the archive and Extract Here.
- Open a terminal:
  > cd Desktop/vmware-tools-distrib
  > sudo ./vmware-install.pl

If this does nothing, or returns an error such as "command not found," run:
  > chmod a+x vmware-install.pl
  > sudo ./vmware-install.pl

Follow all defaults prompts and then restart the machine. You will now see that you have better screen resolution and mouse control. Things such as drag and drop between the host and guest will be possible and the clipboard will be accessible. Update installed software using:
  > sudo apt-get update && sudo soup
  VMware Tools Install: vSphere Client
  Inventory > Virtual Machine > Guest > Install/Upgrade VMware Tools

This should cause a file browser window to launch on the desktop of your SO VM. Follow previous steps of drag and drop simplicity.

Manually assign an Internet Protocol (IP) address to the server. You will likely need to configure your Dynamic Host Configuration Protocol (DHCP) server with a "static range" or ask your admin to give you a static IP that you can have for this. In my test bed network, I have allocated IP addresses to the user devices; the number of devices on my network is fairly static. This means that whereas the machines remain in DHCP mode, I have pinned their media access control (MAC) addresses to specific IP addresses.

I do this so that I will be able to learn the IP address of each machine. I also have taken note and identified every remaining machine and created a dynamic range of 10 IP addresses. This way, if something shows up on my network outside either range, or takes an IP in my free range, it will stick out like a sore thumb:

    local: 192.168.1.237 machine.local.net
    225-230 + 233 are assigned.
    10 - 20 are DHCP, 10 - 13 are assigned

At this stage, your computer already has an IP address. You have a couple of options, possibly ones that you should have taken up front. If you are anything like me, you will run through this process a few times, so the next time you do it you may want to start off right out of the gate, with a static, allocated IP address.

In my case, I am running my SO server on a VM, and it has an IP address that is unique to a local IP subnet created by my host, which is different from my lab subnet.

SO Server VM IP: 192.168.###.###

Setting up a Security Onion Server

Although sometimes it may seem like it, NSM is not about collecting data for the sake of collecting data. It allows you to store information for as long as your policy dictates you need to, and if the need arises, you can perform flawless network forensics on those data. It is important for you to anticipate and understand the net amount of data that enter your network and flow among computers within your network; this will allow you to size SO properly.

If you have successfully installed the SO ISO, you will find that you have some items on your desktop. One of them is a setup onion icon. Double click on the onion and it will launch the setup. It will ask for a password. Each of the next steps corresponds to a step in the install. Sometimes I use screenshots or sidebars to illustrate a point; sometimes I do not. Some items, such as enabling a passive real-time asset detection system (PRADS) or sending HTTP.logs to Sguil (rhymes with squeal) choices, are a matter of preference and workflow. Both PRADS and http_agent are disabled when choosing Best Practices. Items such as this are optional. Items discussed and recommended subsequently are more interesting and have greater bearing on the work of intrusion detection, and so are presented as requirements. The following is based on the 14.04.4.2 version of SO, released in April 2016:

1. The first screen will ask you to configure interfaces. Choose "Yes, configure/etc/network/interfaces!"
2. This is a server only, so choose a management interface.
3. Select "Static". It is okay to use DHCP if this is a test environment, but bear in mind that if its IP address changes at some point, repairing it may be a challenge.

4. Again, this is a server, so only configure a management interface. You would also configure a monitor interface only if this were also (or only) a sensor.
5. Next, the changes you just made will be configured and the setup utility will ask you to reboot. Choose "Yes, reboot!"
6. The server will reboot, and you will need to run SO Setup again. It will tell you "It looks like /etc/network/interfaces has already been configured by this script." Go ahead and choose the option to skip network configuration.
7. Choose "Production Mode"
8. Server
9. The next screen asks "Best Practices" or "Custom." Choose "Best Practices."
10. Choose an Sguil user. I choose to create one called "SOAdmin." It is considered bad form to use your own name when installing systems that others may be using.
11. Enable an IDS engine. We choose Snort.
12. Which IDS rule set? Choose "Emerging Threats GPL." Here, you choose between Suricata or Snort as an IDS. We chose Snort. Results of a comparison of the two projects are posted here: http://www.aldeid.com/wiki/Suricata-vs-snort.[2] Incidentally, *Suricata suricatta* is the scientific name for a meerkat.[3] It (the software, not the animal) is relatively (to Snort) new to the market and is developed by the Open Information Security Foundation.
13. Choose "Yes, proceed with the changes!" as shown in Fig. 5.3.

Now, let us look at some additional information (Fig. 5.4) about where the setup log (var/log/nsm/sosetup.log) and bro logs (/nsm/bro/) can be found. This may be useful later, so it is documented here.

The behind-the-scenes database used in SO is MySQL (see sidebar: "MySQL Data Integrity"). MySQL has a tendency to become corrupted easily owing to its lack of atomicity, consistency, independent, and durable transactions.

In the preceding section you have just installed all the tools you will need to engage in NSM work. These tools make it easy for you to review NSM data from a single interface. They let you look at varying types of NSM data. Now we can begin to examine the way in which the data should be reviewed and analyzed. Next, we will setup a sensor. Of course, you may wish to set up a server-sensor all-in-one solution, but if you want to be able to translate this skill to an enterprise environment, you should begin to learn how to piece it all together, and you will need to

2. Aldeid.com: a wiki about Network and Web Applications Security, Ethical Hacking and Network Forensics.
3. https://en.wikipedia.org/wiki/Meerkat.

MySQL Data Integrity

Data become corrupt *just sitting on disk*, irrespective of *when* the data were written. Such is the nature of magnetic media: tracks are not written with angular perfection. If you are keeping 30 days' worth of data, ideally you would check 30 days, every day. This can put greater load on the system, but if you need to access data from 29 days ago, and find that they are corrupted, you will be truly disappointed that the checks did not go deeper.

SO runs an SQL REPAIR nightly. A daily Cron job stops Sguil and runs a REPAIR procedure against the MySQL tables based on the DAYSTOREPAIR configuration in/etc/nsm/securityonion.conf. However, atabase check, optimization, and repair activities are essential to the proper functioning, health,

and usability of a database. MySQL has built in a client called Mysqlcheck and you can use it to combine CHECK, OPTIMIZE, and REPAIR actions with just one command:

> mysqlcheck -u root -p –auto-repair -c -o securityonion_db

If you have a lot of large databases, invocation of mysqlcheck with the—all—databases option may take a long time to complete. You should work to understand the best practice and most optimal maintenance practice in your environment. The business in which you work may have RTO/RPO. Database corruption that occurs at a deep level that REPAIR does not address may not be a concern for you.

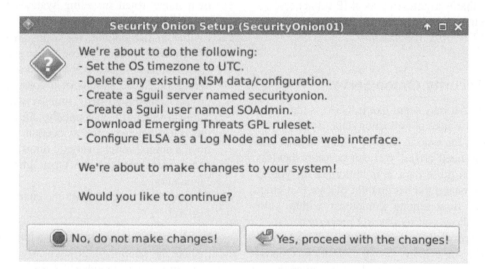

FIGURE 5.3   Summary of Actions. The final setup screen for Security Onion lists the changes it is about to make. Note that this machine will now be running in the Coordinated Universal Time zone (UTC). *ELSA*, Enterprise Log Search and Archive; *GPL*, GNU General Public License; *NSM*, network security monitoring; *OS*, operating system.

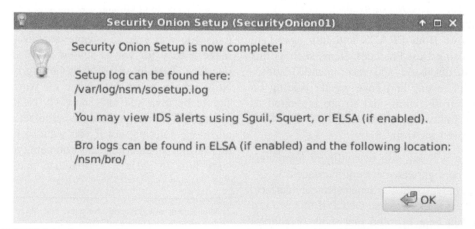

FIGURE 5.4   Summary of logs. *ELSA*, Enterprise Log Search and Archive; *IDS*, intrusion detection system.

understand the plumbing. Ultimately we need to know how much data the system will be piping between server and sensor, and we need to be sure to instrument our environment in such a way that the data that we are collecting do not become a target.

The Tool Set

Before we dive into sensor creation, let us take a quick overview of some of the more instrumental tools in SO and what they do. Each tool has a specialized purpose, but because they are all separate, open source—developed projects by different groups, some of their individual functions overlap. Here, I talk about just a few of the main players in the suite:

Sguil

Pronounced "Squeal", this tool provides a system of managing real-time alerts. From inside Sguil, you can pivot to various other tools on your system to open packet captures.

You interact with Sguil in its capacity to collect and generate traffic alerts gathered from a live network interface.

Sguil performs simple aggregation of similar alert data records and makes certain types of metadata, and related data readily available. It permits queries and review of session data in an alert-centered investigative model. Through a series of right-click context menus, you can pivot to full content data, rendered as text in a transcript, in a protocol analyzer such as Wireshark or in a network forensic tool such as Network Miner.

Sguil exposes these features so analysts can quickly review and classify events. This same interface enables escalation and other incident response decisions.

When you start Sguil, you will be presented with a startup screen as shown in Fig. 5.5. Enter the username and password that you created earlier.

Squert

This is a Web interface that was created to allow easy Web access to the Sguil database. It provides additional tools for research, such as viewing alert data, metadata and other related data; alert aggregation; and classification of data. It is open source, written by Paul Halliday. It is maintained as a GitHub repository at http://github.com/int13h/squert/blob/master/COPYING/.

Netsniff-ng

Netsniff-ng has one job: it writes pcap files to disk. Tools such as Enterprise Log Search and Archive (ELSA) and Sguil allow you to *pivot* from one GUI interface into an interface such as Wireshark. There, you can gain deeper knowledge and information about the conversation.

Snort

This tool monitors network data and generates alerts into Sguil. Snort is a signature-based system that offers powerful tools to conduct session analysis. For example, you can leverage the functionality of rules to something called "flowbits" that can be set to allow you to track the flow of a conversation and check it using a series of rules. The flowbits keyword works with stream preprocessor conversation tracking capabilities. In Fig. 5.6, a panel in Sguil reveals the alert signature and the binary of the packet that tripped the alert.

Bro

Bro is a complete IDS tool originally developed by Vern Paxson. He continues to lead the project with a team of researchers at the International Computer Science Institute in Berkeley, California and the National Center for Supercomputing Applications in Urbana—Champaign, Illinois. In SO, Bro populates data into ELSA. It also provides a

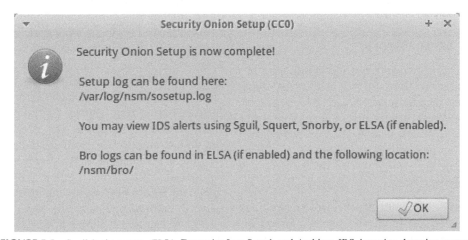

FIGURE 5.5 Sguil login screen. *ELSA*, Enterprise Log Search and Archive; *IDS*, intrusion detection system.

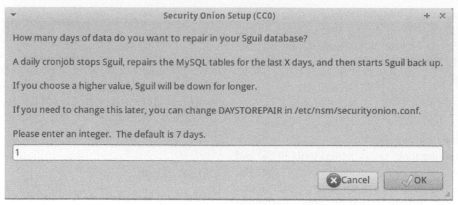

FIGURE 5.6 Viewing alert data in the Sguil interface.

full-featured platform, including its own Turing complete language, Bro, for scripting and functional augmentation. All Bro logs are stored in ELSA, which provides a powerful interface to analyze suspect conversations. You can then pivot to any of these Transmission Control Protocol (TCP) streams in ELSA to capme, which will display the corresponding FPC for the entire stream. Bro also extracts any executables and drops them to a staging directory where you can scan them for viruses.

ELS A

ELSA allows you to slice and dice bro logs as well as other types of logs. It is essentially a log analysis tool that allows you to pivot into other tools for further analysis, and provides a back-end data warehouse for reviewing billions of records.

PF_RING

PF_RING, like Netsniff-NG, captures packets. However, it does not write packets to disk. Bro and Snort both use PF_RING as a source for data to analyze. In addition, it provides a flow-based load balancer to allow running multiple Snort/Suricata/Bro workers to distribute the traffic more evenly across multiple CPU cores.

Planning Your Sensor Array

After the build of the server is completed, it is time to focus on sensors. A powerful server can also run as a sensor. Best Practices suggest that a master server should be in the role of master only, and should not perform any packet capture at all. If you find you need to make a combined server and sensor, you should pick the box monitoring the least amount of traffic.

Planning the Sensor Array

In planning the sensor array, I first drew a diagram of where the sensor would be located. In this diagram, I mirrored all internal network traffic using a Dualcomm 100-megabyte

(MB) tap. They also make a 1-gigabyte (GB) rated box, but because my lab network only has 45 MB inbound and 15 out, only 100 MB was needed. The 100-MB Dualcomm box cost less than half the 1 GB. Ultimately, its throughput was not nearly high enough to support a network with this many devices on it. Even on an Internet connection of only 40 MB per second (Mbps), it was apparent that a bottleneck had been inserted. The 100-Mbps switch is not production ready; that is, it is not suitable for any but the simplest of networks and the slowest of Internet connections.

Make a Disk

Step 1 is to burn a disk. An ISO is a kind of disk "image." An "image" is a binary representation in a file of the bits and bytes that are on the *physical* disk. A familiar example to you might be when one wishes to create a new VM. You use some piece of software to create an ISO. Maybe you downloaded the ISO from a trusted website. Few people are sending out CD/DVDs anymore, so chances are good that you have almost all of your operating system (OS) software in ISO form. If you want to use the ISO, you burn it to an optical disk and then you boot from it.

However, increasingly fewer computers are shipping with CD/DVD ROM drives, and to be frank, there is really no longer a need for them. Optical drives offer unparalleled security when it comes to cost-effective tamper resistance. Solutions such as mechanical write-protected universal serial bus (USB) drives are available from Kanguru and come equipped with Federal Information Processing Standard—compliant, signed firmware that makes them highly resistant to BadUSB. However, they are pricey. If you do not want to pay premium dollars for a USB drive that you must remember to flip a switch on before you use, consider an optical drive solution. CD/DVDs were all the rage of the 1990s, but they are falling the way of the floppy: they are becoming archaic. All computers *do* ship with USB ports, but not all ship with CD-ROM nowadays. Also we can now "burn" our image onto a USB drive, and then we will have ourselves a bootable USB that can be used to install SO onto any computer.

I took a standard, run-of-the-mill Dell E7240 laptop for the purpose of loading SO (Ubuntu) on it. However, the Dell did not have a disk drive. I needed this ISO "burned" to a USB drive. There are applications made for PC to do this, which means you must download a tool from the Internet to complete this. Then you can "burn" the ISO onto a USB drive. One such program is called Your Universal Multiboot Integrator.

Sizing Your Hardware

SO does virtualize well, and there are a number of good reasons to do this, some of which will be touched upon in this section (see sidebar: "Sizing Hardware for Security Onion With a Lot of Load"). Preferably, you will dedicate your host only to SO guests. This is a good security approach and it makes troubleshooting performance issues easier. If, for example, a vulnerability were uncovered in your virtualization platform that allowed a user of a malicious VM to "punch a hole" through to other VMs on the host, an attacker could then compromise your NSM machine.

Switched Port Analyzer or Tap

Whether to SPAN or tap your ports is one of the classic arguments in NSM. Both methods have their pros and cons (See sidebar: "Switched Port Analyzer or Tap Your Ports?").

Sizing Hardware for Security Onion With a Lot of Load

Sizing hardware properly for SO depends a lot on load. Load on a server primarily depends on:
1. the amount of new data flowing in;
2. the amount of simultaneous analysis that will have to be conducted.

There are four areas of consideration when it comes to load:
1. CPU: You should plan based on agents per 200 Mbps of traffic. This allows for the proper number of Snort, Sro, Suricata, Netsniff-ng agents, and others, which are all busier when there is more traffic.[4] Each agent may take up 100% of a single core; the more agents you have, the more cores you will need. In addition, plan on cores for overhead such as OS and task. Generally, performance engineers do not like to see total average CPU across all cores higher than 80%.
2. RAM: Per the SO wiki, located on GitHb, Doug Burks put forth the following guidelines:
   a. 50–500 Mbps: 16–128 GB RAM
   b. 500–1000 Mbps: 128–256 GB RAM or more
3. Disk:
   a. The primary consideration with disks is the size of the array: how many days' worth of data do you need? How much traffic is coming in? In an ideal world, you would store a year's worth of data. Why? Because many breaches are not uncovered for a year. However, with NSM the idea is that you will see the breach as it is occurring and be able to triage quickly and investigate the issue.
   b. Disk speed: A redundant array of independent disks (RAID) configured as a RAID 1+0 is the best redundancy and the best speed. Disk latency is the bane of a database; with potentially massive amounts of data on disk, searching through it can take a long time if disk response is not adequate, which also allows for disk speed comparisons between mechanical and solid-state drives. Tools such as atop, iotop, iostat, and pt-diskstats can be used to cover a broad spectrum of disk performance monitoring with SO. It is up to the analyst to gain a strong understanding of these tools and ensure that the disk fabric can support the load. The best cure

for an ailing database that has been properly tuned at the application level is typically more RAM. After that is more and faster disk.

4. Network: You need to bear in mind that you need an extra interface for management, and then you will have to ensure that you get compatible (8, 10, or 16 GB, twinax, ether, FibreChannel over Ethernet, or straight fiber) cards and that the cards will work with your network.

A busy network will write a lot of data to disk. If you have 4 Gbps of traffic that you are onboarding, and your total disk write capacity is 10 Gbps, that gives you some disk bandwidth for other activity and you can add other network interfaces. Building on ESX also has the advantage of a nice set of monitoring tools that can help pinpoint load issues. Filtering out nuisance traffic at the sensors will help (things such as bittorrent, Twitch, and YouTube might be site traffic you can safely reject); this will improve your disk latency issues but will not improve your network bandwidth. The traffic is still there; it is just punted and not written to disk if you exclude it.

Sizing
Understanding where messages are logged when traffic exceeds capacity is important. In every sensor, there are logs. In these logs (which may be long and numerous) if you explore carefully, you may find messages such as:

Log Entry Excerpt
S5: Session exceeded configured max bytes to queue 1,048,576 using 1,049,688 bytes (client queue). 10.10.62.9 60414–> 10.10.127.9 80 (0): LWstate 0x9 LWFlags 0x406007. This one can be handled by adjusting your the stream5 configuration settings in each sensor's snort.conf.

Basically, what this means is that if you have a server experiencing data load coming in on a continuous basis, and this already creates stress, the added stress of conducting searches or analysis of any sort may render the system unusable for both data collection and analysis tasks.

---

4. https://github.com/Security-Onion-Solutions/security-onion/wiki/Hardware.

Switched Port Analyzer or Tap Your Ports?

Taps may not always be available. For example, if you are tapping Ethernet, the only way to use a tap for this is to plug in something like a Dualcomm device. But (and this is a big but) you may also find that the argument to be one of politics. It may turn out in the end that you do need to SPAN. This is where a top-down approach is essential. C-level should make plans with architects, and that plan should be pushed top-down to be implemented. There is no reason for an NSM technician and an information technology (IT) technician ever to speak to each other. Aside from the extreme differences in architecture, the typical IT mentality will be based on cost savings. Trying to save money while implementing NSM will almost definitely cost more money in time, and in the end you may do it the expensive way anyway.

Setting Up Security Onion on an ESXi Host

Build your VM. It is probable that this will be the only machine you virtualize on this box, but do not forget: ESX has to live there, too.

ESX Steps

If you plan on using snapshots, be aware that there are log files that ESX generates, so leave it ample disk space. The longer you keep a snapshot, the larger this space needs to be. Consider that snapshot logs are like uncommitted transactions: The longer you keep a snapshot, the larger the logs will grow, and performance of your system will suffer. Do not use snapshots to replace backups.

Leave at least 4 GB of RAM for ESX. If you get into a situation where you are running large MySQL queries, your RAM will get used up and if you have left nothing for the host, it will page down to disk and performance will tank.

Horizontal Movement

Imagine a network that encompasses three floors of an office building. Each floor has an intermediate distribution frame (IDF) room, with a main distribution frame (MDF) on the first floor. Each floor is divided into four sections. It is trivial to place servers in each IDF and the MDF and tap into inter-quadrant and interfloor traffic. But how good is that? Is it enough? If a hacker gains access to a single computer within a single quadrant, will he limit his activities to just one quadrant? Will he know whether you are or are not watching?

Chances are good he will not know, but he will find out. He will begin by doing things (some networking event or events) that he knows would trip an alert, and he will do it to a computer right next to him. Then he will expand his reach. Chances are good that once "inside," the hacker will believe he has free reign to do as he pleases and that he has escaped detection. My preference is to tap everything: The sooner you can spot the hacker, the better. In addition, internal users who may understand how your monitoring is configured may leverage the lack of horizontal tracking to exploit systems.

Next, let us look at why you may decide for any number of reasons to set up in a virtual environment (see sidebar: "Setting Up Security Onion on an ESXi Host"). For convenience, virtualizing and running on a dedicated host may be ideal.

Virtual Machine Planner Virtual Disks

Substantial literature exists that will tell you not to use these, but that literature is mostly old VMWare 4 information. These are the best-performing disk types to use. I also set mine up as independent disks. I am not that concerned with virtualization and want my virtual SO machine to behave as much like physical as possible. That being said, I use thick provisioning, lazy zeroed, which will immediately begin to expand the volume but will (I hope) zero it out with opportunistic writes. This means that if I am trying to do other things, it will not interfere. To create the

disk volume, ESX actually writes zeroes to the disk to increase the file size. If you have a storage area network (SAN), you should eagerly zero this because it should be fast. More than likely, your SAN is thin provisioned, but it could also be thick provisioning. You should know your SAN settings. A thin provisioned VM sitting on top of a thin provisioned SAN will likely exacerbate performance problems that may occur when the SAN senses it is running out of space. Some SANs will actually throttle write speeds by as much as 80%, causing serious performance bottlenecks. More information about supported OS and VMware paravirtualized small computer system interfaces can be found at http://tinyurl.com/paravirtual.

Installing the Fiber Cards

Your server/sensor may be needed on a fiber channel. The following procedure applies only if you have fiber channel Peripheral Component Interconnect Express (PCIe) cards that you need to pass through to the guest. Using fiber taps is preferable over SPANs for one reason: If the switch becomes overwhelmed, your SPAN will be the first thing to be sacrificed. Also, your SPAN port that connects you to the server may only be a 1-Gbps port. Your network admin was kind enough to set this up for you, but what he may not bother to tell you is that when you SPAN a 10-Gbps port to a 1-Gbps, any throughput over 1-Gbps just gets truncated. Taps are preferable because no packets will get dropped. To suggest that such a thing is possible is like saying that part of your reflection in a mirror will vanish if you stare at it too intently.

Once you have completed the setup of the VM, it will ask you if you want to edit the settings before creation. Follow this link and choose to add "PCIe Passthrough." If you have more than one card, you will need to do this for each card. You may notice a warning that informs you that some commands will not work once you have created a passthrough. This is not a

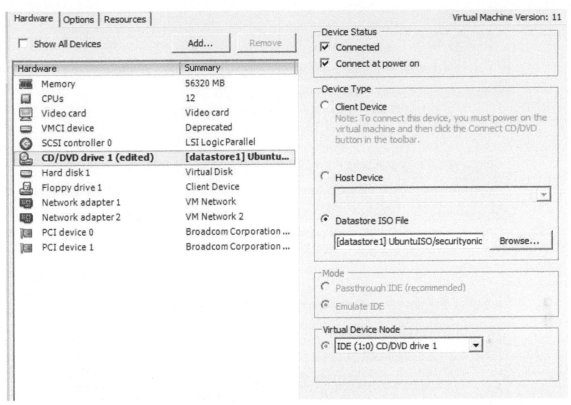

FIGURE 5.7   Setting up a virtual machine.

traditional "VM" compared with what you may find in an enterprise; this loss of mobility is acceptable.

Installing the Operating System

Now that you have configured the VM, it is time to install a guest OS. Edit the settings of the VM, and on the hardware tab, select the CD-ROM device. Choose Datastore ISO file in the panel to the right. Browse to your ISO. If it is not already there, you will need to load it. To upload an ISO:

1. Click on your vHost in the left pane.
2. Go to configuration tab.
3. Click on storage in the left hand of the configuration pane.
4. Right-click on a datastore and select Browse.
5. Create an ISO folder.
6. Upload your ISO file using the browser by clicking on the little can-shaped icon.

7. This file will be stored on your VMFS3 partition and, as is the way of such things, it will take up VM space, so you may want to delete them when you are done.

Once you have loaded your ISO, you can edit your VM by right-clicking on it and going to Edit Settings. Click on the VM and then select Device Status "Connected" and "Connected at power on," and also choose your ISO in the datastore ISO option, as shown in Fig. 5.7.

Configuring Ethernet Adapters

You may have a fair number of Ethernet adapters on your host. Which one maps to the guests adapters? Type > ifconfig at the Linux command line and note the MAC address. Look at the HWaddr in the output:

HWaddr 00:0a:21:oe:ba:11

Next, access ESX, right-click on the guest, edit configuration, and click on the network adapters. You will be able to see a matching MAC address there.

Gotcha: I had two virtual network interface cards (NICs) on one vSwitch when what I needed was two virtual NICs with two vSwitches, one for each card.

Gotcha: Do not let your ESX host have an IP in your DHCP range. When your VM starts up, it might take it. Then you might lose access, and if you do not have an integrated Dell Remote Access Controller, you will be in the server room with a crash cart.

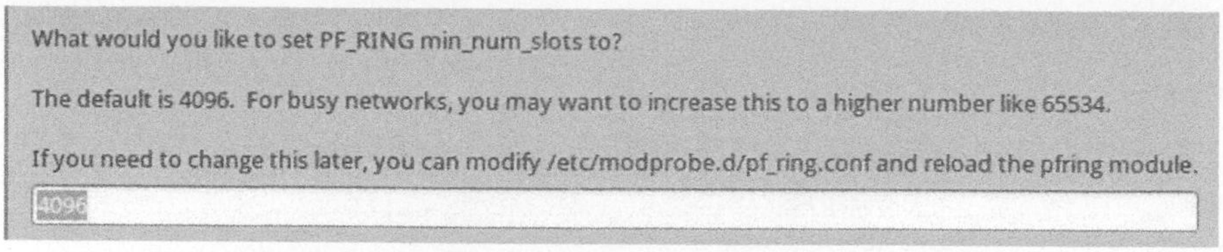

What would you like to set PF_RING min_num_slots to?

The default is 4096. For busy networks, you may want to increase this to a higher number like 65534.

If you need to change this later, you can modify /etc/modprobe.d/pf_ring.conf and reload the pfring module.

4096

FIGURE 5.8   Assign a dedicated number of slots to PF_RING.

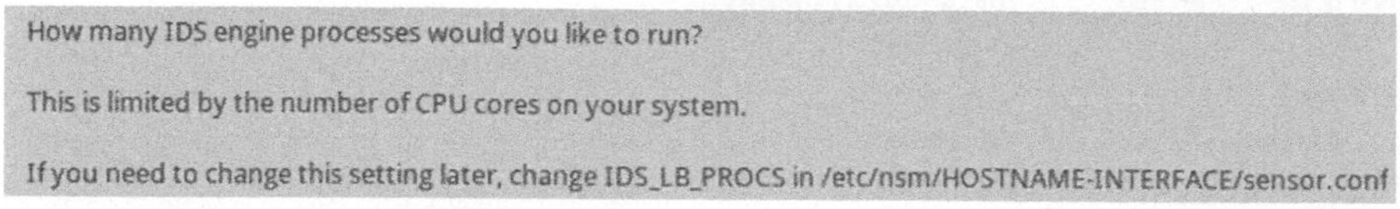

How many IDS engine processes would you like to run?

This is limited by the number of CPU cores on your system.

If you need to change this setting later, change IDS_LB_PROCS in /etc/nsm/HOSTNAME-INTERFACE/sensor.conf

FIGURE 5.9   Setting the intrusion detection system (IDS) engine processes. If you selected Snort as your IDS, this will determine the number of Snort instances per each interface. The current version of Security Onion (14.04.2) will attempt to determine and configure this for you.

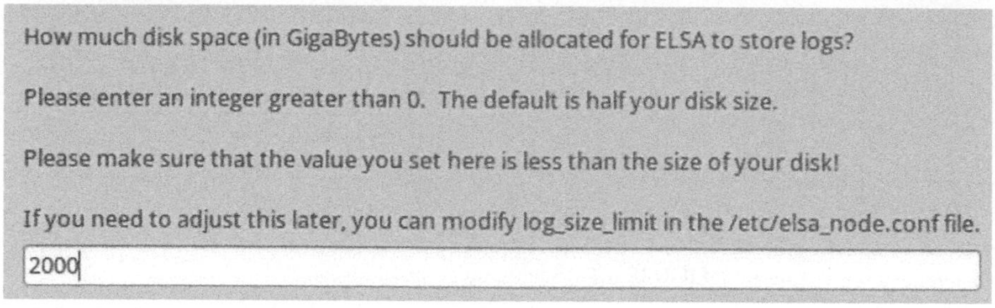

How much disk space (in GigaBytes) should be allocated for ELSA to store logs?

Please enter an integer greater than 0. The default is half your disk size.

Please make sure that the value you set here is less than the size of your disk!

If you need to adjust this later, you can modify log_size_limit in the /etc/elsa_node.conf file.

2000

FIGURE 5.10   Set amount of gigabytes. Here, I am allowing up to 2 terabytes. *ELSA*, Enterprise Log Search and Archive.

It is important that you do not accidentally include your management address in the adapter pool that you are monitoring. It may render the machine unusable if you do.

Security Onion Sensor Setup

We have discussed setting up a master server, and setting up SO on a VM environment. Once the OS is installed, you will access the desktop and run the SO Setup utility; only this time, after choosing a management interface, you will choose to configure a monitoring interface.

Setting PF_RING min_num_slots

Load balancing in PF_RING is achieved through a method of hash analysis that allows the sorting of IP headers into multiple "buckets." PF_RING can then spawn instances of Snort, one for each "ring." This creates efficiency through multiprocessing. Of course, this works best with processors that support multithreaded processes: CPUs that have multiple cores, such as Intel's i7 chip, which has four cores. With HyperThreading enabled, it can handle eight threads. Then, the only setup that seemed to require some math was the PF_RING buffer, as shown in Fig. 5.8.

Each instance of Snort will get its own "bucket" or ring. After all, it is called PF_RING, not PF_BUCKET.

Setting Intrusion Detection System Engine Processes

Most important, understand that the number you set is *each sniffing interface*, as shown in Fig. 5.9. If you set this to 8, and you only have eight cores, you will pummel your CPU. If you are able to add cores later, you can change this.

Enterprise Log Search and Archive has a limit as to how much space it will use. This is configured and can be adjusted later, as shown in Fig. 5.10.

More information about Best Practices and configuring a production sensor of SO can be found at https://github. com/Security-Onion-Solutions/security-onion/wiki/Best-Practices. Upon completing the setup, as shown in Fig. 5.11, and just as with the server setup, SO details the steps it is about to take.

Now that you have SO installed, you may want to check whether you are collecting data in the data directories. As shown in Fig. 5.12, useful screens in the SO setup tell you where to look for things. It is useful to take screenshots and

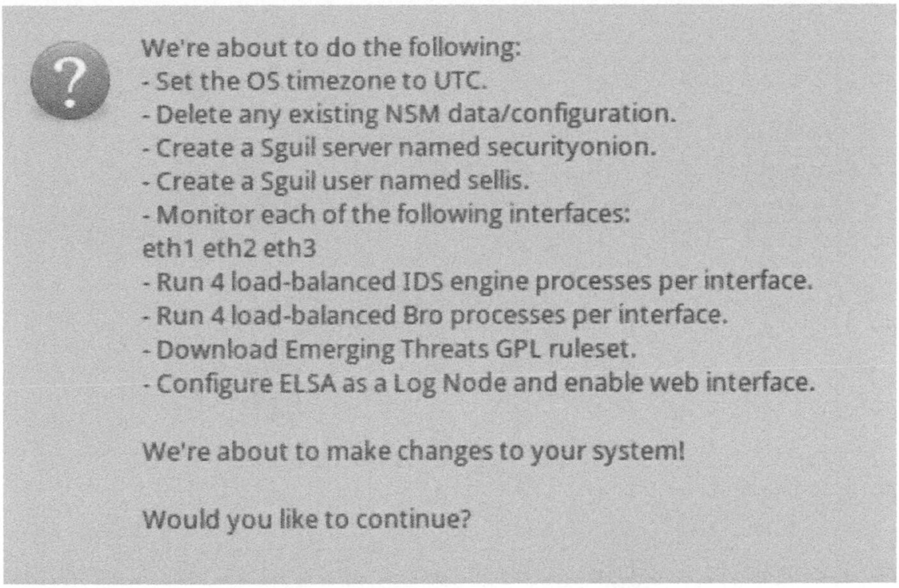

We're about to do the following:
- Set the OS timezone to UTC.
- Delete any existing NSM data/configuration.
- Create a Sguil server named securityonion.
- Create a Sguil user named sellis.
- Monitor each of the following interfaces:
eth1 eth2 eth3
- Run 4 load-balanced IDS engine processes per interface.
- Run 4 load-balanced Bro processes per interface.
- Download Emerging Threats GPL ruleset.
- Configure ELSA as a Log Node and enable web interface.

We're about to make changes to your system!

Would you like to continue?

FIGURE 5.11 The steps of installation. *ELSA*, Enterprise Log Search and Archive; *GPL*, GNU General Public License; *IDS*, intrusion detection system; *NSM*, network security monitoring; *OS*, operating system; *UTC*, Coordinated Universal Time.

make copious notes during installation. Your installation may differ and the setup may change between versions. You should start to see packet capture (pcap) files appearing if you have followed these recommendations.

Management of Storage

Once SO is up and running and collecting data, you may notice that your disks begin to fill quickly: FPC is collecting every single network packet! An hourly Cron job removes any sensor-collected data as storage exceeds 90%. Many production systems will have storage capacity so large that the system could not possibly fill 10% of the drive in 1 h; therefore it may make sense to adjust this time. Conversely, for a smaller system on a busy connection or on a connection that has the capacity to become busy (i.e., if some new activity suddenly floods the sensor with data), it may be worthwhile to modify the CRIT_DISK_USAGE value in /etc/nsm/securityonion.conf.

Data generated by NSM is stored in two primary locations. On the sensor, pcap files are stored in */nsm/sensor_data/%serverName%-%interface%*. For example, on my test deployment, sensor files are located in the directory */nsm/sensor_data/server-eth0* and include the following directories:

- argus
- dailylogs
- portscans
- sancp
- snort-1

- snort-2
- snort-1.stats
- snort-2.stats
- snort.stats

All of these directories are easily accessible from a file manager window.

On the server, data are stored in a MySQL database in the folder */var/lib/mysql*. This folder holds SO databases and will store far fewer data than the sensor's */nsm* folder.

If you navigate to this folder, you will find that you likely cannot access it, that only members of the MySQL group can access this folder, and that being a member of the group is not enough to give you the rights.

The following commands will give you access to this folder. For no reason other than to want to monitor the size of your database, you must have access to this folder from time to time. The easiest way to do this is to run:

Sudo -i

This will drop you into a shell that is running as *root*, which will have permissions for this directory.

5. INSTALLING SECURITY ONION TO A BARE-METAL SERVER

Now that you have mastered installing SO to your test systems, it is time to "go live" with it and get a real proof of concept up and running on your network; collecting real data; and, uncovering any hidden malware on your

---

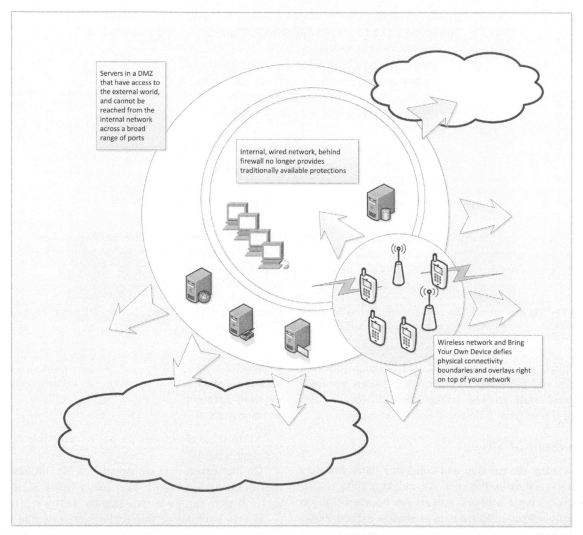

FIGURE 5.12 Useful utilities can give you information and allow you to share information without revealing sensitive information. *DMZ*, demilitarized zone.

Labels in figure:
- Servers in a DMZ that have access to the external world, and cannot be reached from the internal network across a broad range of ports
- Internal, wired network, behind firewall no longer provides traditionally available protections
- Wireless network and Bring Your Own Device defies physical connectivity boundaries and overlays right on top of your network

network. A previous section walked you through how to install SO. My assumption is that you are not going to leap before you look, and that you will run through this on a test VM or a test laptop. I have installed SO on a Dell Latitude E7240, and it was an easy installation. The following section will detail some traps and pitfalls in deploying SO on a campus 3 layer (L3) network where you have dispersed core, distribution, and access layers.

Networks Are Complex

They have evolved over time and the modern campus architecture is modular, redundant, and capable of withstanding outages and moving large volumes of data without interruption. Typically, because many enterprises implement Cisco systems, an Enterprise network is architected into three layers, often shortened into the acronyms L1, L2, and L3 (not to be confused with the layers of the Open

Systems Interconnection network model). These three layers are Core, Distribution, and Access.

The Access Layer

This is what you may think of as "the business end" of the network. It is of particular challenge to NSM methodologies, and this chapter will attempt to derive some sense from how to implement a monitoring solution that works throughout your network without massive cost or terabytes upon terabytes of storage overhead and traffic duplication. Also consider that every network is different, and a three-layer approach is not essential or always recommended. Cisco does not demand or force the network to be assembled in this manner, and for smaller campuses, an L2 model may be sufficient. The Access layer is the internal perimeter. It is where users can plug in printers, PCs, servers, etc. Think of your network as a jelly-filled donut: your users are

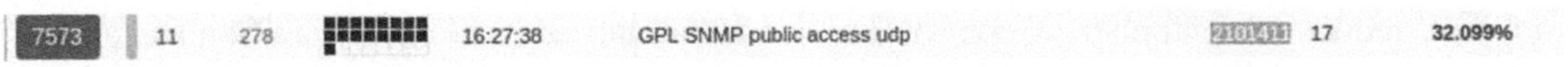

| 7573 | 11 | 278 | | 16:27:38 | GPL SNMP public access udp | 2101411 | 17 | 32.099% |

FIGURE 5.13 Dramatic simplification when it comes to types of networks found in modern campus architectures. Some attack or threat models layer the model of the modern network into four tiers. *GPL SNMP*, General Public License Simple Network Management Protocol.

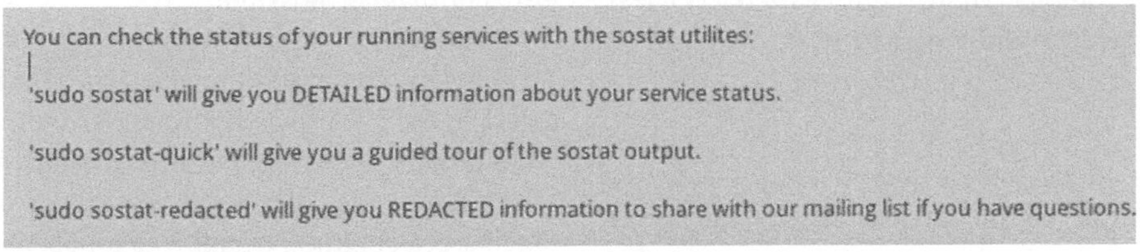

You can check the status of your running services with the sostat utilites:

'sudo sostat' will give you DETAILED information about your service status.

'sudo sostat-quick' will give you a guided tour of the sostat output.

'sudo sostat-redacted' will give you REDACTED information to share with our mailing list if you have questions.

FIGURE 5.14 Checking the status of the running services with the sostat utilities.

the gelatinous mass at the center of it. You may also think of your network as many different structures built on top of each other, expanding over time. Fig. 5.14 is a diagram of a typical enterprise network that has evolved over many years into a practical conglomeration of many networks.

Distribution Layer

Distribution acts as the boundary surface between Core and Access. One oversimplification would be to say that distribution allows for the aggregation and centralization of key distribution components. It reduces the complexity of the network.

Core is the simplest. It provides critical connectivity services and is typically designed to be highly available and always on. Redundancy is an important component of this. Its mission is to provide redundancy, isolation, and backbone connectivity. Typical L3 equipment includes items such as 24-and 48-port switches, and wireless access points.

The diagram in Fig. 5.13 attempts to demonstrate the looseness of some (most) modern networks. This diagram is in stark contrast to typical network diagrams, which often show a single point of access for all systems, connecting them to the Internet. This *connected space*[5] model layers firewalls in a ring, or a sphere (like a run-about ball) wrapped around your network, but only some spheres converge and are placed in more vulnerable positions than others. Multiple trusts may exist that have intrusive rights and weak passwords. It is, of course, not really a sphere, but it is easier to think about it that way. The four-tiered model[6] describes:

1. A perimeter-based firewall
2. A demilitarized zone (DMZ)
3. A wireless zone
4. All internal switches

Over the past few decades, networks have been transforming. DMZ? "Too much trouble to maintain," said the IT technicians and their managers. "Modern firewalls are more than enough to protect us from internal threats," said the IT directors and doers of the time. Besides, they would say, once a DMZ is compromised, they [the hackers] are practically inside. It is just a matter of time. There is some truth in this. As you can see in Fig. 5.13, what protection does the firewall give to the dual-homed host in the employee's pocket? Or to the hacker in the coffee shop across the street, who has accessed via the wireless, using a password he picked up from a conference room whiteboard? Modern networks are multiplexed composites of the four-tiered network. Tapping them? Do your best. The more structure, the better adherence to the four-tiered model that you can get, the stronger and more thorough your taps will be. Legitimate tap products are best. Your tap network should be 100% segregated from the business network. It should be undetectable to anyone on the network.

Traditional thinking is that wireless networks should be treated as untrusted, should connect only via virtual private networks, and should use two-factor authentication. In the military, such edicts could easily be issued. In a modern workplace, such dictatorial viewpoints will bump up against looser styles of networking, and where CISO and CIO philosophies may clash. Many employees do not perceive a difference between authoritarianism and limited wireless network connectivity. Furthermore, in this current climate and age of unrestricted computing, what is to stop me from tethering my computer to my cell phone and using it as the Internet, creating a portal on the network that cannot be seen?. And although most breaches may not come from "the inside," enough do that we need to worry about new devices appearing on our network as well, or the ability of users to attach computers to unknown or unregistered networks. Logging and tracking of events such as this can be done in a security paradigm such as this, but are outside of the scope of this chapter.

If you are fortunate, you will find a network that is well-organized and planned and follows Best Practices.

5. https://en.wikipedia.org/wiki/Connected_space.
6. Bejtlich, Richard. The Tao of Network Security Monitoring: Beyond Intrusion Detection (Kindle Locations 1338–1341). Pearson Education. Kindle Edition.

An efficient network reduces the number of connections necessary through by using additional core equipment.

If your topology (your networking infrastructure) matches that of a bird's nest, deploying successful sensor instrumentation will be expensive and it can be difficult to assess placement. A simpler architecture will be (1) less expensive, and (2) cheaper and easier to tap.

Exercise

Does it make sense to tap on the perimeter (outside the firewall)? In the modern day of scanless attacks, and sheer quantity of attacks, does it lend useful insights to see what attacks are being leveled against a corporate firewall? What are the pros and cons, and how would the information be leveraged?

6. PUTTING IT ALL TOGETHER

The following information about the various tools (see sidebar: "The All But Not All-Inclusive Blended Tools") expands on the previous narrative in the "The Tool Set"

section and adds to a more full understanding of optimization. It blends purpose, optimization, and sizing, because it is helpful to understand what a software program is actually doing on (or to) your machine before you try to think about making sure that it can do its job in the most efficient manner possible.

Historically, Max Transmission Unit was set to 1500 bytes, plus an additional 14 bytes for the Ethernet header and 4 byte FCS brings the frame size up to 1518. Most OS NICs default to this value. There are other headers that would affect that value, of course; virtual local area network ID tagging is a common example that puts the frame at 1522.

You can increase Snort performance by changing the pattern loading strategy from ac-split to ac. Memory usage can get high when this is done, with each Snort instance loading its rule set into memory, as opposed to calling it up from disk as needed.

To arrive at this, I examined our network traffic and saw that my average traffic hovered around 100 Mbps with a peak of 520 Mbps on each of my three monitoring interfaces, for a grand total of 1560 Mbps. I created two

---

The All But Not All-Inclusive Blended Tools

Tool: Bro Intrusion Detection System
Purpose: Protocol Detection, Logging, Alerting, etc.
  Packet Source: PF_RING
  Configuration file: /opt/bro/etc/node.cfg
  Potential packet loss from source to storage:
- at the mirror/SPAN
- at the aggregation point as information is passed to disk
- at the sensor interface: something about the NIC itself
- at PF_RING if the buffer count is too small and the input too high. If processing of the buffers cannot keep up with intake, ring buffers get overwritten and unprocessed information gets lost.
- at Bro. Bro's capture_loss.log shows a measurement of desyncs. It can be a good indicator of upstream packet loss.

Tool: Snort/Suricata
Purpose: Alert IDS
  Packet Source: PF_RING
  Configuration file: /etc/nsm/<sensorname>/sensor.conf
  Potential loss from source to tool:
- at the mirror/SPAN
- going to disk
- at the sensor interface (NIC)
- in the PF_RING buffers
- at Snort: not enough instances of Snort

Tool: Netsniff_ng (Next Generation)
Purpose: FPC to disk
  Packet Source: fast network analyzer, uses packet memory mapped [mmap(2)] mechanisms to bring packets directly from NIC to disk, with no need for transport to userland for analysis.
  Configuration file: not available.
  Potential loss from source to tool:

- at the tap/SPAN
- at the aggregation point
- at the sensor interface
- uses lazy writes (opportunistic cache writing to disk). A busy disk fabric or subsystem can be a problem because the cache fills, and without an opportunity to write it to disk, it will flush the cache.

Tool: PF_RING Tuning
Configuration: min_num_slots
  Default: 4096
  Recommended: 65,534 (increase this, memory permitting)
  Location: /etc/modprobe.d/pf_ring.conf
  Description: Slots store packets, and a slot is a component of the "ring." Slot sizes are dictated by the size of the packet (the caplen). The total ring size potentially could be caplen × min_num_slots, but actual ring size is caplen × used slots. Your PF_RING memory use, then, is the sum of the total sum of rings × caplen × used slots.

Think of the "ring" as a bucket with a hole in the bottom. The bucket acts as a reservoir, or a buffer, so that in the event of a sudden influx of water (packets), water will not flow over the bucket and be lost. The larger the count of slots is, the bigger the bucket is and the more overflow it can handle. Ideally the bucket will never be even half full. In reality, it will always be 80% full. It is up to you, the analyst, to monitor and track this so that you can properly request adequate resources. The buffering comes in when you increase the slot count, effectively replacing the cup with a bucket. You have the same size hole but the bucket can hold much more during the ebb and flow of bursting network traffic. When too many packets get tossed in the bucket, it overflows and those packets are dropped.

agents per interface, which would give me a total of (sustainable) 1200 Mbps, leaving a potential of 350 MB flooding into the buffer every second. It is important to balance the amount of information flowing into the system against its capabilities to process those data.

7. SECURING YOUR INSTALLATION

Some basic steps need to be taken to secure your installation of SO. Not all of these steps are documented, so be mindful that as versions of SO change over time, you will need to modify these steps on your own:

1. Default usernames and passwords are the bane of network security. Most successful attacks occur because someone somewhere either left the door unlocked or left the keys to the house under the doormat. A well-rounded and versatile hacker *tries all known keys first.* Why waste time with social engineering if I can just walk in as though I had been invited? All other forms of attacks are more likely to be seen and to leave behind evidence that can link the hacker to the attack. ELSA, which is part of SO, installs with a default username and password:
   a. Username: ELSA
   b. password: biglog

Fortunately, all communications that use these logins are sealed off from the outside world. You must have SSH access even to see the ports that these communications will use, and if the perpetrators have SSH access, they are so deep inside that they can take any access they want; they are root.

Running Sguil as an Analyst

Now that you have the system built and running, you will want to access it for the purposes of viewing alerts. There are several tools for this, the most useful of which have been summarized here. Sguil is best (and most efficiently) accessed from an analyst VM on your local desktop. It is a thick client, meaning that it executes many transactions against the server and has an application. Running Sguil on the desktop of the master server presents multiple issues. To reduce load on the server and avoid its desktop, run Sguil through an analyst VM on your local machine. Alternatively, you may run it through X Window from a separate, examiner machine, but some functionality may not work as expected.

SO's producer (Doug Burks) recommends that analysts run SO as a client only on a VM; and, that it is the easiest way to monitor and run the tools needed to access and manage a sensor array.[7] Via SSH, anything that can be accomplished via a VM installation of SO "client only" can also be

accomplished, but it may be more sensitive to latency than using a VM, and copying and pasting can be more awkward when running, for example, via SSH X Window on a MacBook. Running a VM can also allow you a safe place to "detonate" things and "safely" interact with external content that may be volatile. You may have to restore your VM to an earlier version in the event of a misstep with something toxic.

Using Sguil via Secure Shell on a Remote PC

On a MAC, getting a terminal window is as easy as hitting ⌘-space bar and typing "Terminal," then enter. This spins up a shell window and you can use SSH to access other machines:

> SSH -X ###.###.###.###

The "X" is *upper* case and it is an important distinction to make. SSH will throw an unusual error back at you if you get this wrong, and it may appear to you as though your X Window version is wrong. ###... is the IP address of the target machine:

> sguil.tk – -d 0

The "-d" switch here is for the purpose of preventing a flood of debugging messages populating your shell. Alternately, update your sguil.conf with "set DEBUG 0" and just run:

> sguil.tk

Sguil will spin up and ask you which interface you want to monitor, and then you will be connected and receiving alert messages. If you are not receiving alerts, either something is broken or you have a remarkably quiet network.

8. MANAGING AN INTRUSION DETECTION SYSTEM IN A NETWORK SECURITY MONITORING FRAMEWORK

Once SO has been completely installed, some post-installation tasks need to be completed to realize the full power and elegance of your solution. The first task, upon completion of your installation of SO, is to check the status of all installed components by typing, at a terminal window:

> sudo service nsm status
For an extremely detailed report, that includes some summary reports of activity:
>sudo sostat

For a quick summary, run "> sudo sostat-quick" for an overview of the sostat output. Typing "> 'sudo

---

7. https://github.com/Security-Onion-Solutions/security-onion/wiki/IntroductionWalkthrough.

Note: The snort.conf file suggests that there are nine steps to creating a custom configuration on a particular sensor NIC.

---

sostat-redacted' will redact any system identifiable information from the output (Fig. 5.14).

To upgrade:

> sudo soup

This is the most efficient upgrade method.

Configuring the Intrusion Detection System

Much customization is needed to get the IDS to a manageable and comprehensive system of alerts. A lot of what you will be doing as an analyst will involve analyzing alerts, so it is important to start with a good rule set.

Rules and Filters

Both Bro and Snort have built in filters that are not necessarily configured out of the SO box for what you want to do. In our initial production proof of concept, we wished to monitor external-facing connections only. Whether you have internal- or external-facing sensors, you should be aware of your IP address ranges and configure your sensors accordingly.

Managing Sensors

Each sensor that you instrument on your network may have multiple NICs that you use as receivers for tapped lines. You may have specific types of traffic on each of these cards, and there will likely be IP address ranges specific to that NIC. It follows that there would be one snort.conf file for each tap. For the most part, you may get away with simply configuring the IP ranges to a large set of everything on your network (if you expect cross-traffic between subnets). However, you may have specific rules or other types of traffic that require special handling (See sidebar: "Special Handling of Sensors").

Sensor Check

You may recall (if you are a *Star Trek* fan) that one of the greatest security tools at the disposal of Starfleet vessels is their sensors. What the sensors are monitoring, what they can detect, and your knowledge of it, are three important things. But how do you see or know about what you cannot see? Here is how I have analyzed sensors.

External Detection

If you plan on probing your externally facing network, first you must know the external IP ranges you are examining. Your Internet provider should be able to provide you with the classless Internet domain routing (CIDR)/IP address of your public-facing network.

Special Handling of Sensors

If you want to increase the number of Snort agents, you need to increase the number of PF_RING instances. First, stop the sensor:

> sudo nsm_sensor_ps-stop
> sudo vi /etc/nsm/$HOSTNAME-$INTERFACE/sensor.conf
\# Change the IDS_LB_PROCS variable to the number that you think will stop dropping packets.
> sudo nsm_sensor_ps-start

To change the actual size of the ring:

> sudo nsm_sensor_ps-stop
> sudo vi /etc/modprobe.d/pf_ring.conf
> sudo nsm_sensor_ps-start

Set the Network Variables

Open a bash (or the shell of your choice) and navigate to the directory where the Snort configuration file resides:

> cd /
> cd etc/nsm/%servername%-eth?/
\#\# %servername% is replaced by your server name, and the question mark "?" indicates the numerical identity of the network card that receives the tap output.
> sudo vim snort.conf

\#At the head of this file you will see a list of the nine steps mentioned in a previous note.

To set the network variables, scroll down (using the arrow keys) and position the cursor on the ipvar line. Remove the IP addresses and add in yours. Other variables include things such as lists of Web servers, Simple Mail Transfer Protocol servers, SSH servers, etc. For the most part, these are set to the $HOME_NET variable, which you set in the *ipvar HOME_NET [ip address ranges here]* command under the \# Step \#1... comment.

Upon completion of configuring the snort.conf file, configure the Bro configuration file at /opt/bro/etc/networks.cfg in a similar fashion. In this file, though, you will list each IP range on a new line.

You must restart NSM services with the command > *sudo nsm_sensor_ps-restart* for the changes to take effect. You must change this at every sensor.

One customized rule you might want to create is to detect Simple Network Management Protocol (SNMP) ping from a particular host. You can then use that host to ping across the full spectrum of your IP addresses. You can analyze the resultant alerts for completeness.

This script can be run from a list of IP addresses that you generate. It will generate a list of UP|DOWN IP addresses that you can then compare with alerts, in which you have set a rule to trip on an event you generate. Use the following to create a shell (.sh) script that you can execute to explore a network:

```
#!/bin/sh
awk '{print $1}' < pingerLoad.txt | while read ipPing;
do
    if ping -c1 $ipPing >/dev/null 2>&1; then
        echo $ipPing IS UP
    else
        echo $ipPing IS DOWN
    fi
done
```

Prerequisites: It does not decode CIDR notation. The user of this must create a file called "pingerLoad.txt" with a single column of all IP addresses you want to check. This shell-script reads the pingerLoad.txt file line by line. It is limited in that only hosts that will respond to ping are testable.

Alternatively, one can use nMap to scan ranges of IP addresses or entire CIDR blocks, and possibly detect servers that are attempting to mask themselves by disabling SNMP. Create this rule to detect external IP addresses:

alert ip ###.###.###.### any -> any any (msg:"MyRule Detect SourceIP Scanning"; flow:established,to_client; sid:51773; rev:1;)

Now, how do you see what you cannot see? Your nMap or bash script scan *should* check every single IP address in the range. An Internet search for CIDR calculator should yield a few respectable calculators that you can use to customize and tailor your nMap script for your network. This particular nMap goes deep, it does so stealthily, and it outputs the results to the file. Using scripts similar to those used in the external detection section, you can then begin to analyze your data, starting with a reconciliation of your nMap data to your Sguil alert data.

The best approach is to use a PostgreSQL database and push the data into it for analysis. Query writing against a static database (one that is not undergoing heavy trans-actions while you are performing queries) is relatively easy, and the amount of data you will be querying iw, in terms of databases, is relatively small. A good understanding of database joins, how to import data, and Boolean logic will go a long way to enhancing your understanding of your network and dramatically increase your ability to glean useful information from it.

Internal Detection

Internal detection differs from external detection only in that you can use a free tool called nMap more easily to "attack" the problem. The same tool would work for an external examination as well; it just becomes more complicated to manage address lists (you do not want to start scanning an IP range accidentally that does not belong to you). Depending on the jurisdiction and where the scan went, someone could get upset by this and it may be illegal; a more advanced understanding of nMap is required.

To begin, first, set up this rule by adding it to the local.rules file. It will alert on an IP address (###.###.###.###) you specify, talking across the sensor:

alert ip ###.###.###.### any -> any any (msg:"MyRule Detect SourceIP Scanning"; flow:established,to_client; sid:51773; rev:1;)

Next, run this nMap. It will ask every computer in this IP address range whether it is a Secure Hypertext Transfer Protocol server. This will successfully trip an alert on each machine to which this machine talks, with the exception of those that it cannot see:

nmap -Pn -v 192.168.0.0/16 | tee 192_all.log

In addition, you can move through your network physically with a laptop. By connecting at each known subnet and acquiring an IP address in it, you can test the IDS on that location by typing:

> curl http://testmyids.com

This is a website that was created with the sole purpose of causing a false positive (FP) in Sguil.

Manual Changes to Rules

If you are interested in tuning, you will spend a lot of time tuning sensors and making changes to rules. The last thing you want is to lose all of your hard work and then have to redo it. Also, you want your rules to go into effect across your entire instrumentation. The following scripts and procedures are designed to explain how the system updates itself. Normally, Salt, a management utility, is running and performing these updates for you.

SO is configured in a server/sensor arrangement, in which one "server" serves as master to the others (sensors). On the sensor server, the primary differentiator is that it houses the MySQL databases that SO uses to retain and catalog data. It can also act as the central location where you make changes to configuration files. Information flows into these databases based on a set of Snort rules. Each sensor can have its own individual rules. Rules on an SO server have a structure.

SO uses Pulled Pork, a Perl script written and marinated by J.J. Cummings. It downloads signatures every night and processes them according to a set of configuration files. In SO, these rules are established in various configuration files, in which you can specify a "state order" by setting, for example, the variable state_order=disable,drop,enable. In this example, you could disable an entire rule set or range of rules, and then enable some of them. PulledPork, a repository available on GitHub, provides the following functions[8]:

- Automated pull, editing, manipulation, and state changes for Snort rule sets
- Checksum verifications of downloaded rules
- Cutomatic generation of updated sid-msg.map file
- Capacity to include your custom local.rules in sid-msg.map file
- Ability to pull down rules and tarballs from custom URLs
- Supports shared objects
- Integrates with IP reputation lists
- Handles simultaneous, multiple rule set downloads
- Logs changes to a changelog
- Instrumental in tuning of rule sets

The configuration file for PulledPork on SO is located at:/etc/nsm/pulledpork/pulledpork.conf. Here is a list of each relevant file for rule manipulation, and its role in that structure. Also included are some useful log and configuration files that may not seem to be immediately useful, but if a rule fails or something else goes wrong, these are all good files to know about:

1. /usr/bin/rule-update
2. /etc/nsm/rules/downloaded.rules
3. /etc/nsm/rules/local.rules
4. /etc/nsm/pulledpork/disablesid.conf
5. /etc/nsm/pulledpork/pulledpork.conf
6. /var/log/nsm/sid_changes.log
7. /etc/nsm/templates/snort/snort.conf
8. /etc/nsm/HOSTNAME-INTERFACE/snort.conf
9. /etc/nsm/rules/bpf.conf
10. /etc/nsm/securityonion.conf
11. /etc/nsm/pulledpork/enablesid.conf
12. /etc/nsm/pulledpork/dropsid.conf
13. /etc/nsm/pulledpork/modifysid.conf
14. /etc/nsm/rules/threshold.conf

/usr/bin/rule-update

This is a script that runs that updates rules throughout SO. If you are not running Salt, it will need to be run on each sensor, starting with the master server first, simply by typing:

>sudo /usr/bin/rule-update

Once it has completed running on the master server, you can run it simultaneously on all other sensors. They go to the master server ("server") for their rule sets.

/etc/nsm/rules/downloaded.rules

This is the file that is read by Snort. Everything else works to manage the content of this file. If you have disabled a rule, it will show up as a commented-out rule in this file.

8. https://github.com/shirkdog/pulledpork.git.

/etc/nsm/rules/local.rules

This is where you put custom rules that you want to go in effect system-wide, After updating this file on the server, run > sudo rule-update on the server. Rule-update is a script that resides in the /usr/bin path. Once it finishes, run it on all sensors to populate. If you are running Salt, this update will be handled automatically.

/etc/nsm/pulledpork/disablesid.conf

By listing rules here in the format of:

Group ID: signature ID

The rule-update script will find the rule in */etc/nsm/rules/downloaded.rules* and put a "#" in front of it, effectively commenting it out of operation.

/etc/nsm/pulledpork/pulledpork.conf

This file contains the configurations that are read when PulledPork runs.

/var/log/nsm/sid_changes.log

PulledPork changelog: This is where all of the new IDs and changes are logged.

/etc/nsm/templates/snort/snort.conf

This file should never be modified. If a change needs to be made to the snort.conf, you need to make it in the /etc/nsm/HOSTNAME-INTERFACE/snort.conf file on each sensor. These files are not inherited from the master. Each interface of each sensor has its own snort.conf and they are not inherited from the master server. Fortunately, modifying files on a Linux server can be relatively easy using sed.

/etc/nsm/HOSTNAME-INTERFACE/snort.conf

This file contains some useful items, such as the ranges of IP addresses and ports to watch, configurable for both internal and external networks. Many rules are designed to trigger when certain traffic from the EXTERNAL_NET is detected. By the default, SO leaves the configuration for both INTERNAL_NET and EXTERNAL_NET at their default values. It is up to you to add in the values for INTERNAL_NET.

/etc/nsm/rules/bpf.conf

This Berkely Packet Filter file can be used to filter IP addresses and CIDR ranges that you wish to ignore. If you perform any sort of network pcap, you will run across things called "primitives," filter aspects that allow you to tune your capture to only see certain traffic. Examples of primitives are "net," "port," "addr," and their respective qualifiers such as "src" and "dst." For example, you can add these lines to the file to prevent capture of all file share traffic from IP address 192.0.2.12 to 0.26; the second line prevents capture of all traffic to and from 203.0.113.68:

> !(src host 192.0.2.12 && dst host 192.0.2.26 && dst
> port 445) &&
> !(host 203.0.113.68)

You can write expressions such as these and place them in this file to modify the behavior and prevent traffic from being captured. Every line except the last one should have "&&" after it. This file is symlinked across all your sensors, so when you change it on the master server, it will change on all servers. The changes will take effect when the daily rule update runs, or you can run it manually.

/etc/nsm/securityonion.conf

This file pertains to configurations such as DAYSTOKEEP and UNCAT_MAX.

/etc/nsm/pulledpork/enablesid.conf

Presumably, this file may act as a "whitelist." This allows you to dictate rules and rule ranges expressly that should be active.

/etc/nsm/pulledpork/dropsid.conf

This file pertains exclusively to an inline deployment of Snort. Traffic that matches the rules listed in this file will be dropped, blocking and logging the packet. Pay attention to state_order when using this file.

/etc/nsm/pulledpork/modifysid.conf

In this file, you can place rules that you have edited. For example, you might constrain a certain rule to fire only under certain conditions, such as when the traffic source is a certain IP address.

/etc/nsm/rules/threshold.conf

This file allows you to make adjustments to certain rules. For example, perhaps you have a machine that is tripping off millions of alerts. It is a machine that you know is running perpetual scans against your network. In MySQL, you can run the following query to generate a list of the alerts:

> SELECT Distinct COUNT(signature_ID) as NumberO-
> fAlerts, signature_ID, signature, inet_ntoa(src_ip)
> FROM event WHERE src_ip = inet_aton
> ('172.17.102.62')
> GROUP BY signature order by 1 desc;

This will give you a nice list of signature IDs. By copying and pasting the list into a program such as Excel, you can manipulate them into the following format:

> suppress gen_id 1, sig_id 2019526, track by_src, ip
> 172.17.102.62

Next, reload the rules.

Log Files

Each instance of Snort that runs will place a log for each session in this directory:

> /var/log/nsm/securityonion/sguild.log
> /var/log/nsm/servername-eth#/

After the Changes

You have made changes and now you want to propagate them to all your sensors. If you are running Salt, it will update the changes in 15 min or less. If you are not manually updating rules, it is a simple matter of first updating the server, by running:

> > sudo /usr/bin/rule-update
> Then, connecting to each sensor and also running:
> > sudo /usr/bin/rule-update
> On each server, then run:
> > sudo /usr/bin/rule-update

Useful File Manipulation Commands

Sometimes you may need to execute commands against configuration files in all sensor folders. Each sensor gets its own folder, so changing those files manually would be excruciating:

> grep -rl matchstring somedir/ | xargs sed -i 's/string1/
> string2/g'
> /etc/nsm/> sudo grep -rl 'ipvar EXTERNAL_NET any' ./
> | sudo xargs sed -i 's/ipvar EXTERNAL_NET any/
> ipvar EXTERNAL_NET !$HOME_NET/g'

The preceding will replace all occurrences of some configuration value in all files named snort.conf where that config value exists. Coincidentally, this is one of the biggest, single noise-reducing tuning changes that can be made. Without it, many forms of innocuous traffic takes shape, such as file share transfers that contain the shellcode attack marker string "CCCCCCCCCCCCCCCCCCCCCCCCC" (many binary files may, coincidentally, contain this string and it is not a shellcode attack).

How to Add Rules

Adding, removing, and changing rules will be an endless pursuit. The syntax for Snort rules, also called signatures, is straightforward and is similar to other signatures used by other sensors, such as Fortinet firewalls. An Internet search for "Fortinet IPS Signature Syntax Guide" will return a result for a PDF guide that is well-written. It is a concise and nonverbose guide on how to use the system and create rules.

How to Disable a Single Rule or Range Rules

Snorts IDS works by processing PF_RING buffers through its agents, which compare that traffic to the signatures that are defined in the alert rules located in the downloaded.rules file. This rule set is at the foundation of SO; for the most part, the alerts you will see are based on that set. Sguil is the tool that is used to review the alerts generated by Snort. At the time of this writing, Snort rules are divided into 54 categories.

Depending on your network and its business purposes, some categories serve little purpose and it is immediately apparent that they should be disabled. For example, on a network serving software developers, who enjoy their social media, and for whom policy controls on the use of social media during the day are nonexistent, the following rule categories are of no use:

- Policy: multimedia: This category will detect violations of your multimedia policy: for example, things such as iTunes. This category contains no alerts on exploits that attempt to leverage the types of vulnerabilities that may be found within multimedia files. Vulnerabilities such as those can be found in the file: multimedia category.
- Policy: social: Violations of social media policy, such as use of peer-to-peer (p2p) communication, Facebook, Twitter, etc., will be found here.
- Policy: other: This category of rules is for activity-violating end-user corporate policy that does not seem to fit into the other categories.

This category, while appearing useful on the surface, may be redundant to other alerting systems and tools:

- Policy: spam: This category is for rules that may indicate the presence of spam on the network.

This category produces a lot of noise on some networks:

- Protocol: Internet Control Message Protocol (ICMP): This category of rules alerts you about the presence of ICMP traffic. It also alerts you if a hacker is attempting to exploit ICMP vulnerabilities in your network. It is least useful on your perimeter. If you are running with sensors on your perimeter, you will want to disable this because it will likely generate thousands of useless alerts. Every hacker in the world is constantly scanning the Internet for externally facing vulnerabilities. Of course, it is possible that you will develop vulnerability in this area. Disable with great caution, and ensure that you have a backup plan.

Additional categories exist for things such as Post Office Protocol and Internet Message Access Protocol. If you think that a rogue email server on your system is a risk you care about, you should leave rules like this enabled. However, in an environment where there may be hundreds of test servers that use these protocols, you may become overwhelmed by the quantity of alerts.

A final good example has to do with server types. If you have no Microsoft servers, for example, disable the Microsoft Alerts. Likewise, if you have no MSSQL servers, who cares if someone is trying to hack in on an MSSQL port? Of course if you do not know what you have on your network, it will be difficult to assess. What if you have a server that runs a product unfamiliar to you and it has SQL at the back end and a default username and password? Now someone has access to your SQL server, and depending on the account they accessed, it may be a short step to remote code execution.

Every network is different, and so there are times when you will want to disable alerts, even entire categories of alerts. The main consideration when disabling a "nuisance" rule is twofold:

1. Consider whether the alert can be lessened by properly configuring the server that is distributing the alert. But for the fact that there are so many of them, would the alert, be actionable?
2. Is the alert consistent with your business rules? For example, if nobody minds that users are using Internet Relay Chat or Skype, alerts of this nature should be disabled.

The best place to perform examinations of alerts at a high level is, arguably, SQUERT. It shows a nice summary of things, and allows you to see more information about the alert, such as the ID and the count of alerts, as well as some useful charts. It follows then, that at an incident response level, on a tuned system, most of the analyst's time will be spent in the Sguil interface, observing alerts as they are generated, evaluating them, and making decisions.

Edit the /etc/nsm/pulledpork/disablesid.conf File

Let us suppose you have completed an analysis of an alert and have decided it is nonsense (more on how to decide this in a later section). It is hoped that by now you have taken to heart the advice to learn a text editor. An Internet search for "vi cheatsheet" will return several useful websites that will get you through what might otherwise be a steep learning curve:

> sudo vi /etc/nsm/pulledpork/disablesid.conf

Prefacing the command with "sudo" ensures that you will be able to make write changes to the file. If you do not use sudo, the file is owned and in use by someone else (SO). Tools such as vi and nano are ubiquitous on Linux machines. Learning how to use them will greatly improve your skills and capabilities.

9. SETTING THE STAGE

Although investigating breaches is fun and exciting, first we have to do some housekeeping. Our house must be in order first, lest you be overwhelmed by FPs and become embroiled in a heated and bitter battle of hurled accusations and false allegations. Have you ever tried to find your keys in a messy house? What you do not want to do is become central to some imbroglio over *legitimate behaviors* on your network. Yes, you are the security guy, but you must step carefully and within the confines of your corporate culture.

Administering security policies to your network cannot "shock" the system. If you have ever taken a houseplant outside into the bitter cold, you will understand exactly what shutting down all external network access will do to productivity at your company. You will not only irritate everyone, you will create a culture where now everyone simply figures out hacks and ways to sidestep your attempts. It is hoped that you do not already have a culture built on sidestepping security; that will be harder to fix. There is an interesting story about a man, a pot of gold, a leprechaun, a bush, and a red ribbon that exemplifies the challenges of the security role nicely.

With that precautionary lecture out of the way, the following section details the underlying policy documentation you need to take and customize for your use, and modify according to your culture. For the sake of completeness of vision, I have provided the entire security suite here, which includes power, physical security, and health and wellness. A well-rounded security architect understands the interlocking nature of all of these systems, and follows or creates an incident response playbook that creates an understanding with the business of how incidents of all types will be managed and handled by the security team.

10. ALERTS AND EVENTS

Now that you have a good foundation for building out an accepted security program and have sensors and servers running, we can take a close look at how you identify, isolate, and remediate certain types of attacks that may occur. For the sake of simplicity, we will focus strictly on alerts and alert or event analysis. Behind every alert lies the underlying event that tripped it. Your job will be to review alerts and make determinations about whether they indicate that a notable event has occurred. There are not enough pages in any book to cover all of the alerts and how they may present in a concerted fashion and definitively underscore an attack in progress. Rather, you are seeing alerts, examining them, and making decisions about next steps, collectively.

Once your sensor array is built, you will begin to see alerts. Many will be false. The biggest unanswered question that surfaces will be, "How do I research and learn about alerts?" It is not easy. The vast majority of alerts that occur are arcane and have little documentation, at best. For example, type into your favorite search engine, "ET POLICY Data POST to an image file (jpg)." The results are cursory (unless you happen to pull up this chapter as a result).

Next, we take a look at the rule as a whole, to see which parts will most likely yield useful information. From the Sguil interface, we see a series of alerts on POST coming from an internal device and going to some external website:

alert tcp $HOME_NET any -> $EXTERNAL_NET $HTTP_PORTS (msg:"ET POLICY Data POST to an image file (jpg)"; flow:to_server,established; **content:"-POST"**; http_method; **content:".jpg"**; http_uri; content:!"upload.wikimedia.org"; **http_uri; pcre:"/\.jpg$/U"** ;reference:url,doc.emergingthreats.net/2010067; classtype:trojan-activity; sid:2010067; rev:9;) /nsm/server_data/securityonion/rules/[sensor-interface]/downloaded.rules: Line 9481

Take special note here of the phrase "http_uri; content:!"upload.wikimedia.org"" in that rule. It is inferable from this (the "!" means "not") that there have been enough false alerts on wikimedia that an exception was added directly into the rule by the publisher. You can edit the rule and add additional exceptions into it as you see fit by adding the rule into the modifysid.conf file. The best course of action is not always simply to disable a rule. In Sguil, right-clicking on the alertID allows you to pivot into the actual conversation:

SRC: POST /attachments/car-parts-sale-wanted-44/2132492583-car-cs-wheels-front-sway-bar-tr_c2.jpg HTTP/1.1
SRC: Host: www.00000000000club.com
SRC: Connection: keep-alive
SRC: Content-Length: 227
SRC: Origin: www.00000000000club.com
SRC: X-Requested-With: XMLHttpRequest
SRC: User-Agent: Mozilla/5.0 (Windows NT 6.1; WOW64) AppleWebKit/537.36 (KHTML, like Gecko) Chrome/49.0.2623.112 Safari/537.36
SRC: Content-Type: application/x-www-form-urlencoded; charset=UTF-8
SRC: Accept: */*
SRC: Referer:

From the preceding, we can use a sandbox to access the URL via a browser or use:

> curl www.00000000000club.com/attachments/car-parts-sale-wanted-44/2132492583-car-cs-wheels-front-sway-bar-tr_c2.jpg

You will need to rebuild the URL manually from the information in the conversation. Once you curl, inspect the code behind the site and examine to see whether an actual "POST to an image file" is occurring. A security analyst will have moderate to good skill in a number of programming languages and a solid understanding of post and get methods used by Web forms.

Note: A sandbox is a VM that we do not care about and that is isolated, so that if its admin credentials are compromised, no harm can come to the other systems you are charged with protecting.

Reconnaissance

Chances are good that once you connect your sensors to the external world, you will see a lot of alerts. The best thing to do is to start with the highest number of alerts, and begin thinking about either disabling the alert or rewriting it and adding some intellectual capital to it, something that many rules are sadly lacking. That may sound like an indictment of the rule sets that come with SO, but it is not. Many of the rules are overwhelming in their complexity and uselessness. Thousands of rules must be removed and hundreds must be modified before your system will make sense for *your* network and before you have a seasoned rule set that fits your network like a glove. All networks are different. The set of rules that trip few FPs on my network might cause a virtual alert landslide on another.

Default Password Breach

Not only do you know you have not yet bothered to change that default password, hackers know it, too. Google, which makes learning how to do our jobs, communicating with the world, and life easier in general, also has conveniently made networking and software documentation inarticulately easy to find.

Table 5.1 lists some common username and password patterns. Note that derivative passwords such as P@55w0rd! are not hard for humans to guess; they are laughably easy for computers to guess.

The Basics

For those of you who need a primer on network intrusion, a sort of "what's all this fuss about?" explanation, let us

provide some explanation about the basic vulnerability of all communications being exploited.

NSM is built on pcap. All network communications are built on hardware that transmits and receives streams of packets. The network card receives the transmission, which is simply a serialized, binary transmission, or impulses. The card translates these into a more useful format, and the OS picks them up from a memory location reserved by the card. A packet capturing application runs beside the OS and reads this same space without (generally) causing interference. There will, of course, be increased load, which is why we typically do not sniff packets directly on a subject/suspect machine. The increase in CPU can alert the user or hacker to your presence. This will either cause him to roll up and vanish without a trace or trip off a larger attack which you are unable to prevent.

Of utmost priority, then, is to develop a capability to see everything an intruder is doing, and without your adversary catching on that you have caught on. It is important to capture side-to-side motion in your network. As you begin to plan your sensor infrastructure, there are a few important considerations:

1. SPANning ports is a perfectly acceptable method of getting packets, with a couple of caveats:
   a. You trust the IT department to do it properly.
   b. You do not mind if the switch gets a heavy load and you lose some packets; even if you are filtering the load and dumping every YouTube packet to dev/null that comes in, it will not matter to the switch. It will drop them indiscriminately. The reference standard here is that you double down on your architecture and ensure that your sensor switches will not drop traffic.
   c. A flooded or poisoned switch may create a packet maelstrom that leaves you with a lot of senseless traffic, and possibly you will miss the one alert you really needed to see. Tools such as EtherFlood, SMAC, Macof, and Technetium MAC Address Changer are readily available tools that use flooding techniques to perform tasks such as Address Resolution Protocol poisoning and session hijacking. Some of these tactics may force the switch to act as a hub, broadcasting all packets for easy intercept.[9]
   d. You do not mind that the switch could potentially be compromised.
2. Traffic that you capture from SPANned ports on switches in access layer is the same as traffic up at the core layer between the core and distribution.
3. Know the internal bandwidth capabilities of your switch. You will need that many ports for your switch.

---

9. **Hacker Techniques, Tools, and Incident Handling** By Sean-Philip Oriyano, President Michael Gregg, (283).

TABLE 5.1 Knowing the Default Username and Password for Many Common Computers and Hardware Simplifies Penetration of a Network

Username	Password
Manufacturer	Password
Manufacturer	[Blank]
Admin	Admin/Admin/adminstat
Admin	[Blank]
Root	Root
Root	[Blank]
Administrator	[Blank]
Product name	Admin/Admin
Product name	Blank
Blank	Blank
Admin	Root
Admin	Password/Password (or some derivative thereof, such as P@55w0rd!
Admin	SysAdmin

Any combination of these two columns will grant access to the vast majority of devices if the password has not been changed. Often, they are not.

4. Know how much your CPU can lift (data).
5. Know the bandwidth write capacity of your sensor's storage.
6. Balance it.

For example, if your CPU can handle 45 Gbps of throughput, your switch can handle 75 Gbps, and your network cards can handle 80 Gbps, you are going to be in trouble because when the switch peaks at 75 Gbps, your sensor will begin to stall, because its CPU will be at 100%. You need two sensors on the switch, or more powerful CPU.

11. SGUIL: TUNING GRAPHICS PROCESSING UNIT RULES, ALERTS, AND RESPONSES

You have installed SO and you are wondering where to start. The best place to start, and where the analyst will always begin, is in Sguil, with alerts. Sguil has six primary functions when it comes to performing NSM analysis:

1. aggregates alerts
2. presents key session and metadata, together with the alert data
3. allows you to use a query builder interface to query and review of alert data
4. allows you to use a query builder interface to query and review of session data
5. allows you to pivot into full packet data

6. provides a management workflow to escalate and classify events.[10]

All of these items are great and most are entirely manageable and make using the software easy and effective. Item 1, however, can be challenging, and will be the focus of this section. The other items, taken in stride with the rest of this chapter, should be relatively self-explanatory. One important item is that right-clicking on the various columns that are within the alert pane in Sguil will yield different context menus. Care should be taken to learn and understand what each column means and what behavior is behind each of the items on the context menu.

If you have installed SO on a busy production system, you will need to trim the number of alerts. There are some 18,000 rules in the GNU General Public License (GPL) rule set, about 10,000 of which most likely are not going to be relevant.

To start, you need to look and see what rules are the noisiest in your environment. Once you get rid of the vast majority of noise, you can be more strategic about how to go about future trimming.

Meanwhile, as you develop your rule set, the alerts will pile up. As you develop your internal rule set, based on your network use and restrictions (or their lack), you can

---

10. Bejtlich, Richard (2013-07-26). The Practice of Network Security Monitoring: Understanding Incident Detection and Response (Kindle Location 3259). No Starch Press. Kindle Edition.

remove alerts from your database by following these simple steps:

1. Edit the SO configuration file. The variables you edit here will be read into the /usr/bin/sguil-db-purge command (bash script) that you will run in Step 4:
   a. vi /etc/nsm/securityonion.conf
   b. change DAYSTOREPAIR=1
   c. DAYSTOKEEP=2 (until the rules are tuned, this will prevent severe buildup of alerts)
   d. UNCAT_MAX=100000 uncategorized events. 100,000 is just an arbitrary starting point of the number of uncategorized events that we want to see on this server at this point. This is a number that, once a proper workflow is in place for handling events, we will not need to worry about. It is also the number of events that will appear in the Sguil interface.

Identifying Nuisance Rules

Rules that trip off thousands of alerts in the system create an almost impenetrable haze of noise. But are such rules that trip off so many alerts actually noise, or do they truly indicate a problem (see Sidebar: "Nuisance Alerts")?

Each of the noisiest rules is then analyzed to see why it is tripping an alert. There are not enough pages in this book and 10 more like it to cover all the Emerging Threat and GPL rules implemented by SO and managed by Snort, and shamefully little is written about each rule on the site. You will need to be prepared to analyze as many as 500 to 600 alerts on your network. That being said, I have included a short discussion here on "how to find out" more. Take the first rule in this list, for example. It is a GPL rule.

In 2015 I was tasked with becoming proficient in SO, of which the Snort IDS is part. Netsniff-ng collects packet data, Snort reviews it, and Sguil gathers its alert data into the SecurityOnion_DB MySQL database, which runs on the MyISAM storage engine, which is little more than an elaborate way of saying "flat files." The data are generally nonrelational and not well-normalized. That being said, the data are small and there are few rows, so it generally queries well.

Nuisance Alerts

To understand nuisance alerts, first you must understand what the rule does and why it fired an alert.

For example, rules often use Perl-Compatible Regular Expressions. To decompose a regular expression, visit: http://www.myezapp.com/apps/dev/regexp/show.ws
At the command line, spin up a MySQL shell:
mysql -uroot -Dsecurityonion_db
This will give you access to run SQL commands directly against the database. If you should forget the name of the database, you can also run:
> mysql
> show databases;
Database:
1. information_schema
2. elsa_web
3. mysql
4. performance_schema
5. securityonion_db
6. syslog
7. syslog_data
8. test
> USE securityonion_db -A
The "-A" will prevent MySQL from aggressively preloading a bunch of information from the database.

Once you use a database, you no longer need to name it explicitly in your SQL syntax. SQL is a nice language for data manipulation, and although ostensibly, it seems easy to use, it is also capable of inflicting a tremendous amount of damage when used incorrectly. For example, forgetting to add a WHERE clause to an update or delete a statement can wipe out most of your data. In addition, a large and complicated SELECT statement can cause a large read from disk that may render the system unresponsive for all users, and may overwhelm the database so completely that it begins to page to disk, which can cause unexpectedly bad performance across all queries, including those that are inserting data.

Run this query to summarize the number of alerts by signature:
SELECT COUNT(*) AS RuleCount, signature, signature_id FROM event WHERE status=0 GROUP BY signature_id ORDER BY RuleCount DESC LIMIT 20;

Note that this query groups by signature_id, which is a number. This will outperform an aggregate of text data. SecurityOnion_db does not rationalize the signature column and stores the entire text of the alert with each row, or event, in the event table.

Hit [ENTER] and the command will run, yielding output something like the output in Table 5.2.

TABLE 5.2 Point in Time Snapshot of How Alerts Are Stacking Up

topAlertsCount	signature	signature_id
17039	GPL SNMP public access udp	2101411
2151	ET POLICY TeamViewer Keep-alive inbound	2008795
2028	ET WEB_CLIENT Possible HTTP 503 XSS Attempt (External Source)	2010527
1878	ET DROP Dshield Block Listed Source group 1	2402000
1824	ET POLICY PE EXE or DLL Windows file download	2000419
1739	ET POLICY TeamViewer Dyngate User-Agent	2009475
1599	ET CHAT Skype User-Agent detected	2002157
1560	GPL ICMP_INFO PING *NIX	2100366
946	ET INFO GENERIC SUSPICIOUS POST to Dotted Quad with Fake Browser 1	2018358
894	ET POLICY Microsoft Online Storage Client Hello TLSv1 Possible...	2014920
894	ET POLICY Microsoft Online Storage Client Hello TLSv1 Possible...	2014919
735	ET INFO Session Traversal Utilities for NAT (STUN Binding Response)	2016150
660	ET POLICY Suspicious inbound to MSSQL port 1433	2010935
579	ET POLICY SSLv3 outbound connection from client vulnerable to...	2019416
571	ET POLICY SSLv3 inbound connection to server vulnerable to...	2019415
531	GPL RPC portmap listing UDP 111	2101280
447	ET SHELLCODE Excessive Use of HeapLib Objects Likely Malicious...	2013222
435	GPL WEB_CLIENT PNG large colour depth download attempt	2103134
432	ET POLICY Data POST to an image file (gif)	2010066
425	ET INFO EXE - Served Attached HTTP	2014520

Understanding the Enterprise Log Search and Archive Database Structure

Where the alert data stored in Sguil is easy to grasp (just look in the Event table, and understand how to use the INET_NTOA and INET_NOTA functions, and you are set), the ELSA data are put together by a drummer of an entirely different beat. For example, see sidebar: "GNU General Public License Simple Network Management Protocol Public Access Uniform Datagram Protocol."

GNU General Public License Simple Network Management Protocol Public Access Uniform Datagram Protocol

The following example will likely be the most common alert. This is in addition to hackers looking to access hardware. For example:

Sample Rule Issue
GPL Shellcode x86...(1,2,3)
1. ...inc ebx NOOP -
2. ...0x90 NOOP unicode
3. ...x86 stealth NOOP

Relevance: Generally considered a noisy alert.
Rule: It is sid 1390, found in the file shellcode,rules f
The full rule text is:

alert ip $EXTERNAL_NET *any* -> $HOME_NET any (msg:"SHELLCODE x86 inc ebx NOOP"; content:"CCCCCCCCCCCCCCCCCCCCCCCC"; classtype:-shellcode-detect; sid:1390; rev:9;)

Response: Disable or adjust port rules to ignore these packets on web ports.

alert ip $EXTERNAL_NET *$SHELLCODE_PORTS* -> $HOME_NET any (msg:"*SRE*:SHELLCODE x86 inc ebx NOOP"; content:"CCCCCCCCCCCCCCCCCCCCCCCC"; classtype:shellcode-detect; sid:1390; rev:9;)

Note: Notice the italicized parts in these rules and definitions. These are the important parts that have changed. The "SRE" in the rule is my initials. It is vital that you mark rules that you have changed. This will ease review of your changes, which should be at least an annual or ongoing activity.

Categories and counts:
cut -d\" -f2 /etc/nsm/rules/downloaded.rules | awk '{print $1, $2}'|sort |uniq -c |sort -nr

Too Many Alerts!

You have now completed installing SO and you feel as if the system is being overwhelmed by alerts of the "GPL SNMP public access UDP" variety. If you have ever had the fortune to sit and watch the senseless hacker traffic that attacks your network, this is the number one alert.

SO downloads and manages signatures on a nightly basis. It uses a tool called "PulledPork" to accomplish this. It is important, then, that you manage rules in a way that will prevent your changes from being overwritten. First, how do we find all of the information about a rule that is needed to disable it? When you click the "Show Rule" check box in the lower right-hand panel of Sguil, the Sguil interface will show you the rule itself. For example:

[ ] Show Packet Data [x] Show Rule
alert tcp $EXTERNAL_NET $HTTP_PORTS -> $HOME_NET any (msg:"ET INFO EXE IsDebugger

Present (Used in Malware Anti-Debugging)"; flow:established,to_client; flowbits:isset,ET.http.binary; content:"IsDebuggerPresent"; content:!"|0d 0a|x-avast"; http_header; classtype:misc-activity; sid:2015744; rev:3;)

With this particular rule, I want to know what "Malware Anti-Debugging" is. Dubugging is a process used by analysts to analyze some malware. It makes sense, then, that if I am the author of malware, I would want to check and see whether a debugger is running in the space where my code (payload) is being detonated. A quick check of the source IP address shows that this alert is from the presumably trusted microsoft.com domain, and that it appears to be a Windows update. I want to know for sure, so I go to /nsm/bro/extracted/ on alerting sensor and look for an executable with a coinciding arrival time. I find one, so I hash it:

> md5sum HTTP-FzzfVZ01QDQwP6O7c.exe

which yields:

e3197b7a33e5a0a7a3abee419eaac477

A lookup on http://www.hashsets.com/nsrl/search/ reveals that the file is a printer driver, so I create an autocat on it and an item in my backlog to automate this process. Further to this, all such alerts could conceivably be handled automatically with a lookup using nsrllookup.[11] Such automations will be common and useful as your NSM solution matures, but detailing them here would be out of the scope of this chapter. A good start would be downloading and installing the nsrllookup tool:

> git clone https://github.com/rjhansen/nsrllookup.git
> sudo ./configure && sudo make && sudo make install

To check to see how noisy a rule or group of rules is, modify the previous query with a WHERE clause as follows:

#grouping by a signature that has a lot of hits that may be "noise" in the system.
SELECT distinct COUNT(signature) as occurrences, signature_id, signature FROM event WHERE signature like 'ET Policy%' GROUP by signature;

The preceding query may burn a lot of CPU. A better query would target a specific signature_ID or source IP address (src_IP).

In a master/sensor SO environment, changes to the configuration file on the server will sync from the master to the sensors via the rule-update script. To disable a rule, access the *disablesid.conf* configuration file and append the signature you want to disable. Enter it in the format

---

11. https://github.com/rjhansen/nsrllookup.

TABLE 5.3 Compartmentalizing the Snort Rule's Constituents

Type	Type Traffic	Source Internet Protocol Address	Port	Traffic Direction	Destination	Port	Message
Alert	ip|tcp	Any	Any	->	Any	Any	(msg:"xxxx")

"gid:sid. Next, run the rule updater on the master and sensor servers. Although the rule only needs be changed on the master, the update needs to be run on each server:

> sudo /usr/bin/rule-update

The preceding update will stop and restart numerous services. It may not be the best idea to run this on a production server during production hours, but because an attack can come at any time, who is to say when "production" begins and ends? It does not; it is random, and ongoing.

If you have millions of alerts and need just to clear the deck and start over, here is one way to do it: In the securityonion.conf file, set DAYSTOKEEP to 1. This will significantly reduce the number of alerts you see. After you have performed some tuning, increase it to the nominal number of days that you want to keep.

Modifying Signatures

How signatures are written, created, and published remains a bit of a mystery. Becoming part of the user community and going to conferences is always the best way to get introduced to people, have conversations, and learn how things work.

Anatomy of a Snort Rule

The following rule is not one that you want to run. It is merely a model example of how rules are constructed in Snort:

alert ip any any -> any any (msg: "IP Packet detected")

Now, let us take this rule and compartmentalize its constituents, as shown in Table 5.3. This rule is for IP, so ports do not matter because all port traffic is IP.

Theory

Someone vastly removed from the real world finds one malformed packet, freaks out about it, and writes a rule. Now, this rule is responsible for 99% of the bogus alerts in my environment.

If your objective is to rewrite bad rules, you are in luck. All of the rules are available in the /etc/nsm/rules/local.rules file. Ultimately, packet filtering is packet filtering is packet filtering, and the way that a packet is constructed does not change just because the filter is different. Fortinet publishes a document on writing signatures that is vastly superior to the manual published by

Snort. Their signature guide can be viewed at: https://video.fortinet.com/uploads/documents/IPS%20Signature%20Syntax%20Guide.pdf.

12. DEVELOPING PROCESS

So far, we have talked a lot about tools and configuring the tools so as to prevent you from experiencing temporary insanity. But how does it all tie together with an attack? How do we pin our various activities to actual command and control stages, and how do we categorize or attain a deep understanding of how the alerts we receive so the actions we take will relate back to those stages? Some authors have called this, and continue to refer to it, as "the kill chain." This indicates that the hacker's end goal is to "kill" the victim. Because this is seldom the case, this author chooses to call it simply "Stages of Command and Control":

1. Motive facilitation: What are the various networks that I could attack that would benefit my agenda?
2. Reconnaissance: Are any of them vulnerable?
3. Probe: attacks that will attempt to leverage known vulnerabilities. Social engineering: easiest to get someone to open the door
4. Gain access
5. Escalate privileges: probe and gain deeper access. This is the same as Steps 2, 3, and 4
6. Reconnaissance and build (discover all internal resources, continue to escalate privileges, install tools, build back doors, cover tracks, deploy roll-up countermeasures)
7. Life cycle: There is no "end game." The hacker's mindset might be one of: "This network is mine, and I will keep it until someone forcibly ejects me; and even then, I'll be back. Unless I get bored. Then I will just go away. Now I set up shop, and continue to build, refine and strengthen my foothold, exfiltrate information securely, and unnoticed or exploit as per my motive." Ultimately, this does not matter that much. If someone is doing donuts on your front lawn, does it matter why? No, you just need to make them stop and then repair the damage and prevent a future attack.

For each of the preceding stages, summarized in Table 5.4, a reasonable defense process must be paired, like a fine wine with a good steak, like Batman and Robin, like Mork and Mindy ... For each of the threat stages, I have paired a corresponding defense activity. Models and lists

TABLE 5.4 Restate How an Attack Might Proceed If You Were Running It: Would You Run Any Reconnaissance or Just Attack?

Motive Facilitation	Threat Modeling
Reconnaissance	Web log and external threat assessment and monitoring.
Probe	Monitoring and alerts
Gain access	Monitoring and alerts, Computer Incident Response Team
Escalate privileges	Controlled access monitoring, privilege escalation notifications
Reconnaissance and build: implement resurrection protocols (persistence)	Process logging monitoring. Computer and memory forensics. Data collection
Life cycle	Analysis of internal, sideways instrumentation. Destruction and replacement of known, infected hardware

are fine, but you should feel free to adapt and make these models your own. Restate them in a way you understand, and which corresponds with your perception of how people operate. You are your own worst enemy; it is time to exploit that fact.

Someone once told me that to detect a counterfeit dollar bill, US Treasury agents would be given the instruction to handle, for countless hours, bills of every denomination that were known to be genuine. Similarly, you must engage in an in-depth examination of your own network. The following list of items can be thought of as a pathway of milestones to network defensibility:

1. Monitoring: You must instrument your network with tap-based sensors in the proper locations as described in this chapter.
2. Inventoried: You know every machine on your network, and who owns it.
3. Assessed: The security team has assessed the risk of the system.
4. Hardened: All systems have a minimal footprint.
5. Current: Emerging threats presented by new vulnerabilities are regularly patched.
6. Maintained: The previous steps are regularly checked and assessed for completeness and quality of operations.

13. UNDERSTANDING, EXPLORING, AND MANAGING ALERTS

Your primary interface to SO will (more than likely) be Sguil. Snort, an IDS, creates alerts that are then inserted into the SecurityOnion_DB. You will use ELSA, Sguil, Squert, and SQL to examine Snort alerts, interpret them, tune them, and then take action when an actual intrusion is detected. It includes useful features such as reverse lookup, transcript views, Wireshark view, and packet view, where you can actually see the packet that tripped the alert.

The interface for Sguil has a few features that are not immediately apparent. You hover over the AlertID and

press two fingers down and hold; you will see an option to view the transcript.

Uniform Datagram Protocol Traffic Alerts

UDP alerts can be somewhat more challenging to investigate because, unlike TCP, there is no distinct "conversation." Essentially, a proper TCP connection can be compared to having a waiter bring you a cup of tea, having him ask you if it is okay, discussing the nuances of tea varieties, and having him bring you cream and sugar. UDP is more like a prisoner in a jail cell getting hit with a fire hose. The prisoner will definitely get a drink of water, but the guard doing the hosing will not really care about it. Similarly, UDP sends a load of packets, does not care whether the prisoner received them and does not send them in any particular order. If sequencing is needed, it is done in the data portion of the packet and interpreted by the application. TCP requires an acknowledgment of receipt (ACK), a synchronization (SYN), and an acknowledgement of the SYN, and then an acknowledgment of the SYN-ACK.

False Alert Analysis

Possibly the greatest skill you can develop is the analysis of false alerts. First, take a look through your events and find one of which (1) there are a lot, and (2) it looks like they could be something potentially dangerous. Begin attacking them one by one. Generally, there will be some alerts that you do not have to dig deep to discover the root cause. For example, a new router is placed on the network and begins immediately spewing SNMP alerts. Your ability to know that the alerts are FPs will depend mostly on your understanding of your current network.

You cannot know that an alert is an FP caused by the device if you neither know what the device is nor know what it is. Automated tools should be implemented that allow you quickly to lookup what an IP address is. This database should be maintained hourly. An internet search for "network inventory software" should provide you with ample results for researching this; you may wish to construct a tool that provides continuous tracking based on the alerts that arrive in the database. Within 15 min of an alert, everything that can be discovered about an IP address on our network should be readily available at my fingertips and can easily be queried, including the phone number of the administrator or owner of the machine.

Case Study

The following case study is of an actual FP from a production system. From this and a few others like it, I developed a framework for analysts to follow when researching alerts. This was the beginning of an alert encyclopedia that could be used to reference each new alert in the system, and provide guidelines for creating consistent criteria that could be used to gauge the seriousness of an actual alert.

Kaaza Alert

Kazaa was known in its time (and today in our collective cultural memory) to be the root of much illicit activity on a network. File-sharing networks were and still are well-known to host many zero-day exploits and malware. Free versions of many types of software, software license crackers, and music files are often embedded with exploits. Everything from illegal downloads, contraband pornography, movie and music sharing, and virus transmission, transpire across p2p networks such as Kazaa. Kazaa itself was sometimes packaged with malware that could render a computer nearly unusable. Therefore, this alert, which occurred in the hundreds, became central to an investigation of it:

    alert udp $EXTERNAL_NET any -> $HOME_NET
    any (msg:"ET P2P Kaaza [sic] Media desktop p2pnet-
    working.exe Activity"; content:"|e30cb0|"; depth:6;
    threshold: type limit, track by_dst, count 1, seconds
    600; reference: url,www.giac.org/practical/GCIH/Ian_-
    Gosling_GCIH.pdf; reference:url,doc.emergingthreats.-
    net/bin/vicw/Main/2000340; classtype:policy-violation;
    sid:2000340;   rev:10;)/nsm/server_data/securityonion/
    rules/interface1- 4/downloaded.rules: Line 9094

It also makes sense that such ad hoc networks can easily be used to exfiltrate data from a network.

From the second word in the rule, "UDP," I know this is UDP traffic, so I need to take a different tack on this investigation, because it is unlikely that reviewing UDP sessions in Wireshark will yield human readable data. Reading the Wireshark packets will be the last step to take if all other avenues lead to nothing or do not provide sufficient evidence for an override. For further analysis, a better understanding of the alert is needed. After carefully

reading this alert, I notice the link: www.giac.org/practical/ GCIH/Ian_Gosling_GCIH.pdf and follow it. It leads to an expired URL. I see a search box on the site, so I search for Ian Gosling and see that he is an examiner whose SANS Institute/Global Information Assurance Certification Certified Incident Handler certification expired in 2007. Next, from the alert, I check the reference URL, "url,doc.e-mergingthreats.net/bin/view/Main/2000340." This reveals little useful information, with the exception that I can see some activity on the alert from October 2011 and with a revision 10 posted in February 2011. It appears to have been some time since the alert has been updated. The following are things to look for:

1. Documentation online about the alert
2. Most recent update of the alert
3. Frequency of updates
4. Known FPs

Tip: You will be doing a lot of Internet searching. Often a seemingly relevant article may not have a date on it. Right-click, view page source, and look for a date. It will often be there, buried in a tag such as "datePublished": "2005-02-10T03:00:00-05:00."

Item: Networking technology and the applications that use them change over time. An old alert like this is an immediate source of skepticism. Nonetheless it is not enough, in and of itself, to dismiss the alert *out of hand*. You must still conduct due diligence because, as a wise man said, the best cons are the oldest cons.

I then begin to review the alert a little more deeply. This occurs from this portion of the rule, called the "signature":

    content:"|e30cb0|"; depth:6;

Therefore, I know it is triggering on the hexidecimal string "e3 0c b0" within the first 6 bytes of the data segment of the packet. That is the extent of it, and although it is a perfectly legitimate signature detection method, I need more information. A review of the emerging threats document shows that the last time this rule was updated was in 2011. An Internet search indicates that as of August 2012, the Kazaa software is no longer supported.

The version of Kazaa targeted by this alert may no longer exist and may not even be compatible with modern computers. Nonetheless, hackers sometimes like to use old tools. Somewhere, it is likely that a few thousand people are still sharing files using old computers. Or perhaps someone built his own engine and resurrected Kazaa after decompiling it or perhaps after having gotten hands on the source code. Perhaps you have nothing but Windows XP computers, upon which this software will still run. The Internet is a big place; the possibilities are endless.

Item: The software is in fact defunct; in fact, much of the concepts behind the software were bridled and crushed by lawsuits that were filed worldwide by the music industry. The whereabouts and activities of the (former?) chief executive officer of Kazaa are unknown. She appears to have vanished from the public eye. Defunct, unsupported software may still be in use, but be skeptical. Ideally, through reconciliation with software logs, you can determine whether a user is actually using the software.

The argument that this is a false alert is pretty convincing at this point, but let us dig deeper, if only for the exercise. Now, let us take a look at the pcap in Wireshark and see what we have.

Sguil allows you to pivot into Wireshark, so I export to a Wireshark file and take a look at it. Now, instead of seeing just the packet that triggered the alert, I can see the entire chain. Sguil does not return only one packet, it returns what appears to be an entire "conversation." Here is a sample of just four sets of bytes from the first 6 bytes in the data segment:

```
80 e0 e3 0a b0 c7
80 60 e3 0b b0 c7
80 e0 e3 0c b0 c7
80 60 e3 0d b0 c7
```

In this string, throughout the capture, the first, third, and fourth bytes remain constant whereas the second alternates between e0 and 60 and the fourth continuously increments hexidecimally. A plausible explanation is that this is a tracking mechanism the application uses to reassemble UDP packets in the application, and that this byte set is part of an identifier number sequence. Here are my observations:

1. The e3 0c b0 content is part of a larger conversation; it is just one packet of 353.
2. The portion of the data header that shows this packet is incremental as I flip through all the packets. I can see that it is incrementing hexidecimally, with a couple of bytes acting as possible conversation indicators.
3. At a deeper byte offset, a 4-byte pattern persists throughout all of the packets. Surely, if this were Kazaa traffic, the writer of the Snort rule would have noticed this other signature.

Still, the purpose of this conversation is unknown, which is bothersome. As part of my investigation, I learn that these IP addresses are part of a known control system that does not involve users doing user-based activities. The devices do not have an accessible "desktop."

Next, I research and see if I can locate an actual sample of Kazaa traffic that would be the most likely source of truth. I find one, but it is TCP. This is UDP.

I notice that for the most part, the alerts are on consistent source and destination ports. Researching the ports reveals only that they are in a range often used by UDP. One port, 443, stands out, though. With these findings, and this categorization tactic, I am able to begin writing a final incident report.

Final Incident Report: Kaaza Alert

The following is a sample of what an incident report may look like. Be prepared: A new system on a large network may require hundreds of investigations, at the end of which you will have developed a truly deep level of intrusion system and network system monitoring understanding.

While reviewing the alerts, a pattern in the port communications seems to present itself. By categorizing the alerts into three categories, based on source ports (SPorts) and destination ports (DPorts), I may be able to see what may be hundreds or thousands of alerts as just three:

1. SPort is 443 and then some high range port for DPort: a wide variety of internal users and mostly resolvable external IPs, either to XO or Google. Per this Web page: https://isc.sans.edu/port.html?port=443, this port is often used for Skype traffic. The Google traffic could be from Chromebooks using QUIC https://en.wikipedia.org/wiki/QUIC.
2. SPort:500(06,08,10,24,28,38,50,56,58) -> DPort (no discernible pattern.): These are all control system IP addresses; also, there are some conversations between employee PCs. I identified one conversation between two people who work in departments within CS (business analyst and customer support) that have heavy interaction. Probable Skype conversation.
3. SPort:8200 -> DPort 56950: this one was an oddball, but a Google search of expert city [source (src) IP] yielded this link, which was helpful: https://lists.emergingthreats.net/pipermail/emerging-sigs/2009-August/003224.html.

In looking through the packets in this conversation (353 packets in the entire conversation of the alert I looked at), I located this string in the data portion of the packet at the beginning of just one packet:

```
80 e0 e3 0c b0 ...
```

Snort triggered on this because in the alert rule, we have content: "|e3 0c b0|"

Looking at previous and subsequent packets in the conversation reveals an incremental pattern at this location in the data segment of the packet, and it was mere coincidence that this pattern occurred. This appears to be just an increment in a numbering scheme of some sort that runs through the entire conversation. Again, there is

TABLE 5.5 Examining All Shellcode Alerts

Counts	Signature
129,651	ET SHELLCODE Possible Call with No Offset TCP Shellcode
66,136	GPL SHELLCODE x86 0x90 NOOP unicode
57,764	GPL SHELLCODE x86 inc ebx NOOP
39,813	ET SHELLCODE Excessive Use of HeapLib Objects Likely Malicious Heap Spray Attempt
33,697	GPL SHELLCODE x86 stealth NOOP
33,528	ET SHELLCODE Possible Call with No Offset UDP Shellcode
14,738	ET SHELLCODE Hex Obfuscated JavaScript Heap Spray 41414141
2892	GPL SHELLCODE x86 0xEB0C NOOP
1483	ET SHELLCODE Common 0a0a0a0a Heap Spray String
768	ET SHELLCODE Possible Encoded %90 NOP SLED
106	ET SHELLCODE Hex Obfuscated JavaScript Heap Spray 0a0a0a0a
71	ET SHELLCODE Possible Backslash Escaped UTF-16 0c0c Heap Spray
53	ET SHELLCODE Possible %41%41%41%41 Heap Spray Attempt
48	ET SHELLCODE Possible %0d%0d%0d%0d Heap Spray Attempt
24	ET SHELLCODE Common %0c%0c%0c%0c Heap Spray String
4	ET SHELLCODE Possible 0x0c0c0c0c Heap Spray Attempt
2	ET SHELLCODE Possible Backslash Escaped UTF-8 0c0c Heap Spray
2	ET SHELLCODE Rothenburg Shellcode
2	GPL SHELLCODE Digital UNIX NOOP

only the one packet in the conversation that has this pattern. We also have the knowledge that more than likely, no version of Kazaa is functional at this date. The software ceased being developed in 2010, and it is highly likely that the executable would not even install properly on a Windows 7, and almost certainly not a Windows 10 box.

Locating an actual Kazaa packet UDP capture was not possible, and the one sample that could be located was unhelpful because it was TCP. I could find no other samples, so I began to think that if we really had Kazaa traffic here, there might be some other alerts in the rules that were better at detecting Kazaa. I took a look then at /etc/nsm/rules/downloaded.rules and found the following additional rules:

- alert udp $HOME_NET 1024:65535 -> $EXTERNAL_NET 1024:65535 (msg:"ET P2P Kazaa over UDP"; content:"KaZaA"; nocase; threshold: type threshold, track by_src,count 10, seconds 60; reference:url,www.kazaa.com/us/index.htm; reference:url, doc.emergingthreats.net/bin/view/Main/2001796; classtype:policy-violation; sid:2001796; rev:5;)

- This one is disabled, though not by us:

    #alert tcp $HOME_NET any -> $EXTERNAL_NET any (msg:"GPL P2P Fastrack kazaa/morpheus traffic"; flow: to_server, established; content:"GET"; depth:4; content:"UserAgent|3A| KazaaClient"; reference:url,www. kazaa.com; classtype:policy-violation; sid:2101699; rev:11;)

- #alert tcp $EXTERNAL_NET any -> $HOME_NET any (msg:"ET DELETED KazaaClient P2P Traffic"; flow: established; content:"Agent|3a| KazaaClient"; nocase; reference:url,www.kazaa.com/us/index.htm; reference:url,doc.emergingthreats.net/bin/view/Main/2001812; classtype:policy-violation; sid:2001812; rev:8;)

I also searched for Kaaza (sic) to see whether there were any more. There were none. My conclusion is that all Kazaa and Kaaza rules should be disabled, with the exception of ones that have never fired before.

Incident Reporting: Sample Incident Report

The following sample report is put together to address a large group of alerts that are occurring among many

---

Shellcode Alerts: Basic Reconnaissance Report

SQL scripts have been included in this report so that you can get a feel for the level of scripting that is required in this system to pull the reports easily:

Report Generated: 2016-05-05 15:50:09
Select now();

Incident Description: Numerous alerts that include the word "shellcode" have been presenting in the system.

Date range, all events: 2016-04-05 00:00:00 - 2016-05-05 15:47:53
SELECT max(timestamp) FROM event
SELECT min(timestamp) FROM event
Keyword: Shellcode
Events Count: 380,691
SELECT count(*) as Shellcode FROM event WHERE signature LIKE '%shellcode%';

Distinct Event Types: 17
SELECT count(ev.signature) FROM (SELECT signature FROM event WHERE signature like '%shellcode%' group by signature) ev. The table of distinct events by conversation (top 50), returns

a distinct list of src and destination (dst) IP address conversations and their respective alerts (Table 5.6).
SELECT:
count(ev.uniqueConvo),
ev.uniqueConvo,
signature,
inet_ntoa(dev.dst_IP),
inet_ntoa(dev.src_IP)
FROM
(SELECT concat(signature,src_ip,dst_ip) uniqueConvo, signature, dst_ip,
inet_ntoa(src_ip) src_IP FROM event WHERE
signature like '%shellcode%') ev
#inet_ntoa(dst_ip) LIKE "10.%"
GROUP by 2 ORDER by 1 DESC;
Alert count by Alert:
SELECT distinct count(*) counts, signature FROM event WHERE signature like '%shellcode%' group by signature order by counts description (desc) (Table 5.5).

List of Shellcode Type Alerts

Most recent occurrence: 2016-05-05 15:47:11
Select max(timestamp) from event where signature like '%shellcode%';
Oldest logged occurrence: 2016-04-05 00:15:51
Select min(timestamp) from event where signature like '%shellcode%';
Computers affected (src IP): 1751
SELECT count(distinct src_ip) from event WHERE signature like '%shellcode%';
Computers affected (dst IP): 1014
SELECT count(distinct dst_ip) from event WHERE signature like '%shellcode%';

Unique conversations: 5270 (count from previous "unique conversation counts")
Other categories (such as ports, actors, common thread): Destination IP address, port 445
Related alerts: there are a total of 87 shellcode type alerts, based on strictly limited visual examination in Sguil; there do not appear to be any other alerts occurring in tandem.
Conclusion: Based on an evaluation of counts grouped by IP addresses that have the most varied alerts, I note that the fileshare is tripping a lot of alerts. In particular, the "ET SHELLCODE Possible Call with No Offset TCP Shellcode" should be escalated and investigated as a probable FP.

---

devices on the network. This much statistical information may be wholly unnecessary for a quieter system with far fewer alerts. For elucidation purposes, this report includes all SQL that was run against the database to summarize the data. This report consists of two parts. First, it details the basic reconnaissance that a junior investigator may conduct. The second part is a brief filed by the senior examiner that details findings and actions taken.

Special Consideration

Bear in mind: Nothing about this analysis is intended to suggest that these rules are wrong, improperly written, dull, or anything less than exciting and highly effective. The intention behind rule analysis is to make determinations about the suitability of a rule in your network and in consideration of *your* traffic patterns. For instructional purposes, these alerts have been selected; in particular,

shellcode alerts (see sidebar: "Shellcode Alerts: Basic Reconnaissance Report") are the focus of this example.

In this case, a pattern emerges. Because it is shellcode, it is probable that a hacker would try many different ways to get a shell (see sidebar: "List of Shellcode Type Alerts"). This list is a candidate to be sorted by IP address and see which IP address has the most distinct alerts. For that, this query needs to be run so that it returns all entries (over 4000), because it may be more interesting to see one computer with one alert against every computer in the network than five computers with 50 alerts against 50 other computers.

Final Note About Report Writing

If report writing seems egregiously tedious, overbearing, and manually intensive, it is because it is. Using the scripts provided here can massively speed up the analysis and help provide direction, but there is more work to do. More script sets like this need to be developed to handle different sets of

TABLE 5.6 Table of Distinct Events by Conversation (Top 50)

Count	Signature	dst_IP	src_IP
30,652	'ET SHELLCODE Possible Call with No Offset TCP Shellcode'	'192.0.70.30'	'192.0.4.49'
20,562	'ET SHELLCODE Possible Call with No Offset TCP Shellcode'	'192.0.100.179'	'192.0.66.163'
14,483	'ET SHELLCODE Excessive Use of HeapLib Objects Likely Malicious Heap Spray Attempt'	'192.0.64.24'	'23.79.193.184'
10,442	'GPL SHELLCODE x86 stealth NOOP'	'192.0.0.37'	'192.0.79.61'
10,382	'GPL SHELLCODE x86 0x90 NOOP unicode'	'192.0.70.30'	'192.0.4.49'
8752	'GPL SHELLCODE x86 inc ebx NOOP'	'192.0.70.30'	'192.0.4.49'
7380	'GPL SHELLCODE x86 inc ebx NOOP'	'192.0.102.37'	'184.106.55.85'
6971	'GPL SHELLCODE x86 stealth NOOP'	'192.0.82.154'	'192.0.72.29'
6434	'ET SHELLCODE Hex Obfuscated JavaScript Heap Spray 41414141'	'192.0.102.32'	'208.111.168.7'
5160	'ET SHELLCODE Hex Obfuscated JavaScript Heap Spray 41414141'	'192.0.102.32'	'208.111.168.6'
4473	'ET SHELLCODE Possible Call with No Offset TCP Shellcode'	'192.0.0.37'	'192.0.79.61'
3565	'ET SHELLCODE Possible Call with No Offset TCP Shellcode'	'192.0.102.15'	'192.0.81.85'
2863	'ET SHELLCODE Possible Call with No Offset UDP Shellcode'	'192.0.50.10'	'192.0.106.33'
2708	'ET SHELLCODE Possible Call with No Offset UDP Shellcode'	'192.0.50.10'	'192.0.74.42'
2517	'GPL SHELLCODE x86 0x90 NOOP unicode'	'192.0.100.11'	'192.0.39.21'
2458	'GPL SHELLCODE x86 0x90 NOOP unicode'	'192.0.100.165'	'172.21.80.52'
2381	'ET SHELLCODE Excessive Use of HeapLib Objects Likely Malicious Heap Spray Attempt'	'192.0.64.28'	'45.55.198.210'
2230	'ET SHELLCODE Possible Call with No Offset UDP Shellcode'	'192.0.50.10'	'192.0.106.49'
2061	'ET SHELLCODE Possible Call with No Offset UDP Shellcode'	'192.0.50.10'	'192.0.106.37'
1991	'ET SHELLCODE Excessive Use of HeapLib Objects Likely Malicious Heap Spray Attempt'	'192.0.98.102'	'23.3.96.83'
1978	'GPL SHELLCODE x86 0x90 NOOP unicode'	'192.0.79.42'	'192.0.0.30'
1975	'GPL SHELLCODE x86 0x90 NOOP unicode'	'192.0.98.169'	'192.0.4.48'
1884	'GPL SHELLCODE x86 inc ebx NOOP'	'192.0.64.159'	'192.0.72.29'
1793	'GPL SHELLCODE x86 0x90 NOOP unicode'	'192.0.102.15'	'192.0.4.48'
1750	'GPL SHELLCODE x86 stealth NOOP'	'192.0.4.42'	'192.168.27.3'
1742	'GPL SHELLCODE x86 0x90 NOOP unicode'	'192.0.90.57'	'192.0.50.10'
1585	'GPL SHELLCODE x86 0x90 NOOP unicode'	'192.0.90.52'	'192.0.50.10'
1533	'GPL SHELLCODE x86 0x90 NOOP unicode'	'192.0.0.37'	'192.0.79.61'
1506	'ET SHELLCODE Possible Call with No Offset UDP Shellcode'	'192.0.50.10'	'192.0.90.57'
1496	'ET SHELLCODE Possible Call with No Offset TCP Shellcode'	'192.0.72.41'	'192.0.80.19'
1444	'GPL SHELLCODE x86 0x90 NOOP unicode'	'192.0.79.41'	'192.0.0.30'
1398	'ET SHELLCODE Possible Call with No Offset TCP Shellcode'	'192.0.72.41'	'192.0.80.161'
1367	'GPL SHELLCODE x86 0x90 NOOP unicode'	'192.0.98.64'	'192.0.4.48'
1346	'GPL SHELLCODE x86 0x90 NOOP unicode'	'192.0.96.45'	'192.0.4.49'
1298	'ET SHELLCODE Possible Call with No Offset TCP Shellcode'	'192.0.96.45'	'192.0.4.49'
1279	'GPL SHELLCODE x86 0x90 NOOP unicode'	'192.0.96.63'	'192.0.72.29'
1266	'ET SHELLCODE Possible Call with No Offset UDP Shellcode'	'192.0.50.10'	'192.0.106.38'

Continued

TABLE 5.6 Table of Distinct Events by Conversation (Top 50)—cont'd

Count	Signature	dst_IP	src_IP
1243	'ET SHELLCODE Possible Call with No Offset UDP Shellcode'	'192.0.50.10'	'192.0.74.35'
1239	'GPL SHELLCODE x86 inc ebx NOOP'	'192.0.96.70'	'192.0.100.80'
1230	'ET SHELLCODE Possible Call with No Offset UDP Shellcode'	'192.0.50.10'	'192.0.74.49'
1202	'GPL SHELLCODE x86 0x90 NOOP unicode'	'192.0.100.80'	'192.0.4.48'
1194	'GPL SHELLCODE x86 stealth NOOP'	'192.0.98.15'	'192.0.72.41'
1120	'ET SHELLCODE Possible Call with No Offset UDP Shellcode'	'192.0.50.10'	'192.0.74.12'
1088	'ET SHELLCODE Possible Call with No Offset TCP Shellcode'	'192.0.98.64'	'192.0.4.48'
1080	'ET SHELLCODE Possible Call with No Offset UDP Shellcode'	'192.0.50.10'	'192.0.106.31'
1067	'ET SHELLCODE Possible Call with No Offset TCP Shellcode'	'192.0.98.169'	'192.0.4.48'
1052	'GPL SHELLCODE x86 0x90 NOOP unicode'	'192.0.68.31'	'192.0.72.29'
1050	'GPL SHELLCODE x86 0x90 NOOP unicode'	'192.0.72.29'	'192.0.102.51'
1047	'GPL SHELLCODE x86 0x90 NOOP unicode'	'192.0.96.170'	'192.0.4.48'
1037	'GPL SHELLCODE x86 0x90 NOOP unicode'	'192.0.102.164'	'192.0.4.48'

Escalated Alert/Incident Investigation Report

The following is an example of an escalated alert/incident investigation report process:

Date Escalated:
Escalated By: Kevin
Date Reviewed:
Reviewed by: Scott Ellis
Root Cause: Reviewing the IP address of the fileshare in Sguil, and I pivot to the TCP conversation and review a handful of the alerts. All are legitimate fileshare conversations. This

alert, 'ET SHELLCODE Possible Call with No Offset TCP Shellcode' is a nuisance alert and should be disabled. Its generic pattern match on the byte pattern (hexidecimal) |E8 00 00 00 00 58| is on a busy network where there are probably billions of bytes flowing through it, far too generic.

Resolution: Alert ET SHELLCODE Possible Call with No Offset TCP Shellcode has been added to the disablesid.conf file on all sensors. Additional reports will be created for each additional shellcode alert as they are examined.

---

circumstances, and a framework needs to be built that will facilitate the process and guide investigations so that alerts can be reviewed, dismissed, and qualified quickly and easily (see Sidebar: "Escalated Alert/Incident Investigation Report").

What a Real Situation Looks Like

To get a good feel for what a real incident looks like, it is helpful to explode something safely that does real damage. To do this, I took my test PC VM and went to a site where I know a nasty download exists. I downloaded it and installed it, and here are the alerts I saw:

- 1   Sensor-eth5-8   57.98946   2016-05-03   18:17:00 192.0.102.20 65483 207.150.194.32 80 6 ET CURRENT_EVENTS Terse alphanumeric executable downloader high likelihood of being hostile
- 1   Sensor-eth5-8   57.98947   2016-05-03   18:17:00 192.0.102.20 65483 207.150.194.32 80 6 ET TROJAN Single char EXE direct download likely Trojan (multiple families)

It is immediately apparent from these two alerts that they are what they say they are, and Snort has done a great job of locating a problem. Was anyone watching?

14. SUMMARY

Trimming your alerts for your network is a repetitious process. From here, for tuning, you would gradually work your way down the list of alerts, starting with the most frequently occurring and working your way down, following the steps and procedures outlined in this chapter. Once you have completed this and the alerts are no longer pouring into your system, you can then use these same steps to examine new, potentially hostile intrusions as you see them in your network.

Very often you may see an onslaught of thousands of alerts. It is extremely important that they all be categorized and treated as groups or even groups within groups. Furthermore, knowing your network, the applications and expected protocols, will be of unparalleled usefulness. To those ends, there are various network devices and inventory programs that produce logs that can be read into a log-reporting database, such as ELSA. A deep discussion of them is beyond the scope of this chapter and the allotted pages, surely of which I have already consumed too many.

NSM is an ongoing discipline. It is a daily grind of staying on top of the alerts, understanding them and your network, and identifying anomalous traffic. Through the use of some automated systems and a strong layer of NSM that bundles together IDS and intrusion prevention system tools, you can ensure that if someone is sniffing around and doing illicit things on your network, it will be as plain to you as a burglar breaking down your front door with a battering ram during Christmas dinner prayers.

Finally, let us move on to the real interactive part of this chapter: review questions/exercises, hands-on projects, case projects, and the optional team case project. The answers and/or solutions by chapter can be found in Appendix K.

CHAPTER REVIEW QUESTIONS/ EXERCISES

True/False

1. True or False? The data with the least greatest usefulness to network security monitoring (NSM) are packet data.
2. True or False? With taps, observing the behavior of a hacker on your network cannot be undertaken.
3. True or False? Once an intruder is aware he is being watched, he may begin to deploy forensic countermeasures, or worse, may begin to take hostages; that is, he may decide to deploy ransomware across your network.
4. True or False? The world of security is characterized by skeptical, hyperparanoid, critical, reality-seeking, hands-on professionals.
5. True or False? Email from friends, business associates, colleagues, and family members are all exploitable avenues of ingress.

Multiple Choice

1. The general preference in the security community is to conduct business from:
   A. Security Onion (SO)
   B. Ubuntu
   C. Secure Shell (SSH)
   D. Linux
   E. GNU Privacy Guard
2. For most of your encryption needs, at least where attachments are concerned, many security professionals choose:
   A. Whale-phishing
   B. Spear-phishing
   C. GNU Privacy Guard
   D. Application-phishing
   E. Bait-phishing
3. What is an encryption suite that you can install at the command line?
   A. Signature
   B. GnuPG

   C. Client side code
   D. LinkedIn.com
   E. Security
4. The work of an intrusion detection analyst must, above all things, include 100%:
   A. Call data
   B. Strategy
   C. Password
   D. Secure communications
   E. Tap
5. SO is capable of operating in a number of different server/sensor configurations, in which one server serves as the "master" server, and then additional servers are deployed to serve as:
   A. UNIX-like systems
   B. Virtual private networks
   C. IP storage
   D. Companies
   E. Sensors

EXERCISE

Problem

Which of the following attributes suggests that the packets below have been crafted?

```
00:03:21.680333    216.164.222.250.1186    >    us.u-
s.us.44.8080: S 2410044679:2410044679 (0) win 512
   00:03:21.810732    216.164.222.250.1189    >    us.u-
s.us.50.8080: S 2410044679:2410044679 (0) win 512
```

Hands-On Projects

Project

What is the most likely reason for choosing to use HEAD requests instead of GET requests when scanning for the presence of vulnerable Web-based applications?

Case Projects

Problem

What is the least effective indicator that the attacker's source address is not spoofed?

Optional Team Case Project

Problem

What is the most likely explanation for "ARP info over-written" messages on a Berkeley Software Distribution—based system?

Chapter 6

Intrusion Detection in Contemporary Environments

Tarfa Hamed, Rozita Dara and Stefan C. Kremer
University of Guelph, Guelph, ON, Canada

1. INTRODUCTION

Over the past two decades, computer systems users have increased. These users bring their own new preferences for how they want to interact with information and each other. These new users are teenagers who want to do things on their phones and tablets, professionals who want to plan or share their experience in their field with others, or people from different levels who want to employ phones in their daily lives. This increase was a reflection to the change in the requirements and needs of our daily life. People are using mobile phones for communication, planning and organizing their private lives, learning, documenting, navigating maps, online banking, and many other purposes. In addition, new mobile devices are characterized by their ease of use, which makes new ways of computing possible. All of this is increasing the number of mobile devices connected to the Internet over time. The latest sales reports indicate that throughout the world, mobile phones sales totaled 446 million units during the second quarter of 2015 and sales increased by 3.9% in the first quarter of 2016 [9].

Moreover, end users look for ways to communicate, obtain and share information, play games, be entertained, and so on. As a result, some providers (big companies) have found ways to provide services either directly for money or for market and attention share. Providers found that it is a good way to increase profit by providing computing systems resources for users for affordable or relatively low costs. Those providers put required computer systems resources on demand for users using virtual machines (VMs). This technology, which is based on virtualization and multi-tenancy, is called cloud computing. Virtualization is an essential technology for minimizing operating costs and increasing elasticity for use [43]. Virtualization technology offers the ability to share hardware resources to run isolated guest operating systems (OSs) [37]. Multitenancy is another major characteristic of cloud computing that enables multiple users to store their data using applications provided by the cloud system [38]. Cloud computing is a technique to maximize computing capability by increasing capacity or appending capabilities efficiently without affording extra expenses of new infrastructure new staff or obtaining licenses for new software [38].

The cost-effectiveness and capabilities offered by cloud computing are in fact the major encouraging factors that attract the attention of many organizations and academic entities [11]. In addition, although mobile phones and tablets are increasing in capabilities, they will never be as computationally powerful or as well-networked as servers will be. Therefore, some services must reside in the cloud, running on servers, but stay accessible to mobile devices. Consequently, that will simultaneously increase the use of mobile devices and cloud computing.

The usefulness of the cloud lies in its ability to store a lot of information and to make it accessible to mobile devices upon demand. Therefore, there is continuous information transmission between mobile devices and the cloud environment. This information is valuable; therefore it has drawn the interest of attackers who want to gain access or disrupt access to that value from legitimate users. In general, there are three main targets in attacking a computing system [7]:

1. **Data**: Target systems may be used to store personal/important data; they may be a good source for information to attackers, such as credit card numbers, private information (driver's license number or birth date), or any

Computer and Information Security Handbook. http://dx.doi.org/10.1016/B978-0-12-803843-7.00006-5

109

other important piece of information (pictures). Therefore, attackers usually try to access this information to remove it, alter it, or gain monetary benefit, blackmail, or any other malicious purpose.

2. **Identity**: Target systems can contain authentication information associated with its owner. Such information can compromise the identity of the owner or organization. An attacker may impersonate the owner or organization to commit some other misbehavior.

3. **Availability**: Attackers may limit access to the system and prevent its legitimate users from obtaining services from it, causing denial of service (DoS).

Although these two technologies, mobile devices and cloud computing, have provided great services to users from different categories (companies, governments, organizations, and individuals), they are also subject to many kinds of attacks that threaten their security. Providing security protection for the two technologies is a subject that attracts researchers from around the world to save the interests of people who use the services offered by those technologies.

However, these two technologies overlap in many aspects. Mobile devices obtain most of their services from the cloud because the devices are limited by power, memory, computation, and connectivity. Therefore, people are witnessing the mobile cloud services era (Fig. 6.1) and it is becoming part of their daily lives. Consequently, any attack that affects the cloud may affect the mobile devices connected to that cloud. Conversely, an infected mobile device with malware can affect the cloud from which it obtains its

service. From the user's perspective, the user might not differentiate whether the cloud system has been compromised or his or her mobile device has been attacked with malware. The user may only discover that his or her credentials have been revealed, pictures have been published, or data have been stolen.

In this chapter we explore intrusion detection systems (IDSs) for this contemporary environment encompassing mobile devices and cloud computing systems. The chapter is organized as follows: Section 2 discusses mobile OSs and briefly explains the most well-known mobile OSs. Section 3 describes malware risks to mobile devices. Section 4 talks about cloud computing models. Attack risks to mobile computing are discussed in Section 5. We talk about the source of attacks on mobile devices in Section 6. Conversely, we discuss the origins of attacks on cloud computing in Section 7. Section 8 is dedicated to classes of mobile malware, whereas Section 9 specifies types of cloud computing attacks. In Section 10, we discuss malware techniques in Android (as a case study). Next, we investigate cloud computing intrusion techniques in Section 11. We provide different examples of smartphone malware in Section 12 and give some examples of cloud attacks in Section 13. Sections 14 and 15 discuss IDSs for mobile devices and cloud computing, respectively. Section 16 is devoted to explaining IDS performance metrics for both mobile device IDSs and cloud computing systems. Finally, in Section 17 we provide a summary of the whole chapter.

2. MOBILE OPERATING SYSTEMS

An OS is a software interface that is responsible for managing and operating hardware units and assisting the user to use those units. For mobile phones, OSs have been developed to enable users to use phones in much the same way as personal computers were used 1 or 2 decades ago. The most well-known mobile OSs are Android, iOS, Windows phone OS, and Symbian. The market share ratios of those OSs are Android 47.51%, iOS 41.97%, Symbian 3.31%, and Windows phone OS 2.57%. There are some other mobile OSs that are less used (BlackBerry, Samsung, etc.) [46]. In the next section, we will briefly explain each of these OSs.

Android Operating System

Android is an open-source mobile OS developed by Google and launched in 2008 [8]. Android is a Linux-based OS that uses Linux 2.6 to provide core services such as security, memory management, process management, network stack, and a driver model. It offers a wide range of libraries that enable the app developers to build different applications. Android applications are usually written in Java programming language [46].

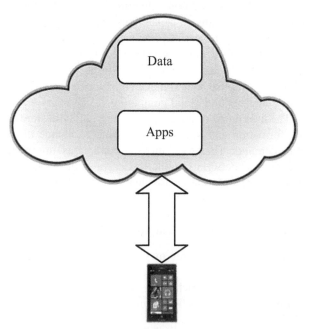

FIGURE 6.1 Mobile–cloud services information exchange.

Apple iOS

Apple iOS is a closed-source code mobile phone OS developed by Apple in 2007; it is used by Apple-only products (iPhone, iPod, and iPad). The iOS architecture is based on three layers incorporated with each other. Cocoa touch is a layer that provides some basic infrastructure used by applications. The second layer is the media layer, which provides audio services, animation video, image formats, and documents in addition to providing two-dimensional (2D) and 3D drawings and audio and video support. The third layer is the core OS, which provides core services such as low-level data types, start-up services, network connection, and access [46].

Symbian Operating System

Symbian OS is an open-source mobile OS written in C++ programming language developed by Symbian Ltd. in 1977; it is mostly used by Nokia phones. Symbian OS consists of multiple layers such as OS libraries, application engines, MKV, servers, Base-kernel, and hardware interface layer. Symbian was the most prevalent mobile device OS until 2010, when it was taken over by Android [46].

Windows Phone Operating System

Windows phone OS is a closed-source code mobile OS developed by Microsoft Corporation and used by multiple smart devices (personal digital assistants, smartphones, and touch devices). Windows phone OS is based on a compact version of .Net framework, which gives it an advantage in developing .Net-oriented mobile applications [46].

We choose to talk about only the two most dominant phone OSs here: Android and iOS. Unlike Android OS, Apple iOS is more immune against malware owing to its closed-source platform and the restricted procedures that Apple follows in apps marketing. Android has become the most susceptible OS to malware because of its open-source platform, the readiness of Android devices to download and install applications from untrusted/unsecured stores.

3. MOBILE DEVICE MALWARE RISKS

Smartphones and tablets have become prevalent in the past few years. In terms of numbers, at the end of 2014 there were around 7 billion active devices worldwide. Because of their enormous distribution, the wide variety of services they offer, and the sensitive information that they store, mobile devices have become a major target of cyber attacks. Smartphones have the great feature of a wide range of connectivity options such as GSM, CDMA, Wi-Fi, global positioning system (GPS), Bluetooth, and NFC. Smartphones also contain personal information such as contacts, messages, social network access, Internet browsing history, and sometimes banking credentials. All of this has attracted the attention of attack developers toward mobile devices. The main enemy of mobile devices is malicious software (malware). Malware is harmful apps that target mobile devices and threaten their security. They are usually disguised as normal and useful apps that users can download and use, but in fact they hide stealthy scripts that carry out different activities in the background that intimidate the user's security. Different risks may threaten a user's security as a result of malware, such as:

- Compromising a user's privacy by stealing sensitive user information such as the user's credit, login history, or password
- Threatening the integrity of the device
- Extracting monetary benefits
- Creating botnets, which are a network of computers that have already been compromised by a robot or bot that executes a wide range of malicious actions for the developer of the botnet
- Mounting aggressive ad campaigns
- Launching DoS

The attackers usually exploit vulnerabilities associated with the mobile devices to launch their attacks. The three main factors of security of any computing system are: **confidentiality, integrity, and availability,** which are also the main factors for mobile device security. **Confidentiality** requires ensuring appropriate protection for confidential or sensitive information stored or processed in the computing system [33]. In other words, sensitive information cannot be accessed by an unauthorized party. **Integrity** requires ensuring the authenticity of data stored in a computing system [33]. The data cannot be modified/altered, removed, or added to by an unauthorized party. **Availability** of data in a computing system's storage imposes provision of the data to the authorized party at any time upon demand [33]. After infecting the mobile device, the attacker can inflict multiple damage by violating different security goals:

- An infected smartphone can record all of the conversations between the user and others, steal images and videos, and send this information to the attack developer without the user's consent. This kind of attack can compromise the user's privacy and compromise confidentiality [7].
- A user's identity is also one of the attacker's targets that can be stolen from a compromised smartphone. The identity can be stolen from the user's sim card or from the phone itself. That can lead to the owner being impersonated to place orders or view bank accounts, or for use of the smartphone as an identity card (where applicable). This action also compromises the user's privacy and confidentiality [7].

- Another action that can compromise the user's privacy is when the attacker removes personal information from the compromised phone (pictures, videos, music, etc.) or removes professional data (contacts, calendars, or personal notes). This action compromises confidentiality [7].
- The integrity of the device is another target of malware, when the attacker can force the compromised phone to make phone calls. For example, malware can use an application program interface (API) function provided by Microsoft called (PhoneMakeCall) only for the Windows phone OS. This function can search for phone numbers from any online source and then call them. This can result in charges to the owner if the call is made to paid services, or it may be more serious if the call is directed to emergency services that disturbs these services. The action compromises integrity [7].
- The attacker can convert the smartphone to a zombie machine, which is a machine that can be controlled by the attacker to send spam messages via short message service (SMS) or email. This kind of attack also threatens the integrity of the device. This action compromises integrity [7].
- The attacker can make the smartphone unusable by preventing its normal operations or preventing its startup. Moreover, the attacker can damage the OS of the phone by deleting the boot scripts, make it unusable by modifying some important files, or run a small code to deplete the battery. This kind of attack also threatens device's availability [7].
- The attacker can steal sensitive information such as the credentials of the smartphone's owner to transfer money to his bank account. This action compromises confidentiality [8].
- Some ad campaigns may attract users to download potentially unwanted apps or malware apps. These apps have hidden malware behavior that can perform multiple damaging actions on the device, such as controlling the device remotely or scanning the device for any vulnerability. This action compromises confidentiality [8].
- Some malware can cause DoS of mobile devices by overwhelming the device's limited central processing unit (CPU), memory, and bandwidth, which results in depriving the legitimate user from using the device's normal functions. This action compromises availability [8].

As we notice from this list of damaging actions that can happen to mobile devices, attackers strive to cause different types damage to mobile devices. This damage also has different levels of severity. In all cases, damage must be identified so that an effective countermeasure can be found.

4. CLOUD COMPUTING MODELS

Cloud computing environments have been constructed in different ways according to the service offered by that environment. In general, there are three different cloud computing models:

1. **Software-as-a-Service (SaaS)**: The cloud service provider (CSP) provides software for the user, which is running and deployed on cloud infrastructure. In this case, the user (consumer) is not responsible for managing or maintaining the cloud infrastructure, including network, servers, OSs, or any other application-related issues. The consumer just uses the software as a service on demand. Google Maps is an example of SaaS [15,41].
2. **Platform-as-a-Service (PaaS)**: The CSP provides a platform to the consumer to deploy consumer-created applications written in any programming language supported by the CSP. The consumer is not responsible for managing or maintaining the underlying infrastructure, such as the network, servers, OSs, or storage. However, the consumer controls the deployed applications and the hosting environment configurations. Google App Engine and Microsoft Azure are examples of PaaS [15,41].
3. **Infrastructure-as-a-Service (IaaS)**: The CSP provides the consumer with the processing, storage, networks, and other essential computing resources to enable the consumer to run his or her software, which can be OSs and applications. This model involves managing the physical cloud infrastructure by the provider. Amazon Web Service (AWS), Eucalyptus, and Open-Nebula are examples of IaaS [15,41].

5. CLOUD COMPUTING ATTACK RISKS

Cloud computing security can be defined as set of techniques, protocols, and controls deployed in the cloud to provide protection to the applications, data, and infrastructure of the cloud computing environment. Cloud data centers have become widely used for a range of always-on services in private, public, and commercial domains. Because of the wide prevalence of cloud computing, it has become a target for many attacks. As mentioned, the three main factors of security are **confidentiality**, **integrity, and availability**, which are also the main goals for cloud computing security. Therefore, any action that compromises one or more of these goals is considered a threat. Vulnerability is a weakness in the system that can be exploited by threats. Putting users' information in the cloud may expose them to many risks, such as:

- Compromise of users' privacy
- Theft of sensitive information

- Malicious insiders
- DoS
- Insecure APIs
- Data loss or leakage

Some of these risks can overlap and can compromise different security goals, depending on the nature of the risks and the target. In this section we will explain the risks behind launching attacks on cloud computing.

Users are really concerned about personal data and are against anything that might lead to an invasion of their privacy. When putting their information on the cloud, users do not want this information to be accessed without their consent, which is against one of the security goals (confidentiality): (1) compromising the user's privacy, and (2) stealing sensitive information, which can fall into the same risk category. Those risks can result from account or service hijacking, which in turn result from phishing, fraud, and software vulnerabilities. Attackers can steal a user's credentials and acquire access to the sensitive domain of deployed cloud computing services. That would result in compromising confidentiality, integrity, and availability of these services. Malicious insider risks can be damaging to the cloud computing environment. By taking advantage of having an insider level of access, they use it to penetrate organizations and assets and commit brand damage, financial losses, and productivity losses. According to the Cloud Security Alliance, a malicious insider was one of the top risks to cloud computing in 2016 [40]. A malicious insider can compromise the goal of confidentiality security. DoS attacks refer to sending a massive number of synchronized connection requests by the attacker to a network for the sake of slowing down servers or creating a barrier for legitimate users willing to access the cloud. According to the Cloud Security Alliance, DoS attacks were among the top risks to cloud computing in 2016 [40]. DoS attacks compromise the availability security goal. Moreover, an insecure API refers to an infirm set of API functions, which are used to connect to the cloud [16,39]. According to the Cloud Security Alliance, an insecure API is also one of the top risks to cloud computing in 2016 [40]. An insecure API compromises all of the security goals: confidentiality, availability, and integrity. Data loss or leakage can also have a negative impact on the business. The CSP can completely lose its brand or reputation in addition to losing the customer's trust owing to this risk. Loss or leakage of data can happen as a result of insufficient authentication, authorization, and audit controls; disposal challenges, data center reliability, and disaster recovery; and inconsistent use of encryption and software keys. Data loss or leakage compromises the security goal of integrity.

6. SOURCE OF ATTACKS ON MOBILE DEVICES

Because of their wide prevalence and the range of services they offer, attacks on mobile devices originate from different sources. In this section we discuss the most common sources of attacks on mobile devices:

- **Professionals**: These could be commercial or military professionals who aim to attack the three targets mentioned previously. Sensitive data from the general public is stolen by these professionals. In addition, they may use the stolen identity to launch other attacks.
- **Thieves**: These use stolen data or identities to obtain an income. Thieves will increase the scope of the attack to increase their prospective income.
- **Black hat hackers**: These particularly target availability. They aim to develop viruses and damaging devices, or steal data from devices.
- **Gray hat hackers**: These particularly reveal vulnerabilities. They aim to disclose the vulnerabilities of the device. However, they do not want to damage or steal data from the device.

7. SOURCE OR ORIGIN OF INTRUSIONS IN CLOUD COMPUTING

Cloud computing systems are also susceptible to many kinds of intrusions that come from different sources. In this section we will explore the different sources of intrusions in cloud computing systems. Intrusions in cloud computing may originate from a VM, a virtual network, a malicious hypervisor, or an outside attack:

- **Attacks from a VM**: In Bahram et al. [2], the authors were able to simulate an attack to subvert VM introspection. They called their attack direct kernel structure manipulation (DKSM) and showed how it can smash existing VM introspection solutions by changing the syntax and semantics of kernel data structures in a running guest.
- **Attacks from a virtual network**: Attackers may exploit vulnerabilities and compromise the VMs to launch a large-scale distributed DoS (DDoS) attack. The attackers start with preliminary actions such as multistep exploitation, low-frequency vulnerability scanning, and converting vulnerable VMs to zombies, and then launch DDoS attacks via these compromised zombies [6]. DDoS attacks usually target the availability of cloud services.
- **Attacks from a malicious hypervisor**: A hypervisor or VM monitor is piece of software responsible for managing the sharing of a hardware platform among different

guest systems. Hypervisors do not have that relatively huge code and have limited communication with the external world. They are supposed to be well-protected and secure. However, it has been observed that hypervisors are not completely secure. For example, Xen, which is a common hypervisor used in Amazon Elastic Compute Cloud (EC2), showed a deficiency as some attacks were able to modify Xen's code and data at runtime and allowed backdoor activity [1]. Compromised hypervisors can lead to catastrophic damage to cloud computing systems if they are not detected and stopped.

- **Attacks from outside the cloud environment**: An attacker may send a huge number of requests to access VMs, disabling the availability of VMs to legitimate users, which is called a DoS attack.

8. CLASSES OF MOBILE MALWARE

Malware that attacks mobile devices is of different types and categories. It is also different in its severity and the damage that it causes. In this section we discuss the most well-known classes of malware that threaten mobile devices [35]:

- **Botnet**: This kind of malware attacks the device by a remote user or a bot-master using a set of commands to make a bot control the device remotely. The constructed network of such devices is called a botnet. The resulting damage is on a different level compared with sending private information to a remote server, launching DoS attacks, or downloading malicious payloads [8].
- **Backdoor**: A backdoor opens on the compromised device, causing it to wait for commands to arrive from an external server or an SMS message. This malware can exploit the root to obtain superuser privileges and avoid antimalware scanners [8].
- **Rootkit**: This malware creates buffer overflow to obtain superuser (root) privileges on the device [35].
- **Worms**: A worm is malware that has the ability to make copies of itself and spread these copies through a network and removable media [8].
- **SMS Trojan**: This malware causes serious damage to the user by: (1) sending stealthy SMS messages without the user's knowledge, making the user subscribe to some premium services; (2) sending spam messages to all of the user's contacts; or (3) obtaining an authentication mechanism for some banking institutions by sending SMS messages to permit unfavorable transactions or banking Trojans [8,35].
- **Spyware**: This kind of malware starts by pretending to be a benign or useful app, but it has an internal

malicious activity [8]. It is characterized by revealing sensitive information from the phone and sending it to an external server. This sensitive information could be the International Mobile Equipment Identity or International Mobile Subscriber Identity, contacts, messages, location, or social network credentials [35].

- **Installer**: This kind of malware installs apps using new authorizations to boost damage to the phone [35].
- **Ransomware**: A kind of malware that blocks the user from accessing the phone by continuously displaying a Web page requesting the user to pay a certain amount of money (ransom) to remove the malware from the device. Another example of this malware is encryption of whole personal data on the phone and the request for a ransom to retrieve the decryption key [35].
- **Trojan**: This kind of malware could be any malware that has behavior different from the previous classes. This kind could modify or remove data from the phone without the owner's consent or it could infect any computer when the phone is connected via a universal serial bus [35].

9. TYPES OF CLOUD COMPUTING ATTACKS

Cloud computing experiences different kinds of attacks that threaten its activity and services. With the increasing use of cloud computing, attacks on cloud computing are also increasing, which raises an issue that needs to be addressed. These attacks target different elements of the cloud such as networks, information, and underlying structure. In general, cloud computing attacks can be categorized into the following classes:

- **Address Resolution Protocol (ARP) spoofing**: ARP is a standard protocol that is responsible for converting the addresses of the network layer to the addresses of the data link layer. This attack involves sending an adjusted ARP reply message to the victim to record the media access control address as if it is of a certain host. This attack leads to a disturbance of regular communication between hosts [13].
- **DoS and DDoS attacks**: DoS and DDoS flooding attacks are major attacks that devastate the *availability* of cloud computing systems. These two attacks aim to prevent intended users from accessing a machine or network resources. DDoS attacks are launched by two or more computers, whereas DoS attacks are launched by one person or computer [21]. Both attacks (Dos and DDoS) usually depend on a recruited device (compromised computer) by a malware named a bot [42]. A DDoS attack is shown in Fig. 6.2.

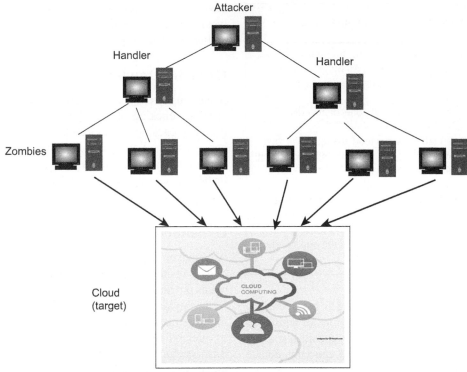

FIGURE 6.2 Distributed denial of service attack on a cloud.

- **Internet Protocol spoofing**: This attack is a major attribute of DDoS attacks to hide the identity of the attacker. As indicated before, DDoS attacks aim to bring down cloud resources and make them unavailable for both cloud providers and cloud users. Hiding the identity of the machine involved in the attack helps the attacker (1) from being easily traced and (2) deceive the cloud provider, to benefit from a service offered only to a trusted host [28].
- **Port scanning**: This attack involves looking into available network protocols or services, to exploit communication channels to launch a subsequent attack. Transmission Control Protocol (TCP) connect scanning is a form of port scanning composed of establishing a TCP connection. The attack involves exchanging multiple packets between the source and the destination. Once the attacker establishes a TCP connection, it still must be determined whether the port is open or not [25].
- **Man-in-the-cloud**: One popular attack experienced in 2015 was the man-in-the-cloud, aimed at storage/synchronization applications such as Dropbox and Google Drive. This attack is based on exploiting synchronization protocols and end-user authentication token of applications. The attack involves accessing

a targeted victim account by using the authentication credentials of the victim without the need to crack the password [11].
- **Insider attacks**: An authorized user (on the client or provider side) may try to gain privileges to perform a malicious activity [14].

10. MALWARE TECHNIQUES IN ANDROID

In this section, we will discuss the techniques malware follows in spreading to users' devices, in addition to stealth techniques employed by Android malware as case studies.

Repackaging Common Apps

Malware developers can use a repackaging technique to make new malware targeting mobile devices. Repackaging involves disassembling or decompiling a common benign app (free or paid) from a trusted app store, inserting and appending the malware code, reassembling the Trojan app, and distributing it through a less common or monitored app store. Malware developers use current reverse-engineering tools to repackage an app (see checklist, "An Agenda For Action For Repackaging An Application").

It has been observed that repackaging is being used to generate a large number of malware versions of legitimate official store apps. Repackaging is now considered a big threat to mobile devices apps because it can contaminate distribution markets.

The *AndroRat APK Binder* is an example of repackaging tools that plant Trojans in legitimate apps and provide them with remote access functionality. The malware developer then can make the infected device send SMS messages, make voice calls, retrieve the device location, and record audio/video using the remote access service.

Drive-by Download

Social engineering can be used by an attacker to trap the user into clicking on a malicious URL of a hostile advertisement, causing the user to download malware onto his or her device. Sometimes a drive-by download may masquerade as a legitimate app and deceive the user into installing an app. *Android/NotCompatible* is common drive-by download malware [8].

Dynamic Payload

An attacker may hide a malicious payload as an executable *apk/jar* inside the *APK* resources. After installing the app, it opens the malware payload and loads *DexClassLoader* API (if the payload is a *jar* file) and executes dynamic code. The malware may persuade the user to install the embedded *apk* by pretending to be a significant update. *BaseBridge* and *Anserverbot* are two malware classes that use this technique. However, other classes of malware do not plant a malicious payload as a resource; instead, they download them from a remote server and bypass detection. *DroidKungFuUpdate* is a notorious example of dynamic payload

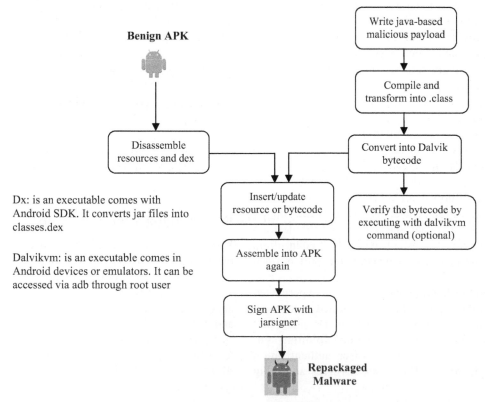

Dx: is an executable comes with Android SDK. It converts jar files into classes.dex

Dalvikvm: is an executable comes in Android devices or emulators. It can be accessed via adb through root user

FIGURE 6.3 App repackaging process. *APK*, Android application package.

malware. Usually, these techniques cannot be detected using static analysis methods [8].

Stealth Malware Techniques

Because Android OS is developed for limited resources (CPU, RAM, battery, etc.), antimalware apps are restricted by these limitations to perform deep inspections on smartphones, unlike their PC counterparts. This limitation is exploited by malware developers to fog malicious payloads into evading commercial antimalware. Stealth techniques include encryption, key permutations, dynamic loading, and reflection code and native code execution; all of these are interesting issues facing signature-based malware detection applications [8].

Colluding Apps

Colluding apps are set of apps that signed with same certificate and share the unique ID. They collude with each other to finalize the intended attack. Together, these apps are malware; however; individually they are benign. For example, malware with READ_SMS permission can read SMS messages and request the colluding assistant with INTERNET permission to send the sensitive information to a remote server. This action compromises the security goal of confidentiality [8].

Privilege Escalation

A mobile device can experience a privilege escalation, when the attack exploits known kernel vulnerabilities to gain root access to the device. In Android, Android-exported components can be exploited to gain root access to critical permissions. This action compromises the confidentiality security goal [8]. Table 6.1 summarizes mobile malware techniques in addition to the security goals compromised and their employed functionality.

11. CLOUD COMPUTING INTRUSIONS TECHNIQUES

Intrusions into cloud computing systems employ different techniques to achieve different goals. In this section we discuss the most well-known techniques used by cloud computing intrusions. These techniques are classified into different categories. We will discuss each category individually.

Reconnaissance Techniques

Reconnaissance involves collecting the maximum possible information about the victim before starting the attack. Usually, this technique is associated with hacking. In the following, we list some reconnaissance techniques [21]:

- **Social engineering**: This technique involves looking for reasoning to gain sensitive information or text by stimulating an individual mind or sense of social norms.
- **Dumpster diving**: This technique involves obtaining sensitive information from trash locations.
- **Usenet tools**: This technique depends on gathering data from company websites, gathering information from employees' social networks, or collecting some useful information from business partners.
- **Domain name system (DNS) reconnaissance—zone transfer**: A DNS server can be a good place for hackers to harvest important information such as an address of a mail server, an address of a web server, operation system information, and even comments.

Denial of Service

This technique is easy to implement but it is difficult to defend against. It is based on targeting the *availability* goal of the cloud security. The technique involves consuming the system resources (CPU, network bandwidth, RAM, or disk space) by sending a huge number of illegitimate

TABLE 6.1 Mobile Malware Techniques, Security Goal Compromised, and Employed Functionality

Malware Technique	Security Goal Compromised	Functionality
Repackaging common apps	Confidentiality + integrity + availability	Insert malicious code into benign application
Drive-by download	Confidentiality	Use social engineering to download malware
Dynamic payload	Confidentiality	Convince user to install embedded *apk* by posing as update
Stealth malware techniques	Confidentiality + availability	Exploit mobile limitation in evading commercial antimalware applications
Colliding apps	Confidentiality	Apps collide with each other to launch attack
Privilege escalation	Confidentiality	Exploiting kernel vulnerabilities to gain root access

requests over the limit the system can handle. That causes legitimate users to become unable to access or use the system. The most common type of DoS attack is DDoS. DDoS depends on using many computers (it can be thousands) to launch the attack instead of one computer (as in the case of DoS) [21].

Account Cracking

An attacker can use some tools to perform password cracking. The attacker can use those tools to crack a hashed password file. Brutus, Web cracker, Obiwan, burp intruder, and burp repeater are some examples of password cracking tools. Different techniques are used by a hacker for password cracking [21]:

- **Dictionary attack**: involves using a dictionary of words against the victim's account
- **Brute force attack**: involves trying every possible combination of characters until the password is cracked
- **Hybrid attack**: basically combines the two attacks (dictionary and brute force)

Structured Query Language Injection

The attacker may concatenate Structured Query Language (SQL) query strings with variables targeting SQL servers that run vulnerable database applications. These vulnerabilities can be exploited by hackers to inject malicious scripts, evade login, and obtain unauthorized access to back-end databases. The rate of SQL injection attacks increased 69% in the second quarter of 2012 compared with the first quarter [5].

Cross-Site Scripting

Cross-site scripting is considered one of the most dangerous categories of attack. It involves injecting malicious scripts such as JavaScript, VBScript, ActiveX, HTML, or flash into a vulnerable active Web page to run the scripts on the victim's Web browser. Some researchers in Germany explained how a cross-site scripting attack can attack the Amazon AWS cloud computing platform. The researchers discovered a vulnerability in Amazon's store that allows hackers to hijack an AWS session and gain access to customers' data [5].

Malware Injection

This attack uses metainformation exchange in cloud computing systems. Usually, metadata exchange is carried out between a *Web server* and a *Web browser*, because in cloud systems the client's request depends on authentication and authorization. The attack involves intruding into these procedures and injecting a malicious code to perform a malicious service. As a result, the cloud service will experience eavesdropping and deadlocks, which in turn increases the waiting time for legitimate users to be served [21]. Table 6.2 lists brief information about the techniques employed by cloud computing attacks, including the name of the technique, the security goal they compromise, and the functionality employed by each technique.

12. EXAMPLES OF SMARTPHONE MALWARE

In this section, we explore some examples of malware that attack mobile devices:

- **Cabir**: This is a computer worm that has the ability to infect smartphones that run the Symbian OS. It is also known as Caribe, SybmOS/Cabir, Symbian/Cabir, and EPOC.cabir. This malware was developed in 2004 [7]. The malware writes the word "Cabire" on the screen of the infected device and uses the Bluetooth connection to propagate to other devices [46].

TABLE 6.2 Techniques Employed by Cloud Computing Attacks, Security Goals Compromised, and Their Functionality

Intrusion Technique	Security Goal Compromised	Functionality
Reconnaissance	Confidentiality	Collecting information about target
Denial of service	Availability	Consuming system's resources to prevent them from access by legitimate users
Account cracking	Confidentiality	Cracking user's passwords
Structured Query Language injection	Confidentiality	Obtaining unauthorized access to database
Cross-site scripting	Confidentiality	Injecting malicious scripts in vulnerable Web pages
Malware injection	Confidentiality + availability	Intruding metainformation exchange into injected malicious code

- **DroidDream**: This is a different generation of malware for Android devices that appeared in 2011. It was able to infect more than 50 apps in the Google Play market. The malware has a sophisticated functionality such as data theft, root exploits, and botnet functionality. The main objective of this malware was to recruit a botnet [30].
- **Commwarrior**: This worm appeared in 2005; it had the ability to infect the Symbian platform OS from multimedia messaging service (MMS). The worm is sent to the victim's device as an archive file named Commwarrior.zip and this file contains another file named Commwarrior.sis. Upon executing this file, Commwarrior starts scanning for nearby devices by Bluetooth or infrared using a random name. Next, it sends an MMS message to the contacts in the compromised phone using different header messages for each contact. The recipient of this MMS will often open it, causing the phone to become infected with this worm [7].
- **Phage**: This is one of the earliest viruses that infected the Palm OS of mobile phones. The virus can be transmitted to the Palm OS via synchronization when it is connected to a PC. After it is transferred to the phone, it starts infecting all of the applications that are on the phone and planting its own code to function without being noticed by the user or being detected by the system [7].
- **Pjapps**: This is a Trojan embedded in an application that contains internal, conventional botnet functionality. This Trojan targets Android devices and is attached with apps from an app market other than Google Play. The main objective of this Trojan is to open a backdoor on the infected device, to make it controllable remotely from a remote server [30].
- **RedBrowser**: This is a Java-based Trojan that can masquerade as a program named "RedBrowser"; it enables the user to visit Wireless Application Protocol (WAP) sites without the need for a WAP connection. It can infect any Java-based mobile phone. Throughout the installation process, the application asks the user for permission to send messages. Upon acceptance, RedBrowser starts sending SMS to paid call centers. In addition, RedBrowser uses the Smartphone's connection to social networks (Facebook, Twitter, etc.) to obtain contact information for the user's friends (based on permission that was given in the beginning) to send them messages without the user's consent [7].
- **WinCE.PmCryptic.A**: This is malware that infects Windows mobile phones. The main objective of the malware developers is to obtain money. It infects memory cards that are inserted in smartphones for better prevalence and to launch a DoS attack [7].
- **CardTrap**: This is a virus that can infect various types of smartphones. The main objective of this virus is to deactivate the system and third-party applications. The virus's malicious activity is to replace the files used to

start the smartphone and their applications, which prevents them from execution. There are different versions of this virus, such as Cardtrap.A, which infects Symbian OS phones. It can also infect the memory card with malware that can infect Windows OS [7].
- **Flexispy**: This is a Trojan that masquerades as an application for Symbian OS phones. The malicious activity of this Trojan is represented in its sending all of the information that is sent and received from the smartphone to a Flexispy server. It was originally developed to protect children and to eavesdrop on unfaithful spouses [7].
- **FakePlayer**: This is an SMS Trojan for the Android platform. It presents as a legal movie player app with a fake Windows Media Player icon. The Trojan sends SMS messages to saved contacts without the user's consent [30].
- **GPS spy:** This is more malware for the Android platform that masquerades as a classic snake game, but it has the ability to collect and send the GPS location of the phone to a remote server without the user's consent [30].
- **Geinimi**: Thi is a Trojan that infects Android mobile phones. The Trojan collects personal information and sends it to a remote server. A new version of this Trojan has the ability to infect legal applications [30].
- **ZitMo**: This is malware that infects Android mobile phones. This Trojan malware has the ability to intercept and forward all SMS messages to a remote server. It also has the ability to infect legitimate applications and works cooperatively with the Zeus banking Trojan to steal banking information [30].
- **NickiBot**: This is Android malware that is controlled remotely by SMS messages from a remote server. This malware has the ability to monitor location, record voice calls, and collect all logs. This malware was discovered in unofficial Android markets [30].
- **RootSmart**: This is Android malware that was noted to interact with a botnet called Android.Bmaster. The malware gains root access on Android-based devices. The malware was discovered in unofficial Android markets [30].

Table 6.3 lists some brief information about this mobile device malware, including names, platforms, and the security goals it compromises.

13. EXAMPLES OF CLOUD ATTACKS

In this section we explore some well-known attacks on cloud computing systems:

- **DKSM**: This attack has the effective ability to destroy and confuse existing VM internal diagnosing. The attack overcomes exiting introspection techniques by manipulating the kernel data structures of the guest

TABLE 6.3 Examples of Mobile Device Malware and Important Related Information

Malware Name	Platform (Operating System)	Compromises
Cabir	Symbian	Confidentiality
DroidDream	Android	Confidentiality
Commwarrior	Symbian	Confidentiality
Phage	Palm	Confidentiality + integrity
Pjapps	Android	Confidentiality
RedBrowser	Any Java-based OS	Confidentiality
WinCE.PmCryptic.A	Windows phone OS	Availability
CardTrap	Symbian	Integrity + availability
Flexispy	Symbian	Confidentiality
FakePlayer	Android	Confidentiality
GPS spy	Android	Confidentiality
Geinimi	Android	Confidentiality
ZitMo	Android	Confidentiality
NickiBot	Android	Confidentiality
RootSmart	Android	Confidentiality

VM on which these techniques depend. This attack has three different approaches: (1) syntax-based manipulation, which involves adding or removing certain fields of kernel data structures; (2) semantics-based manipulation, which involves modifying the semantics of the underlying data structures; and (3) multifaceted combo manipulation, which efficiently integrates the previous two approaches [2].

- **Kernel Beast rootkit on Linux**: This is a kernel rootkit that can hide a loadable kernel module, process (*ps*, *pstree*, *top*, and *lsof*), ports, socket and connections (*netstat* and *lsof*), and files/directory. This rootkit attacks Ubuntu 10.04 32-bit OS VM [17].
- **Hacker Defender rootkit**: This rootkit attacks user-mode Windows OS by manipulating the API of Windows. The main objective of this rootkit is to allow a hacker to hide process, files, and registry key system drivers. Furthermore, it performs port scanning on the network connections. This rootkit was observed to inject into a Windows 7–based guest VM successfully [17].
- **DoS attack**: The main objective of DoS and DDoS attacks is to make the computer or network unavailable to legitimate users by overwhelming the system with huge forged messages. Some sophisticated and powerful tools may be used by attackers to make this attack difficult to detect [17].
- **Nova**: This is an OpenStack attack written in Python. OpenStack is an open-source software platform used in cloud computing; it is particularly deployed as an

IaaS used to manage computer resources. Attackers aim to exploit Nova's network configuration to reach the host on the same virtual network. Attackers may check booted instances to gain a possible connection on the host system by checking the gateway address and performing *ssh* service on it [11].

- **Horizon**: This is a legitimate representation of the OpenStack dashboard. It has an interface to help the user access OpenStack services. However, the default settings of Horizon can be exploited by the attacker by using the assigned cookie to save the session state on the client side and steal the cookie. The attacker can impersonate the target by using the stolen cookie [11].
- **Kelihos**: This malware appeared in 2010; different versions of it have been developed since then. Kelihos can perform different attacks such as phishing and spamming [41]. One of its variants was observed to perform sophisticated avoidance techniques. Moreover, this malware can monitor network traffic for Hypertext Transfer Protocol and File Transfer Protocol to steal sensitive information and spread via TCP port 80. One of the attack variants is named Trojan.Kelihos [23].
- **Zeus:** This malware was developed in 2010. Its developers produced an overabundance of versions since then. In July 2014, it was able to compromise millions of machines and its developers constructed a botnet able to steal sensitive banking information. One of the malware variants could confuse and distort security software installed on a given host. It starts with finding

TABLE 6.4 Examples of Cloud Computing Attacks on Mobile Devices and Related Important Information

Attack Name	Platform (Operating System)	Compromises
DKSM	NA	Integrity
Kernel Beast	Ubuntu	Integrity
Hacker Defender rootkit	Windows	Integrity
DoS attack	All platforms	Availability
Nova	All platforms	Confidentiality
Horizon	All platforms	Confidentiality
Kelihos	All platforms	Confidentiality
Zeus	All platforms	Confidentiality + integrity

one of the main system processes in which to inject itself; it then disrupts antivirus and security applications. That keeps the malware from being undetected by any detection system within the OS. One of the malware variants is named Trojan.Zbot-18 [41].

Table 6.4 shows some brief information about cloud computing attacks, including their names and platforms, and the security goals they compromise.

14. TYPES OF INTRUSION DETECTION SYSTEMS FOR MOBILE DEVICES

Because of continuous increases in malware attacks on mobile devices [35], it has become a necessity to design and implement effective countermeasures. IDSs are the main defense mechanism against any threat that aims to compromise one or more mobile device security goals (confidentiality, integrity, and availability).

There are four major types of IDSs for mobile devices: signature-based, anomaly-based, cloud-based [22], and manual analysis, as shown in Fig. 6.4. A description of each type is provided in this section.

Signature-Based Intrusion Detection System

A signature-based ID is based on extracting signatures from behavioral patterns that are derived from known

malware misbehaviors. These signatures will be compared with the signature of new applications. The Multilevel Anomaly Detector for Android Malware (MADAM) is a signature-based IDSs for smartphones [35]. This IDS, which is designed for Android devices, aims to detect malicious behavioral patterns extracted from several categories of malware. The goal of MADAM was achieved by monitoring five groups of Android features: system calls, SMS, critical API, user activity, and application metadata. In fact, these groups belong to four different levels of abstraction: kernel, application, user, and package. The extracted features are used to detect unusual user and device behavioral patterns. After detecting particular behavioral patterns, it intercepts and blocks malware by applying all of the prespecified hazard procedures for the user and the device. MADAM is designed to assess any newly installed app by inspecting the requested permissions and reputation metadata, such as user scores and download count, and include the app in a suspicious list if it is assessed as risky.

In Shen et al. [36], the authors built a topology graph for every kind of malware family; this graph represents its malicious behavior. The topology graph was constructed for Android applications, which are divided into a number of classes including Android-specific components. Using the application classes, the graph is constructed by making the classes the nodes of the graph; the relationships between components and other classes can be the edges, such as *startActivity*, *startService*, and method invocation.

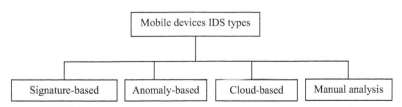

FIGURE 6.4 Types of intrusion detection system (IDS) for mobile devices.

Because two different applications may share part of the program structure, it is not enough to detect malware using the topology graph. Therefore, malware detection can extract API sets in every class to be attributes of nodes of the topology graph. The wisdom behind using API information is that API calls report the implemented function in the classes and may reveal certain malicious behaviors. In this way, malware detectors can distinguish between benign apps and malware.

Anomaly-Based Intrusion Detection System

In contrast to signature-based IDS, anomaly-based IDS in malware detection does not require signatures to detect intrusion. In addition, an anomaly-based IDS can identify unknown attacks depending on the similar behavior of other intrusions. The approach of anomaly-based detection is based on modeling normality to identify occurrences of malware. Consequently, any deviation from this model is considered anomalous. This technique is effective in detecting unknown malware. The anomaly-based model presented in Sanz et al. [34] involved extracting several features from the Manifest file of Android applications, which are *uses-permission* and *uses-features*, to build the model. These features were used to build the normal model of several legitimate applications to detect malicious applications. Other efforts, such as the model proposed in Ghaffari and Abadi [10], used entropy-based anomaly detection to detect clear deviations in the network behavior of Android applications. They used two common entropy measures, sample entropy and modified sample entropy, in detecting Android malware.

Anomaly-based malware detection has attracted researchers in computing systems and network traffic. Different approaches have been used in mobile malware detection, such as statistical-based approaches, data mining based methods, and machine learning techniques. The model presented in Cheng et al. [3] was based on a statistical approach by collecting communication activity information from the smartphone, then conducting joint analysis to detect single-device and system-wide malicious behavior. Machine learning algorithms can also be used in anomaly-based malware detection, such as the model proposed in Peiravian and Zhu [29]. The authors combined permissions and API calls in a machine learning approach to malware. The permission is extracted from each app's profile information, whereas the APIs are extracted from the packed app file by using libraries to represent API calls. By combining permissions and API calls and employing them as features to describe each app, a classifier can be trained to distinguish between benign apps and malware. Deep learning is a new machine learning technique that has proven effective in many applications. Deep learning was used in malware detection in Yuan et al. [47] after the researchers conducted

static and dynamic analysis to extract features from each app. Static analysis extracts features such as required permissions and sensitive APIs, whereas dynamic analysis uses the installation file (the *apk* file) of each app. Deep belief networks architecture and convolutional neural networks were used to construct the online-learning model and characterize Android apps. The learning model consisted of two phases: unsupervised pretraining and supervised back-propagation phases. Their system, *DroidDetector*, has been kept online for user testing and can be used to detect whether a submitted app is malware or benign.

Cloud-Based Intrusion Detection System

Because mobile IDSs consume more CPU and memory in performing their task, and smartphones and other mobile devices have limited energy and computational resources, implementing IDS for smartphones is a challenging task. As a resolution for these problems, a cloud-based IDS has been proposed to detect suspicious behavior or malicious activity on smartphones. The main objectives of such a solution are that it should not be consume resources and should be practical and suitable for implementation. One solutions [13] requires users to install a lightweight agent on their smartphones and register on an online cloud service. This registry involves specifying some information, such as the smartphones' OS, the application installed on the phone, and other relevant information about the device. The next step is to emulate the smartphone in a VM on the cloud using a proxy, which in turn duplicates incoming traffic to the device, and then forwards traffic to the emulation platform (the location of detection). Because the system is developed in the cloud, all registered users can use the system at the same time. The lightweight agent that is installed on the user's registered device will inspect all of the file activity of the system. Whenever the user performs any data transfer activity, the agent will forward the traffic to the cloud through the proxy server. This procedure allows the execution of multiple detection engines in parallel by hosting them on an emulated device. The advantage of using virtualization to run multiple detection engines is that it increases the coverage of malware detection. This approach involves a proactive defense mechanism because it alerts the smartphone user that the file is infected before it is downloaded.

Another cloud-based botnet malware approach, proposed in Jadhav et al. [12], consists of two stages: malware analysis and data clustering. The malware analysis stage is specified for accepting applications from the user and performing malware analysis and data collection. In the clustering stage, the system conducts multilayer clustering depending on data collected in the first stage. The system is characterized by its ability to handle multiple clients at the same time, and by its resource flexibility.

Manual Analysis

A professional auditor can perform manual analysis to detect mobile malware on the server that provides malware service. However, this method is considered to be time-consuming; also, it is not accurate, which may lead to high false negatives. Contemporary malware follows sophisticated techniques and obfuscation methods to avoid detection strategies. It requires considerable time to build the required expertise to accomplish this kind of job.

15. TYPES OF INTRUSION DETECTION SYSTEMS FOR CLOUD COMPUTING

As a countermeasure to the increasing number of attacks on cloud computing systems, IDS has been used to detect malicious activity that may compromise cloud computing security. IDS in a cloud computing environment can be divided into five categories (types): network-based, host-based, hybrid-based, hypervisor, and distributed, as shown in Fig. 6.5.

Network-Based Intrusion Detection System

Network-based IDSs for cloud computing systems are based on capturing network traffic and analyzing it to detect any potential intrusion, such as DoS attacks, port scanning, and botnets. Internally, a network-based IDS can use a signature-based approach and compare the collected information with a signature database to look for a match with an intrusion, or it can work as anomaly-based system and compare current behavior with normal behavior to decide whether there is an attack.

The model proposed in Chou and Wang [4] consists of three parts: *preprocessing*, an *analyzer*, and a *detector*. The preprocessor is responsible for converting audited data from raw packets to connection records with the required features.

The connection records are fed to the analyzer as input and then get labeled with tags as normal or as an anomaly using an unsupervised learning algorithm. The resulting labeled records are then saved in a database. This database is used by the analyzer to train a prediction model and update the existing model to adapt to the environment. The last part is the detector, which loads the resulting prediction model from the analyzer to inspect the records from the preprocessor output. The architecture of the proposed system is depicted in Fig. 6.6.

The cloud computing system uses virtualization technologies to provide different services through VMs. In the proposed cloud platform, a server-agent scheme is used to achieve network intrusion detection. A lightweight agent is placed in each client VM and executed in the background. This agent is responsible for inspecting in real time and transferring data to a server VM. The server VM receives the input connection records and outputs an updated tree

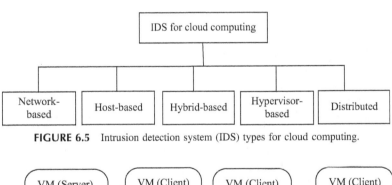

FIGURE 6.5   Intrusion detection system (IDS) types for cloud computing.

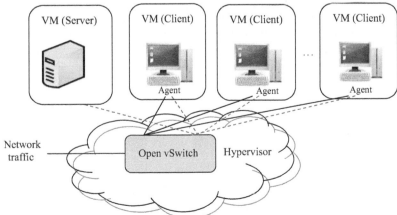

FIGURE 6.6   Platform of the proposed approach in Chou and Wang [4]. *VM*, virtual machine.

file to all client VMs to keep the detection ability of all VMs up to date. It is preferable (for security reasons) to isolate communication between agents and the server VM and make it inaccessible for users accessing services offered by client VMs.

Therefore, an open *vSwitch* is added to administer different networks in the hypervisor, as shown in Fig. 6.6. However, the implemented system in Chou and Wang [4] has some limitations, such as that it is not able to detect attacks that make many connections, such as DoS and probing attacks; instead, it is restricted to detect only rare attacks.

Other work has used network-based IDS to handle a large flow of network traffic; analyze this traffic; and then, generate organized reports by incorporating the results of behavior analysis to identify and detect intrusions on the cloud at an earlier stage. The architecture of the proposed IDS consisted of four major components: traffic capturing, traffic identifier, analyzer, and malicious activity detector. Traffic capturing is responsible for forwarding captured traffic of the network being monitored in the raw format to the next component, which is the traffic identifier. The role of the traffic identifier is to minimize the size of the captured network traffic by extracting a set of features from the raw data. The output of the traffic identifier will be used as input to the analyzer (detection engine). The detection engine used an artificial neural network to look for malicious activity. Once malicious activity is detected, a report will be sent to the administrator to inform about the attack [18].

Host-Based Intrusion Detection System

Host-based intrusion detection (HIDS) is based on gathering information from connected hosts and analyzing them to detect malicious activities. The gathered information can be a system log file, OS data structures, running processes, file access and modification, system and application configuration, or system calls [15]. This kind of IDS is used to protect the integrity of a cloud computing system [31]. However, conventional HIDS cannot be used for intrusion detection in cloud computing. That is because of the internal procedure employed by conventional HIDS; it analyzes the behavior of users in their local contexts. Cloud users are different in terms of the freedom they have in using multiple resources from different domains at the same time or one after the other. The intrusion detection is accomplished from the cloud perspective as an integrated system. Therefore, different approaches are used to overcome this problem. IDS log cloud analysis system is a proposed IDS analysis system for cloud inter-VM and different platforms [43]. The internal architecture is based on Hadoop's MapReduce log file analysis for a cloud computing system. The main characteristics of this design are its scalability and reliability.

Hypervisor-Based Intrusion Detection System

Another type of IDS for cloud computing can be at the hypervisor level. A hypervisor is a software component that serves as the main pillar of virtualization in the cloud computing system. It is responsible for sharing resources to VMs and providing a level for interaction among VMs [17]. The existence of any vulnerability in VMs can be exploited by attackers to initiate various advanced attacks such as a stealthy rootkit, Trojan, and regular DoS and DDoS against those VMs. The attacks launched at the hypervisor level can throw the normal operation of cloud infrastructure into disorder. Therefore, it has become a must to look for an effective strategy to defend against attacks at the hypervisor level to protect the virtualized resources of the guest OS.

The hypervisor and VM-Dependent Intrusion Detection and Prevention System (VMIDPS) for a virtualized cloud environment [17] is one of the proposed hypervisor-based IDSs for virtual environments aimed to provide a robust state of the VM by detecting and then eliminating rootkits. The architecture is composed of four collaborated components to achieve the goal: a *management unit*, a *VMIDPS server*, an *IDPS core*, and a *hypervisor*, as shown in Fig. 6.7.

The first component is the management unit (which is one of the hypervisor's components) and the hypervisor and Intrusion Detection and Prevention System (IDPS) core stay in it. The second component is the VMIDPS-server, which is the complementary part of the IDPS core; it runs on the hypervisor.

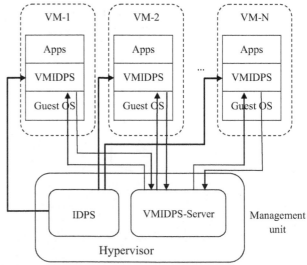

FIGURE 6.7 The architecture of Virtual Machine—Dependent Intrusion Detection and Prevention System (VMIDPS) for virtualized environment. *IDPS*, Intrusion Detection and Prevention System; *OS*, operating system; *VM*, virtual machine.

The management unit is informed by the hypervisor to deploy an IDPS agent onto every launched new VM. Therefore, every IDPS running on a VM is called the VMIDPS. The VMIDPS is responsible for scanning the whole VM to confirm that the system is a safe and in an uninfected state. VMs can give permission to execute a function only if it is confirmed as a safe (robust) system function; otherwise VMIDPS will trigger an alarm to take a suitable action to bring the VM back to a normal state. The VMIDPS integrates different intrusion techniques such as file integrity verification, signature-based intrusion detection, and anomaly-based intrusion detection. These techniques are used to detect multiple types of intrusions (rootkits, viruses, worms, port scans, file alterations, and others). The VMIDPS sends the whole state of the VM to the VMIDPS-server on a regular basis to detect intrusions able to avoid the VM level. A cross-view analysis-based intrusion detection technique is employed to detect intrusions.

Other hypervisor-based IDSs used some performance metrics collected from hypervisors, such as network data transmitted/received, block device read/write requests, and CPU use to detect suspicious activity within the VM and without detailed knowledge of the OS running on that VM. In addition, the proposed hypervisor-based IDS method does not require additional software to be installed on VMs. The framework consists of three major components: a *controller node*, an *end point node*, and a *notification service*.

The *controller node* takes charge of analyzing close to real-time performance data in all of the VMs in the cloud computing environment [27]. The *end point nodes* are responsible for collecting data on every VM running in the cloud environment from the hypervisor and directs the data to the *controller node*. The last component is the *notification service*, which is responsible for signaling a notification when an attack signature is detected. The framework structure is illustrated in Fig. 6.8.

Distributed Intrusion Detection System

A distributed IDS for cloud computing systems is based on deploying IDSs over the network to inspect the traffic for intrusive behavior. Each of these IDSs consists of two components: a *detection component* and a *correlation manager*. The detection component is responsible for inspecting the system's behavior and sending the collected data after representing them in a standard format to the correlation manager. The correlation manager, in turn, gathers data from various IDSs and produces high-level alerts that stimulate a reaction to the attack. The analysis phase can use anomaly-based and signature-based detection techniques to respond to known and unknown attacks.

Modi [24] proposed a distributed IDS for cloud computing. The framework was based on installing network IDSs on each host machine of the cloud to monitor virtual network traffic with the goal of detecting intrusions. The proposed framework consisted of six components: *packet capture, signature detection, network traffic profile generation, anomaly detection, severity calculation,* and an *alert system.* Packet capture is responsible for capturing network traffic and for communication between VMs and between VMs and the host machine for intrusion inspection. The signature detection is used to detect known attacks from real-time captured network traffic data and filter out any intrusive connection. The third component, network traffic profile generation, makes network profiles by extracting some useful network features. It also extracts the virtual local area network (VLAN) ID to identify the VLAN number from where the attacking VM is running. The generated profile is sent to the anomaly detection component, which uses an associative classifier to predict a class label (either normal or intrusion) with all of the received profiles. This classifier is useful for detecting unknown attacks in the network. In case an intrusion is detected, an alert is sent to the severity calculation module,

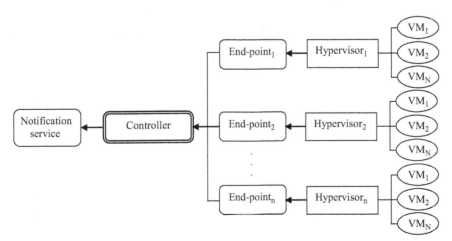

FIGURE 6.8 Conceptual diagram of hypervisor-based cloud intrusion detection system proposed in Nikolai and Wang [28]. *VM*, virtual machine.

which is responsible for identifying distributed attacks from detected intrusions by checking intrusion alerts in the central log server, where intrusion alerts are stored. The last component is the alert system, where alert messages of intrusions are produced. The system stores alert information about each detected intrusion in the network traffic profile log for further learning about the associative classifier.

16. INTRUSION DETECTION SYSTEM PERFORMANCE METRICS

IDS performance is measured by different performance metrics, depending on the goal of the IDS. Some IDSs are concerned about detection accuracy, whereas others are concerned about false negatives. These performance metrics give important information that can be used to compare different proposed IDSs. This section explains the performance metrics of IDSs on both environments: mobile devices and cloud computing.

Intrusion Detection System Performance Metrics in Mobile Devices

IDSs on mobile devices aim to achieve the highest performance in detecting malware and any suspicious activity. Therefore, to evaluate different IDSs and malware detectors, different evaluation metrics have been used. This section discusses the most well-known metrics used by these applications. First, we need to know that IDSs deal with two cases of applications: normal and malicious (malware).

Therefore, the IDS will first need to build a table of all available cases, which is usually called a confusion matrix. The confusion matrix is simply a 2×2 matrix illustrating whether each instance (normal or malicious) has been classified correctly, as shown in Table 6.5. Most evaluation metrics used by IDS and malware detectors extract evaluation metrics from the confusion matrix. Confusion matrix elements are:

- **True positive (TP)**: Its value represents the number of malwares that have been correctly classified as malwares.

- **False negative (FN)**: Its value represents the number of malwares that have been misclassified as normal programs.
- **False positive (FP)**: Its value represents the number of normal applications that have been misclassified as malwares.
- **True negative (TN)**: Its value represents the number of normal applications that have been correctly classified as normal.

After building the confusion matrix, the most well-known evaluation metrics can be extracted as:

- **Accuracy:** Represents the percentage of correctly classified applications compared with the total number of applications. Accuracy is given by Refs. [10,44,45,47]:

$$\text{Accuracy} = \frac{(TP + TN)}{(TP + TN + FP + FN)} \quad (6.1)$$

- **Detection rate or true positive rate (TPR)**: It represents the percentage of correctly classified malwares compared with the total number of malwares [20]. Detection rate is given by Refs. [10,26,44,45]:

$$\text{Detection rate} = \frac{TP}{(TP + FN)} \quad (6.2)$$

- **False alarm rate or false positive rate (FPR)**: It represents the percentage of normal applications incorrectly classified as malwares compared with the total number of normal applications. FPR is given by Refs. [19,44,45]:

$$\text{FPR} = \frac{FP}{(FP + TN)} \quad (6.3)$$

- **False negative rate (FNR)**: It represents the percentage of malwares incorrectly classified as normal compared with the total number of malwares. FNR is given by Refs. [44,45]:

$$FNR = \frac{FN}{(FN + TP)} \quad (6.4)$$

- **True negative rate (TNR) or recall**: It represents the percentage of correctly classified normal applications compared with the total number of normal applications. TNR is given by Refs. [44,45]:

$$\text{TNR} = \frac{TN}{(TN + FP)} \quad (6.5)$$

- **Precision:** Represents the rate of relevant results rather than irrelevant results. Precision is given by Refs. [26,45]:

$$\text{Precision} = \frac{TP}{(TP + FP)} \quad (6.6)$$

TABLE 6.5 Confusion Matrix Built by Any Intrusion Detection System

Classified as	Malicious	Normal
Actual Class		
Malicious	True positive	False negative
Normal	False positive	True negative

- **F-measure**: It represents a combined system performance of both precision and recall. The F-measure is given by Ref. [26]:

$$F - measure = \frac{(2 \times Recall \times Precision)}{(Recall + Precision)} \quad (6.7)$$

- **Error rate**: Some authors measure the error rate of malware detectors as [44,45]:

$$Err = \frac{(FP + FN)}{(FP + FN + TP + TN)} \quad (6.8)$$

- **Receiver operating characteristic (ROC) curve**: The area under the ROC curve is another metric that can be used with IDS for malware. The curve is generated by plotting the TPR against the FPR at different points. In perfect cases, the ROC value is 1. On the contrary, if the probability of distinguishing a normal application from malware is 50%, the area under ROC is 0.5.

Intrusion Detection System Performance Metrics for Cloud Computing

As stated earlier, cloud computing systems are also susceptible to intrusions. Evaluations of IDS for cloud computing systems use some measurements. Some of these measurements are used by IDS mobile devices; others are used only in cloud computing IDS. This section discusses the most well-know IDS evaluation metrics for cloud computing:

- **Accuracy**: It also refers to the percentage of true predictions done by the IDS and is calculated using Eq. (6.1) [18,24,27,41,48].
- **Detection rate or recall**: It also refers to correctly classified intrusions compared with the total number of intrusions and can be calculated using Eq. (6.2) [4,18,24,32].
- **FPR**: This is the same as the FPR in mobile device IDSs; it can be calculated using Eq. (6.3) [4,41,48].
- **FNR**: This is the same as the FNR in mobile device IDSs; it can be calculated using Eq. (6.4) [48].
- **Precision**: This is the same as precision in mobile device IDSs; it can be calculated using Eq. (6.6) [18,24,32,41].
- **F-score (F-measure)**: This is the same as the F-measure in mobile device IDSs; it can be calculated using Eq. (6.7) [18,41].
- **G-mean (geometric mean)**: This represents the rounded measure of the performance of the IDS by considering all outcomes; it can be calculated from [41]:

$$G - Mean = \sqrt{Precision \times Recall} \quad (6.9)$$

IDSs for both mobile devices and cloud computing share the way in which IDS performance is measured. The only difference is that in mobile devices the IDS looks for malware whereas in cloud computing the IDS looks for intrusions or attacks. In both environments, IDSs usually compete in detecting the maximum number of malwares/intrusions to find the suitable reaction against these threats. However, the IDS design also requires a balance to be made between the number of detected threats and false alarms (because false alarms can be disturbing to users).

17. SUMMARY

Technology supporting mobile computation and communication is developing around the clock in a competitive manner to serve people and make their lives easier, safer, more convenient, and secure. However, this competition has many enemies who try to impede this competition in different ways and for different goals (making money, stealing information, damaging competitors, etc.). Cloud computing and mobile devices are two contemporary technologies that aim to make people's lives easier and more convenient. The two technologies have become targets for many kinds of attacks. These attacks differ in their severity, techniques, and goals. Therefore, providing security to these two environments has become a major concern to people. This chapter has discussed the security issues of these two environments. The chapter explored contemporary mobile platforms and cloud computing models. The risks resulting from mobile devices and cloud computing attacks have also been discussed. The chapter laid the foundation for malware techniques employed in Android (as a case study) and those employed by cloud computing intrusions. The chapter also presented several common examples of smartphone malware as well of cloud computing attacks. The chapter explained in detail all of the types of IDSs for mobile devices in addition to all of the types of IDSs for cloud computing systems. The chapter concluded by explaining most of the performance metrics used to evaluate any IDS for both mobile devices and cloud computing systems.

However, intrusion detection designers must keep developing techniques because attacks on computing systems are increasing in their sophistication. IDSs look for intrusions and the intrusions employ evasion techniques to avoid detection by IDSs. Therefore, it can be considered an arm race between malware/intrusion developers and intrusion detection designers.

Finally, let us move on to the real interactive part of this chapter: review questions/exercises, hands-on projects, case projects, and an optional team case project. The answers and/or solutions by chapter can be found in Appendix K.

CHAPTER REVIEW QUESTIONS/ EXERCISES

True/False

1. True or false? The cost-effectiveness and capabilities offered by cloud computing are in fact the major encouraging factors that attract the attention of many organizations and academic entities.
2. True or false? An OS is a hardware interface that is responsible for managing and operating hardware units, and assisting the user to use that unit.
3. True or false? Android is an open-source mobile OS developed by Google and launched in 2000.
4. True or false? Apple iOS is a closed-source code mobile phone OS developed by Apple in 2001 that is used by Apple-only products (iPhone, iPod, and iPad).
5. True or false? Symbian OS is an open-source mobile OS written in C++ programming language developed by Symbian Ltd. in 1977 and used by mostly Nokia phones.

Multiple Choice

1. The CSP provides software to the user, and that software is running and deployed on a cloud infrastructure. What is this called?
   A. Platform-as-a-service (PaaS)
   B. Infrastructure-as-a-service (IaaS)
   C. Compromising a user's privacy
   D. Software-as-a-service (SaaS)
   E. Stealing sensitive information
2. Who uses stolen data or identities to obtain an income?
   A. Thieves
   B. Professionals
   C. Black hat hackers
   D. Gray hat hackers
   E. White hat hackers
3. What is it called when authors are able to simulate an attack to subvert VM introspection?
   A. Attacks from a VM
   B. Attacks from a virtual network
   C. Attacks from a malicious hypervisor
   D. Attacks from outside the cloud environment
   E. All of the above
4. What kind of malware attacks the device by making a bot to control the device remotely by a remote user or a bot-master using a set of commands?
   A. Backdoor
   B. Botnet
   C. Rootkit
   D. Worms
   E. SMS Trojan

5. What is a standard protocol that is responsible for converting the addresses of the network layer to the addresses of the data link layer?
   A. ARP spoofing
   B. DoS and DDoS attacks
   C. IP spoofing
   D. Port scanning
   E. Man-in-the-cloud

EXERCISE

Problem

Why should an organization use intrusion detection, especially when it already has firewalls, antivirus tools, and other security protections on its system?

Hands-on Projects

Project

How can IDSs and vulnerability assessment systems interact?

Case Projects

Problem

What are the limitations of IDSs?

Optional Team Case Project

Problem

How do you go about selecting the best IDS for your organization?

REFERENCES

[1] A.M. Azab, P. Ning, Z. Wang, X. Jiang, X. Zhang, N.C. Skalsky, HyperSentry: enabling stealthy in-context measurement of hypervisor integrity, in: Proceedings of the 17th ACM Conference on Computer and Communications Security, 2010, pp. 38–49.
[2] S. Bahram, X. Jiang, Z. Wang, M. Grace, J. Li, D. Srinivasan, J. Rhee, D. Xu, DKSM: subverting virtual machine introspection for fun and profit, in: Proceedings of the 2010 29th IEEE Symposium on Reliable Distributed Systems, October 2010, pp. 82–91, http://dx.doi.org/10.1109/SRDS.2010.39.
[3] J. Cheng, S.H. Wong, H. Yang, S. Lu, SmartSiren: virus detection and alert for smartphones, in: Proceedings of the 5th International Conference on Mobile Systems, Applications and Services, 2007, pp. 258–271.
[4] H.H. Chou, S.D. Wang, An adaptive network intrusion detection approach for the cloud environment, in: 2015 International Carnahan Conference on Security Technology (ICCST), September 2015, pp. 1–6, http://dx.doi.org/10.1109/CCST.2015.7389649.

[5] T.-S. Chou, Security threats on cloud computing vulnerabilities, Int. J. Comput. Sci. Inf. Technol. 5 (3) (2013) 79.

[6] C.J. Chung, P. Khatkar, T. Xing, J. Lee, D. Huang, Nice: network intrusion detection and countermeasure selection in virtual network systems, IEEE Trans. Dependable Secure Comput. 10 (4) (July 2013) 198–211, http://dx.doi.org/10.1109/TDSC.2013.8.

[7] R. Creutzburg, Wikipedia Handbook of Computer Security and Digital Forensics 2016 – Part I – Computer Security, 2016, http://dx.doi.org/10.13140/RG.2.1.1166.8249.

[8] P. Faruki, A. Bharmal, V. Laxmi, V. Ganmoor, M.S. Gaur, M. Conti, M. Rajarajan, Android security: a survey of issues, malware penetration, and defenses, IEEE Commun. Surveys Tutorials 17 (2) (2015) 998–1022, http://dx.doi.org/10.1109/COMST.2014.2386139.

[9] I. Gartner, Gartner Says Worldwide Smartphone Sales Recorded Slowest Growth Rate since 2013, 2015. Retrieved from: http://www.gartner.com/newsroom/id/3115517.

[10] F. Ghaffari, M. Abadi, DroidMalHunter: a novel entropy-based anomaly detection system to detect malicious android applications, in: 2015 5th International Conference on Computer and Knowledge Engineering (ICCKE), October 2015, pp. 301–306, http://dx.doi.org/10.1109/ICCKE.2015.7365846.

[11] R.M. Jabir, S.I.R. Khanji, L.A. Ahmad, O. Alfandi, H. Said, Analysis of cloud computing attacks and countermeasures, in: 2016 18th International Conference on Advanced Communication Technology (ICACT), January 2016, p. 1, http://dx.doi.org/10.1109/ICACT.2016.7423295.

[12] S. Jadhav, S. Dutia, K. Calangutkar, T. Oh, Y.H. Kim, J.N. Kim, Cloud-based Android botnet malware detection system, in: 2015 17th International Conference on Advanced Communication Technology (ICACT), 2015, pp. 347–352.

[13] H.S. Kang, J.H. Son, C.S. Hong, Defense technique against spoofing attacks using reliable ARP table in cloud computing environment, in: 17th Asia-Pacific Network Operations and Management Symposium (APNOMS) 2015, August 2015, pp. 592–595, http://dx.doi.org/10.1109/APNOMS.2015.7275401.

[14] S.G. Kene, D.P. Theng, A review on intrusion detection techniques for cloud computing and security challenges, in: 2015 2nd International Conference on Electronics and Communication Systems (ICECS), February 2015, pp. 227–232, http://dx.doi.org/10.1109/ECS.2015.7124898.

[15] M. Keshavarzi, Traditional host based intrusion detection systems' challenges in cloud computing, Adv. Comput. Sci. Int. J. 3 (2) (2014) 133–138.

[16] I.M. Khalil, A. Khreishah, S. Bouktif, A. Ahmad, Security concerns in cloud computing, in: 2013 Tenth International Conference on Information Technology: New Generations (ITNG), 2013, pp. 411–416.

[17] M.A. Kumara, C.D. Jaidhar, Hypervisor and virtual machine dependent Intrusion Detection and Prevention System for virtualized cloud environment, in: 2015 1st International Conference on Telematics and Future Generation Networks (TAFGEN), IEEE, May 2015, pp. 28–33.

[18] N.S. Aljurayban, A. Emam, Framework for cloud intrusion detection system service, in: 2015 2nd World Symposium on Web Applications and Networking (WSWAN), March 2015, pp. 1–5, http://dx.doi.org/10.1109/WSWAN.2015.7210298.

[19] H. Kurniawan, Y. Rosmansyah, B. Dabarsyah, Android anomaly detection system using machine learning classification, in: 2015 International Conference on Electrical Engineering and Informatics (ICEEI), August 2015, pp. 288–293, http://dx.doi.org/10.1109/ICEEI.2015.7352512.

[20] J. Liu, H. Wu, H. Wang, A detection method for malicious codes in android apps, in: 10th International Conference on Wireless Communications, Networking and Mobile Computing (WiCOM 2014), September 2014, pp. 514–519, http://dx.doi.org/10.1049/ic.2014.0154.

[21] R. Madhubala, Survey on security concerns in cloud computing, in: 2015 International Conference on Green Computing and Internet of Things (ICGCIoT), IEEE, October 2015, pp. 1458–1462.

[22] T.M. Marengereke, K. Sornalakshmi, Cloud based security solution for android smartphones, in: 2015 International Conference on Circuit, Power and Computing Technologies (ICCPCT), March 2015, pp. 1–6, http://dx.doi.org/10.1109/ICCPCT.2015.7159512.

[23] A.K. Marnerides, M.R. Watson, N. Shirazi, A. Mauthe, D. Hutchison, Malware analysis in cloud computing: network and system characteristics, in: 2013 IEEE Globecom Workshops (GC Wkshps), December 2013, pp. 482–487, http://dx.doi.org/10.1109/GLOCOMW.2013.6825034.

[24] C.N. Modi, in: R.N. Shetty, N. Prasad, N. Nalini (Eds.), Emerging Research in Computing, Information, Communication and Applications: ERCICA 2015, vol. 1, Springer India, New Delhi, 2015, pp. 289–296. Retrieved from: http://dx.doi.org/10.1007/978-81-322-2550-8 28.

[25] H. Mohamed, L. Adil, T. Saida, M. Hicham, A collaborative intrusion detection and prevention system in cloud computing, in: AFRICON, 2013, September 2013, pp. 1–5, http://dx.doi.org/10.1109/AFRCON.2013.6757727.

[26] F.A. Narudin, A. Feizollah, N.B. Anuar, A. Gani, Evaluation of machine learning classifiers for mobile malware detection, Soft Comput. 20 (1) (2016) 343–357.

[27] J. Nikolai, Y. Wang, Hypervisor-based cloud intrusion detection system, in: 2014 International Conference on Computing, Networking and Communications (ICNC), February 2014, pp. 989–993, http://dx.doi.org/10.1109/ICCNC.2014.6785472.

[28] O.A. Osanaiye, Short paper: IP spoofing detection for preventing DDoS attack in cloud computing, in: 2015 18th International Conference on Intelligence in Next Generation Networks (ICIN), February 2015, pp. 139–141, http://dx.doi.org/10.1109/ICIN.2015.7073820.

[29] N. Peiravian, X. Zhu, Machine learning for android malware detection using permission and API calls, in: 2013 IEEE 25th International Conference on Tools with Artificial Intelligence (ICTAI), 2013, pp. 300–305.

[30] H. Pieterse, M.S. Olivier, Android botnets on the rise: trends and characteristics, in: 2012 Information Security for South Africa, August 2012, pp. 1–5, http://dx.doi.org/10.1109/ISSA.2012.6320432.

[31] N.A. Premathilaka, A.C. Aponso, N. Krishnarajah, Review on state of art intrusion detection systems designed for the cloud computing paradigm, in: 2013 47th International Carnahan Conference on Security Technology (ICCST), October 2013, pp. 1–6, http://dx.doi.org/10.1109/CCST.2013.6922049.

[32] T. Probst, E. Alata, M. Kaaniche, V. Nicomette, Automated evaluation of network intrusion detection systems in IaaS clouds, in: 2015 Eleventh European Dependable Computing Conference (EDCC), September 2015, pp. 49–60, http://dx.doi.org/10.1109/EDCC.2015.10.

[33] P. Samarati, S. De Capitani di Vimercati, Cloud Security: Issues and Concerns. Encyclopedia on Cloud Computing, Wiley, New York, 2016.

[34] B. Sanz, I. Santos, X. Ugarte-Pedrero, C. Laorden, J. Nieves, P.G. Bringas, Instance-based anomaly method for android malware detection, in: 2013 International Conference on Security and Cryptography (SECRYPT), July 2013, pp. 1–8.

[35] A. Saracino, D. Sgandurra, G. Dini, F. Martinelli, MADAM: effective and efficient behavior-based android malware detection and

prevention, IEEE Trans. Dependable Secure Comput. PP (99) (2016) 1, http://dx.doi.org/10.1109/TDSC.2016.2536605.

[36] T. Shen, Y. Zhongyang, Z. Xin, B. Mao, H. Huang, Detect android malware variants using component based topology graph, in: 2014 IEEE 13th International Conference on Trust, Security and Privacy in Computing and Communications, 2014, http://dx.doi.org/10.1109/trustcom.2014.52.

[37] Y. Shoaib, O. Das, Pouring Cloud Virtualization Security Inside Out, arXiv preprint arXiv:1411.3771, 2014.

[38] S. Subashini, V. Kavitha, A survey on security issues in service delivery models of cloud computing, J. Network Comput. Appl. 34 (1) (2011) 1–11.

[39] A. Tripathi, A. Mishra, Cloud computing security considerations, in: 2011 IEEE International Conference on Signal Processing, Communications and Computing (ICSPCC), September 2011, pp. 1–5, http://dx.doi.org/10.1109/ICSPCC.2011.6061557.

[40] K. Walker, Cloud Security Alliance Releases the Treacherous Twelve Cloud Computing Top Threats in 2016, 2016. Retrieved from: https://cloudsecurityalliance.org/media/news/cloud-security-alliance-releases-the-treacherous-twelve-cloud-computing-top-threats-in-2016/.

[41] M.R. Watson, N.U.H. Shirazi, A.K. Marnerides, A. Mauthe, D. Hutchison, Malware detection in cloud computing infrastructures, IEEE Trans. Dependable Secure Comput. 13 (2) (March 2016) 192–205, http://dx.doi.org/10.1109/TDSC.2015.2457918.

[42] Q. Yan, F.R. Yu, Q. Gong, J. Li, Software-defined networking (SDN) and distributed denial of service (DDoS) attacks in cloud computing environments: a survey, some research issues, and challenges, IEEE Commun. Surveys Tutorials 18 (1) (2016) 602–622, http://dx.doi.org/10.1109/COMST.2015 .2487361.

[43] S.F. Yang, W.Y. Chen, Y.T. Wang, ICAS: an inter-VM IDS log cloud analysis system, in: 2011 IEEE International Conference on Cloud Computing and Intelligence Systems, September 2011, pp. 285–289, http://dx.doi.org/10.1109/CCIS.2011.6045076.

[44] S.Y. Yerima, S. Sezer, G. McWilliams, I. Muttik, A new Android malware detection approach using bayesian classification, in: 2013 IEEE 27th International Conference on Advanced Information Networking and Applications (AINA), March 2013, pp. 121–128, http://dx.doi.org/10.1109/AINA.2013.88.

[45] S.Y. Yerima, S. Sezer, I. Muttik, High accuracy android malware detection using ensemble learning, IET Inf. Security 9 (6) (2015) 313–320.

[46] M. Yesilyurt, Y. Yalman, Security threats on mobile devices and their effects: estimations for the future, Int. J. Security Its Appl. 10 (2) (2016) 13–26.

[47] Z. Yuan, Y. Lu, Y. Xue, DroidDetector: Android malware characterization and detection using deep learning, Tsinghua Sci. Technol. 21 (1) (February 2016) 114–123, http://dx.doi.org/10.1109/TST.2016.7399288.

[48] M. Zbakh, K. Elmahdi, R. Cherkaoui, S. Enniari, A multi-criteria analysis of intrusion detection architectures in cloud environments, in: 2015 International Conference on Cloud Technologies and Applications (CloudTech), June 2015, pp. 1–9, http://dx.doi.org/10.1109/CloudTech.2015.7336967.

Chapter 7

Preventing System Intrusions

Michael A. West

Truestone Maritime Operations, Martinez, CA, United States

There's a war raging across the globe, and you're right in the middle of it. But while this war doesn't include gunfire and mass carnage, its effects can be thoroughly devastating nonetheless. This war is being waged in cyberspace by people bent on stealing the heart and soul of your business, your company's plans and secrets, or worse, your client names and their financial information.

So how bad is it? Just what are you up against?

Imagine this: You're in charge of security for an advanced movie screening. You've been hired and assigned the daunting task of keeping the advanced screening from being copied and turned into a bootleg version available overseas or on the web. So how do you make sure that doesn't happen (how many times have we heard about this scenario or seen it in the movies)?

First, you might start by controlling access to the theater itself, allowing only the holders of very tightly controlled tickets into the screening. You post a couple of personnel at the door who carefully check every ticket against a list to verify the identity of both the ticket holder and their numbered ticket. Your goal is clear: restrict the viewers and, hopefully, reduce the possibility of someone entering with a counterfeit ticket. But what about the back stage door? While you're busy watching the front door, someone could simply sneak in the back. So, you secure that door and post a guard. But what about the ventilation system (the ventilation system is a favorite Hollywood scenario—remember Tom Cruise in *Mission Impossible*)? So, you secure that too. You also secure the projection room.

Did you think about a ticket holder coming into the theater with a digital recording device? Or a recording device surreptitiously planted just outside the projection room before anyone even entered. Or, worse, someone who rigged up a digital recording system that captures the movie from *inside* the projector and feeds it directly to their computer?

The point is this: No matter how diligent you are at securing your network, there are always people waiting outside who are just as motivated to steal what you're trying to protect as you are trying to keep them from stealing it. You put up a wall; they use a back door. You secure the back door; they come in through a window. You secure the windows; they sneak in through the ventilation system. You secure the ventilation system; they simply bypass the physical security measures and go straight for your users, turning them into unwitting thieves. And so on and so on.

There's a very delicate balance between the need to keep your network secured and allowing user access. Users may be your company's lifeblood, but they are simultaneously your greatest and most necessary asset, and your weakest link.

It almost sounds like an impossible task, doesn't it? It's easy to see how it might seem that way when a casual Internet search reveals no shortage of sites selling hacking tools. In some cases, the hacking tools were written for— and marketed to—those not schooled in programming languages.

When I wrote this chapter three years ago, the cyber world was a very different place. Back then, crackers were simply stealing credit-card numbers and financial data (for example, in January, hackers penetrated the customer database for online shoe store giant Zappos and stole names, email addresses, shipping addresses, phone numbers, and the last four digits of credit-card numbers for over 24 million customers), siphoning corporate proprietary information (also known as industrial espionage), and defacing websites.

In today's world, crackers twice took control of an American satellite called Terra Eos, not just interrupting data flow, but taking full control of the satellite's guidance systems. They literally could have given the satellite

Computer and Information Security Handbook. http://dx.doi.org/10.1016/B978-0-12-803843-7.00007-7

commands to start a de-orbit burn.[1] And there's no shortage of some very simple and readily accessible software tools that allow crackers to sit nearby, say, in a coffee shop and wirelessly follow your web browsing, steal your passwords, or even assume your identity.

Now, who do you think could pull off a feat like that? Most likely, it's not your neighbor's kid or the cyberpunk with just enough skill to randomly deface websites. Many experts believe this effort was well funded, most likely with government sponsorship. The Chinese military believes that attacking the communications links between ground stations and orbiting satellites is a legitimate strategy at the outset of any conflict. If that's the case, then a government-sponsored attack is a frightening prospect.

The moment you established an active web presence, you put a target on your company's back. And like the hapless insect that lands in the spider's web, your company's size determines the size of the disturbance you create on the web—and how quickly you're noticed by the bad guys. How attractive you are as prey is usually directly proportionate to what you have to offer a predator. If yours is an e-commerce site whose business thrives on credit card or other financial information or a company with valuable secrets to steal, your "juiciness" quotient goes up; you have more of value there to steal. And if your business is new and your web presence is recent, the assumption could be made that perhaps you're not yet a seasoned veteran in the nuances of cyber warfare and, thus, are more vulnerable to an intrusion.

Unfortunately for you, many of those who seek to penetrate your network defenses are educated, highly motivated, and quite brilliant at developing faster and more efficient methods of quietly sneaking around your perimeter, checking for the smallest of openings. Most IT professionals know that an enterprise's firewall is relentlessly being probed for weaknesses and vulnerabilities by crackers from every corner of the globe. Anyone who follows news about software understands that seemingly every few months, word comes out about a new, exploitable opening in an operating system or application. It's widely understood that no one—not the savviest network administrator, or the programmer who wrote the software—can possibly find and close all the holes in today's increasingly complex software.

Despite the increased sophistication of today's software applications, bugs and holes exist in those applications, as well as in operating systems, server processes (daemons), and client applications. System configurations can be easily exploited, especially if you don't change the default administrator's password, or if you simply accept default

system settings, or unintentionally leave a gaping hole open by configuring the machine to run in a nonsecure mode. Even Transmission Control Protocol/Internet Protocol (TCP/IP), the foundation on which all Internet traffic operates, can be exploited, since the protocol was designed before the threat of hacking was really widespread. Therefore, it contains design flaws that can allow, for example, a cracker to easily alter IP data.

Once the word gets out that a new and exploitable opening exists in an application (and word *will* get out), crackers around the world start scanning sites on the Internet searching for any and all sites that have that particular opening.

Making your job even harder is the fact that many of the openings into your network are caused by your employees. Casual surfing of online shopping sites, porn sites, and even banking sites can expose your network to all kinds of nasty bugs and malicious code, simply because an employee visited the site. The problem is that, to users, it might not seem like such a big deal. They either don't realize that they're leaving the network wide open to intrusion, or they don't care.

1. SO, WHAT IS AN INTRUSION?

A network intrusion is an unauthorized penetration of your enterprise's network, or an individual machine address in your assigned domain. Intrusions can be passive (in which the penetration is gained stealthily and without detection) or active (in which changes to network resources are effected). Intrusions can come from outside your network structure or inside (an employee, a customer, or business partner). Some intrusions are simply meant to let you know the intruder was there by defacing your website with various kinds of messages or crude images. Others are more malicious, seeking to extract critical information on either a one-time basis or as an ongoing parasitic relationship that continues to siphon off data until it's discovered. Some intruders implant carefully crafted code, such as Trojan-type malicious software (malware), designed to steal passwords, record keystrokes, or open an application's "back door."

Still worse, some high-end crackers can set up phony websites that exactly mimic your company's site, and surreptitiously redirect your unaware users away from your site to theirs (known as a "man in the browser attack"). Others will embed themselves into your network like a tick, quietly siphoning off data until found and rendered inert.

An attacker can get into your system physically (by gaining physical access to a restricted machine's hard drive and/or BIOS), externally (by attacking your web servers or finding a way to bypass your firewall), or internally (your own users, customers, or partners).

---

1. ABC News, November 16, 2011.

2. SOBERING NUMBERS

So how often do these intrusions and data thefts occur? The estimates are staggering: In August of 2009, InfoTech Spotlight reported that "cybercrime costs organizations an average of $3.8 million per year,"[2] and there are thousands of new, fake phishing[3] websites set up online every day. The *APWG Phishing Activity Trends Report* for the first half of 2011 shows that even though unique phishing reports are down 35% (from an all-time high of 40,621 in August of 2009), data-stealing Trojan malware reached an all-time high in the first half of 2011 and comprised almost *half* of all detected malware. And from January to June of 2011, the number of new malware samples hit a whopping 11,777,775—an increase of 13% from the second half of 2010![4]

A March 2010 report by Security Management revealed that the most common Internet fraud complaints are from people whose identities have been compromised.[5] On two occasions, I myself have been the victim of a stolen credit-card number. In one case, a purchase was made at a jewelry store in Texas, and in the other, the purchases were made at a grocery store in the Philippines.

The Federal Bureau of Investigation (FBI) reports receiving over 330,000 identity theft reports, with losses estimated at over $560 million. And McAfee reports estimate business losses topped $1 trillion! Sadly, this number is likely to climb; 72% of newly detected malware are Trojans capable of stealing user information.

Not surprisingly, financial services are still the hardest hit and most frequently targeted sector, and account for almost half of all industry attacks. In the first half of 2011, new and more malevolent types of "Crimeware" (software specifically designed to steal customer information such as credit-card data, Social Security numbers, and customers' financial website credentials) appeared. Patrik Runald, senior manager of Security Research at Websense, has stated: "With cybercrime being an industry generating hundreds of millions of dollars for the bad guys, it's clear that this is a trend we will see for a long time."[6]

Unfortunately, the United States continues to host the highest number of infected phishing sites: Nearly 60% of all malware-infected URLs comes from the United States.

In today's cyber battlefield, attacks are specifically targeting one organization as a prelude to attacking and penetrating others. And if you're an enterprise's IT professional, you need to make a fundamental shift in mind-set away from trying to build the most impressive defenses that money can buy to thinking seriously about defense and detection. The reality is, you have to assume you have been or soon will be compromised.

Even the big boys in cybersecurity aren't immune. In March of 2010, RSA was among hundreds of major companies compromised in a massive, coordinated cyber-attack. The attackers penetrated RSA's formidable defenses and made off with information that RSA said could "reduce the effectiveness" of its widely used SecurID authentication system. In what the cyber security industry refers to as an "advanced persistent threat," the crackers used the information they stole from RSA to attack defense contractor Lockheed Martin.[7]

Whatever the goal of the intrusion—fun, greed, bragging rights, or data theft—the end result will be the same: Someone discovered and exploited a weakness in your network security, and until you discover that weakness—the intrusion entry point—it will continue to be an open door into your environment.

So, just who's out there looking to break into your network?

3. KNOW YOUR ENEMY: HACKERS VERSUS CRACKERS

An entire community of people—experts in programming and computer networking and those who thrive on solving complex problems—have been around since the earliest days of computing. The term *hacker* originated from the members of this culture, and they are quick to point out that it was hackers who built and make the Internet run, and hackers who created the Unix operating system. Hackers see themselves as members of a community that builds things and makes them work. And to those in their culture, the term *cracker* is a badge of honor.

Ask a traditional hacker about people who sneak into computer systems to steal data or cause havoc, and he'll most likely correct you by telling you those people aren't true hackers. (In the cracker community, the term for these types is *cracker*, and the two labels aren't synonymous.) So, to not offend traditional hackers, I'll use the term *crackers* and focus on them and their efforts.

From the lone-wolf cracker seeking peer recognition to the disgruntled former employee out for revenge or the deep pockets and seemingly unlimited resources of a hostile government bent on taking down wealthy capitalists, crackers are out there in force, looking to find the chink in your system's defensive armor.

2. Bright Hub, Cyber Crime Costs/Cyber Crime Losses, September 13, 2010.

3. Phishing is an attempt to steal user information (e.g., usernames, passwords, credit-card information, etc.) by disguising phony websites as legitimate ones the user may be accustomed to accessing.

4. Panda Security, PandaLabs.

5. Uptick in Cybercrime Cost Victims Big in 2009, FBI Report Says, *Security Manage* (March 15, 2010).

6. APWG Phishing Activity Trends Report.

7. CNNMoney, February 28, 2012.

The crackers' specialty—or in some cases, their mission in life—is to seek out and exploit the vulnerabilities of an individual computer or network for their own purposes. Crackers' intentions are normally malicious and/or criminal in nature. They have, at their disposal, a vast library of information designed to help them hone their tactics, skills, and knowledge, and they can tap into the almost unlimited experience of other crackers through a community of like-minded individuals sharing information across underground networks.

They usually begin this life learning the most basic of skills: software programming. The ability to write code that can make a computer do what they want is seductive in and of itself. As they learn more and more about programming, they also expand their knowledge of operating systems and, as a natural course of progression, operating systems' weaknesses. They also quickly learn that, to expand the scope and type of their illicit handiwork, they need to learn HTML—the code that allows them to create phony web pages that lure unsuspecting users into revealing important financial or personal data.

There are vast underground organizations to which these new crackers can turn for information. They hold meetings, write papers, and develop tools that they pass along to each other. Each new acquaintance they meet fortifies their skill set and gives them the training to branch out to more and more sophisticated techniques. Once they gain a certain level of proficiency, they begin their trade in earnest.

They start off simply by researching potential target firms on the Internet (an invaluable source for all kinds of corporate network related information). Once a target has been identified, they might quietly tiptoe around, probing for old forgotten back doors and operating system vulnerabilities. As starting points for launching an attack, they can simply and innocuously run basic DNS queries that can provide IP addresses (or ranges of IP addresses). They might sit back and listen to inbound and/or outbound traffic, record IP addresses, and test for weaknesses by pinging various devices or users.

To breach your network, a cracker starts by creating a chain of exploited systems in which each successful takeover sets the stage for the next. The easiest systems to exploit are those in our homes: Most home users do little to secure their systems from outside intrusions. And a good cracker can implant malware so deeply in a home computer that the owner never knows it's there. Then, when they're asleep or away, the malware takes control of the home computer and starts sending out newly mutated versions to another compromised system. In this way, there are so many compromised systems between them and the intrusion that it sends investigators down long, twisted paths that can include dozens, if not hundreds, of unwittingly compromised systems. Once your network is breached,

they can surreptitiously implant password cracking or recording applications, keystroke recorders, or other malware designed to keep their unauthorized connection alive—and profitable. From there, they sit back and siphon off whatever they deem most valuable.

The cracker wants to act like a cyber-ninja, sneaking up to and penetrating your network without leaving any trace of the incursion. Some more seasoned crackers can put multiple layers of machines, many hijacked, between them and your network to hide their activity. Like standing in a room full of mirrors, the attack appears to be coming from so many locations you can't pick out the real from the ghost. And before you realize what they've done, they've up and disappeared like smoke in the wind.

4. MOTIVES

Though the goal is the same—to penetrate your network defenses—crackers' motives are often different. In some cases, a network intrusion could be done from the inside by a disgruntled employee looking to hurt the organization or steal company secrets for profit.

There are large groups of crackers working diligently to steal credit-card information that they then turn around and make available for sale. They want a quick grab and dash—take what they want and leave. Their cousins are the network parasites—those who quietly breach your network, then sit there siphoning off data.

A new and very disturbing trend is the discovery that certain governments have been funding digital attacks on network resources of both federal and corporate systems. Various agencies from the US Department of Defense to the governments of New Zealand, France, and Germany have reported attacks originating from unidentified Chinese hacking groups. It should be noted that the Chinese government denies any involvement, and there is no evidence that it is or was involved.

5. THE CRACKERS' TOOLS OF THE TRADE

Over the years, the tools available to crackers have become increasingly more sophisticated. How sophisticated?

Most security software products available today have three basic methods of spotting malicious software. First, it scans all incoming data traffic for traces of known malware (pulling malware characteristics from a source database). Then, it looks for any kind of suspicious activity (e.g., vulnerable processes unexpectedly activating or running too long, unusual activity during normally dormant periods, etc.). And finally, the security software checks for indications of information leaving from abnormal paths or processes.

Recently, however, a relatively new and extremely malicious malware program called Zeus has appeared. Designed specifically to steal financial information, Zeus can defeat these methods by not only sitting discreetly and quietly—not drawing attention to itself but also by changing its appearance tens of thousands of times per day. But its most insidious characteristic is that it siphons data off from an infected system using your browser. Called a "man in the browser attack," Zeus implants itself in your browser, settling in between you and a legitimate website (say, the site for the financial institution that manages your IRA), and very capably altering what you see to the point at which you really can't tell the difference. Not knowing the difference, you confidently enter your most important financial details, which Zeus siphons off and sends to someone else. New Zeus updates come out regularly, and, once released, it can take weeks for its new characteristics to become known by security software companies.

Our "Unsecured" Wireless World

Do you think much about the time you spend using a coffee shop's free Wi-Fi signal to surf, check your email, or update your Facebook page? Probably not. But today, the person sitting next to you quietly sipping her coffee and working away on her laptop can now sit back and watch what websites you've visited, then assume your identity and log on to the sites you visited. How? A free program called Firesheep can grab from your web browser the cookies[8] for each site you visit. That cookie contains identifying information about your computer, and site settings for each site you visit plus your customized private information for that site. Once Firesheep grabs that cookie, a malicious user can use it to log on to sites as you, and can, in some cases, gain full access to your account.

You may be asking yourself, "So what does this have to do with my network?" If the unsuspecting user is wirelessly completing a sales transaction or bank transfer when software like Firesheep snatches the browser cookie, the cracker can log back into your site as the compromised user and drain your account.

In years past, only the most experienced and savvy crackers with expensive tools and plenty of time could do much damage to secured networks. But like a professional thief with custom-made lock picks, crackers today can obtain a frightening array of tools to covertly test your network for weak spots. Their tools range from simple password-stealing malware and keystroke recorders (loggers) to methods of implanting sophisticated parasitic software strings that copy data streams coming in from customers who want to perform an e-commerce transaction with your company. Some of the more widely used tools include these:

- *Wireless sniffers.* Not only can these devices locate wireless signals within a certain range, they can siphon off the data being transmitted over the signals. With the rise in popularity and use of remote wireless devices, this practice is increasingly responsible for the loss of critical data and represents a significant headache for IT departments.
- *Packet sniffers.* Once implanted in a network data stream, these tools passively analyze data packets moving into and out of a network interface, and utilities capture data packets passing through a network interface.
- *Port scanners.* A good analogy for these utilities is a thief casing a neighborhood, looking for an open or unlocked door. These utilities send out successive, sequential connection requests to a target system's ports to see which one responds or is open to the request. Some port scanners allow the cracker to slow the rate of port scanning—sending connection requests over a longer period of time—so the intrusion attempt is less likely to be noticed. The usual targets of these devices are old, forgotten "back doors," or ports inadvertently left unguarded after network modifications.
- *Port knocking.* Sometimes network administrators create a secret backdoor method of getting through firewall-protected ports—a secret knock that enables them to quickly access the network. Port-knocking tools find these unprotected entries and implant a Trojan horse that listens to network traffic for evidence of that secret knock.
- *Keystroke loggers.* These are spyware utilities planted on vulnerable systems that record a user's keystrokes. Obviously, when someone can sit back and record every keystroke a user makes, it doesn't take long to obtain things like usernames, passwords, and ID numbers.
- *Remote administration tools.* Programs embedded on an unsuspecting user's system that allow the cracker to take control of that system.
- *Network scanners.* Explore networks to see the number and kind of host systems on a network, the services available, the host's operating system, and the type of packet filtering or firewalls being used.
- *Password crackers.* These sniff networks for data streams associated with passwords, then employ a brute-force method of peeling away any encryption layers protecting those passwords.

---

8. Cookies are bits of software code sent to your browser by websites. They can be used for authentication, session identification, preferences, shopping cart contents, and so on.

6. BOTS

Three years ago, bots were an emerging threat. Now, organized cyber criminals have begun to create and sell kits on the open market that inexperienced nonprogramming crackers can use to create their own botnets. It offers a wide variety of easy to use (or preprogrammed) modules that specifically target the most lucrative technologies. It includes a management console that can control every infected system and interrogate bot-infected machines. If desired, Zeus kit modules are available that can allow the user to create viruses that mutate every time they're implanted in a new host system.

So what are bots? Bots, also known as an Internet bots, web robots, or World Wide Web (WWW) robots, are small software applications running automated tasks over the Internet. Usually, they run simple tasks that a human would otherwise have to perform, but at a much faster rate. When used maliciously, they are a virus, surreptitiously implanted in large numbers of unprotected computers (usually those found in homes), hijacking them (without the owners' knowledge) and turning them into slaves to do the cracker's bidding. These compromised computers, known as *bots*, are linked in vast and usually untraceable networks called *botnets*. Botnets are designed to operate in such a way that instructions come from a central PC and are rapidly shared among other botted computers in the network. Newer botnets are now using a "peer-to-peer" method that, because they lack a central identifiable point of control, makes it difficult if not impossible for law enforcement agencies to pinpoint. And because they often cross international boundaries into countries without the means (or will) to investigate and shut them down, they can grow with alarming speed. They can be so lucrative that they've now become the cracker's tool of choice.

There are all kinds of bots; there are bots that harvest email addresses (spambots), viruses, and worms, filename modifiers, bots to buy up large numbers of concert seats, and bots that work together in botnets, or coordinated attacks on networked computers.

Botnets exist largely because of the number of users who fail to observe basic principles of computer security—installed and/or up-to-date antivirus software, regular scans for suspicious code, and so on—and thereby become unwitting accomplices. Once taken over and "botted," their machines are turned into channels through which large volumes of unwanted spam or malicious code can be quickly distributed. Current estimates are that, of the 800 million computers on the Internet, up to 40% are bots controlled by cyber thieves who are using them to spread new viruses, send out unwanted spam email, overwhelm websites in denial-of-service (DoS) attacks, or siphon off sensitive user data from banking or shopping websites that look and act like legitimate sites with which customers have previously done business.

Bot controllers, also called *herders*, can also make money by leasing their networks to others who need a large and untraceable means of sending out massive amounts of advertisements but don't have the financial or technical resources to create their own networks. Making matters worse is the fact that botnet technology is available on the Internet for less than $100, which makes it relatively easy to get started in what can be a very lucrative business.

7. SYMPTOMS OF INTRUSIONS

As stated earlier, merely being on the web puts a target on your back. It's only a matter of time before you experience your first attack. It could be something as innocent looking as several failed login attempts or as obvious as an attacker having defaced your website or crippled your network. It's important that you go into this knowing you're vulnerable.

Crackers are going to first look for known weaknesses in the operating system (OS) or any applications you are using. Next, they would start probing, looking for holes, open ports, or forgotten back doors—faults in your security posture that can quickly or easily be exploited.

Arguably one of the most common symptoms of an intrusion—either attempted or successful—is repeated signs that someone is trying to take advantage of your organization's own security systems, and the tools you use to keep watch for suspicious network activity may actually be used against you quite effectively. Tools such as network security and file integrity scanners, which can be invaluable in helping you conduct ongoing assessments of your network's vulnerability, are also available and can be used by crackers looking for a way in.

Large numbers of unsuccessful login attempts are also a good indicator that your system has been targeted. The best penetration-testing tools can be configured with attempt thresholds that, when exceeded, will trigger an alert. They can passively distinguish between legitimate and suspicious activity of a repetitive nature, monitor the time intervals between activities (alerting when the number exceeds the threshold you set), and build a database of signatures seen multiple times over a given period.

The "human element" (your users) is a constant factor in your network operations. Users will frequently enter a mistyped response but usually correct the error on the next try. However, a sequence of mistyped commands or incorrect login responses (with attempts to recover or reuse them) can be a signs of brute-force intrusion attempts.

Packet inconsistencies—direction (inbound or outbound), originating address or location, and session characteristics (ingoing sessions versus outgoing sessions)—can also be good indicators of an attack. If a packet has an unusual source or has been addressed to an abnormal port—say, an inconsistent service request—it could be a sign of random system scanning. Packets coming from the outside that have local network addresses that request services on the inside can be a sign that IP spoofing is being attempted.

Sometimes odd or unexpected system behavior is itself a sign. Though this is sometimes difficult to track, you should be aware of activity such as changes to system clocks, servers going down or server processes inexplicably stopping (with system restart attempts), system resource issues (such as unusually high CPU activity or overflows in file systems), audit logs behaving in strange ways (decreasing in size without administrator intervention), or unexpected user access to resources. You should investigate any and all unusual activity at regular times on given days, heavy system use (possible DoS attack), or CPU use (brute-force password-cracking attempts).

8. WHAT CAN YOU DO?

It goes without saying that the most secure network—the one that has the least chance of being compromised—is the one that has no direct connection to the outside world. But that's hardly a practical solution, since the whole reason you have a web presence is to do business. And in the game of Internet commerce, your biggest concern isn't the sheep coming in but the wolves dressed like sheep coming in with them. So, how do you strike an acceptable balance between keeping your network intrusion free and keeping it accessible at the same time?

As your company's network administrator, you walk a fine line between network security and user needs. You have to have a good defensive posture that still allows for access. Users and customers can be both the lifeblood of your business and its greatest potential source of infection. Furthermore, if your business thrives on allowing users access, you have no choice but to let them in. It seems like a monumentally difficult task at best.

Like a castle, imposing but stationary, every defensive measure you put up will eventually be compromised by the legions of very motivated thieves looking to get in. It's a game of move/countermove: You adjust, they adapt. So you have to start with defenses that can quickly and effectively adapt and change as the outside threats adapt.

First and foremost, you need to make sure that your perimeter defenses are as strong as they can be, and that means keeping up with the rapidly evolving threats around you. The days of relying solely on a firewall that simply does firewall functions are gone; today's crackers have figured out how to bypass the firewall by exploiting weaknesses in applications themselves. Simply being reactive to hits and intrusions isn't a very good option either; that's like standing there waiting for someone to hit you before deciding what to do rather than seeing the oncoming punch and moving out of its way or blocking it. You need to be flexible in your approach to the newest technologies, constantly auditing your defenses to ensure

that your network's defensive armor can meet the latest threat. You have to have a very dynamic and effective policy of constantly monitoring for suspicious activities that, when discovered, can be quickly dealt with so that someone doesn't slip something past without your noticing it. Once that happens, it's too late.

Next, and this is also a crucial ingredient for network administrators: You have to educate your users. No matter how good a job you've done at tightening up your network security processes and systems, you still have to deal with the weakest link in your armor—your users. It doesn't do any good to have bulletproof processes in place if they're so difficult to manage that users work around them to avoid the difficulty, or if they're so loosely configured that a casually surfing user who visits an infected site will pass that infection along to your network. The degree of difficulty in securing your network increases dramatically as the number of users goes up.

User education becomes particularly important where mobile computing is concerned. Losing a device, using it in a place (or manner) in which prying eyes can see passwords or data, awareness of hacking tools specifically designed to sniff wireless signals for data, and logging on to unsecured networks are all potential problem areas with which users need to be familiar.

A relatively new tool is the intrusion detection system (IDS). IDSs merge their deep packet scanning with a firewall's blocking can filter capabilities. A good IDS and not only detect intrusion attempts, but also stop the attack before it does any damage.

One type of IDS, known as an inline IDS, can sit between your network's outside interface and your most critical systems. They essentially inspect every data packet headed for those critical systems, sniffing and "tasting" them, then scrubbing out the ones that have suspicious characteristics.

Another type of IDS is based on an application firewall scheme. These types of IDSs sit on all protected servers and are configured to protect specific applications. They are designed to "learn" every aspect of an application—how it interacts with users and the Internet, how the application's features play with each other, and what "customizable" features the application has that may require more detailed configuration—then create a rule for dealing with those aspects. This last point reveals a drawback of application-based IDSs: In order for them to protect all aspects of the application, it has to "know" every aspect of the application. The only way you can configure the IDS to protect every one of the application's functions is to let it "learn" the functions by exercising them. It can't develop a protection rule for a feature with which it's unfamiliar. So thorough testing is needed, or the IDS may miss a particular vulnerability. And if you update the protected application, you'll need to exercise its features again to ensure the IDS knows what it's supposed to protect.

You can also set up a decoy—sort of the "sacrificial lamb"—as bait. Also known as "honey pots," these userless networks are specifically set up to draw in an attacker and gain valuable data on the methods, tools, and any new malware they might be using.

Know Today's Network Needs

The traditional approach to network security engineering has been to try to erect preventative measures—firewalls—to protect the infrastructure from intrusion. The firewall acts like a filter, catching anything that seems suspicious and keeping everything behind it as sterile as possible. However, though firewalls are good, they typically don't do much in the way of identifying compromised applications that use network resources. And with the speed of evolution seen in the area of penetration tools, an approach designed simply to prevent attacks will be less and less effective.

Today's computing environment is no longer confined to the office, as it used to be. Though there are still fixed systems inside the firewall, ever more sophisticated remote and mobile devices are making their way into the workforce. This influx of mobile computing has expanded the traditional boundaries of the network to farther and farther reaches and requires a different way of thinking about network security requirements.

Your network's endpoint or perimeter is mutating—expanding beyond its historical boundaries. Until recently, that endpoint was the user, either a desktop system or laptop, and it was relatively easy to secure those devices. To use a metaphor: The difference between endpoints of early network design and those of today is like the difference between the battles of World War II and the current war on terror. In the World War II battles there were very clearly defined "front lines"—one side controlled by the Allied powers, the other by the Axis. Today, the war on terror has no such front lines and is fought in multiple areas with different techniques and strategies that are customized for each combat theater.

With today's explosion of remote users and mobile computing, your network's endpoint is no longer as clearly defined as it once was, and it is evolving at a very rapid pace. For this reason, your network's physical perimeter can no longer be seen as your best "last line of defense," even though having a robust perimeter security system is still a critical part of your overall security policy.

Any policy you develop should be organized in such a way as to take advantage of the strength of your unified threat management (UTM) system. Firewalls, antivirus, and IDSs, for example, work by trying to block all currently known threats—the "blacklist" approach. But the threats evolve more quickly than the UTM systems can, so it almost always ends up being an "after the fact" game of

catch-up. Perhaps a better, and more easily managed, policy is to specifically state which devices are allowed access and which applications are allowed to run in your network's applications. This "whitelist" approach helps reduce the amount of time and energy needed to keep up with the rapidly evolving pace of threat sophistication, because you're specifying what gets in versus what you have to keep out.

Any UTM system you employ should provide the means of doing two things: specify which applications and devices are allowed and offer a policy-based approach to managing those applications and devices. It should allow you to secure your critical resources against unauthorized data extraction (or data leakage), offer protection from the most persistent threats (viruses, malware, and spyware), and evolve with the ever-changing spectrum of devices and applications designed to penetrate your outer defenses.

So, what's the best strategy for integrating these new remote endpoints? First, you have to realize that these new remote, mobile technologies are becoming increasingly ubiquitous and aren't going away anytime soon. In fact, they most likely represent the future of computing. As these devices gain in sophistication and function, they are unchaining end users from their desks and, for some businesses, are indispensable tools. iPhones, Blackberries, Palm Treos, and other smart phones and devices now have the capability to interface with corporate email systems, access networks, run enterprise-level applications, and do full-featured remote computing. As such, they also now carry an increased risk for network administrators due to loss or theft (especially if the device is unprotected by a robust authentication method) and unauthorized interception of their wireless signals from which data can be siphoned off.

To cope with the inherent risks, you engage an effective security policy for dealing with these devices: Under what conditions can they be used, how many of your users need to employ them, what levels and types of access will they have, and how will they be authenticated?

Solutions are available for adding strong authentication to users seeking access via wireless LANs. Tokens, either of the hardware or software variety, are used to identify the user to an authentication server for verification of their credentials. For example, SafeNet's SafeWord can handle incoming access requests from a wireless access point and, if the user is authenticated, pass them into the network.

Key among the steps you take to secure your network while allowing mobile computing is to fully educate the users of such technology. They need to understand, in no uncertain terms, the risks to your network (and ultimately to the company in general) represented by their mobile devices, and they also need to be aware that their mindfulness of both the device's physical and electronic security is an absolute necessity.

Network Security Best Practices

So, how do you either clean and tighten up your existing network, or design a new one that can stand up to the inevitable onslaught of attacks? Let's look at some basics. Consider the diagram shown in Fig. 7.1.

Fig. 7.1 shows what could be a typical network layout. Users outside the demilitarized zone (DMZ) approach the network via a secure (HTTPS) web or virtual private network (VPN) connection. They are authenticated by the perimeter firewall and handed off to either a web server or a VPN gateway. If allowed to pass, they can then access resources inside the network.

If you're the administrator of an organization that has only, say, a couple dozen users with whom to contend, your task (and the illustration layout) will be relatively easy to manage. But if you have to manage several hundred (or several thousand) users, the complexity of your task increases by an order of magnitude. That makes a good security policy an absolute necessity.

9. SECURITY POLICIES

Like the tedious prep work before painting a room, organizations need a good, detailed, and well-written security policy. Not something that should be rushed through "just to get it done," your security policy should be well thought out; in other words, the "devil is in the details." Your security policy is designed to get everyone involved with your network "thinking along the same lines."

The policy is almost always a work in progress. It must evolve with technology, especially those technologies aimed at surreptitiously getting into your system. The threats will continue to evolve, as will the systems designed to hold them at bay.

A good security policy isn't always a single document; rather, it is a conglomeration of policies that address specific areas, such as computer and network use, forms of authentication, email policies, remote/mobile technology use, and web surfing policies. It should be written in such a way that, while comprehensive, it can be easily understood by those it affects. Along those lines, your policy doesn't have to be overly complex. If you hand new employees something that resembles *War and Peace* in size and tell them they're responsible for knowing its content, you can expect to have continued problems maintaining good network security awareness. Keep it simple.

First, you need to draft some policies that define your network and its basic architecture. A good place to start is by asking the following questions:

- What kinds of resources need to be protected (user financial or medical data, credit-card information, etc.)?
- How many users will be accessing the network on the inside (employees, contractors, etc.)?
- Will there need to be access only at certain times or on a 24/7 basis (and across multiple time zones and/or internationally)?
- What kind of budget do I have?
- Will remote users be accessing the network, and if so, how many?

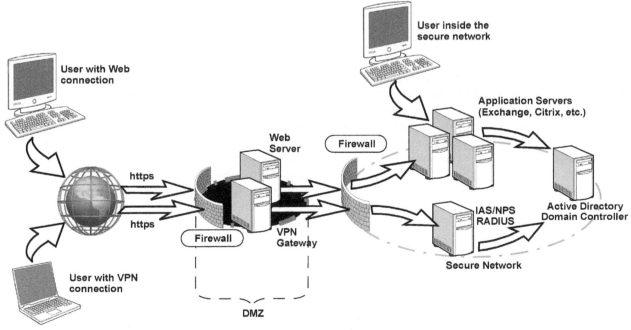

FIGURE 7.1 Network diagram.

- Will there be remote sites in geographically distant locations (requiring a failsafe mechanism, such as replication, to keep data synched across the network)?

Next, you should spell out responsibilities for security requirements, communicate your expectations to your users (one of the weakest links in any security policy), and lay out the role(s) for your network administrator. It should list policies for activities such as web surfing, downloading, local and remote access, and types of authentication. You should address issues such as adding users, assigning privileges, dealing with lost tokens or compromised passwords, and under what circumstances you will remove users from the access database.

You should establish a security team (sometimes referred to as a "tiger team") whose responsibility it will be to create security policies that are practical, workable, and sustainable. They should come up with the best plan for implementing these policies in a way that addresses both network resource protection and user friendliness. They should develop plans for responding to threats as well as schedules for updating equipment and software. And there should be a very clear policy for handling changes to overall network security—the types of connections through your firewall that will and will not be allowed. This is especially important because you don't want an unauthorized user gaining access, reaching into your network, and simply taking files or data.

10. RISK ANALYSIS

You should have some kind of risk analysis done to determine, as near as possible, the risks you face with the kind of operations you conduct (e-commerce, classified/proprietary information handling, partner access, or the like). Depending on the determined risk, you might need to rethink your original network design. Although a simple extranet/intranet setup with mid-level firewall protection might be okay for a small business that doesn't have much to steal, that obviously won't work for a company that deals with user financial data or proprietary/classified information. In that case, what might be needed is a tiered system in which you have a "corporate side" (on which things such as email, intranet access, and regular Internet access are handled) and a separate, secure network not connected to the Internet or corporate side. These networks can only be accessed by a user on a physical machine, and data can only be moved to them by "sneaker-net" physical media (scanned for viruses before opening). These networks can be used for data systems such as test or lab machines (on which, for example, new software builds are done and must be more tightly controlled, to prevent inadvertent corruption of the corporate side), or networks on which the

storage or processing of proprietary, business-critical, or classified information are handled. In Department of Defense parlance, these are sometimes referred to as *red nets* or *black nets*.

Vulnerability Testing

Your security policy should include regular vulnerability testing. Some very good vulnerability testing tools, such as WebInspect, Acunetix, GFI LANguard, Nessus, HFNetChk, and Tripwire, allow you to conduct your own security testing. Furthermore, there are third-party companies with the most advanced suite of testing tools available that can be contracted to scan your network for open and/or accessible ports, weaknesses in firewalls, and website vulnerability.

Audits

You should also factor in regular, detailed audits of all activities, with emphasis on those that seem to be near or outside established norms. For example, audits that reveal high rates of data exchanges after normal business hours, when that kind of traffic would not normally be expected, is something that should be investigated. Perhaps, after checking, you'll find that it's nothing more than an employee downloading music or video files. But the point is that your audit system saw the increase in traffic and determined it to be a simple Internet use policy violation rather than someone siphoning off more critical data.

There should be clearly established rules for dealing with security, use, and/or policy violations as well as attempted or actual intrusions. Trying to figure out what to do after an intrusion, is a bit too late. And if an intrusion does occur, there should be a clear-cut system for determining the extent of damage; isolation of the exploited application, port, or machine; and a rapid response to closing the hole against further incursions.

Recovery

Your plan should also address the issue of recovery after an attack has occurred. You need to address issues such as how the network will be reconfigured to close off the exploited opening. This might take some time, since the entry point might not be immediately discernible. There has to be an estimate of damage—what was taken or compromised, was malicious code implanted somewhere, and, if so, how to most efficiently extract it and clean the affected system. In the case of a virus in a company's email system, the ability to send and receive email could be halted for days while infected systems are rebuilt. And there will have to be discussions about how to reconstruct the network if the attack decimated files and systems.

This will most likely involve more than simply rein-stalling machines from archived backups. Because the compromise will most likely affect normal business oper-ations, the need to expedite the recovery will hamper efforts to fully analyze just what happened.

This is the main reason for preemptively writing a disaster recovery plan and making sure that all departments are represented in its drafting. However, like the network security policy itself, the disaster recovery plan will also be a work in progress that should be reviewed regularly to ensure that it meets the current needs. Things such as new threat notifications, software patches and updates, vulner-ability assessments, new application rollouts, and employee turnover all have to be addressed.

11. TOOLS OF YOUR TRADE

Although the tools available to people seeking unautho-rized entry into your domain are impressive, you also have a wide variety of tools to help keep them out. Before implementing a network security strategy, however, you must be acutely aware of the specific needs of those who will be using your resources.

Simple antispyware and antispam tools aren't enough. In today's rapidly changing software environment, strong security requires penetration shielding, threat signature recognition, autonomous reaction to identified threats, and the ability to upgrade your tools as the need arises.

The following section describes some of the more common tools you should consider adding to your arsenal.

Intrusion Detection Systems (IDSs)

As discussed earlier in the chapter, it's no longer good enough to have solid defenses. You also need to know when you've been penetrated—and the sooner, the better. Statistics paint a dismal picture. According to Verizon's threat report, less than 5% of cybersecurity breaches are detected within hours of the assault, and 80% weren't found for weeks, or months.[9] Bret Hartman, RSA's chief technology officer said, in a recent interview, that there's a new "shift in the level of paranoia to assume that you're always in a state of partial compromise."

A good IDS detects unauthorized intrusions using one of three types of models: anomaly-based, signature-based, and hybrid detection.

- Anomaly-based systems learn what's "normal" for a given network environment, so that they can quickly detect the "abnormal."
- Signature-based systems look for slight variations, or signatures, of suspicious network activity.

9. CNNMoney Tech, February 28, 2012.

- Hybrid detection systems are currently in development which compensate for weaknesses of both anomaly and signature-based systems by combining the best of both.

Firewalls

Your first line of defense should be a good firewall, or better yet, a system that effectively incorporates several security features in one. Secure Firewall (formerly Side-winder) from Secure Computing is one of the strongest and most secure firewall products available, and as of this writing it has never been successfully hacked. It is trusted and used by government and defense agencies. Secure Firewall combines the five most necessary security systems—firewall, antivirus/spyware/spam, VPN, applica-tion filtering, and intrusion prevention/detection systems—into a single appliance.

Intrusion Prevention Systems

A good *intrusion prevention system* (IPS) is a vast improvement over a basic firewall in that it can, among other things, be configured with policies that allow it to make autonomous decisions as to how to deal with application-level threats as well as simple IP address or port-level attacks.

IPS products respond directly to incoming threats in a variety of ways, from automatically dropping (extracting) suspicious packets (while still allowing legitimate ones to pass) to, in some cases, placing an intruder into a "quar-antine" file. IPS, like an application layer firewall, can be considered another form of access control in that it can make pass/fail decisions on application content.

For an IPS to be effective, it must also be very good at discriminating between a real threat signature and one that looks like but isn't one (false positive). Once a signature interpreted to be an intrusion is detected, the system must quickly notify the administrator so that the appropriate evasive action can be taken. The following are types of IPS.

- *Network-based.* Network-based IPSs create a series of choke points in the enterprise that detect suspected intrusion attempt activity. Placed inline at their needed locations, they invisibly monitor network traffic for known attack signatures that they then block.
- *Host-based.* These systems don't reside on the network per se but rather on servers and individual machines. They quietly monitor activities and requests from appli-cations, weeding out actions deemed prohibited in nature. These systems are often very good at identifying post-decryption entry attempts.
- *Content-based.* These IPSs scan network packets, look-ing for signatures of content that is unknown or

unrecognized or that has been explicitly labeled threatening in nature.

- *Rate-based.* These IPSs look for activity that falls outside the range of normal levels, such as activity that seems to be related to password cracking and brute-force penetration attempts, for example.

When searching for a good IPS, look for one that provides, at minimum:

- Robust protection for your applications, host systems, and individual network elements against exploitation of vulnerability-based threats as "single-bullet attacks," Trojan horses, worms, botnets, and surreptitious creation of "back doors" in your network.
- Protection against threats that exploit vulnerabilities in specific applications such as web services, mail, DNS, SQL, and any Voice over IP (VoIP) services.
- Detection and elimination of spyware, phishing, and anonymizers (tools that hide a source computer's identifying information so that Internet activity can be undertaken surreptitiously).
- Protection against brute-force and DoS attacks, application scanning, and flooding.
- A regular method of updating threat lists and signatures.

Application Firewalls

Application firewalls (AFs) are sometimes confused with IPSs in that they can perform IPS-like functions. But an AF is specifically designed to limit or deny an application's level of access to a system's OS—in other words, closing any openings into a computer's OS to deny the execution of harmful code within an OS's structure. AFs work by looking at applications themselves, monitoring the kind of data flow from an application for suspicious or administrator-blocked content from specific websites, application-specific viruses, and any attempt to exploit an identified weakness in an application's architecture. Though AF systems can conduct intrusion prevention duties, they typically employ proxies to handle firewall access control and focus on traditional firewall-type functions. AFs can detect the signatures of recognized threats and block them before they can infect the network.

Windows' version of an application firewall, called Data Execution Prevention (DEP), prevents the execution of any code that uses system services in such a way that could be deemed harmful to data or virtual memory (VM). It does this by considering RAM data as nonexecutable—in essence, refusing to run new code coming from the data-only area of RAM, since any harmful or malicious code seeking to damage existing data would have to run from this area.

The Macintosh Operating System (MacOS) also includes a built-in application firewall as a standard feature. The user can configure it to employ two-layer protection in which installing network-aware applications will result in an OS-generated warning that prompts for user authorization of network access. If authorized, MacOS will digitally sign the application in such a way that subsequent application activity will not prompt for further authorization. Updates invalidate the original certificate, and the user will have to revalidate before the application can run again.

The Linux OS has, for example, an application firewall called AppArmor that allows the administrator to create and link to every application a security policy that restricts its access capabilities.

Access Control Systems

Access control systems (ACSs) rely on administrator-defined rules that allow or restrict user access to protected network resources. These access rules can, for example, require strong user authentication such as tokens or biometric devices to prove the identity of users requesting access. They can also restrict access to various network services based on time of day or group need.

Some ACS products allow for the creation of an *access control list* (ACL), which is a set of rules that define security policy. These ACLs contain one or more *access control entries* (ACEs), which are the actual rule definitions themselves. These rules can restrict access by specific user, time of day, IP address, function (department, management level, etc.), or specific system from which a logon or access attempt is being made.

A good example of an ACS is SafeWord by Aladdin Knowledge Systems. SafeWord is considered a two-factor authentication system in that it uses what the user knows (such as a personal identification number, or PIN) and what the user has (such as a one-time passcode, or OTP, token) to strongly authenticate users requesting network access. SafeWord allows administrators to design customized access rules and restrictions to network resources, applications, and information.

In this scheme, the tokens are a key component. The token's internal cryptographic key algorithm is made "known" to an authentication server when the token's file is imported into a central database.

When the token is assigned to a user, its serial number is linked to that user in the user's record. On making an access request, the authentication server prompts the user to enter a username and the OTP generated by the token. If a PIN was also assigned to that user, she must either prepend or append that PIN to the token-generated passcode. As long as the authentication server receives what it expects, the user is granted whatever access privileges she was assigned.

Unified Threat Management

The latest trend to emerge in the network intrusion prevention arena is referred to as *unified threat management,* or UTM. UTM systems are multilayered and incorporate several security technologies into a single platform, often in the form of a plug-in appliance. UTM products can provide such diverse capabilities as antivirus, VPN, firewall services, and antispam as well as intrusion prevention.

The biggest advantages of a UTM system are its ease of operation and configuration and the fact that its security features can be quickly updated to meet rapidly evolving threats.

Sidewinder by Secure Computing is a UTM system that was designed to be flexible, easily and quickly adaptable, and easy to manage. It incorporates firewall, VPN, trusted source, IPS, antispam and antivirus, URL filtering, SSL decryption, and auditing/reporting.

Other UTM systems include Symantec's Enterprise Firewall and Gateway Security Enterprise Firewall Appliance, Fortinet, LokTek's AIRlok Firewall Appliance, and SonicWall's NSA 240 UTM Appliance, to name a few.

12. CONTROLLING USER ACCESS

Traditionally users—also known as employees—have been the weakest link in a company's defensive armor. Though necessary to the organization, they can be a nightmare waiting to happen to your network. How do you let them work within the network while controlling their access to resources? You have to make sure your system of user authentication knows who your users are.

Authentication, Authorization, and Accounting

Authentication is simply proving that a user's identity claim is valid and authentic. Authentication requires some form of "proof of identity." In network technologies, physical proof (such as a driver's license or another photo ID) cannot be employed, so you have to get something else from a user. That typically means having the user respond to a challenge to provide genuine credentials at the time he or she requests access.

For our purposes, credentials can be something the user knows, something the user has, or something they are. Once they provide authentication, there also has to be authorization, or permission to enter. Finally, you want to have some record of users' entry into your network—username, time of entry, and resources. That is the accounting side of the process.

What the User Knows

Users know a great many details about their own lives—birthdays, anniversaries, first cars, their spouse's name—and many will try to use these nuggets of

information as a simple form of authentication. What they don't realize is just how insecure those pieces of information are.

In network technologies, these pieces of information are often used as fixed passwords and PINs because they're easy to remember. Unless some strict guidelines are established on what form a password or PIN can take (for example, a minimum number of characters or a mixture of letters and numbers), a password will offer little to no real security.

Unfortunately, to hold down costs, some organizations allow users to set their own passwords and PINs as credentials, then rely on a simple challenge-response mechanism in which these weak credentials are provided to gain access. Adding to the loss of security is the fact that not only are the fixed passwords far too easy to guess, but because the user already has too much to remember, she writes them down somewhere near the computer she uses (often in some "cryptic" scheme to make it more difficult to guess). To increase the effectiveness of any security system, that system needs to require a much stronger form of authentication.

What the User Has

The most secure means of identifying users is by a combination of (1) a hardware device in their possession that is "known" to an authentication server in your network, coupled with (2) what they know. A whole host of devices available today—tokens, smart cards, biometric devices—are designed to more positively identify a user. Since a good token is the most secure of these options, let us focus on them here.

Tokens

A *token* is a device that employs an encrypted key for which the encryption algorithm—the method of generating an encrypted password—is known to a network's authentication server. There are both software and hardware tokens. The software tokens can be installed on a user's desktop system, in the cellular phone, or on the smart phone. The hardware tokens come in a variety of form factors, some with a single button that both turns the token on and displays its internally generated passcode; others have a more elaborate numerical keypad for PIN input. If lost or stolen, tokens can easily be removed from the system, quickly rendering them completely ineffective. And the passcodes they generate are of the "one-time-passcode," or OTP, variety, meaning that a generated passcode expires once it's been used and cannot be used again for a subsequent logon attempt.

Tokens are either programmed onsite with token programming software or offsite at the time they are ordered from their vendor. During programming, functions such as a token's cryptographic key, password length, whether a PIN is required, and whether it generates passwords based on internal clock timing or user PIN input are written into the token's memory. When programming is complete, a file containing this information and the token's serial number are imported into the authentication server so that the token's characteristics are known.

A token is assigned to a user by linking its serial number to the user's record, stored in the system database. When a user logs onto the network and needs access to, say, her email, she is presented with some challenge that she must answer using her assigned token.

Tokens operate in one of three ways: time synchronous, event synchronous, or challenge-response (also known as asynchronous).

Time Synchronous

In time synchronous operations, the token's internal clock is synched with the network's clock. Each time the token's button is pressed, it generates a passcode in hash form, based on its internal timekeeping. As long as the token's clock is synched with the network clock, the passcodes are accepted. In some cases (for example, when the token hasn't been used for some time or its battery dies), the token gets out of synch with the system and needs to be resynched before it can be used again.

Event Synchronous

In event synchronous operations, the server maintains an ordered passcode sequence and determines which passcode is valid based on the current location in that sequence.

Challenge-Response

In challenge-response, a challenge, prompting for username, is issued to the user by the authentication server at the time of access request. Once the user's name is entered, the authentication server checks to see what form of authentication is assigned to that user and issues a challenge back to the user. The user inputs the challenge into the token, then enters the token's generated response to the challenge. As long as the authentication server receives what it expected, authentication is successful and access is granted.

The User Is Authenticated, but Is She/He Authorized?

Authorization is independent of authentication. A user can be permitted entry into the network but not be authorized to access a resource. You don't want an employee having access to HR information or a corporate partner getting access to confidential or proprietary information.

Authorization requires a set of rules that dictate the resources to which a user will have access. These permissions are established in your security policy.

Accounting

Say that our user has been granted access to the requested resource. But you want (or in some cases are required to have) the ability to call up and view activity logs to see who got into what resource. This information is mandated for organizations that deal with user financial or medical information or DoD classified information or that go through annual inspections to maintain certification for international operations.

Accounting refers to the recording, logging, and archiving of all server activity, especially activity related to access attempts and whether they were successful. This information should be written into audit logs that are stored and available any time you want or need to view them. The audit logs should contain, at minimum, the following information:

● The user's identity;
● The date and time of the request;
● Whether the request passed authentication and was granted.

Any network security system you put into place should store, or archive, these logs for a specified period of time and allow you to determine for how long these archives will be maintained before they start to age out of the system.

Keeping Current

One of the best ways to stay ahead is to not fall behind in the first place. New systems with increasing sophistication are being developed all the time. They can incorporate a more intelligent and autonomous process in the way the system handles a detected threat, a faster and more easily accomplished method for updating threat files, and configuration flexibility that allows for very precise customization of access rules, authentication requirements, user role assignment, and how tightly it can protect specific applications.

Register for newsletters, attend seminars and network security shows, read white papers, and, if needed, contract the services of network security specialists. The point is, you shouldn't go cheap on network security. The price you pay to keep ahead will be far less than the price you pay to recover from a security breach or attack.

Finally, let's briefly look at how host-based IPS agents offer various intrusion prevention capabilities. The following describes common intrusion prevention capabilities.

13. INTRUSION PREVENTION CAPABILITIES

As previously mentioned, host-based IPS agents offer various intrusion prevention capabilities. Because the capabilities vary based on the detection techniques used by each product, the following activities (see checklist: "An Agenda for Action for Intrusion Prevention Activities") describe the capabilities by detection technique.

14. SUMMARY

This chapter has made it very apparent that preventing network intrusions is no easy task. Like cops on the street—usually outnumbered and underequipped compared to the bad guys—you face enemies with determination, skill, training, and a frightening array of increasingly sophisticated tools for hacking their way through your best defenses. And no matter how good your defenses are today, it's only a matter of time before a tool is developed that can penetrate them. If you know that ahead of time, you'll be much more inclined to keep a watchful eye for what "they" have and what you can use to defeat them.

Your best weapon is a logical, thoughtful, and nimble approach to network security. You have to be nimble—to evolve and grow with changes in technology, never being content to keep things as they are because "Hey, they're working just fine." Well, today's "just fine" will be tomorrow's "What the hell happened?"

Stay informed. There is no shortage of information available to you in the form of white papers, seminars, contract security specialists, and online resources, all dealing with various aspects of network security.

Invest in a good intrusion detection system. You want to know, as soon as possible, that a breach has occurred, what was stolen, and, if possible, where it went.

Have a good, solid, comprehensive, yet easy-to-understand network security policy in place. The very process of developing one will get all involved parties thinking about how to best secure your network while addressing user needs. When it comes to your users, you simply can't overeducate them where network security awareness is concerned. The more they know, the better equipped they'll be to act as allies against, rather than accomplices of, the hordes of crackers looking to steal, damage, hobble, or completely cripple your network.

Do your research and invest in good, multipurpose network security systems. Select systems that are easy to install and implement, are adaptable and quickly

---

An Agenda for Action for Intrusion Prevention Activities

From the organizational perspective, preventing intrusions includes the following key activities (check all tasks completed):

_____1. **Code Analysis**: The code analysis techniques can prevent code from being executed, including malware and unauthorized applications.

_____2. **Network Traffic Analysis**: This can stop incoming network traffic from being processed by the host and outgoing network traffic from exiting it.

_____3. **Network Traffic Filtering**: Working as a host-based firewall, this can stop unauthorized access and acceptable use policy violations (use of inappropriate external services).

_____4. **Filesystem Monitoring**: This can prevent files from being accessed, modified, replaced, or deleted, which could stop malware installation, including Trojan horses and rootkits, as well as other attacks involving inappropriate file access.

_____5. **Removable Media Restriction**: Some products can enforce restrictions on the use of removable media, both Universal Serial Bus (USB-based, or flash drive) and traditional (CD). This can prevent malware or other unwanted files from being transferred to a host and can also stop sensitive files from being copied from the host to removable media.

_____6. **Audiovisual Device Monitoring**: A few host-based IPS products can detect when a host's audiovisual devices, such as microphones, cameras, or IP-based phones, are activated or used. This could indicate that the host has been compromised by an attacker.

_____7. **Host Hardening**: Some host-based intrusion detection and prevention systems (IDPSs) can automatically harden hosts on an ongoing basis. For example, if an application is reconfigured, causing a particular security function to be disabled, the IDPS could detect this and enable the security function.

_____8. **Process Status Monitoring**: Some products monitor the status of processes or services running on a host, and if they detect that one has stopped, they restart it automatically. Some products can also monitor the status of security programs such as antivirus software.

_____9. **Network Traffic Sanitization**: Some agents, particularly those deployed on appliances, can sanitize the network traffic that they monitor. For example, an appliance-based agent could act as a proxy and rebuild each request and response that is directed through it. This can be effective at neutralizing certain unusual activity, particularly in packet headers and application protocol headers.

configurable, can be customized to suit your needs of today as well as tomorrow, and are supported by companies that keep pace with current trends in cracker technology.

Finally, let's move on to the real interactive part of this chapter: review questions/exercises, hands-on projects, case projects, and optional team case project. The answers and/or solutions by chapter can be found in the Online Instructor's Solutions Manual.

CHAPTER REVIEW QUESTIONS/ EXERCISES

True/False

1. True or False? A network intrusion is an authorized penetration of your enterprise's network, or an individual machine address in your assigned domain.
2. True or False? In some cases, a network intrusion could be done from the inside by a disgruntled employee looking to hurt the organization or steal company secrets for profit.
3. True or False? Most security software products available today have two basic methods of spotting malicious software.
4. True or False? Crackers are going to first look for known strengths in the operating system (OS) or any applications you are using.
5. True or False? Finding a device, using it in a place (or manner) in which prying eyes can see passwords or data, awareness of hacking tools specifically designed to sniff wireless signals for data, and logging on to unsecured networks, are all potential problem areas with which users need to be familiar.

Multiple Choice

1. Which devices can locate wireless signals within a certain range, where they can siphon off the data being transmitted over the signals?
   A. Wireless sniffers
   B. Packet sniffers
   C. Port scanners
   D. Port knocking
   E. Keystroke loggers
2. You can expect to have continued problems maintaining good network security awareness. Keep it simple. You need to draft some policies that define your network and its basic architecture. A good place to start is by asking the following questions, except which one?
   A. What kinds of resources need to be protected (user financial or medical data, credit-card information, etc.)?
   B. How many users will be accessing the network on the inside (employees, contractors, etc.)?
   C. Will there need to be access only at certain times or on a 24/7 basis (and across multiple time zones and/or internationally)?
   D. What kind of budget do I have?
   E. Will internal users be accessing the network, and if so, how many?
3. A good IDS detects unauthorized intrusions using three types of models:
   A. Anomaly-based
   B. Signature-based
   C. Network-based
   D. Hybrid detection
   E. Host-based
4. For an IPS to be effective, it must also be very good at discriminating between a real threat signature and one that looks like but isn't one (false positive). Once a signature interpreted to be an intrusion is detected, the system must quickly notify the administrator so that the appropriate evasive action can be taken. The following are types of IPS, except one:
   A. Network-based
   B. Rate-based
   C. Host-based
   D. Backdoor-based
   E. Content-based
5. The latest trend to emerge in the network intrusion prevention arena is referred to as:
   A. Antivirus
   B. Unified threat management
   C. VPN
   D. Firewall services
   E. Antispam

EXERCISE

Problem

Determine how an information system could prevent non-privileged users from circumventing intrusion prevention capabilities.

Hands-On Projects

Project

To safeguard its intellectual property and business, a pharmaceutical company had to keep pace with an increasingly sophisticated threat landscape of malware and viruses, as well as complex security legislation across its multiple sites. Please describe what type of intrusion prevention capabilities/services the company implemented.

Case Projects

Problem

A large medical center sought a powerful security solution that could continuously protect its high-throughput network without compromising network performance. It also required a healthy network: one that is safe from hackers, worms, viruses, and spyware and can compromise the performance of the medical's life-critical applications or the federally mandated confidentiality of its medical records. In addition, the security system needed to be cost-effective and interoperate transparently with the medical center's multivendor infrastructure. In this case project, how would an intrusion prevention system (IPS) provide the pervasive and proactive protection that the medical center required?

Optional Team Case Project

Problem

With so much at stake, companies of all sizes are taking a closer look at IPSs security solutions. In order to sift through the claims and separate the intrusion prevention contenders from the pretenders, the companies need to ask potential vendors a number of obvious basic questions first. Please list the basic IPS questions that a company might ask their vendors?

Chapter 8

Guarding Against Network Intrusions

Thomas M. Chen

City University London, Wales, United Kingdom

1. INTRODUCTION

Virtually all computers today are connected to the Internet through dialup, broadband, Ethernet, or wireless technologies. The reason for ubiquitous Internet connectivity is simple: applications depending on the network, such as email, web, remote login, instant messaging, social networking, and Voice over Internet Protocol (VoIP), have become essential to everyday computing. Unfortunately, the Internet exposes computer users to risks from a wide variety of possible threats. Users have much to lose—their privacy, valuable data, control of their computers, and possibly theft of their identities. The network enables attacks to be carried out remotely from anywhere in the world, with relative anonymity and low risk of traceability.

The nature of network intrusions has evolved over the years. A decade ago, a major concern was fast worms such as Code Red, Nimda, Slammer, and Sobig. More recently, concerns have shifted to spyware, Trojan horses, botnets, and ransomware. Although these other threats still continue to be major problems, the web has become the primary vector for stealthy attacks today.[1]

2. TRADITIONAL RECONNAISSANCE AND ATTACKS

Traditionally, attack methods follow sequential steps analogous to physical attacks, as shown in Fig. 8.1: reconnaissance, compromise, and cover-up[2] (sometimes more steps are identified, depending on how the details of attacks are broken down). Here we are only addressing attacks directed at a specific target host. Some other types of attacks, such

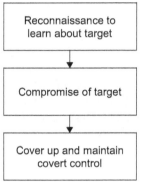

FIGURE 8.1 Steps in directed attacks.

as worms or malicious websites, are not directed at specific targets. Instead, they attempt to hit as many targets as quickly as possible without caring who or what the targets are.

In the first step of a directed attack, the attacker performs reconnaissance to learn as much as possible about the chosen target before carrying out an actual attack. A thorough reconnaissance can lead to a more effective attack because the target's weaknesses can be discovered. One might expect the reconnaissance phase to possibly tip off the target about an impending attack, but scans and probes are going on constantly in the "background noise" of Internet traffic, so systems administrators might ignore attack probes as too troublesome to investigate.

Through pings and traceroutes, an attacker can discover IP addresses and map the network around the target. Pings are Internet Control Message Protocol (ICMP) echo request and echo reply messages that verify a host's IP address and availability. Traceroute is a network mapping utility that takes advantage of the time-to-live (TTL) field in IP packets. It sends out packets with TTL = 1, then TTL = 2, and so on. When the packets expire, the routers along the packets' path report that the packets have been discarded,

---

1. M. Fossi et al., Symantec Global Internet Security Threat Report, vol. 16, 2010. Available at: www.symantec.com.
2. E. Skoudis, Counter Hack Reloaded: A Step-by-Step Guide to Computer Attacks and Effective Defenses, second ed., Prentice Hall, 2006.

returning ICMP "time exceeded" messages and thereby allowing the traceroute utility to learn the IP addresses of routers at a distance of one hop, two hops, and so on.

Port scans can reveal open ports. Normally, a host might be expected to have certain well-known ports open, such as Transmission Control Protocol (TCP) port 80 (HTTP), TCP port 21 (FTP), TCP port 23 (Telnet), or TCP port 25 (SMTP). A host might also happen to have open ports in the higher range. For example, port 12345 is the default port used by the Netbus remote access Trojan horse, or port 31337 is the default port used by the Back Orifice remote access Trojan horse. Discovery of ports indicating previous malware infections could obviously help an attacker considerably.

In addition to discovering open ports, the popular NMAP scanner (www.insecure.org/nmap) can discover the operating system running on a target. NMAP uses a large set of heuristic rules to identify an operating system based on a target's responses to carefully crafted TCP/IP probes. The basic idea is that different operating systems will make different responses to probes to open TCP/User Datagram Protocol (UDP) ports and malformed TCP/IP packets. Knowledge of a target's operating system can help an attacker identify vulnerabilities and find effective exploits.

Vulnerability scanning tests a target for the presence of vulnerabilities. Vulnerability scanners such as SATAN, SARA, SAINT, and Nessus typically contain a database of known vulnerabilities that is used to craft probes to a chosen target. The popular Nessus tool (www.nessus.org) has an extensible plug-in architecture to add checks for backdoors, misconfiguration errors, default accounts and passwords, and other types of vulnerabilities.

In the second step of a directed attack, the attacker attempts to compromise the target through one or more methods. Password attacks are common because passwords might be based on common words or names and are guessable by a dictionary attack, although computer systems today have better password policies that forbid easily guessable passwords. If an attacker can obtain the password file from the target, numerous password-cracking tools are available to carry out a brute-force password attack. In addition, computers and networking equipment often ship with default accounts and passwords intended to help systems administrators set up the equipment. These default accounts and passwords are easy to find on the web (for example, www.phenoelit-us.org/dpl/dpl.html). Occasionally users might neglect to change or delete the default accounts, offering intruders an easy way to access the target.

Another common attack method is an exploit attack code written to take advantage of a specific vulnerability.[3]

Many types of software, including operating systems and applications, have vulnerabilities. Symantec discovered 6253 vulnerabilities in 2010, or 17 vulnerabilities per day on average. Vulnerabilities are published by several organizations such as CERT and MITRE as well as vendors such as Microsoft through security bulletins. MITRE maintains a database of publicly known vulnerabilities identified by common vulnerabilities and exposures (CVE) numbers. The severity of vulnerabilities is reflected in the industry-standard common vulnerability scoring system (CVSS). In the first half of 2011, Microsoft observed that 44% of vulnerabilities were highly severe, 49% were medium-severe, and 7% were low-severe.[4] Furthermore, about 45% of vulnerabilities were easily exploitable.

Historically, buffer overflows have been the most common type of vulnerability.[5] They have been popular because buffer overflow exploits can often be carried out remotely and lead to complete compromise of a target. The problem arises when a program has allocated a fixed amount of memory space (such as in the stack) for storing data but receives more data than expected. If the vulnerability exists, the extra data will overwrite adjacent parts of memory, which could mess up other variables or pointers. If the extra data is random, the computer might crash or act unpredictably. However, if an attacker crafts the extra data carefully, the buffer overflow could overwrite adjacent memory in a way that benefits the attacker. For instance, an attacker might overwrite the return pointer in a stack, causing the program control to jump to malicious code inserted by the attacker.

An effective buffer overflow exploit requires technical knowledge of the computer architecture and operating system, but once the exploit code is written, it can be reused again. Buffer overflows can be prevented by the programmer or compiler performing bounds checking or during runtime. Although C/C++ has received a good deal of blame as a programming language for not having built-in checking that data written to arrays stays within bounds, buffer overflow vulnerabilities appear in a wide variety of other programs, too.

Structured Query Language (SQL) injection is a type of vulnerability relevant to web servers with a database backend.[6] SQL is an internationally standardized interactive and programming language for querying data and managing databases. Many commercial database products support SQL, sometimes with proprietary extensions. Web applications often take user input (usually from a web form)

3. S. McClure, J. Scambray, G. Kutz, Hacking Exposed, third ed., McGraw-Hill, 2001.

4. J. Faulhaber et al., Microsoft Security Intelligence Report, vol. 11. Available at: www.microsoft.com.
5. J. Foster, V. Osipov, N. Bhalla, Buffer Overflow Attacks: Detect, Exploit, Prevent, Syngress, 2005.
6. D. Litchfield, SQL Server Security, McGraw-Hill Osborne, 2003.

and pass the input into an SQL statement. An SQL injection vulnerability can arise if user input is not properly filtered for string literal escape characters, which can allow an attacker to craft input that is interpreted as embedded SQL statements and thereby manipulate the application running on the database.

Servers have been attacked and compromised by toolkits designed to automate customized attacks. For example, the MPack toolkit emerged in early 2007 and is sold commercially in Russia, along with technical support and regular software updates. It is loaded into a malicious or compromised website. When a visitor goes to the site, a malicious code is launched through an iframe (inline frame) within the HTML code. It can launch various exploits, expandable through modules, for vulnerabilities in web browsers and client software.

Metasploit (www.metasploit.com) is a popular Perl-based tool for developing and using exploits with an easy-to-use Web or command—line interface. Different exploits can be written and loaded into Metasploit and then directed at a chosen target. Exploits can be bundled with a payload (the code to run on a compromised target) selected from a collection of payloads. The tool also contains utilities to experiment with new vulnerabilities and help automate the development of new exploits.

Although exploits are commonplace, not all attacks require an exploit. *Social engineering* refers to types of attacks that take advantage of human nature to compromise a target, typically through deceit. A common social engineering attack is *phishing*, used in identity theft.[7] Phishing starts with a lure, usually a spam message that appears to be from a legitimate bank or e-commerce business. The message attempts to provoke the reader into visiting a fraudulent website pretending to be a legitimate business. These fraudulent sites are often set up by automated phishing toolkits that spoof legitimate sites of various brands, including the graphics of those brands. The fraudulent site might even have links to the legitimate website, to appear more valid. Victims are thus tricked into submitting valuable personal information such as account numbers, passwords, and Social Security numbers.

Other common examples of social engineering are spam messages that entice the reader into opening an email attachment. Most people know by now that attachments could be dangerous, perhaps containing a virus or spyware, even if they appear to be innocent at first glance. But if the message is sufficiently convincing, such as appearing to originate from an acquaintance, even wary users might be tricked into opening an attachment. Social engineering attacks can be simple but effective because they target people and bypass technological defenses.

The third step of traditional directed attacks involves cover-up of evidence of the compromise and establishment of covert control. After a successful attack, intruders want to maintain remote control and evade detection. Remote control can be maintained if the attacker has managed to install any of a number types of malicious software: a backdoor such as Netcat; a remote access Trojan such as BO2K or SubSeven; or a bot, usually listening for remote instructions on an Internet relay chat (IRC) channel, such as phatbot.

Intruders obviously prefer to evade detection after a successful compromise, because detection will lead the victim to take remedial actions to harden or disinfect the target. Intruders might change the system logs on the target, which will likely contain evidence of their attack. In Windows, the main event logs are secevent.evt, sysevent.evt, and appevent.evt. A systems administrator looking for evidence of intrusions would look in these files with the built-in Windows Event Viewer or a third-party log viewer. An intelligent intruder would not delete the logs but would selectively delete information in the logs to hide signs of malicious actions.

A *rootkit* is a stealthy type of malicious software (*malware*) designed to hide the existence of certain processes or programs from normal methods of detection.[8] Rootkits essentially alter the target's operating system, perhaps by changing drivers or dynamic link libraries (DLLs) and possibly at the kernel level. An example is the kernel-mode FU rootkit that manipulates kernel memory in Windows 2000, XP, and 2003. It consists of a device driver, msdirectx.sys, that might be mistaken for Microsoft's DirectX tool. The rootkit can hide certain events and processes and change the privileges of running processes.

If an intruder has installed malware for covert control, he will want to conceal the communications between himself and the compromised target from discovery by network-based *intrusion detection systems* (IDSs). IDSs are designed to listen to network traffic and look for signs of suspicious activities. Several concealment methods are used in practice. *Tunneling* is a commonly used method to place packets of one protocol into the payload of another packet. The "exterior" packet serves a vehicle to carry and deliver the "interior" packet intact. Though the protocol of the exterior packet is easily understood by an IDS, the interior protocol can be any number of possibilities and hence difficult to interpret.

Encryption is another obvious concealment method. Encryption relies on the secrecy of an encryption key shared between the intruder and the compromised target.

7. M. Jakobsson, S. Meyers (Eds.), Phishing and Countermeasures: Understanding the Increasing Problem of Electronic Identity Theft, Wiley-Interscience, 2006.

8. G. Hoglund, J. Butler, Rootkits: Subverting the Windows Kernel, Addison—Wesley Professional, 2005.

The encryption key is used to mathematically scramble the communications into a form that is unreadable without the key to decrypt it. Encryption ensures secrecy in practical terms but does not guarantee perfect security. Encryption keys can be guessed, but the time to guess the correct key increases exponentially with the key length. Long keys combined with an algorithm for periodically changing keys can ensure that encrypted communications will be difficult to break within a reasonable time.

Fragmentation of IP packets is another means to conceal the contents of messages from IDSs, which often do not bother to reassemble fragments. IP packets may normally be fragmented into smaller packets anywhere along a route and reassembled at the destination. An IDS can become confused with a flood of fragments, bogus fragments, or deliberately overlapping fragments.

3. MALICIOUS SOFTWARE

Malicious software, or malware, continues to be an enormous problem for Internet users because of its variety and prevalence and the level of danger it presents.[9–11] It is important to realize that malware can take many forms. A large class of malware is *infectious*, which includes viruses and worms. Viruses and worms are self-replicating, meaning that they spread from host to host by making copies of themselves. Viruses are pieces of code attached to a normal file or program. When the program is run, the virus code is executed and copies itself to (or infects) another file or program. It is often said that viruses need a human action to spread, whereas worms are standalone automated programs. Worms look for vulnerable targets across the network and transfer a copy of themselves if a target is successfully compromised.

Historically, several worms have become well-known and stimulated concerns over the possibility of a fast epidemic infecting Internet-connected hosts before defenses could stop it. The 1988 Robert Morris Jr. worm infected thousands of Unix hosts, at the time a significant portion of the Arpanet (the predecessor to the Internet). The 1999 Melissa worm infected Microsoft Word documents and emailed itself to addresses found in a victim's Outlook address book. Melissa demonstrated that email could be a very effective vector for malware distribution, and many subsequent worms have continued to use email, such as the 2000 Love Letter worm. In the 2001−4 interval, several fast worms appeared, notably Code Red, Nimda, Klez, SQL Slammer/Sapphire, Blaster, Sobig, and MyDoom.

An important feature of viruses and worms is their capability to carry a *payload*—malicious code that is executed on a compromised host. The payload can be virtually anything. For instance, SQL Slammer/Sapphire had no payload, whereas Code Red carried an agent to perform a denial-of-service (DoS) attack on certain fixed addresses. The Chernobyl or CIH virus had one of the most destructive payloads, attempting to overwrite critical system files and the system BIOS that is needed for a computer to boot up. Worms are sometimes used to deliver other malware, such as bots, in their payload. They are popular delivery vehicles because of their ability to spread by themselves and carry anything in their payload.

Members of a second large class of malware are characterized by attempts to conceal themselves. This class includes Trojan horses and rootkits. Worms are not particularly stealthy (unless they are designed to be), because they are typically indiscriminate in their attacks. They probe potential targets in the hope of compromising many targets quickly. Indeed, fast-spreading worms are relatively easy to detect because of the network congestion caused by their probes.

Stealth is an important feature for malware because the critical problem for antivirus software is obviously detection of malware. Trojan horses are a type of malware that appears to perform a useful function but hides a malicious function. Thus, the presence of the Trojan horse might not be concealed, but functionality is not fully revealed. For example, a video codec could offer to play certain types of video but also covertly steal the user's data in the background. In the second half of 2007, Microsoft reported a dramatic increase of 300% in the number of Trojan downloaders and droppers, small programs to facilitate downloading more malware later.[1]

Rootkits are essentially modifications to the operating system to hide the presence of files or processes from normal means of detection. Rootkits are often installed as drivers or kernel modules. A highly publicized example was the extended copy protection (XCP) software included in some Sony BMG audio CDs in 2005, to prevent music copying. The software was installed automatically on Windows PCs when a CD was played. Made by a company called First 4 Internet, XCP unfortunately contained a hidden rootkit component that patched the operating system to prevent it from displaying any processes, Registry entries, or files with names beginning with sys. Although the intention of XCP was not malicious, there was concern that the rootkit could be used by malware writers to conceal malware.

A third important class of malware is designed for remote control. This class includes remote access Trojans (RATs) and bots. Instead of *remote access Trojan*, RAT is sometimes interpreted as *remote administration tool* because it can be used for legitimate purposes by systems administrators. Either way, RAT refers to a type of software

9. D. Harley, D. Slade, Viruses Revealed, McGraw-Hill, 2001.
10. E. Skoudis, Malware: Fighting Malicious Code, Prentice Hall PTR, 2004.
11. P. Szor, The Art of Computer Virus Research and Defense, Addison−Wesley, 2005.

usually consisting of server and client parts designed to enable covert communications with a remote controller. The client part is installed on a victim host and mainly listens for instructions from the server part, located at the controller. Notorious examples include Back Orifice, Netbus, and Sub7.

Bots are remote-control programs installed covertly on innocent hosts.[12] Bots are typically programmed to listen to IRC channels for instructions from a "bot herder." All bots under control of the same bot herder form a botnet. Botnets have been known to be rented out for purposes of sending spam or launching a distributed DoS (DDoS) attack.[13] The power of a botnet is proportional to its size, but exact sizes have been difficult to discover.

One of the most publicized bots is the Storm worm, which has various aliases. Storm was launched in January 2007 as spam with a Trojan horse attachment. As a botnet, Storm has shown unusual resilience by working in a distributed peer-to-peer manner without centralized control. Each compromised host connects to a small subset of the entire botnet. Each infected host shares lists of other infected hosts, but no single host has a full list of the entire botnet. The size of the Storm botnet has been estimated at more than 1 million compromised hosts, but an exact size has been impossible to determine because of the many bot variants and active measures to avoid detection. Its creators have been persistent in continually updating its lures with current events and evolving tactics to spread and avoid detection.

Another major class of malware is designed for data theft. This class includes keyloggers and spyware. A keylogger can be a Trojan horse or other form of malware. It is designed to record a user's keystrokes and perhaps report them to a remote attacker. Keyloggers are planted by criminals on unsuspecting hosts to steal passwords and other valuable personal information. It has also been rumored that the Federal Bureau of Investigation (FBI) has used a keylogger called Magic Lantern.

As the name implies, *spyware* is stealthy software designed to monitor and report user activities for the purposes of learning personal information without the user's knowledge or consent. Surveys have found that spyware is widely prevalent on consumer PCs, usually without knowledge of the owners. Adware is viewed by some as a mildly objectionable form of spyware that spies on web browsing behavior to target online advertisements to a user's apparent interests. More objectionable forms of spyware are more invasive of privacy and raise other objections related to stealthy installation, interference with normal web browsing, and difficulty of removal.

Spyware can be installed in a number of stealthy ways: disguised as a Trojan horse, bundled with a legitimate software program, delivered in the payload of a worm or virus, or downloaded through deception. For instance, a deceptive website might pop up a window appearing to be a standard Windows dialogue box, but clicking any button will cause spyware to be downloaded. Another issue is that spyware might or might not display an end-user license agreement (EULA) before installation. If an EULA is displayed, the mention of spyware is typically unnoticeable or difficult to find.

More pernicious forms of spyware can change computer settings, reset homepages, and redirect the browser to unwanted sites. For example, the notorious Cool-WebSearch changed homepages to Coolwebsearch.com, rewrote search engine results, and altered host files, and some variants added links to pornographic and gambling sites to the browser's bookmarks.

Lures and "Pull" Attacks

Traditional network attacks can be viewed as an "active" approach in which the attacker takes the initiative of a series of actions directed at a target. Attackers face the risk of revealing their malicious intentions through these actions. For instance, port scanning, password guessing, or exploit attempts can be readily detected by an IDS as suspicious activities. Sending malware through email can only be seen as an attack attempt.

Security researchers have observed a trend away from direct attacks toward more stealthy attacks that wait for victims to visit malicious websites, as shown in Fig. 8.2.[14] The web has become the primary vector for infecting computers, in large part because email has become better secured. Sophos discovers a new malicious webpage every 14 s, on average.[15]

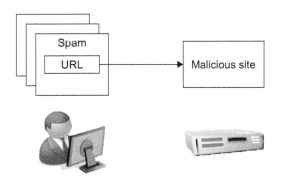

FIGURE 8.2 Stealthy attacks lure victims to malicious servers.

12. C. Schiller et al., Botnets: the Killer Web App, Syngress Publishing, 2007.
13. D. Dittrich, Distributed Denial of Service (DDoS) Attacks/Tools. Available at: http://staff.washington.edu/dittrich/misc/ddos/.
14. J. Scambray, M. Shema, C. Sima, Hacking Exposed Web Applications, second ed., McGraw-Hill, 2006.
15. Sophos, Security Threat Report 2012. Available at: http://www.sophos.com/medialibrary/PDFs/other/SophosSecurityThreatReport2012.pdf.

Web-based attacks have significant advantages for attackers. First, they are stealthier and not as "noisy" as active attacks, making it easier to continue undetected for a longer time. Second, web servers have the intelligence to be stealthy. For instance, web servers have been found that serve up an attack only once per IP address, and otherwise serve up legitimate content. The malicious server remembers the IP addresses of visitors. Thus, a visitor will be attacked only once, which makes the attack harder to detect. Third, a web server can serve up different attacks, depending on the visitor's operating system and browser.

As mentioned earlier, a common type of attack carried out through the web is phishing. A phishing site is typically disguised as a legitimate financial organization or e-commerce business. During the month of June 2011, the Anti-Phishing Working Group found 28,148 new unique phishing sites hijacking 310 brands (www.antiphishing.org).

Another type of web-based attack is a malicious site that attempts to download malware through a visitor's browser, called a *drive-by download*. A web page usually loads a malicious script by means of an iframe (inline frame). It has been reported that most drive-by downloads are hosted on legitimate sites that have been compromised. For example, in June 2007 more than 10,000 legitimate Italian websites were discovered to be compromised with malicious code loaded through iframes. Many other legitimate sites are regularly compromised.

Drive-by downloading through a legitimate site holds certain appeal for attackers. First, most users would be reluctant to visit suspicious and potentially malicious sites but will not hesitate to visit legitimate sites in the belief that they are always safe. Even wary web surfers may be caught off-guard. Second, the vast majority of web servers run Apache (approximately 50%) or Microsoft IIS (approximately 40%), both of which have vulnerabilities that can be exploited by attackers. Moreover, servers with database applications could be vulnerable to SQL injection attacks. Third, if a legitimate site is compromised with an iframe, the malicious code might go unnoticed by the site owner for some time.

Pull-based attacks pose one challenge to attackers: They must attract visitors to the malicious site somehow while avoiding detection by security researchers. One obvious option is to send out lures in spam. Lures have been disguised as email from the Internal Revenue Service, a security update from Microsoft, or a greeting card. The email attempts to entice the reader to visit a link. On one hand, lures are easier to get through spam filters because they only contain links and not attachments. It is easier for spam filters to detect malware attachments than to determine whether links in email are malicious. On the other hand, spam filters are easily capable of extracting and following links from spam. The greater challenge is to determine whether the linked site is malicious.

4. DEFENSE IN DEPTH

Most security experts would agree with the view that perfect network security is impossible to achieve and that any single defense can always be overcome by an attacker with sufficient resources and motivation. The basic idea behind the *defense-in-depth strategy* is to hinder the attacker as much as possible with multiple layers of defense, even though each layer might be surmountable. More valuable assets should be protected behind more layers of defense. The combination of multiple layers increases the cost for the attacker to be successful, and the cost is proportional to the value of the protected assets. Moreover, a combination of multiple layers will be more effective against unpredictable attacks than will a single defense optimized for a particular type of attack.

The cost for the attacker could be in terms of additional time, effort, or equipment. For instance, by delaying an attacker, an organization would increase the chances of detecting and reacting to an attack in progress. The increased costs to an attacker could deter some attempts if the costs are believed to outweigh the possible gain from a successful attack.

Defense in depth is sometimes said to involve people, technology, and operations. Trained security people should be responsible for securing facilities and information assurance. However, every computer user in an organization should be made aware of security policies and practices. Every Internet user at home should be aware of safe practices (such as avoiding opening email attachments or clicking suspicious links) and the benefits of appropriate protection (antivirus software, firewalls).

A variety of technological measures can be used for layers of protection. These should include firewalls, IDSs, routers with access control lists (ACLs), antivirus software, access control, spam filters, and so on. These topics are discussed in more depth later.

The term *operations* refers to all preventive and reactive activities required to maintain security. Preventive activities include vulnerability assessments, software patching, system hardening (closing unnecessary ports), and access controls. Reactive activities should detect malicious activities and react by blocking attacks, isolating valuable resources, or tracing the intruder.

Protection of valuable assets can be a more complicated decision than simply considering the value of the assets. Organizations often perform a risk assessment to determine the value of assets, possible threats, likelihood of threats, and possible impact of threats. Valuable assets facing unlikely threats or threats with low impact might not need much protection. Clearly, assets of high value facing likely threats or high-impact threats merit the strongest defenses. Organizations usually have their own risk management process for identifying risks and deciding how to allocate a security budget to protect valuable assets under risk.

5. PREVENTIVE MEASURES

Most computer users are aware that Internet connectivity comes with security risks. It would be reasonable to take precautions to minimize exposure to attacks. Fortunately, several options are available to computer users to fortify their systems to reduce risks.

Access Control

In computer security, *access control* refers to mechanisms to allow users to perform functions up to their authorized level and restrict users from performing unauthorized functions.[16] Access control includes:

- Authentication of users
- Authorization of their privileges
- Auditing to monitor and record user actions

All computer users will be familiar with some type of access control.

Authentication is the process of verifying a user's identity. Authentication is typically based on one or more of these factors:

- Something the user knows, such as a password or PIN
- Something the user has, such as a smart card or token
- Something personal about the user, such as a fingerprint, retinal pattern, or other biometric identifier

Use of a single factor, even if multiple pieces of evidence are offered, is considered weak authentication. A combination of two factors, such as a password and a fingerprint, called *two-factor* (or *multifactor*) *authentication*, is considered strong authentication.

Authorization is the process of determining what an authenticated user can do. Most operating systems have an established set of permissions related to read, write, or execute access. For example, an ordinary user might have permission to read a certain file but not write to it, whereas a root or superuser will have full privileges to do anything.

Auditing is necessary to ensure that users are accountable. Computer systems record actions in the system in audit trails and logs. For security purposes, they are invaluable forensic tools to recreate and analyze incidents. For instance, a user attempting numerous failed logins might be seen as an intruder.

Vulnerability Testing and Patching

As mentioned earlier, vulnerabilities are weaknesses in software that might be used to compromise a computer.

Vulnerable software includes all types of operating systems and application programs. New vulnerabilities are being discovered constantly in different ways. New vulnerabilities discovered by security researchers are usually reported confidentially to the vendor, which is given time to study the vulnerability and develop a path. Of all vulnerabilities disclosed in 2007, 50% could be corrected through vendor patches.[17] When ready, the vendor will publish the vulnerability, hopefully along with a patch.

It has been argued that publication of vulnerabilities will help attackers. Though this might be true, publication also fosters awareness within the entire community. Systems administrators will be able to evaluate their systems and take appropriate precautions. One might expect systems administrators to know the configuration of computers on their network, but in large organizations, it would be difficult to keep track of possible configuration changes made by users. Vulnerability testing offers a simple way to learn about the configuration of computers on a network.

Vulnerability testing is an exercise to probe systems for known vulnerabilities. It requires a database of known vulnerabilities, a packet generator, and test routines to generate a sequence of packets to test for a particular vulnerability. If a vulnerability is found and a software patch is available, that host should be patched.

Penetration testing is a closely related idea but takes it further. Penetration testing simulates the actions of a hypothetical attacker to attempt to compromise hosts. The goal is, again, to learn about weaknesses in the network so that they can be remedied.

Closing Ports

Transport layer protocols, namely TCP and UDP, identify applications communicating with each other by means of port numbers. Port numbers 1 to 1023 are well known and assigned by the Internet Assigned Numbers Authority (IANA) to standardized services running with root privileges. For example, web servers listen on TCP port 80 for client requests. Port numbers 1024 to 49151 are used by various applications with ordinary user privileges. Port numbers above 49151 are used dynamically by applications.

It is good practice to close ports that are unnecessary, because attackers can use open ports, particularly those in the higher range. For instance, the Sub7 Trojan horse is known to use port 27374 by default, and Netbus uses port 12345. Closing ports does not by itself guarantee the safety of a host, however. Some hosts need to keep TCP port 80 open for HyperText Transfer Protocol (HTTP), but attacks can still be carried out through that port.

---

16. B. Carroll, Cisco Access Control Security: AAA Administration Services, Cisco Press, 2004.

17. IBM Internet Security Systems, X-Force 2007 Trend Statistics, January 2008.

Firewalls

When most people think of network security, firewalls are one of the first things to come to mind. Firewalls are a means of perimeter security protecting an internal network from external threats. A firewall selectively allows or blocks incoming and outgoing traffic. Firewalls can be standalone network devices located at the entry to a private network or personal firewall programs running on PCs. An organization's firewall protects the internal community; a personal firewall can be customized to an individual's needs.

Firewalls can provide separation and isolation among various network zones, namely the public Internet, private intranets, and a demilitarized zone (DMZ), as shown in Fig. 8.3. The semiprotected DMZ typically includes public services provided by a private organization. Public servers need some protection from the public Internet so they usually sit behind a firewall. This firewall cannot be completely restrictive because the public servers must be externally accessible. Another firewall typically sits between the DMZ and private internal network because the internal network needs additional protection.

There are various types of firewalls: packet-filtering firewalls, stateful firewalls, and proxy firewalls. In any case, the effectiveness of a firewall depends on the configuration of its rules. Properly written rules require detailed knowledge of network protocols. Unfortunately, some firewalls are improperly configured through neglect or lack of training.

Packet-filtering firewalls analyze packets in both directions and either permit or deny passage based on a set of rules. Rules typically examine port numbers, protocols, IP addresses, and other attributes of packet headers. There is no attempt to relate multiple packets with a flow or stream. The firewall is stateless, retaining no memory of one packet to the next.

Stateful firewalls overcome the limitation of packet-filtering firewalls by recognizing packets belonging to the same flow or connection and keeping track of the connection state. They work at the network layer and recognize the legitimacy of sessions.

Proxy firewalls are also called application-level firewalls because they process up to the application layer. They recognize certain applications and can detect whether an undesirable protocol is using a nonstandard port or an application layer protocol is being abused. They protect an internal network by serving as primary gateways to proxy connections from the internal network to the public Internet. They could have some impact on network performance due to the nature of the analysis.

Firewalls are essential elements of an overall defensive strategy but have the drawback that they only protect the perimeter. They are useless if an intruder has a way to bypass the perimeter. They are also useless against insider threats originating within a private network.

Antivirus and Antispyware Tools

The proliferation of malware prompts the need for antivirus software.[11] Antivirus software is developed to detect the presence of malware, identify its nature, remove the malware (disinfect the host), and protect a host from future infections. Detection should ideally minimize false positives (false alarms) and false negatives (missed malware) at the same time. Antivirus software faces a number of difficult challenges:

- Malware tactics are sophisticated and constantly evolving.
- Even the operating system on infected hosts cannot be trusted.
- Malware can exist entirely in memory without affecting files.
- Malware can attack antivirus processes.
- The processing load for antivirus software cannot degrade computer performance such that users become annoyed and turn the antivirus software off.

One of the simplest tasks performed by antivirus software is file scanning. This process compares the bytes in files with known signatures that are byte patterns indicative of a known malware. It represents the general approach of signature-based detection. When new malware is captured, it is analyzed for unique characteristics that can be described in a signature. The new signature is distributed as updates to antivirus programs. Antivirus looks for the signature during file scanning, and if a match is found, the signature identifies the malware specifically. There are major drawbacks to this method, however: New signatures require time to develop and test; users must keep their signature files up to date; and new malware without a known signature may escape detection.

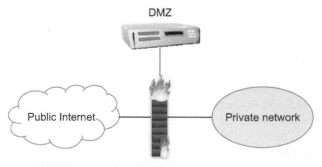

FIGURE 8.3 A firewall isolating various network zones.

Behavior-based detection is a complementary approach. Instead of addressing what malware is, behavior-based detection looks at what malware tries to do. In other words, anything attempting a risky action will come under suspicion. This approach overcomes the limitations of signature-based detection and could find new malware without a signature, just from its behavior. However, the approach can be difficult in practice. First, we must define what is suspicious behavior, or conversely, what is normal behavior. This definition often relies on heuristic rules developed by security experts, because normal behavior is difficult to define precisely. Second, it might be possible to *discern* suspicious behavior, but it is much more difficult to *determine* malicious behavior, because malicious intention must be inferred. When behavior-based detection flags suspicious behavior, more follow-up investigation is usually needed to better understand the threat risk.

The ability of malware to change or disguise appearances can defeat file scanning. However, regardless of its form, malware must ultimately perform its mission. Thus, an opportunity will always arise to detect malware from its behavior if it is given a chance to execute. Antivirus software will monitor system events, such as hard-disk access, to look for actions that might pose a threat to the host. Events are monitored by intercepting calls to operating system functions.

Although monitoring system events is a step beyond file scanning, malicious programs are running in the host execution environment and could pose a risk to the host. The idea of emulation is to execute suspected code within an isolated environment, presenting the appearance of the computer resources to the code, and to look for actions symptomatic of malware.

Virtualization takes emulation a step further and executes suspected code within a real operating system. A number of virtual operating systems can run above the host operating system. Malware can corrupt a virtual operating system, but for safety reasons a virtual operating system has limited access to the host operating system. A "sandbox" isolates the virtual environment from tampering with the host environment, unless a specific action is requested and permitted. In contrast, emulation does not offer an operating system to suspected code; the code is allowed to execute step by step, but in a controlled and restricted way, just to discover what it will attempt to do.

Antispyware software can be viewed as a specialized class of antivirus software. Somewhat unlike traditional viruses, spyware can be particularly pernicious in making a vast number of changes throughout the hard drive and system files. Infected systems tend to have a large number of installed spyware programs, possibly including certain cookies (pieces of text planted by web sites in the browser as a means of keeping them in memory).

Spam Filtering

Every Internet user is familiar with spam email. There is no consensus on an exact definition of spam, but most people would agree that spam is unsolicited, sent in bulk, and commercial in nature. There is also consensus that the vast majority of email is spam. Spam continues to be a problem because a small fraction of recipients do respond to these messages. Even though the fraction is small, the revenue generated is enough to make spam profitable because it costs little to send spam in bulk. In particular, a large botnet can generate an enormous amount of spam quickly.

Users of popular webmail services such as Yahoo! and Hotmail are attractive targets for spam because their addresses might be easy to guess. In addition, spammers harvest email addresses from various sources: websites, newsgroups, online directories, data-stealing viruses, and so on. Spammers might also purchase lists of addresses from companies who are willing to sell customer information.

Spam is more than an inconvenience for users and a waste of network resources. Spam is a popular vehicle to distribute malware and lures to malicious websites. It is the first step in phishing attacks.

Spam filters work at an enterprise level and a personal level. At the enterprise level, mail gateways can protect an entire organization by scanning incoming messages for malware and blocking messages from suspicious or fake senders. A concern at the enterprise level is the rate of false positives, which are legitimate messages mistaken for spam. Users may become upset if their legitimate mail is blocked. Fortunately, spam filters are typically customizable, and the rate of false positives can be made very low. Additional spam filtering at the personal level can customize filtering even further, to account for individual preferences.

Various spam-filtering techniques are embodied in many commercial and free spam filters, such as DSPAM and SpamAssassin, to name two. Bayesian filtering is one of the more popular techniques.[18] First, an incoming message is parsed into tokens, which are single words or word combinations from the message's header and body. Second, probabilities are assigned to tokens through a training process. The filter looks at a set of known spam messages compared to a set of known legitimate messages and calculates token probabilities based on Bayes' theorem (from probability theory). Intuitively, a word such as *Viagra* would appear more often in spam, and therefore the appearance of a Viagra token would increase the probability of that message being classified as spam.

The probability calculated for a message is compared to a chosen threshold; if the probability is higher, the message

---

18. J. Zdziarski, Ending Spam: Bayesian Content Filtering and the Art of Statistical Language Classification, No Starch Press, 2005.

is classified as spam. The threshold is chosen to balance the rates of false positives and false negatives (missed spam) in some desired way. An attractive feature of Bayesian filtering is that its probabilities will adapt to new spam tactics, given continual feedback, that is, correction of false positives and false negatives by the user.

It is easy to see why spammers have attacked Bayesian filters by attempting to influence the probabilities of tokens. For example, spammers have tried filling messages with large amounts of legitimate text (e.g., drawn from classic literature) or random innocuous words. The presence of legitimate tokens tends to decrease a message's score because they are evidence counted toward the legitimacy of the message.

Spammers are continually trying new ways to get through spam filters. At the same time, security companies respond by adapting their technologies.

Honeypots

The basic idea of a *honeypot* is to learn about attacker techniques by attracting attacks to a seemingly vulnerable host.[19] It is essentially a forensics tool rather than a line of defense. A honeypot could be used to gain valuable information about attack methods used elsewhere or imminent attacks before they happen. Honeypots are used routinely in research and production environments.

A honeypot has more special requirements than a regular PC. First, a honeypot should not be used for legitimate services or traffic. Consequently, every activity seen by the honeypot will be illegitimate. Even though honeypots typically record little data compared to IDS, for instance, their data has little "noise," whereas the bulk of IDS data is typically uninteresting from a security point of view.

Second, a honeypot should have comprehensive and reliable capabilities for monitoring and logging all activities. The forensic value of a honeypot depends on the detailed information it can capture about attacks.

Third, a honeypot should be isolated from the real network. Since honeypots are intended to attract attacks, there is a real risk that the honeypot could be compromised and used as a launching pad to attack more hosts in the network.

Honeypots are often classified according to their level of interaction, ranging from low to high. Low-interaction honeypots, such as Honeyd, offer the appearance of simple services. An attacker could try to compromise the honeypot but would not have much to gain. The limited interactions pose a risk that an attacker could discover that the host is a honeypot. At the other end of the range, high-interaction honeypots behave more like real systems. They

have more capabilities to interact with an attacker and log activities, but they offer more to gain if they are compromised.

Honeypots are related to the concepts of black holes or network telescopes, which are monitored blocks of unused IP addresses. Since the addresses are unused, any traffic seen at those addresses is naturally suspicious (although not necessarily malicious).

Traditional honeypots suffer a drawback in that they are passive and wait to see malicious activity. The idea of honeypots has been extended to active clients that search for malicious servers and interact with them. The active version of a honeypot has been called a *honey-monkey* or *client honeypot*.

Network Access Control

A vulnerable host might place not only itself but an entire community at risk. For one thing, a vulnerable host might attract attacks. If compromised, the host could be used to launch attacks on other hosts. The compromised host might give information to the attacker, or there might be trust relationships between hosts that could help the attacker. In any case, it is not desirable to have a weakly protected host on your network.

The general idea of *network access control* (NAC) is to restrict a host from accessing a network unless the host can provide evidence of a strong security posture. The NAC process involves the host, the network (usually routers or switches, and servers), and a security policy, as shown in Fig. 8.4.

The details of the NAC process vary with various implementations, which unfortunately currently lack standards for interoperability. A host's security posture includes its IP address, operating system, antivirus software, personal firewall, and host intrusion detection system. In some implementations, a software agent runs on the host, collects information about the host's security posture, and reports it to the network as part of a request for admission to the network. The network refers to a policy server to compare the host's security posture to the security policy, to make an admission decision.

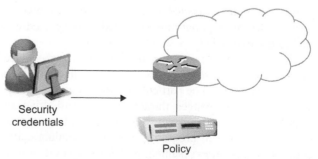

FIGURE 8.4 Network access control.

---

19. The Honeynet Project, *Know Your Enemy: Learning About Security Threats*, second ed., Addison–Wesley, 2004.

The admission decision could be anything from rejection to partial admission or full admission. Rejection might be prompted by out-of-date antivirus software, an operating system needing patches, or firewall misconfiguration. Rejection might lead to quarantine (routing to an isolated network) or forced remediation.

6. INTRUSION MONITORING AND DETECTION

Preventive measures are necessary and help reduce the risk of attacks, but it is practically impossible to prevent all attacks. Intrusion detection is also necessary to detect and diagnose malicious activities, analogous to a burglar alarm. Intrusion detection is essentially a combination of monitoring, analysis, and response.[20] Typically an IDS supports a console for human interface and display. Monitoring and analysis are usually viewed as passive techniques because they do not interfere with ongoing activities. The typical IDS response is an alert to systems administrators, who might choose to pursue further investigation or not. In other words, traditional IDSs do not offer much response beyond alerts, under the presumption that security incidents need human expertise and judgment for follow-up.

Detection accuracy is the critical problem for intrusion detection. Intrusion detection should ideally minimize false positives (normal incidents mistaken for suspicious ones) and false negatives (malicious incidents escaping detection). Naturally, false negatives are contrary to the essential purpose of intrusion detection. False positives are also harmful because they are troublesome for systems administrators who must waste time investigating false alarms. Intrusion detection should also seek to more than identify security incidents. In addition to relating the facts of an incident, intrusion detection should ascertain the nature of the incident, the perpetrator, the seriousness (malicious vs. suspicious), scope, and potential consequences (such as stepping from one target to more targets).

IDS approaches can be categorized in at least two ways. One way is to differentiate host-based and network-based IDS, depending on where sensing is done. A host-based IDS monitors an individual host, whereas a network-based IDS works on network packets. Another way to view IDS is by their approach to analysis. Traditionally, the two analysis approaches are misuse (signature-based) detection and anomaly (behavior-based) detection. As shown in Fig. 8.5, these two views are complementary and are often used in combination.

In practice, intrusion detection faces several difficult challenges: signature-based detection can recognize only incidents matching a known signature; behavior-based

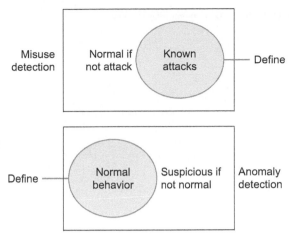

FIGURE 8.5 Misuse detection and anomaly detection.

detection relies on an understanding of normal behavior, but "normal" can vary widely. Attackers are intelligent and evasive; attackers might try to confuse IDS with fragmented, encrypted, tunneled, or junk packets; an IDS might not react to an incident in real time or quickly enough to stop an attack; and incidents can occur anywhere at any time, which necessitates continual and extensive monitoring, with correlation of multiple distributed sensors.

Host-Based Monitoring

Host-based IDS runs on a host and monitors system activities for signs of suspicious behavior. Examples could be changes to the system Registry, repeated failed login attempts, or installation of a backdoor. Host-based IDSs usually monitor system objects, processes, and regions of memory. For each system object, the IDS will usually keep track of attributes such as permissions, size, modification dates, and hashed contents, to recognize changes.

A concern for a host-based IDS is possible tampering by an attacker. If an attacker gains control of a system, the IDS cannot be trusted. Hence, special protection of the IDS against tampering should be architected into a host.

A host-based IDS is not a complete solution by itself. Though monitoring the host is logical, it has three significant drawbacks: visibility is limited to a single host; the IDS process consumes resources, possibly impacting performance on the host; and attacks will not be seen until they have already reached the host. Host-based and network-based IDS are often used together to combine strengths.

Traffic Monitoring

Network-based IDSs typically monitor network packets for signs of reconnaissance, exploits, DoS attacks, and malware. They have strengths to complement host-based IDSs: network-based IDSs can see traffic for a population of

---

20. R. Bejtlich, The Tao of Network Security Monitoring: Beyond Intrusion Detection, Addison–Wesley, 2005.

FIGURE 8.6 IDSs monitoring various network zones.

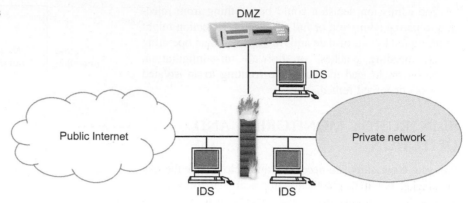

hosts; they can recognize patterns shared by multiple hosts; and they have the potential to see attacks before they reach the hosts.

IDSs are placed in various locations for different views, as shown in Fig. 8.6. An IDS outside a firewall is useful for learning about malicious activities on the Internet. An IDS in the DMZ will see attacks originating from the Internet that are able to get through the outer firewall to public servers. Lastly, an IDS in the private network is necessary to detect any attacks that are able to successfully penetrate perimeter security.

Signature-Based Detection

Signature-based intrusion detection depends on patterns that uniquely identify an attack. If an incident matches a known signature, the signature identifies the specific attack. The central issue is how to define signatures or model attacks. If signatures are too specific, a change in an attack tactic could result in a false negative (missed alarm). An attack signature should be broad enough to cover an entire class of attacks. On the other hand, if signatures are too general, it can result in false positives.

Signature-based approaches have three inherent drawbacks: new attacks can be missed if a matching signature is not known; signatures require time to develop for new attacks; and new signatures must be distributed continually.

Snort is a popular example of a signature-based IDS (www.snort.org). Snort signatures are rules that define fields that match packets of information about the represented attack. Snort is packaged with more than 1800 rules covering a broad range of attacks, and new rules are constantly being written.

Behavior Anomalies

A behavior-based IDS is appealing for its potential to recognize new attacks without a known signature. It presumes that attacks will be different from normal behavior.

Hence the critical issue is how to define normal behavior, and anything outside of normal (anomalous) is classified as suspicious. A common approach is to define normal behavior in statistical terms, which allows for deviations within a range.

Behavior-based approaches have considerable challenges. First, normal behavior is based on past behavior. Thus, data about past behavior must be available for training the IDS. Second, behavior can and does change over time, so any IDS approach must be adaptive. Third, anomalies are just unusual events, not necessarily malicious ones. A behavior-based IDS might point out incidents to investigate further, but it is not good at discerning the exact nature of attacks.

Intrusion Prevention Systems

IDSs are passive techniques. They typically notify the systems administrator to investigate further and take the appropriate action. The response might be slow if the systems administrator is busy or the incident is time-consuming to investigate.

A variation called an *intrusion prevention system* (IPS) seeks to combine the traditional monitoring and analysis functions of an IDS with more active automated responses, such as automatically reconfiguring firewalls to block an attack. An IPS aims for a faster response than humans can achieve, but its accuracy depends on the same techniques as the traditional IDS. The response should not harm legitimate traffic, so accuracy is critical.

7. REACTIVE MEASURES

When an attack is detected and analyzed, systems administrators must exercise an appropriate response to the attack. One of the principles in security is that the response should be proportional to the threat. Obviously, the response will depend on the circumstances, but various options are available. Generally, it is possible to block, slow, modify,

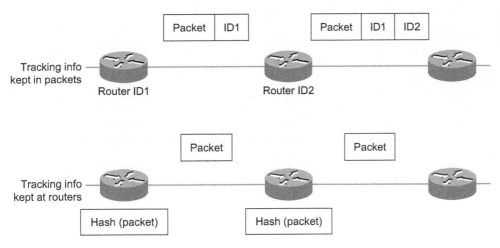

FIGURE 8.7 Tracking information stored at routers or carried in packets to enable packet traceback.

or redirect any malicious traffic. It is not possible to delineate every possible response. Here we describe only two responses: quarantine and traceback.

Quarantine

Dynamic quarantine in computer security is analogous to quarantine for infectious diseases. It is an appropriate response, particularly in the context of malware, to prevent an infected host from contaminating other hosts. Infectious malware requires connectivity between an infected host and a new target, so it is logical to disrupt the connectivity between hosts or networks as a means to impede the malware from spreading further.

Within the network, traffic can be blocked by firewalls or routers with ACLs. ACLs are similar to firewall rules, allowing routers to selectively drop packets.

Traceback

One of the critical aspects of an attack is the identity or location of the perpetrator. Unfortunately, discovery of an attacker in IP networks is almost impossible because:

- The source address in IP packets can be easily spoofed (forged).
- Routers are stateless by design and do not keep records of forwarded packets.
- Attackers can use a series of intermediary hosts (called *stepping stones* or *zombies*) to carry out their attacks.

Intermediaries are usually innocent computers taken over by an exploit or malware and put under control of the attacker. In practice, it might be possible to trace an attack back to the closest intermediary, but it might be too much to expect to trace an attack all the way back to the real attacker.

To trace a packet's route, some tracking information must be either stored at routers when the packet is forwarded

or carried in the packet, as shown in Fig. 8.7. An example of the first approach is to store a hash of a packet for some amount of time. If an attack occurs, the target host will query routers for a hash of the attack packet. If a router has the hash, it is evidence that the packet had been forwarded by that router. To reduce memory consumption, the hash is stored instead of storing the entire packet. The storage is temporary instead of permanent so that routers will not run out of memory.

An example of the second approach is to stamp packets with a unique router identifier, such as an IP address. Thus the packet carries a record of its route. The main advantage here is that routers can remain stateless. The problem is that there is no space in the IP packet header for this scheme.

8. NETWORK-BASED INTRUSION PROTECTION

Network-based IPS components are similar to other types of IPS technologies, except for the sensors. A network-based IPS sensor monitors and analyzes network activity on one or more network segments. Sensors are available in two formats: appliance-based sensors, which are comprised of specialized hardware and software optimized for IPS sensor use, and software-only sensors, which can be installed onto hosts that meet certain specifications.

Network-based IPSs also provide a wide variety of security capabilities. Some products can collect information on hosts such as which operating systems (OSs) they use and which application versions they use that communicate over networks. Network-based IPSs can also perform extensive logging of data related to detected events (see checklist: "An Agenda for Action for Logging Capabilities Activities"); most can also perform packet captures.

An Agenda for Action for Logging Capabilities Activities

As previously stated, network-based IPSs typically perform extensive logging of data related to detected events. This data can be used to confirm the validity of alerts, to investigate incidents, and to correlate events between the IPS and other logging sources. Data fields commonly logged by network-based IPSs includes the following key activities (check all tasks completed):

_____**1.** Timestamp (usually date and time).

_____**2.** Connection or session ID (typically a consecutive or unique number assigned to each TCP connection or to like groups of packets for connectionless protocols).

_____**3.** Event or alert type. In the console, the event or alert type often links to supporting information for the specific vulnerability or exploit, such as references for additional information and associated CVE numbers.

_____**4.** Rating (priority, severity, impact, confidence).

_____**5.** Network, transport, and application layer protocols.

_____**6.** Source and destination IP addresses.

_____**7.** Source and destination TCP or UDP ports, or ICMP types and codes.

_____**8.** Number of bytes transmitted over the connection.

_____**9.** Decoded payload data, such as application requests and responses.

_____**10.** State-related information (authenticated username).

_____**11.** Prevention action performed (if any).

---

9. SUMMARY

To guard against network intrusions, we must understand the variety of attacks, from exploits to malware to social engineering. Direct attacks are prevalent, but a class of *pull attacks* has emerged, relying on lures to bring victims to a malicious website. Pull attacks are much more difficult to uncover and in a way defend against. Just about anyone can become victimized.

Much can be done to fortify hosts and reduce their risk exposure, but some attacks are unavoidable. Defense in depth is a most practical defense strategy, combining layers of defenses. Although each defensive layer is imperfect, the cost becomes harder to surmount for intruders.

One of the essential defenses is *intrusion detection*. Host-based and network-based IDSs have their respective strengths and weaknesses. Research continues to be needed to improve intrusion detection, particularly behavior-based techniques. As more attacks are invented, signature-based techniques will have more difficulty keeping up.

Finally, let's move on to the real interactive part of this chapter: review questions/exercises, hands-on projects, case projects, and optional team case project. The answers and/ or solutions by chapter can be found in Appendix K.

CHAPTER REVIEW QUESTIONS/ EXERCISES

True/False

1. True or False? Traditionally, attack methods do not follow sequential steps analogous to physical attacks.
2. True or False? Malicious software, or malware, is not an enormous problem for Internet users because of its variety and prevalence and the level of danger it presents.
3. True or False? Traditional network attacks can be viewed as an "active" approach in which the attacker takes the initiative of a series of actions directed at a target.
4. True or False? The basic idea behind the *defense-in-depth strategy* is to hinder the attacker as much as possible with multiple layers of defense, even though each layer might be surmountable.
5. True or False? In computer security, *access control* refers to mechanisms to allow users to perform functions up to their unauthorized level and restrict users from performing authorized functions.

Multiple Choice

1. A stealthy type of malicious software (*malware*) designed to hide the existence of certain processes or programs from normal methods of detection is known as a:
   A. Wireless sniffer
   B. Rootkit
   C. Port scanner
   D. Port knocker
   E. Keystroke logger
2. If an intruder has installed malware for covert control, he/she will want to conceal the communications between him- or herself and the compromised target from discovery by:
   A. Network-based IDSs
   B. Tunneling
   C. Multiple time zones
   D. Budgets
   E. Networks
3. What is a commonly used method to place packets of one protocol into the payload of another packet?
   A. Encryption
   B. Signature-based
   C. Tunneling

  D. Hybrid detection
  E. Host-based
4. What is another obvious concealment method?
  A. Infection
  B. Rate
  C. Host
  D. Back door
  E. Encryption
5. What can be a Trojan horse or other form of malware?
  A. Antivirus
  B. Unified threat management
  C. Keylogger
  D. Firewall
  E. Antispam

EXERCISE

Problem

A physical security company has an innovative, patented product, and critical secrets to protect. For this company, protecting physical security and safeguarding network security go hand-in-hand. A web application in the data center tracks the serialized keycodes and allows customers to manage their key sets. The customers include everyone from theft-conscious retail chains to security-sensitive government agencies. In this case project, how would the security company go about establishing solid network security to protect them against intrusions?

Hands-On Projects

Project

A solution services company is also a managed service provider specializing in IT infrastructure, VoIP, wireless

broadband, data centers, and procurement. As part of a customer network security upgrade, how would the company go about establishing a solid network to protect a school district's network from external threats as well as the risk of unauthorized intrusions by users within the network?

Case Projects

Problem

For an international town's 10-person IT staff, upgrading its network security initiative meant expanding its multi-vendor Gigabit and Fast Ethernet network and ensuring that its growing volume of e-government services, including online tax payments, license application filings, and housing services, function without network intrusions. To accomplish this purpose, how would the town go about guarding against increasing waves of computer viruses, malware, and DoS attacks?

Optional Team Case Project

Problem

Intrusion types of systems are put in place to serve business needs for meeting an objective of network security; IDSs and IPSs provide a foundation of technology meets to tracking; and identifying network attacks which detect intrusions through logs of IDS systems and preventing an action through IPS systems. If a company hosts critical systems, confidential data, and strict compliance regulations, then it's a great to use IDS, IPS, or both in guarding network environments. So, what are the basic benefits of IDS and IPS systems?

Chapter 9

Fault Tolerance and Resilience in Cloud Computing Environments

Ravi Jhawar and Vincenzo Piuri
Universita' degli Studi di Milano, Crema, Italy

1. INTRODUCTION

Cloud computing is increasing in popularity over traditional information processing systems. Service providers have been building massive data centers that are distributed over several geographical regions to meet the demand efficiently for their cloud-based services [1−4]. In general, these data centers are built using hundreds of thousands of commodity servers, and virtualization technology is used to provision computing resources [e.g., by delivering virtual machines (VMs) with a given amount of CPU, memory, and storage capacity] over the Internet by following the pay-per-use business model [1]. Leveraging the economies of scale, a single physical host is often used as a set of several virtual hosts by the service provider, and benefits such as the semblance of an inexhaustible set of available computing resources are provided to users. As a consequence, an increasing number of users are moving to cloud-based services for realizing their applications and business processes.

However, the use of commodity components exposes the hardware to conditions for which it was not originally designed [5,6]. Moreover, owing to the highly complex nature of the underlying infrastructure, even carefully engineered data centers are subject to a large number of failures [7−9]. Dependability, security, and privacy in these complex infrastructures therefore become increasingly critical [10−14]. Failures evidently reduce the overall dependability, reliability, and availability of the cloud computing service. As a result, fault tolerance becomes of paramount importance to the users as well as the service providers to ensure correct and continuous system operation even in the presence of an unknown and unpredictable number of failures.

The dimension of risks on the user's applications deployed in the VM instances in a cloud has also changed because the failures in data centers are normally outside the scope of the user's organization. Moreover, traditional ways to achieve fault tolerance require users to have an in-depth knowledge of the underlying mechanisms, whereas, owing to the abstraction layers and business model of cloud computing, the system's architectural details are not widely available to the users. This implies that traditional methods of introducing fault tolerance may not be effective in a cloud computing context, and there is an increasing need to address users' concerns regarding reliability and availability.

The goal of this chapter is to develop an understanding of the nature, numbers, and kind of faults that appear in typical cloud computing infrastructures, how these faults affect user applications, and how faults can be handled in an efficient and cost-effective manner. With this aim, we first describe the fault model of typical cloud computing environments in Section 2 on the basis of the system architecture, the failure characteristics of a widely used server and network components, and analytical models. An overall understanding of the fault model may help researchers and developers to build more reliable cloud computing services. We introduce some basic and general concepts of fault tolerance and summarize parameters that must be taken into account when building a fault-tolerant system in Section 3. A scheme in which different levels of fault tolerance can be achieved by user applications by exploiting the properties of the cloud computing architecture is then presented in Section 4.

In Section 5, we discuss a solution that can function on user applications in a general and transparent manner to tolerate one of the two most frequent classes of faults that appear in the cloud computing environment. In Section 6, we present a scheme that can tolerate the other class of frequent faults while reducing overall resource costs by half compared with existing solutions in the literature. These two techniques, along with the concept of different fault tolerance levels, are used as the basis for developing a methodology and framework that offers fault tolerance as an additional service to user applications (see Section 7). We believe that the notion of offering fault tolerance as a service may serve as an efficient alternative to traditional approaches in addressing users' concerns regarding reliability and availability.

2. CLOUD COMPUTING FAULT MODEL

In general, a failure represents the condition in which the system deviates from fulfilling its intended functionality or the expected behavior. A failure happens as the result of an error: that is, the result of reaching an invalid system state. The hypothesized cause of an error is a fault that represents a fundamental impairment in the system. The notion of faults, errors, and failures can be represented using the following chain [15,16]:

… Fault → Error → Failure → Fault → Error → Failure …

Fault tolerance is the ability of the system to perform its function even in the presence of failures. This implies that it is of utmost importance to understand clearly and define what constitutes correct system behavior so that specifications regarding its characteristics of failure can be provided and consequently a fault-tolerant system be developed. In this section, we discuss the fault model of typical cloud computing environments to develop an understanding of the numbers and causes behind recurrent system failures. To analyze the distribution and impact of faults, we first describe the generic cloud computing architecture.

Cloud Computing Architecture

Cloud computing architecture is composed of four distinct layers, as illustrated in Fig. 9.1 [17]. Physical resources (e.g., blade servers and network switches) are considered to be the lowest layer in the stack, on top of which virtualization and system management tools are embedded to form the infrastructure-as-a-service (IaaS) layer [18]. Note that the infrastructure supporting large-scale cloud deployments is typically the data centers, and virtualization technology is used to maximize the use of physical resources, application isolation, and quality of service. Services offered by IaaS are normally accessed through a set of user-level middleware services, which provide an environment to simplify application development and deployment (e.g., Web 2.0 interfaces, libraries, and programming languages). The layer above the IaaS that binds all user-level middleware tools is referred to as platform-as-a-service (PaaS). User-level applications (e.g., social networks and scientific models) that are built and hosted on top of the PaaS layer comprise the software-as-a-service (SaaS) layer.

Failure in a given layer normally has an impact on services offered by the layers above it. For example, failure in user-level middleware (PaaS) may produce errors in the software services built on top of it (SaaS applications). Similarly, failures in physical hardware or the IaaS layer will have an impact on most PaaS and SaaS services. This implies that the impact of failures on the IaaS layer or the physical hardware is significantly high; hence, it is important to characterize typical hardware faults and develop corresponding fault tolerance techniques.

We describe the failure behavior of various server components based on the statistical information obtained from large-scale studies on data center failures using data mining techniques [6,19] and analyze the impact of component failures on user applications by means of analytical models such as fault trees and Markov chains [20,21]. Similar to server components, we present the behavior of network component failures.

Failure Behavior of Servers

Each server in the data center typically contains multiple processors, storage disks, memory modules, and network interfaces. The study of server failure and hardware repair

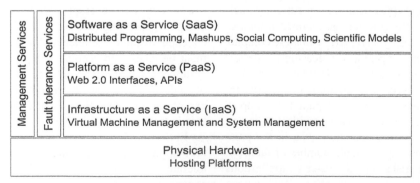

FIGURE 9.1 Layered architecture of cloud computing.

behavior is to be performed using a large collection of servers (approximately 100,000 servers) and corresponding data on part replacement, such as details about server configuration, when a hard disk was issued a ticked for replacement, and when it was actually replaced. Such a data repository, which includes a server collection spanning multiple data centers distributed across different countries, is gathered and described in Vishwanath and Nagappan [6]. Key observations derived from this study are that:

- 92% of machines do not see any repair events, but the average number of repairs for the remaining 8% is two per machine (20 repair/replacement events contained in nine machines were identified over 14 months). The annual failure rate (AFR) is therefore around 8%.
- For an 8% AFR, repair costs are approximately $2.5 million for 100,000 servers.
- About 78% of total faults/replacements were detected on hard disks and 5% on redundant array of inexpensive disks controllers; 3% resulted from memory failures; and 13% of replacements were due to a collection of components (not particularly dominated by a single component failure). Hard disks are clearly the most failure-prone hardware components and the most significant reason behind server failures.
- About 5% of servers experience a disk failure less than 1 year from the date when they are commissioned (young servers) and 12% when the machines are 1 year old; 25% of servers experience hard disk failures when they are 2 years old.
- Interestingly, based on chi-squared automatic interaction detector methodology, none of the following factors were a significant indicator of failure: age of the server, its configuration, location within the rack and workload run on the machine.
- Comparison of the number of repairs per machine (RPM) and the number of disks per server in a group of servers (clusters) indicates that (1) there is a relationship in the failure characteristics of servers that have already experienced a failure, and (2) the number of RPM has a correspondence to the total number of disks on that machine.

Based on these statistics, it can be inferred that robust fault tolerance mechanisms must be applied to improve the reliability of hard disks (assuming independent component failures) to substantially reduce the number of failures. Furthermore, to meet the high availability and reliability requirements, applications must reduce utilization of hard disks that have already experienced a failure (since the probability of seeing another failure on that hard disk is higher).

Failure behavior of servers can also be analyzed based on the models defined using fault trees and Markov chains [20–22]. The rationale behind the modeling is twofold: (1) to capture the user's perspective on component failures,

that is, understand the behavior of user's applications that are deployed in the VM instances under server component failures and (2) to define the correlation between individual component failures and the boundaries on the impact of each failure. An application may have an impact when there is a failure/error either in the processor, memory modules, storage disks, power supply or network interfaces of the server, or the hypervisor, or the VM instance itself. Fig. 9.2A and B illustrate this behavior as a fault tree where the top-event represents a failure in the user's application. Reliability and availability of each server component must be derived using Markov models that are populated using long-term failure behavior information such as the one described in [6].

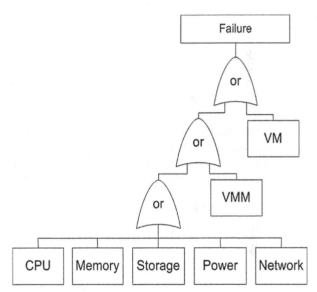

FIGURE 9.2A Fault tree characterizing server failures [20]. *VM*, virtual machine; *VMM*, virtual machine monitor.

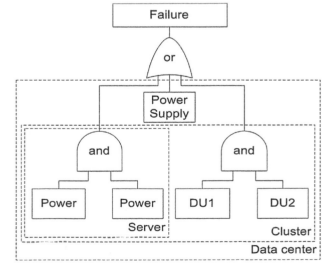

FIGURE 9.2B Fault tree characterizing power failures [20]. *DU*, depleted uranium.

Failure Behavior of the Network

It is important to understand the overall network topology and various network components involved in constructing a data center, so as to characterize network failure behavior. Fig. 9.3A illustrates an example of partial data center network architecture [19,22]. Servers are connected using a set of network switches and routers. In particular, all rack-mounted servers are first connected via a 1-gigabit per second link to a top-of-rack switch (ToR), which is in turn connected to two (primary and backup) aggregation switches (AggSs). An AggS connects tens of switches (ToRs) to redundant access routers (AccRs). This implies that each AccR handles traffic from thousands of servers and routes it to core routers that connect different data centers to the Internet [19–21]. All links in the data centers commonly use Ethernet as the link layer protocol, and redundancy is applied to all network components at each layer in the network topology (except for ToRs). In addition, redundant pairs of load balancers (LBs) are connected to each AggS and mapping between the static Internet Protocol (IP) address presented to users and the dynamic IP addresses of internal servers that process users' requests is performed. Similar to the study on the failure behavior of servers, a large-scale study on network failures in data centers is performed in Gill et al. [19]. A link failure happens when the connection between two devices on a specific interface is down, and a device failure happens when the device is not routing/forwarding packets correctly (e.g., owing to a power outage or hardware crash). Key observations derived from this study are that:

- Among all network devices, LBs are the least reliable (with a failure probability of 1 in 5) and ToRs the most reliable (with a failure rate of less than 5%). The

root causes for failures in LBs are mainly software bugs and configuration errors (as opposed to hardware errors for other devices). Moreover, LBs tend to experience short but frequent failures. This observation indicates that low-cost commodity switches (e.g., ToRs and AggSs) provide sufficient reliability.

- The links forwarding traffic from LBs have the highest failure rates; links higher in the topology (e.g., connecting AccRs) and links connecting redundant devices have the second highest failure rates.
- The estimated median number of packets lost during a failure is 59,000 and the median number of bytes is 25 MB (the average size of lost packets is 423 bytes). Based on prior measurement studies (that observe packet sizes to be bimodal with modes around 200 and 1400 bytes), it is estimated that most lost packets belong to the lower part (e.g., ping messages or ACKs).
- Network redundancy reduces the median impact of failures (in terms of the number of lost bytes) by only 40%. This observation goes against the common belief that network redundancy completely masks failures from applications.

Therefore, overall data center network reliability is about 99.99% for 80% of links and 60% of devices. Similar to servers, Fig. 9.3B represents the fault tree for users' application failure with respect to network failures in the data center. A failure happens when there is an error in all redundant switches: ToRs, AggS, AccR; or, core routers; or, the network links connecting physical hosts. Because the model is designed from the user's perspective, a failure in this context implies that the application is not connected to the rest of the network or gives errors during data transmission. Using this modeling technique, the boundaries on the impact of each network failure can be represented (using server, cluster, and data center–level blocks) and can be used further to increase the fault tolerance of the user's application (e.g., by placing replicas of an application in different failure zones).

3. BASIC CONCEPTS OF FAULT TOLERANCE

In general, the faults we analyzed in Section 2 can be classified in different ways depending on the nature of the system. Because in this chapter we are interested in typical cloud computing environment faults that appear as failures to end users, we classify the faults into two types, similar to other distributed systems:

- *Crash faults* that cause system components to stop functioning completely or to remain inactive during failures (e.g., power outage, hard disk crash)

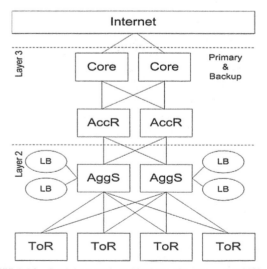

FIGURE 9.3A Partial network architecture of a data center [19]. *AccR*, access router switch; *AggS*, aggregation switch; *LB*, load balancer; *ToR*, top-of-rack switch.

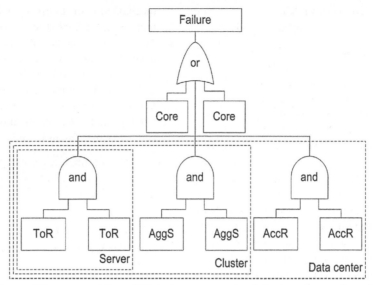

FIGURE 9.3B Fault tree characterizing network failures [20]. *AccR*, access router switch; *AggS*, aggregation switch; *ToR*, top-of-rack switch.

- *Byzantine faults* that lead system components to behave arbitrarily or maliciously during failure, causing the system to behave unpredictably incorrect

As observed previously, fault tolerance is the ability of the system to perform its function even in the presence of failures. It serves as a means to improve the overall system's dependability. In particular, it contributes significantly to increasing the system's reliability and availability.

The most widely adopted methods to achieving fault tolerance against crash faults and Byzantine faults are:

- *Checking and monitoring*: The system is constantly monitored at runtime to validate, verify, and ensure that correct system specifications are being met. This technique, although simple, has a key role in failure detection and subsequent reconfiguration.
- *Checkpoint and restart*: The system state is captured and saved based on predefined parameters (e.g., after every 1024 instructions or every 60 s). When the system undergoes a failure, it is restored to the previously known correct state using the latest checkpoint information (instead of restarting the system from start).
- *Replication*: Critical system components are duplicated using additional hardware, software, and network resources in such a way that a copy of the critical components is available even after a failure happens. Replication mechanisms are mainly used in two formats: active and passive. In active replication, all of the replicas are simultaneously invoked and each replica processes the same request at the same time. This implies that all replicas have the same system state at any given point in time (unless they are designed to function in an asynchronous manner) and it can continue to deliver its service even in case of a single replica failure. In passive replication,

only one processing unit (the primary replica) processes the requests while the backup replicas save the system state only during normal execution periods. Backup replicas take over the execution process only when the primary replica fails.

Variants of traditional replication mechanisms (active and passive) are often applied on modern distributed systems. For example, the semiactive replication technique is derived from traditional approaches in which primary and backup replicas execute all of the instructions but only the output generated by the primary replica is made available to the user. Output generated by the backup replicas is logged and suppressed within the system so that it can readily resume the execution process when the primary replica failure happens. Fig. 9.4A depicts the Markov model of a system that uses an active/semiactive replication scheme with two replicas [20,21]. This model serves as an effective means to derive the reliability and availability of the system because failure behavior of both replicas can be taken into account. Moreover, as described in Section 2, the results of the Markov model analysis can be used to support the fault

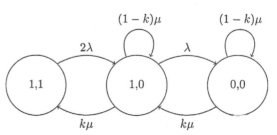

FIGURE 9.4A Markov model of a system with two replicas in active/semiactive replication scheme [20].

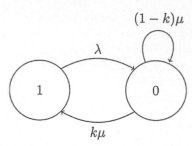

FIGURE 9.4B Markov model of a system with two replicas in passive replication scheme [20].

trees in characterizing the impact of failures in the system. Each state in the model is represented by a pair (x, y), where x = 1 denotes that the primary replica is working and x = 0 implies that it failed. Similarly, y represents the working condition of the backup replica. The system starts and remains in state (1,1) during normal execution, i.e., when both of the replicas are available and working correctly.

A failure in either the primary or the backup replica moves the system to state (0,1) or (1,0) where the other replica takes over the execution process. A single state is sufficient to represent this condition in the model because both replicas are consistent with each other. The system typically initiates its recovery mechanism in state (0,1) or (1,0) and moves to state (1,1) if the recovery of failed replica is successful; otherwise it transits to state (0,0) and becomes completely unavailable. Similarly, Fig. 9.4B illustrates the Markov model of the system for which a passive replication scheme is applied. λ denotes the failure rate, μ denotes the recovery rate, and k is a constant.

Fault tolerance mechanisms are successful to varying degrees in tolerating faults [23]. For example, a passively replicated system can tolerate only crash faults, whereas actively replicated system using $3f + 1$ replicas are capable of tolerating Byzantine faults. In general, mechanisms that handle failures at a finer granularity, offering higher-performance guarantees, also consume higher amount of resources [24,25]. Therefore, the design of fault tolerance mechanisms must take into account a number of factors such as implementation complexity, resource costs, resilience, and performance metrics, and achieve a fine balance of the following parameters:

- *Fault tolerance model*: measures the strength of the fault tolerance mechanism in terms of the granularity at which it can handle errors and failures in the system. This factor is characterized by the robustness of failure detection protocols, state synchronization methods, and strength of the fail-over granularity.
- *Resource consumption*: measures the amount and cost of resources that are required to realize a fault tolerance mechanism. This factor is normally inherent with the granularity of the failure detection and recovery

mechanisms in terms of CPU, memory, bandwidth, input–output, and so on.

- *Performance*: deals with the impact of the fault tolerance procedure on the end-to-end quality of service (QoS) during both failure and failure-free periods. This impact is often characterized using fault detection latency, replica launch latency, and failure recovery latency, and other application-dependent metrics such as bandwidth, latency, and loss rate.

We build on the basic concepts discussed in this section to analyze the fault tolerance properties of various schemes designed for cloud computing environment.

4. DIFFERENT LEVELS OF FAULT TOLERANCE IN CLOUD COMPUTING

As discussed in Section 2, server components in a cloud computing environment are subject to failures affecting user applications, and each failure has an impact within a given boundary in the system. For example, a crash in the pair of aggregate switches may result in the loss of communication among all servers in a cluster; in this context, the boundary of failure is the cluster because applications in other clusters can continue functioning normally. Therefore, while applying a fault tolerance mechanism such as a replication scheme, at least one replica of the application must be placed in a different cluster to ensure that aggregate switch failure does not result in a complete failure of the application. Furthermore, this implies that deployment scenarios (i.e., the location of each replica) are critical to realize the fault tolerance mechanisms correctly. In this section, we discuss possible deployment scenarios in a cloud computing infrastructure, and the advantages and limitations of each scenario.

Based on the architecture of the cloud computing infrastructure, different levels of failure independence can be derived for cloud computing services [26,27]. Moreover, assuming that the failures in individual resource components are independent of each other, fault tolerance and resource costs of an application can be balanced based on the location of its replicas. Possible deployment scenarios and their properties are:

- *Multiple machines within the same cluster:* Two replicas of an application can be placed on the hosts that are connected by a ToR switch, i.e., within a local area network (LAN). Replicas deployed in this configuration can benefit in terms of low latency and high bandwidth but obtain limited failure independence. A single switch or power distribution failure may result in an outage of the entire application, and both replicas cannot communicate to complete the fault tolerance protocol. Cluster level blocks in the fault trees of each resource component (e.g., network failures as shown in Fig. 9.3B) must be combined using a logical AND operator to analyze the overall impact of failures in the system. Note that reliability and availability values for each fault tolerance mechanism with respect to server faults must be calculated using a Markov model.

- *Multiple clusters within a data center:* Two replicas of an application can be placed on the hosts belonging to different clusters in the same data center, i.e., on the hosts that are connected via a ToR switch and AggS. Failure independence of the application in this deployment context remains moderate because the replicas are not bound to an outage with a single power distribution or switch failure. The overall availability of an application can be calculated using cluster level blocks from fault trees combined with a logical OR operator in conjunction with power and network using AND operator.

- *Multiple data centers:* Two replicas of an application can be placed on the hosts belonging to different data centers (connected via a switch, AggS and AccR). This deployment has a drawback with respect to high latency and low bandwidth, but offers a high level of failure independence. A single power failure has least effect on the availability of the application. The data center level blocks from the fault trees may be connected with a logical OR operator in conjunction with the network in the AND logic.

As an example, using the data published in Smith et al. [22] and Kim et al. [28], the overall availability of each representative replication scheme with respect to different deployment levels is obtained as shown in Table 9.1. Availability of the system is highest when the replicas are placed in two different data centers. The value reduces when replicas are placed in two different clusters within the same data center and lowest when replicas are placed inside the same LAN. Overall availability obtained by semiactive replication is higher than semipassive replication and lowest for a simple passive replication scheme.

As described in Section 3, effective implementation of fault tolerance mechanisms requires consideration of the strength of fault tolerance model, resource costs, and performance. Whereas traditional fault tolerance methods require tailoring of each application with an in-depth knowledge of the underlying infrastructure, in a cloud computing scenario, it would also be beneficial to develop methodologies that can generically function on users' applications so that a large number of applications can be protected using the same protocol. In addition to generality, agility in managing replicas and checkpoints to improve the performance, and reduction in resource consumption costs while not limiting the strength of fault tolerance mechanisms are required.

Although several fault tolerance approaches are being proposed for cloud computing services, most solutions that achieve at least one of the required properties described here are based on virtualization technology. Using virtualization-based approaches, it is also possible to deal with both classes of faults that are discussed in Section 3. In particular, in Section 5 we present a virtualization-based solution that provides fault tolerance against crash failures using a checkpointing mechanism. We discuss this solution because it offers two additional, significantly useful properties: (1) fault tolerance is induced independent of the applications and hardware on which it runs. In other words, an increased level of generality is achieved because any application can be protected using the same protocol as long as it is deployed in a VM; and (2) mechanisms such as replication, failure detection, and recovery are applied transparently, not modifying the operating system (OS) or application's source code. Then, in Section 6 we present a virtualization-based solution that uses typical properties of a cloud computing environment to tolerate Byzantine faults using a combination of replication and checkpointing techniques. We discuss this solution because it reduces by nearly half the resource consumption costs incurred by typical Byzantine Fault Tolerance (BFT) schemes during fail-free periods.

5. FAULT TOLERANCE AGAINST CRASH FAILURES IN CLOUD COMPUTING

A scheme that leverages virtualization technology to tolerate crash faults in the cloud in a transparent manner is discussed in this section. The system or user application that must be protected from failures is first encapsulated in a VM (say an active VM or the primary), and operations are performed at the VM level (in contrast to traditional approach of operating at the application level) to obtain paired servers that run in active—passive configuration. Because the protocol is applied at the VM level, this scheme can be used independent of the application and underlying hardware, offering an increased level of generality. In particular, we discuss the design of *Remus* as an example system that offers these properties [29]. Remus

TABLE 9.1 Availability Values (Normalized to 1) for Replication Techniques at Different Deployment Scenarios [20]

	Same Cluster	Same Data Center, Different Clusters	Different Data Centers
Semiactive	0.9871	0.9913	0.9985
Semipassive	0.9826	0.9840	0.9912
Passive	0.9542	0.9723	0.9766

aims to provide high availability to the applications; to achieve this, it works in four phases:

1. Checkpoint the changed memory state at the primary and continue to the next epoch of network and disk request streams.
2. Replicate system state on the backup.
3. Send checkpoint acknowledgment from the backup when complete memory checkpoint and corresponding disk requests have been received.
4. Release outbound network packets queued during the previous epoch upon receiving the acknowledgment.

Remus achieves high-availability by frequently checkpointing and transmitting the state of the active VM onto a backup physical host. The VM image on the backup resides in the memory and may begin execution immediately after a failure in the active VM is detected. The backup only acts like a receptor because the VM in the backup host is not actually executed during fail-free periods. This allows the backup to receive checkpoints concurrently from VMs running on multiple physical hosts (in an N-to-1 style configuration), which provides a higher degree of freedom in balancing resource costs owing to redundancy.

In addition to generality and transparency, seamless failure recovery can be achieved, i.e., no externally visible state is lost in case of a single host failure, and recovery happens rapidly enough that it appears only like a temporary packet loss. Because the backup is only periodically consistent with the primary replica using the checkpoint-transmission procedure, all network output is buffered until a consistent image of the host is received by the backup, and the buffer is released only when the backup is completely synchronized with the primary. Unlike network traffic, the disk state is not externally visible but it has to be transmitted to the backup as part of a complete cycle. To address this, Remus asynchronously sends the disk state to the backup where it is initially buffered in the RAM. When the corresponding memory state is received, complete checkpoint is acknowledged, output is made visible to the user, and the buffered disk state is applied to the backup disk.

Remus is built on Xen hypervisor's live migration machinery [30]. Live migration is a technique using which a complete VM can be relocated onto another physical host in the network (typically a LAN) with a minor interruption to the VM. Xen provides an ability to track a guest's writes to memory using a technique called shadow page tables. During live migration, memory of the VM is copied to the new location while the VM continues to run normally at the old location. The writes to the memory are then tracked and the dirtied pages are transferred to the new location periodically. After a sufficient number of iterations, or when no progress in copying the memory is being made (i.e., when the VM is writing to the memory as fast as the migration process), the guest VM is suspended, remaining dirtied memory along

with the CPU state is copied, and the VM image in the new location is activated. The total migration time depends on the amount of dirtied memory during guest execution, and total downtime depends on the amount of memory remaining to be copied when the guest is suspended. The protocol design of the system, particularly each checkpoint, can be viewed as the final stop-and-copy phase of live migration. The guest memory in live migration is iteratively copied, incurring several minutes of execution time. The singular stop-and-copy (the final step) operation incurs a limited overhead, typically on the order of a few milliseconds.

Whereas Remus provides an efficient replication mechanism, it employs a simple failure detection technique that is directly integrated within the checkpoint stream. A timeout of the backup in response to commit requests made by the primary will result in the primary suspecting a failure (crash and disabled protection) in the backup. Similarly, a timeout of the new checkpoints being transmitted from the primary will result in the backup assuming a failure in the primary. At this point, the backup begins execution from the latest checkpoint. The protocol is evaluated (1) to understand whether the overall approach is practically deployable, and (2) to analyze the kind of workloads that are most amenable to this approach.

Correctness evaluation is performed by deliberately injecting network failures at each phase of the protocol. The application (or the protected system) runs a kernel compilation process to generate CPU, memory, and disk load; and a graphics-intensive client (glxgears) attached to an X11 server is simultaneously executed to generate the network traffic. Checkpoint frequency is configured to 25 ms and each test is performed two times. It is reported that the backup successfully took over the execution for each failure with a network delay of about 1 s when the backup detected the failure and activated the replicated system. The kernel compilation task continued to completion and the glxgears client resumed after a brief pause. The disk image showed no inconsistencies when the VM was gracefully shut down.

Performance evaluation is performed using the SPECweb benchmark, which is composed of a Web server, an application server, and one or more Web client simulators. Each tier (server) was deployed in a different VM. The observed scores decrease the native score up to five times (305) when the checkpointing system is active. This behavior is mainly the result of network buffering; the observed scores are much higher when network buffering is disabled. Furthermore, it is reported that at configuration rates of 10, 20, 30, and 40 checkpoints per second, the average checkpoint rates achieved are 9.98, 16.38, 20.25, and 23.34, respectively. This behavior can be explained with SPECweb's fast memory dirtying, which results in slower checkpoints than desired. The realistic workload hence illustrates that the amount of network traffic generated by the checkpointing protocol is considerably large; as

TABLE 9.2 Resource Consumption Costs Incurred by Well-Known Byzantine Fault Tolerance Protocols [32]

	Practical Byzantine Fault Tolerance [31]	Security Evaluation Program [34]	Zyzzyva [33]	ZZ [32]
Agreement replicas	$3f + 1$	$3f + 1$	$3f + 1$	$3f + 1$
Execution replicas	$3f + 1$	$2f + 1$	$2f + 1$	$(1 + r)f + 1$

consequence, this system is not well-suited for applications that are sensitive to network latencies. Therefore, virtualization technology can largely be exploited to develop general-purpose fault tolerance schemes that can be applied to handle crash faults in a transparent manner.

6. FAULT TOLERANCE AGAINST BYZANTINE FAILURES IN CLOUD COMPUTING

BFT protocols are powerful approaches to obtaining highly reliable and available systems. Despite numerous efforts, most BFT systems have been too expensive for practical use; so far, no commercial data centers have employed BFT techniques. For example, the BFT algorithm presented in Castro and Liskov [31] for asynchronous, distributed, client–server systems requires at least a $3f + 1$ replica (one primary and remaining backup) to execute a three-phase protocol that can tolerate f Byzantine faults. As described in Section 3, systems that tolerate faults at a finer granularity, such as Byzantine faults, also consume high amounts of resources, and as discussed in Section 4, it is critical to consider the resource costs while implementing a fault tolerance solution.

The high resource consumption cost in BFT protocols is most likely caused by the way faults are normally handled. BFT approaches typically replicate the server [state machine replication (SMR)] and each replica is forced to execute the same request in the same order. This enforcement requirement demands the server replicas to reach an agreement on the ordering of a given set of requests even in the presence of Byzantine faulty servers and clients. For this purpose, an agreement protocol referred to as a *Byzantine Agreement* is used. When an agreement on the ordering is reached, service execution is performed and a majority voting scheme is devised to choose the correct output (and to detect the faulty server). This implies that two clusters of replicas are necessary to realize BFT protocols.

When realistic data center services implement BFT protocols, the dominant costs result from the hardware performing service execution and not from running the agreement protocol [32]. For instance, a toy application running *null* requests with the Zyzzyva BFT approach [33] exhibits a peak throughput of 80,000 requests/s whereas a

database service running the same protocol on comparable hardware exhibits almost three times lower throughput. Based on this observation, ZZ, an execution approach that can be integrated with existing BFT SMR and agreement protocols, is presented in Wood et al. [32]. The prototype of ZZ is built on the Base implementation [31] and guarantees BFT while significantly reducing resource consumption costs during fail-free periods. Table 9.2 compares resource costs of well-known BFT techniques. Because ZZ provides an effective balance between resource consumption costs and a fault tolerance model, in this section we subsequently discuss its system design in detail.

The design of ZZ is based on virtualization technology and is targeted to tolerate Byzantine faults while reducing resource provisioning costs incurred by BFT protocols during fail-free periods. The cost reduction benefits of ZZ can be obtained only when BFT is used in the data center running multiple applications so that sleeping replicas can be distributed across the pool of servers and higher peak throughput can be achieved when execution dominates the request processing cost and resources are constrained. These assumptions make ZZ a suitable scheme to be applied in a cloud computing environment. The system model of ZZ makes the following assumptions similar to most existing BFT systems:

- The service is deterministic, or nondeterministic operations in the service can be transformed to deterministic ones using an agreement protocol (i.e., ZZ assumes an SMR-based BFT system).
- The system involves two kinds of replicas (1) *agreement replicas* that assign an order to clients' requests, and (2) *execution replicas* that execute each client's request in the same order and maintain the application state.
- Each replica fails independently and exhibits Byzantine behavior (i.e., faulty replicas and clients may behave arbitrarily).
- An adversary can coordinate faulty nodes in an arbitrary manner, but it cannot circumvent standard cryptographic measures (e.g., collision resistant hash functions, encryption scheme, and digital signatures).
- An upper-bound g on the number of faulty agreement replicas and f execution replicas is assumed for a given window of vulnerability.

- The system can ensure safety in an asynchronous network, but liveness is guaranteed only during periods of synchrony.

Because the system runs replicas inside VMs, to maintain failure independence requires a physical host to deploy at most one agreement and one execution replicas of the service simultaneously. The novelty in the system model is that it considers a Byzantine hypervisor. Note that as a consequence of this replica placement constraint, a malicious hypervisor can be treated simply by considering a single fault in all of the replicas deployed on that physical host. Similarly, an upper bound f on the number of faulty hypervisors is assumed. The BFT execution protocol reduces the replication cost from $2f + 1$ to $f + 1$ based on the following principle:

- A system that is designed to function correctly in an asynchronous environment will provide correct results even if some of the replicas are outdated.
- A system that is designed to function correctly in the presence of f Byzantine faults will, during a fault-free period, remain unaffected even if up to f replicas are turned off.

The second observation is used to commission only an $f + 1$ replica to execute requests actively. The system is in a correct state if the responses obtained from all $f + 1$ replicas are the same. In case of a failure (i.e., when responses do not match), the first observation is used to continue system operation as if the f standby replicas were slow but correct replicas.

To correctly realize this design, the system requires an agile replica wake-up mechanism. To achieve this, the system exploits virtualization technology by maintaining additional replicas (VMs) in a "dormant" state, which are either prespawned but paused VMs or the VM that is hibernated to a disk. There is a trade-off in adopting either method. Prespawned VMs can resume execution in a short span (on the order of a few milliseconds) but consume memory higher resources, whereas VMs hibernated to disks incur greater recovery times but occupy only storage space. This design also raises several interesting challenges, such as: *How can a restored replica obtain the necessary application state that is required to execute the current request? How can the replication cost be made robust to faulty replica or client behavior? Does the transfer of entire application state take an unacceptably long time?*

The system builds on the BFT protocol that uses independent agreement and execution clusters (similar to Yin et al. [34]). Let A represent the set of replicas in the agreement cluster, $|A| = 2g + 1$, that runs the three-phase agreement protocol [31]. When a client c sends its request Q to the agreement cluster to process an operation o with timestamp t, the agreement cluster assigns a sequence number n to the request. The timestamp is used to ensure that each client request is executed only once and a faulty client behavior does not affect other clients' requests. When an agreement replica j learns of the sequence number n committed to Q, it sends a commit message C to all execution replicas.

Let E represent the set of replicas in the execution cluster where $|E| = f + 1$ during fail-free periods. When an execution replica i receives $2g + 1$ valid and matching commit messages from A, in the form of a commit certificate $\{C_i\}$, $i \in A \,|2g + 1$, and if it has already processed all the requests with a sequence lower than n, it produces a reply R and sends it to the client. The execution cluster also generates an execution report ER for the agreement cluster.

During normal execution, the response certificate $\{R_i\}$, $i \in E|f + 1$ obtained by the client matches replies from all $f + 1$ execution nodes. To avoid unnecessary wake ups resulting from a partially faulty execution replica that replies correctly to the agreement cluster but delivers a wrong response to the client, ZZ introduces an additional check as follows: When the replies are not matching, the client resends the same request to the agreement cluster. The agreement cluster sends a reply affirmation RA to the client if it has $f + 1$ valid responses for the retransmitted request. In this context, the client accepts the reply if it receives $g + 1$ messages containing a response digest $\overline{R}$ that matches one of the replies already received. Finally, if the agreement cluster does not generate an affirmation for the client, additional nodes are started.

ZZ uses periodic checkpoints to update the state of newly commissioned replicas and to perform garbage collection on the replica's logs. Execution nodes create checkpoints of the application state and reply logs, generate a checkpoint proof CP, and send it all execution and agreement nodes. The checkpoint proof is in the form of a digest that allows a recovering node to identify the checkpoint data they obtain from potentially faulty nodes; and, the checkpoint certificate $\{CP_i\}$, $i \in E|f + 1$ which is a set of $f + 1$ CP messages with matching digests.

Fault detection in the execution replicas is based on timeouts. Both lower and higher values of timeouts may affect the system's performance. The former may falsely detect failures and the latter may provide a window into the faulty replicas to degrade the system's performance. To set appropriate timeouts, ZZ suggests the following procedure: the agreement replica sets the timeout τ_n to Kt_1 upon receiving the first response to the request with sequence number n; t_1 is the response time and K is a preconfigured variance bound. Based on this trivial theory, ZZ proves that a replica faulty with a given probability p can inflate average response time by a factor of:

$$\max\left(1, \sum_{0 \le m \le f} P(m)I(m)\right)$$

where:

$$P(m) = \binom{f}{m} p^m (1-p)^{f-m}$$

$$I(m) = \max\left(1, \frac{K \cdot E[MIN_{f+1-m}]}{E[MAX_{f+1}]}\right)$$

$P(m)$ represents the probability of m simultaneous failures and $I(m)$ is the response time inflation that m faulty nodes can inflict. Assuming identically distributed response times for a given distribution, $E[MIN_{f+1-m}]$ is the expected minimum time for a set of $f+1-m$ replicas and $E[MAX_{f+1}]$ is the expected maximum response time of all $f+1$ replicas [32]. Replication costs vary from $f+1$ to $2f+1$, depending on the probability of replicas being faulty p and the likelihood of false timeouts π_1. Formally, the expected replication cost is less than $(1+r)f+1$, where $r = 1 - (1-p)^{f+1} + (1-p)^{f+1}\pi_1$. Therefore, virtualization technology can be used effectively to realize BFT mechanisms at significantly lower resource consumption costs.

7. FAULT TOLERANCE AS A SERVICE IN CLOUD COMPUTING

The drawback of the solutions discussed in Sections 5 and 6 is that the user must either tailor its application using a specific protocol (e.g., ZZ) by taking into account the system architecture details or require the service provider to implement a solution for its applications (e.g., Remus). Note that (1) the fault tolerance properties of the application remain constant throughout its life cycle using this methodology, and (2) users may not have all of the architectural details of the service provider's system. However, the availability of a pool of fault tolerance mechanisms that provide transparency and generality can allow the realization of the notion of fault tolerance as a service. The latter perspective to fault tolerance intuitively provides immense benefits.

As a motivating example, consider a user that offers a Web-based e-commerce service to its customers that allows them to pay their bills and manage fund transfers over the Internet. The user implements the e-commerce service as a multitier application that uses the storage service of the service provider to store and retrieve its customer data and compute service to process its operations and respond to customer queries. In this context, a failure in the service provider's system can affect the reliability and availability of the e-commerce service. The implications of a storage server failure may be much higher than a failure in one of the compute nodes. This implies that each tier of the e-commerce application must possess different levels of fault tolerance, and the reliability and availability goals may change over time based on the business demands.

Using traditional methods, fault tolerance properties of the e-commerce application remains constant throughout its life cycle, and hence according to the user's perspective, it is complementary to engage with a third party [the fault tolerance service provider (ftSP)], specify its requirements based on the business needs, and transparently possess desired fault tolerance properties without studying the low-level fault tolerance mechanisms.

The ftSP must realize a range of fault tolerance techniques as individual modules (e.g., separate agreement and execution protocols, and heartbeat-based fault detection technique as an independent module) to benefit from the economies of scale. For example, because failure detection techniques in Remus and ZZ are based on the same principle, instead of integrating the liveness requests within the checkpointing stream, the heartbeat test module can be reused in both solutions. However, realization of this notion requires a technique for selecting appropriate fault tolerance mechanisms based on the user's requirements and a general-purpose framework that can integrate with the cloud computing environment. Without such a framework, individual applications must implement their own solution, resulting in a highly complex system environment. Further in this section, we present a solution that supports ftSP to realize its service effectively.

To abstract low-level system procedures from users, a new dimension to fault tolerance is presented in the literature [21,25,35–39] in which applications deployed in VM instances in a cloud computing environment can obtain desired fault tolerance properties from a third-party as a service. The new dimension realizes a range of fault tolerance mechanisms that can transparently function on user applications as independent modules, and a set of metadata is associated with each module to characterize its fault tolerance properties. The metadata are used to select appropriate mechanisms based on user requirements. A complete fault tolerance solution is then composed using selected fault tolerance modules and delivered to the user's application.

Consider ft_unit to be the fundamental module that applies a coherent fault tolerance mechanism, in a transparent manner, to a recurrent system failure at the granularity of a VM instance. An ft_unit handles the impact of hardware failures by applying fault tolerance mechanisms at the virtualization layer rather than the user's application. Examples of ft_units include the replication scheme for the e-commerce application that uses checkpointing technique such as Remus (ft_unit1), and the node failure detection technique using the heartbeat test (ft_sol2). Assuming that the ftSP realizes a range of fault tolerance mechanisms as ft_units, a two-stage delivery scheme that can deliver fault tolerance as a service is as follows:

The *design stage* starts when a user requests the ftSP to deliver a solution with a given set of fault tolerance properties to its application. Each ft_unit provides a unique set of properties; the ftSP banks on this observation and defines the fault tolerance property p corresponding to each ft_unit as $p = (u, \widehat{p}, A)$, where u represents the ft_unit, $\widehat{p}$ denotes high-level abstract properties such as reliability and availability, and A denotes the set of functional, structural, and operational attributes that characterize the ft_unit u. The set A sufficiently refers to the granularity at which the ft_unit can handle failures, its limitations and advantages, resource consumption costs, and QoS parameters. Each attribute $a \in A$ takes a value $v(a)$ from a domain D_a and a partial (or total) ordered relationship is defined on the domain D_a. The values for the abstract properties are derived using the notion of fault trees and Markov model, as described for the availability property in Table 9.1. An example fault tolerance property for the ft_unit u_1 is $p = (u_1, \widehat{p} = \{reliability = 98.9\%,\ availability = 99.95\%\}, A = \{mechanism = semiactive\_replication, fault\_model = server\_crashes, power\_outage, number\_of\_replicas = 4\})$

Similar to the domain of attribute values, a hierarchy of fault tolerance properties $\leq_p$ is also defined: If P is the set of properties, and given two properties $p_i, p_j \in P$, $p_i \leq_p p_j$ if $p_i \cdot \widehat{p} = p_j \cdot \widehat{p}$ and for all $a \in A$, $v_i(a) \leq v_j(a)$. This hierarchy suggests that all ft_units that hold the property p_j also satisfy the property p_i. Fault tolerance requirements of the users are assumed to be specified as desired properties p_c, and for each user request, the ftSP first generates a short-listed set S of ft_units that match p_c. Each ft_unit within the set S is then compared, and an ordered list based on user requirements is created. An example of the matching, comparison, and selection process is as follows:

As an example, assume that the ftSP realizes three ft_units with properties:

$p_1 = (u_1, A = \{mechanism = heartbeat\_test, time-out\_period = 50 ms, number\_of\_replicas = 3, fault\_model = node\_crashes\})$

$p_2 = (u_2, A = \{mechanism = majority\_voting, fault\_model = programming\_errors\})$

$p_3 = (u_3, A = \{mechanism = heartbeat\_test, time-out\_period = 25 ms, number\_of\_replicas = 5, fault\_model = node\_crashes\})$

respectively. If the user requests fault tolerance support with a robust crash failure detection scheme, the set $S = (u_1, u_3)$ is first generated (u_2 is not included in the set because it does not target server crash failures alone, and its attribute values that contribute to robustness are not defined), and finally after comparing each ft_unit within S, ftSP leverages u_3 because it is more robust than u_1.

Note that each ft_unit serves only as a single fundamental fault tolerance module. This implies that the overall solution ft_sol that must be delivered to the user's application can be obtained by combining a set of ft_units as per specific execution logic. For instance, a heartbeat test–based fault detection module must be applied only after performing replication, and recovery mechanism must be applied after a failure is detected. In other words, ft_units must be used as a process that provides a complete fault tolerance solution, such as:

```
ft sol[
invoke:ft unit(VM-instances replication)
invoke:ft unit(failure detection)
do{
execute(failure detection ft unit)
}while(no failures)
if(failure detected)
invoke:ft unit(recovery mechanism)
]
```

By composing ft_sol using a set of modules on the fly, the dimension and intensity of the fault tolerance support can be changed dynamically. For example, the more robust fault detection mechanism can be replaced with a less robust one in the ft_sol based on the user's business demands. Similarly, by realizing each ft_unit as a configurable module, resource consumption costs can be limited. For example, a replication scheme using five replicas can be replaced with one with three replicas if desired by the user.

The *runtime stage* starts immediately after ft_sol is delivered to the user. This stage is essential to maintain a high level of service because the context of the cloud computing environment may change at runtime, resulting in mutable behavior of the attributes. To this aim, the ftSP defines a set of rules R over attributes $a \in A$ and their values $v(a)$ such that the validity of all of the rules $r \in R$ establishes that the property p is supported by ft_sol (violation of a rule indicates that the property is not satisfied). Therefore, in this stage, the attribute values of each ft_sol delivered to the user's applications is continuously monitored at runtime and the corresponding set of rules is verified using a validation function $f(s, R)$. The function returns true if all rules are satisfied; otherwise it returns false. The matching and comparison process defined for the design stage are used to generate a new ft_sol in case of a rule violation. By continuously monitoring and updating the attribute values, note that the fault tolerance service offers support valid throughout the life cycle of the application (both initially during design time and during runtime).

As an example, for a comprehensive fault tolerance solution ft_sol s_1 with property,

$p_1 = (S_1, \widehat{p} = \{reliability = 98.9\%,\ availability = 99.95\%\ A = \{ mechanism = active\_replication, fault\_detection = heartbeat\_test, number\_of\_replicas = 4, recovery\_time - = 25 ms\})$, a set of rules R that can sufficiently test the validity of p_1 can be defined as:

r_1: number_of_server_inst wances ≥ 3
r_2: heartbeat_frequency $= 5$ ms
r_3: recovery_time ≤ 25 ms

These rules ensure that end reliability and availability are always greater than or equal to 98.9% and 99.95%, respectively.

A conceptual architectural framework, the *Fault Tolerance Manager* (FTM), is also introduced in Jawar et al. [24,25,35] that provides the basis for realizing the design stage and runtime stage of the delivery scheme, and serves as the basis for offering fault tolerance as a service. FTM is inserted as a dedicated service layer between the physical hardware and user applications along the virtualization layer. FTM is built using the principles of service-oriented architectures, where each ft_unit is realized as an individual Web service and ft_sol is created by orchestrating a set of ft_units (Web services) using the business process execution language (BPEL) constructs. This allows the ftSP to satisfy its scalability and interoperability goals. The central computing component, denoted as the FTMKernel, is composed of three main components:

- *Service directory*: It is the registry of all ft_units realized by the service provider in the form of Web services that (1) describes its operations and input—output data structures [e.g., Web Services Description Language (WSDL) and Web Services Conversation Language (WSCL)], and (2) allows other ft_units to coordinate and assemble with it. This component also registers the metadata representing the fault tolerance property of each ft_unit. The service directory matches user preferences and generates the set S of ft_units that satisfy p_c.

- *Composition engine*: It receives an ordered set of ft_units from the service directory as input and generates a comprehensive fault tolerance solution ft_sol as output. In terms of service-oriented architectures, the composition engine is a Web service orchestration engine that exploits BPEL constructs to build a fault tolerance solution.

- *Evaluation unit*: It monitors the composed fault tolerance solutions at runtime using the validation function and the set of rules defined corresponding to each ft_sol. The interface exposed by Web services (e.g., WSDL and WSCL) allows the evaluation unit to validate the rules. If a violation is detected, the evaluation unit updates the present attribute values in the metadata; otherwise, the service continues uninterrupted.

A set of components that provide complementary support to fault tolerance mechanisms is included in the FTM. These components affect the quality of service and support ftSP in satisfying user requirements and constraints. Fig. 9.5 illustrates the overall architecture of the FTM. The functionality of each component is, briefly:

- *Client interface*: This component provides a specification language that allows clients to specify and define their requirements.
- *Resource manager*: This component maintains a consistent view of all computing resources in the cloud to (1) efficiently perform resource allocation during each user request and (2) avoid overprovisioning during failures. The resource manager monitors the working state of

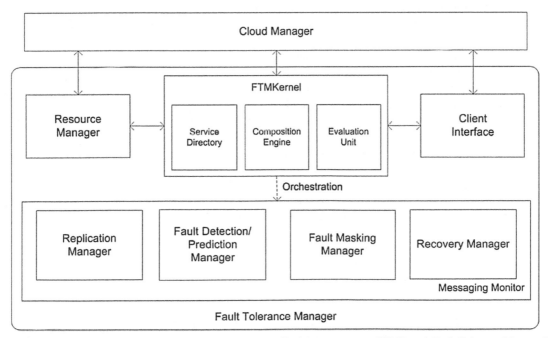

FIGURE 9.5 Architecture of the Fault Tolerance Manager showing all of the components. *FTMKernel*, Fault Tolerance Manager Kernel.

physical and virtual resources and maintains a database of inventory and log information, and a graph representing the topology and working state of all the resources in the cloud.

- *Replication manager*: This component supports the replication mechanisms by invoking the replicas and managing their execution as defined in the ft_unit. The set of replicas that are controlled by a single replication mechanism is denoted as a replica group. The tasks of the replication manager are to make the user perceive a replica group as a single service and to ensure that each replica exhibits correct behavior in the fail-free periods.

- *Fault detection/prediction manager*: This component provides FTM with failure detection support at two different levels. The first level offers failure detection globally to all the nodes in the cloud (infrastructure-centric); the second level provides support only to detect failures among individual replicas in each replica group (user application-centric). This component supports several well-known failure detection algorithms (e.g., gossip-based protocols, heartbeat protocol) that are configured at runtime according to user preferences. When a failure is detected in a replica, a notification is sent to the fault-masking manager and recovery manager.

- *Fault-masking manager*: The goal of this component is to support ft_units that realize fault-masking mechanisms so that the occurrence of faults in the system can be hidden from users. This component applies masking procedures immediately after a failure is detected so as to prevent faults from resulting into errors.

- *Recovery manager*: The goal of this component is to achieve system-level resilience by minimizing the downtime of the system during failures. It supports ft_units that realize recovery mechanisms so that an error-prone node can resume back to a normal operational mode. The support offered by this component is complementary to that of the failure detection/prediction manager and fault-masking manager when an error is detected in the system. The FTM maximizes the lifetime of the cloud infrastructure by continuously checking for the occurrence of faults and by recovering from failures.

- *Messaging monitor*: This component extends through all components of the FTM and offers the communication infrastructure in two different forms: message exchange within a replica group and intercomponent communication within the framework. The messaging monitor integrates Web Services Reliable Messaging standard with other application protocols to ensure correct messaging infrastructure even in the presence of failures. This component is therefore critical in providing maximum interoperability, and serves as a key QoS factor.

For example, consider that at the start of the service, the resource manager generates a profile of all computing

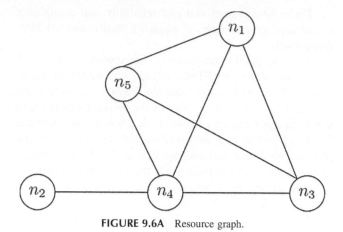

FIGURE 9.6A Resource graph.

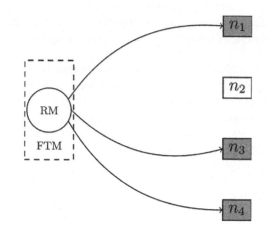

FIGURE 9.6B Nodes selected by the replication manager (RM). *FTM*, Fault Tolerance Manager.

resources in the cloud and identifies five processing nodes $\{n_1, \ldots, n_5\} \in N$ with the network topology represented in Fig. 9.6A. Further consider that the FTMKernel, upon gathering the user's requirements from the client interface, chooses a passive replication mechanism for the e-commerce service. Based on the chosen fault tolerance mechanism (i.e., the set of ft_units that realize the envisioned passive replication scheme), FTMKernel requires the following conditions to be satisfied: (1) the replica group must contain one primary and two backup nodes, (2) the node on which the primary replica executes must not be shared with any other VM instances, (3) all of the replicas must be located on different nodes at all times, and (4) node n_5 must not allow any user-level VM instance (rather it should be used only to run system-level services such as the monitoring unit). An overview of the activities performed by each supporting component in the FTM is as follows:

- The replication manager selects the node n_1 for the primary replica and nodes n_3 and n_4, respectively, for two backup replicas so that a replica group can be formed (Fig. 9.6B). Assume that the replication manager

Replica Group

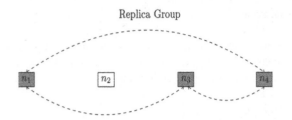

FIGURE 9.6C   Messaging infrastructure created (forms a replica group).

Replica Group

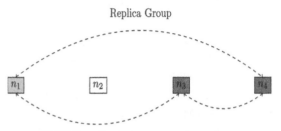

FIGURE 9.6D   Failure detected at node n_1.

synchronizes the state between the replicas by frequently checkpointing the primary and updating the state of backup replicas.

- The messaging manager establishes the infrastructure required to carry out the checkpointing protocol and forms the replica group for the e-commerce service (Fig. 9.6C).
- Assume that the service directory selects a proactive fault tolerance mechanism. As a consequence, the failure detection/prediction manager continuously gathers the state information of nodes n_1, n_3, and n_4, and verifies whether all system parameter values satisfy threshold values (e.g., physical memory use of a node allocated to a VM instance must be less than 70% of its total capacity).
- When the failure detection/prediction manager predicts a failure in node n_1 (Fig. 9.6D), it invokes the fault-masking ft_unit that performs a live migration of the VM instance. The entire OS at node n_1 is moved to another location (node n_2) so that e-commerce customers do not experience an impact of the failure.
- Although the high availability goals are satisfied using the fault-masking manager (Fig. 9.6E), the IaaS may

New Replica Group

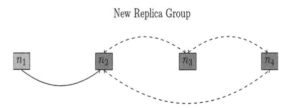

FIGURE 9.6E   Fault-masking performed: virtual machine instance migrated to node n_2.

Replica Group

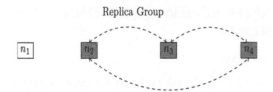

FIGURE 9.6F   Recovery manager brings node n_1 back to a working state.

be affected because the system now consists of only four working nodes. Therefore, the FTM applies robust recovery mechanisms at node n_1 for it to resume to a normal working state, increasing the system's overall lifetime (Fig. 9.6F).

Using the FTM framework, the notion of providing fault tolerance as a service can be realized effectively for the cloud computing environment. Based on the delivery scheme that FTM employs, users can achieve high levels of reliability and availability for their applications without having knowledge about the low-level mechanisms, and dynamically change the fault tolerance properties of its applications (based on the business needs) at runtime.

8. SUMMARY

Fault tolerance and resilience in cloud computing are critical to ensure correct and continuous system operation. We discussed the failure characteristics of typical cloud-based services and analyzed the impact of each failure type on user applications. Because failures in the cloud computing environment arise mainly as a result of crash faults and Byzantine faults, we discussed two fault tolerance solutions, each corresponding to one of these two classes of faults. The choice of fault tolerance solutions was also driven by the large set of additional properties that they offer (e.g., generality, agility, transparency, and reduced resource consumption costs).

We also presented an innovative delivery scheme that leverages existing solutions and their properties to deliver high levels of fault tolerance based on a given set of desired properties. The delivery scheme was supported by a conceptual framework that realized the notion of offering fault tolerance as a service to user applications. Because of the complex nature of cloud computing architecture and the difficulties in realizing fault tolerance using traditional methods, we advocate fault tolerance as a service to be an effective alternative to address users' concerns regarding reliability and availability.

Finally, let us move on to the real interactive part of this chapter: review questions/exercises, hands-on projects, case projects, and the optional team case project. The answers and/or solutions by chapter can be found in Appendix K.

CHAPTER REVIEW QUESTIONS/ EXERCISES

True/False

1. True or False? Crash faults do not cause system components to stop functioning completely or to remain inactive during failures (power outage or hard disk crash).
2. True or False? Byzantine faults do not lead system components to behave arbitrarily or maliciously during failure, causing the system to behave unpredictably incorrect.
3. True or False? The system is rarely monitored at runtime to validate, verify, and ensure that correct system specifications are being met.
4. True or False? The system state is captured and saved based on undefined parameters (after every 1024 instructions or every 60 s).
5. True or False? Critical system components are duplicated using additional hardware, software, and network resources in such a way that a copy of critical components is available even before a failure happens.

Multiple Choice

1. What measures the strength of the fault tolerance mechanism in terms of the granularity at which it can handle errors and failures in the system?
   A. Resource consumption
   B. Performance
   C. Fault tolerance model
   D. Multiple machines within the same cluster
   E. All of the above
2. What factor deals with the impact of the fault tolerance procedure on the end-to-end QoS during both failure and failure-free periods?
   A. Resource consumption
   B. Fault tolerance model
   C. Performance
   D. Multiple machines within the same cluster
   E. All of the above
3. How many replicas of an application can be placed on hosts that are connected by a ToR switch (within a LAN)?
   A. One
   B. Three
   C. Five
   D. Four
   E. Two
4. How many replicas of an application can be placed on hosts belonging to different clusters in the same data center (on hosts that are connected via a ToR switch and AggS)?
   A. One
   B. Three
   C. Five

D. Four
E. Two
5. How many replicas of an application can be placed on hosts belonging to different data centers (connected via a switch), AggS and AccR?
   A. Two
   B. Four
   C. One
   D. Three
   E. Five

EXERCISE

Problem

How secure is a cloud-based platform?

Hands-on Projects

Project

What components go into a cloud architecture?

Case Projects

Problem

How does cloud architecture scale?

Optional Team Case Project

Problem

How do you achieve fault tolerance in a cloud?

ACKNOWLEDGMENTS

This work was supported in part by the EC within the 7FP under Grant Agreement 312797 (ABC4EU) and within the H2020 program under Grant Agreement 644597 (ESCUDO-CLOUD); and the Italian Ministry of Research within PRIN project "GenData 2020" (2010RTFWBH).

REFERENCES

[1] Amazon Elastic Compute Cloud, © 2012, Amazon Web Services, Inc. or its affiliates. http://aws.amazon.com/, 2012.
[2] Azure, © 2012 Microsoft. http://www.windowsazure.com/en-us/, 2012.
[3] Build your business on Google Cloud Platform, © 2012 Google, https://cloud.google.com/, 2012.
[4] HP Helion Eucalyptus Cloud Manager, © 2015 Hewlett-Packard Development Company, L.P., http://www.eucalyptus.com, 2015.
[5] E. Feller, L. Rilling, C. Morin, Snooze: a scalable and autonomic virtual machine management framework for private clouds, in: Proc. of CCGrid'12, Ottawa, Canada, 2012, pp. 482–489.
[6] K. Vishwanath, N. Nagappan, Characterizing cloud computing hardware reliability, in: Proc. of SoCC'10, Indianapolis, IN, USA, 2010, pp. 193–204.

[7] U. Helzle, L.A. Barroso, The Datacenter as a Computer: An Introduction to the Design of Warehouse-scale Machines, first ed., Morgan and Claypool Publishers, 2009.

[8] S. De Capitani di Vimercati, S. Foresti, P. Samarati, Managing and accessing data in the cloud: privacy risks and approaches, in: Proc. of 2012 7th International Conference on Risk and Security of Internet and Systems (CRiSIS 2012), Cork, Ireland, 2012, pp. 1–9.

[9] F. Distante, V. Piuri, Hill-climbing heuristics for optimal hardware dimensioning and software allocation in fault tolerant distributed systems, IEEE Trans. Reliab. 38 (1) (1989) 28–39.

[10] V. Piuri, Design of fault-tolerant distributed control systems, IEEE Trans. Instrum. Meas. 43 (2) (1994) 257–264.

[11] P. Samarati, Data security and privacy in the cloud, in: Proc. of 10th International Conference on Information Security Practice and Experience (ISPEC 2014), Fuzhou, China, 2014, pp. 28–41.

[12] P. Samarati, S. De Capitani di Vimercati, Cloud security: issues and concerns, in: S. Murugesan, I. Bojanova (Eds.), Encyclopedia on Cloud Computing, Wiley, 2016 (to appear).

[13] P. Samarati, S. De Capitani di Vimercati, Data protection in outsourcing scenarios: issues and directions, in: Proceedings of the 5th ACM Symposium on Information, Computer and Communications Security (ASIACCS 2010), Beijing, China, 2010, pp. 1–14.

[14] S. De Capitani di Vimercati, S. Foresti, S. Jajodia, S. Paraboschi, G. Pelosi, P. Samarati, Encryption-based policy enforcement for cloud storage, in: Proc. of 2010 IEEE 30th International Conference on Distributed Computing Systems Workshops (ICDCSW 2010), Genoa, Italy, 2010, pp. 42–51.

[15] B. Selic, Fault Tolerance Techniques for Distributed Systems, IBM Library, 2004. http://www.ibm.com/developerworks/rational/library/114.html.

[16] A. Heddaya, A. Helal, Reliability, Availability, Dependability and Performability: A User-centered View, Tech. Rep, Boston, MA, USA, 1997.

[17] M. Armbrust, A. Fox, R. Griffith, A.D. Joseph, R.H. Katz, A. Konwinski, G. Lee, D.A. Patterson, A. Rabkin, I. Stocia, M. Zaharia, Above the Clouds: A Berkeley View of Cloud Computing, EECS Dept., University of California, Berkeley, 2009. Tech. Rep. UCB/EECS-2009-28.

[18] C.A. Ardagna, R. Jhawar, V. Piuri, Dependability certification of services: a model-based approach, in: Computing, vol. 97(1), Springer, 2013, pp. 51–78.

[19] P. Gill, N. Jain, N. Nagappan, Understanding network failures in data centers: measurement, analysis and implications, ACM Comput. Commun. Rev. 41 (4) (2011) 350–361.

[20] R. Jhawar, V. Piuri, fault tolerance management in IaaS clouds, in: Proc. of 2012 IEEE Conf. in Europe about Space and Satellite Telecommunications (ESTEL 2012), Rome, Italy, 2012, pp. 1–6.

[21] R. Jhawar, V. Piuri, Dependability-oriented resource management schemes for cloud computing data centers, in: S.U. Khan, A.Y. Zomaya (Eds.), Handbook on Data Centers, Springer, 2015, pp. 1285–1305.

[22] W.E. Smith, K.S. Trivedi, L.A. Tomek, J. Ackaret, Availability analysis of blade server systems, IBM Syst. J. 47 (4) (2008) 621–640.

[23] N. Ayari, D. Barbaron, L. Lefevre, P. Primet, Fault tolerance for highly available internet services: concepts, approaches and issues, IEEE Commun. Surv. Tutorials 10 (2) (2008) 34–46.

[24] R. Jhawar, V. Piuri, M. Santambrogio, A comprehensive conceptual system-level approach to fault tolerance in cloud computing, in: Proc. of IEEE International Systems Conference (SysCon 2012), Vancouver, BA, Canada, 2012, pp. 1–5.

[25] R. Jhawar, V. Piuri, M. Santambrogio, Fault tolerance management in cloud computing: a system-level perspective, IEEE Syst. J. (2013) 288–297.

[26] R. Guerraoui, M. Yabandeh, Independent faults in the cloud, in: Proc. of LADIS'10, Zurich, Switzerland, 2010, pp. 12–17.

[27] A. Undheim, A. Chilwan, P. Heegaard, Differentiated availability in cloud computing SLAs, in: Proc. of Grid'11, Lyon, France, 2011, pp. 129–136.

[28] S. Kim, F. Machinda, K. Trivedi, Availability modeling and analysis of virtualized system, in: Proc. of PRDC'09, Shanghai, China, 2009, pp. 365–371.

[29] B. Cully, G. Lefebvre, D. Meyer, M. Feeley, N. Hutchinson, A. Warfield, Remus: high availability via asynchronous virtual machine replication, in: Proc. of NSDI'08, San Francisco, CA, USA, 2008, pp. 161–174.

[30] C. Clark, K. Fraser, S. Hand, J.G. Hansen, E. Jul, C. Limpach, I. Pratt, A. Warfield, Live Migration of virtual machines, in: Proc. of NSDI'05, Boston, MA, USA, 2005, pp. 273–286.

[31] M. Castro, B. Liskov, Practical byzantine fault tolerance, in: Proc. of OSDI'99, New Orleans, LA, USA, 1999, pp. 173–186.

[32] T. Wood, R. Singh, A. Venkataramani, P. Shenoy, E. Cecchet, ZZ and the art of practical BFT execution, in: Proc. of EuroSys'11, Salzburg, Austria, 2011, pp. 123–138.

[33] R. Kotla, L. Alvisi, M. Dahlin, A. Clement, E. Wong, Zyzzyva: speculative byzantine fault tolerance, in: ACM Transactions on Computer Systems, vol. 27(4), 2009, pp. 7.1–7.39.

[34] J. Yin, J.P. Martin, A. Venkataramani, L. Alvisi, M. Dahlin, Separating agreement from execution for byzantine fault tolerant services, in: Proc. of SOSP'03, New York, NY, USA, 2003, pp. 253–267.

[35] R. Jhawar, V. Piuri, P. Samarati, Supporting security requirements for resource management in cloud computing, in: Proc. of the 2012 IEEE International Conference on Computational Science and Engineering (CSE 2012), Paphos, Cyprus, 2012, pp. 170–177.

[36] M. Albanese, S. Jajodia, R. Jhawar, V. Piuri, Reliable mission deployment in vulnerable distributed systems, in: Proc. of the 43rd Annual IEEE/IFIP International Conference on Dependable Systems and Networks Workshop (DSN-rsda 2013), Budapest, Hungary, 2013, pp. 1–8.

[37] M. Albanese, S. Jajodia, R. Jhawar, V. Piuri, Securing mission-centric operations in the cloud, in: S. Jajodia, K. Kant, P. Samarati, V. Swarup, C. Wang (Eds.), Secure Cloud Computing, Springer, New York, 2014, pp. 239–260.

[38] R. Jhawar, V. Piuri, Adaptive resource management for balancing availability and performance in cloud computing, in: Proc. of the 10th International Conference on Security and Cryptography (SECRYPT 2013), Reykjavik, Iceland, 2013, pp. 254–264.

[39] C. Ardagna, E. Damiani, R. Jhawar, V. Piuri, A model-based approach to reliability certification of services, in: Proc. of 2012 IEEE International Conference on Digital Ecosystem Technologies – Complex Environment Engineering (DEST-cee 2012), Campione D'Italia, Italy, 2012, pp. 1–8.

Chapter 10

Securing Web Applications, Services, and Servers

Gerald Beuchelt

Demandware, Inc., Burlington, MA, United States

1. SETTING THE STAGE

The development of a distributed hypertext system in the early 1990s at the CERN in Switzerland was one of the defining moments in making the Internet available to an audience beyond academia and specialized communities. The combination of a simple, yet powerful transport protocol—Hypertext Transfer Protocol (HTTP)—with a specialization of the Standard Generic Markup Language (SGML) made it possible to render complex content on the fly and link related information, even if it was distributed.

Like with many other information systems technologies, the early implementation of the web included only very limited built-in security, especially since the system was initially designed for use within a research facility. However, the growth of the hypertext system at CERN into the World Wide Web (WWW) required much more advanced security controls.

Defining Threats to Your Web Assets

Initially, there were only very few real threats to the WWW: early on, hackers proved their ability and highlighted potential threats to the new environment by defacing web sites. Once commercial transactions (such as online shopping) and other high-value information exchanges were starting to use the web, the number of potential threat actors and threats grew quickly. Today, any public or private web application or service operator will need to perform at least a cursory threat and vulnerability assessment to determine appropriate risk mitigation strategy for their web assets.

Depending on the use cases, the data, and the audience of a web asset, a variety of threat actors should be considered when performing a threat assessment. Among these threat actors one may find a diverse crowd: script kiddies, disgruntled employees, organized crime, hacktivists, terrorists, or foreign intelligence agencies. While their capabilities and credibility as threat actors may vary significantly, they are all credible source of attacks against simple web sites such as nonprofit club home pages, or highly secured commercial targets such as banks or e-commerce sites.

While web assets are typically more accessible than other services (such as file servers or databases), the general approach to performing risk assessment and management is very similar. One useful approach is described in the Special Publication (SP) series of the National Institute for Standards and Technologies (NIST) of the United States. Specifically, SP 800-30 rev. 1 and SP 800-39 describe a comprehensive approach to ensuring threat and risk assessment and mitigation. The reader is strongly encouraged to review these documents for further guidance on implementing their own risk management strategy.

Surveying the Legal Landscape and Privacy Issues

In addition to the embarrassment and potential liability for monetary damage to third parties after exposure to hackers, web operators are often also subject to other regulatory requirements. For example, web sites that store or process personally identifiable information (PII) may be required to disclose their data-handling policies, and may have to restrict access for young children. The legal requirements for website operators vary from country to country, and lack of clearly defined "borders" on the Internet may require compliance with differing, sometimes contradicting regulatory regimes.

Computer and Information Security Handbook. http://dx.doi.org/10.1016/B978-0-12-803843-7.00010-7

Any web operator will minimally need to comply with the terms of service of their service provider and the laws applying to them. For example, US-based providers will need to review their web sites in the light of very diverse laws, including (but not limited to) the Children's Online Privacy Protection Act (COPPA), Sarbanes-Oxley Act (SOX), Health Insurance Portability and Accountability Act (HIPAA), and the Privacy Act. European operators will need to address not only the requirements of their respective local countries, but also the EU Data Protection Directive. In general, any website operator handling information from their employees or customers, visitors, or third parties is well advised to consult with a local law firm that specializes in Internet, compliance, and privacy law.

Web Services Overview

Web services have become a widely used technology in both corporate and Internet applications. Information technology (IT) practitioners such as architects, developers, and administrators have been moving away from traditional client-server architectures to loosely coupled service environments to a number of issues. Service architectures rely on clearly defined interfaces so that service clients and service providers can change their internal architectures independently from each other, allowing decoupling of the development processes for different systems components. This process started in the late 1980s and has been implemented in specialized distributed architectures such as CORBA, COM+, or Java RMI. The success of web technologies in the mid-90s inspired system architects to profile these new platform-agnostic technologies to build distributed systems that can interoperate across vendors and runtime architectures. Web services have been defined in different ways; we will focus in this chapter on the following two principal realizations of distributed services that typically use HTTP for exchanging information:

- Simple Object Access Protocol (SOAP) web services have been popularized in the early 2000s by Microsoft and IBM, and have seen broad adoption across very different platforms. SOAP services are built around the concept of a SOAP envelope, an XML document that contains a SOAP header, and a SOAP body. The header defines the necessary metadata for the SOAP message, including processing instructions and security elements. The SOAP body can—in principle—transport any media type, although the core protocol was originally formulated around XML documents.
- HTTP services have been in use since the early days of the WWW. The original design of the HTTP protocol included not only the well-known operations such as GET (to retrieve data) or POST (to modify data) which are commonly used by web browsers, but also PUT (to

create data) and DELETE (to delete data). In addition, HTTP also supports other operations that allow comprehensive management of the service and the interaction. Roy Fielding formalized the common best practices around creating HTTP services in his dissertation and coined the term Representational State Transfer (REST) to describe the architectural style of well-designed HTTP systems.

The protocols, architecture, and design of web services alone are fairly complex. The reader is expected to have a basic understanding of how HTTP and SOAP work, how they are currently being used, and how they can be created. The goals of this chapter are to provide a general overview of the breadth of web service security, provide an introduction to the subject area, and guide the reader to sources with deeper information.

This chapter addresses both REST HTTP service and SOAP-based web services. Each technology has its strengths and weaknesses and users should clearly enumerate the requirements they have for their web service environment before deciding to implement one or the other. In many complex cases, a hybrid environment will prove to be the best approach (see Sidebar: "Protocol Versions").

Protocol Versions

Within this chapter, we will always reference the latest versions of the protocols referenced. Some of the protocols are backward compatible, since they only add features to the overall specification, but in many instances the protocols break backward compatibility to fix significant security holes. Existing implementations of these security protocols sometime lag behind the latest standardized version [Transport Layer Security (TLS) being one example], but increasingly the standards community works in a much more agile way, where implementation of draft specifications are available and fully supported by vendors (OAuth 2.0 or higher). Depending on the application of web services, the user will need to make a business-requirements and risk-based determination what version of the protocol should be used.

---

2. BASIC SECURITY FOR HTTP APPLICATIONS AND SERVICES

Since HTTP services implementing a REST architectural style (often called "REST Services") are simply using the HTTP stack, all security aspects of HTTP apply. At the same time, there is a critical distinction to web applications: for the latter, the user agent (the software making the HTTP requests) is a web browser, which is event-driven and operated by a human. As such operations such as providing username and password credentials, selecting Public Key Infrastructure (PKI) certificates, or making choices about how to interact with the web server are not complicated for the client. This is all very different if the client user is an agent.

Basic authentication and some other authentication and authorization mechanisms are built into the HTTP stack and the layered protocols supported by most operating systems and clients. At the same time, many of these security mechanisms were created to support end-user facing agents such as web browsers, and often require considerable human interaction in order to work as designed. For example, HTTP Basic Authentication or HTML forms-based authentication with clear-text passwords works well for an end-user that needs to access a website (or web application), but username/password tokens are less ideal for machine-to-machine interactions, since they (1) require a secure store of the secret, but (2) do not offer a particularly high level of security.

This part of the chapter introduces a number of widely available and deployed HTTP mechanisms that may be used to build interoperable, secure machine-to-machine HTTP services. In general, most security mechanism supported by the HTTP specification itself are typically the most interoperable, while layered protocols and mechanisms (such as those provided by the GSS-API and SASL) tend to be less interoperable out of the box.

Basic Authentication

HTTP[1] provides "Basic Authentication"[2] as part of the standard HTTP stack, where the exchange of the credential is performed. For typical web applications, the server denies access to the resources that was requested at the URI, and returns an HTTP status code of 401, including a WWW-Authenticate header, which needs to be set to the "Basic" authentication mechanism. The client then responds with another request to the same resource, but adds a WWW-Authorization header with the Base64 encoding of the username and password. The server can then decode the username and password and verify the credential. While this authentication mechanism is straightforward and very easy to implement, it is only of limited use in environments where HTTP is used for the following machine-to-machine communication:

1. This mechanism transmits the username and password unencrypted. The simple Base64 encoding can be decoded by anyone and must be treated as clear text. As such, this authentication mechanism can only be used in conjunction with a channel protection mechanism (such as TLS) that provides for the confidentiality of the channel.

2. Assigning username/password accounts to machines tends to lead to bad code. Often, developers will hard-code the credential into the code, making changes much harder. Even if a configuration file is used, the username and password are very often not cryptographically protected on disk.

Overall, it is not recommended to rely on username/password credentials (HTTP Basic Authentication) when implementing HTTP services, especially in production environments. Note that other browser-centric authentication mechanisms (such as HTML forms-based authentication) are not usable for client-server authentication in REST architectures.

Transport Layer Security

TLS[3] is based on the Secure Socket Layer (SSL) protocol that was developed in the 1990s by the Netscape Corporation. The basic design requires a X.503 V3 based PKI at least for the server and requires client and server to maintain a session state. Both use PKI to negotiate a session master key: this approach ensures that the asymmetric cryptography is used to introduce client and server and establish a secure channel between the two communication partners. The establishment of the secure session key using symmetric cryptography allows leveraging the efficiency of these mechanisms in bulk encryption transactions.

The SSL/TLS protocol stack (and also its most popular implementation, OpenSSL) have been subject to a large number of significant vulnerabilities in recent years. These were related to transport protocol implementation choices, extension, cipher suite support, and other aspects of design and implementation. The use of any version of SSL high at this time considered to be vulnerable to a number of different attacks and increasingly no longer supported by browsers, other clients, and servers. While most clients and servers today still support TLS 1.0, it is recommended to move to TLS 1.2 to avoid potential security holes. Also the use of strong ciphers is becoming a new standard: new X.509 certificates are now issued with SHA-256 as the default signature algorithm, and most certificates use Rivest, Shamir, and Adelman public/private key pairs with 2048 bit or more for their key lengths. Also, the use of elliptic curve cryptography (ECC) algorithms for asymmetric cryptography is becoming more popular as well.

In general, it is recommended to verify any TLS configuration with an appropriate scanning tool. While there any many commercial and free solutions available, a

1. RFC 2616, "Hyper Text Transfer Protocol—HTTP 1.1", R. Fielding et al., Internet Engineering Task Force, June 1999.
2. RFC 2617, "HTTP Authentication: Basic and Digest Authentication", J. Franks et al., Internet Engineering Task Force, June 1999.

3. RFC 5246, "The Transport Layer Security (TLS) Protocol Version 1.2", T. Dierks et al., Internet Engineering Task Force, August 2008.

popular free web service for testing TLS setups can be found at https://www.ssllabs.com/.

Server Authentication

Every TLS transaction requires the server to authenticate itself to the client. This is typically initiated by the client sending the server a list of supported TLS versions, supported cipher-suites, and other connection information (such as the time or random parameters). Note that this initial request typically requires the client to connect to a port different from the usual port for the protocol. For example, HTTP usually operates on TCP port 80, but the TLS version of HTTP (called HTTPS) is defined to operate on port 443. The server responds with a list including the same information and also the server PKI certificate. The subject identifier of the certificate is typically the web address of the server (such as https://www.example.com), but there are other options such as wildcard certificates or Subject Alternate Name (SAN) certificates as well.[4] The client can then use the server certificate to authenticate the server, and responds with a message that includes a master secret, which is used to generate the session keys. Once the keys are available, the TLS handshake completes with the client and the server starting to use the session keys and shifting to an encrypted communication channel.

Mutual Authentication

Mutual authentication means that both client and server are authenticated to each other, (the client needs to authenticate to the server as well). This is achieved by the server sending a Certificate Request message to the client as part of the handshake. The client will then provide a user certificate to the server. This establishes the identity of the client to the server. While subject identifiers in client certificates can vary, most often they are bound to the user's email address.

Application to REST Services

TLS channel protection adds a number of security features to the communication between a REST client and service, as follows:

1. Server authentication using strong cryptographic methods. The server certificate is bound to the server's

DNS name itself by the subject identifier, thus providing additional protection against DNS attacks.
2. Channel protection. Once the secure channel handshake is complete, the secure channel provides confidentiality to the communication path between client and server. This allows the exchanges of sensitive information including additional authentication and authorization data.
3. REST client libraries can usually make use of operating or runtime systems certificate stores in a very efficient way. Certificate stores typically provide built-in protections of the cryptographic material. Additionally, both client and server systems usually allow fairly simple updates of the certificates when needed.
4. TLS can provide a Message Authentication Code (MAC) for each packet, allowing full integrity protection of the connection.

The only significant drawback of using simple or client-authenticated TLS is the high cost for using a PKI: for cross-enterprise transactions, PKI certificates must be obtained through common trust anchors which may be too expensive in low-value transactions (such as social network interactions). For intraenterprise connections, a custom PKI may be used, but the cost of maintaining this can also be substantial, especially for large enterprises.

GSS-API Negotiated Security

Another way to perform authentication for HTTP-based service and application is through the use of the GSS-API and its security mechanisms. The GSS-API has been defined for C and the Java runtime,[5] and provides a number of standard features:

- Authentication of client–server relationship through a feature complete handshake protocol between client and server.
- Confidentiality and Integrity for the payload of the connection, independent of the protocols encapsulated. This is achieved by wrapping the payload within the structure needed for the GSS-API protected traffic. Note that the capabilities of this feature are strongly dependent on the underlying security mechanism.
- Extensibility and mechanism negotiation through the SPNego pseudo mechanism. This is used by Microsoft to integrate Kerberos with the HTTP protocol for authentication and to provide a smooth browsing experience.

The preceding technology was initially developed in the early 1990s and has a high level of implementation

---

4. SAN certificates have a special multivalued extension (called subjectAlternateName) that permits the certificate to apply to multiple DNS domain names. This can ber very useful for sites that can be reach with different DNS names (such as multicountry sites), or it can be useful for web servers hosting multiple different web sites. Wildcard certificates apply to all hosts of a specific subdomain, such as *.example.com. This subject identifier will many any hostname under example.com. Note that there are no standardized ways of having multilevel wildcard certificates such as *.*.example.com.

5. The C binding is defined in the IETF RFC 2744 and the Java binding is standardized in JSR-72. See http://tools.ietf.org/html/rfc2744 and http://jcp.org/aboutJava/communityprocess/review/jsr072/index.html for more information.

maturity. At the same time, it very focused on traditional client–server environments and encourages a much stronger coupling of the participants than desired for typical web services. For example, when using Kerberos over SPNego as the underlying security mechanism, the administrator will need to ensure that client and server are either part of the same Kerberos realm, or there is an established trust relationship between the two realms. Since this trust and deployment model does not scale to cross-organizational deployments, this approach can only be used effectively within a single administrative domain.

3. BASIC SECURITY FOR SOAP SERVICES

The situation for SOAP-based web services (see Sidebar: "SOAP-based Web Services") is significantly different from basic HTTP services: while SOAP may use the HTTP protocol for transport, it was designed to be transport independent, and as such needs to re-create the entire security stack in a self-contained way. This is achieved by extending the SOAP headers to support security-related information in the WS-Security protocol, and other profiles and protocols that build on top of it.

SOAP-Based Web Services

SOAP version 1.2[6] or higher is a flexible XML-based protocol to exchange information. Originally developed by Microsoft, IBM, and others, SOAP is available today on most web-enabled platforms. Conceptually, SOAP defines an Envelope as the root node of the XML document. The Envelope contains two child elements: the Header and the Body of the SOAP message. The Body typically contains the main payload of the message, which is intended to be an XML-serialized representation of a data model. The Header section of the Envelope may contain metadata about the message, sender, and receiver, and about the transaction itself. The Header is highly customizable and extensible.

SOAP was originally developed as a web service protocol, with an HTTP transport binding. At the same time, the designers of the protocol made sure that the SOAP specification was not dependent on any features of the underlying transport. As a result, SOAP can be used over a large number of transport protocols today, thus providing a consistent way of creating services over a number of different platforms. Such platforms include SMTP, FTP, and message queuing protocols. This flexibility does not come for free, though, since many transport semantics (such as session security, routing, acknowledgments, etc.) that are provided by the underlying transport protocols need to be replicated within the SOAP stack. This can lead to significant performance issues and replication of functionality at different layers.

For this chapter, it is assumed that the reader has a good understanding of the basic SOAP protocol structures.

---

6. "SOAP Version 1.2", M. Gudgin et al., W3C Recommendation, April 2007.

WS-Security Overview

WS-Security[7] (often abbreviated WSS) defines a Header extension to provide a number of features for SOAP-based messages, as follows:

- Signing the message to provide integrity protection and nonrepudiation;
- Encrypting the message to provide message-level confidentiality;
- Attaching arbitrary security tokens to the messages to provide identity of the sender.

It should be noted that since WS-Security is only tied to the SOAP messaging structures, it is completely transport independent and can therefore be used over the SOAP HTTP binding, but also with any other form of SOAP transport. At the same time due to its independence, WS-Security can be combined with the security mechanisms of the underlying transport security.

To provide the various features mentioned in this section, WS-Security leverages the XML Encryption and Signature standards. Users of WS-Security should have a robust understanding of how these standards work, minimally from an API perspective, but ideally also from a protocol point of view. The WSS headers directly use the <Signature>, <KeyInfo>, and <EncryptedData> elements of the XML Signature and Encryption standards, respectively.

For example, a SOAP message may be signed and encrypted at the message-level using WS-Security and transported over an encrypted HTTPS connection as well. For complex situations, where the SOAP message is routed by SOAP intermediaries that sit between the sender and the server, this feature can be used to provide both: (1) secure point-to-point connections between the sender, receiver, and their respective intermediaries using HTTP over TLS, and (2) end-to-end security from the sender to the receiver using message-level encryption.

Protocol Design

As discussed, WS-Security injects a security header as an XML child node into the SOAP Header (see Fig. 10.1). This security header can contain a number of different elements that enable the various features of WSS. Note that the following examples reference the usage of WS-Security with SOAP 1.2 or higher only. The WS-Security specification defines also the use of SOAP 1.1 or higher, but this will be omitted here. The namespace prefixes

---

7. "Web Service Security: SOAP Messaging Framework 1.1", A. Nadlin et al., OASIS Open, November 2006.

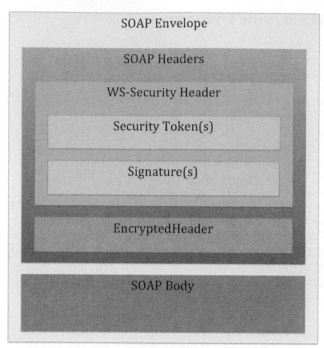

FIGURE 10.1   Simple Object Access Protocol and WS-Security message layout.

below are identical to the ones used in the WSS 1.1 or higher specification. For real implementations they may be different, as long as the XML namespace rules are followed.

The <wsse:Security> is the base WS-Security header element within the <S12:Header> element of the SOAP message. It may contain a number of typical attributes from the SOAP headers, such as mustUnderstand, to indicate the receiver or intermediary must understand the WSS header in order to correctly process the SOAP message. Also, the <Security> header can be extended with any additional attribute or child element, effectively providing a very flexible extension point. It should be noted that open-ended extension points like this—while desirable to protocol implementers and vendors—may introduce significant interoperability issues when being deployed: if vendor-specific extensions are required for operation, environments that require cross-platform interoperability may run into significant difficulties.

In order to enable signature and encryption of arbitrary parts of the SOAP message, the WSS specification introduces the ability to reference nodes of the entire SOAP Envelope using the wsu:Id attribute. Similar to an anchor in an HTML page, an XML element within the message can be tagged with this attribute and then be referenced within the WSS header structures that are used for providing signature and encryption.

Signature is provided through the <ds:Signature> element that may contain the crypto material (such as a <ds:KeyInfo> element) and additional information to provide identification of the type of signer, the signature, and canonicalization[8] algorithm, and references to the signed elements.

For encryption of elements, WSS differentiates between header elements that need to be encrypted and the main SOAP Body (or portions of the body). For the headers, WSS introduces the <wsse:EncryptedHeader> element that may be processed by SOAP intermediaries or the final receiver of the messages. If the SOAP handling system cannot decode the encrypted header it needs to leave it in place. Within the SOAP body, the <xenc:EncryptedData> element is used to wrap encrypted parts of the XML infoset within the overall message structure.

In either case, the WSS header will contain the necessary key information to decrypt the data, similar to how this is handled for signatures. When decrypting, the decrypted elements replace the <xenc:EncryptedData> and <wsse:EncryptedHeader> elements, respectively.

Usage of WS-Security

By itself, WS-Security is only of limited use: it describes how security elements such as tokens and signatures can be incorporated into a SOAP message. It also provides limited instructions on how to protect portions of the message using these security elements.

Authentication With WS-Security

A common use of WS-Security is for authentication of the incoming request. In order to process (an update to an account using a SOAP request), the bank service will need to verify the identity of the invoker (authentication) so that it can apply its authorization policies. For this, the clients will need to attach one or more security tokens to the WS-Security header that prove their users' identity. WS-Security provides for a number of built-in tokens such as <wsse:UsernameToken> or the more generic <wsse:BinarySecurityToken>, but it can also be extended to support other token types as well. Common stacks such as Apache Axis or .NET WCF support these and others such as Security Assertion Markup Language (SAML) or vendor-specific tokens as well (see Sidebar: "Attaching Policies to Web Services").

8. WSS supports both W3C XML Canonicalization and W3C Exclusive XML Canonicalization. Since the later provides a better support for XML namespaces, and is recommended in most situations.

In the easiest case, a simple UsernameToken is used, which can include the password in clear text. Obviously, such a token would typically not be used without protecting the message for confidentiality. Alternatively, a trusted authentication server could sign a UsernameToken or an SAML statement. The service could then decide to trust the authentication server, and not require additional credentials. If an SAML statement is used for authentication, the SAML Token Profile for WS-Security will describe the possible configurations that the server can request from the client.

WS-I Security Profile

As seen earlier, the configuration parameters to simply perform authentication can be very complex. While WS-SecurityPolicy is capable to describe the requirements that the server has, it is impossible even within a fairly rich policy framework to describe all possible parameters for the WS-Security stack. Even though placement of individual XML elements should not matter from an infoset perspective, and most crypto parameters such as algorithms are described in the core specification, tests between different vendors have shown that acceptable interoperability cannot be achieved without a very narrow profile. The WS-I organization (now a subgroup of OASIS Open) created a number of such profiles. The WS-I Basic Security Profile includes very detailed implementation guidance for WS-Security, WS-SecurityPolicy, the various token profiles (username, SAML, X.509 certificate, Kerberos), and SOAP with Attachments. While users of WS-Security are typically not expected to implement these specifications and their profiles, it is important to understand their relevance when creating cross-platform services.

Example for a Web Service Definition Language for WS-Security

The following Fig. 10.2 contains a sample WSDL[9] for a very simple SOAP web service with a single operation. The service requires authentication using a SAML 2.0 or higher Security token using the SAML Token Profile version 1.1 or higher. Note that within this WSDL there is no directive how to utilize the information found within the SAML token for authorization. The SAML statement will contain information that is used for authentication and authorization. How this is used by the application server runtime and the service itself depends on the application server vendor and the service developer, respectively.

4. IDENTITY MANAGEMENT AND WEB SERVICES

Electronic identities are routinely used to access logical and physical resources, and have become a ubiquitous part of our national infrastructure. Identity management systems are responsible for the creation, use, and termination of electronic identities. However, Identity Management as a formal discipline is a fairly new concept.

On the other hand, the advance of web services technologies have far-reaching effects on the Internet and enterprise networks. Web services technology can be implemented in a wide variety of architectures, can coexist with other technologies and software design approaches, and can be adopted in an evolutionary manner without requiring major transformations to legacy applications and databases.

The security challenges presented by the web services approach are formidable and unavoidable. Many of the features that make web services attractive, including greater accessibility of data, dynamic application-to-application connections, and relative autonomy (lack of human intervention) are at odds with traditional security models and controls.

Background

Since web services are intended to implement a distributed architecture, it becomes very important to manage the identities of the participating actors: different systems implementing the services or the clients need to fully understand who they are interacting with in order to make access control decisions that are consistent with the security policies for the systems. While this has been always the case for complex systems, the loosely couple design of web services exacerbates this problem and requires a number of new patterns to address this in a

---

9. For readability, XML namespaces have been removed from the listing.

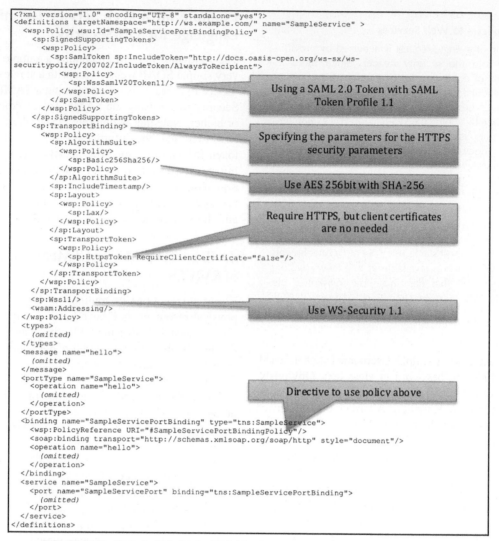

```
<?xml version="1.0" encoding="UTF-8" standalone="yes"?>
<definitions targetNamespace="http://ws.example.com/" name="SampleService" >
  <wsp:Policy wsu:Id="SampleServicePortBindingPolicy" >
    <sp:SignedSupportingTokens>
      <wsp:Policy>
        <sp:SamlToken sp:IncludeToken="http://docs.oasis-open.org/ws-sx/ws-
securitypolicy/200702/IncludeToken/AlwaysToRecipient">
          <wsp:Policy>
            <sp:WssSamlV20Token11/>
          </wsp:Policy>
        </sp:SamlToken>
      </wsp:Policy>
    </sp:SignedSupportingTokens>
    <sp:TransportBinding>
      <wsp:Policy>
        <sp:AlgorithmSuite>
          <wsp:Policy>
            <sp:Basic256Sha256/>
          </wsp:Policy>
        </sp:AlgorithmSuite>
        <sp:IncludeTimestamp/>
        <sp:Layout>
          <wsp:Policy>
            <sp:Lax/>
          </wsp:Policy>
        </sp:Layout>
        <sp:TransportToken>
          <wsp:Policy>
            <sp:HttpsToken RequireClientCertificate="false"/>
          </wsp:Policy>
        </sp:TransportToken>
      </wsp:Policy>
    </sp:TransportBinding>
    <sp:Wss11/>
    <wsam:Addressing/>
  </wsp:Policy>
  <types>
    (omitted)
  </types>
  <message name="hello">
    (omitted)
  </message>
  <portType name="SampleService">
    <operation name="hello">
      (omitted)
    </operation>
  </portType>
  <binding name="SampleServicePortBinding" type="tns:SampleService">
    <wsp:PolicyReference URI="#SampleServicePortBindingPolicy"/>
    <soap:binding transport="http://schemas.xmlsoap.org/soap/http" style="document"/>
    <operation name="hello">
      (omitted)
    </operation>
  </binding>
  <service name="SampleService">
    <port name="SampleServicePort" binding="tns:SampleServicePortBinding">
      (omitted)
    </port>
  </service>
</definitions>
```

Callouts:
- Using a SAML 2.0 Token with SAML Token Profile 1.1
- Specifying the parameters for the HTTPS security parameters
- Use AES 256 bit with SHA-256
- Require HTTPS, but client certificates are no needed
- Use WS-Security 1.1
- Directive to use policy above

FIGURE 10.2   Example Web Service Definition Language for WS-Security protected service.

reliable way. The identity management community created a number of patterns that allow not only simple authentication, but also advanced patterns including:

- Single Sign On (SSO) using mutually trusted identity servers. This idea is based on the SSO mechanisms used for web applications: a user (or machine entity) authenticates once to a trusted identity server, which issues security tokens that can be used to sign into relying parties (sometimes also called service providers). This pattern decouples the process of identification and authentication itself from the use of the authentication and authorization.
- Federations of identity providers. In order to allow cross-organizational access to web services, the concept of an identity federation was introduced. In this pattern the operators of two separate identity servers (such as in Company A and Company B) decide to trust each other's authentication process. This is realized by allowing a client to exchange a security token from the identity server of Company A with a security token from Company B. This allows the client to access services that trust Company B's identity server.
- Complex, distributed authorization. By fully decoupling the authentication process from the authorization to access a resource, web services can allow very flexible authorization mechanisms such as Attribute-Based Access Control (ABAC).

Other patterns, such as privacy preserving authentication and authorization have also been demonstrated and implemented using web services-based identity management technologies. While many of these patterns were pioneered for the SOAP stack, recent developments have brought most them to REST-styled HTTP services. Due to its expressiveness and top-down design, SOAP-based identity management is quite achievable. In real-world implementations, some of the performance issues of XML processing have limited the broad adoption of SOAP-based identity management technologies. The initially less feature-rich REST designs have always leveraged the efficiency of the underlying transport protocols, resulting in a much slower availability of useful patterns, but providing a much better price/performance ratio.

Security Assertion Markup Language

The SAML[10] was created to provide a means for exchanging information about authenticated entities and their attributes between a client (also called service consumer) and a service. Fundamentally, SAML defines a set of security tokens that can hold information about an entities' authentication, their attributes, or their authorization status.[11] In addition, SAML defines a request/response protocol that allows exchanging SAML security tokens in remote procedure call (RPC)-style exchanges.

The SAML protocol stack (see Fig. 10.3) extends from the basic tokens and protocol to include SAML Bindings,

which describe how the SAML protocol can be used with the appropriate token types over different transport mechanisms. The Bindings are then used to build profiles for different SAML system participants such as web browser SSO clients, identity providers, or attribute providers.

Security Assertion Markup Language Token Types

The SAML tokens are supported by many different vendors and can be used with many different protocols, even those that compete with the SAML request/response protocol. The SAML 2.0 or higher specification identifies the following three token types (called "Statements" in the specification):

- SAML Authentication Token. This statement describes how a user (or machine entity) authenticated to a given service. It can contain detailed information about the authentication act, including the time, the subject, and the authentication context.
- SAML Attribute Token. This statement can contain an arbitrary number of clear-text and encrypted attributes about a given subject, as asserted by the identity provider. This statement is the foundation for many ABAC-based authorization schemes.
- SAML Authorization Decision Token. This statement was deprecated by the eXtensible Access Control Markup Language (XACML) protocol at the time of publication of the SAML 2.0 or higher standard. It has been kept within the specification text, but should not be used unless for legacy interoperability purposes.

All tokens require a Subject element to identify the principal of the assertion. This Subject can contain identifiers (such as email addresses or distinguished names) and SubjectConfirmation elements. The use of these fields is specific to the protocols for which the tokens are used. For example, the WS-Security SAML token profile[12] defines two common SubjectConfirmation methods: Holder-of-Key (HOK) and Sender-Vouches.

HOK ensures that the sender of the SOAP message has access to the private key of the Subject by requiring a signature over parts of the message block. This authenticates the subjects and confirms to the web service the identity of the sender. In the Sender-Vouches method, the web service trusts an authentication server to authenticate the client for them, and requires only a signature by that authentication server over the message block.

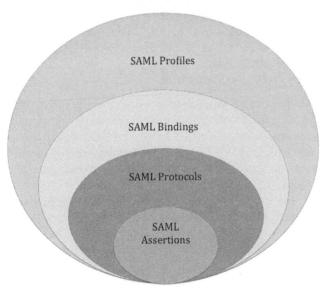

FIGURE 10.3 Security Assertion Markup Language protocol stack.

10. SAML Technology Overview: N. Ragouzis et al., "Security Assertion Markup Language (SAML) V2.0 Technical Overview", OASIS Committee Draft, March 2008. SAML 2.0 Core: S. Cantor et al., "Assertions and Protocols for the OASIS Security Assertion Markup Language (SAML) V2.0" OASIS Standard, March 2005.
11. In SAML 2.0, the authorization token has been deprecated by the XACML protocol.

12. R. Monzillo et al., "Web Service Security: SAML Token Profile 1.1" OASIS Standard, February 2006.

Security Assertion Markup Language Protocol

The SAML protocol (sometime called "SAML-P" to distinguish it from the SAML token format) is an XML-based protocol that implements a request/response patterns for exchanging information. It is completely transport independent, and can therefore be used with a wide variety of system participants. The basic exchange implements a Request message by a client that is answered by a Response. The SAML protocol is self-contained and uses its own mechanism to indicate response status, failures, and other interaction metadata. Similar to SOAP, this independence from the underlying transport results in less effective architecture, since underlying functions such as status codes have to be replicated at the application level. There are a number of interactions defined in the basic SAML specification, as follows:

- SAML Assertion Query. This protocol is used to request specific assertions in about subjects from an authoritative source. This can include authentication, attribute, and authorization decision statements. The response then includes a token for the requested information about the Subject.
- Authentication Request Protocol. An entity can use this protocol when it wishes to obtain a statement for establishing a security context for a principal. Typically, a requester asks to obtain a SAML authentication assertion from an Identity Provider (IdP) during a web service invocation.
- Artifact Resolution. A SAML Artifact is a reference to a SAML statement instead of the statement itself. This protocol is used to resolve a SAML Artifact into an actual SAML assertion.
- Single Logout. While SSO is very desirable from a user experience perspective, single logout is critical from a security perspective. Within the SAML specification stack, this protocol ensures that assertions can be identified as invalidated once a logout was requested. It should be noted that this protocol does not guarantee logout but requires the cooperation of all relying parties.
- Name Identifier Management and Name Identifier Mapping. These protocols are used to create reliable, pseudonymous federations between IdPs in different administrative domains.

These protocols can then be used with different transports. The use of specific transport protocols with the SAML protocol is called a "Binding" and specified in a separate document. SOAP is one of the standards transports, but there are also other browser-centric transport bindings available, as well. The Bindings are used to define "Profiles" which describe complex function systems such as IdPs.

While the SAML protocol is standardized in the core SAML specification it is not implemented by all vendors: while SAML tokens have been popular across the entire identity management landscape, early adopters of the WS-* specifications such as IBM and Microsoft have been using these tokens in with WS-Security, WS-Trust, and WS-Federation. Users will need to make sure what parts of the SAML specification stack (tokens, protocol, bindings, profiles) the vendors support.

Using Security Assertion Markup Language Tokens With WS-*

SAML tokens have been used with other exchange protocols as well. The term "WS-* stack" commonly refers to a set of protocols that build on top of the SOAP platform and enable additional functionality for SOAP-based web services. This includes features such as complex transactions support (WS-AtomicTransactions), reliable delivery (WS-ReliableTransport), and service discovery (Universal Description, Discovery, and Integration, UDDI). Since these are intended to be used in a transport-agnostic way, underlying features of message queuing systems cannot be relied on for guaranteed delivery, but have to be created within the SOAP envelope through SOAP header extensions.

For security, WS-Security defines the most fundamental extension, and many of the other WS-* protocols implementing security functions rely on the WS-Security framework. The use of SAML Tokens with WS-Security is standardized in the SAML Token Profile 1.1 or higher.[9]

WS-Trust Architecture

WS-Trust is an alternative to using some portions of the SAML protocol for creating an environment with a mutually trusted authentication server, a client, and a service. WS-Trust uses WS-Security for wrapping security elements such as security tokens, signatures, and encrypted data blocks.

The mutually trusted entity is in the WS-Trust environment called a Secure Token Service (STS), which responds to token requests (see Fig. 10.4). At a high level, the client (called a requestor) contacts the service (called a relying party) and obtains through the WS-SecurityPolicy of the relying party service the token requirements. These requirements include the acceptable origin of the token (the STS (or list of STS) that are acceptable sources for tokens).

The requestor then proceeds to request such a token from a STS by sending a RequestSecurityToken (RST) message to the STS service endpoint. This request will typically include appropriate forms of authentication (from the requestor to the STS) by providing a security token

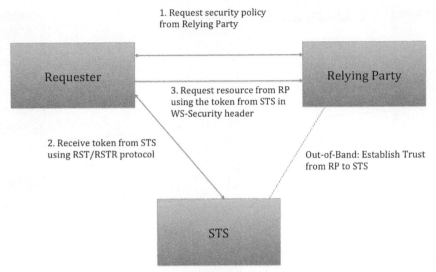

FIGURE 10.4 WS-Trust architecture.

within the WS-Security headers of the WS-Trust RST message.

The STS builds a token to the specification of the requestor and wraps this in the WS-Security header of the RequestSecurityTokenResponse (RSTR) message. The requestor can then proceed to interact with the relying party using the new token.

Building Federations With WS-Federation

Since WS-Trust is only used for building a distributed authorization system, OASIS has created a number of other protocols for the WS-* stack focusing on different functionalities. One of these is the WS-Federation specification which is used to enable the leveraging of security tokens issued by STS form different administrative domains. This means that a client can obtain a token from "their" STS, and use this to access relying parties that usually trust only tokens issued by another STS. The prerequisite for this to work is setting up a federation.

It should be noted that the most significant amount of work for creating a federation is typically not the technical configuration: creating and maintaining the necessary business agreement between two organizations is complex and requires collaboration with legal, finance, and potentially human resources subject matter experts.

Advanced HTTP Security

The basic security functions of HTTP described earlier are sufficient for simple client—server systems, but are hard to manage for complex multiparty interactions. In addition, the most common security transport—TLS—typically requires a comprehensive PKI rollout, especially when using user certificates for mutual authentication.

Typical applications of HTTP applications and services in social networking or cloud environments have use cases that cannot be easily address with basic HTTP authentication schemes. Furthermore, the deployment of PKI in such environments is too expensive or extremely complex: PKI implies a fairly high level of trust in the binding of the credential to a system or the user, which is hard to control in highly dynamic environments.

Based on these constraints a number of large web 2.0 or higher providers (including Google, Twitter, AOL, and others), as well as smaller companies with deep insight into the architectures of dynamic web application and REST-style HTTP services, started in 2004 developing technologies that are complementary to the "heavyweight" SOAP-centric identity management technologies. While initially focused on simple data-sharing use case with limited risk (such as SSO for blog commenting), these technologies have matured to the point where they can be used to secure commercial services and provide a simplified experience for users of social media and other web applications.

OAuth Overview and Use Cases

The OAuth protocol dates back to the early days of social networking sites. The standard use case is for safely sharing user data held at one site with another site. This would occur when site A is a photo-hosting site and site B is a site that makes prints from photos (see Fig. 10.5). In this use case, users have an account at both sites and store their photos at site A. For creating a new set of prints, users will not upload

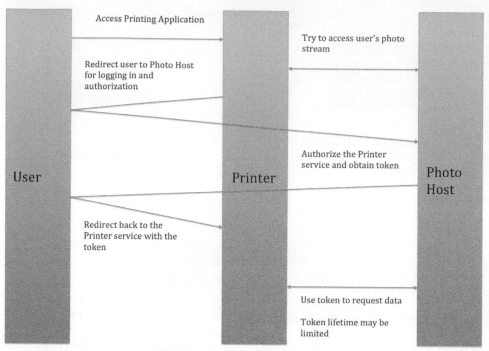

FIGURE 10.5 OAuth basic use case.

or transfer their photos to site B, but instead authorize site B to access their photo stream (or a portion thereof) on site A. This is effectively achieved by initially logging into site B and indicating the location of their photo stream (through a dropdown menu) at site A. When site B now tries to access the photo stream, the users are redirected to the login screen for site A where they need to provide their credentials. Once logged in site A will create a token that site B can use for accessing the users' photo stream and attach this token to the HTTP redirect back to site B. The end state is now that site B has a token that it can use at attach to the HTTP request when obtaining the photos.

The exchange is somewhat more complicated than in the illustration, since the Printer service initially obtains an unauthorized request token in the initial exchange between the Printer and the Photo Host service. The request token is then authorized by the user and provided to the Printer which exchanges it into an access token. The goal for this use case is to keep the accounts at the two services separate while still allowing authorized information sharing between the two sites.

OAuth 2.0 or higher is at the time of writing completed with regards to standardization at the Internet Engineering Task Force (IETF). The final protocol is now available. Most implementations already support OAuth 2.0 or higher; and, updates to implementations for transitioning from the draft versions to the completed version are minor, if any.

OpenID Connect

The original OpenID protocol was built on the concept of using URLs as identifiers for users (a user would use something like "https://example.com/user" for their username). This was intended to solve the problem of discovery in identity management: any dynamic interaction between a user and a service would only be able to leverage identity management protocols, if the relying party and the identity provider had an existing relationship. For well-defined cross-organizational interactions this is quite achievable, but requires to configure the respective IdPs (or STSs), relying parties, and requestors to use the acceptable services for identity management and authorization services.

While the OpenID protocol did solve this problem with the URL identifier, users typically did not accept this scheme, so the large web 2.0 or higher providers such as Google, Twitter, Facebook, AOL, etc. solved this by creating specialized buttons to use for OpenID login. Since most sites desired to support at least the big social networks and identity providers, the login sites often featured more than five specialized login button, leading to the term "NASCAR problem": similar to racing cars in

NASCAR, login sites would be littered with banners from all major login providers.

Additionally, the initial versions of OpenID had a number of significant security issues, leading to the realization that it would be helpful to design a new version of OpenID that could leverage a secure HTTP-based identity transport protocol. The natural choice was OAuth, and OpenID Connect now uses OAuth as its underlying security protocol. Simplified, OpenID Connect creates an identity provider web service and uses OAuth to protect access from relying parties to it.

5. AUTHORIZATION PATTERNS

In addition to the authentication mechanism (such as a password), access control is concerned with how authorization patterns are structured. In some cases, authorization patterns may mirror the structure of the organization, while in others it may be based on the sensitivity level of various documents and the clearance level of the user accessing those documents.

Access Control Models

Early systems implemented fairly simple access control models that rely mostly on the identity of the user and define access control lists (ACLs) that are stored with the resource that is subject to that access control list. This model has sometimes been called "Identity Based Access Control" (IBAC) and has proven to be very efficient and easy to implement. Most modern operating systems support IBAC based access control for file systems access and other security related functions. While fast for small ACLs, very large ACLs are inefficient to evaluate, and the need to store the ACL (which is effectively a security policy for the resource) decentralized with the resources can cause significant lifecycle management problems. Some solutions such as user groups or ACL inheritance have been implemented to mitigate these shortcomings, but overall the limitations of IBAC limit its use for large-scale applications. Other access control models include Role-Based Access Control (RBAC)[13] and ABAC. Core to these models is a better separation of resources and applicable access control policies.

Web services have been pioneering technologies for implementing ABAC models especially through the introduction of the eXtensible Access Control Markup Language (XACML).[14] Since XACML was developed to complement SAML with a flexible authorization system,

it shared some architectural similarities. In fact, the XACML replaces the SAML 2.0 or higher authorization decision statement with its own request response protocol.

eXtensible Access Control Markup Language Overview

Within the XACML model, there are a number of actors that enable the distributed authorization environment. Note that some of these actors can be co-located: certain appliances or access managers allow configurations where PEP, PDP, and PAP are co-located, as discussed in the following components:

- Access requester (or client). This is the entity that initiates a request.
- Policy Enforcement Point (PEP). The PEP intercepts the request from the client to the resources and performs an authorization check. This actor is sometimes integrated with a reverse proxy (a façade service that wraps the resource and replicates the resource's interface to the clients).
- Policy Decision Point (PDP). The PDP performs the actual policy evaluation, based on the information in the request from the PEP, a policy set (the merged set of applicable policies, based on a policy merging systems), configured attribute sources, and other environmental factors (such as time of day, origin or destination of request, etc.).
- Policy Administration Point (PAP). The policy administration point allows the configuration and administration of applicable access control policies. The PDP is configured through the PAP to use a specific set of policies.
- Policy Information Point (PIP). The PIP provides contextual information input into the policies, based on a request from the PDP. If the PIP provides specific attributes for identities, e.g., in the form of a Directory Server, the PIP is sometime also called an Attribute Source (AS).
- Resource. The resource itself provides the service for the client. While XACML is typically used for SOAP services, there is no requirement for the resource to be implemented as a SOAP service. For example, a combined PEP/service façade can be used to expose the functionality of a legacy application to SOAP-enabled clients.

These preceding components and how they related to each other are shown in Fig. 10.6. Conceptually, the Requester tries to access the Resource (typically a SOAP-based web service, but this is not a requirement within XACML) and is intercepted by the PEP. The PEP itself

---

13. The U.S. National Institute of Standards and Technology (NIST) has published a number of documents on RBAC and how it can be implemented. See http://csrc.nist.gov/groups/SNS/rbac/ for more information.
14. XACML is standardized at OASIS Open in the XACML Technical Committee. See here: https://www.oasis-open.org/committees/tc_home.php?wg_abbrev=xacml.

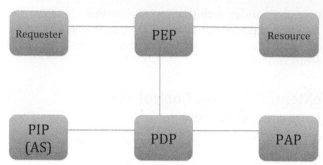

FIGURE 10.6 eXtensible Access Control Markup Language actors overview.

formulates a decision request to the PDP with the information that is available to it, namely metadata from the request and the resource.

With the PDP, the applicable access policies are identified, evaluated, and—if necessary—combined into a single policy decision. Note that XACML defines a rich policy language for describing access control policies in terms of Targets, Rules, and Constraints.

The PDP responds to the PEP in a Result Response with one of the following four possible decisions: Permit, Deny, Indeterminate (no decision was possible, based on the available policies and information), or NotApplicable (the request was not applicable in this context). The response may include additional obligations that need to be abided by. The complete XACML protocol, policy language, result definition, and combination algorithms can be used for very complex situations, and it is beyond the scope of this chapter to describe the details of the XACML protocol.

XACML and SAML for ABAC and RBAC

The core XACML protocol architecture is modeled around the concepts of ABAC: attributes (either provided by an AS or other PIPs providing environmental attributes) are evaluated in the context of a specific request. While most situations will require the identity of the requestor, ABAC can even allow pseudonymous access to resource, as long as the PDP can obtain sufficient information to arrive at a "permit" authorization decision.

The core set of XACML specifications also includes guidance on how an RBAC model can be implemented using XACML. The basic idea is to model role membership through a multivalued attribute. This attribute is then evaluated in the context of access control policies designed to reflect the role-based approach.

At the same time, the technology used to implement the access control model should not be confused with the access control model itself. This means that while XACML is currently the predominant technology to implement ABAC in distributed systems, they should not be equated.

6. SECURITY CONSIDERATIONS

Security considerations are essential to implementing and integrating a comprehensive strategy for managing risk for all IT assets in an organization. This should result in more cost-effective, risk-appropriate security control identification, development, and testing.

Avoiding Common Errors

The flexibility of web-based systems and the ease of implementing new services lead to an early proliferation of web applications and web services. It became obvious pretty quickly that these new technologies resulted in a number of mistakes that were independently made by many developers. Security research groups and organizations started to look into this problem and identified a number of antipatterns and mistakes that were particularly common, and identified measure to counter them. The following gives an overview of two commonly referred to lists of common mistakes and useful controls, respectively.

Open Web Application Security Project (OWASP) Top 10

The Open Web Application Security Project (OWASP) Top 10 list[15] was developed by the OWASP community to enumerate common problems with web applications. This list focuses specifically on web application risks, and deals with both transport issues (HTTP) as well as content problems (HTML) and how content is rendered within browsers. The latter issues are less interesting for developers of web services, since the user agent is typically not a browser, and the data may be represented as HTML, but most often is not. It is updated occasionally to reflect the changing security environment.

Fig. 10.7 shows the 2013 version of the OWASP Top 10. Out of this list only A3, A4, A6, A7, A8, and A9 are highly relevant to web service developers. Since REST-style HTTP service leverage the features of HTTP more heavily than SOAP service using the HTTP transport binding, the former will likely have to pay more attention to avoiding mistakes identified in the list. At the same time, SOAP services operating within standard runtime environment can suffer from issues such as security misconfigurations (A6) or problems with the transport layer protection (A9) just as

---

15. The document is available from https://www.owasp.org/. The last update to the list was done in 2013. At the time of this writing, OWASP is requesting input to the 2016 list, which is scheduled to be released during the second half of 2016.

A1 – Injection
A2 – Broken Authentication and Session Management
A3 – Cross-Site Scripting (XSS)
A4 – Insecure Direct Object References
A5 – Security Misconfiguration
A7 – Insecure Cryptographic Storage – Merged with A9 →
A6 – Sensitive Data Exposure
A7 – Missing Function Level Access Control
A8 – Cross-Site Request Forgery (CSRF)
A9 – Using Known Vulnerable Components
A10 – Unvalidated Redirects and Forwards

FIGURE 10.7   Open Web Application Security Project Top 10 (2010).

easily. In the following, the more pertinent elements form the OWASP top 10 are briefly discussed:

- A1: Injection flaws, such as SQL, OS, and LDAP injection may occur when untrusted data is sent to a web service trying to exploit the underlying business logic.
- A2: Broken Authentication and Session Management. If access to the HTTP resources where the service is host is not protected properly, arbitrary users may invoke the service and cause confidentiality and integrity problems. Authentication issues can arise when the verification of accounts with the user database is compromised, user information is leaked through other channels, or the authentication session parameters are not set properly.
- A4: Insecure Direct Object References. If input of the access URL (for REST-style services) or the content of the SOAP request is not verified through input validation techniques, a malicious user may replace legitimate data references with improper data. For example, if a service call should reference Alice's account for receiving a money transfer, a malicious attacker could try to replace Alice's account number with Eve's, thus redirecting the transfer to a wrong account.
- A5: Security Misconfiguration. This can include default account, unpatched or unmaintained server code, references to old versions of services, etc. Any security misconfiguration can be exploited by attackers to gain access, elevate privileges, or violate confidentiality or integrity of the data.
- A6: Sensitive Data Exposure. Web services can easily expose sensitive data including authentication information, PII, financial, or health data.
- A8: Using Components with Known Vulnerabilities. Web services rely on a large stack of third-party software, including the operating system, format parsers, virtual machines, web servers, application servers, cryptographic libraries, and many other tools. Any known vulnerability in this third-party code may lead to a compromise of the entire service.

Center for Internet Security Top 20 Critical Security Controls

The Center for Internet Security (CIS) Top 20 list of critical security controls[16] enumerates the most important technical and administrative controls to prevent or limit attacks on computer systems. The list was developed by a number of experts from the US government and the commercial sector and condenses a lot of best practices of good systems management. They provide not only a description of implementable countermeasures and system configurations, but include also metrics to measure the effectiveness of the controls within a given environment. Additionally, the CIS Top 20 control description include references to the NIST SP 800-53[17] control set, which is mandatory for many systems operated by the US federal government.

The controls themselves are generic and not specific to web services. At the same time, they can be applied to the architectural concepts, technologies, and deployed systems implementing web services. The complete list is an excellent starting point for any secure system design, but we will focus here on the most applicable controls for securing web service deployments.

Critical Control 3: Secure Configurations for Hardware and Software on Laptops, Workstations, and Servers

This control requires a secure configuration of all system components. This can be implemented by creating standard system images that are hardened against attacks. Such hardening may include disabling nonessential system services, limiting the visibility to network probes, configuring kernel-level security enforcement rules, etc. A secure baseline operating system limits the potential damage that a misconfigured or compromised web service or client can cause.

Critical Control 4: Continuous Vulnerability Assessment and Remediation

The window for attacking weak systems is significantly reduced by continuously monitoring and assessing the vulnerability profile of all deployed systems. With a comprehensive program in place—that should ideally consist of automated and human components—potential

---

16. The list is available at http://www.sans.org/critical-security-controls/— It was formerly know as the SANS Top 20 Critical Security Controls, but transitioned with version 6.0 to the Center for Internet Security.
17. NIST Special Publication (SP) 800-53 (in it current version R4) is a comprehensive list of information security controls and they verification procedures.

weaknesses in the web service application runtime or the implementing code itself can be detected and fixed in near real time. This minimizes the attack window for threat actors significantly.

Critical Control 9: Limitation and Control of Network Ports, Protocols, and Services

It is crucial to have a comprehensive list of allowed port, protocols, and system services for all active and passive network devices. Each individual component must only be allowed to perform its designated function and use the appropriate set of network resources to do so. This way compromised devices can be identified much more easily: if a server designated to provide web service over HTTPS suddenly starts to send out Border Gateway Protocol (BGP) messages, network monitors and intrusion detection and prevention systems can react immediately and take that system off the network to prevent unauthorized routing of data.

Critical Control 11: Secure Configurations for Network Devices Such as Firewalls, Routers, and Switches

Not only the actual business systems such as servers and client, but also the supporting network infrastructure components need to be configured in the most secure way. This control is complementary to Critical Control 3, and should be implemented equivalently.

Critical Control 12: Boundary Defense

Firewalls and other boundary defense technologies have been available for a long time, and despite them having a bad reputation for preventing advanced attacks, they are very useful in preventing certain classes of vulnerabilities. A solid boundary defense also enables close monitoring of data ingress and egress, and allows to inspect and control information flow from the web service to the client and vice versa. Separating the rest of the world from the internal networks also make monitoring of the use of ports, protocols, and service (Critical Control 9) much easier.

Critical Control 17: Security Skills Assessment and Appropriate Training to Fill Gaps

All personnel involved in the creation and maintenance of the web service must be qualified to perform their job functions. While this seems like an ancient IT adage,

many IT architects, developers, and administrators have a hard time staying on top of their field both from an application and security perspective. Security training and evaluations should be part of everyone's responsibility. Exploring the usefulness of relevant security certifications for key staff members may augment this. Overall, only senior-level management sponsorship can ensure the successful implementation of this control.

Critical Control 18: Application Software Security

In the context of the SANS Top 20, this control focuses on the security of the code implementing the service itself. While there are other frameworks available as well, the OWASP Top 10 list (see Fig. 10.7) is a good starting point for assessing the security of the service and client software quality.

Critical Control 20: Penetration Tests and Red Team Exercises

Even the best security engineering teams will make mistakes or miss possible attack vectors when protecting critical resources such as web services. Only a comprehensive penetration test and recurring exercises can expose potential security flaws. More details on creating a test program for web services are explained later in the chapter.

Other Resources

There are many other, often industry specific sets of security controls that can handle web service security. Examples include the American Institute of Certified Public Accountants (AICPA) Service Organization Controls (SOC) 2: "Controls at a Service Organizations Relevant to Security, Availability, Processing Integrity, Confidentiality, or Privacy,"[18] which specify requirements for cloud providers and can have relevance in the context of operating web service on behalf of customers. Another set of applicable security controls includes the NIST SP 800-53 controls,[19] which include SOA controls in their latest revision.

There are other resources that address SOA-specific issues as well. One example is the Common Attack

---

18. See http://www.aicpa.org/soc for more information on the SOC reports.
19. All NIST SPs can be found at http://csrc.nist.gov/publications/PubsSPs.html.

Pattern Enumeration and Classification (CAPEC)[20] that features a catalog of techniques used by attackers to break into systems. While this database is intended to cover all typical attack vectors against systems, it has a specialization for service-oriented issues. The information within the database is typically fairly comprehensive and addresses not only specific attack methodologies, but defines also a framework for classifying these approaches.

Fig. 10.8 provides a sample CAPEC pattern that applies to SOA, in this case on WSDL scanning. It provides a fairly comprehensive set of attributes of this particular attack, and suggests possible mitigation strategies to counter this attack pattern. To use this catalog efficiently, it is recommended that one search the site on specific technologies and develop a list of countermeasures for mitigation.

Testing and Vulnerability Assessment Testing Strategy

As identified in the CIS Top 20 list of Critical Controls and many other documentations of security best practices, testing and continuous monitoring are central to maintaining a secure environment. While tests during the design of a software package such as a service are standard development practices,[21] the deployed service itself should be evaluated in context as well.

Such tests can include simple functional tests that verify the invocation of a service call in the deployed environment (or a mockup of that environment), but they may also include performance tests to ensure that the service behaves correctly under heavy load. There are a number of commercial and open source tools available for performing such test, including the popular soapUI framework[22] or webInject[23] open source projects.

Vulnerability Assessment Tools

In addition to functional testing at development and deploy time web services should undergo at least a vulnerability assessment to determine their actual vulnerabilities (see Sidebar: "Vulnerability Assessment Versus Penetration Testing"). Such a vulnerability assessment is focused on

determining the problems with the exposed service, from a number of different angles.

Vulnerability Assessment Versus Penetration Testing

In the past, Vulnerability Assessment and Penetration Testing have sometimes been used synonymously. While their goals and sometimes the techniques are similar, there is a fundamental difference between the two:

- Vulnerability Assessments are cooperative engagements, where the security expert, the developers, and the administrators are working hand in hand to understand, document, and eliminate vulnerabilities of the exposed services. The assessors should have full access to the source code, the interface definition (such as the WSDL for SOAP services), security documentation, and privileged access to the servers hosting the services. The end goal is a plan to improve the security posture of the deployed service.
- Penetration Tests, on the other hand, are noncooperative exercises, where the owners of the web service are not necessarily aware of the fact that a penetration test is underway. Depending on the rules of engagement, the penetration testers (sometime called "red team") may use a large variety of techniques to gain access or subvert a deployed service, including trying to get physical access to the hosting servers. Furthermore, the red team may operate under rules that allow them to permanently damage the deployed service in order to better understand the potential security impact a real attack may have. While penetration test often result is more in-depth analysis the security posture, most companies will not allow the red team to perform a full-scale attack on production systems.

To perform a comprehensive vulnerability assessment of a service installation, the analyst should be familiar with the base techniques of vulnerability assessments for servers. There are many tools available for performing such an assessment, both commercial as well as open source-based solutions. Specialized Linux distributions such as Kali Linux[24] are specifically designed for vulnerability assessments and testing, and have many of the best tools preinstalled. For HTTP-based systems, testers should minimally employ w3af, MetaSploit, openVAS, and Nessus in addition to other standard tools.

Finally, let's take a brief look at the web applications, services, and servers challenges that still need to be addressed. The following checklist (see checklist: "An Agenda for Action for Security Actions That Web Applications, Services, and Servers Need to Consider") discusses several web applications, services, and servers security

---

20. The CAPEC catalog can be found at http://capec.mitre.org/.

21. This may include Unit testing, continuous builds, and other functional tests to verify the correct functioning of the service. For services, Unit tests may include not only API invocations of the implementing classes, but also explicit calls to the service interfaces exposed on the network. Note that configuring such tests with services that implement security functionality directly (e.g., in-code authorization) may be very complex and not necessarily feasible.

22. See http://www.soapui.org/ for information on using soapUI.

23. WebInject is available form http://www.webinject.org/.

24. See http://www.kali.org/ for more information on Kali Linux.

CAPEC-95: WSDL Scanning

WSDL Scanning

Attack Pattern ID: 95   **Typical Severity:** High   **Status:** Draft

 Description

Summary

This attack targets the WSDL interface made available by a web service. The attacker may scan the WSDL interface to reveal sensitive information about invocation patterns, underlying technology implementations and associated vulnerabilities. This type of probing is carried out to perform more serious attacks (e.g. parameter tampering, malicious content injection, command injection, etc.). WSDL files provide detailed information about the services ports and bindings available to consumers. For instance, the attacker can submit special characters or malicious content to the Web service and can cause a denial of service condition or illegal access to database records. In addition, the attacker may try to guess other private methods by using the information provided in the WSDL files.

Attack Execution Flow

1. The first step is exploratory meaning the attacker scans for WSDL documents. The WDSL document written in XML is like a handbook on how to communicate with the web services provided by the target host. It provides an open view of the application (function details, purpose, functional break down, entry points, message types, etc.). This is very useful information for the attacker.

2. The second step that a attacker would undertake is to analyse the WSDL files and try to find potential weaknesses by sending messages matching the pattern described in the WSDL file. The attacker could run through all of the operations with different message request patterns until a breach is identified.

3. Once an attacker finds a potential weakness, they can craft malicious content to be sent to the system. For instance the attacker may try to submit special characters and observe how the system reacts to an invalid request. The message sent by the attacker may not be XML validated and cause unexpected behavior.

 Attack Prerequisites

A client program connecting to a web service can read the WSDL to determine what functions are available on the server.

The target host exposes vulnerable functions within its WSDL interface.

 Typical Likelihood of Exploit

Likelihood: High

 Methods of Attack

- Analysis
- API Abuse

 Examples-Instances

Description

A WSDL interface may expose a function vulnerable to SQL Injection.

Description

The Web Services Description Language (WSDL) allows a web service to advertise its capabilities by describing operations and parameters needed to access the service. As discussed in step 5 of this series, WSDL is often generated automatically, using utilities such as Java2WSDL, which takes a class or interface and builds a WSDL file in which interface methods are exposed as web services.

Because WSDL generation often is automated, enterprising hackers can use WSDL to gain insight into the both public and private services. For example, an organization converting legacy application functionality to a web services framework may inadvertently pass interfaces not intended for public consumption to a WSDL generation tool. The result will be SOAP interfaces that give access to private methods.

Another, more subtle WSDL attack occurs when an enterprising attacker uses naming conventions to guess the names of unpublished methods that may be available on the server. For example, a service that offers a stock quote and trading service may publish query methods such as requestStockQuote in its WSDL. However, similar unpublished methods may be available on the server but not listed in the WSDL, such as executeStockQuote. A persistent hacker with time and a library of words and phrases can cycle thru common naming conventions (get, set, update, modify, and so on) to discover unpublished application programming interfaces that open doors into private data and functionality.

Source : "Seven Steps to XML Mastery, Step 7: Ensure XML Security", Frank Coyle. See reference section.

 Attacker Skills or Knowledge Required

Skill or Knowledge Level: Low

This attack can be as simple as reading WSDL and starting sending invalid request.

Skill or Knowledge Level: Medium

This attack can be used to perform more sophisticated attacks (SQL injection, etc.)

 Probing Techniques

Description

An attacker can request the WSDL file from the target host by sending a SOAP message.

Description

There are free Vulnerability testing tool, such as WSDigger to perform WSDL scanning - Foundstone's free Web services security tool performs WSDL scanning, SQL injection and XSS attacks on Web Services.

 Solutions and Mitigations

FIGURE 10.8 Sample Common Attack Pattern Enumeration and Classification for Web Service Definition Language scanning.

challenges in detail, including web services discovery, quality of service, quality of protection, and protection from denial of service attacks.

7. CHALLENGES

While many of the web applications, services, and server challenges have been met with existing standards, there are a number of challenges that standards organizations are addressing—particularly in the area of web services discovery and reliability. The Web Services Interoperability Organization (WS-I) acknowledges that there are many challenges that have yet to be addressed. Some examples of these challenges are:

- Repudiation of transactions;
- Secure issuance of credentials;
- Exploitation of covert channels;
- Compromised services;
- Spread of malware, such as viruses and Trojan horses via SOAP messages;
- Denial of service attacks;
- Incorrect service implementations.

An Agenda for Action for Security Actions That Web Applications, Services, and Servers Need to Consider

The items in this section are possible actions that organizations should consider; some of the items may not apply to all organizations. In particular, it is necessary to balance these actions against budget requirements and the potential risks an organization's Web applications, services, and servers may face (check all tasks completed):

_____1. **Replicate Data and Services to Improve Availability**. Since web applications, services, and servers are susceptible to denial-of-service (DoS) attacks, it is important to replicate data and applications in a robust manner. Replication and redundancy can ensure access to critical data in the event of a fault. It will also enable the system to react in a coordinated way to deal with disruptions.

_____2. **Use Logging of Transactions to Improve Non-repudiation and Accountability**. Nonrepudiation and accountability require logging mechanisms involved in the entire Web applications, services, and server transaction. In particular, the level of logging provided by various UDDI registries, identity providers, and individual web services varies greatly. Where the provided information is not sufficient to maintain accountability and nonrepudiation, it may be necessary to introduce additional software or services into the SOA to support these security requirements.

_____3. **Use Threat Modeling and Secure Software Design Techniques to Protect from Attacks**. The objective of secure software design techniques is to ensure that the design and implementation of web applications, services, and server software does not contain defects that can be exploited. Threat modeling and risk analysis techniques should be used to protect the web services application from attacks. Used effectively, threat modeling can find security strengths and weaknesses, discover vulnerabilities, and provide feedback into the security life cycle of the application. Software security testing should include security-oriented code reviews and penetration testing. By using threat modeling and secure software design techniques, web applications, services, and servers can be implemented to withstand a variety of attacks.

_____4. **Use Performance Analysis and Simulation Techniques for End-to-End Quality of Service (QoS) and Quality of Protection**. Queuing networks and simulation techniques have long played critical roles in designing, developing, and managing complex information systems. Similar techniques can be used for quality assured and highly available web applications, services, and servers. In addition to QoS of a single service, end-to-end QoS is critical for most composite services. For example, enterprise systems with several business partners must complete business processes in a timely manner to meet real-time market conditions. The dynamic and compositional nature of web applications, services, and servers makes end-to-end QoS management a major challenge for service-oriented distributed systems.

_____5. **Digitally Sign UDDI Entries to Verify the Author of Registered Entries**. UDDI registries openly provide details about the purpose of a web service as well as how to access it. Web applications, services, and servers use UDDI registries to discover and dynamically bind to web applications, services, and servers at run time. Should an attacker compromise a UDDI entry, it would be possible for requesters to bind to a malicious provider. Therefore, it is important to digitally sign UDDI entries so as to verify the publisher of these entries.

_____6. **Enhance Existing Security Mechanisms and Infrastructure**. Web applications, services, and servers rely on many existing Internet protocols and often coexist with other network applications on an organization's network. As such, many web applications, services, and server security standards, tools, and techniques require that traditional security mechanisms, such as firewalls, intrusion detection systems (IDS), and secured operating systems, are in effect before implementation or deployment of web services applications.

8. SUMMARY

The practices recommended in this chapter are designed to help mitigate the risks associated with web applications, services, and servers. Web applications, services, and servers are important drivers for the software industry. The primary goal of service-oriented computing is to make a collection of software services accessible via standardized protocols whose functionality can be automatically discovered and integrated into applications. While several standards bodies (such as W3C and OASIS) are laying the foundation for web applications, services, and servers, several research problems must be solved to make secure web applications, services, and servers a reality. Service description, automatic service discovery as well as QoS are some of the important problems that need to be solved.

Web applications, services, and servers are increasingly becoming an integral part of organizational IT infrastructures—even though there are still unmet security challenges. To this end, the development and deployment of secure web applications, services, and servers are essential to many organizations' IT infrastructures. However, web applications, services, and servers security standards do not provide all of the required properties to develop robust, secure, and reliable web applications, services, and servers. To adequately support the needs of the web applications, services, and servers based applications, effective risk management and appropriate deployment of alternate countermeasures are essential. Defense-in-depth through security engineering, secure software development, and risk management can provide much of the robustness and reliability required by these applications.

Finally, let's move on to the real interactive part of this Chapter: review questions/exercises, hands-on projects, case projects, and optional team case project. The answers and/or solutions by chapter can be found in Appendix K.

CHAPTER REVIEW QUESTIONS/ EXERCISES

True/False

1. True or False? The development of a distributed hypertext system in the early 1990s at the CERN in Switzerland was one of the defining moments in making the Internet available to an audience beyond academia and specialized communities.
2. True or False? Since HTTP services implementing a REST architectural style (often called "REST Services") are simply using the HTTP stack, all security aspects of HTTP apply.
3. True or False? It should be noted that since WS-Security is only tied to the SOAP messaging structures, it is completely transport independent and can therefore

be used over the SOAP HTTP binding, but also with any other form of SOAP transport.
4. True or False? Since web services are intended to implement a distributed architecture, it becomes very important to manage the identities of the participating actors: different systems implementing the services or the clients need to fully understand who they are interacting with in order to make access control decisions that are consistent with the security policies for the systems.
5. True or False? Most modern operating systems support IBAC-based access control for file systems access and other security related functions.

Multiple Choice

1. SOAP services are built around the concept of a:
   A. SOAP header
   B. SOAP body
   C. SOAP envelope
   D. SOAP message
   E. All of the above
2. The simple Base64 encoding can be decoded by anyone and must be treated as:
   A. Bad code
   B. Clear text
   C. Basic authentication
   D. Server authentication
   E. All of the above
3. What can usually make use of operating or runtime systems certificate stores in a very efficient way?
   A. TLS
   B. PKI
   C. MAC
   D. REST client libraries
   E. Two
4. WS-Security[25] (often abbreviated WSS) defines a Header extension to provide a number of features for SOAP-based messages, except which two?
   A. Signing the message to provide integrity protection and nonrepudiation.
   B. WS-Security can be combined with the security mechanisms of the underlying transport security.
   C. Encrypting the message to provide message-level confidentiality.
   D. Attaching arbitrary security tokens to the messages to provide identity of the sender.
   E. WS-Security leverages the XML Encryption and Signature standards.
5. The identity management community created a number of patterns that allow not only simple authentication,

---

25. "Web Service Security: SOAP Messaging Framework 1.1", A. Nadlin et al., OASIS Open, November 2006.

but also advanced patterns including the following, except which two?

A. Other patterns, such as privacy preserving authentication and authorization.

B. Single Sign On (SSO) using mutually trusted identity servers.

C. Federations of identity providers.

D. SAML Authentication Token.

E. Complex, distributed authorization.

EXERCISE

Problem

When multiple requesters, providers, and intermediaries are participating in a web service transaction, it may be necessary to coordinate them. What are the two different types of mechanisms for coordinating web services?

Hands-On Projects

Project

Because a web service relies on some of the same underlying HTTP and web-based architecture as common web applications, it is susceptible to similar threats and vulnerabilities. Web services security is based on what several important concepts?

Case Projects

Problem

Web services rely on the Internet for communication. Because SOAP was not designed with security in mind, SOAP messages can be viewed or modified by attackers as the messages traverse the Internet. What options are available for securing web service messages?

Optional Team Case Project

Problem

Security decisions must always be made with an understanding of the threats facing the system to be secured. While there are a wealth of security standards and technologies available for securing Web services, they may not be adequate or necessary for a particular organization or an individual service. For that reason, it is important to understand the threats that face web services so that organizations can determine which threats their web services must be secured against. What are the top threats facing web services today?

RESOURCES

[1] The opinions and guidance presented here are those of the author and do not necessarily reflect the positions of The MITRE Corporation, its customers or sponsors, or any part of the U.S. Federal Government.

[2] The document is available from https://www.owasp.org/. The last update to the list was done in 2010.

[3] The list is available at http://www.sans.org/critical-security-controls/.

[4] NIST Special Publication (SP) 800-53 is a comprehensive list of information security controls and they verification procedures.

[5] See http://www.backtrack-linux.org/ for more information on BackTrack.

Chapter 11

UNIX and Linux Security

Gerald Beuchelt

Demandware, Inc., Burlington, MA, United States

1. INTRODUCTION

When UNIX was first booted on a PDP-8 computer at Bell Labs, it already had a basic notion of user isolation, separation of kernel and user memory space, and process security. It was originally conceived of as a multiuser system, and as such, security could not be added on as an afterthought. In this respect, UNIX was different from a whole class of computing machinery that had been targeted for single-user environments.

Linux is mostly a GNU software-based operating system (OS) with a kernel originally written by Linus Torvalds, with many popular utilities from the GNU Software Foundation and other open-source organizations added. GNU/Linux implements the same interfaces as most current UNIX systems, including the Portable Operating System Interface (POSIX) standards. As such, Linux is a UNIX-style OS, even though it was not derived from the original AT&T/Bell Labs UNIX code base.

Debian is a distribution originally developed by Ian Murdock of Purdue University. Debian's express goal is to use only open and free software, as defined by its guidelines. Ubuntu is a derivative Linux distribution based on the Debian system. It emphasizes ease of use and allows beginning users easy access to a comprehensive Linux distribution.

All versions of MacOS X are built on UNIX OSs, namely the Mach microkernel and the University of California's FreeBSD code. Although the graphical user interface and some other systems enhancements are proprietary, MacOS has a XNU kernel and includes most of the command-line utilities commonly found in UNIX OSs.

The examples in this chapter refer to Solaris, MacOS, and Ubuntu Linux, a distribution by Canonical, Inc., built on the popular Debian distribution.

2. UNIX AND SECURITY

As already indicated, UNIX was originally created as a multiuser system. Initially systems were not necessarily networked, but with the integration of the Berkley Software Distribution (BSD) TCP/IP V4 stack in 1984, UNIX-based systems quickly became the backbone of the rapidly growing Internet. As such, UNIX servers started to provide critical services to network users as well.

The Aims of System Security

In general, secure computing systems must guarantee the confidentiality, integrity, and availability of resources. This is achieved by combining different security mechanisms and safeguards, including policy-driven access control and process separation.

Authentication

When a user is granted access to resources on a computing system, it vitally important to establish and verify the identity of the requesting entity. This process is commonly referred to as *authentication* (sometimes abbreviated as *AuthN*).

Authorization

As a multiuser system, UNIX must protect resources from unauthorized access. To protect user data from other users and nonusers, the OS has to put up safeguards against unauthorized access. Determining the eligibility of an authenticated (or anonymous) user to access or modify a resource is usually called *authorization* (sometimes abbreviated as *AuthZ*).

Availability

Guarding a system (including all of its subsystems, such as the network) against security breaches is vital to keep the

Computer and Information Security Handbook. http://dx.doi.org/10.1016/B978-0-12-803843-7.00011-9

system available for its intended use. The *availability* of a system must be properly defined: Any system is physically available, even if it is turned off; however, a shutdown system would not be useful. In the same way, a system that has only the core OS running but not the services that are supposed to run on the system is considered unavailable.

Integrity

Similar to availability, a system that is compromised cannot be considered available for regular service. Ensuring that the UNIX system is running in the intended way is crucial, especially because the system might otherwise be used maliciously by a third party, such as for a relay or member in a botnet.

Confidentiality

Protecting resources from unauthorized access and safeguarding the content is referred to as confidentiality. As long as it is not compromised, a UNIX system will maintain the confidentiality of system user data by enforcing access control policies and separating processes from each other. There are two fundamentally different types of access control: discretionary and mandatory. Users themselves manage the former, whereas the system owner sets the latter. We will discuss the differences later in this chapter.

3. BASIC UNIX SECURITY OVERVIEW

UNIX security has a long tradition, and although many concepts of the earliest UNIX systems still apply, a large number of changes have fundamentally altered the way the OS implements these security principles. One of the reasons why it is complicated to talk about UNIX security is that a lot of variants of UNIX and UNIX-like OSs are on the market. In fact, if you look at only some of the core POSIX standards that have been set forth to guarantee minimal consistency across different UNIX flavors (Fig. 11.1), almost every OS on the market qualifies as UNIX (or, more precisely, POSIX compliant). Examples include not only traditional UNIX OSs such as Solaris, HP-UX, and AIX but also Windows NT—based OSs (such as Windows XP,

The term POSIX stands (loosely) for "Portable Operating System Interface for uniX". From the IEEE 1003.1 Standard, 2004 Edition:

"This standard defines a standard operating system interface and environment, including a command interpreter (or "shell"), and common utility programs to support applications portability at the source code level. This standard is the single common revision to IEEE Std 1003.1-1996, IEEE Std 1003.2-1992, and the Base Specifications of The Open Group Single UNIX Specification, Version 2." Partial or full POSIX compliance is often required for government contracts.

FIGURE 11.1   Various UNIX and Portable Operating System Interface (POSIX) standards.

through the native POSIX subsystem or the Services for Windows extensions) and even z/OS.

Traditional UNIX Systems

Most UNIX systems share some internal features, though: Their approaches to authentication and authorization are similar, their delineation between kernel space and user space goes along the same lines, and their security-related kernel structures are roughly comparable. In the past few years, however, there have been major advancements in extending the original security model by adding role-based access control[1] (RBAC) models to some OSs. In addition to RBAC, most UNIX-based system can support mandatory access control (MAC) models by implementing kernel-level object tagging and rule enforcement. A more detailed discussion of MAC is provided later in this chapter.

Kernel Space Versus User Land

UNIX systems typically execute instructions in one of two general contexts: the kernel or the user space. Code executed in a kernel context has (at least in traditional systems) full access to the entire hardware and software capabilities of the computing environment. Although some systems extend security safeguards into the kernel, in most cases not only can a rogue kernel execution thread cause massive data corruption, it can effectively bring down the entire OS.

Obviously, a normal user of an OS should not wield so much power. To prevent this, user execution threads in UNIX systems are not executed in the context of the kernel but in a less privileged context, the user space, which is sometimes facetiously called "user land." It is common to restrict user-land access to certain more privileged execution commands by switching the operational context of the processor. For example, the common Intel x386 architecture (including the AMD 64 bit extensions) has a ring model in which privileged commands are available only in higher rings. Most OSs execute the kernel in ring 0 and user processes in ring 3.

The UNIX kernel defines a structure called *process* (Fig. 11.2) that associates metadata about the user as well as potentially other environmental factors with the execution thread and its data. Access to computing resources such as memory, input—output (I/O) subsystems, and so on

---

1. RBAC developed in the 1990s as a new approach to access control for computing resources. Authorization to access resources is granted based on role membership and often allows more fine-grained resource control because specific operations (such as "modify file" or "add printer") can be granted to role members. In 2004, the RBAC model was standardized in American National Standard 359—2004 (see also http://csrc.nist.gov/rbac/ for more information).

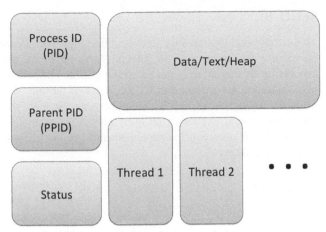

FIGURE 11.2 Kernel structure of a typical UNIX process.

is safeguarded by the kernel; if a user process wants to allocate a segment of memory or access a device, it has to make a system call, passing some of its metadata as parameters to the kernel. The kernel then performs an authorization decision[2] and either grants the request or returns an error. It is then the process's responsibility to react properly to either the results of the access or the error.

If this model of user space process security is so effective, why not implement it for all OS functions, including most kernel operations? The answer is that to a large extent the overhead of evaluating authorization metadata is computation-expensive. If most or all operations (which are, in the classical kernel space, often hardware-related device access operations) are run in user space or in a comparable way, the performance of the OS would suffer severely. There is a class of OS with a microkernel that implements this approach; the kernel implements only the most rudimentary functions (processes, scheduling, and basic security); all other operations, including device access and those typically carried out by the kernel, run in separate user processes. The advantage is a higher level of security and better safeguards against rogue device drivers. Furthermore, new device drivers or other OS functionality can be added or removed without having to reboot the kernel. The performance penalties are so severe, however, that no major commercial OS implements a comprehensive microkernel architecture.[3]

Many modern UNIX-based systems operate in a mixed mode: Whereas many device drivers such as hard drives, video, and I/O systems operate in the kernel space, they also provide a framework for user space drivers. For example, the "Filesystems in User Space" allows additional drivers to be loaded for file systems. This allows the mounting of devices that are not formatted with the default file system types that the OS supports, without having to execute with elevated privileges. It also allows the use of file systems or other hardware drivers in situations in which license conflicts prevent the integration of a file system driver into the kernel (for example, the Common Development and Distribution License ZFS file system into the General Public License Linux kernel).

Semantics of User Space Security

In most UNIX systems, security starts with access control to resources. Because users interact with the systems through processes and files, it is important to know that every user space process structure has two important security fields: the user identifier (UID) and the group identifier (GID). These identifiers are typically positive integers that are unique for each user.[4] Every process that is started[5] by or on behalf of a user inherits the UID and GID values for that user account. These values are usually immutable for the lifetime of the process.

Access to system resources must go through the kernel by calling the appropriate function that is accessible to user processes. For example, a process that wants to reserve some system memory for data access will use the malloc() system call and pass the requested size and an (uninitialized) pointer as parameters. The kernel then evaluates this request, determines whether enough virtual memory (physical memory plus swap space) is available, reserves a section of memory, and sets the pointer to the address where the block starts.

Users who have the UID 0 have special privileges: They are considered *superusers*, able to override many of the security guards that the kernel sets up. The default UNIX superuser is named *root*.

Standard File and Device Access Semantics

File access is a fundamental task, and it is important that only authorized users get read or write access to a given

---

2. In the case of MAC-enabled OSs, the kernel can leverage a rich set of attributes and policies for authorization. In traditional UNIX implementations, this authorization is more limited and often is restricted to the UID.
3. The MACH kernel was an attempt in the 1990s to create a microkernel architecture. It was intended to be the kernel for the open-source GNU OS. Owing its lack of performance it never became popular, and the Linux kernel was most commonly used as the basis for the GNU OS. In fact, what is now known simply as "Linux" should really be called the GNU/Linux, because the vast majority of the initial OS components were taken from the GNU project.
4. If two usernames are associated with the same UID, the OS will treat them as the same user. Their authentication credentials (username and password) are different but their authorization with respect to system resources is the same. This has been used to provide access to the superuser account to different individuals, but malware authors and hackers have also used this method to create and hide privileged access accounts.
5. Processes can be "started" or created in a variety of ways: for example, by calling the fork() system call or by calling the execve() system call to load a new executable file and start it.

file. If any user were able to access any file, there would be no privacy and security could not be maintained, because the OS would not be able to protect its own permanent records, such as configuration information or user credentials. Most UNIX OSs use an identity-based access control (IBAC) model, in which access policies are expressed in terms of the identity of user.

The most common IBAC policy describing who may access or modify files and directories is commonly referred to as an *access control list* (ACL). Note that there is more than just one type of ACL; standard UNIX ACLs are well-known, but different UNIX variants or POSIX-like OSs might implement different ACLs and only define a mapping to the simple POSIX 1003 semantics. A good example is the Windows NTFS ACL or the NFS v4 ACLs. ACLs for files and devices represented though device files are stored within the file system as metadata for the file information itself. This is different from other access control models in which policies may be stored in a central repository.

Read, Write, Execute

From its earliest days, UNIX implemented a simple but effective way to set access rights for users. Normal files can be accessed in three fundamental ways: read, write, and execute. The first two ways are obvious; execution requires a little more explanation. A file on disk may be executed only as a binary program or a script if the user has the right to execute this file. If the execute permission is not set, the system call exec() or execve() to execute a file image will fail. In addition to a user's permissions, there must be a notion of ownership of files and sometimes other resources. In fact, each file on a traditional UNIX file system is associated with a user and a group. The user and group are not identified by their name but by UID and GID.

In addition to setting permissions for the user owning the file, two other sets of permissions are set for files: for the group and for all others. Similar to being owned by a user, a file is also associated with one group. All members of this group[6] can access the file with the permissions set for the group. In the same way, the other set of permissions applies to all users of the system.

Special Permissions

In addition to the standard permissions, there are a few special permissions.

---

6. Users belong to one primary group, identified by the GID set in the password database. However, group membership is actually determined separately through the /etc/group file. As such, a user can be (and often is) a member of more than one group.

SetID Bit

This permission applies only to executable files, and it can be set only for the user or the group. If this bit is set, the process for this program is not set to the UID or GID of the invoking user, but instead the UID or GID of the file. For example, a program owned by the superuser can have the SetID bit set and execution allowed for all users. In this way a normal user can execute a specific program with elevated privileges.

Sticky Bit

When the sticky bit is set on an executable file, its data (specifically the text segment) are kept in memory even after the process exits. This is intended to speed execution of commonly used programs. A major drawback of setting the sticky bit is that when the executable file changes (for example, through a patch), the permission must be unset and the program started once more. When this process exits, the executable is unloaded from memory and the file can be changed.

Mandatory Locking

Mandatory file and record locking refer to a file's ability to have its reading or writing permissions locked while a program is accessing that file. In addition, there might be additional implementation-specific permissions. These depend on the capabilities of the core operating facilities, including the kernel, but also on the type of file system. For example, most UNIX OSs can mount Microsoft DOS-based file allocation table—based file systems, which do not support any permissions or user and group ownership. Because the internal semantics require some values for ownership and permissions, these are typically set for the entire file system.

Permissions on Directories

The semantics of permissions on directories (Fig. 11.3) are different from those on files.

Making a directory readable for everyone:

```
# chmod o+r /tmp/mydir # ls -ld /tmp/mydir
drwxr-xr-x  2 root    root     117 Aug  9 12:12 /tmp/
mydir
```

Setting the SetID bit on an executable, thus enabling it to be run with super-user privileges:

```
# chmod u+s specialprivs # ls -ld specialprivs
-rwsr-xr-x  2 root    root     117 Aug  9 12:12
specialprivs
```

FIGURE 11.3   Examples of chmod for files and directories.

Read and Write

Mapping these permissions to directories is fairly straight-forward: The read permission allows files to be listed in the directory and the write permission allows us to create files. For some applications it can be useful to allow writing but not reading.

Execute

If this permission is set, a process can set its working directory to this directory. Note that with the basic permissions there is no limitation on traversing directories, so a process might change its working directory to a child of a directory, even if it cannot do so for the directory itself.

SetID

Semantics may differ here. For example, on Solaris this changes the behavior for default ownership of newly created files from the System V to the BSD semantics.

Other File Systems

As mentioned, the set of available permissions and authorization policies depends on the underlying OS capabilities, including the file system. For example, the UFS file system in Solaris since version 2.5 allows additional ACLs on a per-user basis. Furthermore, NFS version 4 or higher defines additional ACLs for file access; it is obvious that the NFS server must have an underlying file system capable of recording these additional metadata. Fig. 11.4 exhibits a list of extended file system ACLs available on MacOS-based UFS. This list is similar for FreeBSD and other UFS-based file systems.

Discretionary Versus Mandatory Access Control

The access control semantics described so far establish a "discretionary" access control (DAC) model: any user may determine what type of access he or she wants to give to other specific users, groups, or anybody else. For many applications this is sufficient: for example, for systems that deliver a single network service and do not allow interactive login, the service's ability to determine itself what data will be shared with network users may be sufficient.

In systems that need to enforce access to data based on centralized, system operator—administered policies, DAC may not be sufficient. For example, for systems that need to operate in multilevel security environments, confidentiality of data can be achieved only through a MAC model. A number of MAC implementations for UNIX-based systems are currently available, including Solaris Trusted Extensions for Solaris 10, SELinux for Linux-based OSs, jails for FreeBSD, the sandbox facility for MacOS and iOS, and TrustedBSD for BSD-based distributions.

MAC can be designed and implemented in many different ways. A common approach is to label OS objects in user both and kernel space with a classification level and enforce appropriate MAC policies, such as the Bell—LaPadua (BLP) model for data confidentiality or the Biba model for data integrity.

Many UNIX OSs provide a rudimentary set of MAC options by default: The SELinux-based Linux Security Module interface is part of the core kernel, and some OS vendors such as Red Hat ship their OSs with a minimal set of MAC policies enabled. To operate in a true multilevel security environment, further configuration and often additional software modules are necessary to enable a BLP- or Biba-compliant set of MAC policies.

Whereas MAC-based systems have traditionally been employed in government environments, modern enterprise architectures have a growing need for enforced access control regarding confidentiality or integrity. For example, data leakage protection systems or auditing systems will benefit from certain types of centralized MAC policies. FreeBSD jails are commonly used to isolate subsystems or applications, such as in the popular FreeNAS distribution. Consumer-facing architectures are also increasingly adopting additional application isolation through MAC: iOS applications and many commercial types of MacOS software leverage the sandbox facility to limit process activity.

4. ACHIEVING UNIX SECURITY

Achieving a high level of system security for a UNIX system is a complex process that involves technical, operational, and managerial aspects of system operations. The subsequent list is a cursory overview of some of the most important aspects of securing a UNIX system. To achieve a level of OS security suitable for operating Internet-facing systems or in a mission-critical environment, additional configuration steps should be taken. These need to include all vendor-suggested configuration and standard maintenance procedures, but they should include additional measures. For example, the Center for Internet Security[7] (CIS) publishes "Security Benchmarks" for most major OSs and major software packages. These are freely available from the CIS in the form of PDF document and provide detailed secure configuration options for most OS subsystems. To its participating members, the CIS also makes a Security Content Automation Protocol (SCAP)-compliant configuration scanner and the associated SCAP[8] files available. Other sources for configuration profiles can

---

7. See https://www.cisecurity.org/.
8. SCAP is an NIST standard used to automate security configurations: https://scap.nist.gov/.

```
The following permissions are applicable to all filesystem objects:
        delete   Delete the item.  Deletion may be granted by either this
                 permission on an object or the delete_child right on the
                 containing directory.
        readattr
                 Read an objects basic attributes.  This is implicitly
                 granted if the object can be looked up and not explicitly
                 denied.
        writeattr
                 Write an object's basic attributes.
        readextattr
                 Read extended attributes.
        writeextattr
                 Write extended attributes.
        readsecurity
                 Read an object's extended security information (ACL).
        writesecurity
                 Write an object's security information (ownership, mode,
                 ACL).
        chown    Change an object's ownership.

The following permissions are applicable to directories:
        list     List entries.
        search   Look up files by name.
        add_file
                 Add a file.
        add_subdirectory
                 Add a subdirectory.
        delete_child
                 Delete a contained object.  See the file delete permission
                 above.

The following permissions are applicable to non-directory filesystem
objects:
        read     Open for reading.
        write    Open for writing.
        append   Open for writing, but in a fashion that only allows writes
                 into areas of the file not previously written.
        execute
                 Execute the file as a script or program.

ACL inheritance is controlled with the following permissions words, which
may only be applied to directories:
        file_inherit
                 Inherit to files.
        directory_inherit
                 Inherit to directories.
        limit_inherit
                 This flag is only relevant to entries inherited by subdi-
                 rectories; it causes the directory_inherit flag to be
                 cleared in the entry that is inherited, preventing further
                 nested subdirectories from also inheriting the entry.
        only_inherit
                 The entry is inherited by created items but not considered
                 when processing the ACL.
```

FIGURE 11.4   Excerpt from main page for chmod(1) on MacOS describing the extended file system access control lists.

be obtained through the US Department of Defense Information System Agency (DISA) in the form of SCAP-compliant Security Technical Implementation Guide (STIG)[9] files.

---

9. The DISA STIG can be found here: http://iase.disa.mil/stigs/Pages/index.aspx.

System Patching

Before anything else, it is vitally important to emphasize the need to keep UNIX systems up to date. No OS or other program can be considered safe without being patched up; this point cannot be stressed enough. Having a system with the latest security patches is the first and most often the best line of defense against intruders and other cyber security threats.

All major UNIX systems have a patching mechanism; this is a way to get the system up to date. Depending on the vendor and the mechanism used, it is possible to "back out" of the patches. For example, on Solaris it is usually possible to remove a patch through the patchrm (1 m) command. On Debian-based systems this is not as easy, because in a patch the software package to be updated is replaced by a new version. Undoing this is possible only by installing the earlier package.

Locking Down the System

In general, all system services and facilities that are not needed for regular operation should be disabled or even uninstalled. Because any software package increases the attack surface of the system, removing unnecessary software ensures a better security posture.

Minimizing User Privileges

User accounts that have far-reaching access rights within a system have the ability to affect or damage a large number of resources, potentially including system management or system service resources. As such, user access rights should be minimized by default, in line with the security principle of "least privilege." For example, unless interactive access to the system is absolutely required, users should not be permitted to login.

Detecting Intrusions With Audits and Logs

By default, most UNIX systems log kernel messages and important system events from core services. The most common logging tool is the syslog facility, which is controlled from the /etc/syslog.conf file.

5. PROTECTING USER ACCOUNTS AND STRENGTHENING AUTHENTICATION

In general, a clear distinction must be made between users obtaining a command shell for a UNIX system ("interactive users") and consumers of UNIX network service ("noninteractive users"). In most instances, the former should be limited to administrators who need to configure and monitor the system, especially because interactive access is almost always a necessary first step to obtaining administrative access.[10]

---

10. Most Web applications would never permit end users any OS level of access, to protect the integrity of the environment. Although the Web applications are designed to implement the appropriate authentication and authorization controls, the underlying UNIX environment is designed for administrators and the services themselves. If a user can establish a way to execute system-level commands through the Web interface, it is not hard to create a "Web shell", i.e., a simple client—server environment in which an end user can interact with the OS in an interactive way, typically in the user context of the service user. This is a serious breach and often is used to break into Web applications. A strong Web application security approach is necessary to protect against attacks such as this.

Establishing Secure Account Use

For any interactive session, UNIX systems require the user to log into the system. To do so, the user must present a valid credential that identifies him (he must authenticate to the system). The type of credentials a UNIX system uses depends on the capabilities of the OS software itself and on the configuration set forth by the systems administrator. The most traditional user credential is a username and a text password, but there are many other ways to authenticate to the OS, including Kerberos, SSH-based public and private keys, and X.509 security certificates.

The UNIX Login Process

Depending on the desired authentication mechanism (Fig. 11.5 shows some commonly used authentication systems), the user will have to use different access protocols or processes. For example, console or directly attached terminal sessions usually support only password credentials or smart card logins, whereas a secure shell connection supports only Rivest—Shamir—Adleman (RSA) or digital signature algorithm (DSA)-based cryptographic tokens over the Secure Shell (SSH) protocol.

The login process is a system daemon that is responsible for coordinating authentication and process setup for interactive users. To do this, the login process does the following:

1. Draw or display the login screen.
2. Collect the credential.
3. Present the user credential to any of the configured user databases [typically these can be files, NIS, Kerberos servers, or Lightweight Directory Access Protocol (LDAP) directories] for authentication.

Overview of Unix authentication methods

- Simple: a username and a password are used to login to the operating system. The login process must receive both in cleartext. For the password, the Unix crypt hash is calculated and compared to the value in the password or shadow file.
- Kerberos: The user is supposed to have a ticket- granting ticket from the Kerberos Key Distribution Server (KDC). Using the ticket- granting ticket, he obtains a service ticket for an interactive login to the Unix host. This service ticket (encrypted, time limited) is then presented to the login process, and the Unix host validates it with the KDC.
- LDAP based authentication uses a centralized LDAP directory for authentication and attribute storage.
- PKI based Smartcard: the private key on the smart card is used to authenticate with the system.

FIGURE 11.5 Various UNIX authentication mechanisms. *LDAP*, Lightweight Directory Access Protocol; *PKI*, public key infrastructure.

4. Create a process with the user's default command-line shell, with the home directory as the working directory.
5. Execute system-wide, user, and shell-specific startup scripts.

The commonly available X11 windowing system does not use the text-oriented login process but instead provides its own facility to perform roughly the same kind of login sequence. Access to interactive sessions using the SSH protocol follows a similar general pattern, but the authentication is significantly different from the traditional login process.

Controlling Account Access

Simple configuration files were the first method available to store and manage user account data. Over the course of years many other user databases have been implemented. We examine these here.

Local Files

Originally, UNIX supported only a simple password file for storing account information. The username and the information required for the login process (UID, GID, shell, home directory, password hashes, and General Electric Comprehensive Operating System information) are stored in this file, which is typically at /etc/passwd. This approach is highly insecure because this file needs to be readable by all for a number of different services, which thus exposes the password hashes to potential hackers. In fact, a simple dictionary or even brute force attack can reveal simple or even more complex passwords. To protect against an attack like this, most UNIX variants use a separate file to store the password hashes (/etc/shadow) that is readable and writable only by the system.

Network Information System

The Network Information System (NIS) was introduced in the 1980s to simplify the administration of small groups of computers. Originally, Sun Microsystems called this service Yellow Pages, but the courts decided that this name constituted a trademark infringement on the British Telecom Yellow Pages. However, most commands that are used to administer the NIS still start with the yp prefix (such as ypbind and ypcat).

Systems within the NIS are said to belong to an NIS domain. Although there is no correlation between the NIS domain and the Domain Name System (DNS) of the system, it is common to use DNS-style domain names to name NIS domains. For example, a system with the DNS name system1.sales.example.com might be a member of the NIS domain nis.sales.Example.COM. Note that NIS domains (other than DNS domains) are case sensitive.

```
# /etc/nsswitch.conf

#
# Example configuration of GNU Name Service
Switch functionality.
#
passwd: files nis
group: files nis
shadow: files nis

hosts: files nis dns
networks: files

protocols: db files
services: db files
ethers: db files
rpc: db files
netgroup: nis
```

FIGURE 11.6 Simple example nsswitch.conf for a Debian system.

The NIS uses a simple master—slave server system: The master NIS server holds all authoritative data and uses an Open Network Computing Remote Procedure Call—based protocol to communicate with the slave servers and clients. Slave servers cannot easily be upgraded to a master server, so careful planning of the infrastructure is highly recommended.

Client systems are bound to one NIS server (master or slave) during runtime. The addresses for the NIS master and the slaves must be provided when joining a system to the NIS domain. Clients (and servers) can always be members of only one NIS domain. To use the NIS user database (and other NIS resources, such as automount maps, netgroups, and host tables) after the system is bound, use the name service configuration file (/etc/nsswitch.conf), as shown in Fig. 11.6.

Using Pluggable Authentication Modules to Modify Authentication

These user databases can easily be configured for use on a given system through the /etc/nsswitch.conf file. However, in more complex situations, the administrator might want to fine-tune the types of acceptable authentication methods, such as Kerberos, or even configure multifactor authentication. Traditionally, the pluggableauthenticationmodule (PAM) is configured through the /etc/pam.conf file, but more modern implementations use a directory structure, similar to the System V init scripts. For these systems the administrator needs to modify the configuration files in the /etc/pam.d/directory.

Using the systemauth PAM, administrators can also enforce users to create and maintain complex passwords, including the setting of specific lengths, the minimal number of numeric or nonletter characters, etc. Fig. 11.7 illustrates a typical systemauth PAM configuration.

```
# /etc/pam.d/common-password - password-related modules common to all services
#
# The "nullok" option allows users to change an empty password, else
# empty passwords are treated as locked accounts.  The "sha512" option enables
# salted SHA512 passwords.  Without this option, the default is Unix crypt.
#
# See the pam_unix manpage for other options.
# As of pam 1.0.1-6, this file is managed by pam-auth-update by default.
# See pam-auth-update(8) for details.
# here are the per-package modules (the "Primary" block)
password        [success=1 default=ignore]        pam_unix.so obscure sha512
# here's the fallback if no module succeeds
password        requisite                 pam_deny.so
# prime the stack with a positive return value if there isn't one already;
# this avoids us returning an error just because nothing sets a success code
# since the modules above will each just jump around
password        required                  pam_permit.so
# and here are more per-package modules (the "Additional" block)
password        optional       pam_gnome_keyring.so
# end of pam-auth-update config
```

FIGURE 11.7   Setting the pam parameters on a Ubuntu system through the pluggableauthenticationmodule system.

Noninteractive Access

The security configuration of noninteractive services can vary significantly. In particular, popular network services, such as LDAP, Hypertext TransferProtocol (HTTP), or Windows File Shares, can use a wide variety of authentication and authorization mechanisms that do not even need to be provided by the OS. For example, an Apache Web server or a MySQL database server might use its own user database without relying on any OS services such as passwd files or LDAP directory authentication.

Monitoring how noninteractive authentication and authorization is performed is critically important because most users of UNIX systems will use them in only noninteractive ways. To ensure the most comprehensive control over the system, it is highly recommended to follow the suggestions in Sections 7 and 8 of this chapter to minimize the attack surface and verify that the system makes only a clearly defined set of services available on the network.

Other Network Authentication Mechanisms

In 1983, BSD introduced the rlogin service. UNIX administrators have been using RSH, RCP, and other tools from this package for a long time; they are easy to use and configure and provide simple access across a small network of computers. The login was facilitated through a simple trust model: Any user could create a .rhosts file in her home directory and specify foreign hosts and users from which to accept logins without proper credential checking. Over the rlogin protocol (TCP 513), the username of the rlogin client would be transmitted to the host system, and in lieu of an

authentication, the rshd daemon would simply verify the preconfigured values. To prevent access from untrusted hosts, the administrator could use the /etc/hosts.equiv file to allow or deny individual hosts or groups of hosts (the latter through the use of NIS netgroups).

Risks of Trusted Hosts and Networks

Because no authentication takes place, this trust mechanism should not be used. Not only does this system rely entirely on the correct functioning of the hostname resolution system, there is no way to determine whether a host was actually replaced.[11] Also, although rlogin-based trust systems might work for small deployments, they become extremely hard to set up and operate with large numbers of machines.

Replacing Telnet, rlogin, and File Transfer Protocol Servers and Clients With Secure Shell

The most sensible alternative to traditional interactive session protocols such as Telnet is the SSH system. It is popular on UNIX systems, and pretty much all versions ship with a version of SSH. Where SSH is not available, the open-source package OpenSSH can easily be used instead.[12]

---

11. This could actually be addressed through host authentication, but it is not a feature of the rlogin protocol.
12. "The Open Group Base Specifications Issue 6 IEEE Std 1003.1, 2004 Edition," see [IEEE04]. Copyright © 2001—2004 The IEEE and The Open Group, All Rights Reserved [www.opengroup.org/onlinepubs/009695399/], 2004.

SSH combines the ease-of-use features of the rlogin tools with a strong cryptographic authentication system. On the one hand, it is fairly easy for users to enable access from other systems; on the other hand, the SSH protocol uses strong cryptography to:

- authenticate the connection: that is, establish the authenticity of the user;
- protect the privacy of the connection through encryption;
- guarantee the integrity of the channel through signatures.

This is done using either the RSA or DSA security algorithm, both of which are available for the SSH v2[13] protocol. The cipher (Fig. 11.8) used for encryption can be explicitly selected. It is important to review the cipher suites used for SSH access periodically and update them to the latest cryptographic algorithms.

The user must first create a public/private key pair through the ssh-keygen(1) tool. The output of the key generator is placed in the .ssh subdirectory of the user's home directory. This output consists of a private key file called id_dsa or id_rsa. This file must be owned by the user and is readable only by the user. In addition, a file containing the public key is created, named in the same way, with the extension .pub appended. The public key file is then placed into the .ssh subdirectory of the user's home directory on the target system.

```
$ ssh -Q cipher
3des-cbc
blowfish-cbc
cast128-cbc
arcfour
arcfour128
arcfour256
aes128-cbc
aes192-cbc
aes256-cbc
rijndael-cbc@lysator.liu.se
aes128-ctr
aes192-ctr
aes256-ctr
aes128-gcm@openssh.com
aes256-gcm@openssh.com
chacha20-poly1305@openssh.com
$ ssh host -luser1 -c aes192-cbc
```

FIGURE 11.8 Requesting available ciphers and creating an interactive Secure Shell session to "host" for user1 using the Advanced Encryption Standard cipher with 192 bits.

13. T. Ylonen, C. Lonvick (Eds.) "The Secure Shell (SSH) Authentication Protocol," Network Working Group, Request for Comments: 4252, SSH Communications Security Corp., Category: Standards Track, Cisco Systems, Inc., see [IETF4252]. Copyright © The Internet Society (2006) [http://tools.ietf.org/html/rfc4252], 2006.

Once the public and private keys are in place and the SSH daemon is enabled on the host system, all clients that implement the SSH protocol can create connections. There are four common applications using SSH:

- Interactive session is the replacement for Telnet and rlogin. Using the ssh(1) command line, the sshd daemon creates a new shell and transfers control to the user.
- In a remotely executed script/command, ssh(1) allows a single command with arguments to pass. This way, a single remote command (such as a backup script) can be executed on the remote system as long as this command is in the default path for the user.
- An SSH-enabled file transfer program can be used to replace the standard FTP or FTP over Secure Sockets Layer (SSL) protocol.
- Finally, the SSH protocol is able to tunnel arbitrary protocols. This means that any client can use the privacy and integrity protection offered by SSH. In particular, the X-Window system protocol can tunnel through an existing SSH connection by using the -X command-line switch.

SSH can also be configured to leverage PKCS#11 encoded security certificates: Instead of relying on configuring the appropriate public keys for each user, the SSH daemon can be configured to trust a certificate authority's signature.

Other Authentication Options: Example of One-Time Password

There can be any number of other network-based or local authentication systems including Kerberos v5 or pure LDAPv3-based authentication, but it goes beyond the scope of this chapter to discuss all of them. A slightly arcane but interesting authentication system sometimes used in environments with a high risk of replay attacks (such as public networks) is the use of one-time passwords (OTPs). An implementation commonly found in BSD-based systems, One Time Passwords in Everything (OPIE) is also available on Windows, MacOS, and most Linux distributions.

The basic idea behind OPIE is to create an initial set of single-use passwords and enable their use through insecure channels. Once the OS allowing OPIE authentication has created the user's OTPs, they can be used each time the user logs in. Obviously it would be inconvenient and insecure to write down, e.g., 500 OTPs, so the OPIE system implements two components: a server-side OTP management system and a client-side on-demand generation facility. Once the OPIE database has been initialized, it uses a secret password, a seed (consisting of two letters and five numbers), and the iteration count as input into the OTP generation. Upon interactive login (e.g., through Telnet or

The login process looks like this:
```
$ ssh administrator@freebsd
otp-md5 498 fr1297 ext
Password:
otp-md5 498 fr1297 ext
Password [echo on]: ORE MUDD ROD JULY ORR LIAR
Last login: Wed May 11 10:07:06 2016 from
10.0.248.1
FreeBSD 10.3-RELEASE-p2 (GENERIC) #0: Wed May  4
06:03:51 UTC 2016

Welcome to FreeBSD!

[administrator@freebsd ~]$
```

On the client side, opiekey is used to generate the 497th password with seed fr1297:
```
$ opiekey -f 498 fr1297
Using the MD5 algorithm to compute response.
Reminder: Don't use opiekey from telnet or dial-in
sessions.
Enter secret pass phrase:
ORE MUDD ROD JULY ORR LIAR
```

FIGURE 11.9 OPIE sample used on FreeBSD.

SSH), the user is presented with an OTP challenge consisting of the iteration count and the seed. The user then needs to use a client side tool (opiekey) to create the OTP and enter it for authentication. Because opiekey requires the use of the secret generation password, the client must be trusted. Fig. 11.9 shows an example session.

6. LIMITING SUPERUSER PRIVILEGES

The superuser[14] has almost unlimited power on a UNIX system, which can be a significant problem. On systems that implement mandatory access controls, the superuser account can be configured not to affect user data, but the problem of overly powerful root accounts for standard, DAC-only systems remains. From an organizational and managerial perspective, access to privileged functions on an UNIX OS should be tightly controlled. For example, operators who have access to privileged functions on an UNIX system not only should undergo special training but should be investigated regarding their personal background and trustworthiness. Finally, it may be advisable to enforce a policy according to which operators of critical systems can access privileged functions only with at least two operators present (e.g., through multifactor authentication

---
14. Access to the superuser account may be disabled by default, and administrative access is granted only temporarily to users through the sudo(1) facility.

technologies). There are a number of technical ways to limit access for the root user. Let us look at a few.

Configuring Secure Terminals

Most UNIX systems allow us to restrict root logins to special terminals, typically the system console. This approach is effective, especially if the console or allowed terminals are under strict physical access control. The obvious downside of this approach is that remote access to the system can be limited: Using this approach, access through any Transmission Control Protocol(TCP)/Internet Protocol (IP)-based connection cannot be configured, thus requiring a direct connection such as a directly attached terminal or a modem.

Configuration is different for the various UNIX systems. Fig. 11.10 compares Solaris and Debian.

Gaining Root Privileges With Su

The su(1) utility allows the identity of an interactive session to be changed. This is an effective mediation of the issues that come with restricting root access to secure terminals: Although only normal users can obtain access to the machine through the network (ideally by limiting the access protocols to those that protect the privacy of the communication, such as SSH), they can change their interactive session to a superuser session.

On Solaris simply edit the file /etc/default/login:

```
# Copyright 2004 Sun Microsystems, Inc. All rights reserved.
# Use is subject to license terms.
# If CONSOLE is set, root can only login on that device.
# Comment this line out to allow remote login by root.
CONSOLE=/dev/console
# PASSREQ determines if login requires a password.
#
PASSREQ=YES
# SUPATH sets the initial shell PATH variable for root
#
SUPATH=/usr/sbin:/usr/bin
# SYSLOG determines whether the syslog(3) LOG_AUTH facility should be used
# to log all root logins at level LOG_NOTICE and multiple failed login
# attempts at LOG_CRIT.
#
SYSLOG=YES
# The SYSLOG_FAILED_LOGINS variable is used to determine how many failed
# login attempts will be allowed by the system before a failed login
# message is logged, using the syslog(3) LOG_NOTICE facility. For
example,
# if the variable is set to 0, login will log -all- failed login attempts.
#
SYSLOG_FAILED_LOGINS=5
```

On Debian:

```
# The PAM configuration file for the Shadow 'login' service
#
# Disallows root logins except on tty's listed in /etc/securetty
# (Replaces the 'CONSOLE' setting from login.defs)
auth    requisite pam_securetty.so
# Disallows other than root logins when /etc/nologin exists
# (Replaces the 'NOLOGINS_FILE' option from login.defs)
auth    requisite pam_nologin.so
# Standard Un*x authentication.
@include common-auth
# This allows certain extra groups to be granted to a user
# based on things like time of day, tty, service, and user.
# Please edit /etc/security/group.conf to fit your needs
# (Replaces the 'CONSOLE_GROUPS' option in login.defs)
auth    optional pam_group.so
# Uncomment and edit /etc/security/time.conf if you need to set
# time restrainst on logins.
# (Replaces the 'PORTTIME_CHECKS_ENAB' option from login.defs
# as well as /etc/porttime)
account    requisite pam_time.so
# Uncomment and edit /etc/security/access.conf if you need to
# set access limits.
# (Replaces /etc/login.access file)
account required    pam_access.so
# Sets up user limits according to /etc/security/limits.conf
# (Replaces the use of /etc/limits in old login)
session    required pam_limits.so
# Prints the last login info upon succesful login
# (Replaces the 'LASTLOG_ENAB' option from login.defs)
session    optional pam_lastlog.so
# Standard Un*x account and session
@include common-account
@include common-session
@include common-password1
```

FIGURE 11.10   Restricting root access.

Using Groups Instead of Root

If users should be limited to executing certain commands with superuser privileges, it is possible and common to create special groups of users. For these groups, we can set the execution bit on programs (while disabling execution for all others) and the SetID bit for the owner, in this case the superuser. Therefore, only users of such a special group can execute the given utility with superuser privileges.

Using the sudo(1) Mechanism

The sudo(1) mechanism is by far more flexible and easier to manage than the approach for enabling privileged execution based on groups. Originally an open-source program, sudo(1) is available for most UNIX distributions. The detailed configuration is complex and the manual page is informative.

From a process perspective, sudo(1) allows the execution of specific commands (including command line shells) under a different UID or GID. Although the implementations for various OSs may slightly vary, sudo(1) basically ensures that the command to be executed is created in an appropriate execution environment. Depending on OS and compile-time options, sudo(1) may use the PAM framework, stay alive until the command finishes, or fork the child process. Configuration for sudo(1) is typically performed in the /etc/sudoers file, which can support a number of different options:

- The user may be allowed to execute certain commands as a different user (including root) without authentication.
- Execution of specific commands, all commands, and shells may be permitted.

- Detailed logging and mail notifications can be set.
- Environmental variables and other settings are taken into account.

Fig. 11.11 contains a sample sudoers file from an Ubuntu distribution. Note that this file must be edited with the visudo(8) command to ensure that the respective privileges are set correctly.

7. SECURING LOCAL AND NETWORK FILE SYSTEMS

For production systems, there is an effective way to prevent the modification of system-critical resources by unauthorized users or malicious software. Critical portions of the file systems (such as the locations of binary files, system libraries, and some configuration files) do not necessarily change often.

Directory Structure and Partitioning for Security

In fact, any system-wide binary code should probably be modified only by systems administrators. In these cases, it is effective to partition the file system properly.

Employing Read-Only Partitions

The reason for partitioning the file system properly (Fig. 11.12) is so that only frequently changing files (such as user data, log files, and the like) are hosted on readable file systems. All other storage then can be mounted on read-only partitions.

```
#
# This file MUST be edited with the 'visudo' command as root.
#
# Please consider adding local content in /etc/sudoers.d/ instead of
# directly modifying this file.
#
# See the man page for details on how to write a sudoers file.
#
Defaults     env_reset
Defaults     mail_badpass
Defaults     secure_path="/usr/local/sbin:/usr/local/bin:/usr/sbin:/usr/bin:/sbin:/bin"

# Host alias specification

# User alias specification

# Cmnd alias specification

# User privilege specification
root  ALL=(ALL:ALL) ALL

# Members of the admin group may gain root privileges
%admin ALL=(ALL) ALL

# Allow members of group sudo to execute any command
%sudo ALL=(ALL:ALL) ALL
```

FIGURE 11.11 Example of sudoers file.

The following scheme is a good start for partitioning with read-only partitions:

- Binaries and Libraries: /bin, /lib, /sbin, /usr - read-only
- Logs and frequently changing system data: /var,/usr/var - writable
- User home directories: /home, /export/home - writable
- Additional software packages: /opt, /usr/local - read-only
- System configuration: /etc, /usr/local/etc - writable
- Everything else: Root (/) - read-only

Obviously, this can only be a start and should be evaluated for each system and application. Updating operating system files, including those on the root file system, should be performed in single-user mode with all partitions mounted writable.

FIGURE 11.12 Secure partitioning.

```
$ find / \( -perm -04000 -o -perm -02000\) -type f -xdev -print
```

FIGURE 11.13 Results with Set User ID and Set Group ID set.

Finding Special Files

To prevent inadvertent or malicious access to critical data, it is vitally important to verify the correct ownership and permission set for all critical files in the file system.

Ownership and Access Permissions

The UNIX find(1) command is an effective way to locate files with certain characteristics. In the following, a number of sample command-line options for this utility are given to locate files.

Locate SetID Files

Because executables with the SetID bit set are often used to allow the execution of a program with superuser privileges, it is vitally important to monitor these files on a regular basis.

Another critical permission set is that of world-writable files; there should be no system-critical files in this list, and users should be aware of any files in their home directories that are world-writable (Fig. 11.13). Finally, files and directories that are not owned by current users can be found by the code shown in Fig. 11.14. For groups, just use-nogroup instead.

Locate Suspicious Files and Directories

Malicious software is sometime stored in nonstarted directories such as subdirectories named "..." that will not

```
$ find / -nouser
```

FIGURE 11.14 Finding files without users.

immediately be noticed. Administrators should pay special attention to such files and verify whether the content is part of a legitimate software package. In addition, appropriate end-point monitoring tools (including file integrity monitoring, signature-based antimalware tools, etc.) should be deployed to sensitive or critical systems.

Encrypting File Systems

Setting up encrypting file systems used to be a complex process and the resulting on-demand decryption during runtime was processor- and disk-intensive. As such, encrypting file systems usually were used only for fairly sensitive environments in which loss of mobile devices could result in significant damage to the system owner. However, significant improvements in processing capabilities, including high-performing multicore processors and the easy availability of solid-state disk drives, make the use of encrypting file systems achievable for many systems that do not require extreme throughput.

In general, it is advisable to perform a general risk assessment before deciding on an encryption strategy. It is important to remember that data-at-rest encryption provides significant protection against data exfiltration when the drive is in the adversary's physical possession.[15] The first decision point should be the likely exposure of the system to potential disk drive theft. For example, a system that is

---

15. During runtime, however, the system does access encrypted data and most often has unencrypted access to this information in its volatile system memory. Malware or adversaries that are capable of attacking a running system can grab the unencrypted data from memory and exfiltrate it. This was the technique used by the point of sales attacks against Target and other retailers in 2014 and 2015.

located within a private suite in a secure data center with limited physical access, security guards, and strong access protocols has a significantly lower likelihood of drive theft than does a laptop or other mobile device. The second major evaluation point should be the sensitivity of the data on the system: A simple test or demo system with limited data is less critical than is a mobile point of sales device or laptop used to access and manage health records. Finally, performance, scalability, and commercial constraints will need to be put into perspective as well: Whereas it may be possible to encrypt file systems with a high-performance enterprise resource planning database, it will likely be cost prohibitive.

For UNIX systems, encrypting file systems can typically be injected as kernel drivers into the system call stack. This enables a seamless environment with little or no interaction from regular users. Interaction with the kernel standard device mapper dm-crypt can be through cryptsetup(8), which can be used to create encrypted partitions on any block devices (such as hard drive partitions), but also logical volumes. Most Linux systems offer the possibility of setting up encrypted partitions during the initial installation process to ensure that the root file system can be encrypted. The installation program also uses cryptsetup(8) underneath to create and manage the encrypted file systems. Note that if you encrypt the root file system, the OS will boot from a separate partition to obtain the cryptsetup(8) runtime and then prompt for a decryption password during startup. In addition to the root file system, the user may want to encrypt the swap space, especially when expecting to pause (or "sleep") a mobile device.

Other OSs such as MacOS have built-in support for encrypted file systems as well. For MacOS, enabling FileVault 2 will automatically encrypt the root file systems with a strong symmetric key. This symmetric key is then stored encrypted in the boot partition, and users that have been configured with permission to boot the system can decrypt the disk key with their user password.

8. NETWORK CONFIGURATION

Because many UNIX systems are used as network servers, most users will never log into these systems interactively. Consequently, the most significant threat sources for UNIX-based systems are initially defective or badly configured network services. However, such initial attacks are often used only to get initial interactive access to the system. Once an attacker can access a command line shell, other layers of security must be in place to prevent an elevation of privileges (superuser access).

Basic Network Setup

UNIX user space processes can access networks by calling a variety of functions from the system libraries: namely the socket() system call and related functions. Whereas other

network protocols such as DECNet or IPX may still be supported, the TCP/IP family of protocols has by far most important role in today's networks. As such, we will focus solely on these protocols. A number of files are relevant for configuring access to networks:

- /etc/hostname (and sometimes also /etc/nodename) sets the name under which the system identifies itself. This name is also often used to determine its own IP address based on hostname resolution.
- /etc/protocols defines the available list of protocols such as IP, TCP, Internet Control Message Protocol, and User Datagram Protocol (UDP).
- /etc/hosts and /etc/networks files define what IP hosts and networks are locally known to the system. They typically include the local host definition (which is always 127.0.0.1 for IPv4 networks) and the loopback network (defined to be 127.0.0.0/24), respectively.
- /etc/nsswitch.conf is available on many UNIX systems and allows fine-grained setting of name resolution for a number of network and other resources, including the UIDs and GIDs. Typical settings include purely local resolution (i.e., through the files in the /etc directory), resolution through NIS, host resolution through DNS, user and group resolution through LDAP, etc.
- /etc/resolv.conf is the main configuration file for the DNS resolver libraries used in most UNIX systems. It points to the IP addresses of the default DNS name servers, and may include the local domain name and any other search domains.
- /etc/services (and/or/etc/protocols) contains a list of well-known services and the port numbers and protocol types to which they are bound. Some system commands (such as, e.g., Netstat) use this database to resolve ports and protocols into user-friendly names.

Depending on the UNIX flavor and the version, there are many other network configuration files that apply to the base OS. In addition, many other services that are commonly used on UNIX systems such as HTTP servers, application servers, databases, etc., have their own configuration files that will need to be configured and monitored in deployed systems.

Detecting and Disabling Standard UNIX Services

To protect systems against outside attacks and remove the overall attack surface, it is highly recommended to disable any service not needed to provide intended functionality. To do this, a simple process can be followed that will likely turn off most system services that are not needed:

1. Examine the startup scripts for your system. Startup procedures have been changing significantly for UNIX

systems over time. Early systems used the /etc/inittab to determine runlevels and startup scripts. UNIX System V introduced the /etc/init.d scripts and the symbolic links from the /etc/rc*.d/directories. Most current UNIX systems either still use this technology or implement an interface to start and stop services (such as Solaris). Debian-based distributions have a System V backward compatibility facility. BSD-based systems typically use an and/etc/rc.d-based service management interface. Administrators should determine their startup system and disable any services and feature not required for the function of that system. Ideally, facilities and services not needed should be uninstalled to minimize the potential attack surface for external attacks as well as privilege escalation attacks by running potentially harmful binaries.

2. In addition, administrators can examine processes that are currently running on a given system [e.g., through running the ps(1) command]. Processes that cannot be traced to a particular software package or functionality should be killed and their file images ideally uninstalled or deleted.

3. The netstat(1) command can be used to display currently open network sockets, specifically for TCP and UDP connections. By default, netstat(1) will use the /etc/services and /etc/protocols databases to map numeric values to well-known services. Administrators should verify only those ports are open that are expected to be used by the software installed on the system. In addition, the lsof(1) command with the −i parameter (where implemented) provides a mapping between listen ports or established connections and the associated processes (Fig. 11.15).

Host-Based Firewall

One of the best ways to limit the attack surface for external attackers is to close down all network sockets that are not being actively used by network clients. This is true for systems attached directly to the Internet as well as systems on private networks. The IP stacks of most UNIX systems can be configured to accept only specific protocols (such as TCP) and connections on specific ports (such as port 80). Fig. 11.16 shows how to limit ssh(1) access to systems on a specific IP subnet. Depending on the network stack, this can be achieved with a setting in the System Preferences for MacOS, or the iptables(1) command for Linux systems.

Restricting Remote Administrative Access

If possible, interactive access to UNIX-based systems should be limited to dedicated administrative terminals. This may be achieved by limiting root access to directly attached consoles and terminals or by creating dedicated private networks for the express purpose of allowing remote access through ssh(1), SNMP, or Web administration utilities.

Consoles and Terminals on Restricted Networks

As described previously, root access to a terminal can be limited to specific devices such as terminals or consoles. If the terminals or consoles are provided through TCP/IP-capable terminal concentrators or keyboard−video−mouse switches, interactive network access can be achieved by connecting these console devices through restricted networks to dedicated administrative workstations.

Dedicated Administrative Networks

Similarly, interactive access can be restricted to a small number of workstation and access points through the following technologies:

- Dedicated physical interface or virtual local area network (VLAN) segmentation: If any interactive or

```
# lsof -i
COMMAND       PID      USER    FD    TYPE  DEVICE  SIZE/OFF  NODE  NAME
cupsd         473      root    7u    IPv4  8852      0t0     TCP   localhost:ipp (LISTEN)
avahi-dae     478      avahi   13u   IPv4  8822      0t0     UDP   *:mdns
avahi-dae     478      avahi   14u   IPv6  8823      0t0     UDP   *:mdns
avahi-dae     478      avahi   15u   IPv6  8824      0t0     UDP   *:47625
avahi-dae     478      avahi   16u   IPv6  8825      0t0     UDP   *:34146
cups-brow     707      root    8u    IPv4  9146      0t0     UDP   *:ipp
dnsmasq       1119     nobody  4u    IPv4  10485     0t0     UDP   pc-ubuntu:domain
dnsmasq       1119     nobody  5u    IPv4  10486     0t0     TCP   pc-ubuntu:domain (LISTEN)
sshd          10449    root    3u    IPv4  26816     0t0     TCP   *:ssh (LISTEN)
sshd          10449    root    4u    IPv6  26818     0t0     TCP   *:ssh (LISTEN)
dhclient      10515    root    6u    IPv4  27107     0t0     UDP   *:bootpc
dhclient      10515    root    20u   IPv4  27091     0t0     UDP   *:5443
dhclient      10515    root    21u   IPv6  27092     0t0     UDP   *:18494
sshd          10768    root    3u    IPv4  27787     0t0     TCP   10.0.248.100:ssh->10.0.248.1:65332 (ESTABLISHED)
sshd          10804    gbeuchelt 3u  IPv4  27787     0t0     TCP   10.0.248.100:ssh->10.0.248.1:65332 (ESTABLISHED)
```

FIGURE 11.15 Output of lsof −I to associate processes with established or listening network connections.

```
$ iptables -A INPUT -i eth0 -p tcp -s
192.168.1.0/24 --dport 22 -m state --state
NEW,ESTABLISHED -j ACCEPT
$ iptables -A OUTPUT -o eth0 -p tcp --sport 22 -m
state --state ESTABLISHED -j ACCEPT
```

FIGURE 11.16 Configuration for iptables(1) for allowing ssh(1) connections from Internet Protocol address range 192.168.1.1—192.168.1.254.

administrative access is limited to separate networks, preferably disconnected from operational networks, the potential attack surface is significantly reduced.
- Logical interface: If no physical or VLAN infrastructure is available, UNIX networking stack typically allow the assignment of additional IP addresses to a single physical networking interface. Although it is more susceptible to lower-level attacks, this approach may be sufficient for the effective separation of networks.
- Routing and firewall table design: As a fairly high-level approach, administrators may limit access to specific services from preconfigured IP addresses or networks through careful design of the host-based firewall and the routing tables of the IP stack.
- Yale University has an old but useful UNIX networking checklist at http://security.yale.edu/network/unix.html that describes a number of general security settings for UNIX systems in general, and Solaris specifically. A similar, older checklist is available from Carnegie Mellon University's Software Engineering Institute Computer Emergency Readiness Team (CERT) at https://www.cert.org/tech_tips/unix_configuration_guidelines.html.
- Special topics in system administration that also address security issues such as auditing, configuration management, and recovery can be found on the Usenix website at https://www.usenix.org/lisa/books.

- Apple provides a detailed document on locking down MacOS X 10.6 Server: http://images.apple.com/support/security/guides/docs/SnowLeopard_Server_Security_Config_v10.6.pdf.
- The US Federal Government operates US-CERT at https://www.us-cert.gov, targeted at technical and nontechnical users in both the government and the private sector. In addition to general information, US-CERT provides information from the National Vulnerability Database, security bulletins, and current threat information.

Finally, let us briefly look at how to improve the security of Linux and UNIX systems. The following part of the chapter describes how to modify Linux and UNIX systems and fix their potential security weaknesses.

9. IMPROVING THE SECURITY OF LINUX AND UNIX SYSTEMS

A security checklist should be structured to follow the life cycle of Linux and UNIX systems, from planning and installation to recovery and maintenance. The checklist is best applied to a system before it is connected to the network for the first time. In addition, the checklist can be reapplied on a regular basis, to audit conformance (see checklist: "An Agenda for Action for Linux and UNIX Security Activities").

An Agenda for Action for Linux and UNIX Security Activities

No two organizations are the same, so in applying the checklist, consideration should be given to the appropriateness of each action to your particular situation. Rather than enforcing a single configuration, the following checklist will identify the specific choices and possible security controls that should be considered at each stage, which includes the following key activities (check all tasks completed):

Determine appropriate security:
_____**1.** computer role
_____**2.** assess security needs of each kind of data handled
_____**3.** trust relationships
_____**4.** uptime requirements and impact if these are not met
_____**5.** minimal software packages required for role
_____**6.** minimal net access required for role
Installation:
_____**7.** install from trusted media

_____**8.** install while not connected to the Internet
_____**9.** use separate partitions
_____**10.** install minimal software
Apply all patches and updates:
_____**11.** initially apply patches while offline
_____**12.** verify integrity of all patches and updates
_____**13.** subscribe to mailing lists to keep up to date
Minimize:
_____**14.** network services
_____**15.** disable all unnecessary startup scripts
_____**16.** SetUID/SetGID programs
_____**17.** other
Secure base OS:
_____**18.** physical, console, and boot security
_____**19.** user logons
_____**20.** authentication

Continued

An Agenda for Action for Linux and UNIX Security Activities—cont'd

_____**21.** access control
_____**22.** other: include vendor configuration settings and in-
       dustry best practices such as CIS Benchmarks
Secure major services:
_____**23.** confinement
_____**24.** tcp_wrappers
_____**25.** other general advice for services
_____**26.** SSH
_____**27.** printing
_____**28.** RPC/portmapper
_____**29.** file services NFS/AFS/Samba
_____**30.** the X Window system
_____**31.** DNS service
_____**32.** WWW service
_____**33.** Squid proxy
_____**34.** Concurrent Versions System
_____**35.** Web browsers
_____**36.** FTP service
Add monitoring capability:
_____**37.** syslog configuration
_____**40.** monitoring of logs
_____**41.** enable trusted audit subsystem if available

_____**42.** monitor running processes
_____**43.** host-based intrusion detection
_____**44.** network intrusion detection
Connect to the net:
_____**45.** first put in place a host firewall
_____**46.** position the computer behind a border firewall
_____**47.** network stack hardening/sysctls
_____**48.** connect to network for the first time
Test backup/rebuild strategy:
_____**49.** backup/rebuild strategy
_____**50.** test backup and restore
_____**51.** allow separate restore of software and data
_____**52.** repatch after restoring
_____**53.** process for intrusion response
Maintain:
_____**54.** mailing lists
_____**55.** software inventory
_____**56.** rapid patching
_____**57.** secure administrative access
_____**58.** log book for all sysadmin work
_____**59.** configuration change control
_____**60.** regular audit

---

10. ADDITIONAL RESOURCES

There is a large number of useful tools to assist administrators in managing UNIX systems. This also includes verifying their security.

Useful Tools

The following discussion of useful tools should not be seen as exhaustive, but much more of a simple starting point.

Webmin

Webmin is a useful general-purpose graphical system management interface that is available for a large number of UNIX systems. It is implemented as a Web application running on port 10,000 by default. Webmin allows the management of basic UNIX functionality such as user and group management, network and printer configuration, file system management, and much more. It also comes with modules for managing commonly used services such as OpenLDAP directory server, the BIND DNS server, a number of different mail transfer agents, databases, etc.

Webmin is particularly useful for casually maintained systems that do not require tight configuration management and may expose a Web application interface. It is not recommended to use Webmin on mission critical systems or in environments where systems are exposed to unknown external users (such as on the Internet or on large private networks). Even for systems where Webmin is an acceptable risk, it is recommended to ensure that the Web interface is protected by transport-level security (HTTP with SSL) and preferably restricted to dedicated administration networks or stations.

Nmap

For testing the open ports on a given host or subnet, Nmap is an excellent tool. It allows a given IP address or IP address range to be scanned and to test what TCP and UDP ports are accessible. It is flexible and can easily be extended, but it comes with a number of modules that allow the OSs of an IP responder to be determined based on the fingerprint of the TCP/IP stack responses.

Local Configuration System

Local Configuration System (LCFG) is an effective configuration management system for complex UNIX deployments. It compiles machine-specific and default configurations for all aspects of a given UNIX system into an XML file and distributes these files to the client machines. More information on LCFG can be found at http://www.lcfg.org/.

Further Information

Because this chapter can provide only an introduction to fully securing UNIX-based systems, the following list of resources is recommended for a more in-depth treatment of this topic. Users are also advised to consult vendor-specific information about secure configuration of their products.

By far the most comprehensive guidance on security configuration for UNIX systems is available through the US DISA. DISA and the National Institutes for Standards and Technology (NIST) create, publish, and update STIGs for a number of OSs at http://iase.disa.mil/stigs/os/. Beyond the general STIG for UNIX security, there are vendor-specific STIGs for Red Hat Linux, Solaris, HP-UX, and AIX.

Industry best practices for secure system configurations are published and frequently updated by CIS at https://cisecurity.org/. The Security Benchmarks are freely available in the form of PDF documents that provide detailed recommended settings. Members of the CIS can also download the CIS-CAT tool, which is a Java-based scanner that uses SCAP files, created by the CIS. The SCAP files can also be leverage for other SCAP-compliant configuration scanners.

11. SUMMARY

This chapter covered communications interfaces between HP-UX, Solaris, Linux, and AIX servers and the communications infrastructure (firewalls, routers, etc.). The use of Oracle in configuring and managing HP-UX, Solaris, Linux, and AIX servers to support large databases and applications was also covered.

There was also a discussion of other UNIX systems such as Solaris, Linux, AIX, etc., as well as how to perform alternate information assurance officer duties for HP-UX, Solaris, Linux, and AIX midtier systems. This chapter also showed entry-level security professionals how to provide support for UNIX security error diagnosis, testing strategies, and resolution of problems normally found in SMC Ogden server HP-UX, AIX, Solaris, and Linux environments. In addition, the chapter showed security professionals how to provide implementation of CIS Benchmarks and DISA security requirements (STIG) and UNIX Security Readiness Reviews.

This chapter helped security professionals gain experience in installing and managing applications in UNIX/Sun/Linux/AIX environments. It also showed security professionals how to apply DISA STIG with regard to installing, configuring, and setting up UNIX/Linux environments under mandatory security requirements.

The chapter also showed security professionals how to work with full life-cycle information technology projects, as well as how to obtain proficiency in the environments of J2EE, EJB, Sun Solaris, IBM WebSphere, Oracle, DB/2, Hibernate, JMS/MQ Series, Web Service, SOAP, and XML. It also helped UNIX/Solaris administrators on a large scale with regard to multiuser enterprise systems.

With regard to certification exams, this chapter helped students gain general experience (including operations experience) on large-scale computer systems or multiserver local area networks; broad knowledge and experience with system technologies (including networking concepts, hardware, and software); and the capability of determining system and network and application performance capabilities. It also helped students gain specialized experience in administrating UNIX-based systems and Oracle configuration knowledge, with security administration skills.

Finally, let us move on to the real interactive part of this chapter: review questions/exercises, hands-on projects, case projects, and an optional team case project. The answers and/or solutions by chapter can be found in Appendix K.

CHAPTER REVIEW QUESTIONS/ EXERCISES

True/False

1. True or False? UNIX was originally created as a single-user system.
2. True or False? UNIX security has a long tradition, and although many concepts of the earliest UNIX systems still apply, a large number of changes have fundamentally altered the way the operating system implements these security principles.
3. True or False? Achieving a high level of system security for UNIX system is a complex process that involves technical, operational, and managerial aspects of system operation.
4. True or False? For any interactive session, Linux systems require the user to log into the system.
5. True or False? The superuser has almost unlimited power on a UNIX system, which can be a significant problem.

Multiple Choice

1. When a user is granted access to resources on a computing system, it is of vital importance to establish and verify the identity of the requesting entity. This process is commonly referred to as:
   A. Authorization
   B. Availability
   C. Integrity
   D. Authentication
   E. Confidentiality
2. What allows for the loading of additional drivers for file systems?
   A. File access
   B. Identity-based access control
   C. File systems in user space
   D. Access control list
   E. Metadata

3. The login process is a system daemon that is responsible for coordinating the authentication and process setup for interactive users. To do this, the login process does the following, except which one?
   A. Draw or display the login screen
   B. Collect the credential
   C. Present the user credential to only one of the configured user databases (typically these can be files, NIS, Kerberos servers, or LDAP directories) for authentication
   D. Create a process with the user's default command-line shell, with the home directory as the working directory
   E. Execute system-wide, user, and shell-specific startup scripts
4. What was introduced to simplify the administration of small groups of computers?
   A. Systemauth PAM
   B. NIS
   C. Noninteractive access
   D. Trusted hosts
   E. Trusted networks
5. The most sensible alternative to traditional interactive session protocols such as Telnet is the:
   A. Open-source package OpenSSH
   B. SSH daemon
   C. Secure shell (SSH) system
   D. SSH protocol
   E. SSH-enabled file transfer program

EXERCISE

Problem

On a Tuesday morning, a company support team was alerted by a customer who was trying to download a drive update. The customer reported that the FTP server was not responding to connection attempts. Upon failing to login to the FTP server remotely via the SSH, the support team member walked into a server room only to discover that the machine crashed and was not able to boot. The reason was simple: No OS was found. The company gathered the standard set of network servers (all running some version of UNIX or Linux): Web, email, DNS servers, and a dedicated FTP server, used to distribute hardware drivers for the company inventory. In this case project, how would the company go about implementing an incident response plan?

Hands-On Projects

Project

Despite the risks of viruses and malicious attacks, most Linux Web servers are inadequately protected against intrusion. How would a company go about protecting their Linux Web servers against intrusion?

Case Projects

Problem

Rlogin is a software utility for UNIX-like computer OSs that allows users to login on another host via a network, communicating via TCP port 513. rlogin is most commonly deployed on corporate or academic networks, where user account information is shared among all of the UNIX machines on the network (often using NIS). However, rlogin has serious security problems. Please list rlogin's possible security problems.

Optional Team Case Project

Problem

Brute force attacks against remote services such as SSH, FTP, and Telnet are still the most common form of attack compromising servers facing the Internet. So, how would security administrators go about thwarting these types of attack?

Chapter 12

Eliminating the Security Weakness of Linux and UNIX Operating Systems

Mario Santana

Terremark Worldwide, Inc., Miami, FL, United States

1. INTRODUCTION TO LINUX AND UNIX

A simple Google search for define:unix yields many definitions. This definition comes from Microsoft: "A powerful multitasking operating system developed in 1969 for use in a minicomputer environment; still a widely used network operating system."[1]

What Is UNIX?

UNIX is many things. Officially, it is a brand and an operating system specification. In common usage, the word *UNIX* is often used to refer to one or more of many operating systems that derive from or are similar to the operating system designed and implemented about 41 years ago at AT&T Bell Laboratories. Throughout this chapter, we will use the term *UNIX* to include official UNIX-branded operating systems as well as UNIX-like operating systems such as Berkeley Software Distribution (BSD), Linux, and even Macintosh OS X.

History

Years after AT&T's original implementation, decades of aggressive market wars among many operating system vendors followed, each claiming that its operating system was UNIX. Ever-increasing incompatibilities among these different versions of UNIX were seen as a major deterrent to the marketing and sales of UNIX. As personal computers grew more powerful and flexible, running inexpensive

operating systems such as Microsoft Windows and IBM OS/2, they threatened UNIX as the server platform of choice. In response to these and other marketplace pressures, most major UNIX vendors eventually backed efforts to standardize the UNIX operating system.

UNIX Is a Brand

Since the early 1990s, the UNIX brand has been owned by The Open Group. This organization manages a set of specifications with which vendors must comply to use the UNIX brand in referring to their operating system products. In this way, The Open Group provides a guarantee to the marketplace that any system labeled as UNIX conforms to a strict set of standards.

UNIX Is a Specification

The Open Group's standard is called the Single UNIX Specification. It is created in collaboration with the Institute of Electrical and Electronics Engineers, the International Standards Organization, and others. The specification is developed, refined, and updated in an open, transparent process.

The Single UNIX Specification is composed of several components, covering core system interfaces such as system calls as well as commands, utilities, and a development environment based on the C programming language. Together, these describe a "functional superset of consensus-based specifications and historical practice."[2]

1. Microsoft, Glossary of Networking Terms for Visio IT Professionals, n.d. Retrieved September 22, 2008, from Microsoft TechNet: http://technet. microsoft.com/en-us/library/cc751329.aspx#XSLTsection142121120120.

2. The Open Group, The Single Unix Specification, n.d. Retrieved September 22, 2008, from What Is Unix: www.unix.org/what_is_unix/ single_unix_specification.html.

Lineage

The phrase *historical practice* in the description of the Single UNIX Specification refers to the many operating systems historically referring to themselves as UNIX. These include everything from AT&T's original releases to versions released by the University of California at Berkeley and major commercial offerings by the likes of IBM, Sun, Digital Equipment Corporation, Hewlett–Packard, the Santa Cruz Operation, Novell, and even Microsoft. But any list of UNIX operating systems would be incomplete if it did not mention Linux (Fig. 12.1).

What Is Linux?

Linux is a bit of an oddball in the UNIX operating system lineup. That is because, unlike the UNIX versions released by the major vendors, Linux did not reuse an existing source code. Instead, Linux was developed from scratch by a Finnish university student named Linus Torvalds.

Most Popular UNIX-like Operating System

Linux was written from the start to function similarly to existing UNIX products. Because Torvalds worked on Linux as a hobby, with no intention of making money, it was distributed for free. These factors and others contributed to making Linux the most popular UNIX operating system today.

Linux Is a Kernel

Strictly speaking, Torvalds' pet project has provided only one part of a fully functional UNIX operating system: the kernel. The other parts of the operating system, including the commands, utilities, development environment, desktop environment, and other aspects of a full UNIX operating system, are provided by other parties, including GNU, XOrg, and others.

Linux Is a Community

Perhaps the most fundamentally different thing about Linux is the process by which it is developed and improved. As the hobby project that it was, Linux was released by Torvalds on the Internet in the hope that someone out there might find it interesting. A few programmers saw Torvalds' hobby kernel and began working on it for fun, adding features and fleshing out functionality in a sort of unofficial partnership with Torvalds. At this point, everyone was just having fun, tinkering with interesting concepts. As more and more people joined the unofficial club, Torvalds' pet project ballooned into a worldwide phenomenon.

Today, Linux is developed and maintained by hundreds of thousands of contributors all over the world. In 1996,

Eric S. Raymond[3] famously described the distributed development methodology used by Linux as a bazaar: a wild, uproarious collection of people, each developing whatever feature they most wanted in an operating system, or improving whatever shortcoming most affected them. Yet somehow, this quick-moving community resulted in a development process that was stable as a whole and that produced an amazing amount of progress in a short time.

This is radically different from the way in which UNIX systems typically have been developed. If the Linux community is like a bazaar, other UNIX systems can be described as a cathedral: carefully preplanned and painstakingly assembled over a long time, according to specifications handed down by master architects from previous generations. However, some traditional UNIX vendors have started moving toward a more decentralized, bazaar-like development model similar in many ways to the Linux methodology.

Linux Is Distributions

The open-source movement in general is important to the success of Linux. Thanks to GNU, XOrg, and other open-source contributors, there was an almost complete UNIX already available when the Linux kernel was released. Linux only filled in the final missing component of a no-cost, open-source UNIX. Because most of the other parts of the operating system came from the GNU project, Linux is also known as GNU/Linux.

To actually install and run Linux, it is necessary to collect all of the other operating system components. Because of the interdependency of the operating system components (each component must be compatible with the others), it is important to gather the right versions of all of these components. In the early days of Linux, this was quite a challenge!

Soon, however, someone gathered a self-consistent set of components and made them all available from a central download location. The first such efforts include H. J. Lu's "boot/root" floppies and MCC Interim Linux. These folks did not necessarily develop any of these components; they only redistributed them in a more convenient package. Other people did the same, releasing new bundles called *distributions* whenever a major upgrade was available.

Some distributions touted the latest in hardware support; others specialized in mathematics or graphics or another type of computing; still others built a distribution that would provide the simplest or most attractive user experience. Over time, distributions have become more robust, offering important features such as package management, which allows a user to upgrade parts of the system safely without reinstalling everything else.

3. E. S. Raymond, The Cathedral and the Bazaar, September 11, 2000. Retrieved September 22, 2008, from Eric S. Raymond's homepage: www.catb.org/esr/writings/cathedral-bazaar/cathedral-bazaar/index.html.

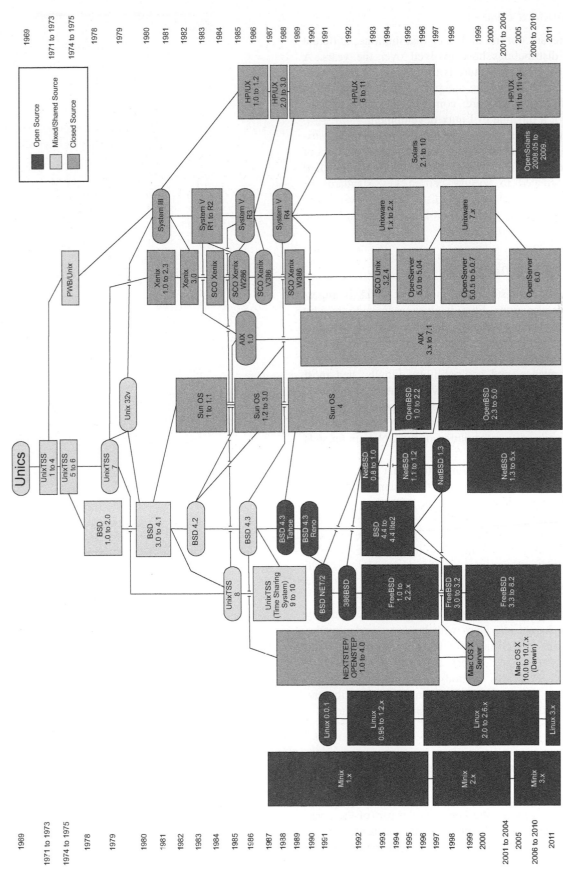

FIGURE 12.1 The simplified UNIX family tree presents a timeline of some of today's most successful UNIX variants. *BSD*, Berkeley Software Distribution.

Linux Standard Base

Today there are dozens of Linux distributions. Different flavors of distributions have evolved over the years. A primary distinguishing feature is the package management system. Some distributions are primarily volunteer community efforts; others are commercial offerings. See Fig. 12.2 for a timeline of Linux development.

The explosion in the number of different Linux distributions created a situation reminiscent of the UNIX wars of previous decades. To address this issue, the Linux Standard Base was created to specify certain key standards of behavior for conforming Linux distributions. Most major distributions comply with the Linux Standard Base specifications.

A Word of Warning

Understanding the history and lineage of UNIX is important for several reasons. First, it gives us insight into why some things work the way they do; often it is for historical reasons. Second, the wide variety of versions allows us to choose one that best fits our needs for security, functionality, performance, and compatibility. Finally, and most important, this understanding shows us that the rich history and many flavors of UNIX make it impossible to treat security as a recipe. Similarly, this chapter cannot possibly cover all details of every variation of the UNIX commands that we will introduce.

Instead of memorizing some steps that will harden a UNIX system, we must understand the underlying concepts and overarching architecture, and be willing to adapt our knowledge to the particular details of whatever version with which we are working. Keep this in mind as you read this chapter, especially as you apply the lessons in it.

System Architecture

The architecture of UNIX operating systems is relatively simple. The kernel interfaces with hardware and provides core functionality for the system. File systems provide permanent storage and access to many other kinds of functionality. Processes embody programs as their instructions are being executed. Permissions describe the actions that users may take on files and other resources.

Kernel

The operating system kernel manages many of the fundamental details with which an operating system needs to deal, including memory, disk storage, and low-level networking. In general, the kernel is the part of the operating system that talks directly to hardware; it presents an abstracted interface to the rest of the operating system components.

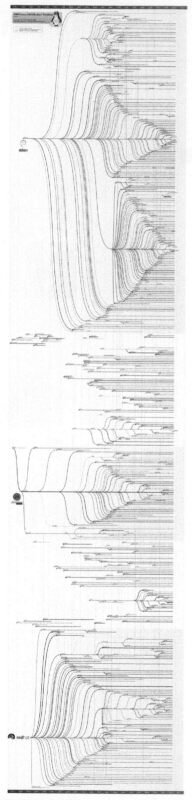

FIGURE 12.2 History of Linux distributions.

Because the kernel understands all of the different sorts of hardware with which the operating system deals, the rest of the operating system is freed from needing to understand all of those underlying details. The abstracted interface presented by the kernel allows other parts of the operating system to read and write files or communicate on the network without knowing or caring about what kinds of disks or network adapter are installed.

File System

A fundamental aspect of UNIX is its file system. UNIX pioneered the hierarchical model of directories that contain files and/or other directories to allow the organization of data into a tree structure. Multiple file systems could be accessed by connecting them to empty directories in the root file system. In essence, this is much like grafting one hierarchy onto an unused branch of another. There is no limit to the number of file systems that can be mounted in this way.

The file system hierarchy is also used to provide more than just access to and organization of local files. Network data shares can also be mounted, just like file systems on local disks. Special files such as device files, first in—first out or pipe files, and others give direct access to hardware or other system features.

Users and Groups

UNIX was designed to be a time-sharing system; as such, it has been a multiuser since its inception. Users are identified in UNIX by their usernames, but internally each is represented as a unique identifying integer called a *user ID*. Each user can also belong to one or more groups. Like users, groups are identified by their names, but they are represented internally as a unique integer called a *group ID*. Each file or directory in a UNIX file system is associated with a user and a group.

Permissions

UNIX has traditionally had a simple permissions architecture, based on the user and group associated with files in the file system. This scheme makes it possible to specify read, write, and/or execute permissions, along with a special permission setting whose effect is context-dependent. Furthermore, it is possible to set these permissions independently for the file's owner; the file's group, in which case the permission applies to all users, other than the owner, who are members of that group; and to all other users. The chmod command is used to set the permissions by adding up the values of all desired permission types, as shown in Table 12.1.

The UNIX permission architecture has historically been the target of criticism because of its simplicity and inflexibility. It is not possible, for example, to specify a different permission setting for more than one user or more than one group. These limitations have been addressed in more recent file system implementations using extended file attributes and access control lists (ACLs).

Processes

When a program is executed, it is represented in a UNIX system as a process. The kernel keeps track of many pieces of information about each process. This information is required for basic housekeeping and advanced tasks such as tracing and debugging. This information represents the user, group, and other data used to make security decisions about a process's access rights to files and other resources.

2. HARDENING LINUX AND UNIX

With a basic understanding of the fundamental concepts of the UNIX architecture, let us take a look at the practical work of securing a UNIX deployment. First, we will review considerations for securing UNIX machines from network-borne attacks. Then we will look at security from a host-based perspective. Finally, we will talk about systems management and how different ways of administering a UNIX system can affect security.

Network Hardening

Defending from network-borne attacks is arguably the most important aspect of UNIX security. UNIX machines are used heavily to provide network-based services running Web sites, domain name servers, firewalls, and many more.

TABLE 12.1 UNIX Permissions and Chmod

Chmod Use	Read	Write	Execute	Special
User	u + r or 0004	u + w or 0002	u + x or 0001	u + s or 4000
Group	u + r or 0040	u + w or 0020	u + x or 0010	u + s or 2000
Other	u + r or 0400	u + w or 0200	u + x or 0100	u + s or 1000

To provide these services, UNIX systems must be connected to hostile networks such as the Internet, where legitimate users can easily access and make use of these services.

Unfortunately, providing easy access to legitimate users makes the system readily accessible to bad actors who would subvert access controls and other security measures to steal sensitive information, change reference data, or simply make services unavailable to legitimate users. Attackers can probe systems for security weaknesses, identify and exploit vulnerabilities, and generally wreak digital havoc with relative impunity from anywhere around the globe.

Minimizing Attack Surface

Every way in which an attacker can interact with the system poses a security risk. Any system that makes available a large number of network services, especially complex services such as the custom Web applications of today, experiences a higher likelihood that inadequate permissions or a software bug or some other error will present attackers with an opportunity to compromise security. In contrast, even an insecure service cannot be compromised if it is not running.

A pillar of any security architecture is the concept of minimizing the attack surface. By reducing the number of enabled network services and the available functionality of those services that are enabled, a system presents a smaller set of functions that can be subverted by an attacker. Other ways to reduce attackable surface areas are to deny network access from unknown hosts when possible and to limit the privileges of running services, to minimize the damage they might be subverted to cause.

Eliminate Unnecessary Services

The first step in reducing an attack surface is to disable unnecessary services provided by a server. In UNIX, services are enabled in one of several ways. The "Internet daemon," or *inetd*, is a historically popular mechanism for managing network services. Like many UNIX programs, inetd is configured by editing a text file. In the case of inetd, this text file is /etc/inetd.conf; unnecessary services should be commented out of this file. Today a more modular replacement for inetd, called *xinetd*, is gaining in popularity. The configuration for xinetd is not contained in any single file but in many files located in the /etc/xinetd.d/ directory. Each file in this directory configures a single service, and a service may be disabled by removing the file or by making the appropriate changes to the file.

Many UNIX services are not managed by inetd or xinetd, however. Network services are often started by the system's initialization scripts during the boot sequence.

Derivatives of the BSD UNIX family historically used a simple initialization script located in /etc/rc. To control the services that are started during the boot sequence, it is necessary to edit this script.

Recent Unices (the plural of UNIX), even BSD derivatives, use something similar to the initialization scheme of the System V or higher family. In this scheme, a "run level" is chosen at boot time. The default run level is defined in /etc/inittab; typically, it is 3 or 5. The initialization scripts for each run level are located in /etc/rc X.d, where X represents the run-level number. The services that are started during the boot process are controlled by adding or removing scripts in the appropriate run-level directory. Some Unices provide tools to help manage these scripts, such as the rcconf command in Debian and derivatives or the chkconfig command in Red Hat Linux and derivatives. Other methods of managing services in UNIX include the Service Management Facility of Solaris 10 or higher. No matter how a network service is started or managed, however, it must necessarily listen for network connections to make itself available to users. This fact makes it possible to positively identify all running network services by looking for processes that are listening for network connections. Almost all versions of UNIX provide a command that makes this a trivial task. The netstat command can be used to list various kinds of information about the network environment of a UNIX host. Running this command with the appropriate flags (usually −lut) will produce a listing of all open network ports, including those that are listening for incoming connections (Fig. 12.3).

Finally, let us take a brief look at how services that are necessary can be configured securely. The following checklist (see checklist: An Agenda for Action When Securing Web Server Activities) presents several points to consider when securing a Web server.

Securely Configure Necessary Services

Every such listening port should correspond to a necessary service that is well understood and securely configured. Although we cannot cover every service that might be run on a UNIX system, we will explore a few of the more common services.

One of the most popular services to run on a UNIX system is a Web server. The Apache Web server is one of the most popular because it is free, powerful, and flexible, with many third-party add-ons to make it even more powerful and flexible. All of this power and flexibility can also make secure Apache configuration a nontrivial exercise.[4]

---

4. Apache.org, Security Tips. Retrieved August 22, 2012 from: http://httpd.apache.org/docs/2.4/misc/security_tips.html.

```
travis ~ # netstat -lut
Active Internet connections (only servers)
Proto Recv-Q Send-Q Local Address          Foreign Address        State
tcp        0      0 *:sunrpc               *:*                    LISTEN
tcp        0      0 *:41182                *:*                    LISTEN
tcp6       0      0 [::]:sunrpc            [::]:*                 LISTEN
tcp6       0      0 [::]:37434             [::]:*                 LISTEN
udp        0      0 *:sunrpc               *:*
udp        0      0 *:725                  *:*
udp        0      0 *:743                  *:*
udp        0      0 *:45308                *:*
udp6       0      0 [::]:sunrpc            [::]:*
udp6       0      0 [::]:725               [::]:*
udp6       0      0 [::]:58154             [::]:*
```

FIGURE 12.3   Output of netstat −lut.

An Agenda for Action When Securing Web Server Activities

The following items are possible actions that organizations should consider; some of the items may not apply to all organizations. Some important points to consider when securing Apache or any other Web server include (check all tasks completed):

_____1. Keep up to date with server software updates.

_____2. Mitigate denial-of-service attacks by maximizing performance and limiting the resources consumed.

_____3. Minimize permissions on Web content directories and files.

_____4. Minimize capabilities for dynamic content.

_____5. When dynamic content (Web applications) is necessary, carefully check the security of the dynamic content scripts.

_____6. Monitor server logs for malicious or anomalous activity.

Another popular service on UNIX servers is the Secure Shell service (SSH). This service enables secure remote access to the UNIX console. To configure it for maximum security, disable the use of passwords and require private key authentication. SSH also allows an administrator to strictly limit which commands can be executed by a given account, a feature that can minimize the risk of SSH accounts used for automated or centralized management functions.

UNIX systems are often used to run database software. These databases can contain sensitive information, in which case they must be carefully configured to secure those data; however, even when the data are of little value, the database server itself can be used as a stepping stone in a larger compromise. That is one reason why it is important to secure any UNIX system and the services it runs. There are many different kinds of database software, and each must be hardened according to its own unique capabilities. From the UNIX point of view, however, the security of any database can be greatly enhanced by using one of the firewall technologies described subsequently, to limit which remote hosts can access the database software.

Host-Based

Obviously, it is impossible to disable all of the services provided by a server. However, it is possible to limit the hosts that have access to a given service. Often it is possible to identify a well-defined list of hosts or subnets that should be granted access to a network service. There are several ways in which this restriction can be configured.

A classical way to configure these limitations is through the *tcpwrappers* interface. The tcpwrappers functionality is to limit the network hosts that are allowed to access services provided by the server. These controls are configured in two text files: /etc/hosts.allow and /etc/hosts.deny. This interface was originally designed to be used by inetd and xinetd on behalf of the services they manage. Today most service-providing software directly supports this functionality.

Another, more robust method of controlling network access is through firewall configurations. Most modern Unices include some form of firewall capability: IPFilter, used by many commercial Unices; IPFW, used by most of the BSD variants; and IPTables, used by Linux. In all cases, the best way to arrive at a secure configuration is to create a default rule to deny all traffic and then to create the fewest, most specific exceptions possible.

Modern firewall implementations are able to analyze every aspect of the network traffic they filter as well as aggregate traffic into logical connections and track the state of those connections. The ability to accept or deny connections based on more than just the originating network address and to end a conversation when certain conditions are met makes modern firewalls a much more powerful control for limiting attack surface than tcpwrappers.

Chroot and Other Jails

Eventually, some network hosts must be allowed to access a service if it is to be useful at all. In fact, it is often necessary to allow anyone on the Internet to access a service, such as a public website. Once a malicious user can access a service, there is a risk that the service will be subverted into executing unauthorized instructions on behalf of the attacker. The potential for damage is limited only by the permissions that the service process has to access resources and to make changes on the system. For this reason, an important security measure is to limit the power of a service to the bare minimum necessary to allow it to perform its duties.

A primary method to achieve this goal is to associate the service process with a user who has limited permissions. In many cases, it is possible to configure a user with few permissions on the system and to associate that user with a service process. In these cases, the service can perform only a limited amount of damage, even if it is subverted by attackers.

Unfortunately, this is not always effective or even possible. Often a service must access sensitive server resources to perform its work. Configuring a set of permissions to allow access to only the sensitive information required for a service to operate can be complex or impossible.

In answer to this challenge, UNIX has long supported the chroot and ulimit interfaces as ways to limit the access that a powerful process has on a system. The chroot interface limits a process's access on the file system. Regardless of actual permissions, a process run under a chroot jail can access only a certain part of the file system. Common practice is to run sensitive or powerful services in a chroot jail and make a copy of only those file system resources that the service needs to operate. This allows a service to run with a high level of system access, yet be unable to damage the contents of the file system outside the portion it is allocated.[5]

The ulimit interface is different in that it can configure limits on the amount of system resources a process or user may consume. A limited amount of disk space, memory, CPU use, and other resources can be set for a service process. This can curtail the possibility of a denial-of-service attack, because the service cannot exhaust all system resources even if it has been subverted by an attacker.[6]

Access Control

Reducing the attack surface area of a system limits the ways in which an attacker can interact and therefore subvert a server. Access control can be seen as another way to reduce the attack surface area. By requiring all users to prove their identity before making use of a service, access control

reduces the number of ways in which an anonymous attacker can interact with the system.

In general, access control involves three phases. The first phase is identification, in which a user asserts his identity. The second phase is authentication, in which the user proves his identity. The third phase is authorization, in which the server allows or disallows particular actions based on permissions assigned to the authenticated user.

Strong Authentication

It is therefore critical for a secure mechanism to be used to prove the user's identity. If this mechanism were to be subverted, an attacker would be able to impersonate a user to access resources or issue commands with whatever authorization level has been granted to that user. For decades, the primary form of authentication has been through the use of passwords. However, passwords have several weaknesses as a form of authentication, and present attackers with opportunities to impersonate legitimate users for illegitimate ends. Bruce Schneier argued for years that "passwords have outlived their usefulness as a serious security device."[7] More secure authentication mechanisms include two-factor authentication and Private Key Infrastructure (PKI) certificates.

Two-Factor Authentication

Two-factor authentication involves the presentation of two of the following types of information by users to prove their identity: something they know, something they have, or something they are. The first factor, something they know, is typified by a password or a personal identification number, some shared secret that only the legitimate user should know. The second factor, something they have, is usually fulfilled by a unique physical token (Fig. 12.4). RSA makes a popular line of such tokens; cell phones, matrix cards, and other alternatives are becoming more common. The third factor, something they are, usually refers to biometrics.

UNIX supports various ways to implement two-factor authentication into the system. Pluggable authentication modules (PAMs) allow a program to use arbitrary authentication mechanisms without needing to manage any of the details. PAMs are used by Solaris, Linux, and other Unices. BSD authentication serves a similar purpose and is used by several major BSD derivatives.

With PAM or BSD authentication, it is possible to configure any combination of authentication mechanisms, including simple passwords, biometrics, RSA tokens, Kerberos, and more. It is also possible to configure a different combination for different services. This kind of

5. W. Richard Stevens, Advanced Programming in the UNIX Environment, Addison—Wesley, Reading, 1992.
6. Ibid.

7. B. Schneier, Real-World Passwords, December 14, 2006. Retrieved October 9, 2008, from Schneier on Security: www.schneier.com/blog/archives/2006/12/realworld_passw.html.

FIGURE 12.4 Physical tokens used for two-factor authentication.

flexibility allows a UNIX security administrator to implement a strong authentication requirement as a prerequisite for access to sensitive services.

Private Key Infrastructure

Strong authentication can also be implemented using a PKI. Secure Socket Layer (SSL) is a simplified PKI designed for secure communications, familiar from its use in securing traffic on the Web. Through use of a similar foundation of technologies, it is possible to issue and manage certificates to authenticate users rather than websites. Additional technologies, such as a trusted platform module or a smart card, simplify the use of these certificates in support of two-factor authentication.

Dedicated Service Accounts

After strong authentication, limiting the complexity of the authorization phase is the most important part of access control. User accounts should not be authorized to perform sensitive tasks. Services should be associated with dedicated user accounts, which then should be authorized to perform only tasks required for providing that service.

Additional Controls

In addition to minimizing the attack surface area and implementing strong access controls, there are several important aspects of securing a UNIX network server.

Encrypted Communications

One of the ways an attacker can steal sensitive information is to eavesdrop on network traffic. Information is vulnerable as it flows across the network, unless it is encrypted.

Sensitive information, including passwords and intellectual property, are routinely transmitted over the network. Even information that is seemingly useless to an attacker can contain important clues to help a bad actor compromise security.

File Transfer Protocol (FTP), World Wide Web (WWW), and many other services that transmit information over the network support the SSL standard for encrypted communications. For server software that does not support SSL natively, wrappers such as *stunnel* provide transparent SSL functionality.

No discussion of UNIX network encryption can be complete without mentioning SSH. SSH is a replacement for Telnet and Remote Shell (RSH), providing remote command-line access to UNIX systems as well as other functionality. SSH encrypts all network communications using SSL, mitigating many of the risks of Telnet and RSH.

Log Analysis

In addition to encrypting network communications, it is important to keep a detailed activity log to provide an audit trail in case of anomalous behavior. At a minimum, the logs should capture system activity such as logon and logoff events as well as service program activity, such as FTP, WWW, or Structured Query Language (SQL) logs.

Since the 1980s, the *syslog* service has been used to manage log entries in UNIX. Over the years, the original implementation has been replaced by more feature-rich implementations such as *syslog-ng* and *rsyslog*. These systems can be configured to send log messages to local files as well as remote destinations, based on independently defined verbosity levels and message sources.

The syslog system can independently route messages based on the facility, or message source, and the level, or message importance. The facility can identify the message as pertaining to the kernel, the email system, user activity, an authentication event, or any of various other services. The level denotes the criticality of the message and can typically be one of *emergency, alert, critical, error, warning, notice, informational*, and *debug*. Under Linux, the *klog* process is responsible for handling log messages generated by the kernel; typically, klog is configured to route these messages through syslog, just like any other process.

Some services, such as the Apache Web server, have limited or no support for syslog. These services typically include the ability to log activity to a file independently. In these cases, simple scripts can redirect the contents of these files to syslog for further distribution and/or processing.

Relevant logs should be copied to a remote, secure server to ensure that they cannot be tampered with. In addition, file hashes should be used to identify any attempt to tamper with the logs. In this way, the audit trail provided by the log files can be depended on as a source of uncompromised information about the security status of the system.

Intrusion Detection System/Intrusion Prevention System

Intrusion detection systems (IDSs) and intrusion prevention systems (IPSs) have become commonplace security items on today's networks. UNIX has a rich heritage of such software, including Snort, Prelude, and OSSEC. Correctly deployed, an IDS can provide an early warning of probes and other precursors to attack.

Host Hardening

Unfortunately, not all attacks originate from the network. Malicious users often gain access to a system through legitimate means, bypassing network-based defenses. Various steps can be taken to harden a UNIX system from a host-based attack such as this.

Permissions

The most obvious step is to limit the permissions of user accounts on the UNIX host. Recall that every file and directory in a UNIX file system is associated with a single user and a single group. User accounts should each have permissions that allow full control of their respective home directories. Together with permissions to read and execute system programs, this allows most of the typical functionality required of a UNIX user account. Additional permissions that might be required include mail spool files and directories as well as crontab files for scheduling tasks.

Administrative Accounts

Setting permissions for administrative users is a more complicated question. These accounts must access powerful system-level commands and resources in the routine discharge of their administrative functions. For this reason, it is difficult to limit the tasks these users may perform. It is possible, however, to create specialized administrative user accounts, and then authorize these accounts to access a well-defined subset of administrative resources. Printer management, website administration, email management, database administration, storage management, backup administration, software upgrades, and other specific administrative functions common to UNIX systems lend themselves to this approach.

Groups

Often it is convenient to apply permissions to a set of users rather than a single user or all users. The UNIX group mechanism allows for a single user to belong to one or more groups and for file system permissions and other access controls to be applied to a group.

File System Attributes and Access Control Lists

It can become unfeasibly complex to implement and manage anything more than a simple permissions scheme using the classical UNIX file system permission capabilities. To overcome this issue, modern UNIX file systems support ACLs. Most UNIX file systems support ACLs using extended attributes that could be employed to store arbitrary information about any given file or directory. By recognizing authorization information in these extended attributes, the file system implements a comprehensive mechanism to specify arbitrarily complex permissions for any file system resource.

ACLs contain a list of *access control entries* (ACEs), which specify the permissions that a user or group has on the file system resource in question. On most Unices, the chacl command is used to view and set the ACEs of a given file or directory. The ACL support in modern UNIX file systems provides a fine-grained mechanism for managing complex permissions requirements. ACLs do not make the setting of minimum permissions a trivial matter, but complex scenarios can now be addressed effectively.

Intrusion Detection

Even after hardening a UNIX system with restrictive user permissions and ACLs, it is important to maintain logs of system activity. As with activity logs of network services, host-centric activity logs track security-relevant events that could show symptoms of compromise or evidence of attacks in the reconnaissance or planning stages.

Audit Trails

Again, as with network activity logs, UNIX has leaned heavily on syslog to collect, organize, distribute, and store log messages about system activity. Configuring syslog for system messages is the same as for network service messages. The kernel's messages, including those generated on behalf of the kernel by klogd under Linux, are especially relevant from a host-centric point of view.

An additional source of audit trail data about system activity is the history logs kept by a login shell such as *bash*. These logs record every command the user issued at the command line. The bash shell and others can be configured to keep these logs in a secure location and to attach timestamps to each log entry. This information is invaluable in identifying malicious activity, both as it is happening and after the fact.

File Changes

Besides tracking activity logs, monitoring file changes can be a valuable indicator of suspicious system activity. Attackers often modify system files to elevate privileges, capture passwords or other credentials, establish backdoors to ensure future access to the system, and support other illegitimate uses. Identifying these changes early can often foil an attack in progress before the attacker is able to cause significant damage or loss.

Programs such as Tripwire and Aide have been around for decades; their function is to monitor the file system for unauthorized changes and raise an alert when one is found. Historically, they functioned by scanning the file system and generating a unique *hash*, or fingerprint, of each file. On future runs, the tool would recalculate the hashes and identify changed files by the difference in the hash. Limitations of this approach include the need to scan the entire file system regularly, which can be a slow operation, as well as the need to secure the database of file hashes from tampering.

Today many UNIX systems support file change monitoring: Linux has dnotify and inotify; Mac OS X has FSEvents, and other Unices have File Alteration Monitor. All of these present an alternative method to identify file changes and review them for security implications.

Specialized Hardening

Many Unices have specialized hardening features that make it more difficult to exploit software vulnerabilities or to do so without leaving traces on the system and/or to show that the system is so hardened. Linux has been a popular platform for research in this area; even the National Security Agency (NSA) has released code to implement its strict security requirements under Linux. Here we outline two of the most popular Linux hardening packages. Other such packages exist for Linux and other Unices, some of which use innovative techniques such as virtualization to isolate sensitive data, but they are not covered here.

GRSec/PAX

The grsecurity package provides several major security enhancements for Linux. Perhaps the primary benefit is the flexible policies that define fine-grained permissions it can control. This role-based access control capability is especially powerful when coupled with grsecurity's ability to monitor system activity over time and generate a minimum set of privileges for all users. In addition, through the PAX subsystem, grsecurity manipulates program memory to make it difficult to exploit many kinds of security vulnerabilities. Other benefits include a robust auditing capability and other features that strengthen existing security features, such as chroot jails.

Security Enhanced Linux

Security Enhanced Linux is a package developed by the NSA. It adds mandatory access control, or MAC, and related concepts to Linux. MAC involves assigning

security attributes as well as system resources such as files and memory to users. When a user attempts to read, write, execute, or perform any other action on a system resource, the security attributes of the user and the resource are both used to determine whether the action is allowed, according to the security policies configured for the system (Fig. 12.5.[8])

Systems Management Security

Now that we have examined hardening a UNIX host from network-borne attacks and hardening it from attacks performed by an authorized user of the machine, we will look at a few systems management issues. These topics arguably fall outside the purview of security as such; however, by taking certain considerations into account, systems management can both improve and simplify the work of securing a UNIX system.

Account Management

User accounts can be thought of as keys to the "castle" of a system. As users require access to the system, they must be issued keys, or accounts, so they can use it. When a user no longer requires access to the system, her key should be taken away or at least disabled.

This sounds simple in theory, but account management in practice is anything but trivial. In all but the smallest environments, it is infeasible to manage user accounts without a centralized account directory where necessary changes can be made and propagated to every server on the network. Through PAM, BSD authentication, and other mechanisms, modern Unices support Lightweight Directory Access Protocol, SQL databases, Windows NT and Active Directory, Kerberos, and myriad other centralized account directory technologies.

Patching

Outdated software is perhaps the number one cause of easily preventable security incidents. Choosing a modern UNIX with a robust upgrade mechanism and history of timely updates, at least for security fixes, makes it easier to keep software up to date and secure from well-known exploits. One of the main differentiating factors between the different UNIX and Linux families is the software management and upgrade system. There are over 50 different package and upgrade management tools in use on the various UNIX flavors.

8. Copyright RedHat, Inc., Introduction to SELinux. Retrieved May 14, 2012 from: http://www.centos.org/docs/5/html/Deployment_Guide-en-US/ch-selinux.html.

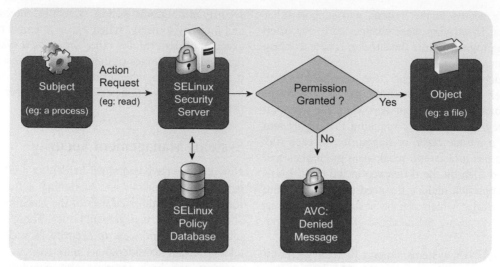

FIGURE 12.5 Security Enhanced Linux (SELinux) decision process. *AVC*, advanced video coding.

Backups

When all else fails, especially when attackers have successfully modified or deleted data in ways that are difficult or impossible to identify positively, good backups will save the day. When backups are robust, reliable, and accessible, they put a ceiling on the amount of damage an attacker can do. Unfortunately, good backups do not help if the greatest damage comes from disclosure of sensitive information; in fact, backups could exacerbate the problem if they are not taken and stored in a secure way.

3. PROACTIVE DEFENSE FOR LINUX AND UNIX

As security professionals, we devote ourselves to defending systems from attack. However, it is important to understand the common tools, mind sets, and motivations that drive attackers. This knowledge can prove invaluable in mounting an effective defense against attack. It is also important to prepare for the possibility of a successful attack and to consider organizational issues so that a secure environment can be developed.

Vulnerability Assessment

A vulnerability assessment looks for security weaknesses in a system. Assessments have become an established best practice, incorporated into many standards and regulations. They can be network-centric or host-based.

Network-Based Assessment

Network-centric vulnerability assessment looks for security weaknesses a system presents to the network. UNIX has a rich heritage of tools for performing network vulnerability assessments. Most of these tools are available on most UNIX flavors.

Nmap is a free, open-source tool for identifying hosts on a network and the services running on those hosts. It is a powerful tool for mapping out the true services being provided on a network. It is also easy to get started with nmap.

Nessus is another free network security tool, although its source code is not available. It is designed to check for and optionally verify the existence of known security vulnerabilities. It works by looking at various pieces of information about a host on the network, such as detailed version information about the operating system and any software providing services on the network. This information is compared to a database that lists vulnerabilities known to exist in certain software configurations. In many cases, Nessus is also capable of confirming a match in the vulnerability database by attempting an exploit; however, this is likely to crash the service or even the entire system. Many other tools are available for performing network vulnerability assessments. Insecure.Org, the folks behind the nmap tool, also maintain a great list of security tools.[9]

Host-Based Assessment

Several tools can examine the security settings of a system from a host-based perspective. These tools are designed to be run on the system that is being checked; no network connections are necessarily initiated. They check things such as file permissions and other insecure configuration settings on UNIX systems.

---

9. Insecure.Org, Top 100 Network Security Tools, 2008. Retrieved October 9, 2008, from: http://sectools.org.

One such tool, *lynis*, is available for various Linux distributions as well as some BSD variants. Another tool is the Linux Security Auditing Tool (*lsat*). Ironically, lsat supports more versions of UNIX than lynis does, including Solaris and AIX.

No discussion of host-based UNIX security would be complete without mentioning *Bastille*. Although lynis and lsat are pure auditing tools that report on the status of various security-sensitive host configuration settings, Bastille was designed to help remediate these issues. Recent versions have a reporting-only mode that makes Bastille work like a pure auditing tool.

Incident Response Preparation

Regardless of how hardened a UNIX system is, there is always a possibility that an attacker, whether a worm, a virus, or a sophisticated custom attack, will successfully compromise the security of the system. For this reason, it is important to think about how to respond to a wide variety of security incidents.

Predefined Roles and Contact List

A fundamental part of incident response preparation is to identify the roles that various personnel will have in the response scenario. The manual, hands-on gestalt of UNIX systems administration has historically forced UNIX systems administrators to be familiar with all aspects of the UNIX systems they manage. These should clearly be on the incident response team. Database, application, backup, and other administrators should be on the team as well, at least as secondary personnel that can be called on as necessary.

Simple Message for End Users

Incident response is a complicated process that must deal with conflicting requirements to bring the systems back online while ensuring that any damage caused by the attack, as well as whatever security flaws were exploited to gain initial access, are corrected. Often, end users without incident response training are the first to handle a system after a security incident has been identified. It is important that these users have clear, simple instructions in this case, to avoid causing additional damage or loss of evidence. In most situations, it is appropriate simply to unplug a UNIX system from the network as soon as a compromise of its security is confirmed. It should not be used, logged onto, logged off from, turned off, disconnected from electrical power, or otherwise tampered with in any way. This simple action has the best chance, in most cases, to preserve the status of the incident for further investigation while minimizing the damage that could ensue.

Blue Team/Red Team Exercises

Any incident response plan, no matter how well designed, must be practiced to be effective. Regularly exercising these plans and reviewing the results are important parts of incident response preparation. A common way to organize such exercises is to assign some personnel (the Red Team) to simulate a successful attack, while other personnel (the Blue Team) are assigned to respond to that attack according to the established incident response plan. These exercises, referred to as Red Team/Blue Team exercises, are invaluable for testing incident response plans. They are also useful for discovering security weaknesses and fostering a sense of esprit des corps among the personnel involved.

Organizational Considerations

Various organizational and personnel management issues can also affect the security of UNIX systems. UNIX is a complex operating system. Many different duties must be performed in the day-to-day administration of UNIX systems. Security suffers when a single individual is responsible for many of these duties; however, that is commonly the skill set of UNIX system administration personnel.

Separation of Duties

One way to counter the insecurity of this situation is to force different individuals to perform different duties. Often, simply identifying independent functions, such as backups and log monitoring, and assigning appropriate permissions to independent individuals is enough. Log management, application management, user management, system monitoring, and backup operations are just some of the roles that can be separated.

Forced Vacations

Especially when duties are appropriately separated, unannounced forced vacations are a powerful way to bring fresh perspectives to security tasks. It is also an effective deterrent to internal fraud or mismanagement of security responsibilities. A more robust set of requirements for organizational security comes from the Information Security Management Maturity Model, including its concepts of transparency, partitioning, separation, rotation, and supervision of responsibilities.[10]

4. SUMMARY

This chapter provides the technical security policies, requirements, and implementation details for eliminating the

---

10. ISECOM 2008, Security Operations Maturity Architecture. Retrieved October 9, 2008, from ISECOM: www.isecom.org/soma.

security weaknesses of Linux and UNIX operating systems. The chapter also contains general requirements for Linux and UNIX operating systems, as well as specific requirements. This chapter may also be used as a guide for enhancing the security configuration of any Linux or UNIX-like system. The chapter also contains all requirements, and check and fix procedures that are expected to be applicable to most Linux and UNIX-like operating systems.

Finally, let us move on to the real interactive part of this chapter: review questions/exercises, hands-on projects, case projects, and the optional team case project. The answers and/or solutions by chapter can be found in the Online Instructor's Solutions Manual.

CHAPTER REVIEW QUESTIONS/ EXERCISES

True/False

1. True or False? UNIX is a brand and an operating system specification.
2. True or False? The architecture of UNIX operating systems is relatively difficult.
3. True or False? Defending from network-borne attacks is arguably the least important aspect of UNIX security.
4. True or False? The first step in reducing an attack surface is to disable unnecessary services provided by a server.
5. True or False? Every listening port should not correspond to a necessary service that is well understood and securely configured.

Multiple Choice

1. What can be seen as another way to reduce the attack surface area?
   A. Dedicated service accounts
   B. PKI
   C. Two-factor authentication
   D. Strong authentication
   E. Access control
2. Information is vulnerable as it flows across the network, unless it is:
   A. Log analyzed
   B. Clear texted
   C. Basically authenticated
   D. Encrypted
   E. All of the above

3. The UNIX group mechanism allows for a single user to belong to one or more:
   A. Attributes
   B. ACLs
   C. Permissions
   D. Groups
   E. Focus groups
4. Even after hardening a UNIX system with restrictive user permissions and ACLs, it is important to maintain logs of:
   A. Audit trails
   B. System messages
   C. System activity
   D. Bash
   E. All of the above
5. An additional source of audit trail data about system activity is the history logs kept by a login shell such as:
   A. Log
   B. File
   C. Password
   D. Bash
   E. All of the above

EXERCISE

Problem

Is Linux a secure operating system?

Hands-on Projects

Project

Is it more secure to compile driver support directly into the kernel, instead of making it a module?

Case Projects

Problem

Why does logging in as root from a remote machine always fail?

Optional Team Case Project

Problem

How do you enable shadow passwords on your Red Hat 4.2 or higher, or 5.x or higher Linux box?

Chapter 13

Internet Security

Intel Corporation, Hillsboro, OR, United States

The Internet, with all its accompanying complications, is integral to our lives. The security problems besetting the Internet are legendary and have become daily annoyances—and worse—to many users. Given the Net's broad impact on our lives and the widespread security issues associated with it, it is worthwhile understanding what can be done to improve the immunity of our communications from attack.

The Internet can serve as a laboratory for studying network security issues; indeed, we can use it to study nearly every kind of security issue. We will pursue only a modest set of questions related to this theme. The goal of this chapter is to understand how cryptography can be used to address some of the security issues affecting communications protocols. To do so, it will be helpful to first understand the Internet architecture. After that we will survey the types of attacks that are possible against communications. With this background we will be able to understand how cryptography can be used to preserve the confidentiality and integrity of messages.

Our goal is modest: It is only to describe the network architecture and its cryptographic-based security mechanisms sufficiently to understand some of the major issues confronting security systems designers and to appreciate some of the major design decisions they have to make to address these issues.

1. INTERNET PROTOCOL ARCHITECTURE

The Internet was designed to create standardized communication between computers. Computers communicate by exchanging messages. The Internet supports message exchange through a mechanism called protocols. Protocols are very detailed and stereotyped rules explaining exactly how to exchange a particular set of messages. Each protocol is defined as a set of automata and a set of message formats. Each protocol specification defines one automaton for sending a message and another for receiving a message. The automata specify the timing of symbols that represent the messages; the automata implicitly define a grammar for the messages, indicating whether any particular message is meaningful or is interpreted by the receiver as gibberish. The protocol formats restrict the information that the protocol can express.

Security has little utility as an abstract, disembodied concept. What the word security should mean depends very much on the context in which it is applied. The architecture, design, and implementation of a system each determine the kind of vulnerabilities and opportunities that exist and which features are easy or hard to attack or defend.

It is fairly easy to understand why this is true. An attack on a system is an attempt to make the system act outside its specification. An attack is different from "normal" bugs that afflict computers and that occur through random interactions between the system's environment and undetected flaws in the system architecture, design, or implementation. An attack, on the other hand, is an explicit and systematic attempt by a party to search for flaws that make the computer act in a way its designers did not intend.

Computing systems consist of a large number of blocks or modules assembled together, each of which provides an intended set of functions. The system architecture hooks the modules together through interfaces, through which the various modules exchange information to activate the functions provided by each module in a coordinated way. These interfaces may be explicit, such as a formal grammar that the automata are supposed to conform, or they may be implicit, as when a parser accepts a larger grammar than is in the specification. An attacker exploits the architecture to compromise the computing system by interjecting inputs into these interfaces that do not conform to the intended specification of inputs into one of the automata. If the targeted module has not been carefully crafted, unexpected inputs can cause it to behave in unintended ways. This

Computer and Information Security Handbook. http://dx.doi.org/10.1016/B978-0-12-803843-7.00013-2
Copyright © 2013 Elsevier Inc. All rights reserved.

implies that the security of a system is determined by its decomposition into modules, which an adversary exploits by injecting messages into the interfaces the architecture exposes. Accordingly, no satisfying discussion of any system is feasible without an understanding of the system architecture. Our first goal, therefore, is to review the architecture of the Internet communication protocols in an effort to gain a deeper understanding of its vulnerabilities.

Communications Architecture Basics

Since communication is an extremely complex activity, it should come as no surprise that the system components providing communication decompose into modules. One standard way to describe each communication module is as a black box with a well-defined service interface. A minimal communications service interface requires four primitives:

- A send primitive, which an application using the communications module uses to send a message via the module to a peer application executing on another networked device. The send primitive specifies a message payload and a destination, as well as a format for how messages are encoded from this information. The communication module responding to the send transmits the message to the specified destination, reporting its requestor as the message source.
- A confirm primitive, to report that the module has sent a message to the designated destination in response to a send request or to report when the message transmission failed, along with any failure details that might be known. It is possible to combine the send and confirm primitives, but network architectures rarely take this approach at their lowest layer. The send primitive is normally defined to allow the application to pass a message to the communications module for transmission by transferring control of a buffer containing the message. The confirm primitive then releases the buffer back to the calling application when the message has indeed been sent. This scheme affects "a conservation of buffers" and enables the communications module and the application using it to operate in parallel, thus enhancing the overall communication performance.
- A listen primitive, which the receiving application uses to provide the communications module with buffers into which it should put messages arriving from the network. Each buffer the application posts must be large enough to receive a message of the maximum expected size. The receiving automata must be carefully designed to respond correctly to arriving messages that are too large for the receive buffer.
- A receive primitive, to deliver a received message from another party to the receiving application. This releases a posted buffer back to the application and usually generates a signal to notify the application of message arrival. The released buffer contains the received message and the (alleged) message source.

Sometimes the listen primitive is replaced with a release primitive. In this model, the receive buffer is owned by the receiving communications module instead of the application, and the application must recycle buffers containing received messages back to the communication module upon completion. In this case the buffer size selected by the receiving module determines the maximum message size. In a moment we will explain how network protocols work around this restriction.

It is customary to include a fifth service interface primitive for communications modules:

- A status primitive, to report diagnostic and performance information about the underlying communications. This might report statistics, the state of active associations with other network devices, and the like.

Communications is affected by providing a communications module black box on systems, connected by a signaling medium. The medium connecting the two devices constitutes the network communications path. The media can consist of a direct link between the devices or, more commonly, several intermediate relay systems between the two communicating endpoints. Each relay system is itself a communicating device with its own communications module, which receives and then forwards messages from the initiating system to the destination system.

Under this architecture, a message is transferred from an application on one networked system to an application on a second networked system as follows:

First, the application sourcing the message invokes the send primitive exported by its communications module. This causes the communications module to (attempt) to transmit the message to a destination provided by the application in the send primitive.

The communications module encodes the message onto the network's physical medium representing a link to another system. If the communications module implements a best-effort message service, it generates the confirm primitive as soon as the message has been encoded onto the medium. If the communication module implements a reliable message service, the communication delays generation of the confirm until it receives an acknowledgment from the message destination. If it has not received an acknowledgment from the receiver after some period of time, it generates a confirm indicating that the message delivery failed.

The encoded message traverses the network medium and is placed into a buffer by the receiving communications module of another system attached to the medium. This communications module examines the destination. The module then examines the destination specified by the message. If the module's local system is not the destination, the module reencodes the message onto the medium representing another link; otherwise the module uses the deliver primitive to pass the message to the receiving application.

Getting More Specific

This stereotyped description of networked communications is overly simplified. Actually, communications are torturously more difficult in real network modules. To overcome this complexity, communications modules are themselves partitioned further into layers, each providing a different networking function. The Internet decomposes communications into five layers of communications modules:

● The physical (PHY) layer
● The Message Authentication Code (MAC) layer
● The network layer
● The transport layer
● The sockets layer

These layers are augmented by a handful of cross-layer coordination modules. The Internet depends on the following cross-layer modules:

● Address Resolution Protocol (ARP)
● Dynamic Host Configuration Protocol (DHCP)
● Domain Naming Service (DNS)
● Internet Control Message Protocol (ICMP)
● Routing

An application using networking is also part of the overall system design, and the way it uses the network has to be taken into consideration to understand system security.

The PHY Layer

The PHY (pronounced "fie") layer is technically not part of the Internet architecture per se, but Ethernet jacks and cables, modems, Wi-Fi adapters, and the like represent the most visible aspect of networking, and no security treatment of the Internet can ignore the PHY layer entirely.

The PHY layer module is medium dependent, with a different design for each type of medium: Ethernet, phone lines, Wi-Fi, cellular phone, OC-768, and the like are based on different PHY layer designs. It is the job of the PHY layer to translate between digital bits as represented on a computing device and the analog signals crossing the specific physical medium used by the PHY. This translation is a physics exercise.

To send a message, the PHY layer module encodes each bit of each message from the sending device as a media-specific signal or wave form, representing the bit value 1 or 0. Once encoded, the signal propagates along the medium from the sender to the receiver. The PHY layer module at the

receiver decodes the medium-specific signal back into a bit. There are often special symbols representing such things as the frame start and frame end symbols, and training symbols to synchronize the receiver with the transmitter. These special symbols provide control only and are distinct from the symbols representing bits. Wave forms different from the defined symbols are undefined and discarded by the receiver.

It is possible for the encoding step at the transmitting PHY layer module to fail, for a signal to be lost or corrupted while it crosses the medium, and for the decoding step to fail at the receiving PHY layer module. It is the responsibility of higher layers to detect and recover from these potential failures.

The MAC Layer

Like the PHY layer, the MAC (pronounced mack) layer is not properly a part of the Internet architecture, but no satisfactory security discussion is possible without considering it. The MAC module is the "application" that uses and controls a particular PHY layer module. A MAC layer is always designed in tandem with a specific PHY (or vice versa), so a PHY–MAC pair together is often referred to as the data link layer.

MAC is an acronym for media access control. As its name suggests, the MAC layer module determines when to send and receive frames, which are messages encoded in a media-specific format. The job of the MAC is to pass frames over a link between the MAC layer modules on different systems.

Although not entirely accurate, it is useful to think of a MAC module as creating *links*, each of which is a communication channel between different MAC modules. It is further useful to distinguish physical links and virtual links. A *physical link* is a direct point-to-point channel between the MAC layers in two endpoint devices. A *virtual link* can be thought of as a shared medium to which more than two devices can connect at the same time. There are no physical endpoints per se; the medium acts as though it is multiplexing links between each pair of attached devices. Some media such as modern Ethernet are implemented as physical point-to-point links but act more like virtual links in that more than a single destination is reachable via the link. This is accomplished by MAC layer switching, which is also called bridging. Timing requirements for coordination among communicating MAC layer modules make it difficult to build worldwide networks based on MAC layer switching, however. Mobile devices such as smartphones, laptops, and notepads also make large-scale bridging difficult, since these devices can shift their attachment points to the network, thus invalidating the data structures used by switches to effect switching. Finally, some media such as Wi-Fi (IEEE 802.11) are shared or broadcast media. In a shared medium all devices can access the channel, and the MAC design must specify an access control policy that the MAC enforces; this behavior is what gives the MAC layer its name. Ethernet was originally a shared medium but evolved into its present switched point-to-point structure in order to simplify medium access control. The access control function of a MAC is always a complex security concern.

A MAC frame consists of a header and a data payload. The frame header typically specifies information such as the source and destination for the link endpoints. Devices attached to the medium via their MAC + PHY modules are identified by MAC addresses. Each MAC module has its own MAC address assigned by its manufacturer and is supposed to be a globally unique identifier. The destination address in a frame allows a particular MAC module to identify frames intended for it, and the source address allows the receiver to identify the purported frame source. The frame header also usually includes a preamble, which is a set of special PHY timing signals used to synchronize the interpretation of the PHY layer data signals representing the frame bits.

The payload portion of a frame is the data to be transferred across the network. The maximum payload size is always fixed by the medium type. It is becoming customary for most MACs to support a maximum payload size of 1500 bytes = 12,000 bits, but this is not universal. The maximum fixed size allows the MAC to make efficient use of the underlying physical medium. Since messages can be of an arbitrary length exceeding this fixed size, a higher-layer function is needed to partition messages into segments of the appropriate length.

As we have seen, it is possible for bit errors to creep into communications as signals representing bits traverse the PHY medium. MAC layers differ a great deal in how they respond to errors. Some PHY layers, such as the Ethernet PHY, experience exceedingly low error rates, and for this reason, the MAC layers for these PHYs make no attempt to more than detect errors and discard the mangled frames. Indeed, with these MACs it is cheaper for the Internet to resend message segments at a higher layer than at the MAC layer. These are called best-effort MACs. Others, such as the Wi-Fi MAC, experience high error rates due to the shared nature of the channel and natural interference among radio sources; experience has shown that these MACs can deliver better performance by retransmitting damaged or lost frames. It is customary for most MAC layers to append a checksum computed over the entire frame, called a frame check sequence (FCS). The FCS allows the receiver to detect bit errors accumulated due to random noise and other physical phenomena during transmission and due to decoding errors. Most MACs discard frames with FCS errors. Some MAC layers also perform error correction on the received bits to remove random bit errors rather than relying on retransmissions.

The Network Layer

The purpose of the network layer module is to represent messages in a media-independent manner and to forward them between various MAC layer modules representing different links. The media-independent message format is called an Internet Protocol, or IP, datagram. The network layer implements the IP layer and is the lowest layer of the Internet architecture per se.

As well as providing media independence, the network layer provides a vital forwarding function that works even for a worldwide network like the Internet. It is impractical to form a link directly between each communicating system on the planet. Indeed, the cabling costs alone are prohibitive—no one wants billions, or even dozens, of cables connecting their computer to other computers—and too many MAC + PHY interfaces can quickly exhaust the power budget for a single computing system. Hence, each machine is attached by a small number of links to other devices, and some of the machines with multiple links comprise a switching fabric. The computing systems constituting the switching fabric are called routers.

The forwarding function supported by the network layer module is the key component of a router and works as follows: When a MAC module receives a frame, it passes the frame payload to the network layer module. The payload consists of an IP datagram, which is the media-independent representation of the message. The receiving network layer module examines the datagram to see whether to deliver it locally or to pass it on toward the datagram's ultimate destination. To accomplish the latter, the network layer module consults a forwarding table to identify some neighbor router closer to the ultimate destination than itself. The forwarding table also identifies the MAC module to use to communicate with the selected neighbor and passes the datagram to that MAC layer module. The MAC module in turn retransmits the datagram as a frame encoded for its medium across its link to the neighbor. This process happens recursively until the datagram is delivered to its ultimate destination.

The network layer forwarding function is based on IP addresses, a concept that is critical to understanding the Internet architecture. An IP address is a media-independent name for one of the MAC layer modules within a computing system. Each IP address is structured to represent the "location" of the MAC module within the entire Internet. This notion of location is relative to the graph comprising routers and their interconnecting links, called the network topology, not to actual geography. Since this name represents a location, the forwarding table within each IP module can use the IP address of the ultimate destination as a sort of signpost pointing at the MAC module with the greatest likelihood of leading to the ultimate destination of a particular datagram.

An IP address is different from the corresponding MAC address already described. A MAC address is a permanent, globally unique identifier, identifying a particular interface on a particular computing device, whereas an IP address can be dynamic due to device mobility. An IP address cannot be assigned by the equipment manufacturer, since a computing device can change locations frequently. Hence, IP addresses are administered and blocks allocated to different organizations with an Internet presence. It is common, for instance, for an Internet service provider (ISP) to acquire a large block of IP addresses for use by its customers.

An IP datagram has a structure similar to that of a frame: It consists of an IP header, which is "extra" overhead used to control the way a datagram passes through the Internet, and a data payload, which contains the message being transferred. The IP header indicates the ultimate source and destinations, represented as IP addresses.

The IP header format limits the size of an IP datagram payload to 64 kilobytes ($2^{16} = 65,536$). It is common to limit datagram sizes to the underlying media size, although datagrams larger than this do occur. This means that normally each MAC layer frame can carry a single IP datagram as its data payload. IP version 4 (IPv4) or higher, still the dominant version deployed on the Internet today, allows fragmentation of larger datagrams to split large datagrams into chunks small enough to fit the limited frame size of the underlying MAC layer medium. IPv4 or higher reassembles any fragmented datagrams at the ultimate destination. IP version 6 (IPv6) or higher, which is becoming more widely deployed due to its widespread use in smartphone networks and Asia, does not support fragmentation and reassembly; this removes from IPv6 or higher one of the attack vectors enabled by IPv4 or higher.

Network layer forwarding of IP datagrams is a best effort and not reliable. Network layer modules along the path taken by any message can lose and reorder datagrams. It is common for the network layer in a router to recover from congestion—that is, when the router is overwhelmed by more receive frames than it can process—by discarding late-arriving frames until the router has caught up with its forwarding workload. The network layer can reorder datagrams when the Internet topology changes, because a new path between source and destination might be shorter or longer than an old path, so datagrams in flight before the change can arrive after frames sent following the change. The Internet architecture delegates recovery from these problems to high-layer modules.

Some applications, such as those utilizing voice and video, do not respond well to reordering because it imposes a severe performance penalty on the application. In order to better accommodate the needs of these types of message traffic, the Internet has begun to implement protocols such as multi protocol label switching, which mimics the switched circuit mechanisms of phone networks. That is, these protocols create flows through the Internet that suppress datagram reordering. Circuit switching uses network resources differently than best-effort forwarding, and network links in the core of the network usually require greater bandwidth for the two technologies to successfully coexist.

The Transport Layer

The transport layer is implemented by TCP and similar protocols. Not all transport protocols provide the same level of service as TCP, but a description of TCP will suffice to help us understand the issues addressed by the transport layer. The transport layer provides a multitude of functions.

First, the transport layer creates and manages instances of two-way channels between communication endpoints. These channels are called connections. Each connection represents a virtual endpoint between a pair of communication endpoints. A connection is named by a pair of IP addresses and port numbers. Two devices can support simultaneous connections using different port numbers for each connection. It is common to differentiate applications on the same host through the use of port numbers.

A second function of the transport layer is to support delivery of messages of arbitrary length. The 64 kilobytes limit of the underlying IP module is too small to carry really large messages, and the transport layer module at the message source chops messages into pieces called segments that are more easily digestible by lower-layer communications modules. The segment size is negotiated between the two transport endpoints during connection setup. The segment size is chosen by discovering the smallest maximum frame size supported by any MAC + PHY link on the path through the Internet used by the connection setup messages. Once this is known, the transmitter typically partitions a large message into segments no larger than this size, plus room for an IP header. The transport layer module passes each segment to the network layer module, where it becomes the payload for a single IP datagram. The destination network layer module extracts the payload from the IP datagram and passes it to the transport layer module, which interprets the information as a message segment. The destination transport reassembles this into the original message once all the necessary segments arrive.

Of course, as noted, MAC frames and IP datagrams can be lost in transit, so some segments can be lost. It is the responsibility of the transport layer module to detect this loss and retransmit the missing segments. This is accomplished by a sophisticated acknowledgment algorithm defined by the transport layer. The destination sends a special acknowledgment message, often piggybacked with a data segment being sent in the opposite direction, for each segment that arrives. Acknowledgments can be lost as well, and if the message source does not receive the acknowledgment within a time window, the source retransmits the unacknowledged segment. This process is repeated a number of times, and if the failure continues, the network layer tears down the connection because it cannot fulfill its reliability commitment.

One reason for message loss is congestion at routers, something blind retransmission of unacknowledged segments will only exacerbate. The network layer is also responsible for implementing congestion control algorithms as part of its transmit function. TCP, for instance, lowers its transmit rate whenever it fails to receive an acknowledgment message in time, and it slowly increases its rate of transmission until another acknowledgment is lost. This allows TCP to adapt to congestion in the network, helping to minimize frame loss.

It can happen that segments arrive at the destination out of order, since some IP datagrams for the same connection could traverse the Internet through different paths due to dynamic changes in the underlying network topology. The transport layer is responsible for delivering the segments in the order sent, so the receiver caches any segments that arrive out of order prior to delivery. The TCP reordering algorithm is closely tied to the acknowledgment and congestion control scheme so that the receiver never has to buffer too many out-of-order received segments and the sender not too many sent but unacknowledged segments.

Segment data arriving at the receiver can be corrupted due to undetected bit errors on the data link and copy errors within routers and the sending and receiving of computing systems. Accordingly, all transport layers use a checksum algorithm called a cyclic redundancy check (CRC) to detect such errors. The receiving transport layer module typically discards segments with errors detected by the CRC algorithm, and recovery occurs through retransmission by the sender when it fails to receive an acknowledgment from the receiver for a particular segment.

The Sockets Layer

The top layer of the Internet, the sockets layer, does not per se appear in the architecture at all. The sockets layer provides a set of interfaces, each of which represents a logical communications endpoint. An application can use the sockets layer to create, manage, and destroy connection instances using a socket as well as send and receive messages over the connection. The sockets layer has been designed to hide much of the complexity of the transport layer, thereby making TCP easier to use. The sockets layer has been highly optimized over the years to deliver as much performance as possible, but it does impose a performance penalty. Applications with very demanding performance requirements tend to utilize the transport layer directly instead of through the sockets layer module, but this comes with a very high cost in terms of software maintenance.

In most implementations of these communications modules, each message is copied twice, at the sender and the receiver. Most operating systems are organized into user space, which is used to run applications, and kernel space, where the operating system itself runs. The sockets layer occupies the boundary between user space and kernel space. The sockets layer's send function copies a message from memory controlled by the sending application into a buffer controlled by the kernel for transmission. This copy prevents the application from changing a message it has posted to send, but it also permits the application and kernel to continue their activities in parallel, thus better utilizing the device's computing resources. The sockets layer invokes the transport layer, which partitions the message buffer into segments and passes the address of each segment to the network layer. The network layer adds its headers to form datagrams from the segments and invokes the right MAC layer module to transmit each datagram to its next hop. A second copy occurs at the boundary between the network layer and the MAC layer, since the data link must be able to asynchronously match transmit requests from the network layer to available transmit slots on the medium provided by its PHY. This process is reversed at the receiver, with a copy of datagrams across the MAC-network layer boundary and of messages between the socket layer and application.

Address Resolution Protocol

The network layer uses ARP to translate IP addresses into MAC addresses, which it needs to give to the MAC layer in order to deliver frames to the appropriate destination.

The ARP module asks the question, "Who is using IP address X?" The requesting ARP module uses a request/response protocol, with the MAC layer broadcasting the ARP module's requests to all the other devices on the same physical medium segment. A receiving ARP module generates a response only if its network layer has assigned the IP address to one of its MAC modules. Responses are addressed to the requester's MAC address. The requesting ARP module inserts the response received in an address translation table used by the network layer to identify the next hop for all datagrams it forwards.

Dynamic Host Configuration Protocol

Remember that unlike MAC addresses, IP addresses cannot be assigned in the factory, because they are dynamic and must reflect a device's current location within the Internet. A MAC module uses DHCP to acquire an IP address for itself to reflect the device's current location with respect to the Internet topology.

DHCP makes the request: "Please configure my MAC module with an IP address." When one of a device's MAC layer modules connects to a new medium, it invokes DHCP to make this request. The associated DHCP module generates such a request that conveys the MAC address of the MAC module, which the MAC layer module broadcasts to the other devices attached to the same physical medium segment. A DHCP server responds with a unicast DHCP response binding an IP address to the MAC address. When it receives the response, the requesting DHCP module passes the assigned IP address to the network layer to configure in its address translation table.

In addition to binding an IP address to the MAC module used by DHCP, the response also contains a number of network configuration parameters, including the address of one or more routers, to enable reaching arbitrary destinations, the maximum datagram size supported, and the addresses of other servers, such as DNS servers, that translate human-readable names into IP addresses.

Domain Naming Service

IP and MAC addresses are efficient means for identifying different network interfaces, but human beings are incapable of using these as reliably as computing devices can. Instead, human beings rely on names to identify the computing devices with which they want to communicate. These names are centrally managed and called domain names. The DNS is a mechanism for translating human-readable names into IP addresses.

The translation from human-readable names to IP addresses happens within the socket layer module. An application opens a socket with the name of the intended destination. As the first step of opening a connection to that destination, the socket sends a request to a DNS server, asking the server to translate the name into an IP address. When the server responds, the socket can open the connection to the right destination, using the IP address provided.

It is becoming common for devices to register their IP addresses under their names with DNS once DHCP has completed. This permits other devices to locate the registering device so that they can send messages to it.

Internet Control Message Protocol

Internet Control Message Protocol (ICMP) is an important diagnostic tool for troubleshooting the Internet. Though ICMP provides many specialized message services, three are particularly important:

- Ping. Ping is a request/response protocol designed to determine the reachability of another IP address. The requestor sends a ping request message to a designated IP address. If the ping message is delivered, the interface using the destination IP address sends a ping response message to the IP address that sourced the request. The responding ICMP module copies the

contents of the ping request into the ping response so that the requestor can match responses to requests. The requestor uses pings to measure the roundtrip time to a destination, among other things.
- Traceroute. Traceroute is another request/response protocol. An ICMP module generates a traceroute request to discover the path it is using to traverse the Internet to a destination IP address. The requesting ICMP module transmits a destination. Each router that handles the traceroute request adds a description of its own IP address that received the message and then forwards the updated traceroute request. The destination sends all this information back to the message source in a traceroute response message.
- Destination unreachable. When a router receives a datagram for which it has no next hop, it generates a "destination unreachable" message and sends it back to the datagram source. When the message is delivered, the ICMP module marks the forwarding table of the message source so that its network layer will reject further attempts to send messages to the destination IP address. An analogous process happens at the ultimate destination when a message is delivered to a network layer, but the application targeted to receive the message is no longer online. The purpose of "destination unreachable" messages is to suppress messages that will never be successfully delivered in order to reduce network congestion.

Routing

The last cross-layer module we'll discuss is routing. Routing is a middleware application to maintain the forwarding tables used by the network layer. Each router advertises itself by periodically broadcasting "hello" messages through each of its MAC interfaces. This allows routers to discover the presence or loss of all neighboring routers, letting them construct the one-hop topology of the part of the Internet directly visible through their directly attached media. The routing application in a router then uses a sophisticated gossiping mechanism to exchange this view of the local topology with their neighbors. Since some of a router's neighbors are not its own direct neighbors, this allows each router to learn the two-hop topology of the Internet. This process repeats recursively until each router knows the entire topology of the Internet. The cost of using each link is part of the information gossiped. A routing module receiving this information uses all of it to compute a lowest-cost route to each destination. Once this is accomplished, the routing module reconfigures the forwarding table maintained by its network layer module. The routine module updates the forwarding table whenever the Internet topology changes, so each network layer can make optimal forwarding decisions in most situations and at the very worst reach any other device that is also connected to the Internet.

There are many different routing protocols, each of which is based on different gossiping mechanisms. The most widely deployed routing protocol between different administrative domains within the Internet is the border gateway protocol (BGP). The most widely deployed routing protocols within wired networks controlled by a single administrative domain are open shortest path first and routing information protocol. Ad hoc on demand distance vector, optimized link state routing, and topology broadcast based on reverse-path forwarding are commonly used in Wi-Fi meshes. Different routing protocols are used in different environments because each one addresses different scaling and administrative issues.

Applications

Applications are the ultimate reason for networking, and the Internet architecture has been shaped by applications' needs. All communicating applications define their own language in which to express what they need to say. Applications generally use the sockets layer to establish communication channels, which they then use for their own purposes.

Since the network modules have been designed to be a generic communications vehicle, that is, designed to meet the needs of all (or at least most) applications, it is rarely meaningful for the network to attempt to make statements on behalf of the applications. There is widespread confusion on this point around authentication and key management, which are the source of many exploitable security flaws.

2. AN INTERNET THREAT MODEL

Now that we have reviewed the architecture of the Internet protocol suite, it is possible to constructively consider the security issues it raises. Before doing so, let's first set the scope of the discussion.

There are two general approaches to attacking a networked computer. The first is to compromise one of the communicating parties so that it responds to queries with lies or otherwise communicates in a manner not foreseen by the system designers of the receiver. For example, it has become common to receive email with virus-infected attachments, whereby opening the attachment infects the receiver with the virus. These messages typically are sent by a machine that has already been compromised, so the sender is no longer acting as intended by the manufacturer of the computing system. Problems of this type are called Byzantine failures, named after the Byzantine Generals problem.

The Byzantine Generals problem imagines several armies surrounding Byzantium. The generals commanding these armies can communicate only by exchanging messages transported by couriers between them. Of course the couriers can be captured and the messages replaced by forgeries, but this is not really the issue, since it is possible to devise message schemes that detect lost messages or forgeries. All the armies combined are sufficient to overwhelm the defenses of Byzantium, but if even one army fails to participate in a coordinated attack, the armies of Byzantium have sufficient strength to repulse the attack. Each general must make a decision as to whether to participate in an attack on Byzantium at dawn or withdraw to fight another day. The question is how to determine the veracity of the messages received on which the decision to attack will be made—that is, whether it is possible to detect that one or more generals have become traitors and so will say their armies will join the attack when in fact they plan to hold back so that their allies will be slaughtered by the Byzantines.

Practical solutions addressing Byzantine failures fall largely within the purview of platform rather than network architecture, although the interconnectivity topology is an important consideration. For example, since viruses infect a platform by buffer overrun attacks, platform mechanisms to render buffer overrun attacks futile are needed. Secure logging, to make an accurate record of messages exchanged, is a second deterrent to these sorts of attacks; the way to accomplish secure logging is usually a question of platform design. Most self-propagating viruses and worms utilize the Internet to propagate, but they do not utilize any feature of the Internet architecture per se for their success. The success of these attacks instead depends on the architecture, design, implementation, and policies of the receiving system. Although these sorts of problems are important, we will rarely focus on security issues stemming from Byzantine failures.

What will instead be the focus of the discussion are attacks on the messages exchanged between computers themselves. As we will see, even with this more limited scope, there are plenty of opportunities for things to go wrong.

The Dolev–Yao Adversary Model

Security analyses of systems traditionally begin with a model of the attacker, and we follow this tradition. Daniel Dolev and Andrew Chi-Chih Yao formulated the standard attack model against messages exchanged over a network. The Dolev-Yao model makes the following assumptions about an attacker:

- Eavesdrop. An adversary can listen to any message exchanged through the network.
- Forge. An adversary can create and inject entirely new messages into the data stream or change messages in flight; these messages are called forgeries.
- Replay. A special type of forgery, called a replay, is distinguished. To replay a message, the adversary resends legitimate messages that were sent earlier.
- Delay and rush. An adversary can delay the delivery of some messages or accelerate the delivery of others.
- Reorder. An adversary can alter the order in which messages are delivered.
- Delete. An adversary can destroy in-transit messages, either selectively or all the messages in a data stream.

This model assumes a very powerful adversary, and many people who do not design network security solutions sometimes assert that the model grants adversaries an unrealistic amount of power to disrupt network communications. However, experience demonstrates that it is a reasonably realistic set of assumptions in practice; examples of each threat abound, as we will see. One of the reasons for this is that the environment in which the network operates is exposed and therefore open to attack by a suitably motivated adversary; unlike memory or microprocessors or other devices internal to a computer, there is almost no assurance that the network medium will be deployed in a "safe" way (Indeed, malware has progressed to the point where internal buses and memories can no longer be considered secure against knowledgeable attackers, which is forcing a migration of network security techniques into the platforms themselves). That is, it is comparatively easy for an attacker to anonymously access the physical network fabric, or at least the medium monitored to identify attacks against the medium and the networked traffic it carries. And since a network is intended as a generic communications vehicle, it becomes necessary to adopt a threat model that addresses the needs of all possible applications.

Layer Threats

With the Dolev—Yao model in hand, we can examine each of the architectural components of the Internet protocol suite for vulnerabilities. We next look at threats each component of the Internet architecture exposes through the prism of this model. The first Dolev—Yao assumption about adversaries is that they can eavesdrop on any communications.

Eavesdropping

An attacker can eavesdrop on a communications medium by connecting a receiver to the medium. Ultimately, such a connection has to be implemented at the PHY layer because an adversary has to access some physical media somewhere to be able to listen to anything at all. This connection to the PHY medium might be legitimate, such as when an authorized device is uncompromised, or illegitimate, such as an illegal wiretap; it can be intentional, as when an eavesdropper installs a rogue device, or unintentional, such as a laptop with wireless capabilities that will by default attempt to connect to any Wi-Fi network within range.

With a PHY layer connection, the eavesdropper can receive the analog signals on the medium and decode them into bits. Because of the limited scope of the PHY layer function—there are no messages, only analog signals representing bits and special control symbols—the damage an adversary can do with only PHY layer functionality is rather limited. In particular, to make sense of the bits, an adversary has to impose the higher-layer frame and datagram formats

onto the received bits. That is, any eavesdropping attack has to take into account at least the MAC layer to learn anything meaningful about the communications. Real eavesdroppers are more sophisticated than this: They know how to interpret the bits as a medium-specific encoding with regard to the frames that are used by the MAC layer. They also know how to extract the media-independent representation of datagrams conveyed within the MAC frames, as well as how to extract the transport layer segments from the datagrams, which can be reassembled into application messages.

The defenses erected against any threat give some insight into the perceived danger of the threat. People are generally concerned about eavesdropping, and it is easy to illicitly attach listening devices to most PHY media, but detection and removal of wiretaps has not evolved into a comparatively large industry. An apparent explanation of why this is so is that it is easier and more cost-effective for an attacker to compromise a legitimate device on the network and configure it to eavesdrop than it is to install an illegitimate device. The evidence for this view is that the antivirus/antibot industry is gigantic by comparison.

There is another reason that an antiwiretapping industry has never developed for the Internet. Almost every MAC module supports a special mode of operation called promiscuous mode. A MAC module in promiscuous mode receives every frame appearing on the medium, not just the frames addressed to itself. This allows one MAC module to snoop on frames that are intended for other parties. Promiscuous mode was intended as a troubleshooting mechanism to aid network administrators in diagnosing the source of problems. However, it is also a mechanism that can be easily abused by anyone motivated to enable promiscuous mode on their own networking devices.

Forgeries

A second Dolev—Yao assumption is that the adversary can forge messages. Eavesdropping is usually fairly innocuous compared to forgeries, because eavesdropping merely leaks information, whereas forgeries cause an unsuspecting receiver to take actions based on false information. Hence, the prevention or detection of forgeries is one of the central goals of network security mechanisms. Different kinds of forgeries are possible for each architectural component of the Internet. We will consider only a few for each layer of the Internet protocol suite, to give a taste of their variety and ingenuity.

Unlike the eavesdropping threat, where knowledge of higher layers is essential to any successful compromise, an attacker with only a PHY layer transmitter (and no higher-layer mechanisms) can disrupt communications by jamming the medium—that is, outputting noise onto the medium in an effort to disrupt communications. A jammer creates signals that do not necessarily correspond to any wave forms corresponding to bit or other control symbols. The goal of a pure PHY layer jammer is denial of service (DoS)—that is, to fill the medium sufficiently so that no communications can take place.

Sometimes it is feasible to create a jamming device that is sensitive to the MAC layer formats above it, to selectively jam only some frames. Selective jamming requires a means to interpret bits received from the medium as a higher-layer frame or datagram, and the targeted frames to jam are recognized by some criterion, such as being sent from or to a particular address. So that it can enable its own transmitter before the frame has been entirely received by its intended destination, the jammer's receiver must recognize the targeted frames before they are fully transmitted. When this is done correctly, the jammer's transmitter interferes with the legitimate signals, thereby introducing bit errors in the legitimate receiver's decoder. This results in the legitimate receiver's MAC layer detecting the bit errors while trying to verify the frame check sequence, causing it to discard the frame. Selective jamming is harder to implement than continuous jamming, but it is also much harder to detect, because the jammer's signal source transmits only when legitimate devices transmit as well, and only the targeted frames are disrupted. Successful selective jamming usually causes administrators to look for the source of the communications failure on one of the communicating devices instead of in the network for a jammer.

There is also a higher-layer analog to jamming, called message flooding. DoS is also the goal of message flooding. The technique used by message flooding is to create and send messages at a rate high enough to exhaust some resource. It is popular today, for instance, for hackers to compromise thousands of unprotected machines, which they use to generate simultaneous messages to a targeted site. Examples of this kind of attack are to completely fill the physical medium connecting the targeted site to the Internet with network layer datagrams—this is usually hard or impossible—or to generate transport layer connection requests at a rate faster than the targeted site can respond. Other variants—request operations that lead to disk I/O or require expensive cryptographic operations—are also common. Message flooding attacks have the property that they are legitimate messages from authorized parties but simply timed so that collectively their processing exceeds the maximum capacity of the targeted system.

Let's turn away from resource-clogging forgeries and examine forgeries designed to cause a receiver to take an unintended action. It is possible to construct this type of forgery at any higher layer: forged frames, datagrams, network segments, or application messages.

To better understand how forgeries work, we need to examine Internet "identities" more closely—MAC addresses, IP addresses, transport port numbers, and DNS names—as

well as the modules that use or support their use. The threats are a bit different at each layer.

Recall that each MAC layer module is manufactured with its own "hardware" address, which is supposed to be a globally unique identifier for the MAC layer module instance. The hardware address is configured in the factory into nonvolatile memory. At boot time, the MAC address is transferred from nonvolatile memory into operational random access memory (RAM) maintained by the MAC module. A transmitting MAC layer module inserts the MAC address from RAM into each frame it sends, thereby advertising an "identity." The transmitter also inserts the MAC address of the intended receiver on each frame, and the receiving MAC layer matches the MAC address in its own RAM against the destination field in each frame sent over the medium. The receiver ignores the frame if the MAC addresses don't match and receives the frame otherwise.

In spite of this system, it is useful—even necessary sometimes—for a MAC module to change its MAC address. For example, sometimes a manufacturer accidentally recycles MAC addresses so that two different modules receive the same MAC address in the factory. If both devices are deployed on the same network, neither works correctly until one of the two changes its address. Because of this problem, all manufacturers provide a way for the MAC module to alter the address in RAM. This can always be specified by software via the MAC module's device driver, by replacing the address retrieved from hardware at boot time.

Since the MAC address can be changed, attacks will find it. A common attack in Wi-Fi networks, for instance, is for the adversary to put the MAC module of the attacking device into promiscuous mode, to receive frames from other nearby systems. It is usually easy to identify another client device from the received frames and extract its MAC address. The attacker then reprograms its own MAC module to transmit frames using the address of its victim. A goal of this attack is usually to "hijack" the session of a customer paying for Wi-Fi service; that is, the attacker wants free Internet access for which someone else has already paid. Another goal of such an attack is often to avoid attribution of the actions being taken by the attacker; any punishment for antisocial or criminal behavior will likely be attributed to the victim instead of the attacker because all the frames that were part of the behavior came from the victim's address.

A similar attack is common at the network layer. The adversary will snoop on the IP addresses appearing in the datagrams encoded in the frames and use these instead of their own IP addresses to source IP datagrams. This is a more powerful attack than that of utilizing only a MAC address, because IP addresses are global; an IP address is an Internet-wide locator, whereas a MAC address is only an identifier on the medium to which the device is physically connected.

Manipulation of MAC and IP addresses leads directly to a veritable menagerie of forgery attacks and enables still others. A very selective list of examples must suffice to illustrate the ingenuity of attackers:

- TCP uses sequence numbers as part of its reliability scheme. TCP is supposed to choose the first sequence number for a connection randomly. If an attacker can predict the first sequence number for a TCP connection, an attacker who spoofs the IP address of one of the parties to the connection can hijack the session by interjecting its own datagrams into the flow that use the correct sequence numbers. This desynchronizes the retry scheme for the device being spoofed, which then drops out from the conversation. This attack seems to have become relatively less common than other attacks over the past few years, since most TCP implementations have begun to utilize better random number generators to seed their sequence numbers.
- An attacker can generate an ARP response to any ARP request, thus claiming to use any requested IP address. This is a common method to hijack another machine's IP address; it is a very effective technique when the attacker has a fast machine and the victim machine has less processing power, and so responds more slowly.
- An attacker can generate DHCP response messages replying to DHCP requests. This technique is often used as part of a larger forgery, such as the evil twin attack, whereby an adversary masquerades as an access point for a Wi-Fi public hot spot. The receipt of DHCP response messages convinces the victim it is connecting to an access point operated by the legitimate hotspot.
- A variant is to generate a DHCP request with the hardware MAC address of another device. This method is useful when the attacker wants to ascribe action it takes over the Internet to another device.
- An attacker can impersonate the DNS server, responding to requests to resolve human-readable names into IP addresses. The IP address in the response messages points the victim to a site controlled by the attacker. This is becoming a common attack used by criminals attempting to commit financial fraud, such as stealing credit card numbers.

Replay

Replay is a special forgery attack. It occurs when an attacker records frames or datagrams and then retransmits them unchanged at a later time.

This might seem like an odd thing to do, but replay attacks are an especially useful way to attack stateful messaging protocols, such as a routing protocol. Since the goal of a routing protocol is to allow every router to know the current topology of the network, a replayed routing message can cause the routers receiving it to utilize out-of-date information.

An attacker might also respond to an ARP request sent to a sabotaged node or to a mobile device that has migrated to another part of the Internet by sending a replayed ARP response. This replay indicates the node is still present, thus masking the true network topology.

Replay is also often a valuable tool for attacking a message encryption scheme. By retransmitting a message, an attacker can sometimes learn valuable information from a message decrypted and then retransmitted without encryption on another link.

A primary use of replay, however, is to attack session start-up protocols. Protocol start-up procedures establish session state, which is used to operate the link or connection and determine when some classes of failures occur. Since this state is not yet established when the session begins, start-up messages replayed from prior instances of the protocol will fool the receiver into allocating a new session. This is a common DoS technique.

Delay and Rushing

Delay is a natural consequence of implementations of the Internet architecture. Datagrams from a single connection typically transit a path across the Internet in bursts. This happens because applications at the sender, when sending large messages, tend to send messages larger than a single datagram. The transport layer partitions these messages into segments to fit the maximum segment size along the path to the destination. The MAC tends to output all the frames together as a single blast after it has accessed the medium. Therefore, routers with many links can receive multiple datagram bursts at the same time. When this happens, a router has to temporarily buffer the burst, since it can output only one frame conveying a datagram per link at a time. Simultaneous arrival of bursts of datagrams is one source of congestion in routers. This condition usually manifests itself at the application by slow communications time over the Internet. Delay can also be intentionally introduced by routers, such as via traffic shaping.

Attackers can induce delays in several ways. We illustrate this idea by describing two different attacks. It is not uncommon for an attacker to take over a router, and when this happens, the attacker can introduce artificial delay, even when the router is uncongested. As a second example, attackers with bot armies can bombard a particular router with "filler" messages, the only purpose of which is to congest the targeted router.

Rushing is the opposite problem: a technique to make it appear that messages can be delivered sooner than can be reasonably expected. Attackers often employ rushing attacks by first hijacking routers that service parts of the Internet that are fairly far apart in terms of network topology. The attackers cause the compromised routers to form a virtual link between them. A virtual link emulates a MAC layer protocol but running over a transport layer connection between the two routers instead of a PHY layer. The virtual link, also called a wormhole, allows the routers to claim they are connected directly by a link and so are only one hop apart. The two compromised routers can therefore advertise the wormhole as a "low-cost" path between their respective regions of the Internet. The two regions then naturally exchange traffic through the compromised routers and the wormhole.

An adversary usually launches a rushing attack as a prelude to other attacks. By attracting traffic to the wormhole endpoints, the compromised routers can eavesdrop and modify the datagrams flowing through them. Compromised routers at the end of a wormhole are also an ideal vehicle for selective deletion of messages.

Reorder

A second natural event in the Internet is datagram reordering. The two most common reordering mechanisms are forwarding table updates and traffic-shaping algorithms. Reordering due to forwarding takes place at the network layer; traffic shaping can be applied at the MAC layer or higher.

The Internet reconfigures itself automatically as routers set up new links with neighboring routers and tear down links between routers. These changes cause the routing application on each affected router to send an update to its neighbors, describing the topology change. These changes are gossiped across the network until every router is aware of what happened. Each router receiving such an update modifies its forwarding table to reflect the new Internet topology.

Since the forwarding table updates take place asynchronously from datagram exchanges, a router can select a different forwarding path for each datagram between even the same two devices. This means that two datagrams sent in order at the message source can arrive in a different order at the destination, since a router can update its forwarding table between the selection of a next hop for different datagrams.

The second reordering mechanism is traffic shaping, which gets imposed on the message flow to make better use of the communication resources. One example is quality of service. Some traffic classes, such as voice or streaming video, might be given higher priority by routers than best-effort traffic, which constitutes file transfers. Higher priority means the router will send datagrams carrying voice or video first while buffering the traffic longer. Endpoint systems also apply traffic-shaping algorithms in an attempt to make real-time applications work better, without gravely affecting the performance of applications that can wait for their data. Any layer of the protocol stack can apply traffic shaping to the messages it generates or receives.

An attacker can emulate reordering any messages it intercepts, but since every device in the Internet must recover from message reordering anyway, reordering

attacks are generally useful only in very specific contexts. We will not discuss them further.

Message Deletion

Like reordering, message deletion can happen through normal operation of the Internet modules. A MAC layer will drop any frame it receives with an invalid frame check sequence. A network layer module will discard any datagram it receives with an IP header error. A transport layer will drop any data segment received with a data checksum error. A router will drop perfectly good datagrams after receiving too many simultaneous bursts of traffic that lead to congestion and exhaustion of its buffers. For these reasons, TCP was designed to retransmit data segments in an effort to overcome errors.

The last class of attack possible with a Dolev–Yao adversary is message deletion. Two message deletion attacks occur frequently enough to be named: black-hole attacks and gray-hole attacks.

Black-hole attacks occur when a router deletes all messages it is supposed to forward. From time to time, a router is misconfigured to offer a zero-cost route to every destination in the Internet. This causes all traffic to be sent to this router. Since no device can sustain such a load, the router fails. The neighboring routers cannot detect the failure rapidly enough to configure alternate routes, and they fail as well. This continues until a significant portion of the routers in the Internet fail, resulting in a black hole: Messages flow into the collapsed portion of the Internet and never flow out. A black-hole attack intentionally misconfigures a router. Black-hole attacks also occur frequently in small-scale sensor, mesh, and peer-to-peer file networks.

A gray-hole attack is a selective deletion attack. Targeted jamming is one type of selective message deletion attack. More generally, an adversary can discard any message it intercepts in the Internet, thereby preventing its ultimate delivery. An adversary intercepting and selectively deleting messages can be difficult to detect and diagnose, and so is a powerful attack. It is normally accomplished via compromised routers.

A subtler, indirect form of message deletion is also possible through the introduction of forwarding loops. Each IP datagram header has a time-to-live (TTL) field, limiting the number of hops that a datagram can make. This field is set to 255 by the initiator and decremented by each router through which the datagram passes. If a router decrements the TTL field to zero, it discards the datagram.

The reason for the TTL field is that the routing protocols that update the forwarding tables can temporarily cause forwarding loops because updates are applied asynchronously as the routing updates are gossiped through the Internet. For instance, if router A gets updated prior to router B, A might believe that the best path to some destination C is via B, whereas B believes the best route to C is via A as the next hop. Messages for C will ping-pong between A and B until one or both are updated with new topology information.

An attacker who compromises a router or forges its routing traffic can intentionally introduce forwarding routes. This causes messages addressed to the destinations affected by the forgery to circulate until the TTL field gets decremented to zero. These attacks are also difficult to detect, because all the routers are behaving according to their specifications, but messages are being mysteriously lost.

Summary

The most striking point to observe about all of the enumerated attacks is that all take advantage of the natural features and structure of the Internet architecture: No one is making any of the protocols misbehave, just "mis-using" the Internet's own features against "legitimate" use. Any I/O channel of any system—and communications over the Internet certainly falls into this bucket—is assumed under the control of an adversary under the Dolev–Yao model. The input parse for any such channel is therefore a programming environment to which we freely grant the adversary access via the language describing protocol messages on the channel. This means our communications architectures necessarily expose our systems to attack, unless we close all possible communications channels. Doing so is impractical because not all people and organizations with which they are affiliated necessarily trust one another for all possible communications, and openness is a necessary condition for our economic models. Vulnerability to attack is therefore a necessary consequence of communications and a judicious mix of security mechanisms with friends and open links with potential business partners is inevitable. Absolutely secure networks and systems have only limited utility.

3. DEFENDING AGAINST ATTACKS ON THE INTERNET

Now that we have a model for thinking about the threats against communication and we understand how the Internet works, we can examine how its communications can sometimes be protected. Here we will explain how cryptography is used to protect messages exchanged between various devices on the Internet and illustrate the techniques with examples.

As might be expected, the techniques vary according to scenario. Methods that are effective for an active session do not work for session establishment. Methods that are required for session establishment are too expensive for an established session. It is interesting that similar methods are used at each layer of the Internet architecture for protecting a session and for session establishment and that each layer defines its own security protocols. Many find the similarity of security solutions at different layers curious and wonder

why security is not centralized in a single layer. We will explain why the same mechanisms solve different problems at different layers of the architecture, to give better insight into what each is for.

Layer Session Defenses

A session is a series of one or more related messages. The easiest and most straightforward defenses protect the exchange of messages that are organized into sessions, so we will start with session-oriented defenses.

Cryptography, when used properly, can provide reliable defenses against eavesdropping. It can also be used to detect forgery and replay attacks, and the methods used also have some relevance to detecting reordering and message deletion attacks. We will discuss how this is accomplished and illustrate the techniques with transport layer security (TLS), IPsec, and 802.11i.

Defending Against Eavesdropping

The primary method used to defend against eavesdropping is encryption. Encryption was invented with the goal of making it infeasible for any computationally limited adversary to be able to learn anything useful about a message that cannot already be deduced by some other means, such as its length. Encryption schemes that appear to meet this goal have been invented and are in widespread use on the Internet. Here we will describe how they are used.

There are two forms of encryption: symmetric encryption, in which the same key is used to both encrypt and decrypt, and asymmetric encryption, in which encryption and decryption use distinct but related keys. The properties of each are different. Asymmetric encryption tends to be used only for applications related to session initiation and assertions about policy (although this is not universally true). The reason for this is that a single asymmetric key operation is generally too expensive across a number of dimensions—computation time, size of encrypted payloads, power consumption—to be applied to a message stream of arbitrary length. We therefore focus on symmetric encryption and how it is used by network security protocols.

A symmetric encryption scheme consists of three operations: key generate, encrypt, and decrypt. The key generate operation creates a key, which is a secret. The key generate procedure is usually application specific; we describe some examples of key generate operations in our discussion of session start-up. Once generated, the key is used by the encrypt operation to transform plaintext messages—that is, messages that can be read by anyone—into ciphertext, which is messages that cannot be read by any computationally limited party who does not possess the key. The key is also used by the decrypt primitive to translate ciphertext messages back into plaintext messages.

There are two kinds of symmetric encryption algorithms. The first type is called a block cipher, and the second a stream cipher. Block and stream ciphers make different assumptions about the environment in which they operate, making each more effective than the other at different protocol layers.

A block cipher divides a message into chunks of a fixed size called blocks and encrypts each block separately. Block ciphers have the random access property, meaning that a block cipher can efficiently encrypt or decrypt any block utilizing an initialization vector in conjunction with the key. This property makes block ciphers a good choice for encrypting the content of MAC layer frames and network layer datagrams, for two reasons. First, the chunking behavior of a block cipher corresponds nicely to the packetization process used to form datagrams from segments and frames from datagrams. Second, and perhaps more important, the Internet architecture models the lower layers as "best-effort" services, meaning that it assumes that datagrams and frames are sent and then forgotten. If a transmitted datagram is lost due to congestion or bit error (or attack), it is up to the transport layer or application to recover. The random access property makes it easy to restart a block cipher anywhere it's needed in the datastream. Popular examples of block ciphers include advanced encryption standard (AES), data encryption standard (DES), and triple data encryption standard (3DES), used by Internet security protocols.

Block ciphers are used by the MAC and network layers to encrypt as follows: First, a block cipher mode of operation is selected. A block cipher itself encrypts and decrypts only single blocks. A mode of operation is a set of rules extending the encryption scheme from a single block to messages of arbitrary length. The most popular modes of operation used in the Internet are counter (CTR) mode and cipher-block chaining (CBC) mode. Both require an initialization vector, which is a counter value for counter mode and a randomly generated bit vector for the CBC mode. To encrypt a message, the mode of operation first partitions the message into a sequence of blocks whose size equals that of the cipher, padding if needed to bring the message length up to a multiple of the block size. The mode of operation then encrypts each block under the key while combining initialization vectors with the block in a mode-specific fashion.

For example, counter mode uses a counter as its initialization vector, which it increments, encrypts, and then exclusive ORs (XORs) the result with the block:

$$\text{counter} \rightarrow \text{counter} + 1; \quad E \leftarrow \text{Encrypt}_{\text{Key}}(\text{counter});$$

$$\text{CipherTextBlock} \leftarrow E \oplus \text{PlainTextBlock}$$

where $\oplus$ denotes exclusive XOR. The algorithm outputs the new (unencrypted) counter value, which is used to encrypt the next block and CipherTextBlock.

The process of assembling a message from a message encrypted under a mode of operation is very simple: Prepend the original initialization vector to the sequence of ciphertext blocks, which together replace the plaintext payload for the message. The right way to think of this is that the initialization vector becomes a new message header layer. Also prepended is a key identifier, which indicates to the receiver which key it should utilize to decrypt the payload. This is important because in many cases it is useful to employ multiple connections between the same pair of endpoints, and so the receiver can have multiple decryption keys to choose from for each message received from a particular source.

A receiver reverses this process: First, it extracts the initialization vector from the data payload, then it uses this and the ciphertext blocks to recover the original plaintext message by reversing the steps in the mode of operation.

This paradigm is widely used in MAC and network layer security protocols, including 802.11i, 802.16e, 802.1ae, and IPsec, each of which utilizes AES in modes related to counter and cipher-block chaining modes.

A stream cipher treats the data as a continuous stream and can be thought of as encrypting and decrypting data one bit at a time. Stream ciphers are usually designed so that each encrypted bit depends on all previously encrypted ones, so decryption becomes possible only if all the bits arrive in order; most true stream ciphers lack the random access property. This means that in principle stream ciphers only work in network protocols when they're used on top of a reliable data delivery service such as TCP. Therefore, they work correctly below the transport layer only when used in conjunction with reliable data links. Stream ciphers are attractive from an implementation perspective because they can often achieve much higher throughputs than block ciphers. RC4 is an example of a popular stream cipher.

Stream ciphers typically do not use a mode of operation or an initialization vector at all, or at least not in the same sense as a block cipher. Instead, they are built as pseudo-random number generators, the output of which is based on a key. The random number generator is used to create a sequence of bits that appear random, called a key stream, and the result is exclusive OR'd with the plaintext data to create ciphertext. Since XOR is an idempotent operation, decryption with a stream cipher is just the same operation: Generate the same key stream and exclusive XOR it with the ciphertext to recover the plaintext. Since stream ciphers do not utilize initialization vectors, Internet protocols employing stream ciphers do not need the extra overhead of a header to convey the initialization vector needed by the decryptor in the block cipher case. Instead, these protocols rely on the ability of the sender and receiver to keep their respective key stream generators synchronized for each bit transferred. This implies that stream ciphers can only be used over a reliable medium such as TCP—that is, a transport that guarantees delivery of all bits in the proper order and without duplication.

TLS is an example of an Internet security protocol that uses the stream cipher RC4. TLS runs on top of TCP, which is a reliable transport and therefore meets one of the preconditions for use of RC4.

Assuming that a symmetric encryption scheme is well designed, its efficacy against eavesdropping depends on four factors. Failing to consider any of these factors can cause the encryption scheme to fail catastrophically.

Independence of Keys

This is perhaps the most important consideration for the use of encryption. All symmetric encryption schemes assume that the encryption key for each and every session is generated independently of the encryption keys used for every other session. Let's parse this thought:

- Independent means selected or generated by a process that is indistinguishable by any polynomial time statistical test from the uniform distribution applied to the key space. One common failure is to utilize a key generation algorithm that is not random, such as using the MAC or IP address of a device or time of session creation as the basis for a key, or even basing the key on a password. Schemes that use such public values instead of randomness for keys are easily broken using brute-force search techniques such as dictionary attacks. A second common failure is to pick an initial key randomly but create successive keys by some simple transformation, such as incrementing the initial key, exclusive OR'ing the MAC address of the device with the key, and so on. Encryption using key generation schemes of this sort are easily broken using differential cryptanalysis and related key attacks.
- Each and every mean each and every. For a block cipher, reusing the same key twice with the same initialization vector can allow an adversary to recover information about the plaintext data from the ciphertext without using the key. Similarly, each key always causes the pseudorandom number generator at the heart of a stream cipher to generate the same key stream, and reuse of the same key stream again will leak the plaintext data from the ciphertext without using the key.
- Methods effective for the coordinated generation of random keys at the beginning of each session constitute a complicated topic. We address it in our discussion of session start-up later in the chapter.

Limited Output

Perhaps the second most important consideration is to limit the amount of information encrypted under a single key. The modern definition of security for an encryption scheme revolves around the idea of indistinguishability of the scheme's output from random. This goes back to a notion of ideal security proposed by Claude E. Shannon (a research mathematician working for Bell Labs). This has a dramatic effect on how long an encryption key may be safely used before an adversary has sufficient information to begin to learn something about the encrypted data.

Every encryption scheme is ultimately a deterministic algorithm using a finite state space, and no deterministic algorithm using a finite state space can generate an infinite amount of output that is indistinguishable from random. This means that encryption keys must be replaced on a regular basis. The amount of data that can be safely encrypted under a single key depends very much on the encryption scheme. As usual, the limitations for block ciphers and stream ciphers are a bit different.

Let the block size for a block cipher be some integer $n > 0$. Then, for any key K, for every string S_1 there is another string S_2 so that:

$$\text{Encrypt}_K(S_2) = S_1 \text{ and } \text{Decrypt}_K(S_1) = S_2$$

This says that a block cipher's encrypt and decrypt operations are permutations of the set of all bit strings whose length equals the block size. In particular, this property says that every pair of distinct n bit strings results in distinct n bit ciphertexts for any block cipher. However, by an elementary theorem from probability called the birthday paradox, random selection of n bit strings should result in a 50 percent probability that some string is chosen at least twice after about $2n/2$ selections. This has a sobering consequence for block ciphers. It says that an algorithm as simple as naïve guessing can distinguish the output of the block cipher from random after about $2n/2$ blocks have been encrypted. This means that an encryption key should never be used to encrypt even close to $2n/2$ blocks before a new, independent key is generated.

To make this specific, DES and 3DES have a block size of 64 bits; AES has a 128-bit block size. Therefore a DES or 3DES key should be used much less than to encrypt $2^{64/2} = 2^{32}$ blocks, whereas an AES key should never be used to encrypt as many as 2^{64} blocks; doing so begins to leak information about the encrypted data without use of the encryption key. As an example, 802.11i has been crafted to limit each key to encrypting 2^{48} before forcing generation of a new key.

This kind of arithmetic does not work for a stream cipher, since its block size is 1 bit. Instead, the length of time a key can be safely used is governed by the periodicity of the pseudorandom number generator at the heart of the stream cipher. RC4, for instance, becomes distinguishable from random after generating about 2^{31} bytes. Note that $31 \approx 32 = \sqrt{256}$, and 256 bytes is the size of the RC4 internal state. This illustrates the rule of thumb that there is a birthday paradox relation between the maximum number of encrypted bits of a stream cipher key and its internal state.

Key Size

The one "fact" about encryption that everyone knows is that larger keys result in stronger encryption. This is indeed true, provided that the generate keys operation is designed according to the independence condition. One common mistake is to properly generate a short key—say, 32 bits long—that is then concatenated to get a key of the length needed by the selected encryption scheme—say, 128 bits. Another similar error is to generate a short key and manufacture the remainder of the key with known public data, such as an IP address. These methods result in a key that is only as strong as the short key that was generated randomly.

Mode of Operation

The final parameter is the mode of operation—that is, the rules for using a block cipher to encrypt messages whose length is different from the block cipher width. The most common problem is failure to respect the documented terms and conditions defined for using the mode of operation.

As an illustration of what can go wrong—even by people who know what they are doing—the cipher-block chaining mode requires that the initialization vector be chosen randomly. The earliest version of the IPsec standard used the cipher-block chaining mode exclusively for encryption. This standard recommended choosing initialization vectors as the final block of any prior message sent. The reasoning behind this recommendation was that, because an encrypted block cannot be distinguished from random if the number of blocks encrypted is limited, a block of a previously encrypted message ought to suffice. However, the advice given by the standard was erroneous because the initialization vector selection algorithm failed to have one property that a real random selection property has: The initialization vector is not unpredictable. A better way to meet the randomness requirement is to increment a counter, prepend it to the message to encrypt, and then encrypt the counter value, which becomes the initialization vector. This preserves the unpredictability property at a cost of encrypting one extra block.

A second common mistake is to design protocols using a mode of operation that was not designed to encrypt multiple blocks. For example, failing to use a mode of operation at all—using the naked encrypt and decrypt operations, with no initialization vector—is itself a mode of operation called electronic code book mode. Electronic code book mode was designed to encrypt messages that never span more than a single block—for example, encrypting keys to distribute for other operations. Using electronic code book mode on a message longer than a single block leaks a bit per block, however, because this mode allows an attacker to disguise when two plaintext blocks are the same or different. A classic example of this problem is to encrypt a photograph using electronic code book mode. The main outline of the

photograph shows through plainly. This is not a failure of the encryption scheme; it is, rather, using encryption in a way that was never intended.

Now that we understand how encryption works and how it is used in Internet protocols, we should ask why it is needed at different layers. What does encryption at each layer of the Internet architecture accomplish? The best way to answer this question is to watch what it does.

Encryption applied at the MAC layer encrypts a single link. Data is encrypted prior to being put on a link and is decrypted again at the other end of a link. This leaves the IP datagrams conveyed by the MAC layer frames exposed inside each router as they wend their way across the Internet. Encryption at the MAC layer is a good way to transparently prevent data from leaking, since many devices never use encryption. For example, many organizations are distributed geographically and use direct point-to-point links to connect sites; encrypting the links connecting sites prevents an outsider from learning the organization's confidential information merely by eavesdropping. Legal wiretaps also depend on this arrangement because they monitor data inside routers. The case of legal wiretaps also illustrates the problem with link layer encryption only: If an unauthorized party assumes control of a router, he or she is free to read all the datagrams that traverse the router.

IPsec operates essentially at the network layer. Applying encryption via IPsec prevents exposure of the datagrams' payload end to end, so the data is still protected within routers. Since the payload of a datagram includes both the transport layer header and its data segments, applying encryption at the IPsec layer hides the applications being used as well as the data. This provides a big boost in confidentiality but also leads to more inefficient use of the Internet, since traffic-shaping algorithms in routers critically depend on having complete access to the transport headers. Using encryption at the IPsec layer also means the endpoints do not have to know whether each link a datagram traverses through the Internet applies encryption; using encryption at this layer simplifies the security analysis over encryption applied at the MAC layer alone. Finally, like MAC layer encryption, IPsec is a convenient tool for introducing encryption transparently to protect legacy applications, which by and large ignored confidentiality issues. A downside of IPsec is that it still leaves data unprotected within the network protocol implementation, and malware can sometimes hook itself between the network and sockets layer to inspect traffic.

The transport layer encryption function can be illustrated by TLS. Like IPsec, TLS operates end to end, but TLS encrypts only the application data carried in the transport data segments, leaving the transport header exposed. Thus, with TLS, routers can still perform their traffic-shaping function, and we still have the simplified security analysis that comes with end-to-end encryption. A second advantage is that TLS protects data essentially from application to application, making malware attacks against the communication channel per se more difficult. There are of course downsides. The first disadvantage of this method is that the exposure of the transport headers gives the attacker greater knowledge about what might be encrypted in the payload. The second disadvantage is that it is somewhat more awkward to introduce encryption transparently at the transport layer; encryption at the transport layer requires cooperation by the application to perform properly. This analysis says that it is reasonable to employ encryption at any one of the network protocol layers because each solves a slightly different problem.

Before leaving the topic of encryption, it is worthwhile to emphasize what encryption does and does not do. Encryption, when properly used, is a read access control. If used correctly, no one who lacks access to the encryption key can read the encrypted data. Encryption, however, is *not* a write access control; that is, it does not guarantee the integrity of the encrypted data. Counter mode and stream ciphers are subject to bit-flipping attacks, for instance. An attacker launches a bit-flipping attack by capturing a frame or datagram, changing one or more bits from 0 to 1 (or vice versa) and retransmitting the altered frame. The resulting frame decrypts to some result—the altered message decrypts to something—and if bits are flipped judiciously, the result can be intelligible. As a second example, CBC mode is susceptible to cut-and-paste attacks, whereby the attack cuts the final few blocks from one message in a stream and uses them to overwrite the final blocks of a later stream. At most, one block decrypts to gibberish; if the attacker chooses the paste point judiciously, for example, so that it falls where the application ought to have random data anyway, this can be a powerful attack. The upshot is that even encrypted data needs an integrity mechanism to be effective, which leads us to the subject of defenses against forgeries.

Defending Against Forgeries and Replays

Forgery and replay detection are usually treated together because replays are a special kind of forgery. We follow this tradition in our own discussion. Forgery detection, not eavesdropping protection, is the central concern for designs to secure network protocol. This is because every accepted forgery of an encrypted frame or datagram is a question whose answer can tell the adversary something about the encryption key or plaintext data. Just as one learns any subject in school, an attacker can learn about the encrypted stream or encryption key faster by asking questions rather than sitting back and passively listening.

Since eavesdropping is a passive attack, whereas creating forgeries is active, turning from the subject of eavesdropping to that of forgeries changes the security goals subtly.

Encryption has a security goal of prevention—to prevent the adversary from learning anything useful about the data that cannot be derived in other ways. The comparable security goal for forgeries would be to prevent the adversary from creating forgeries, which is not feasible. This is because any device with a transmitter appropriate for the medium can send forgeries by creating frames and datagrams using addresses employed by other parties. What is feasible is a form of asking forgiveness instead of permission: Prevent the adversary from creating undetected forgeries.

The cryptographic tool underlying forgery detection is called a message authentication code. Like an encryption scheme, a message authentication code consists of three operations: a key generation operation, a tagging operation, and a verification operation. Also like encryption, the key generation operation, which generates a symmetric key shared between the sender and receiver, is usually application specific. The tagging and verification operations, however, are much different from encrypt and decrypt.

The tagging operation takes the symmetric key, called an authentication key, and a message as input parameters and outputs a tag, which is a cryptographic checksum depending on the key and message to produce its output.

The verification operation takes three input parameters: the symmetric key, the message, and its tag. The verification algorithm recomputes the tag from the key and message and compares the result against the tag with the received message. If the two fail to match, the verify algorithm outputs a signal that the message is a forgery. If the input and locally computed tag match, the verify algorithm declares that the message is authenticated.

The conclusion drawn by the verify algorithm of a message authentication code is not entirely logically correct. Indeed, if the tag is n bits in length, an attacker could generate a random n bit string as its tag and it would have one chance in $2n$ of being valid. A message authentication scheme is considered good if there are no polynomial time algorithms that are significantly better than random guessing at producing correct tags.

Message authentication codes are incorporated into network protocols in a manner similar to encryption. First, a sequence number is prepended to the data that is being forgery protected; the sequence number, we will see, is used to detect replays. Next, a message authentication code tagging operation is applied to the sequence number and message body to produce a tag. The tag is appended to the message, and a key identifier for the authentication key is prepended to the message. The message can then be sent. The receiver determines whether the message was a forgery by first finding the authentication key identified by the key identifier, then by checking the correctness of the tag using the message authentication code's verify operation. If these checks succeed, the receiver finally uses the sequence number to verify that the message is not a replay.

How does replay detection work? When the authentication key is established, the sender initializes to zero the counter that is used in the authenticated message. The receiver meanwhile establishes a replay window, which is a list of all recently received sequence numbers. The replay window is initially empty. To send a replay protected frame, the sender increments his counter by one and prepends this at the front of the data to be authenticated prior to tagging. The receiver extracts the counter value from the received message and compares this to the replay window. If the counter falls before the replay window, which means it is too old to be considered valid, the receiver flags the message as a replay. The receiver does the same thing if the counter is already represented in the replay window data structure. If the counter is greater than the bottom of the replay window and is a counter value that has not yet been received, the frame or datagram is considered "fresh" instead of a replay.

The process is simplest to illustrate for the MAC layer. Over a single MAC link it is ordinarily impossible for frames to be reordered, because only a single device can access the medium at a time; because of the speed of electrons or photons comprising the signals representing bits, at least some of the bits at the start of a frame are received prior to the final bits being transmitted (satellite links are an exception). If frames cannot be reordered by a correctly operating MAC layer, the replay window data structure records the counter for the last received frame, and the replay detection algorithm merely has to decide whether the replay counter value in a received frame is larger than that recorded in its replay window. If the counter is less than or equal to the replay window value, the frame is a forgery; otherwise it is considered genuine. 802.11i, 802.16, and 802.1ae all employ this approach to replay detection. This same approach can be used by a message authentication scheme operating above the transport layer, by protocols such as TLS and Secure Shell (SSH), since the transport eliminates duplicates and delivers bits in the order sent. The replay window is more complicated at the network layer, however, because some reordering is natural, given that the network reorders datagrams. Hence, for the network layer the replay window is usually sized to account for the maximum reordering expected in the "normal" Internet. IPsec uses this more complex replay window.

This works for the following reason: Every message is given a unique, incrementing sequence number in the form of its counter value. The transmitter computes the message authentication code tag over the sequence number and the message data. Since it is not feasible for a computationally bounded adversary to create a valid tag for the data with probability significantly greater than $1/2n$, a tag validated by the receiver implies that the message, including its sequence number, was created by the transmitter. The worst thing that could have happened, therefore, is that the adversary has delayed the message. However, if the sequence number falls within the replay window, the message could not have been delayed longer than reordering due to the normal operation of forwarding and traffic shaping within the Internet.

A replay detection scheme limits an adversary's opportunities to delete and to reorder messages. If a message does not arrive at its destination, its sequence number is never set in the receive window, so it can be declared a lost message. It is easy to track the percentage of lost messages, and if this exceeds some threshold, then communications become unreliable, but more important, the cause of the unreliability can be investigated. Similarly, messages received outside the replay window can also be tracked, and if the percentage becomes too high, messages are arriving out of order more frequently than might be expected from normal operation of the Internet, pointing to a configuration problem, an equipment failure, or an attack. Again, the cause of the anomaly can be investigated. Mechanisms like these are often how attacks are discovered in the first place. The important lesson is that attacks and even faulty equipment or misconfigurations are often difficult to detect without collecting reliability statistics, and the forgery detection mechanisms can provide some of the best reliability statistics available.

Just like encryption, the correctness of this analysis depends critically on the design enforcing some fundamental assumptions, regardless of the quality of the message authentication code on which it might be based. If any of the following assumptions are violated, the forgery detection scheme can fail catastrophically to accomplish its mission.

Independence of Authentication Keys

This is absolutely paramount for forgery detection. If the message authentication keys are not independent, an attacker can easily create forged message authentication tags based on authentication keys learned in other ways. This assumption is so important that it is useful to examine in greater detail.

The first point is that a message authentication key utterly fails to accomplish its mission if it is shared among even three parties; only two parties must know any particular authentication key. This is very easy to illustrate. Suppose A, B, and C were to share a message authentication key, and suppose A creates a forgery-protected message it sends to C. What can C conclude when it receives this message? C cannot conclude that the message actually originated from A, even though its addressing indicates it did, because B could have produced the same message and used A's address. C cannot even conclude that B did not change some of the message in transit. Therefore, the algorithm loses all its efficacy for detecting forgeries if message authentication keys are known by more than two parties. They must be known by at least two parties or the receiver cannot verify that the message and its bits originated with the sender.

This is much different than encryption. An encryption/decryption key can be distributed to every member of a group, and as long as the key is not leaked from the group to a third party, the encryption scheme remains an effective read access control against parties that are not members of the group. Message authentication utterly fails if the key is shared beyond two parties. This is due to the active nature of forgery attacks and the fact that forgery handling, being a detection rather than a prevention scheme, already affords the adversary more latitude than encryption toward fooling the good guys.

So for forgery detection schemes to be effective, message authentication keys must be shared between exactly two communicating devices. As with encryption keys, a message authentication key must be generated randomly because brute-force searches and related key attacks can recover the key by observing messages transiting the medium.

No Reuse of Replay Counter Values with a Key

Reusing a counter with a message authentication key is analogous to reusing an initialization vector with an encryption key. Instead of leaking data, however, replay counter value reuse leads automatically to trivial forgeries based on replayed messages. The attacker's algorithm is trivial: Using a packet sniffer, record each of the messages protected by the same key and file them in a database. If the attacker ever receives a key identifier and sequence number pair already in the database, the transmitter has begun to reuse replay counter values with a key. The attacker can then replay any message with a higher sequence number and the same key identifier. The receiver will be fooled into accepting the replayed message.

This approach implies that known forgery detection schemes cannot be based on static keys. To the contrary, we could attempt to design such a scheme. One could try to checkpoint in nonvolatile memory the replay counter at the transmitter and the replay window at the receiver. This approach does not work, however, in the presence of a Dolev—Yao adversary. The adversary can capture a forgery-protected frame in flight and then delete all successive messages. At its convenience later, the adversary resends the captured message. The receiver, using its static message authentication key, will verify the tag and, based on its replay window retrieved from nonvolatile storage, verify that the message is indeed in sequence and so accept the message as valid. This experiment demonstrates that forgery detection is not entirely satisfactory because sequence numbers do not take timeliness into account. Secure clock synchronization, however, is a difficult problem with solutions that enjoy only partial success. The construction of better schemes that account for timing remains an open research problem.

Key Size

If message authentication keys must be randomly generated, they must also be of sufficient size to discourage brute-force attack. The key space has to be large enough to make exhaustive search for the message authentication key cost prohibitive. Key sizes for message authentication comparable with those for encryption are sufficient for this task.

Message Authentication Code Tag Size

We have seen many aspects that make message authentication codes somewhat more fragile encryption schemes. Message authentication code size is one in which forgery detection can on the contrary effectively utilize a smaller block size than an encryption scheme. Whereas an encryption scheme based on a 128-bit block size has to replace keys every 2^{48} or so blocks to avoid leaking data, an encryption scheme can maintain the same level of security with about a 48-bit message authentication code tag. The difference is that the block cipher-based encryption scheme leaks information about the encrypted data due to the birthday paradox, whereas an attacker has to create a valid forgery based on an exhaustive search due to the active nature of a forgery attack. In general, to determine the size of a tag needed by a message authentication code, we have only to determine the maximum number of messages sent in the lifetime of the key. As a rule of thumb, if this number of messages is bounded by $2n$, the tag need only be $n + 1$ bits long. This is only a rule of thumb because some MACs cannot be safely truncated to this minimal number of bits.

As with encryption, for many it is confusing that forgery detection schemes are offered at nearly every layer of the Internet architecture. To understand the preceding concept, it is again useful to ask what message forgery detection accomplishes at each layer.

If a MAC module requires forgery detection for every frame received, physical access to the medium being used by the module's PHY layer affords an attacker no opportunity to create forgeries. This is a very strong property. It means that the only MAC layer messages attacking the receiver are either generated by other devices authorized to attach to the medium or else are forwarded by the network layer modules of authorized devices, because all frames received directly off the medium generated by unauthorized devices will be discarded by the forgery detection scheme. A MAC layer forgery detection scheme therefore essentially provides a write access control of the physical medium, closing it to unauthorized parties. Installing a forgery detection scheme at any other layer will not provide this kind of protection. Requiring forgery detection at the MAC layer is therefore desirable whenever feasible.

Forgery detection at the network layer provides a different kind of assurance. IPsec is the protocol designed to accomplish this function. If a network layer module requires IPsec for every datagram received, this essentially cuts off attacks against the device hosting the module to other authorized machines in the entire Internet; datagrams generated by unauthorized devices will be dropped. With this forgery detection scheme it is still possible for an attacker on the same medium to generate frames attacking the device's MAC layer module, but attacks against higher layers become computationally infeasible. Installing a forgery detection scheme at any other layer will not provide this kind of protection. Requiring forgery detection at the network layer is therefore desirable whenever feasible as well.

Applying forgery detection at the transport layer offers different assurances entirely. Forgery detection at this level assures the receiving application that the arriving messages were generated by the peer application, not by some virus or Trojan-horse program that has linked itself between modules between protocol layers on the same or different machine. This kind of assurance cannot be provided by any other layer. Such a scheme at the network or MAC layers only defends against message injection by unauthorized devices on the Internet generally or directly attached to the medium, not against messages generated by unauthorized processes running on an authorized machine. Requiring forgery detection at the transport layer therefore is desirable whenever it is feasible.

The conclusion is that forgery detection schemes accomplish different desirable functions at each protocol layer. The security goals that are achievable are always architecturally dependent, and this comes through clearly with forgery detection schemes.

We began the discussion of forgery detection by noting that encryption by itself is subject to attack. One final issue is how to use encryption and forgery protection together to protect the same message. Three solutions could be formulated to this problem. One approach might be to add forgery detection to a message first—add the authentication key identifier, the replay sequence number, and the message authentication code tag—followed by encryption of the message data and forgery detection headers. TLS is an example Internet protocol that takes this approach. The second approach is to reverse the order of encryption and forgery detection: First encrypt, then compute the tag over the encrypted data and the encryption headers. IPsec is an example Internet protocol defined to use this approach. The last approach is to apply both simultaneously to the plaintext data. SSH is an Internet protocol constructed in this manner.

Session Start-up Defenses

If encryption and forgery detection techniques are such powerful security mechanisms, why aren't they used universally for all network communications? The problem is that not everyone is your friend; everyone has enemies, and

in every human endeavor there are those with criminal mind-sets who want to prey on others. Most people do not go out of their way to articulate and maintain relationships with their enemies unless there is some compelling reason to do so, and technology is powerless to change this.

More than anything else, the keys used by encryption and forgery detection are relationship signifiers. Possession of keys is useful not only because they enable encryption and forgery detection but because their use assures the remote party that messages you receive will remain confidential and that messages the peer receives from you actually originated from you. They enable the accountable maintenance of a preexisting relationship. If you receive a message that is protected by a key that only you and I know, and you didn't generate the message yourself, it is reasonable for you to conclude that I sent the message to you and did so intentionally.

If keys are signifiers of preexisting relationships, much of our networked communications cannot be defended by cryptography, because we do not have preexisting relationships with everyone. We send and receive email to and from people we have never met. We buy products online from merchants we have never met. None of these relationships would be possible if we required all messages to be encrypted or authenticated. What is always required is an open, unauthenticated, risky channel to establish new relationships; cryptography can only assure us that communication from parties with whom we already have relationships is indeed occurring with the person with whom we think we are communicating.

A salient and central assumption for both encryption and forgery detection is that the keys these mechanisms use are fresh and independent across sessions. A session is an instance of exercising a relationship to effect communication. This means that secure communications require a state change, transitioning from a state in which two communicating parties are not engaged in an instance of communication to one in which they are. This state change is session establishment.

Session establishment is like a greeting between human beings. It is designed to synchronize two entities communicating over the Internet and establish and synchronize their keys, key identifiers, sequence numbers and replay windows, and, indeed, all the states to provide mutual assurance that the communication is genuine and confidential.

The techniques and data structures used to establish a secure session are different from those used to carry on a conversation. Our next goal is to look at some representative mechanisms in this area. The field is vast, and it is impossible to do more than skim the surface briefly to give the reader a glimpse of the beauty and richness of the subject. Secure session establishment techniques typically have three goals, as described in the following sections of this chapter.

Mutual Authentication

First, session establishment techniques seek to mutually authenticate the communicating parties to each other. To mutually authenticate means that both parties learn the "identity" of the other. It is not possible to know what is proper to discuss with another party without also knowing the identity of the other party. If only one party learns the identity of the other, it is always possible for an imposter to masquerade as the unknown party.

There are a couple of points to make about this issue. The first is what "learn" means. The kind of learning needed for session establishment is the creation of common knowledge: You know both identities, the peer knows both identities, and the peer knows you know both identities (and vice versa). A lower level of knowledge always enables opportunities for subverting the session establishment protocol.

The second point is what an identity is. Identities in session establishment protocols work differently than they do in real life. In session establishment, an identity is a commitment to a key that identifies you or your computing system. That is, an identity commits its sender to utilizing a particular key during session establishment, and the receiver to reject protocol messages generated using other keys.

Key Secrecy

Second, session establishment techniques seek to establish a session key that can be maintained as a secret between the two parties and is known to no one else. The session key must be independent from all other keys for all other session instances and indeed from all other keys. This implies that no adversary with limited computational resources can distinguish the key from one selected uniformly at random. Generating such an independent session key is both harder and easier than it sounds; it is always possible to do so if a preexisting relationship already exists between the two communicating parties, and it is impossible to do so reliably if a preexisting relationship does not exist. Relationships begat other relationships, and nonrelationships are sterile with respect to the technology.

Session State Consistency

Finally, the parties need to establish a consistent view of the session state. This means that they both agree on the identities of both parties; they agree on the session key instance; they agree on the encryption and forgery detection schemes used, along with any associated state such as sequence counters and replay windows; and they agree on which instance of communication this session represents. If they fail to agree on a single shared parameter, it is always possible for an imposter to convince one of the parties that it is engaged in a conversation that is different from its peer's conversation. As with identities, agree means the two establish common knowledge of all of these parameters, and

a session establishment protocol can be considered secure in the Dolev–Yao model only if the protocol proves that both parties share common knowledge of all of the parameters.

Mutual Authentication

There are an enormous number of ways to accomplish the mutual authentication function needed to initiate a new session. Here we examine two approaches that are used in various protocols within the Internet.

A Symmetric Key Mutual Authentication Method

Our old friend the message authentication code can be used with a static, long-lived key to create a simple and robust mutual authentication scheme. Earlier we stressed that the properties of message authentication are incompatible with the use of a static key to provide forgery detection of session-oriented messages. The incompatibility is due to the use of sequence numbers for replay detection. We will replace sequence numbers with unpredictable quantities in order to resocialize static keys. The cost of this resocialization effort will be a requirement to exchange extra messages.

Suppose parties A and B want to mutually authenticate. We will assume that ID_A is B's name for the key it shares with A, whereas ID_B is A's name for the same key B. We will also assume that A and B share a long-lived message authentication key K and that K is known only to A and B. We will assume that A initiates the authentication. A and B can mutually authenticate using a three-message exchange, as follows: For message 1, A generates a random number R_A and sends a message containing its identity ID_A and random number to B:

$$A \rightarrow B: ID_A, R_A \qquad (13.1)$$

The notation $A \rightarrow B: m$ means that A sends message m to B. Here the message being passed is specified as ID_A, R_A, meaning it conveys A's identity ID_A (or, more precisely, the name of the key K) and A's random number R_A. This message asserts B's name for A, to tell B which is the right long-lived key it should use in this instance of the authentication protocol. The random number R_A plays the role of the sequence number in the session-oriented case. It is random in order to provide an unpredictable challenge. If B responds correctly, then this proves that the response is live and was not prerecorded. R_A also acts as a transaction identifier for the response to A's message 1 (it allows A to recognize which response goes with which message 1). This is important in itself, because without the ability to interleave different instances of the protocol A would have to wait forever for any lost message in order to obtain a correct theory.

If B is willing to have a conversation with A at this time, it fetches the correct message authentication key K, generates its own random number R_B, and computes a message authentication code tag T over the message ID_B, ID_A, R_A, R_B, that is, over the message consisting of both names and both random numbers. B appends the tag to the message, which it then sends to A in response to message 1:

$$B \rightarrow A: \text{ID}_B, \text{ID}_A, R_A, R_B, T \qquad (13.2)$$

B includes A's name in the message to tell A which key to use to authenticate the message. It includes A's random number R_A in the message to signal the protocol instance to which this message responds.

The magic begins when A validates the message authentication code tag T. Since independently generated random numbers are unpredictable, A knows that the second message could not have been produced before A sent the first, because it returns R_A to A. Since the authentication code tag T was computed over the two identities ID_B and ID_A and the two random numbers R_A and R_B using the key K known only to A and B, and since A did not create the second message itself, A knows that B must have created message 2. Hence, message 2 is a response from B to A's message 1 for this instance of the protocol. If the message were to contain some other random number than R_A, A would know the message is not a response to its message 1.

If A verifies message 2, it responds by computing a message authentication code tag T' computed over ID_A and B's random number R_B, which it includes in message 3:

$$A \rightarrow B: \text{ID}_A, R_B, T' \qquad (13.3)$$

Reasoning as before, B knows A produced message 3 in response to its message 2, because message 3 could not have been produced prior to message 2 and only A could have produced the correct tag T'. Thus, after message 3 is delivered, A and B both have been assured of each other's identity, and they also agree on the session instance, which is identified by the pair of random numbers R_A and R_B.

A deeper analysis of the protocol reveals that message 2 must convey both identities and both random numbers protected from forgery by the tag T. This construction binds A's view of the session with B's, and this is providing A with B's view of what they know in common. This binding prevents interleaving or man-in-the-middle attacks. As an example, without this binding, a third party, C, could masquerade as B to A and as A to B. Similarly, message 3 confirms the common knowledge: A knows that B knows that A knows ID_A, ID_B, R_A, and R_B if B verifies the third message; similarly, if B verifies message 3, B knows that A knows that B knows the same parameters.

It is worth noting that message 1 is not protected from either forgery or replay. This lack of any protection is an intrinsic part of the problem statement. During the protocol, A and B must transition from a state where they are unsure about the other's identity and have no communication instance instantiating the long-term relationship signified

by the encryption key K to a state where they fully agree on each other's identities and a common instance of communication expressing their long-lived relationship. A makes the transition upon verifying message 2, and there are no known ways to reassure it about B until this point of the protocol. B makes the state transition once it has completed verification of message 3. The point of the protocol is to transition from a mutually suspicious state to a mutually trusted state.

An Asymmetric Key Mutual Authentication Method

Authentication based on asymmetric keys is also possible. In addition to asymmetric encryption, there is also an asymmetric key analog of a message authentication code called a signature scheme. Just like a message authentication code, a signature scheme consists of three operations: key generate, sign, and verify. The key generate operation outputs two parameters, a signing key S and a related verification key V. S's key holder is never supposed to reveal S to another party, whereas V is meant to be a public value. Under these assumptions, the sign operation takes the signing key S and a message M as input parameters and outputs a signature s of M. The verify operation takes the verification key V, message M, and signature s as inputs, and returns whether it verifies that s was created from S and M. If the signing key S is indeed known by only one party, the signature s must have been produced by that party. This is because it is infeasible for a computationally limited party to compute the signature s without S. Asymmetric signature schemes are often called public/private key schemes because S is maintained as a secret, never shared with another party, whereas the verification key is published to everyone.

Signature schemes were invented to facilitate authentication. To accomplish this goal, the verification key must be public, and it is usually published in a certificate, which we will denote as $\text{cert}(\text{ID}_A, V)$, where ID_A is the identity of the key holder of S and V is the verification key corresponding to A. The certificate is issued by a well-known party called a certificate authority. The sole job of the certificate authority is to introduce one party to another. A certificate $\text{cert}(\text{ID}_A, V)$ issued by a certificate authority is an assertion that entity A has a public verification key V that is used to prove A's identity.

As with symmetric authentication, hundreds of different authentication protocols can be based on signature schemes. The following is one example among legions of examples:

$$A \rightarrow B: \text{cert}(\text{ID}_A, V), R_A \qquad (13.4)$$

Here $\text{cert}(\text{ID}_A, V)$ is A's certificate, conveying its identity ID_A and verification key V; R_A is a random number generated by A. If B is willing to begin a new session with A, it responds with the message:

$$B \rightarrow A: \text{cert}(ID_B, V'), R_B, R_A \text{ sig}_B(ID_A, R_B, R_A) \quad (13.5)$$

R_B is a random number generated by B, and $\text{sig}_B(ID_A, R_B, R_A)$ is B's signature over the message with fields ID_A, R_B, and R_A. Including ID_A under B's signature is essential because it is B's way of asserting that A is the target of message 2. Including R_B and R_A in the information signed is also necessary to defeat man-in-the-middle attacks. A responds with a third message:

$$A \rightarrow B: \text{cert}(ID_A, V), R_b, \text{sig}_B(ID_B, R_B) \quad (13.6)$$

A Caveat

Mutual authentication is necessary to establish identities. Identities are needed to decide on the access control policies to apply to a particular conversation, that is, to answer the question, Which information that the party knows is suitable for sharing in the context of this communications instance? Authentication—mutual or otherwise—has very limited utility if the communications channel is not protected against eavesdropping and forgeries.

One of the most common mistakes made by Wi-Fi hotspot operators, for instance, is to require authentication but disable eavesdropping and forgery protection for the subsequent Internet access via the hotspot. This is because anyone with a Wi-Fi radio transmitter can access the medium and hijack the session from a paying customer. Another way of saying this is that authentication is useful only when it's used in conjunction with a secure channel. This leads to the topic of session key establishment. The most common use of mutual authentication is to establish ephemeral session keys using the long-lived authentication keys. We will discuss session key establishment next.

Key Establishment

Since it is generally infeasible for authentication to be meaningful without a subsequent secure channel, and since we know how to establish a secure channel across the Internet if we have a key, the next goal is to add key establishment to mutual authentication protocols. In this model, a mutual authentication protocol establishes an ephemeral session key as a side effect of its successful operation; this session key can then be used to construct all the encryption and authentication keys needed to establish a secure channel. All the session states, such as sequence number, replay windows, and key identifiers, can be initialized in conjunction with the completion of the mutual authentication protocol.

It is usually feasible to add key establishment to an authentication protocol. Let's illustrate this with the symmetric key authentication protocol, based on a message authentication code, discussed previously. To extend the protocol to establish a key, we suppose instead that A and B share two long-lived keys K and K'. The first key K is a message authentication key as before. The second key K' is a derivation key, the only function of which is to construct other keys within the context of the authentication protocol. This is accomplished as follows: After verifying message 2 (from line 2 previously), A computes a session key SK as:

$$SK \leftarrow \text{prf}(K', R_A, R_B, ID_A, ID_B, \text{length}) \quad (13.7)$$

Here prf is another cryptographic primitive called a pseudorandom function. A pseudorandom function is characterized by the properties that (1) its output is indistinguishable from random by any computationally limited adversary and (2) it is hard to invert; that is, given a fixed output O, it is infeasible for any computationally limited adversary to find an input I so that $O \leftarrow \text{prf}(I)$. The output SK of Eq. (13.7) is length bits long and can be split into two pieces to become encryption and message authentication keys. B generates the same SK when it receives message 3. An example of a pseudorandom function is any block cipher, such as AES, in cipher-block chaining MAC mode. CBC MAC mode is just like CBC mode, except all but the last block of encrypted data is discarded.

This construction meets the goal of creating an independent, ephemeral set of encryptions of message authentication keys for each session. The construction creates independent keys because any two outputs of a prf appear to be independently selected at random to any adversary that is computationally limited. A knows that all the outputs are statistically distinct, because A picks the parameter to the prf R_A randomly for each instance of the protocol; similarly for B. And using the communications instances identifiers R_A, R_B along with A and B's identities ID_A and ID_B are interpreted as a "contract" to use SK only for this session instance and only between A and B.

Public key versions of key establishment based on signatures and asymmetric encryption also exist, but we will close with one last public key variant based on a completely different asymmetric key principle called the Diffie—Hellman algorithm.

The Diffie—Hellman algorithm is based on the discrete logarithm problem in finite groups. A group G is a mathematical object that is closed under an associative multiplication and has inverses for each element in G. The prototypical example of a finite group is the integers under addition modulo a prime number p.

The idea is to begin with an element g of a finite group G that has a long period. This means $g^1 = g$, $g^2 = g \times g$, $g^3 = g^2 \times g$, ... Since G is finite, this sequence must eventually repeat. It turns out that $g = gn + 1$ for some integer $n > 1$, and $gn = e$ is the group's neutral element. The element e has the property that $h \times e = e \times h = h$ for every element h

in G, and n is called the period of g. With such an element it is easy to compute powers of g, but it is hard to compute the logarithm of gk. If g is chosen carefully, no polynomial time algorithm is known that can compute k from gk. This property leads to a very elegant key agreement scheme:

$$A \to B: \text{cert}(\text{ID}_A, V), g^a$$
$$B \to A: g^b, \text{cert}(\text{ID}_B, V'), \text{sig}_B(g^a, g^b, \text{ID}_A)$$
$$A \to B: \text{sig}_A(g^b, g^a, \text{ID}_B)$$

The session key is then computed as $SK \leftarrow \text{prf}(K, g^a g^b, \text{ID}_A, \text{ID}_B)$, where $K \leftarrow \text{prf}(0, g^{ab})$. In this protocol, a is a random number chosen by A, b is a random number chosen by B, and 0 denotes the all zeros key. Note that A sends g^a unprotected across the channel to B.

The quantity g^{ab} is called the Diffie–Hellman key. Since B knows the random secret b, it can compute $g^{ab} = (g^a)b$ from A's public value g^a, and similarly A can compute g^{ab} from B's public value g^b. This construction poses no risk because the discrete logarithm problem is intractable, so it is computationally infeasible for an attacker to determine a from g^a. Similarly, B may send g^b across the channel in the clear, because a third party cannot extract b from g^b. B's signature on message 2 prevents forgeries and assures that the response is from B. Since no method is known to compute g^{ab} from g^a and g^b, only A and B will know the Diffie–Hellman key at the end of the protocol. The step $K \leftarrow \text{prf}(0, g^{ab})$ extracts all the computational entropy from the Diffie–Hellman key. The construction $SK \leftarrow \text{prf}(K, g^a g^b, \text{ID}_A, \text{ID}_B)$ computes a session key, which can be split into encryption and message authentication keys as before.

The major drawback of Diffie–Hellman is that it is subject to man-in-the-middle attacks. The preceding protocol uses signatures to remove this threat. B's signature authenticates B to a and also binds g^a and g^b together, preventing man-in-the-middle attacks. Similarly, A's signature on message 3 assures B that the session is with A.

These examples illustrate that it is practical to construct session keys that meet the requirements for cryptography, if a long-lived relationship already exists.

State Consistency

We have already observed that the protocol specified in Eqs. (13.1) through (13.3) achieves state consistency when the protocol succeeds. Both parties agree on the identities and on the session instance. When a session key SK is derived, as in Eq. (13.7), both parties also agree on the key. Determining which parties know which pieces of information after each protocol message is the essential tool for a security analysis of this kind of protocol. The analysis of this protocol is typical for authentication and key establishment protocols.

Finally, allowing Internet access in the workplace can create two challenges: ensuring employee efficiency and mitigating security risks. Since you can't simply take away Internet privileges, you must find a way to boost employee

productivity while maintaining Internet security. So, with the preceding in mind, because of the frequency of poor security practices or far-too-common security failures on the Internet, let's briefly look at the importance of the process that is used to gather all of these faults into an Internet security checklist and give them a suitable solution.

4. INTERNET SECURITY CHECKLIST

Internet security is a fast-moving challenge and an ever-present threat. There is no one right way to secure a website, and all security methods are subject to instant obsolescence, incremental improvement, and constant revision. All public facing websites are open to constant attack. So, are you willing and able to invest the time it takes to administer a dynamic, 24×7, world-accessible, database-driven, interactive, user-authenticated Website? Do you have the time and resources to respond to the constant flow of new Internet security issues? The following high-level checklist helps to answer the preceding questions and addresses a number of far-too-common security failures on the Internet (see checklist: An Agenda for Action in Selecting Internet Security Process Activities.

An Agenda for Action in Selecting Internet Security Process Activities

The following high-level checklist should be addressed in order to find the following Internet security practices helpful (check all tasks completed):

_____**1.** Login pages should be encrypted.

_____**2.** Data validation should be done server-side.

_____**3.** Manage your Website via encrypted connections.

_____**4.** Use strong, cross-platform compatible encryption.

_____**5.** Connect from a secured network.

_____**6.** Don't share login credentials.

_____**7.** Prefer key-based authentication over password authentication.

_____**8.** Maintain a secure workstation.

_____**9.** Use redundancy to protect the Website.

_____**10.** Make sure you implement strong security measures that apply to all systems—not just those specific to Web security.

_____**11.** Validate logins trough SSL encryption.

_____**12.** Do not use clear text protocols to manage your server.

_____**13.** Implement security policies that apply to all systems.

---

5. SUMMARY

This chapter examined how cryptography is used on the Internet to secure protocols. It reviewed the architecture of the Internet protocol suite, for even the meaning of what security means is a function of the underlying system architecture. Next it reviewed the Dolev–Yao model, which describes the threats to which network communications are exposed. In particular, all levels of network protocols are completely exposed to eavesdropping and manipulation by an attacker, so using cryptography properly is a first-class requirement to derive any benefit from its use. We learned that effective security mechanisms to protect session-oriented and session establishment protocols are different, although they can share many cryptographic primitives. Cryptography can be very successful in protecting messages on the Internet, but doing so requires preexisting, long-lived relationships. How to build secure open communities is still an open problem; it is probably an intractable question because a solution would imply the elimination of conflict between human beings who do not know each other.

Finally, let's move on to the real interactive part of this chapter: review questions/exercises, hands-on projects, case projects, and optional team case project. The answers and/or solutions by chapter can be found in the online Instructor's Solutions Manual.

CHAPTER REVIEW QUESTIONS/ EXERCISES

True/False

1. True or False? The Internet was designed to create standardized communication between computers.
2. True or False? Since communication is an extremely complex activity, it should come as no surprise that the system components providing communication decompose into modules.
3. True or False? Practical solutions addressing Byzantine failures fall largely within the purview of platform rather than network architecture, although the interconnectivity topology is an important consideration.
4. True or False? Security analyses of systems traditionally begin with a model of the user.
5. True or False? A user can eavesdrop on a communications medium by connecting a receiver to the medium.

Multiple Choice

1. The Internet supports message exchange through a mechanism called:
   A. Interfaces
   B. Send primitive
   C. Protocols
   D. Confirm primitive
   E. Listen primitive
2. A minimal communications service interface requires the following four primitives, except which one?
   A. Send

   B. Clear
   C. Confirm
   D. Listen
   E. Receive
3. A report of diagnostic and performance information about underlying communications is known as a:
   A. Send primitive
   B. Confirm primitive
   C. Shift cipher
   D. Status primitive
   E. Deliver primitive
4. What is technically not part of the Internet architecture per se?
   A. PHY Layer
   B. Chi-square statistic
   C. Polyalphabetic cipher
   D. Kerckhoff's principle
   E. Unicity distance
5. What is a request/response protocol designed to determine the reachability of another IP address?
   A. Traceroute
   B. Chi-square test
   C. Statistical test
   D. Ping
   E. Destination unreachable

EXERCISE

Problem

How would an organization go about deciding an authentication strategy?

Hands-On Projects

Project

How would an organization go about deciding an authorization strategy?

Case Projects

Problem

When should an organization use message security versus transport security?

Optional Team Case Project

Problem

With regard to a Microsoft-based Internet security system, how would an organization go about using its existing Active Directory infrastructure?

Chapter 14

The Botnet Problem

Nailah Mims

Bright Horizons, Burlington, MA, United States

1. INTRODUCTION

Billions of computers, mobile devices, network appliances, and other equipment that support a variety of information systems communicate through and store data within cyberspace. The National Institute of Standards and Technology (NIST) defines cyberspace as "A global domain within the information environment consisting of the interdependent network of information systems infrastructures including the Internet, telecommunications networks, computer systems, and embedded processors and controllers" [1].

While there are many advantages with respect to the proliferation of devices, easy access to data or information, and such a high level of connectedness, opportunities for the misuse and exploitation of cyberspace and its assets present significant challenges particularly with respect to privacy and security. One of the serious problems affecting cyberspace and its users is the spread of malicious software, also called malware. This chapter will discuss the problem presented by one type of malware in particular called a bot and the extensive botnets which are formed when many bots work together to facilitate cyber-attacks on cyberspace entities.

2. WHAT IS A BOTNET?

A bot is "an automated malware program that scans blocks of network addresses and infects vulnerable computers" [2]. This malware is usually covertly delivered to a host and the bot installed so that it can communicate with a server typically positioned outside of the host's network and run by an attacker. The code is designed to hijack small parts of the machine's resources in order to open communications channels to the attacker's machine, spread to different hosts, and accomplish other clandestine tasks. Collectively, all computers or devices that have been infected by a bot,

along with a machine or machines run by an attacker that act as a central command center, or command and control server that issue commands to the bots, are known as a botnet.

To set up a botnet, an attacker must install or trick a user into installing malicious bot-code to run their computing devices. There are several ways of accomplishing this. The most common approach is by sending a user compromised website links, embedding bot malware in legitimate looking software programs to be downloaded by unsuspecting users in a Trojan horse, or including infected attachments in an email that also appears to be from a reputable entity in a phishing attack. A botnet can be leveraged through the attacker's control to execute a variety of cyber-attacks, in particular, by flooding targeted networks and devices with too much traffic and stealing data from hosts infected with the bots: "Once the botnet is in place, it can be used in distributed denial of service (DDoS) attacks, proxy and spam services, malware distribution, and other organized criminal activity. Botnets can also be used for covert intelligence collection, and terrorists or state-sponsored actors could use a botnet to attack Internet-based critical infrastructure" [2]. Furthermore, as additional machines are infected, these computers and any command and control systems run by the attacker find themselves unwitting members of a botnet that may consist of a few scores of machines or a few million from around the globe.

3. BUILDING A BOTNET

A botnet consists of several key components: the attacker(s) and their command and control computers (c2); a bot and its associated malware and delivery or spreading mechanism; the hosts, also known as zombie machines on which the bot resides; the botnet's purpose; and the communications mechanisms between the infected hosts and the attacker's c2 machines.

The Attacker and Their Command and Control (C2)

The attacker's C2 computer is usually far removed from the security perimeter of a targeted individual or organization while the infected hosts reside on the internal network. It is the central system to which all of the bots report and respond according to whatever instructions are issued. An attacker, who is typically looking to exploit cyberspace and a target's cyberspace assets and data will use the C2 machine to commandeer the hosts that are infected with the bots and instruct them, for instance to send large amounts of a data to another host or network, the latter being the final target. It's important to note, however, that this machine may or may not be the originator of the bot and its associated malware. In many cases, as we will see later, existing malware which already has been designed to steal credentials or log keystrokes has had its functionality modified to include connecting with a command and control server. Thus the C2 machine may not actually be involved in the initial delivery of the bot, since a user may have acquired it by unknowingly downloading the malware on their own.

Another note, which is important as we will see later in the chapter, is this machine is a chokepoint for the botnets. Once located, law enforcement agencies are able to dismantle botnets by taking down the c2 machine. Also, multiple C2 machines may be a part of a botnet which has implications for the persistence of the botnet, even after one server has been taken down.

The Bot Spreads

Setting up a botnet (Fig. 14.1) requires the attacker to install their bots on as many systems as possible. Delivery of the bots is usually accomplished by several direct or indirect methods which have some similarity to the same processes of information gathering, vulnerability exploitation and social engineering tactics an attacker uses to otherwise hack into an organization's network or system. One method of delivery involves pairing the bot with other software, which looks legitimate, a type of malicious code known as a Trojan horse, in order to trick the user into installing the code. The software may be sent to the user via a phishing email and attachment, or may be posted on a compromised website and the user sent the link so once they click on it, the bot is downloaded. Alternatively, attackers may design the bot as a virus or a worm, both types of malware that propagated from machine to machine either automatically or via human intervention. The virus or worm may take advantage of a vulnerability that impacts a particular operating systems or application and thus spread the bots in that manner. In this situation and that of the Trojan horse, an attacker will repurpose existing malware that has been released for a particular vulnerability and modify it with a bot or additional functionality to establish a connection back to the command and control server.

Once the bot is installed on a host, users may inadvertently spread the bots, by forwarding infected e-mails and attachments for instance, or the bots may spread by their built in propagation mechanisms, usually a virus or worm which may scan for additional machines to infect on its own. Each bot in turn establishes a connection out of the target's network across the Internet and back to a command and control (c2) system run by the attacker and depending on the botnet, the other bots.

Hosts/Zombie Machines on Which the Bot Resides

All malicious software associated with the bot will quietly run on the host system until called upon by the command machine, or until discovered and cleaned from the system. The many hosts or zombie machines on which a bot resides represents a significant challenge in resolving botnet problems, given the number of potential hosts are in the millions and potentially billions. It is estimated that over 3 billion people, a significant number that is approaching half of the world's population, are Internet users [3]. Each of these users access the Internet with one or multiple devices and any device with an Internet connection can potentially be a host for a bot. Cisco Systems, Inc. estimates there will be 50 billion devices connected to the Internet by 2020 which has ominous implications for the spread of bots and the increasing size of the botnets they form [4].

The evolution of technology and cyberspace, has seen the rise of the Internet of Things (IoT) (Fig. 14.2), where everything from GPS devices, commercial and industrial systems such as heating, ventilation, and air conditioning (HVAC), household appliances, vehicles, and ever-present mobile devices are now not only attached to the Internet, but also communicate among each other and in some cases executing software programs to do so [4]. The other side of these "things" becoming hosts due to their connection to the Internet is that they may also now become targets.

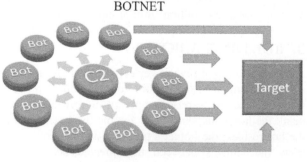

BOTNET

FIGURE 14.1 Botnet overview.

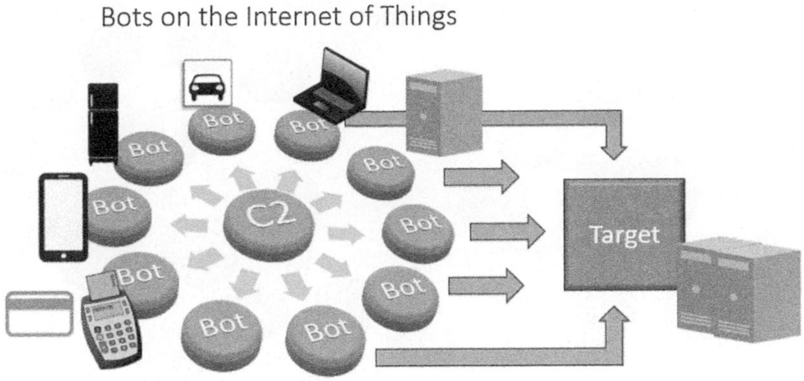

Bots on the Internet of Things

FIGURE 14.2 Botnets and the Internet of Things.

The aforementioned could be infected with bots recruited to attack other industrial systems, appliances, and machines connected to the Internet, as we will see in the next section, to devastating effect. These varied and prolific cyberspace as hosts or targets present global implications for the botnet threat and security operations.

The Botnet's Purpose

A bot, in and of itself, is not necessarily harmful provided the user installs it voluntarily and the bot does what is advertised. For instance, Internet Relay Chat (IRC) and Twitter, which will be discussed in greater detail later, are common applications that make use of bot-like methods to establish and manage communications among many users and their devices. Both require users to download clients or bots and form a network among the hosts with the bots and the communications and channels established are managed by centralized servers. However, like many of the capabilities cyberspace affords and has been noted previously, bot and botnet technology also has many less innocuous uses.

Like with many unauthorized cyberspace activities, a botnet can be set up by a variety of attackers with a variety of motives. The major purposes botnets are built for fall under financial gain, theft of information, or launching denial-of-service (DoS) attacks. The bots may be designed to act autonomously or at the command of the command and control system, and can be tasked to do a variety of things like monitor a user's activities on a computer, steal data, and send it to the attacker's system, capture credentials as users log into portals from their host machines, or even just stay dormant until called by the attacker's systems.

Criminals, can use bot networks to perpetrate fraud—both financial and identity theft—by designing malware that extracts sensitive personal information or the financial data and having it sent to the C2 machine for further exploitation. Attackers can use information gather to pilfer

funds directly, open unauthorized accounts, and if the bots manage to make their way on payment card machines, extract credit card numbers. As they spread, bots may collect sensitive information such as the keys user press as they use their device, monitor the applications they open, web browsing history, credit card information, and user names and passwords. "It can also imitate a legitimate website to lure you into revealing your sensitive information" [5].

DDoS attacks, in which bots installed on many hosts are directed to aim and then send a large amount of traffic to flood and overwhelm a target's cyberspace assets are a significant threat posed by botnets. In this case, the hosts are secondary targets recruited for the attack on a primary target. There are a variety of different flooding techniques that go by names such as pings of death, TCP Flood, Smurf, and Fraggle attacks; but the implications of an attacker not just using a single machine to generate large amounts of data (as what was done in the past, but using multiple machines to do so, as in the case with a botnet) will have significant greater effects in what has been termed an amplified DoS (Fig. 14.3). The overwhelming nature of this type of attack presents is another significant part of the problem with botnets.

Bots Communications

Like many of the cyber-based tools that use Internet technologies and protocols to enhance communication between systems and facilitate information transfer, the setup and implementation of a botnet is usually done through the misappropriation of a communication protocol. Botnets can hijack and repurpose communication and connectivity mechanisms in IRC, HTTP, or take advantage peer-to-peer (P2P) communications in which machines are able to talk directly to each other.

"IRC provides a way of communicating in real time with people from all over the world. It consists of various separate networks (or 'nets') of IRC servers, machines that

Botnet

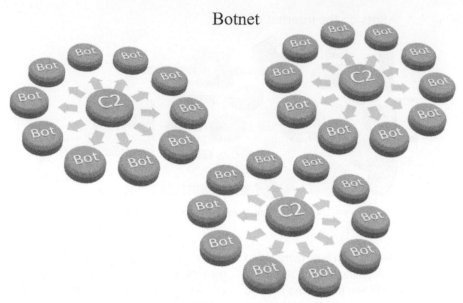

FIGURE 14.3 Botnets amplified.

allow users to connect to IRC. IRC is very similar to text messaging, but designed around communicating with large groups of users instead of one on one" [6]. Furthermore it works on a client–server network model whereby IRC clients connect to an IRC server which in turn connects to other IRC servers to expand the IRC network. In the same way, an attacker will build their botnet with hosts and with one or multiple command and control servers. "You run a client program on your own computer which connects you to a server computer on the Internet. These servers link to many other servers to make up an IRC network, which transport messages from one user (client) to another. In this manner, people from all over the world can talk to each other live and simultaneously" [7].

One key component of IRC are IRC bots. These are a set of scripts or an independent program that connects to IRC as a client, and so appears to other IRC users as another user: "A typical use of bots in IRC is to provide IRC services or a specific functionality within a channel such as to host a chat-based game or provide notifications of external events." However some IRC bots can be used to launch malicious attacks of questionable intent such as DoS, spamming, or exploitation. Additionally, IRC Scripts can be written to flood the IRC network or to generate a flood of activity from the hosts (Fig. 14.4).

There are a variety of protocols and applications that can facilitate the spread of bots in a botnet. You may have noticed that IRC sounds similar to the chat and instant messenger functions integrated in many social networking applications. Indeed, Twitter is remarkably similar to IRC, and its Twitter bots "are, essentially, computer programs that tweet of their own accord. While people access Twitter through its Website and other

clients, bots connect directly to the Twitter mainline, parsing the information in real time and posting at will" [8]. Like IRC, the open-ended and autonomous channels that comprise Twitter make it similarly susceptible to manipulation by bots [6].

4. THE PROBLEM WITH BOTNETS

Using a single computer an attacker can do significant damage to a target's operations, impacting everything from reputation, finances, and ability to perform its mission. Information stolen can include sensitive or confidential files and credentials for any applications and websites a user may have visited. Damages can include disruption of a target's web presence and DoS for critical applications and core hardware devices. Attackers using botnets can recruit thousands, even millions of unsuspecting hosts from around the world in order to accomplish the same and with even greater consequences to the security of data and viability of the infrastructure on which so much of the data relies. One example of the impact of this scenario is what is called an amplified DDoS attack. This type of attack takes the normal methods of a DDoS and multiplies the effect due to the number of hosts that can be recruited to accomplish these attacks [9].

With the spread of devices being able to talk to one another and set up persistent channels of communication, and in addition to their exposure to the Internet and thus vulnerable to malware, botnets have grown to have significant implications for IoT. As mentioned previously, these devices may be either commandeered as a host for a bot or the primary target of botnet activity. Furthermore, the implications for other social media and the automated

IRC

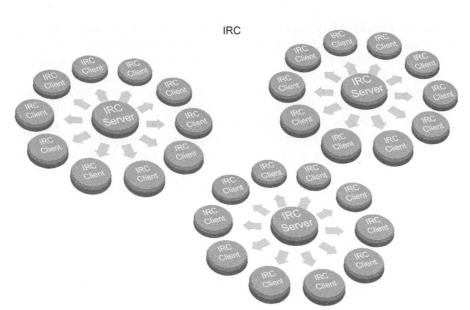

FIGURE 14.4 Internet Relay Chat (IRC) overlay.

functionality that is built into many cyberspace applications make it easy for attackers to pivot users into supporting a botnet and use botnets in their cyber-attacks.

Bots and botnets may thus be used as stand-alone attacks or can be blended with other attack vectors to accomplish malicious activity in cyberspace on behalf of the botnet commander. Click fraud, spam marketing, DDoS, keylogging, and the harvest of credentials and bank account info are popular applications for botnet offenses. Also, like many cyber tools, bots and botnets are available for sale on the darker areas of Internet. Criminals can purchase botnet software and even purchase the services of established botnets, groups of computers that have already been compromised as zombies, to be used to accomplish their nefarious aims.

Botnets could also be useful in a new category of cyber-based attack called an Advanced Persistent Threat (APT). In these attacks, attackers seek to gain access to and then reside on a targeted network for an extended period of time. Additionally, once inside, they move from machine to machine looking for confidential data or other sensitive systems to access and then send stolen information to the attackers undetected over a long period of time. NIST defines the advanced persistent threat as "an adversary that possesses sophisticated levels of expertise and significant resources that allow it to create opportunities to achieve its objectives … [which] … typically include establishing and extending footholds within the information technology infrastructure of the targeted organizations for purposes of exfiltrating information, undermining or impeding critical aspects of a mission, program, or organization; or positioning itself to carry out these objectives in the future (NIST SP800-39).

So, while APTs are typically considered the domain of the more sophisticated and technically advanced hacker groups such as nation-state agencies, a single or small group of attackers could use a botnet to facilitate an APT, which, as has been noted in previous sections, has many of the same characteristics.

We have discussed IRC and Twitter as two applications which can be used by botnets, but botnets can also use other Internet communications mechanisms to spread and communicate with an attacker's c2 system. Botnets may also be built to take advantage of P2P networking. P2P networks comprise of multiple computers that are "connected and share resources without going through a separate server computer … [and] can be an ad hoc connection … [or] permanent infrastructure that links a half-dozen computers in a small office over" [10]. Since these networks eliminate the need for central servers, all computers are able to communicate and share resources as equals and again we can note comparative functionality. Furthermore, given that music file sharing, instant messaging, and other popular applications rely on P2P technology and have been integrated with many web applications in particular, these represent additional avenues for the establishment of botnets. Also problematic are the autonomous functionalities that characterize bots, botnets, and the applications they use, which are often enabled by default. This adds to the challenge of actually guarding against the spread of bots, even as antivirus and antimalware programs are increasingly able to detect the associated malware.

Detecting bots and botnets is straightforward unless they attempt to obfuscate their tracks by opening up legitimately looking channels or similar methods that appear to be legitimate. Antivirus/antimalware, scanning, and logging technologies can identify, block, and remove malware and capture unauthorized connections between computers that are indicative of botnet activity. Furthermore, as we will see in the case studies, disrupting a botnet can be accomplished by seizing the C2 server, or servers that are chokepoints and thus the botnets' weakest link. The characteristic persistent nature of the bots, however, make taking down the expansive botnets they form a significant effort. The case studies in the next section present one

example of the international effort required to dismantle an established botnet and also showcase the familiar challenges of attribution, which is common to other types of cyber-attacks. Furthermore, once the C2 machines are taken down the tens or hundreds of thousands unsuspecting zombie machines must be cleaned of the bot infections, and unaffected machines must be protected in order to prevent the botnet from spreading further (see checklist: "An Agenda For Action For Preventing Botnet Activities").

An Agenda for Action for Preventing Botnet Activities

In order to provide a timely, comprehensive, relevant, and accurate Internet communication security strategy, the following set of preventative botnet activities must be adhered to (check all tasks completed):

Botnet Incident Handler Communications and Facilities

_____1. **Contact information: This includes** phone numbers and email addresses for team members and others within and outside the organization (primary and backup contacts) who may have helpful information, such as antivirus vendors and other incident response teams.

_____2. **On-call information is used** for other teams within the organization, including escalation information.

_____3. **Pagers or cell phones that are** to be carried by team members for off-hour support, onsite communications.

_____4. **Alternate Internet access method which is used** for finding information about new threats, downloading patches and updates, and reaching other Internet-based resources when Internet access is lost during a severe botnet incident.

_____5. **War room is used** for central communication and coordination; if a permanent war room is not necessary, the team should create a procedure for procuring a temporary war room when needed.

Botnet Incident Analysis Hardware and Software

_____6. **Laptops,** which provide easily portable workstations for activities such as analyzing data and sniffing packets.

_____7. **Spare workstations, servers, and networking equipment**, which may be used for trying out botnets in an isolated environment. If the team cannot justify the expense of additional equipment, perhaps equipment in an existing test lab could be used, or a virtual lab

could be established using operating system (OS) emulation software.

_____8. **Blank media,** such as CDs and flash drives, for storing and transporting botnet samples and other files as needed.

_____9. **Packet sniffers and protocol analyzers that are used** to capture and analyze network traffic that may contain botnet activity.

_____10. **Up-to-date, trusted versions of OS executables and analysis utilities, which are** stored on flash drives or CDs, to be used to examine systems for signs of botnet infection (antivirus software, spyware detection and removal utilities, system administration tools, forensics utilities).

Botnet Incident Analysis Resources

_____11. **Port lists** that include commonly used ports and known Trojan horse and backdoor ports.

_____12. **Documentation** for OSs, applications, protocols, and antivirus and intrusion detection signatures.

_____13. **Network diagrams and lists of critical assets,** such as web, email, and File Transfer Protocol (FTP) servers.

_____14. **Baselines** of expected network, system, and application activity.

Botnet Incident Mitigation Software

_____15. **Media,** which includes OS boot disks and CDs, flash drives, OS media, storage media, and application media.

_____16. **Security patches** from OS and application vendors.

_____17. **Disk imaging software and backup images** of OS, applications, and data stored on secondary media.

---

5. BOTNET CASE STUDIES AND KNOWN BOTNETS

In this section we will go over some known instances of established botnets, the crimes they facilitated, and their dismantling by law enforcement agencies. It will largely focus on the recent takedown of the Gameover Zeus botnet

to illustrate many of the characteristics of botnets we have discussed. It will also highlight the challenges faced by security professionals and law enforcement to dismantle what are essentially large unauthorized networks and apprehend the attackers who run the C2 systems that serve as the focal point for their operation and crimes. It is also of note that by all accounts, these bots were created by taking an existing piece of malware, modifying or extending its functionality so it could connect to other computers, setting up a communication with a C2 machine, and sustaining those connections over a period of time primarily for data exfiltration and DoS.

Gameover Zeus

The Gameover Zeus botnet components included legacy malware, a Trojan horse, the bots, and some iterations of a new type of malware called ransomware. Ransomware is just what it sounds like: once a host is infected, the malware will encrypt the files and then an attacker will demand a fee for decryption. Several reports note the bot infections began showing up in 2011, with the virus portion of the botnet, the Trojan horse called Gameover Zeus, having its origins around 2007. The original malware program was designed to be installed on a machine and steal its credentials and the most common targets for this program were banking and other financial institutions [11].

Gameover Zeus included a botnet kit in which users were sent a spam email that contained compromised and spoofed URLs in a tactic known as phishing. When they clicked on the URLs, their computers were infected with the bot and they became another host in the botnet. As later reported by Shadowserver, who is dedicated to researching and dismantling of botnets: "It had become widely distributed and has been used for financial crimes targeting several hundred different banks — both by stealing ordinary credentials and also in real-time hijacking of bank accounts. However, it can also be used for activities as diverse as malware dropping, DDoS attacks, stealing Bitcoins or theft of Skype and other online service credentials" [11].

This botnet ultimately spread across the global cyberspace with over 1 million computers estimated to have been infected, and with the ransomware component included, netted the criminals tens of millions of dollars before being disrupted in 2014 by a global law enforcement effort [12]. A significant portion of their intake came from the ransomware which is called CryptoLocker. As reported: "On Monday June 2nd 2014, the US Department of Justice announced an ongoing operation to take down the infamous Gameover Zeus and CryptoLocker cyber-crimal botnet infrastructures. 'Operation Tovar' was the name given to the joint effort between international law enforcement agencies, such as the FBI, UK NCA and Europol/EC3, plus multiple private partners" [13]. The operation aimed to take down the c2 servers and identify the masterminds behind it, and the investigation discovered the botnet was attributed to a network of cyber criminals with the aim of financial theft. The bots in this case stole credentials and personal and financial information.

Other Botnets

Another example of a botnet is the case attributed to a single attacker whose bot installed adware on vulnerable machines. It was estimated that his botnet attacked more than 400,000 computers in a two-week period, and it was reported to have crippled the network at Seattle's Northwest Hospital in January 2005, shutting down an intensive care unit and disabling doctors' pagers. The botnet also shut down computers at the US Department of Justice, which suffered damage to hundreds of computers worldwide in 2004 and 2005 [14].

One high-profile cyber-attack that was thought perpetrated by botnets occurred in 2014, when Sony PlayStation was severely impacted by a DoS attack thought to be launched by attackers taking advantage of Sony's PlayStation Network. The network is described as " an online service that connects PlayStation 3 and PlayStation 4 video game consoles to the Internet and to over-the-top video services such as Netflix" [15]. In other words, the game consoles were the devices that essentially hosted a bot to facilitate the connections.

Another example is a botnet that has been given the name Pushdo, which in 2010 apparently targeted several government agencies and companies including the CIA, FBI, PayPal, Yahoo, and Twitter. This botnet "Pushdo is using a fake SSL header in the communications sent from the infected zombies to its own command and control server" and attempts to cover its tracks by "sending a flurry of connections to legitimate Web sites could be designed to make sure the command and control server doesn't stand out" [16]. Furthermore, it downloaded different Trojans onto infected machines and has been used to send spam as part of the Cutwail spambot, according to Stewart [16]. This botnet is comprised of about 300,000 infected PCs, and the operators, believed to be located in Eastern Europe, were leasing out its usage to criminals. Interestingly, and pointing to the reuse or repurposing of existing malware, the Gameover Zeus botnet used the same Cutwail spambot to establish its botnet as well.

The case of the Pushdo botnet was one that extended beyond the usual financial motives [17]. This botnet was determined to be a portion of an ongoing case where hacktivists launched DoS attacks against several companies that had publicly cut ties with WikiLeaks. While some groups of activists joined the bot effort voluntarily, reports indicate that thousands of other unwitting machines were recruited for the effort. Furthermore, with respect to the spreading mechanism, "the botnet infects computers via peer-to-peer file sharing systems, but it can spread via Microsoft Messenger and USB sticks." The reports found the PayPal and MasterCard websites were targeted and taken down as a result. This was a critical blow to two entities who rely on their websites as the primary component of their payment processing business.

FIGURE 14.5 Internet Storm Center (ISC) threat map.

PayPal was also targeted by a botnet in 2007 when an attacker used bot-installed host computers to harvest user names, passwords, and financial information. In that case the bot-herder deployed bots to over 250,000 unsuspecting hosts and then spied on the users to capture their credentials as they visited websites such as PayPal. They then used the information to remove victims' funds from their accounts. According to the online publication eWeek, "This was the first time that someone has been charged under the US federal wiretap statute for conduct relating to botnets" [18].

These are just a few examples of real-world botnets to illustrate the nature of the threat. There are ongoing investigations as new botnets are established and there are several organizations that track worldwide botnet activity. One of these is the Internet Storm Center (ISC), which, per its website, "provides a free analysis and warning service to thousands of Internet users and organizations, and is actively working with Internet Service Providers to fight back against the most malicious attackers." Accordingly they manage a map that shows the most recent 30 days of Internet threat activity around the globe. One of the threat categories tracked includes botnet activity on an interactive map posted at https://isc.sans.edu/threatmap.html (Fig. 14.5).

6. SUMMARY

In this chapter, we covered what a bot and botnet is, how they are established, and the problems they pose. A bot is a piece of code created by an attacker designed to infect a target's

machine and perform/respond to whatever commands are sent by the C2 system. We have seen how there are two core problems with botnets: the Internet of many hosts which can all be recruited for or targeted by the botnet, and the fact that individual or small groups of attackers are less limited by the capabilities of their own machines. We saw how simple communications technologies and protocols are ideal carriers for botnets and how the proliferation of these technologies which have been integrated into social media and other applications makes the problems of botnets one that will not go away soon. Essentially, we've seen how technologies that open channels between many users and automatically install scripts or mini programs can be tweaked to install malicious software onto the machines of thousands of unsuspecting users and thus form a botnet. Lastly, we also discussed case studies of real world botnets and the efforts by law enforcement to take them down.

Finally, let's move on to the interactive part of this Chapter: review questions/exercises, hands-on projects, case projects, and optional team case project. The answers and/or solutions by chapter can be found in Appendix K.

CHAPTER REVIEW QUESTIONS/ EXERCISES

True/False

1. True or False? A botnet is a collection of compromised Internet computers being controlled remotely by attackers for malicious and legal purposes.

2. True or False? The person controlling a botnet is known as the botmaster or bot-herder.
3. True or False? Centralized botnets use a double entity (a host or a small collection of hosts) to manage all bot members.
4. True or False? The attacker exploits a vulnerability in a running service to automatically gain access and install his software without any user interaction.
5. True or False? After infection, the bot starts up for the first time and attempts to contact its C&C server(s) in a process known as waiting.

Multiple Choice

1. A collection of compromised Internet computers being controlled remotely by attackers for malicious and illegal purposes is known as a:
   A. Malware
   B. Spyware
   C. Botmaster
   D. Botnet
   E. Bot-herder
2. The botmaster develops his/her bot software, often reusing existing code and adding custom features. This is known as:
   A. Infection
   B. Rallying
   C. Creation
   D. Waiting
   E. Executing
3. Once a victim machine becomes infected with a bot, it is known as a:
   A. Vampire
   B. Werewolf
   C. Ghost
   D. Succubus
   E. Zombie
4. After infection, the bot starts up for the first time and attempts to contact its C&C server(s) in a process known as:
   A. Infection
   B. Creation
   C. Rallying
   D. Waiting
   E. Executing
5. Having joined the C&C network, the bot waits for commands from the botmaster. This is known as:
   A. Infection
   B. Creation
   C. Rallying
   D. Executing
   E. Waiting

EXERCISE

Problem

On a Wednesday morning, a new worm is released on the Internet. The worm exploits a Microsoft Windows vulnerability that was publicly announced 3 weeks before, at which time patches were released. The worm spreads itself through two methods: emailing itself to all addresses that it can locate on an infected host and identifying and sending itself to hosts with open Windows shares. The worm is designed to generate a different attachment name for each copy that it mails; each attachment has a randomly generated filename that uses one of over a dozen file extensions. The worm also chooses from more than 200 email subjects and a similar number of email bodies. When the worm infects a host, it gains administrative rights and attempts to download a DDoS agent from different Internet Protocol (IP) addresses using File Transfer Protocol (FTP). The number of IP addresses providing the agent is unknown. Although the antivirus vendors quickly post warnings about the worm, it spreads very rapidly, before any of the vendors have released signatures. The organization has already incurred widespread infections before antivirus signatures become available 4 h after the worm started to spread. What questions should the botnet incident response team be asking?

Hands-On Projects

Project

On a Monday night, one of the organization's network intrusion detection sensors alerts on a suspected outbound DDoS activity involving a high volume of Internet Control Message Protocol (ICMP) pings. The intrusion analyst reviews the alerts; although the analyst cannot confirm that the alerts are accurate, they do not match any known false positives. The analyst contacts the botnet incident response team so that it can investigate the activity further. Because the DDoS activity uses spoofed source IP addresses, it takes considerable time and effort to determine which host or hosts within the organization are producing it; meanwhile, the DDoS activity continues. The investigation shows that eight servers appear to be generating the DDoS traffic. Initial analysis of the servers shows that each contains signs of a DDoS rootkit. What questions should the botnet incident response team be asking?

Case Projects

Problem

On a Saturday afternoon, several users contact the help desk to report strange popup windows and toolbars in their web browsers. The users' descriptions of the behavior are similar, so the help desk agents believe that the users' systems have been affected by the same thing, and that the most likely cause is web-based malicious mobile code. What questions should the botnet incident response team be asking?

Optional Team Case Project

Problem

Shortly after an organization adopted a new instant messaging platform, its users are hit with a widespread botnet attack that propagates itself through the use of instant messaging. Based on the initial reports from security administrators, the attack appears to be caused by a worm. However, subsequent reports indicate that the attacks also involve web servers and web clients. The instant messaging and web-based attacks appear to be related to the worm because they display the same message to users. What questions should the botnet incident response team be asking?

REFERENCES

[1] NIST Special Publication 800-53 Revision 4, Security and Privacy Controls for Federal Information Systems and Organizations. Joint Task Force Transformation Initiative, April 2013. http://nvlpubs.nist.gov/nistpubs/SpecialPublications/NIST.SP.800-53r4.pdf.

[2] FBI News Blog, Botnets 101—What They Are and How to Avoid Them, 2013. Retrieved from: http://www.fbi.gov/news/news_blog/botnets-101/botnets-101-what-they-are-and-how-to-avoid-them.

[3] Number of internet users 2005—2015 | Statistic, n.d. Retrieved from: http://www.statista.com/statistics/273018/number-of-internet-users-worldwide/.

[4] Internet of Things (IoT), n.d. Retrieved from: http://www.cisco.com/web/solutions/trends/iot/overview.html.

[5] Microsoft, TrojanSpy:Win32/Hesperbot.A, 2015. Retrieved from: https://www.microsoft.com/security/portal/threat/encyclopedia/entry.aspx?Name=TrojanSpy:Win32/Hesperbot.A.

[6] D. Caraballo, J. Lo, The IRC Prelude, 2014. Retrieved from: http://www.irchelp.org/irchelp/new2irc.html.

[7] R. Van Loon (1991) & J. Lo (1997, 2004), An IRC Tutorial. Retrieved from: http://www.irchelp.org/irchelp/irctutorial.html.

[8] R. Dubbin, The Rise of Twitter Bots, The New Yorker, 2013. Retrieved from: http://www.newyorker.com/tech/elements/the-rise-of-twitter-bots.

[9] R. Lemos, Amplified DDoS Attacks Increasingly Use Network Time Service, 2014. Retrieved from: http://www.eweek.com/security/amplified-ddos-attacks-increasingly-use-network-time-service.html.

[10] J. Cope, Computerworld | Peer-to-peer Network, 2002. Retrieved from: http://www.computerworld.com/article/2588287/networking/peer-to-peer-network.html.

[11] The Shadowserver Foundation, Gameover Zeus & Cryptolocker, 2014. Retrieved from: https://goz.shadowserver.org/ & http://blog.shadowserver.org/2014/06/08/gameover-zeus-cryptolocker/.

[12] M. Cooney, Network World | FBI: Operation Bot Roast Finds Over 1 Million Botnet Victims, 2007. Retrieved from: http://www.networkworld.com/article/2291381/lanwan/fbi—operation-bot-roast-finds-over-1-million-botnet-victims.html.

[13] FBI, GameOver Zeus Botnet Disrupted. Collaborative Effort Among International Partners, 2014. Retrieved from: http://www.fbi.gov/news/stories/2014/june/gameover-zeus-botnet-disrupted/.

[14] J.P. Menezes, Why We're Losing the Botnet Battle, 2007. Retrieved from: http://www.networkworld.com/article/2293116/lan-wan/why-we-re-losing-the-botnet-battle.html.

[15] W. Wei, Sony PlayStation Network Taken Down by DDoS Attack, 2014. Retrieved from: http://thehackernews.com/2014/08/sony-playstation-network-taken-down-by_24.html.

[16] E. Mills, Botnet Sends Fake SSL Pings to CIA, PayPal, Others, 2010. Retrieved from: http://www.cnet.com/news/botnet-sends-fake-ssl-pings-to-cia-paypal-others/#!.

[17] R. McMillan, MasterCard, PayPal Reap Botnet Payback Siege for Shunning WikiLeaks, 2010. Retrieved from: http://www.itbusiness.ca/news/mastercard-paypal-reap-botnet-payback-siege-for-shunning-wikileaks/15758.

[18] L. Vaas, Botnet Herder Pleads Guilty to Massive PayPal Scam, 2007. Retrieved from: http://www.eweek.com/c/a/Security/Botnet-Herder-Pleads-Guilty-to-Massive-PayPal-Scam.

Chapter 15

Intranet Security

Bill Mansoor

Information Security Office County of Riverside, Mission Viejo, CA, United States

Headline dramas such as the ones shown in the accompanying sidebar (Intranet Security as News in the Media) (in the mainstream media) are embarrassing nightmares to top brass in any large corporation. These events have a lasting impact on a company's bottom line because the company's reputation and customer trust take a direct hit. Once events such as these occur, customers and current and potential investors never look at the company in the same trusting light again, regardless of remediation measures. The smart thing, then, is to avoid the limelight. The onus of preventing such embarrassing security gaffes falls squarely on the shoulders of the information technology (IT) security chiefs (chief information security officer and security officers), who are sometimes hobbled by unclear mandates from government regulators and a lack of sufficient budgeting to tackle the mandates.

Intranet Security as News in the Media

- "State department contract employees fired, another disciplined for looking at passport file"[1]
- "Laptop stolen with a million customer data records"[2]
- "eBayed [virtual private network] VPN kit hands over access to council network"[3]
- "[Employee] caught selling personal and medical information about ... [Federal Bureau of Investigation] agent to a confidential source ... for $500"[4]
- "Data thieves gain access to TJX through unsecured wireless access point"[5]

1. Jake Tapper, and Radia Kirit, "State Department Contract Employees Fired, Another Disciplined for Looking at Passport File," ABCnews.com, March 21, 2008, http://abcnews.go.com/Politics/story?id=4492773&page=1.
2. Laptop security blog, Absolute Software, http://blog.absolute.com/category/real-theft-reports.
3. John Leyden, "eBayed VPN Kit Hands over Access to Council Network," theregister.co.uk, September 29, 2008, www.theregister.co.uk/2008/09/29/second_hand_vpn_security_breach.
4. Bob Coffield, "Second Criminal Conviction under HIPAA," Health Care Law Blog, March 14, 2006, http://healthcarebloglaw.blogspot.com/2006/03/second-criminal-conviction-under-hipaa.html.
5. "TJX Identity Theft Saga Continues: 11 Charged with Pilfering Millions of Credit Cards," Networkworld.com magazine, August 5, 2008, www.networkworld.com/community/node/30741?nwwpkg = breaches? ap1 = rcb.

However, federal governments across the world are not taking breaches of personal data lightly (see sidebar: TJX: Data Breach With 45 Million Data Records Stolen). In view of a massive plague of publicized data thefts over the past decade, mandates such as the Health Insurance Portability and Accountability Act (HIPAA), Sarbanes–Oxley, and the Payment Card Industry–Data Security Standard (PCI-DSS) Act within the United States have teeth. These laws even spell out stiff fines and personal jail sentences for chief executive officers who neglect data breach issues.

TJX: Data Breach With 45 Million Data Records Stolen

The largest-scale data breach in history occurred in early 2007 at TJX, the parent company for the TJ Maxx, Marshalls, and HomeGoods retail chains.

In the largest identity-theft case ever investigated by the US Department of Justice, 11 people were convicted of wire fraud. The primary suspect was found to perpetrate the intrusion by wardriving and taking advantage of an unsecured Wi-Fi access point to get in and set up a "sniffer" software instance to capture credit card information from a database.

Although the intrusion was earlier believed to have taken place from May 2006 to January 2007, TJX later found that it took place as early as July 2005. The data compromised included portions of credit and debit card transactions for approximately 45 million customers.[6]

6. "The TJX Companies, Inc. Updates Information on Computer Systems Intrusion," February 21, 2007, www.tjx.com/Intrusion_Release_email.pdf.

As seen in the TJX case, intranet data breaches can be a serious issue, affecting a company's goodwill in the open marketplace as well as spawning class action lawsuits.[7] Gone are the days when intranet security was a superficial

7. "TJX Class Action Lawsuit Settlement Site," The TJX Companies, Inc., and Fifth Third Bancorp, Case No. 07–10,162, www.tjxsettlement.com.

exercise; security inside the firewall was all but nonexistent. There was a feeling of implicit trust in the internal user. After all, if you hired that person, training him for years, how could you not trust him?

In the new millennium, the Internet has come of age, and so have its users. The last largely computer-agnostic generation has exited the user scene; their occupational shoes have been filled with the X and Y generations. Many of these young people have grown up with the Internet, often familiar with it since elementary school. It is common today to find young college students who started their programming interests in the fifth or sixth grade.

With such a level of computer expertise in users, the game of intranet security has changed (see sidebar: Network Breach Readiness: Many Are Still Complacent). Resourceful as ever, these new users have gotten used to the idea of being hyperconnected to the Internet using mobile technology such as personal digital assistants (PDAs), smartphones, and firewalled barriers. For a corporate intranet that uses older ideas of employing access control as the cornerstone of data security, such mobile access to the Internet at work needs careful analysis and control. The idea of building a virtual moat around your well-constructed castle (investing in a firewall and hoping to call it an intranet) is gone. Hyperconnected "knowledge workers" with laptops, PDAs, and universal serial bus (USB) keys that have whole operating systems built in have made sure of it.

Network Breach Readiness: Many Are Still Complacent

The level of readiness for breaches among IT shops across the country is still far from optimal. The Ponemon Institute, a security think tank, surveyed some industry personnel and came up with some startling revelations. It is hoped that these statistics will change in the future:

- A total of 85% of industry respondents reported that they had experienced a data breach.
- Of those responding, 43% had no incident response plan in place and 82% did not consult legal counsel before responding to the incident.
- After a breach, 46% of respondents still had not implemented encryption on portable devices (laptops or PDAs) with company data stored on them.[8]

8. "Ponemon Institute Announces Result of Survey Assessing the Business Impact of a Data Security Breach," May 15, 2007, www.ponemon.org/press/Ponemon_Survey_Results_Scott_and_Scott_FINAL1.pdf.

If we could reuse the familiar vehicle advertising tagline of the 1980s, we would say that the new intranet is no longer "your father's intranet." The intranet as just a simple place to share files and list a few policies and procedures has ceased to be. The types of changes can be summed up in the following list of features, which shows that the intranet has become a combined portal as well as a public dashboard. Some of the features include:

- a searchable corporate personnel directory of phone numbers by department. Often the list is searchable only if the exact name is known
- expanded activity guides and a corporate calendar with links for various company divisions
- several Really Simple Syndication (RSS) feeds for news according to divisions such as IT, human resources (HR), finance, accounting, and purchasing
- company blogs (weblogs) by top brass that talk about the current direction of the company in reaction to recent events, a sort of "mission statement of the month"
- a search engine for searching company information, often helped by a search appliance from Google. Microsoft also has its own search software on offer that targets corporate intranets
- one or several "wiki" repositories for company intellectual property, some of which is of a mission-critical nature. Usually granular permissions are applied for access here. One example could be court documents for a legal firm with rigorous security access applied
- a section describing company financials and other mission-critical indicators. This is often a separate Web page linked to the main intranet page
- a "live" section with IT alerts regarding specific downtimes, outages, and other critical time-sensitive company notifications. Often embedded within the portal, this is displayed in a "ticker-tape" fashion or similar to an RSS-type dynamic display

Of course, this list is not exhaustive; some intranets have other unique features not listed here. In any case, intranets these days do a lot more than simply list corporate phone numbers.

Knowledge management systems have presented another challenge to intranet security postures. Companies that count knowledge as a prime protected asset (virtually all companies these days) have started deploying "mashable" applications (apps) that combine social networking (such as FaceBook and LinkedIn), texting, and microblogging (such as Twitter) features to encourage employees to "wikify" their knowledge and information within intranets. One of the bigger vendors in this space, Socialtext, has introduced a mashable wiki app that operates like a corporate dashboard for intranets.[9,10]

---

9. James Mowery, "Socialtext Melds Media and Collaboration," cmswire.com, October 8, 2008, www.cmswire.com/cms/enterprise-20/socialtext-melds-media-and-collaboration-003270.php.

10. Rob Hof, "Socialtext 3.0: Will Wikis Finally Find Their Place in Business?" Businessweek.com magazine, September 30, 2008, www.business-week.com/the_thread/techbeat/archives/2008/09/socialtext_30_i.html.

Socialtext has individual widgets, one of which, "Social-text signals," is a microblogging engine. In the corporate context, microblogging entails sending Short Message Service (SMS) messages to apprise colleagues of recent developments in the daily routine. Examples could be short messages on progress on any major project milestone: for example, joining up major airplane assemblies or getting Food and Drug Administration testing approval for a special experimental drug.

These emerging scenarios present special challenges to security personnel guarding the borders of an intranet. The border as it once existed has ceased to be. One cannot block stored knowledge from leaving the intranet when most corporate mobile users are accessing intranet wikis from anywhere using inexpensive mininotebooks that are given away with cell phone contracts.[11]

If we consider the impact of national and international privacy mandates on these situations, the situation is compounded further for C-level executives in multinational companies who have to come up with responses to privacy mandates in each country in which the company does business. Privacy mandates regarding private customer data have always been more stringent in Europe than in North America, which is a consideration for doing business in Europe.

It is hard enough to block entertainment-related Flash video traffic from time-wasting Internet abuse without blocking a video of last week's corporate meeting at headquarters. Letting in traffic only on an exception basis becomes untenable or impractical because of a high level of personnel involvement needed for every ongoing security change. Simply blocking YouTube.com or Vimeo.com is not sufficient. Video, which has myriad legitimate work uses nowadays, is hosted on all sorts of content-serving (caching and streaming) sites worldwide, which makes it well near impossible to block using Web filters. The evolution of the Internet Content Adaptation Protocol (ICAP), which standardizes website categories for content-filtering purposes, is under way. However, ICAP still does not solve the problem of the dissolving networking "periphery."[12]

Guarding movable and dynamic data, which may be moving in and out of the perimeter without notice, flouting every possible mandate, is a key feature of today's intranet. The dynamic nature of data has rendered the traditional confidentiality, integrity, and availability (CIA) architecture somewhat less relevant. The changing nature

of data security necessitates some specialized security considerations:

- Intranet security policies and procedures (P&Ps) are the first step toward a legal regulatory framework. The P&Ps needed on any of the security controls listed subsequently should be compliant with federal and state mandates (such as HIPAA, Sarbanes–Oxley, European Directive 95/46/EC on the protection of personal data, and PCI-DSS, among others). These P&Ps have to be signed off by top management and placed on the intranet for review by employees. There should be sufficient teeth in all procedural sections to enforce the policy, explicitly spelling out sanctions and other consequences of noncompliance, leading up to discharge.
- To be factual, none of these government mandates spell out details on implementing any security controls. That is the vague nature of federal and international mandates. Interpretation of the security controls is better left after the fact to an entity such as the National Institute of Standards and Technology (NIST) in the United States or the Geneva-based International Organization for Standardization (ISO). These organizations have extensive research and publication guidance for any specific security initiative. Most of NIST's documents are offered as free downloads from its website.[13] ISO security standards such as 27,002–27,005 are also available for a nominal fee from the ISO site.

Once finalized, P&Ps need to be automated as much as possible (one example is mandatory password changes every 3 months). Automating policy compliance takes the error-prone human factor out of the equation (see sidebar: Access Control in the Era of Social Networking). Numerous software tools are available to help accomplish security policy automation.

1. SMARTPHONES AND TABLETS IN THE INTRANET

The proliferation of mobile devices for personal and business use has gained an unprecedented momentum, which only reminds one of the proliferation of personal computers (PCs) at the start of the 1980s. Back then, the rapid proliferation of PCs was rooted in the wide availability of common PC software and productivity packages such as Excel or Borland. Helping with kids' homework and spreadsheets at home was part of the wide appeal.

A large part of the PC revolution was also rooted in the change in interactivity patterns. Interaction using graphical

11. Matt Hickey, "MSI's 3.5G Wind 120 Coming in November, Offer Subsidized by Taiwanese Telecom," Crave.com, October 20, 2008, http://news.cnet.com/8301-17938_105-10070911-1.html?tag=mncol;title.
12. Network Appliance, Inc., RFC Standards white paper for Internet Content Adaptation Protocol (ICAP), July 30, 2001, www.content-networking.com/references.html.
13. National Institute of Standards and Technology, Computer Security Resource Center, http://csrc.nist.gov/.

Access Control in the Era of Social Networking

In an age in which younger users have grown up with social networking sites as part of their digital lives, corporate intranet sites are finding it increasingly difficult to block them from using these sites at work. Depending on the company, some are embracing social networking as part of their corporate culture; others, especially government entities, are actively blocking these sites. Detractors mention as concerns wasted bandwidth, lost productivity, and the possibility of infections with spyware and worms.

However, blocking these sites can be difficult because most social networking and video sites such as Vimeo and YouTube can use port 80 to vector Flash videos into an intranet, which is wide open for Hypertext Transfer Protocol access. Flash videos have the potential to provide a convenient Trojan horse for malware to get into the intranet.

To block social networking sites, one needs to block either the social networking category or the specific URLs (such as YouTube.com) for these sites in the Web-filtering proxy appliance. Flash videos are rarely downloaded from YouTube itself. More often a redirected caching site is used to send in the video. The caching sites also need to be blocked; this is categorized under Content Servers.

user interfaces (GUIs) and mice had made PCs widely popular compared with the Disk Operating System (DOS) character screen. The consumer PC revolution did not really take off until Windows PCs and Mac Classics brought along mice, starting in the early 1990s. It was a quantum leap for ordinary people unfamiliar with DOS commands.

Today, which some now call the post-PC era,[14] the interaction between people and computers has again evolved. The finger (touch) has again replaced keyboards and mice as an input device in smartphones and tablets, which invariably use a mobile-oriented operating system (OS) such as Android or iOS, as opposed to MAC OS, Linux, or Windows. Android and iOS were built from the ground up with the "touch interface" in mind.

This marks a sea change.[15] By the next couple of years, most smartphones will end up with the computing power of a full-size PC that is only 5 years older. These powerful smartphones and portable tablets (such as iPads and Android devices) enabled with multimedia and gaming capabilities are starting to converge toward becoming one and the same device. The increasing speed and functionality for the price ("bang for the buck") will only gather a

more rapid pace as user demand becomes more intense. The success of smartphones and tablet devices over traditional full-size laptops stems from two primary reasons:

1. **the functionality and ease of use of using** "voice," "gesture," **and** "touch" **interfaces.** As opposed to the use of mice and keyboards, voice-enabled, touch, and gesture-based interfaces used in mobile devices offer a degree of ease unseen in traditional laptops.
2. **the availability of customized apps (applications).** Given the number of specialized apps found in the Apple App Store (and Android's equivalent "market"), they offer increased versatility for these new mobile devices compared with traditional laptops. In Apple's case, the closed ecosystem of apps (securely allowed only after testing for security) decreases the possibility of hacking iPads using uncertified apps.

In iPhone 4s, the use of "Siri" as a speech-aware app only portends the increasing ease of use for this class of device.[16] Using Siri, the iPhone can be issued voice commands to set appointments, read back messages, and notify people if one is going to be late, among a myriad other things, all without touching a keypad. In the Android version 4.0 or higher, face recognition authentication using the onboard camera is also an ease-of-use feature. There are bugs in these applications, of course, but they indisputably point to a pattern of interactivity change compared with a traditional laptop. There are a few other trends to watch in the integration of mobile devices in the enterprise:

1. Mobile devices let today's employees stretch work far beyond traditional work hours. Because of rich interactivity and ease of use, these devices blur the boundary between work and play. Companies benefit from this employee availability at nontraditional work hours. The very concept of being at work has changed compared with even 10 years ago.
2. The iteration life cycles of mobile devices are now more rapid. Unlike laptops that had life cycles of almost 3 years, new version of the iPad comes out almost every year with evolutionary changes. This makes it increasingly less feasible for IT to set standardization for mobile devices or even pay for them. IT is left in most cases with supporting these devices. However, IT can put in recommendations about which device it is able or unable to support for feasibility reasons.
3. Because of these cost reasons, it is no longer feasible for most IT departments to dictate the brand or platform of

14. Ina Fried, "Steve Jobs: Let the Post-PC Era Begin," CNET News, June 1, 2010, http://news.cnet.com/8301-13860_3-20006442-56.html?tag=content;siu-container.

15. Associated Press, "Apple Describes Post-PC Era, Surprise of Success," March 7, 2012, http://news.yahoo.com/apple-describes-post-pc-era-surprise-success-212613625.html.

16. "Siri—Your Wish Is Its Command," http://www.apple.com/iphone/features/siri.html.

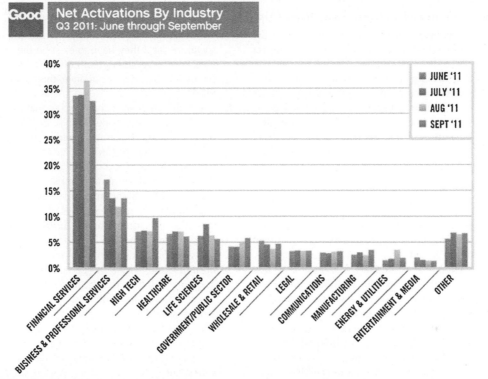

FIGURE 15.1 Net activation by industry. *From http://i.zdneMt.com/blogs/zdnet-good-technology-ios-survey-1.jpg?tag=content;siu-container.*

mobile device that employees use to access the corporate network. It is often a Bring Your Own Device situation. As long as specialized software can be used to partition the personally owned mobile device to store company data safely (which cannot be breached), this approach is feasible.

4. The mobile device that seems to be numerically most ready for the enterprise is the same one that has been the most successful commercially, the Apple iPad. Already in its third iteration in 2012 since the first one came out in 2010, the iPad 3 with its security and VPN features seems to be ready to be managed by most mobile device management (MDM) packages. It has been adopted extensively by executives and sales staff at larger corporate entities.[17] It is also starting to be adopted by state and local government to expedite certain e-government initiatives.[18]

5. Compared with the Apple iPhone, however, Android smartphones generally have had better adoption rates. BlackBerry adoption, however, is on the wane.[19] Smartphones will need to have more specially designed Web pages to cope with interactivity on a smaller screen.

6. According to a major vendor in the MDM space ("Good Technology"), the financial services sector saw the highest level of iPad (iOS) activation, accounting for 46% for the third quarter in 2011, which tripled the amount of activation in any other industry (Fig. 15.1).[20]

When it comes to mobile devices (see sidebar: The Commoditization of Mobile Devices and Impact Upon Businesses and Society) and smartphones, one can reasonably surmise that the act of balancing security versus business considerations has clearly tilted toward the latter. The age of mobile devices is here, and IT has to adapt security measures to conform to it. The common IT security concept of protecting the host may have to convert to protecting the network from itinerant hosts.

17. Rachel King, "SAP CIO Bussman on Tablets and Mobile Strategy for Enterprise," September 19, 2011, http://www.zdnet.com/blog/btl/sap-cio-bussman-on-tablets-and-mobile-strategy-for-enterprise/58247.

18. "BetterHealthChannel—iPhoneandiPadMobileApplication,"Retrieved March 19, 2012, http://www.egov.vic.gov.au/victorian-government-resources/government-initiatives-victoria/health-and-community-victoria/health-victoria/better-health-channel-iphone-and-ipad-mobile-application.html.

19. Brad Reed, "iOS vs. Android vs. BlackBerry OS vs. Windows Phone," Retrieved November 2, 2011, http://www.networkworld.com/news/2011/102011-tech-arguments-android-ios-blackberry-windows-252223.html.

20. Rachel King, "iPad Driving Massive Growth for iOS in Enterprise (Survey)," October 20, 2011, http://www.zdnet.com/blog/btl/ipad-driving-massive-growth-for-ios-in-enterprise-survey/61229?tag=content;siu-container.

The Commoditization of Mobile Devices and Impact Upon Businesses and Society

There are many increasingly visible trends that portend the commoditization of mobile devices and their resulting impact on businesses.

1. The millennial generation is more familiar with mobile technology. Because of the widespread use of smartphones and iPhones as communication devices for computing use (other than simply voice), and now iPads, which have taken their place, familiarity with mobile hardware is far higher than it was for previous generations. The technological sophistication of these devices has forced most of the current generation of young people to be far more tech savvy than previous generations because they have grown up around this mobile communication–enabled environment.

2. Mobile devices are eating into the sales of PCs and laptops. The millennial generation is no longer simply content with traditional bulky PCs and laptops as computing devices. Lightweight devices with pared-down mobile OSs and battery-efficient mobile devices with 10-h lives are quickly approaching the computing power of traditional computers and are also far more portable. The demands of lowered cost, immediacy, and ease of use of mobile devices have caused traditional laptop sales to slow in favor of tablet and iPad sales.

3. Social media use by mobile devices such as FaceBook, Twitter, and Flickr encourage collaboration and have given rise to use of these sites employing nothing other than mobile devices, whereas this was not possible previously. Most smartphones (even an increasingly common class of global positioning system–enabled point-and-shoot cameras) enable upload of images and videos to these sites directly from the device itself using Wi-Fi connections and Wi-Fi–enabled storage media (SD cards). This has engendered a mobile lifestyle for this generation, to which sites such as FaceBook, Twitter, and Flickr are only too happy to cater. Employees using social media represent new challenges to businesses because protection of business data (enforced by privacy-related federal and state regulations and mandates) has become imperative. Business data have

to be separated and protected from personal use of public social media if they have to exist on the same mobile device. Several vendors already offer products that enable this separation. In industry parlance, this area of IT is known as MDM.

4. The mobile hardware industry has matured. Margins have been pared to the bone. Mobile devices have become a buyers' market. Because of wider appeal, it is no longer just the tech savvy (opinion leaders and early adopters) who determine the success of a mobile product. It will be the wider swath of nontechie users looking for attractive devices with a standardized set of often-used functions that will determine the success of a product. Sooner than later, this will force manufacturers to compete based on price rather than product innovation. This downward pressure on price will also make it cost-effective for businesses to adopt these mobile devices within their corporate IT infrastructure. Amazon's Kindle and Barnes & Noble's Nook are both nimbly designed and priced at around a $200 price point compared with the $500 iPad. They have begun to steal some market share from full-featured tablets such as the iPad, but of course enterprise adoption for the cheaper devices remains to be sorted out.

5. Users expect the "cloud" to be personal. In their personal lives, users have become used to customizing their Internet digital persona by being offered limitless choices in doing so. In their use of the business "cloud," they expect the same level of customization. This customization can easily be built into the back end using the likes of Active Directory and collaboration tools such as Microsoft's SharePoint once a user authenticates through the VPN. Customization can be built upon access permissions in a granular manner per user while tracking their access to company information assets. This accumulated data trend can be used later to refine ease of use for remote users using the company portal.

In 2011, Apple shipped 172 million portable computing devices including iPads, iPods, and iPhones. Among these were 55 million iPads. The sales of mostly Android tablets by other manufacturers are also increasing at a rapid pace. By the end of the first decade of the new millennium, it became clear that sales of iPads and tablets made serious dents in the sale of traditional PCs, indicating a shift in consumer preference toward a rapid commoditization of computing. Fig. 15.2 from the Forrester Research consumer PC and Tablet forecast helps illustrate this phenomenon.[21]

Several reasons can be attributed to this shift. The millennial generation was already reinventing the idea of

how business is conducted, and where. Because of increased demands on employee productivity, business had to be conducted in real time at the employee's location (home, hotel, and airport) and not just at the traditional workplace. With gas prices hovering in the United States at around $5.00/gallon (essentially a doubling of prices over the first half-decade of the millennium), traditional 9-to-5 work hours with long commutes are no longer practical. iPads and tablets therefore had become de rigueur not only for field employees but also for workers at headquarters. Instead of imposing rigid 9-to-5 attendance on employees, progressive companies had to let employees be flexible in meeting sales or deliverables on their own deadlines, which improved employee morale and productivity.

Popular devices such as the iPad, Samsung Galaxy Android tablet, and many types of smartphones are already

21. Zack Whittaker, "One Billion Smartphones by 2016, Says Forrester," February 13, 2012, http://www.zdnet.com/blog/btl/one-billion-smartphones-by-2016-says-forrester/69279.

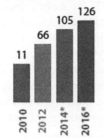
Mobile device adoption explodes

126
105
66
11

2010 2012 2014* 2016*

126 million tablets will be in use with US consumers by 2016.[†]

257 million smartphones will be in use with US consumers by 2016.[‡]

Mobile apps are a **$6.0 billion** market today, growing to **$55.7 billion** by 2015.[§]

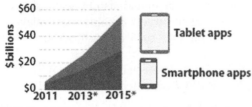

$60
$billions $40
$20
$0

2011 2013* 2015*

Tablet apps

Smartphone apps

FIGURE 15.2 Mobile device adaptation. *From http://i.zdnet.com/blogs/screen-shot-2012-02-13-at-173416.png.*

capable of accessing company intranets using customized intranet apps. This ensures that access to critical company data needed for a sale or demonstration will not stand in the way of closing an important deal. All this had already been enabled by laptops, but the touchpad-enabled tablet eases this process by using more functional media usage and richer interactivity features.

Ultimately, it will matter less what device employees use to access the company portal or where they are, because their identity will be the deciding factor regarding the information to which they will gain access. Companies will do better in providing customized "private cloud environments" for workers accessible from anywhere. Employees may still use PCs while at the office (see sidebar: Being Secure in the

---

Being Secure in the Post—Personal Computer Era

The post-PC era began with the advent of tablets such as iPads as enterprise mobile computing devices. Secure use of tablets in the enterprise presupposes a number of conditions:

1. **Back-end enterprise network infrastructure support has to be ready** and has to be strong to handle mobile devices interacting with Secure Sockets Layer (SSL) VPNs. Specifically, enterprises need to consider each device platform and their unique issues and idiosyncrasies in trying to connect using an SSL VPN. SSL (or Web) VPNs are preferred because IPSec and L2TP VPNs were not known to be easy to implement on mobile devices (especially Android tablets) as SSL VPNs. Point-to-Point Tunneling Protocol (PPTP) VPNs are dated and not known to have sufficient encryption and security compared with SSL VPNs.

Being Secure in the Post—Personal Computer Era—cont'd

2. **Testing of remote access scenarios such as VPNs is critical.** Client Apps for each supported platform (iOS, Android, and Windows Phone) against the existing or proposed VPN appliance will need to be tested thoroughly.
3. **This is fundamentally a new paradigm for delivering applications** (email, dashboards, and databases) to users. Starting with a practical and functional client App from ground zero will be a better philosophy than sticking to existing GUI ideas or concepts. Instead of pretty but nonfunctional interfaces, spare but well-tested and robust mobile interfaces will afford users time savings and efficiency to get their job done quicker. Once they are working reliably, additional functions can be added slowly to the app in successive versions.

Post—Personal Computer Era) and mobile devices while in the field conducting business, but they will increasingly demand the same degree of ease in accessing company data regardless of their location or the means used to access it. The challenge for IT will be to cater to these versatile demands without losing sight of security and protecting privacy.

2. SECURITY CONSIDERATIONS

Many risks need to be resolved when approaching intranet security with regard to mobile devices:

1. **risk of size and portability:** Mobile devices are prone to loss. An Apple staffer's "loss" of a fourth-generation iPhone to a Gizmodo staffer during a personal outing to a bar is well-known. There is no denying that, because of their size, smartphones are easy theft targets in the wrong place at the wrong time. Loss of a few hundred dollars of hardware, however, is nothing when an invaluable client list is lost and falls into a competitor's hands. These are nightmare scenarios that keep chief information officers (CIOs) up at night.
2. **risk of access** via **multiple paradigms:** Mobile devices can access unsafe sites using cellular networks and download malware into storage. The malware, in turn, can bypass the company firewall to enter the company network to wreak havoc. Old paradigms of security by controlling security using perimeter network access are no longer feasible.
3. **social media risks:** By definition, mobile devices are designed in such a way that they can easily access social media sites, which are the new target for malware-propagating exploits. Because they are personal devices, mobile media devices are much more at risk for getting exploits sent to them and being "pwned" (so to speak).

These issues can be approached and dealt with by using a solid set of technical as well as administrative controls:

1. **Establish a customized corporate usage policy for mobile devices.** This policy/procedure must be signed by new hires at orientation and by all employees who ask for access to the corporate VPN using mobile devices (even personal ones). Ideally this should be in the form of a contract and should be signed by the employee before a portion of the employee's device storage is partitioned for access and storage of corporate data. Normally, there should be yearly training highlighting the do's and don'ts of using mobile devices in accessing a corporate VPN. The first thing emphasized in this training should be how to secure company data using passwords and, if cost-effective, two-factor authentication using hardware tokens.

2. **Establish a policy for reporting theft or misplacement.** This policy should identify at the least how quickly one should report thefts of mobile devices containing company data and how quickly remote wipe should be implemented. The policy can optionally detail how the mobile devices feature (app) enabling location of the misplaced stolen device will proceed.

3. **Establish a well-tested SSL VPN for remote access.** Reputed vendors that have experience with mobile device VPN clients should be chosen. The quality, functionality, and adaptability of use (and proven reputation) of the VPN clients should be key in determining the choice of the vendor. The advantage of an SSL VPN compared with IPsec or L2TP for mobile use is well-known. The SSL VPNs should be capable of supporting two-factor authentication using hardware tokens. For example, Cisco's "Cisco AnyConnect Secure Mobility Client" and Juniper's "Junos Pulse App" are free app downloads available within the Apple iTunes App store. Other VPN vendors will have these apps available and they can be tested to see how smooth and functional the access process is.

4. **Establish inbound and outbound malware scanning.** Inbound scanning should occur for obvious reasons, but outbound scanning should also be scanned in case the company's email servers become spam relays and get blacklisted on sites such as Lashback or get blocked to external sites by force.

5. **Establish Wi-Fi Protected Access 2 (WPA2) encryption for Wi-Fi traffic access.** For now, WPA2 is the best encryption available compared with Wireless Equivalent Privacy (WEP) encryption, which is dated and not recommended.

6. **Establish logging metrics and granular controls.** Keeping regular tabs on information asset access by users and configuring alerting on unusual activity (such as large-scale access or exceeded failed-logon thresholds) is a good way to prevent data leakage.

Mobile devices accessing enterprise intranets using VPNs are subject to the same factors as any other device remotely accessing VPNs, namely (Fig. 15.3):

Deployment Scenario

The example depicts a typical deployment with a VPN server/concentrator as well as an authentication server controlling access to enterprise network services.

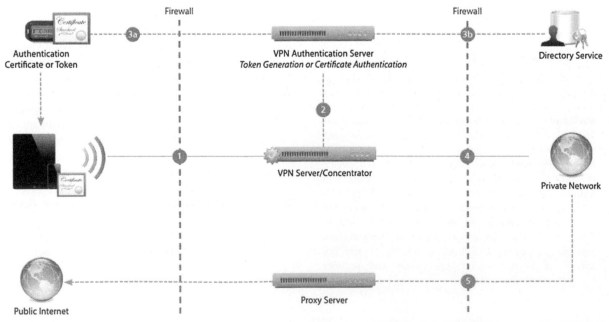

FIGURE 15.3   Mobile device virtual private network (VPN) access to company network using token authentication. *Courtesy: Apple Inc.*

1. protection of data while in transmission
2. protection of data while at rest
3. protection of the mobile device itself (in case it fell into the wrong hands)
4. app security

At a minimum, the following standards are recommended for managing tablets and smartphones with MDM appliances:

1. **protection of data while in transmission:** Transmission security for mobile devices is concerned primarily with VPN security as well as Wi-Fi security. With regard to VPNs, the primary preference for most mobile devices should be for Web-based or SSL VPNs. The reason is that IPsec and L2TP VPN implementations are still buggy as of this writing on all but iOS devices (iPhones and iPads). SSL VPNs can also be implemented as clientless. Regarding Wi-Fi, the choice is simply to configure WPA2 Enterprise using 128-bit Advanced Encryption Standard (AES) encryption for mobile devices connecting via Wi-Fi. Again, MDM appliances can be used to push out these policies to the mobile devices.

2. **protection of data while at rest:** The basis of protecting stored data on a mobile device is the password. The stronger the password is, the harder it is to break the encryption. Some devices (including the iPad) support 256-bit AES encryption. Most recent mobile devices also support remote wipe and progressive wipe. The latter feature will progressively increase the time of the lockout duration until finally initiating an automatic remote wipe of all data on the device. These wipe features are designed to protect company data from falling into the wrong hands. All of these features can be queried and are configurable for mobile devices via either Exchange ActiveSync policies or configuration policies from MDM appliances.

3. **protection of the mobile device:** Passwords for mobile devices have to conform to the same corporate "strong password" policy as for other wired network devices. This means the password length, content (minimum of eight characters, alphanumeric, special characters, etc.), password rotation and expiry (remember: last 3 and every 2–3 months), and password lockout (three to five attempts) have to be enforced. Complete sets of configuration profiles can be pushed to tablets, smartphones, and iPads using MDM appliances specifying app installation privileges, YouTube, and iTunes content ratings permissions, among many others.

4. **App security:** In both Android and iOS, significant changes have been made so that app security has become more bolstered. For example, in both OSs, apps run in their own silos and cannot access other app or system data. Although iPhone apps are theoretically capable of accessing the users' contact information and also their locations in some cases, Apple's signing process for every app that appears in the iTunes app store takes care of this. It is possible on the iOS devices to encrypt data using either software methods such as AES, RC4, 3DES, or hardware-accelerated encryption activated when a lockout occurs. In iOS, designating an app as managed can prevent its content from being uploaded to iCloud or iTunes. In this manner, MDM appliances or Exchange ActiveSync can prevent leakage of sensitive company data.

Although there are many risks in deploying mobile devices within the intranet, with careful configuration these risks can be minimized to the point where the myriad benefits outweigh the risks. One thing is certain: These mobile devices and the efficiency they promise are for real, and they are not going away.

Empowering employees is the primary idea in the popularity of these devices. Corporate IT will only serve its own interest by designing enabling security regarding these devices and letting employees be more productive.

3. PLUGGING THE GAPS: NETWORK ACCESS CONTROL AND ACCESS CONTROL

The first priority of an information security officer in most organizations is to ensure that there is a relevant corporate policy on access controls. Simple on the surface, the subject of access control is often complicated by the variety of ways the intranet is connected to the external world.

Remote users coming in through traditional or SSL (browser-based) VPNs, control over use of USB keys, printouts, and CD-ROMs all require that a comprehensive end-point security solution be implemented.

Past years have seen large-scale adoption of network access control (NAC) products in the midlevel and larger IT shops to manage end-point security. End-point security ensures that whoever is plugging into or accessing any hardware anywhere within the intranet has to comply with the minimum baseline corporate security policy standards. This can include add-on access credentials but it goes far beyond access. Often these solutions ensure that traveling corporate laptops are compliant with a minimum patching level, scans, and antivirus definition levels before being allowed to connect to the intranet.

NAC appliances that enforce these policies often require a NAC fat client to be installed on every PC and laptop. This rule can be enforced during logon using a logon script. The client can also be part of the standard OS image for deploying new PCs and laptops.

Microsoft has built an NAC-type framework into some versions of its client OSs (Vista and XP SP3) to ease compliance with its NAC server product called MS Network Policy Server, which closely works with its Windows 2008 Server product (see sidebar: The Cost of a Data Breach). The company has been able to convince many industry networking heavyweights (notably Cisco and Juniper) to adopt its NAP standard.[22]

The Cost of a Data Breach

As of July 2007, the average breach cost per incident was $4.8 million.

• This works out to $182 per exposed record.
• It represents an increase of more than 30% from 2005.
• As much as 35% of these breaches involved the loss or theft of a laptop or other portable device.
• Up to 70% were due to a mistake or malicious intent by an organization's own staff.
• Since 2005, almost 150 million individuals' identifiable information has been compromised owing to a data security breach.
• As much as 19% of consumers notified of a data breach discontinued their relationship with the business, and a further 40% considered doing so.[23]

---

23. Kevin Bocek, "What Does a Data Breach Cost?" SCmagazine.com, July 2, 2007, www.scmagazineus.com/What-does-a-data-breach-cost/article/35131.

Essentially, the technology has three parts: a policy-enforceable client, a decision point, and an enforcement point. The client could be an XP SP3 or Vista client (either a roaming user or guest user) trying to connect to the company intranet. The decision point in this case would be the Network Policy Server product, checking to see whether the client requesting access meets the minimum baseline to allow it to connect. If it does not, the decision point product would pass this data on to the enforcement point, a network access product such as a router or switch, which would then be able to cut off access.

The scenario would repeat at every connection attempt, allowing the network's health to be maintained on an ongoing basis. Microsoft's NAP page has more details and animation to explain this process.[24]

Access control in general terms is a relationship triad among internal users, intranet resources, and the actions internal users can take on those resources. The idea is to give users only the least amount of access they require to perform their job. Tools used to ensure this in Windows shops employ Active Directory for Windows logon scripting and Windows user profiles. Granular classification is needed for users, actions, and resources to form a logical

---

22. "Juniper and Microsoft Hook Up for NAC work," May 22, 2007, PHYSORG.com, www.physorg.com/news99063542.html.
24. NAP Program details, Microsoft.com, www.microsoft.com/windowsserver2008/en/us/nap-features.aspx.

---

and comprehensive access control policy that addresses who gets to connect to what, yet keeping the intranet safe from unauthorized access or data security breaches. Many off-the-shelf solutions geared toward this market combine inventory control and access control under a "desktop life-cycle" planning umbrella.

Typically, security administrators start with a "deny-all" policy as a baseline before slowly building in the access permissions. As users migrate from one department to another, are promoted, or leave the company, in large organizations this job can involve one person by herself. This person often has a close working relationship with Purchasing, Helpdesk, and HR, getting coordination and information from these departments about users who have separated from the organization and computers that have been surplused, deleting and modifying user accounts and assignments of PCs and laptops.

Helpdesk software usually has an inventory control component that is readily available to Helpdesk personnel to update and/or pull up to access details on computer assignments and user status. Optimal use of form automation can ensure that these details occur (such as deleting a user on the day of separation) to avoid the possibility of an unwelcome data breach.

4. MEASURING RISK: AUDITS

Audits are another cornerstone of a comprehensive intranet security policy. To start an audit, an administrator should know and list what he is protecting, as well as know the relevant threats and vulnerabilities to those resources.

Assets that need protection can be classified as either tangible or intangible. *Tangible assets* are, of course, removable media (USB keys), PCs, laptops, PDAs, Web servers, networking equipment, digital video recording (DVR) security cameras, and employees' physical access cards. *Intangible assets* can include company intellectual property, such as corporate email and wikis, user passwords, and, especially for HIPAA and Sarbanes–Oxley mandates, personally identifiable health and financial information, which the company could be legally liable to protect.

Threats can include the theft of USB keys, laptops, PDAs, and PCs from company premises. This results in a data breach (for tangible assets), weak passwords, and unhardened operating systems in servers (for *intangible assets*).

Once a correlated listing of assets and associated threats and vulnerabilities has been made, we have to measure the impact of a breach, which is known as *risk*. The common rule of thumb to measure risk is:

$$Risk = Value\ of\ asset \times Threat \times vulnerability$$

It is obvious that an Internet-facing Web server faces greater risk and requires priority patching and virus scanning because the vulnerability and threat components are

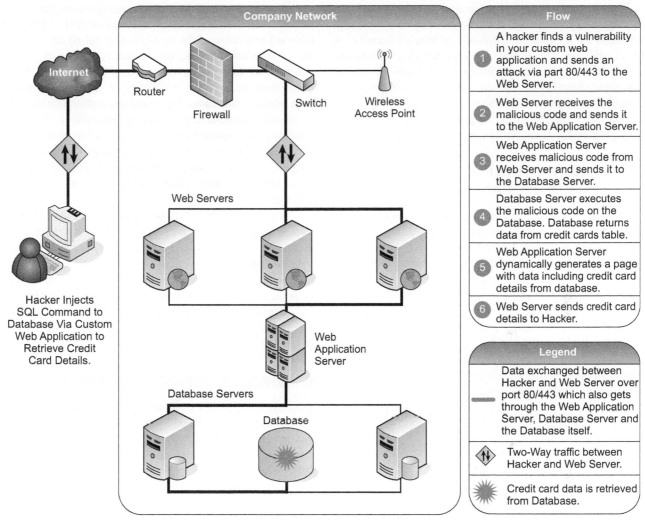

	Company Network		Flow

Internet

Router

Firewall

Switch

Wireless Access Point

Web Servers

Web Application Server

Database Servers

Database

Hacker Injects SQL Command to Database Via Custom Web Application to Retrieve Credit Card Details.

Flow

1. A hacker finds a vulnerability in your custom web application and sends an attack via part 80/443 to the Web Server.

2. Web Server receives the malicious code and sends it to the Web Application Server.

3. Web Application Server receives malicious code from Web Server and sends it to the Database Server.

4. Database Server executes the malicious code on the Database. Database returns data from credit cards table.

5. Web Application Server dynamically generates a page with data including credit card details from database.

6. Web Server sends credit card details to Hacker.

Legend

— Data exchanged between Hacker and Web Server over port 80/443 which also gets through the Web Application Server, Database Server and the Database itself.

↕ Two-Way traffic between Hacker and Web Server.

✴ Credit card data is retrieved from Database.

FIGURE 15.4   Structured Query Language (SQL) injection attack. *From © acunetix.com.*

high in that case (these servers routinely get sniffed and scanned over the Internet by hackers looking to find holes in their armor). However, this formula can standardize the priority list so that the actual audit procedure (typically carried out weekly or monthly by a vulnerability-scanning device) is standardized by risk level. Vulnerability-scanning appliances usually scan server farms and networking appliances only because these are high-value targets within the network for hackers who are looking for either unhardened server configurations or network switches with default factory passwords left on by mistake. To illustrate the situation, look at Fig. 15.4, which illustrates a Structured Query Language (SQL) injection attack on a corporate database.[25]

---

25. "Web Application Security—Check Your Site for Web Application Vulnerabilities," www.acunetix.com/websitesecurity/webapp-security. htm.

Questions for a Nontechnical Audit of Intranet Security

1. Is all access (especially to high-value assets) logged?
2. In case of laptop theft, is encryption enabled so that the records will be useless to the thief?
3. Are passwords verifiably strong enough to comply with the security policy? Are they changed frequently and held to strong encryption standards?
4. Are all tangible assets (PCs, laptops, PDAs, Web servers, and networking equipment) tagged with asset tags?
5. Is the process for surplusing obsolete IT assets secure (that is, are disks wiped for personally identifiable data before surplusing happens)?
6. Are email and Web use logged?
7. Are peer-to-peer (P2P) and instant messaging use controlled?

Based on the answers you get (or do not get), you can start the security audit procedure by finding answers to these questions.

The value of an asset is subjective and can be assessed only by the IT personnel in that organization (see sidebar: Questions for a Nontechnical Audit of Intranet Security). If the IT staff has an Information Technology Infrastructure Library (ITIL) process under way, often the value of an asset will already have been classified and can be used. Otherwise, a small spreadsheet can be created with classes of various tangible and intangible assets (as part of a hardware/software cataloging exercise) and values assigned that way.

5. GUARDIAN AT THE GATE: AUTHENTICATION AND ENCRYPTION

To most lay users, authentication in its most basic form is two-factor authentication, meaning a username and a password. Although adding further factors [such as additional autogenerated personal identification numbers (PINs) and/or biometrics] makes authentication stronger by magnitudes, one can do a lot with just the password within a two-factor situation. Password strength is determined by how hard the password is to crack using a password-cracker application that uses repetitive tries employing common words (sometimes from a stored dictionary) to match the password. Some factors will prevent the password from being cracked easily and make it a stronger password:

- password length (more than eight characters)
- use of mixed case (both uppercase and lowercase)
- use of alphanumeric characters (letters as well as numbers)
- use of special characters (such as !, ?, %, and #)

The access control list (ACL) in a Windows AD environment can be customized to demand up to all four factors in the setting or renewal of a password, which will render the password strong. Before a few years ago, the complexity of a password (the last three items in the preceding list) was favored as a measure of strength in passwords. However, the latest preference as of this writing is to use uncommon passwords, joined-together sentences to form passphrases that are long but do not have much in the way of complexity. Password authentication ("what you know") as two-factor authentication is not as secure as adding a third factor to the equation (a dynamic token password). Common types of third-factor authentication include biometrics (fingerprint scan, palm scan, or retina scan: in other words, "what you are") and token-type authentication (software or hardware PIN—generating tokens: that is, "what you have"). Proximity or magnetic swipe cards and tokens have seen common use for physical premises-access authentication in high-security buildings (such as financial and R&D companies), but not for network or hardware access within IT.

When remote or teleworker employees connect to the intranet via VPN tunnels or Web-based SSL VPNs (the outward extension of the intranet once called an *extranet*), the connection needs to be encrypted with strong Triple Data Encryption Algorithm (3DES) or AES-type encryption to comply with patient data and financial data privacy mandates. The standard authentication setup is usually a username and a password, with an additional hardware token-generated random PIN entered into a third box. Until lately, RSA as a company was one of the bigger players in the hardware-token field; incidentally, it also invented the RSA algorithm for public-key encryption.

As of this writing, hardware tokens cost under $30 per user in quantities of greater than a couple hundred pieces, compared with about a $100 only a decade ago. Most vendors offer free lifetime replacements for hardware tokens. Instead of a separate hardware token, some inexpensive software token generators can be installed within PC clients, smartphones, and BlackBerry devices. Tokens are probably the most cost-effective enhancement to security today.

6. WIRELESS NETWORK SECURITY

Employees using the convenience of wireless to log into the corporate network (usually via laptop) need to have their laptops configured with strong encryption to prevent data breaches. The first-generation encryption type known as WEP was easily deciphered (cracked) using common hacking tools and is no longer widely used. The latest standard in wireless authentication is WPA or WPA2 (802.11i), which offers stronger encryption compared with WEP. Although wireless cards in laptops can offer all of the choices previously noted, they should be configured with WPA or WPA2 if possible.

There are many hobbyists roaming corporate areas looking for open wireless access points (transmitters) equipped with powerful Wi-Fi antennas and wardriving software; a common package is Netstumbler. Wardriving was originally meant to log the presence of open Wi-Fi access points on websites (see sidebar: Basic Ways to Prevent Wi-Fi Intrusions in Corporate Intranets), but there is no guarantee that actual access and use (*piggybacking*, in hacker terms) will not occur, because curiosity is human nature. If there is a profit motive, as in the TJX example, access to corporate networks will take place, although the risk of getting caught and the resulting risk of criminal prosecution will be high. Furthermore, installing a RADIUS server is a must to check access authentication for roaming laptops.

7. SHIELDING THE WIRE: NETWORK PROTECTION

Firewalls are, of course, the primary barrier to a network. Typically rule based, firewalls prevent unwarranted traffic from getting into the intranet from the Internet. These days, firewalls also do some stateful inspections within packets to peer a little into the header contents of an incoming packet, to check validity: that is, to check whether a streaming video packet is really what it says it is, and not malware masquerading as streaming video.

Intrusion prevention systems (IPSs) are a newer type of inline network appliance that uses heuristic analysis (based on a weekly updated signature engine) to find patterns of malware identity and behavior and block malware from entering the periphery of the intranet. The IPS and the intrusion detection system (IDS) operate differently, however.

IDSs are typically *not* sitting inline; they sniff traffic occurring anywhere in the network, cache extensively, and can correlate events to find malware. The downside of IDSs is that unless their filters are modified extensively, they generate copious amounts of false positives, so much so that "real" threats become impossible to sift out of all the noise.

IPSs, in contrast, work *inline* and inspect packets rapidly to match packet signatures. The packets pass through many hundreds of parallel filters, each containing matching rules for a different type of malware threat. Most vendors publish new sets of malware signatures for their appliances every week. However, signatures for common worms and injection exploits such as SQL-slammer, Code-red, and NIMDA are sometimes hardcoded into the application-specific integrated chip that controls the processing for the filters. Hardware-enhancing a filter helps avert massive-scale attacks more efficiently because it is performed in hardware, which is more rapid and efficient compared with software signature matching. Incredible numbers of malicious packets can be dropped from the wire using the former method.

The buffers in an enterprise-class IPS are smaller than those in IDSs and are fast, akin to a high-speed switch to preclude latency (often as low as 200 μs during the highest

Basic Ways to Prevent Wi-Fi Intrusions in Corporate Intranets

1. Reset and customize the default Service Set Identifier (SSID) or Extended Service Set Identifier for the access point device before installation.
2. Change the default admin password.
3. Install a RADIUS server, which checks for laptop user credentials from an Active Directory database (ACL) from the same network before giving access to the wireless laptop. See Figs. 15.5 and 15.6 for illustrated explanations of the process.
4. Enable WPA or WPA2 encryption, not WEP, which is easily cracked.
5. Periodically try to wardrive around your campus and try to sniff (and disable) nonsecured network-connected rogue access points set up by naive users.
6. Document the wireless network by using one of the leading wireless network management software packages made for that purpose.

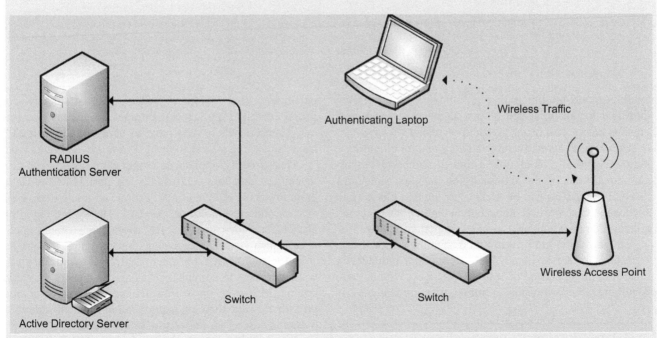

FIGURE 15.5 Wireless Extensible Authentication Protocol authentication using Active Directory and authentication servers.

Basic Ways to Prevent Wi-Fi Intrusions in Corporate Intranets—cont'd

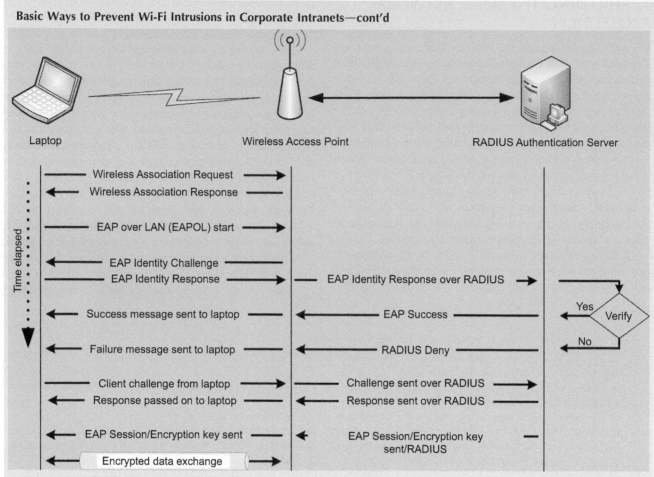

FIGURE 15.6 High-level wireless Extensible Authentication Protocol (EAP) workflow. *LAN*, local area network.

Note: Contrary to common belief, turning off the SSID broadcast will not help unless you are talking about a home access point situation. Hackers have an extensive suite of tools with which to sniff SSIDs for lucrative corporate targets, which will be broadcast anyway when connecting in clear text (unlike the real traffic, which will be encrypted).

load). A top-of-the-line midsize IPS box's total processing threshold for all input and output segments can exceed 5 gigabits per second using parallel processing.[26]

However, to avoid overtaxing CPUs and for efficiency's sake, IPSs usually block only a limited number of important threats out of the thousands of malware signatures listed. Tuning IPSs can be tricky: just enough blocking to silence the false-positive noise but enough to make sure all critical filters are activated to block important threats.

The most important factors in designing a critical data infrastructure are resiliency, robustness, and redundancy regarding the operation of inline appliances. Whether one is talking about firewalls or inline IPSs, redundancy is

paramount (see sidebar: Types of Redundancy for Inline Security Appliances). Intranet robustness is a primary concern where data have to be available on a 24/7 basis.

Most security appliances come with syslog reporting (event and alert logs sent usually via port 514 User Datagram Protocol) and email notification (set to alert beyond a customizable threshold) as standard. The syslog reporting can be forwarded to a security event management appliance, which consolidates syslogs into a central threat console for the benefit of event correlation and forwards warning emails to administrators based on preset threshold criteria. Moreover, most firewalls and IPSs can be configured to forward their own notification email to administrators in case of an impending threat scenario.

For special circumstances in which a wireless-type local area network (LAN) connection is the primary one

26. IPS specification datasheet. "TippingPoint® intrusion prevention system (IPS) technical specifications," www.tippingpoint.com/pdf/resources/datasheets/400918-007_IPStechspecs.pdf.

Types of Redundancy for Inline Security Appliances

1. Security appliances usually have dual power supplies (often hot-swappable) and are designed to be connected to two separate uninterrupible power supply (UPS) devices, thereby minimizing the chances of a failure within the appliance itself. The hot-swap capability minimizes replacement time for power supplies.

2. We can configure most of these appliances to either shut down the connection or fall back to a level 2 switch (in case of hardware failure). If reverting to a fallback state, most IPSs become basically a bump in the wire and, depending on the type of traffic, can be configured to fail open so that traffic remains uninterrupted. Also, inexpensive, small, third-party switchboxes are available to enable this failsafe high-availability option for a single IPS box. The idea is to keep traffic flow active regardless of attacks.

3. IPS or firewall devices can be placed in dual-redundant failover mode, either in active—active (load-sharing) or active—passive (primary—secondary) mode. The devices commonly use a protocol called Virtual Router Redundancy Protocol, in which the secondary pings the primary every second to check live status and assumes leadership to start processing traffic in case pings are not returned from the primary. The switchover is instantaneous and transparent to most network users. Before the switchover, all data and connection settings are fully synchronized at identical states between both boxes to ensure failsafe switchover.

4. Inline IPS appliances are relatively immune to attacks because they have highly hardened Linus/UNIX operating systems and are designed from the ground up to be robust and low-maintenance appliances (logs usually clear themselves by default).

(whether microwave beam, laser beam, or satellite-type connection), redundancy can be ensured by a secondary connection of equal or smaller capacity. For example, in certain northern Alaska towns where digging trenches into the hardened icy permafrost is expensive and rigging wire across the tundra is impractical because of the extreme cold, the primary network connections between towns are always via microwave link, often operating in dual redundant mode.

8. WEAKEST LINK IN SECURITY: USER TRAINING

Intranet security awareness is best communicated to users in two primary ways: during new employee orientation and by ongoing targeted training for users in various departments with specific user audiences in mind. A formal security training policy should be drafted and signed off by management, with well-defined scopes, roles, and responsibilities of various individuals, such as the CIO and the information security officer, and posted on the intranet. New recruits should be given a copy of all security policies to sign off on before they are granted user access. The training policy should also spell out the roles of the HR, compliance, and public relations departments in the training program.

Training can be given using the PowerPoint Seminar method in large gatherings before monthly "all-hands" departmental meetings and also via an emailed Web link to a Flash video format presentation. The latter can also be configured to have an interactive quiz at the end, which should pique audience interest in the subject and help people remember relevant issues.

With regard to topics to be included in the training, any applicable federal or industry mandate such as HIPAA, Sarbanes—Oxley, PCI-DSS, or ISO 27002 should be discussed extensively first, followed by discussions on tackling social engineering, spyware, viruses, and so on.

The topics of data theft and corporate data breaches are frequently in the news. These topics can be discussed extensively, with emphasis on how to protect personally identifiable information in a corporate setting. Password policy and access control topics are always good things to discuss; at a minimum, users need to be reminded to sign off their workstations before going on a break.

9. DOCUMENTING THE NETWORK: CHANGE MANAGEMENT

Controlling the IT infrastructure configuration of a large organization is more about change control than other things. Often the change control guidance comes from documents such as the ITIL series of guidebooks.

After a baseline configuration is documented, change control, a deliberate and methodical process that ensures that any changes are made to the baseline IT configuration of the organization (such as changes to network design, AD design, and so on), is extensively documented and authorized only after prior approval. This is done to ensure that unannounced or unplanned changes are not allowed to hamper the day-to-day efficiency and business functions of the overall intranet infrastructure.

In most government entities, even small changes are made to go through change management (CM); however, management can give managers leeway to approve a certain minimal level of ad hoc change that has no potential to disrupt operations. In most organizations in which mandates are a day-to-day affair, no ad hoc change is allowed unless it goes through supervisory-level CM meetings.

The goal of CM is largely to comply with mandates, but for some organizations, waiting for a weekly meeting can slow things significantly. If justified, an emergency CM meeting can be called to approve a time-sensitive change.

Practically speaking, the CM process works as follows: A formal CM document is filled out (usually a multitab online Excel spreadsheet) and forwarded to the CM ombudsman (maybe a project management person). For some CM form details, see the sidebar: Change Management Spreadsheet Details to Submit to a CM Meeting.

The document must have supervisory approval from the requestor's supervisor before proceeding to the ombudsman. The ombudsman posts this change document on a section of the intranet for all other supervisors and managers within the CM committee to review in advance. Done this way, the CM committee, meeting in its weekly or biweekly change approval meetings, can voice reservations or ask clarification questions of the change-initiating person, who is usually present to explain the change. At the end of the deliberations the decision is then voted on to approve, deny, modify, or delay the change (sometimes with preconditions).

Change Management Spreadsheet Details to Submit to a Change Management Meeting

- name and organizational details of the change requestor
- actual change details, such as the time and duration of the change
- any possible impacts (high, low, or medium) to significant user groups or critical functions
- the amount of advance notice needed for affected users via email (typically 2 working days)
- evidence that the change has been tested in advance
- signature and approval of the supervisor and her supervisor (manager)
- whether and how rollback is possible
- postchange, a "postmortem tab" has to confirm whether the change process was successful, and any revealing comments or notes for the conclusion
- one of the tabs can be an "attachment tab" containing embedded Visio diagrams or word documentation embedded within the Excel sheet to aid discussion

---

If approved, the configuration change is then made (usually within the following week). The postmortem section of the change can then be updated to note any issues that occurred during the change (such as a rollback after change reversal, and the causes).

Some organizations have started to operate the CM collaborative process using social networking tools at work. This allows disparate flows of information, such as emails, departmental wikis, and file-share documents, to belong to a unified thread for future reference.

10. REHEARSE THE INEVITABLE: DISASTER RECOVERY

Possible disaster scenarios can range from the mundane to the biblical in proportion. In intranet or general IT terms, recovering successfully from a disaster can mean resuming critical IT support functions for mission-critical business functions. Whether such recovery is smooth and hassle-free depends on how prior disaster recovery (DR) planning occurred and how this plan was tested to address all relevant shortcomings adequately.

The first task when planning for DR is to assess the business impact of a certain type of disaster on the functioning of an intranet using business impact analysis (BIA). BIA involves certain metrics; again, off-the shelf software tools are available to assist with this effort. The scenario could be a natural hurricane-induced power outage or a human-induced critical application crash. In any one of these scenarios, one needs to assess the type of impact in terms of time, productivity, and finance.

BIAs can take into consideration the breadth of impact. For example, if the power outage is caused by a hurricane or an earthquake, support from generator vendors or the electricity utility could be hard to get because of the large demands for their services. BIAs also need to take into account historical and local weather priorities. Although there could be possibilities of hurricanes occurring in California or earthquakes occurring along the Gulf Coast of Florida, for most practical purposes the chances of those disasters taking place in those locales are pretty remote. Historical data can be helpful for prioritizing contingencies.

Once the business impacts are assessed to categorize critical systems, a DR plan can be organized and tested. Criteria for recovery have two types of metrics: a recovery point objective (RPO) and a recovery time objective (RTO).

In the DR plan, the RPO refers to how far back or "back to what point in time" that backup data have to be recovered. This time frame generally dictates how often tape backups are taken, which again can depend on the criticality of the data. The most common scenario for medium-sized IT shops is daily incremental backups and a weekly full backup on tape. Tapes are sometimes changed automatically by tape backup appliances.

One important thing to remember is to rotate tapes (that is, put them on a life-cycle plan by marking them for expiry) to make sure that tapes have complete data integrity during a restore. Most tape manufacturers have marking schemes for this task. Although tapes are still relatively expensive, the extra amount spent on always having fresh tapes ensures that there are no nasty surprises at the time of a crucial data recovery.

RTO refers to how long it takes to restore backed up or recovered data to its original state for resuming normal business processes. The critical factor here is cost. It will cost much more to restore data within an hour using an online backup process or to resume operations using a hotsite rather than a 5-h restore using stored tape backups. If business process resumption is critical, cost becomes a less important factor.

DR also has to take into account resumption of communication channels. If network and telephone links are not up, having a timely tape restore does little good to resume business functions. Extended campus network links often depend on leased lines from major vendors such as Verizon and AT&T, so having a trusted vendor relationship with agreed-on service level agreement (SLA) standards is a requirement.

Depending on budgets, one can configure DR to happen almost instantly, if so desired, but that is a far more costly option. Most shops with "normal" data flows are okay with business being resumed within the span of about 3—4 h or even a full working day after a major disaster. Balancing costs with business expectations is the primary factor in the DR game. Spending inordinately for a rare disaster that might never happen is a waste of resources. It is fiscally imprudent (not to mention futile) to try to prepare for every contingency possible.

Once the DR plan is more or less finalized, a DR committee can be set up under an experienced DR professional to orchestrate the routine training of users and managers to simulate disasters on a frequent basis. In most shops this means management meeting every 2 months to simulate a DR "war room" (command center) situation and employees going through a mandatory interactive 6-month disaster recovery training, listing the DR personnel to contact.

Within the command center, roles are preassigned, and each member of the team carries out his or her role as though it were a real emergency or disaster. DR coordination is frequently modeled after the US Federal Emergency Management Agency guidelines, an active entity that has training and certification tracks for DR management professionals.

Simulated "generator shutdowns" in most shops are scheduled on a biweekly or monthly basis to see how the systems actually function. The systems can include UPSs, emergency lighting, email and cell phone notification methods, and alarm enunciators and sirens. Because electronics items in a server room are sensitive to moisture damage, gas-based Halon fire-extinguishing systems are used. These Halon systems also have a provision to be tested (often twice a year) to determine their readiness. The vendor will be happy to be on retainer for these tests, which can be made part of the purchasing agreement as an SLA. If equipment is tested on a regular basis, shortcomings and major hardware maintenance issues with major DR systems can easily be identified, documented, and redressed.

In a severe disaster situation, priorities need to be exercised regarding what to salvage first. Clearly, trying to recover employee records, payroll records, and critical business mission data such as customer databases will take precedence. Anything irreplaceable or not easily replaceable needs priority attention.

We can divide the levels of redundancies and backups to a few progressive segments. The level of backup sophistication would, of course, depend on (1) criticality and (2) time-to-recovery criteria of the data involved.

At the basic level, we can opt not to back up any data or not even have procedures to recover data, which means that data recovery would be a failure. Understandably, this is not a common scenario.

More typical is contracting with an archival company of a local warehouse within a 20-mile periphery. Tapes are backed up onsite and stored offsite, with the archival company picking up the tapes from your facility on a daily basis. The time to recover depends on retrieving the tapes from archival storage, getting them onsite, and starting a restore. The advantages here are lower cost. However, the time needed to transport tapes and recover them might not be acceptable, depending on the type of data and the recovery scenario.

Often a "coldsite" or "hotsite" is added to the intranet backup scenario. A coldsite is a smaller and scaled-down copy of the existing intranet data center that has only the most essential pared-down equipment supplied and tested for recovery but not in a perpetually ready state (powered down as in "cold," with no live connection). These coldsites can house the basics, such as a Web server, domain name servers, and SQL databases, to get an informational site started up in very short order.

A hotsite is the same thing as a coldsite, except that in this case the servers are always running and the Internet and intranet connections are "live" and ready to be switched over much more quickly than on a coldsite. These are just two examples of how the business resumption and recovery times can be shortened.

Recovery can be made rapidly if the hotsite is linked to the regular data center using fast leased-line links (such as a DS3 connection). Backups synched in real time with an identical redundantarrayof inexpensivedisks at the hotsite over redundant high-speed data links afford the shortest recovery time.

In larger intranet shops based in defense-contractor companies, sometimes there are requirements for even faster data recovery with far more rigid standards for data integrity. To-the-second real-time data synchronization in addition to hardware synchronization ensure that duplicate sites thousands of miles away can be up and running within a matter of seconds, even faster than a hotsite. Such extreme redundancy typically is needed for critical national databases (that is, air traffic control or customs databases that are accessed 24/7, for example).

At the highest level of recovery performance, most large database vendors offer "zero data loss" solutions, with a variety of cloned databases synchronized across the country that automatically failover and recover in an instantaneous fashion to preserve a consistent status, often free from human intervention. Oracle's version is called Data Guard; most mainframe vendors offer a similar product, varying in their offerings of tiers and features.

The philosophy here is simple: The more dollars you spend, the more readiness you can buy. However, the expense has to be justified by the level of criticality for the availability of the data.

11. CONTROLLING HAZARDS: PHYSICAL AND ENVIRONMENTAL PROTECTION

Physical access and environmental hazards are relevant to security within the intranet. People are the primary weak link in security (as previously discussed), and controlling the activity and movement of authorized personnel and preventing access to unauthorized personnel fall within the purview of these security controls. This important area of intranet security must first be formalized within a management-sanctioned and published P&P.

Physical access to data center facilities (as well as IT working facilities) is typically controlled using card readers. These were scanning types in the past 2 decades but are increasingly being converted to near-field or proximity-type access card systems. Some high-security facilities (such as bank data centers) use smartcards, which use encryption keys stored within the cards for matching keys.

Some important and commonsense topics should be discussed within the subject of physical access. First, disbursal of cards needs to be a deliberate and high-security affair requiring the signatures of at least two supervisory-level people who can be responsible for the authenticity and actual need to access credentials for a person to specific areas.

Access card permissions need to be highly granular. An administrative person probably will never need to be in the server room, so that person's access to the server room should be blocked. Areas should be categorized and cataloged by sensitivity, and access permissions granted accordingly.

Physical data transmission access points to the intranet have to be monitored via DVR and closed-circuit cameras if possible. Physical electronic eavesdropping can occur to unmonitored network access points in both wireline and wireless ways. There have been known instances of thieves intercepting LAN communication from unshielded Ethernet cable (usually hidden above the plenum or false ceiling for longer runs). All a data thief needs is to place a tap box and a miniature (Wi-Fi) wireless transmitter at entry or exit points to the intranet to copy and transmit all communications. At the time of this writing, these transmitters are the size of a USB key. The miniaturization of electronics has made data theft possible for part-time thieves. Spy store sites give determined data thieves plenty of workable options at relatively little cost.

Using a DVR solution to monitor and store access logs to sensitive areas and correlating them to the timestamps on the physical access logs can help forensic investigations in case of a physical data breach malfeasance, or theft. It is important to remember that DVR records typically rotate and are erased every week. One person has to be in charge of the DVR so records are saved to optical disks weekly before they are erased. DVR tools need some tending to because their sophistication level often does not come up to par with other network tools.

Written or PC-based sign-in logs must be kept at the front reception desk, with timestamps. Visitor cards should have limited access to private and/or secured areas. Visitors must provide official identification and log times coming in and going out, as well as names of persons to be visited and the reason for their visit. If possible, visitors should be escorted to and from the specific person to be visited, to minimize the chances of subversion or sabotage.

Entries to courthouses and other special facilities have metal detectors, but these may not be needed for every facility. The same goes for bollards and concrete entry barriers, to prevent car bombings. In most government facilities where security is paramount, even physical entry points to parking garages have special personnel (usually deputed from the local sheriff's department) to check under cars for hidden explosive devices.

Contractor laptops must be registered and physically checked in by field support personnel. If these laptops are going to be plugged into the local network, the laptops need to be virus-scanned by data-security personnel and checked for unauthorized utilities or suspicious software (such as hacking utilities, Napster, or other P2P threats).

Supply of emergency power to the data center and the servers has to be robust to protect the intranet from corruption caused by power failures. Redundancy has to be exercised all the way from the utility connection to the servers themselves. This means there has to be more than one power connection to the data center (from more than one substation/transformer, if it is a larger data center).

There has to be provision of an alternate power supply (a ready generator to supply some, if not all, power requirements) in case of a power failure.

Power supplied to the servers has to come from more than one single UPS, because most servers have two removable power inputs. Data center racks typically have two UPSs on the bottom supplying power to two separate power strips on both sides of the rack for this redundancy purpose (for seamless switchover). In case of a power failure, the UPSs instantly take over the supply of power and start beeping, alerting personnel to shut down servers gracefully. UPSs usually have reserve power for brief periods (less than 10 min) until the generator kicks in, relieving the UPS of the large burden of the server power loads. Generators come on trailers or are skid-mounted and are designed to run as long as fuel is available in the tank, which can be about 3–5 days, depending on the model and capacity to generate (in thousands of kilowatts).

Increasingly, expensive, polluting batteries have made UPSs in larger data centers fall out of favor compared with flywheel power supplies, which are a cleaner, battery-less technology to supply interim power. Maintenance of this technology is half as costly as UPS, and it offers the same functionality. Provision has to be made for rechargeable emergency luminaires within the server room, as well as all areas occupied by administrators, so the entry and exit are not hampered during a power failure.

Provision for fire detection and firefighting must also be made. As mentioned previously, Halon gas fire-suppression systems are appropriate for server rooms because sprinklers will inevitably damage expensive servers if the servers are still turned on during sprinkler activation.

Sensors have to be placed close to the ground to detect moisture from plumbing disasters and resultant flooding. Master shutoff valve locations for water have to be marked and identified and personnel need to be periodically trained on performing shutoffs. Complete environmental control packages with cameras geared toward detecting any type of temperature, moisture, and sound abnormality are offered by many vendors. These sensors are connected to monitoring workstations using Ethernet LAN cabling. Reporting can occur through emails if customizable thresholds are met or exceeded.

12. KNOW YOUR USERS: PERSONNEL SECURITY

Users working within intranet-related infrastructures have to be known and trusted. Often data contained within the intranet is highly sensitive, such as new product designs and financial or market-intelligence data gathered after much research and at great expense.

Assigning personnel to sensitive areas in IT entails attaching security categories and parameters to the positions, especially within IT. Attaching security parameters to a position is akin to attaching tags to a photograph or blog. Some parameters will be more important than others, but all describe the item to some extent. The categories and parameters listed on the personnel access form should correlate to access permissions to sensitive installations such as server rooms. Access permissions should be compliant to the organizational security policy in force at the time. Personnel, especially those who will be handling sensitive customer data or individually identifiable health records, should be screened before hiring, to ensure that they do not have felonies or misdemeanors on their records.

During transfers and terminations, all sensitive access tools should be reassessed and reassigned (or deassigned, in case termination happens) for logical and physical access. Access tools can include such items as encryption tokens, company cell phones, laptops or PDAs, card keys, metal keys, entry passes, and any other company identification provided for employment. For people who are leaving the organization, an exit interview should be taken. System access should be terminated on the hour after former personnel have ceased to be employees of the company.

13. PROTECTING DATA FLOW: INFORMATION AND SYSTEM INTEGRITY

Information integrity protects information and data flows while they are in movement to and from users' desktops to the intranet. System integrity measures protect the systems that process the information (usually servers such as email or file servers). Processes to protect information can include antivirus tools, IPS and IDS tools, Web-filtering tools, and email encryption tools.

Antivirus tools are the most common security tools available to protect servers and users' desktops. Typically, enterprise-level antivirus software from larger vendors such as Symantec and McAfee will contain a console listing all machines on the network and will enable administrators to see graphically (color or icon differentiation) which machines need virus remediation or updates. All machines will have a software client installed that does some scanning and reporting of the individual machines to the console. To save bandwidth, the management server that contains the console will be updated with the latest virus (and spyware) definition from the vendor. Then it is the management console's job to update the software client slowly in each computer with the latest definitions. Sometimes the client itself will need an update, and the console allows this to be done remotely.

IDS detects malware within the network from the traffic and communication malware used. Certain patterns of behavior are attached to each type of malware, and those signatures are what IDSs are used to match. Currently,

IDSs are mostly defunct. The major problems with IDSs were that (1) IDSs used to produce too many false positives, which made sifting out actual threats a huge, frustrating exercise; and (2) IDSs had no teeth: that is, their functionality was limited to reporting and raising alarms. IDS devices could not stop malware from spreading because they could not block it.

Compared with IDSs, IPSs have seen much wider adoption across corporate intranets because IPS devices sit inline processing traffic at the periphery and can block traffic or malware, depending on a much more sophisticated heuristic algorithm than IDS devices. Although IPSs are mostly signature based, there are experimental IPS devices that can stop threats not on signature, but based only on suspicious or anomalous behavior. This is good news because the numbers of "zero-day" threats are on the increase, and their signatures are mostly unknown to the security vendors at the time of infection.

Web-filtering tools have become more sophisticated as well. A decade ago, Web filters could block traffic to specific sites only if the URL matched. Today, most Web filter vendors have large research arms that try to categorize specific websites under certain categories. Some vendors have realized the enormity of this task and have allowed the general public to contribute to this effort. The website www.trustedsource.org is an example; a person can go in and submit a single or multiple URLs for categorization. If they are examined and approved, the site category will then be added to the vendor's next signature update for their Web filter solution.

Web filters not only match URLs, they also do a fair bit of packet examining these days, just to make sure that a JPEG frame is indeed a JPEG frame and not a worm in disguise. The categories of websites blocked by a typical midsized intranet vary, but some surefire blocked categories would be pornography, erotic sites, discrimination/hate, weapons/illegal activities, and dating/relationships.

Web filters are not just there to enforce the moral values of management. These categories, if not blocked at work, openly enable an employee to offend another employee (especially pornography or discriminatory sites) and are fertile grounds for a liability lawsuit against the employer.

Finally, email encryption has been in the news because of various mandates such as Sarbanes–Oxley and HIPAA. Both mandates specifically mention email and communication encryption to encrypt personally identifiable financial or patient medical data while in transit. California (among other states) has adopted a resolution to discontinue fund disbursements to any California health organization that does not use email encryption as a matter of practice. This has caught many Californian companies and local government entities unaware because email encryption software is relatively hard to implement. The toughest challenge yet is to train users to get used to the tool. Email encryption works by entering a set of credentials to access the email rather than just getting email pushed to the user, as within the email client Outlook.

14. SECURITY ASSESSMENTS

A security assessment (usually done on a yearly basis for most midsized shops) not only uncovers various misconfigured items on the network and server-side sections of IT operations, it also serves as a convenient blueprint for IT to activate necessary changes and get credibility for budgetary assistance from the accounting folks.

Typically, most consultants take 2–4 weeks to conduct a security assessment (depending on the size of the intranet), and they primarily use open-source vulnerability scanners such as Nessus. GFI LANguard, Retina, and Core Impact are other examples of commercial vulnerability-testing tools. Sometimes testers also use other proprietary suites of tools (special open-source tools such as the Metasploit Framework or Fragrouter) to conduct "payload-bearing attack exploits," thereby evading the firewall and the IPS to gain entry. In the case of intranet Web servers, cross-site scripting attacks can occur (see sidebar: Types of Scans Conducted on Servers and Network Appliances During a Security Assessment).

Types of Scans Conducted on Servers and Network Appliances During a Security Assessment
- firewalls and IPS device configuration
- regular and SSL VPN configuration
- Web server hardening (most critical; available as guides from vendors such as Microsoft)
- Demilitarized zone (DMZ) configuration
- email vulnerabilities
- domain name server anomalies
- database servers (hardening levels)
- network design and access control vulnerabilities
- internal PC health such as patching levels and incidence of spyware, malware, and so on

The results of these penetration tests are usually compiled as two separate items: (1) as a full-fledged technical report for IT, and (2) as a high-level executive summary meant for and delivered to top management to discuss strategy with IT after the engagement.

15. RISK ASSESSMENTS

Risk is defined as the probability of loss. In IT terms we are talking about compromising data CIA. Risk management is a way to manage the probability of threats causing an impact. Measuring risks using a risk assessment exercise is the first step toward managing or mitigating a risk. Risk assessments can identify network threats, their probabilities, and their impacts. The reduction of risk can be achieved by reducing any of these three factors.

Regarding intranet risks and threats, we are talking about anything from threats such as unpatched PCs getting viruses and spyware (with hidden keylogging software) to network-borne denial-of-service attacks and even large, publicly embarrassing Web vandalism threats, such as someone being able to deface the main page of the company website. The last is a high-impact threat but is mostly perceived to be a remote probability, unless, of course, the company has experienced this before. Awareness among vendors as well as users regarding security is at an all-time high because security is a high-profile news item.

Any security threat assessment needs to explore and list exploitable vulnerabilities and gaps. Many midsized IT shops run specific vulnerability assessment (VA) tools in-house on a monthly basis. eEye's Retina Network Security Scanner and Foundstone's scanning tools appliance are two examples of VA tools that can be found in use at larger IT shops. These tools are consolidated on ready-to-run appliances that are usually managed through remote browser-based consoles. Once the gaps are identified and quantified, steps can be taken to mitigate these vulnerabilities gradually, minimizing the impact of threats.

In intranet risk assessments, we identify primarily Web server and database threats residing within the intranet, but we should also be mindful about the periphery to guard against breaches through the firewall or IPS.

Finally, making intranet infrastructure and applications can be a complex task. This gets more complex and even confusing when information is obtained from different sources that are normally found at security conferences around the world. Frequently, these conference sources give a high-level overview, talking about generic compliance, but none gives a full picture and details that are required for quick implementation. So, with the preceding in mind, and because of the frequency of poor security practices or far-too-common security failures on the intranet, let us briefly look at an intranet security implementation process checklist.

16. INTRANET SECURITY IMPLEMENTATION PROCESS CHECKLIST

With this checklist, you get all of your questions in one place. This not only saves time, it is also cost-effective. The following high-level checklist lists all of the questions that are typically raised during the implementation process (see checklist: An Agenda for Action for Intranet Security Implementation Process Activities).

An Agenda for Action for Intranet Security Implementation Process Activities

The following high-level checklist should be addressed to find the following intranet security implementation process questions helpful (check all tasks completed):

_____ 1. How do you validate the intranet?
_____ 2. How do you validate Web applications?
_____ 3. How do you ensure and verify accuracy of file transfer through emails?
_____ 4. Does one need third-party certificates for digital signatures?
_____ 5. How do you ensure limited and authorized access to closed and open systems?
_____ 6. How can one safely access the company intranet while traveling?
_____ 7. How do you best protect the intranet from Internet attacks?
_____ 8. How do you handle security patches?
_____ 9. Does the stakeholder expect to be able to find a procedure using a simple search interface?
_____ 10. How many documents will be hosted?
_____ 11. What design will be used (centralized, hub and spoke, etc.)?
_____ 12. Who will be involved in evaluating projects?
_____ 13. What is the budget?
_____ 14. Who will be responsible for maintaining the site after it goes "live"?

---

17. SUMMARY

It is true that the level of Internet hyperconnectivity among Generation X and Y users has mushroomed, and the network periphery that we used to take for granted as a security shield has been diminished largely because of the explosive growth of social networking and the resulting connectivity boom. However, with the various new types of incoming application traffic [Voice Over Internet Protocol, Session Initiation Protocol, and Extensible Markup Language (XML) traffic] to their networks, security administrators need to stay on their toes and deal with these new protocols by implementing newer tools and technology. One example of new technology is the application-level firewall to connect outside vendors to intranets (also known as an XML firewall, placed within a DMZ) that protects the intranet from malformed XML and Simple Object Access Protocol message exploits coming from outside sourced applications.[27]

---

27. Latest standard (version 1.1) for SOAP message security standard from OASIS, a consortium for Web Services Security, www.oasisopen.org/committees/download.php/16790/wss-v1.1-spec-os-SOAPMessageSecurity.pdf.

We can say that with the myriad security issues facing intranets today, most IT shops are still well-equipped to defend themselves if they assess risks and, most important, train their employees regarding data security practices on an ongoing basis. The problems with threat mitigation remain largely a matter of meeting gaps in procedural controls rather than technical measures. Trained and security-aware employees are the biggest deterrent to data thefts and security breaches.

Finally, let us move on to the real interactive part of this chapter: review questions/exercises, hands-on projects, case projects, and the optional team case project. The answers and/or solutions by chapter can be found in the Online Instructor's Solutions Manual.

CHAPTER REVIEW QUESTIONS/ EXERCISES

True/False

1. True or false? In the corporate context, microblogging entails sending SMS messages to apprise colleagues of recent developments in the daily routine.
2. True or false? Popular devices like the iPad, Samsung Galaxy Android tablet, and many types of smartphones are capable of accessing company intranets using customized intranet apps.
3. True or false? Many risks need to be resolved when approaching intranet security concerning mobile devices.
4. True or false? Mobile devices accessing enterprise intranets using VPNs have to be subject to the same factors as any other device remotely accessing VPNs.
5. True or false? While there are few risks in deploying mobile devices within the Intranet, with careful configuration these risks can be increased to the point where the myriad benefits outweigh the risks.

Multiple Choice

1. The intranet, as just a simple place to share files and list a few policies and procedures, has ceased to be. The types of changes can be summed up in the following list of features, which shows that the intranet has become a combined portal as well as a public dashboard. Some of the features include the following, except which one?
   A. a corporate personnel directory of phone numbers by department
   B. several RSS feeds for news according to divisions such as IT, HR, finance, accounting, and purchasing

   C. a search engine for searching company information, often helped by a search appliance from Google
   D. a section describing company financials and other mission-critical indicators
   E. a "live" section with IT alerts regarding specific downtimes, outages, and other critical time-sensitive company notifications
2. Intranet security P&Ps are:
   A. the functionality and ease of use of using voice, gesture, and touch interfaces
   B. the first step toward a legal regulatory framework
   C. the availability of customized apps
   D. the change in the very concept of "being at work" compared with even 10 years ago
   E. the more rapid iteration life cycles of mobile devices
3. The millennial generation is more familiar with:
   A. PCs and laptops
   B. social media
   C. mobile technology
   D. mobile hardware industry
   E. cloud
4. Back-end enterprise network infrastructure support has to be ready and has to be strong to handle mobile devices interacting with:
   A. iPads
   B. IPSec
   C. L2TP VPNs
   D. SSL VPNs
   E. PPTP VPNs
5. What policy/procedure must be signed by new hires at orientation and by all employees who ask for access to the corporate VPN using mobile devices (even personal ones)?
   A. WPA2 encryption for Wi-Fi traffic access
   B. inbound and outbound malware scanning
   C. a well-tested SSL VPN for remote access
   D. a policy for reporting theft or misplacement
   E. a customized corporate usage policy for mobile devices

EXERCISE

Problem

How can an organization prevent security breaches to its intranet?

Hands-on Projects

Project

How would an organization handle an intranet attack?

Case Projects

Problem

How would an organization go about handling unauthorized access of an intranet?

Optional Team Case Project

Problem

How would an organization go about handling the misuse of user privileges on an intranet?

Chapter 16

Local Area Network Security

Pramod Pandya

CSU Fullerton, Fullerton, CA, United States

Note: This chapter is available in its entirety online at store.elsevier.com/product.jsp?isbn= 9780128038437 (click the Resources tab at the bottom of the page).

1. ABSTRACT

With an ever-increasing amount of information being transmitted electronically, it is important for security to be considered in every phase of local area network design and maintenance. Although much emphasis has been placed on things such as wireless networks and remote access, it is imperative that the core local area network not be overlooked.

Because the wired local area network is the nervous system of an organization's information systems, great care must be taken to secure it properly. This chapter begins by looking at the implications for wired local area network infrastructure security. Next, local area network segmentation and traffic isolation will be discussed. Using segmentation and isolation, there is an increased opportunity for security boundaries. Another concept that will be discussed is the security of the local area network equipment. The local area network is functional only if the core equipment is operational, so securing equipment is an important part of any security strategy. Finally, restriction of local area network access will be investigated and an organizational approach will be discussed. Because more and more users need access to local area network resources, there must be a way to identify and restrict who is allowed on the network and what access they are granted. In wired local area network infrastructure security, organizations must remember that they are only as secure as their weakest point. By carefully considering the various aspects of local area network security during design, these weak points can be reduced and the overall security of the network increased. Although it is impossible to be 100% secure and still be functional, by using some general guidelines to secure the wired local area network, many threats to the network can be reduced, if not eliminated.

2. CONTENTS

Chapter 17

Wireless Network Security

Chunming Rong[1], Gansen Zhao[2], Liang Yan[1], Erdal Cayirci[1] and Hongbing Cheng[1]

[1]University of Stavanger, Stavanger, Norway; [2]Sun Yat-sen University, Guangzhou, China

With the rapid development of technology in wireless communication and microchips, wireless technology has been widely used in various application areas. The proliferation of wireless devices and wireless networks in the past decade shows the widespread use of wireless technology.

Wireless networks are a general term to refer to various types of networks that communicate without the need of wire lines. Wireless networks can be broadly categorized into two classes based on the structures of the networks: wireless ad hoc networks and cellular networks. The main difference between these two is whether a fixed infrastructure is present.

Three of the well-known cellular networks are the global system for mobile communication (GSM) network, the code division multiple access (CDMA) network, and the 802.11 wireless LAN. The GSM network and the CDMA network are the main network technologies that support modern mobile communication, with most of the mobile phones and mobile networks that are built based on these two wireless networking technologies and their variants. As cellular networks require fixed infrastructures to support the communication between mobile nodes, deployment of the fixed infrastructures is essential. Further, cellular networks require serious and careful topology design of the fixed infrastructures before deployment, because the network topologies of the fixed infrastructures are mostly static and will have a great impact on network performance and network coverage.

Wireless ad hoc networks do not require a fixed infrastructure; thus it is relatively easy to set up and deploy a wireless ad hoc network (Fig. 17.1). Without the fixed infrastructure, the topology of a wireless ad hoc network is dynamic and changes frequently. It is not realistic to assume a static or a specific topology for a wireless ad hoc network. On the other hand, wireless ad hoc networks need to be self-organizing; thus mobile nodes in a wireless ad hoc network can adapt to the change of topology and establish cooperation with other nodes at runtime.

Besides the conventional wireless ad hoc networks, there are two special types that should be mentioned: wireless sensor networks and wireless mesh networks. Wireless sensor networks are wireless ad hoc networks, most of the network nodes of which are sensors that monitor a target scene. The wireless sensors are mostly deprived devices in terms of computation power, power supply, bandwidth, and other computation resources. Wireless mesh networks are wireless networks with either a full mesh topology or a partial mesh topology in which some or all nodes are directly connected to all other nodes. The redundancy in connectivity of wireless networks provides great reliability and excellent flexibility in network packet delivery.

1. CELLULAR NETWORKS

Cellular networks require fixed infrastructures to work (Fig. 17.2). A cellular network comprises a fixed infrastructure and a number of mobile nodes. Mobile nodes connect to the fixed infrastructure through wireless links. They may move around from within the range of one base station to outside the range of the base station, and they can move into the ranges of other base stations. The fixed infrastructure is stationary, or mostly stationary, including base stations, links between base stations, and possibly other conventional network devices such as routers. The

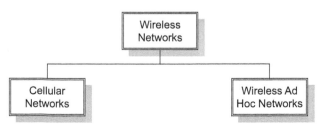

FIGURE 17.1 Classification of wireless networks.

Computer and Information Security Handbook. http://dx.doi.org/10.1016/B978-0-12-803843-7.00017-X

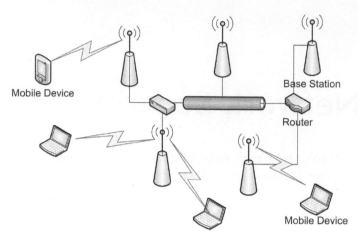

FIGURE 17.2 Cellular networking.

links between base stations can be either wired or wireless. The links should be more substantial than those links between base stations and mobile nodes in terms of reliability, transmission range, bandwidth, and so on.

The fixed infrastructure serves as the backbone of a cellular network, providing high speed and stable connection for the whole network, compared to the connectivity between a base station and a mobile node. In most cases, mobile nodes do not communicate with each other directly without going through a base station. A packet from a source mobile node to a destination mobile node is likely to be first transmitted to the base station to which the source mobile node is connected. The packet is then relayed within the fixed infrastructures until reaching the destination base station to which the destination mobile node is connected. The destination base station can then deliver the packet to the destination mobile node to complete the packet delivery.

Cellular Telephone Networks

Cellular telephone networks offer mobile communication for most of us. With a cellular telephone network, base stations are distributed over a region, with each base station covering a small area. Each part of the small area is called a *cell*. Cell phones within a cell connect to the base station of the cell for communication. When a cell phone moves from one cell to another, its connection will also be migrated from one base station to a new base station. The new base station is the base station of the cell into which the cell phone just moved.

Two of the technologies are the mainstream for cellular telephone networks: GSM and CDMA.

GSM is a wireless cellular network technology for mobile communication that has been widely deployed in most parts of the world. Each GSM mobile phone uses a pair of frequency channels, with one channel for sending data and another for receiving data. Time division multiplexing (TDM) is used to share frequency pairs by multiple mobiles.

CDMA is a technology developed by a company named Qualcomm and has been accepted as an international standard. CDMA assumes that multiple signals add linearly, instead of assuming that colliding frames are completely garbled and of no value. With coding theory and the new assumption, CDMA allows each mobile to transmit over the entire frequency spectrum at all times. The core algorithm of CDMA is how to extract data of interest from the mixed data.

802.11 Wireless LANs

Wireless LANs are specified by the IEEE 802.11 series standard [1], which describes various technologies and protocols for wireless LANs to achieve different targets, allowing the maximum bit rate from 2 Mbps to 248 Mbps. Wireless LANs can work in either access point (AP) mode or ad hoc mode, as shown in Fig. 17.3. When a wireless LAN is working in AP mode, all communication passes through a base station, called an access point. The AP then passes the communication data to the destination node, if it is connected to the AP, or forwards the communication data to a router for further routing and relaying. When working in ad hoc mode, wireless LANs work in the absence of base stations. Nodes directly communicate with other nodes within their transmission range, without depending on a base station.

One of the complications that 802.11 wireless LANs incur is medium access control in the data link layer. Medium access control in 802.11 wireless LANs can be either distributed or centralized control by a base station. The distributed medium access control relies on the Carrier Sense Multiple Access (CSMA) with Collision Avoidance (CSMA/CA) protocol. CSMA/CA allows network nodes to compete to transmit data when a channel is idle and uses the Ethernet binary exponential backoff algorithm to decide a waiting time before retransmission when a collision occurs. CSMA/CA can also operate based on MACAW

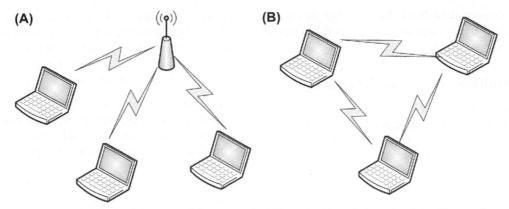

FIGURE 17.3 (A) A wireless network in access point (AP) mode; (B) a wireless network in ad hoc mode.

(Multiple Access with Collision Avoidance for Wireless) using virtual channel sensing. Request packets and clear-to-send (CTS) packets, are broadcast before data transmission by the sender and the receiver, respectively. All stations within the range of the sender or the receiver will keep silent in the course of data transmission to avoid interference on the transmission.

The centralized medium access control is implemented by having the base station broadcast a beacon frame periodically and poll nodes to check whether they have data to send. The base station serves as a central control over the allocation of the bandwidth. It allocates bandwidth according to the polling results. All nodes connected to the base station must behave in accordance with the allocation decision made by the base station. With the centralized medium access control, it is possible to provide quality-of-service guarantees because the base station can control on the allocation of bandwidth to a specific node to meet the quality requirements.

2. WIRELESS AD HOC NETWORKS

Wireless ad hoc networks are distributed networks that work without fixed infrastructures and in which each network node is willing to forward network packets for other network nodes. The main characteristics of wireless ad hoc networks are as follows:

- Wireless ad hoc networks are distributed networks that do not require fixed infrastructures to work. Network nodes in a wireless ad hoc network can be randomly deployed to form the wireless ad hoc network.
- Network nodes will forward network packets for other network nodes. Network nodes in a wireless ad hoc network directly communicate with other nodes within their ranges. When these networks communicate with network nodes outside of their ranges, network packets will be forwarded by the nearby network nodes; and, other nodes that are on the path from the source nodes to the destination nodes.

- Wireless ad hoc networks are self-organizing. Without fixed infrastructures and central administration, wireless ad hoc networks must be capable of establishing cooperation between nodes on their own. Network nodes must also be able to adapt to changes in the network, such as the network topology.
- Wireless ad hoc networks have dynamic network topologies. Network nodes of a wireless ad hoc network connect to other network nodes through wireless links. The network nodes are mostly mobile. The topology of a wireless ad hoc network can change from time to time, since network nodes move around from within the range to the outside, and new network nodes may join the network, just as existing network nodes may leave the network.

Wireless Sensor Networks

A wireless sensor network is an ad hoc network mainly comprising sensor nodes, which are normally used to monitor and observe a phenomenon or a scene. The sensor nodes are physically deployed within or close to the phenomenon or the scene. The collected data will be sent back to a base station from time to time through routes dynamically discovered and formed by sensor nodes.

Sensors in wireless sensor networks are normally small network nodes with very limited computation power, limited communication capacity, and limited power supply. Thus a sensor may perform only simple computation and can communicate with sensors and other nodes within a short range. The life spans of sensors are also limited by the power supply.

Wireless sensor networks can be self-organizing, since sensors can be randomly deployed in some inaccessible areas. The randomly deployed sensors can cooperate with other sensors within their range to implement the task of monitoring or observing the target scene or the target phenomenon and to communicate with the base station that collects data from all sensor nodes. The cooperation might involve finding a route to transmit data to a specific destination, relaying data from one neighbor to another neighbor when the two neighbors are not within reach of each other, and so on.

Wireless Multimedia Sensor Networks

Wireless multimedia sensor networks (WMSNs), developed based on wireless sensor networks, are the networks of wireless, interconnected smart devices that enable processing video and audio streams, still images, and scalar sensor data. WMSNs will enable the retrieval of multimedia streams and will store, process in real-time, correlate, and fuse multimedia content captured by heterogeneous sources. The characteristics of a WMSN diverge consistently from traditional network paradigms, such as the Internet and even from scalar sensor networks. Most potential applications of a WMSN require the sensor network paradigm to be rethought to provide mechanisms to deliver multimedia content with a predetermined level of quality of service (QoS). Whereas minimizing energy consumption has been the main objective in sensor network research, mechanisms to efficiently deliver application-level QoS and to map these requirements to network-layer metrics, such as latency and jitter, have not been primary concerns. Delivery of multimedia content in sensor networks presents new, specific system design challenges, which are the object of this article. Therefore, there is a potential to enable many new applications, including Multimedia Surveillance Sensor Networks, Traffic Avoidance, Enforcement, and Control Systems Advanced Health Care Delivery. Environmental and Structural Monitoring and Industrial Process Control.

Internet of Things

The Internet of Things (IoT) is an emerging global Internet-based information architecture facilitating the exchange of goods and services in global supply-chain networks, the connection of physical things to the Internet makes it possible to access remote sensor data and to control the physical world from a distance. The applications of IoT are based on real physical objectives. For example, the lack of certain goods would automatically be reported to the provider which in turn immediately causes electronic or physical delivery. From a technical point of view, the IoT architecture is based on data communication tools, primarily Radio-Frequency Identification (RFID) tagged items. The IoT has the purpose of providing an IT-infrastructure facilitating the exchanges of "things" in a secure and reliable manner. The most popular industry proposal for the new IT-infrastructure of the IoT is based on an Electronic Product Code (EPC), introduced by EPCglobal and GS1. The "things" are physical objects carrying RFID tags with a unique EPC; the infrastructure can offer and query EPC Information Services (EPCIS) both locally and remotely to clients. Since some important business processes are concerned, a high degree of reliability about IoT is needed. Generally, the following security and privacy requirements are necessary for IoT:

1. Resilience to attacks: IoT system has to avoid single points of failure and should adjust itself to node failures.
2. Data authentication: Retrieved address and object information must be authenticated is a principle for efficient applications.
3. Access control: Information providers of IoT must be able to implement access control scheme on their confidential data.
4. Client privacy: there should be suitable measures to prevent others retrieving clients' private information and data.

Mesh Networks

One of the emerging technologies of wireless network are wireless mesh networks (WMNs). Nodes in a WMN include mesh routers and mesh clients. Each node in a WMN works as a router as well as a host. When it's a router, each node needs to perform routing and to forward packets for other nodes when necessary, such as when two nodes are not within direct reach of each other and when a route to a specific destination for packet delivery is required to be discovered.

Mesh routers may be equipped with multiple wireless interfaces, built on either the same or different wireless technologies, and are capable of bridging different networks. Mesh routers can also be classified as access mesh routers, backbone mesh routers, or gateway mesh routers. Access mesh routers provide mesh clients with access to mesh networks; backbone mesh routers form the backbone of a mesh network; and a gateway mesh router connects the backbone to an external network.

Each mesh client normally has only one network interface that provides network connectivity with other nodes. Mesh clients are not usually capable of bridging different networks, which is different from mesh routers.

Similar to other ad hoc networks, a wireless mesh network can be self-organizing. Thus nodes can establish and maintain connectivity with other nodes automatically, without human intervention. Wireless mesh networks can divided into backbone mesh networks and access mesh networks.

3. SECURITY PROTOCOLS

Wired Equivalent Privacy (WEP) was defined by the IEEE 802.11 standard [1]. WEP is designed to protect linkage-level data for wireless transmission by providing confidentiality, access control, and data integrity, to provide secure communication between a mobile device and an access point in a 802.11 wireless LAN.

4. WIRED EQUIVALENT PRIVACY

Implemented based on shared key secrets and the Rivest Cipher 4 (RC4) stream cipher [2], WEP's encryption of a frame includes two operations (Fig. 17.4). It first produces a checksum of the data, and then it encrypts the plaintext and the checksum using RC4:

- *Checksumming.* Let *c* be an integrity checksum function. For a given message *M*, a checksum *c(M)* is calculated and then concatenated to the end of *M*, obtaining a plaintext $P = <M, c(M)>$. Note that the checksum *c(M)* does not depend on the shared key.
- *Encryption.* The shared key *k* is concatenated to the end of the initialization vector (IV) *v*, forming $<v,k>.<v,k>$ is then used as the input to the RC4 algorithm to generate a keystream $RC4(v,k)$. The plaintext *P* is exclusive-or ed (XOR, denoted by $\oplus$) with the keystream to obtain the ciphertext: $C = P \oplus RC4(v,k)$.

Using the shared key *k* and the IV *v*, WEP can greatly simplify the complexity of key distribution because it needs only to distribute *k* and *v* but can achieve a relatively very long key sequence. IV changes from time to time, which will force the RC4 algorithm to produce a new key sequence, avoiding the situation where the same key sequence is used to encrypt a large amount of data, which potentially leads to several types of attacks [3,4].

WEP combines the shared key *k* and the IV *v* as inputs to seed the RC4 function. 802.11B [1] specifies that the seed shall be 64 bits long, with 24 bits from the IV *v* and 40 bits from the shared key *k*. Bits 0 through 23 of the seed contain bits 0 through 23 of the IV *v*, and bits 24 through 63 of the seed contain bits 0 through 39 of the shared key *k*. When a receiver receives the ciphertext *C*, it will XOR the ciphertext *C* with the corresponding keystream to produce the plaintext *M'* as follows:

$$M' = C \oplus RC4(k, v) = (P \oplus RC4(k, v)) \oplus RC4(k, v) = M$$

Wi-Fi Protected Access (WPA) and WPA2

Wi-Fi Protected Access (WPA) is specified by the IEEE 802.11i standard. The standard is aimed at providing a stronger security compared to WEP and is expected to tackle most of the weakness found in WEP [5–7].

WPA

WPA has been designed to target both enterprise and consumers. Enterprise deployment of WPA is required to be used with IEEE 802.1x authentication, which is responsible for distributing different keys to each user. Personal deployment of WPA adopts a simpler mechanism, which allows all stations to use the same key. This mechanism is called the Pre-Shared Key (PSK) mode.

The WPA protocol works in a similar way to WEP. WPA mandates the use of the RC4 stream cipher with a

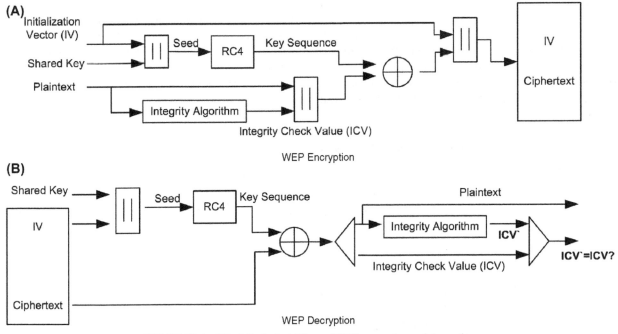

FIGURE 17.4 Wired Equivalent Privacy (WEP) encryption and decryption.

128-bit key and a 48-bit initialization vector (IV), compared with the 40-bit key and the 24-bit IV in WEP.

WPA also has a few other improvements over WEP, including the Temporal Key Integrity Protocol (TKIP) and the Message Integrity Code (MIC). With TKIP, WPA will dynamically change keys used by the system periodically. With the much larger IV and the dynamically changing key, the stream cipher $RC4$ is able to produce a much longer keystream. The longer keystream improved WPA's protection against the well-known key recovery attacks on WEP, since finding two packets encrypted using the same key sequences is literally impossible due to the extremely long keystream.

With MIC, WPA uses an algorithm named Michael to produce an authentication code for each message, which is termed the MIC. The message integrity code also contains a frame counter to provide protection over replay attacks.

WPA uses the Extensible Authentication Protocol (EAP) framework [8] to conduct authentication. When a user (supplicant) tries to connect to a network, an authenticator will send a request to the user asking the user to authenticate herself using a specific type of authentication mechanism. The user will respond with corresponding authentication information. The authenticator relies on an authentication server to make the decision regarding the user's authentication.

WPA2

WPA2 is not much different from WPA. Though TKIP is required in WPA, Advanced Encryption Standard (AES) is optional. This is aimed to provide backward compatibility for WPA over hardware designed for WEP, as TKIP can be implemented on the same hardware as those for WEP, but AES cannot be implemented on this hardware. TKIP and AES are both mandatory in WPA2 to provide a higher level of protection over wireless connections. AES is a block cipher, which can only be applied to a fixed length of data block. AES accepts key sizes of 128, 196, and 256 bits.

Besides the mandatory requirement of supporting AES, WPA2 also introduces supports for fast roaming of wireless clients migrating between wireless access points. First, WPA2 allows the caching of a Pair-Wise Master Key (PMK), which is the key used for a session between an access point and a wireless client; thus a wireless client can reconnect a recently connected access point without having to reauthenticate. Second, WPA2 enables a wireless client to authenticate itself to a wireless access point that it is moving to while the wireless client maintains its connection to the existing access point. This reduces the time needed for roaming clients to move from one access point to another, and it is especially useful for timing-sensitive applications.

SPINS: Security Protocols for Sensor Networks

Sensor nodes in sensor networks are normally low-end devices with very limited resources, such as memory, computation power, battery, and network bandwidth.

Perrig et al. [9] proposed a family of security protocols named SPINS, which were specially designed for low-end devices with severely limited resources, such as sensor nodes in sensor networks. SPINS consists of two building blocks: Secure Network Encryption Protocol (SNEP) and the "micro" version of the Timed, Efficient, Streaming, Loss-tolerant Authentication Protocol (μTESLA). SNEP uses symmetry encryption to provide data confidentiality, two-party data authentication, and data freshness. μTESLA provides authentication over broadcast streams. SPINS assumes that each sensor node shares a master key with the base station. The master key serves as the base of trust and is used to derive all other keys.

Secure Network Encryption Protocol

As illustrated in Fig. 17.5, SNEP uses a block cipher to provide data confidentiality and message authentication code (MAC) to provide authentication. SNEP assumes a shared counter C between the sender and the receiver and two keys, the encryption key K_{encr} and the authentication key K_{mac}. For an outgoing message D, SNEP processes it as follows:

- The message D is first encrypted using a block cipher in counter mode with the key K_{encr} and the counter C, forming the encrypted text $E = \{D\} <K_{encr}, C>$.
- A message authentication code is produced for the encrypted text E with the key K_{mac} and the counter C, forming the MAC $M = MAC(K_{mac}, C|E)$ where $MAC()$ is a one-way function and $C|E$ stands for the concatenation of C and E.
- SNEP increments the counter C.

To send the message D to the recipient, SNEP actually sends out E and M. In other words, SNEP encrypts D to E

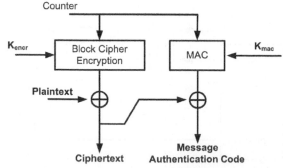

FIGURE 17.5 Sensor Network Encryption Protocol (SNEP).

using the shared key K_{encr} between the sender and the receiver to prevent unauthorized disclosure of the data, and it uses the shared key K_{mac}, known only to the sender and the receiver, to provide message authentication. Thus data confidentiality and message authentication can both be implemented.

The message D is encrypted with the counter C, which will be different in each message. The same message D will be encrypted differently even it is sent multiple times. Thus semantic security is implemented in SNEP. The MAC is also produced using the counter C; thus it enables SNEP to prevent replying to old messages.

Timed, Efficient, Streaming, Loss-tolerant Authentication Protocol

TESLA [10−12] was proposed to provide message authentication for multicast. TESLA does not use any asymmetry cryptography, which makes it lightweight in terms of computation and overhead of bandwidth.

μTESLA is a modified version of TESLA, aiming to provide message authentication for multicasting in sensor networks. The general idea of μTESLA is that the sender splits the sending time into intervals. Packets sent out in different intervals are authenticated with different keys. Keys to authenticate packets will be disclosed after a short delay, when the keys are no longer used to send out messages. Thus packets can be authenticated when the authentication keys have been disclosed. Packets will not be tampered with while they are in transit since the keys have not been disclosed yet. The disclosed authentication keys can be verified using previous known keys to prevent malicious nodes from forging authentication keys.

μTESLA has four phases: sender setup, sending authenticated packets, bootstrapping new receivers, and authenticating packets. In the sender setup phase, a sender generates a chain of keys, K_i ($0 \le i \le n$). The keychain is a one-way chain such that K_i can be derived from K_j if $i \le j$, such as a keychain K_i ($i = 0, \ldots, n$), $K_i = F(K_{i+1})$, where F is a one-way function. The sender also decides on the starting time T_0, the interval duration T_{int}, and the disclosure delay d (unit is interval), as shown in Fig. 17.6.

To send out authenticated packets, the sender attaches a MAC with each packet, where the MAC is produced using a key from the keychain and the data in the network packet. μTESLA has specific requirements on the use of keys for producing MACs. Keys are used in the same order as the key sequence of the keychain. Each of the keys is used in one interval only. For the interval $T_i = T_0 + i \times T_{int}$, the key K_i is used to produce the MACs for the messages sent out in the interval T_i. Keys are disclosed with a fixed delay d such that the key K_i used in interval T_i will be disclosed in the interval T_{i+d}. The sequence of key usage and the sequence of key disclosure are demonstrated in Fig. 17.6.

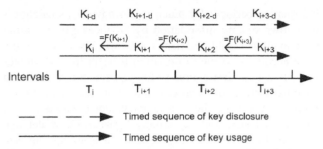

FIGURE 17.6 Sequences of intervals, key usages, and key disclosure.

To bootstrap a new receiver, the sender needs to synchronize the time with the receiver and needs to inform the new receiver of a key K_j that is used in a past interval T_j, the interval duration T_{int}, and the disclosure delay d. With a previous key K_j, the receiver will be able to verify any key K_p where $j \le p$ using the one-way keychain's property. After this, the new receiver will be able to receive and verify data in the same way as other receivers that join the communication prior to the new receiver.

To receive and authenticate messages, a receiver will check all incoming messages if they have been delayed for more than d. Messages with a delay greater than d will be discarded, since they are suspect as fake messages constructed after the key has been disclosed. The receiver will buffer the remaining messages for at least d intervals until the corresponding keys are disclosed. When a key K_i is disclosed at the moment T_{i+d}, the receiver will verify K_i using K_{i-1} by checking if $K_{i-1} = F(K_i)$. Once the key K_i is verified, K_i will be used to authenticate those messages sent in the interval T_i.

5. SECURE ROUTING

Secure Efficient Ad Hoc Distance (SEAD) [13] vector routing is a design based on Destination-Sequenced Distance Vector (DSDV) routing [14]. SEAD augments DSDV with authentication to provide security in the construction and exchange of routing information.

Secure Efficient Ad Hoc Distance

Distance vector routing works as follows. Each router maintains a routing table. Each entry of the table contains a specific destination, a metric (the shortest distance to the destination), and the next hop on the shortest path from the current router to the destination. For a packet that needs to be sent to a certain destination, the router will look up the destination from the routing table to get the matching entry. Then the packet is sent to the next hop specified in the entry.

To allow routers to automatically discover new routes and maintain their routing tables, routers exchange routing information periodically. Each router advises its neighbors of its own routing information by broadcasting its routing table to all its neighbors. Each router will update its routing table according to the information it hears from its neighbors. If a new destination is found from the information advertised by a neighbor, a new entry is added to the routing table with the metric recalculated based on the advertised metric and the linking between the router and the neighbor. If an existing destination is found, the corresponding entry is updated only when a new path that is shorter than the original one has been found. In this case, the metric and the next hop for the specified destination are modified based on the advertised information.

Though distance vector routing is simple and effective, it suffers from possible routing loops, also known as the counting to infinity problem. DSDV [14] is one of the extensions to distance vector routing to tackle this issue. DSDV augments each routing update with a sequence number, which can be used to identify the sequence of routing updates, preventing routing updates being applied in an out-of-order manner. Newer routing updates are advised with sequence numbers greater than those of the previous routing updates. In each routing update, the sequence number will be incremented to the next even number. Only when a broken link has been detected will the router use the next odd sequence number as the sequence number for the new routing update that is to be advertised to all its neighbors. Each router maintains an even sequence number to identify the sequence of every routing update. Neighbors will only accept newer routing updates by discarding routing updates with sequence numbers less than the last sequence number heard from the router.

SEAD provides authentication on metrics' lower bounds and senders' identities by using the one-way hash chain. Let H be a hash function and x be a given value. A list of values is computed as follows:

$$h_0, h_1, h_2, ..., h_n$$

where $h_0 = x$ and $h_{i+1} = H(h_i)$ for $0 \leq i \leq$ n. Given any value h_k that has been confirmed to be in the list, to authenticate if a given value d is on the list or not one can compute if d can be derived from h_k by applying H a certain number of times, or if h_k can be derived from d by applying H to d a certain number of times. If either d can be derived from h_k or h_k can be derived from d within a certain number of steps, it is said that d can be authenticated by h_k.

SEAD assumes an upper bound $m - 1$ on the diameter of the ad hoc network, which means that the metric of a routing entry will be less than m. Let h_0, h_1, h_2, ..., h_n be a hash chain where $n = m \times k$ and $k \in Z^+$. For an update with the sequence number i and the metric value of j, the value $h_{(k-i)m+j}$ is used to authenticate the routing update entry. By using $h_{(k-i)m+j}$ to authenticate the routing update

entry, a node is actually disclosing the value $h_{(k-i)m+j}$ and subsequently all h_p where $p \geq (k-i)m+j$, but not any value h_q where $q \leq (k-i)m+j$.

Using a hash value corresponding to the sequence number and metric in a routing update entry allows the authentication of the update and prevents any node from advertising a route to some destination, forging a greater sequence number or a smaller metric. To authenticate the update, a node can use any given earlier authentic hash value h_p from the same hash chain to authenticate the current update with sequence number i and metric j. The current update uses the hash value $h_{(k-i)m+j}$ and $(k-i)m+J \leq P$, thus h_p can be computed from $h_{(k-i)m+j}$ by applying H for $(k-i)m+j-p$ times.

The disclosure of $h_{(k-i)m+j}$ does not disclose any value h_q where $q \leq (k-i)m+j$. Let a fake update be advised with a sequence number p and metric q, where $p \geq i$ and $q \leq j$, or $q \leq j$. The fake update will need to use the hash value $h_{(k-P)m+q}$. If the sequence number p is greater than i or the metric q is less than j, $(k-p)m+q<(k-i)m+j$. This means that a hash value $h_{(k-p)m+q}$ that has not been disclosed is needed to authenticate the update. Since the value $h_{(k-p)m+q}$ has not been disclosed, the malicious node will not be able to have it to fake a routing update.

Ariadne

Ariadne [15] is a secure on-demand routing protocol for ad hoc networks. Ariadne is built on the Dynamic Source Routing protocol (DSR) [16].

Routing in Ariadne is divided into two stages: the route discovery stage and the route maintenance stage. In the route discovery stage, a source node in the ad hoc network tries to find a path to a specific destination node. The discovered path will be used by the source node as the path for all communication from the source node to the destination node until the discovered path becomes invalid. In the route maintenance stage, network nodes identify broken paths that have been found. A node sends a packet along a specified route to some destination. Each node on the route forwards the packet to the next node on the specified route and tries to confirm the delivery of the packet to the next node. If a node fails to receive an acknowledgment from the next node, it will signal the source node using a ROUTE ERROR packet that a broken link has been found. The source node and other nodes on the path can then be advised of the broken link.

The key security features Ariadne adds onto the route discovery and route maintenance are node authentication and data verification for the routing relation packets. Node authentication is the process of verifying the identifiers of nodes that are involved in Ariadne's route discovery and route maintenance, to prevent forging routing packets. In route discovery, a node sends out a ROUTE REQUEST packet to perform a route discovery. When the ROUTE REQUEST packet reaches the destination node, the destination node verifies the originator identity before responding. Similarly, when the source node receives a ROUTE REPLY packet, which is a response to the ROUTE REQUEST packet, the source node will also authenticate the identity of the sender. The authentication of node identities can be of one of the three methods: TELSA, digital signatures, and MAC.

Data verification is the process of verifying the integrity of the node list in route discovery for the prevention of adding and removing nodes from the node list in a ROUTE RQUEST. To build a full list of nodes for a route to a destination, each node will need to add itself into the node list in the ROUTE REQUEST when it forwards the ROUTE REQUEST to its neighbor. Data verification protects the node list by preventing unauthorized adding of nodes and unauthorized removal of nodes.

6. AUTHENTICATED ROUTING FOR AD HOC NETWORKS

Authenticated Routing for Ad Hoc Networks (ARAN) [17] is a routing protocol for ad hoc networks with authentication enabled. It allows routing messages to be authenticated at each node between the source nodes and the destination nodes. The authentication that ARAN has implemented is based on cryptographic certificates.

ARAN requires a trusted certificate server, the public key of which is known to all valid nodes. Keys are assumed to have been established between the trusted certificate server and nodes. For each node to enter into a wireless ad hoc network, it needs to have a certificate issued by the trusted server. The certificate contains the IP address of the node, the public key of the node, a time stamp indicating the issue time of the certification, and the expiration time of the certificate. Because all nodes have the public key of the trusted server, a certificate can be verified by all nodes to check whether it is authentic. With an authentic certificate and the corresponding private key, the node that owns the certificate can authenticate itself using its private key.

To discover a route from a source node to the destination node, the source node sends out a route discovery packet (RDP) to all its neighbors. The RDP is signed by the source node's private key and contains a nonce, a time stamp, and the source node's certificate. The time stamp and the nonce work to prevent replay attacks and flooding of the RDP.

The RDP is then rebroadcast in the network until it reaches the destination. The RDP is rebroadcast with the signature and the certificate of the rebroadcaster. On receiving an RDP, each node will first verify the source's signature and the previous node's signature on the RDP.

On receiving an RDP, the destination sends back a reply packet (REP) along the reverse path to the source after validating the RDP. The REP contains the nonce specified in the RDP and the signature from the destination node.

The REP is unicast along the reverse path. Each node on the path will put its own certificate and its own signature on the RDP before forwarding it to the next node. Each node will also verify the signatures on the RDP. An REP is discarded if one or more invalid signatures are found on the REP.

When the source receives the REP, it will first verify the signatures and then the nonce in the REP. A valid REP indicates that a route has been discovered. The node list on a valid REP suggests an operational path from the source node to the destination node that is found.

As an on-demand protocol, nodes keep track of route status. If there has been no traffic for a route's lifetime or a broken link has been detected, the route will be deactivated. Receiving data on an inactive route will force a node to signal an error state by using an error (ERR) message. The ERR message is signed by the node that produces it and will be forwarded to the source without modification. The ERR message contains a nonce and a time stamp to ensure that the ERR message is fresh.

7. SECURE LINK STATE ROUTING PROTOCOL

Secure Link State Routing Protocol (SLSP) [18] is a secure routing protocol for an ad hoc network building based on link state protocols. SLSP assumes that each node has a public/private key pair and has the capability of signing and verifying digital signatures. Keys are bound with the MAC and the IP address, allowing neighbors within transmission range to uniquely verify nodes if public keys have been known prior to communication.

In SLSP, each node broadcasts its IP address and the MAC to its neighbor with its signature. Neighbors verify the signature and keep a record of the pairing IP address and the MAC. The Neighbor Lookup Protocol (NLP) of SLSP extracts and retains the MAC and IP address of each network frame received by a node. The extracted information is used to maintain the mapping of MACs and IP addresses.

Nodes using SLSP periodically send out link state updates (LSUs) to advise the state of their network links. LSU packets are limited to propagating within a zone of their origin node, which is specified by the maximum number of hops. To restrict the propagation of LSU packets, each LSU packet contains the zone radius and the hops traversed fields. Let the maximum hop be R; X, a random number; and H be a hash function. *Zone-radius* will be initialized to $H^R(X)$ and *hops−traversed* be initialized to $H(X)$. Each

LSU packet also contains a *TTL* field initialized as $R - 1$. If $TTL < 0$ or $H(hops-traversed) = zone\text{-}radius$, a node will not rebroadcast the LSU packet. Otherwise, the node will replace the *hops−traversed* field with $H(hops-traversed)$ and decrease *TTL* by one. In this way, the hop count is authenticated. SLSP also uses signatures to protect LSU packets. Receiving nodes can verify the authenticity and the integrity of the received LSU packets, thus preventing forging or tampering with LSU packets.

8. KEY ESTABLISHMENT

Because wireless communication is open and the signals are accessible by anyone within the vicinity, it is important for wireless networks to establish trust to guard the access to the networks. Key establishment builds relations between nodes using keys; thus security services, such as authentication, confidentiality, and integrity can be achieved for the communication between these nodes with the help of the established keys.

The dynamically changing topology of wireless networks, the lack of fixed infrastructure of wireless ad hoc and sensor networks, and the limited computation and energy resources of sensor networks, have all added complication to the key establishment process in wireless networks.

Bootstrapping

Bootstrapping is the process by which nodes in a wireless network are made aware of the presence of others in the network. On bootstrapping, a node gets its identifying credentials that can be used in the network the node is trying to join. Upon completion of the bootstrapping, the wireless network should be ready to accept the node as a valid node to join the network.

To enter a network, a node needs to present its identifying credential to show its eligibility to access the network. This process is called preauthentication. Once the credentials are accepted, network security associations are established with other nodes.

These network security associations will serve as further proof of authorization in the network. Security associations can be of various forms, including symmetric keys, public key pairs, hash key chains, and so on. The security associations can be used to authenticate nodes. Security associations may expire after a certain period of time and can be revoked if necessary. For example, if a node is suspected of being compromised, its security association will be revoked to prevent the node accessing the network. The actual way of revocation depends on the form of the security associations.

Bootstrapping in Wireless Ad Hoc Networks

Wireless ad hoc networks bring new challenges to the bootstrapping process by their lack of a centralized security infrastructure. It is necessary to build a security infrastructure in the bootstrapping phase. The trust infrastructure should be able to accept nodes with valid credentials to enter the network but stop those nodes without valid credentials from joining the network and establish security association between nodes within the network.

To build such a trust infrastructure, we can use any one of the following three supports: prior knowledge, trusted third parties, or self-organizing capability. Prior knowledge is information that has been set on valid nodes in advance, such as predistributed secrets or preset shared keys. This information can be used to distinguish legitimate nodes from malicious ones. Only nodes with prior knowledge will be accepted to enter the network. For example, the predistributed secrets can be used to authenticate legitimate nodes, so the network can simply reject those nodes without the predistributed secrets so that they can't enter the network.

Trusted third parties can also be used to support the establishment of the trust infrastructure. The trusted third party can be a Certificate Authority (CA), a base station of the wireless network, or any nodes that are designated to be trusted. If trusted third parties are used, all nodes must mutually agree to trust them and derive their trust on others from the trusted third parties. One of the issues with this method is that trusted third parties are required to be available for access by all nodes across the whole network, which is a very strong assumption for wireless networks as well as an impractical requirement.

It is desirable to have a self-organizing capability for building the trust infrastructure for wireless networks, taking into account the dynamically changing topology of wireless ad hoc networks. Implementing a self-organizing capability for building the trust infrastructure often requires an out-of-band authenticated communication channel or special hardware support, such as tamper-proof hardware tokens.

Bootstrapping in Wireless Sensor Networks

Bootstrapping nodes in wireless sensor networks is also challenging for the following reasons:

- *Node capture.* Sensor nodes are normally deployed in an area that is geographically close or inside the monitoring environment, which might not be a closed and confined area under guard. Thus sensor nodes are vulnerable to physical capture because it might be difficult to prevent physical access to the area.
- *Node replication.* Once a sensor node is compromised, it is possible for adversaries to replicate sensor nodes by using the secret acquired from the compromised node. In this case, adversaries can produce fake legitimate node that cannot be distinguished by the network.
- *Scalability.* A single-sensor network may comprise a large number of sensor nodes. The more nodes in a

wireless sensor network, the more complicated it is for bootstrapping.

- *Resource limitation.* Sensor nodes normally have extremely limited computation power and memory as well as limited power supply and weak communication capability. This makes some of the deliberate algorithms and methods not applicable to wireless sensor networks. Only those algorithms that require a moderate amount of resources can be implemented in wireless sensor networks.

Bootstrapping a sensor node is achieved using an incremental communication output power level to discover neighbors nearby. The output power level is increased step by step from the minimum level to the maximum level, to send out a HELLO message. This will enable the sensor node to discover neighbors in the order of their distance from the sensor node, from the closest to the farthest away.

Key Management

Key management schemes can be classified according to the way keys are set up (Fig. 17.7). Either keys are managed based on the contribution from all participating nodes in the network or they are managed based on a central node in the network. Thus key management schemes can be divided into contributory key management schemes, in which all nodes work equally together to manage the keys, and distributed key management schemes, in which only one central node is responsible for key management [19].

Classification

The distributed key management scheme can be further divided into symmetric schemes and public key schemes. Symmetric key schemes are based on private key cryptography, whereby shared secrets are used to authenticate legitimate nodes and to provide secure communication between them. The underlying assumption is that the shared secrets are known only to legitimate nodes involved in the interaction. Thus proving the knowledge of the shared

secrets is enough to authenticate legitimate nodes. Shared secrets are distributed via secure channels or out-of-band measures. Trust on a node is established if the node has knowledge of a shared secret.

Public key schemes are built on public key cryptography. Keys are constructed in pairs, with a private key and a public key in each pair. Private keys are kept secret by the owners. Public keys are distributed and used to authenticate nodes and to verify credentials. Keys are normally conveyed in certificates for distribution. Certificates are signed by trusted nodes for which the public keys have been known and validated. Trust on the certificates will be derived from the public keys that sign the certificates. Note that given $g^i \ (mod \ p)$ and $g^j \ (mod \ p)$, it is hard to compute $g^{i*j} \ (mod \ p)$ without the knowledge of i and j.

Contributory Schemes

Diffie-Hellman (D-H) [20] is a well-known algorithm for establishing shared secrets. The D-H algorithm's strength depends on the discrete log problem: It is hard to calculate s if given the value $g^s \ (mod \ p)$, where p is a large prime number.

Diffie-Hellman Key Exchange

D-H was designed for establishing a shared secret between two parties, namely node A and node B. Each party agrees on a large prime number p and a generator g. A and B each choose a random value i and j, respectively. A and B are then exchanged with the public values $g^i \ (mod \ p)$ and $g^j \ (mod \ p)$. On the reception of $g^j \ (mod \ p)$ from B, A is then able to calculate the value $g^{j \times i} \ (mod \ p)$. Similarly, B computes $g^{i \times j} \ (mod \ p)$. Thus a shared secret, $g^{i \times j} \ (mod \ p)$, has been set up between A and B.

9. INGEMARSSON, TANG, AND WONG

Ingemarsson, Tang, and Wong (ING) [21] extends the D-F key exchange to a group of n members, $d_1, ..., d_n$. All group members are organized in a ring, where each member has a left neighbor and a right neighbor. Node d_i has a right

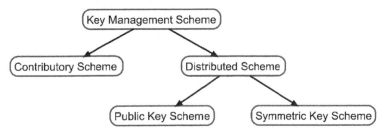

FIGURE 17.7 Key management schemes.

neighbor d_{i-1} and a left neighbor d_{i+1}. Note that for node d_i, its right neighbor is d_{i+1}; for node d_{i+1}, its left neighbor is d_i.

Same as the D-F algorithm, all members in an ING group assume a large prime number p and a generator g. Initially, node d_i will choose a random number r_i. At the first round of key exchange, node d_i will compute $g^{r_i} \pmod p$ and send it to its left neighbor d_{i+1}. At the same time, node d_i also receives the public value $g^{r_{i-1}} \pmod p$ from its right neighbor d_{i-1}. From the second round on, let q be the value that node d_i received in the previous round, node d_i will compute a new public value $q^{d_i} \pmod p$. After $n-1$ rounds, the node d_i would have received a public value, $g^k \pmod p$ where $k = \prod_{m=1}^{i-1} r_m \times \prod_{s=i+1}^{n} r_s$, from its right neighbors. With the public value received at the $n-1$th round, the node d_i can raise it to the power of r_i to compute the value $g^l \pmod p$ where $l = \prod_{m=1}^{n} r_m$.

Hypercube and Octopus

The hypercube protocol [22] assumes that there are 2^d nodes joining to establish a shared secret and all nodes are organized as a d-dimensional vector space $GF(2)^d$ Let $b_1, \ldots, b_d$ be the basic of $GF(2)^d$. The hypercube protocol takes d rounds to complete:

- In the first round, every participant $v \in GF(2)^d$ chooses a random number r_v and conducts a D-H key exchange with another participant $v + b_1$, with the random values r_v and r_{v+b_1}, respectively.
- In the ith round, every participant $v \in GF(2)^d$ performances a D-H key exchange with the participant $v + b_i$, where both v and $v + b_i$ use the value generated in the previous round as the random number for D-H key exchange.

This algorithm can be explained using a complete binary tree to make it more comprehensible. All the nodes are put in a complete binary tree as leaves, with leaves at the 0-level and the root at the d-level. D-H key exchanges are performed from the leaves up to the root. The key exchange takes d rounds:

- In the first round, each leaf chooses a random number k and performs a D-H key exchange with its sibling leaf, which has a random number j, and the resulting value $g^{k \times j} \pmod p$ is saved as the random value for the parent node of the above two leaves.
- In the ith round, each node at the $i-1$ level performs a D-H key exchange with its sibling node using the random numbers m and n, respectively, that they received in the previous round. The resulting value $g^{m \times n} \pmod p$ is saved as the random value for the parent node of the above two nodes.

After d rounds, the root of the complete binary tree contains the established shared secrets. The hypercube protocol assumes that there are 2^d network nodes. The octopus protocol removes the assumption and extends the hypercube protocol to work with an arbitrary number of nodes. Thus the octopus protocol can be used to establish a shared key for a node set containing an arbitrary number of nodes.

Distributed Schemes

A partially distributed threshold CA scheme [23] works with a normal public key infrastructure (PKI) system where a CA exists. The private key of the CA is split and distributed over a set of n server nodes using a (k,n) secret-sharing scheme [24]. The (k,n) secret-sharing scheme allows any k or more server nodes within the n server nodes to work together to reveal the CA's private key. Any set of nodes with fewer than k nodes will not be able to reveal the CA's private key. With the threshold signature scheme [25], any k of the n nodes can cooperate to sign a certificate. Each of the k nodes produces a piece of the signature on the request of signing a given certificate. With all the k pieces of the signature, a valid signature, which is the same as the one produced using the CA's private key, can be produced by combining the k pieces of the signature.

Partially Distributed Threshold Certificate Authority Scheme

In this way, the partial distributed threshold CA scheme can avoid the bottleneck of the centralized CA of conventional PKI infrastructures. As long as there are at least k of the n nodes available, the network can always issue and sign new certificates. Attacks to any single node will not bring the whole CA down. Only when an attack manages to paralyze $n-k$ or more nodes will the CA's signing service not be available.

To further improve the security of the private key that is distributed over the n nodes, proactive security [26] can be imposed. Proactive security forces the private key shares to be refreshed periodically. Each refreshment will invalidate the previous share held by a node. Attacks on multiple nodes must complete within a refresh period to succeed. To be specific, only when an attack can compromise k or more nodes within a refresh period can the attack succeed.

While conventional PKI systems depend on directories to publish public key certificates, it is suggested that certificates should be disseminated to communication peers when establishing a communication channel with the partial distributed threshold CA scheme. This is due to the fact that the availability of centralized directories cannot be guaranteed in wireless networks. Therefore it is not realistic to assume the availability of a centralized directory.

Self-Organized Key Management (PGP-A)

A self-organized key management scheme (PGP-A) [27] has its basis in the Pretty Good Privacy (PGP) [28] scheme. PGP is built based on the "web of trust" model, in which all nodes have equal roles in playing a CA. Each node generates its own public/private key pair and signs other nodes' public keys if it trusts the nodes. The signed certificates are kept by nodes in their own certificate repositories instead of being published by centralized directories in the X.509 PKI systems [29].

PGP-A treats trust as transitive. So, trust can be derived from a trusted node's trust on another node, that is, if node A trusts node B, and node B trusts node C, then A should also trust C if A knows the fact that node B trusts node C.

To verify a key of a node u, a node j will merge its certificate repository with those of j's trusted nodes, and those of the nodes trusted by j's trusted nodes, and so forth. In this way, node j can build up a web of trust in which node j is at the center of the web and j's directly trusted nodes as node j's neighbors. Node l is linked with node k if node k trusts node l. Node j can search the web of trust built as above to find a path from j to u. If such as path exists, let it be a sequence of nodes S: $node_i$ where $i = 1, ..., n$, n be the length of the path, and $node_1 = j$ and $node_n = u$. This means that $node_i$ trust $node_{i+1}$ for all $i = 1, ..., n-1$. Therefore u can be trusted by j. The path S represents a verifiable chain of certificates. PGP-A does not guarantee that a node u that should be trusted by node j will always be trusted by node j, since there are chances that the node j fails to find a path from node j to node u in the web of trust. This might be due to the reason that node j has not acquired enough certificates from its trusted nodes to cover the path from node j to node u.

Self-Healing Session Key Distribution

The preceding two key management schemes are public key management schemes. The one discussed here, a self-healing session key distribution [30], is a symmetric key management scheme. In such a scheme, keys can be distributed either by an online key distribution server or by key predistribution. A key predistribution scheme normally comprises the key predistribution phase, the shared-key discovery phase, and the path key establishment phase.

In the key predistribution phase, a key pool of a large number of keys is created. Every key can be identified by a unique key identifier. Each network node is given a set of keys from the key pool. The shared-key discovery phase begins when a node tries to communicate with the others. All nodes exchange their key identifiers to find out whether there are any keys shared with others. The shared keys can then be used to establish a secure channel for communication. If no shared key exists, a key path will need to be discovered. The key path is a sequence of nodes with which all adjacent nodes share a key. With the key path, a message can travel from the first node to the last node securely, by which a secure channel can be established between the first node and the last node.

The self-healing session key distribution (S-HEAL) [30] assumes the existence of a group manager and preshared secrets. Keys are distributed from the group manager to group members. Let h be a polynomial, where for a node i, node i knows about $h(i)$. Let K be the group key to be distributed, K is covered by h in the distribution: $f(x) = h(x) + K$. The polynomial $f(x)$ is the information that the group manager sends out to all its group members. For node j, node j will calculate $K = f(j) - h(j)$ to reveal the group key. Without the knowledge of $h(j)$, node j will not be able to recover K.

To enable revocation in S-HEAL, the polynomial $h(x)$ is replaced by a bivariate polynomial $s(x,y)$. The group key is covered by the bivariate polynomial $s(x,y)$ when it is distributed to group members, in the way that $f(N,x) = s(N,x) + K$. Node i must calculate $s(N,i)$ to recover K. The revocation enabled S-HEAL tries to stop revoked nodes to calculate $s(N,i)$, thus preventing them to recover K.

Let s of degree t; then $t + 1$ values are needed to compute $s(x,i)$. Assuming that $s(i,i)$ is predistributed to node i, node i will need another t values to recover $s(N,i)$, namely $s(r_1,x), ..., s(r_t,x)$. These values will be disseminating to group members together with the key update. If the group manager wants to revoke node i, the group manager can set one of the values $s(r_1,x), ..., s(r_t,x)$ to $s(i,x)$. In this case, node i obtains only t values instead of $t + 1$ values. Therefore, node i will not be able to compute $s(x,i)$, thus it will not be able to recover K. This scheme can only revoke maximum t nodes at the same time.

Now, let's take a very brief look at wireless network security management countermeasures. Security comes at a cost: either in dollars spent on security equipment, in inconvenience and maintenance, or in operating expenses. Some organizations may be willing to accept risk because applying various management countermeasures may exceed financial or other constraints.

10. MANAGEMENT COUNTERMEASURES

Management countermeasures ensure that all critical personnel are properly trained on the use of wireless technology. Network administrators need to be fully aware of the security risks that wireless networks and devices pose. They must work to ensure security policy compliance and to know what steps to take in the event of an attack (see checklist: "An Agenda for Action when Implementing Wireless Network Security Policies").

Management countermeasures for securing wireless networks begin with a comprehensive security policy. A security policy, and compliance therewith, is the foundation on which other countermeasures (the operational and technical) are rationalized and implemented. Finally, the most important countermeasures are trained and aware users.

An Agenda for Action when Implementing Wireless Network Security Policies

The items below are possible actions that organizations should consider; some of the items may not apply to all organizations. A wireless network security policy should be able to do the following (check all tasks completed):

_____**1.** Identify who may use WLAN technology in an organization.

_____**2.** Identify whether Internet access is required.

_____**3.** Describe who can install access points and other wireless equipment.

_____**4.** Provide limitations on the location of and physical security for access points.

_____**5.** Describe the type of information that may be sent over wireless links.

_____**6.** Describe conditions under which wireless devices are allowed.

_____**7.** Define standard security settings for access points.

_____**8.** Describe limitations on how the wireless device may be used, such as location.

_____**9.** Describe the hardware and software configuration of any access device.

_____**10.** Provide guidelines on reporting losses of wireless devices and security incidents.

_____**11.** Provide guidelines on the use of encryption and other security software.

_____**12.** Define the frequency and scope of security assessments.

---

11. SUMMARY

Organizations should understand that maintaining a secure wireless network is an ongoing process that requires greater effort than for other networks and systems. Moreover, it is important that organizations more frequently assess risks and test and evaluate system security controls when wireless technologies are deployed. Maintaining a secure wireless network (and associated devices) requires significant effort, resources, and vigilance, and involves the following steps:

- Maintaining a full understanding of the topology of the wireless network.
- Labeling and keeping inventories of the fielded wireless and handheld devices.
- Creating frequent backups of data.
- Performing periodic security testing and assessment of the wireless network.
- Performing ongoing, randomly timed security audits to monitor and track wireless and handheld devices.

- Applying patches and security enhancements.
- Monitoring the wireless industry for changes to standards to enhance to security features and for the release of new products.
- Vigilantly monitoring wireless technology for new threats and vulnerabilities.

Organizations should not undertake wireless deployment for essential operations until they understand and can acceptably manage and mitigate the risks to their information, system operations, and risk to the continuity of essential operations. As described in this chapter, the risks provided by wireless technologies are considerable. Many current communications protocols and commercial products provide inadequate protection and thus present unacceptable risks to organizational operations. Agencies must proactively address such risks to protect their ability to support essential operations before deployment. Furthermore, many organizations poorly administer their wireless technologies. Some examples include deploying equipment with factory default settings; failing to control or inventory their access points; not implementing the security capabilities provided; and not developing or employing a security architecture suitable to the wireless environment (firewalls between wired and wireless systems, blocking unneeded services/ports, using strong cryptography, etc.). To a large extent, most of the risks can be mitigated. However, mitigating these risks requires considerable tradeoffs between technical solutions and costs. Today, the vendor and standards community is aggressively working toward more robust, open, and secure solutions for the near future.

Finally, let's move on to the real interactive part of this Chapter: review questions/exercises, hands-on projects, case projects, and optional team case project. The answers and/or solutions by chapter can be found in the Online Instructor's Solutions Manual.

CHAPTER REVIEW QUESTIONS/ EXERCISES

True/False

1. True or False? Wireless networks are a general term to refer to various types of networks that communicate without the need of wire lines.
2. True or False? Cellular networks require fixed infrastructures to work.
3. True or False? Wireless ad hoc networks are distributed networks that work without fixed infrastructures and in which each network node is willing to forward network packets for other network nodes.
4. True or False? WEP is designed to protect linkage-level data for wireless transmission by providing confidentiality,

access control, and data integrity, to provide secure communication between a mobile device and an access point in a 802.11 wireless LAN.
5. True or False? The WPA standard is aimed at providing a stronger security compared to WEP and is expected to tackle most of the weakness found in WEP.

Multiple Choice

1. Personal deployment of WPA adopts a simpler mechanism, which allows all stations to use the same key. This mechanism is called the:
   A. *RC*4 stream cipher
   B. Temporal Key Integrity Protocol (TKIP)
   C. Pre-Shared Key (PSK) mode
   D. Message Integrity Code (MIC)
   E. Extensible Authentication Protocol (EAP) framework
2. What are low-end devices with very limited resources, such as memory, computation power, battery, and network bandwidth?
   A. SPINS
   B. Sequences of intervals
   C. Key usages
   D. Sensor nodes
   E. All of the above
3. Secure Efficient Ad hoc Distance (SEAD) vector routing is a design based on a:
   A. Secure on-demand routing protocol
   B. ROUTE RQUEST
   C. Message Authentication Code (MAC)
   D. Authenticated Routing for Ad hoc Networks (ARAN)
   E. Destination-Sequenced Distance Vector (DSDV) routing
4. What requires a trusted certificate server, where the public key is known to all valid nodes?
   A. ARAN
   B. RDP
   C. REP
   D. ERR
   E. All of the above
5. What is a secure routing protocol for an ad hoc network building based on link state protocols?
   A. Neighbor Lookup Protocol (NLP)
   B. Secure Link State Routing Protocol (SLSP)
   C. Bootstrapping protocol
   D. Preauthentication protocol
   E. All of the above

EXERCISE

Problem

What is WEP?

Hands-On Projects

Project

What is a WEP key?

Case Projects

Problem

Organization A is considering implementing a WLAN so that employees may use their laptop computers anywhere within the boundaries of their office building. Before deciding, however, Organization A has its computer security department perform a risk assessment. The security department first identifies WLAN vulnerabilities and threats. The department, assuming that threat-sources will try to exploit WLAN vulnerabilities, determines the overall risk of operating a WLAN and the impact a successful attack would have on Organization A. The manager reads the risk assessment and decides that the residual risk exceeds the benefit the WLAN provides. The manager directs the computer security department to identify additional countermeasures to mitigate residual risk before the system can be implemented. What are those additional countermeasures?

Optional Team Case Project

Problem

Organization C is considering purchasing mobiles devices for its sales force of 300 employees. Before making a decision to purchase the mobiles devices, the computer security department performs a risk assessment. What did the computer security department find out from the risk assessment?

REFERENCES

[1] L. M. S. C. of the IEEE Computer Society, Wireless LAN Medium Access Control (MAC) and Physical Layer (PHY) Specifications, Technical Report, IEEE Standard 802.11, 1999 ed., 1999.
[2] R.L. Rivest, The RC4 Encryption Algorithm, RSA Data Security, Inc., March 1992. Technical Report.
[3] E. Dawson, L. Nielsen, Automated cryptanalysis of XOR plaintext strings, Cryptologia 20 (2) (April 1996).
[4] S. Singh, The Code Book: The Evolution of Secrecy from Mary, Queen of Scots, to Quantum Cryptography, Doubleday, 1999.
[5] W.A. Arbaugh, An Inductive Chosen Plaintext Attack Against WEP/WEP2, IEEE Document 802.11—01/230, May 2001.
[6] J.R. Walker, Unsafe at Any Key Size; an Analysis of the WEP Encapsulation, IEEE Document 802.11—00/362, October 2000.
[7] N. Borisov, I. Goldberg, D. Wagner, Intercepting Mobile Communications: The Insecurity of 802.11, MobiCom, 2001.
[8] B. Aboba, L. Blunk, J. Vollbrecht, J. Carlson, E.H. Levkowetz, Extensible Authentication Protocol (EAP), Request for Comment, Network Working Group, 2004.

[9] A. Perrig, R. Szewczyk, V. Wen, D. Culler, J.D. Tygar, SPINS: security protocols for sensor networks, in: MobiCom '01: Proceedings of the 7th Annual International Conference on Mobile Computing and Networking, 2001.

[10] A. Perrig, R. Canetti, D. Xiaodong Song, J.D. Tygar, Efficient and secure source authentication for multicast, in: NDSS 01: Network and Distributed System Security Symposium, 2001.

[11] A. Perrig, J.D. Tygar, D. Song, R. Canetti, Efficient authentication and signing of multicast streams over lossy channels, in: SP '00: Proceedings of the 2000 IEEE Symposium on Security and Privacy, 2000.

[12] A. Perrig, R. Canetti, J.D. Tygar, D. Song, RSA CryptoBytes, 5, (2002).

[13] Y.-C. Hu, D.B. Johnson, A. Perrig, SEAD: secure efficient distance vector routing for mobile wireless ad hoc networks, in: WMCSA '02: Proceedings of the Fourth IEEE Workshop on Mobile Computing Systems and Applications, IEEE Computer Society, Washington, DC, 2002.

[14] C.E. Perkins, P. Bhagwat, Highly dynamic destination-sequenced distance-vector routing (DSDV) for mobile computers, SIGCOMM Comput. Commun. Rev. 24 (4) (1994) 234—244.

[15] Y.-C. Hu, A. Perrig, D. Johnson, Ariadne: a secure on-demand routing protocol for ad hoc networks, Wire. Netw. J. 11 (1) (2005).

[16] D.B. Johnson, D.A. Maltz, Dynamic Source Routing in Ad Hoc Wireless Networks Mobile Computing, Kluwer Academic Publishers, 1996.

[17] K. Sanzgiri, B. Dahill, B.N. Levine, C. Shields, E.M. Belding-Royer, A secure routing protocol for ad hoc networks, in: 10th IEEE International Conference on Network Protocols (ICNP'02), 2002.

[18] P. Papadimitratos, Z.J. Haas, Secure Link State Routing for Mobile Ad Hoc Networks, Saint-w, 00, 2003.

[19] E. Cayirci, C. Rong, Security in Wireless Ad Hoc, Sensor, and Mesh Networks, John Wiley & Sons, 2008.

[20] W. Diffie, M.E. Hellman, New directions in cryptography, IEEE Trans. Inf. Theory IT-22 (6) (1976) 644—654.

[21] I. Ingemarsson, D. Tang, C. Wong, A conference key distribution system, IEEE Trans. Inf. Theory 28 (5) (September 1982) 714—720.

[22] K. Becker, U. Wille, Communication complexity of group key distribution, in: ACM Conference on Computer and Communications Security, 1998.

[23] L. Zhou, Z.J. Haas, Securing ad hoc networks, IEEE Netw. 13 (1999) 24—30.

[24] A. Shamir, How to share a secret, Comm. ACM 22 (11) (1979).

[25] Y. Desmedt, Some Recent Research Aspects of Threshold Cryptography, ISW, 1997, pp. 158—173.

[26] R. Canetti, A. Gennaro, D. Herzberg, Naor, proactive security: long-term protection against break-ins, CryptoBytes 3 (1) (Spring 1997).

[27] S. Capkun, L. Buttyán, J.-P. Hubaux, Self-organized public-key management for mobile ad hoc networks, IEEE Trans. Mob. Comput. 2 (1) (2003) 52—64.

[28] P. Zimmermann, The Official PGP User's Guide, The MIT Press, 1995.

[29] ITU-T, Recommendation X.509, ISO/IEC 9594—8, Information Technology: Open Systems Interconnection — The Directory: Public-key and Attribute Certificate Frameworks, fourth ed., ITU, 2000.

[30] J. Staddon, S.K. Miner, M.K. Franklin, D. Balfanz, M. Malkin, D. Dean, Self-healing key distribution with revocation, in: IEEE Symposium on Security and Privacy, 2002.

Chapter 18

Wireless Sensor Network Security: The Internet of Things

Harsh Kupwade Patil[1] and Thomas M. Chen[2]

[1]*Southern Methodist University, Dallas, Texas, USA;* [2]*Swansea University, Wales, United Kingdom*

1. INTRODUCTION TO WIRELESS SENSOR NETWORKS

Advances in microelectronic mechanical systems and wireless communication technologies have led to the proliferation of wireless sensor networks (WSNs). A WSN can be broadly described as a network of nodes that makes a collaborative effort to sense certain specified data around its periphery, and thereby controls the surrounding environment. A typical sensor network consists of a large number of low-cost, low-powered sensor nodes that are deployable in harsh operating environments [1]. Because of their varied applications in civilian and military sectors, including habitat monitoring, air and water quality management, hazard and disaster monitoring, health care, remote sensing, and smart homes, WSNs have become popular. Fig. 18.1 depicts a typical WSN in which sensor nodes are distributed in an ad hoc, decentralized fashion. Usually, WSNs are connected to a legacy network [Internet Protocol (IP) network or third-generation (3G) network] using one or more sink nodes or base stations. Routing in a WSN is typically carried out in a hop-by-hop fashion.

In general, WSN protocols should be designed to minimize energy consumption and prolong the lifetime of the network. Information gathering in a WSN is done by asking for information regarding a specific attribute of the phenomena or by asking for statistics about a specific area of the sensor field. This requires a protocol that can handle requests for a specific type of information, which includes data-centric routing and data aggregation. The last important characteristic of WSNs is that the position of the nodes may not be engineered or predetermined, and therefore must provide data routes that are self-organizing.

Although WSNs have gained a lot of popularity, there are some serious limitations when implementing security. WSNs present extreme resource limitations in available storage (memory) space, computing, battery life, and bandwidth. Hence, sensor networks present major challenges for integrating traditional security techniques in such resource-constrained networks [2]. In addition, the ad hoc, decentralized nature of WSNs poses even greater challenges to applying conventional security mechanisms. Researchers must take all of these constraints into consideration while providing adequate security to WSNs.

Wireless Sensor Network Architecture and Protocols

Most traditional networks (IP networks) are built on the principles of the Open System Interconnection (OSI) model. However, a WSN operates in a resource-constrained environment and therefore deviates somewhat from the traditional OSI model. A WSN protocol stack is usually composed of six layers: an application layer, middleware, transport, network, data link, and physical layer. In addition to these six layers that are mapped to each sensor node, three more planes span across the entire sensor network and have more visibility to address issues such as mobility, power, and task management, as shown in Fig. 18.2.

Application Layer

The application layer aims to create an abstraction of the main functions of the sensing application, thereby making the lower software and hardware levels transparent to the end user. The application layer can involve several processes running simultaneously, and handles user requests

Computer and Information Security Handbook. http://dx.doi.org/10.1016/B978-0-12-803843-7.00018-1

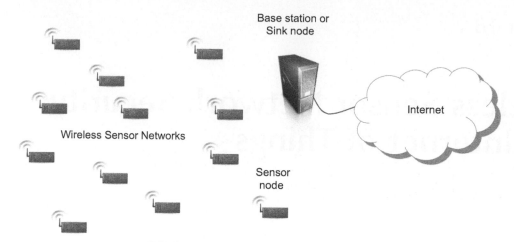

FIGURE 18.1 A typical wireless sensor network.

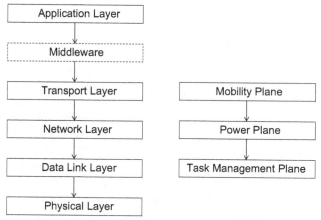

FIGURE 18.2 Wireless sensor network protocol stack.

relating to data aggregation, location finding, sleep—awake cycle control, time synchronization, authentication, encryption, key distribution, and other security measures. It also defines the order and format of message exchange between the two communication parties.

Middleware

The middleware layer provides an application program interface for applications running in the higher layer, and may involve complex functionalities such as resource sharing and task management.

Transport Layer

The transport layer is responsible for flow and congestion control. It also performs error control to detect corrupted frames that arrive from lower layers. Owing to the severe operating environment and lesser transmission power, it is difficult to achieve high end-to-end link reliability compared with traditional wireless networks. In addition, the transport layer performs fragmentation of sender data and reassembly of received data frames.

Network Layer

The network layer's primary goals are to perform routing and self-configuration. It is responsible for link failures and provides regular updates to neighboring nodes. However, ensuring network connectivity at all times is a major challenge because of dynamically changing network topology. The routing protocols in WSN are different from traditional routing protocols because of the need to optimize network life by performing intelligent routing.

Data Link Layer

The data link layer is an interface between the network and physical layer. It is further subdivided into two protocol sublayers: medium access control (MAC) and logical link control (LLC). The MAC module has a critical role in conserving network life by efficiently and fairly allocating medium access to the contending nodes. The LLC is on top of the MAC layer and is responsible for cyclic redundancy check, sequencing information, and adding appropriate source and destination information. In addition, the data link layer is responsible for multiplexing of data streams and data frame detection.

Physical Layer

The physical layer is responsible for converting digital bits into analog symbols, and vice versa. It involves modulation and demodulation, frequency selection, power control, and symbol synchronization. WSNs usually operate in the frequency range between 915 MHz and 2.4 GHz. It is recommended to use a lower-frequency band that has lower attenuation than higher-frequency bands. However, with the limited availability of the bandwidth in lower frequencies, WSNs may be forced to operate at higher frequencies. The environment in which sensors are operating has a major role in signal attenuation. Thus, sensors placed on the ground or floating on water tend to experience greater attenuation and consequently require higher transmit power. The choice of modulation scheme is one of the prime factors in deciding the transmit power. The modulation scheme decides the bit error rate (BER), spectrum efficiency, and number of bits per symbol. For example, an M-ary modulation scheme is able to transmit more bits per symbol than other binary modulation schemes such as phase shift keying. However, M-ary schemes result in higher BER and require more transmit power than binary modulation schemes. Hence binary modulation schemes are more applicable to WSNs. As mentioned earlier, there are three planes that span across the entire sensor network:

- *Mobility plane:* Sensor nodes can be attached to moving objects such as animals, vehicles, or people, which will lead to a dynamic network topology. If sensor nodes are mobile, the mobility plane in cooperation with the network layer is responsible for maintaining the list of active neighboring nodes. It is also responsible for interacting periodically with other neighboring nodes' mobility planes, so that it can create and maintain a table of active, power-efficient routes.
- *Power plane:* The power plane focuses on the awareness of power at each horizontal and vertical layer. It is responsible for shutting off the sensors if they are not participating in any routing decisions or if the sensing activity is complete. Power planes of each node work collectively on determining efficient routes to sink nodes and maintaining the sleep—awake cycles of sensor nodes.
- *Task management plane:* The task management plane is responsible for achieving a common goal by taking properties of each layer and across each layer in a power-aware manner.

Vulnerabilities and Attacks on Wireless Sensor Networks

A taxonomy of possible attacks on WSNs is shown in Fig. 18.3. They can be broadly divided into attacks on privacy, control, or availability. It is also useful to classify attacks as passive or active. In passive attacks, an attacker is able to intercept and monitor data between communicating nodes, but does not tamper or modify packets. This is obviously a threat to privacy if packet contents can be read. Even in the case of encrypted data, the attacker can find useful information by analyzing headers of packets, their sizes, and the frequency of transmissions. In WSNs, reconnaissance can also be carried out to understand information exchange between communicating nodes, particularly at data aggregation points. Eavesdropping can also discover routing information for exploitation.

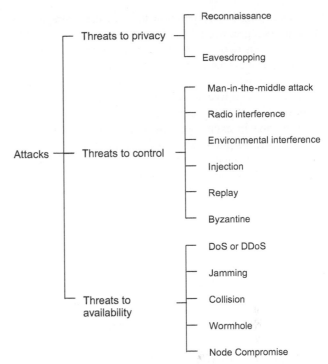

FIGURE 18.3 Taxonomy of attacks on wireless sensor networks. *DoS*, denial of service; *DDoS*, distributed denial of service.

Active Attacks

In active attacks, the attacker takes actions to participate in communications (control and data) and may modify, delete, reorder, replay, or spoof messages. Some other active attacks include node capturing, tampering with routing information, and resource exhaustion attacks. In an attack unique to WSNs, the attacker can modify the surrounding environment, which could affect the sensed phenomena.

2. THREATS TO PRIVACY

In WSNs, threats to privacy can be further classified into reconnaissance and eavesdropping.

Reconnaissance

Reconnaissance refers to intelligent gathering or probing to access the vulnerabilities in a network, to launch a full-scale attack later. Reconnaissance attacks can be further classified into active and passive. Passive reconnaissance attacks include the collection of network information through indirect or direct methods, but without probing the target; active reconnaissance attacks involve the process of gathering traffic with the intention of eliciting responses from the target.

Eavesdropping

Eavesdropping is the act of listening secretly to a private conversation. However, in the context of WSNs, eavesdropping is an operation to learn the aggregate data that are being collected by the entire network. Eavesdropping between two specific sensor nodes may not help the attacker in understanding the entire network thoroughly. It can be further classified into active and passive eavesdropping. An active eavesdropper sends queries to other nodes in an attempt to instigate them to respond to his queries, and in exchange will be able to comprehend the precise task assigned to the nodes in the network. Usually, the attacker launches a man-in-the-middle attack to infiltrate the network by forcing himself into the active path. A passive eavesdropper listens to all traffic sent over the broadcast medium. It may be difficult to detect a passive eavesdropping attack, because the attacker is not carrying out any actions beyond listening.

Threats to Control

The nodes in the network are unaware that the entire flow control is being handled by the attacker.

Man-in-the-Middle Attack

The man-in-the-middle attack is one of the classical attacks that can be executed in a WSN environment. The attacker tries to establish an independent connection between a set of nodes and the sink node. The nodes in the network are unaware that the entire flow control is being handled by the attacker. He can be in either a passive or active state. In a passive state, he simply relays every message among the nodes with the intention of performing an eavesdropping attack. In an active state, he can tamper with the intercepted data in an attempt to break authentication. The attack can be executed at the physical, data link, network, and application layers [3].

Radio Interference

Given the increasing number of wireless technologies using the same open spectrum band (2.4 GHz, 5 GHz, or 900 MHz), there is bound to be radio interference. For example, in a dense urban environment, where cordless phones share the same spectrum, there is a sharp degradation of individual node performance owing to radio interference. Similar problems can be experienced in sensor networks with the increase in sensor nodes per network. Such interference can cause transmitted bits to become unintelligible and ultimately dropped by the receiver [4]. Hence, radio interference similar to jamming could lead to a denial of service (DoS) attack.

Injection Attack

After an attacker has stealthily intruded into the WSN network, he may impersonate a few of the sensor nodes (or even sink nodes) and thereby inject malicious data into the network. The malicious data might be false advertisement of neighbor-node information to other nodes, leading to impersonation of sink nodes and aggregation of all data.

Replay Attack

A replay attack is a common attack in WSNs, whereby an attacker is able to intercept user data and retransmit user data at a later time. This attack is particularly effective in breaking weak authentication schemes, which do not consider the timestamp when authenticating nodes. This attack is also effective during shared-key distribution processes.

Byzantine Attack

In a Byzantine attack, the outside adversary is able to take full control of a subset of authenticated nodes that can be further used to attack the network from the inside. Such attacks by malicious behavior are known as Byzantine attacks. Some examples of Byzantine attacks are black holes, wormholes, flood rushing, and overlay network wormholes.

Black Hole Attacks

In black hole attacks, the attacker drops packets selectively, or all control and data packets that are routed through him. Therefore, any packet routed through this intermediate malicious node will experience partial or total data loss.

Flood Rushing Attack

A flood rushing attack is common to wireless networks and exploits the flood duplicate suppression technique. In this attack, the attacker attempts to overthrow the existing routing path by sending a flood of packets through an alternate route, which will result in discarding the legitimate route in favor of the adversarial route. Usual authentication schemes cannot prevent this attack because the adversaries are authenticated nodes.

Wormhole Attack

In a wormhole attack, two conniving sensor nodes tunnel control and data packets between each other, with the intention of creating a shortcut in the WSN. Such a low-latency tunnel between the two conniving nodes will likely increase the probability of its being selected as an active path. This type of attack is closely related to the sinkhole attack, because one of the conniving nodes could falsely advertise to be the sink node and thereby attract more traffic than usual. One of the main differences between a Byzantine wormhole and a traditional wormhole is that in a Byzantine wormhole, the tunnel exists between two compromised nodes, whereas in a traditional wormhole, two legitimate nodes are tricked into believing that a secure tunnel exists between them.

Byzantine Overlay Network Wormhole Attack

A Byzantine overlay network wormhole attack is a variant of wormhole attack and occurs when the wormhole attack is extended to multiple sensor nodes; resulting in an overlay of compromised nodes. It provides a false illusion to honest nodes that they are surrounded by legitimate nodes, resulting in frequent reuse of the adversarial path.

Sybil Attack

The Sybil attack was first introduced by Douceur [5] while studying security in peer-to-peer networks; later, Karlof and Wagner [6] showed that this type of attack poses a serious threat to routing mechanisms in WSNs. Sybil is an impersonation attack in which a malicious node masquerades as a set of nodes by claiming false identities, or generating new identities in the worst case [7]. Such attacks can be easily executed in a WSN environment because the nodes are invariably deployed in an unstructured and distributed environment, and communicate via radio transmission. They are especially detrimental in applications such as data aggregation, voting systems, reputation evaluation, and geographic routing. Using a Sybil attack in location-aware routing, it is possible to be in multiple locations at the same time.

Sinkhole Attack

In a sinkhole attack, the adversary impersonates a sink node and attracts the whole of traffic to a node or a set of nodes. Similar to a black hole attack, the attacker takes control of a few compromised nodes and advertises false routing information to its neighbors, thereby luring all traffic to him.

Threats to Availability

Because of threats to the WSN, some portion of the network or some of the functionalities or services provided by the network could be damaged and unavailable to participants of the network. For instance, some sensors could die earlier than their expected lifetimes. Thus, availability service ensures that the necessary functionalities or the services provided by the WSN are always carried out, even in the case of attacks.

Denial of Service Attack

A DoS attack occurs when an attacker floods the victim with bogus or spoofed packets with the intent of lowering the response rate of the victim. An extension of a DoS attack is a distributed DoS (DDoS) attack, in which an attacker takes control of multiple nodes in the network, leading to a distributed flood attack against the victim. In the worst-case scenario, it makes the victim totally unresponsive. For instance, in a WSN environment where nodes have limited computational capacity, a DoS attack from a resource-abundant adversary can overwhelm the nodes by flooding packets, which will exhaust communication bandwidth, memory, and processing power. From an attacker's point of view, this attack is also useful in wireless networks where nodes are required to deliver time-critical data. Jamming the wireless links can also lead to a DoS attack (discussed subsequently).

HELLO Flood Attack

One common technique to discover neighbors is to send HELLO packets. If a node receives a HELLO packet, it indicates that it is within the range of communication. However, a laptop-class adversary could easily send HELLO packets with sufficient power to convince the sensor nodes that it is in proximity of communication and may be a potential neighbor. The adversary could also impersonate a sink node or a cluster node.

Jamming

Jamming is one of the most damaging types of attacks in WSN and is a direct way to compromise the entire wireless network. The attacker jams a spectrum band with a powerful transmitter, and prevents any member of the network in the affected area from transmitting or receiving any packet. Jamming attacks can be divided into constant jamming and sporadic jamming. Sporadic jamming can be effective at times when a change in 1 bit of a data frame will force the receiver to drop it. In this kind of attack, it is difficult for the victim to identify whether his band is being jammed intentionally or owing to channel interference, and his immediate reaction is usually to increase his transmitting power, thereby depleting resources at a faster rate. Jamming attacks target the physical and MAC layers. Four types of jamming attacks (random, reactive, deceptive, and constant) leading to DoS are discussed by Xu et al. [8]. They conclude that detection schemes can be complex with reference to differentiating malicious attacks from link impairment.

Collision Attacks

Collision attacks target the MAC layer to cause costly exponential back-off. Whenever collision occurs, the nodes should retransmit packets affected by collision, thus leading to multiple retransmissions. The amount of energy spent by the attacker is much less than the energy expended by the sensor nodes, which can exhaust batteries. Collision attacks can be categorized under resource exhaustion attacks.

Node Compromise

Node compromise is one of the most common and detrimental attacks in WSN. Because sensors can be deployed in harsh environments such as a battlefield, an ocean bed, or the edge of an active volcano, they are easily susceptible to capture by a foreign agent. In case of a battlefield scenario, the enemy could make an effort to dig into nodes with the intention of extracting useful data (extracting private keys in sensor nodes). Furthermore, it could be reprogrammed and launched into a battlefield to operate on behalf of the enemy.

Attacks Specific to Wireless Sensor Networks

In attacks on a beaconing protocol, a beaconing protocol uses a breadth-first spanning tree algorithm to broadcast routing updates. The sink node periodically broadcasts updated routing information to its immediate neighboring nodes. These neighboring nodes then rebroadcast this information to their immediate neighbors, and the process continues recursively. During this process, each intermediate node makes a note of its parent node (the parent node is the first node that was able to make contact with its subordinate node and relay the routing information). When all the active nodes are operational, they should send all the sensed data to their parent node. However, this protocol is vulnerable to many attacks. For example, a simple impersonation attack, leading to a sinkhole attack, can totally compromise the entire network [6,9].

Authentication can be used to prevent such impersonation attacks, but it does not prevent a laptop-class adversary from launching a selective forwarding attack, an eavesdropping attack, or a black hole attack. The attacker creates a wormhole between two conniving laptop-class adversaries. The two laptops are placed near the sink node and the targeted area, respectively. The laptop near the sink node attracts its entire neighbor's traffic and simply tunnels these authenticated messages to its colluder. The laptop attacker, close to the sink node, has a passive role in forwarding these messages. Because of his furtive nature, it is difficult for his neighbors to detect whether he is malicious. Once the authenticated messages reach the remote laptop adversary, he could launch a black hole attack or a selective forwarding attack.

Let us consider a situation in which digital signatures are being used for authentication and, while the routing updates are in progress, the sink node's private key is leaked. As soon as the sink node realizes that its private key is being compromised, it immediately broadcasts a new public key. All the nodes in close proximity to the sink node will update their local copy of the sink node's public key. The laptop close to the sink node will perform the same operation and convey this information to its colluding laptop. The remote laptop can now easily impersonate the sink node and launch a sinkhole attack. In addition, he can further create routing loops, which is a resource-exhaustion attack.

Attacks on Geographic- and Energy-Aware Routing

Geographic- and energy-aware routing (GEAR) proposes a location- and energy-aware, recursive routing algorithm to address the problem of uneven energy consumption in routing in WSNs [10]. In GEAR, every node gauges the energy levels of its neighbors along with the distance from the target before making a routing decision. In such situations, a laptop-class attacker can advertise that he has larger energy levels than his neighboring node and attract all traffic to him. Thenceforth, he can execute a Sybil, black hole, or selective forwarding attack.

As attacks on WSN become more sophisticated, the demand for new security solutions is continually increasing. Hence, an array of new security schemes has been designed and implemented [11,12]. Most of these schemes have been designed to provide solutions on a layer-by-layer basis rather than on a per-attack basis; in doing so, they have left a gap between layers that may lead to cross-layer attacks.

Physical and Data Link Layer Security

Data link layer security handles communications on the physical network components. Controls at this level protect a specific physical link. Because each physical link must be secured separately, controls at this level are not feasible for protecting connections that involve several links, including most connections across the Internet.

Security Measures in Physical Layer

To prevent radio interference or jamming, two common techniques are frequency-hopping spread spectrum (FHSS) and direct-sequence spread spectrum (DSSS). In FHSS, the signal is modulated at frequencies such that it hops from one frequency to another in a seemingly random fashion at a fixed time interval. The transmitter and the corresponding receiver hop between frequencies using the same pseudo-random code for modulation and demodulation. If an eavesdropper intercepts an FHSS signal, he will not be able to demodulate the signal without prior knowledge of the spreading signal code. Furthermore, spreading the signal across multiple frequencies will considerably reduce interference.

In DSSS, a spreading code is used to map each data bit in the original signal to multiple bits in the transmitted signal. The pseudorandom code (spreading code) spreads the input data across a wider frequency range compared with the input frequency. In the frequency domain, the output signals appear as noise. Because the pseudorandom code provides a wide bandwidth to the input data, it allows the signal power to drop below the noise threshold without losing information. Therefore, this technique is hard for an eavesdropper to detect, owing to lower energy levels per frequency and more tolerance to interference.

Security Measures in Data Link Layer

Data link layer security has an important role in providing hop-by-hop security. Its protocols are useful in handling fair channel access, neighbor-node discovery, and frame error control. Legacy security protocols such as Secure Socket Layer (SSL) or Internet Protocol Security cannot be applied directly to WSN because they do not provide data aggregation or allow in-network processing, which are prime requirements in designing security protocols.

To prevent DoS attacks on WSN, it is proposed that each intermediate node in the active routing path perform an authentication and integrity check. However, if a few intermediate nodes in the active path have very low-energy levels, and if they are forced to perform authentication checks, they would expend all their energy and disrupt the active path. On the other hand, if we look at end-to-end authentication in WSN, it is more energy-efficient, because the sink node (resource-abundant) is the only node that performs authentication and integrity checks. Nevertheless, this scheme is vulnerable to many types of security attacks (black hole, selective forwarding, and eavesdropping). Hence there is a need for adaptive schemes that consider the energy levels of each node when deciding on the authentication schemes.

Early security approaches focused on symmetric keying techniques, and authentication was achieved using message authentication code (MAC). One common MAC scheme is a cipher block chaining message authentication code. However, this scheme is not secure for variable-length input messages. Hence the end user (sensor nodes) has to pad the input messages to be equal to a multiple of the block cipher. Therefore, each node has to waste energy, padding input data. To overcome this issue, other block cipher models such as CTR and OCB have been proposed. With reference to confidentiality, symmetric encryption schemes used to protect WSNs are Data Encryption Standard, Advanced Encryption Standard (AES), RC5, and Skipjack (block ciphers) and RC4 (a stream cipher). Usually, block ciphers are preferred over stream ciphers because they allow authentication and encryption.

A few proposed link-layer security frameworks include TinySec, Sensec, SNEP, MiniSec, SecureSense [12,13], and, ZigBee Alliance [14]. However, these schemes have limitations. For example, in Tinysec a single key is manually programmed into all the sensor nodes in the network. A simple node-capture attack on any one of these nodes may result in leakage of the secret key and compromise of the entire network. A need for a stronger keying mechanism is needed to secure TinySec. In addition, TinySec requires padding for input messages that are less than 8 bytes. It uses block cipher to encrypt messages; for messages that are less than 8 bytes, the node will have to use extra energy to pad the message before encrypting.

3. CRYPTOGRAPHIC SECURITY IN WIRELESS SENSOR NETWORKS

In general, any cryptographic security suite should ensure authentication, integrity, confidentiality, availability, access control, and nonrepudiation (see checklist: "An Agenda for Action When Implementing a Security Suite"). In addition, physical security is absolutely necessary to avoid tampering or destruction of nodes. Therefore, construction of tamper-resistant sensor nodes is imperative. However, such tamper-resistant schemes incur a higher manufacturing cost and are restricted to applications that are not only critical but that use fewer nodes.

Authentication

In all WSN applications, authentication and encryption are fundamental security requirements and are useful in mitigating impersonation attacks. They are also useful in preventing the ever-increasing DoS and DDoS attacks on resource-constrained environments such as WSNs. Three scenarios exist in WSNs that require authenticated communications:

- sink node to sensor nodes, and vice versa
- sensor node with other sensor nodes
- outside user and sensor nodes

Most of the time, critical applications in WSN require a message to be sent as promptly as possible. The intermediate nodes between the sender and receiver are responsible for relaying the message to the receiver. If one of the nodes is compromised, the malicious node can inject falsified packets into the network while routing messages. Such an act could lead to falsified distribution of such messages, and in turn deplete the energy levels of other honest nodes. Hence there is a need to filter messages as early as possible by authenticating every message, consequently conserving relaying energy.

In most WSN applications, the sensor nodes are expected to aggregate, process, store, and supply sensed data upon the end user's query. For example, in a military application, soldiers would require constant interaction with motion sensors that detect movement along the border.

An Agenda for Action When Implementing a Security Suite

A construction of tamper-resistant sensor nodes is absolutely necessary. However, such tamper-resistant schemes come at a higher manufacturing cost and are restricted to applications that are not only critical but use fewer nodes, and that can do the following when implementing a security suite (check all tasks completed):

_____**1.** *Authentication:* The main objective of authentication is to prevent impersonation attacks. Hence, authentication can be defined as the process of ensuring that the identity of the communicating entity is what it claims to be.

_____**2.** *Integrity:* The goal of integrity is to affirm that the data received are not altered by an interceptor during communication (by insertion, deletion, or replay of data) and, are exactly as they were sent by the authorized sender. Usually, cryptographic methods such as digital signatures and hash values are used to provide data integrity.

_____**3.** *Confidentiality:* The goal of confidentiality is to protect the data from unauthorized disclosure. A common approach to achieving confidentiality is by encrypting user data.

_____**4.** *Availability:* The goal of availability is to ensure that the system (network) resources are available and usable by an authorized entity, upon request. It tries to achieve survivability of the network at all times.

_____**5.** *Access control:* The goal of access control is to enforce access rights to all resources in its system. It tries to prevent unauthorized use of system and network resources. Access control is closely related to authentication attributes. It has a major role in preventing leakage of information during a node-compromise attack. One conventional approach to access control is to use threshold cryptography. This approach hides data by splitting them into a number of shares. To retrieve the final data, each share should be received through an authenticated process.

_____**6.** *Nonrepudiation:* Nonrepudiation can best be explained with an example. Let Alice and Bob be two nodes who wish to communicate with each other. Let Alice send a message to Bob. Later, Alice claims that she did not send a message to Bob. Hence, the question that arises is how Bob should be protected if Alice denies involvement in any form of communication with Bob. Nonrepudiation aims to achieve protection against communicating entities that deny that they ever participated in any sort of communication with the victim.

In such situations, a large number of mobile or static end users could query the sensor nodes for sensed data. Usually, such interactions are realized through broadcast/multicast operations. Therefore, in such situations, a broadcast authentication mechanism is required before the query is sent. Furthermore, access control is also required, which would allow the authorized user to access only data to which he is entitled. Broadcast authentication was first addressed in µTESLA [12]. In this scheme, users are assumed to be a few trustworthy sink nodes. This scheme uses one-way hash functions and the hash preimages are used as keys to the MAC algorithm.

However, the messages are transmitted through a wireless medium, which consumes a considerable amount of time. In addition, the hop-by-hop routing nature of WSN further creates a delay in transmission. Hence there is an increased need for rapid generation and verification of signature schemes.

Existing symmetric schemes such as µTESLA and its variants use message authentication codes to gain efficiency in terms of processing and energy consumption. However, these symmetric schemes experience delayed authentication and sluggish performance for large-scale networks and are susceptible to DoS attacks owing to late authentication. Furthermore, multiple senders cannot send authenticated broadcast messages simultaneously. For example, if a single node is interested in broadcasting a message, it would have to send a Unicast message to its respective sink node, which would then broadcast the message to all other nodes on its behalf. Because of resource constraint, asymmetric schemes (for example, digital signatures that would require public key certificates) were pronounced inefficient. To address this problem, new avenues are being explored to introduce authentication in public key cryptography in WSN [14].

Lightweight Public Key Infrastructure for WSN

Although the applicability of public key infrastructure (PKI)-based approaches has been deemed inappropriate for a resource constraint environment such as WSN, security researchers have been proposing new lightweight PKI-based approaches for WSN. For instance, a simplified version of SSL has been proposed [15]. Although this SSL version has less overhead compared with the usual SSL/Transport Layer Security protocol, it is still not directly applicable to mobile sensor nodes because it would lead to increased communication and computational overhead. For instance, in an ad hoc mobile sensor network, the nodes keep changing their location, and any change in their position would compel them to initiate the SSL protocol before informing their neighbors of their new location. In addition, schemes such as TinyPK have been designed that are in conjunction with TinySec and facilitate authentication and key agreement between sensor nodes [16].

However, TinyPK implements a Diffie—Hellman key exchange protocol that is susceptible to an active man-in-the-middle attack.

Huang et al. [17] proposed hybrid architecture for authenticated key establishment of a session key between a leaf node and a sink node or an end user. This protocol leverages the difference in the computational and communication capabilities between the leaf node and the resource abundant device (sink node or end user). During the inception of the protocol, both parties exchange certificates issued by a certificate authority to extract each other's public keys. However, the corresponding private keys are discovered after both parties run the protocol. This step in this protocol can easily be exploited by an adversary by replaying a valid certificate that would result in a DoS attack. As a result, the nodes are forced to perform expensive computations and waste their resources and bandwidth. In addition, a serious vulnerability was shown in the scheme of Huang et al in which an end user can easily discover the long-term private key of a leaf node after having one normal run of the protocol [18].

To expunge the transmission of public key certificates, Ren et al. [19] proposed a hybrid authentication scheme (HAS) for a multiuser broadcast authentication scheme in WSN. Each sensor node is preloaded with the required PKI of the end user using the Bloom filter and Merkle hash tree [20,21]. However, HAS with the Merkle hash tree does not facilitate user scalability (a new user can only be added into the network after revocation of the old user).

Key Management in Wireless Sensor Network

As mentioned previously, WSNs have diverse applications and operate in harsh environments. These characteristics present difficulties for traditional key management. In addition, the lack of a priori information about the network topology makes key management complex. Key distribution provides communication secrecy (confidentiality) and authentication among sensor nodes, and key revocation refers to the task of removing compromised keys from the network. Key distribution can be further divided into symmetric and asymmetric key distribution protocols.

Considerable work has been done in proposing new symmetric key distribution protocols in WSNs, but less effort has been invested in the area of asymmetric key distribution algorithms in WSNs, which have low computational and storage requirements. Significant work has been done to show the applicability of implementing binary-field algorithms on sensor nodes [22]. Consequently, such implementations have resulted in considerable reductions in computational time and memory access. In general, key distribution schemes in WSNs can be broadly classified into four classes: symmetric key algorithms,

trusted server mechanisms, random key predistribution schemes, and public key algorithms.

Symmetric Key Algorithms

In this class, a single shared key is used to perform the encryption and decryption operations in a communication network.

Fully Pairwise-Shared Keys

In the fully pairwise-shared keys scheme, every node in the network shares a unique, preshared, symmetric key with every other node in the network. The keys are preloaded into the sensor nodes before deployment. Hence, in a network of n nodes, there would be a total of $n(n-1)/2$ unique keys. Subsequently, every node stores $n-1$ keys, one for each of the other nodes in the network. The compromise of a few sensor nodes will not result in the complete collapse of the entire network. However, the applicability of this approach in large sensor networks is not pragmatic, because each node would need to store $n-1$ keys, thus resulting in the rapid exhaustion of its limited memory space. In addition, nodes usually communicate with their immediate one-hop neighbors, thereby eliminating the need to establish unique keys with every node in the network. Although symmetric key algorithms are limited in terms of key distribution, they provide basic cryptographic primitives, which can be used in combination with asymmetric key cryptographic algorithms.

Trusted Server Mechanisms

In this category, key distribution is done via centralized trusted servers, which are usually static in nature. In WSN, the sink node or the base station can act as a key distribution center (KDC). Usually, unique symmetric keys are shared between the sink node and the ordinary nodes. If two nodes were to communicate with each other, they would first authenticate with the base station, after which the base station would generate a link key and send it securely to both parties.

An example of a base station—mediated key agreement protocol is the Security Protocol for Sensor Networks [12]. Using this protocol, only one unique single key is preloaded in every node of the network. Hence, a node capture will not result in the total compromise of the network. In addition, centralized revocation is possible through authenticated unicasts from the trusted base station. The main drawback of this scheme is that the trusted base station represents a single point of compromise for security information, and may also induce a focused communication load centered on the base station, which may lead to early battery exhaustion for the nodes closest to the base station.

Another concern is that certain networks do not have a suitable, highly functional, and tamper-proof device that can be used as a secure KDC.

λ-Secure n × n Key Establishment Schemes

Now, let us address the problem of key distribution and key establishment [23,24] between all pairs of n principals. Although these schemes were originally intended for group keying in traditional networks, and not for sensor networks, they are included here because of their relevance to the development of subsequent key distribution schemes for sensor networks. The schemes of both Blom and Blundo et al. have an important resiliency property, the λ-secure property: The coalition of no more than λ-compromised sensor nodes reveals nothing about the pairwise key between any two noncompromised nodes.

The main advantage of this class of schemes is that they allow a parameterizable trade-off between security and memory overhead. Whereas the full pairwise scheme involves the storage of $O(n)$ keys at each node and is n-secure, this class of schemes allows the storage of $O(\lambda)$ keys in return for a λ-secure property, and it is perfectly resilient to node compromise until $\lambda + 1$ nodes have been compromised, at which point the entire network's communications are compromised.

Random Key Predistribution Schemes

In this method, the keys are predistributed by preloading random keying material on sensor nodes with the intention of establishing a common secret key between the communicating entities. Upon deployment, these nodes carry out a lookup process to see whether a shared key exists between them. Because keys are preloaded in a random manner, certain set of nodes may not share a common key. In such cases, nodes could make use of their immediate neighbors who share keys as bridges between the nodes that do not share a common key. One of the early, key-sharing algorithms using random graph theory was proposed by Eschenauer and Gligor [25].

Random Key Predistribution Schemes

In the basic random key predistribution scheme, let m denote the number of distinct cryptographic keys that can be stored on the key ring of a sensor node. This scheme is divided into three phases as follows:

Phase I: Key Predistribution

In this initialization phase, a random pool (set) of keys Q is picked from the total possible key space. In addition, for each node, m keys are randomly selected from the key pool Q and stored into the node's memory. Each of the m keys has identifiers that will be used to map the keys by the receiving nodes during the discovery phase of this scheme (discussed in the next section). This set of m keys is called the node's key ring. The number of keys in the key pool $|Q|$ (key pool size) is chosen such that any two random subsets of size m in Q will share at least one key, with some probability p.

Phase II: Shared-Key Discovery

On deployment, neighboring sensor nodes begin the discovery process to find out whether they share a common key; if they do, they establish a secure link. There could be many modes for the discovery phase, such as broadcasting the list of identifiers existing in their key ring in clear text or through a challenge-response mechanism. If the probability p is chosen correctly for the network's neighbor density, the resultant graph of secure links will be connected with some high probability. The remaining links in the graph are then filled in by routing key establishment messages along this connected network of initial secure links. From a security perspective, although this approach does not reveal important information to the adversary, it is still susceptible to a passive traffic analysis attack.

Phase III: Path-Key Establishment

Upon completing the discovery phase, if two nodes in the network discover that they do not share a key, they send an encrypted message to neighbors with whom they share a key, with a request to secure connection with the unshared node. This model assumes that after the completion of Phase II, many keys exist in each key ring that can be used for third-party path-key establishment. Hence, the neighboring nodes generate pairwise keys for nodes that do not directly share a key.

Let us now find this probability p that any two nodes with key ring sizes m in the network share at least one common key from the pool Q. Let p' be the probability that two nodes do not share a key between them. Then, p is defined as

$$p = 1 - p' \tag{18.1}$$

In this case, keys from the key ring are drawn from Q without replacement. The total number of possible key rings t_1 is shown below:

$$t_1 = \frac{Q!}{m!(Q-m)!} \tag{18.2}$$

Now, the total number of possible key rings that do not share a key with a particular key ring t_2 is the number of key rings drawn from the remaining $Q - m$ unused keys in the pool:

$$t_2 = \frac{(Q-m)!}{m!(Q-2m)!} \tag{18.3}$$

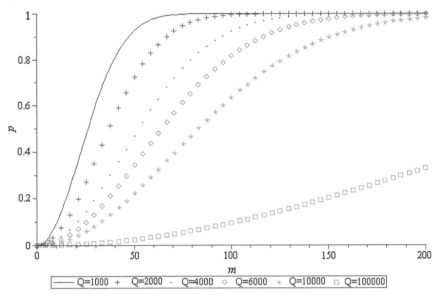

FIGURE 18.4   Probability of sharing at least one shared key using Eschenauer and Gligor's scheme.

Then, the probability that no key is shared between any two rings is t_2/t_1. Hence, the probability p is

$$p = 1 - \frac{t_2}{t_1} = 1 - \frac{((Q-m)!)^2}{Q!(Q-2m)!} \tag{18.4}$$

Usually, the value of p is very large compared with m, and using Sterling's approximation for $n!$, the value of p is

$$p = 1 - \frac{\left(1 - \dfrac{m}{Q}\right)^{2(Q-m+0.5)}}{\left(1 - \dfrac{2m}{Q}\right)^{(Q-2m+0.5)}} \tag{18.5}$$

Fig. 18.4 shows the value of p for different values of Q and m. We observe that with an increase in Q, there is a negligible increase in the key ring size m for the same value of p. For example, for $p = 0.5$ and $Q = 6000$, the value of $m = 68$. Subsequently, if the pool size is increased to 10,000, for the same value of $p = 0.5$, m is only increased to 95.

In this scheme, all nodes use the same key pool Q. This implies that the security of the network is gradually eroded as keys from Q are compromised by an adversary that captures more and more nodes. The number of exposed keys is roughly linear to the number of nodes compromised. This characteristic of the basic scheme motivated a search for key predistribution schemes that have better resiliency to node capture.

Q-Composite Key Scheme

The basic scheme was extended by the q-composite key scheme [26]. Instead of designing for a given probability p of sharing a single key, the parameters are altered such that any two nodes have a given probability p of sharing at least

q different keys from the key pool. All q keys are used in the generation of the key, which encrypts communications between sensor nodes; hence to eavesdrop on the secured link, the adversary now has to compromise all q keys instead of just one. As q increases, it is exponentially harder for the attacker to break a link by taking possession of a given set. However, increasing the probability of overlap in this fashion naturally involves reducing the size of the key pool Q. Thus, the smaller key-pool size makes the scheme more vulnerable to an adversary that is capable of compromising larger numbers of sensor nodes.

The key predistribution phase of this model is similar to *Phase 1 n*, the basic random key predistribution scheme, with the only exception being the key-pool size Q. In the shared key discovery phase, each node must find nodes that share all common keys with each other. The discovery mechanism is similar to that of Phase II. Although a broadcast-based approach is susceptible to an eavesdropping attack, alternative methods that are slower but more secure are suggested where the nodes use the Merkle puzzle for key discovery [20]. After the discovery phase, each node would be able to recognize its immediate neighboring nodes with which it would share at least q keys. Subsequently, each node could establish a link between nodes that share at least q keys by hashing the keys in some canonical order.

In this scheme, the key pool size $|Q|$ has a critical role because with a larger Q, the probability of any two nodes sharing at least q keys would be much less. Consequently, after bootstrapping, the network may not be connected. On the contrary, if $|Q|$ is small, the security of the network is compromised. Hence $|Q|$ should be such that the probability of sharing at least q key should be greater than or equal to the probability of successfully achieving a key setup with any of its neighbors. The approach used to

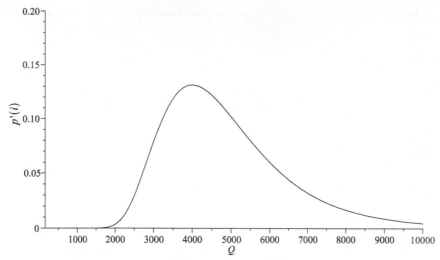

FIGURE 18.5 Key-pool set $|Q|$ selection based on $p'(i)$ for $m = 200$ and $i = 10$.

calculate the probability of any two nodes sharing exactly i keys $p'(i)$ is similar to calculating p, as shown in Eq. (18.4), and is given as

$$p'(i) = \frac{\binom{|Q|}{i}\binom{|Q| - i}{2(m - i)}\binom{2(m - i)}{m - i}}{\binom{|Q|}{m}^2} \qquad (18.6)$$

For example, in Fig. 18.5, we find the value of $|Q|$ for a given m and i. In this case, for $m = 200$ and $i = 10$, we achieve a maximum $p'(i)$ for $|Q| = 3900$.

In general, random key predistribution presents a desirable trade-off between the insecurity of using a single network-wide key and the impractical high memory overhead of using unique pairwise keys. Its main advantage is that it provides much lower memory overhead than the full pairwise keys scheme while being more resilient to node compromise than the single-network-wide key scheme. Furthermore, it is fully distributed and does not require a trusted base station. Main disadvantages to this approach are the probabilistic nature of the scheme, which makes it difficult to provide the guarantee of the initial graph of secure links being connected under nonuniform conditions or sparse deployments. Furthermore, because keys can be shared among a large number of nodes, this class of schemes does not provide high resilience against node compromise and subsequent exposure of node keys.

The random pairwise key scheme [26] is a hybrid of the random key predistribution scheme and the full pairwise key scheme. In the analysis of random key predistribution, it was deduced that as long as any two nodes can form a secure link with at least a probability p, the entire network will be connected with secure links with high probability. Based on this observation, Chan et al. noted that it is not necessary to perform full pairwise key distribution to achieve a network in which any two nodes can find a secure pathway to each other. Instead of preloading unique pairwise keys in each node, the random pairwise key scheme preloads unique pairwise keys from each node. The m keys of a key ring are a small, random subset of the possible unique keys that this node could share with the other n nodes in the network. Using the same reasoning as the random key predistribution scheme, as long as these m keys provide some sufficient probability p of enabling any two neighboring nodes to establish a secure link, the resultant graph of initial secure links will have a high probability of being connected. The remaining links are then established using this initial graph exactly as in the random key predistribution scheme.

Chan et al. [26] presents a preliminary initial distributed node revocation scheme that makes use of the fact that possessing unique pairwise keys allows nodes to perform node-to-node identity authentication. Each of the m nodes that shares a unique pairwise key with the target node (the node's participants) carries a preloaded vote it can use to signify a message that the target is compromised. These m votes form a Merkle hash tree with leaves [20]. To vote against the target node, a node performs a network-wide broadcast of its vote (its leaf in the Merkle hash tree) along with the $\log m$ internal hash values, which will allow the other participants of the target to verify that this leaf value is part of the Merkle hash tree. Once at least t participants of a given target have voted, and the votes have been verified by the other m participants using the Merkle hash tree, all m nodes will erase any pairwise keys shared with the target, thus revoking it from the network.

The random pairwise key scheme inherits both strengths and weaknesses from the full pairwise keys scheme and the random key distribution scheme. Under the random pairwise keys scheme, nodes captured do not reveal information to the rest of the network, and central revocation can be accomplished by just unicasting to each of the nodes that share keys with the revoked node. It also involves a much lower memory overhead than the full pairwise keys scheme. Unfortunately, like the random key predistribution schemes, it is probabilistic and cannot be guaranteed to work in nonuniform or sparse deployments.

Multispace Key Schemes

This class of schemes is a hybrid between random key predistribution and the λ-secure $n \times n$ key establishment schemes [27]. Recall that in random key predistribution, a key pool is first selected from the universe of possible keys. Each sensor node is then preloaded with a set of keys from the key pool such that any two nodes possess some chosen probability p of sharing enough keys to form a secure link. Multispace key schemes use the same basic notion of random key predistribution but use key spaces, in which individual keys are used in random key predistribution. Hence, the key pool is replaced by a pool of key spaces and each node randomly selects a subset of key spaces from the pool of key spaces, such that any two nodes will have some common key space with probability p. Each key space represents a unique instance of a different λ-secure $n \times n$ key establishment scheme [23]. If two nodes possess the same key space, they can then perform the relevant λ-secure $n \times n$ key establishment scheme to generate a secure session key.

The main advantage of multispace schemes is that node compromise under these schemes reveals much less information to the adversary than occurs with the random key predistribution schemes. However, they retain the disadvantage of being probabilistic in nature (no guarantee of success in nonuniform or sparse deployments); furthermore, they experience the threshold-based sudden security failure mode that is a characteristic of λ-secure schemes. Other schemes have combined λ-secure schemes with constructions other than random key-space selection. Liu and Ning [28], in particular, describe a deterministic grid-based construction in which key spaces are used to perform intermediary-based key establishment between nodes.

Deterministic Key Predistribution Schemes

One drawback of the random key distribution approach is that it does not guarantee success. Researchers have proposed using combinatorial design techniques to allocate keys to nodes in such a way as to always ensure key sharing between any two nodes [29,30]. The amount of memory required per node is typically some fractional power of the overall supported network size [$O(\sqrt{n})$]. The main drawback of these schemes is that the same keys are shared among many nodes, leading to weaker resistance to node compromise. Chan et al. [26] proposed a deterministic scheme using peer nodes as intermediaries in key

establishment with similar memory overheads. Compared with the combinatorial design approach, this scheme trades increased communication cost for greater resistance against node compromise.

Public Key Algorithms

Although symmetric key cryptographic primitives provide computational and storage efficiency in WSN, bootstrapping keys between nodes is challenging and requires a prekey distribution (discussed in previous sections). However, prekey distribution requires physical access to nodes, which may not be possible in ad hoc, decentralized networks in which remote nodes keep adding and or dropping from the network. Hence, scalability and security (physical attack such as a node capture) were some early concerns raised during such prekey distribution activities. The past decade saw enormous interest in implementing asymmetric key cryptographic solutions in WSN. The reason was that it simplifies key management and revocation, which could not be achieved with symmetric key cryptography. However, the dependence on PKI and the use of digital certificates (X.509v3 certificates) proved to be resource intensive (larger certificate sizes, increased communication overhead and complex path chain validation processes) in the WSN paradigm [14,22]. Consequently, non−PKI-based schemes such as identity-based cryptography, certificate-less public key cryptographic implementations with and without pairings, and the elliptic curve Qu-Vanstone Implicit Certificate Scheme seem more promising and expunge the need for certificates [31−34]. Moreover, mathematical realization of identity-based cryptographic implementations include computational number-theoretic primitive pairing and nonpairing based schemes. However, identity-based schemes still have the classical key escrow problem [14].

Of late, cryptanalysts have found security deficiencies in pairing-friendly schemes based on binary elliptic curves [35,36]. Hence, most pairing implementations rely on prime curves as opposed to binary curves. As a logical progression, WSN implementations have focused on escrow-less authenticated key agreement schemes based on elliptic curve cryptography (strengthened Menezes−Qu−Vanstone [37]).

4. SECURE ROUTING IN WIRELESS SENSOR NETWORKS

Routing consists of two steps: (1) discovering a suitable route between a packet's source and destination, and (2) forwarding packets along this discovered route. In traditional (IP or 3G networks) networks, routing operations are dedicated to special nodes, namely routers. However, WSNs consist of resource-constrained devices operating in an ad hoc decentralized manner that requires all of the network operations to be done by these ordinary sensor nodes. Some real-time applications (remote-sensing operations) require the routing protocols to facilitate the timely delivery of messages. However, such applications are too resource-intensive in WSNs and require routing protocols that can balance the energy consumption of the entire network. Furthermore, the number of nodes operating in a WSN scenario is much larger than conventional networks. Consequently, there is a need for the mass production of low-cost nodes. However, with the increase in the number of sensor nodes to meet the current demand for sensor applications, construction of each node to be tamper resistant would be expensive. As a result, nodes could be susceptible to a node-capture attack. Hence, routing protocols used in traditional networks cannot be applied directly to a resource-constrained environment such as WSN. New routing protocols taking into account energy use have been sought for WSNs [38].

5. ROUTING PROTOCOLS IN WIRELESS SENSOR NETWORKS

Routing protocols in WSN can be broadly classified into proactive, reactive, hybrid, and location-aware routing protocols [39]. In a proactive routing scheme, each node maintains an up-to-date routing table by frequently querying its immediate neighbors for routing information. An example of such a scheme is the Destination Sequenced Distance Vector (DSDV) routing protocol [40]. However, one of the major drawbacks with such schemes is the additional overhead owing to frequent routing updates.

In contrast, reactive routing involves on-the-fly route establishment and is demand driven. It is based on a request–response model. The initial discovery phase, to find the destined node, could involve flooding, and the response phase establishes the transient active routing path. Examples include ad hoc on-demand distance vector routing and dynamic source routing [41,42].

Various hybrid protocols use the node-discovery method of the proactive routing protocol, along with the on-the-fly routing-path establishment method to produce a hybrid version of the protocol. Zone Routing Protocol is an example of such a hybrid scheme [43]. In position-aware routing protocols, the nodes select the geographically closest neighboring node when making routing decisions. An example of such a protocol is the GEAR protocol [10]. However, GEAR does not take security into consideration.

Selective-Forwarding Attack in Wireless Sensor Networks

Many routing protocols in WSN use a breadth-first spanning-tree algorithm to broadcast routing updates [7,44]. The sink node periodically broadcasts updated routing information to its immediate cluster heads. These cluster heads then rebroadcast this information to their immediate neighbors, and the process continues recursively. During this process, each intermediate node makes a note of its parent node, in which the parent node is the first node that was able to make contact with its subordinate node and relay the routing information. When all the active nodes are operational, they should send all the sensed data to their parent node. However, this protocol is vulnerable to many attacks.

Cross-Layer Design in Wireless Sensor Networks

A flurry of cross-layer design schemes have been proposed for WSNs. Because the fusion of secure networking and wireless communication occupies the center stage in sensor networks, the traditional layered protocol architecture is being reconsidered. Although the layered approach is traditionally used in wired networks, it has been argued that the same approach cannot be directly applied in resource-constrained wireless ad hoc networks such as WSNs. As an alternative, security researchers have proposed several cross-layer design schemes for the ad hoc environment [45]. Unlike the layering approach, in which protocols at each layer are designed independently, cross-layer designs aim to exploit the dependence between different protocol layers to achieve maximum performance gains.

In the current state of the art in cross-layer design schemes for ad hoc wireless networks, several diverse interpretations exist. One of the main reasons for such varied explanations is that the design effort is largely dominated by researchers who have made independent efforts in designing different layers of the stack. Many of the cross-layer designs depend on other cross-layer designs, and hence raise the fundamental question of the coexistence of different cross-layer design proposals. In addition, the question of time synchronization between various cross-layer schemes and the roles each layer of the stack has is an active area of research.

The wireless medium allows richer modalities of communication than wired networks. For example, nodes can use the inherent broadcast nature of the wireless medium and cooperate with each other. Employing modalities such as node cooperation in protocol design also calls for cross-layer design. The goal of designing security solutions with a cross-layer design approach is a new paradigm for security research.

The main objective of security solutions in a network is to provide security services such as authentication, integrity, confidentiality, and availability to users. In wireless ad hoc networks, because of the unreliable nature of the shared radio medium, attackers can launch varying attacks ranging from passive reconnaissance attacks to active man-in-the-middle attacks. Routing in WSN is hop by hop and assumes a trusted, cooperative environment as intermediate nodes act as relays. However, compromised intermediate nodes can launch varying routing attacks, such as black hole, wormhole, flood rushing, and selective-forwarding attacks. In this section, we review the existing state of the art in the cross-layer design from a security perspective. In addition, as an example, we look at a cross-layer key distribution mechanism.

Cross-layer interactions among layers can be categorized in different ways: for example, lower to upper (violation in the flow control from bottom to top), upper to lower (violation in the flow control from top to bottom), and lower and upper. In all of these cases, new interfaces will be created between layers. In addition, cross-layer designs can be categorized by integrating adjacent layers, design coupling without interfaces, and horizontal calibrations.

Lower to Upper

The requirement of information from the lower layer to the upper layer at runtime results in the creation of a new interface between these two layers. In this case, the lower layers update necessary information to the appropriate upper layers via the interface. For example, the data link layer is made aware of the transmit power and the BER information by the physical layer so that it can adjust its error-correction mechanism. Subsequently, the transport layer can inform the application layer about the Transmission Control Protocol (TCP) packet loss because it would help the upper layer in the stack (application layer) to adjust its transmitting rate. In addition, self-adaptation loops should not be part of a cross-layer design approach because they do not require new interfaces to be created between the necessary lower and upper layers. For example, in an auto-rate fallback mechanism for rate selection in a wireless networking environment with multirate physical layers, the MAC layer rate selection depends on the received acknowledgment that is observable at the MAC layer. Hence this mechanism would not qualify as a cross-layer design approach because there is no need to create new interfaces for rate adaption.

Upper to Lower

The upper layers provide updated information to the necessary lower layers via an interface. For example, if the application layer senses a delay or loss of data, a direct notification to the data link layer by the application layer would help adapt its error correction mechanism. In addition, delay-sensitive packets could be treated with priority. As proposed by Larzon, Bodin, and Schelen [46], lower-to-upper

information flow is treated as notifications (the lower layer notifies the upper layer about the underlying network condition), whereas the upper-to-lower information flow is treated as hints (upper layers provide hints to the lower layers on the means to process application data).

Lower and Upper

In this case, both the upper and lower layers are at liberty to transmit notifications about their current state and send queries to the other layers. During runtime, layers executing different tasks can collaborate with each other on an iterative loop basis, resulting in back-and-forth communication between them. For example, a back-and-forth information flow between layers is seen in a proposal to solve the multiple access problem for contention-based wireless ad hoc networks using joint scheduling and suggesting a distributed power control algorithm for such networks [47]. In addition, direct communication between layers at runtime could indicate the advantage of making the variables at each layer visible to the other layers of the stack. However, one disadvantage of this approach would be in managing the shared memory spaces between the layers when variables and internal states are shared between different layers.

Integration of Adjacent Layers

The formation of a superlayer by combining two or more adjacent layers would result in a new cross-layer design scheme. The resulting layer would simply provide the union of the services that were provided by the individual layers. For example, a collaborative design of the data link and physical layer would suffice to produce a superlayer. From a network security perspective, a superlayer that combines network and data link layer would help prevent advanced Address Resolution Protocol poisoning attacks.

Design Coupling Without Interfaces

Coupling two or more layers during the design phase would avoid creating extra interfaces at runtime that could result in a new cross-layer design approach. However, in deployed networks, one of the architectural challenges would be to integrate the coupled layer with already existing fixed layers.

Vertical and Horizontal Calibration Across Layers

Vertical calibration refers to the efficient use of parameters across different layers of the vertical stack. The parameters set at the application level could dictate terms to the lower layers, and vice versa. For example, the transport protocol

[TCP or User Datagram Protocol (UDP)] chosen at the transport layer would assert reliable or unreliable communication and would directly affect the layers below it. Consequently, the joint adjustment at different layers of the vertical stack would result in a more holistic performance of the system than the adjustment of individual parameters.

Horizontal Calibration

Horizontal calibration could be useful in a resource-constraint environment such WSNs. In this case, not only individual parameters pertaining to that layer are taken into consideration; parameters pertaining to other compatriot layers are also considered. For example, while routing packets, if the network level state of intermediate nodes is taken into consideration, it would be easy to detect non-active nodes and could subsequently result in an energy-efficient routing protocol. However, challenges exist in case the participating nodes do not adhere to the same cross-layer approach as the initiating node.

6. WIRELESS SENSOR NETWORKS AND INTERNET OF THINGS

Over the past 4 decades, the Internet has grown exponentially from the private network of a few nodes to a worldwide public network of billions of nodes. In 1999, Kevin Ashton coined the expression the "Internet of Things" (IoT) to refer to the trend toward interconnected "things" that collect data through sensing and performing computations on the sensor data. IoT is a broad term without a unique definition but involves disparate "things" ranging from mundane physical objects to complex biosensors that are capable of (1) sensing/actuation, (2) connecting through the Internet, and (3) processing [48].

The evolution of IoT can be categorized into four phases, as shown in Fig. 18.6. The first phase witnessed the emergence of radio-frequency identification (RFID) and bar codes, which simplified inventory management in

manufacturing, retail, pharmaceutical, and other industries. In addition, it provided a rudimentary form of tracking and identification. Although RFID is a well-established technology for low-cost identification and tracking, WSNs bring richer capabilities for sensing and actuation. The second phase involved the connectivity of WSNs to the Internet (through gateway nodes). WSNs cover a broad range of applications and provide better support for IoT applications [49–51]. This phase paved the way for new civilian and military applications. In the third phase, a new wave of IoT solutions will leverage the next generation of sensors, generating data on a scale enabling big data analysis. Finally, the fourth phase will bridge the gap in connectivity among different sectors (consumer, health care, industrial, transportation, retail, military, energy, and buildings) to provide a seamless interaction of everything.

Many current WSNs are non-IP based and proprietary (ZigBee, WAVE2M, and WirelessHart), but they are information silos with limited connectivity to the external world [52,53]. The current trend is toward IP connectivity between WSNs and the Internet to make an IoT [49]. Smart objects will use open standards and unique IP addresses [54]. However, the multitude of application domains for IoT means that there is no single strategy for realizing the vision of the IoT. Standardization of the IoT is currently one of the main obstacles to widespread adoption [55].

Internet of Things Protocols

The Internet Engineering Task Force (IETF) and Institute of Electrical and Electronics Engineers (IEEE), among other organizations, are working on standards for the IoT protocol stack [56]. A view of a representative protocol stack is shown in Fig. 18.7 (additional protocols might be used as well).

Application Layer

The Constrained Application Protocol (CoAP) is a proposal developed by the IETF Constrained RESTful

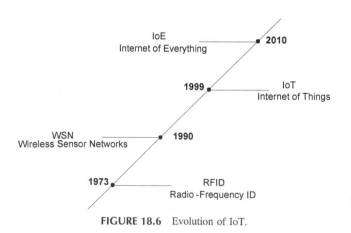

FIGURE 18.6 Evolution of IoT.

Application layer	CoAP
Transport layer	UDP
Network layer	IPv6, 6LoWPAN, RPL
Data link/MAC layer	IEEE 802.15.4 MAC
Physical layer	IEEE 802.15.4 PHY

FIGURE 18.7 Internet of Things protocol stack. *CoAP*, Constrained Application Protocol; *IEEE*, Institute of Electrical and Electronics Engineers; *MAC*, medium access control; *PHY*, Physical Layer; *UDP*, User Datagram Protocol.

Environments working group for an application layer protocol for interoperability among resource-constrained IoT devices. It is designed specifically for special environments, typically of an IoT, that have strict constraints in terms of limited energy resources, high packet loss rates, and limited hardware capabilities. CoAP consists of a subset of Hypertext Transport Protocol functionalities that have been redesigned considering the low processing power and energy consumption constraints of small embedded devices. CoAP defines short messages encoded in a simple binary format and exchanged by default UDP port 5683 [57]. Application layer protocol metadata can be compressed without compromising application interoperability, in conformance with the representational state transfer architecture of the Web.

Transport Layer

The Transport Layer Protocol is UDP, which is used by many application protocols that do not need connections. UDP adds only error detection and multiplexing above the IP.

Network Layer

Communication through the Internet necessarily makes use of IP. The IP for Smart Objects Alliance actively promotes IPv6-embedded devices for machine-to-machine applications. Given the expected huge number of IoT devices, IPv6 (version 6) is necessary because the address space in IPv4 is only 32 bits (or 4 billion addresses). The address space in IPv6 is 128 bits, allowing for 3.4×10^{38} addresses. It is sometimes pointed out that IPv6 allows 6.5×10^{23} addresses for every square meter of the Earth's surface. Moreover, IPv6 allows network autoconfiguration and stateless operation.

The IETF IPv6 over low-power wireless personal area network (WPAN) (6LoWPAN) work group has come up with a number of recommendations to adapt IPv6 for use over IEEE 802.15.4 networks. The 6LoWPAN architecture is made up of low-power wireless area networks (LoWPANs) that are connected to other IP networks through edge routers. The edge router has an important role because it routes traffic in and out of the LoWPAN while handling 6LoWPAN compression and NeighborDiscovery for the LoWPAN. Recommendations include:

- overview [RFC 4919]
- IPv6 packet transmission over IEEE 802.15.4 networks [RFC 4944, 6282, 6775]
- IPv6 compression header [RFC 6282]
- neighbor discovery [RFC 6775]
- routing requirements [RFC 6606]
- use cases [RFC 6568]

Routing in 6LoWPAN environments has been addressed by the IETF Routing Over Low power and Lossy networks working group [58]. Its main recommendation is

Routing Protocol for Low-Power and Lossy Networks (RPL) [RFC 6550]. RPL supports point-to-point, point-to-multipoint, and multipoint-to-point traffic flows. RPL can support different types of applications running in a WSN. Secure versions of the various routing control messages are defined, as well as three basic security modes. Not exactly a routing protocol, RPL is more of a framework that is adaptable to the requirements of particular IoT application domains. Application-specific profiles are already defined to identify the corresponding routing requirements of applications.

Medium Access Control and Physical Layers

Various physical communications can be used for IoT, but the main technology is IEEE 802.15.4, which covers the physical layer, and MAC, for low-rate wireless personal area networks [59]. Security is provided only at the MAC layer, which supports various security modes as an option to the application layer. Available security modes are different in their security guarantees and the size of the integrity data employed [58]. Security services in the MAC layer include access control, data encryption, frame integrity, and sequential freshness. It is assumed that keys are generated, transmitted, and stored by the upper layers in a secure manner. Advanced security features (key management and authentication) are the responsibility of higher protocol layers.

ZigBee is an emerging technology for reliable, cost-effective, low-power wireless network promoted by the ZigBee Alliance. The physical and MAC layers are defined by the IEEE 802.15.4 standard, whereas the network and application layers of the stack are defined by the ZigBee specification. The ZigBee specification provides authentication using a common network key; data freshness using counters; message integrity; and encryption using 128-bit AES network level or device level.

Internet of Things Security

The IoT will have billions to trillions of "things" communicating with each other, humans, and virtual entities. The openness of the system, combined with the physical and virtual accessibility of objects from anywhere, means that security will be a major problem [60]. Security must be concerned with all possible attack vectors, which could be numerous. It is a system without any real borders, and therefore traditional perimeter defenses cannot be used. Attackers can be "internal" and "external" at the same time [61]. The state of the art in IoT security is at an early stage, and solutions are currently limited. An examination of some possible threats [61] includes:

- DoS attacks to exhaust service provider resources and network bandwidth, or attacks against the wireless communication infrastructure (jamming the channels)

- physical attacks to compromise "things"
- eavesdropping on various communication channels
- capture of things to extract their information
- attacks to gain control of an IoT device or the services that the device is providing

As usual, IoT security must provide the usual assurances in terms of confidentiality, integrity, authentication, and nonrepudiation [58]. Privacy and anonymity may be particularly important for social acceptance of future IoT applications. Availability and resilience will be additional requirements in light of possible DoS and physical attacks.

Privacy

Privacy is essential for social acceptance of the IoT given that so much sensory data will be collected. Mechanisms to ensure an appropriate level of control over personally identifiable information could be complex [61]. At the same time, the edge intelligence principle offers hope that privacy will be easier, because every IoT device has more control over the data it generates and processes.

Authentication

The problem of managing identity and authentication in the IoT is challenging: that is, considering that multiple entities (data sources, service providers, and information processing systems) need to authenticate each other to create trustable services [61].

Access Control

Access control is as challenging for the IoT as for any distributed system [61]. A service may be constructed by aggregating several services and data sources from different locations and contexts. All of these information providers will have their own access control policies and permission systems.

Key Management

PKI and identity-based cryptography (IBC) have been proposed as infrastructures for public key cryptography. IBC is the best choice for WSNs because there is no certificates problem, but IBC does not scale to large networks [62]. Hence PKI is needed for the scale of IoT.

Fault and Intrusion Tolerance

With a population of billions of things, it would be realistic to expect that some things will become faulty or compromised by intrusions. In case of faults, things may stop working but that should not bring down the entire system [61]. In case of intrusions, things may continue to work but might send inaccurate or even manipulated data. The overall system must be able to continue to operate satisfactorily even if some things are compromised and data are problematic.

Self-healing

In the event of attacks bringing down part of the system, ideally the system should be able to detect the attack, carry out diagnostics, respond with countermeasures, and repair the damage. All these must be performed in a lightweight manner owing to the low capacity and resources of devices [60].

7. SUMMARY

The past decade has witnessed a surge in low-power, resource-constrained networks such as WSN. With their growing popularity, security concerns regarding WSNs have arisen and the need for effective countermeasures is greater than ever. In this chapter, we review WSN architectures, possible threats and attacks, and their countermeasures. In particular, we focus on the Holy Grail, key management, and later, authentication in WSN. Consequently, we foresee that the legacy layered approach to security can lead to security gaps and calls for the need for cross-layer designs. Finally, because the emergence of IoT and WSN are part of the IoT ecosystem, we survey different IoT protocols and their related threats and attacks. As IoT frameworks mature, security, privacy, fault-tolerant methods, and trust models need advancement to meet the growing need for the IoE.

Finally, let us move on to the real interactive part of this chapter: review questions/exercises, hands-on projects, case projects, and the optional team case project. The answers and/or solutions by chapter can be found in Appendix K.

CHAPTER REVIEW QUESTIONS/ EXERCISES

True/False

1. True or False? Although WSNs have gained little popularity, there are some serious limitations when implementing security.
2. True or False? WSNs operate in a resource-constrained environment and therefore deviate from the traditional OSI model.
3. True or False? In WSNs, threats to privacy can be further classified into reconnaissance.
4. True or False? The man-in-the-middle attack is not one of the classical attacks that can be executed in a WSN environment.
5. True or False? Because of threats to the WSN, some portion of the network or some of the functionalities or services provided by the network could be damaged and available to participants of the network.

Multiple Choice

1. The middle layer provides one of the following for applications existing in the upper layers:
   - A. RC four-stream cipher
   - B. Temporal Key Integrity Protocol (TKIP)
   - C. Application Program Interface
   - D. Message Integrity Code (MIC)
   - E. Extensible Authentication Protocol (EAP) framework
2. Which of the following is responsible for flow and congestion control?
   - A. Middle Layer
   - B. Network Layer
   - C. Transport Layer
   - D. Data link Layer
   - E. All of the above
3. What allows organizations to reason about attacks at a level higher than a simple list of vulnerabilities?
   - A. Secure on-demand routing protocol
   - B. Taxonomy
   - C. Message Authentication Code (MAC)
   - D. Authenticated Routing for Ad hoc Networks (ARAN)
   - E. Destination-Sequenced Distance Vector (DSDV) routing
4. In what type of attack is the attacker is able to intercept and monitor data between communicating nodes, but does not tamper or modify packets for fear of raising suspicion of malicious activity among the nodes?
   - A. Active attack
   - B. Privacy attack
   - C. Eavesdropping attack
   - D. Man-in-the-middle attack
   - E. Passive attack
5. What occurs when an attacker floods the victim with bogus or spoofed packets with the intent of lowering the response rate of the victim?
   - A. HELLO Flood attack
   - B. Denial-of-service attack
   - C. Sinkhole attack
   - D. Sybil attack
   - E. All of the above

EXERCISE

Problem

What is wireless sensor networking data acquisition?

Hands-on Projects

Project

What is the difference between the Wi-Fi NI CompactDAQ chassis and a wireless sensor node?

Case Projects

Problem

How do you add wireless sensors to your hardwired security system?

Optional Team Case Project

Problem

How do you install window sensors for a wireless burglar alarm?

REFERENCES

[1] I.F. Akyildiz, W. Su, Y. Sankarasubramaniam, E. Cayirci, Wireless sensor networks: a survey, Comput. Networks 38 (2002) 393—422.

[2] Y. Zhou, Y. Fang, Y. Zhang, Securing wireless sensor networks: a survey, IEEE Commun. Surv. Tutorials 10 (2008) 6—28.

[3] M. Anand, Z.G. Ives, I. Lee, Quantifying Eavesdropping Vulnerability in Sensor Networks, Departmental Papers, Department of Computer & Information Science, University of Pennsylvania, 2005.

[4] W. Xu, W. Trappe, Y. Zhang, Defending wireless sensor networks from radio interference through channel adaptation, ACM Trans. Sens. Network 4 (August 2008).

[5] J.R. Douceur, The Sybil attack, in: In First International Workshop on Peer-to-Peer Systems (IPTPS '02), 2002.

[6] C. Karlof, D. Wagner, Secure routing in wireless sensor networks: attacks and countermeasures, in: First International Workshop on Sensor Network Protocols and Applications, 2003, pp. 113—127.

[7] J. Newsome, E. Shi, D. Song, A. Perrig, The Sybil attack in sensor networks: analysis & defenses, in: Third International Symposium on Information Processing in Sensor Networks, IPSN, 2004, pp. 259—268.

[8] W. Xu, W. Trappe, Y. Zhang, T. Wood, The feasibility of launching and detecting jamming attacks in wireless networks, in: Presented at the Proceedings of the 6th ACM International Symposium on Mobile Ad Hoc Networking and Computing, Urbana-Champaign, IL, USA, 2005.

[9] Z. Sun, X-g. Zhang, H. Li, A. Li, The application of TinyOS beaconing WSN routing protocol in mine safety monitoring, in: International Conference on Mechtronic and Embedded Systems and Applications, MESA, 2008, pp. 415—419.

[10] Y. Yu, R. Govindan, D. Estrin, Geographical and Energy Aware Routing: A Recursive Data Dissemination Protocol for Wireless Sensor Networks, Tech Report, 2001.

[11] M. Healy, T. Newe, E. Lewis, Security for wireless sensor networks: a review, in: SAS 2009 — IEEE Sensors Applications Symposium, 2009, pp. 80—85.

[12] A. Perrig, R. Szewczyk, J. Tygar, V. Wen, D. Culler, SPINS: security protocols for sensor, Wireless Networks 8 (2002) 521—534.

[13] C. Karlof, N. Sastry, D. Wagner, TinySec: a link layer security architecture for wireless sensor networks, in: Second ACM Conference on Embedded Networked Sensor Systems, 2004, pp. 162—175.

[14] H. Kupwade Patil, S.A. Szygneda, Security for Wireless Sensor Networks Using Identity-based Cryptography, CRC Press, 2012.

[15] A.S. Wander, N. Gura, H. Eberle, V. Gupta, S.C. Shantz, Energy analysis of public-key cryptography for wireless sensor networks, in: Third IEEE International Conference on Pervasive Computing and Communications, 2005, pp. 324–328.

[16] R. Watro, D. Kong, S. Cuti, C. Gardiner, C. Lynn, P. Kruus, TinyPK: securing sensor networks with public key technology, in: 2nd ACM Workshop on Security of Ad Hoc and Sensor Networks, 2004, pp. 59–64.

[17] Q. Huang, J. Cukier, H. Kobayashi, B. Liu, J. Zhang, Fast authenticated key establishment protocols for organizing sensor networks, in: Workshop on Sensor Networks and Applications (WSNA), 2003, pp. 141–150.

[18] X. Tian, D. Wong, R. Zhu, Analysis and improvement of an authenticated key exchange protocol for sensor networks, Commun. Lett. 9 (2005) 970–972.

[19] K. Ren, W. Lou, Y. Zhang, Multi-user broadcast authentication in wireless sensor networks, in: Proceedings of Sensor, Mesh and Ad Hoc Communications and Networks, 2012, pp. 223–232.

[20] R.C. Merkle, Protocols for public key cryptosystems, in: Symposium on Security and Privacy, 1980, pp. 122–134.

[21] M. Mitzenmacher, Compressed bloom filters, Trans. Networking 10 (2002).

[22] D. Aranha, R. Dahab, J. López, L. Oliveira, Efficient implementation of elliptic curve cryptography in wireless sensors, Adv. Math. Commun. 4 (2010) 169–187.

[23] R. Blom, An optimal class of symmetric key generation systems, in: Advances in Cryptology: Proceedings of Eurocrypt '84, 1984, pp. 335–338.

[24] C. Blundo, A.D. Santis, A. Herzberg, S. Kutten, Perfectly-secure key distribution for dynamic conferences, in: Advances in Cryptology - Crypto '92, 1992, pp. 471–486.

[25] L. Eschenauer, V.D. Gligor, A key management scheme for distributed sensor networks, in: Proceedings of the 9th ACM Conference on Computer and Communication Security, 2002.

[26] P. Chan, D. Song, Random key pre-distribution schemes for sensor networks, in: Proceedings of the 2003 IEEE Symposium on Security and Privacy, 2003, pp. 197–213.

[27] W. Du, J. Deng, Y. Han, P. Varshney, A pairwise key pre-distribution scheme for wireless sensor networks, in: Proceedings of the Tenth ACM Conference on Computer and Communications Security (CCS 2003), 2003, pp. 42–51.

[28] D. Liu, P. Ning, Establishing pairwise keys in distributed sensor networks, in: Proceedings of the 10th ACM Conference on Computer and Communications Security (CCS 2003), 2003, pp. 52–61.

[29] J. Lee, D. Stinson, Deterministic key predistribution schemes for distributed sensor networks, Lect. Notes Comput. Sci. 3357 (2005) 294–307.

[30] S. Camtepe, B. Yener, Combinatorial design of key distribution mechanisms for wireless sensor networks, IEEE Trans. Networking 15 (2007) 346–358.

[31] S.S. Al-Riyami, K.G. Paterson, Certificateless public key cryptography, in: C.-S. Laih (Ed.), Advances in Cryptology – ASIACRYPT 2003: 9th International Conference on the Theory and Application of Cryptology and Information Security, Taipei, Taiwan, November 30 – December 4, 2003. Proceedings, Springer Berlin Heidelberg, Berlin, Heidelberg, 2003, pp. 452–473.

[32] J. Baek, R. Safavi-Naini, W. Susilo, Certificateless public key encryption without pairing, in: J. Zhou, J. Lopez, R.H. Deng, F. Bao (Eds.), Information Security: 8th International Conference, ISC 2005, Singapore, September 20–23, 2005. Proceedings, Springer Berlin Heidelberg, Berlin, Heidelberg, 2005, pp. 134–148.

[33] B. Lee, C. Boyd, E. Dawson, K. Kim, J. Yang, S. Yoo, Secure key issuing in ID-based cryptography, in: Presented at the Proceedings of the Second Workshop on Australasian Information Security, Data Mining and Web Intelligence, and Software Internationalisation, vol. 32, 2004. Dunedin, New Zealand.

[34] D.R.L. Brown, R. Gallant, S.A. Vanstone, Provably secure implicit certificate schemes, in: P. Syverson (Ed.), Financial Cryptography: 5th International Conference, FC 2001 Grand Cayman, British West Indies, February 19–22, 2001 Proceedings, Springer Berlin Heidelberg, Berlin, Heidelberg, 2002, pp. 156–165.

[35] F. Göloğlu, R. Granger, G. McGuire, J. Zumbrägel, On the function field sieve and the impact of higher splitting probabilities, in: R. Canetti, J.A. Garay (Eds.), Advances in Cryptology – CRYPTO 2013: 33rd Annual Cryptology Conference, Santa Barbara, CA, USA, August 18-22, 2013. Proceedings, Part II, Springer Berlin Heidelberg, Berlin, Heidelberg, 2013, pp. 109–128.

[36] A. Joux, A new index calculus algorithm with complexity $L(1/4+o(1))$ in small characteristic, in: T. Lange, K. Lauter, P. Lisoněk (Eds.), Selected Areas in Cryptography – SAC 2013: 20th International Conference, Burnaby, BC, Canada, August 14–16, 2013, Revised Selected Papers, Springer Berlin Heidelberg, Berlin, Heidelberg, 2014, pp. 355–379.

[37] A.P. Sarr, P. Elbaz-Vincent, J.-C. Bajard, A new security model for authenticated key agreement, in: J.A. Garay, R. De Prisco (Eds.), Security and Cryptography for Networks: 7th International Conference, SCN 2010, Amalfi, Italy, September 13–15, 2010. Proceedings, Springer Berlin Heidelberg, Berlin, Heidelberg, 2010, pp. 219–234.

[38] J.N. Al-Karaki, A.E. Kamal, Routing techniques in wireless sensor networks: a survey, Wireless Commun. 11 (2004) 6–28.

[39] Y. Xiao, X. Shen, D. Du, Wireless Network Security, Springer, 2007.

[40] C. Perkins, P. Bhagwat, Highly dynamic destination sequenced distance-vector routing for mobile computers, ACM's Comput. Commun. Rev. (1994) 234–244.

[41] C. Perkins, E. Royer, Ad-hoc on-demand distance vector routing, in: Proc. of the 2nd IEEE Workshop on Mobile Computing Systems and Applications, 1999, pp. 90–100.

[42] D. Johnson, D. Maltz, Dynamic source routing, Mobile Comput. (1996) 153–181.

[43] Z. Haas, M. Pearlman, The performance of query control scheme for the zone routing protocol, Trans. Networking (2001) 427–438.

[44] S. Kuo-Feng, W. Wei-Tong, C. Wen-Chung, Detecting Sybil attacks in wireless sensor networks using neighboring information, Comput. Networks 53 (December 2009) 3042–3056.

[45] S. Shakkottai, T.S. Rappaport, P.C. Karlsson, Cross-layer design for wireless networks, in: Communications Magazine, 2003, pp. 74–80.

[46] L.-A. Larzon, U. Bodin, O. Schelen, Hints and notifications, in: Wireless Communications and Networking Conference, 2002, pp. 635–641.

[47] T. ElBatt, A. Ephremides, Joint scheduling and power control for wireless ad hoc networks, IEEE Trans. Wireless Commun. 3 (2004) 74—85.

[48] R. Want, B.N. Schilit, S. Jenson, Enabling the Internet of Things, Computer 48 (2015) 28—35.

[49] L. Mainetti, L. Patrono, A. Vilei, Evolution of wireless sensor networks towards the Internet of Things: a survey, in: Software, Telecommunications and Computer Networks (SoftCOM), 2011 19th International Conference on, 2011, 2011, pp. 1—6.

[50] P. Eugster, V. Sundaram, X. Zhang, Debugging the Internet of Things: the case of wireless sensor networks, IEEE Software 32 (2015) 38—49.

[51] M.T. Lazarescu, Design of a WSN platform for long-term environmental monitoring for IoT applications, IEEE J. Emerging Sel. Top. Circuits Syst. 3 (2013) 45—54.

[52] A. McGibney, A.E. Rodríguez, S. Rea, Managing wireless sensor networks within IoT ecosystems, in: Internet of Things (WF-IoT), 2015 IEEE 2nd World Forum on, 2015, 2015, pp. 339—344.

[53] Z. Sheng, S. Yang, Y. Yu, A.V. Vasilakos, J.A. Mccann, K.K. Leung, A survey on the ietf protocol suite for the internet of things: standards, challenges, and opportunities, IEEE Wireless Commun. 20 (2013) 91—98.

[54] S. Hong, D. Kim, M. Ha, S. Bae, S.J. Park, W. Jung, et al., SNAIL: an IP-based wireless sensor network approach to the internet of things, IEEE Wireless Commun. 17 (2010) 34—42.

[55] L. Atzori, A. Iera, G. Morabito, The Internet of Things: a survey, Comput. Networks 54 (2010) 2787—2805.

[56] M.R. Palattella, N. Accettura, X. Vilajosana, T. Watteyne, L.A. Grieco, G. Boggia, et al., Standardized protocol stack for the Internet of (important) Things, IEEE Commun. Surv. Tutorials 15 (2013) 1389—1406.

[57] C. Bormann, A.P. Castellani, Z. Shelby, CoAP: an application protocol for billions of tiny internet nodes, IEEE Internet Comput. 16 (2012) 62—67.

[58] J. Granjal, E. Monteiro, J.S. Silva, End-to-end transport-layer security for Internet-integrated sensing applications with mutual and delegated ECC public-key authentication, in: IFIP Networking Conference, 2013, 2013, pp. 1—9.

[59] IEEE P802.15.4e/D7.0, September 2011, based on IEEE P802.15.4-2011, IEEE Draft Standard for Local and Metropolitan Area Networks Part 15.4: Low Rate Wireless Personal Area Networks (LR-wpans) Amendment to the MAC Sub-layer, 2011, pp. 1—233.

[60] J.A. Stankovic, Research directions for the internet of things, IEEE Internet Things J. 1 (2014) 3—9.

[61] R. Roman, J. Zhou, J. Lopez, On the features and challenges of security and privacy in distributed internet of things, Comput. Networks 57 (2013) 2266—2279.

[62] F. Li, P. Xiong, Practical secure communication for integrating wireless sensor networks into the internet of things, IEEE Sens. J. 13 (2013) 3677—3684.

Chapter 19

Security for the Internet of Things

William Stallings

Independent consultant, Brewster, MA, USA

1. INTRODUCTION

The Internet of Things (IoT) is primarily driven by deeply embedded devices [1]. These devices are low-bandwidth, low-repetition data capture, and low-bandwidth data-usage appliances that communicate with each other and provide data via user interfaces. Embedded appliances, such as high-resolution video security cameras, video VoIP phones, and a handful of others, require high-bandwidth streaming capabilities. Yet countless products simply require packets of data to be intermittently delivered. With reference to the end systems supported, the Internet has gone through roughly four generations of deployment culminating in the IoT:

1. **Information technology (IT)**: Personal computers (PCs), servers, routers, firewalls, and so on, bought as IT devices by enterprise IT personnel, primarily using wired connectivity.
2. **Operational technology (OT)**: Machines/appliances with embedded IT built by non-IT companies, such as medical machinery, supervisory control and data acquisition (SCADA), process control, and kiosks, bought as appliances by enterprise OT personnel and primarily using wired connectivity.
3. **Personal technology**: Smartphones, tablets, and eBook readers bought as IT devices by consumers (employees) exclusively using wireless connectivity and often multiple forms of wireless connectivity.
4. **Sensor/actuator technology**: Single-purpose devices bought by consumers, IT, and OT personnel exclusively using wireless connectivity, generally of a single form, as part of larger systems.

Scope of the Internet of Things (IoT)

It is the fourth generation of the Internet that is usually thought of as the IoT, and which is marked by the use of billions of embedded devices. ITU-T Y.2060 [2] provides the following definitions that suggest the scope of IoT:

- **IoT**: A global infrastructure for the information society, enabling advanced services by interconnecting (physical and virtual) things based on existing and evolving interoperable information and communication technologies.
- **Thing**: With regard to the IoT, this is an object of the physical world (physical things) or the information world (virtual things), which is capable of being identified and integrated into communication networks.
- **Device**: With regard to the IoT, this is a piece of equipment with the mandatory capabilities of communication and the optional capabilities of sensing, actuation, data capture, data storage, and data processing.

Y.2060 characterizes the IoT as adding the dimension "Any THING communication" to the information and communication technologies which already provide "any TIME" and "any PLACE" communication (see Fig. 19.1). McEwen [3] condenses the elements of the IoT into a simple equation:

$$\text{Physical Objects} + \text{Controllers, Sensors, Actuators} + \text{Internet} = \text{IoT}$$

This equation neatly captures the essence of the IoT. An instance of the IoT consists of:

- A collection of physical objects, each of which contains a microcontroller that provides intelligence;
- A sensor that measures some physical parameter and/or an actuator that acts on some physical parameter;
- A means of communicating via the Internet or some other network.

Computer and Information Security Handbook. http://dx.doi.org/10.1016/B978-0-12-803843-7.00019-3

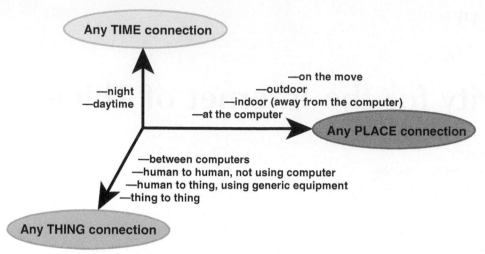

FIGURE 19.1 The new dimension introduced in the Internet of Things (IoT).

One item not covered in the equation, and referred to in the Y.2060 definition, is a means of identification of an individual thing, usually referred to as a tag. Typically, this is done by radio-frequency identification (RFID). RFID is a data collection technology that uses electronic tags attached to items to allow the items to be identified and tracked by a remote system. The tag consists of an RFID chip attached to an antenna.

Note that although the term IoT is always used in the literature, a more accurate description would be a "network of things." A smart home installation, for example, consists of a number of things in the home that are interconnected via Wi-Fi or Bluetooth with some central controller. In a factory or farm setting, there may be a network of things enabling enterprise applications to interact with the environment and run applications to exploit the network of things. In these examples, it is usually but not invariably the case that remote access over the Internet is available. Whether or not such Internet connection is available, the collection of smart objects at a site, plus any other local compute and storage device, can be characterized as a network or an IoT.

Layers of the Internet of Things (IoT)

Both the business and technical literature often focus on two elements of the IoT—the things that are connected, and the Internet that interconnects them. It is better to view the IoT as a massive system, which consists of five layers:

- **Sensors and actuators**: These are the things. Sensors observe their environment and report back quantitative measurements of such variables as temperature, humidity, presence or absence of some observable, and so on. Actuators operate on their environment, such as changing a thermostat setting or operating a valve.

- **Connectivity**: A device may connect via either a wireless or wired link into a network to send collected data to the appropriate data center (sensor) or receive operational commands from a controller site (actuator).
- **Capacity**: The network supporting the devices must be able to handle a potentially huge flow of data.
- **Storage**: There needs to be a large storage facility to store and maintain backups of all the collected data. This is typically a cloud capability.
- **Data analytics**: For large collections of devices, "big data" is generated, requiring a data analytics capability to process the data flow.

All of the preceding layers are essential to an effective use of the IoT concept.

2. ITU-T INTERNET OF THINGS (IOT) REFERENCE MODEL

Given the complexity of an IoT, it is useful to have an architecture that specifies the main elements and their interrelationship. An IoT architecture can have the following benefits:

1. It provides the IT or network manager with a useful checklist with which to evaluate the functionality and completeness of vendor offerings.
2. It provides guidance to developers as to which functions are needed in an IoT and how these functions work together.
3. It can serve as a framework for standardization, promoting interoperability and cost reduction.

This part of the chapter is an overview of the IoT architecture developed by ITU-T, and defined in Y.2060. Unlike most of the other IoT reference models and architectural models in the literature, the ITU-T model goes into detail about the actual physical components of the IoT ecosystem. This is a useful treatment because it makes visible the elements in the IoT ecosystem that must be interconnected, integrated, managed, and made available to applications. This detailed specification of the ecosystem drives the requirements for the IoT capability.

An important insight provided by the model is that the IoT is in fact not a network of physical things. Rather, it is a network of devices that interact with physical things, together with application platforms, such as computers, tablets, and smartphones, that interact with these devices. Thus, we begin our overview of the ITU-T model with a discussion of devices. Table 19.1 lists definitions of key terms used in Y.2060.

TABLE 19.1 Y.2060 Internet of Things (IoT) Terminology

Communication network: An infrastructure network that connects devices and applications, such as an IP-based network or Internet.

Thing: An object of the physical world (**physical things**) or the information world (**virtual things**), which is capable of being identified and integrated into communication networks.

Device: A piece of equipment with the mandatory capability of communication and the optional capabilities of sensing, actuation, data capture, data storage, and data processing.

Data-carrying device: A device attached to a physical thing to indirectly connect the physical thing with the communication networks. Class 3, 4, and 5 RFID tags are examples.

Data-capturing device: A reader/writer device with the capability to interact with physical things. The interaction can happen indirectly via data-carrying devices, or directly via data carriers attached to the physical things.

Data carrier: A battery-free data-carrying object attached to a physical thing that can provide information to a suitable data-capturing device. This category includes bar codes and QR codes attached to physical things.

Sensing device: Detects or measures information related to the surrounding environment and convert it into digital electronic signals.

Actuating device: Converts digital electronic signals from the information networks into operations.

General device: A general device has embedded processing and communication capabilities and may communicate with the communication networks via wired or wireless technologies. General devices include equipment and appliances for different IoT application domains, such as industrial machines, home electrical appliances, and smart phones.

Gateway: A unit in the Internet of Things (IoT) which interconnects the devices with the communication networks. It performs the necessary translation between the protocols used in the communication networks and those used by devices.

Devices

The unique aspect of an IoT compared to other network systems is the presence of a number of physical things and devices other than computing or data processing devices. Fig. 19.2, adapted from one in Y.2060, shows the types of devices in the ITU-T model. The model views an IoT as functioning as a network of devices that are tightly coupled with things. Sensors and actuators interact with physical things in the environment. Data-capturing devices read data from and/or write data to physical things via interaction with a data-carrying device or a data carrier attached or associated in some way with a physical object.

The model makes a distinction between data-carrying devices and data carriers. A data-carrying device is a device in the Y.2060 sense. A device at minimum is capable of communication and may include other electronic capabilities. An example of a data-carrying device is an RFID tag. By contrast, a data carrier is an element attached to a physical thing for the purpose of identification of providing some other sort of information. Y.2060 notes that technologies used for interaction between data-capturing devices and data-carrying devices or data carriers include radio frequency, infrared, optical, and galvanic driving. Examples of each include:

- **Radio frequency**: An RFID tag is an example.
- **Infrared**: Infrared badges arc in use in military, hospital, and other settings where the location and movement of personnel needs to be tracked. Examples include infrared reflective patches used by the military and battery-operated badges that emit identifying information. The latter can include a button that must be pressed so that the badge can be used as a means of passing through a portal, and a badge that automatically repeats the signal as a means of tracking personnel. Remote control devices used in the home or other settings to control electronic devices can also easily be incorporated into an IoT.
- **Optical**: Bar codes and QR codes are examples of identifying data carriers that can be read optically.
- **Galvanic driving**: An example of this is implanted medical devices that use the conductive properties of the body [4]. In implant-to-surface communication, galvanic coupling is used to send signals from an implanted device to electrodes on the skin. This scheme uses very little power and reduces the size and complexity of the implanted device.

The final type of device shown in Fig. 19.2 is the general device. These are devices with processing and communications capability that can be incorporated into an IoT. A good example is smart home technology that can integrate virtually every device in the home into a network for central or remote control.

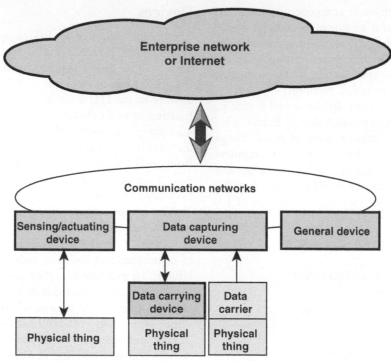

FIGURE 19.2 Types of devices and their relationships with physical things.

Fig. 19.3 provides an overview of the elements of interest in an IoT. The various ways that physical devices can be connected are shown on the left-hand side of the figure. It is assumed that one or multiple networks support communication among the devices.

Fig. 19.3 introduces one additional IoT-related device: the gateway. At minimum, a gateway functions as a protocol translator. Gateways address one of the greatest challenges in designing an IoT, which is connectivity, both among devices and between devices and the Internet or enterprise network. Smart devices support a wide variety of wireless and wired transmission technologies and networking

protocols. Further, these devices typically have limited processing capability. Y.2067 [5] lays out the requirements for IoT gateways, which generally fall into three categories:

1. The gateway supports a variety of device access technologies, enabling devices to communicate with each other and across an Internet or enterprise network with IoT applications. The access schemes could include, for example, ZigBee, Bluetooth, and Wi-Fi.
2. The gateway supports the necessary networking technologies for both local and wide area networking. These could include Ethernet and Wi-Fi on the premises, and

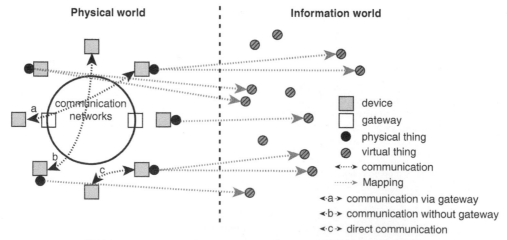

FIGURE 19.3 Technical overview of the Internet of Things (IoT) (Y.2060).

cellular, Ethernet, DSL, and cable access to the Internet and wide area enterprise networks.

3. The gateway supports interaction with application, network management, and security functions.

The first two requirements involve protocol translation between different network technologies and protocol suites. The third requirement is generally referred to as an IoT agent function. In essence, the IoT agent provides higher-level functionality on behalf of IoT devices, such as organizing and/or summarizing data from multiple devices to pass on to IoT applications, implementing security protocols and functions, and interacting with network management systems.

At this point, it should be noted that the term communication network is not directly defined in the Y.206x series of IoT standards. The communication network or networks supports communication among devices and may directly support application platforms. This may be the extent of a small IoT, such as a home network of smart devices. More generally, the device network(s) connect to enterprise networks or the Internet for communication with systems that host apps and servers that host databases related to the IoT.

We can now return to the left-hand side of Fig. 19.3, which illustrates the communication possibilities among devices. The first possibility is for communication between devices via the gateway. For example, a sensor or actuator with Bluetooth capability could communicate with a data-capturing device or general device that uses Wi-Fi by means of the gateway. The second possibility is communication across the communication network without a gateway. For example, all of the devices in a smart home network may use Bluetooth and could be managed from a Bluetooth-enabled computer, tablet, or smartphone. The third possibility is devices that communicate directly with each other through a separate local network and then (not shown in the figure) communicate through the communication network via a local network gateway. An example of this third possibility is the

following: A number of low-power sensor devices could be deployed in an extended area, such as farmland or a factory. These could communicate with one another to pass data on toward a device connected to a gateway to the communication network.

The right-hand side of Fig. 19.3 emphasizes that each physical thing in an IoT may be represented in the information world by one or more virtual things but a virtual thing can also exist without any associated physical thing. Physical things are mapped to virtual things stored in databases and other data structures. Applications process and deal with virtual things.

The Reference Model

Fig. 19.4 depicts the ITU-T IoT reference model, which consists of four layers as well as management capabilities and security capabilities that apply across layers. We have so far been considering the device layer. In terms of communications functionality, the device layer includes, roughly, the open systems interconnection (OSI) physical and data link layers. We now look at the other layers.

The **network layer** performs two basic functions. Networking capabilities refer to the interconnection of devices and gateways. Transport capabilities refer to the transport of IoT service and application specific information as well as IoT-related control and management information. Roughly, these correspond to OSI network and transport layers.

The **service support and application support layer** provides capabilities that are used by applications. Generic support capabilities can be used by many different applications. Examples include common data processing and database management capabilities. Specific support capabilities are those that cater for the requirements of a specific subset of IoT applications.

The **application layer** consists of all the applications that interact with IoT devices. The **management capabilities**

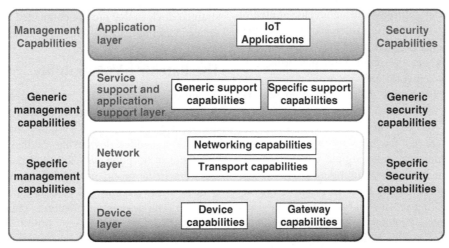

FIGURE 19.4   ITU-TY.2060 Internet of Things (IoT) reference model.

layer covers the traditional network-oriented management functions of fault, configuration, accounting, and performance management. Y.2060 lists the following as examples of generic management capabilities:

- **Device management**: such as device discovery, authentication, remote device activation and deactivation, configuration, diagnostics, firmware and/or software updating, device working status management.
- **Local network topology management**: such as network configuration management.
- **Traffic and congestion management**: such as the detection of network overflow conditions and the implementation of resource reservation for time-critical and/or life-critical data flows.

Specific management capabilities are tailored to specific classes of applications. An example is smart grid power transmission line monitoring.

The **security capabilities layer** includes generic security capabilities that are independent of applications. Y.2060 lists the following as examples of generic security capabilities:

- **Application layer**: authorization, authentication, application data confidentiality and integrity protection, privacy protection, security audit, and antivirus;
- **Network layer**: authorization, authentication, user data and signaling data confidentiality, and signaling integrity protection;
- **Device layer**: authentication, authorization, device integrity validation, access control, data confidentiality, and integrity protection.

Specific security capabilities relate to specific application requirements, such as mobile payment security requirements.

3. INTERNET OF THINGS (IOT) SECURITY

IoT is perhaps the most complex and undeveloped area of network security. To see this, consider Fig. 19.5, which shows the main elements of interest for IoT security. At the center of the network are the application platforms, data storage servers, and network and security management systems. These central systems gather data from sensors, send control signals to actuators, and are responsible for managing the IoT devices and their communication networks. At the edge of the network are IoT-enabled devices, some of which are quite simple constrained devices and some of which are more intelligent unconstrained devices. As well, gateways may perform protocol conversion and other networking service on behalf of IoT devices.

Fig. 19.5 illustrates a number of typical scenarios for interconnection and the inclusion of security features.

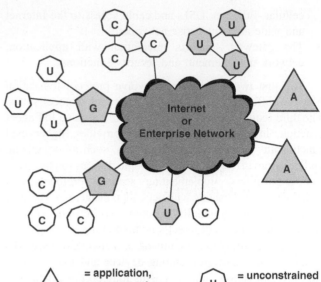

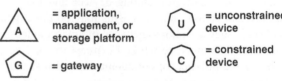

FIGURE 19.5   Internet of Things (IoT) security: elements of interest.

The shading in Fig. 19.5 indicates the systems that support at least some of these functions. Typically, gateways will implement secure functions, such as TLS and IPsec. Unconstrained devices may or may not implement some security capability. Constrained devices generally have limited or no security features. As suggested in the figure, gateway devices can provide secure communication between the gateway and the devices at the center, such as application platforms and management platforms. However, any constrained or unconstrained devices attached to the gateway are outside the zone of security established between the gateway and the central systems. As shown, unconstrained devices can communicate directly with the center and support security functions. However, constrained devices that are not connected to gateways have no secure communications with central devices.

The Patching Vulnerability

In an often-quoted 2014 article, security expert Bruce Schneier stated that we are at a crisis point with regard to the security of embedded systems, including IoT devices [6]. The embedded devices are riddled with vulnerabilities and there is no good way to patch them. The chip manufacturers have strong incentives to produce their product with its firmware and software as quickly and cheaply as possible. The device manufacturers choose a chip based on price and features and do very little if anything to the chip software and firmware. Their focus is the functionality of the device itself. The end user may have no means of patching the system or, if so, little information about when and how to patch. The result is that the hundreds of millions of Internet-connected devices in the IoT are vulnerable to attack. This is certainly a problem with sensors, allowing attackers to insert false data into the network. It is potentially a graver threat with actuators, where the attacker can affect the operation of machinery and other devices.

Internet of Things (IoT) Security and Privacy Requirements Defined by ITU-T

ITU-T Recommendation Y.2066 [7] includes a list of security requirements for the IoT. This list is a useful baseline for understanding the scope of security implementation needed for an IoT deployment. The requirements are defined as being the functional requirements during capturing, storing, transferring, aggregating, and processing the data of things, as well as to the provision of services which involve things. These requirements are related to all of the IoT actors. The requirements are:

- **Communication security**: Secure, trusted, and privacy-protected communication capability is required, so that unauthorized access to the content of data can be prohibited, integrity of data can be guaranteed and privacy-related content of data can be protected during data transmission or transfer in IoT.
- **Data management security**: Secure, trusted, and privacy-protected data management capability is required, so that unauthorized access to the content of data can be prohibited, integrity of data can be guaranteed and privacy-related content of data can be protected when storing or processing data in IoT.
- **Service provision security**: Secure, trusted, and privacy protected service provision capability is required, so that unauthorized access to service and fraudulent service provision can be prohibited and privacy information related to IoT users can be protected.
- **Integration of security policies and techniques**: The ability to integrate different security policies and techniques is required, so as to ensure a consistent security control over the variety of devices and user networks in IoT.
- **Mutual authentication and authorization**: Before a device (or an IoT user) can access the IoT, mutual authentication and authorization between the device (or the IoT user) and IoT is required to be performed according to predefined security policies.
- **Security audit**: Security audit is required to be supported in IoT. Any data access or attempt to access IoT applications are required to be fully transparent, traceable, and reproducible according to appropriate regulation and laws. In particular, IoT is required to support security audit for data transmission, storage, processing, and application access.

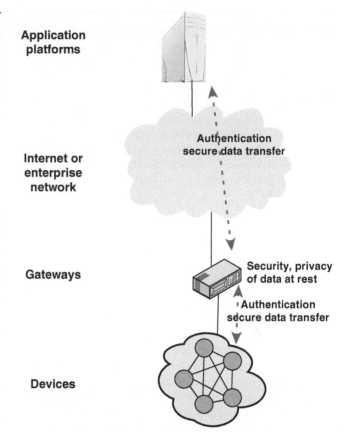

FIGURE 19.6   Internet of Things (IoT) gateway security functions.

A key element in providing security in an IoT deployment is the gateway. Y.2067 details specific security functions that the gateway should implement, some of which are illustrated in Fig. 19.6 (see checklist: "An Agenda for Action for Implementing Specific Security Functions by the Gateway").

Some of these requirements may be difficult to achieve when they involve providing security services for constrained devices. For example, the gateway should support security of data stored in devices. Without encryption capability at the constrained device, this may be impractical to achieve.

Note that the Y.2067 requirements make a number of references to privacy requirements. Privacy is an area of growing concern with the widespread deployment of IoT-enabled things in homes, retail outlets, and vehicles and humans. As more things are interconnected, governments and private enterprises will collect massive amounts of data about individuals, including medical information, location and movement information, and application usage.

An Internet of Things (IoT) Security Framework

Cisco has developed a framework for IoT security [8] that serves as a useful tool for designing and implementing

---

An Agenda for Action for Implementing Specific Security Functions by the Gateway

Implementing specific security functions by the gateway includes the following key activities (check all tasks completed):

____**1.** Support identification of each access to the connected devices.

____**2.** Support authentication with devices. Based on application requirements and device capabilities, it is required to support mutual or one-way authentication with devices. With one-way authentication, either the device authenticates itself to the gateway or the gateway authenticates itself to the device, but not both.

____**3.** Support mutual authentication with applications.

____**4.** Support the security of the data that are stored in devices and the gateway, or transferred between the gateway and devices, or transferred between the gateway and applications; support for the security of these data based on security levels.

____**5.** Support mechanisms to protect privacy for devices and the gateway.

____**6.** Support self-diagnosis and self-repair as well as remote maintenance.

____**7.** Support firmware and software update.

____**8.** Support auto configuration or configuration by applications. The gateway is required to support multiple configuration modes, e.g., remote and local configuration, automatic and manual configuration, and dynamic configuration based on policies.

IoT-related security protocols. Fig. 19.7 illustrates the security environment related to the logical structure of an IoT. The framework consists of the following levels:

- **Smart objects/embedded systems**: Consists of sensors, actuators, and other embedded systems at the edge of the network. This is the most vulnerable part of an IoT. The devices may not be in a physically secure environment and may need to function for years. Availability is certainly an issue. Also network managers need to be concerned about the authenticity and integrity of the data generated by sensors and about protecting actuators and other smart devices from unauthorized use. Privacy and protection from eavesdropping may also be requirements.

- **Fog/edge network**: This level is concerned with the wired and wireless interconnection of IoT devices. In addition, a certain amount of data processing and consolidation may be done at this level. A key issue of concern is the wide variety of network technologies and protocols used by the various IoT devices and the need to develop and enforce a uniform security policy.

- **Core network**: The core network level provides data paths between network center platforms and the IoT devices. The security issues here are those confronted in traditional core networks. However, the vast number of endpoints to interact with and manage creates a substantial security burden.

- **Data center/cloud**: This level contains the application, data storage, and network management platforms. IoT does not introduce any new security issues at this level, other than the necessity of dealing with huge numbers of individual endpoints.

Within this four-level architecture, the Cisco model defines four general security capabilities that span multiple levels:

- **Role-based security**: role-based access control (RBAC) systems assign access rights to roles instead of individual users. In turn, users are assigned to different roles, either statically or dynamically, according to their responsibilities. RBAC enjoys widespread commercial use in cloud and enterprise systems and is a well-understood tool that can be used to manage access to IoT devices and the data they generate.

- **Antitamper and detection**: This function is particularly important at the device and fog network levels but also extends to the core network level. All of these levels may involve components that are physically outside the area of the enterprise that is protected by physical security measures.

- **Data protection and confidentiality**: These functions extend to all level of the architecture.

- **Internet protocol protection**: Protection of data in motion from eavesdropping and snooping is essential between all levels.

Fig. 19.7 maps specific security functional areas across the four layers of the IoT model. The Cisco White Paper also proposes a secure IoT framework that defines the components

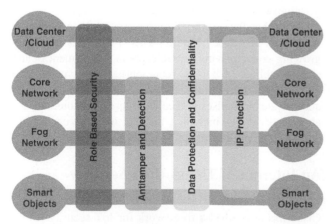

FIGURE 19.7 Internet of Things (IoT) security environment.

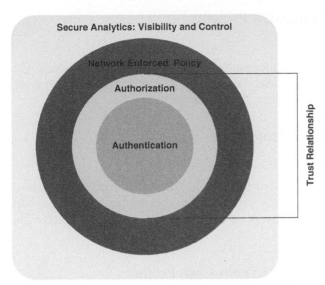

FIGURE 19.8 Secure Internet of Things (IoT) framework.

of a security facility for an IoT that encompasses all the levels, as shown in Fig. 19.8. The four components are:

- **Authentication**: Encompasses the elements that initiate the determination of access by first identifying the IoT devices. In contrast to typical enterprise network devices, which may be identified by a human credential (e.g., username and password or token), the IoT endpoints must be fingerprinted by means that do not require human interaction. Such identifiers include RFID, x.509 certificates, or the MAC address of the endpoint.
- **Authorization**: Controls a device's access throughout the network fabric. This element encompasses access control. Together with the authentication layer, it establishes the necessary parameters to enable the exchange of information between devices and between devices and application platforms and enables IoT-related services to be performed.
- **Network enforced policy**: Encompasses all elements that route and transport endpoint traffic securely over the infrastructure, whether control, management, or actual data traffic.
- **Secure analytics, including visibility and control**: This component includes all the functions required for central management of IoT devices. This involves, firstly, visibility of IoT devices, which simply means that central management services are securely aware of the distributed IoT device collection, including identity and attributes of each device. Building on this visibility is the ability to exert control, including configuration, patch updates, and threat countermeasures.

An important concept related to this framework is that of trust relationship. In this context, trust relationship refers to the ability of the two partners to an exchange to have confidence in the identity and access rights of the other. The authentication component of the trust framework provides a basic level of trust, which is expanded with the authorization component. The Cisco White Paper gives the example that a car may establish a trust relationship with another car from the same vendor. That trust relationship, however, may only allow cars to exchange their safety capabilities. When a trusted relationship is established between the same car and its dealer's network, the car may be allowed to share additional information such as its odometer reading and last maintenance record.

4. SUMMARY

Computer and network security protocols, technologies, and policies have developed and matured over the past decades, tailored to the needs of enterprises, governments, and other users. Although there is an ongoing arms race between attackers and defenders, it is possible to build a powerful network security facility. The sudden explosion of IoT networks with millions to billions of devices poses an unprecedented security challenge. A model and framework such as that of Figs. 19.7 and 19.8 can serve as a foundation for the design and implementation of an IoT security facility.

Finally, let's move on to the real interactive part of this Chapter: review questions/exercises, hands-on projects, case projects, and optional team case project. The answers and/or solutions by chapter can be found in Appendix K.

CHAPTER REVIEW QUESTIONS/ EXERCISES

True/False

1. True or False? The IoT is primarily driven by deeply embedded devices.
2. True or False? It is the fourth generation of the Internet that is usually thought of as the IoT, and which is marked by the use of billions of embedded devices.
3. True or False? Both the business and technical literature often focus on two elements of the Cloud Security Alliance—the things that are connected, and the Internet that interconnects them.
4. True or False? Given the complexity of an IoT, it is not useful to have an architecture that specifies the main elements and their interrelationship.
5. True or False? The unique aspect of an IoT, compared to other network systems, is the presence of a number of physical things and devices other than computing or data processing devices.

Multiple Choice

1. What is an example of a radio frequency?
   A. Infrared
   B. Optical
   C. Galvanic driving
   D. Gateway
   E. RFID tag

2. What supports a variety of device access technologies, enabling devices to communicate with each other and across an Internet or enterprise network with IoT applications?
   A. Ethernet
   B. Wi-Fi
   C. DSL
   D. Gateway
   E. All of the above
3. What performs two basic functions?
   A. Network layer
   B. Service support layer
   C. Application support layer
   D. Application layer
   E. All of the above
4. What is known as device discovery, authentication, remote device activation and deactivation, configuration, diagnostics, firmware and/or software updating, and device working status management?
   A. Local network topology management
   B. Device management
   C. Traffic and congestion management
   D. Framework management
   E. All of the above
5. What includes generic security capabilities that are independent of applications?
   A. Application layer
   B. Network layer
   C. Security capabilities layer
   D. Device layer
   E. All of the above

EXERCISE

Problem

Who is responsible for coordinating the security for the 16 critical infrastructure sectors?

Hands-On Projects

Project

As the number of connected objects in the IoT grows, what will the potential risk of successful intrusions and increases in costs from those incidents be?

Case Projects

Problem

The interconnectivity of IoT devices may also provide entry points through which hackers can access other parts of a network. Please elaborate on how to solve this problem.

Optional Team Case Project

Problem

How can Access be used for destruction of IoT objects?

REFERENCES

[1] W. Stallings, Foundations of Modern Networking: SDN, NFV, QoE, IoT, and Cloud, Pearson, Indianapolis, 2016.
[2] ITU-T, Overview of the Internet of Things. Y.2060, June 2012.
[3] A. McEwen, H. Cassimally, Designing the Internet of Things, Wiley, New York, 2013.
[4] J. Ferguson, A. Redish, Wireless communication with implanted medical devices using the conductive properties of the body, Expert Rev. Med. Devices 6 (4) (2011). www.expert-reviews.com.
[5] ITU-T, Common Requirements and Capabilities of a Gateway for Internet of Things Applications. Y.2067, June 2014.
[6] B. Schneier, The Internet of Things Is Wildly Insecure—And Often Unpatchable, Wired, January 6, 2014.
[7] ITU-T, Common Requirements of the Internet of Things. Y.2066, June 2014.
[8] J. Frahim, et al., Securing the Internet of Things: A Proposed Framework, Cisco White Paper, March 2015.

Chapter 20

Cellular Network Security

Peng Liu, Thomas F. LaPorta and Kameswari Kotapati
Penn State University, State College, PA, United States

1. INTRODUCTION

Cellular networks are high-speed, high-capacity voice and data communication networks with enhanced multimedia and seamless roaming capabilities for supporting cellular devices. With the increase in popularity of cellular devices, these networks are used for more than just entertainment and phone calls. They have become the primary means of communication for finance-sensitive business transactions, lifesaving emergencies, and life-/mission-critical services such as E-911. Today these networks have become the lifeline of communications.

A breakdown in a cellular network has many adverse effects, ranging from huge economic losses due to financial transaction disruptions; loss of life due to loss of phone calls made to emergency workers; and communication outages during emergencies such as the September 11, 2001, attacks. Therefore, it is a high priority for cellular networks to function accurately.

It must be noted that it is not difficult for unscrupulous elements to break into a cellular network and cause outages. The major reason for this is that cellular networks were not designed with security in mind. They evolved from the old-fashioned telephone networks that were built for performance. To this day, cellular networks have numerous well-knownand unsecured vulnerabilities providing access to adversaries. Another feature of cellular networks is network relationships (also called dependencies) that cause certain types of errors to propagate to other network locations as a result of regular network activity. Such propagation can be very disruptive to a network, and in turn it can affect subscribers. Finally, Internet connectivity to cellular networks is another major contributor to cellular networks' vulnerability because it gives Internet users direct access to cellular network vulnerabilities from their homes.

To ensure that adversaries do not access cellular networks and cause breakdowns, a high level of security must be maintained in cellular networks. However, though great efforts have been made to improve cellular networks in terms of support for new and innovative services, greater number of subscribers, higher speed, and larger bandwidth, very little has been done to update the security of cellular networks. Accordingly, these networks have become highly attractive targets to adversaries, not only because of their lack of security but also due to the ease with which these networks can be exploited to affect millions of subscribers.

In this chapter, we analyze the security of cellular networks. Toward understanding the security issues in cellular networks, the rest of the chapter is organized as follows. We present a comprehensive overview of cellular networks with a goal of providing a fundamental understanding of their functioning. Next we present the current state of cellular network security through an in-depth discussion on cellular network vulnerabilities and possible attacks. In addition, we present a cellular network specific attack taxonomy. Finally, we present a review of current cellular network vulnerability assessment techniques and conclude with a discussion.

2. OVERVIEW OF CELLULAR NETWORKS

The current cellular network is an evolution of the early-generation cellular networks that were built for optimal performance. These early-generation cellular networks were proprietary and owned by reputable organizations. They were considered secure due to their proprietary ownership and their closed nature, that is, their control infrastructure was unconnected to any public network (such as the Internet) to which end subscribers had direct access. Security was a nonissue in the design of these networks.

Recently, connecting the Internet to cellular networks has not only imported the Internet vulnerabilities to cellular networks, it has also given end subscribers direct access to the control infrastructure of a cellular network, thereby opening the network. Also, with the increasing demand for these networks, a large number of new network operators

Computer and Information Security Handbook. http://dx.doi.org/10.1016/B978-0-12-803843-7.00020-X

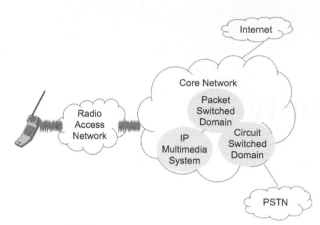

FIGURE 20.1 Cellular network architecture.

have come into the picture. Thus, the current cellular environment is no longer a safe, closed network but rather an insecure, open network with many unknown network operators having nonproprietary access to it. Here we present a brief overview of the cellular network architecture.

Overall Cellular Network Architecture

Subscribers gain access to a cellular network via radio signals enabled by a radio access network, as shown in Fig. 20.1. The radio access network is connected to the wireline portion of the network, also called the core network. Core network functions include servicing subscriber requests and routing traffic. The core network is also connected to the Public Switched Telephone Network (PSTN) and the Internet, as illustrated in Fig. 20.1 [1].

The PSTN is the circuit-switched public voice telephone network that is used to deliver voice telephone calls on the fixed landline telephone network. The PSTN uses Signaling System No. 7 (SS7), a set of telephony signaling protocols defined by the International Telecommunication Union (ITU) for performing telephony functions such as call delivery, call routing, and billing. The SS7 protocols provide a universal structure for telephony network signaling, messaging, interfacing, and network maintenance. PSTN connectivity to the core network enables mobile subscribers to call fixed network subscribers, and vice versa. In the past, PSTN networks were also closed networks because they were unconnected to other public networks.

The core network is also connected to the Internet. Internet connectivity allows the cellular network to provide innovative multimedia services such as weather reports, stock reports, sports information, chat, and electronic mail. Interworking with the Internet is possible using protocol gateways, federated databases, and multiprotocol mobility managers [2]. Interworking with the Internet has created a new generation of services called cross-network services. These are multivendor, multidomain services that use a combination of Internet-based data and data from the cellular

network to provide a variety of services to the cellular subscriber. A sample cross-network service is the Email Based Call Forwarding Service (CFS), which uses Internet-based email data (in a mail server) to decide on the call-forward number (in a call-forward server) and delivers the call via the cellular network.

From a functional viewpoint, the core network may also be further divided into the circuit-switched (CS) domain, the packet-switched (PS) domain, and the IP Multimedia Subsystem (IMS). In the following, we further discuss the core network organization.

Core Network Organization

Cellular networks are organized as collections of interconnected network areas, where each network area covers a fixed geographical region (as shown in Fig. 20.2). At a particular time, every subscriber is affiliated with two networks: the home network and the visiting network.

Every subscriber is permanently assigned to the home network (of his device), from which they can roam onto other visiting networks. The home network maintains the subscriber profile and his current location. The visiting network is the network where the subscriber is currently roaming. It provides radio resources, mobility management, routing, and services for roaming subscribers. The visiting network provides service capabilities to the subscribers on behalf of the home environment [3].

The core network is facilitated by network servers (also called service nodes). Service nodes are composed of (1) a variety of data sources (such as cached read-only, updateable, and shared data sources) to store data such as subscriber profile and (2) service logic to perform functions such as computing data items, retrieving data items from data sources, and so on.

Service nodes can be of different types, with each type assigned specific functions. The major service node types in the circuit-switched domain include the Home Location Register (HLR), the Visitor Location Register (VLR), the Mobile Switching Center (MSC), and the Gateway Mobile Switching Center (GMSC) [4].

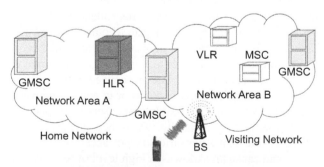

FIGURE 20.2 Core network organization.

All subscribers are permanently assigned to a fixed HLR located in the home network. The HLR stores permanent subscriber profile data and relevant temporary data such as current subscriber location (pointer to VLR) of all subscribers assigned to it. Each network area is assigned a VLR. The VLR stores temporary data of subscribers currently roaming in its assigned area; this subscriber data is received from the HLR of the subscriber. Every VLR is always associated with an MSC. The MSC acts as an interface between the radio access network and the core network. It also handles circuit-switched services for subscribers currently roaming in its area. The GMSC is in charge of routing the call to the actual location of the mobile station. Specifically, the GMSC acts as interface between the fixed PSTN network and the cellular network. The radio access network comprises a transmitter, receiver, and speech transcoder called the base station (BS) [5].

Service nodes are geographically distributed and serve the subscriber through collaborative functioning of various network components. Such collaborative functioning is possible due to the intercomponent network relationships (called dependencies). A dependency means that a network component must rely on other network components to perform a function. For example, there is a dependency between service nodes to service subscribers. Such a dependency is made possible through signaling messages containing data items. Service nodes typically request other service nodes to perform specific operations by sending them signaling messages containing data items with predetermined values. On receiving signaling messages, service nodes realize the operations to perform based on values of data items received in signaling messages. Further, dependencies may exist between data items so that received data items may be used to derive other data items. Several application layer protocols are used for signaling messages.

Examples of signaling message protocols include Mobile Application Part (MAP), ISDN User Part (ISUP), and Transaction Capabilities Application Part (TCAP) protocols.

Typically in a cellular network, to provide a specific service a preset group of signaling messages is exchanged between a preset group of service node types. The preset group of signaling messages indicates the operations to be performed at the various service nodes and is called a signal flow. In the following, we use the call delivery service [6] to illustrate a signal flow and show how the various geographically distributed service nodes function together.

Call Delivery Service

The call delivery service is a basic service in the circuit-switched domain. It is used to deliver incoming calls to any subscriber with a mobile device regardless of their location. The signal flow of the call delivery service is illustrated in Fig. 20.3. The call delivery service signal flow comprises MAP messages SRI, SRI_ACK, PRN, and PRN_ACK; ISUP message IAM; and TCAP messages SIFIC, Page MS, and Page.

Fig. 20.3 illustrates the exchange of signal messages between different network areas. It shows that when a subscriber makes a call using his mobile device, the call is sent in the form of a signaling message IAM to the nearest GMSC, which is in charge of routing calls and passing voice traffic between different networks. This signaling message IAM contains data items such as called number that denotes the mobile phone number of the subscriber receiving this call. The called number is used by the GMSC to locate the address of the HLR (home network) of the called party. The GMSC uses this address to send the signaling message SRI.

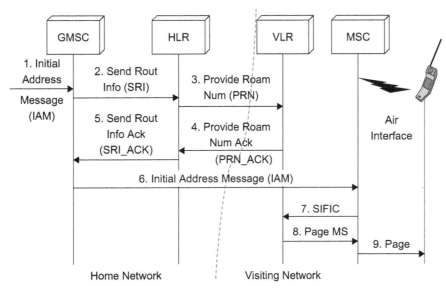

FIGURE 20.3   Signal flow in the call delivery service.

The SRI message is an intimation to the HLR of the arrival of an incoming call to a subscriber with called number as mobile phone number. It contains data items such as the called number and alerting pattern. The alerting pattern denotes the pattern (packet-switched data, short message service, or circuit-switched call) used to alert the subscriber receiving the call. The HLR uses the called number to retrieve from its database the current location (pointer to VLR) of the subscriber receiving the call. The HLR uses this subscriber location to send the VLR the message PRN. The PRN message is a request for call routing information (also called roaming number) from the VLR where the subscriber is currently roaming. The PRN message contains the called number, alerting pattern, and other subscriber call profile data items.

The VLR uses the called number to store the alerting pattern and subscriber call profile data items and assign the roaming number for routing the call. This roaming number data item is passed on to the HLR (in message PRN_ACK), which forwards it to the GMSC (in message SRI_ACK). The GMSC uses this roaming number to route the call (message IAM) to the MSC where the subscriber is currently roaming. On receipt of the message IAM, the MSC assigns the called number resources for the call and also requests the subscriber call profile data items, and alerting pattern for the called number (using message SIFIC) from the VLR, and receives the same in the Page MS message. The MSC uses the alerting pattern in the incoming call profile to derive the page type data item. The page type data item denotes the manner in which to alert the mobile station. It is used to page the mobile subscriber (using message Page). Thus subscribers receive incoming calls irrespective of their locations.

If data item values are inaccurate, a network can misoperate and subscribers will be affected. Hence, accurate functioning of the network is greatly dependent on the integrity of data item values. Thus signal flows allow the various service nodes to function together, ensuring that the network services its subscribers effectively.

3. THE STATE OF THE ART OF CELLULAR NETWORK SECURITY

This part of the chapter presents the current state of the art of cellular network security. Because the security of a cellular network is the security of each aspect of the network, that is, radio access network, core network, Internet connection, and PSTN connection, we detail the security of each in detail.

Security in the Radio Access Network

In a cellular network, the radio access network uses radio signals to connect the subscriber's cellular device with the core network. Hence it would seem that attacks on the radio access network could easily happen because anyone with a transmitter/receiver could capture these signals. This was

very true in the case of early-generation cellular networks (first and second generations), where there were no guards against eavesdropping on conversations between the cellular device and BS; cloning of cellular devices to utilize the network resources without paying; and cloning BSs to entice users to camp at the cloned BS in an attack is called a false base station attack, so that the target user provides secret information to the adversary.

In the current generation (third-generation) of cellular networks, all these attacks can be prevented because the networks provide adequate security measures. Eavesdropping on signals between the cellular device and BS is not possible, because cipher keys are used to encrypt these signals. Likewise, replay attacks on radio signals are voided by the use of nonrepeating random values. Use of integrity keys on radio conversations voids the possibility of deletion and modification of conversations between cellular devices and BSs. By allowing the subscriber to authenticate a network, and vice versa, this generation voids the attacks due to cloned cellular devices and BSs. Finally, as the subscriber's identity is kept confidential by only using a temporary subscriber identifier on the radio network, it is also possible to maintain subscriber location privacy [7].

However, the current generation still cannot prevent a denial-of-service (DoS) attack from occurring if a large number of registration requests are sent via the radio access network (BS) to the visiting network (MSC). Such a DoS attack is possible because the MSC cannot realize that the registration requests are fake until it attempts to authenticate each request and the request fails. To authenticate each registration request, the MSC must fetch the authentication challenge material from the corresponding HLR. Because the MSC is busy fetching the authentication challenge material, it is kept busy and the genuine registration requests are lost [7]. Overall there is a great improvement in the radio network security in the current third-generation cellular network.

Security in Core Network

Though the current generation of a cellular network has seen many security improvements in the radio access network, the security of the core network is not as improved. Core network security is the security at the service nodes and security on links (or wireline signaling message) between service nodes.

With respect to wireline signaling message security, of the many wireline signaling message protocols, protection is only provided for the Mobile Application Part (MAP) protocol. The MAP protocol is the cleartext application layer protocol that typically runs on the security-free SS7 protocol or the IP protocol. MAP is an essential protocol and it is primarily used for message exchange involving subscriber location management, authentication, and call handling. The reason that protection is provided for only the MAP protocol is that it carries authentication material and other subscriber-specific confidential data; therefore, its security was considered top priority and was standardized [8–10]. Though protection for other signaling message protocols was also considered important, it was left as an improvement for the next-generation networks [11].

Security for the MAP protocol is provided in the form of the newly proposed protocol called Mobile Application Part Security (MAPSec), when MAP runs on the SS7 protocol stack, or Internet Protocol Security (IPSec) when MAP runs on the IP protocol. Both MAPSec and IPSec protect MAP messages on the link between service nodes by negotiating security associations. Security associations comprise keys, algorithms, protection profiles, and key lifetimes used to protect the MAP message. Both MAPSec and IPSec protect MAP messages by providing source service node authentication and message encryption to prevent eavesdropping, MAP corruption, and fabrication attacks.

It must be noted that though MAPSec and IPSec are deployed to protect individual MAP messages on the link between service nodes, signaling messages typically occur as a group in a signal flow, and hence signaling messages must be protected not only on the link but also in the intermediate service nodes. Also, the deployment of MAPSec and IPSec is optional; hence if any service provider chooses to omit MAPSec/IPSec's deployment, the efforts of all other providers are wasted. Therefore, to completely protect MAP messages, MAPSec/IPSec must be used by every service provider.

With respect to wireline service nodes, while MAPSec/IPSec protects links between service nodes, there is no standardized method for protecting service nodes [7]. Remote and physical access to service nodes may be subject to operator's security policy and hence could be exploited (insider or outsider) if the network operator is lax with security. Accordingly, the core network suffers from the possibility of node impersonation, corruption of data sources, and service logic attacks. For example, unauthorized access to HLR could deactivate customers or activate customers not seen by the building system. Similarly, unauthorized access to MSC could cause outages for a large number of users in a given network area.

Corrupt data sources or service logic in service nodes have the added disadvantage of propagating this corruption to other service nodes in a cellular network [12–14] via signaling messages. This fact was confirmed by a security evaluation of cellular networks [13] that showed the damage potential of a compromised service node to be much greater than the damage potential of compromised signaling messages. Therefore, it is of utmost importance to standardize a scheme for protecting service nodes in the interest of not only preventing node impersonation attacks but also preventing the corruption from propagating to other service nodes.

In brief, the current generation core networks are lacking in security for all types of signaling messages, security for MAP signaling messages in service nodes, and a standardized method for protecting service nodes. To protect all types of signaling message protocols and ensure that messages are secured not only on the links between service nodes but also on the intermediate service nodes (that is, secured end to end), and prevent service logic corruption from propagating to other service nodes, the End-to-End Security (EndSec) protocol was proposed [13].

Because signaling message security essentially depends on security of data item values contained in these messages, EndSec focuses on securing data items. EndSec requires every data item to be signed by its source service nodes using public key encryption. By requiring signatures, if data items are corrupt by compromised intermediate service nodes en route, the compromised status of the service node is revealed to the service nodes receiving the corrupt data items. Revealing the compromised status of service nodes prevents corruption from propagating to other service nodes, because service nodes are unlikely to accept corrupt data items from compromised service nodes.

EndSec also prevents misrouting and node impersonation attacks by requiring every service node in a signal flow to embed the PATH taken by the signal flow in every EndSec message. Finally, EndSec introduces several control messages to handle and correct the detected corruption. Note that EndSec is not a standardized protocol.

Security Implications of Internet Connectivity

Internet connectivity introduces the biggest threat to the security of cellular networks. This is because cheap PC-based equipment with Internet connectivity can now access gateways connecting to the core network (of a cellular network). Therefore, any attack possible in the Internet can now filter into the core network via these gateways. For example, Internet connectivity was the reason for the slammer worm to filter into the E-911 service in Bellevue, Washington, making it completely unresponsive [15]. Other attacks that can filter into the core network from the Internet include spamming and phishing of short messages [16].

We expect low-bandwidth DoS attacks to be the most damaging attacks brought on by Internet connectivity [16–18]. These attacks demonstrate that by sending just 240 short messages per second, it is possible to saturate a cellular network and cause the MSC in charge of the region to be flooded and lose legitimate short messages per second. Likewise, it shows that it is possible to cause a specific user to lose short messages by flooding that user with a large number of messages, causing a buffer overflow. Such DoS attacks are possible because the short message delivery time in a cellular network is much greater than the short message submission time using Internet sites [17].

Also, short messages and voices services use the same radio channel, so contention for these limited resources may still occur and cause a loss of voice service. To avoid loss of voice services due to contention, separation of voice and data services on the radio network (of a cellular network) has been suggested [14]. However, such separation requires major standardization and overhaul of the cellular network and is therefore unlikely be implemented very soon. Other minor techniques such as queue management and resource provisioning have been suggested [17].

Though such solutions could reduce the impact of short message flooding, they cannot eliminate other types of low-bandwidth, DoS attacks such as attacks on connection setup and teardown of data services. The root cause for such DoS attacks from the Internet to the core network of a cellular network was identified as the difference in the design principles of these networks. Though the Internet makes no assumptions on the content of traffic and simply passes it on to the next node, the cellular network identifies the traffic content and provides a highly tailored service involving multiple service nodes for each type of traffic [18].

Until this gap is bridged, such attacks will continue, but bridging the gap itself is a major process because either the design of a cellular network must be changed to match the Internet design, or vice versa, which is unlikely to happen soon. Hence a temporary fix would be to secure the gateways connecting the Internet and core network. As a last note, Internet connectivity filters attacks not only into the core network, but also into the PSTN network. Hence PSTN gateways must also be guarded.

Security Implications of PSTN Connectivity

PSTN connectivity to cellular networks allows calls between the fixed and cellular networks. Though the PSTN was a closed network, the security-free SS7 protocol stack on which it is based was of no consequence. However, by connecting the PSTN to the core network that is in turn connected to the Internet, the largest open public network, the SS7-based PSTN network has "no security left" [19].

Because SS7 protocols are plaintext and have no authentication features, it is possible to introduce fake messages, eavesdrop, cause DoS by traffic overload, and incorrectly route signaling messages. Such introduction of SS7 messages into the PSTN network is very easily done using cheap PC-based equipment. Attacks in which calls for 800 and 900 numbers were rerouted to 911 servers so that legitimate calls were lost are documented [20]. Such attacks are more so possible due to the IP interface of the PSTN service nodes and web-based control of these networks.

Because PSTN networks are to be outdated soon, there is no interest in updating these networks. So, they will remain "security free" until their usage is stopped [19].

So far, we have addressed the security and attacks on each aspect of a cellular network. But an attack that is common to all the aspects of a cellular network is the cascading attack.

Next we detail the cascading attack and present the corresponding vulnerability assessment techniques.

4. CELLULAR NETWORK ATTACK TAXONOMY

In this part of the chapter, we present a cellular network specific attack taxonomy. This attack taxonomy is called the three-dimensional taxonomy because attacks are classified based on the following three dimensions: (1) adversary's physical access to the network when the attack is launched; (2) type of attack launched; and (3) vulnerability exploited to launch the attack.

The three-dimensional attack taxonomy was motivated by a cellular network specific abstract model, which is an atomic model of cellular network service nodes. It enables better study of interactions within a cellular network and aids in derivation of several insightful characteristics of attacks on the cellular network.

The abstract model not only led to the development of the three-dimensional attack taxonomy that has been instrumental in uncovering (1) cascading attacks, a type of attack in which the adversary targets a specific network location but attacks another location, which in turn propagates the attack to the target location, and (2) cross-infrastructure cyber-attack, a new breed of attack in which a cellular network may be attacked from the Internet [21]. In this part of the chapter we further detail the three-dimensional attack taxonomy and cellular network abstract model.

Abstract Model

The abstract model dissects functionality of a cellular network to the basic atomic level, allowing it to systematically isolate and identify vulnerabilities. Such identification of vulnerabilities allows attack classification based on vulnerabilities, and isolation of network functionality aids in extraction of interactions between network components, thereby revealing new vulnerabilities and attack characteristics.

Because service nodes in a cellular network comprise sophisticated service logic that performs numerous network functions, the abstract model logically divides the service logic into basic atomic units, called agents (represented by the elliptical shape in Fig. 20.4). Each agent performs a single function. Service nodes also manage data, so the abstract model also logically divides data sources into data units specific to the agents they support. The abstract model also divides the data sources into permanent (represented by the rectangular shape in Fig. 20.4) or cached (represented by the triangular shape in Fig. 20.4) from other service nodes.

The abstract model eveloped for the CS domain is illustrated in Fig. 20.4. It shows agents, permanent, and cached data sources for the CS service nodes. For example, the subscriber locator agent in the HLR is the agent that tracks

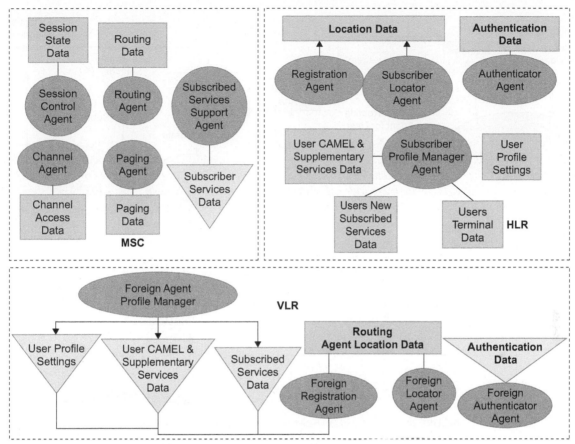

FIGURE 20.4 Abstract model of circuit-switched service nodes.

the subscriber location information. It receives and responds to location requests during an incoming call and stores a subscriber's location every time they move. This location information is stored in the location data source. Readers interested in further details may refer to Refs. [21,22].

Abstract Model Findings

The abstract model led to many interesting findings. We outline them as follows:

Interactions

To study the network interactions, service nodes in signal flows (call delivery service) were replaced by their corresponding abstract model agents and data sources. Such an abstract-model signal flow based on the call delivery service is shown in Fig. 20.5.

In studying the abstract model signal flow, it was observed that interactions happen (1) between agents typically using procedure calls containing data items; (2) between agents and data sources using queries containing data items; and (3) between agents belonging to different service nodes using signaling messages containing data items.

The common behavior in all these interactions is that they typically involve data items whose values are set or modified in agents or data source, or it involves data items passed between agents, data sources, or agents and data sources. Hence, the value of a data item not only can be corrupt in an agent or data source, it can also be easily passed on to other agents, resulting in propagation of corruption. This propagation of corruption is called the cascading effect, and attacks that exhibit this effect are called cascading attacks. In the following, we present a sample of the cascading attack.

Sample Cascading Attack

In this sample cascading attack, cascading due to corrupt data items and ultimately their service disruption are illustrated in Fig. 20.6. Consider the call delivery service explained previously. Here the adversary may corrupt the roaming number data item (used to route the call) in the VLR. This corrupt roaming number is passed on in message PRN_ACK to the HLR, which in turn passes this information to the GMSC. The GMSC uses the incorrect roaming number to route the call to the incorrect MSC_B, instead of the correct MSC_A. This results in the caller losing the call or receiving a wrong-number call. Thus corruption cascades and results in service disruption.

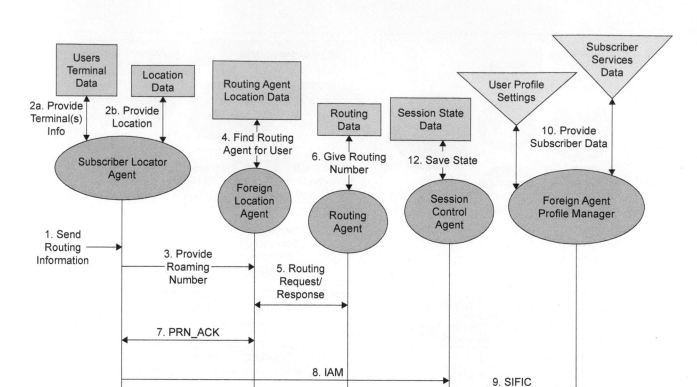

FIGURE 20.5 Abstract model-based signal flow for the call delivery service.

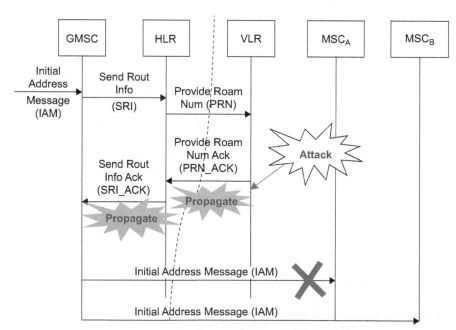

FIGURE 20.6 Sample cascading attacks in the call delivery service.

The type of corruption that can cascade is system-acceptable incorrect value corruption, a type of corruption in which corrupt values taken on system-acceptable values, albeit incorrect values. Such a corruption can cause the roaming number to be incorrect but a system-acceptable value.

Note that it is easy to cause such system-acceptable incorrect value corruption due to the availability of web-sites that refer to proprietary working manuals of service nodes such as the VLR [23,24]. Such command insertion attacks have become highly commonplace, the most infamous being the telephone tapping of the Greek government and top-ranking civil servants [25].

Cross-Infrastructure Cyber Cascading Attacks

When cascading attacks cross into cellular networks from the Internet through cross-network services, they're called cross-infrastructure cyber cascading attacks. This attack is illustrated on the CFS in Fig. 20.7.

As the CFS forwards calls based on the emails received, corruption is shown to propagate from the mail server to a call-forward (CF) server and finally to the MSC. In the attack, using any standard mail server vulnerabilities, the adversary may compromise the mail server and corrupt the email data source by deleting emails from people the victim is expecting to call. The CF server receives and caches incorrect email from the mail server.

When calls arrive for the subscriber, the call-forwarding service is triggered, and the MSC queries the CF server on how to forward the call. The CF server checks its incorrect email cache, and because there are no emails from the caller, it responds to the MSC to forward the call to the victim's voicemail when in reality the call should have been forwarded to the cellular device. Thus the effect of the attack on the mail server propagates to the CF service nodes. This is a classic example of a cross-infrastructure cyber cascading attack, whereby the adversary gains access to the cross-network server, and attacks by modifying data in the data source of the cross-network server. Note that it has become highly simplified to launch such attacks due to easy accessibility to the Internet and subscriber preference for Internet-based cross-network services.

Isolating Vulnerabilities

From the abstract model, the major vulnerable-to-attacks network components are: (1) data sources; (2) agents (more generally called service logic); and (3) signaling messages. By exploiting each of these vulnerabilities, data items that

are crucial to the correct working of a cellular network can be corrupted, leading to ultimate service disruption through cascading effects.

In addition, the effect of corrupt signaling messages is different from the effect of corrupt data sources. By corrupting data items in a data source of a service node, all the subscribers attached to this service node may be affected. However, by corrupting a signaling message, only the subscribers (such as the caller and called party in case of call delivery service) associated with the message are affected. Likewise, corrupting the agent in the service node can affect all subscribers using the agent in the service node. Hence, in the three-dimensional taxonomy, a vulnerability exploited is considered as an attack dimension, since the effect on each vulnerability is different.

Likewise, the adversary's physical access to a cellular network also affects how the vulnerability is exploited and how the attack cascades. For example, consider the case when a subscriber has access to the air interface. The adversary can only affect messages on the air interface. Similarly, if the adversary has access to a service node, the data sources and service logic may be corrupted. Hence, in the three-dimensional taxonomy, the physical access is considered a category as it affects how the vulnerability is exploited and its ultimate effect on the subscriber.

Finally, the way the adversary chooses to launch an attack ultimately affects the service in a different way. Consider a passive attack such as interception. Here the service is not affected, but it can have a later effect on the subscriber, such as identity theft or loss of privacy. An active attack such as interruption can cause complete service disruption. Hence, in the three-dimensional taxonomy, the attack means are considered a category due the ultimate effect on service. In the next part of the chapter, we detail the cellular network specific three-dimensional taxonomy and the way the previously mentioned dimensions are incorporated (see checklist: "An Agenda for Action when Incorporating The Cellular Network Specific Three-Dimensional Attack Taxonomy").

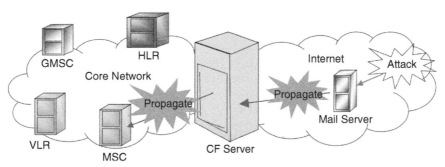

FIGURE 20.7 Cross-infrastructure cyber cascading attacks on call-forward service.

An Agenda for Action when Incorporating the Cellular Network Specific Three-Dimensional Attack Taxonomy

The three dimensions in the taxonomy include Dimension I: Physical Access to the Network, Dimension II: Attack Categories, and Dimension III: Vulnerability Exploited. In the following, we outline each dimension (check all tasks completed):

_____**1.** Dimension I—Physical Access to the Network: In this dimension, attacks are classified based on the adversary's level of physical access to a cellular network. Dimension I may be further classified into single infrastructure attacks (Level I–III) and cross-infrastructure cyber-attacks (Level IV–V):

_____**a.** Level I: Access to air interface with physical device. Here the adversary launches attacks via access to the radio access network using standard inexpensive "off-the-shelf" equipment [26]. Attacks include false base station attacks, eavesdropping, and man-in-the-middle attacks and correspond to attacks previously mentioned.

_____**b.** Level II: Access to links connecting core service nodes. Here the adversary has access to links connecting to core service nodes. Attacks include disrupting normal transmission of signaling messages and correspond to message corruption attacks previously mentioned.

_____**c.** Level III: Access core service nodes. In this case, the adversary could be an insider who managed to gain physical access to core service nodes. Attacks include editing the service logic or modifying data sources, such as subscriber data (profile, security and services) stored in the service node and corresponding to corrupt service logic, data source, and node impersonation attacks previously mentioned.

_____**d.** Level IV: Access to links connecting the Internet and the core network service nodes. This is a cross-infrastructure cyber-attack. Here the adversary has access to links connecting the core network and Internet service nodes. Attacks include editing and deleting signaling messages between the two networks. This level of attack is easier to achieve than Level II.

_____**e.** Level V: Access to Internet servers or cross-network servers. This is a cross-infrastructure cyber-attack. Here the adversary can cause damage by editing the service logic or modifying subscriber data (profile, security, and services) stored in the cross-network servers. Such an attack was previously outlined earlier in the chapter. This level of attack is easier to achieve than Level III.

_____**2.** Dimension II—Attack Type: In this dimension, attacks are classified based on the type of attack. The attack categories are based on Stallings's [27] work in this area:

_____**a.** Interception. The adversary intercepts signaling messages on a cable (Level II access) but does not modify or delete them. This is a passive attack. This affects the privacy of the subscriber and the network operator. The adversary may use the data obtained from interception to analyze traffic and eliminate the competition provided by the network operator.

_____**b.** Fabrication or replay. In this case, the adversary inserts spurious messages, data, or service logic into the system, depending on the level of physical access. For example, via a Level II access, the adversary inserts fake signaling messages; and via a Level III access, the adversary inserts fake service logic or fake subscriber data into this system.

_____**c.** Modification of resources. Here the adversary modifies data, messages, or service logic. For example, via a Level II access, the adversary modifies signaling messages on the link; and via a Level III access, the adversary modifies service logic or data.

_____**d.** Modification of resources. Here the adversary modifies data, messages, or service logic. For example, via a Level II access, the adversary modifies signaling messages on the link; and via a Level III access, the adversary modifies service logic or data.

_____**e.** Denial of service. In this case, the adversary takes actions to overload a network results in legitimate subscribers not receiving service.

_____**f.** Interruption. Here the adversary causes an interruption by destroying data, messages, or service logic.

_____**3.** Dimension III—Vulnerability Exploited: In this dimension, attacks are classified based on the vulnerability exploited to cause the attack. Vulnerabilities exploited are explained as follows:

_____**a.** Data. The adversary attacks the data stored in the system. Damage is inflicted by modifying, inserting, and deleting the data stored in the system.

_____**b.** Messages. The adversary adds, modifies, deletes, or replays signaling messages.

_____**c.** Service logic. Here the adversary inflicts damage by attacking the service logic running in the various cellular core network service nodes.

_____**d.** Attack classification. In classifying attacks, we can group them according to Case 1: Dimension I versus Dimension II, and Case 2: Dimension II versus Dimension III. Note that the Dimension I versus Dimension III case can be transitively inferred from Case 1 and Case 2.

TABLE 20.1 Sample Case 1 Classification

	Interception	Fabrication/ Insertion	Modification of Resources	Denial-of-Service	Interruption
Level I	• Observe time, rate, length, source, and destination of victim's locations.	• Using modified cellular devices, the adversary can send spurious registration messages to the target network.	• With a modified base station and cellular devices, the adversary modifies conversations between subscribers and their base stations.	• The adversary can cause denial-of-service (DoS) by sending a large number of fake registration messages.	• Jam victims' traffic channels so that victims cannot access the channels.
	• With modified cellular devices, eavesdrop on victim.	• Likewise, using modified base stations, the adversary can signal victims to camp at their locations.			• Broadcast at a higher intensity than allowed, thereby hogging the bandwidth.

Table 20.1 shows a sample tabulation of Level I attacks grouped in Case 1. For example, with Level I access an adversary causes interception attacks by observing traffic and eavesdropping. Likewise, fabrication attacks due to Level I access include sending spurious registration messages. Modification of resources due to Level I access includes modifying conversations in the radio access network. DoS due to Level I access occurs when a large number of fake registration messages are sent to keep the network busy so as to not provide service to legitimate subscribers. Finally, interruption attacks due to Level I access occur when adversaries jam the radio access channel so that legitimate subscribers cannot access the network. For further details on attack categories, refer to Ref. [22].

5. CELLULAR NETWORK VULNERABILITY ANALYSIS

Regardless of how attacks are launched, if attack actions cause a system-acceptable incorrect value corruption, the corruption propagates, leading to many unexpected cascading effects. To detect remote cascading effects and identify the origin of cascading attacks, cellular network vulnerability assessment tools were developed.

These tools, including the Cellular Network Vulnerability Assessment Toolkit (CAT) and the advanced Cellular Network Vulnerability Assessment Toolkit (aCAT) [12,28], receive the input from users regarding which data item(s) might be corrupted and output an attack graph. The CAT attack graph not only shows the network location and service where the corruption might originate, it also shows the various messages and service nodes through which the corruption propagates.

An attack graph is a diagrammatic representation of an attack on a real system. It shows various ways an adversary can break into a system or cause corruption and the various ways in which the corruption may propagate within the system. Attack graphs are typically produced manually by red teams and used by systems administrators for protection. CAT and aCAT attack graphs allow users to trace the effect of an attack through a network and determine its side effects, thereby making them the ultimate service disruption.

Cellular networks are at the nascent stage of development with respect to security, so it is necessary to evaluate security protocols before deploying them. Hence, aCAT can be extended with security protocol evaluation capabilities into a tool [13] called Cellular Network Vulnerability Assessment Toolkit for evaluation (eCAT). eCAT allows users to quantify the benefits of security solutions by removing attack effects from attack graphs based on the defenses provided. One major advantage of this approach is that solutions may be evaluated before expensive development and deployment.

It must be noted that developing such tools—CAT, aCAT, and eCAT—presented many challenges: (1) cellular networks are extremely complex systems; they comprise several types of service nodes and control protocols, contain hundreds of data elements, and support hundreds of services; hence developing such toolkits requires in-depth working knowledge of these systems; and (2) every cellular network deployment comprises a different physical configuration; toolkits must be immune to the diversity in physical configuration; and finally (3) attacks cascade in a network due to regular network activity as a result of dependencies; toolkits must be able to track the way that corruption cascades due to network dependencies.

The challenge of in-depth cellular network knowledge was overcome by incorporating the toolkits with cellular network specifications defined by the Third Generation Partnership Project (3GPP) and is available at no charge [29]. The 3GPP is a telecommunications standards body formed to produce, maintain, and develop globally applicable "technical specifications and technical reports" for a third-generation mobile system based on evolved GSM core networks and the radio access technologies that they support [24].

Usage of specifications allows handling of the diversity of physical configuration, as specifications detail the functional behavior and not the implementation structure of a cellular network. Specifications are written using simple flow-like diagrams called the Specification and Description Language (SDL) [30], and are referred to as *SDL specifications*. Equipment and service providers use these SDL specifications as the basis for their service implementations.

Corruption propagation is tracked by incorporating the toolkits with novel dependency and propagation models to trace the propagation of corruption. Finally, Boolean properties are superimposed on the propagation model to capture the impact of security solutions.

CAT is the first version of the toolkit developed for cellular network vulnerability assessment. CAT works by taking user input of seeds (data items directly corrupted by the adversary and the cascading effect of which leads to a goal) and goals (data parameters that are derived incorrectly due to the direct corruption of seeds by the adversary) and uses SDL specification to identify cascading attacks. However, SDL is limited in its expression of relationships and inexplicit in its assumptions and hence cannot capture all the dependencies; therefore CAT misses several cascading attacks.

To detect a complete set of cascading effects, CAT was enhanced with new features, to aCAT. The new features added to aCAT include (1) a network dependency model that explicitly specifies the exact dependencies in a cellular network; (2) infection propagation rules that identify the reasons that cause corruption to cascade; and (3) a small amount of expert knowledge. The network dependency model and infection propagation rules may be applied to SDL specifications and help alleviate their limited expression capability. The expert knowledge helps capture the inexplicit assumptions made by SDL.

In applying these features, aCAT captures all those dependencies that were previously unknown to CAT, and thereby aCAT was able to detect a complete set of cascading effects. Through extensive testing of aCAT, several interesting attacks were found and the areas where SDL is lacking was identified.

To enable evaluation of new security protocols, aCAT was extended to eCAT. eCAT uses Boolean probabilities in attack graphs to detect whether a given security protocol can eliminate a certain cascading effect. Given a security protocol, eCAT can measure effective coverage, identify the types of required security mechanisms to protect the network, and identify the most vulnerable network areas. eCAT was also used to evaluate MAPSec, the new standardized cellular network security protocol. Results from MAPSec's evaluation gave insights into MAPSec's performance and the network's vulnerabilities. In the following, we detail each toolkit.

Cellular Network Vulnerability Assessment Toolkit (CAT)

In this part of the chapter, we present an overview of CAT and its many features. CAT is implemented using the Java programming language. It is made up of a number of subsystems (as shown in Fig. 20.8). The knowledge base contains the cellular network knowledge obtained from SDL specifications. SDL specifications contain simple flowchart-like diagrams. The flowcharts are converted into data in the knowledge base. The integrated data structure is similar to that of the knowledge base; it holds intermediate attack graph results.

The graphical user interface subsystem takes user input in the form of seeds and goals. The analysis engine contains algorithms (forward and midpoint) incorporated with cascading effect detection rules. It explores the possibility of the user input seed leading to the cascading effect of the user input goal, using the knowledge base, and outputs the cascading attack in the form of attack graphs.

Using these attack graphs, realistic attack scenarios may be derived. Attack scenarios explain the effect of the attack on the subscriber in a realistic setting. Each attack graph may have multiple interpretations and give rise to multiple scenarios. Each scenario gives a different perspective on how the attack may affect the subscriber.

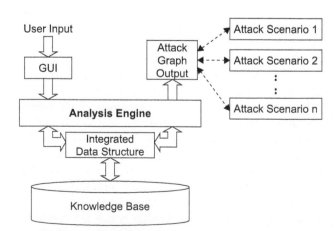

FIGURE 20.8 Architecture of Cellular Network Vulnerability Assessment Toolkit (CAT). *GUI*, graphical user interface.

Cascading Effect Detection Rules

The Cascading Effect Detection Rules were defined to extract cascading effects from the SDL specifications contained in the knowledge base. They are incorporated into the algorithms in the analysis engine. These rules define what constitutes propagation of corruption from a signaling message to a block, and vice versa, and propagation of corruption within a service node. For example, when a service node receives a signaling message with a corrupt data item and stores the data item, it constitutes propagation of corruption from a signaling message to a block. Note that these rules are high level.

Attack Graph

The CAT attack graph may be defined as a state transition showing the paths through a system, starting with the conditions of the attack, followed by attack action, and ending with its cascading effects. In Fig. 20.9, we present the CAT attack graph output, which was built using user input of ISDN Bearer Capability as a seed and Bearer Service as goal. The attack graph constitutes nodes and edges. Nodes represent states in the network with respect to the attack, and edges represent network state transitions. For description purposes, each node has been given a node label followed by an alphabet, and the attack graph has been divided into layers.

Nodes may be broadly classified as conditions, actions, and goals, with the conditions of the attack occurring at the lowest layer and the final cascading effect at the highest layer. In the following, we detail each node type.

Condition Nodes

Nodes at the lowest layer typically correspond to the conditions that must exist for the attack to occur. These condition nodes directly follow from the taxonomy. They are an adversary's physical access, target service node, and vulnerability exploited. For example, the adversary has access to links connecting to the GMSC service node, that is, Level II physical access; this is represented as Node A in the attack graph. Likewise, the adversary corrupts data item ISDN Bearer Capability in the IAM message arriving at the GMSC. Hence the target of the attack is the GMSC and is represented by Node B. Similarly, the adversary exploits vulnerabilities in a message (IAM); and, this is represented by Node D in the attack graph.

The CAT attack graphs show all the possible conditions for an attack to happen. In other words, we see not only the corruption due to the seed ISDN Bearer Capability in the signaling message, but also IAM arriving at the GMSC. But, there are also other possibilities, such as the corruption of the goal Bearer Service in the signaling message SIFIC, represented by Node M.

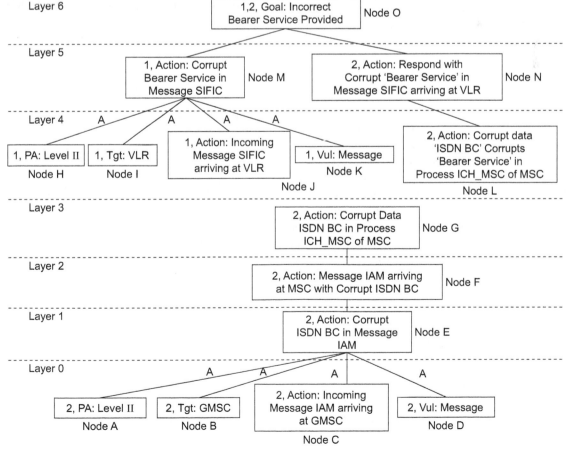

FIGURE 20.9 Cellular Network Vulnerability Assessment Toolkit (CAT) attack graph output.

Action Nodes

Nodes at higher layers are actions that typically correspond to effects of the attack propagating through the network. Effects typically include propagation of corruption between service nodes, such as from MSC to VLR (Node N), propagation of corruption within service nodes such as ISDN Bearer Capability corrupting Bearer Service (Node L), and so on. Actions may further be classified as adversary actions, normal network operations, or normal subscriber activities. Adversary actions include insertion, corruption, or deletion of data, signaling messages, or service logic represented by Node E. Normal network operations include sending (Node N) and receiving signaling messages (Node E). Subscriber activity may include updating personal data or initiating service.

Goal Nodes

Goal nodes typically occur at the highest layer of the attack graph. They indicate corruption of the goal items due to the direct corruption of seeds by the adversary (Node A).

Edges

In our graph, edges represent network transitions due to both normal network actions and adversary actions. Edges help show the global network view of adversary action. This is the uniqueness of our attack graph. Transitions due to adversary action are indicated by an edge marked by the letter A (edges connecting Layer 0 and Layer 1). By inclusion of normal network transitions in addition to the transitions caused by the adversary, our attack graph shows not only the adversary's activity but also the global network view of the adversary's action. This is a unique feature of the attack graph.

Trees

In the graph, trees are distinguished by the tree numbers assigned to its nodes. For example, all the nodes marked with number 2 belong to Tree 2 of the graph. Some nodes in the graph belong to multiple trees. Tree numbers are used to distinguish between AND and OR nodes in the graph. Nodes at a particular layer with the same tree number(s) are AND nodes. For example, at Layer 4, Nodes H, I, J, and K are AND nodes; they all must occur for Node M at Layer 5 to occur. Multiple tree numbers on a node are called OR nodes. The OR node may be arrived at using alternate ways. For example, Node O at Layer 6 is an OR node, the network state indicated by Node O may be arrived at from Node M or Node N.

Each attack tree shows the attack effects due to corruption of a seed at a specific network location (such as signaling message or process in a block). For example, Tree 1 shows the attack due to the corruption of the seed Bearer Service at the VLR. Tree 2 shows the propagation of the seed ISDN Bearer Capability in the signaling message IAM. These trees show

that the vulnerability of a cellular network is not limited to one place but can be realized due to the corruption of data in many network locations.

In constructing the attack graph, CAT assumes that an adversary has all the necessary conditions for launching the attack. The CAT attack graph format is well suited to cellular networks because data propagates through the network in various forms during the normal operation of a network; thus an attack that corrupts a data item manifests itself as the corruption of a different data item in a different part of the network after some network operations take place.

Attack Scenario Derivation

The CAT attack graph is in cellular network semantics, and realistic attack scenarios may be derived to understand the implications of the attack graph. Here we detail the principles involved in the derivation of realistic attack scenarios:

End-User Effect

Goal node(s) are used to infer the end effect of the attack on the subscriber. According to the goal node in Fig. 20.9, the SIFIC message to the VLR has incorrect goal item Bearer Service. The SIFIC message is used to inform the VLR the calling party's preferences such as voice channel requirements and request the VLR to set up the call based on the calling party and receiving party preferences.

If the calling party's preferences (such as Bearer Service) are incorrect, the call setup by the VLR is incompatible with the calling party, and the communication is ineffective (garbled speech). From the goal node, it can be inferred that Alice, the receiver of the call, is unable to communicate effectively with Bob, the caller, because Alice can only hear garbled speech from Bob's side.

Origin of Attack

Nodes at Layer 0 indicate the origin of the attack, and hence the location of the attack may be inferred. The speech attack may originate at the signaling messages IAM, or the VLR service node.

Attack Propagation and Side Effects

Nodes at all other layers show the propagation of corruption across the various service nodes in the network. From other layers in Fig. 20.9, it can be inferred that the seed is the ISDN bearer capability and the attack spreads from the MSC to the VLR.

Example Attack Scenario

Using these guidelines, an attack scenario may be derived as follows. Trudy, the adversary, corrupts the ISDN Bearer Capability of Bob, the victim, at the IAM message arriving at the GMSC. The GMSC propagates this corruption to the MSC, which computes, and hence corrupts, the Bearer

Service. The corrupt Bearer Service is passed on to the VLR, which sets up the call between Bob, the caller, and Alice, the receiver. Bob and Alice cannot communicate effectively because Alice is unable to understand Bob.

Though CAT has detected several cascading attacks, its output to a great extent depends on SDL's ability to capture data dependencies. SDL is limited in its expression capability in the sense that it does not always accurately capture the relationship between data items, and in many cases, SDL does even specify the relationship. Without these details CAT may miss some cascading effects due to loss of data relationships. CAT's output to a minor extent also depends on user input in the sense that to accurately capture all the cascading effect of a seed, the user's input must comprise all the seeds that can occur in the cascading effect; otherwise the exact cascading effect is not captured. To alleviate CAT's inadequacies, aCAT was developed.

Advanced Cellular Network Vulnerability Assessment Toolkit (aCAT)

In this section, we present aCAT, an extension of CAT with enhanced features. These enhanced features include (1) incorporating expert knowledge to compensate for the lacking caused by SDL's inexplicit assumptions; expert knowledge added to the knowledge base with the SDL specifications; (2) defining a network dependency model that accurately captures the dependencies in a cellular network; the network dependency model is used to format the data in knowledge base, thereby clarifying the nature of the network dependency; and (3) defining infection propagation rules that define fine-grained rules to detect cascading attacks; these infection propagation rules are incorporated into the analysis engine, which comprises the forward, reverse, and combinatory algorithms. aCAT is also improved in terms of its user input requirements. It requires as input either seeds or goals, whereas CAT required both seeds and goals.

In principle, cascading attacks are the result of propagation of corruption between network components (such as signaling messages, caches, local variables, and service logic) due to dependencies that exist between these network components. Hence, to uncover these attacks, the network dependency model and infection propagation (IP) rules were defined. In the following, we detail the network dependency model and infection propagation model using Fig. 20.10.

Network Dependency Model

The network dependency model accurately defines fine-grained dependencies between the various network components. Given that service nodes comprise agents and data sources (from the abstract model), the dependencies are defined as follows. In interagent dependency, agents communicate with each other using agent invocations (as shown by 6 in Fig. 20.10) containing data items. Thus, agents are related to each other through data items. Likewise, in agent to data source dependency, agents communicate with data sources using Read and Write operations containing data items. Therefore, agents and data items are related to each other through data items. Within agents, derivative dependencies define relationships between data items. Here data items are used as input to derive data items using derivation operations such as AND, OR operations. Therefore, data items are related to each other through derivation operation. For further detail on the network dependency model, refer to Ref. [12].

Infection Propagation (IP) Rules

These are fine-grained rules to detect cascading effects. They are incorporated into the algorithms in the analysis engine. An example of the IP rule is that an output data item in the AND dependency is corrupt only if both the input data items are corrupt (as shown by 9 in Fig. 20.10). Likewise, an output data item in the OR dependency is corrupt if a single input data item is corrupt (as shown by 8 in Fig. 20.10). Similarly, corruption propagates between agents when the data item used to invoke the agent is corrupt, and the same data item is used as an input in the derivative dependency whose output may be corrupt (as shown by 6, 8 in Fig. 20.10). Accordingly, corruption propagates from an agent to a data source if the data item written to the data source is corrupt (as shown by 4 in Fig. 20.10). Finally, corruption propagates between service nodes if a data item used in the signaling message between the service nodes is corrupt, and the corrupt data item is used to derive corrupt output items or the corrupt data item is stored in the data source (as shown by 1, 3 or 1, 4 in Fig. 20.10) [12].

With such a fine-grained dependency model and infection propagation rules, aCAT was very successful in identifying cascading attacks in several key services offered by a cellular network, and it was found that aCAT can indeed identify a better set of cascading effects in comparison to CAT. aCAT has also detected several interesting and unforeseen cascading attacks that are subtle and difficult to identify by other means. These newly identified cascading attacks include the alerting attack, power-off/power-on attack, mixed identity attack, call redirection attack, and missed calls attack.

Alerting Attack

In the following we detail aCAT's output, a cascading attack called the alerting attack, shown in Fig. 20.11. From goal nodes (Node A at Level 5, and Node C at Level 4) in the alerting attack, it can be inferred that the Page message has incorrect data item page type. The Page message is

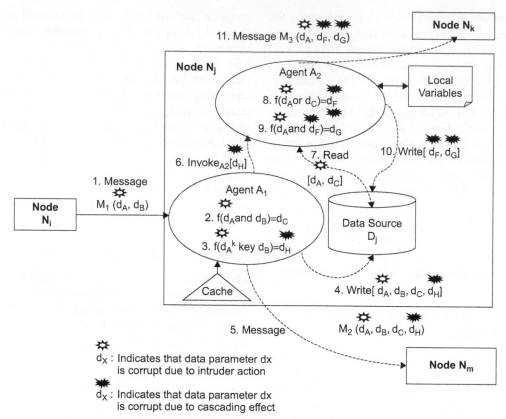

FIGURE 20.10 Network dependency model.

used to inform subscribers of the arrival of incoming calls, and "page type" indicates the type of call. "Page type" must be compatible with the subscriber's mobile station or else the subscriber is not alerted. From the goal node it may be inferred that Alice, a subscriber of the system, is not alerted on the arrival of an incoming call and hence does not receive incoming calls. This attack is subtle to detect because network administrators find that the network processes the incoming call correctly and that the subscriber is alerted correctly. They might not find that this alerting pattern is incompatible with the mobile station itself.

Also, nodes at Level 0 indicate the origin of the attack as signaling messages SRI, PRN, the service nodes VLR, or the HLR. From the other levels it may be inferred that the seed is the alerting pattern that the adversary corrupts in the SRI message and the attack spreads from the HLR to the VLR and from the VLR to the MSC. For more details on these attacks, refer to Ref. [12].

Cellular Network Vulnerability Assessment Toolkit for Evaluation (eCAT)

In this part of the chapter, we present eCAT an extension to aCAT. eCAT was developed to evaluate new security

protocols before their deployment. Though the design goals and threat model of these security protocols are common knowledge, eCAT was designed to find (1) the effective protection coverage of these security protocols in terms of percentage of attacks prevented; (2) the other kinds of security schemes required to tackle the attacks that can evade the security protocol under observation; and (3) the most vulnerable network areas (also called hotspots) [13].

eCAT computes security protocol coverage using attack graphs generated by aCAT and Boolean probabilities in a process called attack graph marking and quantifies the coverage using coverage measurement formulas (CMF). Attack graph marking also identifies network hotspots and exposes if the security protocol being evaluated protects these hotspots. eCAT was also used to evaluate MAPSec, as it is a relatively new protocol, and evaluation results would aid network operators.

Boolean Probabilities

Boolean probabilities are used in attack graphs to distinguish between nodes eliminated (denoted by 0, or shaded node in attack graph) and nodes existing (denoted by 1, or unshaded node in attack graph) due to the security protocol under

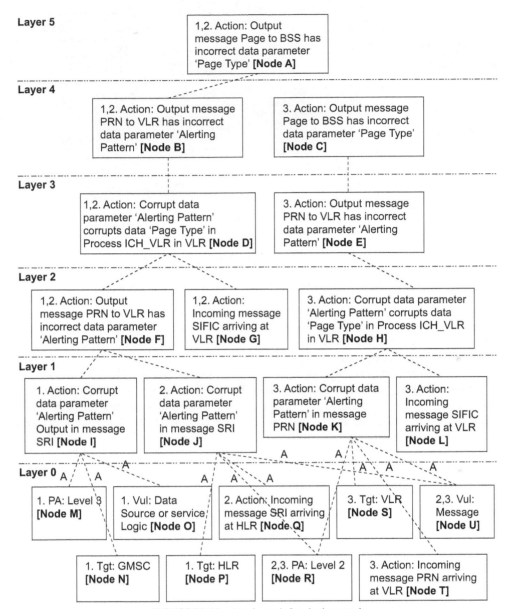

FIGURE 20.11 Attack graph for alerting attack.

evaluation. By computing Boolean probabilities for each node in the attack graph, eCAT can extract the attack effects that may be eliminated by the security protocol under evaluation.

Attack Graph Marking

To mark attack graphs, user input of Boolean probabilities must be provided for Layer 0 nodes. For example, if the security protocol under evaluation is MAPSec, then because MAPSec provides security on links between nodes, it eliminates Level 2 physical access. For example, consider the attack graph generated by eCAT shown in Fig. 20.12. Here, Node 5 is set to 0, while all other nodes are set to 1.

eCAT uses the input from Layer 0 nodes to compute the Boolean probabilities for the rest of the nodes starting from

Layer 1 and moving upward. For example, the Boolean probability of the AND node (Node 18) is the product of all the nodes in the previous layer with the same tree number. Because Node 5 has the same tree number as Node 18, and Node 5's Boolean probability is 0, Node 18's Boolean probability is also 0. This process of marking attack graphs is continued until Boolean probability of all the nodes is computed till the topmost layer.

Hotspots

Graph marking also marks the network hotspots in the attack graph. With respect to the attack graph, hotspots are the Layer 0 nodes with the highest tree number count. For example in Fig. 20.12, Node 3 and Node 4

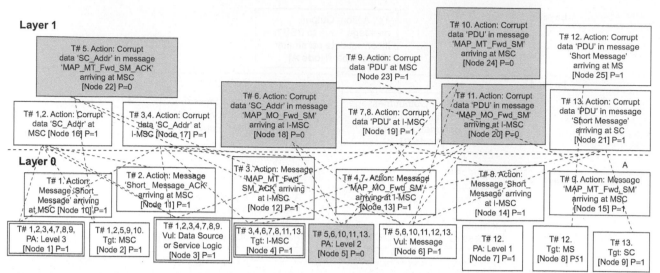

FIGURE 20.12   Fragment of a marked attack graph generated by Cellular Network Vulnerability Assessment Toolkit for evaluations (eCAT).

are the hotspots. A high tree number count indicates an increased attractiveness of the network location to adversaries. This is because by breaking into the network location indicated by the hotspot node, the adversary has a higher likelihood of success and can cause the greatest amount of damage.

Extensive testing of eCAT on several of the network services using MAPSec has revealed hotspots to be "Data Sources and Service Logic." This is because a corrupt data source or service logic may be used by many different services and hence cause many varied cascading effects, spawning a large number of attacks (indicated by multiple trees in attack graphs). Thus attacks that occur due to exploiting service logic and data source vulnerabilities constitute a major portion of the network-wide vulnerabilities and so a major problem. In other words, by exploiting service logic and data sources, the likelihood of attack success is very high. Therefore, data source and service logic protection mechanisms must be deployed. It must be noted that MAPSec protects neither service logic nor data sources; rather, it protects MAP messages.

Coverage Measurement Formulas

The CMF comprises the following set of three formulas to capture the coverage of security protocols: (1) effective coverage, to capture the average effective number of attacks eliminated by the security protocol; the higher the value of Effective Coverage the greater the protection the security protocol; (2) deployment coverage, to capture the coverage of protocol deployments; and (3) attack coverage, to capture the attack coverage provided by the security protocol; the higher this value, the greater is the security solution's efficacy in eliminating a large number of attacks on the network.

Extensive use of CMF on several of the network services has revealed that MAPSec has an average network-wide attack coverage of 33%. This may be attributed to the fact that message corruption has a low spawning effect. Typically a single message corruption causes a single attack, since messages are typically used by a single service. Hence MAPSec is a solution to a small portion of the total network vulnerabilities.

Finally, in evaluating MAPSec using eCAT, it was observed that though MAPSec is 100% effective in preventing MAP message attacks, it cannot prevent a successfully launched attack from cascading. For MAPSec to be truly successful, every leg of the MAP message transport must be secured using MAPSec. However, the overhead for deploying MAPSec can be high, in terms of both processing load and monetary investment. Also, as MAP messages travel through third-party networks en route to their destinations, the risk level of attacks without MAPSec is very high. Hence, MAPSec is vital to protect MAP messages.

In conclusion, because MAPSec can protect against only 33% of attacks, it alone is insufficient to protect the network. A complete protection scheme for the network must include data source and service logic protection.

6. SUMMARY

Next to the Internet, cellular networks are the most highly used communication network. It is also the most vulnerable, with inadequate security measures making it a most attractive target to adversaries that want to cause communication outages during emergencies. As cellular networks are moving in the direction of the Internet, becoming an amalgamation of several types of diverse networks, more attention must be paid to securing these networks. A push from government agencies requiring mandatory security standards for operating cellular networks would be just the momentum needed to securing these networks.

Of all the attacks discussed in this chapter, cascading attacks have the most potential to stealthily cause major network misoperation. At present there is no standardized scheme to protect from such attacks. EndSec is a good solution for protecting from cascading attacks, since it requires every data item to be signed by the source service node. Because service nodes are unlikely to corrupt data items and they are to be accounted for by their signatures, the possibility of cascading attacks is greatly reduced. EndSec has the added advantage of providing end-to-end security for all types of signaling messages. Hence, standardizing EndSec and mandating its deployment would be a good step toward securing the network.

Both Internet and PSTN connectivity are the open gateways that adversaries can use to gain access and attack the network. Because the PSTN's security is not going to be improved, at least its gateway to the core network must be adequately secured. Likewise, since neither the Internet's design nor security will be changed to suit a cellular network, at least its gateways to the core network must be adequately secured.

Finally, because a cellular network is an amalgamation of many diverse networks, it has too many vulnerable points. Hence, the future design of the network must be planned to reduce the number of vulnerable network points and reduce the number of service nodes that participate in servicing the subscriber, thereby reducing the number of points from which an adversary may attack.

Finally, let's move on to the real interactive part of this Chapter: review questions/exercises, hands-on projects, case projects and optional team case project. The answers and/or solutions by chapter can be found in the Online Instructor's Solutions Manual.

CHAPTER REVIEW QUESTIONS/ EXERCISES

True/False

1. True or False? Cellular networks are high-speed, high-capacity voice and data communication networks with enhanced multimedia and seamless roaming capabilities for supporting cellular devices.
2. True or False? The current cellular network is an evolution of the early-generation cellular networks that were built for optimal performance.
3. True or False? It would seem that attacks on the radio access network could not easily happen, because anyone with a transmitter/receiver could capture these signals.
4. True or False? Though the current generation of a cellular network has seen many security improvements

in the radio access network, the security of the core network is not as improved.
5. True or False? Internet connectivity introduces the biggest threat to the security of cellular networks.

Multiple Choice

1. Cellular networks are organized as collections of interconnected:
   A. Message Integrity Codes (MIC)
   B. Temporal Key Integrity Protocols (TKIP)
   C. Application Program Interfaces
   D. Network Areas
   E. Extensible Authentication Protocol (EAP) framework
2. The core network is facilitated by network servers, which are also called?
   A. Middle Layers
   B. Network Layers
   C. Transport Layers
   D. Service Nodes
   E. All of the above
3. What is a basic service in the circuit-switched domain?
   A. Secure on-demand routing protocol service
   B. Taxonomy service
   C. Caller delivery service
   D. Authenticated Routing for Ad hoc Networks (ARAN) service
   E. Destination-Sequenced Distance Vector (DSDV) routing service
4. The cloning of cellular devices to utilize the network resources without paying; and cloning BSs to entice users to camp at the cloned BS in an attack, is called a:
   A. False base station attack
   B. Privacy attack
   C. Eavesdropping attack
   D. Man-in-the-Middle Attack
   E. Passive attack
5. What introduces the biggest threat to the security of cellular networks?
   A. HELLO Flood connectivity
   B. Denial-of-service attack connectivity
   C. Internet connectivity
   D. Sybil connectivity
   E. All of the above

EXERCISE

Problem

What are the limitations of cellular network security?

Hands-On Projects

Project

What are the security issues in cellular networks?

Case Projects

Problem

What types of attacks are cellular networks open to?

Optional Team Case Project

Problem

What additional security mechanisms are available to cellular networks?

REFERENCES

[1] 3GPP, Architectural Requirements, Technical Standard 3G TS 23.221 V6.3.0, 3G Partnership Project, May 2004.

[2] K. Murakami, O. Haase, J. Shin, T.F. LaPorta, Mobility management alternatives for migration to mobile internet session-based services, IEEE J. Sel. Areas Commun. (J-SAC) 22 (June 2004) 834–848.

[3] 3GPP, 3G Security, Security Threats and Requirements, Technical Standard 3G TS 21.133 V3.1.0, 3G Partnership Project, December 1999.

[4] 3GPP, Network Architecture, Technical Standard 3G TS 23.002 V3.3.0, 3G Partnership Project, May 2000.

[5] V. Eberspacher, GSM Switching, Services and Protocols, John Wiley & Sons, 1999.

[6] 3GPP, Basic Call Handling – Technical Realization, Technical Standard 3GPP TS 23.018 V3.4.0, 3G Partnership Project, April 1999.

[7] 3GPP, a Guide to 3rd Generation Security, Technical Standard 3GPP TR 33.900 V1.2.0, 3G Partnership Project, January 2001.

[8] B. Chatras, C. Vernhes, Mobile application part design principles, in: Proceedings of XIII International Switching Symposium, vol. 1, June 1990, pp. 35–42.

[9] J.A. Audestad, The Mobile Application Part (Map) of GSM, Technical Report, Telektronikk 3.2004, Telektronikk, March 2004.

[10] 3GPP, Mobile Application Part (MAP) Specification, Technical Standard 3GPP TS 29.002 V3.4.0, 3G Partnership Project, April 1999.

[11] K. Boman, G. Horn, P. Howard, V. Niemi, Umts security, Electron. Commun. Eng. J. 14 (5) (October 2002) 191–204.

[12] K. Kotapati, P. Liu, T.F. LaPorta, Dependency Relation-Based Vulnerability Analysis of 3G Networks: Can it Identify Unforeseen Cascading Attacks?, Special Issue of Springer Telecommunications Systems on Security, Privacy and Trust for Beyond 3G Networks, March 2007.

[13] K. Kotapati, P. Liu, T.F. LaPorta, Evaluating MAPSec by marking attack graphs, ACM/Kluwer J. Wire. Netw. J. (WINET) 12 (March 2008).

[14] K. Kotapati, P. Liu, T.F. LaPorta, EndSec: an end-to-end message security protocol for cellular networks, IEEE workshop on security, privacy and authentication in wireless networks (SPAWN 2008), in: IEEE International Symposium on a World of Wireless Mobile and Multimedia Networks (WOWMOM), June 2008.

[15] D. Moore, V. Paxson, S. Savage, C. Shannon, S. Staniford, N. Weaver, Inside the slammer worm, IEEE Secur. Privacy 1 (4) (2003) 33–39.

[16] W. Enck, P. Traynor, P. McDaniel, T.F. LaPorta, Exploiting open functionality in sms-capable cellular networks, in: CCS '05: Proceedings of the 12th ACM Conference on Computer and Communications Security, ACM Press, 2005.

[17] P. Traynor, W. Enck, P. McDaniel, T.F. LaPorta, Mitigating attacks on open functionality in SMS-capable cellular networks, in: MobiCom '06: Proceedings of the 12th Annual International Conference on Mobile Computing and Networking, ACM Press, 2006.

[18] P. Traynor, P. McDaniel, T.F. LaPorta, On attack causality in internet-connected cellular networks, in: USENIX Security Symposium (SECURITY), August 2007.

[19] T. Moore, T. Kosloff, J. Keller, G. Manes, S. Shenoi, Signaling system 7 (SS7) network security, in: Proceedings of the IEEE 45th Midwest Symposium on Circuits and Systems, August 2002.

[20] G. Lorenz, T. Moore, G. Manes, J. Hale, S. Shenoi, Securing SS7 telecommunications networks, in: Proceedings of the 2001 IEEE Workshop on Information Assurance and Security, June 2001.

[21] K. Kotapati, P. Liu, Y. Sun, T.F. LaPorta, A taxonomy of cyber attacks on 3G networks, in: Proceedings IEEE International Conference on Intelligence and Security Informatics, Springer-Verlag, May 2005.

[22] K. Kotapati, Assessing Security of Mobile Telecommunication Networks (Ph.D. dissertation), Penn State University, August 2008.

[23] Switch, 5ESS Switch, www.alleged.com/telephone/5ESS/.

[24] Telcoman, Central Offices, www.thecentraloffice.com/.

[25] V. Prevelakis, D. Spinellis, The Athens affair, IEEE Spectr. (July 2007).

[26] H. Hannu, Signaling Compression (SigComp) Requirements & Assumptions, RFC 3322 (Informational), January 2003.

[27] W. Stallings, Cryptography and Network Security: Principles and Practice, Prentice Hall, 2000.

[28] K. Kotapati, P. Liu, T.F. LaPorta, CAT – a practical graph & SDL based toolkit for vulnerability assessment of 3G networks, in: Proceedings of the 21st IFIP TC-11 International Information Security Conference, Security and Privacy in Dynamic Environments, SEC 2006, May 2006.

[29] 3GPP2 3GPP, Third Generation Partnership Project, 2006. www.3gpp.org/.

[30] J. Ellsberger, D. Hogrefe, A. Sarma, SDL, Formal Object-Oriented Language for Communicating Systems, Prentice Hall, 1997.

Chapter 21

Radio Frequency Identification Security

Chunming Rong[1], Gansen Zhao[2], Liang Yan[1], Erdal Cayirci[1] and Hongbing Cheng[1]
[1]University of Stavanger, Stavanger, Norway; [2]Sun Yat-sen University, Guangzhou, P.R. China

1. RADIO FREQUENCY IDENTIFICATION INTRODUCTION

Generally, a radio frequency identification (RFID) system consists of three basic components: RFID tags, RFID readers, and a back-end database:

- *RFID tags or RFID transponders:* These are the data carriers attached to objects. A typical RFID tag contains information about the attached object, such as an identifier (ID) of the object and other related properties of the object that may help to identify and describe it.
- *The RFID reader or the RFID transceiver:* These devices can read information from tags and may write information into tags if the tags are rewritable.
- *Back-end database:* This is the data repository responsible for the management of data related to the tags and business transactions, such as ID, object properties, reading locations, reading time, and so on.

Radio Frequency Identification System Architecture

Fig. 21.1 illustrates RFID systems architecture. Tags are attached to or embedded in objects to identify or annotate them. An RFID reader send out signals to a tag to request information stored on the tag. The tag responds to the request by sending back the appropriate information. With the data from the back-end database, applications can then use the information from the tag to proceed with the business transaction related to the object.

Tags

In RFID systems, objects are identified or described by information on RFID tags attached to the objects. An RFID tag basically consists of a microchip that is used for data storage and computation and a coupling element for communicating with the RFID reader via radio frequency communication, such as an antenna. Some tags may also have an on-board battery to supply a limited amount of power.

RFID tags can respond to radio frequencies sent out by RFID readers. On receiving the radio signals from an RFID reader, an RFID tag either send back the requested data stored on the tag or write the data into the tag, if the tag is rewritable. Because radio signals are used, RFID tags do not require line of sight to connect with the reader and precise positioning, as do bar codes. Tags may also generate a certain amount of electronic power from the radio signals they receive, to power the computation and transmission of data.

RFID tags can be classified based on four main criteria: power source, type of memory, computational power, and functionality.

A basic and important classification criterion of RFID tags is to classify tags based on power source. Tags can be categorized into three classes: active, semiactive, and passive RFID.

Active RFID tags have on-board power sources, such as batteries. Active RFID tags can proactively send radio signals to an RFID reader and possibly to other tags [1] as well. Compared with tags without on-board power, active tags have longer transmission range and are more reliable. Active tags can work in the absence of an RFID reader. On the other hand, the on-board power supply increases the costs of active tags.

Semiactive RFID tags also have on-board power sources to power their microchips, but they use RFID readers' energy field to actually transmit their data [2] when responding to incoming transmissions. Semiactive tags have the middle transmission range and cost.

Computer and Information Security Handbook. http://dx.doi.org/10.1016/B978-0-12-803843-7.00021-1

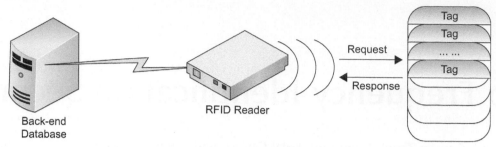

FIGURE 21.1   Radio frequency identification (RFID) system architecture.

TABLE 21.1 Tags Classified by Power Source

Power Source	Active Tags	Semiactive Tags	Passive Tags
On-board power supply	Yes	Yes	No
Transmission range	Long	Medium	Short
Communication pattern	Proactive	Passive	Passive
Cost	Expensive	Medium	Cheap

Passive RFID tags do not have internal power sources and cannot initiate communications. Passive RFID tags generate power from radio signals sent out by an RFID reader in the course of communication. Thus passive RFID tags can work only in the presence of an RFID reader. Passive tags have the shortest transmission range and the cheapest cost. The differences among active, semiactive, and passive tags are shown in Table 21.1.

RFID tags can be classified into three categories according to the type of memory that a tag uses: read-only, write-once/read-many, and fully rewritable. The information on read-only tags cannot be changed in the life cycle of the tags. Write-once/read-many tags can be initialized with application-specific information. The information on fully rewritable tags can be rewritten many times by an RFID reader.

According to the computational power, RFID tags can be classified into three categories: basic, symmetric key, and public key. Basic tags do not have the ability to perform cryptography computation. Symmetric key tags and public key tags have the ability to perform symmetric key and public–key cryptography computation, respectively.

RFID tags can also be classified according to their functionality. In 2003, the Massachusetts Institute of Technology (MIT) Auto-ID Center defined five classes of tags according to their functionality [1]: 0, 1, 2, 3, 4. Every class has different functions and different requirements for tag memory and power resources. Class 0 tags are passive and do not contain memory. They only announce their presence and offer electronic article surveillance (EAS) functionality. Class 1 tags are typically passive. They have read-only or write-once/read-many memory and can only offer identification functionality. Class 2 tags are mostly semiactive and active. They have fully rewritable memory and can offer data-logging functionality. Class 3 tags are semiactive and active tags. They contain on-board environmental sensors that can record temperature, acceleration, motion, or radiation and require fully rewritable memory. Class 4 tags are active tags and have fully rewritable memory. They can establish ad hoc wireless networks with other tags because they are equipped with wireless networking components.

Radio Frequency Identification Readers

An RFID reader (transceiver) is a device used to read information from and possibly also write information into RFID tags. An RFID reader is normally connected to a back-end database to send information to that database for further processing.

An RFID reader consists of two key functional modules: a high-frequency (HF) interface and a control unit. The HF interface can perform three functions: generate the transmission power to activate the tags, modulate the signals for sending requests to RFID tags, and receive and demodulate signals received from tags. The control unit of an RFID reader has also three basic functions: control communication between the RFID reader and RFID tags, encode and decode signals, and communicate with the back-end server to send information to the back-end database or execute commands from the back-end server. The control unit can perform more functions in the case of complex RFID systems, such as executing anticollision algorithms in the case of communicating with multitags, encrypting requests sent by the RFID reader and decrypting responses received from tags, and performing authentication between RFID readers and RFID tags [4].

RFID readers can provide high-speed tag scanning. Hundreds of objects can be dealt with by a single reader within a second; thus it is scalable enough for applications such as supply chain management, in which a large number of objects need to be dealt with frequently. RFID readers need only to be placed at every entrance and exit. When products enter or leave the designated area by passing through an entrance or exit, RFID readers can instantly identify the products and send the necessary information to the back-end database for further processing.

Back-End Database

The back-end database is in the back-end server that manages information related to the tags in an RFID system. Every object's information can be stored as a record in the database, and the information on the tag attached to the object can serve as a pointer to the record.

The connection between an RFID reader and a back-end database can be assumed to be secure, no matter via whether it is wireless link, because constraints for readers are not tight and security solutions such as Secure Sockets Layer/ Transport Layer Security can be implemented for them [2].

Radio Frequency Identification Standards

Currently, because different frequencies are used for RFID systems in various countries and many standards are adopted for different kinds of application, there is no agreement on a universal standard that is accepted by all parties. Several kinds of RFID standards [6] are being used today. These standards include contactless smart cards, item management tags, RFID systems for animal identification, and electronic product code (EPC) tags. These standards specify the physical layer and the link layer characteristics of RFID systems but do not cover the upper layers.

Contactless smart cards can be classified into three types according to their communication ranges. The International Organization for Standardization (ISO) standards for them are ISO 10536, ISO 14443, and ISO 15693. ISO 10536 sets the standard for close-coupling smart cards, for which the communication range is about 0–1 cm. ISO 14443 sets the standard for proximity-coupling smart cards, which have a communication range of about 0–10 cm. ISO 15693 specifies vicinity-coupling smart cards, which have a communication range of about 0–1 m. The proximity-coupling and vicinity-coupling smart cards have been implemented with some cryptography algorithms such as 128-bit Advanced Encryption Standard (AES), triple Data Encryption Standard, and Secure Hash Algorithm1 and challenge-response authentication mechanisms to improve system security [3].

Item management tag standards include ISO 15961, ISO 15962, ISO 15963, and ISO 18000 series [8]. ISO 15961 defines the host interrogator, tag functional commands, and other syntax features of item management. ISO 15962 defines the data syntax of item management, and

ISO 15963 is "Unique Identification of RF [Radio Frequency] tag and Registration Authority to Manage the Uniqueness." For the ISO 18000 standards series, Part 1 describes the reference architecture and parameters definition; Parts 2–7 the parameters for air interface communications below 135 kHz, at 13.56 MHz, at 2.45 GHz, and at 860, 960, and 433 MHz, respectively.

Standards for RFID systems for animal identification include ISO 11784, ISO 11785, and ISO 14223 [2]. ISO 11784 and ISO 11784 define the code structure and technical concepts for radio frequency identification of animals. ISO 14223 includes three parts: air interface, code and command structure, and applications. These kinds of tags use low frequency for communication and have limited protection for animal tracking [3].

The EPC standard was created by the MIT Auto-ID, which is an association of more than 100 companies and university laboratories. The EPC system is currently operated by EPCglobal [8]. A typical EPC network has four parts [2]: the electronic product code, the identification system that includes RFID tags and RFID readers, the Savant middleware, and the object naming service (ONS). First- and second-generation EPC tags cannot support strong cryptography to protect the security of the RFID systems because of the limitation of computational resources, but both can provide a kill command to protect the privacy of the consumer [3].

EPC tag encoding includes a Header field followed by one or more Value fields. The Header field defines the overall length and format of the Value fields. There are two kinds of EPC format: EPC 64-bit format and EPC 96-bit format. In a recent version [9], the 64-bit format was removed from the standard. As shown in Table 21.2, both formats include four fields: a header (8 bits), an EPC manager number (28 bits), an object class (24 bits), and a serial number (36 bits). The header and the EPC manager number are assigned by EPCglobal [8], and the object class and the serial number are assigned by the EPC manager owner. The EPC header identifies the length, type, structure version, and generation of the EPC. The EPC manager number is the entity responsible for maintaining the subsequent partitions of the EPC. The object class identifies a class of objects. The serial number identifies the instance.

TABLE 21.2 Electronic Product Code (EPC) Basic Format

Header	EPC	Object Class	Serial
	Manager		Number
	Number		

Radio Frequency Identification Applications

Increasingly more companies and organizations have begun to use RFID tags rather than traditional bar codes because RFID systems have many advantages over traditional bar code systems. First, information stored in RFID tags can be read by RFID readers without a line of sight, whereas bar codes can be scanned only within the line of sight. Second, the distance between a tag and a reader is longer compared with the bar code system. For example, an RFID reader can read information from a tag at a distance as long as 300 feet, whereas the read range for a bar code is typically no more than 15 feet. Third, RFID readers can scan hundreds of tags in seconds. Fourth, because most RFID tags are produced using silicon technology, more functions can be added to them, such as large memory for more information storage and the calculation ability to support various kinds of encryption and decryption algorithms, so privacy can be better protected and the tags cannot be easily cloned by attackers. In addition, information stored in the bar code cannot be changed after being imprinted on the bar code, whereas for RFID tags with rewritable memory, information can be updated when needed.

With these characteristics and advantages, RFID has been widely adopted and deployed in various areas. Currently, RFID can be used in passports, transportation payments, product tracking, lap scoring, animal identification, inventory systems, RFID mandates, promotion tracking, human implants, libraries, schools and universities, museums, and social retailing. These myriad applications of RFID can be classified into seven classes according to the purpose of identifying items [10]: asset management, tracking, authenticity verification, matching, process control, access control, and automated payment. Table 21.3 lists the identification purposes of various application types.

Asset management involves determining the presence of tagged items and helping manage item inventory. One possible application of asset management is EAS. For example, every good in a supermarket is attached to an EAS tag, which will be deactivated if it is properly checked out. Then RFID readers at the supermarket exits can detect unpaid goods automatically when they pass through.

Tracking is used to identify the location of tagged items. If the readers are fixed, a single reader can cover only one area. To track the items effectively, a group of readers is needed, together with a central system to deal with the information from different readers.

Authenticity verification methods are used to verify the source of tagged items. For example, by adding a cryptography-based digital signature in the tag, the system can prevent tag replication to make sure that a good is labeled with the source information.

TABLE 21.3 Radio Frequency Identification Application Purpose

Application Type	Identification Purpose
Asset management	Determine item presence
Tracking	Determine item location
Authenticity verification	Determine item source
Matching	Ensure affiliated items are not separated
Process control	Correlate item information for decision making
Access control	Person authentication
Automated payment	Conduct financial transaction

Matching is used to ensure that affiliated items are not separated. Samples for matching applications include mothers and their newborn babies to match each other in the hospital and for airline passengers to match their checked luggage and so prevent theft.

Access control is used for person authentication. Buildings may use contactless RFID card systems to identify authorized people. Only those authorized people with the correct RFID card can authenticate themselves to the reader to open a door and enter a building. Using a car key with RFID tags, a car owner can open his own car automatically, another example of RFID's application to access control.

Process control involves decision making by correlating tagged item information. For example, RFID readers in different parts of an assembly line can read the information on the products, which can be used to help production managers make suitable decisions.

Automated payment is used to conduct financial transactions. Applications include payment for toll expressways and at gas stations. These applications can improve the speed of payment to hasten the processing of these transactions.

2. RADIO FREQUENCY IDENTIFICATION CHALLENGES

RFID systems have been widely deployed in some areas. Perhaps this happened beyond the expectations of RFID researchers and RFID service providers. There are many limitations of the RFID technology that restrain the deployment of RFID applications, such as the lack of universal standardization of RFID in the industry and concerns about security and privacy problems that may affect the privacy and security of individuals and organizations. Security and privacy issues pose a huge challenge for RFID applications. Here we briefly summarize some of the challenges facing RFID systems.

Counterfeiting

As described earlier in the chapter, RFID tags can be classified into three categories based on the equipped computation power: basic, symmetric key, and public key. Symmetric key and public key tags can implement cryptography protocols for authentication with private key, and public keys, respectively. Basic tags are not capable of performing cryptography computation. Although they lack the capability to perform cryptography computation, they are most widely used for applications such as supply chain management and travel systems. With the widespread application of fully writable or even reprogrammable basic tags, counterfeiters can easily forge basic tags in real-world applications, and these counterfeit tags can be used in multiple places at the same time, which can cause confusion.

The counterfeiting of tags can be categorized into two areas based on the technique used to tamper with tag data: modifying tag data and adding data to a blank tag. In real-world applications, we face counterfeit threats such as [3]:

- The attacker can modify valid tags to make them invalid or modify invalid tags to make them valid.
- The attacker can modify a high-priced object's tag as a low-priced object or modify a low-priced object's tag as a high-priced object.
- The attacker can modify an object's tag to be the same as tags attached to other objects.
- The attacker can create an additional tag for personal reasons by reading the data from an authorized tag and adding these data to a blank tag in real-world applications, such as in a passport or a shipment of goods.

Sniffing

Another main issue of concern in deploying RFID systems is the sniffing problem. It occurs when third parties use a malicious and unauthorized RFID reader to read the information on RFID tags within their transmission range. Unfortunately, most RFID tags are indiscriminate in their responses to reading requests transmitted by RFID readers and do not have access control functions to provide protection against an unauthorized reader. Once an RFID tag enters a sufficiently powered reader's field, it receives the reader's requests via radio frequency. As long as the request is well formed, the tag will reply to the request with the corresponding information on the tag. Then the holder of the unauthenticated reader may use this information for other purposes.

Tracking

With multiple RFID readers integrated into one system, the movements of objects can be tracked by fixed RFID readers [4]. For example, once a specific tag can be associated with a particular person or object, when the tag enters a reader's field, the reader can obtain the specific identifier of the tag, and the presence of the tag within the range of a specific reader implies specific location information related to the attached person or object. With location information coming from multiple RFID readers, an attacker can follow movements of people or objects. Tracking can also be performed without decrypting the encrypted messages coming from RFID readers [2]. Generally, the more messages the attacker describes, the more location or privacy information can be obtained from the messages.

One way to track is to generate maps of RFID tags with mobile robots [5]. A sensor model is introduced to compute the likelihood of tag detections, given the relative pose of the tag with respect to the robot. In this model a highly accurate FastSLAM algorithm is used to learn the geometrical structure of the environment around the robots, which are equipped with a laser range scanner; then it uses the recursive Bayesian filtering scheme to estimate the posterior locations of the RFID tags, which can be used to localize robots and people in the environment with the geometrical structure of the environment learned by the FastSLAM algorithm.

There is another method to detect the motion of passive RFID tags that are within a detecting antenna's field. The response rate at the reader is used to study the impact of four cases of tag movements that can provide prompt and accurate detection and the influence of the environment. The idea of multiple tags/readers is introduced to improve performance. The movement-detection algorithms can be improved and integrated into the RFID monitoring system to localize the position of the tags. The method does not require the modification of communication protocols or the addition of hardware. In real-world applications, the following tracking threat exists: The attacker can track the potential victim by monitoring the movement of the person and performing some illegal actions against the potential victim [13].

Now, let us take a brief look at denial of service (DoS) threats. Availability enables a Web services application to detect a DoS attack, continue operation as long as possible, and then gracefully recover and resume operations afterward. There is a need for techniques to replicate data and services to ensure continuity of operations in the event of a fault or threat (see checklist: "An Agenda for Action When Thwarting Denial of Service Threats"). There is also a need for management and monitoring solutions to provide service performance and availability monitoring to meet certain service-level objectives.

An Agenda for Action When Thwarting DoS Threats

DoS takes place when RFID readers or back-end servers cannot provide excepted services. DoS attacks are easy to accomplish and difficult to guard against [13]. The following are nine DoS threats (check all tasks completed):

_____**1.** *Killing tags to make them disabled to disrupt readers' normal operations.* EPCglobal had proposed that tags have a "kill" command to destroy them and protect consumer privacy. If an attacker knows the password of a tag, it can "kill" the tag easily in real-world applications. Now Class 0, Class 1 Generation 1, and Class 1 Generation 2 tags are all equipped with the kill command.

_____**2.** Carry a blocker tag that can disrupt communication between an RFID reader and RFID tags. A blocker tag is a cheap, passive RFID device that can simulate many basic RFID tags at one time and render specific zones private or public. An RFID reader can communicate with only a single RFID tag at any specific time. If more than one tag responds to a request coming from the reader at the same time, "collision" happens. In this case, the reader cannot receive the information sent by the tags, which makes the system unavailable to authorized users.

_____**3.** Carry a special absorbent tag that can be tuned to the same radio frequencies used by legitimate tags. The absorbent tag can absorb the energy or power generated by radio frequency signals sent by the reader, and the resulting reduction in the reader's energy may make the reader unavailable to communicate with other tags.

_____**4.** Remove, physically destroy, or erase information on tags attached to or embedded in objects. The reader will not communicate with the dilapidated tags in a normal way.

_____**5.** *Shielding RFID tags from scrutiny using a Faraday cage.* A Faraday cage is a container made of a metal enclosure that can prevent reading radio signals from the readers [6].

_____**6.** Carry a device that can actively broadcast more powerful return radio signals or noises than the signals responded to by the tags so as to block or disrupt the communication of any nearby RFID readers and make the system unavailable to authorized users. The power of the broadcast is so high that it could cause severe blockage or disruption of all nearby RFID systems, even those in legitimate applications where privacy is not a concern [6].

_____**7.** *Perform a traditional Internet DoS attack and prevent back-end servers from gathering EPC numbers from the readers.* The servers do not receive enough information from the readers and cannot provide the additional services from the server.

_____**8.** Perform a traditional Internet DoS attack against the ONS. This can deny the service.

_____**9.** Send URL queries to a database and make the database busy with these queries. The database may then deny access to authorized users.

Other Issues

Besides the four basic types of attack (counterfeiting, sniffing, tracking, and DoS) in real-world applications, some other threats to RFID systems exist.

Spoofing

Spoofing attacks take place when an attacker successfully poses as an authorized user of a system [13]. Spoofing attacks are different from counterfeiting and sniffing attacks, although they are all falsification types of attack. Counterfeiting takes place when an attacker forges the RFID tags that can be scanned by authorized readers. Sniffing takes place when an attacker forges authorized readers that can scan the authorized tags to obtain useful information. However, the forging object of spoofing is an authorized user of a system. The following spoofing threats exist in real-world applications [13]:

- *The attacker can pose as an authorized EPC global Information Service ONS user.* If the attacker successfully poses as an authorized ONS user, he can send queries to the ONS to gather EPC numbers. Then, from the EPC numbers, the attacker may easily obtain location, identification, or other privacy information.

- *The attacker can pose as an authorized database user in an RFID system.* The database stores the complete information from the objects, such as manufacturer, product name, read time, read location, and other privacy information. If the attacker successfully poses as an authorized database user and an authorized user of ONS, he can send queries to the ONS to obtain the EPC number of one object, and then get complete information on the object by mapping the EPC number to the information stored in the database.

- *The attacker can also pose as an ONS server.* If the attacker's pose is successful, he can easily use the ONS server to gather EPC numbers, respond to invalid requests, deny normal service, and even change the data or write malicious data to the system.

Repudiation

Repudiation takes place when a user denies doing an action or no proof exists to prove that the action has been implemented [13]. There are two kinds of repudiation threats:

- The sender or the receiver denies performing the send and receive actions. A nonrepudiation protocol can be used to resolve this problem.
- The owner of the EPC number or the back-end server denies that it has the information from the objects to which the tags are attached.

Insert Attacks

Insert attacks take place when an attacker inserts some system commands to the RFID system where data are normally expected [15]. In real-world applications, the following attack exists: A system command rather than valid data is carried by a tag in its data storage memory.

Replay Attacks

Replay attacks take place when an attacker intercepts communication signals between an RFID reader and an RFID tag and records the tag's response. Then the RFID tag's response can be reused if the attacker detects that the reader sends requests to the other tags for querying [16]. There, the following two threats exist:

- The attacker can record communication between proximity cards and a building access reader and play it back to access the building.
- The attacker can record the response that an RFID card in a car gives to an automated highway toll collection system, and the response can be used when the car of the attacker wants to pass the automated toll station.

Physical Attacks

Physical attacks are strong attacks that physically obtain tags and have unauthorized physical operations on the tags. However, it is fortunate that physical attacks cannot be implemented in public or on a widespread scale, except for Transient Electromagnetic Pulse Emanation Standard attacks. There, the following physical attacks exist [1,17]:

- *probe attacks*: The attacker can use a probe directly attached to the circuit to obtain or change information on tags.
- *material removal*: The attacker can use a knife or other tools to remove tags attached to objects.
- *energy attacks*: The attacks can be either of the contact or contactless variety. It is required for contactless energy attacks to be close enough to the system.
- *radiation imprinting*: The attacker can use an X-ray band or other radial bands to destroy the data unit of a tag.
- *circuit disruption*: The attacker can use strong electromagnetic interference to disrupt tag circuits.

- *clock glitch*: The attacker can lengthen or shorten clock pulses to a clocked circuit and destroy normal operations.

Viruses

Viruses are old attacks that threaten the security of all information systems, including RFID systems. RFID viruses always target the back-end database in the server, perhaps destroying and revealing the data or information stored in the database. There, the following virus threats exist:

- An RFID virus destroys and reveals data or information stored in the database.
- An RFID virus disturbs or even stops normal services provided by the server.
- An RFID virus threatens the security of communications between RFID readers and RFID tags or between back-end database and RFID readers.

Social Issues

Because of security challenges in RFID, many people do not trust RFID technologies and fear that they could allow attackers to purloin their privacy information.

Weis [16] presented two main arguments. These arguments make some people choose not to rely on RFID technology, and regard RFID tags as the "mark of the beast." However, security issues cannot prevent the success of RFID technology.

The first argument is that RFID tags are regarded as the best replacement for current credit cards and all other ways of paying for goods and services. However, RFID tags can also serve as identification. The replacement of current ways of paying by RFID tag requires people to accept RFID tags instead of credit cards, and they cannot sell or buy anything without RFID tags.

There is a second argument [16]: "Since RFID tags are also used as identification, they should be implanted to avoid losing the ID or switching it with someone. Current research has shown that the ideal location for the implant is indeed the forehead or the hand, since they are easy to access and unlike most other body parts they do not contain much fluid, which interferes with the reading of the chip."

Comparison of All Challenges

Previously in this chapter we introduced some challenges that RFID systems face. Every challenge or attack can have a different method or attack goal, and the consequences for the RFID system after an attack may also be different. In this part of the chapter, we briefly analyze the challenges according to attack methods, attack goals, and the consequences for RFID systems after attacks (Table 21.4).

TABLE 21.4 Comparison of All Challenges or Attacks in Radio Frequency Identification (RFID) Systems

Challenge or Attack	Attack Method	Attack Goal	Direct Consequence
Counterfeiting	Forge tags	Tag	Invalid tags
Sniffing	Forge readers	Reader	Reveals information
Tracking	Monitor movement of objects	Objects of RFID system	Tracks movement of object
Denial of service	Radio frequency jamming, kill normal command, physical destroy, etc.	Reader, back-end database or server	Denies normal services
Spoofing	Pose as authorized user	User	Invalid operations by invalid user
Repudiation	Deny action or no proof that action was implemented	Tag, reader, back-end database or server	Deniable actions
Insert attacks	Insert invalid command	Tag	Invalid operations by invalid commands
Replay attacks	Reuse response of tags	Communication between RFID tags and readers	Invalid identification
Physical attacks	Physical operations on tag	Tag	Disrupts or destroys communication between RFID tags and readers
Virus	Insert invalid data	Back-end database or server	Destroys data or service of system
Social issues	Social attitude	Psychology of potential user	Restricts widespread application

The first four challenges are the four basic challenges in RFID systems that correspond to the four basic use cases. *Counterfeiting* happens when counterfeiters forge RFID tags by copying information from a valid tag or adding some well-formed format information to a new tag in the RFID system. *Sniffing* happens when an unauthorized reader reads information from a tag, and the information may be used by attackers. *Tracking* happens when an attacker who holds some readers unlawfully monitors the movements of objects attached by an RFID tag that can be read by those readers. *DoS* happens when the components of RFID systems deny the RFID service.

The last seven challenges or attacks can always happen in RFID systems (Table 21.4). *Spoofing* happens when an attacker poses as an authorized user of an RFID system on which the attacker can perform invalid operations. *Repudiation* happens when a user or component of an RFID system denies the action it performed and there is no proof that the user did perform the action. *Insert attacks* happen when an attacker inserts some invalid system commands into the tags and some operations may be implemented by the invalid command. *Replay attacks* happen when an attacker intercepts the response of the tag and reuses the response for another communication. *Physical attacks* happen when an attacker performs some physical operations on RFID tags and these attacks disrupt communications between the RFID readers and tags. A *virus* is the

security challenge of all information systems; it can disrupt the operations of RFID systems or reveal the information in those systems. *Social issues* involve users' psychological attitudes that can influence the users' adoption of RFID technologies for real-world applications.

3. RADIO FREQUENCY IDENTIFICATION PROTECTIONS

According to their computational power, RFID tags can be classified into three categories: basic, symmetric key, and public key. In the next part of the chapter, we introduce some protection approaches to these three kinds of RFID tags.

Basic Radio Frequency Identification System

Prices have been one of the biggest factors to be considered when we are making decisions about RFID deployments. Basic tags are available for the cheapest price, compared with symmetric key tags and public key tags. Because of the limited computation resources built into a basic tag, these tags are not capable of performing cryptography computations. This imposes a huge challenge on implementing protections into basic tags; cryptography has been one of the most important and effective methods to implementing protection mechanisms. Several approaches have been proposed to tackle this issue.

Most approaches to security protection for basic tags focus on protecting consumer privacy. A usual method is by tag killing, proposed by EPCglobal. In this approach, when the reader wants to kill a tag, it sends a kill message to the tag to deactivate it permanently. Together with the kill message, a 32-bit tag-specific personal identification number (PIN) code is also sent to the object tag, to avoid killing other tags. Upon receiving this kill message, a tag will deactivate itself, after which the tag will become inoperative. Generally, tags are killed when the tagged items are checked out in shops or supermarkets. This is similar to removing tags from the tagged items when they are purchased. It is an efficient method of protecting the privacy of consumers, because a killed tag can no longer send out information.

The disadvantage of this approach is that it will reduce the postpurchase benefits of RFID tags. In some cases, RFID tags need to be operative only temporarily. For example, RFID tags used in libraries and museums to tag books and other items need to work at all times and should not be killed or be removed from the tagged items. In these cases, instead of being killed or removed, tags can be made temporarily inactive. When a tag needs to be reawakened, an RFID reader can send a wakeup message to the tag with a 32-bit tag-specific PIN code, which is sent to avoid waking up other tags. This also results in the management of PIN codes for tags, which brings some inconvenience.

Another approach to protecting privacy is tag relabeling, which was first proposed by Sarma et al. [7]. In this scheme, to protect consumers' privacy, identifiers of RFID tags are effaced when tagged items are checked out, but the information on the tags will be kept for later use. Inoue and Yasuuran [8] proposed that consumers store the identifiers of the tags and give each tag a new identifier. When needed, people can reactivate the tags with the new identifiers. This approach allows users to manage tagged items throughout the items' life cycle. A third approach is to allocate each tag a new random number at each checkout; thus attackers cannot rely on the identifiers to collect information about customers [9]. This method does not solve the problem of tracking [9]. To prevent tracking, random numbers need to be refreshed frequently, which will increase the burden on consumers. Juels proposed a system called the *minimalist system* [10], in which every tag has a list of pseudonyms, and for every reader query, the tag will respond with a different pseudonym from the list and return to the beginning of the list when this list is exhausted. It is assumed that only authorized readers know all of these tag pseudonyms. Unauthorized readers that do not know these pseudonyms cannot identify the tags correctly. To prevent unauthorized readers from getting the pseudonyms list by

frequent query, the tags will response to an RFID reader's request with a relatively low rate, which is called *pseudonym throttling*. Pseudonym throttling is useful, but it cannot provide a high level of privacy for consumers, because with the tag's small memory, the number of pseudonyms in the list is limited. To tackle this problem, the protocol allows an authorized RFID reader to refresh a tag's pseudonyms list.

Juels and Pappu [11] proposed to protect consumers' privacy by using tagged banknotes. The proposed scheme used public key cryptography to protect the serial numbers of tagged banknotes. The serial number of a tagged banknote is encrypted using a public key to generate a ciphertext, which is saved in the memory of the tag. Upon receiving a request for the serial number, the tag will respond with this ciphertext. Only law enforcement agencies know the related private key and can decrypt this ciphertext to recover the banknote's serial number. To prevent tracking of banknotes, the ciphertext will be reencrypted periodically. To avoid the ciphertext of a banknote being reencrypted by an attacker, the tagged banknote can use an optical write—access key. A reader that wants to reencrypt this ciphertext needs to scan the write—access key first. In this system only one key pair, a public key and a private key, is used. However, this is not enough for the general RFID system. Using multiple key pairs will impair the privacy of RFID systems, because if the reader wants to reencrypt the ciphertext, it needs to know the corresponding public key of this tag.

Thus, a universal reencryption algorithm was introduced [12]. In this approach, an RFID reader can reencrypt the ciphertext without knowing the corresponding public key of a tag. The disadvantage of this approach is that attackers can substitute the ciphertext with a new ciphertext, so the integrity of the ciphertext cannot be protected. By signing the ciphertext with a digital signature, this problem can be solved [13], because only the authenticated reader can access the ciphertext.

Floerkemeier et al. [14] introduced another approach to protect consumer privacy by using a specially designed protocol. In their approach, they first designed the communication protocol between RFID tags and RFID readers. This protocol requires an RFID reader to provide information about the purpose and the collection type for the query. In addition, a privacy-enforcing device called a *watchdog tag* is used in the system. This watchdog tag is a kind of sophisticated RFID tag that is equipped with a battery, a small screen, and a long-range communication channel. A watchdog tag can be integrated into a personal digital assistant (PDA) or a cell phone and can decode the messages from an RFID reader and display them on the screen for the user to read. With a watchdog tag, a user can know not only the information from the RFID readers in the vicinity of the tag but also the ID, the query purpose, and the collection type of the requests sent by the RFID readers. With this information, the user is able to identify unwanted communications between tags and an RFID reader, which makes this method useful for users to avoid the reader ID spoofing attack.

Rieback, Crispo, and Tanebaum [15] proposed another privacy-enforcing device called RFID Guardian, which is also a battery-powered RFID tag that can be integrated into a PDA or a cell phone to protect user privacy. RFID Guardian is actually a user privacy protection platform in RFID systems. It can also work as an RFID reader to request information from RFID tags, or it can work like a tag to communicate with a reader. RFID Guardian has four different security properties: auditing, key management, access control, and authentication. It can audit RFID readers in its vicinity and record information about the RFID readers, such as commands, related parameters, and data, and provide these kinds of information to the user. Using this information, the user can sufficiently identify illegal scanning. In some cases, a user might not know or could forget the tags in his vicinity. With the help of RFID Guardian, the user can detect all the tags within radio range. Then the user can deactivate the tags according to his choice.

For RFID tags that use cryptography methods to provide security, one important issue is key management. RFID Guardian can perform two-way RFID communications and can generate random values. These features are useful for key exchange and key refresh. Using the features of coordination of security primitives, context awareness, and tag reader mediation, RFID Guardian can provide access control for RFID systems [15]. Also, using two-way RFID communication and standard challenge-response algorithms, RFID Guardian can provide off-tag authentication for RFID readers.

Another approach to privacy protecting was proposed by Juels, Rivest, and Szydlo [6]. In this approach, a cheap, passive RFID tag is used as the blocker tag. Because this blocker tag can simulate many RFID tags at the same time, it is difficult for an RFID reader to identify the real tag carried by the user. The blocker tag can both simulate all the possible RFID tags and simulate only a select set of the tags, which makes it convenient for the user to manage the RFID tags. For example, the user can tell the blocker tag to block only the tags that belong to a certain company. Another advantage of this approach is that if the user wants to reuse these RFID tags, unlike the "killed" tags that need to be activated by the user, the user only needs to remove the blocker tag. Because the blocker tag can shield the serial numbers of the tags from being read by RFID readers, it can also be used by attackers to disrupt proper operation of an RFID system. A thief can also use the blocker tag to shield the tags attached to the commodities in shops and take them out without being detected.

Radio Frequency Identification System Using Symmetric Key Cryptography

Symmetric key cryptography, also called *secret key cryptography* or *single key cryptography*, uses a single key to perform both encryption and decryption. Because of the limited amount of resources available on an RFID chip, most available symmetric key cryptographs are too costly to be implemented on an RFID chip. For example, a typical implementation of AES needs about 2000–3000 gates. This is not appropriate for low-cost RFID tags. It is possible to implement AES only in high-end RFID tags. A successful case of implementing a 128-bit AES on high-end RFID tags has been reported [16].

Using the Symmetric Key to Provide Authentication and Privacy

Symmetric key cryptography can be applied to prevent tag cloning in RFID systems using a challenge and response protocol. For example, if a tag shares a secret key K with a reader and the tag wants to authenticate itself to the reader, it will first send its identity to the reader. The reader will then generate a nonce N and send it to the tag. The tag will use this nonce and the secret K to generate a hash code $H = h(K, N)$ and send this hash code to the reader. The reader can also generate a hash code $H' = h(K, N)$ and compare these two codes to verify this tag. Using this scheme, it is difficult for an attacker to clone the tags without knowing the secret keys.

Different kinds of symmetric key cryptography protocol-based RFID tags have been used in daily life. For example, an RFID device that uses this symmetric key challenge-response protocol, called a digital signature transponder, was introduced by Texas Instruments. This transponder can be built into cars to prevent car theft and can be implemented into wireless payment devices used in filling stations.

One issue of RFID systems that use symmetric key cryptography is key management. To authenticate itself to an RFID reader, each tag in the system should share a different secret key with the reader, and the reader needs to keep all of the keys of these tags. When a tag wants to authenticate itself to an RFID reader, the reader needs to know the secret key shared between them. If the reader does not know the identification of the tag in advance, it cannot determine which key can be used to authenticate this tag. If the tag sends its identification to the reader before the authentication for the reader to search the secret key, the privacy of the tag cannot be protected, because other readers can also obtain the identification of this tag.

To tackle this problem, one simple method is *key searching*. The reader will search all of the secret keys in its memory to find the right key for the tag before authentication. There are some protocols proposed for the key search for RFID tags. One general kind of key search scheme [4] has been proposed. In this approach, the tag first generates a random nonce N and hashes this N using its secret key K to generate the hash code. Then it sends both this hash code and N to the reader. Using this nonce N, the reader will generate the hash code with all of the secret keys and compare them with the received hash code from the tag. If there is a match, it means it found the right key. In this scheme, because the nonce N is generated randomly every time, the privacy of the tag can be protected.

The problem with this approach is that if there are a large number of tags, the key searching will be costly. To reduce the cost of the key searching, a modification of this scheme was proposed [17]; in Haehnel et al. [5], using this approach, a scheme called *tree of secret* is used. Every tag is assigned to a leaf in the tree, and every node in the tree has its secret key. This way the key search cost for each tag can be reduced, but it will add some overlap to the sets of keys for each tag.

Another approach to reducing the cost of key searching is for the RFID tags and RFID reader to keep synchronized with each other. In this kind of approach, every tag will maintain a counter for the reader query times. For each reader's query, the tag should respond with a different value. The reader will also maintain counters for all of the tags' responses and maintain a table of all possible response values. Then, if the reader and tags can keep synchronized, the reader can know the approximate current counter number of the tags. When the reader receives a response from a tag, it can search the table and quickly identify this tag.

Other Symmetric Key Cryptography-Based Approaches

In addition to the basic symmetric key challenge-response protocol, some symmetric key cryptography-based approaches have been proposed to protect the security and privacy of RFID systems.

One approach is called Yet Another Trivial RFID Authentication Protocol (YA-TRAP), proposed by Tsudik [18]. In this approach, a technique for the inexpensive untraceable identification of RFID tags is introduced. Here *untraceable* means it is computationally difficult to gather information about the identity of RFID tags from the interaction with them. In YA-TRAP, for the purpose of authentication, only minimal communication between the reader and tags is needed, and the computational burden on the back-end server is small.

The back-end server in the system is assumed to be secure and maintains all tag information. Each tag should be initialized with three values: K_i, T_0, and T_{max}. K_i is both the ID and the cryptographic key for this tag. The size of K_i depends on the number of tags and the secure authentication requirement; in practice, 160 bits is enough. T_0 is the initial timestamp of this tag. The value of T_0 of each tag does not

need to vary. This means that a group of tags can have the same T_0. T_{max} is the maximum value of T_0, and a group of tags can also have the same T_{max} value. In addition, each tag has a seeded pseudorandom number generator.

YA-TRAP works as follows: First, each tag should store a timestamp T_t in its memory. When an RFID reader wants to interrogate an RFID tag, it will send the current timestamp T_r to this tag. Receiving T_r, the tag will compare T_r with the timestamp value it stores and with T_{max}. If $T_r < T_t$ or $T_r > T_{max}$, this tag will respond to the reader with a random value generated by the seeded pseudorandom number generator. Otherwise, the tag will replace T_t with T_r and calculate $H_r = HMACK_i(T_t)$, and then send H_r to the reader. Then the reader will send T_r and H_r to the back-end server. The server will look up its database to find whether this tag is a valid tag. If it is not, the server will send a tag-error message to the reader. If this is a valid tag, the server will send the meta-ID of this tag or the valid message to the reader, according to different application requirements. Because the purpose of this protocol is to minimize interaction between the reader and tags and minimize the computation burden of the back-end server, it has some vulnerability. One of them is that the adversary can launch a DoS attack to the tag. For example, the attack can send a timestamp $t < T_{max}$, but this t is wildly inaccurate with the current time. In this case, the tag will update its timestamp with the wrong time and the legal reader cannot get access to this tag.

Jechlitschek [16] proposed another approach called *deterministic hash locks* [4]. In this scheme, the security of RFID systems is based on the one-way hash function. During initialization, every tag in the system will be given a meta-ID, which is the hash code of a random key. This meta-ID will be stored in the tag's memory. Both the meta-ID and the random key are also stored in the back-end server. After initialization, all the tags will enter the locked state. When they stay in the locked state, tags will respond only with the meta-ID when interrogated by an RFID reader. When a legitimate reader wants to unlock a tag, as shown in Fig. 21.2, it will first send a request to the tag. After receiving the meta-ID from the tag, the reader will send this meta-ID to the back-end server. The back-end server will search in its database using this meta-ID to get the random key. Then it will send this key to the reader, and the reader will send it to the tag. Using this random key, the tag will hash this key and compare the hash code with its

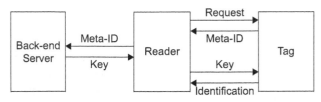

FIGURE 21.2 Tag unlock. *Meta-ID*, meta-identifier.

meta-ID. The tag will unlock itself and send its actual identification to the reader if these two values match. Then the tag will return to the locked state to prevent hijacking of illegal readers. Because the illegal reader cannot contact the back-end server to get the random key, it cannot get the actual identification of the tag.

One problem with deterministic hash locks is that when the tag is queried, it will respond with its meta-ID. Because the meta-ID of the tag is static and cannot change, the tag can be tracked easily. To solve this problem, Weis, Sarma, Rivest, and Engels proposed the Randomized Hash Locks protocol to prevent tracking of the tag. In this protocol, each tag is equipped with not only the one-way hash function but also a random number generator. When the tag is requested by a reader, it will use the random number generator to generate a random number and will hash this random number together with its identification. The tag will respond with this hash code and the random number to the reader. After receiving this response from the tag, the reader will get all identifications of the tags from the back-end server. Using these identifications, the reader will perform a brute force search by hashing the identification of each tag together with the random number and compare the hash code. If there is a match, the reader can know the identification of the tag. In this approach, the tag response to the reader does not depend on the request of the reader, which means that the tag is vulnerable to replay attack. To avoid this, Juels and Weis proposed a protocol called Improved Randomized Hash-Locks [19].

Radio Frequency Identification System Using Public Key Cryptography

Symmetric key cryptography can provide security for RFID systems, but it is more suitable to for implementation in a closed environment. If the shared secret keys between them are leaked, it will impose a big problem for the security of RFID systems. Public key cryptography is more suitable for open systems, because both RFID readers and tags can use their public keys to protect the security of RFID systems. In addition, using public key cryptography cannot prevent leakage of information to the eavesdropper attack during communication between reader and tags, and it also can provide digital signatures for both the readers and tags for authentication. In the public key cryptography system, an RFID reader does not need to keep all of the secret keys for each tag and does not need to search the appropriate key for each tag as it does in a symmetric key cryptography system. This will reduce the system burden for key management. Although public key cryptography has some advantages over symmetric key cryptography, it is commonly accepted that public key cryptography is computationally more expensive than symmetric key cryptography. Because of the limitations of memory and computational power of the ordinary RFID tags, it is difficult for the public key cryptography to be implemented in RFID systems. Research shows that some kinds of public key—based cryptographies such as elliptic curve and hyperelliptic curve are feasible to be implemented in high-end RFID tags [20].

Authentication With Public Key Cryptography

Basically, two different kinds of RFID tag authentication methods use public key cryptography: online authentication and offline authentication [21].

For the authentication of RFID tags in an online situation, the reader is connected with a database server. The database server stores a large number of challenge-response pairs for each tag, which makes it difficult for the attacker to test all of the challenge-response pairs during a limited period. During the challenge-response pair enrollment phase, the physical unclonable function part of RFID systems will be challenged by a Certification Authority with a variety of challenges, and accordingly it will generate responses for these challenges. The physical unclonable function is embodied in a physical object and can give responses to the given challenges [20]. Then these generated challenge-response pairs will be stored in the database server.

In the authentication phase, when a reader wants to authenticate a tag, first the reader will send a request to the tag for its identification. After getting the ID of the tag, the reader will search the database server to get a challenge-response pair for this ID and send the challenge to the tag. After receiving the challenge from the reader, the tag will challenge its physical unclonable function to get a response for this challenge and then send this response to the reader. The reader will compare this received response with the response stored in the database server. If the difference between these two responses is less than a certain predetermined threshold, the tag can pass the authentication. Then the database server will remove this challenge-response pair for this ID.

One paper [20] details how the authentication of RFID tags works in an offline situation using public key cryptography. To provide offline authentication for the tags, a physical unclonable function (PUF) Certification Identification—based scheme is proposed. In this method, a standard identification scheme and a standard signature scheme are used. Then the security of RFID systems depends on the security of the PUF, the standard identification scheme, and the standard signature scheme. For the standard identification scheme, an elliptic curve discrete log based on Okamoto's Identification protocol [22] is used. This elliptic curve discrete log protocol is feasible for implementation in the RFID tags.

Identity-Based Cryptography Used in Radio Frequency Identification Networks

An identity-based cryptographic scheme is a kind of public key—based approach that was first proposed by Shamir [23] in 1984. To use identity-based cryptography in RFID systems, because both the RFID tags and the reader have identities, it is convenient to use their own identities to generate their public keys.

An RFID system based on identity-based cryptography should be set up with the help of a private key generator (PKG). When the reader and tags enter the system, each is allocated a unique identity stored in their memory. The process of key generation and distribution in the RFID system that uses identity-based cryptography is shown in Fig. 21.3:

1. PKG generates a "master" public key, *PUpkg*, and a related "master" private key *PRpkg* and saves them in its memory.
2. The RFID reader authenticates itself to the PKG with its identity, *IDre*.
3. If the reader can pass the authentication, PKG generates a unique private key, *PRre*, for the reader and sends this private key together with *PUpkg* to reader.
4. When an RFID tag enters the system, it authenticates itself to the PKG with its identity, *IDta*.
5. If the tag can pass the authentication, PKG generates a unique private key, *PRta*, for the tag and sends *PRta* together with *PUpkg* and the identity of the reader, *IDre*, to the tag.

After this process, the reader can know its private key, *PRre*, and can use *PUpkg* and its identity to generate its public key. Every tag entered into the system can know its own private key and can generate a public key of its own and a public key of the reader.

If an RFID tag is required to transmit messages to the reader in security, because the tag can generate the reader's public key, *PUre*, it can use this key, *PUre* to encrypt the message and transmit this encrypted message to the reader. As shown in Fig. 21.4, after receiving the message from the tag, the reader can use its private key, *PRre*, to decrypt the message. Because only the reader can know its private key, *PRre*, the security of the message can be protected.

Fig. 21.5 illustrates the scheme for the reader to create its digital signature and verify it. First, the reader will use the message and the hash function to generate a hash code, and then it uses its private key *PRre* to encrypt this hash code to generate the digital signature and attach it to the original message and send both the digital signature and message to the tag. After receiving them, the RFID tag can use the public key of the reader *PUre* to decrypt the digital signature to recover the hash code. By comparing this hash code with the hash code generated from the message, the RFID tag can verify the digital signature.

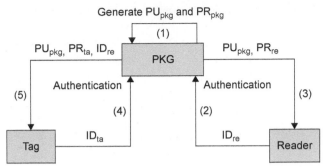

FIGURE 21.3 Key generation and distribution. *PKG*, private key generator.

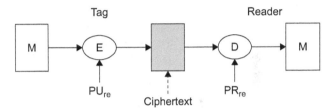

FIGURE 21.4 Message encryption.

Fig. 21.6 illustrates the scheme for the RFID tag to create its digital signature and verify it. In RFID systems, the reader cannot know the identity of the tag before reading it from the tag. The reader cannot generate the public key of the tag, so the general protocol used in identity-based networks cannot be used here. In our approach, first, the tag will use its identity and its private key, *PRta*, to generate a digital signature. When the tag needs to authenticate itself to the reader, it will add this digital signature to its identity, encrypt it with the public key of the reader, *PUre*, and send it to the reader; only the reader can decrypt this ciphertext and get the identity of the tag and the digital signature. Using the tag identity, the reader can generate the tag's public key, *PUta*. Then the reader can use this public key to verify the digital signature.

As mentioned, the most important problem for the symmetric key approach in RFID systems is key management. The RFID tags need a great deal of memory to store all of the secret keys related to each tag in the system for message decryption. Also, if the RFID reader receives a message from a tag, it cannot know which tag this message is from and therefore cannot know which key it can use to decrypt the message. The reader needs to search all of the keys until it finds the right one. In RFID systems using identity-based cryptography, every tag can use the public key of the reader to generate the ciphertext that can be decrypted using the reader's private key, so the reader does not need to know the key of the tags; all it needs to keep is its own private key.

FIGURE 21.5 A digital signature from a reader.

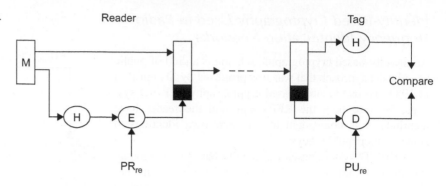

FIGURE 21.6 A digital signature from a tag.

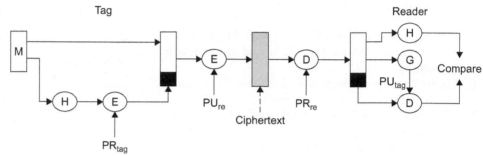

In some RFID applications such as epassports and visas, tag authentication is required. However, the symmetric key approach cannot provide digital signatures for RFID tags to authenticate them to RFID readers. By using an identity-based scheme, the tags can generate digital signatures using their private keys and store them in the tags. When they need to authenticate themselves to RFID readers, they can transmit these digital signatures to the reader, and the reader can verify them using the tags' public keys.

In identity-based cryptography RFID systems, because the identity of the tags and reader can be used to generate public keys, the PKG does not need to keep the key directory, so it can reduce the resource requirements. Another advantage of using identity-based cryptography in RFID systems is that the reader does not need to know the public keys of the tags in advance. If the reader wants to verify the digital signature of an RFID tag, it can read the identity of the tag and use the public key generated from the identity to verify the digital signature.

An inherent weakness of identity-based cryptography is the key escrow problem. However, in RFID systems that use identity-based cryptography, because all devices can be within one company or organization, the PKG can be highly trusted and protected, and the chance of key escrow can be reduced.

Another problem of identity-based cryptography is revocation. For example, people always use their public information such as their names or home addresses to generate their public key. If a person's private keys are compromised by an attacker, because public information cannot be changed easily, this will make it difficult to regenerate new public keys. In contrast, in RFID systems the identity of the tag is used to generate the public key. If the private key of one tag has been compromised, the system can allocate a new identity to the tag and use this new identity to create a new private key to the tag effortlessly.

4. SUMMARY

Like any information technology, RFID presents security and privacy risks that must be carefully mitigated through management, operational, and technical controls to realize the numerous benefits the technology has to offer. When practitioners adhere to sound security engineering principles, RFID technology can help a wide range of organizations and individuals realize substantial productivity gains and efficiencies. These organizations and individuals include hospitals and patients, retailers and customers, and manufacturers and distributors throughout the supply chain. This chapter provided detailed coverage of RFID technology, the associated security and privacy risks, and recommended practices that will enable organizations to realize productivity improvements while safeguarding sensitive information and protecting the privacy of individuals. Whereas RFID security is a rapidly evolving field with a number of promising innovations expected in coming years, these guidelines focus on controls that are commercially available today.

Finally, let us move on to the real interactive part of this chapter: review questions/exercises, hands-on projects, case projects, and the optional team case project. The answers and/or solutions by chapter can be found in the Online Instructor's Solutions Manual.

CHAPTER REVIEW QUESTIONS/ EXERCISES

True/False

1. True or False? Data carriers attached to objects are called RFID tags.
2. True or False? Currently, because different frequencies are used for RFID systems in various countries and many standards are adopted for different kinds of application, there is an agreement on a universal standard that is accepted by all parties.
3. True or False? Increasingly more companies and organizations have begun to use RFID tags rather than traditional bar codes because RFID systems have many advantages over traditional bar code systems.
4. True or False? RFID tags can be classified into three categories based on the equipped computation power: basic, symmetric key, and public key.
5. True or False? Another main issue of concern in deploying RFID systems is the sniffing problem.

Multiple Choice

1. Besides the four basic types of attack (counterfeiting, sniffing, tracking, and DoS) in real-world applications, other threats exist to RFID systems, such as:
   A. Spoofing
   B. Temporal Key Integrity Protocols
   C. Application program interfaces
   D. Network areas
   E. Extensible Authentication Protocol framework
2. What happens when counterfeiters forge RFID tags by copying the information from a valid tag or adding some well-formed format information to a new tag in the RFID system?
   A. Middle layers
   B. DoS
   C. Tracking
   D. Sniffing
   E. Counterfeiting
3. What tags are available for the cheapest price, compared with symmetric key tags and public key tags?
   A. Symmetric key tags
   B. Public key tags
   C. Basic tags
   D. Authenticated routing tags
   E. All of the above
4. What uses a single key to perform both encryption and decryption?
   A. False base cryptography
   B. Symmetric key cryptography
   C. Eavesdropping cryptography
   D. Man-in-the-middle cryptography
   E. Passive cryptography
5. What can provide security for RFID systems but is more suitable for implementation in a closed environment?
   A. HELLO Flood connectivity
   B. DoS attack connectivity
   C. Internet connectivity
   D. Symmetric key cryptography
   E. All of the above

EXERCISE

Problem

What provisions are made for code security?

Hands-on Projects

Project

How can you ensure the security of EPC data?

Case Projects

Problem

Personnel and asset tracking in a health care environment is a hypothetical case study to illustrate how RFID security might be implemented in practice. Although the case study is fictional, it is intended to resemble real-world activities, including how decision makers address common and expected RFID security problems and their solutions. The case study does not cover *all* of the aspects of RFID system engineering or operations that an organization may encounter in its RFID implementation, but rather a representative sample of salient issues. The case study follows.

The Fringe Science Research Center (FSRC) is a health care facility dedicated to the study of highly contagious diseases: those transmitted through casual human contact. The Center has 80 beds for patient care, a radiology unit with four rooms of sophisticated imaging equipment, and eight laboratories with various diagnostic and research capabilities. The Center confronts the same management issues as many hospitals, including locating portable diagnostic equipment when needed and accounting for missing assets. Another important concern is the ability to locate patients and staff quickly as they move about the facility. Poor asset management results in higher costs, reduced efficiency, and lower quality of care.

The mission of the FSRC also leads to specialized requirements. To prevent unnecessary outbreaks of disease and understand how transmission occurs, FSRC needs to track interactions among its staff, patients, and visitors. These tracked interactions provide useful information to researchers about who came into contact with whom and at what time. In addition, the FSRC must alert caregivers of disease-specific protocols when they are in close proximity to particular patients, including prohibiting staff contact in some cases. It must track blood, urine, and stool samples from patient to laboratory. Finally, the FSRC would like to track the history of in-house diagnostic equipment and trace how the equipment is used to support patients throughout each day. Currently, paper processes are used to achieve these objectives, but they are labor-intensive and error-prone, sometimes with fatal consequences.

FSRC executives tasked the FSRC's chief information officer (CIO) to use RFID technology to improve the FSRC's traditional asset management function, as well as meet its specialized requirements. Working with the FSRC executives, how did the CIO go about commissioning a project to reengineer FSRC business practices by using RFID technology as a primary tool to improve organizational performance?

Optional Team Case Project

Problem

Supply chain management of hazardous materials is also a hypothetical case study to illustrate how RFID security might be implemented in practice. Although the case study is fictional, it is intended to resemble real-world activities, including how decision makers address common and expected RFID security problems and their solutions. The case study does not cover *all* of the aspects of RFID system engineering or operations that an organization may encounter in its RFID implementation, but rather a representative sample of salient issues. The case study follows.

The RAD Corporation oversees the movement of radioactive research materials among production facilities, national laboratories, military installations, and other relevant locations. RAD oversight of the supply chain for these materials involves many of the same issues as in nearly any other supply chain. RAD wants to know who is in possession of what quantity of materials at any given time. It also wants to locate materials at a site quickly, without having to search through numerous containers to find them. Bar code technology does not provide that capability.

Some of RAD's requirements are more unique. For instance, much of the transported radionuclide material must be closely monitored because extreme temperatures or excessive vibration can make it useless for its intended applications. Consequently, RAD wants temperature and vibration sensors to measure environmental conditions and record readings continuously on the tag. In addition, the handling of RAD-regulated materials is a US Department of Homeland Security issue. If the materials were to fall into unauthorized hands, they could endanger public welfare. So, with the preceding in mind, how would RAD's project team go about conducting a risk assessment?

REFERENCES

[1] Auto-ID Center, Draft Protocol Specification for a Class 0 Radio Frequency Identification Tag, February 2003.

[2] P. Peris-Lopez, J.C. Hernandez-Castro, J. Estevez-Tapiador, A. Ribagorda, RFID systems: a survey on security threats and proposed solutions, in: 11th IFIP International Conference on Personal Wireless Communications — PWC06, Volume 4217 of Lecture Notes in Computer Science, Springer-Verlag, September 2006.

[3] T. Phillips, T. Karygiannis, R. Huhn, Security standards for the RFID market, IEEE Secur. Privacy (November/December 2005) 85—89.

[4] S. Weis, S. Sarma, R. Rivest, D. Engels, in: Security and Privacy Aspects of Low-Cost Radio Frequency Identification Systems, Springer-Verlag, 2003, pp. 454—469.

[5] D. Haehnel, W. Burgard, D. Fox, K. Fishkin, M. Philipose, Mapping and localization with WID technology, in: International Conference on Robotics & Automation, 2004.

[6] A. Juels, R.L. Rivest, M. Syzdlo, The blocker tag: selective blocking of RFID tags for consumer privacy, in: V. Atluri (Ed.), 8th ACM Conference on Computer and Communications Security, 2003, pp. 103—111.

[7] S.E. Sarma, S.A. Weis, D.W. Engels, RFID Systems Security and Privacy Implications, Technical Report, MITAUTOID-WH-014, AutoID Center, MIT, 2002.

[8] S. Inoue, H. Yasuura, RFID privacy using user-controllable uniqueness, in: RFID Privacy Workshop, MIT, November 2003.

[9] N. Good, J. Han, E. Miles, D. Molnar, D. Mulligan, L. Quilter, J. Urban, D. Wagner, Radio frequency ID and privacy with information goods, in: Workshop on Privacy in the Electronic Society (WPES), 2004.

[10] A. Juels, C. Blundo, S. Cimato, Minimalist cryptography for low-cost RFID tags, in: C. Blundo, S. Cimato (Eds.), The Fourth International Conference on Security in Communication Networks — SCN 2004, Vol. 3352 of Lecture Notes in Computer Science, Springer-Verlag, 2004, pp. 149—164.

[11] A. Juels, R. Pappu, in: Squealing Euros: Privacy Protection in RFID-Enabled Banknotes, Springer-Verlag, 2003, pp. 103—121.

[12] P. Golle, M. Jakobsson, A. Juels, P. Syverson, Universal re-encryption for mixnets, in: T. Okamoto (Ed.), RSA Conference-cryptographers' Track (CT-RSA), 2964, 2004, pp. 163—178.

[13] G. Ateniese, J. Camenisch, B. de Madeiros, Untraceable RFID tags via insubvertible encryption, in: 12th ACM Conference on Computer and Communication Security, 2005.

[14] C. Floerkemeier, R. Schneider, M. Langheinrich, Scanning with a Purpose Supporting the Fair Information Principles in RFID Protocols, 2004.

[15] M.R. Rieback, B. Crispo, A. Tanenbaum, C. Boyd, J.M.G. Nieto, RFID guardian: a battery-powered mobile device for RFID privacy management, in: C. Boyd, J.M.G. Nieto (Eds.), Australasian Conference on Information Security and Privacy — ACISP 2005, Vol. 3574 of Lecture Notes in Computer Science, Springer-Verlag, 2005, pp. 184—194.

[16] M. Feldhofer, S. Dominikus, J. Wolkerstorfer, Strong authentication for RFID systems using the AES algorithm, in: M. Joye, J.-J. Quisquater (Eds.), Workshop on Cryptographic Hardware and Embedded Systems CHES 04, Vol. 3156 of Lecture Notes in Computer Science, Springer-Verlag, 2004, pp. 357–370.

[17] D. Molnar, D. Wagner, B. Pfitzmann, P. McDaniel, Privacy and security in library RFID: issues, practices, and architecturesACM Conference on Communications and Computer Security, in: B. Pfitzmann, P. McDaniel (Eds.), ACM Conference on Communications and Computer Security, ACM Press, 2004, pp. 210–219.

[18] G. Tsudik, YA-TRAP: yet another trivial RFID authentication protocol, in: Fourth Annual IEEE International Conference on Pervasive Computing and Communications Workshops (PERCOMW'06), 2006, pp. 640–643.

[19] A. Juels, S. Weis, Defining strong privacy for RFID, in: Pervasive Computing and Communications Workshops, 2007.

[20] P. Tuyls, L. Batina, D. Pointcheval, RFID tags for anticounterfeiting Topics in Cryptology-CT-RSA 2006, in: D. Pointcheval (Ed.), Topics in Cryptology-CT-rsa 2006, Springer-Verlag, 2006.

[21] L. Batina, J. Guajardo, T. Kerins, N. Mentens, P. Tuyls, I. Verbauwhede, Public-key cryptography for RFID-tags, in: Printed Handout of Workshop on RFID Security, RFIDSec06, 2006, pp. 61–76.

[23] T. Okamoto, E.F. Brickell, Provably secure and practical identification schemes and corresponding signature schemesAdvances in Cryptology | CRYPTO'92, Vol. 740 of LNCS, in: E.F. Brickell (Ed.), Advances in Cryptology | CRYPTO'92, Vol. 740 of LNCS, Springer-Verlag, 1992, pp. 31–53.

[23] A. Shamir, Identity-based cryptosystems and signature scheme, in: Advances in Cryptology: Proceedings of CRYPTO 84, LNCS, 1984, pp. 47–53.

Chapter 22

Optical Network Security

Lauren Collins
Winning Edge Communications, Frankfort, IL, United States

Note: This chapter is available in its entirety online at store.elsevier.com/product.jsp?isbn= 9780128038437 (click the Resources tab at the bottom of the page).

1. ABSTRACT

Fault and attack survivability issues concerning security in all optical networks require a new approach that takes into consideration the physical characteristics of optical networks. Furthermore, unlike the case in which electronic networks regenerate signals at every node, attack detection and isolation schemes may not have access to the overhead bits used to transport supervisory information between regenerators or switching sites to perform their functions. This chapter presents an analysis of attack and protection problems in optical networks. It also proposes a conceptual framework for modeling attack problems and protection schemes for optical networks.

2. CONTENTS

Optical Network Security

Lauren Collins

ABSTRACT

CONTENTS

Chapter 23

Optical Wireless Security

Scott R. Ellis
kCura Corporation, Chicago, IL, United States

Note: This chapter is available in its entirety online at store.elsevier.com/product.jsp?isbn= 9780128038437 (click the Resources tab at the bottom of the page).

1. ABSTRACT

Optical wireless systems provide a high degree of physical security, if only because the signals are difficult to intercept. They typically take place high above ground. This, in and of itself, helps protect it from tampering and intrusion. Furthermore, optical wireless networking transmissions occur on the physical, or layer 1, level. Optical and copper cables are far more vulnerable to unauthorized access. The level of difficulty of interception of optical wireless signals that use narrow beam technology makes this form of network communication the most appealing choice for establishing communications between remote locations. This chapter focuses on free space optics and the security that has been developed to protect its transmission, and presents an overview of the basic technology. Security of communications is thought of primarily as having to do with the security of the data itself. Of secondary, yet no less important interest is the physical security. Tapping into communication links that traverse public space is difficult to detect, and cabling and fiber are vulnerable once they leave the building and enter basements, attics, tunnels, and other untended locations. The topic of optical wireless security is one of physical security. On the physical layer, it is one of the most secure forms of communication. On a higher, protocol level, technologies such as Advanced Encryption Standard 128 or 256 provide excellent security and can be implemented with optical systems in the same manner as any other system with no special considerations.

2. CONTENTS

Computer and Information Security Handbook. http://dx.doi.org/10.1016/B978-0-12-803843-7.00023-5

Part II

Managing Information Security

Chapter 24

Information Security Essentials for Information Technology Managers: Protecting Mission-Critical Systems

Albert Caballero

HBO Latin America, Surfside, FL, United States

1. INTRODUCTION

Information security involves the protection of organizational assets from the disruption of business operations, modification of sensitive data, or disclosure of proprietary information. The protection of this data is usually described as maintaining the confidentiality, integrity, and availability (CIA) of an organization's assets, operations, and information. Beyond that, information security must become a design consideration at the core of every infrastructure, application, and system. It is no longer sufficient to look at information security as maintaining the three basic tenants of CIA. While these core concepts remain the holy grail of security, the protection mechanisms needed to ensure that these three tenants are sustained in any environment can take many forms. Information security controls must have situational awareness and must be implemented with customized tactics and varying methodologies to be effective. One philosophy security professionals can adopt which transcends the three basic tenants listed in this section is to consider every aspect of implementation in three fundamental areas: Attack Resiliency, Incident Readiness, and Security Maturity depicted in Fig. 24.1.

Attack resiliency helps protect core business assets from internal and external attacks by implementing strong technical controls and adhering to industry best practices. When considering how to protect assets and data it is important to make the distinction between on-premise, public cloud, private cloud, and hybrid environments. When protecting assets that are in a public cloud the traditional protection mechanisms will not suffice, and in many cases they will not apply because the subscriber will have little or no access to the underlying infrastructure or operating systems. When building a private cloud infrastructure the data owners remain autonomous and are responsible for all of their own security operations, which can be a double-edged sword. If there isn't a highly skilled and experienced IT team with a supporting security design architect, or if the IT organization is not able to perform, automate, and deliver at the level of a service provider then it is easy to let potentially dangerous considerations fall by the wayside.

Incident readiness is a key strategic component that can help in early detection of security breaches or incidents. When a security breach is detected it is common for an organization to call in professional help from the outside to assist with incident response and recovery, especially if they run their own private or hybrid cloud environment. A common issue is that when the third party is engaged and appears on-site to help, the first thing they do is request relevant information such as log data, packet captures, and forensic images. If an organization has not put the necessary controls in place before the security incident occurs, then it often happens that all traces of the breach are overwritten or deleted by the time it's investigated. Tools that perform functions such as capturing event logs and vulnerability data, network packet inspection, end point recording, and live response will help build the visibility needed to effectively identify and respond to security incidents whenever they are discovered.

Even today, organizations have not reached a level of security maturity that will significantly deter attackers from compromising their data. Building a mature information security program with a comprehensive, risk-based, and business-aligned strategy is necessary for other controls to

Computer and Information Security Handbook. http://dx.doi.org/10.1016/B978-0-12-803843-7.00024-7

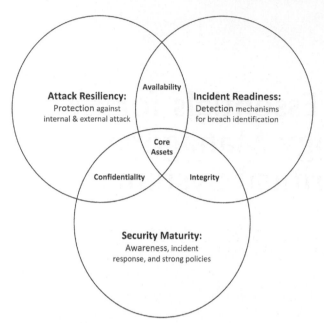

FIGURE 24.1 Information security strategy.

be effective. Among the items that are part of mature information security programs are policies that make sense, a detailed incident response plan, and an all-inclusive user awareness program. Information security management as a field is ever increasing in demand and responsibility as most organizations are spending larger percentages of their IT budgets in attempting to manage risk and mitigate intrusions. For information security managers, it is critical to maintain a clear perspective of all the areas of business that require protection.

Through collaboration with other business units, security managers must work security into the processes of each area within the organization, as security is not an IT issue, it is a business issue. The evolution of what it means to embark on this security journey as an information security manager is depicted in Fig. 24.2 [12]. We have moved from an ad-hoc and infrastructure-based mentality to compliance-based and

threat-based. The next evolution must consist of a risk-based paradigm that strives to be aligned with the business. Securing the organization's technical infrastructure can no longer provide complete protection for assets, nor will it protect other things that are not dependent on technology for their existence or protection, such as the people and business. Thus, the organization that does not evolve into a business-aligned security strategy will ultimately be lulled into a false sense of security relying solely on the perception of what is important without taking into account what is truly core to the business.

2. PROTECTING MISSION-CRITICAL SYSTEMS

Information security is a business issue in that the entire organization must frame and solve security problems based on its own strategic drivers, not solely on technical controls aimed to mitigate certain types of attack. Information security goes beyond technical controls and encompasses people, technology, policy, and operations in a way that few other business objectives do. At the core of any organization are its mission-critical systems. These are systems without which the mission of the business cannot be accomplished. The major components to protecting these systems are detailed throughout this chapter; however, there are some key components that must be understood for the continuity of any organization. Some of these key components include understanding the business goals, operational risk, threat strategy, and risk management techniques needed for success. The design and implementation of these techniques are typically based on a paradigm of protect, detect, and react. This means that in addition to incorporating protection mechanisms, organizations need to include detection tools that allow them to react and recover quickly from inevitable attacks. Fig. 24.3 depicts a business-aligned security strategy that addresses all of these areas in a control framework provided by Optiv Security [13].

FIGURE 24.2 The security journey: a business-aligned strategy.

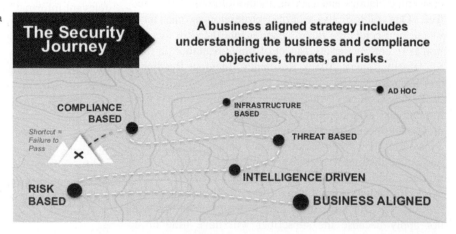

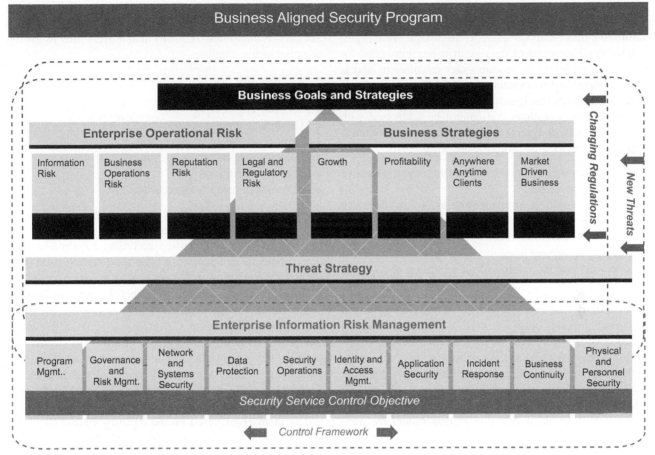

FIGURE 24.3 Business-aligned security program.

Information Risk Management

Risk is, in essence, the likelihood of something going wrong and compromising the ability of an organization to conduct business. Due to the ramifications of such risk, an organization should try to reduce the risk to an acceptable level. This process is known as information risk management. Risk to an organization and its information assets, similar to threats, comes in many different forms. Some of the most common risks to organizations other than cyber-attacks are:

- Physical damage: Fire, water, vandalism, power loss, and natural disasters.
- Human interaction: Accidental or intentional action or inaction that can disrupt productivity.
- Equipment malfunctions: Failure of systems and peripheral devices.
- Internal and external attack: Hacking, cracking, hacktivism, distributed denial-of-service (DDoS), etc.
- Misuse of data: Sharing trade secrets; fraud, espionage, and theft.

- Loss of data: Intentional or unintentional loss of information through destructive means.
- Application error: Computation errors, input errors, and buffer overflows.

The idea of risk management is that threats of all kinds must be identified, classified, and evaluated to calculate their damage potential. This is easier said than done. During risk analysis there are several units that can help measure risk. Before risk can be measured though, the organization must identify the vulnerabilities and threats against its mission-critical systems in terms of business continuity. During risk analysis, an organization tries to evaluate the cost for each security control that helps mitigate the risk. If the control is cost-effective relative to the exposure of the organization, then the control is put in place. Risk is traditionally defined as a product of threat, vulnerability, and potential impact:

$$\text{Risk} = \text{Threat} \times \text{Vulnerability} \times \text{Impact}.$$

When assessing the cost of a potential risk there are two primary types of analysis: quantitative and qualitative. Quantitative risk analysis attempts to assign meaningful numbers to all elements of the risk. It is recommended for large, costly projects that require exact calculations and is typically performed to examine the viability of a project's cost or time objectives. Quantitative risk analysis provides answers to three questions that cannot be addressed with deterministic risk and project management such as traditional cost estimating or project scheduling [19]:

1. What's the probability of meeting the project objective given all known risks?
2. How much could the overrun or delay be, and therefore how much contingency do we need for the organization's desired level of certainty?
3. Where in the project is the most risk, given the model of the project and the totality of all identified and quantified risks?

Qualitative risk analysis does not assign numerical values but instead opts for general categorization by severity levels. Where little or no numerical data is available for a risk assessment, the qualitative approach is the most appropriate. The qualitative approach does not require heavy mathematics; instead, it thrives more on the people participating and their backgrounds. Qualitative analysis enables classification of risk that is determined by wide experience and knowledge captured within the process. Ultimately it is not an exact science, so the process will count on expert opinions for its base assumptions. The assessment process uses a structured and documented approach. It is also quite common to calculate risk as a single loss expectancy (SLE) or annual loss expectancy (ALE) by project or business function to determine cost over time.

3. INFORMATION SECURITY ESSENTIALS FOR INFORMATION TECHNOLOGY MANAGERS

In the information security industry there have been several initiatives to attempt to define security management and how to apply it. There are many universities that have begun to offer bachelor's and master's degrees in the area of information security. These typically consist of coursework in Management Information Systems, Computer Sciences, or Electrical Engineering. In addition to traditional educational institutions there are organizations such as the SANS Institute [16] that have built extensive curriculums and certifications around information security practices that are truly world class. Another example of an organization that has developed a Common Body of Knowledge (CBK) that is comprehensive and has proven to be complete enough to lay down a solid foundation for

most security professionals is ISC2 [11]. They offer a certification called the Certified Information Systems Security Professional (CISSP) that covers the following domains of knowledge:

- Security and risk management
- Asset security
- Security engineering
- Communications and network security
- Identity and asset management
- Security assessment and testing
- Security operations
- Software development security

In addition to individual certification there must be guidelines to turn this knowledge into actionable skills that can be measured and verified according to some international standard or framework. The most widely used standards for maintaining and improving information security is ISO/IEC 27002, a standard published by the International Organization for Standardization (ISO) and by the International Electrotechnical Commission (IEC), titled Information Technology—Security techniques—Code of practice for information security management [7]. Also publishing security standards is the National Institute of Standards and Technologies (NIST) [10]. That being said, compliance requirements have also become standards in and of themselves based on the industry a particular business operates in. For example, healthcare organizations must abide by the Health Insurance Portability and Accountability Act (HIPAA) and if you store consumer credit card information then there are the standards established by Visa and MasterCard for the Payment Card Industry (PCI). All of these security standards and compliance requirements are ultimately designed to help mitigate the risk of threats. So what are the most common threats and attacks an information security manager should be aware of?

Common Threats and Attacks

Threats to information systems come in many flavors, some with malicious intent, and others with unexpected surprises. Threats can be deliberate acts of espionage, extortion, or sabotage; however, more often than not it happens that the biggest threats can be forces of nature (hurricane, flood) or acts of human error. It is easy to become consumed in attempting to anticipate and mitigate every threat, but this is simply not possible. Threat agents are threats only when they are provided the opportunity to take advantage of vulnerability, and ultimately there is no guarantee that the vulnerability will be exploited. Therefore, determining which threats are important can only be done from within the context of your organization. The process by which a threat can actually cause damage to your organization is as

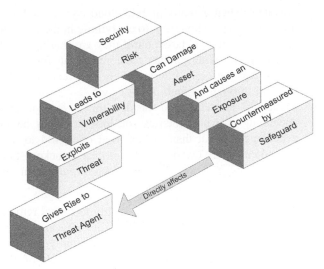

FIGURE 24.4 The threat process.

follows: A threat agent gives rise to a threat that exploits a vulnerability and can lead to a security risk that can damage your assets and cause an exposure. This can be countermeasured by a safeguard that directly counteracts the threat agent. Fig. 24.4 shows the building blocks of the threat process.

Threats are exploited with a variety of attacks, some technical, others not so much. Organizations that focus on the technical attacks and neglect items such as policies and procedures or employee training and awareness are setting information security up for failure. The mantra that the IT department, or even the security department, by itself can secure an organization is as antiquated as black-and-white

television. Most threats today are a mixed blend of automated information gathering, social engineering, and combined exploits, giving the perpetrator endless vectors through which to gain access.

We've all heard the sequence of events depicted in Fig. 24.5. Step one, an attacker targets a victim and identifies vulnerability. This does not necessarily have to be a technical vulnerability in an application or system that gets exploited. In fact, often it is an end user's credential that gets compromised through email phishing or some other low-tech mechanism. Once the vulnerability gets exploited the attacker gains access to some asset. This can be an asset like a web server, drive repository, cloud resource, or email inbox. Initial access may be at a user level but by monitoring user activity, data points, and network behavior inside the victim's environment it's only a matter of time before they gain privileged access and are able to compromise the entire infrastructure.

Once privileged access is gained it is game over and the attacker can choose to steal, destroy, or leak data as they see fit. One common goal is disruption of commerce such as defacing a website or denial-of-service (DoS), if that's the case, then it is usually attributed to hacktivists who want to call out some ethical or political ideal that is in conflict with their own. If the intent is identity theft, monetary gain, or fraud then it is quite possible you are dealing with organized crime and notifying the authorities may be a reasonable option. It could also be that they are after intellectual property or conducting some sort of cyber espionage in which case you may be dealing with a competitor, nation-state, or well-funded group with strategic objectives.

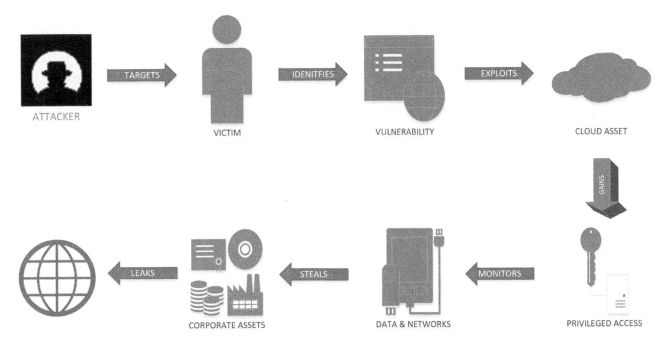

FIGURE 24.5 Targeting victims and exploiting vulnerability.

We have observed a disturbing trend from business disruption and theft to the destruction of data and infrastructure. During the Sony Pictures Entertainment breach of 2014 the goal was to decimate the company and destroy its infrastructure, compromising the identity and reputation of executives. This is a paradigm shift to what we have seen in the past and seems to have been a concerted effort between well-funded, organized attackers and disgruntled employees. It is important for every organization to try and avoid becoming a target for this type of deliberate attack because it is easier to accomplish and more destructive than most people would like to admit. Some of the security threats we should be concerned about, especially if cloud computing is introduced, are [4]:

- Data breaches: The ultimate goal is unauthorized access to company data. The motives or intent of the attacker once a data breach is successful may vary, but in every case this is step one in a successful attack. Data breaches may originate in the cloud or a user system and quickly propagate internally or vice versa, but data protection is paramount in this interconnected, Internet of Things (IoT) world we live in.
- Data loss: Losing data due to an attack is one thing; however, there is a real possibility that simply by virtue of having data in a public cloud environment an organization can experience unexpected data loss. The possibilities are many but anything from a disruption of service on the provider's end to an incompatibility in the interfaces between providers it becomes inevitable that during migration or access there could be some data that is lost and must be recreated.
- Account or service hijacking: This is not a new threat; however, using the cloud for mission-critical services may lead to added exposure. Cloud services are all managed by some account somewhere, and usually by several accounts. Both the subscriber and the provider have individuals that manage the cloud service instance and therefore there are more people that have access to the data and related services than would otherwise.
- Nonsecure APIs: Nowadays application programming interfaces (APIs) equate to remote desktop sessions in traditional IT infrastructures. They are the primary mechanism by which you manage, provision, and modify a specific environment. The problem arises when an administrator does not properly secure their APIs and do not require the proper authorization when performing administrative tasks. This can lead to unauthorized and even unauthenticated privileged access to what would otherwise be restricted management activities.
- DoS: The potential for a DoS attack continues to be a threat to all environments but the issue becomes more

prevalent when a shared public cloud service is being used. An organization may do everything in their power to avoid becoming a target but if they are sharing cloud infrastructure with another customer that for some reason has become a target then they can also be affected through no fault of their own.
- Malicious insiders: The insider threat is real and depending on which metrics you look at it may be an even bigger threat than the external one. Add to this the potential of dealing with internal attackers that may not even work for your own organization its possible for this threat to increase.

Examples of attacks vary from highly technical remote exploits over the Internet to social engineering an administrative assistant to reset a password or simply walking right through an unprotected door in the back of the building. All scenarios have the potential to be equally devastating to the security of the organization. The following are some of the most common attacks.

- Malicious code (malware): Malware is a broad category; however, it is typically software designed to infiltrate or damage a computer system without the owner's informed consent.
- Social engineering: The art of manipulating people into performing actions or divulging information. Similar to a confidence trick or simple fraud, the term typically applies to trickery to gain information or computer system access; in most cases, the attacker never comes face to face with the victim.
- Industrial espionage: Industrial espionage describes activities such as theft of trade secrets, bribery, blackmail, and technological surveillance as well as spying on commercial organizations and sometimes governments.
- Spam, phishing, and hoaxes: Spamming and phishing, although different, often go hand in hand. Spamming is the abuse of electronic messaging systems to indiscriminately send unsolicited bulk messages, many of which contain hoaxes or other undesirable contents such as links to phishing sites. Phishing is the criminally fraudulent process of attempting to acquire sensitive information such as usernames, passwords, and credit card details by masquerading as a trustworthy entity in an electronic communication.
- DoS and DDoS: These are attempts to make a computer resource unavailable to its intended users. Although the means and motives for a DoS attack may vary, it generally consists of the concerted, malevolent efforts of a person or persons to prevent an Internet site or service from functioning efficiently or at all, temporarily or indefinitely.
- Botnets: The term botnet is generally used to refer to a collection of compromised computers (called zombies) running software, usually installed via worms, Trojan

Threat Detection Maturity Model

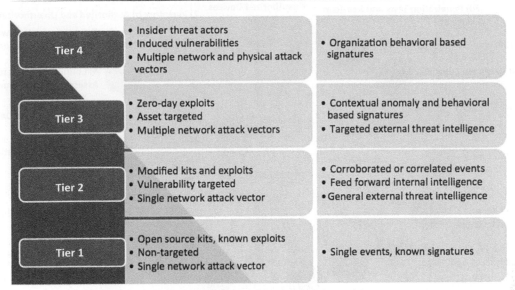

FIGURE 24.6 Threat detection maturity model.

horses, or backdoors, under a common command-and-control infrastructure.

Fig. 24.6 [18] depicts a Threat Detection Maturity Model evaluating the sophistication of attacks and what an organization needs to do to be able to detect such events. The higher the level of attack sophistication the more mature an organization's threat detection model needs to be.

4. SYSTEMS AND NETWORK SECURITY

Systems and network security is at the core of every information security strategy. Though physical security is extremely important and a breach could render all your systems and network security safeguards useless, without hardened systems and networks, anyone from the comfort of their own living room can take over your network, access your confidential information, and disrupt your operations. In many cases when an attacker gains access to a system, the first order of business is escalation of privileges. This means that the attacker gets in as a regular user and attempts to find ways to gain administrator or root privileges. The host system is the core of where data sits and is accessed, so it is therefore also the main target of many intruders. Regardless of the operating system that is selected to run certain applications and databases, the principles of hardening systems are the same and apply to all server systems as well as network devices, as we will see in the upcoming sections. Fig. 24.7 describes the top 20 controls necessary for a secure infrastructure according to SANS Institute [8].

The System

Some of the specific steps required to maintain host systems in as a secure state as possible are as follows:

- OS hardening: Guidelines by which a base operating system goes through a series of checks to make sure no unnecessary exposures remain open and that security features are enabled where possible. There is a series of organizations that publish OS hardening guides for various platforms.
- Removing unnecessary services: In any operating system there are usually services that are enabled but have no real business need. It is necessary to go through all the services of your main corporate image, on both the server side and client side, to determine which services are required and which would create a potential vulnerability if left enabled.
- Vulnerability management: All vendors release updates for known issues on some kind of schedule. Part of host-based security is making sure that all required vendor patches, at both the operating system and the application level, are applied as quickly as business operations allow on some kind of regular schedule. There should also be an emergency patch procedure in case there is an outbreak and updates need to be pushed out of sequence.
- Endpoint protection: Antivirus is dead—or at least many professionals believe it to be. Today antivirus programs are still required and used by most organizations but in reality they detect around 50% of potential malware on systems. It is important to familiarize

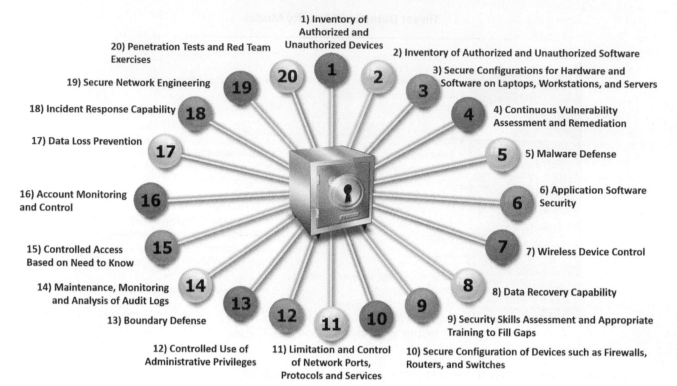

FIGURE 24.7 Top 20 information security controls.

yourself with technologies such as application whitelisting, behavior analysis, and endpoint forensics for true protection of the host operating system.

- Intrusion detection systems (IDS): Although many seem to think IDS is a network security function, there are many good host-based IDS applications, both commercial and open source, that can significantly increase security and act as an early warning system for possibly malicious traffic and/or files for which the anti virus does not have a definition.
- Firewalls: Host-based firewalls are not as popular as they once were because many big vendors such as Symantec, McAfee, and Checkpoint have moved to a host-based client application that houses all security functions in one and many operating systems include a built-in firewall. That being said there is another trend in the industry to move toward application-specific firewalls like those designed to run on a web or database server, for example.
- Data encryption: One item often overlooked is encryption of data while it is at rest. Many solutions have recently come onto the market that offer the ability to encrypt sensitive data such as credit card and Social Security numbers that sit on your file server or inside a database. This is a huge protection in the case of information theft or data leakage.
- Backup and restore: Without the ability to back up and restore both servers and clients in a timely fashion, an

issue that could be resolved in short order can quickly turn into a disaster; for example, something called ransomware is gaining popularity and it can be impossible to regain access to your data if you do not keep a viable backup available. Backup procedures should be in place and restored on a regular basis to verify their integrity.
- Event logging: Event logs are significant when you're attempting to investigate the root cause of an issue or incident. In many cases, logging is not turned on by default and needs to be enabled after the core installation of the host operating system or server services. The OS hardening guidelines for your organization should require that logging be enabled and centralized.

The Network

The network is the communication highway for everything that happens between all the systems. All data at one point or another passes over the wire and is potentially vulnerable to snooping or spying by the wrong person. The controls implemented on the network are similar in nature to those that can be applied to host systems; however, network-based security can be more easily classified into two main categories: detection and prevention. We will discuss security-monitoring tools in another section; for now the main functions of network-based security are to either detect a potential incident based on a set of events or prevent a known attack. Most network-based security devices can perform some detection or protection functions in one of two ways: signature or anomaly based (behavior analysis). Signature based detection and prevention is similar to antivirus signatures that look for known traits of a particular attack or malware. Anomaly or behavior-based systems can make decisions based on what is expected to be "normal" on the network or based on a certain set of mathematical algorithms, usually after a period of being installed in what is called "learning" or "monitor" mode, called machine learning.

Intrusion detection is the process of monitoring the traffic occurring on networks and analyzing them for signs of possible incidents that are violations or imminent threats to computer security policies, acceptable-use policies, and standard security practices. Incidents have many causes, such as malware (e.g., worms, spyware), attackers gaining unauthorized access, or even authorized users who misuse their privileges attempting to gain additional privileges for which they are not authorized. The most common detection technologies and their security functions on the network are as follows:

- Packet sniffing and network recording: These tools are used quite often by networking teams to troubleshoot connectivity issues; however, they can be a security professional's best friend during investigations and root-cause analysis. When properly deployed and maintained, a packet capture device on the network allows security professionals to reconstruct data and reverse engineer malware in a way that is simply not possible without a full packet capture of the communications.
- Intrusion detection systems: In these systems, appliances or servers monitor network traffic and run it through a rules engine to determine whether it is malicious according to its signature set. If the traffic is deemed malicious, an alert will fire and notify the monitoring system.
- Anomaly detection systems (machine learning): Aside from the actual packet data traveling on the wire, there are also traffic trends that can be monitored on the switches and routers to determine whether unauthorized or anomalous activity is occurring. With Net-flow and S-flow data that can be sent to an appliance or server, aggregated traffic on the network can be analyzed and can alert a monitoring system if there is a problem. Anomaly detection systems are extremely useful when there is an attack for which the IDS does not have a signature or if there is some activity occurring that is suspicious.

Intrusion prevention is a system that allows for the active blocking of attacks while they are in-line on the network, before they even get to the target host. There are many ways to prevent attacks or unwanted traffic from coming into your network, the most common of which is

known as a firewall. Although a firewall is mentioned quite commonly and a lot of people know what a firewall is, there are several different controls that can be put in place in addition to a firewall that can seriously help protect the network. Here are some common prevention technologies:

- Firewalls: The purpose of a firewall is to enforce an organization's security policy at the border of two networks. Typically, most firewalls are deployed at the edge between the internal network and the Internet (if there is such a thing) and are configured to block (prevent) any traffic from going in or out that is not allowed by the corporate security policy.
- Packet filtering: The most basic type of firewalls perform what is called stateful packet filtering, which means that they can remember which side initiated the connection, and rules (called access control lists, or ACLs) can be created based not only on IPs and ports but also depending on the state of the connection (whether the traffic is going into or out of the network).
- Secure socket layer (SSL) Proxies: The main difference between proxies and stateful packet-filtering firewalls is that proxies have the ability to terminate and reestablish connections between two end hosts, acting as a proxy for all communications and adding a layer of security and functionality to the regular firewalls. SSL is a certificate-based encryption technology that allows for the encryption of web traffic; that being said, SSL effectively disables the ability of most security devices to see an attack when it is happening. Due to this blinding of in-line security tools by SSL, SSL proxies have become a critical part of a security strategy. By terminating and reestablishing connections in and out of a network an SSL proxy can read the data being transferred and act as a protection mechanism that is no longer blind to encrypted communications.
- Application layer firewalls: Application firewalls have become increasingly popular; they are designed to protect certain types of applications (web or database) and can be configured to perform a level of blocking that is much more intuitive and granular, based not only on network information but also application-specific variables so that administrators can be much more precise in what they are blocking. In addition, app firewalls can typically be loaded with server-side SSL certificates, allowing the appliance to decrypt encrypted traffic, a huge benefit to a typical proxy or stateful firewall.
- Intrusion prevention systems: An intrusion prevention system (IPS) is software that has all the capabilities of an intrusion detection system and can also attempt to stop possible incidents using a set of conditions based on signatures or anomalies while in-line and in real time.

Businesses today tend to communicate with many other business entities, not only over the Internet but also through private networks or guest access connections directly to the organization's network, whether wired or wireless. Business partners and contractors conducting business communications obviously tend to need a higher level of access than public users but not as extensive as permanent employees, so how does an organization handle this phenomenon? External parties working on internal projects are also classified as business partners. Some general rules for users to maintain security control of external entities and maintain personal protection of their own data and identity are:

● Access to a user's own IT system must be protected in such a way that system settings can only be changed subject to authentication.

● Unauthorized access to in-house resources including data areas (shares, folders, mailboxes, calendar, etc.) must be prevented in line with their need for protection. In addition, the necessary authorizations for approved data access must be defined.

● Users are not permitted to operate resources without first defining any authorizations (such as no global sharing). In particular, those users who are system managers of their own resources must observe this rule.

● Users of an IT system must lock the access links they have opened (for example, by enabling a screensaver or removing the chip card from the card reader), even during short periods of absence from their workstations.

● When work is over, all open access links must be properly closed or protected against system/data access (such as if extensive compilation runs need to take place during the night).

● Deputizing roles for access to the user's own system or data resources must be made in agreement with the manager and the acting employee.

● Employees must ensure that their protection resources cannot be subject to snooping while data required for authentication is being entered (e.g., password entry during login).

● Employees must store all protection resources and records in such a way that they cannot be subjected to snooping or stealing.

● Personal protection resources must never be made available to third parties.

● In the case of chip cards, SecurID tokens, or other protection resources requiring a personal identification number (PIN), the associated PIN (PIN letter) must be stored separately.

● Loss, theft, or disclosure of resources must be reported immediately.

● Protection resources subject to loss, theft, or snooping must be disabled immediately.

5. APPLICATION SECURITY

Web and application security has come to center stage because websites and other public-facing applications have had so many vulnerabilities reported that it is often trivial to find some part of the application that is vulnerable to one of the many exploits out there. When an attacker compromises a system at the application level, often it is trivial to take advantage of the capabilities it has to offer, including querying the back-end database or accessing proprietary information. In the past it was not as necessary to implement security during the development phase of an application, and since most security professionals are not programmers, that worked out just fine; however, due to factors such as rushing software releases and complacency where users expect buggy software and to have to apply patches, there is a trend toward inserting security earlier in the development process.

Web Security

Web security is unique to every environment; any application and service that the organization wants to deliver to the customer will have its own way of performing transactions. Static websites with little content or searchable areas pose the least risk, but they also offer less functionality. Implementing something like a shopping cart or content delivery on your site opens up new, unexpected aspects of security. Among the things that need to be considered are whether it is worth developing the application in-house or buying one off the shelf, relying on someone else for the maintenance and updating. With some of these thoughts in mind, here are some of the biggest threats and defenses associated with having a public website:

● Vandalism
● Financial fraud
● Privileged access
● Theft of transaction information
● Theft of intellectual property
● DoS attacks
● Input validation errors
● Path or directory traversal
● Unicode encoding
● URL encoding
● Web application firewalls
● IPSs
● SYN proxies on the firewall

An integrated approach to application security in the organization is required for successful deployment and maintenance of all applications. A corporate initiative to define, promote, assure, and measure the security of critical business applications would greatly enhance an organization's overall security. Some of the biggest obstacles, as

OWASP Top 10 – 2010 (Previous)	OWASP Top 10 – 2013 (New)
A1 – Injection	A1 – Injection
A3 – Broken Authentication and Session Management	A2 – Broken Authentication and Session Management
A2 – Cross-Site Scripting (XSS)	A3 – Cross-Site Scripting (XSS)
A4 – Insecure Direct Object References	A4 – Insecure Direct Object References
A6 – Security Misconfiguration	A5 – Security Misconfiguration
A7 – Insecure Cryptographic Storage – Merged with A9 →	A6 – Sensitive Data Exposure
A8 – Failure to Restrict URL Access – Broadened into →	A7 – Missing Function Level Access Control
A5 – Cross-Site Request Forgery (CSRF)	A8 – Cross-Site Request Forgery (CSRF)
<buried in A6: Security Misconfiguration>	A9 – Using Known Vulnerable Components
A10 – Unvalidated Redirects and Forwards	A10 – Unvalidated Redirects and Forwards
A9 – Insufficient Transport Layer Protection	Merged with 2010-A7 into new 2013-A6

FIGURE 24.8   Open web application security project (OWASP) top 10 application threats.

mentioned in the previous section, are that security professionals are not typically developers, so this means that all too often, application security is left to IT or research and development (R&D) personnel, which can lead to gaping holes. Components of an application security program consist of:

- People: Security architects, managers, technical leads, developers, and testers.
- Policy: Integrate security steps into your SDLC and ADLC; have security baked in, not bolted on. Find security issues early so that they are easier and cheaper to fix. Measure compliance; are the processes working? Inventory and categorize your applications.
- Standards: Which controls are necessary, and when and why? Use standard methods to implement each control. Provide references on how to implement and define requirements.
- Assessments: Security architecture and design reviews, security code reviews, application vulnerability tests, risk acceptance review, external penetration test of production applications, white-box philosophy. Look inside the application, and use all the advantages you have such as past reviews, design documents, code, logs, interviews, and so on. Attackers have advantages over you; don't tie your hands.
- Training: Take awareness and training seriously. All developers should be performing their own input

validation in their code and need to be made aware of the risks involved in sending unsecure code into production.

An organization that has been advocating open standards is the Open Web Application Security Project (OWASP). They publish security standards and threat documentation that has become the benchmark in application security. To better understand what are the top risks in application security it is also important to know what are the most common threats to an application; Fig. 24.8 shows the OWASP top 10 application security threats [14].

SecDevOps

DevOps is a newer programming methodology, which has sprung from the concept of agile development incorporating quicker turnaround and advocating a shortening of the development lifecycle. That being said, if DevOps is implemented without consideration for security it is also likely to produce less secure code and allow for more vulnerable applications. That is why it is critical to incorporate security into the organization's DevOps strategy, referred to as SecDevOps. SecDevOps takes into consideration which protection mechanisms can be implemented in each stage of the development lifecycle so that secure coding is built into the process and does not remain an afterthought. Fig. 24.9 depicts the DevOps lifecycle [6] as

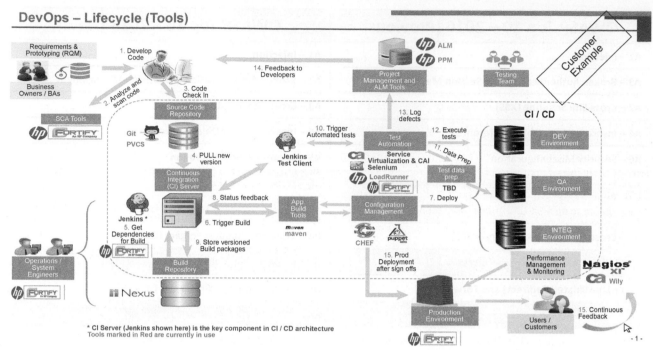

FIGURE 24.9 DevOps lifecycle with built-in security.

described by Hewlett Packard, showing each step in the process and how their particular security technologies can help. That being said, the most important places where security is commonly implemented are as follows:

- Static code analysis: The act of reviewing the actual code of every application at the time of development or when it is checked in to the versioning system.
- Dynamic code analysis: The act of scanning a live website or application once it is running (usually in staging or QA) for vulnerabilities that may not have been identified by simply looking at the written code when it's compiled.
- Runtime application protection: Usually implemented by running a security agent on the actual web server once it is in production to monitor for unauthorized activity or anomalous behavior by the application itself.

6. CLOUD SECURITY

The cloud has so many usage models that every cloud experience is different and security cannot be assessed based on one set of standards or single reference architecture. There are many cloud security reference architectures published that are use-case specific and take into account different business requirements. For example, it is possible that an organization is looking to build out an Infrastructure as a Service (IaaS) to run windows-based servers in a traditional IT operation. This typically requires well-known deployment architecture and can fit into traditional security management models. More complex

use cases may involve deploying a Platform as a Service (PaaS) or Software as a Service (SaaS) environment that is PCI compliant or adheres to NIST government standards. This type of environment may hold cardholder or employee data. If this is the case then more customized security reference architectures with advanced security controls is required [17].

Public Cloud

There are many core ideas and characteristics behind the architecture of the public cloud, but possibly the most alluring is the ability to create the illusion of infinite capacity. Whether its one server or thousands, the performance appears to perform the same, with consistent service levels that are transparent to the end user. This is accomplished by abstracting the physical infrastructure through virtualization of the operating system so that applications and services are not locked into any particular device, location, or hardware. Cloud services are also on demand, which is to say that you only pay for what you use and should therefore drastically reduce the cost of computing for most organizations. Investing in hardware and software that is underutilized and depreciates quickly, is not as appealing as leasing a service, that with minimal upfront costs, an organization can deploy as an entire infrastructure.

Server, network, storage, and application virtualization are the core components that most cloud providers specialize in delivering. These different computing resources make up the bulk of the infrastructure in most organizations, so it is easy to see the attractiveness of the solution. In the cloud, provisioning these resources is fully automated and scale up and down quickly. To understand how each provider protects and configures each of the major architecture components of the cloud, it is critical for an organization to be able to assess and compare the risk involved in utilizing that provider or service. Make sure to request that the cloud provider furnish information regarding the reference architecture in each of the following areas of their infrastructure:

- Compute: Physical servers, OS, CPU, memory, disk space, etc.
- Network: VLANs, DMZ, segmentation, redundancy, connectivity, etc.
- Storage: LUNs, ports, partitioning, redundancy, fail-over, etc.
- Virtualization: Hypervisor, geolocation, management, authorization, etc.
- Application: Multitenancy, isolation, load-balancing, authentication, etc.

An important aspect of pulling off this type of elastic and resilient architecture is commodity hardware. A cloud provider needs to be able to provision more physical servers, hard drives, memory, network interfaces, and just about any operating system or server application transparently and efficiently. To be able to do this, servers and storage need to be provisioned dynamically and they are constantly being reallocated to and from different customer environments with minimum regard for the underlying hardware. As long as the service level agreements for up time are met and the administrative overhead is minimized, the cloud provider does little to guarantee or disclose what the infrastructure looks like. It is incumbent upon the subscriber to ask and validate the design characteristics of every cloud provider they contract services from. There are many characteristics that define a cloud environment; please see Fig. 24.10 providing a comprehensive list of cloud design characteristics.

Most of the key characteristics can be summarized in the list that follows [15].

- On demand: The always-on nature of the cloud allows for organizations to perform self-service administration and maintenance, over the Internet, of their entire infrastructure without the need to interact with a third party.
- Resource pooling: Cloud environments are usually configured as large pools of computing resources such as CPU, RAM, and storage from which a customer

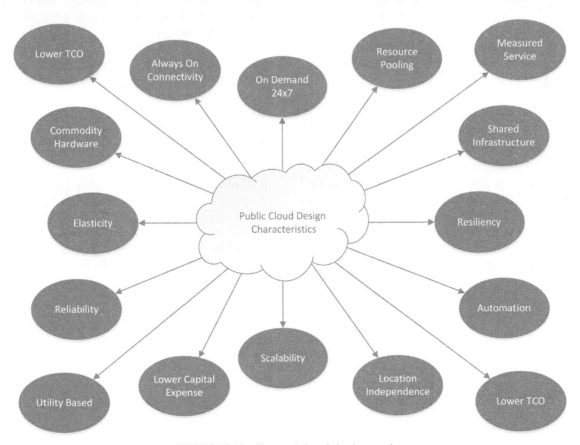

FIGURE 24.10 Characteristics of cloud computing.

can choose to use or leave to be allocated to a different customer.

- Measured service: The cloud brings tremendous cost savings to the end user due to its pay-as-you-go nature; therefore, it is critical for the provider to be able to measure the level of service and resources each customer utilizes.
- Network connectivity: The ease with which users can connect to the cloud is one of the reasons why cloud adoption is so high. Organizations today have a mobile workforce, which require connectivity for multiple platforms.
- Elasticity: A vital component of the cloud is that it must be able to scale up as customers demand it. A subscriber may spin up new resources seasonally or during a big campaign and bring them down when no longer needed. It is the degree to which a system can autonomously adapt capacity over time.
- Resiliency: A cloud environment must always be available as most service agreements guarantee availability at the expense of the provider if the system goes down. The cloud is only as good as it is reliable so it is essential that the infrastructure be resilient and delivered with availability at its core.
- Multitenancy: A multitenant environment refers to the idea that all tenants within a cloud should be properly segregated from each other. In many cases a single instance of software may serve many customers so for security and privacy reasons it is critical that the provider takes the time to build in secure multitenancy from the bottom up. A multitenant environment focuses on the separation of tenant data in such a way as to take every reasonable measure to prevent unauthorized access or leakage of resource between tenants.

The most significant cloud security challenges revolve around how and where the data is stored as well as whose responsibility is it to protect. In a more traditional IT infrastructure or private cloud environment the responsibility to protect the data and who owns it is clear. When a decision is made to migrate services and data to a public cloud environment certain things become unclear and difficult to prove and define. The most pressing challenges to assess are [3]:

- Data residency: This refers to the physical geographic location where the data stored in the cloud resides. There are many industries that have regulations requiring organizations to maintain their customer or patient information within their country of origin. This is especially prevalent with government data and medical records. Many cloud providers have data centers in several countries and may migrate virtual machines or replicate data across disparate geographic regions

causing cloud subscribers to fail compliance checks or even break the law without knowing it.

- Regulatory compliance: Industries that are required to meet regulatory compliance such as HIPAA or security standards such as those in the PCI typically have a higher level of accountability and security requirements than those who do not. These organizations should take special care of what cloud services they decide to deploy and that the cloud provider can meet or exceed these compliance requirements. Many cloud providers today can provision part of their cloud environment with strict HIPAA or PCI standards enforced and monitored but only if you ask for it, and at an additional cost, of course.
- Data privacy: Maintaining the privacy of users is of high concern for most organizations. Whether employees, customers, or patients, personally identifiable information is a high valued target. Many cloud subscribers do not realize that when they contract a provider to perform a service that they are also agreeing to allow that provider to gather and share metadata and usage information about their environment.
- Data ownership: Many cloud services are contracted with stipulations stating that the cloud provider has permission to copy, reproduce, or retain all data stored on their infrastructure, in perpetuity—this is not what most subscribers believe is the case when they migrate their data to the cloud.
- Data protection: This isn't always clear unless it is discussed before engaging the service. Many providers do have security monitoring available but in most cases it is turned off by default or costs significantly more for the same level of service. A subscriber should always validate that the provider can protect the company's data just as effectively, or even more so than the company itself.

If these core challenges with public cloud adoption are not properly evaluated then there are some potential security issues that could crop up. On the other hand, these issues can be avoided with proper preparation and due diligence. The type of data and operations in your unique cloud instance will determine the level of security required.

Private Cloud

Private cloud security requires all the components of a traditional defense in depth strategy for protecting mission-critical systems. In addition to these best practices there are implications and challenges unique to a private cloud that should be considered. If it is determined that the data being stored in the private cloud is mission critical then more advanced security techniques may be required. It is an orchestration of operations, development, and security that needs to be delicately handled so that one of these critical aspects are not overlooked and easily exploited. The goal is for an organization to develop an advanced security architecture design that addresses each of these implications [1,2].

- Virtualization: A core capability of virtualization is to abstract the hardware from the software allowing multiple instances of the software to emulate stand-alone hardware. This means that one physical system may house many servers, which all communicate and interact with each other on a virtual network over shared resources. Visibility into this virtualized computing infrastructure is important.
- Infrastructure: Lifecycle management of hardware components, temperature controls, datacenter security, storage arrays, and network devices are all factors when building a resilient infrastructure. At each of these layers there is a need to make decisions that will determine the availability and reliability of your cloud.
- Platform: Whether it is a resource intensive back-end database or high transaction web application the platform that is being built on top of the infrastructure should be independently assessed. There will need to be basic security controls baked into the design before implementation to ensure a more robust platform.
- Software: Software applications require unique security testing to assure that the developer has not written vulnerable code. With commercial applications vulnerability scans and penetration testing can be performed. When the software is developed in house more robust options which perform static and dynamic analysis of the code from development through production should be assessed.
- Network: In cloud implementations the perimeter of the network is completely redefined. An organization's IT team must literally think outside of the box and assume that the entire Internet and every object connecting to it is now its own perimeter. Public network connectivity and interoperability with other clouds usually comes hand in hand with the deployment of a new private cloud.
- Data: Data classification, security, and separation together help design a data protection strategy. Once data is properly classified it can be separated into zones and properly protected at the level of security it deserves.
- Client security: Endpoint protection takes on a whole new meaning in the cloud. The end systems that are connecting to the cloud vary tremendously from tablets and phones to other cloud platforms, software applications, and business partners. There should be a clear strategy on how to implement client security for all types of connections the cloud environment is designed to handle.

- Security monitoring and auditing: Monitoring all events from every system in the private cloud, from hardware to hypervisor and up through applications is a critical component of security. Most organizations do not take the time to properly plan and implement a robust, centralized logging solution.
- Incident response: Once an issue is identified, performing incident response, gathering forensic data, and analyzing security information may not be as straightforward as in a traditional IT infrastructure. There are areas in a cloud that may demand different capture techniques and analysis methods to arrive at root cause.
- Legal issues: An organization that is geographically dispersed and running data centers in multiple countries needs to be aware of the laws, regulations, and compliance standards that apply in each region. Most countries have different laws governing the seizure of corporate data and storing personal employee data outside of the country. Aside from international regulations there may also be contractual obligations that dictate how data should be stored and transferred.
- Attacker profiles: Building a baseline for the activity of authenticated users helps define what the profile of an attacker may look like. An attacker must become an authenticated user to effect any damage on the infrastructure; therefore, security must be implemented assuming the attacker will already have privileged access.

7. DATA PROTECTION

Data security is at the core of what needs to be protected in terms of information security and mission-critical systems. Ultimately it is the data that the organization needs to protect, and usually data is exactly what perpetrators are after. Whether trade secrets, customer information, or a database of Social Security numbers—the data is where it's at! To be able to properly classify and restrict data, the first thing to understand is how data is accessed. A subject accesses data, whether that is a person, process, or another application, and what is accessed to retrieve the data is called an object. Both subjects and objects can be a number of things acting in a network; depending on what action they are taking at any given moment. Various data classification models are available for different environments. Some security models focus on the confidentiality of the data (such as Bell—La Padula) and use different classifications. For example, the US military uses a model that goes from most confidential (Top Secret) to least confidential (Unclassified) to classify the data on any given system. On the other hand, most corporate entities prefer a model whereby they classify data by business unit (HR, Marketing, R&D) or use terms such as Company Confidential to define items that should not be shared with the public. Other security models focus on the integrity of the data (for example, Bipa); yet others are expressed by mapping security policies to data classification (for example, Clark-Wilson). In every case there are areas that require special attention and clarification.

Three main access control models are in use today: Role-Based Access Control (RBAC), Discretionary Access Control (DAC), and Mandatory Access Control (MAC). In RBAC, the job function of the individual determines the group he is assigned to and determines the level of access he can attain on certain data and systems. IT personnel, in accordance with policies and procedures, usually define the level of access for each user. In DAC, the end user or creator of the data object is allowed to define who can and who cannot access the data; this has become less popular in recent history but is making a comeback with shared cloud resources and data drives. MAC is more of a militant style of applying permissions, where permissions are the same across the board to all members of a certain level or class within the organization. The following are data security "need to knows":

- Authentication versus authorization: It's crucial to understand that simply because someone becomes authenticated does not mean that they are authorized to view certain data. There needs to be a means by which a person, after gaining access through authentication, is limited in the actions they are authorized to perform on certain data (i.e., read-only permissions).
- Encryption of data: This is important for the security of both the organization and its customers. Usually the most important item that an organization needs to protect, aside from trade secrets, is its customer's personal data. If there is a security breach and the data that is stolen or compromised was previously encrypted, the organization can feel more secure in that the collateral damage to their reputation and customer base will be minimized.
- Data leakage prevention and content management: An area of data security that has proven extremely useful in preventing sensitive information from leaving an organization. With this technology, a security administrator can define the types of documents, and further define the content within those documents, that cannot leave the organization and quarantine them for inspection before they hit the public Internet.
- Secure email systems: One of the most important and overlooked areas of data security. With access to the mail server, an attacker can snoop through anyone's email. Password files, company confidential documents, and contacts for all address books are only some of the things that a compromised mail server can reveal about an organization, not to mention root/administrator access to a system in the internal network.

8. WIRELESS AND MOBILE SECURITY

Wireless networking enables devices with wireless capabilities to use information resources without being physically connected to a network. A wireless local area network (WLAN) is a group of wireless networking nodes within a limited geographic area that is capable of radio communications. WLANs are typically used by devices within a fairly limited range, such as an office building or building campus, and are usually implemented as extensions to existing wired local area networks to provide enhanced user mobility. Since the beginning of wireless networking, many standards and technologies have been developed for WLANs. One of the most active standards organizations that address wireless networking is the Institute of Electrical and Electronics Engineers (IEEE). Like other wireless technologies, WLANs typically need to support several security objectives. This is accomplished through a combination of security features built into the wireless networking standard. Some common security objectives for WLANs are as follows:

- Access control: Restrict the rights of devices or individuals to access a network or resources within a network.
- Confidentiality: Ensure that unauthorized parties cannot read communication.
- Integrity: Detect any intentional or unintentional changes to data that occur in transit.
- Availability: Ensure that devices and individuals can access a network and its resources whenever needed.

Typically there are two means by which to validate the identities of wireless devices attempting to connect to a WLAN: open-system authentication and shared-key authentication. Neither of these alternatives are secure. The security provided by the default connection means is unacceptable; all it takes for a host to connect to your system is a Service Set Identifier (SSID) for the access point (which is a name that is broadcast in the clear) and, optionally, a MAC Address. The SSID is clearly not intended as an access control feature. A possible threat against confidentiality is network traffic analysis. Eavesdroppers might be able to gain information by monitoring and noting which parties communicate at particular times. Also, analyzing traffic patterns can aid in determining the content of communications; for example, terminal emulation or instant messaging might cause short bursts of activity, whereas steady streams of activity might be generated by videoconferencing. More sophisticated analysis might be able to determine the operating systems in use based on the length of certain frames. Other than encrypting communications, IEEE 802.11, like most other network protocols, does not offer any features that might thwart network traffic analysis, such as adding random lengths of padding to messages or sending additional messages with randomly generated data. Once a system is able to successfully authenticate to an access point it will be treated as any other node on the network.

Data integrity checking for messages transmitted between hosts and access points does exist and is designed to reject any messages that have been changed in transit, such as by a man-in-the-middle attack. Individuals who do not have physical access to the WLAN infrastructure can cause a DoS for the WLAN. Another threat is known as jamming, which involves a device that emits electromagnetic energy on the WLAN's frequencies. The energy makes the frequencies unusable by the WLAN, causing a DoS. Jamming can be performed intentionally by an attacker or unintentionally by a non-WLAN device transmitting on the same frequency. Yet another threat against availability is flooding, which involves an attacker sending large numbers of messages to an access point at such a high rate that it cannot process them causing a partial or total DoS. These threats are difficult to counter in any radio-based communications; thus, the IEEE 802.11 standard does not provide any defense against jamming or flooding. Also, attackers can establish rogue access points; if a system mistakenly attaches to a rogue access point instead of a legitimate one, this could make the legitimate WLAN effectively unavailable to users. Some of the general rules for mobile systems that can be put into place to enhance security controls and extended self-protection are as follows.

- A mobile IT system must be safeguarded against theft (that is, secured with a cable lock, locked away in a cupboard, or kept physically near the owner).
- The data from a mobile system using corporate proprietary information must be safeguarded as appropriate (e.g. encryption). In this connection, CERT rules in particular are to be observed.
- The software provided by the organization for system access control may only be used on the organization's own mobile IT systems.
- A mobile IT system must be operated in an unprotected open network only for the duration of a secure access link to the organization's own network. The connection establishment for the secure access link must be performed as soon as possible, at least within 5 min.
- Simultaneous operation on open networks (protected or unprotected) and the organization's own networks is forbidden at all times.
- Remote access to company internal resources must always be protected by means of strong authentication.
- For the protection of data being transferred via a remote access link, strong encryption must always be used.

Mobile devices have so much built-in functionality that they have become equally powerful as laptops, and equally as susceptible to attack as well. Many of the same threats that exist for client systems apply to mobile phones and tablets; many times these devices are running the same operation systems. To address all the vulnerabilities introduced by mobile devices there is a need for a strong Mobile Device Management platform, which can implement policies on all managed devices restricting data usage, location tracking, and app installation. Some of the most common attacks seen on mobile devices are:

- Social engineering
- Exploitation of social networking
- Mobile botnets
- Exploitation of mobile applications
- Exploitation of m-commerce.

9. IDENTITY AND ACCESS MANAGEMENT

Identity and Access Management (IAM) involves tracking the behavior and actions of each individual and asset in the IT environment, specifically your system administrators and mission-critical assets. This is specifically challenging due to the always-on nature and broad connectivity characteristics of our interconnected systems. IAM enables individuals to access the correct resources at the right times for the proper reasons, which requires significant systems integration so that all platforms have the situational awareness necessary to properly enforce policy. If properly implemented, IAM can drastically increase visibility and security. Some of the key characteristics of a standard IAM strategy include:

- Authentication and authorization: Strong authentication mechanisms with proper access rights must be implemented with more scalable and available solutions that include functionality covering cloud and mobile assets as well.
- RBAC: Without RBACs, it would be impossible to maintain separation of duties, control privileged access, or security against internal attacks.
- Single sign-on: The ability to have a single location that will authenticate cloud users to any number of back-end applications and services becomes more critical every day. Also, applications and services that are running with local users should be integrated into a centralized authentication system.
- Federation of services: Federated services are often used in cloud and hybrid deployments, typically to extend the functionality of an internal network into the cloud. This common requirement is seen when deploying cloud-based technologies that need to leverage Microsoft Active Directory or other internal authentication services.

FIGURE 24.11 Identity and access management
(IAM) key components.

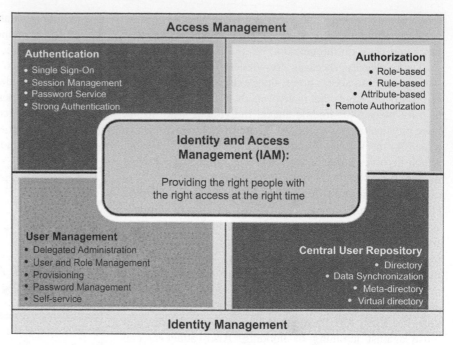

Fig. 24.11 describes key components of an IAM strategy.

10. SECURITY OPERATIONS

Security operation management is the next evolution to a constant presence of security-aware personnel who actively monitor and research events. A substantial number of suspicious events occur within most enterprise networks and computer systems every day and go completely undetected. Only with an effective security-monitoring strategy, incident response plan, and security validation in place will an optimal level of security be attained. The idea is to automate and correlate as much as possible between both events and vulnerabilities to build intelligence into security tools so that they alert you if a known bad set of events has occurred or a known vulnerability is actually being attacked. The main responsibility of security operations is incident management. Incidents can be classified as anything from a combination of interesting events that are generated by one system to a widespread security breach across the entire organization. A strong security operations team is needed to understand and distill security data from all the disparate systems to properly identify and respond to incidents. It is essential to orchestrate people, process, and technology for proper incident analysis and breach response with focused workflows and intuitive dashboards.

Some core elements to good security operations management are as follows [2]:

- Monitor and audit extensively
- Automate security operations
- Apply security best practices
- Understand that isolation is key
- Assume attackers are authenticated and authorized
- Assume all data locations are accessible
- Use strong cryptographic technologies
- Limit routing and enforce segmentation

Security Monitoring

Security monitoring involves real-time or near real-time monitoring of events and activities happening on all mission-critical systems. To properly monitor an organization for security events that can lead to an incident or an investigation, usually an organization uses a Security Information and Event Management (SIEM) tool. Security analysts and managers must filter through tons of event data identifying and focusing on only the most interesting events.

Understanding the regulatory and forensic impact of event and alert data in any given enterprise takes planning and a thorough understanding of the quantity of data the system will be required to handle (see checklist: "An Agenda for Action When Implementing a Critical Security

Mechanism"). The better logs can be stored, understood, and correlated, the better the possibility of detecting an incident in time for mitigation. Responding to incidents, identifying anomalous or unauthorized behavior, and securing intellectual property have never been more important.

An Agenda for Action When Implementing a Critical Security Mechanism

Without a solid log management strategy it becomes nearly impossible to have the necessary data to perform a forensic investigation, and without monitoring tools, identifying threats and responding to attacks become much more difficult. For an incident response and forensics investigation to be successful, it is important that certain mechanisms be in place; for example, an organization may want to implement some of the following (check all tasks completed):

_____1. Securely acquire and store raw log data for as long as possible from as many disparate devices as possible while providing search and restore capabilities of these logs for analysis.

_____2. Monitor interesting events coming from all important devices, systems, and applications in as near real time as possible.

_____3. Run regular vulnerability scans and correlate these vulnerabilities to intrusion detection alerts or other interesting events, identifying high-priority attacks as they happen and minimizing false positives.

_____4. Aggregate and normalize event data from unrelated network devices, security devices, and application servers into usable information.

_____5. Analyze and correlate information from various sources such as vulnerability scanners, IDS/IPS, firewalls, servers, and so on, to identify attacks as soon as possible and help respond to intrusions more quickly.

_____6. Conduct network forensic analysis on historical or real-time events through visualization and replay of events.

_____7. Create customized reports for better visualization of your security posture.

_____8. Increase the value and performance of existing security devices by providing a consolidated event management and analysis platform.

_____9. Improve the effectiveness and help focus IT risk management personnel on the events that are important.

Security monitoring is a key component in gaining the visibility necessary to identify incidents quickly and having the information necessary to respond and remediate. Monitoring any environment is difficult but there are additional challenges that crop up in the cloud which are not easily overcome, primarily when it comes to monitoring parts of the infrastructure that are in the control of the provider and not of the data owner or subscriber. One major challenge in gaining visibility into what's happening in your cloud environment is the inability to analyze network traffic and perform basic packet capture or install intrusion detection systems. As an alternative to monitoring activity in this fashion there have been new cloud access security technologies that leverage APIs to constantly query a particular cloud service to log every activity that happens in that instance of the cloud. With this type of monitoring activity there are Indicators of Compromise (IoC) that can be identified and reported as anomalies. In addition to calling out these anomalies, such as logging in with the same credentials at the same time from geographically disparate regions, these security technologies can also implement some machine-learning algorithms to trend the behavior of every user and alert when something out of the ordinary happens.

Every cloud provider publishes a subset APIs that allows subscribers to query the cloud instance for different data the problem arises when the subscriber has a need to monitor more granular information that what the provider's API support. If sufficiently granular security information is available it can be compared to activity provided by threat feeds and watch lists which can provide insight into malicious behavior that has been observed in other customer and cloud environments. These technologies and techniques should be implemented in addition to the regular security-monitoring tools that are used to monitor traditional IT infrastructures. Some of the important cloud security-monitoring techniques that should be considered for implementation above and beyond traditional controls is as follows:

- Secure APIs: Secure APIs are automated queries that allow for the monitoring of cloud activities and actions.
- Cloud Access Security Brokers (CASB): CASBs are platforms that leverage secure cloud APIs for many cloud services enabling subscribers to have a centralized location for the monitoring and inspection of all their cloud events.
- Anomaly detection: Methodologies for identifying and alerting on activities that are not considered normal and have never been seen before in an effort to prevent a security breach before it gets out of control.
- Machine learning: This is the automation of longstanding techniques that have been used to identify anomalies in the past. The correlation of events was largely manual in the past but many platforms have incorporated the ability to automatically develop anomaly criteria without user intervention.

- Threat intelligence: This term refers to threat feeds, watch lists, and other mechanisms by which threats to a particular environment have been identified and are communicated to end users, security tools, and customers.
- Behavioral detection: It is common for many security tools nowadays to first learn the behavior of users, systems, and networks before they start generating alerts for unauthorized activity. This type of behavioral detection goes beyond the blanket anomaly and creates a profile for each object using the cloud. Where it might be normal for an administrator to transfer 10 GB of data every day to and from the cloud and no alarm sounds a typical end user performing the same action would fire an alarm because they have never performed that type of action before.

Validating Effectiveness

The process of validating security effectiveness comprises making sure that the security controls that you have put in place are working as expected and that they are truly mitigating the risks they claim to be mitigating. There is no way to be sure that your network is not vulnerable to something if you haven't validated it yourself. Ensuring that the information security policy addresses your organizational needs and assessing compliance with your security policy across all systems, assets, applications, and people is the only way to have a concrete means of validation. Here are some areas where actual validation should be performed—in other words, these are areas where assigned IT personnel should go with policy in hand, log in, and verify the settings and reports before the auditors do:

- Verifying operating system settings
- Reviewing security device configuration and management
- Establishing ongoing security tasks
- Maintaining physical security
- Auditing security logs
- Creating an approved application list
- Reviewing encryption strength
- Providing documentation and change control

Validating security with internal as well as external vulnerability assessments and penetration tests is a good way to measure an increase or decrease in overall security, especially if similar assessments are conducted on a regular basis. There are several ways to test security of applications, hosts, and network devices. With a vulnerability assessment, usually limited scanning tools are used to determine vulnerabilities that exist in the target systems. Then a report is created and the manager reviews a holistic picture of security. With authorized penetration tests it's a little different. In that case the data owner is allowing

someone to use just about any means within reason (in other words, many different tools and techniques) to gain access to the system or information. A successful penetration test does not typically provide the remediation steps that a vulnerability assessment does; rather, it is a good test of how difficult it would be for someone to truly gain access if he were trying.

Incident Response

An incident response plan (IRP) is a detailed set of processes and procedures that anticipate, detect, and mitigate the impact of an unexpected event. Before an incident can be responded to there is the challenge of determining whether an event is a routine system event or an actual incident. This requires that there be some framework for incident classification (the process of examining a possible incident and determining whether or not it requires a reaction). Initial reports from end users, intrusion detection systems, host- and network-based malware detection software, and systems administrators are all ways to track and detect incident candidates. When a threat becomes a valid attack, it is classified as an information security incident if it is directed against specific people or information assets, has a realistic chance of success, and threatens the confidentiality, integrity, or availability of core assets. Incident response planning is composed of six major phases:

- Preparation: Planning and readying in the event of a security incident.
- Identification: To identify a set of events that have some negative impact on the business and can be considered a security incident.
- Containment: During this phase the security incident has been identified and action is required to mitigate its potential damage.
- Eradication: After it's contained, the incident must be eradicated and studied to make sure it has been thoroughly removed from the system.
- Recovery: Bringing the business and assets involved in the security incident back to normal operations.
- Lessons learned: A thorough review of how the incident occurred and the actions taken to respond to it where the lessons learned get applied to future incidents.

The preparation phase requires detailed understanding of information systems and the threats they face; so to perform proper planning an organization must develop predefined responses that guide users through the steps needed to properly respond to an incident. Predefining incident responses enables rapid reaction without confusion or wasted time and effort, which can be crucial for the success of an incident response. Identification occurs once an actual incident has been confirmed and properly classified as an incident that requires action. At that point the IR team moves from identification to containment. In the containment phase, the IR team and others take a number of actions. These steps to respond to an incident must occur quickly and may occur concurrently, including notification of key personnel, the assignment of tasks, and documentation of the incident. Containment strategies focus on two tasks: first, stopping the incident from getting any worse, and second, recovering control of the system if it has been hijacked. Once the incident has been contained and system control regained, eradication can begin, and the IR team must assess the full extent of damage to determine what must be done to restore the system. Immediate determination of the scope of the breach of CIA of information is called an incident damage assessment. Those who document the damage must be trained to collect and preserve evidence in case the incident is part of a criminal investigation or results in legal action.

At the moment that the extent of the damage has been determined, the recovery process begins to identify and resolve vulnerabilities that allowed the incident to occur in the first place. The IR team must address the issues found and determine whether they need to install and/or replace the safeguards that failed to stop or limit the incident or were missing from system in the first place. Finally, a discussion of lessons learned should always be conducted to prevent future similar incidents from occurring and review what could have been done differently.

11. POLICIES, PLANS, AND PROGRAMS

A quality information security program begins and ends with properly implemented information security policy. Policies are the least expensive means of control and often the most difficult to implement. An information security policy is a plan that influences and determines the actions taken by employees who are presented with a policy decision regarding information systems. Other components related to a security policy are practices, procedures, and guidelines, which attempt to explain in more detail the actions that are to be taken by employees in any given situation. For policies to be effective, they must be properly disseminated, read, understood, and agreed to by all employees as well as backed by upper management. Without upper management support, a security policy is bound to fail. Most information security policies should contain at least:

- Statement of purpose with overview of the corporate philosophy on security
- Information about shared responsibility by all members of the organization
- Information technology elements needed to define or enforce controls
- The organization's responsibilities defining the organizational structure

Entering and accessing information systems to any degree within any organization must be controlled. What's more, it is necessary to understand what is allowed and what's not; if those parameters are clearly defined, the battle is half won. Of course not every organization is working in a high-security or regulated industry, so it's understandable that some of the following statements may not apply to your organization; however, there should be a good, clear reason as to why they are not. The following are some important thoughts to consider when thinking about security maturity:

- Are policies and procedures developed and implemented that address allowing authorized and limiting unauthorized physical access to electronic information systems and the facility or facilities in which they are housed?
- Do the policies and procedures identify individuals (workforce members, business associates, contractors, etc.) with authorized access by title and/or job function?
- Do the policies and procedures specify the methods used to control physical access, such as door locks, electronic access control systems, security officers, or video monitoring?
- Have we established procedures that allow restoration of lost data under the disaster recovery plan and in the event of an emergency?
- Have we implemented policies and procedures to safeguard the facility and the equipment therein from unauthorized physical access, tampering, and theft?
- Are there access control and validation procedures in place to control and validate a person's access to systems and facilities based on their role or function including control of access to software programs for testing and revision?

Some basic rules must be followed when you're shaping a policy:

- Never conflict with the local or federal law
- Your policy should be able to stand up in court
- It must be properly supported and administered by management
- It should contribute to the success of the organization
- It should involve end users of information systems from the beginning

Contingency Planning

Contingency planning is necessary in several ways for an organization to be sure it can withstand some sort of security breach or disaster. Among the important steps required to make sure an organization is protected and able to respond to a security breach or disaster are business impact analysis, disaster recovery planning, and business continuity planning. These contingency plans are interrelated in several ways and need to stay that way so that a response team can change from one to the other seamlessly if there is a need. Business impact analysis must be performed in every organization to determine exactly which business process is deemed mission-critical and which processes would not seriously hamper business operations should they be unavailable for some time. An important part of a business impact analysis is the recovery strategy that is usually defined at the end of the process. If a thorough business impact analysis is performed, there should be a clear picture of the priority of each organization's highest-impact, therefore riskiest, business processes and assets as well as a clear strategy to recover from an interruption in one of these areas.

Business continuity planning (BCP) ensures that critical business functions can continue during a disaster and is most ultimately managed by the CEO of the organization. The BCP is usually activated and executed concurrently with disaster recovery planning (DRP) when needed and reestablishes critical functions at alternate sites (DRP focuses on reestablishment at the primary site). BCP relies on identification of critical business functions and the resources to support them using several continuity strategies, such as exclusive-use options like hot, warm, and cold sites or shared-use options like time-share, service bureaus, or mutual agreements. DRP is the preparation for and recovery from a disaster. Whether natural or manmade, it is an incident that has become a disaster because the organization is unable to contain or control its impact, or the level of damage or destruction from the incident is so severe that the organization is unable to recover quickly. The key role of DRP is defining how to reestablish operations at the site where the organization is usually located. Some key consideration in a properly designed DRP include:

- Clear delegation of roles and responsibilities
- Execution of alert roster and notification of key personnel
- Clear establishment of priorities
- Documentation of the disaster
- Action steps to mitigate the impact
- Alternative implementations for various systems components
- DRP must be tested regularly

Security Education, Training, and Awareness

Security Education, Training, and Awareness (SETA) is a process by which all users of an organization have an opportunity to enhance their knowledge of information security in an effort to protect themselves and organizational assets. There are three major areas of a SETA program: education, training, and awareness. When implemented properly a SETA program is a continuum that is designed to address different populations of users as they continue to learn and grow within the organization, all of which are essential for the protection of people, information, and assets. Without a properly implemented SETA program an organization is more likely to experience a data breach and will be less prepared to handle an incident when it happens. Among the principal goals and benefits of SETA are to enhance the protection of assets, improve the morale and motivation of individuals, and increase executive awareness in the importance of fostering a security culture within the organization. Fig. 24.12 describes the IT Security Learning Continuum according to NIST [9].

Computer users in every organization, school, or agency are a critical aspect to the defense and protection of sensitive data and secure operations. Users can quickly become the Achilles heel of any security organization because there is no predicting how they will behave given a certain set of circumstances. A single user that is duped by an attacker into clicking a malicious link or revealing their username and password can defeat all the security technologies that may be in place. To avoid becoming a victim of social engineering, phishing attacks, or any number of subversive techniques that take advantage of human nature a SETA program is as important as any technical security control. With a properly designed and implemented SETA program an information security team can help change the behavior of the average user and promote a security culture that has a healthy dose of skepticism when encountering potentially risky situations. From designing the SETA program to developing and delivering the material, each component should be well thought out and planned so as to make sure that participation is encouraged and people remain engaged.

Security education is a formal curriculum created for the purpose of educating individuals in a broad array of security topics that will build a body of knowledge essential for a career in information security. This is most useful for people that do not have extensive backgrounds or experience in security and can benefit from formal coursework to establish a baseline of knowledge they can build on. Security training is more tactical and is usually tailored to an individual or group that has specific roles and responsibilities within an organization. This type of training tends to be outsourced and acquired by going outside of the organization so that subject matter experts that have mastered that specific area of information security may provide it. Security awareness is likely the most critical aspect of SETA at the workplace and is the least used method for general knowledge transfer. SETA programs can drastically decrease the likelihood of a security breach and can transform user behavior and corporate culture by developing a more conscientious and savvy user

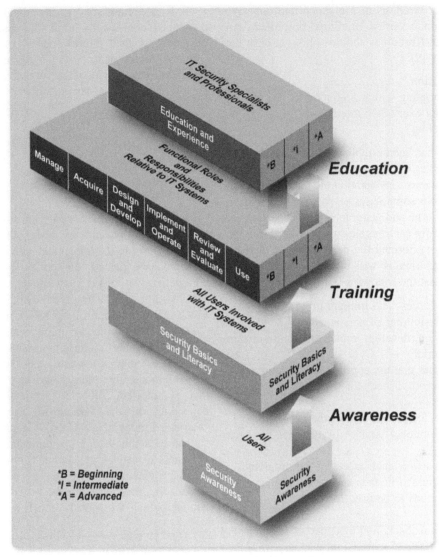

FIGURE 24.12 The IT security learning continuum.

population. There are some basic tenants associated with security awareness that are fundamentally different from security education or training. For example, security awareness focuses more on people than on technology, it assures general accessibility to all users, and it defines key learning objectives that are simple, relatable, and deliverable with minimal technical jargon. Unlike security education, which covers a comprehensive body of knowledge, or training that is specialized and technical, security awareness should speak to all users and focus on individual accountability.

The single most effective mechanism to limit risky behavior and prevent unauthorized activity is to raise the awareness of all individuals, thereby limiting the liability of the organization and changing the culture of the company. The higher the level of risk that individuals manage, the higher the level of security awareness and training they

must be provided. As part of the design of the SETA program there's usually a central authority that needs to authorize the program and establish a policy, which defines minimum requirements. A SETA Policy requires executive support and the best way to get executive support is to include them in the process. A good way to involve the executives of an organization with information security initiatives is to form an Information Security Council. An Information Security Council is a group of key stakeholders in an organization that meet on a regular basis to discuss corporate and operational risk. Having a team of individuals that have the power to implement significant change within an organization is crucial in maintaining strategic support and defining a direction that aligns with the goals of the organization. Another important aspect of an effective SETA Policy is that Human Resources participate with the delivery of information security briefings in a planned and cohesive manner. Information security briefings promoted and delivered by Human Resources should follow at least the following frequency [9]:

- New hire orientation
- Initial security briefing within 3—6 months
- Refresher briefing every 3—6 months
- Termination briefing

Once the policy has been established and executives as well as HR are involved there should be a needs assessment performed that takes into consideration the nuances of each organizational unit. In some cases, especially those in an organization that is large and geographically dispersed, the budget may come from each organizational unit. Once the needs assessment is performed the next step is to develop the plan on how the training will be delivered. The plan should include at least the following components [5]:

- Scope of the awareness and training program
- Roles and responsibilities of personnel
- Who should design, develop, implement, and maintain the training material
- Who should ensure that the appropriate users attend
- Goals to be accomplished for each aspect of the program
- Target audiences for each aspect of the program
- Mandatory and optional courses or material for each target audience
- Learning objectives for each aspect of the program
- Topics to be addressed in each session or course
- Deployment methods to be used for each aspect of the program
- Documentation, feedback, and evidence of learning
- Evaluation and update of material for each aspect of the program
- Frequency that each target audience should be exposed to material

Next, we will define the type of training material that will be developed. A significant amount of topics can be selected for material to be developed and it will largely be based on the type of industry, organizational unit, and individual roles. A relevant question that can be asked is, "What do we want all agency personnel to be aware of regarding IT Security?" [9] Among the initial topics that are commonly chosen for developing material for are:

- Password usage and management
- Email security and phishing awareness
- Social engineering and social media
- Laptop, tablet, and mobile security
- Incident response and compliance
- Viruses, worms, and malicious code
- Data security and encryption

It is important to organize the training that will be developed not just by topic but also by organizational elements so that the awareness program and training addresses every aspect of the organization in a fair and complete way. Some of the organizational elements that should be considered are as follows:

- Personnel security
- Administrative security
- Physical security
- Operations security
- Internal security
- Special investigations

Implementing a SETA program can only be as effective as the planning put into the design and development of the program. Prior to the implementation of SETA there should be emphasis placed on policy and strategy with a comprehensive needs assessment and program plan. Fig. 24.13 provides a graphic showing the stages leading up to the implementation of the SETA program [9].

Once it is time to implement it is important to communicate the plan appropriately and to carry out effective techniques for delivering the awareness material. The communication plan should be mapped to the strategy that is selected, such as centralized or decentralized depending on the makeup of the organization. In a centralized model the CIO or IT security program manager should take the lead in communicating the plan to the managers of each organizational unit that then communicates the plan to their staff. The unit manager can then return ideas and topics to the program manager as nominations, which will narrow down the types of awareness

FIGURE 24.13 Key steps leading to security education, training, and awareness (SETA) program implementation.

training that will ultimately be provided. In a decentralized strategy the CIO or IT security manager will disseminate the strategy and policy of the organization and then the organizational managers will take it upon themselves to gather topic nominations, decide what will be covered, and deliver the training within their respective units. Once it is decided how the strategy will be implemented then there are some techniques that can be used to actually deliver the content. Some of the techniques used to deliver an engaging security awareness program include [9]:

- Computer-based training
- Phishing awareness emails
- Video campaigns
- Posters and banners
- Lectures and conferences
- Regular newsletters
- Brochures and flyers
- Trinkets (coffee cups, pens, pencils, T-shirts)
- Bulletin boards
- Corporate events (lunches, all day, off-site)

Regardless of the techniques chosen to deliver the material it is important that the following features are maintained throughout each of the methods or techniques implemented:

- Ease of use
- Scalability
- Accountability
- Industry support

Postimplementation, there should be a mechanism by which feedback is returned to the program managers. These feedback mechanisms can consist of traditional surveys during the delivery of the content, evaluation forms, focus groups, or a number of other methods. Defining key metrics that will help measure the effectiveness of the training is the final stage of implementation and can provide valuable information to keep the security program up to date and current.

12. SUMMARY

Security is a process, and it is also a mindset: a mindset that must be turned on prior to implementation and continually reassessed throughout the entire lifecycle of every IT system within the organization. A significant amount of emphasis has been placed on proper planning and security design by shedding some light on all the implications regarding protecting mission-critical systems. An understanding of all the layers of security that can be implemented and recognizing where they are best implemented is critical to the success of any information security program. Many security breaches can be directly traced back to an area of the infrastructure where activity is not properly

monitored and logged or policy is not enforced due to some coverage gaps in security instrumentation. Analyzing every situation from many different angles is the nature of most security professionals and of upmost importance when protecting mission-critical systems.

Everyday security incidents occur, small and large, and many go unnoticed and unreported. Most organizations will experience a security breach at some point and it can take months for them to identify the issue, especially if it happens outside of their corporate environment. The organizations and security professionals that understand this will be better prepared when it occurs. To become as incident-ready as possible before a breach occurs and to be able to provide consistent and effective methods for the identification, response, and recovery of security incidents is critical. Every organization needs to also maintain a level of security maturity performing due diligence and producing strong policies around their data and operations before leveraging a public cloud service. With the technologies, standards, and services available, combined with the constant compromise between security and privacy, we are in for an interesting cyber future.

Finally, let's move on to the real interactive part of this Chapter: review questions/exercises, hands-on projects, case projects, and optional team case project. The answers and/or solutions by chapter can be found in Appendix K.

CHAPTER REVIEW QUESTIONS/ EXERCISES

True/False

1. True or False? Information security management as a field is ever decreasing in demand and responsibility because most organizations spend increasingly larger percentages of their IT budgets in attempting to manage risk and mitigate intrusions, not to mention the trend in many enterprises of moving all IT operations to an Internet-connected infrastructure, known as enterprise cloud computing.
2. True or False? Information security is a business problem in the sense that the entire organization must frame and solve security problems based on its own strategic drivers, not solely on technical controls aimed to mitigate one type of attack.
3. True or False? In defining required skills for information security managers, the ISC has arrived at an agreement on 10 domains of information security that is known as the Common Body of Knowledge (CBK).
4. True or False? Threats to information systems come in many flavors, some with malicious intent, others with supernatural powers or expected surprises.
5. True or False? Threats are exploited with a variety of attacks, some technical, others not so much.

Multiple Choice

1. The art of manipulating people into performing actions or divulging confidential information is known as:
   A. Malware
   B. Industrial espionage
   C. Social engineering
   D. Spam
   E. Phishing
2. What describes activities such as theft of trade secrets, bribery, blackmail, and technological surveillance as well as spying on commercial organizations and sometimes governments?
   A. Spam
   B. Phishing
   C. Hoaxes
   D. Industrial espionage
   E. Denial-of-Service
3. What is the abuse of electronic messaging systems to indiscriminately send unsolicited bulk messages, many of which contain hoaxes or other undesirable contents such as links to phishing sites?
   A. Spamming
   B. Phishing
   C. Hoaxes
   D. Distributed Denial-of-Service
   E. All of the Above
4. What is the criminally fraudulent process of attempting to acquire sensitive information such as usernames, passwords, and credit card details by masquerading as a trustworthy entity in an electronic communication?
   A. Splicing
   B. Phishing
   C. Bending
   D. FSO
   E. Cabling
5. What requires that an individual, program, or system process is not granted any more access privileges than are necessary to perform the task?
   A. Administrative controls
   B. Principle of Least Privilege
   C. Technical controls
   D. Physical controls
   E. Risk analysis

EXERCISE

Problem

What is continuous monitoring?

Hands-On Projects

Project

If your information system is subject to continuous monitoring, does that mean it does not have to undergo security authorization?

Case Projects

Problem

Why is continuous monitoring not replacing the traditional security authorization process?

Optional Team Case Project

Problem

What is front-end security and how does it differ from back-end security?

REFERENCES

[1] Bill Loeffler (Publisher) and Jim Dial (Last Revision), Private Cloud Principles, Concepts, and Patterns, MicrosoftTechnet Article, Microsoft Corp, 2013, http://social.technet.microsoft.com/wiki/contents/articles/4346.private-cloud-principles-concepts-and-patterns.aspx.

[2] Bill Loeffler (Publisher) and Jim Dial (Last Revision), Private Cloud Security Operations Principles, MicrosoftTechnet Article, Microsoft Corp, 2013, http://social.technet.microsoft.com/wiki/contents/articles/6658.private-cloud-security-operations-principles.aspx.

[3] B. Lowans, N. MacDonald, C. Casper, Five Cloud Data Residency Issues that Must Not Be Ignored, Gartner, Inc., Stamford, CT, 2012, pp. 13−25. https://www.gartner.com/doc/2288615.

[4] Cloud Security Alliance Top Threats Working Group, The Notorious Nine Cloud Computing Top Threats in 2013, 2013, pp. 8−21. https://downloads.cloudsecurityalliance.org/initiatives/top_threats/The_Notorious_Nine_Cloud_Computing_Top_Threats_in_2013.pdf.

[5] Department of Homeland Security Management Directive System, Security Education, Training, and Awareness Program Directive, 2004. https://www.dhs.gov/sites/default/files/publications/mgmt_directive_11053_security_education_training_and_awareness_program_directive.pdf.

[6] DevOps Lifecycle. HP Enterprise Solutions. Slide 6.

[7] ISO 17799 Security Standards. ISO Website, http://www.iso.org/iso/home.htm.

[8] J. Pescatore, Ask the Expert Webcast: The Critical Security Controls, slide 7, SANS, Bethesda, MD, 2013, http://www.slideshare.net/Lancope/lancope-webcast-022014-cs-cs-lancope.

[9] M. Wilson, J. Hash, Building and Information Technology Security Awareness and Training Program, National Institute of Standards and Technology, 2003. http://csrc.nist.gov/publications/nistpubs/800-50/NIST-SP800-50.pdf.

[10] NIST Computer Security Special Publications. NIST Website, http://csrc.nist.gov/publications/PubsSPs.html.

[11] Official (ISC)2 CBK Training Seminars for the CISSP. (ISC) 2 website: https://www.isc2.org/cissp-training.aspx.

[12] Optiv Cyber Security Solutions, The Security Journey: A Business Aligned Strategy, Slide 8, 2016, https://www.optiv.com/.

[13] Optiv Cyber Security Solutions, Security Controls Framework, Slide 11, 2016, https://www.optiv.com/.

[14] OWASP Top 10 Project. OWASP Website, https://www.owasp.org/index.php/Category:OWASP_Top_Ten_Project.

[15] P. Mell, T. Grance, NIST National Institute of Standards and Technologies. The NIST Definition of Cloud Computing, Computer Security Division, Gaithersburg, MD, 2011, pp. 5–7. http://nvlpubs.nist.gov/nistpubs/Legacy/SP/nistspecialpublication800-145.pdf.

[16] SANS Institute Website https://www.sans.org/.

[17] Security Awareness Program Special Interest Group — PCI Security Standards Council, PCI Data Security Standard (PCI DSS) 1.0, 2014. https://www.pcisecuritystandards.org/documents/PCI_DSS_V1.0_Best_Practices_for_Implementing_Security_Awareness_Program.pdf.

[18] Slide 5, Threat Detection Maturity Model, Reliaquest, 2014.

[19] L. Galway, Quantitative Risk Analysis for Project Management, A Critical Review, WR-112-RC, February 2004. Rand.org Website, http://www.rand.org/pubs/working_papers/2004/RAND_WR112.pdf.

Chapter 25

Security Management Systems

Jim Harmening

Computer Bits, Inc., Chicago, IL, United States

1. SECURITY MANAGEMENT SYSTEM STANDARDS

To give organizations a starting point to develop their own security management systems, the International Organization for Standardization (ISO) and the International Electrotechnical Commission (IEC) developed a family of standards known as the Information Security Management System-27000:2016 Family of Standards. Starting with ISO/IEC-27001, this group of standards gives organizations the ability to certify their security management systems. For more details, see www.iso.org. As an alternative, some organizations are following the SANS 20 Critical Security Controls (http://www.sans.org/critical-security-controls/) set of 20 critical security controls that leads you through a 20-step audit process for your organization.

The ISO/IEC-27001 certification process takes place in several stages. The first stage is an audit of all documentation and policies that currently exist for a system. The documentation is usually based directly on the requirements of the standard, but it does not have to be. Organizations can come up with their own sets of standards, as long as all aspects of the standard are covered. The second stage actually tests the effectiveness of the existing policies. The third stage reassesses the organization to make sure it still meets the requirements. This third stage keeps organizations up to date over time because standards for security management systems change. This certification process is based on a Plan–Do–Check–Act iterative process created by W. Edward Deming in the 1950s:

Plan the security management system and create the policies that define it. **Do** implement the policies in your organization. **Check** to ensure the security management system's policies are protecting the resources they were meant to protect. **Act** to respond to incidents that breach the implemented policies.

Certifying your security management system helps ensure that you keep the controls and policies constantly up to date to meet certification requirements. Becoming certified also demonstrates to your partners and customers that your security management systems will help keep your business running smoothly if network security events were to occur.

Although the ISO/IEC-27000 Family of Standards allows for businesses optionally to get certified, the Federal Information Security Management Act (FISMA) requires all government agencies to develop security management systems. The process of complying with FISMA is similar to the process of implementing the ISO-27000 Family of Standards.

The first step of FISMA compliance is to determine what constitutes the system you are trying to protect. Next, you need to perform risk assessment to determine what controls you will need to put in place to protect your system's assets. The last step is actually implementing the planned controls. FISMA then requires mandatory yearly inspections to make sure an organization stays in compliance.

One advantage of the Sans 20 Critical Security Controls is the 20 individual touchstones that can be acted upon by the organization. It starts with some basic audit information. In Step 1, you inventory all authorized and unauthorized devices. This may mean accessing each workstation and reviewing the system logs to identify whether a universal serial bus (USB), music, or headphones have been plugged into the computer. The second step is to audit the software in the same way. Many times users will download software and not know they have violated their organization's information technology (IT) policies. These two basic checks need to be done annually for some organizations and more frequently for others. For more details, access the SANS.ORG website.

Computer and Information Security Handbook. http://dx.doi.org/10.1016/B978-0-12-803843-7.00025-9

2. TRAINING REQUIREMENTS

Many security management system training courses for personnel are available over the Internet. These courses provide information for employees setting up security management systems and for those using the computer and network resources of the company that are referenced in the policies of the security management system. Training should include creating company security policies and user roles that are specific to the organization. Planning policies and roles ahead of time will prevent confusion in the event of a problem, because everyone will know their responsibilities. Documenting these roles is also important.

3. PRINCIPLES OF INFORMATION SECURITY

The act of securing information has been around for as long as the idea of storing information. Over time, three main objectives of information security have been defined:

- *confidentiality:* Information is available only to the people or systems that need access to it. This is done by encrypting information that only certain people are able to decrypt or denying access to those who do not need it. This might seem simple at first, but confidentiality must be applied to all aspects of a system. This means preventing access to all backup locations and even log files if those files contain sensitive information.
- *integrity:* Information can be added or updated only by those who need to update those data. Unauthorized changes to data cause them to lose integrity, and access to information must be cut off to everyone until the information's integrity is restored. Allowing access to compromised data will cause those unauthorized changes to propagate to other areas of the system.
- *availability:* Information needs to be available in a timely manner when requested. Access to no data is just as bad as access to compromised data. No process can be performed if the data on which the process is based are unavailable.

4. ROLES AND RESPONSIBILITIES OF PERSONNEL

All personnel who come into contact with information systems need to be aware of the risks from improper use of those systems. Network administrators need to know the effects of each change they make to their systems and how that affects the overall security of that system. They also need to be able to control access to those systems efficiently in case of emergencies, when quick action is needed.

Users of those systems need to understand what risks can be caused by their actions and how to comply with

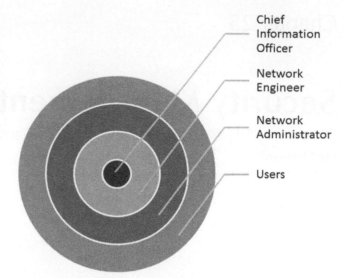

FIGURE 25.1 Who is in charge of your data?

company policy. Several roles should be defined within the organization (Fig. 25.1): Who is in charge of your data?

- *chief information officer/director of IT:* This person is responsible for creating and maintaining the security policies for your organization.
- *network engineer:* This person is responsible for the physical connection of your network and the connection of your network to the Internet. He or she is also responsible for the routers, firewalls, and switches that connect your organization.
- *network administrator:* This person handles all other network devices within the organization, such as servers, workstations, printers, copiers, tablets, video conference, smartphones, and wireless access devices. Server and workstation software is also the responsibility of the network administrator.
- *end users:* These people are allowed to operate the computer in accordance with company policies, to perform their daily tasks. They should not have administrator access to their personal computers or, especially, servers.

There are also many other specific administrators some companies might require. These are Microsoft Exchange Administrators, Database Administrators, and Active Directory Administrators, to name a few. These administrators should have specific tasks to perform and a specific scope in which to perform them that is stated in the company policy.

5. SECURITY POLICIES

Each organization should develop a company policy detailing the preferred use of company data, software, and equipment. An example of a policy is: No person shall transfer any data to any device that was not purchased by the company. This policy can help prevent unauthorized access to company data. Some companies ban all removable media within the organization. The object is to define a policy that is understandable to the users who are affected by it.

Security policies should govern how the computer is to be used on a day-to-day basis. Often, computer users are required to have Internet access to do research pertaining to their jobs. This is not hard to restrict in a specialized setting such as a law firm, where only a handful of sites contain pertinent information. In other cases, it can be nearly impossible to restrict all websites except the ones that contain information that applies to the organization or research. In those cases, it is imperative to have company policies that dictate what websites users are able to visit and for what purposes. When unrestricted Internet access is allowed, it is a good practice to use software that will track the websites a user visits to make sure they are not breaking company policy. Many companies create a white list of allowable sites; other companies use a blacklist to prevent certain sites from being accessed. Some of the more advanced firewalls give a list of categories that are allowed or blocked. For example, SonicWALL firewall and Network Security Appliances give you the ability to purchase a subscription to block unwanted viruses, worms, and malware.

A policy is only as good as its implementation. Care should be given as to how security is communicated to each worker. One option is to have a training class on security followed with a test. If the user does not get the test correct, he must take the training again.

Furthermore, a security policy needs to make sense. Articulating why a security policy is in place and having practices to ensure compliance are challenges for any size organization. Making security a priority from the top of an organization down to the line workers will ensure the success of the policy.

6. SECURITY CONTROLS

Three types of security controls need to be implemented for a successful security policy to be put into action: physical, technical, and administrative.

Physical controls consist of things such as magnetic swipe cards, radio-frequency identification, or biometric security to prevent access to stored information or network resources. Physical controls consist of environmental controls such as heating, ventilation and air conditioning units, power generators, and fire suppression systems. One of the most common failures is people when leave their computers on and another person uses the computers to gain access to information or data they should not be allowed to access. Many companies employ password screen savers or require a computer to be "locked" before a workstation is

left. Another common security measure is to encrypt the drives on a computer. Many vendors have whole-disk encryption. When you encrypt a disk it prevents data from being accessed from a stolen laptop or computer.

Technical controls can also be called software or system control; they are used to limit access to network resources and devices that are used in the organization. They can be individual usernames and passwords used to access individual devices or access control lists (ACLs) that are part of a network operating system. Many organizations are putting in password expiration dates of 30—60 days and even account deletion for accounts not accessed for more than 90 days. In addition, passwords that contain numbers, upper and lowercase letters, and special characters and have a length that exceeds 12 characters are required by some organizations to ensure stronger passwords. Short passwords are susceptible to brute force hacking, which tries every combination to break into a computer. There are also tables that contain the most commonly used passwords. Stay away from words or two-word passwords. For sure, stay away from princess, king, password, 123, 456, 1234, qwerty, dragon, baseball, football, etc.

Administrative controls consist of policies created by an organization that determine how they will work. These controls guide employees by describing how their jobs are to be done and what resources they are supposed to use to do them. This is probably the weakest section of each company's policies. The lack of written policies makes implementing security difficult. More organizations should spend time setting up their policies and keeping their employees up to date on what expectations they have for each employee.

7. NETWORK ACCESS

The first step in developing a security management system is to document the network resources and which group of users may access those resources. Users should have access only to the resources that they need to complete their jobs efficiently. An example of when this will come in handy is when the president of the company wants access to every network resource and then his computer becomes infected with a virus that starts infecting all network files. Organizing who has access and who does not is important (Fig. 25.2). Network access is complicated. "Do not get be behind the fence" makes us aware that planning at the beginning can save time in the long run. ACLs should be planned ahead of time and then implemented on the network to avoid complications with the network ACL hierarchy.

An ACL dictates which users have access to certain network resources. Network administrators usually have access to all files and folders on a server. Department administrators will have access to all files used by their

FIGURE 25.2 Network access is complicated. Don't get caught behind the fence.

departments. End users will have access to a subset of the department files they need to perform their jobs. ACLs are developed by the head of IT for an organization and the network administrator, and implemented by the network administrator.

Implementing ACLs prevents end users from being able to access sensitive company information and helps them perform their jobs better by not giving them access to information that can act as a distraction. Access control can apply to physical access as well as electronic access. Access to certain networking devices could cause an entire organization to stop functioning for a period of time, so access to those devices should be carefully controlled.

The use of Remote Authentication Dial in User Service is an added layer of security to your network. Many of these systems employ a random number generator key fob that displays a random number and changes it every 30–60 s. With this extra step of user authentication, a person can combine a private key along with the random number to access the network. For example, an RSA SecureID token generates an eight-digit number; combined with the user's own four-digit private password, an administrator can stop unauthorized access to the system.

8. RISK ASSESSMENT

Before security threats can be blocked, all risks must first be identified and assessed (see checklist: "An Agenda for Action When Identifying and Assessing Risks"). Risk assessment forms the foundation of a good security management system. Network administrators must document all aspects of the network setup. This documentation should provide information on the network firewall, Wi-Fi access points, printers, servers, workstations, and any other devices physically or wirelessly connected to the network.

An Agenda for Action When Identifying and Assessing Risks

The most time should be spent documenting how the private computer network will be connected to the Internet for Web browsing and email. Some common security risks that should be identified and assessed are (check all tasks completed):

_____1. USB storage devices: devices that can be used to copy proprietary company data off the internal network. Many organizations use software solutions to disable unused USB ports on a system; others physically block the connections.

_____2. Remote control software: Services such as GoToMyPc or Log Me In do not require special router or firewall configuration to enable remote access.

_____3. Email: Filters should be put in place to prevent sensitive company information from simply being emailed outside the organization.

_____4. General Internet use: There is always the possibility of downloading a malicious virus from the Internet unless all but trusted and necessary websites are restricted to internal users. This can be accomplished by a content-filtering firewall or Web proxy server.

_____5. Laptops: Lost laptops pose a large security risk, depending on the type on data stored on them.

Policies need to be put in place to determine what types of information can be stored on these devices and what actions should be taken if a laptop is lost.

_____6. Peer-to-peer applications: Peer-to-peer applications that are used to download illegal music and software cause a risk because the files that are downloaded are not coming from known sources. People who download an illegal version of an application could be downloading a worm that can affect the entire network.

_____7. Television/digital video recorder/Blu-Ray devices: With the expansion of technology, even televisions have Internet access and storage.

_____8. Voice Over Internet Protocol (VoIP) telephones: The proliferation of VoIP telephones brings another device into our network environment. Some companies prefer to have their phones on a separate physical network, which prevents slow response times and bad phone quality; others have routers and switches that will prioritize the traffic of the phone calls to maintain good phone quality.

9. INCIDENT RESPONSE

Knowing what to do in case of a security incident is crucial to being able to track down what happened and how to make sure it never happens again. When a security incident is identified, it is imperative that steps are taken so that forensic evidence is not destroyed in the investigation process. Forensic evidence includes the content of all storage devices attached to the system at the time of the incident and even the contents stored in the memory of a running computer. Using an external hard drive enclosure to browse the content of the hard drive of a compromised system will destroy the date and timestamps a forensic technician can use to tie together various system events.

When a system breach or security issue has been detected, it is recommended to consult someone familiar with forensically sound investigation methods. If forensic methods are not used, it can lead to evidence not being admissible in court if the incident results in a court case.

There are specific steps to take with a computer system, depending on the type of incident that occurred. Unless a system is causing damage to itself by deleting files or folders that can be potential evidence, it is best to leave the system running but disconnected from the network, for the forensic investigator. The forensic investigator will:

- *document what is on the screen by photographing it.* He will also photograph the actual computer system and all cable connections. Do not forget about any peripherals that may contain storage. Many modern printers and routers have internal storage or connections for USB storage drives.
- *capture the contents of the system's memory.* This is done using a small utility installed from a removable drive that will create a forensic image of what is in the system's physical memory. This can be used to document Trojan activity. If memory is not imaged and the computer was used to commit a crime, the computer's user can claim that a malicious virus, which was running only in memory, was responsible.
- *turn off the computer.* If the system is running a Windows workstation operating system such as Windows Vista Workstation or Windows Azure, the forensic technician will pull the plug on the system. If the system is running a server operating system such as Windows Server 2008, Windows 7 Server, Windows Server 2012, Windows 8 and 10 or a Linux or UNIX-based operating system such as Red Hat, Fedora, or Ubuntu, the investigator will properly shut down the system.
- create a forensic image of the system's hard drive. This is done using imaging software and usually a hardware write-blocker to connect the system's hard drive to the imaging computer. A hardware write-blocker is used to prevent the imaging computer from writing anything at all to the hard drive. By default, Windows will create

a recycle bin on the new volume that it is able to mount, which would cause the evidence to lose forensic value. Investigators are then able to search through the system without making changes to the original media.

10. SUMMARY

Organizations interested in implementing a comprehensive security management system should start with a good roadmap. Fig. 25.3 ("Don't get struck by lightning. Implement ISO/IEC-27000) cautions us to have a good plan and execute the plan. Information is the key to security. By documenting all business processes that are critical to an organization and then analyzing the risks associated with them, you can get a better understanding of how to thwart threats to your systems. Each business should implement controls that can protect those processes from external and internal threats.

Physical security as well as virtual security should be considered. Internet threats are not usually the cause of someone with malicious intent but rather someone who accidentally downloads a Trojan or accidentally moves or deletes a directory or critical file. For a plan to work in the long run, you must perform annual recursive checking of the policies your organization has put in place. Then adjust for new technologies that need to be protected or new ways that external threats can damage your network. The easiest way to implement security management systems is to use the Plan−Do−Act−Check process to step though the necessary procedures. A locked door, a good password, and good supervision of employees are key to good security management.

Finally, let us move on to the real interactive part of this chapter: review questions/exercises, hands-on projects, case

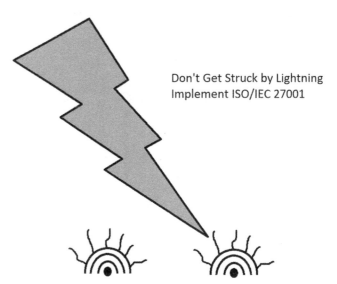

Don't Get Struck by Lightning
Implement ISO/IEC 27001

FIGURE 25.3 Don't get struck by lightning. Implement International Organization for Standardization (ISO)/International Electrotechnical Commission (IEC)-27000.

projects, and the optional team case project. The answers and/or solutions by chapter can be found in the Online Instructor's Solutions Manual.

CHAPTER REVIEW QUESTIONS/EXERCISES

True/False

1. True or False? To give organizations a starting point to develop their own security management systems, the International Organization for Standardization (ISO) and the International Electrotechnical Commission (IEC) developed a family of standards known as the Information Security Management System-27,000 Family of Standards.
2. True or False? Training should include creating company security policies and creating user roles that are specific to the organization.
3. True or False? The act of securing information has not been around for as long as the idea of storing information.
4. True or False? All personnel who come into contact with information systems need to be aware of the risks from improper use of those systems.
5. True or False? Each organization should not develop a company policy detailing the preferred use of company data or company software.

Multiple Choice

1. ____what is on the screen by photographing it?
   A. Capture
   B. Turn off
   C. Document
   D. Create
   E. All of the above
2. ____the contents of the system's memory?
   A. Turn off
   B. Document
   C. Create
   D. Capture
   E. All of the above
3. ____the computer?
   A. Capture

   B. Create
   C. Document
   D. Distribute
   E. Turn off
4. ____a forensic image of the system's hard drive?
   A. Create
   B. Turn off
   C. Capture
   D. Document
   E. All of the above
5. Devices that can be used to copy proprietary company data off the internal network are known as:
   A. Remote control software
   B. Email
   C. USB storage
   D. General Internet use
   E. Risk analysis

EXERCISE

Problem

Why should an organization certify its security management system?

HANDS-On Projects

Project

How does ISO/IEC-27001 (BS 7799) relate to other security management system standards (ISO-9001 and 14001)?

Case Projects

Problem

Why should an organization invest in implementing a short message service and certifying it using ISO/IEC-27001 (BS 7799-2)?

Optional Team Case Project

Problem

How is risk assessment related to ISO/IEC-27001 (BS 7799)?

Chapter 26

Policy-Driven System Management

Henrik Plate[1], Cataldo Basile[2] and Stefano Paraboschi[3]

[1]SAP Research Sophia-Antipolis, Mougins, France; [2]Politecnico di Torino, Torino, Italy; [3]Universitá degli studi di Bergamo, Bergamo, Italy

1. INTRODUCTION

This chapter begins with a high-level view of security management and the development of security concepts, followed by an introduction of core concepts and terms relevant to policy-based management (PBM) in particular, the layering of policies with different abstraction levels in a so-called policy hierarchy. Sections 3 and 4 explain high-level security objectives and principles, policies, and technologies relevant to the various policy abstraction levels and architecture layers in more detail, thereby putting particular focus on access control policies, related enforcement technologies, and selection criteria when touching lower abstraction levels. Section 5 summarizes the policy-related functionality of a small selection of existing products and technologies. Because the large-scale deployment of a policy-based computing system does not yet exist, all of the examples provide focus on selected aspects of PBM. Section 6 explains the approach of two research projects on the subject matter: Ponder, a project conducted in the early 1990s, considered a forerunner in this research domain; and Policy and Security Configuration Management (PoSecCo), an ongoing European Union research project that relates PBM to organizational structures and processes, seeking to optimize and semiautomate the policy refinement process, and supporting policy-based configuration audits. The products and projects introduced in Sections 5 and 6 will be positioned with regard to the security life-cycle phases covered, policy types and abstraction levels supported, and architecture layers concerned. Note that we put special emphasis on access control (AC), and leave other security-related topics and technologies aside (privacy or Digital Rights Management).

2. SECURITY AND POLICY-BASED MANAGEMENT

This section briefly summarizes today's practice with regard to security management, followed by a description of its deficiencies and an explanation of how PBM can help overcome them. Thereafter, we explain basic concepts of PBM and conclude with a short summary of autonomic computing, which aims at policy-based self-management of future information systems.

System Architecture and Security Management

Information technology (IT) systems are traditionally structured according to several architecture layers; each layer offers a number of security capabilities that can support organizations in reaching desired security objectives. Architectures that exemplify the layered structure of IT systems are the three-tier architecture of Web applications or the cloud computing reference architecture [1]. Typical architecture layers are composed of, for instance, user front ends, software services, andzxapplications that implement the business logic, platform services that provide a runtime environment, or infrastructure services that offer connectivity or computing resources.

Ideally, capabilities offered on different layers are combined in a complementary manner to implement *defense in depth*, a security principle recommending the setup of multiple, complementary lines of defense against malicious attacks or other threats to security. Because many

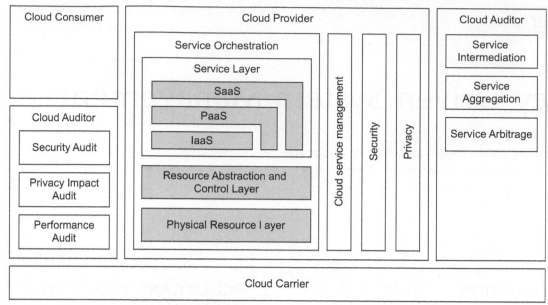

FIGURE 26.1   National Institute of Standards and Technology cloud computing reference architecture [1]. *IaaS*, infrastructure as a service; *PaaS*, platform as a service; *SaaS*, software as a service.

of the security mechanisms[1] employed on different layers do not work in isolation but affect each other, security is typically seen to be orthogonal to the various technology layers to have a holistic view of security (Fig. 26.1). This view is also supported by the IT Infrastructure Library[2] (ITIL), a widely adapted methodology for the management of IT services, which aims to overcome IT silos, specialized people, expertise, and tools that focus on the management of system slices (databases or networks).

High-level security objectives, common controls, as well as processes regarding the design, implementation, and operation of an information security management system and a security concept are described in various standards and guidelines (the International Organization for Standardization (ISO) 27000 series of standards as well as national adaptations[3]). These processes structure the design of secure systems in several phases that generally follow the idea of the plan—do—check—act cycle introduced by Deming [3].

The *plan* phase starts with the specification of security objectives and the definition of protection requirements by C-level executives, data protection (DP) officers, or business stakeholders. Larger organizations and those known to have special requirements can do this on the basis of a comprehensive risk analysis, whereas others follow a best-practice approach. Other sources of high-level objectives are composed of general laws and regulations (Sarbanes—Oxley Act or privacy laws) or industry-specific standards such as those from the US Food and Drug Administration, or the Data Security Standard (DSS) authored by the Payment Card Industry (PCI), which is relevant for every organization that stores or processes cardholder information [4].

Once those high-level objectives are defined, suitable security controls need to be identified and assessed by means of a cost—benefit analysis; as a result, some of the controls will be selected for implementation. This activity is complicated by the fact that the security capabilities of controls residing on different architecture layers can overlap and even conflict. Application servers, for instance, also support Internet Protocol (IP) address filtering.[4] Firewalls, as another example, emerged to analyze application-level communication protocols.

The *do* phase sees the implementation of security controls, which includes, among other activities, the transformation of high-level policies to a representation that can be interpreted by the security mechanisms selected. Here, system and security administrators knowledgeable in the various technologies enter the scene. The *check* phase concerns the performance review and monitoring of security mechanisms as to understanding whether they are still suitable to meet the initial objectives (design

---

1. Note that we use the terms *security mechanism* and *security control* interchangeably to denote a technical security capability provided by software or hardware components. In other contexts, the term *security control* typically has a broader meaning, and denotes technical and nontechnical measures to reach a given security objective.
2. http://www.itil-officialsite.com.
3. The Federal Office for Information Security (BSI) in Germany, for example, maintains the standard BSI 100-1 to describe general requirements for an Information Security Management System in greater detail and following a more didactic approach [2].

4. The Apache HTTP Server, for example, supports AC rules with conditions over source IP addresses or domain names.

Policy-Driven System Management **Chapter | 26** **429**

effectiveness) and whether they work as designed (operation effectiveness). Finally, the *act* phase covers continuous improvements of the security mechanisms in reaction to (small) requirement and system changes.

The Promise of Policy-Based Management

Security management as performed today involves a variety of stakeholders with different job functions, expertise, and objectives, and the use of different tools and terminology. Human-centric processes, however, are the main contributor to the significant increase of costs related to system management. On average, 70% of IT budgets are spent to maintain and manage current IT infrastructures [5]. Despite significant spending, many organizations "cannot prove enforcement [of security policies] or it is prohibitively expensive to do so" [6]. At the same time, human intervention is prone to errors, in particular when it comes to repetitive tasks involving low-level technology aspects. A series of studies shows that inaccurate configuration settings are among the most common reasons for insecure and incompliant systems, many times leading to actual data breaches [7,8]. A UK security report, for instance, found that, "whilst many of the organizations investigated actually had firewalls installed, poor configuration of these devices rendered most of them useless" [9]. Moreover, "in over 96% of cases, … PCI DSS was not adequately adhered to." Inaccurate configurations are typically introduced during the implementation and operations phase of a security concept, for instance, when configurations are altered to reflect system or business process changes.

In light of this, the promise of PBM with regard to system management is twofold. On the one hand, it aims to reduce management costs by automating activities that require human intervention. On the other hand, it aims to improve service quality (in part through avoiding human failure). Both goals should be achieved by sparing humans from low-level and repetitive tasks that relate to technical implementation details of IT systems.

One property of policy-based systems that contributes to these goals is the fact that security decision rules of system elements are not represented by hard-coded algorithms, which would result in modifications or replacements of system elements whenever security rules change. Policy-based systems instead rely on declarative statements made available to and interpreted by the respective system element. This separation of policy specification and enforcement is cost-beneficial and increases the flexibility to adapt a system to changing security requirements.

PBM aligns well with the security life cycle, because both follow a top–down approach that starts with the specification of high-level objectives and ends with the enforcement of low-level policies by security mechanisms. In PBM, high-level security objectives that control overall system behavior are still given by humans, but subsequent steps related to the selection, implementation, and operation of appropriate mechanisms become more and more automated.

To reach its goals, PBM must address the following problems: the identification, assessment, and selection of appropriate security mechanisms, the refinement of higher-level policies to lower-level representations until selected enforcement mechanisms can interpret them, the analysis and resolution of policy conflicts occurring on several abstraction levels, within and across policy enforcement mechanisms, and, finally, the organization of policies and their distribution to enforcement devices.

Policy Basics

Generally speaking, a *policy* is a "definite goal, course or method of action to guide and determine present and future decisions" [10]. The term *policy* is broadly used in the domain of computer science and information security, and denotes many different things (firewall policies, access control policies, acceptable use policies, or security policies). Sometimes the term refers to a single policy rule; in other contexts it refers to a collection of such rules.

For our purposes, a policy constrains the behavior of computing systems. More formally, following Agrawal et al. [11], a policy is defined over a target system that is associated with a number of attributes that have a certain type, and all of which together determine the system state. The behavior of a system is then defined as a continuous ordered set of states in which order is imposed by time. Considering the set of all possible behaviors, a policy represents a set of constraints on the possible behaviors (it defines a subset of acceptable behaviors). Based on this generic definition, in Agrawal et al. [11] policies are classified into different types, in particular *configuration constraint policies* that constrain the values of configurable system attributes, *metric constraint policies* that constrain observable but not directly influenceable attributes, *action policies* that, upon the observation of a given state, trigger operations to reach a desired target state, and *alert policies* that notify users as soon as the system state satisfies certain conditions.

A password policy, for instance, that demands a certain password length and complexity can be considered a configuration constraint policy over attributes belonging to an authentication mechanism. An access control policy, for instance, can be considered an action policy in which the condition is defined over attributes of the subject, resource, or other entities, and the action is either to deny or allow.

Although the generality of this definition covers a broad range of policies, many more specific definitions were created for single-policy application domains. In that context, *policy information models* are often used to visualize the constituting policy elements and their structural relationships. Condition-

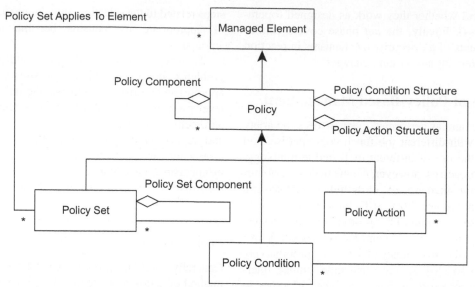

FIGURE 26.2 Common Information Model policy model [12].

action (CA) and embedded and communications alliance (ECA) thus represent basic policy models in which a single action or set of actions is executed upon certain conditions.[5] The Common Information Model (CIM) Policy Model, for instance, uses Unified Modeling Language (UML) to model the structure of CA policies that can be associated with CIM managed elements (Fig. 26.2).[6]

Security-related information models such as for AC typically specify conditions under which a subject can perform an operation defined over a target (or resource). Upon first sight, typical AC policy models seem to differ from the CA–ECA models mentioned before. However, this is because event and action are not made explicit, but exist implicitly in the form of the access request issued by the subject, and the deny or allow action that determines whether access can be granted.

Information models are useful for illustrating the conceptual structure of policies, but *policy languages* are required to represent concrete policies. A plethora of such languages exist, ranging from natural language for the expression of high-level policies on the one hand to precise mathematical models to support computer-based reasoning on the other. In many cases, the syntax and vocabulary of a policy language are tailored to a specific application domain, and some languages were designed without explicitly denoting the underlying information model. eXtensible Access Control Markup Language (XACML), for instance, is a widely used eXtensible Markup Language (XML)-based language for expressing access control policies. CIM–Simple Policy

Language (SPL), for instance, can be used to represent CIM policies according to the CIM Policy Model.

Policy Hierarchy and Refinement

The PBM approach naturally leads to a so-called policy continuum [13], a hierarchy of policies that are subject to different abstraction levels. Such policies undergo an iterative refinement process that transforms high-level and abstract policies into lower-level representations that can be eventually interpreted by enforcement mechanisms situated in a given IT system.

The highest policy abstraction level is typically referred to as business view [14], goal policies [15,16],[7] corporate policies [17], or high-level user-specified policies [11]. Such policies use business terms and relate to, for instance, corporate goals, business-critical risks, or regulatory and legal requirements. They abstract from the IT system in question and often specify goals without detailing how to attain them. They are typically authored by management and business users who neither need nor want to depend on technology when specifying business goals. Because they are independent from the IT system, business policies typically remain more stable than lower-level representations that are more exposed to system changes. Business policies are often written in an informal and possibly ambiguous way (with the support of spreadsheets and policy documents, and so they are seldom subject to automated reasoning that supports the detection of policy conflicts).

---

5. The ECA model also specifies the event that triggers the evaluation.
6. The CIM is a DMTF standard that uses an object-oriented approach to model computing systems and is widely used in IT management systems.

7. Although in White et al. [16] utility function policies are considered the highest policy level, we consider them here as metapolicies that define the relative importance of goal policies.

The PCI—DSS requirement, which demands the use of "strong cryptography and security protocols to safeguard cardholder data during transmission over public networks," is a typical example of a high-level business policy [4]. It merely states an objective without prescribing a specific enforcement technology, and it remains agnostic of a given IT system. "Response time must not exceed 2 s" is another example of a high-level goal policy [16], because it does not specify suitable actions to improve the response time once the threshold is reached.

The number of intermediate abstraction levels following business policies varies among classification schemes. In White et al. [16], for instance, action policies are presented that specify how a goal policy can be reached, and in Agrawal et al. [11], a distinction is made between abstract, technology-independent and concrete, technology-specific policies as intermediate levels. Common to the transformation of higher to lower abstraction levels is that policies are enriched step-by-step with additional details, which thereby keeps the policy structure intact. Policy goals are substituted with actions and mechanisms that support reaching the goal. To enforce the PCI—DSS requirement, for instance, one has to specify the security technology to be used [Secure Socket Layer (SSL)/Transport Layer Security (TLS) or IPsec]. As another example, the action policy "Increase CPU share by 5% if response time exceeds 2 s" refines this goal policy using the form CA. Moreover, policy components such as subjects, targets, conditions, and actions become refined and enriched until they correspond to identifiable elements in a given IT system. Logical roles, for instance, are substituted with technical roles used in the respective system components; or logical names for computers or groups of computers become substituted with IP addresses or address ranges. The kind of lower-level information to be enriched depends on the enforcement mechanism chosen (IP addresses for network-level firewalls vs. protocols or URLs for application-level firewalls), whereas the actual information is determined by the system in question.

The lowest policy abstraction level is typically referred to as executable or deployment policies [11], or policy mechanism information [15]. These policies can be deployed into and interpreted by a given system component, which then acts as a policy enforcement point. The format or language to express executable policies depends on technologies and vendors. Typical examples for executable policies are, for instance, configuration parameters that establish the use of TLS for Internet-facing Web applications that process cardholder data, or a configuration rule that increases or decreases the priority of operating system processes depending on response time changes. System management tools typically focus on a subset of policy representations instead of taking a holistic view of the entire policy hierarchy. Microsoft Group Policy, for instance, concentrates only on the executable policy layer but does not support policy analysis or translation of upper-layer policy representations. Security architecture professional (SAS) Access Control, as another example, supports concrete policies for role-based access control systems and their translation to vendor-specific representations on the executable policy layer.

Policy Organization and Conflicts

Larger systems make it impractical to specify policies for individual system elements. Accordingly, PBM must support the grouping of both policies and system elements to facilitate the scoping of policies (the specification of system elements to which a given set of policies should apply). System management is typically structured by administrative domains that govern a subset of the entire system, which is organized in a hierarchical fashion. This hierarchy is then used to group system elements and policies.

Microsoft Group Policy, for instance, supports the linking of policies to a hierarchy of domains, sites, and organizational units. In Sloman [15], the term *managed domain* was introduced to denote a collection of managed objects that are grouped for management purposes. In Agrawal et al. [11], the use of roles is presented as a means to creating group policies. Policies for Web servers can be created, distributed, and evaluated as a group.

Once a set of policies is somehow structured and assigned to managed elements, the system has to determine which policy or policies should be evaluated in the course of a given event. This selection is supported by different strategies, sometimes considering the entire set of policies and sometimes terminating the search as soon as an applicable policy is found. Policies assigned to tree structures allow, for instance, preference of more specific over more general policies, or vice versa. A strategy implemented by most firewalls is to order policy rules, evaluate the first one with matching conditions, and ignore the rest. Other means are to prioritize policies and evaluate the one with the highest priority in case several policies have matching conditions, or to specify metapolicies.

Moreover, a group of policies may be subject to anomalies and conflicts. A (modal) policy conflict between, for instance, firewall policy rules arises if two rules have overlapping conditions (on the source IP address) but conflicting actions (allow and deny). As another example, a modal conflict between obligation and access control policies exists if a subject is obliged to perform a given action but does not have the required authorization [18]. Such conflicts are relatively easy to spot in case they concern just one enforcement point (a firewall) but are more complex if several enforcement points are concerned. Accordingly, continuing the firewall example, a classification is presented in Al-Shaer et al. [19] of intrafirewall and interfirewall policy conflicts (conflicts that arise from the interpretation of policy rules by a single firewall and those that result from a sequence of policy evaluations performed by several firewalls). Furthermore, conflicts can also occur between policies targeting different architecture layers, which are again more difficult to identify and require a holistic view on policies. More details on policy conflicts can be found in Chapter 55.

Policy Distribution

Once refined to low-level representations (executable policies according to the terminology used by Agrawal et al. [11]), policies need to be distributed to system elements that need to evaluate and enforce them at system runtime. To overcome problems inherent in manual deployment, a variety of tools support administrators in the automated deployment of policies in large-scale distributed systems.

Such tools include, on the one hand, tailor-made configuration scripts that copy configuration files by, for instance, means of Secure Shell connections. This category of tools is also composed of, on the other hand, configuration management systems such as SAP Solution Manager or HP OpenView, which maintains central configuration repositories, support versioning, and implement ITIL-defined workflows to prevent unauthorized and erroneous configuration changes. Other examples are Local Configuration, a large-scale UNIX configuration system that facilitates configuration management in UNIX environments, and Microsoft Group Policy, which supports Windows environments. Configuration management systems increase the correctness and consistency of configuration information, speed deployment processes, and support a variety of other security-related activities such as IT audits. However, they do not yet free humans from the burden of dealing with low-level details of system management, because the initial specification of low-level configuration parameters is still left to administrators. In other words, they cover neither high-level policy representations nor the translation from abstract policies to concrete configuration parameters.

Generic Policy Architecture

Policy-based systems require a set of common functionalities related to the creation, storage, distribution, and enforcement of policies. The standardization bodies Internet Engineering Task Force (IETF) and Distributed Management Task Force, Inc. (DMTF) started defining a generic architecture for policy-based systems [20], which was subsequently refined and now represents a common basis for policy-related work, thereby abstracting from specific technologies, vendors, or types of policies.

In this generic architecture, the policy administration point (PAP) provides a user interface to allow end users to create, translate, validate, and manage policies that will be stored in a policy repository. At system runtime, a policy decision point (PDP) identifies and evaluates applicable policies provided by the repository to decide whether appropriate actions need to be taken. In the course of policy evaluation, a policy information point (PIP) supplies complementary information required to take a policy decision. Finally, the so-called policy enforcement point (PEP) is responsible for ensuring that the outcome of policy decisions is enforced in the system.

The runtime interaction of these components can be illustrated as the example of an access request to a protected resource (Fig. 26.3). Here, the PEP mediates any access request of a user to a protected resource. The PEP sends a corresponding request to the PDP, providing identifiers of the authenticated user and the protected resource. The PDP searches for applicable policies and seeks complementary information from the PIP: for instance, user-role assignments stored in a Lightweight Directory Access Protocol directory. The PDP terminates the policy evaluation by deciding whether access to this resource should be denied or granted to the user in question, which in turn is enforced

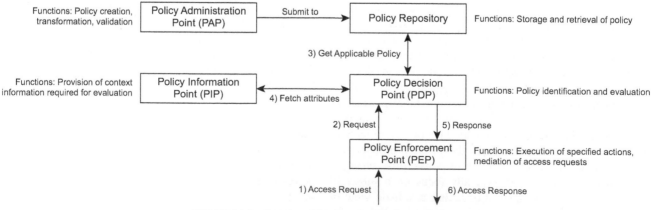

FIGURE 26.3 Generic architecture of policy-based systems.

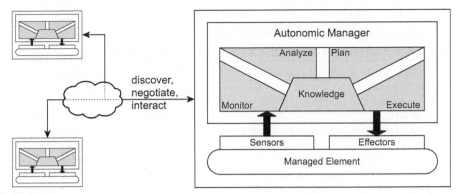

FIGURE 26.4 Monitor, Analyze, Plan, Execute, and Knowledge reference model for autonomic elements.

by the PEP. The preceding could be implemented with the help of, for instance, XACML, which not only specifies a language for defining AC policies but also defines a protocol for the interaction of PEP and PDP.

Note that most security mechanisms, including some of those presented later in this chapter, implement several of these policy-related functions in an integrated manner rather than supporting a clean, protocol-based separation as outlined by the generic architecture. Firewalls, for instance, typically integrate the functionalities of PEP, PDP, and repository, which is motivated by significant performance advantages compared with the communication of possibly distributed components.

Autonomic Computing

The term *autonomic computing* was coined by IBM to denote computing systems that manage themselves [21]. Inspired by biological and social systems, autonomic (computing) systems are composed of autonomic elements (aka agents) that autonomously enforce high-level policies with which they were provided by humans or other system elements, and thereby discover, interact, and negotiate with other autonomic elements. Two of the four self-management properties stipulated by IBM are *self-protection* and *self-healing*. Self-protection refers to the capability of autonomic systems to detect and correlate distributed events that result from attacks, cascading failures, or problematic changes inadvertently introduced by users, and to react appropriately to defend the system against security compromise. Self-healing concerns the detection, diagnosis, and correction of localized problems that result from software bugs or hardware failures. The correction of a software bug could result, for instance, in the search, application, and test of software patches. The contribution of IBM's autonomic computing manifesto [22] does not primarily concern technology; the foundation was already laid, but it gives perspective to the future and long-term development of IT as a means to tie several research domains to a bigger context, and to address nontechnical questions that emerge when IT components behave in an autonomous fashion.

As illustrated by Fig. 26.4, an autonomic element is composed of autonomic manager, which seeks to enforce the policy by observing and manipulating one or several managed elements under its control. Managed elements essentially correspond to software as it exists; all of the security mechanisms presented in Section 5 can be managed elements. The autonomic manager monitors managed elements by using sensors, analyzes such information, and, when necessary, plans appropriate actions that are executed through effectors. In the course of policy distribution, and in contrast to existing distribution technologies, the autonomic manager receives a high-level policy that must be refined to lower-level representations understood by its managed elements. Policy translation as well as the analysis and planning phases of the Monitor, Analyze, Plan, Execute, Knowledge control loop are guided by a knowledge base populated by the agent developer. In case managed elements do not provide a required security capability by themselves, a software agent may also act as a policy enforcement point. Ponder, for instance, relies on agents to enforce authorization policies specified over the target managed element.

Accreditation

The following checklist addresses accreditation criteria for security and policy-based management (see checklist: An Agenda for Action When Addressing Accreditation Criteria for Security and Policy-Based Management) systems. The numbering of this checklist generally follows the numbering of other checklists found in the rest of the book, as well as other tasks that must be completed.

- All items on this checklist should be addressed.
- Place an "X" beside each item that represents a nonconformity (formerly called a deficiency).
- Place a "C" beside each item for which you are making a comment.
- Place an "OK" beside each item that you observed or verified at the laboratory.

An Agenda for Action When Addressing Accreditation Criteria for Security and Policy-Based Management

All organizations must adhere to the following accreditation process (check all tasks completed):

_____**1.** The management system documentation was most recently reviewed on _____. Changes and additions required by the reviewers were made by the laboratory.

_____**2.** The management system documentation was adequate for *continuation of the assessment process.*

_____**3.** Changes and additions to the management system documentation, which were required by the reviewers, were made by the laboratory.

_____**4.** The initial on-site visit was conducted on _____.

_____**5.** Resolutions of findings from the initial on-site visit will be reviewed during the assessment visit.

_____**6.** The results of the initial evaluations have been read and will be reviewed during the assessment visit.

_____**7.** The laboratory should establish and maintain policies and procedures for maintaining laboratory impartiality and integrity in evaluating the conduct of information technology security evaluations.

_____**8.** When conducting evaluations under the National Information Assurance Partnership (NIAP) Common Criteria Scheme, the laboratory policies and procedures should ensure that:

_____**a.** Laboratory staff members cannot both develop and evaluate the same protection profile, security target, or IT product.

_____**b.** Laboratory staff members cannot provide consulting services for and then participate in the evaluation of the same protection profile, security target, or IT product.

_____**9.** The laboratory should have physical and electronic controls augmented with an explicit policy and set of procedures for maintaining separation, both physical and electronic, between the laboratory evaluators and laboratory consultants, product developers, system integrators, and others who may have an interest in and/or may unduly influence the evaluation outcome.

_____**10.** The management system should include policies and procedures to ensure the protection of proprietary information.

_____**11.** The protection of proprietary information protection should specify how proprietary information will be protected from persons outside the laboratory, from visitors to the laboratory, from laboratory personnel without the need to know, and from other unauthorized persons.

_____**12.** The management system requirements are designed to promote laboratory practices that ensure the technical accuracy and integrity of the security evaluation and adherence to quality assurance practices appropriate to common criteria testing.

_____**13.** The laboratory should maintain a management system that fully documents the laboratory's policies and practices, and the specific steps taken to ensure the quality of the IT security evaluations.

_____**14.** The reference documents, standards, and publications should be available for use by laboratory staff developing and maintaining the management system and conducting evaluations.

_____**15.** Each applicant and accredited laboratory should have written and implemented procedures.

_____**16.** Records should be kept of all management system activities.

_____**17.** The procedures for review of contracts should include procedures to ensure that the laboratory has adequate staff and resources to meet its evaluation schedule and complete evaluations in a timely manner.

_____**18.** The laboratory should maintain a functional record-keeping system that is used to track each security evaluation.

_____**19.** Records should be easily accessible and contain complete information for each evaluation.

_____**20.** Required records of evaluation activities should be traceable to common criteria evaluator actions and common evaluation methodology work units.

_____**21.** Computer-based records should contain entries indicating the date created and the individual(s) who performed the work, along with any other information required by the management system.

_____**22.** Entries in laboratory notebooks should be dated and signed or initialed.

_____**23.** All records should be maintained in accordance with laboratory policies and procedures and in a manner that ensures record integrity.

_____**24.** There should be appropriate backups and archives.

_____**25.** There must be enough evaluation evidence in the records so that an independent body can determine what evaluation work was actually performed for each work unit and can concur with the verdict.

_____**26.** Records should include evaluator notebooks, records relating to the product, work-unit level records, and client-site records.

_____**27.** Laboratory records should be maintained, released, or destroyed in accordance with the laboratory's proprietary information policy and contractual agreements with customers.

_____**28.** Records covering the following are required:

_____**a.** All quality system activities

_____**b.** Staff training dates and competency reviews

_____**c.** All audits and management reviews

_____**d.** Creation of and changes to evaluation procedures and methodology

An Agenda for Action When Addressing Accreditation Criteria for Security and Policy-Based Management—cont'd

_____e. Acceptance/rejection of products submitted for evaluation

_____f. Complete tracking of multiple versions of evaluation evidence and evaluation technical reports

_____g. Complete tracking of evaluation activities to the work-unit level, including initial analysis, verdicts, and any subsequent changes to those verdicts (based on modifications of evidence or additional analysis)

_____h. Source code, binary executables, data, and configuration information sufficient to reproduce any testing performed during the evaluation must be retained; this includes source code and binary executables for any test tools (when available) along with test data and configuration information/files

_____i. Calibration records for any equipment when reported results include an estimate of error

_____j. Calibration records should include the range of calibration, the resolution of the instrument and its allowable error, calibration date and schedule, date and result of last calibration, identity of the laboratory individual or external service responsible for calibration, and source of reference standard and traceability

_____k. Configuration of all test equipment used during an evaluation along with analysis of that equipment to confirm the suitability of test equipment to perform the desired testing

_____29. The internal audit should cover the laboratory management system and the application of the management system to all laboratory activities.

_____30. The audit should cover compliance with contractual and laboratory management system requirements.

_____31. Audits should cover all aspects of the evaluation activities, including the evaluation work performed.

_____32. In the case in which only one member of the laboratory staff is competent to conduct a specific aspect of a test method, and performing an audit of work in this area would result in that person auditing his or her own work, audits may be conducted by another staff member.

_____33. The audit should cover the evaluation methodology for that test method and should include a review of documented procedures and instructions, adherence to procedures and instructions, and review of previous audit reports.

_____34. External experts may also be used in these situations.

_____35. The most recent internal audit report should be available for review during on-site assessments.

_____36. The laboratory shall perform at least one complete internal audit prior to the first full on-site assessment.

_____37. A partial internal audit should be performed before the initial on-site assessment.

_____38. The records should be reviewed before or during the on-site assessment visit.

_____39. The most recent management review report should be available for review during on-site assessments.

_____40. The laboratory should perform at least one management review before the first full on-site assessment.

_____41. A management review should be performed before the initial on-site assessment.

_____42. The records should be reviewed before or during the on-site assessment visit.

_____43. The quality manual should contain, or refer to, documentation that describes and details the laboratory's implementation of procedures covering all of the technical requirements.

_____44. The laboratory should maintain a competent administrative and technical staff appropriate for common criteria-based IT security evaluations.

_____45. The laboratory should maintain position descriptions, training records, and resumes for responsible supervisory personnel and laboratory staff members who have an effect on the outcome of security evaluations.

_____46. The laboratory should maintain a list of personnel designated to fulfill requirements, including the laboratory director, an authorized representative, approved signatories, evaluation team leaders, and senior evaluators.

_____47. The laboratory should also identify a staff member as a quality manager who has overall responsibility for the management system, the quality system, and maintenance of the management system documents.

_____48. An individual may be assigned or appointed to serve in more than one position; however, to the extent possible, the laboratory director and the quality manager positions should be independently staffed.

_____49. When key laboratory staff is added, the notification of changes should include a current resume for each new staff member.

_____50. Laboratories should document the required qualifications for each staff position.

_____51. The staff information may be kept in the official personnel folders or in separate official folders that contain only the information that the assessors need to review.

_____52. Laboratory staff members who conduct IT security evaluation activities should have a bachelor of

Continued

An Agenda for Action When Addressing Accreditation Criteria for Security and Policy-Based Management—cont'd

science in computer science, computer engineering, or a related technical discipline or equivalent experience.

____53. Laboratory staff collectively should have knowledge or experience in the following areas: operating systems, data structures, design/analysis of algorithms, database systems, programming languages, computer systems architectures, and networking.

____54. In addition, the laboratory staff should have knowledge or experience in any specific technologies for which an evaluation is conducted.

____55. The laboratory should have a detailed, documented description of its training program for new and current staff members.

____56. Each new staff member should be trained for assigned duties.

____57. The training program should be updated and current staff members should be retrained when the common criteria, common evaluation methodology, or scope of accreditation change, or when the individuals are assigned new responsibilities.

____58. Each staff member may receive training for assigned duties through on-the-job training, formal classroom study, attendance at conferences, or another appropriate mechanism.

____59. Training materials that are maintained within the laboratory should be kept up to date.

____60. Staff members should be trained in the following areas:

    ____a. general knowledge of test methods including generation of evaluation reports

    ____b. computer science concepts

    ____c. computer security concepts

    ____d. working knowledge of common criteria

    ____e. working knowledge of common methodology

____61. The laboratory should annually the competence of each staff member review for each test method the staff member is authorized to conduct.

____62. The staff member's immediate supervisor, or a designee appointed by the laboratory director, should conduct an assessment and an observation of performance annually for each staff member.

____63. A record of the annual review of each staff member should be dated and signed by the supervisor and the employee.

____64. A description of competency review programs should be maintained in the management system.

____65. Individuals hired to perform common criteria testing activities are sometimes referred to as "subcontractors."

____66. To that end, all individuals performing evaluation activities must satisfy all requirements, irrespective of the means by which individuals are compensated.

____67. The records for each staff member who have an effect on the outcome of evaluations should include a position description, resume/curriculum vitae/biography (matching person to job), duties assigned, annual competence review, and training records and training plans.

____68. To maintain confidentiality and impartiality, the laboratory should maintain proper separation between personnel conducting evaluations and other personnel inside the laboratory or outside the laboratory, but inside the parent organization.

____69. The laboratory should have adequate facilities to conduct IT security evaluations.

____70. This (Checklist Number 69) includes laboratory facilities for security evaluation, staff training, record keeping, document storage, and software storage.

____71. A protection system should be in place to safeguard customer proprietary hardware, software, test data, electronic and paper records, and other materials.

____72. The protection system should protect the proprietary materials and information from personnel outside the laboratory, visitors to the laboratory, laboratory personnel without a need to know, and other unauthorized persons.

____73. Laboratories should have systems (firewall and intrusion detection) in place to protect internal systems from untrustworthy external entities.

____74. If evaluation activities are conducted at more than one location, all locations should meet the requirements and mechanisms should be in place to ensure secure communication among all locations.

____75. The laboratory should have regularly updated protection for all systems against viruses and other malicious software (malware).

____76. The laboratory should have an effective backup system to ensure that data and records can be restored in the event of their loss.

____77. If the laboratory is conducting multiple simultaneous evaluations, it should maintain a system of separation between the products of different customers and evaluations.

____78. This (Checklist Number 77) includes the product under evaluation, the test platform, peripherals, documentation, electronic media, manuals, and records.

____79. Public key infrastructure—enabled electronic mail capability is required for communications.

____80. Internet access also is required to obtain revisions to the common criteria, common evaluation methodology, guidance, and interpretations.

____81. Evaluation activities will be conducted outside the laboratory, and the management system should include appropriate procedures for conducting security evaluation activities at customer sites or other off-site locations.

An Agenda for Action When Addressing Accreditation Criteria for Security and Policy-Based Management—cont'd

_____82. The customer site procedures should explain how to secure the site, where to store records and documentation, and how to control access to the test facility.

_____83. If the laboratory is conducting its evaluation at the customer site or other location outside the laboratory facility, the environment should conform to the requirements for the laboratory environment, as appropriate.

_____84. If a customer's system on which an evaluation is conducted is potentially open to access by unauthorized entities during the evaluation, the evaluation laboratory should control the evaluation environment.

_____85. This (Checklist Number 84) is to ensure that the systems are in a defined state compliant with the requirements for the evaluation before starting to perform evaluation work, and that the systems ensure that unauthorized entities do not gain access to the system during the evaluation.

_____86. The test methods of ISO/IEC 17025 are analogous to the evaluation methodology using the common criteria (CC), the common evaluation methodology (CEM), and additional laboratory-developed methodology.

_____87. The version of the CC and CEM to be used in each evaluation should be established in consultation with NIAP and the sponsor.

_____88. For the purposes of achieving product validation through the CC scheme, laboratories may be required to comply with both international interpretations and NIAP-specified guidance.

_____89. The CC, CEM, guidance and interpretations, and the laboratory's procedures for conducting security evaluations should be maintained up to date and be readily available to the staff.

_____90. The laboratory should have documented procedures for conducting security evaluations using the CC and CEM, and for complying with guidance or interpretations.

_____91. The laboratory should ensure that documented procedures are followed.

_____92. Security evaluations may be conducted at the customer site, the laboratory, or another location that is mutually agreed to.

_____93. When evaluation activities are conducted outside the laboratory, the laboratory should have additional procedures to ensure the integrity of all tests and recorded results.

_____94. The additional procedures should also ensure that the same requirements that apply to the laboratory and its facility are maintained at the nonlaboratory site.

_____95. When exceptions to the evaluation methodology are deemed necessary for technical reasons, and to ensure that the new methodology continues to meet all requirements and policies, the customer

should be informed, and details of these exceptions should be described in the evaluation report.

_____96. The laboratory should maintain on-site systems adequate to support IT security evaluations in keeping with the tests for which it is seeking accreditation.

_____97. The laboratory should have electronic report generation capability.

_____98. The laboratory should document and maintain records of all test equipment or test suites used during CC testing.

_____99. The laboratory is responsible for configuration and operation of all equipment within its control.

_____100. Computer systems and other platforms used during the conduct of testing should be under configuration control.

_____101. The laboratory should have procedures to ensure that any equipment (hardware and software) used for testing is in a known state before its use for testing.

_____102. Measurement traceability is required when applicable.

_____103. The equipment used to conduct security evaluations should be maintained in accordance with the manufacturer's recommendations or with internally documented laboratory procedures, as applicable.

_____104. Test equipment refers to software and hardware products or other assessment mechanisms used by the laboratory to support the evaluation of the security of an IT product.

_____105. Laboratories should calibrate their test equipment.

_____106. In CC testing, calibration means verification of correctness and suitability.

_____107. Any test tools used to conduct security evaluations that are not part of the unit under evaluation should be studied in isolation to make sure they correctly represent and assess the test assertions they make.

_____108. Test tools should also be examined to ensure they do not interfere with the conduct of the test and do not modify or affect the integrity of the product under testing in any way.

_____109. Laboratories should have procedures that ensure appropriate configuration of all test equipment.

_____110. Laboratories should maintain records of the configuration of test equipment and all analysis to ensure the suitability of test equipment to perform the desired testing.

_____111. For CC testing, "traceability" is interpreted to mean that security evaluation activities are traceable to the underlying CC requirements and work units in the CEM.

_____112. Test tools and evaluation methodology demonstrate that the tests they conduct and the test assertions they make are traceable to specific criteria and methodology.

_____113. The laboratory should use documented procedures for sampling.

Continued

Managing Information Security

An Agenda for Action When Addressing Accreditation Criteria for Security and Policy-Based Management—cont'd

_____**114.** Whenever sampling is used during an evaluation, the laboratory should document its sampling strategy, the decision-making process, and the nature of the sample.

_____**115.** Sampling should be part of the evaluation record.

_____**116.** The laboratory should protect products under evaluation and calibrated tools from modification, unauthorized access, and use.

_____**117.** The laboratory should maintain separation between and control over items from different evaluations to include the product under evaluation, its platform, peripherals, and documentation.

_____**118.** When the product under evaluation includes software components, the laboratory should ensure that configuration management mechanisms are in place to prevent inadvertent modifications to software components during the evaluation process.

_____**119.** The laboratory should have procedures to ensure proper retention, disposal, or return of software and hardware after completion of the evaluation.

_____**120.** The laboratory should have procedures for conducting a final review of evaluation results and laboratory records of the evaluation before their submission to the customer.

_____**121.** The laboratory should issue evaluation reports of its work that accurately, clearly, and unambiguously present the evaluator analysis, test conditions, test setup, test and evaluation results, and all other required information.

_____**122.** Evaluation reports should provide all necessary information to permit the same or another laboratory to reproduce the evaluation and obtain comparable results.

_____**123.** There may be two types of evaluation reports: (1) reports that are to be submitted, and (2) reports that are produced under contract and are intended for use by the customer.

_____**124.** The evaluation report should contain sufficient information for the exact test conditions and results to be reproduced at a later time if a reexamination or retest is necessary.

_____**125.** Reports intended for use only by the customer should meet customer laboratory contract obligations and be complete.

_____**126.** The electronic version should have the same content as the hard-copy version and use an application format (Adobe PDF or Microsoft Word).

_____**127.** Evaluation reports that are delivered in electronic form via electronic mail shall be digitally signed or have a message authentication code applied to ensure the integrity of the report and the identity of the laboratory that produced the report.

_____**128.** The laboratory should provide a secure means of conveying the necessary information for the verification of the signature or the message authentication code.

_____**129.** Confidentiality mechanisms should be employed to ensure that the evaluation report cannot be disclosed to anyone other than the intended recipient(s).

_____**130.** Each applicant and accredited laboratory should have written and implemented procedures.

_____**131.** Implementation is used here to mean that the appropriate management system and technical documents were written, experts and expertise were obtained, training was conducted, activity was conducted, activity was audited, and a management review was conducted.

_____**132.** Procedures are an integral part of the laboratory management system and should be included for all aspects of the laboratory operation.

_____**133.** A laboratory should implement all procedures that are required to meet the accreditation requirements.

_____**134.** Failure to have implemented procedures may lead to suspension of accreditation.

_____**135.** General procedures for the following activities are required and should be implemented before accreditation can be granted:

_____**a.** internal audits and management review
_____**b.** writing and implementing procedures
_____**c.** writing and implementing instructions
_____**d.** staff training and individual development plans
_____**e.** contract review
_____**f.** staff members who work at home and at alternate work sites outside the laboratory (telecommuting)
_____**g.** referencing National Voluntary Laboratory Accreditation Program (NVLAP) accreditation and use of the NVLAP logo

_____**136.** The following program-specific procedures should be implemented before the activity is undertaken, as well as procedures for writing common methodology work unit–level instructions before an evaluation is conducted:

_____**a.** writing a work plan for an evaluation
_____**b.** selecting the members of an evaluation team
_____**c.** writing an evaluation technical report
_____**d.** writing an observation report
_____**e.** conducting an evaluation at a customer's site (if the laboratory offers such services)
_____**f.** conducting evaluations for specific technologies (firewalls, operating systems, and biometric devices)
_____**g.** vulnerability analysis
_____**h.** conducting independent testing
_____**i.** requesting and incorporating interpretations
_____**j.** working with NIAP or other validators during an evaluation
_____**k.** records and record keeping for evaluations

3. CLASSIFICATION AND LANGUAGES

The availability of tools for policy-based security management will support the realization of all classical security objectives such as confidentiality, integrity, and availability. Indeed, in most cases, the design of a secure system separately considers each of the objectives, whereas a holistic view is needed to capture the interdependencies that exist among separate security services. For instance, the specification of authorizations requires the availability of adequate authentication services, and in the construction of a secure information system, it is the direct responsibility of the security designer to manage the integration between authentication and authorization. This dependency can be automatically implemented by PBM, with strong guarantees about its correct realization.

An important aspect of the design and implementation of a secure information system is the correct consideration of the security principles. They represent fundamental guidelines derived from experience. One of the most well-known security principles is the "least privilege" principle, which claims that elements of a system should only be authorized to execute the minimum set of actions that are required to fulfill the specified tasks. A crucial obstacle to realizing this principle is the difficulty in managing security policies. For instance, most Web applications and Web services use a single account to access the data stored in the database supporting the application, and the presence of a single vulnerability in the Web application may jeopardize the protection of the complete database content. Finer granularity controls and the application of "defense in depth" are services made available by tools for policy-based security management that permit better compliance with the "least privilege" principle.

The realization of policy-based security management has to consider the collection of approaches and solutions offered by current technology. AC is one of the critical components in the realization of a secure system, and many different models have been proposed to organize and support AC policies. The level of support of the high-level security requirements strongly depends on the features of the AC model that the underlying technological system is able to support. For instance, the high-level requirements can use the concept of "role," in a way consistent with the features of the role-based-access control (RBAC) model, but the underlying system may not offer native support to it; then the tool will be responsible for introducing a mapping from the high-level RBAC policies to the specific model supported by the system.

Next, the main security objectives are presented. Then, well-known security principles are presented; for each of them we describe how the realization of a policy-based security management can help achieve them in realizing a secure information system. Finally, the major AC models are described, and it will be shown how a modern approach to policy-based security management can flexibly support them.

Security Objectives

In computer security, the acronym CIA describes the basic security objectives of *confidentiality*, *integrity*, and *availability*, which a secure system is typically designed to support. These three basic objectives are the basis for realizing a large variety of security functions and satisfying the security requirements of most applications. In some applications there is the need to support only part of them, but a secure system is applicable to concrete scenarios only if all three of them are offered by the system and can immediately be adopted when the need arises.

Confidentiality is the property that is typically associated with the use of encryption. Indeed, when the concern about security derives from the transmission on a channel of sensitive information, encryption represents the crucial technology that is able to protect the information content of the transferred information from being readable by adversaries who have access to the communication channel. In information systems, the confidentiality of information stored within the system is mostly realized using the AC services, which are responsible for monitoring every access to a protected resource. Only read accesses that are consistent with the policy will be allowed by the system. In some cases, encryption can support the realization of an AC policy for read operations, but this is reserved for information systems with outsourced resources or for representation of data at the low level (hard disks support the encryption of the information contained in them).

Integrity is arguably the most important security service in the design of business applications. Integrity guarantees that all information stored and sent along communication channels is not manipulated by unauthorized users without detection. Integrity in network traffic commonly relies on the use of hash functions, message authentication codes, encryption functions, and digital signatures. Integrity for services requires that the function of the service not be manipulated (supported by code signing) and that only authenticated users that have been authorized to invoke a given service are actually able to have their service requests processed by the system. The critical aspect for achieving integrity protection is that the access policy is configured in a way consistent with security requirements.

Availability focuses on the resistance against attacks that aim to disrupt the offer of services. As a security service, this aspect is particularly important for military applications. In the business environment, this is typically considered together with safety and reliability aspects and represents the property that the system is able to provide the services continuously, independently from the variety of threats, owing to adversaries or random events that may make the system inoperable. There may be specific business scenarios in which the security aspect is extremely relevant (such as Web application providers that are victims of flooding attacks by adversaries who want to blackmail the service owners), but in most cases the scope is the complete collection of all possible malfunctions that can block the system.

Beyond CIA, other services are often added in this classification as basic security services, but they can typically be considered as variants or combinations of the main services. *Authenticity* can be considered a variant of integrity, in which resources and services have to prove their origin and users have to prove the control of a specified identity. *Accountability* is also a variant of integrity, in which the goal is to guarantee that actions on the system are always recorded without loss and associated with the verified identity of the user. In this way, *nonrepudiability* can also be guaranteed, because users cannot deny that they were responsible for the actions they executed on the system.

Security Principles

Security principles denote the basic guidelines that should be used when designing a secure system. Experience shows that a crucial success factor in the design of a secure system is the correct consideration of security principles. Vulnerabilities and attacks in most cases can be ascribed to the inadequate application of some principle.

Several classifications of these principles exist. A classical and seminal analysis is the one by Saltzer and Schroeder [23], which lists the following principles: least privilege, economy of mechanism, separation of privilege, psychological acceptability, fail-safe defaults, complete mediation, open design, and least common mechanism.

The *least privilege* principle requires the set of authorizations that each user gets in the system to be the minimum set that permits the user to execute his or her role. The same principle can be adopted for the configuration of the privileges of programs and services. The idea is that the *need-to-know* approach has to be used when giving access to resources or services. A critical requirement to apply the principle correctly is to have available an expressive authorization language that permits a fine-grained definition of the boundaries of the access domain of each user and process. The critical obstacle to applying this principle, when a flexible AC language is available, is the difficulty in forecasting the domain of resources precisely that the user will need to access in executing his tasks. The application of PBM offers great support to realizing this principle, because the policy is specified in a more abstract and structured way and limitations to the access of users can be better delineated. Application of the defense-in-depth approach is a variant of this principle that receives significant support from the advanced support of PBM.

The *economy of mechanism* principle establishes that the protection has to be obtained with a mechanism that is as simple as possible; otherwise it becomes harder to guarantee that the system is able to protect the resource. This principle becomes harder to respect in modern information systems, in which resources are typically stored in a layered system. For example, a sensitive credit card number can be used by an application, which stores it in a database, which stores it into a table stored on a disk managed by an operating system, which may be executed in a virtual machine running in parallel with a multitude of other processes; each layer may offer to the adversary its own opportunities to bypass the protection offered by the application. The protection then depends on the robust implementation at every layer. The use of encryption can mitigate the problem, but its adoption is far from trivial in most circumstances. PBM helps to have a consistent representation of an access policy across the multiple layers, increasing the strength at each layer.

The *separation of privilege* principle clarifies that greater protection can be obtained by requiring distinct actors for the execution of an action. In this way the system is more robust against breaches of trust in the principles legitimately receiving access privileges. An AC model supporting separation of duty constraints supports this principle. PBM can support separation of duty constraints even when the underlying access model does not offer native support to this construct.

The *psychological acceptability* principle states that the security solution has to be understandable by the users, both in its design and during its use. PBM offers clear support to this principle in the design phase, because it offers a way to understand the variety of security configurations that characterize a modern information system.

The *fail-safe defaults* principle suggests the use of a secure default configuration, in which in the absence of further information access has to be denied. The use of abstract policies can support the system-level specification of default protective actions that will be enforced by all of the elements in the system.

The *complete mediation* principle requires that every access to a protected resource must be monitored and verified for consistency with the access policy. The complete coverage of accesses offered by PBM can provide more robust guarantees that each access path is captured by the system.

The *open design* principle establishes that the security of the system must not depend on the obscurity of its design; rather, it has to depend on knowledge of a few well-managed secrets. In PBM, the availability of a high-level description of the policy limits the reliance on the assumption that the system can be protected by keeping hidden the protection measures. Instead, modern security practices are promoted.

The *least common mechanism* principle concerns the design of solutions in which a single resource or piece of software is used to mediate access for different users. Any vulnerability in such an element can then lead to a compromise of the system. PBM helps realize this privilege because it simplifies the configuration in a consistent way for multiple devices.

Access Control Models

AC commonly denotes the combination of the authentication, authorization, and auditing services. Each of the three services is organized into two parts: a policy directing how the system resources should be accessed, and a mechanism responsible for implementing the policy. Of the six components, the one that mostly characterizes the AC system is the *authorization policy.*

The authorization policy, given an access request produced by a user with the intention of executing a specific action on a resource, has the goal of specifying whether the request has to be authorized. Many proposals have emerged for representing the authorization policy. The design of the authorization policy has to balance the requirements of expressivity carefully with the strict efficiency constraints that limit the amount of computational resources that can be dedicated to processing each access request. There are a few long-term trends, clearly visible in the evolution of IT technology, that have a specific impact. The evolution of computer systems is significantly increasing the amount of computational resources available to process an access request; the application of AC increasingly occurs in distributed systems where the delay caused by network access can support a more complex evaluation; and application requirements are becoming more complex and require the evaluation of sophisticated conditions. These trends lead to a progressive increase in the amount of resources available to process each access request and to a corresponding enrichment of the AC models used to represent the authorization policies. We summarize the evolution of these models, describing their main features. Each model typically extends previous proposals and offers specific new functionalities.

The classical AC model, which is still the basis of most operating systems and databases, is the discretionary AC (DAC) model, which starts from the assumptions that users have the ability to manage the information they access without restrictions, and users are able to specify the access policy for the resources they create. The access policy can be represented by (subject, resource, action) triples that describe each permitted action. The elements of the policy can be organized by resource (offering access control lists) or subject (offering capabilities). This AC model presents a number of variants; for instance, a user can transfer the privileges he received; also, programs can be configured to give to users who invoke the program the privileges of the owner of the program.

A first evolution of the DAC model was represented by the mandatory AC (MAC) models, which establish policies that restrict the set of operations that users can apply over the

resources they are authorized to access. The most famous of these models is the Bell—LaPadula model [24], which was designed with inspiration from the approaches used to protect information in military and intelligence environments, classifying resources according to their secrecy level, and giving users clearance to access resources up to a certain level; restrictions are then imposed on the flow of information. The restrictions guarantee that information will not flow from a high level to a low level, independent of the actions of the users. Alternative MAC models have been defined supporting integrity (the Biba model [25]) and protection of conflict of interest requirements (the Chinese Wall model [26]). When applied to real systems, all of these models showed significant shortcomings, mostly owing to their rigidity; the presence of covert channels in real systems limited the robustness of the approach. The idea of establishing restrictions on the operations of a resource that depend on properties of resources and users is an advanced aspect that characterizes AC solutions.

The RBAC model [27] assumes that the assignment of privileges to users is mediated by the specification of roles. Roles represent functions in an organization, which require a collection of privileges to execute their tasks. Users are assigned a role depending on the organizational function that is given to them. The model is particularly interesting for large enterprises, in which this structure of the access policy greatly facilitates the management of the security requirements. The evolution of the access policy can be better controlled, with a clear strategy to support the evolution of the required resource privileges and of the organization. The use of roles in general requires two kinds of authorization: system authorization specifying the privileges a role should acquire and role authorization specifying the subjects that can enact the defined roles. This increase in structural complexity is in most cases mitigated by a significant reduction in the size of the policy and by easier management. The RBAC model has been successful and has been adopted in many environments, with dedicated support in the Structured Query Language 3 standard and modern operating systems.

A modern family of solutions is represented by attribute-based AC (ABAC) models. These models assume that authorizations can express conditions on properties of the resource and the subject. For instance, assuming that each resource has an attribute that denotes the identifier of the subject that created the resource, a single authorization can specify the ownership privilege for all creators of every resource; this would either require an ad hoc mechanism in the AC module or the creation of a distinct authorization for every resource. Advantages are evident in terms of flexibility and expressive power of the ABAC model. The main obstacle to its adoption in real systems has always been worry about the performance impact of such a solution. In the scenario of AC for cooperating Web services, this worry is mitigated by the high cost of each access that makes acceptable the cost required to evaluate predicates on resource and user properties. The XACML proposal is a notable example of a language that supports an ABAC model. The evolution of AC solutions is expected to lead to wider adoption of ABAC models.

Another family of authorization models focuses on specification of the constraint that different users have to be involved in executing a task. This is consistent with the "separation of privilege" principle presented earlier, which urges the design of secure systems to be robust against breaches of trust, by making critical actions executable only with the cooperation of a defined number of distinct users. The classical example is the withdrawal at a bank of an amount larger than a given threshold, which requires the cooperation of a bank teller and the supervision of the branch director. The damage that can be done by a corrupt or blackmailed bank employee is then limited.

Several models have been proposed for representation of these AC restrictions, commonly called Separation of Duty (SoD) constraints. The design of such a model typically occurs extending a role-based model, specifying different privileges for roles that are required in the execution of a given process, and then imposing that the same subject cannot enact two roles. There are two variants of SoD conflicts: static and dynamic. Static SoD assumes the roles to be rigidly assigned to users, who will always enact the same role in every action. Dynamic SoD assumes that the conflict has to be evaluated within the domain of a specific action instance, where distinct users have to enact conflicting roles. The same user may enact conflicting roles as long as they are enacted in different action instances. Static SoD is the model receiving greater support, typically at the level of policy definition, with the availability of techniques that permit the identification of assignments of privileges to users that may violate the constraint. SAP AC, for instance, supports the detection of static SoD conflicts during role design and provisioning. Dynamic SoD requires robust support from the execution system, and this remains a critical requirement. Dynamic SoD requires some robust way to keep track of the history of access within an action. An extensive analysis of these issues appears in Chapter 59.

We note again that PBM can offer the opportunity to use a sophisticated high-level policy model for the design of the policy, taking the responsibility for mapping the high-level representation to the concrete AC model that the system responsible for the implementing the system can offer. This is one advantage of using such an approach. The PoSecCo project, described later in the chapter, offers an abstract flexible policy language, with support for RBAC and ABAC models. This policy can be translated into a collection of policies for the low-level systems that are used in the IT infrastructure,

each with its own restrictions. This represents an interesting approach to applying modern AC models in a scenario where common network protocols, operating systems, database management systems, Web servers, and application servers are used.

To conclude this analysis, we want to quickly present the concept of *obligation*, which presents specific features that clearly distinguish it from the concept of authorization presented earlier. Obligations are ECA policies that serve to determine future actions a subject has to perform (on a target) as a reaction to specific events. As noted by Sloman [28], obligation policies are enforced at the subject, whereas AC policies are enforced at the resource side. They also differ from the provisional AC model proposed by Jajodia [29], which extends traditional yes–no AC answers by saying that subjects must cause a set of conditions to be evaluated to true "prior" to authorizing a request. Obligations are used in many management fields such as quality of service (increase resources if a service-level agreement is not satisfied), privacy management (delete user information after 6 months), auditing (raise an alarm if some events occur), dynamic network reconfiguration based on security or network events [activate backup links in case of distributed denial of access (DDoS)], and activity scheduling (periodic backups). Complex events can be specified from basic events using event expressions managed also using external monitoring or event services and reused in many policies. Because of their operative and temporal nature, obligations are used not only in security-relevant policies but also for workflow management. Unlike AC, obligations policies are often unenforceable; that is, the system cannot ensure that each obligation will actually be fulfilled by the subject [30]. There is a lack of security controls able to enforce obligations. Even if ad hoc agents have been proposed sometimes [31] and some tool is available, to be practically used, obligation policies are often mapped to other enforceable authorization mechanisms [32].

4. CONTROLS FOR ENFORCING SECURITY POLICIES IN DISTRIBUTED SYSTEMS

The fulfillment of high-level security objectives in distributed systems goes beyond the specification of AC policies and their enforcement, which is typically done at the end point (close to the resource that requires protection). Complications that arise in distributed systems result from the topological arrangement and interaction of system elements over trustworthy and untrustworthy networks. The satisfaction of CIA properties in distributed systems can primarily count on two different categories of security controls: firewalls that separate network portions with different security levels provide security checks before allowing incoming and outgoing network traffic and communication protection mechanisms such as virtual private networks (VPNs) that allow two end points to communicate securely over untrustworthy networks. Next, the difficulty in choosing the "best" security control in a given context, as well as an alternative firewall and communication protection technologies, is explained in much more detail.

Criteria for Control Selection

As previously described, the planning phase of the security life cycle requires the identification and selection of appropriate security controls. However, evaluating the alternatives is not an easy task because different control technologies have different features, performance, management costs, and security implications. First, there is a large availability of security controls. They may be available at the end points (personal firewalls or channel protection mechanisms) or in the infrastructure (VPN gateways or border firewalls).

Firewalls are displaced in many points of corporate networks to separate the internal network in portions at different security levels (the administrator's from the guests' subnet). Firewalls have different functionalities, as explained in the next section, which can be used to enforce different policies, but they have different performance. Performance critical elements often run on dedicated appliances, as often happens for the border firewalls, the main elements of defense, because they separate the internal network from the remainder of the (unsecured) Internet. Filtering capabilities are also available at the operating system level (iptables in Linux), or they can be freely installed to be used for host protection (personal firewall) or to implement a filtering mechanism (forwarding firewall). Best practices suggest discarding disallowed traffic as soon as possible: that is, as close as possible to the source. However, other factors need to be carefully considered: for instance, the performance, or the trustworthiness of the control to configure, based on the vendor/product reputation and on an analysis of historical data of vulnerabilities (number, seriousness, and exposure time) [33]. As previously anticipated, firewall configurations are an ordered list of rules; the action enforced is the one taken from the first matching rule. Software-based implementations of the resolution algorithm have linear processing time, which means that the higher the number of rules, the higher the overhead and the lower the performance. Therefore, optimizing the rule set is mandatory to have reasonable performance. Hardware-based implementations use expensive hardware and sophisticated algorithms [34] (content-addressable memories to improve performance to a constant time; that is, the firewall takes more or less the same time regardless of the rule set size). However, when the hardware resources are saturated, no other rules can be added. For instance, Netscreen 100 products allow the specification of no more than 733 rules. More expensive appliances need to be bought if more rules are needed; thus, in this case, the optimization of the rule set may also reduce the expenses.

Enforcement of a communication protection policy shares the same decisional problems, but it is even worse because of the availability of different technologies working at different levels of the ISO—Open Systems Interconnection stack. The most well-known solutions are IPsec, which works at the network layer, the TLS protocol, which works up to the transport layer, and Web Service Security (WS-Security), which prescribes how to protect Simple Object Access Protocol (SOAP) messages using XML Signature and XML Encryption. In most cases, these protections are available directly in the kernel (IPsec), in the server software (TLS), and in the application containers (WS-Security). Therefore, the decision regarding the most appropriate one does not depend on availability but on other considerations such as the efficiency of the solution, the configuration and management costs, the ease of use for clients, and overall security. These technologies can be divided into channel protection, when the protection is applied to data during the transmission and is valid up to the other communication party, and message protection, when the protection is applied to data before being transmitted [WS-Security and Secure/Multipurpose Internet Mail Extensions (S/MIME)] so that the communication medium becomes irrelevant. The decision between channel and message protection is also sensitive and requires a careful analysis of the systems to be configured. This difficulty can be exemplified with the help of, for instance, WS-Security. This technology can be used to encrypt sensitive information exchanged by Web services and is considered secure, because application data remain encrypted along the entire communication channel, whereas application data protected by TLS are often subject to TLS offloading, which results in unencrypted data exchange within a service providers' network. The choice to use WS-Security, however, must consider the potential impact on other security mechanisms in place. It can, for instance, inhibit the work of application-level or content inspection firewalls. It can also prevent data leakage prevention systems to detect the leakage of sensitive information in outbound calls. Moreover, message protection technologies have worse performance compared with channel protection ones. Fig. 26.5 presents a logical view of the techniques available at the different layers together, and illustrates the possibility of nesting them. Note that practically, implementation of WS-Security is typically offered by plug-ins or modules of the application services (Rampart is the security module of Axis2).

In addition to these considerations, distributed systems are intrinsically redundant for availability purposes. Together with duplicated functionalities, many backup

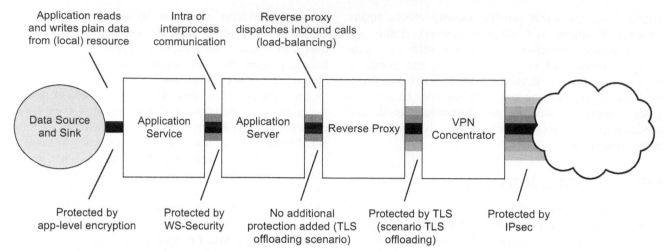

FIGURE 26.5 Logical view of data protection offered by different technologies in Web service environments (scenario of secure socket layer offloading). *TLS*, transport layer security; *VPN*, virtual private network.

solutions are available to connect different end points, even if they may be disabled. Redundant controls are often used in combinations (configured with the same policy) to mitigate the risk of attacks in case one of the controls has some vulnerability. In other words, the decision is not only about the main security controls (and subsequently configuring them) but also about having backup solutions that cope with failures or attacks.

Another aspect that complicates the selection of security controls is that they cannot be considered in isolation. In general, every time a security control blocks or alters the information transmitted (changing the addresses), as for network address translation (NAT) and packet enveloping, or the content, such as encrypted communications, there is a risk that another control is hampered; thus, another high-level policy is not enforced.

Other parameters that need to be considered when selecting and configuring security controls are management costs (including the configuration costs), deployment costs, efforts related to the creation of the initial configuration [controls provided with a graphical user interface (GUI) are often preferred to a script-based approach], or efforts related to implement configuration changes (automatic remote deployment systems are preferred to manual ones). Moreover, the expressiveness of the policy is important. Depending on the layer where each solution works, security controls can decide based on MAC or IP addresses and ports, up to application layer information as users, and roles or other semantically rich information.

Automatic or semiautomatic tool support would significantly facilitate the selection and evaluation of appropriate security controls and their configuration. The PoSecCo project, for instance, proposes an optimized control selection and configuration generation starting from end-to-end requirements.

Firewall Technologies

An overview of firewall types is given by the National Institute of Standards and Technology (NIST) in Scarfone and Hoffman [35]. The simplest firewall feature is *packet filtering*, which makes decisions about each received packet based on information in IP and transport headers. Rules for packet filters are sometimes referred to as five-tuples, because they include conditions on IP source and destination addresses, source and destination ports, and the IP protocol field. Packet filters are efficient and often work at wire speed even without dedicated hardware. However, they cannot be used to express complex filtering policies [to allow File Transfer Protocol (FTP) in passive mode], and in general, compared with more sophisticated firewalls, more rules are needed to specify the same policy. However, many studies proved that their performance is seriously affected by the quality of the rule set. Reducing overlapping rules (that match the same packets) and eliminating redundant ones (never activated rules) [36,37], together with a careful rule reordering based on traffic profile [38], strongly increase the overall performance.

Stateful inspection improves packet filters by tracking connection states at the transport layer, by examining certain values of Transmission Control Protocol (TCP) headers and maintaining a *state table*. State values are used to take decisions [allowing all of the TCP packets from an "established" connection (responses) or "related" connection (FTP data connections)], or blocking packets that do not comply with the TCP protocol specification. Some controls that implement the stateful inspection are also able to track other protocols [permit domain name system (DNS) response only after DNS query], and Internet Control Message Protocol echo-reply only after an echo-request. Stateful inspection may enforce bandwidth control (to limit the number of connections allowed to a given destination, or the packet rate per destination address or port base). Currently, stateful firewalls are the most frequently used technology as they allow sufficiently expressive policies, but they are also appropriate where performance is critical (for border protection) because they are often sold with dedicated hardware appliances. As stated previously, analyzing the rule set and optimizing it allows organizations to save money as less expensive hardware can be bought.

Another capability is the *stateful protocol analysis*, also known as *deep packet inspection*: that is, the ability to read the data and reconstruct the state of application layer protocols. Elements able to perform deep packet inspection are often referred to as *application firewalls*. Because of the large variety of application protocols, these security controls can be "customized" to a specific protocol to perform a more focused analysis; therefore they are named specialized application firewalls, the most widespread of which is the Web application firewall (WAF). The WAF can block traffic depending on the values of Hypertext Transfer Protocol (HTTP) properties and fields (e.g., they can filter email messages that contain attachments of a given type), or block possibly harmful protocol operations, as is often the case for the FTP "put" command or HTTP unsafe methods (TRACK, TRACE, DELETE). In addition, application firewalls are able to check traffic compliance to protocol standards or to a set of harmless implementations ["Request for Comments (RFC) compliance"] and to identify unexpected sequences of commands. Application firewalls enable fine-grained decisions (to allow or deny access to Web pages), not only considering their URLs but also checking whether Java or ActiveX is used, or filter TLS connections from or to end points whose certificates have been issued by an untrustworthy certification authority. At the application level, information is often represented in the form of strings (MIME objects, URLs, or filenames). For this reason, conditions are often formulated using regular expressions.

An improved type of application firewall is the *application-proxy gateway*, which enforces an AC policy using a proxy agent. It accepts incoming connections and uses circuit relay services to forward allowed ones. It hides details about an internal network, because its address is the only visible one. In addition, it keeps track of authenticated users, thus permitting the specification of rules that prescribe the maximum number of users allowed, or the maximum number of connections on a per-user base. More precisely, the proxy is named a "tunneling proxy" if it does not modify requests and responses after a successful authentication, "forward proxy" if it retrieves the resource on behalf of the client (and it belongs to the client's network), and "reverse proxy" if it answers to client requests on behalf of a server or a set of servers (and it belongs to the servers' network). Finally, some firewalls support *content inspection*, that is, the ability to analyze and make decisions based on the payload of application protocols.

These components are the bricks needed to create more complex firewall architectures that achieve a better level of protection. For instance, the screened subnet presented in Cheswick et al. [39] creates an intermediate level of protection between internal and external networks by creating a demilitarized zone (DMZ) with limited access to the internal network, where services to be provided to the external network are usually put (Fig. 26.6).

As the firewalls separate network portions at different security levels, they often implement NAT functionality. NAT is the functionality that changes IP addresses and ports into the received packets. When source IP addresses are modified, the mapping can be one-to-one, if every IP address is statically changed, or many-to-one, when an entire network is mapped on one or a few (public) IP addresses. In the latter case, TCP/User Datagram Protocol (UDP) port numbers are also modified to perform the required multiplexing; for this reason, this technique is named network address and port translation. Unlike circuit relay, the NAT does not break the IP stack because the change is made transparently. First proposed to avoid IPv4 address exhaustion, now it is commonly used to hide private networks, but it introduces drawbacks to the connectivity quality and requires careful configuration. On the other hand, it can be useful to masquerade the actual IP address of publicly available services or when load balancing systems

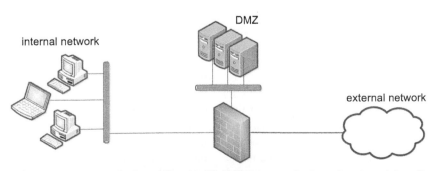

FIGURE 26.6 Screened subnet with a demilitarized zone created using a three-legged firewall.

are used that forward requests to a pool of services. In that case, the destination NAT is used. For Web servers and Web services, another technique is used that permits associating the resources with URLs in a dynamic way, both to expose "fancy URLs" usable by the search engines and to redirect content.

Although the importance of a correct configuration of filtering devices is easily understood for the security of the internal network, a "polite" configuration of firewalls can produce a significant impact on the security of the entire Internet. To this purpose, two best practices have been proposed: *ingress filtering* and *egress filtering*. Ingress filtering is a technique that consists of accepting packets from the outside only if they actually come from the networks that they claim to be from. According to RFC 2827 [40], systematic ingress filtering starting at the periphery of the Internet would reduce or permit mapping DDoS attacks. Packet filtering at source IP level is usually enough to enforce it. Egress filtering consists of configuring the filtering infrastructure to block unauthorized or malicious traffic from the internal network. It can be implemented using a packet filter that verifies that the source IP address in all packets is within the allocated IP block used by the company, or in more advanced ways using proxies that authenticate users before allowing them to access the Internet.

Channel and Message Protection Technologies

This part of the chapter presents two channel protection technologies: IPsec, which works at Layer 3, and the TLS protocol, which works at Layer 4, and two message protection technologies, WS-security, which protects SOAP objects (used by Web services), and S/MIME, which protects MIME email messages. IPsec is a suite of protocols that offers various security services for traffic at the IP layer, for both the IPv4 and IPv6 protocols. The protection is guaranteed by means of two security protocols, the Authentication Header (AH) and the Encapsulating Security Payload (ESP). AH guarantees the integrity and symmetric authentication of IP packets; both the payload and the nonvariable fields of the header. ESP may provide the integrity, authentication, and confidentiality of IP packets payload (but not of the header). Both optionally provide an antireplay service by maintaining a window with the last 32 or 64 packets. These protocols can be used in two modes: *transport* and *tunnel*. The transport mode is between two network nodes to provide security services to upper layers, and therefore protects only the payload. This type of configuration is named end-to-end security (Fig. 26.7A). In tunnel mode, a secure channel is established between two end points, the gateways, each of which is associated with the IP addresses of the subnet they control. When packets arrive at one gateway from a subnet and are directed to the other, they are first encapsulated in a new packet exchanged between the gateways (by means of IP in IP); then its payload (that is, the entire original packet) is protected. This type of configuration is named basic VPN (Fig. 26.7C). In addition, IPsec in tunnel mode can be used to secure the remote access (to allow a user to connect to a gateway without knowing his IP address a priori via user-level authentication), as shown in Fig. 26.7B. The connections to protect are specified by means of a security policy stored in the Security Policy Database. The details to protect a connection are summarized by means of a Security Association (SA). An SA is a univocally identified set of parameters that characterize a unidirectional connection, including symmetric cryptographic algorithms, keys, the selected protocol (AH or ESP), and a lifetime. The SA can be manually written by administrators or negotiated using an ad hoc key management solution, the Internet Key Exchange (IKE) protocol [41], and are stored in a Security Association Database. A prior offline agreement is needed to write or negotiate the SA and configure IPsec accordingly. In some cases, vendors provide software for simplified remote client configuration (Cisco VPN client). In general, IPsec has good performance but it has high management costs. IKE supports certificate-based user authentication; a granular policy can be enforced.

TLS is a suite of protocols that allow a client and a server to authenticate each other, to negotiate the security services to enforce and the cryptographic keys before starting to exchange data at the application layer in a client-server scenario. It was first issued by Netscape as SSL, and then absorbed with minor (but security-relevant) revisions by the IETF as TLS [42]. TLS works at the transport layer; that is, it is encapsulated in a reliable transport protocol, like TCP. In addition, there exists the Datagram TLS that guarantees the same security properties with datagram protocols, like UDP [43] and Datagram Congestion Control Protocol [44]. The protection is summarized using a cipher suite, a string that indicates the peer authentication and key exchange algorithm, the hash algorithm used to calculate the message authentication code (HMAC for TLS, and keyed digest for SSL), and the encryption algorithm (TLS RSA WITH AES 128 CBC SHA). The cipher suites are negotiated using the TLS Handshake Protocol, which also supports server authentication using X.509 certificates. It optionally supports server-requested client authentication. Because the TLS Handshake Protocol is expensive both computationally and in terms of exchanged data, a resume functionality exists based on a session identification mechanism. The protection is applied to application data by the TLS Record Protocol, which divides the application data into blocks to protect them, optionally compresses them, calculates the message authentication code, ciphers it, and adds the TLS record header before transmitting each block. The main advantage of TLS over IPsec is that it requires less configuration effort on the client side, because

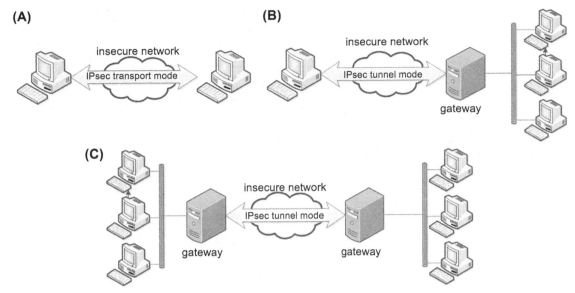

FIGURE 26.7 IPsec.

the TLS client is available in every browser together with a list of trusted certification authorities. Nevertheless, its performance is a little worse [45]. For remote access, TLS VPN permits two types of use: the clientless approach, when an authenticated user can select a set of predefined resources from a Web page, and the thin client, when by means of an ActiveX- or Java-based plug-in an authenticated user can run other applications across the VPN. However, TLS VPNs are subject to other security issues; for instance, because they allow a Web-based approach, they are more vulnerable to password-cracking attacks, they may be the vector for malware to the internal network, and, if split tunneling is used, they may allow a compromised remote machine to become a router for the internal network. In addition, they may increase the risk of exposure owing to keystroke loggers, open sessions, or cached data on shared machines, because they easily allow connections anywhere, including from public machines.

As anticipated previously, when there is the risk of offloading (for instance, in the case of email systems where relaying servers temporarily store the emails before forwarding them to the user's inbox) channel protection solutions working at the network and transport layer are not enough. In fact, the assumption that all the intermediaries and the end point are trusted no longer holds. In this case, the protection needs to be applied directly to the exchanged messages. The emails, represented with the MIME format, are protected with the S/MIME [46]. S/MIME applies senders' authentication, message integrity, nonrepudiation of origin, privacy, and data security using X.509 certificates. S/MIME-protected messages are conveyed using an ad hoc MIME type, the application/pkcs7-mime. There are two types of protected messages for security purposes: the "enveloped-data," when data are ciphered with a session

key that is then encrypted with the public keys taken from the certificates of all of the recipients, and the "signed-data," when data are signed with the private key of the sender's certificate. Message protections can be nested in any order; however, available implementations include the enveloped-only, signed-only, or signed-then-enveloped messages. S/MIME messages are represented using the Cryptographic Message Syntax format [47], an extension of PKCS#7.

Analogously, in the case of Web services, a SOAP-level security mechanism has been made available, WS-Security. It has been defined as a SOAP extension protocol that specifies how to sign or encrypt messages using XML Signature and XML Encryption. In addition, it can be used to transport credentials (like X.509 certificates) and security tokens (like Security Assertion Markup Language assertions or Kerberos tokens) that can also be associated with messages. WS-Security can be used to enforce an end-to-end security at the application layer when Web services are used. Using WS-Security is computationally expensive owing to the use of cryptographic algorithms, and it increases the size of the messages. Compared with TLS or IPsec, it is significantly less performing, but it allows for more granular application of the protection, because it can be applied to single XML fields and to enforce more sophisticated authentication and authorization policies. Because of the granularity of the enforcement, configuring and managing changes with WS-Security may require significantly more effort than channel protection techniques, which poses a major burden on administrators.

5. PRODUCTS AND TECHNOLOGIES

This section introduces a small and diverse selection of mature technologies and products related to PBM, which

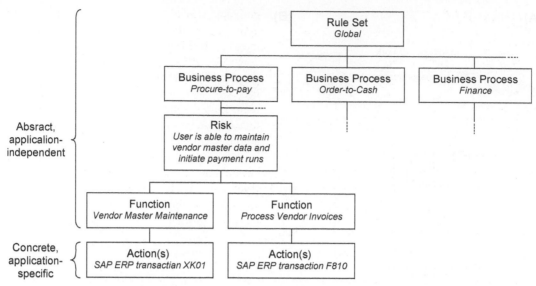

FIGURE 26.8 Example risk specified in SAP's access control.

can now be used to improve system security and compliance. Note that none of them takes a holistic view of PBM. Instead, each example looks at different facets of system security and works with different abstraction levels of security policy. The solutions from SAP, Microsoft, and Cisco exemplify the state-of-the-art in managing authorizations for enterprise applications, end point security, and network security devices, respectively. XACML has been selected as an example for policy specification languages, while acknowledging its increasing adoption by industry. Moreover, it was specifically created for dealing with AC, whereas other languages such as Ponder and CIM-SPL are general-purpose languages. Finally, Security Enhanced Linux (SELinux) is a prominent open-source example for the policy-based configuration of operating systems.

SAP Access Control

SAP Access Control is an enterprise software application that enables organizations to control access and prevent fraud across enterprise applications while minimizing the time and cost of compliance. The solution is centered on a repository of access and authorization-based risks related to single or multiple functions executed in the course of business processes. Each business function is linked to one or several actions that implement the respective functionality in a given enterprise application. Users can specify their own risk rules or rely on a standard rule set for business processes implemented by standard enterprise resource planning applications from SAP, Oracle, and others. A typical SoD risk related to the business process Procure-to-Pay is, for instance, that single users within the same organizational unit have permission to both maintain

vendor master data and initiate payment runs, which could be misused to perform fraud (Fig. 26.8).

The rule set is the basis for the analysis and reporting of risks caused by the assignment of authorizations to roles and users, respectively performed at the design and runtime of an enterprise-wide authorization concept. At design time, SAP Access Control supports the management of roles from multiple SAP or non-SAP systems with a single unified role repository; any new or changed role is subject to risk analysis to prevent SoD violations within a single role. Role design is further supported by approval workflows and role refinement according to organizational hierarchies, and eventually results in the automated generation and deployment of technical roles in the respective target application. At runtime, risk analysis is performed during (de)provisioning workflows to detect SoD violations that could result from the assignment of multiple roles to a given user. Such workflows are triggered by human resources events (such as result from a new hire) or self-services, include approval steps, and eventually result in the automated provisioning of roles (and identities) to all systems concerned.

SAP Access Control focuses on the design and operation of authorization concepts for the application layer. The definition of risks and subsequently roles is subject to the design phase of a security concept, whereas the mapping of generic business functions to the respective applications and authorizations as well as the support of change and provisioning workflows belongs to the implementation and operations phases. With regard to policy abstraction levels, one can distinguish abstract and application-independent business functions and roles on the one hand, and the concrete and application-specific counterparts on the other.

Microsoft Group Policy

Microsoft Group Policy is a technology that facilitates the management of configuration settings in Windows environments. More specifically, domain-based Group Policy supports centralized configuration management and scales up to IT networks that span across multiple sites and domains, thereby relying on Active Directory Domain Services.

Although it can be used to configure all kinds of features, Group Policy is particularly useful for the enforcement of security policies concerning password policies or the setup of end point firewalls. Settings governed by Group Policy cannot be modified by standard users; this ensures that security-relevant settings remain as specified and cannot be changed advertently or inadvertently. Technically, a so-called Group Policy Object (GPO) is composed of policy settings, each of which prescribes a desired value for a given software configuration parameter. GPOs are linked to a hierarchy of domains, sites, and organizational units determining to which systems and users a GPO applies (Fig. 26.9). The settings are deployed in regular intervals and manifest primarily in the Windows registry. Group Policy supports inheritance, whereas more specific GPOs prevail over GPOs that are linked to upper-level hierarchy nodes. Policy settings that concern systems are applied after startup, whereas user-related settings apply after logon.

Fig. 26.9 displays the Group Policy Management Console, which administrators use to associate GPOs with hierarchy elements. The Default Domain Policy, for instance, is a GPO associated with the entire company domain, which renders the contained policy settings applicable to all users and systems in the entire domain. On the right-hand side, it becomes visible that this GPO is composed of mainly security-related settings (the minimum password length as specified in the registry). Settings can be maintained with the help of the Group Policy Management Editor; further tools extend Group Policy with regard to approval workflows, delegation, or role-based administration.

With regard to the notion of policy abstraction levels, Group Policy does not support the specification of high-level policies, but works on the level of concrete and software-specific configuration parameters that determine the behavior of a given software feature.

Cisco

Cisco, a leading provider of computer network hardware, offers products to enforce, manage, and monitor the security of network infrastructures for clouds and data centers, and generally for medium to large enterprise networks. It sells a set of modular appliances for network security, including the Adaptive Security Appliances series, the Catalyst series, and the IOS series, which can be expanded with firewalls (stateful, application layer, and content inspection), IPsec- and TLS-based VPN components, and intrusion prevention systems, to scale and reach the company needs. These tools also permit the dynamic definition of zones to partition the network according to security levels (to create DMZs) and the definition of NAT rules. It also freely provides VPN clients to allow remote access to IPsec VPNs.

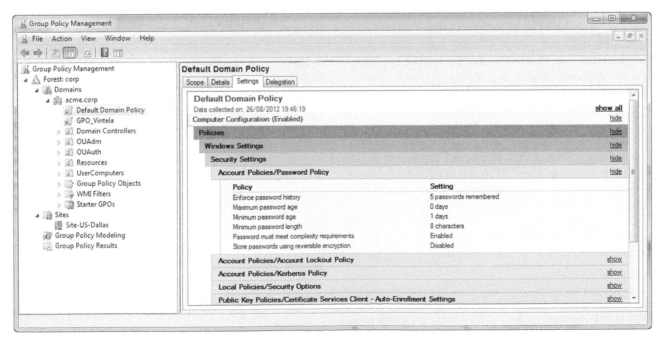

FIGURE 26.9 Microsoft group policy management console.

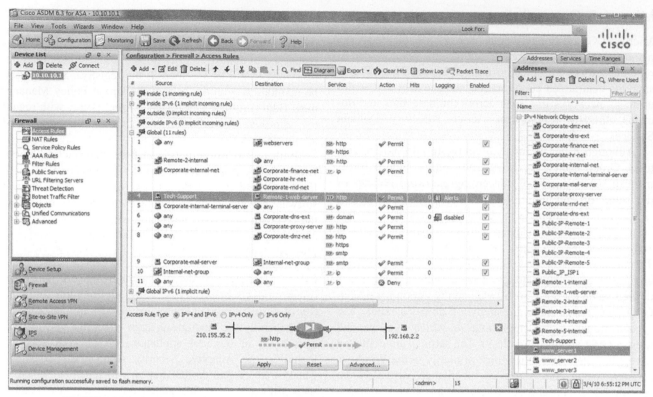

FIGURE 26.10 Cisco Adaptive Security Device Manager graphical user interface-based firewall appliance management.

All of the Cisco devices can be configured using a command-line script-based approach, which they themselves declared as "cumbersome" [48]. For this reason, they also provide Web-based or stand-alone user-friendly applications that allow administrators to simplify the configuration, troubleshooting, and central management of appliances. For instance, the Adaptive Security Device Manager, with a representative interface presented in Fig. 26.10, provides setup wizards and administration tools, together with dashboards that provide an at-a-glance view of appliance status, and debugging tools such as packet trace and packet capture. Alternatively, the Cisco Security Manager provides a set of tools to perform policy deployment and enforcement in larger environments. Another example is the Easy VPN that allows the central management (and pushing) of channel protection configurations through an Easy VPN server. These tools only cover Cisco appliances and cannot be used with products of other vendors or open-source products.[8]

Cisco products efficiently cover demands for the traditional administration of policies at the lowest abstraction layer, that is, the Executable Policy Layer,[9]

with some features of the upper layer, the Concrete Policy Layer. Thusx, in this context, a policy is a collection of rules to configure Cisco appliances, graphically represented in a GUI or represented as a collection of command-line instructions. Human errors and inconsistencies, the leading factor to move toward a PBM approach, may be reduced because of a more efficient data representation and management [the reuse of low-level security rules and objects (IP addresses, ports, and URLs)], because of the availability of simple integrated debugging tools, such as packet capture, ping, and trace route, or because of the integration with intrusion prevention systems. However, high-level specifications are not supported. Today this status is common to all of the companies producing security appliances.

XACML

XACML is the outcome of the work of an Organization for the Advancement of Structured Information Standards committee. The XACML Committee released version 1.0 in 2003 [50]. Version 3.0 or higher was expected to be approved in 2013. The goal of the language is to define an XML representation of AC policies, focusing on the description of authorizations.

The main goal of XACML is to offer a platform-independent representation of access control policies to facilitate the representation and exchange among systems

---

8. A step toward the multiproduct multivendor management of security controls is Firewall Builder [49], which permits support of Cisco devices as well as other open-source firewalls such as iptables and pf with a single GUI and a set of translation and deployment scripts.

9. http://www.cisco.com/en/US/products/ps6121/index.html.

of the AC restrictions that systems have to apply. XACML is a member of a large family of specifications that offer an XML schema for the portable representation of information to be shared in a distributed system.

The model behind the language assumes that the basic building block is a rule, which is associated with a resource, a subject, and an action. Rules are structured in policies, and policies build policy sets. The specification of the elements of the rules and policies can use the XPath language, supporting the representation of flexible predicates on resource and subject properties. Based on this, XACML can be considered an example of an ABAC model, with the possibility of defining compact policies. This choice is consistent with the general architecture of a policy management system described in Fig. 26.3, with the roles of PEP, PDP, PIP, and PAP.

XACML can be considered a successful initiative; a lot of interest is dedicated to it in the research and industrial community. Systems exist that are able to evaluate XACML policies and implement the components of the XACML architecture; many prototypes have been built that use a variant of XACML to manage advanced policies (for obligations, delegations, and privacy profiles [51]). The most significant industrial use of XACML is to offer a representation of the internal policies of a system in a format that can be understood by other components. An interesting opportunity is the realization of a family of adapters able to create the AC configuration of a real system, starting from an XACML policy. The XACML Committee has worked on the definition of a variety of profiles that define restrictions and introduce terms for the definition of polices that make them processable by automatic tools. Currently, however, there is support for only a limited number of systems. An interesting profile is one for the representation of RBAC policies [52].

The XACML language has an interesting role in the design of a PBM system, because it can be used to represent policies in a portable way, using the services of ad hoc translators to map the XACML policy to the concrete implementation. Also, the ability of some profiles to map a high-level view of the policy to the concrete setting is consistent with the goals of the approach advocated in this chapter. It is not clear whether XACML will emerge as the central component for the realization of such architectures, but certainly it deserves careful consideration in this area.

SELinux

SELinux is the outcome of a project initially sponsored by the National Security Agency with the aim of improving the protection of the Linux operating system. The first implementation was made available in 2000. The module was initially offered as a default option in a few distributions; since version 2.6 or higher of the Linux kernel, SELinux has been a stable part of the operating system.

SELinux enriches the native discretionary model that characterizes UNIX-like operating systems. Limitations of this model have been known for a long time and SELinux introduced an additional layer of protection. The approach took inspiration from classical mandatory models and looked at the experience from use of these models. This led to an offer of higher expressivity and the possibility of flexibly controlling the behavior of the system. Initial experience with the use of SELinux demonstrated the difficulty of putting an additional layer of AC in an existing system: Users encountered frequent situations in which the new AC services were blocking the execution of legitimate applications. Progressively, the technology evolved and policies were greatly refined. Today the presence of SELinux in a system that uses only standard applications and modules does not exhibit anomalies, at the same time offering increased protection against misuse.

The approach used by SELinux relies on the idea of associating a context with three components (role, user name, and domain) with users and processes of the system. Labels with the same structure are assigned to resources in the system. Processes typically inherit the context of the user that invoked the process, except when an explicit policy rule permits a change in the running context. A policy defines the compatibility rules among contexts and labels. Typically, processes are only authorized to access resources characterized by a label compatible with the process context (in the same domain). Specific resources that may need to be accessed by a variety of processes will be associated with less restrictive rules. In general, the SELinux policy permits a rigid compartmentalization to be built among the resources of a system, which greatly limits the possibility that vulnerability in some process or protocol would lead to the manipulation of a critical resource and the consequent compromise of the system.

An interesting feature of SELinux is the way the policy is defined and applied. A policy language is used to express the policy that a system must follow. Tools are also offered that assist the administrator in designing the policy. The policy is then compiled, a low-level configuration is produced, and each element is then associated with the resources that will be protected. The compilation phase is introduced to improve the performance and distribute the policy to all elements of the system responsible for the protection. This approach is consistent with the idea of using a high-level representation of the policy valid for the whole system, which is then mapped to a low-level configuration to realize its objectives. This can be considered a realization at the level of a single system of the PBM approach, which has as its goal the security management of distributed systems. The success of SELinux can be considered a valid demonstration of the advantages of such an approach. The Security

Enhancements for Android initiative has started, which aims to improve the security of the Android environment by adapting the SELinux approach.

6. RESEARCH PROJECTS

Policies and policy-based management have been a research topic for several decades; because of their ambition as well as technological advancements, they will remain so for a number of years. This section introduces the approaches of two publicly funded projects to PBM. First, we will introduce Ponder, a project conducted in the early 1990s that is considered a forerunner in the use of policies for system management. Second, we will describe PoSecCo, a project started in 2010, which looks at optimization problems related to policy refinement, the embedding of PBM into organizational processes, as well as policy-based audits. One important difference between the two is that Ponder relies on agents to enforce AC policies, whereas PoSecCo discovers and uses standard security capabilities available in virtually every given system.

Ponder

Ponder is a generic policy framework that was developed by the Policy Research Group of Imperial College in London. It features a policy specification language [28] and a toolkit with a management console tool for dynamically managing policies using policy enforcement agents. Its goal is to support security and management policy specification in large-scale distributed systems.

The Ponder language is *declarative* and *object-oriented*. Everything is represented by an object interface, and policies are written in terms of interface methods. It includes grouping constructs and policy inheritance useful for scalability purposes in large systems. The basic policy types in Ponder are (positive and negative) authorization, refrain, obligation, and delegation policies. Metapolicies are also supported to constrain the acceptable types of policies in the system. Policies can be specified directly as instances or as reusable parameterized, template-like policy types from which multiple instances can be created by passing the actual parameters.

In Ponder, administrators create and edit policies using an administration tool, which includes a policy compiler that transforms policies to policy classes that are stored in a policy server that acts as a central point of management. Policies can be loaded, unloaded, enabled, and disabled. The description of the system to manage is made using *domains*. A domain is a file system—like hierarchy used to group objects such as users, resources, services, and devices into categories for management purposes with parent—children policy propagation methods. A *domain service* keeps track of objects in the domain hierarchy and is responsible for evaluating policy subject and target sets at runtime. As domains change dynamically, the domain server maintains the references to all installed policies that apply to each subdomain. When the domain hierarchy changes, the relevant policy objects are notified of the change.

Enforcement is left to a set of enforcement agents. When policies are loaded, policy objects distribute enforcement classes to the enforcement agents, which are destroyed when policies are unloaded. On the other hand, the enforcement classes react to enable and disable events. In case of authorization policies, the enforcement agent is the access controller of the target object, and for obligation and refrain policies, it is the subject policy management agent. Policy management agents of obligation policies register themselves to receive certain events from the *event server* that collects system events and notifies the registered event subscribers so that obligation policies can be triggered. The Ponder architecture is shown in Fig. 26.11.

Ponder presented some limitations in flexibility owing to the centralized management of the enforcement. For this reason, Ponder2 was developed. Ponder2 provides a new framework for an event-based enforcement in which management services implement self-management cells that interact with each other through asynchronous events. It is composed of an application programming interface (API), a shell that can be used to perform various maintenance actions, and a compiler/interpreter for PonderTalk, the Ponder2 management and policy specification language based on SmallTalk. Ponder2 inherits from its ancestor the authorization and obligation policy models, but it acts differently by giving more emphasis to the dynamic aspects of a system. For example, it supports changes, activation,

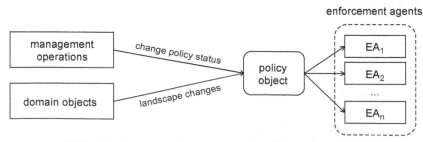

FIGURE 26.11   Ponder reference architecture. *EA*, enforcement agent.

and deactivation of policies while the system is running, without requiring the system to stop.

Policy and Security Configuration Management

The research project PoSecCo[10] focuses on securing shared IT systems that are used by service providers to deliver to end users business (application) services, which consist of elements that are in parts operated internally and in other parts provided by outsourcing or cloud providers. Because the project relies on off-the-shelf security capabilities (to enforce security policies), rather than developing new kinds of policy enforcement points, it bridges the gap between policy-related research and purist policy systems on the one hand and today's IT systems and management practice on the other hand. This approach aims to render research results more applicable to real-world systems and is accompanied by the consideration of economic and organizational considerations around the design and runtime of a security concept.

System and Security Model

The policy hierarchy of PoSecCo consists of five layers, four of which correspond to different abstraction levels linked to a functional counterpart; the fifth represents concrete configuration information for security mechanisms. Fig. 26.12 visualizes the relationships between functional and security models belonging to the different abstraction levels and mentions how each model is built.

A *business policy* represents a high-level requirement provided by management or stemming from laws, regulations, or customers. Business policies are associated with risks that express the probability of a threat to affect assets or asset classes negatively [53]. The latter are generic concepts that can be linked to arbitrary elements of the *business model*, which in turn is composed of general business concepts relevant for organizations (institution, business service, customer, organizational role, and business information). Business policies have a defined structure and can be organized in a hierarchy, but the core is represented in natural language. Business policies are typically created by business and legal stakeholders (management or DP officers). No dedicated policy language exists to represent business policies, and the semiformal nature of business policies hampers automated reasoning.

An *IT security policy* represents an AC or DP policy that contributes to the fulfillment of one or several business policies. They are specified over concepts of the *IT service model*, which describes the interaction of logical IT resources to realize a given business service. Logical IT resources abstract software components present in an actual system, which allows the specification of security policies without considering implementation details. IT security policies are again specified by humans, in particular by security architects, who have the required knowledge to specify appropriate AC or DP policies. IT security policies (as well as lower-level policy representations) are represented by means of an ontology [Web Ontology Language—Description Logic (OWL-DL)], which allows the automation of reasoning tasks (conflict or enforceability analysis).

A *logical association* specifies a security property over two system elements that represent end points of a communication link. As such, they refine an IT security policy to the level of the real system, which is described by the *infrastructure model*. This topology-aware representation of an IT security policy represents the basis for the search and selection of security capabilities that are suitable for enforcing a given policy. A policy demanding a "secure channel" between two communication end points, for instance, can be enforced by several capabilities offered "along the way" (the capability of VPN concentrators to establish a VPN connection), or the capability of an application server to support SSL/TLS. The refinement to logical associations and the discovery of suitable enforcement mechanisms is again done with the help of ontology. Every security mechanism found is then assessed by performance, cost, and security functions that aim to choose the "best" alternative.

Once a human chooses one (or several) security mechanisms proposed for implementation, a so-called abstract configuration is created, which configures a capability in a vendor and product-independent manner. The abstract configuration again becomes transformed into a concrete configuration that is understood by the device offering the respective capability. Its representation or format is hence determined by the respective system element.

The policy hierarchy is constructed during the *plan* and *do* phases of the classical security life cycle and terminates with the deployment of concrete configurations. The hierarchy will then be used to deal with ongoing requirement and system changes at operations time.

System architecture. The PoSecCo architecture (Fig. 26.13) is centered on a model repository called Model Versioning and Evolution (MoVE),[11] which has been chosen to manage all functional and security models. Each is stored and in a version independent of each other, but related concepts can be associated by cross-model links. The model repository offers a coarse-grained XMI interface for reading and writing entire models, as well as fine-grained create, read, update, and delete operations for

---

10. Policy and security configuration management, http://www.posecco.eu.

11. Model versioning and evolution, http://move.q-e.at/.

Functional Models   Policy Hierarchy/Security Models

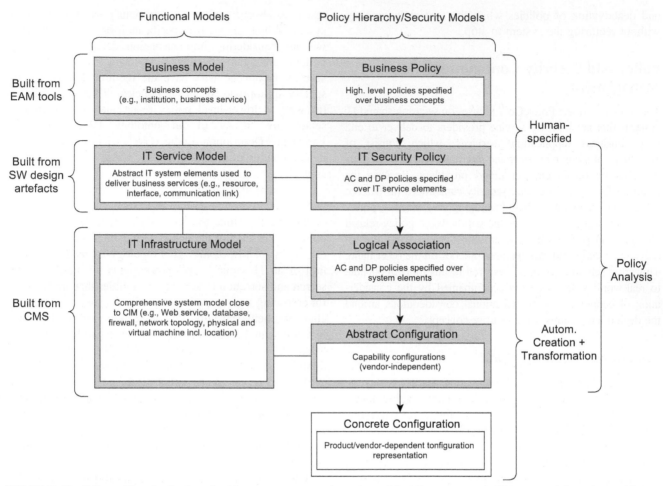

FIGURE 26.12   Policy and Security Configuration Management system and security models. *AC*, access control; *CIM*, common information model; *DP*, data protection; *IT*, information technology.

manipulating single-model elements. Moreover, it supports the definition of state machines for single classes, in which state changes result in corresponding events that can be used to trigger other actions. Finally, MoVE offers an Object Constraint Language (OCL) interface to query the models.

The business and IT service models of PoSecCo are created by interfacing Enterprise Architecture Management systems and by reading software design artifacts (UML component diagrams). The infrastructure model is built by using the Web-Based Enterprise Management (WBEM) standards from DMTF to read information from configuration management systems (CMS). Such tools represent an important building block of ITIL and commonly support CIM, which is in large part equivalent to the PoSecCo infrastructure model. CMS are also expected to transform and deploy the abstract configuration as soon as it has been completed at the end of the policy refinement process.

The policy hierarchy will then be constructed by so-called *PoSecCo applications* in a top-down manner, each using the MoVE API to read and manipulate model elements of its respective abstraction layer. Orchestration of

these applications in the course of the plan and implementation phases of the security life cycle is realized by means of an event bus.[12] The change in policies on each abstraction layer results in state transitions that persist in MoVE and also are published to topics to which other PoSecCo applications can subscribe. The successful harmonization of IT policies by the application of *Policy Specification and Harmonization*, for instance, leads to a state transition from *UNVERIFIED* to *VERIFIED*, which is notified to the application *Policy Refinement and Optimization* for the continuation of the policy refinement.

Requirements Engineering

This PoSecCo application offers a Web-based environment for the specification, management, and monitoring of

---

12. An event bus is a middleware component supporting the publish/subscribe communication model, in which software components do not directly interact with each other, but communicate through events or messages mediated by the event bus. Events are produced (published) by a source component and consumed by one or multiple target components.

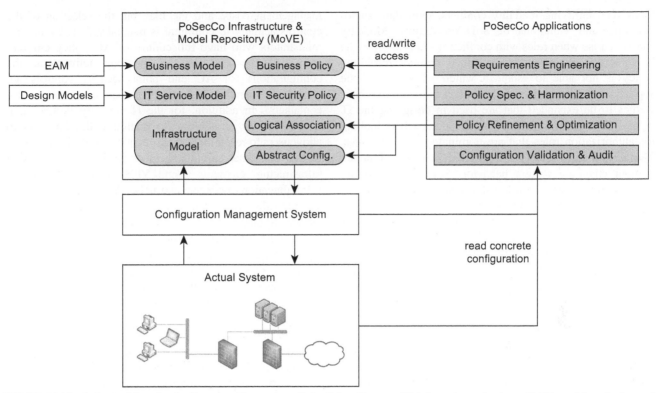

FIGURE 26.13 Policy and Security Configuration Management (PoSecCo) architecture. *IT*, information technology; *MoVE*, model versioning and evolution. *EAM*, enterprise asset management.

hierarchically organized security requirements (business policies in terms of PoSecCo). Requirements can be linked to various stakeholders within an organization to express responsibility, accountability, or interest, which allows the hierarchy of requirements to be tied to the organizational structure. Different fulfillment models allow specifying under which conditions a requirement is considered fulfilled, partially fulfilled, or not fulfilled, and whether such state changes can happen in an automated fashion or require human confirmation (which is limited in time to force the continuous revalidation of requirements). Furthermore, different reporting views allow users to monitor requirements, to see the compliance rate of organizational units with given laws or regulations.

Policy Specification and Harmonization

This application offers the administrator access to the set of requirements specified in the previous phase and supports him or her in constructing a collection of instances of the IT Security Policy model able to represent the requirements. The IT Security Policy model focuses on representing AC and DP requirements. The AC part supports the high-level formal description of the authentication and authorization profiles of applications.

For the authentication profile, the model considers the description of a variety of authentication techniques. The most common solution is to use usernames and passwords, but richer solutions based on certificates, hardware tokens, and cryptographic credentials are supported. The model distinguishes between "direct" authentication solutions, in which the system managing the authentication phase and verifying the correctness of the claimed identity of the user is the same that will offer the services, and "indirect" authentication solutions, in which some support is received by external systems responsible for the secure retrieval of the protected credential for the complete execution of the authentication phase.

For the authorization profile, the IT Security Policy model permits the representation of modern AC models. The central concepts of this part are system authorization and role authorization. These two constructs are integrated, and the possibility is offered of expressing declarative restrictions on the subject and the resource of an authorization. Authorizations have a sign, positive or negative; in general, DAC, MAC, RBAC, and ABAC models can be represented. The expressivity of the authorization model is loosely comparable to what can be achieved with XACML, even if the different assumptions about the structure of subjects and resources do not permit a formal containment relationship to be established between models.

Once the IT policy has been defined, reasoning services are offered to verify whether the policy satisfies a number of consistency constraints. The checks that are supported focus on identifying modality conflicts, redundant authorizations, and violations of SoD constraints. Modality conflicts arise when rules with conflicting signs apply to the same access request and a specified conflict resolution policy is not able to establish which rules have to be applied. The detection requires subject and resource hierarchies to be expanded that are used in designing the IT Policy. Redundant authorizations are detected by looking for authorization rules that are dominated by other rules. These redundant rules can be omitted from the IT policy without changing system behavior. SoD constraints are specified using negative role authorizations, and violations are detected by identifying subjects that are able to acquire two roles denoted as conflicting. All checks are implemented thanks to the use of Semantic Web tools, translating the IT policy into an OWL representation and then invoking adequate reasoning services. The outcome of this phase is a harmonized IT policy that is passed to the next phase.

Policy Refinement and Optimization

The harmonized IT Security Policy is the input, together with the landscape to configure, to the refinement phase that produces abstract configurations for the security controls available in the landscape. The Policy Refinement and Optimization application is a modular framework that drives the administrator in all refinement phases and allows him or her to make informed decisions and provide missing information. In fact, the Policy Refinement and Optimization application allows different refinement strategies to be selected (prefer the enforcement of security at the application layer or message protection over channel protection, or use infrastructure rather than the end point controls), or a manual selection of the devices to configure for each IT Security Policy.

The refinement is performed in two phases: ontology-based refinement and landscape configuration. During ontology refinement, the IT Security Policy is enriched according to the landscape information using specialized ontologies that characterize the meaning of security concepts for each policy type (AC vs. DP) and for each device type (databases vs. operating systems). Moreover, the generated configurations are further adapted for the control that will actually enforce it (Windows vs. Linux AC policies) to simplify the transformation from abstract to concrete configurations. In addition, the ontology permits automatic reasoning about the target landscape (to classify an element according to the security level), to capture the complex dependencies among all entities involved in policy enforcement and identify possible issues. Depending on the IT Security Policy to refine and the chosen strategy, available controls are proposed for configuration according to their policy expressiveness and enforcement granularity,

management costs, and the like, but the selection of the controls actually to configure is manually done by the administrators who have full control of AC policy enforcement. At the end of the ontology refinement, the configurations for AC end point security controls are generated (operating systems, databases, and Web service containers). In addition, for the IT Security Policies that require further refinement (to configure the firewalls to allow users to reach the services they are authorized to use), for the ones that administrators decided to enforce using infrastructure elements (using VPN gateways to protect communications between two networks), or for those that are not enforceable with end point security, the ontology refinement outputs the logical associations that are the input for the landscape configuration phase.

The landscape configuration takes into account all information about the target landscape, including all infrastructure controls and the entire network topology. Because at this level many different alternatives are usually available (different available controls, different configuration modes, different paths, etc.), the selection of controls to configure and the rules to configure them are decided through an optimization process that decides not only based on single-control configuration but also at the global landscape level. Many target functions can be selected by the administrator to maximize the overall performance, to minimize the risk exposure, and other balanced combinations. In addition, the entire process can be customized with additional constraints; for instance, it is possible to implement defense in depth, to configure at least two redundant controls. For example, the best practice for firewall configuration imposed to block prohibited traffic as soon as possible may force the use of the border firewall to implement most of the IT policy. According to security and performance considerations, the Policy Refinement and Optimization application can move some of the rules from the border firewall to the periphery to avoid performance degradation. Another example concerns channel protection controls, in which it is possible to avoid redundant channels or to aggregate end-to-end connections into basic VPNs according to the trustworthiness of the involved networks to improve performance. At the end of these phases, all missing abstract configurations are generated. The set of abstract configurations is provided to Configuration Management Systems, which are expected first to transform them into the representation required by the respective system element and then to deploy this concrete configuration to enforce the policy.

Configuration Validation and Audit

The deployment of concrete configuration marks the end of the implementation phase of the security life cycle. The PoSecCo application *Configuration Validation and Audit* then checks the presence of a concrete configuration to validate the *operation effectiveness* of implemented security controls. This is achieved by using and extending the Security Content Automation Protocol, a collection of standards developed by the NIST to foster the standardized representation, exchange, and automated processing of security knowledge. Open Vulnerability Assessment Language (OVAL), in particular, is used to check whether the PoSecCo-generated configuration is in place. Configuration discrepancies will be reflected by policy state changes on upper abstraction levels. The PCI–DSS requirement to protect cardholder data, for instance, linked to the concrete configuration of a server's SSL feature, will enter the state *UNDER ANALYSIS* during the assessment of a configuration discrepancy, and *NOT FULFILLED* in case the assessment concludes that the discrepancy affects security up to a point where the originating requirement is no longer fulfilled (in case MD5 instead of SHA1 is used as a hash algorithm). Within that context, OVAL has been extended to support the checking of application-level configurations in distributed environments and to abstract check specifications from the way the configuration is actually collected [54].

Operation effectiveness is one element of common IT audits, but in itself it is not sufficient to check whether a control framework put into place by an organization addresses all security objectives and requirements. It is complemented by a check of the framework's *design effectiveness* to see whether planned controls are in principle suitable to reach the desired objectives (independent of the question of whether they have been implemented and properly configured). PoSecCo will support auditors and other stakeholders in this activity by allowing them to explore a subset of the models stored in MoVE and to formulate OCL queries. The subset defined depends on the actual audit scope: for example, a given business service and all connected elements. As an example, an auditor could query the model to check whether cardholder data are transmitted over communication links without a corresponding data protection policy. Finally, the model will also be used to generate draft audit programs that refer to OVAL checks for concrete configuration; these programs can be further enriched by auditors before the automated execution in the auditee's system. Here, the aim is to overcome today's audit practice of taking samples, but to enable complete and automated validation of all relevant configurations.

7. SUMMARY

This chapter briefly sketched different aspects of policy-based system management. It outlines achievements made since the late 1980s, when policies were first considered for system management purposes concerning areas such as policy information models, specification languages, and policy refinement and conflict detection. Some of this work culminated in international standards that fostered a broader adoption of PBM. IBM succeeded in establishing the vision of autonomic computing that forecasts the long-term development of future IT systems founded on mature and broadly applied policy technologies and techniques. This vision drives technology researchers from academia and industry; it also serves as a vehicle to discuss nontechnical matters related to autonomous and self-managing IT systems (ethical and socioeconomic questions).

We observe that policy concepts are increasingly adopted by commercial products used in real-life systems. It comes without surprise that this application started by looking into single domains (network management), specification of AC policies, and system management. This restricted focus facilitates implementation and already suffices to realize economic benefits and service quality improvements. As yet, however, no implementation of a PBM system exists that takes a holistic view of the many different kinds of policies at their various abstraction levels and that considers the interdependencies of security mechanisms at various architecture layers. Moreover, today's application of PBM primarily targets the management of administrative domains belonging to one organizational entity, whereas new technologies and business models, such as virtualization and cloud services, result in the collaboration of many organizations across all layers of the application stack.

As such, at least two major technical challenges need to be addressed to move toward autonomous systems: (1) the detection of policy conflicts across architectural layers (see Chapter 59), and (2) the policy-based negotiation and collaboration of system elements that belong to different organizational entities (business partners). Efforts in the latter direction include working on the high-level description of nonfunctional service properties and requirements, including security, which represents the basis for discovery and negotiation capabilities. This topic also stretches across compositional security, which investigates the preservation of security properties when systems are constructed from smaller components (with given properties).

We believe that the further development and increased adoption of policy technology by the IT industry strongly depends on the use of common specification languages, protocols, and architectures. Whereas typical problems related to standardization also apply to the area of PBM (long-running standardization processes are sometimes outpaced by technological developments or undermined by strong market participants who seek to establish proprietary technology), we observe that past standardization efforts related to policies prove to be successful. The DMTF standards CIM and WBEM are broadly supported by state-of-the-art tools for system management.

Finally, let us move on to the real interactive part of this chapter: review questions/exercises, hands-on projects, case projects, and the optional team case project. The answers and/or solutions by chapter can be found in the Online Instructor's Solutions Manual.

CHAPTER REVIEW QUESTIONS/ EXERCISES

True/False

1. True or False? Policy-driven system management or policy-based management (PBM) is a research domain that aims to automatize the management of small-scale computing systems.
2. True or False? IT systems are not traditionally structured according to several architecture layers, each layer offering a number of security capabilities that can support organizations in reaching desired security objectives.
3. True or False? Security management as performed today involves a variety of stakeholders with different job functions, expertise, and objectives, and using different tools and terminology.
4. True or False? Generally speaking, a policy is a definite goal, course, or method of action to guide and determine present and future decisions.
5. True or False? The approach of PBM naturally leads to a so-called policy continuum, a hierarchy of policies that are subject to the same abstraction levels.

Multiple Choice

1. What makes it impractical to specify policies for individual system elements?
   A. Smaller systems
   B. Larger systems
   C. Management systems
   D. Network systems
   E. All of the above
2. What increases the correctness and consistency of configuration information, speeds deployment processes, and supports a variety of other security-related activities such as IT audits?
   A. Smaller systems
   B. Larger systems
   C. Configuration management systems
   D. Network systems
   E. All of the above
3. What requires a set of common functionalities related to the creation, storage, distribution, and enforcement of policies?
   A. Smaller systems
   B. Larger systems

   C. Policy-based systems
   D. Configuration management systems
   E. Network systems
4. What term has been coined by IBM to denote computing systems that manage themselves?
   A. Autonomic computing
   B. Self-protection
   C. Self-healing
   D. Autonomic elements
   E. All of the above
5. An important aspect in the design and implementation of a secure information system is the correct consideration of:
   A. Remote control software
   B. Email
   C. Universal serial bus storage
   D. Security principles
   E. Risk analysis

EXERCISE

Problem

How long does ISO certification/accreditation take?

Hands-on Projects

Project

What happens after ISO certification/accreditation?

Case Projects

Problem

What if an organization has an accident, incident, or complaint?

Optional Team Case Project

Problem

What is the difference between major and minor nonconformance?

ACKNOWLEDGMENTS

This work was partially funded by the European Community in the scope of the research project PoSecCo (Project No. 257129), under the Information and Communication Technologies (ICT) theme of the Seventh Framework Program for R&D (FP7). The PoSecCo general approach, methodology, and architecture stem from the joint efforts of all consortium partners. The work by Stefano Paraboschi was partially supported by the PRIN 2008 Project PEPPER (2008SY2PH4).

REFERENCES

[1] F. Liu, J. Tong, J. Mao, R. Bohn, J. Messina, L. Badger, NIST Cloud Computing Reference Architecture, National Institute of Standards and Technology (NIST), 2011.

[2] BSI: Standard 100—1: Information Security Management Systems (ISMS), 2008. URL: https://www.bsi.bund.de/SharedDocs/Downloads/EN/BSI/Publications/BSIStandards/standard_100-1_e_pdf.pdf.

[3] W.E. Deming, Out of the Crisis, MIT Center for Advanced Engineering Study, 1986.

[4] PCI Security Standards Council LLC: PCI DSS Requirements and Security Assessment Procedures, 2010.

[5] IBM, IBM Corporate Strategy Analysis of IDC Data, 2007.

[6] K. Kark, L.M. Orlov, S. Bright, How to Manage Your Information Security Policy Framework, 2006.

[7] W.H. Baker, A. Hutton, C.D. Hylender, C. Novak, C. Porter, B. Sartin, et al., 2009 Data Breach Investigations Report, 2009. URL, http://www.verizonbusiness.com/resources/security/reports/2009_databreach_rp.pdf.

[8] J. Williams, D. Wichers, Top 10 Most Critical Web Application Security Risks, 2010. URL, https://www.owasp.org/index.php/Top_10_2010-A6.

[9] C. Maple, A. Philips, UK security Breach Investigations Report 2010, 2010. URL, http://www.7safe.com/breach_report/Breach_report_2010.pdf.

[10] E.A. Westerinen, RFC 3198—Terminology for Policy-Based Management, 2001. URL, http://www.ietf.org/rfc/rfc3198.

[11] D. Agrawal, S. Calo, K.W. Lee, J. Lobo, D. Verma, Policy Technology for Self-Managing Systems, IBM Press, 2009.

[12] Moore, RFC 3460—Policy Core Information Model (PCIM) Extensions, 2003. URL, http://www.ietf.org/rfc/rfc3460.

[13] J. Strassner, How policy empowers business-driven device management, in: Proceedings of the Third International Workshop on Policies for Distributed Systems and Networks (POLICY'02). POLICY '02, IEEE Computer Society, Washington, DC, USA, 2002.

[14] R. Boutaba, I. Aib, Policy-based management: a historical perspective, J. Netw. Syst. Manage. 15 (4) (2007) 447—480.

[15] M. Sloman, Policy driven management for distributed systems, J. Netw. Syst. Manage. 2 (1994) 333—360.

[16] S.R. White, J.E. Hanson, I. Whalley, D.M. Chess, J.O. Kephart, An architectural approach to autonomic computing, in: International Conference on Autonomic Computing, 2004, pp. 2—9.

[17] R. Wies, Policy definition and classification: aspects, criteria, and examples, in: IEEE/IFIP Workshop on Distributed Systems Operations and Management, 1994, pp. 10—12.

[18] E. Lupu, M. Sloman, Conflicts in policy-based distributed systems management, Softw. Eng. IEEE Trans. 25 (6) (1999) 852—869.

[19] E. Al-Shaer, H. Hamed, R. Boutaba, M. Hasan, Conflict classification and analysis of distributed firewall policies, Sel. Areas Commun. IEEE J. 23 (10) (2005) 2069—2084.

[20] G. Waters, J. Wheeler, A. Westerinen, L. Rafalow, R. Moore, Policy Framework Architecture (IETF Internet-Draft <draft-ietf-policy-arch-00.txt>), 1999.

[21] M.C. Huebscher, J.A. McCann, A survey of autonomic computing—degrees, models, and applications, ACM Comput. Surv. 40 (3) (2008) 7:1—7:28.

[22] P. Horn, Autonomic Computing: IBMs Perspective on the State of Information Technology, 2001. URL, http://researchweb.watson.ibm.com/autonomic/manifesto/autonomic_computing.pdf.

[23] J.H. Saltzer, M.D. Schroeder, The protection of information in computer systems, Proc. IEEE 63 (9) (1975) 1278—1308.

[24] D.E. Bell, L.J. LaPadula, Technical Report MTR-2547, Secure Computer Systems: Mathematical Foundations, vol. 1, MITRE Corp, Bedford, MA, 1973.

[25] K.J. Biba, Integrity Considerations for Secure Computer Systems, Technical Report ESD-TR-76—372, USAF Electronic systems division, Bedford, MA, 1977 (Also available through National Technical Information Service, Springfield, VA, NTIS AD-A039324.).

[26] D.F.C. Brewer, M.J. Nash, The Chinese wall security policy, IEEE Symp. Secur. Priv. (1989) 206—214.

[27] D. Ferraiolo, R. Kuhn, Role-based access control, in: Fifteenth NIST-NCSC National Computer Security Conference, 1992, pp. 554—563.

[28] N. Damianou, N. Dulay, E. Lupu, M. Sloman, The ponder policy specification language, in: Proceedings of the International Workshop on Policies for Distributed Systems and Networks. POLICY '01, Springer-Verlag, London, UK, 2001.

[29] S. Jajodia, M. Kudo, V.S. Subrahmanian, Provisional Authorizations E-Commerce Security and Privacy, Springer, 2001.

[30] K. Irwin, T. Yu, W.H. Winsborough, Assigning responsibilities for failed obligations, in: Proceedings of the IFIPTM Joined ITrust and PST Conference on Privacy, Trust Management and Security (ITrust), June 2008, pp. 327—342.

[31] P. Gama, P. Ferreira, Obligation policies: an enforcement platform, in: Proceedings of the Sixth IEEE International Workshop on Policies for Distributed Systems and Networks. POLICY '05, IEEE Computer Society, Washington, DC, USA, 2005.

[32] N. Li, H. Chen, E. Bertino, On practical specification and enforcement of obligations, in: Proceedings of the Second ACM Conference on Data and Application Security and Privacy. CODASPY '12, ACM, New York, NY, USA, 2012.

[33] S. Bugiel, L.V. Davi, S. Schulz, Scalable trust establishment with software reputation, in: Proceedings of the Sixth ACM Workshop on Scalable Trusted Computing. STC '11, ACM, New York, NY, USA, 2011.

[34] D. Taylor, J. Turner, Scalable Packet Classification Using Distributed Crossproducting of Field Labels, Dept. of Computer Science and Engineering, George Washington University, Washington, DC, 2004. Tech. Rep. WUCSE-2004-38.

[35] K. Scarfone, P. Hoffman, NIST Special Publication 800—41: Guidelines on Firewalls and Firewall Policy, National Institute of Standards and Technology (NIST), 2009.

[36] E. Al-Shaer, H. Hamed, Modeling and management of firewall policies, IEEE Trans. Netw. Serv. Manage. 1 (1) (2004) 2—10.

[37] C. Basile, A. Cappadonia, A. Lioy, Network-level access control policy analysis and transformation, IEEE/ACM Trans. Netw. 20 (4) (2012) 985—998.

[38] A. El-Atawy, T. Samak, E. Al-Shaer, H. Li, Using Online Traffic Statistical Matching for Optimizing Packet Filtering Performance, INFOCOM, 2007.

[39] W.R. Cheswick, S.M. Bellovin, A.D. Rubin, Firewalls and Internet Security; Repelling the Wily Hacker, second ed., Addison-Wesley, Reading, MA, 2003.

[40] P. Ferguson, D. Senie, Network Ingress Filtering: Defeating Denial of Service Attacks Which Employ IP Source Address Spoofing, RFC 2827 (Best Current Practice). Updated by RFC 3704, 2000.

[41] D. Harkins, D. Carrel, The Internet Key Exchange (IKE), RFC 2409 (Proposed Standard). Obsoleted by RFC 4306, updated by RFC 4109, 1998.

[42] T. Dierks, E. Rescorla, The Transport Layer Security (TLS) Protocol Version 1.2, RFC 5246 (Proposed Standard). Updated by RFCs 5746, 5878, 6176, 2008.

[43] E. Rescorla, N. Modadugu, Datagram Transport Layer Security Version 1.2, RFC 6347 (Proposed Standard), 2012.

[44] T. Phelan, Datagram Transport Layer Security (DTLS) over the Datagram Congestion Control Protocol (DCCP), RFC 5238 (Proposed Standard), 2008.

[45] A. Alshamsi, T. Saito, A technical comparison of IPsec and SSL, in: Proceedings of the 19th International Conference on Advanced Information Networking and Applications—Volume 2. AINA '05, IEEE Computer Society, Washington, DC, USA, 2005.

[46] B. Ramsdell, S. Turner, Secure/Multipurpose Internet Mail Extensions (S/MIME) Version 3.2 Message Specification, RFC 5751 (Proposed Standard), 2010.

[47] R. Housley, Cryptographic Message Syntax (CMS), RFC 5652 (Standard), 2009.

[48] Cisco Systems, Inc., Cisco adaptive security device manager, http://www.cisco.com/en/US/products/ps6121/index.html.

[49] NetCitadel LLC, Firewall builder 5 user's guide, http://www.fwbuilder.org/.

[50] S. Godik, T. Moses (Eds.), eXtensible Access Control Markup Language (XACML) Version 1.0, 2003.

[51] C.A. Ardagna, S.D.C. di Vimercati, S. Paraboschi, E. Pedrini, P. Samarati, M. Verdicchio, Expressive and deployable access control in open web service applications, IEEE Trans. Serv. Comput. 4 (2) (2011) 96—109.

[52] XACML Profile for Role Based Access Control (RBAC), 2004.

[53] F. Innerhofer-Oberperer, R. Breu, M. Hafner, Living security—collaborative security management in a changing world, in: Parallel and Distributed Computing and Networks/720. Software Engineering, 2011.

[54] M. Casalino, M. Mangili, H. Plate, S. Ponta, Detection of Configuration Vulnerabilities in Distributed (Web) Environments, 2012.

Chapter 27

Information Technology Security Management

Rahul Bhaskar and Bhushan Kapoor

California State University, Fullerton, CA, United States

Note: This chapter is available in its entirety online at store.elsevier.com/product.jsp?isbn= 9780128038437 (click the Resources tab at the bottom of the page).

1. ABSTRACT

Information technology (IT) security management can be defined as a process that enables organizational structure and technology to protect an organization's IT operations and assets against internal and external threats, intentional or otherwise. The principal purpose of IT security management is to ensure confidentiality, integrity, and availability of IT systems. Fundamentally, security management is a part of the risk management process and business continuity strategy in an organization.

2. CONTENTS

Computer and Information Security Handbook. http://dx.doi.org/10.1016/B978-0-12-803843-7.00027-2

Chapter 28

The Enemy (The Intruder's Genesis)

Pramod Pandya
CSU Fullerton, Fullerton, CA, United States

Note: This chapter is available in its entirety online at store.elsevier.com/product.jsp?isbn= 9780128038437 (click the Resources tab at the bottom of the page).

1. ABSTRACT

It is estimated that global IP traffic on the Internet will reach an annual rate of 1.3 zettabytes by 2016 as more people connect to the Internet by mobile devices. Global IP traffic in 2011 was about 369 exabytes, or 0.369 zettabytes. Furthermore, the number of devices that will be connected to the Internet would reach around 19 billion. The reality of threat to the Internet security will be extremely critical to all individual, corporate, and government users. The Internet was envisioned to support primarily educational and research activities to share information and knowledge. In the early 21st century, social media networks such as Facebook have overshadowed the dot-com on the Internet. Hence the nature of Internet security has now become synonymous with cybersecurity. Government agencies are currently in the process of creating a formal set of governance to define cybersecurity and courses of actions to be taken to defend against cyberattacks.

2. CONTENTS

Computer and Information Security Handbook. http://dx.doi.org/10.1016/B978-0-12-803843-7.00028-4

Chapter 29

Social Engineering Deceptions and Defenses

Scott R. Ellis

kCura Corporation, Lake Bluff, IL, United States

1. INTRODUCTION

More than ever in the history of computing, unknown attacks threaten enterprise data. Data exist everywhere and come in from everywhere, and the idea of a "perimeter," a wall that you can defend, has crumbled and is gone. End point to end point encryption has become prevalent, so the risk to physical devices increases. More than ever, hackers will attempt access to physical devices when other means fail.

If someone asks the question, "Why would someone do that?" as a response to a defense proposition, the only answer is, "It doesn't matter. What matters is that someone *could* do that." You have to build awareness, probe for weaknesses, and show how the exploit works and that it is successful. Often, penetration testers will suggest that an attack is possible when in fact it is not. The "brilliant hacker" defense is not good enough. You have to hone your skills and become good enough to demonstrate that what you suspect is in fact true. It is one thing to tell the director of information technology that someone *could* pass the hash and step into domain admin; it is an entirely different matter to display the domain admin password on a slide in a pen-test readout.

2. COUNTER-SOCIAL ENGINEERING

The examples listed in this chapter suggest solutions on a layered model of counter-social engineering. This section proposes that a model to counter-social engineering exists and is in common use but has been poorly defined and has not been canonized critically. In the first layer, we have "at a glance" security. If something fails this test, precaution is highly advised. For example, if someone I do not know tries to tailgate me into the office, I politely ask whether they would not mind using a badge to enter. On the surface, I make the assumption that the person is in fact a valid employee or has authorized access.

The SANS Institute published a document about social engineering. In it, they discussed layers of defense and the three layers of threat, or risk, that people perceive. This chapter seeks to exploit and expound upon those three layers, and develop a layered style of defense that has proven results to reduce risk and can easily be taught to others. The three levels of perception of risk to victims are that:

1. There is risk
2. There is risk to others around me
3. There is risk to me

Taking these three stages and arming the potential victim with a series of tests and defensive strategies for each stage allows for a flexible three-layered strategy that can cope with most known attacks and should prepare for unknown ones. The oldest tricks, the ones that have been employed by confidence game (con) men for centuries, are well-known for only one reason: They are effective against the vast majority of humans.

Ultimately, the greatest challenge, and the challenge most often not discussed, is that of moving people from Level 2 to Level 3. This can be accomplished most successfully by demonstrating the vulnerability *indirectly*. In other words, it is one thing for you to demonstrate to team members that you can send email from their computer when they walk away and leave it unlocked; It is another thing if you hire an external consultant to do it and leave their calling card on the user's computer. Ultimately, a pseudo-"sting" is the best form of inoculation against all forms of

Computer and Information Security Handbook. http://dx.doi.org/10.1016/B978-0-12-803843-7.00029-6

attacks. In this author's experience, no amount of training can replace an actual demonstration of vulnerability.[1]

3. VULNERABILITIES

Before diving into aspects of defense, it is useful to detail the vulnerabilities. This section defines and explains the various human weaknesses that an attacker will exploit.

Strong Effect

Sex, drugs, alcohol, anger, joy, sadness, and any range of strong emotions in between present an opportunity for exploitation to the social engineer (SE). Used car salesmen, real estate agents, insurance agents, and recruiters master these techniques as well, playing on and using human empathy to exaggerate and leverage your emotions. It behooves anyone to learn these tactics that are used by others for the sole purpose of exploiting you and enriching themselves. Forewarned is forearmed. Attacks such as "The Vixen," "You may already be a winner," "Earn thousands of dollars in your spare time," etc., are all designed to hit you where you might be hurting and promise to solve your problems. At the time of this writing, several seemingly pyramid scheme health food subscriber networks are making wild promises of cash earned in your spare time. One boast is, "We just had 5000 people at an event in Dallas. In 20 months Team Awesome has grown to 90,000 people and $130 million in sales." Being too emotional to do the math is bank for the scammers. An average of $1444.44/year revenue is probably not a distant second to the average amount of money that each of those "members" has sunk into product that they are trying to sell, product that is sitting in the trunk of their car or collecting dust in their garage.

Overloading

Imagine a receptionist at her desk. A man approaches and explains that he needs to gain access, when in walks someone else needing a more mundane task. Like what? A delivery, perhaps? The receptionist is then preoccupied with a man needing to check the conference room that he was in yesterday for the phone that he lost. It might have fallen behind the credenza, you see, and probably nobody would see it. Meanwhile, the receptionist buzzes in a "divert man." She was overloaded.

When people have too much information to process, they become passive. Politician stump speeches are famous for this, and veteran courtroom lawyers use it, too: Throw

enough manure at a wall, and some of it will stick. Bombard your constituents or your jury with a plethora of "facts," and some of them will stick. The veteran SE knows which ones will stick and tailors his argument accordingly; when you act, it is because you have responded according to his plan. Now, do not get haughty: we are all vulnerable. The only necessary ingredient that the SE needs to tweak you into doing his bidding is *your desire*.

Reciprocation and Obligation

From complex to simple, reciprocation and obligation (vulnerabilities) depend on the basic goodness inherent in human nature: We want to help those who help us. Take, for example, when an employee uses a badge to enter at a door. An SE, right on his heels, pulls the door open with a smile, and a nice "How ya doin'?" The employee says, "Thank you," and does not challenge as the SE walks in behind him.

Yield begets yield. Small concessions on the part of the SE lead to larger concessions on the part of the victim. One victim, a nerdy Air Force enlisted man, finds himself friends with Mr. Popular (SE). It is not long before he is running errands for the SE, paying for his drinks and chauffeuring him around, and finally when SE is dishonorably discharged from the service (unbeknownst to the victim), the victim gives the SE $5000 in cash for a motorcycle, a motorcycle that the SE promised he owned and for which he would get the title to him next week. The need for acceptance and friendship is a key vulnerability that SEs exploit. The need to obligate someone who has helped you underpins the morality of civilization. Deceptive friendships leverage these principles of reciprocation and obligation.

Deceptive Relationships

Imagine a man who throws some roofing nails onto a road. He then just waits until someone has a blowout. Kind stranger that he is, he reluctantly accepts the $50 cash the poor old lady offers him after he changes her tire for her … never mind you that he caused the blowout.

The preceding is reverse social engineering: Cause the problem and then fix it. Now you are the hero. Be cautious of people who are too friendly. Friends are not always friends, and a clever SE will be friends with you long before he asks "a favor."

Mob Rule

Mob rule is a unique engineering feat and typically will require one or more "shills" who are in on it. It depends on controlling and engineering a crowd to accomplish a specific purpose. From the physical world perspective, riots, protests, concerts, and large conferences can provide

1. B.J. Sagarin, R.B. Cialdini, W.E. Rice, S.B. Serna, Dispelling the illusion of invulnerability: the motivations and mechanisms of resistance to persuasion. J. Personal. Soc. Psychol. 83 (3) Sept 2002 526–541 (533).

opportunities for mob rule social engineering. An electronic equivalent could be an email that intimates that all of your peers will be at a "free" conference, the point of which ultimately results in knowledge gained about you for the purposes of prequalifying you as a lead or enticing you to purchase a useless service. Condominium time share sales events, weekend wellness conferences, and multilevel marketing sales events are good examples of mob rule being leveraged to achieve objectives.

Deceptive Relationships

Fake preachers, nuns, and doctors all exert moral authority. *Even an atheist* will respect the moral authority of a man with a white collar. In cyberspace, moral authority is conferred by an association with Microsoft, Cisco, EMC, or other big names. The countless spam mail this author has received from one large networking appliance manufacturer is surpassed only by those claiming to be affiliated with it. These emails are only ever blocked and deleted; most of them will contain an "unsubscribe" link, but the main purpose of this is to verify and validate your existence. Your action of unsubscribing merely lets scammers know that they need to move on and try a different tactic with you. Eventually they will find something you want; it is a numbers game to them.

4. USING A LAYERED DEFENSE APPROACH

We have discussed the individual vulnerabilities that SEs and scammers employ. Now we must develop a state-of-mind system of defenses that will allow us to still enjoy life but also to trip off our perimeter alerts when we are being scammed. To do this, we must begin to think of the world around us as a threat; and, incorporate a series of questions within those places in our minds where we interface with others. We must begin to think in three specific layers.

Layer 1 Test: Initial Contact: Known Entity

We understand from the SANS article that there are threats in the world, there are threats that might affect people we know, and there are threats that affect us. Layer 1 is any point of potential interaction with you. Every contact with you should meet these criteria. In this scenario, we will judge an interaction and make our decisions based on the outcome. Layer 1 is composed of three litmus tests:

1. The person communicating to you is known to you.
2. The method of communication is established and known.
3. The topic of conversation is customary.

A vendor I frequently use contacted me. When my phone rang, the proper number appeared on the caller ID. The caller is the vendor's office manager and I had had previous albeit infrequent conversations with her. It is not common for this vendor to contact me via phone. It is far more common for them just to come to my house. The vendor's office manager was requesting that I pay, in full and in cash, a recent bill of $2500. The owner, Ethan, required an infusion of cash owing to the lateness of the season starting and various unstated seasonal "start-up" costs.

In 10 years of my relationship with this vendor, the owner has never requested cash. I denied the request, stating I would be happy to pay by check in full at any time.

This contact then passed the first aspect of a Layer 1 contact; it arguably barely passed the second, and then failed the third litmus. Alternatively, for the third aspect, could I have requested that the owner come by my house, and that I would give the cash to him personally? No; the reason might seem like extreme paranoia to you, but even for a known contact with whom transactions of this amount are frequent, the following could also be true: He could be under duress somehow. One solution would be to have a prearranged signal with all of your associates, a way for them to communicate to you that they are under duress.

The order of the day is to streamline and functionalize your paranoia. Finally, always understand what is at risk. In this scenario, $2500 is at risk. This it more money than most people want to lose. Always know your level of acceptable loss.

Layer 2 Test: The Meet

Let us assume for the sake of exploring this model that your transaction has survived Layer 1, and at the prearranged time your doorbell rings. You grab the $2500 and head for the door. (Or do you?) You see two men standing at the door. Neither of them is Ethan.

Layer 2 is physical interaction, and covers how to conduct oneself with physical security in mind (see sidebar: "Physical: Interaction and Security"). As you approach the door, you see that Ethan is standing at the door and has four men with him who are unknown to you. Layer 2 then proceeds with aspects that are similar to those in Layer 1.

Layer 3: Engaged in the Con (How to Exit)

A wise man named Marty Becker, an attorney with the firm Becker and Gurian, once said to me, "Scott, honesty is not the best policy." A little surprised, I asked, "It's not?" He replied, "No! It's the only policy." Your transaction has translated through Layers 1 and 2 unscathed. All is well, right? Or perhaps you are well into a deep, long con. You have realized you are in a con, and now you need to exit. You have a few choices here, and again I will discuss three aspects that can act as a litmus test. If the transaction cannot pass these tests, you are being socially hacked. Get out,

---

Physical: Interaction and Security

1. The person communicating with you is known to you:
   a. I walk to the door, and there are two strangers standing there. My first question to myself is, "Why am I holding $2500 in my hand?" My second question is, "How do I get out of this?" You lie, and you stick to your lie, and you ensure your lie is bulletproof.
   b. "Hey guys, I know you are here to pick up the money, but sadly my air conditioning blew out last night. The repairman actually just left, and I had to give him the money to fix it, and I'm drained now. Thanks for stopping by. Tell Ethan I'm sorry and will catch up with him later."

2. The method of transacting is well-known and customary:
   a. Even if it were normal for you to hand Ethan $2500 at your front door, it is not normal for you to hand it to two strangers. What is going on here?
   b. Familiar with the rules of antisocial engineering, you entertain the two men at the door. Curious, you ask them, "What is going on? Why does Ethan need cash?" Now, the con begins. The reality is that Ethan is deep in debt to Colombian drug lords and his landscaping business and the trust he has built with his clients over the years is his exit strategy. However, the story these men will tell you is not reality.
   c. You are about to experience a variation on the "Spanish Prisoner" con.
   d. The men explain to you that Ethan has been kidnapped. The attempts to get cash are attempts to get ransom. They assure you that Ethan is okay, but that they need to raise $100,000 in cash. Ethan, they assure you, has the cash and can pay you back, and will pay you back with interest. Because of banking rules, they simply cannot extract enough cash from Ethan's account without raising alerts (and you know this to be true). They sense that you are honest, so they ask you how much you can give and what you would want for interest. You are a kind person and insist that you do not want any part of

it, that they should immediately contact the authorities. Unfortunately, they tell you, Ethan is an illegal immigrant from Norway. Any contact with the authorities would not only risk Ethan's life but could end up with him being deported. Their response? If you could just give an additional $2000, Ethan will provide landscaping services for free for 2 years. If you can give an additional $4000, he will make you a partner. They may describe for you some ideas about a multilevel marketing scheme whereby you bring in more customers and sign others up to the same deal.
   e. At this point, you fall back to the story from 1.b. You have no money and cannot help them. You contact the Federal Bureau of Investigation and relay to them the entirety of what just happened. If you do not, if somehow this story has merit and you fall for it, you are into Layer 3: engaged in the con.

3. You gain nothing. In any transaction, if it is too good to be true, it probably is not. Wealth is *earned* by most, and if it feels like a con, it likely is. There is an old saying: "You can't con an honest man." Typically, fraudsters will try to enroll you in some aspect of their scheme, and what they will ask you to do will border on unethical behavior. The bigger the con, the more dishonesty and complicity is needed. For example, a short-change artist can easily trick an honest person. Perhaps the rule applies only to the long con (and the older the con, the better.) In any kind of con, whether it is a variation of the badger or the Spanish Prisoner, as just illustrated, the hook will be an unbelievable deal for you. Remember (and this is important), some people have nothing to lose. A man with nothing to lose is a dangerous creature. I once bought a motorcycle for $200 only to find that when I went to the bank to get the title, $2000 was still owed. The man who sold it to me? He sold it to me on his last day on the base. Unbeknownst to me, he had been dishonorably discharged. Fortunately, the credit union was happy to work out an arrangement with me.

---

seek help, or cut your losses. This may involve changing your phone number or moving if the fraudsters are that deep into your life.

Presumably, the transaction passed Level 1 and 2 security checks. Now, 3 weeks have passed and you have not heard a peep from Ethan, and your lawn has been completely untended. You are fairly certain that your $4500 is gone. This is a deep, long con, and it worked on you. What now? Depending on how deep the con was perpetrated, the following options are available to you. If you have followed the layered approach outlined here, recompense may be a reasonable expectation: payment for services rendered or for services to be rendered.

Unfortunately, your recourse is limited. Your con man has vanished and gone back to Denmark or some other country with nonexistent extradition, or to a place where

extradition for $4500 just is not going to happen. Here are the three final steps you should have taken that could have prevented it:

1. Never, ever engage in illegal activity, even on the periphery. In some jurisdictions, even paying a ransom could be a crime.
2. Get it in writing. Take photos of those involved.
3. Demand collateral. The promise of a motorcycle is not nearly as good as the keys in hand. Granted, there may be other keys to the bike, but a disc brake motorcycle lock is an easy and cheap thing to purchase.

These have been illustrations of physical cons. Understand this: Digital cons are the same. They work the same. Variations of just about every con, from the Spanish Prisoner/Nigerian Princess to the Pig in the Poke con all exist in digital format. These physical representations have been provided because they deliver real-world experience that translates well to digital hacks.

5. ATTACK SCENARIOS

These scenarios all leverage one or more of the previously described vulnerabilities. Can you match the vulnerabilities with the attacks?

6. SUSPECT EVERYONE: NETWORK VECTOR

In this vector, the end goal is to obtain network credentials via either physical or network intrusion, with an unwitting assist from someone on the inside. The following scenarios depict things that might be going on in any office, anywhere, without anyone's knowledge, that could make even the humblest of business endeavors a target. Here are a couple of things that may convert an innocuous network into a target-rich environment:

Ron, in accounting, is a nephew to an eccentric billionaire named John who recently passed away. Sam, a law clerk in John's estate attorney's office, has large gambling debt. John has discussed some of the firm's cases online. His gambling "friends" whom he met online assure him that if they could just get access to Ron's computer, a big payout to him would be forthcoming.

Sue and Bob are going through a nasty divorce. Bob knows where Sue works and he also knows that she has been keeping quiet about their marital woes. Bob also is certain that Sue has a little nest egg hidden away, and if he could just search her desk at work, he would find it.

Let us explain a few ways in which an attack may occur. These exercises are designed to get you thinking about the different ways that an attacker may leverage the good in others to do evil.

The Distraction

It is 8:50 a.m. A woman stands outside of an office building on a busy street. A man (let's call him "Joe") with a big smile on his face thanks her as she hands him something, and he walks away. Tiffany nears and the woman smiles and says "Can you take a quick 2 min survey for a $50 gift card to [insert Tiffany's favorite restaurant here]?" Tiffany looks at her watch. In 10 min, the office doors will open automatically. "Two minutes? Sure."

Of course, the survey takes exactly 11 min to complete, and Joe accesses the office right as the doors automatically unlock. How did he know the door would unlock? He'd been trying them for the last five days, in 4 min increments starting at 8 a.m. This is just one of any number of different attacks he will carry out to gain

physical access. Solution: Doors should never be programmed to open automatically.

The Water Bottle Attack (Trojan Device)

Water bottles are ubiquitous. An inside hacker or an accomplice could leave wireless logging devices inserted into water bottles in various conference rooms, hunting for domain admin credentials. The water bottle could drift from conference room to room, seemingly left there by a forgetful employee. Other Trojan devices include wall chargers and wireless keyboards. Solution: Admin personnel sweep for and remove unauthorized items from conference rooms every day as part of assigned duties.

Forgotten Badge

Hacker Max chooses a target and he determines that she works on the 27th floor and arrives every day at exactly 7:30 a.m. He has already hacked elevator security and has a permanent working badge, but he still needs to get past the second layer of defense, the office door system. Over a period of 3 weeks he has ridden the elevator with her exactly six times. On the sixth time, he makes small talk with her, making a joke about how they are like "elevator buddies." He complained that his schedule is "too predictable" and that she must be stalking him. She laughs. Two days later, on the seventh time, he complains that he forgot his badge. Would she be so kind as to let him in on the 30th floor? Admin is not yet in and cannot issue him a temporary badge. Admin is on the 31st floor. Joe is wearing a suit and appears to be a successful attorney. He is possibly a partner in this big law firm.

"Of course," she replies. He is in.

Solution: Instead, she says "Of course," and pulls out her cell phone. Once she gets to the 31st floor, at the door, she asks, "What is your last name? I just need to verify you with security really quickly." Everyone in the firm has the on-call security number on speed dial. She catches a photo of him as he bails out and heads for the stairwell. His photo is circulated corporate-wide within minutes, and security files a police report. Corporate policy is so tight that even if the senior named partner himself is requesting badgeless access, security, which is a 24/7 operation, must be contacted for off-hours access.

The Tailgate

Max's attempt failed but he has friends, and they very much want to read some sensitive files about a high-profile divorce. Hacker William, with a load of files in his hands, gets on the elevator at the 22nd floor with Sharon (never mind that he came out of the stairwell). He asks her to hit the button for the 30th floor for him. She was already going

FIGURE 29.1 Set your wireless network always to ask before joining.

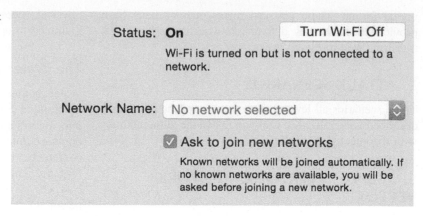

there and had already pressed 30. She smiles politely. On the 30th floor, she politely holds the door open for him and he walks right in. He ditches the files in a restroom trash can and heads to the senior partner's office. He knows the senior partner is on vacation because he has been spamming him for months and finally received his out-of-office reply. This is not a law firm where people are wearing suits? It is easy enough to get any T-shirt or polo shirt printed up. Look closely at shirts. Know your corporate swag as well as the marketing guy who designed it. When someone shows up wearing a shirt that is *just not quite the right color*, you will know something is amiss.

Solution: Disable the capability for out-of-office replies. Security should receive an alert from the door security system that a door was held open, and this should be an unusual enough occurrence that they examine the footage. A notification must be sent to Sharon and her manager that tailgating is not permitted. Depending on the corporate culture, this can be phrased as either a polite reminder that holding doors open forces security to review security camera footage, or it can be a stern warning that a second offense will result in immediate termination.

The Interview

A promising candidate is coming in for an interview. Typically, an interview can be a long process with multiple teams interviewing the more promising candidates. This candidate inserts a thumb-sized Power over Ethernet wireless device into a network port on the underside of a phone's computer extension jack. This device creates a wireless ad hoc network. Such a device can literally be inserted anywhere on a network.

Solution: Lock down all network access. No unauthenticated devices may persist on the network. Unauthorized devices are "dumped." Conduct interviews in interview rooms. These are rooms that sometimes have external access to the reception area and have a backdoor that the candidate cannot open. As you can see in the floor plan in Fig. 29.1, the candidate has zero access to resources besides a refrigerator and a potted plant, and cannot leave the interview room and wander.

Faux Vixen/Reynard

It is not hard to find a beautiful head shot of a beautiful person and then hide behind that person, fabricating a fake persona from LinkedIn, Facebook, etc. It is a simple matter to accumulate hundreds of friends on Facebook. By posing as a recruiter, one security analyst[2] created an online persona, Robin Sage, and was able to make connections and get invited to speak at conferences; one of the "victims" went so far as to send the vixen documents for "her" to review. Glamorous head shots of female recruiters on LinkedIn are a dime a dozen. Are they all real? The male version of this exploit is called a "Reynard."

Dropped Drive

This can take several forms. In the past, inserting media into your computer would automatically launch certain types of files on the media. Microsoft learned the error of this and corrected it, but a universal serial bus (USB) drive in the parking lot or lobby still can be surprisingly effective. Add an enticing filename, such as "corporate earnings 2016 Q2.xlsx.exe" or "C-Level payroll.xlsx.exe" to improve hit success. Additional forms include "lost" hard drives and lost memory cards. A "lost" camera with a dead (or missing) battery may lead a person to pull the card and look at it to see if he can determine the owner.

Phishing

Email from friends, business associates, colleagues, and family members are all exploitable avenues of ingress. The mass phisher casts a wide net. He shoots out millions

2. T. Ryan, Getting in Bed with Robin Sage, BlackHat USA, 2010.

of emails from the hundred most common names. Chances are good that one of your friends has one of those names, and maybe the email will strike a chord and will resonate with you in a familiar way. You will actually think that the email is from your friend.

But what if it was more targeted? What if the email comes from your boss? Spear-phishing and whale-phishing are more targeted: The attacker actually knows who he is after. In whale-phishing, the targeted employee will be one with access to bank account passwords and tokens and/or classified information, such as contact lists and sales projections. In one corporation, the chief financial officer (CFO) received an email from the chief executive officer (CEO), requesting wired funds. The CFO immediately identified the email as a forgery because the signature was incorrect. *How* the CEO signs his emails has remained unchanged for years, and this email had a signature block that matched the rest of the employees in the company.

One way, then, to "fingerprint" emails at a cursory level is to enforce the uniqueness of signatures. It could be an image or just a nickname. For example, one person may consistently sign his emails with just his initials "~ABC" whereas another may sign with all lowercase initials, "~abc." The key is to be consistent at the individual level. One supervisor may sign with just his or her Twitter handle. Thus, inconsistency across the corporation level is critical to preventing fraudsters from forging emails. Here, Layer 2 protection would be the questioning of authenticity. This surface-level authentication is by no means foolproof, but it adds a layer of complexity to the attack, and the goal is not to stop the attacker but to make it increasingly difficult, enough so that the attacker will move on to easier targets.

Everything is fake. This is the solution. Any message you receive from anyone unexpectedly (for example, a Facebook message from someone who has never messaged you before but suddenly wants you to visit a link) must be suspected of fraud. In addition, policy and training are crucial. The CEO should never send an email to someone suggesting that they transfer funds to a strange account, ever. If he does, it is either a forgery or he is under duress.

7. POLICY AND TRAINING

How, then, does internal policy protect corporate assets? Without training (see checklist: "An Agenda for Action for Developing and Deploying a Good Training Program for Protecting Corporate Assets"), it does little. Employees notoriously do not read employee handbooks. They all know that the employee handbook is merely a corporate indemnification designed to reduce exposure of the kind inherent in hiring and firing practices in America today.

An Agenda for Action for Developing and Deploying a Good Training Program for Protecting Corporate Assets

A good training program should be short and cover the following points (check all tasks completed):

_____**1.** Assets at risk, including personal exposure to risk when employees do not practice proper Internet security

_____**2.** Reporting: Employees should report anything suspicious.

_____**3.** Password practices (16 characters at least; complex passwords): One security expert was overheard saying that a simple password 16 characters long, with no complexity requirements, was better than a short password with complexity. I dared him to let me scan his network of several thousand computers for *passwordpassword*. He declined my offer. Ideally, a random phrase with some special characters is best. Something that is hard for a person to guess is not necessarily hard for a computer to guess. It takes mere moments to run through every possible variation of the word "password."

_____**4.** Wireless safety: Unadulterated connecting to wireless networks is a hacker's dream. You come to them. You connect to your neighborhood coffee shop, a national chain. Someone at the same coffee shop with a wireless network in his backpack has named his wireless network with a service set identifier (SSID) of "national chain." Your phone, or worse, your computer, automatically connects to "known" networks unless you check the box as shown in Fig. 29.1 (MacBook). What are the standards by which it determines "known?"

_____**5.** Physical security: If you could change one thing to improve security, what would it be?

_____**6.** What the security team and administration will never do, what you should never do:

_____**a.** If Security needs to access your system owing to a suspected breach, they will change the password and then instruct you to change it when they have finished. They will not ask you for your password over the phone, not ever. No one will.

_____**b.** Request unencrypted sensitive data. You should neither request sensitive data nor send it unencrypted. This is the biggest challenge and requires a massive mindset and culture shift.

_____**7.** Close your training with methods of contact and who should be contacted if the trainee experiences any of the following:

_____**a.** Phishing emails

_____**b.** Possible breach

_____**c.** Physical security

_____**d.** News alerts

FIGURE 29.2 Clean out your known networks periodically. Anyone with these service set identifier names may be able to trick you into joining them with no password.

Preferred Networks:	
Network Name	Security
Black Tern	WPA/WPA2 Personal
Karl Knauz Guest	None
Google Starbucks	None
dd-wrt	None
Salamander	WPA2 Personal
SpottedSalamander	WPA2 Personal

+ −   Drag networks into the order you prefer.

A computer "knows" a network by two things: The network SSID (its name), and the password. If the network has no password and you have joined it, the biggest danger by far to you is that your computer will join the network with no prompting. The rogue network can then act as a proxy, fooling you into accessing popular banking sites, accepting bad certificates, entering your passwords, etc. Whenever your computer connects automatically to a network and there is no password, exercise extreme caution, especially in heavily populated areas where the attacker can operate at low risk and with high dividends. Hackers like to buy and sell large lists. Bigger is better. Note in the network list in Fig. 29.2, taken from an actual computer, the number of insecure connections that exist.

8. PHYSICAL ACCESS

Through one of these routes, a skilled operative has gained physical access to what are supposed to be secure facilities. What can he access? Here is a quick punch list of the resources that a skilled intruder will attempt to exploit.

You must presume that once he has gained access, he will first seek to:

1. Create a more sustainable breach by:
   a. Locating where your badges are stored
   b. Hacking into your badging system
   c. Gaining an impression of a key
   d. Getting copies of stolen keys made. Stamping "Do Not Duplicate" carries no legal protection or enforcement. If a locksmith duplicates the key and stamps his mark on one side, such a stamp is merely a guarantee that he *might* stamp "Do Not Duplicate" on the other side without asking your permission.
   e. Sitting in your lunch room every day, eating.
   f. Walking the hallways, seeking to gain familiarity with the physical layout and getting people used to seeing him.
   g. Knowing who is on vacation and who is unresponsive to emails, and where the most likely place is that he can sit without getting caught.

h. Being able to bypass your camera systems. He will seek a hidden stairwell access, service corridor, or other access door that can provide backdoor access. He may even put an elevator into service mode and set up shop.

Once he has infiltrated sustainably, or if a one time visit is his goal, he will seek to exploit as much as possible while on premise. He will:

1. Photograph any papers or manuals he finds out in the open or in unlocked desk drawers
2. Photograph any whiteboard with writing on it
3. Plant listening devices and possibly join all conference room phones to a conference line of his choice that is muted and set to record
4. Attack via any chink in your armor, *anything* electronic that you have around:
   a. Charging stations
   b. Security controls (for example, a sign-in "sheet" run by an iPad, on the network, that is always on)
   c. Externally networked cameras
   d. Lighting controls that you might not even know are controlled via a vulnerable wireless device
   e. If it has a light-emitting-diode in it or is powered by electricity, it might be on your network and it might be vulnerable. If it is, the attacker will find it.

It is no coincidence that network penetration testers who work for companies such as Mandiant and NCC also conduct physical penetration tests for companies. The adroit computer security professional cannot only exploit via remote code execution or phishing attack, he or she is also skilled at gaining physical access through key impressioning, bumping (where legal: check your jurisdiction. In some places, the mere possession of a bump key is considered evidence of a crime), lock picking, safe-cracking, sweet-talking her way in, tailgating, eavesdropping, and physical network exploitation.

9. SUMMARY

Security is not foolproof, and there are fools everywhere. This is less about findings and conclusions and more about "and the moral of the story is ..." Teaching security to nonparanoid, trusting, nonsecurity conscientious people is *hard*. Nobody wants to believe that this level of deception exists in the world, and this is precisely why it is so successful.

Reports on the Internet vary, and many lack citable sources, but a failure rate of 20% to 90% of certain types of engineered attacks (such as the dropped USB attack) is reasonable. Humans are *curious* and *helpful*. It is a deadly combination.

The goal of this chapter, then, was not to show you how to raise your security to 100%. It was to show you that the biggest weakness has been, and always will be, people. The solution is not to train the people to be better. It is to design a system that they cannot bypass and one that you can observe and watch.

Training people so that they do not allow tailgating without a badge swipe may reduce tailgate access by some unknown, probably small, percentage. Installing an archway that sounds an alarm if they fail to do so, and takes a flash photo of them, causing a security response, is far more effective. *Prevention eventually fails*[3] but people always fail. If we rely on the general population of employees to provide a defense, it will fail. Highly visible security cameras will definitely create an ambience of security and will deter some intruders. This is prevention only. More effective is someone actually watching the cameras, creating incidents, and responding to them.

The moral of the story here is that to prevent a socially engineered attack, someone has to be paying attention, watching for it, and conducting an incident response. It is a real conundrum, but by reducing the number of people in the equation, you can decrease the quantity of potential failures. Understanding prevention, then, will lead to an end game of enhanced ability to insert monitoring points at the right locations in an environment.

Finally, let us move on to the real interactive part of this chapter: review questions/exercises, hands-on projects, case projects, and the optional team case project. The answers and/or solutions by chapter can be found in Appendix K.

CHAPTER REVIEW QUESTIONS/ EXERCISES

True/False

1. True or False? Mob rule is a unique engineering feat and typically will require one or more "shills" who are in on it.

---
3. R. Bejtlich. The Tao of Network Security Monitoring: Beyond Intrusion Detection (Kindle Location 343), Pearson Education, Kindle Edition.

2. True or False? From complex to simple, reciprocation and obligation (vulnerabilities) depend on the basic goodness inherent in human nature.
3. True or False? Small concessions on the part of the SE lead to larger concessions on the part of the victim.
4. True or False? Layer 3 is physical interaction, and covers how to conduct oneself with physical security in mind.
5. True or False? Email from friends, business associates, colleagues, and family members are all exploitable avenues of ingress.

Multiple Choice

1. Spear-phishing and whale-phishing are more:
   A. Switched
   B. Penetrated
   C. Promotional
   D. Power-shelled
   E. Targeted
2. In what type of phishing is the targeted employee the one with access to bank account passwords and tokens and/or classified information, such as contact lists and sales projections?
   A. Whale-phishing
   B. Spear-phishing
   C. Valid-phishing
   D. Application-phishing
   E. Bait-phishing
3. One way to "fingerprint" emails at a cursory level is to enforce the uniqueness of:
   A. Signatures
   B. Fabrics
   C. Client side codes
   D. LinkedIn.com
   E. Security
4. A computer "knows" a network by two things: the network SSID (its name) and the:
   A. Call data
   B. Strategy
   C. Password
   D. Protocol
   E. Tap
5. It is no coincidence that network penetration testers also conduct physical penetration tests for:
   A. UNIX-like systems
   B. VPNs
   C. IP storage
   D. Companies
   E. Servers

EXERCISE

Problem

What type of individuals are SEs?

Hands-on Projects

Project

What are your thoughts on heuristic thinking?

Case Projects

Problem

What are the physiological triggers of social engineering?

Optional Team Case Project

Problem

What are the social engineering attack vectors and how are they used?

Chapter 30

Ethical Hacking

Scott R. Ellis

kCura Corporation, Chicago, IL, United States

1. INTRODUCTION

Ethical hacking is the discipline of leveraging and combining together known vulnerabilities and may involve an element of social engineering (talking or phishing your way to access) in the most responsible way possible. A typical ethical hacking engagement is called a "Network penetration (pen) test" and will usually involve a physical element as well. A good hacker, then, can also attack doors, open them, and gain access without doing any damage to the door, whether by means of lock picking, shimming, or subverting the computerized badging system.

In this chapter, which is written in an immersive style, you will be encouraged to create an interactive environment and step through some beginner scanning, testing, and hacking scenarios of your own system. This will provide you with an in-depth knowledge of both system setup, maintenance, and intrusion patterns. For example, you will learn that a popular utility called "metasploit" regularly contacts the Internet for updates. Snort, an intrusion detection system (IDS) tool, throws an alert when it sees this behavior. This sort of behavior, and many more like it, are just some of the things you will learn as you both maintain and hack around in systems you own.

We will begin by setting up Kali on your own workstation or as a VM. We will then discuss five attack vectors, how to execute them, how they work, and how they can be detected and defeated. This chapter will not focus on perimeter, but rather it will focus on sensor arrays and instrumentation of systems—instrumentation that bypasses the typical layers that hackers operate on, and focuses on the underlying physical layer: a hacker can't change and alter what he doesn't know you have, and what he thinks he is doing in silence. Meanwhile, your layer 1 physical taps are storing all network traffic and analyzing it in the

background. Chapter 5 provides an in-depth overview on getting started with network security monitoring. This chapter will refer to it often, but assumes you have read through that chapter, and/or are able to construct your own network security monitoring solution.

Many courses offered on ethical hacking provide information and sections on attack motives. It is often mistakenly believed that by knowing the mind of your enemy you can then defeat him. This may bear some semblance of truth when the actual enemy is known; then, things like reconnaissance and covert operations can yield useful information. In the world of espionage and counterespionage, where we are generally aware of which nation-states we least wish to have our secrets, this might make a grain of sense. In the sphere of system intrusions, you don't know who the attacker is. You cannot know his motive—if you even know she was there, maybe then you can piece something together if you can determine what they took. If it's high enough profile, maybe they will tell you what their motive is. Very likely, it may appear to be extortion. But even in cases of extortion, this may just be a side benefit: the hacker has probably already extracted all the immediately available value from the engagement. Now, he is just putting the icing on his cake by demanding money from you. For all you know, a competitor hired the hacker to simply throw a wrench into your works. You don't know. Even if the hacker gets caught and sent to prison, you still might not get to know.

The correct approach, then, is to study all possible attack vectors, to not assume what the attacker will or won't do, and to not attribute any motives to him or her. Can he get in? Yes: fix the vulnerability. The endless discussions that revolve around questions such as "is it easy? How many people can do it? What motive would someone have to have that would instigate an attack like this?" are not

Computer and Information Security Handbook. http://dx.doi.org/10.1016/B978-0-12-803843-7.00030-2

productive. If you can execute the attack and show that the vulnerability is real, then it should be fixed.

2. HACKER'S TOOLBOX

Countless times, I've been in my workshop, crafting one thing or another, when I've found myself saying, "If only I had a tool that could do X…" For example, I needed to drill a very deep, very narrow hole into a major structural component of a five-octave marimba I was building at the time. Fortunately, I knew what tool to go buy (an auger bit). This section will attempt to transfer enough knowledge to you so that you will have that capability: think of a tool that should exist, find it, download it, and use it. Chances are great, as you are starting out, that someone has already written the tool you seek.

Kali

Kali is your attack platform. You may have a Mac or a Windows box, but you should not use these for anything attack related—they are best suited to host your Kali instance in a virtual machine (VM).

The official Kali download is available at www.kali.org. Kali is maintained and funded by Offensive Security, and is quite simple to setup and run. Ideally, run it on a VM with dedicated CPU, memory, network connection, and disk. Kali is based on a rolling release of Debian. What this means is that the OS is upgraded whenever a new patch is out. This is similar to the DevOps notion of continuous deployment. To install, I chose the most recent version of Debian x64 listed in the OS choices screen in VMWare, and then chose "graphical install" from the install menu. For more complete installation instructions, visit the Kali site at: http://docs.kali.org/installation/kali-linux-hard-disk-install.

Later, we will use Kali to manage an attack against a Windows PC. Before that, we will examine various attack vectors.

Metasploit

Metasploit is a software program that provides full exploit to p@wn lifecycle management. It is a framework, which means that you will need to develop a level of understanding of how to use the tool. Metasploit allows you to develop and deploy exploits against target systems (see checklist, "An Agenda for Developing and Deploying Exploits Against Target Systems").

Nmap

Nmap is a community managed tool that allows users to script and deploy very deep and intensive network scans.

An Agenda for Developing and Deploying Exploits Against Target Systems

Using Metasploit, you can do the following (check all tasks completed):

_____**1.** Choose the exploit you wish to use.

_____**2.** Scan to see if the target system is vulnerable to that exploit (optional).

_____**3.** Choose the payload to deploy once the exploit has succeeded.

_____**4.** Choose an encoding that will prevent IDS or IPS from detecting what you are doing. If you can execute your exploit without throwing a Snort alert, you will bypass most detection systems. Ideally, load every rule set you can get your hands on into Snort. See "Chapter 5: Detecting System Intrusions" for more information on what someone might be doing to monitor their network for intrusions (possibly the best advice you will get in this chapter!).

_____**5.** Execute: Inject your payload through the vulnerability and p@wn the system.

It is the tool of choice for network administrators, pen testers, and hackers (black and white hat). Its primary purpose in life is network examination and enumeration. Network administrators may use it to explore a machine they have discovered on their network that is doing strange things, and by hackers that want to locate vulnerable machines that they can attack. It is included in many Linux and Unix operating systems (OSs), and is a top download at the Freshmeat.Net repository.[1] The wide user base is important as it practically ensures that development of the product will continue and that bugs will be found and repaired. One note about Nmap that is worth mentioning: It is kind of chatty with the user. It does offer normal output, XML output, and grepable output (deprecated). Yes, "grepable" actually is a word! You will want to learn to pipe grep and cut commands to tailor the output to your needs [see Sidebar: "List of All IP Addresses in a classless inter-domain routing (CIDR)"].

Here are some sample Nmap commands: They are command line interface (CLI) issued instructions, so each one is proceeded with a ">" as a CLI prompt. A full listing of commands can be found at: http://nmap.org/nsedoc/. Bear in mind: Nmap must be used responsibly. Some of its commands (From the manual (man) for Nmap page: > man nmap) can flood systems or cause systems to crash.

---

1. https://nmap.org/.

List of All IP Addresses in a CIDR

For example, listing out ALL IP addresses in a CIDR range such as:

> nmap -sL -n 192.0.17.0/30

This will cause Nmap to spool out a list of every IP address in that subnet, active on your network or not, in the form of:

Nmap scan report for 192.0.17.0

Nmap scan report for 192.0.17.1

... etc.

For piping into a file, you would want:

> nmap -sL -n 192.0.2.1/32 192.0.1.0/30 | grep 'Nmap scan report for' | cut -f 5 -d ' ' > IPAddys.txt

Use >> IPAddys.txt to append to the file.

From the Nmap site, we also have this interesting output format:

-oS <*filespec*> (ScRipT KIdd|3 oUTpuT)

"Script kiddie output is like interactive output, except that it is post-processed to better suit the l33t HaXXorZ who previously looked down on Nmap due to its consistent capitalization and spelling. Humor impaired people should note that this option is making fun of the script kiddies before flaming me for supposedly 'helping them'."

Nmap ("Network Mapper") is an open source tool for network exploration and security auditing. It was designed to rapidly scan large networks, although it works fine against single hosts. Nmap uses raw IP packets in novel ways to determine what hosts are available on the network, what services (application name and version) those hosts are offering, what OSs (and OS versions) they are running, what type of packet filters/firewalls are in use, and dozens of other characteristics. While Nmap is commonly used for security audits, many systems and network administrators find it useful for routine tasks such as network inventory, managing service upgrade schedules, and monitoring host or service uptime.

Originally written by Gordon Lyon, it easily answers the following question: What IP addresses can you find on the local network? Because of the tendency of Nmap to make some noise on a network, system administrators may not take kindly to you running these scripts. Either request permission, or only run them in an air-gapped, lab environment.

For example, the -P0 (that's a zero) flag causes Nmap to skip the process that discovers hosts by pinging it and goes straight into scanning ports. You can also customize the ports to scan. If you are on a Windows network, for example, you may scan for port 445. Most Windows machines will respond to this unless administrators have specifically locked it down. Even better, try port 135, which is the Server Message Block (SMB) and is used by pretty much everyone: > sudo nmap -sP -PS445,135 ipAddress/

CIDR. You'd of course replace ipAddress/CIDR with real numbers.

> **NOTE:** Nmap will conduct ARP/Neighbor Discovery (-PR) against targets on a local network even when other -P* options are specified. This scan is almost always usually faster, and more effective.

Once you have a list of IP addresses that you know are live, you can begin to deepen your understanding with things like OS fingerprinting and full port scans. Armed with the knowledge provided by these tools, you can search for unauthorized servers running illicit network services on a network, and remove any that pose a threat.

Burp

Developed by portswigger, Burp acts as an IDS. That is, you can use it to falsify and format the form submission inputs to the server however you like. With it, you can bypass any JavaScript form field scrubbing that may occur. This is precisely why Javascript input validation is useless, from the security perspective. Typically, the only input a server will need is the form inputs in the proper submit format. Burp provides this. Additionally, Burp, as a suite, includes the aforementioned proxy along with a spider, a scanner, and intruder, sequencer, and a repeater.

Spider

The Burp spider passively crawls all site content. It identifies forms, broken links, cookies, and creates a detailed sitemap of what it finds.

Scanner

Burp's vulnerability scanner scans an application for known vulnerabilities. The open web application security project (OWASP) seeks to document and provide information about vulnerabilities and types of attacks. Ostensibly, the Burp suite's vulnerability scanner can automate the detection of vulnerabilities such as those described by the OWASP Top 10 at: https://www.owasp.org/index.php/Top_10_2013-Top_10.

Powershell

I list this tool last because the other tools, up to now, have been focused on getting you to where you have powershell access on the machine. A tutorial located at: http://www.irongeek.com/i.php?page=videos/hack3rcon5/h01-intro-to-powershell-scripting-for-security[2] will provide you with a very thorough introduction to this tool. Now is when you bookmark this page, and go watch this video.

Powershell will allow you to pull down and create the tools you need to penetrate more deeply, enumerate the network, and spread your reach and control. It allows you to interact directly with the system at a level that would typically require additional downloads to the system of executables and scripts: Items that may be detected by virus scanning systems. Powershell provides:

- Access into Windows APIs.
- It's object oriented.
- Redefined how Microsoft does development.
- Allows you to bypass security frameworks, mostly excluded.

If you can get Powershell access on a PC, you have a powerful tool at your disposal. What other advantages does Powershell provide (think: commandlets)?

3. ATTACK VECTORS

Attack vectors are like windows and doors to your house. A criminal (or possibly even raccoons) can access your house any number of ways, and it makes sense to understand the tools of the common burglar as well as you understand tools for network intrusion—there are similarities, and the two trades have significant overlap. A criminal that can both access the most secure parts of a high-rise office and hack into their most secure systems is, indeed, a very real creature and a persistent threat. However, it makes even more sense to think of your attackers like raccoons trying to get into your house. Any opening big enough, and they are in your attack. It's only a matter of time, then, before they gain access to the house at large.

Public Information

Enumerate the enemy. Have you ever Googled yourself? Social engineering is a key part of any penetration test because it is a key tactic used by hackers. Corporate entities store vast amounts of information online. Marketing companies such as Rain King go to great lengths to enumerate their victims based on your Internet browsing activity and other investigative tactics. The information gathered by advertiser tracking cookies can reveal sensitive information about corporate

strategy. It's not a stretch of the imagination to deduce that, by knowing your browsing history and your job title, your interests may reveal the following:

- Mergers
- IPOs
- Acquisitions
- New technology initiatives
- Software in use

LinkedIn.com lists positions held by employees; and, your list of friends on Facebook may not be as private as you think. Advanced techniques include purchasing ads on the Internet—once I can get ads onto millions of websites, and can get data back on who is clicking what ads, I can begin to work out, for example, what companies will be working on certain high-profile projects. Using a manufactured identity, I received a rip-sheet from Rain-King that detailed what some would consider to be sensitive information—all gleaned from what Rain King had managed to glean from its hordes of data. The nonvirtual equivalent would be if the garbage company were to root through all of your trash, making note of what products you used, and selling that information to the highest bidders. Next thing you know, 10—20 salesmen are knocking on your door, and all of them know that you are building a prototype electric car in your garage.

While there are other search engines, the most information is available about Google, and books have been written about leveraging it to cull for information. For example, try searching for:

[default password site:s2sys.com type:pdf]

This string searches every PDF on the website s2sys.com for the terms "default password." S2 manufactures a popular line of door control systems. For accessing a corporation's private space with no questions asked, you most certainly want the door to unlock for you when you approach it with a fake badge. At the time of this writing, S2 publishes an installation manual that lists the default admin account and password. I reiterate: the overlap between physical burglar and black-hat hacker is not imagined. Every movie or TV show that illustrates a hacker easily commandeering cameras and remotely opening physical doors is very real. The "Star Wars" movies are about nothing if they aren't about negligent security practices by the Empire, how to exploit them, and how fear does very little to prevent hackers (the Rebel Alliance) from penetrating its weak defenses. In one scene, a little robot rolls up to a port on a wall, plugs in, and in short order can access just about any system (note that it does not set a delayed "self-destruct" which surely would have ended the movie too early). In other scenes, shooting a door security panel with a blaster causes the door to open.

---

2. Brandon Morris, Hack3rcon 5.

In other words, Google can be used to find things that, really, we aren't supposed to be able to find. Google hacking is the first skill that most hackers should practice.

Public Website

For many corporations, the lines between public Internet website and internal network are blurry or just nonexistent. Hacking into a website that faces the public may be the quickest avenue of ingress. On a corporate network, network administrators often place servers and workstations in one of three configurations:

1. A demilitarized zone (DMZ)
2. Network Address Translation
3. A hybrid of both

Very seldom will you ever see a physical server residing on the Internet with a public IP address.

Note that once a hacker gains access to a website through some vulnerability, his work is not yet completed. Often, a DMZ network is 100% isolated from the corporate network; to traverse to the DMZ, employees use a VPN. If the hacker was targeting the corporate network, he missed by a mile. Bear in mind, though, that missing by a mile is not that far off the mark when the target is so large the hacker can use a tool such as mimikatz to scrape passwords from memory, which will likely yield a duplication of passwords on the corporate network.

Historically, a typical attack against a website would involve a full round of reconnaissance scans. These take time, though. Many attacks now simply attempt the exploit, with no provocation. Hackers take aim and fire, and it may be for as simple a reason as you have a cool Twitter handle, and they want it.

Password Attack

It is not uncommon, even, to find a list of passwords stored right on the desktop of a server. As a third tier support technician, I'd sometimes spend hours on the phone, elbows deep in some of the world's largest data centers. A password bank was never too far out of reach for many system admins, and duplication of passwords between administrator accounts in a DMZ and a back office system is not uncommon.

> **TIP**: Password security is the Achilles heel of all computing systems.

Port Scanning

Hacking a public website often revolves first around deep port scans. What ports are open? Sometimes an open remote desktop protocol (RDP) port will have administrator access and a simple password, such as "Password" or "test123"—passwords that were often created during initial setup with the good intention of changing it later.

Structured Query Language (SQL) Injection

Structured Query Language (SQL) databases are at the core of a great many systems. Any application that wishes to communicate with a database must do so through what is called a "connection string."

Information entered into a website, for example, gets processed by a program that runs on the web server, probably as some sort of application pool. When the application receives the correct instruction, such as a form submission on a website, it takes the post of data, puts it into a container, makes a connection to the database, and queries the database appropriately.

The idea behind SQL injection is to either cause data to return to your screen, or to elevate privileges to the point that you can turn on the xp_cmdshell option on a Microsoft SQL Server, and then use this extended stored procedure to execute shell commands against the OS. For example, the shell can be used to issue a series of commands designed to download (via FTP) the executable of your choice, and then run it.

To enable xp_cmdshell (if it isn't enabled already), you must get the following SQL statement to run. It is an advanced option, so first you need to enable advanced options to run on the server:

```
EXEC sp_configure 'show advanced options', 1;
RECONFIGURE;
```

Now you can enable the vulnerability:

```
EXEC sp_configure 'xp_cmdshell', 1;
RECONFIGURE;
```

Detect Impersonation

In MS SQL, a user privilege called "impersonation" allows us to pivot to a successful SQL injection attack. Not all users in SQL have the capability reconfigure advanced options.

Often, to make code more modular and to enable software to do database things, developers will use the EXECUTE AS functionality of SQL and then use impersonation to access those commands on demand. For example, activities such as creating new databases, accessing system-related database information, and creating new logins may be activities that are nice to automate in the application.

You may find that no accounts offer this holy grail of access. The SQL account being used to run the application you are hacking, however, may have permission to grant itself impersonation. If you can inject the following SQL and get a response back, it will tell you the best candidate for SQL impersonation:

```
USE Master;
SELECT distinct b.name
FROM sys.server_permissions serper
INNER JOIN sys.server_principals serpri
ON serper.grantor_principal_id = serpri.principal_id
WHERE serper.permission_name = 'IMPERSONATE';
```

The preceding will query the system tables for permissions. SQL injection can be a powerful tool and through it you can escalate, achieve command line access, and take over a server. In the absence of being able to escalate privileges, simply being able to execute SQL and echo query results back to the command line can lead to serious exposure for a company. Such a finding is typically, always, a critical finding that companies take very seriously.

Grant Impersonation

All SQL servers ship installed with an account called "sa". This account may be disabled. If it is, then you simply need to iterate through all the accounts that exist. SQL has WHILE and IF logic structures that work much like any other language. For example:

```
GRANT IMPERSONATE ON LOGIN::sa to
[targetAccount];
```

"TargetAccount" is the account under which your current context runs. All software that wishes to interact with a database must have at least one user, known to the software that can access SQL and run queries.

Known Vulnerabilities

Most of ethical hacking is not about discovering new vulnerabilities. Using your Kali distribution, use Nmap to scan your network for known vulnerabilities. Metasploit has provided a very nice, exploitable disk image called (conveniently) "metasploitable" and it can be downloaded. For example:

https://sourceforge.net/projects/metasploitable/files/Metasploitable2/.

4. PHYSICAL PENETRATIONS

Part of any hackers toolset will be a pickset. Hackers have a very special and unique job attribute: The act of industrial espionage may mean, sometimes, that the only way to access a system covertly is to gain physical access to the systems. There are many methods of gaining access to a physical system. In other words, just because I think I can hook a door latch because there is a gap under the door, is that enough to report the vulnerability?

Philosophically, the pen tester has a unique philosophy, one which, if held by most people, would result in visits to a psychiatrist and a subsequent regime of daily medication. We know, and believe, and act, with all our heart and soul, as though an attacker is on the inside. We work and act under a philosophy of extreme paranoia. However, lest this philosophy drive us to the edge of reason, we also embrace an attitude of "What will be will be." We can tell people about the vulnerability. They can tell us we are crying wolf, but that is one thing we never do. We never "cry wolf." We tell it like it is, and examine the facts before making and sharing conclusive decisions.

Mindset of a Pen Tester

Consider a building. The building has many floors, and a dark, fully enclosed, windowless service vertical at its center. Inside this massive vertical, each floor has building equipment (HVAC stuff) in an enclosed room, which is locked from the inside, it is locked to egress. You find, every now and then, this door (door number one) is cracked open. Wondering at why this door would ever be left open, you enter it to investigate. You pass into an HVAC power and cooling equipment room. You note that this door is not locked to ingress.

At the back of this room is another door (door number two), and on the door are printed large red letters "NOT AN EXIT." You exit door number two anyway and find yourself on a platform fabricated from a metal grate. You check the door, and see that it has no lock, and the handle turns freely. You will be able to re-enter. Nonetheless, you leave the door propped open. It's kind of scary in here. You turn on a powerful flashlight and see that you have entered into some sort of large, vertical ventilation shaft. You note, as you look upward and downward, that each floor above and below you seems to also have "Not an Exit" access onto their own respective "balconies" into this shaft.

Looking up, you can see a skylight in the distance. Looking down, beyond the reach of your light, you see more balconies, and then nothing but darkness. If you had a rope ladder, you could easily climb down to the next balcony. Beside you, you see a column, rising upward and descending downward into the darkness. Behind you, the door leading into the office space (door number two) is unsecured. The door leading into the column, door number three, is secured.

What is behind door number three? Maybe you can't find out, and knowing what is behind door number two is completely irrelevant. It could be a staircase. Alternatively, someone could rappel down from above, in complete secrecy, and walk into the space through door number one. Door number two, unsecured, doesn't have a lock in it. Arguments can and will go back and forth in a situation about how to secure the upper floors, how to pry open door number two and find out what is behind it, etc. The simplest solution is to put a lock on door number one. A lot of energy and time can and will be wasted if you get into philosophical arguments. At the end of the day, the solution is simple: put a lock on the door.

5. SUMMARY

Ethical hacking is a continuous, repeating process. In terms of a physical analogy, software is like a house that is always being added on to. Doors get changed on a regular basis. New doors are added between rooms. New doors are added that lead to the outside world, at ground level, where they have added new rooms. The goal of the ethical hacker is to call out problems with old and new construction, and to find interesting new ways to access systems that have previously been overlooked.

Finally, let's move on to the real interactive part of this Chapter: review questions/exercises, hands-on projects, case projects, and optional team case project. The answers and/or solutions by chapter can be found in Appendix K.

CHAPTER REVIEW QUESTIONS/ EXERCISES

True/False

1. True or False? Ethical hacking is the discipline of leveraging and combining together known vulnerabilities and may involve an element of social engineering (talking or phishing your way to access) in the most responsible way possible.
2. True or False? Nmap is a community managed tool that allows users to script and deploy very deep and intensive network scans.
3. True or False? Developed by portswigger, Burp acts as an intrusion detection system.
4. True or False? The Burp spider passively crawls all site content.
5. True or False? Burp's vulnerability scanner scans an application for unknown vulnerabilities.

Multiple Choice

1. What tool will allow you to pull down and create the tools you need to penctrate more deeply, enumerate the network, and spread your reach and control?
   A. SAN switch
   B. Penetration
   C. Promotional email
   D. Powershell
   E. Data controller
2. What is a key part of any penetration test because it is a key tactic used by hackers?
   A. Social engineering
   B. Location technology
   C. Valid
   D. Application
   E. Bait

3. What lists positions held by employees, where your list of friends on Facebook may not be as private as you think?
   A. Data minimization
   B. Fabric
   C. Client side code
   D. LinkedIn.com
   E. Security
4. Hacking into a website that faces the public may be the quickest avenue of:
   A. Call data floods
   B. Greedy strategies
   C. Ingress
   D. SAN protocols
   E. Taps
5. Often, a DMZ network is 100% isolated from the corporate network; to traverse to the DMZ, employees use a:
   A. UNIX-like system
   B. VPN
   C. IP storage access
   D. Configuration file
   E. Server policy

EXERCISE

Problem

Does it matter if an ethical hacker writes a script kiddy that runs a tool if the target system gets compromised anyway?

Hands-On Projects

Project

What types of Ethical Hacking techniques and technology can an organization employ?

Case Projects

Problem

Some ethical hackers argue that disclosure of information that governments or corporations try to keep secret will ultimately provide more good than harm by making those governments and corporations truly accountable and allowing citizens or shareholders to demand change when needed. Do you agree?

Optional Team Case Project

Problem

Do all of us have an absolute right to access all the information available on the Internet?

Chapter 31

What Is Vulnerability Assessment?

Almantas Kakareka

Demyo, Inc., Sunny Isles Beach, FL, United States

1. INTRODUCTION

In computer security, the term *vulnerability* is applied to a weakness in a system that allows an attacker to violate the integrity of that system. Vulnerabilities may result from weak passwords, software bugs, a computer virus or other malicious software (malware), a script code injection, or unchecked user input, just to name a few.

A security risk is classified as vulnerability if it is recognized as a possible means of attack. A security risk with one or more known instances of a working or fully implemented attack is classified as an *exploit*. Constructs in programming languages that are difficult to use properly can be large sources of vulnerabilities.

Vulnerabilities always existed, but when the Internet was in its early stage they were not used and exploited as often. The media did not report news of hackers who were getting put in jail for hacking into servers and stealing vital information.

Vulnerability assessment may be performed on many objects, not only computer systems/networks. For example, a physical building can be assessed so that it will be clear what parts of the building have kinds of flaws. If the attacker can bypass the security guard at the front door and get into the building via a back door, it is definitely vulnerability. Actually, going through the back door and using that vulnerability is called an *exploit*. The physical security is one of the most important aspects to be taken into account. If the attackers have physical access to the server, the server is no longer yours! Just stating, "Your system or network is vulnerable" does not provide useful information. Vulnerability assessment without a comprehensive report is pretty much useless. A vulnerability assessment report should include:

- identification of vulnerabilities
- a risk rating of each vulnerability (critical, high, medium, or low)
- quantity of vulnerabilities

FIGURE 31.1 One critical vulnerability affects the entire network.

It is enough to find one critical vulnerability, which means the whole network is at risk, as shown in Fig. 31.1.

Vulnerabilities should be sorted by severity and then by servers or services. Critical vulnerabilities should be at the top of the report and should be listed in descending order: that is, critical, then high, medium, and low.

2. REPORTING

Reporting capability is of growing importance to administrators in a documentation-oriented business climate where you must not only be able to do your job, you must also provide written proof of how you have done it. In fact, respondents to Sunbelt's survey[1] indicated that flexible and prioritizing reporting was their number one favorite feature.

A scan might return hundreds or thousands of results, but the data are useless unless they are organized in a way that can be understood. That means that ideally you will be able to sort and cross-reference the data, export them to other programs and formats (such as Comma Separated Values, HyperText Markup Language, Extensible Markup Language, Multiple-Hypothesis Tracking, MDB, Excel,

---

1. Vulnerability Assessment Scanning: Why Sunbelt Network Security Inspector (SNSI)? Sunbelt Software, [http://img2.insight.com/graphics/uk/content/microsite/sunbelt/sunbelt_network_security_inspector_whitepaper.pdf], February 2004.

Word, and/or various databases), view it in different ways, and easily compare it with the results of earlier scans.

Comprehensive, flexible, and customizable reporting is used within your department to provide a guideline of technical steps you need to take, but that is not all. Good reports also give you the ammunition you need to justify to management the costs of implementing security measures.

3. THE "IT WILL NOT HAPPEN TO US" FACTOR

Practical matters aside, chief executive officers, chief information officers, and administrators are all human beings and thus subject to normal human tendencies, including the tendency to assume that bad things happen to "other people," not us. Organizational decision makers assume that their companies are not likely targets for hackers ("Why would an attacker want to break into the network of Widgets, Inc., when they could go after the Department of Defense or Microsoft or someone else who is much more interesting?").

4. WHY VULNERABILITY ASSESSMENT?

Organizations have a tremendous opportunity to use information technology (IT) to increase productivity. Securing information and communications systems will be a necessary factor in taking advantage of all of this increased connectivity, speed, and information. However, no security measure will guarantee a risk-free environment in which to operate. In fact, many organizations need to provide easier user access to portions of their information systems, thereby increasing potential exposure. Administrative error, for example, is a primary cause of vulnerabilities that can be exploited by a novice hacker, whether an outsider or insider in the organization. Routine use of vulnerability assessment tools along with immediate response to identified problems will alleviate this risk. It follows, therefore, that routine vulnerability assessment should be a standard element of every organization's security policy. Vulnerability assessment is used to find unknown problems in the systems. The main purpose of vulnerability assessment is to find out what systems have flaws and take action to mitigate the risk. Some industry standards such as Payment Card Industry Data Security Standard (PCI DSS) require organizations to perform vulnerability assessments on their networks. The sidebar "PCI DSS Compliance" gives a brief look.

Payment Card Industry Data Security Standard Compliance

PCI DSS was developed by leading credit card companies to help merchants be secure and follow common security criteria to protect sensitive customers' credit card data. Before that, every credit card company had a similar standard to protect customer data on the merchant side. Any company that does transactions via credit cards needs to be PCI compliant. One of the requirements to be PCI compliant is to test security systems and processes regularly. This can be achieved via vulnerability assessment. Small companies that do not process a lot of transactions are allowed to do self-assessment via questionnaire. Big companies that process a lot of transactions are required to be audited by third parties.[2]

5. PENETRATION TESTING VERSUS VULNERABILITY ASSESSMENT

There seems to be a certain amount of confusion within the security industry about the difference between penetration testing and vulnerability assessment. They are often classified as the same thing, but in fact they are not. Penetration testing sounds a lot more exciting, but most people actually want a vulnerability assessment and not a penetration test, so many projects are labeled as penetration tests when in fact they are 100% vulnerability assessments.

A penetration test mainly consists of a vulnerability assessment, but it goes one step further. A penetration test is a method for evaluating the security of a computer system or network by simulating an attack by a malicious hacker. The process involves an active analysis of the system for any weaknesses, technical flaws, or vulnerabilities. This analysis is carried out from the position of a potential attacker and will involve active exploitation of security vulnerabilities. Any security issues that are found will be presented to the system owner, together with an assessment of their impact and often with a proposal for mitigation or a technical solution.

A vulnerability assessment is what most companies generally do, because the systems they are testing are live production systems and cannot afford to be disrupted by active exploits that might crash the system. Vulnerability assessment is the process of identifying and quantifying vulnerabilities in a system. The system being studied could be a physical facility such as a nuclear power plant, a computer system, or a larger system (for example, the communications infrastructure or water infrastructure of a region). Vulnerability assessment has many things in common with risk assessment. Assessments are typically performed according to the following steps:

1. cataloging assets and capabilities (resources) in a system
2. assigning quantifiable value and importance to resources

---

2. PCI Security Standards Council, Copyright© 2006−2013 PCI Security Standards Council, LLC. All rights reserved. [www.pcisecuritystandards.org], 2013.

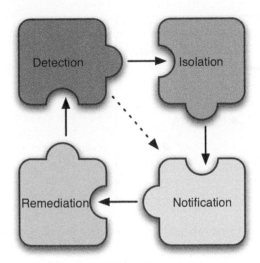

FIGURE 31.2 Vulnerability mitigation cycle.

3. identifying the vulnerabilities or potential threats to each resource
4. mitigating or eliminating the most serious vulnerabilities for the most valuable resources

This is generally what a security company is contracted to do, from a technical perspective: not actually to penetrate the systems but to assess and document the possible vulnerabilities and recommend mitigation measures and improvements. Vulnerability detection, mitigation, notification, and remediation are linked, as shown in Fig. 31.2.[3]

6. VULNERABILITY ASSESSMENT GOAL

The theoretical goal of network scanning is elevated security on all systems or establishing a network-wide minimal operation standard (Fig. 31.3 shows how usefulness is related to ubiquity):

● host-based intrusion prevention system
● network-based intrusion detection system
● antivirus
● network-based intrusion prevention system

7. MAPPING THE NETWORK

Before we start scanning the network we have to find out what machines are alive on it. Most scanners have a built-in network mapping tool, usually the Nmap network mapping tool running behind the scenes. The Nmap Security Scanner is a free and open-source utility used by millions of people for network discovery, administration, inventory, and security auditing. Nmap uses raw Internet Protocol (IP) packets in novel ways to determine what hosts are available

on a network, what services (application name and version) those hosts are offering, what operating systems they are running, what type of packet filters or firewalls are in use, and more. Nmap was named "Information Security Product of the Year" by *Linux Journal* and *Info World*. It was also used by hackers in the movies *Matrix Reloaded*, *Die Hard 4*, and *Bourne Ultimatum*. Nmap runs on all major computer operating systems, plus the Amiga. Nmap has a traditional command–line interface, as shown in Fig. 31.4; zenmap is the official Nmap security scanner graphical user interface (GUI) (Fig. 31.5).

It is a multiplatform (Linux, Windows, Mac OS X, BSD, etc.), free, open-source application that aims to make Nmap easy for beginners to use while providing advanced features for experienced Nmap users. Frequently used scans can be saved as profiles to make them easy to run repeatedly. A command creator allows interactive creation of Nmap command lines. Scan results can be saved and viewed later. Saved scan results can be compared with one another to see how they differ. The results of recent scans are stored in a searchable database.

Gordon Lyon (better known by his nickname, Fyodor) released Nmap in 1997 and continues to coordinate its development. He also maintains the Insecure.Org, Nmap.Org, SecLists.Org, and SecTools.Org security resource sites and has written seminal papers on operating system (OS) detection and stealth port scanning. He is a founding member of the Honeynet project and coauthored the books *Know Your Enemy: Honeynets* and *Stealing the Network: How to Own a Continent*. Gordon is president of Computer Professionals for Social Responsibility, which has promoted free speech, security, and privacy since 1981.[4]

Some systems might be disconnected from the network. Obviously, if the system is not connected to any network it will have a lower priority for scanning. However, it should not be left in the dark and not be scanned at all, because there might be other nonnetwork-related flaws: for example, a FireWire exploit that can be used to unlock the Windows XP SP2 system. Exploits work like this: An attacker approaches a locked Windows XP SP2 station, plugs a FireWire cable into it, and uses special commands to unlock the locked machine. This technique is possible because FireWire has direct access to RAM. The system will accept any password and unlock the computer.[5]

8. SELECTING THE RIGHT SCANNERS

Scanners alone do not solve the problem; using scanners well helps solve *part* of the problem. Start with one scanner

---

3. Darknet, © Darknet–The Darkside 2000–2013. [www.darknet.org.uk/2006/04/penetration-testing-vs-vulnerability-assessment/], 2013.

4. insecure.org, http://insecure.org/fyodor/.
5. N. Patel, Windows Passwords Easily Bypassed Over Firewire, © 2013 AOL Inc. All rights reserved. [http://www.engadget.com/2008/03/04/windows-passwords-easily-bypassed-over-firewire/], March 4, 2008.

Emergent
Dominant
Firewalls
HIPS
Usefulness
NIPS
AV
NIDS
Esoteric
Dormant
Ubiquity

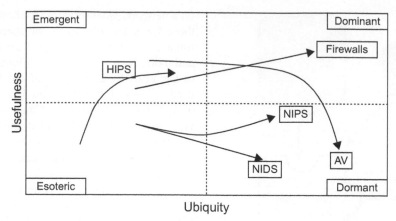

FIGURE 31.3 Usefulness–ubiquity relationship. *AV*, antivirus; *HIPS*, host-based intrusion prevention system; *NIDS*, network-based intrusion detection system; *NIPS*, network-based intrusion prevention system.

sh-3.2# nmap -sV scanme.nmap.org
Starting Nmap 5.61TEST4 (http://nmap.org) at 2012-02-25 15:08 EST
Nmap scan report for scanme.nmap.org (74.207.244.221)
Host is up (0.17s latency).
Not shown: 994 closed ports
PORT STATE SERVICE VERSION
22/tcp open ssh OpenSSH 5.3p1 Debian 3ubuntu7 (protocol 2.0)
25/tcp filtered smtp
80/tcp open http Apache httpd 2.2.14 ((Ubuntu))
646/tcp filtered ldp
1720/tcp filtered H.323/Q.931
9929/tcp open nping-echo Nping echo
Service Info: OS: Linux; CPE: cpe:/o:linux:kernel
Service detection performed. Please report any incorrect results at http://
Nmap done: 1 IP address (1 host up) scanned in 11.31 seconds
sh-3.2#

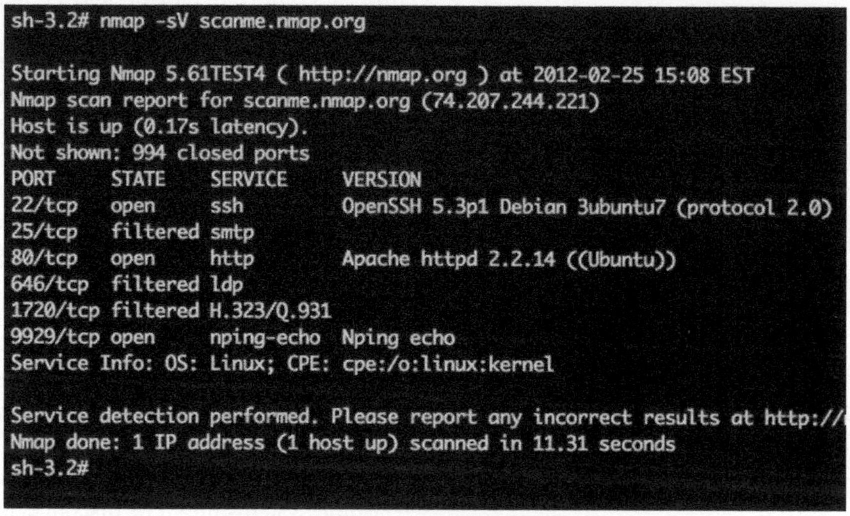

FIGURE 31.4 Nmap command-line interface.

Zenmap
Scan Tools Profile Help
Target: scanme.nmap.org
Profile: Intense scan
Scan
Cancel
Command: nmap -T4 -A -v scanme.nmap.org
Hosts
Services
Nmap Output
Ports / Hosts
Topology
Host Details
Scans
OS
Host
scanme.nmap.
Port Protocol State Service Version
22 tcp open ssh OpenSSH 5.3p1 Debian 3ubuntu7 (protocol 2.0)
25 tcp filtered smtp
80 tcp open http Apache httpd 2.2.14 ((Ubuntu))
646 tcp filtered ldp
1720 tcp filtered H.323/Q.931
9929 tcp open nping-echo Nping echo
Filter Hosts

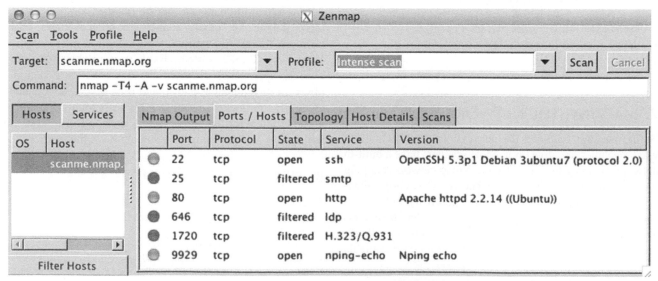

FIGURE 31.5 Zenmap graphical user interface.

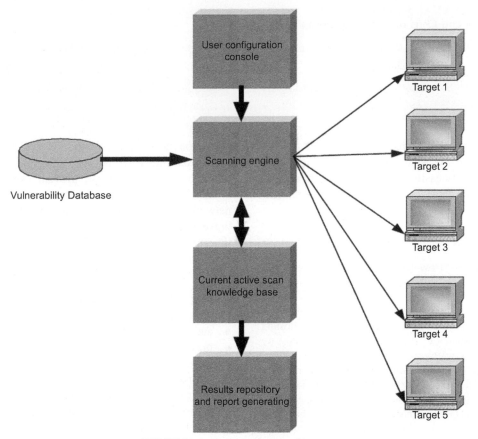

FIGURE 31.6 Typical scanner architecture.

but consider more than one. It is a good practice to use more than one scanner. This way you can compare results from a couple of them. Some scanners are more focused on particular services. Typical scanner architecture is shown in Fig. 31.6.

For example, Nessus is an outstanding general-purpose scanner, but Web application-oriented scanners such as HP Web Inspect or Hailstorm will do a much better job of scanning a Web application. In an ideal situation, scanners would not be needed because everyone would maintain patches and tested hosts, routers, gateways, workstations, and servers. However, the real world is different; we are humans and we tend to forget to install updates, patch systems, and/or configure systems properly. Malicious code will always find a way into your network! If a system is connected to the network, that means there is a possibility that this system will be infected at some time in the future. The chances might be higher or lower depending on the system's maintenance level. The system will never be 100% secure. There is no such thing as 100% security; if well maintained, it might be 99.9999999999% secure, but never 100%. There is a joke that says, if you want to make a computer secure, you have to disconnect it from the network and power outlet and then put it into a safe and lock it. This system will be *almost* 100% secure (although not useful), because social engineering cons may call your

employees and ask them to remove that system from the safe and plug it back into the network.[6,7]

9. CENTRAL SCANS VERSUS LOCAL SCANS

The question arises: Should we scan locally or centrally? Should we scan the whole network at once, or should we scan the network based on subdomains and virtual local area networks? Table 31.1 shows pros and cons of each method.

With localized scanning and central scanning verification, central scanning becomes a verification audit. The question again arises, should we scan locally or centrally? The answer is both. Central scans give overall visibility into the network. Local scans may have higher visibility into the local network. Centrally driven scans serve as the baseline. Locally driven scans are critical to vulnerability reduction. Scanning tools should support both methodologies. Scan

6. Hewlett–Packard Development Company, L.P. © 2013 Hewlett–Packard Development Company, L.P. [http://www.hpenterprisesecurity.com/], 2013.
7. Cenzic Desktop: Application Security for Cloud and Web, © 2012 Cenzic, Inc. All rights reserved. Cenzic, Inc., 655 Campbell Technology Parkway, Suite #100Campbell, CA 95,008. [http://www.cenzic.com/products/desktop/index.html], 2013.

TABLE 31.1 Pros and Cons of Central Scans and Local Scans

	Centrally Controlled and Accessed Scanning	Decentralized Scanning
Pros	Easy to maintain	Scan managers can scan at will
Cons	Slow; most scans must be queued	Patching of scanner is often overlooked

managers should be empowered to police their own area and enforce policy. So what will hackers target? Script kiddies will target any easily exploitable system; dedicated hackers will target some particular network/organization (see sidebar, "Who Is the Target?").

Who Is the Target?

"We are not a target." How many times have you heard this statement? Many people think that they do not have anything to hide, they do not have secrets, and thus nobody will hack them. Hackers are after not only secrets but also resources. They may want to use your machine for hosting files, use it as a source to attack other systems, or just try some new exploits against it.

If you do not have juicy information, you might not be a target for a skilled hacker, but you will always be a target for script kiddies. In hacker culture terms, *script kiddie* describes an inexperienced hacker who is using available tools, usually with a GUI, to do any malicious activity. Script kiddies lack technical expertise to write or create any tools by themselves. They try to infect or deface as many systems as they can with the least possible effort. If they cannot hack your system or site in a couple of minutes, usually they move on to an easier target. It is different with skilled hackers, who seek financial or other benefits from hacking the system. They spend a lot of time just exploring the system and collecting as much information as possible before trying to hack it. The proper way of hacking is with data mining and writing scripts that will automate the whole process, thus making it fast and hard to respond to.

---

10. DEFENSE IN DEPTH STRATEGY

Defense in depth is an information assurance strategy in which multiple layers of defense are placed throughout an IT system. Defense in depth addresses security vulnerabilities in personnel, technology, and operations for the duration of the system's life cycle. The idea behind this approach is to defend a system against any particular attack using several varying methods. It is a layering tactic, conceived by the National Security Agency as a comprehensive approach to information and electronic security. Defense in depth was originally a military strategy that seeks to delay, rather than prevent, the advance of an attacker by yielding space to buy time. The placement of

protection mechanisms, procedures, and policies is intended to increase the dependability of an IT system in which multiple layers of defense prevent espionage and direct attacks against critical systems. In terms of computer network defense, defense in depth measures only should not prevent security breaches, they should give an organization time to detect and respond to an attack, thereby reducing and mitigating the impact of a breach. Using more than one of the following layers constitutes defense in depth:

- physical security (deadbolt locks)
- authentication and password security
- antivirus software (host based and network based)
- firewalls (hardware or software)
- demilitarized zones
- intrusion detection systems (IDSs)
- intrusion prevention systems
- packet filters (deep packet inspection appliances and stateful firewalls)
- routers and switches
- proxy servers
- virtual private networks
- logging and auditing
- biometrics
- timed access control
- proprietary software/hardware not available to the public

11. VULNERABILITY ASSESSMENT TOOLS

There are many vulnerability assessment tools. Popular scanning tools according to www.sectools.org are listed here.

Nessus

Nessus is one of the most popular and capable vulnerability scanners, particularly for UNIX systems. It was initially free and open source, but they closed the source code in 2005 and removed the free "Registered Feed" version in 2008. It now costs $1200 per year, which still beats many of its competitors. A free "Home Feed" is also available, although it is limited and licensed only for home network use. Nessus is constantly updated, with more than 46,000 plug-ins. Key features include remote and local (authenticated) security checks, a client/server architecture with a Web-based interface, and an embedded scripting language for writing your own plug-ins or understanding the existing ones. The open-source version of Nessus was forked by a group of users who still develop it under the OpenVAS name.

GFI LANguard

This is a network security and vulnerability scanner designed to help with patch management, network and software audits, and vulnerability assessments. The price is based on the number of IP addresses you wish to scan. A free trial version of up to five IP addresses is available.

Retina

Retina is a commercial vulnerability assessment scanner by eEye. Like Nessus, Retina's function is to scan all hosts on a network and report on any vulnerabilities found. It was written by eEye, which is well known for security research.

Core Impact

Core Impact is not cheap (be prepared to spend at least $30,000), but it is widely considered to be the most powerful exploitation tool available. It sports a large, regularly updated database of professional exploits and can do neat tricks such as exploiting one machine and then establishing an encrypted tunnel through that machine to reach and exploit other boxes. Other good options include Metasploit and Canvas.

Internet Security Systems Internet Scanner

Application-level vulnerability assessment Internet Scanner started off in 1992 as a tiny open-source scanner by Christopher Klaus. Now he has grown Internet Security Systems (ISS) into a billion-dollar company with myriad security products.

X-Scan

A general scanner for scanning network vulnerabilities, X-Scan is a multithreaded, plug-in—supported vulnerability scanner. X-Scan includes many features, including full Nessus Attack Scripting Language support, detecting service types, remote OS type/version detection, weak user—password pairs, and more. You may be able to find newer versions available at the X-Scan site if you can deal with most of the page being written in Chinese.

12. SECURITY AUDITOR'S RESEARCH ASSISTANT

Security Auditor's Research Assistant is a vulnerability assessment tool that was derived from the infamous

Security Administrator Tool for Analyzing Networks (SATAN) scanner. Updates are released twice a month and the company tries to leverage other software created by the open-source community (such as Nmap and Samba).

QualysGuard

A Web-based vulnerability scanner delivered as a service over the Web, QualysGuard eliminates the burden of deploying, maintaining, and updating vulnerability management software or implementing ad hoc security applications. Clients securely access QualysGuard through an easy-to-use Web interface. QualysGuard features more than 5000 unique vulnerability checks, an inference-based scanning engine, and automated daily updates to the QualysGuard vulnerability knowledge base.

13. SECURITY ADMINISTRATOR'S INTEGRATED NETWORK TOOL

Security Administrator's Integrated Network Tool (SAINT) is another commercial vulnerability assessment tool (like Nessus, ISS Internet Scanner, or Retina). It runs on UNIX and used to be free and open source but is now a commercial product.

14. MICROSOFT BASELINE SECURITY ANALYZER

Microsoft Baseline Security Analyzer (MBSA) is an easy-to-use tool designed for the IT professional that helps small and medium-sized businesses determine their security state in accordance with Microsoft security recommendations, and offers specific remediation guidance. Built on the Windows Update Agent and Microsoft Update infrastructure, MBSA ensures consistency with other Microsoft management products, including Microsoft Update, Windows Server Update Services, Systems Management Server, and Microsoft Operations Manager. Apparently, on average, MBSA scans over three million computers each week.[8]

15. SCANNER PERFORMANCE

A vulnerability scanner can use a lot of network bandwidth, so you want the scanning process to be completed as quickly as possible. Of course, the more vulnerabilities in the database and the more comprehensive the scan, the longer it will take, so this can be a trade-off. One way to

8. SecTools.Org: Top 125 Network Security Tools. SecTools.Org, [www.sectools.org], 2013.

An Agenda for Action for the Use of Network Scanning Countermeasures

Here is a checklist of network scanning countermeasures and for when a commercial firewall is in use (check all tasks completed):

_____**1.** Filter inbound Internet Control Message Protocol (ICMP) message types at border routers and firewalls. This forces attackers to use full-blown Transmission Control Protocol (TCP) port scans against all of your IP addresses to map your network correctly.

_____**2.** Filter all outbound ICMP type 3 unreachable messages at border routers and firewalls to prevent User Datagram Protocol (UDP) port scanning and fire-walking from being effective.

_____**3.** Consider configuring Internet firewalls so that they can identify port scans and throttle the connections accordingly. You can configure commercial firewall appliances (such as those from Check Point, NetScreen, and WatchGuard) to prevent fast port scans and synchronization floods being launched against your networks. On the open-source side, many tools such as port sentry can identify port scans and drop all packets from the source IP address for a given period of time.

_____**4.** Assess the way that your network firewall and IDS devices handle fragmented IP packets by using fragtest and fragroute when performing scanning and probing exercises. Some devices crash or fail under

conditions in which high volumes of fragmented packets are being processed.

_____**5.** Ensure that your routing and filtering mechanisms (both firewalls and routers) cannot be bypassed using specific source ports or source-routing techniques.

_____**6.** If you house publicly accessible File Transfer Protocol services, ensure that your firewalls are not vulnerable to stateful circumvention attacks relating to mal-formed PORT and PASV commands.

If a commercial firewall is in use, ensure the following:

_____**7.** The latest firmware and latest service pack are installed.

_____**8.** Antispoofing rules have been correctly defined so that the device does not accept packets with private spoofed source addresses on its external interfaces.

_____**9.** Investigate using inbound proxy servers in your environment if you require a high level of security. A proxy server will not forward fragmented or mal-formed packets, so it is not possible to launch FIN scanning or other stealth methods.

_____**10.** Be aware of your own network configuration and its publicly accessible ports by launching TCP and UDP port scans along with ICMP probes against your own IP address space. It is surprising how many large companies still do not undertake even simple port-scanning exercises properly.

---

increase performance is to use multiple scanners on the enterprise network, which can report back to one system that aggregates the results.

16. SCAN VERIFICATION

The best practice is to use few scanners during your vulnerability assessment, and then use more than one scanning tool to find more vulnerabilities. Scan your networks with different scanners from different vendors and compare the results. Also consider penetration testing; that is, hire white- or gray-hat hackers to hack your own systems.

17. SCANNING CORNERSTONES

All orphaned systems should be treated as hostile. Something in your organization that is not maintained or touched poses the largest threat. For example, say that you have a Web server and you inspect every byte of dynamic HyperText Markup Language and make sure it has no flaws, but you totally forget to maintain the Simple Mail Transfer Protocol (SMTP) service with open relay that it is also running. Attackers might not be able to deface or harm your Web page, but they will be using the SMTP server to send out spam emails via your server. As a result, your

company's IP ranges will be put into spammer lists such as spamhaus and spamcop.[9,10]

18. NETWORK SCANNING COUNTERMEASURES

A company wants to scan its own networks, but at the same time the company should take countermeasures to protect itself from being scanned by hackers. Here is a checklist of countermeasures (see checklist: "An Agenda for Action for the Use of Network Scanning Countermeasures") to use when you are considering technical modifications to networks and filtering devices to reduce the effectiveness of network scanning and probing undertaken by attackers.

19. VULNERABILITY DISCLOSURE DATE

The time of disclosure of vulnerability is defined differently in the security community and industry. It is most commonly referred to as "a kind of public disclosure of security

---

9. The Spamhaus Project Ltd., © 1998—2013 The Spamhaus Project Ltd. All rights reserved. [www.spamhaus.org], 2013.
10. Cisco Systems, Inc., ©1992—2010 Cisco Systems, Inc. All rights reserved. [www.spamcop.net], 2010.

information by a certain party." Usually vulnerability information is discussed on a mailing list or published on a security website and results in a security advisory afterward. A mailing list named "Full Disclosure Mailing List" is a perfect example of how vulnerabilities are disclosed to the public. It is a must read for any person interested in IT security. This mailing list is free of charge and is available at http://seclists.org/fulldisclosure/.

The *time of disclosure* is the first date on which security vulnerability is described on a channel where the disclosed information on the vulnerability has to fulfill the following requirements:

- The information is freely available to the public.
- The vulnerability information is published by a trusted and independent channel/source.
- The vulnerability has undergone analysis by experts such that risk rating information is included upon disclosure.

The method of disclosing vulnerabilities is a topic of debate in the computer security community. Some advocate immediate full disclosure of information about vulnerabilities once they are discovered. Others argue for limiting disclosure to the users placed at greatest risk and releasing full details only after a delay, if ever. Such delays may allow those notified to fix the problem by developing and applying patches, but they can also increase the risk to those not privy to full details. This debate has a long history in security; see full disclosure and security through obscurity. A new form of commercial vulnerability disclosure has taken shape, as some commercial security companies offer money for exclusive disclosures of zero-day vulnerabilities. Those offers provide a legitimate market for the purchase and sale of vulnerability information from the security community.[11]

From the security perspective, a free and public disclosure is successful only if the affected parties obtain the relevant information before potential hackers; if they did not, the hackers could take immediate advantage of the revealed exploit. With security through obscurity, the same rule applies but this time rests on the hackers finding the vulnerability themselves, as opposed to being given the information from another source. The disadvantage here is that fewer people have full knowledge of the vulnerability and can aid in finding similar or related scenarios.

It should be unbiased to enable a fair dissemination of security-critical information. Most often a channel is considered trusted when it is a widely accepted source of security information in the industry (such as the Community Emergency Response Team, SecurityFocus, Secunia, and www.exploit-db.com). Analysis and risk rating ensure

the quality of the disclosed information. The analysis must include enough details to allow a concerned user of the software to assess his individual risk or take immediate action to protect his assets.

Find Security Holes Before They Become Problems

Vulnerabilities can be classified into two major categories:

- those related to errors made by programmers in writing the code for the software;
- those related to misconfigurations of the software's settings that leave systems less secure than they could be (improperly secured accounts, running of unneeded services, etc.).

Vulnerability scanners can identify both types. Vulnerability assessment tools have been around for many years. They have been used by network administrators and misused by hackers to discover exploitable vulnerabilities in systems and networks of all kinds. One of the early well-known UNIX scanners, SATAN, later morphed into SAINT. These names illustrate the disparate dual nature of the purposes to which such tools can be put.

In the hands of a would-be intruder, vulnerability scanners become a means of finding victims and determining those victims' weak points, like an undercover intelligence operative who infiltrates the opposition's supposedly secure location and gathers information that can be used to launch a full-scale attack. However, in the hands of those who are charged with protecting their networks, these scanners are a vital proactive defense mechanism that allows you to see your systems through the eyes of the enemy and take steps to lock the doors, board up the windows, and plug up seldom used passageways through which the "bad guys" could enter, before they get a chance.

In fact, the first scanners were designed as hacking tools, but this is a case in which the bad guys' weapons have been appropriated and used to defend against them. By "fighting fire with fire," administrators gain a much-needed advantage. For the first time, they are able to battle intruders proactively. Once the vulnerabilities are found, we have to remove them (see sidebar, "Identifying and Removing Vulnerabilities").

20. PROACTIVE SECURITY VERSUS REACTIVE SECURITY

There are two basic methods of dealing with security breaches:

- The *reactive method* is passive; when a breach occurs, you respond to it, doing damage control at the same

---

11. C. McNab, Network Security Assessment, O'Rielly, Chapter 4: IP Network Scanning. [www.trustmatta.com/downloads/pdf/Matta_IP_Network_Scanning.pdf], pp. 36–72, 2013.

Identifying and Removing Vulnerabilities

Many software tools can aid in the discovery (and sometimes removal) of vulnerabilities in a computer system. Although these tools can provide an auditor with a good overview of possible vulnerabilities present, they cannot replace human judgment. Relying solely on scanners will yield false positives and a limited-scope view of the problems present in the system.

Vulnerabilities have been found in every major operating system including Windows, Mac OS, various forms of UNIX and Linux, and OpenVMS. The only way to reduce the chance of a vulnerability being used against a system is through constant vigilance, including careful system maintenance (e.g., applying software patches), best practices in deployment (e.g., the use of firewalls and access controls), and auditing during development and throughout the deployment life cycle.

time you track down how the intruder or attacker got in and cut off that means of access so it will not happen again.

- The *proactive method* is active; instead of waiting for the hackers to show you where you are vulnerable, you put on your own hacker hat in relation to your own network and set out to find the vulnerabilities yourself, before anyone else discovers and exploits them.

The best security strategy employs both reactive and proactive mechanisms. IDSs, for example, are reactive in that they detect suspicious network activity so that you can respond to it appropriately.

Vulnerability assessment scanning is a proactive tool that gives you the power to anticipate vulnerabilities and keep out attackers instead of spending much more time and money responding to attack after attack. The goal of proactive security is to prevent attacks before they happen, thus decreasing the load on reactive mechanisms. Being proactive is more cost-effective and usually easier; the difference can be illustrated by contrasting the time and cost required to clean up after vandals break into your home or office with the effort and money required simply to install better locks that will keep them out.

Despite the initial outlay for vulnerability assessment scanners and the time spent administering them, potential return on investment is high in the form of time and money saved when attacks are prevented. *Threat intelligence* is another example of proactive security methods. The goal of threat intelligence is to monitor dark corners of Internet for hacks, exploits, and malicious code being sent to your networks. For example company XYZ, Inc. receives threat intelligence information that one of their Web server's administrator-level access is for sale in Russian underground forums. For this company it will be so much cheaper to shut down the server as soon as

possible, so there will be the least amount of damage done.[12]

21. VULNERABILITY CAUSES

The following are examples of vulnerability causes:

- password management flaws
- fundamental operating system design flaws
- software bugs
- unchecked user input

Password Management Flaws

The computer user uses weak passwords that could be discovered by brute force. The computer user stores the password on the computer where a program can access it. The user has so many accounts on different websites that it is impossible to have a different password and still remember it. The result: the user uses the same password on many websites (déjà vu, anyone?).

Fundamental Operating System Design Flaws

The operating system designer chooses to enforce suboptimal policies on user/program management. For example, operating systems with policies such as *default permit* grant every program and every user full access to the entire computer. This operating system flaw allows viruses and malware to execute commands on behalf of the administrator.

Software Bugs

The programmer leaves an exploitable bug in a software program. The software bug may allow an attacker to misuse an application through (for example) bypassing access control checks or executing commands on the system hosting the application. Also, the programmer's failure to check the size of data buffers, which then can be overflowed, can cause corruption of the stack or heap areas of memory (including causing the computer to execute code provided by the attacker).

Unchecked User Input

The program assumes that all user input is safe. Programs that do not check user input can allow unintended direct execution of commands or Structured Query Language (SQL) statements (known as buffer overflows, SQL

---

12. Threat Intelligence, © 2013 Demyo, Inc., Demyo, Inc. [http://demyo.com/services/threat-intelligence/], 2013.

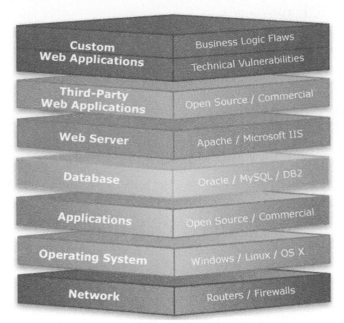

FIGURE 31.7 Vulnerabilities with the biggest impact.

injection, or other nonvalidated inputs). For example, a form on the Web page is asking how old you are. A regular user would enter 32; a hacker would try −3.2, which is somewhat legitimate input. The goal for entering bogus data is to find out how an application reacts and to monitor for input validation flaws. The biggest impact on the organization would be if vulnerabilities were found in core devices on the network (routers, firewalls, etc.), as shown in Fig. 31.7.

22. DO IT YOURSELF VULNERABILITY ASSESSMENT

If you perform credit card transactions online, you are most likely PCI DSS compliant or working on getting there. In either case, it is much better to resolve compliancy issues on an ongoing basis rather than stare at a truckload of problems as the auditor walks into your office. Although writing and reviewing policies and procedures is a big part of reaching your goal, being aware of the vulnerabilities in your environment and understanding how to remediate them are just as important. For most small businesses, vulnerability assessments sound like a lot of work and time that you just do not have. What if you could have a complete understanding of all vulnerabilities in your network and a fairly basic resolution for each, outlined in a single report within a couple of hours? Sound good? What if I also told you that the tool that can make this happen is currently free and does not require an IT genius to run it? Sounding better?

It is not pretty and it is not always right, but it can give you some valuable insight into your environment. Tenable's Nessus vulnerability scanner is one of the most widely used tools in professional vulnerability assessments today. In its default configuration, all you need to do is provide the tool with a range of IP addresses and click Go. It will then compare its database of known vulnerabilities against the responses it receives from your network devices, gathering as much information as possible without killing your network or servers, usually. It does have some dangerous plug-ins that are disabled by default, and you can throttle down the amount of bandwidth it uses to keep the network noise levels to a minimum. The best part about Nessus is that it is well documented, and used by over 75,000 organizations worldwide, so you know you are dealing with a trustworthy product. I urge you to take a look Tenable's enterprise offerings as well. You might be surprised at how easy it is to perform a basic do-it-yourself vulnerability assessment:

- Tenable's Nessus: www.nessus.org
- Tenable Network Security: www.tenablesecurity.com

23. SUMMARY

Network and host-based vulnerability assessment tools are extremely useful in determining what vulnerabilities might exist on a particular network. However, these tools are not useful if the vulnerability knowledge base is not kept current. Also, these tools can only take a snapshot of the systems at a particular point in time. Systems administrators will continually update code on the target systems and will continuously add or delete services and configure the system. All found vulnerabilities should be promptly patched (especially critical ones).

Finally, let us move on to the real interactive part of this chapter: review questions/exercises, hands-on projects, case projects, and the optional team case project. The answers and/or solutions by chapter can be found in the Online Instructor's Solutions Manual.

CHAPTER REVIEW QUESTIONS/ EXERCISES

True/False

1. True or False? Reporting capability is of growing importance to administrators in a documentation-oriented business climate where you must not only be able to do your job, you must also provide written proof of how you have done it.
2. True or False? Organizations have a tremendous opportunity to use information technologies to increase their productivity.
3. True or False? PCI DSS stands for Payment Card Information Data Security Standard.
4. True or False? There seems to be a certain amount of confusion within the security industry about the

similarities between penetration testing and vulnerability assessment.

5. True or False? The theoretical goal of network scanning is elevated security on all systems or establishing a network-wide minimal operation standard.

Multiple Choice

1. What runs on all major computer operating systems, plus the Amiga?
   A. Nmap
   B. Zenmap
   C. Security scanner GUI
   D. More popular phase
   E. Attack phase

2. What is an outstanding general-purpose scanner, although Web application-oriented scanners such as HP Web Inspect or Hailstorm will do a much better job of scanning a Web application?
   A. Nessus
   B. SATAN
   C. Central
   D. Local
   E. User-level rootkit scan

3. With localized scanning and central scanning verification, central scanning becomes a:
   A. Stateful firewall
   B. Virus
   C. Methodology
   D. Verification audit
   E. User-level rootkit

4. What is an information assurance strategy in which multiple layers of defense are placed throughout an IT system?
   A. Physical security
   B. Authentication and password security
   C. Defense in depth
   D. Antivirus software
   E. Firewall rootkit

5. What is one of the most popular and capable vulnerability scanners, particularly for UNIX systems?
   A. Nessus
   B. GFI LANguard
   C. Retina
   D. Core Impact
   E. ISS Internet Scanner

EXERCISE

Problem

What will happen if a vulnerability is exploited, and who exploits vulnerabilities?

Hands-on Projects

Project

Will scanning interrupt or affect the servers?

Case Projects

Problem

What is Open Vulnerability and Assessment Language (OVAL)?

Optional Team Case Project

Problem

How is OVAL different from commercial vulnerability scanners?

Chapter 32

Security Metrics: An Introduction and Literature Review

George O.M. Yee

Carleton University, Ottawa, Ontario, Canada

Note: This chapter is available in its entirety online at store.elsevier.com/product.jsp?isbn= 9780128038437 (click the Resources tab at the bottom of the page).

1. ABSTRACT

This chapter provides an introduction to and a literature review for security metrics. It begins by describing the need for security metrics, followed by a discussion of the nature of security metrics, including what makes a good security metric, what security metrics have been used in the past, and how security metrics can be scientifically based. This presentation is followed by suggestions for starting a security metrics program within an organization and a discussion of the feasibility of an intelligent security dashboard driven by metrics. The chapter concludes with a literature review that summarizes security metrics publications (including research papers) where one could obtain more information.

2. CONTENTS

Security Metrics: An Introduction and Literature Review

George O.M. Yee

1. ABSTRACT

Chapter 33

Security Education, Training, and Awareness

Albert Caballero

HBO Latin America, Surfside, FL, United States

1. SECURITY EDUCATION, TRAINING, AND AWARENESS (SETA) PROGRAMS

Security Education, Training, and Awareness (SETA) is a program that targets all users in an organization to help them become more aware of information security principles as is appropriate for their jobs. Without a SETA program an organization runs the risk of easy infiltration by simple virtue of their employee's ignorance on how to securely perform basic IT tasks. A SETA program not only has the bottom-line effect of raising the difficulty for attackers to infiltrate an organization, but can also decrease cyber-risk insurance premiums, help meet regulatory standards, and set the tone for the secure business practices of an entire industry. All users have a responsibility to help secure the business and should therefore be given an opportunity to learn how to better protect themselves and their company's assets with appropriate information security training. It is important for every employee to understand their role in security, so the goal of a SETA program should be participation and motivation.

If implemented well, a SETA program is a continuum of training that begins with the most general for all users and becomes more targeted and in-depth depending on the role of each individual or group. The most basic level of a SETA program, and likely the most important, starts with awareness. Security awareness is the general information security training that is delivered to all users. The goal is to create a culture of security awareness across the entire organization and should therefore speak to all users focusing on individual accountability so that everyone maintains a certain level of skepticism when finding themselves in a situation that is unorthodox or out of the ordinary. It is these special exceptions and social manipulations that are typically leveraged by attackers to gain a foothold and some level of

access from which to pivot and expand unauthorized access further into an organization. For example, something as simple as letting someone into the building without proper ID, clicking on a mail attachment that is not expected, or sharing your password with a coworker could end up being the demise of an entire business costing tens of thousands of dollars or more in recovery efforts. Fig. 33.1

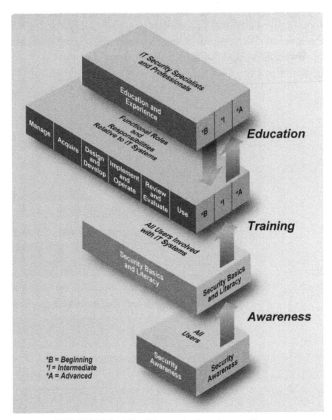

*B = Beginning
*I = Intermediate
*A = Advanced

FIGURE 33.1 The IT security learning continuum.

Computer and Information Security Handbook. http://dx.doi.org/10.1016/B978-0-12-803843-7.00033-8

below describes the IT Security Learning Continuum according to the National Institute of Standards and Technology (NIST) [2].

The next level in a properly implemented SETA program is training. Security training is more targeted and tactical typically based on the responsibility of each employee and helps develop more advanced skills, increasing the understanding on how to securely perform their specific job functions. There are two methodologies by which to effectively deliver this type of security training: functional and skill-based. Functional information security training is specialized training based on the role of an employee. For example, a network firewall administrator will likely require training on the type of firewalls that are in production by any particular company such as Checkpoints, Palo Alto, or Cisco; whereas, an infrastructure administrator will likely need security training in Windows Active Directory and ITIL Change Management procedures—all critical aspects of running a safe computing environment. Skill-based training will take into account the current skill level (beginner, intermediate, or advanced) of the employee when delivering technical training. An individual that has been a firewall administrator for several years will likely benefit much from an advanced course in firewall hardening tactics whereas a person that may have had a security education but no real world experience will need to start at a beginner class that addresses basic management and implementation of the specific firewalls being administered. Ultimately, the higher the level of risk that individuals manage the higher the level of awareness and training they must be provided as depicted in Fig. 33.2 [2].

Many times this type of training requires a level of technical expertise that is not available within a typical organization so it is necessary to go outside of the company to institutions like SANS.org and ISC2 for advanced and highly technical information security training that can be delivered to small groups or individuals that need it, not to the entire organization as security awareness would be. Today, a Security Education is possible by enrolling in a formal curriculum that is purpose built to teach all the fundamental concepts required to build a career in information security. Many universities and colleges have begun to create curriculums that will offer bachelor's and master's degrees on information security. These degree programs are good for students that are fresh out of high school or adults which would like to retrain in this fast-growing field; however, many of these programs do little to expose students to real world information security practices. The most important aspect of developing a proper security education program should be to map to real world scenarios and job functions in areas that are in high demand. Some of these fundamentals areas of study should include:

- Information security and risk management
- Network communication analysis, design, and security
- Software development and embedded operating system (OS) security
- Ethical hacking and application security
- Social engineering and SETA
- Mission-critical infrastructure
- Identity and access management
- Digital and mobile forensics
- Data security standards and regulatory compliance
- Malware analysis and reverse engineering

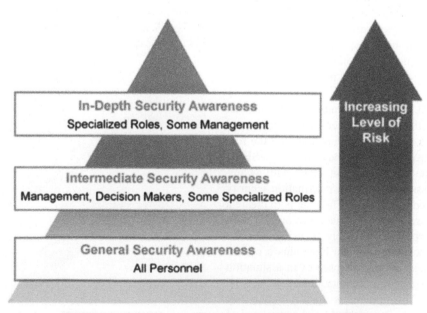

FIGURE 33.2 Depth of security awareness, training, and education.

2. USERS, BEHAVIOR, AND ROLES

Users in every organization are critical to the defense and protection of sensitive data and secure operations. No matter what technical controls are implemented from firewalls to intrusion detection systems it only takes one user clicking on the wrong link or tripping over the wrong wire and a true disaster or outbreak can occur. This is why all users need to have clearly defined roles and their behavior must be modified so as to think twice before taking an action that may lead to nefarious consequences. This can only be done with SETA. It is increasingly important throughout the SETA program to maintain user engagement high in order to raise morale and reward the appropriate behavior while discouraging risky behavior.

Understanding user behavior and motivation is key to a successful SETA program. As a security professional it is necessary to be both an evangelist and a leader. To be an effective leader there is a need to implement proven techniques and strategies in modifying user behavior whenever possible. Although there are certain innate qualities present in most leaders there is also a training management process that should be understood and practiced to enhance leadership skills to more effectively influence the way users behave under certain circumstances. Behavioral management is an important aspect of this and needs planning that should occur at three levels. First, at an individualized level where support is provided one on one, which is most effective with users that have a high level of responsibility within the organization by way of managing other users (such as managers and executives) or by their administrative duties (such as network and system administrators). Next, there is classroom or group support, which can also be referred to as business units or departments depending on the organization. For example, the Human Resources department may have quite different security awareness needs than the Operations or Legal department. There should be customized training sessions based on these user groups that address their specific needs. Finally there is school-wide or organization-wide support, which addresses general security awareness topics that are common across the entire organization. Fig. 33.3 shows the levels to consider when planning a behavior management strategy in a classroom or business environment [4].

Defining roles and responsibilities is part of the best practices needed to understand how to best design and develop a SETA program that will engage the right people and encourage the desired behavior. As part of these best practices the Payment Card Industry Data Security Standards (PCI DSS) has defined the roles described in Fig. 33.4 below. This maps somewhat to the traditional

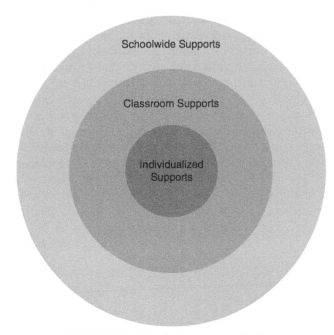

FIGURE 33.3 Behavior management planning.

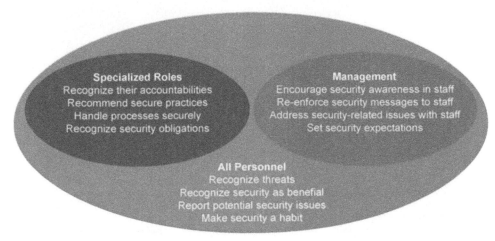

FIGURE 33.4 Security awareness roles for organizations.

behavioral management techniques used in higher education institutions. All personnel need to be able to recognize security threats and potentially risky behavior. Management needs to reinforce and support these initiatives, while security professionals need to understand what they are held accountable for and recognize their security obligations [6].

3. SECURITY EDUCATION, TRAINING, AND AWARENESS (SETA) PROGRAM DESIGN

The ultimate purpose of a SETA program is to change the behavior of users (and, this cannot be done without engaging them in a way that is memorable and effective), it is important that the design of the program be well thought out. For users to be engaged there needs to be a variety of training opportunities that are both interactive and innovative with a campaign that is all inclusive, in other words, does not leave anyone out. From managers and executives in any organization to temps and interns, security awareness is essential for designing and developing an effective SETA program.

Designing and developing a SETA program requires thought, organization, and planning making sure to keep the mission and culture of the organization in mind. To be successful it needs to support the business needs while making the users feel relevant and connected to the subject matter. During the design process the needs of the organization are identified and an effective, organization-wide program is developed. Without organizational buy-in, proper funding,

and established priorities it becomes extremely difficult to implement a valuable program. While designing the program there are three major components to consider: policy, strategy, and implementation. Policy is extremely important and is typically centralized with requirements being established organization-wide and applying to all users. Depending on the organization there may be a need to have either a distributed or centralized strategy for implementation depending on the size of the organization, budget allocations, and geography of the users.

The training strategy typically benefits from customization based on the different groups needing training although there should be some consistency in the actual training material covered. Ideally, implementation will be highly customized and take into consideration not just the organizational culture but also that of the employee's region, department, and function. There are several different strategies available when creating a SETA program. One of these is a centralized training strategy where there is a top-down effect that can be effective, especially if there is support from upper management. If a centralized strategy is too difficult to implement due to organizational, cultural, or geographical differences then it would make sense to simply write a general policy for the entire organization and let each logical division handle the design and delivery of the material. This is most common where there are language barriers such as a multinational organization or multiple business units that have different core businesses such as a holding company. See Fig. 33.5 for an

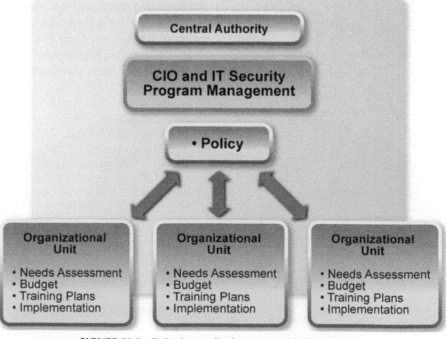

FIGURE 33.5 Fully decentralized strategy and implementation.

example of a fully decentralized SETA program where each organizational unit has a high level of input into the design of the program [2].

Regardless of the strategy selected for implementation there always needs to be a central authority that authorizes, supports, and establishes executive support for the program. That being said, there is also the consideration that these types of training programs are not the core competency of most information security groups. The delivery of these types of programs are best designed and developed by the departments that are in charge of developing other training programs such as Human Resources, Risk and Compliance, or Employee Training, if they exist. There is also a large impact on an organization at the highest level if a committee or council of key stake holders is put together to support the initiatives put forth by the central authority. Having a team of individuals that have the power to implement significant change within an organization is crucial in maintaining strategic support and defining a direction that aligns with the goals of the organization. Information security training should follow the frequency defined below [1]:

- New hire orientation
- Initial security briefing within 3—6 months
- Refresher briefing every 3—6 months
- Termination briefing

4. SECURITY EDUCATION, TRAINING, AND AWARENESS (SETA) PROGRAM DEVELOPMENT

Once the design of the program has been approved the content will need to be developed and this will indeed involve more security staff. There is a significant amount of topics that can be selected for information security training but to overwhelm users is quite easy so the organization should typically begin with a short list of pertinent topics that apply to all users. Remember that security awareness is organization wide and it's not until we refer to security staff and some other types of technical personnel that we do not need to define the training and education piece or the program. Also, the security awareness portion because it needs to be general and applicable to every user it requires less in-depth expertise than other types of training and can usually be developed in house. Among the initial topics that are commonly chosen for developing material for are:

- Password security
- Email phishing
- Social engineering
- Mobile device security
- Sensitive data security
- Business communications

As part of the development of the program it is important to define the content that will be delivered but also develop some of the materials and collateral that will be used to help communicate the content. There are many different techniques that can be used to deliver an engaging security awareness program. The most effective is usually a combination of different techniques whereby creating a security awareness campaign that delivers propaganda and content in ways that are innovative, engaging, and all-inclusive. Some of the different materials and techniques that can be used include:

- Computer-based training
- Phishing awareness emails
- Video campaigns
- Posters and banners
- Lectures and conferences
- Regular newsletters
- Brochures and flyers
- Corporate events

5. IMPLEMENTATION AND DELIVERY

Implementing and delivering a SETA program effectively is critical to the security of every organization. As mentioned it only takes one user that is not aware of how to handle a malicious email or a social engineering phone call to cost an organization a tremendous amount of damage and money. How well a SETA program is implemented and delivered depends largely on the design and development of the program. Both design and development are key steps in the proper building of an effective program and if there are misfires in executive support, program design, or content development it can significantly hamper how much users learn. It is valuable to spend a good amount of time and emphasis on the corporate policy to make sure it is well-written and communicated correctly. Immediately after having figured out the language on the policy it helps to perform a needs assessment. A needs assessment before the implementation of the SETA program will likely bring to light some unexpected needs and improve the results of the program after and during implementation. Some of the steps involved in implementing any training program include:

1. Identifying program scope, goals, and objectives.
2. Identify the training staff and target audiences.
3. Motivate management and employees.
4. Administer, maintain, and evaluate the program.

When it is finally time to implement, communication is key. There should be a communication plan that is mapped to the overall strategy. When implementing the SETA program and communication plan it is important that it is delivered not just by topic but also by business unit, department, and geolocation. Regardless of the implementation techniques

Metric	Training Effectiveness Indicator
Operational Metrics	
Reduced system downtime and network or application outages	Consistent, approved change-management processes; fewer malware outbreaks; better controls
Reduction in malware outbreaks and PC performance issues related to malware	Fewer opened malicious e-mails; increased reports from personnel of malicious e-mails
Increase in reports of attempted e-mail or phone scams	Better recognition by personnel of phishing and other social-engineering attempts
Increase in reporting of security concerns and unusual access	Increased understanding by personnel of risks
Increase in the number of queries from personnel on how to implement secure procedures	Better awareness by personnel of potential threats
DLP scanning and network traces are active but not detecting cardholder data outside the CDE	Better understanding by personnel of potential threats
Vulnerability scans are active and detect high or critical vulnerabilities	Decrease in time between detection and remediation
Vulnerabilities are addressed or mitigated in a timely manner	Better understanding by personnel of potential threats and risks to sensitive information
Training Program Metrics	
Increase in number personnel completing training	Attendance tracking and performance evaluations
Increase in number of employees with privileged access who have received required training	Attendance tracking and performance evaluations
Increase in personnel comprehension of training material	Feedback from personnel; quizzes and training assessments

FIGURE 33.6   Metrics defining training effectiveness.

chosen, it is important to deliver the material in ways that take into consideration the following key aspects:

- Ease of use
- Scalability
- Accountability
- Industry support

After implementation there should be ways that feedback can be returned to the program managers. These feedback mechanisms can consist of traditional surveys during the delivery of the content, evaluation forms, focus groups, or a number of other methods. Defining key metrics that will help measure the effectiveness of the training is the final stage of implementation and can provide valuable information to keep the security program up to date and

current. The table shown in Fig. 33.6 below is a good template that can be used as a starting point to define some powerful metrics for a SETA program [6].

6. TECHNOLOGIES AND PLATFORMS

In the effort to enable an effective SETA program, there are several technologies that can be leveraged to help in the process. One of the most effective ways of training personnel is with a behavioral management tool (see Fig. 33.7) such as ThreatSIM by Wombat Security, Phishme, or other Learning Management Systems (LMS) available from other vendors. ThreatSIM is a platform that allows administrators to measure and monitor the delivery of emails to users and can be used to craft fake phishing

FIGURE 33.7 Behavioral management training platform.

emails that can be customized by department or region. This allows you to evaluate vulnerability to different threat vectors based on user groups and regions. It is also possible to deliver standard or customized teachable moments to employees who fall for mock attacks. This allows for brief, focused, just in time teaching with messages that focus practical guidance in avoiding future threats [7].

7. SUMMARY

A SETA program targets all users in an organization with programs specific to their positions, roles, and level of expertise to minimize the likelihood and impact of a security breach. Security education is the concept that information security personnel require higher education to be competent at their positions and to achieve a common body of knowledge that prepares them to enter the workforce. Security training is tactical and helps technology and operations staff receive highly specialized, formal training that helps everyone manage their roles and responsibilities better as well as be more effective at understanding their own accountability. Security awareness gets the word out to all personnel and helps everyone focus on building a security culture and a mature information security practice. The principal goal of a SETA program is that technology leaders, executive management, and all personnel get the appropriate security knowledge based on their roles and responsibilities (see checklist: " An Agenda for Action Plan for Other Important Goals of a Security Education, Training, and Awareness (SETA) Program").

Every aspect of security is a process, indicating that a one-time security briefing or training session will not suffice when attempting to implement real security. Ongoing and continuous training is part of any major endeavor. At the pace with which security breaches are increasing in number and sophistication it is necessary to adopt these methods when it comes to security training. Fig. 33.8 below describes an ongoing process that when implemented properly will help build a continuous training methodology that will be effective for a long time to come [7].

Now, let's move on to the real interactive part of this Chapter: review questions/exercises, hands-on projects, case projects, and optional team case project. The answers and/or solutions by chapter can be found in Appendix K.

An Agenda for Action Plan for Other Important Goals of a Security Education, Training, and Awareness (SETA) Program

Some of the other important goals of a SETA program should include at least the following key activities (check all tasks completed):

_____**1.** Increase awareness of the need to protect people, assets, and resources.

_____**2.** Develop the skills and knowledge necessary to perform jobs more securely.

_____**3.** Hold employees accountable for their actions by communicating security policy to all users.

_____**4.** Provide better protection of assets by helping employees recognize real and potential security concerns.

_____**5.** Improve morale by providing information that is personally useful, such as how to avoid scams, phishing, and identity theft.

_____**6.** Save money by reducing the number and extent of security breaches.

_____**7.** Motivate employees to improve their behaviors and incorporate security concerns into their decision-making.

_____**8.** Protect customer and corporate information by building a security culture.

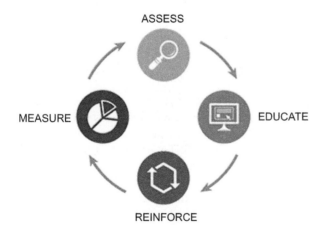

FIGURE 33.8 Continuous training methodology.

CHAPTER REVIEW QUESTIONS/ EXERCISES

True/False

1. True or False? Security Education, Training, and Awareness (SETA) is a process by which all users of an organization have an opportunity to enhance their knowledge of information security in an effort to protect themselves and organizational assets.

2. True or False? Security education is an informal curriculum created for the purpose of educating individuals in a broad array of security topics that will build a body of knowledge essential for a career in information security.

3. True or False? Understanding user behavior and motivation is key to a successful SETA program.

4. True or False? Because the ultimate purpose of a SETA program is to change the behavior of users (and, this can be done without engaging them in a way that is memorable and effective), it is important that the design and development of the program be well thought out.

5. True or False? Implementing a SETA program can only be as effective as the planning put into the design and development of the program.

Multiple Choice

1. One of the techniques used to deliver an engaging security awareness program includes?
   A. Username
   B. Password
   C. Validations
   D. Security systems
   E. Computer-based training

2. Regardless of the techniques chosen to deliver the material, which feature is maintained throughout each of the methods or techniques implemented?
   A. Attack
   B. Choking
   C. Ease of use
   D. Security
   E. Questionnaire

3. What platform allows administrators to measure and monitor the delivery of emails to users and can be used to craft fake phishing emails that can be customized by department or region?
   A. Devices
   B. ThreatSIM
   C. Data
   D. Backups
   E. All of the above

4. What concept is required by information security personnel that requires higher education to be competent for their positions and to achieve a common body of knowledge that prepares them to enter the workforce?
   A. Security education
   B. Private plan
   C. Secure plan
   D. Virtual plan
   E. All of the above

5. What gets the word out to all personnel and helps everyone focus on building a security culture and a mature information security practice?
   A. Monitoring
   B. Securing
   C. Governing
   D. Security awareness
   E. All of the above

EXERCISE

Problem

How do you go about developing a security education training and awareness (SETA) program?

Hands-On Projects

Project

Where can you find existing security awareness training that your employees can take?

Case Projects

Problem

What type of cyber security training is available in order to brush up on your security knowledge and skills?

Optional Team Case Project

Problem

How can you improve the SETA program in your organization?

REFERENCES

[1] Department of Homeland Security Management Directive System, Security Education, Training, and Awareness Program Directive, 2004. https://www.dhs.gov/sites/default/files/publications/mgmt_directive_11053_security_education_training_and_awareness_program_directive.pdf.

[2] M. Wilson, J. Hash, Building and Information Technology Security Awareness and Training Program, National Institute of Standards and Technology, 2003. http://csrc.nist.gov/publications/nistpubs/800-50/NIST-SP800-50.pdf.

[3] Deleted in review.

[4] R.C. Martella, J.R. Nelson, N.E. Marchand-Martella, M. O'Reilly, Comprehensive Behavior Management: Individualized, Classroom, and Schoolwide Approaches, SAGE Publications, Inc., 2012, pp. 2–5.

[5] Deleted in review.

[6] Security Awareness Program Special Interest Group – PCI Security Standards Council, PCI Data Security Standard (PCI DSS) 1.0, 2014. https://www.pcisecuritystandards.org/documents/PCI_DSS_V1.0_Best_Practices_for_Implementing_Security_Awareness_Program.pdf.

[7] Wombat Security Technologies Website, 2016. https://www.wombatsecurity.com/.

Chapter 34

Risk Management

Sokratis K. Katsikas

University of Piraeus, Piraeus, Greece

Integrating security measures with the operational framework of an organization is neither a trivial nor an easy task. This explains to a large extent the low degree of security that information systems operating in contemporary businesses and organizations enjoy. Some of the most important problems that security professionals face when confronted with the task of introducing security measures in businesses and organizations are:

- the difficulty of justifying the cost of security measures
- the difficulty of establishing communication between technical and administrative personnel
- the difficulty of ensuring active participation of users in the effort to secure the information system and in committing higher management to supporting the effort continuously
- the widely accepted erroneous perception of information systems security as a purely technical issue
- the difficulty of developing an integrated, efficient, and effective information systems security plan
- identifying and assessing the organizational impact that the implementation of a security plan entails

The difficulty of justifying the cost of the security measures, particularly those of a procedural and administrative nature, stems from the very nature of security itself. Indeed, justification of the need for a security measure can be proved only "after the (unfortunate) event," whereas at the same time, there is no way to prove that already implemented measures can adequately cope with a potential new threat. This cost not only pertains to acquiring and installing mechanisms and tools for protection, it includes the cost of human resources, of educating and making users aware, and of carrying out tasks and procedures relevant to security.

The difficulty of expressing the cost of security measures in monetary terms is a fundamental factor that makes communication between technical and administrative personnel difficult. An immediate consequence of this is the difficulty of securing the continuous commitment of higher management to support the security enhancement effort. This becomes even more problematic when organizational and procedural security measures are proposed. Both management and users are concerned about the impact of these measures in their usual practice, particularly when the widely accepted concept that security is purely a technical issue is put into doubt.

Moreover, protecting an information system calls for an integrated, holistic study that will answer questions such as: Which elements of the information system do we want to protect? Which, among these, are the most important ones? What threats is the information system facing? What are its vulnerabilities? What security measures must be put in place? Answering these questions gives a good picture of the current state of the information system with regard to its security. As research[1] has shown, developing techniques and measures for security is not enough, because the most vulnerable point in any information system is the human user, operator, designer, or other human. Therefore, the development and operation of secure information systems must equally consider and take into account both technical and human factors. At the same time, the threats that an information system faces are characterized by variety, diversity, complexity, and continuous variation. As the technological and societal environment continuously evolves, threats change and evolve, too. Furthermore, both information systems and threats against them are dynamic; hence the need for continuous monitoring and managing of the information system security plan.

The most widely used methodology that aims to deal with these issues is information systems risk management. This methodology adopts the concept of risk that originates

---

1. E.A. Kiountouzis, S.A. Kokolakis, An analyst's view of information systems security, in: S.K. Katsikas, D. Gritzalis (Eds.), Information Systems Security: Facing the Information Society of the 21st Century, Chapman & Hall, 1996.

Computer and Information Security Handbook. http://dx.doi.org/10.1016/B978-0-12-803843-7.00034-X

in financial management and substitutes the unachievable and immeasurable goal of fully securing the information system with the achievable and measurable goal of reducing the risk that the information system faces to that within acceptable limits.

1. THE CONCEPT OF RISK

The concept of risk originated in the 17th century with the mathematics associated with gambling. At that time, risk referred to a combination of the probability and magnitude of potential gains and losses. During the 18th century, risk, which was seen as a neutral concept, still considered both gains and losses and was employed in the marine insurance business. In the 19th century, risk emerged in the study of economics. The concept of risk, which was thus seen more negatively, caused entrepreneurs to call for special incentives to take the risk involved in investment. By the 20th century, a total negative connotation was understood when referring to outcomes of risk in engineering and science, with particular reference to the hazards posed by modern technological developments.[2,3]

Within the field of information technology (IT) security, risk R is calculated as the product of P, the probability of an exposure occurring a given number of times per year times C, the cost or loss attributed to such an exposure: that is, $R = P \times C$.[4]

The most recent standardized definition of risk comes from the International Organization for Standardization (ISO),[5] which defines risk as "the effect of uncertainty on objectives." This definition, which is different from the past definition (2008) of the same standard, is the result of the process of aligning definitions within the ISO 27000 series of standards with those within the ISO 31000 series. Notwithstanding that this alignment facilitates the treatment of risk regardless of its kind (IT security, environmental, etc.) within an enterprise, it does not directly convey the true meaning of risk within the IT security context. Within this context, it makes much more sense to retain the older standardized definition of risk as "the potential that a given threat will exploit vulnerabilities of an asset or group of assets and thereby cause harm to the organization."

To complete this definition, definitions of the terms *threat*, *vulnerability*, and *asset* are in order. These are as follows: A threat is "a potential cause of an incident, that may result in harm to system or organization." A vulnerability is "a weakness of an asset or group of assets that can be exploited by one or more threats." An asset is "anything that has value to the organization, its business operations and their continuity, including information resources that support the organization's mission."[6] In addition, harm results in impact, which is "an adverse change to the level of business objectives achieved."[7] The relationships among these basic concepts are depicted in Fig. 34.1.

2. EXPRESSING AND MEASURING RISK

Information security risk "is measured in terms of a combination of the likelihood of an event and its consequence." Because we are interested in events related to information security, we define an information security event as "an identified occurrence of a system, service or network state indicating a possible breach of information security policy or failure of safeguards, or a previously unknown situation that may be security relevant."[8] In addition, an information security incident is "indicated by a single or a series of unwanted information security events that have a significant probability of compromising business operations and threatening information security." These definitions actually invert the investment assessment model, in which an investment is considered worth making when its cost is less than the product of the expected profit times the likelihood of the profit occurring. In our case, risk R is defined as the product of likelihood L of a security incident occurring times impact I that will be incurred to the organization owing to the incident: that is, $R = L \times I$.[9]

To measure risk, we adopt the fundamental principles and scientific background of statistics and probability theory, particularly of the area known as Bayesian statistics, after the mathematician Thomas Bayes (1702−1761), who formalized the namesake theorem. Bayesian statistics is based on the view that the likelihood of an event happening in the future is measurable. This likelihood can be calculated if the factors affecting it are analyzed. For example, we are able to compute the probability of our data being stolen as a

2. M. Gerber, R. von Solms, Management of risk in the information age, Comput. Secur. 24 (2005) 16−30.

3. M. Douglas, Risk as a forensic resource, Daedalus 119 (4) (1990) 1−17.

4. R. Courtney, Security risk assessment in electronic data processing, in: The AFIPS Conference Proceedings of the National Computer Conference 46, AFIPS, Arlington, 1977, pp. 97−104.

5. ISO/IEC, Information Technology—Security Techniques—Information Security Risk Management, ISO/IEC 27005:2011 (E).

6. British Standards Institute, Information Technology—Security Techniques—Management of Information and Communications Technology Security—Part 1: Concepts and Models for Information and Communications Technology Security Management, BS ISO/IEC 13335-1:2004.

7. ISO/IEC, Information Technology—Security Techniques—Information Security Risk Management, ISO/IEC 27005:2008 (E).

8. British Standards Institute, Information Technology—Security Techniques—Information Security Incident Management, BS ISO/IEC TR 18044:2004.

9. R. Baskerville, Information systems security design methods: implications for information systems development, ACM Comput. Surv. 25 (4) (1993) 375−414.

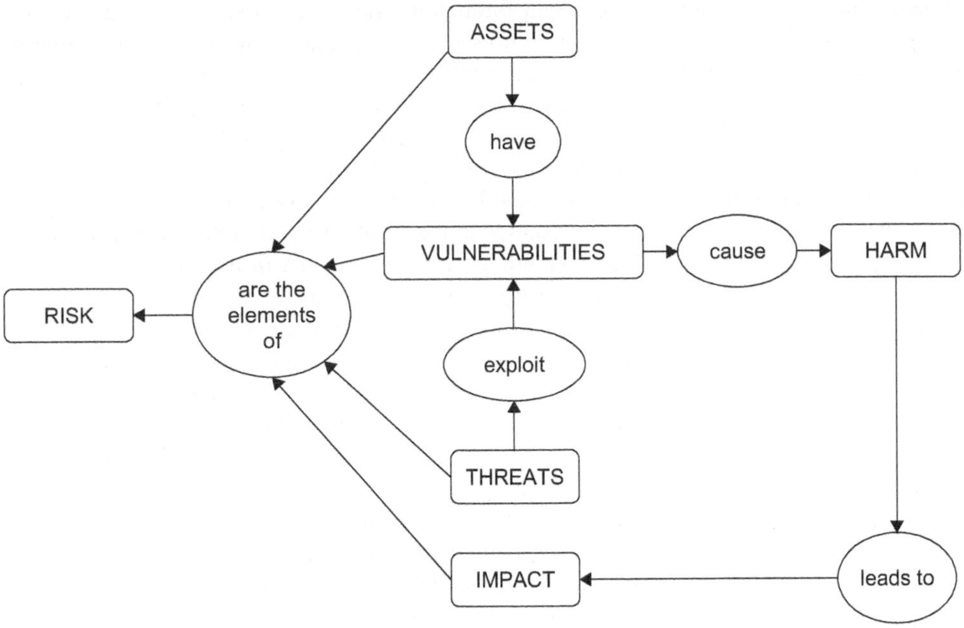

FIGURE 34.1 Risk and its related concepts.

function of the probability an intruder will attempt to intrude into our system and the probability that he will succeed. In risk analysis terms, the former probability corresponds to the likelihood of the threat occurring and the latter corresponds to the likelihood of the vulnerability being successfully exploited. Thus, risk analysis assesses the likelihood that a security incident will happen, by analyzing and assessing the factors that are related to its occurrence, namely the threats and the vulnerabilities. Subsequently, it combines this likelihood with the impact resulting from the incident occurring to calculate the system risk. Risk analysis is a necessary prerequisite for subsequently treating risk. Risk treatment pertains to controlling the risk so that it remains within acceptable levels. Risk can be reduced by applying security measures; it can be shared, by outsourcing or by insuring; it can be avoided; or it can be accepted, in the sense that the organization accepts the likely impact of a security incident.

The likelihood of a security incident occurring is a function of the likelihood that a threat appears and the likelihood that the threat can exploit the relevant system vulnerabilities successfully. The consequences of the occurrence of a security incident are a function of the likely impact the incident will have on the organization as a result of the harm that the organization assets will sustain. Harm, in turn, is a function of the value of the assets to the organization. Thus, risk R is a function of four elements: (1) V, the value of the assets; (2) T, the severity and likelihood of appearance of the threats; (3) V, the nature and extent of the vulnerabilities and the likelihood that a threat can successfully exploit them; and (4) I, the likely impact of the harm should the threat succeed: that is, $R = f(A, T, V, I)$.

If the impact is expressed in monetary terms, the likelihood is dimensionless, and then risk can be also expressed in monetary terms. This approach has the advantage of making the risk directly comparable to the cost of acquiring and installing security measures. Because security is often one of several competing alternatives for capital investment, the existence of a cost–benefit analysis that would offer proof that security will produce benefits that equal or exceed its cost is of great interest to the management of the organization. Of even more interest to management is an analysis of the investment opportunity costs: that is, its comparison with other capital investment options.[10] However, expressing risk in monetary terms is not always possible or desirable, because harm to some kinds of assets (human life) cannot (and should not) be assessed in monetary terms. This is why risk is usually expressed in nonmonetary terms, on a simple dimensionless scale.

Assets in an organization are usually diverse. Because of this diversity, it is likely that some assets that have a known monetary value (hardware) can be valued in the local currency, whereas others of a more qualitative nature (data or information) may be assigned a numerical value based on the organization's perception of their value. This value is assessed in terms of the assets' importance to the organization or their potential value in different business opportunities. The legal and business requirements are also taken into account, as are the impacts to the asset itself and to the

10. R. Baskerville, Risk analysis as a source of professional knowledge, Comput. Secur. 10 (1991) 749–764.

related business interests resulting from loss of one or more of the information security attributes (confidentiality, integrity, or availability). One way to express asset values is to use the business impacts that unwanted incidents, such as disclosure, modification, nonavailability, and/or destruction, would have on the asset and the related business interests that would be directly or indirectly damaged. An information security incident can affect more than one asset or only a part of an asset. Impact is related to the degree of success of the incident. Impact is considered to have either an immediate (operational) effect or a future (business) effect that includes financial and market consequences. An immediate (operational) impact is either direct or indirect.

A direct impact may result because of the financial replacement value of a lost (part of) asset or the cost of acquisition, configuration, and installation of the new asset or backup, or the cost of suspended operations resulting from the incident until the service provided by the asset(s) is restored. An indirect impact may result because financial resources needed to replace or repair an asset would have been used elsewhere (opportunity cost), or owing to the cost of interrupted operations or to potential misuse of information obtained through a security breach, or because of the violation of statutory or regulatory obligations or of ethical codes of conduct.

These considerations should be reflected in the asset values. This is why asset valuation (particularly of intangible assets) is usually done through impact assessment. Thus, impact valuation is not performed separately, but is embedded within the asset valuation process.

The responsibility for identifying a suitable asset valuation scale lies with the organization. Usually, a three-value scale (low, medium, and high) or a five-value scale (negligible, low, medium, high, and very high) is used.[11]

Threats can be classified as deliberate or accidental. The likelihood of deliberate threats depends on the motivation, knowledge, capacity, and resources available to possible attackers and the attractiveness of assets to sophisticated attacks. On the other hand, the likelihood of accidental threats can be estimated using statistics and experience. The likelihood of these threats might also be related to the organization's proximity to sources of danger, such as major roads or rail routes, and factories dealing with dangerous material such as chemical materials or oil. Also the organization's geographical location will affect the possibility of extreme weather conditions. The likelihood of human error (one of the most common accidental threats) and equipment malfunction should also be estimated. As already noted, the responsibility for identifying a suitable threat valuation scale lies with the organization. What is important here is that the interpretation of the levels be

consistent throughout the organization and clearly convey the differences between the levels to those responsible for providing input to the threat valuation process. For example, if a three-value scale is used, the value *low* can be interpreted to mean that it is not likely that the threat will occur; there are no incidents, statistics, or motives that indicate that this is likely to happen. The value *medium* can be interpreted to mean that it is possible that the threat will occur, there have been incidents in the past or statistics or other information that indicate that this or similar threats have occurred sometime before, or there is an indication that there might be some reasons for an attacker to carry out such an action. Finally, the value *high* can be interpreted to mean that the threat is expected to occur, there are incidents, statistics, or other information that indicate that the threat is likely to occur, or there might be strong reasons or motives for an attacker to carry out such an action.

Vulnerabilities can be related to the physical environment of the system, to the personnel, management, and administration procedures and security measures within the organization, to the business operations and service delivery, or to the hardware, software, or communications equipment and facilities. Vulnerabilities are reduced by installed security measures. The nature and extent as well as the likelihood of a threat successfully exploiting the three former classes of vulnerabilities can be estimated based on information on past incidents, on new developments and trends, and on experience. The nature and extent as well as the likelihood of a threat successfully exploiting the latter class, often termed technical vulnerabilities, can be estimated using automated vulnerability-scanning tools, security testing and evaluation, penetration testing, or code review. As in the case of threats, the responsibility for identifying a suitable vulnerability valuation scale lies with the organization. If a three-value scale is used, the value *low* can be interpreted to mean that the vulnerability is hard to exploit and the protection in place is good. The value *medium* can be interpreted to mean that the vulnerability might be exploited but some protection is in place. The value *high* can be interpreted to mean that it is easy to exploit the vulnerability and there is little or no protection in place.

3. THE RISK MANAGEMENT METHODOLOGY

The term *methodology* means an organized set of principles and rules that drives action in a particular field of knowledge. A *method* is a systematic and orderly procedure or process for attaining some objective. A *tool* is any instrument or apparatus that is necessary to the performance of some task. Thus, methodology is the study or description of methods. A methodology is instantiated and materializes by a set of methods, techniques, and tools. A methodology does not

---

11. British Standards Institute, ISMSs—Part 3: Guidelines for Information Security Risk Management, BS 7799-3:2006.

An Agenda for Action for the Risk Management Framework

A risk-based approach to security control selection and specification considers effectiveness, efficiency, and constraints owing to applicable laws, directives, executive orders, policies, standards, or regulations. The following activities related to managing organizational risk (also known as the Risk Management Framework) are paramount to an effective information security program and can be applied to both new and legacy information systems within the context of the system development life cycle and the enterprise architecture (check all tasks completed):

_____**1.** Categorize the information system and the information processed, stored, and transmitted by that system based on an impact analysis.

_____**2.** Select an initial set of baseline security controls for the information system based on the security categorization, tailoring and supplementing the security control baseline as needed based on organization assessment of risk and local conditions.

_____**3.** Implement the security controls and document how the controls are deployed within the information system and environment of operation.

_____**4.** Assess the security controls using appropriate procedures to determine the extent to which the controls are implemented correctly, operating as intended, and producing the desired outcome with respect to meeting the security requirements for the system.

_____**5.** Authorize information system operations based on a determination of the risk to organizational operations and assets, individuals, other organizations, and the nation, resulting from operation of the information system and the decision that this risk is acceptable.

_____**6.** Monitor and assess selected security controls in the information system on an ongoing basis including assessing security control effectiveness, documenting changes to the system or environment of operation, conducting security impact analyses of the associated changes, and reporting the security state of the system to appropriate organizational officials.

TABLE 34.1 Risk Management Constituent Processes

ISO/IEC 27005:2011 (E)	BS 7799-3:2006	SP 800–30
Context establishment	Organizational context	
Risk assessment	Risk assessment	Risk assessment
Risk treatment	Risk treatment and management decision making	Risk mitigation
Risk acceptance		
Risk communication and consultation	Ongoing risk management activities	
Risk monitoring and review		Evaluation and assessment

BS, British Standard; *IEC*, International Electrotechnical Commission; *ISO*, International Organization for Standardization; *SP*, Special Publication.

describe specific methods; nevertheless, it specifies several processes that need to be followed. These processes constitute a generic framework (see checklist: "An Agenda for Action for the Risk Management Framework"). They may be broken down into subprocesses or combined, or their sequence may change. However, every risk management exercise must carry out these processes in some form or another.

Risk management consists of six processes: context establishment, risk assessment, risk treatment, risk acceptance, risk communication and consultation, and risk monitoring and review. This is more or less in line with the approach in which four processes are identified as the constituents of risk management: putting information security risks in the organizational context, risk assessment, risk treatment, and management decision making and ongoing risk management activities. Alternatively, risk management

is composed of three processes: risk assessment, risk mitigation, and evaluation and assessment.[12] Table 34.1 depicts the relationships among these processes.

Context Establishment

The context establishment process receives as input all relevant information about the organization. Establishing the context for information security risk management determines the purpose of the process. It involves setting basic criteria to be used in the process, defining the scope and boundaries of the process, and establishing an appropriate organization

---

12. G. Stoneburner, A. Goguen, A. Feringa, Risk Management Guide for Information Technology Systems, National Institute of Standards and Technology, Special Publication SP 800-30, 2002.

operating the process. The output of the context establishment process is the specification of these parameters.

The purpose may be to support an information security management system (ISMS); to comply with legal requirements and provide evidence of due diligence; to prepare for a business continuity plan; to prepare for an incident reporting plan; or to describe the information security requirements for a product, service, or mechanism. Combinations of these purposes are also possible.

Basic criteria include risk evaluation, impact, and risk acceptance. When setting risk evaluation criteria, the organization should consider the strategic value of the business information process; the criticality of the information assets involved; legal and regulatory requirements and contractual obligations; operational and business importance of the attributes of information security; and stakeholders' expectations and perceptions, and negative consequences for goodwill and reputation. Impact criteria specify the degree of damage or costs to the organization caused by an information security event. Developing impact criteria involves considering the level of classification of the impacted information asset; breaches of information security; impaired operations; loss of business and financial value; disruption of plans and deadlines; damage to reputation; and breach of legal, regulatory, or contractual requirements. Risk acceptance criteria depend on the organization's policies, goals, and objectives, and the interest of its stakeholders. When developing risk acceptance criteria, the organization should consider business criteria, legal and regulatory aspects, operations, technology, finance, and social and humanitarian factors.

The scope of the process needs to be defined to ensure that all relevant assets are taken into account in the subsequent risk assessment. Any exclusion from the scope needs to be justified. In addition, the boundaries need to be identified to address risks that might arise through these boundaries. When defining the scope and boundaries, the organization needs to consider its strategic business objectives, strategies, and policies; its business processes; its functions and structure; applicable legal, regulatory, and contractual requirements; its information security policy; its overall approach to risk management; its information assets; its locations and their geographical characteristics; constraints that affect it; expectations of its stakeholders; its sociocultural environment; and its information exchange with its environment. This involves studying the organization (its main purpose, its business; its mission; its values; its structure; its organizational chart; and its strategy). It also involves identifying its constraints. These may be of a political, cultural, or strategic nature; they may be territorial, organizational, structural, functional, personnel, budgetary, technical, or environmental constraints; or they could be constraints arising from preexisting processes. Finally, it entails identifying legislation, regulations, and contracts.

Setting up and maintaining the organization for information security risk management fulfills part of the requirement to determine and provide the resources needed to establish, implement, operate, monitor, review, maintain, and improve an ISMS.[13] The organization to be developed will bear responsibility for developing the information security risk management process suitable for the organization; for identifying and analyzing the stakeholders; for defining roles and responsibilities of all parties, both external and internal to the organization; for establishing the required relationships between the organization and stakeholders, interfaces to the organization's high-level risk management functions, as well as interfaces to other relevant projects or activities; for defining decision escalation paths; and for specifying records to be kept. Key roles in this organization are the senior management, the chief information officer, the system and information owners, the business and functional managers, the information systems security officers, the IT security practitioners, and the security awareness trainers (security/subject matter professionals). Additional roles that can be explicitly defined are those of the *risk assessor* and of the *security risk manager*.

Risk Assessment

This process is composed of three subprocesses: risk identification, risk analysis, and risk evaluation. The process receives as input the output of the context establishment process. It identifies, quantifies, or qualitatively describes risks and prioritizes them against the risk evaluation criteria established within the course of the context establishment process and according to objectives relevant to the organization. It is often conducted in more than one iteration, the first of which is a high-level assessment aiming to identify potentially high risks that warrant further assessment; the second and possibly subsequent iterations entail further in-depth examination of potentially high risks revealed in the first iteration. The output of the process is a list of assessed risks prioritized according to risk evaluation criteria.

Risk identification seeks to determine what could happen to cause a potential loss and to gain insight into how, where, and why the loss might happen. It involves a number of steps, such as identification of assets, identification of threats, identification of existing security measures, identification of vulnerabilities, and identification of consequences. Input to the subprocess is the scope and boundaries for the risk assessment to be conducted, an asset inventory, information on possible threats, documentation of existing security measures, possibly preexisting risk treatment implementation plans, and the list of business processes. The output of the subprocess is a list of assets to

13. ISO/IEC, Information Security Management—Specification with Guidance for Use, ISO 27001.

be risk-managed together with a list of business processes related to these assets; a list of threats on these assets; a list of existing and planned security measures, their implementation, and usage status; a list of vulnerabilities related to assets, threats, and already installed security measures; a list of vulnerabilities that do not relate to any identified threat; and a list of incident scenarios with their consequences, related to assets and business processes.

Two kinds of assets can be distinguished: *primary assets*, which include business processes and activities and information; and *supporting assets*, which include hardware, software, network, personnel, site, and the organization's structure. Hardware assets are composed of data-processing equipment (transportable and fixed), peripherals, and media. Software assets are composed of the operating system; service, maintenance, or administration software; and application software. Network assets are composed of media and supports, passive or active relays, and communication interfaces. Personnel assets are composed of decision makers, users, operation/maintenance staff, and developers. Site assets are composed of the location (and its external environment, premises, zone, essential services, and communication and utilities characteristics) and the organization (and its authorities, structure, the project or system organization and its subcontractors, suppliers, and manufacturers).

Threats are classified according to their type and origin. Threat types are physical damage (fire, water, or pollution); natural events (climatic, seismic, or volcanic phenomena); loss of essential services (failure of air-conditioning, loss of power supply, or failure of telecommunication equipment); disturbance caused by radiation (electromagnetic radiation, thermal radiation, or electromagnetic pulses); compromise of information (eavesdropping, theft of media or documents, or retrieval of discarded or recycled media); technical failures (equipment failure, software malfunction, or saturation of the information system); unauthorized actions (fraudulent copying of software, corruption of data, or unauthorized use of equipment); and compromise of functions (error in use, abuse of rights, or denial of actions). Threats are classified according to origin into deliberate, accidental, or environmental. A deliberate threat is an action aimed at information assets (remote spying or illegal processing of data); an accidental threat is an action that can accidentally damage information assets (equipment failure or software malfunction); and an environmental threat is any threat that is not based on human action (a natural event or loss of power supply). Note that a threat type may have multiple origins.

Vulnerabilities are classified according to the asset class to which they relate. Therefore, vulnerabilities are classified as hardware (susceptibility to humidity, dust, or soiling; or unprotected storage); software (no or insufficient software testing, or lack of an audit trail); network (unprotected communication lines or insecure network architecture); personnel (inadequate recruitment processes or lack of security awareness); site (location in an area susceptible to flood, or unstable power grid); and organization (lack of regular audits or lack of continuity plans).

Risk analysis is done either quantitatively or qualitatively. Qualitative analysis uses a scale of qualifying attributes to describe the magnitude of potential consequences (low, medium, or high) and the likelihood these consequences will occur. Quantitative analysis uses a scale with numerical values for both consequences and likelihood. In practice, qualitative analysis is used first, to obtain a general indication of the level of risk and to reveal the major risks. It is followed by a quantitative analysis of the major risks identified.

Risk analysis involves a number of steps, such as assessing consequences (through valuating assets), assessing incident likelihood (through valuating threat and vulnerability), and determining the risk level. We discussed valuating assets, threats, and vulnerabilities in an earlier section. Input to the subprocess is the output of the risk identification subprocess. Its output is a list of risks with value levels assigned.

Having valuated assets, threats, and vulnerabilities, we should be able to calculate the resulting risk if the function relating these to risk is known. Establishing an analytic function for this purpose is probably impossible and certainly ineffective. This is why, in practice, an empirical matrix is used for this purpose. Such a matrix links asset values and threat and vulnerability levels to the resulting risk; an example this is shown in Table 34.2. In this example, asset values are expressed on a scale of 0 to10, whereas threat and vulnerability levels are expressed on a scale of low—medium—high. Risk values are expressed on a scale of 1 to 7. When linking the asset values and the threats and vulnerabilities, consideration needs to be given to whether the threat—vulnerability combination could cause problems to confidentiality, integrity, and/or availability. Depending on the results of these considerations, the appropriate asset value(s) should be chosen: that is, the one that has been selected to express the impact of a loss of confidentiality, integrity, or availability. Using this method can lead to multiple risks for each asset, depending on the particular threat—vulnerability combination considered.

Finally, the risk evaluation process receives as input the output of the risk analysis process. It compares the levels of risk against the risk evaluation criteria and risk acceptance criteria that were established within the context establishment process. The process uses the understanding of risk obtained by the risk assessment process to make decisions about future actions. These decisions include whether an activity should be undertaken and sets priorities for risk treatment. The output of the process is a list of risks prioritized according to the risk evaluation criteria, in relation to the incident scenarios that lead to those risks.

Risk Treatment

When the risk is calculated, the risk assessment process finishes. However, our actual ultimate goal is to treat the

TABLE 34.2 Example Risk Calculation Matrix

Asset Value	Level of Threat								
	Low (L)			Medium (M)			High (H)		
	Level of Vulnerability								
	L	M	H	L	M	H	L	M	H
0	0	1	1	1	2	2	2	3	3
1	1	1	2	2	2	3	3	3	3
2	1	1	2	2	2	3	3	3	3
3	2	2	2	3	3	3	3	4	4
4	2	2	3	3	3	4	4	4	5
5	2	3	3	4	4	4	4	5	5
6	3	3	4	4	4	4	4	5	6
7	3	3	4	5	5	5	5	5	6
8	3	3	4	5	6	6	6	6	6
9	3	4	4	5	6	6	6	7	7
10	3	4	5	5	6	6	6	7	7

risk. The risk treatment process aims to select security measures to reduce, retain, avoid, or transfer the risks and to define a risk treatment plan. The process receives as input the output of the risk assessment process and produces as output the risk treatment plan and the residual risks subject to the acceptance decision by the management of the organization.

Options available to treat risk are to modify it, retain it, avoid it, or share it. Combinations of these options are also possible. Factors that might influence the decision are the cost each time the incident related to the risk happens; how frequently it is expected to happen; the organization's attitude toward risk; the ease of implementation of the security measures required to treat the risk; the resources available; the current business/technology priorities; and organizational and management politics.

For all risks for which the option to modify the risk has been chosen, appropriate security measures should be implemented to reduce the risks to the level that has been identified as acceptable, or at least as much as is feasible toward that level. The questions then arise: How much can we reduce the risk? Is it possible to achieve zero risk?

Zero risk is possible when either the cost of an incident is zero or the likelihood of the incident occurring is zero. The cost of an incident is zero when the value of the implicated asset is zero or the impact to the organization is zero. Therefore, if one or more of these conditions is found to hold during the risk assessment process, it is meaningless to take security measures. On the other hand, the likelihood

of an incident occurring being zero is not possible because the threats faced by an open system operate in a dynamic and hence highly variable environment, as contemporary information systems do, and the causes that generate them are extremely complex; human behavior, which is extremely difficult to predict and model, has an important role in securing information systems, and the resources that a business or organization has at its disposal are finite.

When faced with a nonzero risk, our interest focuses on reducing the risk to acceptable levels. Because risk is a nondecreasing function in all of its constituents, security measures can reduce it by reducing these constituents. Because the asset value cannot be reduced directly,[14] it is possible to reduce risk by reducing the likelihood of the threat occurring or the likelihood of the vulnerability being exploited successfully or the impact if the threat succeeds. Which of these ways (or a combination of them) an organization chooses to adopt to protect its assets is a business decision and depends on the business requirements, the environment, and the circumstances in which the organization needs to operate. There is no universal or common approach to the selection of security measures. A possibility

---

14. As we will see later, it is possible to indirectly reduce the value of an asset. For example, if sensitive personal data are stored and the cost of protecting them is high, it is possible to decide that such data are too costly to continue storing. This constitutes a form of risk avoidance. As another example, we may decide that the cost for protecting our equipment is too high and to resort to outsourcing. This is a form of risk sharing.

is to assign numerical values to the efficiency of each security measure, on a scale matching that in which risks are expressed, and to select all security measures that are relevant to the particular risk and have an efficiency score at least equal to the value of the risk. Several sources provide lists of potential security measures.[15] It is important to document the selected security measures in supporting certification; it enables the organization to track implementation of the selected security measures.

When considering modifying (reducing) a risk, several constraints may appear. These may be related to the time frame, financial or technical issues, the way the organization operates or its culture, the environment within which the organization operates, the applicable legal framework or ethics, the ease of use of the appropriate security measures, the availability and suitability of personnel, to the difficulties of integrating new and existing security measures. Owing to the existence of these constraints, it is likely that some risks will exist for which either the organization cannot install appropriate security measures or the cost of implementing appropriate measures will outweigh the potential loss from the incident occurring related to the risk. In these cases, a decision may be made to retain the risk and live with the consequences if the incident related to the risk occurs. These decisions must be documented so that management is aware of its risk position and can knowingly retain the risk. The importance of this documentation has led risk acceptance to be identified as a separate process. A special case for which particular attention must be paid is when an incident related to a risk is deemed to be highly unlikely to occur but if it occurred, the organization would not survive. If such a risk is deemed to be unacceptable but too costly to reduce, the organization could decide to share it.

Risk sharing is an option in which it is difficult for the organization to reduce the risk to an acceptable level or the risk can be more economically shared with a third party. Risks can be shared using insurance. In this case, the question of what is a fair premium arises.[16] Another possibility is to use third parties or outsourcing partners to handle critical business assets or processes if they are suitably qualified for doing so. Combining both options is also possible; in this case, the fair premium may be determined.[17]

Risk avoidance describes any action in which business activities or ways to conduct business are changed to avoid a risk occurring. For example, risk avoidance can be achieved by not conducting certain business activities, by moving assets away from an area of risk, or by deciding not to process particularly sensitive information. Risk avoidance entails the organization to accept consciously that the impact is likely to occur if an incident occurs. However, the organization chooses not to install the required security measures to reduce the risk. There are several cases in which this option is exercised, particularly when the required measures contradict the culture and/or the policy of the organization.

After the risk treatment decision(s) have been taken, there will always be remaining risks. These are called *residual risks*. Residual risks can be difficult to assess, but at least an estimate should be made to ensure that sufficient protection is achieved. If the residual risk is unacceptable, the risk treatment process should be repeated.

Once the risk treatment decisions have been taken, activities to implement these decisions need to be identified and planned. The risk treatment plan needs to identify limiting factors and dependencies, priorities, deadlines and milestones, resources, including any necessary approvals for their allocation, and the critical path of the implementation.

Risk Communication and Consultation

Risk communication is a horizontal process that interacts bidirectionally with all other processes of risk management. Its purpose is to establish a common understanding of all aspects of risk among all the organization's stakeholders. Common understanding does not come automatically, because it is likely that perceptions of risk vary widely owing to differences in assumptions, needs, concepts, and concerns. Establishing a common understanding is important, because it influences decisions to be taken and the ways in which such decisions are implemented. Risk communication must be made according to a well-defined plan that should include provisions for risk communication under both normal and emergency conditions.

Risk Monitoring and Review

Risk management is an ongoing, never-ending process that is assigned to an individual, a team, or an outsourced third party, depending on the organization's size and operational characteristics. Within this process, implemented security measures are regularly monitored and reviewed to ensure that they function correctly and effectively and that changes in the environment have not rendered them ineffective. Because there is a tendency over time for the performance of any service or mechanism to deteriorate, monitoring is intended to detect this deterioration and initiate corrective

15. British Standards Institute, Information Technology—Security Techniques—Information Security Incident Management, BS ISO/IEC 17799:2005.

16. C. Lambrinoudakis, S. Gritzalis, P. Hatzopoulos, A.N. Yannacopoulos, S.K. Katsikas, A formal model for pricing information systems insurance contracts, Comput. Stand. Interfaces 27 (2005) 521–532.

17. S. Gritzalis, A.N. Yannacopoulos, C. Lambrinoudakis, P. Hatzopoulos, S.K. Katsikas, A probabilistic model for optimal insurance contracts against security risks and privacy violation in IT outsourcing environments, Int. J. Inf. Secur. 6 (2007) 197–211.

action. Maintenance of security measures should be planned and performed on a regular, scheduled basis.

Results from an original security risk assessment exercise need to be reviewed regularly for change, because several factors could change the originally assessed risks. Such factors may be the introduction of new business functions, a change in business objectives and/or processes, a review of the correctness and effectiveness of the implemented security measures, the appearance of new or changed threats and/or vulnerabilities, or changes external to the organization. After all of these different changes have been taken into account, the risk should be recalculated and *necessary* changes to the risk treatment decisions and security measures should be identified and documented.

Regular internal audits should be scheduled and conducted by an independent party that does not need to be from outside the organization. Internal auditors should not be under the supervision or control of those responsible for the implementation or daily management of the ISMS. In addition, audits by an external body are not only useful, they are essential for certification.

Finally, complete, accessible, and correct documentation and a controlled process to manage documents are necessary to support the ISMS, although the scope and detail will vary from organization to organization. Aligning these documentation details with the documentation requirements of other management systems, such as ISO 9001, is certainly possible and constitutes good practice. Fig. 34.2 summarizes different processes within the risk management methodology, as we discussed earlier.

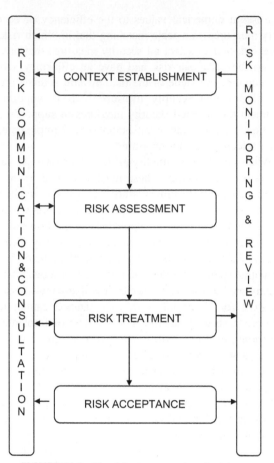

FIGURE 34.2 The risk management methodology.

Integrating Risk Management into the System Development Life Cycle

Risk management must be totally integrated into the system development life cycle. This cycle consists of five phases: initiation, development or acquisition, implementation, operation or maintenance, and disposal. Within the initiation phase, identified risks are used to support the development of the system requirements, including security requirements and a security concept of operations. In the development or acquisition phase, the risks identified can be used to support the security analyses of the system that may lead to architecture and design trade-offs during system development. In the implementation phase, the risk management process supports the assessment of the system implementation against its requirements and within its modeled operational environment. In the operation or maintenance phase, risk management activities are whenever major changes are made to a system in its operational environment. Finally, in the disposal phase,

risk management activities are performed for system components that will be disposed of or replaced to ensure that the hardware and software are properly disposed of, that residual data are appropriately handled, and that system migration is conducted in a secure and systematic manner.

Critique of Risk Management as a Methodology

Risk management as a scientific methodology has been criticized as being shallow. The main reason for this strong and probably unfair criticism is that risk management does not provide for feedback of the results of the selected security measures or of the risk treatment decisions. In most cases, although the trend has already changed, information systems security is a low-priority project for management until some security incident happens. Then, and only then, does management seriously engage in an effort to improve security measures. However, after a while, the problem stops being at the center of interest, and what remains is a number of security measures, some specialized hardware and software, and an operationally more complex system. Unless an incident happens again, there is no way for management to know whether the efforts were really worthwhile. After all, in many cases the information system had operated for years in the past without problems, without the security improvements that the security professionals recommended.

The risk management methodology, as stated, is based on the scientific foundations of statistical decision making. The Bayes theorem, on which the theory is based, pertains to the statistical revision of a priori probabilities, providing a posteriori probabilities, and is applied when a decision is sought based on imperfect information. In risk management, the decision for quantifying an event may be a function of additional factors other than the probability of the event itself occurring. For example, the probability that a riot will occur may be related to the stability of the political system. Thus, the calculation of this probability should involve quantified information relevant to the stability of the political system. The overall model accepts the possibility that any information ("The political system is stable") may be inaccurate. Compared with this formal framework, risk management, as applied by the security professionals, is simplistic. Indeed, by avoiding the complexity that accompanies the formal probabilistic modeling of risks and uncertainty, risk management looks more like a process that attempts to guess rather than formally predict the future on the basis of statistical evidence.

Finally, the risk management methodology is highly subjective in assessing the value of assets, the likelihood of threats occurring, the likelihood of vulnerabilities being successfully exploited by threats, and the significance of the impact. This subjectivity is frequently obscured by the formality of the underlying mathematical-probabilistic models, the systematic way in which most risk analysis methods work, and the objectivity of the tools that support these methods.

If indeed skepticism about the scientific soundness of the risk management methodology is justified, the question becomes crucial: Why, then, has risk management as a practice survived for so long? There are several answers to this question.

Risk management is an important instrument for designing, implementing, and operating secure information systems because it systematically classifies and drives the process of deciding how to treat risks. In doing so, it facilitates a better understanding of the nature and operation of the information system, thus constituting a means to document and analyze the system. Therefore, it is necessary for supporting the efforts of the organization's management to design, implement, and operate secure information systems.

Traditionally, risk management has been seen by security professionals as a means to justify to management the cost of security measures. Nowadays, it not only does

that, it also fulfills legislative and/or regulatory provisions that exist in several countries, which demand information systems to be protected in a manner commensurate with the threats they face.

Risk management constitutes an efficient means of communication between technical and administrative personnel, as well as management, because it allows us to express the security problem in a language comprehensible by management, by viewing security as an investment that can be assessed in terms of cost–benefit analysis. In addition, it is flexible, so it can fit into several scientific frameworks and be applied either by itself or combined with other methodologies. It is the most widely used methodology for designing and managing information systems security and has been applied successfully in many cases.

Finally, an answer frequently offered by security professionals is that there simply is no other efficient way to carry out the tasks that risk management does. Indeed, it has been proved in practice that simply by using methods of management science, law, and accounting, it is not possible to reach conclusions that can adequately justify risk treatment decisions.

Risk Management Methods

Many methods for risk management are available today. Most are supported by software tools. Selecting the most suitable method for a specific business environment and the needs of a specific organization is important, albeit difficult, for a number of reasons[18]:

- There is a lack of a complete inventory of all available methods, with all their individual characteristics.
- No commonly accepted set of evaluation criteria exists for risk management methods.
- Some methods cover only parts of the whole risk management process. For example, some methods only calculate the risk without covering the risk treatment process. Some others focus on a small part of the whole process (e.g., disaster recovery planning). Some focus on auditing the security measures, and so on.
- Risk management methods differ widely in the analysis level that they use. Some use high-level descriptions of the information system under study; others call for detailed descriptions.
- Some methods are not freely available to the market, a fact that makes their evaluation difficult, if at all possible.

18. R. Moses, A European standard for risk analysis, in: Proceedings, 10th World Conference on Computer Security, Audit and Control, Elsevier Advanced Technology, 1993, pp. 527–541.

In 1991 the National Institute of Standards and Technology (NIST) compiled a comprehensive report on risk management methods and tools.[19] Recognizing the need for a homogenized and software-supported risk management methodology for use by European businesses and organizations, in 1993 the European Commission assigned a similar project to a group of companies. Part of this project's results was the creation of an inventory and the evaluation of all available risk management methods at the time.[20] In 2006 the European Network and Information Security Agency repeated the endeavor. Although some results toward an inventory of risk management/risk assessment methods have been made available,[21] the process is ongoing.[22] Some of the most widely used risk management methods are briefly described in the sequel.

The Central Communication and Telecommunication Agency (CCTA) Risk Analysis and Management Methodology (CRAMM)[23] is a method developed by the British government organization CCTA, now renamed the Office of Government Commerce. CRAMM was first released in 1985. Currently CRAMM is the UK government's preferred risk analysis method, but CRAMM is also used in many countries outside the United Kingdom. CRAMM is especially appropriate for large organizations such as government bodies and industry. CRAMM provides a staged and disciplined approach embracing both technical and nontechnical aspects of security. To assess these components, CRAMM is divided into three stages: asset identification and valuation, threat and vulnerability assessment, and countermeasure selection and recommendation. CRAMM enables the reviewer to identify the physical, software, data, and location assets that make up the information system. Each of these assets can be valued. Physical assets are valued in terms of their replacement cost. Data and software assets are valued in terms of the impact that would result if the information were to be unavailable, destroyed, disclosed, or modified. CRAMM covers the full range of deliberate and accidental threats

that may affect information systems. This stage concludes by calculating the level of risk. CRAMM contains a large countermeasure library consisting of over 3000 detailed countermeasures organized into over 70 logical groupings. The CRAMM software uses the measures of risks determined during the previous stage and compares them against the security level (a threshold level associated with each countermeasure) to identify whether the risks are sufficiently large to justify the installation of a particular countermeasure. CRAMM provides a series of help facilities, including backtracking, what-if scenarios, prioritization functions, and reporting tools, to assist with implementing countermeasures and actively managing identified risks. CRAMM is ISO/International Electrotechnical Commission (IEC) 17799, ISO/IEC 27001, Gramm–Leach–Bliley Act, and Health Insurance Portability and Accountability Act (HIPAA) compliant.

MAGERIT is an open methodology for risk analysis and management developed by the Spanish Ministry of Public Administration, offered as a framework and guide to the public administration. Given its open nature, it is also used outside the administration. MAGERIT was first released in 1997. Version 2 was published in 2005 and is structured into three books. Book I (Methodology) describes the core steps and basic tasks to carry out a project for risk analysis and management, the formal description of the project, and application to the development of information systems. It provides a large number of practical clues as well as the theoretical foundations, together with some other complementary information. Book II (Catalog of Elements) provides standard elements and criteria for information systems and risk modeling: asset classes, valuation dimensions, valuation criteria, typical threats, and safeguards to be considered. It also describes reports containing findings and conclusions (value model, risk map, safeguard evaluation, risk status, deficiencies report, and security plan), thus contributing to achieve uniformity. Book III (Practical Techniques) describes techniques frequently used to carry out risk analysis and management projects, such as tabular and algorithmic analysis; threat trees, cost–benefit analysis, data-flow diagrams, process charts, graphical techniques, project planning, working sessions (interviews, meetings, and presentations), and Delphi analysis.[24] Application of MAGERIT is supported by the software PILAR/EAR, which exploits and increases its potentialities and effectiveness.[25]

19. NIST, Description of Automated Risk Management Packages that NIST/NCSC Risk Management Research Laboratory Have Examined, March 1991. Available at: http://w2.eff.org/Privacy/Newin/New_nist/risktool.txt.
20. INFOSEC 1992, Project S2014—Risk Analysis, Risk Analysis Methods Database, January 1993.
21. ENISA Technical Department (Section Risk Management), Risk Management: Implementation Principles and Inventories for Risk Management/Risk Assessment Methods and Tools, June 2006. Available at: http://www.enisa.europa.eu/activities/risk-management/current-risk/risk-management-inventory/files/deliverables/risk-management-principles-and-inventories-for-risk-management-risk-assessment-methods-and-tools/at_download/fullReport.
22. Risk Management, © 2005–2012 by the European Network and Information Security Agency (ENISA), ENISA – European Network and Information Security Agency, P.O. Box 1309, 71,001 Heraklion, Crete, Greece, 2012. http://www.enisa.europa.eu/activities/risk-management.
23. CRAMM, © Siemens Enterprise 2011, 2012. www.cramm.com.
24. Ministerio de Administraciones Publicas, MAGERIT—version 2, Methodology for Information Systems Risk Analysis and Management, Book I – The Method. Available at: http://administracionelectronica.gob.es/?_nfpb=true&_pageLabel=PAE_PG_CTT_Area_Descargas&langPae=es&iniciativa=184.
25. EAR/PILAR Environment for the Analysis of Risk, 2012. http://www.pilar-tools.com/en/index.html.

The methodological approach offered by Expression des Besoins et Identification des Objectifs de Sécurité (EBIOS)[26] provides a global and consistent view of information systems security. It was first released in 1995. The method takes into account all technical entities and nontechnical entities. It allows all personnel using the information system to be involved in security issues and offers a dynamic approach that encourages interaction among the organization's various jobs and functions by examining the complete life cycle of the system. Promoted by the Direction Centrale de la Sécurité des Systèmes d' Information of the French government and recognized by the French administrations, EBIOS is also a reference in the private sector and outside France. The EBIOS approach consists of five phases. Phase 1 deals with context analysis in terms of global business process dependence on the information system. Security needs analysis, and threat analyses are conducted in Phases 2 and 3. Phases 4 and 5 yield objective diagnostics on risks. The necessary and sufficient security objectives (and further security requirements) are then stated, proof of coverage is furnished, and residual risks made explicit. Local standard bases (German IT-Grundschutz) are easily added on to its internal knowledge bases and catalogs of best practices. EBIOS is supported by a software tool developed by the Central Information Systems Security Division (France). The tool helps the user to produce all risk analysis and management steps according to the EBIOS method and allows all of the study results to be recorded and the required summary documents to be produced. EBIOS is compliant with ISO/IEC 27001, ISO/IEC 13335 (GMITS), ISO/IEC 15408 (Common Criteria), ISO/IEC 17799, and ISO/IEC 21827, and is consistent with the ISO/IEC 31000, ISO/IEC 27005, and ISO/IEC 27001 standards.

The Information Security Forum's (ISF's) Standard of Good Practice[27] provides a set of high-level principles and objectives for information security together with associated statements of good practice. The Standard of Good Practice is split into five distinct aspects, each of which covers a particular type of environment: security management, critical business applications, computer installations, networks, and systems development. Fundamental Information Risk Management (FIRM) is a detailed method for monitoring and controlling information risk at the enterprise level. It has been developed as a practical approach to monitor the effectiveness of information security. As such, it enables

information risk to be managed systematically across enterprises of all sizes. It includes comprehensive implementation guidelines, which explain how to gain support for the approach and get it up and running. The Information Risk Scorecard is an integral part of FIRM. The Scorecard is a form used to collect a range of important details about a particular information resource such as the name of the owner, criticality, the level of threat, business impact, and vulnerability. The ISF's Information Security Status Survey is a comprehensive risk management tool that evaluates a wide range of security measures used by organizations to control the business risks associated with their IT-based information systems. Simple to Apply Risk Analysis (SARA) is a detailed method for analyzing information risk in critical information systems. Simplified Process for Risk Identification (SPRINT) is a relatively quick and easy-to-use method for assessing business impact and analyzing information risk in important but not critical information systems. The full SPRINT method is intended for application to important but not critical systems. It complements the SARA method, which is better suited to analyzing risks associated with critical business systems. SPRINT first helps decide the level of risk associated with a system. After the risks are fully understood, SPRINT determines how to proceed and, if the SPRINT process continues, culminates in the production of an agreed plan of action for keeping risks within acceptable limits. SPRINT can identify the vulnerabilities of existing systems and the safeguards needed to protect against them, and define the security requirements for systems under development and the security measures needed to satisfy them. The method is compliant with ISO/IEC 17799. The method was revised in 2011, which aligns with requirements for ISMS set out in ISO 27001 and provides a wider and deeper coverage of ISO 27002 controls topics. It particularly covers many new topics such as cloud computing, information leakage, consumer devices, and security governance. Furthermore, the 2011 Standard provides full coverage of COBIT v4 topics and offers substantial alignment with other relevant standards and legislation such as Payment Card Industry (PCI)−Data Security Standard (DSS) and the Sarbanes−Oxley Act.

IT-Grundschutz (IT baseline protection)[28] provides a method for an organization to establish an ISMS. It was first released in 1994. The full method, to which we will come back in Section 5, describes an ISMS composed of a governance structure and a suite of information security controls ranging from technological, organizational, and sociological to infrastructural (physical) in nature. In its present form the IT-Grundschutz is composed of several

26. EBIOS 2010 − Expression of Needs and Identification of Security Objectives, © French Network and Information Security Agency (FNISA) 2012, 2012. http://www.ssi.gouv.fr/en/the-anssi/publications-109/methods-to-achieve-iss/ebios-2010-expression-of-needs-and-identification-of-security-objectives.html.
27. Information Security Forum, The Standard of Good Practice for Information Security, 2007 and 2011. Available at: https://www.securityforum.org/downloadresearch/downloadsogp/.

28. IT-Grundschutz, © Federal Office for Information Security (BSI). All rights reserved, 2012. https://www.bsi.bund.de/ContentBSI/EN/Topics/ITGrundschutz/itgrundschutz.html.

parts, so the methods are separate from the catalog of threats. The part describing the risk analysis method is BSI Standard 100-3 "Risk Analysis Based on IT-Grundschutz," which uses the catalogs to specify security controls for "normal" systems that are assumed to have "normal" risks, using risk analysis only to identify additional risk and control requirements for "high" or "very high" systems. The IT security process suggested by IT-Grundschutz consists of the following steps: initialization of the process; definition of IT security goals and business environment; establishment of an organizational structure for IT security; provision of necessary resources; creation of the IT security concept; IT structure analysis; assessment of protection requirements; modeling; IT security check; supplementary security analysis; implementation planning and fulfillment; maintenance, monitoring, and improvement of the process; and IT-Grundschutz Certification (optional). IT-Grundschutz is supported by a software tool named *Gstool*,[29] which was developed by the Federal Office for Information Security (BSI). The method is compliant with ISO/IEC 17799 and ISO/IEC 27001.

Méthode Harmonisée d'Analyze de Risques Informatiques (MEHARI)[30] is a method designed by security experts of the Club de la Sécurité Informatique Français (CLUSIF) that replaced the earlier CLUSIF-sponsored MARION and MELISA methods. It was first released in 1996. It proposes an approach for defining risk reduction measures suited to the organization objectives. MEHARI provides a risk assessment model and modular components and processes, and enhances the ability to discover vulnerabilities through audit and to analyze risk situations. MEHARI includes formulas facilitating threat identification and threat characterization and optimal selection of corrective actions. MEHARI provides accurate indications for building security plans based on a complete list of vulnerability control points and an accurate monitoring process in a continual improvement cycle. It is compliant with ISO/IEC 17799 and ISO/IEC 13335.

The Operationally Critical Threat, Asset, and Vulnerability Evaluation (OCTAVE)[31] method, developed by the Software Engineering Institute of Carnegie Mellon University, defines a risk-based strategic assessment and planning technique for security. It was first released in 1999. OCTAVE is self-directed in the sense that a small team of people from the operational (or business) units and the IT department work together to address the security needs of the organization. The team draws on the knowledge of many employees to define the current state of security, identify risks to critical assets, and set a security strategy. OCTAVE is different from typical technology-focused assessments in that it focuses on organizational risk and strategic, practice-related issues, balancing operational risk, security practices, and technology. The OCTAVE method is driven by operational risk and security practices. Technology is examined only in relation to security practices. OCTAVE-S is a variation of the method tailored to the limited means and unique constraints typically found in small organizations (less than 100 people). OCTAVE Allegro is tailored for organizations focused on information assets and a streamlined approach. The Octave Automated Tool has been implemented by the Advanced Technology Institute to help users implement the OCTAVE method.

Callio Secura 17799[32] was first released in 2001. It is a multiuser Web application with database support that lets the user implement and certify an ISMS and guides the user through each step leading to ISO 27001/17799 compliance and British Standard (BS) 7799-2 certification. Moreover, it provides document management functionality as well as customization of the tool's databases. It also carries out audits for other standards, such as Control Objectives for Information and Related Technologies (COBIT), HIPAA, and Sarbanes–Oxley, by importing the user's own questionnaires. Callio Secura is compliant with ISO/IEC 17799 and ISO/IEC 27001.

COBRA[33] is a standalone application for risk management from C&A Systems Security. It is a questionnaire-based Windows PC tool, using expert system principles and a set of extensive knowledge bases. It has also embraced the functionality to deliver other security services optionally, such as checking compliance with the ISO 17799 security standard or with an organization's own security policies. It can be used to identify threats and vulnerabilities; it measures the degree of actual risk for each area or aspect of a system and directly links this to the potential business impact. It offers detailed solutions and recommendations to reduce risks and provides business as well as technical reports. It is compliant with ISO/IEC 17799.

Alion's product CounterMeasures[34] performs Web-based enterprise risk management based on the US-NIST 800 series and Office of Management and Budget (OMB) Circular A-130 USA standards. The user standardizes the evaluation criteria and, using a "tailor-made" assessment

29. IT-Grundschutz Tool – Performance features, © Federal Office for Information Security (BSI). All rights reserved, 2012. https://www.bsi.bund.de/ContentBSI/EN/Topics/ITGrundschutz/ITGrundschutzGSTOOL/gstool.html.
30. MEHARI: Information Risk Analysis and Management Methodology, Club de la securite de l' information francais, https://www.clusif.asso.fr/en/production/mehari/.
31. OCTAVE, © 1995–2012 Carnegie Mellon University, 2012. www.cert.org/octave/.
32. Callio, © 2003–2009 ACinfotec Co. Ltd. All rights reserved, 2012. http://www.acinfotec.com/callio.php.
33. Security Risk Analysis & Assessment, and ISO 27000 Compliance, 2012. www.riskworld.net/method.htm.
34. Countermeasures Risk Analysis Products and Services, © 2012 Alion Science and Technology Corporation, 2012. www.countermeasures.com.

checklist, the software provides objective evaluation criteria to determine security posture and/or compliance. CounterMeasures is available in both networked and desktop configurations. It is compliant with the NIST 800 series and OMB Circular A-130 USA standards.

Proteus[35] is a product suite from InfoGov. It was first released in 1999. Through its components the user can perform gap analysis against standards such as ISO 17799 or create and manage an ISMS according to ISO 27001 (BS 7799-2). *Proteus* Enterprise is a fully integrated Web-based information risk management, compliance, and security solution that is fully scalable. Using *Proteus* Enterprise, companies can perform any number of online compliance audits against any standard and compare them. They can then assess how deficient compliance security measures affect the company both financially and operationally by mapping them onto its critical business processes. *Proteus* then identifies risks and mitigates those risks by formulating a work plan, maintaining current and demonstrable compliance status with regulators and senior management alike. The system works with the company's existing infrastructure and uses RiskView to bridge the gap between the technical/regulatory community and senior management. *Proteus* is a comprehensive system that includes online compliance and gap analysis, business impact, risk assessment, business continuity, incident management, asset management, organization roles, policy repository, and action plans. Its compliance engine supports any standard (international, industry, and corporate specific) and is supplied with a choice of comprehensive template questionnaires. The system is fully scalable and can size from a single user up to the largest of multinational organizations. The product maintains a full audit trail. It can perform online audits for both internal departments and external suppliers. It is compliant with ISO/IEC 17799 and ISO/IEC 27001.

CORAS[36] is a method for conducting security risk analysis. CORAS provides a customized language for threat and risk modeling and comes with detailed guidelines explaining how the language should be used to capture and model relevant information during the various stages of the security analysis. In this respect, CORAS is model-based. The Unified Modeling Language (UML) is typically used to model the target of the analysis. To document intermediate results and present overall conclusions, special CORAS diagrams are used, which are inspired by UML. The CORAS method provides a computerized tool designed to support documenting, maintaining, and reporting analysis results through risk modeling. In the CORAS method a security risk analysis is conducted in eight steps: preparations for the analysis; customer presentation of the target; refining the target description using asset diagrams; approval of the target description; Risk identification using threat diagrams; risk estimation using threat diagrams; risk evaluation using risk diagrams; and risk treatment using treatment diagrams. The method is supported by a software tool.[37]

RiskWatch for Information Systems and ISO 17799[38] is the RiskWatch company's solution for information system risk management. Other relevant products in the same suite are RiskWatch for Financial Institutions, RiskWatch for HIPAA Security, RiskWatch for Physical and Homeland Security, RiskWatch for University and School Security, and RiskWatch for North American Electric Reliability Corporation and C-TPAT-Supply Chain. The RiskWatch for Information Systems and ISO 17799 tool conducts automated risk analysis and vulnerability assessments of information systems. All RiskWatch software is fully customizable by the user. It can be tailored to reflect any corporate or government policy, including incorporation of unique standards, incident report data, penetration test data, observation, and country-specific threat data. Every product includes information security as well as physical security. Project plans and simple workflow make it easy to create accurate and supportable risk assessments. The tool includes security measures from the ISO 17799 and US-NIST 800-26 standards, with which it is compliant.

The Security by Analysis (SBA) method[39] is a concept that has existed since the beginning of the 1980s. It is more of a way of looking at analysis and security work in computerized businesses than a fully developed method. It could be called the "human model" concerning risk and vulnerability analyses. The human model implies a strong confidence in knowledge among staff and individuals within the analyzed business or organizations. It is based on the idea that those who work with everyday problems, regardless of position, are better qualified to pinpoint the most important problems and to suggest the solutions. SBA is supported by three software tools. Every tool implements its own method, but they are all based on the same concept: gathering a group of people who represent the necessary breadth of knowledge. SBA Check is primarily a tool for

---

35. Proteus Enterprise, © Information Governance Limited, Information Governance Limited PO Box 634, Farnham, Surrey, GU9 1HR, UK, 2012. www.infogov.co.uk.

36. The CORAS Method, 2012. Sourceforge.net, http://coras.sourceforge.net/index.html.

37. The CORAS Tool, 2012. Sourceforge.net, http://coras.sourceforge.net/coras_tool.html.

38. RiskWatch International, Copyright © 2012 Risk Watch International, All Rights Reserved, Risk Watch International, 1237 N. Gulfstream Ave., Sarasota, FL 34236, USA, 2012. www.riskwatch.com/index.php?option=com_content&task=view&id=22&Itemid=34.

39. The SBA Method, Copyright © 2002 Norendal International All Rights Reserved, Norendal International PO Box 13 Cockermouth CA13 0GQ, UK, 2012. www.thesbamethod.com.

anyone working with or responsible for information security issues. The role of analysis leader is central to the use of SBA Check. The analysis leader is in charge of ensuring that analysis participants' knowledge of the operation is brought to bear during the analysis process in a way that is relevant, so that the description of the current situation and opportunities for improvement retain their consistent quality. SBA Scenario is a tool that evaluates business risks methodically through quantitative risk analysis. The tool also evaluates which actions are correct and financially motivated through risk management. SBA Project is an IT support tool and a method that identifies conceivable problems in a project and provides suggestions for conceivable measures to deal with those problems. Analysis of participants' views and knowledge is used as a basis to provide a good picture of the risk in the project.

4. RISK MANAGEMENT LAWS AND REGULATIONS

Many nations have adopted laws and regulations containing clauses that pertain directly or indirectly to aspects of information systems risk management. Similarly, a large number of international laws and regulations exist. In the following, a brief description of such documents is given with an international scope directly relevant to information systems risk management.[40]

"Regulation (EC) No 45/2001 of the European Parliament and of the Council of 18 December 2000 on the protection of individuals with regard to the processing of personal data by the Community institutions and bodies and on the free movement of such data"[41] requires that any personal data processing activity by Community institutions undergoes a prior risk analysis to determine the privacy implications of the activity and to determine appropriate legal, technical, and organizational measures to protect such activities. It also stipulates that such activity is effectively protected by measures, which must be state of the art, taking into account the sensitivity and privacy implications of the activity. When a third party is charged with the processing task, its activities are governed by suitable and enforced agreements. Furthermore, the regulation requires the European Union's (EU's) institutions and bodies to take similar precautions with regard to their

telecommunications infrastructure, and to inform users properly of any specific risks of security breaches.

The European Commission's Directive on Data Protection went into effect in October 1998 and prohibits the transfer of personal data to non-EU nations that do not meet the European "adequacy" standard for privacy protection. The United States takes an approach to privacy different from that of the EU; it uses a sectoral approach that relies on a mixture of legislation, regulation, and self-regulation. The EU, however, relies on comprehensive legislation that, for example, requires the creation of government data protection agencies, registration of data bases with those agencies, and, in some instances, prior approval before personal data processing may begin. The Safe Harbor Privacy Principles[42] aim to bridge this gap by providing that an EU-based entity self-certifies its compliance with them.

The "Commission Decision of 15 June 2001 on standard contractual clauses for the transfer of personal data to third countries, under Directive 95/46/EC", the "Commission Decision of 27 December 2004 amending Decision 2001/497/EC as regards the introduction of an alternative set of standard contractual clauses for the transfer of personal data to third countries," and the "Commission Decision of 5 February 2010 on standard contractual clauses for the transfer of personal data to processors established in third countries under Directive 95/46/EC of the European Parliament and of the Council"[43] provide a set of voluntary model clauses that can be used to export personal data from a data controller who is subject to EU data protection rules to a data processor outside the EU who is not subject to these rules or to a similar set of adequate rules. Upon acceptance of the model clauses, the data controller warrants that the appropriate legal, technical, and organizational measures ensure the protection of the personal data. Furthermore, the data processor must agree to permit auditing of its security practices to ensure compliance with applicable European data protection rules.

The HIPAA of 1996[44] is a US law with regard to health insurance coverage, electronic health, and requirements for the security and privacy of health data. Title II of HIPAA, known as the Administrative Simplification provisions, requires the establishment of national standards for electronic health care transactions and national identifiers for providers, health insurance plans, and employers. Per the requirements of Title II, the Department of Health and Human Services promulgated five rules regarding

40. J. Dumortier, H. Graux, Risk Management/Risk Assessment in European Regulation, International Guidelines and Codes of Practice, ENISA, June 2007. Available at: http://www.enisa.europa.eu/activities/risk-management/current-risk/laws-regulation/downloads/risk-management-risk-assessment-in-european-regulation-international-guidelines-and-codes-of-practice.

41. Official Journal of the European Communities, 12.1.2001, EN, L 8/1−8/22, 2001. Available at: http://eur-lex.europa.eu/LexUriServ/LexUriServ.do?uri=OJ:L:2001:008:0001:0022:en:PDF.

42. export.gov. Helping U.S. Companies export, 2012. http://export.gov/safeharbor/eu/eg_main_018476.asp.

43. Official Journal of the European Union, 12.2.2010, EN, L 39/5−39/18, 2010.

44. LegalArchiver.org, www.legalarchiver.org/hipaa.htm, 2012.

Administrative Simplification: the Privacy Rule, the Transactions and Code Sets Rule, the Security Rule, the Unique Identifiers Rule, and the Enforcement Rule. The standards are meant to improve the efficiency and effectiveness of the US health care system by encouraging the widespread use of electronic data interchange.

The "Directive 2002/58/EC of the European Parliament and of the Council of 12 July 2002 concerning the processing of personal data and the protection of privacy in the electronic communications sector (Directive on privacy and electronic communications)"[45] requires any provider of publicly available electronic communications services to take appropriate legal, technical and organizational measures to ensure the security of its services; inform his subscribers of any particular risks of security breaches; take the necessary measures to prevent such breaches; and indicate the likely costs of security breaches to the subscribers.

The "Directive 2006/24/EC of the European Parliament and of the Council of 15 March 2006 on the retention of data generated or processed in connection with the provision of publicly available electronic communications services or of public communications networks and amending Directive 2002/58/EC"[46] requires affected providers of publicly accessible electronic telecommunications networks to retain certain communications data to be specified in their national regulations, for a specific amount of time, under secured circumstances in compliance with applicable privacy regulations; to provide access to this data to competent national authorities; to ensure data quality and security through appropriate technical and organizational measures, shielding it from access by unauthorized individuals; to ensure its destruction when it is no longer required; and to ensure that stored data can be promptly delivered on request from the competent authorities.

The "Regulation (EC) No 1907/2006 of the European Parliament and of the Council of 18 December 2006 concerning the Registration, Evaluation, Authorization and Restriction of Chemicals, establishing a European Chemicals Agency, amending Directive 1999/45/EC and repealing Council Regulation (EEC) No 793/93 and Commission Regulation (EC) No 1488/94 as well as Council Directive 76/769/EEC and Commission Directives 91/155/EEC, 93/67/EEC, 93/105/EC and 2000/21/EC"[47] implants risk management obligations by imposing a reporting obligation on producers and importers of articles covered by the regulation, with regard to the qualities of certain chemical substances, which includes a risk assessment and obligation to examine how such risks can be managed. This information is to be registered in a central database. It also stipulates that a Committee for Risk Assessment within the European Chemicals Agency established by the Regulation is established, and requires that the information provided to be kept up to date with regard to potential risks to human health or the environment, and for such risks to be adequately managed.

The "Council Framework Decision 2005/222/JHA of 24 February 2005 on attacks against information systems"[48] contains conditions under which legal liability can be imposed on legal entities for conduct of certain natural persons of authority within the legal entity. Thus, the Framework decision requires that the conduct of such figures within an organization to be monitored adequately, also because the decision states that a legal entity can be held liable for acts of omission in this regard. In addition, the decision defines a series of criteria under which jurisdictional competence can be established. These include the competence of a jurisdiction when a criminal act is conducted against an information system within its borders.

The "Organisation for Economic Co-operation and Development Guidelines for the Security of Information Systems and Networks: Toward a Culture of Security" (25 July 2002)[49] aim to promote a culture of security; raise awareness about the risk to information systems and networks (including the policies, practices, measures, and procedures available to address those risks and the need for their adoption and implementation); foster greater confidence in information systems and networks and the way in which they are provided and used; create a general frame of reference; promote cooperation and information sharing; and promote the consideration of security as an important objective. The guidelines state nine basic principles underpinning risk management and information security practices. No part of the text is legally binding, but noncompliance with any of the principles indicates a breach of risk management good practices that can potentially incur liability.

The "Basel Committee on Banking Supervision—Risk Management Principles for Electronic Banking"[50] identify

45. Official Journal of the European Communities, 31.7.2002, EN, L 201/37−201/47, 2002. Available at: http://eur-lex.europa.eu/LexUriServ/LexUriServ.do?uri=OJ:L:2002:201:0037:0037:EN:PDF.
46. Official Journal of the European Union, 13.4.2006, EN, L 105/54−105/63, 2006. Available at: http://eur-lex.europa.eu/LexUriServ/LexUriServ.do?uri=OJ:L:2006:105:0054:0063:EN:PDF.
47. Official Journal of the European Union, 30.12.2006, EN, L 396/1−396/849. Available at: http://eurlex.europa.eu/LexUriServ/LexUriServ.do?uri=OJ:L:2006:396:0001:0849:EN:PDF.
48. Official Journal of the European Union, 16.3.2005, EN, L 69/67−69/71. Available at: http://eurlex.europa.eu/LexUriServ/LexUriServ.do?uri=CELEX:32005F0222:EN:NOT.
49. Organisation for economic co-operation and development, OECD Guidelines for the Security of Information Systems and Networks: Toward a Culture of Security, © OECD 2002. Available at: http://www.oecd.org/sti/interneteconomy/15582260.pdf.
50. Basel Committee on Banking Supervision, Risk Management Principles for Electronic Banking, July 2003. Available at: www.bis.org/publ/bcbs98.pdf.

14 Risk Management Principles for Electronic Banking to help banking institutions expand their existing risk oversight policies and processes to cover their e-banking activities. The Risk Management Principles fall into three broad and often overlapping categories of issues that are grouped to provide clarity: board and management oversight; security controls; and legal and reputational risk management. The Risk Management Principles are not put forth as absolute requirements or even "best practice," nor do they attempt to set specific technical solutions or standards relating to e-banking. Consequently, the Risk Management Principles and sound practices are expected to be used as tools by national supervisors and to be implemented with adaptations to reflect specific national requirements and individual risk profiles where necessary.

The "Commission Recommendation 87/598/EEC of 8 December 1987, concerning a European code of conduct relating to electronic payments"[51] provides a number of general nonbinding recommendations. This includes an obligation to ensure that privacy is respected and that the system is transparent with regard to potential security or confidentiality risks, which must obviously be mitigated by all reasonable means.

The "Public Company Accounting Reform and Investor Protection Act of 30 July 2002" (commonly referred to as *Sarbanes-Oxley* and often abbreviated to *SOX* or *Sarbox*)[52] although indirectly relevant to risk management, is discussed here owing to its importance. The Act is a US federal law passed in response to a number of major corporate and accounting scandals including those affecting Enron, Tyco International, and WorldCom (now MCI). These scandals resulted in a decline of public trust in accounting and reporting practices. The legislation is wide ranging and establishes new or enhanced standards for all US public company boards, management, and public accounting firms. Its provisions range from additional corporate board responsibilities to criminal penalties, and require the Securities and Exchange Commission to implement rulings on requirements to comply with the new law. The first and most important part of the Act establishes a new quasipublic agency, the Public Company Accounting Oversight Board (www.pcaobus.org), which is charged with overseeing, regulating, inspecting, and disciplining accounting firms in their roles as auditors of public companies. The Act also covers issues such as auditor independence, corporate governance, and enhanced financial disclosure.

The "Office of the Comptroller of the Currency—Electronic Banking Guidance"[53] is fairly high level. It should be indicative of the subject matter to be analyzed and assessed by banking institutions, rather than serve as a yardstick to identify actual problems.

The PCI—DSS[54] provides central guidance allowing financial service providers that rely on payment cards to implement the necessary policies, procedures, and infrastructure to safeguard their customer account data adequately. PCI DSS has no formal binding legal power. Nevertheless, considering its origins and the key participants, it holds significant moral authority, and noncompliance with the PCI DSS by a payment card service provider may indicate inadequate risk management practices.

The "Directive 2002/65/EC of the European Parliament and of the Council of 23 September 2002 concerning the distance marketing of consumer financial services and amending Council Directive 90/619/EEC and Directives 97/7/EC and 98/27/EC (the 'Financial Distance Marketing Directive')"[55] requires that, as a part of the minimum information to be provided to a consumer before concluding a distance financial services contract, the consumer must be clearly and comprehensibly informed of any specific risks related to the service concerned.

5. RISK MANAGEMENT STANDARDS

Various national and international, de jure, and de facto standards exist that are related, directly or indirectly, to information systems risk management. In the following, we briefly describe the most important international standards that are directly related to risk management.

The ISO/IEC 27000 series of standards has been reserved for a family of information security management standards derived from British Standard BS 7799. Several standards within the series have already been published; others are in various stages of development. A comprehensive presentation and discussion of these standards is provided by the ISO 27001 security home.[56] Within this series, the "ISO/IEC 27001:2005—Information technology—Security techniques—Information security management

51. Official Journal of the European Communities, 24.12.87, EN, No L 365/72—365/76. Available at: http://eurlex.europa.eu/LexUriServ/LexUriServ.do?uri=CELEX:31987H0598:EN:pdf.

52. US Public Law 107-204-July 30, 2002, 116 STAT.745. Available at: http://www.gpo.gov/fdsys/pkg/PLAW-107publ204/pdf/PLAW-107publ204.pdf.

53. Office of the Comptroller of the Currency, US Department of the Treasury, 2012. www.occ.treas.gov/netbank/ebguide.htm.

54. PCI Security standards council, Copyright © 2006—2012 PCI Security Standards Council, LLC, All rights reserved, PCI Security Standards Council, LLC401 Edgewater Place Suite 600, Wakefield, MA, USA 01880, 2012. https://www.pcisecuritystandards.org/security_standards/documents.php.

55. Official Journal of the European Communities, 9.10.2002, EN, L 271/16—271/271/24. Available at: http://eurlex.europa.eu/LexUriServ/LexUriServ.do?uri=CELEX:32002L0065:EN:pdf.

56. ISO 27001 Security. Information Security Standards, Copyright © 2012 IsecT Ltd., Castle Peak, 1262 Taihape Road, RD9 Hastings 4179, New Zealand, 2012. http://www.iso27001security.com/index.html.

systems—Requirements" standard is designed to ensure the selection of adequate and proportionate security measures that protect information assets and give confidence to interested parties. The standard covers all types of organizations (commercial enterprises, government agencies, and not-for-profit organizations) and specifies requirements for establishing, implementing, operating, monitoring, reviewing, maintaining, and improving a documented ISMS within the context of the organization's overall business risks. Furthermore, it specifies requirements for implementing security measures customized to the needs of individual organizations or their parts. Its application in practice is often combined with related standards, such as BS 7799-3:2006, which provides additional guidance to support the requirements given in ISO/IEC 27001:2005.

The "ISO/IEC 27005:2011—Information technology—Security techniques—Information security risk management" standard[57] provides guidelines for information security risk management. It supports the general concepts specified in ISO/IEC 27001 and is designed to assist the satisfactory implementation of information security based on a risk management approach. ISO/IEC 27005:2011 is applicable to all types of organizations (commercial enterprises, government agencies, and nonprofit organizations) that intend to manage risks that could compromise the organization's information security. ISO/IEC 27005 revised and superseded the Management of Information and Communications Technology Security standards ISO/IEC TR 13335-3:1998 plus ISO/IEC TR 13335-4:2000. The standard describes the risk management methodology without specifying, recommending, or even naming a specific method.

The "ISO 31000:2009 Risk management—principles and guidelines" standard provides principles and generic guidelines on risk management.[58] The standard is not sector or industry specific, and it can be used by any public, private, or community enterprise, association, group, or individual. It can be applied to any type of risk, whatever its nature, whether having positive or negative consequences. This also means that the standard is not specific to information security or even to IT risks. It is intended for ISO 31000:2009 to be used to harmonize risk management processes in existing and future standards. It provides a common approach in support of standards dealing with specific risks and/or sectors, and does not replace those standards.

The IEC 31010:2009 "Risk management—risk assessment techniques" is a supporting standard for ISO 31000 and provides guidance on the selection and application of systematic techniques for risk assessment. The standard treats risk assessment as an integral part of risk management, helping managers understand risks that could affect

the achievement of business objectives and assess the adequacy and effectiveness of various risk mitigation controls. It covers risk assessment concepts as well as processes and a range of techniques.[59]

ISO Guide 73:2009 provides the definitions of generic terms related to risk management. It aims to encourage a mutual and consistent understanding of, and a coherent approach to, the description of activities relating to the management of risk, and the use of uniform risk management terminology in processes and frameworks dealing with the management of risk. For principles and guidelines on risk management, reference is made to ISO 31000:2009.[60]

The "BS 7799-3:2006—Information security management systems—Guidelines for information security risk management" standard was the predecessor of ISO/IEC 27005. It gives guidance to support the requirements given in BS ISO/IEC 27001:2005 regarding all aspects of an ISMS risk management cycle and is therefore typically applied in conjunction with this standard in risk assessment practices. This includes assessing and evaluating the risks, implementing security measures to treat the risks, monitoring and reviewing the risks, and maintaining and improving the system of risk treatment. The focus of this standard is effective information security through an ongoing program of risk management activities. This focus is targeted at information security in the context of an organization's business risks. With the proliferation of ISO/IEC 27005, it is expected that BS 7799-3 will eventually be withdrawn.

In Section 3 we discussed BSI Standard 100-3, i.e., the part of IT-Grundschutz (IT baseline protection)[61] that describes the risk analysis method. BSI Standard 100-1 ISMS is an overview of the IT-Grundschutz approach to developing and implementing an ISMS. BSI Standard 100-2 IT-Grundschutz Methodology is basically about governance of information security within the organization using an ISMS. BSI Standard 100-4 *Business Continuity Management* explains how to establish and maintain a business continuity management system. BSI IS audit guideline *Information Security Audit (IS Audit), a guideline for IS audits based on IT-Grundschutz*, is primarily aimed at IS auditors working for German federal agencies. IT-Grundschutz Catalogs contains detailed advice on information security threats, controls, etc.

The "ISF Standard of Good Practice" standard, which we discussed as a risk management method in Section 3, is a commonly quoted source of good practices and serves as a resource for the implementation of information security policies and as a yardstick for auditing such systems and/or

57. ISO/IEC, Information Technology — Security Techniques — Information Security Risk Management, 2011.
58. ISO, Risk Management — Principles and Guidelines, 2009.
59. ISO/IEC, IEC 31010:2009 Risk Management — Risk Assessment Techniques, 2009.
60. ISO, ISO Guide 73:2009 Risk Management — Vocabulary, 2009.
61. IT-Grundschutz, Copyright © Federal Office for Information Security (BSI). All rights reserved, 2012. https://www.bsi.bund.de/ContentBSI/EN/Topics/ITGrundschutz/itgrundschutz.html.

the surrounding practices. The standard covers six distinct aspects of information security, each of which relates to a particular type of environment. The standard focuses on how information security supports an organization's key business processes.

The US General Accounting Office "Information security risk assessment: practices of leading organizations" guide[62] is intended to help federal managers implement an ongoing information security risk assessment process by providing examples, or case studies, of practical risk assessment procedures that have been successfully adopted by four organizations known for their efforts to implement good risk assessment practices. More important, based on the case studies, it identifies factors important to the success of any risk assessment program, regardless of the specific methodology employed.

The US-NIST Special Publication (SP) 800-30 "Risk management guide for information technology systems," developed by NIST in 2002, provides a common foundation for experienced and inexperienced, technical, and nontechnical personnel who support or use the risk management process for their IT systems. Its guidelines are for use by federal organizations that process sensitive information, and are consistent with the requirements of OMB Circular A-130, Appendix III. The guidelines may also be used by nongovernmental organizations on a voluntary basis, even though they are not mandatory and binding standards.

Finally, the US-NIST SP 800-39 "Managing Information Security Risk: Organization, Mission and Information System View" standard[63] provides guidelines for managing risk to organizational operations, organizational assets, individuals, other organizations, and the nation resulting from the operation and use of information systems. It provides a structured yet flexible approach for managing that portion of risk resulting from the incorporation of information systems into the mission and business processes of organizations.

6. SUMMARY

The information systems risk management methodology was developed with an eye to guiding the design and the management of security of an information system within the framework of an organization. It aims to analyze and assess the factors that affect risk, subsequently treat the risk, and continuously monitor and review the security plan. Central concepts of the methodology are those of the threat, the vulnerability, the asset, the impact, and the risk. The

operational relationship of these concepts materializes when a threat exploits one or more vulnerabilities to harm assets, an event that will affect the organization. Once the risks are identified and assessed, they must be treated, that is, modified, shared, avoided, or retained. Treating the risks is done on the basis of a carefully designed security plan, which must be continuously monitored, reviewed, and amended as necessary. Many methods implementing the whole or parts of the risk management methodology have been developed. Although most of them closely follow the methodology as described in pertinent international standards, they differ considerably in their underlying philosophy and their specific steps. The risk management methodology has been and is being applied internationally with considerable success and enjoys universal acceptance. However, it has several disadvantages that should be seriously considered in the process of applying it. Particular attention must be paid to the subjectivity of its estimates, which is often obscured by the formality of the underlying probabilistic models and the systematic nature of most risk management methods. Subjectivity in applying the methodology is unavoidable and should be accepted and consciously managed. A number of international laws and regulations contain provisions for information system risk management, in addition to national provisions. The risk management methodology is standardized by international organizations.

Finally, let us move on to the real interactive part of this chapter: review questions/exercises, hands-on projects, case projects, and the optional team case project. The answers and/or solutions by chapter can be found in the Online Instructor's Solutions Manual.

CHAPTER REVIEW QUESTIONS/ EXERCISES

True/False

1. True or False? Information security risk "is measured in terms of a combination of the likelihood of an event and not its consequence."
2. True or False? The likelihood of a security incident occurring is a function of the likelihood that a threat appears and of the likelihood that the threat can successfully exploit the relevant system vulnerabilities.
3. True or False? The term *methodology* means an organized set of principles and rules that drives action in a particular field of knowledge.
4. True or False? The context establishment process receives as input all relevant information about the organization.
5. True or False? Risk identification seeks to determine what could happen to cause a potential loss and to gain insight into how, where, and why the loss might happen.

62. U.S. General Accounting Office, Information Security Risk Assessment: Practices of Leading Organizations, 1999.
63. NIST, Managing Information Security Risk: Organization, Mission and Information System View, US NIST SP 800-39, 2011. Available at: http://csrc.nist.gov/publications/nistpubs/800-39/SP800-39-final.pdf.

Multiple Choice

1. What are classified according to the asset class to which they relate?
   A. Qualitative analysis
   B. Vulnerabilities
   C. Promotional email
   D. Malformed request denial of service (DoS)
   E. Data controller
2. When the risk is calculated, the _____ process finishes.
   A. Network attached storage (NAS)
   B. Risk assessment
   C. Valid
   D. Load-based DoS
   E. Bait
3. What is a horizontal process that interacts bidirectionally with all other processes of risk management?
   A. Data minimization
   B. Fabric
   C. Target access
   D. Risk communication
   E. Security
4. What is an ongoing, never-ending process that is assigned to an individual, a team, or an outsourced third party, depending on the organization's size and operational characteristics?
   A. Risk management
   B. Greedy strategy
   C. Ports
   D. Storage Area Network protocol
   E. Taps

5. What must be totally integrated into the system development life cycle?
   A. Irrelevant
   B. Tape library
   C. Internet Protocol storage access
   D. Configuration file
   E. Risk management

EXERCISE

Problem

What is continuous monitoring?

Hands-on Projects

Project

If an organization's information system is subject to continuous monitoring, does that mean it does not have to undergo security authorization?

Case Projects

Problem

Why is continuous monitoring not replacing the traditional security authorization process?

Optional Team Case Project

Problem

What is front-end security and how does it differ from back-end security?

Chapter 35

Insider Threat

William F. Gross

Gross Security, LLC, Spencer, WV, United States

1. INTRODUCTION

William James is credited as saying, "A chain is no stronger than its weakest link, and life is after all a chain." In security and technology circles, the human is often declared the weakest link, and with good cause. From a penetration tester's perspective, which is oddly congruent with a malicious attacker's perspective, compromising a valuable zero-day exploit to gain access to the victim's network remains less desirable than any of dozens of easier methods. Likewise, attacking a firewall to find a vulnerability is a fool's errand because the device is inherently robust to its task. The "weakest link" human, however, presents a vulnerable attack surface. Consider the story of Kevin Mitnick, perhaps the most famous of hackers: Although he is technologically savvy, a quick read of his book, *The Art of Deception*, reveals that most of his success came not from mastery of the command line but from social engineering: exploiting the human link in the security chain [22]. The proliferation of a computer in every home is still only one-half of a generation old; moreover, as the technological marvel of computation power increases, so does the inherent complexity of the systems and software. Companies, motivated by profit, rush to market products without adequate security controls in place. Technology's influence on society is undeniable and in fact paradigm shifting. Our lexicon contains new words such as cybersecurity and cyberspace, although die-hard technology professionals point out that we are not keeping our "cybers" secure, but instead our information. Legal scholars declare that the cyberspace debate over "threats, vulnerabilities, and responsibilities" is incomplete [2]. When stories of data loss, theft, and breach dominate headlines, one can reasonably conclude that the workforce tasked with cybersecurity needs continued attention as to its capacity and capabilities [1].

2. DEFINING INSIDER THREAT

In August 2000, the Defense Advance Research Agency (RAND Corporation's National Defense Research Institute) hosted a conference on insider threats and discussed the need to develop threat models and compile information on incidents providing a database of metrics [3]. The participants recognized the need for greater analysis, definition, and control measures to respond adequately to activity from insider threats. Roughly 1 year later, the United States experienced the world's single greatest terrorism attack, which brought the subject of security to the forefront of conversation.

The Department of Homeland Security, established in response the attacks of 9/11 [21] and Presidential Policy Directive PPD-21 [20], divided the nation into 16 critical infrastructure sectors, "whose assets, systems, and networks, whether physical or virtual, are considered so vital to the United States that their incapacitation or destruction would have a debilitating effect on security, national economic security, national public health or safety, or any combination thereof." When examining the role of the military in protecting the American economy, cyberspace exists as a man-made domain and reflects many characteristics of sea and land domains as they relate to commerce and trade [2].

A Working Definition

So, what exactly is an insider threat? According to the RAND Corporation's 2000 workshop, an insider is "Any authorized user who performs unauthorized actions that result in loss of control of computational assets" [3]. The report expounds on the definition with the term "attributes," including, "access, knowledge, privileges, skills, risk, tactics, motivation, and process."

Computer and Information Security Handbook. http://dx.doi.org/10.1016/B978-0-12-803843-7.00035-1

However, analyzing the term "insider threat" reveals some conundrums. First, the concept of an insider implies a distinct, almost physical boundary. With the advent of mobile computers, teleworkers, outsourcing, contractors, and the myriad of technologies to support these disregarded entities, the concept of a physical boundary blurs. Second, the fundamental definition of an insider is a binary condition: he is or is not an insider. In a rule-based system in which rules determine whether a person is an insider, the varying degrees of "insiderness" must be accounted for. If the rules applied to paper documents, the janitor is also an insider [18].

Insider Threat Costs

What are the costs associated with insider threats and how do they compare with other malicious activity? In early 2000, the average cost of a penetration was reported at $56,000, compared with $2.7 million for an insider attack [3]. Another estimate of the cost of insider threats to the world economy is $300 billion to $1 trillion in 2013 [6]. The percent change of these two estimates is 37,036,937%! Some figures show the average business to experience over 100 attacks per year, costing $11.6 million [7]. It is easy to understand why the damage from the insider threat remains the most costly: The insider naturally possesses a certain level of trust and therefore access to the systems and information exploited. A discussion of cost must include ancillary costs beyond the value placed on the information stolen. In terms of other cost categories, ancillary costs include loss from business interruption, fixing the original problem, investigations by state and federal agencies, fines, and litigation [7].

Case Study: Snowden

Edward Snowden is a technology specialist and former employee of Dell and the Central Intelligence Agency (CIA), and later a contractor for Booz Hamilton working for the National Security Agency (NSA), who in 2013 became a world-famous whistle-blower of NSA surveillance when he leaked thousands of highly classified documents detailing the agency's massive and global data collection efforts. A careful analysis of the Snowden case reveals interesting behaviors consistent with the insider threat model:

- He had little formal education; instead, he obtained industry certifications.
- He became a security guard at a facility requiring guards to undergo background checks and obtain high-level security clearance.
- He gained unprecedented access to classified information as a computer and network administrator of those systems.
- He compiled the leaked information over several years.
- At one point, he took a job with lesser pay that gave him access to information he wanted but could not access in his current job.

- "Taken in its entirety, the Snowden archive led to an ultimately simple conclusion: the US government had built a system that has as its goal the complete elimination of electronic privacy worldwide" [23].

3. MOTIVATIONS OF THE INSIDER THREAT ACTORS

The root causes of insider threat behavior are varied and not easily quantified into simple statements. The seminal work, Computer Emergency Response Teams (CERT) *Guide to Insider Threats* (2012) takes a comprehensive look at motivations behind malicious actors. The CERT team created a database of information from past insider events and used queries to establish patterns. One interesting distinction followed an all too common thread: To avoid embarrassment and publicity, managers often choose to settle problems with insider threat activity quietly [2]. As previously discussed, the costs to a business include much more than the actual information itself. Damage to a company's reputation and goodwill, although difficult to quantify in dollars, can be catastrophic. Often, an insider's motives include revenge, ego gratification, challenge, anger, and sense of entitlement [3].

Trust

Naturally, insiders hold a position of trust [3]; you must allow them certain privilege, authority, and access to accomplish their assigned tasks. Other, subtler threats exist, too: Insiders often witness behaviors and social interactions of colleagues and may be able to leverage these activities in exploits. Another unintended consequence of this trust relationship occurs when an employee fulfills multiple rolls. By "wearing many hats," the insider is granted access to different systems, files, and folders. Depending on the access model in use, the complex combination of permissions for the multiple functions may grant insiders access where they may not otherwise have been granted.

Personality

Often the personality types best suited for complex logical programming are social introverts. The type prefers predictability of computers over the unpredictability of social interactions [3]. This personality becomes more susceptible to insider behavior, because he does not normally possess the coping skills of other people.

Human Resources Role

The human resources (HR) department bears a measure of responsibility for preventing insider threat behavior. Does the company have a background check policy for initial hires, or promotions of increasing responsibility? A well-written and legally approved acceptable use policy, renewed annually, establishes criteria for good and bad behavior when the employee uses the company's phone, Internet, and data-processing resources. Initial and routine employee screening, or a lack thereof, was cited in several cases, especially for ancillary employees such as consultants and contractors [3].

Theft of Intellectual Property

For the purpose of selling it outright, the theft of intellectual property remains a surprisingly small fraction of insider crime. Instead, the primary motivation for theft of intellectual property is to provide it to a foreign government, starting or enhancing a competing business, or new employment. Another unusual misconception is the role of computer administrators as data thieves. Although they have an unusually high degree of access, their incidence of theft is small. Instead, primary insiders who steal intellectual property are "scientists, engineers, programmers, or salespeople" [17]. Theft is often accomplished during normal work hours by those with authorized access to the data stolen. Distinguishing authorized access from malicious activity is therefore more difficult.

Growth

Long-term detection of insider threats is complicated by two trends: first, the increasingly technological savvy of the population, and second, the availability and staggering capacities of information vectors such as universal serial bus drives, cellular phones, and encrypted chat apps. As a society becomes more dependent on data and more information becomes digital, there is a greater potential for the incidence of theft. Consider the X-ray; the days when a physician handled a large sheet of film against a backlit viewing box are fading; instead, X-ray data are digitized, stored in a database, and transmitted electronically while being handled by several clinicians and stored in electronic medical record systems composed of servers and databases. In this case, the X-ray, as a piece of information, often resides in multiple locations, each with complex access rules and authorities for the various medical staff allowed to interact with these data.

Stuxnet

A careful analysis of the Stuxnet malware revealed that the delivery mechanism was human: in particular, an Iranian nuclear scientist's laptop and memory sticks. Processing nuclear material for use in energy plants and weapons requires purification by industrial centrifuges. The Stuxnet malware attacked the Supervisory Control and Data Acquisition system, an industrial control system used to manage the centrifuge's speeds and cycles. In this case, the malware made tiny pressure adjustments and speed control changes, thus ruining the work by causing vibrations, and in some cases spinning the centrifuge out of control [8].

4. INSIDER THREAT INDICATORS

People change over time. The once trusted employee may experience some significant change in his life that would induce him to criminal behavior. Certain indicators to look for include:

- financial issues: unexplained wealth or debt, garnishments, bankruptcy, or repossessions
- foreign influences: short/frequent travel overseas, or new or ongoing relationships with foreign nationals
- changes in marital status or cohabitation
- legal issues: arrests, trials, or convictions
- addictive behaviors: drugs, gambling, or alcohol
- suspicious activity or behavior: unauthorized copying or transmitting of confidential, proprietary, or trade secret material
- possession of unauthorized camera, recording, or telecommunication devices
- abnormal intranet browsing or access to areas and files not otherwise authorized
- use or installation of hacking, password cracking, or other tools
- a desire to work additional projects with increased responsibility and access
- willingness or working late evenings or weekend hours with little or no supervision

5. EXAMPLES OF INSIDER THREATS

One unnamed US-based company presented an interesting case study. Over a period of 2 years, the company moved toward a telecommuting workforce and implemented a virtual private network concentrator to facilitate remote connections. The network staff decided to monitor the traffic on the concentrator and began noticing anomalous activity in the logs: in particular, a regular and daily connection from Asia. The employee kept regular office hours but somehow managed to connect from China. Confounding the issue was the additional security provided to employees: the company implemented multifactor authentication and issued access tokens. Security investigators discovered that the employee outsourced his job to a third-party contractor and FedExed his token. The employee even had good performance reviews. When examining his workstation, the security team found that this employee spent his day surfing Reddit, eBay, Facebook, and LinkedIn. At the end of each day, he would submit an update email to management detailing the work effort of his outsourced programmer [15].

A study by Carnegie Mellon University examined 23 insider threat incidents by 26 insiders between 1996 and

2002. Although a little dated, the findings are interesting. Most incidents were not sophisticated, planned in advance, motivated by financial gain, detected by other people in the company, and conducted while on the job. However, the perpetrators were dissimilar [12].

6. IMPACTS

The financial impact of insider theft can be devastating. Tens or hundreds of millions of dollars have been lost to foreign countries, proprietary data have been compromised, and business lose heavily when competing products flood the market place. In fact, "more than half of our theft of intellectual property cases involved trade secrets" [17]. Another interesting point was that the preponderance of intellectual property theft is not in the information technology (IT) space as one would expect; instead, the statistic reveals that only 50% involves IT.

7. ANALYSIS: RELEVANCE

According to the 2015 Verizon Data Breach Digest, analysis of over 500 cybersecurity incidents in 40 countries revealed social tactics used in 20% of confirmed data breaches. The insider threat is easily classified as malicious or innocuous; deception in the form of email, in person, and through phone calls leads the way [15].

During the 3-year period of 2013−2015, financial motivations took the majority of insider and privilege misuse at 63%; in fact, end users such as bank employees with access to personally identifiable information exceed system administrators with similar access. Likewise, analysis of the 2015 report on insider threats revealed [15]:

- a frequency rate of 12%
- time to discovery and time to containment as great as months
- a pattern of privilege misuse
- motivations of financial gain, espionage, and grudge
- industries most affected to be financial services, health care, and the public sector

HData Exfiltration Methods

How does information leave the premises? The top three avenues are remote network access, email, and removable media. Other avenues include paper documents, file transfer via File Transfer Protocol (FTP) or other cloud-based storage solutions, and using a corporate laptop to transfer data from the network to the laptop and removing the data outside the workplace [17].

Fusion

An analysis of threat information, similar to the concept of data mining, provides behavioral predictability; one example is intrusion detection systems. A combination of correlating alerts, analysis of known attack methodologies feeds predictive algorithms to identify and detect malicious behavior. They are especially useful in multistage cyberattacks [4].

Weibull Hazard Model

A 2015 study of insider threats to financial institutions blends activity theory with survival modeling in a Weibull hazard model. After analyzing 7 months of field data, the study illustrated the utility of routine activity theory-based risk assessments. The study also revealed the difficulty in predicting human behavior because an insider, when new to an organization, is unfamiliar with security practices and is less likely to make unauthorized attempts. However, as the insider becomes more acclimated with process and procedures, he may be more inclined to act nefariously [10]. Motivators for insider threat behavior include [17]:

- financial gain by selling to a competitor
- giving to his home country
- establishing a competing business
- bringing to a new employer

8. MANAGE AND MITIGATE THE INSIDER THREAT

The System Administration, Networking and Security Institute publishes a top 20 list of critical security controls. Oddly, the first item on the list is the most obvious: "inventory of authorized and unauthorized devices" [18]. To protect something, you must first be aware of its existence. One technique to identify critical assets is solutions including data loss prevention systems, digital rights management tools, and digital watermarking [17]; each solution carries potential implementation hurdles. Imagine trying to identify critical data files across a large organization, using network attached storage or cloud-based data repositories. Did the well-intentioned scientist in the R&D department bring in a small office or home officeWi-Fi access point to make his work easier? Protecting assets begins with knowing what and where they are, which also allows the "protector" to identify rogue data, processes, and equipment.

Detection

Modern attacks are often complex, exploiting multiple vulnerabilities. The attacker gains a foothold in the organization, perhaps on an unimportant and therefore unmonitored machine such as a printer, postage machine, or old and unpatched server. From there, the attacker pivots and escalates his authority to compromise the true objective successfully. Therefore, identification and analysis of seemingly inconsequential data must be synthesized without overwhelming the security tool with false positives and false negatives. Another powerful tool in detecting attack behaviors is the human eye. As the saying goes, "A picture is worth a thousand words," and so, too, the adage applies to the study of cyber behavior. One tool is attack graphs; they provide a visual framework [5]. Using various graph-based approaches, one group of scientists is able to discover anomalous patterns in data sets indicative of insider threat activity [14]. Creating abstract art with algorithms of various data points allows the human eye to see patterns; when the patterns change, something is changing in the original data. Another type of detection is simply human observation. An example is a small company with 42 employees installed a network monitoring and filtration device. After gathering data for several months, the IT technician ran a report showing aggregate use of the Internet and numbers of emails. Interestingly, one employee's use of the email and Internet systems was egregiously disproportionate to the norm. In this case the employee was taking online college classes during work hours and was one of those people who forwarded chain letters and humorous email messages. In addition, her office arrangement put her monitor facing away from her office door such that any person entering her office would need to walk around her desk to see her monitor, which gave her time to switch between screens. Her office furniture arrangement was unique in the organization.

Insider threats would not be possible without the human component. The study of human behavior is a science unto itself. Changes in workplace behavior are indicators. Possessiveness, dissatisfaction, and sense of entitlement all contribute to an insider's decision to steal data. Nontechnical employees discovered the theft in 72% of cases [17].

Time Frame

When do attacks from insiders occur? Most insider theft occurs 30 days before or after the termination event, so the full period to study is actually 2 months in duration [17].

Technical Controls

Least privilege is a control mechanism in which the user is granted only enough access and authority to accomplish his assigned duties. In the case of Edward Snowden, least privilege was not used and could potentially have made a huge difference [9].

Data Leakage Tools

Data leakage tools are a suite of applications that can alert administrators of emails with large attachments, protecting documents from copying, tracking document copy processes to removable media, preventing email to Hotmail- or Gmail-type accounts, and preventing connections such as cloud storage, FTP, or email to foreign governments or IP addresses [17].

Monitoring

Another power tool to prevent an insider threat is monitoring of network activity. Commercial solutions include products such as Zenoss, Solarwinds, and Fortinet. The solutions are often a combination of software and hardware that monitor or restrict traffic by port, protocol, or IP address. For example, one contractor used his personal email account to steal intellectual property and was later arrested, sentenced to 26 years in prison, and fined $850,000. In another case, an employee changing jobs was found to have downloaded proprietary documents valued at $400 million from his former employer [17]. The methods of data exfiltration are usually simple and often include personal email, thumb drives or other removable media, and cloud service file storage. A network traffic monitor tool can be configured to block and/or alert when these types of technologies are accessed.

Access Controls

Access controls generally fall into three categories: mandatory access control, discretionary access control, and role-based access control (RBAC). A study by the University of Pittsburg recommends a framework that extends RBAC by blending a risk management component. Looking for behaviors outside their normal job functions, called technical precursors, the system reduces the user's trust level, ultimately requiring intervention by a third party [11].

In a study by CERT, almost 75% of intellectual property theft was from insiders with authorized access to the material they stole; however, not all should have had access [17]. An organization's security polices often develop slowly over time and do not keep pace with the growth of the company and value of the intellectual property and information it processes. Employee transfers between departments must also be scrutinized carefully.

Another interesting roadblock to security policy implementation is the perceived insult to employee trust. Among vocal concerns of tightened security policy are:

- Why, all of a sudden, are we blocking access to personal Webmail?
- I've never had to sign an acceptable use agreement before!
- Why can't I install software anymore?

Taking away authority and access from employees as part of security program implementation requires buy-in from management and experiences the same hurdles as other corporate culture changes.

Multifactor Authentication

Multifactor authentication is an authentication process that uses at least two of the following three components: what you have, what you are, and what you know. What you have is something like a memory card, access token, or other device. What you are is a form of biometric information such as a retinal, palm or fingerprint scan held in a reference file. What you know is the most common form and consists of usernames, passwords, and answers to personal questions. By requiring at least two of the three components, the access level is considered "safe/secure" [13].

Computer Emergency Response Team Recommendations

At the RSA Conference in 2012, the Software Engineering Institute of Carnegie Mellon University proposed a top 10 list for "Winning the Battle Against Insider Threats." Please see the following checklist: "An Agenda for Action for 'Winning the Battle Against Insider Threats'" [16]:

"An Agenda for Action for 'Winning the Battle Against Insider Threats'"

The following is a "top 10 list for winning the battle against insider threats." Check all steps completed:

_____ 1. #10 Learn from past incidents [16].
_____ 2. #9 Focus on protecting the crown jewels [16].
_____ 3. #8 Use your current technologies differently [16].
_____ 4. #7 Mitigate threats from trusted business partners [16].
_____ 5. #6 Recognize concerning behaviors as a potential indicator [16].
_____ 6. #5 Educate employees regarding potential recruitment [16].
_____ 7. #4 Pay close attention at resignation/termination [16].
_____ 8. #3 Address employee privacy issues with general counsel [16].
_____ 9. #2 Work together across the organization [16].
_____ 10. #1 Create an insider threat program now [16]!

Other Human Resource Deterrents

Other policy and procedure implementations can affect the ability of insider threat. Among them are segregation of duties; background checks for new hires and promotions to positions of increasing responsibility; mandatory vacations; overlapping responsibilities; password policies on age, length, reuse, and complexity; and multifactor authentication.

Employment Controls

Acceptable use agreements are a type of employment control that modestly helps with the insider threat. These documents typically spell out company policy with regard to use of the Internet, telephones, email, and other data systems in the organization. The documents should indicate that ignorance is no defense. They should clearly spell out copyright concerns, trademark issues, and trade secrets, and clearly define obscene or offensive data as defined by the Communications Decency Act of 1996, versus consumer data as defined by the Fair Credit Reporting Act [19]. When properly developed in coordination with an attorney, these agreements become legally binding and should clearly define access, acceptable use, and misuse. The penalties can be enormous. For example, the Electronic Communications Privacy Act provides for fines including up to 2 years' imprisonment and $250,000 to individuals and businesses. Another component of acceptable use agreements, especially for the new hire, is a paragraph containing a promise the new employee is not bringing in any data, trade secrets, or insider information from a previous employer [17]. Employees should receive regular oral and written reminders of security policies, as well as frequent, annual, and refresher training about the company's security policy and procedures [19].

9. SUMMARY

As our culture changes with increasingly reliance on IT for basic life essentials, more consideration is due to protecting assets. Even the criminal justice system struggles to keep up; consider the worldwide damage of millions of dollars by the "I Love You" virus, written by a man in the Philippines, who was arrested and later released because there was no law on the books to prosecute him. Flaws in software, discovered and harnessed as zero-day exploits, redefine the scale of threat from the outsider; consider, then, the potential for damage from the already trusted insider, who has physical and logical assess to company assets. The threat posed by insiders is real and growing. Companies would be wise the heed the number one rule of CERT's recommendations: "Create an insider threat program now!" [16].

Finally, let us move on to the real interactive part of this chapter: review questions/exercises, hands-on projects, case projects, and the optional team case project. The answers and/or solutions by chapter can be found in Appendix K.

CHAPTER REVIEW QUESTIONS/EXERCISES

True/False

1. True or False? Edward Snowden is a technology specialist and former employee of Dell and the CIA and later a contractor for Booz Hamilton working for the NSA, who in 2015 became a world-famous whistle-blower of NSA surveillance when he leaked thousands of highly classified documents detailing the agency's massive and global data collection efforts.
2. True or False? The root causes of insider threat behavior are varied and not easily quantified into simple statements.
3. True or False? Naturally, insiders hold a position of trust; you must allow them certain privilege, authority, and access to accomplish their assigned tasks.
4. True or False? Often the personality types least suited for complex logical programming are social introverts.
5. True or False? The HR department bears a measure of responsibility for preventing insider threat behavior.

Multiple Choice

1. For the purpose of selling it outright, the theft of intellectual property remains a surprisingly small fraction of:
   A. Platform as a Service
   B. Infrastructure as a Service
   C. Compromising a user's privacy
   D. Software as a Service
   E. Insider crime
2. A study by Carnegie Mellon University examined 23 insider threat incidents by 26 insiders between:
   A. 1996 and 2002
   B. 1988 and 1995
   C. 2003 and 2009
   D. 2010 and 2016
   E. All of the above
3. An analysis of threat information, similar to the concept of data mining, provides behavioral predictability; one example is:
   A. Intrusion prevention systems
   B. Intrusion detection systems
   C. Attacks from a malicious hypervisor
   D. Attacks from outside the cloud environment
   E. All of the above
4. A 2015 study of insider threats to financial institutions blends activity theory with survival modeling in a:
   A. Backdoor
   B. Botnet
   C. Rootkit
   D. Weibull hazard model
   E. Short message service Trojan
5. The System Administration, Networking and Security Institute publishes a top 20 list of:
   A. Address Resolution Protocol spoofing
   B. Denial of service and distributed denial of service attacks
   C. Critical security controls
   D. Port scanning
   E. Man-in-the-cloud

EXERCISE

Problem

How does one go about developing and issuing minimum standards and guidance for implementing insider threat program capabilities throughout an organization?

Hands-on Projects

Project

Who should be principally responsible for establishing a process to gather, integrate, centrally analyze, and respond to a potential insider threat?

Case Projects

Problem

What should the organization's top management do with regard to insider threat information integration, analysis, and response?

Optional Team Case Project

Problem

Who should ensure that personnel assigned to an insider threat program are fully trained?

REFERENCES

[1] D.L. Burley, J. Eisenberg, S.E. Goodman, Would cybersecurity professionalization help address the cybersecurity crisis? Commun. ACM 57 (2) (2014) 24−27, http://dx.doi.org/10.1145/2556936.
[2] M.G. Martemucci, Unpunished insults—the looming cyber barbary wars, Case West. Reserve J Int. Law 47 (2015) 53−62.
[3] R. Anderson, T. Bozek, T. Longstaff, W. Meitzler, M. Skroch, K. VanWyk. Research on Mitigating the Insider threat to information system #2. Proceedings of a Workshop Held August 2000. Rand Corp.
[4] S. Yang, A. Stotz, J. Jolsopple, M. Sudit, M. Kuhl, High level information fusion for tracking and projection of multistage cyber attacks, J. Inf. Fusion 10 (1) (January 2009) 107−121.
[5] D. Ha, S. Upadhyaya, H. Ngo, S. Pramanik, R. Chinchani, S. Mathew, Insider threat analysis using information-centric modeling, in: P. Craiger (Ed.), Advances in Digital Forensics III.

DigitalForensics 2007. IFIP — The International Federation for Information Processing, vol. 242, Springer, New York, NY, 2007.

[6] A. Piper, Businesswide Cybersecurity, Internal Auditor 71 (3) (2014) 38—43.

[7] J. Reinhard, Cybersecurity. Threats to the Organization's Data, Systems and Devises Present a Challenge to the Entire Business, Not Just the IT Department, Internal Auditor (June 2014) 39.

[8] P.W. Singer, STUXNET and its hidden lessons on the ethics of cyberweapons, Case West. Reserve J. Int. Law 47 (2015) 79—86.

[9] M. Middleton-Leal, Edward Snowden and the power of the privileged insider, Engineering & Technology (17509637) 8 (9) (2013) 29.

[10] W. Jingguo, M. Gupta, H.R. Rao, Insider threats in a financial institution: analysis of attack-proneness of information systems applications, MIS Quarterly 39 (1) (2015) 91—112.

[11] N. Baracaldo, J. Joshi, A trust-and-risk aware RBAC framework: tackling insider threat, in: SACMAT, ACM, Newark, NJ, 2012.

[12] M. Randazzo, M. Keeney, E. Kowalski, Insider Threat Study: Illicit Cyber Activity in the Banking and Finance Sector, Technical Report, Carnegie Mellon Software Engineering Institute, June 2005.

[13] B. Winterberg, Cybersecurity: hitting a moving target, J. Financ. Plann. 28 (7) (2015) 34—35.

[14] W. Eberle, J. Graves, L. Holder, Insider threat detection suing a graph based approach, J. Appl. Secur. Res. 6 (2011) 32—81. Taylor and Francis Group.

[15] Verizon Data Breach Digest, 2015.

[16] D. Cappelli, The CERT top 10 list for winning the battle against insider threats, in: CERT Insider Threat Center Software Engineering Institute Carnegie Mellon University, RSA Conference, 2012.

[17] D. Cappelli, A. Moore, R. Trzeciak, The CERT Guide to Insider Threats. How to Prevent, Detect and Respond to Information Technology Crimes (Theft Sabotage, Fraud).

[18] M. Bishop, C. Gates, Defining the Insider Threat, ACM, 2008.

[19] M.A. Williams, C.A. Bequai, Management's pitfalls in cyberspace: a primer, SAM Adv. Manage. J. (07497075) 79 (1) (2014) 12—25.

[20] Retrieved https: www.whitehouse.gov/the-press-office/2013/02/12/ presidential-policy-directive-critical-infrastructure-security-and-resil.

[21] Retrieved https: www.dhs.gov/critical-infrastructure-sectors.

[22] K.D. Mitnick, W.L. Simon, The Art of Deception: Controlling the Human Element of Security, John Wiley & Sons, 2011.

[23] G. Greenwald, No Place to Hide: Edward Snowden, the NSA, and the US Surveillance State, Macmillan, 2014.

Part III

Disaster Recovery Security

Chapter 36

Disaster Recovery

Scott R. Ellis and Lauren Collins
kCura Corporation, Chicago, IL, United States

1. INTRODUCTION

In almost every organization, when a technology-oriented task is at hand and where no one knows who would handle the request, it typically lands in the information technology department (IT). Whether the task consists of a special, faulty light bulb or a backup for a grease stop in the kitchen sink, organizations rely heavily on the IT department to know the unknown, and to fix anything that breaks.

Disaster recovery (DR), not unlike the plugged sink, is another task that many organizations fail to consider until after much of the technology groundwork has been laid, the corporation is profitable, and suddenly someone realizes that *not* having a DR site is a serious risk to the business. It is at this time that they begin to consider and ponder what a strategy might look like that enables the business to continue to run in the event of Force Majeure or some other disaster, such as if a hacker came in and tore their system down or somehow seized control of it.

Hardware, physical or virtual, must be acquired and configured to capture the environment as it currently sits—and it must be able to continue with its synchronization. Whether this is by the minute, hour, day, or week is a business decision. In fact, much of the DR strategy is driven by business continuity requirements. In the event of a disaster, there must be a plan in place that considers which individuals will act in the event of a disaster. Those individuals must know what constitutes a disaster and the roles must be defined for those individuals.

2. MEASURING RISK AND AVOIDING DISASTER

A key component of a DR plan is for the committee to assess conceivable risks to the organization that could result in the disasters or emergency situations themselves. All events must be considered, and the impact must also be reflected upon so that the organization has the ability to continue and deliver business as usual. Quantitative and qualitative risks are considered separately in a DR plan; however, both come together when determining how an organization's reputation and earnings should be managed in the event of a disaster. Risk is assessed on an inherent and residual basis, allowing an entity to understand the extent to which potential events might impact objectives from two perspectives: likelihood and impact.

Assessing Risk in the Enterprise

Enterprise Risk Management (ERM) is not a template that can be given to every company to meet their needs and fit their business structure. Proper risk assessment identifies the risks throughout the organization and specifies the external and internal sources that the organization may face. The organization engages members from each organizational unit [Executives, Human Resources (HR), Finance, etc.], and asks questions such as "What do you perceive to be the largest risks to the company in terms of significance and likelihood?" and "What do you perceive to be the biggest risks within your control?" After a common understanding is met and all are aware of the risks, such risk assessments should be linked to strategic objectives as shown in Fig. 36.1.

Once the company has an understanding of the top risks that can impact the organization, the executive team determines the company's risk appetite and risk tolerance. Risk appetite is the amount of risk, on a comprehensive level, that an entity is willing to accept in pursuit of value. Risk tolerance, on the other hand, is the range of acceptable variation around the company's objectives. The key is to determine the degree of maturity that meets the needs of your organization.

Steps in the Risk Process

There are five steps to consider for a company to come out ahead when a disaster hits to avoid risk and protect your

Computer and Information Security Handbook. http://dx.doi.org/10.1016/B978-0-12-803843-7.00036-3

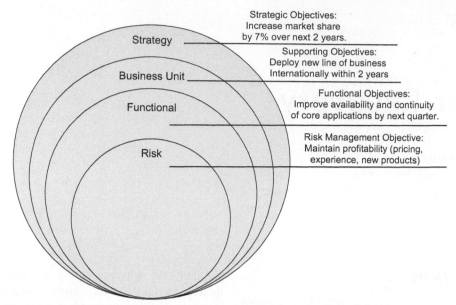

FIGURE 36.1 Risk assessments are linked to strategic objectives in an organization as a whole to allow a company to understand the risks in the organization, the company's risk appetite, and risk tolerance.

data. The following checklist (see checklist: An Agenda for Action for Risk Assessment) is a list of these steps, from assessment to planning, architecting, specifying, and implementing a full-bodied DR solution.

Downtime presents serious consequences for businesses, no matter what their function may be. It is difficult, if not impossible, to recoup lost revenue and rebuild a corporate reputation that is damaged by an outage. While

---

An Agenda for Action for Risk Assessment

Steps in risk assessment (check all tasks completed):

_____**1.** Discover the potential threats:

_____**a.** Environmental (tornado, hurricane, flood, earthquake, fire, landslide, epidemic).

_____**b.** Organized or deliberate disruption (terrorism, war, arson).

_____**c.** Loss of utilities or services (electrical power failure, petroleum shortage, communications services breakdown).

_____**d.** Equipment or system failure (internal power failure, air conditioning failure, production line failure, equipment failure).

_____**e.** Security threat (leak of sensitive information, loss of records or data, cyber-crime).

_____**f.** Supplementary emergency situations (workplace violence, public transportation disruption, health and safety hazard).

_____**2.** Determine requirements:

_____**a.** Prioritize processes

_____**b.** Determine recovery objectives

_____**c.** Plan for common incidents

_____**d.** Communicate the plan

_____**e.** Choose individuals who will test plan regularly and act in the event of a disaster

_____**3.** Understand DR options:

_____**a.** Determine how far to get the data out of the data center.

_____**b.** Will the data center be accessible at the same time as the disaster.

_____**c.** Determine the process to backup and/ or replicate data off-site.

_____**d.** Determine the process to recreate an environment off-site.

_____**4.** Audit providers:

_____**a.** Compare list of providers with internal list of requirements.

_____**b.** Understand range of data protection solutions offered.

_____**c.** Assess proximity (power grid/communications and contingencies).

_____**d.** Data center hardening features and their DR contingencies.

_____**5.** Record findings, implement/test, and revise if/as necessary:

_____**a.** Documentation is the heart of your plan.

_____**b.** Test and adjust plan as necessary, and record findings.

_____**c.** As the environment changes and business needs change, revise the plan and test again.

4. True or False? Downtime presents moderate consequences for businesses, no matter what their function may be.
5. True or False? A business impact assessment is a solution that determines critical business processes based on their impact during a disruption.

Multiple Choice

1. An organization must have a thorough understanding of the _____ and the tolerance of a business outage to define objectives to succeed in the event of an outage.
   A. qualitative analysis
   B. vulnerabilities
   C. critical business processes
   D. malformed request DoS
   E. data controller
2. There are challenges associated with managing a _____, coupled with the technology each department integrates into that infrastructure.
   A. network attached storage (NAS)
   B. risk assessment
   C. valid
   D. high-density infrastructure
   E. bait
3. There are many types of _____ that can occur in business.
   A. data minimization
   B. fabric
   C. disasters
   D. risk communication
   E. security
4. Once a disaster recovery plan has been created that includes both fail and no-fail infrastructure circumstances, a plan must be made that allows for varying degrees of:
   A. risk management
   B. greedy strategy
   C. infrastructure failure
   D. SAN protocol
   E. taps

5. What are equipment or data or communications that are not functioning for such a length of time as to render irreparable damage to business revenues or relationships?
   A. Irrelevant
   B. Tape library
   C. IP storage access
   D. Configuration file
   E. Unusable

EXERCISE

Problem

What are the differences among a Continuity of Operations Plan (COOP), a Business Continuity Plan (BCP), a Critical Infrastructure Protection (CIP) Plan, a Disaster Recovery Plan (DRP), an Information System Contingency Plan (ISCP), a Cyber Incident Response Plan, and an Occupant Emergency Plan (OEP)?

Hands-On Projects

Project

What type of alternate site should an organization choose as a disaster recovery strategy?

Case Projects

Problem

When an event occurs, who should be notified?

Optional Team Case Project

Problem

With what other activities should the ISCP and the recovery solutions be coordinated?

Chapter 37

Disaster Recovery Plans for Small and Medium Businesses (SMBs)

William F. Gross, Jr.

Gross Security, LLC, Spencer, WV, United States

1. INTRODUCTION

Thanks in part to technological marvels like the Internet and modern transportation, the world is more connected than ever before. The term globalization refers to the integration and interaction of people and national economies, culture, and ideologies. With this global interconnectedness comes new and creative threats. Consider, for example, the classic email scam where a wealthy persecuted foreign national needs help moving a large sum of money into the US, or a North Korean attack against the American power grid.

Events like the terrorist attacks of 9/11 and Hurricanes Andrew and Sandy remind us the threat contains both natural and human-caused components. Hurricane Katrina demonstrated the federal government's lack of preparation. Consider, too, the upsurge in popularity of reality TV shows like Survivor, Doomsday Preppers, and The Colony, show a macabre audience. A positive result of this cultural change is businesses are now rethinking sustainability, especially considering the threat may be a well-funded nation state hacker team.

Although the actual classification of "small" in small and medium business (SMB) varies by industry and is sometimes based on numbers of employees or company revenues, the assumption made is that large businesses have the resources, shareholder interest, and, therefore, wisdom and willingness to prepare. However, SMBs may find disaster planning intimidating due to lack of resources, assets, or staff experience. Moreover, planning for catastrophic events should move from a data loss focus in the server room to the mainstream lines of the business. Modern thinking suggests disaster recovery (DR) is not the same thing as business continuity and the idea of DR reaches far beyond just the data center processing function and data repositories [1].

2. IDENTIFYING THE NEED FOR A DISASTER RECOVERY PLAN

In 1992, Hurricane Andrew cost the insurance industry almost $20 billion [1]. In the wake of Hurricane Andrew, one fruit and vegetable business, who previously declined additional product insurance, lost hundreds of thousands of dollars because the power failed and their pr duct spoiled without refrigeration. They now insure their produce to preclude a similar loss [2].

The World Trade Center bombing in 1993 prompted many businesses to examine their disaster recovery plan (DRP) strategies. After 9/11, Morgan Stanley was back up and running on the following Monday when the stock markets opened, with their service offerings to their clients nearly identical as the day before the attacks, even in the face of significant losses [3]. Sadly, other businesses ceased to exist. The cost of a basic disaster plan is affordable, but an extremely detailed plan could be cost prohibitive for most businesses [4]. The alternative is equally dismal: "73% of firms hit by a disaster wind up shutting down" [5].

3. RECOVERY

The process of recovery includes the development of a comprehensive plan that addresses:

- Assessment of disaster impacts on personnel, process, and facilities
- Developing recovery plans and procedures
- Restoration operations and supporting resources [4]

A DRP is a response to a particular event, and therefore, a tactical process, whereas business continuity plans or business recovery plans are strategic: they address repair to a damaged facility, disruption in the supply chain, and the flow of goods and services to customers [6].

The first step for an SMB to create a DRP involves choosing a team; they must be qualified to address the needs of the business. Suggested personnel include a member of the C staff, a financial rep, someone from human resources, a senior member of the information technology (IT) staff, a risk or insurance person, legal counsel, and a media/public relations voice. Having a representative cross-section of the business ensures all business needs are considered; having a company executive ensures the team wields enough power to accomplish the company's planning goals. Many small businesses may not have the requisite expertise in house and should consider consultant services for their disaster planning needs [7]. It is also wise to get your advice from someone not selling solutions.

4. THREAT ANALYSIS

After the massive earthquake in 1971 in the San Fernando Valley, the state government adopted seven pieces of legislation focused on seismic safety in land-use planning. Planning exclusively for specific disasters welcomes the Murphy factor: an unforeseen event and, therefore, an unprepared business. However, if the business resides in geographic areas prone to wildfires, earthquake, or hurricanes, for example, these specific threats remain worthy of consideration. In other words, the preceding analogy is similar to a company's risk assessment, which identifies exceptional risk, such as a company that produces rocket fuel. In the California example, studies conducted after the legislation was implemented showed reduced seismic damage [8].

If you live near an ocean, planning for a hurricane or tsunami seems intuitive, and indeed the team should consider obvious threats both natural and human-caused. However, focusing on the obvious tends to overshadow the equally threatening but less obvious. A better technique for disaster planning is to consider business impacts. Storms, accidents, terrorism, and overloads are all reasons the business may suddenly be without electricity. We need a way to consider how the lack of electricity impacts the business expressed as intensity, measured in dollars over time. Another important consideration is business reputation. If the bank floods, is your money safe?

5. METHODOLOGY

Current philosophy on properly developing DRPs begins with two components: Business Impact Analysis (BIA) and testing the plan. Both elements are important.

The BIA examines every division of the company and details several key items:

- How long the organization can survive without critical assets;
- Identify business functions, then prioritize and identify which are critical;
- Vulnerability, specifically which business functions are susceptible to natural disasters;
- Estimated cost of loss for business functions over time.

These data become the building blocks of the DRP. The true value of the BIA is the unbiased look at process, loss, and cost [9]. Regardless, if a tornado damages the office building, or the disaster is a result of fire or flood, the BIA provides a look at the loss of function irrespective of the cause. The team building the plan carefully considers the value of utilities, space, personnel, and business process, and the financial impact of each loss over different periods of time. For example, a chemical plant manufacturing solid rocket fuel in a single facility has enormous risk of fire; this type of disaster would devastate the business. Accordingly, the company may consider alternate mitigation and fire reduction strategies beyond those required by local and state municipalities.

Hot, Warm, and Cold Sites

Another consideration for the SMB is a backup site, generally referred to as hot, warm, or cold site. Although definitions vary slightly, a cold site has none of the equipment or additional services; the time to take a cold site live is measured in weeks. A warm site has facilities such as HVAC, but is missing the data processing equipment used in daily operations; the expectation is a warm site can be fully operational in a matter of days. A hot site is a live mirror image of the business operations that can be fully operational in a few hours. Cost increases exponentially from cold to hot and based on the nature of the company's resources [10,11].

For most SMB, the cost of a hot site and in many cases, the warm site, is prohibitive. A good DRP, utilizing the BIA, will identify critical assets, processes, and functions and recommend a course of action to preserve the business's viability even during catastrophic events.

Exposures and Vulnerabilities

Other factors to consider in plan development include a financial component. Will you have necessary cash flow available? Operational considerations include having alternate retail or manufacturing spaces far enough away to escape the disaster, but close enough to service your clients. Staffing and data resources play a part, too: do you need an alternate staff or data center? It is likely the disaster event impacts the employees personally. Consider, too, the psychological impacts. You want your employees to feel safe and free from exposure to health, danger, and safety risks from the work product [4].

Derivative Loss

Another important point for the disaster team to consider is the effect of derivative loss, also known as a cascading effect [12]. Complexity and interconnectedness of systems introduce unforeseen disruptions. As the disaster plan is implemented, weaknesses in the plan's ability to address interoperability of the original systems become readily apparent. For example, many organizations have a patch management system in place and in some cases, an old server running an oddly critical utility cannot be patched. Moving into the recovery phase, it is discovered that the operating system is no longer available for the old server, and the original utility application, now so desperately needed, was originally deployed on 3.5″ media and the backup servers have the data, but not the application.

Key Elements of the Plan

The plan should start with a statement of its purpose, scope, and expectations. Key roles, members, positions, and responsibilities should be well documented. The business services identified as critical should be listed as well as recovery priorities and objectives. The plan should also contain lists detailing complete contact information of vendors, suppliers, creditors, and business-to-business (B2B) relationships. Relying on automation to retrieve such data is a potential failure point. Finally, the plan should detail activities for recovery, how they proceed, and considerations during recovery operations [13].

6. TRAIN AND TEST THE PLAN

While the development and refinement of a plan seems to be a monumental task, the process is only partially complete. The US Army uses the slogan, "Train as you fight," which essentially means training should be safe but as realistic as possible. Regardless of the scope and depth of intelligence and wisdom in creating the plan, a simple hands-on test will reveal flaws. In one case, a community bank developed and documented their DRP, which included moving to an alternate location. At the insistence of their consultant, the testing team, normally comprised of a vice president, disaster consultant, and IT admin included a new member for testing the plan: a lobby teller. Including a nonplanner in the testing phase gives a fresh and untainted perspective. The team proudly took their preparations to the alternate site, established telephony and data communications and handed the "working" bank lobby over to the teller, who is the ultimate end user. She immediately began her daily routine of logging into various systems, printing reports, and counting cash drawers, only to find several critical failures the original team could not have predicted without live testing.

Any DRP should be validated with regular live testing, using the alternate processes, disaster site resources, and especially the people and teams who routinely do this type of work. The event should simulate a real disaster as closely as possible, while keeping safety in mind. Training is expensive, too, in terms of dollars and time; consider the impact of that same bank lobby without the normal staff during the test period, and the need to rotate all staff through the training event. However, the intangible rewards surface when reviewing the results of the test (see checklist: "An Agenda for Action for Implementing the Main Objectives of a DR Test"). Employee buy-in helps by making them feel important to the DR process. Training gives employees a sense of purpose and it helps alleviate confusion and fear during any stressful and emotionally draining real event.

An Agenda for Action for Implementing the Main Objectives of a Disaster Recovery (DR) Test

The main objectives of a DR test include the following (Check All Tasks Completed):

_____**1.** Test the processes and procedures for recovery.
_____**2.** Ensure everyone is familiar with the plan.
_____**3.** Validate the plan.
_____**4.** Prove the usability of the recovery site.
_____**5.** Discover if the plan objectives are realistic.
_____**6.** Detail improvements to the plan [13].

---

7. COMMUNICATION

If you listen to any news report about some terrific event, a common theme emerges: people interviewed often comment, "I didn't know what was happening." Communication becomes increasingly important during a crisis event and the DR team should consider this component carefully. Notification procedures that define who needs to know what, when, and how are fulfilled by maintaining a list of customers, suppliers, investors, creditors, government agencies, banks, insurance companies, and vendors, with contact information and organized in a prioritized list, containing phone numbers and physical and email addresses [4]. Other alternate communication ideas include:

- Maintaining an alternate web server with dark pages arranged in templates.
- Have preprinted press releases with blanks for dates.
- Acquire and test alternate cellular networks, Internet service providers (ISP), mobile hotspots, and other connection methods.

Social Media

A 2015 study by the *Journal of Physical Security* concluded that social media as a tool for managing emergencies is viable but needs further study. Emergency management professionals need further guidance on privacy and security issues for using social media as a crisis tool [14]. With virtually every teenager and adult carrying a video camera, email, and texting device in the form of a smartphone, the volume of information about a particular event could easily become staggering; moreover, a DR official would need guidelines to authenticate the veracity of information. Over 76% of respondents to an American Red Cross survey indicated they expected a response from authorities within 3 h of their posting social media requests for help [15]. Conversely, social media offers an ideal platform for officials to communicate messages such as public service announcements, instructions, directions, and immediate feedback to stakeholders.

8. RECOVERY

Planning for recovering from a disaster involves several considerations. First is Recovery Time Objective (RTO), defined as the time between formal implementation of the DRP and when key services are resumed. Second, is the Recovery Point Objective (RPO), or an expression of the amount of data that can be lost. The RPO can be expressed as never, one day, one week, or more, and this critical decision should drive the data backup services, schedule, and locations. Another key term for planners is the Maximum Tolerable Period of Disruption (MTPD), which is how long the business will survive from the point of initial disruption [13].

9. SUMMARY

All business must adapt to changing economic conditions. We are growing accustomed to hearing employers say "do more with less" and "wear multiple hats" as ways of expressing a need to streamline, consolidate, and improve profitability. In the realm of disaster preparations, business continuity, and business impact analyses, SMB often struggle to justify the expense of even a modest plan when faced with the crushing costs of fully functional hot sites, thoroughly developed plans, and regular training events. Natural disasters notwithstanding, and now thanks to the Internet, the attack vector to all businesses became global seemingly overnight. While SMB bemoan the cost of contingency planning as something unforeseen, unpredictable, and therefore not tangible, the lessons learned from natural and human-caused disasters in the last decade close the case against the need for disaster planning. Even a modest plan with mediocre testing is better than the unprepared company facing a real crisis, under severe stress, trying to make strategic decisions. It is much better to prepare in the quiet and still of a fully functioning conference room where cooler heads prevail.

Finally, let's move on to the real interactive part of this Chapter: review questions/exercises, hands-on projects, case projects, and optional team case project. The answers and/or solutions by chapter can be found in Appendix K.

CHAPTER REVIEW QUESTIONS/ EXERCISES

True/False

1. True or False? Although the actual classification of "small" in SMB varies by industry and is sometimes based on numbers of employees or company revenues, the assumption made here is that small businesses have the resources, shareholder interest, and, therefore, wisdom and willingness to prepare.
2. True or False? A DRP is a response to a particular event and, therefore, a tactical process; whereas business continuity plans or business recovery plans are strategic: they address repair to a damaged facility, disruption in the supply chain, and the flow of goods and services to customers.
3. True or False? Past philosophy on properly developing DRPs begins with two components: Business Impact Analysis (BIA) and testing the plan.
4. True or False? The true value of the BIA is the unbiased look at process, loss, and cost.
5. True or False? Another consideration for the SMB is a backup site, generally referred to as hot, warm, or cold.

Multiple Choice

1. Other factors to consider in plan development include a:
   A. Platform-as-a-Service (PaaS)
   B. Financial component
   C. Compromising user's privacy
   D. Software-as-a-Service (SaaS)
   E. Insider crime
2. Another important point for the disaster team to consider is the effect of derivative loss, also known as a:
   A. Key element of a plan
   B. Cascading effect
   C. Purpose
   D. Scope
   E. All of the above
3. Any DRP should be validated with regular live testing, using the alternate processes, disaster site resources, and especially the people and teams who routinely do this type of:
   A. IPS
   B. IDS
   C. Work
   D. Attack
   E. All of the above
4. Emergency management professionals need further guidance on privacy and security issues for using social media as a:
   A. Backdoor
   B. Botnet

C. Rootkit

D. Crisis tool

E. SMS Trojan

5. What is an expression of the amount of data that can be lost:

A. Maximum Tolerable Period of Disruption

B. SMB

C. Critical security control

D. Port scanning

E. Recovery Point Objective

EXERCISE

Problem

How should SMBs go about planning for DR in advance?

Hands-On Projects

Project

How should SMBs go about preparing a DRP?

Case Projects

Problem

How should SMBs go about creating a preparedness program?

Optional Team Case Project

Problem

How should SMBs go about testing their business systems?

REFERENCES

[1] F. Alonso, J. Boucher, R.H. Colson, Business continuity plans for disaster response, CPA J. 71 (11) (2001) 60.

[2] N. Opiela, When misfortune brings a client to your door, J. Financ. Plann. 14 (2) (2001) 58–64.

[3] M. Barrier, Preparing for the worst (cover story), Intern. Aud. 58 (6) (2001) 57.

[4] S. Weier, Managing effective disaster recovery (cover story), CPA J. 71 (12) (2001) 22.

[5] N. Pekala, Back to business, J. Prop. Manag. 67 (6) (2002) 44.

[6] M. Morganti, A Business Continuity Plan Keeps You in Business, vol. 78, ©2001 Factory Mutual Insurance Co. Reprinted with permission from Record—The Magazine of Property Conservation, Third Quarter 2001, 2001.

[7] J.A. Gerber, E.R. Feldman, Is your business prepared for the worst? J. Account. 193 (4) (2002) 61–64.

[8] A.C. Nelson, S.P. French, Plan quality and mitigating damage from natural disasters, J. Am. Plan. Assoc. 68 (2) (2002) 194.

[9] K. Bandyopadhyay, The role of business impact analysis and testing in disaster recovery planning by health maintenance organizations, Hosp. Top. 79 (1) (2001) 16.

[10] E. McCarthy, Tech tools for disaster recovery, J. Financ. Plann. 20 (2) (2007) 28–34.

[11] S. Harris, CISSP All-in-One Exam Guide, McGraw-Hill, Inc., 2010.

[12] J. Pu, Y.Y. Haimes, Risk management for Leontief-based interdependent systems, Risk Anal. 24 (5) (2004) 1215–1229, http://dx.doi.org/10.1111/j.0272-4332.2004.00520.x.

[13] C. Bradbury, DISASTER! Creating and managing an effective recovery plan, Manager: Br. J. Adm. Manag. 62 (2008) 14–16.

[14] T. Jordan, W. Preining, G.D. Curry, J.J. Leflar, M. Glasser, R. Loyear, J. Sorbron, J. Phys. Secur. 8 (2) (2015) 15–36.

[15] C. Wardell III, Y. San Su, 2011 Social Media Emergency Management Camp, CNA Analysis Solutions, 2011.

Part IV

Security Standards and Policies

Part IV

Security Standards and Policies

Chapter 31 Security, Certification and Standards Implementation
Keith Lewis

Chapter 33 Security Policies and Plans Development

Chapter 38

Security Certification and Standards Implementation

Keith Lewis

Keller Graduate School of Management, kCura, Chicago, IL, United States

1. INTRODUCTION: THE SECURITY COMPLIANCE PUZZLE

Safeguarding consumer data and company information systems have evolved into a science over the years. The biggest challenge is making sure the public is fully protected by supporting and enforcing security design frameworks with regulatory requirements for industry leaders and management teams to follow. Thanks to standard institutions working closely with government agencies to plan laws and regulations, these frameworks and validation controls ensure a reliable and robust approach toward overall security design, once implemented.

To begin putting the puzzle together, you must start with identifying the level of security your company wants to address. Is it customer or employee data (see Fig. 38.1) that you are trying to protect, only? Is it subscriber data? Medical data? Personal social media information? Computer network design? Financial or credit card information? These are just some of the areas a security assessment initiative reviews with the goal to produce the best mitigation recommendations possible so strong process controls can be put into place on a foundation of compliance that everyone can follow. Assessment exercises require both an internal and external exercise of audit activity to validate the current security strengths and weaknesses of your company or organization.

2. THE AGE OF DIGITAL REGULATIONS

As the digital age grew in the late 1990s through the 2000s, the lack of controls in security, accountability, and data integrity became more evident when industry scandals such as WorldCom and Enron [1] took center stage and fraudulent practices became apparent. It became clear that more process

control and system validations needed to come into focus as the volume of customer and information data stored in companies began to grow exponentially every year.

Laws and the shoring up of missing or existing regulations were paramount during these times to bring back public confidence in the large-sized industries caught up in these public scandals, but they also were the foundation for establishing reliable and credible compliance standards for all levels of companies who manage data information systems. The laws created during these times required the following areas of standardization, best practices, and audit compliance validations:

- Security Controls validated through Security Audit Compliance reporting
- Ongoing compliance process management ensuring the integrity of the process lifecycle
- Assessment reviews to identify risks and their required remediation in process, data management, and technology infrastructure designs
- Monthly, Quarterly, and Annual reporting assessing a company's potential material weakness in their organization [2]

While the laws mostly established during the early 2000s were targeted at business integrity best practices, many did not take into account the digital technology challenges to maintain these quality standards the industries were tasked to put into place. Additional standards, certifications, and best practice controls and reporting were strongly needed in the underlying structured enterprises that supported these business infrastructures and heavily relied on digital technologies. These standardizations are now used for all businesses to ensure that security, data integrity (see Fig. 38.2), and customer confidence is being monitored, maintained, and used daily.

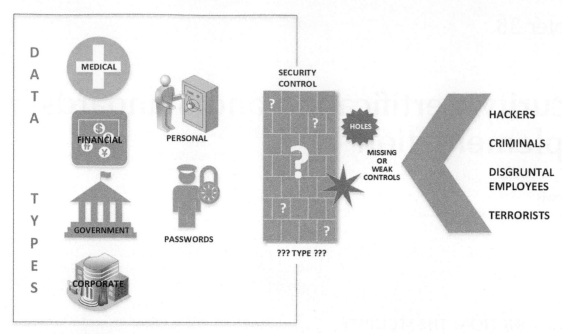

FIGURE 38.1   Identifying the level of security your company wants to address for its customer or employee data.

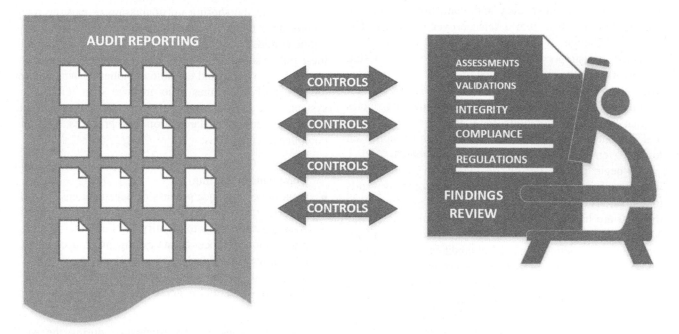

FIGURE 38.2   Standardizations that are now being used for all businesses to ensure that security, data integrity, and customer confidence are being monitored, maintained, and used daily.

3. SECURITY REGULATIONS AND LAWS: TECHNOLOGY CHALLENGES

Now, let's look at some of the major regulatory acts that impact Information Technology Specialists on a daily basis. The major regulatory acts are shown below:

- HIPAA: Health Insurance Portability and Accountability Act
- PCI DSS: Payment Card Industry Data Security Standard
- FISMA: Federal Information Security Management Act of 2002
- SOX: The Sarbanes-Oxley Act of 2002

HIPAA: Health Insurance Portability and Accountability Act

This law was established to protect healthcare-related information for both electronic Protected Health Information (ePHI) data and standard Protected Health Information materials for patients and people who have healthcare plans managed by service providers in the healthcare industry. Technology and procedure security reviews are required on a frequent basis to validate the security controls needed to secure this information, especially for digital electronic data information. Companies are required to have audit specialists, both internal and external, to do annual assessments ensuring security technologies such as data encryption, data retention, secure database systems, and the administration tracking needed, so these types of information are not potentially compromised due to lack of control systems and access approvals [3].

PCI DSS: Payment Card Industry Data Security Standard

With the continuing use of credit card services worldwide, the Cardholder Information Security Program (CISP) was established by MasterCard and VISA to protect domestic and global customer interests by establishing required security standards. This was needed so customers using their commerce services were strongly protected when credit card identification and financial account transactions occurred over various types of security devices such as input Pin Entry Devices (PED), or security chip cards also referred as "Chip Cards." These standards now manage credit card security guidelines for VISA, MasterCard, Discoverer, American Express, and JCB International. These devices must adhere to the strongest security requirements for PCI certification compliance. From ATMs to credit-card readers, to Secure Socket Layer (SSL) transports and updated Certificate of Authority solutions, PCI DSS and compliance plays an important part in ensuring credit card information security for customer information systems (see checklist: "An Agenda for Action for Technology Standards of Focus for PCI DSS") [4].

An Agenda for Action for Technology Standards of Focus for PCI DSS

Technology Standards of Focus for PCI DSS includes the following key activities (check all tasks completed):

_____**1.** Control objectives and PCI DSS requirements

_____**2.** Secure network connectivity

_____**3.** Cardholder data privacy and protection

_____**4.** Security vulnerability protection program (virus protection, malware defenses, etc.)

_____**5.** Strengthen access controls

_____**6.** Risk assessments, archived, and real-time monitoring systems

_____**7.** Security policy governance

FISMA: Federal Information Security Management Act of 2002

This important legislation passed in 2002 as a United States Federal law under Title III focused on the country's federal agency offices on the importance of standardizing security systems. This helped establish the support for institutes which govern standards and best practices in these areas, such as the National Institute Standards of Technology (NIST). The NIST currently manages the National Vulnerability Database, the Information Security Automation Program, and many other standard setting services and initiatives that are shared beyond the Federal Government agency infrastructure environments. This act has helped create frameworks for the government and commercial industries to use that helps measure risk and vulnerabilities against cost-effective cyber security solutions to help mitigate these potential weaknesses in an organization's network [5].

SOX: The Sarbanes-Oxley Act of 2002

This law was established due to the multiple fraudulent cases being discovered during the early 2000s. The focus of Section 404 that requires an annual report review for all public businesses with corporation entities that must provide at the end of year Finding Reports. This report goes to the public and corporate shareholders, an overall credibility assessment from external auditing services verifying financial reports that are managed by strong security technologies with external audit validations to assess annual reviews of existing security controls put into place. The SOX law did not clarify a detailed technological approach on how to achieve these compliance quality assurances, a structure of best practice security policies needed to be established. These controls included framework controls such as COBIT, ISO standards, Information Systems Audit and Control Association (ISACA), ITIL, and other charter groups to bridge the gulf between oversight objectives from the SOX act to tangible process and solutions IT management environments [6].

Regulations and Laws: The International Challenge

Not all standard institutes interpret laws and regulations at a global or international level when it comes to security standards. Each country's interpretation of law or regulation is based on the many factors such as:

1. A specific country's interpretation of the law or regulation and the level of risk and severity it implies for their governmental, commercial, or public interests.

TABLE 38.1 Framework Toolsets

Framework Toolset	Providers	Primary Use
COBIT (control objectives for information and related technology) [8]	ISACA (Information Systems Audit and Control Association)	Connecting business goals and objectives with Information Technology (IT) goals through process control management
ISO 17799 (ISO: International organization for standardization) [8]	ISO/IEC (IEC: International Electrotechnical Commission)	Foundation framework planning for creating a security project or program structure
ITIL (information technology infrastructure library)	United Kingdom office of government commerce	IT service management, workflow, and process controls. End-to-end lifecycle technology and process management
CSC (Critical security controls)	SANS and CISC (SANS: The SANS Institute) (CISC: center for internet security)	Important framework security controls used for overall network security validation objectives for information technology centers and their computer environments
ISO/IEC 27002	ISO/IEC (IEC: International Electrotechnical Commission)	Security standard frameworks published for IT governance audit and support management communities [8]

2. International treaties can be a factor when it comes to regulatory requirements with companies or governments using security standards that may or may not comply with these guidelines or restrictions.
3. Continent, federal, state, province, county, city, village, or any governing body type can also have different requirements based on those areas of legal acceptance and law interpretation for those specific locations.
4. Audit frequencies, policies, and report types can also have unique complexities for how security assessments and controls are managed on a regular basis [7].

4. IMPLEMENTATION: THE COMPLIANCE FOUNDATION

One of the most difficult challenges a business can face is trying to get a handle on how to plan out an implementation project for audit controls and compliances. Luckily, there are many resources both on the Internet and through Subject Matter Expert (SME) services who can provide all the frameworks you need, based on the size of your organization and the unique security requirements your company must take on. Standard support institutes such as ISACA have preplanned frameworks and summary plans for best practices on how to create and manage an IT Governance team who can take on the compliance challenges and recommendations for both approach and methodology as you structure out your teams. ISACA's Information Technology Assurance Framework (ITAF) that you can download free from ISACA's website can help your implementation team get a good head start on how you want to plan out your project to bring a solid compliance governance framework into your company or organization.

Getting to Industry Compliance: Best Practice Framework Tools

Based on the compliance goals your company is trying to achieve, there is a wide variety of best practice framework tools from standard institutes available for businesses. Each has a range of strengths and benefits based on the type of business organization. Some of the frequently used Framework Toolsets in industries today are shown in Table 38.1.

Information Technology (IT) Governance: The Keepers to the IT Compliance Kingdom

When your company or organization decides to implement the controls needed in sustaining an IT Compliance structure-lifecycle, it will need dedicated resources to keep these objectives on track on an ongoing basis. This is where IT Governance comes in. IT Governance provides the stability and accountability management needed to ensure security controls, process procedures, and overall infrastructure integrity with making sure security systems are operating efficiently and effectively. Key target goals for this include:

- The Initiation/Implementation Process: Turning Chaos-to-Order
- Accountability and Security Ownership: The Process and Technology Stakeholders
- Repeatable and Dependable with predictable output: Confidence with Input/Output integrity
- Security Definition Library for Business Processes and Security Controls: Security Definitions

- Support Management Controlled: Security controls and procedures work as-designed from Security Definition Library

The IT Governance and the management support team works closely with each Technology Champion in their respective areas of support. For example, for the creation of security controls related to database systems, an IT Database Manager, and Database Administrator will help (during the "Initiation and Implementation" phase) to define the necessary process controls. Administration password such as a shared system-related "admin" account that multiple team members know about has periodic audit trail event tracking capabilities so that such changes are recorded and justified through change or incident management requests. Using the database administration control, for example, could consist of:

1. IT Governance (see Fig. 38.3) working with IT Database administration team to define the technology and process controls needed to mitigate a potential security risk. For example, a shared access administration account.
2. The IT Database administration team would work with the IT Governance team and create a monitoring or audit report that appears on a regular basis (e.g., daily, weekly, monthly, etc.), that displays any database updates or changes that occurred for the specific database in question.
3. These report changes showing "any" shared account activity would need a corresponding change or incident management ticket request number that justified the activity noted in the report.
4. The change or incident management ticket noted in this reported must have a business justification, management approval, and evidence of some sort that demonstrates an artifact of nonmalicious intent for these recorded changes.

Information Technology (IT) Governance: Who's Watching the Watchers

Using the database example for a shared database system administration account helps ensure security permissions are taken into account and have not been compromised with regular audit trail capturing and security system activity report reviews in the control process. This example shows how passive security control management works. More proactive audit controls for more powerful access accounts such as Microsoft Domain Admin user or firewall administrator account should require not only audit activity capturing but immediate support department alert notification for any unplanned system activity that may look like planned or unplanned maintenance tasks. What's great about audit reviews shared by IT Governance, and IT Support teams is also taking the time necessary to work on shoring up new or existing security control processes to safeguard an organization's system environment.

IT Governance managers and security auditors work together with IT Support to create, update, or identify the needed documentation for control procedures created by defined security policies that try to take into account all levels of industry-proven best practice Framework Toolsets available by standard institutes such as SANS or ISO/IEC.

Information Technology (IT) Governance: The Audit Experience

When security controls are defined, agreed upon, and implemented to help safeguard an organization's environment, sometimes the audit control experience can be overwhelming. Especially if the policy and security control process put into place turns out to be overcomplicated or more than ongoing system support teams can handle. For example, let's say a network team has worked with IT

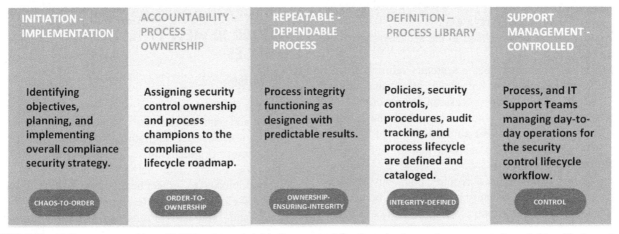

IT GOVERNANCE – COMPLIANCE MANAGEMENT ROLE

INITIATION - IMPLEMENTATION	ACCOUNTABILITY - PROCESS OWNERSHIP	REPEATABLE - DEPENDABLE PROCESS	DEFINITION – PROCESS LIBRARY	SUPPORT MANAGEMENT - CONTROLLED
Identifying objectives, planning, and implementing overall compliance security strategy.	Assigning security control ownership and process champions to the compliance lifecycle roadmap.	Process integrity functioning as designed with predictable results.	Policies, security controls, procedures, audit tracking, and process lifecycle are defined and cataloged.	Process, and IT Support Teams managing day-to-day operations for the security control lifecycle workflow.
CHAOS-TO-ORDER	ORDER-TO-OWNERSHIP	OWNERSHIP-ENSURING-INTEGRITY	INTEGRITY-DEFINED	CONTROL

FIGURE 38.3 IT Governance working with IT Database administration team to define the technology and process controls needed to mitigate a potential security risk.

RL-No.	Control Section	Control No.	Control Description	Request-Type Description	Process Owner	Test Category	Date Requested	Date Due	Current Status	Additional notes
				Client Information Request Listings - Report						
1	Networking	1.1	Wi-Fi Guest Password periodic changing required	Configuration Validation	Fred Smith - Network Manager	Review	1/1/2016	2/1/2016	Request submitted	
2	Networking	1.2	Firewall Rulesets - Daily Updating	Configuration Validation	Fred Smith - Network Manager	Review	1/1/2016	2/1/2016	Request submitted	

FIGURE 38.4 Audit control toolsets commonly used by audit professionals are known as Provided by the Client (PBC) reporting.

Governance to help implement a firewall update policy that must be reported on through monthly reporting. This monthly report requires both an automated process and a support technician's manual intervention to enter the update changes to the firewall system. If the support technician at 2:00 a.m. in the morning updates blocking or opens up a port to correct a business communication problem on the Internet, and he or she forgets to update their manual task for this, that's a negative strike against the control process originally put into place.

When negative strikes are discovered during a regular audit review activity, a correction must be immediately identified and put into place to safeguard the environment and also make sure the control process weakness is resolved. During an internal audit review, there can be many of these that sometimes can test management's patience due to unforeseen costs in material, times, and resources needed to allocate to the problem that may have been originally poorly implemented.

Auditor activities consist mostly of two types: internal and external. The internal audit activity will be an outside auditing service hired by your company, coming onsite to your business and running assessment reporting and system validation activities to report back to IT Governance and IT Management teams the strengths and weaknesses found in the predefined or missing controls. These audit tasks from the audit professionals can consist of:

1. Document Reviews:
   a. Missing or existing policy or procedure security documentation related to the security control being reviewed.
   b. Security audit trail logs and reports related to the security control being reviewed.
2. Security role reviews related to the security control being reviewed.
   a. For example, why does a secretary administrator in the company have high-level Microsoft Domain Admin security group access on her account?
   b. Another example could be why does the business role of an account give all accountants in this security group access to an external firewall logging system.
   c. Security role reviews require both business and accountable functionality justification to be accepted in an review audit report.

Provided by the Client (PBC) Reporting

Audit control toolsets commonly used by audit professionals are known as Provided by the Client (PBC) reporting (see Fig. 38.4). This is a system questionnaire that support teams are required to have knowledge of for compliance reviews. Auditors will take the answers from this report, analyze it, and work with the process support teams to see if corrections are needed and what the risk magnitude is for any open process weaknesses discovered.

5. SUMMARY

External auditors do the same thing as internal auditors, but they will be the final providers in security control integrity testing. Internal auditors are usually the teams that help with a trial practice run for the year, so the support teams can get their control vulnerabilities identified and mitigation put into place before the final external audit report findings are scheduled and thoroughly completed. The year's final external audit findings report is normally shared with executive management. If any serious security weaknesses are discovered, a corporation is normally required to report these results in an annual shareholder's financial report as a "material weakness." Such findings cannot only jeopardize the company's reputation and integrity to its shareholders and the public but also cost the business millions of dollars in customer confidence damage control.

Finally, let's move on to the real interactive part of this Chapter: review questions/exercises, hands-on projects, case projects, and optional team case project. The answers and/or solutions by chapter can be found in Appendix K.

CHAPTER REVIEW QUESTIONS/ EXERCISES

True/False

1. True or False? Assessment exercises require both an internal and external exercise of audit activity to validate the current security strengths and weaknesses of your company or organization.
2. True or False? The Sarbanes-Oxley Act of 2002 was established to protect healthcare related information for both electronic Protected Health Information (ePHI) data and standard Protected Health Information

materials for patients and people who have healthcare plans managed by service providers in the healthcare industry.

3. True or False? With the continuing use of credit card services worldwide, the Cardholder Information Security Program (CISP) was established by American Express to protect domestic and global customer interests by establishing required security standards.

4. True or False? The HIPPA legislation passed in 2002 as a United States Federal law under Title III focused on the country's federal agency offices on the importance of standardizing security systems.

5. True or False? The SOX law was established due to the multiple fraudulent cases being discovered during the early 2000s.

Multiple Choice

1. What requires both an internal and external exercise of audit activity to validate the current security strengths and weaknesses of your company or organization?
   A. Strong process controls
   B. Assessment exercises
   C. Mitigation recommendations
   D. Current security strengths
   E. All of the above

2. What law was established to protect healthcare related information for both electronic Protected Health Information (ePHI) data and standard Protected Health Information materials for patients and people who have healthcare plans managed by service providers in the healthcare industry?
   A. HIPAA
   B. PCI DSS
   C. FISMA
   D. SOX
   E. All of the above

3. Not all standard institutes interpret laws and regulations at a global or international level when it comes to:
   A. Risk and severity
   B. International Treaties
   C. Security standards
   D. Different requirements
   E. All of the above

4. What can help your implementation team get a good head start on how you want to plan out your project to bring a solid compliance governance framework into your company or organization?
   A. Framework Toolsets
   B. ISO/IEC
   C. ISACA's ITAF
   D. ITIL
   E. All of the above

5. What provides the stability and accountability management needed to ensure security controls, process procedures, and overall infrastructure integrity with making sure security systems are operating efficiently and effectively?
   A. Role-based Security Access
   B. Security
   C. Governance
   D. Information Technology Governance
   E. All of the above

EXERCISE

Problem

Stemming from the organizational level, what processes throughout an organization examine security posture and compliance with mandates?

Hands-On Projects

Project

How does an organization ensure that its security standards and guidelines are technically correct and implementable?

Case Projects

Problem

Can an organization prioritize its recommended security controls to establish which controls should be deployed first?

Optional Team Case Project

Problem

Are there automated tools to support implementation and efficient and affordable generation of certification and accreditation evidence?

REFERENCES

[1] J.R. Emshwiller, R. Smith, 24 Days: How Two Wall Street Journal Reporters Uncovered the Lies that Destroyed Faith in Corporate America or Infectious Greed (Harper Information), 2003.
[2] PCAOB Auditing Standard No 5, PCAOB Release No 2007-005, May 24, 2007.
[3] HIPAA. http://www.dhcs.ca.gov.
[4] PCI DSS. https://www.pcisecuritystandards.org/pci_security/.
[5] FISMA. https://www.dhs.gov/fisma/.
[6] SOX. http://www.soxlaw.com/.
[7] B. Boczek, International Law: A Dictionary, Scarecrow Press, 2005.
[8] ISACA. https://www.isaca.org.

Chapter 39

Security Policies and Plans Development

Keith Lewis

Keller Graduate School of Management, kCura, Chicago, IL, United States

1. INTRODUCTION: POLICIES AND PLANNING: SECURITY FRAMEWORK FOUNDATION

When building a solid house of security frameworks (Fig. 39.1), a strong foundation backed by fortified support points is required or the structure is bound to collapse at the first stressful experience. This is the reason why it is so important to have a well-planned security policy implementation base to be put into place, backed by business needs, legal compliance, and senior management support. Security policy creation is based primarily on [1]:

- The business or organization's functional purpose

- Data management type (e.g., customer data, PII data, etc.)
- Level of security risks identified through audit assessments
- Legal compliance regulation requirements
- Financial budgetary and staffing resource limitations enabled to support implementing and supporting ongoing security measures on a regular basis

Security Policy Security Points: Brick Fortification

Each security policy reviewed and implemented is our "brick" (Fig. 39.2) in the fortification for the defense-in-depth

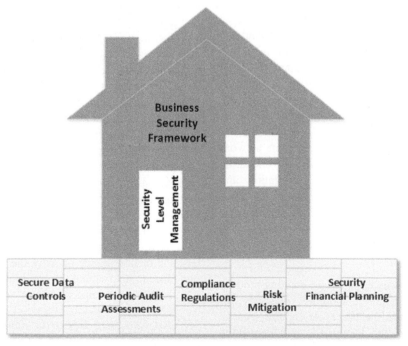

FIGURE 39.1 Business security frameworks.

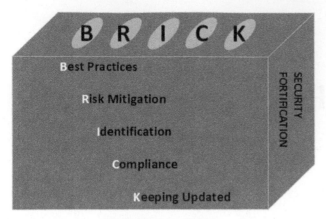

FIGURE 39.2 BRICK

strategy needed to achieve a well-rounded overall design of security that best fits the business or organization's needed to mitigate risks from criminal elements and potential internal malicious internal resource retaliation. Using the brick analogy, the following rules for brick component considerations should be focused on:

- "B" for Best Practices
- "R" for Risk Assessments
- "I" for Identity Management
- "C" for Compliance
- "K" for Keeping Security Points updated

"B" for Best Practices

By leveraging the existing framework plans used by industry today, negates the need for "reinventing" the wheel; thus, minimizing the need to achieve optimal implementation planning; and, not spending a lot of time and resources for creating solutions from the ground up. For example, defense-in-depth best practices take into consideration People, Technologies, and Operations that frames out the importance of many different types of process and technology areas an organization must protect. This includes activities of Security Awareness, implementing Facility Countermeasures, System Security Administration, Social Engineering, defenses on network communication boundaries, server, and workstation infrastructures, and continuous detection, mitigation, and notification to security support personnel from the manager, to facilities, to the IT technology support teams managing that specific security area's environment.

"R" for Risk Assessments

Risk assessments are not only essential for creating security policies, but also are required monthly, quarterly, or annually. This is to ensure the life cycle for the security policy is being followed and supported, and identifying whether the policies are providing the risk mitigation originally identified that needs to be updated or not from recently discovered vulnerabilities.

"I" for Identity Management

Whether it's content data information or personal account information, the risk potentials always start at the Identity Management (IDM) level for security frameworks. Authentication, Authorization, and Account Provisioning is a continuous technical and business management process, that if compromised at the administration level, can give hackers the "keys to the kingdom" to permission roles or system administration account access. There are many other technical hacking methodologies, such as the "man in the middle" attacks that takes, for example, processes which covertly alters data transports between two system contact points giving the false impression they are securely connecting with each other. While this interception hack methodology relies on technology behavior limitations, the end goal is to grab and control the permission account level so the hacker can gain access to the data needed to circumvent and compromise the targeted system during the attack [2].

"C" for Compliance

Support for technology measures required to manage implemented security policy controls and procedures can be very expensive in hardware and software purchasing; ongoing annual support licensing to keep the systems up to date; and audit and assessment reviews to ensure these systems are as fortified as modern designs can make them. Resources allocated to support these security controls must also be considered and must be weighted with the security IT Governance body and senior management teams so that the value of security investments are balanced against the level of risks that are mitigated. When it comes to these kinds of business challenges, legal and security compliance requirements will help cost justify these important types of security investments while also maintaining a focused perspective in keeping the business and customer data secure with the latest solutions available in the industry, today. What can drive this at a corporate level is the annual fiscal report to shareholders where, thanks to Sarbanes-Oxley, accounting auditors are required to report preexisting "material weakness" potentials found during the fiscal year that could impact the credibility of company integrity and financial statement irregularities [1]. Based on how large the corporation is, sometimes these types of negative findings could impact a company's reputation costing the organization millions of dollars. However, compliance is not only to be used for mandating the importance of control security investments, but also should be used in ensuring a baseline of acceptance on why the policy needs to be put into place to help secure the environment and defining what it will take to accomplish this.

"K" for Keeping Security Points Updated

One of the biggest challenges companies must continuously work on is keeping their security environments, policies, and procedures as updated as possible due to innovative hackers, criminals, or disgruntled employees taking advantage of legacy security holes that come from out-of-date solutions or bad security patching that may appear from time to time that requires immediate attention. Process and procedures can also become out of date, such as social engineering attacks that could fool a help desk administration technician into giving a hacker permission access to a system because they are using out-of-date support scripts that haven't been reviewed and improved upon to avoid these types of risks. Keeping security process, procedures, and physical environments as up to date as possible requires regularly scheduled audit assessment reviews and remediation. Many other security control mapping formats can also be leveraged for creating and developing security control implementations [3] such as ISACA CoBIT Process Mapping, or the SANS CIS Security Controls Matrix assessment tool sets.

2. CIA: NOT THE CENTRAL INTELLIGENCE AGENCY

Whenever someone new to security best practices hears or reads on the importance of CIA best practices, immediately thoughts of super spies come to mind as this acronym is most commonly used for the United States "Central Intelligence Agency" department. CIA for security best practices stands for Confidentiality, Integrity, and Availability [2] when it comes to thinking about, developing, and implementing a new security control policy into your computer environments. This helps IT Governance support and management personnel get a good understanding from the ground up, on what level of security must be focused on and its importance to the organization that justifies the cost needed to implement it, at a fundamental level. The CIA Triad (Fig. 39.3) that comes in many forms and addendum types is still used as a baseline to begin security control policy planning, today [4].

Confidentiality

Levels of privacy for confidentiality can stem from a user's private account information such as medical data, social security number information, or birth date; or it can also be interpreted at an administration technology level for security roles group information such as permissions and access to folders in various types of computer file shares. Protecting both data content information and access to this type of information must be carefully analyzed and planned for when evaluating a new or existing security control process procedure. Identifying who is the owner of these security control processes, from a database administrator to a systems administrator, and who or what validates their security access must also be identified and entered into the control. The overall importance of this part of the CIA Triad is to identify, designate, or restrict appropriate access and authorization rights on specific information to the correct users requiring it on the system.

Integrity

This part of the CIA Triad takes into account the authenticity of the data information stored in a security-type container such as a database or directory service and that any changes to the data are fully approved by a data validation owner. This owner can be a database administrator, system administrator, business application administrator, accountant, or anyone who has been given designated authorization rights to manage the ongoing content data population to these systems. For example, if a program calculates department earnings on an income report and enters this value into a spreadsheet but a valid adjustment must be made to offset a correction, a change control tracking process must be initiated and validated to ensure the credibility of this value change is verified and approved. This change would be tracked and recorded so periodic audit sampling review would be available to assessment teams.

Availability

System access for public use, restricted or limited use, administrative use, or device access must be available with the correct permission and authorization security settings put into place. These access control activities must be carefully monitored to ensure no malicious intent is attempting to compromise the system. Attacks such as denial-of-service (DoS) attacks in progress, that are attempting to crash and bring down the system, must be immediately identified and mitigated to protect system access and availability [4]. Defined security control policies help remediate these situations ahead of time to help keep these systems safe and secure.

3. SECURITY POLICY STRUCTURE

While it's important to take into consideration preexisting and proven security control policy templates and formats available by the many standard institutes or audit assessment organizations in the industry today, it's even more important that the

FIGURE 39.3 Confidentiality, Integrity, and Availability (CIA) triad.

An Agenda for Action for Creating Control Security Policies for an Organization

Creating control security policies for an organization includes the following key activities (check all tasks completed):

_____**1.** Policy Category Type
    _____**a.** Scope
    _____**b.** Policy Summary Statement
_____**2.** Policy Statement Agreement
_____**3.** Definition Management
    _____**a.** User Access
    _____**b.** Administrative Access
    _____**c.** Service Access
    _____**d.** Device Access
    _____**e.** Confidential and Sensitive Information Agreement
_____**4.** Policy (Business Process and Department Security Owner)
    _____**a.** Applicability Management
    _____**b.** Security Roles
    _____**c.** Adhering Standards (if applicable)
    _____**d.** Requirements
        _____**i.** Logical Access Controls (Login Credentials)
            _____**(a)** Security Validation and Verification
            _____**(b)** Third-party Service Management
        _____**ii.** Hardware Security Requirements (Requiring Network Connectivity)
            _____**(a)** Valid Registration for Network Devices
            _____**(b)** Network Identity Configurations
            _____**(c)** Equipment removal lifecycle
            _____**(d)** Server Identity Configurations
            _____**(e)** Security Configuration
        _____**iii.** Software Security Requirements (Server or Workstation)
            _____**(a)** Virus Protection
            _____**(b)** Firewall Application
            _____**(c)** Legally purchased and licensed software
            _____**(d)** Software Patching Lifecycle Update Capability
            _____**(e)** End-Point Integrity System Validation
            _____**(f)** Secure and Encrypted Data Link Connectivity (as needed)
            _____**(g)** Secure and Encrypted Storage File Management Systems
    _____**e.** Prohibited Activities (End User License Agreement (EULA) and Preagreement Requirement)
        _____**i.** General Unacceptable System Usage
        _____**ii.** Commercial Usage
        _____**iii.** Illegal Software or Copyright Usage
        _____**iv.** Inappropriate Email Usage
        _____**v.** Network Monitoring: Prohibited Usage
        _____**vi.** Production Operations: Server Network
        _____**vii.** Wireless Remote Infrastructure
    _____**f.** Security Policy Enforcement: Statement
    _____**g.** Access Exception Statement
        _____**i.** Access Roles and Responsibilities
        _____**ii.** Privacy Exception
    _____**h.** Security Breach Management
        _____**i.** Monitoring
        _____**ii.** Escalation Procedures
            _____**(a)** Notification Workflow
            _____**(b)** Remediation Implementation: Reactive
            _____**(c)** Remediation Implementation: Passive
    _____**i.** Data Backup and Recovery: Continuity Summary
    _____**j.** Security Training: Educational Awareness Program (if applicable)
    _____**k.** Security Control Policy: Ownership Agreement
        _____**i.** Digital or Physical Signature Approval (IT Governance)
        _____**ii.** Digital or Physical Signature Approval (Process and Technology Owner)
    _____**l.** Effective Date: Implementation
        _____**i.** Digital or Physical Signature Approval (e.g., CFO, CIO, etc.)
    _____**m.** Policy Revision: Monthly, Quarterly, or Yearly
        _____**i.** Digital or Physical Signature Approval (e.g., CFO, CIO, etc.)

---

security policy covers the company-specific risk mitigation objective. This is why external party resources for both internal or external audit system and procedures assessment reviews are so important to help define new policies as well as update and improve on existing ones to provide a more secure environment. With this noted, there is a common structure most businesses and government institutes will utilize when creating control security policies for their organization (see checklist: "An Agenda for Action for Creating Control Security Policies for an Organization") [1,2,4].

Policy Category Type

The policy category type is defined by the security business function type; the security policy control leveraging process; and procedures by technology or staff administration that protect and remediates the identified security risk. For example, a policy category could be "New Hire: Service Level Agreement" with onboarding security controls in place to manage the security requirement. The scope and purpose of the security control are normally summarized in this section. Policy category types are usually associated with control ID numbers to be referenced in audit matrix reference assessments [3].

Policy Statement Agreement

The policy statement agreement goes into more detail on what the policy can and cannot due to remediate the risk it attempts to manage. This agreement shows the benefit and limitations to the process owners agree are consistent with the understanding of the lifecycle management needs for the control. This provides clear expectations on original control intent and design boundaries for this type of security policy.

Definition Management

A policy definition, and who or what it applies to, is defined in this section of the policy documentation. The audience for the user, administrative, technical service, equipment, or interface device access is clearly defined for the Definition Management section. The Confidential and Sensitive Information Agreement in the form of a restated EULA is defined and related to the in-scope audience using the system, and will be noted in this section, as well (if applicable).

Policy (Business Process and Department Security Owner)

In this section, we discuss the overall policy core structure that takes into account applicability, security roles, the importance of adhering to required company-based or regulatory security standards, as well as support and technology requirements that constitute the security control policy in its entirety. It goes over into even more detail on what lifecycle activities are needed to manage the control on a daily basis. Audit frequency to support the lifecycle is also defined in this section. Prohibited activities are fully explained with enforcement consequences also defined depending on the type of illicit usage being noted. Access exceptions, security breach response escalation, and overall incident management will be summarized in this section for the security policy control requirement.

Business continuity with backup and data recovery planning is referenced to ensure the lifecycle of the process is fully protected in case of data loss due to a security breach incident.

4. SECURITY POLICY: SIGN OFF APPROVAL

After audit assessments help create new controls or update existing ones by reporting both internal and external audit assessor findings to the IT Governance and security department, management support teams who own the process, digital or physical sign-off agreements will be completed once review and remediation activities are finalized. Executive management sign off is normally required on a yearly basis to approve annual fiscal public information updates.

5. SUMMARY

A Security Steering Committee (SSC) or administration body of managers and support staff make up the review board for security planning and solution implementations to help safeguard the company or organization's computer network or facilities environments. The SSC will normally convene on a regular basis to ensure security focus for control policy management is being followed and adhered to. This committee also works with the support staff and business process owners to schedule regular audit reviews with frequency based on a company's unique business cycle. The review audit findings help define the security project planning objectives for departments or enterprise-wide initiatives depending on the administrative controls or procedures it impacts. In the early phases of project requirements during a Systems Development Life Cycle (SDLC) project review, security required documentation dependencies must be filled out to help clearly define what scope, if any, a technology project initiative may or may not impact on a security level. This will ensure that existing or lacking security policy controls flow upstream to IT Governance to keep newly implemented or updated technology project initiatives visible so they follow the security standards of the business [4].

Finally, let's move on to the real interactive part of this Chapter: review questions/exercises, hands-on projects, case projects, and optional team case project. The answers and/or solutions by chapter can be found in Appendix K.

CHAPTER REVIEW QUESTIONS/ EXERCISES

True/False

1. True or False? When building a solid house of security frameworks, a strong foundation backed by fortified

support points is required, or the structure is bound to collapse at the second stressful experience.

2. True or False? Each security policy reviewed and implemented is a "brick" in the fortification for the defense-in-depth strategy needed to achieve a well-rounded overall design of security that best fits the business or organization's needed to mitigate risks from criminal elements and potential internal malicious internal resource retaliation.

3. True or False? Leveraging the existing framework plans used by the industry today optimizes the need for "reinventing" the wheel, which minimizes the need to achieve optimal implementation planning and to spend a lot of time and resources creating solutions from the ground up.

4. True or False? Risk assessments are not only essential for creating security policies but also are required monthly, quarterly, or annually.

5. True or False? Whether it's content data information or personal account information, the risk potentials always ends at the Identity Management (IDM) level for security frameworks.

Multiple Choice

1. What is one of the biggest challenges companies must continuously work on?
   A. Strong process controls
   B. Assessment exercises
   C. Keeping their security environments, policies, and procedures as updated as possible
   D. Current security strengths
   E. All of the above

2. What acronym with regards for security best practices, stands for Confidentiality, Integrity, and Availability?
   A. CAA
   B. CIA
   C. CMA
   D. COX
   E. All of the above

3. Levels of privacy for _____ can stem from a user's private account information such as medical data, social security number information, birth date, etc.
   A. Risk and severity
   B. International Treaties
   C. Security standards
   D. Confidentiality
   E. All of the above

4. What part of the CIA Triad takes into account the authenticity of the data information stored in a security-type container such as a database or directory service?

A. Framework Toolsets
B. Confidentiality
C. ISACA's ITAF
D. ITIL
E. Integrity

5. Attacks such as _____ attacks in progress, that are attempting to crash and bring down the system, must be immediately identified and mitigated to protect system access and availability.
   A. Role-based Security Access
   B. Security
   C. Governance
   D. Information Technology Governance
   E. Denial-of-Service (DoS)

EXERCISE

Problem

What is a cyber-security framework core and how is it used?

Hands-On Projects

Project

What is the difference between using, adopting, and implementing a cyber-security framework?

Case Projects

Problem

How would an organization go about developing and creating a common language and encourage the use of a cyber-security framework as a process and risk management tool, rather than a set of static compliance requirements?

Optional Team Case Project

Problem

How can an organization use a cyber-security framework?

REFERENCES

[1] R. Johnson, M. Merkow, Security Policies and Information Issues, Jones and Bartlett Learning, 2010.
[2] L. Hayden, IT Security Metrics: A Practical Framework for Measuring Security & Protecting Data, first ed., McGraw-Hill Companies, 2010.
[3] ISACA. < https://www.isaca.org>.
[4] SANS. < http://www.sans.org/security-resources/policies/>.

Part V

Cyber, Network, and Systems Forensics Security and Assurance

Chapter 40

Cyber Forensics

Scott R. Ellis

kCura Corporation, Chicago, IL, United States

1. WHAT IS CYBER FORENSICS?

Definition: Cyber forensics is the acquisition, preservation, and analysis of electronically stored information (ESI) in such a way that ensures its admissibility for use as evidence, exhibits, or demonstratives in a court of law.

Rather than discussing at great length what cyber forensics is (the rest of the chapter will take care of that), for the sake of clarity, let us define what cyber forensics is *not*. It is not an arcane ability to tap into a vast, secret repository of information about every single thing that ever happened on, or to, a computer. Often it involves handling hardware in unique circumstances and doing things with both hardware and software that typically are not things that the makers or manufacturers intended (see sidebar: "Angular Momentum").

Not every single thing a user ever did on a computer is 100% knowable beyond a shadow of a doubt or even beyond reasonable doubt. Some things are certainly *knowable* with varying degrees of certainty, and there is nothing that can happen on a computer through the use of a keyboard and a mouse that cannot be replicated with a software program or macro of some sort. It is fitting, then, that many of the arguments of cyber forensics become philosophical, and that *degrees of certainty* exist and beg definition, such as: How heavy is the burden of proof? Right away, lest arrogant thoughtlessness prevail, anyone undertaking a study of cyber forensics must understand the core principles of what it means to be in a position of authority and to what varying degrees of certainty an examiner may attest without finding he has overstepped his mandate (see sidebar, "Angular Momentum"). Sections 11 and 12 in this chapter and the article "Cyber Forensics and Ethics, Green Home Plate Gallery View" address these concerns as they relate to ethics and testimonial work.

Angular Momentum

Hard drive (HD) platters spin very fast. The 5¼-inch floppy disk of the 1980s has evolved into heavy metallic platters that spin at ridiculous speeds. If your car wheels turned at 10,000 rpm, you would zip along at 1000 mph. Some HDs spin at 15,000 rpm. That is really fast. Although HD platters will not disintegrate (as CD-ROMs have been known to do), anecdotal evidence suggests that in larger, heavier drives, the bearings can become so hot that they liquefy, effectively stopping the drive in its tracks. Basic knowledge of surface coating magnetic properties tells us that if the surface of an HD becomes overly hot, the basic magnetic properties, the "zeroes and ones" stored by the particulate magnetic domains, will become unstable. The stability of these zeroes and ones maintains the consistency of the logical data stored by the medium. The high speeds of large, heavy HDs generate heat and ultimately result in drive failure.

Forensic technicians are often required to handle HDs, sometimes while they have power attached to them. For example, a computer may need to be moved while it still has power attached to it. Here is where a note about angular momentum becomes necessary: A spinning object translates pressure applied to its axis of rotation 90 degrees from the direction of the force applied to it. Most HDs are designed to park the heads at even the slightest amount of detected *g*-shock. They claim to be able to withstand thousands of "*g*'s," but this simply means that if the HD were parked on a neutron star it would still be able to park its heads. This is a relatively meaningless, static attribute. Most people should understand that if you drop your computer, you may damage the internal mechanics of an HD, and if the platters are spinning, the drive may be scored. Older drives, those that are more than 3 years old, are especially susceptible to damage. Precautions should be taken to keep older drives vibration free and cool.

With very slight, gentle pressures, a spinning HD can be handled much as you would handle a gyro and with little

Computer and Information Security Handbook. http://dx.doi.org/10.1016/B978-0-12-803843-7.00040-5

potential for damage. It can be handled in a way that will not cause the heads to park.

Note: Older drives are the exception, and any slight motion at all can cause them to stop functioning.

Most HDs have piezoelectric shock detectors that will cause the heads to park the instant a certain *g*-shock value is reached. Piezoelectrics work under the principle that when a force is exerted along a particular axis, certain types of crystals will emit an electrical charge. Just like their pocket-lighter counterparts, they do not always work and eventually become either desensitized or oversensitized; if the internal mechanism of the HD is out of tolerance, the shock detector may either work or it will not park the heads correctly and the heads will shred the surface of the platters. Or, if it does work, it may thrash the surface anyway as the heads park and unpark during multiple, repeated shocks. A large, heavy drive [such as a 1-terabyte (TB) drive] will behave exactly as would any heavy disk spinning about an axis: just like a gyro (Fig. 40.1). So, when a vector of force is applied to a drive and it is forced to turn in the same direction as the vector, instead of its natural 90 degrees offset, the potential for damage to the drive increases dramatically.

Such is the case of a computer mounted in brackets inside a PC in transit. The internal, spinning platters of the drive try to shift in opposition to the direction the external drive turned; it is an internal tug of war. As the platters attempt to lean forward, the drive leans to the left instead. If there is any play in the bearings, the cushion of air that floats the drive heads can be disrupted and the surface of the platters can scratch. If you must move a spinning drive (and sometimes you must), be careful, go slowly, and let the drive do all the work. If you must transport a running HD, ensure that the internal drive is rotating about the x axis: that it is, horizontally mounted inside the computer, and that there is an external shock pad. Some PCs have vertically mounted drives.

Foam padding beneath the computer is essential. If you are in the business of transporting running computers that have been seized, a floating platform of some sort would not be a bad idea. A lot of vibrations, bumps, and jars can shred less durably manufactured HDs. This author once shredded his own laptop HD by leaving it turned on, carrying it 15 city blocks, and then for an hour-long ride on the train. You can transport and move computers your entire life and not

have an issue. But the one time you do, it could be an unacceptable and unrecoverable loss.

Never move an older computer. If the computer cannot be shut down, the acquisition of the computer must be completed onsite. Anytime a computer is to be moved while it is running, everyone involved in the decision-making process should sign off on the procedure and be aware of the risk.

Lesson learned: Always make sure that a laptop put into standby mode has actually gone into standby mode before closing the lid. Windows can be tricky like that sometimes.

2. ANALYSIS OF DATA

Never underestimate the power of a maze. Maze experts generally agree on two types of mazes: unicursive and multicursive. In the unicursive maze, the maze has only one answer; you wind along a path and with a little patience you end up at the end. Multicursory mazes, according to the experts, are full of wrong turns and dead ends.

However, the fact of the matter is that when one sets foot into a multicursive maze, one need only recognize that it is two unicursory mazes put together, with the path through the maze being the seam. If you take the unicursory tack and simply *always stay to the right (or the left*, as long as you are consistent), you will traverse the entire maze and have no choice but to traverse and complete it successfully.

This is not a section about mazes, but they are analogous in that there are two approaches to cyber forensics: one that churns through every last bit of data and one that takes shortcuts. This is called *analysis*. Often as a forensic analyst, the sheer amount of data that need to be sifted will seem enormous and unrelenting. However there is a path that, if you know it, you can follow it through to success. Here are a few guidelines on how to go about conducting an investigation. For starters, we talk about a feature that is built into most forensic toolsets. It allows the examiner to "reveal all" in a fashion that can place hundreds of thousands of files at the fingertips for examination. It can also create a bad situation, legally and ethically.

Cyber Forensics and Ethics, Green Home Plate Gallery View[1]

A simplified version of this article was published on the Chicago Bar Association blog in late 2007. This is the original version, unaltered.

EnCase is a commonly used forensic software program that allows a cyber forensic technologist to conduct an investigation of a forensic hard disk copy. One of the functions of the software is something known as "green

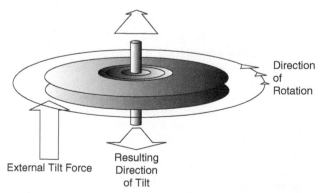

FIGURE 40.1 A spinning object distributes applied force differently from a stationary object. Handle operating hard drives with extreme care.

1. Cyber forensics and ethics, Green Home Plate Gallery View, Chicago Bar Association Blog, September 2007.

home plate gallery view." This function allows the forensic technologist to create, in *plain view*, a gallery of every single image on the computer.

In EnCase, the entire folder view structure of a computer is laid out just as in Windows Explorer, with the exception that to the left of every folder entry are two boxes. One is shaped like a square, and the other like a little "home plate" that turns green when you click on it; hence the "green home plate." The technical name for the home plate box is "Set Included Folders." With a single click, every single file *entry* in that folder and its subfolders becomes visible in a table view. An additional option allows the examiner to switch from a table view of entries to a gallery view of *thumbnails*. Both operations together create the "green home plate gallery view" action.

With two clicks of the mouse, the licensed EnCase user can gather up every single image that exists on the computer and place it into a single scrollable thumbnail gallery. In a court-ordered investigation in which the search may be for text-based documents such as correspondence, green home plate gallery view has the potential of being *misused* to search the computer visually for imaged/scanned documents. I emphasize *misused* because ultimately, this action puts every single image on the computer in *plain view*. It is akin to policemen showing up for a domestic abuse response with an x-ray machine in tow and x-raying the contents of the whole house.

Because this action enables one to view every single image on a computer, including those that may have nothing to do with the forensic search at hand, it raises a question of ethics, and possibly even legality. Can a forensic examiner green home plate gallery view without reasonable cause?

In terms of a search in which the search or motion specifically authorized searching for text-based "documents,"

green home plate gallery view is not the correct approach, nor is it the most efficient. The action exceeds the scope of the search and it may raise questions regarding the violation of rights and/or privacy. To some inexperienced examiners, it may seem to be the quickest and easiest route to locating all documents on a computer. More experienced examiners may use it as a quick litmus test to "peek under the hood" to see whether there are documents on the computer.

Many documents that are responsive to the search may be in the form of image scans or PDFs. Green home plate gallery view renders them visible and available, just for the scrolling. Therein lies the problem: If anything incriminating turns up, it also has the ring of truth in a court of law when the examiner suggests that he was innocently searching for financial documents when he inadvertently discovered, in *plain view*, offensive materials that were outside the scope of his original mandate. But just because something has the ring of truth does not mean that the bell has been rung.

For inexperienced investigators, green home plate gallery view (Fig. 40.2) may truly seem to be the only recourse, and it may also be the one that has yielded the most convictions. However, because there is a more efficient method to capture and detect text, one that can protect privacy and follows the constraints of the search mandate, it should be used.

Current forensic technology allows us, through electronic file signature analysis, sizing, and typing of images, to capture and export every image from the subject file system. Next, through optical character recognition (OCR), the experienced professional can detect every image that has text and discard those that do not. In this manner, images are protected from being viewed, the subject's privacy is protected, and all images with text are located efficiently. The resultant set can then be hashed and reintroduced into

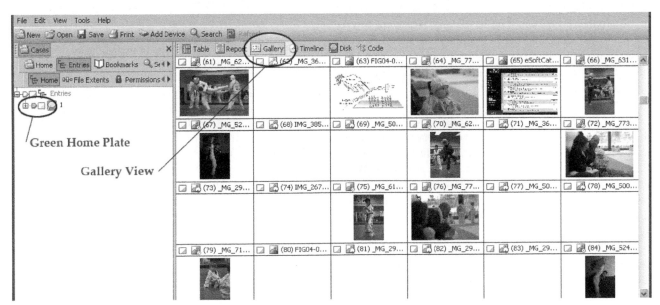

FIGURE 40.2 Green home plate gallery view.

EnCase as single files, hashed, and indexed so that the notable files can be bookmarked and a report generated.

Technically, this is a more difficult process because it requires extensive knowledge of imaging, electronic file signature analysis, automated OCR discovery techniques, and hash libraries. However, to a trained technician, this is actually faster than green home plate gallery view, which may yield thousands of images and may take hundreds of hours to review accurately.

In practice, the easiest way is seldom the most ethical way to solve a problem; neither is it always the most efficient method to get a job done. Currently, many similar scenarios exist within the discipline of cyber forensics. As the forensic technology industry grows and evolves, professional organizations may eventually emerge that will provide codes of ethics and some syncretism with regard to these issues. For now, however, it falls on attorneys to retain experienced cyber forensic technologists who place importance on developing appropriate ethical protocols. Only when these protocols are in place can we successfully understand the breadth and scope of searches and prevent possible violations of privacy.

Database Reconstruction

A disk that hosts an active database is a busy place. Again and again throughout this chapter, a single recurring theme will emerge: Data that have been overwritten cannot, by any conventionally known means, be recovered. If they could be, Kroll Ontrack and every other giant in the forensics business would be shouting this service from the rooftops and charging a premium price for it. Experimentally, accurate statistics on the amount of data that will be overwritten by the seemingly random action of a write head may be available, but most likely it functions by rules that are different for every system based on the amount of use, the size of the files, and the size of the unallocated clusters. Anecdotally, the formula goes something like this: The rules change under any given circumstances, but this story goes a long way toward telling how much data will be available:

On a server purposed with storing surveillance video, there are three physical HDs. Drive C serves as the operating system (OS) disk and program files disk; Drives E and F, 350 gigabytes (GB) each, serve as storage disks. When the remote DVR units synchronize each evening, every other file writes to every other disk of the two storage drives. Thirty-day-old files automatically get deleted by the synchronization tool.

After 8 months of use, the entire unallocated clusters of each drive, 115 GB on one drive and 123 GB on the other, are completely filled with Moving Picture Experts Group format (MPG) data. An additional 45 GB of archived deleted files is available to be recovered from each drive.

In this case, the database data were MPG movie files. In many databases, the data, the records (as the database indexes and grows and shrinks, and is compacted and optimized), will grow to populate the unallocated clusters. Database records found in the unallocated clusters are not an indicator of deleted records. Database records that exist in the unallocated clusters that do not exist in the live database *are* a sign of deleted records.

Lesson learned: Do not believe everything you see. Check it out and be sure. Get second, third, and fourth opinions when you are uncertain.

3. CYBER FORENSICS IN THE COURT SYSTEM

Cyber forensics is one of the few cyber-related fields in which the practitioner will be found in the courtroom on a given number of days of the year. With that in mind, the following sections are derived from the author's experiences in the courtroom, the lessons learned there, and the preparation leading up to giving testimony. To most lawyers and judges, cyber forensics is a mysterious black art. It is as much a discipline of the art to demystify and explain results in plain English as it is to conduct an examination. It was with special consideration of the growing prevalence of the use of ESI in the courtroom, and the general unfamiliarity with how it must be handled as evidence, that spawned the idea for the sidebar "Preserving Digital Evidence in the Age of Electronic Discovery."

Preserving Digital Evidence in the Age of Electronic Discovery[2]

Society has awakened to the realities of being immersed in the digital world. With that, the harsh realities of how we conduct ourselves in this age of binary processing are taking form in terms of new laws and new ways of doing business. In many actions, both civil and criminal, digital documents are the new "smoking gun." With federal laws that open the floodgates of accessibility to your digital media, the sanctions for mishandling such evidence have become a fact of law and a major concern.

At some point, most of us (any of us) could become involved in litigation. Divorce, damage suits, patent infringement, intellectual property theft, and employee misconduct are just some examples of cases we see. When it comes to digital evidence, most people simply are not sure of their responsibilities. They do not know how to handle the requests for and subsequent handling of the massive amounts of data that can be crucial to every case. Like the proverbial smoking gun, "digital evidence" must be handled properly.

A friend forwarded us an article about a case ruling in which a routine email exhibit was found inadmissible owing to authenticity and hearsay issues. What we should take away from that ruling is that ESI, just like any other evidence, must clear standard evidentiary hurdles. Whenever ESI is offered as evidence, the following evidence rules must be considered.

In most courts, there are four types of evidence. Cyber files that are extracted from a subject machine and presented in court typically fall into one or more of these types:

- *Documentary evidence* is paper or digital evidence that contains human language. It must meet the authenticity requirements outlined subsequently. It is also unique in that it may be disallowed if it contains hearsay. Emails fall into the category of documentary evidence.
- *Real evidence* must be competent (authenticated), relevant, and material. For example, a computer that was involved in a court matter would be considered real evidence provided that it has not been changed, altered, or accessed in a way that destroyed the evidence. The ability to use these items as evidence may be contingent on this fact, and that is why cyber or digital media must be preserved.
- *Witness testimony*. With ESI, the technician should be able to verify how he retrieved the evidence and that the evidence is what it purports to be; and he should be able to speak to all aspects of computer use. The witness must both remember what he saw and be able to communicate it.
- *Demonstrative evidence* uses things such as PowerPoint, photographs, or cyber-aided design drawings of crime scenes to demonstrate or reconstruct an event. For example, a flowchart that details how a person goes to a website, enters her credit card number, and makes a purchase would be considered demonstrative.

For any of these items to be submitted in court, each must pass the admissibility requirements of relevance, materiality, and competence to varying degrees. For evidence to be *relevant*, it must make the event it is trying to prove either more or less probable. A forensic analyst may discover a certain Web page on the subject's HD that shows the subject visited a website where flowers are sold and that he made a purchase. In addition to perhaps a credit card statement, this shows that it is more probable that the subject of an investigation visited the site on his computer at a certain time and location.

Materiality means that something not only proves the fact (it is relevant to the fact that it is trying to prove) but is also *material* to the issues in the case. The fact that the subject of the investigation purchased flowers on a website may not be material to the matter at hand.

Finally, *competency* is the area in which the forensic side of things becomes most important. Assuming that the purchase of flowers from a website is material (perhaps it is a stalking case), how the evidence was obtained and what happened to it afterward will be put under a microscope by both the judge and the party objecting to the evidence. The best evidence collection experts are trained professionals with extensive experience in their field. The best attorneys will understand this and will use experts when and where needed. Spoliation results from mishandled ESI, and spoiled data are generally inadmissible. It rests upon everyone involved in a case [information technology (IT) directors, business owners, and attorneys] to get it right. Cyber forensics experts cannot undo damage that has been done,

but if involved in the *beginning*, they can prevent it from happening.

2. Scott R. Ellis, Preserving digital evidence in the age of ediscovery, Daily Southtown (2007).

4. UNDERSTANDING INTERNET HISTORY

Of the many aspects of user activity, the Internet history is usually of the greatest interest. In most investigations, people such as those who work in human resources (HR), employers, and those in law enforcement seek to understand the subject's use of the Internet. What websites did he visit? When did he visit them? Did he visit them more than once? The article "What Have You Been Clicking on?" (see sidebar) seeks to demystify the concept of temporary Internet files (TIF).

What Have You Been Clicking on?

You have probably heard the rumor that whenever you click on something on a webpage, you leave a deeply rooted trail behind you for anyone (with the right technology) to see. In cyber forensics, just as in archeology, these pieces a user leaves behind are called *artifacts*. An artifact is a thing made by a human. It tells the story of a behavior that happened in the past.

On your computer, that story is told by metadata stored in databases as well as by files stored on your local machine. They reside in numerous places, but this article will address just three: Internet history, Web cache, and TIF. Because Internet Explorer (IE) was developed when bandwidth was precious, storing data locally prevents a browser from having to retrieve the same data every time the same Web page is visited. Also, at the time, no established technology existed that could show data on a local machine through a Web browser without first putting the file on the local machine. Essentially, a Web browser was a piece of software that combined File Transfer Protocol (FTP) and document-viewing technology into one application platform, complete with its own protocol, Hypertext Transfer Protocol (HTTP).

In IE, press **Ctrl + H** to view your history. This will show a list of links to all sites that were viewed over a period of 4 weeks. The history database stores only the name and date the site was visited. It holds no information about files that may be cached locally. That is the job of the Web cache.

To go back further in history, an Internet history viewer is needed. A Google search for "history.dat viewer" will turn up a few free tools.

The Web cache database, index.dat, is located in the TIF folder; it tracks the date, the time the Web page downloaded, the original Web page filename, and its local name and location in the TIF. Information stays in the index.dat for a long time, much longer than 4 weeks. You will notice that if you set your computer date back a few weeks and then press **Ctrl + H**, you can always pull the last 4 weeks of data for as long as you have had your computer (and not cleared your cache). Using a third-party viewer to view the Web cache shows you with certainty the date and origination of a Web page. The Web cache is a detailed inventory of everything in the TIF. Some history viewers will show Web cache information, too.

The TIF is a set of local folders where IE stores Web pages your computer has downloaded. Typically, the size varies depending on user settings. However, websites are usually small, so 500 megabytes (MB) can hold thousands of Web pages and images! Viewing these files may be necessary. Web mail and financial and browsing interests are all stored in the TIF. However, malicious software activity such as pop-ups, exploits, viruses, and Trojans can cause many strange files to appear in the TIF. For this reason, files that are in the TIF should be compared with their entry in the Web cache. Time stamps on files in the TIF may or may not accurately show when a file was written to disk. System scans period-ically alter Last Accessed and Date Modified time stamps! Because of HD caching and delayed writing, the Date Created time stamp may not be the actual time the file arrived. Cyber forensics uses special tools to analyze the TIF, but much is still left to individual interpretations.

Inspection of all of the user's Internet artifacts, when intact, can reveal what a user was doing and whether a click trail exists. Looking just at time stamps or IE history is not enough. Users can easily delete IE history, and time stamps are not always accurate. Missing history can disrupt the trail. Missing Web cache entries or time stamp–altering system scans can destroy the trail. Any conclusions are best not preceded by a suspended leap through the air (you may land badly and trip and hurt yourself). Rather, check for viruses and bad patching, and get the artifacts straight. If there is a click trail, it will be revealed by the Web cache, the files in the TIF, and the history. Bear in mind that when pieces are missing, the reliability of the click trail erodes, and professional examination may be warranted.

5. TEMPORARY RESTRAINING ORDERS AND LABOR DISPUTES

A temporary restraining order (TRO) will often be issued in intellectual property or employment contract disputes. The role of the forensic examiner in a TRO may be multifold, or it may be limited to a simple, one-time acquisition of an HD. Often when an employee leaves an organization under less than amicable terms, accusations will be fired in both directions and the resulting lawsuit will be a many-headed beast. Attorneys on both sides may file motions that result in forensic analysis of emails, user activity, and possible contract violations as well as extraction of information from financial and customer relationship management databases.

Divorce

Typically the forensic work done in a divorce case will involve collecting information about one of the parties to be used to show that trust has been violated. Dating sites, pornography, financial sites, expatriate sites, and email should be collected and reviewed.

Patent Infringement

When one company begins selling a part that is patented by another company, a lawsuit will likely be filed in federal court. Subsequently, the offending company will be required to produce all the invoices relating to sales of that product. This is where a forensic examiner may be required. The infringed-on party may find through their own research that a company has purchased the part from the infringer and that the sale has not been reported. A thorough examination of the financial system will reveal all of the sales. It is wise when doing this sort of work to contact the financial system vendor to get a data dictionary that defines all of the fields and the purpose of the tables.

Invoice data are easy to collect. They will typically reside in just two tables: a header and a detail table. These tables will contain customer codes that will need to be joined to the customer table, so knowing some Structured Query Language (SQL) will be a great help. Using the database server for the specific database technology of the software is the reference standard for this sort of work. Getting the collection to launch into VMware is the ulti-mate standard, but sometimes an image will not want to boot. Software utilities such as Live View do a great job of preparing the image for deployment in a virtualized environment.

When to Acquire and When to Capture Acquisition

When a forensics practitioner needs to capture the data on a hard disk, he or she does so in a way that is forensically sound. This means that through any actions on the part of the examiner, no data on the HD are altered and a complete and total copy of the surface of the HD platters is captured. Here are some common terms used to describe this process:

- collection
- mirror
- ghost
- copy
- acquisition

Any of these terms is sufficient to describe the process. The one that attorneys typically use is *mirror*, because they seem to understand it best. A "forensic" acquisition simply means that the drive was write-protected by either a software or hardware write blocker while the acquisition was performed.

Acquisition of an entire HD is the standard approach in any case that will require a deep analysis of the behaviors and activities of the user. It is not always the standard procedure. However, most people will agree that a forensic procedure must be used whenever information is copied from a PC. Forensic, enterprise, and electronic discovery (ediscovery) cases all vary in their requirements for the amount of data that must be captured. In discovery, much of what is located on a computer may be deemed "inaccessible," which is really just fancy lawyer talk for "it costs too much to get it." Undeleting data from hundreds of computers in a single discovery action in a civil case would be a rare thing to happen and would take place only if massive malfeasance were suspected. In these cases, forensic creation of logical evidence files allows the examiner to capture and copy relevant information without altering the data.

Creating Forensic Images Using Software and Hardware Write Blockers

Both software and hardware write blockers are available. Software write blockers are versatile and come in two flavors. One is a module that "plugs" into the forensic software and can generally be used to write block any port on the computer. The other method of software write blocking is to use a forensic boot disk. This will boot the computer from the HD. Developing checklists that can be repeatable procedures is an ideal way to ensure solid results in any investigation.

Software write blockers are limited by the port speed of the port they are blocking, plus some overhead for the write-blocking process. But then, all write blockers are limited in this manner.

Hardware write blockers are normally optimized for speed. Forensic copying tools such as Logicube and Tableau are two examples of hardware write blockers, although many companies make them. Logicube will both hash and image a drive at a rate of about 3 GB/min. They are small and portable and can replace the need for bulky PCs on a job site. There are also appliances and large enterprise software packages that are designed to automate and alleviate the labor requirements of large discovery/disclosure acquisitions that may span thousands of computers.

Live Capture of Relevant Files

Before conducting any sort of a capture, all steps should be documented and reviewed with counsel before proceeding. Preferably, attorneys from both sides on a matter and the judge agree to the procedure before it is enacted. Whenever a new procedure or technique is introduced late on the job site, if auditors or observers are present, the attorneys will argue, which can delay the work by several hours. Most forensic software can be loaded to a universal serial bus (USB) drive and launched on a live system with negligible forensic impact to the operating environment. Random access memory (RAM) captures are more popular; currently this is the only way to capture an image of physical RAM. Certain companies are rumored to be creating physical RAM write blockers. Launching a forensic application on a running system will destroy a substantial amount of physical RAM as well as the paging file. If either RAM or the paging file is needed, the capture must be done with a write blocker.

Once the forensic tool is launched, either with a write blocker or on a live system, the local drive may be previewed. The examiner may be interested only in Word documents, for example. Signature analysis is a lengthy process in preview mode, as are most searches. A better method, if subterfuge is not expected is thus: Filtering the table pane by extension produces a list of all documents. "Exporting" them will damage the forensic information, so instead you need to create a logical evidence file. Using EnCase, a user can create a condition to view all .DOC files and then dump the files into a logical evidence file in about 30 s. Once the logical evidence file is created, it can be used later to create a CD-ROM. Special modules are available that will allow an exact extraction of native files to CD to allow further processing for a review tool.

Redundant Array of Independent (or Inexpensive) Disks

Acquiring an entire redundant array of independent (or inexpensive) disks (RAID) set disk by disk and then reassembling them in EnCase is probably the easiest way to deal with a RAID and may be the only way to capture a software RAID. Hardware RAIDs can be most efficiently captured using a boot disk. This allows the capture of a single volume that contains all unique data in an array. It can be trickier to configure, and as with everything, practice makes perfect. Be sure you understand how it works. The worst thing that can happen is that the wrong disk or an unreadable disk gets imaged and the job has to be redone at your expense.

File System Analyses

File allocation table (FAT)12, FAT16, and FAT32 are all types of file systems. Special circumstances aside, most forensic examiners will find themselves regularly dealing with either FAT or New Technology File System (NTFS) file systems. FAT differs from NTFS primarily in the way it stores information about how it stores information. Largely, from the average forensic examiner's standpoint, little about the internal workings of these file systems is relevant. Most modern forensic software will do the work of reconstructing and extracting information from these systems, at the system level, for you. Nonetheless, an understanding of these systems is critical because at any given time, an examiner *just might* need to know it. The following are some examples showing where you might need to know about the file system:

- rebuilding RAID arrays
- locating lost or moved partitions
- discussing more advanced information that can be gleaned from entries in the master file table (MFT) or FAT

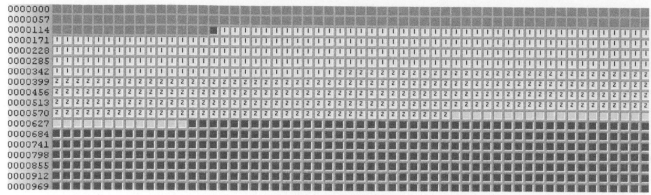

FIGURE 40.3   Sector view.

The difference between FAT12, 16, and 32 is in the size of each item in the FAT. Each has a correspondingly sized entry in the FAT. For example, FAT12 has a 12-bit entry in the FAT. Each 12-bit sequence represents a cluster. This places a limitation on the file system regarding the number of file extents available to a file. The FAT stores the following information:

- fragmentation
- used or unused clusters
- a list of entries that correspond to each cluster on the partition
- marks a cluster as used, reserved, unused, or bad
- cluster number of the next cluster in the chain

Sector information is stored in the directory. In the FAT file system, directories are actually files that contain as many 32-byte slots as there are entries in the folder. This is also where deleted entries from a folder can be discovered. Fig. 40.3 shows how the sector view is represented by a common forensic analysis tool.

New Technology File System

NTFS is a significant advancement in terms of data storage. It allows for long filenames, almost unlimited storage, and a more efficient method of accessing information. It also provides for much greater latency in deleted files: that is, deleted files stick around a lot longer in NTFS than they do in FAT. The following items are unique to NTFS. Instead of keeping the filenames in folder files, the entire file structure of NTFS is retained in a flat file database called the MFT:

- improved support for metadata
- advanced data structuring improves performance and reliability
- improved disk space use with a maximum disk size of 7.8 TB, or 2^{64} sectors; sector sizes can vary in NTFS and are most easily controlled using a third-party partitioning tool such as Partition Magic.
- greater security

Role of the Forensic Examiner in Investigations and File Recovery

The forensic examiner is at his best when he is searching for deleted files and attempting to reconstruct a pattern of user behavior. The sidebar "Oops! Did I Delete That?" first appeared in the Chicago *Daily Southtown* column "Bits You Can Use." In addition, this section includes a discussion of data recovery and an insurance investigation article (see sidebar, "Don't Touch That Computer! Data Recovery Following Fire, Flood, or Storm").

Oops! Did I Delete That?

The file is gone. It's not in the recycle bin. You've done a complete search of your files for it, and now the panic sets in. It's vanished. You may have even asked people to look through their email because maybe you sent it to them (you didn't). Oops. Now what?

Hours, days, maybe even years of hard work seem to be lost. Wait! Don't touch that PC! Every action you take on your PC at this point may be destroying what is left of your file. It's not too late yet. You've possibly heard that things that are deleted are never really deleted, but you may also think that it will cost you thousands of dollars to recover deleted files once you've emptied the recycle bin. Suffice it to say, unless you are embroiled in complicated ediscovery or forensic legal proceedings where preservation is a requirement, recovering some deleted files for you may cost no more than a tune-up for your car.

Now the part where I told you: "Don't touch that PC!" I meant it. Seriously: Don't touch that PC. The second you realize you've lost a file, stop doing anything. Don't visit any websites. Don't install software. Don't reformat your HD, do a Windows repair, or install undelete software. In fact, if it's not a server or running a shared database application, pull the plug from the back of the PC. Every time you "write" to your HD, you run the risk that you are destroying your lost file. In the case of one author we helped, 10 years of a book were "deleted." With immediate professional help, her files were recovered.

Whether you accidentally pulled your USB drive from the slot without stopping it first (corrupting your MFT), intentionally deleted it, or have discovered an "OS not found" message when you booted your PC, you need your files back and you need them now. However, if you made the mistake of actually overwriting a file with a file that has the same name and thereby replaced it, "Abandon hope all ye who enter here." Your file is trashed, and all that may be left are some scraps of the old file, parts that didn't get overwritten but can be extracted from file slack. If your HD is physically damaged, you may also be looking at an expensive recovery.

Here's the quick version of how deleted files become "obliterated" and unrecoverable:

Step 1: The MFT that contains a reference to your file marks the deleted file space as available.

Step 2: The actual sectors where the deleted file resides *might* be either completely or partially overwritten.

Step 3: The MFT record for the deleted file is overwritten and destroyed. Any ability to *easily* recover your deleted file at this point is lost.

Step 4: The sectors on the PC that contain your deleted file *are* overwritten and eventually only slight traces of your lost file remain. Sometimes the MFT record may be destroyed before the actual sectors are overwritten. This happens a lot, and these files are recoverable with a little extra work.

It's tremendously amazing how fast this process can occur. It's equally amazing how slowly this process can occur. Recently I retrieved hundreds of files from a system that had periodically been deleting files, and new files were written to the disk on a daily basis. Yet recovery software successfully recovered hundreds of complete files from nearly 6 months ago! A lot of free space on the disk contributed to this success. A disk that is in use and is nearly full will be proportionally less likely to contain old, deleted files.

The equipment and training investment to perform these operations is high, so expect that labor costs will be higher, but you can also expect some degree of success when attempting to recover files that have been accidentally deleted. Let me leave you with two dire warnings: Disks that have experienced surface damage (scored platters) are unrecoverable with current technology. And never, ever, ever disrupt power to your PC when it's performing a defrag. The results are disastrous.

Don't Touch That Computer! Data Recovery Following Fire, Flood, or Storm

Fire, flood, earthquakes, landslides, and other catastrophes often result in damaged cyber equipment, and loss of electronic data. For claims managers and adjusters, this data loss can manifest in an overwhelming number of insurance claims, costing insurers millions of dollars each year.

The improper handling of computers immediately after a catastrophic event is possibly one of the leading causes of data loss, and once a drive has been improperly handled, the chances of data retrieval plummet. Adjusters often assume a complete loss, when in fact there are methods that can save or salvage data on even the most damaged computers.

Methods to Save or Salvage Data

One of the first steps toward salvaging cyber data is to focus on preserving the HD. HDs are highly precise instruments, and warping of drive components by even fractions of a millimeter will cause damage to occur in the very first moments of booting up. During these moments the drive head can shred the surface of the platters, rendering the data unrecoverable.

HDs are preserved in different ways, depending on the damaging event. If the drive is submerged in a flood, the drive should be removed and resubmerged in clean, distilled water and shipped to an expert. It is important that this be done immediately. HD platters that are allowed to corrode after being exposed to water, especially if the drive experienced seepage, will oxidize and data will be destroyed. A professional can completely disassemble the drive to ensure that all of its parts are dry, determine what level of damage has already occurred, and then decide how to proceed with the recovery. Care must always be taken during removal from the site to prevent the drive from breaking open and being exposed to dust.

Fire or Smoke Damage

After a fire or a flood, the HD should not be moved; under no circumstances should it be powered up. A certified cyber forensic expert with experience in handling damaged drives should be contacted immediately. Typically, these experts will be able to dismantle the drive and move it without causing further damage. They are able to assess the external damage and arrive at a decision that will safely triage the drive for further recovery steps. Fire-damaged drives should never be moved or handled by laymen.

Shock Damage

Shock damage can occur when someone drops a computer or it is damaged via an automobile accident; in more catastrophic scenarios, shock damage can result when servers fall through floors during a fire or are damaged by bulldozers that are removing debris. This type of crushing damage often results in bending of the platters and can be extensive. As in fire and flood circumstances, the drive should be isolated and power should not be applied.

A drive that has been damaged by shock presents a unique challenge: From the outside, the computer may look fine. This is typical of many claims involving laptop computers damaged during an automobile collision. If the computer consultant can verify that the drive was powered down at the time the accident occurred, most will be comfortable attempting to power up a drive that has been in a collision, to begin the data capture process. At the first sign of a change in the dynamics of the drive, a head clicking or a drive spinning down, power will be cut from the drive and the restoration will continue in a clean room where the drive will be opened up and protected from harmful dust.

The Importance of Off-Site Cyber Backup

One of the best ways to maximize cyber data recovery efforts is to have off-site cyber backup. For adjusters arriving at the scene, this should be one of the first questions asked. An offsite backup can take many forms. Some involve the use of special data centers that synchronize data constantly. There are companies that provide this service. Other backups, for smaller companies, may be as mundane (but effective) as removing a tape backup of critical data from the site on a daily basis. With proper rotation and several tapes, a complete backup of data is always off site. Prices for these services vary widely depending on how much data need to be backed up, and how often.

Case Studies

Scenario 1

John ran a home-based IT business. After his home burned down, John posted an insurance claim for a $500,000 loss for lost income, damaged cyber equipment, and lost wages. He also charged the insurance company $60,000 for the 3 months he spent recovering data from the drives. Because he was able to recover only 25% of the data, he posted an additional claim for the cost of reconstructing the websites he hosted from his home.

For the cyber forensic consultant, this case raised several questions. As an IT professional, John should have known better than to touch the HD and attempt to recover any of the data himself. Also, when a claimant intentionally or unintentionally inflicts damage on his or her own property after an event, who is responsible? After a thorough evaluation of the circumstances and intense questioning of the claimant, the claim was eventually reduced to a substantially smaller amount.

Scenario 2

Sammie's Flowers had 113 retail outlets and one central headquarters where they kept photography, custom software, catalog masters, and the like. There was no off-site backup. Everything was on CD-ROMs or on the HD of the company's server.

One night, lightning struck the headquarters building and it burned down. An IT appraiser lacking the appropriate cyber forensic skills evaluated the cyber equipment after the fire. No attempts were made to recover data from the HDs or to start the computers; because of their damaged physical condition, they were simply thrown into a Dumpster.

One year later, the insured filed a claim for $37 million. Under the terms of the insured's policy, coverage for valuable papers and business personal property was most pertinent to the case. The policy limit for valuable papers is small and easily reached. The coverage limit for business personal property, on the other hand, *will* cover the $37 million claim, if the court decides that the cyber data that were lost qualify as "business-valuable papers." Although this case is still pending, the cost of resolving this claim could be astronomic; if a cyber data recovery expert had been consulted, the claim amount could have been reduced by millions.

Scenario 3

Alisa, a professional photographer, was in a car accident that damaged her laptop computer. She had been using the PC at a rest stop before the accident and later reported to the adjuster that when she booted it up after the accident she heard "a strange clicking and clacking sound." Unfortunately for Alisa, that was the sound of data being destroyed. She posted a $500,000 claim to her insurance company under her business policy, including the cost of 2000 lost images and the cost of equipment, site, model, and agency

fees for a one-day photography shoot. If the PC, which had a noticeable crack in it caused by the accident, had been professionally handled, the chances are good that the data could have been recovered and the claim would have been significantly reduced.

Cyber equipment is always at risk of being damaged, whether by flood, fire, lightning, or other catastrophic means. However, damage does not always equal data loss. Indeed, companies and their adjusters can be quick to write off damaged storage media, when in fact recovery may be possible. By taking the immediate measures of protecting the computers from touch and power and by calling in professional cyber forensic experts to assess the damage, insurers can reap the benefits in reduced claim amounts.

Password Recovery

The following is a short list of the types and ways in which passwords can be recovered. Many useful tools that can be downloaded from the Internet for free will crack open system files that store passwords. Software programs such as Peachtree (a financial database), Windows 8, certain FTP programs, and the like store passwords in a way that allows easy retrieval.

Recovering license keys for software is often an important step in reconstructing or virtualizing a disk image. Like passwords, without a valid license key the software will not work. There are a number of useful programs that can recover software license keys from the registry of a computer that can be found with a quick Google search. Understanding the mind of the user can also be helpful in locating things such as password storage tools or simply thinking to search a computer for the word *password*. A tremendous number of websites will pass the password down to a client machine through the Password field in Hyper Text Markup Language (HTML) documents. Some developers have wised up to this "feature" and they strip it out before it comes down, but most of them do it on the client side. This means that with the proper intercepting tool, the password can be captured midstream on its way down to the client before it gets stripped out.

Password cracking can be achieved with a minimal amount of skill and a great deal of patience. Having some idea of what the password is before cracking it will be helpful. You can also purchase online services as well as software tools that will strip the password right out of a file, removing it completely. Word documents are particularly vulnerable, and zip files are particularly invulnerable. However, there is a method (and a free download) that can figure out the password of a zip file if a sample of a file that is known to be in the zip can be provided.

File Carving

In most investigations, the first place a file system examination begins is with live files. Live files are those files that still have MFT entries. Link file, trash bin, Outlook Temporary (OLK) folders, recent items, International Organization for Standardization lists, Internet history, TIF, and thumb databases all constitute a discernible, unique pattern of user activity. As such, they hold particular interest. By exploring these files, an examiner can make determinations about file origins, the use of files, the distribution of files, and of course the current location of the files. However, sometimes the subject has been clever and removed all traces of activity. Or the suspect item may be a server, used merely as a repository for the files. Or maybe someone just wants to recover a file that he deleted a long, long time ago (see sidebar, "Oops! Did I Delete That?").

When such a need arises, the vast graveyard called *unallocated clusters* could hold the last hope that the file can be recovered. By searching the unallocated clusters using a search tool designed for such things, and by using a known keyword in the file, one may locate the portion within the unallocated clusters where a file used to reside. Typically, search hits will be stored under a tab or in a particular area of the forensic toolset, and they may be browsed, one by one, along with a small excerpt from the surrounding bits. By clicking on the search hit, another pane of the software window may show a more expanded view of the hit location. If it is a document with text, that is great, and you may see other words that were also known to have been in the target file. Now, on TV shows such as *CSI*, of course the document is always there, and by running some reverse 128-bit decryption sequencer to an inverted 12-bit decryption sequencer that reloops the hashing algorithm through a 256-bit decompiler by rethreading it into a multiplexing file marker, detectives can just right click and say "Export this," and the file will print out, even if it is not on the computer that is being examined and never was. (Yes, I made all of that up.)

In the real world, more often than not, we find that our examinations are spurred and motivated and wholly created by someone's abject paranoia. In these cases, no amount of digging will ever create the evidence that they want to see. That leaves only the creative use of time stamps on documents to attempt to create an aroma of guilt about the subject piece. Sometimes we find that even after rooting through 300 GB of unallocated clusters, leaving no stone unturned, the *file just is not there*. But sometimes, all pessimism aside, we find little bits and pieces of interesting things all salted around throughout the unallocated clusters.

The first place to turn is the automated carvers. By familiarizing ourselves with the hexadecimal patterns of file signatures (and I have provided a nice table for you here), we may view the hex of the unallocated clusters in a hex editor or in the hex pane of the examination tool. Or possibly we already know the type of file. Let us say that we know the type of file because our clients told us that they only use Word as their document editor. We scroll to

the beginning of the section of text, which might look like this:

Figure sample file signature
From the text pane view of EnCase:
ÐÏ·à¡±á···············>···þÿ········
From the Hex view:
00 00 00 00 00 00 00 00 00 00 00 00 00 00 00 4F 6F
70 73
21 20 20 44 69 64
20 49 20 64 65 6C 65 74 65 20 74 68 61 74 3F 0D
42 79
20 53 63 6F 74 74 20
52 2E 20 45 6C 6C 69 73 0D 73 65 6C 6C 69 73 40
75 73
2E 72 67 6C 2E 63 6F
6D 0D 0D 54 68 65 20 66 69 6C 65 20 69 73 20 67
6F 6E
65 2E 20 20 49 74 92
73 20 6E 6F 74 20 69 6E 20 74 68 65 20 72 65 63
79 63
6C 65 20 62 69 6E 2E
20 59 6F 75 92 76 65 20 64 6F 6E 65 20 61 20 63
6F 6D
70 6C 65 74 65 20 73

Scrolling down in the text pane, we then find the following:
············Oops! Did I delete that? By Scott R. Ellis The file is gone. It's not in the recycle bin. You've ....

By simply visually scanning the unallocated clusters, we can pick up where the file begins and, if the file signature is not in the provided list of signatures or if for some reason the carving scripts in the forensic software are incorrectly pulling files, they may need to be manually set up. Truly, for Word files, that is all you need to know. You need to be able to determine the end and the beginning of a file. Some software will ignore data in the file before and after the beginning and end of file signatures. This is true for very many file types; I cannot tell you which ones because I have not tried them all. There are some file types that need a valid end-of-file (EOF) marker, but most do not. However, if you *do not* capture the true EOF (sensible marker or no), the file may look like garbage or all the original formatting will be scrambled or it will not open. Some JPEG viewers (such as Adobe Photoshop) will throw an error if the EOF is not found. Others, such as IE, will not even notice. Here is the trick, and it is a trick, and do not let anyone tell you differently; they might not teach this in your average university cyber forensics class: Starting with the file signature, highlight as many of the unallocated clusters *after* the file signature that you think would possibly be big enough to hold the entire file size. Now double that, and export it as raw data. Give it a .DOC extension and open it in Word. *Voilá!* The file has been reconstructed. Word will know where the document ends and it will show you that document. If you happen to catch a few extra documents at the end, or a JPG or whatever, Word will ignore them and show only the first document.

Unless some sort of drastic "wiping action" has taken place, as in the use of a third-party utility to delete data, I have almost always found that a great deal of deleted data are *immediately* available in EnCase (forensic software) within 20—25 min after a hard disk image is mounted, simply by running "recover folders" and sitting back and waiting while it runs. This is especially true when the drive has not been used at all since the time the data were deleted. Preferably, counsel will have taken steps to ensure that this is the case when a computer is the prime subject of an investigation. Often this is not the case, however. Many attorneys, IT, and HR directors "poke around" for information all on their own.

It is conceivable that up to 80% of deleted data on a computer may be readily available, without the necessity of carving, for up to 2 or 3 years, as long as the computer has not seen extreme use (large amounts of files, or large amounts of copying and moving of very large files) that could conceivably overwrite the data.

Even so, searching unallocated clusters for file types typically does not require the creation of an index. Depending on the size of the drive, it may take 4 or 5 h for the carving process to complete, and it may or may not be entirely successful, depending on the type of files that are being carved. For example, MPEG videos do not carve well at all, but there are ways around that. DOC and XLS files usually carve out nicely.

Indexing is something that is done strictly for the purpose of searching massive amounts of files for large numbers of keywords. We rarely use EnCase to search for keywords; we have found it better to use Relativity, our review environment, to allow people who are interested in keywords to do the keyword searching themselves as they perform their review. Relativity is built on an SQL platform on which indexing is a known and stable technology.

In other words (as in the bottom line), spending 15—25 min with a drive, an experienced examiner can provide a succinct answer as to how long it would take to provide the files that they want. Likely, the answer could be, "Another 30 min and it will be yours." Including time to set up, extract, and copy to disk, if everything is in perfect order, 2 h is the upper limit. This is based on the foundation that the deleted data for which they are looking were deleted in the past couple of weeks of the use of the computer. If they need to go back more than a couple of months, an examiner may end up carving into the unallocated clusters to find "lost" files. These are files for which part of or all of the MFT entry has been obliterated and portions of the files themselves may be overwritten.

Carving is considered one of the consummate forensic skills. Regardless of the few shortcuts that exist, carving requires a deep, disk-level knowledge of how files are stored, and it requires a certain intuition that cannot be "book taught." Examiners gain this talent from years of looking at raw disk data. Regardless, even the most efficient and skilled of carvers will turn to their automated carving tools. Two things at which carving tools excel is carving out images and print spool files (enhanced metafiles). What are they really bad at? The tools I use do not even begin to work properly to carve out email files. General regular program (GREP) searching does not provide for branching logic, so you cannot locate a qualified email header every single time, and capture the end of it. The best you can do is to create your own script to carve out the emails. GREP does not allow for any sort of true logic that would be useful or even efficient at capturing something as complex as the many variations of email headers that exist, but it does allow for many alterations of a single search term to be formulated with a single expression. For example, the words *house, housing, houses,* and *housed* all could be searched for with a single statement such as "hous[(e)|(es)|(ing)|(ed)]." GREP can be useful but it is not really a shortcut. Each option added to a GREP statement doubles the length of time the search will take to run. Searching for *house(s)* has the same run time as two separate keywords for *house* and *houses.* It also allows for efficient pattern matching. For example, if you wanted to find all phone numbers on a computer for three particular area codes, you could formulate a GREP expression like this. Using a test file and running the search each time, an expression can be built that finds phone numbers in any of three area codes:

> *(708)|(312)|(847) Checks for the three area codes [\(]?(708)|(312)|(847)[\-\)\ ]? Checks for parentheses and other formatting*
> *[\(]?(708)|(312)|(847)[\-\)\ ]?###[\-\ ]?#### Checks for the rest of the number*

This statement will find any 10-digit string that is formatted like a phone number, as well as any 10-digit string that contains one of the three area codes. This last option, to check for any 10-digit number string, if run against an entire OS, will likely return numerous results that are not phone numbers. The question marks render the search for phone number formatting optional.

The following are the characters that are used to formulate a GREP expression. Typically, the best use of GREP is its ability to formulate pattern-matching searches. In GREP, the following symbols are used to formulate an expression:

- . The period is a wildcard and means a space must be occupied by any character.
- * The asterisk is a wildcard that means any character or no character. It will match multiple repetitions of the character as well.

? The character preceding the question mark must repeat 0 or 1 time. It provides instructions as to how to search for the character or grouping that precedes it.

+ This is like the question mark, only it *must* exist at least one or more times.

Matches a number.

[·] Matches a list of characters. *[hH]i* matches *hi* and *Hi* (but not *hHi!*).

∧ This is a "not" and will exclude a part from a string.

[−] A range of characters such as (a−z) will find any single letter, a through z.

\ This will escape the standard GREP search symbols so that it may be included as part of the search. For example, a search string that has the (symbol in it (such as a phone number) needs to have the parentheses escaped so that the string can be included as part of the search.

| This is an "or." See previous sample search for area codes.

\x Searches for the indicated hex string.

Preceding a hex character with \x marks the next two characters as hexadecimal characters. Using this to locate a known hex string is more efficient than relying on it to be interpreted from Unicode or Unicode Transformation Format.

Most forensic applications have stock scripts included that can carve for you. Many of the popular cyber forensics applications can carve for you. They have scripted modules that will run, and all you have to do is select the signature you want, and *voilá*, it carves it right out of the unallocated clusters for you. Sounds pretty slick, and it is slick... when it works. The problem is that some files, such as MPEG video, do not have a set signature at the beginning and end of each file. So how can we carve them? Running an MPEG carver will make a mess. It is a far better thing to do a "carve" by locating MPEG data, highlighting it, exporting it to a file, and giving it an MPEG extension.

Things to Know: How Time Stamps Work

Let us take an example: Bob in accounting has been discovered to be pilfering from the cash box. A forensics examiner is called in to examine his cyber system to see whether he has been engaging in any activities that would be against company policy and to see whether he has been accessing areas of the network that he should not be. They want to know what he has been working on. A quick examination of his PC turns up a very large cache of pornography. A casual glance at the Entry Modified time stamp shows that the images were created nearly 1 year before Bob's employment, so automatically the investigator disregards the images and moves on to his search for evidence of copying and deleting sensitive files to his local

machine. The investigator begins to look at the deleted files. His view is filtered, so he is not looking at anything but deleted files. He leaves the view in "gallery" view so that he can see telltale images that may give clues as to any websites used during the time frame of the suspected breaches. To his surprise, the investigator begins seeing images from that porn cache. He now notices that when a deleted file is overwritten, in the gallery view of the software the image that overwrote the deleted file is displayed. He makes the logical conclusion that the Entry Modified time stamp is somehow wrong.

On a Windows XP machine, an archive file is extracted. Entry Modified time stamps are xx:xx:xx, even though the archive was extracted to the file system on yy:yy:yy. Normally when a file is created on a system, it takes on the system date as its Date Created time stamp. Such is not the case with zip files.

Entry Modified, in the world of cyber forensics, is that illustrious time stamp that has cinched many a case. It is a hidden time stamp that users never see and few actually know about. As such, they cannot change it. A little-known fact about the Entry Modified time stamp is that it is constrained. It can be no later than the Date Created time stamp. (This is not true in Vista.) When a zip file is created, the Date Created and Date Modified time stamps become the same.

Experimental Evidence

Examining and understanding how time stamps behave on individual PCs and OSs provide some of the greatest challenges facing forensic examiners. This is not the result of any great difficulty, but rather because of the difficulty in clearly explaining it to others. This examiner once read a quotation from a prosecutor in a local newspaper that said, "We will clearly show that he viewed the image on three separate occasions." In court the defense's expert disabused her of the notion she held that Last Written, Last Accessed, Entry Modified, and Date Created time stamps were convenient little recordings of user activity. Rather, they are references mostly used by the OS for its own arcane purposes. Table 40.1 compares the three known Windows time stamps with the four time stamps in EnCase.

XP

A zip file was created using a file with a Date Created time stamp of 12/23/07 10:40:53AM (ID 1 in Table 40.2). It was then extracted and the time stamps were examined.

Using Windows XP compressed folders, the file was then extracted to a separate file on a different system (ID 2 in Table 40.2). Date Created and Entry Modified time stamps, upon extraction, inherited the original Date Created time stamp of 12/23/12 10:40:53AM and Last Accessed of 04/28/13 01:56:07PM.

TABLE 40.1 Comparison of Three Known Windows Time Stamps With Four EnCase Time Stamps

Windows	EnCase	Purpose
Date Created	Date Created	Typically this is the first time a file appeared on a system. It is not always accurate.
Date Modified	Last Written	Usually this is the time when a system last finished writing or changing information in a file.
Last Accessed	Last Accessed	This time stamp can be altered by any number of user and system actions. It should not be interpreted as the file having been opened and viewed.
Not available	Entry Modified	This is a system pointer that is inaccessible to users through the Explorer interface. It changes when the file changes size.

TABLE 40.2 Date Created Time Stamp

ID	Name	Last Accessed	File Created	Entry Modified
1	IMG_3521.CR2	04/28/08 01:56:07PM	12/23/07 10:40:53AM	03/15/08 09:11:15AM
2	IMG_3521.CR2	04/28/08 01:56:07PM	12/23/07 10:40:53AM	04/28/08 01:57:12PM

The system Entry Modified (not to be confused with Date Modified) became 04/28/13 01:57:12PM.

Various OSs can perform various operations that will alter the Entry Modified time stamp en masse (Table 40.3). For example, a tape restoration of a series of directories will create a time stamp adjustment in Entry Modified that corresponds to the date of the restoration. The original file is on another system somewhere and is inaccessible to the investigator (because he does not know about it).

In Table 40.3, Entry Modified becomes a part of a larger pattern of time stamps after an OS event. On a computer on

TABLE 40.3 Altering the Entry Modified Time Stamp

ID	Name	Last Accessed	File Created	Entry Modified
1	IMG_3521.CR2	04/28/08 01:56:07PM	12/23/07 10:40:53AM	03/15/08 09:11:15AM
2	IMG_3521.CR2	05/21/08 03:32:01PM	12/23/07 10:40:53AM	05/21/08 03:32:01PM

which most of the time stamps have an Entry Modified time stamp that is sequential to a specific time frame, it is now more difficult to determine when the file actually arrived on the system. As long as the date stamps are not inherited from the overwriting file by the overwritten file, examining the files that were overwritten by ID2 (Table 40.3), can reveal a No Later Than time. In other words, the file could not have appeared on the system before the file that it overwrote.

Vista

A zip file was created using a file with a Date Created time stamp of dd:mm:yyyy(a) and a date modified of dd:mm:yy(a). Using Windows Vista compressed folders, the file was then extracted to a separate file on the same system. Date Modified time stamps, on extraction, inherited the original time stamp of dd:mm:yyyy(a), but the Date Created time stamp reflected the true date. This is a significant change from XP. There are also tools available that will allow a user to mass-edit time stamps. Forensic examiners must always bear in mind that there are some savvy users who research and understand antiforensics.

Email Headers and Time Stamps, Email Receipts, and Bounced Messages

There is much confusion in the ediscovery industry and in cyber forensics in general about how best to interpret email time stamps. Although it might not offer the perfect "every case" solution, this section reveals the intricacies of dealing with time stamps and how to interpret them correctly.

Regarding sources of email, Simple Mail Transfer Protocol (SMTP) has to relay email to its own domain. HELO/EHLO allows a user to connect to the SMTP port and send email.

As most of us are aware, in 2007 the US Congress enacted the Energy Policy Act of 2005 (http://www.epa.gov/oust/fedlaws/publ_109-058.pdf, Section 110, Daylight Savings). This act was passed into law by President George W. Bush on August 8, 2005. Among other provisions, such as subsidies for wind energy, reducing air pollution, and providing tax breaks to homeowners for making energy-conserving changes to their homes, it amended the Uniform Time Act of 1966 by changing the start and end dates for Daylight Savings Time beginning in 2007. Previously, clocks would be set ahead by an hour on the first Sunday of April and set back on the last Sunday of October. The new law changed this as follows: Starting in 2007 clocks were set ahead 1 h on the first Sunday of March and then set back on the first Sunday in November. Aside from the additional confusion facing everyone when we review email and attempt to translate Greenwich Mean Time (GMT) to a sensible local time, probably the only true noteworthy aspect of this law is the extra daylight time afforded to children trick-or-treating on Halloween. Many observers questioned whether the act actually resulted in a net energy savings.

In a world of remote Web-based email servers, it has been observed that some email sent through a Web mail interface will bear the time stamp of the time zone where the server resides. Either your server is in the Central Time zone or the clock on the server is set to the wrong time/time zone. Servers that send email mark the header of the email with the GMT stamp numerical value (noted in bold in the example that follows) as opposed to the actual time zone stamp. For example, instead of saying 08:00 CST, the header will say 08:00 (−0600). The GMT differential is used so that every email client interprets that stamp based on the time zone and time setting of itself and is able to account for things such as Daylight Savings Time offsets. This is a dynamic interpretation; if I change the time zone of my computer, it will change the way Outlook *shows* me the time of each email, but it does not actually physically change the email itself. For example, if an email server is located in Colorado, every email I send appears to have been sent from the Mountain Time zone. My email client interprets the Time Received of an email based on when my server received the mail, *not* when my email client down-loads the email from my server.

If a server is in the Central Time zone and the client is in Mountain Time, the normal Web mail interface will not be cognizant of the client's time zone. Hence those are the times you will see. I checked a Web mail account on a server in California that I use and it does the same thing. Here I have broken up the header to show step by step how it moved. Here is, first, the entire header in its original context, followed by a breakdown of how I interpret each transaction in the header:

```
**********************************
```

Received: from p01c11m096.mxlogic.net (208.65.144. 247) by mail.us.rgl.com
(192.168.0.12) with Microsoft SMTP Server id 8.0.751.0; Fri, 30 Nov 200721:03:15-0700
Received: from unknown [65.54.246.112] (EHLO bay0-omc1-s40.bay0.hotmail.com)
by p01c11m096.mxlogic.net (mxl_mta-5.2.0-1) with ESMTP id 23cd0574.3307895728.120458.00-105.p01c11m096. mxlogic.net (envelope-from
<timezone32@hotmail.com>); Fri, 30 Nov 2007 20:59:46-0700 (MST)
Received: from BAY108-W37 ([65.54.162.137]) by bay0-omc1-s40.bay0.hotmail.com
with Microsoft SMTPSVC(6.0.3790.3959); Fri, 30 Nov 2007 19:59:46-0800
Message-ID: <BAY108-W374BF59F8292A9D2C95 F08BA720@phx.gbl>

Return-Path: timezone32@hotmail.com
Content-Type: multipart/alternative;   boundary = "=_reb-r538638D0-t4750DC32"
X-Originating-IP: [71.212.198.249]
From: Test Account <timezone3@hotmail.com>
To: Bill   Nelson   <attorney@attorney12345.com>, Scott
Ellis <sellis@us.rgl.com>
Subject: FW: Norton Anti Virus
Date: Fri, 30 Nov 2007 21:59:46 -0600
Importance: Normal
In-Reply-To: <BAY108-W26EE80CDDA1C4C632124 ABA720@phx.gbl>
References: <BAY108-W26EE80CDDA1C4C632124 ABA720@phx.gbl>
MIME-Version: 1.0
X-OriginalArrivalTime: 01 Dec 2007 03:59:46.0488 (UTC) FILETIME=[9CAC5B80:01C833CE]
X-Processed-By: Rebuild v2.0-0
X-Spam: [F=0.0038471784; B=0.500(0);
spf =0.500; CM=0.500; S=0.010(2007110801);
MH=0.500(2007113048); R=0.276(1071030201529);
SC=none; SS=0.500]
X-MAIL-FROM: <timezone3@hotmail.com>
X-SOURCE-IP: [65.54.246.112]
X-AnalysisOut: [v=1.0 c=0 a=Db0T9Pbbji75CibVO CAA:9
a = rYVTvsE0vOPdh0IEP8MA:]
X-AnalysisOut: [7   a=TaS_S6-EMopkTzdPlCr4MVJ L5D QA:4
a=NCG-xuS670wA:10 a = T-0]
X-AnalysisOut:[QtiWyBeMA:10a=r9zUxlSq4yJzx Rie7pAA:7
a=EWQMng83CrhB0XWP0h]
X-AnalysisOut: [vbCEdheDsA:4 a=EfJqPEOeqlMA:10 a=37WNUvjkh6kA:10]

```
*******************************
```

Looks like a bunch of garbage, right? Here it is, step by step, transaction by transaction, in reverse chronological order:

1. My server in Colorado receives the email (GMT differential is in bold):
   Received: from p01c11m096.mxlogic.net (208.65.144. 247) by mail.us.rgl.com
   (192.168.0.12) with Microsoft SMTP Server id 8.0.751.0; Fri, 30 Nov 2007 21:03:15 -0700
2. Before that, my mail-filtering service in Colorado receives the email:
   Received: from unknown [65.54.246.112] (EHLO bay0-omc1-s40.bay0.hotmail.com) by p01c11m096. mxlogic.net (mxl_mta-5.2.0-1) with ESMTP id

*23cd0574.3307895728.120458.00-105.p01c11m096.
mxlogic.net (envelope-from
<timezone3@hotmail.com>); Fri, 30 Nov 2007
20:59:46 -0700 (MST)*

a. The email server receives the sender's email in this next section. On most networks, the mail server is rarely the same machine on which a user created the email. This next item in the header of the email shows that the email server is located in the Pacific Time zone. 65.54.246.112, the x-origin stamp, is the actual Internet Protocol (IP) address of the computer that sent the email:

*Received: from BAY108-W37 ([65.54.162.137]) by
bay0-omc1-s40.bay0.hotmail.com
with Microsoft SMTPSVC(6.0.3790.3959); Fri, 30
Nov 2007 19:59:46 -0800
Message-ID: <BAY108-W374BF59F8292A9D2C95
F08BA720@phx.gbl>
Return-Path: timezone310@hotmail.com*

b. This content was produced on the server where the Web mail application resides. Technically, the email was created on the Web client application with only one degree of separation between the originating IP and the sender IP. By examining the order and type of IP addresses logged in the header, a trail can be created that shows the path of mail servers that the email traversed before arriving at its destination. This machine is the one that is likely in the Central Time zone, because it can be verified by the -0600 in the following. The X-originating IP address is the IP address of the sender's external Internet connection IP address in her house and the X-Source IP address is the IP address of the Web mail server she logged into on this day. This IP address is also subject to change because they have many Web mail servers as well. In fact, comparisons with older emails sent on different dates show that it is different. Originating IP address is also subject to change because a digital subscriber line or cable Internet is likely a dynamic account, but it (likely) will not change as frequently as the X-source:

*Content-Type: multipart/alternative; boundary=
"=_ reb-r538638D0-t4750DC32"
X-Originating-IP: [71.212.198.249]
From: Test Account <@hotmail.com>
To: Bill Nelson <attorney@attorney12345.com>,
Scott
Ellis <sellis@us.rgl.com>
Subject: FW: Norton Anti Virus
Date: Fri, 30 Nov 2007 21:59:46 -0600
Importance: Normal*

*In-Reply-To: <BAY108-W26EE80CDDA1C4C632
124 ABA 720@phx.gbl>
References: <BAY108-W26EE80CDDA1C4C632
124 ABA7 20@phx.gbl>
MIME-Version: 1.0
X-OriginalArrivalTime: 01 Dec 2007 03:59:46.0488
(UTC) FILETIME= [9CAC5B80:01C833CE]
X-Processed-By: Rebuild v2.0-0
X-Spam: [F=0.0038471784; B=0.500(0);
spf=0.500;
CM=0.500; 5=0.010(2007110801); MH=0.500
(2007113 048); R=0.276(1071030201529);
SC=none; SS=0.500]
X-MAIL-FROM: <timezone310@hotmail.com>
X-SOURCE-IP: [65.54.246.112]
X-AnalysisOut: [v=10c=0a=Db0T9Pbbji75Cib
VOCAA:9
a=rYVTvsE0vOPdh0IEP8MA:]
X-AnalysisOut:[7a=TaS_S6-
EMopkTzdPlCr4MVJL5DQA:4
a=NCG-xuS670wA:10a=T-0]
X-AnalysisOut: [QtiWyBeMA:10 a = r9zUxlS-
q4yJzxRie 7p AA:7 a = EWQMng83CrhB0XWP0h]
X-AnalysisOut: [vbCEdheDsA:4 a = EfJq-
PEOeqlMA:10 a = 37WNUvjkh6kA:10]*
From: *Test Account [mailto:timezone310@hotmail.
com*
Sent: *Friday, November 30, 2007 10:00 PM*
To: *Bill Nelson; Scott Ellis*
Subject: *FW: Norton Anti Virus*
*Bill and Scott,
By the way, it was 8:57 my time when I sent the last
email, however, my hotmail shows that it was 9:57
pm. Not sure if their server is on Central time or
not. Scott, can you help with that question? Thanks.
Anonymous*
From:*timezone3@hotmail.com*
To:*attorney@attorney12345.com;   sellis@us.rgl.
com*
CC:*timezone310@hotmail.com*
*Subject: Norton Anti Virus
Date: Fri, 30 Nov 2007 21:57:16 -0600
Bill and Scott,
I am on the computer now and have a question for
you. Can you please call me?
Anonymous*

Steganography "Covered Writing"

Steganography tools provide a method that allows a user to hide a file in plain sight. For example, there are a number of stego software tools that allow the user to hide one image inside another. Some of these do it by simply appending the "hidden" file at the tail end of a JPEG file and then add a pointer to the beginning of the file. The most common way that steganography is discovered on a machine is by detecting the steganography software on the machine. Then comes the arduous task of locating 11 of the files that may possibly contain hidden data. Other, more manual stego techniques may be as simple as hiding text behind other text. In Microsoft Word, text boxes can be placed right over the top of other text, formatted in such a way as to render the text undetectable to a casual observer. Forensic tools will allow the analyst to locate this text, but upon opening the file the text will not be readily visible. Another method is to hide images behind other images using the layers feature of some photo enhancement tools, such as Photoshop.

StegAlyzerAS is a tool created by Backbone Security to detect steganography on a system. It works by both searching for known stego artifacts as well as by searching for the program files associated with over 650 steganography toolsets. Steganography hash sets are also available within the National Institute of Standards and Technology database of hash sets. Hash sets are databases of Message Digest algorithm 5 (MD5) hashes of known unique files associated with a particular application.

6. FIRST PRINCIPLES

In science, *first principles* refer to going back to the most basic nature of a thing. For example, in physics, an experiment is *ab initio* (from first principles) if it only subsumes a parameterization of known irrefutable laws of physics. The experiment of calculation does not make assumptions through modeling or assumptive logic.

First principles, or *ab initio*, may or may not be something that a court will understand, depending on the court and the types of cases it tries. Ultimately the best evidence is that which can be easily duplicated. In observation of a compromised system in its live state, even if the observation photographed or videoed may be admitted as evidence but the events viewed cannot be duplicated, the veracity of the events will easily be questioned by the opposition.

During an investigation of a defendant's PC, an examiner found that a piece of software on the computer behaved erratically. This behavior had occurred after the computer had been booted from a restored image of the PC. The behavior was photographed and introduced in court as evidence. The behavior was mentioned during a cross-examination and had not originally been intended as use for evidence; it was simply something that the examiner recalled seeing during his investigation, that the list of files a piece of software would display would change. The prosecution was outraged because this statement harmed his case a great deal. The instability and erratic behavior of

the software were the underpinnings of the defense. The examiner, in response to the prosecutor's accusations of ineptitude, replied that he had a series of photographs that demonstrated the behavior. The prosecutor requested the photos, but the examiner did not have them in court. He brought them the next day, at which time, when the jury was not in the room, the prosecutor requested the photos, reviewed them, and promptly let the matter drop.

It would have been far more powerful to have produced the photographs at the time of the statement; but it may have also led the prosecution to an *ab initio* effort, one that may have shown that the defense expert's findings were irreproducible. In an expert testimony, the more powerful and remarkable a piece of evidence is, the more likely it is to be challenged by the opposition. It is an intricate game because such a challenge may ultimately destroy the opposition's case, because a corroborative result would only serve to increase the veracity and reliability of the expert's testimony. Whether you are defense, prosecution, or plaintiff, the strongest evidence is that which is irrefutable and relies on first principles. Aristotle defined it as those circumstances in which "for the same (characteristic) simultaneously to belong and not belong to the same (object) in the same (way) is impossible." In less obfuscating, 21st-century terms, the following interpretation is applicable: One thing cannot be two different things at the same time in the same circumstance; there is only one truth, and it is self-evidentiary and not open to interpretation. For example, when a computer HD is imaged, the opposition may also image the same HD. If proper procedures are followed, there is no possible way that different MD5 hashes could result. Black cannot be white.

The lesson learned? Never build your foundation on irreproducible evidence. To do so is tantamount to building the case on "circumstantial" evidence.

7. HACKING A WINDOWS XP PASSWORD

There are very many methods to decrypt or "hack" a Windows password. This section lists some of them. One of the more interesting methods of cracking passwords using forensic methods is to hack the Active Directory. It is not covered here, but suffice it to say that there is an awesome amount of information stored in the Active Directory file of a domain server. With the correct tools and settings in place, Bitlocker-locked PCs can be accessed and passwords can be viewed in plaintext with just a few simple, readily available scripts.

Net User Password Hack

If you have access to a machine, this is an easy thing, and the instructions to do it can easily be found on YouTube.

Type **net users** at the Windows command line. Pick a user. Type **net user***username*** *. (You have to type the asterisk or it will not work.) Regardless of your privileges, you will then be allowed to change any password, including the local machine administrator password.

Lanman Hashes and Rainbow Tables

- The following procedure can be used to "reverse-engineer" the password from where it is stored in Windows. Lan Manager [or Lanman (LM)] has been used by Windows, in versions before Windows Vista, to store passwords that are shorter than 15 characters. The vast majority of passwords are stored in this format. LM hashes are computed via a short series of actions. The following items contribute to the weakness of the hash.
- Password is converted to all uppercase.
- Passwords longer than seven characters are divided into two halves. By visual inspection of the hash, this allows us to determine whether the second half is padding. We can do this by viewing all the LM hashes on a system and observing whether the second halves of any of the hashes are the same. This will speed the process of decrypting the hash.
- There is no salt. In cryptography, *salt* is random bits that are thrown in to prevent large lookup tables of values from being developed.

Windows will store passwords using the Lanman hash. Windows Vista changed this. For all versions of Windows except Vista, about 70 GB of what are called *rainbow tables* can be downloaded from the Internet. Using a tool such as the many that are found on Backtrack will capture the actual hashes that are stored for the password on the physical disk. Analysis of the hashes will show whether the hashes are in use as passwords. Rainbow tables, which can be downloaded from the Web in a single 70-GB table, are simply lookup tables of every possible iteration of the hashes. By entering the hash value, the password can be easily and quickly reverse-engineered and access to files can be gained. A favorite method of hackers is to install command-line software on remote machines that will allow access to the Lanman hashes and will send them via FTP to the hacker. Once the hacker has admin rights, he owns the machine.

Password Reset Disk

Emergency Boot CD is a Linux-based tool that allows you to boot a computer that has an unknown password. Using this command-line tool, you can reset the administrator password easily. It will not tell you the plaintext of the password, but it will clear it so that the machine can be accessed through something like VMware with a blank password.

Memory Analysis and the Trojan Defense

One method to retrieve passwords and encryption keys is through memory analysis: physical RAM. RAM can be acquired using a variety of relatively nonintrusive methods. HBGary.com offers a free tool that will capture RAM with minimal impact. In addition to extracting encryption keys, RAM analysis can be used to defeat or corroborate the Trojan defense. The Responder tool from HBGary (single-user license) provides in-depth analysis and reporting on the many malicious software (malware) activities that can be detected in a RAM environment. The Trojan defense is commonly used by innocent and guilty parties to explain unlawful actions that have occurred on their computers. The following items represent a brief overview of the types of things that can be accomplished through RAM analysis:

- A hidden driver is a 100% indicator of a bad guy. Hidden drivers can be located through analysis of the physical memory.
- Using tools such as FileMon, TCPView, and RegMon, you can usually readily identify malware infections. There is a small number of advanced malware that is capable of doing things such as rolling up completely (poof, it's gone!) when it detects the presence of investigative tools, or that is capable of escaping a virtualized host. All the same, when conducting a malware forensic analysis, be sure to isolate the system from the network.
- RAM analysis using a tool such as HBGary's Responder can allow reverse-engineering of processes that are running and can uncover potential malware behavioral capabilities. As this science progresses, a much greater ability to detect malware easily and quickly is expected.

User Artifact Analysis

There is nothing worse than facing off against an opposing expert who has not done his artifact analysis on a case. Because of an increasing workload in this field, experts are often taking shortcuts that make more work for everyone in the long run. In life and on computers, the actions people take leave behind artifacts. The following is a short list of artifacts that are readily viewed using any method of analysis:

- recent files
- OLK files
- shortcuts
- TIF
- My Documents
- desktop
- Recycle Bin
- email
- Exchangeable image file format (EXIF) data

Users create all of these artifacts, either knowingly or unknowingly, and aspects of them can be reviewed and understood to indicate that certain actions on the computer took place. For example, a folder in My Documents called "fast trains" that contains pictures of Europe's TGV and surrounding countryside, TIF sites that show the user booking travel to Europe, installed software for a Casio Exilim digital camera, EXIF data that show the photos were taken with a Casio Exilim, and email confirmations and discussions about the planned trip all work together to show that the user of that account on that PC likely took a trip to Europe and took the photos. Not that there is anything wrong with taking pictures of trains, but if the subject of the investigation is a suspected terrorist and he has ties with a group that was discovered to be planning an attack on a train, this evidence would be very valuable.

It is the sum of the parts that matters the most. A single image of a train found in the user's TIF would be virtually meaningless. Multiple pictures of trains in his TIF could also be meaningless; maybe he likes trains or maybe someone sent him a link that he clicked to take him to a website about trains. *It is likely he will not even remember having visited the site.* It is the forensic examiner's first priority to ensure that all user artifacts are considered when making a determination about any behavior.

Recovering Lost and Deleted Files

Unless some sort of drastic "wiping action" has taken place, as in the use of a third-party utility to delete data or if the disk is part of a RAIDed set, I have almost always found that deleted data are *immediately* available in EnCase (forensic software I use) within 20—25 min after a hard disk image is mounted. This is especially true when the drive has not been used at all since the time the data were deleted.

Software Installation

Nearly every software installation will offer to drop one on your desktop, in your Start menu, and on your quick launch tool bar at the time of program installation. Whenever a user double-clicks on a file, a link file is created in the Recent folder located at the root of Documents and Settings. This is a hidden file.

Recent Files

In Windows XP (and similar locations exist in other versions), link files are stored in the Recent folder under Documents and Settings. Whenever a user double-clicks on a file, a link file is created. Clicking the Start button in Windows and navigating to the My Recent Documents link will show a list of the last 15 documents on which a user has clicked. What most users do not realize is that the C:\Documents and Settings\$user name$\Recent folder will

potentially reveal *hundreds* of documents that have been viewed by the user. This list is indisputably a list of documents that the user has viewed. Interestingly, in Windows 2000, if the Preserve History feature of the Windows Media Player is turned off, no link files will be created. The only way to make any legitimate determination about the use of a file is to view the Last Accessed time, which has been shown in several cases to be inconsistent and unreliable in certain circumstances. Be careful when using this time stamp as part of your defense or prosecution. It is a loaded weapon, ready to go off.

Start Menu

The Start menu is built on shortcuts. Every item in the Start file has a corresponding .LNK file. Examining Last Accessed or Date Created time stamps may shed light on when software was installed and last used.

Email

Extracting email is an invaluable tool for researching and finding out thoughts and motives of a suspect in any investigation. Email can be extracted from traditional client-based applications such as Outlook Express, Lotus Notes, Outlook, Eudora, and Netscape Mail, as well as from common Web mail apps such as Gmail, Hotmail, Yahoo Mail, and Excite. For example, reviewing log files from server-based applications such as Outlook Web mail can show a user accessing and using his Web mail after employment termination. It is important for companies to realize that they should terminate access to such accounts the day a user's employment is terminated.

Internet History

Forensic analysis of a user's Internet history can reveal much useful information. It can also show the exact code that may have downloaded on a client machine and resulted in an infection of the system with a virus. Forensic examiners should actively familiarize themselves with the most recent, known exploits.

Typed URLs is a registry key. It will store the last 10 addresses that a user has typed into a Web browser address field. I once had a federal agent try to say that everything that appeared in the drop-down window was a "typed" URL. This is not the case. The only definitive source of showing the actual typed URLs is the registry key. One look at the screen shown in Fig. 33.4 should clearly demonstrate that the user never would have "typed" all of those entries. Yet that is exactly what a Department of Homeland Security agent who sat on the witness stand swore under oath to be true. In Fig. 40.4, simply typing in **fil** spawns a list of URLs that were never typed but rather are the result of either the user having opened a file or a program having opened one.

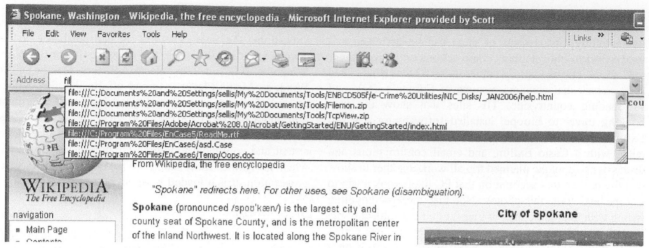

FIGURE 40.4 Spawning a list of URLs that were never typed (the Google one is deleted).

The highlighted file entered the history shown as a result of installing the software, not as a result of the user "typing" the filename. Many items in the history wind their way into it through regular software use, with files being accessed as an indirect result of user activity.

8. NETWORK ANALYSIS

Many investigations require a hands-off approach in which the only forensics that can be collected is network traffic. Every machine is assigned an IP address and a media access control (MAC) address. It is like an IP address on layer 3, but the MAC address sits on layer 2. It is like a phone number in that it is unique. Software that is used to examine network traffic is categorized as a *sniffer*. Tools such as Wireshark and Colasoft are two examples of sniffers. They can be used to view, analyze, and capture all of the IP traffic that comes across a port.

Switches are not promiscuous, however. To view the traffic coming across a switch, you can put a hub in line with the traffic (between the target and the switch) and plug the sniffer into the hub with it, or ports can be spanned. Spanning, or mirroring, allows one port on a switch to copy and distribute network traffic in a way such that the sniffer can see everything. The argument could be made in court that the wrong port was accidentally spanned, but this argument quickly falls apart because all network packets contain both the machine and the IP address of a machine. Address Resolution Protocol poisoning is the practice of spoofing another user's IP address, however. This would be the smartest defense, but if a hub is used on a switched port, with the hub wired directly to the port, a greater degree of forensic certainty can be achieved. The only two computers that should be connected to the hub are the examiner and target machines.

Protocols

In the world of IP, the various languages of network traffic that are used to perform various tasks and operations are called *protocols*. Each protocol has its own special way of organizing and forming its packets. Unauthorized protocols viewed on a port are a good example of a type of action that might be expected from a rogue machine or employee. Depending on the sniffer used, network sniffing for email (SMTP and Post Office Protocol) traffic and capturing it can allow the examiner to view live email traffic coming off the target machine. Viewing the Web (HTTP) protocol allows the examiner to capture images and text from websites that the target is navigating in real time.

Analysis

Once the capture of traffic has been completed, analysis must take place. Colasoft offers a packet analyzer that can carve out and filter out the various types of traffic. A good deal of traffic can be eliminated as just "noise" on the line. Filters can be created that will capture the specific protocols, such as Voice Over IP (VoIP). Examination of the protocols for protocol obfuscation can (if it is not found) eliminate the possibility that a user has a malware infection, and it can identify a user who is using open ports on the firewall to transmit illicit traffic. They sneak legitimate traffic over open ports, masking nefarious activities over legitimate ports, knowing that the ports are open. This can be done with whitespace inside an existing protocol, with HTTP, VoIP, and many others. The thing to look for, which will usually be clearly shown, is something like:

VOIP > SMTP

This basically means that VOIP is talking to a mail server. This is not normal.[3]

Another thing to look for is protocols coming off a box that is not purposed for that task. It is all context: who should be doing what with whom. Why is the workstation

---

3. M.J. Staggs, FireEye, Network Analysis talk at CEIC 2008.

suddenly popping a Domain Name System server? A real-world example is when a vehicle comes screaming into your neighborhood. Two guys jump out and break down the door of your house and grab your wife and kids and drag them out of the house. Then they come and get you. Seems a little fishy, right? But it is a perfectly normal thing to have happen if the two guys are firefighters, the vehicle is a fire truck, and your house is on fire.

9. CYBER FORENSICS APPLIED

This section details the various ways in which cyber forensics is applied professionally. By no means does this cover the extent to which cyber forensics is becoming one of the hottest computer careers. It focuses on the consulting side of things, with less attention to corporate or law enforcement applications. Generally speaking, the average forensic consultant handles a broader variety of cases than do corporate or law enforcement disciplines, with broader applicability.

10. TRACKING, INVENTORY, LOCATION OF FILES, PAPERWORK, BACKUPS, AND SO ON

These items are all useful areas of knowledge in providing consultative advisement to corporate, legal, and law enforcement clients. During the process of discovery and warrant creation, knowledge of how users store and access data at a deep level is critical to success.

Testimonial

Even if the work does not involve the court system directly (for example, a technician who provides forensic backups of computers and is certified), someday you may be called to provide discovery in a litigation matter. Subsequently, you may be required to testify.

Experience Needed

In cyber forensics, the key to a successful technologist is experience. Nothing can substitute for experience, but a good system of learned knowledge that represents at least the past 10 years is welcome.

Job Description, Technologist

Practitioners must possess extreme abilities in adapting to new situations. The environment is always changing.
 Job description:
 Senior Forensic Examiner and eDiscovery Specialist Prepared by Scott R. Ellis, November 1, 2007.

- Forensics investigative work that includes imaging HDs, extracting data and files for ediscovery production, development of custom scripts as required to extract or locate data. On occasion this includes performing detailed analyses of user activity, images, and language that may be of an undesirable, distasteful, and potentially criminal format. For this reason, a manager must be notified immediately upon the discovery of any such materials
- Creation of detailed reports that lay out findings in a meaningful and understandable format. All reports will be reviewed and okayed by manager before delivery to clients
- Use of software tools such as FTK, EnCase, VMware, Recovery for Exchange, IDEA, LAW, and Relativity
- Processing ediscovery and some paper discovery
- Be responsive to opportunities for publication such as papers, articles, blog, or book chapter requests. All publications should be reviewed by manager and marketing before being submitted to requestor
- Use technology such as servers, email, time reporting, and scheduling systems to perform job duties and archive work in client folders
- Managing lab assets (installation of software, Windows updates, antivirus, maintaining backup strategy, hardware installation, tracking hardware and software inventory)
- Some marketing work
- Work week will be 40 h/week, with occasional weekends as needed to meet customer deadlines
- Deposition or testimony as needed
- Occasional evenings and out of town to accommodate client schedules for forensic investigative work
- Occasional evenings and out of town to attend seminars, continuing and professional education or technology classes as suggested by self or by manager, and marketing events
- Other technology-related duties as may be assigned by manager in the support of the company mission as it relates to technology or forensic technology matters

Job Description Management

A manager in cyber forensics is usually a working manager. He is responsible for guiding and developing staff as well as communicating requirements to the executive level. His work duties will typically encompass everything mentioned in the previous description.

Commercial Uses

Archival, ghosting images, data duplicator command, recover lost partitions, etc., are all applications of cyber forensics at a commercial level. Data recovery embraces a great many practices typically attributed to cyber forensics. Archival and retrieval of information for any number of purposes, not just litigation, are required, as is a forensic level of system knowledge.

Solid Background

To become a professional practitioner of cyber forensics, there are three requirements for a successful career. Certainly there are people, such as many who attain certification through law-enforcement agencies, who have skipped or completely bypassed the professional experience or scientific training necessary to be a true cyber forensic scientist. That is not to degrade the law enforcement forensic examiner. His mission is traditionally different from that of a civilian, and these professionals are frighteningly adept and proficient at accomplishing their objective, which is to locate evidence of criminal conduct and prosecute in court. Their lack of education in the traditional sense should never lead one to a desultory conclusion. No amount of parchment will ever broaden a mind; the forensic examiner must have a broad mind that eschews constraints and boxed-in thinking.

The background needed for a successful career in cyber forensics is much like that of any other except that, as a testifying expert, publication will give greater credence to a testimony than even the most advanced pedigree. The exception would be the cyber forensic scientist who holds a doctorate and happened to write her doctoral thesis on just the thing that is being called into question on the case. Interestingly, at this time, this author has yet to meet anyone with a doctorate (or any university degree, for that matter), in cyber forensics. We can then narrow the requirements to these three items. Coincidentally, these are also the items required to qualify as an expert witness in most courts:

- education
- programming and experience
- publications

The weight of each of these items can vary. To what degree depends on who is asking, but suffice it to say that a deficiency in any area may be overcome by strengths in the other two. The following sections provide a more in-depth view of each requirement.

Education/Certification

A strong foundation at the university level in mathematics and science provides the best mental training that can be obtained in cyber forensics. Of course, anyone with an extremely strong understanding of computers can surpass and exceed any expectations in this area. Of special

consideration are the following topics. The best forensic examiner has a strong foundation in these areas and can qualify not just as a forensic expert with limited ability to testify as to the functions and specific mechanical abilities of software, but as a cyber expert who can testify to the many aspects of both hardware and software.

Understand how database technologies, including MS SQL, Oracle, Access, My SQL, and others, interact with applications and how thin and fat clients interact and transfer data. Where do they store temporary files? What happens during a maintenance procedure? How are indexes built, and is the database software disk aware?

Programming and Experience

Background in cyber programming is an essential piece. The following software languages must be understood by any well-rounded forensic examiner:

- Java
- JavaScript
- ASP/.NET
- HTML
- XML
- Visual Basic
- SQL

Develop a familiarity with the purpose and operation of technologies that have not become mainstream but have a devoted cult following. At one time such things as virtualization, Linux, and even Windows lived on the bleeding edge, but from being very much on the "fringe," they have steadily become more mainstream.

- If it runs on a computer and has an installed base of greater than 10,000 users, it is worth reviewing.
- Internet technologies should be well understood. JavaScript, Java, HTML, ASP, ASPRX, cold fusion, databases, etc., are all Internet technologies that may end up at the heart of a forensic examiner's investigation.
- Experience: Critical to either establishing oneself in a career as a corporate cyber forensic examiner or as a consultant, experience working in the field provides the confidence and knowledge base needed to complete a forensic examination successfully. From cradle to grave, from initial interviews with the client to forensic collection, examination, reporting, and testifying, experience will guide every step. No suitable substitute exists. Most forensic examiners come into the career later in life after serving as a network or software consultant. Some arrive in this field after years in law enforcement in which almost anyone who can turn on a computer winds up taking some cyber forensic training.

Communications

- Cyber forensics is entirely about the ability to look at a cyber system and subsequently explain, in plain English, the analysis. A typical report may consist of the following sections:
- summary
- methodology
- narrative
- health care information data on system
- user access to credit card numbers
- date range of possible breach and order handlers
- distinct list of operators
- Russell and Crist Handlers
- all other users logged in during Crist/Russel logins
- Login failures activity coinciding with account activity
- all users:
- user access levels: possible ingress/egress
- audit trail
- login failures
- conclusion
- contacts/examiners

Each section represents actual tables, images, and calculated findings, or it represents judgments, impressions, and interpretations of those findings. Finally, the report should contain references to contacts involved in the investigation. A good report conveys the big picture and translates findings into substantial knowledge without leaving trailing questions asked and unanswered. Sometimes findings are arrived at through a complex procedure such as a series of SQL queries. Conclusions that depend on such findings should be as detailed as necessary so that opposing experts can reconstruct the findings without difficulty.

Almost any large company requires some measure of forensic certified staff. Furthermore, the forensic collection and ediscovery field continues to grow. Virtually every branch of law enforcement (the Federal Bureau of Investigation, the Central Intelligence Agency, the Department of Homeland Security, and state and local agencies) all use cyber forensics to some degree. Accounting firms and law firms of almost any size greater than 20 need certified forensic and ediscovery specialists that can support their forensic practice areas as well as grow business.

Publications

Publishing articles in well-known trade journals goes a long way toward establishing credibility. The following things are nearly always true:

- A long list of publications not only creates in a jury the perception that the expert possesses special knowledge that warrants publication; it also shows the expert's ability to communicate. Articles published on the Internet typically do not count unless they are from well-known publications that have a printed publication as well as an online magazine.
- Publishing in and of itself creates a certain amount of risk. Anything that an expert writes, says, or posts online may come back to haunt him in court. Be sure to remember to check, double-check, and triple-check anything that could be of questionable interpretation.
- When you write, you get smarter. Writing forces an author to conduct research and refreshes the memory on long unused skills.

Getting published in the first place is perhaps the most difficult task. Make contact with publishers and editors at trade shows. Ask around, and seek to make contact and establish relationships with published authors and bloggers. Most important, always seek to gain knowledge and deeper understanding of the work.

11. TESTIFYING AS AN EXPERT

Testifying in court is difficult work. As with any type of performance, the expert testifying must know her material inside and out. She must be calm and collected and have confidence in her assertions. Often, degrees of uncertainty may exist within a testimony. It is the expert's duty to convey those "gray" areas with clarity and alacrity. She must be able to speak of things confidently in terms of degrees of certainty and clear probabilities, using language that is accessible and readily understood by the jury.

In terms of degrees of certainty, often we find ourselves discussing the "degree of difficulty" of performing an operation. This is usually when judges ask whether an operation has occurred through direct user interaction or through an automated, programmatic, or normal maintenance procedure. For example, it is well within the normal operation of complex database software to reindex or compact its tables and reorganize the way the data are arranged on the surface of the disk. However, it is not within the normal operation of the database program to obliterate itself and all its program, help, and system files completely 13 times over a period of 3 weeks, all in the time leading up to requests for discovery from the opposition. Such information, when forensically available, will then be followed by the question of "Can we know *who* did it?" And that question, if the files exist on a server where security is relaxed, can be nearly impossible to answer.

Degrees of Certainty

Most cyber forensic practitioners ply their trade in civil court. A typical case may involve monetary damages or loss. From a cyber forensics point of view, evidence that you have extracted from a computer may be used by the attorneys to establish liability, that the plaintiff was damaged by the actions of the defendant. Your work may be the lynchpin of the entire case. You cannot be wrong. The burden to prove the amount of damages is less stringent once you have established that damage was inflicted, and because a single email may be the foundation for that proof, its provenance should prevail under even the most expert scrutiny. Whether the damage was inflicted may become a point of contention that the defense uses to pry and crack open your testimony.

The following sections may prove useful in your answers. The burden of proof will fall on the defense to show that the alleged damages are not accurate. Three general categories of "truth" can be used to clarify for a judge, jury, or attorney the weight of evidence. See the section on "Rules of Evidence" for more on things such as relevance and materiality.

Generally True

Generally speaking, something is generally true if under normal and general use the same thing always occurs. For example, if a user deletes a file, generally speaking it will go into the recycle bin. This is not true if:

- the user holds down a Shift key when deleting;
- the recycle bin option "Do not move files to the recycle bin. Remove files immediately when deleted" is selected;
- An item is deleted from a server share or from another computer that is accessing a local user share.

Reasonable Degree of Certainty

If it smells like a fish and looks like a fish, generally speaking, it is a fish. However, without dissection and DNA analysis, there is the possibility that it is a fake, especially if someone is jumping up and down and screaming that it is a fake. Short of expensive testing, one may consider other factors. Where was the fish found? Who was in possession of the fish when it was found? We begin to rely on more than just looking at the fish to see whether it is a fish.

Cyber forensic evidence is much the same (see checklist: "An Agenda for Action for Retrieval and Identification of Evidence"). For example, in an employment dispute, an employee may be accused of sending sensitive and proprietary documents to her personal Web mail account. The employer introduces forensic evidence that the files were

---

An Agenda for Action for Retrieval and Identification of Evidence

The computer forensics specialist should ensure that the following provisional list of actions for retrieval and identification of evidence is adhered to (check all tasks completed):

____1. Protect the subject computer system during the forensic examination from any possible alteration, damage, data corruption, or virus introduction.

____2. Discover all files on the subject system. This includes existing normal files, deleted yet remaining files, hidden files, password-protected files, and encrypted files.

____3. Recover all (or as much as possible) discovered deleted files.

____4. Reveal (to the greatest extent possible) the contents of hidden files as well as temporary or swap files used by both the application programs and the OS.

____5. Access (if possible and legally appropriate) the contents of protected or encrypted files.

____6. Analyze all possibly relevant data found in special (and typically inaccessible) areas of a disk. This includes but is not limited to what is called unallocated space on a disk (currently unused, but possibly the repository of previous data that are relevant evidence), as well as slack space in a file (the remnant area at the end of a file in the last assigned disk cluster that is unused by current file data, but once again may be a possible site for previously created and relevant evidence).

____7. Print out an overall analysis of the subject computer system, as well as a list of all possibly relevant files and discovered file data.

____8. Provide an opinion of the system layout; the file structures discovered; any discovered data and authorship information; any attempts to hide, delete, protect, and encrypt information; and anything else that has been discovered and appears to be relevant to the overall computer system examination.

____9. Provide expert consultation and/or testimony, as required.

---

sent from her work email account during her period of employment on days when she was in the office.

Pretty straightforward, right? Not really. Let us go back in time to 2 months before the employee was fired. Let us go back to the day after she got a bad performance review and left for the day because she was so upset. Everyone knew what was going on, and they knew that her time was limited. Two weeks later she filed an Equal Employment Opportunity Commission complaint. The IT manager in this organization, a seemingly mild-mannered, helpful savant, was getting ready to start his own company as a silent partner in competition with his employer. He wanted information. His partners wanted information in exchange for a 20% stake. As an IT manager, he had administrative rights and could access the troubled employee's email account and began to send files to her Web mail account. As an IT administrator, he had system and network access that would easily allow him to crack her Web mail account and determine the password. All he had to do was spoof her login page and store it on a site where he could pick it up from somewhere else. If he was particularly interested in keeping his own home and work systems free of the files, he could wardrive her house, hack her home wireless (lucky for him, it was unsecured), and then use terminal services to access her home cyber, log into her Web mail account (while she was home), and view the files to ensure that they appeared as "read." This scenario may seem farfetched but it is not; this is not hard to do.

For anyone with the IT manager's level of knowledge, lack of ethics, and opportunity, this was likely the *only* way that he would go about stealing information. There is no other way that would leave him so completely out of the possible running of suspects.

There is no magic wand in cyber forensics. The data are either there or they are not, despite what Hollywood says about the subject. If an IT director makes the brash decision to reinstall the OS on a system that has been compromised and later realizes he might want to use a forensic investigator to find out what files were viewed, stolen, or modified, he cannot just dial up his local forensics technician and have him pop in over tea, wave his magic wand, and recover all the data that were overwritten. Here is the raw, unadulterated truth: If you have 30 GB of unallocated clusters and you copy the DVD *Finding Nemo* onto the drive until the disk is full, nobody (and I really mean this), *nobody* will be able to extract a complete file from the unallocated clusters. Sure, they might find a couple of keyword hits in file slack and maybe, just maybe, if the stars align and Jupiter is in retrograde and Venus is rising, maybe they can pull a tiny little complete file out of the slack or out of the MFT. Small files, less than 128 bytes, are stored directly in the MFT and will not ever make it out to allocated space. This can be observed by viewing the $MFT file.

When making the determination "reasonable degree of forensic certainty," *all* things must be considered. Every possible scenario that could occur must flash before the forensic practitioner's eyes until only the most reasonable answer exists, an answer that is supported by all of the evidence, not just part of it. This is called *interpretation*, and it is a weighing of whether a preponderance of

evidence actually exists. The forensic expert's job is not to decide whether a preponderance of evidence exists. His job is to present the facts and his interpretation of the individual facts, fairly and truthfully. Questions an attorney might ask a cyber forensics practitioner on the stand are:

- Did the user delete the file?
- Could someone else have done it?
- Could an outside process have downloaded the file to the computer?
- Do you know for certain how this happened?
- Did you see Mr. Smith delete the files?
- How do you know he did?
- Is it not true, Mr. Expert, that you are being paid to be here today?

These are not "yes or no" questions. Here might be the answers:

- I am reasonably certain he did.
- Owing to the security of this machine, it is very unlikely that someone else did it.
- There is evidence to strongly indicate that the photos were loaded to the computer from a digital camera, not the Internet.
- I am certain, without doubt, that the camera in Exhibit 7a is the same camera that was used to take these photos and that these photos were loaded to the computer while username CSMITH was logged in.
- I have viewed forensic evidence that strongly suggests that someone with Mr. Smith's level of access and permissions to this system did, in fact, delete these files on December 12, 2009.
- I am not sure I did not just answer that.
- I am an employee of The Company. I am receiving my regular compensation and today is a normal workday for me.

Be careful, though. Reticence to answer in a yes or no fashion may be interpreted by the jury as uncertainty. If certainty exists, say so. However, it is always better to be honest and admit uncertainty than to attempt to inflate one's own ego by expressing certainty when none exists. Never worry about the outcome of the case. You cannot care about the outcome of the trial. Guilt or innocence cannot be a factor in your opinion. You must focus on simply answering the questions in front of you that demand to be answered.

Certainty Without Doubt

Some things on a computer can happen only in one fashion. For example, if a deleted item is found in the recycle bin, there are steps that must be taken to ensure that "it is what it is":

- Was the user logged in at the time of deletion?
- Are there link files that support the use or viewing of the file?

- Was the user with access to the user account at work that day?
- What are the permissions on the folder?
- Is the deleted file in question a system file or a user-created file located in the user folders?
- Is the systems administrator beyond reproach or outside the family of suspects?

If all of these conditions have been met, you may have arrived at certainty without doubt. Short of reliable witnesses paired with physical evidence, it is possible that there will always be other explanations, and that uncertainty can exist to some degree. It is the burden of the defense and the plaintiff to understand and resolve these issues and determine whether, for example, hacker activity is a plausible defense. I have added the stipulation of reliable witnesses because, in the hands of a morally corrupt forensic expert with access to the drive and a hex editor, a computer can be undetectably altered. Files can be copied onto an HD in a sterile manner that, to most trained forensic examiners, could appear to be original. Even advanced users are capable of framing the evidence in such a way as to render the appearance of best evidence, but a forensic examination may lift the veil of uncertainty and show that data have been altered, or that something *is not quite right*. For example, there are certain conditions that can be examined that can show with certainty that the time stamps on a file have been somehow manipulated or are simply incorrect, and it is likely that the average person seeking to plant evidence will not know these tricks (Table 40.4). The dates on files that were overwritten may show that "old" files overwrote newer files. This is impossible.

As shown here, the file kitty.jpg overwrites files that appear to have been created on the system after it. Such an event may occur when items are copied from a CD-ROM or unzipped from a zip file.

TABLE 40.4 Example of Forensic View of Files Showing Some Alteration or Masking of Dates

Filename	Date Created	File Properties	Original Path
Kitty.jpg	5/12/2007	File, Archive	
summaryReport.doc	7/12/2007	File, Deleted, Overwritten	Kitty.jpg
Marketing_flyer.pdf	2/12/2008	File, Deleted, Overwritten	Kitty.jpg

12. BEGINNING TO END IN COURT

In most courts in the world, the accuser goes first and then the defense presents its case. This is for the logical reason that if the defense goes first, nobody would know what they are talking about. The Boulder Bar has a Bar manual located at www.boulder-bar.org [4] that provides a more in-depth review of the trial process than can be presented here. Most states and federal rules are similar, but nothing here should be taken as legal advice; review the rules for yourself for the courts where you will be testifying. The knowledge is not necessary, but the less you seem to be a fish out of water, the better. This section *does not* replace true legal advice; it is strictly intended for the purpose of education. The manual located at the Boulder Bar website was created for a similar reason that is clearly explained on the site. The manual was specifically developed without "legalese," which makes it easy to understand.

Defendants, Plaintiffs, and Prosecutors

When someone, an individual or an organization, decides it has a claim of money or damages against another individual or entity, a claim is filed in court. The group filing the claim is the plaintiff; the other parties are the defendants. Experts may find themselves working for strictly defendants, strictly plaintiffs, or a little bit of both. In criminal court, charges are "brought" by an indictment, complaint, information, or a summons and complaint.

Pretrial Motions

Before the actual trial, there may be very many pretrial motions and hearings. When a motion is filed, such as when the defense in a criminal case is trying to prevent certain evidence from being seen or heard by the jury, a hearing is called and the judge decides whether the motion has merit. In civil court, it may be a hearing to decide whether the defense has been deleting, withholding, or committing other acts of discovery abuse. Cyber forensic practitioners will find that they may be called to testify at any number of hearings before the trial, and then they may not be needed at the trial, or the defense and plaintiff may reach a settlement and there will be no trial at all.

Trial: Direct and Cross-examination

Assuming that there is no settlement or plea agreement, a case will go to trial. The judge will first ask the prosecutor or plaintiff whether they want to make an opening statement. Then the defense will be asked. Witnesses will be called, and if it is the first time appearing in the particular trial as an expert,

4. Boulder Bar, www.boulder-bar.org/bar_media/index.html.

the witness will be qualified, as discussed in a moment. The party putting on the witness will conduct a direct examination and the other side will likely cross-examine the witness afterward. Frequently the two sides will have reviewed the expert report and will ask many questions relating directly to it. "Tricks" may be pulled by either attorney at this point. Certain prosecutors have styles and techniques that are used in an attempt to either rattle the expert's cage or simply intimidate him into a state of nervousness so that he will appear uncertain and unprepared. These prosecutors are not interested in justice. They are interested in winning because their career rotates around their record of wins/losses.

Rebuttal

After a witness has testified and undergone direct examination and cross-examination, the other side may decide to bring in an expert to discuss or refute. The defendant may then respond to the prosecution's witness in *rebuttal*. In criminal court, when the state or the government (sometimes affectionately referred to by defense attorneys as "The G") brings a case against an individual or organization, the attorneys that prosecute the case are called the state's attorney, district attorney, assistant U.S. attorney, or simply prosecutor.

Surrebuttal

This is the plaintiff (or prosecutor's!) response to rebuttal. Typically the topics of surrebuttal will be limited to those topics that are broached in rebuttal, but the rules for this are probably best left to attorneys to decipher; this author has occasionally been asked questions that should have been deemed outside the bounds of the rebuttal. This could most likely be attributed to a lack of technical knowledge on the part of the attorneys involved in the case.

Testifying: Rule 702: Testimony by Experts

Rule 702 is a federal rule of civil procedure that governs expert testimony. The judge is considered the "gatekeeper," and she alone makes the decision as to whether the following rule is satisfied:

If scientific, technical, or other specialized knowledge will assist the trier of fact to understand the evidence or to determine a fact in issue, a witness qualified as an expert by knowledge, skill, experience, training, or education, may testify thereto in the form of an opinion or otherwise, if (1) the testimony is based upon sufficient facts or data, (2) the testimony is the product of reliable principles and methods, and (3) the witness has applied the principles and methods reliably to the facts of the case (U.S. Courts, Federal Rules of Evidence, Rule 702).

There are certain rules for qualifying as an expert. In court, when an expert is presented, both attorneys may question the expert on matters of background and expertise. This process is referred to as *qualification*, and if an "expert" does not meet the legal definition of expert, he may not be allowed to testify. This is a short list of items that will be asked when qualifying as an expert witness:

- How long have you worked in the field?
- What certifications do you hold in this field?
- Where did you go to college?
- Did you graduate? What degrees do you have?
- What are your publications?

You may also be asked if you have testified in other proceedings. It is important always to be honest when on the stand. Perjury is a serious crime and can result in jail time. All forensics experts should familiarize themselves with Federal Rules 701−706 as well as understand the purpose, intent, and results of a successful *Daubert* challenge, in which an expert's opinion or the expert himself may be challenged, and if certain criteria are met, may have his testimony thrown out. It is accepted and understood that experts may have reasonably different conclusions given the same evidence.

When testifying, stay calm (easier said than done). If you have never done it, approaching the bench and taking the witness stand may seem like a lot of fun. In a case in which a lot is on the line and it all depends on the expert's testimony, nerves will shake and cages will be rattled. The best advice is to stay calm. Drink a lot of water. According to ex−Navy Seal Mike Lukas, drinking copious amounts of water will dilute the affect of adrenalin in the bloodstream.

Testifying in a stately and austere court of law may seem as if it is the domain of professors and other ivory tower enthusiasts. However, it is something that pretty much anyone can do who has a valuable skill to offer, regardless of educational background. Hollywood often paints a picture of the expert witness as a consummate professorial archetype bent on delivering "just the facts." It is true that expert witnesses demand top dollar in the consulting world. Much of this is for the reason that a great deal is at stake once the expert takes the stand. There is also a high inconvenience factor. When on the stand for days at a time, one simply cannot take phone calls, respond to emails, or perform work for other clients. There is a certain amount of business interruption that the fees must make up for somehow.

Testifying is interesting. Distilling weeks of intense, technical investigation into a few statements that can be understood by everyone in the courtroom is no small task. It is a bit nerve wracking, and one can expect to have high blood pressure and overactive adrenalin glands for the day. Drinking lots of water will ease the nerves better than anything (nonpharmaceutical). It can have other side effects, however, but it is better to be calm and ask the judge for a short recess as needed than to have shaky hands and a trembling voice from nerves. Caffeine is a bad idea.

Correcting Mistakes: Putting Your Head in the Sand

The interplay of examiner and expert in the case of cyber forensics can be difficult. Often the forensic examiner can lapse into speech and explanations that are so common-place to her that she does not realize she is speaking fluent geek-speak. The ability to understand how she sounds to someone who does not understand technology must be cultivated. Practice by explaining to a 6-year-old what it is that you do.

Direct Testimony

Under direct questioning, your attorney will ask questions to which you will know the answer. A good expert will, in fact, have prepared a list of questions and reviewed the answers with the attorney and explained the context and justification for each question thoroughly. If it is a defense job, you will likely go first and testify as to what your investigation has revealed. Avoid using big words and make eye contact with the jury if you feel you need to explain something to them; but generally speaking, you should follow the attorney's lead. If she wants you to clarify something for the jury, you should do so, and at that time you should look at the jury. Generally, the rule of thumb is to look at the attorney who asked you the question. If the judge says, "Please explain to the jury…" then by all means, look at the jury.

Cross-examination

The purpose of a cross-examination is to get the testifying expert to make a mistake or to discredit him. Sometimes (rarely) it is actually used to understand and clarify things further that were discussed in a direct. In most cases, the attorney will do this by asking you questions about your experience or about the testimony the expert gave under direct. However, there is another tactic that attorneys use. They ask a question that is completely unrelated to the topic you talked about. They know that the vast majority of time you spend is on the issues in your direct. For example, you may give a testimony about Last Accessed time stamps. Your entire testimony may be about Last Accessed time stamps. It may be the only issue in the case of which you are aware. Then, upon cross-examination, the attorney asks a question about the behavior of the mail icon that appears on each line next to the subject line in an email. "Great," the expert thinks. "They recognize my expertise and are asking questions."

Stop. They are about to ask you an arcane question about a behavior in a piece of software in the hope that you are overconfident and will answer from the hip and get the answer wrong. Because if you get this wrong, then everything else you said must be wrong, too. *Whenever* you are asked a question that does not relate to your previous testimony, pause. Pause for a long time. Give your attorney time to object. He might not know that he should object, but the fact is that you might get the answer wrong and even if there is no doubt in your mind that you know the answer, you should respond that you had not prepared to answer that question and would like to know more details. For example, what is the version of the software? What is the OS? What service pack? If it is Office, what Office service pack? You need to make it clear that you need more information before you answer the question because, frankly, if the opposition goes down this road, they will try to turn *whatever* you say into the wrong answer.

As a forensic examiner, you may find yourself thinking that the reason they are asking these questions in such a friendly manner is because they forgot to ask their own expert and are trying to take advantage of your time, because possibly this came up in a later conversation. This could well be the case. Maybe the counselor is not trying to trip up the expert. Maybe the Brooklyn Bridge *can* be purchased for a dollar, too.

What is the best response to a question like this? If you give it a 10 count and your attorney has not objected, and the asking attorney has not abandoned the question, you may have to answer. There are many schools of thought about this. It is best to understand that a number of responses can facilitate an answer to difficult questions. One such response might be, "That is not really a forensics question" (if it is not), or "I am not sure how that question relates back to the testimony I just gave." Or, if it is a software question, you can say, "Different software behaves differently, and I do not think I can answer that question without more details. I do not typically memorize the behavior of every piece of software, and I am afraid that if I answer from memory I may not be certain." At the end of the day, the expert should speak only to what he knows *with certainty*. There is very little room for error. Attorneys can back pedal a certain amount to "fix" a mistake, but a serious mistake can follow you for a long time and can hamper future testimony. For example, if you make statements about time stamps in one trial, and then in the next trial you make statements that interpret them differently, there is a good chance that the opposition will use this against you.

Fortunately, when cyber forensic experts testify in a defense trial, the testimony can last a number of hours. Great care is usually taken by the judge to ensure that understanding of all of the evidence is achieved. This can create a long transcript that is difficult to read, understand, and recall with accuracy. For this reason, rarely will bits and pieces of testimony be used against a testifying expert in a future trial. This is not, of course, to say that it cannot or will not happen.

It is important, in terms of both setting expectations and understanding legal strategy, for an expert witness to possess passable knowledge of the trial process. Strong familiarity with the trial process can benefit the expert and the attorneys as well as the judge and the court reporter.

13. SUMMARY

Computers have appeared in the course of litigation for quite a few years. In 1977, there were 291 U.S. federal cases and 246 state cases in which the word *computer* appeared and which were sufficiently important to be noted in the Lexis database. In 2012, according to industry analysts, those figures in the United States have risen dramatically, to 3,250,514 U.S. federal cases and 2,750,177 state cases in which the word *cyber* appeared. In the United Kingdom, there were only 20 in 1977, with a rise to 220,372 in 2012. However, as early as 1968, the computer's existence was considered sufficiently important for special provisions to be made in the English Civil Evidence Act.

The following description is designed to summarize the issues rather than attempt to give a complete guide. As far as one can tell, noncontentious cases tend not to be reported, and the arrival of computers in commercial disputes and in criminal cases did not create immediate difficulties. Judges sought to allow cyber-based evidence on the basis that it was no different from forms of evidence with which they were already familiar: documents, business books, weighing machines, calculating machines, films, and audio tapes. This is not to say that such cases were without difficulty; however, no completely new principles were required. Soon, though, it became apparent that many new situations were arising and that analogies with more traditional evidential material were beginning to break down. Some of these were tackled in legislation, as with the English 1968 Act and the U.S. Federal Rules of Evidence in 1976. However, many were addressed in a series of court cases. Not all of the key cases deal directly with computers. Nonetheless, they have a bearing on them because they relate to matters that are characteristic of cyber-originated evidence. For example, cyber-originated evidence or information that is not immediately readable by a human being is usually gathered by a mechanical counting or weighing instrument. The calculation could also be performed by a mechanical or electronic device.

The focus of most of this legislation and judicial activity was determining the admissibility of the evidence. The common law and legislative rules are those that have arisen as a result of judicial decisions and specific law. They extend beyond mere guidance. They are rules that a court must follow; the thought behind these rules may have been to impose standards and uniformity in helping a court test authenticity, reliability, and completeness. Nevertheless, they have acquired a status of their own and in some cases prevent a court from making ad hoc common sense decisions about the quality of evidence. The usual effect is

that once a judge has declared evidence inadmissible (that is, failing to conform to the rules), it is never put to a jury; for a variety of reasons that will become apparent shortly. It is not wholly possible for someone interested in the practical aspects of computer forensics (that is, the issues of demonstrating authenticity, reliability, completeness, or the lack thereof) to separate out the legal tests.

Finally, let us move on to the real interactive part of this chapter: review questions/exercises, hands-on projects, case projects, and the optional team case project. The answers and/or solutions by chapter can be found in the Online Instructor's Solutions Manual.

CHAPTER REVIEW QUESTIONS/ EXERCISES

True/False

1. True or False? Cyber forensics is the acquisition, preservation, and analysis of electronically stored information (ESI) in such a way that ensures its admissibility for use as evidence, exhibits, or demonstratives in a court of law.
2. True or False? EnCase is a commonly used forensic software program that does not allow a cyber forensic technologist to conduct an investigation of a forensic hard disk copy.
3. True or False? On a server purposed with storing surveillance video, there are three physical hard drives.
4. True or False? Cyber forensics is one of the many cyber-related fields in which the practitioner will be found in the courtroom on a given number of days of the year.
5. True or False? A temporary restraining order (TRO) will often be issued in intellectual property or employment contract disputes.

Multiple Choice

1. Typically the forensic work done in a _____ will involve collecting information about one of the parties to be used to show that trust has been violated.
   A. Security incident
   B. Security breach
   C. Computer virus
   D. Divorce case
   E. Security policy
2. When one company begins selling a part that is _____ by another company, a lawsuit will likely be filed in federal court.
   A. Assigned
   B. Breached
   C. Detected
   D. Patented
   E. Measured

3. When a forensics practitioner needs to capture the data on a hard disk, he or she does so in a way that is:
   A. Forensically acquired
   B. Forensically mirrored
   C. Forensically sound
   D. Forensically imaged
   E. Forensically booted

4. Before conducting any sort of a capture, all steps should be documented and reviewed with a _____ before proceeding
   A. Observer
   B. Investigator
   C. Counsel
   D. Forensic expert
   E. Judge

5. Are FAT12, FAT16, FAT32 and FAT64 file systems types; or, is FAT64 the only file system type?
   A. FAT12
   B. FAT16
   C. FAT32
   D. FAT64
   E. All of the above

EXERCISE

Problem

Does cyber forensics ensure that computer evidence is properly handled; as well as, the preservation and authentication of cyber data.

Hands-on Projects

Project

How long does data recovery take?

Case Projects

Problem

Are there instances in which data cannot be recovered?

Optional Team Case Project

Problem

What can an organization do to protect its data and minimize the chances of losing data?

Chapter 41

Cyber Forensics and Incidence Response

Cem Gurkok
Terremark Worldwide, Inc., Miami, FL, United States

1. INTRODUCTION TO CYBER FORENSICS

Cyber forensics and incident response go hand in hand. Cyber forensics reduces the occurrence of security incidents by analyzing the incident to understand, mitigate, and provide feedback to the actors involved. To perform incident response and related activities, organizations should establish an incident plan, a computer security incident response team (CSIRT) or a computer emergency response team (CERT) to execute the plan and associated protocols.

Responding to Incidents

In an organization there is a daily occurrence of events within the IT infrastructure, but not all of these events qualify as incidents. It is important for the incident response team to be able to distinguish the difference between events and incidents. Generally, incidents are events that violate an organization's security policies, end user agreements, or terms of use. SANS (sans.org) defines an incident as an adverse event in an information system or network, or the threat of an occurrence of such an event. Denial-of-service (DoS) attacks, unauthorized probing, unauthorized entry, destruction or theft of data, and changes to firmware or operating systems (OSs) can be considered incidents.

Generally, incident response handling is composed of incident reporting, incident analysis, and incident response. Incident reporting takes place when a report or indications of an event is sent to the incident response team. The team then performs an incident analysis by examining the report, available information, evidence, or artifacts related to the event to qualify the event as an incident, correlate the data, and assess the extent of damage, source, and plan potential solutions. Once the analysis is over, the team responds to mitigate the incident by containing and eradicating the incident. This is followed by the creation of a detailed report about the incident.

Applying Forensic Analysis Skills

Forensic analysis is usually applied to determine who, what, when, where, how, and why an incident took place. The analysis may include investigating crimes and inappropriate behavior, reconstructing computer security incidents, troubleshooting operational problems, supporting due diligence for audit record maintenance, and recovering from accidental system damage. The incident response team should be trained and prepared to be able to collect and analyze the related evidence to answer these questions. Data collection is a very important aspect of incident response since evidence needs to be collected in a forensically sound manner to protect its integrity and confidentiality. The incident responder needs to have the necessary skills and experience to be able to meet the collection requirements.

Forensic analysis is the process where the collected data is reviewed and scrutinized for the lowest level of evidence (deleted data in slack space) it can offer. The analysis may involve extracting email attachments, building timelines based on file times, review of browser history, in-memory artifact review, decryption of encrypted data, and malware reverse engineering. Once the analysis is complete, the incident responder will produce a report describing all the steps taken starting from the initial incident report until the end of the analysis. One of the most important skills a forensic analyst can have is note-taking and logging, which becomes very important during the reporting phase and, if it ever comes to it, in court. These considerations related to forensics should be addressed in organizational policies. The forensic policy should clearly define the responsibilities and roles of the actors involved. The policies should also address the types of activities that should be undertaking under certain circumstances and the handling of sensitive information.

Distinguishing Between Unpermitted Corporate and Criminal Activity

We previously defined incidents as events that are not permitted by a certain organization's policies. The incident response team should also be aware of several federal laws that can help them to identify criminal activity to ensure that the team does not commit a crime while responding to the incident. Some of these federal laws include:

- The Foreign Intelligence Surveillance Act of 1978
- The Privacy Protection Act of 1980
- The Computer Fraud and Abuse Act of 1984
- The Electronic Communications Privacy Act of 1986
- Health Insurance Portability and Accountability Act of 1996 (HIPAA)
- Identity Theft and Assumption Deterrence Act of 1998
- The USA PATRIOT Act of 2001

When an incident response team comes across incidents relevant to these laws, they should consult with their legal team. They should also contact appropriate law enforcement agencies.

2. HANDLING PRELIMINARY INVESTIGATIONS

An organization should be prepared beforehand to properly respond to incidents and mitigate them in the shortest time possible. An incident response plan should be developed by the organization and tested on a regular basis. The plan should be written in an easily understood and implemented fashion. The incident response team and related staff should also be trained on an ongoing basis to keep them up to date with the incident response plan, latest threats, and defense techniques.

Planning for Incident Response

Organizations should be prepared for incidents by identifying corporate risks, preparing hosts and the network for containment and eradication of threats, establishing policies and procedures that facilitate the accomplishment of incident response goals, and creating an incident response team and an incident response toolkit to be used by the incident response team.

Communicating with Site Personnel

All departments and staff that have a part in an incident response should be aware of the incident response plan and should be regularly trained on its content and implementation. The plan should include the mode of communication with the site personnel. The site personnel should clearly log all activity and communication, including the date and time in a central repository that is backed up regularly. This information should be reviewed by all of the incident response team members to assure all players are on the same page. Continuity and the distribution of information within the team is critical in the swift mitigation of an incident. An incident response team leader should be assigned to an incident and should make sure all team members are well informed and acting in a coordinated fashion.

Knowing Your Organization's Policies

An organization's policies will have an impact on how incidents are handled. These policies are usually very comprehensive and effective computer forensics policies that include considerations, such as contacting law enforcement, performing monitoring, and conducting regular reviews of forensic policies, guidelines, and procedures. Banks, insurance companies, law firms, governments, and health care institutions have such policies. Generally policies should allow the incident response team to monitor systems and networks and perform investigations for reasons described in the policies. Policies may be updated frequently to keep up with the changes to laws and regulations, court rulings, and jurisdictions.

Forensics policies define the roles and responsibilities of the staff involved including users, incident handlers, and IT staff. The policy indicates when to contact internal teams or reach out to external organizations. It should also discuss how to handle issues arising from jurisdictional conflicts. Policies also discuss the valid use of antiforensics tools and techniques (sanitation and privacy versus malicious use, such as hiding evidence). How to maintain the confidentiality of data and the retention time of the data is also governed by organizational policies.

Minimizing Impact on Your Organization

The goals of incident response include minimizing disruption to the computer and network operations, and minimizing the exposure and compromise of sensitive data. To be able to meet these goals, incident response preparedness, planning, and proper execution following related policies is crucial. Incident response teams should minimize the down times of business critical systems once the evidence has been gathered and the systems have been cleared of the effects of the incident. Incident response teams should also identify an organization's risks and work with appropriate teams to continuously test and eliminate any vulnerability. Red team—blue team exercises, where a team plays the role of malicious people and the other team as incident responders, can provide good training for the staff and expose previously unknown risks and vulnerabilities. To minimize the impact of incidents, organizations should also establish and enforce security policies and procedures, gain management support for security policies and incident response, keep systems updated and patched, train IT staff and end users, implement a strong credential policy, monitor network traffic and system logs, implement and routinely test a backup policy.

Identifying the Incident Life Cycle

SANS (sans.org) defines the phases of the incident life cycle in Fig. 41.1.

Preparation

It's a matter of when, rather than if, an incident will happen. Therefore, it has become a top priority for an organization to be prepared for an incident. To be prepared, an organization must establish security plans and controls, make sure these plans and controls are continuously reviewed and updated to keep up with the evolving threats, and make sure they are enforced in case of an incident. Organizations should be prepared to act swiftly to minimize the impact of any incident to maintain business continuity. Incident response teams should continuously train, test, and update the incident response plan to keep their skills honed.

Detection, Collection, and Analysis

The detection of an incident involves the observance and reporting of security or IT department staff members, customers of irregularities, or suspicious activities. Once an event has been reported and escalated to the incident response team, the event is evaluated to determine if it warrants classification as an incident. If the event has been classified as an incident, the incident response team should move in to perform data collection on the affected systems that will later be used for analysis. During collection, it is important to work in accordance with the organization's policies and procedures and preserve a valid chain of custody. The person involved in collecting the data should make sure that the integrity of the data is maintained on both the original and working copies of the evidence. Once the relevant information has been captured, the incident response team should analyze the data to determine who, what, when, where, how, and why an incident took place.

Containment, Eradication, and Recovery

Once the involved systems and offending vectors have been analyzed, the incident response team should move in to contain the problem and eradicate it. It is crucial to contain an incident as fast as possible to minimize its impact on the business. This can be as easy as disconnecting the system from the network or as hard as isolating a whole server farm from the production environment. Containment and eradication should strive to protect service integrity, sensitive data, hardware, and software. The recovery phase depends on the extent of the incidence. For example, an intrusion that was detected while it was affecting a single user is easier to recover from in comparison to an intrusion where the lateral movement of the intruder is extensive. Most of the time, recovery involves backing up the unaffected data to use on the new systems. OSs and applications are usually installed fresh to avoid any type of contamination.

Postincident Activity

The postincident phase involves documenting, reporting, and reviewing the incident. Documentation actually starts as soon as an event has been classified as an incident. The report should include all of the documentation compiled during the incident, the analysis methods and techniques, and all other findings. The person writing the report should keep in mind that the report might someday be used by law enforcement or in court. Finally, the incident response team should go over the report with the IT department and other involved parties to discuss how to improve he infrastructure to prevent similar incidents.

Capturing Volatile Information

Computer systems contain volatile data that is temporarily available either till a process exits or a system is shutdown. Therefore, it is important to capture this data before making any physical or logical changes to the system to avoid tampering with evidence. Many incident responders have destroyed memory-only resident artifacts by shutting down a system in the name of containment.

Volatile data is available as system memory (including slack and free space), network configuration, network connections and sockets, running processes, open files,

FIGURE 41.1   Incident response life cycle.

login sessions, and OS time. System memory can be captured by using sampling tools (MoonSols Windows Memory Toolkit, GMG Systems' KnTDD) as a file and analyzed with the Volatility Framework to obtain the volatile data previously mentioned. The volatile data can also be captured individually with tools that are specific for each data type. The Microsoft Windows Sysinternals suite provides an extensive set of tools that can capture volatile data, such as login sessions, Registry, process information, service information, shares, and loaded dynamic-link libraries (DLLs).

3. CONTROLLING AN INVESTIGATION

To control an investigation, the incident response team should have a forensics investigation plan, a forensics toolkit, and documented methods to secure the affected environment. An investigator should always keep in mind that the evidence collected, and the analysis performed might be presented in court or used by law enforcement. Related documentation should be detailed and contain dates and times for each activity performed. To avoid challenges to the authenticity of evidence investigators should be able to secure the suspect infrastructure, log all activity, and maintain a chain of custody.

Collecting Digital Evidence

It is important to an investigator to preserve data related to an incident as soon as possible to avoid the rapid degradation or loss of data in digital environments. Once the affected systems have been determined, volatile data should be captured immediately followed by nonvolatile data, such as system users and groups, configuration files, password files and caches, scheduled jobs, system logs, application logs, command history, recently accessed files, executable files, data files, swap files, dump files, security software logs, hibernation files, temporary files, and complete file listing with times.

Chain of Custody and Process Integrity

The incident response team should be committed to collect and preserve evidence using methods that can support future legal or organizational proceedings. A clearly defined chain of custody is necessary to avoid allegations of tampering evidence. To accomplish this task the team should keep a log of every entity who had physical custody of the evidence, document all of the actions performed on the evidence with the related date and time, make a working copy of the evidence for analysis, verify the integrity of the original and working copy, and store the evidence in secured location when not in use [2]. Also before touching a physical system, the investigator should take a photograph of it. To ensure the integrity of the

process a detailed log should be kept of all the collection steps, information about every tool used in the incident response process.

Advantages of Having a Forensics Analysis Team

Forensic analysis is usually thought in the context of crime investigations. Nowadays, due to the increase in computer-related malicious activity and growing digital infrastructure, forensic analysis is involved in incident response, operational troubleshooting, log monitoring, data recovery, data acquisition, audits, and regulatory compliance. Therefore, organizations can no longer rely on law enforcement due to resource and jurisdictional limitations. A violation of organizational policies and procedures might not concern law enforcement leaving the organization to its own devices. It has become evident to organizations that maintaining capabilities to perform forensic analysis has become a business requirement to satisfy organizational and customer needs. While it may make sense for some organizations to maintain an internal team of forensic analysts, some might find it more beneficial to hire outside parties to carry out this function. Organizations should take cost, response time, and data sensitivity into consideration before making this decision [2]. Keeping an internal forensic analysis team might reduce cost depending on the scale of the incident, provide faster response due to familiarity with the infrastructure, and prevent sensitive data from being viewed by third parties.

Legal Aspects of Acquiring Evidence: Securing and Documenting the Scene

Securing the physical scene and documenting it should be one of the first steps an incident responder should take. This involves photographing the system setup, cabling, general area, collecting and documenting all cables and attached devices, write-protecting all media, using antistatic packaging for transportation, maintaining proper temperature for stored devices, avoiding exposure to excessive electromagnetic fields, and logging all access to the area. The incident response team should keep an inventory of evidence-handling supplies (chain of custody forms, notebooks, evidence storage bags, evidence tape), blank media, backup devices, and forensics workstations.

Processing and Logging Evidence

The goal of an investigation is to collect and preserve evidence that can be used for internal proceedings or court of law. Investigators should be able prove that the evidence has not been tampered with. To be able to accomplish this the incident response team members should receive training specifically addressing these issues and should practice these skills on an ongoing basis to stay sharp.

To properly process and log evidence, investigators should keep the evidence within a secured and controlled environment where all access is logged, and should document the collected evidence and its circulation among investigative entities. We cannot stress how important it is to associate each activity with a date and time.

4. CONDUCTING DISC-BASED ANALYSIS

To be able to process evidence in a manner that is admissible in a court of law, a lab and accompanying procedures should be established. This will ensure that the data integrity is not breached and the data remains confidential: in other words, the evidence remains forensically sound.

Forensics Lab Operations

To ensure forensic soundness, an investigator's process needs to be reliable, repeatable, and documented. To have a controlled and secure environment for the investigator to follow these steps, a forensic lab becomes a necessity.

The lab should be established in a physically secure building that is monitored 24/7, should have a dedicated staff, should have regularly upgraded and updated workstations dedicated to forensic analysis with related software installed, and should have a disaster recovery plan in place.

Acquiring a Bit-Stream Image

Acquiring a bit-stream image involves producing a bit-by-bit copy of a hard drive on a separate storage device. By creating an exact copy of a hard drive, an investigator preserves all data on a disc, including currently unused and partially overwritten sectors. The imaging process should not alter the original hard drive to preserve the copy's admissibility as evidence. Selecting a proper imaging tool is crucial to produce a forensically sound copy. The National Institute of Standards and Technology (NIST) lists the requirements for a drive imaging tool as follows [2]:

- The tool shall make a bit-stream duplicate or an image of an original disc or a disc partition on fixed or removable media.
- The tool shall not alter the original disc.

- The tool shall be able to access both integrated development environment (IDE) and small computer standard interface (SCSI) discs.
- The tool shall be able to verify the integrity of a disc image file.
- The tool shall log input/output (I/O) errors.
- The tool's documentation shall be correct.

The imaging of a hard drive can be performed using specialized hardware tools or by using a combination of computers and software.

Specialized Hardware

The Image MASSter Solo series hard drive duplicators generally support serial advanced technology attachment, IDE, Universal Serial Bus (USB), external serial advanced technology attachment, universal serial advanced technology attachment, serial-attached SCSI hard drives and flash memory devices. They can hash the disc images besides providing write-blocking to ensure the integrity of the copies. The imaging process can be either disc-to-disc or disc-to-file.

The Digital Intelligence Forensic Duplicator units have the same properties as the Image MASSter Solo series. But, they provide access to different hard drive formats through their protocol modules.

Software: Linux

The dd or dcfldd has been fully tested and vetted by NIST as a forensic imaging tool. It is a freeware utility for any Linux-based system and can copy every sector of hard drives. The software program dcfldd is dd-based and enhances dd's output by providing status and time-to-completion output as the disc gets imaged and can split the output to smaller chunks. It can also hash the output to ensure data integrity. The following command, as seen in Table 41.1, will read block sizes of 512 bytes, produce 2 GB chunks of a disc device defined as /dev/sdb, and will calculate the MD5 hashes every 2 GB to ensure integrity. The hash values will be written to a file named md5.og. In the event of a read error, dcfldd will write zeroes in the copy.

Windows The AccessData Forensic Toolkit (FTK) Imager tool is a commercial disc-imaging tool distributed by AccessData. FTK supports storage of disc images in EnCase's file format, as well as in bit-by-bit (dd) format.

TABLE 41.1 Creating an Image of a Drive

```
$ dcfldd if=/dev/sdb hash=md5 hashwindow=2G md5log=md5.log  hashconv=after bs=512

conv=noerror,sync split=2G splitformat=aa of=driveimage.dd
```

On the other hand, the Guidance EnCase tool is a commercial disc imaging tool distributed by Guidance Software. Disc images are stored in the proprietary EnCase Evidence File Format, which contains compressed data prefixed with case metadata and contains hashes if the image data.

Enabling a Write Blocker

Write blockers are hardware- or software-based tools that allow the acquisition of hard drive images while preventing any data from being written to the source hard drive, therefore ensuring the integrity of the data involved. Write blockers can do this by only allowing read commands to pass through by blocking write commands or by letting only specific commands through. While copying data with a hardware write blocker, the source and destination drives should both be connected to the write-blocking device and in case of a software blocker, the blocking software should be activated first before copying [1]. After imaging is performed with a write blocker, calculating the hashes of both the source and destination images is essential to ensure data integrity. Some hardware write blockers that are used in the industry is as follows:

- Tableau Forensic Bridges
- WiebeTech WriteBlocker

Establishing a Baseline

It is important to maintain the integrity of the data being analyzed throughout the investigation. When dealing with disc drives, to maintain integrity, calculating the hashes of the analyzed images becomes crucial. Before copying or performing any analysis, the investigator should take a baseline hash of the original drives involved. The hash could be either just MD5 or a combination of MD5, SHA-1, and SHA-512. The baseline hash can be compared with hashes of any copies that are made thereafter for analysis or backup to ensure that the integrity of the evidence is maintained.

Physically Protecting the Media

After making copies of the original evidence hard drives, they should be stored in a physically secure location, such as a safe in a secured storage facility. These drives could be used as evidence in the event of prosecution. The chain of custody should also be maintained by labeling the evidence and keeping logs of date, time, and persons the evidence has come in contact with. During transportation, the hard drives should be placed in antistatic bags and should not be exposed to harsh environmental conditions. If possible, photographs of the evidence should be taken whenever they are processed, starting from the original location to the image acquisition stages.

Disc Structure and Recovery Techniques

Once a forensically sound copy has been made of the evidence, we can proceed to analyzing its contents. There are different kinds of storage media: hard disc drives (HDD), solid state drives (SSD), digital video discs (DVD), compact discs (CD), flash memory, and other kinds. An investigator needs to be mindful about how each media stores data differently. For example, while data in the unused space on an HDD is stored as long as new data is not written, the data in the unused space of an SSD is destroyed within minutes of switching it on. This difference in retaining data makes it difficult to obtain a forensically sound image and recovering data (see checklist: "An Agenda for Action for Data Recovery").

An Agenda for Action for Data Recovery

The cyber forensic specialist should ensure that the following provisional list of actions for data recovery are adhered to (check all tasks completed):

_____1. Make sure you are ready and have procedures in place for disasters like floods, tornadoes, earthquakes, and terrorism when they strike.

_____2. Make sure you are ready and have a plan in place to take periodic image copies and send them offsite.

_____3. Perform change accumulation to reduce the number of logs required as input to the recovery, which saves time at the recovery site. However, performing this step consumes resources at the home site.

_____4. Evaluate your environment to decide how to handle the change accumulation question/problem in action/task #3.

_____5. Make sure you have procedures in place to implement your plan.

_____6. Check your assets to make sure they're ready as part of your plan.

_____7. Make sure you build your recovery job control language (JCL) correctly. JCL is tricky, and you need to get it exactly right. Data integrity and your business rely on this task.

_____8. Make sure you clean your remote console data sets. It can take hours if done manually, and it's an error-prone process. When your system is down, can you afford to make mistakes with this key resource?

_____9. Make sure you test your plan. There's a lot to think about. In the real world, there's much more.

_____10. Make sure your plan works before you are required to use it!

_____11. Make sure that you have procedures in place to deal with issues of increased availability, shrinking expertise, and growing complexity, failures of many types, and the costs of data management and downtime.

Disc Geometry Components

With regards to HDD geometry: The surface of each HDD platter is arranged in concentric magnetic tracks on each side. To make accessing data more efficient, each track is divided into addressable sectors or blocks as seen in Fig. 41.2. This organization is known as formatting. Sectors typically contain 512 bytes or 2048 bytes of data in addition to the address information. Newer HDDs use 4096 byte sectors. The HDD controller uses the format and address information to locate the specific data processed by the OS.

Now, with regards to SSD geometry: Compared to HDDs, SSDs store data in 512 kilobyte sectors or blocks, which are in turn divided into 4096 byte long pages. These structures are located in arrays of NAND (Negated AND or NOT AND) transistors.

Inspecting Windows File System Architectures

File systems, including Windows, can be defined in six layers: physical (absolute sectors), data classification (partitions), allocation units (clusters), storage space management (file allocation table [FAT] or master file table [MFT]), information classification (folders), and application level storage (files). Knowing these layers will guide the investigator as to what tool is needed to extract information from the file system. Windows file systems have gone through an evolution starting from FAT and continuing to New Technology File System (NTFS).

File Allocation Table (FAT)

FAT has been available widely on Windows systems starting with the MS-DOS OS. This file system has incarnations, such as FAT12, FAT16, FAT32, and exFAT. The volume is organized into specific sized chunks based on the version numbering of the file system. FAT12 has a cluster size of 512 bytes to 8 kilobytes whereas FAT16 has cluster sizes ranging from 512 bytes to 64 kilobytes. FAT32 file systems can support disc sizes up to two terabytes using cluster sizes ranging from 512 bytes to 32 kilobytes. FAT file systems begin with the boot sector and procced with FAT areas 1 and 2, the root directory, files, and other directories. FAT provides a table to the OS as to which cluster in the volume is used for a file or folder. In a FAT file system, file deletion is accomplished by overwriting the first character of the object's name with 0xE5 or 0x00 and by setting the table entry of the related clusters to zero. FAT file times are stored by using the local system's time information.

New Technology File System (NTFS)

As the name suggests, NTFS was developed to overcome the limitations inherent in the FAT file system. These limitations were the lack of access control lists (ACLs) on file system objects, journaling, and compression, encryption, named streams, rich metadata, and many other features. The journaling features of NTFS make it capable of recovering itself by automatically restoring the consistency of the file system when an error takes place [2]. It also should be noted that NTFS file times are stored in the Universal Coordinated Time (UTC) compared to FAT where the OS's local time is used. There are mainly two artifacts in NTFS that interests a forensics investigator: MFT and alternate data stream (ADS).

Master File Table (MFT)

MFT or $MFT can be considered one of the most important files in the NTFS file system. It keeps records of all files in a volume, the files' location in the directory, the physical location of the files in on the drive, and file metadata. The metadata includes file and folder create dates, entry modified dates, access dates, last written dates, physical and logical file size, and ACLs of the files. The file and directory metadata is stored as an MFT entry that is 1024 bytes in size. The first 16 entries in the MFT belong to system files, such as the MFT itself. From a forensics investigator perspective, entries are very interesting because when a file is deleted an entry gets marked as unallocated while the file content on the drive remains intact. The file name in the MFT entry can be overwritten due to MFT tree structure reorganization so most of the time file names are not maintained. File data eventually is overwritten as the unallocated drive space gets used.

Alternate Data Streams (ADS)

NTFS supports multiple data streams for files and folders. Files are composed of unnamed streams that contain the actual file data besides additional named streams (mainfile.txt:one-stream). All streams within a file share the file's metadata, including file size. Since the file size does not change with the addition of ADSs, it becomes difficult to detect their existence. Open source forensics tools, such as The Sleuth Kit (TSK) can be used to parse MFT entries and reveal the existence of ADSs. Specifically, the TSK command fls can be used to list the files and the associated ADSs.

 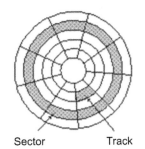

Zone Density Recording   Sector   Track

FIGURE 41.2 Physical structure of a drive.

TABLE 41.2 Listing Files From a Raw Disc Image

```
$ fls -o 63 -rp evidence-diskimage.dd

r/r 11315-158-1:    ads-folder/ads-file.txt

r/r 11315-158-4:    ads-folder/ads-file.txt:suspicious.exe

r/r 11315-158-3:    ads-folder/host.txt:another-stream
```

TABLE 41.3 Extracting a File From a Raw Image With Its Inode

```
$ icat -o 63 evidence-diskimage.dd 11315-158-4 >  suspicious.exe
```

Locating and Restoring Deleted Content

Files can be fully or partially recovered depending on the method of deletion, time elapsed since the deletion, and drive fragmentation. A deleted or unlinked file is one whose MFT entry has been marked as unallocated and is no longer present in the user's view. The file can be recovered based on the metadata still present in the MFT entry given that too much time has not passed since the deletion. TSK can be used to parse the MFT to locate and recover these files. The investigator would need to execute the command fls to get a listing of the deleted file's inode and use that inode to extract the file data with the command icat.

Orphaned files' MFT entries, on the other hand, are no longer fully intact, and therefore the related metadata, such as the file name, might not be available. On the other hand, the file's data may still be recovered using the same method used for deleted files.

Unallocated files' MFT entries have been reused and/or unlinked. In this scenario, the only way to recover the file would be to "carve" the data out of the unallocated drive space. Carving involves using tools (foremost, scalpel) that recognize specific file formats, such as headers and footers to find the beginning and end of the file and extract the data.

Overwritten files' MFT entries and content have been reallocated or reused. Complete recovery would not be possible. Fragments of the file can be recovered by searching through the unallocated spaces on the drive with tools, such as grep.

5. INVESTIGATING INFORMATION-HIDING TECHNIQUES

Hidden data can exist due to regular OS activities or deliberate user activities. This type of data includes ADS,

information obscured by malicious software, data encoded in media (steganography), hidden system files, and many others.

Uncovering Hidden Information

Collection of hidden data can be a challenge for an investigator. The investigator needs to be aware of the different data hiding techniques to employ the proper tools.

Scanning and Evaluating Alternate Data Streams

Open source forensics tools, such as TSK can be used to parse MFT entries and reveal the existence of ADSs. Specifically, the TSK command fls can be used to list the files and the associated ADSs as seen in Table 41.2.

In this example, we can see that the file ads-file.txt contains two streams named suspicious.exe and another-stream. The numbers seen in the beginning of each listing is the inode. This value identifies each file and folder in the file system. We should note that 63 bytes were skipped starting from the beginning of the drive since that data belongs to the master boot record (MBR). To extract the file data from the file system, the TSK command icat can be used in combination with the inode values as seen in Table 41.3.

Executing Code From a Stream

Malicious software can attempt to hide its components in ADSs to obscure themselves from investigators. Such components could be executable files. Executable ADSs can be launched with the Windows start command or by other scripting languages, such as VBScript or Perl by referring to the ADS file directly: start ads-file.jpg:suspicious.exe. Executable hidden in ADSs can be automatically launched on system startup by defining it to do so in the Windows registry key "HKEY_LOCAL_MACHINE\-Software\Microsoft\Windows\CurrentVersion\Run"   by creating a string value containing the full path of the ADS file.

Steganography Tools and Concepts

Steganography is the science of hiding secret messages in nonsecret messages or media in a manner that only the person who is aware of the mechanism can successfully find and decode. Messages can be hidden in images, audio files, videos, or other computer files without altering the actual presentation or functionality. While steganography is about hiding the message and its transmission, cryptography only aims to obscure the message content itself through various algorithms. Steganography can be performed by using the least significant bits in image files, placing comments in the source code, altering the file header, spreading data over a sound file's frequency spectrum, or hiding encrypted data in pseudorandom locations in a file. There are several tools that perform steganography:

- S-Tools is a freeware steganography tool that hides files in BMP, GIF, and WAV files. The message can be encrypted with algorithms, such as IDEA, DES, 3DES, and MDC before being hidden in the images.
- Spam Mimic is a freeware steganography tool that embeds messages in spam email content. This tool would be useful when real spam messages are numerous and the fake spam message would not wake any suspicion.
- Snow is a freeware steganography tool that encodes message text by appending white space characters to the end of lines. The tool's name stands for and exploits the steganographic nature of whitespace. It also can employ ICE encryption to hide the content of the message in case of the detection of steganography. While most of the time it's visually undetectable, it can be discovered by a careful investigator or a script looking for this tool's artifacts.
- OutGuess is an open source tool that hides messages in the redundant bits of data sources. OutGuess can use any data format as a medium as long as a handler is provided.

Detecting Steganography

During an incident, an investigator might suspect that steganography has been used by the suspect due to an admission, a discovery of specific tools, or other indicators. Traces of the use of steganography tools can be found in the recently used files (MRU) key, the USERASSIST key, and the MUICache key in the Windows registry; prefetch files, web browser history, and deleted file information in the file system; and in the Windows Search Assistant utility. File artifacts generated by these tools can also be a good indicator of the tools' use.

The presence of files (JPEG, MP3) that present similar properties but different hash values might also generate suspicion. The investigator might be able to discover such pairs of carrier and processed files to apply discovery algorithms to recover the hidden messages. Steganalysis tools can also be used to detect the presence of steganography:

- Stegdetect is an open source steganalysis tool that is capable of detecting steganographic content in images that have been generated by JSteg, JPHide, Invisible Secrets, OutGuess, F5, Camouflage, and appendX.
- StegSpy is a freeware steganalysis tool that can currently identify steganography generated by the Hiderman, JPHideandSeek, Masker, JPegX, and Invisible Secrets tools.
- Stegbreak is used to launch dictionary attacks against JSteg-Shell, JPHide, and OutGuess 0.13b generated messages.

Scavenging Slack Space

File slack or slack space refers to the bytes between the logical end of a file and the end of the cluster the file resides in. Slack space is a source of information leak, which can result in password, email, registry, event log, database entries, and word processing document disclosures. File slack has the potential of containing data from the system memory. This can happen if a file can't fill the last sector in a cluster and the Windows OS uses randomly selected data from the system memory (RAM slack) to fill the gap. RAM slack can contain any information loaded into memory since the system was turned on. The information can include file content resident in memory, usernames, passwords, and cryptographic keys. File slack space can also be used to hide information by malicious users or software, which can get challenging if the investigator is not specifically looking for such behavior. Volume slack is the space that remains on a drive when it's not used by any partition. This space can contain data if it was created as a result of deleting a partition. While the partition metadata no longer exists, its contents still remain on the drive. Partition slack is the area between the ending of a logical partition and the ending of a physical block the partition is located in. It is created when the number of sectors in a partition is not a multiple of the physical block size. Registry slack is formed when a registry key is deleted and the size value is changed to a positive value. Normally, key sizes are negative values when read as signed integer. The registry key data still remains on the drive. Jolanta Thomassen created a Perl script called "regslack" to parse registry hives and extract

TABLE 41.4 Inspecting File Headers

```
$ file hidden.pdf

hidden.pdf: PE32 executable for MS Windows (GUI) Intel 80386 32-bit
```

```
Example of a PDF Header:

0000000: 2550 4446 2d31 2e36 0a25 e4e3 cfd2 0a31   %PDF-1.6.%.....1
```

```
Example of a Windows Executable Header:

0000000: 4d5a 9000 0300 0000 0400 0000 ffff 0000   MZ..............
```

deleted keys by exploiting the negative to positive conversion information.

Inspecting Header Signatures and File Mangling

Users or malware with malicious intent can alter or mangle file names or the files themselves to hide files that are used to compromise systems or contain data that has been gathered as a result of their malicious actions. These techniques include but are not limited to renaming files, embedding malicious files in regular files (PDF, Doc, Flash), binding multiple executables in a single executable, and changing file times to avoid event time−based analysis. For example, a malicious Windows executable "bad.exe" can be renamed to "interesting.pdf" and be served by a web page to an unsuspecting user. Depending on the web browser, the user would get prompted with a dialog that asks them if they would like to run the program and most of the time the user will dismiss the dialog by clicking the OK button. To analyze a file disguised in different file extensions, a header based file type checker, such as the Linux "file" command or the tool TrID (also available in Windows) can be used. Table 41.4 provides a sample of the malware Trojan.Spyeye hidden in a file with an Acrobat PDF document extension being detected by the tool file.

Combining Files

Combining files is a very popular method among malware creators. Common file formats, such as Microsoft Office files, Adobe PDF, and Flash files can be used as containers to hide malicious executables. One example is a technique where a Windows executable is embedded in a PDF file as an object stream and marked with a compression filter. The stream is usually obfuscated with XOR. The Metasploit Framework provides several plugins to generate such files for security professionals to conduct social engineering in the form of phishing attacks. The example in Table 41.5 uses Metasploit to generate a PDF file with an embedded executable file.

To discover such embedding, an investigator can use Didier Stevens's tool PDF-parser to view the objects in a PDF file.

Binding Multiple Executable Files

Binding multiple executable files provides the means to pack all dependencies and resource files a program might need while running into a single file. This is advantageous since it permits a malicious user to leave a smaller footprint on a target system and makes it harder for an investigator to locate the malicious file. Certain tools, such as the WinZip Self-Extractor, nBinder, or File Joiner can create one executable file by archiving all related files whose execution will be controlled by a stub executable. When executed, the files will be extracted and the contained program will be launched automatically. Some of these file binders can produce files that can't be detected by some antiviruses and if downloaded and ran by an unsuspecting user, it can result in a system compromise.

File Time Analysis

File time analysis is one of the most used techniques by investigators. File times are used to build a story line that could potentially reveal how and when an event on a system caused a compromise. The file time of a malicious executable could be linked to a user's browser history to find out which sites were visited before the compromise occurred.

The problem with this type of analysis is that sometimes the file times can be tampered with and can't be relied upon as evidence. The tool Timestomp, created by James Foster and Vincent Liu, allows for the deletion or modification of file MACE times (modified, accessed, created, entry modified in MFT times) in the MFT's $STANDARD_INFORMATION attribute. Timestomp can't change the file MACE times in the

TABLE 41.5 Creating a Malicious PDF File With the Metasploit Framework

```
msf > use exploit/windows/fileformat/adobe_pdf_embedded_exe

msf exploit(adobe_pdf_embedded_exe) > set FILENAME evil.pdf

FILENAME => evil.pdf

msf exploit(adobe_pdf_embedded_exe) > set PAYLOAD windows/meterpreter/reverse_tcp

PAYLOAD => windows/meterpreter/reverse_tcp

msf exploit(adobe_pdf_embedded_exe) > set INFILENAME ./base.pdf

INFILENAME => ./base.pdf

[*] Please wait while we load the module tree...

....

INFILENAME => ./base.pdf

payload => windows/meterpreter/bind_tcp

[*] Reading in './base.pdf'...

[*] Parsing './base.pdf'...

[*] Parsing Successful.

[*] Using 'windows/meterpreter/bind_tcp' as payload...

[*] Creating 'evil.pdf' file...

[+] evil.pdf stored at .../local/evil.pdf
```

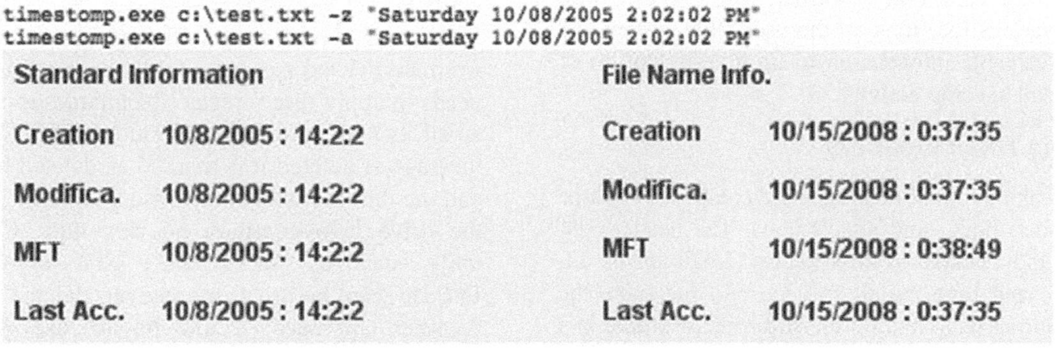

```
timestomp.exe c:\test.txt -z "Saturday 10/08/2005 2:02:02 PM"
timestomp.exe c:\test.txt -a "Saturday 10/08/2005 2:02:02 PM"
```

Standard Information		File Name Info.	
Creation	10/8/2005 : 14:2:2	Creation	10/15/2008 : 0:37:35
Modifica.	10/8/2005 : 14:2:2	Modifica.	10/15/2008 : 0:37:35
MFT	10/8/2005 : 14:2:2	MFT	10/15/2008 : 0:38:49
Last Acc.	10/8/2005 : 14:2:2	Last Acc.	10/15/2008 : 0:37:35

FIGURE 41.3 Changing timestamps as a result of time stomping.

MFT's $FILE_NAME attribute because this attribute is meant to be modified by Windows system internals only. This time tampering method can be defeated by using Mark McKinnon's MFT Parser tool to view all eight-file times to detect discrepancies as seen in Fig. 41.3.

Executable compile times can also be used as a data point during timeline analysis. The open source Python module pefile can be used to extract this information from the executable header. For example, if malicious software changes MACE times to a future date, but keeps its original

TABLE 41.6 Compilation Time of an Executable Extracted With Pefile

```
Compilation timedatestamp: 2010-03-23 23:42:40

Target machine: 0x14C (Intel 386 or later processors and compatible processors)

Entry point address: 0x000030B1
```

compile time, this can be flagged as suspicious by an investigator as seen in Table 41.6.

6. SCRUTINIZING EMAIL

While many noncommercial users are favoring webmail nowadays, most corporate users are still using local email clients, such as Microsoft Outlook or Mozilla Thunderbird. Therefore, we should still look at extracting and analyzing email content from local email stores. Email message analysis might reveal information about the sender and recipient, such as email addresses, IP addresses, data and time, attachments, and content.

Investigating the Mail Client

An email user will generally utilize a local client to compose and send their message. Depending on the user's configuration, the sent and received messages will exist in the local email database. Deleted e-mails can be also stored locally for some time depending on the user's preferences. Most corporate environments utilize Microsoft Outlook. Outlook will store the mail in a portable storage table (PST) or offline storage table (OST) format. Multiple PST files can exist in various locations on the user's file system and can provide valuable information to an investigator about the user's email-specific activity.

Interpreting Email Headers

Generally speaking, email messages are composed of three sections: header, body, and attachments. The header contains source and destination information (email and IP addresses), date and time, email subject, and the route the email takes during its transmission. Information stored in a header can either be viewed through the email client or through an email forensics tool such as libpff (an open source library to access email databases), FTK, or EnCase.

The "Received" line in Table 41.7 email header shows that the email was sent from IP address 1.1.1.1. An investigator should not rely on this information as concrete evidence because it can be easily changed by a malicious sender (email spoofing). The time information in the header might also be incorrect due to time zones, user system inaccuracies and tampering.

Recovering Deleted E-mails

While most users treat e-mails as transient, the companies they work for have strict data retention policies that can enforce the storage of email, sometimes indefinitely. User emails usually are stored in backup archives or electronic-discovery systems to provide means for analysis in case there is an investigation. The email servers also can keep messages in store although the users remove them from their local systems. Therefore, it has become somewhat difficult for a corporate user to delete an email permanently. Recovery is usually possible from various backup systems. In cases where there is no backup source and users delete an email from their local system, we need to perform several steps on the user's storage drive depending on the level of deletion:

- If the user deletes the message, but does not empty the deleted messages folder, the user can move the messages from the deleted folder to the original folder quite easily.
- If the user deletes the email message and removes it from the deleted messages folder, then the investigator needs to apply disc forensics techniques to recover the email. In case of a Microsoft Outlook PST file, when a message is deleted it is marked as deleted by Outlook and the data remains on the disc unless the location on the drive is overwritten by new data. Commercial tools, such as AccessData's FTK or Guidance's EnCase can be used to recover deleted messages. Another approach would be to use Microsoft's "Scanpst.exe" tool. To apply this technique, the investigator should first backup the PST and then deliberately corrupt the PST file with the command "DEBUG <FILE.pst> -f 107 113 20 -q." If the file is too large and there is insufficient system memory, then the investigator should use a hex editor to make the changes marked in red in the PST file as shown in Fig. 41.4.

TABLE 41.7 An Email Header

```
Return-Path: <example_from@acme.edu>

X-SpamCatcher-Score: 1 [X]

Received: from [1.1.1.1] (HELO acme.edu)

      by fe3.acme.edu (CommuniGate Pro SMTP 4.1.8)

      with ESMTP-TLS id 61258719 for example_to@mail.acme.edu;

Mon, 23 Aug 2004 11:40:10 -0400

Message-ID: <4129F3CA.2020509@acme.edu>

Date: Mon, 23 Aug 2005 11:40:36 -0400

From: Jim Doe <example_from@acme.edu>

User-Agent: Mozilla/5.0 (Windows; U; Windows NT 5.1; en-US;

rv:1.0.1) Gecko/20020823 Netscape/7.0

X-Accept-Language: en-us, en

MIME-Version: 1.0

To: John Doe <example_to@mail.acme.edu>

Subject: Sales Development Meeting

Content-Type: text/plain; charset=us-ascii; format=flowed

Content-Transfer-Encoding: 7bit
```

```
Offset     0  1  2  3  4  5  6  7  8  9  A  B  C  D  E  F
00000000  21 42 44 4E 4B E7 0A 20 20 20 20 20 20 20 20 20   !BDNKç.
00000010  20 20 20 20 D0 00 00 00 04 00 00 00 01 00 00 00   □...........
00000020  B3 93 07 00 00 00 00 00 F8 7E 27 00 D2 D8 00 00   ³".....ø~'.ÒØ..
00000030  09 35 01 00 09 2A 01 00 00 36 01 00 28 6E 04 00   .5...*...6..(n..
00000040  84 37 01 00 00 36 01 00 00 36 01 00 E0 DA 00 00   „7...6...6..àÚ..
```

FIGURE 41.4 Manipulating a PST file for recovery.

Once the PST file has been corrupted, then the "Scanpst.exe" tool should be located on the drive. And it should also be executed to repair the file as seen in Fig. 41.5.

7. VALIDATING EMAIL HEADER INFORMATION

Email header information can be tampered with by users that wish to not disclose their source information or by malicious users that would like to fake the origin of the message to avoid detection and being blocked by spam filters. Email header information can be altered by spoofing by using an anonymizer (removes identifying information), and using a mail relay server.

Detecting Spoofed Email

A spoofed email message is a message that appears to be from an entity other than the actual sender entity. This can be accomplished by altering the sender's name, email address, email client type, and/or the source IP address in the email header. Spoofing can be detected by looking at the "Received" and "Message-ID" lines of the header. The "Received" field will have each email server hop the message that was taken before it had been received by the email client. An investigator can use the email server IP addresses in the header to get their host names from their Domain Name System (DNS) records and verify them by comparing to the actual outgoing and incoming email

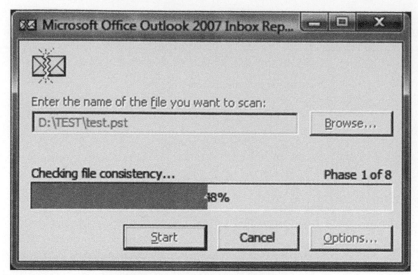

FIGURE 41.5 Use of the Scanpst.exe tool.

servers' information. The "Message-ID" field uniquely identifies a message and is used to prevent multiple deliveries. The domain information in the "Message-ID" field should match the domain information of the sender's email address. If this is not the case, the email is most probably spoofed. An investigator should also look out for different "From" and "Reply-To" email addresses, and unusual email clients displayed in the "X-Mailer" field.

Verifying Email Routing

Email routing can be verified by tracing the hops an email message has taken. This can be accomplished by verifying the "Received" field information through DNS records and if possible obtaining email transaction logs from the email servers involved. The "Message-ID" information can be searched for in the logs to make sure that the message has actually traveled the route declared in the "Received" field.

8. TRACING INTERNET ACCESS

Knowing the path a perpetrator has taken becomes very valuable when an investigator is building a case to present in court. It adds credibility to the claim and solidifies the storyline by connecting the events. For example, knowing the path an attacker has taken to steal a company's source code can reveal the extent of the compromise (loss of domain credentials, customer information leakage, and intellectual property loss), show intent, and prevent the same attack from happening. Tracing Internet access can also be valuable in the case of employees viewing content not compliant with work place rules.

Inspecting Browser Cache and History Files

An investigator can use various data points to trace a perpetrator's activity by analyzing the browser cache and web history files in the gathered evidence. Every action of a user on the Internet can generate artifacts. The browser cache contains files that are saved locally as a result of a user's web browsing activity. The history files contain a list of visited URLs, web searches, cookies, and bookmarked websites. These files can be located in different folders depending on the OS, OS version, and browser type.

Exploring Temporary Internet Files

A browser cache stores multimedia content (images, videos), and web pages (HTML, JavaScript, CSS) to increase the load speed of a page when viewed the next time. For the Internet Explorer web browser on Windows XP and 2003, the cache files can be located in the folder "Documents and Settings\%username%\Local Settings\Temporary Internet Files," in Windows Vista/7/2008 they are located in the folder "Users\%username%\AppData\ Local\Microsoft\Windows\Temporary Internet Files":

- On Windows XP/2003, Mozilla Firefox stores the cached files in the folder "C:\Documents and Settings\%username\Local Settings\ Application Data\Mozilla\Firefox\Profiles," and for Windows Vista/7/2008 in "C:\Users\%username%\AppData\Roaming\Mozilla\Firefox\ Profiles."
- On Windows XP/2003 Google Chrome web browser stores the cached files in the folder "C:\Documents and Settings\%username\Application Data\ Google\-Chrome\Default\Cache," and for Windows Vista/7/

2008 in "C:\Users\%username%\AppData\Local\Google\Chrome\ Default\Cache."

- The MAC times of these cached files can be used during a timeline analysis to find when certain artifacts, such as malware, get dropped by malicious or compromised websites. Malicious executable PDF files or Java files can be located in the cache unless the cache is cleared by the user or malware.

Visited URLs, Search Queries, Recently Opened Files

The Internet Explorer web browser stores the visited URL, search query, and opened file information in the file "index.dat" accompanied by last modified and last accessed, and expiration times. This file on Windows XP/2003 systems can be located in the folder "Documents and Settings\%username%\Local Settings\Temporary Internet Files\Content.IE5," and in Windows Vista/7/2008 systems it is located in the folder "Users\%username%\AppData\Local\Microsoft\Windows\Temporary Internet Files\Content.IE5." The "index.dat" file contains a LEAK record, which is a record that remains when it's marked as deleted, but can't be deleted due to a related temporary internet file (TIF) still being used.

Mozilla Firefox stores the URL, search, and open files-related history in a SQLite 3 database file Places.sqlite.

These files on Windows XP/2003 systems can be located in the folder "C:\Documents and Settings\%username\Local Settings\ Application Data\Mozilla\Firefox\Profiles," and in Windows Vista/7/2008 systems it is located in the folder "C:\Users\%username%\AppData\Roaming\Mozilla\Firefox\Profiles."

Google Chrome also stores its user activity data in SQLite 3 database files. These files on Windows XP/2003 systems can be located in the folder "C:\Documents and Settings\%username\Application Data\ Google\Chrome\default," and in Windows Vista/7/2008 systems it is located in the folder "C:\Users\%username%\AppData\Local\Google\Chrome\ default."

All three browsers' history files, cookies, and cache files can be parsed and interpreted by log2timeline, a tool created by Kristinn Gudjonsson. Log2timeline is capable of parsing multiple data sources and producing a timeline with, including but not limited to, file MAC times, registry write times, and Windows event logs. The tool can be pointed to a raw drive image (dd image) and as a result it can produce a "super" timeline in CSV format for all pursuable time-based data sources as seen Fig. 41.6 and Table 41.8.

Researching Cookie Storage

Internet Explorer cookies can be found in the folder "Documents and Settings\%username%\ Cookies" in

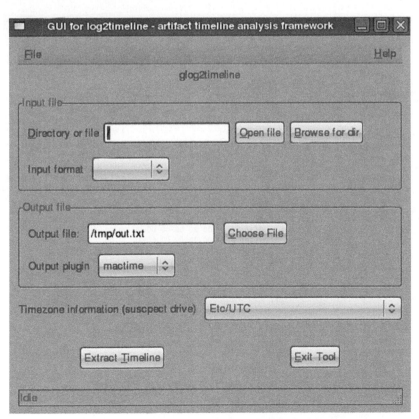

FIGURE 41.6 Graphical user interface (GUI) for log2timeline.

TABLE 41.8 Using Log2timeline From the Command Line

```
log2timeline -p -r -f win7 -z EST5EDT /storage/disk-image001.dd -w supertimeline001.csv
```

Windows XP/2003 systems and in Windows Vista/7/2008 systems in "Users\%username%\AppData\Roaming\ Microsoft\Windows\Cookies." The cookies are stored in plain text format.

Mozilla Firefox stores its cookies in a SQLite 3 database Cookies.sqlite located in the folder "C:\Documents and Settings\%username\Local Settings\ Application Data\Mozilla\Firefox\Profiles," and in Windows Vista/7/ 2008 systems, it is located in the folder "C:\Users\%username%\AppData\Roaming\Mozilla\Firefox\Profiles."

Google Chrome stores its cookies in a SQLite 3 database file "C:\Documents and Settings\%username\Application Data\ Google\Chrome\default\Cookies" in Windows XP/2003 systems, and in the file "C:\Users\%username %\AppData\Local\Google\Chrome\ default\Cookies" in Windows Vista/7/2008 systems. The cookies files of all three browser types can be parsed and viewed by the tool log2timeline as previously mentioned.

Reconstructing Cleared Browser History

It is possible to come across cleared browser histories during an investigation. The user could have deliberately deleted the files to hide their web browsing activity or a malware could have removed its traces to avoid detection and analysis. Nevertheless, an investigator will look into various locations on the suspect system to locate the deleted browser history files. The possible locations are unallocated clusters; cluster slack, page files, system files, hibernation files, and system restore points. Using AccessData's FTK Imager on the suspect drive or drive image, an investigator could promptly locate the orphaned files and see if the browser files are present there. The next step would be to use the FTK Imager to look at the unallocated spaces, which should end up being a time-consuming analysis as seen in Fig. 41.7. If the drive has not been used too much, an investigator has a high chance of locating the files in the unallocated space.

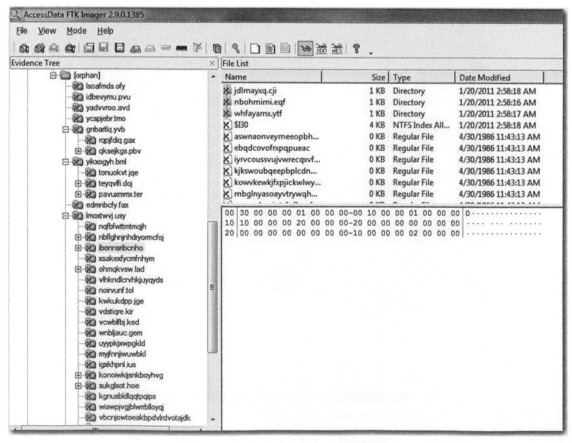

FIGURE 41.7   Use of AccessData FTK Imager.

Auditing Internet Surfing

Knowing what employees are browsing on the web while they are at work has become necessary to prevent the employees from visiting sites that host malicious content (sites with exploits and malware), content that is not compliant with work place rules, and content that is illegal. Employees can use the web to upload confidential corporate information, which can cause serious problems for the employer.

Tracking User Activity

User activity can be tracked by using tools that monitor network activity, DNS requests, local user system activity, and proxy logs. Network activity, on the other hand, can be monitored by looking at netflows. A netflow is a network protocol developed by Cisco Systems for monitoring IP traffic. It captures source and destination IP addresses, IP protocol, source and destination ports, and IP type of service.

Local user system activity can be monitored by installing specific agents on the users' systems that can report their activity back to a centralized server. Spector-Soft offers a product called Spector 360 that can be installed on user system and a central server. The agents on the user systems can track user browser activity by hooking into system application program interfaces (APIs) and enforce rules set by the employer.

DNS requests can be monitored at the corporate DNS server level or by looking at network traffic. When a user requests a web page with its domain name, the name gets translated to an IP address via DNS. User activity can be tracked by monitoring for domains that are not approved by the employer or domains hosting illegal content in the DNS server's logs.

Most corporate environments utilize a proxy server to funnel web traffic through. A proxy server acts as the middle man for requests from users seeking resources from external servers. This position of the proxy server permits tracking user browsing activity and can be used to filter or block certain behavior. Content protected by Secure Socket Layer (SSL) protocol can also be tracked by proxies, by setting the proxy up as an intercept proxy. Squid is one of the most popular open source proxies available and can carry out the necessary functions to track and block user activity.

Uncovering Unauthorized Usage

Unauthorized web usage can take multiple forms, such as downloading or viewing noncompliant or illegal content, uploading confidential information, launching attacks on other systems, and more. Once the unauthorized usage has been detected by the previously mentioned means, an investigator can focus on the user's system to corroborate the unauthorized activity. This can be done by analyzing browser history files and related file system activities. Building a "super" timeline with the tool log2timeline can become very useful to find the created cache and cookie files and the browser history entries around the same time the unauthorized activity was detected.

9. SEARCHING MEMORY IN REAL TIME

Analyzing memory in real time can provide very crucial information about activities of malware or a hacker that would be otherwise unavailable if only looking at a system's drives. This information can be network connections and sockets, system configuration settings, collected private information (user names, passwords, credit card numbers), memory-only resident executables, and much more. Real-time analysis involves analyzing volatile content and therefore requires swift action by the investigator. The investigator has to quickly act to capture an image of the memory using tools, such as MoonSols Windows Memory Toolkit, GMG Systems' KnTDD, or F-response. F-response is different from the other memory imaging tools since it provides real-time access to the target systems memory. Real-time access can reduce the time to analyze by permitting the investigator to analyze the memory right away without waiting for the whole memory to be downloaded into a file. You can read more about F-response at www.f-reponse.com.

Comparing the Architecture of Processes

Generally speaking, Windows architecture uses two access modes, which are user and kernel modes. The user mode includes application processes, such as programs and protected subsystems. The protected subsystems are named so because each of these is a separate process with its own protected virtual address space in memory. The kernel mode is a privileged mode of functioning in which the application has direct access to the virtual memory. This includes the address spaces of all user mode processes and applications and the associated hardware. The kernel mode is also called as the protected mode, or Ring 0:

- Windows processes are generally composed of an executable program, consisting of initial code and data, a private virtual address space, system resources that are accessible to all threads in the process, a unique identifier, called a process ID (PID), at least one thread of execution, and a security context (an access token).
- A Windows thread is what Windows uses for execution within a process. Without threads, the program used by the process cannot run. Threads consist of contents of the registers representing the state of the processor, two stacks (one for the thread for executing

kernel-mode instructions, and one for user mode), private storage area used by the subsystems, run-time libraries and DLLs, and a unique identifier named a thread ID.

- DLLs are set of callable subroutines linked together as a binary file that can be dynamically loaded by applications that use the subroutines. Windows user-mode entities utilize DLLs extensively. Using DLLs are advantageous for an application since they can share DLLs. Windows ensures that there is only one copy of a DLL in memory. Each DLL has its own import address table (IAT) in its compiled form.

Identifying User and Kernel Memory

Windows refers to Intel's linear memory address space as a virtual address space (VAS) since Windows uses the disc space structure to manage physical memory. In other words, 2 GB of VAS is not a one-to-one match to physical memory. Thirty-two-bit Windows divides VAS into user space (linear addresses 0x00000000 − 0x7FFFFFFF, 2 GB) and kernel space (linear addresses 0x80000000 − 0xFFFFFFFF, 2 GB) where user space gets the lower end of the address range and kernel space gets the upper end of the address space. To get an idea of how user space is arranged, we can use the !peb command in the Windows debugger. A list of loaded kernel modules can be obtained by running the command 'lm n' in the Windows debugger.

Inspecting Threads

While it is assumed that user and kernel code are restricted to their own address spaces, a thread can jump from user space to kernel space by the instruction SYSENTER and jump back with the instruction SYSEXIT. Malicious threads can also exist within valid kernel or other user processes. Such hidden or orphan kernel threads can be detected using the Volatility Framework with the plugin threads, which are shown in Table 41.9.

Discovering Rogue Dynamic-Link Libraries (DLLs) and Drivers

DLLs can be used for malicious purposes by injecting them through AppInit_DLLs registry value, SetWindowsHookEx() API call, and using remote threads via the CreateRemoteThread() Windows API call. Injected DLLs can be detected using the Volatility Framework's apihooks plugin. The plugin provides detailed information regarding the DLLs loaded, such as IAT, process, hooked module, hooked function, from−to instructions, and hooking module as seen in Table 41.10.

The Volatility Framework plugin malfind can find hidden or injected DLLs in user memory based on Virtual Address Descriptor (VAD) tags and page. The use of the malfind plugin to discover injected code is shown in Table 41.11.

The plugin dlllist in the Volatility Framework can also be used to list all DLLs for a given process in memory and find DLLs injected with the CreateRemoteThread and LoadLibrary technique. This technique does not hide the DLL and therefore will not be detected by the plugin malfind as seen in Table 41.12.

Employing Advanced Process Analysis Methods

Processes can be analyzed using tools, such as the Windows Management Instrumentation (WMI), and walking dependency trees.

Evaluating Processes with Windows Management Instrumentation (WMI)

WMI is a set of extensions to the Windows Driver Model that provides an OS interface where components can provide information and notifications. The WMI classes Win32_Process can help collect useful information about processes. The Windows command wmic extends WMI for operation from several command-line interfaces and through batch scripts without having to rely on any other programming language. The command wmic uses class aliases to query related information. It can be executed remotely as well as locally by specifying target node or host name and credentials. Various commands that can be used to extract various process-related information through wmic are shown in Table 41.13.

WMI output can be used to get a clean baseline of a system to periodically run comparisons. The comparisons can show any new process that has appeared on the system, and can help to update the baseline if the new process is a known one.

Walking Dependency Trees

Viewing the dependencies of a process can provide valuable information about the functionality a process contains. A process's dependencies may be composed of various Windows modules, such as executables, DLLs, object linking and embedding control extension (OCX) files; SYS files (mostly real-mode device drivers). Walking a dependency tree means to explore a process's dependencies in a hierarchal view, such as a tree. The free tool Dependency Walker provides an interface that presents such a view, which is shown in Fig. 41.8.

It lists all of the functions that are exported by a given Windows module, and the functions that are actually being called by other modules. Another view displays the minimum set of required files, along with detailed information

TABLE 41.9 Use of the Threads Plugin

```
$ python vol.py threads -f /memory_samples/tigger.vmem -F OrphanThread

Volatile Systems Volatility Framework 2.2_alpha

[x86] Gathering all referenced SSDTs from KTHREADs...

Finding appropriate address space for tables...

------

ETHREAD: 0xff1f92b0 Pid: 4 Tid: 1648

Tags: OrphanThread,SystemThread

Created: 2010-08-15 19:26:13

Exited: 1970-01-01 00:00:00

Owning Process: System

Attached Process: System

State: Waiting:DelayExecution

BasePriority: 0x8

Priority: 0x8

TEB: 0x00000000

StartAddress: 0xf2edd150 UNKNOWN

ServiceTable: 0x80552180

  [0] 0x80501030

  [1] 0x00000000

  [2] 0x00000000

  [3] 0x00000000

Win32Thread: 0x00000000

CrossThreadFlags: PS_CROSS_THREAD_FLAGS_SYSTEM

0xf2edd150 803d782aeff200    CMP BYTE [0xf2ef2a78], 0x0

0xf2edd157 7437              JZ 0xf2edd190

0xf2edd159 56                PUSH ESI

0xf2edd15a bef0d0edf2        MOV ESI, 0xf2edd0f0

0xf2edd15f ff35702aeff2      PUSH DWORD [0xf2ef2a70]

0xf2edd165 ff                DB 0xff

0xf2edd166 15                DB 0x15

0xf2edd167 0c                DB 0xc

...
```

TABLE 41.10 Use of the Apihooks Plugin to Detect Hooking

```
$ python vol.py -f coreflood.vmem -p 2015 apihooks

Volatile Systems Volatility Framework 2.1_alpha

**************************************************************************

Hook mode: Usermode

Hook type: Import Address Table (IAT)

Process: 2015 (IEXPLORE.EXE)

Victim module: iexplore.exe (0x400000 - 0x419000)

Function: kernel32.dll!GetProcAddress at 0x7ff82360

Hook address: 0x7ff82360

Hooking module: <unknown>


Disassembly(0):

0x7ff82360 e8fbf5ffff          CALL 0x7ff81960

0x7ff82365 84c0                TEST AL, AL

0x7ff82367 740b                JZ 0x7ff82374

0x7ff82369 8b150054fa7f        MOV EDX, [0x7ffa5400]

0x7ff8236f 8b4250              MOV EAX, [EDX+0x50]

0x7ff82372 ffe0                JMP EAX

0x7ff82374 8b4c2408            MOV ECX, [ESP+0x8]

...
```

about each file including a full path to the file, base address, version numbers, machine type, and debug information. Dependency Walker can be used in conjunction with the tool Process Explorer (a free Microsoft tool) to detect malicious DLLs. This can be achieved by comparing the DLL list in Process Explorer to the imports displayed by the Dependency Walker.

Auditing Processes and Services

Auditing changes in process and service properties as well as their counts on a system can provide valuable information to an investigator about potentially malicious activity. Rootkits, viruses, Trojans, and other malicious software can be detected by auditing process and service creation or deletion across a period of time. This technique is frequently used in malware behavioral analysis in

sandboxes. We can audit Windows processes and services by using tools that utilize system APIs or system memory for live analysis. To view information through the system APIs we can use the tool Process Hacker. The Process Hacker provides a live view of processes and services that are currently being executed or present on the system. It provides an interface to view and search process information in detail, such as process privileges, related users and groups, DLLs loaded, handles opened, and thread information, which is shown in Fig. 41.9. Service information can also be viewed in the services tab. Process and service information can be saved periodically and compared across time to detect any suspicious variations.

System memory can also be analyzed with the Volatility Framework for audit purposes. Periodic memory samples can be obtained using tools, such as F-response, MoonSols Windows Memory Toolkit, or GMG Systems' KnTDD. The

TABLE 41.11 Use of the Malfind Plugin to Discover Injected Code

```
$ python vol.py -f zeus.vmem malfind -p 1645

Volatile Systems Volatility Framework 2.1_alpha


Process: explorer.exe Pid: 1645 Address: 0x1600000

Vad Tag: VadS Protection: PAGE_EXECUTE_READWRITE

Flags: CommitCharge: 1, MemCommit: 1, PrivateMemory: 1, Protection: 6


0x01600000  b8 35 00 00 00 e9 cd d7 30 7b b8 91 00 00 00 e9   .5......0{......

0x01600010  4f df 30 7b 8b ff 55 8b ec e9 ef 17 c1 75 8b ff   O.0{..U......u..

0x01600020  55 8b ec e9 95 76 bc 75 8b ff 55 8b ec e9 be 53   U....v.u..U....S

0x01600030  bd 75 8b ff 55 8b ec e9 d6 18 c1 75 8b ff 55 8b   .u..U......u..U.


0x1600000 b835000000         MOV EAX, 0x35

0x1600005 e9cdd7307b         JMP 0x7c90d7d7

0x160000a b891000000         MOV EAX, 0x91

0x160000f e94fdf307b         JMP 0x7c90df63

0x1600014 8bff               MOV EDI, EDI

0x1600016 55                 PUSH EBP
```

Volatility Framework plugin pslist can be used to audit processes while the plugin svcscan can be used to audit services.

Investigating the Process Table

The process table (PT) is a data structure kept by the OS to help context switching, scheduling, and other activities. Each entry in the PT, called process context blocks (PCB), contains information about a process, such as process name and state, priority, and PID. The exact content of a context block depends on the OS. For example, if the OS supports paging, then the context block contains a reference to the page table. While to a user a process is identified by the PID, in the OS the process is represented by entries in the PT. The process control block is a large data structure that contains information about a specific process. In Linux this data structure is called task_struct whereas in Windows it is called an EPROCESS structure. Each EPROCESS structure contains a LIST_ENTRY structure called ActiveProcessLinks, which contains a link to the previous (Blink) EPROCESS structure and the next (Flink) EPROCESS structure.

A listing of processes represented in the PT can be obtained by using the plugin pslist in the Volatility Framework. This plugin generates its output by walking the doubly linked list. Certain malware or malicious users can hide processes by unlinking them from this linked list by performing direct kernel object manipulation (DKOM). To detect this kind of behavior, the Volatility Framework plugin psscan can be used since it relies on scanning the memory to detect pools similar to that of an EPROCESS structure instead of walking the linked list.

Discovering Evidence in the Registry

We have already covered one method to inject code into a process. Another method is to add a value in the AppInit_DLLs registry key (HKEY_LOCAL_MACHINE\-Software\Microsoft\Windows NT\CurrentVersion\Windows\AppInit_DLLs) that makes a new process to load a DLL of malicious origin (table XXX).

AppInit_DLLs is a mechanism that allows an arbitrary list of DLLs to be loaded into each user mode process on

TABLE 41.12 Use of the Dlllist Plugin to Detect DLL Injection

```
$ python vol.py dlllist -f sample.vmem -p 468

Volatile Systems Volatility Framework 2.2_alpha

************************************************************************

wuauclt.exe pid:    468

Command line : "C:\WINDOWS\system32\wuauclt.exe"

Service Pack 2


Base            Size Path
----------  ---------- ----

0x00400000    0x1e000 C:\WINDOWS\system32\wuauclt.exe

0x7c900000    0xb0000 C:\WINDOWS\system32\ntdll.dll

0x7c800000    0xf4000 C:\WINDOWS\system32\kernel32.dll

0x77c10000    0x58000 C:\WINDOWS\system32\msvcrt.dll

0x76b20000    0x11000 C:\WINDOWS\system32\ATL.DLL

0x77d40000    0x90000 C:\WINDOWS\system32\USER32.dll

0x77f10000    0x46000 C:\WINDOWS\system32\GDI32.dll

0x77dd0000    0x9b000 C:\WINDOWS\system32\ADVAPI32.dll

0x77e70000    0x91000 C:\WINDOWS\system32\RPCRT4.dll

...
```

TABLE 41.13 List of Windows Management Instrumentations (WMI) Commands to Get Process Information

`wmic /node: /user: process where get ExecutablePath,parentprocessid`	Find the path to a specific running executable and its parent process (for all, leave off 'where name=')
`wmic /node: /user: process where get name,processid,commandline,creationdate`	Find command-line invocation of a specific executable as well as the creation time for the process (for all, leave off 'where name=').
`wmic startup list full`	Find all files loaded at start-up and the registry keys associated with autostart.
`wmic process list brief | find "cmd.exe"`	Search for a specific process name, such as cmd.exe

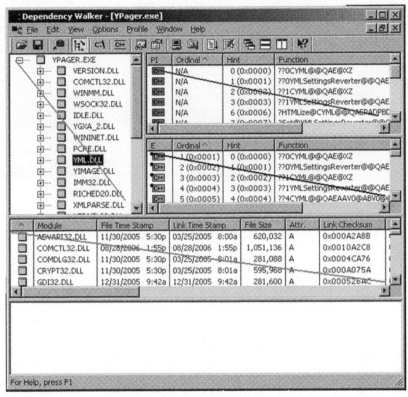

FIGURE 41.8   Using the Dependency Walker.

the system. Although a code-signing requirement was added in Windows 7 and Windows Server 2008 R2, it is still being utilized by various malicious software to hide and persist on a system.

The Volatility Framework can also be used to analyze the registry that has been loaded to memory. The plugins that are available from the Volatility Framework for registry analysis are shown in Table 41.14.

A listing of services can be obtained from the registry in memory from the registry key "HKEY_LOCAL_MACHI-NE\SYSTEM\CurrentControlSet\Services." This key contains the database of services and device drivers that get read into the Windows service control manager's (SCM) internal database. SCM is a remote procedure call (RPC) server that interacts with the Windows service processes.

Other registry keys that might be of interest are the keys located in the registry key "HKEY_LOCAL_MACHINE\ SOFTWARE\ Microsoft\ Windows\CurrentVersion." The keys that are part of the autostart registries are "Run," "Run-Once," "RunOnceSetup," "RunOnceEx," "RunServices," and "RunServicesOnce". Malware can set values in these keys to persist across system restarts and get loaded during system start up.

Deploying and Detecting a Rootkit

Rootkits are composed of several tools (scripts, binaries, and configuration files) that permit malicious users to

hide their actions on a system so they can control and monitor the system for an indefinite time. Rootkits can be installed either through an exploit payload or installed after system access has been achieved. Rootkits are usually used to provide concealment, command and control (C2), and surveillance. A rootkit most of the time will try to hide system resources, such as processes, Registry information, files, and network ports. API hooking is a popular rootkit technique that intercepts system calls to make the OS report inaccurate results that conceal the presence of the rootkit. To skip all of the system-level subversion, we can look into the memory directly to detect rootkits. The Volatility Framework provides various plugins to detect rootkit concealment techniques as seen in Table 41.15:

10. SUMMARY

In this chapter we have seen the importance of having a well-documented incident response plan and process, and having an incident response team that is experienced in cyber forensics analysis. Besides having these important components, an organization needs to have strong policies and procedures that back them. Incident response is not only about countering the incident, but also about learning from it and improving on the weaknesses exposed. We should always keep in mind that preparedness is paramount since it is a matter of when rather than if an incident will strike.

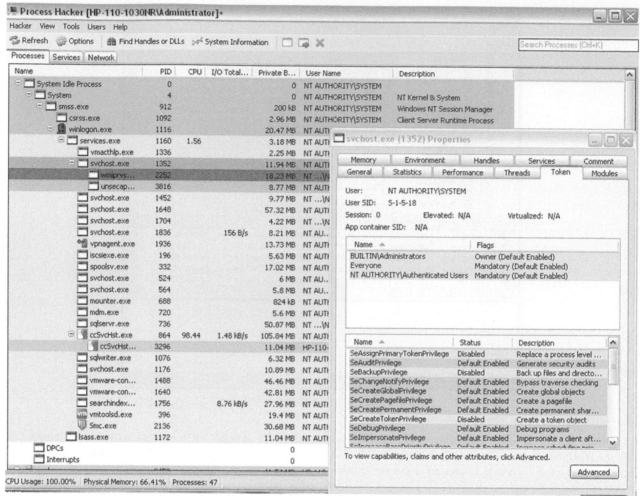

FIGURE 41.9 Using Process Hacker to view process and service information.

TABLE 41.14 List of Volatility Framework Plugins to Extract Registry Information From Memory

hivescan	Finds the physical address of CMHIVE structures, which represent a registry hives in memory.
hivelist	Takes a physical address of one CMHIVE, returns the virtual address of all hives, and their names.
printkey	Takes a virtual address of a hive and a key name (e.g., 'ControlSet001\Control'), and display the key's timestamp, values, and subkeys.
hashdump	Dump the LanMan and NT hashes from the registry.
lsadump	Dump the LSA secrets (decrypted) from the registry.
cachedump	Dump any cached domain password hashes from the registry.

Looking into the near future, the amount of data that needs to be gathered and analyzed is increasing rapidly and as a result we are seeing the emergence of big-data analytics tools that can process disparate data sources to deal with large cases. Tomorrow's incident response teams will need to be skilled in statistical analysis as well as forensics to be able to navigate in this increasingly hostile and expanding cyberspace. As you can see, incident response and cyber forensics needs to be a step ahead of the potential causes of threats, risks, and exploits.

Finally, let's move on to the real interactive part of this Chapter: review questions/exercises, hands-on projects,

TABLE 41.15 List of Volatility Framework Plugins to Detect Rootkit Hooking

Rootkit Technique	The Volatility Framework Plugin
IAT (import address table) hooks	apihooks: detect overwritten IAT entry for a PE file
EAT (export address table) hooks	apihooks
Inline application program interface (API) hooks	apihooks
IDT (interrupt descriptor table) hooks	idt: detects overwritten IDT entries that point to malicious interrupts ot processor exceptions
Driver IRP (I/O request packets) hooks	driverirp: detects overwritten IRP function table entries (modified to monitor buffer data)
SSDT (system service descriptor table) hooks	ssdt: detects hooking of pointers to kernel mode functions in the SSDT that occurs per thread
Hiding with orphan threads in kernel	threads: detects orphan threads that can unlinking or unloading its driver

case projects, and optional team case project. The answers and/or solutions by chapter can be found in Appendix K.

CHAPTER REVIEW QUESTIONS/ EXERCISES

True/False

1. True or False? Cyber forensics and incident response go hand in hand.
2. True or False? In an organization there is a daily occurrence of events within the IT infrastructure, but not all of these events qualify as incidents.
3. True or False? Forensic analysis is not usually applied to determine who, what, when, where, how, and why an incident took place.
4. True or False? When an incident response team comes across incidents relevant to these laws, they should consult with their legal team.
5. True or False? An organization should be prepared beforehand to properly respond to incidents and mitigate them in the longest time possible.

Multiple Choice

1. How do incident response and cyber forensics fit together?
   A. They don't
   B. Incident response helps cyber forensics in analyzing evidence
   C. Cyber forensics provides answers to questions that need to be answered for proper incident response
   D. None of the above
   E. All of the above
2. Which option might be classified as an incident?
   A. Phishing attack
   B. Unauthorized access
   C. Intellectual property theft
   D. Denial of service attack
   E. All of the above
3. Which one should be considered volatile data and captured immediately?
   A. Configuration files
   B. Database files
   C. Documents
   D. System memory
   E. All of the above
4. Which considerations would be involved in monitoring employee email?
   A. Technical factors
   B. Legal factors
   C. Organizational factors
   D. All of the above
   E. None of the above
5. Which tool can be used to extract the MFT of a Windows system from a drive?
   A. The Sleuth Kit
   B. The Volatility Framework
   C. The KntDD
   D. Truecrypt
   E. All of the above

EXERCISE

Problem

How does an organization ship their hard drives?

Hands-On Projects

Project

How does an organization get their data back?

Case Projects

Problem

As an exercise to practice what you have learned in this chapter, you will analyze your own Windows workstation:

1. Create an image of your disc drive and save it to an external drive using AccessData FTK Imager.
2. Create a memory sample from your system using MoonSols Windows Memory Toolkit and save it to an external drive.
3. Create a super timeline of the disc image using log2timeline and list the files created within 24 h.
4. Using the Volatility Framework, get a list of the following objects from the memory sample: processes, DLLs, modules, services, connections, sockets, API hooks.

Optional Team Case Project

Problem

When should an organization consider using a computer forensic examiner?

REFERENCES

[1] Disk Imaging Tool Specification, NIST, 2001.
[2] Guide to Integrating Forensic Techniques into Incident Response, NIST, 2006.

Chapter 42

Securing e-Discovery

Scott R. Ellis

kCura Corporation, Chicago, IL, United States

Few if any corporations are exempt from litigation. For some, the risk of litigation far outweighs the cost associated with managing and structuring their internal information systems in such a way as to facilitate discovery actions. In other words, the cost of doing "business as usual" in the event of large-scale litigation can actually bankrupt a company. Preparedness to respond swiftly and accurately to discovery requests can prevent costly processing and overly inclusive review. In the legal industry, any request for information typically arrives in the form of a court-ordered "discovery request." Essentially, when one organization sues another, each is allowed to request the disclosure of any relevant documents relating to the litigated matter. For some corporations, these actions occur daily. For them, adhering to some sort of framework of security that allows them to engage and respond to such requests quickly becomes extremely important. Many models exist that outline and assist in defining the entire process of electronic discovery, such as the Electronic Discovery Reference Model (EDRM).[1] This chapter does not aspire to redefine, reorganize, or even correct or suggest a need for correction in any such model.

The field of e-discovery relates to litigation as a whole (see checklist: "An Agenda for Action for Discovery of Electronic Evidence"). At some point, most aspects of civil lawsuits will brush up against the EDRM, whether civil or criminal. There has been deeper adoption and application of the Federal Rules of Civil Procedure (FRCP) by criminal courts as well. Cultivating an understanding of the FRCP therefore becomes a necessity for any attorney who wishes to practice law in the federal court system.

It thus follows that corporations should also develop a similar, if not deeper, awareness of the EDRM life cycle. Although this chapter acknowledges and makes reference

to regulatory and legal compliance requirements, it does not seek to explain them or detail them. Such legal, risk, and compliance issues are going to be industry dependent. First on any e-discovery manager's list should be the need to discover whether data (and what data!) should be preserved beyond the scope of immediate purposefulness. Fig. 42.1 presents the basic diagram of the EDRM life cycle.

When one organization sues another, both may become subject to a court requirement that they preserve any information pertaining to the matter. Even a letter from an opposing attorney requesting that the defendant secure and "hold" any documents that may pertain to the matter (and even in the case of a threatening letter that does not specifically request a hold when the circumstances indicate a reasonable likelihood of litigation) may trigger a need to preserve information, because litigation may be imminent. In the United States, the process of collecting, processing, reviewing, and producing this body, this collective corpus of "documents" that may contain email, images, executables, databases, text files, documents, spreadsheets, structured systems, and so on, which may be relevant to the litigation, is commonly called "discovery." Essentially, *anything*, any potentially relevant information that exists in electronic form, is fair game. Furthermore, in some industries there may be regulatory compliance laws that dictate the length of time that data must be preserved. One such example is Sarbanes–Oxley (SOX),[2] which states:

> *Whoever knowingly alters, destroys, mutilates, conceals, covers up, falsifies, or makes a false entry in any record, document, or tangible object with the intent to impede, obstruct, or influence the investigation or proper administration of any matter within the jurisdiction of any department or agency of the United States or any case filed*

---

1. EDRM (edrm.net).

2. Section 802(a) of the SOX, 18 USC 1519.

An Agenda for Action for Discovery of Electronic Evidence

The cyber forensics specialist should ensure that the following are adhered to (check all tasks completed):

_____**1.** Do not alter discovered information.

_____**2.** Always back up discovered information.

_____**3.** Document all investigative activities.

_____**4.** Accumulate the computer hardware and storage media necessary for the search circumstances.

_____**5.** Prepare the electronic means needed to document the search.

_____**6.** Ensure that specialists are aware of the overall forms of information evidence that are expected to be encountered as well as the proper handling of this information.

_____**7.** Evaluate the current legal ramifications of information discovery searches.

_____**8.** Back up the information discovery file or files.

_____**9.** Start the lab evidence log.

_____**10.** Mathematically authenticate the information discovery file or files.

_____**11.** Proceed with the forensic examination.

_____**12.** Find the MD5 message digest for the original information discovery file or files.

_____**13.** Log all message digest values in the lab evidence log.

_____**14.** When forensic work is complete, regenerate the message digest values using the backups on which work was performed; log these new values alongside the hashes that were originally generated. If the new values match the originals, it is reasonable to conclude that no evidence tampering took place during the forensic examination of the information file(s).

_____**15.** Briefly compare the physical search and seizure with its logical (data-oriented) counterpart, information discovery.

---

under title 11, or in relation to or contemplation of any such matter or case, shall be fined under this title, imprisoned not more than 20 years, or both.

There are, in fact, *criminal* penalties for getting this wrong, in addition to civil monetary sanctions. Technologists should be aware that the regulations exist, and they should ensure that their organizations are compliant by working with a qualified law firm or legal department. Mountains of this sort of regulatory legalese exist. Whether it applies to your organization is important to the work and the level of security detailed in this chapter and to its implementation. Understanding all of the challenges of regulatory compliance in your organization will likely be a departmental or cross-departmental responsibility; that is, an entire department or team will provide oversight of this increasingly important aspect of conducting business.

The EDRM model and its accompanying diagram represent just *one* way of how data may flow from an information system to a discovery information system, to a courtroom. The large box in Fig. 42.2 represents the confines of a discovery information system. Shaded boxes represent zone boundaries where information may move from one vendor to another. Dotted line boxes are used to refer to areas of interest or to break out details or suggest technologies. In this example, overlapping zones identify areas of functionality where data are passed from one vendor to the next. Some vendors service Zones 1–6, but in this example each zone represents a different vendor handling data. A similar, real diagram of a corporate EDRM would attach a similar diagram, complete with vendor names and data transfer protocols, to an EDRM procedure document for each and every case in which data may be processed using different vendors. For security

purposes, it is wisest to keep the number of vendors to a minimum, with set and established data conduits.

There are disparate, often overlapping zones in this diagram because it is common for multiple vendors to be involved in processing data in a lawsuit. This is done because few vendors perform the work required in all zones. From start to finish, from standard information management strategies through presenting data in the courtroom, few if any can do everything and do it well. Even fewer corporations manage any of this work internally. Later, this chapter will refer back to the numbers on the boxes and will describe the various security measures taken at each zone interface, as well as the benefits of shifting certain work to fewer vendors or moving certain tasks to internal, corporate information technology (IT). Some of this fragmentation can also be attributed to the defibrillating effect of the change in the Federal Rules on the entire paper discovery industry in 2006. Many of these small e-discovery shops already existed but were amped up by the sudden demand for their services. So, rather than use the EDRM as one (and perhaps the most accurate) example, this chapter:

1. Explains it from an industry insider perspective;
2. Collates issues of performance, urgency, accuracy, risk, and security to a zoned model that underpins the EDRM;
3. Explains the real need for organizations to secure certain operations internally;
4. Provides examples through real-world experiences of flawed discovery and what should have been done differently; and
5. Discusses how security *from* the information, as well as security *of* it, has a critical role throughout much of the EDRM.

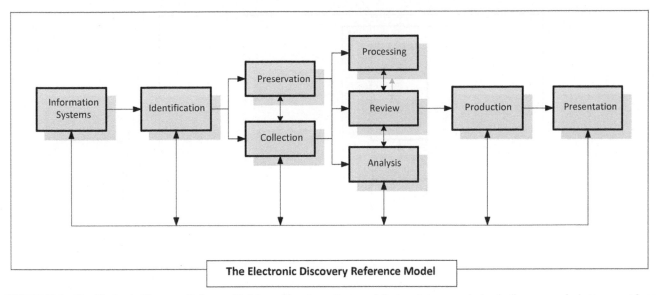

FIGURE 42.1 The Electronic Discovery Reference Model provides a loose framework for how to manage electronic discovery and what to expect from a process viewpoint.

1. INFORMATION MANAGEMENT

The framework of the EDRM begins with information management. Much in the same way that a model for e-discovery exists, an information governance reference model exists as well that pays particular attention to the needs of an IT management organization that concerns itself, and prepares itself, for possible future litigation. To be successful, information management must consider all stakeholders in an environment; it must apply successful collaboration across all groups in an enterprise; it must consider the security of the data and protection of systems; and it must engage IT to implement the procedures and guidelines created. It must also be secure. There is no worse feeling than the sinking sensation you will feel than when anonymous hacks your systems and posts your entire discovery database online, along with your chief executive officer's (CEO's) email box.

2. LEGAL AND REGULATORY OBLIGATION

Certain types of organizations are more likely than others to be prone to litigation. This means that they must operate at a heightened sense of awareness as it pertains to e-discovery processes. In particular, law firms have both ethical and legal obligations to protect client confidential data. Guidelines pertaining to the security requirements and the specific safeguards required by law all are outlined in the FRCP. This chapter is not meant to replace that. Rather, it seeks to familiarize its readers with the basic flow of information throughout a lawsuit so that proper security can be executed. Without knowledge and deep understanding of the inner workings of a lawsuit and the functions that are

required for the successful management of it, security will surely fail.

Securing the Field of Play

This chapter is titled "Securing E-Discovery," but it has much broader-reaching implications. Just about any organization may be subject to litigation. What, then, is a security model if it is one that does not anticipate litigation? A security model that does not anticipate the possible need to collect large amounts of data, port it into other systems, and ensure that the data are relevant risks being unresponsive to a request from the court and possible noncompliance with an order from a judge. Much in the same way that not knowing the speed limit will not get you out of a ticket, not knowing how or where your data are stored will not prevent a judge from sending someone else to your offices to show you how your systems interoperate. This person will be an expert, probably chosen by the opposition, and interviewed by the judge, and you will be paying his bill, which may be as much as $400/h or higher. What follows are several steps to:

- Assess, evaluate, and remediate the current state of security and discovery preparedness;
- Get things in order; and
- Set the stage for data collection and effective response to a discovery request.

Step 1: Examine the Information Management Environment

Are you secure? Your internal systems may be a mess of disparate data and IT fiefdoms, but first, let us close the doors

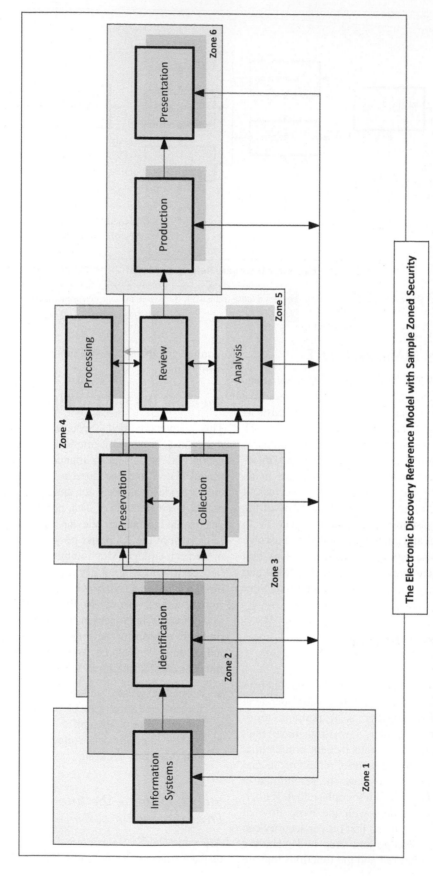

The Electronic Discovery Reference Model with Sample Zoned Security

FIGURE 42.2 Underpinning the Electronic Discovery Reference Model with zone security throughout the electronic discovery life cycle.

and staunch the flow. Areas where sensitive data or easily obtained access to sensitive data stores should be secured:

- Physical security: Common areas such as lunchrooms that may have external access should never be unstaffed. Reception areas that have front door access or may have corridors that lead to other areas should also be secured with as follows:
  - Biometric security for physical access to sensitive data areas
  - Background checks
  - A visible photo badge policy
  - A visitor policy that includes visible visitor photo ID badges
- Data center International Organization for Standardization 9001 security.
- Firewalls should be configured with the most minimal access possible.
- Antivirus should be nonintrusive and should aim at points of ingress. File repositories should run scheduled scans. Virus signature databases are frequently updated; a file that is clean today may trip an alert after a signature update. Entire system scans should be scheduled jobs that run during nightly or weekly maintenance.
- Acceptable use policy: Users are the number one incursion vector. Ensure that your acceptable use policy is well-formed and *understood.*
- Response plans: What do we do when someone we do not know tries to tailgate us into the office? What do we do when tables are suddenly missing in our database?

Step 2: Measure: How Secure Is the System?

Penetration testing should be performed against the enterprise systems. Any organization that wishes to conduct collections must understand that sensitive data will be copied and corralled into a new area. This area should be secured. If any one of these steps is not followed, as an IT director you will almost certainly come into work and find that the penetration team has placed a chocolate cake on your desk and changed your desktop image. The organization that will conduct the penetration testing should be testing the following things:

1. Internal, physical penetration: Can they put someone at a desktop and access the system? Can they insert "malicious" code into your system? This may be as simple as accessing the basic input—output system of a machine, changing the boot order, and booting a new machine on your network
2. Penetration testing of any and all external facing software, especially websites
3. Internal penetration testing: Can internal systems be breached by someone sitting at a desktop, with varying levels of access?
4. Penetration testing of any critical Software as a Service (SAAS) system. For example, if the testers can trick the human resources (HR) director into logging into a spoofed or cross-site scripted payroll site that contains sensitive employee data, a flaw exists in your security system.
5. Penetration testing of known services that protect essential data: Ensure that they cannot be hacked easily. Many methods for hacking services such as Amazon Cloud or ADP are easy to spot. All SAAS providers should have implemented or be in the process of implementing two-factor authentication. If they are not, your data should not be there and should be moved.
6. Examine the virtual local area network architecture in both virtual and physical topologies. Virtual switches offer a whole host of challenges of which many IT administrators are unaware.
7. Socially engineered attacks: Most attacks have a social component. The attacker knows what he wants, he knows who works at the company, and he knows their name, too. Or it may be completely impersonal, and the hacker simply saw an email address he liked and wanted to play with it.
8. Stolen and lost access badges: The easiest way to access a building is if you have a radio-frequency identification (RFID) pass. Criminals know that the badges that workers wear can get them unquestioned access to a building. As a bonus, the badges are easy to steal (people wear them dangling from their clothing and often even drop them on the street; this author has found at least three potentially all-access badges on the streets of Chicago.) Badges can certainly contain a photo; but name, workplace, address, and so on should be encoded in the chip. There should be a mail-to address on the card that *is not* the same as the location to which the card grants access.

Step 3: Remediate Issues

Number 4 is perhaps the most important item in this list. Most penetrations that result in loss of data are socially engineered and at some stage will include some social element. Someone will receive an email with a link that will take the user to a spoofed Web page where the users will log in, thinking they are logging into their own systems.

Example

Mattie, an internal HR director, uses a custom-built payroll system that is built on top of a known technology. The password reset notifications sent out by the system *always look the same.* The hacker is aware of the system used. Perhaps he used to be an employee or a contractor. Perhaps he saw it on the software vendor's website and thought that Mattie's company was a client. He then culled Mattie's name from a published employee directory. Or maybe he worked out her email address by calling and asking questions about employment. It does not matter. He gets in by sending Mattie an email that appears to be from an internal email address. Its header has been forged. The email claims that multiple attempts have been made to log in using Employee x's login, and she will need to reset the password. The email provides a link to the "system." Mattie follows the link, sees her internal login screen, enters HER login information, and is immediately redirected to her internal login screen. She blinks and says to herself, "That's odd, didn't I just log in?"

Mattie is pretty savvy. Her company has a security training program. She immediately logs in and changes her password, and then reports the incident. The hacker had her login credentials momentarily, and if not for her quick thinking, he would have used them to export the entire payroll successfully, which he then would have held hostage or simply posted on the Internet.

How do you stop this sort of thing from happening? Spam filters may be able to trap these emails, but what if it comes in on a personal account? Most people would just raise their eyebrows and say, "That's interesting," and chances are good they would not follow it, but you cannot count on it. One step would be not to give the outside world access to internal, sensitive systems. Then the redirect would fail, and even if the hacker traps the sign-on, he has to breach the physical location. Another way to prevent it would be to ensure two-factor authentication.

There are loopholes in any external-facing system. Wherever a human being interfaces with an electronic system, this is an avenue of ingress that can be exploited. A seemingly secure operation such as entering a password and checking a fob on a keychain or a text message on a cell phone to access a system has a weakness. There is a password that remains constant, which means it can be observed or logged, and there is a keychain or cell phone that can be stolen, cloned, or replaced. In addition, many different types of accounts can be *linked* together now, and hackers can daisy chain enough information together from the different password hints provided by these accounts that they can successfully leapfrog right into secure areas.

Gaining access to one employee's Twitter account could conceivably be the single breach a hacker needs to be able to gain access to all of corporate systems, especially if the victim has access to everything and passwords set to automatic on his laptop, has linked password recovery of corporate accounts to both personal and work email addresses, and is someone who has an active part in the online community and a high level of visibility.

Here are some security items that should be ensured in each zone. Later, this chapter will explain the specific vulnerabilities of each zone while describing how to collapse the zones to more manageable, securable corridors:

1. Examine the security policy *as it exists today*. Do not just document how it should be and tell everyone how

it should be. Rather, show them how it is and tell them what to stop doing. Better yet, *stop them*. Do not allow employees to use their work email addresses in any non-work related capacity. Do not let them use their personal email addresses on corporate systems.
2. Do not allow employees to use their personal email addresses as password recovery points for any work-related systems.
3. Office systems should never be accessed from personal laptops, which may be unsecured or may have lapsed antivirus. If circumstances necessitate this allowance, provide licenses to antivirus and firewall technologies to employees for free. After all, they are accessing work systems and ostensibly performing work while at home from personal systems. If the corporation cannot see the wisdom in providing security, disallow it and take the productivity hit.
4. Enforce work–personal email uniqueness. Somebody1@website1.com should not be under the same user as somebody1@website2.com. For example, your work email and personal email address prefixes must be different.
5. Do use encrypted tunnels, Advanced Encryption Standard (AES) 256 entire-drive encryption, and secure messenger services for moving sensitive data.

Securing e-discovery data will be challenging, and there will be many hurdles to overcome. Human behavior (changing it) presents the greatest challenge. Infallible controls must be put into place to protect these data, because they will likely represent the most sensitive data in the organization. Successful information management will facilitate the identification and securing of relevant data. Relevancy will have a key part in this process. Take the approach that there is an existing compromise, that there is already someone in your network. Minimize risk of exposure as much as possible: They cannot get what is not there.

Identification

The EDRM model breaks identification into a separate phase of e-discovery from information management. This was perhaps for ease and beautification of the EDRM diagram. From a fountainhead perspective, information management most certainly belongs in this position on the EDRM diagram. However, from a physical management perspective, information management encompasses the entire spectrum of the EDRM life cycle, with each segment along the way underscored by an information management system. Securing e-discovery then becomes a matter of interfacing and connecting to disparate information management systems that are designed to perform different tasks, or it becomes a matter of absorbing those systems into the collective corporate information system.

For very large or highly litigated corporations faced with a new lawsuit every day, it is not a matter of whether they will save money by bringing e-discovery internally; it is a matter of *how much*. By doing this, by bringing the identification systems in-house, corporations can then create a security cordon that contains the team infrastructure, the software used to identify relevant data, and the access and permission controls to the identification system, which should tie directly to its users. Typically this would be the internal legal department. This cordoned system can then act as a launch pad for secure transmission corridors to vendors for further data processing.

For many corporations and many IT experts however, the term *legal hold* means little. From a high level, few corporations will be faced with litigation on a daily basis. There are several reasons for this:

1. They are not big enough to make it worthwhile.
2. They are transparent in what they do already.
3. They do not think that anything they are doing could ever cause a lawsuit to be filed.
4. They never thought they would need to sue another company.
5. The corporation is able to settle quickly any matters that arise.
6. It is a shell corporation, and the owners are untraceable.
7. Economically, the corporation would collapse after just one discovery motion, so they declare bankruptcy and fold.
8. They have not made yet anyone angry.

Generally, companies such as these do not concern themselves with e-discovery. However, some of them should. Item 3, in particular, causes many companies to be caught unawares. Some people simply do not realize that copying someone else's product is illegal, and they will even brag about it to complete strangers. These people are heading the wrong way down a one-way track. Any organization with revenues in the millions of dollars is likely doing something on a scale about which someone will notice, take offense, and file a suit.

Note: The Sedona Conference is an organization composed of leading judges and attorneys who provide guidelines and frameworks for the proper conduct of legal hold, as well as other e-discovery activities.

When faced with a litigation hold requirement, business stakeholders should inform their technologists of as many details of the lawsuit as possible. Key stakeholders in a legal action are:

- Officers of the corporation
- In-house counsel or other representation
- IT directors
- Managers of custodians

Each of these people should understand what makes a potential lawsuit. This will better enable both the attorneys and the information technologist to work together to produce the relevant documents.[3] What makes a potential lawsuit? Let us take a look[4]:

1. Something happens that causes loss of income, life, or injuries.
2. The corporation or person knew the potentially dangerous condition existed and had a legal duty to safeguard the damaged party.
3. The corporation did nothing and was not in the process of remedying it, and prevention would have been the normal practice of a "reasonably prudent party."

Many types of lawsuits fit this scenario. One example[5] would be of a school that runs its own bus service and offers safety training to its kindergarten children every year on the third day of school. Because it occurs at the end of the day on the third day of school, it means the children have *already* ridden the bus five times with no safety training. At the same time, prevailing practices among similar schools require safety training before using the bus.

Note: Optionally, what can make a lawsuit even stronger is if the corporation tried to hide what happened. Best-case scenario (for the plaintiff, not the defendant!) would be a case in which the plaintiff is awarded punitive damages owing to intentional misconduct. The author includes this information in part because it is interesting, and in part as a warning. Punitive damages may involve multiplying monetary damages, such as a tripling of the award.

One year, an incident occurs on the first day of school in which an older child convinces one of the kindergarteners that he needs to exit the bus at the next stop through the rear exit door while the bus is moving. He attempts to do it but is stopped by the bus driver. The parent of the child writes an angry letter to the school and advises the staff that they should be providing safety training *before* the kindergarteners are ever allowed on the bus. The school fears a

---

3. This is not to be interpreted as legal advice, but is based on the courtroom and work life experiences of the author, working and testifying within the federal and state judiciaries of the United States and with litigating attorneys for over a dozen years.
4. It follows, then, that a deeper understanding of the entire motivation and rationale behind these lawsuits will enable a system security architect to better anticipate and understand the nature of what is happening, and what is about to happen, to him, or rather, what is about to happen to his security model. The following examples closely parallel several of the lawsuits within which this author served as an expert witness. For exemplification and clarity, certain aspects of the cases, including the overall nature of each, have been changed. Where applicable, references to actual cases have been included for further study.
5. This and any other stories, unless referencing actual cases, are completely fictionalized accounts. Names, situations, and places have been changed.

lawsuit (even though no loss occurred) and the parent is put on an internal watch list as "litigious."

The school then thanks the parent for the letter but does nothing. The school fails actually to respond to the threat. This is because the school administrators did not understand the rules discussed earlier. Now, this incident is not actionable because there was no loss to society. However, a year passes by and on the first day of school the incident recurs, with the same, older child, and this time it leads to the injury of a kindergarten child and a lawsuit is filed. The parent of the child in the first incident informs the parent of the child in the second incident, and even provides him with a copy of the email he had sent. The email letter becomes the centerpiece in the lawsuit, but the school denies that the email was ever sent.

The plaintiffs are granted access to the school, and over a single weekend they create exact duplicate copies of every personal computer (PC) and server in the district. The judge in the case is convinced that the school network in its entirety was instrumental in the incident, and FRCP 37 covers this. Whether criminal charges will be filed remains on the table.

Unbeknownst to the defendants, the judge issues a civil search warrant that allows civilian experts (employed by the plaintiffs) to access the site and make forensic copies of all digital media located on the premises. This *includes* any thumb drives that employees may happen to be carrying on their person! To ensure that this civil search warrant is carried out, arrival on site is heralded by 20 black sport utility vehicles, a squad of fully armored and M16 rifle—carrying Federal US Marshals, which pulls up into the school parking lot at 3 p.m. on a Friday afternoon when school is being let out. The school computer system administrator is located and ordered by Federal Marshals to relinquish complete and total access, passwords, tokens, and so on. Now enter the e-discovery and forensic experts who will take the school's information systems apart piece by piece, and make forensic copies of every hard drive. They will render the entire school's information system subject to discovery.[6] Upon inspection of the systems, the experts locates a deleted copy of the email and dozens of

other complaints about the school safety system in general, all of which create sensational drama in front of the jury, and result in a judgment against the district of many millions of dollars.[7]

This situation plays out in courtrooms around the world on a daily basis. Companies are simply aggregations of humans trying to make money. Sometimes they engage in activities that are unsafe or illegal in an effort to save money (or make money). Sometimes these activities are activities that put others at risk.

A less distressing, and also fictional, example would be the case of *HappyFlyers v. MadFlyers*. MadFlyers is a small company that manufactures model remote control helicopters. Unfortunately, their engineer retires (he is not very good anyway), sales are slipping, and everyone is buying the competition's (Happy Flyers) helicopters, even though they are more expensive. MadFlyers CEO Gerardo Gutierrez purchases one of the Happy Flyers choppers and says, "What the heck!" and sends it off to his chop shop in China, where they reverse engineer it and make a near exact replica. MadFlyers then sells thousands of the helicopters for half the price. Unbeknownst to Gerardo, the CEO of Happy Flyers hears about this, visits one of his shops, and purchases one of the knock-off choppers. In addition, Gerardo is not the only one who copies the helicopter. Six other manufacturers also feel the heat and similarly copy patented sections of the Happy Flyers copter. Also unbeknownst to Gerardo is that he has crossed paths with a patent house. Basically, Happy Flyers is a shell company owned by a holding corporation that owns and protects many patents. The only actual work it does is to search the marketplace for potential violations of the patents it owns and new patents to purchase, and to file lawsuits when violations are found.

Gerardo finds himself subpoenaed and is asked to settle for an undisclosed amount. Of the seven companies that were targeted in this patent infringement suit, MadFlyers refuses to admit what they did. They claim they sold "only five or six" of the helicopters. They also claim that they are working to pull and find all the invoices from their system, but they are having trouble accessing it. Again and again, Gerardo claims the system is difficult to access and that reports cannot be run, that he has to go to the warehouse and do them one at a time, and so on. Ultimately, the judge allows an independent and neutral forensic examiner, escorted by Federal Marshals, to enter the Mad Flyers warehouse facility in California, where several servers and PCs are imaged.

Subsequently, in court, the expert testimony reveals that he uncovered nearly a million dollars' worth of sales of the phony copter and that the sales were recovered from the database as orphan line item records, meaning that the original order had been deleted, but because someone had

---

6. *Covad v. Revonet*: In a landmark decision, Mag. Judge Facciola reduced Revonet's arguments to dust when he ordered that the entire network was relevant to the action and ordered them to allow a team of Covad forensic experts to enter the Revonet Sioux Falls location and create exact, forensic copies of all PCs, laptops, and servers. Over 125 forensic images were created at a cost of many thousands of dollars. Ultimately, Revonet declared bankruptcy. Revonet failed to provide a believable and reliable basis for determining that only particular subsidiary databases contained relevant documents, thereby rendering the entire networked database, and this included all PCs, subject to the other party's expert forensic handling and searching for relevant documents (US District Court for the District of Columbia, Civil Action 06-1892-CKK-JMF, Document 95, Filed 05/27/2009).

---

7. Remember, this entire account is a fictionalized amalgamation of many cases and experiences of the author.

gone into the back end of the sales/order system to do it, and had done it incorrectly, the detail of each order remained behind, while from the front end, it would most likely appear that the sales never existed. The judge orders both parties to retire to a conference room and settle this matter, and he warns the defendant that *he will not like* the judgment that will be handed out should he fail to come back into the courtroom without a settlement. They settle for an undisclosed amount.

Identification thus becomes a matter of asking a number of questions. First, one must understand what is happening to him or her in a lawsuit, and the degree to which uncooperativeness will aggravate the situation and make the judge angry. Angry federal judges are not fun people. Do not make them angry. To facilitate the litigation hold process, many companies use legal hold software to manage the custodians and administer legal holds. A typical legal hold product will allow the legal hold administrator to perform the following identifications, and then inform the owners of the data, the *custodians*, to *hold* any and all relevant data to the matter. One piece of software, titled "Method," offers the following capabilities, which guide the hold administrator to input the correct information:

1. It will initiate the process of identifying *who the custodians are*: the people who have the data that are material or relevant[8] to the lawsuit.
2. Where are the data?
3. Are there backups, are there thumb drives floating around, etc.?
4. It will provide instructions for next actions.

The role of a security architect, a system administrator, a CIO, a chief technology officer, a technology director, and the like goes beyond simple security and encompasses a holistic security model and a level of awareness that demands attention to the facts at hand. This means that in the model laid out in Fig. 42.1, the interfaces of each zone must be identified and assessed. Mechanisms must be in place to deal with the movement of data, and the administrator must be equipped with a responsible, responsive

plan that he or she can engage when litigation becomes apparently imminent. The EDRM model may take different shapes and forms in differing types of litigation and reflect that no two IT infrastructures are built in the same way. In fact, we expect to see vast variations within just one information management system.

This chapter seeks to impart an understanding of the EDRM as it relates to information security. To do this, it underpins the structure of a lawsuit with the structure of a zoned security model, which will also vary substantially from one organization to the next and even from one lawsuit to the next. The point of this chapter is to provide an acceptable, sufficiently adaptable model whereby the flows of information between zones, and the type of information in motion, may be fully understood and modeled. Through a demonstration of how risk can be mitigated by adjusting the activities, the reader of this chapter should begin to understand how malleable this model is and how the various decisions made to hire vendors, purchase licenses for internal use, and hire internal or external counsel can have a deep impact on the overall security model.

Identification Integration

From a security standpoint, then, how do we plan? By securing information identified as relevant internally, and by developing policies and procedures that govern how information is retained, we can respond quickly and accurately to any demand for disclosure. In addition, we can do it while minimizing the risk of exposing the data in a vulnerable environment or unintentionally releasing data. A corporation can then prevent unauthorized delivery of sensitive personal and corporate information into the hands of strangers. This section is entitled "Identification Integration" because it discusses how to integrate an identification system into the information management segment of the EDRM. Ultimately, it is most secure for all zones to be collapsed into this segment because this is where the corporation can maintain the most complete control over the security of its information.

When the identification process is executed internally, as in Fig. 42.3, observe how the entirety of Zone 2 becomes encapsulated by Zone 1. Zone 3 then collapses into a simple, manageable form, leaving us with a fathomable disconnect between Zones 2 and 4. Zone 3 can then be treated as a secured conduit. Often, however, companies have no internal resources to which to turn when faced with e-discovery requests. E-discovery is a relatively new field that experienced a surge of growth and acceptance in December 2006 with the new FRCP, which finally formalized the consideration of electronic evidence and codified it into law. Since 2006, hundreds of companies that specialize in e-discovery management sprang into

---

8. Two words often confused with one another are *material* and *relevant*. Here is an example of this confusion: Elaine alleges that she remembers witnessing a certain event at a certain time and what she was wearing because it rained on Tuesday. Elaine, while walking outside on Tuesday, got soaking wet. She preserved her dress to prove that it rained on Tuesday. The dress is material in that it will be offered to prove a specific issue in the case. Elaine's testimony would then be relevant, because she will testify that she wore the dress on Tuesday, and it became wet because it rained. Relevancy tends to tie together one or more material facts. For example, testimony to prove that the dress is a dress, or that the dress is wet, would not be relevant. However, any information pertaining to the purchase of the dress, the type of dress, documentation about how wet it was, and so on might be deemed as being *responsive* to the matter, which means the documents are eligible for evaluation in the process of admitting evidence, and means they are "discoverable."

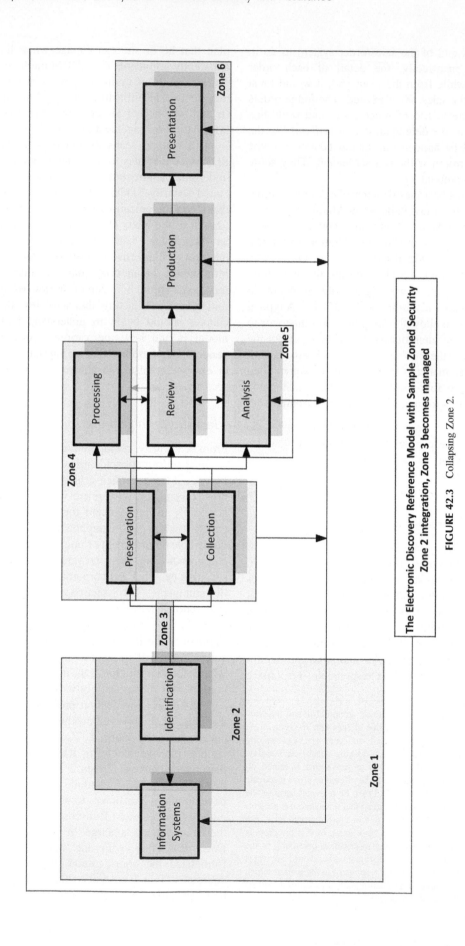

The Electronic Discovery Reference Model with Sample Zoned Security Zone 2 integration, Zone 3 becomes managed

FIGURE 42.3   Collapsing Zone 2.

existence. Many of these companies possess vast experience in the field, but some are simply once specialized in paper discovery and scrambled to hire anyone who has even a modicum of knowledge of the process so that they do not collapse along with the paper industry. They have populated their staff with "experts" who have insufficient skills in searching and culling techniques, and lack significant expertise in deploying infrastructure to support the Big Data lawsuits of this decade.

Such companies are not easily identified; they possess all of the tools and all of the staff, and they may even host large cases for big-name clients. However, software vendors that publish effective software solutions exist, and they may have some sort of "best of breed" programs. In these programs, clients are tested by the vendor to ensure that they possess the capability to manage the program successfully. Vendors will list these best of breed companies on their websites in special areas. The best software vendors will participate in programs such as Gartner's Magic Quadrant study. Every year, Gartner publishes a study of the competing players in almost all of the major technology markets. A firm grasp of the principles put forth in this chapter will provide the background needed to build a successful and defensible corporate EDRM implementation.

Securing Zone 1

Zone 2 in this model is now subsumed by Zone 1. This is not to say that the information in Zone 2 inherits the permissions of Zone 1. It still maintains its own rules, but it can do so using the same framework of information security that secures Zone 1. Security managers of Zone 1 may also manage items in Zone 2 because they have internalized the function of identification. Perhaps they have hired internal counsel and installed an appliance that allows them to capture and cull information that is deemed relevant. Perhaps the identification process was as simple as walking over to Joe's desk, pulling the plug on his PC, taking it to a secure area, and bagging and tagging it. When securing a computer that may be a pivotal item in a court case, standard, forensically sound procedures should always be used to secure it. Any further reads and writes to the drive will be deemed suspicious. Chapter 40 in this book, on cyber forensics, provides much greater detail on the procedures that should be used here.

Zone 2 notwithstanding, Zone 1 must then adopt some new standards of data security. In terms of defensibility, data must be preserved in a way that is customary and necessary for continued business operations. It makes no sense for some companies to retain 7 years' worth of email. For some companies, however, this may be necessary. Zone 1, the information management phase, encompasses all that a business must do simply to operate securely day to

day. When developing a model of security that incorporates e-discovery, consider that there is a new model of need. Consider that businesses have a hierarchy of needs similar to that of Maslow's.

In getting it right [like Maslow's hierarchy of needs (Fig. 42.4)], enterprises should focus on the most important tasks first: start at the bottom of the triangle and work toward the top. It makes no sense to be worrying about the nuances of converting .eml files to eXtensible Markup Language for more efficient storage if you do not know where all of your backup tapes are going or if your backups are even completing successfully.

Each layer of the triangle describes the phase of development. The items at the bottom of the triangle *must* be executed effectively before implementing process. Process that you implement on top of a fragmented or incomplete backup and the retention strategy will be forced to change or adapt later, and change is costly. Failure in this may also have deadly business consequences. Losing all of your responsive data in a lawsuit could be a business-ending event:

- **Evolution**: finding better ways to improve what you are doing. Be faster, better, and stronger. Do more in-house and do it more efficiently.
- **Process**: defining and understanding your information flow.
- **Standardization**: things such as making sure everyone uses the same software, stores information in the same places, and uses approved technology for information transmittals. Ensuring that the policies carried out on the bottom rung are understood, make sense, and adhere to business best practices.

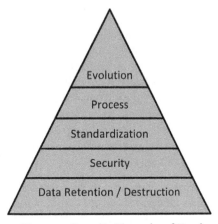

e-Discovery Security Hierarchy of Needs

FIGURE 42.4 Getting it right. Like Maslow's hierarchy of needs, enterprises need to focus on the most important tasks first: Start at the bottom of the triangle and work toward the top. It makes no sense to worry about the nuances of converting .eml files to eXtensible Markup Language for more efficient storage if you do not know where all of your backup tapes are going or even if your backups are completing successfully.

- **Security**: ensuring that you know your data are not walking out your front (or back) door.
- **Data retention/destruction**: ensuring that you are keeping what you want to keep, destroying what you do not want, and backing up data at risk.

Starting at the bottom and working up the pyramid, provide architects with a scalable model of data security. Alternatively, starting at the top and working to the bottom is similar to folding one's clothes before washing them. It makes little sense.

Securing Zone 2

Securing Zone 2 once it has been collapsed into Zone 1 then becomes a matter of definition. The breadth and scope of the discovery and the manner in which potentially relevant information will be identified all scream for a comprehensive plan. This plan should detail the steps needed to identify the following items of information:

1. Custodians.
2. Keywords or time periods of relevancy. Discerning this may be a matter of conducting interviews and documenting the location of data.
3. Do backups exist? What format?
4. Is all information accessible? Inaccessible information or data that have been destroyed *after they became apparent that litigation was likely* will present special challenges. It is important that all IT personnel understand that tampering with evidence may have dire consequences.

This phase is about identification. As it relates to security, the following items should be of interest and should be secured from distribution:

1. Have a strategy plan. All items should be marked with the words "Confidential" and "Attorneys' Eyes Only."
2. Create an Identification Team roster.
3. Plans and spreadsheets that detail source lists should be stored securely. Applications that can track media should be created.
4. Access to software used to initiate a legal hold should be password protected and only team members trained in its use should access it.

All information pertaining to litigation should be treated with the same amount of security with which one would handle sensitive financial data, if not more so. In the end, emails collected may contain data relating to *all* aspects of the enterprise, from logistical data to personal messages sent by the CEO to his administrative assistant; there could truly be sensitive data released to the opposition. In the event of a "no holds barred" judgment? All data could go to the opposition … all of it. When it comes to the deeply

probative nature of a lawsuit, there can be no doubt that at some point, information from many sources may be culled. Here are some helpful tips:

- Build a solid identification system from the start. This will allow system administrators to respond rapidly and securely, with only responsive data.
- Create a solid but not overly restrictive communication system that raises corporate awareness. Inform corporate system users that the corporate system should not be used for personal communication.
- See to it that employees shred and destroy any personal emails they have sent.
- For employees' personal communication, make sure they use their own personal devices. In today's highly equipped society, there is no reason to use the corporate system for anything personal.
- Make it group policy at the corporate-wide level to delete temporary Internet files upon exiting the application.
- Consider that some interrelay chat messaging systems can be configured to save and send missed chats as emails, and create a policy that covers how these chat logs should be treated.
- Be aware of "cloud" data: data that a corporation may have created and is potentially relevant, but could be stored in a third-party SAAS system. Are these data easily exported? Can they be accessed and exported with custom queries?

Keeping personal communication off the enterprise system has several benefits. Aside from the inherent security benefit (users may launch harmful attachments from personal emails that are not scanned by the corporate email system), consider that with a security awareness program:

- The amount of potentially discoverable data will be reduced;
- The potential exposure to harmful and misleading personal conversations diminishes or disappears; and
- The program itself raises awareness that users should not write any emails that they would not want to be made publicly available.

A strong security policy will allow the legal hold team to perform their work within a predefined and secure framework. An "anything goes" policy, although seemingly employee friendly, can have disastrous results: When the professional, corporate system commingles with employees' personal lives, the amount of data increases and the opportunities for email from disgruntled employees who have their own interpretations that they may willingly be sharing with those outside the organization, on the corporate system, increase. Keeping to the hierarchy and defining this stage of the EDRM within the corporation is critical to securing this zone. Creating a responsive and secure information identification program *within* the information management system is essential to maintaining the utmost security of corporate data. When Zone 2 is subsumed by Zone 1, a secure conduit can be opened for the movement of data and for the subsequent integration of all zones into a secure work flow. The alternative to assimilation of Zone 2 by Zone 1 is that outside consultants be granted unfettered access to entire systems, and that it be secure.

Many possible vendor arrangements can be made when dealing with the identification of data. Ultimately, whichever configuration is arrived at must meet several rules of e-discovery security[9]:

1. Information must always be encrypted when transmitted over the Internet.
2. Data cannot be lost: Create multiple backups and have a disaster recovery (DR) site as well. In the end, there is no such thing as a real "backup" of electronic data. There are only redundant points of failure.
3. Data can be accessed only by authorized personnel.
4. Data have not been changed or altered maliciously, which can be verified independently. This verification can be accomplished easily using methods that are well known in the e-discovery industry. An e-discovery vendor's sales team may not be up to speed on this, but their technical staff should know all about it.
5. Stored or archived data are encrypted. Data stored outside your system should reside on encrypted systems. A bankruptcy of the firm or vendor hosting your e-discovery data could mean that your data reside on systems that will be sold at auction.
6. Data can easily be located and destroyed when no longer needed.

Once these rules are understood, we are ready to delve deeper into the EDRM life cycle and discuss the transition of data from Zone 2 to Zone 3 in preservation, collection, and processing. Zone 3, then, becomes a securable conduit with easily established secure data transfer protocols, and security experts can shift their focus to battening down Zone 4.

Securing Zone 4: Preservation, Collection, and Processing

In the EDRM, preservation refers primarily to the act of requesting that all custodians cease and desist any and all deletion activities and any automatic deletion procedures respecting potentially responsive data. Effectively, though, the end result of the act of preservation, collection, and

processing is that data are preserved. Until data have actually been collected, logged, and securely stored, they have not been preserved in the traditional sense of the word.

Preservation

Typically, at the outset of litigation, or when litigation is reasonably likely, a requirement called a "legal hold" or "litigation hold" will apply. In a sense, this is the order that triggers identification. Some organizations should have the ability to pull the requested data immediately; for others, however, the criticality of collection matters little. Once data have been identified, they then must be preserved in a forensic manner. This necessitates a discussion on metadata. You cannot preserve and secure data if you do not know what the data are, where they are, or what data are necessary to be captured. Often at the heart of this debate lies a conversation about *metadata* and about data *forensics*.

What Are Metadata?

Metadata are data about data. For example, this chapter includes the following metadata, which can be derived using programs such as EnCase or FTK, which are forensic analysis tools.

As can be seen in Table 42.1, these metadata includes operating system (OS) information such as file created, modified, accessed, and last written. These timestamps may be important because they will provide timeline data when investigating some sort of breach. One such example would be an employee accessing documents during her tenure as an employee versus her accessing the file systems after termination. Chapter 40 includes a description of these timestamps and what they mean. These metadata must be preserved. Other items that may fall into the category of "metadata" to be preserved include drafts, outlines, and all their subsequent markup, hidden text, track changes, and so on. As can be seen in Table 42.2, a much more extensive list can be produced using a software tool to extract and compile the data into a structure format.[10]

Ultimately, these tables demonstrate that a lot of data can be considered *metadata*. Whether are actually metadata is a philosophical argument. Regardless, a comprehensive policy can prevent the accumulation of this sort of data.

Note: Some companies set up all of their documents so that upon sending through email, all sensitive track changes data are removed.

What Is Data Forensics?

The word "forensic" means that the data meet or exceed the standards required in a court of law for the information to be presented as evidence. Information, when properly

---

9. These items are derived from the Health Insurance Portability and Accountability Act (Pub.L. 104–191, 110 Stat. 1936, enacted Aug. 21, 1996), which is not specific to e-discovery. In the end, it is up to organizations to make certain that they have complied with whatever standards are applicable in their industry.

10. The data used in this example are from the Word document for this chapter.

TABLE 42.1 Listing of Some of Operating System Metadata That Can Be Derived From EnCase

Metadata	Item
Filename	Chapter 64.docx
File ext	Docx
File category	Document
Description	File, archive
Last accessed	09/27/2012 04:34:03 PM
File created	09/27/2012 04:34:03 PM
Last written	09/25/2012 08:32:27 AM
Entry Modified	09/27/2012 04:34:03 PM
Logical size	418,950
Physical size	421,888
Starting extent	0D-C10609788
File extents	1
Physical location	44,717,031,424
Physical sector	87,337,952
Full path	C:\User\Chapter 64 - Securing eDiscover\Chapter 64.docx

preserved, must comply with several rules to be admissible. Not least among the rules is the need for proof that the information was not altered. There are two ways in which this can be accomplished. For civilian organizations, the preferred method is to hash the data and preserve the resulting hash. A hash is an algorithm that reads *all* of the data on disk and creates a unique identifier. Nothing but a perfect copy of the data would result in the same hash. In other areas, the witness is enough. Ideally, the following scenario will provide sufficient proof of preservation to allow admissibility to court. Bear in mind, though, that exceptions abound. Just because one of these rules is broken does not mean that the evidence will not be admitted. Certain judges in any court, where the judge has the ultimate authority to decide law, may even allow a hard drive to be admitted that had neither chain of custody nor a hash that matched the original drive's hash.[11] Ultimately, it boils down to the judge's interpretation of the rules of evidence and how they may be applicable to electronic data:

1. The hard drive or files are acquired using a forensically proven method and hashed.
2. Paperwork that describes where the files were found and how the files were captured must be created and stored in a secure location with the images.

3. A witness must be available who can say that she personally collected the files and stored them.

These rules protect the electronically stored information (ESI) from tampering or even accidental destruction. These rules must be followed during a collection activity. Collection is the actual practice of data forensics in motion. Remember, though, that data can become corrupt just sitting on a disk.

Collection

Collection is the logical successor to identification; in the EDRM diagram, preservation shows a double-sided arrow pointing between collection and preservation. Preservation applies first in the sense that the litigation hold requires responsive data to be preserved rather than deleted. Collection is an activity, collected records are the result of that activity, and the collected records themselves must be preserved. Whether true preservation occurs wholly depends on whether the rules mentioned in the previous section were followed and whether the collection is properly conducted. Securing the data is entirely critical to both. This creates a zone that cannot and should not be integrated with other zones. It should stand alone as an entity unto itself. A collection activity may manifest in several scenarios; each has unique security requirements:

- The ESI collected is stored internally.
- The ESI was collected by your staff from a remote location.
- The ESI is being collected from your location by the opposing counsel's vendors.

Each of these scenarios requires special treatment. Security approaches will vary within each circumstance. Many products are used to do this work; they fall into several categories:

1. Boot device only
2. Network boot only
3. Network collection (this includes use of a crossover)
4. Direct or drive-to-drive acquisition

Each of these options will allow for two types of collections. Which is needed depends on the case and type of litigation. If there is a possibility that locating a deleted file can alter the outcome of the case, choose Option 2 unilaterally:

1. Logical files
2. Physical disk image

Physical disk images present a unique concern in the world of security. To a certain extent, a hard drive acts as a recording device. However, if there is a lot of churn on the PC, if many files are created and deleted, the files

---

11. *US v. Gore.*

TABLE 42.2 Metadata That Can Be Extracted From a Document

Metadata Field	Data
Time zone field	1038662
Processing custodian	1038663
Originating processing set	2352
Control number	REL000000020
Virtual path	
Level	1
Container ID	
Container name	
Container extension	
File path	\\server\FileShare\dan\INV\0\5.DOCX
Processing duplicate hash	05D5DD668238B1DF9D18B57DF5469DCCB343-D6859556FEB2CF21ACBD2452A272
Processing errors	
Extracted text	\\server\FileShare\dan\INV\INTERMEDIATE\0\5.TXT
OutsideInFileId	1336
OutsideInFileType	Microsoft word 2010
Folder path	
ChildControlNumbers	REL000000021; REL000000022; REL000000023; REL000000024; REL000000025; REL000000026
Author	Ellis
Comments	
EmailConversation	
ConversationFamily	
EmailConversationIndex	
CreatedOn	9/28/2012 14:30
LastModified	9/28/2012 16:43
LastPrinted	
EmailReceivedOn	
EmailSentOn	
FileExtension	DOCX
DocumentSubject	
EmailBCCSmtp	
EmailKeywords	
EmailCCSmtp	
EmailSenderSmtp	
EmailSubject	
EmailToSmtp	
Email/DomainParsedFrom	
Email/DomainParsedTo	
Email/DomainParsedCC	

Continued

TABLE 42.2 Metadata That Can Be Extracted From a Document—cont'd

Metadata Field	Data
Email/DomainParsedBCC	
HiddenText	TRUE
FileName	Chapter 64 Securing eDiscovery Final.docx
FileSize	588,272
FileType	Microsoft Office word open XML format
RelativityGroupId	REL000000020
EmailImportance	
MD5Hash	9AC20F60696D0ECC861D3893F9AFC5A0
AttachmentCount	6
OtherProps	Office/LastAuthor = Ellis; Office/Revision =;
	InternalCreatedOn = 9/28/2012 2:30:00 PM;
	LastSaved = 9/28/2012 4:43:00 PM; Office/EmbeddedItems = True;
	TrackChanges = True
ParentDate	
ParentControlNumber	
SHA1Hash	B2E8BA743F154EE1687B9011572907A3C5636A57
SHA256Hash	BF6B62AE6B5CFB4F274640C6123949063FBEA-9C233A26FB443FCE4AE6483E11D

This extraction was performed using a tool called Relativity Processing.

have the potential to multiply like rabbits. Imagine that the hard drive is like an onion slice, only with millions of concentric rings. If the hard drive is frequently defragmented, the layers of the onion build up over time. Often, what happens in the world of IT is that a user will "fill up" her hard drive. When this happens, the IT support technician, or perhaps the user, will clean up the computer by deleting files. Perhaps she will delete 50 gigabytes (GB) of data from accumulated logs, windows temporary files, and email. That night, defragmentation runs and all of the files that were on the outer ring of the drive are moved inward, filling the space where the deleted files previously existed, and leaving copies out on the outer edges. Windows Delete *does not* overwrite the file. It only marks the space as free. The deleted file is easily recovered using a tool that can examine the master file table. To even the most incompetent of forensic examiners, there are now copies of her files that can easily be located. Because she deleted so much data (perhaps a Windows log file had grown out of control at some point), it will be some time before the data reach that outer ring and overwrite it. Defragmentation is good but must be followed by a secure wipe of the unallocated clusters.

Data Retention Policies

This leads us directly into data retention policies, which require that the security administrator understand the nature and location of any sensitive data, and ensure that a sound and responsible policy be formulated around them. It dovetails into collection because ultimately, the data that exist may be data that get collected. A rigorous data retention policy will prevent the exposure of outdated and irrelevant files.

Deleted files are a security concern because they may still be extant. The following items present deleted data security challenges:

1. Email databases.
2. Structured Query Language (SQL) log files. Often, SQL log files are not maintained properly. See the sidebar: "Managing Structured Query Language Server Log Files" for directions on how to keep the logs in such a way that they will remain efficient and continually overwrite themselves. It is common to find an unmaintained log that contains 150 GB of past transactions. Left to its own devices, SQL will allow a log file to grow interminably, or until disk space runs out.
3. Decommissioned servers.

4. Old backup tapes.
5. Forgotten share locations. The author of this chapter once located 1 year of database versions. The database was central to the case.
6. Internet Explorer cache files. This is the backstage pass to a full-blown, no-holds-barred collection order by the judge. Unless regularly cleaned, Internet cache files will grow to be large and will contain a recorded history of user activity. Many companies use online tools for contact management. Thus, the Internet history may contain a record going back several years of every contact created in the system.
7. Local drives. Users like to save files where they know they can find them. Most users have been bitten by IT enough times to want to make certain that they keep their most important files on a local drive.
8. Shadow copies, versioning
9. Partial files in file slack. When a file writes to a Windows cluster, it takes the whole cluster. You cannot store two files in one extant. However, if one file takes up an entire sector and then just 1 byte of the next sector, if another file (deleted) lived in that next sector, it would be recoverable. It is difficult to recover these files, but in the normal course of an examination of a PC, a forensic investigator will stumble across many items of interest. Because of deletion activity and defragmentation, many, many copies of a single file may exist. When that file gets deleted and partially overwritten, it may still exist in dozens, if not hundreds, of other places.
10. Decommissioned laptops and PCs.
11. Hard drive upgrades. Regardless of being slated for destruction, stacks of hard drives become discoverable when a legal hold is issued.
12. Personal digital assistants and tablets.
13. Digital cameras.
14. Smart media cards.
15. CDs, DVDs, universal serial bus (USB) thumb drives, digital audio and video tapes, voice mail, and surveillance servers.

There are many enterprise software packages available that handle secure deletion. Secure deletion means at least one complete overwriting of the data. Some organizations operate at a heightened level of anxiety and may require as many as 35 overwrites of the data. Gutmann theorized that 35 overwrites of data are required to obliterate the data fully from the surface of the drive. In terms of meeting modern security requirements, this is probably excessive. The Gutmann algorithm, devised by Peter Gutmann and Colin Plumb, targeted certain types of drives of a certain track density, and so they suggested that near perfect obliteration of any residual magnetic data could be accomplished by writing a series of 35 patterns over the disk regions being deleted. The patterns are designed specifically for three different types of drive data-encoding techniques that were prevalent in the 1980s.[12]

Managing Structured Query Language Log Files

- Ensure that log file backups are set to run at least once every hour. Consider running them more often in the following scenarios:
- You want to recover with less than 1 h of data loss.
- More data can be written to the log file in 1 h than is desirable.
- The amount of data written to the log file in 1 h causes the log file to fill up the drive. SQL marks the log file as reusable once it is backed up, so it should not grow too large.

  Note: Some single transactions in processing software are large and may result in log file growth through multiple-transaction log backups. This can prevent successful log backups.

- Ensure that the growth of the log files is set to at least 512 megabytes (MB).
- In certain situations, many gigabytes of data may pour into a log file before the next scheduled log backup marks space as available. Unanticipated growth can also occur when extremely large transactions run. If this occurs, use some sort of log file size monitoring tool to control the size.
- When necessary, grow the log file size in anticipation of any large influx of new data.

To this date, no software or hardware product exists that can read the outer edges of a disk track and recompile overwritten data on a modern hard drive, unless, of course, one believes in a secret government facility that nobody knows exists that hosts an array of scanning probe microscopes, as well as scientists and analysts. Secure deletion thus means at least one complete overwriting of the data and includes file slack (regions of sectors that are not being used by the file) and unallocated clusters. Doing it twice would be advisable; if there are two station points in the workflow, it will ensure at least some protection from human error.

Some organizations operate at a higher level of anxiety and may require as many as 35 overwrites of the data, using the Gutmann algorithm. The reason for this level of deletion was perhaps owing to misunderstanding of the theory and an article published by Peter Gutmann. In his article, he described the potential to recover data from the outer edges of tracks using scanning probe microscopy and the potential to recover overwritten data through a form of error-canceling read in which the calculated signal from the current data is subtracted

---

12. P. Gutmann, Secure deletion of data from magnetic and solid-state memory, Sixth USENIX Security Symposium Proceedings, San Jose, CA, Jul. 22–25, 1996. http://www.cs.auckland.ac.nz/~pgut001/pubs/secure_del.html.

from the signal that is actually read, with the difference caused by the influence of previously written data.[13]

The procedure itself (the use of a robot-controlled drive mechanism and an oscilloscope to collect data from an 80-MB disk pack) has in fact been accomplished, and it was verified that the data did have the appearance of a true bit stream that could then be further analyzed for comparative data.[14] This would be a challenging operation, but it is conceivable that if portions of the files are known, it could be extended to "decrypt" three or four passes at different locations in the same track. However, modern drives are far denser, and owing to the use of advanced recording techniques, the potential for this sort of attack to be successful is extremely unlikely.[15]

Ultimately, there are software products that can perform truly secure deletion on modern drives with just one pass. In addition, secure deletion should take place as part of the defragmentation routine. In any security-conscious enterprise, secure wiping of the unallocated clusters should always happen *after* a defragmentation.

There are only two ways to destroy electronically stored data. You can overwrite the media using software, or you can physically destroy the hard drive. Solid-state drives present unique challenges as well.[16] For the physical-destruction option, any severe deformation, perforation, or incineration of the platters will suffice. Commercially available products such as diskstroyer have received good reviews.

Thus, the security of collection is not just about the security of how the collected data are stored. This will be discussed in the next few sections. Rather, it begins with the security of the data themselves that are being collected: You most know where data live, and you must work to ensure that you know what data are being taken. It also means that the data must be stored in such a way as to take all possible and reasonable precautions to prevent data loss. Data loss, whenever it occurs, must be fully documented and explained, and it must not have occurred owing to human error or willful neglect. This also means the data must be securable and identifiable.

The practice of collection can be divided into two categories: internal and external. Internal collection occurs when an organization looks inward and investigates itself using staff or consultant data forensic examiners. The motivation to perform the work stems from internal concerns, such as incidents involving earlier misconduct by a terminated employee; and there are internal stakeholders.

An external collection occurs in litigation, where many parties may be involved.

Internal Collection

Many large corporations have their own internal forensic groups. However, even large corporations may turn to specialized forensic experts when unique circumstances arise. An internally conducted collection, though, will be one in which staff employees, who are members of the enterprise domain, perform the work of securing, copying, and storing the discoverable information. A number of methods are employed:

1. Appliances are installed throughout the network.
2. Enterprise software allows administrators to capture everything from individual files to entire disk images, remotely, with two options:
   a. Systems are monitored for breaches in security policy; when a breach is detected, the user system is locked down and the evidence is collected.
   b. Systems are not monitored, and collections are conducted only when suspicious behavior is observed or upon employee termination.
3. Physical collection: The drive is harvested, imaged, and stored, and then a standard disk image is redeployed to the machine.

In each of these methods, the end result is that a large amount of redundant data must be secured and preserved, possibly for a very, very long time. Lawsuits can last many years, or regulatory compliance may require retention of up to a decade. It follows, then, that the location, nature (matter), and status of all data should be tracked carefully. These data should be secured at a much higher level than other data in the enterprise, because it is most likely a corporate espionage gold mine of all of the business's most sensitive data:

- Two-factor authentication
- Physical access with surveillance and biometric access controls
- AES 256-bit encryption when possible
- Hardware and data destruction policies
- Group-based access by matter

Often, internal forensic examiners provide advice and expertise in externally related matters; but often, depending on the matter at hand, these examiners will work tangentially with external consultants on projects that involve externally driven litigation.

External Collection

When external adversarial forces are at play, enterprises often choose to involve external collection experts. Ostensibly, this shift stabilizes liability and planning from internal sources, which are already taxed with managing internal risk, to an outside firm. These external firms

13. Email from Peter Gutmann to author, dated 10/5/2012.
14. C. Fenton, Digital Archeology with Drive-Independent Data Recovery, ELEN E9002 Research Project Final Report, Summer 2011. http://tinyurl.com/3jhe2os.
15. Email from Peter Gutmann to author, dated 10/5/2012.
16. http://www.cs.auckland.ac.nz/~pgut001/pubs/secure_del.html#recommendations.

should be experienced and should be able to integrate their tools easily to your systems for a speedy and accurate collection of data. They are often managed by in-house counsel in tandem with external counsel. In the small world of e-discovery vendors, the vendors selected by both sides likely will have worked together in the past. Interview any potential vendor carefully.

Occasionally a court will allow a plaintiff's staff ESI specialists to conduct an on-site collection, even at the protest of the opposing defense's argument. It does happen, but it is not the normal course of events. A corporation that responds and complies with discovery requests in a timely fashion, demonstrating cooperation, will not face sanctions. Typically, by the time it comes to the "other side," which is allowed to put its experts in the living room of an exemployee or the data center of the opposition, things have become combative in the courtroom. The reason for this is usually the utter failure of one side or the other to adhere to the bottom layer of the e-Discovery Security Hierarchy of Needs. This short list details some of the reasons why a judge may allow the opposition's experts full access to the other side's data center:

1. Failure to produce relevant documents on the agreed-to timeline
2. Failure to produce relevant documents in the agreed-upon format
3. Denial that any relevant documents exist
4. Failure to appear
5. Refusal to pay costs associated with discovery, or claims of financial destitution
6. Failure to provide a believable and reliable basis for determining whether something is or is not relevant.

All of this exemplifies the need for a robust backup and data retention policy. Acceptable use policies are also an important part of this. Zone 3, as shown in Fig. 42.3, becomes a matter of physical or encrypted tunnel transport of data. Often, the amount of data involved in a collection can approach many terabytes or petabytes in size. Movement of such large volumes of data, when they require processing, becomes infeasible. Fortunately, with proper encryption, moving the data via hard drives, using accepted shipping methods, provides adequate security. Backups of data should be retained, and pass-phrases that allow access to the data should be transmitted securely. If the need to transport dozens of drives via courier arises, ensure that the courier has a copy of the order upon his person and in the hardened transport case, with the drives.

Collection "Don'ts"

Enterprises faced with litigation for the first time often make severe mistakes. A good example of a first-time litigation is that in which an employee storms out of the

investors' Office of Alice Rabbit and Hole, and the next week begins working for a rival investment firm, Tweedle Dee and Dum. Suddenly, clients that were long-time loyal customers are dropping their accounts with Alice and moving to … yes, the Tweedle, where the exemployee now works. Later, the CEO of Alice receives a brochure, passed along from a client. It outlines a new pricing structure for the opposing firm's services that mirror the work being done at Alice, work that the exemployee participated in developing. The brochure appears to be the same layout with only a few slight differences.

The CEO calls his IT director and demands an explanation. The IT director panics, saying, "I'll get to the bottom of this!" and immediately goes to access the exemployee's laptop. She finds it on the workbench of an IT associate, halfway through a reload of the OS. She halts the work. Next, she browses the network to the exemployee's share and begins to browse the directory contents, searching for content that the user should not have had in her drive area, files that were thought to be restricted to marketing. She finds interesting files, and then she connects a hard drive to her network and copies all of Alice's files to the hard drive. Then, thinking to herself, "Gee, I could really use all that space she was hogging," she deletes all of the exemployee's files from the network share.

Ultimately, Alice may still have a case until, of course, a private investigator discovers that the exemployee and the IT director had had an affair. The case would have been far simpler and easier to execute if an intact laptop had been available, a laptop that may have shown evidence of the exemployee using webmail to airlift files from the corporate network. Furthermore, it would have been prudent to have a protocol in place to handle disgruntled employee departures. The CEO should have instructed his IT director to engage the protocol, which would have resulted in forensic-quality images of everything the exemployee had ever touched. Now, there will be a long drawn-out legal battle that will be costly because Alice Rabbit and Hole essentially have a weakened position.

Processing

One might think that once the data have been identified, properly collected, and shipped, the heavy lifting is completed. It is in fact only just beginning. The following searches may now need to be executed against a data set that is largely unstructured. Processing takes unstructured data and structures them so that future searches may be executed efficiently. Processing software provides, at a minimum, the following functionality:

- File types;
- Although a collection may have targeted spreadsheets and documents, to be thorough the effort may have swept up files that are not the correct file type; or the

collection technologies may have used targeted areas such as unallocated clusters, compressed files, or entire file systems, and the types of files that were of interest may not have become apparent until later in the EDRM life cycle. The processing tool will recognize these files and will not process them;

- Date range culling;
- Database conversion;
- Files stored in databases, or information stored in databases, present unique challenges. A customer database that uses a Web interface to access the data may require a design team to recreate pages that display the information, which can then be reviewed, or they may simply be required to search the database. This requires that the database server be hosted by the processing agent;
- Keyword searches;
- Custodian organization;
- Deencrypting of encrypted files: the ability to enter passwords or "try" lists of passwords;
- It will remove National Institute of Science and Technology (NIST) items (De-NIST). Earlier, file hash values were discussed as being unique identifiers for a file that possesses certain content. As passwords are broken, unusual compression algorithms unlocked, and hidden files uncovered, standard system and program files may be uncovered (this may be conducted multiple times, any step of the way);
- Deduplication Customized lists of hash values are created and duplicates are removed. There are three ways to do this: globally, by custodian, and by family or child. When the context of the item does not matter, global deduplication is best. If the context, such as the location of the file, who sent it, and its location matter, dedupe families only. Often, users will have local archives of files that will contain large volumes of copies. A 5- to 6-terabyte corpus can easily be reduced through deNISTing and deduplication.

Some combination of all of these may be necessary. For example, after identifying that any email sent by an employee during a certain date range may be relevant, further analysis may be needed.

Securing the Processing Architecture: Zone 4

In Fig. 42.3, Zone 4 encapsulates preservation, collection, and processing. Each of these items requires special treatment. In reality, preservation is a process that begins with identification, issuing a legal hold, and collecting the data; and data must be "processed" each step of the way. Data are not truly preserved until they have been securely copied, logged, and moved to a staging area where they can be accessed and reviewed at a high level for relevancy. In Fig. 42.5, the upside-down triangle represents a funnel.

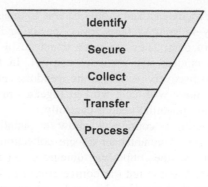

FIGURE 42.5 The preservation effort does not end with a simple backup and archive of the data. Throughout the Electronic Discovery Reference Model cycle, the act of preserving metadata and file integrity remains important.

The EDRM is actually a drawn-out preservation and display process, and as we move through it, the amount of data being manipulated should shrink. However, sometimes things happen. For example, perhaps many compressed archives will be discovered, or deleted partitions recovered. There may be momentary bursts of data. Recall also that the entire process is cyclical. There may be many separate requests for disclosure in a single case. Storage and sizing become major challenges of e-discovery architects, and securing the storage becomes a great challenge for security architects.

As storage bursts, emergency measures may need to be executed to meet deadlines. If emergency protocols do not exist, they cannot be executed. An example of an emergency protocol would be to have agreements with companies that sell storage and servers to execute on preauthorized purchase orders within 24 h. This is normal, and hardware vendors are prepared for such requests because they also tie into DR strategies.

In both planned and unplanned situations, servers will get moved, disk arrays transferred, and storage area network fabrics rearchitected. An adept security plan considers this contingency, is adaptable, and provides for extremely rapid scaling of the environment. This is not a "let us budget it for Q3" item. This is a "We need it, and we need it now, or we could get fined a million dollars" situation or, from the law firm or vendor perspective, "We need it, and we need it now, or we are going to lose an $85 million a year client." This sort of work occurs not only in small businesses across the world but in the very largest enterprises that exist.

When all is said and done, British Petroleum and the *Deepwater Horizon* case will likely involve thousands of people and many terabytes of data, and will involve many millions of dollars, if not over a billion, in legal costs alone. Duplicative work can double and triple costs. Deficiencies in process can create even greater inefficiencies.

In 2007, this author was involved in managing the electronic data for a large class action lawsuit that involved a consumer loss. Thousands of consumers had a home remodeling component that had failed owing to manufacturing defects. The e-discovery included thousands of joint photographic expert group digital photographs. Nearly all of the photos were far larger than needed; a short experiment proved that the images could be reduced in size with no discernible loss of quality. Simply observing that 80 GB of images could be reduced in size to 10 GB can reduce storage costs by eight times! Why is this important to security? Properly securing e-discovery includes ensuring manageability of the data. Data that boom in size rapidly begin to break down the barriers of security. Escalating costs cause corners to be cut and will leach funds away from the security budget. In the e-discovery industry, all-hands-on-deck emergencies are common if not daily events at many firms. Maintaining security should be the first priority. New servers introduced should be sanitized of any data and disjoined from other security groups, and should not have outbound Internet access.

The processing arena should be cordoned through demilitarized technologies, as shown in Fig. 42.6. Differing technologies have differing methods of access. At every step of the way, intrusion detection systems, intrusion prevention, and virus and malicious software detection systems should be dovetailed with each processing step. Fig. 42.6 provides a sample configuration of how different servers may be tied to security cordons that are designed to minimize the risk of infected files being inadvertently viewed, which in turn can inadvertently execute malicious code. Staging areas, which are large disk repositories where data are stored as they are being accessed and manipulated, tangentially allow for other processes to be used to scan and monitor these areas.

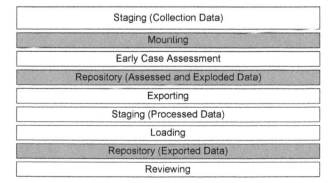

FIGURE 42.6 Each *shaded area* represents either a static location or the process that creates the data that reside in that repository. *Shaded areas* indicate key areas where virus scanning activities may take place.

Staging (Collection Data)

Fig. 42.6 introduced the concept of staging and the issue of having a secure staging area. In large litigation cases, collected files can arrive in many formats. Also, depending on the vendor, the work that remains to be done may differ. For the sake of simplicity, in this diagram, the assumption is that many forensic images of disks have arrived and have been stored on a high-capacity storage array.

Mounting

Subsequently, for processing, the forensic images are mounted as drive letters. At this time, performing a virus scan is not necessary. The files are read-only: If a virus was found, nothing could be done except to make note of it and exclude it, or mark it for manual review if it is a relevant file. In fact, depending on the method and software used to process the data, this is one of the options. However, at this stage, forensic tools are used to cull the data, and viruses that exist in system files may be ignored if they are in uninteresting locations. As part of culling, other processes may simply export all data from the mounted layer to a secondary staging area, and then may scan the entire area and quarantine infected files. Infected files may, of course, include files that are relevant. A virus scanning utility that allows for cleansing of the infected files should be used.

Early Case Assessment

During the assessment process, the risk increases of a user coming into contact with a virus. Decommissioned hard drives, unflushed quarantine directories, USB drives, thumb drives, spam email, and so on all can rise to the surface. In particular, as the processing tool fails, one may come into direct contact with the file that failed, and the reason for the failure may be that the file is infected. As the early case assessment software service searches files, relevant files may be loaded into RAM by an unsuspecting user wishing to review a file. The file may be infected and may not appear in the viewer properly, so the user may choose to access the file and open it. When this happens, the virus is triggered, and a malicious hacker receives a notification on his bootleg cell phone that one of his viruses has been activated. Imagine his delight when, upon accessing the servers, he discovers that he has complete control over all of the electronic data of a highly sensitive litigation. Perhaps it is a merger. Perhaps it is a high-profile divorce, or bankruptcy, or product liability.

In addition, technicians working with the files may erroneously believe that the processing software *failed* to process the file. They will not realize that the file is infected, and they may actually spread the virus by sending it to the software vendor. All files that are identified as suspect during processing should be quarantined and scanned before further evaluation.

Security around these areas cannot be tight enough. These systems should not have Internet access, and there should be double-layered, interwoven defenses of firewalls, intrusion detection, and intrusion prevention, even in disconnected systems. Some viruses are merely designed to infect other files and/or inflict damage. Once activated, nothing is to stop the virus from wreaking havoc on the servers. The infected files may have to be produced to the opposition in the lawsuit. Imagine how unhappy they will be if they discover that their entire network became infected by files in the production they received from opposing counsel. Referring back to Fig. 42.2, outside Zone 1, Zone 4 presents the greatest security challenges.

Processing

In this step of the EDRM, by now potentially relevant data have been identified. It may be a handful of files or it may be millions of files. The current atmosphere of e-discovery is one of "more is less," and so the discipline finds itself faced with issue of "Big Data." The end result of processing is that a "package" is created, or a series of them, that contains all of the natives and all of the metadata information extracted from the natives. This includes something called "extracted text." Extracted text is nothing more than the body of language encapsulated in a file. For example, in this chapter the extracted text would include all of the alphanumeric characters with no formatting. It would also include any hidden comments, track changes, and markup notes. This will all be stored as Unicode, so that special characters may be preserved and later searched. This package of data, which may actually be many terabytes, will then be transmitted to a new location. This new location may be internal to the corporation, to a law firm, or to a vendor data center. Review and analysis represent a major shift, or interface, where large amounts of data are likely to shift into a different area. That is, a copy of everything processed is now ready to be looked at and loaded into a hosted review tool.

Securing Zone 5: Hosting/Review

For some organizations, the hosted review may be integrated within the processing cordon. However, for many it is not, so this chapter treats it as though the data will be moving to a separate entity, either internal or external to the organization. Once the package has been received in the hosting review center, it must be loaded to the review software. Some software processing platforms may integrate directly with the review tool. For example, the software product Relativity includes a processing package: data may be pumped directly, SQL server to SQL server, from the processing center to the hosted review

platform. Antivirus scans should continue, for two reasons. First, this system will likely be connected to the Internet. Large-scale litigation requires many reviewers, and these many review shops are located all over the world. The enterprise data are about to go global. Second, virus definitions are frequently updated. A file that scanned "virus free" yesterday may not actually be virus free and may just be a time bomb waiting to be set off.

More Is Less

This returns us to the "more is less" philosophy prevalent in e-discovery culture in 2012. This philosophy is being countered by developments in automated review. In the sidebar "Relativity-Assisted Review," Constantine Pappas discusses assisted review, which is a way to eliminate documents programmatically from the potentially relevant population of documents. This sort of technology may often reduce the cost of analysis as well as the amount of data that need to be reviewed by humans. If exposure is measured by surface area, an increase in the volume of documents in e-discovery effectively increases that surface area. Primarily, this is because additional computer systems will need to be set up (more Web servers for a hosted review) and because of an increase in human eyes that are performing the review. By leveraging predictive coding tools *before* releasing all of the data, exposure may be significantly reduced. The exposure here is the exposure of sensitive corporate data to hundreds of reviewers. Fewer reviewers mean more security and less potential that someone will steal corporate data. It also means that if the system is hacked, fewer files will escape. Exposure is not curtailed but it is certainly reduced.

Software products that provide review services should be secure. They will have received "A" ratings from security auditing service companies. In response to security concerns, security consulting firms work diligently to ensure that proper security precautions are integrated into the platform for things such as:

- JavaScript injection
- SQL injection
- Cross-site scripting
- At least AES 256 encryption of website and installers
- Federal Information Processing Standard
- Signed
- Secure session cookies

In addition, any security manager or software provider should be cognizant of new threats. Frequently, clients and peers, along with blogs and journals, are great sources of information. Keeping an eye out and seriously considering all threats or descriptions of potential threats, regardless of the source of information, can mean the difference between correcting a potential SQL injection vulnerability and having it remain to be discovered by a hacker.

Relativity-Assisted Review

Relativity-Assisted Review is a workflow process designed to save time and money during the e-discovery phase of a lawsuit or investigation. The process captures human decisions on sample sets of documents and in turn applies those decisions to other documents in the same database that meets a predetermined conceptual similarity threshold. It is an iterative workflow divided into phases called rounds. The number of rounds necessary to complete the project varies depending on validation criteria and other case-specific variables.

The tool employs text analytics categorization, specifically an engine called Latent Semantic Indexing. First, the documents to be categorized are indexed; these analytics indexes typically filter out email header information and other repeated content that could otherwise serve to confound effective machine learning.

Once the index has been created, a sample set of documents is generated. A random statistical sample is often employed, although it is also common to choose known documents that are believed to be excellent candidates for machine learning. Sampling by this latter method is called judgmental sampling.

Human reviewers will then apply values to a designation field (typically as either Responsive or Nonresponsive) for each sample document. Once all documents in the sample set have been reviewed, they are submitted for Categorization by the system. When Categorization is complete, the categorized documents are then sampled into new validation rounds, which human reviewers check for accuracy. Each instance in which a reviewer corrects the system is called an overturn, and the process of sampled validation review and Categorization is repeated until the overturn rate reaches an acceptable level or no longer changes. This effect is called stabilization and indicates completion of the Assisted Review phase of the discovery project.

Ultimately, the "More Is Less" process can greatly reduce the costs and time required to review a large number of records. This is accomplished by being able to isolate and either deprioritize or disregard the Nonresponsive population, which is typically an overwhelming majority of most data sets. In addition, the tool amplifies human expertise, taking each coding decision and multiplying it many times over. This process greatly augments both consistency and decision-making transparency compared with traditional linear review. Review tools, even Web-based ones, are most often secured in one of the following methods:

1. Simple forms security over Hyper Text Transfer Protocol Secure to a Web server.

2. Two-factor authentication with an integration of the application with something like Rivest–Shamir–Adleman encryption.
3. Portal-based access. One organization, Juniper, uses Uniform Resource Locator rewriting to control access to Web-based applications, adding an additional layer of token-based authentication security to an already secure application.
4. Thin-client remote access. Remote desktop access uses something like Citrix to allow users server-next-door speeds when using the Web-based tool. It also prevents information from being downloaded to users' machines. This may assist with compliance to some safe harbor rules and for overseas access and review of data. Some countries, such as the United Kingdom, have stringent policies about disclosure of motherland data to overseas entities.
5. Site-based security: Vendors own and control the review arenas, and the machines are locked down so that data cannot be loaded to a thumb drive. Users view documents in a basic dumb-terminal setup.

Consider the flowchart in Figs. 42.7 and 42.8. In this flowchart, the ease with which an infiltrator can secure administration access is described. At times, these e-discovery systems contain extremely sensitive data.

Review and analysis are in the same vertical in the EDRM. Essentially, they are one and the same: Analysis often takes place exclusively in the review platform. However, whereas there are many things that many review platforms can do, there are many things that they cannot. Not all review platforms can perform:

- Entity relationship mapping
- Voice recognition
- Threading
- Benford's law
- Gap analysis
- Deduplication
- Managing projects
- Bypassing painful load file management
- Audio and visual searching

Often, once documents have been coded by reviewers, data must be exported from the review platform and into some sort of analysis tool or another. These data may still be considered proprietary to the corporate entity and should remain under the same controls as any other data. A good review application will have permission-based security on various functions, such as the ability to download natives or export data to Excel spreadsheets. Security will consider many different software products to have special requirements and require varying levels of security permissions on the network.

Review platforms also must have storage capacity, and the same storage capacity issues can occur here that come

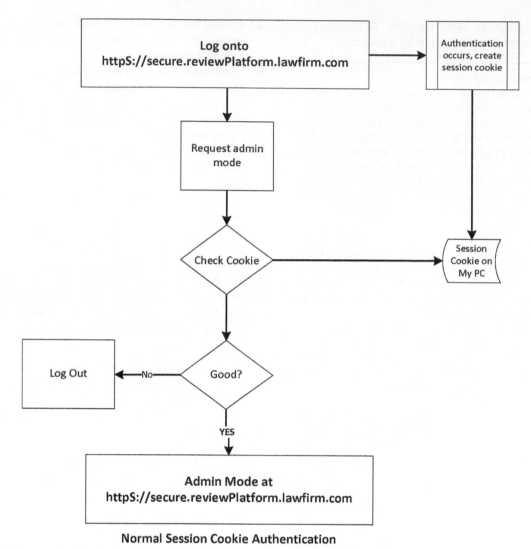

Normal Session Cookie Authentication

FIGURE 42.7 In a normal authentication, the cookie is generated by the browser and shared with the server. Subsequently, the browser is authenticated using the same cookie. *PC*, personal computer.

up in processing. In addition, there are in fact virus threats even at this stage, where one would think that everything had already been scanned three or four times.

Consider the zeroth-day threat, in which a threat is considered to be occurring on the "zeroth" day when as of yet it has not been discovered. It is true that files that are in the repository of a review platform most likely have already been scanned, so continual scanning of a file repository would be overkill if you have other intrusion countermeasures in place. Use something like a network intrusion prevention system for the Web and two-factor authentication on any other types of access. The reason for the scanning shown on the review repository in Fig. 42.6 is to address zeroth-day threats that could be lurking.

The term *zeroth* day is, in reality, somewhat misleading. This author once had a desktop that scanned clean by antivirus tool A (I *knew* it was infected). Scanning the

machine again using Antivirus tool B (and then C, D, E, and F) also revealed nothing. The only thing to do was to shut the machine down and preserve it. A month later, using the same scanning tools but with updated definitions, a scan located the virus.

Sometimes the scanners we are using just do not yet have the definitions. *Do* require scanning of an adequately protected file repository when virus definitions are updated. In particular, be cognizant of virus definitions that cover loose files. Scanning the file repository in a targeted way can reduce the load on the system. For example, when an antivirus company releases a signature update that specifically addresses infected Excel spreadsheets, scan all spreadsheets with that particular signature.

Scanning activities should also occur in a staging area whenever new loads of files arrive, regardless of the source, but especially ones that have been processed

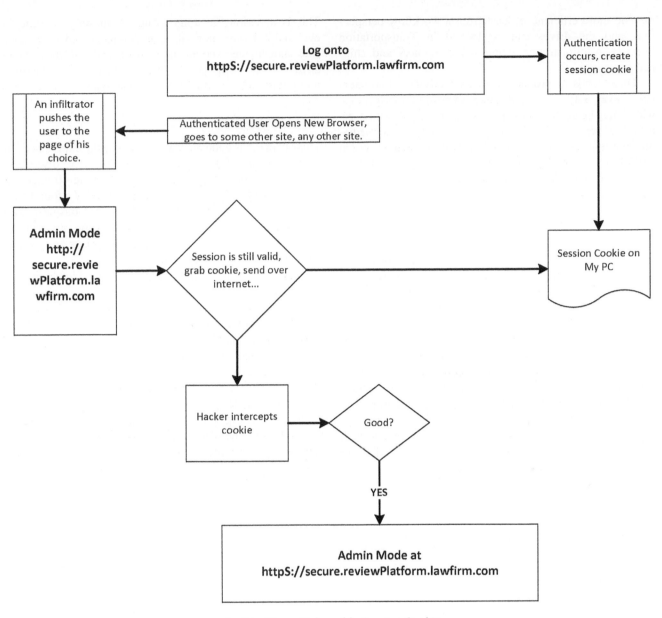

Surf Jacking a Vulnerable Session Cookie

FIGURE 42.8 In a poorly secured application, the cookie becomes vulnerable to "surf-jacking," in which a malicious user can seize control of a session. *PC*, personal computer.

without regard to any sort of an EDRM security zone model. This chapter puts forth a zoned security model that underpins the entire EDRM: Any processing vendor that operates as though it is an island should be cause for concern.

Securing Zone 6: Production and Presentation

These two areas of the EDRM are zoned together in this model. In this model, there are two types of production.

The first kind is called a "disclosure" in some countries. In the United States, it is just "discovery." Effectively, the first kind of production is the release of information in the format agreed to in the prediscovery "meet and confer" conference with the opposing counsel. Production data that are to be delivered to the opposing counsel should be delivered in a compressed and encrypted format. 7Zip is one such tool that is both free and effective. It allows for compressing in several different formats and offers all of the flexibility needed to compress large amounts of data. Alternatively, whole-drive encryption may be more efficient, at least from a workflow perspective, and the drives can be locked in Transportation Security Administration—approved containers and shipped overnight.

Other kinds of production include privilege log, attorneys' eyes-only logs, and other same-side productions, which may be delivered to other counsels, expert witnesses, or other vendors for further processing. Use a media-tracking application in conjunction with a labeling system (RFID or bar code) to control media. Knowledge of the location and who has handled or come into contact with e-discovery will determine the source of a security weakness; it will also help with the continued, ongoing assessment of risk.

In the EDRM, the presentation vertical simply refers to courtroom technologies and the presentation of documents and other information. Several software products will allow things such as video, document, and transcript presentation via a projector. In the past, law firms would spend thousands of dollars on large, printed foam-board charts and graphs to make their points to juries and judges. This trend has declined, with more and more attorneys bringing laptops into the courtroom. Few courts are not media ready, wired for sound, with microphone and video, and with strategically placed monitors and projectors.

The quality of monitors, however, should be checked, as should all systems. Some courtrooms are slow to upgrade and either will not have monitors available or will make available monitors that are of such poor quality that they can hardly be viewed. This may swing the decision as to whether a mobile network should be set up in the courtroom. There will rarely be hard-wired network access available, although there may be a public wireless point that will likely be shared. Secure wireless access by ensuring that a software firewall exists on any laptops that will be entering the court room.

Security

Zone 6 security thus involves thorough tracking of media and securing any deliveries of data or findings to a separate vendor entity for processing into a more presentable format. At this stage, the e-discovery process is complete. It is show time. If the documents are in the production, they will soon be out of the control of the enterprise. Questioning and ensuring the security of these documents should not be overlooked: The attorneys may not know or even think to worry about this. It is up to the director of e-discovery at the originating corporate level to follow the progress, to ensure security at every touch point, and to ensure that a program is in place that educates attorneys as to the importance of data security and what they can do to help. Insist on encryption and secure storage of delivered productions.

This is a reasonable thing to do. Requesting "attorney's eyes only" is also normal. Confidentiality and nondisclosure agreements should be signed and understood by anyone who will come into contact with sensitive, proprietary, and confidential corporate data.

3. SUMMARY

This chapter has endeavored to condense the experiences of over a decade of forensic, litigation, security, discovery, and software design and use cases into some 40 pages. It has attempted to do this in such a way as to lay a foundation of understanding. Through learning the business and understanding the ins and outs of it, a proper security framework for individually unique enterprises and unique legal cases can be established.

The industry is rapidly changing. New technologies are emerging, and companies such as kCura, Recommind, and AccessData, which were once microshops, are growing and absorbing more of the EDRM's functions into their offerings. As these platforms grow, they will inevitably become more robust and will offer the full life cycle in one product or suite. Ultimately, the organizations that are suing each other will experience the greatest security when the data can be kept and processed in as few disparate locations as possible.

The preceding will be achieved only by consolidating and collapsing the security zones to the point at which there only exist the corporate information system and a legal system whereby attorneys are able to present their work securely in a court of law. If the EDRM can be run in such a way that *only* responsive data leave the building, the surface area of exposure shrinks and security increases.

Finally, let us move on to the real interactive part of this chapter: review questions/exercises, hands-on projects, case projects, and an optional team case project. The answers and/or solutions by chapter can be found in the Online Instructor's Solutions Manual.

CHAPTER REVIEW QUESTIONS/ EXERCISES

True/False

1. True or False? The field of e-discovery does not relate to litigation as a whole.
2. True or False? The framework of the EDRM begins with information security.
3. True or False? Certain types of organizations are more likely than others to be prone to litigation.
4. True or False? There are loopholes in any external facing system.
5. True or False? The EDRM model breaks identification into the same phase of e-discovery as information management.

Multiple Choice

1. Finding better ways to improve what you are doing is known as:
   A. process
   B. standardization
   C. data retention
   D. evolution
   E. security

2. Defining and understanding your information flow is known as:
   A. evolution
   B. standardization
   C. data retention
   D. process
   E. security

3. Making sure everyone uses the same software, stores information in the same places, and uses approved technology for information transmittals is known as:
   A. evolution
   B. data retention
   C. standardization
   D. process
   E. security

4. Ensuring that you know your data are not walking out your front (or back) door is known as:
   A. security
   B. data retention
   C. standardization
   D. process
   E. evolution

5. Ensuring that you are keeping what you want to keep, destroying what you do not want, and backing up data at risk is known as:
   A. security
   B. data retention
   C. standardization
   D. data destruction
   E. all of the above

EXERCISE

Problem

Can an organization's internal IT staff conduct an investigation and extract electronic evidence?

Hands-on Projects

Project

What happens to electronic information after it is deleted?

Case Projects

Problem

What can an organization do immediately to safeguard the integrity and admissibility of electronic evidence?

Optional Team Case Project

Problem

What is spoliation, and how can an organization protect against it?

Chapter 43

Network Forensics

Yong Guan

Iowa State University, Ames, IA, United States

Note: This chapter is available in its entirety online at store.elsevier.com/product.jsp?isbn= 9780128038437 (click the Resources tab at the bottom of the page).

1. ABSTRACT

Today's cyber-criminal investigator faces a formidable challenge: tracing network-based cyber criminals. The possibility of becoming a victim of cyber-crime is the number-one fear of billions of people. This concern is well founded. The findings in the annual Computer Security Institute/Federal Bureau of Investigation Computer Crime and Security Surveys confirm that cyber-crime is real and continues to be a significant threat. Trace-back and attribution are performed during or after cyber violations and attacks to identify where an attack originated, how it propagated, and what computer(s) and person(s) are responsible and should be held accountable. The goal of network forensics capabilities is to determine the path from a victimized network or system through any intermediate systems and communication pathways, back to the point of attack origination or the person who is accountable. In some cases, the computers launching an attack may themselves be compromised hosts or be controlled remotely. Attribution is the process of determining the identity of the source of a cyber-attack. Types of attribution can include both digital identity [computer, user account, Internet Protocol (IP) address, or enabling software] and physical identity (the actual person using the computer from which an attack originated). Cyber-crime has become a painful side effect of the innovations of computer and Internet technologies. With the growth of the Internet, cyber-attacks and crimes are happening every day and everywhere. It is very important to build the capability to trace and attribute attacks to the real cyber criminals and terrorists, especially in this large-scale human-built networked environment. In this chapter, we discuss the current network forensic techniques in cyber-attack trace-back. We focus on the current schemes in IP spoofing trace-back and stepping-stone attack attribution. Furthermore, we introduce the trace-back issues in Voice over Internet Protocol, botmaster, and online fraudsters.

2. CONTENTS

Chapter 44

Microsoft Office and Metadata Forensics: A Deeper Dive

Rich Hoffman

UnitedLex, Overland Park, KS, United States

1. INTRODUCTION

I am a firm believer that every document and forensic image have a story to tell and every case has three possible outcomes:

1. I found the evidence needed.
2. I was not smart enough to find it.
3. The absence of evidence fails to support the allegations.

The challenge is how can you honestly tell the difference between outcome 2 and 3? How do you know you have been thorough enough to know that the evidence does not exist? Therefore, I begin every examination as if it only has the first two possible outcomes.

In other words, to uncover evidence, specialists should gain a background of the suspect and offense, and determine a set of terms for the examination. Search expressions should be developed in a systematic fashion, such as using contact names that may be relevant. By proceeding systematically, the specialist creates a profile for potential leads that may unveil valuable findings (see checklist, "An Agenda for Action for the Analysis of Extracted Metadata").

2. IN A PERFECT WORLD

Every case has its own unique challenges. To limit variables, utilize the same methods as the custodian or suspect used. With each version and update to Microsoft Office, things can change. Always test using the same version of Microsoft Office as the custodian or suspect used. You should test your theory many times on multiple machines. Your goal is to limit the variables and make the conclusion obvious. Keep in mind, the lawyers reviewing your findings, as well as the opposing counsel's client and forensic examiner, will often see things differently. Your experience

---

An Agenda for Action for the Analysis of Extracted Metadata

The following are recommendations for the analysis of extracted metadata (check all tasks completed):

_____1. **Ownership and possession:** Identify the individuals who created, modified, or accessed a file, and the ownership and possession of questioned metadata by placing the subject with the device at a particular time and date; locating files of interest in nondefault locations; recovering passwords that indicate possession or ownership; and identifying contents of files that are specific to a user.

_____2. **Application and file analysis:** Identify information relevant to the investigation by examining file content, correlating files to installed applications, identifying relationships between files (email files to email attachments), determining the significance of unknown file types, examining system configuration settings, and examining file metadata (documents containing authorship identification).

_____3. **Timeframe analysis:** Determine when events occurred on the system to associate usage with an individual by reviewing any logs present and the date/time stamps in the file system, such as the last modified time. Besides call logs, the date/time and content of messages and email can prove useful. Such metadata can also be corroborated with billing and subscriber records kept by the service provider.

_____4. **Data hiding analysis:** Detect and recover hidden metadata that may indicate knowledge, ownership, or intent by correlating file headers to file extensions to show intentional obfuscation; gaining access to password-protected, encrypted, and compressed files; gaining access to steganographic information detected in images; and gaining access to reserved areas of metadata storage outside the normal file system.

Computer and Information Security Handbook. http://dx.doi.org/10.1016/B978-0-12-803843-7.00044-2

and thorough testing will enable you to high five your coworkers in the end.

In a perfect world where the document is opened and saved on one workstation, the document "Content created" metadata field starts the moment a new document is opened and will be BEFORE the file system created date and time. The file system created date will set to the date and time when the document is saved onto the workstation for the first time. The document "Date last saved" metadata field and file system modified date should match perfectly. In this perfect world, the document "Revision number" metadata field for a newly saved document will be 1. However, if the document has been opened, changed and resaved, the revision number will increase with each occurrence. Once the document has been changed and saved, subsequent use of the save button will not change the "Revision number" metadata field unless alterations have been made to the document.

Last Printed

The document "Last printed" metadata field is an often unreliable field for investigations. This field does not change every time the document is printed. When an existing document is opened and printed with no changes made, the application does not ask to save the document on exit. If the document is closed without saving, the last printed date and time is not updated. Furthermore, if a new document is created from an existing document or template, the last printed date and time will be carried over from the original document. The document "Last printed" metadata field is not very reliable because it is only updated and accurate when the document is changed, printed, and saved after each printing.

Accessing or Modifying Office Metadata

Office metadata is typically accessed through the details tab with a right click on the document and selecting properties. It is also accessible within the document by selecting "File," "Properties," and "Advanced Properties" with the document open. The "Advanced Properties" section allows the changing of the "Hyperlink base" and "Keywords" metadata fields which are not accessible from the details tab. Editing the metadata through the "Advanced Properties" section will require saving of the document which will change the file system last modified date and the "Date last saved" metadata field. Additionally, the custodian or suspect can change the Microsoft Office "User name" and "Initials" in the application's "Options" settings which is accessible with a document opened. The "User name" filed is responsible for the information in the "Author" and "Last saved by" metadata fields.

It is important to understand that if the custodian or suspect modifies any metadata fields from the details tab, the "Date last saved" metadata field will not change but the file system modified date will. The option to remove "Last saved by" and "Program name" are not editable through the details tab without using the "Remove Properties and Personal Information" feature accessible from the details tab. This feature does not allow alteration of the metadata fields, only deletion. This will create a copy of the document with only the file system modified date changed with all available or selected metadata fields that are checked removed:

- Create a copy with all possible properties removed
- Remove the following properties from this file:
  - Title
  - Subject
  - Tags
  - Categories
  - Comments
  - Authors
  - Last saved by
  - Revision number
  - Version number
  - Program name
  - Company
  - Manager
  - Content status
  - Content type
  - Language

Listed in Table 44.1 are the fields that can be easily modified by the user. These metadata fields can be modified through the details tab with a right click on the document and selecting properties. It is also accessible within the document by selecting "File", "Properties," and "Advanced Properties" with the document open.

The fields in Table 44.2 are automatically modified by the Microsoft Office applications. With the exception of the "Program name" and "Total editing time" metadata fields, they cannot be modified by the custodian or suspect.

The metadata fields in Table 44.3 are provided from the file system. These are not changeable by the custodian or suspect with the exception of the file system "Date created" and "Date modified" fields. Those modified fields can be changed by moving the document to a new source; thus, creating a copy or editing and, saving the document.

3. MICROSOFT EXCEL

Oh, Excel, why do you hate me? For those who love it, Excel moves into their house and they cuddle while watching movies. For people like me, I want to find the creators of Excel and talk bad about them behind their backs. It is the only option I have as I'm not a tough kid.

TABLE 44.1 Easily Modified Metadata Fields by the Custodian or Suspect

Property Type	Property Name	Can Be Changed?
Standard	Author	Yes
Standard	Category:	Yes
Standard	Comments	Yes
Standard	Company	Yes
Standard	Content status	Yes
Standard	Content type	Yes
Standard	Hyperlink base	Yes
Standard	Keywords	Yes
Standard	Language	Yes
Standard	Manager	Yes
Standard	Revision number	Yes
Standard	Subject	Yes
Standard	Tags	Yes
Standard	Title	Yes
Standard	Version number	Yes

When an Excel document is changed, it does not always mean the custodian or suspect opened, made changes and saved the document. One example is if a document is created with Excel 2003 and the Microsoft Office application is later upgraded to Excel 2007. After the upgrade,

TABLE 44.2 The Fields That Are Automatically Updated by the Application

Property Type	Property Name	Can Be Changed?
Auto update	Content created	No
Auto update	Character count	No
Auto update	Date last saved	No
Auto update	Last printed	No
Auto update	Last saved by	No
Auto update	Line count	No
Auto update	Links dirty?	No
Auto update	Pages	No
Auto update	Paragraph count	No
Auto update	Program name	No
Auto update	Scale	No
Auto update	Template	No
Auto update	Total editing time	No
Auto update	Word count	No

TABLE 44.3 The Fields That Are Provided by the File System

Property Type	Property Name	Can Be Changed?
File system	Availability	No
File system	Computer	No
File system	Date accessed	No
File system	Date created	No
File system	Date modified	No
File system	Offline status	No
File system	Shared with	No
File system	Size	No

when an existing document is opened, Excel 2007 makes small changes to the document that does not ask the user to save. Thus, the file is altered without any user action other than opening the document. Additionally, Excel will sometimes ask the user to save even though no changes have been made to the document. Some examples include:

- There is a volatile function used in the Excel document. A volatile function is one that causes recalculation of the formula in a cell.
- A formula that contains a link to a formula in another workbook that uses volatile functions.
- Linked pictures.
- Iterative formulas that use circular references that cause your functions to repeat until a specific numeric condition is met.
- Charts that are embedded into worksheets but have their source data in another workbook.
- Visual basic for applications code that updates the workbook.
- Excel formulas such as a date formula such as NOW() or TODAY().

4. EXAMS!

Now, to the fun stuff. The following forensic examinations (Exams 44.1–44.3) will all tell stories. Try to find this story before you read the answer. You won't have all data available from a full forensic image, but you will have what was provided for the case—a single document. Some of this could be easily found by the experienced examiner. However, I will bet that even the experienced examiner will be scratching their head. This part of the chapter will contain actual data for you to download. Good luck!

All exams can be performed with or without a forensic application. The exam data is contained in an AccessData image file (AD1). This will require AccessData FTK

EXAM 44.1 Forensic Examination

Problem

The client contacted you to validate the date of the document produced by opposing counsel. The case hinges on whether or not this document was created in June 2012. In a January 2015 deposition, the opposing counsel's client stated that this document is the original and was created in June 2012. They also stated that this document was copied directly to a thumb drive from the original source and delivered to opposing counsel on January 8, 2015. This thumb drive was delivered directly to you which was acquired using a write blocker and is waiting examination. The client is in the Central Time Zone (CST). Use one of the two links to download Exam 1:

- www.publishingcompany.com/nameofbook/Exam1.zip
- www.richhoffman.com/Exam1.zip

Answers

Don't read this until you have completed Exam 1! You will never be able to go back in time to the point when you did not know the answer. Honestly, why watch the football game when you know the end score? Last warning… don't read on!

Desired outcome: The client wishes to prove that the created date of this document is <u>NOT</u> in June 2012.

Below is the important document metadata and file system fields:

"Validate Word Dates.doc" File System Information:
Created: Tuesday, June 12, 2012, 2:27:16 PM
Modified: Tuesday, June 12, 2012, 2:27:17 PM
"Validate Word Dates.doc" Metadata Information:
Content created: 06/12/2012, 2:27 PM
Date last saved: 06/12/2012, 2:27 PM
Last Printed: 1/8/2015, 9:01 AM
Revision number: 2
Total editing time: 00:00:00

Findings

1. Yes, the file system created and modified dates of this document are in June 2012, precisely 1 s apart. This would appear to support opposing counsel's claim of the document's June 2012 created date. However, it should be a red flag that the file system created and modified dates are almost exact! If this was the original document, the "Content created" metadata filed would start the instant the document was opened. The "Date last saved" metadata field would be later when the document was first saved.

2. In the January 2015 deposition, the deposed claimed the document is the original, created in June 2012, copied directly to a thumb drive from the original source and delivered to opposing counsel on January 8th, 2015. It is VERY important to obtain background information for your cases. The case NEVER starts and finishes with only the digital evidence delivered. The "Revision number 2" metadata filed with the file system created date and the "Content created" metadata field match perfectly. This does not support what was stated in the deposition.
   a. Three scenarios that would explain the "Revision number 2":
      i. Revision number changes when saving the document twice in the normal course of use. This would have different "Content created" and "Date last saved" metadata fields date and time. This would also have a "Total editing time" that is not 00:00:00. This is NOT the case here.
      ii. If you create a NEW UNSAVED document and close the application before it is saved for the first time. The

application will ask "Want to save your changes to …?" If you select "Save," this will create a document with identical file system created and modified dates with a "Revision number 2." It will skip 1 in this scenario even though this is the first time the document was saved. However, the "Content created" metadata field in this scenario would be set to the moment the document was opened and the "Date last saved" metadata filed would match the file system modified date. They would be different. This is NOT the case here.
      iii. A previously saved document was opened and "File," "Save As" was used. This will create a document with the "Revision number 2," "Total editing time" of 00:00:00 and matching "Content created" and "Date last saved" metadata fields. This is what happened!

Facts

1. Fact: This document or the one it was created from WAS printed on a workstation on 1/8/2015, 9:01 AM according to the clock set on the workstation. This document MUST have first been changed, printed, and saved for that "Last Printed" date to be recorded.
2. Fact: The file system created and modified dates and the "Content created" and "Date last saved" metadata fields are all 6/12/2012, 2:27 PM. This document was "SAVED AS" onto a new location on 6/12/2012, 2:27 PM according to the clock set on that workstation and the "Revision number" metadata filed.
3. If the document was copied to a thumb drive like the deposed claimed it will traditionally bring with it the file system modified date but WILL change the file system created date unless an application such as Robocopy/Xcopy is used to preserve it. It appears that an application was used to preserve the file system created date or the document was saved directly to the thumb drive.

Conclusion

Dates on the workstation were changed to create this document. The printed date is AFTER the document "Date last saved" metadata field and the file system last modified dates. This is simply not possible for this to be the original document because the "Date last printed" metadata file requires a document save which will change the "Date last saved" metadata field. This, in turn, would cause a change to the file system modified dates. This document was created from an existing document that was last printed on 1/8/2015, 9:01 AM as that document must have been last saved after the "Last printed" date.

Additional Information

- This document was created using Microsoft Word 2013 and saved as DOC and not DOCX. The DOCX extension is used by Word 2007, 2010, and 2013 for Windows and Word 2008 and 2011 for OSX.
- The "Date last saved" metadata field should ALWAYS match the file system modified date. If this is NOT the case, red flags should rise.
- If a document is opened and not changed, it could be printed 100 times and when closed the last printed date will be exactly as it was before it was opened and printed. The ONLY time the "Last printed" metadata filed will change is if the document is CHANGED, PRINTED AND SAVED. If all three of these do not occur, the "Last Printed" date will NOT be changed.

EXAM 44.2 Forensic Examination

Problem

A law firm has contacted you to validate their client's document before this goes to court. This document will be delivered to opposing counsel's forensic examiner and it is important that it was created in November 2011 and last modified in July 2013. This document CANNOT Be outside of those dates or the case falls apart. Most importantly, if something is missed, opposing counsel's forensic examiner will eat you alive in court. This document was collected from opposing counsel's client file server called STORAGE01 using AccessData FTK Imager on 4/29/2016. During collection, it was noticed that all files stored with this document have different file system created and modified dates. The client is in the Central Time Zone (CST).

During the onsite visit, the following was obtained:

- Counsel's client has had the same server since March 2010.
- The document in question has not been moved since the document was created and last saved.
- Counsel's client has had no data loss or issues with the server.

Use one of the two links to download Exam 2:

www.publishingcompany.com/nameofbook/Exam2.zip

www.richhoffman.com/Exam2.zip

Answers

Don't read this until you have completed exam 2! I noticed that some of you did not download Exam 1 because I am tracking the number of downloads compared to the number of books sold. We are short, people! Last warning... don't read on!

For review, our client needs the created date of this document to be in November 2011 and last modified in July 2013.

Below is the important document information:

"**Your Company.docx**" File System Information:

Created: Tuesday, April 26, 2016, 7:10:53 AM

Modified: Sunday, July 7, 2013, 10:10:06 AM

"**Your Company.docx**" Metadata Information:

Content created: 11/26/2011, 5:58 AM

Date last saved: 7/7/2013, 10:10 AM

Revision number: 1

Total editing time: 14139:12:00

Findings

1. The metadata "Content created" and "Date last saved" dates are what is needed for this case.
2. The file system created date is April 26, 2016.
3. The document was collected on April 27, 2016, the day after the document file systems created date.
4. The file system modified date and time is the same as the "Date last saved" metadata filed date and time. This appears the document was saved normally.
5. The metadata "Total editing time" is 14139:12:00.

Facts

1. The file system created date is 4/26/2016. NOTE! When a document is saved in an alternate location such as the server, the file system created date will match the date/time of the alternate location and NOT the date/time of the workstation. The document metadata fields WILL match the time of the workstation.
2. The metadata "Total editing time" is 14139:12:00. The "Content created" metadata filed is 11/26/2011, 5:58 AM, and the "Last saved date" metadata field is 7/7/2013, 10:10 AM. NOTE! The time between both the "Content created" and "Date last saved" is 589 days, 4 h, and 12 min. This is 1 h off but is because of daylight saving time.

Conclusion

The day before the document was collected, opposing counsel's client set the clock back on the workstation and saved the document on the server. During this time, the document was left open when the date and time on the workstation was set back.

Additional Information

- Time travel should be left only to those with a DeLorean and a Flux Capacitor.

Imager to extract the document which is downloadable from: www.accessdata.com.

5. ITEMS OUTSIDE OF OFFICE METADATA

The following information will assist in determining what to look for outside of the document metadata. This information can change with each release of the operating system and office application. Simply, know what is available.

OAlerts.evtx

OAlerts are gold! These will assist in determining user activity as they include all messages that pop up with the Office applications. Listed below is the location of the OAlerts.evtx and some of the alerts (C:\Windows\System32\winevt\Logs\OAlerts.evtx):

- "Before deleting the e-mail account containing your personal mail, contacts, and calendar data, you must create a new location for your data."
- "Are you sure you want to remove this profile from the system?"
- "The connection to Microsoft Exchange is unavailable. Outlook must be online or connected to complete this action."
- "This will be permanently deleted."
- "Delete this folder and everything in it?"

EXAM 44.3 Forensic Examination

Problem

You were contacted to validate the date of a document produced by opposing counsel. A forensic report was also included from opposing counsel's forensic expert that validated the 2009 creation date. This is your biggest client and the creation date of this document must be in 2009 or they stated they will need to take this to someone else. This is a huge concern as you are not as friendly or good looking as the forensic company across the street. However, this one appears to be a loss for you with opposing counsel's expert report, and you have told your realtor it is time to move into a smaller place. This document was delivered to you in an AccessData forensic image by opposing counsel and is waiting examination. The client is in the Central Time Zone (CST).

Use one of the two links to download Exam 3:
www.publishingcompany.com/nameofbook/Exam3.zip
www.richhoffman.com/Exam3.zip

Answers

Don't read this until you have completed exam 3! This is my favorite exam and if you don't download and attempt this examination you will break my heart. Download this or do not expect an invite to my birthday party. This exam stumps most of the examiners and it is time to step up to the plate. Last warning… don't read on!

For review, your financial well-being and the client need the created date of this document to be in 2009. Below is the important document information:

"Validate Word Dates.doc" File System Information:
Created: Wednesday, March 4, 2009, 2:53:46 PM
Modified: Tuesday, April 14, 2009, 8:32:58 PM
"Validate Word Dates.doc" Metadata Information:
Revision number: 10
Content created: 3/4/2009, 1:53 PM
Date last saved: 4/14/2009, 8:32 PM
Last printed: 3/19/2009, 6:31 PM
Total editing time: 01:33:00

Findings

1. The file system created date is 1 h different from the "Content created" metadata field.
2. The file system modified date and "Date last saved" metadata field match perfectly.
3. The document metadata appears to indicate normal use.
4. Inside the document is the image of the company logo in the document header.

Facts

1. This appears to have been saved on a server or network-attached storage (NAS) because of the drive letter it was collected from.
2. The file system creation date and the "Date last saved" metadata field date and time is 1 h apart. This is most likely due to daylight saving time which begins on the second Sunday of March and ends on the first Sunday of November. In 2009 daylight saving time began on Sunday, March 8. With daylight saving time the clock moves ahead 1 h in March, whereas it moves back 1 h in November. It appears that the workstation has daylight saving enabled and the server or NAS does not.
3. The EXIF data of the JPEG of the company logo saved in the document header shows this image was saved using Adobe Photoshop CS5 using a Windows machine on 2/20/2015, 2:32 PM.
4. Your work should NOT stop here! Look online and find that Adobe Photoshop CS5 was not released until May 2010!

Conclusion

There is NO way this Microsoft Word document could be created on April 14, 2009. The image's EXIF data show this document was created on February 20, 2015 using Adobe Photoshop CS5. This document was created 5 years, 11 months, 16 days, 39 min and 51 s before the image was created. Additionally, Adobe Photoshop CS5 was not available for purchase for 1 year and 56 days after this Microsoft Word document was created. This can only be accomplished by setting the clock back on the computer and falsifying the document.

Document 3 Additional Information

- ALWAYS keep in mind that opposing council's forensic examiner is often hired to examine the data that supports opposing counsel's case ONLY. A forensic examiner is not typically asked to perform hours of examination on dates that the client and counsel's client are sure of. Remember that the opposing forensic examiner is your peer and is no better or worse then you. They are often placed in a bad situation because of the items they were asked to examine. Keep yourself in check!
- You can save an image as a JPG or TIF in Office 2010 and older and see the EXIF data natively if the image contains any. Right click on the image and select "Save as." Often, the MD5 of the file will be identical to the file placed in the document.
- If an image is large, the office application will often shrink it, changing the image.

- "Everything in the 'Deleted Items' folder will be permanently deleted."
- "A folder with this name already exists. Use another name."
- "Move 'Outlook folder name' to your Deleted Items folder?"

- "If you continue, you'll lose your changes to the attachment 'document name.xxx' opened from the message 'RE: Subject of email'."
- "We can't find 'http://site/document.xxx.' Please make sure you're using the correct location or web address."
- "Want to save your changes to 'document name'?"

Outlook Auto Archiving Registry Settings

Outlook can create an archive portable storage table (PST) for items that used to exist in the default PST or in the Exchange server. This will remove the Outlook items and they will not be available in the master PST or Exchange server. Additionally, the archive PST could be available in an alternate location such as a network share. Is Auto Archiving Enabled/Disabled (HKCU\Software\Microsoft\Office\##.#\Outlook\Preferences\):

- If DWORD "DoAging" exists- AutoArchiving is/has been enabled
- If DWORD "DoAging" = 1 — enabled, 0 — disabled
- If DWORD "DoAging" does not exist — AutoArchive has never been enabled (Default)

Outlook Cached Exchange Mode

Outlook cached Exchange is a copy of the items available on the Exchange server stored on the workstation. The offline storage table (OST) or Offline Outlook Data File is very similar to the PST or Outlook Data File. The following sidebar ("Outlook Cached Exchange Mode") shows how to find if Outlook cached Exchange Mode is enabled.

Volume Shadow Copy Service (VSS)/ Previous Versions

Volume Shadow Copy Service (VSS) or Previous Versions can save snapshots of data at different points in time. VSS creates manual or automatic copies of volumes or files even when they are in use. VSS was first added to Windows XP and Windows Server 2003. This is the first place I go for recovery. If a user forensically overwrites data, VSS can often bring it back if enabled. The sidebar ("Registry Key") will show if VSS is enabled with any snapshots that exist and files not included.

Windows/Mac Backup

The Windows Backup application keeps track of the items added or modified and adds them to the existing backup. What is being backed up? The schedule and total

---

Outlook Cached Exchange Mode
Outlook 2003/2007:
    HKCU\Software\Microsoft\Windows NT\Current Version\Windows Messaging Subsystem\Profiles\13dbb0c8aa05101a9bb000aa002fc45a\
        Key "00036601"
        Enabled value "84 01 00 00"
        Enabled with Public Folders/Favorites "84 05 00 0"
        Disabled value "04 00 00 00"
    Outlook 2010/2013:
    HKCU\Software\Microsoft\Windows NT\ CurrentVersion\Windows Messaging Subsystem\Profiles\Outlook\
    Search for the key "00036601". It may be found in multiple places as Outlook 2010 allows for multiple exchange accounts (thus multiple OSTs). Outlook 2013 is not in the above location so search for the above key.
        Enabled value "84 19 00 00"
        Enabled with Public Folders/Favorites "84 05 00 00"
        Disabled value "04 10 00 00"
    Warning: With the default configuration of Outlook 2013 it will only synchronizes 12 months of email to the Offline Outlook Data (.OST) file. If the user has the default Outlook settings, email older than 12 months will exist ONLY on the Exchange server and not on the workstation's OST. In this case, an export of the data on the Exchange server or an export from the Exchange server must be performed. The offline synchronizing limitation using Outlook 2013 does not affect the following items:
- Calendar
- Contacts
- Tasks
- Journal
- Notes
- Outbox
- Shared or delegate

Registry Key
VSS Enabled/Disabled:
    HKLM\SOFTWARE\Microsoft\Windows NT\CurrentVersion\SystemRestore\RPSessionInterval.
    Disabled "0"
    Enabled "1"
    Files NOT included in VSS Snapshot:
    HKLM\SYSTEM\ControlSet001\Control\BackupRestore\FilesNotToSnapshot.
- VSS requires the NTFS file system.
- By default, Windows 7 disables VSS on SSD drives.
- Windows Vista VSS can take up to 15 percent of the size of the volume or a maximum of 30 percent of the free disk space, whichever is less.
- Windows 7 with hard drives over 64 GB, VSS can take up to 5 percent of the size of the volume or a maximum of 10 GB of disk space, whichever is less. On computers with hard drives of 64 GB or less, VSS can take at most 3 percent of the disk space.
- Windows 8 is lacking the feature for the user to access the VSS data. However, forensic applications that do not use the Windows API to access VSS will have the ability to access the VSS data.
- VSS will run every 24 h with Windows Vista and every week with Windows 7 by default. If you see VSS restore points outside of the default times, look for other reasons this happened, such as:
  - VSS created by the user.
  - VSS is created before a Windows update.
  - VSS is create before an unsigned driver is installed.
  - VSS can be created during the install/uninstall of a program if the application requests.

size of the backup can be changed by the end user, as shown below:

Is Backup Enabled:
HKLM\SOFTWARE\Microsoft\Windows\
CurrentVersion\WindowsBackup\
Enabled "ValidConfig (1)"
Data being backed up:
HKLM\SOFTWARE\Microsoft
\Windows\CurrentVersion\WindowsBackup
\ScheduleParams\Rules.
Backup Destination:
HKLM\SOFTWARE\Microsoft\Windows
\CurrentVersion\WindowsBackup\ScheduleParams
\TargetDevice

Roaming Profiles or Folder Redirection

Roaming Profiles will redirect a copy of the workstations user's data onto the server. This will require the workstation to be connected to the location roaming profiles is storing the data in order to synchronize. This feature can be enabled by the server through active directory or by the end user. This will contain a copy of the user's data both on the server and the workstation. If viewing a user profile that does not appear to contain the typical user folders, look in the following location:

\WINDOWS\CSC

CD/DVD Temporary Burn Folder

To create a CD/DVD it will be required to have a CD/DVD burner and recordable CD/DVD media. There are many third party applications for CD/DVD burning but this will concentrate on the applications included with the Windows and Mac operating systems. The locations to look for files as Windows/Mac creates a copy of the data being burned to CD/DVD are shown below:

Windows XP:
\Documents and Settings\%profile%\Local Settings\
Application Data\Microsoft\CD Burning.
Windows Vista, 7/8/10:
\Users\%profile
%\AppData\Local\Microsoft\Windows\Burn\
Mac:
\var\log\system.log \Users\%profile%\Library\
Logs\DiscRecording.log.

6. SUMMARY

Microsoft Office files are everywhere. Often, hundreds to tens of thousands of documents will exist in email, workstations, and server shares. Due to their heavy everyday use, it is no wonder these files are often the reason for the investigation. Many document reviewers and attorneys will often take the document's metadata and file system data at face value. They often do not fully understand the story this document wants to tell. However, an experienced examiner can be able to understand what is possible and what should be to assist in telling what potentially happened with this document. Always keep in mind that everyone will see this story differently. Based on the experience, the examiner requests, and the research, the story can be found. Find it!

Finally, let's move on to the real interactive part of this Chapter: review questions/exercises, hands-on projects, case projects, and optional team case project. The answers and/or solutions by chapter can be found in Appendix K.

CHAPTER REVIEW QUESTIONS/ EXERCISES

True/False

1. True or False? To uncover evidence, specialists should gain a background of the suspect and offense, and determine a set of terms for the examination.
2. True or False? In a perfect world where the document is closed and saved on one workstation, the document "Content created" metadata field starts the moment a new document is opened and will be BEFORE the file system created date and time.
3. True or False? The document "Last printed" metadata field is an often unreliable field for investigations.
4. True or False? Office metadata is typically accessed through the details tab with a left click on the document and selecting properties.
5. True or False? When an Excel document is changed, it does not always mean the custodian or suspect opened, made changes, and saved the document.

Multiple Choice

1. What causes recalculation of the formula in a cell?
   A. Privacy-enhancing technology
   B. Location technology
   C. Volatile function
   D. Technical improvement
   E. Web technology
2. All exams can be performed with or without a:
   A. Privacy-enhancing technology
   B. Location technology
   C. Forensic application
   D. Web
   E. Web technology
3. Before deleting the email account containing your personal mail, contacts, and calendar data, you must create a new location for your:
   A. Access control
   B. Data
   C. XML-based language
   D. Certification authority
   E. Security

4. Outlook can create an archived PST for items that used to exist in the default PST or in the:
   A. Access control models
   B. Exchange server
   C. Privacy-aware access control
   D. Privacy preferences
   E. Taps
5. Outlook cached Exchange is a copy of the items available on the Exchange server stored on the:
   A. Release policy
   B. Access control policy
   C. Workstation
   D. Intellectual property
   E. Social engineering

EXERCISE

Problem

How does an organization go about using metadata forensics?

Hands-on Projects

Project

How does an organization go about accessing file metadata forensics?

Case Projects

Problem

Why is metadata so important to an investigation?

Optional Team Case Project

Problem

What is the advantage of processing metadata electronically rather than in paper form for discovery purposes?

Chapter 45

Hard Drive Imaging

John Benjamin Khan
University of Massachusetts Boston, Boston, MA, United States

1. INTRODUCTION

Hard drive imaging has been the mainstay of digital forensics for many years. It has been articulated by many organizations that the forensic image of a hard drive is designed to get that bit-for-bit image of the entire contents of a hard drive. That concept is drilled into digital examiners; vendors have built tools around that concept; and the National Institute of Technology and Standards (NIST) has built a whole department around the science of hard drive imaging—thus, the subject matter of this chapter covers this information:

- Hard Disc Drives
- Solid State Drives
- Hardware Tools
- Software Tools
- Techniques

2. HARD DISC DRIVES

Hard Disc Drives are electromechanical devices where computer systems store information. This information can be inculpatory or incriminating evidence in an investigation; or it can serve sentimental value when recovered. Within the last decade, Solid State Drives have emerged to take the place of Hard Disc Drives. Solid State Drives are digital mediums that achieve the same task where a traditional Hard Disc Drive would have been used. In other words, they are two different birds of the same tree.

A Hard Disc Drive is made up of many components: metal alloy platter, a head that moves by an arm mounted to an actuator, which interconnects to an outer circuit board that connects to the motherboard of a computer system, or encased to a Universal Serial Bus (USB) adapter if it is external. At a minimum, of course, there are many iterations of this technology as it has been in use for many

years. It may even be necessary to research the design of the Hard Disc Drive you are either investigating or performing a recovery on. On several occasions it was necessary to replace the outer circuit board of the Hard Disc Drive to getting it working again.

Doing such requires a Hard Disc Drive from the same manufacturer and model. Therefore, it is good to have a cache of Hard Disc Drives in your arsenal. Depending on your level of skill, some electronic engineering can also come in handy when dealing with Hard Disc Drives. It is also important to know that depending on the type of system you are working on, multiple Hard Disc Drives may be involved and can be from different manufacturers. So hoarding Hard Disc Drives can be beneficial.

3. SOLID STATE DRIVES

As stated before, Solid State Drives are digital mediums that achieve the same task where a traditional Hard Disc Drive would have been used. Depending on the manufacturer or unless specified otherwise, Solid State Drives utilize a form of Flash memory: either NOR or NAND, both of which should be researched for a further understanding of how their functions differ in achieving the same task.

Unlike a Hard Disc Drive, there are no mechanical parts in a Solid State Drive. This is usually made up of a circuit board with electrical components attached. Despite serving the same task, there are few, if any, interchangeable parts, meaning once it goes bad it is rendered useless. If you have electrical engineering experience, you may be able to desolder modules and solder them to another circuit board of the same make and model or perform some other manipulation to extract data, if possible. This is similar to swapping the platters of a Hard Disc Drive.

Unlike a Hard Disk Drive that stores data on the platter, Solid State Drives move data throughout cells that are composed of Flash modules. Because of this movement, it is

Computer and Information Security Handbook. http://dx.doi.org/10.1016/B978-0-12-803843-7.00045-4

near impossible to determine physically where the requested data is. So electrical engineering and reverse engineer skills can work hand in hand when dealing with such devices.

4. HARDWARE TOOLS

In a field where expectations and standards can change case-by-case or person-to-person, you must establish an arsenal of many tools, especially hardware. You may want to hoard a couple old legacy systems and newer computer systems. Although software emulators such as virtual machines might give you the options to match the specs of the machine under investigation or recovery, it may not be able to suffice the components of a physical machine. Aside from being able to recreate the system you must first figure out how to acquire a Forensic image of the drive.

Depending on the situation and nature of the case you will have to make, the decision must be made to either leave the system on or power off to make a Forensic image of the drive. It is a complicated decision, but in regards to the nature of Solid State Drives, it is better to leave the system on and use the data migration software that some manufacturers provide with their Solid State Drives to copy the drive. However, a physical duplicator can suffice for both Hard Disc Drives and Solid State Drives for a physical forensic copy.

There are many manufacturers of physical duplicators: some indicate their capacity limitations and some can make more than one copy. Some work well with specific file systems and others are not biased. Adapters and converters are always good to have since there are variations to the common Serial Advanced Technology Attachment and USB connections. Bear in mind form factors and power configurations of the drives themselves. You will want to make sure you are able to support various sizes and capacity.

5. SOFTWARE TOOLS

Not all hardware has Write Blocking capabilities, and software alone should not be trusted for this. For instance, some operating systems (OSs) themselves have ways for users to enable read-only modes on attached drives. To do this on Microsoft's Windows [1] System requires a registry hack that can be implemented by yourself, or you can download the registry files from online. Possessing a few common OSs can also come in handy in both physical and virtual environments. With that being said, I would like to interject that Apple makes the most forensically friendly computer-based OS. However, it requires adding their hardware to your arsenal, which would be a good thing if you support Apple's Mac OSX [2].

Despite being a forensically friendly system, you may encounter a situation where you cannot power off the system and remove the hard drive. So Black Bag Technologies Macquisition [3] will be a necessary tool to have in your software arsenal. Bear in mind the objective of a

Computer Forensic investigation or Data Recovery, because your selection of tools will vary and you will need to provide validation either to a courtroom or investigator (see checklist: "An Agenda for Action for Hard Drive Imaging Tool Test Process"). A Hash Analysis will be needed in order to do this. Some tools have this feature built in but not all tools do. It is a best practice to provide both MD5 and SHA1 Hash values for individual files and Forensic image files of drives. Guidance Software's EnCase [4] Forensic software has the ability to do both once the image or drive is processed.

An Agenda for Action for Hard Drive Imaging Tool Test Process

After a hard drive imaging specification has been developed and a tool selected, follow the test process in this checklist (check all tasks completed):
_____1. Acquire the tool to be tested.
_____2. Review the tool documentation.
_____3. Select relevant test cases depending on features supported by the tool.
_____4. Develop test strategy.
_____5. Execute tests.
_____6. Produce test report.
_____7. Steering Committee reviews test report.
_____8. Vendor reviews test report.
_____9. Post support software to the web.
_____10. Post test report to the web.

Perhaps you may not have a budget for the aforementioned software but will have to make use of free software. PassMark Software's OSForensics [5] has some limitations in the free version but has similar capabilities as Guidance Software's EnCase such as a drive imaging function within one Graphical User Interface. Although Access Data's FTK [6] Imager is a standard for creating Forensic image file(s) of drives. We live in an environment with no respect to standards and therefore have to make use of nonstandard means of achieving the same task.

6. TECHNIQUES

Say a small business owner loses their password to the security camera system and gives you the hard drive to find any suspicious video footage. You do not have access to proprietary software but have a similar security camera DVR and a good amount of time on your hands. Having never seen such a drive before, you are familiar with the manufacturer and you take from your arsenal a drive of the same capacity and other matching characteristics and create a physical copy. Once done, you put the original hard drive in a sandwich bag and write the date you received it and the date and time you created the physical image.

A Computer Forensic investigator can sometimes become a Data Recovery specialist and vice versa. Continuing along with my example. After numerous attempts with a couple tools you have no luck extracting anything from the copy of the drive. Thus, a little progress can be made by creating a Forensic image file of the original drive, and then running that file through more tools such as Piriform's Recuva [7]; but then, when you get a video file, the video file only plays in VideoLAN's VLC media player [8].

So you then deem Piriform's Recuva as a stepping stone, mount the Forensic image file to PassMark Software's OSForensics, and use the deleted file and data carving tool to search for video files. Then hours later, you let the small business owner know that the timestamps on the video files do not match the time of when the suspicious activity took place. Do not underestimate yourself, but make sure you are following what will be applicable to the law in legal proceedings that require Computer Forensic investigations and efficient Data Recovery.

7. SUMMARY

This chapter covered how the firmware and modules of hard drive imaging tools, contain programs and configuration settings that are needed by the hard drive to operate. There are a very small number of tools that can read or modify the service area of hard drive imaging. So, for the time being, this is not an everyday threat to digital forensic examiners cases. It is something, however, that organizations need to be aware of now and in the future. Testimony about the imaging of hard drives needs to carry the caveat that organizations are imaging the user-accessible area of the hard drive. Organizations should not be looking at a bit-for-bit image of the entire hard drive. Data can be written to the service area, but those areas of the hard disk drive are not accessible when utilizing the forensically imaged current industry tools. The current forensic imaging tools do not allow for imaging outside of the user-accessible area and will not in the foreseeable future.

Finally, let's move on to the interactive part of this Chapter: review questions/exercises, hands-on projects, case projects, and optional team case projects. The answers and/or solutions by chapter can be found in Appendix K.

CHAPTER REVIEW QUESTIONS/ EXERCISES

True/False

1. True or False? Hard Disc Drives are electromechanical devices where computer systems store information.
2. True or False? A Hard Disc Drive is made up of many components: metal alloy platter, a head that moves by an arm that is mounted to an actuator, which interconnects to an outer circuit board that connects to the motherboard of a computer system or encased to a USB adapter if it is external.
3. True or False? Depending on the type of system you are working on, multiple Hard Disc Drives may be involved and can be from the same manufacturers.
4. True or False? Solid State Drives are digital media that achieve the same task where a traditional Hard Disc Drive would have been used.
5. True or False? Unlike a Hard Disc Drive, there are no mechanical parts in a Solid State Drive.

Multiple Choice

1. Unlike a Hard Disk Drive that stores data on the platter, Solid State Drives move data throughout its cells that are composed of:
   A. Google Authenticators
   B. MOTPs
   C. Mobile OTPs
   D. Flash modules
   E. All of the above
2. In a field where expectations and standards can change case-by-case or person-to-person, you must establish an arsenal of many tools, especially:
   A. Hardware
   B. Risk assessments
   C. Scales
   D. Access
   E. Active monitoring
3. Depending on the situation and nature of the case you will have to make, the decision must be made to either leave the system on or power off to make a Forensic image of the:
   A. Drive
   B. Text message
   C. Worm
   D. Log
   E. All of the above
4. There are many manufacturers of physical duplicators; some indicate their capacity limitations and some can make more than just one
   A. Token
   B. Copy
   C. Paper
   D. Metal
   E. All of the above
5. Some operating systems themselves have ways for users to enable read-only modes on:
   A. Systems security plans
   B. TrustPlus

C. Attached drives
D. Client devices
E. All of the above

EXERCISE

Problem

How does an organization go about creating a forensic hard drive image?

Hands-On Projects

Project

What is the purpose of hard drive imaging? How does an organization go about imaging a hard drive?

Case Projects

Problem

What is the purpose of hard drive cloning? How does an organization go about cloning a hard drive?

Optional Team Case Project

Problem

How would an organization go about reimaging a hard drive?

REFERENCES

[1] https://www.microsoft.com/en-us/windows, 2016.
[2] Apple, 1 Infinite Loop, Cupertino, CA 95014, http://www.apple.com/osx/, 2016.
[3] https://www.blackbagtech.com/software-products/macquisition.html, 2016.
[4] Guidance Software, Inc., 1055 E. Colorado Blvd., Pasadena, CA 91106-2375 United States, https://www.guidancesoftware.com/encase-forensic, 2016.
[5] PassMark Software Pty Ltd., Level 5, 63 Foveaux St, Surry Hills, NSW 2010, Australia, http://www.osforensics.com/, 2016.
[6] AccessData, 588 West, 400 South, Suite 350, Lindon, UT 84042, http://accessdata.com/solutions/digital-forensics/forensic-toolkit-ftk, 2016.
[7] http://www.piriform.com/recuva, 2016.
[8] VideoLAN, 18, rue Charcot, 75013 Paris, France, http://www.videolan.org/vlc/index.html, 2016.

Part VI

Encryption Technology

Chapter 46

Data Encryption

Bhushan Kapoor and Pramod Pandya

CSU Fullerton, Fullerton, CA, United States

Note: This chapter is available in its entirety online at store.elsevier.com/product.jsp?isbn= 9780128038437 (click the Resources tab at the bottom of the page).

1. ABSTRACT

The Internet evolved over the years as a means for users to access information and exchange emails. Later, once the bandwidth became available, businesses exploited the Internet's popularity to reach customers online. It has been reported that organizations that store and maintain customers' private and confidential records were compromised on many occasions by hackers breaking into data networks and stealing records from storage media. We have come across headline-grabbing security breaches regarding laptops with sensitive data being lost or stolen, and the Feds have encrypted around 1 million laptops with encryption software loaded to secure data such as names and Social Security numbers. This chapter is about security and the role of cryptographic technology in data security. Securing data while they are in storage or in transition from an unauthorized access is a critical function of information technology. If compromised, all forms of electronic commerce (ecommerce) activities such as online credit card processing, purchasing stocks, and banking data processing would lead to businesses losing billions of dollars in revenues as well as customer confidence lost in ecommerce.

2. CONTENTS

Chapter 47

Satellite Encryption

Daniel S. Soper
California State University, Fullerton, CA, United States

1. INTRODUCTION

For virtually all of human history, the communication of information was relegated to the surface of Earth. Whether written or spoken, transmitted by land, by sea, or by air, all messages had one thing in common: they were, like those who created them, inescapably bound to the terrestrial surface. In February 1945, however, the landscape of human communication was forever altered when an article by the highly influential science fiction writer Arthur C. Clarke proposed the extraordinary possibility that artificial satellites placed into orbit above Earth could be used to facilitate mass communication on a global scale. A year later, a Project RAND report concluded that "A satellite vehicle with appropriate instrumentation [could] be expected to be one of the most potent scientific tools of the 20th century," and that "The achievement of a satellite craft would produce repercussions comparable to the explosion of the atomic bomb." It was only 12 short years after Clarke's historic prediction that mankind's first artificial satellite, Sputnik 1, was transmitting information from orbit back to Earth. In the decades that followed, satellite technology

evolved rapidly from its humble beginnings to become an essential tool for such diverse activities as astronomy, commerce, communications, scientific research, defense, navigation, and the monitoring of global climate conditions. In the 21st century, satellites are helping to fuel globalization, and societies everywhere are relying heavily on the power of satellite technology to enable the modern lifestyle. It is for these reasons that satellite communications must be protected. Before examining satellite encryption in particular, however, a brief review of satellite communication in general may be useful.

For communications purposes, modern satellites can be classified into two categories: those that communicate exclusively with the surface of Earth (which will be referred to here as "Type 1" satellites), and those that communicate not only with the surface of Earth, but also with other satellites or spacecraft (which will be referred to here as "Type 2" satellites). The distinction between these two types of satellite communication is depicted in Fig. 47.1.

As shown in Fig. 47.1, there are several different varieties of communications links that a particular satellite may

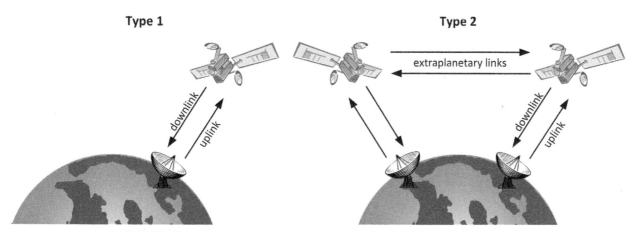

Type 1   **Type 2**

extraplanetary links

FIGURE 47.1 Comparison of Type 1 and Type 2 satellite communication capabilities.

Computer and Information Security Handbook. http://dx.doi.org/10.1016/B978-0-12-803843-7.00047-8

support. Classifying satellites as Type 1 or Type 2 provides us with a useful framework for understanding and discussing basic satellite communications capabilities, and allows us to gain insight into the sort of communications links that may need to be protected. In the case of Type 1 satellites, the spacecraft may support uplink capabilities, downlink capabilities, or both. An uplink channel is a communications channel through which information is transmitted from the surface of Earth to an orbiting satellite or other spacecraft. By contrast, a downlink channel is a communications channel through which information is transmitted from an orbiting satellite or other spacecraft to the terrestrial surface. While Type 2 satellites may possess the uplink and downlink capabilities of a Type 1 satellite, they are also capable of establishing links with spacecraft or other Type 2 satellites for purposes of extraplanetary communication. Type 2 satellites that can act as an intermediary between other spacecraft and the terrestrial surface can be classified as relay satellites. Note that whether a particular link is used for sending or receiving information depends upon the perspective of the viewer. From the ground, for example, an uplink channel is used to send information, but from the perspective of the satellite, the uplink channel is used to receive information.

2. THE NEED FOR SATELLITE ENCRYPTION

Depending on the type of satellite communications link that needs to be established, substantially different technologies, frequencies, and data encryption techniques may be required in order to secure a satellite-based communications channel. The reasons for this lie as much in the realm of human behavior as they do in the realm of physics. Broadly speaking, it is not unreasonable to conclude that satellite encryption would be entirely unnecessary if every human being were perfectly trustworthy. That is to say, the desire to

protect our messages from the possibility of extraterrestrial interception and decipherment notwithstanding, there would be no need to encrypt satellite communications if only those individuals entitled to send or receive a particular satellite transmission actually attempted to do so. In reality, however, human beings, organizations, and governments commonly possess competing or contradictory agendas, thus implying the need to protect the confidentiality, integrity, and availability of information transmitted via satellite.

Keeping such human behavioral concerns in mind, we can also understand the need for satellite encryption from a physical perspective. Consider, for example, a Type 1 communications satellite that has been placed into orbit above Earth's equator. Transmissions from the satellite to the terrestrial surface (the downlink channel) would commonly be made by way of a parabolic antenna. Although such an antenna facilitates focusing the signal, the signal nevertheless disperses in a conical fashion as it departs the spacecraft and approaches the surface of the planet. The result is that the signal may be made available over a wider geographic area than would be optimally desirable for security purposes. As with terrestrial radio, in the absence of encryption, anyone within range of the signal who possesses the requisite equipment could receive the message. In this particular example, the geographic area over which the signal would be dispersed would depend both on the focal precision of the parabolic antenna, and the altitude of the satellite above Earth. These concepts are illustrated in Fig. 47.2.

Because the sender of a satellite message may have little or no control over to whom the transmission is theoretically available, protecting the message requires that its contents be encrypted. For similar reasons, extraplanetary transmissions sent between Type 2 satellites must also be protected. After all, with thousands of satellites orbiting the planet, the chances of an intersatellite communication being intercepted are quite good!

Fixed Altitude, Variable Focal Precision

Variable Altitude, Fixed Focal Precision

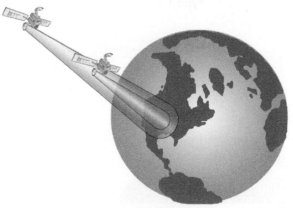

FIGURE 47.2 Effect of altitude and focal precision on satellite signal dispersion.

Aside from these considerations, the sensitivity of the information being transmitted must also be taken into account. Different entities possess different motivations for wanting to ensure the security of messages transmitted via satellite. An individual, for example, may want her private telephone calls or bank transaction details to be protected. An organization may likewise want to prevent its proprietary data from falling into the hands of its competition while a government may want to protect its military communications and national security secrets from being intercepted or compromised by an enemy. As is the case with terrestrial communications, the sensitivity of the data being transmitted via satellite must dictate the extent to which those data are protected. If the emerging global Information Society is to fully capitalize on the benefits of satellite-based communication, its citizens, organizations, and governments must be assured that their sensitive data are not being exposed to unacceptable risk. In light of these considerations, satellite encryption will almost certainly play a key role in the future advancement of mankind.

3. IMPLEMENTING SATELLITE ENCRYPTION

It was noted earlier in this chapter that information can be transmitted to or from satellites using three general types of communication links: surface-to-satellite links (uplinks), satellite-to-surface links (downlinks), and intersatellite or interspacecraft links (extraplanetary links). Technological considerations notwithstanding, the specific encryption mechanism used to secure a transmission depends not only on which of these three types of links is being utilized, but also on the nature and purpose of the message being transmitted. For purposes of simplicity, the value of transmitted information can be classified along two dimensions: high-value and low-value. The decision as to what constitutes high-value and low-value information largely depends on the perspective of the beholder—after all, one person's trash is another person's treasure. Nevertheless, establishing this broad distinction allows satellite encryption to be considered in the context of the conceptual model shown in Fig. 47.3.

As shown in Fig. 47.3, any satellite-based communication can be classified into one of six possible categories.

Each of these categories will be addressed later in the chapter by considering the encryption of both high-value and low-value data in the context of the three types of satellite communication links. Before considering the specific facets of encryption pertaining to satellite uplink, extraplanetary, and downlink transmissions, however, an examination of several of the more general issues associated with satellite encryption may be useful.

General Satellite Encryption Issues

One of the problems common to all forms of satellite encryption relates to signal degradation. Satellite signals are typically sent over long distances using comparatively low-power transmissions, and must frequently contend with many forms of interference, including terrestrial weather, solar and cosmic radiation, and many other forms of electromagnetic noise. Such disturbances can cause errors or gaps to emerge in the signal that carries a satellite transmission from its source to its destination. Depending on the encryption algorithm chosen, this situation can be particularly problematic for encrypted satellite transmissions, since the entire encrypted message may be irretrievably lost if even a single bit of data is out of place. To resolve this problem, a checksum or cryptographic hash function may be applied to the encrypted message to allow errors to be identified and reconciled upon receipt. This approach comes at a cost, however; appending checksums or error-correcting code to an encrypted message increases the length of the message, and by extension increases the time required for the message to be transmitted. The result, of course, is that a satellite's actual overall communications capacity is commonly lower than its theoretical capacity, due to the extra burden that is placed on its limited resources by this communications overhead.

Another common problem associated with two-way encrypted satellite communications relates to establishing the identity of the sender of a message. Most modern satellites, for example, are designed to receive and respond to signals that control their onboard functions. Such satellites need to be certain that the control signals they receive from the ground originate from an authorized source. In addition to control signals, senders of other types of satellite transmissions commonly need to be authenticated as well.

Type of Satellite Communications Link

Data Value	Uplink	Downlink	Extraplanetary Link
High-Value	Category 01	Category 03	Category 05
Low-Value	Category 02	Category 04	Category 06

FIGURE 47.3 Satellite communications categories as a function of data value and type of link.

An intelligence agency receiving a satellite transmission from one of its operatives, for example, needs to establish that the transmission is genuine. To establish the identity of the sender, the message needs to be encrypted in such a way that from the recipient's perspective, only a legitimate sender could have encoded the message. The sender, of course, also wants to ensure that the message is protected while in transit, and thus desires that only an authorized recipient would be able to decode the message upon receipt. Both parties to the communication must therefore agree to use an encryption algorithm that serves to identify the authenticity of the sender while affording a sufficient level of protection to the message while it is in transit to its destination. Although keyless encryption algorithms may satisfy these two criteria, such algorithms are usually avoided in satellite communications, since the satellite may become useless if the keyless encryption algorithm were to be compromised, and satellites are expensive to replace. This problem also extends to the terrestrial equipment used to encrypt satellite signals prior to transmission and decrypt those signals after receipt. Keyed encryption algorithms are therefore typically used to protect information transmitted via satellite. Even keyed methods of encryption can be problematic when it comes to satellite communications, however.

To gain insight into the problems associated with keyed encryption, one might first consider the case of a symmetrically keyed encryption algorithm, wherein the same key is used to both encode and decode a message. If party A wants to communicate with party B via satellite using this method, then both A and B must agree on a secret key in advance of the communication. As long as the key remains secret, it also serves to authenticate both parties. If party A also wants to communicate with party C, however, then A and C must agree on their own unique secret key, otherwise party B could masquerade as A or C, and vice-versa. A keyed encryption approach to two-way satellite communication thus requires that each party establish a unique secret key with every other party with whom they would like to communicate. To further compound this problem, each party must obtain all of its secret keys in advance, because possession of an appropriate key is a necessary prerequisite to establishing a secure communications channel with another party.

To resolve these issues, an asymmetrically keyed encryption algorithm may be adopted, wherein the key used to encrypt a message is different from the key used to decrypt the message. Such an approach requires each party to maintain only two keys, one of which is kept private, and the other of which is made publicly available. If party A wants to send party B a secure transmission, A first asks B for her public key, which can be transmitted over an unsecured connection. Party A then encodes a secret message using B's public key. The message is secure because only B's private key can decode the message. To authenticate herself to B, party A needs only to reencode the entire message using her own private key before transmitting the message to B. Upon receiving the message, B can establish whether it was sent by A, because only A's private key could have encoded a message that can be decoded with A's public key. This process is depicted in Fig. 47.4.

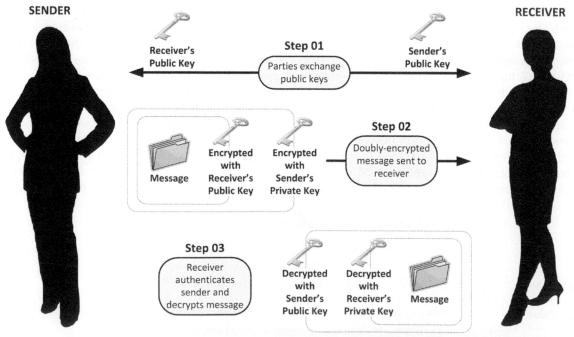

FIGURE 47.4 Ensuring sender identity and message security with asynchronously keyed encryption.

Unfortunately, even this approach to secure two-way satellite communication is not entirely foolproof. To understand why, consider how a malicious party M might interject himself between A and B in order to intercept the secure communication. To initiate the secure transmission, A must request B's public key over an unsecure channel. If this request is intercepted by M, then M can supply A with his own (that is, M's) public key. A will then encrypt the message with M's public key, after which she will reencrypt the result of the first encryption operation with her own private key. A will then transmit the encrypted message to B, which will once again be intercepted by M. Using A's public key in conjunction with his own private key, M will be able to decrypt and read the message. A will not know that the message has been intercepted, and B will not know that a message was even sent. Note that intercepting a secure communication is particularly easy for M if he owns or controls the satellite through which the message is being routed. In addition to the risk of interception, asynchronously keyed encryption algorithms are typically at least 10,000 times slower than synchronously keyed encryption algorithms—a situation that may place an enormously large burden on a satellite's limited computational resources. Until a means is developed of dynamically and securely distributing synchronous keys, satellite-based encryption will always require trade-offs among security, computational complexity, and ease of implementation.

Uplink Encryption

Protecting a transmission that is being sent to a satellite from at or near the surface of Earth requires much more than just cryptographic techniques; to wit, encrypting the message itself is a necessary but insufficient condition for protecting the transmission. The reason for this is that the actual transmission of the encrypted message to the satellite is but the final step in a long chain of custody that begins when the message is created and ends when the message is successfully received by the satellite. Along the way, the message may pass through many people, systems, or networks, the control of which may or may not reside entirely in the hands of the sender. If one assumes that the confidentiality and integrity of the message have not been compromised as the message has passed through all of these intermediaries, then but two primary security concerns remain: the directional accuracy of the transmitting antenna, and the method used to encrypt the message. In the case of the former, the transmitting antenna must be sufficiently well-focused to allow the signal to be received by—and ideally *only* by—the target satellite. With thousands of satellites in orbit, a strong potential exists for a poorly focused transmission to be intercepted by another satellite, in which case the only remaining line of defense for a message is the strength of the encryption algorithm

with which it was encoded. For this reason, a prudent sender should always assume that their message could be intercepted while in transit to and from the satellite, and should implement message encryption accordingly.

When deciding upon which encryption method to use, the sender must simultaneously consider the value of the data being transmitted, the purpose of the transmission, and the technological and computational limitations of the target satellite. A satellite's computational and technological capabilities are a function of its design specifications, its current workload, and any degradation that has occurred since the satellite was placed into orbit. These properties of the satellite can therefore be considered constraints—any encrypted uplink communications must work within the boundaries of these limitations. That said, the purpose of the transmission also features prominently in the choice of which encryption method to use. Here we must distinguish between two types of transmissions: commands, which instruct the satellite to perform one or more specific tasks, and transmissions-in-transit, which are intended to be retransmitted to the surface or to another satellite or spacecraft. Not only are command instructions of high-value, but they are also not typically burdened with the same low-latency requirements of transmissions-in-transit. Command instructions should therefore always be highly encrypted, because control of the satellite could be lost if they were to be intercepted and compromised. What remains, then, are transmissions-in-transit, which may be of either high-value, or of low-value. One of the basic tenants of cryptography states that the value of the data should dictate the extent to which the data are protected. As such, minimal encryption may be acceptable for low-value transmissions-in-transit. For such transmissions, adding an unnecessarily complex layer of encryption may increase the computational burden on the satellite, which in turn may delay message delivery and limit the satellite's ability to perform other tasks simultaneously. High-value transmissions-in-transit should be protected with a robust encryption scheme that reflects the value of the data being transmitted. The extent to which a highly encrypted transmission-in-transit will negatively impact a satellite's available resources depends upon whether or not the message needs to be processed before being retransmitted. If the message is simply being relayed through the satellite without any additional processing, then the burden on the satellite's resources may be comparatively small. If, however, a highly encrypted message needs to be processed by the satellite prior to retransmission (if the message needs to be decrypted, processed, and then reencrypted), the burden on the satellite's resources may be substantial. Processing high-value, highly encrypted transmissions-in-transit may therefore vastly reduce a satellite's throughput capabilities when considered in conjunction with its technological and computational limitations.

Extraplanetary Link Encryption

Before a signal is sent to the terrestrial surface, it may need to be transmitted across an extraplanetary link. Telemetry from a remote spacecraft orbiting Mars, for example, may need to be relayed to scientists by way of an Earth-orbiting satellite. Alternatively, a television signal originating in China may need to be relayed around Earth by several intermediary satellites in order to reach its final destination in the United States. In such circumstances, several unique encryption-related issues may arise, each of which is associated with the routing of an extraplanetary transmission through one or more satellite nodes. Perhaps the most obvious of these issues is the scenario that arises when the signal transmitted from the source satellite or spacecraft is not compatible with the receiving capabilities of the target. For example, the very low-power signals transmitted from a remote exploratory spacecraft may not be detectable by a particular listening station on the planet's surface, or the data rate or signal modulation with which an extraplanetary transmission is sent may not be supported by the final recipient. In this scenario, the intermediary satellite through which the signal is being routed must act as an interpreter or translator of sorts, a situation which is illustrated in Fig. 47.5.

From an encryption perspective, the situation illustrated in Fig. 47.5 implies that the intermediary satellite may need to decrypt the extraplanetary message and reencrypt it using a different encryption scheme prior to retransmission. A similar issue may arise for legal or political reasons. Consider, for example, a message that is being transmitted from one country to another by way of several intermediary satellites. The first country may have no standing policies regarding the encryption of messages sent via satellite, while the second country may have policies that strictly regulate the encryption standards of messages received via satellite.

In this case, one or more of the orbiting satellites may need to alter the encryption of a message in transit in order to satisfy the legal and regulatory guidelines of both countries.

Downlink Encryption

Several different issues impact the way in which information is protected as it is transmitted from orbiting satellites to the surface of Earth. As with uplink encryption, the technological and computational capabilities of the spacecraft may constrain the extent to which a particular message can be protected. If, for example, an older communications satellite does not possess the requisite hardware or software capabilities to support a newly developed downlink encryption scheme, then that scheme simply cannot be used with the satellite. Similarly, if the utilization of a particular encryption scheme would reduce the efficiency or message-handling capacity of a satellite to a level that is deemed unacceptable, then the satellite's operators may choose to prioritize capacity over downlink security. The precision with which a satellite is able to focus a downlink transmission may also impact the choice of encryption scheme—as noted earlier in this chapter, a widely dispersed downlink signal can be more readily intercepted than can a signal transmitted with a narrow focus. While each of these computational and technological limitations must be considered when selecting a downlink encryption scheme, they are by no means the only factors requiring consideration.

Unlike uplink signals, which can only originate from the surface of the planet, messages to be transmitted over a downlink channel can come from one of three different sources: the terrestrial surface, from another spacecraft, or from the satellite itself. The source of the message to be broadcast to the planet's surface plays a critical role in determining the method of protection for that message.

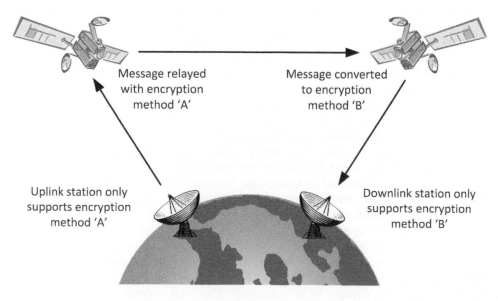

FIGURE 47.5 In-transit translation of encrypted messages in satellite communication.

Message relayed with encryption method 'A'

Message converted to encryption method 'B'

Uplink station only supports encryption method 'A'

Downlink station only supports encryption method 'B'

Consider, for example, a message that originates from the surface or from another spacecraft. In this case, one of two possible scenarios may exist. First, the satellite transmitting the message to Earth may be serving only as a simple signal repeater or amplifying transmitter; that is to say, the message is already encrypted upon receipt, and the satellite is simply relaying the previously encrypted message to the surface. In this case, the satellite transmitting the downlink signal has very little to do with the encryption of the message, and only the integrity of the message and the retransmission capabilities of the satellite at the time the message is received need be considered. In the second scenario, a satellite may need to filter a message or alter its encryption method prior to downlink transmission. For example, a satellite may receive signals that have been optimized for extraplanetary communication from a robotic exploration spacecraft in the far reaches of the solar system. Prior to retransmission, the satellite may need to decrypt the data, process it, and then reencrypt the data using a different encryption scheme more suited to a downlink transmission. In this case, the technological capabilities of the satellite, the timeliness with which the data need to be delivered, and the value of the data themselves dictate the means through which those data are protected prior to downlink transmission.

Finally, one might consider the scenario in which the data being transmitted to the terrestrial surface originate from the satellite itself, rather than from the surface or from another spacecraft. Such data can be classified as either telemetry, relating to the status of the satellite, or as information that the satellite has acquired or produced while performing an assigned task. In the case of the former, telemetry relating to the status of the satellite should always be highly protected, as it may reveal details about the satellite's capabilities, inner workings, or control systems if it were to be intercepted and compromised. In the case of the latter, however, the value of the data that the satellite has acquired or produced should dictate the extent to which those data are protected. Critical military intelligence, for example, should be subjected to a much higher standard of encryption than data that are comparatively less valuable. In the end, a satellite operator must weigh many factors when deciding upon the extent to which a particular downlink transmission should be protected. It is tempting to conclude that the maximum level of encryption should be applied to every downlink transmission. Doing so, however, would unnecessarily burden satellites' limited resources, and would vastly reduce the communications capacity of the global satellite network. Instead, a harmonious balance needs to be sought between a satellite's technological and computational capabilities, and the source, volume, and value of the data that it is asked to handle. Only by achieving such a balance can the maximum utility of a satellite be realized.

4. PIRATE DECRYPTION OF SATELLITE TRANSMISSIONS

As a general rule, it is reasonable to assume that encrypted satellite messages contain content that is important or valuable in some way. After all, why would a sender go to the trouble of encrypting a message if its contents were not of value? Unfortunately, the fact that encrypted satellite transmissions contain valuable information is sufficient motivation for some individuals, organizations, and governments to attempt to decrypt and benefit from such information, even if they are not its intended recipients. In the world of encrypted satellite communications, this problem of pirate signal decryption is compounded by two additional factors. First, the dispersive nature of satellite-to-ground transmissions—as illustrated in Fig. 47.2—creates an environment in which many people other than the intended recipient have access to the encrypted signal. This is, of course, also one of the great benefits of satellite communication, since it allows providers of commercial services such as satellite-based television and radio to ensure that their signals are available to as many potential customers as possible. Second, equipment designed to receive satellite signals is, at least in the developed world, both abundant and relatively inexpensive.

As opposed to satellite transmitters or transceivers—both of which can send messages to satellites—the vast majority of the satellite communications devices in use today are classified simply as receivers, which can receive satellite transmissions but cannot send them. These differences are illustrated in Fig. 47.6.

There are literally hundreds of millions of Global Positioning System (GPS) devices, commercial satellite television receivers, and satellite radio devices in use in the world today, and while all are designed to receive satellite signals, only a tiny fraction can actually send them. When

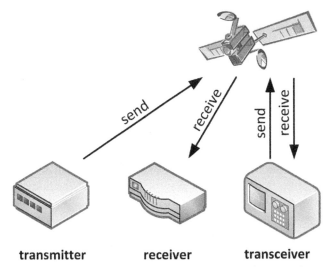

FIGURE 47.6 Communications capabilities of satellite transmitters, receivers, and transceivers.

viewed through the eyes of a signal pirate, the combination of these factors makes encrypted satellite transmissions a very tempting target. There are three reasons for this: First, since the encrypted signal is already available, no additional effort (such as physical wiretapping) is required in order to gain access to the signal itself. Second, since compatible receiving equipment is relatively inexpensive and widely available, acquiring the equipment necessary to receive an encrypted satellite signal is not at all difficult for most would-be pirates. Finally, although pirating encrypted satellite transmissions is illegal in many countries, the fact that most satellite communications devices are simple receivers that cannot transmit any information back to the sender means that the probability of a signal pirate being detected and subsequently punished is quite low.

Since signal piracy has become a rampant phenomenon in the realm of commercial satellite communications, a survey of the history of satellite signal piracy should prove useful. As described earlier in this chapter, modern digital satellite communication relies on keyed encryption algorithms for message security. In this model, the sender first encodes a message by running the digital data through an encryption algorithm with a chosen key. The resulting encrypted data are then relayed to the receiver by way of a satellite transmission, after which the receiver can decrypt the message using the appropriate key. Anyone wishing to access the encrypted satellite transmission must therefore satisfy three conditions if he or she is to be successful. First, the receiver must have access to the encrypted signal. This typically means that the receiver must possess compatible receiving equipment, and must be geographically located within the satellite's signal dispersion zone. Next, the receiver must know which encryption algorithm was used to encode the message. This is usually not a significant problem, since the encryption algorithm is typically embedded within the hardware or software of the receiving device. Finally, presuming that the first two conditions have been met, the receiver must apply the proper key in order to unlock the encrypted digital message. It is toward this final condition that efforts aimed at signal piracy are most often directed.

Circuit-Based Security

Since most satellite receivers are not capable of two-way communication, they are also generally not capable of negotiating a new key with the sender of the encrypted message in real-time. The sender of the message must therefore find some other way of supplying its authorized receivers with the proper key, and many different approaches have been developed with this problem in mind. In early secure satellite communications, the means of decoding encrypted transmissions were often built directly into the receiving devices themselves in the form of fixed solid-state circuitry. The "key" in these cases would be the

one unique circuit design that would allow a given message to be decrypted. Anyone who owned such a receiver could therefore decode the encrypted transmission, and the sender maintained security by regulating who was given access to compatible receiving devices.

From a security perspective, this early approach was plagued by several obvious flaws. First, anyone able to clone the circuitry of the receiving device would have immediate access to the encrypted message. Circuit components and circuit design knowledge were quite rare in the early days of satellite communication, but it was not long until a would-be signal pirate with a little knowledge could walk into his or her local electronics supply store and buy everything needed to build a simple satellite receiver. Since the security of this approach depended on maintaining the secrecy of the circuit design, the entire system would be compromised as soon as knowledge of that design was made available outside of the circle of authorized recipients. The security of the system could thence only be restored by replacing all of the legitimate receivers with new receivers that contained a different unique circuitry key. If only a few people were authorized to receive the encrypted messages, then replacing the compromised devices might not be terribly problematic. If thousands or even millions of people were authorized to receive the encrypted messages, however, then replacing all of the compromised receivers could be a financially and logistically daunting prospect. Clearly, a better approach was needed.

Removable Security Cards

The next major evolutionary step in secure satellite communications arrived with the introduction of removable security cards. In this model, the receiving devices themselves were of a generalist design inasmuch as they could receive satellite messages encrypted with any number of algorithms or keys. Decoding the encrypted message, however, required that a proprietary security card be inserted into the receiver. It was thus the security card and not the receiver itself which contained the proper circuitry for decrypting the signal. This approach had three major advantages. First, service offerings could be readily stratified into multiple layers. A satellite television customer who wanted to purchase a premium movie channel, for example, could be sent a security card capable of decrypting that channel. Second, the security cards could be rotated according to some predefined schedule. Secret military communications, for example, might use a different security card every day or every week in order to enhance the overall security of the system. Third, if the security of the decryption circuitry were ever compromised, the sender would only need to replace the security cards themselves. This would, of course, be much less expensive than replacing all of the receivers completely.

Unfortunately, this security card—based approach suffered from many of the same fundamental flaws as earlier approaches. Namely, an aspiring signal pirate could gain access to the encrypted signal simply by cloning the circuitry of the security card. Once successful, the pirate could rest comfortably knowing that the probability he or she would be detected was virtually zero. This problem came to a head when the first several generations of security cards developed by direct broadcast satellite television companies were cracked almost immediately after being released. Not only did this create a great deal of embarrassment and bad press for these companies, but it also spawned a lively and flourishing black market for pirated satellite security cards. Eventually, a new generation of security cards that incorporated what are known as application-specific integrated circuits (ASICs) was released in order to combat this problem. As the name implies, an ASIC is an integrated circuit that is designed for a very specific purpose—in this case, to decode encrypted satellite signals. Since integrated circuits are much smaller than standard circuitry and can contain thousands if not millions of logic gates, reverse-engineering an ASIC's circuit pathways is an extremely difficult task that requires highly specialized equipment such as a circuit probe or an electron microscope. While the introduction of ASICs all but eliminated the black market for cloned satellite security cards, signal piracy is still prevalent today as pirates have found ways of tinkering with or reprogramming existing cards to allow them to illicitly receive premium or restricted content. There is little reason to believe that this long-lived battle between signal pirates and satellite content providers will end anytime soon.

5. SATELLITE ENCRYPTION POLICY

Given the rapid adoption of satellite communications and the potential security implications associated therewith, many governments and multinational coalitions are increasingly establishing policy instruments with a view toward controlling and regulating the availability and use of satellite encryption in both the public and private sectors. Such policy instruments have wide-reaching economic, political, and cultural implications that commonly extend well beyond national boundaries. One might, for example, consider the export controls placed on satellite encryption technology by the United States government, which many consider to be the most stringent in the world. Broadly, these export controls were established in support of two primary objectives. First, the maintenance of a restrictive export policy allows the government to review and assess the merits of any newly developed satellite encryption technologies that have been proposed for export. If the export of those technologies is ultimately approved, the government will possess a detailed understanding of how the technologies operate, potentially allowing for their encryption schemes to be defeated if deemed necessary. Second, such controls allow the government to prevent satellite encryption technologies of particularly high merit from leaving the country, especially if the utilization of those technologies by foreign entities would interfere with US intelligence-gathering activities. Although these stringent controls may appear to be a legacy of the xenophobic policies of the Cold War, they are nevertheless still seen as prudent measures in a world where information and communication technologies can be readily leveraged to advance extreme agendas. Unfortunately, such controls have potentially negative economic implications, insofar as US firms may be barred from competing in the increasingly lucrative global market for satellite communication technologies.

The establishment and maintenance of satellite encryption policy also needs to be considered in the context of satellite systems of global import. Consider, for example, the NAVSTAR GPS, whose constellation of satellites enables anyone with a GPS receiver to accurately determine their current location, time, elevation, velocity, and direction of travel anywhere on or near the surface of Earth. In recent years, GPS capabilities have been incorporated into the navigational systems of automobiles, ocean-going vessels, trains, commercial aircraft, military vehicles, and many other forms of transit all over the world. Despite its worldwide use, the NAVSTAR GPS satellites are currently operated by the 2nd Space Operations Squadron of the US Air Force, implying that satellite encryption policy decisions related to the GPS system are controlled by the US Department of Defense. One of the options available to the United States government through this arrangement is the ability to selectively or entirely block the transmission of civilian GPS signals while retaining access to GPS signals for military purposes. Additionally, the United States government reserves the right to introduce errors into civilian GPS signals, thus making them less accurate. Since the US government exercises exclusive control over the GPS system, users all over the world are forced to place a great deal of trust in the goodwill of its operators, and in the integrity of the encryption scheme for the NAVSTAR uplink channel. Given the widespread use of GPS navigation, a global catastrophe could ensue if the encryption scheme used to control the NAVSTAR GPS satellites were to be compromised. Because the GPS system is controlled by the US military, the resiliency and security of this encryption scheme cannot be independently evaluated.

In the reality of a rapidly globalizing and interconnected world, the effectiveness of national satellite encryption policy efforts may not be sustainable in the long run. Satellite encryption policies face the same legal difficulties as so many other intrinsically international issues; to wit, outside of international agreements, the ability of a specific country to enforce its laws extends only so far as its geographic boundaries. This problem is particularly relevant in the context of satellite communications, since the satellites themselves orbit Earth, and hence do not lie within the geographic boundaries of any one nation. Considered in conjunction with the growing need of governments to share intelligence resources and information with their allies, future efforts targeted toward satellite encryption policy-making may increasingly fall under the auspices of international organizations and multinational coalitions.

Finally, let's briefly look at Satellite Encryption Service (SES). SES provides dedicated and reliable satellite encryption–based transmission for specific data networks and mission critical applications, where landline access may not be available, as well as wideband video broadcast transmission. The connection from the satellite Earth station to the Service Delivery Platform (SDP) is included in this service.

6. SATELLITE ENCRYPTION SERVICE (SES)

SES can be used as dedicated transmission service for voice, data, and video traffic transmission and wideband broadcast applications, such as broadband distance learning and broadcast of data/multimedia files. The service provides full-duplex, half-duplex, and simplex (broadcast) encrypted transmissions using C-band, Ku-band, and Ka-band satellites.

SES provides dedicated and ad-hoc (reservation-based) encrypted satellite transmission. This transmission can be used by any application services at a customer specified bandwidth between two or more distance learning, broadcast-quality National Television System Committee (NTSC) video and associated audio, digital compressed video, and associated audio, including encrypted communications specified end points. The connection between the locations receiving this encryption service is permanently established unless a service request for modification, move, or disconnect is received.

This encryption service can be used for applications such as voice, data, video, and multimedia, and may include government end-to-end encrypted communications. As previously stated, SES also provides reservation-based wideband encrypted satellite broadcast transmission that can be used for numerous applications.

SES connects to and interoperates with specified permanent or temporary locations (SDPs, such as private branch exchange, Multiplexer, router, video codec, Earth station, and Voltage Security Assessment Tool, both fixed and transportable/deployable). This results in a satellite encryption strategy being guided by a set of precutover activities (see checklist: "An Agenda for Action for Satellite Encryption Service [SES] Precutover Activities").

7. THE FUTURE OF SATELLITE ENCRYPTION

Despite the many challenges faced by satellite encryption, the potential advantages afforded by satellites to mankind

are so tantalizing and alluring that the utilization of satellite-based communication can only be expected to grow for the foreseeable future. As globalization continues its indefatigable march across the terrestrial surface, access to secure, high-speed communications will be needed from even the most remote and sparsely populated corners of the globe. Satellites by their very nature are well-positioned to meet this demand, and will therefore play a pivotal role in interconnecting humanity and enabling the forthcoming global Information Society. Furthermore, recent developments in the area of quantum cryptography promise to further improve the security of satellite-based encryption. This rapidly advancing technology allows the quantum state of photons to be manipulated in such a way that the photons themselves can carry a synchronous cryptographic key. The parties involved in a secure communication can be certain that the cryptographic key has not been intercepted, because eavesdropping upon the key would introduce detectable quantum anomalies into the photonic transmission. By using a constellation of satellites in low Earth orbit, synchronous cryptographic keys could be securely distributed via photons to parties wishing to communicate, thus resolving the key exchange problem. The parties could then establish secure communications using more traditional satellite channels. The further development and adoption of technologies such as quantum cryptography ensures that satellite-based communication has a bright and secure future.

There are, of course, risks to relying heavily on satellite-based communication. Specifically, if the ability to access critical satellite systems fails due to interference or damage to the satellite, disastrous consequences may ensue. What might happen, for example, if interference from a solar flare were to disrupt the constellation of global positioning satellites? What might happen if a micrometeoroid storm were to damage all of the weather satellites monitoring the progress of a major hurricane? What might happen to a nation's ability to make war if antisatellite weapons were deployed to destroy its military communications and intelligence-gathering satellites? Questions such as these highlight the risks of relying too heavily on artificial satellites. Nevertheless, as the costs associated with building, launching, and operating satellites continue to decline, the utilization of satellite technology will, for the foreseeable future, become an increasingly common part of the human experience.

8. SUMMARY

This chapter focused on encrypted satellite data transmissions (uplink and downlink) in the critical national infrastructure and private industry. Over the last 16 years, the federal government and corporations have become increasingly reliant on the commercial satellite communications industry. Today, the satellite industry is providing encrypted voice, data, and video services in support of

An Agenda for Action for Satellite Encryption Service (SES) Precutover Activities

In order to provide timely, comprehensive, relevant, and accurate satellite encryption strategy, the following set of precutover activities must be adhered to (check all tasks completed):

Administrative

_____**1.** Has a Hierarchy Code (HC) been provided to the vendor?

_____**2.** Have local contacts (recommend at least two per location) been identified and contact information provided?

_____**3.** Has a Project Specific Transition Plan Identifier been assigned?

_____**4.** Note (P_OPS) in the Service Request Number (SRN) if this is parallel encryption service.

Preordering/Design Decisions

_____**5.** Has the vendor developed the functional and performance specifications for Satellite Encryption Service (SES) systems and Sensor Evolutionary Developments (SEDs) in accordance with requirements? This task will include the development of the operational concept for SES within the overall network architecture.

_____**6.** Has the vendor identified all necessary interfaces between the wireline and wireless systems and SES?

_____**7.** Has the vendor defined the contours of the SES coverage to make and receive calls?

_____**8.** Has the vendor presented a plan to continue to provide any changes to satellite footprints for each satellite system providing the coverage?

_____**9.** Determine the Parallel Operations Period—all orders for parallel service will have to be so noted in the SRN.

_____**10.** Fall-back plan: Has the vendor provided a detailed fall-back/back-out plan to all stakeholders?

Site Preparation

_____**11.** Has the vendor conducted site surveys at all locations if required and provided site survey reports?

_____**12.** Has the vendor delivered an acceptable, detailed, system design? This design plan, at a minimum, will address network topology, configuration, addressing (fleet mapping), coverage, availability, reliability, scalability, security, Service Enabling Devices (SEDs), and disaster recovery requirements.

User Training

_____**13.** Has the vendor provided any required training and documentation for users?

Installation

_____**14.** Has the vendor managed the SEDs required for the installation and operation of the SES to include ensuring that SEDs are transported to the appropriate site of deployment and/or stored until installation is complete?

Network Management

_____**15.** Has the vendor submitted a detailed, overall management plan for the SES to include operational support?

Documentation

_____**16.** Has the vendor provided all required documentation (Systems Specifications Document, System Design Document, and Test Documentation when completed)?

Execute Tests

_____**17.** Have the Network Management Organization and vendor reviewed the results of this testing to ensure all is ready for the actual cutover?

_____**18.** Conduct precutover testing.

governmental and commercial operations, including national security and emergency preparedness (NS/EP) missions. The commercial industry is also supplying the majority of the encrypted satellite communications used for military and surveillance operations along and outside the border of Iran and within Afghanistan. As part of the critical national infrastructure, encrypted satellite networks provide unparalleled coverage of remote geographical areas and difficult terrain. They complement terrestrial networks also used to provide NS/EP communications support.

The terrestrial components of encrypted satellite networks contain many of the same subsystems found in other communications networks. As a result, encrypted satellite and terrestrial networks share similar cyber vulnerabilities

and mitigation measures. However, because satellites must be controlled remotely from Earth, satellite operators take special care to mitigate two risks: (1) remote introduction of a false spacecraft command; and (2) a malicious third party preventing the spacecraft from executing authorized commands or interfering with satellite telemetry reception.

Satellite operators use redundant and geographically diverse facilities to protect terrestrial infrastructure from human-made and natural threats and to ensure continuity of encrypted critical satellite network functions. Ground stations are connected by redundant, path-diverse, cryptographically secured communications links and employ preventative measures such as buffer zones and robust security systems to protect from attack. Further, operators maintain personnel security procedures, including background checks, employee badges, logged entry and exit, and on-site security guards as part of their best practice security efforts.

Consistent with government policy, most satellite companies use the National Security Agency-approved satellite command uplink encryption for satellites supporting US government services. As operators replace their older, legacy satellites that are technically incapable of encrypting commands, newer satellites are likely to be fully compliant with the government's policy direction.

Finally, let's move on to the real interactive part of this Chapter: review questions/exercises, hands-on projects, case projects, and an optional team case project. The answers and/or solutions by chapter can be found in the Online Instructor's Solutions Manual.

CHAPTER REVIEW QUESTIONS/ EXERCISES

True/False

1. True or False? Depending on the type of satellite communications link that needs to be established, substantially different technologies, frequencies, and data encryption techniques may be required in order to secure a satellite-based communications channel.
2. True or False? For purposes of simplicity, the value of transmitted information can be classified along three dimensions: high-value, medium-value, and low-value.
3. True or False? One of the problems common to all forms of satellite encryption relates to signal degradation.
4. True or False? Protecting a transmission that is being sent to a satellite from at or near the surface of Earth requires much more than just cryptographic techniques; to wit, encrypting the message itself is a necessary but insufficient condition for protecting the transmission.
5. True or False? Before a signal is sent to the terrestrial surface, it may need to be transmitted across an extraplanetary link.

Multiple Choice

1. For communications purposes, modern satellites can be classified into two categories:
   A. Type 1
   B. Type 2
   C. Type 3
   D. Type 4
   E. Type 5
2. Any satellite-based communication can be classified into one of:
   A. Two possible categories

   B. Six possible categories
   C. Four possible categories
   D. Eight possible categories
   E. Seven possible categories
3. In addition to the risk of interception, asynchronously keyed encryption algorithms are typically at least:
   A. 10,000 times slower than synchronously keyed encryption algorithms
   B. 20,000 times slower than synchronously keyed encryption algorithms
   C. 30,000 times slower than synchronously keyed encryption algorithms
   D. 40,000 times slower than synchronously keyed encryption algorithms
   E. 50,000 times slower than synchronously keyed encryption algorithms
4. As opposed to satellite transmitters or transceivers—both of which can send messages to satellites—the vast majority of the satellite communications devices in use today are classified simply as:
   A. Devices
   B. Signals
   C. Transmissions
   D. Receivers
   E. Messages
5. What is an integrated circuit that is designed for a very specific purpose:
   A. ASIC
   B. NAVSTAR
   C. GPS
   D. SES
   E. SDP

EXERCISE

Problem

How would you go about breaking the encryption algorithms known as A5-GMR-1 and A5-GMR-2 that are used to secure civilian communications between mobile phones and satellites based on the GMR-1 and GMR-2 satphone standards?

Hands-On Projects

Project

Finding the right satellite encryption solution is critical for financial services providers in order to meet compliance requirements. A bank needed a cost-effective, secure, and reliable way to back up its data files, and faced a decision between choosing a hardware solution or finding the right software that would work on their system. What motivated the bank's search for a satellite encryption solution and what approach did it take to find that solution?

Case Projects

Problem

This case study illustrates a need for a new satellite receiver platform with a unique encryption system. Please identify what type of platform should be developed.

Optional Team Case Project

Problem

A commercial satellite encryption communications solutions and hardware company had run into major impediments on both cost and delivery. Please identify how the company redesigned their commercial grade satellite receiver to achieve an increase in delivery at a reduced cost.

Chapter 48

Public Key Infrastructure

Terence Spies

Hewlett Packard Enterprise, Cupertino, CA, United States

The ability to create, manipulate, and share digital documents has created a host of new applications (email, word processing, and e-commerce websites) but also created a new set of problems, namely, how to protect the privacy and integrity of digital data when stored and transmitted. The invention of public key cryptography in the 1970s [8] pointed the way to a solution to those problems: most important, the ability to encrypt data without a shared key and the ability to "sign" data, ensuring its origin and integrity. Although these operations are conceptually straightforward, they both rely on the ability to bind a public key (which is typically a large essentially random number) reliably with an identity sensible to the application or user (for example, a globally unique name, a legal identifier, or an email address.) Public key infrastructure (PKI) is the umbrella term used to refer to the protocols and machinery used to perform this binding.

The most important security protocols used on the Internet rely on PKI to bind names to keys, a crucial function that allows authentication of users and websites. A set of attacks in 2011 called into question the security of the PKI architecture [18,19], especially when governmental entities might be tempted to subvert Internet security assumptions. A number of interesting proposed evolutions of the PKI architecture have been proposed as potential countermeasures to these attacks. Even in the face of these attacks, PKI remains the most important and reliable method of authenticating networked entities.

1. CRYPTOGRAPHIC BACKGROUND

To understand how PKI systems function, it is necessary to grasp the basics of public key cryptography. PKI systems enable the use of public key cryptography and also use public key cryptography as the basis for their operation. Although there are thousands of varieties of cryptographic algorithms, we can understand PKI operations by looking at only two: signature and encryption.

Digital Signatures

The most important cryptographic operation in PKI systems is the digital signature. If two parties are exchanging some digital document, it may be important to protect those data so that the recipient knows that the document has not been altered since it was sent, and that any document received was indeed created by the sender. Digital signatures provide these guarantees by creating a data item, typically attached to the document in question that is uniquely tied to the data and the sender. The recipient then has some verification operation that confirms that the signature data matches the sender and the document.

Fig. 48.1 illustrates the basic security problem that motivates signatures. An attacker controlling communications between the sender and receiver can insert a bogus document, fooling the receiver. The aim of the digital signature is to block this attack by attaching a signature that can only be created by the sender, as shown in Fig. 48.2.

Cryptographic algorithms can be used to construct secure digital signatures. These techniques (for example, the Rivest–Shamir–Adleman (RSA) Algorithm or Digital Signature Algorithm) all have the same three basic operations, as shown in Table 48.1.

Public Key Encryption

Variants of the three operations used to construct digital signatures can also be used to encrypt data. Encryption uses a public key to scramble data in such a way that only the holder of the corresponding private key can unscramble it (Fig. 48.3).

Public key encryption is accomplished with variants of the same three operations used to sign data, as shown in

Computer and Information Security Handbook. http://dx.doi.org/10.1016/B978-0-12-803843-7.00048-X

FIGURE 48.1 Block diagram of altering an unsigned document.

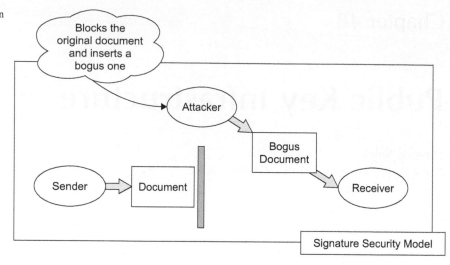

FIGURE 48.2 Block diagram showing prevention of an alteration attack via a digital signature.

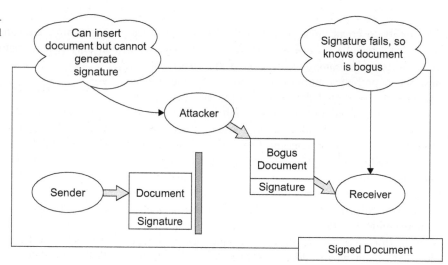

TABLE 48.1 Three Fundamental Digital Signature Operations

Key generation	Using some random source, the sender creates a public and private key, called K_{public} and $K_{private}$. Using K_{public}, it is cryptographically difficult to derive $K_{private}$. The sender then distributes K_{public} and keeps $K_{private}$ hidden.
Signing	Using a document and $K_{private}$, the sender generates the signature data.
Verification	Using the document, the signature, and K_{public}, the receiver (or any other entity with these elements) can test that the signature matches the document and could be produced only with the $K_{private}$ matching K_{public}.

Table 48.2. Note that in actual implementations, the algorithms used to encrypt and sign may be different.

The security of signature and encryption operations depends on two factors: first, the ability to keep the private key private; and, second, the ability to tie a public key reliably to an application or user identity. If a private key is known to an attacker, he can then perform the signing operation on arbitrary bogus documents, and can also decrypt any document encrypted with the matching public key. The same attacks can be performed if an attacker can convince a sender or receiver to use a bogus public key.

PKI systems are built to distribute public keys securely, thereby preventing attackers from inserting bogus public keys. They do not directly address the security of private keys, which are typically defended by measures at a particular end point, such as keeping the private key on a

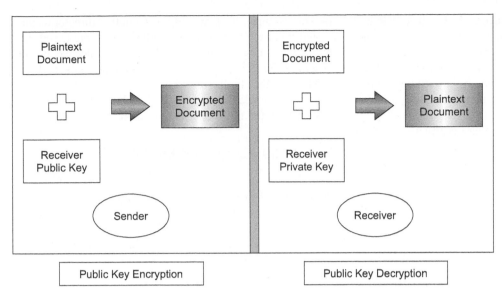

FIGURE 48.3 The public key encryption and decryption process.

| Public Key Encryption | Public Key Decryption |

TABLE 48.2 Three Fundamental Public Key Encryption Operations

Key generation	Using some random source, the sender creates a public and private key, called K_{public} and $K_{private}$. Using K_{public}, it is cryptographically difficult to derive $K_{private}$. The sender then distributes K_{public} and keeps $K_{private}$ hidden.
Encryption	Using a document and K_{public}, the sender encrypts the document.
Decryption	The receiver uses $K_{private}$ to decrypt the document.

smart card, encrypting private key data using operating system facilities, or other, similar mechanisms. The remainder of this section will detail the design, implementation, and operation of public key distribution systems.

2. OVERVIEW OF PUBLIC KEY INFRASTRUCTURE

PKI systems solve the problem of associating meaningful names with essentially meaningless cryptographic keys. For example, when encrypting an email, the user will typically specify a set of recipients that should be able to decrypt that mail. The user will want to specify these as some kind of name (email address or a name from a directory), not as a set of public keys. In the same way, when signed data are received and verified, the user will want to know what user signed the data, not what public key correctly verified the signature. (By way of contrast, some systems such as the Bitcoin currency protocol use keys directly as identities and thereby avoid some of the complexities associated with PKI-based designs.) The design goal of PKI systems is to connect user identities securely and efficiently to the public keys used to encrypt and verify data.

The original Diffie–Hellman article [8] that outlined public key cryptography proposed that this binding would be done through storing public keys in a trusted directory. Whenever users wanted to encrypt data other users, they would consult the "public file" and request the public key corresponding to some users. The same operation would yield the public key needed to verify the signature on signed data. The disadvantage of this approach is that the directory must be online and available for every new encryption and verification operation. (Although this older approach was never widely implemented, variants of this approach are now reappearing in newer PKI designs. For more information, see the section on Alternative Public Key Infrastructure Architectures.)

PKI systems solve this online problem and accomplish identity binding by distributing "digital certificates," data structures that contain an identity and a key, bound together by a digital signature. They may also provide a mechanism to check the validity of these certificates. Certificates, which were first invented by Kohnfelder in 1978, are essentially a digitally signed message from some authority stating that "Entity X is associated with public key Y." Communicating parties can then rely on this statement (to the extent that they trust the authority signing the certificate) to use the public key Y to validate a signature from

X or to send an encrypted message to X. Because time may pass and identities may change between when the signed certificate was produced and when someone uses that certificate, it may be useful to have a validation mechanism to check that the authority still stands by a particular certificate. We will describe PKI systems in terms of producing and validating certificates.

There are multiple standards that describe how certificates are formatted. The X.509 standard, promulgated by the International Telecommunication Union (ITU) [12], is the most widely used and is the certificate format used in the Transport Layer Security/Secure Socket Layer (TLS/SSL) protocols for secure Internet connections, and the Secure/Multipurpose Internet Mail Extensions (S/MIME) standards for secured email. The X.509 certificate format also implies a particular model of how certification works. Other standards have attempted to define alternate models of operation and associated certificate models. Among the other standards that describe certificates are: Pretty Good Privacy (PGP) and the Simple Public Key Infrastructure (SPKI) [spki]. In this section, we will describe the X.509 PKI model and then describe how these other standards attempt to remediate problems with X.509.

3. THE X.509 MODEL

The X.509 model is the most prevalent standard for certificate-based PKIs, although the standard has evolved such that PKI-using applications on the Internet are mostly based on the set of Internet Engineering Task Force (IETF) standards that have evolved and extended the ideas in X.509. X.509-style certificates are the basis for SSL, TLS, many virtual private networks, the US Federal Government PKI, and many other widely deployed systems.

The History of X.509

A quick historical preface here is useful to explain some of the properties of X.509. X.509 is part of the X.500 directory standard owned by the ITU Telecommunications Standardization Sector. X.500 specifies a hierarchical directory useful for the X.400 set of messaging standards. As such, it includes a naming system (called "distinguished naming") that describes entities by their position in some hierarchy. A sample X.500/X.400 name might look like this:

- CN = Joe Davis, OU = Human Resources, O = WidgetCo, C = US

This name describes a person with a Common Name (CN) of "Joe Davis" that works in an Organizational Unit (OU) called "Human Resources," in an Organization called "WidgetCo" in the United States. These name components were intended to be run by their own directory components

(so, for example, there would be "Country" directories that would point to "Organizational" directories, etc.), and this hierarchical description was ultimately reflected in the design of the X.509 system. Many of the changes made by IETF and other bodies that have evolved the X.509 standard were made to reconcile this hierarchical naming system with the more distributed nature of the Internet.

The X.509 Certificate Model

The X.509 model specifies a system of Certifying Authorities (CAs) that issue certificates for end entities (users, websites, or other entities that hold private keys). A CA-issued certificate will contain (among other data) the name of the end entity, the name of the CA, the end entity's public key, a validity period, and a certificate serial number. All of this information is signed with the CA's private key. (Additional details on the information in a certificate and how it is encoded is in Section 6.) To validate a certificate, a relying party uses the CA's public key to verify the signature on the certificate, checks that the time falls within the validity period, and may also consult a server associated with the CA to ensure that the CA has not revoked the certificate.

This process leaves out on important detail: Where did the CA's public key come from? The answer is that another certificate is typically used to certify the public key of the CA. This "chaining" action of validating a certificate by using the public key from another certificate can be performed any number of times, allowing for arbitrarily deep hierarchies of CAs. Of course, this must terminate at some point, typically at a self-signed certificate that is trusted by the relying party. Trusted self-signed certificates are typically referred to as "root" certificates. Once the relying party has verified the chain of signatures from the end-entity certificate to a trusted root certificate, it can conclude that the end-entity certificate is properly signed, and then move onto whatever other validation steps (proper key usage fields, validity dates in some time window, etc.) are required to trust the certificate fully. Fig. 48.4 shows the structure of a typical certificate chain.

One other element is required for this system to function securely: CAs must be able to "undo" a certification action. Whereas a certificate binds an identity to a key, there are many events that may cause that binding to become invalid. For example, a CA operated by a bank may issue a certificate to a newly hired person that gives that user the ability to sign messages as an employee of the bank. If that person leaves the bank before the certificate expires, the bank needs some way to undo that certification. The physical compromise of a private key is another circumstance that may require invalidating a certificate. This is accomplished by a validation protocol in which (in the abstract) a user examining a certificate can ask the CA

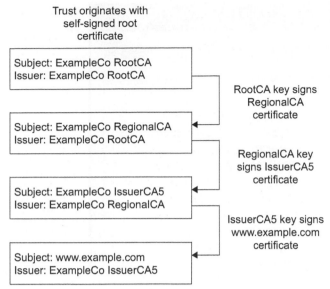

Trust originates with
self-signed root
certificate

Subject: ExampleCo RootCA
Issuer: ExampleCo RootCA

RootCA key signs
RegionalCA
certificate

Subject: ExampleCo RegionalCA
Issuer: ExampleCo RootCA

RegionalCA key
signs IssuerCA5
certificate

Subject: ExampleCo IssuerCA5
Issuer: ExampleCo RegionalCA

IssuerCA5 key signs
www.example.com
certificate

Subject: www.example.com
Issuer: ExampleCo IssuerCA5

FIGURE 48.4 Sample X.509 certificate chain. *CA*, Certifying Authority.

whether a certificate is still valid. In practice, revocation protocols are used that delegate processing revocation checks to a dedicated set of servers.

Root certificates are critical to the process of validating public keys through certificates. They must be inherently trusted by the application, because no other certificate signs these certificates. This is most commonly done by installing the certificates as part of the application that will use the certificates under a set of root certificates. For example, Internet Explorer uses X.509 certificates to validate keys used to make TLS/SSL connections. Internet Explorer has a large set of root certificates installed that can be examined by opening the Internet Options menu item and selecting "Certificates" in the "Content" tab of the Options dialogue. A list like the one in Fig. 48.5 will appear.

In Windows, the list of allowed root certificates for a given computer can be viewed in the Control Panel under Administrative Tools/Manage Computer Certificates. Both certificate dialogues can also be used to inspect these root certificates. Microsoft Root certificate details are shown in Fig. 48.6. The meaning of these fields will be explored in subsequent sections.

4. X.509 IMPLEMENTATION ARCHITECTURES

Although in theory the Certification Authority is the entity that creates and validates certificates, in practice it may be desirable or necessary to delegate the actions of user authentication and certificate validation to other servers. The security of the CA's signing key is crucial to the security of a PKI system. By limiting the functions of the server that holds that key, it should be subject to less risk of

disclosure or illegitimate use. The X.509 architecture defines a delegated server role, the Registration Authority (RA), which allows delegation of authentication. Subsequent extensions to the core X.509 architecture have created a second delegated role, the Validation Authority (VA), which owns answering queries about the validity of a certificate after creation.

An RA is typically used to distribute the authentication function needed to issue a certificate without needing to distribute the CA key. The RA's function is to perform the authentication needed to issue a certificate, and then send a signed statement containing the fact that it performed the authentication, the identity to be certified, and the key to be certified. The CA validates the RA's message and issues a certificate in response.

For example, a large multinational corporation wants to deploy a PKI system using a centralized CA. It wants to issue certificates on the basis of in-person authentication, so it needs some way to distribute authentication to multiple locations in different countries. Copying and distributing the CA signing key creates a number of risks, not only because the CA key will be present on multiple servers, but also because of the complexities of creating and managing these copies. Sub-CAs could be created for each location, but this requires careful attention to controlling the identities allowed to be certified by each sub-CA (otherwise, an attacker compromising one sub-CA could issue a certificate for any identity he liked.) One possible way to solve this problem is to create RAs at each location and have the CA check that the RA is authorized to authenticate a particular employee when a certificate is requested. If an attacker subverts a given RA signing key, he can request certificates for employees in the purview of that RA, but it is straightforward, once discovered, to deauthorize the RA, solve the security problem, and create a new RA key.

VAs are given the ability to revoke certificates (the specific methods used to effect revocation are detailed in the X.509 Revocation Protocols section) and offload that function from the CA. Through judicious use of RAs and VAs, it is possible to construct certification architectures in which the critical CA server is accessible to only a small number of other servers, and network security controls can be used to reduce or eliminate threats from outside network entities.

5. X.509 CERTIFICATE VALIDATION

X.509 certificate validation is a complex process that can be done to several levels of confidence. This section will outline a typical set of steps involved in validating a certificate, but it is not an exhaustive catalog of the possible methods that can be used. Different applications will often require different validation techniques, depending on the application's security policy. It is rare for an application to

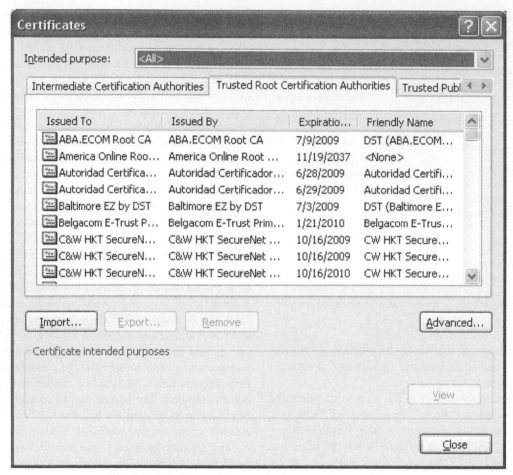

FIGURE 48.5   Microsoft Internet Explorer trusted root certificates.

implement certificate validation, because there are several application program interfaces and libraries available to perform this task. Microsoft CryptoAPI, OpenSSL, and Java JCE all provide certificate validation interfaces. The Server-based Certificate Validity Protocol (SCVP) can also be used to validate a certificate. However, all of these interfaces offer a variety of options, and understanding the validation process is essential to using these interfaces properly.

Although a complete specification of the certificate validation process would require hundreds of pages, we supply a sketch of what happens during certificate validation. It is not a complete description and is purposefully simplified. The certificate validation process typically proceeds in three steps and typically takes three inputs. The first is the certificate to be validated, the second is any intermediate certificates acquired by the applications, and the third is a store containing the root and intermediate certificates trusted by the application. The following steps are a simplified outline of how certificates are typically validated. In practice, the introduction of bridge CAs and other nonhierarchical certification models have led to more

complex validation procedures. IETF Request for Comments (RFC) 3280 [11] presents a complete specification for certificate validation, and RFC 4158 [7] presents a specification for constructing a certification path in environments where nonhierarchical certification structures are used.

Validation Step 1: Construct the Chain and Validate Signatures

The contents of the target certificate cannot be trusted until the signature on the certificate is validated, so the first step is to check the signature. To check the signature, the certificate for the authority that signed the target certificate must be located. This is done by searching the intermediate certificates and certificate store for a certificate with a Subject field that matches the Issuer field of the target certificate. If multiple certificates match, the validator can search the matching certificates for a Subject Key Identifier extension that matches the Issuer Key Identifier extension in the candidate certificates. If multiple certificates still match, the most recently issued candidate certificate can be

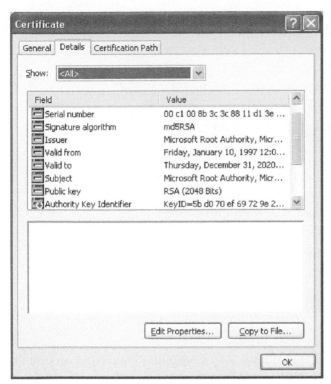

FIGURE 48.6   View of the fields in an X.509 certificate using Microsoft Internet Explorer.

used. (Note that, because of potentially revoked intermediate certificates, multiple chains may need to be constructed and examine through Steps 2 and 3 to find the actual valid chain.) Once the proper authority certificate is found, the validator checks the signature on the target certificate using the public key in the authority certificate. If the signature check fails, the validation process can be stopped, and the target certificate deemed invalid.

If the signature matches and the authority certificate is a trusted certificate, the constructed chain is then subjected to Steps 2–4. If not, the authority certificate is treated as a target certificate, and Step 1 is called recursively until it returns a chain to a trusted certificate or fails.

Constructing the complete certificate path requires that the validator be in possession of all certificates in that path. This requires that the validator keep a database of intermediate certificates or that the protocol using the certificate supplies the needed intermediates. The SCVP provides a mechanism to request a certificate chain from a server, which can eliminate these requirements. The SCVP protocol is described in more detail in a subsequent section.

Step 2: Check Validity Dates, Policy and Key Usage

Once a chain has been constructed, various fields in the certificate are checked to ensure that the certificate was issued correctly and that it is currently valid. The following checks should be run on the candidate chain:

The certificate chain times are correct. Each certificate in the chain contains a validity period with a not before and not after time. For applications outside validating the signature on a document, the current time must fall after the not before time and before the not after time. Some applications may require "time nesting," meaning that the validity period for a certificate must fall entirely within the validity period of the issuer's certificate. It is up to the policy of the application if it treats out-of-date certificates as invalid or treats it as a warning case that can be overridden by the user. Applications may also treat certificates that are not yet valid differently from certificates that have expired.

Applications that are validating the certificate on a stored document may have to treat validity time as the time when the document was signed, as opposed to the time when the signature was checked. There are three cases of interest. The first, and easiest, is where the document signature is checked, and the certificate chain validating the public key contains certificates that are currently within their validity time interval. In this case, the validity times are all good, and verification can proceed. The second case is where the certificate chain validating the public key is currently invalid because one or more certificates are out of date and the document is believed to be signed at a time when the chain was out of date. In this case, the validity times arc all invalid, and the user should be at least warned.

The ambiguous case arises when the certificate chain is currently out of date but the chain is believed to have been valid with respect to time when the document was signed. Depending on its policy, the application can treat this case in several different ways. It can assume that the certificate validity times are strict, and fail to validate the document. Alternatively, it can assume that the certificates were good at the time of signing, and validate the document. The application can also take steps to ensure that this case does not occur, by using a time-stamping mechanism in conjunction with signing the document, or provide some mechanism for resigning documents before certificate chains expire.

Once the certificate chain has been constructed, the verifier must also verify that various X.509 extension fields are valid. Some common extensions that are relevant to the validity of a certificate path are:

- BasicConstraints: This extension is required for CAs, and limits the depth of the certificate chain below a specific CA certificate.
- NameConstraints: This extension limits the namespace of identities certified underneath the given CA certificate. This extension can be used to limit a specific CA to issuing certificates for a given domain or X.400 namespace.

TABLE 48.3 Data Fields in an X.509 CRL

Version	Specifies the format of the CRL. Current version is 2.
SignatureAlgorithm	Specifies the algorithm used to sign the CRL
Issuer	Name of the Certifying Authority issuing the CRL
thisUpdate	Time from when this CRL is valid
nextUpdate	Time when the next CRL will be issued

CRL, Certificate Revocation List.

TABLE 48.4 Format of a Revocation Record in an X.509 CRL

Serial Number	Serial number of a revoked certificate
Revocation date	Date the revocation is effective
CRL extensions	[Optional] specifies why the certificate is revoked

CRL, Certificate Revocation List.

- KeyUsage and ExtendedKeyUsage: These extensions limit the purposes for which a certified key can be used. CA certificates must have KeyUsage set to allow certificate signing. Various values of ExtendedKeyUsage may be required for some certification tasks.

Step 3: Consult Revocation Authorities

Once the verifier has concluded that it has a suitably signed certificate chain with valid dates and proper KeyUsage extensions, it may want to consult the revocation authorities named in each certificate to check whether the certificates are currently valid. Certificates may contain extensions that point to Certificate Revocation List (CRL) storage locations or to Online Certificate Status Protocol (OSCP) responders. These methods allow the verifier to check that a CA has not revoked the certificate in question. The next section details these methods in more detail. Note that each certificate in the chain may need to be checked for revocation status. The next section on certificate revocation details the mechanisms used to revoke certificates.

6. X.509 CERTIFICATE REVOCATION

Because certificates are typically valid for a significant period of time, it is possible that during the validity period of the certificate a key may be lost or stolen, an identity may change, or some other event may occur that causes a certificate's identity binding to become invalid or suspect. To deal with these events, it must be possible for a CA to revoke a certificate, typically by some kind of notification that can be consulted by applications examining the validity

of a certificate. Two mechanisms are used to perform this task: CRLs and the OCSP.

The original X.509 architecture implemented revocation via a CRL. A CRL is a periodically issued document containing a list of certificate serial numbers that are revoked by that CA. X.509 has defined two basic CRL formats, V1 and V2. When CA certificates are revoked by a higher-level CA, the serial number of the CA certificate is placed on an Authority Revocation List (ARL), which is formatted identically to a CRL. CRLs and ARLs, as defined in X.509 and IETF RFC 3280, are ASN.1 encoded objects that contain the information shown in Table 48.3.

This header is followed by a sequence of revoked certificate records. Each record contains the information shown in Table 48.4.

The list of revoked certificates is optionally followed by a set of CRL extensions that supply additional information about the CRL and how it should be processed. To process a CRL, the verifying party checks that the CRL has been signed with the key of the named issuer, and that the current date is between the thisUpdate time and the nextUpdate time. This time check is crucial because if it is not performed, an attacker could use a revoked certificate by supplying an old CRL where the certificate had not yet appeared. Note that expired certificates are typically removed from the CRL, which prevents the CRL from growing unboundedly over time.

The costs of maintaining and transmitting CRLs to verifying parties has been repeatedly identified as an important component of the cost of running a PKI system [3,13], and several alternative revocation schemes have been proposed to lower this cost. The cost of CRL

Note: CRLs can only revoke certificates on time boundaries determined by the nextUpdate time. If a CA publishes a CRL every Monday, for example, a certificate that is compromised on a Wednesday will continue to validate until its serial number is published in the CRL on the following Monday. Clients validating certificates may have downloaded the CA's CRL on Monday and are free to cache the CRL until the nextUpdate time occurs. This caching is important because it means that the CRL is downloaded only once per client per publication period rather than for every certificate validation. However, it has the unavoidable consequence of having a potential time lag between a certificate becoming invalid and its appearance on a CRL. The online certificate validation protocols detailed in the next section attempt to solve this problem.

distribution was also a factor in the emergence of online certificate status-checking protocols such as OCSP and SCVP.

Delta Certificate Revocation Lists

In large systems that issue many certificates, CRLs can potentially become lengthy. One approach to reducing the network overhead associated with sending the complete CRL to every verifier is to issue a Delta CRL along with a Base CRL. The Base CRL contains the complete set of revoked certificates up to some point in time, and the accompanying Delta CRL contains only the additional certificates added over some time period. Clients that are capable of processing the Delta CRL can then download the Base CRL less frequently and download the smaller Delta CRL to obtain recently revoked certificates. Delta CRLs are formatted identically to CRLs but have a critical extension added in the CRL that denotes that they are a Delta, not Base CRL. IETF RFC 3280 [11] details how Delta CRLs are formatted, and the set of certificate extensions that indicate that a CA issues Delta CRLs.

Online Certificate Status Protocol

The OSCP was designed with the goal of reducing the costs of CRL transmission and eliminating the time lag between certificate invalidity and certificate revocation inherent in CRL-based designs. The idea behind OCSP is straightforward. A CA certificate contains a reference to an OSCP server. A client validating a certificate transmits the certificate serial number, a hash of the issuer name, and a hash of the subject name to that OSCP server. The OSCP server checks the certificate status and returns an indication as to the current status of the certificate. This removes the need to download the entire list of revoked certificates and also allows for essentially instantaneous revocation of invalid certificates. It has the design trade-off of requiring that

clients validating certificates have network connectivity to the required OCSP server.

OSCP responses contain the basic information as to the status of the certificate in the set of "good," "revoked," or "unknown." They also contain a thisUpdate time, similar to a CRL, and are signed. Responses can also contain a nextUpdate time, which indicates how long the client can consider the OSCP response definitive. The reason the certificate was revoked can also be returned in the response. OSCP is defined in IETF RFC 2560 [14].

7. SERVER-BASED CERTIFICATE VALIDITY PROTOCOL

The X.509 certificate path construction and validation process requires a nontrivial amount of code, the ability to fetch and cache CRLs, and, in the case of mesh and bridge CAs, the ability to interpret CA policies. The SCVP [9] was designed to reduce the cost of using X.509 certificates by allowing applications to delegate the task of certificate validation to an external server. SCVP offers two levels of functionality: Delegated Path Discovery (DPD), which attempts to locate and construct a complete certificate chain for a given certificate, and Delegated Path Validation (DPV), which performs a complete path validation, including revocation checking, on a certificate chain. The main reason for this division of functionality is that a client can use an untrusted SCVP server for DPD operations, because it will validate the resulting path itself. Only trusted SCVP servers can be used for DPV, because the client must trust the server's assessment of a certificate's validity.

SCVP also allows certificates to be checked according to some defined certification policy. They can be used to centralize policy management for an organization that wishes all clients to follow some set of rules with respect to what set of CAs are trusted, what certification policies are trusted, etc. To use SCVP, the client sends a query to an SCVP server, which contains the following parameters:

- *QueriedCerts.* This is the set of certificates for which the client wants the server to construct (and optionally validate) paths.
- *Checks.* The Checks parameter specifies what the client wants the server to do. The checks parameter can be used to specify that the server should build a path, should build a path and validate it without checking revocation, or should build and fully validate the path.
- *WantBack.* The WantBack parameter specifies what the server should return from the request. This can range from the public key from the validated certificate path (in which case the client is fully delegating certificate validation to the server) to all certificate chains that the server can locate.

- **ValidationPolicy.** The ValidationPolicy parameter instructs the server how to validate the resultant certification chain. This parameter can be as simple as "use the default RFC 3280 validation algorithm" or it can specify a wide range of conditions that must be satisfied. Some of the conditions that can be specified with this parameter are:
  - **KeyUsage and Extended Key Usage.** The client can specify a set of KeyUsage or ExtendedKeyUsage fields that must be present in the end-entity certificate. This allows the client to accept, for example, only certificates that are allowed to perform digital signatures.
  - **UserPolicySet.** The client can specify a set of certification policy Object Identifier (OIDs) that must be present in the CAs used to construct the chain. CAs can assert that they follow some formally defined policy when issuing certificates and this parameter allows the client to accept only certificates issued under some set of these policies. For example, if a client wanted to accept only certificates acceptable under the Medium Assurance Federal Bridge CA policies, it could assert that policy identifier in this parameter. For more information on policy identifiers, see the section on X.509 Extensions.
  - **InhibitPolicyMapping.** When issuing bridge or cross-certificates, a CA can assert that a certificate policy identifier in one domain is equivalent to some other policy identifier within its domain. By using this parameter, the client can state that it does not want to allow these policy equivalences to be used when validating certificates against values in the UserPolicySet parameter.
  - **TrustAnchors.** The client can use this parameter to specify some set of certificates that must be at the top of any acceptable certificate chain. By using this parameter, a client could, for example, say that only VeriSign Class 3 certificates were acceptable in this context.
  - **ResponseFlags.** This specifies various options as to how the server should respond (if it needs to sign or otherwise protect the response) and if a cached response is acceptable to the client.
  - **ValidationTime.** The client may want a validation performed as if it were a specific time, so that it can find whether a certificate was valid at some point in the past. Note that SCVP does not allow for "speculative" validation in terms of asking whether a certificate will be valid in the future. This parameter allows the client to specify the validation time to be used by the server.
  - **IntermediateCerts.** The client can use this parameter to give additional certificates that can potentially be used to construct the certificate chain. The server is

not obligated to use these certificates. This parameter is used where the client may have received a set of intermediate certificates from a communicating party, and is not certain whether the SCVP server has possession of these certificates.
  - **RevInfos.** Like the IntermediateCerts parameter, the RevInfos parameter supplies extra information that may be needed to construct or validate the path. Instead of certificates, the RevInfos parameter supplies revocation information such as OSCP responses, CRLs, or Delta CRLs.

8. X.509 BRIDGE CERTIFICATION SYSTEMS

In practice, large-scale PKI systems proved to be more complex than could easily be handled under the X.509 hierarchical model. For example, Polk and Hastings [15] identified a number of policy complexities that presented difficulties when attempting to build a PKI system for the US Federal Government. In this case, certainly one of the largest PKI projects ever undertaken, they found that the traditional model of a hierarchical certification system was simply unworkable. They stated:

> The initial designs for a federal PKI were hierarchical in nature because of government's inherent hierarchical organizational structure. However, these initial PKI plans ran into several obstacles. There was no clear organization within the government that could be identified and agreed upon to run a governmental "root" CA. While the search for an appropriate organization dragged on, federal agencies began to deploy autonomous PKIs to enable their electronic processes. The search for a "root" CA for a hierarchical federal PKI was abandoned, due to the difficulties of imposing a hierarchy after the fact.

Their proposed solution to this problem was to use a "mesh CA" system to establish a Federal Bridge Certification Authority. This Bridge architecture has since been adopted in large PKI systems in Europe and the financial services community in the United States. The details of the European Bridge CA can be found at http://www.bridge-ca.org. This part of the chapter will detail the technical design of bridge CAs, and the various X.509 certificate features that enable bridges.

Mesh Public Key Infrastructures and Bridge Certifying Authorities

Bridge CA architectures are implemented using a nonhierarchical certification structure called a mesh PKI. The classic X.509 architecture joins together multiple PKI systems by subordinating them under a higher-level CA. All certificates chain up to this CA, and that CA essentially

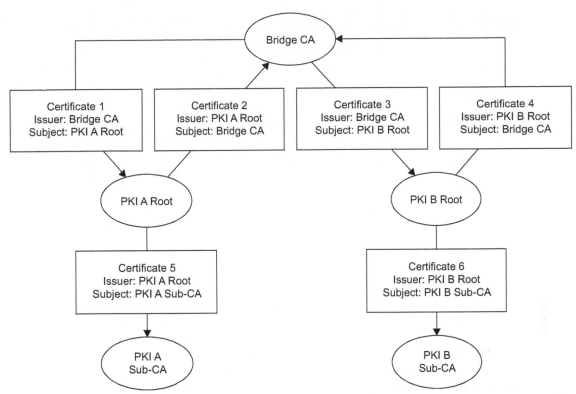

FIGURE 48.7   Showing the structure of two public key infrastructures (PKIs) connected via a bridge Certifying Authority (CA).

creates trust between the CAs below it. Mesh PKIs join together multiple PKI systems using a process called "cross-certification" that does not create this type of hierarchy. To cross-certify, the top-level CA in a given hierarchy creates a certificate for an external CA called the Bridge CA. This bridge CA then becomes, in a manner of speaking, a sub-CA under the organization's CA. However, the Bridge CA also creates a certificate for the organizational CA, so it can also be viewed as a top level CA certifying that organizational CA.

The end result of this cross-certification process is that if, two organizations, A and B have joined the same bridge CA, the can both create certificate chains from their respective trusted CAs through the other organization's CA to end-entity certificates that it has created. These chains will be longer than traditional hierarchical chains but have the same basic verifiable properties. Fig. 48.7 shows how two organizations might be connected through a bridge CA, and what the resultant certificate chains look like.

In the case illustrated in Fig. 48.7, a user that trusts certificates issued by PKI A (that is, PKI A Root is a "trust anchor") can construct a chain to certificates issued by the PKI B Sub-CA, because it can verify Certificate 2 via its trust of the PKI A Root. Certificate 2 then chains to Certificate 3, which chains to Certificate 6. Certificate 6 then is a trusted issuer certificate for certificates issued by the PKI B Sub-CA.

Mesh architectures create two significant technical problems: path construction and policy evaluation. In a hierarchical PKI system, there is only one path from the root certificate to an end-entity certificate. Creating a certificate chain is as simple as taking the current certificate, locating the issuer in the subject field of another certificate, and repeating until the root is reached (completing the chain) or no certificate can be found (failing to construct the chain.) In a mesh system, there can be cyclical loops where this process can fail to terminate with a failure or success. This is not a difficult problem to solve, but it is more complex to deal with than the hierarchical case.

Policy evaluation becomes much more complex in the mesh case. In the hierarchical CA case, the top-level CA can establish policies that are followed by Sub-CAs, and these policies can be encoded into certificates in an unambiguous way. When multiple PKIs are joined by a bridge CA, these PKIs may have similar policies but may be expressed by different names. PKI A and PKI B may both certify "medium assurance" CAs that perform a certain level of authentication before issuing certificates, but may have different identifiers for these policies. When joined by a bridge CA, clients may reasonably want to validate certificates issued by both CAs, and understand the policies under which that those certificates are issued. The Policy-Mapping technique allows similar policies under different names from disjoint PKIs to be translated at the bridge CA.

TABLE 48.5 Data Fields in an X.509 Version 3 Certificate

Version	Version of Standard Used to Format Certificate
Serial number	A number, unique relative to the issuer, for this certificate
Signature algorithm	The specific algorithm used to sign the certificate
Issuer	Name of the authority issuing the certificate
Validity	The time interval for which this certificate is valid
Subject	The identity being certified
Subject public key	The key being bound to the subject
Issuer unique ID	Obsolete field
Subject unique ID	Obsolete field
Extensions	A list of additional certificate attributes
Signature	A digital signature by the issuer over the certificate data

Although none of these problems is insurmountable, they increase the complexity of certificate validation code and helped drive the invention of server-based validation protocols such as SCVP. These protocols delegate path discovery and validation to an external server rather than require applications to integrate this functionality. This may lower application complexity, but the main benefit of this strategy is that questions of acceptable policies and translation can be configured at one central verification server rather than distributed to every application doing certificate validation.

9. X.509 CERTIFICATE FORMAT

The X.509 standard (and the related IETF RFCs) specify a set of data fields that must be present in a properly formatted certificate, a set of optional extension data fields that can be used to supply additional certificate information, how these fields must be signed, and how the signature data are encoded. All of these data fields (mandatory fields, optional fields, and the signature) are specified in Abstract Syntax Notation (aka ASN.1), a formal language that allows for exact definitions of the content of data fields and how those fields are arranged in a data structure. An associated specification, Determined Encoding Rules (DER), is used with specific certificate data and the ASN.1 certificate format to create the actual binary certificate data. The ASN.1 standard is authoritatively defined in ITU Recommendation X.693. (For an introduction to ASN.1 and DER, see [kaliski].)

X.509 V1 and V2 Format

The first X.509 certificate standard was published in 1988 as part of the broader X.500 directory standard. X.509 was intended to provide public key–based access control to an

X.500 directory, and defined a certificate format for that use. This format, which is now referred to as X.509 v1, defined a static format containing an X.400 Issuer name (the name of the CA), an X.400 Subject name, a validity period, the key to be certified, and the signature of the CA. Whereas this basic format allowed for all basic PKI operations, the format required that all names be in the X.400 form and it did not allow for any other information to be added to the certificate. The X.509 v2 format added two more Unique ID fields but did not fix the primary deficiencies of the v1 format. As it became clear that name formats would have to be more flexible and certificates would have to accommodate a wider variety of information, work began on a new certificate format.

X.509 V3 Format

The X.509 certificate specification was revised in 1996 to add an optional extension field that allows a set of optional additional data fields to be encoded into the certificate (Table 48.5). This change may seem minor, but in fact it allowed certificates to carry a wide array of information useful for PKI implementation, and also for the certificate to contain multiple, non-X.400 identities. These extension fields allow for key usage policies, CA policy information, revocation pointers, and other relevant information to live in the certificate. The V3 format is the most widely used X.509 variant and is the basis for the certificate profile in RFC 3280 [11] issued by the IETF.

X.509 Certificate Extensions

This section is a partial catalog of common X.509 V3 extensions. There is no existing canonical directory of V3 extensions, so there are undoubtedly extensions in use outside this list. The most common extensions are defined in RFC 3280 [11], which contains the IETF certificate profile, which are used by S/MIME and many SSL/TLS implementations. These extensions address a number of deficiencies in the base X.509 certificate specification, and which in many cases are essential for constructing a practical PKI system. In particular, the Certificate Policy, Policy Mapping, and Policy Constraints extensions form the basis for the popular bridge CA architectures.

Authority Key Identifier

The Authority Key Identifier extension identifies which specific private key owned by the certificate issuer was used to sign the certificate. The use of this extension allows a single issuer to use multiple private keys and unambiguously identifies which key was used. This allows issuer keys to be refreshed without changing the issuer name and enables handling events such as an issuer key being compromised or lost.

Subject Key Identifier

Like the Authority Key Identifier, the Subject Key Identifier extension indicates which subject key is contained in the certificate. This extension provides a way to identify quickly which certificates belong to a specific key owned by a subject. If the certificate is a CA certificate, the Subject Key Identifier can be used to construct chains by connecting a Subject Key Identifier with a matching Authority Key Identifier.

Key Usage

A CA may wish to issue a certificate that limits the use of a public key. This may lead to an increase in overall system security by segregating encryption keys from signature keys, and even segregating signature keys by use. For example, an entity may have a key used for signing documents and a key used for decryption of documents. The signing key may be protected by a smart card mechanism that requires a personal identifier number per signing, whereas the encryption key is always available when the user is logged in. The use of this extension allows the CA to express that the encryption key cannot be used to generate signatures, and notifies communicating users that they should not encrypt data with the signing public key. The key usage capabilities are defined in a bit field, which allows a single key to have any combination of the defined capabilities (see checklist, "An Agenda for Action to Define Key Usage Capabilities").

Subject Alternative Name

This extension allows the certificate to define non-X.400–formatted identities for the subject. It supports a variety of namespaces, including email addresses, Domain Name System names for servers, Electronic Document Interchange party names, Uniform Resource Identifiers, and Internet Protocol (IP) addresses, among others.

An Agenda for Action to Define Key Usage Capabilities

The currently defined key usage capabilities/bits that need to be completed are as follows (check all tasks completed):

_____1. *digitalSignature*: The key can be used to generate digital signatures.

_____2. *nonRepudiation*: Signatures generated from this key can be traced back to the signer in such a way that the signer cannot deny generating the signature. This capability is used in electronic transaction scenarios where it is important that signers cannot disavow a transaction.

_____3. *keyEncipherment*: The key can be used to wrap a symmetric key that is then used to bulk encrypt data. This is used in communications protocols and applications such as S/MIME, in which an algorithm such as Advanced Encryption Standard (AES) is used to encrypt data, and the public key in the certificate is then used to encipher that AES key. In practice, almost all encryption applications are structured in this manner, because public keys are generally unsuitable for the encryption of bulk data.

_____4. *dataEncipherment*: The key can be used to encrypt data directly. Because of algorithmic limitations of public encryption algorithms, the keyEncipherment technique is nearly always used instead of directly encrypting data.

_____5. *keyAgreement*: The key can be used to create a communication key between two parties. This capability can be used in conjunction with the encipherOnly and decipherOnly capabilities.

_____6. *keyCertSign*: The key can be used to sign another certificate. This is a crucial key usage capability because it essentially allows creation of sub-certificates under this certificate, subject to basic-Constraints. All CA certificates must have this usage bit set, and all end-entity certificates must NOT have it set.

_____7. *cRLSign*: The key can be used to sign a CRL. CA certificates may have this bit set or they may delegate CRL creation to a different key, in which case this bit will be cleared.

_____8. *encipherOnly*: When the key is used for keyAgreement, the resultant key can be used only for encryption.

_____9. *decipherOnly*: When the key is used for keyAgreement, the resultant key can be used only for decryption.

Policy Extensions

Three important X.509 certificate extensions (Certificate Policy, Policy Mapping, and Policy Constraints) form a complete system for communicating CA policies regarding how certificates are issued or revoked, and how CA security is maintained. They are interesting in that they communicate information that is more relevant to business and policy decision making than the other extensions that are used in the technical processes of certificate chain construction and validation. As an example, a variety of CAs run multiple Sub-CAs that issue certificates according to a variety of issuance policies, ranging from "Low Assurance" to "High Assurance." The CA will typically formally define in a policy document all of its operating policies, state them in a practice statement, define an ASN.1 OID that names this policy, and distribute it to parties that will validate those certificates. The policy extensions allow CAs to attach a policy OID to its certificate, translate policy OIDs among PKIs, and limit the policies that can be used by Sub-CAs.

Certificate Policy

The Certificate Policy extension, if present in an issuer certificate, expresses the policies that are followed by the CA, both in terms of how identities are validated before certificate issuance and how certificates are revoked, as well as the operational practices that are used to ensure integrity of the CA. These policies can be expressed in two ways: as an OID, which is a unique number that refers to one given policy, and as a human-readable Certificate Practice Statement (CPS). One Certificate Policy extension can contain both the computer-sensible OID and a printable CPS. One special OID has been set aside for "AnyPolicy," which states that the CA may issue certificates under a free-form policy.

IETF RFC 2527 [6] gives a complete description of what should be present in a CA policy document and CPS. More details on the 2527 guidelines are given in the PKI Policy Description section.

Policy Mapping

The Policy Mapping extension contains two policy OIDs: one for the Issuer domain and the other for the Subject domain. When this extension is present, a validating party can consider the two policies identical, which is to say, the Subject OID, when present in the chain below the given certificate, can be considered to be the same as the policy named in the Issuer OID. This extension is used join together two PKI systems with functionally similar policies that have different policy reference OIDs.

Policy Constraints

The Policy Constraints extension enables a CA to disable policy mapping for CAs farther down in the chain, and to require explicit policies in all of the CAs below a given CA.

10. PUBLIC KEY INFRASTRUCTURE POLICY DESCRIPTION

In many application contexts, it is important to understand how and when CAs will issue and revoke certificates. Especially when bridge architectures are used, an administrator may need to evaluate a CA's policy to determine how and when to trust certificates issued under that authority. For example, the US Federal Bridge CA maintains a detailed specification of its operating procedures and requirements for bridged CAs at the US Chief Information Officers office website (http://www.cio.gov/fpkipa/documents/FBCA_CP_RFC3647.pdf). More information about the Federal Bridge CA can be found at http://www.idmanagement.gov. Many other commercial CAs, such as VeriSign, maintain similar documents.

To make policy evaluation easier and more uniform, IETF RFC 2527 [6] specifies a standard format for CAs to communicate their policy for issuing and revoking certificates. This specification divides a policy specification document into the following sections:

- **Introduction**: This section describes the type of certificates that the CA issues, the applications in which those certificates can be used, and the OIDs used to identify CA policies. The Introduction also contains the contact information for the institution operating the CA.
- **General Provisions**: This section details the legal obligations of the CA, any warranties given as to the reliability of the bindings in the certificate, and details as to the legal operation of the CA, including fees and relationship to any relevant laws.
- **Identification and Authentication**: This section details how certificate requests are authenticated at the CA or RA, and how events such as name disputes or revocation requests are handled.
- **Operational Requirements**: This section details how the CA will react in case of key compromise, how it renews keys, how it publishes CRLs or other revocation information, how it is audited, and what records are kept during CA operation.
- **Physical, Procedural, and Personnel Security Controls**: This section details how the physical location of the CA is controlled and how employees are vetted.
- **Technical Security Controls**: This section explains how the CA key is generated and protected though its life cycle. CA key generation is typically done through an

audited, recorded key generation ceremony to assure certificate users that the CA key was not copied or otherwise compromised during generation.

- *Certificate and CRL Profile*: The specific policy OIDs published in certificates generated by the CA are given in this section. The information in this section is sufficient to accomplish the technical evaluation of a certificate chain published by this CA.
- *Specification Administration*: The last section explains the procedures used to maintain and update the certificate policy statement itself.

These policy statements can be substantial documents. The Federal Bridge CA policy statement is at least 93 pages long, and other certificate authorities have similarly exhaustive documents. The aim of these statements is to provide enough legal backing for certificates produced by these CAs so that they can be used to sign legally binding contracts and automate other legally relevant applications.

11. PUBLIC KEY INFRASTRUCTURE STANDARDS ORGANIZATIONS

The PKI X.509 (PKIX) Working Group was established in the fall of 1995 with the goal of developing Internet standards to support X.509-based PKIs. These specifications form the basis for numerous other IETF specifications that use certificates to secure various protocols, such as S/MIME (for secure email), TLS [for secured Transmission Control Protocol (TCP) connections], and Internet Protocol Security (for securing internet packets).

Internet Engineering Task Force Public Key Infrastructure X.509

The PKIX working group has produced a complete set of specifications for an X.509-based PKI system. These specifications span 36 RFCs; at least eight more RFCs are being considered by the group. In addition to the basic core of X.509 certificate profiles and verification strategies, the PKIX drafts cover the format of certificate request messages, certificates for arbitrary attributes (rather than for public keys), and a host of other certificate techniques.

Other IETF groups have produced a group of specifications that detail the use of certificates in various protocols and applications. In particular, the S/MIME group, which details a method for encrypting email messages, and the SSL/TLS group, which details TCP/IP connection security, use X.509 certificates.

In May 2015, the IETF established the Automated Certificate Management Environment (ACME) working group to build protocols that would simplify the issuance of certificates with the goal of making encrypted network connections easier to establish and thus, it was hoped, more

commonplace. The ACME group published a draft RFC for the ACME protocol, which enables a CA to establish domain ownership and create certificates with little or no user intervention. This protocol was then used to create the "Let's Encrypt" CA, which issues zero-cost certificates using ACME. Websites can use Let's Encrypt (https://letsencrypt.org) to provision certificates automatically and thereby enable encryption with no need to pay a commercial CA. This approach has proven popular, with more than a million certificates issued in the first year of operation. Several commercial CAs have followed with offerings of low- or zero-cost domain authentication certificates, and this approach may lead to wider use of encrypted SSL/TLS connections for Web communications.

SDSI/SPKI

The Simple Distributed Security Infrastructure (SDSI) group was chartered in 1996 to design a mechanism for distributing public keys that would correct some of the perceived complexities inherent in X.509. In particular, the SDSI group aimed to build a PKI architecture [sdsi] that would not rely on a hierarchical naming system, but would instead work with local names that would not have to be enforced to be globally unique. The eventual SDSI design, produced by Ron Rivest and Butler Lampson, has a number of unique features:

- *Public key-centric design.* The SDSI design uses the public key itself (or a hash of the key) as the primary identifying name. SDSI signature objects can contain naming statements about the holder of a given key, but the names are not intended to be the "durable" name of a entity.
- *Free-form namespaces.* SDSI imposes no restrictions on what form names must take and imposes no hierarchy that defines a canonical namespace. Instead, any signer may assert identity information about the holder of a key, but no entity is required to the use (or believe) the identity bindings of any other particular signer. This allows each application to create a policy about who can create identities, how those identities are verified, and even what constitutes an identity.
- *Support for groups and roles.* The design of many security constructions (access control lists, for example) often includes the ability to refer to groups or roles instead of the identity of individuals. This allows access control and encryption operations to protect data for groups, which may be more natural in some situations.

The SPKI group was started at nearly the same time, with goals similar to the SDSI effort. In X, the two groups were merged, and the SDSI/SPKI 2.0 specification was produced, incorporating ideas from both architectures.

Internet Engineering Task Force Open Pretty Good Privacy

The PGP public key system, created by Phillip Zimmermann, is a widely deployed PKI system that allows for the signing and encryption of files and email. Unlike the X.509 PKI architecture, the PGP PKI system uses the notion of a "Web of Trust" to bind identities to keys. The Web of Trust (WoT) [1] replaces the X.509 idea of identity binding via an authoritative server with identity binding via multiple semitrusted paths.

In a WoT system, the end user maintains a database of matching keys and identities, each of which is given two trust ratings. The first trust rating denotes how trusted the binding is between the key and the identity, and the second denotes how trusted a particular identity is to "introduce" new bindings. Users can create and sign a certificate, and import certificates created by other users. Importing a new certificate is treated as an introduction. When a given identity and key in a database are signed by enough trusted identities, that binding is treated as trusted.

Because PGP identities are not bound by an authoritative server, there is also no authoritative server that can revoke a key. Instead, the PGP model states that the holder of a key can revoke that key by posting a signed revocation message to a public server. Any user seeing a properly signed revocation message then removes that key from the database. Because revocation messages must be signed, only the holder of the key can produce them, so it is impossible to produce a false revocation without compromising the key. If an attacker does compromise the key, production of a revocation message from that compromised key actually improves the security of the overall system, because it warns other users not to trust that key.

12. PRETTY GOOD PRIVACY CERTIFICATE FORMATS

To support the unique features of the WoT system, PGP invented a flexible packetized message format that can encode encrypted messages, signed messages, key database entries, key revocation messages, and certificates. This packetized design, described in IETF RFC 2440, allows a PGP certificate to contain a variable number of names and signatures, as opposed to the single-certification model used in X.509.

A PGP certificate (known as a transferable public key) contains three main sections of packetized data. The first section contains the main public key itself, potentially followed by some set of relevant revocation packets. The next section contains a set of User ID packets, which are identities to be bound to the main public key. Each User ID packet is optionally followed by a set of Signature packets,

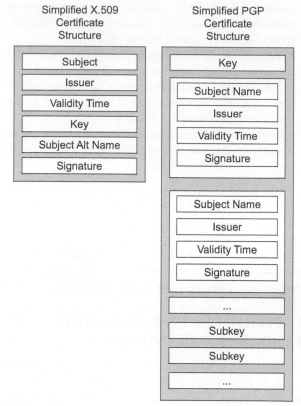

FIGURE 48.8 Comparing X.509 and Pretty Good Privacy (PGP) certificate structures.

each of which contains an identity and a signature of the User ID packet and the main public key. Each of these Signature packets essentially forms an identity binding. Because each PGP certificate can contain any number of these User ID/Signature elements, a single certificate can assert that a public key is bound to multiple identities (for example, multiple email addresses that correspond to a single user), certified by multiple signers. This multiple signer approach enables the WoT model. The last section of the certificate is optional and may contain multiple subkeys, which are single-function keys (for example, an encryption-only key) also owned by the holder of the main public key. Each of these subkeys must be signed by the main public key.

PGP Signature packets contain all information needed to perform a certification, including time intervals for which the signature is valid. Fig. 48.8 shows how the multiname, multisignature PGP format differs from the single-name, single-signature X.509 format.

13. PRETTY GOOD PRIVACY PUBLIC KEY INFRASTRUCTURE IMPLEMENTATIONS

The PGP PKI system is implemented in commercial products sold by the PGP Corporation and several open source projects including Gnu Privacy Guard and OpenPGP. Thawte offers a WoT service that connects people with "WoT notaries" that can build trusted introductions. PGP Corporation operates a PGP Global Directory that contains PGP keys along with an email confirmation service to make key certification easier. The OpenPGP group (www. openpgp.org) maintains IETF specification (RFC 2440) for the PGP message and certificate format.

14. WORLD WIDE WEB CONSORTIUM

The World Wide Web Consortium standards group published a series of standards on encrypting and signing eXtensible Markup Language (XML) documents. These standards, XML Signature and XML Encryption, have a companion PKI specification called XML Key Management Specification (XKMS).

The XKMS specification describes a meta-PKI that can be used to register, locate, and validate keys that may be certified by an outside X.509 CA, a PGP referrer, an SPKI key signer, or the XKMS infrastructure itself. The specification contains two protocol specifications: XML Key Information Service Specification (X-KISS) and XML Key Registration Service Specification (X-KRSS). X-KISS is used to find and validate a public key referenced in an XML document, and X-KRSS is used to register a public key so that it can be located by X-KISS requests.

15. IS PUBLIC KEY INFRASTRUCTURE SECURE?

PKI has formed the basis of Internet security protocols such as S/MIME for securing email, and SSL/TLS protocols for securing communications between clients and Web servers. The essential job of PKI in these protocols is to bind a name such as an email address or domain name to a key that is controlled by that entity. As seen in this chapter, that job boils down to a CA issuing a certificate for an entity. The security of these systems then rests on the trustworthiness of the CAs trusted within an application. If a CA issues a set of bad certificates, the security of the entire system can be called into question.

The issue of a subverted CA was largely theoretical until attacks on the Comodo and DigiNotar CAs [18,19] in 2011. Both of these CAs discovered that an attacker had bypassed their internal controls and obtained certificates for prominent Internet domains (google.com, yahoo.com) These certificates were revoked, but the incident caused the major browser vendors to revisit their policies about what CA roots are trusted, and the removal of many CAs. In the case of DigiNotar, these attacks ultimately led to the bankruptcy of the company.

By attacking a CA and obtaining a false certificate for a given domain, the attacker can set up a fake version of the domain's website and, using that certificate, create secure connections to clients that trust that CA's root certificate. This secure connection can be used as a "man-in-the-middle" server that reveals all traffic between the client (or clients) and the legitimate website.

Can these attacks be prevented? There are research protocols such as "Perspectives" [20] that attempt to detect false certificates that might be signed by a legitimate CA. These protocols use third-party repositories to track what certificates and keys are used by individual websites. A change that is noticed by only some subset of users may indicate an attacker using a certificate to gain access to secured traffic.

In 2015, the IETF published RFC 7469, which specifies "certificate pinning," a method to allow websites to specify an acceptable key or certificate that cannot be changed outside a specified time window. The pinning method (which is now implemented in several browsers) prevents a rogue CA from publishing illegitimate certificates for a given site. To pin a certificate, the site sends a hash that must match the SubjectPublicKeyInfo field of a certificate in the site's certificate chain. Although a malicious actor could spoof this field, it would fool only browsers that had not visited the legitimate site. Once a browser has seen the pinning data, it will refuse to connect to sites with nonconforming certificate chains. Pinning can also be used in other protocols by providing a way to communicate an essentially permanent constraint on the certificate chain used to validate an entity. Pinning has become more popular over time and may evolve into a standard mechanism to limit CA-based attacks on Internet protocols.

Some other products that rely on PKI certification have introduced new features to make these attacks harder to execute. Google's Chrome browser also has incorporated security features [21] intended to foil attacks on PKI infrastructure. The Mozilla Foundation, owners of the Firefox browser, have instituted an audit and review system that requires all trusted CAs to attest that they have specific kinds of security mechanisms in place to prevent the issuance of illegitimate certificates.

As a general principle, systems built to rely on PKI for security should understand the risks involved in CA compromise, and also understand how critical it is to control exposure to these kinds of attacks. One simple mechanism for doing this is to restrict the number of CAs that are trusted by the application. The large number of roots trusted by the average Web browser is large, which makes auditing of the complete list of CAs difficult.

16. ALTERNATIVE PUBLIC KEY INFRASTRUCTURE ARCHITECTURES

PKI systems have proven to be remarkably effective tools for some protocols, most notably SSL, which has emerged as the dominant standard for encrypting Internet traffic. Deploying PKI systems for other types of applications or as a general key management system has not been as successful. The differentiating factor seems to be that PKI keys for machine end-entities (such as websites) do not encounter usability hurdles that emerge when issuing PKI keys for human end-entities. Peter Guttman [notdead] has a number of overviews of PKI that present the fundamental difficulties of classic X.509 PKI architectures. Alma Whitten and Doug Tygar [17] published "Why Johnny Can't Encrypt," a study of various users attempting to encrypt email messages using certificates. This study showed substantial user failure rates resulting from the complexities of understanding certificate naming and validation practices. A subsequent study [10] showed similar results when using X.509 certificates with S/MIME encryption in Microsoft Outlook Express. Most of the research on PKI alternatives has focused on making encryption easier to use and deploy.

17. MODIFIED X.509 ARCHITECTURES

Some researchers have proposed modifications or redesigns of the X.509 architecture to make obtaining a certificate easier, and lower the cost of operating applications that depend on certificates. The goal of these systems is often to allow internet based services to use certificate based signature and encryption service without requiring the user to consciously interact with certification services or even understand that certificates are being used.

Perlman and Kaufman's User-Centric Public Key Infrastructure

Perlman and Kaufman proposed the "User-centric PKI" [Perlman], which allows the user to act as his own CA, with authentication provided through individual registration with service providers. It has several features that attempt to protect user privacy by allowing the user to pick what attributes are visible to a specific service provider.

Guttman's Plug and Play Public Key Infrastructure

Guttman's proposed "Plug and Play PKI" [gutmann-pnp] provides for similar self-registration with a service provider and adds location protocols to establish how to contact certifying services. The goal is to build a PKI that provides a reasonable level of security and that is essentially transparent to the end user.

Callas' Self-assembling Public Key Infrastructure

In 2003, Jon Callas [5] proposed a PKI system that would use existing, standard PKI elements bound together by a "robot" server that would examine messages sent between users, and attempt to find certificates that could be used to secure the message. In the absence of an available certificate, the robot would create a key on behalf of the user, and send a message requesting authentication. This system has the benefit for speeding deployment of PKI systems for email authentication, but loses many of the strict authentication attributes that drove the development of the X.509 and IETF PKI standards.

18. ALTERNATIVE KEY MANAGEMENT MODELS

PKI systems can be used for encryption as well as digital signatures, but these two applications have different operational characteristics. In particular, systems that use PKIs for encryption require an encrypting party to have the ability to locate certificates for its desired set of recipients. In digital signature applications, a signer only requires access to his own private key and certificate. The certificates required to verify the signature can be sent with the signed document, so there is no requirement for verifiers to locate arbitrary certificates. These difficulties have been identified as factors contributing to the difficulty of practical deployment of PKI-based encryption systems such as S/MIME.

In 1984, Adi Shamir [16] proposed an Identity-Based Encryption (IBE) system for email encryption. In the identity-based model, any string can be mathematically transformed into a public key, typically using some public information from a server. A message then can be encrypted with this key. To decrypt, the message recipient contacts the server and requests a corresponding private key. The server is able to derive a private key mathematically, which is returned to the recipient. Shamir disclosed how to perform a signature operation in this model, but did not give a solution for encryption.

This approach has significant advantages over the traditional PKI model of encryption. The most obvious is the ability to send an encrypted message without locating a certificate for a given recipient. There are other points of differentiation:

- *Key recovery.* In the traditional PKI model, if a recipient loses the private key corresponding to a certificate, all messages encrypted to that certificate's public key cannot be decrypted. In the IBE model, the server can recompute lost private keys. If messages must be recoverable for legal or other business reasons, PKI systems typically add mandatory secondary public keys to which senders must encrypt messages.

- *Group support.* Because any string can be transformed into a public key, a group name can be supplied instead of an individual identity. In the traditional PKI model, groups are either done by expanding a group to a set of individuals at encrypt time or by issuing group certificates. Group certificates pose serious difficulties with revocation, because individuals can only be removed from a group as often as revocation is updated.

In 2001, Boneh and Franklin gave the first fully described secure and efficient method for IBE [4]. This was followed by a number of variant techniques, including Hierarchical Identity-Based Encryption (HIBE) and Certificateless Encryption. HIBE allows multiple key servers to be used, each of which controls part of the namespace used for encryption. Certificateless [2] Encryption adds the ability to encrypt to an end user using an identity, but in such a way that the key server cannot read messages. IBE systems have been commercialized and are the subject of standards under the IETF (RFC 5091) and the Institute of Electrical and Electronics Engineers(1363.3).

19. SUMMARY

A PKI is the key management environment for public key information about a public key cryptographic system. As discussed in this chapter, there are three basic PKI architectures based on the number of Certificate Authorities (CAs) in the PKI, in which users of the PKI place their trust (known as a user's trust point), and the trust relationships between CAs within a multi-CA PKI.

The most basic PKI architecture is one that contains a single CA that provides the PKI services (certificates, certificate status information, etc.) for all users of the PKI. Multiple CA PKIs can be constructed using one of two architectures based on the trust relationship between CAs. A PKI constructed with superior–subordinate CA relationships is called a hierarchical PKI architecture. Alternatively, a PKI constructed of peer-to-peer CA relationships is called a mesh PKI architecture.

Directory Architectures

As discussed in this chapter, early PKI development was conducted under the assumption that a directory infrastructure (specifically a global X.500 directory) would be used to distribute certificates and CRLs. Unfortunately, the global X.500 directory did not emerge, which resulted in PKIs being deployed using various directory architectures based on how directory requests are serviced. If the initial directory cannot service a request, the directory can forward the request to other known directories using directory

chaining. Another way a directory can resolve an unserviceable request is to return a referral to the initiator of the request indicating a different directory that might be able to service the request. If the directories cannot provide directory chaining or referrals, pointers to directory servers can be embedded in a PKI certificate using the Authority Information Access and Subject Information Access extensions. In general, all PKI users interface to the directory infrastructure using the Lightweight Directory Access Protocol regardless of how the directory infrastructure is navigated.

Bridge Certification Authorities and Revocation Modeling

Bridge Certification Authorities provide the means to leverage the capabilities of existing corporate PKIs as well as federal PKIs. PKIs are being fielded in increasing size and numbers, but operational experience to date has been limited to a relatively small number of environments. As a result, there are still many unanswered questions about the ways in which PKIs will be organized and operated in large-scale systems. Some of these questions involve the ways in which individual certification authorities (CAs) will be interconnected. Others involve the ways in which revocation information will be distributed.

Most of the proposed revocation distribution mechanisms have involved variations of the original CRL scheme. Examples include the use of segmented CRLs and Delta CRLs. However, some schemes do not involve the use of any type of CRL (online certificate status protocols and hash chains).

A model of certificate revocation presents a mathematical model for describing the timings of validations by relying parties. The model is used to determine how request rates for traditional CRLs change over time. This model is then extended to show how request rates are affected when CRLs are segmented. This chapter also presented a technique for distributing revocation information, overissued CRLs. Overissued CRLs are identical to traditional CRLs but are issued more frequently. The result of overissuing CRLs is to spread out requests from relying parties and thus to reduce the peak load on the repository.

A more efficient use of Delta CRLs employs the model described in a model of certificate revocation to analyze various methods of issuing Delta CRLs. It begins with an analysis of the "traditional" method of issuing Delta CRLs and shows that under some circumstances, issuing Delta CRLs in this manner fails to provide the efficiency gains for which Delta CRLs were designed. A new method of issuing Delta CRLs, sliding window Delta CRLs, was presented. Sliding window Delta CRLs are similar to traditional Delta CRLs, but provide a constant amount of historical information. Whereas this does not affect the request rate for

Delta CRLs, it can significantly reduce the peak request rate for base CRLs. The chapter provided an analysis of sliding window Delta CRLs along with advice about how to select the optimal window size to use when issuing Delta CRLs.

Finally, let us move on to the real interactive part of this chapter: review questions/exercises, hands-on projects, case projects, and the optional team case project. The answers and/or solutions by chapter can be found in Appendix K.

CHAPTER REVIEW QUESTIONS/ EXERCISES

True/False

1. True or False? The most important security protocols used on the Internet do not rely on PKI to bind names to keys, a crucial function that allows authentication of users and websites.
2. True or False? To understand how PKI systems function, it is not necessary to grasp the basics of public key cryptography.
3. True or False? The most important cryptographic operation in PKI systems is the digital signature.
4. True or False? Using RSA, variants of the three operations used to construct digital signatures can also be used to encrypt data.
5. True or False? PKI systems solve the problem of associating meaningful names with essentially meaningless cryptographic keys.

Multiple Choice

1. What model is the most prevalent standard for certificate-based PKIs?
   A. X.510
   B. SPKI
   C. TLS
   D. X.509
   E. S/MIME
2. What model specifies a Web of Trust system for certifying user email encryption keys?
   A. PGP
   B. X.509
   C. SPKI
   D. X.512
   E. ASN.1
3. Although in theory the _____ is the entity that creates and validates certificates, in practice it may be desirable or necessary to delegate the actions of user authentication and certificate validation to other servers.
   A. Evolution
   B. Residue class
   C. Peer-to-peer (P2P)
   D. Certification Authority
   E. Security
4. What process would typically NOT be done as part of certificate validation?
   A. Expiration checking
   B. Revocation checking
   C. Parity checking
   D. Extension checking
   E. Constraint checking
5. The contents of the target certificate cannot be trusted until the integrity of those contents is validated, so the first step is to check the:
   A. Physical world
   B. Data retention
   C. Standardization
   D. Permutation
   E. Signature

EXERCISE

Problem

What are some complexities associated with issuing certificates for end users (in an application such as S/MIME) as opposed to machines (as in TLS)?

Hands-on Projects

Project

Describe the major differences between symmetric key distribution systems and public key systems such as PKI.

Case Projects

Problem

How does PKI provide management and control?

Optional Team Case Project

Problem

What are the core components of a PKI?

REFERENCES

[1] A. Abdul-Rahman, The PGP Trust Model, EDI-Forum, April 1997. Available at: http://www.cs.ucl.ac.uk/staff/F.AbdulRahman/docs/.
[2] S.S. Al-Riyami, K. Paterson, Certificateless public key cryptography, in: C.S. Laih (Ed.), Advances in Cryptology — Asiacrypt 2003, Lecture Notes in Computer Science, vol. 2894, Springer-Verlag, 2003, pp. 452—473.

[3] S. Berkovits, S. Chokhani, J.A. Furlong, J.A. Geiter, J.C. Guild, Public Key Infrastructure Study: Final Report, Produced by the MITRE Corporation for NIST, April 1994.

[4] D. Boneh, M. Franklin, Identity-based encryption from the Weil Pairing, SIAM J. Comput. 32 (3) (2003) 586–615.

[5] J. Callas, Improving message security with a self-assembling PKI, in: 2nd Annual PKI Research Workshop Pre-proceedings, Gaithersburg, MD, April 2003. http://citeseer.ist.psu.edu/callas03 improving.html.

[6] S. Chokhani, W. Ford, Internet X.509 Public Key Infrastructure: Certificate Policy and Certification Practices Framework, IETF RFC 2527, March 1999.

[7] M. Cooper, Y. Dzambasow, P. Hesse, S. Joseph, R. Nicholas, Internet X.509 Public Key Infrastructure: Certification Path Building, IETF RFC 4158, September 2005.

[8] W. Diffie, M.E. Hellman, New directions in cryptography, IEEE Trans. Inform. Theory IT-22 (6) (1976) 644–654.

[9] T. Freeman, R. Housely, A. Malpani, D. Cooper, W. Polk, Server Based Certificate Validation Protocol (SCVP), IETF RFC 5055, December 2007.

[10] S. Garfinkel, R. Miller, Johnny 2: a user test of key continuity management with S/MIME and outlook express, in: Symposium on Usable Privacy and Security, 2005.

[11] R. Housely, W. Ford, W. Polk, D. Solo, Internet X.509 Public Key Infrastructure Certificate and Certificate Revocation List Profile, IETF RFC 3280, April 2002.

[12] ITU-T Recommendation X.509 (1997 E): Information Technology – Open Systems Interconnection – the Directory: Authentication Framework, June 1997.

[13] S. Micali, Efficient Certificate Revocation, Technical Report TM-542b, MIT Laboratory for Computer Science, March 22, 1996, http://citeseer. ist.psu.edu/micali96efficient.html.

[14] M. Myers, R. Ankeny, A. Malpani, S. Galperin, C. Adams, X.509 Internet Public Key Infrastructure: Online Certificate Status Protocol – OCSP, IETF RFC 2560, June 1999.

[15] W.T. Polk, N.E. Hastings, Bridge Certification Authorities: Connecting B2B Public Key Infrastructures, White paper, US Nat'l Institute of Standards and Technology, 2001. Available at: http://csrc. nist.gov/groups/ST/crypto_apps_infra/documents/B2B-article.pdf.

[16] A. Shamir, Identity-based cryptosystems and signature schemes, in: Advances in Cryptology – Crypto '84, Lecture Notes in Computer Science, vol. 196, Spring-Verlag, 1984, pp. 47–53.

[17] A. Whitten, J.D. Tygar, Why Johnny can't encrypt: a usability evaluation of pgp 5.0, in: Proceedings of the 8th USENIX Security Symposium, August 1999.

[18] Fake DigiNotar Web Certificate Risk to Iranians, BBC News, September 5, 2011. Retrieved: http://www.bbc.co.uk/news/ technology-14789763.

[19] R. Richmond, An Attack Sheds Light on Internet Security Holes, New York Times, April 6 , 2011. Retrieved: http://www.nytimes. com/2011/04/07/technology/07hack.html?ref=stuxnet.

[20] D. Wendlandt, D.G. Andersen, A. Perrig, Perspectives: improving SSH-style host authentication with multi-path probing, in: USENIX Annual Technical Conference, 2008, pp. 321–334.

[21] New Chromium Security Features, June 2011, The Chromium Blog, June 14, 2011. Retrieved: http://blog.chromium.org/2011/06/new-chromium-security-features-june.html.

Chapter 49

Password-Based Authenticated Key Establishment Protocols

Jean Lancrenon[1], Dalia Khader[2], Peter Y.A. Ryan[2] and Feng Hao[3]

[1]*Interdisciplinary Centre for Security, Reliability and Trust, Luxembourg-Kirchberg, Luxembourg;* [2]*University of Luxemburg, Coudenhove-Kalergi, Luxembourg;* [3]*Newcastle University, Newcastle Upon Tyne, Netherlands*

Note: This chapter is available in its entirety online at store.elsevier.com/product.jsp?isbn= 9780128038437 (click the Resources tab at the bottom of the page).

1. ABSTRACT

If two parties wish to safely communicate over an insecure channel, one method they may use is to first run an authenticated key exchange protocol over this channel so as to jointly and secretly construct a cryptographically strong session key that can serve to subsequently secure further bulk communication. This chapter is an introduction to the design of such key exchange protocols when the only secret information shared a priori by both parties is a simple, short password. After a brief description of authenticated key exchange in general, we explain the security challenges faced in the password-based case and illustrate our exposition with three concrete password-authenticated key exchange protocols.

2. CONTENTS

Chapter 45

Password-Based Authenticated
Key Establishment Protocols

ABSTRACT

Chapter 50

Context-Aware Multifactor Authentication Survey

Emin Huseynov and Jean-Marc Seigneur

University of Geneva, Carouge, Switzerland

1. INTRODUCTION

Multifactor authentication was described in 1988 in US Patent 4,720,860, where the second factor was presented as "nonpredictable code" [1]. The first implementations of such systems were based on isolated hardware devices generating such codes. In this type of system, that device can be regarded as a context for additional authentication factors. Thus, the idea of using context to replace or deliver additional authentication factors is not new and was used in a large number of projects. We will review a few of them to illustrate the principle of context-aware multifactor authentication.

It is important first to define what is meant by context. The definitions of context may vary depending on the research areas, but broadly, context refers to different ambient conditions of objects that are parts of the authentication mechanism. Authors also define context as information that characterizes situations of objects that are considered relevant to the user—application interaction [2]. Context is typically the location, identity, and state of people, groups, and computational and physical objects. In our work the following examples can be shown as context factors:

- A carried device (classic multifactor authentication)
- Environmental (sound, light, images, videos, and ambient temperature)
- Internal [biometrics, Internet Protocol (IP) address, global positioning system (GPS)]

Some of these factors, such as physical location (proximity to a certain device) will be used as the primary factor, but others will be used as additional verification or protection mechanisms in combination with the primary factor. An example of such a combination is transmitting a physical location together with the exact ambient temperature of a beacon device to the authenticating server that can then be verified with the same data submitted by the client trying to authenticate, to improve the security of the process and minimize data forgery and replay attack possibilities.

Section 2 reviews classic method of two-factor authentication, Section 3 presents modern approaches, and Section 4 provides a comparative summary of some of the reviewed methods in the context of user experience and security.

2. CLASSIC APPROACH TO MULTIFACTOR AUTHENTICATION

Multifactor authentication using carried devices (a hardware token or an application on a mobile device) as a context was among the first implementations of strong security. We consider this context to be classic and review some of the most commonly used variations of such systems in this section.

Hardware Tokens

One-time passwords (OTP), as generated by a standalone hardware token, can be considered a classic method of multifactor authentication. In this example, this hardware device is serving as a proximity context proving the user has access to a physical device. For our survey, the type of the algorithms used to generate an OTP is not critical; however, we can review a number of modern hardware types to compare with each other. Most token producers are moving or have already moved to hash message authentication code (HMAC)-based [HMAC-based OTP(HOTP)]

Computer and Information Security Handbook. http://dx.doi.org/10.1016/B978-0-12-803843-7.00050-8

standard [30], and in most of cases its time-based variant, time-based OTP (TOTP) and the principle of TOTP hardware or software tokens are exactly the same; therefore we review some of the tokens that do not use TOTP as their algorithm. Hardware tokens can be of two types: (1) disconnected tokens, separate devices that have no direct connection to client system (users have to type the OTPs manually using keyboards); and (2) connected tokens, which transmit the generated OTPs to the client via a physical connection, usually universal serial bus (USB).

SecurID

RSA SecurID is one of the oldest hardware tokens on the market and used to be a de facto standard for two-factor authentication (Fig. 50.1). It uses RSA proprietary algorithms to generate OTPs. It is still popular, but after a security breach in 2011 [3], it is no considered secure by end users.

Yubico

Yubico offers a number of products that appear to achieve the real minimum of a user's interaction that is required to submit a second factor [4] and can be shown as examples of connected tokens (Fig. 50.2). Yubico's Nano and Neo hardware tokens are designed to send generated OTPs via near field communication (NFC) or USB (emulating

FIGURE 50.1   Hardware token for two-factor authentication.

FIGURE 50.2   Yubico connected tokens.

keyboard input). These devices are indeed making two-factor authentication much easier for end users; however there are still some disadvantages. It is impossible to use the USB-based token on most mobile devices without additional equipment, and the activity range of NFC tokens is limited to 15 cm [5]. Furthermore, the number of accounts each token can use is limited to a maximum of two keys per device.

Software Tokens

Software tokens are applications running on a computer device, usually mobile devices. Modern mobile operating systems allow complex and powerful mobile applications to be created, so software tokens provide additional features such as multiple profiles, Quick Response (QR) code-based enrollment, and cloud backup. However, the main functionality of software tokens (generation of OTPs) is supported even on models that are not defined as "smartphones." This section reviews a variety of such applications under different platforms.

MobileOTP

MobileOTP (MOTP) was one of the first software tokens designed for two-factor authentication. The first version of MOTP was published in 2003 and was intended to be run primarily on regular phones with Java support (not smartphones) [6]. OTP codes generated by MOTP are alphanumeric codes generated based on the MD5 hash of a secret seed, current timestamp, and a personal identification number (PIN) code entered by the end user each time OTP needs to be generated. MOTP has the same level of security [7]; however, it was originally designed to work on ordinary cell phones (now called "conventional"), and therefore it lacks some features, especially the enrollment process designed to be done in the "client-to-server" direction. This means than the unique key (secret) needs to be generated on the device and then entered to the user's profile on the authentication server (Radius, Database or plaintext configuration files; there are hundreds of server side realizations done for MOTP). Fig. 50.3 shows photos of MOTP Java applications (MIDlets) running on a Nokia 3510 phone.

Google Authenticator

Google Authenticator (Fig. 50.4) is a mobile application that uses TOTP or HOTP algorithms as described by Request for Comments (RFC) 6238 [8]. The algorithm of OTP generation is based on an HMAC-Secure Hash Algorithm 1 hash of a secret key and a counter value (timestamp in the case of TOTP). The enrollment process, which is different from MOTP, is server to client, and in most cases it is based on a QR code with manual entry in case the device does not have a camera.

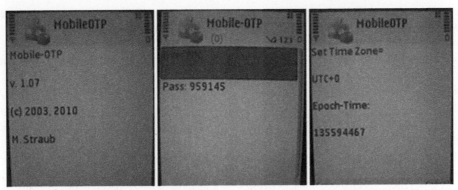

FIGURE 50.3 MobileOTP version 1.07 running on a Nokia 3510.

FIGURE 50.4 Google Authenticator mobile application for Android.

Google Authenticator is available on Android, Blackberry, and Apple iOS platforms. A number of applications with similar functionalities exist on alternative platforms [9].

Comparison of MobileOTP and Google Authenticator

Let us review the difference between Google Authenticator and Mobile OTP. Google Authenticator uses an HOTP-based TOTP algorithm, which is similar to MOTP but different from MOTP. With TOTP-based systems, the key is generated on the server and then shown to the client during the enrollment process. In particular with Google Authenticator, the key is shown as a QR code to be scanned by the app, which makes the enrollment process extremely easy. This, in our opinion, is the main advantage of Google Authenticator, and this is why such systems are becoming popular. However, there are some more key factors that are different, as shown in Table 50.1.

Other Software Token Alternatives

Most of other software tokens use push-notifications to deliver OTP to the user's mobile device. In this case, the OTP is generated on a central server, which then sends this information over a cellular or Wi-Fi network to end users.

TABLE 50.1 Google Authenticator Compared With MobileOTP

	MobileOTP	Google Authenticator (TOTP)
OTP generation algorithm	MD5-based	HMAC-Secure Hash Algorithm 1–based
OTP validity time[a]	10 s	30 s
Additional PIN protection[b]	Yes	No
Key generation	Client side	Server side
Easy enrollment (with QR)	No	Yes
RFC based	No	Yes

HMAC, hash message authentication code; OTP, one-time password; PIN, personal identification number; QR, Quick Response; RFC, Request for Comments; TOTP, time-based one-time password.
[a]OTP regeneration interval on the client, the server side algorithm can be set to accept previous OTPs by adjusting the timestamp used: a loop from [time ()-300) to [time ()] will accept OTPs generated during an interval of 300 s. For example, Google seems to be accepting the current and one previous OTP.
[b]With MobileOTP, a PIN is basically a portion of the key and is stored only on the server. Users only have to remember it and type in the client app whenever an OTP is needed. With Google Authenticator TOTP algorithm keys stored both on client and server sides need to be equal. As per the comparison table, the advantage of MobileOTP-based systems would be an additional layer of protection (PIN), although some may regard this as an inconvenience. At the same time, the lack of PIN code protection (or at least the possibility of having one) is the main shortcoming of Google Authenticator.

Most such apps use TOTP as a fallback method in case the device is not online. There are alternative apps that offer additional PIN code protection to standard TOTP profiles.

Alternative Types of Strong Authentication

Although HOTP/TOTP is the standard algorithm described by the Internet Engineering Task Force for implementing two-factor authentication, other technologies provide the same level of security using different approaches and algorithms. We will not review the proprietary systems providing such strong authentication, but will cover open-source strong authentication tokens.

Short Message Service—Based Strong Authentication

A common technology used to deliver OTPs is text messaging. Because text messaging is a ubiquitous communication channel directly available in nearly all mobile handsets and, through text-to-speech conversion, to any mobile or landline telephone, text messaging has the great potential to reach all consumers with a low total cost to implement. The implementation is simple: the authentication service creates a random value (usually digits-only PIN), and transmits it to the user's mobile phone (in some implementations this can be done via landline numbers). Then, the user enters the code received, which serves as the second factor for the authentication.

Paper Token

A number of implementations of strong authentication use a list of OTPs that are printed on a piece of paper. The logic behind it is simple: Both the server and client have a list of numbered passwords, and when logging in, the server chooses a password and prompts the user to enter it [10]. Fig. 50.5 illustrates an example of a real-life paper token—based production system [11]. The login page that is shown randomly selects a password to be entered. The user

has a laminated piece of paper with these passwords, which is used to find the requested password.

Paper-Based Token Printed by Automated Teller Machine

A similar approach is used in the electronic banking system of AzeriCard. In its implementation, the lists of passwords are printed out from participant banks' automated teller machines (ATMs). As per user instructions published on the website [12], "To connect to an 'Internet Banking' system, it is necessary to obtain a list of one-time passwords in any of the information kiosks or ATMs of the Bank. To do this, in the ATM menu, select 'Payment,' then 'Services,' then 'A list of IB passwords," and the machine will print out a list similar to the one shown in Fig. 50.6. Although access to this list is secured with the additional factor of the banking card and its PIN code, this can be regarded as another example of paper-based strong authentication.

3. MODERN APPROACHES TO MULTIFACTOR AUTHENTICATION

Multifactor authentication is an area in which new inventions frequently appear. In this section, we will review methods, techniques, and products that were designed to replace, complement, simplify, or strengthen classic methods.

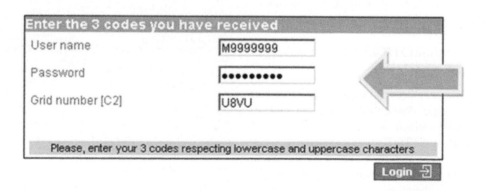

FIGURE 50.5 Example of a paper token—based system.

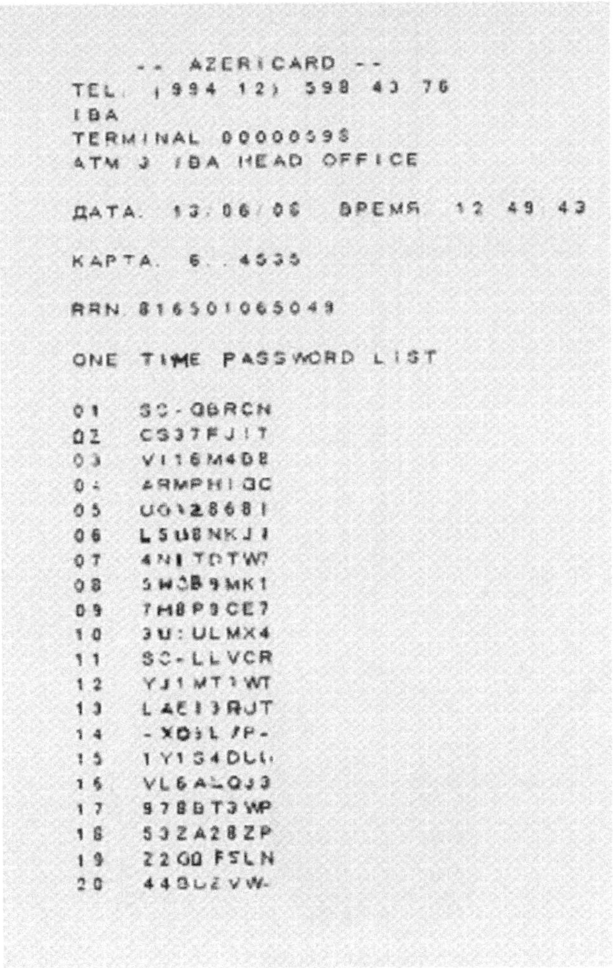

```
          - - AZERICARD - -
     TEL.  (994 12)  398 43 76
     IBA
     TERMINAL  00000398
     ATM 3 IBA HEAD OFFICE

     ДATA.  13.06.06  ВPEMЯ  12 49 43

     KAPTA.  6. .4533

     RRN  816501065049

     ONE TIME PASSWORD LIST

     01    SC-QBRCN
     02    CS37FJIT
     03    VI16M4D8
     04    ARMPHIJC
     05    UG128681
     06    LSU8NKJI
     07    4NITDTW?
     08    5H3B9MK1
     09    7H8P9CE7
     10    3U:ULMX4
     11    SC-LLVCR
     12    YJ1MT1WT
     13    LAEI9RJT
     14    -XD3L/P-
     15    1Y1S4DLU
     16    VL6ALQJ3
     17    978BT3WP
     18    53ZA28ZP
     19    22G0FSLN
     20    443L2VW-
```

FIGURE 50.6 One-time password list printed by an automated teller machine.

Static or Pseudodynamic Context

The context factors reviewed next do not change frequently enough to qualify as strong security factors. We will review them to illustrate and compare them with other, more secure context factors.

Internet Protocol Address

It may sound controversial, but any type of authentication over a Transmission Control Protocol (TCP)/IP network already has the possibility of context-aware authentication: the IP address of the client device. Thus, restricting access to an IP address or a range of an IP addresses theoretically can be regarded as a context factor. Furthermore, because IP address databases also have associations with countries, cities, and in some cases particular buildings, they can also be considered proximity context factors.

However, it is relatively easy to forge or spoof IP addresses, so using IP address restriction itself cannot

provide a satisfactory level of security. In some cases, this method can complement other methods to provide an acceptable security level. In the following example, it is used in conjunction with OTP to secure plain File Transfer Protocol (FTP) connections.

One-Time Password—File Transfer Protocol

As a protocol, FTP is known to be insecure by design and is not recommended. It should be replaced by Secured FTP or Secure Sockets LayerFTP; however, in some situations users prefer to keep using the standard plaintext FTP. OTP-FTP [13] is an attempt to make the plaintext FTP protocol as secure as possible by introducing a Web panel protected with two-factor authentication that generates a temporary session password for an FTP user and restricts access to a specific IP address. In this example, IP address is a context factor used as an additional protection mechanism.

Global Positioning System Coordinates as Security Context Factor

In some cases, access to a certain resource is restricted to a geographic location. This idea is presented in the "Secure Spatial Authentication Using Cell Phones" report [14]. The main principle is that the cell phones send GPS coordinates to both the authentication server and the cellular network, which are then compared and validated if these coordinates match. The report states that for this concept to be secure, a "using a tamper proof GPS module" should be used, which would be hard to ensure, and GPS coordinates would be easy to forge with special devices.

Ambient Temperature as a Context

A number of Bluetooth low energy (BLE) devices are equipped with temperature sensors, so it is technically possible to verify the ambient temperature when authorizing a user. Estimote devices are an example of such a device [15]. The logic behind it is simple (Fig. 50.7): the device is equipped with a temperature sensor that sends the current temperature both to the client via BLE and to the authentication server via an IP/Internet connection. Because the sensor has a high accuracy level and the current temperature may keep changing, the ambient temperature may be a constantly changing factor and can serve as a dynamic second factor.

Disadvantages of this method are obvious: In addition to hardware requirements and the accuracy level of the sensor, there is a narrow attack window inherent in the nature of the factor itself (in most areas ambient temperature stays constant and does not change significantly). However, in some cases this may be a convenient method (for outdoor areas with frequently changing temperatures).

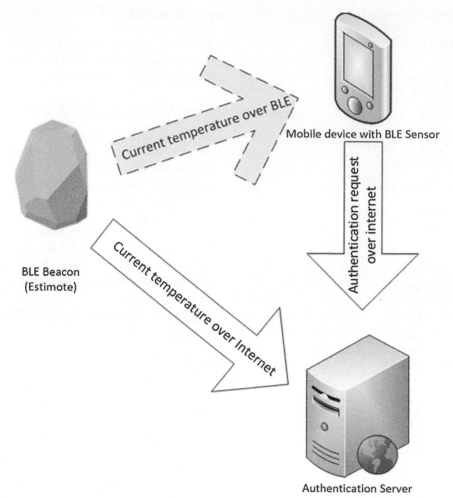

FIGURE 50.7 Temperature-based context-aware authentication with Bluetooth low energy (BLE) beacon.

Face and Voice Recognition as a Context

A number of services provide application program interfaces (APIs) to integrate users' faces and/or voice recognition as a second authentication factors. Face2.in [16] and KeyLemon [17] provide APIs as well as additional integration components (such as WordPress plugins) to enable this.

Biometrics is also relied upon in more critical areas such as online banking. Wells Fargo [18] implemented biometric logins to their online banking system using a mobile application. The application, shown in Fig. 50.8, uses both voice and face recognition to identify users.

Although using biometrics as a context in multifactor authentication significantly increases the overall security level, these factors (the user's face and voice) cannot be considered dynamic; in fact, the entropy level of these factors allows to them to be called more static factors. Some vendors try to increase entropy by asking users to move or blink their eyes, but this can easily be circumvented by using a good-quality photo of the user's face [19] and recorded voice samples to generate a voice verification response.

Dynamic Context

The context factors reviewed in this section are dynamic. In addition, they provide higher security because the attack vector is minimal, especially compared with static factors.

Bluetooth Low Energy Beacons

A user's physical location is one example of a context. Being close to a device can verify the location as well. A number of techniques use BLE (Bluetooth 4.0) to determine proximity to a device. BLE beacons periodically broadcast sets of data that includes the unique ID of a device as well as additional parameters (major ID, minor ID, and others) that can be used to deliver OTP data to end users' devices.

Authy Authy Bluetooth is a TOTP-based implementation of two-factor authentication. Because it is based on BLE protocol, the use of Authy Bluetooth [20] is limited to

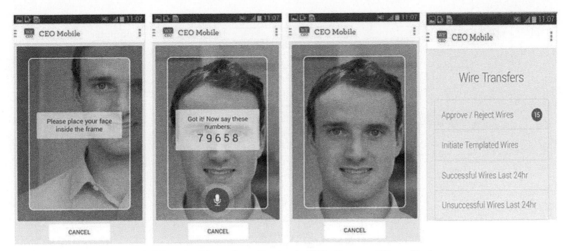

FIGURE 50.8 Biometric verification in Wells Fargo mobile application.

situations in which both a client access system (a laptop) and the system running the token (a mobile phone with the Authy app) support the BLE protocol. For this reason, Authy Bluetooth is supported only on recent Mac devices as clients, iPhone 4s and above, plus Android devices running version 4.4.4 and above with BLE support as a mobile device. In addition, the current implementation can hardly be considered a system with "minimal user interaction," because users need to: launch the Authy application and select an account, and after the current OTP is copied to clipboard, users are advised to paste it to the form requiring the OTP.

Bluetooth Low Energy One-Time Password Tokens Another system with a similar implementation was proposed by Rijswijk-Deij [21], in which TOTP broadcasts are emitted by a BLE-based token beacon device. This concept may be further developed using Eddystone, an open beacon format announced by Google [22].

SAASPASS Authentication using a virtual iBeacon as a second factor has been used in the product offered by SAASPASS [23]. Installed on a user's smartphone, the application automatically transmits the generated OTP to a special connector (currently available only for Macs). This connector searches for BLE packets transmitted in the near or immediate range, and if the packet parameters match, it passes the values gathered to the application (a browser) emulating keyboard keys. The drawbacks of these systems are that BLE is supported only on limited types of devices and Bluetooth is usually not activated on devices, because users often perceive it to be a battery hog.

Wi-Fi

A number of concepts use Wi-Fi as a proximity context. Wi-Fi can indeed be a good (or in some cases better)

alternative to BLE given the range and wider spread, especially as far as hardware is concerned.

Wi-Fi Proximity A system based on WIFI Service Set Identifier (SSID) was proposed by Namiot [24], in which SSID is used as a context-aware application concept. This report describes using the information exchanged between access points and client devices to determine proximity data, and using this proximity data to send promotional information, similar to Apple's iBeacon technology but based on Wi-Fi rather than BLE. This report uses the similar concept of employing Wi-Fi SSID to relay information, but it does not provide security analysis because the system is not intended to be used as a security mechanism.

Wireless Fidelity One-Time Password This solution implements two-factor authentication without affecting the user's experience, by introducing minimum user interaction based on standard Wi-Fi [25]. The main idea is to create a dynamically changing SSID that has OTP encrypted in it. Client devices only need to "see" the name of the network without connecting to it and use a special shared encryption key to decrypt the OTP broadcasted via SSID.

Sound as a Context

A few projects employ sound as the context. A common prerequisite for using these projects is to have a device equipped with a microphone and a speaker.

Sound-Proof In Sound-Proof [26] the second authentication factor is based on verification of the user's phone's presence near the main device (Fig. 50.9). The system compares ambient noise recorded by the main system (a laptop) with sound recorded by the mobile phone. This comparison is triggered by a push notification (the ambient sound does not need to be recorded all of the time); it is done

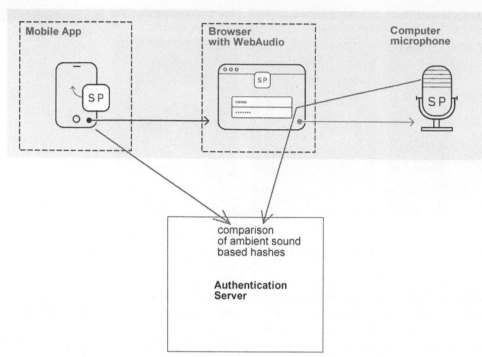

FIGURE 50.9 Sound-based authentication example. *SP*, Sound-Proof.

only for a short time when the second factor is requested by the system. In case there is no ambient sound at all (which is presented as a very rare case), the system suggests that the user "clears the throat" to generate some sound.

SlickLogin This concept is similar to Sound-Proof, but instead of relying on ambient sound, the mobile application generates inaudible sounds (ultrasound) that is captured by the main system's microphone and sent to the server for comparison [27].

4. COMPARATIVE SUMMARY

We have reviewed a variety of modern multifactor authentication systems. Each method has advantages and disadvantages. Although some methods are more secure, others are more convenient for end users. We compared MOTP and Google Authenticator in the previous section; in this section we will compare and evaluate some multifactor authentication methods, taking into account aspects of their security and user experience.

The principle to be used in the surveyed research is often based on beacons of different types. The main idea is that beacons transmit the same set of data to both the client and the authentication server. Based on the results of the comparison, the server accepts or denies the authentication request. Surveyed research uses existing beacon technologies to determine the proximity factor, such as BLE beacons (Eddystone or iBeacon) as well as innovative types, such as Wi-Fi SSID broadcast beacons, ultrasound, and

Light Fidelity [28]. BLE beacons will be enhanced with additional context factors such as temperature and humidity. As surveyed earlier, biometrics-based authentication has also been used as a context (based on face recognition). This has been done for comparison purposes only, because it does not really fall under determined two-factor authentication, as the second factor in this case (the user's face or voice) is also static. A diagram of all varieties of context factors is shown in Fig. 50.10.

User Experience

As far as the user's experience is concerned, the ideal authentication mechanism should require no additional actions from users. This concept is described in the "Zero Interaction Authentication" report [29] and can be applied equally to multifactor authentication. In Table 50.2 we use this approach to evaluate the techniques reviewed in this report from the point of view of the user's experience. In addition to desktop systems, the user's experiences with mobile devices are also compared.

Security

To evaluate the security level of different token types (Table 50.3), we will review the attack type that can be applied to them and probability of the attack succeeding (see checklist: "An Agenda for Action for Token Threat/ Attack Mitigation Mechanisms"). It is assumed that the first factor (username and password) has already been

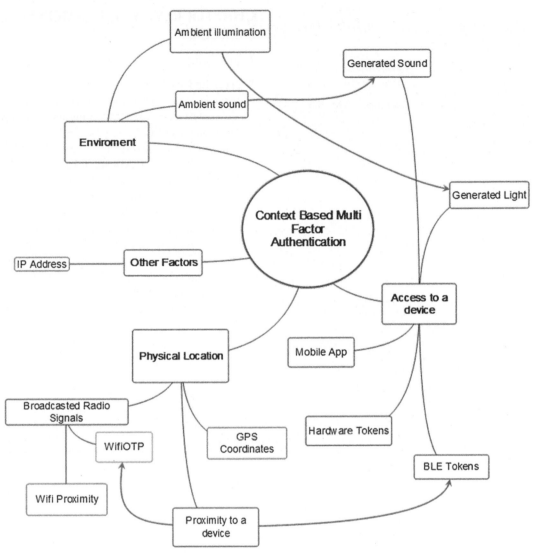

FIGURE 50.10   Diagram of context types as factors for multifactor authentication. *IP*, Internet Protocol; *WifiOTP*, Wi-Fi one-time password.

compromised. The security level is evaluated based on both the attack vector and probability.

Security Comparison Summary

Based on the comparison of security and user experience, we can provide a comparison summary (Table 50.4) of different token types when used on a desktop system. To simplify the comparison, we will compare a few classic and a few modern tokens and use the lowest ratings given in previous comparisons. The score will be calculated as an average of security and user experience ratings.

5. SUMMARY

Implementing multifactor authentication is a balance of security and user experience. Ideal multifactor authentication

should simplify the user's interaction by minimizing or completely eliminating actions required to add a factor or factors for authentication. We have reviewed a number of existing multifactor authentication systems and critically evaluated them from the points of view of security and the user's experience. As an outcome of this review, we created a comparative summary of different methods that clearly show pros and cons of each system. This brings us to the conclusion that although classic methods are still secure and usable, modern methods provide the same or better security while significantly improving the user's experience.

Finally, let us move on to the real interactive part of this chapter: review questions/exercises, hands-on projects, case projects, and the optional team case project. The answers and/or solutions by chapter can be found in Appendix K.

TABLE 50.2 Token Types Comparison Based on User Experience

Token Type	User Experience: Scale of 1–10 (10 = high)	
	Desktop	Mobile
Classic hardware tokens	1	1
Connected token (universal serial bus keyboard emulation)	9	1
Software tokens	1	2
Push notification based tokens with Internet access	8	8
Tokens with Bluetooth low energy[a] broadcasts	9	2
Wi-Fi one-time password tokens[b]	9	8–10[c]

[a]*Provided both client system and token are equipped with BLE modules.*
[b]*Only requires a Wi-Fi module to be present and enabled on the device*
[c]*On Android platforms only. 8: when using WifiOTP in standard apps with the Android keyboard method by users with multiple keyboards installed. 9: the same for users with a single keyboard. 10: with specially adapted apps.*

CHAPTER REVIEW QUESTIONS/ EXERCISES

True/False

1. True or False? Multifactor authentication using carried devices (a hardware token or an application on a mobile device) as a context was among the first implementation of strong security.
2. True or False? Two-time passwords (OTPs) generated by a standalone hardware token can be considered a classic method of multifactor authentication.
3. True or False? Yubico offers a number of products that appear to be achieving the real minimum of a user's interaction required to submit a second factor, and can be shown as an examples of connected tokens.
4. True or False? Software tokens are applications running on a computer device, usually standalone devices.
5. True or False? MobileOTP (MOTP) is one of the first software tokens designed for three-factor authentication.

An Agenda for Action for Token Threat/Attack Mitigation Mechanisms

The token-related mechanisms that assist in mitigating the threats/attacks that are examined in this checklist include (check all tasks completed):

_____1. Theft: Use multifactor tokens that need to be activated through a PIN or biometric.

_____2. Duplication: Use tokens that are difficult to duplicate, such as hardware cryptographic tokens.

_____3. Discovery: Use methods in which responses to prompts cannot easily be discovered.

_____4. Eavesdropping: Use tokens with dynamic authenticators in which knowledge of one authenticator does not assist in deriving a subsequent authenticator.

_____5. Eavesdropping: Use tokens that generate authenticators based on a token input value.

_____6. Eavesdropping: Establish tokens through a separate channel.

_____7. Offline cracking: Use a token with a high-entropy token secret.

_____8. Offline cracking: Use a token that locks up after a number of repeated failed activation attempts.

_____9. Phishing or pharming: Use tokens with dynamic authenticators in which knowledge of one authenticator does not assist in deriving a subsequent authenticator.

_____10. Social engineering: Use tokens with dynamic authenticators in which knowledge of one authenticator does not assist in deriving a subsequent authenticator.

_____11. Online guessing: Use tokens that generate high-entropy authenticators.

_____12. Multiple factors: Make successful attacks more difficult to accomplish.

_____13. Employ physical security mechanisms to protect a stolen token from duplication.

_____14. Impose password complexity rules to reduce the likelihood of a successful guessing attack.

_____15. Employ system and network security controls to prevent an attacker from gaining access to a system or installing malicious software.

_____16. Perform periodic training to ensure the subscriber understands when and how to report compromise (or suspicion of compromise) or otherwise recognize patterns of behavior that may signify an attacker attempting to compromise the token.

_____17. Employ out-of-band techniques to verify proof of possession of registered devices (cell phones).

TABLE 50.3 Token Types Comparison Based on Security Strength

Token Type	Attack Vector and Method	Exploit Probability	Security Level: Scale (10 = high)
Disconnected hardware token	Trojan/keylogger on client systems	Only in real time via man-in-the-browser attacks	10
Universal serial bus connected hardware tokens	Trojan/keylogger on client systems	Only in real time via man-in-the-browser attacks	10
Push notification-based "online" software tokens	Compromised mobile devices	Can be exploited by intercepting notifications on mobile operating system level	8
"Offline"[a] software tokens	Compromised mobile devices	Can be exploited if secret hash from token app has been stolen	5
Wi-Fi OTP	Trojan/keylogger on client systems	Only in real time via man-in-the-browser attacks	10
BLE-broadcast OTP	Intercepting BLE broadcasts	Probability is minimal because physical proximity is required	9

BLE, Bluetooth low energy; *OTP*, one-time password.
[a]*Using OTP generation based on HOTP or MobileOTP.*

TABLE 50.4 Overall Token Types Comparison

Token Type	Security	User Experience	Score
Classic hardware tokens	10	1	5.5
Time-based OTP Mobile applications	5	2	3.5
Push notification-based mobile applications	8	8	8
Bluetooth low energy–based mobile applications	9	2	5.5
Wi-Fi OTP	10	9	9.5

OTP, one-time password.

Multiple Choice

1. What is a mobile application that uses TOTP or HOTP algorithms as described by RFC 6238?
   A. Google Authenticator
   B. MOTP
   C. Mobile OTP
   D. Apple iOS platform
   E. All of the above

2. Most other software tokens, are using _____ to deliver OTP to the user's mobile device.
   A. Push notifications
   B. Risk assessments
   C. Scales
   D. Access
   E. Active monitoring

3. A common technology used for the delivery of OTPs is:
   A. Organizations
   B. Text messaging
   C. Worms
   D. Logs
   E. All of the above

4. There are a number of implementations of strong authentication that use a list of one-time passwords that are printed on a piece of:
   A. Token
   B. Wood
   C. Paper
   D. Metal
   E. All of the above

5. It may sound controversial, but any type of authentication over a TCP/IP network already has the possibility of context-aware authentication: the IP address of the:
   A. Systems security plan
   B. TrustPlus
   C. Denial of service

D. Client device

E. All of the above

EXERCISE

Problem

How does an organization go about using tokens with regards to multistage authentication?

Hands-on Projects

Project

Under certain circumstances, it may be desirable to raise the assurance level of an electronic authentication session between a subscriber and a relaying party in the middle of the application session. How does an organization go about doing this?

Case Projects

Problem

Based on attacks, how would an organization go about categorizing the different types of authentication factors that comprise the token?

Optional Team Case Project

Problem

How would an organization go about categorizing credentials (objects that bind identity to a token)?

REFERENCES

[1] K.P. Weiss, SecurID. RSA Security Inc., 1988 U.S. Patent 4720860. http://www.google.com/patents/US4720860.

[2] A.K. Dey, G.D. Abowd, D. Salber, A conceptual framework and a toolkit for supporting the rapid prototyping of context-aware applications, Hum. Comput. Interact. 16 (2) (2001) 97–166.

[3] M.J. Schwartz, RSA SecurID Breach Cost $66 Million, Information Week, July 2011. http://www.informationweek.com/news/security/attacks/231002833.

[4] Yubico | Trust the Net with YubiKey Strong Two-Factor Authentication, 2011. https://www.yubico.com/.

[5] M. Abel, RFC 4729-IETF Tools, 2006. https://tools.ietf.org/html/rfc4729.

[6] Mobile-OTP: Strong Two-factor Authentication with Mobile Phones, 2005. http://motp.sourceforge.net/.

[7] This Elaboration — Mobile-OTP, 2011. http://motp.sourceforge.net/md5.html.

[8] J. Rydell, RFC 6238-IETF Tools, 2011. https://tools.ietf.org/html/rfc6238.

[9] Google Authenticator — AlternativeTo, 2013. http://alternativeto.net/software/google-authenticator/.

[10] Paper Token: Gutenberg's Version of One Time Passwords, 2010. http://www.quuxlabs.com/blog/2010/09/paper-token-gutenbergs-version-of-one-time-passwords/.

[11] Procedure to Follow to Use the Secured Access of the Website, 2011. http://www.lamutuelle.org/amfiweb/free/documents/Information_acces_securise_anglais.pdf.

[12] User Manual — Internet Banking, 2013. https://www.hbservice.com/instructions/Instruction1-engl.htm.

[13] Как сделать обычный сервер ЕТО Цокнастоящему безоЦасным и одновременно удобным, 2013. http://habrahabr.ru/post/205152/.

[14] A. Durresi, et al., Secure spatial authentication using cell phones. Availability, Reliability and Security, 2007. ARES 2007. The Second International Conference on 10 April 2007 543–549.

[15] Estimote SDK Updated with Accelerometer and Temperature Sensor Support, 2014. http://blog.estimote.com/post/81380655308/estimote-sdk-updated-with-accelerometer-and.

[16] FACE2.in, 2015. https://face2.in/.

[17] KeyLemon — Face Recognition Technology, 2009. https://www.keylemon.com/.

[18] Wells Fargo to Roll Out Biometric Logins by June | Bank Innovation, 2016. http://bankinnovation.net/2016/01/wells-fargo-to-roll-out-biometric-logins-by-june/.

[19] Q. Xiao, Security issues in biometric authentication, in: Information Assurance Workshop, 2005. IAW'05. Proceedings from the Sixth Annual IEEE SMC 15 June 2005, 2005, pp. 8–13.

[20] Two-Factor Authentication ● Authy, 2012. https://www.authy.com/.

[21] R. van Rijswijk-Deij, Simple Location-Based One-time Passwords.

[22] Beacons | Google Developers, 2015. https://developers.google.com/beacons/?hl=en.

[23] Bluetooth, BLE, Two-factor Authentication | SAASPASS, 2014. https://www.saaspass.com/about/bluetooth-ble-two-factor-authentication.html.

[24] D. Namiot, Network proximity on practice: context-aware applications and Wi-Fi proximity, Int. J. Open Inf. Technol. 1 (3) (2013).

[25] E. Huseynov, J.-M. Seigneur, WifiOTP: Pervasive Two-factor Authentication Using Wi-fi SSID Broadcasts, 2015.

[26] N. Karapanos, et al., Sound-Proof: Usable Two-factor Authentication Based on Ambient Sound, arXiv preprint arXiv:1503.03790, 2015.

[27] Google Acquires SlickLogin, the Sound-based Password Alternatives, 2014. http://techcrunch.com/2014/02/16/google-acquires-slicklogin-the-sound-based-password-alternative/.

[28] Z. Zhou, et al., Lifi: line-of-sight identification with wifi. INFOCOM, 2014 Proceedings IEEE 27 April 2014 2688–2696.

[29] H.T.T. Truong, et al., Comparing and fusing different sensor modalities for relay attack resistance in zero-interaction authentication. Pervasive Computing and Communications (PerCom), 2014 IEEE International Conference on 24 March 2014 163–171.

[30] D. M'Raihi, M. Bellare, F. Hoornaert, D. Naccache, O. Ranen, HOTP: An HMAC Based One-time Password Algorithm, RFC 4226, IETF, 2005.

Chapter 51

Instant-Messaging Security

Samuel J.J. Curry

Arbor Networks, Burlington, MA, United States

1. WHY SHOULD I CARE ABOUT INSTANT MESSAGING?

When considering instant messaging (IM), it is important to realize that it is first and foremost a technology; it is not a goal in and of itself. Like an ERP[1] system, an email system, a database, a directory, or a provisioning system, IM must ultimately serve the business: it is a means to an end. The end should be measured in terms of *quantifiable* returns and should be put in context. Before engaging in an IM project, you should be clear about why you are doing it. The basic reasons you should consider IM are:

- Employee satisfaction
- Improving efficiency
- Performing transactions (some business transactions have been built, as you'll see later, to use IM infrastructures; those who do this are aware of it and those who have not seen it before are frequently horrified)
- Improving communications
- Improving response times and timelines

Business decisions revolve around the principle of acceptable risk for acceptable return, and as a result, your *security* decisions with respect to IM are effectively *business* decisions. To those of you reading this with a security hat on, you've probably experienced the continued rapprochement of security and business in your place of work (and in some cases the splitting of security into both a technical and a business discipline): IM is no exception to that. So let's look at IM, trends, the business around it, and then the security implications.

2. WHAT IS INSTANT MESSAGING?

IM is a technology in a continuum of advances (q.v.) that have arisen for communicating and collaborating over the Internet. The most important characteristic of IM is that it has the appearance of being in "real time," and for all intents and purposes it is in real time.[2] Of course, some IM systems allow for synchronization with folks who are offline and come online later through buffering and batching delivery, although these aren't really "instant" messaging (ironically, this is coming back with the advent of some features in social networking applications and environments like Facebook).

IM technologies predate the Internet, with many early mainframe systems and bulletin board systems (BBS) having early chat-like functionality, where two or more people could have a continuous dialogue. In the post-mainframe world, when systems became more distributed and autonomous, chatting and early IM technologies came along, too. In the world of the Internet, two basic technologies have evolved: communications via a central server and communications directly between two peers. Many IM solutions involve a hybrid of these two basic technologies, maintaining a directory or registry of users that then enable a peer-to-peer (P2P) connection.

Some salient features that are relevant for the purposes of technology and will be important later in our approaches to securing IM are as follows:

- *Simultaneity.* IM is a real time or "synchronous" form of communication—real-time opportunity and real-time risk.

---

2. The debate over what constitutes real time is a favorite in many technical circles and is materially important when dealing with events and their observation in systems in which volumes are high and distances and timing are significant. When dealing with human beings and the relatively simple instances of whom we interact with and our perceptions of communications, it is far simpler to call this "real time" than "near real time."

---

1. Enterprise resource planning (ERP) is a category of software that ties together operations, finance, staffing, and accounting. Common examples include SAP and Oracle software.

Computer and Information Security Handbook. http://dx.doi.org/10.1016/B978-0-12-803843-7.00051-X

- *Recording.* IM transactions are a form of written communication, which means that there are logs and sessions can be captured. This is directly analogous to email, although it can be hard to instrument in a P2P connection.
- *Nonrepudiation.* IM usually involves a dialogue and the appearance of nonrepudiation by virtue of an exchange, but there is no inherent nonrepudiation in most IM infrastructures. For example, talking to "Bobby" via IM does not in any way prove that it is registered to "Bobby" or is actually "Bobby" at the time you are talking to the other user.
- *Lack of confidentiality and integrity.* There is no guarantee that sessions are private or unaltered in most IM infrastructures without the implementation of effective encryption solutions.
- *Availability.* Most companies do not have guaranteed service-level agreements around availability and yet they depend on IM, either consciously or unknowingly, and suffer the costs of supporting the service when it fails.

Most users of an IM infrastructure also treat IM as an informal form of communication. It's also not subject to the normal rules of behavior, formatting, and formality of other forms of business communication, such as letters, memoranda, and email.

3. THE EVOLUTION OF NETWORKING TECHNOLOGIES

Over time, technology changes and, usually, advances. Advancements in this context generally refer to being able to do more transactions with more people for more profit. Of course, generalizations of this sort tend to be true on the macroscopic level only since at the microscopic level the tiny deltas in capabilities, offerings, and the vagaries of markets drive many small changes, some of which are detrimental. However, over the long term and at the macroscopic level, advances in technology enable us to do more things with more people more easily and in closer to real time.

There are more than a few laws that track the evolution of some distinct technology trends and the positive effects that are expected. A good example of this is Moore's Law, which has yet to be disproven and has proven true since the 1960s. Moore's Law, put simply, postulates that the number of transistors that can be effectively integrated doubles roughly every two years, and the resultant computing power or efficiency increases along with that. Most of us in technology know Moore's Law, and it is arguable that we as a society depend on it for economic growth and stimulus: There is always more demand for more computing power (or has been to date and for the foreseeable future). A lesser-known further example is Gilder's Law[3] (which has since been disproven)

---

3. www.netlingo.com/lookup.cfm?term=Gilder's%20Law.

that asserts that a similar, related growth in available bandwidth occurs over time.

Perhaps the most important "law" with respect to networks and for IM is Metcalfe's Law, which states that the value of a telecommunications network increases exponentially with a linear increase in the number of users. (Actually, it states that it is proportional to the square of the users on the network.)

Let's also assume that over time the value of a network will increase; the people who use it will find new ways to get more value out of it. The number of connections or transactions will increase, and the value and importance of that network will go up. In a sense, it takes time once a network has increased in size for the complexity and number of transactions promised by Metcalfe's Law to be realized. What does all this have to do with IM? Let's tie it together:

- Following from Moore's Law (and to a lesser extent Gilder), computers (and their networks) will get faster and therefore more valuable—and so connecting them in near real time (of which IM is an example of real-time communications) is a *natural occurrence* and will *increase value.*
- Following from Metcalfe, over time networks will become increasingly valuable to users of those networks.

In other words, IM as a phenomenon is really a tool for increasing connections among systems and networks and for getting more value. For those of us in the business world, this is good news: using IM, we should be able to realize more value from that large information technology (IT) investment and should be able to do more business with more people more efficiently. That is the "carrot," but there is a stick, too: It is not all good news, because where there is value and opportunity, there is also threat and risk.

4. GAME THEORY AND INSTANT MESSAGING

Whenever gains or losses can be quantified for a given population, game theory applies. Game theory is used in many fields to predict what is basically the *social* behavior or organisms in a system: people in economics and political science, animals in biology and ecology, and so on. When you can tell *how much* someone stands to gain or lose, you can build reasonably accurate predictive models for how they will behave; and this is in fact the foundation for many of our modern economic theories. The fact of the matter is that now that the Internet is used for business, we can apply game theory to human behavior with Internet technologies, too, and this includes IM.

On the positive side, if you are seeing more of your colleagues, employees, and friends adopt a technology, especially in a business context, you can be reasonably sure that there is some gain and loss equation that points to an increase in value behind the technology. Generally, people should not go out of their way to adopt technologies simply for the sake of adopting them on a wide scale (though actually, many people do just this and then suffer for it; technology adoption on a wide scale and over a long period of time generally means that something is showing a return on value). Unfortunately, in a business context, this may not translate into more business or more value for the business. Human beings not only do things for quantifiable, money-driven reasons, but they also do things for moral and social reasons.

Let's explore the benefits of adopting IM technology within a company, and then we can explore the risks a little more deeply.

Your Workforce

Whether you work in an IT department or run a small company, your employees have things they need to do: process orders, work with peers, manage teams, talk to customers and to partners. IM is a tool they can and will use to do these things. Look at your workforce and their high-level roles: Do they need IM to do their jobs? IM is an entitlement within a company, not a right. The management of entitlements is a difficult undertaking, but it isn't without precedent. For older companies, you probably had to make a decision similar to the IM decision with respect to email or Internet access. The first response from a company is usually binary: Allow everyone or disallow everyone. This reactionary response is natural, and in many cases some roles are denied entitlements such as email or Internet access on a regular basis. Keep in mind that in some industries, employees make the difference between a successful, aggressively growing business and one that is effectively in a "maintenance mode" or, worse, is actively shrinking. In the remainder of this chapter, we outline factors in your decision making, as follows with the first factor.

Factor #1

Do your employees need IM? If so, which employees need IM and what do they need it for?

Examples of privileged IM entitlement include allowing developers, brokers, sales teams, executives, operations, and/or customer support to have access. *Warning*: If you provide IM for some parts of your company and not for others, you will be in a situation in which some employees have a privilege that others do not. This will have two, perhaps unintended, consequences:

- Employees without IM will seek to get it by abusing backdoors or processes to get this entitlement.

- Some employees will naturally be separated from other employees and may become the object of envy or of resentment. This could cause problems.

We have also touched on employee satisfaction, and it is important to understand the demographics of your workplace and its social norms. It is important to also consider physical location of employees and general demographic considerations with respect to IM because there could be cultural barriers, linguistic barriers, and, as we will see later, generational ones, too.

Factor #2

Is IM important as a job satisfaction component?

Economists generally hold that employees work for financial, moral, and social reasons. Financial reasons are the most obvious and, as we've seen, are the ones most easily quantified and therefore subject to game theory; companies have money, and they can use it to incentivize the behaviors they want. However, human beings also work on things for moral reasons, as is the case with people working in nonprofit organizations or in the open-source movement. These people work on things that matter to them for moral reasons.

However, the social incentives are perhaps the most important for job satisfaction. In speaking recently with the CIO of a large company that banned the use of external IM, the CIO was shocked that a large number of talented operations and development people refused lucrative offers on the grounds that IM was disallowed with people outside the company. This led to a discussion of the motivators for an important asset for this company: attracting and keeping the right talent. The lesson is that if you want to attract the best, you may have to allow them to use technologies such as IM.

After you have determined whether or not IM is needed for the job (Factor #1), interview employees on the uses of IM in a social context: With whom do they IM and for what purposes? Social incentives include a large number of social factors, including keeping in touch with parents, siblings, spouses, and friends but also with colleagues overseas, with mentors, and for team collaboration, especially over long distances.

Generational Gaps

An interesting phenomenon is observable in the generation now in schools and training for the future: They multitask frequently. Generational gaps and their attendant conflicts are nothing new; older generations are in power and are seen to bear larger burdens, and younger generations are often perceived in a negative light. Today IM may be at the forefront of yet another generational conflict.

If you've observed children recently, they do more all at once than adults have done in the past 20 years. This is a generation that grows up in a home with multiple televisions, multiple computers, cell phones from a young age, Power-Point in the classroom, text messaging, email,[4] and IM.

The typical older-generation values in a generational conflict that we must watch out for are assuming that the younger generation is inherently more lazy, is looking for unreasonable entitlement, wants instant gratification, or is lacking in intelligence and seasoning. If you catch yourself doing this, stop yourself and try to empathize with the younger folks. Likewise, the younger generation has its pitfalls and assumptions; but let's focus on the younger, emerging generation, because they will soon be entering the workforce. If you find yourself assuming that multitasking and responding to multiple concurrent stimuli is distracting and likely to produce a lack of efficiency, stop and run through a basic question: Is what's true for you immediately true for the people you are interacting with? This leads to Factors 3 and 4.

Factor #3

Does IM improve or lessen efficiency?

With respect to IM, does IM (and the interruptions it creates) have to mean that someone is less efficient, or could they be more efficient because of it? As we've seen, it is possible that many younger employees can have multiple IM conversations and can potentially get a lot more done in less time compared to either sending out multiple emails or waiting for responses. In many respects, this question is similar to the questions that the BlackBerry raised when it was introduced to the workforce, and there are three ways that it can be answered:

- In some cases, jobs require isolation and focus, and a culture of IM can create conditions that are less effective.
- In some cases, it doesn't matter.
- In some cases, some employees may be much more effective when they receive maximum stimulus and input.

Factor #4

Will this efficiency change over time, or is it in fact different for different demographics of my workforce?

Consider generational differences and the evolution of your workforce. This may all be moot, or there may be a de facto acceptance of IM over time, much as there was with email and other, older technologies in companies. It is interesting to note that younger, newer companies never consider the important factors with respect to IM because *they culturally assume it is a right.* This assumption may form the basis of some real conflicts in the years to come. Imagine companies

that shut off new technologies being sued over "cruel and unusual" work conditions because they are removing what employees assume to be a right. Of course, this conflict is small now, but it is important to have a process for dealing with new technologies within the corporation rather than being blindsided by them as they emerge or, worse, as a new generation of users find themselves cut off from stimuli and tools that they consider necessary for their job or for their quality of life. In the end, the first four factors should help you define the following three items:

- Do you need IM as a company?
- Why do employees need it?
  - To do their jobs?
  - To improve efficiency?
  - To do more business?
  - To work with peers?
  - To improve employee satisfaction?
- Who needs it?

Without answers to these questions, which are all about the workforce as a whole, the role of IM will not be easily understood nor established within the company.

Transactions

Some companies have taken a bold step and use IM infrastructure for actual business processes. These are typically younger, fast-growing companies that are looking for more real-time transactions or processes. They typically accept a higher level of risk in general in exchange for greater potential returns. The unfortunate companies are the ones that have built product systems and processes on an IM infrastructure *unknowingly* and now have to deal with potentially unintended consequences of that infrastructure.

How does this happen? The infrastructures for IM on the Internet are large, ubiquitous, and fairly reliable, and it is natural that such infrastructures will get used. As we saw in the section on the evolution of Internet technologies, users will find ways to increase complexity and the value of networks over time, in essence fulfilling Metcalfe's Law. This is why some companies find that a small team using IM (where a built in business process on an IM application has grown fast, with real-time response times for some processes) has now reached the point where sizable business and transactions are conducted over IM.

Factor #5

Does your company have a need or dependency on IM to do business?

If this is the case, you need to understand immediately which applications and infrastructures you rely on. You

---

4. To my amusement, my goddaughter, who is 11, recently told me that "email was old fashioned" and she couldn't believe that I used it so heavily for work!

should begin a process for examining the infrastructure and mapping out the business processes:

- Where are the single points of failure?
- Where does liability lie?
- What is availability like?
- What is the impact of downtime on the business?
- What is the business risk?
- What are your disaster recovery and business continuity options?

The answers to these questions will lead to natural action plans. They will also follow the basic rule of acceptable risk for acceptable return, unless you find you have a regulatory implication (in which case, build action plans immediately).

Factor #6

Are you considering deploying a technology or process on an IM infrastructure?

If this is the case, you need to understand immediately which applications and infrastructures you will rely on. You should begin a process for understanding the infrastructure and quantifying and managing the business risk. Again, make sure, as with the workforce, that you in fact need the IM infrastructure in the first place.

5. THE NATURE OF THE THREAT

There are some clear threats, internal and external, and both inadvertent and malicious. These different threats call for the implementation of different countermeasures. Fig. 51.1 shows a simple grid of the populations that a security professional will have to consider in the context of their security postures for IM.

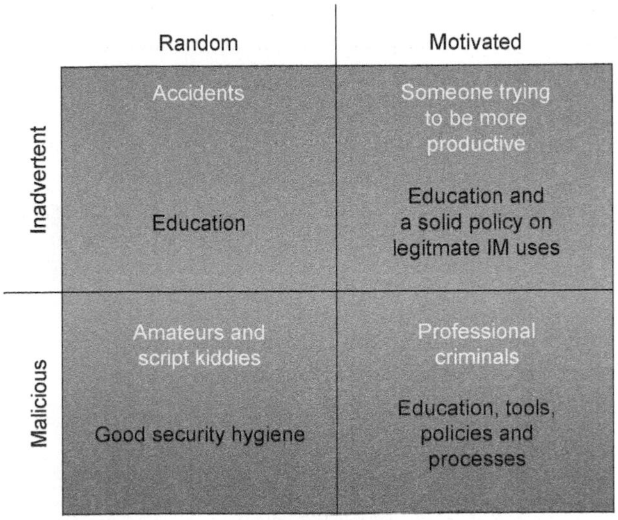

FIGURE 51.1 Populations that present a corporate risk and the correct responses to each.

Malicious Threat

We've looked at the good guys, who are basically looking within the company or are perhaps partners looking to use a powerful, real-time technology for positive reasons: more business with more people more efficiently. Now it is time to look at the bad guys: black hats.[5]

In the "old days," black hats were seen to be young kids in their parents' basements, or perhaps a disgruntled techie with an axe to grind. These were people who would invest a disproportionate amount of time in an activity, spending hundreds of hours to gain fame or notoriety or to enact revenge. This behavior led to the "worm of the week" and macro-viruses. They were, in effect, not a systematic threat but were rather background noise. We will calls these folks "amateurs" for reasons that will become clear.

There have also always been dedicated black hats, or "professionals," who plied their trade for gain or as mercenaries. These folks were at first in the minority and generally hid well among the amateurs. In fact, they had a vested interest in seeing the proliferation of "script kiddies" who could "hack" easily: This activity created background noise against which their actions would go unnoticed. Think of the flow of information and activity, of security incidents as a CSI scene where a smart criminal has visited barber shops, collected discarded hair from the floors, and then liberally spread them around the crime scene to throw off the DNA collection of forensic investigators. This is what the old-world professionals did and why they rejoiced at the "worms of the week" that provided a constant background noise for them to hide their serious thefts.

Now we come to the modern age, and the professionals are in the majority. The amateurs have grown up and found that they can leave their parents' basements and go out and make money working for real organizations and companies, plying their skills to abuse the Internet and systems for real gain. This is what led to the proliferation of spyware; and because it is an *economic* activity, we can quantify losses and gains for this population and can begin to apply game theory to predicting their behaviors and *the technologies that they will abuse for gain.*

There is a new category as well around the *Advanced Persistent Threat* (APT).[6] These attackers are likewise professionals and highly motivated by a mission. They are also well funded and include both nation states and hacktivists looking for key intelligence and access: economic, military or political access, information, and control.

5. This term was a difficult one to choose. I opted not to go with crackers or hackers but rather with black hats because that is the most neutral term to refer to malicious computer exploiters.
6. I prefer Josh Corman's term of Advanced Persistent Adversary since this most accurately reflects the human nature of this class of threat. However, I will use APT as the more common term of the day.

On the one hand, the bad guys are now a vested interest, as has been well documented[7] and analyzed; they are a sustained, real, commercial interest and present a clear and present risk to most IT infrastructures. On the other hand, there are well-funded APTs that are specifically determined to break in and achieve their mission, which you are empowered and responsible for stopping. Keep in mind the following general rules about these online miscreants:

- It is not about ego or a particular trick; they are not above using or abusing any technology.
- They do what they do to make money or to achieve their mission. This is your money, your IP and your trust they are threatening. They are a risk to you and to your company.
- They are sophisticated; they have supply and distribution agreements and partners, they have SLAs[8] and business relationships, they have allies and enemies, and they even have quality labs, alliances, and conferences. They are not merely immature adults or precocious adolescents.

In general, online criminals will seek to exploit IM if they can realize value in the target and if they can efficiently go after it. IM represents a technology against which it is easy for black hats to develop exploits, and even relatively small returns [such as a 1% click rate on *spam instant messaging* (SPIM)] would have enormous potential value.

Factor #7

Does the value to the company of information and processes carried over IM represent something that is a valuable target (because it can either affect your business or realize a gain)? Do you have information or processes that are valuable to your customers or partners? This should include the ability to blackmail employees and partners: Can someone learn things about key employees that they could use to threaten or abuse employees and partners?

The answer to this question will help put in perspective the potential for IM technology to be abused.

Factor #8

If the IM technology were abused or compromised, what would be the risk to the business or to a customer or partner?

SPIM, worms, viruses, spyware, Trojans, rootkits, backdoors, and other threats can spread over IM as readily as email, file shares, and other transmission vectors—in fact, it is arguable that it can spread more readily via IM.

Will an incident over IM cause an unacceptable risk to the business? This should be answered in the same way as "Will an incident over email cause an unacceptable risk to the business?" For most organizations the answer should always be yes.

Vulnerabilities

Like any form of software (or hardware), IM applications and infrastructure are subject to vulnerabilities and weaknesses from poor configuration and implementation. Most of these applications do not have the same degree of rigor around maintenance, support, and patching as other enterprise software applications. As a result, it is important to have processes for penetration testing and security audits and to establish a relationship, if possible, with manufacturers and distributors for enterprise caliber support. In many cases, the total cost of ownership of an IM infrastructure and applications may rise considerably to make up for this lack. For this reason, using the freeware services may be a temptation, but the risks may quickly outweigh the savings.

Man-in-the-Middle Attacks

A man-in-the-middle attack is a class of attack in which a third party acts as a legitimate or even invisible broker. As shown in Fig. 51.2, an attacker is posing to each user in an IM transaction as a legitimate part of the process while in fact recording or relaying information. This is a common attack philosophy, and without basic mutual authentication or encryption tools, it is inexpensive for black hats to carry out in a wide-scale manner.

As a security professional, it is possible to monitor IM protocols and the IP addresses with which they communicate, allowing IM to and from only certain recognized hubs. Even this is not perfect, because "X-in-the-middle" attacks in their most generic form can include everything from Trojans and keyloggers to line taps. It is also

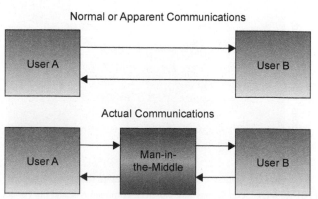

FIGURE 51.2 Normal versus man-in-the-middle communications.

7. www.rsa.com/blog/blog. aspx#Security-Blog.
8. Service-level agreement.

possible to monitor communications among peers, although effectively looking for man-in-the-middle attacks in this way is difficult.

Phishing and Social Engineering

Social engineering is the practice of fooling someone into giving up something they wouldn't otherwise surrender through the use of psychological tricks. Social engineers rely on the normal behavior of people presented with data or a social situation to respond in a predictable, human way. An attack of this sort will rely on presenting trusted logos and a context that seems normal but is in fact designed to create a vulnerability that the social engineer can exploit. This is relevant to IM because people can choose IM identities *similar to ones with whom the user normally communicates.* The simplest attack of all is to get an identity that is similar to a boss, sibling, friend, or spouse and then provide information to get information. Employees should be educated to always directly check with end users to ensure that they are in fact communicating with whom they believe they are communicating.

Knowledge Is the Commodity

It goes without saying that knowledge of business trans-actions is itself something that can be turned to profit. The contents of a formula, the nature of an experiment, the value and type of a financial transaction are all important to competitors and to speculators. Stock values rise and fall on rumors of activity, and material knowledge of what is happening can be directly translated into profit.

There are companies, organizations, and individuals that launder money and reap huge profits on the basis of insider information and intellectual property, and the bad guys are looking for exactly this information. Know what is being communicated and educate your employees about the open, real-time, and exposed nature of IM. Make sure that you have solid policies on what is acceptable to commu-nicate over IM.

Factor #9

What intellectual property, material information, corporate documents, and transaction data are at risk over IM?

Make sure that you know what people use IM for and, if you do not have the means to control it, consider denying access to IM or implementing content-filtering technologies. With false positives and technology failing to track context of communications, do not rely heavily on a technological answer; make sure you have educational options and that you document use of IM in your environment.

Data and Traffic Analysis

The mere presence of communications is enough, in some circumstances, to indicate material facts about a business or initiative. This is particularly well understood by national governments and interests with "signals intelligence." You do not have to know what someone is saying to have an edge. This has been seen throughout history, with the most obvious and numerous examples during World War II: If you know that someone is communicating, that is in effect intelligence.

Communicating with a lawyer, making a trade, and the synchronizing in real time of that information with public data may construe a material breach if it's intercepted. Wherever possible, artificial traffic levels and data content flags to the outside world should be used to disguise the nature and times of communication for transactions that indicate insider information or transactions that you otherwise wouldn't want the world to know about.

Factor #10

What do transaction types and times tell people about your business? Is it acceptable for people to have access to this information?

Some of the most important events in history have occurred because of intelligence not of what was said, but rather how, and, most importantly, why a communication occurred.

Unintentional Threats

Perhaps the most insidious threat isn't the malicious one; it is the inadvertent one. Employees are generally seeking to do more work more efficiently. This is what leads to them using their public, web-based emails for working at home rather than only working in the office. Very often people who are working diligently do something to try to work faster, better, or in more places and they inadvertently cause a business risk. These are, in effect, human behaviors that put the company at risk, and the answer is both an educational one and one that can benefit from the use of certain tools.

Intellectual Property Leakage

Just as employees shouldn't leave laptops in cars or work on sensitive documents in public places such as an airport or coffee shop, they also should not use public IM for sensitive material. Intellectual property leakage of source code, insider information, trade secrets, and so on are major risks with IM when used incorrectly, although it should be noted that when deployed correctly, such transactions can be done safely over IM (when encrypted and appropriate, with the right mutual authentication).

Inappropriate Use

As with web browsing and email, inappropriate use of IM can lead to risks and threats to a business. In particular, IM is an informal medium. People have their own lingo in IM, with acronyms[9] peculiar to the medium (B4N = bye for now, HAND = have a nice day, IRL = in real life, and so on). The very informal nature of the medium means that it is generally not conducted in a businesslike manner; it is more like our personal interactions and notes. When the social glue of an office becomes less business-oriented, it can lead to inappropriate advances, commentary, and exposure. Outlining inappropriate use of IM, as with any technology, should be part of the general HR policy of a company, and correct business use should be part of a regular regimen of business conduct training.

Factor #11

What unintended exposure could the company face via IM? Which populations have this information and require special training, monitoring, or protection?

Make sure that your company has a strategy for categorization and management of sensitive information, in particular personally identifiable information, trade secrets, and material insider information.

Regulatory Concerns

Last, but far from least, are the things that simply must be protected for legal reasons. In an age where customer information is a responsibility, not a privilege, where credit card numbers and Social Security numbers are bartered and traded and insider trading can occur in real time (sometimes over IM), it is imperative that regulatory concerns be addressed in an IM policy. If you can't implement governance policies over IM technology, you might have to ban IM use until such time as you can govern it effectively—and you very well may have to take steps to actively root out and remove IM applications, with drastic consequences for those who break the company's IM policy. Examples of these are common in financial institutions, HR organizations, and healthcare organizations.

Factor #12

Do you have regulatory requirements that require a certain IM posture and policy?

No matter how attractive the technology, you may not be able to adopt IM if the regulatory concerns aren't addressed. If you absolutely need it, the project to adopt compliant IM will be driven higher in the priority queue;

but the basic regulatory requirement and penalties could be prohibitive if this isn't done with utmost care and attention.

Remember also that some countries have explicit regulations about monitoring employees. In some jurisdictions, in Europe and Asia in particular, it is *illegal to monitor employee behavior and actions*. This may seem alien to some in the United States, but multinationals and companies in other regions must conform to employee rights requirements.

6. COMMON INSTANT MESSAGING APPLICATIONS

IM is a fact of life. Now it is time to decide which applications and infrastructures your company can and will be exposed to. You most likely will want to create a policy and to track various uses of IM and develop a posture and educational program about which ones are used in which contexts. You will want to review common IM applications in the consumer or home user domain because they will find their ways into your environment and onto your assets. For example, many people install IM applications for personal use on laptops that they then take out of the company environment; they aren't using them at work, but those applications are on systems that have company intellectual property and material on them and they are used on insecure networks once they leave the building.

Consumer Instant Messaging

Numbers of subscribers are hard to come by in a consistent manner, although some analyst firms and public sites present disparate numbers. Wikipedia has a current view and commentary on relative sizes of IM networks and concentrations that are worth examining and verifying in a more detailed fashion. The major IM programs are AIM at 100 million, Yahoo! Messenger at 248 million, Windows Live Messenger/MSN at 330 million users, Skype at 882 million, and Tencent at a staggering 900 million (which is up enormously from the first edition of this book). There is also a good comparison of the technologies and infrastructure in use with various tools as well. Others include a host of smaller applications such as ICQ (at 50 million) continue to proliferate.

It is important to keep in mind who owns the infrastructures for private IM applications. In effect, the IM backbone passes information in the clear (unless an encryption program is used), and the owners of the infrastructure can see and collect data on who is communicating with whom, how, and what they are saying.

It could, for instance, with respect to quarterly earnings or an investigation or lawsuit, be materially important to know with whom the CFO is communicating and at what times. As a result, companies are well advised to educate employees on the risks of IM in general and the acceptable

---

9. A good source on these is found at AOL: www.aim.com/acronyms.adp.

uses for certain applications. It may be acceptable to talk to your husband or wife on Yahoo! or QQ, but is it acceptable to talk to your lawyer that way?

Enterprise Instant Messaging

Some companies, such as IBM and Microsoft, offer IM solutions for internal use only. These are readily deployed and allow for good, real-time communications within the company. They of course do not address the issues of bridging communications with the outside world and the general public, but they are good for meeting some needs for improved productivity and efficiency that are clearly business related. The risk that these pose is in complacency—assuming that the IM application is exclusively used within the organization. Very often, they are used from public places or from private homes and even in some cases from employee-owned assets. As such, the ecosystem for remote access should be carefully considered.

Instant-Messaging Aggregators

There are some programs, such as Trillian,[10] for pulling together multiple IM applications. The danger here is similar to many applications that aggregate passwords or information: They should be legitimate companies, such as Cerulean Studios, with real privacy and security policies. Many illegitimate applications pose as IM aggregators, especially "free" ones, and are really in the business of establishing a spyware presence on PCs, especially corporate-owned PCs. To be clear, there are real, legitimate IM aggregators with real value, and you should look to do business with them, read their end user license agreements (EULAs), and deploy and manage them correctly. There are also *illegitimate* companies and organizations that manufacture spyware but that pose as IM aggregators; these will come into your environment via well-meaning end users.

Most *illegitimate* applications should be caught with antispyware applications (note that some antivirus applications have antispyware capabilities; verify that this is the case with your vendor) that are resident on PCs, but there are some basic steps you should make sure that your security policies and procedures take into account:

- Make sure that you have antivirus and antispyware software that is up to date and active.
- Make sure that end users know the risks of these applications, especially on noncorporate systems (home or user-owned systems).
- Make sure you survey communications into and out of the network for "phone home," especially encrypted

communications, and that you have a standard policy and procedure on what course of action to take should suspicious communications be discovered.

Backdoors: Instant Messaging via Other Means (HTML)

Some IM applications have moved to HTML-based integrations with their network. The reason is obvious: This is a way around the explicit IM protocols being blocked on corporate networks. Employees want to keep using their IM tools for personal or professional reasons, and they are finding workarounds. The obvious counter to this is HTML content filtering, especially at the gateways to networks. If your policy disallows IM, make sure the content-filtering blacklists are sensitive to IM IP addresses and communications. Many IM applications will actively scan for ports that are available on which they can piggyback communications, meaning that if you have any permissive rules for communications, the IM application will find it.

Mobile Dimension

Computing platforms and systems keep getting smaller and converging with their larger cousins; personal digital assistants (PDAs) and phones are everywhere, and most major IM networks have an IM client for BlackBerry, cell phones, and the like. On corporate-owned assets with the latest generation of mobile technologies, it is fairly simple to lock down these applications to conform to the corporate IM policy. In some instances, however, it is more complex, especially in situations where PDAs are employee-owned or managed. In these cases, you actually have a larger potential problem and need a PDA and phone policy; the IM policy is secondary to that.

7. DEFENSIVE STRATEGIES

There are four basic postures that you can take within your company with respect to IM (actually this applies to all end-user applications more generally, although it needs to be rationalized for IM in particular):

- *Ban all IM.* This is the least permissive and most likely to fail over time. It is normally only advisable in cases of extremely high risk and in businesses that are very resistant to technology. This will be the hardest to enforce socially if not technically.
- *Allow internal IM.* This is the most common first step, but it demands a careful understanding and policies and procedures to enforce the ban on *external* or consumer IM.
- *Allow all IM.* Outright allowing all IM is not a common first policy, though some companies on due consideration may consider it.

---

10. Manufactured by Cerulean Studios: http://www.ceruleanstudios.com.

- *Create a sophisticated IM policy.* This is the most difficult to do, but a sophisticated and granular IM policy, integrated with classic security measures, asset management, and a rigorous information policy, is the hallmark of a mature security organization. Incidentally, many of these exist already. It is not necessary to reinvent all of them if these sorts of policies have already been worked through and are a web search away.

8. INSTANT-MESSAGING SECURITY MATURITY AND SOLUTIONS

Companies will likely go through an evolution of the security policy with respect to IM. Many (particularly older companies) begin with a ban and wind up over time settling on a sophisticated IM policy that takes into account asset policies, information policies, human behavior, risk, and corporate goals around employee satisfaction, efficiency, and productivity.

Asset Management

Many asset management solutions such as CA Unicenter, IBM Tivoli, and Microsoft SMS manage systems and the software they have. They are most effective for managing corporate-owned assets; make sure that employees have the right tools, correctly licensed and correctly provisioned. They also make sure that rogue, unlicensed software is minimized and can help enforce IM applications bans as in the case of a "ban of all IM" policy or a ban on external or consumer IM.

Built-in Security

Enterprise IM applications are generally the most readily adopted of solutions within a company or organization. Many of these IM platforms and "inside the firewall" IM applications provide some built-in security measures, such as the ability to auto-block inbound requests from unknown parties. Many of these features are good for hardening obvious deficiencies in the systems, but by themselves they do not typically do enough to protect the IM infrastructure.

Keep in mind also that "inside the firewall" is often misleading; people can readily sign on to these applications via virtual private network from outside the firewall or even from home computers, with a little work. Make sure the access policies and security features built into internal applications are understood and engaged correctly.

It is also generally good to ensure that strong authentication (multifactor authentication) is used in cases where people will be gaining remote access to the internal IM application. You want to make sure that the employee in question is in fact the employee and not a family member, friend, or someone who has broken into the employee's home or hotel room.

Content Filtering

A class of relatively new security products has arisen over the past few years specifically designed to do content filtering on IM. These are still not widely adopted and, when adopted, apply to only a limited set of users. Most companies that use these tools are those with strong regulatory requirements and then only to a limited set of users who expose the company most. The most common examples are insiders in financial firms or employees who can access customer data. Real-time leaks in a regulated or privileged environment are generally the most serious drivers here.

Classic Security

The perimeter is dead—long live the Internet. It is almost hackneyed these days to say that perimeter-centric security is dead; firewalls and intrusion detection systems aren't the solution. In many ways, modern security is about proving a negative—it can't be done. Human beings seeking to do better at their jobs, to communicate with friends and family, or to actively invade and bypass security will find new ways and new vectors around existing security controls. Having said that, it is important to realize that our job as security professionals is to first remove the inexpensive and easy ways to get around security controls and then to efficiently *raise the security bar* for getting at what matters: the information. It is important to do a real, quantitative analysis of your cost threshold for the controls you are going to put in place and the amount by which it raises the bar and compare these to the risk and likelihood of loss.

In this regard, the traditional software for perimeter security *still serves a purpose*; in fact, many of these vendors are quite innovative at adding new features and new value over time. The classic products of proxies, corporate firewalls, virtual private networks, intrusion detection, and antimalware continue to raise the bar for the most simple and inexpensive attack vectors and for stopping inadvertent leakage. This is true of adding layered protection to IM, and the classic security products should be leveraged to raise the security bar (that is, to lower basic business risk). They won't solve the problem, but it is important to use them in a layered approach to reducing business risk.

Compliance

Some industries have strict regulations that require that information be handled in certain ways. These industries have no choice but to comply or face punitive and legal damages and increased risk to their business. It is vital to consult with auditors and compliance departments regarding the implications of IM on corporate compliance.

Also, explicitly keep in mind employee rights legislation that may prohibit monitoring employees' IM communications. There are jurisdictions in which this kind of monitoring is illegal.

Data Loss Prevention

There is a new class of data loss prevention (DLP) product that can discover, classify, categorize, monitor, and enforce information-centric policies (at endpoint, network, datacenter, and "gateway" touchpoints) for a user population—either the whole company or a subset of the workforce population. There are tradeoffs to be made among applications of this type, in particular when it comes to false positives (wrongly identifying information as sensitive) and efficiency at particular times (filtering HR information during benefits enrollment periods or filtering financial-related information at the close of a quarter). This class of product can be massively powerful for enforcing the policy as a useful tool, but its efficiency and impact on *employee* efficiency need to be carefully applied. Further, the vital discovery, classification, and categorization features should be well understood, as should monitoring and enforcement applications.

Logging

Security information and event management (SIEM) systems are only as effective as what they instrument. In combination with content-filtering and DLP, this technology can be extremely effective. The best "real-world" analogy is perhaps insider trading. It is not impossible to commit insider trading, but it isn't as widespread as it could be because the Securities and Exchange Commission (and other regulatory bodies outside the United States) has effective logging and anomaly detection and reporting functions to catch transgressors. Logging in the form of SIEM on the right controls is both a good measure for active protection and a deterrent; just be sure to mention in your education processes that this is happening, to realize the deterrence benefit.

Anomaly Detection

Going beyond even correlation in a SIEM context, it's possible to look for patterns and trends in data—neural networks, Bayesian engines, and other correlation engines can be used to determine baselines, reveal deviation from baselines, and spot anomalies. The most effective of these will also tie into a risk analysis engine and should inform authentication and authorization engines in your company. The general direction of authentication technologies is toward establishing context, "continuous" authentication, and a constant estimation of the likely risk inherent in someone whenever they do a transaction of any sort.

Archival

In conjunction with regulatory requirements, you may have either a process or audit requirement to keep logs for a certain period of time. Archival, storage, and retrieval systems are likely to form an important part of your post-event analysis and investigation and forensics policies and may actually be legally required for regulatory purposes.

9. PROCESSES

The lifeblood of any policy is the process and the people who enforce that policy. You will need a body of processes and owners that is documented and well maintained. Some of the processes you may need include, but aren't limited to, the following.

Instant-Messaging Activation and Provisioning

When someone is legitimately entitled to IM, how specifically do they get access to the application? How are they managed and supported? If you have IM, you will have issues and will have to keep the application and service current and functioning.

Application Review

Make sure that you know the state of the art in IM. Which applications have centralized structures, and what nations and private interests host these? Which applications are poorly written, contain weaknesses, or, worse, have remote control vulnerabilities and are potentially spyware?

People

Make sure your IT staff and employees know the policies and why they matter. Business relevance is the best incentive for conformity. Work on adding IM to the corporate ethics, conduct, information, and general training policies.

Revise

Keep the policy up to date and relevant. Policies can easily fall into disuse or irrelevance, and given the nature of advances in Internet technologies, it is vital that you regularly revisit this policy on a quarterly or semiannual basis. Also ensure that your policy is enforceable; a policy that is not enforceable or is counterintuitive is useless.

Audit

Be sure to audit your environment. This is not auditing in the sense of a corporate audit, although that may also be a requirement, but do periodic examinations of network traffic for sessions and traffic that are out of policy. IM will leave proprietary protocol trails and even HTML trails in the network. Look, in particular, for rogue gateways and rogue proxies that have been set up by employees to work around the corporate policy.

10. SUMMARY

Remember game theory with respect to your workforce and business; people will find ways to do more with the tools, networks, and systems at their disposal. They will find ways to use ungoverned technology, such as IM, to do more things with more people more efficiently. The siren call of real-time communications is too much to resist for a motivated IT department and a motivated workforce who want to do more with the tools that are readily available to them.

Let's review a few lists and what you must consider in formulating an IM security policy—and remember that this must always be *in service* to the business. In the following sidebar, "The 12 Factors," consider the factors and the posture in which these put you and your company.

Now consider your responses to these factors in the context of your employees, your partners, your competitors, and the active threats your company will face. Next, consider the basic risks and returns and the infrastructure that you deploy:

- Where are the single points of failure?
- Where does liability lie?
- What is availability like?
- What is the impact of downtime on the business?
- What is the business risk?
- What are your disaster recovery and business continuity options?

Last, consider regulatory requirements and the basic business assets you must protect. You will most likely have to create or update your security policy to consider IM (see checklist, "An Agenda for Action for Regulatory Requirements and the Basic Business Assets That Must Be Protected").

IM, like any other technology, can serve the business or be a risk to it. The best situation of all is where it is quantified like any other technology and helps promote the ability to attract talent and keep it while serving the business—driving more business with more people more efficiently and while minimizing risk for business return.

The 12 Factors

Factor #1: Do your employees need IM? If so, which employees need IM and *what do they need it for?*

Factor #2: Is IM important as a job satisfaction component?

Factor #3: Does IM improve or lessen efficiency?

Factor #4: Will this efficiency change over time, or is it in fact different for different demographics of my workforce?

Factor #5: Does your company have a need or dependency on IM to do business?

Factor #6: Are you considering deploying a technology or process on an IM infrastructure?

Factor #7: Does the value to the company of information and processes carried over IM represent something that is a valuable target (because it can either affect your business or realize a gain)? This should include the ability to blackmail employees and partners; can someone learn things about key employees that they could use to threaten or abuse employees and partners?

Factor #8: If the IM technology were abused or compromised, what would be the risk to the business?

Factor #9: What intellectual property, material information, corporate documents, and transaction information is at risk over IM?

Factor #10: What do transaction types and times tell people about your business? Is it okay for people to have access to this information?

Factor #11: What unintended exposure could the company face via IM? Which populations have this information and require special training, monitoring, or protection?

Factor #12: Do you have regulatory requirements that require a certain IM posture and policy?

Example Answers to Key Factors

Let's take the example of Acme Inc., as shown in the sidebar, "Acme Inc.'s Answers to the 12 Factors." Acme is a publicly traded company that has international offices and groups that span geographies.

Giving answers to these simple questions mean that the scope of risk and the business relevance is known. These answers can now be used to formulate a security policy and begin the IT projects that are needed for enforcement and monitoring.

Finally, let's move on to the real interactive part of this Chapter: review questions/exercises, hands-on projects, case projects, and optional team case project. The answers and/or solutions by chapter can be found in the Online Instructor's Solutions Manual.

An Agenda for Action for Regulatory Requirements and the Basic Business Assets That Must Be Protected

This will mean having a posture on the following items, at a minimum (check all tasks completed):

_____**1.** You must have formal, written policies for each of the following:
   _____**a.** Intellectual property identification, monitoring, and protection
   _____**b.** Sensitive information identification, monitoring, and protection
   _____**c.** Entitlements by role for IM specifically
   _____**d.** Legitimate, accepted uses for IM and specifically prohibited ones (if any)
   _____**e.** Monitoring of IM traffic
   _____**f.** Enforcement of IM policies
   _____**g.** Logging of IM traffic
   _____**h.** Archival of IM logs
   _____**i.** Regulatory requirements and needs and the processes to satisfy them around IM

_____**2.** Education
   _____**a.** With respect to IM
   _____**b.** With respect to regulations
   _____**c.** With respect to intellectual property
   _____**d.** With respect to social engineering
   _____**e.** About enforcement, monitoring, and archival requirements (remember that these can have a deterrence benefit)

_____**3.** Applications
   _____**a.** Dealing with consumer IM and the applications employees will try to use
   _____**b.** Internal, enterprise IM applications
   _____**c.** Asset management

_____**4.** Processes
   _____**a.** Provisioning IM and accounts
   _____**b.** Deprovisioning (via asset management processes) illegal IM clients
   _____**c.** Revoking IM entitlements and accounts

_____**5.** Do you have basic security hygiene configured correctly for an environment that includes IM?
   _____**a.** Asset management software
   _____**b.** Firewalls and proxies
   _____**c.** Intrusion detection systems
   _____**d.** Antimalware
   _____**e.** Virtual private networks and remote access
   _____**f.** Strong authentication
   _____**g.** Authorization

_____**6.** Advanced security
   _____**a.** Monitoring and enforcement with DLP
   _____**b.** Monitoring and SIEM
   _____**c.** Anomaly and pattern detection

Acme Inc.'s Answers to the 12 Factors

Factor #1: Do your employees need IM? If so, which employees need IM and *what do they need it for?*

Yes! All online working employees should have IM to allow for increased internal communications.

Factor #2: Is IM important as a job satisfaction component? Yes!

Factor #3: Does IM improve or lessen efficiency? IM should improve efficiency by allowing employees to get immediate answers/results and to be able to pull groups together quickly, compared to emails.

Factor #4: Will this efficiency change over time, or is it in fact different for different demographics of my workforce? Efficiency should grow as adoption and comfort levels with IM technologies grow.

Factor #5: Does your company have a need for or dependency on IM to do business?

IM cannot be used for external business transactions or discussions.

Factor #6: Are you considering deploying a technology or process on an IM infrastructure?

Yes. We would need to implement an internal tool to perform IM services.

Factor #7: Does the value to the company of information and processes carried over IM represent something that is a valuable target (because it can either affect your business or realize a gain)? This should include the ability to blackmail employees and partners; can someone learn things about key employees that they could use to threaten or abuse employees and partners?

Yes. All IM communications must remain internal.

Factor #8: If the IM technology were abused or compromised, what would be the risk to the business? Data loss: intellectual property.

Business plan loss: Sensitive information that we can't afford to let the competition see.

Customer data theft: Some Personally Identifiable Information (PII), but all customer-related information is treated as PII.

Factor #9: What intellectual property, material information, corporate documents, and transaction information is at risk over IM?

All internal data would be at risk.

Factor #10: What do transaction types and times tell people about your business? Is it okay for people to have access to this information?

Data will always remain on a need-to-know basis and the IM implementation must not result in the loss of data.

Factor #11: What unintended exposure could the company face via IM? Which populations have this information and require special training, monitoring, or protection? Unintentional internal transfer of restricted data to internal staff without the required internal clearances.

Factor #12: Do you have regulatory requirements that require a certain IM posture and policy? We are under PCI, HIPAA, ISO 27001, and SAS70 Type II guidelines.

CHAPTER REVIEW QUESTIONS/ EXERCISES

True/False

1. True or False? When considering IM, it is important to realize that it is first and foremost a technology; it is not a goal in and of itself.
2. True or False? IM is a technology in a continuum of advances (q.v.) that have arisen for communicating and collaborating over a local area network.
3. True or False? Perhaps the most important "law" with respect to networks and for instant messaging is Metcalfe's Law, which states that the value of a telecommunications network increases exponentially with a linear increase in the number of users. (Actually, it states that it is proportional to the square of the users on the network.)
4. True or False? Whenever gains or losses can be quantified for a given population, game theory does not apply.
5. True or False? Whether you work in an IT department or run a small company, your employees have things they need to do: process orders, work with peers, manage teams, talk to customers and to partners. IM is a tool they can and will use to do these things.

Multiple Choice

1. Employees without _____ will seek to get it by abusing backdoors or processes to get this entitlement.
   A. XM
   B. IMS
   C. IM
   D. EM
   E. EXO
2. Some companies have taken a bold step and use _____ for actual business processes.
   A. Metcalfe's Law
   B. Malicious threat
   C. Spyware
   D. IM infrastructure
   E. APT

3. Like any form of software (or hardware), IM applications and infrastructure are subject to _____ and weaknesses from poor configuration and implementation.
   A. Evolution
   B. Residue class
   C. Vulnerabilities
   D. Certification Authority
   E. Security
4. A _____ attack is a class of attack in which a third party acts as a legitimate or even invisible broker.
   A. Trojan horse
   B. X-in-the-middle
   C. Man-in-the-middle
   D. keylogger
   E. tap
5. What is the practice of fooling someone into giving up something they wouldn't otherwise surrender through the use of psychological tricks?
   A. Phishing
   B. IM identity
   C. Knowledge
   D. Intellectual property
   E. Social engineering

EXERCISE

Problem

How does IM differ from email?

Hands-On Projects

Project

How does one manage their IM content?

Case Projects

Problem

What are the current best practices for capturing IM?

Optional Team Case Project

Problem

How can one schedule IM content?

Part VII

Privacy and Access Management

Chapter 52

Online Privacy

Chiara Braghin and Marco Cremonini
University of Milan, Crema, Italy

1. THE QUEST FOR PRIVACY

In an article published in The New York Times on June 16, 2012, the journalist Natasha Singer opened her piece with a messianic tone: "It knows who you are. It knows where you live. It knows what you do" [1]. This undisclosed "it," she continued, "peers deeper into American life than the F.B.I. or the I.R.S., or those prying digital eyes at Facebook and Google." True that, after the NSA scandal of 2013 that unveiled the surveillance practices of intelligence agencies, the winner of the contest for the thirstiest of citizen's personal data is now more open, but for sure the subject of the New York Times' article is still a strong contender. "It" was the *data broker industry*, the group of companies that supplies valuable information services on citizens mostly to the advertising sector, always looking for better tailored and targeted online ads. But, before delving into more details about the struggle between privacy values and business dynamics or technological advancements in current online ecosystem, it is useful to look at the invasion of citizens' privacy in perspectives.

Is the data broker industry another offspring of the Internet era, post-dotcom failures and 9/11, like personal data guzzling behemoths from Silicon Valley, or massive online surveillance programs carried out by states? In other words, could an analysis of *online* privacy just start from the inception of the online world? The answer is no. Online privacy has its roots much earlier than online threats to privacy, or the establishment of Internet-based data-centric corporations. The data broker industry in combination with advertisers have figured out, way before the Internet-era, that citizens' personal data were a treasure waiting to be discovered and to become the core of their business. The ability in analyzing personal data and behaviors and extracting business value has been the key for building a giant and enormously influent industrial sector. On the other side, data brokers and advertisers had the merit of

having shaped our Western societies as we know them, contributing to the expansion of commerce and of the economy, to the fortune of many enterprises, and in general to our wealth. The same is true now, when we consider Internet-centric corporations, which are driving forces of innovation and wealth. Therefore, discussing about online privacy, without aiming to embrace an activist agenda, is certainly not a matter of separating the good from the evil, or just pinpointing those violating privacy without trying to consider the whole multifaceted scenario. This is also true for governmental agencies which have incurred in abuses and unacceptable practices, but still remain agencies of democratic governments and of free and open societies in charge of fundamental tasks for ensuring national security and contrasting criminals. It is important to clearly state this in order to correctly frame the discourse, since, in the words of the just-approved European Union's General Data Protection Regulation [2], "The processing of personal data should be designed to serve mankind. The right to the protection of personal data is not an absolute right; it must be considered in relation to its function in society and be balanced with other fundamental rights, in accordance with the principle of proportionality."

As it often happens when a debate heats up, the extremes speak louder and, about privacy, the extremes are those that advocate the ban of the disclosure of whatever personal information and those that say that all personal information is already out there, therefore privacy is dead. Supporters of a generalized deployment and use of anonymizing technologies built around inaccessible cryptographic technology represent one extreme. Those promulgating a ban on the use of anonymity and even its weaker version, pseudonymity, are examples of another extreme. However, these are just the extremes: in reality, privacy in the digital society is a fluid concept that such radical positions cannot fully contain. Indeed, even those supporting

Computer and Information Security Handbook. http://dx.doi.org/10.1016/B978-0-12-803843-7.00052-1

full anonymity recognize that there are several limitations to its adoption, either technical or functional. On the other side, even the most skeptical cannot avoid dealing with privacy issues, either because of laws and norms, or because of common sense.

Understanding online privacy implies the search of a difficult trade-off among often-contrasting interests and rights, it implies considering the huge impact that modern digital technologies have on our society and on the relationships between business and social welfare, between companies, governments, and the citizens. It implies capturing a moving target that depends on the dynamics of our society, which is not simply defined by a collection of rights, but by a combination of rights and interests that must coexist.

The Origin of the Concept

Looking at the origin of the privacy concept, Aristotle's distinction between the public sphere of politics and the private sphere of the family is often considered the root. The distinction between public and private sphere has been one of the most debated in modern political science and philosophy. Goldschmidt, for instance, a renowned political scientist of last century, speaking about democratic values of Western societies, mentioned "two disturbing tendencies: first, a tendency toward too much publicity with a consequent disregard of the individual's right of privacy; and second, a tendency toward too little publicity, with a consequent increase of secrecy in areas hitherto considered public" [3].

With respect to the social transformations brought by market forces eroding citizens' privacy, the German philosopher, Jurgen Habermas, in one of his most influential works [4]—an account of how the liberal public sphere took shape at the time of a developing market economy—wrote that "the family now evolved even more into a consumer of income and leisure time, into the recipient of publicly guaranteed compensations and support services. Private autonomy was maintained not so much in functions of control as in functions of consumption [...]. As a result, there arose the illusion of an intensified privacy in an interior domain whose scope had shrunk to comprise the conjugal family only insofar as it constituted a community of consumers."

It is remarkable for our chapter on online privacy to highlight that, despite the radically changed characteristics of the context, the debate on the concept of privacy continued during the 20th century for the shrinking domain of privacy on the one side and the tendency toward over-secrecy on the other. The concept of privacy has always been enmeshed with the definition of public realm, the interests of the industrial sector, the state's monopoly of power, the extension and limitations of property rights, and more recently with the rise of human rights movements. This complicated network of relationships still exists today for online privacy, although with different proportions among the forces, and must be considered.

Another fundamental constituent of the definition of privacy is how it is framed by law scholars. Here, the fundamental reference is to Supreme Court Judges Warren and Brandais, who in 1890 published in the Harvard Law Review a famous article titled "The Right to Privacy" [5]. In online privacy literature, this article is often referred to as the first account of an unmistakable definition of privacy as the "right to be let alone" (actually, the expression was coined by Judge Cooley several years earlier [6,7]). The "right to be let alone" indeed resonates with the modern understanding of privacy, for the ever growing difficulty, if not impossibility, to be effectively let alone with our always-on connectivity. It is, however, not correct to decontextualize that phrase and transport it to our digital world, because the meaning of the "to be let alone" has changed and does not refer to the same problem, then and today. Margaret Kohn in her book *Brave New Neighborhoods: The Privatization of Public Space* [8] gives a useful and detailed account of the struggle between public and private spaces, and how it evolved from late 19th century to the political movements of the 20th century. It is in those turbulent years and in that quickly evolving context that the phrase "right to be let alone" was coined, and it is strictly dependent to the then-evolving meaning of the concept of *property* and of *protection*, mainly from government threatening citizens' liberty. With the words of Judges Warren and Brandais: "[...] now the right to life has come to mean the right to enjoy life, − the right to be let alone; the right to liberty secures the exercise of extensive civil privileges; and the term 'property' has grown to comprise every form of possession − intangible, as well as tangible" [5]. It is the concept of property that "has grown to comprise every form of possession" the motivation for the right to be let alone. The assailants from which citizens should be defended by a new privacy tort law are "instantaneous photographs and newspaper enterprise," "unauthorized circulation of portraits of private persons," and "numerous mechanical devices threaten to make good the prediction that 'what is whispered in the closet shall be proclaimed from the house-tops.'" [5]. Privacy laws should then enforce once again the saying "My home is my castle," that is, the sovereignty over one's private sphere, and the property of tangible and intangible possessions. This is for the concept of property, as declared by Judges Warren and Brandais, but it should not be overlooked by the fact that there was a second pillar to the new right to privacy: the protection of citizens' private spheres from oppressive laws. It is to clarify and contextualize this aspect that Margaret Kohn's book [8] is useful, for its analysis of the historical tension between private and public spaces and the link with the *free speech* movement. In late 19th century, at the time of Judges Warren and Brandais' paper, laws limiting speeches critic with the government were still actively enforced by courts, but the discontent with such remnants of 18th century was growing. It was in the first few years of the beginning of the 1900s, that abolitionists driven by the International Workers of the World (IWW) association erupted in public protests, asking for the end of ordinances forbidding free speaking on the street. Margaret Kohn writes, "For the IWW, the right to free speech was not an abstract principle; it was an indispensable precondition to their struggle for radical political and economic change. Reviled by the mainstream press, the IWW relied on street speaking to spread its message." The right to privacy as a civil right, consequence of the right to maintain a public sphere void of external invasions from oppressive laws or attacks from the press for exercising free speech and then political activism, critical analysis and even radical protest gains a much deeper meaning than the simple "right to be let alone" as an extension of the property rights. More than a century after the IWW protests against the ban of free speaking along the streets, Julie Cohen, a law scholar, recently discussed the consequence of the reduction of privacy in our technology-centered society in terms of political freedom and the ability to innovate by infusing new ideas. The parallel with the historical analysis of free speech movements by Margaret Kohn is striking. Here is an excerpt from Cohen's *What Privacy Is For* [9]: "I will argue that freedom from surveillance, whether public or private, is foundational to the practice of informed and reflective citizenship. Privacy therefore is an indispensable structural feature of liberal democratic political systems. Freedom from surveillance also is foundational to the capacity for innovation [...]."

The roots of the modern right to privacy are both in the private sphere, as the extension of one's property right to intangible possessions, and in the public sphere, as the protection from those attempting to limit citizens' free speech. Privacy has thus both an individual dimension and a social value; it is a matter of human and of civil rights, and an economic and a political matter. Today, analyses of online privacy and considerations about the role of technology and of the new role of IT corporations must consider that multiple nature of privacy.

The Many Definitions of Privacy

Daniel J. Solove put it bluntly in his *A Taxonomy of Privacy* [10]: "Privacy seems to be about everything, and therefore it appears to be nothing." Privacy as a concept traverses many disciplines and areas of expertise, and for this reason has accumulated dozens of different definitions, often with no common, and sometimes conflicting, elements. Several commentators have lamented the lack of coherence or of meaning of the concept, and this has probably contributed to a general inhomogeneity of privacy-related studies. Posner called the term privacy a *misnomer* [11], a term that tries to catch too many meanings and for this misses its significance. Turning again to Margaret Kohn's book, we can find the notion of *cluster concept* or *term*, that is a term that has multiple and sometimes contradictory definitions, so it can be defined only by a list of criteria, possibly weighted, being no one of those necessary or sufficient [8]. Privacy, like game, public space, democracy, and probably even security, are examples of cluster concepts.

Analyses of online privacy issues clearly suffer from this situation: Most of privacy scholars, activists, and policymakers agree that privacy is a right, even a Constitutional right; some seem also to have a strong opinion about the nature of such a right. Many instead look as if they do not know which kind of right it should be, and overall there is no agreement over the fundamental nature of privacy among legal scholars, economists, computer scientists, social scientists, and policymakers.

Solove introduced a taxonomy of activities affecting privacy rather than attempting a definition. These activities are divided in groups: information collection, information processing, information dissemination, and invasion of privacy. For example, surveillance belongs to information collection, secondary use to information aggregation, disclosure to information dissemination, and intrusions to invasion of privacy [10].

Smith et al. in Ref. [12] presents a classification of *information* privacy research, first by distinguishing it from *physical* privacy, a difference that often is not made when generic invasions of privacy are referred. *Online* privacy, the subject of this chapter, clearly refers to information privacy, being personal information disseminated online by users of networked services, the target of data collection. However, it must not be ignored that violation of information privacy may lead to violation of personal privacy, when, for example, the gathering of personal information about the habits of an individual allows her physical surveillance. For information privacy, they introduce two broad categories: *value-based* and *cognate-based* [12]. In the first case, privacy is seen as a human-right belonging to the society's moral value system. This approach is very close to the origins of privacy as previously discussed and to the distinction between public and private sphere. The digital society has blurred the traditional lines between what is considered private and what is public, not just by expanding the domain of public information over private ones (think to the role of social networks, for example), but also vice versa, increasing even more the tendency to privatize large parts of what were once public spaces (the online equivalent of private malls replacing public squares could be the prevalence of corporate owned and regulated discussion boards, or to put it with a metaphor, "There's no Central Park on the Web"). Legal scholars have widely adopted a value-based approach to information privacy. Economists did too, in general, but with the difference that privacy become a *commodity* that, in principle, could be traded [13,14]. This has brought to a so-called *privacy paradox*, in which the elevated moral value of privacy does not seems to reflect into a correspondent economic value [15–18]. In his book *Free Culture* [19], Lessig provided an excellent explanation of the difference between privacy in the physical and in the digital world: "The highly inefficient architecture of real space means we all enjoy a fairly robust amount of privacy. That privacy is guaranteed to us by friction. Not by law [...] and in many places, not by norms [...] but instead, by the costs that friction imposes on anyone who would want to spy. [...] Enter the Internet, where the cost of tracking browsing in particular has become quite tiny. [...] The friction has disappeared, and hence any 'privacy' protected by the friction disappears, too."

With the cognate-based approach, instead, privacy is conceptualized as related to the individual's mind, perception, and cognition. Psychologists and cognitive scientists have discussed privacy for decades; however, for online privacy, the most relevant conceptualization is to consider privacy as a problem of *control* of access to self. This view has inspired some of the most important policies for data protection and privacy preservation, those whose pillar is to provide individuals with instruments to control the access and usage of personal information. More details on privacy policies and control will be discussed in a following section of this chapter.

2. TRADING PERSONAL DATA

Citizens' personal data are regularly traded. This is neither a secret nor the peculiar by-product of the Internet-based economy. On the contrary, personal data and their trading, direct or indirect, has been the core business of a whole industrial sector of the US economy for many decades. It was the 1970s when the US Federal Trade Commission (FTC) promulgated the Fair Credit Reporting Act (FCRA), which sought to regulate how consumer data must be used by consumer reporting agencies in decisions about credit, employment, insurance, housing, and the like. At that time, a market for the collection, trading, and usage of citizens' information was already established. However, the FCRA did not cover the trade of citizens' data for advertising or other goals different than financial credit. It was only in late 1990s that other business-oriented practices involving customer data began to be analyzed.

Privacy and Data Brokers

The FTC has actively monitored data broker practices, and its reports have shed a light on such a crucial while elusive industrial segment of the digital society with enormous implications for online privacy. In 2012, it published the document, "Protecting Consumer Privacy in an Era of Rapid Change" [20], addressing the data broker sector and specifically those not regulated by the FCRA. Data brokers were categorized as those having an activity: (1) subject to the FCRA; (2) not subject to FCRA and collecting data for marketing purposes; (3) not subject to FCRA and collecting data for purposes other than marketing, for instance to detect frauds or locate people. Then, in 2014, a new report titled "Data Brokers—A Call for Transparency and Accountability" was published [21]. To date, it represents one of the most comprehensive analysis of the data broker industry. The characteristics of nine data brokers are described. Their names are unknown for almost everybody (Acxiom, Corelogic, Datalogix, eBureau, ID Analytics, Intelius, PeekYou, Rapleaf, and Recorded Future), but their activity has involved nearly every US consumer and many others internationally. These companies manage consumers' data—usually bought from other data brokers or from companies directly collecting them from individuals—and produce derived data for satisfying their clients business needs in terms of marketing, risk mitigation, and people search. Citizens are normally unaware and never specifically informed of their personal data being used for these purposes. Data may include bankruptcy information, voting registration, consumer purchase data, web browsing activities, warranty registrations, and other from everyday online and offline activity [21]. Data sources are heterogeneous; from publicly available blogs and social media to commercial sources, for example, about the purchasing history of customers or online service registrations. Data updates are commanded by data brokers according to their cost–benefit assessment: The more frequent the update, the higher the classification accuracy and costs. For this reason, some personal data might be inaccurate even for a long time, without the individual able to know about that and about possible consequences of misalignment.

Typically, data brokers compile commercial categories and group customers with similar behaviors. Such categories may look fancy to those not accustomed to advertising practices. Examples of categories could be: Soccer Moms, Urban Scramble, Rural Everlastings, or Thrifty Elders [21]. Bizarre as they may sound, categories like these are useful for targeting *quality buyers*, as profiled citizens are dubbed by a very active online advertising company [22].

Another data broker activity is to develop models to predict behaviors. In this case a subset of customers is specifically analyzed for its purchase behavior and that knowledge is applied to predict future purchases of other customers with similar characteristics. This may also involve sensitive information like those related to health, pregnancy, and medicine consumption. In particular, privacy abuses of health data have been the subject of several journalistic investigations [23,24] and scientific research [25,26], which unveiled some commercial practices that most citizens completely ignore but strongly oppose when informed. For instance, the severity of medical privacy invasion came shockingly to light in 2013 with the Congressional testimony of Pam Dixon of World Privacy Forum [27]. In that occasion, Dixon presented evidence that lists of patients suffering from mental illness to sexual dysfunctions, cancer and HIV/AIDS, to name just a few examples, were commonly traded. Even more outrageously, lists of rape victims were publicly advertised and sold.

Opting out of data broker profiling is often impractical, at least. Since data brokers typically do not interact directly with consumers, even those offering clear opt-out procedures are unlikely to be known by consumers willing to exercise their choice. Many data brokers instead provide murky opt-out procedures or simply do not care of providing any. In Dixon Congressional testimony, it was mentioned that in a sample of 352 data brokers, just 128 provided an opt-out procedure. In some cases—for example, when consumers are profiled to calculate a credit score—it is practically impossible to be deleted from a score list. In other situations, the opt-out choice is made difficult to exercise due to clauses such as the request of a motivation to be approved or of a fee. Therefore, opting-out of data broker profiling, when permitted, is likely to be incomplete, does not imply deletion of personal data, and does not involve third parties, it may be costly, hard to find, and there is no guarantee that it is not just temporary [27]. The conclusion of the Federal Trade Commission is disheartened: "In the nearly two decades since the Commission first began to examine data brokers, little progress has been made to improve transparency and choice" [21].

3. CONTROL OF PERSONAL DATA

Some privacy advocates maintain that the US's Fair Information Practice Principles (FIPPs) require data subjects be notified that their personal data will be shared; even if the data being shared will be deidentified; and even if there is no legal obligation to notify the subjects. However, current US policy and law gives organizations considerable latitude in the control and uses that can be made of personal data. These policies were typically developed based on an attempt to balance the societal benefit resulting from the control and use of personal data with the perceived risks to subjects that might result from having the control of personal data reidentified. Because these risks may change as technology evolves, it is important to periodically review policies regarding the control and use of personal data.

Privacy and Big Data

In *Big Data and Privacy: A Technological Perspective* [28], the US President's Council of Advisors on Science and Technology addressed many of the critical issues arising from the conflicting relationship between big data and privacy. A discussion about the historical roots, the promises (and also the hype), and the huge amount of research and investments for big data cannot be presented in the limited space of this chapter. For simplicity, we mention the observation contained in Ref. [28], which has the merit of highlight two important dimensions of big data: "Big data is big in two different senses. It is big in the quantity and variety of data that are available to be processed. And, it is big in the scale of analysis (termed 'analytics') that can be applied to those data, ultimately to make inferences and draw conclusions." This observation is useful because the two dimensions of big data are also the two dimensions of privacy problems with big data: personal information is collected and stored and many sensitive inferences can be produced from those data. Beneficial uses of big data are real and already tangible in many areas, certainly a lot more to come in future years. On the other side, harmful consequences are real and already tangible with respect to privacy. Addressing privacy problems derived by big data has vast implications that will inevitably invest the political sphere, as well as market strategies and global digital innovation. Big data, as observed in Ref. [28], are also "rapidly changing the distinction between government and the private sector as potential threats to individual privacy." It is not just corporations or data brokers that have the motivations and the power to amass enormous amount of personal information and run powerful analytics over them; it is not just governmental intelligence agencies or the police that want to keep an eye on citizens by accessing their digital trails. It is the public sector as a whole that may revolutionize public services by exploiting big data and obtaining more efficiency, personalization, and reducing the gap with citizen needs. In all these cases, individual privacy is inevitably in danger. It sounds paradoxical not to be able to enjoy clearly beneficial uses of big data without suffering clearly detrimental consequences in terms of privacy. With this respect, a discussion of big data paradoxes having some ties with privacy has been presented by Richards and King [29]. The first paradoxical situation is called the *transparency paradox*: the fact that all sorts of personal information are collected, but the operations of big data companies are almost completely shielded from public scrutiny by commercial and legal secrecy. This observation is valid for almost all big data initiatives and is dangerously similar to one of the criticism to the data broker industry, typically characterized by opacity and lack of public scrutiny. The second paradox is the *identity paradox*: big data aims to identify people through their personal and behavioral data, but at the same time threatens people's identity. Once a certain profile for an individual emerges from data, it is almost impossible for the individual to modify it in order to better reflect his/her own perception of self. In other words, it is likely to see a relevant gap between one's definition of herself and the definition produced by big data. The third paradox is called the *power paradox*. Big data initiatives are supposed to have a transformative power on our vision of the world and of society, thanks to the information and inferences we could learn from such a mass of data. However, big data power is not evenly distributed and most of all is not in the hands of ordinary people, those which produce the majority of data. Big data tends to benefit corporations, powerful intermediaries, and the few with the training and knowledge necessary to extract informative value from the data. Big data have already been exploited to overcome citizens' privacy, either for commercial or political reasons. Therefore, with respect to privacy, the three big data paradoxes could be reinterpreted as: opacity and lack of scrutiny of big data organizations; lack of control on personal identities; and asymmetric distribution of power in exploiting big data. Barocas and Nissenbaum in Ref. [30] approached the relationship between privacy and big data from a different angle by discussing *anonymity* and *consent* in a world of big data. More on consent will be discussed in the next section; here we consider anonymity in particular. "Anonymity obliterates the link between data and a specific person not so much to protect privacy but, in a sense, to bypass it entirely," wrote Barocas and Nissenbaum, pointing to the specific role that anonymity plays in the context of privacy management. Anonymity is the preferred choice for the Internet presence of many privacy advocates both decades ago [31] and today [32]. Anonymity is sometimes celebrated as the only safe harbor for ordinary people in the battle for preserving privacy from the prying eyes of data brokers, Internet corporations, social networks and governments. *Anonymous*, the much hyped hacktivist collective, built part of its narrative on the populistic notion of absence of identity of its members and lack of organizational hierarchy [33]. Regardless of whether anonymity is considered a fundamental requirement for online freedom and equality or an inacceptable concealment [34,35], it is certainly in danger of being weakened, if not suppressed, in a world of big data. Even more worrisome is the fact that anonymization techniques, based on the concept of Personal Identifiable Information (PII) and that have been considered the perfect solution to satisfy both privacy and openness requirements for data to be made public (Open Data), proved weak against reidentification attempts based on the ever-increasing availability of personal data [36–38]. Successful reidentification of anonymized archives has been documented against medical, urban planning, education, and public utility data, among the others.

In addition to reidentification, the concept of *anonymous identifier* was introduced by Barocas and Nissenbaum [30] as a persistent identifier not based on name or other PII

such as home address or birth date. Anonymous identifiers are those typically implemented for online advertising by means of cookies or cookie-less techniques such as browser fingerprinting (more on these techniques in following sections). This denotes a shift in the notion of anonymity, from the classical approach based on PII and enforced by privacy regulations to that of online advertisers, which may claim to record just anonymous information because they are not interested in PII (the customer name or birth date, etc.). They need to place the right banner to the right user to produce a "quality buyer"; this is why they need data broker categories of customers, rather than PII. To this regard, the advent of big data decreases the effectiveness of anonymity-oriented solutions to privacy problems.

Informed Consent and the Perception of Privacy Control

One of the pillars of modern data protection and privacy management is the notion of *control*. Privacy as control of personal information is a foundational principle as powerful as the "right to be left alone" of Warren and Brandais. Even more important for our chapter, the idea of providing citizens with the right to control the usage and dissemination of personal data is at the core of most online privacy initiatives, regulations, and proposals. Citizens of the digital world, customers of Internet merchants, and users of online services should be able to decide which PII to release, to whom, for which purposes, and for how long based on the privacy control theory. It was Alan Westin in 1967 to define privacy as "the claim of individuals, groups, or institutions to determine for themselves when, how, and to what extent information about them is communicated to others" [39]. However, like the many developments in the decades following the days of the small Kodak cameras used to peek into people's private life demonstrated, the "right to be left alone" and the theory of privacy control are much more difficult to achieve and complex to analyze than initially believed. The same Alan Westin recognized the intrinsic complex nature of privacy by writing in 2003 an historical overview of how the concept of privacy changed, reflecting social and political events and issues in the last four decades [40].

Le Métayer and Lazaro examined the issue of control applied to privacy in more detail and introduced the distinction between *structural/objective* control and *individual/subjective* control [41]. The former is related to the notion of surveillance exercised by public or private organizations over citizens' life and behavior. The latter describes the privacy approach aiming at letting individuals free to define their own digital identity in a self-management fashion. The privacy as control approach falls in the individual/subjective category and has been connected to both a liberal vision of citizenship and a market-oriented definition of privacy as a *property right* [42]. "Consent should be given by a clear affirmative action establishing a freely given, specific, informed and unambiguous indication of the data subject's agreement to personal data relating to him or her being processed," states the new EU Data Protection Regulation [2]. Individual consent is the main pillar of the newest and probably the strictest privacy regulation to date, as well as back in the 1970s after Alan Westin articulated his principles [39] that were used in developing the FIPPs [43]. The *Individual Participation* principle recites: "Organizations should involve the individual in the process of using PII and, to the extent practicable, seek individual consent for the collection, use, dissemination, and maintenance of PII." As sound the principle of individual consent for data protection could be in theory, its practical application has demonstrated many intrinsic limits, in addition to the subterfuges adopted by those harvesting personal data in order to keep individuals unaware of their practices. Daniel Solove wrote that "Consent legitimizes nearly any form of collection, use, or disclosure of personal data" [44]. This stark declaration has several reasons, among them that cognitive limitations have been reported in many social science research, resulting in an extreme difficulty for individuals to make rational choices about cost and benefits for a complex and often unclearly defined matter as personal privacy in the rich and interactive online environment. Given the number of parties collecting data, the potential secondary usages, and the number of online services we are used to interacting with, it is virtually impossible to make an informed, specific, and unambiguous choice in all cases. It would be simply overwhelming. On the other hand, current examples of informed consent are often blatantly ineffective. Take, for instance, the case of the current, so-called, *Cookie Law* in the European Union. The *ePrivacy* directive [45] establishes that for a website it is possible to use cookies (only session cookies are exempted) only after a user has explicitly gave her consent. As a result, all European web sites, starting from 2015, exhibit a banner with a long and mostly incomprehensible disclaimer and consent request to all users at their first visit. The consent in some case must be given by clicking on an "accept" button, but most of the time it can be given indirectly by just scrolling to the page or clicking outside the banner. It is evident that in this case the presumed privacy control is just illusory. The privacy-as-control approach based on informed consent runs into an unsolved and often neglected dilemma: if people have to be fully informed, then the choice becomes unmanageable in practice, otherwise if the choice is made simple (often oversimplified) then people are asked to decide without understanding the matter. The problem of privacy as control does not scale well, and today a solution is still missing. Furthermore, privacy as control can even backfire in the case of advertising. One well-known problem

that advertisers face is *reactance*, which is the emotional reaction of consumers that start behaving in the opposite way an advertising intends if they perceive an ad as intrusive or coercive. Studies have discovered that one effective way for advertisers to mitigate the reactance effect is to improve the perception of privacy control, because, even if the actual control is partial, consumers' confidence increases and advertising is more effective [46]. The *perception* of control is, most of the time, the true artifact of privacy initiatives, not an effective control of one's own personal data.

4. PRIVACY AND TECHNOLOGIES

In this section, we address the privacy issues in the context of different technologies: at the application level, we describe the techniques used to profile user's habits and the possible countermeasures. Then, we deal with privacy enhancing technologies that help to defend against traffic analysis. Finally, we investigate the problem of privacy in mobile health applications.

Tracking User's Habits

Offering customers personalized services and targeted advertisements is probably the most fundamental mainstay of today's Internet economy. The obvious drawback is the inevitable erosion of users' privacy. Indeed, collecting a user's web browsing history gives a lot of information on a person: The pages a user visits can reveal her location, interests, medical conditions, financial challenges, and a lot more. Correlating the access to different pages gives an even more accurate picture of the person.

At the moment, there are many techniques that can be used to track users' browsing habits: They fall into the *stateful* (or explicit) category, if they rely on a website's ability to store a state on the user's machine, or into the *stateless* category otherwise. Historically, the first tracking technique is the one based on *HTTP cookies*. The others have been introduced in order to bypass the user ability to disable cookies, in the hope of limiting privacy invasion. In this section we give a brief overview of the most commonly used techniques and discuss the possible countermeasures.

HTTP Cookies

Cookies have originally been introduced in order to remember stateful information such as items added in a shopping cart of an online store, users' language preferences, or the fact that a user has logged into a website when browsing within a same domain [47]. A cookie is a small piece of data that is sent to the user the first time she visits a website (using the `Set-Cookie` header in the server HTTP response) and is stored in the user's browser folder. Then, every time the user visits the same website, the browser sends the cookie back to the server (using the `Cookie` header in the HTTP response). Cookies may expire when the user quits the browser (in this case they are called session cookies), or they may be permanent cookies and live until their expiration date. Obviously, the more they last the more the user's profile will be enriched. Originally, a cookie contained all state information. Now, it is common that the cookie is a unique identifier and all the data (with no space limit) is stored at the server side. Data can be contents in a shopping chart, the user's log-in name or the fact that the user has logged in (and she does not need to authenticate for each protected page she accesses), user's preferences such as language preferences, or tracking data, such as what pages and content she has looked at, and when she visited.

If the cookie is set by the website accessed by the user, it is called a *first-party cookie*; if the cookie is set by some other domain embedded in the top-level page, it is called a *third-party cookie*. Third-party cookies are common since web pages are increasingly composed of content from different unrelated third-party websites dealing with advertising, analytics, weather forecast, social networking, etc.

For example, we might have a user visiting the site www.dailynews.com to read the news of the day. At her first visit, the site sets a first-party cookie. If the site contains an advertisement banner from ad.someservice.com, this is a third-party site which produces a third-party cookie belonging to the advertisement's domain. If the user, after reading the news, visits an online bookshop that contains another advertisement from ad.someservice.com, the browser sends the cookie to the domain. Now, ad. someservice.com knows the user is interested in reading the news and in buying books (and probably which kind of books). Each time the user bumps into a site with advertisement banners from ad.someservice.com (or visits the site itself), the third-party site will profile the user by recording when and where she saw an ad, whether she clicked on it, and so forth including physical information like the IP address and information about the navigation history. However, notice that also first-party cookies may be used to collect user's information, and that the number of cookies per site may be tremendously high: more than 100 [48,49].

Flash Cookie and Cookie Respawning

The term *Flash cookie* (or *local shared object*) is used to refer to the local shared objects (LSOs) created by the Adobe Flash plug-in. Flash cookies are commonly used to view Flash-based animations and videos. Like HTTP cookies, they store information on the user's computer, containing the same information of HTTP cookies plus other Flash-specific data, such as the place where the user stopped playing a video, or the video volume preferences. Unlike HTTP cookies, Flash cookies are stored in a specific file and they are managed through Adobe Flash player settings, and cannot be deleted in the same way as HTTP cookies. Thus, many users are unaware of Flash cookies, and of their persistence even when HTTP cookies are deleted. Moreover, being browser-independent, they allow cross-browser tracking.

Flash cookies have caused controversy since they may be used to recreate deleted HTTP cookies (such a process is called *respawning*, and cookies are called *zombie cookies*). In the paper "Flash Cookies and Privacy" [50], the authors surveyed the top 100 web sites according to QuantCast in July of 2009, and found that more than half of them used Flash cookies. Moreover, they found that Flash cookies were frequently employed to track users that had explicitly attempted to prevent cookie tracking, by using the Flash cookie to regenerate an HTTP cookie that had been deleted. More curious is the fact that from the website pool used in the research, only four of them disclosed the presence of Flash cookies in their privacy policy.

Entity Tag

An Entity Tag (ETag) [51] is an opaque identifier assigned by a web server to a specific version of a resource found at a URL. It is one of the mechanisms used by the HTTP protocol for web cache validation to help browsers avoid loading the same data repeatedly. For example, if a user visits a web page with an image, the image will be downloaded and stored on her computer. When the image is sent the first time, the server can send an ETag along with it, which the browser stores. The next time the users visits the page, the browser may send the ETag within the request. If the image did not change (the ETag sent by the browser matches the one stored by the server), thus the browser does not download the image again. The ETag can also be used as a unique identifier to a database entry containing previous browsing habits.

In their follow up study on Flash cookies and privacy [52], the authors found that ETags were used also for cookie respawning. They highlighted that ETag tracking and respawning is particularly problematic from the user perspective, since the technique is able to generate unique tracking identifiers even when the user blocks HTTP, Flash, and HTML5 cookies. In order to block this tracking method, the user would have to clear the cache between each website visit, since even in private browsing mode ETags can track the user during a browser session.

Other Stateful Techniques

HTML5 local storage allows web applications to store data locally within the user's browser. Unlike cookies, the storage limit is far larger (at least 5 MB) and information is never transferred to the server.

HTTP header enrichment allows a mobile operator to annotate HTTP connections via the use of a wide range of request headers. This technique has received significant press coverage since it came out that AT&T and Verizon were using it to produce a unique tracking identifier [53]. Given the negative media coverage, AT&T stopped using it, whereas Verizon continued in its practice (even when users opted out of the advertising program) until it was found that somebody else, the tech company Turn, was using the Verizon number to respawn user's deleted cookies. One study highlighted that there are still other mobile operators using header enrichment to track users [54].

Device Fingerprinting

Device fingerprinting is a stateless tracking technique that works by collecting a set of system attributes to compose a signature that, for each possible device and value of the attributes, should be stable and unique. The attribute may include the device's screen size, the versions of installed software, the list of installed fonts, the time zone, browser plug-ins, and operating system version. For web tracking, the process of collecting the attributes is done through the browser by means of a script, or through traffic analysis. The first experiment on web device fingerprinting dates back to 2010 [55]: The attributes logged by the system included the user's screen size, time zone, browser plug-ins, and set of installed system fonts, and the results showed that, of 470,000 voluntary users participating to the experiment, 84% of their browsers produced unique fingerprints (94% if you count those that supported Flash or Java). A most recent approach is called *canvas fingerprinting* [56]. This technique works by exploiting the HTML5 canvas element: The browser is forced to create a hidden image that is then converted to a digital token. Since almost every machine will render the image slightly differently it can be used as a unique identifier. As reported in Refs. [57,58], device fingerprinting is increasingly used by advertising and antifraud companies. A sneaky fingerprinting technique has been publicly discussed; it is called *AudioContext fingerprinting* and it exploits the Audio API to find a unique response to be used as an identifier. Englehardt and Narayanan discuss this and other modern fingerprinting techniques in a preliminary technical paper [59].

Countermeasures

Due to the rising concerns about privacy, new tools and browser features aimed at privacy protection during web surfing are available. None can block some of the more sophisticated tracking techniques:

- *Opt out cookies*. These are particular cookies created by a specific website that will block future cookies coming from the same site. It is an option that most third-party

ad-serving companies offer. The drawback of this technique is the fact that they are cookies and browser specific (they do not cover the usage of other methods to profile users and if you change browser, you need to opt-out again). Moreover, opting out does not mean that the user will no longer receive online advertising (that, for some users, may be annoying), it means that ads will not be targeted based on the user's browsing history.

- *Browser's cookies settings*. All browsers allow the user to manage her cookies. The options that most browsers give include deleting specific cookies or all cookies (first-party and third-party), enabling or disabling cookies (first-party or third-party), and deciding when cookies expire. Blocking all cookies would not be very helpful since it would make the navigation almost impossible (a user could not log automatically into her account), but blocking third-party cookies can be a first safe step.

- *Private browsing*. Also called *Incognito Mode* or *InPrivate Browsing*, depending on the browser. It turns off the web history and enables only the cookies necessary for the site to work, but blocks third-party cookies. At the end of the session, all cookies are deleted. It is intended to be used for hiding activities on a shared computer, rather than actually remaining invisible online.

- *Browser add-ons*. Independent developers started producing privacy-preserving extensions that users could add to their browsers. Today, the most popular extension to Mozilla's Firefox browser is AdBlock Plus [60], which rejects both ads and third-party cookies used for tracking. Recently developed tools like Ghostery [61] and Mozilla's Lightbeam [62] reveal the number of trackers on each website and show how these trackers collaborate between seemingly unrelated sites.

- *Do Not Track (DNT)*. DNT is an HTTP header field that the browser may put in the HTTP requests to indicate that the user does not want to be tracked. At present, all browsers support the header, but there are no legal requirements for accomplishing the user's request when it is enabled. At present, there is a W3C Tracking Preference Expression (DNT) Working Group that is trying to standardize DNT [63].

Privacy Enhancing Technologies for Anonymity

Privacy enhancing technologies (PETs) is a general term for a set a computer tools, applications, protocols and mechanisms aiming at protecting and enhancing the privacy of user's PII. Examples of existing PETs ranges from communications anonymizer to languages for privacy-aware access control and privacy preferences, or to obfuscation techniques for location-privacy in ubiquitous computing.

In this section, we focus on PETs for anonymity to see how it is possible to provide *anonymity, unobservability,* and *unlinkability* when being online (how a user is able to keep secret not only the information she exchanges, but also the fact that she is exchanging information and with whom). Such a problem has to do with traffic analysis, and it requires ad hoc solutions. Traffic analysis is the process of intercepting and examining messages to deduce information from patterns in communication. It can be performed even when messages are encrypted. In general, the greater the number of messages analyzed, the more can be inferred from the traffic. The core of these technologies is based on hiding each correlation between input and output data in order to protect the identity of the end user (see checklist, "An Agenda for Action for Protecting One's Identity").

An Agenda for Action for Protecting One's Identity

You'll want to protect the privacy of your personal information while you're online. Here's a checklist of some of the most important things you can do to protect your identity and prevent others from easily getting your personal information (check all tasks completed):

_____1. Check a site's privacy policy before you enter any personal information and know how it will be used.

_____2. Make sure you have a secure Internet connection, by checking for the unbroken key or closed lock icon in your browser, before you enter any personal information onto a webpage.

_____3. Only give a credit card number when buying something.

_____4. Register your credit cards with your card provider's online security services, such as Verified by Visa and MasterCard SecureCode.

_____5. Use just one credit card for online purchases; if possible, use an account with a low spending limit or small available balance.

_____6. Don't use a debit card for your online purchases. Credit cards are better because bank-provided security guarantees apply to credit cards, so an unauthorized charge is limited to $50.

_____7. Don't select the "remember my password" option when registering online.

_____8. Change your passwords every 60–90 days and don't use personal information as your password; instead, use a string of at least five letters, numbers, and punctuation marks.

_____9. Don't store your passwords near your computer or in your purse or wallet.

_____10. Don't give more information than a site requires.

_____11. Keep your antivirus software up to date to reduce the risk of malicious code running on your PC.

_____12. Don't go online unless you have a personal firewall enabled to add a layer of protection to your PC by stopping unknown connections to your PC.

_____13. Don't reply directly to email messages asking for personal information.

_____14. Type web addresses directly into your web browser instead of clicking on email links.

_____15. Get antivirus and antispam filtering software and keep it up to date by using its automatic update feature, if your service provider or employer doesn't provide it for you.

_____16. Check out online retailers' ratings at BizRate and the Better Business Bureau and the before buying.

Onion Routing and TOR

TOR [64], the second-generation onion routing protocol [65], is intended to provide real-time bidirectional *anonymous connections* that are resistant to both eavesdropping and traffic analysis in a way that is transparent to applications. Onion routing works beneath the application layer, replacing socket connections with anonymous connections and without requiring any change to proxy-aware Internet services or applications. It consists of a fixed infrastructure of onion routers, where each router has a longstanding socket connection to a set of neighboring ones. Only a few routers, called *onion router proxies*, know the whole infrastructure topology. In onion routing, instead of making socket connections directly to a responding machine, initiating applications make a socket connection to an onion routing proxy that builds an anonymous connection through several other onion routers to the destination. In this way, the onion routing network allows the connection between the initiator and responder to remain anonymous. Although the protocol is called onion routing, the routing that occurs during the anonymous connection is at the application layer of the protocol stack, not at the IP layer.

TOR is also an effective *circumvention tool* (a tool to bypass Internet filtering in order to access content blocked by governments or corporations). All circumvention tools use the same approach to circumvent network filtering: They proxy connections through third-party sites that are not filtered themselves.

Other Network Anonymity Services

Other approaches offer some possibilities for providing anonymity and privacy, but they are still vulnerable to different types of attacks. For instance, many of these approaches are designed for web access only; being protocol-specific, these approaches may require further development to be used with other applications or Internet services, depending on the communication protocols used in those systems.

David Chaum [66,67] introduced the idea of *mix networks* in 1981 to enable unobservable communication between users of the Internet. Mix nodes are intermediate nodes that may reorder, delay, and pad incoming messages to complicate traffic analysis. A mix node stores a certain number of incoming messages that it receives and sends them to the next mix node in a random order. Thus, messages are modified and reordered in such a way that it is nearly impossible to correlate an incoming message with an outgoing message. Messages are sent through a series of mix nodes and encrypted with mix keys. If participants exclusively use mixes for sending messages to each other, their communication relations will be unobservable, even if the attacker records all network connections. Also, without additional information, the receiver does not have any clue about the identity of the message's sender. As in onion routing, each mix node knows only the previous and next node in a received message's route. Hence, unless the route only goes through a single node, compromising a mix node does not enable an attacker to violate either the sender nor the recipient privacy. Mix networks are not really efficient, since a mix needs to receive a large group of messages before forwarding them, thus delaying network traffic. However, onion routing has many analogies with this approach, and an onion router can be seen as a real-time Chaum mix.

Reiter and Rubin [68] proposed an alternative to mixes, called *crowds*, a system to make only browsing anonymous: It aims at hiding from web servers and third-party information about either the user or the information she retrieves. This is obtained by preventing a web server from learning any information linked to the user, such as the IP address or domain name, the page that referred the user to its site, or the user's computing platform. The approach is based on the idea of "blending into a crowd," that is, hiding one's actions within the actions of many others. Before making any request, a user joins a crowd of other users. Then, when the user submits a request, it is forwarded to the final destination with probability p and to some other member of the crowd with probability $1 - p$. When the request is eventually submitted, the end server cannot identify its true initiator. Even crowd members cannot identify the initiator of the request, since the initiator is indistinguishable from a member of the crowd that simply passed on a request from another.

Freedom network [69] is an overlay network that runs on top of the Internet, that is, on top of the application layer. The network is composed of a set of nodes called

anonymous Internet proxies, which run on top of the existing infrastructure. As for onion routing and mix networks, the Freedom network is used to set up a communication channel between the initiator and the responder, but it uses different techniques to encrypt the messages sent along the channel.

Anonymous Remailers

An anonymous remailer is a system that provides sender anonymity for emails. The basic idea is that a mail server receives messages and then forwards them without revealing where they originally came from. There are different types of anonymous remailer servers. A *Type-0* remailer (or *Pseudonymous* remailer) removes the server address, sets a random pseudonym to the sender and sends the message to the intended recipient. In this way, the recipient may send a message back to the sender. The server keeps a list containing the matching of the pseudonyms to sender real email addresses. The remailer is vulnerable to traffic analysis; moreover, if the server is compromised and an attacker is able to obtain the matching list all the senders are revealed.

Type-I remailers (or *Cypherpunk* remailers) were developed to deal with the problems highlighted above. The basic idea is the same: The remailer receives the message, removes the sender address, and then sends it to the recipient, but there are some changes: (1) the message may be encrypted with the remailer public key; (2) the remailer does not keep any log that could be used to identify senders; and (3) the message is not sent directly to the recipient but to a *chain* of remailers. In this way, a single remailer does not know both the sender and the recipient. The drawback is that it is not possible to reply to the message and that they are still vulnerable to some kinds of attack. For this reason, Type-II (or Mixmaster) and Type-III (or Mixminion) remailers have been proposed, but they are not really used in practice since they require specially customized software in order to send mails.

Privacy in Mobile Health Applications

In recent years, there has been a proliferation of mobile health (*mHealth*) applications on smartphones. mHealth applications are programs that use smartphone's inbuilt tools, such as the Global Positioning System (GPS), accelerometer, microphone, speaker, and camera to automatically detect and measure health-related behaviors. In order to measure and upload physiological data, a number of applications may also synchronize wirelessly with other wearable devices, such as wristband sensor, heart rate sensor, belt sensor, shoe sensor, glucometers, blood pressure cuffs, or smart clothing with wearable sensing technologies. Most of the popular mobile health and fitness applications focus on self-monitoring physiological markers relevant to a person's health status and for encouraging physical activity and healthy diets. Depending on the data collected, mHealth applications may cover a wide range of uses, including patient health and fitness self-management tools, remote and continuous monitoring of patients by caregivers, reminder systems improving glycemic control in patients with diabetes by prompting the users to take medications and check their blood glucose, symptom monitoring in asthma and heart disease, supporting smoking cessation, an effective source of health information, helping to monitor, improve, and manage fitness activities, weight goals, diet, pregnancy, and sleep.

They have the potential to reduce the cost of healthcare in a period in which many countries are facing the problem of an aging population with chronic diseases such as obesity, diabetes, and high pressure by encouraging healthy behaviors to prevent or reduce health problems, and by supporting chronic disease self-management that may reduce the number of healthcare visits. The efficiency of mHealth applications has been evaluated in a variety of domains, including different clinical areas and countries [70]. The results confirm the effectiveness in improving clinical outcomes. As a consequence, some insurance companies are now using application data to lower premiums, and the number of applications available for the different mobile platforms is growing [71].

However, several concerns exist about privacy and security in mHealth applications, since they could contain highly personal information, such as social interactions, location, emotional status, blood type, fingerprints, DNA profile, or other potentially sensitive health conditions [72,73]. To achieve the necessary minimal privacy (and security) requirements mHealth applications have to: (1) secure the data during the communication between the possible external sensor and the phone, and during the (possible) transfer to a cloud environment; (2) secure the data (and processing) inside the phone; and (3) be transparent on how data is managed and by whom (collected, stored, and transferred).

To this aim, some considerations need to be done: Many companies have significant commercial interests in collecting clients' private health data and sharing them with insurance companies, research institutions, or even the government agencies. On the other hand, from the user's point of view, third-party use of personal health information could lead to possible employment discrimination, loss of insurance coverage, higher insurance premiums, or other privacy intrusions. Traditional privacy protection mechanisms by simply removing clients' personal identity information (such as names or Social Security numbers) or by using anonymization techniques fail to serve as an effective way in dealing with privacy of mHealth systems due to the increasing amount and diversity of PII. Moreover, the

settings of smartphones may allow applications to access and share more information that people realize (and that are willing to let them do) [74]. Although existing privacy laws such as the Health Insurance Portability and Accountability Act (HIPAA) [75] provide a baseline protection for personal health records, they are generally considered not applicable or transferable to cloud computing environments. More health information than users may realize is not subject to HIPAA's regulatory regime. Besides, the current law is more focused on protection against adversarial intrusions while there is little effort on protecting clients from business collecting private information.

The results of some recent studies on the security issues of mHealth applications are not encouraging and show how mobile applications should improve transparency for end users about their commercial data practices:

- According to some empirical analysis of a large amount of the most frequently rated and commonly used applications for iOS and Android, most applications did not have a privacy policy. When present, the policy either did not focus on the app but on the services offered by the developer, or required college-level literacy, or did not adequately address the purpose of collection, transfer, storage, and destruction of user's data, and who exactly the information was shared with, or which specific permissions were given to the application [76,77].
- In 2014 the US FTC published an analysis of 12 popular mHealth applications [78]: They found that the applications were sending the device's screen size, device model, and language setting to 76 different third parties, whereas only a subset received exact information like the phone's Unique Device Identifier (UDID), the phone's media access control address (MAC address) and its International Mobile Station Equipment Identity (IMEI), or a user's personal information (not only a user's running routes, eating habits, sleeping patterns, and the cadence of how they walk, but also gender, geolocation, and zip codes). The results are in line with an older study of the Privacy Rights Clearinghouse [79] that investigated into 43 paid fitness applications and found that a large percentage of those apps did not have privacy policies and only 13% of them encrypted all data between the app and the developer's website. In addition, a third of the apps were found transmitting user information to a party not disclosed by the developer or the developer's website [80].

Currently, most health and fitness applications allow users to share their accomplishments with friends on social media (Facebook, Twitter, Pinterest, Instagram, etc.). If, on the one hand, this practice can be seen positively as a way to obtain social support and to promote friendly competition, on the other hand, from a privacy perspective, users are intentionally sharing data that should remain confidential.

5. SUMMARY

In this chapter, we have discussed some fundamentals of online privacy, including its diverse historical roots and the enduring difficulty in establishing accepted definitions. The very nature of the concept of privacy requires such an enlarged perspective because it often appears indefinite, being constrained into the tradeoff between the undeniable obligation of protecting the private space of individuals and the manifest utility, in many contexts, of making personal information available to the public or to the business. The digital society and the global interconnected infrastructure eased accessing and spreading of personal information; therefore, developing technical means and defining norms and fair usage procedures for privacy protection are now more demanding than in the past.

We presented in some details the case of the data broker industry, because of its relatively lesser media exposition and involvement in the public discourse than the much-debated cases of state-based surveillance and Internet corporations for which the user is the product. Discussing the characteristics of the data broker industry, let us also to make a connection between different epochs: before and after the advent of the Internet.

We also discuss the central problem of the informed consent given by individuals as the main pillar of most current privacy policies and regulations. This lead us to show the intrinsic complexity of the current scenario. Online privacy is involved with the IT markets and its economics, with human cognitive limitations and the difficulty facing decisions under uncertainty, with problems of scalability of solutions aiming at providing individuals with controls.

We presented the techniques that are currently used to profile a user's online behavior and the possible counter-measures. Furthermore, we investigated the important issue of anonymity on the Internet in order to let individuals access online services and interact with remote parties in an anonymous way, which has been the goal of many efforts for years, by describing some important technologies and tools that are available and are gaining popularity. Then, we covered the issue of privacy in the context of mobile health applications, highlighting the security and privacy risks emerging in this context, both because of the type of data collected, and of the fact that privacy issues on mobile applications have not been fully addressed yet.

To conclude, whereas privacy on the Internet and digital society does not look to be in good shape, the augmented sensibility of individuals to its erosion, the many scientific and technological efforts to introduce novel solutions, and a better knowledge of the problem with the help of fresh data contribute to stimulating the need for better protection and fairer use of personal information. For this reason, it is likely that Internet privacy will remain an important topic in the years to come and more innovations toward better management of privacy issues will emerge.

Finally, let's move on to the real interactive part of this Chapter: review questions/exercises, hands-on projects, case projects, and optional team case project. The answers and/or solutions by chapter can be found in Appendix K.

CHAPTER REVIEW QUESTIONS/ EXERCISES

True/False

1. True or False? Privacy in today's digital society is one of the most debated and controversial topics.
2. True or False? As it often happens when a debate heats up, the extremes speak louder and, about privacy, the extremes are those that advocate the ban of the disclosure of whatever personal information, and those that say that all personal information is already out there and so therefore privacy is alive.
3. True or False? Threats to individual privacy have become publicly appalling since July 2012, when the California Security Breach Notification Law [8] went into effect.
4. True or False? The existence of strong economic factors that influence the way privacy is managed, breached, or even traded off has not been recognized.
5. True or False? The relationship between privacy and business has been examined from several angles by considering which incentives could be ineffective for integrating privacy with business processes and, instead, which disincentives make business motivations to prevail over privacy.

Multiple Choice

1. With respect to the often difficult relation between business goals and privacy requirements, a special attention should be given to _____ business and the many tools and mechanisms that have been developed to improve the knowledge about customers, their habits, and preferences in order to offer to them purchase suggestions and personalized services.
   A. Privacy-enhancing technology
   B. Location technology
   C. Web-based
   D. Technical improvement
   E. Web technology
2. Technical improvements of _____ and location technologies have fostered the development of online applications that use the private information of users (including physical position of individuals) to offer enhanced services?

A. Privacy-enhancing technology
B. Location technology
C. Web-based
D. Web
E. Web technology

3. What systems have been introduced for regulating and protecting access to resources and data owned by parties?
   A. Access control
   B. XACML
   C. XML-based language
   D. Certification Authority
   E. Security

4. The importance gained by privacy requirements has brought with it the definition of _____ that are enriched with the ability of supporting privacy requirements.
   A. Access control models
   B. Languages
   C. Privacy-Aware Access Control
   D. Privacy preferences
   E. Taps

5. What governs access/release of services/data managed by the party (as in traditional access control)?
   A. Release policies
   B. Access control policies
   C. Data handling policies
   D. Intellectual property
   E. Social engineering

EXERCISE

Problem

What should I know about privacy policies?

Hands-on Projects

Project

How can I protect my privacy when shopping online?

Case Projects

Problem

How can I prevent web sites from sharing my web browsing habits?

Optional Team Case Project

Problem

How can I prevent my computer from keeping a history of where I browse?

REFERENCES

[1] N. Singer, You for Sale: Mapping, and Sharing, the Consumer Genome, The New York Times, June 16, 2012. Available at: www.nytimes.com/2012/06/17/technology/acxiom-the-quiet-giant-of-consumer-databasemarketing.html.

[2] Regulation (EU) 2016/679-General Data Protection Regulation, Official Journal of the European Union, 2016. Available at: http://ec.europa.eu/justice/data-protection/reform/files/regulation_oj_en.pdf.

[3] M.L. Goldschmidt, Publicity, privacy and secrecy, West. Political Q. (1954) 401–416.

[4] J. Habermas, The Structural Transformation of the Public Sphere: An Inquiry into a Category of Bourgeois Society, MIT press, 1991.

[5] S.D. Warren, L.D. Brandeis, The right to privacy, Harv. Law Rev. 4 (5) (1890).

[6] T.M. Cooley, Cooley on Torts, 29, 2d ed., 1888.

[7] K. Gormley, One hundred years of privacy, Wis. Law Rev. 1335 (1992).

[8] M. Kohn, Brave New Neighborhoods: The Privatization of Public Space, Routledge, 2004.

[9] J.E. Cohen, What privacy is for, Harv. Law Rev. 126 (2012) 1904.

[10] D.J. Solove, A taxonomy of privacy, Univ. Pa. Law Rev. (2006) 477–564.

[11] R.A. Posner, Right of privacy, Ga. Law Rev. 12 (3) (1978) 393–422.

[12] J.H. Smith, T. Dinev, H. Xu, Information privacy research: an interdisciplinary review, MIS Q. 35 (4) (2011) 989–1016.

[13] C.J. Bennett, In defence of privacy: the concept and the regime, Surveill. Soc. 8 (4) (2011) 485.

[14] J. Angwin, Has Privacy Become a Luxury Good?, The New York Times, March 3, 2014. http://www.nytimes.com/2014/03/04/opinion/has-privacy-become-a-luxury-good.html.

[15] H. Xu, X.R. Luo, J.M. Carroll, M.B. Rosson, The personalization privacy paradox: an exploratory study of decision making process for location-aware marketing, Decis. Support Syst. 51 (1) (2011) 42–52.

[16] S. Utz, N. Kramer, The privacy paradox on social network sites revisited: the role of individual characteristics and group norms, Cyberpsychol. J. Psychosoc. Res. Cyberspace 3 (2) (2009).

[17] A. Acquisti, J. Leslie, G. Loewenstein, What is privacy worth, Workshop on Information Systems and Economics (WISE), 2009.

[18] A. Acquisti, C.R. Taylor, L. Wagman, The Economics of Privacy, 2015. SSRN 2580411.

[19] L. Lessig, Free Culture: How Big Media Uses Technology and the Law to Lock Down Culture and Control Creativity, Penguin, 2004.

[20] US Federal Trade Commission, Protecting Consumer Privacy in an Era of Rapid Change: Recommendations for Businesses and Policymakers, 2012. Available at: http://ftc.gov/os/2012/03/120326privacyreport.pdf.

[21] US Federal Trade Commission, Data Brokers – A Call for Transparency and Accountability, US Federal Trade Commission, Washington, DC, May 2014. Available at: https://www.ftc.gov/system/files/documents/reports/data-brokers-call-transparency-accountability-report-federal-trade-commission-may-2014/140527databrokerreport.pdf.

[22] Rubicon Project, The Advertising Automation Cloud, 2016. Available at: https://rubiconproject.com/.

[23] L. Beckett, Everything We Know about What Data Brokers Know about You, Pro Publica, 2014. Available at: https://www.propublica.org/article/everything-we-know-about-what-data-brokers-know-about-you.

[24] A. Tanner, How Data Brokers Make Money off Your Medical Records, Scientific American, 2016. Available at: http://www.scientificamerican. com/article/how-data-brokers-make-money-off-your-medical-records/.

[25] B. Kaplan, Selling health data, Camb. Q. Healthc. Ethics 24 (03) (2015) 256–271.

[26] M. Huesch, M. Ong, B.D. Richman, Could Data Broker Information Threaten Physician Prescribing and Professional Behavior?, CESR-Schaeffer Working Paper, 2015.

[27] P. Dixon, Congressional Testimony: What Information Do Data Brokers Have on Consumers?, World Privacy Forum, 2013. Available at: https://www.worldprivacyforum.org/2013/12/testimony-what-information-do-data-brokers-have-on-consumers/.

[28] President's Council of Advisors on Science and Technology, Big Data and Privacy: A Technological Perspective, Report to the President, May 2014.

[29] N.M. Richards, J.H. King, Three paradoxes of big data, Stanf. Law Rev. Online 66 (September 2013) 41. Available at: http://www.stanfordlawreview.org/online/privacy-and-big-data/three-paradoxes-big-data.

[30] S. Barocas, H. Nissenbaum, Big data's end run around anonymity and consent, in: J. Lane, V. Stodden, S. Bender, H. Nissenbaum (Eds.), Privacy, Big Data, and the Public Good: Frameworks for Engagement, Cambridge University Press, NY, 2014.

[31] K. Rigby, Anonymity on the Internet Must Be Protected, Ethics and Law on the Electronic Frontier, MIT, 1995. Available at: http://groups.csail.mit.edu/mac/classes/6.805/student-papers/fall95-papers/rigby-anonymity.html.

[32] J. Card, Anonymity Is the Internet's Next Big Battleground, The Guardian, 2015. Available at: http://www.theguardian.com/media-network/2015/jun/22/anonymity-internet-battleground-data-advertisers-marketers.

[33] G. Coleman, Hacker, Hoaxer, Whistleblower, Spy: The Many Faces of Anonymous, Verso Book, 2015.

[34] D. Davenport, Anonymity on the Internet: why the price may be too high, Commun. ACM 45 (4) (2002) 33–35.

[35] K. Ruogu, S. Brown, S. Kiesler, Why do people seek anonymity on the internet?: Informing policy and design, in: Proceedings of the SIGCHI Conference on Human Factors in Computing Systems, ACM, 2013.

[36] A. Narayanan, V. Shmatikov, Myths and fallacies of personally identifiable information, Commun. ACM 53 (6) (2010) 24–26.

[37] P. Ohm, Broken promises of privacy: responding to the surprising failure of anonymization, UCLA Law Rev. 57 (2010) 1701.

[38] A. Narayanan, E.W. Felten, No Silver Bullet: De-identification Still Doesn't Work, White Paper, 2014. Available at: http://randomwalker.info/publications/no-silver-bullet-de-identification.pdf.

[39] A.F. Westin, Privacy and Freedom, Athenum, New York, 1967.

[40] A.F. Westin, Social and political dimensions of privacy, J. Soc. Issues 59 (2) (2003) 431–453.

[41] D. Le Métayer, C. Lazaro, Control over personal data: true remedy or fairy tale? Scripted J. Law Technol. Soc. 12 (1) (2015).

[42] J.B. Baron, Property as control: the case of information, Mich. Telecommun. Technol. Law Rev. 20 (2012).

[43] United States Department of Health, Education and Welfare, Records, Computers and the Rights of Citizens, Report of the Secretary's Advisory Committee on Automated Personal Data Systems, 1973. Available at: https://www.justice.gov/opcl/docs/rec-com-rights.pdf.

[44] D.J. Solove, Privacy self-management and the consent dilemma, Harv. Law Rev. 126 (1880) 2013.

[45] Directive on privacy and electronic communications, Official Journal L 201 (2002) 0037–0047. Available at: http://eur-lex.europa.eu/LexUriServ/LexUriServ.do?uri=CELEX:32002L0058:EN: HTML.

[46] C.E. Tucker, Social networks, personalized advertising, and privacy controls, J. Mark. Res. 51 (5) (2014) 546–562.

[47] Request for Comments 6265, HTTP State Management Mechanism, April 2011.

[48] J.R. Mayer, J.C. Mitchell, Third-party web tracking: policy and technology, in: Proc. of the 2012 IEEE Symposium on Security and Privacy, 2012, pp. 413–427.

[49] F. Roesner, T. Kohno, D. Wetherall, Detecting and defending against third-party tracking on the web, in: Proc. of the 9th USENIX Conference on Networked Systems Design and Implementation (NSDI'12), 2012, pp. 155–168.

[50] A. Soltani, S. Canty, Q. Mayo, L. Thomas, C.J. Hoofnagle, Flash cookies and privacy, in: AAAI Spring Symposium: Intelligent Information Privacy Management, 2010, pp. 158–163.

[51] Request for Comments 7232, Hypertext Transfer Protocol (HTTP/1.1): Conditional Requests, 2014.

[52] M.D. Ayenson, D. Wambach, J. Dietrich, A. Soltani, N. Good, C.J. Hoofnagle, Flash Cookies and Privacy II: Now with HTML5 and ETag Respawning, 2011. Available at: SSRN 1898390.

[53] J. Angwin, M. Tigas, Zombie Cookie: The Tracking Cookie that You Can't Kill, ProPublica, January 14, 2015.

[54] N. Vallina-Rodriguez, S. Sundaresan, C. Kreibich, V. Paxson, Header enrichment or ISP enrichment?: emerging privacy threats in mobile networks, in: Proc. of the 2015 ACM SIGCOMM Workshop on Hot Topics in Middleboxes and Network Function Virtualization (HotMiddlebox '15), 2015.

[55] P. Eckersley, How unique is your browser?, in: Proc. of the 10th Privacy Enhancing Technologies Symposium (PETS), 2010, pp. 1–17.

[56] K. Mowery, H. Shacham, Pixel perfect: fingerprinting canvas in HTML5, in: Proc. of W2SP 2012, 2012.

[57] N. Nikiforakis, A. Kapravelos, W. Joosen, C. Kruegel, F. Piessens, G. Vigna, Cookieless monster: exploring the ecosystem of web-based device fingerprinting, in: Proc. of the IEEE Symposium on Security and Privacy, 2013, pp. 541–555.

[58] G. Acar, C. Eubank, S. Englehardt, M. Juarez, A. Narayanan, C. Diaz, The Web never forgets: persistent tracking mechanisms in the wild, in: Proc. of CCS 2014, 2014.

[59] S. Englehardt, A. Narayanan, Online Tracking: A 1-Million-Site Measurement and Analysis Draft, May 18, 2016. Technical Paper, 2016.

[60] Adblock Plus. Available at: https://adblockplus.org/.

[61] Ghostery. Available at: https://www.ghostery.com/.

[62] Lightbeam for Firefox. Available at: https://www.mozilla.org/en-US/lightbeam/.

[63] Tracking Preference Expression (DNT), W3C Candidate Recommendation, Available at: https://www.w3.org/TR/tracking-dnt/, August 2015.

[64] R. Dingledine, N. Mathewson, P. Syverson, Tor: the second-generation onion router, in: Proc. of the 13th Conference on USENIX Security Symposium (SSYM'04), vol. 13, 2014, pp. 303–320.

[65] P. Reed, P. Syverson, D. Goldschlag, Anonymous connections and onion routing, IEEE J. Sel. Areas Commun. 16 (4) (1998) 482–494.

[66] D. Chaum, Untraceable electronic mail, return address, and digital pseudonyms, Commun. ACM 24 (2) (1981) 84–88.

[67] O. Berthold, H. Federrath, S. Köpsell, Web MIXes: a system for anonymous and unobservable Internet access, in: Anonymity 2000, LNCS, vol. 2009, 2000, pp. 115–129.

[68] M.K. Reiter, A.D. Rubin, Anonymous web transactions with crowds, Commun. ACM 42 (2) (1999) 32–48.

[69] P. Boucher, A. Shostack, I. Goldberg, Freedom System 2.0 Architecture, White Paper, Zero Knowledge Systems, Inc., 2000.

[70] C. Free, G. Phillips, L. Galli, L. Watson, L. Felix, P. Edwards, et al., The effectiveness of mobile-health technology-based health behaviour change or disease management interventions for health care consumers: a systematic review, PLoS Med. 10 (1) (2013).

[71] J.P. Higgins, Smartphone applications for patients' health and fitness, Am. J. Med. 129 (1) (2015) 11–19.

[72] A. Raij, A. Ghosh, S. Kumar, M. Srivastava, Privacy risks emerging from the adoption of innocuous wearable sensors in the mobile environment, in: Proc. of the SIGCHI Conference on Human Factors in Computing Systems (CHI '11), 2011, pp. 11–20.

[73] S. Kumar, W.J. Nilsen, A. Abernethy, A. Atienza, K. Patrick, M. Pavel, D. Hedeker, Mobile health technology evaluation: the mHealth evidence workshop, Am. J. Prev. Med. 45 (2) (2013) 228–236.

[74] A. Porter Felt, E. Chin, S. Hanna, D. Song, D. Wagner, Android permissions demystified, in: Proc. of the 18th ACM Conference on Computer and Communications Security (CCS '11), 2011, pp. 627–638.

[75] US Department of Health and Human Services, Health Insurance Portability and Accountability Act of 1996 (HIPAA). Pub. L. 104-191, 1996.

[76] M. Rowan, M. Dehlinger, A privacy policy comparison of health and fitness related mobile applications, in: Proc. the International Conference on Emerging Ubiquitous Systems and Pervasive Networks (EUSPN-2014), vol. 37, 2014, pp. 348–355.

[77] A. Sunyaev, T. Dehling, P.L. Taylor, K.D. Mandl, Availability and quality of mobile health app privacy policies, Am. J. Med. 22 (e1) (2015) e28–33.

[78] J. Ho, A snapshot of data sharing by select health and fitness apps, in: Seminar on Privacy Implications of Consumer Generated and Controlled Health Data, 2014. Washington, DC.

[79] L. Ackerman, Mobile Health and Fitness Applications and Information Privacy – Report to California Consumer Protection Foundation, Privacy Rights Clearinghouse, 2013.

[80] K. Park, I. Weber, M. Cha, C. Lee, Persistent sharing of fitness app status on Twitter, in: Proc. of the ACM Conference on Computer-Supported Cooperative Work & Social Computing (CSCW '16), 2016, pp. 184–194.

Chapter 53

Privacy-Enhancing Technologies

Simone Fischer-Hbner and Stefan Berthold
Karlstad University, Karlstad, Sweden

Privacy is considered as a core value and is recognized either explicitly or implicitly as a fundamental human right by most constitutions of democratic societies. In Europe, the foundations for the right to privacy of individuals were embedded in the European Convention on Human Rights and Fundamental Freedoms of 1950 (Art. 8) and the Charter of Fundamental Rights of the European Union in 2009 (Art. 7 & 8). The importance of privacy protection was recognized by the Organization for Economic Cooperation and Development (OECD) with the publication of the OECD Privacy Guidelines in 1980 [1], which served as the foundation for many national privacy laws and were updated in 2013 [2].

1. THE CONCEPT OF PRIVACY

Privacy as a social and legal issue has for a long time been a concern of social scientists, philosophers, and lawyers. The first definition of privacy by legal researchers was given by the two American lawyers Samuel D. Warren and Louis D. Brandeis in their famous Harvard Law Review article "The Right to Privacy" [3], in which they defined privacy as "the right to be let alone." At that time, the risks of modern technology in the form of photography used by the yellow press to infringe privacy of individuals was the motivation of Warren and Brandeis to discuss the individuals' right to privacy.

In the age of modern computing, an early and often referred to definition of privacy was given by Alan Westin: "Privacy is the claim of individuals, groups and institutions to determine for themselves, when, how and to what extent information about them is communicated to others" [4]. Even though according to Westin's definition, natural persons (humans) as well as legal persons (groups and institutions) have a right to privacy, in most legal systems, privacy is defined as a basic human right that only applies to natural persons.

In general, the concept of personal privacy has several dimensions. This article will mainly address the dimension of informational privacy, which can be defined, similarly as by Westin and by the German Constitutional Court in its Census decision[1], as the right to informational self-determination (the right of individuals to determine for themselves when, how, to what extent information about them is communicated to others). Furthermore, so-called spatial privacy can be defined as another dimension of the concept of privacy, which also covers the "right to be let alone," where spatial privacy is defined as the right of individuals to control what is presented to their senses [5]. Further dimensions of privacy, which will, however, not be the subject of this chapter, are territorial privacy which concerns the setting of limits on intrusion into the domestic, work place, and other environments (public spaces), and bodily privacy which concerns the protection of people's physical selves by protecting a person against undue interference, such as physical searches, drug testing, or information violating his/her moral sense (see [6,7]).

Data protection is concerning the protection of personal data in order to guarantee privacy and is only a part of the concept of privacy. Privacy, however, is not an unlimited or absolute right, as it can be in conflict with other rights or legal values, and because individuals cannot participate fully in society without revealing personal data. Nevertheless, even in cases where privacy need to be restricted, the very core of privacy still needs to be protected, and for this reason, privacy and data protection laws have the objective to define fundamental privacy principles that need to be enforced if personal data is collected, stored, or processed.

2. LEGAL PRIVACY PRINCIPLES

In this section, we give an overview to internationally well accepted, basic legal privacy principles, for which also PETs implementing these principles have been developed.

---

1. German Constitutional Court, Census decision, 1983 (BVerfGE 65, 1).

These principles are part of the EU Data Protection Directive 95/46/EC [8] newly adopted EU General Data Protection Regulation 2016/679 (GDPR) [9], which will replace the EU Data Protection Directive and will enter into force in all member states in May 2018. It defines a single set of modernized privacy rules, and which will in May 2018 be directly valid across the EU. The Directive and the GDPR are important legal instruments for privacy protection in Europe, as do not only codify general privacy rules for Europe, but also reflect the basic privacy principles of the OECD privacy guidelines and of the US Federal Trade Commission's (FTC) Fair Information Practice Principles (even going beyond them). Below we list some of the most relevant legal privacy principles that can be technically enforced by different types of PETs:

1. Legitimacy
2. Purpose specification and purpose binding (also called purpose limitation)
3. Data minimization
4. Transparency and rights of the data subjects
5. Security

Legitimacy

Personal data processing has to be legitimate (according to Art. 7 EU Directive 95/46/EC and Art. 6 GDPR), which is usually the case if the data subject[2] has given his/her unambiguous (and informed) consent, if there is a legal obligation, or contractual agreement (cf. the Collection Limitation Principle of the OECD Guidelines). The requirement of informed consent poses special challenges for the design of user interfaces (UIs) for PETs.

Purpose Specification And Purpose Binding

Personal data must be collected for specified, explicit and legitimate purposes and may not be further processed in a way incompatible with these purposes (Art.6 I b EU Directive 95/46/EC and Art. 5 (1) b GDPR). The purpose limitation principle is of key importance for privacy protection, as the sensitivity of personal data does not only depend on how "intimate" the details are, which the personal data are describing, but is also mainly influenced by the purposes of data processing and context of use. For this reason, the data processing purposes need to be specified in advance by the law maker or by the data processor before obtaining the individual's consent and personal data may later not be (mis-)used for any other purposes (cf. Purpose Specification and Use Limitation Principles of the OECD Guidelines). Privacy policy languages and tools (discussed in Section 7) have the objective to enforce this principle.

Data Minimization

The processing to personal data must be limited to data that are adequate, relevant, and not excessive (Art.6 I (c) EU Directive 95/46/EC and Art. 5 (1) c GDPR). Besides, data should not be kept in a personally identifiable form any longer than necessary (Art.6 I (e) EU Directive 95/46/EC—cf. Data Quality Principle of the OECD Guidelines, which requires that data should be relevant to the purposes for which they are to be used). In other words, the collection of personal data and extend to what personal data are used should be minimized, because obviously privacy is best protected if no personal data at all (or at least as little data as possible) are collected or processed. The data minimization principle derived from the Directive also serves as a legal foundation for PETs (see checklist, "An Agenda for Action for Privacy-Enhancing Technologies") that aim at protecting "traditional" privacy goals, such as anonymity, pseudonymity, or unlinkability for users and/or other data subjects.

An Agenda for Action for Privacy-Enhancing Technologies

The Privacy-Enhancing Technology (PET) concept (check all tasks completed):

_____**1.** Enforces making sparing use of data.
_____**2.** Makes privacy the default.
_____**3.** Transfers control to individuals.
_____**4.** Sends tags to a secure mode automatically.
_____**5.** Can prove that automatic activation of secure mode always works
_____**6.** Prevents eavesdropping of tag-reader communication.
_____**7.** Protects individuals from producer.
_____**8.** Protects individuals from retailer.
_____**9.** Protection includes in-store problem.
_____**10.** Protects tag in secure mode against presence-spotting.
_____**11.** Does not require individuals to take active protection measures.
_____**12.** Does not interfere with active protection measures.
_____**13.** Avoids creation and use of central database(s).
_____**14.** Avoids creation and use of databases at all.
_____**15.** Enables functionality after point-of-sale in a secure way.
_____**16.** Can be achieved without changing radio-frequency identification (RFID) physical technology.
_____**17.** Does not make tags much more expensive.
_____**18.** Does not introduce additional threats to privacy.
_____**19.** Introduces additional benefits for privacy.
_____**20.** Provides benefits for the retailer.

---

2. A data subject is a person about whom personal data is processed.

Transparency and Rights of the Data Subjects

Transparency of data processing means informing a data subject about the purposes and circumstances of data processing, who is requesting personal data, how the personal data flow, where and how long the data are stored, what type of rights and controls the data subject has in regard to his personal data. The Directive 95/46/EC and the GDPR provide data subjects with respective information rights according to Art. 10 and Art. 14 respectively. Transparency is a prerequisite for informational self-determination, as "a society, in which citizens can no longer know who does, when, and in which situations know what about them, would be contradictory to the right of informational self-determination."[3] Further rights of the data subjects include the right of access to data (Art.12 (a) EU Directive 95/46/EC, Art. 15 GDPR), the right to correction, erasure, or blocking of incorrect or illegally stored data (Art.12 (b) EU Directive 95/46/EC, Art. 16 GDPR, cf. Openness and Individual Participation Principle of the OECD Guidelines), as well as the right to be forgotten and the right to data portability (Art. 17, 20 GDPR). Transparency-enhancing tools and tools for enforcing data subject rights will be discussed in Section 7.

Security

The data controller needs to implement appropriate technical and organizational security mechanisms to guarantee the confidentiality, integrity, and availability of personal data (Art.17 EU Directive 95/46/EC, Art. 32 GDPR, cf. Security Safeguards Principle of the OECD Guidelines). Classical security mechanisms, such as authentication, cryptography, access control, or security logging, which need to be implemented for technical data protection, will however not be discussed in this chapter. The new GDPR includes specifically the principle of data protection/privacy by design and by default (Art. 25), requiring building PETs already into the initial system design.

3. CLASSIFICATION OF PRIVACY-ENHANCING TECHNOLOGIES (PETS)

PETs can be defined as technologies that are enforcing legal privacy principles in order to protect and enhance privacy of users of information technology (IT) and/or data subjects (see [10]). While many fundamental PET concepts for achieving data minimization were already introduced, mostly by David Chaum, in the eighties (see [11−13]), the term "Privacy-enhancing Technologies" was first introduced in 1995 in a report on PETs, which was jointly

published by the Dutch Registratiekamer and the Information and Privacy Commissioner in Ontario/Canada [14].

PETs can basically be divided into three different classes: The first class comprises PETs for enforcing the legal privacy principle of data minimization by minimizing or avoiding the collection and use of personal data of users or data subjects. These types of PETs are providing the "traditional" privacy goals of anonymity, unlinkability, unobservability, and pseudonymity, which will be elaborated in the next section. This class of PETs can be further divided dependent on whether data minimization is achieved on communication level or application level. Examples for some of the most prominent data minimization technologies will be presented in Section 6.

While data minimization is the best strategy for protecting privacy, there are many occasions in daily life when individuals simply have to reveal personal data, or when users want to present themselves by disseminating personal information (on social networking sites). In these cases, privacy of the individuals concerned still needs to be protected by adhering to other relevant legal privacy requirements. The second class of PETs therefore comprises technologies that enforce legal privacy requirements, such as informed consent, transparency, right-to-data subject access, purpose specification and purpose binding and security, in order to safeguard the lawful processing of personal data. In this article, so-called "transparency-enhancing technologies" will be discussed, which are PETs enforcing or promoting informed consent and transparency. Besides, we will refer to privacy models and privacy authorization languages for enforcing the principle of purpose binding.

The third class of PETs comprises technologies that are combining PETs of the first and second class. An example is provided by privacy-enhancing identity management technologies as the ones that have been developed within the EU FP6 project PRIME (Privacy and Identity Management for Europe) [14]. The PRIME architecture supports strong privacy by default by anonymizing the underlying communication and achieving data minimization on application level by the use of anonymous credential protocols. Besides, privacy presentation and negotiation tools, privacy authorization language for enforcing negotiated policies, and tools allowing users to "track" and access their data that they released to remote services sides, ensure the technical enforcement of all privacy requirements mentioned in the section above.

4. TRADITIONAL PRIVACY GOALS OF PRIVACY-ENHANCING TECHNOLOGIES (PETS)

In this section, privacy goals for achieving data minimization are defined, which we call "traditional privacy goals, as early PETs that were developed already in the eighties

---

3. German Constitutional Court, Census decision, 1983 (BVerfGE 65, 1).

followed these goals. Data minimization as an abstract strategy describes the avoidance of unnecessary or unwanted data disclosures. The most fundamental information that can be disclosed about an individual is who he is (an identifier, or which observable events he is related to). If this information can be kept secret, the individual remains anonymous. Pfitzmann and Hansen, who pioneered the technical privacy research terminology, define anonymity as follows: Anonymity of a subject means that the subject is not identifiable within a set of subjects, the anonymity set [15].

By choosing the term "subject," Pfitzmann and Hansen aim to define the term anonymity as general as possible. The subject can be any entity defined by facts (names or identifiers), or causing observable events (by sending messages). If an adversary cannot narrow down the sender of a specific message to less than two possible senders, the actual sender of the message remains anonymous. The two or more possible senders in question form the anonymity set. The anonymity set, and particularly its size, will be the first privacy metrics discussed in the Section 5.

An adversary that discovers the relation between a fact or event and a subject identifies the subject. Relations cannot only exist between facts or events and subjects, but may exist between facts, actions, and subjects. An adversary, may for instance, discover that two messages have been sent by the same subject, without knowing this subject. The two messages would be part of the equivalence relation [16] which is formed by all messages that have been sent by the same subject. Knowing this equivalence relation (and maybe even others) helps the adversary to identify the subject. Pfitzmann and Hansen define the inability of the adversary to discover these equivalence relations as unlinkability: Unlinkability of two or more items of interest [IOIs (subjects, messages, actions), …] from an attacker's perspective means that within the system (comprising these and possibly other items), the attacker cannot sufficiently distinguish whether these IOIs are related or not [15]. A special type of unlinkability is the unlinkability of a sender and recipient of a message (or so-called relationship anonymity), which means that the relation of who is communicating with whom is kept secret.

Data minimization can also be implemented through obfuscating the presence of facts and events. The idea is that adversaries who are unable to detect the presence of facts or events cannot link them to subjects. Pfitzmann and Hansen define this privacy goal as undetectability: Undetectability of an IOI from an attacker's perspective, means that the attacker cannot sufficiently distinguish whether it exists or not [15].

The strongest privacy goal in data minimization is unobservability, which combines undetectability and anonymity. Unobservability of an item of IOI means:

- Undetectability of the IOI against all subjects uninvolved in it; and
- Anonymity of the subject(s) involved in the IOI even against the other subject(s) involved in that IOI [15].

The third and last way to implement data minimization, apart from obfuscating the facts, the events (undetectability, unobservability), or the relation between them and the subjects (unlinkability), is the use of pseudonyms in the place of subjects. Pseudonyms may be random numbers, e-mail addresses, or (cryptographic) certificates, etc. In order to minimize the disclosed information, pseudonyms must not be linkable to the subject. The corresponding privacy goal is pseudonymity: Pseudonymity is the use of pseudonyms as identifiers [15].

Pseudonymity is related to anonymity as both concepts aim at protecting the real identity of a subject. The use of pseudonyms, however, allows to maintain a reference to the subject's real identity (for accountability purposes [17]). A trusted third party could, for instance, reveal the real identities of misbehaving pseudonymous users. Pseudonymity also enables a user to link certain actions under one pseudonym. For instance, a user could reuse the same pseudonym in an online auction system (such as eBay) for building up a reputation.

The degree of anonymity protection provided by pseudonyms depends on the amount of personal data of the pseudonym holder that can be linked to the pseudonym, and on how often the pseudonym is used in various contexts/for various transactions. The best privacy protection can be achieved if for each transaction a new so-called transaction pseudonym is used that is unlinkable to any other transaction pseudonyms and at least initially unlinkable to any other personal data items of its holder (see also [15]).

5. PRIVACY METRICS

Privacy metrics aim to quantify the effectiveness of schemes or technologies with regard to the privacy goals defined in the previous section. A simple metrics for measuring anonymity is the anonymity set [15]. The anonymity set comprises all subjects that may have caused an event that is observed by the adversary. The subjects in the set cover up for each other against the adversary. The adversary can thus not hold a single subject responsible for the observed event as long as the set size of the anonymity set is greater than one. Greater set sizes are useful for protecting against (stronger) adversaries that would accept false positives up to a certain threshold among the subjects that are held responsible. In this case, the set size has to exceed such a threshold.

The anonymity set size is also related to the metrics in k-anonymity [18]. K-anonymity is defined as a property or a requirement for databases that must not leak sensitive private information, and was also applied as a anonymity metrics in location-based services [19] and in Voice over Internet Protocol (VoIP) [20,21]. The underlying assumption is that database tables store two kinds of attributes, the first kind is identifying information, and the second is sensitive information. The claim is that the database table is anonymous if every search for identifying information results in a group of at least k candidate records. The k in k-anonymity is thus the privacy parameter which determines the minimum group size. Groups of candidate records form anonymity sets of identifiers in the database table.

The k-anonymity as a privacy property and k as a metrics are not undisputed. In particular, the fact that k-anonymity only depends on the identifying information in the database table (it is independent of the sensitive information), leads to remaining privacy risks [22]. A simple attack building on the k-anonymity's blindness for sensitive information is described in [23]. The trick is to search for candidate groups where the sensitive attribute has a constant value for all candidates. The sensitive attribute value is immediately disclosed for all records in the candidate group, thus, privacy is breached. A solution to these risks is a new privacy property, l-diversity, with the privacy parameter l. The claim of l-diversity is that a database table is anonymous if the diversity of sensitive attribute values is at least l (>1) in every candidate group. In some cases, l-diversification would not sufficiently protect from attribute disclosure or would be too difficult to establish. A third property, t-closeness [24], is solving this problem. T-closeness restricts the distribution of sensitive information within a candidate group. The claim is that a database table is anonymous if the distribution of sensitive information within each candidate group differs from the table's distribution at most up to a threshold t.

All these privacy metrics with the exception of the anonymity set are tailored to static database tables. Changes in the dataset are possible, but the privacy properties have to be reestablished afterward. T-closeness as one of the latest developed properties in this category is a close relative to information-theoretic privacy metrics. Information-theoretic metrics measure the information that an adversary learns by observing an event or a system (all observable events in a communication system). The information always depends on the knowledge the adversary had before his observation, the a priori knowledge. Knowledge is expressed as a probability distribution over the events. For a discrete set of events

$X = \{x_1, x_2, \ldots, x_n\}$ and the probability mass function Pr: $X \rightarrow [0,1]$, Shannon [25] defines the self-information of x_i, $1 \leq i \leq n$, as

$$I(x_i) = -\log_2 \Pr(x_i).$$

The self-information $I(x_i)$ is what an adversary learns when he observes the event x_i with his a priori knowledge about all possible events encoded in the probability mass function Pr. The self-information takes the minimal value zero for $\Pr(x_i) = 1$ (the adversary will learn minimal information from observing x_i), if he is a priori certain that x_i will be observed. The self-information approaches infinity for $\Pr(x_i) \rightarrow 0$(the more information the adversary learns), the less likely the observed events are. The expected self-information of a system with the events X is the entropy of the system. Shannon defines the entropy as

$$H(X) = \sum_{x_i \in X} \Pr(x_i) \cdot I(x_i).$$

The entropy is maximal when the distribution of all events is uniform ($\Pr(x_i) = \frac{1}{n}$ for all $1 \leq i \leq n$). The maximal entropy is thus

$$H_{max} = -\log_2 \frac{1}{n} = \log_2 n.$$

The entropy is minimal when one event x_i is perfectly certain ($\Pr(x_i) = 1$ and $\Pr(x_j) = 0$ for all $x_j \in X$ and $x_j \neq x_i$). The "degree of anonymity" is the entropy of the communication system in question [26,27]. This degree of anonymity measures the anonymity of message's sender within the communication system. When the adversary learns the actual sender of the message, he will learn the self-information $I(x_i)$ where each $x_i \in X$ encodes the fact that one specific subject is the sender of the message. The probability distribution Pr encodes the a priori knowledge of the adversary about the sender. A uniform distribution (maximal entropy), indicates minimal a priori knowledge (maximal sender anonymity). Absolute certainty, on the other hand (minimal entropy), indicates perfect a priori knowledge (minimal sender anonymity). The degree of anonymity can be used to compare communication systems with different features (numbers of subjects) when normalized [26] with max entropy H_{max} and otherwise without normalization [27].

The same entropy-based metrics can be applied to measure the anonymity provided by facts about a subject [28]. The adversary's a priori knowledge, encoded in the probability mass function Pr, comprises how well a feature vector with facts about a subject fits to each subject $x_i \in X$. The adversary learns the self-information $I(x_i)$ when learning that the feature vector applies to the subject x_i. The entropy $H(X)$ can be seen as the confusion of the adversary before he learns the subject that the feature vector is applying to.

The entropy can be used to calculate the expected anonymity set size, which is $2^{H(X)}$. The expected anonymity set size is equal to the anonymity set size, if Pr corresponds to the uniform distribution (if the message [26,27] or feature vector [28] is not more or less linkable to one subject than to any other subject in X). The anonymity set size can be seen as an overestimation of the expected anonymity set size, if Pr does not correspond to the uniform distribution (some subjects are more linkable than others in the anonymity set). In this case, the expected anonymity set size or the degree of anonymity is the more accurate metrics.

Metrics that are based on entropy have the disadvantage that the a priori knowledge Pr of the adversary has to be known when evaluating the metrics. When this a priori knowledge can be derived from publicly available observations (message routing data in a network [26,27]), the metrics are easy to apply. If the Pr depends on personal information which is not available to nonadversaries [28], the metrics are hard to evaluate without additional tools being effective (legal transparency tools).

6. DATA MINIMIZATION TECHNOLOGIES

In this section, we will present the most relevant PETs for minimizing data on both communication and application level. It is important to note that applications (such as eCommerce applications) can only be designed and used anonymously if their users cannot be identified on a communication level (via their IP addresses). Hence, anonymous communication is a prerequisite for achieving anonymity, more generally or data minimization, on application level.

Anonymous Communication

Already in 1981, David Chaum presented the Mix net protocol for anonymous communication, which has become the fundamental concept for many practical anonymous communication technologies that have been broadly used for many years. In this section, we will provide an overview to anonymous communication technologies that we think are most relevant from a practical and a scientific point of view.

DC Network

David Chaum's Dining Cryptographer (DC) network protocol [29] is an anonymous communication protocol, which is, even though it cannot be easily used in practice, still very interesting from a scientific perspective. It provides unconditional sender anonymity, recipient anonymity, and unobservability, even if we assume a global adversary who can observe all communication in the network, and hence, it can guarantee the strongest anonymity properties of all known anonymous communication protocols. DC nets are based on binary superposed sending. Before any message can be sent, each participant in the network (user station) has to exchange via a secure channel a random bit stream with at least one other user station. These random bit streams serve as secret keys and are at least as long as the messages to be sent. For each single sending step (round), every user station adds modulo 2 (superposes) all the key bits it shares and its message bit, if there is one. Stations that do not wish to transmit messages send zeros by outputting the sums of their key bits (without any inversions). The sums are sent over the net and added up modulo 2. The result, which is broadcasted to all user stations, is the sum of all sent message bits, because every key bit was added twice (see Fig. 53.1). If exactly one participant transmits a message, the message is successfully broadcasted as the result of the global sum to each participant. Collisions are easily detected (as the message sent by a user and the one which is broadcasted back to him will be different) and have to be resolved, for example, by retransmitting the message after a random number of rounds.

In theory, superposed sending provides in the information-theoretic sense perfect (unconditional) sender anonymity and unobservability, as the fact that someone is sending a meaningful message (and not only zeros) is hidden by a one-time pad encryption. From a metrics perspective, all senders in the DC network form the

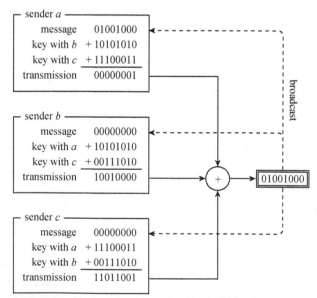

FIGURE 53.1 A Dining Cryptographer (DC) network with three users. Sender "a" sends a message, but from observing the communication in the network alone. The adversary cannot tell whether it was sent by a, b, or c (and not even if a meaningful message was sent at all).

anonymity set. No user is more likely to be the sender of the message than any other user for an outside adversary. Perfect recipient anonymity can be achieved by reliable broadcast. However, the DC network and the one-time pad share the same practical shortcomings which have prevented that they can be broadly used: the security of DC networks depends on the perfect randomness of keys and the secure distribution of keys. Moreover, each key is to be used only once and the keys need to be perfectly unavailable to the adversary (the adversary may not get hold of the keys before or after the message has been sent).

Mix Nets

Mix nets [13] are more practical than DC networks, but do not provide security against adversaries with unlimited resources. Nevertheless, most anonymity networks (Mixmaster, Tor, Onion Routing, and AN.ON), build on the mix net concept. A mix is a relay or proxy server that performs four steps to hide the relation between incoming and outgoing messages (see Fig. 53.2):

1. Duplicates (replayed messages) are discarded. Without this functionality, an adversary could launch a replay attack by sending two identical messages, which will be forwarded as two identical output messages by the mix. The adversary could thus link these messages and therefore "bridge over" the mix.
2. All messages are (randomly) delayed (by temporarily storing them in a buffer). Without this functionality (if messages were immediately forwarded), the anonymity set for one message would be reduced to one sender (no anonymity at all).
3. All messages are recoded. This is usually done by cryptography. Without this functionality, the adversary could link the input with the output messages by comparing the contents of the messages.
4. The sending sequence of delayed messages is determined independently of the receiving sequence. Without the delay and reordering of messages, an adversary could link the input to the output messages by a time correlation attack (he could be sure that the first message in is the first message out).

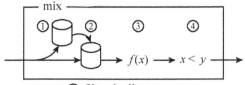

① filter duplicates
② delay messages
③ recode messages
④ reorder messages

FIGURE 53.2 Processing steps within a mix.

5. Mixes can be used to achieve unlinkability of sender and recipient, sender anonymity as well as recipient anonymity. For achieving the latter two properties, different recoding functions are used. For providing sender anonymity, asymmetric cryptography is used. The mix user (or more precisely his machine) encrypts the message m with the public key e_R of the recipient and achieves $enc_{e_R}(m)$. He then encrypts $enc_{e_R}(m)$ together with the address of the recipient and a nonce with public key e_1 of the mix and sends the resulting message $enc_{e_1}(r_1, A_R, enc_{e_R}(m))$ to the mix. Adding the nonce is necessary to achieve nondeterministic encryption, which prevents that an adversary can monitor the output message $enc_{e_R}(m)$ and address A_R of the recipient and then simply encrypt both values with the public key of the mix and compare it with the messages that were sent to the mix. Moreover, it prevents the mix from discarding one of two messages when identical contents are intended to be sent. The mix decrypts the message with its private key, discards the nonce and sends $enc_{e_R}(m)$ to the address A_R of the recipient.

6. Using a single mix can only provide anonymity if it is fully trustworthy and cannot be compromised. For improving security, several mixes can be used in a chain or a "cascade." Let us assume that the sender (or more precisely his machine) choses a chain of n mixes with addresses A_i and public keys e_i, $i = 1...n$. The sender will first add layers of encryptions using the public keys of the mixes in the path in reverse order. Each layer includes the message to be forwarded by the mix, the address to which the message should be sent (next mix in the chain or the final recipient) plus a nonce to be discarded. The resulting message $enc_{e_1}(r_1, A_2, enc_{e_2}(...enc_{e_n}(r_n, A_R, enc_{e_R}(m))...))$ is sent to the first mix (with the address A_1). Each mix on the path decrypts the message with its privacy key, and thereby gets a nonce that is discarded as well as an encrypted message and address to which it sends this message. The last mix in the path finally sends $enc_{e_R}(m)$ to the recipient. Unlinkability of sender and recipient can in principle be provided also in presence of an adversary who monitors all communication lines, as long as the crypto operations cannot be broken and one mix in the path is trustworthy (one mix which is not controlled by the adversary). Fig. 53.3 illustrates how sender anonymity can be achieved with a path consisting of two mixes.

For achieving recipient anonymity, symmetric cryptography is used as recoding function[4]. The recipient first

---

4. In the following, we will use capital letters and curly brackets for the symmetric encryption function ENC.

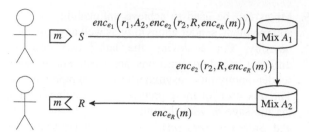

FIGURE 53.3 Sender anonymity with two mixes.

chooses a sequence of n mixes with addresses A_i and public keys e_i, $i = 1...n$, a sequence of m symmetric encryption keys k_j, $j = 0...n$, and a label L_R and creates an anonymous return address $R_S = (k_0, A_1, R_1)$, which contains a symmetric key k_0, the address of the first mix A_1 in the chain and another anonymous return address R_1, which is calculated according to the following scheme:

$$R_j = enc_{e_i}(k_j, A_{j+1}, R_{j+1}) \text{ for } j = 1...n,$$

where A_{n+1} is the address of the recipient and $R_{n+1} = L_R$.

The recipient makes the anonymous return address available to the sender, who uses key k_0 to encrypt his message m. The encrypted message $ENC_{k_0}\{m\}$ is then sent along with the return address R_1 to the first mix A_1. The first mix decrypts $R_1 = enc_{e_i}(k_1, A_2, R_2)$, encrypts $ENC_{k_0}\{m\}$ with the symmetric key k_1, and sends the encrypted message $ENC_{k_1}\{ENC_{k_0}\{m\}\}$ along with R_2 to the next mix with the address A_2. This is repeated for all mixes along the path. The last mix in the path finally forwards $ENC_{k_n}\{...ENC_{k_1}\{ENC_{k_0}\{m\}\}...\}$ and L_R to the recipient. The label L_R of the return address indicates to the recipient which sequence of symmetric keys he has to use to decrypt the message.

The two schemes above provide either sender or recipient anonymity. By combining both schemes, it is possible for two communication partners to communicate anonymously in both directions. Suppose that Alice anonymously sends a message including an anonymous return address to a discussion forum. Bob can then anonymously send his reply via a self-chosen sequence of mixes to the first mix used in the anonymous return address. If Bob's message also contains an anonymous return address, Alice can reply as well in the same manner. Thus, Alice and Bob can communicate without knowing each other's identities.

The mix net protocol was invented by Chaum back in 1981 for high-latency communication such as e-mail communication. In the mid-nineties, when interactive Internet services became broadly used, low-latency anonymous communication protocols were developed. The most broadly used low-latency protocols AN.ON and Onion Routing/Tor, which are based on the mix net concept, will be briefly presented in the next sections.

AN.ON

AN.ON [30] is an anonymity service which was developed and operated since the late nineties at the Technical University of Dresden. As it aims at providing a network of mixes for low-latency traffic routing, symmetric cryptography is replacing asymmetric cryptography where possible (asymmetric cryptography is only used to exchange symmetric session keys between mixes and users). Moreover, low latency requires that message delays are reduced, and in fact, AN.ON mixes implement practically no message delay. The downside of reducing delays is that the size of the message buffer in the mixes and thus the anonymity set decreases. In order to increase the size of anonymity sets, AN.ON provides standard routes through the mix network, the so-called mix cascades. A mix cascade typically contains a sequence of two or three mixes and every message sent to the cascade runs through the mixes in the same order as any other message sent to the same cascade. Predefined and stable mix cascades have a number of advantages over dynamic routing:

1. Mixes can be audited and certified with regard to their performance, their geographical position, the legislation in which they operate, and the operator (the company or the governmental institution operating the mix infrastructure).
2. Cascades can be designed to cross different nations, different legislations, and different operators in order to enjoy the protection of the most liberal regulation; they can also be designed to provide a certain performance.
3. Security measures focus on a small number of mixes while the costs can be distributed to a large number of users.

The disadvantages of implementing mix cascades include:

1. Each mix is a possible bottleneck and thus needs to provide a stable and high bandwidth installation, as one mix going offline stops all cascades in which it was involved.
2. Setting up and operating mixes is expensive due to the considerable organizational overhead for establishing mix cascades and due to the high performance requirements.

Onion Routing/Tor

Onion routing [31] is a low-latency mix-based routing protocol, which was developed in the nineties at the Naval Research Laboratory. It provides anonymous socket connections by means of proxy servers. Onion Routing uses the mix net concept of layers of public key encryption (the so-called "onion") to build up an anonymous bidirectional virtual circuit between communication partners. The initiator's proxy (for the service being requested) constructs a "forward onion," which encapsulates a series of routing nodes ("mixes") forming a path to the responder, and sends it with a create command to the first node. Each layer of the onion is encrypted with the public key of each node on the path and contains symmetric crypto function/key pairs as a payload. After sending the onion, the anonymous path is established and the initiator's proxy sends data through this anonymous connection. The symmetric function/key pairs are applied by each node on the path to crypt data that will be sent along the virtual circuit. All information (onions, data, and network control) are sent through the Onion Routing network in uniform-seized cells. All cells arriving at an onion router within a fixed time interval are mixed together to reduce correlation by network insiders. Reply onions, which correspond to untraceable return addresses, allow for a responder to send back anonymously a reply after its original circuit is broken.

Since individual routing nodes in each circuit only know the identities of adjacent nodes, and since the nodes further encrypt multiplexed virtual circuits, traffic analysis is made difficult. However, if the first node behind the initiator's proxy and the last node of the circuit cooperate, they will be able to determine the source and recipient of communication through the number of cells sent over this circuit or through the duration for that the virtual circuit was used.

Tor [32], the second-generation of onion routing, has added several improvements. In particular, it provides forward secrecy, (once that the session keys are deleted, they cannot be obtained any longer), even if all communication has been wiretapped the long-term secret keys of the onion routers ("mixes") become compromised. Therefore, instead of using hybrid encryption for distributing symmetric session keys, the Diffie-Hellman key negotiation protocol is used, which provides forward secrecy. The sender and the first onion router OR_1 exchange random bits as session keys and use the Diffie-Hellman handshake of the TLS connection (Fig. 53.4). The symmetric session key shared by the first onion router OR_1 with the second onion router OR_2 is negotiated by means of a separate Diffie-Hellman handshake. The first half of the handshake g^{x_2} is encrypted with the public key of OR_2 (to prevent man in the middle attacks) and $enc_{OR_2}(g^{x_2})$ is then sent through OR_1 to OR_2 (Fig. 53.5). On the transport from the sender to OR_1, the message is protected by encryption with the symmetric key k_1. The onion router OR_2 replies to OR_1 with the second half of the handshake (g^{y_2} and a hash over the negotiated session key $k_2 = g^{x_2 y_2}$. OR_1 encrypts the reply of OR_2 with the session key k_1 and forwards the reply to the sender). Only the sender and OR_1 are now in possession of k_1 and only the sender and OR_2 are now in possession of k_2. The communication between sender and OR_2 can now be encrypted with k_2. Once a circuit has been established, the symmetric encryption with the negotiated session keys is applied by each node on the path to crypt data that will be sent along the circuit (Figs. 53.6 and 53.7). The advantages of Tor over AN.ON are as follows:

1. Tor provides forward secrecy.
2. It is easy to setup new onion routers ("mixes"), which are run by many volunteers all over the world.
3. There are lower performance requirements for each "mix".
4. Each mix is a possible bottleneck, however in Tor, "mixes" that do not perform can be excluded from the dynamic routing.

The disadvantages include:

1. Anyone can setup "mixes" independent of their performance (bandwidth, latency, security).
2. There is no audit or certification, thus a lack of reliable data about legislation and operator.

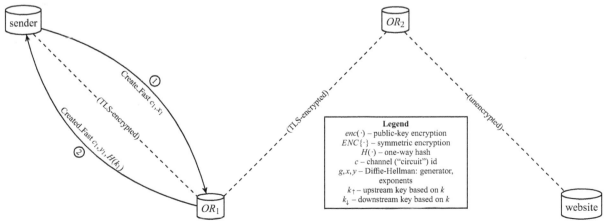

FIGURE 53.4 Tor circuit construction (1) fast create [32].

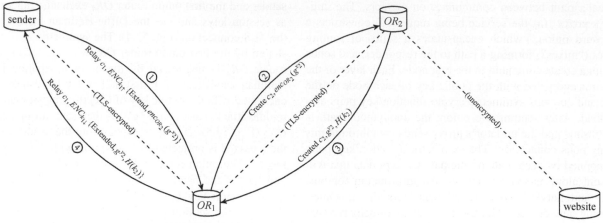

FIGURE 53.5 Tor circuit construction (2) extend/create [32].

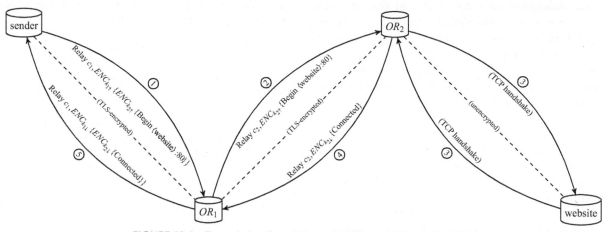

FIGURE 53.6 Transmission Control Protocol (TCP) handshake via Tor [32].

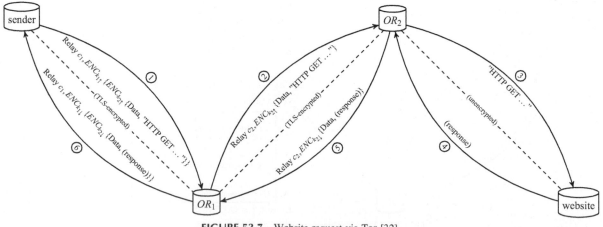

FIGURE 53.7 Website request via Tor [32].

3. Bridging the "mixes" and thus breaching anonymity by controlling the entry node and the exit node is easier for adversaries, since they can easily setup their own new nodes. In particular, an adversary can easily try to attract user traffic by establishing a few well-performing exit nodes and a lot of stable intermediate mix nodes that eventually become entry nodes [33].

Data Minimization at Application Level

Even if the communication channel is anonymized, users can still reveal personal and identifying data on application level—often, users have to reveal more personal data than needed. Hence, data minimization techniques are also needed on the application level. Many of such data minimization techniques are based on cryptographic protocols (see also [34] for an overview). The classical types of privacy-protecting cryptography which have already been applied for decades are of course encryption schemes themselves. However, there are a number of more recent crypto schemes for protecting data and authenticating information, which are variations or extensions of basic crypto schemes, with "surprising properties" that can offer in many cases better data minimization properties [34]. In this chapter, some of the most relevant examples of — mainly cryptographic—mechanisms for protecting privacy at application level will be given.

Blind Signatures and Anonymous eCash

Blind signatures are an extension of digital signatures and provide privacy by allowing someone to obtain a signature from a signer on a document without the signer seeing the actual content of the "blinded" document that he is signing. Hence, if the signer is later presented with the signed "unblinded" document, he cannot relate it with the signing session and with the person on behalf whom he has signed the document. Blind signatures were invented by David Chaum as a basic building block for anonymous eCash. They can be also use to achieve anonymity of other applications, such as eVoting, and are also used as basic building block for other privacy crypto protocols, such as anonymous credentials.

David Chaum has invented protocols based on blind signatures [11,35,36], which allow electronic money to flow perfectly tracelessly from the back through consumer and merchant before returning to the bank. Chaum's cryptographic "online" payment protocol based on blind signatures can be summarized as follows (see also Fig. 53.8):

Let (e, n) be the bank's private key indicating a certain value of a signature under this key (in this example: one dollar) and (d, n) the bank's public key[5]. f is a suitable one-way function. Electronic money has the form $(x, f(x)^d$

$(mod\ n))$, where the one-way function is needed to prevent forgery of electronic money (see also [37] for more explanations):

1. The customer Alice (his computer) first generates a bank note number x (of at least 100 digits) at random and (in essence) multiplies it with a blinding factor r, which he has also chosen at random: $B = r^e \cdot f(x) (mod\, n)$. He then signs the blinded bank note number with his private key and sends it to the bank.

2. The bank verifies and removes Alice's signature. Then, it signs the blinded note (and thereby creates the blinded signature) with its "worth one dollar" signature: $B^d(mod\ n) = (r^e \cdot f(x))^d(mod\ n) = r \cdot f(x)^d(mod\ n)$. The bank then withdraws one dollar from his account and returns the note with the blind signature.

3. Alice divides out the blinding factor and thereby extracts: $C = \frac{B^d}{r}(mod\, n) = f(x)^d(mod\ n)$ from B. For paying the online merchant Bob one dollar, Alice sends him the pair $(x, f(x)^d\ (mod\ n))$.

4. Bob verifies the bank's signature and immediately contacts the bank for verifying that the note has not already been spent.

5. The bank verifies it signature, checks the note against a list of those notes already spent and credits Bob's account by one dollar.

The blind signature scheme provides (unconditional) anonymity of the electronic money: even if the bank and the merchant cooperate, they cannot determine who spent the notes. Since the bank does not know the blinding factors, it cannot correlate the note it was signing blindly for Alice with the note that was spent (however, Alice's identity is only protected, if he also uses an anonymized communication channel and if he does not reveal personally identifying information, such as a personal delivery address).

In addition to the online eCash protocol version (where the bank needs to be constantly online for checking whether notes have already been spent), a protocol for offline electronic money is presented by Chaum [28]. With the offline protocol, a user remains unconditionally anonymous as long as he spends each bank note only once. If, however, a note is spent twice, the bank will get enough information to identify the spender's account. Disappointingly, there has been a lack of adoption of anonymous eCash (attempts of commercial deployment of Chaum's schemes failed in the late nineties) and today, there are still no widely deployed anonymous electronic payment services.

Zero-Knowledge Proofs

A zero-knowledge proof is defined as an interactive proof, in which a prover can prove to a verifier that a statement is true without revealing anything else than the veracity of the

---

5. Using the RSA encryption scheme.

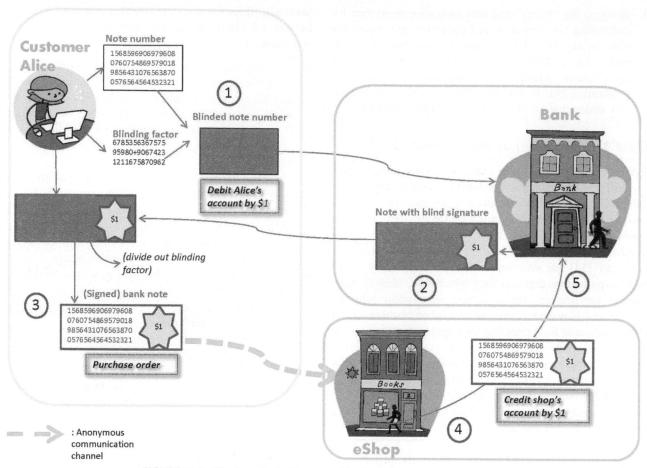

FIGURE 53.8 The flow of eCash's untraceable electronic money (see also [36]).

statement. Zero-knowledge proofs were first presented in 1985 by Goldwasser [38]. The following three properties must be fulfilled by a zero-knowledge proof:

1. *Completeness*: if the statement is true, the honest verifier will be convinced of this fact by an honest prover.
2. *Soundness*: if the statement is false, no cheating prover can convince the honest verifier that it is true, except with some very small probability.
3. *Zero-knowledge*: if the statement is true, no cheating verifier learns anything other than this fact.

Zero-knowledge proofs are building blocks for data minimizing technologies, such as anonymous credential systems. The anonymous credential protocol IdeMix is, for example, based on proofs of knowledge, in which a prover proofs that that he knows a secret value or that he is able to solve some number theoretic problem, which would contradict the assumption that the problem cannot be solved by a polynomially bounded Turing machine.

Anonymous Credentials

A traditional credential (often also called certificate or attribute certificate) is a set of personal attributes, such as

birth date, name, or personal number, signed (and thereby certified) by the certifying party (the so-called issuer), and bound to its owner by cryptographic means (by requiring the user's secret key to use the credential). In terms of privacy, the use of (traditional or anonymous) credentials is better than the direct request to the certifying party, as this prevents the certifying party from profiling the user. Traditional credentials require, however, that all attributes are disclosed together if the user wants to prove certain properties, so that the verifier can check the issuer's signature. This makes different uses of the same credential linkable to each other. Besides, the verifier and issuer can link the different uses of the user's credential to the issuing of the credential.

Anonymous credentials (also called private certificates) were first introduced by Chaum [11] and later enhanced by Brands [39] and by Camenisch and Lysyanskaya [40] and have stronger privacy properties than traditional credentials. Microsoft's U-Prove technology based on Brands' protocols and IBM's IdeMix technology based on the credential protocols by Camenisch et al. are currently the practically most relevant anonymous credential technologies.

Anonymous credentials allow the user to essentially "transform" the certificate into a new one that contains only a subset of attributes of the original certificate (it allows proving only a subset of its attributes to a verifier—selective disclosure property). Instead of revealing the exact value of an attribute, anonymous credential systems also enable the user in the transformation to apply any mathematical function to the (original) attribute value, allowing him to prove only attribute properties without revealing the attribute itself. Besides with the IdeMix protocol by Camenisch et al., the issuer's signature is also transformed in such a way that the signature in the new certificate cannot be linked to the original signature of the issuer [34]. Hence, different credential uses cannot be linked by the verifier and/or issuer (unlinkability property). Cryptographically speaking, with IdeMix, the user is basically using a zero-knowledge proof to convince the verifier of possessing a signature generated by the issuer on a statement containing the subset of attributes.

Fig. 53.9 provides an example scenario how data minimization can be achieved in an identity management online transaction: First, user Alice obtains an anonymous driving license credential issued by the Swedish Road authority (the so-called identity provider) with personal attributes typically stored in the license including her birth date. Later, he would like to purchase a video from an online shop (the so-called relying party, which is also the verifier in this scenario), which is only permitted for adults. After sending a service request, the online shop will answer her with a data request for a proof that he is older than 18. Alice can now take advantage of the selective disclosure

feature of the anonymous credential protocol to prove with her credential just the fact that he is older than 18 without revealing her birth date or any other attributes of her credential. If Alice later wants to purchase another video which is only permitted for adults at the same video online shop, he can use the same anonymous credential for a proof that he is over 18. If the IdeMix protocol is used, the video shop is unable to recognize that the two proofs are based on the same credential. Hence, the two rental transactions cannot be linked to the same person.

Private Information Retrieval

Private Information Retrieval (PIR) allows a user to retrieve an item (record) from a database server without revealing which item he is interested in (privacy of the item of interest is provided). A typical application example is a patent database, from which inventors would like to retrieve information without revealing their interests. A trivial approach would be to simply download the entire database and to make a local selection, which would be too costly, bandwidth-wise. In [41], one of the first PIR solutions was introduced, which requires the existence of $t+1$ non-cooperating identical database servers (with n records each). To each server, one n-bit query vector (out of a set of $t+1$ query vectors) is sent via an encrypted channel, where each bit represents one record of the queried database: if the bit is one then the record is selected, otherwise not. The user creates t of the query vectors randomly. The remaining $t+1^{st}$ vector is calculated by (exclusive operator) XOR-ing (superposing) all random vectors and flipping the bit

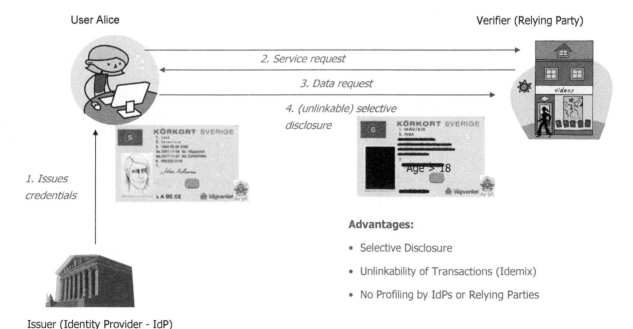

User Alice   **Verifier (Relying Party)**

2. Service request

3. Data request

4. (unlinkable) selective disclosure

1. Issues credentials

Age > 18

Advantages:

• Selective Disclosure

• Unlinkability of Transactions (Idemix)

• No Profiling by IdPs or Relying Parties

Issuer (Identity Provider - IdP)

FIGURE 53.9 Example for achieving data minimization for an online transaction by the use of anonymous credentials.

representing the record of interest. To each database, one of the query vectors is sent. All selected records are superposed (XOR-ed). The result is exactly the requested database item. If each of the bits in the t random query vectors are set to 1 with a probability of 0.5, then an adversary who has access to at most t of the requests or responses associated with the query vectors will gain no information about the database item that the user is retrieving.

A disadvantage of a multidatabase solution is however that several identical databases must be obtained. Especially updates are complex, as changes should take place simultaneously. Besides information-theoretic PIR scheme with database replication, several single-database (computational) PIR schemes have been subsequently developed and advanced (see for instance [42,43] for surveys and references). Oblivious transfer [43] is private information retrieval, where additionally the user may not learn any item other than the one that he requested.

7. TRANSPARENCY-ENHANCING TOOLS

As we elaborated, transparency is a basic legal principle. Moreover, it is also an important social trust factor, as trust in an application can be enhanced if procedures are clear, transparent and reversible, so that users feel in control [44]. Transparency-enhancing technologies provide tools to the end users, or their proxies acting on behalf of the user's interests (such as data protection commissioners), for making personal data processing more transparent to them.

Classification

Transparency-enhancing tools (TETs) for privacy purposes can be classified into categories as follows (see also [45]):

1. TETs that provide information about the intended data collection and processing to the data subject, in order to enhance the data subject's privacy.
2. TETs that provide the data subject with an overview of what personal data have been disclosed to which data controller under which policies.
3. TETs that provide the data subject, or his proxy, online access to his personal data, to information on how his data have been processed and whether this was in line with privacy laws and/or negotiated policies, and/or to the logic of data processing in order to enhance the data subject's privacy.
4. TETs that provide "counter profiling" capabilities to the data subject, helping his to "guess" how his data match relevant group profiles, which may affect his future opportunities or risks.

TETs of the first and last categories are also called ex ante TETs, as they provide transparency of any intended data processing to the data subjects before they are releasing any personal data. TETs of the second and third categories provide transparency in regard to the processing of personal data, which the user has already disclosed, and are therefore called ex post TETs.

Ex Ante Transparency-Enhancing Tools

Examples of ex ante TETs are privacy policy languages tool and Human Computer Interaction (HCI) components that make privacy policies of services sides more transparent, such as the Platform for Privacy Preferences (P3P) language [46] and P3P user agents, such as the privacy bird[6]. P3P enables websites to express their privacy policy (basically stating what data are requested by whom, for what purposes and how long the data will be retained) in a standard (machine-readable XML) format that can be retrieved automatically and interpreted easily by user agents and matched with the user's privacy preferences. Thus, P3P user agents enable users to be better informed of a Website's data handling practices (in both machine- and human-readable formats).

Recently developed visualization technique for displaying P3P-based privacy policies are based on the metaphor of a "Nutrition Label" assuming that people already understand other nutrition, warning and energy labeling, which consequently can also allow users to find and digest policy-related information with a proposed privacy label design more accurately and quickly (see [47]).

A more advanced policy language, the PrimeLife Policy Language (PPL), was developed in the EU FP7 project PrimeLife [48]. PPL is a language to specify not only privacy policies of data controllers but also of third parties to whom (so-called downstream controllers) to whom data are further forwarded as well as privacy preferences of users. It is based on two widespread industry standards, eXtensible Access Control Markup Language (XACML) and Security Assertions Markup Language (SAML). The data controller and downstream data controller have policies basically specifying which data are requested from the user, for which purposes and obligations (under the obligation that the data will be deleted after a certain time period). PPL allows specifying both uncertified data requests as well as certified data requests based on proofs of the possession of (anonymous IdeMix or traditional X.509) credentials that fulfill certain properties. The user's preferences allow expressing for each data item to which data controller and downstream data controllers the data can be released and how the user expects his data to be treated. The PPL engine conducts an automated matching of the data controller's policy and the user's preferences, which can result in a mutual agreement concerning the usage of data in form of a

---

6. http://www.privacybird.org/.

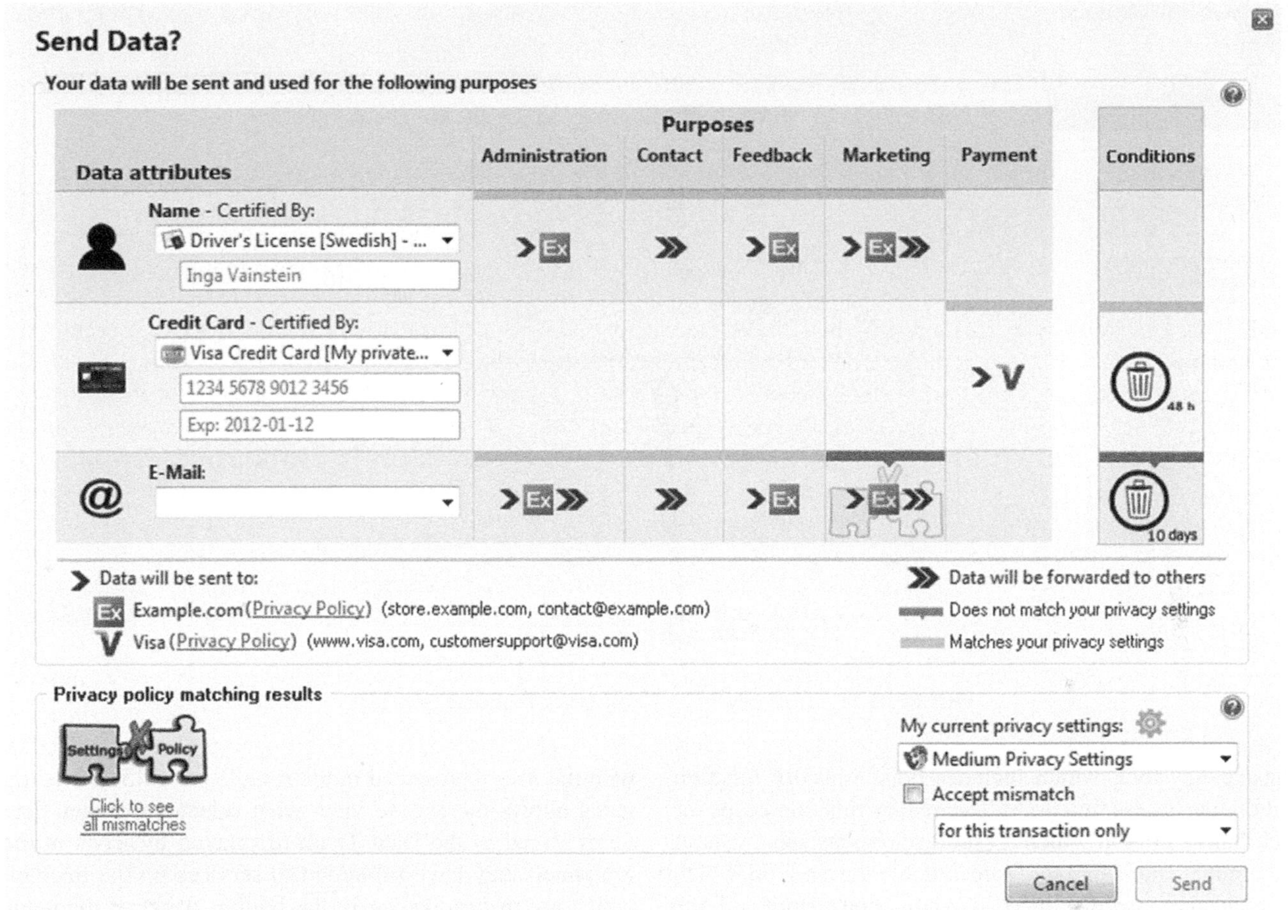

Send Data?

Your data will be sent and used for the following purposes

Purposes

| Data attributes | Administration | Contact | Feedback | Marketing | Payment | Conditions |

Name - Certified By:
Driver's License [Swedish] - ...
Inga Vainstein

Credit Card - Certified By:
Visa Credit Card [My private...]
1234 5678 9012 3456
Exp: 2012-01-12

E-Mail:

Data will be sent to:
Ex Example.com (Privacy Policy) (store.example.com, contact@example.com)
V Visa (Privacy Policy) (www.visa.com, customersupport@visa.com)

Data will be forwarded to others
Does not match your privacy settings
Matches your privacy settings

Privacy policy matching results

Settings Policy

Click to see all mismatches

My current privacy settings:
Medium Privacy Settings
Accept mismatch
for this transaction only

Cancel   Send

FIGURE 53.10 "Send Data?" PrimeLife Policy Language (PPL) user interface [50].

so-called sticky policy, which should be enforced by the access control systems at the backend sides and will "travel" with the data that are transferred to downstream controllers. The Accountability Policy Language A-PPL extends PPL by allowing users to define additional accountability obligations and rules on data retention, locations, logging and notifications [49].

As PPL has many features that P3P does not provide (downstream data controllers, credential selection for certified data, obligations), the design of usable A-PPL/PPL user interfaces provides many challenges. The "Send Data?" user interfaces for letting the PPL engine interact with the user for displaying the result of policy matches, identity/credential selection and obtaining informed consent for disclosing selected certified und uncertified data items were developed and presented [50]. Fig. 53.10 depicts an example PPL "Send Data?" dialog.

The PPL user interfaces follow the Art. 29 Data Protection Working Party recommendation of providing policy information in a multilayered format [51] for making policies more understandable and usable. According to this recommendation, a short privacy notice on the top layer offers individuals the core information required under Art.

10 EU Directive 95/46/EC, including at least the identity of the service provider and the purpose of data processing. In addition, a clear indication (in form of URLs—in our example, the "privacy policy" URLs of the two data controllers) must be given as to how the individuals can access the other layers presenting the additional information required by Art. 10 and national privacy laws.

Ex Post Transparency-Enhancing Tools[7]

An important transparency-enhancing tool falling into the categories 2 and 3 of our classification is the Data Track that has been developed in the PRIME[8],PrimeLife,[9] and A4Cloud[10] projects [52–55]. The Data Track is a user side

7. This section corresponds to some parts to Section 2.4.2 that the leading author has contributed to ENISA's study on "Privacy, Accountability and Trust — Challenges and Opportunities" published in 2011 [63].
8. EU FP6 project PRIME (Privacy and Identity Management for Europe), www.prime-project.eu.
9. EU FP7 project PrimeLife (Privacy and Identity Management for Life), www.primelife.eu.
10. EU FP7 project A4Cloud (Accountability for the Cloud), http://www.a4cloud.eu/.

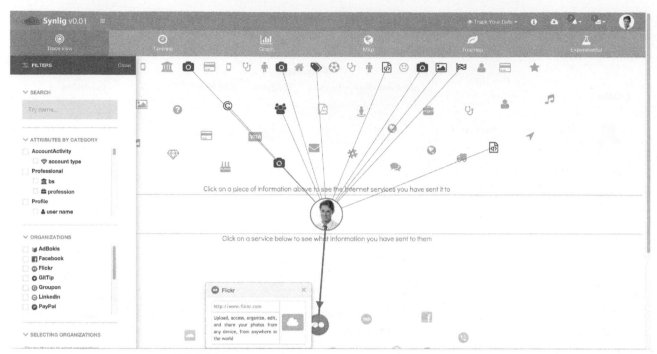

FIGURE 53.11 Trace view of the Transparency Tool Data Track [55].

transparency tool, which includes both a history function and Online access functions. The history function keeps for each transaction, in which a user discloses personal data to a communication partner, a record for the user on which personal data are disclosed to whom (the identity of the controller), for which purposes, which credentials and/or pseudonyms have been used in this context as well as the details of the negotiated or given privacy policy. These transaction records are either stored at the user side or centrally (in the Cloud—see [56]) in a secure and privacy-friendly manner. User-friendly search functionalities, which allow the user to easily get an overview about who has received what data about him/her, are included as well. The online access functions allow end users to exercise their rights to access their data at the remote services sides on-line. By this, they can compare what data have been disclosed by them to a services side with what data are still stored by the services side. This allows them to check whether data have been changed, processed or deleted (in accordance with data retention periods of the negotiated or given privacy policy). online access is granted to a user if he can provide a unique transaction ID (currently implemented as a larger random number), which is shared between the user (stored in his Data Track) and the services side for each transaction of personal data disclosure. This allows in principle also anonymous or pseudonymous users to access their data.

Within the A4Cloud project, a graphical UI was developed for the Data Track including a so-called trace view (see Fig. 53.11), which is divided into three panels

with the user represented in the middle panel [57]. The top panel allows the user to view what selected personal data items stored in the Data Track (displayed by icons in the top panel) they have submitted to services on the Internet, which are in turn shown in the bottom panel of the interface. If users click on one or many Internet service icons in the bottom panel, they will be shown arrows pointing to the icons symbolizing data items that those services have about them; in other words they can see a trace of the data that services have about them. Analogously, by selecting and clicking on icons of data items (on the top), they will be shown arrows pointing to the Internet services that have received those data items.

A user can also exercise online access functions by clicking on the cloud icon next to the service provider's logo, and see what data the service provider has actually stored about him, which it either received explicitly or implicitly from the user or derived about him. Related data tracking and control tools for end users are in contrast to the Data Track usually restricted to specific applications, cannot be used directly to track data along cloud chains or are not under complete control of the users. Examples are Mozilla's Lightbeam[11] that uses interactive visualizations to show the first and third party sites that a user is interacting with on the web, and Google Dashboard[12], which grants its users access to a summary of the data stored with a Google account

---

11. Mozilla. Lightbeam add-on for Firefox, https://www.mozilla.org/en-US/lightbeam/.
12. Google dashboard, https://www.google.com/settings/dashboard.

including account data and the users' search query history, which are however only a part of the personal data that Google processes. It does not provide any insight how these data provided by the users (the users' search queries) have subsequently been processed by Google. Besides, access is provided only to authenticated Google users.

Further examples of transparency tools that allow users to view and control how their personal data have been processed and to check whether this is in compliance with a negotiated or given privacy policy are based on secure logging systems that usually extend the Kelsey-Schneier log [58] and protect the integrity and the confidentiality of the log data. Such a secure logging system and an automated privacy audit facility are key components of a privacy evidence approach proposed by [59]. This privacy evidence system allows a user to inspect all log entries that are recording actions of that user with a special view tool and allows to send the log view created by that tool to the automated privacy audit component, which compares the log view with the privacy policy and to construct privacy evidence. This privacy evidence provides an indication to the user whether the privacy policy has been violated.

Unlinkability of log entries, which means that they should in particular not be stored in the sequence of their creation, is needed to prevent that an adversary can correlate the log with other information sources such as other external logs, which could allow him to identify data subjects to whom the entries refer (cf. [60]). Also anonymous access is needed to prevent that an adversary can observe who views which log entries and by this conclude to whom the log entries refer. Wouters et al. [61] have presented such a secure and privacy-friendly Logging for eGovernment Services. It, however, addresses unlinkability of logs between logging systems in eGovernment rather than the unlinkability of log entries within a log. Moreover, it does not address insider attacks, nor does it allow anonymous access to log entries.

Within the PrimeLife project, a secure logging system has been developed, which addresses these aspects of unlinkability of log entries and anonymous user access. In particular, it fulfills the following requirements (see [60]):

- Only the data subject can decrypt log entries after they have been committed to the log.
- A user can check the integrity of his log entries. A service provider can check the integrity of the whole log file.
- It is not possible for an attacker to secretly modify log entries, which have been committed to the log before the attacker took over the system (forward integrity).
- It is practically impossible to link log entries, which refer to the same user.
- For efficiency reasons, it should be possible for a data subject to read his log entries without the need to download and/or fully traverse the whole log database.

The need and requirements of tools which can anticipate profiles (category 4 of our definition above) have been analyzed within studies of the FIDIS project (see for instance [62]). To the best of our knowledge, there are no practical transparency-enhancing tools fulfilling the requirements. In academia, promising approaches [63,64] have been formulated and are subject of research.

8. SUMMARY

This chapter has provided an introduction to the area of Privacy-enhancing technologies. We presented the legal foundation of PETs and provided a classification of PETs as well as a selection of some of the most relevant PETs. Following the Privacy by Design paradigm, for effectively protecting privacy, privacy protection should be incorporated into the overall system design (it should be embedded throughout the entire system life cycle).

While technical PET solutions have existed for many years for solving many practical privacy issues, they have not been adopted widely by either industry or users. The main factors contributing to this problem are low demand by industry, which rather is under competitive business pressure to exploit and monetize user data, low user awareness in combination with a lack of easily usable, efficient PET implementations (see also [65]). While this chapter is contributing to a technical computer security handbook and has thus focused on the technical (and partly legal) aspects of PETs, clearly also the economic, social and usability aspects of PETs need further attention in future.

Finally, let's move on to the real interactive part of this Chapter: review questions/exercises, hands-on projects, case projects, and optional team case project. The answers and/or solutions by chapter can be found in Appendix K.

CHAPTER REVIEW QUESTIONS/ EXERCISES

True/False

1. True or False? Data protection is concerning the protection of personal data in order to guarantee privacy and is only a part of the concept of privacy.
2. True or False? Personal data processing has to be legitimate, which is according to Art. 7 EU Directive 95/46/ EC usually the case if the data subject[13] has given his ambiguous (and informed) consent, if there is a legal obligation, or contractual agreement (cf. the Collection Limitation Principle of the OECD Guidelines).
3. True or False? Personal data must be collected for specified, explicit and legitimate purposes and may be

---

13. A data subject is a person about whom personal data is processed.

further processed in a way incompatible with these purposes (Art.6 I b EU Directive 95/46/EC).

4. True or False? The processing to personal data must not be limited to data that are adequate, relevant and not excessive (Art.6 I (c) EU Directive 95/46/EC).

5. True or False? Transparency of data processing means informing a data subject about the purposes and circumstances of data processing, who is requesting personal data, how the personal data flow, where and how long the data are stored, what type of rights and controls the data subject has in regard to his personal data.

Multiple Choice

1. What needs to install appropriate technical and organizational security mechanisms to guarantee the confidentiality, integrity, and availability of personal data (Art.17 EU Directive 95/46/EC)?
   A. Privacy-enhancing technology
   B. Location technology
   C. Web-based
   D. Technical improvement
   E. Data controller

2. What can be defined as technologies that are enforcing legal privacy principles in order to protect and enhance privacy of users of information technology (IT) and/or data subjects?
   A. Information technology
   B. Location technology
   C. Web-based
   D. Privacy-enhancing technologies
   E. Web technology

3. What as an abstract strategy describes the avoidance of unnecessary or unwanted data disclosures?
   A. Data minimization
   B. XACML
   C. XML-based language
   D. Certification authority
   E. Security

4. What aim to quantify the effectiveness of schemes or technologies with regard to the privacy goals defined in the previous section.
   A. Privacy metrics
   B. Languages
   C. Privacy-Aware Access Control
   D. Privacy preferences
   E. Taps

5. What is a prerequisite for achieving anonymity, more generally or data minimization, on the application level?
   A. Release policies
   B. Anonymous communication
   C. Data handling policies
   D. Intellectual property
   E. Social engineering

EXERCISE

Problem

Why now? Why is the National Strategy for Trusted IDs in Cyberspace needed?

Hands-On Projects

Project

Won't having a single password and credential be less secure and private than having many usernames and passwords?

Case Projects

Problem

Who will make sure that companies follow the rules?

Optional Team Case Project

Problem

Will new laws be needed to create the Identity Ecosystem?

REFERENCES

[1] OECD, Guidelines on the Protection of Privacy and Transborder Flows of Personal Data, September 1980.
[2] OECD, Guidelines on the Protection of Privacy and Transborder Flows of Personal Data (Revised), 2013.
[3] S.D. Brandeis, L.D. Warren, The right to privacy, Harv. Law Rev. (5) (1890) 193–220.
[4] A. Westin, Privacy and Freedom, Atheneum, New York, 1967.
[5] G. Hogben, Annex A, in: PRIME Project Deliverable D14.0a - PRIME Framework V0, June 2004.
[6] Global Internet Liberty Campaign, PRIVACY AND HUMAN RIGHTS - An International Survey of Privacy Laws and Practice, [Online]. Available: http://gilc.org/privacy/survey/.
[7] R. Rosenberg, The Social Impact of Computers, Academic Press, 1992.
[8] European Union, Directive 95/46/EC of the European Parliament and of the Council of 24 October 1995 on the protection of individuals with regard to the processing of personal data and on the free movement of such data, Off. J. L (281) (1995).
[9] E. Commission, Regulation (EU) 2016/679 of the European Parliament and of the Council of 27 April 2016 on the protection of natural persons with regard to the processing of personal data and on the free movement of such data, and repealing Directive 95/46/EC, Off. J. Eur. Union L 119/1 (2016) L 119/1–L 119/88.
[10] S. Fischer-Hübner, Anonymity, in: Encyclopedia of Database Systems, Springer, Heidelberg, 2009, pp. 90–91.
[11] D. Chaum, Security without identification: card computers to make big brother obsolete, Inform. Spektrum 10 (1987) 262–277.
[12] D. Chaum, The dining cryptographers problem: unconditional sender and recipient untraceability, J. Cryptol. 1 (1) (Jan. 1988) 65–75.

[13] D. Chaum, Untraceable electronic mail, return addresses, and digital pseudonyms, Commun. ACM 24 (2) (Feb. 1981) 84–88.

[14] Registratiekamer & Information and Privacy Commissioner of Ontairo, Privacy-enhancing Technologies: The Path to Anonymity, Achtergrondstudies en Verkenningen 5B, Vol. I & II, August 1995. Rijswijk.

[15] A. Pfitzmann, M. Hansen, Anonymity, Unlinkability, Undetectability, Unobservability, Pseudonymity, and Identity Management - a Consolidated Proposal for Terminology, 2010 [Online]. Available: http://dud.inf.tu-dresden.de/Anon_Terminology.shtml.

[16] S. Steinbrecher, S. Köpsell, Modelling unlinkability, in: Workshop on Privacy Enhancing Technologies, 2003.

[17] Common Criteria for Information Technology Security Evaluation, Version 3.1, Part 2: Security Functional Requirements, Common Criteria Project, September 2006 [Online]. Available: www.common criteriaportal.org.

[18] L. Sweeney, K-anonymity: a model for protecting privacy, Int. J. Uncertain. Fuzziness Knowledge-Based Sys. 10 (5) (2002) 571–588.

[19] M. Gruteser, D. Grunwald, Anonymous usage of location-based services through spatial and temporal cloaking, in: Proceedings of the 1st International Conference on Mobile Systems, Applications and Services (MobiSys), 2003.

[20] W. Wang, M. Motani, V. Srinivasan, Dependent link padding algorithms for low latency anonymity systems, in: Proceedings of the 15th ACM Conference on Computer and Communications Security (CCS), 2008.

[21] M. Srivatsa, A. Iyengar, L. Liu, Privacy in VoIP networks: a k-anonymity approach, in: Proceedings of the IEEE INFOCOM 2009, 2009.

[22] A. Narayanan, V. Shmatikov, Robust De-anonymization of large sparse datasets, in: Proceedings of the IEEE 29th Symposium on Security and Privacy, Oakland, CA, USA, 2008.

[23] A. Machanavajjhala, D. Kifer, J. Gehrke och, M. Ventikasubramaniam, l-Diversity: privacy beyond k-anonymity, in: ACM Transactions on Knowledge Discovery from Data, vol. 1, 2007.

[24] N. Li, T. Li och, S. Venkatasubramanian, t-Closeness: privacy beyond k-Anonymity and l-Diversity, in: Proceedings of the IEEE 23rd International Conference on Data Engineering, 2007.

[25] C.E. Shannon, A mathematical theory of communications, Bell Sys. Tech. J. 27 (1948) 379–423, 623-656.

[26] C. Diaz, S. Seys, J. Claessens, B. Preneel, Towards measuring anonymity, in: Workshop on Privacy Enhancing Technologies, 2002.

[27] A. Serjantov, G. Danezis, Towards an information theoretic metric for anonymity, in: Workshop on Privacy Enhancing Technologies, 2002.

[28] S. Clauss, A framework for quantification of linkability within a privacy-enhancing identity management system, in: Emerging Trends in Information and Communication Security (ETRICS), 2006.

[29] D. Chaum, The dining cryptographers problem: unconditional sender and recipient untraceabilit, J. Cryptol. 1 (1) (Jan. 1988) 65–75.

[30] http://anon.inf.tu-dresden.de, [Online]. [Använd 29 August 2012].

[31] D.M. Goldschlag, M.G. Reed och, P.F. Syverson, Hiding routing information, in: Information Hiding, 1996.

[32] R. Dingledine, N. Mathewson, P. Syverson, Tor: The Second-Generation Onion Router, Naval Research Lab, Washington DC, 2004.

[33] R. Böhme, G. Danezis, C. Díaz, S. Köpsell, A. Pfitzmann, On the PET workshop panel "mix cascades versus peer-to-peer: is one concept superior?", in: Workshop on Privacy-Enhancing Technologies (PET) 2004, 2005.

[34] J. Camenisch, M. Dubovitska, M. Kohlweiss, J. Lapon, G. Neve, Cryptographic mechanisms for privacy, in: Privacy and Identity Management for Life, Springer, Heidelberg, 2011, pp. 117–134.

[35] D. Chaum, A. Fiat, M. Naor, Untraceable electronic cash, in: Advances in Cryptology - Crypto'88, 1988.

[36] D. Chaum, Achieving electronic privacy, Sci. Am. (1992) 76–81.

[37] S. Fischer-Hübner, in: IT-security and Privacy - Design and Use of Privacy-Enhancing Security Mechanisms, Springer LNCS, Heidelberg, 2001.

[38] S. Goldwasser, S. Micali, C. Rackoff, The knowledge complexity of interactive proof systems, in: Proceedings of the 17th ACM Symposium on Theory of Computing, 1985, pp. 291–304.

[39] S. Brands, Rethinking Public Key Infrastructure and Digital Certificates – Building in Privacy, PhD thesis, Institute of Technology, Eindhoven, 1999.

[40] J. Camenisch, A. Lysyanskaya, Efficient non-transferable anonymous multi-show credential system with optional anonymity revocation, in: Advances in Cryptology - Eurocrypt 2001, vol. 2045, 2001, pp. 93–118.

[41] D. Cooper, K. Birman, Preserving privacy in a network of mobile computers, in: Proceedings of the 1995 IEEE Symposium on Security and Privacy, Oakland, May 1995.

[42] R. Ostrovsky och, W. Skeith, A survey of single-database private information retrieval: techniques and applications, in: Public Key Cryptography–pkc 2007, Springer, 2007.

[43] H. Lipmaa, Oblivious Transfer or Private Information Retrieval, [Online]. Available: http://www.cs.ut.ee/~lipmaa/crypto/link/protocols/oblivious.php.

[44] R. Leenes, M. Lips, R. Poels, M. Hoogwout, User aspects of privacy and identity management in online environments: towards a theoretical model of social factors, in: PRIME Framework V1 (Chapter 9) Project Deliverable, 2005.

[45] H. Hedbom, A survey on transparency tools for privacy purposes, in: Proceedings of the 4th FIDIS/IFIP Summer School, Published by Springer, 2009., Brno, September 2008.

[46] W3C, P3P – The Platform for Privacy Preferences 1.1 (P3P1.1) Specification, 2006 [Online]. Available: http://www.w3.org/P3P/.

[47] P. Kelley, L. Cesca, J. Bresee, L. Cranor, Standardizing privacy notices: an online study of the nutrition label approach, in: Proceedings of the 28th International Conference on Human Factors in Computing Systems, ACM, 2010, p. 1573.

[48] PrimeLife, Privacy and Identity Management in Europe for Life - Policy Languages, [Online]. Available: http://primelife.ercim.eu/results/primer/133-policy-languages.

[49] M. Azraoui, K. Elkhiyaoui, M. Önen, K. Bernsmed, A. Santana De Oliveira, J. Sendor, A-PPL: an accountability policy language, in: Data Privacy Management, Autonomous Spontaneous Security, and Security Assurance, Springer, 2015.

[50] J. Angulo, S. Fischer-Hübner, E. Wästlund och, T. Pulls, Towards usable privacy policy display & management for PrimeLife, Inf. Manag. Comput. Secur. (Emerald) 20 (1) (2012) 4–17.

[51] Opinion on More Harmonised Information Provisions. 11987/04/EN WP 100, Article 29 Data Protection Working Party, November 25, 2004, [Online]. Available: http://ec.europa.eu/justice_home/fsj/privacy/docs/wpdocs/2004/wp100_en.pdf..

[52] J.S. Pettersson, S. Fischer-Hübner, M. Bergmann, Outlining "Data Track": privacy-friendly data maintenance for end-users, in: Advances in Information Systems Development, Springer, US, 2007, pp. 215–226.

[53] S. Fischer-Hübner, H. Hedbom och, E. Wästlund, Trust and assurance HCI, in: Privacy and Identity Management for Life, Springer, Berlin Heidelberg, 2011, pp. 245–260.

[54] E. Wästlund och, S. Fischer-Hübner, End user transparency tools: UI prototypes, in: PrimeLife Deliverable D4.2.2, June 2010. www.primelife.eu.

[55] S. Fischer-Hübner, J. Angulo, F. Karegar, P. Tobias, Transparency, privacy and trust – technology for tracking and controlling my data disclosures: does this work?, in: Darmstadt, Proceedings of the IFIPTM 2016 Conference, 2016.

[56] T. Pulls, Privacy-friendly cloud storage for the data track: an educational transparency tool, in: NordSec - 17th Nordic Conference on Secure IT Systems Will Be Held at Blekinge Institute of Technology, Karlskrona, October 2012.

[57] J. Angulo, S. Fischer-Hübner, T. Pulls, E. Wästlund, Usable transparency with the data track: a tool for visualizing data disclosures, in: Proceedings of the 33rd Annual ACM Conference Extended Abstracts on Human Factors in Computing Systems, 2015.

[58] B. Schneier, J. Kelsey, Cryptographic support for secure logs on untrusted machines, in: The Seventh USENIX Security Symposium Proceedings, USENIX Press, 1998, pp. 53–62.

[59] S. Sackmann, J.A.R. Strüker, Personalization in privacy-aware highly dynamic systems, Commun. ACM 49 (9) (September 2006).

[60] H. Hedbom, T. Pulls, P. Hjärtquist, A. Lavén, Adding secure transparency logging to the PRIME core, in: 5th IFIP WG 9.2,9.6/11.7,11.4,11.6/PrimeLife International Summer School, Revised Selected Papers, Published by Springer in 2010, Nice, France, 2009.

[61] K. Wouters, K. Simoens, D. Lathouwers, B. Preneel, Secure and privacy-friendly logging for eGovernment services, in: 3rd International Conference on Availability, Reliability and Security (ARES 2008), IEEE, 1091-1096, 2008.

[62] M. Hildebrandt, Biometric behavioral profiling and transparency enhancing tools, in: FIDIS Deliverable D 7.12, 2009. www.fidis.net.

[63] S. Berthold, R. Böhme, Valuating privacy with option pricing theory, in: T. Moore, D.J. Pym, C. Ioannidis (Eds.), Economics of Information Security and Privacy, Springer, 2010, pp. 187–209.

[64] S. Berthold, Towards a formal language for privacy options, in: Privacy and Identity Management for Life, 6th IFIP WG 9.2,9.6/11.7, 11.4, 11.6/PrimeLife International Summer School 2010, Revised Selected Papers, 2011.

[65] S. Fischer-Hübner, C.J. Hoofnagle, I. Krontiris, K. Rannenberg och, M. Waidner, Online privacy: towards informational self-determination on the internet (Dagstuhl perspectives workshop 11061), Dagstuhl Manif. 1 (1) (2011) 1–20.

Chapter 54

Personal Privacy Policies[1]

George O.M. Yee[1] and Larry Korba[2]
[1]Carleton University, Ottawa, ON, Canada; [2]National Research Council of Canada, Ottawa, ON, Canada

Note: This chapter is available in its entirety online at store.elsevier.com/product.jsp?isbn= 9780128038437 (click the Resources tab at the bottom of the page).

1. ABSTRACT

The rapid growth of the Internet has been accompanied by similar growth in the availability of Internet electronic services (e-services) such as online booksellers and stockbrokers. This proliferation of e-services has in turn fueled the need to protect the personal privacy of e-service users or consumers. This chapter proposes the use of personal privacy policies to protect privacy. It is evident that the content must match the user's privacy preferences as well as privacy legislation. It is also evident that the construction of a personal privacy policy must be as easy as possible for the consumer. Furthermore, the content and construction must not result in negative unexpected outcomes (an unexpected outcome that harms the user in some manner). The chapter begins with the derivation of policy content based on privacy legislation, followed by a description of how a personal privacy policy may be constructed semi-automatically. It then shows how to specify policies so that negative unexpected outcomes can be avoided. Finally, it describes our Privacy Management Model, which explains how to use personal privacy policies to protect privacy, including what is meant by a "match" of consumer and service provider policies and how nonmatches can be resolved through negotiation. Hence, it has become hard for individuals to manage and control their personal spheres. Both legal and technical means are needed to protect privacy and to (re)establish individuals' control. This chapter provides an overview of the area of privacy-enhancing technologies (PETs), which protect privacy by technically enforcing legal privacy principles. It starts by defining the legal foundations of PETs, and presents a classification of PETs as well as a definition of traditional privacy properties that PETs address and metrics for measuring the level of privacy that PETs provide. Then, a selection of the most relevant PETs is presented.

2. CONTENTS

---

1. NRC Paper number: NRC 50334.

Chapter 55

Detection of Conflicts in Security Policies

Cataldo Basile[1], Matteo Maria Casalino[2], Simone Mutti[3] and Stefano Paraboschi[3]

[1]*Politecnico di Torino, Torino, Italy;* [2]*SAP Research Sophia-Antipolis, Mougins, France;* [3]*Universita degli studi di Bergamo, Bergamo, Italy*

1. INTRODUCTION

The evolution of information systems is continuously increasing the capabilities and range of offered services, leading to infrastructures that see the participation of a larger number of users, a greater level of integration among separate systems, and a correspondingly larger impact of possible misbehaviors. Security solutions are available to protect the correct delivery of services, but these solutions have to adapt to the increasing complexity of system architectures. In this scenario, the management of security becomes a critical task. The goal is not only part of natural business practices; it is also required to show compliance with respect to the many regulations promulgated by governments.

In modern information systems, a particular area of security requirement is access control management, with security policies that describe how resources and services should be protected. These policies offer a classification of the actions on the system that distinguishes them into authorized and forbidden, depending on a variety of parameters. Given the critical role of security and their large size and complexity, concerns arise about the policy's correctness. It is no longer possible to rely on the security designer to guarantee that the policy correctly represents how the system should protect access to resources.

Examples will be used to support the explanation and try to make the description self-contained. We want to provide an understanding of what we perceive as the main applications of these techniques.

The chapter is organized as follows. Section 2 introduces the concept of conflict in a security policy; then the resolution of conflicts is discussed and the relationship with separation of duty constraints is illustrated. Section 3 presents conflicts that arise in executing a security policy; the example of security policies for Java EE is used as an example. Section 4 offers an extensive analysis of conflict detection for network policies; significant attention is dedicated to this area, because it represents the domain in which there is large experience in the use of conflict detection. Section 5 illustrates how Semantic Web technology can support the detection of conflicts in generic policies. Section 6 presents a few concluding remarks.

2. CONFLICTS IN SECURITY POLICIES

A typical top-down representation of the protection of an information system might consist of the five layers shown in Fig. 55.1.

Security Requirements

Security requirements are a high-level, declarative representation of the rules according to which access control must be regulated. Security requirements largely ignore details of the system used to deliver the service, but focus on business concepts. This layer uses terminology and levels of detail typical of managers that are commonly expressed using natural language. For this reason, formal consistency verification cannot be applied automatically to security requirements, and so human intervention will be required to complete the task.

Policies

Policies represent how business requirements are mapped to the systems used for service provisioning. Policies can be defined at different levels, and the use of higher-level specification requires an approach to be adopted, possibly associated with a software tool, that supports the generation of lower-level representations.

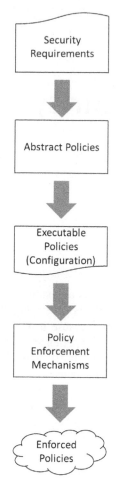

FIGURE 55.1 Top-down representation of the protection of an information system.

Abstract Policies

Abstract policies provide a formal representation of access control and its behavior. A policy may state, for instance, that an internal database storing credit card information must not be accessible from the Internet. It is declarative because it does not detail the actual mechanism used to enforce this policy. First, the policy is intended to define the desired behavior of the services. Because the policy will apply to abstract service definitions (services that are not yet instantiated), the specification cannot use full topological details.

Executable Policies

Executable policies describe the access control policy in a way that can immediately be processed by an access control component. Executable policies can be considered the security configuration of a system and are expressed in the specific language that a system recognizes. For instance, a policy for a relational Data Base Management System

(DBMS) will typically be expressed by a sequence of Structured Query Language (SQL) statements.

Policy Enforcement Mechanisms

Policy enforcement mechanisms correspond to the low-level functions that implement the executable policies. It is convenient in the design and analysis of the system to separate the consideration of the policies (abstract and executable) from the mechanisms responsible for enforcing them, because each has its own weaknesses and threats.

Research has proposed multiple approaches for policy specification. Proposals have often been characterized by direct integration with the languages and models of the modern Web scenario. These models include industry standards such as eXtensible Access Control Markup Language (XACML) [1], which is interesting because it can be characterized as a mostly abstract policy language but it is also associated with tools that are able to process it directly, which makes it an executable policy. There are other abstract policy languages that a computer can directly process, such as rule-based policy notation using an if-then-else format, or proposals based on the representation of policies using Deontic logic for obligation and permissibility rules. Academic efforts produced solutions ranging from theoretical languages such as the one proposed by Jajodia et al. [2] to executable policy languages such as Ponder [3]. In the Semantic Web area proposals have emerged such as Rei [4] and KAoS [5]. Policy languages based on Semantic Web technologies allow policies to be described over heterogeneous domain data and promote a common understanding among participants who might not use the same information model.

A crucial advantage of using a formal policy representation, particularly at the abstract level, is the possibility of the early identification of anomalies. Security policies in real systems often exhibit contradictions (inconsistencies in the policy that can lead to an incorrect realization of the security requirements) and redundancies (elements of the policy that are dominated by other elements, increasing the cost of security management without providing benefits to the users or applications). The availability of a high-level and complete representation of the security policies supports the construction of services for the analysis of the policies able to identify these anomalies and possibly suggest corrections. A classical taxonomy of conflicts is shown in Fig. 55.2.

As depicted in Fig. 55.2, conflicts can be divided into two categories: (1) *intrapolicy* conflicts that may exist within a single policy and (2) *interpolicy* conflicts that may exist between at least two policies. For each category we have the following subcategories: (1) contradictory, (2) redundant, and (3) irrelevant.

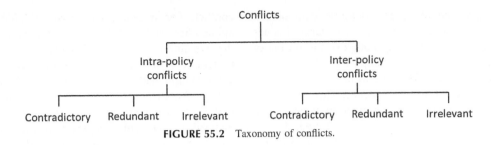

FIGURE 55.2   Taxonomy of conflicts.

Contradictory

Contradictory conflicts arise when principals are authorized to do an action a on a resource r by a positive authorization, and are forbidden to do the same action a on the resource r by a negative authorization. In this case, the two authorizations are said to be incompatible. For example, in Fig. 55.3, Authorization 1 is in conflict with Authorization 3. In fact, Authorization 1 states that Alice can read file1, and Authorization 3 states that Alice cannot read file1.

Contradictory authorizations make the policy inconsistent. The security administrator has to be alerted to correct this error by editing or removing the conflict. In network policies, a classification is introduced that further refines this type of conflict.

Redundant

Redundant conflicts arise when an authorization is dominated by other authorizations and does not contribute to the policy (its removal would not modify the behavior of the system). Given two authorizations, a_1 and a_2, with the same action and sign, let us call p_i (respectively, r_i) the principals (respectively, resources) associated, directly or indirectly, with a_i. If $p_2 \subseteq p_1$ and $r_2 \subseteq r_1$ and a_2 is not involved in any conflict with other authorizations, then a_2 is redundant with respect to a_1 and can be safely removed from the policy without modifying the behavior of the system. For example, in Fig. 55.3, Authorization 2 is redundant with respect to Authorization 4 because Authorization 4 dominates (it is expressed on the folder) Authorization 2 (it is expressed on file1, but it is contained in the folder).

#	Sign	User	Action	Resource
1	+	Alice	read	file1
2	+	Bob	write	file2
3	-	Alice	read	file1
4	+	Bob	write	folder (contains file1 and file2)

FIGURE 55.3   Examples of contradictory and redundant conflicts.

Irrelevant

Irrelevant conflicts occur when the conflict can never manifest itself in a system. This may happen when specification of the elements of the authorizations cannot lead to activation of all of the authorizations involved in the conflict. Recognizing that a conflict is irrelevant may be hard, depending on the expressive power of the language used to represent authorizations. Examples are presented in Section 4 in a discussion of conflicts in network policies.

This classification is a starting point for evaluating the conflicts. In the next section we present some examples of conflicts and discuss introducing techniques to resolve conflicts to be able to solve contradictions in the policy.

Conflict Resolution

Security policies in real systems often exhibit conflicts and redundancies. The availability of a high-level and complete representation of the security policies supports the construction of services for the analysis of the policies able to identify these anomalies and possibly suggest corrections. Contradictions in the policy are also called *modality conflicts*. They arise when principals are authorized to do an action a on a resource r by a positive authorization, and are forbidden to do the same action a on resource r by a negative authorization.

In this case, the two authorizations are said to be *incompatible*. An example was presented earlier with Authorizations 1 and 3 in Fig. 55.3.

In the literature and in systems, several criteria have been proposed and implemented to manage this kind of conflict at the time policy execution [6] with the aim of removing ambiguity in the policy and solving the conflict. In that regard, consider the case of a generic network firewall device in which packet filtering rules are evaluated in a given order, and as such, any conflict among them (more than one rule matching to the same packet) is deterministically solved by evaluating the result dictated by the first matching rule. The rules that handle the composition of authorizations to solve the conflicts do not necessarily have to be fixed. More sophisticated languages are in fact equipped with specific constructs to instruct the policy evaluator to apply one of several possible composition strategies. The XACML language [1], for instance, defines so-called combining algorithms to compose the results of different access control rules. Examples of the available options are the *"deny-overrides"* algorithm, in which rules prescribing access denial take precedence. This means that in case of conflict, the negative authorization always wins, so a forbidden action will never be permitted. In the example presented in Fig. 55.3, this means that Authorization 3, which is negative for subject Alice, has priority over Authorization 1, so Alice is not allowed to read file1. Another strategy that sees extensive adoption in operating systems is the *"first-applicable"* one, in which rules are evaluated in order, such as in the case of a network firewall mentioned earlier. In a similar fashion, the Apache Web server access control configuration language permits specification of the order of priority of rule evaluation. For example, the "Order allow, deny" directive determines the priority of permissions over denials.

Other important criteria are those based on identification of a dominance relationship among rules. This is represented by the criterion *"most specific wins,"* which states that when one authorization dominates the other, the more specific wins. In most cases this represents an adequate and flexible solution. A critical problem of this approach is that specificity may not always be defined for conflicting authorizations, for a variety of reasons.

A first case is represented by the authorizations supporting a hierarchy for any element of the (<*subject, action, resource*>) triple, with the possibility of being contained in more than one ancestor. For example, for a given action and resource, Authorization *A3* has a positive sign and is applied to Group *G1*, and Authorization *A4* has a negative sign and is applied to Group *G2*, with *G1* and *G2* not contained one into the other and with User *u* belonging to both groups. In this situation, the *"most specific wins"* does not solve the conflict. A second case occurs when containment hierarchies are possible on more than one element. For example, Authorization *A5* has a positive sign and applies to User *u* when accessing elements in Resource Group *RG*; Authorization *A6* has a negative sign and applies to User group *UG* when accessing Element *r*; if *u* is a member of *UG* and *r* is included in *RG*, the *"most specific wins"* criterion is not able to manage the conflict. Other solutions have been proposed that rely on the explicit specification of a priority for each authorization. If a partial order is specified using the same priority for sets of authorizations, the possibility of unresolved conflicts remains. If priorities build a total order on authorizations, conflicts would be solved, but it appears difficult to assign priorities efficiently that are consistent with the application semantics.

An option that can solve all of the conflicts is to combine multiple resolution criteria, applying each one only after the previous ones were not able to solve the conflict. For instance, the *"most specific wins"* can be applied first, and the *"deny overrides"* can be used to solve the remaining conflicts. In most cases this solution is preferable to identification of some fixed ordering of the authorization that is not consistent with the semantics of the policy. Another option that has a significant potential, particularly when dealing with abstract policies that will be mapped to executable policies, is to use the *"most specific wins"* criterion as a first step and let the conflict detection solutions notify the security administrator of the remaining conflicts, to modify the policy or introduce an ad hoc solution. Support for this approach can be found by using Semantic Web tools, as discussed in Section 5.

Separation of Duty

The conflicts presented until now derive from the presence of positive and negative authorizations in the same policy that can be applied to the same access request. A different kind of conflict derives from the definition in the security policy of constraints that the authorizations have to satisfy. An important class of constraints is *separation of duty* (*SoD*). These constraints follow the common best practice for which sensitive combinations of permissions should not be held by the same individual, to avoid violating business rules. The purpose of this constraint is to discourage fraud by spreading the responsibility and authority for an action or task, thereby raising the risk involved in committing a fraudulent act, by requiring the involvement of more than one individual. The idea of SoD existed long before the information age and is extensively used in some areas such as the banking industry and the military. *Role-based access control* can be adapted to express this kind of constraint because the role hierarchy allows easy mapping of real-world business rules to the access control model.

A well-known example is the process of creating and approving purchase orders. If a single person creates and approves purchase orders, it is easy and tempting for him to create and approve a phony order and pocket the money. If different people must create and approve orders, committing fraud requires a conspiracy of at least two people, which significantly lowers the risk.

The two main categories of SoD are (1) static SoD and (2) dynamic SoD (Fig. 55.4). The former category (also known as strong exclusion) is the simplest way to implement SoD. Given two roles, $role_1$ and $role_2$, static SoD between these two roles means that a User *u* must not exist who can activate both $role_1$ and $role_2$. For instance, if *Order Creator* and *Order Approver* are strongly exclusive roles, no one who may assume the Order Creator role would be allowed to assume the Order Approver role; on the other hand, no one who may assume the *Order Approver* role would be allowed to assume the *Order Creator* role.

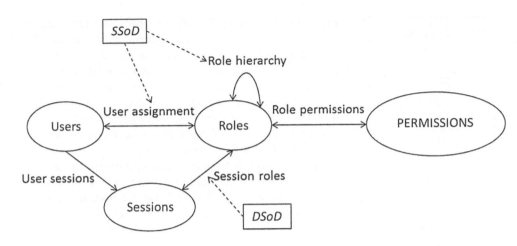

FIGURE 55.4 National Institute of Standards and Technology role-based access control model. *DSoD,* dynamic separation of duty; *SSoD,* static separation of duty.

The latter category (also known as weak exclusion) states that "A principal may be a member of any two exclusive roles, but he must not activate both at the same time." This definition implies that the system will keep precise track of each task. Before doing any task, the system will check that the SoD is not violated. Dynamic SoD allows users to perform roles that would be strongly exclusive in static systems.

Violations of the SoD constraints policy are another kind of conflict. Support for this conflict can be adequately provided by implementing conflict detection services, which are able to notify the security designer of inconsistencies in the policy. Resolution of such a conflict will typically require revising the policy, restricting the user's ability to enact conflicting roles, or modifying the specification of the constraint. The efficient identification of these violations can use ad hoc solutions. An interesting option is represented by the use of Semantic Web tools, as discussed in Section 5.

3. CONFLICTS IN EXECUTABLE SECURITY POLICIES

So far, we have focused on how conflicts have been studied in the context of abstract security policies, in which the specific details of implementing policy enforcement mechanisms are not part of the model. Therefore they are not assumed to introduce any possible issue into the policy evaluation.

In this section we instead consider the case of concrete policy evaluation frameworks, in which an *evaluation algorithm* determines the effect of a given policy according to:

- An executable representation of the policy
- Context-dependent information

The executable policy can be seen as the configuration of the security enforcement mechanism, and it can be referred to as its *security configuration.* A security configuration is typically expressed according to a respective *configuration language.* The semantics of this language is ultimately given by the evaluation algorithm that computes the result of a configuration at operations time. As a consequence, configuration authors need to have a thorough understanding of the semantics evaluation, such that they can configure the behavior of the enforcing mechanism exactly according to the policy they want the system to implement.

Security configuration languages and corresponding evaluation semantics typically incorporate mechanisms to cope with conflicts that may arise at the evaluation stage. This can be achieved, on the one hand, by constraining the expressiveness of the configuration language so that some inconsistencies are syntactically ruled out; for instance, contradictions in the policy (see Section 2) cannot occur in the case of an access control configuration language that allows only specifying collections of positive (respectively, negative) authorization rules. On the other hand, solutions to resolve the conflicting situations can be included in the evaluation semantics. For example, the rules that determine the semantics of the composition of different constructs of the language can be designed to handle conflicts by applying a predetermined strategy, as discussed earlier.

Although policy conflicts are sorted out in the evaluation semantics of security configuration languages, errors still can be introduced by inexperienced configuration authors. As a matter of fact, the gap of abstraction that lies between a security configuration and the corresponding enforced abstract policy is similar to the difference between a program's source code and the behavior realized by an interpreter while executing the program (Fig. 55.5). As such, policies that enforce unintended security properties can stem from misconfigured security enforcement devices: for instance bugs in the program's source code producing incorrect runtime behavior.

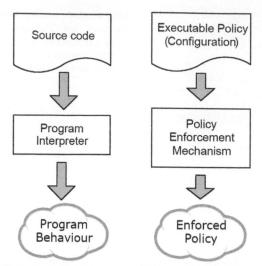

FIGURE 55.5 Analogy between program interpretation and the low portion of Fig. 55.1.

To solve this issue, researchers have been studying the characteristics of security policy languages and their semantics to:

- Identify in particular counterintuitive corner-cases or anomalous situations that likely stem from misconfigurations
- Propose models to detect and possibly solve such misconfigurations automatically

In the following we discuss these issues in the scenario of Java Enterprise Edition (EE). The treatment will also use some concrete examples of the security configuration language.

Java Enterprise Edition Access Control

The Java Enterprise Edition (Java EE) platform consists of a set of application program interfaces (APIs) and a runtime environment that allows development and execution of distributed Web-based applications. The basic execution model of a Java EE Web application is depicted in Fig. 55.6. Hypertext Transfer Protocol (HTTP) requests coming over the network are processed by the Java EE application server and abstracted to *HttpServlet Request* Java objects, which constitute the input of the Web application. Web applications are composed of *Web Components*, dealing with the client's requests and computing responses, and *JavaBeans Components*, which can be optionally involved to encapsulate the business logic of large-scale Web applications.

The interface between the Web Components and the application server, providing their execution environment, is standardized in the Java EE Servlet Specification [7]. This document establishes a contract between application server implementations on one side and Web applications on the other, prescribing, among others, a number of mechanisms to deal with security in Java EE Web applications.

Such mechanisms belong to two categories: programmatic security and declarative security. Programmatic security describes functionalities that developers can use through an API to implement security within their application's code. Declarative security refers instead to the enforcement of security properties (such as HTTP-based access control) achieved not through dedicated source code in the application, but rather through the declarative specification of security configurations. In the latter case, the enforcement of security at runtime is completely transparent to the Web application's developer. When the Web application is deployed within the application server, it comes together with a configuration file, the so-called deployment descriptor, in which security and several other aspects of the Web application's runtime environment are configured. Analogous mechanisms are likewise available for JavaBeans Components, as described in a dedicated specification [8].

Because we are interested in discussing examples of security configuration languages, in this section we focus on declarative security. We first provide an overview of its evaluation semantics and then examine different approaches to the analysis of Java EE security configurations.

FIGURE 55.6 Execution model of a Java Enterprise Edition Web application [7]. *Http*, Hypertext Transfer Protocol.

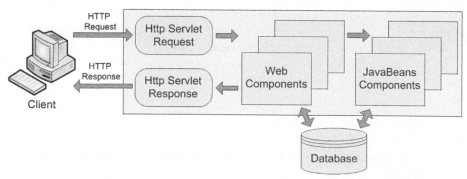

The deployment descriptor of Web Components is an eXtensible Markup Language (XML) document that conforms to a grammar (XML schema) defined as part of the Servlet Specification. The security-related fragment of this grammar is the subtree rooted at the *security constraint* XML tag.

Every security constraint associates a set of resources [i.e., Uniform Resource Locators (URLs) of the Web application] with the required security properties. Two categories of security properties can be configured: *authorization constraints*, which are access control on URLs, and *user data constraints*, which stand for confidentiality or integrity requirements on data exchanged between the client and the Web application. Access control is configured by associating URL patterns and a (possibly empty) set of HTTP methods to at most one authorization constraint: that is, the set of roles allowed to access the mentioned resources. Wild cards are allowed in the definition of both URL patterns and granted roles: in particular (1) the special role name '*' is shorthand for all the roles defined inside the deployment descriptor, and (2) entire URL hierarchies can be specified with URL patterns ending with the '/*' wildcard.

Similarly, requirements for data confidentiality or integrity are specified by associating URL patterns and HTTP methods with one or more transport guarantee XML nodes, containing either the CONFIDENTIAL or INTEGRAL keywords.

According to the informal semantics from Rubinger et al. [9], to have access granted, a user must be a member of *at least one of the roles* named in the security constraint (or implied by '*') that matches her or his HTTP request. An empty authorization constraint means that *nobody* can access the resources, whereas access is granted to *any* (possibly unauthenticated) user in case the authorization constraint is omitted. Unauthenticated access is also allowed by default to any unconstrained resources. An intuitively insignificant syntactic difference, such as omitting the authorization constraint instead of specifying an empty one, corresponds to a major gap in semantics: *allow all* or *deny all* behaviors, respectively, are obtained.

In case the same URL pattern and HTTP method occur in different security constraints, they have to be conceptually composed, because they apply to overlapping sets of resources. Concerning access control, if two nonempty authorization constraints are composed, the result is the *union* of the two sets of allowed roles. If one of the two allows unauthenticated access, the composition does so as well. In contrast, if one of the sets of roles is empty, their composition is empty; that is, the *intersection* of the two sets is performed in this case. Constraints on more specific URL patterns (*/a/b*) always override more general ones (*/a/**). The composition of user data constraints, instead, is always the union of the single requirements.

The following snippet is an example of two overlapping security constraints. As a result of their composition, no access is granted to the URL hierarchies '*' and '*/acme/ wholesale/**' via the *DELETE* and *PUT HTTP* methods. Access to '*/acme/wholesale/**' via *GET* is restricted to users with the role *SALESCLERK*. HTTP requests with any method other than the aforementioned are instead granted to anyone:

```
<security-constraint>
<web-resource-collection>
<url-pattern>/*</url-pattern>
<url-pattern>/acme/wholesale/*</url-pattern>
<http-method>DELETE</http-method>
<http-method>PUT</http-method>
</web-resource-collection>
<auth-constraint/>
</security-constraint>
<security-constraint>
<web-resource-collection>
<url-pattern>/acme/wholesale/*</url-pattern>
<http-method>GET</http-method>
<http-method>PUT</http-method>
</web-resource-collection>
<auth-constraint>SALESCLERK</auth-constraint>
</security-constraint>
```

It is suggested [10] that the evaluation semantics of security constraints for Java EE Web Components is partly counterintuitive, specifically in its fragments concerning composition, which is where the rules to deal with conflicts are encoded, as argued earlier. The peculiar handling of unconstrained HTTP methods and the fact that more specific URL patterns should override less specific ones, for instance, may lead to unexpected behaviors, as illustrated in the following example.

Let us consider again a couple of security constraints introduced previously. According to the earlier interpretation, the *HTTP DELETE* requests to the URL */acme* are denied, because the first constraint applies. In contrast, requests to the same URL but through any unconstrained method, such as *GET*, are allowed to anyone.

We now assume that a system administrator, wanting to deny *GET* requests to the URL */acme*, added the following constraint:

```
<security-constraint>
<web-resource-collection>
<url-pattern>/acme</url-pattern>
<http-method>GET</http-method>
</web-resource-collection>
<auth-constraint/>
</security-constraint>
```

Because this new constraint is the most specific for the URL */acme*, and it does not specify any behavior for methods other than *GET*, it introduces a side effect by allowing requests that were previously denied. For example, the *DELETE* requests to */acme* become *allowed to anyone* after introducing this constraint. This behavior is particularly counterintuitive because the new constraint does not include a reference to the *DELETE* method, which is nevertheless affected. Also, although apparently it specifies *access denial* (empty authorization constraint), it implicitly carries *access permission* semantics for every unconstrained method.

Al-Shaer and Hamed [10] argue for the need for a formal characterization of the semantics of security constraints, which can be used as a reference to check the correctness of the behavior of both application server implementations and Web application configurations. Hence, they propose a set-theoretic model that captures the expressiveness of Java EE Web Components' authorization constraints, in which resources form a set ordered according to the URL tree hierarchy and sets of roles, ordered by inclusion, form a lattice of permissions.

4. CONFLICTS IN NETWORK SECURITY POLICIES

The identification of conflicts in security policies has been investigated especially in the scenario of the configuration of computer networks. This area of security sees significant industrial interest; it is currently one of the most critical components in the protection of an information system from external threats and relies on a protection model that is well understood and adequate to realizing a number of ad hoc solutions. Thus, we consider it interesting to analyze solutions that have been devised to detect policy conflicts in this scenario. The analysis will give a more precise understanding of problems that can be faced when managing conflicts in a real system. The results of work in this area provide important guidelines that can drive the design of this functionality in the different scenarios in which security policies are defined. First, we will consider the configuration of firewalls. Then, we will analyze how the configuration of channel protection solutions can identify other kinds of conflicts in the policy.

Filtering Intrapolicy Conflicts

Firewalls are devices used to separate parts of networks parts that have different security levels; in fact, they are able to enforce an authorization policy that selects the traffic to be allowed according to a security policy expressed as a set rules, often named the access control list (ACL). The rules are composed by a *condition* clause, formed by a series of predicates over some packet header fields, and an action clause, determining the action to be enforced, typically allowing or denying the traffic.

When a new packet arrives at one of the firewall network interfaces, the values from its headers are used to evaluate the condition clause predicates [10,11]. A packet matches a rule if all of the predicates of the rule are true. If a packet matches only one rule, the action enforced is taken of its action clause. However, in an ACL a packet can match more than one rule; therefore rules are prioritized and the action from the matching rule at the highest priority is enforced. This approach is often named the "*first applicable*" resolution strategy, based on ordering rules by priority and starting from the one with the highest priority; the action enforced is the one from the first matching rule. However, hardware-based approaches use ad hoc algorithms and fast memories that speed up the matching process considerably. In practice, the ACL is not scanned linearly, because the action is selected by fast look-up algorithms [12]. It also may happen that a packet does not match any of the ACL rules. In that case, a default action is enforced; typically, the traffic is denied and the packet is dropped.

Firewalls are categorized according to their capabilities or the layer at which they work (that is, the headers they can consider). The simplest firewall capability is the *packet filter*, working at the network and transport International Organization of Standardization/Open System Interconnection (ISO/OSI) layer, which makes decisions based on five fields: the Internet Protocol (IP) address and ports of the source and destination, and the IP protocol type. Packet filters do not maintain state information [distinguishing packets that belong to an established Transmission Control Protocol (TCP) connection], and they are also referred to as *stateless firewalls*.

A firewall that performs the stateful packet inspection is named a *stateful firewall*, and it usually maintains information about the TCP state, but also about other stateless protocols (Internet Control Message Protocol echo-request echo-reply sequences) or stateful application-layer protocols [understanding the opening of File Transfer Protocol (FTP) data ports in active or passive mode]. At the highest level of the ISO/OSI stack, there are the *application firewalls*. Because application protocols are heterogeneous, application firewalls are usually tailored to one or more specific protocols to perform a more focused analysis. The most widespread one is the Web Application Firewall, which observes HTTP properties and fields, including Multipurpose Internet Mail Extension objects, and, if integrated with the Web service it protects, can also circumvent common attacks and vulnerability exploits. In addition, application firewalls are able to check the "RFC compliance" that verifies whether the protocol traffic is consistent with the standards or with a set of nonharmful implementations. Therefore, the condition clause of stateful and application firewalls also contains predicates over state information and application protocol fields.

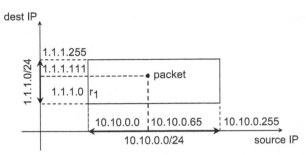

FIGURE 55.7 Geometric representation of a rule and a packet. *IP,* Internet Protocol.

Condition clauses are not just modeled as logical predicates; in fact, many works represent them as using geometrical models that are proven equivalent. According to the geometric view, every packet is a point in a decision space composed by many dimensions, one for each field for which it is possible to state a condition. A rule thus becomes a hyperrectangle. For instance, the decision space of packet filters is often named five-tuple space. A packet matches a rule if it is in the rule hyperrectangular area. For instance, a simple bidimensional case is represented in Fig. 55.7.

Because firewalls are a major security shield against attacks and intrusions, their correct configuration has always worried administrators. However, most firewalls are poorly configured, as Wool highlighted in a study in 2004 whose trend was confirmed [13,14]. Historically, three approaches are used to verify the correctness of intrafirewall policies: manual testing, query-based approaches, and the use of conflict and anomaly analysis tools. Companies have been using complex distributed systems with many firewalls and redundant controls; therefore, all of these approaches have been designed or extended to interfirewall policies analysis.

In interfirewall policy analysis, verification of the correctness of the action enforced by a firewall is extended to a more general case, evaluating actual reachability by analyzing the actions enforced by all of the firewalls encountered in a communication path.

Manual Testing

Manual testing is the first and simplest case. It can be performed by actually trying a set of connections to verify whether they succeed and comparing them with the authorization policy, or using software able to probe hosts, servers, and other devices for open ports and available features: that is, the vulnerability scanner. Many scanners are available for this purpose, mostly as open-source software such as Nmap [15], Amap [16], and Nessus [17]. They are sophisticated and can be used to detect more complex cases (to recognize operating system and software

fingerprints, or to distinguish filtered ports from closed ones) or to identify known vulnerabilities. This approach is time-consuming and requires an effort that is beyond the administrator's possibilities, especially in large networks. In addition, it requires actual deployment of the policy and physical access to the network, which may also be flooded by probe packets that may interfere with normal network functioning. Although scanners' output is detailed, they need a further step to be compared with the firewall policy and to know if it has been correctly implemented.

5. QUERY-BASED CONFLICT DETECTION

The first attempts to overcome the limitations of the manual approach consisted of representing a firewall policy using an abstract format to perform queries and figure out actual firewall behavior by evaluating the action it would enforce instead of trying the connections. Firewall queries can be considered questions concerning firewall behavior [16]. Examples of questions of interest to administrators are: "Which clients can access the server s1?" and "Which server is reachable from the Internet?" This query-based approach easily extends to the analysis of firewalls in distributed systems. In fact, firewall questions can be easily extended to more general reachability problems.

Querying a firewall requires an abstract representation of the policy it implements and an abstract representation of the issued question. One major theoretical problem is the query aggregation. In fact, the number of cases to be considered, for instance, to answer previous questions, is too large: For a five-tuple IPv4 packet filter there are 2^{104} different packets, potentially corresponding to cases to consider.[1] It is critical to use IP address ranges instead of single addresses and port intervals, merging adjacent intervals. The aggregation of the results is also complex and computationally expensive, because the union of rectangles is not always a rectangle.

The first tool produced was Fang [18], a simulation-based engine that performs simple query aggregation. Its successor, Firewall Analyzer (formerly known as Lumeta) [19,20], also provided standard queries and import functionalities to automate the analysis and facilitate the job of the administrators. Another early work from Hazelhurst [21] concentrated on a simple query-based analysis.

Liu proposed Structured Firewall Query Language (SFQL) and an associated intrafirewall query engine [22], which he extended to an analysis of corporate networks composed of packet filters with network address and port translation capabilities (Network Address Translation and Network Address and Port Translation) [11]. SFQL is a SQL-like language that permits specifying queries in a

---

1. 32 bits for source and destination IPv4 addresses, 16 bits for ports, and 8 for the protocol type.

compact and familiar syntax. Assuming that D is the field name for the destination address, S for source address, N for the destination port, and P for the protocol type, the following query answers the following question: "Which are the IP (source) addresses of computers that can reach the Web service s_1 available at 10.0.0.1:80/TCP?" Please see the following lines of code:

```
Select S
from firewall
where {S ∈ all} ∧
{D ∈ 10.0.0.1} ∧
{N ∈ {80}} ∧
{P ∈ {TCP}} ∧
{decision = accept}
```

The main limitation of the firewall querying approach is that the questions at issue are selected by administrators who have to identify the meaningful queries, write them correctly, aggregating if needed the results of more queries (similarly to the SQL union clause), and analyze the results, which may be large. However, they "often do not know what to query" [18]. In the literature, only the Firewall Analyzer addressed this problem, proposing a set of standard queries.

Conflict Detection by Anomaly Classification

A different method to identify whether the firewall policy is correct consists of performing an exhaustive analysis of the ACL, to detect all the situations that may be evidence of a misconfiguration. Although the terms *conflict* and *anomaly* are often used synonymously, in this field they have different meanings: a *conflict* is an occurrence that may stop the correct working (having two matching rules in a router that allows for only one matching rule at the time); an *anomaly* is a particular relation between one or more ACL rules that administrators have to consider, because it may be the evidence of specification mistakes, but that is perfectly allowed by the examined control.

Sloman [6,23,24] initially introduced the concept of conflicting policy, but the methods he presented are not directly applicable to firewall policies and in general to all of the low-level configurations. Many seminal articles present solutions for an analysis of packet filtering. First works concentrated on efficient representations of the ACL, because conflicting rules decrease performance or were not allowed in devices owing to the limited computation capabilities.

The approaches are mainly equivalent, even if they use different rule representations. Hazelhurst presented solutions based on binary decision diagrams (BDDs) [21], Hari [25] proposed the use of tries, Baboescu [26], the use of bit

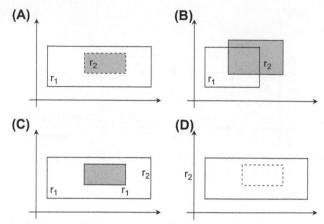

FIGURE 55.8 Al-Shaer's rule-pair anomaly classification for packet filters.

vectors, and Srinivasan [27], the Tuple Space Search classification algorithm.

The first formalization of the anomaly concept was proposed by Al-Shaer, who focused on the intrapolicy analysis of packet filters [10]. He introduced the concept of anomaly, defined as "the existence of two or more filtering rules that may match the same packet, or the existence of a rule that can never match any packet," and identified five rule-pair anomaly types: *shadowing, correlation, generalization*, and *irrelevance*, and presented an algorithm to discover and manage anomalies in ordered rule lists. Given two rules, r_1 and r_2, where r_1 is the highest-priority rule, the rule-pair anomalies are:

1. *Shadowing anomaly*: r_2 is shadowed when r_1 matches all of the packets that r_2 matches, so that r_2 will never be activated (Fig. 55.9B);
2. *Correlation anomaly*: r_1 and r_2 are correlated if (1) they enforce different actions; (2) there exists some packet matching both r_1 and r_2; and (3) there exists some packet matching r_1 but not r_2, and vice versa (Fig. 55.8B);
3. *Generalization anomaly*[2]: r_2 is a generalization of r_1 if (1) they enforce different actions; and (2) all the packets matching r_1 also match r_2, but not the contrary (Fig. 55.8C);
4. *Redundancy anomaly*: r_2 is redundant if r_1 matches the same packets and enforces the same action as r_2, so the removal of r_2 will not change the policy behavior (Fig. 55.9A);
5. *Irrelevance anomaly*: A rule is irrelevant if does not match any packet that could pass through the firewall. It does not concern relations between rules, but rather between a rule and the enforcing device.

---

2. In Basile et al. [28] this is named an exception.

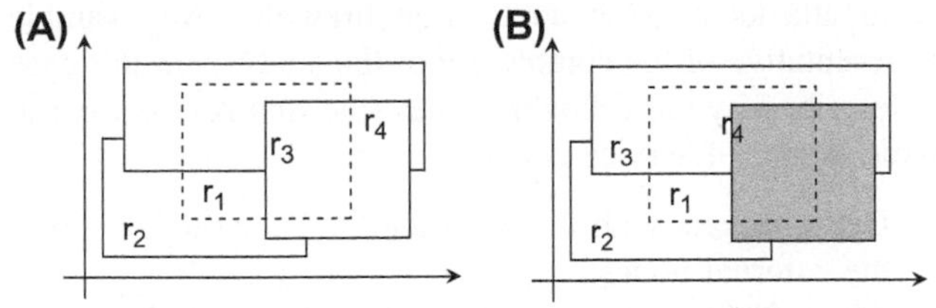

(A)

(B)

FIGURE 55.9 Multirule anomaly classification.

For instance, with reference to Table 55.1, r_1 is a generalization of r_2, and r_2 shadows r_3, makes r_4 redundant, and is correlated to r_5. Finally, r_6 is irrelevant if the traffic from IP address 5.5.5.5 cannot reach the firewall interfaces.

Al-Shaer's classification is limited because it detects only anomalies in rule pairs; anomalies that arise when more rules are considered are not discussed. Basile [28,29] generalized Al-Shaer's classification to multirule anomalies: that is, anomalies that involve more than two rules. The firewall policies are categorized as *conflicting* when at least two rules contradict each other (that includes the correlation, generalization, and shadowing anomalies), and suboptimal when the removal of one or more rules does not affect the behavior of the firewall (that includes shadowing and redundancy). Suboptimality is caused by *hidden rules* (rules that are never activated regardless of the number of rules that hide them). Hidden rules are further classified as *general redundant* if all of the rules hiding them enforce the same action (as presented in Fig. 55.9A) and *general shadowed*, if at least one enforces a different action (as presented in Fig. 55.9B).

A More In-Depth View of Packet Filter Conflict Analysis

Al-Shaer's classification is the starting point for several works that tried to improve the identification of the anomalies using different techniques. Bouhoula [30] used rule field logical relations permitting the analysis of different firewall rule formats, not only the five-tuples. Thanasegaran

[31] used bit vectors that support the detection of rule-pair anomalies more efficiently and the definition of new fields, but they fail to express conditions effectively on ordered fields (ranges of port numbers). Ferraresi [32] presented a slightly alternative conflict classification and a proven correct algorithm that produces a conflict-free rule list. Other works propose rule set optimization by redundancy removal. Gouda [33] provided algorithms to verify the consistency, completeness, and compactness of packet filters, and Liu [34] introduced techniques to detect redundancy based on Firewall Decision Diagrams. Alfaro [35] proposed a set of algorithms to remove anomalies between packet filters and network intrusion detection systems in distributed systems, implemented in the Mirage tool [36]. Hu [37] also introduced an ontology-based anomaly management framework that delegates set operations to BDDs. A completely different approach was presented by Bandara [38], who used argumentation logic and achieved excellent performance. A complementary approach is represented by Liu's Firewall Compressor [39], which minimizes the ACL size by manipulating the specified rules to obtain an equivalent ACL with a minimal number of rules. Redundant and shadowed rules disappear but correlated rules are not examined. The compressed ACL serves only deployment purposes because it is no longer manageable by the administrators.

Stateful Firewall Analysis

Anomaly analysis of stateful firewalls is a less explored field. It is difficult to share the optimism of Buttyàn [40], who stated that "stateful is not harder than stateless." Their scenario is oversimplified because they added one single field to the five-tuple decision space to describe all possible states. The stateful case is harder for at least two reasons: There are new anomalies that do not appear in the stateless case, and it is computationally more complex because many fields need to be considered. Gouda and Liu [41] presented a model of stateful firewalls that maps the stateful filtering functionalities to the packet filter case to use available

TABLE 55.1 Sample Filtering Policy With Anomalies

	Priority	Source IP	Source Port	Destination IP	Destination Port	Protocol	Action
r_1	1	10.0.0.64/28	Any	1.1.1.64/28	80	TCP	DENY
r_2	2	10.0.0.0/24	Any	1.1.1.0/24	80	TCP	ALLOW
r_3	3	10.0.0.2	Any	1.1.1.1	80	TCP	DENY
r_4	4	10.0.0.250	Any	1.1.1.1	80	TCP	ALLOW
r_5	5	10.0.0.16/24	Any	1.1.1.16/24	80	TCP	DENY
r_6	6	5.5.5.5	Any	6.6.6.6	Any	Any	ALLOW

IP, Internet Protocol; TCP, Transmission Control Protocol.

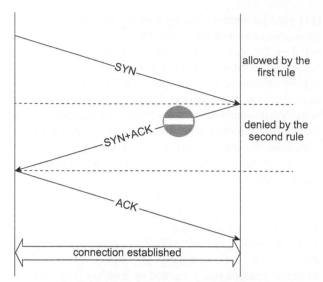

FIGURE 55.10 Blocked three-way handshake.

detection algorithms. For this reason, they model stateful firewalls using two components: the stateful section and the stateless section. The stateful section inspects the transport headers and maintains a *state table* that associates each of the connections observed with a set of Boolean variables: for example, the established state for TCP connections. A set of (hard-coded) *stateful rules* regulates how the state table is updated according to previous states and received packets. The stateless section is simply a packet filter that includes predicates over the Boolean variables in the state table; the anomalies found are Al-Shaer's. Cuppens [42] extended Al-Shaer's classification, adding stateful conflicts, such as situations connected to the specific protocol state machines: for example, rules that deny TCP setup and termination for allowed connections, or rules that block allowed, related FTP connections.

Finally, there is currently no extensive work to detect anomalies in application firewalls, if we exclude the effort to validate the factory-provided regular expressions used to avoid attacks in Web application firewalls. An example representative of the complexity of the analysis in this case is described by the following rules (the first rule is used to avoid denial of service attacks):

1. Deny packets with the SYN and ACK set to true from the external nodes;
2. Allow TCP connections from the internal node having IP 1.1.1.1 to the external server 2.2.2.2 (in the Internet).

These rules are apparently disjointed because one poses a condition with different values of IP addresses and TCP flags. However, according to the TCP specification, the three-way handshake cannot be terminated; the result is thus that the connection from 1.1.1.1 to 2.2.2.2 is forbidden (Fig. 55.10).

Interfirewall Analysis

Al-Shaer [43] also provided the first classification of anomalies in distributed systems. He considered the case of two serially connected stateless firewalls, named, respectively, upstream and downstream firewalls. Assuming *fwu* is the upstream firewall and *fwd* is the downstream firewall, four anomaly types are identified:

- *Shadowing anomaly*: occurs if *fwu* blocks traffic accepted by *fwd* (Fig. 55.11A);
- *Spuriousness anomaly*: occurs if *fwu* permits traffic denied by *fwd* (Fig. 55.11B);
- *Redundancy anomaly*: occurs if *fwu* denies traffic already blocked by *fwu* (Fig. 55.11C);
- *Correlation anomaly*: occurs when a rule *ru* in *fwu* and a rule *rd* in *fwd* are correlated (Fig. 55.11D).

Another work that addresses conflict analysis in distributed systems is presented in Gouda and Lin [41]. This work defines for every pair of nodes in the network two separate end-to-end policies: the allowed packets, named accept property, and the denied packets, named discard property. Based on an abstract representation of the

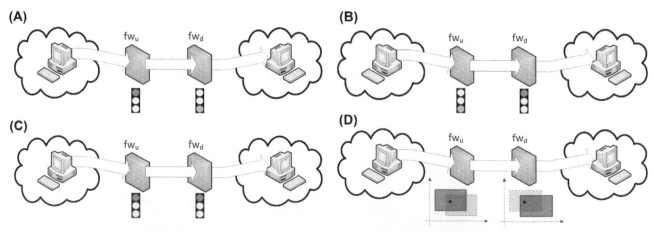

FIGURE 55.11 Al-Shaer's rule-pair anomaly classification for distributed packet filters.

firewall ACL, the Firewall Decision Diagram [31], they calculate the effects on the communication between two nodes n_1 and n_2, by superposing the actions taken by all of the cascading firewalls encountered in the path between n_1 and n_2. Then, they compare the results with the accept and discard properties; a conflict arises when an accept or discard property is not satisfied. Finally, a tool able to detect Al-Shaer's anomalies in distributed systems is FIREMAN, which also checks whether a distributed policy complies with an end-to-end policy [42].

Channel Protection Conflicts

The configuration of secure channels is also an error-prone activity; thus administrators need assistance and conflict detection mechanisms. A few differences can be highlighted with respect to the filtering case: The number of rules is usually orders of magnitude less than in the firewall case. However, they enforce more complex actions, they may enforce more than one action in case of multiple matches, and they have more complex dependencies on the actual distributed system topology.

Different technologies are available to protect channels, and these technologies work at different levels of the ISO/OSI stack. The most well-known solutions are Internet Protocol Security (IPsec), which works at the network layer, and the Transport Layer Security (TLS) protocol, which works up to the transport layer. IPsec allows the creation of secure communication channels between two end points. IPsec can enforce authentication and integrity of IP payload and header using the Authentication Header (AH) protocol, and confidentiality, authenticity, and integrity of the IP payload using the Encapsulating Security Payload (ESP). These end points can be the communicating peers (client and server or two peers) or two gateways used to allow two subnets or two offices to be securely connected over a public/insecure network (the Internet) and to establish a virtual private network (VPN). Also, TLS is used as the base protocol to create VPNs; when this technology is employed, the terms *OpenVPN* or *clientless VPN* are used. These techniques have many similarities from the configuration point of view; therefore they share the same anomalous situations. However, only IPsec VPNs have received attention from researchers, nevertheless, the results for IPsec VPNs are easily extendable to the OpenVPN scenario.

Internet Protocol Security Intrapolicy Conflict Detection

The IPsec configuration rules (the security policy) are stored in the local Security Policy Database (SPDB). These rules select the traffic to be protected by means of (condition clause) predicates on the source and destination IP addresses, IP protocol type fields, and traffic direction (in—out). Three

types of anomalies can be found in this scenario: (intrapolicy) local anomalies (intrapolicy) topology-dependent local anomalies, and interpolicy anomalies.

Local anomalies are analogous to the packet filter scenario (see checklist: "An Agenda for Action for Developing Security Policies for Packet Filtering") and they can be identified using the same techniques (only a simple adaptation is needed). It is not surprising that Al-Shaer [10] proposed the application of its classification for packet filters for intra-IPsec policy analysis [44], extending an early work from Fu et al. [45].

An Agenda for Action for Developing Security Policies for Packet Filtering

IPsec can perform host-based packet filtering to provide limited firewall capabilities for end systems. You can configure IPsec to permit or block specific types of unicast IP traffic based on source and destination address combinations and specific protocols and specific ports. For example, nearly all of the systems illustrated in the following checklist can benefit from packet filtering to restrict communication to specific addresses and ports. You can strengthen security by using IPsec packet filtering to control exactly the type of communication that is allowed between systems (check all tasks completed):

_____1. The internal network domain administrator can assign an Active Directory-based IPsec policy (a collection of security settings that determines IPsec behavior) to block all traffic from the perimeter network (also known as a demilitarized zone or screened subnet).

_____2. The perimeter network domain administrator can assign an Active Directory-based IPsec policy to block all traffic to the internal network.

_____3. The administrator of the computer running Microsoft SQL Server on the internal network can create an exception in the Active Directory-based IPsec policy to permit SQL protocol traffic to the Web application server on the perimeter network.

_____4. The administrator of the Web application server on the perimeter network can create an exception in the Active Directory-based policy to permit SQL traffic to the computer running an SQL server on the internal network.

_____5. The administrator of the Web application server on the perimeter network can also block all traffic from the Internet, except requests to TCP port 80 for the HTTP and TCP port 443 for HTTP Secure Protocol (HTTP over Secure Sockets Layer/TLS Protocol), which are used by Web services. This provides additional security for traffic allowed from the Internet in case the firewall was misconfigured or compromised by an attacker.

_____6. The domain administrator can block all traffic to the management computer but allow traffic to the perimeter network.

The anomaly types are the same: Shadowed, redundant, correlated, and generalized rule pairs can be found in an IPsec SPDB. However, the effort required for the analysis is greater. The main difference is that the actions that can be enforced using IPsec are more complex, because confidentiality, authenticity, and integrity (of the IP payload only using ESP, or IP payload and header using AH) can be selected. Moreover, cryptographic algorithms need to be evaluated and compared. For instance, is it better to protect a channel using "ESP with hash message authentication code (HMAC)-SHA1 and Advanced Encryption Standard (AES) 256" or a channel using "ESP with reserve component 2128 encapsulated in AH with HMAC-MD5"? The answer is not easy and depends on the requirements specified at the business level.

Together with the previous anomalies, other types of anomaly appear from the analysis of a local SPDB, with the intrapolicy channel overlapping and multitransform anomalies. These anomalies depend on the possibility of applying in the same SPDB more than one transformation; choosing the correct order, modes, and algorithms becomes crucial.

Overlapping occurs when an SPDB contains more than one rule with the same source s and destination d that uses different tunneling devices, g_1 and g_2 (Fig. 55.12). For instance, if the SPDB contains the following rules:

- (short tunnel) tunnel to g_1 with protection p_1
- (long tunnel) tunnel to g_2 with protection p_2

and is applied in this order, the following communications are performed:

1. $s \rightarrow g_2$ protected with p_1 and p_2
2. $g_2 \rightarrow g_1$ protected with p_1 (p_2 is removed at g_2)
3. $g_1 \rightarrow d$ with no protection

Therefore, the rule order matters. In fact, if the rules are applied in the opposite order, the communications are, as expected:

1. $s \rightarrow g_1$ protected with p_1 and p_2
2. $g_1 \rightarrow g_2$ protected with p_2 (p_1 is removed at g_1)
3. $g_2 \rightarrow d$ with no protection

This anomaly can also occur with a transport transform (instead of the long tunnel) followed by a tunnel (short tunnel). Applying more than one transformation increases the risk of reducing the protection level. In fact, it is not always true that the combination of more transformations results in a stronger protection. Moreover, because the application of each transformation requires computational resources, using more than one transformation must be justified from the security point of view. The multitransform anomaly occurs when a weaker protection is applied after a stronger one. For instance, applying ESP after AH reduces the overall security because ESP transport does not provide IP header protection. On the other hand, applying AH after ESP is often justified to preserve the header integrity. In addition, a multitransform anomaly may also occur when the increase of cost—benefit in terms of security is not justified, as when one is applying ESP with AES 256 after having applied ESP with AES 128. Resolving these anomalies is delicate. Every case needs to be considered individually, because the "protection strength" needs to be measured and compared with the performance loss, but an official measure does not exist and every organization may have its own evaluation criteria.

Internet Protocol Security Interpolicy Conflict Detection

Together with the explicit deny action, communications can also be blocked in case of misconfigurations or if the peer authentication fails, if the *security association* defining the algorithms and keys to use to protect the channel is not available and nonnegotiable, or if there is more than one security association when a unique security association is expected. Therefore, the types of anomaly are analogous to those presented in distributed systems. In fact, IPsec communications can be shadowed (block traffic already blocked by the upstream device) and spurious (allow traffic already blocked by the upstream device).

In addition, it is possible to highlight *interpolicy channel overlapping*, presenting the same mechanism as the intrapolicy case but involving more than two elements. To protect communication between Source s and Destination d, there are three gateways, g_1, g_2, and g_3, which are encountered in this order by packets from s to d (Fig. 55.13). The following policy is enforced:

- s creates a secure channel (transport mode) to g_2 with protection p_1.
- g_1 creates a tunnel to g_3 with protection p_2.

FIGURE 55.12 Internet Protocol Security intrapolicy overlapping conflict.

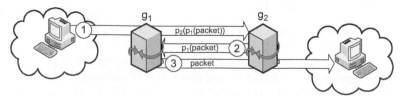

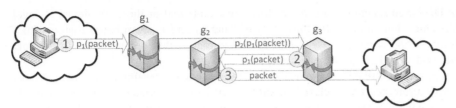

FIGURE 55.13 To protect communication between sources and Destination d, there are three gateways: g_1, g_2, and g_3.

Therefore, the resulting communications are:

1. $s \rightarrow g_1$ protected with p_1
2. $g_1 \rightarrow g_3$ protected with p_1 and p_2
3. $g_3 \rightarrow g_2$ protected with p_1 (p_2 is removed at g_3)
4. $g_2 \rightarrow d$ with no protection

IPsec devices are managed by different people who often work in different units; therefore interpolicy conflicts are relatively frequent. Sun et al. [46] proposed a new architecture that stores all of the IPsec policy centrally and offers access via a manager that also enforces an access control policy. In addition, the proposed work aims to manipulate the SPDB automatically to avoid or recover some of the anomalies presented before.

6. SEMANTIC WEB TECHNOLOGY FOR CONFLICT DETECTION

The term *Semantic Web* refers to both a vision and a set of technologies. The vision is articulated, in particular by the World Wide Web Consortium (W3C), as an extension to the current idea of the Web in which knowledge and data could be published in a form easy for computers to understand and reason with. Doing so would support more sophisticated software systems that share knowledge, information, and data on the Web just as people do by publishing text and multimedia. Under the stewardship of the W3C, a set of languages, protocols, and technologies has been developed to realize this vision partially, to enable exploration and experimentation, and to support the evolution of the concepts and technology. The current set of W3C standards is based on Resource Description Framework (RDF) [47], a language that provides a basic capability of specifying graphs with a simple interpretation as a *semantic network* and serializing them in XML and several other popular Web systems (e.g., JavaScript Object Notation). Because it is a graph-based representation, RDF data are often reduced to a set of triples in which each represents an edge in the graph or, alternatively, a binary predicate. The Web Ontology Language (OWL) [48] is a family of knowledge representation languages based on Description Logic (DL) [49] with a representation in RDF. OWL supports the specification and use of ontologies that consist of terms representing individuals, classes of individuals, properties, and axioms that assert constraints over them.

The use of OWL to describe and verify the properties of policies offers several important advantages that are particularly critical in distributed environments possibly involving coordination across multiple organizations. First, most policy languages define constraints over classes of targets, objects, actions, and other kinds of information (location). A substantial part of the development of a policy is often devoted to the precise specification of these classes. This is especially important if the policy is shared among multiple organizations that must adhere to or enforce the policy, even though they have their own native schemas or data models for the domain in question. The second advantage is that OWL's grounding in logic facilitates the translation of policies expressed in OWL to other formalisms, either for further analysis or for execution.

Semantic Web technology offers an extensive collection of tools that can be used to model and represent policy conflicts. Several approaches can be adopted, with different profiles in terms of abstractness and efficiency. There are three main approaches to discover conflicts: standard reasoners, ad hoc reasoning methods, and rule-based inferencing. In the next subsections we characterize these three alternatives.

Use of Standard Reasoners

The standard reasoner is one of the core elements of an ontology-based system. Starting from the information contained in the ontology described in OWL, it is able to perform several tasks (it is able to check the consistency and validity of the ontology, classify its information, answer queries, and generate inferences) using a variety of techniques derived from the work of the artificial intelligence community.

In particular, standard DL reasoning performed with regard to a formal ontology can check complex consistency constraints in the model. Such constraints are different from the usual ones from database and Unified Modeling Language (UML)-like systems. In OWL-DL, which is the portion of OWL restricted to the expressivity of DL, we can express:

- Constraints on properties, domains, and ranges
- Definitions of concepts (classes) in terms of relationships with other elements
- Boolean operations on classes

One of the main differences between DL-based schema definitions and UML or Entity relationship definitions concerns the constraints on property domains and ranges. Properties can be defined in a general way, and their behavior in terms of range type can be precisely described while refining the ontology concepts. This promotes the definition and reuse of high-level properties without losing the ability to force precise typing. In this way, the resolution of some conflicts can be explicitly expressed in the policy without the need to rely on an external conflict resolution option or implicit priorities. For instance, authorizations associated with a subject administrator can be denoted as having higher priority, dominating in possible conflicts with other authorizations.

Ad Hoc Reasoning Methods

Standard *DL* reasoners can answer complex questions and verify structural and nonstructural constraints. Furthermore, DL-based language expressiveness often exceeds classical solutions (such as UML for design and SQL for data storage models). This supports the description and verification of more complex structural constraints. For example, if we consider the approach used in Finin et al. [50], in which the roles are represented as individuals of the class Role, the *roleHierarchy*: *Role* → *Role* property[3] is used to connect each role to its direct subroles and the *canHaveRole+*: *Identity* → *Role* property is used to represent the roles that each identity (user) can activate, directly or indirectly, thanks to the presence of positive role authorizations. Thus, *roleHierarchy* (r_1, r_2) means that role r_1 is a superrole of r_2. Its transitive closure *canBe+*: *Role* → *Role* can be used to identify all the direct or indirect subroles. The subrole (as well as its inverse superrole) relationship is not a containment and does not define a taxonomy on identities (a superrole of Role R is intended to be more privileged than R and is available to a more restricted set of identities).

With these tools it is possible, for instance, to offer an immediate management of SoD constraints. The user role assignment relation is represented using role authorizations, which specialize authorizations with the specification of the role that the principal is allowed or forbidden to assume. An SoD constraint between Role r_1 and r_2 then can be expressed using a negative role authorization r_{auth} that forbids Role r_1 from enacting Role r_2. SoD constraints are enforced both at the role hierarchy level (in this way we directly prevent a Role r_1 from being declared superrole of another Role r_2, such that r_1 and r_2

are in an SoD constraint) and at the user hierarchy level (to prevent two Roles r_1 and r_2 from being assigned to a user, directly or indirectly, that are involved in an SoD constraint).

To show a more concrete example, we assume that class *RoleAuthorization* ⊆ Authorization represents the role authorizations, and properties *grantedTo*: *RoleAuthorization* → *Principal* and *enabledRole*: *RoleAuthorization* → *Role* are used to represent, respectively, the role enabled by the role authorization and the principal to which the role is assigned. To keep track of all SoD conflicts on roles, we can define a class *SoDOnRole* ⊆ *Role*. SoD constraints on the role hierarchy can be expressed adding to the ontology the following set of axioms:

$$\forall auth \in RoleAuthorization: sign(auth, -),$$

$$grantedTo(auth, r_1), enabledRole(auth, r_2)$$

$$SoDOnRole \equiv \exists canBe + .\{r_1\} \cap \exists canBe + .\{r_2\}$$

The interpretation of these axioms is that for each negative role authorization, there is an instance in class SoDOnRole only if there exists a single role that belongs to r_1 and to r_2. We can thus enforce the SoD at the role hierarchy level simply by adding the axiom *SoDOnRole* ⊆ ⊥ to the ontology, which declares as consistent the ontology only if the class is empty.

In a way similar to what we have done for the identification of SoD conflicts at the role hierarchy level, we can define a class *SoDOnUser* ⊆ *Identity* that keeps track of the conflicts on the user hierarchy. We then express SoD constraints using the following axioms:

$$\forall auth \in RoleAuthorization: sign(auth, -),$$

$$grantedTo(auth, r_1), enableRole(auth, r_2)$$

$$SoDOUser \equiv \exists canHaveRole$$

$$+ .\{r_1\} \cap \exists canHaveRole + .\{r_2\}$$

and to enforce the SoD constraints we simply have to add to the ontology the axiom *SoDOnUser* ⊆ ⊥.

This approach can easily be extended to handle other kinds of SoD constraints, such as *Permission-based SoD* (which requires that no user be allowed to do both Actions a_1 and a_2) or *Object-based SoD* (which requires that no user can access both Resources res_1 and res_2). However, DL systems, as well as *Semantic Web* tools in general, are designed and implemented with a focus on knowledge management services, such as knowledge integration, schema matching, and instance retrieval. Such a specialization raises some limitations on the use of pure DL reasoning in real scenarios, in which reasoning must be carried out on a well-defined and complete description of a closed system.

---

3. The notation "*R*: *A* → *B*" has to be interpreted according to DL conventions. It states that *A* and *B* are, respectively, the domain and the range of Property *R*, with no further constraints about the functionality or completeness of *R*.

Closed World Assumption

Closed World Assumption (CWA) reasoning is a generally accepted requirement in model-driven systems. Conversely, DL reasoners usually work under the Open World Assumption. This means that the facts asserted in the model (about the layout topology or the authorization policies) are not assumed to be complete. Obviously, this can become a problem if model characteristics are described in terms of the existence of some properties or some relationships between model elements.

Reasoning on Complex Property Paths

Reasoning on complex property paths (commutatively of nontrivial graphs), creates uncertainty of the formal logics the language is based on. Checking the closure of complex paths is beyond the expressive power of classical database systems, but unfortunately it is sometimes necessary to check structural constraints. This is the case, for example, for the consistency loop in Fig. 55.14, which states that:

an authorization of executing an action must be assigned to a resource (Database) that runs on a system (DBMS) compatible with the action type (Select, Create, Delete).

Unique Name Assumption

Unique Name Assumption is a commonly accepted assumption in most model-driven tools. It consists of assuming that different names will always denote different elements in the model. This is usually not true in DL reasoners because of the essential nature of knowledge integration problems. In fact, in the Semantic Web scenario, different authors may describe the same entities (both shared conceptualizations and physical objects), assigning a new name, generally in the form of a Uniform Resource Identifier, defined independently from other users.

These properties must be considered carefully when applying DL and Semantic Web tools to the detection of policy conflicts. The obstacles introduced can be solved as long as attention is paid to them. Misbehaviors of the system can be observed otherwise.

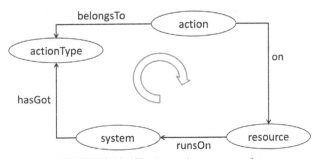

FIGURE 55.14 Simple consistency constraint.

Rule-Based Inferencing

Rule inference reasoning is widely used in knowledge management systems. Some combinations of theorem-proving systems (such as DL ones) and rule inference systems have been proposed to address some limitations of decidable theorem-proving systems.

Semantic Web Rule Language (SWRL) is the W3C standard proposal for integrating rule-based inferencing into systems that represent knowledge as a set of RDF triples and introducing some limitations to the use of the rules, to preserve joint system decidability. In a real scenario, the main advantage of combining rules and classical theorem-proving systems is the support for complex property chains. In fact, even if some *OWL* profiles introduce the support for the chaining of properties (aka roles in DL terminology), this may not be sufficient to express some complex topological properties. For example, the simple consistency loop shown in Fig. 55.14 is not enforceable at the schema level using only DL axioms. To perform a consistency check on Fig. 55.14, a simple SWRL rule like this one is needed:

$$on\ (\ ?\ a_1, ?\ r_1)\ ,\ belongsTo\ (\ ?\ a_1, ?\ act_1)\ ,\ runsOn\ (\ ?\ r_1, ?\ s_1),\ hasGot\ (\ ?\ s_1, ?\ act_2)\ ,\ differentFrom\ (\ ?\ act_1, ?\ act_2)\ -> Error\ (\ ?\ a_1,\ Error)$$

This SWRL rule verifies whether there is an Action a_1 belonging to Action type act_1 that is applied to Resource r_1, which runs on Service s_1, which has an Action type act_2; if act_1 and act_2 are verified to be incompatible (using the *differentFrom* predicate), an instance of class Error is created, recording a_1. Essentially, using this rule we can verify that all the *system* instances on which the action is granted are compatible with the *actionType*. Violations are recorded into Error.

As a technical note, we observe that as a general outcome of the adoption of the *Open World Assumption*, even if we could enforce the existence of the loops, we would not be able to require that such loops be explicitly stated into the assertional part of the semantic model (*A-box*). At the opposite end, owing to decidability issues (DL safe rules), the rule-based component of the language operates in a kind of CWA limited to the nodes. This means that a forward chaining rule can be triggered by any property derived by the reasoning, but involving only nodes that are explicitly named in the A-box. Then, we can operate only on nodes and properties explicitly stated in the semantic model. Furthermore, rules can freely combine as antecedent triple patterns to capture complex topological structures, and this solves the lack of complex property chains of *DLs*. This means that we can check for loops, or for the absence of loops, by adding custom rules to the ontology. However, SWRL safe rules can consume only positive knowledge, so they can be used directly to detect errors that consist of the existence of some structure in the ontology: that is, the existence of a loop.

Semantic Web technology offers an interesting potential for detecting conflicts in a variety of settings. Integration with a rich environment of tools, open source and commercial, together with the increasing familiarity that users are acquiring with them, make this option particularly interesting for the realization of sophisticated conflict-detection solutions. These approaches support the flexible definition and identification of conflicts, going beyond the classifications introduced in this chapter and adapting the model to the specific requirements of every application scenario.

7. SUMMARY

The detection and management of conflicts in security policies is an important topic for both the research and industrial communities. The chapter was not exhaustive in its treatment of the topic, although it is extensive. The goal was to focus on the detection of conflicts, considering abstract and executable policies, and illustrating in greater detail the detection of policy conflicts in computer networks, which is the area that sees the greater industrial support. Support in industrial products can be expected to appear in the near future for security policies in other scenarios and at a variety of abstraction levels. The discussion of Semantic Web technology has shown how this family of tools can be applied to this task, offering a strategy that can be particularly interesting for deployment in real systems.

We expect that conflict detection techniques will become common components of tools for the design and configuration of security. The Policy and Security Configuration Management project described in Chapter 26 aims to realize a policy-based security management; it represents an interesting example of such a system.

Finally, let us move on to the real interactive part of this chapter: review questions/exercises, hands-on projects, case projects, and the optional team case project. The answers and/or solutions by chapter can be found in the Online Instructor's Solutions Manual.

CHAPTER REVIEW QUESTIONS/ EXERCISES

True/False

1. True or False? The evolution of information systems is continuously increasing the capabilities and range of offered services, leading to infrastructures that see the participation of a larger number of users, a greater level of integration among separate systems, and a correspondingly larger impact of possible misbehaviors.

2. True or False? A typical top-down representation of the protection of an information system might consist of five layers.

3. True or False? Security requirements are a low-level, declarative representation of the rules according to which access control must be regulated.

4. True or False? Policies represent how security requirements are mapped to the systems used for service provisioning.

5. True or False? Abstract policies provide a formal representation of access control and its behavior.

Multiple Choice

1. What describes the access control policy in a way that can be immediately processed by an access control component?
   A. Privacy-enhancing technology
   B. Location technology
   C. Web-based
   D. Executable policies
   E. Data controller

2. What mechanisms correspond to the low-level functions that implement the executable policies?
   A. Policy enforcement
   B. Location technology
   C. Valid
   D. Privacy-enhancing technologies
   E. Web technology

3. What conflicts arise when principals are authorized to do an Action a on a Resource r by a positive authorization, and are forbidden to do the same Action a on the Resource r by a negative authorization?
   A. Data minimization
   B. *XACML*
   C. Private information
   D. Contradictory
   E. Security

4. What conflicts arise when an authorization is dominated by other authorizations and does not contribute to the policy (its removal would not modify the behavior of the system)?
   A. Privacy metrics
   B. Retention time
   C. Redundant
   D. Privacy preferences
   E. Taps

5. What conflicts occur when the conflict can never manifest itself in a system?
   A. Irrelevant
   B. Anonymous communication
   C. Data-handling policies
   D. Disclose-to
   E. Social engineering

EXERCISE
Problem
What is meant by the phrase "where technically feasible"?

Hands-on Projects
Project
What is meant by the phrase "reasonable business judgment"?

Case Projects
Problem
What is meant by *data, documents, documentation, logs, and records*? What are the differences between these terms?

Optional Team Case Project
Problem
What are some sample security policy test procedures?

ACKNOWLEDGMENTS
This work was partially funded by the European Community in the scope of the research project PoSecCo (Project No. 257129), under the Information and Communication Technologies theme of the Seventh Framework Program for R&D (FP7). The work by Stefano Paraboschi was partially supported by the PRIN 2008 project PEPPER (2008SY2PH4) and the PRIN 2010-11 Project GenData-2020.

REFERENCES
[1] A. Anderson, eXtensible Access Control Markup Language (XACML), Identity, 2006. http://www.oasis-open.org/committees/xacml/.
[2] S. Jajodia, P. Samarati, V.S. Subrahmanian, A logical language for expressing authorizations, in: Proceedings of the 1997 IEEE Symposium on Security and Privacy (SP '97), IEEE Computer Society, Washington, DC, USA, 1997.
[3] N. Damianou, N. Dulay, E. Lupu, M. Sloman, The ponder policy specification language, in: POLICY '01 Proceedings of the International Workshop on Policies for Distributed Systems and Networks, Springer-Verlag, London, UK, 2001.
[4] L. Kagal, T. Finin, A. Joshi, A policy language for a pervasive computing environment, POLICY '03, in: Proceedings of the 4th IEEE International Workshop on Policies for Distributed Systems and Networks, IEEE Computer Society, Washington, DC, USA, 2003.
[5] G. Tonti, J.M. Bradshaw, R. Jeffers, R. Montanari, N. Suri, A. Uszok, Semantic web languages for policy representation and reasoning: a comparison of KAoS, Rei, and Ponder, in: D. Fensel, K.P. Sycara, J. Mylopoulos (Eds.), International Semantic Web Conference, Springer, 2003, pp. 419–437.
[6] E. Lupu, M. Sloman, Conflicts in policy-based distributed systems management, IEEE Trans. Software Eng. 25 (6) (1999) 852–869.
[7] N. Coward, Y. Yoshida, Java servlet specification version 2.4, Tech. Rep. (2003).
[8] M. Casalino, R. Thion, M.S. Hacid, S. Fischer-Hbner, S. Katsikas, G. Quirchmayr, Access control configuration for J2EE web applications: a formal perspective, in: S. Fischer-Hbner, S. Katsikas, G. Quirchmayr (Eds.), Trust, Privacy and Security in Digital Business, Lecture Notes in Computer Science, vol. 7449, Springer, Berlin Heidelberg, 2012, pp. 30–35.
[9] A. Rubinger, B. Burke, R. Monson-Haefel, Enterprise JavaBeans 3.1, in: Java Series, O'Reilly Media, Incorporated, 2010.
[10] E. Al-Shaer, H. Hamed, Modeling and management of firewall policies, IEEE Trans. Network Serv. Manage. 1 (1) (2004) 2–10.
[11] A.R. Khakpour, A.X. Liu, Quantifying and querying network reachability, in: Proc. of the 2010 IEEE 30th Int. Conf. on Distributed Computing Systems, Washington, DC, USA, 2010, pp. 817–826.
[12] D. Taylor, Survey and taxonomy of packet classification techniques, ACM Comput. Surv. 37 (3) (2005) 238–275.
[13] A. Wool, A quantitative study of firewall configuration errors, Computer 37 (2004) 62–67.
[14] A. Wool, Trends in firewall configuration errors: measuring the holes in swiss cheese, IEEE Internet Comput. 14 (2010) 58–65.
[15] Insecure.Com LLC: Network mapper. http://nmap.org/.
[16] The Hachers Choice, Amap. http://thc.org/thc-amap/.
[17] T.N. Security, Nessus vulnerability scanner. http://www.tenable.com/products/nessus/nessus-product-overview.
[18] A. Mayer, A. Wool, E. Ziskind, Fang: a firewall analysis engine, in: Proc. of the 2000 IEEE Symposium on Security and Privacy, Washington, DC, USA, 2000, pp. 177–187.
[19] A. Wool, Architecting the lumeta firewall analyzer, in: Proc. of the 10th Conference on USENIX Security Symposium, vol. 10, 2001, p. 7. Berkeley, CA, USA.
[20] A. Mayer, A. Wool, E. Ziskind, Offline firewall analysis, Int. J. Inf. Secur. 5 (3) (2006) 125–144.
[21] S. Hazelhurst, A. Attar, R. Sinnappan, Algorithms for improving the dependability of firewall and filter rule lists, in: Proc. of the 2000 Int. Conf. on Dependable Systems and Networks, Washington, DC, USA, 2000, pp. 576–585.
[22] A.X. Liu, M.G. Gouda, Firewall policy queries, IEEE Trans. Parallel Distrib. Syst. 20 (2009) 766–777.
[23] J.D. Moffett, M.S. Sloman, Policy conflict analysis in distributed system management, J. Organ. Comput. 4 (1) (1993) 1–22.
[24] M. Sloman, Policy driven management for distributed systems, J. Network Syst. Manage. 2 (4) (1994) 333–360.
[25] H. Adiseshu, S. Suri, G.M. Parulkar, Detecting and resolving packet filter conflicts, INFOCOM (2000) 1203–1212.
[26] F. Baboescu, G. Varghese, Fast and scalable conflict detection for packet classifiers, Comput. Networks 42 (6) (2003) 717–735.
[27] V. Srinivasan, S. Suri, G. Varghese, Packet classification using tuple space search, in: Proc. of the Conference on Applications, Technologies, Architectures, and Protocols for Computer Communication, New York, NY, USA, 1999, pp. 135–146.
[28] C. Basile, A. Cappadonia, A. Lioy, Geometric interpretation of policy specification, in: IEEE Policy 2008, New York, NY, 2008, pp. 78–81.
[29] C. Basile, A. Cappadonia, A. Lioy, Network-level access control policy analysis and transformation, IEEE/ACM Trans. Networking (2012).

[30] M. Benelbahri, A. Bouhoula, Tuple based approach for anomalies detection within firewall filtering rules, in: ISCC 2007, Aveiro, Portugal, 2007, pp. 63–70.

[31] S. Thanasegaran, Y. Yin, Y. Tateiwa, Y. Katayama, N. Takahashi, A topological approach to detect conflicts in firewall policies, in: IPDPS 2009, Rome, Italy, 2009, pp. 1–7.

[32] S. Ferraresi, S. Pesic, L. Trazza, A. Baiocchi, Automatic conflict analysis and resolution of traffic filtering policy for firewall and security gateway, in: ICC '07, Glasgow, Scotland, 2007, pp. 1304–1310.

[33] M.G. Gouda, X.Y.A. Liu, Firewall design: consistency, completeness, and compactness, in: Proc. of the 24th Int. Conf. on Distributed Computing Systems (ICDCS '04), Washington, DC, USA, 2004, pp. 320–327.

[34] A.X. Liu, M.G. Gouda, Complete redundancy detection in firewalls, in: Proc. of the 19th Annual IFIP WG 11.3 Working Conference on Data and Applications Security, 2005, pp. 193–206.

[35] J.G. Alfaro, N. Boulahia-Cuppens, F. Cuppens, Complete analysis of configuration rules to guarantee reliable network security policies, Int. J. Inf. Secur. 7 (2) (2008) 103–122.

[36] J. Garcia-Alfaro, F. Cuppens, N. Cuppens-Boulahia, S. Preda, MIRAGE: a management tool for the analysis and deployment of network security policies, in: Proc. of the 5th Int. Workshop on Data Privacy Management, 2011, pp. 203–215.

[37] H. Hu, G.J. Ahn, K. Kulkarni, Ontology-based policy anomaly management for autonomic computing, in: D. Georgakopoulos, J.B.D. Joshi (Eds.), CollaborateCom, 2011, pp. 487–494.

[38] A.K. Bandara, A.C. Kakas, E.C. Lupu, A. Russo, Using argumentation logic for firewall configuration management, Integr. Network Manage. (2009) 180–187.

[39] A.X. Liu, E. Torng, C.R. Meiners, Firewall compressor: an algorithm for minimizing firewall policies, INFOCOM (2008) 176–180.

[40] L. Buttyan, G. Pék, T.V. Thong, Consistency verification of stateful firewalls is not harder than the stateless case, Infocommun. J. 54 (2–3) (2009) 1–8.

[41] M.G. Gouda, A.X. Liu, A model of stateful firewalls and its properties, in: Proc. of the IEEE Int. Conf. on Dependable Systems and Networks (DSN-05), Yokohama, Japan, 2005.

[42] F. Cuppens, N. Cuppens-Boulahia, J. Garca-Alfaro, T. Moataz, X. Rimasson, Handling stateful firewall anomalies, in: Information Security and Privacy Research—27th IFIP TC 11 Information Security and Privacy Conference, SEC 2012, Heraklion, Crete, Greece, June 4–6, 2012, Proceedings, vol. 376, 2012, pp. 174–186.

[43] E. Al-Shaer, H. Hamed, R. Boutaba, M. Hasan, Conflict classification and analysis of distributed firewall policies, IEEE JSAC 23 (10) (2005) 2069–2084.

[44] H. Hamed, E. Al-Shaer, W. Marrero, Modeling and verification of IPsec and VPN security policies, ICNP '05, in: Proceedings of the 13th IEEE International Conference on Network Protocols, IEEE Computer Society, Washington, DC, USA, 2005.

[45] Z. Fu, S.F. Wu, H. Huang, K. Loh, F. Gong, I. Baldine, et al., IPsec/VPN security policy: correctness, conflict detection, and resolution, in: POLICY, 2001, pp. 39–56.

[46] H.M. Sun, S.Y. Chang, Y.H. Chen, B.Z. He, C.K. Chen, The design and implementation of IPsec conflict avoiding and recovering system, in: TENCON 2007 – 2007 IEEE Region 10 Conference, 2007, pp. 1–4.

[47] O. Lassila, R.R. Swick, Resource Description Framework (RDF) Model and Syntax Specification, 1999.

[48] S. Bechhofer, F. van Harmelen, J. Hendler, I. Horrocks, D.L. McGuinness, P.F. Patel-Schneider, et al., OWL Web Ontology Language Reference, Technical report, W3C, 2004, http://www.w3.org/TR/owl-ref/.

[49] F. Baader, D. Calvanese, D.L. McGuinness, D. Nardi, P.F. Patel-Schneider, Description logic handbook, in: F. Baader, D. Calvanese, D.L. McGuinness, D. Nardi, P.F. Patel-Schneider (Eds.), Description Logic Handbook, Cambridge University Press, 2003.

[50] T. Finin, A. Joshi, L. Kagal, J. Niu, R. Sandhu, W. Winsborough, et al., ROWLBAC: representing role based access control in OWL, in: Proc. of SACMAT, ACM, 2008.

Chapter 56

Supporting User Privacy Preferences in Digital Interactions

Sara Foresti and Pierangela Samarati
Università degli Studi di Milano, Crema, Italy

1. INTRODUCTION

The advancements in Information and Communications Technology (ICT) allow users to take more and more advantage of the availability of online services (and resources) that can be accessed anywhere and at any time. In such a scenario, the server providing the service and the requesting user may be unknown to each other. As a consequence, traditional access control systems [1] based on the preliminary identification and authentication of users requesting access to a service cannot be adopted, and are usually not suited to open scenarios (e.g., Refs. [2–5]). The solutions proposed to allow servers to regulate access to the services they offer, while not requiring users to manage a huge number of accounts, rely on attribute-based access control mechanisms (e.g., Refs. [3,4,6–16]). Policies regulating access to services define conditions that the requesting client must satisfy to gain access to the service of interest. Upon receiving a request to access a service, the server will not return a yes/no reply but it will send to the client the conditions that she must satisfy to be authorized to access the service. To prove to the server the possession of the attributes required to gain the access, the client releases digital certificates (i.e., *credentials*) signed by a trusted third party, the certification authority, who declares under its responsibility that the certificate holder possesses the attributes stated in the certificate. Practically, credentials are the digital representation of paper certificates (e.g., ID card, passport, credit card). The adoption of credentials in access control has several advantages. First, credential-based access control enables clients to conveniently access web services, without the need to remember a different *<username, password>* pair for each system with which she wants to interact. Second, it offers better protection against adversaries interested in improperly acquiring users' access privileges.

The use of credentials to enforce access control restrictions in open environments has been widely studied in the last 15 years. Most attention has, however, been devoted to the server-side of the problem, proposing a number of novel policy languages for specifying access control rules (e.g., Refs. [4,6–8,14–16]); policy engines, for the evaluation of access requests and the enforcement of policy restrictions (e.g., Refs. [13,14,16,17]); and strategies for communicating access conditions to the requesting clients, possibly engaging a negotiation protocol (e.g., Refs. [13,14,16–20]). Since the interacting parties are assumed to be unknown to each other, the client may not know which attributes/credentials to release to gain access to the service of interest. As a consequence, the server should send to the client its policy, which may be considered sensitive and therefore needs to be adequately protected before being disclosed. Most of the current approaches implicitly assume that clients adopt an approach symmetric to the one used by servers for regulating access to the sensitive information certified by their credentials. Although expressive and powerful, these solutions do not fully support the specific protection requirements of the clients. In fact, clients are interested in a solution that is expressive and flexible enough to support an intuitive and user-friendly definition of the sensitivity/privacy levels that they perceive as characterizing their data. These preferences are used to choose which credentials to release when more than one subset of credentials satisfy the access control policy defined by the server (e.g., to buy medicine, a patient needs to prove her identity by releasing either her identity card or her passport).

This chapter provides an overview of the privacy issues arising in open environments, both from the client's and the server's point of view, and illustrates some solutions proposed to overcome these problems. The remainder of this chapter is organized as follows. Section 2 introduces basic concepts and describes the desiderata of privacy-aware access control systems operating in open environments. Sections 3–6 illustrate some recent proposals that permit clients to specify privacy preferences that are then used to determine which credentials to disclose to gain access to a service of interest. Section 7 focuses on the server side of the problem, describing approaches that permit to regulate the disclosure of sensitive access control policies. Section 8 presents some open issues that still need to be addressed. Finally, Section 9 presents our concluding remarks.

2. BASIC CONCEPTS AND DESIDERATA

In this section, we first describe the concepts at the basis of the proposals that we will describe in the following. Then, we discuss the desiderata that an attribute-based access control system should satisfy to effectively support both client and server privacy preferences.

Client Portfolio

The information that a client can provide to a server to gain access to a service are organized in a *portfolio* including both *credentials* signed by third parties and certifying client properties, and *declarations* stating uncertified properties uttered by the client [7]. Each credential c in the client portfolio is characterized by: a unique identifier $id(c)$, an issuer $issuer(c)$, a set of attributes $attributes(c)$, and a credential type $type(c)$. The type of a credential determines the set of attributes it certifies. Credential types are traditionally organized in a rooted *hierarchy*, where intermediate nodes represent abstractions defined over specific credential types that correspond to the leaves of the hierarchy [21]. Formally, a hierarchy H of credential types is a pair $(T, \leq_{isa})$, where T is the set of all credential types and abstractions defined over them, and $\leq_{isa}$ is a partial order relationship on T. Given two credential types t_i and t_j, $t_i \leq_{isa} t_j$ if t_j is an abstraction of t_i. For instance, *photo_id* is an abstraction of credential types *id_card* and *passport* (i.e., $id\_card \leq_{isa} photo\_id$ and $passport \leq_{isa} photo\_id$). The root of the hierarchy is node *, representing any credential type. We note that

declarations are usually modeled as a type of credentials, signed by the client herself. Fig. 56.1 illustrates an example of a hierarchy of credential types.

The hierarchy of credential types is a knowledge shared between the client and the server. In fact, while a client knows exactly the different instances of credential types composing her portfolio, the server formulates its requests over credential types since it cannot be aware of the instances composing the client portfolio. We note that a client may possess different credentials of the same type (e.g., she can have more than one credit card).

Depending on the cryptographic protocol used for their generation, credentials can be classified as atomic or nonatomic. Atomic credentials are the most common kind of credentials used today in distributed systems (e.g., X.509 certificates) and can only be released as a whole. As a consequence, even if an atomic credential certifies attributes that are not required to gain access to a service, if the client decides to release it, these attributes will be disclosed to the server. Nonatomic credentials have been proposed as a successful approach to limit data disclosure (e.g., U-Prove, Idemix, and HM12 [22–24]). Credentials generated adopting these technologies permit the client to selectively release a subset of the attributes certified by the credential (as well as the existence of the credential itself). Note that the release of an attribute (or a set thereof) certified by a nonatomic credential entails the disclosure of the existence in the client portfolio of the credential itself. Clearly, declarations are nonatomic credentials.

Attributes within credentials are characterized by a *type*, a *name*, and a *value* (e.g., attribute *Name* of type *Name* with value *Bob*), which can either depend only on the client or on the specific credential certifying the attribute. In the first case, the attribute is *credential-independent* since its value is the same, independently from the credential certifying it (e.g., Name and DoB are credential-independent attributes). In the second case, the attribute is *credential-dependent* since its value depends not only on the credential holder, but also on the specific instance of the credential certifying it (e.g., attribute type *CCNum*, representing the credit card number, is a credential-dependent attribute since each credit card has a different number).

For instance, Table 56.1 illustrates an example of client portfolio composed of four atomic and three non-atomic credentials. In Table 56.1, credential-independent attributes are in roman, while credential-dependent attributes are in *italic*.

Disclosure Policies

Attribute-based access control restricts access to server service depending on the attributes and credentials that the requesting client discloses to the server. The policy regulating access to services is therefore defined over attributes and credentials provided by clients. Since the server may not know the

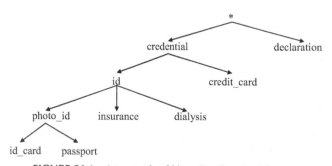

FIGURE 56.1 An example of hierarchy of credential types.

TABLE 56.1 An Example of Client Portfolio

id(c)	Atomic	type(c)	attributes(c)
MyIdCard	✔	id_card	Name, DoB, City
MyPassport		passport	Name, DoB, Country
MyVISA	✔	credit_card	Name, *VISANum, VISALimit*
MyAmEx	✔	credit_card	Name, *AmExNum, AmExLimit*
MyDialysis		dialysis	Name, City
MyInsurance	✔	insurance	Name, *Company, Coverage*
MyDecl		declaration	Name, DoB, City, Country, *VISANum, VISALimit, AmExNum, AmExLimit, Company, Coverage*, e-mail

requesting client and therefore ignore the credential instances in her portfolio, the access control policy is defined considering only the hierarchy of credential types, which represents a common knowledge to the interacting parties. An access control policy is defined as a Boolean formula composed of basic conditions *cond* of the form ($term_1$ *o* -$term_2$), where *o* is a predicate operator (e.g., $>$, $<$, $=$), and $term_1$ and $term_2$ are its operands. The operands of a basic condition can be either constant values, or (certified or declared) attributes represented by terms of the form *c.a*, where *c* is a variable representing a credential and *a* is the name of the attribute. For instance, basic condition *Coverage*$>$10,000 USD requires that the coverage offered by insurance is higher than 10,000 USD to access the service. The server may also define restrictions on the type of credentials that should certify the requested attributes and/or require that a set of attributes in the policy are certified by the same credential. As an example, policy (*type(c)* $=$ *insurance*) $\land$ (*c.Company* $\neq$ 'A') $\land$ (*c.Coverage* $>$ 10,000 USD) requires that attributes *Company* and *Coverage* are certified by the same credential *c*, of type *insurance*.

Trust Negotiation

Since clients and servers operating in open environments are assumed to be unknown to each other, they interact to build a trust relationship that permits the client to gain access to a service offered by the server. This trust relationship is built step by step through the exchange of credentials. Since credentials may certify sensitive information, their release is often regulated, like for services, by access control policies. Usually, these conditions require the release by the counterpart of another credential (or set thereof). As an example, a user agrees to release the certificate stating her dialysis condition to a server only if the server proves (through a certificate) to be a medical institution or a pharmacy recognized by the Health Ministry.

To gain access to a service, the client and the server must then find a sequence of certificates exchange, called strategy,

satisfying the access control policies of both parties. For instance, with reference to the above example, a successful strategy that permits the user to buy the medicine of interest consists of the following steps: (1) the patient sends her request to the pharmacy; (2) the pharmacy answers with a request for a certificate proving that the user has a nephrological disease; (3) the client, in turn, asks the pharmacy the certificate proving that it is recognized by the Health Ministry; (4) the pharmacy releases to the client the requested certificate; (5) the client then discloses to the pharmacy her dialysis certificate; (6) finally, the server grants access to the service. Different approaches have been proposed in the literature to identify a successful trust negotiation strategy (e.g., Refs. [13,14,16–20]) that depends not only on the policies defined by the parties and on the credentials at their disposal, but also on their choice of disclosure/nondisclosure of their data. As an example, an eager strategy would disclose a credential as soon as the policy regulating its release is satisfied, while a more parsimonious strategy permits the release of a credential only if there exists a successful strategy that will finally grant the client access to the service. It is interesting to note that, given the policies and credentials of the interacting client and server, there may exist more than one successful strategy. For instance, with reference to the portfolio in Table 56.1, policy (*type(c)* $=$ *id*) $\land$ (*c.DoB* $<$ 01/01/1994) can be satisfied by the client releasing either credential *MyIdCard* or *MyPassport*. Although all the successful strategies may seem equivalent, this is generally not true. Both the client and the server may prefer to release a credential over another one because they perceive a different sensitivity level associated with the information that credentials certify. For instance, the client may prefer to release her *id_card* over her *passport*.

Client Privacy Preferences

Given the server request, the client needs to determine which credentials and/or attributes to disclose to satisfy it. This task becomes harder if different subsets of credentials and/or attributes in the client portfolio can be used to fulfill the server policy, since the client needs to choose among them. Ideally, the choice should be driven by the sensitivity level that the client perceives for her credentials and attributes, as she will be more willing to disclose less sensitive portfolio components. It is therefore necessary to provide clients with a flexible and effective system that automatically determines the release strategy that better satisfies her privacy preferences. To this purpose, a flexible and expressive model for representing privacy preferences needs to be defined. We now illustrate the main desiderata that a privacy-aware access control system should satisfy:

- *Fine-grained preference specification.* The privacy preferences associated with attributes and credentials in the client portfolio reflect the sensitivity perceived by the credential owner for the personal information represented by the attribute/credential. The model should support the definition of privacy preferences for each instance of attribute and credential in the client portfolio, meaning that different instances of the same credential type (and credential-dependent attribute) might be associated with different privacy preferences. For instance, with reference to the portfolio in Table 56.1, the client may prefer to release VISA credit card instead of AmEx.

- *Inheritance of privacy preferences.* To provide flexibility in the definition of privacy preferences and a user-friendly mechanism for their specification, the model should take advantage of the hierarchy of credential types characterizing the client portfolio. When the client portfolio is composed of a huge number of attributes and credentials, it might be difficult for the client to specify a different preference value for each credential and attribute. Privacy preferences associated with abstractions of credential types could, however, be inherited by all its specifications, if not overwritten by a more specific preference value, thus reducing the client overhead. For instance, with reference to the hierarchy of credential types in Fig. 56.1 and the portfolio in Table 56.1, the client may specify a single privacy preference associated with credential type *photo_id*, which is automatically inherited by credentials *MyId-Card* and *MyPassport*.

- *Partial order relationship and composition operator.* The domain of privacy preferences should be characterized by a (partial) order relationship $\geqslant$ that permits to precisely determine whether a given piece of personal information is more or less sensitive than another. The domain should also be characterized by a composition operator $\oplus$, which permits to compute the privacy preference value characterizing the release of a set of attributes and/or credentials. As an example, if the domain of privacy preferences is the set of positive integer numbers, the partial order relationship could be the "greater than" relationship (i.e., $\geq$), while the composition operator could be the sum operator (i.e., $+$).

- *Sensitive associations.* In different scenarios, the combined release of a set of attributes and/or credentials is considered more (or less) sensitive than the release of each portfolio component singularly taken. For instance, with reference to the portfolio in Table 56.1, the client may consider the combined release of attributes *DoB* and *City* more sensitive than the release of each of the two attributes, since their combination could be exploited to infer the identity of the client [25,26]. On the other hand, she may value the release of *City* and *Country* less sensitive than the release of the two attributes singularly taken, due to the dependency between the values of the two attributes. As a consequence, the model should support the definition of a privacy preference value for the combined release of a set of attributes and/or credentials that is different from the result of the combination of the privacy preferences of the items in the set.

- *Disclosure constraints.* There are situations where the client needs to specify restrictions on the combined release of portfolio components, since she wants to keep the association among a subset of attributes and/or credentials confidential, or limit their combined release. For instance, with reference to the portfolio in Table 56.1, the client may not be willing to release credential *MyDialysis* together with attribute *DoB*, to prevent the server from exploiting this information for data mining purposes (e.g., to analyze the age of people with nephrologic diseases).

- *Context-based preferences.* The privacy preferences associated with attributes and credentials may vary depending on the context in which their release is requested (i.e., depending on the requested service and/or on the server providing it). For instance, the client may be more willing to release her dialysis certificate to a pharmacy for buying a medicine than to a hotel for booking a room.

- *History-based preferences.* The preference of the client toward disclosing one credential (attribute, respectively) over another one may depend on the history of past interactions with the server offering the service. As a matter of fact, if the server already knows the attributes and credentials released by the client during a previous interaction, the client may be more willing to release the same (or a different) set of portfolio components. For instance, with reference to the portfolio in Table 56.1, assume that the client released credential *MyVISA* to a server to buy a service. When interacting again with the same server to buy another service, the client may prefer to use the same credit card, instead of releasing also credential *MyAmEx*.

- *Proof of possession.* Thanks to novel technologies, clients can release proofs of possession of certificates and proofs of the satisfaction of conditions (e.g., Refs. [22–24,27]). As a consequence, the model should also permit the client to specify privacy preferences associated with proofs (besides attributes and credentials on which proofs are defined). For instance, with reference to the portfolio in Table 56.1, the client may consider more sensitive the release of her *DoB* than the release of a proof that she is at least 18.
- *User-friendly preference specification.* The definition of privacy preferences should be easy for the client who may not be familiar with access control systems. As a consequence, it is necessary to provide clients with interfaces that permit to easily define preferences without introducing inconsistencies.

Server Privacy Preferences

With attribute-based access control, servers regulate access to their services based on the attributes and certificates presented by the requesting client. Upon receiving an access request, the server needs to communicate to the client the policy that she should satisfy to possibly gain access to the service. The access control policy could however be sensitive and the server may not be willing to disclose it completely to the client: while the communication of the complete policy favors the privacy of the client (since she can avoid disclosing her attributes and credentials if they would not satisfy the conditions in the policy), the communication of the attributes involved in the policy only favors the privacy of the server (since the specific conditions are not disclosed). Also, different portions of the same policy may be subject to different confidentiality requirements. For instance, assume that a pharmacy grants to clients access to the online medicine purchase service only if the insurance coverage of the clients is higher that 10,000 USD and the insurance company is not in the pharmacy black list. The pharmacy might not mind disclosing the fact that only clients with insurance coverage greater than 10,000 USD can access its services, but it does not want to reveal its black list. The system managing the disclosure of server policies should satisfy the following desiderata:

- *Disclosure policy.* The server should be able to define, at a fine-granularity level, how policy release should be regulated.
- *Policy communication.* The communication of the access control policy regulating access to the requested service to the client should guarantee that privacy requirements are satisfied and that the client has enough information to determine the set of attributes and/or credentials she needs to disclose to possibly gain access to the service.

It is therefore necessary to define a mechanism that adequately transforms the access control policy before communicating it to the client.
- *Integration with client mechanisms.* The approach designed to regulate policy release should be integrated with the one designed to manage the release of portfolio components at the client side.

Note that in a negotiation process, both the client requesting access to a service and the server providing it possess a portfolio and regulate the disclosure of credentials and attributes composing it according to their access control policy.

3. COST-SENSITIVE TRUST NEGOTIATION

A solution that takes disclosure preferences into consideration in attribute-based access control has been introduced in Ref. [28]. The authors propose to associate a *sensitivity cost* $w(c)$ with each credential c in the client (and server) portfolio, and with each access control policy p regulating credentials disclosure and access to services. A policy p is defined as a Boolean formula over the credentials in the counterparty's portfolio. Boolean variable representing credential c in policy p is *true* if c has already been disclosed; it is *false* otherwise. The sensitivity cost associated with credential c (policy p, respectively) models how much the credential's owner (party who defined the policy, respectively) values the release of the credential (policy, respectively) and the disclosure of the sensitive information that the credential certifies. Intuitively, a client (server, respectively) is more willing to disclose credentials (policies, respectively) with lower sensitivity cost and, vice versa, she prefers to keep credentials (policies, respectively) with high sensitivity cost confidential. For instance, Table 56.2 (Table 56.3, respectively) illustrates an example of client portfolio (server portfolio, respectively). For each credential, the table reports the policy regulating its disclosure, the sensitivity cost of the credential, and the

TABLE 56.2 An Example of Client Portfolio and Policies Regulating Its Disclosure

id(c)	w(c)	Policy p Regulating c	w(p)
MyIdCard	2	TRUE	0
MyPassport	4	TRUE	0
MyCreditCard	10	POS_register	5
MyDialysis	20	pharmacy_register	10
MyInsurance	15	pharmacy_register	10

TABLE 56.3 An Example of Server Portfolio and Policies Regulating Its Disclosure

id(c)	w(c)	Policy p Regulating c	w(p)
MyPOSRegister	2	TRUE	0
MyPharmacyRegister	5	passport ∨ id_card	4

sensitivity cost of it policy. Constant value TRUE is used in policy definition to model the case when the release of a credential is free, that is, it is not regulated by a policy (the portfolio in Table 56.2 is a simplified version of the portfolio in Table 56.1).

The goal of the client and the server engaging a negotiation protocol is that of *minimizing* the sensitivity cost of the credentials and policies exchanged during a successful negotiation strategy. This optimization problem can be formulated as follows [28].

Problem 1: Minimum Sensitivity Cost Problem

Let C_s be the set of server credentials and services; P_s be the set of policies regulating the disclosure of server credentials and access to services; C_c be the set of client credentials; P_c be the set of policies regulating the disclosure of client credentials; $w : C_s \cup P_s \cup C_c \cup P_c \rightarrow \mathbf{R}$ be the sensitivity cost function; and $s \in C_s$ be the service requested by the client. Find an exchange sequence of credentials and policies such that:

1. s is released to the client;
2. the policy regulating the disclosure of each credential released to the counterpart is satisfied before credential release;
3. the sum of the sensitivity costs of released credentials and policies is minimum.

The problem of computing a Minimum Sensitivity Cost strategy is NP-hard [28] and therefore any algorithm that solves it at optimum has exponential cost in the size of its input (i.e., the number of credentials and policies in $C_s \cup P_s \cup C_c \cup P_c$). In Ref. [28] the authors propose two different heuristic approaches for computing a good (although nonoptimal) solution to the problem. These heuristics have polynomial computational complexity and can be adopted when policies can be freely disclosed, and when they are associated with a sensitivity cost, respectively.

Nonsensitive Policies

The solution proposed for the simplified scenario where policies are not associated with a sensitivity cost (i.e., they can be freely released) is based on the definition of a *policy graph* modeling the policies regulating credential disclosure at both the client and server side. A policy graph $G(V,A,w)$ is defined as a weighted graph with:

- a vertex v_c for each credential c in $C_s \cup C_c$;
- a vertex v_s for each service s in C_s;
- a vertex v_T for constant value TRUE;
- a vertex v for each disjunction in the policies regulating credential release;
- an edge (v_i,v_j), with v_i and v_j vertexes representing credentials, if the release of the credential represented by v_i is a necessary condition to gain access to the credential represented by v_j;
- an edge (v_i,v_j), with v_i a vertex representing a credential and v_j a vertex representing a disjunction, if v_i is one of the clauses of the disjunction represented by v_j.

The weight of a vertex representing a credential corresponds to the sensitivity cost of the credential it represents, while other vertexes do not have weight. For instance, consider the access control policies in Tables 56.2 and 56.3 and service *MedicineBooking*, regulated by policy $p = dialysis \vee (id\_card \wedge (credit\_card \vee insurance))$. Fig. 56.2A illustrates the policy graph modeling the access control policies in the system.

The first step of the negotiation process consists in disclosing the policies regulating credential release and access to services at the client and at the server side. This information permits to correctly build the policy graph. Note that this disclosure is permitted thanks to the assumption that policies are not sensitive in this simplified scenario. The Minimum Sensitivity Cost problem then translates into the equivalent problem of determining a *Minimum Directed Acyclic Graph* for the policy graph, starting at vertex v_T (representing value TRUE) and ending at the vertex v_s representing the requested service s. Formally, a Minimum Directed Acyclic Graph is defined as follows.

Definition 1: Minimum Directed Acyclic Graph

Let $G(V,A,w)$ be a policy graph, v_T be the vertex representing value TRUE, and v_s be the vertex representing service s. A directed acyclic graph starting at v_T and ending at v_s is a sub-graph $G'(V',A',w)$ of G such that:

1. G' is acyclic;
2. $v_T, v_s \in V'$;
3. $\nexists (v_i, v_T) \in A', v_i \in V'$;
4. $\nexists (v_s, v_i) \in A', v_i \in V'$;

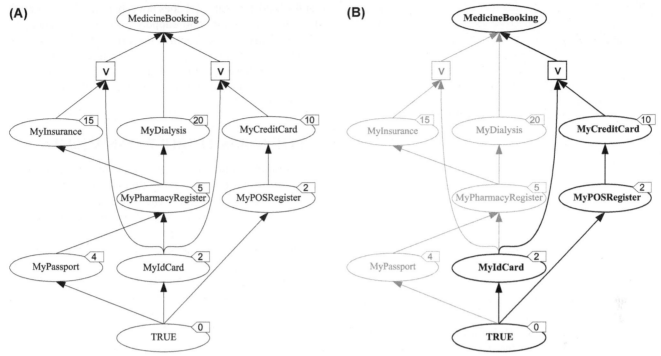

FIGURE 56.2 Policy graph for the policies in Table 56.2 and in Table 56.3 (A), and Minimum Directed Acyclic Graph for the *MedicineBooking* service (B).

5. $\forall v_i \in V'$, $\exists v_T | v_i$, where $v_T | v_i$ is a path starting at v_T and ending at v_i;
6. $\forall v_i \in V'$, $\forall (v_i, v_j) \in A$, where v_i represents a credential, $(v_i, v_j) \in A'$, $v_j \in V'$;
7. $\nexists G''(V'', A'', w)$ that satisfies all the previous conditions and such that $\sum_{v \in V''} w(v) < \sum_{v \in V'} w(v)$.

It is easy to see that a directed acyclic graph starting at v_T and ending at v_s represents a successful negotiation strategy for service s. Therefore, the Minimum Sensitivity Cost problem and the problem of computing a Minimum Directed Acyclic Graph from vertex v_T to vertex v_s are equivalent. The heuristic algorithm proposed in Ref. [28] is based on a variation of the well-known Dijkstra algorithm [29]. In Ref. [28] the authors experimentally prove that the proposed algorithm computes an optimal solution in most cases. For instance, consider the policy graph in Fig. 56.2A and assume that the client is interested in the *MedicineBooking* service. Fig. 56.2B illustrates a Minimum Directed Acyclic Graph for the *MedicineBooking* service with cost 14, where the vertexes and edges in the policy graph that also belong to the Minimum Directed Acyclic Graph are in black, while the other vertexes and edge are in gray.

Sensitive Policies

The solution proposed in Ref. [28] for the more complex scenario where both credentials and policies regulating their release are associated with a sensitivity cost is based on a *greedy strategy* that consists of two steps. During the first step, the interacting parties adopt an eager strategy (i.e., each party discloses to the counterpart the name of a credential as soon as the policy for its release is satisfied) to mutually exchange the name and sensitivity cost associated with credentials that could be useful for identifying a successful negotiation strategy with minimum cost. If this first step finds such a strategy, the client and the server start the second step of the protocol, which consists in enforcing the strategy discovered during the first step. For instance, with reference to the policy graph in Fig. 56.2A, the first step consists of the sequence of releases illustrated in Fig. 56.3. First, the client and the server reveals to each other the name and sensitivity cost of credentials whose release is not regulated by a policy, that is, *MyIdCard* and *MyPassport* for the client and *MyPOSRegister* for the server. These releases satisfy the policy regulating the release of *MyCreditCard* at the client side and *MyPharmacyRegister* at the server side, whose names and sensitivity costs are disclosed. These releases, in turn, satisfy the policies regulating the disclosure of credentials *MyInsurance* and *MyDialysis* at the client side and service *MedicineBooking* at the server side. The exchange then represents a successful negotiation strategy. Note that the edges in Fig. 56.3 are labeled with the cumulative sensitivity cost of the negotiation process (e.g., *MyCreditCard* is associated with cost $12 = w(MyCreditCard) + w(MyPOSRegister)$). The successful

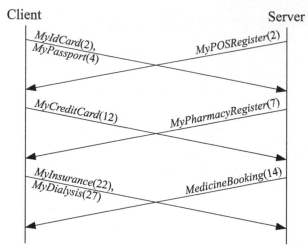

FIGURE 56.3 Sequence of exchanges between the client and the server to determine a successful negotiation strategy.

negotiation strategy computed by the first step is enforced during the second step of the protocol. Therefore, the server first discloses credential *MyPOSRegister* and the client releases *MyIdCard*. When the client receives the credential from the server, she discloses *MyCreditCard*, thus gaining access to the *MedicineBooking* service. The overall sensitivity cost of the strategy is 14.

Open Issues

It is interesting to note that, although effective, the model and algorithms proposed in Ref. [28] suffer from some limitations. A first drawback is that the proposed approach assumes that the disclosure of access control policies does not need to be regulated, while also policy release may be subject to restrictions. Also, this solution assumes that the objective of a privacy-aware negotiation protocol is that of minimizing the overall sensitivity cost of credentials and policies disclosed during the negotiation process. However, the goal of the two parties may be different. For instance, with reference to our example, the pharmacy offering the *MedicineBooking* service may not be interested in minimizing the sensitivity cost of the policies and credentials it needs to disclose to offer the service. On the contrary, the patient wants to minimize the sensitivity cost of the credentials she must disclose to the pharmacy. We also note

that the model in Ref. [28] does not satisfy all the desiderata illustrated in Section 2 to support privacy preferences in attribute-based access control scenarios. In fact, it only supports the definition of privacy preferences as sensitivity costs, which have a numerical domain characterized by a total order relationship (i.e., $\geq$) and by a composition operator (i.e., $+$).

4. POINT-BASED TRUST MANAGEMENT

The problem of minimizing the amount of sensitive information disclosed by a trust negotiation protocol has been also addressed in Ref. [30], where the authors propose a point-based trust management model. This model assumes that policies regulating access to services and release of credentials are based on the definition of quantitative measures. More precisely, the server associates a number pt of points with each credential type t. This value represents the trustworthiness perceived by the server for the credential issuer (i.e., credentials issued by a more reliable party will be associated with a higher number of points and vice versa). To restrict the access to its services, the server then associates a threshold thr with each service. To gain access to a service s, the client must disclose a subset of credentials in her portfolio such that the sum of the points of the released credentials is higher than or equal to the threshold fixed by the server for s. Analogously, the client associates a privacy score ps with each credential in her portfolio, which represents how much she values the release of the credential to an external server. The higher the privacy value of a credential, the lower the client's willingness in its release. As a consequence, a client who is interested in accessing a service s must determine a subset of credentials in her portfolio that satisfies the threshold fixed by the server for s, while minimizing the privacy score of released credentials. Table 56.4 illustrates an example of points and privacy scores associated by the server and the client, respectively, to the credentials composing the client's portfolio.

Since the server policy might be considered sensitive, the server does not reveal the threshold associated with its services to the client. Analogously, the client does not reveal to the counterpart the privacy scores she associates with the credentials in her portfolio. As a consequence, when a client

TABLE 56.4 An Example of Points pt and Privacy Scores ps Associated by the Server and the Client, Respectively, to the Credential in the Client Portfolio

	id_card	passport	credit_card	dialysis	insurance
pt	1	1	2	3	2
ps	2	4	10	20	15

requests access to a service, she needs to identify a subset of the credentials in her portfolio that satisfies the server threshold (i.e., the access control policy regulating the release of the service) without knowing it and without revealing to the server credentials' privacy scores. More formally, the Credential Selection problem is an optimization problem that can be formulated as follows [30].

Problem 2: Credential Selection Problem

Let $C = \{c_1, ..., c_n\}$ be the set of credentials in the client portfolio; $pt(type(c_i))$ be the points associated by the server with credential type $type(c_i)$, $i = 1, ..., n$; $ps(c_i)$ be the privacy score associated by the client with credential c_i, $i = 1, ..., n$; s be the service requested by the client; and thr be the release threshold associated with s. Find a subset $D \subseteq C$ of credentials s.t.:

1. $\sum_{c \in D} pt(type(c)) \geq thr$;

2. $\nexists D' \subseteq C$ s.t. $\sum_{c \in D'} pt(type(c)) \geq thr$ and
   $\sum_{c \in D'} ps(c) < \sum_{c \in D} ps(c)$.

The first condition states that the subset of credentials in the client portfolio must satisfy the server policy, while the second condition states that the sensitive information disclosed is minimum. For instance, with reference to the points and privacy scores in Table 56.4, let us assume that the server offering service s (*MedicineBooking* in our example) defines a threshold $thr = 3$. The release of her *id_card* and of her *credit_card* permits the client to gain access to the service of interest (pt (*id_card*) $+ pt$ (*credit_card*) $= 3 \geq thr$), while minimizing the overall privacy score of released information (ps (*id_card*) $+ ps$ (*credit_card*) $= 12$).

Dynamic Programming Algorithm

The Credential Selection problem is NP-hard and can be rewritten into a knapsack problem, where each credential c can be inserted into the knapsack with weight $pt(type(c))$ and value $ps(c)$ [30]. Since the knapsack algorithm maximized the value of the items inserted in the knapsack to satisfy its capacity, while the goal of the client is that of minimizing the sensitivity of the credentials necessary to reach the threshold of interest, the solution to the Credential Selection problem is computed by inserting in the knapsack those credentials that will not be released. Intuitively, the knapsack problem is complementary to our problem and therefore the approach in Ref. [30] finds the complementary solution to the Credential Selection problem by exploiting a known dynamic programming algorithm for the knapsack problem [29]. The knapsack capacity KC is computed as the complementary of the threshold fixed by the server with respect to the clients portfolio, that is, $KC = \sum_{c \in C} pt(type(c)) - thr$, which is the difference between the sum of points associated with credential types in the client's portfolio and the threshold fixed by the server to gain access to the service. With reference to the example above, $KC = (1 + 1 + 2 + 3 + 2) - 3 = 6$.

The dynamic programming solution to the knapsack problem is based on the definition of a matrix M with $n + 1$ rows, where n is the number of items that can be inserted into the knapsack (i.e., credentials in our scenario), and $KC + 1$ columns. All the cells in the first row and in the first column of the matrix are set to zero (i.e., $M[i,0] = 0$, $i = 0, ..., n$, and $M[0,j] = 0$, $j = 0, ..., KC$). The value of the other cells in the matrix is computed according to the following formula:

$$M[i,j] = \begin{cases} M[i-1,j], & j < pt(type(c_i)) \\ max(M[i-1,j], M[i-1, i - pt(c_i)] + ps(c_i)), & j \geq pt(type(c_i)) \end{cases}$$

The values of the cells in the matrix are computed, in the order, starting from top to bottom and from left to right (i.e., by increasing value of i and j, respectively). Each cell in the matrix represents the total value of the knapsack, obtained inserting (a subset) of the items preceding the current element in the matrix without exceeding the knapsack capacity. It is obtained as the current value of the knapsack either including or not including the current element.

Table 56.5 illustrates the matrix computed considering points and privacy scores in Table 56.4. The first row in the

TABLE 56.5 An Example of Dynamic Programming Matrix for the Portfolio in Table 56.4

	0	1	2	3	4	5	6
0	0	0	0	0	0	0	0
id_card	0	2	2	2	2	2	2
passport	0	4	6	6	6	6	6
credit_card	0	4	10	14	16	16	16
dialysis	0	4	14	20	24	30	34
insurance	0	4	15	20	29	35	39

matrix represents an empty knapsack. Cells $M[id\_card,1]$, ..., $M[id\_card,6]$ in the first row model the insertion of credential id_card in the empty knapsack. As a consequence, the knapsack has weight 2. Cell $M[passport,2]$ is obtained by comparing the solution represented by cell $M[id\_card,2]$ (which models a knapsack including only id_card) with the solution $M[id\_card] \cup \{passport\}$ obtained by inserting also credential $passport$ into the knapsack. The weight of the two alternative solutions is, respectively, 2 and $2 + 4 = 6$. Since $6 > 2$, $M[passport,2]$ is set to 6 and it represents a knapsack including credentials id_card and $passport$. The other cells in the matrix are computed in the same way.

The optimal solution to the knapsack problem is represented by the value in cell $M[n,KC]$, which represents the value of the knapsack obtained trying to insert all the candidate elements in the knapsack without exceeding its capacity. To determine the elements that belong to the optimal solution, it is necessary to keep track of which item has been inserted at each step. For instance, consider the matrix in Table 56.5, cell $M[insurance,6] = 39$ is as the sum of the cells in gray in the table, that is, it represent a solution including credentials $passport$, $dialysis$, and $insurance$. Since the credentials included in the knapsack are not disclosed, the credentials disclosed by the client to gain the access are id_card and $credit\_card$ that, as already noted, satisfy the threshold fixed by the server for the $MedicineBooking$ service while minimizing privacy scores.

The traditional dynamic programming algorithm described above for the knapsack problem assumes that the client knows the points assigned by the server to credential types (or that the server knows the privacy scores that the client associates with the credentials in her portfolio). Since this assumption does not hold in the considered scenario, in Ref. [30] the authors propose to enhance the basic algorithm to permit the client and the server to interact with each other for computing a solution to the knapsack problem without the need for the client and the server to reveal to each other their secret parameters. The proposed solution consists of a secure two-party dynamic-programming protocol, which relies on homomorphic encryption to provide privacy guarantees to sensitive information [31,32].

Open Issues

The model and algorithm introduced in Ref. [30] suffer from different shortcomings. First of all, the client and the server must share, as a common knowledge, the set of possible credentials on which the negotiation process should be based. Such knowledge may, however, put the privacy of the server policy at risk. The proposed model also assumes that the access control policy defined by the server consists of a threshold value, but in many real-world

scenarios the server needs to define more expressive policies. Furthermore, the focus of the proposal, as well as the model in Ref. [28], is more on the negotiation process than on the management of the privacy preferences of the interacting parties. The solution in Ref. [30] represents however an important step toward the definition of a privacy-aware access control model, even if it does not satisfy all the desiderata described in Section 2. In fact, this approach only supports the definition of privacy preferences as privacy scores, which have a numerical domain characterized by a total order relationship (i.e., $\geq$) and by a composition operator (i.e., $+$).

5. LOGICAL-BASED MINIMAL CREDENTIAL DISCLOSURE

The solutions in Refs. [28,30], are based on the assumption that privacy preferences can be expressed as numerical values, defined over a domain characterized by a total order relationship and an additive operator (as defined, for instance, in Ref. [33]). While this assumption permits to easily integrate privacy preferences with traditional negotiation processes, the usability of the resulting system may be limited. In fact, it might not be easy for the final user to express her privacy preferences through numeric values, also because the adoption of numeric preference values may cause unintended side effects (e.g., dominance relationships are not explicitly defined, but are implied by the values assigned to the portfolio components). To overcome these limitations, in Refs. [34,35] the authors propose to adopt qualitative (instead of quantitative) preference values. The solution proposed in Ref. [34] is based on the assumption that credentials are singleton (i.e., certify one attribute only) and that the policy defined by the server is publicly available. The goal of the approach is to determine, among the successful negotiation strategies, the one that better suits the client preferences (i.e., the set of credentials that minimizes the amount of sensitive information disclosed to the server to gain access to the requested service). When the number of successful strategies is limited, the client can explicitly choose the one she prefers. However, when the number of credentials in the client portfolio increases and the server policy becomes complex, the number of successful trust negotiation strategies may grow quickly. For instance, assume that the client portfolio is composed of credentials {$Name$, DoB, $City$, $VISANum$, $VISALimit$, $AmExNum$, $AmExLimit$, $Insurance$, $InsCoverage$, $Dialysis$}, and that the policy regulating access to the $MedicineBooking$ service is (($Name \land (DoB \lor City) \lor Dialysis \lor Insurance) \land ((VISANum \land VISALimit) \lor (AmExNum \land AmExLimit) \lor (InsCoverage \land DoB))$). There are 12 strategies that satisfy the access control policy. It is therefore necessary to define a mechanism that permits to exploit qualitative disclosure preferences defined by the client to limit the number of strategies among which she is explicitly asked to choose.

Qualitative Preferences

Given the set $C = \{c_1, \ldots, c_n\}$ of credentials in the client portfolio, the release of a subset of credentials is modeled as a binary n-dimension vector D, where $D[i] = 1$ if c_i is released and $D[i] = 0$ otherwise, $i = 1, \ldots n$. For instance, with reference to the previous example, Table 56.6 summarizes the subsets of portfolio credentials satisfying the policy regulating service *MedicineBooking*. Disclosure D_1 represents the release of $\{Name, DoB, VISANum, VISALimit\}$.

The model proposed in Ref. [34] permits to specify privacy preferences at different granularity levels. Dominance relationship $>_i$ defines disclosure preferences for credential c_i. Usually, credential-level preferences state that $0 >_i 1$, $i = 1, \ldots n$, meaning that the client prefers not to disclose credential c_i. To compare the disclosure of different subsets of credentials in the client portfolio, credential-level preferences are composed according to the Pareto composition operator $>_P$. A disclosure set D_i dominates, according to the Pareto composition, a disclosure set D_j if, for each credential c_l in the portfolio, either $D_i[l] >_l D_j[l]$ or $D_i[l] =_l D_j[l]$, meaning that D_i releases a proper subset of the credentials in D_j. For instance, consider the disclosure sets in Table 56.6, $D_3 >_P D_6$ since $D_3[DoB] >_{DoB} D_6[DoB]$, that is, $D_6 = D_3 \cup \{DoB\}$.

The most interesting kind of preferences modeled by the solution in Ref. [34] is represented by amalgamated preferences, which compare the release of sets of credentials that are not related by a subset−containment relationship. Amalgamated preferences are of the form $c_i \rightarrow c_j$, meaning

that the client prefers to release credential c_i over credential c_j. This preference defines a dominance relationship, denoted $>_{\{i,j\}}^{(1,0)(0,1)}$, among disclosure sets. More formally, disclosure set D_k dominates, according to amalgamated preference $c_i \rightarrow c_j$, disclosure set D_l if $D_k[i] = 1$, $D_k[j] = 0$, $D_l[i] = 0$, $D_l[j] = 1$, and $D_k[x] = D_l[x]$, for all $x \neq i$, $x \neq j$. For instance, consider the disclosure sets in Table 56.6 and amalgamated preference *Insurance* $\rightarrow$ *Dialysis*, then $D_{10} >_{\{Insurance,Dialysis\}}^{(1,0)(0,1)} D_7$ since they both disclose credentials *VISANum* and *VISALimit*, but D_{10} releases *Insurance* while D_7 releases *Dialysis*. Analogously, $D_{11} >_{\{Insurance,Dialysis\}}^{(1,0)(0,1)} D_8$ and $D_{12} >_{\{Insurance,Dialysis\}}^{(1,0)(0,1)} D_9$. Note that the binary subvectors on the top of the dominance operator can be any pair of binary subvectors of the same length. Amalgamated preferences can be conveniently represented through a graph, whose vertexes model credentials and whose edges represent disclosure preferences among them. Note that, to avoid inconsistencies in the definition of privacy preferences, the disclosure graph must be acyclic. The model in Ref. [34] permits also to specify conditions associated with preferences, meaning that a dominance relationship holds only if the associated condition is satisfied (e.g., only if a given credential has already been disclosed). For instance, the client may prefer to release credential *Insurance* over her *Name* if credential *InsCoverage* has already been released (since the server is aware of the fact that the client has subscribed an insurance). These conditions are graphically represented by labels associated with the edges of the preference graph. Fig. 56.4 illustrates an example of graph representing amalgamated preferences for the portfolio in our example. Consider the

TABLE 56.6 Disclosure Strategies that Satisfy the Access Control Policy of Service *MedicineBooking*

	Name	DoB	City	VISANum	VISALimit	AmExNum	AmExLimit	Insurance	InsCoverage	Dialysis
D_1	1	1	0	1	1	0	0	0	0	0
D_2	1	1	0	0	0	1	1	0	0	0
D_3	1	1	0	0	0	0	0	0	1	0
D_4	1	0	1	1	1	0	0	0	0	0
D_5	1	0	1	0	0	1	1	0	0	0
D_6	1	1	1	0	0	0	0	0	1	0
D_7	0	0	0	1	1	0	0	0	0	1
D_8	0	0	0	0	0	1	1	0	0	1
D_9	0	1	0	0	0	0	0	0	1	1
D_{10}	0	0	0	1	1	0	0	1	0	0
D_{11}	0	0	0	0	0	1	1	1	0	0
D_{12}	0	1	0	0	0	0	0	1	1	0

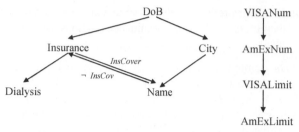

FIGURE 56.4 An example of a set of amalgamated preferences.

disclosure sets in Table 56.6, according to the preferences in the graph, $D_1 \succ^{(1,0)(0,1)}_{\{DoB,City\}} D_4$ and $D_2 \succ^{(1,0)(0,1)}_{\{DoB,City\}} D_5$ since the disclosure of *DoB* is preferred to the disclosure of *City*. Also, $D_{12} \succ^{(1,0)(0,1)}_{\{Insurance,Name\}} D_3$ since credential *InsCoverage* has already been released and therefore the client prefers to release *Insurance* instead of *Name*.

Both the dominance relationship defined by the Pareto composition and the dominance relationships induced by amalgamated preferences permit to compare disclosure sets that differ only for the release of the subset of credentials on which the dominance relationship has been defined. However, it may happen that two disclosure sets cannot be compared considering one dominance relationship only, but they can be compared combining two or more disclosure preferences. For instance, consider the graph in Fig. 56.4 and the disclosure sets in Table 56.6. Disclosure sets D_1 and D_2 cannot be directly compared, but it is immediate to see that D_1 dominates D_2 by combining amalgamated preferences *VISANum* → *AmExNum* and *VISALimit* → *AmExLimit*. In fact, D_1 discloses the attributes of VISA credit card, while D_2 discloses the attributes of AmEx credit card. In Ref. [34] the authors propose to incrementally compose certificate-level and amalgamated preferences. The transitive closure of all the preferences in the system permits to define a complete preference relationship, denoted $\succ\succ$, which summarizes all the preference relationships expressed by the client. As a consequence, given the access control policy p regulating the release of the service requested by the client, the approach in Ref. [34] permits to limit the set of successful disclosure strategies among which the client needs to choose. In fact, the choice can be restricted to the optimal disclosure sets, that is, to the sets of credentials in the client portfolio that satisfy p and that are not dominated by another disclosure set that satisfies p. More formally, the set of optimal disclosure sets is defined as follows [34].

Definition 2: Optimal Disclosure Sets

Let $C = \{c_1, ..., c_n\}$ be the set of credentials in the client portfolio; s be the service requested by the client; p be the access control policy regulating the release of s; $\mathscr{D} = \{D_1, ..., D_m\}$ be the set of disclosure sets that satisfy

p, with $D_i \subseteq C$, $i = 1, ..., n$; and $\succ\succ$ be a complete preference relationship over C. An optimal disclosure set $\mathscr{D}_{\succ\succ}$ of $\mathscr{D}$ wrt $\succ\succ$ is defined as: $\mathscr{D}_{\succ\succ} = \{D \in \mathscr{D} | \nexists\ D' \in \mathscr{D}, D' \succ\succ D\}$.

The disclosure sets in $\mathscr{D}_{\succ\succ}$ are optimal and cannot be compared with respect to the disclosure preferences defined by the client (i.e., they are equivalent according to client preferences). To finally decide which set of credentials to disclose to the server, the client needs to choose, among the negotiation strategies in $\mathscr{D}_{\succ\succ}$, the one she prefers to disclose. For instance, with reference to the disclosure sets in Table 56.6 and the preferences in Fig. 56.4, $\mathscr{D}_{\succ\succ} = \{D_1, D_{10}, D_{12}\}$.

Open Issues

The solution proposed in Ref. [34] has the great advantage over the approaches discussed in Section 2 and 3 of modeling and managing qualitative preferences. In fact, it permits to specify privacy preferences at the attribute granularity, and it defines a partial order relationship and different composition operators over the domain of privacy preferences, therefore resulting easy to use for the client. However, it still needs to be enhanced to comply with all the desiderata that a privacy-aware access control system should satisfy (see Section 2). The main shortcoming from which the proposal in Ref. [34] suffers is that it requires the client intervention in the choice of the set of credentials to disclose among the successful strategies in the optimal set. Also, the proposed model assumes that each credential in the client portfolio certifies one attribute only, while often credentials include a set of attributes that cannot be singularly released (i.e., atomic credentials).

6. PRIVACY PREFERENCES IN CREDENTIAL-BASED INTERACTIONS

The first solution that formally models the client portfolio to permit the client to specify fine-grained privacy preferences, as well as constraints on the disclosure of portfolio components, has been proposed in Ref. [21]. One of the main advantages of the portfolio modeling in Ref. [21] is that it permits to represent both atomic and nonatomic credentials, declarations, and the attributes composing them, clearly distinguishing between credential-dependent and credential-independent attributes. As a consequence, this modeling permits to easily associate privacy preferences with each credential and attribute in the client portfolio. More precisely, the client portfolio is modeled as a bipartite graph $G(V_C \cup V_A, E_{CA})$ with a vertex for each credential and each attribute in the portfolio and an edge connecting each credential to the attributes it certifies. It is important to note that each credential-independent attribute is represented by a vertex in G, while each credential-dependent attribute is represented by several vertexes (one for each credential certifying it). For instance, Fig. 56.5 illustrates the graph representing the portfolio in Table 56.1, where we distinguish atomic credentials by attaching all the edges incident to the vertex representing the credential to a black semicircle. The label of vertexes representing credentials is of the form *id*:type, where *id* is the identifier of the credential and *type* is its type. The label of vertexes representing attributes is of the form name:value.

Sensitivity Labels

The client can define her privacy preferences at a fine-granularity level by associating a sensitivity label with each credential and attribute (or combinations thereof) in her portfolio. These labels represent how much the client values the disclosure of the portfolio components. The domain Λ of sensitivity labels can be any set of values characterized by a partial order relationship $\succcurlyeq$, and a composition operator $\oplus$. This generic definition of sensitivity labels captures different methods for expressing preferences. For instance, sensitivity labels could be positive integer values, where the order relationship $\succcurlyeq$ is the traditional $\geq$ relationship and the composition operator can either be the sum (i.e., $+$) or the maximum. In the example, for simplicity, we will consider numerical sensitivity labels. Labeling function λ associates a sensitivity label in Λ with each credential c, with each attribute a in the client portfolio, and possibly with subsets thereof. Fig. 56.6 illustrates the portfolio graph in Fig. 56.5, extended by associating each vertex with its sensitivity label and by including new vertexes that represent associations and disclosure constraints. The semantics of the sensitivity labels associated with portfolio components can be summarized as follows:

- $\lambda(a)$: defines the sensitivity of attribute a singularly taken and reflects how much the client values its disclosure. For instance, with reference to the portfolio graph in Fig. 56.6, $\lambda\,(VISANum) \geq \lambda\,(DoB)$ since the client considers the number of her VISA more sensitive than her date of birth.
- $\lambda(c)$: defines the sensitivity of the existence of credential c. This label reflects how much the client values the additional information carried by the credential itself, independently from the attributes it certifies. For instance, with reference to the portfolio graph in Fig. 56.6, λ (*MyDialysis*) reflects the sensitivity associated by the client with the credential certifying her nephrological disease, independently from the fact that this credential also certifies attributes *Name* and *City*. Clearly, the existence of the credential itself has a sensitivity that goes beyond the demographical information it certifies.

The sensitivity label associated with the combined release of a set of credentials and attributes generally corresponds to the composition through operator $\oplus$ of the sensitivity labels of each portfolio component in the released set. For instance, the release of atomic credential *MyIdCard* has sensitivity label $\lambda(MyIdCard) \oplus \lambda(Name) \oplus \lambda (DoB) \oplus \lambda(City)$. There are however cases where the combined release of some portfolio components may cause a higher or lower information disclosure than the sensitivity label obtained composing the labels of the released credentials and attributes. To capture these situations, the model in Ref. [21] permits the client to specify sensitivity labels for subsets of portfolio components, representing how much the client values the release of the *association* of their values. The sensitivity labels of associations must then be considered when composing the sensitivity labels of the attributes and/or credentials in the association. Graphically, associations are represented by additional vertexes in the portfolio graph, connected to the attributes and/or credentials composing the associations. In particular, the following two kinds of associations are modeled:

- *Sensitive views* model situations where the combined release of a set of portfolio components carries more information than the composition of the sensitive labels

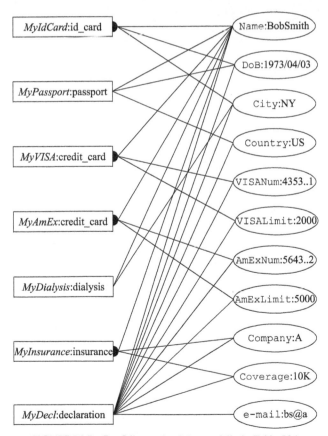

FIGURE 56.5 Portfolio graph of the portfolio in Table 56.1.

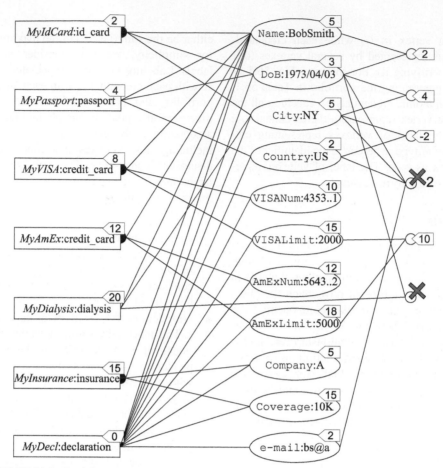

FIGURE 56.6 Portfolio graph in Fig. 56.5 extended with sensitivity labels, associations, and constraints.

of its components. For instance, with reference to the portfolio graph in Fig. 56.6, $\lambda(\{DoB, City\}) = 4$ models the additional sensitivity carried by the combined release of the two attributes.

- *Dependencies* model situations where the combined release of a set of portfolio components carries *less* information than the composition of the sensitive labels of its components. For instance, with reference to the portfolio graph in Fig. 56.6, $\lambda(\{City, Country\}) = -2$ represents the sensitivity to be removed when the two attributes are released together, since the knowledge of the *City* where a user leaves permits to easily infer her *Country*. The sensitivity label associated with a dependency $\mathscr{A} = \{c_i, \ldots, c_j, a_k, \ldots, a_l\}$ can assume any value, provided the sensitivity label of the combined release of all the credentials and attributes in $\mathscr{A}$ dominates the sensitivity label of the most sensitive element in $\mathscr{A}$ (i.e., $\lambda(c_i) \oplus \ldots \oplus \lambda(c_j) \oplus \lambda(a_k) \oplus \ldots \oplus \lambda(a_l) \oplus \lambda(\mathscr{A}) \geqslant \max(\lambda(x), x \in \mathscr{A})$).

In addition to sensitivity labels associated with credentials, attributes, and subsets thereof, the client may need to specify disclosure constraints that cannot be expressed through sensitivity labels. To this purpose, in Ref. [36] the

authors extend the original model introduced in Ref. [21] with the following two kinds of constraints:

- *Forbidden views* represent subsets of portfolio components whose combined release is prohibited. For instance, with reference to the portfolio graph in Fig. 56.6, forbidden view $\{DoB, MyDialysis\}$ prevents the combined release of attribute *DoB* and credential *MyDialysis* and is graphically represented by a cross-shaped vertex connected with the attribute and credential in the constraint.
- *Disclosure limitations* represent subsets of portfolio components characterized by restrictions of the form at most n elements in the set can be jointly disclosed. For instance, with reference to the portfolio graph in Fig. 56.6, disclosure limitation $\{Name, City, Country, e\text{-}mail\}_2$ permits to release at most two attributes in the set and is graphically represented by a cross-shaped vertex with label 2 and connected with all the attributes in the set.

Disclosure

Given the client portfolio, it is important to note that not all the subsets of portfolio components represent a valid disclosure, that is, not all the sets of credentials and attributes can be communicated to the server to gain access to the requested service. First of all, a subset D of portfolio components represents a *disclosure* only if it satisfies the following three conditions:

1. *Certifiability*: each disclosed attribute is certified by at least a credential, whose existence is disclosed as well (i.e., $\forall a \in D, \exists c \in Ds.t.a \in attributes(c)$).
2. *Atomicity*: if an attribute certified by an atomic credential is disclosed, all the attributes in the credential are disclosed (i.e., $\exists c \in Ds.t.c$ is atomic, $\forall a \in attributes(c), a \in D$).
3. *Association exposure*: if all the attributes and/or credentials composing an association are disclosed, then the association itself is disclosed (i.e., $\forall x \in \mathscr{A}, x \in D$ then $\mathscr{A} \in D$).

These conditions permit to easily take into account both atomic and non-atomic credentials, as well as associations, in the computation of the sensitivity label characterizing the disclosure of a set of credentials and attributes. For instance, consider the portfolio graph in Fig. 56.6. An example of disclosure D is represented in Fig. 56.7A, where released elements are reported in black while nonreleased elements are reported in gray. Fig. 56.7B represents instead a subset of the portfolio components that does not represent a disclosure, since it violates the above properties. The *sensitivity* of a disclosure D is computed by composing the sensitivity label of all the credentials, attributes, and associations composing it. For instance, the sensitivity of the disclosure in Fig. 56.7A is $\lambda(D) = \lambda$ (*MyPassport*) $+ \lambda$ (*MyVISA*) $+ \lambda$ (*MyDecl*) $+ \lambda$ (*Name*) $+ \lambda$ (*DoB*) $+ \lambda$ (*VISANum*) $+ \lambda$ (*VISALimit*) $+ \lambda$ (*e-mail*) $+ \lambda$ ({*Name,DoB*}) $= 4 + 8 + 0 + 5 + 3 + 10 + 15 + 2 + 2$ $= 49$. A disclosure is said to be *valid* if it does not violate disclosure constraints. Only valid disclosures can be released. For instance, the disclosure in Fig. 56.7A is valid, while the one in Fig. 56.7C is not valid since it violates forbidden view {*DoB,MyDialysis*}.

Given the server policy p regulating the disclosure of the service of interest, it is necessary to determine a minimum disclosure (i.e., a valid disclosure with minimum sensitivity label) satisfying p. In Ref. [21], the authors assume that server policies are formulated as Boolean formulas composed of terms of the form $t.\{a_i, ..., a_j\}$ in disjunctive normal form. A clause $t.\{a_i, ..., a_j\}$ in the server policy requires the disclosure of a credential c of type t that certifies attributes $\{a_i, ..., a_j\}$. A valid disclosure D satisfies a term $t.\{a_i, ..., a_j\}$ if $\exists c \in Ds.t.type(c) \leq_{isa} t$ and $\{a_i, ..., a_j\} \subseteq attributes(c)$. For instance, assume that the policy regulating access to the *MedicineBooking* service is $id.\{Name\} \wedge credit\_card.\{Name, Number,Limit\} \wedge *.\{DoB,e\text{-}mail\}$. The disclosure in Fig. 56.7A satisfies the policy and grants the client access to the requested service: term $id.\{Name\}$ is satisfied by the release of attribute *Name*

from credential *MyIdCard*; term *credit_card*.{*Name, Number,Limit*} is satisfied by the release of atomic credential *MyVISA*; and term **.{DoB,e-mail}* is satisfied by the release of attribute *DoB* from credential *MyIdCard* and by the declaration of attribute *e-mail*. Formally, the minimum disclosure problem can then be formulated as follows.

Problem 3: Minimum Disclosure Problem

Let $C = \{c_1, ..., c_n\}$ be the set of credentials in the client portfolio; $A = \{a_1, ..., a_m\}$ be the set of attributes in the client portfolio; $(T, \leq_{isa})$ be the hierarchy of credential types; $\mathbb{A}$ be the set of sensitive associations; $\mathbb{F}$ be the set of forbidden views; $\mathbb{L}$ be the set of disclosure limitations; λ be the labeling function; and p be the server policy. Find a subset $D \subseteq C \cup A$ such that:

1. $\forall a \in D, \exists c \in Ds.t.a \in attributes(c)$ (certifiability);
2. $\exists c \in Ds.t.c$ is atomic, $\forall a \in attributes(c), a \in D$ (atomicity);
3. $\forall x \in \mathscr{A}, x \in D$ then. $\mathscr{A} \in D$ (association exposure);
4. $\forall f \in \mathbb{F}, f \nsubseteq D$ (forbidden views satisfaction);
5. $\forall l_i \in \mathbb{L}, \nexists l' \subseteq Ds.t.|l'| \geq i$, with i the threshold fixed by constraint l_i (disclosure limitation satisfaction);
6. $\exists$ a clause $t_1.\{a_{i1}, ..., a_{j1}\} \wedge ... \wedge t_l.\{a_{il}, ..., a_{jl}\}$ in p such that for each term $t.\{a_i, ..., a_j\}$ in the clause, $\exists c \in Ds.t.type(c) \leq_{isa} t$ and $\{a_i, ..., a_j\} \subseteq attributes(c)$ (policy satisfaction);
7. $\nexists D'$ satisfying all the conditions above and such that $\lambda(D) > \lambda(D')$.

For instance, the disclosure in Fig. 56.7A represents a minimal disclosure for our example.

The problem of computing a minimal disclosure is NP-hard [21]. In Ref. [21] the authors propose a graph-based heuristic algorithm to compute a minimal disclosure (i.e., a disclosure that, although not minimal, has a low sensitivity label). In Ref. [36] the authors define a modeling of the problem as an instance of the Max-SAT problem, and use Max-SAT solvers to compute an optimum solution in a limited computational time.

The model in Ref. [21] has been extended in Ref. [37] to permit the client to complement her privacy preferences with context-based restrictions that limit the disclosure of credentials on the basis of the context of her request. In the same paper, the authors also propose to take the history of past interactions into account in the choice of the set of credentials and attributes to disclose for gaining access to the requested service.

Open Issues

The modeling of the client portfolio proposed in Ref. [21] permits the client to specify sensitivity labels at the attribute granularity level and to take advantage of new constructs for taking sensitive associations and disclosure constraints

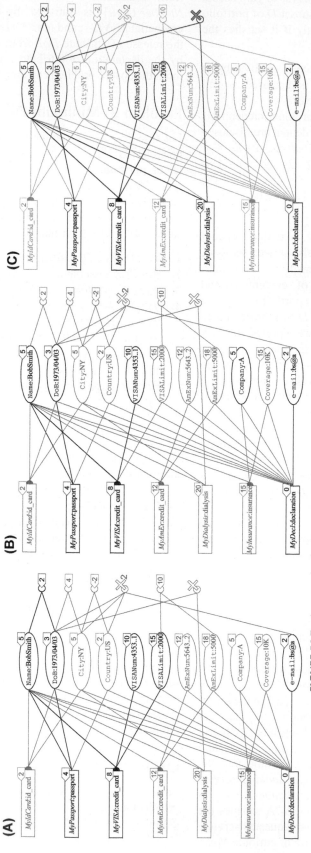

FIGURE 56.7 An example of valid disclosure (A), arbitrary subset of portfolio elements (B), and nonvalid disclosure (C).

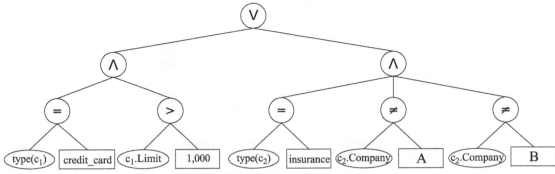

FIGURE 56.8 An example of a policy tree.

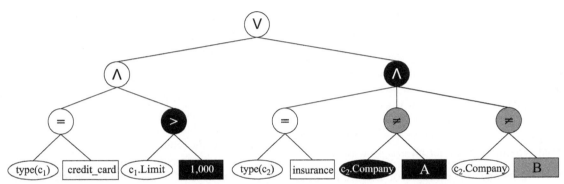

FIGURE 56.9 An example of coloring for the policy tree in Fig. 56.8.

into consideration in the choice of the set of portfolio components to disclose. This approach leaves however space to further improvements. Sensitivity labels modeling privacy preferences may not be easy to define for final users. In fact, as already noted in Ref. [34], it is hard to associate a quantitative value with each portfolio component (and possible subset thereof), while it would be easier to define a partial order relationship between subsets of portfolio components.

7. FINE-GRAINED DISCLOSURE OF SENSITIVE ACCESS POLICIES

In Ref. [38], the authors address the problem of regulating the disclosure of access control policies, by proposing a model that permits the server to specify a disclosure policy regulating if and how an access control policy should be communicated to the client. To this purpose, the approach in Ref. [38] models access control policies as policy trees. Policy tree $T(N)$ representing policy p has a node for each operator, attribute, and constant value in p. The internal nodes of the tree represent operators, whose operands are represented by the sub-trees rooted at its children. For instance, Fig. 56.8 represents the policy tree of $p = (type(c_1) = credit\_card \wedge c_1.Limit > 1000)$

$\vee$ $(type(c_2) = insurance$ $\wedge$ $c_2.Company \neq$ 'A' $\wedge$ $c_2.Company \neq$ 'B').

Disclosure Policy

The disclosure policy regulating the release of a policy p to a client regulates the visibility of each node in the policy tree $T(N)$. The disclosure policy is formally defined as a coloring function $\gamma{:}N \rightarrow \{green, yellow, red\}$ that associates with each node n in the policy tree a color in the set $\{green, yellow, red\}$, thus obtaining a *colored policy tree* $T(N, \gamma)$. The semantics of the colors, with respect to the client visibility of a node, can be summarized as follows:

- *green*: the node is released;
- *yellow*: the label of the node is removed (i.e., the operator, attribute, or constant value it represents) before its release, while its presence in the tree and its children are preserved;
- *red*: the label of the node is removed and possibly also its presence in the tree.

As an example, Fig. 56.9 illustrates a possible coloring regulating the disclosure of the policy tree in Fig. 56.8. In the figure, *green* nodes are white, *yellow* nodes are gray, and *red* nodes are black.

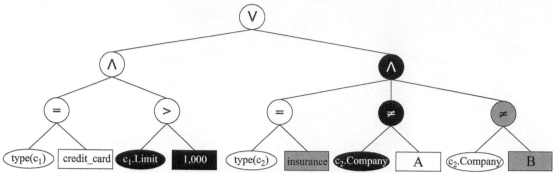

FIGURE 56.10 An example of non-well-defined colored policy tree.

Although the server can decide to associate an arbitrary color with each node in the tree, a disclosure policy is well-defined if it is meaningful. More precisely, a disclosure policy is well defined if it satisfies the following conditions.

1. If a leaf node representing a constant value is *green*, then its sibling (which represents an attribute) is *green* and its parent (which represents an operator) is not *red*.
2. If a node representing an operator is *green*, at least one of its children must be either *green* or *yellow*.
3. The nodes in a subtree representing a condition on credential type must be either all *green* or all *red*.

Fig. 56.10 illustrates an example of non-well-defined coloring for the policy tree in Fig. 56.8. In fact, since only node 'A' is *green* in the subtree representing condition $c_2.Company \neq$ 'A', the server would disclose value 'A' instead of the condition. Analogously, only node > is *green* in the sub-tree of condition $c_1.Limit >$ 1,000, the server would disclose the operator > only to the client. Finally, node *insurance* is *yellow* in the sub-tree of condition $type(c_2) = insurance$, while the other nodes are *green*. The disclosed condition would then only release operand $type(c_2)$ and operator =, which does not give to the client any information to possibly gain access to the service.

Policy Communication

When the client sends a request for accessing a service to the server, the server transforms its access control policy into a client policy view according to the disclosure policy. The colored policy tree $T(N, \gamma)$ regulating policy disclosure is therefore transformed into an equivalent client policy tree view by: (1) removing the label of *yellow* and *red* nodes; (2) removing unnecessary *red* leaves; and (3) collapsing internal *red* nodes in a parent-child relationship in a single *red* node. To this purpose, the server visits the tree following a post-order strategy and applies, in the order, the following three classes of transformation rules:

- *Prune rules*. These rules remove unnecessary leaf nodes. Two kinds of prune rules can be applied on an internal node *n* whose children are leaf nodes.

- *Red predicate rule*. If *n* is *red*, all its *red* children are removed. For instance, consider the colored policy tree in Fig. 56.9, according to this rule node representing constant value 1000 is removed.
- *Red children rule*. If all the children of *n* are *red*, they are removed and the color of node *n* is set to *red*. For instance, consider the colored policy tree in Fig. 56.9, according to this rule the nodes representing attribute *Company* and constant value 'A' in condition $(c_2.Company \neq$ 'A') are removed. Also, the color of the node representing operator $\neq$ is set to red.
- *Collapse rule*. This rule operates on internal *red* nodes and removes their non-leaf *red* children. For instance, consider the colored policy tree in Fig. 56.9, the node representing operator $\neq$ in condition $(c_2.Company \neq$ 'A') is removed since its parent (i.e., the second child of the root node) is *red*.
- *Hide label rule*. This rule removes the labels of *yellow* and *red* nodes.

Fig. 56.11 illustrates the client policy tree view obtained applying the transformation rules described above to the colored policy tree in Fig. 56.9.

The disclosure of a client policy tree view may be meaningless for the client, since it may not represent in a "fair way" the server access control policy [38]. Intuitively, a client policy tree view fairly represents the server policy if it includes at least a subset of attributes that permit the access control policy evaluation. In fact, in this case, the client can decide whether to release the requested attributes to possibly gain access to the service of interest. Clearly, the server should disclose only fair policies. For instance, the policy view represented by the tree in Fig. 56.11 is fair, since all the attributes and credential types in the original policy are preserved in the client view. The client can decide whether to release either one of her credit cards or her insurance to possibly gain access to the *MedicineBooking* service.

Open Issues

The solution proposed in Ref. [38] to protect the confidentiality of access control policies, while permitting the

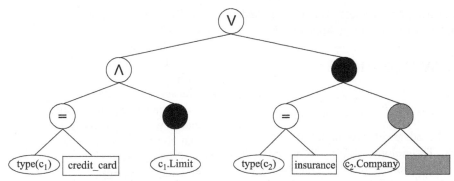

FIGURE 56.11   Policy tree view of the colored policy tree in Fig. 56.9.

client—server interaction in open environments, is effective and permits the definition of disclosure restrictions at a fine granularity level. However, this proposal represents only a first step in the definition of an effective system regulating policy disclosure. In fact, the proposed model permits to check whether a disclosure policy generates a fair client policy tree view but it does not propose an approach for possibly revising the disclosure policy when the client policy tree view is not fair (and therefore prevents the definition of a successful negotiation strategy). Also, the model could be extended to consider the disclosure of proofs of possession and/or proofs of satisfaction of condition.

8. OPEN ISSUES

The enforcement of access privileges in open environments taking into account both client privacy preferences and policy confidentiality requirements still present different open issues that need to be addressed. In the following, we illustrate the most relevant still open issues:

- *Inheritance of privacy preferences.* Most of the solutions proposed in the literature assume that the client associates a preference with each credential and/or attribute in her portfolio. Although the solution in Ref. [21] uses the hierarchy of credential types for checking whether the disclosure of a subset of the portfolio components satisfies a given server request, it does not consider this hierarchy in the definition of privacy preferences. An interesting open issue consists in exploiting the hierarchy of credential types to make the definition of privacy preferences more user-friendly.
- *Proof of possession.* The values modeling privacy preferences are traditionally associated with credentials and/ or attributes and express how much their owner values their release. Recent technologies however permit to release proofs of possession of credentials and proofs of satisfaction of conditions defined on attributes. The release of a proof is usually considered less sensitive than the release of the credential/attribute on which

the proof is based. This different disclosure risk should therefore be adequately modeled.
- *Shared knowledge.* Attribute-based access control solutions traditionally assume that the hierarchy of credential types and attribute names represent a common knowledge for the server and the client. However, this assumption does not always hold in real-life scenarios, where there may be mismatches due also to the fact that servers refer to credential and attribute types while clients refer to their instances. Access control models should be extended to handle this problem.
- *Integration.* Both the solutions developed to support client privacy preferences and the solutions proposed to protect the confidentiality of server policies do not consider the privacy requirements of the counterpart. It is therefore important to study new models that consider both the client and the server privacy needs.
- The approaches proposed in the literature for the support of client privacy preferences present advantages and disadvantaged complementary to each other. For instance, the solution in Ref. [34] has the advantage of usability, while the approach in Ref. [21] supports sensitive associations and disclosure constraints. An interesting open issue is therefore the definition of a model that combines the advantages of all the proposed approaches.

9. SUMMARY

We have analyzed the privacy issues that may arise in open scenarios where the client accessing a service and the server offering it may be unknown to each other and need to exchange information to build a trust relationship. We have illustrated both the problem of taking client privacy preferences into account in credential disclosure, and the problem of maintaining the confidentiality of server access control policies. For each of these problems, we have described some recent approaches for their solution and illustrated some open issues that still need to be addressed.

Finally, let's move on to the real interactive part of this chapter: review questions/exercises, hands-on projects, case projects, and optional team case project. The answers and/ or solutions by chapter can be found in Appendix K.

CHAPTER REVIEW QUESTIONS/ EXERCISES

True/False

1. True or False? The advancements in Information and Communications Technology (ICT) allow users to take more and more advantage of the availability of on-line services (and resources) that can be accessed anywhere and at any time.

2. True or False? The information that a client can provide to a server to gain access to a service are organized in a portfolio including both credentials signed by third parties and certifying client properties, and declarations stating certified properties uttered by the client.

3. True or False? Attribute-based access control restricts access to server service depending on the attributes and credentials that the requesting client discloses to the server.

4. True or False? Since clients and servers operating in open environments are assumed to be unknown to each other, they interact to the aim of building a trust relationship that permits the client to gain access to a service offered by the server.

5. True or False? Given the server request, the client needs to determine which credentials and/or attributes to disclose to satisfy it.

Multiple Choice

1. With _____, servers regulate access to their services based on the attributes and certificates presented by the requesting client?
   A. Privacy-enhancing technology
   B. Location technology
   C. Attribute-based access control
   D. Executable policies
   E. Data controller

2. The goal of the client and the server engaging a negotiation protocol is that of _____ the sensitivity cost of the credentials and policies exchanged during a successful negotiation strategy.
   A. Policy enforcement
   B. Location technology
   C. Valid
   D. Minimizing
   E. Web Technology

3. The solution proposed for the simplified scenario where policies are not associated with a sensitivity cost (they can be freely released) is based on the definition of a _____ modeling the policies regulating credential disclosure at both the client and server side.

A. Data minimization
B. *XACML*
C. Policy graph
D. Contradictory
E. Security

4. The solution for the more complex scenario where both credentials and policies regulating their release are associated with a sensitivity cost is based on a _____ that consists of two steps.
   A. Privacy metrics
   B. Greedy strategy
   C. Redundant
   D. Privacy preferences
   e. Taps

5. Since the _____ might be considered sensitive, the server does not reveal the threshold associated with its services to the client.
   A. Irrelevant
   B. Anonymous communication
   C. Data handling policies
   D. Disclose-to
   E. Server policy

EXERCISE

Problem

If an organization uses a distributed access control system, do they have to give up other access control methods or security measures?

Hands-On Projects

Project

Who does an organization have to trust with regards to a distributed access control system?

Case Projects

Problem

Exactly how is a user authenticated?

Optional Team Case Project

Problem

Do all distributed access control system users have to have client certificates issued by the same certificate authority?

ACKNOWLEDGMENTS

We would like to thank Sabrina De Capitani di Vimercati for suggestions and comments on the chapter organization and presentation. This work was partially supported by the EC within the 7FP under grant agreement

312797 (ABC4EU) and within the H2020 program under grant agreement 644579 (ESCUDO-CLOUD), and by the Italian Ministry of Research within PRIN project "GenData 2020" (2010RTFWBH).

REFERENCES

[1] P. Samarati, S. De Capitani di Vimercati, Access control: policies, models, and mechanisms, in: R. Focardi, R. Gorrieri (Eds.), Foundations of Security Analysis and Design, Volume of 2171 of LNCS, Springer-Verlag, 2001.

[2] S. Cimato, M. Gamassi, V. Piuri, R. Sassi, F. Scotti, Privacy-aware biometrics: design and implementation of a multimodal verification system, in: Proc. of ACSAC 2008, Anaheim, CA, USA, December 2008.

[3] S. De Capitani di Vimercati, S. Foresti, S. Jajodia, P. Samarati, Access control policies and languages in open environments, in: T. Yu, S. Jajodia (Eds.), Secure Data Management in Decentralized Systems, Springer-Verlag, 2007.

[4] S. De Capitani di Vimercati, P. Samarati, S. Jajodia, Policies, models, and languages for access control, in: Proc. of the Workshop on Databases in Networked Information Systems, Aizu-Wakamatsu, Japan, March 2005.

[5] M. Gamassi, V. Piuri, D. Sana, F. Scotti, Robust fingerprint detection for access control, in: Proc. of RoboCare 2005, Rome, Italy, May 2005.

[6] C.A. Ardagna, S. De Capitani di Vimercati, S. Paraboschi, E. Pedrini, P. Samarati, M. Verdicchio, Expressive and deployable access control in open web service applications, IEEE TSC 4 (2) (April—June 2011) 6—109.

[7] P. Bonatti, P. Samarati, A uniform framework for regulating service access and information release on the web, JCS 10 (3) (2002) 241—272.

[8] P. Bonatti, P. Samarati, Logics for authorizations and security, in: J. Chomicki, R. van der Meyden, G. Saake (Eds.), Logics for Emerging Applications of Databases, Springer-Verlag, 2003.

[9] S. De Capitani di Vimercati, S. Foresti, S. Jajodia, S. Paraboschi, G. Psaila, P. Samarati, Integrating trust management and access control in data-intensive web applications, ACM TWEB 6 (2) (May 2012) 6:1—6:43.

[10] S. De Capitani di Vimercati, S. Foresti, S. Jajodia, P. Samarati, Access control policies and languages, IJCSE 3 (2) (2007) 94—102.

[11] S. De Capitani di Vimercati, S. Foresti, P. Samarati, Recent advances in access control, in: M. Gertz, S. Jajodia (Eds.), Handbook of Database Security: Applications and Trends, Springer-Verlag, 2008.

[12] V.C. Hu, D. Richard Kuhn, D.F. Ferraiolo, Attribute-based access control, IEEE Comput. 2 (48) (2015) 85—88.

[13] K. Irwin, T. Yu, Preventing attribute information leakage in automated trust negotiation, in: Proc. of ACM CCS 2005, Alexandria, VA, USA, November 2005.

[14] A.J. Lee, M. Winslett, J. Basney, V. Welch, The Traust authorization service, ACM TISSEC 11 (1) (February 2008) 1—33.

[15] T. Ryutov, L. Zhou, C. Neuman, T. Leithead, K.E. Seamons, Adaptive trust negotiation and access control, in: Proc. of SACMAT 2005, Stockholm, Sweden, June 2005.

[16] T. Yu, M. Winslett, K.E. Seamons, Supporting structured credentials and sensitive policies trough interoperable strategies for automated trust, ACM TISSEC 6 (1) (February 2003) 1—42.

[17] J. Li, N. Li, W.H. Winsborough, Automated trust negotiation using cryptographic credentials, in: Proc. of ACM CCS 2005, Alexandria, VA, USA, November 2005.

[18] K.E. Seamons, M. Winslett, T. Yu, Limiting the disclosure of access control policies during automated trust negotiation, in: Proc. of NDSS 2001, San Diego, CA, USA, April 2001.

[19] W. Winsborough, K.E. Seamons, V. Jones, Automated trust negotiation, in: Proc. of DISCEX 2000, Hilton Head Island, SC, USA, January 2000.

[20] T. Yu, M. Winslett, A unified scheme for resource protection in automated trust negotiation, in: Proc. of the IEEE Symposium on Security and Privacy 2003, Berkeley, CA, USA, May 2003.

[21] C.A. Ardagna, S. De Capitani di Vimercati, S. Foresti, S. Paraboschi, P. Samarati, Minimizing disclosure of private information in credential-based interactions: a graph-based approach, in: Proc. of PASSAT 2010, Minneapolis, MN, USA, August 2010.

[22] S. Brands, Rethinking Public Key Infrastructure and Digital Certificates—Building in Privacy, MIT Press, 2000.

[23] J. Camenisch, A. Lysyanskaya, An efficient system for non-transferable anonymous credentials with optional anonymity revocation, in: Proc. of EUROCRYPT 2001, Innsbruck, Austria, May 2001.

[24] J. Hajny, L. Malina, Unlinkable attribute-based credentials with practical revocation on smart-cards, in: Proc of CARDIS 2012, Graz, Austria, November 2012.

[25] S. De Capitani di Vimercati, S. Foresti, G. Livraga, P. Samarati, Data privacy: definitions and techniques, Int. J. Uncertain. Fuzz. 20 (6) (December 2012) 793—817.

[26] P. Samarati, Protecting respondents' identities in microdata release, IEEE TKDE 13 (6) (November/December, 2001) 1010—1027.

[27] C.A. Ardagna, J. Camenisch, M. Kohlweiss, R. Leenes, G. Neven, B. Priem, P. Samarati, D. Sommer, M. Verdicchio, Exploiting cryptography for privacy-enhanced access control: a result of the PRIME project, JCS 18 (1) (2010) 123—160.

[28] W. Chen, L. Clarke, J. Kurose, D. Towsley, Optimizing cost-sensitive trust-negotiation protocols, in: Proc. of INFOCOM 2005, Miami, FL, USA, March 2005.

[29] T.H. Cormen, C.E. Leiserson, R.L. Rivest, C. Stein, Introduction to Algorithms, third ed., MIT Press, 2009.

[30] D. Yao, K.B. Frikken, M.J. Atallah, R. Tamasia, Private information: to reveal or not to reveal, ACM TISSEC 12 (1) (October 2008) 1—27.

[31] I. Damgrad, M. Jurik, A generalisation, a simplification and some applications of Paillier's probabilistic public-key system, in: Proc. of PKC 2001, Cheju Island, Korea, February 2001.

[32] P. Paillier, Public-key cryptosystems based on composite degree residuosity classes, in: Proc. of EUROCRYPT 1999, Prague, Czech Republic, May 1999.

[33] S.E. Whang, H. Garcia-Molina, A model for quantifying information leakage, in: Proc. of SDM 2012, Anaheim, CA, USA, April 2012.

[34] P. Kärger, D. Olmedilla, W.-T. Balke, Exploiting preferences for minimal credential disclosure in policy-driven trust negotiations, in: Proc. of SDM 2008, Atlanta, GA, USA, August 2008.

[35] Z.J. Oster, G.R. Santhanam, S. Basu, V. Honavar, Model checking of qualitative sensitivity preferences to minimize credential disclosure, in: Proc. of FACS 2012, Mountain View, CA, USA, September 2012.

[36] C.A. Ardagna, S. De Capitani di Vimercati, S. Foresti, S. Paraboschi, P. Samarati, Supporting privacy preferences in credential-based interactions, in: Proc. of WPES 2010, Chicago, IL, USA, October 2010.

[37] C.A. Ardagna, S. De Capitani di Vimercati, S. Foresti, S. Paraboschi, P. Samarati, Minimising disclosure of client information in credential-based interactions, IJIPSI 1 (2/3) (2012) 205–233.

[38] C.A. Ardagna, S. De Capitani di Vimercati, S. Foresti, G. Neven, S. Paraboschi, F.-S. Preiss, P. Samarati, M. Verdicchio, Fine-grained disclosure of access policies, in: Proc. of ICICS 2010, Barcelona, Spain, December 2010.

Chapter 57

Privacy and Security in Environmental Monitoring Systems: Issues and Solutions

Sabrina De Capitani di Vimercati, Angelo Genovese, Giovanni Livraga, Vincenzo Piuri and Fabio Scotti
Università degli Studi di Milano, Crema, Italy

1. INTRODUCTION

Environmental monitoring systems allow the study of physical phenomena and the design of prediction and reaction mechanisms for dangerous situations. In its general form, a monitoring system consists of a certain number of sensors designed to measure different physical quantities, one or more processing nodes, and a communication network. The sensors provide output analogical signals that are conditioned and converted into the digital domain. The digital signals are then transmitted to the computing devices, which aggregate the obtained data to enable us to understand the measured phenomenon.

These systems are becoming increasingly important for keeping the state of the environment under control. In fact, they have a fundamental role in detecting new environmental issues and providing evidence that can help prioritize environmental policies. Such systems are also useful to better understand the relationship between the environment, economical activities, and daily life and health of people. For instance, weather affects agricultural prosperity and the well-being of forests, whereas environmental pollution affects human health and reduces the quality of water, land, cultivation, and forests. There is thus great interest in monitoring the environment to associate possible effects with observed phenomena and predict critical or dangerous situations. For instance, we know there is a direct link between exposure to particulate matter (PM) $\leq 10\,\mu\text{m}$ (PM_{10}) and $PM_{2.5}$ and the different pathologies of vascular systems. Moreover, natural resource management and preservation can greatly benefit from using monitoring systems to observe this status and its evolution so as to initiate conservation actions when needed. Similarly, natural disaster detection, observation, and eventually prediction can be based on monitoring geographical areas of interest. Another sector in which these systems are becoming highly significant is the monitoring of critical infrastructure, in particular encompassing railways, highways, gas pipelines, and electric energy distribution networks.

In the past several years, environmental monitoring systems have been subject to fundamental changes owing to rapid advancements in technology as well as the development of global information infrastructure such as the Internet, which allows the easy and rapid diffusion of information worldwide. As an example, advances in spectral and spatial resolution, new satellite technology, and progress in communication technologies have improved the level of detail of satellite Earth observations, making available high-resolution spatial and spectral data. Although such technological developments have the positive effect of expanding the application fields in which environmental data can be used successfully, there is also a negative effect related to increased misuse of environmental data and systems. As a matter of fact, seemingly innocuous environmental information can lead to privacy concerns. For instance, ambient environmental monitoring data could be used to identify small geographic areas. Property owners identified in the vicinity of a hazardous waste site or other pollution sources could experience decreased property values or increased insurance costs.

In this chapter, we aim to provide a comprehensive analysis of main security and privacy issues that can arise when collecting, processing, and sharing environmental data. The main contribution of this chapter is an analysis of security and privacy issues that involve both the infrastructure of environmental monitoring systems and the data collected and disseminated, along with possible countermeasures for mitigating them. The remainder of the chapter is organized as follows. Section 2 discusses the different kinds of systems and architectures used for environmental monitoring. Section 3 presents what kinds of environmental data are typically collected and analyzed. Section 4 illustrates main security and privacy issues related to the collection, processing, and sharing of environmental data. Section 5 discusses how such security and privacy risks can be counteracted by adopting suitable protection techniques. Finally, Section 6 concludes the chapter.

2. SYSTEM ARCHITECTURES

Environmental monitoring systems have evolved from a simple computer with sensors to composite structures that include specialized subcomponents addressing particular data collection issues. These systems are typically classified by considering the system architecture, the geographical extension of the monitored phenomenon, or the number of functions performed by the system.

Based on the system architecture, environmental monitoring systems can be classified as *centralized*, *distributed*, and *remote sensing systems* [1]. Centralized systems are composed of a single processor or controller, a limited number of sensors, and a simple output presentation interface (a single value on a display). Data are collected by sensors and transmitted to the processing unit that performs data analysis and feature extraction required by the application, and stores all relevant information as specified by the application itself. They may have small dimensions and be easily transported. Examples of centralized environmental monitoring systems are radiation detectors, gas detectors, and laboratory equipment. Centralized systems include monitoring systems based on a single observation point and systems that use robotic architectures to monitor hostile or remote environments [2].

Distributed systems are composed of a high number of sensing nodes and can exploit distributed computing and storing abilities. A sensing node contains a limited number of sensors, a processing unit, and a network communication channel. Sensing nodes collect data and may perform some local processing; they route data and information toward some processing nodes in the distributed structure. Some nodes have interfaces to deliver the results of their elaborations and storage devices to save acquired sensor data and processed information. Sensing nodes are deployed in a fixed position or may be mobile onboard robots to explore the environment [3]. Some intelligence may be distributed in sensing and processing nodes to provide local ability for data processing to extract knowledge as near to sensors as possible, reducing transmitted data or taking earlier local actions [4]. Sensing nodes can have self-configuration capabilities to adapt their operation to the environment and allow for easier deployment, especially when environmental conditions are harsh or humans cannot reach the

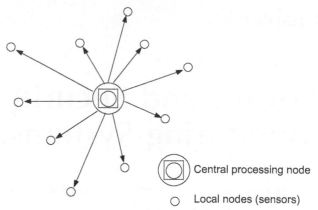

FIGURE 57.1 Sensor network with a central processing node.

monitored place. Mechanisms are also introduced for effecting automatic network configuration if nodes are added or removed [4], for determining whether node measurements are not necessary and thus saving energy, or for allowing nodes to move when a more suitable position is found [5]. Self-calibration techniques are used to set the operating parameters [6]. The distributed structures may limit costs and may affect the environment (using small and inexpensive sensors, shorter and cheaper sensor connections, small low-cost processing units for real-time operation, and possibly wireless transmission for limited interconnection costs).

In the simplest network topology, a central node processes data (Fig. 57.1); although continuous data transmission from sensing nodes leads to higher energy consumption, adjacent nodes may measure redundant or highly correlated data, and scalability may be limited owing to computational and bandwidth issues.

To overcome these problems, hierarchical sensor networks have been used. These networks are usually composed of three levels: *local nodes* (sensors), *intermediate nodes* (local aggregation centers, gateways, or base stations), and a *central processing* node. Some nodes may coordinate some sensors (cluster) by performing synchronization and data fusion [4] (Fig. 57.2). Computation is distributed in the hierarchical structure to create abstract views of the environment at different abstraction levels and compact the information by extracting the relevant knowledge as locally as possible. Local processing should be performed carefully to avoid possible erroneous interpretation of corresponding data at higher levels. Appropriate data aggregation techniques must be adopted to achieve a global understanding of the measured phenomena while avoiding data loss and redundant transmissions [7].

Communications are a critical aspect of sensor networks. They can be wired, as in conventional architectures, or wireless (as in wireless sensor networks). Use of cables to power sensors and transmit the data can create difficulties. Low-power communication protocols and wireless

Instead, active systems send a signal to the object to be monitored and measure the reflected pulse (radar, light detection and ranging, and laser altimeters). Remote sensing techniques can be merged with terrestrial sensor networks to integrate local data with large-scale observations to enhance the observation quality [10].

Environmental monitoring systems can also be classified according to their geographical extension as *large-scale*, *regional*, or *localized* monitoring systems [11]. Large-scale environmental monitoring systems are deployed when there is the need to cover a vast geographical area, such as several countries, or even the whole Earth globe. They are typically based on distributed networks or remote sensing, and they are used, for example, for monitoring seismic activity [12–14], geophysics [15], earth pollution [16,17],

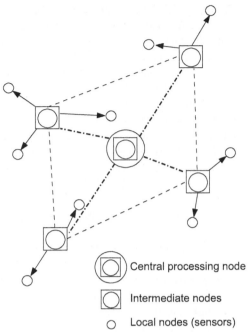

FIGURE 57.2 Hierarchical sensor network.

- Central processing node
- Intermediate nodes
- Local nodes (sensors)

interconnections are often used [8]. In these architectures, the geographical position of nodes may not be known a priori: global positioning systems (GPSs) or geographic information systems are used to trace the positions of data collected from sensors.

Sensing can be performed using sensors for the specific quantities to be measured and placed locally at the point in which the measure has to be taken. In some environments, direct local sensing may be difficult or even impossible owing to costs or environmental/operating conditions. To overcome this problem, for some quantities indirect measures can be taken by observing the point of interest from some distance. Visual sensor networks are an example of this approach: Their nodes are equipped with image-capturing devices and use image-based monitoring techniques. However, they require more complex devices, greater memory use, higher bandwidth, and nodes with more power consumption. Hierarchical sensor network architectures, consisting of heterogeneous nodes, can be used to reduce the costs and computational load [9].

Remote sensing systems are based on signals and images acquired by sensors installed on artificial satellites or aircraft and are used for vast geographical phenomena. These systems can capture several types of quantities at a significant distance, for example, by aircraft or artificial satellites. Such systems can be passive or active. In the first case, the sensors only detect quantities naturally produced by the object (the radiations of the reflected sunlight emitted by the objects). Many passive sensors can be used according to the chosen wavelength and signal dimension (radiometers, multispectral, and hyperspectral imaging).

An Agenda for Action for Privacy and Security of Environmental Compliance Monitoring Systems

The Environmental Protection Agency's (EPA's) national compliance monitoring program is responsible for maximizing compliance with federal environmental statutes dealing with the prevention and control of air pollution, water pollution, hazardous waste, toxic substances, and pesticides. Under these statutes, the EPA and its regulatory partners monitor activities under 44 separate statutory programs. The statutory and regulatory requirements of these programs apply to approximately 41 million regulated entities, such as sewage treatment plants, gas stations, and hospitals. The EPA regulates chemicals and monitors compliance with environmental laws and regulations designed to reduce pollution to protect public health and the environment. Without compliance with the environmental requirements, the promulgation of laws and regulations has little impact. Compliance monitoring consists of a variety of activities including (check all tasks completed):

_____**1.** Conducting compliance inspections, civil investigations, and evaluations under the air program

_____**2.** Determination of facility/site compliance status

_____**3.** Entry of results of activities into national data systems

_____**4.** Response to citizen complaints

_____**5.** Participation in development of rules to ensure they are enforceable

_____**6.** Development of compliance monitoring tools such as inspection checklists/guides

_____**7.** Procurement and dissemination of new compliance monitoring technologies such as remote sensing and hand-held computers

_____**8.** Development and delivery of training for compliance monitoring personnel

_____**9.** Support in developing enforcement cases

_____**10.** Development of state, tribal, local, and international compliance monitoring capacity

_____**11.** Funding and oversight of regional, state, and tribal compliance monitoring programs global water quality [18], wildfire [19], meteorological data [20—23], arctic ice and snow [20,24], desert sand storms [25], or their combinations (see checklist: An Agenda for Action for Privacy and Security of Environmental Compliance Monitoring Systems) [26—29].

Regional monitoring systems typically cover areas such as cities, forests, and regions. They are used, for example, to monitor water quality [30], air quality [31,32], meteorological information [33—36], regional oceanographic processes [33,36], and wildfires [37—41].

Localized systems are used to monitor localized points: for example, lakes, volcanoes, indoor environments, and buildings. Several practical cases are available: for example, for the quality of the water in lakes, rivers, or small bays [42—44]; the state of glaciers [45]; underwater currents [46]; air quality in small environments [47—49], and urban pollution (noise [50] and radiation [51]). Localized systems are also used for disaster prevention (for active volcanoes [52], landslides [53], and critical infrastructures [54,55]).

More complex measurement systems, called *heterogeneous sensor networks* [11], have been created by integrating combinations of subsystems of these types, with different scales and functions, especially when applications use systems already deployed in the environment of interest or when quantities must be measured in a heterogeneous setting. Some examples of this kind of system are the UK Climate Change Network [21,23] for land and aquatic places in the United Kingdom, the Global Earth Observation System [28] for different environmental processes all over the world, and Project Orion [56] for oceans. Heterogeneous systems may combine information from local sensor networks with satellite information: for example, linking local sensor networks on a planetary scale [10] or aggregating local imaging data with satellite imaging techniques [57].

Environmental monitoring systems are also characterized by the type of functionalities performed [11]. In *monofunction systems*, measured quantities are directed to provide knowledge for a single application, as in monitoring volcanoes [52] or buildings [55]. In *multiple-function systems*, data are collected (possibly in subsets of different types from different locations) and used by different applications and even for different global purposes, thus integrating various monitoring systems into a single infrastructure ([58]. Multiple-function systems also support environmental monitoring, border control, and surveillance applications while [26,27] dealing with climate and resource monitoring, topography, and disaster prevention).

3. ENVIRONMENTAL DATA

Before describing the security and privacy issues that characterize an environmental monitoring system, it is important to clarify what kinds of environmental data typically can be collected and possibly released to the public. Different data types are used in environmental monitoring systems, depending on the context. The used sensors can, in fact, measure data related to different physical quantities: movement, speed, acceleration, force, pressure, humidity, radiation, luminosity, chemical concentration, audio, video, and so on. Usually, the acquired data consist of monodimensional or multidimensional signals (images/frame sequences). The data used by large-scale environmental monitoring systems are inherent in the physical quantities chosen to measure a single phenomenon, and the data are captured and aggregated at a high frequency to perform continuous monitoring of the phenomenon.

In most cases, the geographical positions of the measuring nodes are fixed, known a priori, and released publicly. For instance, the system described in Hoogenboom [34] was composed of 192 measurement stations with fixed and known positions, and performed continuous monitoring of air temperature, humidity, precipitation, solar radiation, wind speed and direction, and atmospheric pressure. The system described in Refs. [12,14] was composed by more than 150 measurement stations with fixed and known positions, and measured data from seismographs. The system proposed in Refs. [16,17] used different UV radiation detectors to perform continuous monitoring of radiation. In the case of regional or localized environmental monitoring networks with multiple functions, nodes may not have fixed or known a priori positions; they are equipped with GPS devices, use wireless transmission techniques, and are powered using batteries. For this reason, the data transmission frequency is often smaller than the one used in large-scale environmental monitoring systems. For instance, the system described in Refs. [33,36] performed continuous monitoring of the waves along the coasts of Louisiana and the Mexican Gulf, measuring the wave height, their period, the direction of propagation, the water level, and the direction and speed of the currents. Different kinds of nodes with wireless transmission capabilities can be used. For instance, a volcano monitoring system is described in Werner-Allen [52] and uses nodes with infrasound sensors and GPS devices. An experimental visual sensor network for fire monitoring is proposed in Genovese et al. and Li et al. [37,40].

At a high level, the life cycle of environmental data can be divided into three macrosteps: *collection, storage*, and *publication*. Data are collected from the environment and stored at the sensor and/or processing nodes. The format of the stored data depends on the specific purpose for which such data have been collected. Authorized parties can access the environmental data for analysis or other purposes. The environmental data (or a subset of them) can then be made available publicly or semipublicly. The data are typically published in the form of *macrodata* (tables reporting aggregated information about an environmental phenomenon) or *microdata* (records reporting data related to specific physical measurements) [59].

In the remainder of this chapter, we illustrate some security and privacy risks that may arise in the data life cycle. To fix ideas and to clarify the following discussion, we refer our examples to a scenario characterized by a localized network in the city of San Francisco, which is under the control of the local municipality. The system is distributed and the sensor nodes are organized according to a centralized configuration. The collected data are stored at a processing node, PN. *Alice* is an adversary who tries to violate the monitoring system and discover sensitive information. We also consider a fictitious factory, A, which improperly releases pollutants and production rejects into the environment.

4. SECURITY AND PRIVACY ISSUES IN ENVIRONMENTAL MONITORING

Environmental monitoring systems and the data they collect can be vulnerable to security and privacy risks [60]. In particular, security risks are related to the threats that can undermine the *confidentiality*, *integrity*, and *availability* of both the data and the monitoring systems in their entirety (e.g., system architecture and communication infrastructure). Conversely, privacy risks are related to threats that can allow an adversary to use the environmental data for *inferring sensitive information*, which is not intended for disclosure and should be kept private. Security and privacy risks are not independent: They are often correlated, and an adversary can exploit a security violation for breaching data privacy. As an example, suppose that *Alice* successfully violates the physical security of processing node PN, causing a security violation that can allow her to access private information related to the pollutant levels in the air of San Francisco. This security violation can allow *Alice* to infer pathologies of the citizens of a given area of the city, therefore violating their privacy.

In this section, we present and illustrate through examples the main security and privacy risks that can arise in the context of environmental monitoring. Note that in the following discussion, we consider neither the classical security problems related to failures of systems and applications owing to errors nor the reliability and dependability aspects characterizing the system; our goal is to focus on less well-known security and privacy issues.

Security Risks

Broadly speaking, in our environmental monitoring scenario, security risks are related to all threats that can: (1) damage the infrastructure of the monitoring system; (2) violate communication channels connecting different components of the monitoring system; or (3) allow unauthorized parties to intrude into the monitoring system for malicious purposes. We now describe these threats in detail.

Damages to the System Infrastructure

Any attack performed with the aim of physically damaging the monitoring system can put at risk the confidentiality, integrity, and availability of the collected environmental data. For instance, suppose that the local municipality of San Francisco wants to build a new playground for children; to determine the safest location, it analyzes the collected environmental data to discard polluted areas of the city. Suppose also that *Alice* maliciously damages the sensor nodes close to Factory A, to hide evidence of the pollutants and production rejects release. Clearly, this compromises the collection of the environmental data, because these sensor nodes become unavailable (data availability violation). An analysis of the partial environmental data available to the local municipality can erroneously identify an area close to Factory A as the safest area for building the new playground. If this were to happen, children would be exposed to pollutants and production rejects. The same risks apply when all sensor nodes are working properly but the processing node gets attacked and becomes unavailable: In this case, the analysis of the environmental data would not be based on the latest measurements of the sensor nodes, and the results might be compromised. Note that these attacks can affect any of the three steps of the environmental data life cycle, because similar problems arise when an adversary succeeds in compromising the nodes collecting data (collection step), the database where environmental data are stored (storage step), or the systems where they are published (publication step).

Violation of the Communication Channels

All communication channels connecting the different components of a sensor network can represent a possible target for an adversary. In particular, the adversary might be a *passive adversary* (that is, she could be interested only in monitoring the communication channels to observe information that she would not be able to access) or an *active adversary* (that is, she could attempt to delete or modify data transmitted on such channels). These two scenarios configure two "classical" security attacks, which can intuitively violate the confidentiality and integrity of the data. Besides such attacks, an adversary can also be interested in monitoring the *accesses* performed on the data by the authorized parties, to discover some sensitive information about them. For instance, the fact that an authorized party accesses data related to the concentration of particulates reveals that the party is interested in discovering the polluted areas. If the party is a building constructor, this may imply that the party is interested in building a new apartment complex, and therefore the adversary can speculate on the costs of the lands. Effective protection of data access also requires the protection of *access patterns*: An adversary should not be able to see whether two accesses performed by two different parties aimed at the same data. For instance, *Alice* should not be able to see whether two competitors are interested in performing similar analyses on the environmental data. If so, *Alice* would be able to sell this knowledge to one of the two competitors. Note how the latter two attack scenarios configure two examples of a security violation, causing a privacy breach.

Unauthorized Access

Environmental data should be available only to users and parties authorized by the data owner. Clearly, restrictions on accesses to environmental data apply only when such data are not publicly released. Unauthorized accesses can possibly involve the database where environmental data are stored after their collection and analysis, or the sensor nodes. The storage server can be a local server, under the control of the data owner, or an external third-party storage server. In the first case, the server can be considered trusted (data can be safely stored), and access control should only be enforced against users requesting access to the stored data. In the second case, the external storage server is not considered trusted, and therefore access restrictions should also take into account the fact that the server itself should not be able to access the stored data. An adversary intruding into sensor nodes can be interested in accessing raw data to update them, or to inject false data so that tampered data are sent to the processing node. For instance, *Alice* can be interested in manipulating the measurements performed by the sensor nodes close to Factory A to reduce the concentration of a specific harmful substance. An adversary intruding into the storage servers is clearly interested in accessing environmental data after their collection, normalization, and analysis. Note that collected data can also be stored together with other datasets and, as a consequence, the adversary can discover correlations and dependencies among these different datasets. In all these cases, both data confidentiality and integrity are at risk.

Privacy Risks

Privacy risks are related to all threats that can allow an adversary to infer sensitive information from the collected environmental data. Such inferences can be *direct*, that is, caused by observations in the data collection (an adversary observing production rejects can discover confidential details of the productive processes of a company) or indirect (studies on the presence of polluting substances in geographical areas or workplaces can be correlated with studies on the relationship between correlating pollutants and diseases, revealing possible illnesses of individuals living in those areas). Inferred sensitive information can involve individuals, the environmental area on which data have been collected, and also areas close to or correlated with it. As an example, the knowledge that some geographical areas are polluted with harmful substances can also affect individuals who live in other areas if they own properties in the polluted areas. In fact, because of such knowledge, the value of their properties could decrease. Privacy risks can occur when environmental data are made publicly available (publication step) or when they are (properly or improperly) accessed; they can be a consequence of data correlations and associations, observations of data evolutions, unusual data, or knowledge of users' locations.

Data Correlation and Association

A possible means through which sensitive information can be inferred is represented by natural correlations existing among different phenomena. To illustrate, consider a life and sickness insurance company in San Francisco. Suppose that a third-party organization releases a study illustrating the relationship existing between pollutants and rare diseases. Suppose also that the insurance company accesses this study. By analyzing environmental data collected by the local municipality and comparing them with the study, the insurance company can decide to increase the risk associated with citizens living in polluted areas of San Francisco and recompute their insurance policies. In addition to correlation, the association of environmental data with other information coming from different sources can also be exploited to infer sensitive information. For instance, suppose that *Alice* can access a collection of data recording the medical histories of a community of patients. *Alice* might then link such data with airborne pollution studies (by exploiting city and county zones that are used to identify populations exposed to specific airborne pollutants) and thereby violate patients' privacy.

Data Evolutions

To obtain more meaningful data, sensor nodes can perform several measurements of quantities of interest over time. For instance, a measuring station can continuously record the noise level in a given area of a city. Although a high number of samples allows for better analysis of a given phenomenon, such repeated measurements can open the door to possible inference channels leaking sensitive information. For instance, suppose that *Alice* wants to discover the timetable of the freight trains traversing the railroad in San Francisco, which is kept secret by the local train company. Suppose also that environmental monitoring of the local municipality includes measurements of the noise pollution in the city. Having access to the measurements collected close to the railway, *Alice* can notice peaks in the noise levels and correlate this information with the public timetables of passenger trains, thus reconstructing the freight trains' timetable.

Unusual Data

Intuitively, if the measurements obtained from an environmental monitoring system deviate from what is expected or considered to be usual, a high risk of sensitive information inference can arise. To illustrate, suppose that the results of the environmental monitoring of the San Francisco city area show a high level of radioactivity. If the neighbor cities do not show such a high level of radioactivity, these values can be considered surprising and may witness the existence of a neighbor location storing radioactive material (nuclear weapons, or rejects of nuclear power plants). Otherwise, if the same level of radioactivity is observed in other cities as well, the radioactivity in San Francisco can be the result of some peculiarities of the soil.

Users' Locations

Mobile phones and smartphones are portable computers that many users have and increasingly carry with them at all times. In the near future, we can imagine that our phones will be equipped with sensors and applications specifically targeted to environmental monitoring, leading to *pervasive* environmental monitoring in which the sensing will be performed directly by users who will collect data related to the locations they visit. Because users move around space, measurements have to be tagged with the location in which they have been captured. An adversary able to track the movements of a given user can violate her privacy, discovering her frequent addresses (home and workplace),

usual movements (from home to work), and habits, and accordingly, can infer sensitive information about her. For instance, suppose that *Alice* gains access to the set of location-tagged environmental measurements performed by her colleague *Bob* with his smartphone. *Alice* can notice that *Bob* visits a clinic for cardiovascular diseases every day, and can discover that *Bob* or one of his relatives or close friends has a heart problem.

5. COUNTERMEASURES

We now describe possible countermeasures that can be adopted to avoid or mitigate the security and privacy risks described in the previous section. In the remainder of this chapter, we will refer our examples to the environmental data in Table 57.1, reporting a possible example of a collection of noise and PM_{10} values measured in the San Francisco area. Each row reports the GPS coordinates of the node that performed the measurement, personal information (name, date of birth, and ZIP code) of the owner of the area in which the sensor node is placed, and the noise and PM_{10} values measured by the node, expressed in decibels and micrograms per cubic meter, respectively.

Counteracting Security Risks

Security risks related to the system architecture can be prevented by hardening the physical security of the whole system architecture and by adopting intrusion detection systems [61]. Fault-tolerance solutions can also be helpful when an adversary turns out to be successful and some parts of the system report damages. For instance, a simple solution for ensuring the availability of data stored in the processing node consists of replicating the data on several machines, possibly located in different sites. Classical attacks on communication channels can be prevented by

TABLE 57.1 Example of a Collection of Environmental Data

| Sensor Position | Owner Personal Data | | | PM_{10} | Noise |
	Name	DoB	ZIP		
37.739404−122.483128	Arnold	21/06/1980	94,210	60	40
37.748313−122.583017	Bob	12/06/1980	94,211	60	42
37.737222−122.451906	Carol	07/06/1980	94,152	42	60
37.746131−122.442895	David	26/06/1980	94,112	30	51
37.735048−122.533784	Emma	01/07/1970	95,113	50	38
37.744957−122.534673	Fred	10/07/1970	95,141	20	40
37.733864−122.625562	George	05/07/1970	95,217	35	43
37.742772−122.416451	Hillary	12/07/1970	95,235	38	61

DoB, date of birth; *PM*, particulate matter.

encrypting the traffic, although lightweight solutions appear to be suitable for an environmental monitoring scenario in which data measurements are typically performed by sensor nodes with limited computational capabilities [62]. More challenging are the problems of ensuring appropriate protection against nonclassical attacks that analyze data access and access patterns, and of enforcing access restrictions under the assumption that the set of authorized users can dynamically change and might not be known a priori. In the remainder of this section, we illustrate possible strategies that can be adopted to address these two issues.

Protecting Environmental Data Access Patterns

The problem of protecting data access and access patterns from external observers and the storage server itself has been mainly studied in the database field [63]. A possible solution to the problem of ensuring that an adversary cannot infer sensitive information from observations of access to data is to change the physical location (blocks of the hard disk) where data are stored at each access. The technique in Ref. [63] goes in this direction, enabling authorized parties to access the stored data while guaranteeing: (1) *content* confidentiality (data privacy is maintained); (2) *access* confidentiality (the fact that access aims at a specific data item is protected); and (3) *pattern* confidentiality (the fact that two different accesses aim at the same data items is protected) from any observer, including the storage server itself. The technique is originally proposed in scenarios of data outsourcing, but it nicely fits a scenario in which a collection of environmental data needs to be stored and maintained private, and each access to certain information is performed by a request issued by a *trusted client*, directly interacting with the storage server.

Adopting this proposal, content, access, and pattern confidentiality are guaranteed by organizing data in an ad hoc data structure called a *shuffle index*. Such a shuffle index assumes data to be organized in an unchained B+ tree and encrypts data at the node level, so that real (plaintext) values are protected from the (possibly untrusted) storage server. In the B+ tree, data are indexed over a candidate key defined for the data collection, and actual data items are stored in the leaves of the tree according to their index values. Accesses to the data items stored in the tree are based on the value of the associated indexes. Note that, to avoid improper leakage of information to the storage server, the B+ tree includes no links from one leaf to the next. The rationale behind this is that such links would expose the order relationship among index values in different nodes.

Data encryption ensures content confidentiality whereas access and pattern confidentiality are safeguarded by the client by means of: (1) hiding the real (target) request

within cover (fake) requests; (2) caching target searches recently performed by users; and (3) shuffling, at each request, the content among blocks stored at the server. These three strategies work as follows:

- Cover searches hide a request in a set of fake ones, thus introducing confusion on the requested target. Cover searches are executed in parallel to the target search, and the number of cover searches can be customized to tune the offered protection level.
- Cache keeps the client from searching in the B+ tree for the same target in two close queries. The client maintains a local copy of the nodes forming a path in the B+ tree reaching a target value. The size of the cache determines the number of last target searches that are maintained in the cache itself.
- Shuffling implies modifying the data structure at every access and shuffling content among its blocks. The shuffling operation destroys the one-to-one correspondence otherwise existing between a block and the node of the B+ tree stored in it. In this way, repeated accesses to the same node might actually refer to searches for different data items, whereas different accesses to different nodes might refer to searches for the same data item.

Enforcing Access Restrictions on Environmental Data

To prevent unauthorized access to the system, an access control mechanism is needed. A peculiarity of the environmental monitoring scenario is that the set of users authorized to access collected environmental data is typically dynamic and may not be known a priori. For instance, consider the monitoring of air pollutants in the area of San Francisco. The collected and analyzed data could be accessed for analysis by the local municipality, but also by young researchers of local universities, which may have collaborations with other universities and therefore be part of a dynamic research group. According to this observation, the identity of users accessing the data may not always be known in advance, and traditional identity-based access control techniques [64] might not be applicable. To overcome this problem, attribute-based access control might represent a viable solution [65]. In this case, rather than considering users' identities, authorizations stating who can access what data are defined by taking into consideration properties (age, nationality, and occupation) of the authorized parties. For instance, suppose that the local municipality of San Francisco aims to give access to the collected environmental data only to US citizens. To this aim, the access control policy might grant access to users showing that they hold a US passport regardless of their identity. Attribute-based access control has been introduced as a means of enforcing this kind of access restriction in open environments. It is based on the assumption that typically each interacting party (e.g., a client and a server) has a portfolio of *credentials* and *declarations*, either issued and certified by trusted authorities or self-declared by the party herself [65]. More precisely, a credential includes a list (possibly empty) of certified attributes of the form ⟨attribute name, attribute value⟩ representing the subject's attributes (e.g., name and surname contained in an electronic passport), the issuer's public key, the subject's public key, a validity period, and a digital signature. Declarations are pairs of the form ⟨attribute name, attribute value⟩ specifying the party's attributes (the professional status communicated by a user during a registration process) and are produced by the party itself, with no certification from a legal authority. A common assumption underlying attribute-based access control systems is that the set of credentials and declarations that can be released by a party is stored in a profile associated with the party itself.

Attribute-based authorizations involve a *subject*, an *object*, and a set of *actions* to which the authorization refers. A *subject* can be defined as a Boolean formula over declarations and/or credentials. Analogously, an *object* can be defined as a Boolean formula of *predicates* specifying given conditions on the metadata associated with objects. An authorization therefore states that all subjects with a profile that satisfies the conditions in the *subject* field can perform *actions* on the objects whose metadata satisfy the conditions in the *object* field [65]. An authorization might also contain other elements imposing further conditions on the authorization, such as the purpose of access or generic conditions that must be satisfied by the access request. For instance, consider the environmental data in Table 57.1. To read (action) a specific set of PM_{10} measurements in the San Francisco area (object) collected from a certain set of ZIP codes (condition to be satisfied by the object profile), an authorization can require the proof of majority age and a US nationality (conditions to be satisfied by the subject's profile).

When an access request is submitted to the storage server (service provider), it is evaluated with respect to the authorizations applicable to it. An access request is allowed if the conditions for the required access are satisfied; it is denied if none of the specified conditions that might grant the requested access can be fulfilled. However, it may happen that the currently available information is insufficient to determine whether the access request should be granted or denied. In such cases, additional information is needed and the requester receives an undefined response with a list of requests that she must fulfill to gain access.

Counteracting Privacy Risks

To protect environmental data from inferences, it is necessary to adopt techniques limiting the analysis that an adversary can perform on them, and obfuscating correlations, associations, and dependencies among them. As previously mentioned, these kinds of inferences can arise whenever environmental data are properly or improperly accessed (when they are stored or outsourced), or when they are made publicly available. In the first case, the privacy of environmental data can be protected by adopting privacy-enhancing solutions devised for data storage and outsourcing (e.g., encryption and fragmentation). In the latter case, solutions investigated in the context of privacy-preserving data publishing can be adopted. In the remainder of this section, we will discuss some of these possible solutions and provide a brief overview of how location privacy can be ensured in the context of environmental monitoring.

Encrypting Stored and Outsourced Environmental Data

Properly storing and maintaining a collection of environmental data that can include, for example, raw data, analysis results, and evidence of correlations among environmental factors is not a trivial problem because of possible inferences that can arise when accessing such data. Ensuring an appropriate degree of data privacy is of paramount importance, especially when the storage server is not trusted for accessing the data. Clearly, storing environmental data in an *encrypted form* can represent an intuitive solution to guarantee protection against inferences. In fact, an encrypted data collection will be accessible for analysis only to authorized users: that is, those who are provided by the data owner with a decryption key.

Ensuring proper access to encrypted data is, however, a challenging problem, because different users are typically authorized to access different portions of the stored data. To ensure that all authorized parties can access *all and only* the data for which they have the appropriate authorization, data encryption can be combined with access control, leading to a peculiar kind of encryption usually referred to as *selective encryption* [66,67]. By adopting selective encryption, the keys with which data items are encrypted are regulated by the authorizations holding on to the data, and different data items are encrypted with different keys, mapping an *authorization policy* into an equivalent *encryption policy*. As a consequence, an authorization to access a data item translates into knowledge of the key with which the data item is encrypted (for efficiency reasons, selective encryption is typically assumed to use symmetric encryption). An intuitive solution for enforcing selective encryption consists of encrypting each data item with a different key and providing each user with a set of keys, including all of those used to encrypt the data items she can access. Such a naïve solution is, however, not viable in practice owing to the unacceptable key management burden left to users: Each user would be required to manage as many keys as the number of data items she is authorized to access. This issue can be conveniently overcome by adopting *key derivation* methods. Basically, a key derivation method allows the computation of an encryption key starting from another key and some public information [66]. Adopting a key derivation technique, each user in the system is provided with a unique key. The set of keys in the system is then built in such a way that, starting from her own key and according to a *key derivation structure*, each user can compute all and only the keys needed to decrypt the resources she can access.

Among the possible key derivation strategies, *token-based* key derivation [66] results are particularly appealing for storing or outsourcing (environmental) data. In fact, this solution minimizes the amount of reencrypting and rekeying required to enforce changes and updates to the authorization policy. Broadly speaking, token-based key derivation works as follows. Given a key k_i in the set of keys of the system, identified by public label l_i, a different key k_j can be derived from k_i and l_j through a so-called *token* $d_{i,j}$, computed as $k_j \oplus h(k_i, l_j)$, where $\oplus$ is the bitwise xor operator and h is a cryptographic function (e.g., a secure hash function). Note that the key derivation can be iteratively applied via a chain of tokens, and, because tokens are public pieces of information, all tokens defined in the system are stored in a public catalog. For instance, given three different keys k_i, k_j, and k_h, and two tokens $d_{i,j}$ and $d_{j,h}$, a user who knows (or can derive) key k_i can first use $d_{i,j}$ to derive k_j and, from k_j and $d_{j,h}$, she can then derive k_h. The effect of providing a user with a set $K = \{k_1, \ldots, k_n\}$ of keys is therefore conveniently obtained by providing the user with a single key $k_i \in K$ and publishing a set of tokens allowing the (direct or indirect) derivation of all keys $k_j \in K$, $i \neq j$. In this way, the user can derive all of the n encryption keys while having to worry about only a single one.

To implement updates in the authorization policy regulating access to the stored data (insertion/deletion of a user or data item and granting/revoking of a permission), a subset of the keys and of the tokens defined in the system must be updated, and some data items must accordingly be reencrypted. To limit computational burden, the solution in Ref. [66] proposes a two-layer encryption strategy called *overencryption*. By adopting overencryption, policy updates can be performed on encrypted resources themselves without the need to decrypt them. In this way, the storage server itself can directly manage policy updates.

Fragmenting Stored or Outsourced Environmental Data

When encryption results are too heavy or when encrypting the whole data is overdue, alternative solutions can be adopted. In fact, if what is sensitive is the data association

instead of specific data values, solutions based on the vertical fragmentation of the data can be adopted. The intuition is simple: When the joint visibility of some pieces of information is sensitive, such pieces of information are split into different portions that are not joinable. Fragmentation can be adopted by itself or coupled with encryption. For instance, suppose that the collected environmental data include information about the concentration of a pollutant in an area, the area, and the owner of the properties within the area. Suppose also that the data holder wants to protect the identities of the owners of polluted properties. Such a collection of environmental data can easily be split in two fragments: One fragment includes the concentration of the pollutant and the corresponding area (with the information about the properties' owner possibly encrypted) and the other fragment includes information about the owners.

Data fragmentation has been deeply studied in the context of data outsourcing and publication to fragment vertically the set of attributes composing the schema of a relation to be outsourced or published in such a way as to satisfy all confidentiality constraints defined by the data holder. Confidentiality constraints are subsets of attributes composing the original schema. Depending on the number of attributes involved, confidentiality constraints can be classified as: (1) *singleton constraints*, stating that the values of the attribute involved in the constraint are sensitive and cannot be released (the Social Security numbers of patients hospitalized for a given respiratory disease caused by PM_{10} exposure are sensitive per se and should be kept private); and (2) *association constraints*, stating that the association among the values of the attributes in the constraint is sensitive and cannot be released (the association between the name and the respiratory illness of a patient can be considered sensitive and should be protected from disclosure). Several fragmentation techniques have been proposed in the literature; these techniques can be classified based on how they fragment the original relation schema and whether they adopt encryption.

The first strategy [68] couples fragmentation with encryption and is based on the assumption that fragments can be stored on two noncommunicating servers. When some confidentiality constraints cannot be solved by fragmentation, at least one attribute appearing in such constraints is encrypted. This technique strictly relies on the absence of communications between the servers storing the fragments. However, because collusions among servers can restore the original relation schema compromising the protection of sensitive data, alternative techniques have been proposed to enforce confidentiality constraints.

The technique in Ref. [69] enforces confidentiality constraints coupling fragmentation with encryption while removing the assumption of the absence of communication among storage servers. This technique satisfies singleton

- c_0 = {SensorPosition}
- c_4 = {Name, Noise}
- c_1 = {Name, DoB}
- c_5 = {DoB, ZIP, PM10}
- c_2 = {Name, ZIP}
- c_6 = {DoB, ZIP, Noise}
- c_3 = {Name, PM10}

FIGURE 57.3 Example of confidentiality constraints.

constraints by encrypting the values of the involved attributes. Association constraints are satisfied by adopting either fragmentation (storing the involved attributes in different fragments) or encryption (encrypting at least one of the involved attributes). However, this technique favors fragmentation over encryption: If a confidentiality constraint can be satisfied via encryption or fragmentation, such a constraint will be enforced with fragmentation. To ensure that no sensitive association can be reconstructed, each attribute must appear in the clear in at most one fragment. This makes the different fragments not joinable, and therefore all fragments might also be stored on a single storage server. Also, to guarantee the possibility of authorized users running queries against the data collection, at the physical level each fragment stores all attributes of the original relation schema either in the clear or encrypted, so that no confidentiality constraint is violated. For instance, consider the environmental data reported in Table 57.1, and suppose that there are seven confidentiality constraints ($c_0 \dots c_6$), as reported in Fig. 57.3.

Intuitively, these confidentiality constraints state that: (1) the list of the sensor GPS positions is considered sensitive (c_0); (2) the association of the landowners' names with any other information in the relation is considered sensitive ($c_1 \dots c_4$); and (3) attributes date of birth and ZIP code can be exploited to infer the identity of the landowners, and therefore their associations with the collected noise and PM_{10} values are considered sensitive (c_5 and c_6).

Table 57.2 represents a possible fragmentation of Table 57.1 satisfying all defined confidentiality constraints.

Attribute Enc_T contains the encrypted version of all attributes appearing in the original relation but not in the clear in the fragment. Note that attribute SensorPosition is the only attribute not appearing in the clear in any fragment, because it is the only attribute involved in a singleton. Therefore, attribute Enc_T of the first fragment on the left-hand side in Table 57.2 includes in encrypted form the set {SensorPosition, DoB, ZIP, PM10, Noise} of attributes. Similarly, attribute Enc_T of the second and third fragment in Table 57.2 includes the sets {SensorPosition, Name } and {SensorPosition, Name, DoB, ZIP} of attributes, respectively.

Favoring fragmentation over encryption, the technique in Ref. [69] aims to limit the overhead conveyed by encryption. There are, however, situations calling for a complete departure from encryption. The technique in Ref. [70] avoids the use of encryption and relies solely on fragmentation to satisfy confidentiality constraints. The assumption is that the data owner is willing to store a limited portion of the data whenever needed to enforce confidentiality constraints. In this context, confidentiality constraints are satisfied by storing (at least) one attribute for each constraint on the data owner side. This fragmentation technique builds a pair of fragments, one stored on the data owner and the other one at the external storage server. Assuming that the storage capacity of the data owner is limited, each attribute of the original schema should appear in only one fragment to avoid replication of attributes that are already stored on the server side. To illustrate, consider the environmental dataset in Table 57.1 and the set of confidentiality constraints in Fig. 57.3, in which there is possible fragmentation where attributes SensorPosition, Name, and ZIP are stored on the data owner side, whereas attributes DoB, PM10, and Noise are stored externally. Note that, unlike fragmentation in Table 57.2, no attribute is

TABLE 57.2 Example of Fragmentation (Multiple Fragments)

Name	Enc_T	DoB	ZIP	Enc_T	PM₁₀	Noise	Enc_T
Arnold	Gfg5656d!	21/06/1980	94,210	Jhfdshjew	60	40	Jr8kds32j-
Bob	Dfgh45rer	12/06/1980	94,211	Hde832a8	60	42	Jhu2982nd
Carol	Fg9324gd	07/06/1980	94,152	Jw92[oq\	42	60	Njef9832m
David	Hd72pjc"L	26/06/1980	94,112	He82n1-x	30	51	Ne983mvs
Emma	543rfet4[f	01/07/1970	95,113	Nhw92d3	50	38	J[NJ9,PDH
Fred	2q34rxa1q	10/07/1970	95,141	9832ie9f	20	40	Jd0wKL34
George	Jkr8478'q	05/07/1970	95,217	Hj282nf2	35	43	/.USHSD8
Hillary	0932hjdfk	12/07/1970	95,235	83jdpvjw	38	61	[/'jdipw8m

DoB, date of birth; *PM*, particulate matter.

encrypted (all attributes belonging to the original schema appear in the clear in exactly one fragment).

By adopting this technique, we see that the execution of queries involving attributes stored in the two fragments requires the two fragments to have a common key attribute to guarantee a lossless join property (attribute T_Id in the fragments in Table 57.3). To increase the utility of fragmented data, the fragmentation process can also take into consideration visibility constraints, expressing views of data that the fragmentation should satisfy. Visibility constraints permit the expression of different needs of visibility, such as visibility over the values of a single attribute, visibility over the association among the values of the attributes, or alternative visibility over different attributes [71]. Furthermore, fragments can be complemented with a sanitized release of the sensitive associations broken by fragmentation. Such a release takes the form of loose associations, defined in a way to guarantee a specified degree of privacy. A loose association reveals some information about the association broken by fragmentation by hiding tuples participating in the associations in groups, and providing information about the associations only at the group level (in contrast to the tuple level) [71,72].

Protecting Published Environmental Data

When environmental data are publicly released, the possible countermeasures for their protection depend on the format of the data themselves (see Section 3). In the following, we illustrate how it is possible to publish environmental data while ensuring appropriate privacy protection in the cases of both macrodata and microdata.

Publishing Environmental Macrodata

If environmental data are published through macrodata tables, they are released as aggregate values and do not contain information specifically related to single individuals or single environmental measurements. However, sensitive information can still be leaked. For instance, consider a macrodata table reporting the concentration of a pollutant during the day and night for each county of a given region. The cells of the macrodata table that contain a high value can be considered sensitive because they indicate that the persons living in the highly polluted counties may have a high probability of experiencing specific illnesses. The content of these cells therefore needs to be protected somehow.

A macrodata table can be protected before or after tabulation. In the first case, the objective is to apply some protection techniques to the collected data (data swapping, sampling or noise addition) so that the computed aggregate values can be considered safe. In the latter case, the protection techniques typically operate in two steps because they first discover sensitive cells: that is, cells that can be easily associated with a specific respondent, and then protect them [59]. We now describe how sensitive cells can be discovered and protected.

Detecting Sensitive Cells Sensitive cells can be identified according to different strategies [72]. An intuitive strategy is the so-called *threshold rule*, according to which a cell is sensitive if the number of respondents who contribute to the value stored in the cell is less than a given threshold. The (n,k) *rule* states that a cell is sensitive if less than n respondents contribute to more than $k\%$ of the total cell value. Other examples of techniques are the *p-percent rule* and the *pq rule*. According to the *p-percent rule*, a cell is sensitive if the total value of the cell minus the largest reported value v_1 minus the second largest reported value v_2 is less than $(p/100)v_1$ (the reported value of some respondents can be estimated too accurately). The *pq rule* is similar to the *p-percent rule* but takes into consideration the value q representing how accurately a respondent can estimate another respondent's sensitive value $(p < q < 100)$.

TABLE 57.3 Example of Fragmentation (No Encryption, Two Fragments)

T_Id	Sensor Position	Name	ZIP	T_Id	DoB	PM$_{10}$	Noise
1	37.739404−122.483128	Arnold	94,210	1	21/06/1980	60	40
2	37.748313−122.583017	Bob	94,211	2	12/06/1980	60	42
3	37.737222−122.451906	Carol	94,152	3	07/06/1980	42	60
4	37.746131−122.442895	David	94,112	4	26/06/1980	30	51
5	37.735048−122.533784	Emma	95,113	5	01/07/1970	50	38
6	37.744957−122.534673	Fred	95,141	6	10/07/1970	20	40
7	37.733864−122.625562	George	95,217	7	05/07/1970	35	43
8	37.742772−122.416451	Hillary	95,235	8	12/07/1970	38	61

DoB, date of birth; *PM*, particulate matter.

TABLE 57.4 Example of Environmental Microdata Table

Sensor Position	Name	DoB	ZIP	PM₁₀
	Owner Personal Data			
37.739404−122.483128	Arnold	21/06/1980	94,210	60
37.748313−122.583017	Bob	12/06/1980	94,211	60
37.737222−122.451906	Carol	07/06/1980	94,152	42
37.746131−122.442895	David	26/06/1980	94,112	30
37.735048−122.533784	Emma	01/07/1970	95,113	50
37.744957−122.534673	Fred	10/07/1970	95,141	20
37.733864−122.625562	George	05/07/1970	95,217	35
37.742772−122.416451	Hillary	12/07/1970	95,235	38

DoB, date of birth; PM, particulate matter.

Protecting Sensitive Cells Once detected, sensitive cells can be protected by applying several techniques. *Cell suppression, rounding, roll-up categories, sampling, controlled tabular adjustment (CTA) function,* and *confidential edit* are examples of protection techniques. In particular, cell suppression consists of protecting a cell by removing its value (*primary suppression*). However, if some partial (marginal) totals of the table are revealed or publicly known, it might still be possible to redetermine the value of a suppressed cell or restrict the uncertainty about it. To counteract this risk, additional cells can be suppressed (*secondary suppression*). The rounding technique modifies the original value of a sensitive cell by rounding it up or down to a near multiple of a chosen base number. The roll-up categories technique modifies the original macrodata table so that a less detailed (of smaller size) table is released. Sampling implies that rather than through a census, the macrodata table is obtained through a sample survey. The CTA technique consists of replacing the value of a sensitive cell with a different value that is not considered sensitive with respect to the rule chosen to detect sensitive cells. In a subsequent step, linear programming techniques are used to adjust the values of the nonsensitive cells selectively. The rationale behind a confidential edit is to compute the macrodata table on a dataset that is being slightly modified with respect to the original collection. In particular, a sample of the original records is selected and matched (i.e., a set of records with the same values on a specific set of attributes) in other geographical regions, and the attributes of the matching records are then swapped.

Publishing Environmental Microdata

Microdata tables contain specific information related to single entities (called respondents). To illustrate, consider the environmental data reported in Table 57.1, and suppose

that the local municipality of San Francisco decides to release the PM₁₀ values in the area publicly. Table 57.4 illustrates a microdata table that the municipality can prepare from the collected data and can then release publicly. Intuitively, the publication of a microdata table increases privacy risks, and extreme attention has to be devoted to ensuring that no sensitive information is improperly leaked as a result of the release of such a table. In particular, in our example, the municipality must protect the fact that a given individual lives in an area with a high concentration of PM₁₀ because an adversary may infer that individuals living in such areas have a high probability of experiencing respiratory diseases.

Before publishing an environmental microdata table, all explicit identifiers have to be removed (or encrypted). For instance, Table 57.5 is a deidentified version of Table 57.4. In Table 57.5, the name of the landowners and the GPS position of the sensing devices (which would univocally identify the associated owner) have been removed by replacing them with value ***.

A deidentified table does not provide a guarantee of anonymity: In fact, besides identifiers, other attributes such as race, ZIP code, or gender (usually referred to as *quasiidentifiers*) can exist that might be linked to publicly available information to reidentify respondents. For instance, consider the public voter list reported in Table 57.1 and the deidentified microdata in Table 57.5, in which there is only one landowner born on 21/06/1980 and living in the 94,210 area. If this combination is unique in the external world as well, it identifies the first tuple of the microdata in Table 57.5 as pertaining to Adam Doe, 1201 Main Street, San Francisco 94,210, thus revealing that Adam is the owner of an area where the level of PM₁₀ is 60 μg/m³.

Effective protection of data privacy can be achieved by adopting techniques that, for example, generalize the data

TABLE 57.5 Example of Deidentified Environmental Microdata Table

Owner Personal Data				
Sensor Position	Name	DoB	ZIP	PM$_{10}$
***	***	21/06/1980	94,210	60
***	***	12/06/1980	94,211	60
***	***	07/06/1980	94,152	42
***	***	26/06/1980	94,112	30
***	***	01/07/1970	95,113	50
***	***	10/07/1970	95,141	20
***	***	05/07/1970	95,217	35
***	***	12/07/1970	95,235	38

DoB, date of birth; *PM*, particulate matter.

while preserving data truthfulness: k-anonymity is the pioneering technique in this direction [73]. k-Anonymity enforces the well-known protection requirement, typically applied by statistical agencies, demanding that any released information should be indistinguishably related to no less than a certain number of respondents. This general requirement is reformulated in the context of k-anonymity as follows: *Each release of data must be such that every combination of values of quasiidentifiers can be indistinctly matched to at least k respondents.* Because typically each respondent is assumed to be represented by at most one tuple in the released table, and vice versa (each tuple includes information related to one respondent only), a microdata table satisfies the k-anonymity requirement if and only if: (1) each tuple in the released table cannot be related to less than k individuals in the population; and (2) each individual in the population cannot be related to less than k tuples in the table. Taking a safe approach, a microdata table is said to be k-anonymous if each combination of values of the quasiidentifier in the table appears with at least k occurrences. In this way, each respondent cannot be associated with less than k tuples in the table, and each tuple cannot be related to less than k respondents in the

population, guaranteeing the satisfaction of the k-anonymity requirement.

To guarantee data truthfulness, k-anonymity is typically achieved by applying *generalization* and *suppression* over quasiidentifying attributes. Generalization substitutes the original values with more general values. For instance, the date of birth can be generalized by removing the day, or the day and month of birth. Suppression consists of removing information from the microdata table. As an example, suppose that the quasiidentifier for Table 57.5 is composed of attributes DoB and ZIP. Table 57.7 represents a possible 2-anonymous version of the environmental data in Table 57.5. The 2-anonymous version has been produced by generalizing the date of birth of the landowners (releasing only the month and year) and the ZIP code (releasing only the first three digits of the code). It is easy to see that comparing the 2-anonymous table with the voter list in Table 57.6 and adversary cannot determine which one between the first two tuples is related to Adam Doe, because both share the same combination of attributes DoB and ZIP. More precisely, each combination of values for attributes DoB and ZIP appears in the table with (at least) two different.

The k-Anonymity has been designed to counteract *identity disclosure*; that is, it represents an effective solution to protect the identities of the respondents of a microdata table. The original definition of k-anonymity has been extended to counteract the risk that sensitive information is leaked when releasing a microdata table (*attribute disclosure*). As an example, ℓ-diversity [74] and t-closeness [75] are two well-known extensions of k-anonymity, which slightly modify the k-anonymity requirement to ensure that neither identities nor sensitive information related to a respondent can be leaked when releasing a microdata table. The basic idea behind these approaches is to extend the k-anonymity requirement considering not only quasiidentifiers but also sensitive attribute values when computing a privacy-preserving microdata table. To illustrate, consider the 2-anonymous microdata in Table 57.7. Although an adversary cannot precisely identify the tuple of Adam Doe between the first two in the table, they both share the same value for the PM$_{10}$ measurement. As a consequence, the adversary is still able to discover that Adam Doe is the owner of a highly polluted area. Table 57.8 illustrates a

TABLE 57.6 Example of Public Voter List

Name	DoB	Address	ZIP	City	Job
...	...	...	...	...	...
Arnold Doe	21/06/1980	1201, Main Street	94,210	San Francisco	Dentist
...	...	...	...	...	...

DoB, date of birth.

TABLE 57.7 Example of 2-Anonymous Microdata Table

Owner Personal Data				
Sensor Position	Name	DoB	ZIP	PM_{10}
***	***	**/06/1980	942**	60
***	***	**/06/1980	942**	60
***	***	**/06/1980	941**	42
***	***	**/06/1980	941**	30
***	***	**/07/1970	951**	50
***	***	**/07/1970	951**	20
***	***	**/07/1970	952**	35
***	***	**/07/1970	952**	38

DoB, date of birth; PM, particulate matter.

TABLE 57.8 Example of 3-Diverse Microdata Table

Owner Personal Data				
Sensor Position	Name	DoB	ZIP	PM_{10}
***	***	**/**/1980	94***	60
***	***	**/**/1980	94***	60
***	***	**/**/1980	94***	42
***	***	**/**/1980	94***	30
***	***	**/**/1970	95***	50
***	***	**/**/1970	95***	20
***	***	**/**/1970	95***	35
***	***	**/**/1970	95***	38

DoB, date of birth; PM, particulate matter.

3-diverse version of the microdata in Table 57.5, obtained by generalizing the date of birth to the year of birth, and the ZIP code by releasing only the first two digits. In this case, the tuple of Adam Doe can be one of the first four tuples of the table, but because these tuples assume three (hence the 3-diversity) different values for the PM_{10} concentration, the adversary cannot determine which is the concentration associated with Adam Doe's area.

The k-Anonymity, ℓ-diversity, and t-closeness have been modified and/or extended to suit particular releasing scenarios characterized by particular assumptions, constraints, and privacy requirements, such as multiple table releases [76,77], data republication [78], nonpredefined or dynamic quasiidentifiers [79], and customizable privacy protection [80].

Protecting the Privacy of Location Information in Environmental Data

The problem of protecting users' positions and movements has gained increasing interest owing to the proliferation of mobile devices equipped with location capabilities and location-based services [81]. This has led to the definition of different techniques to protect location information, which can be nicely adapted to the scenario of pervasive environmental monitoring. In the remainder of this section, we will survey three different classes of works that can be adopted in this scenario for protecting users' privacy.

The first class of works aims to protect the privacy of anonymous users communicating with a location-based service provider whenever their real identities are not relevant to the service provision [81]. The goal of these techniques is to avoid the possibility of *reidentifying* users observing their position. Because in traditional location-based services users communicate with the service provider posing queries associated with their position, the intuition is that of ensuring that the same location will be shared by at least a certain number of different users. These techniques guarantee indistinguishability of users typically by enforcing the requirement of k-anonymity [72], specifically tailored to fit the location-based scenario. In our environmental context, instead of issuing queries to a service provider, users communicate some environmental measurements: This translates to the requirement that a same sensed location should be shared by at least a certain number of different sensing users.

The second class of works aims to obfuscate the real position of the users in scenarios in which users are not made anonymous and must provide their real identity to the service provider. The idea is that of *degrading the accuracy* of the location measurement. An intuitive strategy might consist of hiding the real position of a user with a set of other n fake positions, characterized by the same probability [82]. A different strategy is based on adopting some *obfuscation operators*, with the goal of balancing the accuracy of the position and the privacy requirements of the users. For instance, the technique in Ardagna et al. [83] equates privacy with respect to the accuracy of the location measurement, because the more accurate the measurement is, the less privacy there is. The defined obfuscation operators change the radius, or the center, of the original location measurement and are used to degrade the accuracy of the location measurement in such a way that for each user, her privacy preferences are satisfied.

The third class of works focuses on *path privacy*, and aims to release a path shared by multiple users to make them indistinguishable [84]. For instance, these solutions are based on a dynamic grouping of users [85], and protect path privacy enforcing a modified version of k-anonymity that requires all k users associated with a specific location to remain grouped together as time passes. A different solution is instead based on the release of fake (simulated) locations [86]. This technique adopts probabilistic models of driving behaviors, applied for creating realistic driving trips, and GPS noise to decrease the precision of the starting point of a trip, and is therefore more suitable for scenarios in which environmental sensing devices are placed on vehicles.

6. SUMMARY

In this chapter, we provided an overview of the systems and architectures used for environmental monitoring. We also presented an overview of the main security and privacy issues in environmental monitoring systems and discussed possible countermeasures for mitigating such issues. Our work can help in a better understanding of the security and privacy issues that characterize environmental monitoring systems, and in designing novel environmental systems and applications that guarantee the privacy-aware collection, management, and dissemination of environmental data.

Finally, let us move on to the real interactive part of this chapter: review questions/exercises, hands-on projects, case projects, and the optional team case project. The answers and/or solutions by chapter can be found in the Online Instructor's Solutions Manual.

CHAPTER REVIEW QUESTIONS/ EXERCISES

True/False

1. True or False? Environmental monitoring systems allow the study of physical phenomena and the design of prediction and reaction mechanisms to dangerous situations.
2. True or False? Environmental monitoring systems have evolved from a simple computer with sensors to composite structures that include specialized components addressing particular data collection issues.
3. True or False? Before describing the security and privacy issues that characterize an environmental monitoring system, it is fundamental to clarify what kinds of environmental data can be typically collected and possibly released to the public.
4. True or False? Environmental monitoring systems and the data they collect cannot be vulnerable to security and privacy risks.
5. True or False? Any attack performed with the aim of physically damaging the monitoring system can put at risk the confidentiality, integrity, and availability of the collected environmental data.

Multiple Choice

1. All _____ connecting the different components of a sensor network can represent a possible target for an adversary.
   A. Privacy-enhancing technologies
   B. Location technologies
   C. Communication channels
   D. Executable policies
   E. Data controllers
2. What should be available only to users and parties authorized by the data owner?
   A. Policy enforcement
   B. Location technology
   C. Valid
   D. Environmental data
   E. Web technology
3. Which of the following are related to all threats that can allow an adversary to infer sensitive information from the collected environmental data?
   A. Data minimization
   B. eXtensible Access Control Markup Language
   C. Privacy risks
   D. Contradictory
   E. Security
4. A possible means through which _____ can be inferred is represented by the natural correlations existing among different phenomena.
   A. Privacy metrics
   B. Greedy strategy
   C. Sensitive information
   D. Privacy preferences
   E. Taps
5. To obtain more meaningful data, _____ can perform several measurements of quantities of interest over time.
   A. Irrelevant
   B. Sensor nodes
   C. Data-handling policies
   D. Disclose-to
   E. Server policy

EXERCISE

Problem

What is the difference between data gathered by stationary and deployable monitors?

Hands-on Projects

Project

What are the EPA's radiation air monitoring capabilities?

Case Projects

Problem

Are near—real time radiation air monitors able to cover the whole United States?

Optional Team Case Project

Problem

What are deployable monitors? What do they measure?

ACKNOWLEDGMENTS

This work was supported in part by the Italian Ministry of Research within the PRIN 2008 project "PEPPER" (2008SY2PH4), and by the Università degli Studi di Milano within the "UNIMI per il Futuro—5 per Mille" project "PREVIOUS."

REFERENCES

[1] F. Amigoni, A. Brandolini, V. Caglioti, V.D. Lecce, A. Guerriero, M. Lazzaroni, Agencies for perception in environmental monitoring, IEEE Trans. Instrum. Meas. 55 (4) (2006) 1038—1050.

[2] M. Dunbabin, L. Marques, Robots for environmental monitoring: significant advancements and applications, IEEE Robotics Autom. Mag. 19 (1) (March 2012) 24—39.

[3] A. Rodic, D. Katie, G. Mester, Ambient intelligent robot-sensor networks for environmental surveillance and remote sensing, (2009).

[4] M. Tubaishat, S. Madria, Sensor networks: an overview, IEEE Potentials 22 (2) (2003) 20—33.

[5] T. Wong, T. Tsuchiya, T. Kikuno, A self-organizing technique for sensor placement in wireless micro-sensor networks, (2004).

[6] H. Leung, S. Chandana, S. Wei, Distributed sensing based on intelligent sensor networks, IEEE Circuits Syst. Mag. 8 (2) (2008) 38—52.

[7] C.Y. Chong, S.P. Kumar, Sensor networks: evolution, opportunities and challenges, IEEE Proc. 91 (8) (2003).

[8] ZigBee Allianz, [Online]. Available: <http://www.zigbee.org>.

[9] P. Kulkarni, D. Ganesan, P. Shenoy, Q. Lu, SensEye: a multitier camera sensor network, in: Proc. of Multimedia 2005, Singapore, 2005.

[10] D. Aksoy, A. Aksoy, Satellite-linked sensor networks for planetary scale monitoring, in: Proc. of VTC 2004, Los Angeles, CA, USA, 2004.

[11] J.K. Hart, K. Martinez, Environmental sensor networks: a revolution in the earth system science? Earth Sci. Rev. 78 (3—4) (2006) 177—191.

[12] R. Butler, T. Lay, K. Creager, P. Earl, K. Fischer, J. Gaherty, The global seismographic network surpasses its design goal, EOS 85 (23) (2004) 225—229.

[13] NOAA Center for Tsunami Research, DART (Deep-ocean Assessment and Reporting of Tsunamis), [Online]. Available: http://nctr.pmel.noaa.gov/Dart.

[14] Global Seismographic Network, [Online]. Available: http://www.iris.edu/hq/programs/gsn.

[15] Hawaii Institute of Geophysics and Planetology, [Online]. Available: http://www.higp.hawaii.edu/.

[16] G. Bernhard, C. Booth, J. Ehramjian, Real-time UV and column ozone from multi-channel UV radiometers deployed in the national science foundation's UV monitoring network, in: Ultraviolet Ground- and Space-based Measurements, Models, and Effects III: Proceedings of SPIE, vol. 5156, 2003, pp. 167—178.

[17] NSF Polar Programs UV Monitoring Network, [Online]. Available: http://uv.biospherical.com/.

[18] GEMSTAT Global Environment Monitoring System, [Online]. Available: http://www.gemstat.org/.

[19] J. Vogelmann, J. Kost, B. Tolk, S. Howard, K. Short, X. Chen, Monitoring landscape change for LANDFIRE using multi-temporal satellite imagery and ancillary data, IEEE J. Sel. Topics Appl. Earth Observations Remote Sens 4 (2) (June 2011) 252—264.

[20] G. Schaefer, R. Paetzold, SNOTEL (SNOwpack TELemetry) and SCAN (Soil Climate Analysis Network), in: Automated Weather Stations for Applications in Agriculture and Water Resources Management: Current Use and Future Perspectives, March 2000.

[21] UK climate change network, [Online]. Available: http://www.ecn.ac.uk.

[22] J. Kimball, L. Jones, K. Zhang, F. Heinsch, K. McDonald, W. Oechel, A satellite approach to estimate land CO2 atmosphere exchange for boreal and arctic biomes using MODIS and AMSR-E, IEEE Trans. Geosci. Remote Sens. 47 (2) (February 2009) 569—587.

[23] A. Lane, The UK environmental change network database: an integrated information resource for long-term monitoring and research, J. Environ. Manage. 51 (1) (1997) 87—105.

[24] S. Ngheim, P. Clemete-Colon, Arctic sea ice mapping with satellite radars, IEEE Aerosp. Electron. Syst. Mag. 24 (11) (November 2009) 41—44.

[25] J. Qu, X. Hao, M. Kafatos, L. Wang, Asian dust storm monitoring combining terra and aqua MODIS SRB measurements, IEEE Geosci. Remote Sens. Lett. 3 (4) (October 2006) 484—486.

[26] M. Shimada, T. Tadono, A. Rosenqvist, Advanced land observing satellite (ALOS) and monitoring global environmental change, IEEE Proc. 98 (5) (May 2010) 780—799.

[27] A. Rosenqvist, M. Shimada, N. Ito, M. Watanabe, ALOS PALSAR: a pathfinder mission for global-scale monitoring of the environment, IEEE Trans. Geosci. Remote Sens. 45 (11) (November 2007) 3307—3316.

[28] National Oceanic and Atmospheric Administration NOA, United States Department of Commerce, Global Earth Observation System, [Online]. Available: http://www.noaa.gov/eos.html.

[29] United States environmental protection agency, national environmental monitoring initiative, [Online]. Available: http://www.epa.gov/cludygxb/html/choices.htm.

[30] King county natural resources and parks, [Online]. Available: http://www.kingcounty.gov/environment/dnrp.aspx.

[31] M. Carotta, G. Martinelli, L. Crema, C. Malagu, M. Merli, G. Ghiotti, Nanostructured thick-film gas sensors for atmospheric pollutant monitoring: quantitative analysis on field tests, Sens. Actuators B 76 (2001) 336—342.

[32] G. Andria, G. Cavone, V.D. Lecce, A. Lanzolla, Model characterization in measurements of environmental pollutants via data correlation of sensor outputs, IEEE Trans. Instrum. Meas. 54 (3) (June 2005) 1061—1066.

[33] WAVCIS Wave-Current-Surge Information System for Coastal Louisiana, [Online]. Available: http://www.wavcis.lsu.edu.

[34] G. Hoogenboom, The Georgia automated environmental monitoring network, Southeastern Climate Rev. 4 (1993) 12—18.

[35] Chesapeake Bay Observatory System, [Online]. Available: http://www.cbos.org.

[36] G. Stone, X. Zhang, J. Li, A. Sheremet, Coastal observing systems: key to the future of coastal dynamics investigations, GCAGS/GCSSEPM Trans. 53 (2003) 783–799.

[37] A. Genovese, R. Donida Labati, V. Piuri, F. Scotti, Wildfire smoke detection using computational intelligence techniques, in: IEEE International Conference on Computational Intelligence for Measurement Systems and Applications (CIMSA 2011), Ottawa, Canada, 2011.

[38] A. Genovese, R. Donida Labati, V. Piuri, F. Scotti, Virtual environment for synthetic smoke clouds generation, in: IEEE International Conference on Virtual Environments, Human-Computer Interfaces and Measurement Systems (VECIMS 2011), Ottawa, Canada.

[39] Z. Liu, A. Kim, Review of recent developments in fire detection technologies, J. Fire Prot. Eng. 13 (2) (May 2003) 129–149.

[40] Q. Li, Q. Hao, K. Zhang, Smart wireless video sensor network for fire alarm, in: Proc. of WiCOM 2010, Chengdu, China, 2010.

[41] B. Son, Y.-S. Her, J.-G. Kim, A design and implementation of forest-fires surveillance system based on wireless sensor networks for South Korea mountains, IJCSNS Int. J. Comput. Sci. Network Secur. 6 (9B) (September 2006).

[42] J. Tschmelak, G. Proll, J. Riedt, J. Kaiser, P. Kraemmer, L. Bárzaga, Automated water analyser computer supported system (AWACSS) part I: project objectives, basic technology immunoassay development, software design and networking, Biosens. Bioelectron. 20 (8) (2005) 1499–1508.

[43] T. Bendikov, J. Kim, T. Harmon, Development and environmental applications of a nitrate selective microsensor based on doped polypyrrole films, in: 204th Meeting of the Electrochemical Society, 2003.

[44] C. Alippi, R. Camplani, C. Galperti, M. Roveri, A robust, adaptive solar-powered WSN framework for aquatic environmental monitoring, IEEE Sens. J. 11 (1) (January 2011) 45–55.

[45] K. Martinez, J. Hart, R. Ong, Environmental sensor networks, Computer 37 (8) (2004) 50–56.

[46] G. Acar, A. Adams, ACMENet: an underwater acoustic sensor network protocol for real-time environmental monitoring in coastal areas, Radar, Sonar Navigation, IEE Proc. 153 (4) (August 2006) 365–380.

[47] K. Persaud, Smart gas sensor for monitoring environmental changes in closed systems: results from the MIR space station, Sens. Actuators B 2–3 (55) (1999) 118–126.

[48] A. Kumar, I. Singh, S. Sud, Energy efficient and low-cost indoor environment monitoring system based on the IEEE 1451 standard, IEEE Sens. J. 11 (10) (October 2011) 2598–2610.

[49] J. Guevara, F. Barrero, E. Vargas, J. Becerra, S. Toral, Environmental wireless sensor network for road traffic applications, Intell. Transport Syst. IET 6 (2) (June 2012) 177–186.

[50] S. Santini, A. Vitaletti, Wireless Sensor Networks for Environmental Noise Monitoring, in: GI/ITG KuVS Fachgespraech Drahtlose Sensornetze, July 2007, pp. 98–101.

[51] L. Ioriatti, M. Martinelli, F. Viani, M. Benedetti, A. Massa, Realtime distributed monitoring of electromagnetic pollution in urban environments, in: Geoscience and Remote Sensing Symposium, 2009 IEEE International, IGARSS 2009, 2009.

[52] G. Werner-Allen, J. Johnson, M. Ruiz, J. Lees, M. Welsh, Monitoring volcanic eruptions with a wireless sensor network, in: Proc. of EWSN 2005, Istanbul, Turkey, 2005.

[53] M.V. Ramesh, Real-time wireless sensor network for landslide detection, in: Proceedings of the 2009 Third International Conference on Sensor Technologies and Applications, Washington, DC, USA, 2009.

[54] L. Buttyan, D. Gessner, A. Hessler, P. Langendoerfer, Application of wireless sensor networks in critical infrastructure protection: challenges and design options, IEEE Wireless Commun. 17 (5) (October 2010) 44–49.

[55] T. Harms, S. Sedigh, F. Bastianini, Structural health monitoring of bridges using wireless sensor networks, IEEE Instrum. Meas. Mag. 13 (6) (December 2010) 14–18.

[56] ORION Project, [Online]. Available: http://orion.lookingtosea.ucsd.edu.

[57] E. Bradley, M. Toomey, C. Still, D. Roberts, Multi-scale sensor fusion with an online application: integrating GOES, MODIS, and webcam imagery for environmental monitoring, IEEE J. Sel. Topics Appl. Earth Observations Remote Sens. 3 (4) (December 2010) 497–506.

[58] P. Ferraro, M. Bauersachs, J. Burns, G. Bataller, A system for the measurement of the Amazon, IEEE Aerosp. Electron. Syst. Mag. 22 (8) (August 2007) 9–19.

[59] V. Ciriani, S. De Capitani di Vimercati, S. Foresti, P. Samarati, T. Jajodia, S. Yu, Microdata protectionSecure data management in decentralized systems, in: T. Jajodia, S. Yu (Eds.), Secure Data Management in Decentralized Systems, Springer-Verlag, 2007.

[60] S. De Capitani di Vimercati, G. Livraga, V. Piuri, F. Scotti, Privacy and security in environmental monitoring systems, in: Proc. of ESTEL 2012, Rome, Italy, 2012.

[61] W. Stallings, Network Security Essentials: Applications and Standards, fourth ed., Prentice Hall Press, Upper Saddle River, NJ, 2010.

[62] C. Castelluccia, A.C.-F. Chan, E. Mykletun, G. Tsudik, Efficient and provably secure aggregation of encrypted data in wireless sensor networks, ACM TOSN 5 (3) (2009) 1–36.

[63] S. De Capitani di Vimercati, S. Foresti, S. Paraboschi, G. Pelosi, P. Samarati, Efficient and private access to outsourced data, in: Proc. of ICDCS 2011, Minneapolis, MN, USA, 2011.

[64] S. De Capitani di Vimercati, P. Samarati, Access control in federated systems, in: Proc. of NSPW, Lake Arrowhead, CA, USA, 1996.

[65] C. Ardagna, M. Cremonini, S. De Capitani di Vimercati, P. Samarati, A privacy-aware access control system, JCS 16 (4) (2008).

[66] S. De Capitani di Vimercati, S. Foresti, S. Jajodia, S. Paraboschi, P. Samarati, Encryption policies for regulating access to outsourced data, ACM TODS 35 (2) (2010) 1–46.

[67] S. De Capitani di Vimercati, S. Foresti, S. Jajodia, S. Paraboschi, P. Samarati, A data outsourcing architecture combining cryptography and access control, in: Proc. of CSAW 2007, Fairfax, VA, USA, 2007.

[68] G. Aggarwal, M. Bawa, P. Ganesan, H. Garcia-Molina, K. Kenthapadi, R. Motwani, et al., Two can keep a secret: a distributed architecture for secure database services, in: Proc. of CIDR 2005, Asilomar, CA, USA, 2005.

[69] V. Ciriani, S. De Capitani di Vimercati, S. Foresti, S. Jajodia, S. Paraboschi, P. Samarati, Combining fragmentation and encryption to protect privacy in data storage, ACM TISSEC 13 (9) (2010).

[70] V. Ciriani, S. De Capitani di Vimercati, S. Foresti, S. Jajodia, S. Paraboschi, P. Samarat, Keep a few: outsourcing data while maintaining confidentiality, in: Proc. of ESORICS 2009, Saint-Malo, France, 2009.

[71] S. De Capitani di Vimercati, S. Foresti, S. Jajodia, S. Paraboschi, P. Samarati, Fragments and loose associations: respecting privacy in data publishing, PVLDB 3 (1) (2010) 1370–1381.

[72] Federal Committee on Statistical Methodology, Statistical Policy Working Paper 22, second ed., 2005. Washington, DC.

[73] P. Samarati, Protecting respondents' identities in microdata release, IEEE TKDE 13 (6) (2001) 1010–1027.

[74] A. Machanavajjhala, D. Kifer, J. Gehrke, M. Venkitasubramaniam, l-diversity: privacy beyond k-anonymity, ACM TKDD 1 (1) (2007) 3–52.

[75] N. Li, T. Li, S. Venkatasubramanian, t-Closeness: privacy beyond k-anonymity and l-diversity, in: Proc. of ICDE 2007, Istanbul, Turkey, 2007.

[76] K. Wang, B. Fung, Anonymizing sequential releases, in: Proc. of KDD 2006, Philadelphia, PA, USA, 2006.

[77] M. Nergiz, C. Clifton, A. Nergiz, Multirelational k-anonymity, in: Proc. of ICDE 2007, Istanbul, Turkey, 2007.

[78] X. Xiao, Y. Tao, M-invariance: towards privacy preserving re-publication of dynamic datasets, in: Proc. of SIGMOD 2007, Beijing, China, 2007.

[79] M. Terrovitis, N. Mamoulis, P. Kalnis, Privacy-preserving anonymization of set-valued data, PVLDB 1 (1) (2008) 115–125.

[80] Frikken, Y. Zhang, Yet another privacy metric for publishing microdata, in: Proc. of WPES 2008, Alexandria, VA, USA, 2008.

[81] C. Bettini, S. Jajodia, P. Samarati, X.S. Wang (Eds.), vol. LNCS 5599, Springer, 2009.

[82] M. Duckham, L. Kulik, A Formal Model of Obfuscation and Negotiation for Location Privacy, Munich, Germany, 2005.

[83] C. Ardagna, M. Cremonini, S. De Capitani di Vimercati, P. Samarati, An obfuscation-based approach for protecting location privacy, IEEE TDSC 8 (1) (2011) 13–27.

[84] C.-Y. Chow, M.F. Mokbel, Trajectory privacy in location-based services and data publication, SIGKDD Explorations Newsl. 13 (11) (2011) 19–29.

[85] C.-Y. Chong, M.M. Chow, Enabling private continuous queries for revealed user locations, in: Proc. of SSTD 2007, Boston, MA, USA, 2007.

[86] J. Krumm, Realistic driving trips for location privacy, in: Proc. of Pervasive 2009, Nara, Japan, 2009.

Chapter 58

Virtual Private Networks

James T. Harmening

Computer Bits, Inc., Chicago, IL, United States

With the incredible advance of the Internet, it has become more and more popular to set up virtual private networks (VPNs) within organizations. Two types of VPNs are typically employed. The first will connect two separate local area networks (LANs), in different locations, to each other; while the second is a single remote computer connecting through the Internet, back to the home network. VPNs have been around for many years and have branched out into more and more varieties. (See Fig. 58.1 for a high-level view of a VPN.) Once only the largest of organizations would utilize VPN technology to connect multiple networks over the Internet's "public networks," but now VPNs are being used by many small businesses as a way to allow remote users access to their business networks from home or while traveling.

Consultants have changed their recommendations from dial-in systems and leased lines to VPNs for several reasons. Security concerns were once insurmountable, forcing the consultants to set up direct dial-in lines. Not that the public telephone system was much more secure, but it gave the feeling of security and with the right setup, dial-in systems approach secure settings. Sometimes they utilized automatic callback options and had their own encryption. Now, with advanced security, including random-number generator logins, a network administrator is far more likely to allow access to their network via a VPN. High-speed Internet access is now the rule instead of the exception. Costs have plummeted for the hardware and software to make the VPN connection as well. The proliferation of vendors, standardization of Internet Protocol (IP) networks, and ease of setup all played a role in the increasingly wide use and acceptance of VPNs.

The key to this technology is the ability to route communications over a public network to allow access to office servers, printers, or data warehouses in an inexpensive manner. As high-speed Internet connections have grown

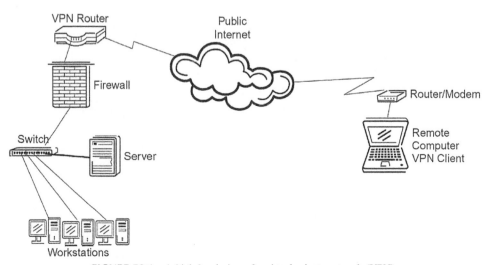

FIGURE 58.1   A high-level view of a virtual private network (VPN).

Computer and Information Security Handbook. http://dx.doi.org/10.1016/B978-0-12-803843-7.00058-2

and become prevalent throughout the world, VPNs over the public Internet have become common. Even inexpensive hotels are offering free Internet access to their customers. This is usually done through Wi-Fi connections, thus causing some concern for privacy, but the connections are available. Moreover, the iPhone, Android, Windows, Blackberry, and other multifunction web-enabled phones are giving mobile users access to the Internet via their phones. Some of the best ways to access the Internet is via a USB or wireless Hotspot from the major phone companies. These dedicated modem cards allow users to surf the Internet as long as they are in contact with the cell towers of their subscribing company.

One of the sources of our information on the overview of VPNs is James Yonan's talk at Linux Fest Northwest in 2004. You can read the entire presentation online at openvpn.net. Although over a decade old, his words still ring true today.

"Fundamentally, a VPN is a set of tools which allow networks at different locations to be securely connected, using a public network as the transport layer" [1]. This quote from Yonan's talk states the basic premise incredibly well. Getting two computers to work together over the Internet is a difficult feat, but making two different computer networks be securely connected together via the public Internet is pure genius. By connecting different locations over the Internet, many companies cut out the cost of dedicated circuits from the phone companies. Some companies have saved thousands of dollars by getting rid of their Integrated Services Digital Network (ISDN) lines, too. Once thought of as the high-speed (128,000 bits per second, or 128 kb) Holy Grail, it is now utilized mainly by antiquated videoconferencing systems that require a direct sustained connection, but the two endpoints aren't usually known much prior to the connection requirement. The ISDN lines are often referred to as glorified fast dial-up connections. Some companies utilize multiple ISDN connections to get higher-quality voice or video.

Not all VPNs had security in the early days. Packets of information were transmitted as clear text and could be easily seen. To keep the network systems secure, the information must be encrypted. Throughout the past 25 years, different encryption techniques have gained and lost favor. Some are too easy to break with the advanced speed of current computers; others require too much processing power at the router level, thus making their implementation expensive. This is one of those areas where an early technology seemed too expensive, but through time and technological advancements, the hardware processing power has caught up with requirements of the software. Encryption that seems secure in our current environments is often insecure as time passes. With supercomputers doing trillions of computations a second, we are required to make sure that the technology employed in our networks is up to the task. There are many different types of encryption, as discussed later in the chapter.

Early in the VPN life-cycle, the goal for organizations was to connect different places or offices to remote computer systems. This was usually done with a dedicated piece of hardware at each site. This "point-to-point" setup allowed for a secure transmission between two sites, allowing users access to computer resources, data, and communications systems. Many of these sites were too expensive to access, so the advent of the point-to-point systems allowed access where none existed. Now multinational companies set up VPNs to access their manufacturing plants all over the world.

Accounting, order entry, and personnel databases were the big driving forces for disparate locations to be connected. Our desire to have more and more information and faster and faster access to information has driven this trend. Now individuals at home are connecting their computers into the corporate network either through VPN connections or Secure Sockets Layer (SSL)-VPN web connections. This proliferation is pushing vendors to increase security, especially in unsecure or minimally secure environments. Giving remote access to some users, unfortunately, makes for a target to hackers and crackers.

1. HISTORY

Like many innovations in the network arena, the telephone companies first created VPNs. AT&T, with its familiar "Bell logo" (see Fig. 58.2), was one of the leading providers of Centrex systems. The goal was to take advantage of different telephone enhancements for conferencing and dialing extensions within a company to connect to employees. Many people are familiar with the Centrex systems that the phone companies offered for many years.

With Centrex the phone company did not require you to have a costly private branch exchange (PBX) switching computer system onsite. These PBXs were big, needed power, and cost a bundle of money. By eliminating the PBX and using the Centrex system, an organization could keep costs down yet have enhanced service and flexibility of the advanced phone services through the telephone company PBX.

FIGURE 58.2 AT&T logo; the company was often referred to as Ma Bell.

The primary business of the phone companies was to provide voice service, but they also wanted to provide data services. Lines from the phone company from one company location to another (called leased lines) offered remote data access from one part of a company to another.

Many companies started utilizing different types of software to better utilize their leased lines. In the early days, the main equipment was located centrally, and all the offices connected to the "hub" (see Fig. 58.3). This was a good system and many companies still prefer this network topography, but times are changing. The phone company usually charged for their circuits taking into consideration the distances between locations. With this in mind, instead of having a hub-and-spoke design, some companies opted to daisy-chain their organization together, thus trying to limit the distance they would have to pay for their leased lines. So a company would have a leased line from New York to Washington, DC, another from DC to Atlanta, and a third from Atlanta to Miami. This would cut costs over the typical hub-and-spoke system of having all the lines go through one central location (see Fig. 58.4).

With the proliferation of the Internet and additional costs for Internet connections and leased-line connections, the companies pushed the software vendors to make cheap connections via the Internet. VPNs solved their problems and had a great return on investment (ROI). Within a year,

the cost of the VPN equipment paid for itself through eliminating the leased lines. Though this technology has been around for years, some organizations still rely on leased lines due to a lack of high-speed Internet in remote areas.

In 1995, Internet Protocol Security (IPsec) was one of the first attempts at bringing encryption to the VPN arena. One of the early downfalls of this technology was its complexity and requirement for fast processors on the routers to keep up with the high bandwidths. In 1995, according to IETF.org, "at least one hardware implementation can encrypt or decrypt at about 1 Gbps" [2]. Yes, one installation that cost thousands of dollars.

Fortunately, Moore's Law has been at work, and today our processing speeds are high enough to get IPsec working on even small routers. Moore's Law is named after Intel cofounder Gordon Moore, who wrote in 1965: "the number of transistors on a chip will double about every 2 years" [3]. This doubling of chip capacity allows for more and more computing to be done.

Another issue with early IPsec is that it is fairly inflexible, with differing IP addresses. Many home and home office computers utilize dynamic IP addresses. You may get a different IP address each time you turn on your computer and connect to the Internet. The IPsec connection will have to be reestablished and may cause a hiccup in

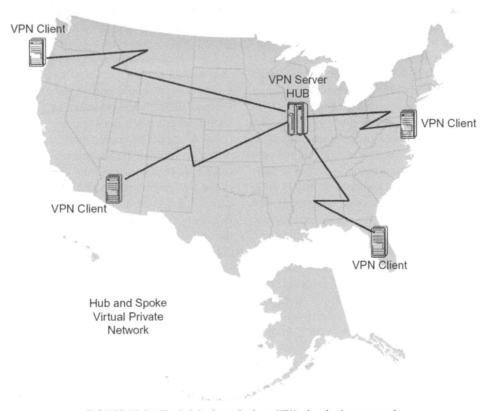

FIGURE 58.3 The hub in the early days. *VPN*, virtual private network.

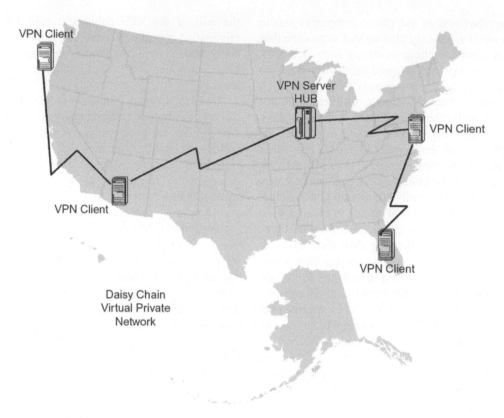

FIGURE 58.4   One central location for the hub-and-spoke system. *VPN*, virtual private network.

your transmissions or the requirement that a password be reentered. This seems unreasonable to most users.

Another difficulty is the use of Network Address Translation (NAT) for some networks. Each computer on the network has the same IP address as far as the greater VPN Client Internet is concerned. This is in part because of the shortage of legal IP addresses available in the IPv4 address space. As we move closer and closer to the IPv6 or higher address space model, some of these issues will be moot. Soon, every device we own, including our refrigerators, radios, and heating systems, will have a static IP address. Maybe even our kitchen sinks will. Big Brother is coming, but won't it be cool to see what your refrigerator is up to? Want that ice cold beer a bit cooler, get on your smartphone and tell the refrigerator you are on your way!

In the late 1990s, Linux began to take shape as a great test environment for networking. A technology called tun, short for tunnel, allows data to be siphoned through the data stream to create virtual hardware. From the operating system perspective it looks like point-to-point network hardware, even though it is virtual hardware. Another technology, called tap, looks like Ethernet traffic but also uses virtual hardware to fool the operating system into thinking it is real hardware.

These technologies utilize a program running in the user area of the operating system software in order to look like a file. They can read and write IP packets directly to and from this virtual hardware, even though the systems are connected via the public Internet and could be on the other side of the world. Security is an issue with the tun/tap method. One way to build in security is to utilize the Secure Shell protocol (SSH) and transport the data via a User Datagram Protocol (UDP) or Transmission Control Protocol (TCP) packet sent over the network.

It is important to remember that IP is an unreliable protocol. There are collisions on all IP networks; high traffic times give high collisions and lost packets, but the protocol is good at resending the packets so that eventually all the data will get to its destination. On the other hand, TCP is a reliable protocol. So, like military and intelligence, we have the added problem of a reliable transportation protocol (TCP) using an unreliable transportation (IP) method.

So, how does it work if it is unreliable? Well, eventually all the packets get there; TCP makes sure of that, and they are put in order and delivered to the other side. Some may have to be retransmitted, but most won't and the system should work relatively quickly.

One way that we can gain some throughput and added security is by utilizing encapsulation protocols. Encapsulation allows you to stuff one kind of protocol inside another type of protocol. The idea is to encapsulate a TCP packet inside a UDP packet. This forces the application to worry about dropped packets and reliability instead of the TCP network layer, since UDP packets are not a reliable packet protocol. This really increases speed, especially during peak network usage times. So, follow this logic: The IP packets are encrypted, then encapsulated and stored for transport via UDP over the Internet. On the receiving end the host system receives, decrypts, and authenticates the packets and then sends them to the tap or tun virtual adapter at the other end, thus giving a secure connection between the two sides, with the operating system not really knowing or caring about the encryption or transport methods. From the OS point of view, it is like a data file being transmitted; the OS doesn't have to know that the hardware is virtual. It is just as happy thinking that the virtual data file is real—and it processes it just like it processes a physical file locally stored on a hard drive.

OpenVPN is just one of many Open Source VPNs in use today. Use your favorite Internet search engine and you will see a great example of a VPN system that employs IPsec.

IPsec is another way to ensure security on your VPN connection. IPsec took the approach that it needed to replace the IP stack and do it securely. IPsec looks to do its work in the background, without utilizing operating system CPU cycles. This is wonderful for its nonimpact on servers, but it then relies heavily on the hardware.

A faster-growing encryption scheme involves SSL VPN; we will talk about it later in this chapter. This scheme gives the user access to resources like a VPN but through a web browser. The end user only needs to install the browser plug-ins to get this VPN up and working, for remote access on the fly. One example of this SSL type of VPN is LogMeIn Rescue [4]. It sets up a remote control session within the SSL layer of the browser. It can also extend resources out to the remote user without initiating a remote-control session.

Finally, the future for standardizing Transport Layer Security (TLS)-based, user-space VPNs is growing quickly. With the ability to prevent eavesdropping before the transmissions begin, future VPN sessions will be even more secure. The Internet Engineering Task Force (IETF) has a charter describing the work being done on the TLS standard (https://tools.ietf.org/wg/tls/charters). The current version is 1.2 and in 2015 work started on version 1.3. With all these schemes and more, we should take a look at who is in charge of helping to standardize the hardware and software requirements of the VPN world.

2. WHO IS IN CHARGE?

For all this interconnectivity to actually work, there are several organizations that publish standards and work for cooperation among vendors in the sea of computer networking change. In addition to these public groups, there are also private companies that are working toward new protocols to improve speed and efficiency in the VPN arena.

FIGURE 58.5 Logo for the Internet Engineering Task Force (IETF).

The two biggest public groups are the Internet Engineering Task Force (www.ietf.org; see Fig. 58.5) and the Institute of Electrical and Electronic Engineers (www. IEEE.org; see Fig. 58.6). Each group has its own way of doing business and publishes its recommendations and standards.

As the IEEE website proclaims, the group's "core purpose is to foster technological innovation and excellence for the benefit of humanity." This is a wonderful and noble purpose. Sometimes they get it right and sometimes input and interference from vendors get in the way of moving technology forward—or worse yet, vendors go out and put up systems that come out before the specifications get published, leaving humanity with different standards. This has happened several times on the wireless networking standards group. Companies release their implementation of a standard prior to final agreement by the standards boards.

The group's vision is stated thus: "IEEE will be essential to the global technical community and to technical professionals everywhere, and be universally recognized for the contributions of technology and of technical professionals in improving global conditions" [5].

The Internet Engineering Task Force (IETF) is a large, open international community of network designers, operators, vendors, and researchers concerned with the evolution of the Internet architecture and the smooth operation of the Internet. It is open to any interested individual. The IETF Mission Statement is documented in RFC 3935. According to the group's mission statement, "The goal of the IETF is to make the Internet work better" [6].

Finally, we can't get away from acronyms unless we include the United States Government. An Organization called the American National Standards Institute (ANSI; www.ansi.org) an over 90-year-old organization with responsibilities that include writing voluntary standards for

FIGURE 58.6 Logo for the Institute of Electrical and Electronics Engineers (IEEE).

FIGURE 58.7 The American National Standards Institute (ANSI) logo.

the marketplace to have somewhere to turn for standardizing efforts to improve efficiencies and interoperability (see Fig. 58.7).

There are many standards for many physical things, such as the size of a light bulb socket or the size of an outlet on your wall. These groups help set standards for networking. Two international groups that are represented by ANSI are the International Organization for Standardization (ISO) and International Electrotechnical Commission (IEC).

These organizations have ongoing workgroups and projects that are tackling the various standards that will be in use in the future releases of the VPN standard. They also have the standards written for current interoperability. However, this does not require a vendor to follow the standards. Each vendor can and will implement parts and pieces of standards, but unless they meet all the requirements of a specification, they will not get to call their system compatible.

There are several Institute of Electrical and Electronics Engineers (IEEE) projects relating to networking and the advancement of interconnectivity. If you are interested in networking, the 802 family of workgroups is your best bet. Check out www.ieee802.org.

3. VIRTUAL PRIVATE NETWORK TYPES

There are many different types of VPN's that rely on different transport protocols and different encryption standards. As our world changes and we have more and more cloud-based services we will see VPN's used on devices from tablets to cell phones. When choosing a VPN, you should consider security, speed, and reliability. What type of data will be coming over your VPN? Are you using audio only? Or are you sending video too? Do you have large data files or are you doing remote printing? Knowing the type of data you will be transporting is critical in picking the correct VPN type.

Internet Protocol Security

As we talked about earlier, this encryption standard for VPN access is heavy on the hardware for processing the encryption and decrypting the packets. This protocol

operates at the Layer 3 level of the Open Systems Interconnection (OSI) model. The OSI model dates to 1982 by ISO [7]. IPsec is still used by many vendors for their VPN hardware.

One of the weaknesses of VPNs we mentioned earlier is also a strength. Because the majority of the processing work is done by the interconnecting hardware, the application doesn't have to worry about knowing anything about IPsec at all.

There are two modes for IPsec. First, the transport mode secures the information all the way to each device trying to make the connection. The second mode is the transport mode, which is used for network-to-network communications. The latest standard for IPsec came out in 2005. One of the downsides to IPsec is its complexity at the kernel level. With one buffer overflow, you can wreak havoc on the transmitted data.

Layer 2 Tunneling Protocol

Layer Tunneling Protocol was released in 1999; then to improve the reliability and security of Point-to-Point Tunneling Protocol (PPTP), Layer 2 Tunneling Protocol (L2TP) was created. It really is a layer 5 protocol because it uses the session layer in the OSI model.

This was more cumbersome than PPTP and forced the users at each end to have authentication with one another. It also has weak security; thus, most implementations of the L2TP protocol utilize IPsec to enhance security.

There is a 32-bit header for each packet that includes flags, versions, Tunnel ID, and Session IDs. There is also a space for the packet size.

Because this is a very weak protocol, some vendors combined it with IPsec to form L2TP/IPsec. In this implementation you take the strong, secure nature of IPsec as the secure channel, and the L2TP will act as the tunnel.

This protocol is a server/user setup. One part of the software acts as the server and waits for the user side of the software to make contact. Because this protocol can handle many users or clients at a time, some Asymmetric Digital Subscriber Line (ADSL) providers use this L2TP protocol and share the resources at the telephone central office. Their modem/routers utilize L2TP to phone home to the central office and share a higher capacity line out to the Internet.

For more information, see the IETF.org publication RFC 2661. You can delve deeper into the failover mode of L2TP or get far more detail on the standard.

L2TPv3 or Higher

This is the draft advancement of the L2TP for large carrier-level information transmissions. In 2005, the draft protocol was released; it provides additional security features, improved encapsulation, and the ability to carry data links

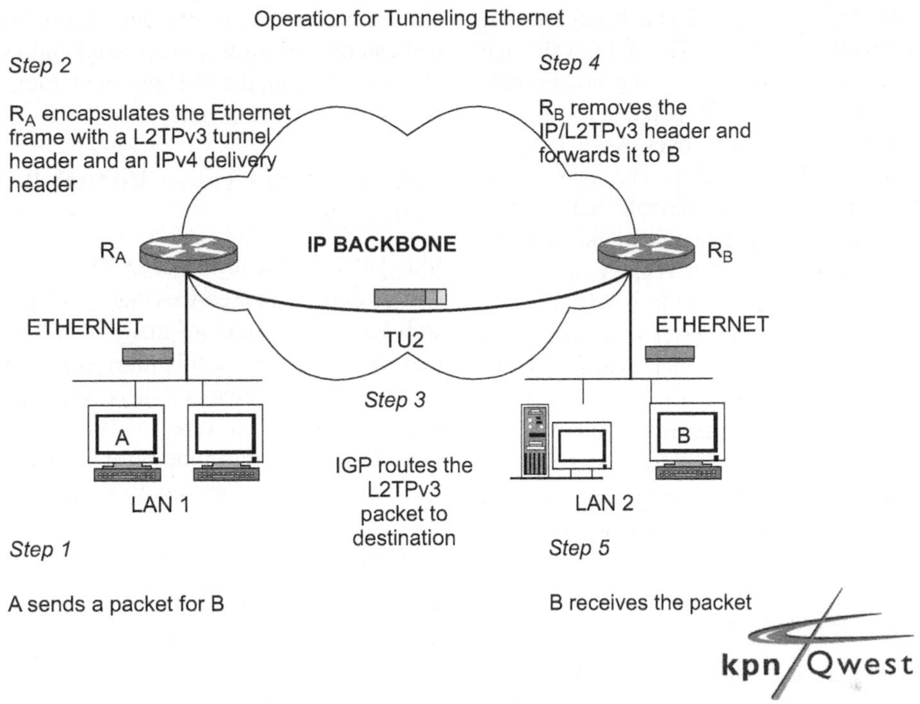

Operation for Tunneling Ethernet

Step 2

R_A encapsulates the Ethernet frame with a L2TPv3 tunnel header and an IPv4 delivery header

Step 4

R_B removes the IP/L2TPv3 header and forwards it to B

R_A **IP BACKBONE** R_B

ETHERNET ETHERNET

TU2

Step 3

IGP routes the L2TPv3 packet to destination

LAN 1 LAN 2

Step 1

A sends a packet for B

Step 5

B receives the packet

kpn Qwest

FIGURE 58.8 The operation for tunneling Ethernet using the L2TPv3 protocol. *LAN*, local area network.

other than simply PPP over an IP network (Frame Relay, Ethernet, ATM). Fig. 58.8 shows the operation for tunneling Ethernet using the L2TPv3 or higher protocol and was taken from Psuedo-Wire Services and L2TPv3 or higher from KPN/Quest [7].

Layer 2 Forwarding

Cisco's Layer 2 Forwarding protocol is used for tunneling the link layer (layer 2 in the OSI model). This protocol allows for virtual dial-up that allows for the sharing of modems, ISDN routers, servers, and other hardware.

This protocol was popular in the mid-to-late 1990s and was utilized by Shiva's products to share a bank of modems to a network of personal computers. This was a fantastic cost savings for network administrators wanting to share a small number of modems and modem lines to a large user group. Instead of having 50 modems hooked up to individual PCs, you could have a bank of eight modems that could be used during the day to dial out and connect to external resources, becoming available at night for workers to dial back into the computer system for remote access to corporate data resources.

For those long-distance calls to remote computer systems, an employee could dial into the office network. For security and billing reasons, the office computer system would dial back to the home user. The home user would access a second modem line to dial out to a long distance computer system. This would eliminate all charges for the

home user except for the initial call to get connected. RFC 2341 on IETF.org gives you the detailed standard [8].

Point-to-Point Tunneling Protocol Virtual Private Network

PPTP was created in the 1990s by Microsoft, Ascend, 3COM, and a few other vendors, in order to try and serve the user community. This VPN protocol allowed for easy implementation with Windows machines because it was included in Windows. It made for fairly secure transmissions, though not as secure as IPsec. Although Microsoft has a great deal of influence in the computing arena, the IPsec and L2TP protocols are the standards-based protocols that most vendors use for VPNs.

Under PPTP, Microsoft has implemented Microsoft Point-to-Point Encryption (MPPE) Protocol, which allows encryption keys of 40−128 bits. The latest updates were done in 2003 to strengthen the security of this protocol. A great excerpt from Microsoft TechNet for Windows NT 4.0 or higher Server explains the process of PPTP extremely well; check out http://technet.microsoft.com/en-us/library/cc768084.aspx for more information.

Multiprotocol Label Switching

Multiprotocol Label Switching (MPLS) is another system for large telephone companies or huge enterprises to get great response times for VPN with huge amounts of data.

This protocol operates between layer 2 and layer 3 of the OSI model we have mentioned before. The IETF web page with the specifications for the label switching architecture can be found at www.ietf.org/rfc/rfc3031.txt.

This protocol has big advantages over Asynchronous Transfer Mode (ATM) and Frame Relay. The overhead is lower and with the ability to have variable length data packets, audio and video will be transmitted much more efficiently. Another big advantage over ATM is the ATM requirement that the two endpoints have to handshake and make a connection before any data is ever transmitted.

The name MPLS came from the underlying way in which the endpoints find each other. The switches using this technology find their destination through the lookup of a label instead of the lookup of an IP address. Label Edge Routers are the beginning and ending points of an MPLS network. The big competitor for future network expansion is L2TPv3 or higher.

Multipath Virtual Private Network

Ragula Systems Development Company created Multipath Virtual Private Network (MPVPN) to enhance the quality of service of VPNs. The basic concept is to allow multiple connections to the Internet at both endpoints and use the combination of connections to create a faster connection. So if you have a T1 line and a DS3 at your office, you can aggregate both lines through the MPVPN device to increase your response times. The data traffic will be load balanced and will increase your throughput.

Secure Shell Protocol

This protocol lets network traffic run over a secured channel between devices. SSH uses public-key cryptography. Tatu Ylönen from Finland created the first version of SSH in 1995 to thwart password thieves at his university network. The company he created is called SSH Communications Security and can be reached at www.ssh.com (see Fig. 58.9).

Utilizing public-key cryptography is a double-edged sword. If an inside user authenticates an attacker's public key, you have just let them into the system, where they can deploy man-in-the-middle hacks. Also, the intent for this security system was to keep out the bad guys at the gate.

FIGURE 58.9 Secure Shell (SSH) communications security logo.

Once a person is authenticated, she is in and a regular user and can deploy software that would allow a remote VPN to be set up through the SSH protocol. Future versions of SSH may prevent these abuses.

Secure Socket Layer Virtual Private Network

SSL VPN isn't really VPN at all. It's more of an interface that gives users the services that look like VPN through their web browsers. There are many remote-control applications that take advantage of this layer in the web browser to gain access to users' resources. It is sometimes referred to as a Hybrid VPN. This type of VPN is usually the most expensive to implement because it allows for many different types of clients and servers to be connected together.

Transport Layer Security

TLS, the successor to SSL, is used to prevent eavesdropping on information being sent between computers. When using strong encryption algorithms, the security of your transmission is almost guaranteed.

Both SSL and TLS work very much the same way. First, the sessions at each endpoint contact each other for information about what encryption method is going to be employed. Second, the keys are exchanged. These could be (Ron Rivest, Adi Shamir, and Leonard Adleman) RSA, elliptic curve Diffie—Hellman (ECDH), security rollup package (SRP), or pre-shared key.

Finally, the messages are encrypted and authenticated, sometimes using Certificate of Authorities Public Key list. When you utilize SSL and TLS you may run into a situation where the server certificate does not match the information held in the Certificate of Authorities Public Key list. If this is the case, the user may override the error message or may choose not to trust the site and end the connection.

The whole public key/private key encryption is able to take place behind the scenes for a few reasons. During the beginning phase of the connection, the server, and requesting computer generate a random number. Random numbers are combined and encrypted using the private keys. Only the owner of the public key can unencrypt the random number that is sent using their private key.

TLS is growing every year. One of the limiting factors is the size of the hash value in the final message is truncated to 96 bits. So even though it could be using a 256 bit hash, the transmission cuts it to 96 bits. In the future we may see something that addresses this.

Datagram Transport Layer Security

Datagram Transport Layer Security is an implementation of TLS that allows for tunneling over UDP. It is used in OpenConnect VPN and Cisco's now unsupported

AnyConnect VPN. OpenConnect was created in order to interface with Cisco's AnyConnect VPN's. Cisco has dropped its offering so the OpenConnect community developed an application that integrates into several routers; with a firmware upgrade the device can now route network traffic using the VPN protocol.

4. AUTHENTICATION METHODS

Currently, usernames and passwords are the most common authentication method employed in the VPN arena. We may transport the data through an SSL channel or via a secured and encrypted transport model, but when it comes to gaining access to the system resources, most often you will have to log into the VPN with a username and password.

As we talked about earlier, there are some edge-based systems that require a dongle, and a random number is generated on gaining access to the login screen. These tiered layers of security can be a great wall that will thwart a hacker's attempt to gain access to your network system in favor of going after easier networks. Not all authentication methods are the same. We will talk about a few different types of protection schemes and point out weaknesses and strengths. With each type of encryption we are concerned with its veracity along with concerns over the verification and authentication of the data being sent. Transmission speeds and overhead in encrypting and decrypting data are another consideration, but as mentioned earlier, Moore's Law has helped a great deal.

Hashing

Using a computer algorithm to mix up the characters in your encryption is fairly common. If you have a secret and want another person to know the answer, but you are fearful that it will be discovered, you can mix up the letters.

Hash Message Authentication Code

Keyed Hash Message Authentication Code (HMAC) is a type of encryption that uses an algorithm in conjunction with a key. The algorithm is only as strong as the complexity of the key and the size of the output. For HMAC either 128 or 160 bits are used.

This type of Message Authentication Code (MAC) can be defeated. One way is by using the birthday attack. To ensure that your data is not deciphered, choose a strong key; use upper- and lowercase letters, numbers, and special characters. Also use 160 bits when possible.

Message Digest 5

Message Digest 5 is one of the best file integrity checks available today. It is also used in some encryption schemes, though the veracity of its encryption strength is being challenged.

The method uses a 128-bit hash value. It is represented as a 32-digit hexadecimal number. A file can be "hashed" down to a single 32-digit hex number. The likelihood of two files with the same hash is 2128 but with the use of rainbow tables and collision theory, there have been a few successes in cracking this encryption. As Tim Callan points out in his January 5, 2009 blog post, "Considering that it took the original researchers four tries over at least a month to successfully accomplish their attack against the RapidSSL brand, we're fully confident that no malicious organization had the opportunity to use this information against RapidSSL, or any other certificate authority authorized by VeriSign."

Secure Hash Algorithm

Secure Hash Algorithm was designed by the US National Security Agency (NSA). There is also SHA-224, SHA-256, SHA-384, and SHA-512. The number of bits in SHA-1 is 160. The others have the number of bits following the SHA.

SHA-1 is purported to have been compromised, but the veracity of the reports has been challenged. In any case, the NSA has created the SHA-224 to SHA-512 specification to make it even more difficult to crack. At the Rump Session of CRYPTO 2006, Christian Rechberger and Christophe De Cannière claimed to have discovered a collision attack on SHA-1 that would allow an attacker to select at least parts of the message.

The basic premise is the same as the MD5 hash: The data is encrypted utilizing a message digest. This method is the basis for several common applications including SSL, PGP, SSH, S/MIME, and IPsec.

NIST announced Keccak as the winner of the SHA-3 Cryptographic Hash Algorithm Competition on October 2, 2012 Check the NIST website at http://csrc.nist.gov/groups/ST/hash/sha-3/index.html for details about the five-year competition. SHA-3 is described by some as a sponge. Data gets absorbed into the sponge on the sending end and then ringed out on the other end. For those who are interested in encryption you can check the NIST site for more information.

5. SYMMETRIC ENCRYPTION

Symmetric encryption requires that both the sender and receiver have the same key and each computes a common key that is subsequently used. Two of the most common symmetric encryption standards are known as Data Encryption Standard (DES) and Advanced Encryption Standard (AES). Once AES was released, DES was withdrawn as a standard and replaced with 3-DES, often referred to as Triple DES and TDES.

3-DES takes DES and repeats it two more times. So it is hashed with the 56-bit algorithm and password, and then done twice more. This prevents more brute-force attacks, assuming a strong key is used. Some VPN software is based on these symmetric keys, as we have discussed before.

Finally, a system of shared secrets allows encryption and decryption of data. This can either be done as a pre-shared password, which is known by both ends prior to communication, or some kind of key agreement protocol where the key is calculated from each end using a common identifier or public key.

6. ASYMMETRIC CRYPTOGRAPHY

The biggest example of asymmetric cryptography for VPNs is in the RSA protocol. Three professors at MIT, Ron Rivest, Adi Shamir, and Leonard Adelman (thus RSA), came up with the RSA encryption algorithm, which is an implementation of public/private key cryptography. Anyone who wants to spend a bit of time can review the math behind the encryption at www.muppetlabs.com/ ~breadbox/txt/rsa.html. The RSA protocol is one of the coolest and most secure means of transmitting data. Not only is it used for transmission of data, but a person can also digitally sign a document with the use of RSA secure systems.

Although these systems have been around for a while, they are becoming more and more prevalent. For example, some states will allow accountants who sign up with them to transmit income tax forms electronically as long as they digitally sign the returns. The federal government also allow electronic signatures and passed the E-SIGN Act, Public Law No. 106−229 in June of 2000.

The RSA algorithm uses two large random prime numbers. Prime number searching has been a pastime for many mathematical scientists. As the prime number gets larger and larger, its use for privacy and security systems is increased. Thus, many search for larger prime numbers. Through the use of these numbers and a key, the data is secured from prying eyes.

When you are in a public system and don't have the luxury of knowing the keys in advance, there are ways to create a key that will work. This system is very interesting and is known as the exponential key exchange because it uses exponential numbers in the initial key exchange to come to an agreed-on cipher.

7. EDGE DEVICES

As with any system, having two locked doors is better than one. With the advent of many remote computing systems, a new type of external security has come into favor. For instance, the setting up an edge device, allows for a unique username and password, or better yet, a unique username and a random password that only the user and the computer system knows.

These edge systems often employ authentication schemes in conjunction with a key fob that displays a different random number every 30−60 s. The server knows what the random number should be based on the time and only authenticates the person into the edge of the network if the username and password match. Once into the edge network, the user is prompted for a more traditional username and password to gain access to data, email, or applications under his username.

Another popular implantation of a two-step encryption system is Google Authenticator. Based upon IETF RFC6238, the application utilizes HMAC-SHA-1 (HOTP algorithm) along with a time difference (TOTP algorithm) and HMAC-SHA-256 or HMAC-SHA-512 in order to get a six-digit number as a secondary key to gain access in the two-step passwords. The Time difference is unique and only known by the originating application and thus ensuring a random number. We all know that the SHA-256 is 64 digits long and SHA-512 is 128 digits long. The algorithm only takes six digits in order to make it reasonable for a person to enter. After logging into the Edge device, a picture of a three-dimensional QR code (see Fig. 58.10) is displayed on the screen, using the Google Authenticator application, you scan the code and get your six-digit number for your one-time use password. You can download the application to your phone or computer in order to set up a system for a secondary single-use password for online applications that utilize a secondary one-use password. Examples of sites utilizing Authenticator include Salesforce.com, Microsoft.com, Barracuda SSL VPN, and Amazon Web Services.

8. PASSWORDS

Your system and data are often only as good as the strength of your password. The weakest of passwords entails a single word or name. An attacker using common dictionary attacks will often break a weak password. For example, using the word password is usually broken very quickly.

Using multiple words or mixing spelling and upper and lowercase will make your weak password a bit stronger. PasswOrd would be better. Adding numbers increases your passwords veracity. P2ssw9rd decreases your chance of

FIGURE 58.10   Example of a QR code.

getting hacked. Add in a few special characters and your password gets even more secure, as with P2#$w9rd.

But to get even stronger you need to use a password over 12 characters made up of upper and lowercase letters, numbers, and special characters: P2#$w9rd.34HHlz. Stay away from acronyms. There are even some systems that don't allow any word from the English language to be used in any part of the password.

Another way to keep your VPNs secure is to only allow access from fixed IP addresses. If the IP address isn't on the allowable list, you don't allow the computer in, no matter what. There is a unique Media Access Control (MAC) address for each network card. This is another fixed ID that can be used to allow or disallow computers onto your VPN. The problem with this method is that both IP and MACs can be spoofed. So, if a person gets his hands on a valid MAC ID, he can get around this bit of security.

Some VPN systems will allow you to log in with a username and password, and then it will connect to a pre-defined IP address. So even if your passwords are stolen, unless the person knows the predefined IP address of the callback, they can't get into your system. This idea is a throwback to the dial-in networks that would allow a person to dial in, connect with their username and password, and then promptly disconnect and call the person's computer system back. It was an extra 2 min on the front end, but a great added level of security.

Finally, biometrics are beginning to play a role in authentication systems. For example, instead of a password, your fingerprint is used. Some systems use voiceprint, hand geometry, retinal eye scan, or facial geometry. We can foresee the day when a DNA reader uses your DNA as your password. Like a bloodhound who is able to follow you by the scent of the dead skin falling off your body (www. mythbusters.com), a sniffer device may be employed to analyze the DNA falling off your body. Homeland Security already has a commercial Rapid DNA product that can test DNA samples in 90 min.

9. HACKERS AND CRACKERS

One of the inherent problems with remote access is security; Duane Dunston asked James Lonan from www. LinuxSecurity.com, "One of my major gripes with IPSec is that it adds a lot of complexity to the kernel. Complexity is really the enemy of security. The problem with putting complex security software in the kernel is that you ignore an important security principle: never design secure systems so that the failure of one component results in a catastrophic security breach. A single buffer overflow exploit in kernel space results in total system compromise — why not move the complexity into user space where the code might run in an empty chroot jail as user 'nobody?' At least with this approach, a code insertion exploit can

be more readily contained" (http://www.linuxsecurity.com/content/view/117363/49/).

Some good ways to prevent hackers and crackers from getting into your system is to enable the best security levels that your hardware has to offer. If you can utilize 512 or 256-bit encryption methods, then use them. If you can afford a random-number generated edge security system, then use it.

Have your users change their VPN passwords frequently, especially if they are utilizing public Internet portals. Don't expect your local library to have the security that your own internal company has. If you access your VPN from an insecure public Internet hotspot, then make sure you change your VPN password. Don't give out your VPN password for other people to use. This can cause you great difficulties if something sinister happens to the network and the connection is traced back to your username and password.

Another way to secure your network is to deactivate accounts that have not been used for 30 days. Yes, this can be a pain, but if a person is not regularly accessing the system, then maybe they don't need access in the first place.

Finally, remove stale VPN accounts from the system. One of the biggest problems with unauthorized VPN access is the employee who has retired but her account never got disabled. Maybe her logon and email were removed, but IT didn't remove her VPN account. Put in checks and balances on accounts.

10. MOBILE VIRTUAL PRIVATE NETWORK

We have become a mobile computing society. We have smartphones, iPads, Android Tablets, netbooks, laptops, and cars, just to name a few of the things we carry that can connect to the Internet. With this connectivity comes challenges to the VPN world. Having a policeman or fireman connected back to the station's computers while on the road can cause subnets to change, cell towers to change, phone carrier's to change not only the speed, but also the protocol for data service. Imagine having to deal with this, all while keeping a secure data connection to the office. Some vehicles are even equipped with radios that can transmit data through their own private network. Or the health professional who does well-care or sick care visit's throughout the community and needs to enter information about their visit as they go. How does the VPN keep the connection, let alone keep it secure?

Host Identity Protocol (HIP) is the technology now being employed to keep us connected on our mobile devices. At this point the IETF has a standard (https://tools.ietf.org/html/rfc7401). Each vendor uses this technology a little bit differently. But the market has pushed them to do so.

The basic premise is to have the tunnel bound to an IP address that is static on the phone, that static IP is used even though the tunnels change and go through different subnets and even different carriers. The VPN software does all the security and handshaking when the changes occur, thus leaving the user free to think they have a steady connection no matter where they are traveling.

Think of some of the security risks as well as the speed problems. This harkens back to the days where an application had to be written with transmission speeds in mind—think more text, less graphics. Think reusable graphics on different form pages, so the browser doesn't have to download them each time a page is changed. Now we have people flying at 400-plus miles an hour "online".

Finally, let's briefly look at VPN deployments. Organizations planning VPN deployments should identify and define requirements, and evaluate several products to determine their fit into the organization.

11. VIRTUAL PRIVATE NETWORK DEPLOYMENTS

VPN products vary in functionality, including protocol and application support. They also vary in breadth, depth, and completeness of features and security services. Some recommendations and considerations are included the following checklist: "An Agenda For Action For VPN Deployments."

12. SUMMARY

This chapter assisted organizations in understanding VPN technologies and in designing, implementing, configuring, securing, monitoring, and maintaining SSL VPN solutions. The chapter also provided a phased approach to VPN planning and implementation that can help in achieving successful SSL VPN deployments. It also provided a comparison with other similar technologies such as IPsec VPNs and other VPN solutions.

Finally, let's move on to the real interactive part of this chapter: review questions/exercises, hands-on projects, case projects, and optional team case project. The answers and/ or solutions by chapter can be found in the Online Instructor's Solutions Manual.

CHAPTER REVIEW QUESTIONS/ EXERCISES

True/False

1. True or False? All VPNs had security in the early days.
2. True or False? ATT, with its familiar "Bell logo," was one of the leading providers of Centrex systems.
3. True or False? In the early days, the main equipment was located locally, and all the offices connected to the "hub."

An Agenda for Action for Virtual Private Network Deployments

Some of the cryptographic requirements, including allowable hash functions and certificate key lengths, have changed. Therefore, organizations who want to provide VPN services must ensure that their systems are upgradeable to the cipher suites and key lengths, and that their SSL VPN vendors guarantee that such upgrades will be available early enough for testing and deployment in the field. Thus, the following set of VPN deployments activities must be adhered to (check all tasks completed):

_____1. VPN manageability features such as status reporting, logging, and auditing should provide adequate capabilities for the organization to effectively operate and manage the SSL VPN and to extract detailed usage information.

_____2. The SSL VPN high availability and scalability features should support the organization's requirements for failover, load balancing, and throughput.

_____3. State and information sharing is recommended to keep the failover process transparent to the user.

_____4. VPN portal customization should allow the organization to control the look and feel of the portal and to customize the portal to support various devices such as personal digital assistants (PDA) and smartphones.

_____5. SSL VPN authentication should provide the necessary support for the organization's current and future authentication methods and leverage existing authentication databases.

_____6. VPN authentication should also be tested to ensure interoperability with existing authentication methods.

_____7. The strongest possible cryptographic algorithms and key lengths that are considered secure for current practice should be used for encryption and integrity protection unless they are incompatible with interoperability, performance, and export constraints.

_____8. SSL VPNs should be evaluated to ensure they provide the level of granularity needed for access controls.

_____9. Access controls should be capable of applying permissions to users, groups, and resources, as well as integrating with endpoint security controls.

_____10. Implementation of endpoint security controls is often the most diverse service among VPN products.

_____11. Endpoint security should be evaluated to ensure it provides the necessary host integrity checking and security protection mechanisms required for the organization.

_____12. Not all SSL VPNs have integrated intrusion prevention capabilities. Those that do should be evaluated to ensure they do not introduce an unacceptable amount of latency into the network traffic.

4. True or False? The encryption standard for VPN access is heavy on the software for processing the encryption and decrypting the packets.
5. True or False? Secure Socket Layer (SSL) VPN is really VPN.

Multiple Choice

1. What is another system for large telephone companies or huge enterprises to get great response times for VPNs with huge amounts of data?
   A. PPTP VPN
   B. L2F
   C. MPLS
   D. L2TPv3
   E. L2TP
2. What allows multiple connections to the Internet at both endpoints and use the combination of connections to create a faster connection?
   A. MPLS
   B. SSH
   C. MPVPN
   D. SSL-VPN
   E. TLS
3. What is used to prevent eavesdropping on information being sent between computers?
   A. SSL
   B. TLS
   C. RSA
   D. ECDH
   E. SRP
4. What are two of the most common authentication methods employed in the VPN arena?
   A. Usernames
   B. Encryption
   C. Random numbers
   D. Decryption
   E. Passwords
5. What is a type of encryption that uses an algorithm in conjunction with a key?
   A. MAC
   B. HMAC
   C. MD5
   D. SHA-1
   E. DES

EXERCISE

Problem

The problem described in this exercise is how do you connect remote users to a single main office. A medium-sized organization has a large population of users that work from remote locations once to several days each week. The organization is research-oriented, and many of these users require access to a broad range of internal IT resources to conduct their research. These resources include email, calendar, file sharing services, and secure shell access on a variety of hosts. The organization already offers remote access services in the form of a host-to-gateway IPsec solution. This works successfully, but has required significant IT labor resources to install and support the client software on user hosts. The current solution also does not provide remote access for hosts based in public locations such as hotels and kiosks. So, how does the organization implement a complementary remote access architecture?

Hands-On Projects

Project

A health care company formed from the merger of two large health care companies started to experience a succession of network stability issues. This was a big concern for the company. Strong network availability is a crucial business requirement for the company, as it predominantly operates in a moderate client environment. If users cannot connect to the central server, they cannot access either the applications or the data that are essential for them to do their jobs. After a competitive evaluation of multiple telecommunications services, what did the company decide to do with regards to replacing its existing point-to-point connections with an Virtual Private Network (VPN)?

Case Projects

Problem

This case study illustrates how a leading building construction company needed a highly scalable and flexible telecommunications solution. So, how would the company go about meeting all of its telecommunications requirements and ensure business continuity in order to back up its vital systems in the event of an unforeseen disaster?

Optional Team Case Project

Problem

An engineering company developed a site-to-site virtual private network (VPN). How was the company's VPN solution able to cut networking costs dramatically by integrating security applications with other platform components to create a tightly integrated, multilayer security perimeter?

REFERENCES

[1] J. Yonan, The User-space VPN and OpenVPN, Copyright 2003 James Yonan. All Rights Reserved. 5980 Stoneridge Drive, Suite 103, Pleasanton, CA 94588 United States, 2003.

[2] P. Metzger, P. Karn, W.A. Simpson, The ESP DES-cbc Transform, Network Working Group, March 1995. RFC 1829.

[3] IEEE Mission and Vision 2001 L Street, NW. Suite 700 Washington, DC 20036-4910 USA www.ieee.org/web/aboutus/visionmission.html Copyright 2012 IEEE.

[4] H. Alvestrand, A Mission Statement for the IETF, Network Working Group, October 2004. RFC3935.

[5] A. Valencia, M. Littlewood, T. Kolar, Cisco Layer Two Forwarding (Protocol) "L2F", Network Working Group, May 1998. RFC2341.

[6] E. Rosen, A. Viswanathan, R. Callon, Multiprotocol Label Switching Architecture, Network Working Group, January 2001. RFC 3031.

[7] T. Callan, MD5 Hack Interesting, but Not Threatening, Security Focus, January 5, 2009.

[8] D. Dunston, In This Article, Duane Dunston Gives a Brief Introduction to OpenVPN and Interviews its Founder James Yonan, Linux Security, October 2006. www.linuxsecurity.com/content/view/117363/49.

RESOURCES

[1] www.openvpn.net/papers/BLUG-talk/2.html. Copyright James Yonan 2003.

[2] http://tools.ietf.org/html/draft-ietf-ipsec-esp-des-cbc-03. (The ESP DES-CBC Transform).

[3] www.intel.com/technology/mooreslaw/Gordon. Moore 1965.

[4] www.logmein.com.

[5] www.ieee.org/web/aboutus/visionmission.html. Copyright IEEE 2008.

[6] www.ietf.org/rfc/rfc3935.txt. Copyright the internet society 2004.

[7] http://en.wikipedia.org/wiki/Open_Systems_Interconnection.

[8] www.ripe.net/ripe/meetings/ripe-42/presentations/ripe42-eofpseudowires2/index.htmlKPN/QuestPseudo-wire. Services and L2TPv3 presentation 5/14/2002.

[9] www.ietf.org/rfc/rfc2341.txt.

[10] http://en.wikipedia.org/wiki/MD5#Vulnerability.

[11] http://en.wikipedia.org/wiki/SHA-1#Cryptanalysis_and_validation.

Chapter 59

Identity Theft

Markus Jakobsson[1] and Alex Tsow[2,a]
[1]*Indiana University, Bloomington, IN, United States;* [2]*The MITRE Corporation, Mclean, VA, Unites States*

Note: This chapter is available in its entirety online at store.elsevier.com/product.jsp?isbn= 9780128038437 (click the Resources tab at the bottom of the page).

1. ABSTRACT

This chapter focuses on identity manipulation tactics in email and Web pages. It describes the effects of features ranging from URL plausibility to trust endorsement graphics on a population of 398 subjects. The experiment presents these trust indicators in a variety of stimuli, since reactions vary according to context. In addition to testing specific features, the test gauges the potential of a tactic that spoofs third-party contractors rather than a brand itself. The results show that indeed graphic design can change authenticity evaluations and that its impact varies with context. We expected that authenticity-inspiring design changes would have the opposite effect when paired with an unreasonable request, but our data suggest that narrative strength, rather than underlying legitimacy, limits the impact of graphic design on trust and that these authenticity-inspiring design features improve trust in both legitimate and illegitimate media. Thus, it is not what is said that matters but how it is said: An eloquently stated unreasonable request is more convincing than a poorly phrased but quite reasonable request.

2. CONTENTS

---

[a] The author's affiliation with The MITRE Corporation is provided for identification purposes only, and is not intended to convey or imply MITRE's concurrence with, or support for, the positions, opinions or viewpoints expressed by the author.

Computer and Information Security Handbook. http://dx.doi.org/10.1016/B978-0-12-803843-7.00059-4

Chapter 60

VoIP Security

Harsh Kupwade Patil[1], Dan Wing[2] and Thomas M. Chen[3]

[1]*Southern Methodist University, Dallas, TX, United States;* [2]*Cisco Systems, San Jose, CA, United States;*
[3]*Swansea University, Wales, United Kingdom*

1. INTRODUCTION

H.323 and *Session Initiation Protocol* (SIP) are the two standardized protocols for the realization of Voice over Internet Protocol (VoIP).[1,2] The multimedia conference protocol H.323 of the International Telecommunication Union (ITU) consists of multiple separate protocols such as the H.245 for control signaling and H.225 for call signaling. H.323 is difficult to implement because of its complexity and the bulkiness that it introduces into the client application.[3] In contrast, SIP is simpler than H.323 and also leaner on the client-side application. SIP uses the human-readable protocol (ASCII) instead of H.323's binary signal coding.

Voice Over Internet Protocol Basics

SIP is the *Internet Engineering Task Force* (IETF) standard for multimedia communications in an IP network. It is an application layer control protocol used for creating, modifying, and terminating sessions between one or more SIP *user agents* (UAs). It was primarily designed to support user location discovery, user availability, user capabilities, and session setup and management.

In SIP, the end devices are called UAs, and they send SIP requests and SIP responses to establish media sessions, send and receive media, and send other SIP messages (to send short text messages to each other or subscribe to an event notification service). A UA can be a SIP phone or SIP client software running on a personal computer (PC) or personal digital assistant (PDA).

Typically, a collection of SIP UAs belongs to an administrative domain, which forms an SIP network. Each administrative domain has a SIP proxy, which is the point of contact for UAs within the domain and for UAs or SIP proxies outside the domain. All SIP signaling messages within a domain are routed through the domain's own SIP proxy. SIP routing is performed using *Uniform Resource Identifiers* (URIs) for addressing UAs. Two types of SIP URIs are supported: the SIP URI and the TEL URI. A SIP URI begins with the keyword *sip* or *sips*, where *sips* indicates that the SIP signaling must be sent over a secure channel, such as TLS.[4] The SIP URI is similar to an email address and contains a user's identifier and the domain at which the user can be found. For example, it could contain a username such as *sip:alice@example.com*, a global E.164 telephone number[5] such as *sip:11-972-310-9882@example.com;user=phone*, or an extension such as *sip:1234@example.com*. The TEL URI only contains an E.164 telephone number and does not contain a domain name, for example, *tel:+1.408.555.1234*.

A SIP proxy server is an entity that receives SIP requests, performs various database lookups, and then forwards ("proxies") the request to the next-hop proxy server. In this way, SIP messages are routed to their ultimate destination. Each proxy may perform some specialized function, such as external database lookups, authorization checks, and so on. Because the media does not flow through the SIP proxies—but rather only SIP signaling—SIP proxies are no longer needed after the call is established. In many SIP proxy designs, the proxies are stateless,

1. ITU-T Recommendation H.323, Packet-Based Multimedia Communications System, 1998. www.itu.int/rec/T-REC-H.323-200606-I/en.
2. J. Rosenberg, H. Schulzrinne, G. Camarillo, J. Peterson, R. Sparks, M. Handley, E. Schooler, SIP: Session Initiation Protocol, IETF RFC 3261, June 2002.
3. H. Schulzrinne, J. Rosenberg, A Comparison of SIP and H.323 for Internet telephony, in: Proceedings of NOSSDAV, Cambridge, UK, July 1998.

4. S. Fries, D. Ignjatic, On the applicability of various MIKEY modes and extensions, IETF Draft, March 31, 2008.
5. F. Audet, The use of the SIPS URI scheme in the Session Initiation Protocol (SIP), IETF Draft, February 23, 2008.

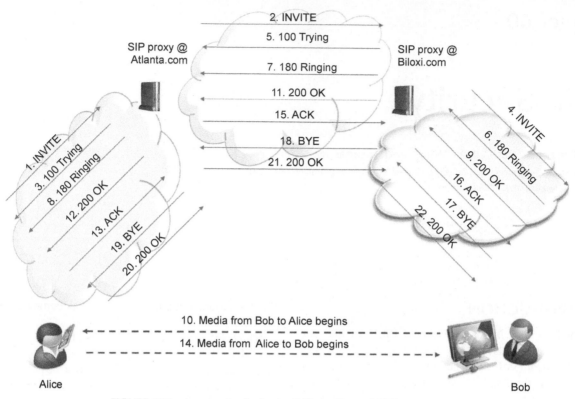

FIGURE 60.1 An example of a Session Initiation Protocol (SIP) session setup.

which allows alternative intermediate proxies to resume processing for a failed (or overloaded) proxy. One type of SIP proxy called a *redirect server* receives a SIP request, performs a database query operation, and returns the lookup result to the requester (which is often another proxy). Another type of SIP proxy is a SIP *registrar server*, which receives and processes registration requests. Registration binds a SIP (or TEL) URI to the user's device, which is how SIP messages are routed to a user agent. Multiple UAs may register the same URI, which causes incoming SIP requests to be routed to all of those UAs, a process termed *forking*, which causes some interesting security concerns.

The typical SIP transactions can be broadly viewed by looking at the typical call flow mechanism in a SIP session setup, as shown in Fig. 60.1. The term *SIP trapezoid* is often used to describe this message flow where the SIP signaling is sent to SIP proxies and the media is sent directly between the two UAs.

If Alice wants to initiate a session with Bob, she sends an initial SIP message (*INVITE*) to the local proxy for her domain (Atlanta.com). Her *INVITE* has Bob's URI (bob@ biloxi.com) as the Request-URI, which is used to route the message. Upon receiving the initial message from Alice, her domain's proxy sends a provisional 100 *Trying* message to Alice, which indicates that the message was received without error from Alice. The Atlanta.com proxy looks at

the *SIP Request-URI* in the message and decides to route the message to the Biloxi.com proxy. The Biloxi.com proxy receives the message and routes it to Bob. The Biloxi.com proxy delivers the *INVITE* message to Bob's SIP phone, to alert Bob of an incoming call. Bob's SIP phone initiates a provisional 180 *Ringing* message back to Alice, which is routed all the way back to Alice; this causes Alice's phone to generate a ringback tone, audible to Alice. When Bob answers his phone a 200 *OK* message is sent to his proxy, and Bob can start immediately sending media ("Hello?") to Alice. Meanwhile, Bob's 200 OK is routed from his proxy to Alice's proxy and finally to Alice's UA. Alice's UA responds with an *ACK* message to Bob and then Alice can begin sending media (audio and/or video) to Bob. Real-time media is almost exclusively sent using the Real-time Transport Protocol (RTP).[6] At this point the proxies are no longer involved in the call and hence the media will typically flow directly between Alice and Bob. That is, the media takes a different path through the network than the signaling. Finally, when either Alice or Bob want to end the session, they send a *BYE* message to their proxy, which is routed to the other party and is acknowledged.

---

6. H. Schulzrinne, R. Frederick, V. Jacobson, RTP: A transport protocol for real-time applications, IETF RFC 1889, January 1996.

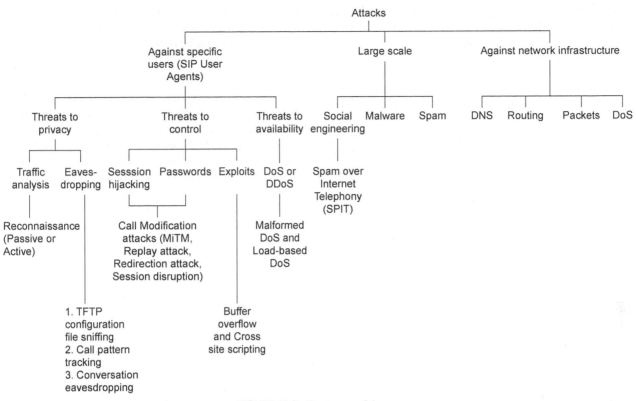

FIGURE 60.2 Taxonomy of threats.

One of the challenging tasks faced by the industry today is secure deployment of VoIP. During the initial design of SIP, the focus was more on providing new dynamic and powerful services along with simplicity rather than security. For this reason, a lot of effort is under way in the industry and among researchers to enhance SIP's security. The subsequent sections of this chapter deal with these issues.

2. OVERVIEW OF THREATS

Attacks can be broadly classified as attacks against specific users (SIP UAs), large scale (VoIP is part of the network), and against network infrastructure (SIP proxies or other network components and resources necessary for VoIP, such as routers, DNS servers, and bandwidth).[7] This chapter does not cover attacks against infrastructure; the interested reader is referred to the literature.[8] The subsequent parts of this chapter deal with the attacks targeted toward the specific host and issues related to social engineering. The taxonomy of attacks is shown in Fig. 60.2.

7. T. Chen, C. Davis, An overview of electronic attacks, in: H. Nemati (Ed.), Information Security and Ethics: Concepts, Methodologies, Tools and Applications, Idea Group Publishing, 2008.
8. A. Chakrabarti, G. Manimaran, Internet Infrastructure Security: a Taxonomy, vol. 16, IEEE Network, December 2002, pp. 13–21.

Reconnaissance of Voice Over Internet Protocol Networks

Reconnaissance refers to intelligent gathering or probing to assess the vulnerabilities of a network, to successfully launch a later attack; it includes *footprinting* the target (also known as *profiling* or *information gathering*). The two forms of reconnaissance techniques are passive and active. Passive reconnaissance attacks include the collection of network information through indirect or direct methods but without probing the target; active reconnaissance attacks involve generating traffic with the intention of eliciting responses from the target. Passive reconnaissance techniques would involve searching for publicly available SIP URIs in databases provided by VoIP service providers or on webpages, looking for publicly accessible SIP proxies or SIP UAs. Examples include *dig* and *nslookup*. Although passive reconnaissance techniques can be effective, they are time intensive.

If an attacker can watch SIP signaling, the attacker can perform number harvesting. Here, an attacker passively monitors all incoming and outgoing calls to build a database of legitimate phone numbers or extensions within an organization. This type of database can be used in more advanced VoIP attacks such as signaling manipulation or Spam over Internet Telephony (SPIT) attacks.

Active reconnaissance uses technical tools to discover information on the hosts that are active on the target network. The drawback to active reconnaissance, however, is that it can be detected. The two most common active reconnaissance attacks are call walking attacks and port-scanning attacks.

Call walking is a type of reconnaissance probe in which a malicious user initiates sequential calls to a block of telephone numbers to identify what assets are available for further exploitation. This is a modern version of *wardialing*, common in the 1980s to find modems on the Public Switched Telephone Network (PSTN). Performed during nonbusiness hours, call walking can provide information useful for social engineering, such as voicemail announcements that disclose the called party's name.

SIP UAs and proxies listen on UDP/5060 and/or TCP/5060, so it can be effective to scan IP addresses looking for such listeners. Once the attacker has accumulated a list of active IP addresses, he can start to investigate each address further. The Nmap tool is a robust port scanner that is capable of performing a multitude of types of scans.[9]

In addition, honeypots and honeynets are becoming increasingly popular, as it would help detect, prevent, or prepare to respond to attacks. A honeypot is a trap where vulnerabilities are deliberately introduced to lure attackers (hackers) and then analyze their activity (probing, security attack, or compromise). While a honeynet is a collection of honeypots, in the domain of VoIP, honeynets can be useful in preventing SPIT and VoIP Phishing (Vishing).

Denial of Service

A denial-of-service (DoS) attack deprives a user or an organization of services or resources that are normally available. In SIP, DoS attacks can be classified as malformed request DoS and load-based DoS.

Malformed Request Denial of Service

In this type of DoS attack, the attacker would craft a SIP request (or response) that exploits the vulnerability in a SIP proxy or SIP UA of the target, resulting in a partial or complete loss of function. For example, it has also been found that some UAs allow remote attackers to cause a DoS ("486 Busy" responses or device reboot) via a sequence of SIP INVITE transactions in which the Request-URI lacks a username.[10] Attackers have also shown that the IP implementations of some hard phones are vulnerable to IP fragmentation attacks [CAN-2002-0880] and Dynamic Host Configuration Protocol (DHCP)-based DoS attacks [CAN-2002-0835], demonstrating that normal infrastructure

protection (such as firewalls) is valuable for VoIP equipment. DoS attacks can also be initiated against other network services such as DHCP and DNS, which serve VoIP devices.

Load-Based Denial of Service

In this case, an attacker directs large volumes of traffic at a target (or set of targets) and attempts to exhaust resources such as the central processing unit (CPU) processing time, network bandwidth, or memory. SIP proxies and session border controllers (SBCs) are primary targets for attackers because of their critical role of providing voice service and the complexity of the software running on them.

A common type of load-based attack is a flooding attack. In case of VoIP, we categorize flooding attacks into these types:

- Control packet floods
- Call data floods
- Distributed DoS attack

Control Packet Floods

In this case, the attacker will flood SIP proxies with SIP packets, such as INVITE messages, bogus responses, or the like. The attacker might purposefully craft authenticated messages that fail authentication to cause the victim to validate the message. The attacker might spoof the IP address of a legitimate sender so that rate limiting the attack also causes rate limiting of the legitimate user as well.

Call Data Floods

The attacker will flood the target with RTP packets, with or without first establishing a legitimate RTP session, in an attempt to exhaust the target's bandwidth or processing power, leading to degradation of VoIP quality for other users on the same network or just for the victim. Other common forms of load-based attacks that could affect the VoIP system are buffer overflow attacks, TCP SYN flood, User Datagram Protocol (UDP) flood, fragmentation attacks, smurf attacks, and general overload attacks. Though VoIP equipment needs to protect itself from these attacks, these attacks are not specific to VoIP.

A SIP proxy can be overloaded with excessive legitimate traffic—the classic "Mother's Day" problem when the telephone system is most busy. Large-scale disasters (earthquakes) can also cause similar spikes, which are not attacks. Thus, even when not under attack, the system could be under high load. If the server or the end user is not fast enough to handle incoming loads, it will experience an outage or misbehave in such a way as to become ineffective at processing SIP messages. This type of attack is very difficult to detect because it would be difficult to sort the legitimate user from the illegitimate users who are performing the same type of attack.

---

9. http://nmap.org/.

10. The common vulnerability and exposure list for SIP. http://cve.mitre.org/cgibin/cvekey.cgi?keyword=SIP.

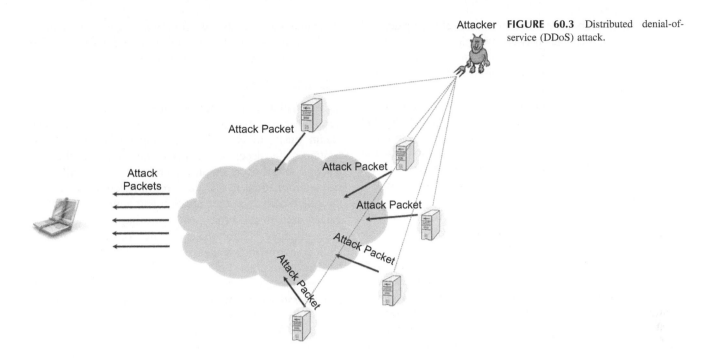

Attacker **FIGURE 60.3** Distributed denial-of-service (DDoS) attack.

Distributed Denial-of-Service Attack

Once an attacker has gained control of a large number of VoIP-capable hosts and formed a "zombies" network under the attacker's control, the attacker can launch interesting VoIP attacks, as illustrated in Fig. 60.3. Each zombie can send up to thousands of messages to a single location, thereby resulting in a barrage of packets, which incapacitates the victim's computer due to resource exhaustion.

Loss of Privacy

The four major eavesdropping attacks are:

● Trivial File Transfer Protocol (TFTP) configuration file sniffing
● Traffic analysis
● Conversation eavesdropping

Trivial File Transfer Protocol Configuration File Sniffing

Most IP phones rely on a TFTP server to download their configuration file after powering on. The configuration file can sometimes contain passwords that can be used to directly connect back to the phone and administer it or used to access other services (such as the company directory). An attacker who is sniffing the file when the phone downloads this configuration file can glean through these passwords and potentially reconfigure and control the IP phone. To thwart this attack vector, vendors variously encrypt the configuration file or use HTTPS and authentication.

Traffic Analysis

Traffic analysis involves determining who is talking to whom, which can be done even when the actual conversation is encrypted, and can even be done (to a lesser degree) between organizations. Such information can be beneficial to law enforcement and for criminals committing corporate espionage and stock fraud.

Conversation Eavesdropping

An important threat for VoIP users is eavesdropping on a conversation. In addition to the obvious problem of confidential information being exchanged between people, eavesdropping is also useful for credit-card fraud and identity theft. This is because some phone calls—especially to certain institutions—require users to enter credit-card numbers, PIN codes, or national identity numbers (Social Security numbers), which are sent as Dual-Tone Multifrequency (DTMF) digits in RTP. An attacker can use tools like Wireshark, Cain & Abel, voice over misconfigured Internet telephones (vomit), VoIPong, and Oreka to capture RTP packets and extract the conversation or the DTMF digits.[11]

Man-in-the-Middle Attacks

The man-in-the-middle attack is a classic form of an attack where the attacker has managed to insert himself between the

11. D. Endler, M. Collier, Hacking VoIP Exposed: Voice Over IP Security Secrets and Solutions, McGraw-Hill, 2007.

two hosts. It refers to an attacker who is able to read, and modify at will, messages between two parties without either party knowing that the link between them has been compromised. As such, the attacker has the ability to inspect or modify packets exchanged between two hosts, insert new packets, or prevent packets from being sent to hosts. Any device that handles SIP messages as a normal course of its function could be a man-in-the-middle: a compromised SIP proxy server or session border controller. If SIP messages are not authenticated, an attacker can also compromise a DNS server or use DNS poisoning techniques to cause SIP messages to be routed to a device under the attacker's control.

In a conventional enterprise network, VoIP phones are configured with different Virtual Local Area Network (VLAN) addresses as opposed to data devices. In such situations, the attacker would initially access the network by connecting his laptop to the existing data VLAN and then hop to the designated voice VLAN. This attack can be achieved in two ways: switch spoofing or double tagging. If a network switch is configured for autotrunking, the attacker converts it to a switch that needs to trunk. In the second method, the attacker sends data from one switch to another by sending frames with two 802.1Q headers (one for the victim's switch and the other for the attacking switch). The victim's switch accepts any incoming frames, while the target switch forwards the second frame (embedded with a false-tag) to the destination host based on the VLAN identifier present in the second 802.1Q header. Once, inside the desired voice VLAN, the attacker could Address Resolution Protocol (ARP) poison the designated phones that would result in a man-in-the-middle attack.

Replay Attacks

Replay attacks are often used to impersonate an authorized user. A replay attack is one in which an attacker captures a valid packet sent between the SIP UAs or proxies and re-sends it at a later time (perhaps a second later, perhaps days later). As an example with classic unauthenticated telnet, an attacker that captures a telnet username and password can replay that same username and password. In SIP, an attacker would capture and replay valid SIP requests. (Capturing and replaying SIP responses is usually not valuable, as SIP responses are discarded if their Call-ID does not match a currently outstanding request, which is one way SIP protects itself from replay attacks.)

If RTP is used without authenticating Real-time Transport Control Protocol (RTCP) packets and without sampling synchronization source (SSRC), an attacker can inject RTCP packets into a multicast group, each with a different SSRC, and force the group size to grow exponentially. A variant on a replay attack is the cut-and-paste attack. In this scenario, an attacker copies part of a captured packet with a generated packet. For example, a security

credential can be copied from one request to another, resulting in a successful authorization without the attacker even discovering the user's password.

Impersonation

Impersonation is described as a user or host pretending to be another user or host, especially one that the intended victim trusts. In case of a phishing attack, the attacker continues the deception to make the victim disclose his banking information, employee credentials, and other sensitive information. In SIP, the From header is displayed to the called party, so authentication and authorization of the values used in the From header are important to prevent impersonation. Unfortunately, call forwarding in SIP (called *retargeting*) makes simple validation of the From header impossible. For example, imagine Bob has forwarded his phone to Carol and they are in different administrative domains (Bob is at work, Carol is his wife at home). Then Alice calls Bob. When Alice's INVITE is routed to Bob's proxy, her INVITE will be retargeted to Carol's UA by rewriting the Request-URI to point to Carol's URI. Alice's original INVITE is then routed to Carol's UA. When it arrives at Carol's UA, the INVITE needs to indicate that the call is from Alice. The difficulty is that if Carol's SIP proxy were to have performed simplistic validation of the From in the INVITE when it arrived from Bob's SIP proxy, Carol's SIP proxy would have rejected it—because it contained Alice's From. However, such retargeting is a legitimate function of SIP networks.

Redirection Attack

If compromised by an attacker or via a SIP man-in-the-middle attack, the intermediate SIP proxies responsible for SIP message routing can falsify any response. In this section, we describe how the attacker could use this ability to launch a redirection attack. If an attacker can fabricate a reply to a SIP INVITE, the media session can be established with the attacker rather than the intended party. In SIP, a proxy or UA can respond to an INVITE request with a 301 Moved Permanently or 302 Moved Temporarily Response. The 302 Response will also include an Expires header line that communicates how long the redirection should last. The attacker can respond with a redirection response, effectively denying service to the called party and possibly tricking the caller into communicating with, or through, a rogue UA.

Session Disruption

Session disruption describes any attack that degrades or disrupts an existing signaling or media session. For example, in the case of a SIP scenario, if an attacker is able to send failure messages such as BYE and inject them into the signaling path, he can cause the sessions to fail when there is no legitimate reason why they should not continue.

For this to be successful, the attacker has to include the Call-ID of an active call in the BYE message. Alternatively, if an attacker introduces bogus packets into the media stream, he can disrupt packet sequence, impede media processing, and disrupt a session. Delay attacks are those in which an attacker can capture and resend RTP SSRC packets out of sequence to a VoIP endpoint and force the endpoint to waste its processing cycles in resequencing packets and degrade call quality. An attacker could also disrupt a Voice over Wireless Local Area Network (WLAN) service by disrupting IEEE 802.11 WLAN service using radio spectrum jamming or a Wi-Fi Protected Access (WPA) Message Integrity Check (MIC) attack. A wireless access point will disassociate stations when it receives two invalid frames within 60 s, causing loss of network connectivity for 60 s. A 1-min loss of service is hardly tolerable in a voice application.

Exploits

Cross-Site Scripting (XSS) attacks are possible with VoIP systems because call logs contain header fields, and administrators (and other privileged users) view those call logs. In this attack, specially crafted From (or other) fields are sent by an attacker in a normal SIP message (such as an INVITE). Then later, when someone such as the administrator looks at the call logs using a web browser, the specially crafted From causes an XSS attack against the administrator's web browser, which can then do malicious things with the administrator's privileges. This can be a damaging attack if the administrator has already logged into other systems (HR databases, the SIP call controller, the firewall) and her web browser has a valid cookie (or active session in another window) for those other systems.

Social Engineering

SPIT is classified as a social threat because the callee can treat the call as unsolicited, and the term *unsolicited* is strictly bound to be a user-specific preference, which makes it hard for the system to identify this kind of transaction. SPIT can be telemarketing calls used for guiding callees to a service deployed to sell products. IM spam and presence spam could also be launched via SIP messages. IM spam is very similar to email spam; presence spam is defined as a set of unsolicited presence requests for the presence package. A subtle variation of SPIT called *vishing* is an attack that aims to collect personal data by redirecting users toward an interactive voice responder that could collect personal information such as the PIN for a credit card. From a signaling point of view, unsolicited communication is technically a correct transaction.

Unfortunately, many of the mechanisms that are effective for email spam are ineffective with VoIP, for many

reasons. First, the email with its entire contents arrives at a server before it is seen by the user. Such a mail server can therefore apply many filtering strategies, such as Bayesian filters, URL filters, and so on. In contrast, in VoIP, human voices are transmitted rather than text. To recognize voices and to determine whether the message is spam or not is still a very difficult task for the end system. A recipient of a call only learns about the subject of the message when he is actually listening to it. Moreover, even if the content is stored on a voice mailbox, it is still difficult for today's speech recognition technologies to understand the context of the message enough to decide whether it is spam or not.

One mechanism to fight automated systems that deliver spam is to challenge such suspected incoming calls with a Turing test. These methods include:

- *Voice menu.* Before a call is put through, a computer asks the caller to press certain key combinations, for example, "Press #55."
- *Challenge models.* Before a call is put through, a computer asks the caller to solve a simple equation and to type in the answer, for example, "Divide 10 by 2."
- *Alternative number.* Under the main number a computer announces an alternative number. This number may even be changed permanently by a call management server. All these methods can even be enforced by enriching the audio signal with noise or music. This prevents SPIT bots from using speech recognition.

Such Turing tests are attractive, since it is often hard for computers to decode audio questions. However, these puzzles cannot be made too difficult, because human beings must always be able to solve them.

One of the solutions to the SPIT problem is the whitelist. In a whitelist, a user explicitly states which persons are allowed to contact him. A similar technique is also used in Skype; where Alice wants to call Bob, she first has to add Bob to her contact list and send a contact request to Bob. Only when Bob has accepted this request can Alice make calls to Bob.

In general, whitelists have an introduction problem, since it is not possible to receive calls by someone who is not already on the whitelist. Blacklists are the opposite of whitelists but have limited effectiveness at blocking spam because new identities (which are not on the blacklist) can be easily created by anyone, including spammers.

Authentication mechanisms can be used to provide strong authentication, which is necessary for strong whitelists and reputation systems, which form the basis of SPIT prevention. Strong authentication is generally Public Key Infrastructure (PKI) dependent. Proactive publishing of incorrect information, namely SIP addresses, is a possible way to fill up spammers' databases with existing contacts. Consent-based communication is the other solution. Address obfuscation could be an alternative wherein spam bots are unable to identify the SIP URIs.

3. SECURITY IN VOICE OVER INTERNET PROTOCOL

Much existing VoIP equipment is dedicated to VoIP, which allows placing such equipment on a separate network. This is typically accomplished with a separate VLAN. Depending on the vendor of the equipment, this can be automated using Cisco Discovery Protocol (CDP), Link Layer Discovery Protocol (LLDP), or 802.1x, all of which will place equipment into a separate "voice VLAN" to assist with this separation. This provides a reasonable level of protection, especially within an enterprise where employees lack much incentive to interfere with the telephone system.

Preventative Measures

However, the use of VLANs is not an ideal solution because it does not work well with softphones that are not dedicated to VoIP, because placing those softphones onto the "voice VLAN" destroys the security and management advantage of the separate network. A separate VLAN can also create a false sense of security that only benign voice devices are connected to the VLAN. However, even though 802.1x provides the best security, it is still possible for an attacker to gain access to the voice VLAN (with a suitable hub between the phone and the switch). Mechanisms that provide less security, such as CDP or LLDP, can be circumvented by software on an infected computer. Some vendors' Ethernet switches can be configured to require clients to request inline Ethernet power before allowing clients to join certain VLANs (such as the voice VLAN), which provides protection from such infected computers. But, as mentioned previously, such protection of the voice VLAN prevents deployment of softphones, which is a significant reason that most companies are interested in deploying VoIP.

Eavesdropping

To counter the threat of eavesdropping, the media can be encrypted. The method to encrypt RTP traffic is Secure RTP (SRTP; RFC3711), which does not encrypt the IP, UDP, or RTP headers but does encrypt the RTP payload (the "voice" itself). SRTP's advantage of leaving the RTP headers unencrypted is that header compression protocols (cRTP,[12] ROHC[13]) and protocol analyzers (looking for RTP packet loss and (S)RTCP reports) can still function with SRTP-encrypted media.

The drawback of SRTP is that approximately 13 incompatible mechanisms exist to establish the SRTP keys. These mechanisms are at various stages of deployment, industry acceptance, and standardization. Thus at this point in time it is unlikely that two SRTP-capable systems from different vendors will have a compatible SRTP keying mechanism. A brief overview of some of the more popular keying mechanisms is provided here.

One of the popular SRTP keying mechanisms, Security Descriptions, requires a secure SIP signaling channel (SIP over TLS) and discloses the SRTP key to each SIP proxy along the call setup path. This means that a passive attacker, able to observe the unencrypted SIP signaling and the encrypted SRTP, would be able to eavesdrop on a call. S/MIME is SIP's end-to-end security mechanism, which Security Descriptions could use to its benefit, but S/MIME has not been well-deployed and, due to specific features of SIP (primarily forking and retargeting), it is unlikely that S/MIME will see deployment in the foreseeable future.

Multimedia Internet Keying (MIKEY) has approximately eight incompatible modes defined; these allow establishing SRTP keys.[4] Almost all these MIKEY modes are more secure than Security Descriptions because they do not carry the SRTP key directly in the SIP message but rather encrypt it with the remote party's private key or perform a Diffie-Hellman exchange. Thus, for most of the MIKEY modes, the attacker would need to actively participate in the MIKEY exchange and obtain the encrypted SRTP to listen to the media.

Zimmermann Real-time Transport Protocol (ZRTP)[14] is another SRTP key exchange mechanism, which uses a Diffie-Hellman exchange to establish the SRTP keys and detects an active attacker by having the users (or their computers) validate a short authentication string with each other. It affords useful security properties, including perfect forward secrecy and key continuity (which allows the users to verify authentication strings once, and never again), and the ability to work through SBCs.

In 2006, the IETF decided to reduce the number of IETF standard key exchange mechanisms and chose DTLS-SRTP. DTLS-SRTP uses Datagram TLS (a mechanism to run TLS over a nonreliable protocol such as UDP) over the media path. To detect an active attacker, the TLS certificates exchanged over the media path must match the signed certificate fingerprints sent over the SIP signaling path. The certificate fingerprints are signed using SIP's identity mechanism.[15]

12. T. Koren, S. Casner, J. Geevarghese, B. Thompson, P. Ruddy, Enhanced Compressed RTP (CRTP) for Links with High Delay, IETF RFC 3545, July 2003.
13. G. Pelletier, K. Sandlund, Robust Header Compression Version 2 (ROHCv2): Profiles for RTP, UDP, IP, ESP and UDP-Lite, IETF RFC 5225, April 2008.
14. P. Zimmermann, A. Johnston, J. Callas, ZRTP: Media Path Key Agreement for Secure RTP, IETF Draft, July 9, 2007.
15. J. Peterson, C. Jennings, Enhancements for Authenticated Identity Management in the Session Initiation Protocol (SIP), IETF RFC 4474, August 2006.

A drawback with SRTP is that it is imperative (for some keying mechanisms) or very helpful (with other keying mechanisms) for the SIP user agent to encrypt its SIP signaling traffic with its SIP proxy. The only standard for such encryption, today, is SIP over TLS which runs over TCP. To date, many vendors have avoided TCP on their SIP proxies because they have found SIP-over-TCP scales worse than SIP-over-UDP. It is anticipated that if this cannot be overcome we may see SIP-over-DTLS standardized. Another viable option, especially in some markets, is to use IPsec ESP (encapsulating security payload) to protect SIP.

Another drawback of SRTP is that diagnostic and troubleshooting equipment cannot listen to the media stream. This may seem obvious, but it can cause difficulties when technicians need to listen to and diagnose echo, gain, or other anomalies that cannot be diagnosed by examining SRTP headers (which are unencrypted) but can only be diagnosed by listening to the decrypted audio itself.

Identity

As described in the "Threats" section, it is important to have strong identity assurance. Today there are two mechanisms to provide for identity: P-Asserted-Identity,[16] which is used within a trust domain (within a company or between a service provider and its paying customers) and is simply a header inserted into a SIP request, and SIP identity,[16] which is used between trust domains (between two companies) and creates a signature over some of the SIP headers and over the SIP body.

SIP identity is useful when two organizations connect via SIP proxies, as was originally envisioned as the SIP architecture for intermediaries between two organizations—often a SIP service provider. Many of these service providers operate SBCs rather than SIP proxies for a variety of reasons. One of the drawbacks of SIP identity is that an SBC, by its nature, will rewrite the SIP body (specifically the m = /c = lines), which destroys the original signature. Thus, an SBC would need to rewrite the From header and sign the new message with the SBC's own private key. This effectively creates hop-by-hop trust; each SBC that needs to rewrite the message in this way is also able to manipulate the SIP headers and SIP body in other ways that could be malicious or could allow the SBC to eavesdrop on a call. Alternative cryptographic identity mechanisms are being pursued, but it is not yet known whether this weakness can be resolved.

Traffic Analysis

The most useful protection from traffic analysis is to encrypt your SIP traffic. This would require the attacker to gain access to your SIP proxy (or its call logs) to determine who you called.

Additionally, your (S)RTP traffic itself could provide useful traffic analysis information. For example, someone may learn valuable information just by noticing where (S)RTP traffic is being sent (the company's in-house lawyers are calling an acquisition target several times a day). Forcing traffic to be concentrated to a device can help prevent this sort of traffic analysis. In some network topologies this can be achieved using a Network Address Translation (NAT), and in all cases it can be achieved with an SBC.

Reactive

An intrusion prevention system (IPS) is a useful way to react to VoIP attacks against signaling or media. An IPS with generic rules and with VoIP-specific rules can detect an attack and block or rate-limit traffic from the offender.

Intrusion Prevention System (IPS)

Because SIP is derived from and related to many well-deployed and well-understood protocols (HTTP), IDS/IPS vendors are able to create products to protect against SIP quite readily. Often an IDS/IPS function can be built into a SIP proxy, SBC, or firewall, reducing the need for a separate IDS/IPS appliance. An IDS/IPS is marginally effective for detecting media attacks, primarily to notice an excessive amount of bandwidth is being consumed and to throttle it or alarm the event.

A drawback of IPS is that it can cause false positives and deny service to a legitimate endpoint, thus causing a DoS in an attempt to prevent a DoS. An attacker, knowledgeable of the rules or behavior of an IPS, may also be able to spoof the identity of a victim (the victim's source IP address or SIP identity) and trigger the IPS/IDS into reacting to the attack. Thus, it is important to deny attackers that avenue by using standard best practices for IP address spoofing[17] and employing strong SIP identity. Using a separate network (VLAN) for VoIP traffic can help reduce the chance of false positives, as the IDS/IPS rules can be more finely tuned for that one application running on the voice VLAN.

Rate Limiting

When suffering from too many SIP requests due to an attack, the first thing to consider doing is simple rate

16. C. Jennings, J. Peterson, M. Watson, Private Extensions to the Session Initiation Protocol (SIP) for Asserted Identity Within Trusted Networks, IETF RFC 3325, November 2002.

17. P. Ferguson, D. Senie, Network ingress filtering: Defeating denial of service attacks which employ IP source address spoofing, IETF 2827, May 2000.

limiting. This is often naïvely performed by simply rate limiting the traffic to the SIP proxy and allowing excess traffic to be dropped. Though this does effectively reduce the transactions per second the SIP proxy needs to perform, it interferes with processing of existing calls to a significant degree. For example, a normal call is established with an INVITE, which is reliably acknowledged when the call is established. If the simplistic rate limiting were to drop the acknowledgment message, the INVITE would be retransmitted, incurring additional processing while the system is under high load. A separate problem with rate limiting is that both attackers and legitimate users are subject to the rate limiting; it is more useful to discriminate the rate limiting to the users causing the high rate. This can be done by distributing the simple rate limiting toward the users rather than doing the simple rate limiting near the server.

On the server, a more intelligent rate limiting is useful. These are usually proprietary rate-limiting schemes, but they attempt to process existing calls before processing new calls. For example, such a scheme would allow processing the acknowledgment message for a previously processed INVITE; process the BYE associated with an active call, to free up resources; or process high-priority users' calls (the vice president's office is allowed to make calls, but the janitorial staff is blocked from making calls).

By pushing rate limiting toward users, effective use can be made of simple packet-based rate limiting. For example, even a very active call center phone does not need to send 100 Mb of SIP signaling traffic to its SIP proxy; even 1 Mb would be an excessive amount of traffic. By deploying simplistic, reasonable rate limiting very near the users, ideally at the Ethernet switch itself, bugs in the call processing application or malicious attacks by unauthorized software can be mitigated.

A similar situation occurs with the RTP media itself. Even high-definition video does not need to send or receive 100 Mb of traffic to another endpoint and can be rate-limited based on the applications running on the dedicated device. This sort of policing can be effective at the Ethernet switch itself, or in an IDS/IPS (watching for excessive bandwidth), a firewall, or SBC.

Challenging

A more sophisticated rate-limiting technique is to provide additional challenges to a high-volume user. This could be done when it is suspected that the user is sending spam or when the user has initiated too many calls in a certain time period. A simple mechanism is to complete the call with an interactive voice response system that requests the user to enter some digits ("Please enter 5, 1, 8 to complete your call"). Though this technique suffers from some problems (it does not work well for hearing-impaired users or if the caller does not understand the IVR's language), it is effective at reducing the calls per second from both internal and external callers.

4. FUTURE TRENDS

Certain SIP proxies have the ability to forward SIP requests to multiple UAs. These SIP requests can be sent in parallel, in series, or a combination of both series and parallel. Such proxies are called *forking proxies*.

Forking Problem in Session Initiation Protocol

The forking proxy expects a response from all the UAs who received the received the request; the proxy forward only the "best" final response back to the caller. This behavior causes a situation known as the *heterogeneous error response forking problem* (HERFP), which is illustrated in Fig. 60.4.[18]

Alice initiates an INVITE request that includes a body format that is understood by UAS2 but not UAS1. For example, the user account control (UAC) might have used a MIME type of multipart/mixed with a session description and an optional image or sound. As UAC1 does not support this MIME format, it returns a 415 (Unsupported Media Type) response. Unfortunately the proxy has to wait until all the branches generate the final response and then pick the "best" response, depending on the criteria mentioned in RFC 3261. In many cases the proxy has to wait a long enough time that the human operating the UAC abandons the call. The proxy informs the UAS2 that the call has been canceled, which is acknowledged by UAS2. It then returns the 415 (Unsupported Media Type) back to Alice, which could have been repaired by Alice by sending the appropriate session description.

Security in Peer-to-Peer Session Initiation Protocol

Originally, SIP was specified as a client/server protocol, but recent proposals suggest using SIP in a peer-to-peer (P2P) setting.[19] One of the major reasons for using SIP in a P2P setting is its robustness, since there is no centralized control. As defined, "peer to peer (P2P) systems are distributed systems without any centralized control or hierarchical organization." This definition defines pure P2P systems. Even though many networks are considered P2P, they employ central authority or use supernodes. Early systems used

18. H. Schulzrinne, D. Oran, G. Camarillo, The Reason Header Field for the Session Initiation Protocol (SIP), IETF RFC 3326, December 2002.
19. K. Singh, H. Schulzrinne, Peer-to-peer Internet telephony using SIP, in: 15th International Workshop on Network and Operating Systems Support for Digital Audio and Video, June 2005.

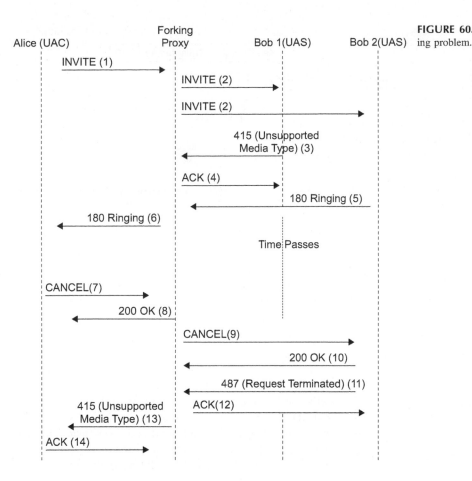

Alice (UAC)   Forking Proxy   Bob 1(UAS)   Bob 2(UAS)

INVITE (1)
INVITE (2)
INVITE (2)
415 (Unsupported Media Type) (3)
ACK (4)
180 Ringing (5)
180 Ringing (6)

Time Passes

CANCEL(7)
200 OK (8)
CANCEL(9)
200 OK (10)
487 (Request Terminated) (11)
ACK(12)
415 (Unsupported Media Type) (13)
ACK (14)

FIGURE 60.4 The heterogeneous error response forking problem.

flooding to route messages, which was found to be highly inefficient. To improve lookup time for a search request, structured overlay networks have been developed that provide load balancing and efficient routing of messages. They use distributed hash tables (DHTs) to provide efficient lookup.[20] Examples of structured overlay networks are CAN, Chord, Pastry, and Tapestry.[21–24]

We focus on Chord Protocol because it is used as a prototype in most proposals for P2P-SIP. Chord has a ring-based topology in which each node stores at most $\log(N)$ entries in its finger table, which is like an application-level routing table, to point to other peers. Every node's IP address is mapped to an m bit chord identifier with a predefined hash function h. The same hash function h is also used to map any key of data onto a key ID that forms the distributed hash table. Every node maintains a finger table of $\log(N) = 6$ entries, pointing to the next-hop node location at distance 2^{i-1} (for $i = 1,2...m$) from this node identifier. Each node in the ring is responsible for storing the content of all key IDs that are equal to the identifier of the node's predecessor in the Chord ring. In a Chord ring each node n stores the IP address of m successor nodes plus its predecessor in the ring. The m successor entries in the routing table point to nodes at increasing distance from n. Routing is done by forwarding messages to the largest node-ID in the routing table that precedes the key ID until the direct successor of a node has a longer ID than the key ID.

Singh and Schulzrinne envision a hierarchical architecture in which multiple P2P networks are represented by a DNS domain. A global DHT is used for interdomain routing of messages.

20. H. Balakrishnan, M. FransKaashoek, D. Karger, R. Morris, I. Stoica, Looking up data in P2P systems, Commun. ACM 46 (2) (February 2003).
21. S. Ratnasamy, P. Francis, M. Handley, R. Karp, S. Shenker, A scalable content-addressable network, in: Proceedings of ACM SIGCOMM, 2001.
22. I. Stoica, R. Morris, D. Karger, M. F Kaashoek, H. Balakrishnan, Chord: A scalable peer-to-peer lookup service for internet applications, in: Proceedings of the 2001 Conference on Applications, Technologies, Architectures, and Protocols for Computer Communication, 2001, pp. 149–160.
23. A. Rowstron, P. Druschel, Pastry: Scalable, decentralized object location and routing for large-scale peer-to-peer systems, in: IFIP/ACM International Conference on Distributed Systems Platforms (Middleware), Heidelberg, Germany, 2001, pp. 329–350.
24. B.Y. Zhao, L. Huang, J. Stribling, S.C. Rhea, A.D. Joseph, J.D. Kubiatowicz, Tapestry: A resilient global-scale overlay for service deployment, IEEE J. Sel. Areas Commun. 22 (1) (January 2004) 41–53.

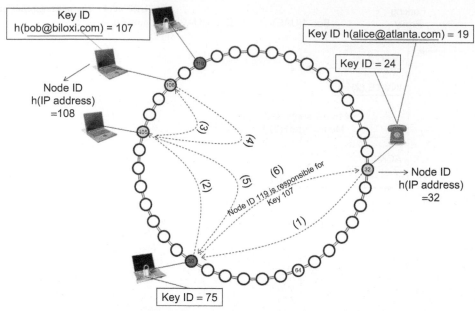

FIGURE 60.5 Man-in-the-middle attack.

Join/Leave Attack

Security of structured overlay networks is based on the assumption that joining nodes are assigned node-IDs at random due to random assignment of IP addresses. This could lead to a join/leave attack in which the malicious attacker would want to control O(logN) nodes out of N nodes as search is done on O(logN) nodes to find the desired key ID. With the adoption of IPv6, the join/leave attack can be more massive because the attacker will have more IP addresses. But even with IPv4, join/leave attacks are possible if the IP addresses are assigned dynamically. Node-ID assignment in Chord is inherently deterministic, thereby allowing the attacker to compute node-IDs in advance where the attack could be launched by spoofing IP addresses. A probable solution would be to authenticate nodes before allowing them to join the overlay, which can involve authenticating the node before assigning the IP address.

Attacks on Overlay Routing

Any malicious node within the overlay can drop, alter, or wrongly forward a message it receives instead of routing it according to the overlay protocol. This can result in severe degradation of the overlay's availability. Therefore an adversary can perform one of the following:

Registration Attacks

One of the existing challenges to P2P—SIP registration is to provide confidentiality. This also includes message integrity to registration messages.

Man-in-the-Middle Attacks

Let's consider the case where a node with ID 80 and a node with ID 109 conspire to form a man-in-the-middle attack, as shown in Fig. 60.5. The honest node responsible for the key is node 180. Let's assume that a recursive approach is used for finding the desired key ID, wherein each routing node would send the request message to the appropriate node-ID until it reaches the node-ID responsible for the desired key ID. The source node (node 30) will not have any control nor can it trace the request packet as it traverses through the Chord ring. Therefore node 32 will establish a dialogue with node 119, and node 80 would impersonate node 32 and establish a dialogue with node 108. This attack can be detected if an iterative routing mechanism is used wherein a source node checks whether the hash value is closer to the key ID than the node-ID it received on the previous hop.[25] Therefore, the source node (32) would get suspicious if node 80 redirected it directly to node 119, because it assumes that there exists a node with ID lower than key ID 107.

Attacks on Bootstrapping Nodes

Any node wanting to join the overlay needs to be bootstrapped with a static node or cached node or discover the bootstrap node through broadcast mechanisms (SIP-multicast). In any case, if an adversary gains access to

25. M. Srivatsa, L. Liu, Vulnerabilities and security threats in structured overlay networks: A quantitative analysis, in: Proceedings of 20th Annual Computer Science Application Conference, Tucson, December 6—10, 2004, pp. 251—261.

the bootstrap node, the joining node can easily be attacked. Securing the bootstrap node is still an open question.

Duplicate Identity Attacks

Preventing duplicate identities is one of the open problems whereby a hash of two IP addresses can lead to the same node-ID. The Singh and Schulzrinne approach reduces this problem somewhat by using a P2P network for each domain. Further, they suggest email-based authentication in which a joining node would receive a password via email and then use the password to authenticate itself to the network.

Free Riding

In a P2P system there is a risk of free riding in which nodes use services but fail to provide services to the network. Nodes use the overlay for registration and location service but drop other messages, which could eventually result in a reduction of the overlay's availability. The other major challenges that are presumably even harder to solve for P2P—SIP are as follows:

- Prioritizing signaling for emergency calls in an overlay network and ascertaining the physical location of users in real time may be very difficult.
- With the high dynamic nature of P2P systems, there is no predefined path for signaling traffic, and therefore it is impossible to implement a surveillance system for law enforcement agencies with P2P—SIP.

End-to-End Identity With Session Border Controllers

As discussed earlier,[16] End-to-End Identity with SBCs provides identity for SIP requests by signing certain SIP headers and the SIP body [which typically contains the Session Description Protocol (SDP)]. This identity is destroyed if the SIP request travels through an SBC, because the SBC has to rewrite the SDP as part of the SBC's function (to force media to travel through the SBC). Today, nearly all companies that provide SIP trunking (Internet telephony service providers, ITSPs) utilize SBCs. In order to work with[16] those SBCs, one would have to validate incoming requests (which is new), modify the SDP and create a new identity (which they are doing today), and sign the new identity (which is new). As of this writing, it appears unlikely that ITSPs will have any reason to perform these new functions.

A related problem is that, even if we had end-to-end identity, it is impossible to determine whether a certain identity can rightfully claim a certain E.164 phone number in the From header. Unlike domain names, which can have their ownership validated (the way email address validation is performed on myriad websites today), there is no de facto or written standard to determine whether an identity can rightfully claim to "own" a certain E.164.

It is anticipated that as SIP trunking becomes more commonplace, SIP spam will grow with it, and the growth of SIP spam will create the necessary impetus for the industry to solve these interrelated problems. Solving the end-to-end identity problem and the problem of attesting E.164 ownership would allow domains to immediately create meaningful whitelists. Over time these whitelists could be shared among SIP networks, end users, and others, eventually creating a reputation system. But as long as spammers are able to impersonate legitimate users, even creating a whitelist is fraught with the risk of a spammer guessing the contents of that whitelist (your bank, family member, or employer).

Session Initiation Protocol Security Using Identity-Based Cryptography

Authentication in SIP has been a major concern, and existing authentication schemes depend on PKI or shared secrets (passwords). Although PKI has existed for decades, the cost of maintaining the infrastructure has prevented enterprises from harnessing it to its fullest potential. In a PKI, the certificates contain a preset expiration date and if the validity date expires, or if the sender refreshes his keys, then the end user (callee) would have to obtain a new certificate from a public key repository. This retrieval process would involve the onerous task of certificate path construction and path validation processes. In such cases, Identity-based cryptography can be extremely useful as it eliminates the generation and maintenance of public key certificates. The basic idea behind an identity-based cryptosystem is that end users can choose an arbitrary string (SIP URI) which represents their identity to compute their public key. As a result, it expunges the need for certificates from Certificate Authority (CA).[26] In addition, concatenation of user identity and Universally Unique Identifier (UUID) to generate a public key would greatly simplify the revocation process.

5. SUMMARY

With today's dedicated VoIP handsets, a separate voice VLAN provides a reasonable amount of security. Going forward, as nondedicated devices become more commonplace, more rigorous security mechanisms will gain

26. D. Berbecaru, A. Lioy, M. Marian, On the complexity of public key certificate validation, in: Proceedings of the 4th International Conference on Information Security, Lecture Notes in Computer Science, vol. 2200, Springer-Verlag, 2001, pp. 183—203.

importance. This will begin with encrypted signaling and encrypted media and will evolve to include spam protection and enhancements to SIP to provide cryptographic assurance of SIP call and message routing.

As VoIP continues to grow, VoIP security solutions (see checklist, "An Agenda for Action for VoIP's Security Challenges") will have to consider consumer, enterprise, and policy concerns. Some VoIP applications commonly installed on PCs, such as Skype, may be against corporate security policies. One of the biggest challenges with enabling encryption is with maintaining a PKI and the complexities involved in distributing public key certificates that would span to end users[27] and key synchronization between various devices belonging to the same end user agent.[28]

An Agenda for Action for Voice Over Internet Protocol's Security Challenges

The following are some tips for ensuring a secure VoIP (check all tasks completed):

_____1. Choose the VoIP protocols carefully.
_____2. Turn off unnecessary protocols.
_____3. Remember that each element in the VoIP infrastructure, accessible on the network like any computer, can be attacked.
_____4. Divide and conquer works well for VoIP networks.
_____5. Authenticate remote operations.
_____6. Separate VoIP servers and the internal network.
_____7. Make sure the VoIP security system can track the communications ports by reading inside the signaling packets to discover the ports selected and enable two endpoints to send media packets to each other.
_____8. Use NAT, even if in some cases it poses a special problem for VoIP. NAT converts internal IP addresses into a single, globally unique IP address for routing across the Internet.
_____9. Use a security system that performs VoIP-specific security checks.

Using IPsec for VoIP tunneling across the Internet is another option; however, it is not without substantial overhead.[29] Therefore, end-to-end mechanisms such as SRTP are specified for encrypting media and establishing session keys.

27. C. Jennings, J. Fischl, Certificate Management Service for the Session Initiation Protocol (SIP), IETF Draft, April 5, 2008.
28. Z. Anwar, W. Yurcik, R. Johnson, M. Hafiz, R. Campbell, Multiple Design Patterns for Voice Over IP (VoIP) Security, IPCCC 2006, April 10–12, 2006, pp. 485–492.
29. H.K. Patil, D. Willis, Identity-Based Authentication in the Session Initiation Protocol, IETF Draft, February 17, 2008.

VoIP network designers should take extra care in designing intrusion detection systems that are able to identify never-before-seen activities and react according to the organization's policy. They should follow industry best practices for securing endpoint devices and servers. Current softphones and consumer-priced hardphones use the "haste-to-market" implementation approach and therefore become vulnerable to VoIP attacks. Therefore VoIP network administrators may evaluate VoIP endpoint technology, identify devices or software that will meet business needs and can be secured, and make these the corporate standards. With P2P–SIP, the lack of central authority makes authentication of users and nodes difficult. Providing central authority would dampen the spirit of P2P–SIP and would conflict with the inherent features of distributed networks. A decentralized solution such as the reputation management system, where the trust values are assigned to nodes in the network based on prior behavior, would lead to a weak form of authentication because the credibility used to distribute trust values could vary in a decentralized system. Reputation management systems were more focused on file-sharing applications and have not yet been applied to P2P–SIP.

Finally, let's move on to the real interactive part of this Chapter: review questions/exercises, hands-on projects, case projects, and optional team case project. The answers and/or solutions by chapter can be found in the Online Instructor's Solutions Manual.

CHAPTER REVIEW QUESTIONS/ EXERCISES

True/False

1. True or False? H.323 and *Session Initiation Protocol* (SIP) are the two substandardized protocols for the realization of VoIP.
2. True or False? SIP is the *Internet Engineering Task Force* (IETF) substandard for multimedia communications in an IP network.
3. True or False? Attacks can be broadly classified as attacks against specific users (SIP UAs), large scale (VoIP is part of the network) and against network infrastructure (SIP proxies or other network components and resources necessary for VoIP, such as routers, DNS servers, and bandwidth).
4. True or False? *Reconnaissance* refers to intelligent gathering or probing to assess the vulnerabilities of a network, to successfully launch a later attack; it includes *footprinting* the target (also known as *profiling* or *information gathering*).
5. True or False? A denial-of-service (DoS) attack deprives a user or an organization of services or resources that are not normally available.

Multiple Choice

1. In what type of DoS attack would the attacker craft a SIP request (or response) that exploits the vulnerability in a SIP proxy or SIP UA of the target, resulting in a partial or complete loss of function?
   A. Privacy-enhancing technology
   B. Location technology
   C. Promotional email
   D. Malformed request DoS
   E. Data controller

2. In what case would an attacker direct large volumes of traffic at a target (or set of targets) and attempt to exhaust resources such as the CPU processing time, network bandwidth, or memory?
   A. Policy enforcement
   B. Location technology
   C. Valid
   D. Load-Based DoS
   E. Bait

3. In what case, would the attacker flood SIP proxies with SIP packets, such as INVITE messages, bogus responses, or the like?
   A. Data minimization
   B. XACML
   C. Control packet floods
   D. Strong narrative
   E. Security

4. What is it called when the attacker floods the target with RTP packets, with or without first establishing a legitimate RTP session, in an attempt to exhaust the target's bandwidth or processing power, leading to degradation of VoIP quality for other users on the same network or just for the victim?
   A. Call data floods
   B. Greedy strategy

C. Sensitive information
D. Phishing
E. Taps

5. Most IP phones rely on a TFTP server to download their _____ after powering on?
   A. Irrelevant
   B. Sensor nodes
   C. Crimeware
   D. Configuration file
   E. Server policy

EXERCISE

Problem

What are some of the disadvantages of VoIP?

Hands-on Projects

Project

Can one use their existing network equipment (routers, hubs, etc.) for a VoIP network?

Case Projects

Problem

What is a VoIP "softphone"?

Optional Team Case Project

Problem

Will a VoIP system continue to function during a power failure or cable outage?

Part VIII

Storage Security

Chapter 61

SAN Security

John McGowan[1], Jeffrey S. Bardin[2] and John McDonald[1]
[1]Dell EMC, Hopkinton, MA, United States; [2]Treadstone 71 LLC, Barre, MA, United States

Note: This chapter is available in its entirety online at store.elsevier.com/product.jsp?isbn= 9780128038437 (click the Resources tab at the bottom of the page).

1. ABSTRACT

One thing to consider is that the most probable avenue of attack in a storage area network (SAN) is through the hosts connected to the SAN. There are potentially thousands of host, application, and operating system—specific security considerations that are beyond the scope of this chapter but should be followed as your systems and application administrators properly configure their owned devices.

Information security is an aspect of security that seeks to protect data confidentiality, data integrity, and access to the data, is an established commercial sector with a wide variety of vendors marketing mature products and technologies, such as VPNs, firewalls, antivirus, and content management. Recently there has been a subtle development in security. Organizations are expanding their security perspectives to secure not only end-user data access and the perimeter of the organization but also the data within the datacenter. Several factors drive these recent developments. The continuing expansion of the network and the continued shrinking of the perimeter expose datacenter resources and the storage infrastructure to new vulnerabilities. Data aggregation increases the impact of a security breach. IP-based storage networking potentially exposes storage resources to traditional network vulnerabilities. Recently the delineation between a back-end datacenter and front-end network perimeter is less clear. Storage resources are potentially becoming exposed to unauthorized users inside and outside the enterprise. In addition, as the plethora of compliance regulations continues to expand and become more complicated, IT managers are faced with addressing the threat of security breaches from both within and outside the organization. Complex international regulations require a greater focus on protecting not only the network but the data itself. This chapter describes best practices for enhancing and applying security of SANs.

2. CONTENTS

Chapter 62

Storage Area Networking Security Devices

Robert Rounsavall

Trapezoid, Inc., Miami, FL, United States

1. WHAT IS STORAGE AREA NETWORKING (SAN)?

The Storage Network Industry Association (SNIA)[1] defines Storage Area Networking (SAN) as a data storage system consisting of various storage elements, storage devices, computer systems, and/or appliances, plus all the control software, all communicating in efficient harmony over a network. Put in simple terms, a SAN is a specialized high-speed network attaching servers and storage devices, and for this reason it is sometimes referred to as "the network behind the servers." A SAN allows "any-to-any" connections across the network, using interconnected elements such as routers, gateways, switches, and directors. It eliminates the traditional dedicated connection between a server and storage as well as the concept that the server effectively "owns and manages" the storage devices. It also eliminates any restriction to the amount of data that a server can access, currently limited by the number of storage devices attached to the individual server. Instead, a SAN introduces the flexibility of networking to enable one server or many heterogeneous servers to share a common storage utility, which may comprise many storage devices including standard disk drives and flash storage. Additionally, the storage utility may be located far from the servers that use it.

The SAN can be viewed as an extension to the storage bus concept, which enables storage devices and servers to be interconnected using similar elements to those used in local area networks (LANs) and wide area networks (WANs). SANs can be interconnected with routers, hubs, switches, directors, and gateways. A SAN can also be shared between servers and/or dedicated to one server. It can be local or extended over geographical distances.

2. STORAGE AREA NETWORKING (SAN) DEPLOYMENT JUSTIFICATIONS

Perhaps a main reason SANs have emerged as the leading advanced storage option is because they can often alleviate many if not all of the data storage "pain points" of Information Technology (IT) managers. For quite some time, IT managers have been in a predicament in which some servers such as database servers, run out of hard disk space rather quickly, whereas other servers, such as application servers, tend not to need a whole lot of disk space and usually have storage to spare. When a SAN is implemented, the storage can be spread throughout servers on an as-needed basis. The following are further justifications and benefits for implementing a storage area network:

- They allow for more manageable, scalable, and efficient deployment of mission critical data.
- SAN designs can protect resource investments from unexpected turns in the economic environment and changes in market adoption of new technology.
- SANs help with the difficulty of managing large disparate islands of storage from multiple physical and virtual locations.
- SANs reduce the complexity of maintaining scheduled backups for multiple systems and difficulty in preparing for unscheduled system outages.
- The inability to share storage resources and achieve efficient levels of subsystem utilization is avoided.
- SANs help us understand how to implement the plethora of storage technology alternatives, including

1. Storage Network Industry Association, http://www.snia.org/.

Computer and Information Security Handbook. http://dx.doi.org/10.1016/B978-0-12-803843-7.00062-4

appropriate deployment of Fiber Channel (FC) as well Internet small computer systems interface (iSCSI), Fiber Channel over IP (FCIP) and Infiniband.

- SANs allow us to work with restricted budgets and increasing costs of deploying and maintaining them, despite decreasing prices for physical storage in terms of average street price per terabyte.

In addition to all these benefits, the true advantage of implementing a SAN is that it enables the management of huge quantities of email and other business critical data such as that created by many enterprise applications, such as customer relationship management (CRM), enterprise resource planning (ERP), and others. The popularity of these enterprise applications, regulatory compliance, and other audit requirements have resulted in an explosion of information and data that have become the lifeblood of these organizations, greatly elevating the importance of a sound data storage strategy. Selecting a unified architecture that integrates the appropriate technologies to meet user requirements across a range of applications is central to ensuring storage support for mission-critical applications. Then matching technologies to user requirements allows for optimized storage architecture, providing the best use of capital and IT resources.

3. THE CRITICAL REASONS FOR STORAGE AREA NETWORKING (SAN) SECURITY

SAN security is important because there is more concentrated, centralized, high-value data at risk than in normal distributed servers with built-in, smaller-scale storage solutions. On a SAN you have data from multiple devices and multiple parts of the network shared on one platform. This typically fast-growing data can be consolidated and centralized from locations all over the world. SANS also store more than just data; with the large-scale adoption of server virtualization, multiple operating system (OS) images and the data they create are being retrieved from and enabled by SANs.

Why Is Storage Area Networking (SAN) Security Important?

Some large-scale security losses have occurred by intercepting information incrementally over time, but many breaches involve access or loss of data from the corporate SAN. A wide range of adversaries can attack an organization simply to access its SAN, which is where all the company data rests. Common adversaries who will be looking to access the organization's main data store are:

- Financially motivated attackers and competitors
- Identity thieves

- Criminal gangs
- State-sponsored attackers
- Internal employees
- Curious business partners

If one or some of these perpetrators were to be successful in stealing or compromising the data in the SAN, and if it was publicly disclosed that your customer data had been compromised, it could directly impact your organization monetarily and cause significant losses in terms of:

- Reputation
- Time lost
- Forensics investigations
- Overtime for IT
- Business litigation
- Perhaps even a loss of competitive edge—for example, if the organization's proprietary manufacturing process is found in the wild.

4. STORAGE AREA NETWORKING (SAN) ARCHITECTURE AND COMPONENTS

In its simplest form, a SAN is a number of servers attached to a storage array using a switch. Fig. 62.1 is a diagram of the major components of a SAN.

Storage Area Networking (SAN) Switches

Specialized switches called SAN switches are at the heart of a typical SAN. Switches provide capabilities to match the number of host SAN connections to the number of connections provided by the storage array. Switches also provide path redundancy in the event of a path failure from host server to switch or to switch or from storage array to switch. SAN switches can connect both servers and storage devices and thus provide the connection points for the fabric of the SAN. Sometimes modular switches are interconnected to create a fault-tolerant fabric. For larger SAN fabrics, director-class switches provide a larger port capacity (64−128 ports per switch) and built-in fault tolerance. The type of SAN switch, its design features, and its port capacity all contribute to its overall capacity, performance, and fault tolerance. The number of switches, types of switches, and manner in which the switches are interconnected define the topology of the fabric.

Network Attached Storage (NAS)

Network attached storage (NAS) is file-level data storage providing data access to many different network clients. The Business Continuity Planning (BCP) defined in this category address the security associated with file-level storage systems/ecosystems. They cover the Network File System (NFS), which is often used by Unix and

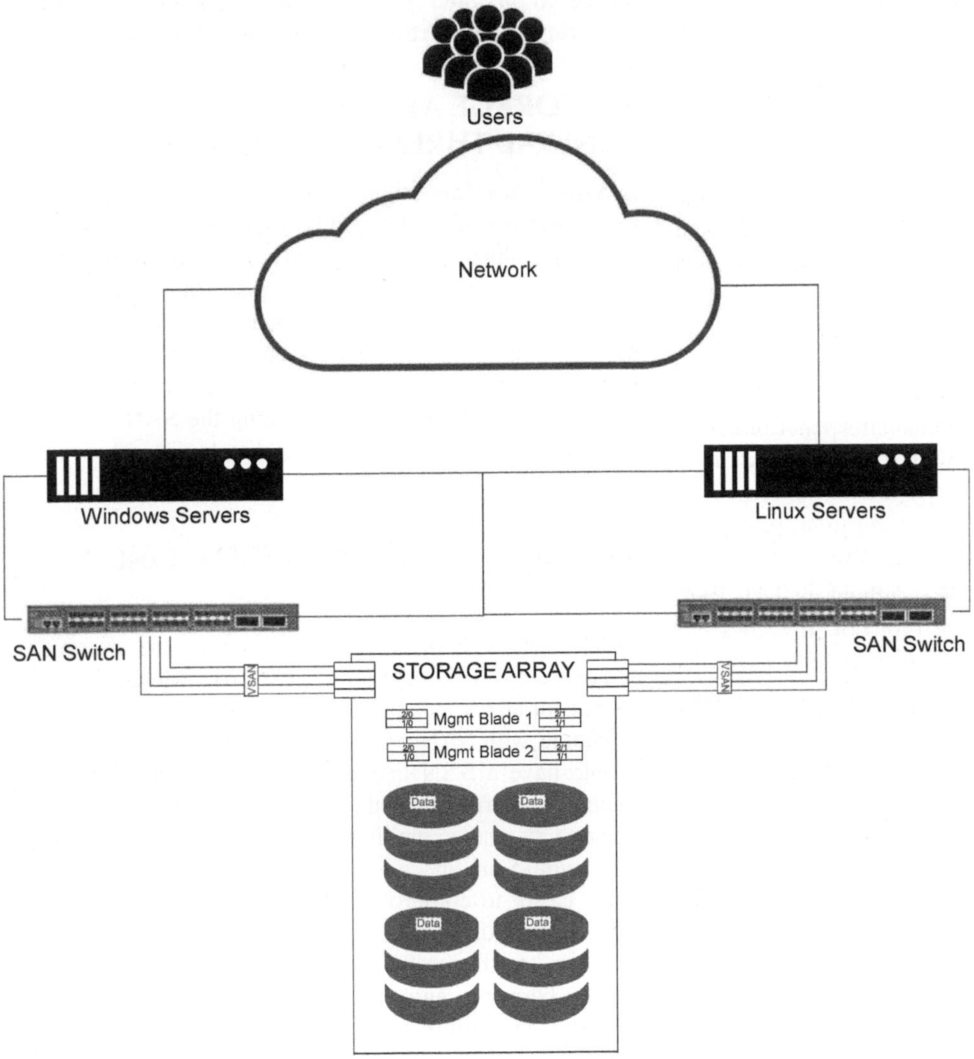

FIGURE   62.1 Storage   Area
Networking (SAN) diagram.

Linux (and their derivatives) clients as well as SMB/CIFS
which is frequently used by Windows clients.

Fabric

When one or more SAN switches are connected, a fabric is
created. The fabric is the actual network portion of the
SAN. Special communications protocols such as FC,
iSCSI, and Fiber Channel over Ethernet (FCoE) are used to
communicate over the entire network. Multiple fabrics may
be interconnected in a single SAN, and even for a simple
SAN it is not unusual for it to be composed of two fabrics
for redundancy.

HBA and Controllers

Host servers and storage systems are connected to the SAN
fabric through ports in the fabric. A host connects to a
fabric port through a Host Bus Adapter (HBA) and the
storage devices connect to fabric ports through their controllers. Each server may host numerous applications that
require dedicated storage for applications processing.
Servers need not be homogeneous within the SAN
environment.

Protocols, Storage Formats, and Communications

The following protocols and file systems are other important components of a SAN:

- Block-Based IP Storage (IP)
- Secure iSCSI
- Secure FCIP
- Fiber Channel Storage (FCS)
- Secure FCP

- Secure FC Storage Networks
- SMB/CIFS
- NFS
- Online Fixed Content

Block-Based IP Storage (IP)

Block-based IP storage is implemented using protocols such as iSCSI, Internet Fiber Channel Protocol (iFCP), and FCIP. The protocols are used to transmit SCSI commands over IP networks.

Secure iSCSI

Internet SCSI or iSCSI, which is described in IETF RFC 3720, is a connection-oriented command/response protocol. The protocol runs over TCP and is used to access disk, tape, and other devices.

Secure FCIP

Fiber Channel over TCP/IP (FCIP), defined in IETF RFC 3821, is a pure FC encapsulation protocol. It allows the interconnections of islands of FC storage area networks through IP-based networks to form a unified storage area network.

Fiber Channel Storage (FCS)

FC is a gigabit-speed network technology. It is used for block-based storage. The Fiber Channel Protocol (FCP) is the interface protocol used to transmit SCSI on this network technology.

Secure FCP

FC entities (host bus adapters or HBAs, switches, and storage) can contribute to the overall secure posture of a storage network. This contribution is done by employing mechanisms such as filtering and authentication.

Secure Fiber Channel Storage Networks

A SAN is architected to attach remote computer storage devices (such as disk arrays, tape libraries, and optical jukeboxes) to servers in such a way that, to the OS, the devices appear as though they're locally attached. These SANs are often based on a FC fabric topology that uses FCP.

SMB/CIFS

SMB/CIFS is a network protocol. Its most common use is sharing files, especially in Microsoft OS environments.

Network File System (NFS)

NFS is a client/server application, communicating with a remote procedure call (RPC) based protocol. It enables file systems physically residing on one computer system or NAS

device to be used by other computers in the network, appearing to users on the remote host as just another local disk.

5. STORAGE AREA NETWORKING (SAN) GENERAL THREATS AND ISSUES

A SAN is a prime target of all attackers due to the gold mine of information that can be attained by accessing it. A threat is defined as any potential danger to information or systems. These are the same threats that exist in any network and they are also applicable to a storage network because Windows and Unix servers are used to access and manage the SAN. For this reason, it is important to take a defense-in-depth approach to securing the SAN.

This section covers the general threats and issues related to SANs.

Storage Area Networking (SAN) Cost: A Deterrent to Attackers

Unlike many network components such as servers, routers, and switches, SANs are quite expensive, which does raise the bar for attackers a little bit. There are not huge numbers of people with SAN protocol expertise, and not too many people have a SAN in their home lab, unless they are a foreign government that has dedicated resources to researching and exploiting these types of vulnerabilities. Why would anyone go to the trouble when it would be much easier to compromise the machines of these people who manage the SANs or the servers that are themselves connected to the SAN?

The barrier to entry to directly attack the SAN is high; however, the ability to attack the management tools and administrators who access the SAN is not. Most are administered via web interfaces, software applications, or command-line interfaces. An attacker simply has to gain root or administrator access on those machines to be able to attack the SAN.

Physical Level Threats, Issues, and Risk Mitigation

There can be many physical risks involved in using a SAN. It is important to take them into consideration when planning and investing in a storage area network:

- Locate the SAN in a secure datacenter
- Ensure that proper access controls are in place
- Cabinets come with locks; use them
- Periodically audit the access control list
- Verify whether former employees can access the location where the SAN is located
- Perform physical penetration and social engineering tests on a regular basis

Physical Environment

The SAN must be located in an area with proper ventilation and cooling. Ensure that your datacenter has proper cooling and verify any service-level agreements with a third-party provider with regard to power and cooling.

Hardware Failure Considerations

Ensure that the SAN is designed and constructed in such a way that if a piece of hardware fails, it does not cause an outage. Schedule failover testing on a regular basis during maintenance windows.

Secure Sensitive Data on Removable Media to Protect "Externalized Data"

Many of the data breaches that fill the newspapers and create significant embarrassments for organizations are easily preventable and involve loss of externalized data such as backup media. To follow are some ideas to avoid unauthorized disclosure while data is in transit:

- Offsite backup tapes of sensitive or regulated data should be encrypted as a general practice and must be encrypted when leaving the direct control of the organization; encryption keys must be stored separately from data.
- Use only secure and bonded shippers if not encrypted. (Remember that duty-of-care contractual provisions often contain a limitation of liability limited to the bond value. The risk transfer value is often less than the data value).
- Secure sensitive data transferred between datacenters.
- Sensitive/regulated data transferred to and from remote datacenters must be encrypted in flight.
- Secure sensitive data in third-party datacenters.
- Sensitive/regulated data stored in third-party datacenters must be encrypted prior to arrival (both in-flight and at-rest).
- Secure your data being used by eDiscovery tools.

Know Thy Network (or Storage Network)

It is not only a best practice but critical that the SAN is well documented. All assets must be known. All physical and logical interfaces must be known. Create detailed physical and logical diagrams of the SAN. Identify all interfaces on the SAN gear. Many times, people overlook the network interfaces for the out-of-band management. Some vendors put a sticker with login and password physically on the server for the out-of-band management ports. Ensure that these are changed. Know what networks can access the SAN and from where. Verify all entry and exit points for data, especially sensitive data such as financial information or Personally Identifiable Information (PII). If an auditor

asks, it should be simple to point to exactly where that data rests and where it goes on the network.

Use Best Practices For Disaster Recovery And Backup

Guidelines such as the NIST Special Publication 800-34[2] outline best practices for disaster recovery and backup. The seven steps for contingency planning are outlined below:

1. *Develop the contingency planning policy statement.* A formal department or agency policy provides the authority and guidance necessary to develop an effective contingency plan.
2. *Conduct the business impact analysis (BIA).* The BIA helps identify and prioritize the critical IT systems and components. A template for developing the BIA is also provided to assist the user.
3. *Identify preventive controls.* Measures taken to reduce the effects of system disruptions can increase system availability and reduce contingency life-cycle costs.
4. *Develop recovery strategies.* Thorough recover strategies ensure that the system may be recovered quickly and effectively following a disruption.
5. *Develop and IT contingency plan.* The contingency plan should contain detailed guidance and procedures for restoring a damaged system.
6. *Plan testing, training, and exercises.* Testing the plan identifies planning gaps, whereas training prepares recovery personnel for plan activation; both activities improve plan effectiveness and overall agency preparedness.
7. *Plan maintenance.* The plan should be a living document that is updated regularly to remain current with system enhancements.

Logical Level Threats, Vulnerabilities, and Risk Mitigation

Aside from the physical risks and issues with SANs, there are also many logical threats. Some of the threats that face a SAN are as follows:

- *Internal threats (malicious).* A malicious employee could access the sensitive data in a SAN via management interface or poorly secured servers.
- *Internal threats (nonmalicious).* Not following proper procedure such as using change management could bring down a SAN. A misconfiguration could bring down a SAN. Poor planning for growth could limit your SAN.

2. Contingency Planning Guide for Federal Information Systems http://nvlpubs.nist.gov/nistpubs/Legacy/SP/nistspecialpublication800-34r1.pdf.

- *Outside threats.* An attacker could access your SAN data or management interface by compromising a management server, a workstation, or laptop owned by an engineer, or other server that has access to the SAN.

The following section of the chapter deals with protecting against these threats.

Begin With a Security Policy

Having a corporate information security policy is essential. Companies should already have such policies, and they should be periodically reviewed and updated. If organizations process credit cards for payment and are subject to the Payment Card Industry (PCI)[3] standards, they are mandated to have a security policy. Federal agencies subject to certification and accreditation under guidelines such as the Federal Information Security Management Act (FISMA)[4] must also have security policies.

Is storage covered in the corporate security policy? Some considerations for storage security policies include the following:

- Identification and classification of sensitive data such as PII, financial, trade secrets, and business critical data
- Data retention, destruction, deduplication, and sanitization
- User access and authentication

Instrument the Network With Security Tools

Many of the network security instrumentation devices such as IDS/IPS have become a commodity, required for compliance and a minimum baseline for any IT network. The problem with many of those tools is that they are signature based and only provide alerts and packet captures on the offending packet alerts. Adding tools such as full packet capture and network anomaly detection systems can allow a corporation to see attacks that are not yet known. They can also find attacks that bypass the IDS/IPSs and help prove to customers and government regulators whether or not the valuable data was actually stolen from the network.

Intrusion Detection and Prevention Systems (IDS/IPS)

Intrusion detection and prevention systems can detect and block attacks on a network. Intrusion prevention systems are usually inline and can block attacks. A few warnings about IPS devices:

- Their number-one goal is to not bring down the network.
- Their number-two goal is to not block legitimate traffic.

Time after time, attacks can slip by these systems. They will block low-hanging fruit, but a sophisticated attacker can trivially bypass IDS/IPS devices. Commercial tools include Palo Alto Networks, Cisco Sourcefire, and Fortinet. Open-source tools include Snort and Bro.

Network Traffic Pattern Behavior Analysis

Intrusion detection systems and vulnerability scanning systems are only able to detect well-known vulnerabilities. A majority of enterprises have these systems as well as log aggregation systems but are unable to detect zero-day threats and other previously compromised machines. One answer to help solve this problem is NetFlow[5] data. NetFlow data shows all connections into and out of the network. There are commercial and open-source tools. Commercial tools include Arbor Networks[6] and Cisco Cyber Threat Defense Solution[7] (Formerly Lancope). Open source tools include NFDUMP[8] and ARGUS.[9]

Full Network Traffic Capture and Replay

Full packet capture tools allow security engineers to record and play back all the traffic on the network. This allows for validation of IDS/IPS alerts and validation of items that NetFlow or log data is showing. Commercial tools include Niksun[10], RSA Security Analytics[11] (Formerly NetWitness), and NetScout. Open-source tools include Wireshark,[12] which is a GUI-based tool, and TCPDUMP, which is a command-line interface-based tool.

Secure Network and Management Tools

It is important to secure the network and management tools. If physical separation is not possible, then at a very minimum, logical separation must occur. For example:

- Separate the management network with a firewall.
- Ensure user space and management interfaces are on different subnets/VLANs.

3. Payment Card Industry Security Standards Council, https://www.pcisecuritystandards.org/pci_security/.
4. Federal Information Security Management Act, http://csrc.nist.gov/groups/SMA/fisma/overview.html.
5. Cisco Systems NetFlow Version nine RFC, https://www.ietf.org/rfc/rfc3954.txt.
6. Arbor Networks, https://www.arbornetworks.com/.
7. Cisco Cyber Threat Defense Solution, http://www.cisco.com/c/en/us/solutions/collateral/enterprise-networks/threat-defense/data_sheet_c78-700868.html.
8. NFDUMP tool set, http://nfdump.sourceforge.net/.
9. Argus NetFlow Tool, http://qosient.com/argus/.
10. Niksun Full Packet Capture, https://www.niksun.com/.
11. RSA Security Analytics, https://www.rsa.com/en-us/products-services/security-operations/security-analytics.
12. Wireshark Packet Capture Tool, https://www.wireshark.org/.

- Use strong communication protocols such as SSH, SSL, and VPNs to connect to and communicate with the management interfaces.
- Have a local technician or datacenter operators connect the line only when remote dial in access is needed, and then disconnect when done.
- Log all external maintenance access.

Restrict Remote Support

Best practice is to not allow remote support; however, many SANs have a "call home" feature that allows them to call back to the manufacturer for support. Managed network and security services are commonplace. If remote access for vendors is mandatory, take extreme care. Here are some things that can help make access to the SAN safe:

- Disable the remote "call home" feature in a SAN until needed.
- Do not open a port in the firewall and give direct external access to the SAN management station.
- If outsourcing management of a device, ensure that there is a VPN set up and verify that the data is transmitted encrypted.
- On mission critical systems, do not allow external connections. Have internal engineers connect to the systems and use a tool such as WebEx or GoToMeeting to allow the vendor to view while the trusted engineer controls the mouse and keyboard.

Attempt to Minimize User Error

It is not uncommon for a misconfiguration to cause a major outage. Not following proper procedure can cause major problems. Not all compromises are due to malicious behaviors; some may be due to mistakes made by trusted personnel.

Establish Proper Patch Management Procedures

Corporations today are struggling to keep up with all the vulnerabilities and patches for all the platforms they manage. With all the different technologies and OSs it can be a daunting task. Mission-critical storage management gear and network gear cannot be patched on a whim whenever the administrator feels like it. There are websites dedicated to patch management software. Microsoft Windows Software Update Services (WSUS) is a free tool that only works with Windows. Other commercial tools can assist with cross-platform patch management deployment and automation:

- Schedule updates.
- Live within the change window.
- Establish a rollback procedure.

- Test patches in a lab if at all possible. Use virtual servers if possible to save cost.
- Purchase identical lab gear if possible. Many vendor sell "nonproduction" lab gear at more than a 50% discount. This allows for test scenarios and patching in a nonproduction environment without rolling into production.
- After applying patches or firmware, validate to make sure that the equipment was actually correctly updated.

Use Configuration Management Tools

Many large organizations have invested large amounts of money in network and software configuration management tools to manage hundreds or thousands of devices around the network. These tools store network devices and software configurations in a database format and allow for robust configuration management capabilities. A commercial example is HP's Network Management Solution,[13] and Puppet Labs[14] has both open source and commercial offerings for network and configuration management automation.

Set Baseline Configurations

If a commercial tool is not available, there are still steps that can be taken. Use templates such as the ones provided by the Center for Internet Security (CIS). They offer security templates for multiple OSs, software packages and network devices. They are free of charge and can be modified to fit the needs of the organization. For example:

- Create a base configuration for all production devices.
- Check with the vendor to see if they have baseline security guides. Many of them do internally and will provide them on request.
- Audit the baseline configuration.
- Script and automate as much as possible.

Center for Internet Security

The CIS[15] is a not-for-profit organization that helps enterprises reduce the risk of business and ecommerce disruptions resulting from inadequate technical security controls and provides enterprises with resources for measuring information security status and making rational security investment decisions.

---

13. HP Network Management Solution, http://www8.hp.com/us/en/software-solutions/network-management/index.html.
14. Puppet Labs commercial and open source tools, https://puppet.com/product/open-source-projects.
15. Center for Internet Security (CIS), https://www.cisecurity.org/.

Vulnerability Scanning

PCI and other compliance frameworks requirements include both internal and external vulnerability scanning. An area that is commonly overlooked when performing vulnerability scans is the proprietary devices and appliances that manage the SAN and network. Many of these have web interfaces and run web applications on board. The following are vulnerability scanning considerations:

- Use the Change Management/Change Control process to schedule the scans. Even trained security professionals who are good at not causing network problems sometimes cause network problems.
- Know exactly what will be scanned.
- Perform both internal and external vulnerability scans.
- Scan the web application and appliances that manage the SAN and the network.
- Use more than one tool to scan.
- Document results and define metrics to know whether vulnerabilities are increasing or decreasing.
- Set up a scanning routine and scan regularly with updated tools.

System Hardening

System hardening is an important part of SAN security. Hardening includes all the SAN devices and any machines that connect to it as well as management tools. There are multiple organizations that provide hardening guides for free that can be used as a baseline and modified to fit the needs of the organization:

- Do not use shared accounts. If all engineers use the same account, there is no way to determine who logged in and when.
- Remove manufacturers' default passwords.
- If supported, use central authentication such as RADIUS.
- Use the principle of least privilege. Do not give all users on the device administrative credentials unless they absolutely need them. A user just working on storage does not need the ability to reconfigure the SAN switch.

Management Tools

There have been instances of management applications with vulnerabilities that the vendor refuses to fix or denies that they are vulnerabilities. They usually surface after a vulnerability scan or penetration test. When vulnerabilities are found, there are steps that can be taken to mitigate the risk:

- Contact the vendor regardless. The vendor needs to know that there are vulnerabilities and they should correct them.

- Verify if they have a hardening guide or any steps that can be taken to mitigate the risk.
- Physically or logically segregate the tools and apply strict access control lists or firewall rules.
- Place it behind an intrusion prevention device.
- Place behind a web application firewall, if a web application.
- Audit and log access very closely.
- Set up alerts for logins that occur outside normal hours.
- Use strong authentication if available.
- Review the logs.

Separate Areas of the Storage Area Networking (SAN)

In the world of security, a defense-in-depth strategy is often employed with an objective of aligning the security measures with the risks involved. This means that there must be security controls implemented at each layer that may create an exposure to the SAN system. Most organizations are motivated to protect sensitive (and business/mission critical) data, which typically represents a small fraction of the total data. This narrow focus on the most important data can be leveraged as the starting point for data classification and a way to prioritize protection activities. The best way to be sure that there is a layered approach to security is to address each aspect of a SAN one by one and determine the best strategy to implement physical, logical, and virtual access controls.

Physical

Segregating the production of some systems from other system classes is crucial to proper data classification and security. For example, if it is possible to physically segregate the quality assurance data from the research and development data, there is a smaller likelihood of data leakage between departments and therefore out to the rest of the world. Physical separation can typically be done at the storage, network, and compute layers by reconfiguring the SAN. Prior to the reconfiguration, all departments or groups of data would reside in the same storage area with the same access. After reconfiguration, each group would have their data only on specified disks within the storage area network. The data would only be accessible by certain compute servers, and the data would only travel over specific network cables on the SAN. Examples follow.

Storage Reconfiguration

Storage area network segmentation can be achieved by assigning separate physical disks to a department or "tenant." Fig. 62.2 depicts a SAN prior to physical disk reconfiguration.

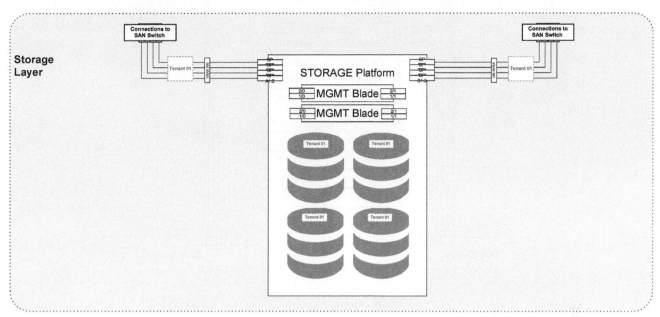

FIGURE 62.2 Pre-reconfiguration.

After reconfiguration, separate disks are assigned to separate departments or tenants. There are some tradeoffs in usable storage; however, the ability to isolate data down to the department can significantly increase the security of the data. Fig. 62.3 depicts a SAN after reconfiguration: Different disks are assigned to each department.

Compute Layer Segmentation

Typically all the compute servers or blades in a chassis such as the Cisco Unified Computing System that connect

to a SAN are assigned to one department or "tenant". The following diagrams depict the before (see Fig. 62.4) and after (see Fig. 62.5) of segmenting the compute servers or blades so that different servers are assigned to different departments or tenants.

Network Reconfiguration

Along with storage and compute reconfiguration, at times it is possible to reconfigure the network components so that data from one department or tenant only travels over the

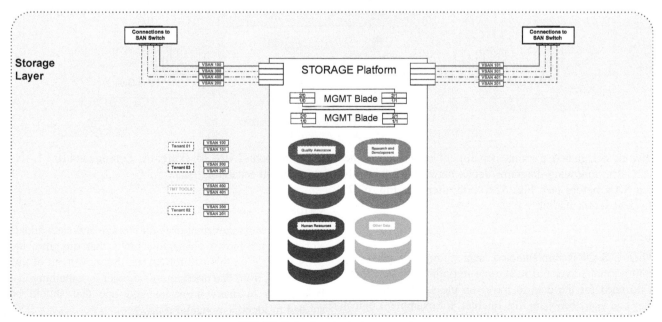

FIGURE 62.3 Postphysical segmentation.

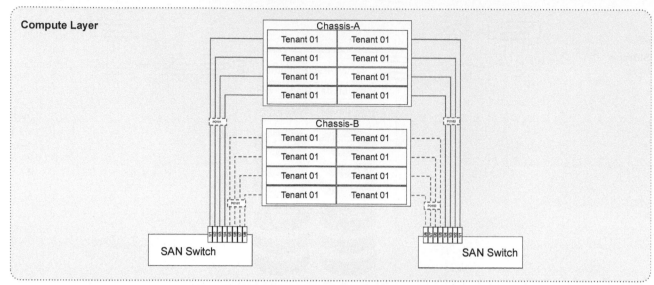

FIGURE 62.4 Precompute segmentation.

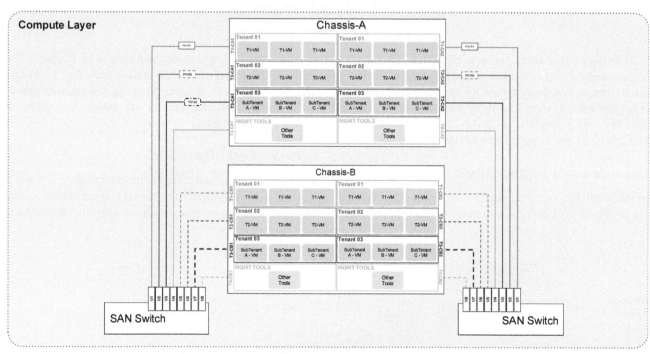

FIGURE 62.5 Postcompute segmentation.

network designated for that department or tenant on the SAN. The following diagrams depict network components of a SAN before (see Fig. 62.6) and after (see Fig. 62.7) physical segmentation.

Logical

When a SAN is implemented, segregating storage traffic from normal server traffic is quite important because there is no need for the data to travel on the same switches as your end users browsing the Internet, for example. Logical

Unit Numbers (LUN) Masking, FC Zoning, and IP VLANs can assist in separating data.

Virtual

One of the most prevalent uses for storage area networks is storing of full-blown virtual machines that run from the SAN itself. With this use for SANs, the movement of virtual servers from one data store to another is something that is required in many scenarios and one that should be studied to identify potential risks.

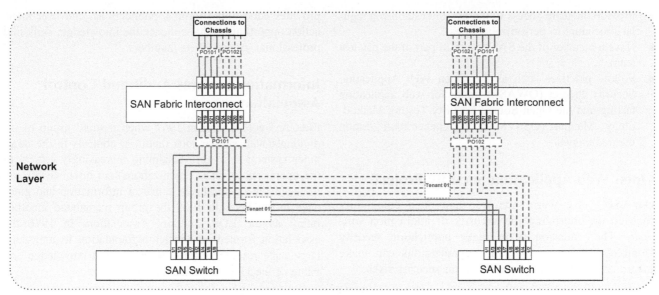

FIGURE 62.6 Prenetwork segmentation.

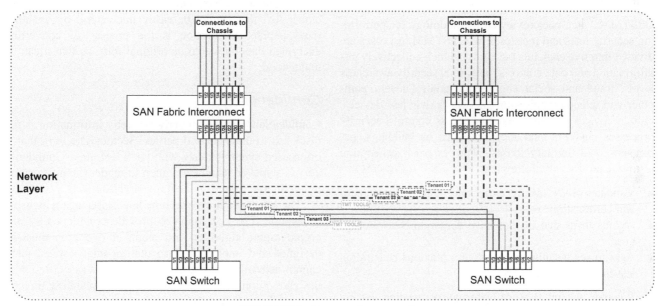

FIGURE 62.7 Postnetwork segmentation.

Penetration Testing

Penetration testing, like vulnerability scanning, has become a regulatory requirement. Now corporations can be heavily fined for losing data and not complying with these regulations. Penetration testing the SAN may be difficult due to the high cost of entry, as noted earlier. Most people don't have a SAN in their lab to practice pen testing.

Environments with custom applications and devices can be sensitive to heavy scans and attacks. Inexperienced people could inadvertently bring down critical systems. The security engineers who have experience working in these environments choose tools depending on the environment.

They also tread lightly so that critical systems are not brought down. Boutique security firms might not have capital available to purchase a SAN so that their professional services personnel can do penetration tests on SANs. With the lack of skilled SAN technicians currently in the field, it is not likely that SAN engineers will be rapidly moving into the security arena. Depending on the size of the organization, there are things that can be done to facilitate penetration testing successfully. An internal penetration testing team does the following:

- Have personnel cross-train and certify on the SAN platform in use.

- Provide the team access to the lab and establish a regular procedure to perform a pen test.
- Have a member of the SAN group as part of the pen test team.
- Follow practices such as the Open Web Application Security Project (OWASP) guide for web application testing and the Open Source Security Testing Methodology Manual (OSSTMM) for penetration testing methodologies.

Open Web Application Security Project

OWASP[16] is a worldwide free and open community focused on improving the security of application software. Their mission is to make application security "visible" so that people and organizations can make informed decisions about application security risks.

Open Source Security Testing Methodology Manual

OSSTMM[17] is a peer reviewed methodology for performing security tests and metrics. The OSSTMM test cases are divided into five channels (sections), which collectively test information and data controls, personnel security awareness levels, fraud and social engineering control levels, computer and telecommunications networks, wireless devices, mobile devices, physical security access controls, security processes, and physical locations such as buildings, perimeters, and military bases. The external penetration testing team does the following:

- Validates SAN testing experience through references and certification.
- Avoids firms that do not have access to SAN storage gear.
- Asks to see a sanitized report of a previous penetration test that included a SAN.

Whether an internal or external penetration testing group, it is a good idea to belong to one of the professional security associations in the area, such as the Information Systems Security Association (ISSA) or Information Systems Audit and Control Association (ISACA).

Information Systems Security Association

ISSA[18] is a not-for-profit, international organization of information security professionals and practitioners. It provides educational forums, publications, and peer interaction opportunities that enhance the knowledge, skill, and professional growth of its members.

Information Systems Audit and Control Association

ISACA[19] got its start in 1967 when a small group of individuals with similar jobs (auditing controls in the computer systems that were becoming increasingly critical to the operations of their organizations) sat down to discuss the need for a centralized source of information and guidance in the field. In 1969 the group formalized incorporating as the EDP Auditors Association. In 1976 the association formed an education foundation to undertake large-scale research efforts to expand the knowledge and value of the IT governance and control field.

Encryption

Encryption is the conversion of data into a form called cipher text that cannot be easily understood by unauthorized people. Decryption is the process of converting encrypted data back into its original form so that it can be understood.

Confidentiality

Confidentiality is the property whereby information is not disclosed to unauthorized parties. Secrecy is a term that is often used synonymously with confidentiality. Confidentiality is achieved using encryption to render the information unintelligible except by authorized entities.

The information may become intelligible again by using decryption. For encryption to provide confidentiality, the cryptographic algorithm and mode of operation must be designed and implemented so that an unauthorized party cannot determine the secret or private keys associated with the encryption or be able to derive the plaintext directly without deriving any keys.

Data encryption can save a company time, money, and embarrassment. There are countless examples of lost and stolen media, especially hard drives and tape drives. A misplacement or theft can cause major headaches for an organization. Take, for example, the University of Miami[20]:

> *A private offsite storage company used by the University of Miami has notified the university and a container and carrying Computer back-up tapes as patient information was stolen. The tapes were in a transport case that was*

16. Open Web Application Security Project, https://www.owasp.org/index.php/Main_Page.
17. Open Source Security Testing Methodology Manual, http://www.isecom.org/research/.
18. Information Systems Security Association, http://www.issa.org/.

19. Information Systems Audit and Control Association, https://www.isaca.org/Pages/default.aspx.
20. Data Loss Notification from the University of Miami, http://www6.miami.edu/dataincident/index.htm.

stolen from a vehicle contracted by the storage company on March 17 in downtown Coral Gables, the company reported. Law enforcement is investigating the incident as one of a series of petty thefts in the area.

Shortly after learning of the incident, the university determined it would be unlikely that a thief would be able to access the backup tapes because of the complex and proprietary format in which they were written. Even so, the university engaged leading computer security experts at Terremark Worldwide to independently ascertain the feasibility of accessing and extracting data from a similar set of backup tapes.

Anyone who has been a patient of a University of Miami physician or visited a UM facility since January 1, 1999 is likely included on the tapes. The data included names, addresses, social security numbers, or health information. The university will be notifying by mail the 47,000 patients whose data may have included credit card or other financial information regarding bill payment.

Even though it was unlikely that the person who stole the tapes had access to the data or could read the data, the university still had to notify 47,000 people that their data may have been compromised. Had the drives been encrypted, they would not have been in the news at all and no one would have had to worry about personal data being compromised.

Deciding What to Encrypt

Deciding what type of data to encrypt (see checklist, "An Agenda for Action for the Encryption of Data") and how best to do it can be a challenge. It depends on the type of data that is stored on the SAN. Encrypt backup tapes as well.

An Agenda for Action for the Encryption of Data

There are two main types of encryption to focus on: data in transit and data at rest. SNIA put out a white paper called Encryption of Data At-Rest: Step-by-Step Checklist, which outlines nine steps for encrypting data at rest[21] (Check All Tasks Completed):

_____**1.** Understand confidentiality drivers.
_____**2.** Classify the data assets.
_____**3.** Inventory data assets.
_____**4.** Perform data flow analysis.
_____**5.** Determine the appropriate points of encryption.
_____**6.** Design encryption solution.
_____**7.** Begin data realignment.
_____**8.** Implement solution.
_____**9.** Activate encryption.

21. www.snia.org/forums/ssif/knowledge_center/white_papers.

Many of the vendors implement encryption in different ways. NIST SP 800-57r4[22] Recommendation for Key Management contains best practices for key management and information about various cryptographic ciphers.

Type of Encryption to Use

The type of encryption used should contain a strong algorithm and be publicly known. Algorithms such as advanced encryption standard, Rivest, Shamir, and Adelman (RSA), and secure hash algorithm are known and tested. All the aforementioned encryption algorithms have been tested and proven to be strong if properly implemented. Organizations should be wary of vendors saying that they have their own "unknown" encryption algorithm. Many times it is just data compression or a weak algorithm that the vendor wrote by itself. Though it sounds good in theory, the thousands of mathematicians employed by the NSA spend years and loads of computer power trying to break well-known encryption algorithms.

Proving That Data Is Encrypted

A well-architected encryption plan should be transparent to the end user of the data. The only way to know for sure that the data is encrypted is to verify the data. Data at rest can be verified using forensic tools such as dd[23] for Linux or the free FTK Imager[24] from Access Data. Data in transit can be verified by network monitoring tools such as Wireshark.

Turn on event logging for any encryption hardware or software. Make sure it is logging when it turns on or off. Have a documented way to verify that the encryption was turned on while it had the sensitive data on the system.

Encryption Challenges and Other Issues

No method of defense is perfect. Human error and computer vulnerabilities do pose encryption challenges. A large financial firm had personal information on its network, including 34,000 credit cards with names and account numbers. The network administrator had left the decryption key on the server. After targeting the server for a year and a half, the attacker was able to get the decryption key and was finally able to directly query the fully encrypted database and pull out 34,000 cards.

---

22. NIST Special Publication 800-57 Part one Revision four Recommendation for Key Management, http://nvlpubs.nist.gov/nistpubs/SpecialPublications/NIST.SP.800-57pt1r4.pdf.
23. Linux man page for the "dd" command, http://man7.org/linux/man-pages/man1/dd.1.html.
24. Access Data FTK Imager download, http://accessdata.com/product-download.

Logging

Logging is an important consideration when it comes to SAN security. There are all sorts of events that can be logged. When a security incident happens, having proper log information can mean the difference between solving the problem and not knowing whether your data was compromised. NIST has an excellent guide to security log management.[25] The SANS institute has the six categories of critical log reports.[26]

There are multiple commercial vendors as well as open source projects for log management. Log management has evolved from standalone syslog server to complex architectures for Security Event/Information Management (SIEM). In addition to log data, they can take in data from IDSs, vulnerability assessment products, and many other security tools to centralize and speed up the analysis and processing of huge amounts of logs. More of a difference is being made between SIEM and audit logging. The former is geared toward looking at events of interest on which to take action; the latter is geared to compliance. In today's legal and compliance environment an auditor will ask an enterprise to immediately provide logs for a particular device for a time period such as the previous 90 days. With a solid log management infrastructure, this request becomes trivial and a powerful tool to help solve problems. NIST SP 800-92 makes the following recommendations:

- Organizations should establish policies and procedures for log management.
- Organizations should prioritize log management appropriately throughout the organization.
- Organizations should create and maintain a log management infrastructure.
- Organizations should provide proper support for all staff with log management responsibilities.
- Organizations should establish standard log management operational processes.

Policies and Procedures

To establish and maintain successful log management activities, an organization should develop standard processes for performing log management. As part of the planning process, an organization should define its logging requirements and goals.

Prioritize Log Management

After an organization defines its requirements and goals for the log management process, it should then prioritize the requirements and goals based on the organization's perceived reduction of risk and the expected time and resources needed to perform log management functions.

Create and Maintain a Log Management Infrastructure

A log management infrastructure consists of hardware, software, networks, and media used to generate, transmit, store, analyze, and dispose of log data. Log management infrastructures typically perform several functions that support the analysis of security log data.

Provide Support for Staff With Log Management Responsibilities

To ensure that log management for individual systems is performed effectively throughout the organization, the administrators of those systems should receive adequate support.

Establish a Log Management Operational Process

The major log management operational process typically includes configuring log sources, performing log analysis, initiating responses to identified events, and managing long-term storage.

What Events Should Be Logged for Storage Area Networking (SAN)?

For storage networks the same type of data should be collected as for other network devices, with focus on the storage management systems and any infrastructure that supports the SAN, such as the switches and servers. According to the SANS institute, the top six critical log reports are as follows:

- Authentication and Authorization Reports
- System and Data Change Reports
- Network Activity Reports
- Resource Access Reports
- Malware Activity Reports
- Critical Errors and Failure Reports

Authentication and Authorization Reports These reports identify successful and failed attempts to access various systems at multiple user privilege levels (authentication). This also includes specific privileged user activities and attempts to use privileged capabilities (authorization).

25. NIST SP800-92 Guide to Computer Security Log Management, http://csrc.nist.gov/publications/nistpubs/800-92/SP800-92.pdf.
26. SANS six Critical Log Reports, http://www.sans.edu/research/security-laboratory/article/6toplogs.

System and Data Change Reports These reports identify various system and critical security changes to various information system and networked assets. This also includes configuration files, accounts, regulated and sensitive data, and other components of the system or applications.

Network Activity Reports These reports identify system suspicious events and potentially dangerous network activities. This also includes activities that need to be tracked for regulatory and/or PCI compliance.

Resource Access Reports These reports identify various system, application, and database resource access patterns across the organization. It can also be used for both activity audit, trending, and incident detection.

Malware Activity Reports These reports summarize various malicious software activities. This also includes events likely related to malicious software.

Critical Errors and Failure Reports These reports summarize various significant errors and failure indications. Very often, these are with direct security significance.

Suspicious or Unauthorized Network Traffic Patterns Suspect traffic patterns can be described as unusual or unexpected traffic patterns on the local network. This not only includes traffic entering the local network but traffic leaving the network as well. This report option requires a certain level of familiarity with what is "normal" for the local network. With this in mind, administrators need to be knowledgeable of local traffic patterns to make the best use of these reports. With that said, there are some typical traffic patterns that can be considered to be highly suspect in nearly all environments.

6. SUMMARY

The financial and IT resource benefits of consolidating information onto a storage area network are compelling, and our dependence on this technology will continue to grow as our data storage needs grow exponentially. With this concentration and consolidation of critical information come security challenges and risks that must be recognized and appropriately addressed. In this chapter we covered these risks as well as the controls and processes that should be employed to protect the information stored on a SAN. Finally, we have emphasized why encryption of data at rest and in flight is a critical protection method that must be employed by the professional SAN administrator. Our intention is for you to understand all these risks to your SAN and to use the methods and controls described here to

prevent you or your company from becoming a data loss statistic.

Finally, let's move on to the real interactive part of this Chapter: review questions/exercises, hands-on projects, case projects, and optional team case project. The answers and/or solutions by chapter can be found in Appendix K.

CHAPTER REVIEW QUESTIONS/ EXERCISES

True/False

1. True or False? The Storage Network Industry Association (SNIA)[1] defines a SAN as a data storage system consisting of various storage elements, storage devices, computer systems, and/or appliances, plus some of the control software, all communicating in efficient harmony over a network.
2. True or False? Perhaps a main reason SANs have emerged as the leading storage option is because they can often alleviate many if not all the data storage "pain points" of IT managers.
3. True or False? SAN security is important because there is more concentrated, centralized, high-value data at risk than in normal distributed servers with built-in, smaller-scale storage solutions.
4. True or False? Some large-scale security gains have occurred by intercepting information incrementally over time, but the vast majority of breaches involve access or loss of data from the corporate SAN.
5. True or False? In its advanced form, a SAN is a number of servers attached to a storage array using a switch.

Multiple Choice

1. Specialized switches called _____ are at the heart of a typical SAN. Switches provide capabilities to match the number of host SAN connections to the number of connections provided by the storage array.
   A. SAN switches
   B. Location technology
   C. Promotional email
   D. Malformed request DoS
   E. Data controller
2. What is file-level data storage providing data access to many different network clients?
   A. Network attached storage (NAS)
   B. Location technology
   C. Valid
   D. Load-Based DoS
   E. Bait

3. When one or more SAN switches are connected, a _____ is created.
   A. Data minimization
   B. Fabric
   C. Target access
   D. Strong narrative
   E. Security
4. Host servers and storage systems are connected to the SAN fabric through _____ in the fabric.
   A. Call data floods
   B. Greedy strategy
   C. Ports
   D. SAN protocol
   E. Taps
5. What is a storage device that is designed to hold, manage, label, and store data to tape?
   A. Irrelevant
   B. Tape library
   C. IP storage access
   D. Configuration file
   E. Server policy

EXERCISE

Problem

What is block level access?

Hands-On Projects

Project

What is a Storage Array?

Case Projects

Problem

When should an organization use a SAN solution?

Optional Team Case Project

Problem

Does a SAN Connected server need to be located in a Data Center?

Part IX

Cloud Security

Chapter 63

Securing Cloud Computing Systems

Cem Gurkok

Terremark Worldwide, Inc., Miami, FL, United States

1. CLOUD COMPUTING ESSENTIALS: EXAMINING THE CLOUD LAYERS

Cloud computing is composed of several layers, such as public, private, hybrid, and community deployment models: SPI, or Software as a Service (SaaS), Platform as a Service (PaaS), and Infrastructure as a Service (IaaS) service models. The National Institute of Standards and Technology (NIST) Model of Cloud Computing is shown in Fig. 63.1 (Visual Model of NIST Working Definition of Cloud Computing, http://www.csrc.nist.gov/groups/SNS/cloud-computing/index.html).

Infrastructure as a service (IaaS) provides online processing, data storage capacity, or network capacity on a virtualized environment. It offers the ability to provision processing, storage, networks and other basic computing resources; allowing the customer to install and run their software, which can involve operating systems (OSs) and applications. IaaS customers buy these resources as a fully outsourced service. IaaS provides a set of application programming interfaces, which allows management and other forms of interaction with the infrastructure by consumers. Amazon, Terremark, and Rackspace are typical IaaS providers.

Platform as a service (PaaS), sits on top of IaaS. It provides an application development and deployment environment in the cloud. PaaS offers the ability to deploy applications by utilizing computer programming languages and tools available from the service provider. The service provider offers developers application building blocks to configure a new business application. This provides all of the facilities required to support the complete life cycle of building and delivering web applications and services entirely available from the Internet. Google App Engine, Microsoft Azure, Engine Yard, and Collabnet are some PaaS providers.

Software as a service (SaaS) is built on IaaS and PaaS. It serves business applications utilized by individuals or enterprise and it can also be referred to as on demand software. SaaS offers the most popular cloud applications to almost everyone that is online. Salesforce.com, Google Docs, and Microsoft Online Services are all popular consumer and enterprise-directed SaaS applications. The applications are accessible from various client devices through a thin client interface such as a web browser.

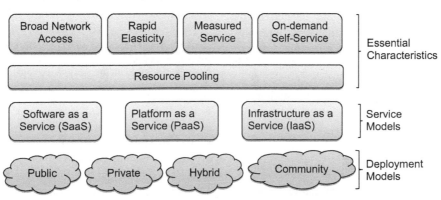

FIGURE 63.1 National Institute of Standards and Technology model of cloud computing [1].

Computer and Information Security Handbook. http://dx.doi.org/10.1016/B978-0-12-803843-7.00063-6

TABLE 63.1 Deployment Model's Responsibilities

Model/Infrastructure	Managed by	Owned by	Location	Used by
Public	External CSP	External CSP	Off-site	Untrusted
Private	Customer or external CSP	Customer or external CSP	On-site or off-site	Trusted
Hybrid	Customer and external CSP	Customer and external CSP	On-site and off-site	Trusted and untrusted

CSP, Content service provider

Analyzing Cloud Options in Depth

Table 63.1 shows us that different cloud deployment models have varying management, ownership, locations, and access levels.

Public

Public cloud is an offering from one service provider to many clients who share the cloud processing resources concurrently. Public cloud clients share applications, processing power, network resources, and data storage space. Differing levels of segregation is provided depending on the resource.

Private

A private cloud hosts one enterprise as a user. Various departments may be present in the cloud, but all are in the same enterprise. Private clouds often employ virtualization within an enterprise's existing computer servers to improve computer utilization. A private cloud also includes provisioning and metering facilities that enable fast deployment and removal where applicable. This model is similar to the conventional IT outsourcing models, but can exist as an enterprise's internal delivery model also. A variety of private cloud implementations have emerged:

- *Dedicated private cloud*: These are hosted within a customer-owned data center or at a collocation facility, and operated by internal IT departments.
- *Community private cloud*: These are located at the premises of a third party; owned, managed, and operated by a vendor who is bound by customized service level agreements (SLAs) and contractual clauses with security and compliance requirements.
- *Managed private cloud*: In this implementation, the infrastructure is owned by the customer and management is performed by a third party.

Virtual Private

A virtual private cloud is a private cloud that exists within a shared or public cloud also called the "Intercloud."

The Intercloud comprises several interconnected clouds and legacy infrastructure. Amazon Web Services provides Amazon Virtual Private Cloud, which allows the Amazon Elastic Compute Cloud service to be connected to legacy infrastructure over an IPsec virtual private network connection. Google App Engine provides similar functionality via their Secure Data Connector product.

Hybrid

A hybrid cloud is a combination of two or more of the previously mentioned deployment models. Each of the three cloud deployment models has specific advantages and disadvantages relative to the other deployment models. A hybrid cloud leverages the advantage of the other cloud models, providing a more optimal user experience. By utilizing the hybrid cloud architecture, users are able to obtain degrees of fault tolerance combined with locally immediate usability without dependency on Internet connectivity.

Establishing Cloud Security Fundamentals

Security in cloud computing, for the most part, is no different than security in a regular IT environment. However, due to the different deployment models as described above, cloud environments present different risks to an organization. European Network and Information Security Agency (ENISA) generally groups the risks into policy and organizational risks, technical risks, legal risks, and general risks and describes them as follows [2]:

Policy and Organizational Risks

Now, let's look at the following policy and organizational risks:

- Lock-in
- Loss of governance
- Compliance challenges
- Loss of business reputation due to co-tenant activities
- Cloud service termination or failure
- Cloud provider acquisition
- Supply chain failure

Lock-In

The potential dependency on a particular cloud provider, depending on the provider's commitments, may lead to a catastrophic business failure should the cloud provider go bankrupt or the content and application migration path to another provider is too costly. There is little or no incentive for cloud providers to make migrating to another provider easy if not contractually bound to do so.

Loss of Governance

By using cloud infrastructures, the client necessarily cedes control to the cloud provider on a number of issues which may affect security. This could have a potentially severe impact on the organization's strategy and therefore on the capacity to meet its mission and goals. The loss of control and governance could lead to the impossibility of complying with the security requirements, a lack of confidentiality, integrity and availability of data, and a deterioration of performance and quality of service, not to mention the introduction of compliance challenges.

Compliance Challenges

Certain companies migrating to the cloud might have the need to meet certain industry standards or regulatory requirements, such as the Payment Card Industry Data Security Standard (PCI DSS). Migrating to the cloud could compromise these business needs if the cloud provider cannot provide evidence of their own compliance to the relevant requirements or if the provider does not permit audits by the customer.

Loss of Business Reputation Due To Co-Tenant Activities

Resource sharing can give rise to problems when the shared resources' reputation becomes tainted by a bad neighbor's activities. This would also include that certain measures are taken to mitigate, such as internet protocol (IP) address blocking and equipment confiscation.

Cloud Service Termination or Failure

If the cloud provider faces the risk of going out of business due to financial, legal, or other reasons, the customer could suffer from loss or deterioration of service delivery performance, and quality of service, as well as a loss of investment.

Cloud Provider Acquisition

The acquisition of the cloud provider could increase the possibility of a strategic change and may put previous agreements at risk. This could make it impossible to comply with existing security requirements. The final impact could be damaging for crucial assets, such as the organization's reputation, customer or patient trust, and employee loyalty and experience.

Supply Chain Failure

A cloud computing provider can outsource certain specialized tasks of its infrastructure to third parties. In such a situation the level of security of the cloud provider may depend on the level of security of each one of the links and the level of dependency of the cloud provider on the third party. In general, a lack of transparency in the contract can be a problem for the whole system.

Technical Risks

Let's continue now by taking a look at the following technical risks:

- Resource exhaustion
- Resource segregation failure
- Abuse of high privilege roles
- Management interface compromise
- Intercepting data in transit, data leakage
- Insecure deletion of data
- Distributed denial of service (DDoS)
- Economic denial of service (EDoS)
- Encryption and key management (Loss of encryption keys)
- Undertaking malicious probes or scans
- Compromise of the service engine
- Customer requirements and cloud environment conflicts

Resource Exhaustion

Inaccurate modeling of customer demands by the cloud provider can lead to service unavailability, access control compromise, and economic and reputation losses due to resource exhaustion. The customer takes a level of calculated risk in allocating all the resources of a cloud service, because resources are allocated according to statistical projections.

Resource Segregation Failure

This class of risks includes the failure of mechanisms separating storage, memory, routing, and even reputation between different tenants of the shared infrastructure (guest-hopping attacks, SQL injection attacks exposing multiple customers' data, and side-channel attacks). The likelihood of this incident scenario depends on the cloud model adopted by the customer. It is less likely to occur for private cloud customers compared to public cloud customers.

Abuse of High Privilege Roles

The malicious activities of an insider could potentially have an impact on the confidentiality, integrity, and availability of all kinds of data, IP, services, and therefore indirectly on the organization's reputation, customer trust, and the experiences of employees. This can be considered especially important in the case of cloud computing due to the fact that cloud architectures necessitate certain roles, which are extremely high-risk. Examples of such roles include the cloud provider's system administrators and auditors and managed security service providers dealing with intrusion detection reports and incident response.

Management Interface Compromise

The customer management interfaces of public cloud providers are Internet accessible and mediate access to larger sets of resources (than traditional hosting providers). They also pose an increased risk especially when combined with remote access and web browser vulnerabilities.

Intercepting Data in Transit, Data Leakage

Cloud computing, being a distributed architecture, implies more data in transit than traditional infrastructures. Sniffing, spoofing, man-in-the-middle, side channel, and replay attacks should be considered as possible threat sources.

Insecure Deletion of Data

Whenever a provider is changed, resources are scaled down, physical hardware is reallocated, and data may be available beyond the lifetime specified in the security policy. Where true data wiping is required, special procedures must be followed and this may not be supported by the cloud provider.

Distributed Denial of Service

A common method of attack involves saturating the target environment with external communications requests, such that it cannot respond to legitimate traffic, or responds so slowly as to be rendered effectively unavailable. This can result in financial and economic losses.

Economic Denial of Service

EDoS destroys economic resources; the worst-case scenario would be the bankruptcy of the customer or a serious economic impact. The following scenarios are possible: An attacker can use an account and uses the customer's resources for his own gain or in order to damage the customer economically. The customer has not set effective limits on the use of paid resources and experiences unexpected loads on these resources. An attacker can use a public channel to deplete the customer's metered resources. For example, where the customer pays per HTTP request, a DDoS attack can have this effect.

Encryption and Key Management (Loss of Encryption Keys)

This risk includes the disclosure of secret keys (SSL, file encryption, customer private keys) or passwords to

malicious parties. It also includes the loss or corruption of those keys, or their unauthorized use for authentication and nonrepudiation (digital signature).

Undertaking Malicious Probes or Scans

Malicious probes or scanning, as well as network mapping, are indirect threats to the assets being considered. They can be used to collect information in the context of a hacking attempt. A possible impact could be a loss of confidentiality, integrity, and availability of service and data.

Compromise of the Service Engine

Each cloud architecture relies on a highly specialized platform and the service engine. The service engine sits above the physical hardware resources and manages customer resources at different levels of abstraction. For example, in IaaS clouds this software component can be the hypervisor. Like any other software layer, the service engine code can have vulnerabilities and is prone to attacks or unexpected failure. Cloud providers must set out a clear segregation of responsibilities that articulates the minimum actions customers must undertake.

Customer Requirements and Cloud Environment Conflicts

Cloud providers must set out a clear segregation of responsibilities that articulates the minimum actions customers must undertake. The failure of the customers to properly secure their environments may pose a vulnerability to the cloud platform if the cloud provider has not taken the necessary steps to provide isolation. Cloud providers should further articulate their isolation mechanisms and provide best practice guidelines to assist customers to secure their resources.

Legal Risks

Now, let's look at the following legal risks:

- Subpoena and eDiscovery
- Varying jurisdiction
- Data protection
- Licensing

Subpoena and eDiscovery

In the event of the confiscation of physical hardware as a result of subpoena by law-enforcement agencies or civil suits, the centralization of storage as well as shared tenancy of physical hardware means many more clients are at risk of the disclosure of their data to unwanted parties. At the same time, it may become impossible for the agency of a single nation to confiscate "a cloud" given pending advances around long-distance hypervisor migration.

Varying Jurisdiction

Customer data may be held in multiple jurisdictions, some of which may be high risk or subject to higher restrictions. Certain countries are regarded as high risk due to their unpredictable legal frameworks and disrespect of international agreements. In these cases customer data can be accessed by various parties without the customer's consent. On the other hand, other countries can have stricter privacy laws and might require that certain data cannot be stored or tracked.

Data Protection

It has to be clear that the cloud customer will be the main person responsible for the processing of personal data, even when such processing is carried out by the cloud provider in its role of external processor. While some cloud providers, such as SAE 16 compliant ones, provide information about their data processing and security activities, others are opaque about these and can cause legal problems for the customer. There may also be data security breaches which are not notified to the controller by the cloud provider. In some cases there might be customers storing illegal or illegally obtained data, which might put the cloud provider and other customers at risk.

Licensing

Licensing conditions, such as per-seat agreements, and online licensing checks may become unworkable in a cloud environment. For example, if software is charged on a per instance basis every time a new machine is instantiated then the cloud customer's licensing costs may increase exponentially even though they are using the same number of machine instances for the same duration.

General Risks

Let's continue by looking at the following general risks:

- Network failures
- Privilege escalation
- Social engineering
- Loss or compromise of operational and security logs or audit trails
- Backup loss
- Unauthorized physical access and theft of equipment
- Natural disasters

Network Failures

This risk is one of the highest risks since it directly affects service delivery. It exists due to network misconfiguration, system vulnerabilities, lack of resource isolation, and poor or untested business continuity (BC) and disaster recovery (DR) plans. Network traffic modification can also be a risk for a customer and cloud provider if provisioning isn't done properly or there are no traffic encryption or vulnerability assessments.

Privilege Escalation

Although there is a low probability of exploitation, privilege escalation can cause loss of customer data, and access control. A malicious entity can therefore take control of large portions of the cloud platform. The risk manifests itself due to authentication, authorization, and other access control vulnerabilities, hypervisor vulnerabilities (cloud-bursting), and misconfiguration.

Social Engineering

This risk is one of the most disregarded since most technical staff focus on the nonhuman aspects of their platforms. The exploitation of this risk has caused loss of reputation for cloud service providers, such as Amazon and Apple, due to the publicity of the events. This risk can be easily be minimized by security awareness training, proper user provisioning, resource isolation, data encryption, and proper physical security procedures.

Loss or Compromise of Operational and Security Logs or Audit Trails

Operational logs can be vulnerable due to lack of policy or poor procedures for logs collection. This would also include retention, access management vulnerabilities, user deprovisioning vulnerabilities, lack of forensic readiness, and OS vulnerabilities.

Backup Loss

This high impact risk affects company reputation, all backed up data, and service delivery. It also occurs due to inadequate physical security procedures, access management vulnerabilities, and user deprovisioning vulnerabilities.

Unauthorized Physical Access and Theft of Equipment

The probability of malicious actors gaining access to a physical location is very low, but in the event of such occurrence, the impact to the cloud provider and its customers is very high. It can affect company reputation, and data hosted on premises and the security risk it brings is due to inadequate physical security procedures.

Natural Disasters

This risk is often ignored but can have a high impact on the businesses involved in the event of its occurrence. If a business has a poor or untested continuity and DR plan or lacks one, their reputation, data, and service delivery can be severely compromised.

Other Cloud Security Concepts

Finally, let's look at the following other cloud security concepts:

- Incident response (IR), notification, and remediation
- Virtualization
- External accreditations

Incident Response, Notification, and Remediation

IR is a set of procedures for an investigator to examine a computer security incident. Although cloud computing brings change on many levels, certain characteristics of cloud computing bear more direct challenges to IR activities than others. The on demand self-service nature of cloud computing environments makes it hard or even impossible to receive cooperation from the cloud service provider when handling a security incident. Also the resource pooling practiced by cloud services, in addition to the rapid elasticity offered by cloud infrastructures, may dramatically complicate the IR process, especially the forensic activities carried out as part of the incident analysis. Resource pooling as practiced by cloud services causes privacy concerns for co-tenants regarding the collection and analysis of telemetry and artifacts associated with an incident (e.g., logging, netflow data, memory, machine images) without compromising the privacy of co-tenants. The cross-border nature of cloud computing might cause the IR team to run into legal and regulatory hurdles due to limitations placed on what data can be accessed and used in investigations.

Virtualization

Virtualization brings with it all the security concerns of the guest OS, along with new virtualization-specific threats. A cloud service provider and customers would need to address virtual device hardening, hypervisor security, intervirtual device attacks, performance concerns, encryption, data comingling, data destruction, virtual device image tampering, and in-motion virtual devices.

Rather than have a cloud service provider respond to numerous contract requests to ensure all risks are covered, there are a number of external accreditations that providers can obtain that will provide evidence that they have both implemented appropriate security controls and follow sound security practices. One of these is the Statement on Auditing Standards (SAS) number 70, commonly known as an SAS 70 audit, which was originally published by the American Institute of Certified Public Accountants (AICPA). In 2011, Statement on Standards for Attestation Engagements (SSAE) No. 16 went into effect and replaced SAS 70 as the guidance for performing a service auditor's examination. SSAE 16 established a new attestation standard (AT 801) to provide the professional guidance. The audit is for service organizations and is designed to ensure that the company has sufficient controls and defenses when they are hosting or processing data belonging to one of their customers. A company that has an SSAE 16 certificate has been audited by an external auditor and the control objectives and activities have been found to be acceptable per SSAE 16 requirements. When considering cloud providers, customers should also look beyond SSAE 16. In other words, the certification comes only after a lengthy and rigorous in-person audit that ensures the service provider adheres to their procedures. Cloud providers, such as Verizon, Rackspace, Microsoft Azure, and Amazon, are SSAE 16 certified.

Determining When Security Goals Require a Private Cloud

While the low cost and elastic nature of cloud computing can be beneficial for customers, due to security concerns the deployment method needs to be carefully selected. The security concerns that a potential customer needs to pay attention to are as follows:

- *Data protection (network and storage)*: Sensitive and personal data, such as medical, human resources, e-mail, government communications will traverse the cloud environment. Securing this data in transit and storage will be important from contractual, legal and regulatory perspectives.
- *Confidentiality*: Business processes and related information that are crucial to a company's survival may be utilized in a cloud environment. Any leakage of that information caused by voluntary communication by the cloud service provider or the cloud environment's security breach may jeopardize the customer's business and services.
- *Intellectual property*: It is important to determine who will own the intellectual property rights deployed in a cloud environment prior to engaging in cloud computing activities, and further determine the use that the parties can make of the objects of such rights.
- *Professional negligence*: The customer may be exposed to contractual and tortuous liability to its customers based on negligence due to functions outsourced to the cloud service provider.
- *Outsourcing services and changes in operational control*: A customer may select working with a cloud service provider due to its perceived qualities. If the cloud service provider decides to outsource these services, security concerns could arise due to the lack of information regarding the processes and their qualities that are adopted by the third parties.

A private cloud deployment model would address all of these concerns by providing an environment that is owned and managed by the customer or trusted third party, located on-premise or at a trusted location, and can only be accessible by trusted resources. Certain government entities and financial institutions prefer private cloud deployments due to the level of control and physical separation they provide. The progression of risk assumption in cloud service models is shown in Fig. 63.2.

2. SOFTWARE AS A SERVICE: MANAGING RISKS IN THE CLOUD

In SaaS environments the service levels, privacy, compliance, security controls, and their scope are negotiated into the contracts for service. Therefore, a SaaS customer has the least tactical responsibility compared to the other cloud service models for implementing and managing security solutions.

Centralizing Information With SaaS to Increase Data Security

SaaS storage is always accessed via a web-based user interface or a client/server application. Data is entered into the system via the web interface and stored within the SaaS application. SaaS may consume database systems, object and file storage, or dedicated IaaS storage volumes. Data is tagged and encrypted in the SaaS application and generally managed by the provider if natively supported. Data passes through an encryption proxy before being sent to the SaaS application. This proxy can be implemented by the customer or the cloud service provider. This single point of exit and entry provides the means to easily monitor and control data being processed. Since data will be residing in a heterogeneous environment, the provider will need to encrypt data at a customer level and use separate database instances.

Implementing and Managing User Authentication and Authorization

In a SaaS environment authentication and authorization is managed with a federated ID management solution (a.k.a. single sign on, or SSO). Federation is the use of Security

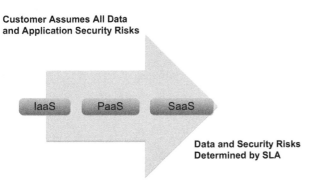

Customer Assumes All Data and Application Security Risks

IaaS   PaaS   SaaS

Data and Security Risks Determined by SLA

FIGURE 63.2   Risk assumption in cloud service models.

Assertion Markup Language (SAML) to offer portability to disparate and independent security domains with some organizations extending their Directory Service (DS) environment via a gateway product that will handle SAML assertions. Other organizations will consume native SAML assertions from an identity service. The following steps will be taken in a simplified SSO approach:

1. The user attempts to access the SaaS provider and will need to do so with some form of identifying information. For example, in the event the SaaS platform is Web based, the identifying information may be in the form of encrypted data in the URL or a cookie.
2. That information will be authenticated against the customer's user directory via a direct web service call.
3. The customer's user directory will then reply back with an assertion containing authorization and authentication information.
4. The resulting request is either fulfilled or denied based on the authentication and authorization of the assertion.

Permission and Password Protection

In a SaaS environment the provider will offer a comprehensive password protection and permissions system. Password granting and password management (including read, write, delete options) should be clear and straightforward. Passwords will be required to change periodically to random values and will be stored in an encrypted and replicated manner.

Permissions will be assignable at different levels (workgroup, folder, subfolder), depending on the data the employee needs to access and requestor's permissions will be validated with every access request as described in the authorization steps. The SaaS platform will capture event logs to track what data was accessed by whom at a given time.

Negotiating Security Requirements With Vendors

Service levels, security, governance, compliance, and liability expectations of the service and provider are contractually stipulated, managed to, and enforced when an SLA is offered to the consumer by the cloud provider. There are two types of SLAs: negotiable and nonnegotiable. When a nonnegotiable SLA is offered, the provider administers those portions stipulated in the agreement. An SLA generally comprises the parties involved, dates, scope of agreement, service hours, security, availability, reliability, support, performance metrics, and penalties.

Identifying Needed Security Measures

The security risks that were previously mentioned need to be identified and addressed by the consumer and stipulated in the SLA. Security departments should be engaged during the establishment of SLAs and contractual obligations to ensure that security requirements are contractually enforceable. SaaS providers that generate extensive customer-specific application logs and provide secure storage as well as analysis facilities will ease the burden on the customer. SLAs should cover data protection, BC and recovery, incident response, eDiscovery, data retention, and removal [3].

Establishing a Service Level Agreement

Since multiple organizations are involved, SLAs and contracts between the parties become the primary means of communicating and enforcing expectations for responsibilities. It is important to note that the SLAs must be such that the cloud provider informs customers in a timely and reliable manner to allow for agreed actions to be taken. The customer should make sure that SLA clauses are not in conflict with promises made by other clauses or clauses from other providers [3].

SLAs may carry too much business risk for a provider, given the actual risk of technical failures. From the customer's point of view, SLAs may contain clauses which turn out to be detrimental—for example, in the area of intellectual property, an SLA might specify that the cloud provider has the rights to any content stored on the cloud infrastructure.

Ensuring SLAs Meet Organizational Security Requirements

Contracts should provide for third-party review of SLA metrics and compliance (e.g., by a mutually selected mediator). The need to quantify penalties for various risk scenarios in SLAs and the possible impact of security breaches on reputation motivate more rigorous internal audit and risk assessment procedures than would otherwise exist. The frequent audits imposed on cloud providers tend to expose risks which would not otherwise have been discovered, having therefore the same positive effect.

3. PLATFORM AS A SERVICE: SECURING THE PLATFORM

A customer's administrator has limited control and accountability in a PaaS environment. With PaaS, securing the platform falls onto the provider, but both securing the applications developed against the platform and developing them securely belong to the customer. Customers need to trust the provider to offer sufficient control, while realizing that they will need to adjust their expectations for the amount of control that is reasonable within PaaS.

PaaS should provide functionality to allow customers to implement intrusion or anomaly detection and should allow the customers to send select events or alerts to the cloud provider's security monitoring platform. PaaS should provide encryption in the application, between client and application, in the database and proxies, and any API that deals with the hosted data. PaaS providers generally permit their customers to perform vulnerability assessments and penetration tests on their systems.

Restricting Network Access Through Security Groups

The segregation through security groups are illustrated in Fig. 63.3.

Firewalls are traditionally used for network separation, and when used together with network controls, a firewall can become an extra supporting layer. This is particularly helpful when multiple subnets profit from a shared service, such as a directory.

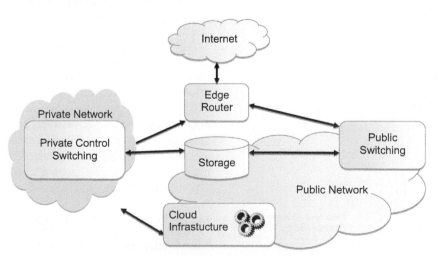

FIGURE 63.3 Segregation through security groups.

In a PaaS environment security groups (SG) can act as a firewall allowing the customer to choose which protocols and ports are open to computers over the Internet. In Amazon EC2, a security group is a set of ACCEPT firewall rules for incoming packets that can apply to TCP, UDP, or ICMP. When an instance is launched with a given SG, firewall rules from this group are activated for this instance in EC2's internal distributed firewall [4].

Configuring Platform-Specific User Access Control

The cloud service provider is responsible for handling access to the network, servers, and application platforms in the PaaS model. On the other hand, the customer is responsible for the access control of the applications that they deploy. Application access control includes user access management, such as user provisioning and authentication. Amazon identity and access management lets customer define users and their access levels, entity roles and permissions, and provides access to federated users within the customer's existing enterprise systems. An example of user access control in PaaS is shown in Fig. 63.4.

Integrating With Cloud Authentication and Authorization Systems

User access control support is not uniform across cloud providers, and offered features may differ. A PaaS provider may provide a standard API like OAuth (an open standard for authorization) to manage authentication and access control to applications. Google supports a hybrid version of an OpenID (an open, decentralized standard for user authentication and access control) and OAuth protocol that combines the authorization and authentication flow in fewer steps to enhance usability. The customer could also

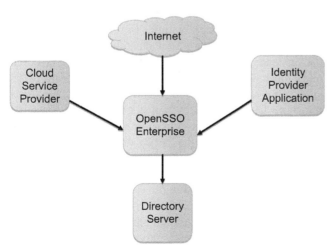

FIGURE 63.4 User access control in Platform as a Service.

delegate authentication to the customer's identity provider if the cloud provider supports federation standards, such as SAML. Microsoft announced the "Geneva" Claims-Based Access Platform that is compliant with SAML 2.0 standards or higher. The platform's objective is to aid developers in delegating authentication, authorization, and personalization so they don't have to implement these futures themselves.

Compartmentalizing Access to Protect Data Confidentiality

When data is stored with a PaaS provider, the provider assumes partial responsibility as the data custodian. Although the responsibilities for data ownership and data custodianship are segregated, the data owner is still accountable for ensuring that data is suitably safeguarded by the custodian, as seen in Fig. 63.5. In a PaaS environment compartmentalizing access provides data confidentiality since users are prevented from being able to access certain information because they do not need access to it to perform their job functions and they have not been given formal approval to access this data (least privilege design).

Securing Data in Motion and Data at Rest

Data at rest denotes data stored in computer systems, including files on an employee's laptop, company files on a server, or copies of these files on an off-site tape backup. Securing data at rest in a cloud is not drastically different than securing it outside a cloud environment. A customer deploying in a PaaS environment needs to find the risk level acceptable and make sure that the cloud provider is the primary custodian of the data.

Data in motion indicates data that is transitioning from storage, such as a file or database entry, to another storage format in the same or to a different system. Data in motion can also include data that is not permanently stored. Because data in motion only exists in transition (computer memory, between end points), its integrity and confidentiality must be ensured. The risk of third party observation of the data in motion exists. Data may be cached on intermediate systems, or temporary files may be created at either end point. The best method to protect data in motion is to apply encryption.

Identifying Your Security Perimeter

With the acceptance of cloud services, an organization's security perimeter has evolved to become more dynamic and has moved beyond the control of the traditional IT department. Cloud computing has extended an organization's network, system, and application realms into the cloud service provider's domain.

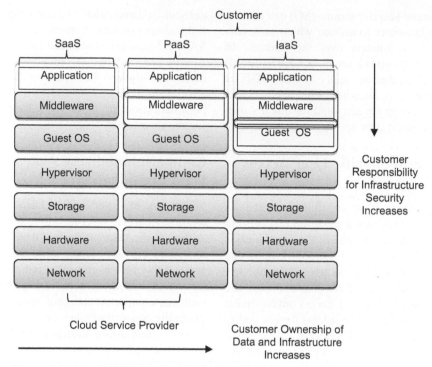

FIGURE 63.5 Ownership in different service models.

The Jericho Forum, an Open Group consortium of IT security officers, has addressed deperimeterization. In the view of the Jericho Forum, it is essential to pinpoint the components that are critical to the customer's operation and ensure that those are sufficiently secured, regardless of the source of the threat. In a completely deperimeterized environment every component will be sufficiently secured to ensure that confidentiality, integrity, and availability of the data is maintained.

Techniques for Recovering Critical Data

A PaaS customer should review the available options for backup and recovery of their critical data and understand the different options available to secure the data transfer in case of an emergency. The customer should also ensure backups and other copies of logs, access records, and any other pertinent information, which may be required for legal and compliance reasons, can be migrated. Data validation should be an automated or user-initiated validation protocol that allows the customer to check their data at any time to ensure the data's integrity. The cloud provider should implement fast SLA-based data recovery. The SLA should be negotiated upfront, and the customer should pay for the SLA required to ensure that there is no conflict of interest. No data, file, or system disk should take more than 30 min to recover. PaaS providers can offer one or more of the options below:

- Basic backup and restore
- Pilot light
- Warm standby
- Multisite

Basic Backup and Restore

PaaS providers can offer storage space on their own platform where the transfer of data is performed over the network. The storage service enables snapshots of the data to be transparently copied into the storage systems. Some providers permit the transfer of large data sets by shipping the storage devices directly.

Pilot Light

The notion of the pilot light is an analogy that originates from the gas heater. In a gas heater, a small flame that is always burning can rapidly kindle the entire heater to warm up a house when desired. This situation is comparable to a backup and restore scenario. Nevertheless, the customer must make sure that the critical core components of the system are already configured and running in PaaS environment (the pilot light). When it's time for recovery, the customer would quickly provision a full-scale production environment based on the critical core components. The pilot light method will provide the customer with a shorter recovery time than the backup and restore option, because the core components of the system already exist, are running, and are continuously updated. There remains some installation and configuration tasks that need to be performed by the customer to fully recover the applications. The PaaS environment allows customers to automate the provisioning and configuration of the resources, which can save time and minimize human errors.

Warm Standby

The warm standby option extends the pilot light components and preparation. The recovery time decreases further because some services are always operating. After identifying the business-critical components, the customer would duplicate these systems in the PaaS environment and configure them to be always running. This solution is not configured to handle a maximum production load, but it provides all of the available functions. This option may be utilized for testing, quality assurance, and internal use. In case of a catastrophe, additional resources are rapidly added to handle the production load.

Multisite

The multisite option exists in the PaaS environment as well as on the customer's on-site infrastructure where both are running. The recovery point selected will determine the data replication method that the customer employs. Various replication methods exist, such as synchronous or asynchronous. A domain name system (DNS) load-balancing service can be used to direct production traffic to the backup and production sites. Part of the traffic will go to the infrastructure in PaaS, and the rest will go to the on-site infrastructure. In case of a catastrophe, the customer can adjust the DNS configuration and send all traffic to the PaaS environment. The capacity of the PaaS service can be rapidly increased to handle the full production load. PaaS resource bursting can be used to automate this process if available from the provider. The customer may need to deploy application logic to detect the failure of the primary site and divert the traffic to the parallel site running in PaaS. The cost of this option is determined by resource consumption.

4. INFRASTRUCTURE AS A SERVICE

Unlike PaaS and SaaS, IaaS customers are primarily responsible for securing the hosts provisioned in the cloud.

Locking Down Cloud Servers

Unlike PaaS and SaaS, IaaS customers are accountable for securing the systems provisioned in the cloud environment. Knowing that most IaaS services available today implement virtualization at the host level, host security in IaaS could be classified as follows:

Virtualization Software Security

Virtualization software is the software that exists on top of hardware and provides customers the capability to create and delete virtual instances. Virtualization at the host level can be achieved by utilizing virtualization models, such as paravirtualization (specialized host OS, hardware, and hypervisor), OS-level virtualization (FreeBSD jails, Solaris Containers, Linux-VServer), or hardware-based virtualization (VMware, Xen). In a public IaaS environment, customers cannot access the hypervisor because it is administered solely by the cloud services provider. Cloud services providers should implement the essential security controls, including limiting physical and logical access to the hypervisor and the other virtualization layers. IaaS customers need to comprehend the technology and access controls implemented by the cloud services provider to guard the hypervisor. This will aid the customer to recognize the compliance needs and gaps in relation to the host security standards, policies, and regulations. To show the weakness of the virtualization layer, during Black Hat 2008 and Black Hat DC 2009 Joanna Rutkowska, Alexander Tereshkin, and Rafal Wojtczuk from Invisible Things Lab showed various methods to compromise the Xen hypervisor's virtualization, including the "Blue Pill" attack.

Customer Guest Operating System or Virtual Instance Security

The virtual incarnation of an OS is created over the virtualization layer and it's usually configured to be exposed to the Internet. Customers have complete access to their virtual machines. Public IaaS systems can be exposed to security threats, such as the theft of keys used to access hosts (e.g., SSH private keys), the attack of exposed vulnerable services (e.g., FTP, NetBIOS, SSH), the hijacking of insecure accounts (i.e., weak or no passwords), and the deployment of malware as software or embedded in the OS.

Ensuring the Cloud Is Configured According to Best Practices

Cloud computing is still subject to conventional security best practices, but cloud services providers and their customers may find it difficult in adopting these practices since they are not tailored to the cloud space. The security best practices for cloud computing has been maturing rapidly lately through the contribution of the players involved in cloud computing, such as hardware manufacturers, software providers, cloud providers, and customers. The key best practices are as follows and can be seen in Fig. 63.6:

- Policy
- Risk management
- Configuration management and change control
- Auditing
- Vulnerability scanning
- Segregation of duties
- Security monitoring

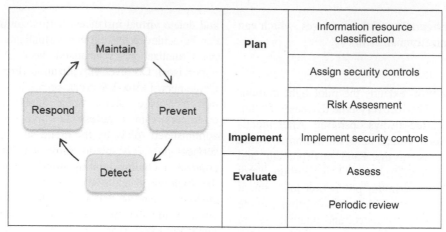

FIGURE 63.6 Cloud computing key best practices.

Policy

It is a best practice for cloud services providers and their customers to define a solid policy for cloud security. This policy should include all security-related aspects of information security, including staff, information, infrastructure, hardware, and software. Policies are crucial to provide organizational direction. To succeed, they must be available and visible across the organization, they must have the backing of management, and they must assign responsibilities. Policies should be updated as continuously, and they should be accompanied by the use of standards, procedures, and guidelines that enable the implementation of policy.

Risk Management

The goals of risk management best practices are to assess, address, and mitigate security risks in a cloud environment. This should be done in the context of determining the risks from a business standpoint. Choosing security controls and monitoring their efficacy are part of risk management. Basically, a best practice for risk management is to begin with an understanding and assessment of the risks one faces (risk analysis) and orient the selection of security controls along with appropriate security practices and procedures toward managing risks.

Configuration Management and Change Control

It is a best practice to have a configuration and change management process that can govern proposed changes. This would also include identifying possible security consequences and providing assurance that the current operational system is correct in version and configuration.

Auditing

In auditing, the customer should seek to verify compliance, review the efficacy of controls, and validate security processes. The customer should follow a schedule in auditing, regularly evaluate security controls, use automated and manual processes to validate compliance to a policy, regularly use third-party vulnerability assessment services, and manually examine system logs to validate effectiveness of the security monitoring systems.

Vulnerability Scanning

It is a best practice to perform periodic cloud infrastructure vulnerability scanning. This should encompass all cloud management systems, servers, and network devices. The purpose of vulnerability scanning is to locate any new or existing vulnerability so that the related risk may be reduced or eliminated.

Segregation of Duties

It is a best practice to limit the privileges that users have to the level that is necessary for them to perform their duties. This comes from the idea of separation of duties, which in turn originates from the principle of least privilege.

Security Monitoring

It is a best practice to automate the collection of security logs from all network devices, servers, and applications. These logs should be kept in their original formats to preserve a legal record of all activity and to so that they can be queried in an event of an alert. The purposes of security monitoring are to detect threats, expose bugs, keep a legal record of activity, and enable forensics. Most likely sources of security events are OS logs (event logs and syslogs), application logs, intrusion detection and prevention logs, antivirus logs, netflow logs, network device logs, and storage equipment logs. These security events are aggregated in streams and redirected via the network to a central collection service, usually a Security Information and Event Management (SIEM) system. Once these events are collected, they should be subject to an ongoing correlation and analysis process, usually performed by a Security Operation Center (SOC). The events get escalated as they are evaluated and assigned alert levels and priorities. The security monitoring lifecycle is shown in Fig. 63.7.

Confirming Safeguards Have Been Implemented

Once the IaaS environment has been implemented it should go through a continuous evaluation in the form of change management and periodic evaluation in the form of control review. The outcome of these evaluations would be to remedy the issues and to continue the evaluation process. The following can be used as a generalized checklist to evaluate the IaaS environment:

- *Foundations of security*
  - Policies, standards, and guidelines
  - Transparency
  - Employee security
  - External providers
- *Business concerns*
  - BC
  - DR
  - Legal considerations
  - Resource planning
- *Layers of defense*
  - Software assurance
  - Authentication
  - Key management
  - Cryptography
  - Network security
  - Hypervisor and virtual machine security
  - Identity and access management

- *Operational security*
  - Operational practices
  - Incident response management
  - Data center: physical security, power and networking, asset management

Networking

The primary factor in determining whether to use private, public, or hybrid cloud deployments is the risk level an organization can tolerate. Though various IaaS providers implement virtual network zoning, they may not be the same as an internal private cloud that employs stateful inspection and other network security services. If the customer has the budget to afford the services of a private cloud, their risks will decline, given they have a private cloud that is internal to their network. In some instances, a private cloud located at a cloud provider's facility can help satisfy security requirements, but will be dependent on the provider's capabilities and maturity. Confidentiality risk can be reduced by using encryption for data-in-transit. Secure digital signatures can make it more difficult for malicious players to tamper with data and therefore ensure the integrity of data. The cloud service provider should provide the following information to the customer:

- Data and access control threats
- Access and authentication controls
- Information about security gateways (firewalls, web application firewalls, service oriented architecture, and application programming interface)
- Secure services like DNSSEC, NTP (network time protocol), OAuth, SNMP (simple network management protocol), and management network segmentation
- Traffic and network flow monitoring capabilities

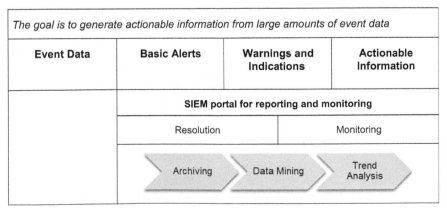

FIGURE 63.7 Security monitoring lifecycle.

- Hypervisor integration availability
- Security products (IDS/IPS, server tier firewall, file integrity monitoring, DLP, antivirus, antispam)
- Security monitoring and incident response capabilities
- Denial-of-service (DoS) protection and mitigation capabilities

Operating Systems

The ease of self-provisioning new virtual instances on an IaaS platform creates a possibility that insecure virtual servers may be created. Secure-by-default configuration should be implemented by default by mirroring or surpassing industry best practices. Securing a virtual instance in the cloud requires solid operational security procedures supported by automation of procedures. The following steps can be used to evaluate host and VM security:

- Use of a hardened system configuration. A best practice for cloud applications is to build hardened virtual machine images that have only the configuration sufficient to support the application stack. Limiting the abilities of the basic application stack not only limits the server's attack surface, but also greatly decreases the number of updates needed to maintain a secure application stack.
- Keeping track of the available virtual machine images and OS versions that are offered for cloud hosting. The IaaS provider offers some of these VM images through their infrastructure. If a virtual machine image from the IaaS provider is utilized, it should go through the same security verification and hardening process for systems within the enterprise infrastructure. The best substitute for the customer is to build their own image that matches the security standards of the internal trusted systems.
- Maintenance of the integrity of the hardened image.
- Securing the private keys required to access hosts in the cloud.
- Separation of the cryptographic keys from the cloud where the data is hosted. The exception to this would be when the keys are necessary for decryption, and this would be limited to the duration of the decryption activity. If the application needs a key to continuously encrypt and decrypt, it may not be feasible to protect the key since it will be hosted with the application.
- No credentials should be placed in the virtual machine images except for a key to decrypt the file system.
- Password-based authentication should not be permitted for remote access.
- Passwords should be required to execute administrative functions.
- A host firewall should be installed and only the minimum ports necessary to support the services should be open to public.

- Only the needed services should be run and the unused services (e.g., turn off FTP, print services, network file services, and database services if they are not required) should be turned off.
- A host-based intrusion detection system (IDS) should be installed.
- System and event logs should be logged to a dedicated log aggregator. The log server should be isolated with strong access controls.
- Ensure a system to provide patching images in the cloud, both online and offline, is available.
- Ensure isolation between different customers (network and data) is provided.

Applications

The integrity and security of a cloud environment is dependent on the integrity of its components. Software is a primary route for vulnerabilities and exploits. IaaS providers, such as Amazon EC2 and Terremark, handle the applications on customer virtual machines as black boxes. This makes the providers completely independent of the operations and management of the customer's applications. Therefore, customers bear the full responsibility for securing their applications deployed in the cloud.

Web applications installed on a public cloud should be designed with an Internet-facing threat model and protected with typical security measures against web application vulnerabilities, such as listed in the Open Web Application Security Project (OWASP) Top 10 web application security risks. Following common security development practices, they should also be periodically audited for vulnerabilities. Security should be embedded into the software development life cycle. It's the customer's responsibility to keep their applications and runtime platform up-to-date to protect their systems from a compromise. It is in the customer's best interest to design and implement applications with the least-privileged access model.

Developers creating applications for IaaS clouds should develop their own mechanisms for authentication and authorization. Similar to traditional identity management implementations, cloud applications should also be designed to use delegated authentication services offered by an enterprise identity provider. If in-house implementations of authentication, authorization, and accounting are not properly designed, they can become a weakness. Cloud customers should avoid using in-house authentication, authorization, and accounting solutions when possible.

Scanning for and Patching Vulnerabilities

Penetration testing and vulnerability assessments of cloud infrastructure should be carried out on a periodic basis. Usually the customer may not have the specialized skills and expertise to perform these tests, and therefore, the customer should work with a third party that is professional and has the necessary skills and certifications. Penetration testing should be geared toward the entire cloud infrastructure and not only individual components. Security is only as good as the weakest link.

A penetration test and vulnerability assessment can uncover multiple vulnerabilities, not all of which can or should be fixed. Newly found vulnerabilities need to be classified by their severity. Generally, a vulnerability that is categorized as critical should be addressed to safeguard the entire cloud. Instead, vulnerabilities categorized as having low and medium severity may be accepted as reasonable risks. Vulnerabilities that are not addressed need to have their residual risk evaluated and then accepted by the customer. If it is found that the same vulnerability exists across all servers with the virtual machine image, then this should be fixed in the golden virtual machine image.

Vulnerability scanning has additional benefits. If one collects scan data against the same targets and stores the scan results in a database, configuration errors and attack trends can be detected by analysis of this data over time. Likewise, use of a database to store scan results makes these immediately available to auditors and automated tools for compliance and other security checking.

Controlling and Verifying Configuration Management

The relationship between configuration management and security control procedures is an often-neglected one in commercial implementations of Internet-facing systems. The root cause is typically a process failure in configuration management or change control (CC). A recognition of this is found in NIST SP 800-64, Security Considerations in the Information System Development Life Cycle, which states: "Changes to the hardware, software, or firmware of a system can have a significant impact on the security of the system ... changes should be documented, and their potential impact on security should be assessed regularly." Configuration management and change management should be well defined and provide a structured method for causing technical and administrative changes. They should also provide assurances that the information technology resources in operation are correct in their version and configuration. Configuration management and change management are essential to controlling and managing an accurate inventory of components and changes.

Vulnerability assessments can be used to confirm the configuration management data. When issues that have not been previously identified are discovered, more thorough investigation becomes necessary.

Most of the time, cloud providers are responsible for the vulnerability, patch, and configuration administration of the infrastructure (hosts, storage, networks, and applications). Cloud providers should assure their customers of their technical vulnerability management program using ISO/IEC 27002 type control and assurance frameworks.

IaaS configuration management and change control focuses on infrastructure managed by the cloud provider, as well as the customer infrastructure interfacing with the IaaS environment. Therefore the provider should be responsible for systems, networks, hypervisors, employee systems, and storage and management applications owned and operated by the provider and third parties. Instead, IaaS customers are responsible for their virtual servers, image standardization, configuration standardization, configuration management of the customer environment, and network access policies.

5. LEVERAGING PROVIDER-SPECIFIC SECURITY OPTIONS

Due to the elastic model of services delivered via the cloud, customers need only pay for the amount of security they require, such as the number of workstations to be protected or the amount of network traffic monitored and not for the supporting infrastructure and staffing to support the various security services. A security-focused provider offers greater security expertise than is typically available within an organization. Finally, outsourcing administrative tasks, such as log management, can save time and money, allowing an organization to devote more resources to its core competencies. The security options that are provided by various cloud providers are as follows:

- Network security
- Multifactor authentication
- Identity and access management
- Data loss prevention
- Encryption
- BC and DR
- Web security
- Email security
- Security assessments
- Intrusion management, detection, and prevention
- Security information and event management

Defining Security Groups to Control Access

The conventional model of network zones and tiers has been supplanted in public clouds with security groups, security domains, or virtual data centers that have logical boundaries between tiers but are less exact and offer less protection than the earlier model. A security group acts as a firewall that controls the traffic allowed into a group of instances. When the customer launches a virtual instance, they can assign it to one or more security groups. For each security group, the customer adds rules that govern the allowed inbound traffic to instances in the group. All other inbound traffic is discarded. The customer can modify rules for a security group at any time. The new rules are automatically enforced for all existing and future instances in the group. The default security group usually allows no inbound traffic and allows all outbound traffic. A virtual instance can have as many security groups as needed.

Filtering Traffic by Port Number

Each security group rule enables a specific source to access the instances in the group using a certain protocol (TCP, UDP, ICMP) and destination port or ports. For example, a rule could allow a source IP address 1.1.1.1 to access the instances in the group on TCP port 80 (the protocol and destination port).

Discovering and Benefiting From the Provider's Built-In Security

Some IaaS providers have the mentioned security options built into their systems. Amazon EC2 provides their customers with identity and access management (IAM) policies, and SGs. Other providers such as Terremark have multifactor authentication built into their enterprise cloud solutions besides IAM and SG. These built-in features decrease the time to launch a secure environment and reduces the cost further.

Protecting Archived Data

The same three information security principles are associated with data stored in the cloud as with data stored elsewhere: confidentiality, integrity, and availability.

Confidentiality

Confidentiality is usually provided by encrypting customer data. Data can be at the volume storage level or object storage level.

Volume storage encryption prevents snapshot cloning or exposure, exploration by the cloud provider, and exposure due to physical loss of drives. IaaS volumes can be encrypted using instance managed encryption (instance managed, keys stored in volume and protected by a secret or key pair), externally managed encryption (instance managed, keys are managed externally, provided on request), or proxy encryption (external software or appliance managed).

Object or file storage encryption allows the user to implement a virtual private storage (VPS). Like a virtual private network, a VPS allows the use of a public shared infrastructure while still protecting data, since only those

with encryption keys can read the data. The objects can be encrypted by standard tools, by the application using the data, or by a proxy before being placed in storage.

IaaS providers can also offer IAM policies and Access Control Lists (ACLs) to further protect stored data. The transfer of data is also protected by provider implemented SSL or VPN connections.

Integrity

Besides the confidentiality of data, the customer also needs to consider the integrity of their data. Confidentiality does not mean integrity. Data can be encrypted for confidentiality reasons, but the customer might not have a method to validate the integrity of that data. IaaS providers should regularly check for integrity by keeping track of data checksums and repair data if corruptions are detected by using redundant data. Data in transfer should also be checksum validated to detect corruption.

Availability

Supposing that a customer's data has preserved its confidentiality and integrity, the customer should also be worried about the availability of their data. Customers should be concerned about three main threats: network-based attacks, the cloud service provider's own availability, and backups or redundancy. Availability is usually stated in the SLA and customers pay for varying levels of availability based on their risk tolerances. IaaS providers may provide redundant storage (geographic and systemic), versioning, and high bandwidth connectivity to prevent problems arising from availability issues.

6. ACHIEVING SECURITY IN A PRIVATE CLOUD

In private clouds, computing and storage infrastructure are dedicated to a single organization and are not shared with any other organization. However, just because they are private does not mean that they are more secure.

Taking Full Responsibility for Security

The security management and day-to-day operation of the environment are relegated to internal IT or to a third party with contractual SLAs. The risks faced by internal IT departments still remain. Private cloud security should be considered from different perspectives:

- *Infrastructure security*: This perspective includes physical access and data leakage concerns (loss of hard drives), energy supply security, facility security, network security, hardware security (hardware cryptography modules, trusted protection modules), compute security (process, memory isolation), storage security, operation system security, virtualization security, and update security (hypervisor, virtual machines).

- *Platform security*: This perspective includes user experience security, application framework security, data security, development environment security, and update security.
- *Software security*: This perspective includes application security (multitenant partitioning, user permissions), and update security.
- *Service delivery security*: This perspective includes connection security (SSL, authentication), and service end-point security (traditional network security).
- *User security*: This perspective includes making sure that the users and the systems they are using to access the private cloud are trusted and secured.
- *Legal concerns*: This perspective includes governance issues, compliance issues (PCI DSS, HIPPA), data protection (personally identifiable information), and legal agreements (SLA, terms of use, user license agreements).

The advantages of a private cloud in the context of security become apparent mostly when compared to a public cloud implementation.

Managing the Risks of Public Clouds

Though a public cloud deployment is suitable for most uses that are nonsensitive, migrating sensitive, mission critical, or proprietary data into any cloud environment that is not certified and designed for handling such data introduces high risk. A customer should first select a cloud deployment model and then make sure that sufficient security controls are in place. These actions should be followed by a reasonable risk assessment:

- *Data and encryption*: If the data is stored unencrypted in the cloud, data privacy is at risk. There is the risk for unauthorized access either by a malicious employee on the cloud service provider side or an intruder gaining access to the infrastructure from the outside.
- *Data retention*: When the data is migrated or removed by the cloud provider or customer, there may be data residues that might expose sensitive data to unauthorized parties.
- *Compliance requirements*: Various countries have varying regulations for data privacy. Because some public cloud providers don't provide information about the location of the data, it is crucial to consider the legal and regulatory requirements about where data can be stored.
- *Multitenancy risks*: The shared nature of public cloud environments increases security risks, such as unauthorized viewing of data by other customers using the same hardware platform. A shared environment also presents resource competition problems whenever one

of the customers uses most of the resources either due to need or due to being exposed to targeted attacks, such as DDoS.

- *Control and visibility*: Customers have restricted control and visibility over the cloud resources because the cloud provider is responsible for administering the infrastructure. This introduces additional security concerns that originate from the lack of transparency. Customers need to rethink the way they operate as they surrender the control of their IT infrastructure to an external party while utilizing public cloud services.
- *Security responsibility*: In a cloud the vendor and the user share the responsibility of securing the environment. The amount of responsibility shouldered by each party can change depending on the cloud model adopted.

Identifying and Assigning Security Tasks in Each SPI Service Model: SaaS, PaaS, and IaaS

Security-related tasks tend to be the highest for the cloud provider in a SaaS environment, whereas an IaaS environment shifts most of the tasks to the customer. Please see the following:

- SaaS
  - *Attack types*: Elevation of privilege, cross-site scripting attack (XSS), cross-site request forgery (CSRF), SQL injection, encryption, open redirect, buffer overflows, connection polling, canonicalization attacks, brute force attacks, dictionary attacks, token stealing.
  - *Provider security responsibilities*: Identity and access management, data protection, security monitoring, security management, authentication, authorization, role-based access control, auditing, intrusion detection, incident response, forensics.
  - *Consumer security responsibilities*: Other than assessing the risk of being in a cloud environment, the customer has little to do in SaaS environment.
- PaaS
  - *Attack types*: Data tampering, buffer overflows, canonicalization attacks, SQL injection, encryption, disclosure of confidential data, elevation of privilege, side-channel attacks (VM-to-VM)
  - Provider security responsibilities: Security monitoring, security management, authentication, authorization, role-based access control, auditing, intrusion detection, incident response, forensics
  - *Customer security responsibilities*: Identity and access management, data protection
- IaaS
  - *Attack types*: Data tampering, side-channel attacks (VM-to-VM, VM-to-host or host-to-VM),

encryption, network traffic sniffing, physical access, brute force attacks, dictionary attacks

- *Provider security responsibilities*: Role-based access control, auditing, intrusion detection, incident response, forensics
- *Customer security responsibilities*: Identity and access management, data protection, security monitoring, security management, authentication, authorization

Selecting the Appropriate Product

While evaluating cloud computing products, customers usually want to know about how secure the implementation is; if the cloud provider is meeting best practices for security; how well does the cloud provider meet discreet controls and requirements; and how does the product compare with other similar services.

Comparing Product-Specific Security Features

To be able to compare cloud providers we need to define a set of metrics and standards. Based on the previous discussions of risk and cloud security coverage we can use the following:

- *Organizational security*: Staff security, third-party management, and SLAs
- *Physical security*: Physical access controls, access to secure areas, environmental controls
- *Identity and access management*: Key management, authorization, authentication
- *Encryption*: Connection encryption [secure socket layer (SSL), virtual private network (VPN)], stored data encryption
- *Asset management and security*: Asset inventory, classification, destruction of used media
- *BC and DR management*: Recovery point objective and recovery time objective information, information security during DR and BC, recovery priority, dependencies
- *Incident management*: Existence of a formal process, detection capabilities, real-time security monitoring, escalation procedures, statistics
- *Legal concerns and privacy*: Audits, certifications, location of data, jurisdiction, subcontracting, outsourcing, data processing, privacy, intellectual property

The vendors that provide the highest transparency into their services will have higher coverage of metrics and a possible higher score compared to the one with less documentation. Some vendors will lack the specific feature or will not document it properly and therefore will not have a score for the specific metric.

Considering Organizational Implementation Requirements

Besides comparing the cloud provider's products, the customers also need to be well aware of their organization's security requirements and how they align with the cloud provider's offerings. The customers should check for the following organizational requirements to see if they apply:

- Data:
  - Separation of sensitive and nonsensitive data: Segregate sensitive data from nonsensitive data into separate databases in separate security groups when hosting an application that handles highly sensitive data.
  - Encryption of nonroot file systems: Use only encrypted file systems for block devices and nonroot local devices.
  - Encryption of file system key: Pass the file system key encrypted at start up.
  - Signing of content in storage.
  - Secure handling of decryption keys and forced removal after use: Decryption keys should be in the cloud only for the duration of use.
- Applications:
  - No dependence on a specific virtual machine system (OS or other cloud services).
  - Source address filtering of network traffic: Only allow needed traffic, such as HTTP and HTTPS.
  - Encryption of network traffic.
  - Strong authentication of network based access: Authentication should be performed using keys with mutual authentication.
  - Use of host-based firewall.
  - Installation of a network-based intrusion detection system (NIDS).
  - Installation of a host-based intrusion detection system (HIDS).
  - Usage of hardening tools: Usage of hardening tools, such as Bastille Linux, SELinux should be possible.
  - System design for patch roll out: System should be designed to easily patch and relaunch instances.
  - Support of SAML or other identity and access management systems.
- Other:
  - Compliance support: Presence of SSAE 16, Payment Card Industry (PCI) Data Security Standard (DSS), and other compliance certifications.
  - Regular full backups stored in remote secure locations.
  - Instance snapshots in case of a security breach.
  - Role segregation: The infrastructure should be segmented based on roles (development, production).

- Regular verification of cloud resources configuration: This is especially important since cloud resources can be managed via different channels [web console and application programming interfaces (APIs)]. Thus if, for example, the web console access has been hacked, this might not be visible immediately to the customer if normally management is only done via APIs. Therefore, some type of intrusion detection for the cloud resource management is needed.
- No credentials in end-user devices.
- Secure storage and generation of credentials.
- Security groups: Use security groups (i.e., named set of firewall rules) to configure IP traffic to and from instances completely in order to isolate every tier, even internally to the cloud.

Virtual Private Cloud

A virtual private cloud (VPC) can offer public cloud users the privacy of a private cloud environment. In a VPC, while the infrastructure remains public, the cloud provider lets the customer to define a virtual network by letting them select their own subnets, IP address ranges, route tables, and network gateways. Optionally, VPNs are provided to further secure the virtual networks. Stored data can also be protected by assigning ACLs.

Simulating a Private Cloud in a Public Environment

VPCs utilize VPNs to secure communication channels by creating protected, virtually dedicated conduits within the cloud provider network. This eradicates the necessity to specify intricate firewall rules between the application in the cloud and the enterprise, because all locations would be linked by a private network isolated from the public Internet. VPNs form the construct of a private network and address space used by all VPN endpoints. Because VPNs can use specific IP addresses, the cloud provider can permit customers to utilize any IP address ranges without conflicting with other cloud customers. A VPC can contain many cloud data centers, but it appears as a single collection of resources to the customer.

Google Secure Data Connector

A secure data center (SDC) provides data connectivity and allows IT administrators to control the services and data that are available in Google Apps (a web-based office suite). SDC builds a secure link by encrypting connections between Google Apps and customer networks. Google Apps is the only external service that can make requests over the secured connection. SDC can filter the types of requests that can be routed. The filters can limit which

gadgets, spreadsheets, and App Engine applications may access which internal systems. Filters can also be used to limit user access to resources. SDC implements OAuth Signed Fetch that adds authentication information to requests that are made through SDC. OAuth can be used by the customer to validate requests from Google and provide an additional layer of security to the SDC filters.

Amazon Virtual Private Cloud

Amazon VPC lets their customers to cut out a private section of their public cloud where they can launch services in a virtual network. Using the Amazon VPC, the customer can delineate a virtual network topology that is similar to a traditional network where the customer can specify its own private IP address range, segregate the IP address range into private and public subnets, administer inbound and outbound access using network access control lists, store data in the Amazon S3 storage service and set access permissions, attach multiple virtual network interfaces, and bridge the VPC with onsite IT infrastructure with a VPN to extend existing security and management policies.

Industry-Standard, Virtual Private Network-Encrypted Connections

A customer might simply want to extend their organization's perimeter into the external cloud computing environment by using a site-to-site VPN and operating the cloud environment making use of their own directory services to control access. Companies such as Terremark and Rackspace offer site-to-site VPN solutions to extend the existing IT infrastructure into their clouds so that customers can securely use solutions deployed in the cloud (collaboration solutions, testing and development, data replication, DR).

The Hybrid Cloud Alternative

A hybrid cloud can be created by combining any of the three cloud types: public, private, and virtual private. Hybrid clouds are formed when an organization builds a private cloud and wants to leverage its public and VPCs in conjunction with its private cloud for a particular purpose. An example of a hybrid cloud would be a website where its core infrastructure is only accessible by the company, but specific components of the website are hosted externally, such as high bandwidth media (video streaming or image caching). Nevertheless, some requirements can thwart hybrid cloud acceptance. For example, financial services companies, such as banks, might not be able comply with regulations if customer data is hosted at a third-party site or location, regardless of the security controls. Governments also might not be able to take the risk of being compromised in case of a hybrid cloud breach.

Connecting On-Premises Data With Cloud Applications

Data transferred to the cloud should be encrypted both when on the cloud and during transfer (with SSL, VPN). The employed encryption service should provide well-thought-out encryption key management policies to guarantee data integrity. Also, the customer should retain encryption key ownership to maintain separation of duties between their business and the other cloud service providers. This permits the customer to use their encryption throughout their private and public clouds and therefore lets the customer avoid vendor lock-in and to move between cloud providers.

Securely Bridging With Virtual Private Cloud

As the name suggests, a VPC does not deliver a fully private infrastructure, but a virtually private infrastructure. Servers created in the customer's VPC are allocated from the same shared resources that are used by all other provider customers. Hence, the customer still has to consider extra security measures in the cloud, both for networking (interserver traffic) and data in shared storage.

To be able to securely bridge existing infrastructure with VPCs, the customer would need to employ tools, such as CloudSwitch or Vyatta. These tools provide data isolation for the data circulating between the in-house data center and the VPCs using data encryption and therefore applying an additional layer of security. For example, CloudSwitch isolates all network and storage access to data at the device level with AES-256 encryption. It also utilizes roles and permissions-based access to enforce corporate policies.

Dynamically Expanding Capacity to Meet Business Surges

Cloudbursting is the dynamic arrangement of an application operating on a private cloud to use public clouds to meet a sudden unforeseen demand, such as a tax services company's need to meet increasing traffic associated with tax filing deadlines. The benefit of this type of hybrid cloud usage is that the customer only pays for the additional computing resources when they are in demand. To utilize cloudbursting, a customer would need to address workload migration (ability to clone the application environment with tools such as Chef, Puppet, CFEngine, Cloudify), data synchronization (maintaining real-time data copies), and network connectivity.

7. MEETING COMPLIANCE REQUIREMENTS

Cloud providers recognize the difficulty of meeting a wide range of customer requirements. To build a model that can scale, the cloud provider needs to have solid set of controls that can benefit all of its customers. To achieve this goal, the cloud provider can use the model of governance, risk, and compliance (GRC). GRC acknowledges that compliance is an ongoing activity, which requires a formal written compliance program. The cloud provider should undergo a continuous cycle of risk assessment, identifying the key controls, monitoring and testing to identify gaps in controls (Security Content Automation Protocol, or SCAP, Cybersecurity Information Exchange Framework, or CYBEX, GRC-XML), reporting, and improving on the reported issues. The cycle of compliance evaluation is shown in Fig. 63.8.

Managing Cloud Governance

Governance is the set of processes, technologies, customs, policies, laws, and institutions affecting the way an enterprise is directed, administered, or controlled. Governance also comprises the relationship between the stakeholders and the goals of the company. Governance includes auditing supply chains, board and management structure and process, corporate responsibility and compliance, financial transparency and information disclosure, and ownership structure and exercise of control rights. A key factor in a customer's decision to engage a corporation is the confidence that expectations will be met. For cloud services, the interdependencies of services should not hinder the customer from clearly identifying the responsible parties. Stakeholders should carefully consider the monitoring mechanisms that are appropriate and necessary for the company's consistent performance and growth.

Customers should review the specific information security governance structure and processes, as well as specific security controls, as part of their due diligence for future cloud providers. The provider's security governance processes and capabilities should be evaluated to see if they are consistent with the customer's information security management processes. The cloud provider's information security controls should be risk-based and clearly support the customer's management processes. The loss of control and governance could cause noncompliance with the security requirements, a lack of confidentiality, integrity, and availability of data, and a worsening of performance and quality of service.

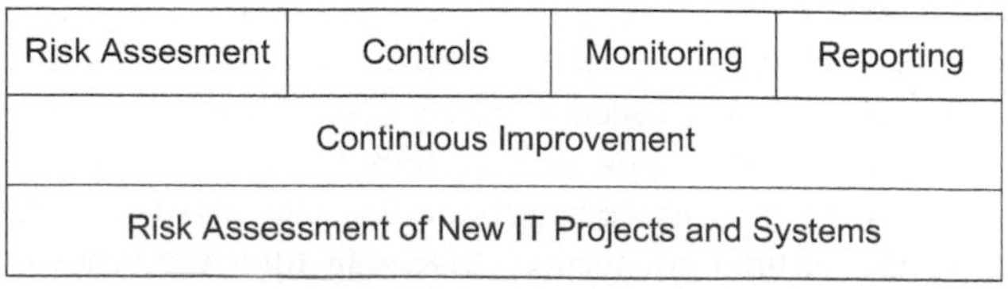

Risk Assesment	Controls	Monitoring	Reporting
Continuous Improvement			
Risk Assessment of New IT Projects and Systems			

FIGURE 63.8 Cycle of compliance evaluation.

Retaining Responsibility for the Accuracy of the Data

Laws and regulations will usually determine who in an organization should be responsible and held accountable for the accuracy and security of the data. If the customer is storing Health Insurance Portability and Accountability Act (HIPAA) data, then the customer must have a security-related post created to ensure compliance. The Sarbanes–Oxley Act assigns the Chief Financial Officer (CFO) and Chief Executive Officer (CEO) joint responsibility for the financial data. The Gramm-Leach-Bliley Act (GLBA) casts a wider net, making the entire board of directors responsible for security. The Federal Trade Commission (FTC) is less specific by only requiring a certain individual to be responsible for information security in a company.

Verifying Integrity in Stored and Transmitted Data

One of the main difficulties in cloud computing is tracking the location of data during processing. Having control over the data's creation, transfer, storage, use, and destruction becomes crucial. Using-data mining tools and solid IT operational practices will be key to managing data. Although host-level security can be tackled, host-to-host communication and its integrity are harder to secure due to the volume and dynamic nature of data in transition. Although traditional security scanners can be used, real-time reporting provides a better assessment. Thus, an IT GRC solution would display a general view of important metrics to provide a summary of site security and reliability. This solution can keep track of version management and integrity verification of backed up and in-transit data.

Demonstrating Due Care and Due Diligence

Before signing a contract with a cloud provider, a customer should assess its specific requirements. The range of the services, along with any limitations, regulations, or compliance requirements should be identified. Any services that will be deployed to the cloud should also be graded as to their importance to the business. A customer should consider if cloud computing is a true core business of the provider, if the provider is financially sound, if the provider is outsourcing, if the physical security of the facilities meet customer needs, if the provider's BC and DR plans are consistent with the customer's needs, if the operations team is technically competent, if they have a verifiable track record, and if the provider offers any indemnifications. Performing due diligence will reduce the negotiation time and ensure that the correct level of security is in place for the customer.

Supporting Electronic Discovery

Electronic discovery (eDiscovery) refers to discovery in civil litigation of information in an electronic format. Due to the nature of a cloud environment, a customer might not be able to apply or use eDiscovery tools regularly used. The customer also might not have the capability or administrative permissions to search or access all of the data existing in the cloud. Therefore, the customer will need to take into consideration the additional time and expense that will result from performing eDiscovery in a cloud environment.

The customer must make clear in the contractual agreement what the cloud provider needs to do if they are contacted to provide data to a third party, such as law enforcement. The customer might want to contest the request due to the confidentiality of the data or due to an unreasonable request.

Preserving a Chain of Evidence

Chain of evidence or chain of custody refers to the chronological documentation showing seizure, custody, control, transfer, analysis, and disposition of evidence. There are several issues around the responsibilities and limits that affect customers and providers with regard to collecting legally admissible evidence for prosecution. Identifying the actors is difficult enough with an evidence chain where responsibility for collecting data is shared between the provider and tenant. One party may be the custodian of the data, while the other is the legal owner. Maintaining a chain of evidence can be difficult due to the possibility of compromising the privacy of other cloud customers, unsynchronized log times, and data tampering in open environments, such as public clouds.

Assuring Compliance With Government Certification and Accreditation Regulations

Cloud providers face an increasingly complex variety of compliance requirements from their customers, such as industry standards, regulations, and customer frameworks. Relevant audit frameworks should be used when designing the cloud provider's security control set and periodic external audits should address the most relevant aspects of these controls.

Health Insurance Portability and Accountability Act

Cloud providers and customers that handle protected health information (PHI) are required to comply with the security and privacy requirements established in support of HIPAA. The HIPAA security and privacy rules focus on health plans, health care clearinghouses, health care providers, and system vendors. HIPAA requires that PHI is sufficiently protected when entrusted to third parties, such as cloud providers. The level of security should be kept up to standard across all environments. HIPAA addresses administrative safeguards, workforce security, information access management, security awareness and training, security incident procedures, contingency plans, evaluations, physical safeguards (facility and user devices), and technical safeguards (access control, audit control and integrity, authentication, encryption).

Sarbanes-Oxley

As a reaction to substantial financial reporting fraud in the early 2000s, the Sarbanes-Oxley Act of 2002 (SOX) was passed and signed into law. As a result of SOX, public company CFOs and CEOs are required to certify the efficacy of their internal controls over financial reporting (ICOFR) on a quarterly and annual basis. Management is required to do a yearly assessment of its ICOFR. Third-party auditors are required to provide an opinion about the efficacy of the management's ICOFR at the company's fiscal year end. SOX also influenced the creation of the Public Company Accounting Oversight Board (PCAOB), which was tasked with instituting audit standards. PCAOB Auditing Standard No. 2 pointed to the significance of information technology general controls (ITGCs).

SOX emphasizes the efficacy of an organization's financial reporting process, accounting and finance processes, other vital business, and controls over IT systems that have a material influence on financial reporting. SOX includes internally administered and outsourced systems that can substantially affect financial reporting. A customer using a SaaS environment might make the cloud provider relevant to their SOX scope if financial information is processed in the cloud. Cloud providers need to be clear about their own and the customer's responsibilities about processing information and ensure robust processes for user management/segregation of duties, systems development, program and infrastructure change management, and computer operations exist. Cloud providers also need to be concerned about physical security; stored and in-transit data; passwords; remote access; provider access to data; data disclosure; other customers accessing the data; data location (data centers, replicas, backups); shared resources; loss of governance; and isolation failures.

Data Protection Act

The Data Protection Act of 1998 is a United Kingdom (UK) Act of Parliament. The Act defines UK law on the processing of data on identifiable living people (see checklist: "An Agenda for Action for Complying With the Data Protection Act Activities").

An Agenda for Action for Complying With the Data Protection Act Activities

All UK businesses holding personal data about third parties (customers) must comply with the Data Protection Act. The act's principles are as follows (check all tasks completed):

_____1. Personal data shall be processed fairly and lawfully and, in particular, shall not be processed unless:
  _____a. At least one of the conditions in Schedule 2 is met; and
  _____b. In the case of sensitive personal data, at least one of the conditions in Schedule 3 is also met.
_____2. Personal data shall be obtained only for one or more specified and lawful purposes, and shall not be further processed in any manner incompatible with that purpose or those purposes.
_____3. Personal data shall be adequate, relevant, and not excessive in relation to the purpose or purposes for which they are processed.
_____4. Personal data shall be accurate and, where necessary, kept up to date.
_____5. Personal data processed for any purpose or purposes shall not be kept for longer than is necessary for that purpose or those purposes.
_____6. Personal data shall be processed in accordance with the rights of data subjects under this Act.
_____7. Appropriate technical and organizational measures shall be taken against unauthorized or unlawful processing of personal data and against accidental loss or destruction of, or damage to, personal data.
_____8. Personal data shall not be transferred to a country or territory outside the European Economic Area unless that country or territory ensures an adequate level of protection for the rights and freedoms of data subjects in relation to the processing of personal data.

Payment Card Industry Data Security Standard

Organizations that deal with credit card transactions are required to comply with PCI DSS. The compliance is ensured by third-party assessments and self-assessments depending on the volume of credit card processing transactions. PCI DSS contains 12 high-level requirements:

1. Install and maintain a firewall configuration to protect cardholder data.
2. Do not use vendor-supplied defaults for system passwords and other security parameters.
3. Protect stored cardholder data.
4. Encrypt transmission of cardholder data across open, public networks.

5. Use and regularly update antivirus software.
6. Develop and maintain secure systems and applications.
7. Restrict access to cardholder data based on the business's need to know.
8. Assign a unique ID to each person with computer access.
9. Restrict physical access to cardholder data.
10. Track and monitor all access to network resources and cardholder data.
11. Regularly test security systems and processes.
12. Maintain a policy that addresses information security.

Customers processing or storing cardholder data in a cloud provider need to ensure that the cloud provider and other third parties comply with PCI DSS as well. If the cloud provider has services including processing of credit card transactions, it is crucial that the cloud provider transparently explains its information flows and how it segregates its credit card processing and storage activities from others. This approach would limit the extent of the infrastructure that would be subject to PCI DSS. The main objectives of PCI DSS are to ensure the protection of cardholder data, avert breaches, and rapidly contain a breach. These objectives are valid for cloud computing environments as well.

Limiting the Geographic Location of Data

Cloud customers need to ensure that the providers employed outside of their country of residence and jurisdiction have sufficient security controls in place, including their primary and backup sites as well as any intermediate sites that the data crosses. The data protection laws of the European Union (EU) states and other countries are complex and have numerous requirements. The EU stipulates that the data controller and processor must notify entities that the data will be sent and processed in a country other than a member state. They must also have contracts approved by the Data Protection Authority before these activities can be performed. The customer also needs to be aware of the cloud provider subcontracting any data-related functionality since the third parties involved might host or transfer data outside of the customer's jurisdiction.

Following Standards for Auditing Information Systems

Due to multitenancy and shared environments, it becomes difficult to conduct an audit without the cloud provider breaching the confidentiality of other customers sharing the infrastructure. In such cases, the cloud provider should adopt a compliance program based on standards such as

ISO 27001 and provide assurance via SysTrust or ISO certification to its customers. Some audit frameworks are:

- *SSAE 16*: This framework involves the audit of controls based on control objectives and control activities (defined by the cloud provider). The auditor provides opinion on the design, operational status, and operating effectiveness of controls. SSAE 16 intends to cover services that are relevant for purposes of customers' financial statement audits.
- *SysTrust*: This framework involves the audit of controls based on defined principles and criteria for security, availability, confidentiality, and processing integrity. SysTrust applies to the reliability of any system.
- *WebTrust*: This framework involves the audit of controls based on defined principles and criteria for security, availability, confidentiality, processing integrity, and privacy. WebTrust applies to online or e-commerce systems.
- *ISO 27001*: This framework involves the audit of an organization's Information Security Management System (ISMS).

Negotiating Third-Party Provider Audits

When customers engage an audit provider, they should involve proper legal, procurement, and contracts teams within their organization. The customer should consider specific compliance requirements and, when negotiating, must agree on how to collect, store, and share compliance evidence (audit logs, activity reports, system configurations). If the standard terms of services do not address the customer's compliance needs, they would need to be negotiated. Contracts should include the involvement of a third party for the review of SLA metrics and compliance (by a mutually selected mediator). Customers should prefer auditors that have expertise in cloud computing that are familiar with the assurance challenges of cloud computing environments. Customers should request the cloud provider's SSAE 16 SOC2 (Statements on Standards for Attestation Engagements No. 16 Service Organization Control 2) or ISAE 3402 Type 2 (International Standard on Assurance Engagements 3402 Type 2) reports to provide a starting point of reference for auditors. SSAE 16 SOC2 provides a standard benchmark by which two data center audit reports can be compared and the customer can be assured that the same set of criteria was used to evaluate each. An ISAE 3402 Type 2 Report is known as the report on the description, design, and operating effectiveness of controls at a service organization.

8. PREPARING FOR DISASTER RECOVERY

To make sure of the availability of cloud services, business continuity (BC) and disaster recovery (DR) address a broad set of activities that are performed. BC is based on standards, policies, guidelines, and procedures that facilitate continuous operation irrespective of the incidents. DR is a subsection of BC and is concerned about data and IT systems.

Implementing a Plan to Sustain Availability

A content service provider (CSP) should have a formal DR plan in place to assure the provider's viability against natural disasters, human errors, and malicious behavior. This plan should be continuously tested to ensure preparedness and should not compromise the security of the cloud in an event of a disaster.

Customers should review their contracts with the cloud provider and third parties to confirm and verify that the DR controls and certifications are in place. Customers could also conduct on-site assessments if found necessary. The cloud provider should inform the customer in advance about any DR tests.

Reliably Connecting to the Cloud Across the Public Internet

There may be a substantial amount of latency between the customer's processing and the data stored in the cloud. Contingent on the amount of data being handled, this can result in unacceptable performance. If users access the data in the cloud, the latency may also cause an intolerable user experience. Wide area network optimization between the customer and the cloud provider should be in place so that the cloud enables full data mobility at reduced bandwidth, storage utilization, and cost. These performance issues might be managed with a combination of increased bandwidth or by traffic management. An alternative method is to utilize a cloud storage gateway. An issue to contemplate with a cloud storage gateway is the difference between tiering and caching. The gateways that use the caching method use cloud storage as their primary storage location. On the other hand, the gateways that utilize the tiering method use on-site storage as their primary storage and the cloud storage as their secondary storage.

Anticipating a Sudden Provider Change or Loss

Some CSPs will unavoidably cease operating, thereby making access to the data in the cloud an issue. Access to data might also be jeopardized if the provider or third party dealing with data breaches the contract and does not provide the promised services. When this happens, the customer's efforts should be directed toward finding a replacement cloud provider and confidentially removing and transferring the data from the defunct provider. It is important to clearly state the handling of data in case of bankruptcy or breach of contract in the SLA. Confidential data should be removed properly without leaving any trace.

Archiving Software as a Service Data Locally

Customers should perform regular extractions and backups to a format that is provider agnostic and make sure metadata can be preserved and migrated. It is also important to understand if any custom tools will have to be developed or if the provider will provide the migration tools. For legal and compliance reasons the customer should ensure that backups and copies of logs, access records, and any other pertinent information are included in the archive as well.

Addressing Data Portability and Interoperability in Preparation for a Change in Cloud Providers

Depending on the application, it is important to integrate with applications that may be present in other clouds or on traditional infrastructure. Interoperability standards either enable or become a barrier to interoperability, and permit maintenance of the integrity and consistency of an organization's information and processes. SLAs should address the steps to change providers from a portability perspective. The customer should have a good understanding of the cloud provider's APIs, hypervisors, application logic, and other restrictions and build processes to migrate to and handle different cloud architectures. Security should be maintained across migrations. Authentication and IAM mechanisms for user or process access to systems now must operate across all components of a cloud system. Using open standards for identity such as SAML will help to ensure portability. Encryption keys should be stored locally. When moving files and their metadata to new cloud environments the customer should ensure copies of file metadata are securely removed to prevent this information from remaining behind and opening up a possible opportunity for compromise.

Exploiting the Cloud for Efficient Disaster Recovery Options

Besides providing all the advantages discussed in this chapter, cloud computing has brought advantages in the form of online storage. This feature can be leveraged for backup and DR and can reduce the cost of infrastructure, applications and overall business processes. Many cloud storage providers guarantee reliability and availability of their service. The challenges to cloud storage, cloud backup, and DR in particular involve mobility, information transfer, availability, assuring BC, scalability, and metered payment. Cloud DR solutions are built on the foundation of three fundamentals: a virtualized storage infrastructure, a scalable file system, and a self-service DR application that responds to customers' urgent business needs. Some vendors that provide cloud storage services are Amazon, Google, Terremark, and Rackspace.

Achieving Cost-Effective Recovery Time Objectives

Recovery Time Objective (RTO) is the maximum amount of time that is acceptable for restoring and regaining access to data after a disruption. To keep RTO low, cloud-based DR requires ongoing server replication, making network bandwidth an important consideration when adopting this approach. To keep bandwidth requirements and related costs low, customers need to identify their critical systems and prioritize them in their DR plan. Focusing on a narrower set of systems will make DR more efficient and more cost-effective by keeping complexity and network bandwidth low.

Employing a Strategy of Redundancy to Better Resist Denial of Service

A DoS, or DDoS, is a type of network-based attack that attempts to make computer or network resources unavailable to their intended users. Customers and cloud providers should ensure that their systems have effective security processes and controls in place so they can withstand DoS attacks. The controls and processes should have the ability to recognize a DoS attack and utilize the provider's local capacity and geographical redundancies to counter the attack's excessive use network bandwidth (SYN or UDP floods), CPU, memory, and storage resources (application attacks).

Techniques such as cloudbursting can be used to mitigate the unexpected increase in resource consumption. Third-party cloud-based DDoS mitigation services (e.g., Akamai, Verisign) can be used to offload server functionality, defend the application layer, offload infrastructure functions, obfuscate infrastructure, protect DNS services, and failover gracefully when an attack is overwhelming.

9. SUMMARY

We have seen that cloud computing offers a service or deployment model for almost every type of customer and each flavor comes with its own security concerns. Advantages offered by cloud solutions need to be weighed with the risks they entail. While public clouds are great for commercial customers, federal customers or other customers dealing with sensitive data need to consider private or hybrid cloud solutions. We have also seen the importance of embodying customer security requirements in SLAs to protect interests for compliance, DR, and other concerns. While delegation of resource management and procurement is a great advantage of cloud computing, customers are still accountable for the security and privacy of the deployed systems and data.

Cloud computing is a new technology that is still emerging. The challenges that appear in the realm of security are being addressed by security experts. If an organization plans to move to a cloud environment, they should do so with caution and weigh the risks to be able to enjoy the low-cost flexibility offered by this empowering technology.

Finally, let's move on to the real interactive part of this Chapter: review questions/exercises, hands-on projects, case projects, and optional team case project. The answers and/or solutions by chapter can be found in Appendix K.

CHAPTER REVIEW QUESTIONS/ EXERCISES

True/False

1. True or False? SaaS, PaaS, and IaaS are SPI models.
2. True or False? The risk-based approach is recommended for organizations considering the cloud.
3. True or False? The data and resources asset(s) is supported by the cloud.
4. True or False? A customer hosts its own application and data while hosting a part of the functionality in the cloud. This service model is referred to as SaaS.
5. True or False? A customer's first step in evaluating its risks while considering a cloud deployment would be to select the data or function that's going to be hosted in the cloud.

Multiple Choice

1. In the criteria to evaluate a potential cloud service model or provider, a customer should consider:
   A. Comfort level for moving to the cloud
   B. Level of control at each SPI cloud model
   C. Importance of assets to move to the cloud
   D. Type of assets to move to the cloud
   E. All of the above
2. Which attack type can affect an IaaS environment?
   A. Cross-site-request-forgery attacks
   B. Side-channel attacks (VM-to-VM)
   C. Token stealing
   D. Canonicalization attacks
   E. All of the above
3. What should a cloud customer prefer for DR?
   A. High RTO, low cost
   B. Low RTO, high cost
   C. Low RTO, low cost, all data
   D. Backup critical data with a low RTO and cost
   E. All of the above
4. Which deployment model is suitable for customers who need the flexibility and resources of a public cloud but also need to secure and define their networks?
   A. Hybrid
   B. Private

   C. Secured
   D. Virtual Private
   E. All of the above
5. What does an SLA cover?
   A. Service levels
   B. Security
   C. Governance
   D. Compliance
   E. All of the above

EXERCISE

Problem

Does the cloud solution offer equal or greater data security capabilities than those provided by your organization's data center?

Hands-on Projects

Project

Have you taken into account the vulnerabilities of the cloud solution?

Case Projects

Problem

As a project to build a small cloud environment, how do you setup a VPC environment on the Amazon EC2 platform?

Optional Team Case Project

Problem

Have you considered that incident detection and response can be more complicated in a cloud-based environment?

REFERENCES

[1] Guidelines on Security and Privacy in Public Cloud Computing, NIST Special Publication 800−144.
[2] Cloud Computing: Benefits, Risks and Recommendations for Information Security, The European Network and Information Security Agency, 2009.
[3] Security Guidance for Critical Areas of Focus in Cloud Computing v3.0, Cloud Security Alliance, 2011.
[4] Amazon Virtual Private Cloud. http://aws.amazon.com/vpc/.

Chapter 64

Cloud Security

Edward G. Amoroso
TAG Cyber LLC, United States

1. CLOUD OVERVIEW: PUBLIC, PRIVATE, HYBRID

Modern enterprise organizations have begun to include cloud computing in support of data center operations, application provisioning, and service deployment. Cloud adoption has been especially aggressive in small and medium sized businesses, which are especially attracted to cloud economics. Larger organizations are moving toward cloud more slowly, owing to inevitable regulatory and compliance issues that arise with any sort of outsourced arrangement. Meanwhile, Internet and mobile service providers view cloud technology as an effective means to reduce cost and deploy on-demand products.

Three categories of cloud services in use are *public*, *hybrid*, and *private* (Fig. 64.1). A *public cloud* makes services available to the general public over the Internet. Examples include Dropbox File Hosting Service and Amazon Web Services, both of which use shared infrastructure resources across multiple customers to reduce cost and support on-demand expansion. A *private cloud* uses a firewall-based perimeter to keep the resources of one user logically

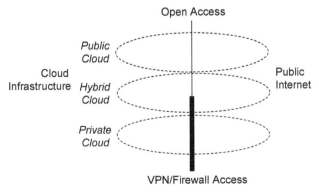

FIGURE 64.1 Three categories of cloud. *VPN*, virtual private network.

separated from all others. The enterprise networks of larger companies, for example, often include private clouds implemented using VMWare or OpenStack software. Such private clouds are made separate from the Internet using a perimeter network. A *hybrid cloud* combines use of public and private clouds in a variety of different arrangements. Internet service providers, for example, offer hybrid cloud services to customers who want increased expansion flexibility. Enterprise architects create hybrid cloud arrangement to optimize the strengths of different public and private offerings.

Users of public and hybrid clouds have different options for the specific types of services made available by their providers. The most common examples include *Software-as-a-Service* (SaaS), *Platform-as-a-Service* (PaaS), and *Infrastructure-as-a-Service* (IaaS). Each of these options is characterized by on-demand operation, which allows for utility computing for end users, an efficient model that optimizes budget. *SaaS* offerings involve applications being licensed and delivered to users over the Internet using a financial subscription model. *PaaS* offerings involve support for users to develop, operate, and maintain their own Web applications without having to manage the underlying compute, hosting, and network infrastructure. *IaaS* offerings involve the provision of virtual machines to users over the Internet. Each of these cloud services shares essential elements that define cloud computing, as defined by the National Institute of Standards and Technology (NIST) [1]:

- *On-demand self-service*: involves users having the ability to obtain services without lengthy provisioning processes by providers
- *Broad network access*: involves the ability for users to access services from a broad geographic and logical network perspective such as with the Internet
- *Resource pooling*: involves services that are bundled together and shared to reduce cost and increase flexibility of use and operation

Computer and Information Security Handbook. http://dx.doi.org/10.1016/B978-0-12-803843-7.00064-8

- *Rapid elasticity*: involves the ability for users to obtain additional (or fewer) resources quickly as needed
- *Measured service*: involves service operation that is closely monitored and measured so as to control pricing

The definition of cloud services by NIST conspicuously omits any definition of required security capability. Groups such as the Cloud Security Alliance (CSA) have tried to fill this gap with guidance on best practices for the protection of cloud-resident data and for optimization of security in cloud operations [2]. Nevertheless, not only is community agreement on security best practices for cloud operations missing, many organizations, particularly large financial service firms, view any use of public or even hybrid clouds as potentially having fatal, inherent security risks.

2. CLOUD SECURITY THREATS

Security threats to cloud services and infrastructure can be identified using traditional threat taxonomy measures (Fig. 64.2). Specifically, hierarchical threat modeling can be used with the familiar confidentiality, integrity, availability model as the hierarchical root, and the cloud infrastructure taxonomy of data, services, and infrastructure as the second root. This two-level model produces a six-node threat model that helps highlight specific areas of focus in addressing cloud infrastructure threats. The six-node model becomes 18 nodes when the third level breaks down threats into public, hybrid, and private.

Each node in the cloud threat taxonomy provides a hint as to the types of concerns an enterprise should have with respect to the use of cloud infrastructure. Experience suggests that the highest risk (probability of attack combined with damage consequence) is associated with three cloud threat categories:

- *Cloud data secrecy*: adversaries covet unauthorized access to private, proprietary, and secret data stored in cloud

- *Cloud system integrity*: proper operation of cloud systems and virtual operation represent a significant target
- *Cloud infrastructure availability*: the denial of service threat is intense for cloud provisioning, access, and use

Although these threats are of comparable intensity for public, hybrid, and private clouds, the manner in which countermeasures are deployed will differ substantially for each case. Private cloud security, for example, will rely heavily on existing perimeter and traditional enterprise controls; public clouds, in contrast, will rely on the feature functionality associated with the cloud provider, including multifactor authentication for user access. These security safeguards are obviously not specific to cloud protection.

Several security technologies and architectural approaches have emerged, however, that focus on the specific threats to public, hybrid, and private clouds. The next few sections provide a more detailed view of several popular approaches in use by enterprise security teams today.

3. INTERNET SERVICE PROVIDER CLOUD VIRTUAL PRIVATE NETWORK PEERING SERVICES

A common security concern with respect to public or hybrid cloud data, services, and infrastructure is the network access path that exists between enterprise gateways and cloud access points. Public or hybrid clouds that are accessible on the Internet, for example, are particularly vulnerable to distributed denial of service attacks. Similarly, data being transferred to and from public or hybrid clouds are vulnerable to prying eavesdroppers with sniffers.

One technique commonly deployed involves the use of private peering connections by Internet service providers (ISPs) from customer virtual private networks (VPNs) into public or hybrid cloud network infrastructure. The technique is most useful for enterprise users of

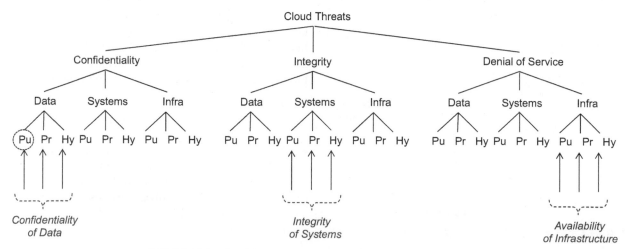

FIGURE 64.2   Cloud threat taxonomy. *Hy*, hybrid; *Pr*, private; *Pu*, public.

ISP-provided multiprotocol label switching (MPLS) networks with VPN capabilities. The ISP uses prearranged peering connections with popular clouds so that an MPLS VPN can include the public cloud as a private node (Fig. 64.3).

This technique clearly reduces the attack surface for public cloud use, especially with respect to denial of service attacks originating on the Internet. It also keeps data sharing activity to the peered public cloud contained to the enterprise VPN. The technique does not, however, prevent the *overall* public cloud infrastructure being peered with from being attacked, because hackers will still have access from Internet-facing gateways. Thus, denial of service attacks, for example, can still have an effect. The technique also does not reduce the likelihood of advanced persistent threats (APTs) being performed through perimeter networks for the purpose of stealing sensitive data going to or from the public cloud over the private peering link.

4. CLOUD ACCESS SECURITY BROKERS

The Internet-facing architecture for public and hybrid clouds lends well to a policy-based, front-end access mediation function. With the front door to public cloud infrastructure such as Amazon Web Services essentially wide open to anyone with Internet connectivity, it is imperative that such access mediation provide strong protection from unauthorized attempts to gather sensitive cloud-resident data or modify cloud systems and applications. Enterprise security teams set policy for such access, and cloud systems should have the ability to enforce this policy.

In response to this requirement, the cybersecurity industry has begun to see the emergence of a functional component called a *cloud access security broker (CASB)* [3]. The CASB (Fig. 64.4) is generally involved as a man-in-the-middle filter through which any type of cloud access, data transfer, download, or other operation must be mediated. The CASB might provide arbitration services, where it has an active role in the protocol; it can provide adjudication services, where it serves as a third party to resolve disputes; or it can serve as a front-end authentication component, where reported identities are validated and access is controlled based on roles, privileges, and security policy.

The decision to implement the CASB as a forward or reverse proxy presents unique challenges in each case. Forward proxies are established by an enterprise to protect users in their communications with the external world. Most commonly used by the enterprise security team in conjunction with a firewall to enforce access policy, forward proxies are most compatible with modern perimeter-based enterprise networks. When the enterprise perimeter begins to blur, forward proxy deployment becomes more challenging. Reverse proxies, on the other hand, are used to protect servers from incoming threats. Users desiring access to a resource inside a reverse proxy will have to negotiate such access first, which turns out to be an excellent means for protecting public clouds from hackers on the Internet.

5. CLOUD ENCRYPTION

Encryption requirements for stored sensitive data can be found in virtually every cybersecurity compliance framework relevant to the enterprise. This stands to reason given the preponderance of data leaks that have occurred as a result of unauthorized access to unencrypted data such as

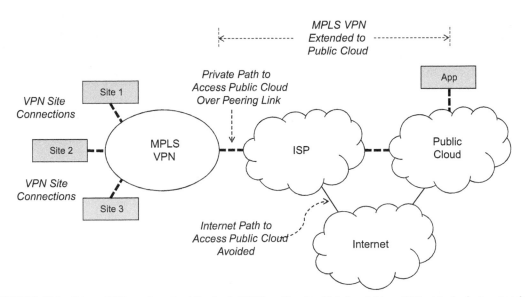

FIGURE 64.3 Private VPN peering of public cloud. *MPLS*, multiprotocol label switching; *VPN*, virtual private network.

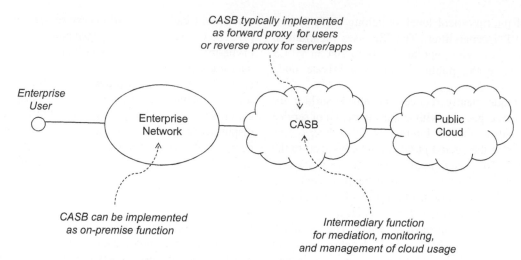

FIGURE 64.4   Cloud access security broker (CASB) network architecture.

personal medical records, credit cards, and contact information. With the evolution to cloud technology and services, it becomes more challenging to meet such encryption requirements, especially in public and hybrid cloud services. The main practical issues with respect to implementing stored data encryption are as follows:

- *Encryption algorithm*: The selected encryption algorithm should have documented assurance of secure design and implementation. This can be achieved via compliance processes such as the National Security Agency (NSA) Suite A/B process, which includes algorithms such as the Advanced Encryption Standard.
- *Key management*: The key management approach should also follow standards to the degree possible with sufficient documented assurance of correct design. The NSA Suite A/B process includes several methods such as Elliptic Curve Cryptography for key management.
- *Data masking*: The ability to mask values in cloud storage is generally not achieved through cryptographic means, but will be an increasingly important feature in secure cloud data storage.

Cloud encryption, key management, masking, and other data features are implemented in cloud via a data-centric protection model. That is, rather than relying on external access protections such as perimeter or CASB functions, data-centric approaches tightly bind security protections to the actual data. Traditional digital rights management works in this manner with permissions, access controls, and other protections tightly connected to the asset.

The result of any data-centric protection model is that data can travel outside an enterprise local area network or other well-defined network to external infrastructure such as the Internet with no drop in secrecy protection. Cloud encryption works in precisely this manner; data can be created, encrypted, and then safely placed in a public or hybrid cloud.

A common implementation approach, although certainly not the only practical method, involves a cloud encryption gateway (Fig. 64.5) that intercepts cloud ingress and egress traffic, often as part of a forward or reverse proxy, and encrypts it before it is stored or sent over an untrusted network. The key management for such a gateway solution requires coordination with user clients and with any disaster recovery management systems that could demand access to data in an emergency.

A common debate with respect to encrypted data stored in cloud is the degree to which the cloud storage provider is obliged to maintain key information for retrieval. Obviously, in cases where disaster occurs and information must be retrieved, having assistance from the storage provider is essential. The challenge is that so much political controversy exists around third-party access to encrypted information that service providers take different approaches to key management. Larger companies can manage their own keys and recovery processes, but smaller companies and individuals will need assistance.

6. CLOUD SECURITY MICROSEGMENTATION

A creative approach to the provision of security for cloud workloads is known as a microsegment. Driven by the degradation of the enterprise perimeter as an effective data

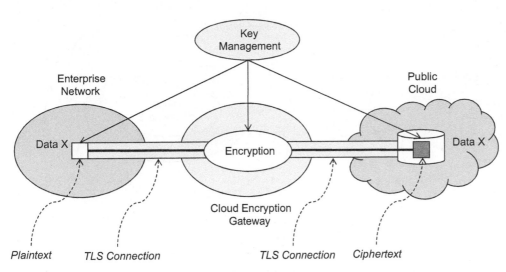

FIGURE 64.5 Typical cloud encryption gateway approach. *TLS*, transport layer security.

protection solution, security technologists have begun to harness the power of virtual provisioning to augment the dynamic creation of virtual machines with the dynamic creation of *virtual security* for the virtual machines. The result is a microperimeter wrapped around cloud workloads with only the protections required for that workload.

The security model for cloud microsegments is based on the automated exchanges that exist in cloud computing between virtual workload processes across application programming interfaces. Presumably a policy would exist for read, write, and execute-type operations between processes, and enforcement would be performed at the edge of the microsegment (Fig. 64.6), perhaps with augmented continual monitoring inside the workload, as one would find with a vulnerability scanning solution.

The advantages of microsegments include all of the familiar benefits of virtualization including reduced hardware costs and increase provisioning cycle times. In addition, the concept of microsegmentation allows for perimeter design that can be tailored to the specific needs of the cloud workload being protected. This can greatly simplify perimeter network design because workloads will always have more modest requirements than an entire enterprise network. The segmentation approach thus reduces the need for massively complex perimeter networks in favor of more focused and more distributed microperimeters protecting cloud workloads.

A desired implication of cloud security microsegmentation, and one that remains to be determined in practice, is a dramatic reduction in APTs. Traditional enterprise networks are vulnerable to the so-called east—west traversal risk, in which an adversary gains unauthorized access to the enterprise and then uses this access to scan for valued assets to steal. With microsegments, the potential for such east—west traversal is reduced, and hence the APT threat would appear to be reduced in commensurate fashion.

7. CLOUD SECURITY COMPLIANCE

A major hurdle for many enterprise teams desiring to move assets into cloud computing and infrastructure is the compliance obligation that comes with any shift in design. Great amounts of time and effort have been spent by virtually every chief information security officer team in virtually every sector to demonstrate compliance of their infrastructure with a plethora of compliance framework requirements. Regulatory, audit, and compliance oversight teams have been particularly tough on enterprise teams, given the repeat data loss attacks experienced by so many customers.

In response to this compliance obligation, groups have formed to support the development of proper security design and operations for cloud systems. The most prominent group supporting security best practice in cloud is the CSA. Driven by corporate and government members, the CSA provides a certification process called CSA Security, Trust, and Assurance Registry (STAR) [4] that allows cloud offerings to transparently document their security practices and features for customers. The CSA STAR is based on two fundamental constructs:

- *Cloud Controls Matrix*: lays out in a structured manner the cloud security controls in place for a given offering
- *Continuous Assessments Initiative Questionnaire*: supports users and auditors with question and answer information that can be useful in cloud security assurance activities.

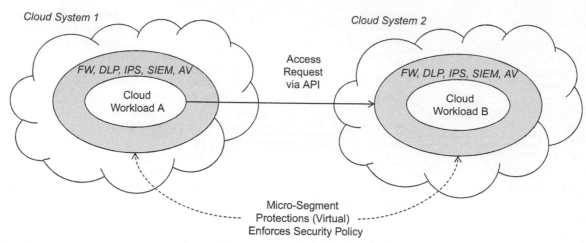

FIGURE 64.6 Intercloud workload policy enforcement at microsegment edge. *API*, application programming interface; *AV*, antivirus; *DLP*, data loss prevention; *FW*, firewall; *IPS*, intrusion protection system; *SIEM*, security information and event management.

These types of assurance functions from CSA are valuable because they provide confidence that as data move from existing perimeter controls to more distributed, virtual protection in public and hybrid clouds, the security controls will meet or even exceed the current levels. Such assurance for CSA STAR can be done in various ways. So-called "Level 1" involves a self-assessment that is documented and provided to customers. "Level 2" assessments involve third parties offering attestation, certification, assessment, and even continuous monitoring.

Finally, the risk-based approach to security control selection and specification considers effectiveness, efficiency, and constraints owing to applicable laws, directives, executive orders, policies, standards, or regulations. Although the framework is flexible and easily adaptable in most cases, it assumes a traditional information technology environment and requires some customization to address the unique characteristics of cloud-based services (see checklist: "An Agenda for Action for Addressing the Unique Characteristics of Cloud-Based Services").

An Agenda for Action for Addressing the Unique Characteristics of Cloud-Based Services

Addressing the unique characteristics of cloud-based services includes the following key activities (check all tasks completed):

_____**1.** Categorize the information system or service migrated to the cloud, and the information processed, stored, and transmitted by that system based on an impact analysis.

_____**2.** Identify security requirements for the information system or service migrated to the cloud, and perform a risk assessment, including a confidentiality, integrity, and availability analysis to identify security components that are appropriate for the system.

_____**3.** Select the baseline security controls.

_____**4.** Select the cloud ecosystem architecture that best fits the analysis performed in Activity 2 for the information system or service migrated to the cloud.

_____**5.** Assess service provider(s) based on their authorization-to-operate (ATO).

_____**6.** Identify the security controls needed for the cloud-based information system or service already implemented by the cloud provider.

_____**7.** Negotiate the implementation of additional security components and controls identified as necessary for this system or service.

_____**8.** When applicable, identify the security controls that remain within the cloud consumer's responsibility, and implement them.

_____**9.** Authorize the use of the selected cloud provider (and cloud broker, when applicable) for hosting the cloud-based information system or service.

_____**10.** Negotiate a service agreement (SA) and service level agreement (SLA) that reflects the negotiation performed in Activity 7.

_____**11.** Monitor the cloud provider (and the cloud broker when applicable) to ensure that all SA and SLA terms are met and that the cloud-based information system maintains the necessary security posture.

_____**12.** Directly monitor the security components and associated controls under the cloud consumer's direct responsibility.

8. SUMMARY

The future of cloud security is mixed, depending on one's perspective. For vendors offering cloud security solutions, the future is bright, with the potential for explosive growth in demand for cloud encryption, cloud access security brokers, cloud workload security, and so on. For enterprise security managers, the future carries with it the obligation to transfer architectural controls from perimeters and local area networks to varied combinations of public, private, and hybrid clouds. This is the correct architectural decision, but it carries with it a great deal of transitional risk, simply because so much will be changing. The group that should experience the biggest jolt with respect to cloud security, however, will be the compliance and regulatory community. Naturally conservative as a group, this community will have to achieve considerable comfort through training and experience before it will sanction public clouds fully acceptable from a security risk perspective. The irony, as they no doubt have already realized, is that the alternative, namely maintenance of the current enterprise perimeter risk, is a worse choice.

Finally, let us move on to the real interactive part of this chapter: review questions/exercises, hands-on projects, case projects, and the optional team case project. The answers and/or solutions by chapter can be found in Appendix K.

CHAPTER REVIEW QUESTIONS/ EXERCISES

True/False

1. True or False? The definition of cloud services by NIST conspicuously adds a definition of required security capability.
2. True or False? Security threats to cloud services and infrastructure can be identified using nontraditional threat taxonomy measures.
3. True or False? Each node in the cloud threat taxonomy provides a hint as to the types of concerns an enterprise should have with respect to the use of cloud infrastructure.
4. True or False? Several security technologies and architectural approaches have emerged that focus on specific threats to public, hybrid, and private clouds.
5. True or False? A common security concern with respect to public or hybrid cloud data, services, and infrastructure is the network access path that exists between enterprise gateways and cloud access points.

Multiple Choice

1. One technique commonly being deployed involves the use of _____ by Internet service providers (ISPs) from customer virtual private networks (VPNs) into public or hybrid cloud network infrastructure:
   A. Private peering connections
   B. Interface security connections
   C. Data integrity connections
   D. Payment Card Industry security connections
   E. Audit assurance connections
2. The cybersecurity industry has begun to see the emergence of a functional component called a:
   A. Man-in-the-middle filter
   B. Front-end authentication component
   C. Forward proxy
   D. Forward proxy deployment
   E. Cloud access security broker
3. What requirements for stored sensitive data can be found in virtually every cybersecurity compliance framework relevant to the enterprise?
   A. Algorithm
   B. Encryption
   C. Management
   D. Data
   E. All of the above
4. What should have documented assurance of secure design and implementation?
   A. Key management
   B. Data masking
   C. Encryption algorithm
   D. Framework planning
   E. All of the above
5. A common implementation approach, although certainly not the only practical method, involves a cloud encryption gateway that intercepts cloud ingress and egress traffic, often as part of a forward or reverse proxy, and encrypts it before it is stored or sent over a(n):
   A. Trusted network
   B. Local area network
   C. Wireless area network
   D. Untrusted network
   E. All of the above

EXERCISE

Problem

Does the cloud solution offer data security capabilities equal to or greater than those provided by your organization's data center?

Hands-on Projects

Project

Have you taken into account the vulnerabilities of the cloud solution?

Case Projects

Problem

Have you considered that incident detection and response can be more complicated in a cloud-based environment?

Optional Team Case Project

Problem

Have you considered that metrics collection, and system performance and security monitoring are more difficult in the cloud?

REFERENCES

[1] NIST Special Publication 800-145, The NIST Definition of Cloud Computing, September 2011.

[2] Cloud Security Alliance Overview, https://www.cloudsecurityalliance. org/.

[3] Cloud Access Security Brokers (CASBs), Gartner IT Glossary, https://www.gartner.com/it-glossary/.

[4] Cloud Security Alliance, Security, Trust, and Assurance Registry, https://www.cloudsecurityalliance.org/.

Chapter 65

Private Cloud Security

Keith Lewis

kCura, Chicago, IL, United States

1. INTRODUCTION: PRIVATE CLOUD SYSTEM MANAGEMENT

Companies and organizations are increasingly shifting their computer infrastructure resources from on-premises (on-prem) to off-premises (off-prem) cloud service models. By moving toward these off-site solution services, businesses can take advantage of increased scalability while reducing on-prem support costs that extensively increase along with on-site support personnel and hardware service providers to manage these systems. This includes the costs of housing, power, heating, ventilation, and air conditioning management, and security that take a larger bite out of a company's budget every year, to help support them. Public and private cloud system services (Fig. 65.1) are off-prem solutions that can make these types of solutions significantly cost-effective for growing companies and the services they provide to their customers. Public cloud services usually provide physical and hardware administrative and maintenance control from a third-party service provider. This provider resides on the Internet; private cloud services do the same, except that the physical server and relevant network devices are fully managed by the customer only while leveraging the equipment at dedicated remote data center sites (off-prem) to take advantage of system housing needs. Private cloud security has the advantage of fully controlling host equipment, firewall defensive systems, CPU and memory resource allocation, Web server management, direct database instance management, and many other aspects normally associated with on-prem data center facilities [1]. This type of model best fits larger companies that have infrastructure support budgets to maintain this type of control because of company compliance requirements, depending on the nature of the business. With private cloud environments comes the importance of managing security points remotely over the Internet or through private service provider networks using the same encryption and security levels as an on-prem location; however, the risks of cloud vulnerabilities must be fully taken into account because these kinds of solutions can fall victim, as well.

2. FROM PHYSICAL TO NETWORK SECURITY BASE FOCUS

Traditional data centers on-prem required the security focus to start at the physical level. This includes physical security access from the door to the data center to local security camera surveillance systems, accessing the individual racks housing the server or network switches, routers, and application equipment that had to be fully managed by local on-prem personnel with information technology (IT) system administrators. With a focus on private cloud security, the physical security housing aspect is under the ownership of the remote site service provider. However, network connectivity, physical server or virtual environments, network systems, and other remote systems are fully under the control of IT support groups remotely connecting to these systems. Depending on the type of service agreement you have with a cloud vendor, maintenance of physical equipment off-prem can also be the full responsibility of an IT system administrator or engineer coming to the location and replacing or changing out equipment. Normally, public cloud services maintain these areas of support, but mostly private cloud environments require these types of micromanagement tasks to support these environments securely on an ongoing basis [2].

Private cloud security has a strong dependency on remote daily interactions, from system integrity monitoring

Computer and Information Security Handbook. http://dx.doi.org/10.1016/B978-0-12-803843-7.00065-X

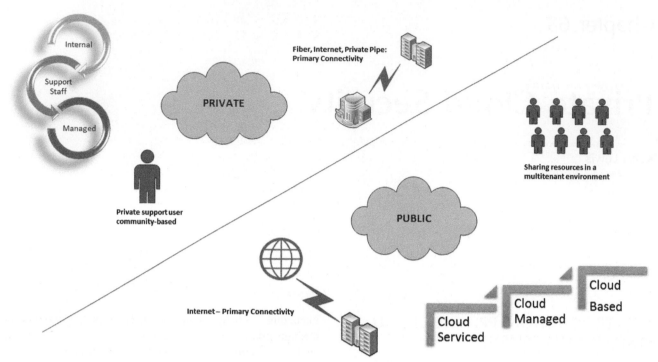

FIGURE 65.1 Private versus public clouds.

to firewall intrusion alerts and server or application access alert notifications. This includes certificate of authority—based management for Web services or capacity alert notification; a network security—based focus is the higher priority to ensure connectivity communication is always at a premium for IT support teams. Existing IP address segment and virtual local area network (LAN) management structures should remain the same, at a network level, other than IP range changes needed to accommodate a private security cloud infrastructure. Most network configurations on the remote internal LAN should not be seriously affected moving into this model or managing the solution on a regular basis. There are important security points that require security control audit reviews, especially with remote data center site management service agreements (see checklist: "An Agenda for Action for Creating Important Security Points That Require Security Control Audit Reviews").

Most private cloud providers working with large companies will have dedicated, walled-off room areas in data centers to manage multitenant environments for security purposes. However, some cloud service providers rely more on rack space or closet security facilities. What normally defines these types of services is the overall cost or level of security the customer and vendor agrees upon with the service provider that best fits their company or organization's security needs. Also, regulatory standards of compliance such as the Health Insurance Portability and Accountability Act can have a significant part in identifying

---

An Agenda for Action for Creating Important Security Points That Require Security Control Audit Reviews

Creating important security points that require security control audit reviews includes the following key activities (check all tasks completed):

_____**1.** In-place security policy process and procedures for off-prem access (Fig. 65.2) to the physical data center for regular maintenance visits requiring a company's engineer or business partner vendors to service equipment, if required

_____**2.** Isolated remote data center access pointed to be in place and regularly monitored, such as locked server racks, access to the same equipment area shared by other companies, or equipment security monitoring services

_____**3.** Escorted access through the off-prem data center for non—company related personnel, such as other companies possibly sharing the same floor or computer room but not the same rack space in which your company equipment currently resides

_____**4.** Approved scheduled visits by senior management or company authorized personnel for any off-prem onsite visits to the cloud data center location.

_____**5.** Backbone network infrastructure fully secured from physical access except for authorized personnel from the cloud service provider or company network engineering support teams

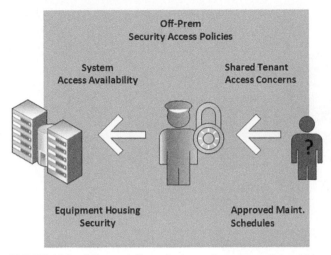

FIGURE 65.2 Off-prem (off-premises) security access policies. *Maint,* maintenance.

the level of physical security you require for your private cloud physical security needs [3].

3. BENEFITS OF PRIVATE CLOUD SECURITY INFRASTRUCTURES

Some benefits a company can have with working within a private cloud security infrastructure are having a large amount of resource and process control over the environments that are housed off-prem. For example, the IT systems support team is limited to using only security methodologies that a public cloud-based security services would force on a customer, which could potentially limit the compatibility or effectiveness of a customized business application solution unique to the company's services. If a company's Web services use a particular set of protocols, port ranges, and routing configurations for their public Internet-facing business solution, but the public cloud provider requires a different network standard that forces a customer to change this configuration, this could greatly affect the way delivered and supported because the customer makes extensive efforts to accommodate the service provider, and not the other way around. Having the freedom to manage your systems in a private cloud security level avoids this. There are many advantages to having private cloud control management during audit reviews, implementing network tunneling solutions, and other unique company solution-based legacy systems that may not be ready to adhere to public cloud security requirement solutions or communication services. Capacity and elasticity are more easily controlled and maintained by IT support personnel than by going through extensive service agreements or technology planning with a public cloud service vendor [5].

4. PRIVATE CLOUD SECURITY STANDARDS AND BEST PRACTICES

Institutes such as the Cloud Security Alliance (CSA) are leading technology standards organizations that serve to provide industry support for cloud security awareness for both public and private based environments. Governments, businesses, educational institutes, nonprofit organizations, and other cloud-based entities greatly benefit from certified subject matter experts and CSA chapter organizations that provide thorough security matrix assessment plans to cover a large spectrum of cloud-based security needs. Next are some of the best practice planning tools they can provide an IT governance committee and IT security department to implement and maintain ongoing cloud-based services for private cloud security environments [3]:

Cloud Controls Matrix

This tool provides security experts and auditors with Domain and Control ID specification structures that will greatly benefit private security cloud infrastructures through audit assessment reviews (Fig. 65.3). Examples of security controls that map to physical, networking, computational resources, storage management, or application support for architecture relevance are areas such as:

- application security
- interface security
- data integrity
- audit assurance
- business continuity
- change control and configuration management
- data center security asset management
- identity management
- cloud service delivery models such as Software-as-a-Service (SaaS), Platform-as-a-Service (PaaS), and Infrastructure-as-a-Service (IaaS)

The Payment Card Industry (PCI) Security Standards Council also provides a wealth of security cloud-based guidelines companies and organizations that can leverage and take advantage of public and private security cloud environments that must use card payment solutions for customer user transactions to cloud-based service providers. The PCI Data Security Standard is normally provided by cloud special interest groups working in collaboration with the PCI Security Standards Council. These standards are updated and published on a regular basis. This gives payment card security support personnel frameworks needed to ensure a reliable and secure cloud security environment for their company or organization and keep the focus on any regulatory requirement. These requirements are what finance departments must adhere to when working with technology solution providers and local

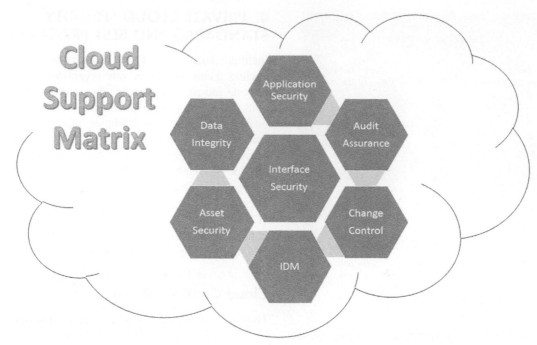

FIGURE 65.3 Cloud support matrix. *IDM*, identity management.

IT support administration staff. Private security cloud subject matter experts who could also benefit from these guidelines are [4]:

- merchant-related businesses and service providers
- cloud service providers
- security audit assessors
- public or private security cloud IT support departments
- IT governance departments

5. "AS-A-SERVICE" UNIVERSE: SERVICE MODELS

Cloud solutions have given security a new landscape of risk mitigation challenges with the multiple benefits they provide. With private cloud security, these types of security challenges are more owned by the customer and their business solutions provider than the cloud infrastructure provider. IaaS, PaaS, and SaaS are industry-proven service models supported by standard institutes with framework-planning publications companies, and organizations can take advantage when implementing and supporting these types of services in the cloud [6,7].

Infrastructure-as-a-Service

The IaaS service model provides infrastructure services to customers with "on-demand" functionality such as servers, network equipment, software, and virtual environments. This helps customers avoid housing and purchasing these

environments with all of the additional on-prem support costs that would be associated with them. This would include paying for unused performance functionality that on-demand solutions allow only for paying for services that are needed; and, being used, instead of purchasing larger, possibly bloated environments that are not being fully used. Private cloud security challenges in these types of environments are sometimes the same as those for on-prem data centers, except the facilities security ownership is provided by the cloud service provider and not maintained at the local office level. However, private cloud security models in IaaS service models still must be fully maintained in mandating and defining what their company considers the security risk level and mitigation its cloud service provider should own and not own at the off-prem facilities level. Network communication security over the cloud is still the responsibility of the customer IT support staff because they manage and support these devices. These devices can be the router, firewall, and equipment-based session levels of security directly; except for power needs, most cloud services are responsible for their switch-room security or data center access permission ownership using regular customer-area shared service model security standards.

Platform-as-a-Service

The PaaS service model provides service delivery at the platform level, again using the benefits for on-demand service capabilities. Whereas IaaS delivers holistic environment solutions at an enterprise level for data center infrastructure functionality, PaaS focuses on platform-specific services such as an application platform and its pertaining database or Web service layer environments. PaaS delivers development changes or ongoing patch maintenance requirements to support and maintain the platform environment solution. Because of technical support complexity for PaaS in problem management, incident management, and change and release management, security responsibilities are normally shared evenly with the customer and the cloud service provider.

Software-as-a-Service

The SaaS service model delivers more at the software, application, and computational resource level, leveraging on-demand service delivery functionality. It normally provides on-demand as a turnkey-type service solution to help with cost savings on additional hardware equipment, software installations, and day-to-day operational support maintenance costs that include license and resource tracking. The cloud service provider in public cloud security models mostly does the security management; in private cloud security environments, administrative responsibilities are a shared agreement between the customer and cloud vendor, similar to the PaaS service model [7].

6. PRIVATE CLOUD SERVICE MODEL: LAYER CONSIDERATIONS

The intricacies of security layer point considerations for creating and managing an effective private cloud security model can be vast. Areas of importance when it comes to identifying required technical layers can be [8]:

- *Client layer considerations*: These layers must ensure that identity management protection is fully managed by using authentication, authorization, and account provisioning work flows as effectively as possible.
- *Software layer considerations*: This layer has to take into account the application's compatibility with encrypted network communication sessions. If the software is not programmed to accommodate secure socket layer sessions, the performance and function can be poor or open to compromise to innovative hackers if the application fails in midstream during protocol communication transports.
- *Platform layer considerations*: With added complexity to manage a private cloud environment comes the designing and architecting equipment platform response timing behavior with its application layer. If unknown performance latency is introduced into the environment, Botnet attacks or denial of service attacks can easily cripple the systems by overwhelming these negative system response times.

7. PRIVACY OR PUBLIC: THE CLOUD SECURITY CHALLENGES

Going to a cloud service model does not improve the simplicity of security. Most of the time, it adds even more complexity and challenges to the overall security process, as follows:

- **Monitoring**: more network end points to monitor carefully in a shared network communication environment that is more Internet/demilitarized zone facing
- **Complexity**: with more dependency on encrypted sessions, file transport communication, filtering out a multitenant activity against your own, ensuring optimal protocol and security appliances are working at peak, and effective efficiency will be more difficult than single-location/backbone infrastructure housing
- **Data replication**: enterprise distribution service models benefit from cloud designs; however, security encapsulation support can become "watered down" if all the distribution points on the Internet are not fully monitored with ongoing risk assessment evaluations held periodically to ensure secure shared service environments are being protected holistically
- **Trust**: the cloud service provider takes on most of the physical back-end hardware security protection residing in their infrastructures for both public and private service models. If an organization depends on government regulation—set security standards, full disclosure and security service agreements must be evaluated and completed to ensure the cloud environment being used has met all legal requirement criteria set by these regulations. Preproject security initiatives identify this early on before the design and implementation process to make sure security is strongly taken into consideration.

8. SUMMARY

This chapter has provided an overview of the security of private clouds; challenges facing private cloud computing; and recommendations that organizations should consider when outsourcing data, applications, and infrastructure to a private cloud environment. The chapter has also provided insights into threats, technology risks, and safeguards related to private cloud environments to help organizations make informed decisions about the use of this technology.

In addition, private cloud computing and the other deployment models are a viable choice for many applications and services. However, accountability for security in private cloud deployments cannot be delegated to a cloud provider and remains an obligation for the organization to fulfill.

Finally, let us move on to the real interactive part of this chapter: review questions/exercises, hands-on projects, case projects, and the optional team case project. The answers and/or solutions by chapter can be found in Appendix K.

CHAPTER REVIEW QUESTIONS/ EXERCISES

True/False

1. True or False? Traditional data centers on-prem required the security focus to start at the metaphysical level.
2. True or False? Most private cloud providers working with large companies will mostly have dedicated, walled-off room areas in data centers to manage multi-tenant environments for security purposes.
3. True or False? Some of the benefits a company can have with working in a private cloud security infrastructure are having a large amount of resource and process control over environments that are housed off-prem.
4. True or False? Institutes such as the Cloud Security Alliance (CSA) are leading technology standards organizations that serve to provide industry support for cloud security awareness for both public and private based environments.
5. True or False? The Cloud Controls Matrix tool provides security experts and auditors with Domain and Control ID specification structures that will not greatly benefit private security cloud infrastructures through audit assessment reviews.

Multiple Choice

1. Examples of security controls that map to physical, networking, computational resources, storage management, or application support for architecture relevance are areas such as the following, except which one:
   A. Application security
   B. Interface security
   C. Data integrity
   D. PCI security standards
   E. Audit assurance
2. What provides a wealth of security cloud-based guidelines companies and organizations that can leverage and take advantage of public and private security cloud environments, and that must use card payment solutions for customer user transactions to cloud-based service providers?
   A. Business continuity
   B. Change control and configuration management
   C. PCI Security Standards Council
   D. Data center security asset management
   E. All of the above
3. Private security cloud subject matter experts who could also benefit from the standards guidelines are:
   A. Merchant-related businesses and service providers
   B. Cloud service providers
   C. Security audit assessors
   D. Public or private security cloud IT support departments
   E. All of the above

4. Cloud solutions have given security a new landscape of _____ challenges with the multiple benefits they provide as well as:
   A. Risk mitigation
   B. Security
   C. Service models
   D. Framework planning
   E. Infrastructure services
5. What provides infrastructure services with "on-demand" functionality such as servers, network equipment, software, and virtual environments to customers?
   A. PaaS service model
   B. IaaS service model
   C. SaaS service model
   D. Private cloud security model
   E. Private cloud service model

EXERCISE

Problem

What are the main issues with private cloud security?

Hands-on Projects

Project

What are some of the differences between public and private cloud security offerings?

Case Projects

Problem

Does secure private cloud computing change your network security approach?

Optional Team Case Project

Problem

Where should you host your secure private cloud?

REFERENCES

[1] P.W. Singer, A. Friedman, Cybersecurity and Cyberwar, Oxford University and Press, 2014.
[2] C. McNab, Network Security Assessment, third ed., O'Reilly Media, 2016.
[3] CSA. http://cloudsecurityalliance.org.
[4] PCI DSS. https://www.pcisecuritystandards.org/pci_security/.
[5] FISMA. https://www.dhs.gov/fisma/.
[6] ISACA. https://www.isaca.org.
[7] NIST. http://nvlpubs.nist.gov/nistpubs/Legacy/SP/nistspecialpublication800-144.pdf.
[8] Microsoft Technet. http://social.technet.microsoft.com/wiki/contents/articles/6642.a-solution-for-private-cloud-security.aspx.

Chapter 66

Virtual Private Cloud Security

Keith Lewis

kCura, Chicago, IL, United States

1. INTRODUCTION: VIRTUAL NETWORKING IN A PRIVATE CLOUD

Imagine setting up a network perimeter of protection at the local data center that resides at your office or business location, setting up subnets, configuring routers, and managing network address translation (NAT) systems and overall connectivity, designing your Transmission Control Protocol (TCP)/Internet Protocol (IP) network security fabric to ensure private network access while giving your business or organization internet access. Now imagine that all these things no longer reside at your local office data center but exist on a cloud service provider system, remotely at another location, along with your private cloud infrastructure systems. This is what virtual private cloud (VPC) infrastructure entails, similar to local network perimeter design. Let us take an electronic commerce (e-commerce) website as an example. Let us say that your web servers must reside on public-facing systems on the Internet. However, the e-commerce database or authentication identity management systems must stay private on your private cloud network. On your VPC environment, you as the network engineer would set up IP subnets for these devices that are published for all Internet users to access; however, a proxy system using an NAT server safely routes and translates external to internal IP address information safely to your private network. This is the overall concept covering the importance of VPC cloud security planning.

VPC environments (Fig. 66.1) require security management for IP subnets, access control list support, routing table management, and gateway administration that can be managed by a company's network engineers or a cloud server provider's network support teams. Some benefits to using a VPC solution are the ease of scalability and elasticity in accessing equipment resources provided by your cloud provider versus purchasing and setup costs involved in local data center installations. The logical concepts of computer network security, however, stay the same as you would have from publishing Web services to your employee or customer base over the Internet using local networks, except that your environment completely resides at a remote cloud location. Another security layer that is different from a local data center is the private pipe connectivity used by employees or support teams, which accesses the company's computer resources from their office area to the cloud provider.

2. SECURITY CONSOLE: CENTRALIZED CONTROL DASHBOARD MANAGEMENT

When you need to access and set up security equipment on your network, often you need to log in through terminal emulation protocols, separate operating system environments, and multiple unique configuration setups. Many of these support chores are optimized into simple security console control panels provided through large cloud services such as Amazon AWS, VMWare vCloud, Rackspace, and Microsoft Cloud. Enterprise-level systems such as Microsoft Azure give extensive VPC functionality by leveraging Platform-as-a-Service and Infrastructure-as-a-Service concepts for delivering networked data center deployment, development, and administration systems that rely on a VPC network security foundation. Using a Web-based configuration application in a secure connection, all of the resource allocations as well as security group settings are easily available for setting up VPC connectivity [1]. Easily set-up configuration and security functions in these single-managed type consoles can be [3]:

- IP subnet management
- NAT configuration gateway settings
- security group support management

Computer and Information Security Handbook. http://dx.doi.org/10.1016/B978-0-12-803843-7.00066-1

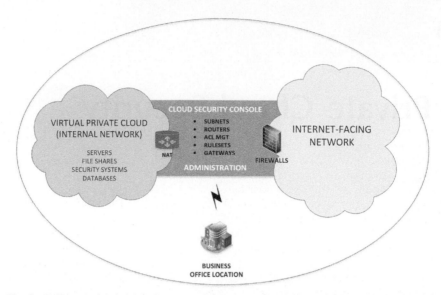

FIGURE 66.1 Cloud security console administration. *ACL MGT*, access control list management; *NAT*, network address translation.

- access control list settings
- routing table setups
- elastic TCP/IP configuration control
- inbound/outbound security object management
- instance support management
- bandwidth threshold management
- protocol control settings
- Internet route mapping rule management
- Layer 7 protection filtering support

- VPN communication management

3. SECURITY DESIGNS: VIRTUAL PRIVATE CLOUD SETUPS

Most VPC configurations can be based on "geographic" location designations. In our example, Chicago will be used for our VPC setup (Fig. 66.2) (see checklist: "An Agenda for Action for a Virtual Private Cloud Setup Approach").

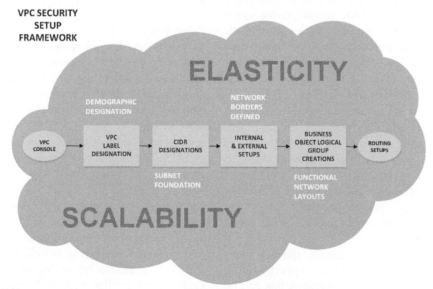

FIGURE 66.2 Virtual private cloud (VPC) security setup framework. *CIDR*, Classless Interdomain Routing.

An Agenda for Action for a Virtual Private Cloud Setup Approach

A step-by-step approach to a VPC setup [2,3] includes the following key activities (check all tasks completed):

_____1. Log into your VPC management console.

_____2. Specify a name for the overall VPC instance, such as "Chicago Northwest VPC."

_____3. Now, as needed, populate your Classless Interdomain Routing (CIDR) block specification information (10.173.0.0/16). Ensure that your range is large, similar to a "Class B" in case you need room for growth in your zones. This allows growth and extensive IP range allocation options to take advantage of larger entities that may, for example, use reserve lookup zones that may be needed to support classless IP address ranges.

_____4. Now, set up your internal and external configurations securely. These should be separate and independent subnet settings to ensure proper communication delegation.

_____5. External subnets normally face the Internet, housing server systems such as Firewalls or low-risk Web services and network appliances.

_____6. Internal subnets would be private-cloud facing. We would need to allocate CIDR settings for both internal and external configurations. Your subnet size and availability settings will vary based on the infrastructure framework requirement your network engineers are trying to build. Servers and platforms such as databases or file shares would normally reside in the internal subnet configuration.

_____7. After both the primary internal and external subnet frameworks have been set up and clearly defined, we can focus on unique business-related topology subnets. Specific subnet segregated networks can be:

_____a. Development Network: For managing development, staging, and release server management systems (production would be fully blocked from these environments at an IP address level, except for code migration or platform upgrade implementation channels)

_____b. Production Network: some Web tier-level servers may be Internet public facing or reside in a subnet zone that safely allows the website access to demilitarized zone Internet users. Depending on the topology and load to support the platform, this layer could be using a Cisco F5 Load Balancer or a Domain Naming Service (DNS) "round robin" configuration to ensure optimal system performance, security, and fail-over or fault tolerance systems

_____c. Directory Services Network: Dynamic Host Control Protocol, DNS, or domain servers would normally reside in these subnet definition regions. For DNS forwarding or any hostname translations during reverse IP address lookups or unique segment considerations, you want to make sure your cloud service provider has DNS services available to your private or external network fabric in case they are needed for optimal system performance, security, and fail-over or fault tolerance systems

_____d. VPC demographic-only subnet configuration creation may need to be considered as well, in case your company or organization is supporting other VPC locations that require secure communication over the private networks of external Internet-facing perimeters. Systems that would use this would be, for example, backup-recovery transport systems, standby database replication systems, virtual private network (VPN) servicing systems, and other important backbone enterprise-level, support-related systems ensuring encryption layers are implemented and safely delegated to authentication hosting systems

_____8. Routing table routing updates, subnet linking to these tables, and default route settings will be the last ongoing support maintenance required for VPC design creation.

---

4. SECURITY OBJECT GROUP ALLOCATIONS: FUNCTIONAL CONTROL MANAGEMENT PRACTICES

Most VPC configurations can be based on "geographic" location designations. Technicians and administrators alike can get lost in the multiple subnet designs that come easily to advanced network engineers. Having this capability allows more efficient network creation and easier ongoing support management throughout the lifecycle of VPC environments. For example, an administrator easily can tie in a subnet created and dedicated only to the database infrastructure domains and zones on your VPC infrastructure. The control console that cloud providers implement allows all of their customers to group these network route access points easily by security object group label allocation versus the need to know [3], configure, and hard-code updates to a static routing table that already has the IP address infrastructure in place. This gives tremendous value to support teams just to pick and choose these dedicated-grouped configurations without the need to rack, unrack, repatch cable, or configure multiple device systems when everything is centralized in a VPC's central control console Web application. Group allocation configuration in these systems also can take advantage of presetting protocol rule sets to allow or deny specific types of stack protocol traffic for both your internal and external subnet configurations.

5. VIRTUAL PRIVATE CLOUD PERFORMANCE VERSUS SECURITY

Businesses are looking for faster and more efficient cloud network solutions to meet the demands of needing larger customer capacity, agile systems or service platform implementation, and affordable infrastructures to Big Data. The problem with more massive environments with a higher focus on performance use could give hackers the coverage needed to slip into flawed topology designs at the network level. Cloud service providers normally provide another layer of holistic security along with the security business will implement on their own when customers set up and manage their VPC enterprise networks. This additional layer of security provided by cloud service providers could come in the form of firewall servers, layered NAT systems with choke router configurations, and strict protocol rule sets to their entire customer base to ensure that common attacks such as Botnet strategies or mass distributed denial of service (DDoS) attacks do not compromise their customer VPC base. Common cloud hack attacks can come in the form of:

- denial of service attacks
- service traffic hijacking attacks
- account hijacking
- simple support negligence
- identity management vulnerabilities

Denial of Service Attacks

When it comes to cloud infrastructure attacks, hacking communities are coming together to orchestrate collaborative efforts to take down systems with DDoS attacks. This hack generates thousands of automatic response requests to which the system attempts to reply, but it can be overwhelmed owing to the sheer volume of intake caused by these digital assaults. Coordinated efforts in communication and security design architectures must be shared with both cloud service provider and its customers so that an effective network security strategy can be devised to safeguard both environments from these types of hacking storms [4].

Service Traffic Hijacking Attacks

Service traffic hijacking attacks can potentially be found in service programming design weaknesses where a hacker will exploit flaws and mimic, take over, or redirect services that are accessed by regular customers without their knowledge. Software vulnerabilities are one of the largest concerns with VPC security support teams. Constant vigilance and due diligence are needed to ensure security patching is as up-to-date as possible so that there is confidence in the overall network access frameworks. Routing table rule sets can only do so much when it comes to attempting to route specific traffic in source-to-destination port range locations. Protocol rule set management is also just as effective if managed properly. For example, network engineers would not want to allow clear text File Transfer Protocol communication flow through an unsecured and unencrypted part of the VPC network where hacking sniffer systems easily can capture and exploit clear text packet information.

Account Hijacking

The Internet browser is an important portal window to the Internet, but it is also a bridge for hackers to leverage their malicious software plugins or search-installed toolbars that can easily capture or cache sensitive and private account information and forward it on to the digital criminal community. Phishing activities from hackers can come in the form of a malicious email that is designed to fool a user into running a dangerous script or take him to a bogus website where a fake duplicated login can easily be captured and used to steal login usernames, passwords, and private security multifactor information. These types of risks are still relevant in VPC environments, and industry standard frameworks with defense in depth strategies should always be strongly considered as regular audit reviews that take these concerns into account.

Simple Support Negligence

Another major type of security risk for VPC security networks is poorly designed or managed setup implementations: for example, not keeping a strongly monitored Certificate of Authority management system in place with updated Web service certificates that ensure Secure Sockets Layer capabilities. Expired certificates, wildcard certificate setups, and other types of security holes all can be identified by engineers or system designers that did not create or managing these systems efficiently and correctly, or Internet Protocol Security encryption/decryption strategies that did not take into account tunneling-point gateway weaknesses owing to active or standby settings configured incorrectly.

Identity Management Vulnerabilities

Authentication, Authorization, and Accounting (AAA) provisioning technologies using stack protocol technologies such as Security Access Markup Language or coded-hash fields over encrypted network communication channels can be at risk if poorly designed. Hacks such as "Pass the Hash" that use LanMan or NT LAN Manager to steal user or administrator passwords can easily flow into compromised server systems if the application layer that manages Initial Decision Maker/AAA systems is not hardened for these attacks.

6. SUMMARY

This chapter covered VPC security as a hybrid model of cloud computing in which a private cloud security solution is provided within a public cloud provider's security infrastructure. VPC security is a cloud computing security service in which a public cloud provider isolates a specific portion of public cloud security infrastructure to be provisioned for private use. The VPC security infrastructure is managed by a public cloud vendor. However, resources allocated to VPC security are not shared with any other customer.

VPC security was introduced specifically for customers interested in taking advantage of the benefits of cloud computing, but who have concerns regarding certain aspects of the cloud. Common concerns involve privacy, security, and the loss of control of proprietary data. In response to this customer need, many public cloud vendors designed a VPC security offering as part of a vendor's public security infrastructure, but with dedicated cloud servers, virtual networks, cloud storage, and private ID addresses, all of which are reserved for a VPC customer. Finally, VPC security is sometimes referred to as private cloud security. However, there is a slight difference, because VPC security is private cloud security sourced over a third-party vendor's security infrastructure rather than over an enterprise's information technology security infrastructure.

Finally, let us move on to the real interactive part of this chapter: review questions/exercises, hands-on projects, case projects, and the optional team case project. The answers and/or solutions by chapter can be found in Appendix K.

CHAPTER REVIEW QUESTIONS/ EXERCISES

True/False

1. True or False? Virtual Private Cloud environments require security management for IP subnets, access control list support, routing table management, and gateway administration that can be managed by a company's network engineers or a cloud server provider's network support teams.
2. True or False? When you need to access and set up your security equipment on your network, often you need to

log in through terminal emulation protocols, separate operating system environments, and multiple unique configuration setups.
3. True or False? Most VPC configurations can be based on "geographic" location designations.
4. True or False? Authentication, Authorization, and Account Provisioning technologies utilizing stack protocol technologies such as Security Access Markup Language, or coded-hash fields over encrypted network communication channels can be at risk if poorly designed.
5. True or False? Businesses are looking for faster and more efficient cloud network solutions to meet the demands of needing larger customer capacity, agile system or service platform implementation, and affordable infrastructures to Big Data.

Multiple Choice

1. What is used to manage development, staging, and release server management systems?
   A. Application security
   B. Interface security
   C. Development network
   D. Payment Card Industry security standards
   E. Audit assurance
2. What may be Internet public facing or reside in a subnet zone that safely allows website access to demilitarized zone Internet users?
   A. Business continuity
   B. Change control and configuration management
   C. Web-tier level servers
   D. Data center security asset management
   E. All of the above
3. What would normally reside in subnet definition regions?
   A. . Dynamic Host Control Protocol
   B. DNS
   C. Domain servers
   D. Directory Services Network
   E. All of the above
4. What may need to be considered in case your company or organization supports other VPC locations that require secure communication over the private networks of external Internet-facing perimeters?
   A. Risk mitigation
   B. Security
   C. Service models
   D. Framework planning
   E. VPC demographic-only subnet configuration creation
5. What will be the last ongoing support maintenance required for VPC design creation?
   A. Routing table routing updates
   B. Subnet linking to tables

C. Default route settings
D. VPC design creation
E. All of the above

EXERCISE

Problem

What are the five phases of the VPC security life cycle?

Hands-On Projects

Project

What technical security considerations are most important for designing virtualization solutions?

Case Projects

Problem

After the security virtualization solution has been designed, the next step is to implement and test a prototype of the design before putting the solution into production. What aspects of the solution should be evaluated?

Optional Team Case Project

Problem

What operational processes are particularly important for maintaining virtualization security?

REFERENCES

[1] T. Mather, S. Kumaraswamy, S. Latif, Cloud Security and Privacy, O'Reilly, 2009.
[2] R. Samani, B. Honan, J. Reavis, CSA Guide to Cloud Computing, Elsevier Inc., 2015.
[3] Amazon AWS. https://aws.amazon.com/.
[4] Rackspace. https://www.rackspace.com/en-us/cloud/private.

Part X

Virtual Security

Chapter 67

Protecting Virtual Infrastructure

Edward G. Amoroso

TAG Cyber LLC, United States

1. VIRTUALIZATION IN COMPUTING

The concept of *virtualization* in computing arose from the ability of one operating system (OS) to execute another OS as an application. To the end user, this approach created the virtual illusion that the guest OS, referred to as a *virtual machine*, was the real one. The true power of virtualization became evident when data center operators realized that they could run multiple virtual machines on one OS, thus reducing the underlying usage-per-unit-cost of the underlying hardware.

For traditional data center operators, this approach initially caused anxiety, because so many professional system administrators have been trained over the years to run their systems at low utilization to avoid overload outages. However, the economics of modern computing have changed owing to the unabashed zeal the Internet and Web companies have applied to running virtual machines at the lowest cost, in the smallest space, and with the smallest energy use. This in turn has created a situation in which essentially 100% of enterprise systems are moving in the direction of virtual data center operation.

Computing virtualization can be implemented in multiple ways (Fig. 67.1). On client systems, it can be achieved by logically isolating applications from the underlying OS and hardware. For servers, it is done through special hardware emulation software called a *hypervisor* that orchestrates the operation of virtual machines, in addition to creating an abstract interface to the underling hardware. Specific applications such as file storage and application hosting have also been subjected to virtualization implementation, but usually through virtual machine operation on the underlying server. In all cases, virtualization emulates the underlying hardware that is being shared by multiple guests.

The motivation for virtualization in data centers and other computing environments has clearly been driven by economics and utility. The lower costs of operation, the flexibility of maintenance, and the potential for almost unbounded scaling have made the technique popular with chief information officers (CIOs) and other information technology (IT) decision makers. However, these benefits are usually explained in the context of the perceived drawbacks that emerge in the context of security. That is, virtualization is often viewed as introducing the following security weaknesses:

- *Attack platform*: By providing malicious offensive actors with limitless attack platform capability, virtualization contributes to the overall cybersecurity threat.

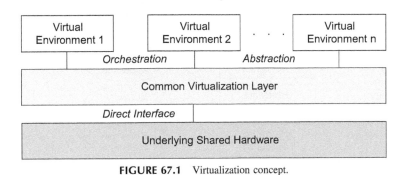

FIGURE 67.1 Virtualization concept.

Computer and Information Security Handbook. http://dx.doi.org/10.1016/B978-0-12-803843-7.00067-3

- *Hypervisor attack target*: Because virtual machines reside on common hypervisor infrastructure, the result is a high-value attack target that serves as a single point of failure.
- *Low-availability attack threshold*: Virtualization economics encourage higher use in data centers, which has the effect of lowering the attack threshold for denial of service attacks.

While the preceding weaknesses are valid, the good news is that just as virtualization can assist the offensive, it can also assist the defense, possibly even in ways that adjust the balance of power toward the defender. One reason for this shift is that the defenders control and maintain the virtualization infrastructure, whereas attackers must reside within the constraints with which they are presented. This advantage of combining security with system control and management is central to the deployment of virtualization as a security advantage.

2. VIRTUAL DATA CENTER SECURITY

The traditional data center has always been constructed from racked, customized hardware appliances controlled by top-of-rack switches. The norm in such environments is low-resource use on hardware to ensure headroom in case of overload situations. It has traditionally been considered neither unusual nor problematic that most of data center traffic involves so-called east—west traffic that originates and terminates with equipment in the data center. Maintenance in such environments usually has been driven by hardware/software troubleshooting, followed by fixes being done during scheduled time windows, usually either late at night or during periods of low customer use.

Traditional data center operation began to be questioned by CIOs when Web companies of the 1990s began to demonstrate effective, robust operation using data centers (Fig. 67.2) that were constructed and based on many different principles. That is, Web companies used orchestration software to adjust and recover from underlying

hardware problems. This allowed much higher system use, which implied lower costs. In addition, Web companies were software companies, and as such, enthusiastically replaced hardware/software functions such as top-of-rack switches with more virtual constructs such as software-defined network (SDN) controllers.

Today, almost all data centers either have completed the transition or are in the process of transitioning to this more software-based approach. With such virtualization has come the obligation to address security risks that emerge with the increased software dependency. Such security protections include the following:

- *Security process overlays for development and operations (dev/ops)*: Software appliances for the modern virtual data center are constructed using a dev/ops model. Security process overlays are common in modern dev/ops to include penetration testing, security code reviews, and other process enhancements to reduce the likelihood of vulnerabilities in delivered code.
- *Compliance requirements for virtual infrastructure*: Compliance and regulatory concerns have held back innovation in many IT environments because existing audits on traditional equipment and infrastructure have to be completely redone with virtualization. Modern virtual solutions from vendors such as VMWare come with enhanced security features and services that will make recertification much easier than in the past.
- *Vendor attention to security requirements*: Vendors providing virtual solutions previously focused on reduced cost and streamlined provisioning but have since increases their attention to security and assurance features in their virtual appliances.

In addition to these newer protections for virtual products, several more substantive advantages have emerged with respect to virtualization in the data center and other computing environments. These security capabilities include hypervisor security, virtual machine security inheritance, microsegments, and containers.

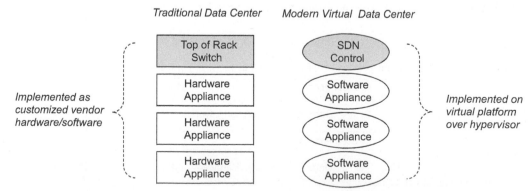

FIGURE 67.2 Evolution of data center toward virtualization. *SDN*, software-defined network.

3. HYPERVISOR SECURITY

The most important functional component in any virtual infrastructure is the hypervisor. Ensuring that the underlying hypervisor is sufficiently secure is an important first step toward overall virtualization security. The US National Institute for Standards and Technology (NIST) published a guide for securing the hypervisor that serves as a useful reference on 22 best practices in this area [1]. Some of the more important techniques recommended in the NIST guide include:

- *Hypervisor configuration*: As with traditional OSs, hypervisors can be configured properly or improperly. Example hypervisor misconfiguration problems include rogue virtual machines gaining too much access to underlying hardware resources.
- *Hypervisor patch and vulnerability management*: As with any software, hypervisors are likely to become subject to required patches and vulnerability updates, so hypervisor administrators must put commensurate processes in place.
- *Privileged operation execution management*: Because hypervisors sit between guest OSs and the underlying hardware, privileged operations must be managed carefully during execution.

Enterprise IT and security staff should not be surprised by these types of recommendations for securing hypervisors, because they closely match the types of OS security recommendations that have been around for years. As a general rule, if a heuristic, tool or procedure is in place to protect an OS, something comparable has probably been proposed to protect the hypervisor (see checklist: "An Agenda for Action for Implementing Security Recommendations for the Hypervisor") [1].

4. ENTERPRISE SEGMENTATION

One of the most exciting trends in cybersecurity is the notion of virtualized containment to protect workloads from attacks. Each virtual container thus becomes a so-called microsegment and offers a useful alternative to the types of network segmentation that enterprise security teams are most likely trying to implement. The motivation for such segmentation is the risk of east—west enterprise traversal by malicious actors.

A network segmentation approach will generally involve the establishment of different enterprise network domains within a perimeter-defined infrastructure (Fig. 67.3). Each domain will be separated by a physical demilitarized zone (DMZ) segment, which will include the usual list of hardware-based protections such as firewalls and intrusion

---

An Agenda for Action for Implementing Security Recommendations for the Hypervisor

The following security recommendations for the hypervisor itself include the following key activities (check all tasks completed):

_____**1.** Install all updates to the hypervisor as they are released by the vendor.

_____**2.** Restrict administrative access to the management interfaces of the hypervisor.

_____**3.** Protect all management communication channels using a dedicated management network, or make sure the management network communications is authenticated and encrypted using validated cryptographic modules.

_____**4.** Synchronize the virtualized infrastructure to a trusted authoritative time server.

_____**5.** Disconnect unused physical hardware from the host system.

_____**6.** Disconnect unused network interface controllers from any network.

_____**7.** Disable all hypervisor services such as clipboard or file sharing between the guest OS and the host OS unless they are needed.

_____**8.** Disable all hypervisor services such as clipboard- or file-sharing between the guest OS and the host OS unless they are needed.

_____**9.** Consider using introspection capabilities to monitor the security of each guest OS.

_____**10.** Consider using introspection capabilities to monitor the security of activity occurring between guest OSs.

_____**11.** Carefully monitor the hypervisor itself for signs of compromise.

---

prevention appliances. Operating many different network segments reduces the east—west traversal threat but is not convenient to manage, administer, or support. In stark contrast, by creating enterprise segmentation using virtualization, the advantages of east—west attack prevention can be obtained without the commensurate management, administration, and support challenges.

Implementing virtual segmentation on an enterprise network requires design decisions regarding the scale and size of the segments. On one end of the spectrum, the segmentation could be dynamic and fine-grained, in which segments are small and created on-demand, and could be physically scattered across disparate underlying hypervisor support. On the other end of the spectrum, the virtual segments could be more substantial and more stable, perhaps supporting a complex cloud workload over a sustained period.

Regardless of the size and scale decision, advantages of using virtualization to segment a network are substantial,

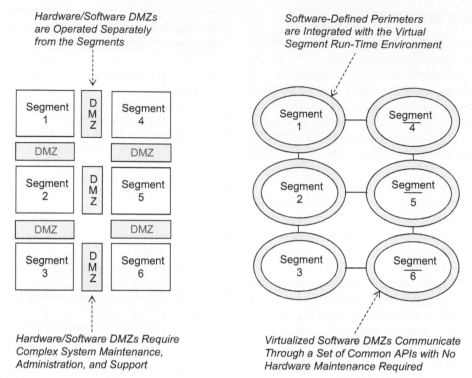

Hardware/Software DMZs
are Operated Separately
from the Segments

Software-Defined Perimeters
are Integrated with the Virtual
Segment Run-Time Environment

Hardware/Software DMZs Require
Complex System Maintenance,
Administration, and Support

Virtualized Software DMZs Communicate
Through a Set of Common APIs with No
Hardware Maintenance Required

FIGURE 67.3 Network versus virtual enterprise segmentation. *API*, application program interface; *DMZ*, demilitarized zone.

including the ability to change components quickly in the virtual DMZ, the ability to gain immediate telemetry from multiple devices, and the ability to quickly patch and restore components that are vulnerable. In virtual environments operating SDN technology, the SDN controller can provide holistic oversight of these maintenance activities.

5. ACTIVE CONTAINERIZED SECURITY

A powerful security technique that uses virtualization involves the creation of a dynamic run-time environment for the purposes of testing or validating some security property. This is most commonly performed for malicious software (malware) detection, in which the suspicious payload is carried off to a virtual environment for safe detonation (Fig. 67.4). The advantage is that if the payload is truly dangerous, the virtual container will ensure that no ill effects are felt beyond the container walls.

This approach was pioneered by vendors such as Fire-Eye and has since become a commonly found protection in every enterprise network. The challenge to such a method, however, is that bad actors have access to the same virtual container technology as the good guys. Thus, they can thus their malware so as to design it to work around the boundaries created by the container. This type of problem is also relevant to containers on end points that try to build a virtual fence around browsing sessions. Bad actors have highly available and realistic test beds on which to design

their attacks. This does not invalidate containers as a powerful technique but rather highlights the cat-and-mouse nature of using virtualization to detect cyber attacks.

6. VIRTUAL ABSORPTION OF VOLUME ATTACKS

Denial of service attacks have become the scourge of enterprise network managers simply because the physics of botnet power seem unbounded, given the enormous number of vulnerable end points that exist on the Internet. Security experts have tried for years to develop solutions that would block, divert, or filter large amounts of traffic being aimed at computing infrastructure, but the problem always remains that eventually the amount of deployed security capability runs out. That is, if 10 gigabits per second (Gbps) of protection is deployed, then an attacker succeeds at 10.1 Gbps; similarly, if 20 Gbps of protection is deployed, then an attacker succeeds at 20.1 Gbps, and so on.

Virtualization changes the defensive equation in a substantive manner by allowing the defender to expand the protection solution dynamically before, during, or after an attack. That is, if 10 Gbps is deployed in virtual protection, and an attacker exceeds this threshold by 0.1 Gbps, then the defender can dynamically provision additional protection on the fly. Virtualization effectively allows the defender to absorb denial of service attacks through rapid provisioning (Fig. 67.5).

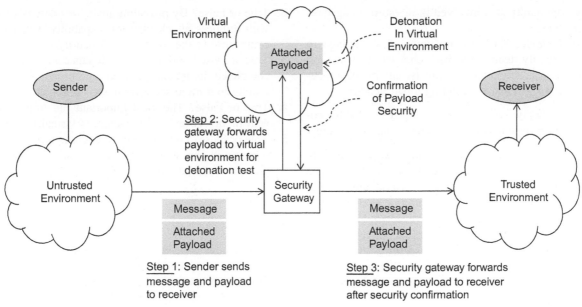

FIGURE 67.4 Virtual detonation for security testing.

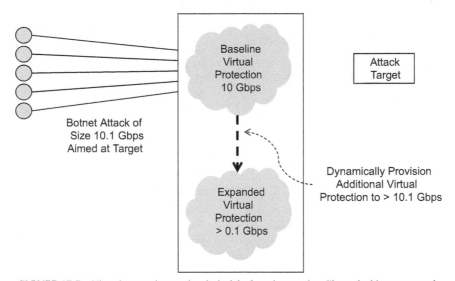

FIGURE 67.5 Virtual expansion to absorb denial of service attacks. *Gbps*, gigabits per second.

The advantages of dynamic virtualization also extend to the malicious attacker, of course, in which virtual machines can be created to expand the size of a botnet using virtual machines or even containers. However, this does not change the equation as dramatically for the offense because botnet creation has always been essentially an unbounded activity. Virtualization would thus seem to benefit the defender in a more substantive manner.

7. OPEN SOURCE VERSUS PROPRIETARY SECURITY CAPABILITIES

In the context of security virtualization, the traditional debate about whether open source or proprietary software is more secure will certainly be relevant to virtual protections.

The leading virtual OS is OpenStack, and the leading proprietary OSs are VMWare and Citrix. Both approaches have their clear pros and cons, but one thing is certain: open source is no longer just the purview of hackers and hobbyists. Critically essential services are often developed using open source software, so the debate must be done on functional and assurance grounds rather than based on any momentum view of the status quo. Stated briefly, the security advantages of using open source software are:

- *Increased code scrutiny*: Open source code is developed within a community, and is therefore exposed to an increased, wider level of scrutiny than proprietary code.
- *Community vulnerability management*: When vulnerabilities are found in open source software, the entire

usage community gets involved in recommending fixes and patches.

- *Diffused blame*: Sadly, many companies continue to blame security teams for bad choices of software; open source selection tends to diffuse any blame a security team might have in selecting a bad vendor.

Correspondingly, the security advantages of using proprietary software products from a commercial vendor are:

- *Hidden vulnerabilities*: One would expect that any complex piece of proprietary code will eventually be retired with multiple hidden, buried vulnerabilities that never required patching, because no one ever noticed.
- *Commercial-quality incentives*: Proprietary software is created by companies with financial incentives to maintain a proper level of quality and security.
- *Clearer legacy source*: Proprietary code from a vendor clarifies legacy development and supply chain issues to a degree.

These pros and cons of open security versus "security through obscurity" are well known but deserve to be highlighted here simply because virtualization increases software dependency and hence highlights the debate. Local enterprise security teams will have to decide for themselves.

8. SUMMARY

Because virtualization has been used in practice only for several years, many of the theoretical, foundational issues of cybersecurity have not yet been applied to the use of virtual machines. Security research issues such as inheritance, for example, will require attention in the security modeling community to avoid future problems. When a hypervisor provisions a new virtual machine, for example, the inheritance privileges the new virtual machine obtains follow simple provisioning rules. However, to ensure proper least privilege and segregation of duty management, inheritance from hypervisors to guest OSs might be an excellent way to orchestrate policy. SDN controllers can perform such orchestration as well. The challenge is that the research community has not yet caught up with virtualization, and it will need to accelerate the pace in coming years.

Finally, let us move on to the real interactive part of this chapter: review questions/exercises, hands-on projects, case projects, and the optional team case project. The answers and/or solutions by chapter can be found in Appendix K.

CHAPTER REVIEW QUESTIONS/ EXERCISES

True/False

1. True or False? The concept of *virtualization* in computing arose from the ability of one OS to execute another OS as an application.

2. True or False? By providing malicious defensive actors with limitless attack platform capability, virtualization contributes to the overall cybersecurity threat.
3. True or False? Today, almost all data centers have either completed the transition or are in the process of transitioning to a more software-based approach.
4. True or False? The most important functional component in any virtual infrastructure is virtualization.
5. True or False? One of the most exciting trends in cybersecurity is the notion of hypervisor containment to protect workloads from attacks.

Multiple Choice

1. Open source code is developed within a community and is therefore exposed to an increased, wider level of scrutiny than proprietary code. What is this called?
   A. Community vulnerability management
   B. Increased code scrutiny
   C. Diffused blame
   D. Hidden vulnerabilities
   E. All of the above
2. One would expect that any complex piece of proprietary code will eventually be retired with multiple hidden, buried vulnerabilities that never required patching, because no one ever noticed. What is this called?
   A. Hidden vulnerabilities
   B. Commercial-quality incentives
   C. Clearer legacy source
   D. Attack platform
   E. All of the above
3. By providing malicious offensive actors with limitless attack platform capability, virtualization contributes to the overall cybersecurity threat. What is this called?
   A. Hypervisor attack target
   B. Low-availability attack threshold
   C. Attack platform
   D. Security process overlays for dev/ops
   E. All of the above
4. Software appliances for the modern virtual data center are constructed today by using:
   A. Security process overlays for dev/ops
   B. Compliance requirements for virtual infrastructure
   C. Vendor attention to security requirements
   D. A dev/ops model
   E. All of the above
5. As with traditional operating systems, hypervisors can be configured properly or improperly. What is this called?
   A. Hypervisor patch and vulnerability management
   B. Privileged operation execution management
   C. Increased code scrutiny
   D. Community vulnerability management
   E. Hypervisor configuration

EXERCISE

Problem

What are the security requirements for the hypervisor?

Hands-on Projects

Project

What are the security requirements for the guest operating system (OS)?

Case Projects

Problem

Virtualization provides simulation of hardware such as storage and network interfaces. This infrastructure is as important to the security of a virtualized guest OS as real hardware infrastructure is to an OS running on a physical computer. Many virtualization systems have features to provide access control to the virtual hardware, particularly storage and networking. Access to virtual hardware should be strictly limited to the guest OSs that will use it. Please explain further.

Optional Team Case Project

Problem

What are the secure virtualization planning and deployment life cycle phases?

REFERENCE

[1] NIST Special Publication 800-125, Guide to Security for Full Virtualization Technologies, January 2011.

Chapter 68

Software-Defined Networking and Network Function Virtualization Security

Edward G. Amoroso

TAG Cyber LLC, United States

1. INTRODUCTION TO SOFTWARE-DEFINED NETWORKING

Since its inception, an important technical aspect of wide-area routing over Internet infrastructure has been *decentralized control*. Routers have been designed from the beginning to support protocols as stand-alone entities accepting, processing, and routing packets *independently* based on locally observed and remotely obtained forwarding data. This decision to enable decentralized control has made it possible for many different infrastructure owners to participate in routing; some obviously do a better job than others.

With the exponential growth of the Internet over the past 2 decades, packet forwarding has become so complex that network designers have had to find ways to simplify this massively distributed system. One approach to simplification involves returning network control functions to increased centralization, not unlike how systems such as Signaling System 7 controlled traditional time division multiplexing. This approach to network centralization, which separates control functions from packet forwarding, is called *software-defined networking* (SDN) and is being implemented by service providers in the cloud. The specific construct used to realize centralized network management is called an *SDN controller* (Fig. 68.1) [1].

Many network security practitioners initially rejected the cloud aspect of SDN, citing concerns about weak data protection and sloppy operations in popular public cloud offerings. These same practitioners began to realize, however, the security advantages of distributing data outside their increasingly ineffective perimeter networks. Each time a major corporation with a traditional perimeter was attacked successfully, overall confidence in private enterprise network security was reduced. As a result, the idea of securely stitching infrastructure across heterogeneous cloud infrastructure began to look better, especially when the cloud was properly managed and appropriately secured by the Internet service provider (ISP).

Furthermore, the ever-increasing requirements for higher-performance routers began to wane with the distribution inherent in cloud architectures. With the shift from perimeter-based enterprise networks to distributed clouds, the topology of the typical enterprise began to disperse and network function virtualization (NFV) became feasible at manageable throughput levels. Security functions could also be virtualized this way, resulting in a virtual perimeter across public, hybrid, and private systems.

With this industry shift to SDN and NFV has come the inevitable requirement to identify the security issues that emerge, both positive and negative. Certain aspects of the shift create generic security considerations, such as the potential for vulnerabilities to be introduced as a result of architectural changes. Such generic considerations are unavoidable in every aspect of technology owing to ongoing rapid changes, so these are not considered relevant to the SDN and NFV security discussion.

However, substantive security issues must be addressed by network and security experts to manage risk properly. As will be shown subsequently, these issues have both positive and negative consequences for enterprise and service provider security; but as will also be shown, the vast majority of implications are overwhelmingly positive, which is obviously good news for enterprise security managers.

Computer and Information Security Handbook. http://dx.doi.org/10.1016/B978-0-12-803843-7.00068-5

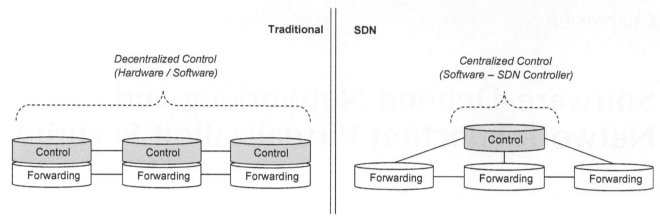

Traditional | **SDN**

Decentralized Control (Hardware / Software)

Centralized Control (Software – SDN Controller)

FIGURE 68.1 Centralized control in software-defined networking (SDN).

2. SOFTWARE-DEFINED NETWORKING AND NETWORK FUNCTION VIRTUALIZATION OVERVIEW

The architecture of an SDN system, whether it is used for Internet service provision or data center operation, always includes the following three functional layers (Fig. 68.2):

- *SDN application plane*: SDN services and applications reside at this layer; many common network security functions such as intrusion detection will be included here as SDN applications.
- *SDN control plane*: The overall control of the SDN resides at this layer and is commonly implemented in a functional component known as the SDN controller, which can be viewed informally as the "brains" of the network.
- *SDN data plane*: The underlying network infrastructure resides here with all of the requisite forwarding devices. NFV involves these devices being virtualized in software.

These components are typically arranged on cloud operating systems such as OpenStack, with application programming interfaces (APIs) to realize network programmability. This is another benefit that comes with SDN and NFV.

To combat any single point of failure weaknesses, most SDN control functions are distributed regionally and logically across the ISP infrastructure. This is an important

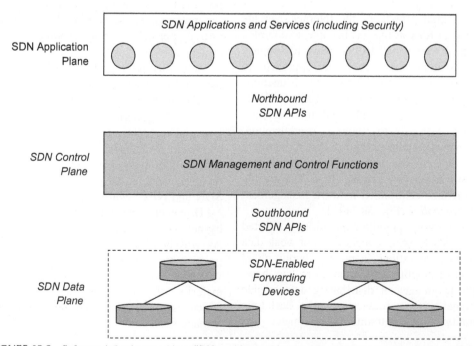

SDN Application Plane — *SDN Applications and Services (including Security)*

Northbound SDN APIs

SDN Control Plane — *SDN Management and Control Functions*

Southbound SDN APIs

SDN Data Plane — *SDN-Enabled Forwarding Devices*

FIGURE 68.2 Software-defined networking (SDN) architectural layers. *API*, application programming interface.

point because so many ISPs have struggled with distributed denial of service (DDOS) attacks. By scattering SDN control functions into a distributed system, the likelihood of forced outages by malicious actors is greatly reduced.

An additional implementation issue with SDN and NFV implementation is the commonality introduced at the hypervisor and underlying hardware/system layers (Fig. 68.3). That is, if the underlying cloud infrastructure lacks diversity, with a single hypervisor or hardware solution supporting 100% of the telecommunications functionality, a so-called *horizontal* cascading attack could rip through lower-level cloud support infrastructure and create service problems at the higher SDN layers.

The cascading attack risk for hypervisors, operating systems, and hardware is clearly an issue that requires mitigation. Security enhancement techniques being used by ISPs to deal with this horizontal threat include the following:

- *Hypervisor, operating system, and hardware diversity*: The underlying infrastructure supporting any SDN, NFV, or cloud service can certainly be diversified. The challenge is that an inverse relationship exists between costs savings and diversity of underlying support infrastructure. Given the critical nature of SDN and NFV to essential services in society, introduction of diversity at the lower layers seems justified.
- *Monitoring algorithms*: Web companies of the 2000s, including Google, Amazon.com, Twitter, and Facebook, demonstrated that algorithms could be used to compensate for underlying hardware failures in practical business settings. Computer scientists postulated such algorithms in classrooms for decades before that, but with the real experiences of Web companies, SDN and NFV deployments will require such distributed algorithms for handing hardware problems.

- *Support containerization*: A major research and development initiative has involved the development of cryptographically secure containers to separate workloads from their real computing environment. Virtual machines make containers a reality by supporting the on-demand creation of dynamically provisioning computing support, which is precisely how a container works. The challenge is to ensure that hackers cannot break through the container.

An additional important consideration in assessing the risk of horizontal cascading attacks is that the existing *vertical* threat to modern telecommunications is arguably comparable, if not worse. That is, criticisms of SDN and NFV operating over horizontally nondiverse hypervisors, systems, and hardware are often made in ignorance of the current telecommunications infrastructure that operates across the globe.

Specifically, in virtually every current ISP infrastructure, components of the network service environment include vertically integrated provision of some vendor solution. For example, if some vendor Alpha provides a network function such as routing or switching that is deployed by a telecommunications provider, the potential exists that a weakness found in vendor Alpha's software could result in a vertically cascading attack through the entire deployment. This is true for all deployed vendors, Alpha, Bravo, etc., and is exacerbated by the fact that most vendors control all vertical stack elements in the service provision from the operating system up through the application layer.

With SDN and NFV, the likelihood that multiple vendor solutions are made available and used across layers is increased simply because virtualization supports diversity. That is, by deploying virtual components with well-defined

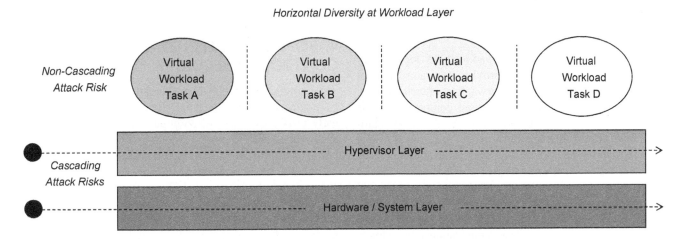

FIGURE 68.3 Cascading risk to hypervisor and hardware/system layers.

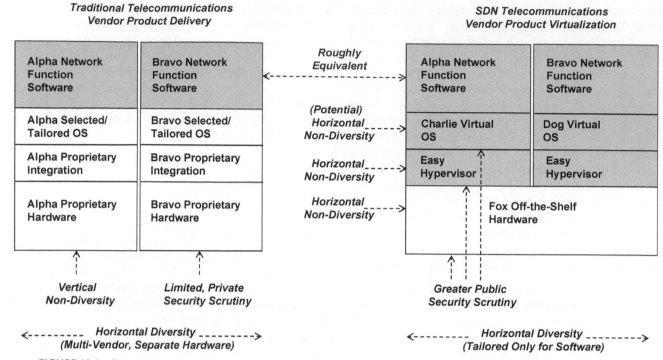

FIGURE 68.4 Comparing modern vertical with hypervisor horizontal threats. *OS*, operating system; *SDN*, software-defined networking.

APIs, the vertical cascading threat can be considerably reduced. As a result, it is reasonable to suggest that SDN and NFV do not introduce additional cascading risk, but instead shift security risk from vertical to horizontal. The implication of this vertical to horizontal shift is that security solutions for SDN and NFV in carrier infrastructure and data centers will have to make the appropriate adjustments as suggested in the preceding discussion (Fig. 68.4).

3. SOFTWARE-DEFINED NETWORKING AND NETWORK FUNCTION VIRTUALIZATION FOR INTERNET SERVICE PROVIDERS

As carriers and network managers adopt SDN for telecommunication service control and provisioning, and NFV for appropriate virtualization of forwarding functions, the argument can be made that the overall complexity of the resultant infrastructure is greatly reduced. End-to-end provisioning of telecommunications, for example, moves from a complex assortment of hardware and software components being chained together through protocols across wireless or wired interfaces, to a collection of dynamically generated software objects communicating through flexible APIs. Experts may disagree about the specific functional advantages of virtual software-based telecommunications, but almost every expert would agree that SDN is simpler than current wired and wireless communications over hardware.

The security implication of this is straightforward: Perhaps the most basic tenet of computer security that has existed since the early days of the US Government Orange Book (with trusted computing base minimization) is the current compliance-obsessed enterprise in which duties must be segregated and privileges must be minimized through system simplifications [2]. The simplification associated with NFV is also obvious; the forwarding devices that remain after SDN control functions are centralized and have become much simpler than the current state-of-the-art router or switch. The security implications here are obvious as well, from improved threat identification to simpler patching.

4. SOFTWARE-DEFINED NETWORKING CONTROLLER SECURITY

The introduction of SDN controllers to carrier infrastructure is reminiscent of the original signaling systems found in early circuit-switched telecommunications. By combining and virtualizing the control function from distributed endpoint forwarding devices into a common control element, the ability to obtain more holistic, instantaneous, and accurate views of network infrastructure become feasible (Fig. 68.5).

For security protection activities such as DDOS mitigation across a large network, the holistic views from an SDN controller reduce the likelihood of unknown collateral damage from changed, filtered, or blocked network routes.

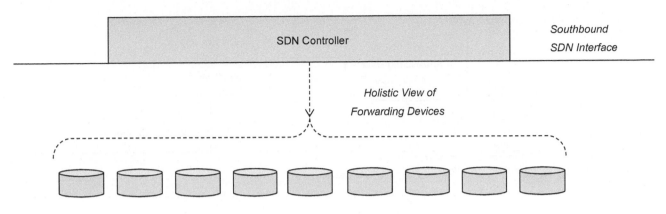

Network Forwarding Devices (Logical and Geographical Distribution)

FIGURE 68.5   Holistic software-defined networking (SDN) controller view of network.

The holistic views also enable the possibility of more accurate snapshot visualizations of current distributed status, rather than an estimation of the current state through distributed protocols.

An additional advantage enabled by SDN controllers is the potential to perform security analytics at the control layer for telecommunications. Modern cybersecurity experts have come to accept that traditional signature-based whit-e and blacklisting, as with antivirus and firewall solutions, do not work well for detecting advanced attacks. Instead, heuristic approaches to collecting data, analyzing and correlating the data, and then deriving actionable intelligence provide much better security. The biggest challenge to security analytic methods involves collecting accurate, meaningful data. SDN controllers have an excellent vantage point for such collection on the southbound interface to forwarding devices. By creating security analysis applications that communicate with the controller via the northbound interface, SDN operators create an effective solution for security analysis across virtual network infrastructure (Fig. 68.6).

The result of the holistic network perspective combined with embedded SDN security analytics support is a desirable cybersecurity capability not found natively in any service provider or data center fabric. To obtain such capability today would require the installation of a comprehensive network monitoring function, feeding some separate Big Data repository used by analysts with a separate correlation tool. SDN integrates these functions natively.

5. IMPROVED PATCHING WITH SOFTWARE-DEFINED NETWORKING

A significant security challenge in the modern data center and service provider infrastructure environment involves the timely patching of vulnerable systems with a minimum of downtime and collateral damage. Most current patching solutions for operating systems, applications, network functions, and other software systems rely on highly imperfect processes to identify an inventory of target systems accurately for patching and ensure that the resulting patched system will not cause problems.

By virtualizing network functions into an SDN environment, the possibility emerges that patching can be done more systematically by using a "remove and replace" method. This works by creating an offline clean image of the patched network function, which then can be used to replace the corresponding unpatched virtual network function wholly.

In theory, because these are *software* replace operations, the process should be a simple provisioning exercise, compared with the more complex arrangement of patching systems that combine hardware, software, and firmware implementations (Fig. 68.7). Such software provisioning can be automated, which will further streamline the patching methodology and reduce cycle time.

A benefit to removing components that are potentially unpatched is that they can be delivered to forensic analysts essentially intact for review and investigation. In the case of a security incident in which some function is deemed the offender, replacement of the virtual appliance or component also provides the ability to streamline incident response and forensics by offering up the offending software to the analysis lab unchanged.

6. DYNAMIC SECURITY SERVICE CHAINING IN SOFTWARE-DEFINED NETWORKING

One of the most consequential features inherent in SDN services for ISPs is the real-time nature of on-demand provisioning into the virtual work stream. Whereas traditional ISP networking would require an integration project

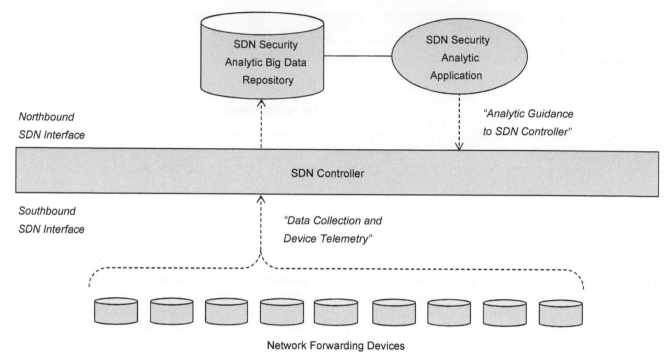

FIGURE 68.6 Software-defined networking (SDN) controller-coordinated security analysis.

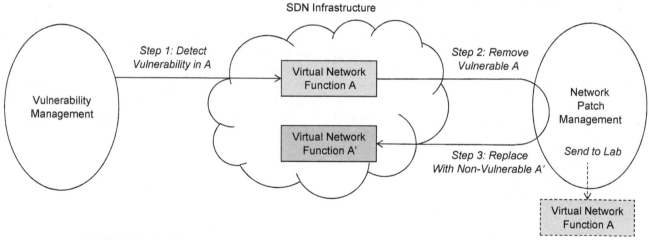

FIGURE 68.7 Patching via removal and replacement of network functions. *SDN*, software-defined networking.

to select, procure, install, test, and deploy new hardware/software-based system functions, SDN relies on virtual functions that do not require the same treatment. In particular, software-based functions in SDN can be integrated through APIs that provide an open entry to the network infrastructure.

Such integration in real-time is called *service chaining*, and the technique represents the future of real-time network security. That is, enterprise and individuals users of ISP services desiring security for some procured service will

simply self-purchase the required capability through a point-and-click portal. The result is a dynamic, on-demand managed security services environment in which users can tailor their security functionality to meet their perceived needs.

The implementation of SDN service chaining (Fig. 68.8) is done via a preprovisioned virtual appliance positioned in the SDN cloud and pretested for use by customers who need commensurate protection (see checklist: "An Agenda for Action for Implementing Software-Defined Networking

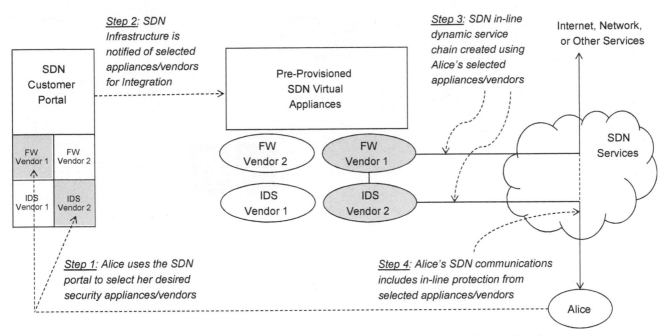

FIGURE 68.8   Software-defined networking (SDN) service chaining. *FW*, firewall; *IDS*, intrusion detection system.

An Agenda for Action for Implementing Software-Defined Networking Service Chaining

Benefits for users of dynamic service chaining embedded in ISP operations on cybersecurity include the following key activities (check all tasks completed):

_____**1.** *Real-time response*: SDN users under cyber attack can immediately provision security solutions in response without the need for lengthy hardware procurement and installation.

_____**2.** *Defense in depth*: SDN users can feasibly install multiple layers of protection, possibly from diverse vendors, to increase their depth of security coverage without undue time and cost.

_____**3.** *Rapid defensive adjustment*: Defensive posture can be adjusted quickly and easily, before, during, or after an attack using a portal, rather than having to change hardware.

Service Chaining"). The experience would be something like a point-on-the-logo interface to provision firewalls, attack detection, behavioral analytics, data leakage prevention, and the like.

Nonsecurity advantages of SDN (reduced cost, faster hardware integration, and simpler operations) are so prominent that the security benefits are often missed. Over time, however, the security protective aspect of SDN service chaining will likely become the most important driver for adopting SDN for business wireless and wired communications.

7. FUTURE VIRTUALIZED MANAGEMENT SECURITY SUPPORT IN SOFTWARE-DEFINED NETWORKING

SDN service chaining offers an obvious means for supporting managed security customers in an efficient manner. That is, rather than the existing approach to managed security services (Fig. 68.9) with on-premise and network-based solutions, SDN offers a more streamlined means for virtualizing the management, monitoring, and usage of security appliances. The approach also provides a means for network security operations to be performed in an integrated manner with underlying telecommunications service management.

The implication for such a major shift in management security support is that managed, on-premise support of appliance-based security capabilities will become a less desirable means for outsourcing security. Furthermore, the economics of integrating security into the telecommunications infrastructure are advantageous for both the ISP and the enterprise security team, who might be able to shift their security budget allocation into their more generic telecommunications bill.

8. SUMMARY

The future of SDN and NFV security will be driven by attractive virtualization economics and utility. As the early regulatory barriers to virtualized network services are gradually cleared, more ISPs, enterprise customers, and

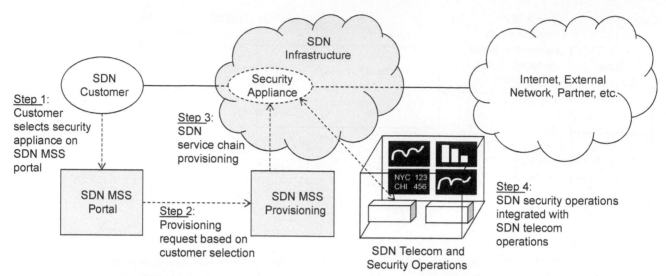

FIGURE 68.9 Managed software-defined networking (SDN) security services. *MSS*, management security support.

even consumers will build on their early experiences to drive increased use of both SDN and NFV. Hackers will certainly notice this trend, so one can expect a commensurate increase in offensive attacks and probes against virtual network infrastructure and services. In the long run, by virtualizing infrastructure, defenders increase their chances of keeping up with innovations in offense, and the result of SDN and NFV migration will be an improved security equation for everyone.

Finally, let us move on to the real interactive part of this chapter: review questions/exercises, hands-on projects, case projects, and the optional team case project. The answers and/or solutions by chapter can be found in Appendix K.

CHAPTER REVIEW QUESTIONS/ EXERCISES

True/False

1. True or False? Since its inception, an important technical aspect of wide-area routing over Internet infrastructure has been *decentralized control.*
2. True or False? To combat two points of failure weaknesses, most SDN control functions are distributed regionally and logically across the ISP infrastructure.
3. True or False? As carriers and network managers adopt SDN for telecommunication service control and provisioning, and NFV for appropriate virtualization of forwarding functions, the argument can be made that the overall complexity of the resultant infrastructure is greatly reduced.
4. True or False? The introduction of SDN controllers to carrier infrastructure is reminiscent of the original

signaling systems found in early circuit-switched telecommunications.
5. True or False? A significant security challenge in the modern data center and service provider infrastructure environment involves the timely patching of vulnerable systems with a maximum of downtime and collateral damage.

Multiple Choice

1. By virtualizing network functions into an SDN environment, the possibility emerges that patching can be done more systematically by using:
   A. Community vulnerability management
   B. Increased code scrutiny
   C. Diffused blame
   D. Hidden vulnerabilities
   E. A remove and replace method
2. One of the most consequential features inherent in SDN services for ISPs is the real-time nature of on-demand provisioning into the:
   A. Virtual work stream
   B. Commercial-quality incentives
   C. Clearer legacy source
   D. Attack platform
   E. All of the above
3. Since its inception, an important technical aspect of wide-area routing over Internet infrastructure has been:
   A. Hypervisor attack target
   B. Decentralized control
   C. Attack platform
   D. Security process overlays for dev/ops
   E. All of the above

4. Routers have been designed from the beginning to support protocols as stand-alone entities accepting, processing, and routing packets _____ based on locally observed and remotely obtained forwarding data.
   A. Security process overlays for dev/ops
   B. Compliance requirements for virtual infrastructure
   C. Independently
   D. Dev/ops model
   E. All of the above
5. The approach to network centralization, which separates control functions from packet forwarding, is called _____ and is being implemented by service providers in the cloud.
   A. Hypervisor patch and vulnerability management
   B. Privileged operation execution management
   C. Increased code scrutiny
   D. Software-defined networking (SDN)
   E. Hypervisor configuration

EXERCISE

Problem

Why are SDN and NFV so important?

Hands-on Projects

Project

What might be an obstacle to implementing SDN and/or NFV security?

Case Projects

Problem

What are the three important differences among secure-software defined networking (SDN), network virtualization (NV), and network function virtualization (NFV)?

Optional Team Case Project

Problem

What is the role of security in SDN and NFV?

REFERENCES

[1] P. Goransson, C. Black, Software Defined Networks — A Comprehensive Approach, Elsevier Science, 2014.
[2] U.S. Department of Defense Computer Security Center, Trusted Computer System Evaluation Criteria (TCSEC), DoD-STD-001−83, 1983.

Part XI

Cyber Physical Security

Part XI

Cyber Physical Security

Chapter 68 Physical Security Essentials
William Stallings

Chapter 69 Biometrics
David Martin

Chapter 69

Physical Security Essentials

William Stallings

Independent Consultant, Brewster, MA, United States

Platt [2] distinguishes three elements of information system (IS) security:

- **Logical security:** protects computer-based data from software-based and communication-based threats.
- **Physical security:** also called **infrastructure security.** Protects ISs that house data and the people who use, operate, and maintain the systems. Physical security also must prevent any type of physical access or intrusion that can compromise logical security.
- **Premises security:** also known as corporate or facilities security. Protects the people and property within an entire area, facility, or building(s); usually required by laws, regulations, and fiduciary obligations. Premises security provides perimeter security, access control, smoke and fire detection, fire suppression, some environmental protection, and usually surveillance systems, alarms, and guards.

This chapter is concerned with physical security, with some overlapping areas of premises security. We begin by looking at physical security threats and then consider physical security prevention measures.

1. OVERVIEW

For ISs, the role of physical security is to protect the physical assets that support the storage and processing of information. Physical security involves two complementary requirements. First, physical security must prevent damage to the physical infrastructure that sustains the IS. In broad terms, that infrastructure includes the following:

- **IS hardware:** including data processing and storage equipment, transmission and networking facilities, and offline storage media. We can include in this category supporting documentation

- **Physical facility:** the buildings and other structures housing the system and network components
- **Supporting facilities:** These facilities underpin the operation of the IS. This category includes electrical power, communication services, and environmental controls (heat, humidity, etc.)
- **Personnel:** Humans involved in the control, maintenance, and use of the ISs

Second, physical security must prevent misuse of the physical infrastructure that leads to the misuse or damage of the protected information. The misuse of the physical infrastructure can be accidental or malicious. It includes vandalism, theft of equipment, theft by copying, theft of services, and unauthorized entry.

Fig. 69.1, which is based on Ref. [1], suggests the overall context in which physical security concerns arise. The central concern is the information assets of an organization. These information assets provide value to the organization that possesses them, as indicated by the upper four items in the figure. In turn, the physical infrastructure is essential to providing for the storage and processing of these assets. The lower four items in the figure are the concern of physical security. Not shown is the role of logical security, which consists of software- and protocol-based measures for ensuring data integrity, confidentiality, and so forth.

The role of physical security is affected by the operating location of the IS, which can be characterized as static, mobile, or portable. Our concern in this chapter is primarily with static systems, which are installed at fixed locations. A mobile system is installed in a vehicle, which serves the function of a structure for the system. Portable systems have no single installation point but may operate in a variety of locations, including buildings, vehicles, or in the open. The nature of the system's installation determines the nature and severity of the threats of various types, including fire, roof leaks, unauthorized access, and so forth.

Computer and Information Security Handbook. http://dx.doi.org/10.1016/B978-0-12-803843-7.00069-7

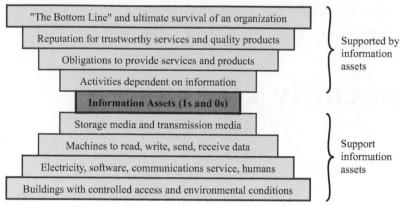

FIGURE 69.1 Context for information assets.

2. PHYSICAL SECURITY THREATS

In this section, we first look at the types of physical situations and occurrences that can constitute a threat to ISs. There are a number of ways in which such threats can be categorized. It is important to understand the spectrum of threats to ISs so that responsible administrators can ensure that prevention measures are comprehensive. We organize the threats into the following categories:

- Environmental threats
- Technical threats
- Human-caused threats

We begin with a discussion of natural disasters, which are a prime source of environmental threats but not the only one. Then we look specifically at environmental threats, followed by technical and human-caused threats.

Natural Disasters

Natural disasters are the source of a wide range of environmental threats to data centers, other information processing facilities, and their personnel. It is possible to assess the risk of various types of natural disasters and take suitable precautions so that catastrophic loss from natural disaster is prevented.

Table 69.1 lists six categories of natural disasters, the typical warning time for each event, whether personnel evacuation is indicated or possible, and the typical duration of each event. We comment briefly on the potential consequences of each type of disaster.

A **tornado** can generate winds that exceed hurricane strength in a narrow band along the tornado's path. There is substantial potential for structural damage, roof damage, and loss of outside equipment. There may be damage from wind and flying debris. Off site, a tornado may cause a temporary loss of local utility and communications. Off-site damage is typically followed by quick restoration of services.

Depending on its strength, a **hurricane** may also cause significant structural damage and damage to outside

equipment. Off site, there is the potential for severe region-wide damage to public infrastructure, utilities, and communications. If on-site operation must continue, emergency supplies for personnel as well as a backup generator are needed. Furthermore, the responsible site manager may need to mobilize private poststorm security measures such as armed guards.

A major **earthquake** has the potential for the greatest damage and occurs without warning. A facility near the epicenter may experience catastrophic, even complete

TABLE 69.1 Characteristics of Natural Disasters

	Warning	Evacuation	Duration
Tornado	Advance warning of potential; not site specific	Remain at site	Brief but intense
Hurricane	Significant advance warning	May require evacuation	Hours to a few days
Earthquake	No warning	May be unable to evacuate	Brief duration; threat of continued aftershocks
Ice storm/ blizzard	Several days warning generally expected	May be unable to evacuate	May last several days
Lightning	Sensors may provide minutes of warning	May require evacuation	Brief but may recur
Flood	Several days warning generally expected	May be unable to evacuate	Site may be isolated for extended period

ComputerSite Engineering, Inc.

destruction, with significant and long-lasting damage to data centers and other IS facilities. Examples of inside damage include the toppling of unbraced computer hardware and site infrastructure equipment, including the collapse of raised floors. Personnel are at risk from broken glass and other flying debris. Off site, near the epicenter of a major earthquake, the damage equals and often exceeds that of a major hurricane. Structures that can withstand a hurricane, such as roads and bridges, may be damaged or destroyed, preventing the movement of fuel and other supplies.

An **ice storm** or **blizzard** can cause some disruption of or damage to IS facilities if outside equipment and the building are not designed to survive severe ice and snow accumulation. Off site, there may be widespread disruption of utilities and communications and roads may be dangerous or impassable.

The consequences of **lightning** strikes can range from no impact to disaster. The effects depend on the proximity of the strike and the efficacy of grounding and surge protector measures in place. Off site, there can be disruption of electrical power, and there is the potential for fires.

Flood is a concern in areas that are subject to flooding and for facilities that are in severe flood areas, at low elevation. Damage can be severe, with long-lasting effects and the need for a major cleanup operation.

Environmental Threats

This category encompasses conditions in the environment that can damage or interrupt the service of ISs and the data they house. Off site, there may be severe region-wide damage to the public infrastructure; in the case of severe hurricanes, it may take days, weeks, or even years to recover from the event.

Inappropriate Temperature and Humidity

Computers and related equipment are designed to operate within a certain temperature range. Most computer systems should be kept between 10 and 32°C (50 and 90°F). Outside this range, resources might continue to operate but produce undesirable results. If the ambient temperature around a computer gets too high, the computer cannot cool itself adequately and internal components can be damaged. If the temperature gets too cold, the system can undergo thermal shock when it is turned on, causing circuit boards or integrated circuits to crack. Table 69.2 indicates the point at which permanent damage from excessive heat begins.

Another temperature-related concern is the internal temperature of equipment, which can be significantly higher than room temperature. Computer-related equipment comes with its own temperature dissipation and cooling mechanisms, but these may rely on, or be affected by, external conditions. Such conditions include excessive ambient temperature, interruption of supply of power or

TABLE 69.2 Temperature Thresholds for Damage to Computing Resources

Component or Medium	Sustained Ambient Temperature at Which Damage May Begin
Flexible disks, magnetic tapes, etc.	38°C (100°F)
Optical media	49°C (120°F)
Hard disk media	66°C (150°F)
Computer equipment	79°C (175°F)
Thermoplastic insulation on wires carrying hazardous voltage	125°C (257°F)
Paper products	177°C (350°F)

Data taken from National Fire Protection Association.

heating, ventilation, and air-conditioning (HVAC) services, and vent blockage.

High humidity also poses a threat to electrical and electronic equipment. Long-term exposure to high humidity can result in corrosion. Condensation can threaten magnetic and optical storage media. Condensation can also cause a short circuit, which in turn can damage circuit boards. High humidity can also cause a galvanic effect that results in electroplating, in which metal from one connector slowly migrates to the mating connector, bonding the two together.

Very low humidity can also be a concern. Under prolonged conditions of low humidity, some materials may change shape, and performance may be affected. Static electricity also becomes a concern. A person or object that becomes statically charged can damage electronic equipment by an electric discharge. Static electricity discharges as low as 10 V can damage particularly sensitive electronic circuits, and discharges in the hundreds of volts can create significant damage to a variety of electronic circuits. Discharges from humans can reach into the thousands of volts, so this is a nontrivial threat. In general, relative humidity should be maintained between 40% and 60% to avoid the threats from both low and high humidity.

Fire and Smoke

Perhaps the most frightening physical threat is fire. It is a threat to human life and property. The threat is not only from the direct flame but also from heat, release of toxic fumes, water damage from fire suppression, and smoke damage. Furthermore, fire can disrupt utilities, especially electricity.

The temperature resulting from fire increases with time, and in a typical building, fire effects follow the curve shown in Fig. 69.2. The scale on the right-hand side of the

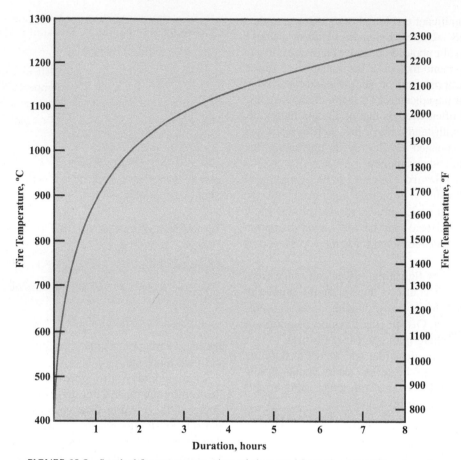

FIGURE 69.2 Standard fire temperature–time relations used for testing of building elements.

figure shows the temperature at which various items melt or are damaged and therefore indicates how long after the fire is started that such damage occurs.

Smoke damage related to fires can also be extensive. Smoke is an abrasive. It collects on the heads of unsealed magnetic disks, optical disks, and tape drives. Electrical fires can produce an acrid smoke that may damage other equipment and may be poisonous or carcinogenic.

The most common fire threat is from fires that originate within a facility; as discussed subsequently, a number of preventive and mitigating measures can be taken. A more uncontrollable threat is faced from wildfires, which are a plausible concern in the western United States, portions of Australia (where the term *bushfire* is used), and a number of other countries.

Water Damage

Water and other stored liquids in proximity to computer equipment pose an obvious threat. The primary danger is an electrical short, which can happen if water bridges a circuit board trace carrying voltage and a trace carrying ground. Moving water, such as in plumbing, and weather-created water from rain, snow, and ice also pose threats. A pipe

may burst from a fault in the line or from freezing. Sprinkler systems, despite their security function, are a major threat to computer equipment and paper and electronic storage media. The system may be set off by a faulty temperature sensor, or a burst pipe may cause water to enter the computer room. For a large computer installation, an effort should be made to avoid sources of water from one or two floors above. An example of a hazard from this direction is an overflowing toilet.

Less common, but more catastrophic, is floodwater. Much of the damage comes from the suspended material in the water. Floodwater leaves a muddy residue that is extraordinarily difficult to clean up.

Chemical, Radiological, and Biological Hazards

Chemical, radiological, and biological hazards pose a growing threat, both from intentional attack and from accidental discharge. None of these hazardous agents should be present in an IS environment, but either accidental or intentional intrusion is possible. Nearby discharges (from an overturned truck carrying hazardous materials) can be introduced through the ventilation system or open windows and, in the case of radiation, through perimeter walls. In addition, discharges in the vicinity can disrupt work by causing evacuations to be ordered. Flooding can also introduce biological or chemical contaminants.

In general, the primary risk of these hazards is to personnel. Radiation and chemical agents can also cause damage to electronic equipment.

Dust

Dust is a prevalent concern that is often overlooked. Even fibers from fabric and paper are abrasive and mildly conductive, although generally equipment is resistant to such contaminants. Larger influxes of dust can result from a number of incidents, such as a controlled explosion of a nearby building and a windstorm carrying debris from a wildfire. A more likely source of influx comes from dust surges that originate within the building caused by construction or maintenance work.

Equipment with moving parts, such as rotating storage media and computer fans, is the most vulnerable to damage from dust. Dust can also block ventilation and reduce radiational cooling.

Infestation

One of the less pleasant physical threats is infestation, which covers a broad range of living organisms, including mold, insects, and rodents. High-humidity conditions can lead to the growth of mold and mildew, which can be harmful to both personnel and equipment. Insects, particularly those that attack wood and paper, are also a common threat.

Technical Threats

This category encompasses threats related to electrical power and electromagnetic emission.

Electrical Power

Electrical power is essential to the operation of an IS. All of the electrical and electronic devices in the system require power, and most require uninterrupted utility power.

Power utility problems can be broadly grouped into three categories: undervoltage, overvoltage, and noise.

An **undervoltage** occurs when the IS equipment receives less voltage than is required for normal operation. Undervoltage events range from temporary dips in the voltage supply to brownouts (prolonged undervoltage), and to power outages. Most computers are designed to withstand prolonged voltage reductions of about 20% without shutting down and without operational error. Deeper dips or blackouts lasting more than a few milliseconds trigger a system shutdown. Generally, no damage is done but service is interrupted.

Far more serious is an **overvoltage**. A surge of voltage can be caused by a utility company supply anomaly, by some internal (to the building) wiring fault, or by lightning. Damage is a function of intensity and duration, and the effectiveness of any surge protectors between your equipment and the source of the surge. A sufficient surge can destroy silicon-based components, including processors and memories.

Power lines can also be a conduit for **noise**. In many cases, these spurious signals can endure through the filtering circuitry of the power supply and interfere with signals inside electronic devices, causing logical errors.

Electromagnetic Interference

Noise along a power supply line is only one source of electromagnetic interference (EMI). Motors, fans, heavy equipment, and even other computers generate electrical noise that can cause intermittent problems with the computer you are using. This noise can be transmitted through space as well as nearby power lines.

Another source of EMI is high-intensity emissions from nearby commercial radio stations and microwave relay antennas. Even low-intensity devices such as cellular telephones can interfere with sensitive electronic equipment.

Human-Caused Physical Threats

Human-caused threats are more difficult to deal with than the environmental and technical threats discussed so far. Human-caused threats are less predictable than other types of physical threats. Worse, human-caused threats are specifically designed to overcome prevention measures and/or seek the most vulnerable point of attack. We can group such threats into the following categories:

- **Unauthorized physical access:** Those who are not employees should not be in the building or building complex at all unless accompanied by an authorized individual. Not counting personal computers and workstations, IS assets such as servers, mainframe computers, network equipment, and storage networks are generally housed in restricted areas. Access to such areas is usually restricted to only a certain number of employees. Unauthorized physical access can lead to other threats such as theft, vandalism, or misuse.
- **Theft:** This threat includes theft of equipment and theft of data by copying. Eavesdropping and wiretapping also fall into this category. Theft can be at the hands of an outsider who has gained unauthorized access or by an insider.
- **Vandalism:** This threat includes destruction of equipment and destruction of data.
- **Misuse:** This category includes improper use of resources by those who are authorized to use them, as

970 PART | XI Cyber Physical Security

well as use of resources by individuals not authorized to use the resources at all.

3. PHYSICAL SECURITY PREVENTION AND MITIGATION MEASURES

In this section, we look at a range of techniques for preventing, or in some cases simply deterring, physical attacks. We begin with a survey of some techniques for dealing with environmental and technical threats and then move on to human-caused threats.

One general prevention measure is the use of cloud computing. From a physical security viewpoint, an obvious benefit of cloud computing is that there is a reduced need for IS assets on site and a substantial portion of data assets are not subject to on-site physical threats. See Chapter 8 for a discussion of cloud computing security issues.

Environmental Threats

We discuss these threats in the same order.

Inappropriate Temperature and Humidity

Dealing with this problem is primarily a matter of having environmental-control equipment of appropriate capacity and appropriate sensors to warn of thresholds being exceeded. Beyond that, the principal requirement is the maintenance of a power supply, discussed subsequently.

Fire and Smoke

Dealing with fire involves a combination of alarms, preventive measures, and fire mitigation. Martin provides the following list of necessary measures [4]:

1. Choice of site to minimize likelihood of disaster. Few disastrous fires originate in a well-protected computer room or IS facility. The IS area should be chosen to minimize fire, water, and smoke hazards from adjoining areas. Common walls with other activities should have at least a 1-h fire-protection rating;
2. Air conditioning and other ducts designed so as not to spread fire. There are standard guidelines and specifications for such designs;
3. Positioning of equipment to minimize damage;
4. Good housekeeping. Records and flammables must not be stored in the IS area. Tidy installation of IS equipment is crucial;
5. Hand-operated fire extinguishers readily available, clearly marked, and regularly tested;
6. Automatic fire extinguishers installed. Installation should be such that the extinguishers are unlikely to cause damage to equipment or danger to personnel;

7. Fire detectors. The detectors sound alarms inside the IS room and with external authorities, and start automatic fire extinguishers after a delay to permit human intervention;
8. Equipment power-off switch. This switch must be clearly marked and unobstructed. All personnel must be familiar with power-off procedures;
9. Emergency procedures posted;
10. Personnel safety. Safety must be considered in designing the building layout and emergency procedures;
11. Important records stored in fireproof cabinets or vaults;
12. Records needed for file reconstruction stored off the premises;
13. Up-to-date duplicate of all programs stored off the premises;
14. Contingency plan for use of equipment elsewhere in case the computers are destroyed;
15. Insurance company and local fire department should inspect the facility.

To deal with the threat of smoke, the responsible manager should install smoke detectors in every room that contains computer equipment as well as under raised floors and over suspended ceilings. Smoking should not be permitted in computer rooms.

For wildfires, the available countermeasures are limited. Fire-resistant building techniques are costly and difficult to justify.

Water Damage

Prevention and mitigation measures for water threats must encompass the range of such threats. For plumbing leaks, the cost of relocating threatening lines is generally difficult to justify. With knowledge of the exact layout of water supply lines, measures can be taken to locate equipment sensibly. The location of all shutoff valves should be clearly visible or at least clearly documented, and responsible personnel should know the procedures to follow in case of an emergency.

To deal with both plumbing leaks and other sources of water, sensors are vital. Water sensors should be located on the floor of computer rooms as well as under raised floors, and should cut off power automatically in the event of a flood.

Other Environmental Threats

For chemical, biological, and radiological threats, specific technical approaches are available, including infrastructure design, sensor design and placement, mitigation procedures, personnel training, and so forth. Standards and techniques in these areas continue to evolve.

As for dust hazards, the obvious prevention method is to limit dust through the use and proper maintenance of filters and regular IS room maintenance. For infestations, regular pest control procedures may be needed, starting with maintaining a clean environment.

Technical Threats

To deal with brief power interruptions, an uninterruptible power supply (UPS) should be employed for each piece of critical equipment. The UPS is a battery backup unit that can maintain power to processors, monitors, and other equipment for a period of minutes. UPS units can also function as surge protectors, power noise filters, and automatic shutdown devices when the battery runs low.

For longer blackouts or brownouts, critical equipment should be connected to an emergency power source such as a generator. For reliable service, a range of issues need to be addressed by management, including product selection, generator placement, personnel training, testing and maintenance schedules, and so forth.

To deal with electromagnetic interference, a combination of filters and shielding can be used. The specific technical details will depend on the infrastructure design and the anticipated sources and nature of the interference.

Human-Caused Physical Threats

The general approach to human-caused physical threats is physical access control. Based on Ref. [1], we can suggest a spectrum of approaches that can be used to restrict access to equipment. These methods can be used in combination:

1. Physical contact with a resource is restricted by restricting access to the building in which the resource is housed. This approach is intended to deny access to outsiders but does not address the issue of unauthorized insiders or employees.
2. Physical contact with a resource is restricted by putting it in a locked cabinet, safe, or room.
3. A machine may be accessed but it is secured (perhaps permanently bolted) to an object that is difficult to move. This will deter theft but not vandalism, unauthorized access, or misuse.
4. A security device controls the power switch.
5. A movable resource is equipped with a tracking device so that a sensing portal can alert security personnel or trigger an automated barrier to prevent the object from being moved out of its proper security area.
6. A portable object is equipped with a tracking device so that its current position can be monitored continually.

The first two of these approaches isolate the equipment. Techniques that can be used for this type of access control include controlled areas patrolled or guarded by personnel, barriers that isolate each area, entry points in the barrier (doors), and locks or screening measures at each entry point.

Physical access control should address not just computers and other IS equipment but also locations of wiring used to connect systems, the electrical power service, the HVAC equipment and distribution system, telephone and communications lines, backup media, and documents.

In addition to physical and procedural barriers, an effective physical access control regime includes a variety of sensors and alarms to detect intruders and unauthorized access or movement of equipment. Surveillance systems are frequently an integral part of building security, and special-purpose surveillance systems for the IS area are generally also warranted. Such systems should provide real-time remote viewing as well as recording.

Finally, the introduction of Wi-Fi changes the concept of physical security in the sense that it extends physical access across physical boundaries such as walls and locked doors. For example, a parking lot outside of a secure building provides access via Wi-Fi.

4. RECOVERY FROM PHYSICAL SECURITY BREACHES

The most essential element of recovery from physical security breaches is redundancy. Redundancy does not undo breaches of confidentiality such as the theft of data or documents, but provides for recovery from loss of data. Ideally, all of the important data in the system should be available off site and updated as near to real time as is warranted based on a cost—benefit trade-off. With broadband connections almost universally available, batch encrypted backups over private networks or the Internet are warranted and can be carried out on whatever schedule is deemed appropriate by management. At the extreme, a *hot site* can be created off site that is ready to take over an operation instantly and has available to it a near—real time copy of operational data.

Recovery from physical damage to the equipment or the site depends on the nature of the damage and, importantly, the nature of the residue. Water, smoke, and fire damage may leave behind hazardous materials that must be meticulously removed from the site before normal operations and the normal equipment suite can be reconstituted. In many cases, this requires bringing in disaster recovery specialists from outside the organization to do the cleanup.

5. THREAT ASSESSMENT, PLANNING, AND PLAN IMPLEMENTATION

We have surveyed a number of threats to physical security and a number of approaches to prevention, mitigation, and recovery. To implement a physical security program, an organization must conduct a threat assessment to determine the amount of resources to devote to physical security and the allocation of those resources against the various threats. This process also applies to logical security.

Threat Assessment

In this subsection, we follow Platt [2] in outlining a typical sequence of steps that an organization should take:

1. **Set up a steering committee.** The threat assessment should not be left only to a security officer or to IS management. All of those who have a stake in the security of the IS assets, including all of the user communities, should be brought into the process.
2. **Obtain information and assistance.** Historical information concerning external threats, such as flood and fire, is the best starting point. This information often can be obtained from government agencies and weather bureaus. In the United States, the Federal Emergency Management Agency (FEMA) can provide much useful information. FEMA has a number of publications available online that provide specific guidance regarding a wide variety of physical security areas (fema.gov/business/index.shtm). The committee should also seek expert advice from vendors, suppliers, neighboring businesses, service and maintenance personnel, consultants, and academics.
3. **Identify all possible threats.** List all possible threats, including those specific to IS operations as well as those that are more general, covering the building and the geographic area.
4. **Determine the likelihood of each threat.** This is clearly a difficult task. One approach is to use a scale of 1 (least likely) to 5 (most likely) so that threats can be grouped to suggest where attention should be directed. All of the information from Step 2 can be applied to this task.
5. **Approximate the direct costs.** For each threat, the committee must estimate not only the threat's likelihood but also its severity in terms of consequences. Again a relative scale of 1 (low) to 5 (high) in terms of costs and losses is a reasonable approach. For both Steps 4 and 5, an attempt to use a finer-grained scale or to assign specific probabilities and specific costs is likely to produce the impression of greater precision and knowledge about future threats than is possible.
6. **Consider cascading costs.** Some threats can trigger consequential threats that add still more impact costs. For example, a fire can cause direct flame, heat, and smoke damage as well as disrupt utilities and result in water damage.
7. **Prioritize the threats.** The goal here is to determine the relative importance of the threats as a guide to focusing

resources on prevention. A simple formula yields a prioritized list:

$$\text{Importance} = \text{Likelihood} \times [\text{Direct Cost} + \text{Secondary Cost}]$$

where the scale values (1−5) are used in the formula.
8. **Complete the threat assessment report.** The committee can now prepare a report that includes the prioritized list, with commentary on how the results were achieved. This report serves as the reference source for the planning process that follows.

Planning and Implementation

Once a threat assessment has been done, the steering committee, or another committee, can develop a plan for threat prevention, mitigation, and recovery. The following is a typical sequence of steps an organization could take:

1. **Assess internal and external resources.** These include resources for prevention as well as response. A reasonable approach is again to use a relative scale from 1 (strong ability to prevent and respond) to 5 (weak ability to prevent and respond). This scale can be combined with the threat priority score to focus resource planning.
2. **Identify challenges and prioritize activities.** Determine specific goals and milestones. Make a list of tasks to be performed, by whom and when. Determine how you will address the problem areas and resource shortfalls that were identified in the vulnerability analysis.
3. **Develop a plan.** The plan should include prevention measures and equipment needed and emergency response procedures. The plan should include support documents, such as emergency call lists, building and site maps, and resource lists.
4. **Implement the plan.** Implementation includes acquiring new equipment, assigning responsibilities, conducting training, monitoring plan implementation, and updating the plan regularly.

6. EXAMPLE: A CORPORATE PHYSICAL SECURITY POLICY

To give the reader a feeling for how organizations deal with physical security, we provide a real-world example of a physical security policy. The company is a European Union−based engineering consulting firm that specializes in the provision of planning, design, and management services for infrastructure development worldwide. With interests in transportation, water, maritime, and property, the company is undertaking commissions in over 70 countries from a network of more than 70 offices.

Fig. 69.3 is extracted from the company's security standards document. For our purposes, we have changed the name of the company to *Company* wherever it appears in the document. The company's physical security policy relies heavily on International Organization for Standardization 17,799 (*Code of Practice for Information Security Management*).

7. INTEGRATION OF PHYSICAL AND LOGICAL SECURITY

Physical security involves numerous detection devices such as sensors and alarms, and numerous prevention devices and measures such as locks and physical barriers. It should be clear that there is much scope for automation and for the integration of various computerized and electronic devices. Clearly, physical security can be made more effective if there is a central destination for all alerts and alarms and if there is central control of all automated access control mechanisms such as smart card entry sites.

From the point of view of both effectiveness and cost, there is increasing interest not only in integrating automated physical security functions but in integrating, to the extent possible, automated physical security and logical security functions. The most promising area is that of access control. Examples of ways to integrate physical and logical access control include the following:

- Use of a single ID card for physical and logical access. This can be a simple magnetic-strip card or a smart card;
- Single-step user/card enrollment and termination across all identity and access control databases;
- A central ID-management system instead of multiple disparate user directories and databases;
- Unified event monitoring and correlation.

As an example of the utility of this integration, suppose that an alert indicates that Bob has logged on to the company's wireless network (an event generated by the logical access control system) but did not enter the building (an event generated from the physical access control system). Combined, these two events suggest that someone is hijacking Bob's wireless account.

For the integration of physical and logical access control to be practical, a wide range of vendors must conform to standards that cover smart card protocols, authentication and access control formats and protocols, database entries, message formats, and so on. An important step in this direction is Federal Information Processing Standard (FIPS) 201-2 [*Personal Identity Verification (PIV) of Federal Employees and Contractors*], issued in 2013. The standard defines a reliable, government-wide PIV system for use in applications such as access to federally controlled facilities and ISs. The standard

specifies a PIV system within which common identification credentials can be created and later used to verify a claimed identity. The standard also identifies federal government-wide requirements for security levels that depend on risks to the facility or information being protected.

Fig. 69.4 illustrates the major components of FIPS 201-2–compliant systems. The PIV front end defines the physical interface to a user who is requesting access to a facility, which could be either physical access to a protected physical area or logical access to an IS. The **PIV front end subsystem** supports up to three-factor authentication; the number of factors used depends on the level of security required. The front end uses a smart card, known as a PIV card, which is a dual-interface contact and contactless card. The card holds a cardholder photograph, X.509 certificates, cryptographic keys, biometric data, and the cardholder unique identifier (CHUID). Certain cardholder information may be read-protected and require a personal identification number (PIN) for read access by the card reader. In the current version of the standard, the biometric reader is a fingerprint reader or an iris scanner.

The standard defines three assurance levels for verification of the card and the encoded data stored on the card, which in turn lead to verifying the authenticity of the person holding the credential. A level of *some confidence* corresponds to use of the card reader and PIN. A level of *high confidence* adds a biometric comparison of a fingerprint captured and encoded on the card during the card-issuing process and a fingerprint scanned at the physical access point. A *very high confidence* level requires the process just described to be completed at a control point attended by an official observer.

The other major component of the PIV system is the **PIV card issuance and management subsystem**. This subsystem includes the components responsible for identity proofing and registration, card and key issuance and management, and the various repositories and services (public key infrastructure directory and certificate status servers) required as part of the verification infrastructure.

The PIV system interacts with an **access control subsystem**, which includes components responsible for determining a particular PIV cardholder's access to a physical or logical resource. FIPS 201-1 standardizes data formats and protocols for interaction between the PIV system and the access control system.

Unlike the typical card number/facility code encoded on most access control cards, the FIPS 201 CHUID takes authentication to a new level through the use of an expiration date (a required CHUID data field) and an optional CHUID digital signature. A digital signature can be checked to ensure that the CHUID recorded on the card was digitally signed by a trusted source and that the CHUID data have not been altered since the card was signed. The CHUID expiration date can be checked to verify that the card has not expired. This is independent from whatever

5. Physical and Environmental security

5.1. Secure Areas

5.1.1. **Physical Security Perimeter** - Company shall use security perimeters to protect all non-public areas, commensurate with the value of the assets therein. Business critical information processing facilities located in unattended buildings shall also be alarmed to a permanently manned remote alarm monitoring station.

5.1.2. **Physical Entry Controls** - Secure areas shall be segregated and protected by appropriate entry controls to ensure that only authorised personnel are allowed access. Similar controls are also required where the building is shared with, or accessed by, non-Company staff and organisations not acting on behalf of Company.

5.1.3. **Securing Offices, Rooms and Facilities** - Secure areas shall be created in order to protect office, rooms and facilities with special security requirements.

5.1.4. **Working in Secure Areas** - Additional controls and guidelines for working in secure areas shall be used to enhance the security provided by the physical control protecting the secure areas.

> *Employees of Company should be aware that additional controls and guidelines for working in secure areas to enhance the security provided by the physical control protecting the secure areas might be in force. For further clarification they should contact their Line Manager.*

5.1.5. **Isolated Access Points** - Isolated access points, additional to building main entrances (e.g. Delivery and Loading areas) shall be controlled and, if possible, isolated from secure areas to avoid unauthorised access.

5.1.6. **Sign Posting Of Computer Installations** - Business critical computer installations sited within a building must not be identified by the use of descriptive sign posts or other displays. Where such sign posts or other displays are used they must be worded in such a way so as not to highlight the business critical nature of the activity taking place within the building.

5.2. Equipment Security

5.2.1. **Equipment Sitting and Protection** - Equipment shall be sited or protected to reduce the risk from environmental threats and hazards, and opportunity for unauthorised access.

5.2.2. **Power Supply** - The equipment shall be protected from power failure and other electrical anomalies.

5.2.3. **Cabling Security** - Power and telecommunication cabling carrying data or supporting information services shall be protected from interception or damage commensurate with the business criticality of the operations they serve.

5.2.4. **Equipment Maintenance** - Equipment shall be maintained in accordance with manufacturer's instruction and/or documented procedures to ensure its continued availability and integrity.

5.2.5. **Security of Equipment off-premises** - Security procedures and controls shall be used to secure equipment used outside any Company's premises

> *Employees are to note that there should be security procedures and controls to secure equipment used outside any Company premises. Advice on these procedures can be sought from the Group Security Manager.*

5.2.6. **Secure Disposal or Re-use of Equipment** - Information shall be erased from equipment prior to disposal or reuse.

> *For further guidance contact the Group Security Manager.*

5.2.7. **Security of the Access Network** - Company shall implement access control measures, determined by a risk assessment, to ensure that only authorised people have access to the Access Network (including: cabinets, cabling, nodes etc.).

5.2.8. **Security of PCs** - Every Company owned PC must have an owner who is responsible for its general management and control. Users of PCs are personally responsible for the physical and logical security of any PC they use. Users of Company PCs are personally responsible for the physical and logical security of any PC they use, as defined within the Staff Handbook.

5.2.9. **Removal of "Captured Data"** - Where any device (software or hardware based) has been introduced to the network that captures data for analytical purposes, all data must be wiped off of this device prior to removal from the Company Site. The removal of this data from site for analysis can only be approved by the MIS Technology Manager.

FIGURE 69.3 Company's physical security policy.

5.3. General Controls

5.3.1. Security Controls - Security Settings are to be utilised and configurations must be controlled

No security settings or software on Company systems are to be changed without authorisation from MIS Support

5.3.2. **Clear Screen Policy** - Company shall have and implement clear-screen policy in order to reduce the risks of unauthorised access, loss of, and damage to information.

This will be implemented when all Users of the Company system have Windows XP operating system.

When the User has the Windows XP system they are to carry out the following:

- *Select the Settings tab within the START area on the desktop screen.*

- *Select Control Panel.*

- *Select the icon called DISPLAY.*

- *Select the Screensaver Tab.*

- *Set a Screen saver.*

- *Set the time for 15 Mins.*

- *Tick the Password Protect box; remember this is the same password that you utilise to log on to the system.*

Staff are to lock their screens using the Ctrl-Alt-Del when they leave their desk

5.3.3. **Clear Desk Policy** – Staff shall ensure that they operate a Clear Desk Policy

Each member of staff is asked to take personal and active responsibility for maintaining a "clear desk" policy whereby files and papers are filed or otherwise cleared away before leaving the office at the end of each day

5.3.4. **Removal of Property** - Equipment, information or software belonging to the organisation shall not be removed without authorisation.

Equipment, information or software belonging to Company shall not be removed without authorisation from the Project Manager or Line Manager and the MIS Support.

5.3.5. **People Identification** - All Company staff must have visible the appropriate identification whenever they are in Company premises.

5.3.6. **Visitors** - All Company premises will have a process for dealing with visitors. All Visitors must be sponsored and wear the appropriate identification whenever they are in Company premises.

5.3.7. **Legal Right of Entry** - Entry must be permitted to official bodies when entry is demanded on production of a court order or when the person has other legal rights. Advice must be sought from management or the Group Security Manager as a matter of urgency.

FIGURE 69.3 cont'd

expiration date is associated with cardholder privileges. Reading and verifying the CHUID alone provide only some assurance of identity because they authenticate the card data, not the cardholder. The PIN and biometric factors provide identity verification of the individual.

Fig. 69.5, adapted from Ref. [3], illustrates the convergence of physical and logical access control using FIPS 201-2. The core of the system includes the PIV and access control system as well as a certificate authority for signing CHUIDs. The other elements of the figure provide examples of the use of the system core for integrating physical and logical access control.

If the integration of physical and logical access control extends beyond a unified front end to an integration of system elements, a number of benefits accrue, including the following [3]:

- Employees gain a single, unified access control authentication device; this cuts down on misplaced tokens, reduces training and overhead, and allows seamless access.
- A single logical location for employee ID management reduces duplicate data entry operations and allows for immediate and real-time authorization revocation of all enterprise resources.
- Auditing and forensic groups have a central repository for access control investigations.
- Hardware unification can reduce the number of vendor purchase-and-support contracts.

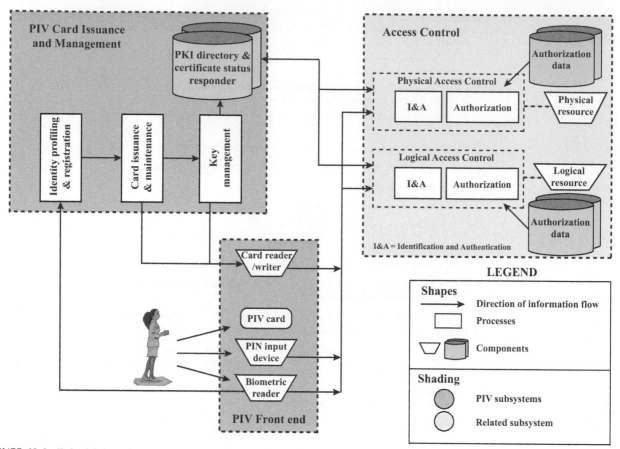

FIGURE 69.4 Federal Information Processing Standard FIPS 201 personal identity verification (PIV) system model. *PIN*, personal identification number; *PKI*, public key infrastructure.

- Certificate-based access control systems can leverage user ID certificates for other security applications, such as document electronic signing and data encryption.

Finally, let us briefly look at a physical security checklist. The effectiveness of the recommendations in the physical security checklist is most useful when initiated as part of a larger plan to develop and implement security policy throughout an organization.

8. PHYSICAL SECURITY CHECKLIST

Although it may be tempting simply to refer to the following checklist as your security plan, to do so would limit the effectiveness of the recommendations. Some recommendations and considerations are included the following checklist: "An Agenda for Action for Physical Security."

9. SUMMARY

Physical security requires that building site(s) be safeguarded in a way that minimizes the risk of resource theft and destruction. To accomplish this, decision makers must be concerned about building construction, room assignments, emergency procedures, regulations governing equipment placement and use, power supplies, product handling, and relationships with outside contractors and agencies.

The physical plant must be satisfactorily secured to prevent people who are not authorized to enter the site and use equipment from doing so. A building does not need to feel like a fort to be safe. Well-conceived plans to secure a building can be initiated without adding undue burden on your staff. After all, if they require access, they will receive it, as long as they were aware of, and abide by, the organization's stated security policies and guidelines. The only way to ensure this is to demand that before any person is given access to your system, they have first signed and returned a valid security agreement. This necessary security policy is too important to permit exceptions.

Finally, let us move on to the real interactive part of this chapter: review questions/exercises, hands-on projects, case projects, and the optional team case project. The answers and/or solutions by chapter can be found in Appendix K.

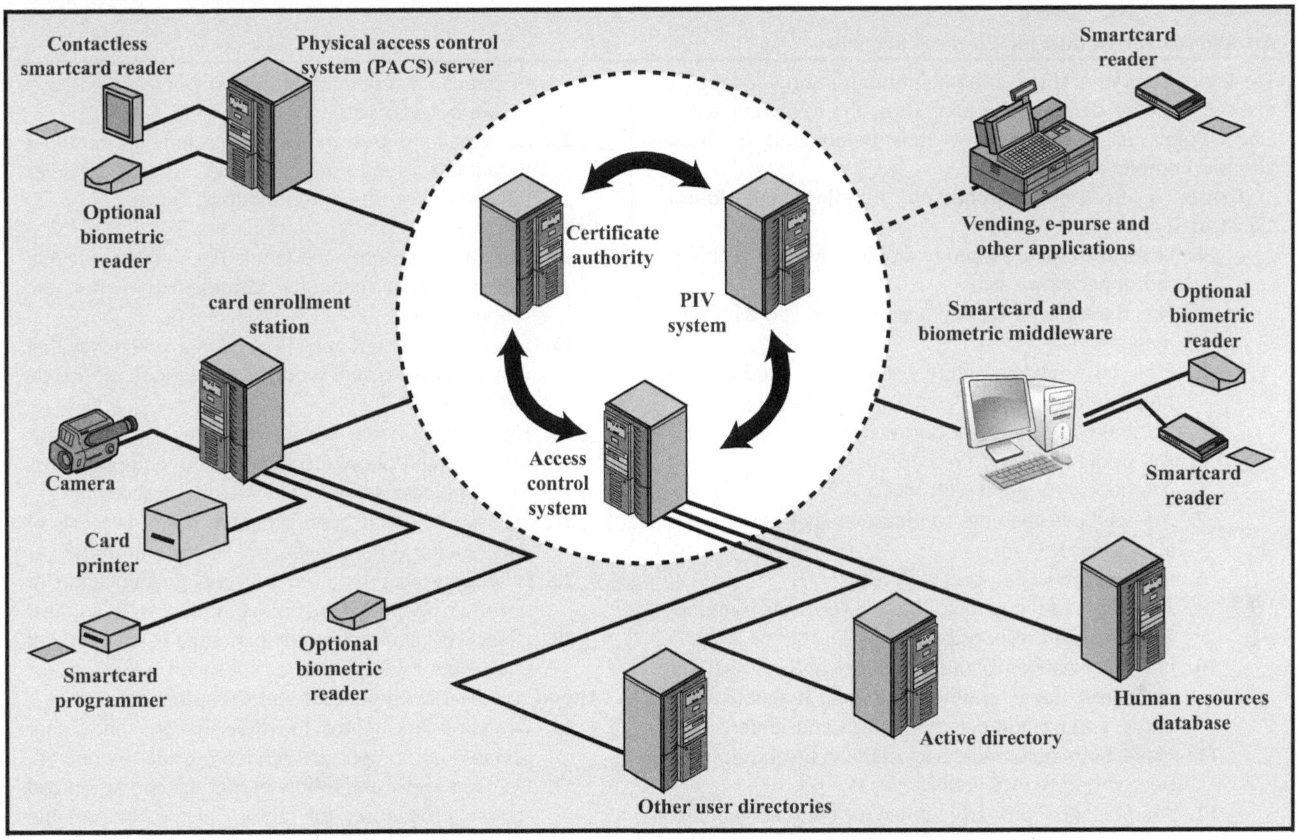

FIGURE 69.5   Convergence example. *PIV*, personal identity verification.

CHAPTER REVIEW QUESTIONS/ EXERCISES

True/False

1. True or False? Information system hardware includes data processing and storage equipment, transmission and networking facilities, and online storage media.
2. True or False? Physical facility includes the buildings and other structures housing the system and network components.
3. True or False? Supporting facilities underscores the operation of the information system.
4. True or False? Personnel are humans involved in the control, maintenance, and use of the information systems.
5. True or False? It is possible to assess the risk of various types of natural disasters and take suitable precautions so that catastrophic loss from natural disaster is achieved.

Multiple Choice

1. What are the three elements of information system (IS) security?
   A. Logical security
   B. Physical security
   C. Maritime security
   D. Premises security
   E. Wireless security
2. In broad terms, which of the following is not included in the critical infrastructure?
   A. Environmental threats
   B. Information system hardware
   C. Physical facility
   D. Supporting facilities
   E. Personnel
3. Which of the following are threats?
   A. Environmental
   B. Natural
   C. Technical
   D. Access
   E. Human-caused
4. Which of the following is not a human-caused threat?
   A. Unauthorized physical access
   B. Theft
   C. Vandalism
   D. Decryption
   E. Misuse
5. Dealing with fire involves a combination of alarms, preventive measures, and fire mitigation. Which of the following is not a necessary measure?
   A. Choice of site to minimize likelihood of disaster

An Agenda for Action for Physical Security

The brevity of a checklist can be helpful but in no way does it make up for the detail of the text. Thus, the following set of Check Points for Physical Security must be adhered to (check all tasks completed):

Create a Secure Environment: Building and Room Construction:

_____1. Does each secure room or facility have low visibility (no unnecessary signs)?

_____2. Has the room or facility been constructed with full-height walls?

_____3. Has the room or facility been constructed with a fireproof ceiling?

_____4. Are there two or fewer doorways?

_____5. Are doors solid and fireproof?

_____6. Are doors equipped with locks?

_____7. Are window openings to secure areas kept as small as possible?

_____8. Are windows equipped with locks?

_____9. Are keys and combinations to door and window locks secured responsibly?

_____10. Have alternatives to traditional lock and key security measures (bars, antitheft cabling, magnetic key cards, and motion detectors) been considered?

_____11. Have both automatic and manual fire equipment been properly installed?

_____12. Are personnel properly trained for fire emergencies?

_____13. Are acceptable room temperatures always maintained (between 50 and 80°F)?

_____14. Are acceptable humidity ranges always maintained (between 20% and 80%)?

_____15. Are eating, drinking, and smoking regulations in place and enforced?

_____16. Has all nonessential, potentially flammable material (curtains and stacks of computer paper) been removed from secure areas?

Guard Equipment:

_____17. Has equipment been identified as critical or general use, and segregated appropriately?

_____18. Is equipment housed out of sight and reach from doors and windows, and away from radiators, heating vents, air conditioners, and other duct work?

_____19. Are plugs, cabling, and other wires protected from foot traffic?

_____20. Are up-to-date records of all equipment brand names, model names, and serial numbers kept in a secure location?

_____21. Have qualified technicians (staff or vendors) been identified to repair critical equipment if and when it fails?

_____22. Has contact information for repair technicians (telephone numbers, customer numbers, and maintenance contract numbers) been stored in a secure but accessible place?

_____23. Are repair workers and outside technicians required to adhere to the organization's security policies concerning sensitive information?

Rebuff Theft:

_____24. Has all equipment been labeled in an overt way that clearly and permanently identifies its owner (the school name)?

_____25. Has all equipment been labeled in a covert way that only authorized staff would know to look for (inside the cover)?

_____26. Have steps been taken to make it difficult for unauthorized people to tamper with equipment (by replacing case screws with Allen-type screws)?

_____27. Has security staff been provided up-to-date lists of personnel and their respective access authority?

_____28. Is security staff required to verify identification of unknown people before permitting access to facilities?

_____29. Is security staff required to maintain a log of all equipment taken in and out of secure areas?

Attend to Portable Equipment and Computers:

_____30. Do users know not to leave laptops and other portable equipment unattended outside the office?

_____31. Do users know and follow proper transportation and storage procedures for laptops and other portable equipment?

Regulate Power Supplies:

_____32. Are surge protectors used with all equipment?

_____33. Are UPSs in place for critical systems?

_____34. Have power supplies been "insulated" from environmental threats by a professional electrician?

_____35. Has consideration been given to the use of electrical outlets so as to avoid overloading?

_____36. Are the negative effects of static electricity minimized through the use of antistatic carpeting, pads, and sprays as necessary?

Protect Output:

_____37. Are photocopiers, fax machines, and scanners kept in open view?

_____38. Are printers assigned to users with similar security clearances?

_____39. Is every printed copy of confidential information labeled as "confidential"?

_____40. Are outside delivery services required to adhere to security practices when transporting sensitive information?

_____41. Are all paper copies of sensitive information shredded before being discarded?

B. Positioning of equipment to minimize damage

C. Good housekeeping

D. Fire detectors

E. Physical contact

EXERCISE

Problem

A company's physical security team analyzed physical security threats and vulnerabilities for its systems. What type of vulnerabilities did the company focus on?

Hands-on Projects

Project

An engineering company operating within a highly regulated industry, in which privacy and compliance are of paramount importance, wanted to compare itself relative to its peers in physical security provision and establish a baseline from which to quantify improvement. Please identify the best practices; compare organizational and outsourcing models; compare security technologies used; and, calibrate investment in physical security against its peers.

Case Projects

Problem

This case study illustrates how a company uses intelligent video processing (a subsystem of its video surveillance system) to detect intrusions at land ports of entry. Virtual fences are integrated into each facility to complement both the facility's perimeter physical security system (composed of a combination of fences, gates, and barriers) and the video surveillance system. What should happen if these virtual fences are breached?

Optional Team Case Project

Problem

A company wants to further develop its access control system (ACS) use of video, proximity-based ID cards, biometrics, radio-frequency ID, Voice Over Internet Protocol, and remotely controlled gates for manned and unmanned access control. What does the company need to do to develop its ACS further?

REFERENCES

[1] M. Michael, Physical security measures, in: H. Bidgoli (Ed.), Handbook of Information Security, Wiley, New York, 2006.

[2] F. Platt, Physical threats to the information infrastructure, in: S. Bosworth, M. Kabay (Eds.), Computer Security Handbook, Wiley, New York, 2002.

[3] J. Forristal, Physical/Logical Convergence, Network Computing, November 23, 2006.

[4] J. Martin, Security, Accuracy, and Privacy in Computer Systems, Prentice Hall, Englewood Cliffs, NJ, 1973.

Chapter 70

Biometrics

Luther Martin

Voltage Security, Cupertino, CA, United States

Note: This chapter is available in its entirety online at store.elsevier.com/product.jsp?isbn= 9780128038437 (click the Resources tab at the bottom of the page).

1. ABSTRACT

This chapter explains why designing biometric systems is actually a very difficult problem. The problem has been made to look easier than it actually is by the way the technology has been portrayed in movies and on television. Biometric systems are typically depicted as being easy to use and secure, whereas encryption that would actually take billions of years of super-computer time to defeat is often depicted as being easily bypassed with minimal effort. This portrayal of biometric systems may have increased expectations well past what current technologies can actually deliver, and it is important to understand the limitations of existing biometric technologies and to have realistic expectations of the security that such systems can provide in the real world.

2. CONTENTS

Part XII

Practical Security

Chapter 71

Online Identity and User Management Services

Tewfiq El Maliki[1] and Jean-Marc Seigneur[2]

[1]*University of Geneva, Megève, France;* [2]*University of Geneva, Carouge, Switzerland*

1. INTRODUCTION

Mobile computing is becoming easier, more attractive, and even cost-effective: the mobile devices carried by roaming users offer more computing power and functionalities, including sensing and providing location awareness [1]. A lot of computing devices are also deployed in the environments where the users evolve; for example, intelligent home appliances or RFID-enabled fabrics. In this ambient intelligent world, the choices of identity mechanisms will have a large impact on social, cultural, business, and political aspects. Moreover, the Internet of Things (Iot) will generate more complicated privacy problems [2]. Identity has become a burden on the online world. When it is stolen it engenders a massive fraud, principally in online services, which generate a lack of confidence in doing business for providers and frustration for users.

Therefore, the whole of society would suffer from the demise of privacy, which is a real human need. As people have hectic lives and cannot spend their time administering their digital identities, we need consistent identity management platforms and technologies enabling usability and scalability, among others [3]. In this chapter, we survey how the requirements have evolved for mobile user-centric identity management and their associated technologies.

The chapter is organized as follows. First, we present the evolution of identity management requirements. Section 4 surveys how the different, most advanced identity management technologies fulfill present-day requirements. Section 5 covers "social login" that is the major identity management technical solution that has emerged after writing the first version of this book chapter and that has gained a stronger user adoption than the other solutions surveyed in Section 4, although a few of them are explored

with the "social login". Section 6 discusses how mobility can be achieved in the field of identity management in an ambient intelligent/ubiquitous computing world.

2. EVOLUTION OF IDENTITY MANAGEMENT REQUIREMENTS

In this section, we first define what we mean by a digital identity. Later in the chapter, we summarize all the different requirements and detail the most important ones in the following subsections, namely, privacy, usability, and mobility.

Digital Identity Definition

A digital identity is a representation of an entity in a specific context [4]. For a long time, a digital identity was considered as the equivalent of our real-life identity which indicates some of our attributes:

- Who we are, name, citizenship, birthday;
- What we like, our favorite reading, food, clothes, etc.;
- What our reputation is, whether we are honest, without any problems, etc.

A digital identity was seen as an extended identity card or passport containing almost the same information. However, it [5] has been argued that the link between the real-world identity and a digital identity is not always mandatory. For example, on eBay what matters is to know whether the seller's digital identity reputation has been remarkable and that the seller can prove that she controls that digital identity. It is less important to know that her real-world national identity is from the Bermuda Islands, where suing anybody is rather unlikely to succeed. It should be underlined that in a major identity management

Computer and Information Security Handbook. http://dx.doi.org/10.1016/B978-0-12-803843-7.00071-5

initiative [6], a digital identity is defined as "the distinguishing character or personality of an individual. An identity consists of traits, attributes, and preferences upon which one may receive personalized services. Such services could exist online, on mobile devices at work, or in many other places," that is, without mentioning a mandatory link to the real-world identity behind the digital identity.

The combination of virtual world with ubiquitous connectivity has changed the physical constraints to an entirely new set of requirements as the associated security issues, such as phishing, spam, and identity theft, has emerged. They are aggravated by the mobility of the user, the temporary and anonymity of cyber relationships. We are moving toward a new virtual world with implications for humans. Therefore, we are facing the problem of determining the identity of our interlocutor and the accuracy of his/her claims. Simply using strong authentication will not resolve all these security issues. Digital identity management is a key issue that will ensure not only the service and functionality expectations but also security and privacy.

Identity Management Overview

A model of identity can be seen as follows [7]:

- Users who want to access a service
- Identity provider (IdP): is the issuer of user identity
- Service provider (SP): is the relay party imposing an identity check
- Identity (Id): is a set user's attributes
- Personal authentication device (PAD): device holding various identifiers and credentials and could be used for mobility

Fig. 71.1 lists the main components of identity management. The relationship between entities, identities, and identifiers are shown in Fig. 71.2, which illustrates that an entity, such as a user, may have multiple identities, and each identity may consist of multiple attributes that can be unique or nonunique identifiers.

Identity management refers to "the process of representing, using, maintaining, deprovisioning and authenticating entities as digital identities in computer networks".

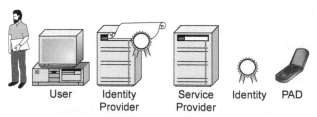

FIGURE 71.1 Identity management main components.

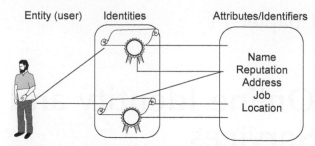

FIGURE 71.2 Relationship between identities, identifiers, and entity.

Authentication is the process of verifying claims about holding specific identities. A failure at this stage will threaten the validity in the entire system. The technology is constantly finding stronger authentication using claims based on:

- Something you know: password, personal identification number (PIN)
- Something you have: one-time password
- Something you are: your voice, face, fingerprint (biometrics)
- Your position
- Some combination of the four

The back trace report [3] has highlighted some interesting points to meet the challenges of identity theft and fraud:

- Developing risk calculation and assessment methods
- Monitoring user behavior to calculate risk
- Building trust and value with the user or consumer
- Engaging the cooperation of the user or consumer with transparency and without complexity or shifting the liability to the consumer
- Taking a staged approach to authentication deployment and process challenges, using more advanced technologies

Digital identity should mange three connected vertexes: usability, cost, and risk as illustrated in Fig. 71.3.

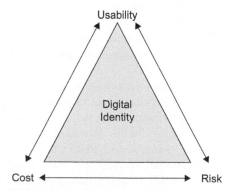

FIGURE 71.3 Digital identity environment to manage.

The user should be aware of the risk he/she is facing if his/her device/software's security is compromised. The usability is the second aspect that should be guaranteed to the user unless he/she will find the system difficult, which could be a source of a security problem. Indeed, a lot of users, when they are flooded by passwords, write them down and hide them in a discreet place under their keyboard. Furthermore, the difficulty to deploy and manage a large number of identities discourages the use of identity management system. The cost of a system should be well-studied and balanced related to risk and usability. Many systems such as a one-time password token are not widely used because they are too costly for a widespread deployment for large institutions. Traditionally, identity management was seen as service-provider centric as it was designed to fulfill the requirements of SP, such as cost effectiveness and scalability. The users were neglected in many aspects because they were forced to memorize difficult or too many passwords. Identity management systems are elaborated to deal with the following core facets [8]:

- Reducing identity theft: The problem of identity theft is becoming a major one, mainly in the online environment. The providers need a more efficient system to tackle this problem.
- Management: The amount of digital identities per person will increase, so the users need convenient support to manage these identities and the corresponding authentication.
- Reachability: The management of reachability allows users to handle their contacts to prevent misuse of their addresses (spam) or unsolicited phone calls.
- Authenticity: Ensuring authenticity with authentication, integrity, and nonrepudiation mechanisms can prevent identity theft.
- Anonymity and pseudonymity: providing anonymity prevent from tracking or identifying the users of a service.
- Organizational personal data management: a quick method to create, modify, and delete work accounts is needed, especially in big organizations.

Without improved usability of identity management [8], for example, weak passwords set up by users on many websites, the number of successful attacks will remain high. To facilitate interacting with unknown entities, simple recognition rather than authentication of a real-world identity has been proposed, which usually involves manual enrollment steps [5]. Usability is indeed enhanced if there is no manual task needed. There might be a weaker level of security but that level may be sufficient for some actions, such as logging into a mobile game platform. Single Sign-On (SSO) is the name given to the

requirements of eliminating multiple password issues and dangerous passwords. When we use multiple user IDs and passwords just to use the emails systems and file servers at work, we feel the inconvenience that comes from having multiple identities. The second problem is the scattering of identity data which causes problems for the integration of IT systems. Moreover, it simplifies the end-user experience and enhances security via identity-based access technology.

Microsoft first largest identity management system was Passport Network. It was a very large and widespread Microsoft Internet service to be an IdP for the MSN and Microsoft properties, and to be an IdP for the Internet. However, with Passport, Microsoft was suspected by many persons of intending to have an absolute control over the identity information of Internet users and thus exploiting them for its own interests. Passport failed to become the Internet identity management tool. Since then, Microsoft has clearly understood that an identity management solution cannot succeed unless some basic rules are respected [9]. That's why Microsoft's Identity Architect, Kim Cameron, has stated the seven laws of identity. His motivation was purely practical in determining the prerequisites of successful identity management system. He formulated the essential principles to maintain privacy and security.

1. User control and consent over the handling of their data
2. Minimal disclosure of data, and for specified purpose
3. Information should only be disclosed to people who have a justifiable need for it
4. The system must provide identifiers for both bilateral relationships between parties, and for incoming unsolicited communications
5. It must support diverse operators and technologies
6. It must be perceived as highly reliable and predictable
7. There must be a consistent user experience across multiple identity systems and using multiple technologies

Most systems do not fulfill the majority of these tests; particularly, they are deficient in fine-tuning the access control over identity to minimize disclosure of data. The formulated Cameron's principles are very clear but they are not enough explicit to compare finely identity management systems. That's why we will define explicitly the identity requirements.

Privacy Requirement

Privacy is a central issue, due to the fact that the official authorities of almost all countries have legal strict policies related to identity. It is often treated in the case of identity management because the management deals with personal information and data. Therefore, it is important to give a definition. Alan F. Westin defines privacy as "the claim of individuals, groups and institutions to determine for themselves, when, how and to what extent information about them is communicated to others" [2]. However, we will use Cooley's broader definition of privacy [10]: "the right to be let alone," because it also emphasizes the problems related to disturbing the user's attention, for example, by email spam.

User Centricity

The evolution of the identity management system is toward the simplification of user experience and reinforcing authentication. It is well known that a poor usability implies the weakness of authentication. Mainly, federated management has responded to some of these requirements by facilitating the use and the managing of identifiers and credentials in the boundary of a federated domain. Nevertheless, it is improbable that only one federated domain will subsist. Moreover, different levels of sensitivity and risks of different services will need different kinds of credentials. It is obvious that we should give users support and atomization of the identity management on the user's side.

A new paradigm must be introduced to solve the problems of usability, scalability, and universal SSO. Therefore, a user-oriented paradigm has emerged which is called user-centric identity management. The word user controlled management [8] is the first used to explain user-centric management model. Federated identity management systems keep strong end-user controls over how identity information is disseminated among members of the federation. This new paradigm gives the user full control over his/her identity by notifying of the information collected and by guaranteeing his/her consent for any type of manipulation over collected information. A user control and consent is also defined as the first law in Cameron's Laws of Identity [9]. A user-centric identity management system supports the user's control and considers user-centric architecture and usability aspects. There is no uniform definition but "user-centric identity management is understood to mean digital identity infrastructure where an individual end-user has substantially independent control over the dissemination and use of their identifier(s) and personally-identifiable information (PII)" [11] (see Fig. 71.4). We can also give this definition of user centricity.

In user-centric identity management the user has the full control over his/her identity and consistent user experience during all transaction when accessing his/her services.

In other terms it means that it allows the user to keep at least some or total control over his/her personal data. One of the principles of user-centric identity is the idea that the user of a Web service should have full control over his/her

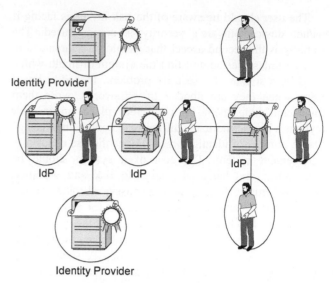

FIGURE 71.4 Identity provider (IdP) centric and user-centric models.

identity information (see checklist: "An Agenda for Action for the User-Centric Identity Paradigm").

An Agenda for Action for the User-Centric Identity Paradigm

A lot of technology discussions and solutions have been focusing on SP and rarely on user's perspectives. User-centric identity paradigm is a real evolution because it moves information technology architecture forward for the users with the following advantages. These are as follows (check all tasks completed):

_____**1.** Empower the total control of users over their privacy.

_____**2.** Usability, as users are using the same identity for each identity transaction.

_____**3.** Give a consistent user's experience thanks to uniformity of identity interface.

_____**4.** Limit identity attacks (phishing).

_____**5.** Limit reachability/disturbances, such as spam.

_____**6.** Review policies on both sides when necessary: IdPs and SPs (websites).

_____**7.** Huge scalability advantages as the IdP does not have to get any prior knowledge about the SP.

_____**8.** Assure secure conditions when exchanging data.

_____**9.** Decouple digital identity from applications.

_____**10.** Pluralism of operators and technologies.

The user-centricity approach allows the user to gain access anonymously as he/she detains the full control on his/her identity. Of course, full anonymity [22] and unlinkability may lead to increased misuse by anonymous users. Then, pseudonymity is an alternative more suitable to the e-commerce environment. In this regard, anonymity must be guaranty at the application and at network levels. Some frameworks have been proposed to ensure user-centric anonymity using the concepts of One-task Authorization key and Binding Signature [22].

Usability Requirement

The security is also compromised with the proliferation of the user's password and even by its weakness. Indeed, some users note their passwords on scratch pads, because their memorization poses problem. The recent Federal Financial Institutions Examination Council (FFIEC) guidance on authentication in online banking reports that "Account fraud and identity theft are frequently the result of single factor (Id/password) authentication exploitation" [12]. From then on, the security must be user oriented as he/her is the effective person concerned with it and a lot of attacks take advantage of the lack of awareness of user attacks (i.e., spoofing, pharming, and phishing) [13]. Without strong control and improved usability [14] of identity management some attacks will be always possible. To facilitate interacting with unknown entities, simple recognition, rather than authentication of a real-world identity, which usually involves manual enrollment steps in the real-world, has been proposed [5]. Usability is indeed enhanced if there is no manual task needed. There might be a weaker level of security reached but that level may be sufficient for some actions, such as, logging to a mobile game platform.

Single Sign-On (SSO) is the name given to the requirements of eliminating multiple password issues and a dangerous password. When we use multiple user IDs and passwords just to use the email systems and file servers at work, we feel the pain that comes from having multiple identities. The second problem is the scattering of identity data which causes problem for the integration of IT systems. Moreover, it simplifies the end-user experience and enhances security via identity-based access technology. Therefore, we offer these features:

- Flexible authentication
- Directory independence
- Session and password management
- Seamless

3. THE REQUIREMENTS FULFILLED BY IDENTITY MANAGEMENT TECHNOLOGIES

This section provides an overview of identity management solutions from Identity 1.0 to Identity 2.0 and how they address the requirements introduced in Section 2. We will

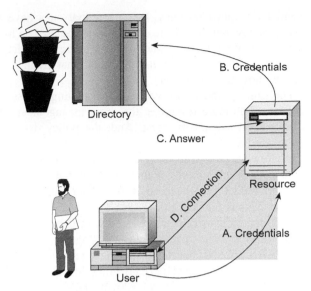

FIGURE 71.5 Identity 1.0 principle.

focus on related standards eXtensible resource identifier (XRI) and Light-Weight Identity (LID) issued from Yadis project and platforms mainly ID-WSF, OpenID, Higgins, InfoCard, and Simple eXtensible Identity Protocol (SXIP). At the end, we treat the identity management in the field of mobility.

Evolution of Identity Management

This section provides an overview of almost all identity management 1.0 (See Fig. 71.5). First of all, we describe the silo model, then different kinds of centralized model and the federated identity management.

4. IDENTITY MANAGEMENT 1.0

In the real world, I use my identity card to prove who I am. How about the online world?

The first digital identity appeared when the user was associated with the pair (username, password) or any other shared secret. This method is used for authentication when connecting to an account or a directory. It proves your identity if you follow the guidelines strictly, otherwise there is no proof. In fact, it is a single authority using opaque trust decision without any credentials (cryptographic proofs), choice, or portability.

In the context of web access, the user must enroll for every nonrelated service, generally with different user interfaces, and follow diverse policies and protocols. Thus, the user has a nonconsistent experience and deals with different identity copies. In addition, some problems related to privacy have also emerged. Indeed, our privacy was potentially invaded by sites. It is clear that sites have a privacy policy, but there is no control from the user on his/ her identity. What are the conditions for using these data? How can we improve our privacy? And to what granularity will we allow them to use it?

The same problem is revealed when having access to resources. The more resources, the more management we have. It is an asymmetric trust. And, the policy decision maybe opaque.

It allows access with an opaque trust decision and a single centralized authority without a credentials choice. It is a silo model [15] because it is neither portable nor scalable. This is Identity 1.0.

The identity management appeared with these problems in the 1980s. The fist identity management system was the Rec. X.500, developed by the International Tele-communication Union (ITU) [1], covering directory services like Directory Access Protocol (DAP). The International Organization for Standardization (ISO) was also associated with the development of the standard. Like a lot of ITU standards, this one was very heavy and complex. A light version appeared in the 1990s for DAP, called Lightweight Directory Access Protocol (LDAP), which was standardized by the Internet Engineering Task Force (IETF) and adopted by Netscape. Microsoft invented an equivalent called Active Directory, and for users, they introduced Passport. It is also the ITU which standardized X.509 for identities related to certificates. It is the format currently recognized. It is a small file, generated by an authority of certification.

If there is a loss or a usurpation of the certificate, it can always be revoked by the authority of certification. This is for a single user, but what about business corporations who have automated their procedures and have a proliferation of applications with deprovisioning but are still in a domain-centric model? What about resources shared between domains?

Silo Model

The main identity management system deployed currently in the world of the Internet is known as the silo model, as shown in Fig. 71.6. Indeed, the IdP and SP are mixed up and they share the same space. The identity management environment is put in place and operated by a single entity for a fixed users' community.

Users of different services must have different accounts and therefore reenter the same information about their identity, which increases the difficulty of management. Moreover, the users are overloaded by identity and password to memorize which produces a significant barrier to usage.

A real problem is the forgetfulness of passwords due to the infrequent use of some of these data. This can obviously

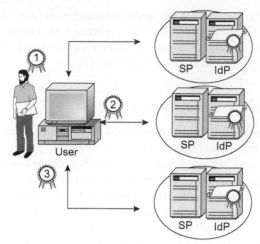

FIGURE 71.6 Identity silo model.

lead to a higher cost of service provisions. This is for single users, but what about enterprises that have automated their procedures and have a proliferation of applications with deprovisioning but are still in a domain-centric model? What about resources shared between domains?

The silo model is not interoperable and is deficient in many aspects. That's why the federated identity manage-ment model is now emerging and it is very appreciated by enterprises. A federated identity management system con-sists of software components and protocols that handle in a decentralized manner the identity of individuals throughout their identity life cycle [16].

Solution by Aggregation

Aggregating identity information and finding the relation-ship between identity records is important to aggregate identity. There are some alternatives:

- The first approach consolidates authentication and attri-butes in only one site and is called a centralized manage-ment solution like Microsoft Passport. This solution avoids the redundancies and inconsistencies in the silo model and gives the user a seamless experience [7]. The evolution was as follows [15,16]:
  - Building a single central identity data store which is feasible only for small organizations.
  - Creating a meta-directory that synchronizes data from other identity data stored elsewhere.
  - Creating a virtual directory (VD) that provides a sin-gle integrated view of the identity data stored.
  - An SSO identity model which allows users to be authenticated by one SP.
- The second approach decentralizes the responsibility of IdP to multiple such IdPs which can be selected by the end users. This is a federated system where some attri-

butes of identity are stored in distributed IdPs. A federated directories model, by linking identity data stored together, has emerged. Protocols are defined in several standards such as in Shibboleth [17], web services (WS) federation language 2003.

Centralized Versus Federation Identity Management

Microsoft Passport is a centralized system, entirely controlled by Microsoft and closely tied to other Microsoft products. Individuals and companies have proven to be reluctant adopters of a system so tightly controlled by one dominant company.

Centrally managed repositories in centralized identity infrastructures can't solve the problem of cross-organizational authentication and authorization. This approach has several drawbacks as the IdP does not only become a single point of failure but may also not be trusted. That's why Microsoft Passport was not successful. In contrast, the federation identity will leave the identity resources in their various distributed locations but produce a federation that links them to solve identity duplication, provision, and management.

A Simple Centralized Model

A relatively simple centralized identity management model is to build a platform that centralizes identities. A separate entity acts as an exclusive user credentials provider for all SPs. This approach merges both authentication and attributes in only one site. This architecture, which could be called a common user identity management model, is illustrated in Fig. 71.7. All identities for each SP are gathered to a unique identity management site (IdP). SPs have to provide each identity to IdP.

In this environment, users can have access to all SPs using the same set of identifiers and credentials. A centralized certificate authority (CA) could be implemented with a Public Key Infrastructure (PKI) or Simple Public Key Infrastructure (SPKI) [18]. This architecture is very efficient in a close domain where users could be identified by a controlled email address. Although such architecture seems to be scalable, the concentration of privacy related information has a lot of difficulties in social acceptance in terms of privacy [4].

Metadirectories (MDs)

SPs can share certain identity-related data on a metalevel. This can be implemented by consolidating all SPs' specific identities to a metaidentifier linked to credentials.

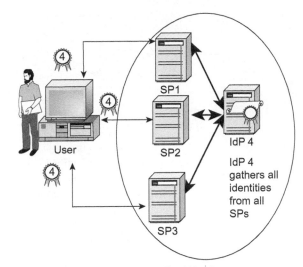

FIGURE 71.7 Simple centralized identity management.

There are collections of directories information from various directory sources. We aggregated them to provide a single view of data. Therefore, we can show these advantages:

- A single point of reference provides an abstraction boundary between application and the actual implementation.
- A single point of administration avoids the multiple directories, too.
- Redundant directory information can be eliminated, reducing the administration tasks.

This approach can be seen from the user's point of view to his/her password as synchronization across multiple SPs. Thus, the password is automatically changed with all the others.

This architecture can be used in large enterprises where all services are linked to a metadirectory (MD), as shown in Fig. 71.8. In this case, the ease-of-use is clear as the administration is done by a single authority.

Virtual Directories (VDs)

VDs are directories that are not located in the same physical structure as the web home directory, but look as if they were to web clients. The actual directories may be at a completely different location in the physical directory structure; for example, on another hard disk or on a remote computer. They are similar in concept to MDs in that they provide a single directory view from multiple independent directories. They differ in the means used to accomplish this goal. MD software agents replicate and synchronize data from various directories in what might be batch processes. In contrast, VD provide a single view of multiple directories using real-time queries based on mapping from

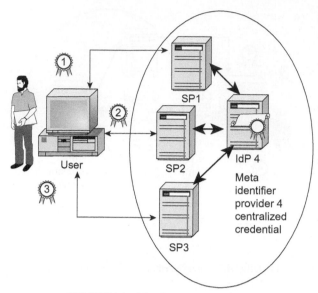

FIGURE 71.8 Metadirectory (MD) model.

fields in the virtual scheme to fields in the physical schemes of the real directories.

Single Sign-On (SSO)

We use multiple user's IDs and passwords just to use the email systems and file servers at work and we feel pain from managing multiple identities. The second problem is the scattering of identity data which causes problem for the integration of IT systems.

SSO (see Fig. 71.9) is a solution proposed to eliminate multiple password issues and dangerous password. Moreover, it simplifies the end-user experience and enhances security via identity-based access technology. Therefore, it offers these features:

- Flexible authentication
- Seamless
- Directory independence
- Session and password management

Federated Identity Management

We have seen different approaches to manage user's identity; they are not clearly interoperable and are deficient in unifying standard-based frameworks. On one hand, maintenance of privacy and identity control are fundamental when offering identity to users, on the other hand, the same users ask for more easy to use and rapid access. The balance of the two sides leads to federated network identity. That's why these environments are now emerging. A federated

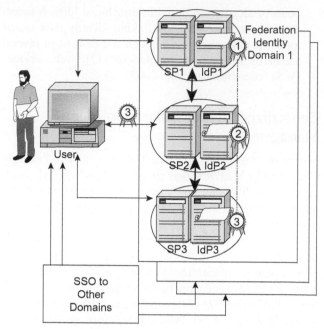

FIGURE 71.9 Single Sign-On (SSO) model.

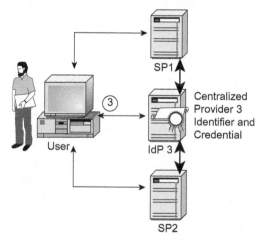

FIGURE 71.10 Federated identity management model.

identity management system (See Fig. 71.10) consists of software components and protocols that handle the identity of individuals throughout their identity life cycle.

This architecture gives the user the illusion that there is a single identifier authority. Even though the user has many identifiers, he doesn't need to know exactly all of them. Only one identifier is enough to have access to all services in the federated domain.

Each SP is responsible for the name space of his users and all SPs are federated by linking the identity domains. Thus, the federated identity model is based on a set of SPs called a circle of trust by the Liberty Alliance. This set of

SPs follows an agreement on mutual security and authentication in order to allow SSO. Indeed, the federated identity management combines SSO and authorization tools using a number of mutual SPs' technologies and standards. This practice makes the recognition and entitlement of user identities by other SPs easy. Fig. 71.10 shows the set of federated domains and the possibility for other SPs to have access to the same user with different identifiers.

The essential difference between federated identity systems and centralized identity management is that there is no single entity that operates the identity management system. Federated systems support multiple IdPs and a distributed and partitioned store for identity information. Therefore, a federated identity network allows a simplified sign-on to users by giving rapid access to resources, but it doesn't require the user's personal information to be stored centrally. With this identity network approach, users authenticate themselves once and can control how their personal information and preferences are used by the SPs.

Federated identity standards, like those produced by the Liberty Alliance [19], provide SSO over all offered services and enable users to manage the sharing of their personal information through identity and SPs as well as the use of personalized services in order to give access to convergent services. The interoperability between disparate security systems is assumed by an encapsulation layer through a trust domain which links a set of trusted SPs.

However, there are some disadvantages with federated identity management. The first one is the lack of privacy of the user as his/her personal attributes and information can be mapped using correlation between identifiers. Anonymity could be violated. The second one is the scalability of users as they have access to the network from different domains by authentication to their relative IdPs. Therefore, the problem of passwords will continue across multiple federated domains.

A major challenge is to integrate all these components into a distributed network and to deal with these drawbacks. This challenge cannot be taken up without new paradigms and supported standards.

The evolution of identity management system works toward simplifying the user experience and reinforcing authentication. It is very known that a poor usability implies the weakness of authentication. A new paradigm should be introduced to solve those problems while still being compatible at least with federated identity management.

That is why a user-centric identity management has emerged [7,15]. This paradigm is embraced by multiple industry products and initiative such as Microsoft

CardSpace [20], SXIP [21], and Higgins Trust Framework [22]. This is Identity 2.0.

Identity 2.0

The user of Internet services is overwhelmed with identities. He/she is seldom able to transfer his/her identity from one site to another. The reputation that he/she gains in one network is useful to transfer to other networks. Nevertheless, he/she cannot profit from his/her constructed reputation and he/she should rebuild his/her identity and reputation another time, and so on. The actual systems don't allow users to decide about the sharing of their attributes related to their identity with other users. This causes a lack of privacy control. Some solutions propose an advanced social system that would model the social interaction like the real world.

The solutions must be easy to use and enable users to share the credentials among many services and must be transparent from the end-user perspective. The principle of modern identity is to separate the acquisition process from the presentation process. It is the same for the identification process and authorization process. Moreover, it provides scalability and privacy. Doing so, we can have more control on my identity.

The scale, security, and usability advantages of user-centric identity are what make it the underpinning for Identity 2.0. The main objective of Identity 2.0 protocol is to provide users with full control over their virtual identities. An important aspect of Identity 2.0 is protection against web attacks like phishing as well as the inadvertent disclosure of confidential information while enabling convenient management.

Identity 2.0 would allow users to use one identity respecting transparency and flexibility. It is focused around the user and not around directory or IdP. It requires identified transactions between users and the relaying party using credentials, thus providing more traceable transactions. To maximize the privacy of users, some credentials could be given to the users in advance. Doing so, the IdP could not easily know when the user is utilizing the credentials.

Identity 2.0 (See Fig. 71.11) endorses completely the paradigms of user-centric identity management enabling the full control of user on his/her identity. SP will therefore be required to change their approaches by including request and authentication of users' identity. Identity 2.0 systems are interested in using the concept of a user's identity as credentials about the user, from their attributes like their name, address, to less traditional things like their desires, customer service history, and other attributes that are usually not so much associated with a user identity.

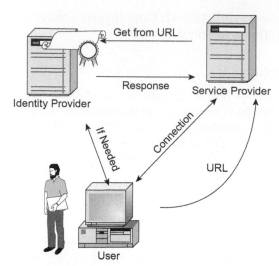

FIGURE 71.11 URL-based Identity 2.0.

Identity 2.0 Initiatives

When a website collects data from users he cannot confirm whether or not the collected data is pertinent and reliable as the users often enter nonsense information into online forms. This is due to the lack of website to control and verify the users' data. Furthermore, due to the law limitation on the requested data, the website cannot provide true customized services even though users require them. On the other side, users have no direct control on what the website will do with their data. In addition, users enter the same data many times when accessing the different websites for the first time. Doing so, they have a huge difficulty to manage their large number of identities.

To mitigate these problems, different models of identity management have been considered. One such model, Identity 2.0, proposes an Internet-scalable and user-centric identity architecture that mimics real world interactions.

Many research labs have collaborated to develop the Identity 2.0 Internet-based identity management services. It is based on the concept of user-centric identity management, supporting enhanced identity verification and privacy, and user consent and control over any access to personal information for Internet-based transactions. There are various Identity 2.0 initiatives:

1. LID
2. XRI
3. Security Assertion Markup Language (SAML)
4. Shibboleth
5. Identity Web Services Framework (ID-WSF)
6. OpenID
7. Microsoft's CardSpace (formerly InfoCard)
8. SXIP
9. Higgins

FIGURE 71.12 Extensible resource identifier (XRI) layers.

Light-Weight Identity (LID)

Like LDAP, LID is under the principle of simplicity because many existing identity schemes are too complicated to be largely adoptable. It simplifies more complex protocol; but instead of being less capable due to fewer features, it has run success that their more complex predecessors lacked. This was because their simplification reduced the required complexity to the point where many people could easily support them, and that was one of the goals of LID.

LID is a set of protocols capable of representing and using digital identities on the Internet in a simple manner, without relying on any central authority. LID is the original URL-based identity protocol, and part of the OpenID movement.

LID supports digital identities for humans, human organizations and non-humans (software agents, things, Websites, etc.) It implements Yadis, a meta-data discovery service and is pluggable on all levels.

Extensible Resource Identifier (XRI) and XRI Data Exchange (XDI)

We have XRI (see Fig. 71.12) and XRI Data Exchange (XDI), which is a fractional solution without WS integrated. They are open standards as they are royalty-free open standards. XRI is about addressing. XDI is about a data sharing protocol and uses XRI. Both XRI and XDI are being developed under the support of OASIS. I-name and I-number registry services for privacy-protected digital addressing use XRI. It can be used as an identifier for persons, machines, and agents.

XRIs offer a human-friendly form of persistent identifier. That's why it is a convenient identifier for an SSO system. They support both persistent and reassignable identifiers in the same syntax and establish global context symbols. Moreover, they enable identification of the same logical resource across multiple contexts and multiple versions of the same logical resource.

XDI is a Secure Distributed Data Sharing Protocol. It is also an architecture and specification for privacy-controlled data exchange where all data is identified using XRIs. The XDI platform includes explicit specification for caching with both push and pull synchronization. XDI universal

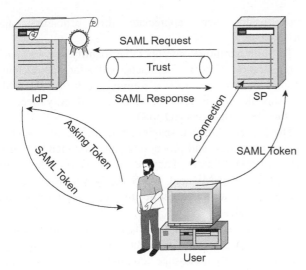

FIGURE 71.13 Security Assertion Markup Language (SAML) token exchange.

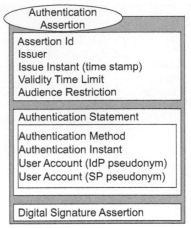

FIGURE 71.14 Security Assertion Markup Language (SAML) assertion.

schema can represent any complex data and have the ability of cross context addressing and linking.

SAML

SAML is an OASIS specification [23] that provides a set of rules for the structure of identity assertions, protocols to move assertions, bindings of protocols for typical message transport mechanisms, and profiles. Indeed, SAML (see Fig. 71.13) is a set of XML and Simple Object Access Protocol (SOAP)-based services and formats for the exchange of authentication and authorization information between security systems.

The initial versions of SAML v1.0 and v1.1 define protocols for SSO, delegated administration, and policy management. The most recent version is SAML 2.0. It is now a common language to the majority platform to change secure unified assertion. SAML is very useful and simple as it is based on XML. An assertion is a datum produced by a SAML authority referring to authentication, attribute information, or authorizations applying to the user with respect to a specified resource.

This protocol (see Fig. 71.14) enables interoperability between security systems (Browser SSO, WS Security, etc.). Other aspects of federated identity management as permission-based attribute sharing are also supported.

SAML is sometimes criticized for its complexity of the specifications and the relative constraint of its security rules. Recently, the SAML community has shown significant interest in extending SAML to reach less stringent requirements for low-sensitivity use cases. The advantages of SAML are robustness of its security and privacy model, and the guarantee of its interoperability between multiple vendor implementations through the Liberty Alliance's Conformance Program.

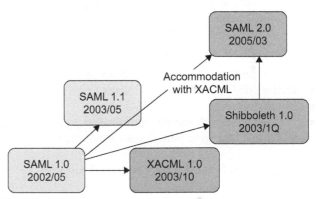

FIGURE 71.15 Convergence between Security Assertion Markup Language (SAML) and Shibboleth.

Shibboleth

Shibboleth [17] is a project which goal is to allow universities to share the web resources subject to control access. Thereafter, it allows interoperation between institutions using it. It develops architectures, policy structure, practical technologies, and an open source implementation. It is building components for both the IdPs and the reliant parties. The key concept includes "federated" management identity whose meaning is almost the same as the Liberty term's [24]. Access control is fundamentally based on user attributes, validated by SAML Assertions. In Fig. 71.15, we can see the evolution of SAML, Shibboleth, and XML Access Control Markup Language (XACML) [25].

Identity Web Services Framework (ID-WSF)

In 2001, a business alliance called Liberty Alliance was formed to serve as an open standards organization for federated identity management [19,26]. Its goals are to

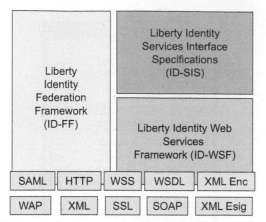

FIGURE 71.16 High-level overview of the Liberty Alliance architecture.

guarantee interoperability, support privacy, and promote adoption of its specifications, guidelines, and best practices. The key objectives of the Liberty Alliance (see Fig. 71.16) are to:

- Enable users to protect their privacy and identity
- Enable SPs' to manage their clients
- Provide an open federated SSO
- Provide a network identity infrastructure that supports all current emerging network access devices

Roadmap to Interoperable Federated Identity Services

The Liberty Alliance's work in the first phase is to enable federated network identity management. It offers, among others, SSO and linking accounts in the set of SPs in the boundary of the circle of trust. This work of this phase is referred to as Identity Federation Framework (ID-FF).

In the second phase, the specifications offer enhancing identity federation and interoperable identity-based web services. This body is referred to as Identity Web Services Framework (ID-WSF). This framework involves support of the new open standard such as WS-Security developed in OASIS. ID-WSF is a platform for the discovery and invocation of identity services—WS associated with a given identity. In the typical ID-WSF use case, after a user authenticates to an IdP this fact is asserted to an SP through SAML-based SSO. Embedded within the assertion is information that the SP can optionally use to discover and invoke potentially numerous and distributed identity services for that user. For some scenarios which present an unacceptable privacy risk, it suggests the possibility of a user's identity being exchanged without their consent or even knowledge. ID-WSF has a number of policy mechanisms to guard against this risk, but ultimately, it is worth noting that many identity transactions (automated bill payments) already occur without the user's active real-time

consent—and users appreciate this efficiency and convenience.

To build additional interoperable identity services such as registration services, contacts, calendar, geolocation services, and alert services, it's envisaged to use ID-WSF. This specification is referred to as the Identity Services Interface Specifications (ID-SIS).

The Liberty Alliance specifications define the protocol messages, profiles, and processing rules for identity federation and management. They rely heavily on other standards such as SAML and WS-Security which is another OASIS specification that defines mechanisms implemented in SOAP headers.

These mechanisms are designed to enhance SOAP messaging by providing a quality of protection through message integrity, message confidentiality, and single message authentication. Additionally, Liberty has contributed portions of its specification back into the technical committee working on SAML. Other identity management enabling standards include:

- Service Provisioning Markup Language (SPML)
- XACML
- XML Key Management Specification (XKMS)
- XML Signature
- XML Encryption

The WS protocol specifications (WS-*) are a set of specifications that is currently under development by Microsoft and IBM. It is a part of a larger effort to define a security framework for WS, the result of proposals are often referred to as WS-*. It includes specifications as WS-Policy, WS-Security Conversation, WS-Trust, and WS-Federation. This last one has functionality for enabling pseudonyms and attribute-based interactions. Therefore, WS-Trust's has the ability to ensure security tokens as a means of brokering identity and trust across domain boundaries [4].

The Liberty Alliance is developing and delivering specification that enables federate network identity management. Fig. 71.16 shows an overview of the Liberty Alliance architecture as describe in the introduction to the Liberty Alliance identity architecture.

OpenID 2.0

Brad Fitzpatrick is at the origin of the development of the OpenID 1.0. The intent of the OpenID framework is to specify layers that are independent and small enough to be acceptable and adopted by the market [11]. OpenID is basically providing simple attribute sharing for low-value transactions. It does not depend on any preconfigured trust model. The version 1.0 has a deal with http-based URL authentication protocol. OpenID authentication 2.0

is becoming an open platform that supports both URL and XRI user identifiers. In addition, it would like to be modular, lightweight, and user-oriented. Indeed, OpenID auth. 2.0 allows user to choose/control/manage his/her identity address. Moreover, the user chooses his/her IdP and has a large interoperability of his/her identity, and he/she can dynamically use new services with attribute verification and a good reputation without any loss of features. No software is required on the user's side as the user interacts directly with the IdP's site. This approach jeopardizes the user identity because it could be hacked or stolen. Moreover, the user has no ability to examine tokens before they are sent.

At the beginning of identity management each technology came with its own futures without any interest for others. Later, the OpenID 1.0 community has realized the importance of integrating other technologies as OASIS XRDS which is useful for his simplicity and extensibility.

OpenID Stack

The first layer is for supporting users' identification. Using the URL or XRI form, we can identify an user. URL uses IP or DNS resolution and is unique and ubiquitously supported. It can be as a personal digital address as used by bloggers even though it is not yet largely used.

XRI is being developed under the support of OASIS and is about addressing. I-names are a generic term for XRI authority names that provide abstract identifiers for the entity to which they are assigned. They can be used as the entry point to access data under the control of that authority. Like a domain name, the physical location of the information is transparent to the requester.

OpenID 2.0 provides a private digital address to allow a user to be only identified in specific conditions. This is guaranty the user privacy in a public domain.

Discovery

Yadis is used for identity service discovery for URLs and XRI resolution protocol for XRIs. The both use OASIS format called Extensible Resource Description Sequence (XRDS). The protocol is simple and describes any type of service.

Authentication

This service lets a user prove his/her URL or I-name using credentials (cryptographic proof). This protocol is explained in Fig. 71.17. The OpenID doesn't need a centralized authority for enrollment and it is therefore a federated identity management. With the OpenID 2.0 the IdP offers the user the option of selecting a digital address

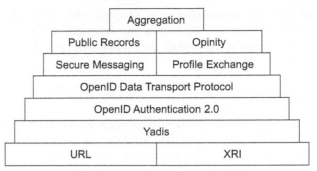

FIGURE 71.17 OpenID protocol stack.

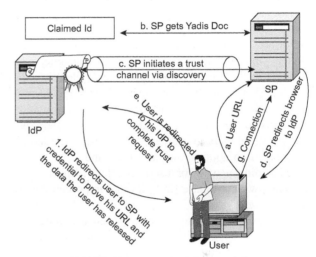

FIGURE 71.18 OpenID 1.1 protocol flow.

to send to the SP. To ensure anonymity, IdP can randomly generate a digital address used specially for this SP.

Data Transport

This layer ensures the data exchange between the IdP and SP. It supports push-and-pull methods and it is independent from authentication procedures. Therefore, the synchronization of data and secure messaging and other service will be enabled. The data formats are those defined by SAML, SDI (XRI Data interchange) or any other data formats. This approach will enable evolution of the OpenID platform.

The four layers construct the foundation of the OpenID ensuring user centricity (see Fig. 71.18). There are three points to guarantee this paradigm:

1. User choose his/her digital identity
2. User choose IdP
3. User choose SP

OpenID is decentralized and well founded and at the same time simple, easy to use, and to deploy. It provides open development process and SSO for the web and ease of integration into scripted web platforms (Drupal, WordPress, etc.). You can learn about OpenID at openidenabled.com also the community of OpenId can be joined at opened.net.

InfoCard

Rather than invent another technology for creating and representing digital identities, Microsoft has adopted the federated user-centric identity metasystem. This is a serious solution that provides a consistent way to work with multiple digital identities. Using standard protocols that anyone can implement on any platform, the identity metasystem allows the acquisition and use of any kind of security tokens to convey identity.

"InfoCard" is the Microsoft's codename for this new technology that tackles the problem of managing and disclosing identity information. InfoCard implements the core of the Identity Metasystem, using open standard protocols to negotiate, request, and broker identity information between trusted IdPs and SPs. "InfoCard" is a technology that helps developers to integrate a consistent identity infrastructure into applications, websites, and WS.

By providing a way for users to select identities and more, Windows CardSpace [20] plays an important part in the identity metasystem.

It provides the consistent user experience required by the identity meta-system. It is specifically hardened against tampering and spoofing to protect the end user's digital identities and maintain end-user control. Windows Card-Space enables users to provide their digital identities in a familiar, secure, and easy way.

In the terminology of Microsoft, the relying party is in our model SP. To prove an identity over a network, the user emitted credentials which are some proofs about his/her identity. For example, in the simplest digital identity the user name is the identity while the password is said to be the authentication credential. In the terminology of Microsoft and others, there are called security token and contain one or more claims. Each claim contains information about the users, like the user name or home address, etc. In addition, security token encloses prove that the claims are correctly emitted by the real user and are belonging to him. This could be done cryptographically using different forms such as X.509 certificates and Kerberos tickets, but unfortunately, they are not practical enough to convey a different kind of claim. The standard SAML as seen before is the indicated one for this purpose as it can be used to define security tokens. Indeed, SAML token could enclose any desired information and thus become as largely useful in the network to show and control digital identity. CardSpace runs on Windows Vista,

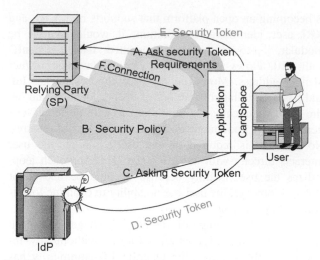

FIGURE 71.19 Interactions among the users, identity providers (IdPs), and relying party.

XP, Server 2003, and Server 2008, based on .NET3, and also uses WS protocols:

- WS-Trust
- WS-Policy
- WS-SecurityPolicy
- WS-MetaDataExchange

CardSpace runs in a self-virtual desktop on the PC. It locks out other processes and reduces the possibility of intercepting information by spyware.

Fig. 71.19 shows that the architecture is fitting exactly to the principle of Identity 2.0. The user access one of any of his/her relying parties (SPs) using an application that supports CardSpace.

When the choice is made, the application asks for the required security token of this specific SP that will answer the SP policy. It contains information about the claims and the accepted token formats. Once this is done, the application passes these requirements to CardSpace which asks the security token from an appropriate IdP.

Once this security token has been received, CardSpace transmits via application to the relying party. The relying party can then use this token to authenticate the user.

Please note that each identity is emitted by an IdP and is stored at the user side. It contains the emitter, the kind of security token he/she can issue and the details about the claims' enclose. All difficulties are hidden to the user as he/she has only to choose one of InfoCard when the process of authentication is launched. Indeed, once the required information is returned and passed to CardSpace, the system displays the card selection matching the requirements on screen. In this regard, the user has a consistent experience as all applications based on CardSpace will have the same interface, and the user does not have to worry about the protocol used to express the identity's security token. The PIN number is entered by the user and the choice of his/her card is done in a private Windows desktop to prevent locally running processes.

Simple eXtensible Identity Protocol (SXIP) 2.0

In 2004, The SXIP 1.0 grew from efforts to build a balanced online identity solution that met the requirements of the entire online community. Indeed, SXIP 2.0 is the new generation of the SXIP 1.0 protocol that was a platform that gives users control over their online identities and enables online communities to have a richer relationship with their membership. SXIP 2.0 defines entities' terminology as:

- Homesite: URL-based identity given by IdP.
- Membersite: SP that uses SXIP 2.0.
- User: equivalent to the user in our model.

SXIP [21] was designed to address the principles defined by the Identity 2.0 model (see Fig. 71.20), which proposes an Internet-scalable and user-centric identity architecture that mimics real-world interactions.

If an SP has integrated an SXIP to a website, which is easily done by using SDKs, it becomes a Membersite. When a subscriber of SXIP would like to access this Membersite:

1. Types his/her URL address and clicks on [SXIP in]
2. Types his/her URL identity issued by IdP (called Homesite)

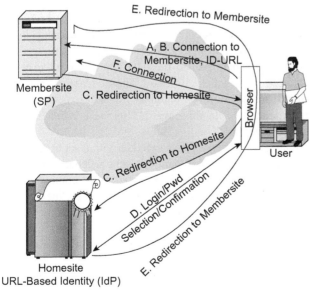

FIGURE 71.20 Simple eXtensible Identity Protocol (SXIP) entities interactions.

3. Browser is redirected to the Homesite
4. Enters his/her username and password, and being informed that the Membersite has requested data, selects the related data and verifies it, then selects to automatically release data for another visit to this Membersite and confirms
5. Browser is redirected to the Membersite
6. Gains access to the content of the site

SXIP 2.0 is a platform based on a fully decentralized architecture providing an open and simple set of processes for exchanging identity information. SXIP 2.0 has significantly reduced the problems resulting from moving identity data form one site to another. It is URL-based protocol that allows a seamless user experience and fits exactly to user-centric paradigm. In that sense, the user has full control on his/her identity and has an active role in the exchange of his/her identity data. Therefore, he/she can profit from portable authentication to connect many websites. Doing so, the user has more choice and convenience when exchanging his/her identity data, which enables, indirectly, websites to offer enhanced services to their subscribers.

SXIP 2.0 provides the following features:

- Decentralized architecture: SXIP 2.0 is completely decentralized and is a federated identity management. The online identity is URL-based and the user identity is separated from the authority that issues the identifiers for this identity. In this regard, we can easily move the location of the identity data without losing the associated identifier.
- Dynamic discovery: a simple and dynamic discovery mechanism ensures that users are always informed online about their home sites that are exporting identity data.
- Simple implementation: SXIP 2.0 is open source using different high level development languages such as Perl, Python, PHP, and Java. Therefore, the integration of SXIP 2.0 into a website is effortless. It does not require PKI as it uses a URL-based protocol that do not need it.
- Support for existing technologies: SXIP 2.0 uses simple web browsers, the primary client and means of data exchange, providing users with choice in the release of their identity data.
- Interoperability: SXIP 2.0 can coexist with other URL-based protocols.
- Richer data at an Internet scale: SXIP 2.0 messages consist of lists of simple name value pairs. It can exchange simple text, use SAML and third-party claims in one exchange, and present them in many separate exchanges. In addition, the IdP is not bothersome every time identity is requested.

Finally, by using SXIP 2.0, websites can also be authoritative about users for data, such as third-party claims. Those are keys to build online reputation, further enriching the online exchange of identity data.

Higgins

Higgins [27] is a project supported principally by IBM and it is a part of IBM's Eclipse open source foundation. It will also offer libraries for Java, C, and C++, and plug-ins for popular browsers. It is really an open source trust framework which goals are to support existing and new applications that give users more convenience, privacy, and control over their identity information. The objective is to develop an extensible, platform-independent, identity protocol-independent, software framework that provides a foundation for user-centric identity management. Indeed, it enables applications to integrate identity, profiles, and relationship across heterogenous systems.

The main goals of Higgins as an identity management system are interoperability, security, and privacy within a decoupled architecture. This system is user-centric based on a federated identity management. The user has the ability to use a pseudonym or simply reply anonymously in case you would not give your name.

We use the term context to cover a range of underlying implementations. A context can be thought of as a distributed container-like object that contains digital identities of multiple people or processes. The platform intends to address four challenges:

- The need to manage multiple contexts
- The need for interoperability
- The need to respond to regulatory, public, or customer pressure to implement solutions based on trusted infrastructure that offers security and privacy
- The lack of common interfaces to identity/networking systems

Higgins matches exactly the user-centric paradigms because it offers consistent user experience based on card icons for the management and release of identity data. Thereby, there is less vulnerability to phishing and other attacks. Moreover, user privacy is enabled by sharing only what is needed. Thus, the user has a full control on his/her personal data. Identity Attribute Service enables aggregation and federation of identity systems and even silos. For enterprises, it integrates all data related to identity, profile, reputation, and relationship information across and among complex systems.

Higgins is a trust framework that enables users and enterprises to adopt, share across multiple systems and integrate to new or existing application, digital identity, profiles, and cross-relationship information. In fact, it facilitates as well the integration of different identity management systems as the management of identity, profile, reputation, and relationship data across repositories. Using context providers, directories, and communications technologies (Microsoft/IBM WS-*, LDAP, email, etc.) can be plugged into the Higgins framework. Higgins has become an Eclipse plug-in, and is a project of the Eclipse Foundation. Any application developed with Higgins will enable users to share identity with other users under a strict control.

Higgins is beneficial for developers, users, and enterprise. Higgins relieves the developers from knowing all the details of multiple identity systems, thanks to one API that supports many protocols and technologies: CardSpace, OpenID, XRI, LDAP, etc. An application written to the Higgins API can integrate the identity, profile, and relationship information across these heterogenous systems. The goal of the framework is to be useful in the development of applications accessed through browsers, rich clients, and WS. Thus, the Higgins Project is supported by IBM and Novell and thwart Microsoft's Info-Card project.

The Higgins framework intends to define in terms of service descriptions, messages, and port types consistent with an Service-Oriented Architecture (SOA) model and to develop a Java binding and implementation as an initial reference. Applications can use Higgins to create a unified, virtual view of identity, profile, and relationship information. A key focus of Higgins is providing a foundation for new "user-centric identity" and personal information management applications.

Finally, Higgins provides a virtual integration, user-centric federated management model, and trust brokering that are applied to identity, profile, and relationship information. Furthermore, Higgins provides common interfaces to identity, and thanks to the data context, it encloses an enhanced automation process. Those features are also offered across multiple contexts, disparate systems, and implementations. In this regard, Higgins is a full interoperable framework.

The Higgins service acts together with a set of so-called context providers which can represent a department, association, informal network, and so on. A context is the environment of Higgins and digital identities, the policies and protocols that govern their interactions. Context providers adjust existing legacy systems to the framework, or implement new ones. Context providers may also contain the identities of a machine or human. A context encloses a group of digital identities and their related claims and links. A context maintains a set of claims about properties and values (name, address, etc.). It is like a security token for

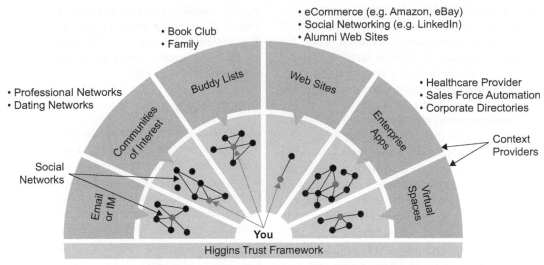

FIGURE 71.21 Higgins Trust Framework and context [22].

Cardspace. The set of profile properties, the set of roles, and the access rights for each role are defined by and controlled by the Context Provider.

Context providers act as adapters to existing systems. Adapter providers can connect, for example, to LDAP servers, identity management systems like CardSpace, mailing list, and social networking systems. A Higgins context provider (see Fig. 71.21) has the ability to implement the context interface and thus empower the applications layered on top of Higgins.

At the moment, SPs have to choose between so many authentications and identity management systems and users are left to face the inconvenience of a variety of digital identities. The main initiatives have different priorities and some unique advantages, while overlapping in many areas. The most pressing requirements for users are interoperability, usability, and centricity. Thanks to Higgins, the majority of identity requirements are guaranteed. Therefore, using it, the user is free to visit all websites without being worried about the identity management system used by the provider.

5. SOCIAL LOGIN AND USER MANAGEMENT

At the time of the writing of the second version of this chapter (end of 2012), none of the identity management technologies surveyed earlier in the chapter have reached major user adoption. A few of them have been discontinued. For example, SXIP went bankrupt [28]. Others have moved very slowly. Higgins has only released a partial implementation of its vision and seems on hold. Liberty Alliance moved to a new initiative called the

Kantara initiative [19]. However, a new type of solutions which was not really expected at time of writing the first version of the chapter, has emerged and gained a quite large user adoption. This type of solution is provided by major online social networks that have reached mass market very fast and where users have spent time configuring their profile. Then, those major online networks have built on top of previously surveyed standard identity management technological building blocks to facilitate logging to other websites and online services with the identities managed on their services. The good news is that most of them have based their work on OpenID. Therefore, although OpenID is less known by the greater public, it still exists underneath. They are also extensively relying on OAuth [29] that was built when OpenID was investigated for Twitter [30]. It is also possible to authenticate through OAuth but OAuth goes beyond OpenID regarding authorizations (in addition to authentication). The major online social network providers that have created tools to allow their users to easily log into other websites and services include Facebook [31], Twitter, LinkedIn [32], and Google [33].

The websites and services that use the "social login" tools of one of these providers provide an easier access to their service to users who already have an account on this external provider. With a few confirming clicks, the user has joined the new service without having to spend time filling out her personal information again. Although this solution has gained large adoption because it fulfilled the user-friendliness requirement, there are still a few flaws remaining.

First, there is concern about the privacy protection requirement. For example, based on Facebook privacy bugs and issues due to privacy protection laws in different countries, one cannot claim that a Facebook user is really under control of her personal data disclosed to Facebook. It does not correspond to a user-centric approach. Thus, the website or service that reuses Facebook identity management service does not really fulfill the privacy requirement discussed in this chapter. The same privacy issues apply to the other "social login" providers.

The second issue concerns allowing users who may not have an account in one of the chosen "social login" providers to still login. Although the "social login" providers have created tools to connect their identity management system to another website or service, adding multiple login forms to a website or service takes times and may confuse the user as many forms may be possible for registering. In addition, most "social login" providers often change their Application Programming Interface (API) without backward compatibility. Thus, the website or service may lose its registration functionality for some time before it can apply the required changes.

It is why a new type of providers has emerged on top of these "social login" providers. Those providers do the hard work to maintain a tool that allows a user to create an account with all the "social login" providers as well as store and manage users information on behalf of the service or website that uses this tool. The owners of websites and services install this tool on their website or service without having to worry when one of the "social login" providers change their API. The price of allowing a user to create an account with any of the main online social network providers without having to maintain each "social login" module has to be weighed against the subscription price to one of these user management providers such as Janrain [34], OneAll [35], LoginRadius [36], or Gigya [37].

6. IDENTITY 2.0 FOR MOBILE USERS

In this section, we discuss identity management in the realm of mobile computing devices. These devices are used more and more, and have different constraints than fixed desktop computers.

Introduction

The number of devices such as mobile phones, smart cards, and RFIDs [38] is increasing daily and becoming huge. Mobile phones have attracted particular interest because of their large penetration and pervasiveness that exceeds that of personal computers. Furthermore, the emergence of both IP-TV and wireless technology has facilitated the proliferation of intelligent devices, mobile phones, RFIDs, and other forms of information technology

that are developing at a rapid speed. These devices include a fixed identifier that could be linked to the user's identity. This identifier provides a mobile identity which takes into account information about the location and the mobile user's personal data [39].

Mobile Web 2.0

Mobile Web 2.0 as a content-based service is an up-to-date offering of services within the mobile network. As the number of people having access to mobile devices exceeds those using a desktop computer, mobile web will be a key factor for the next generation network. At the moment, mobile web suffers from lack of interoperability and usability due to the small screen size and lower computational capability. Fortunately, these limitations are only temporary and within 5 years they will be easily overcome. There will be convergence in the next generation public networks toward the mobile network which will bring mobility to the forefront. Thus, mobile identity management (MIDM) will play a central role in addressing issues such as usability, privacy, and security, which are key challenges for researchers in the mobile network. Since the initial launch of mobile WS, customers have increasingly turned to their wireless phones to connect with family and friends and also to obtain the latest news and information or even to produce content with their mobile and then publish them. Mobile Web 2.0 [23] is the enforcement of evolution and will enhance the experience of users by providing connections in an easier and more efficient way. For this reason, it will be welcome by the key actors as a well-established core service identity management for the next generation mobile network. This MIDM will be used not only to identify, acquire, access, and pay for services but also to offer context-aware services as well as location-based services.

Mobility

The mobile identity may not be stored at the same location but could be distributed among many locations, authorities, and devices. Indeed, identity is mobile in many respects [1]:

1. There is a device mobility where a person is using the same identity while using different devices
2. There is a location mobility where a person is using the same devices while changing the location
3. There is context mobility where a person is receiving services based on different societal roles: as a parent, as a professional, and so on

The three kind of mobility are not isolated but they interacted more often and became concurrently modified creating much more complex situations that what implied from single mode. MIDM addresses three main challenges:

(1) usability via context awareness; (2) trust based on the perception of secure operation; and (3) the protection of privacy [1].

Evolution of Mobile Identity

MIDM is in its infancy. Global system for mobile communication (GSM) networks, for example, provide management of SIM identities as a kind of MIDM, but they do not meet all the requirements for a complete MIDM. Unlike static identity already implemented in Web 2.0 identity, dynamic aspects, such as the user's position or the temporal context, gain increasing importance for new kinds of mobile applications [40].

Mobile identity (MID) infrastructure solutions have evolved over time and can be classified into three solutions. The first proposed solution is just an extension of wired identity management to mobile Internet. This is the widespread solution, which is limited to the users of mobile devices running the same operating system (OS) as a wired solution. This limitation is expected to evolve over time mainly with the large deployment of WS. Some specifications, such as Liberty Alliance specifications, have been developed for identity management including mobility. However, several limitations are observed when the MID system is derived from fixed context. These limitations are principally due to the assumptions during their design and they do not match well with the extra requirements of mobility [1].

Many improvements such as interoperability, privacy, and security are to be operated. Also, older centralized PKI must be replaced by a modern trust management system or at least a decentralized PKI.

The second solution is capable of providing an alternative to the prevalent Internet derived MID infrastructure. This consists of either connected (cellular phones) or unconnected (smart cards) mobiles devices.

The third one consists of using implantable radio-frequency identification (RFID) devices. This approach is expected to increase rapidly even if the market penetration is smaller than cellular phones.

In addition, the sensitivity risk of data related to different applications and services are seldom at the same level and the number of identifiers used by a person is constantly increasing. Thus, there is a real need for different kinds of credentials associated with different kinds of applications. Indeed, a tool at the user side capable of managing the credentials and identities is inevitable. With the increasing capacity of CPU power and the spreading number of mobile phones with a SIM card, mobile phones can be considered a PAD. They can hold securely the users' credentials, password, and even identities. Therefore, we

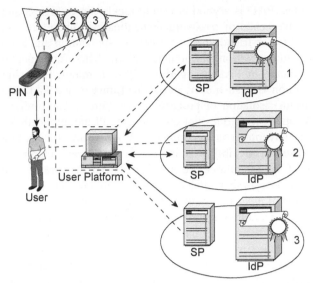

FIGURE 71.22 Integration of a personal authentication device (PAD) in the silo model.

introduced a new efficient identity management device at the user side that is able to facilitate memorization on the one hand, and strengthen security by limiting the number of passwords and their weakness on the other hand. All wired identity management can be deployed using PAD. In addition, many different authentication architectures become possible and easy to implement such as dual channel authentication.

Personal Authentication Device (PAD) as Solution to Strong Authentication

PAD is a tamper-resistant hardware device which could include smart card and sensors or not. As it is used for authentication it is called a PAD [41]. This term has been used in the context of security by Wong et al. [42]. The approach is the same and the only change so far is the performance of the mobile device. This is the opportunity to emphasize the user centricity as the PAD could strengthen the user experience and to facilitate the automation and system support of the identity management at the user side. Fig. 71.22 illustrated the combination of PAD and silo model. The user stores his/her identity in the PAD. Whenever he/she would like to connect to an SP,

1. He/she authenticates her/himself with a PIN code to use the PAD.
2. The user choose the password to be used for his/her connection to the specific SP.
3. The user launches and logs to the specific SP by entering his/her username and the password.

The PAD is a good device to tackle the weakness and inconvenience of password authentication. Therefore, we have a user-friendly and user-centric application and even introducing stronger authentication. The fundamental advantage of PAD comparing with a common PC using common OSs such as Windows or Linux is that PAD has a robust isolation of processes. Therefore, compromising one application does not compromise all the applications. This advantage is becoming less important for mobile phones; as flexibility is introduced by manufacturers, a lot of vulnerabilities are also introduced. We have seen many viruses for mobile phones and for RFID. This vulnerability can compromise authentication and even biometrics authentication. That's why we should be very vigilant in implementing security in PAD devices. An ideal device is the USB stick running a standalone OS, and integrating a biometric reader and mobile network access. One can find some of them with a fingerprint reader for a reasonable price.

Two main categories can group many authentication architectures that could be implemented in a PAD. There are single and dual channel authentications. Therefore, the cost, the risk, and the inconvenience could be tackled at the same time.

Fig. 71.23 illustrates the principle of single channel authentication, which is the first application of the PAD. Fig. 71.24 illustrates the second principle of dual-channel authentication, which is more secure.

Different Kinds of Strong Authentication Through a Mobile Personal Authentication Devices (PADs)

The mobile network, mainly GSM, can help to overcome a lot of security vulnerabilities such as phishing or man-in-the-middle attacks. It attracts all business that would like to deploy double channel authentication but are worried about cost and usability. The near-ubiquity of the mobile network has made feasible the utilization of this approach and even being adopted by some banks.2

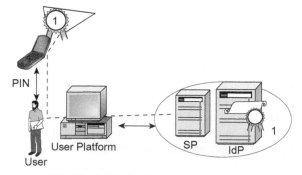

FIGURE 71.23 Single channel authentication.

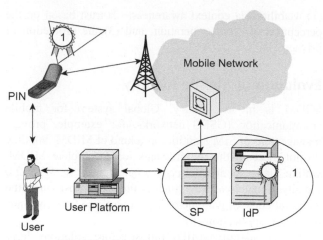

FIGURE 71.24 Dual channel authentication.

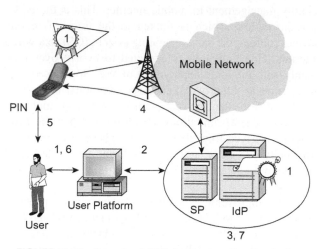

FIGURE 71.25 Scenario of SMS double channel authentication.

SMS-Based One-Time Password (OTP)

The main advantages in a mobile network are the facility and usability to send and receive SMSs. Moreover, they could be used to setup and download a Java program to the mobile device. In addition, mobile devices are using smart cards that can securely calculate and store claims.

The cost is minimized by adopting a mobile device using SMS to receive a one-time password (OTP) instead of a special hardware that can generate an OTP. The scenario implemented by some banks is illustrated in Fig. 71.25. First of all, the user switches his/her mobile phone and enters his PIN code, then:

1. The user logs into his online account by entering his/her username and password (U/P)
2. The website received the U/P
3. The server verifies the U/P
4. The server sends an SMS message with OTP
5. The user reads the message

6. The user enters the OPT into the online account
7. The server verifies the OPT and gives access

The problem with this approach is the fact that the cost is assumed by the SP. In addition, some drawbacks are very common, mainly in some developing countries, such as lack of coverage and SMS latency. Of course, the man-in-the-middle attack is not overcome by this approach.

Soft Token Application

In this case, the PAD is used as a token emitter. The application is previously downloaded. SMS could be sent to the user in order to set up the application that will play the role of soft token.

The scenario is exactly identical to the SMS but only the user generates his/her OTP using the soft token instead of waiting for an SMS message. The cost is less than the SMS-based OTP. This approach is a single channel authentication that is not dependent on mobile network coverage neither on his latency. Furthermore, the man-in-the-middle attack is not tackled.

Full Option Mobile Solution

We have seen in the two previous scenarios that the man-in-the-middle attack is not addressed. It exists as a counterattack to this security issue consisting of using the second channel to completely control all the transactions over the online connection. Of course, the security of this approach is based on the assumption that it is difficult for an attacker to steal the user's personal mobile phone or to attack the mobile network. We have developed an application to encrypt the SMS message which minimizes the risk of attacks. The scenario is illustrated in Fig. 71.26 and it is as follows:

1. The user logs in to the online account using a token
2. The server receives the token

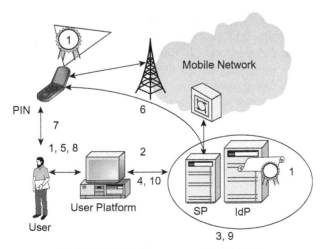

FIGURE 71.26 Secure transaction via SMS.

3. The server verifies the token
4. The access is given to the service
5. The user requests a transaction
6. An SMS message is sent with the requested transaction and a confirmation code
7. The user verifies the transaction
8. He enters the confirmation code
9. The server verifies and executes the transaction
10. The server sends a transaction confirmation

Future of Mobile User-Centric Identity Management in an Ambient Intelligence (AmI) World

Ambient intelligence (AmI) manifests itself through a collection of everyday devices incorporating computing and networking capabilities that enable them to interact with each other, make intelligent decisions, and interact with users through user-friendly multimodal interfaces. AmI is driven by users' needs and the design of its capabilities should be driven by users' requirements.

AmI technologies are expected to combine concepts of ubiquitous computing and intelligent systems putting humans in the center of technological developments. Indeed, the Internet extension to home and mobile networks, the multiplication of modes of connection will make the individual the central point. Therefore, the identity is a challenge in this environment and will guarantee the infatuation with AmI. Moreover, AmI will be part of the future environment where we shall be surrounded by mobile devices which will be more and more used for mobile interactions with things, places, and people.

The low-cost and the shrinking size of sensors as well as the ease of deployment will aid ambient intelligence research efforts for rapid prototyping. Evidently, a sensor combined with unique biometric identifiers is becoming more frequently utilized to access a system and supposedly provide proof of a person's identity and thus accountability for subsequent actions. To explore these new AmI technologies, it is easier to investigate a scenario related to ubiquitous computing in an ambient intelligence environment.

Ambient Intelligence (AmI) Scenario

A person having a mobile device, Global Positioning System (GPS) device (or equivalent), and an ad-hoc communication network connected to sensors, visits an intelligent environment supermarket and would like to acquire some merchandise. We illustrate below how this person can benefit from mobile identity.

When this person enters the supermarket, he/she is identified by means of his/her mobile device or implemented RFID tag and a special menu is displayed to him/her. His/her profile, related to his/her context identity, announces a discount if there is one.

The members of this person's social network could propose a connection if they are present and even guide the person to a location. Merchandise on display could communicate with his/her device to show prices and details. Location-based services could be offered to quickly find his/her specific articles.

The device could help this person find diabetic foods or any restrictions associated with specific articles. A secure web connection could be initiated to give more information about purchases and the user account.

An adaptive screen could be used by the supermarket to show the person information that is too extensive for the device screen. Payment could be carried out using payment identity stored in his/her device and even a biometric identity to prevent identity theft.

Identity information and profiling should be portable and seamless for interoperability. The identity must be managed to ensure user control. Power and performance management in this environment is a must. The concept of authentication between electronic devices is also highlighted.

In order to use identity management, the user needs an appropriate tool to facilitate the management for the disclosure of personal data. A usable and secure tool should be proposed to help even inexperienced users manage their general security needs when using the network.

We need MIDM, which is a concept that allows the user to keep his or her privacy, depending on the situation. By using identity management, the user's device acts in a similar way to the user. In different contexts, the user presents a different appearance. Devices controlled by identity management change their behavior similar to the way in which a user would.

Requirements for Mobile User-Centric Identity Management in an AmI World

As the network evolution is toward mobility with the proliferation of ubiquitous and pervasive computing systems, the importance of identity management to build trust relationships in the context of electronic and mobile (e/m) government and business is evident [43,44]. Therefore, all these systems require advanced, automated identity management systems in order to be cost-effective and easy to use.

Several mobile devices such as mobile phones, smart cards, and RFID are used for mobility. As mobile devices have fixed identifiers, they are essentially providing a mobile identity that can be linked to a user. Mobile identity takes into account location data of mobile users in addition to their personal data. A court decision in the United Kingdom has established as proof of location of the

accused the location trace of his mobile phone which implies a de facto recognition of the identity of a citizen as the identity of her mobile telephones [1].

That is why MIDM is necessary to empower mobile users to manage their mobile identities to enforce their security and privacy interests. MIDM is a special kind of identity management. For this purpose, mobile users must be able to control the disclosure of their mobile identity dependent on the respective SP and also their location via MIDM systems.

Ambient Intelligence emphasizes the principles of secure communication anywhere, anytime, with anything. The evolution of AmI will directly influence identity management with this requirement to ensure mutual interaction between users and things. Being anywhere will imply more and more mobility, interoperability, and profiling. Being anywhere at any time will imply online as well as offline connection as the network does not have 100% coverage and will imply power as well as performance management in order to optimize battery use. With anything will imply sensor use, biometrics, and RFID interaction; and securely implies more and more integration of privacy, authentication, anonymity, and prevention of identity theft.

From multilateral security [45,46], Jendricke [27] has derived privacy principles for MIDM and we have completed them below with a few other important principles. Management systems are as follows:

1. Context-detection
   a. Sensors
   b. Biometrics
   c. RFID
2. Anonymity
3. Security
   a. Confidentiality
   b. Integrity
   c. Nonrepudiation
   d. Availability
4. Privacy
   a. Protection of location information
5. Trustworthiness
   a. Segregation of power, separating knowledge, integrating independent parties
   b. Using open source
   c. Trusted seals of approval
6. Law Enforcement/Liability
   a. Digital evidence
   b. Digital signatures
   c. Data retention
7. Usability
   a. Comfortable and informative user interfaces
   b. Training and education
   c. Reduction of system complexity
   d. Raising awareness

8. Affordability
    a. Power of market: produce multimedia integrated modeling system (MIMS) that are competitive and are able to reach a remarkable penetration of market
    b. Using open source building blocks
    c. Subsidies for development, use, operation, etc.
9. Power management: the energy provided by the batteries of mobile devices is limited and that energy must be used with care on energy-friendly applications and services
10. Online and offline identity proof
11. Small screen size and lower computational capability
12. Interoperability
    a. Identity needs to be portable to be understood by any device.

7. SUMMARY

The Internet is being used more and more, but the fact that the Internet has not been developed with an adequate identity layer is a major security risk. Password fatigue and online fraud are a growing problem and are damaging user confidence. However, it is a difficult problem to solve both from a technical and a business point of view. Users are not prepared to pay themselves for identity management and expect the SP should provide it to them. It is the reason that a number of major initiatives trying to provide a more adequate identity layer for the Internet surveyed in this chapter and already present in the first version of this chapter have been discontinued due to a failing business model—for example, SXIP. If user involvement takes too long or requires retyping personal information, many users may not take the time to join the new service. "Social login" provided by online social networks has emerged as the main identity management solution adopted by the users to log in to new websites and services because users do not have to type their personal information again. It has been to the detriment to the privacy of the users, but it is clear that it does not worry users because they are not able to take into account the effect of this privacy leak in the long term. They prefer accessing the service they want to use, such as Facebook, even if it may impact their privacy in the long term. Thus, although "social login" does not fulfill all identity management requirements that have been presented in this chapter since its first version, "social login" has won over many other identity management initiatives, even if a few of them are still used underneath, e.g., OpenId. User management providers listed in Section 4 and aggregating several "social login" solutions for websites and services are promising. Another development concerns MIDM, and those new user management providers may also play an importation role in this respect.

Finally, let's move on to the real interactive part of this chapter: review questions/exercises, hands-on projects, case projects, and optional team case project. The answers and/or solutions by chapter can be found in the Online Instructor's Solutions Manual.

CHAPTER REVIEW QUESTIONS/ EXERCISES

True/False

1. True or False? A digital identity is a representation of an entity in a general context.
2. True or False? Identity management refers to "the process of representing, using, maintaining, deprovisioning, and authenticating entities as digital identities in computer networks."
3. True or False? Privacy is a central issue, due to the fact that the official authorities of almost all countries have legal strict policies related to identity.
4. True or False? The evolution of the identity management system is away from the simplification of user experience and reinforcing authentication.
5. True or False? The security is also compromised with the proliferation of the user's password and even by its strength.

Multiple Choice

1. The main identity management system deployed currently in the world of the Internet is known as the?
    A. Federated identity management model
    B. Identity life cycle
    C. Aggregate identity
    D. Executive management model
    E. Silo model
2. _____ in centralized identity infrastructures, can't solve the problem of cross-organizational authentication and authorization?
    A. Centrally managed repositories
    B. Information system auditors
    C. IT personnel
    D. Systems administrators
    E. All of the above
3. A relatively simple _____ model is to build a platform that centralizes identities?
    A. Common user identity management
    B. Simple centralized identity management
    C. Unique identity management
    D. MD
    E. Executive management
4. What provides an abstraction boundary between application and the actual implementation?
    A. Single point of administration
    B. Redundant directory information

C. Single point of reference

D. Business impact analysis

E. All of the above

5. What directories are not located in the same physical structure as the web home directory, but look as if they were to web clients?

A. Single Sign-On

B. Seamless

C. Session

D. Virtual

E. Flexible

EXERCISE

Problem

What is a digital identity?

Hands-On Projects

Project

Why would a bank issue digital identities?

Case Projects

Problem

Does the digital identity capture the physical signature of the person?

Optional Team Case Project

Problem

What if I am already using digital certificates or credentials?

REFERENCES

[1] G. Roussos, U. Patel, Mobile Identity Management: An Enacted View, Birkbeck College, University of London, City University, London, 2003.

[2] A. Westin, Privacy and Freedom, Athenaeum, New York, NY, 1967.

[3] J. Madelin, et al., BT Report on: Comprehensive Identity Management Balancing Cost, Risk and Convenience in Identity Management, 2007.

[4] T. Miyata, A survey on identity management protocols and standards, IEICE Trans. Inf. Syst. (2006).

[5] J.-M. Seigneur, Trust, Security and Privacy in Global Computing (Ph.D. thesis), Trinity College, Dublin, 2005.

[6] Introduction to the Liberty Alliance Identity Architecture. Rev. 1.0, March 2003.

[7] A.B. Spantzel, User Centricity: A Taxonomy and Open Issues, IBM Zurich Research Laboratory, 2006.

[8] Identity Management Systems (IMS): Identification and Comparison Study, Independent Center for Privacy Protection (ICPP) and Studio Notarile Genghini (SNG), 2003.

[9] K. Cameron, Laws of Identity, 5/12/2005.

[10] T.M. Cooley, A Treatise on the Law of Torts, Callaghan, Chicago, 1888.

[11] David Recordon VeriSign Inc, Drummond Reed, OpenID 2.0: A Platform for User-Centric Identity Management, 2006.

[12] Federal Financial Institutions Examination Council, Authentication in an Internetbanking Environment, October 2005. http://www.ffiec.gov/press/pr101205.htm.

[13] A. Erzberg, A. Gbara, TrustBar: Protecting (Even Naïve) Web Users from Spoofing and Phishing Attacks, 2004. http://wwwcs.biu.ac.il/~erzbea/papaers/ecommerce/spoofing.htm.

[14] Introduction to Usability, 2005. http://www.usabilityfirst.com/intro/index.tx1.

[15] A. Jøsang, S. Pope, User centric identity management, in: AusCERT Conference, 2005.

[16] A. Jøsang, Usability and Privacy in Identity Management Architectures, AISW 2007, Ballarat, Australia, 2007.

[17] Internet2, Shibboleth Project, 2016. http://shibboleth.Internet2.edu.

[18] C. Esslison, et al., RFC 2693—SPKI Certification Theory, IETF, September 1999. http://www.ietf.org/rfc/rfc2693.txt.

[19] Kantara Initiative, 2016. http://kantarainitiative.org/.

[20] Microsoft, a Technical Ref. for Infocard in Windows, 2005. http://msdn.microsoft.com/winfx/reference/infocard/.

[21] J. Merrells, SXIP Identity, DIX: Digital Identity Exchange Protocol. Internet Draft, March 2006.

[22] Higgings Trust Framework Project, 2006. http://www.eclipse.org/higgins/.

[23] A. Jaokar, T. Fish, Mobile Web 2.0, a Book, 2007.

[24] Liberty Developer Tutorial, 2003. http://www.projectliberty.org/resources/LAP_DIDW_Oct-15_2003_jp.pdf.

[25] XACML, 2016. http://www.oasis-open.org/committees/tc_home.php?wg_abbrev=xacml.

[26] Liberty Alliance, Liberty ID-FF Architecture Overview, Liberty Alliance Project, 2005.

[27] U. Jendricke, et al., Mobile Identity Management, UBICOMP, 2002.

[28] Sxip bankruptcy, 2016. http://techcrunch.com/2008/05/22/identity-20-startup-sxips-into-the-deadpool/.

[29] IETF OAuth, 2016. <https://www.ietf.org/mailman/listinfo/oauth>.

[30] Twitter, 2016. http://www.twitter.com.

[31] Facebook, 2016. http://www.facebook.com.

[32] LinkedIn, 2016. http://www.linkedin.com.

[33] Google, 2016. http://www.google.com.

[34] Janrain, 2016. http://www.janrain.com.

[35] OneAll, 2016. http://www.oneall.com.

[36] LoginRadius, 2016. http://www.loginradius.com.

[37] Gigya, 2016. http://www.gigya.com.

[38] S. Garfinkel, B. Rosenberg, RFID, Applications, Security and Privacy, Addison Wesley, Boston, 2006.

[39] S.A.Weis et al.,Security and privacy aspects of low-Cost radio frequency identification systems in Proceedings of the First International Conference on Security in Pervasive Computing March 2003.

[40] M. Hoffmann, User-Centric Identity Management in Open Mobile Environments, Fraunhofer-Institute for Secure Telecooperation (SIT).

[41] A. Jøsang, Trust Requirements in Identity Management, AISW, 2005.

[42] Wong, et al., Polonius: an identity authentication system, in: Proceedings of the 1985 IEEE Symposium on Security and Privacy, 1985.

[43] MyGrocer Consortium, Mygrocer Whitepaper, 2002.

[44] M. Wieser, The computer for the twenty-first century, Sci. Am. (1991).

[45] K. Rannenberg, Multilateral security? a concept and examples for balanced security, in: Proc. of the Ninth ACM New Security Paradigms Workshop, 2000.

[46] K. Reichenbach, et al., Individual management of personal reachability in mobile communications, in: Proc. of the IFIP TC11 (Sec'97), 1997.

Chapter 72

Intrusion Prevention and Detection Systems

Christopher Day
Terremark Worldwide, Miami, FL, United States

1. WHAT IS AN "INTRUSION" ANYWAY?

Information security is concerned with the confidentiality, integrity, and availability of information systems (ISs) and the information or data they contain and process. Thus, an "intrusion" is any action taken by an adversary that has a negative impact on the confidentiality, integrity, or availability of that information. Given such a broad definition of "intrusion," it is instructive to examine a number of commonly occurring classes of IS intrusions.

2. PHYSICAL THEFT

Having physical access to a computer system allows an adversary to bypass most security protections put in place to prevent unauthorized access. By stealing a computer system, the adversary has all of the physical access he or she could want, and unless the sensitive data on the system are strongly encrypted (see sidebar: "Definition of Encryption"), the data are likely to be compromised. This issue is most prevalent with laptop loss and theft. Given the processing and storage capacity of even low-cost laptops, a great deal of sensitive information can be put at risk if a laptop containing these data is stolen. In May 2006, it was revealed that over 26 million military veterans' personal information, including names, Social Security numbers, addresses, and some disability data were on a Veteran Affairs staffer's laptop that was stolen from his home [2a]. The stolen data were of the type often used to commit identity theft; owing to the large number of veterans who were affected, there was a great deal of concern about

this theft and the lack of security regarding such a sensitive collection of data. In another example, in May 2012 it was revealed that an unencrypted laptop containing medical records for 2159 patients was stolen from a Boston Children's Hospital staffer who was traveling overseas for a conference [2b].

Definition of Encryption

Encryption is the process of protecting the content or meaning of a message or other kinds of data [3]. Modern encryption algorithms are based on complex mathematical functions that scramble the original clear-text message or data in such a way that makes them difficult or impossible for an adversary to read or access without the proper key to reverse the scrambling. The encryption key is typically a large number of values that are fed into the encryption algorithm and scramble and unscramble the data being protected, and without which it is extremely difficult or impossible to decrypt encrypted data. The science of encryption is called cryptography and is a broad and technical subject.

---

3. ABUSE OF PRIVILEGES (THE INSIDER THREAT)

An insider is an individual who has some level of authorized access to the IS environment and systems because of his role in the organization. The level of access can range from that of a regular user to a system administrator with nearly unlimited privileges. When an

Computer and Information Security Handbook. http://dx.doi.org/10.1016/B978-0-12-803843-7.00072-7

insider abuses his privileges, the impact can be devastating. Even a relatively limited-privilege user is starting with an advantage over an outsider owing to his knowledge of the IS environment, critical business processes, and potential knowledge of security weaknesses or "soft spots." An insider may use his access to steal sensitive data such as customer databases, trade secrets, national security secrets, or personally identifiable information (PII) (see sidebar: "Definition of Personally Identifiable Information"). Because he is a trusted user, and given that many IDSs are designed to monitor for attacks from outsiders, an insider's privileged abuse can go unnoticed for a long time, compounding the damage. In 2010, US soldier Bradley Manning allegedly used his legitimate access to the Secret Internet Protocol Router Network to pass classified information to the whistle-blower website WikiLeaks in what has been described as the largest known theft of classified information in US history [4]. An appropriately privileged user may also use his access to make unauthorized modifications to systems that can undermine the security of the environment. These changes can range from creating "backdoor" accounts used to preserve access in the event of termination to installing so-called "logic bombs," which are programs designed to cause damage to systems or data at some predetermined time, often as a form of retribution for some real or perceived sleight.

Definition of Personally Identifiable Information

PII is a set of information such as a name, address, Social Security number, financial account number, credit card number, and driver's license number. This class of information is considered particularly sensitive owing to its value to identify thieves and others who commit financial crimes such as credit card fraud. Most states in the United States have some form of data breach disclosure law that imposes a burden of notification on any organization that experiences unauthorized access, loss, or theft of unencrypted PII. All current laws provide a level of "safe harbor" for organizations that experience a PII loss if the PII was encrypted. California's SB1386 was the first and arguably most well known of disclosure laws.

---

4. UNAUTHORIZED ACCESS BY OUTSIDER

An outsider is considered to be anyone who does not have authorized access privileges to an IS or environment. To gain access, the outsider may try to gain possession of valid system credentials via social engineering or even by guessing username and password pairs in a brute force attack. Alternatively, the outsider may attempt to exploit vulnerability in the target system to gain access. Often the result of successfully exploiting system vulnerability leads to some form of high-privileged access to the target, such as an "Administrator" or Administrator-equivalent account on a Microsoft Windows system or "root" or root-equivalent account on a UNIX or Linux-based system. Once an outsider has this level of access on a system, he or she effectively "owns" that system and can steal data or use the system as a launching point to attack other systems.

5. MALICIOUS SOFTWARE INFECTION

Malicious software (malware) can be generally defined as "a set of instructions that run on your computer and make your system do something that allows an attacker to make it do what he wants it to do" [5]. Historically, malware (see sidebar: "Classifying Malware") in the form of viruses and worms was more of a disruptive nuisance than a real threat, but it has been evolving as the weapon of choice for many attackers owing to the increased sophistication, stealth, and scalability of intrusion-focused malware. Today we see malware being used by intruders to gain access to systems, search for valuable data such as PII and passwords, monitor real-time communications, provide remote access/control, and automatically attack other systems, just to name a few capabilities. Using malware as an attack method also provides the attacker with a "standoff" capability that reduces the risk of identification, pursuit, and prosecution. By "standoff" we mean the ability to launch malware via a number of anonymous methods such as an insecure, open public wireless access point, and once the malware has gained access to the intended target or targets, manage the malware via a distributed command and control system such as Internet Relay Chat, website pages, dynamic Domain Name Server (DNS), as well as completely novel mechanisms. Not only does the command and control network help mask the location and identity of the attacker, it also provides a scalable way to manage many compromised systems at once, maximizing results for the attacker. In some cases the number of controlled machines can be astronomical, such as with the Storm worm infection which, depending on the estimate, ranged somewhere between 1 and 10 million compromised systems [6]. These large collections of compromised systems are often referred to as "bot-nets."

Classifying Malicious Software

Malware takes many forms, but it can be roughly classified by function and replication method:

- *Virus*: Self-replicating code that attaches itself to another program. It typically relies on human interaction to start the host program and activate the virus. A virus usually has a limited function set and its creator has no further interaction with it once released. Examples are Melissa, Michelangelo, and Sobig.
- *Worm*: Self-replicating code that propagates over a network, usually without human interaction. Most worms take advantage of a known vulnerability in systems and compromise those that are not properly patched. Worm creators have begun experimenting with updatable code and payloads, such as that seen with the Storm worm [5]. Examples are Code Red, SQL Slammer, and Blaster.
- *Backdoor*: A program that bypasses standard security controls to provide an attacker access, often in a stealthy way. Backdoors rarely have self-replicating capability and are installed manually by an attacker after compromising a system to facilitate future access or by other self-propagating malware as payload. Examples are Back Orifice, Tini, and netcat (netcat has legitimate uses as well).
- *Trojan horse*: A program that masquerades as a legitimate, useful program while performing malicious functions in the background. Trojans are often used to steal data or monitor user actions and can provide a backdoor function as well. Examples of two well-known programs that have had Trojaned versions circulated on the Internet are tcpdump and Kazaa.
- *User-level rootkit*: Trojan/backdoor code that modifies operating system software so the attacker can maintain privileged access on a machine but remain hidden. For example, the rootkit will remove malicious processes from user-requested process lists. This form of rootkit is called user-level because it manipulates operating system components employed by users. This form of rootkit often can be uncovered by the use of trusted tools and software, because the core of the operating system is unaffected. Examples of user-level rootkits are the Linux Rootkit family and FakeGINA.
- *Kernel-level rootkit*: Trojan/backdoor code that modifies the core or kernel of the operating system to provide the intruder with the highest level of access and stealth. A kernel-level rootkit inserts itself into the core of the operating system, the kernel, and intercepts system calls, and thus can remain hidden even from trusted tools brought onto the system from the outside by an investigator. Effectively, nothing the compromised system tells a user can be trusted, and detecting and removing kernel-level rootkits is difficult and often requires advanced technologies and techniques. Examples are Adore and Hacker Defender.

- *Blended malware*: Forms of malware combining features and capabilities discussed into one program. For example, one might see a Trojan horse that, once activated by the user, inserts a backdoor employing user-level rootkit capabilities to stay hidden and provide a remote handler with access. Examples of blended malware are Lion and Bugbear.

6. ROLE OF THE "ZERO-DAY"

The Holy Grail for vulnerability researchers and exploit writers is to discover a previously unknown and exploitable vulnerability, often referred to as a zero-day exploit (pronounced "zero-day" or "oh-day"). Because others have not discovered the vulnerability, all systems running the vulnerable code will be unpatched and possible targets for attack and compromise. The danger of a given zero-day is a function of how widespread the vulnerable software is and what level of access it gives the attacker. For example, a reliable zero-day for something as widespread as the ubiquitous Apache Web server that somehow yields root or Administrator-level access to the attacker is far more dangerous and valuable than an exploit that works against an obscure point-of-sale system used by only a few hundred users (unless the attacker's target is that very set of users).

In addition to having a potentially large, vulnerable target set to exploit, the owner of a zero-day also has the advantage that most intrusion detection and prevention systems (IDPSs) [1] will not trigger on the exploit precisely because it has never been seen before and the various IDS/intrusion prevention system (IPS) technologies will not yet have signature patterns for the exploit. We will discuss this issue in more detail later.

This combination of many unpatched targets and the potential ability to evade many forms of IDPSs make zero-days a powerful weapon in the hands of an attacker. Many legitimate security and vulnerability researchers explore software systems to uncover zero-days and report them to the appropriate software vendor in the hope of preventing malicious individuals from finding and using them first. Those who intend to use zero-days for illicit purposes guard the knowledge of a zero-day carefully lest it become widely and publicly known and effective countermeasures, including vendor software patches, can be deployed.

One of the more disturbing issues regarding zero-days is their lifetimes. The lifetime of a zero-day is the amount of time between the discovery of the vulnerability and public disclosure through vendor or researcher announcement, mailing lists, and so on. Because of the nature of zero-day discovery and disclosure, it is difficult to obtain reliable statistics on lifetimes, but one vulnerability research organization claims their studies indicate an average zero-day lifetime of 348 days [7]. Hence, if malicious attackers have a high-value zero-day in hand, they may have almost a year to put it to most effective use. If used in a stealthy manner so as not to tip off system defenders, vendors, and researchers, this sort of zero-day can yield many high-value compromised systems for the attackers. Although there has been no official substantiation, there has been a great deal of speculation that the "Titan Rain" series of attacks against sensitive US Government networks between 2003 and 2005 used a set of zero-days against Microsoft software [8,9].

7. THE ROGUE'S GALLERY: ATTACKERS AND MOTIVES

Now that we have examined some of the more common forms of computer system intrusion, it is worthwhile to discuss those who are behind these attacks and attempt to understand their motivations. The appropriate selection of intrusion detection and prevention technologies depends on the threat being defended against, the class of adversary, and the value of the asset being protected.

Although it is always risky generalizing, those who attack computer systems for illicit purposes can be placed into a number of broad categories. At a minimum this gives us a "capability spectrum" of attackers to begin to understand motivations and therefore threats.

Script Kiddy

The pejorative term "script kiddy" is used to describe those who have little or no skill at writing or understanding how vulnerabilities are discovered and exploits written but download and use other's exploits available on the Internet to attack vulnerable systems. Typically, script kiddies are not a threat to a well-managed, patched environment because they are usually relegated to using publicly known and available exploits for which patches and detection signatures exist.

Joy Rider

This type of attacker is often represented by those with potentially significant skills in discovering vulnerabilities and writing exploits but who rarely have real malicious intent when they access systems for which they are not authorized. In a sense they are "exploring" for the pleasure of it. However, although their intentions are not directly malicious, their actions can represent a major source of distraction and cost to system administrators who must respond to the intrusion especially if the compromised

system contained sensitive data such as PII for which a public disclosure may be required.

Mercenary

Since the late 1990s there has been a growing market for those who possess the skills to compromise computer systems and are willing to sell them and those willing to purchase these skills [10]. Organized crime is a large consumer of these services, and computer crime has seen a significant increase in both frequency and severity over the past decade, primarily driven by direct, illicit financial gain and identity theft [11]. In fact, these groups have become so successful that a full-blown market has emerged including support organizations offering technical support for rented botnets and online trading environments for the exchange of stolen credit card data and PII. Stolen data have a tangible financial value, as shown in Table 72.1, which indicates dollar value ranges for various types of PII.

Nation-State Backed

Nations performing espionage against other nations do not ignore the potential for intelligence gathering via information technology systems. Sometimes this espionage takes the form of malware injection and system compromises such as the previously mentioned Titan Rain attack; other times it may take the form of electronic data interception of unencrypted email and other messaging protocols. A number of nations have developed or are developing an information warfare capability designed to impair or incapacitate an enemy's Internet-connected systems, command-and-control systems, and other information technology capability [12]. These sorts of capabilities were demonstrated in 2007 against Estonia, allegedly by Russian sympathizers, who used a sustained series of denial of service attacks designed to make certain websites unreachable as well as interfere with online activities such as email and mission-critical systems such as telephone exchanges [13].

8. A BRIEF INTRODUCTION TO TRANSMISSION CONTROL PROTOCOL/ INTERNET PROTOCOL

Throughout the history of computing, there have been numerous networking protocols, the structured rules computers use to communicate with each other, but none have been as successful and become as ubiquitous as the Transmission Control Protocol/Internet Protocol (TCP/IP) suite of protocols. TCP/IP is the protocol suite used on the Internet and the vast majority of enterprise and government networks have implemented TCP/IP on their networks.

TABLE 72.1 Personally Identifiable Information Values

Goods and Services	Percentage (%)	Range of Prices
Financial accounts	22	$10–$1000
Credit card information	13	$0.40–$20
Identity information	9	$1–$15
eBay accounts	7	$1–$8
Scams	7	$2.5–$50/week for hosting $25 for design
Mailers	6	$1–$10
Email addresses	5	$0.83–$10/MB
Email passwords	5	$4–$30
Drop (request or offer)	5	10–50% of drop amount
Proxies	5	$1.50–$30

Complied from Miami Electronic Crimes Task Force and Symantec Global Internet Security Threat Report (2008).

Owing to this ubiquity almost all attacks against computer systems are designed to be launched over a TCP/IP network and thus most IDPSs are designed to operate with and monitor TCP/IP-based networks. Therefore, to understand the nature of these technologies better, it is important to have a working knowledge of TCP/IP. Although a complete description of TCP/IP is beyond the scope of this chapter, there are numerous excellent references and tutorials for those interested in learning more [14,15]. Three features that have made TCP/IP so popular and widespread are [16]:

1. Open protocol standards that are freely available. This and independence from any particular operating system or computing hardware means TCP/IP can be deployed on nearly any computing device imaginable.
2. Hardware, transmission media and device independence. TCP/IP can operate over numerous physical devices and network types such as Ethernet, Token Ring, optical, radio, and satellite.
3. A consistent and globally scalable addressing scheme. This ensures that any two uniquely addressed network nodes can communicate (notwithstanding any traffic restrictions implemented for security or policy reasons) with each other even if those nodes are on different sides of the planet.

9. TRANSMISSION CONTROL PROTOCOL/INTERNET PROTOCOL DATA ARCHITECTURE AND DATA ENCAPSULATION

The best way to describe and visualize the TCP/IP suite is to think of it as a layered stack of functions, as shown in Fig. 72.1.

Each layer is responsible for a set of services and capabilities provided to the layers above and below it. This layered model allows developers and engineers to modularize the functionality in a given layer and minimize the impacts of changes on other layers. Each layer performs a series of functions on data as it is prepared for network transport or received from the network. How those functions are performed internal to a given layer is hidden from the other layers, and as long as the agreed-upon rules and standards are adhered to with regard to how data are passed from layer to layer, the inner workings of a given layer are isolated from any other.

The Application Layer is concerned with applications and processes, including those that users interact with such as browsers, email, instant messaging, and other network-aware programs. There may also be numerous

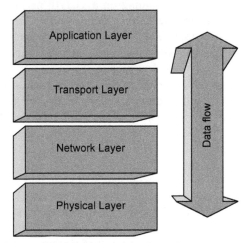

FIGURE 72.1 Transmission Control Protocol/Internet Protocol data architecture stack.

applications in the Application Layer running on a computer system that interact with the network, but users have little interaction with such as routing protocols.

The Transport Layer is responsible for handling data flow between applications on different hosts on the network. There are two Transport protocols in the TCP/IP suite: the Transport Control Protocol (TCP) and the User Datagram Protocol (UDP). TCP is a connection or session-oriented protocol that provides a number of services to the application described earlier, such as reliable delivery via Positive Acknowledgment with Retransmission, packet sequencing to account for out-of-sequence receipt of packets, receive buffer management, and error detection. In contrast, UDP is a low-overhead, connectionless protocol that provides no delivery acknowledgment or other session services. Any necessary application reliability must be built into the application, whereas with TCP the application need not worry about the details of packet delivery. Each protocol serves a specific purpose and allows maximum flexibility to application developers and engineers. There may be numerous network services running on a computer system, each built on either TCP or UDP (or, in some cases, both) so both protocols use the concept of *ports* to identify a specific network service and direct data appropriately. For example, a computer may be running a Web server and standard Web services are offered on TCP port 80. That same computer could also be running an email system using the Simple Mail Transport Protocol (SMTP), which is by standard offered on TCP port 25. Finally, this server may also be running a DNS on both TCP and UDP port 53. As can be seen, the concept of ports allows multiple TCP and UDP services to be run on the same computer system without interfering with each other.

The Network Layer is primarily responsible for packet addressing and routing through the network. The IP manages this process within the TCP/IP protocol suite. One important construct found in IP is the concept of an IP address. Each system running on a TCP/IP network must have at least one unique address for other computer systems to direct traffic to it. An IP address is represented by a 32-bit number that is usually represented as four integers ranging from 0 to 255 separated by decimals such as 192.168.1.254. This representation is often referred to as a *dotted quad*. The IP address actually contains two pieces of information in it: the network address and the node address. To know where the network address ends and the node address begins, a *subnet mask* is used to indicate the number of bits in the IP address assigned to the network address and is usually designated as a slash and a number such as "/24." If the example address of 192.168.1.254 has a subnet mask of /24, we know that the network address is 24 bits or 192.168.1, and the node address is 254. If we were presented with a subnet mask of /16, we would know the network address is 192.168 whereas the node address is 1.254. Subnet masking allows network designers to construct subnets of various sizes ranging from two nodes (a subnet mask of /30) to literally millions of nodes (a subnet of /8) or anything in between. The topic of subnetting and its impact on addressing and routing is a complex one; the interested reader is referred to Stevens [14] for more detail.

The Physical Layer is responsible for interaction with the physical network medium. Depending on the specifics of the medium, this may include functions such as collision avoidance, the transmission and reception of packets or datagrams, basic error checking, and so on. The Physical Layer handles all of the details of interfacing with the network medium and isolates the upper layers from the physical details.

Another important concept in TCP/IP is that of data encapsulation. Data are passed up and down the stack as they travel from a network-aware program or application in the Application Layer, are packaged for transport across the network by the Transport and Network Layer, and eventually are placed on the transmission medium (copper or fiber-optic cable, radio, satellite, and so on) by the Physical Layer. As data are handed down the stack, each layer adds its own header (a structured collection of fields of data) to the data passed to it by the layer above. Fig. 72.2 illustrates three important headers: the IP header, the TCP header, and the UDP header. The various headers are where layer-specific constructs such as IP address and TCP or UDP port numbers are placed so the appropriate layer can access this information and act on it accordingly.

The receiving layer is not concerned with the content of the data passed to it, only that the data are given to it in a way compliant with the protocol rules. The Physical Layer places the completed packet (the full collection of headers and application data) onto the transmission medium for handling by the physical network. When a packet is received, the reverse process occurs. As the packet travels up the stack, each layer removes its respective header, inspects the header content for instructions regarding which upper layer in the protocol stack to hand the remaining data, and passes the data to the appropriate layer. This process is repeated until all TCP/IP headers have been removed and the appropriate application is handed the data. The encapsulation process is illustrated in Fig. 72.3.

To best illustrate these concepts, let us explore a simplified example. Fig. 72.4 illustrates the various steps in this example. Assume a user, Alice, wishes to send an email to her colleague, Bob, at cool company.com:

1. Alice launches her email program and types in Bob's email address, *bob@coolcompany.com*, as well as her message to Bob. Alice's email program constructs a properly formatted SMTP-compliant message, resolves Cool Company's email server address using a DNS query, and passes the message to the TCP component of the Transport Layer for processing.

IP, Version 4 Header

4-bit version	4-bit header length	8-bit type of service	16-bit total packet length (value in bytes)	
16-bit IP/fragment identification			3-bit flags	13-bit fragment offset
8-bit time to live (TTL)		8-bit protcol ID	16-bit header checksum	
32-bit source IP address				
32-bit destination IP address				
options (if present)				
data (inlcuding upper layer headers)				

TCP Header

16-bit source port number			16-bit destination port number	
32-bit sequence number				
32-bit acknowledgement number				
4-bit TCP header length	6-bit reserved	6-bit flags	16-bit window size	
16-bit TCP checksum			16-bit urgent pointer	
options (if present)				
data (if any)				

UDP Header

16-bit source port number	16-bit destination port number
16-bit UDP length (header plus data)	16-bit UDP checksum
data (if any)	

(sourced from Request for Comment (RFC) 791, 793, 768)

FIGURE 72.2 Internet Protocol (IP), Transmission Control Protocol (TCP), and User Datagram Protocol (UDP) headers.

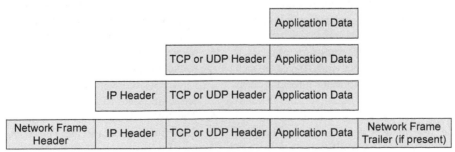

FIGURE 72.3 Transmission Control Protocol/Internet Protocol (TCP/IP) encapsulation. *UDP*, User Datagram Protocol.

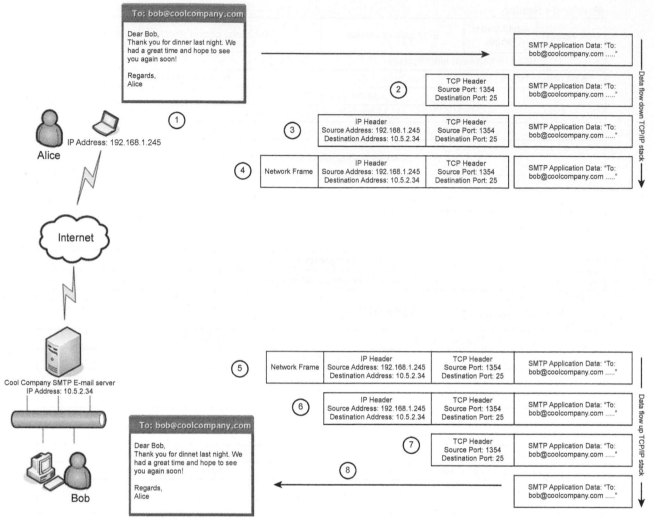

FIGURE 72.4 Application and network interaction example. *IP*, Internet Protocol; *SMTP*, Simple Mail Transport Protocol; *TCP*, Transmission Control Protocol.

2. The TCP process adds a TCP header in front of the SMTP message fields including such pertinent information as the source TCP port (randomly chosen as a port number greater than 1024, in this case 1354), the destination port (port 25 for SMTP email), and other TCP-specific information such as sequence numbers and receive buffer sizes.

3. This new data package (SMTP message plus TCP header) is then handed to the Network Layer and an IP header is added with such important information as the source IP address of Alice's computer, the destination IP address of Cool Company's email server, and other IP-specific information such as packet lengths, error-detection checksums, and so on.

4. This complete IP packet is then handed to the Physical Layer for transmission onto the physical network medium, which will add network layer headers as appropriate. Numerous packets may be needed to fully

transmit the entire email message depending on the various network media and protocols that must be traversed by the packets as they leave Alice's network and travel the Internet to Cool Company's email server. The details will be handled by the intermediate systems and any required updates or changes to the packet headers will be made by those systems.

5. When Cool Company's email server receives the packets from its local network medium via the Physical Layer, it removes the network frame and hands the remaining data to the Network Layer.

6. The Network Layer strips off the IP header and hands the remaining data to the TCP component of the Transport Layer.

7. The TCP process removes and examines the TCP header to examine the destination port (again, 25 for email), among other tasks, and finally hand the SMTP message to the SMTP server process.

8. The SMTP application performs further application-specific processing as well delivery to Bob's email application by starting the encapsulation process all over again to transit the internal network between Bob's PC and the server.

It is important to understand that network-based computer system attacks can occur at every layer of the TCP/IP stack, and thus an effective intrusion detection and prevention program must be able to inspect at each layer and act accordingly. Intruders may manipulate any number of fields within a TCP/IP packet to attempt to bypass security processes or systems including the application-specific data, all in an attempt to gain access and control of the target system.

10. SURVEY OF INTRUSION DETECTION AND PREVENTION TECHNOLOGIES

Now that we have discussed the threats and those who pose them to ISs, and have examined the underlying protocol suite in use on the Internet and enterprise networks, we are prepared to explore the various technologies available to detect and prevent intrusions. Although technologies such as firewalls, a robust patching program, and disk and file encryption can be part of a powerful intrusion prevention program, these are considered static preventative defenses and will not be discussed here. In this section, we will discuss various dynamic systems and technologies that can assist in detecting and preventing attacks on ISs.

11. ANTIMALICIOUS SOFTWARE

We have discussed malware and its various forms. Antimalware software, which typically used to be referred to as antivirus software, is designed to analyze files and programs for known signatures or patterns in the data that make up the file or program and indicates that malicious code is present. This signature scanning is often accomplished through a multitiered approach in which the entire hard drive of the computer is scanned sequentially during idle periods and any file accessed is scanned immediately to prevent dormant code in a file that has not been scanned from becoming active. When an infected file or malicious program is found, it is prevented from running and is either quarantined (moved to a location for further inspection by a system administrator) or simply deleted from the system. There are also appliance-based solutions that can be placed on the network to examine certain classes of traffic such as email before being delivered to the end systems.

In any case, the primary weakness of the signature-based scanning method is that if the software does not have a signature for a particular piece of malware, the malware will be effectively invisible to the software and will be able to run without interference. A signature may not exist because a particular instance of the antimalware software may not have an up-to-date signature database or the malware may be new or modified so as to avoid detection. To overcome this increasingly common issue, more sophisticated antimalware software will monitor for known-malicious behavioral patterns instead of, or in addition to, signature-based scanning. Behavioral pattern monitoring can take many forms such as observing the system calls all programs make and identifying patterns of calls that are anomalous or known-malicious. Another common method is to create a white list of allowed known-normal activity and to prevent all other activity or at least prompt the user when a non–while listed activity is attempted. Although these methods overcome some limitations of the signature-based model and can detect malware previously not seen, they come with the price of higher false-positive rates and/or additional administrative burdens.

Although antimalware software can be evaded by new or modified malware, it serves a useful purpose as a component in a defense-in-depth strategy, as illustrated in Fig. 72.5. A well-maintained antimalware infrastructure will detect and prevent known forms, freeing up resources to focus on other threats, but it can also be used to speed and simplify containment and eradication of a malware infection once an identifying signature can be developed and deployed.

12. NETWORK-BASED INTRUSION DETECTION SYSTEMS

For many years, network-based IDSs (NIDSs) have been the workhorse of information security technology and in many ways have become synonymous with intrusion detection [17]. NIDSs function in one of three modes: signature detection, anomaly detection, and hybrid. A signature-based NIDS operates by passively examining all network traffic flowing past its sensor interface or interfaces and examines TCP/IP packets for signatures of known attacks, as illustrated in Fig. 72.6.

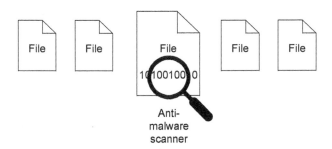

FIGURE 72.5 Antimalicious software (antimalware) file scanning.

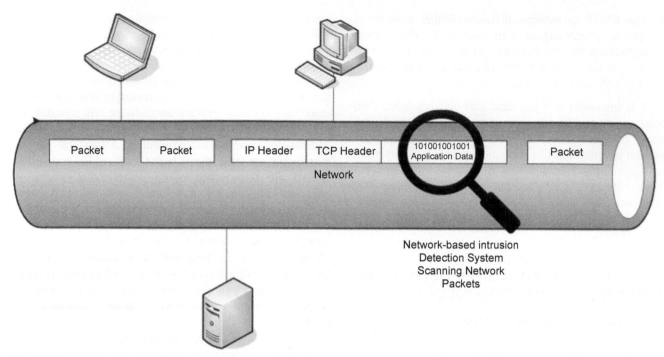

FIGURE 72.6 Network intrusion detection system device scanning packets flowing past sensor interface. *IP*, Internet Protocol; *TCP*, Transmission Control Protocol.

TCP/IP packet headers are also often inspected to search for nonsensical header field values sometimes used by attackers in an attempt to circumvent filters and monitors. In much the same way that signature-based antimalware software can be defeated by never before seen malware or malware sufficiently modified no longer to possess the signature used for detection, signature-based NIDS will be blind to any attack for which it does not have a signature. This can be a serious limitation, but signature-based NIDSs are still useful owing to most systems' ability for the operator to add custom signatures to sensors. This allows security and network engineers to deploy monitoring and alarming capability rapidly on their networks in the event they discover an incident or are suspicious about certain activity. Signature-based NIDSs are also useful to monitor for known-attacks and ensure none of those are successful at breaching systems, which frees up resources to investigate or monitor other, more serious threats.

NIDSs designed to detect anomalies in network traffic build statistical or baseline models for the traffic they monitor and raise an alarm about any traffic that deviates significantly from those models. There are numerous methods for detecting network traffic anomalies; one of the most common involves checking traffic for compliance with various protocol standards such as TCP/IP for underlying traffic and application layer protocols such as Hypertext Transfer Protocol for Web traffic, SMTP for email, and so on. Many attacks against applications or the underlying network attempt to cause system malfunctions by violating the protocol standard in ways unanticipated by the system developers and with which the targeted protocol handling layer does not deal properly. Unfortunately, there are entire classes of attacks that do not violate a protocol standard and thus will not be detected by this model of anomaly detection. Another model commonly used is to build a model for user behavior and generate an alarm when a user deviates from the "normal" patterns. For example, if Alice never logs into the network after 9 p.m. and suddenly a log-on attempt is seen from Alice's account at 3 a.m., this would constitute a significant deviation from normal usage patterns and generate an alarm. Some main drawbacks of anomaly detection systems are defining the models of what is normal and what is malicious, defining what a significant enough deviation is from the norm to warrant an alarm, and defining a sufficiently comprehensive model or models to cover the immense range of behavioral and traffic patterns that are likely to be seen on any given network. Because of this complexity and the relative immaturity of adaptable, learning anomaly detection technology, few production-quality systems are available today. However, because it does not rely on static signatures, the potential of the successful implementation of an anomaly detection NIDS for detecting zero-day attacks and new or custom malware is so tantalizing that much research continues in this space.

A hybrid system takes the best qualities of both signature-based and anomaly detection NIDSs and integrates them into a single system to attempt to overcome the weaknesses of both models. Many commercial NIDSs implement a hybrid model by using signature matching owing to its speed and flexibility while incorporating some level of anomaly detection to flag suspicious traffic for closer examination by those responsible for monitoring the NIDS alerts, at a minimum.

Aside from the primary criticism of signature-based NIDSs their depending on static signatures, common additional criticisms of NIDS are that they tend to produce a lot of false alerts either as a result of imprecise signature construction or because of poor tuning of the sensor to match the environment better, poor event correlation resulting in many alerts for a related incident, the inability to monitor encrypted network traffic, difficulty dealing with very high-speed networks such as those operating at 10 gigabits per second, or no ability to intervene during a detected attack. This last criticism is a driving reason behind the development of IPSs.

13. NETWORK-BASED INTRUSION PREVENTION SYSTEMS

Whereas NIDS are designed to monitor traffic passively and raise alarms when suspicious traffic is detected, network IPSs (NIPSs) are designed to go one step further and actually try to prevent the attack from succeeding. This is typically achieved by inserting the NIPS device inline with the traffic it is monitoring. Each network packet is inspected and passed only if it does not trigger some sort of alert based on a signature match or anomaly threshold. Suspicious packets are discarded and an alert is generated.

In contrast to the passive monitoring of NIDSs, the ability to intervene and stop known attacks is the greatest benefit of NIPSs. However, NIPSs have the same drawbacks and limitations as discussed for NIDSs, such as heavy reliance on static signatures, the inability to examine encrypted traffic, and difficulties with very high network speeds. In addition, false alarms are much more significant because the NIPS may discard that traffic even though it is not really malicious. If the destination system is business or mission critical, this action could have a significant negative impact on the function of the system. Thus, great care must be taken to tune the NIPS during a training period when there is no packet discard before allowing it to begin blocking any detected malicious traffic.

14. HOST-BASED INTRUSION PREVENTION SYSTEMS

A complementary approach to network-based intrusion prevention is to place the detection and prevention system on the system requiring protection as an installed software package. Host-based IPSs (HIPSs), although often using some of the same signature-based technology found in NIDSs and NIPSs, also take advantage of being installed on the protected system to protect by monitoring and analyzing what other processes on the system are doing at a detailed level. This process monitoring is similar to that which we discussed in the antimalware software section and involves observing system calls, interprocess communication, network traffic, and other behavioral patterns for suspicious activity. Another benefit of HIPS is that encrypted network traffic can be analyzed after the decryption process has occurred on the protected system, thus providing an opportunity to detect an attack that would have been hidden from an NIPS or NIDS device monitoring network traffic.

Again, as with NIPS and NIDS, HIPS is only as effective as its signature database, anomaly detection model, or behavioral analysis routines. Also, the presence of an HIPS on a protected system incurs processing and system resource usage overhead, and on a busy system this overhead may be unacceptable. However, given the unique advantages of HIPS, such as being able to inspect encrypted network traffic, it is often employed as a complement to NIPS and NIDS in a targeted fashion, and this combination can be effective.

15. SECURITY INFORMATION MANAGEMENT SYSTEMS

Modern network environments generate a tremendous amount of security event and log data via firewalls, network routers and switches, NIDS/NIPS, servers, antimalware systems, and so on. Envisioned as a solution to help manage and analyze all of this information, security information management (SIM) systems have evolved to provide data reduction and reduce the sheer quantity of information that must analyzed and event correlation capabilities that assist a security analyst in making sense of it all [18]. A SIM system not only acts as a centralized repository for such data, it helps organize them and provides an analyst with the ability to perform complex queries across this entire database. One of the primary benefits of a SIM system is that data from disparate systems are normalized into a uniform database structure, thus allowing an analyst to investigate suspicious activity or a known incident across different aspects and elements of the information technology environment. Often an intrusion will leave various types of "footprints" in the logs (see checklist: "An Agenda for Action for Logging Capabilities") of different systems involved in the incident; bringing these together and providing a complete picture for the analyst or investigator is the job of the SIM.

An Agenda for Action for Logging Capabilities

Network-based IDPSs typically perform extensive logging of data related to detected events. These data can be used to confirm the validity of alerts, investigate incidents, and correlate events between the IDPS and other logging sources. Data fields commonly logged by network-based IDPSs include the following (check all tasks completed):

_____1. Timestamp (usually date and time)

_____2. Connection or session ID (typically a consecutive or unique number assigned to each TCP connection or to like groups of packets for connectionless protocols)

_____3. Event or alert type

_____4. Rating (priority, severity, impact, and confidence)

_____5. Network, transport, and application layer protocols

_____6. Source and destination IP addresses

_____7. Source and destination TCP or UDP ports, or Internet Control Message Protocol types and codes

_____8. Number of bytes transmitted over the connection

_____9. Decoded payload data such as application requests and responses

_____10. State-related information (authenticated username)

_____11. Prevention action performed (if any)

_____12. Most network-based IDPSs can also perform packet captures. Typically this is done once an alert has occurred, either to record subsequent activity in the connection or to record the entire connection if the IDPS has been temporarily storing the previous packets.

Even with modern and powerful event correlation engines and data reduction routines, however, a SIM system is only as effective as the analyst examining the output. Fundamentally, SIM systems are a reactive technology like NIDS, and because extracting useful and actionable information from them often requires a strong understanding of the various systems sending data to the SIM, the analyst's skill set and experience become critical to the effectiveness of the SIM as an IDS [19]. SIM systems also have a significant role during incident response, because often, evidence of an intrusion can be found in the various logs stored on the SIM.

16. NETWORK SESSION ANALYSIS

Network session data represents a high-level summary of "conversations" occurring between computer systems [20]. No specifics about the content of the conversation such as packet payloads is maintained but various elements about the conversation are kept and can be useful when investigating an incident or as an indicator of suspicious activity.

There are a number of ways to generate and process network session data, ranging from vendor-specific implementations such as Cisco's NetFlow [21] to session data reconstruction from full traffic analysis using tools such as Argus [22]. However the session data are generated, a number of common elements constitute the session, such as the source IP address, source port, destination IP address, destination port, timestamp information, and an array of metrics about the session such as bytes transferred and packet distribution.

Using the collected session information, an analyst can examine traffic patterns on a network to identify which systems are communicating with each other and identify suspicious sessions that warrant further investigation. For example, a server configured for internal use by users and having no legitimate reason to communicate with addresses on the Internet will cause an alarm to be generated if a session or sessions suddenly appear between the internal server and external addresses. At that point the analyst may suspect a malware infection or other system compromise and investigate further. Numerous other queries can be generated to identify sessions that are abnormal in some way or another, such as excessive byte counts, excessive session lifetime, or unexpected ports being used. When run over a sufficient timeframe, a baseline for traffic sessions can be established and the analyst can query for sessions that do not fit the baseline. This sort of investigation is a form of anomaly detection based on high-level network data versus the more granular types discussed for NIDS and NIPS.

Another common use of network session analysis is to combine it with a honeypot or honeynet (see sidebar: "Honeypots and Honeynets"). Any network activity seen on these systems other than known-good maintenance traffic such as patch downloads is by definition suspicious because there are no production business functions or users assigned to these systems. Their sole purpose is to act as a lure for an intruder. By monitoring network sessions to and from these systems, an early warning can be raised without necessarily needing to perform a complex analysis.

Honeypots and Honeynets

A honeypot is a computer system designed to act as a lure or trap for intruders. This is most often achieved by configuring the honeypot to look like a production system possibly containing valuable or sensitive information and providing legitimate services but in actuality neither the data nor the services are real. A honeypot is carefully monitored, and because there is no legitimate reason for a user to be interacting with it, any activity seen targeting it is immediately considered suspicious. A honeynet is a collection of honeypots designed to mimic a more complex environment than one system can support [23].

17. DIGITAL FORENSICS

Digital forensics is the "application of computer science and investigative procedures for a legal purpose involving the analysis of digital evidence" [24]. Less formally, digital forensics is the use of specialized tools and techniques to investigate various forms of computer-oriented crime including fraud, illicit use such as child pornography, and many forms of computer intrusions.

Digital forensics as a field can be divided into two subfields: network forensics and host-based forensics. Network forensics focuses on the use of captured network traffic and session information to investigate computer crime. Host-based forensics focuses on the collection and analysis of digital evidence collected from individual computer systems to investigate computer crime. Digital forensics is a vast topic; a comprehensive discussion is beyond the scope of this chapter. Interested readers are referred to Jones [25] for more detail.

In the context of intrusion detection, digital forensic techniques can be used to analyze a suspected compromised system in a methodical manner. Forensic investigations are most commonly used when the nature of the intrusion is unclear, such as those perpetrated via a zero-day exploit, but in which the root cause must be fully understood either to ensure the exploited vulnerability is properly remediated or to support legal proceedings. Owing to the increasing use of sophisticated attack tools and stealthy and customized malware designed to evade detection, forensic investigations are becoming increasingly common, and sometimes only a detailed and methodical investigation will uncover the nature of an intrusion. The specifics of the intrusion may also require a forensic investigation such as those involving the theft of PII in regions covered by one or more data breach disclosure laws.

18. SYSTEM INTEGRITY VALIDATION

The emergence of powerful and stealthy malware, kernel-level rootkits, and so-called clean-state attack frameworks that leave no trace of an intrusion on a computer's hard drive have given rise to the need for technology that can analyze a running system and its memory and provide a series of metrics regarding the integrity of the system. System integrity validation (SIV) technology is still in its infancy and an active area of research, but it primarily focuses on live system memory analysis and the notion of deriving trust from known-good system elements [26]. This is achieved by comparing the system's running state including the processes, threads, data structures, and modules loaded into memory, with the static elements on disk from which the running state was supposedly loaded. Through a number of cross-validation processes, discrepancies between what is running in memory and what should

be running can be identified. When properly implemented, SIV can be a powerful tool for detecting intrusions, even those using advanced techniques.

19. SUMMARY

It should be clear that intrusion detection and prevention is not a single tool or product but a series of layered technologies coupled with appropriate methodologies and skill sets. Each technology surveyed in this chapter has its own specific strengths and weaknesses, and a truly effective intrusion detection and prevention program must be designed to play to those strengths and minimize the weaknesses. Combining NIDS and NIPS with network session analysis and a comprehensive SIM, for example, helps to offset the inherent weakness of each technology as well as provide the information security team with greater flexibility to bring the right tools to bear for an ever-shifting threat environment.

An essential element in a properly designed intrusion detection and prevention program is an assessment of the threats faced by the organization and a valuation of the assets to be protected. There must be an alignment of the value of the information assets to be protected and the costs of the systems put in place to defend them. The program for an environment processing military secrets and needing to defend against a hostile nation state must be far more exhaustive than that for a single server containing no data of real value that must simply keep out assorted script kiddies.

For many organizations, however, their ISs are business and mission critical enough to warrant considerable thought and planning with regard to the appropriate choices of technologies, how they will be implemented, and how they will be monitored. Only through flexible, layered, and comprehensive intrusion detection and prevention programs can organizations hope to defend their environment against current and future threats to information security.

Finally, let us move on to the real interactive part of this chapter: review questions/exercises, hands-on projects, case projects, and the optional team case project. The answers and/or solutions by chapter can be found in the Online Instructor's Solutions Manual.

CHAPTER REVIEW QUESTIONS/ EXERCISES

True/False

1. True or False? Information security is concerned with the integrity and availability of information systems and the information or data they contain and process.
2. True or False? Having physical access to a computer system allows an adversary to bypass most security protections put in place to prevent unauthorized access.

3. True or False? An insider is an individual who, owing to his role in the organization, has some level of authorized access to the IS environment and systems.

4. True or False? An outsider is considered anyone who does not have authorized access privileges to an information system or environment.

5. True or False? Malware can be generally defined as "a set of instructions that run on your computer and make your system do something that allows an attacker to make it do what he wants it to do."

Multiple Choice

1. What is a self-replicating code that attaches itself to another program?
   A. Worm
   B. Virus
   C. Backdoor
   D. Trojan horse
   E. User-level rootkit

2. What is a self-replicating code that propagates over a network, usually without human interaction?
   A. Backdoor
   B. Virus
   C. Worm
   D. Trojan horse
   E. User-level rootkit

3. What is a program that bypasses standard security controls to provide an attacker access, often in a stealthy way?
   A. Trojan horse
   B. Virus
   C. Worm
   D. Backdoor
   E. User-level rootkit

4. What is a program that masquerades as a legitimate, useful program while also performing malicious functions in the background?
   A. Trojan horse
   B. Virus
   C. Worm
   D. Backdoor
   E. User-level rootkit

5. What is the Trojan/backdoor code that modifies operating system software so the attacker can maintain privileged access on a machine but remain hidden?
   A. Trojan horse
   B. Virus
   C. Worm
   D. Backdoor
   E. User-level rootkit

EXERCISE

Problem

How do intrusion detection systems (IDSs) work?

Hands-on Projects

Project

Why should an organization use an IDS, especially when it already has firewalls, antivirus tools, and other security protections on its system?

Case Projects

Problem

What are the different types of IDSs?

Optional Team Case Project

Problem

How does one go about selecting the best IDS for one's organization?

REFERENCES

[1] NIST, 100 Bureau Drive, Stop 1070, Gaithersburg, MD 20899–1070, [US Department of Commerce, 1401 Constitution Avenue, NW, Washington, DC 20230], NIST Special Publication on Intrusion Detection Systems, 2006.

[2] [a] M. Bosworth, VA Loses Data on 26 Million Veterans, consumeraffairs.com, 2006. http://www.consumeraffairs.com/news04/2006/05/va_laptop.html;
[b] B. Prince, Stolen Laptop Exposes Boston Hospital Patient Data, darkreading.com, 2012. http://www.darkreading.com/compliance/167901112/security/attacks-breaches/240001031/stolen-laptop-exposes-boston-hospital-patient-data.html.

[3] B. Schneier, Applied Cryptography, Wiley, 1996.

[4] S. Fishman, Bradley Manning's Army of One, New York Magazine, July 3, 2011.

[5] E. Skoudis, Malware: Fighting Malicious Code, Prentice Hall, 2003.

[6] P. Gutman, World's Most Powerful Supercomputer Goes Online, Full Disclosure, 2007. http://seclists.org/fulldisclosure/2007/Aug/0520.html.

[7] J. Aitel, The IPO of the 0-day, 2007. http://www.immunityinc.com/downloads/0day_IPO.pdf.

[8] M.H. Sachs, Cyber-Threat Analytics, 2006. www.cyber-ta.org/downloads/files/Sachs_Cyber-TA_ThreatOps.ppt.

[9] J. Leyden, Chinese Crackers Attack US.Gov, The Register, 2006. http://www.theregister.co.uk/2006/10/09/chinese_crackers_attack_us/.

[10] P. Williams, Organized Crime and Cyber-Crime: Implications for Business, 2002. http://www.cert.org/archive/pdf/cybercrime-business.pdf.

[11] C. Wilson, Botnets, Cybercrime, and Cyberterrorism: Vulnerabilities and Policy Issues for Congress, 2008. http://fas.org/sgp/crs/terror/RL32114.pdf.

[12] M. Graham, Welcome to Cyberwar Country, USA, WIRED, 2008. http://www.wired.com/politics/security/news/2008/02/cyber_command.

[13] M. Landler, J. Markoff, Digital Fears Emerge after data Siege in Estonia, New York Times, 2007.

[14] R. Stevens, TCP/IP Illustrated, Volume 1: The Protocols, Addison-Wesley Professional, 1994.

[15] D.E. Comer, Internetworking with TCP/IP Vol. 1: Principles, Protocols, and Architecture, fourth ed., Prentice Hall, 2000.

[16] C. Hunt, TCP/IP Network Administration, third ed., O'Reilly Media, Inc., 2002.

[17] S. Northcutt, Network Intrusion Detection, third ed., SAMS, 2002.

[18] J.L. Bayuk, Stepping through the InfoSec Program, ISACA, 2007.

[19] B. Schneier, Security information management systems (SIMS), in: Schneier on Security, October 20, 2004. http://www.schneier.com/blog/archives/2004/10/security_inform.html.

[20] R. Bejtlich, The Tao of Network Security Monitoring: Beyond Intrusion Detection, Addison-Wesley Professional, 2004.

[21] Cisco Website, Cisco IOS NetFlow. http://www.cisco.com/web/go/netflow.

[22] Argus Website, Argus − Auditing Network Activity, August 13, 2012. http://qosient.com/argus/.

[23] Honeynet Project Website, The Honeynet Project, 2012. www.honeynet.org.

[24] K. Zatyko, Commentary: Defining Digital Forensics, Forensics Magazine, 2007. http://www.forensicmag.com/articles.asp?pid=130.

[25] K. Jones, Real Digital Forensics: Computer Security and Incident Response, Addison-Wesley Professional, 2005.

[26] Volatile Systems Website, Volatile Systems, 2012. www.volatilesystems.com.

Chapter 73

Transmission Control Protocol/Internet Protocol Packet Analysis

Pramod Pandya

CSU Fullerton, Avante, CA, United States

Note: This chapter is available in its entirety online at store.elsevier.com/product.jsp?isbn= 9780128038437 (click the Resources tab at the bottom of the page).

1. ABSTRACT

To manage network security, you need an in-depth understanding of the Transmission Control Protocol/Internet Protocol (TCP/IP) stack. This chapter will discuss how TCP/IP packets are constructed and analyzed, to interpret applications that use the TCP/IP stack. The intrusion detection principle relies on being able to analyze the packets and detect a potential attack or an attack in progress. We will introduce the Internet model to develop the argument to support packet data networking for local and wide area networks that include the Internet.

2. CONTENTS

Transmission Control Protocol/Internet Protocol Packet Analysis

Pramod Pandya

1. ABSTRACT

2. CONTENTS

Chapter 74

Firewalls

Errin W. Fulp

Wake Forest University, Winston-Salem, NC, United States

Note: This chapter is available in its entirety online at store.elsevier.com/product.jsp?isbn= 9780128038437 (click the Resources tab at the bottom of the page).

1. ABSTRACT

The purpose of the firewall and its location is to have network connections traverse the firewall, which can then stop any unauthorized packets. A simple firewall will filter packets based on IP addresses and ports. A useful analogy is filtering your postal mail based only on the information on the envelope. You typically accept any letter addressed to you and return any letter addressed to someone else. This act of filtering is essentially the same for firewalls. This chapter refers to the secure network as the internal network; the insecure network is the external network. The remainder of this chapter provides an overview of firewall policies, designs, features, and configurations. Of course, technology is always changing, and network firewalls are no exception. However, the intent of this chapter is to describe aspects of network firewalls that tend to endure over time.

2. CONTENTS

Computer and Information Security Handbook. http://dx.doi.org/10.1016/B978-0-12-803843-7.00074-0

Firewalls

Colin W. Pyle

ABSTRACT

CONTENTS

Chapter 75

Penetration Testing

Roman Zabicki and Scott R. Ellis
kCura, Chicago, IL, United States

1. WHAT IS PENETRATION TESTING?

Penetration testing is testing that looks for security flaws to exploit. A typical penetration test would look for vulnerabilities that could lead to major security problems such as the ability to impersonate users, steal passwords, or delete all data in the system.

Penetration tests are generally timeboxed, and for good reason. There is not enough time to perform every test that you can imagine. Even if the software passed every test you could think of, that still does not mean the software is safe. Absence of proof of vulnerability is not proof of absence of *any* vulnerability; you might have just missed something. Because there is no way to be certain that a test has covered everything, the usual approach is to set a time limit and prioritize the most important tests first.

Penetration testing is often tedious. A successful penetration test often requires trying a great many inputs before finding one input that causes the system to misbehave. Thomas Edison famously described his progress inventing light bulbs with the phrase, "I have not failed. I have found 10,000 things that don't work." That could have applied to penetration testing just as easily as to light bulb invention. Just as Edison did not know in advance whether there was a way to build a light bulb, penetration testers do not know in advance whether there is a way to compromise a computer system. The exploratory nature of penetration testing means that sometimes there is no substitute for making a lot of attempts. In addition, much of this exploration takes place at the edges of acceptable input for the system. By sending a computer program inputs that are intentionally difficult to process, a penetration tester can sometimes slow down or even crash the system under test.

Penetration testing is not automatable. The entire point of the test is to find the cracks, the things that slipped through, that no one considered. An automated check could

protect you against the problems you knew about yesterday, but it cannot help find new vulnerabilities tomorrow.

"But no one would ever do that!" A large part of successful penetration testing is thinking up things that no legitimate user would ever do. For example, a legitimate user of an accounting program would never have a first name consisting of the letter "A" repeated 10,000 times. However, a penetration tester should test what happens when he sets his first name that way. In a program written in a language without memory management, such a name could lead to a buffer overflow exploit. A buffer overflow is a vulnerability common to programs written in languages such as C and C++. A buffer overflow occurs when a program sets aside a chunk of memory called a buffer to store data, but when the time comes to store data in that buffer, the data do not fit, so they overflow and overwrite adjacent memory. This ability to overwrite memory with arbitrary attacker-controlled data gives the attacker control over the program. This control is equivalent to giving the attacker the ability to run a program of his own creation on the vulnerable computer.

Penetration testing is an enjoyable career. It is challenging and requires a wide range of technical knowledge and skills including programming, networking, cryptography, and creativity. The worst part, however, is that sometimes you see that a program has flaws but you are unable to exploit them. When this happens, you are left with worry but are not armed with the facts you would need to convince development to make changes.

2. WHY WOULD YOU DO IT?

It can be difficult to allocate resources for penetration testing, but the effort spent will pay great dividends. It is important to find the security flaws before criminals do.

There are significant financial, reputational, and productivity costs associated with a breach. IBM's 2015 Cost

Computer and Information Security Handbook. http://dx.doi.org/10.1016/B978-0-12-803843-7.00075-2

of Data Breach Study [1] found that the average cost of a data breach is $3.8 million, which is a 23% increase just from 2013. If your organization is the victim of a breach, development productivity may grind to a halt while you repair your systems. Finally, your customers and potential customers may start to look elsewhere.

Customers are becoming increasingly security-savvy. It is common for customers to want to see professional security audits of any software they bring into their organization. This means hiring an expensive security team.

Conventional wisdom in software development says that the cost of a bug goes up dramatically when the bug is found in production, and so it is with security. If you can find vulnerabilities during internal testing, the cost to fix it will be lower than if you had found it in production. If you can prevent the creation of vulnerabilities in the first place, you will save even more. Thus, it is important to understand the causes of vulnerabilities, not just the symptoms, and respond to vulnerability findings with architectural changes that will prevent similar vulnerabilities in the future.

In other words, the following examples show how multiple technical techniques can complement one another and how the selection of techniques can relate to risk

concerns with regard to vulnerabilities. These examples are intended as illustrations rather than as recommended combinations of techniques for organizations' assessments of vulnerabilities. Each case is different, and organizations should evaluate the requirements and objectives of each vulnerability assessment when determining an appropriate combination of techniques (see checklist: "An Agenda for Action for Determining an Appropriate Combination of Techniques").

3. HOW DO YOU DO IT?

Think, "Hello world," not "Destroy all partitions with fdisk." That is, test whether you have compromised a system by doing something innocuous such as popping up an alert box, not something damaging such as wiping out a file system. At first glance, this achievement may seem underwhelming. Why should anyone care about something so trivial? Penetration testers intentionally pick nonharmful demonstrations of their capabilities so as not to impede further testing. Also, full weaponization takes time that is better spent on further exploration. Once a tester can demonstrate the ability to insert code that does

---

An Agenda for Action for Determining an Appropriate Combination of Techniques

Organizations often use a combination of techniques to achieve an in-depth security assessment while maintaining an acceptable level of risk to systems and networks. Nontechnical techniques may be used instead of, or in addition to, technical techniques; many assessments use a combination of nontechnical and technical techniques (check all tasks completed):

_____1. Identify technical weaknesses in a system's security architecture and security configuration while minimizing risk from the assessment itself:

    _____**a. Documentation review**. Identify policy and procedure weaknesses and security architecture flaws.

    _____**b. Ruleset and security configuration review**. Identify deviations from organizational security policies in the forms of systems network security architecture and system security flaws.

    _____**c. Wireless scanning**. Identify rogue wireless devices within the proximity of the system and additional security architecture weaknesses related to the wireless networks used by the system.

    _____**d. Network discovery and vulnerability scanning**. Identify all active hosts within the system and their known vulnerabilities.

_____2. Identifying and validating technical weaknesses in a system's security architecture and security configura

tion validation will include attempts to exploit selected vulnerabilities:

    _____**a. Ruleset and security configuration review**. Identify deviations from organizational security policies in the forms of systems network security architecture and system security flaws.

    _____**b. Network discovery and vulnerability scanning**. Identify all active hosts within the system and their known vulnerabilities.

    _____**c.** Penetration test with social engineering. Validate vulnerabilities in the system.

_____3. Identifying and validating technical weaknesses in a system's security architecture and security configuration from an external attacker's viewpoint validation will include attempting to exploit some or all vulnerabilities. Evaluate the effectiveness of the organization's audit capabilities for attacks against the system.

    _____**a. External penetration testing**. Perform external network discovery, port scanning, vulnerability scanning, and attacks to identify and validate system vulnerabilities.

    _____**b. Log review**. Review security control audit logs for the system to determine their effectiveness in capturing information related to external penetration testing activities.

something innocuous such as popping up an alert box, it should be assumed that with time they could do something malicious.

Leave time for remediation. This is a tricky bit of time management. Penetration testing needs to take place after development is finished, but it should be expected that most penetration tests will need to be followed up by a remediation effort. Do not be tempted to start a test before development is finished because new, untested features could contain vulnerabilities.

Fix the underlying problem, not the symptom. Consider a development teams who learns that its application has a cross-site scripting vulnerability. What would happen if instead of fixing the root of the vulnerability, it chose instead to blacklist the word "alert?" This is not a robust solution. An adversary could still execute malicious Java-Script that, for instance, submitted forms in the target Web application. Receiving feedback that penetration testers have found vulnerabilities is painful, but the pain should motivate the development of a cure, not the development of a Band-Aid. The development team in this example is like a person in a gym who uses bad form when lifting weights. The point of this exercise is not to move the barbell; it is to get stronger. If you cheat while doing curls and get your legs and back into it, you have cheated your biceps out of the work it needed to get stronger. You have also ruined your ability to compare this workout with previous workouts and to see your progress. Similarly, if you quickly code up a way to stop the specific diagnostic that the penetration test used, you are still vulnerable to a real attack, but you have removed the ability to check your progress and see when it is fixed. The objective of the penetration test is not just to stop the alert, it is to stop all real-life attacks.

When vulnerabilities are found, think about whether there are other places in the application that do similar things and might be vulnerable to similar attacks. When thinking about remediation, ask yourself if there is a way to fix it once and reuse a shared method or class throughout the application so that there is only one code path worry about.

Prepare Your Test Environment

In preparing your test environment, users and administrators sometimes modify settings to make their systems more secure, resistant to attack, or more compliant with policies and other requirements. Although this can be viewed as positive, changes made under these circumstances are generally maintained only for the duration of the test, after which the systems are returned to their previous configurations. Providing no advance notice of testing to users and administrators helps to address this challenge. Many organizations perform occasional unannounced tests to supplement their announced tests.

Web Application Firewalls

If you have one, disable it for the test. Yes, an attacker would have to go through it, but an attacker has more time than your penetration testers do. Also, a real-life attacker may know weaknesses in your firewall that you do not know, so it may be that your firewall does not provide you with as much protection as you think. With sufficient time, many such defenses can be bypassed. You should build your application as though it has to defend itself and cannot rely on firewalls for safety. The point of the test is to find flaws in your Web application, not to find flaws in a commercial firewall. Therefore, you do not want to do anything to impede the feedback to be gained from the test.

Source Code

Allow source code access during a penetration test. Yes, a real attacker might not have it, but again a real attacker has unlimited time, whereas penetration testers have tight time constraints.

Also, are you sure the adversary does not have it? Insecure source code repositories, compromise of development network, disgruntled current and former employees, and insecure backups are just a few ways an adversary can gain access to source code. If you distribute your application to clients for them to run on their own computers, you should consider your source code as available to an attacker anyway. Executables can be reversed and should be thought of as providing the same information as the source code.

Source code auditing is a useful practice but different from penetration testing. In the context of a penetration test, do not focus on reading the source. Consider it a way to give a high-level view of a system or to answer specific questions raised during testing. For example, use the source to see whether it imports a library with known issues or whether there is a hard-coded encryption key. Do not spend penetration testing time on reading through all the source looking for logic flaws.

Source code access is no silver bullet. It is easy to sink a lot of time into reading through code that is poorly written or overly complex. Another common mistake is to read a version of the code that does not correspond to the executable being tested. This can waste a tremendous amount of time.

Administrative Tasks

If the penetration testers are not the developers of the system, make sure they have been shown basic administration tasks on the application. In particular, make sure they know where the logs are and that they can restart the application if it crashes or becomes unresponsive. The latter is particularly important because they certainly may crash it. It is worthwhile to assign an expert to help the penetration testers in case the system becomes unstable, because you do not want to waste testing time if they break the system.

Legality

Make sure you only perform penetration tests on systems and data you have permission to test! One way to do this is to build your own servers to test. Another way is to perform penetration tests on dedicated training sites listed at the end of the chapter. Even if you have permission, local laws and regulations may prohibit certain activities that may be deemed as wiretapping. Be sure you understand what you are allowed to do, even with permission, in the relevant jurisdictions including yours, the system's, and the users'. If you test a system containing live data, ensure that you understand the data stored in the system, and that your client understands that if you are successful, you may view sensitive data.

Staffing

Generally, companies use two ways to perform a penetration test: They will either keep an internal team on staff full-time to do the testing or retain a third-party testing team. There are pluses and minuses to both approaches. Often, companies chose a mix of both and see the advantage of having an external set of eyes reviewing things.

An internal team will have an opportunity to get to know the application better than a third party team would. An internal team has more time with the project. This extra time may allow for things such as turning vulnerability findings into automated tests that run as part of the build process. This ensures that a fixed vulnerability *stays fixed*. An internal team has an opportunity to work more closely with the development team to establish safe coding practices. However, it is difficult to staff such a team.

An external team, by definition, has a wider breadth of experience. It has worked with a greater variety of applications; it has a greater breadth of experience with vulnerabilities (seeing others' mistakes) and can bring fresh insights to the project.

Primarily, there are two types of penetration testing engagements: that in which you know everything there is to know about the system, and that in which you know nothing except perhaps a URL or a business name. In the former, you develop an approach that, you hope, covers all of the bases over time and results in a regular suite of tests that you develop and repeat against the system with the eventual outcome that all known (and maybe a couple of previously unknown) exploits are attempted. So, is the end goal always Structured Query Language (SQL) injection? Or, is it cracking weak ciphers? And is it passing and intercepting session tokens? These are difficult if not impossible questions to answer specifically. The answer that works is "All of the above," and then some [1].

Assemble Your Toolkit

Before we begin diving into specific tests, let us spend a few paragraphs talking about our tool set. What follows is a list of tools that are commonly useful in penetration tests. This list shows a preference for Web-based technologies because so much software is written for the Web. Whatever the architecture (embedded, mobile, Web, stand-alone, etc.), it is important to have tools to show what is actually happening, not just what the graphical user interface (GUI) shows you.

Linux/Mac

For throwing together quick scripts, there is no substitute for the file-centric design of a UNIX-like system. What is more, many network tools that are available for UNIX-like systems work well with UNIX's pipe redirection. Consider using a Kali virtual machine on your workstation of choice. Kali is a Linux distribution built especially for penetration testing and ethical hacking. It comes with many of the tools you would want already installed. If you run it as a virtual machine, you have a degree of protection in case you break something.

Python/Ruby

You will frequently need to script requests or modify requests, and so on. The ability to write short programs to do this is extremely useful. These two languages are fairly popular in the penetration testing community, so familiarity will make more examples and libraries available to you. Any programming language is fine, however.

Burp

Burp is probably the most popular Web proxy for penetration testers. It sits between your browser and any website you visit. It records all communication between them and allows modification and playback. It is ubiquitous, powerful, programmable, and reasonably priced. Even the free version is powerful. It shows you what actually happened on the network, not just the GUI. It is ubiquitous for Web app pen testers. It is well-supported and has a large community of users.

HttPie/Curl

There are two nice ways to interact with websites or Web services via the command line. They are both good exploratory tools in case someone tells you, "Here's our open Web api. It's RESTful. Have at it." Curl is more widely used but HttPie has nicely formatted output. Both of these tools can work through a Web proxy such as Burp.

4. EXAMPLES OF PENETRATION TEST SCENARIOS

Penetration test scenarios should focus on locating and targeting exploitable defects in the design and implementation of an application, system, or network. Tests should reproduce both the most likely and most damaging attack patterns, including worst-case scenarios such as malicious actions by administrators. Because a penetration test scenario can be designed to simulate an inside attack, an outside attack, or both, external and internal security testing methods are considered. If both internal and external testing are to be performed, external testing usually occurs first.

Structured Query Language Injection

With a little understanding of how relational databases work, we can understand a common attack vector: SQL injection. This is an attack that gives the attacker control over the database. This happens because of a bug in the system that allows attacker input to be treated as code to execute rather than data to store.

Relational databases are typically queried with statements written in SQL. In a relational database, data are stored in tables. A table can be thought of as a grid with rows and columns, like a spreadsheet. There is generally one table for each noun in the system. A row in a table represents an instance of that noun in the system. A column in a table represents an attribute of the noun being modeled.

Let us look at an example. A database for a typical online forum would have one user table named Users (Table 75.1) to store all of the users, one posts table to store all of the posts, etc. A simplified user table might include one column for username, one for email address, and one for time of last login.

Now that we have a table with data in it, how do we search through the data to get just the rows we want? We use SQL statements to query the table. The following SQL statement would return a user whose email address is george@whitehouse.gov:

SELECT * FROM Users WHERE Email = 'george @whitehouse.gov'

Let us break down that statement as shown in the sidebar: "Breaking Down the Statement."

TABLE 75.1 Users		
Username	Email	LastLogin
gwashington	george@whitehouse.gov	July 4, 1776
alincoln	abe@whitehouse.gov	February 12, 1862

Breaking Down the Statement
SELECT: A keyword in SQL. It means to get all of the data described by the rest of the statement. Use SELECT statements when you want to search the database.

*: A wildcard meaning that every column in the table should be returned. Instead of the wildcard, we could explicitly list columns to be returned.

FROM: A keyword in SQL. It indicates that the table to be queried is coming up next.

Users: The name of the table to query.

WHERE: A keyword in S0051L. It means that the criterion of which rows to return is coming up next.

Email = 'george@whitehouse.gov': It means that only rows where the email column is george@whitehouse.gov should be returned. The single quotation marks are used to delimit the email address to match.

So the query we looked at would return a single row, George Washington's row.

It is fine to write a query like that, but it is not useful. That one hard-coded query will only return George Washington's user data. It would be nice to extend that query and expose it through a Web interface so that users could search for user data by typing in an email address of a user in the system. Here is pseudocode for a naive implementation of a search by a user-supplied email address, as shown in the sidebar: "Pseudocode for a Naive Implementation."

Pseudocode for a Naive Implementation
String emailAddress = getEmailAddressFromUser Request();
executeQuery("SELECT * FROM Users WHERE Email = ' + emailAddress + '");
So if a user typed in abe@whitehouse.gov, the resulting SQL statement would be:
SELECT * FROM Users WHERE Email = 'abe@ whitehouse.gov'
Similarly, if a user typed in whharrison@whitehouse.gov, the resulting SQL statement would be:
SELECT * FROM Users WHERE Email =' whharrison@whitehouse.gov'
But what if we had a malicious user who did not enter a legitimate email address, but instead typed in:
' OR Email != '
That is a strange-looking "email address," but our program would dutifully concatenate it to create the following SQL statement:
SELECT * FROM Users WHERE Email ='' OR Email != ''
The WHERE clause in this statement is a tautology: a statement that is true by definition. We do not have to know which email addresses are in the table to know that each one is either equal to the empty string or not equal to the empty string. So when the database interprets this query, it will return every row in the table [1,2].

The vulnerability shown in the sidebar, "Pseudocode for a Naive Implementation," is called an SQL injection. Because the code takes input from the user and executes it as part of an SQL statement, the attacker can execute arbitrary SQL. From here, it is straightforward for an attacker to craft malicious "email addresses" that abuse this search functionality to perform arbitrary SQL commands. SQL is a powerful language that does much more than just querying a single table. SQL statements can join data together from multiple tables, insert data, modify data, and delete data. In general, SQL injection means that an attacker has complete control of the database. This is a dire outcome from seemingly innocuous search functionality.

To prevent this, a developer should never take input from a user and concatenate it into an SQL statement. Instead a developer should use prepared statement functionality that is part of nearly every relational database system. With a prepared statement, no string concatenation takes place. Instead, an SQL statement is built up with placeholder tokens, something like this:

SELECT * FROM Users WHERE Email = ?

The application code then sends the SQL with placeholders along with a list of data that the database will use in place of the placeholders. The power of this approach is that the SQL and the data are always kept separate. This means that the attacker's input never gets executed as SQL. Instead, the attacker's input is always treated as data. If an attacker inserts a long string, that will result in the database rejecting it because it was expecting a date.

One reason SQL injection is so devastating is that most of the time a Web application will have a single database account to perform all of the database work. Once the application has been tricked into performing SQL on behalf of the attacker, it does so in a database context that has full permissions on the entire database. For this reason, it is worth considering creating multiple database users to do work on behalf of a single Web application. This way, if a query in one part of the application is broken, only some of the tables would be under the control of the attacker. This adds complexity to the system, however, so it should be done carefully. This is not a replacement for using prepared statements. Whereas proper use of prepared statements prevents the problem, use of multiple database users merely reduces the impact of the problem.

Injections are a common method of attack and can show up in many parts of a system. The essence of an injection attack is a program taking user-supplied data and combining them with executable code. That code does not have to be SQL. It could also be JavaScript, or commands executed in a shell such as a Bourne Again Shell (bash). It is important to maintain a separation between code and user-supplied data. If that separation is not maintained, an attacker will be able to execute code on the server in the

context of the application. To prevent this, make sure that user-supplied data are never concatenated directly into an executable statement. If the user-supplied data are to be used with SQL, use prepared statements. If they are going to be used with something else, translate appropriately. For instance, if user-supplied data are going to be used as part of a JavaScript statement, you can use a well-tested library to strip out JavaScript special characters.

Another part of the defense is to have easily reusable code for the dynamic parts of the system. If the easiest way to build the functionality just happens to be the safe way, the developers on the team are more likely to get it right. Also, you do not want to duplicate the effort to research how to use user-supplied data in a search, for instance. Once that research has been done, be sure to share that knowledge with the team in the form of reusable code.

Misplaced Trust in Attacker-Controlled (Client Side) Code

Another common source of security flaws is misplaced trust in client side code. Developers spend a lot of time thinking about the flow of execution in client side code that they write. Therefore, it is easy to slip into thinking that client side code will always work the way they have planned. But anything that happens on the client side is under control of the adversary. With just an intercepting Web proxy or a Hypertext Transfer Protocol client library, an attacker can modify or altogether bypass any client side code. One way to keep this in mind is to use the phrase "attacker-controlled" whenever one might otherwise use the phrase "client side."

To see how trust in client side code can be abused, we will consider a Web application with a page that contains a button that should be enabled only for administrative users. A naive implementation of this might be to include the markup for this button every time the page is loaded regardless of who is logged in, and then disable the button in JavaScript if the user is not an administrative user. An attacker could modify the JavaScript by using an intercepting Web proxy and reenable the button even though the server had sent JavaScript to disable it.

One solution to this would be to put server side code in place that includes the button in the markup only when the currently logged-in user has the appropriate permissions. This is a good first step because it keeps the attacker even from seeing the button exists. It is not sufficient, however; if the attacker were able to guess the name of the button or has previous knowledge of it, he would be able to submit a request to the server that included the button click even though the page he loaded *did not* have a button present. An attacker would be able to accomplish this again by using an intercepting Web proxy. A programmatic Web client or a command line client such as Curl or HTTPie would also be able to do this. These methods intercept the post from the attacker-controlled browser, allow it to be modified by the attacker, and then sent up to the host, which cannot tell the difference.

A robust solution to this problem enforces the permissioning on the server side, where an attacker cannot interfere. There is nothing wrong with putting restrictions on the client side for usability's sake, but it has to be enforced on the server side. If the server gets a request that contains the privileged button for a nonadministrative user, the server must reject the request.

Custom Cryptography

Cryptography is notoriously difficult to get right. If you find custom cryptography during a penetration test, you will almost certainly find vulnerabilities. Breaking cryptography is too broad a subject to cover here. Rather than fail in the attempt to do so, I will leave you with several quotations from security experts whom I find illuminating:

> Schneier's law [2], which comes to us from cryptographer and author Bruce Schneier, states [1,2]:

> *Anyone, from the most clueless amateur to the best cryptographer, can create an algorithm that [they themselves] can't break. It's not even hard. What is hard is creating an algorithm that no one else can break, even after years of analysis. And the only way to prove that is to subject the algorithm to years of analysis by the best cryptographers around.*

This sums up nicely why custom cryptography is so dangerous. Custom cryptography has not gone through that analysis. As a side note, it is interesting that the roots of this quotation date back to Charles Babbage, who said [3]:

> *One of the most singular characteristics of the art of deciphering is the strong conviction possessed by every person, even moderately acquainted with it, that he is able to construct a cipher which nobody else can decipher.*

Security expert Thomas Ptacek set out to illustrate how easy it is to write fatally flawed cryptography by putting together a fantastic series of cryptography challenges [4]. As he wrote in the introduction to the site:

> *The current state of crypto software security is similar to the state of software security in the 1990s. Specifically: until around 1995, it was not common knowledge that software built by humans might have trouble counting. As a result, nobody could size a buffer properly, and humanity incurred billions of dollars in cleanup after a decade and a half of emergency fixes for memory corruption vulnerabilities.*

> *Counting is not a hard problem. But cryptography is. There are just a few things you can screw up to get the size of a buffer wrong. There are tens, probably hundreds, of obscure little things you can do to take a cryptosystem that should be secure even against an adversary with more CPU cores than there are atoms in the solar system, and make it solvable with a Perl script and 15 seconds. Don't take our word for it: do the challenges and you'll see.*

If you have an interest in cryptography, I cannot recommend Cryptopals highly enough. It is fun and eye-opening. You will learn about many implementation choices that seem harmless but turn out to be show stoppers.

5. SUMMARY

The pen tester's education is never completed. There is always more to learn. Your mission as a pen tester is to find strange new bugs that you can exploit, seek out new software weaknesses, and boldly find new vulnerabilities that nobody ever would have expected to see. To do this, you must constantly educate yourself, be willing to explore and try new things, expand your skills, and above all, have fun!

Finally, let us move on to the real interactive part of this chapter: review questions/exercises, hands-on projects, case projects, and the optional team case project. The answers and/or solutions by chapter can be found in Appendix K.

CHAPTER REVIEW QUESTIONS/ EXERCISES

True/False

1. True or False? Penetration testing is testing that finds security flaws to exploit.
2. True or False? It can be difficult to allocate resources for penetration testing, but the effort spent will pay few dividends.
3. True or False? When vulnerabilities are found, think about whether there are other places in the application that do similar things and might be vulnerable to similar attacks.
4. True or False? In preparing your test environment, users and administrators sometimes modify settings to make their systems more secure, resistant to attack, or more compliant with policies and other requirements.
5. True or False? A real-life attacker may know weaknesses in your firewall that you do not know, so it may be that your firewall does not provide you with as much protection as you think.

Multiple Choice

1. Allow source code access during a:
   A. Storage area network (SAN) switch test
   B. Penetration test
   C. Promotional email test

    D. Malformed request denial of service test

    E. Data controller test

2. If the penetration testers are not the developers of the system, make sure they have been shown basic administration tasks on the:

    A. Network attached storage (NAS)

    B. Location technology

    C. Valid

    D. Application

    E. Bait

3. Another common source of security flaws is misplaced trust in:

    A. Data minimization

    B. Fabric

    C. Client side code

    D. Strong narrative

    E. Security

4. If you find custom cryptography during a penetration test, you will almost certainly find:

    A. Call data floods

    B. Greedy strategies

    C. Vulnerabilities

    D. SAN protocols

    E. Taps

5. For throwing together quick scripts, there is no substitute for the file-centric design of a:

    A. UNIX-like system

    B. Tape library

    C. Internet Protocol storage access

    D. Configuration file

    E. Server policy

EXERCISE

Problem

Who within an organization is authorized to conduct penetration testing?

Hands-on Projects

Project

What would an organization's penetration testing logistics look like?

Case Projects

Problem

How should an organization handle sensitive data?

Optional Team Case Project

Problem

What should an organization do in the event of an incident?

REFERENCES

[1] IBM. http://www.ibm.com/security/data-breach/.

[2] B. Schneier. https://www.schneier.com/blog/archives/2011/04/schneiers_law.html.

[3] C. Babbage. http://www-history.mcs.st-and.ac.uk/history/Extras/Babbage_deciphering.html.

[4] T. Ptacek. http://www.cryptopals.com.

Chapter 76

System Security

Lauren Collins
Winning Edge Communications, New Lennox, IL, United States

Note: This chapter is available in its entirety online at store.elsevier.com/product.jsp?isbn= 9780128038437 (click the Resources tab at the bottom of the page).

1. ABSTRACT

Computer security is one division of technology; it is often referred to as information security and is applied to the systems we work on as well as the networks that transmit the data. The term computer security often necessitates cooperative procedures and appliances by which such sensitive and confidential information and services are secure from an attack by unauthorized activities, usually achieved by treacherous individuals. Hackers plan events to take place on systems unexpectedly and usually target an audience or targeted data set that was well thought out and carefully planned. This chapter objective includes familiarizing yourself with how to protect your information from harm, and also presents ways to make your data readily available for access to an intended audience of users. The author believes a real-world perspective of hardware security is crucial to building secure systems in practice, but it has not been sufficiently addressed in the security research community. Many of the sections in this chapter strive to cover this gap.

2. CONTENTS

Computer and Information Security Handbook. http://dx.doi.org/10.1016/B978-0-12-803843-7.00076-4

Chapter 77

Access Controls

Lauren Collins

Winning Edge Communications, New Lennox, IL, United States

1. INFRASTRUCTURE WEAKNESSES: DISCRETIONARY ACCESS CONTROL (DAC), MANDATORY ACCESS CONTROL (MAC), AND ROLE-BASED ACCESS CONTROL (RBAC)

The dichotomy between types of companies and implementing layers of security led to the use of three types of access control mechanisms: discretionary access control (DAC), mandatory access control (MAC), and role-based access control (RBAC).

Discretionary Access Control

DAC, also known as file permissions, is the access control in Unix and Linux systems. Whenever you have seen the syntax drwxr-xs-x, it is the ugo abbreviation for owner, group, and other permissions in the directory listing. Ugo is the abbreviation for user access, group access, and other system user's access, respectively. These file permissions are set to allow or deny access to members of their own group, or any other groups. Modification of file, directory, and devices are achieved using the chmod command. Tables 77.1 and 77.2 illustrate the syntax to assign or remove permissions. Permissions can be assigned using the character format:

```
Chmod [ugoa] [+-=] [rwxXst] fileORdirectoryName
```

In DAC, usually the resource owner will control who can access resources. Everyone has administered a system in which they decide to give full rights to everyone so that it is less to manage. The issue with this approach is that users are allowed not only to read, write, and execute files, but also to delete any files they have access to. This author has so often seen system files deleted in error by users, or simply by the user's lack of knowledge. This is an instance where DAC could be seen as a disadvantage, or less advantageous.

Mandatory Access Control

MAC regulates user process access to resources based on an organizational security policy. This particular policy is a collection of rules that specify what types of access are allowed on a system. System policy is associated with MAC comparably to how firewall rules are associated with firewalls. Security-enhanced Linux (SELinux) is a Linux kernel implementation of a supple MAC mechanism called type enforcement. These policies restrict users and processes to the minimal amount of privilege required to perform tasks. Type enforcement uses a type identifier and

TABLE 77.1 Notation to Add, Remove Access, and How to Explicitly Assign Access

+	add access
−	remove access
=	access explicitly assigned

TABLE 77.2 Notation for File Permissions

r	Permission to read file
	Permission to read a directory (also requires "x")
w	Permission to delete or modify a file
	Permission to delete or modify files in a directory
x	Permission to execute a file/script
	Permission to read a directory (also requires "r")
s	Set user or group ID on execution
u	Permissions granted to the user who owns the file
t	Set sticky bit. Execute file/script as a user root for regular user

Computer and Information Security Handbook. http://dx.doi.org/10.1016/B978-0-12-803843-7.00077-6

assigns it to every user and object; these authorizations are defined in an SELinux policy.

The SELinux implementation of MAC exercises a type of enforcement mechanism that necessitates every subject and object be assigned an identifier. We will use the terms subject and object for this example. Consider the subject as a user or a process, and the object as a file or a process. Characteristically, a subject cannot access an object unless the type identifier assigned to the subject is authorized to access the object. The default policy is to deny all access that is not specifically allowed. Authorization is determined by rules defined in the SELinux policy. The following is an example of rule-granting access:

```
allow httpd_t httpd_sys_content_t : file (ioctol
read getattr lock);
```

where the subject http daemon is assigned the type identifier of httpd_t and is granted permissions ioctol, read, gettattr, and lock for any file object assigned in the type identifier httpd_sys_content_t. Basically, the http daemon is allowed to read a rule that is assigned the type identifier httpsd_sys_content_t. This is a simpler rule; there are thousands of rules, varying in complexity. There are also many types of identifiers for use with subjects and objects. SELinux adds type enforcement to standard Linux distributions. To access an object, the user must have both the appropriate file permissions (DAC) and the correct SELinux access. ELinux security context covers three capacities:

1. The user
2. The role
3. The type identifier

By running the ls command with the -Z switch, conventional file information is displayed along with the security context for each element in the subdirectory. See the following example, where the security context for the index.html file encompasses user_u as the user, object_r as the role, and httpd_sys_content_t as the type identifier:

```
[web_admin@localhost html]$ls -Z index.html -rw-r-r-
web_admin web_admin user_u:object_r:httpd_sys_con-
tent_t index.html
```

Role-Based Access Control

RBAC is a method whereby only authorized users can gain access to an environment and the sessions contained in the environment, as shown in Fig. 77.1. Some refer to RBAC as role-based security due to the roles an organization creates to assign permissions to users, who perform specific functions, and such users acquire their roles and rights when their account is created. In Active Directory, either the users are in a department that assigns rights by department or the users have customized access based off

their role to perform a job function. Referring to the model in Fig. 77.1, use the following conventions:

- Subject (S)—person or agent
- Role (R)—job function
- Permission (P)—authorization to access a resource or utility
- Session (SE)—mapping, including S, R, and/or P
- Subject Assignment (SA)
- Permission Agent (PA)
- Partial Instructional Role Hierarchy (RH)—$\geq$(where $x \geq y$ requires x to inherit permissions of y)
  1. Subjects are allowed multiple roles.
  2. Roles are allowed to contain multiple subjects.
  3. Roles are allowed to assign multiple permissions.
  4. Permissions can be allocated to multiple roles.
  5. Operations can be allocated to multiple permissions.
  6. Permissions can be allocated many operations.

Whereas a constraint positions a provisional rule on the possibility of inherited permissions from contrasting rules, it can thus be utilized to attain applicable partitions of duties. As such, a user should not be permitted to both create a login or to empower such an account creation. RBAC is comprised of three principal guidelines:

1. Role assignment: A subject can implement permission once the subject has been designated or has allocated a role.
2. Role authorization: A subject's dynamic role requires permission for the subject. Refer to rule 1, above, which warrants users only inherit roles for which they are sanctioned.
3. Permission authorization: A subject can employ permission merely if the permission is approved for the subject's functional role. Refer to rules 1 and 2; rule 3 confirms users can only carry out permissions for which they are allowed.

Several additional controls can be applied on top of the former three rules, and roles can be combined in a hierarchy where higher-level roles consider permissions retained by subroles. In larger organizations, typically those with over 500 users, administrators tend to combine MAC or DAC.

As previously mentioned, RBAC can be referred to as an adaptable secure access control. RBAC diverges from access control lists (ACLs) in that it appoints permissions to exclusive operations for users to perform their job functions, rather than to low-level data objects. Let's say an access control list could be utilized to allow or deny write access to a certain file system, but it is unable to dictate how that file could be changed.

As an example, in financial systems, an operation may seek to create a new trading account or to create a new database for a particular trading product. The assignment of

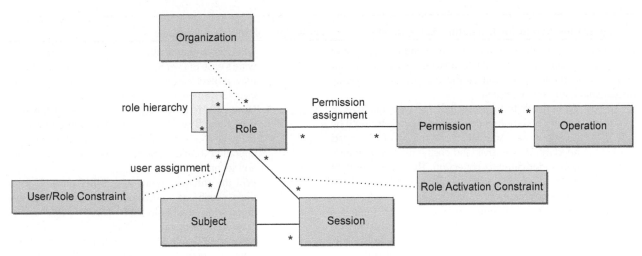

FIGURE 77.1   Role-based access control model that restricts environment access to authorized users.

the permission to perform a particular operation is meaningful in this instance, since the operations are so granular with meaning to an application. You would not want college interns creating new trading accounts utilizing real money and would prefer that only an administrator of the risk department had those rights. Even concerning trading limits, imagine if traders could go into the application and raise their trading limits themselves. Risk controls are put into place to protect assets and rights.

RBAC is well suited to separate liabilities, ensuring that more than two people are involved in authorizing critical operations. Integrating RBAC benefits access control policies and aids the information technology (IT) infrastructure where Active Directory, SQL Server, and any other proprietary applications are concerned.

Logical Access Controls

Logical access control tools are used for credentials, validation, authorization, and accountability in an infrastructure and the systems within. These components enforce access control measures for systems, applications, processes, and information. This type of access control can also be embedded inside an application, operating system, database, or infrastructure administrative system. Physical access control is a mechanical form and can be thought of as physical access to a room with a key. The line is often unclear whether or not an element can be considered physical or logical access control. Physical access is controlled by software, the chip on an access card, and an electric lock grant access through software. Thus, physical access should be considered a logical access control. A benefit of having logical access controlled centrally in a system allows for a user's physical access permissions to be instantaneously revoked or amended.

For example, when an employee is fired, his or her badge access can be disabled, as can the employee's multiple system access accounts. Persons in possession of the proper access card, the appropriate security level, and in some cases a personal identification number (PIN) are granted entry to a room once the credentials are checked against a database.

Physical Access Controls

Physical access control is a mechanical form and can be thought of as physical access to a room with a key. The line is often unclear whether or not an element can be considered a physical or a logical access control. When physical access is controlled by software, the chip on an access card and an electric lock grants access through software (see checklist: An Agenda for Action for Evaluating Authentication and Access Control Software Products), which should be considered a logical access control. That being said, incorporating biometrics adds another layer to gain entry into a room. This is considered a physical access control. Identity authentication is based on a person's physical characteristics. The most common physical access controls are used at hospitals, police stations, government offices, data centers, and any area that contains sensitive equipment and/or data.

A significant element surrounding physical access controls as opposed to conventional security solutions is its capacity to capture multifaceted and detailed images of physical traits, encode such traits in files, and evaluate sets of data within seconds. Homeowners are now considering this layer of security since loved ones and belongings are sacred, and this layer of security is not possible to forge. Physical access controls not only enhance security but also allow for efficiency, only requiring one form of authentication, a physical trait (fingerprint, retina, palm of hand). This eliminates the risk of a card being stolen or a PIN being hacked.

An Agenda for Action for Evaluating Authentication and Access Control Software Products

Before one starts evaluating authentication and access control software products, they'll need to answer several questions about the technology, as well as the organization's specific needs (check all tasks completed):

_____1. **What needs to be protected?** The type and level of protection required depends on the assets you'll be safeguarding. After all, national security secrets need more extensive (and costly) protection than a public domain data collection. This is an important matter you will need to discuss with a security professional.

_____2. **Which type of authentication is best?** There are four basic ways of authenticating users: asking for something only the authorized user knows (such as a password), testing for the presence of something only the authorized user has (like a smart card), obtaining some nonforgeable biological or behavioral measurement of the user (like a fingerprint), or determining that the user is located at a place where only the authorized user can enter. The best (and most effective) solutions require a combination of two or more authentication methods.

_____3. **Is the software compatible with existing systems and devices?** The solution must be compatible with current operating systems and applications. Compatibility is a particularly big concern with biometric systems, since existing hardware and applications often must be adapted and/or reprogrammed to work with these tools.

_____4. **Does it offer an acceptable trade-off between security and convenience?** Organizations must balance the value of the information being protected

with the authentication and access control software's ease of use. Solutions that are difficult to use may protect systems, but only at the expense of user convenience and productivity.

_____5. **How easy is it to upgrade and expand the software?** You'll want a product that you can use for many years. Over that time span, it will need to be upgraded to accommodate new security practices and technologies.

_____6. **Will the software work with other types of solutions, such as antifraud and user behavior-monitoring technologies?** These days, access control is often a part of a multifaceted enterprise security initiative. It's important to know if the software you're looking at plays well with others.

_____7. **What are the product's management features?** Authentication and access control software products are notoriously difficult to set up and maintain. Look for management features that are straightforward and easy to understand.

_____8. **Has the software ever been defeated? If so, how?** If the product has ever been hacked, you'll want to know what steps the vendor has taken to make its technology more secure.

_____9. **How much does the software cost?** Don't look at the license fee alone. The total product cost includes acquisition, customization, deployment, management, user training, extra hardware, productivity impact, and maintenance. Ask vendors for detailed statements, policies, and prices for each of these factors.

---

2. STRENGTHENING THE INFRASTRUCTURE: AUTHENTICATION SYSTEMS

Authentication might involve confirming the identity of a person or software program (see checklist: An Agenda for Action for Evaluating Authentication and Access Control Software Products). The introduction to this chapter mentioned three categories authentication may fall under. Whether it is knowledge specific to a user, a piece of information the user has, or the position the user is in, each of them aims to verify the user's identity. Each authentication factor covers a range of elements used to authenticate or verify a person's identity prior to being granted access. Examples include a computer approving a transaction request, electronically signing a document or other work product, administrators granting authority to users with management approval, and a chain of authority that must be established to keep the controls in place and consistent.

Security investigations have determined that the standard for verification must include components from at least two factors, and preferably three. Three authentication factors are as follows:

1. *Ownership factors*: something tangible the user has (ID card, security token, software token, phone, or cell phone)
2. *Knowledge factors*: a piece of information the user knows (password, pass phrase, PIN, or a challenge response, such as a security question only the user knows the answer to)
3. *Physical factors*: a physical trait of an individual (fingerprint, retinal pattern, signature, voice, or another biometrical identifier)

A common example of a two-factor authentication is when one uses his or her ATM card and has to enter a PIN. Some organizations not only require a username and password to authenticate to the virtual private network (VPN) but also give employees a token with a random set of numbers that change every 30 s. The author has visited multiple data center facilities, and while some differ in their choice of the second authentication factor, all data centers require two-factor authentication. While one data center may require use of a badge and your pointer finger fingerprint, others may use a PIN along with a biometric hand scan. Additionally, a handful of facilities include a third factor for authentication, a mantrap. The mantrap screens the person's height, weight, facial features, and retina. These facilities institute higher security standards and are generally financial or governmental collocation sites.

Kerberos and Challenge-Handshake Authentication Protocol (CHAP)

Kerberos is a secure method for authenticating a request for a service in a network. Kerberos was developed in the Athena Project at the Massachusetts Institute of Technology (MIT). Based on the name of the Needham—Schroeder protocol, Kerberos is named after a three-headed dog who guarded the gates of Hades in Greek mythology. Kerberos lets a user request an encrypted "ticket" from an authentication process that can then be used to request a particular service from a server. The user's password does not have to pass through the network. MIT offers a download for both the client and server versions of Kerberos, or you can buy a copy.

One weakness is that Kerberos requires the continuous availability of a central server. Knock out the Kerberos server and no one can log in. This problem can be mitigated by using multiple Kerberos servers. The technology is also sensitive to clock settings and won't work properly unless the clocks of the involved hosts are synchronized. Default configuration requires that clock times be no more than 10 min apart. Additionally, the administration of the protocol is not standardized and differs between server implementations. And since the secret keys for all users are stored on the central server, a compromise of that server will jeopardize all users' secret keys.

Big data is a hot subject these days, and without question an increasing number of enterprise information security teams are going to be asked about the security-related ramifications of big data projects. There are many issues to look into, but here are a few ideas to make the big data environment more secure during architecture and implementation phases:

1. Create data controls as close to the data as possible, since much of this data isn't "owned" by the security team. The risk of having big data traversing your network is that you have large amounts of confidential data—such as credit-card data, Social Security numbers, and personally identifiable information (PII)—residing in new places and being used in new

ways. Also, you're usually not going to see terabytes of data siphoned from an organization, but you should be concerned about the search for patterns to find the content in these databases. Keep the security as close to the data as possible and don't rely on firewalls, intrusion prevention systems (IPSs), data loss prevention (DLP), or other systems to protect the data.

2. Verify that sensitive fields are indeed protected by using encryption so that when the data is analyzed, manipulated, or sent to other areas of the organization, you're limiting risk of exposure. All sensitive information needs to be encrypted once you have control over it.

3. After you've made the move to encrypt data, the next logical step is to concern yourself with key management. There are a few new ways to perform key management, including creating keys on an as-needed basis so you don't have to store them.

4. In Hadoop designs, review the Hadoop Distributed File System (HDFS) permissions of the cluster and verify that all access to HDFS is authenticated. When first implemented, Hadoop frameworks were notoriously bad at performing authentication of users and services. This allows users to impersonate as a user the cluster services themselves. You can be authenticated to the Hadoop framework using Kerberos, which can be used with HDFS access tokens to authenticate to the name node.

Challenge-Handshake Authentication Protocol (CHAP) is an authentication scheme used by Point-to-Point Protocol (PPP) hosts to authorize the identity of remote users and clients. CHAP occasionally validates the identity of the client by using a three-way handshake. This occurs simultaneously as the initial link is established, and can take place randomly at any time. Substantiation is based on a shared secret—for example, the user or client's password. Steps in the CHAP authentication scheme are as follows (reference Table 77.3):

1. Once the link has been established, the authenticator sends a "challenge" message to the peer.

2. The peer then responds with a determined value using a one-way hash function on the challenge and the secret combined.

3. The authenticator checks the response against the expected answer, or calculation of the expected hash value. If the values match, the authenticator acknowledges the authentication. If it does not match, the connection is terminated.

Randomly, the Authenticator Sends Another Challenge to the Peer and Repeats the Steps Mentioned Above

The ID chosen for the random challenge is also used in the corresponding response, success, and failure

TABLE 77.3 Authentication Scheme Used by CHAP Packets.

	CHAP Packets					
Description	1 Byte	1 Byte	2 Bytes	1 Byte	Variable	Variable
Challenge	Code = 1	ID	Length	Response length	Challenge value	Name
Response	Code = 2	ID	Length	Response length	Response value	Name
Success	Code = 3	ID	Length		Message	
Failure	Code = 4	ID	Length		Message	

packets. A new challenge with a new ID must be different from the last challenge with another ID. If the success or failure is lost, the same response can be sent again and will trigger the same success or failure indication. For MD5 as hash, the response value is MD5(ID||secret||challenge), the MD5 for the concatenation of ID, secret, and challenge.

Wireless Security Access Controls

The IT Department has just been notified that the company wishes to allow personnel to access the company network from personal devices. A common approach to achieve this is to create separately named networks, Service Set Identifiers (SSIDs), and corresponding Virtual Local Area Networks (VLANs) inside your wired network. Segregating VLANs will separate the traffic between the other network traffic. Public wireless can be placed on a separate VLAN rather than private wireless, and there could also be a Mobile Wireless VLAN added to separate laptop wireless traffic from mobile devices.

However, you still want network access protection and a secure and simple way for key personnel to register their own devices for secure access to a private wireless network. Ask your wireless vendor if it sells a visitor management feature or a registration portal capable of walking personal devices through authorization and Wi-Fi provisioning. Another method for network access protection and wireless access control could be using a Mobile Device Manager (MDM) to drive these tasks.

WPA2-Personal requires every device to supply a Preshared Key (PSK) derived from a passphrase. For example, devices on your trading floor might be required to supply the same random string of 20 characters known only to your IT department and configured during deployment. This method is often combined with MAC address filtering, so that only known devices with the right PSK are granted access. However, MAC address filters are easily bypassed, as are PSKs that are too short or too easy to guess. WPA2-Enterprise requires every device to

complete an 802.1X log-on process that can support various authentication methods. For example, each device on your trading floor might be required to prove its identity with a unique digital certificate. Alternatively, each device might be required to supply a unique username and password configured during deployment and known only to your IT department. With this Wi-Fi access control method, you will be able to tell which individual machines are logged on. When used with certificates, WPA2-Enterprise is less vulnerable to password sharing and reuse, which are common problems when employees know a valid username/password or PSK and simply configure those into personal devices.

3. SUMMARY

Although only the most commonly used access mechanisms are discussed in this chapter, many extensions, combinations, and different mechanisms are possible. Trade-offs and limitations are involved with all mechanisms and access control designs, so it is the user's responsibility to determine the best-fit access control mechanisms that work for their business functions and requirements.

Also included in this chapter are the most commonly used access control policies. Since access control policies are targeted to specific access control requirements, unlike access control mechanisms, specific limitations cannot be inherently associated with them. And like access control mechanisms, it is up to the users to select the best policies for their needs. In addition to the limitations and issues, quality biometrics depends not only on the consideration of administration cost, but also on the flexibility of the mechanism helping the user in assessing or selecting among access control systems.

Finally, let's move on to the real interactive part of this chapter: review questions/exercises, hands-on projects, case projects, and optional team case project. The answers and/or solutions by chapter can be found in the Online Instructor's Solutions Manual.

CHAPTER REVIEW QUESTIONS/ EXERCISES

True/False

1. True or False? The dichotomy between types of companies and implementing layers of security led to the use of three types of access control mechanisms: denial of access control, mandatory access control, and role-based access control.
2. True or False? Discretionary access control (DAC), also known as file permissions, is the access control in Unix and Windows systems.
3. True or False? Mandatory access control (MAC) regulates user process access to resources based on an organizational security policy.
4. True or False? Role-based access control (RBAC) is a method whereby only authorized users can lose access to an environment and the sessions contained in the environment.
5. True or False? Role-based access controls tools are used for credentials, validation, authorization, and accountability in an infrastructure and the systems within.

Multiple Choice

1. What is a mechanical form and can be thought of as physical access to a room with a key?
   A. Qualitative analysis
   B. Vulnerabilities
   C. Spoofing
   D. Physical access control
   E. DHS
2. What might involve confirming the identity of a person or software program?
   A. Firewall
   B. Risk assessment
   C. Scale
   D. Authentication
   E. Bait
3. What is a secure method for authenticating a request for a service in a network?
   A. Organizations
   B. Fabric
   C. Kerberos
   D. Web application firewall
   E. Security
4. What requires every device to supply a Preshared Key (PSK) derived from a passphrase?
   A. Cabinet-level state office
   B. Denial-of-service attack
   C. WPA2-Personal
   D. SAN protocol
   E. Taps
5. What is an authentication scheme used by Point-to-Point Protocol (PPP) hosts to authorize the identity of remote users and clients?
   A. Systems security plan
   B. Consumer privacy protection
   C. IP storage access
   D. Vulnerability
   E. Challenge-Handshake Authentication Protocol (CHAP)

EXERCISE

Problem

Which type of authentication is best?

Hands-On Projects

Project

Is the access control and authentication software compatible with existing systems and devices?

Case Projects

Problem

Does access control and authentication software offer an acceptable trade-off between security and convenience?

Optional Team Case Project

Problem

How easy is it to upgrade and expand access control and authentication software?

Chapter 78

Endpoint Security

Keith Lewis
kCura, Chicago, IL, United States

1. INTRODUCTION: ENDPOINT SECURITY DEFINED

To begin, what is an Endpoint? It's accessed by computer devices such as PC desktops, laptops, servers, appliances, workstations, tablets, mobile devices, VoIP devices, and any other physical computer-based tool your company or organization are currently using to support your business needs. Protection is the priority for Endpoint security (EPS) solutions (see Fig. 78.1) when it comes to potential threats that could impact these devices. These preventative functions include:

- Virus protection
- Antimalware protection systems
- Packet variant prevention systems
- Encryption protection
- Data loss and recovery systems
- Browser exploits protection
- Application whitelist capabilities
- Behavior monitoring
- Cyber threat protection
- Mobile and desktop system protection
- Multilayer network protection
- Prevention, detection, analysis with immediate response functionality
- Passive and active (real-time) capabilities

Essentially, protection is the prevention of any logical, physical, or network-based activity intent on malicious objectives to steal or cause harm to your computer data information or device functionality. Using EPS solutions as the digital "watchdog, shield, and doctor" role for your computer devices will help secure and safeguard these systems [1].

2. ENDPOINT SOLUTION: OPTIONS

Computer network infrastructures must have organized and secured framework methodologies when remote computers

such as laptops or wireless enabled devices connect to them. Using industry-supported toolsets such as Symantec, Kaspersky, Sophos, Bitdefender, McAfee, TrendMicro, or Microsoft System Center Endpoint protection systems [2] are some of the highly rated systems available today. This is the foundation and philosophy of architecture computer network design when it comes to EPS. This network security framework and approach helps deliver to your network engineering teams more support alternatives with control features when it comes to managing the security for these devices connecting to your network. Predicting and securing possible infection routes for a viruses or malware attack to take advantage of is key for an effective defense-in-depth approach encompassing all network communication access points on your company or organization's topology [3].

Hackers attempting to infiltrate your network systems would have limited access point potentials to break into, thanks to EPS Planning Risk Management. Customer and employee user authorization security group settings that are setup to use role-based configuration profiles can also leverage and benefit from EPS solutions for easier-to-manage security and support coverage.

3. STANDARD REQUIREMENTS: SECURITY DECISIONS

EPS requires equipment and software standards and the permission structures surrounding them before giving someone access to your corporate environment. An example of this could be giving only specific employees or vendors tunneled access using your Virtual Private Network (VPN) solution that requires the computer accessing this network to have the latest in signature and application virus security protection. This type of security should also prevent a user over VPN from trying to access a Linux system versus a Microsoft PC system, depending on your company's operating system (OS) support

Computer and Information Security Handbook. http://dx.doi.org/10.1016/B978-0-12-803843-7.00078-8

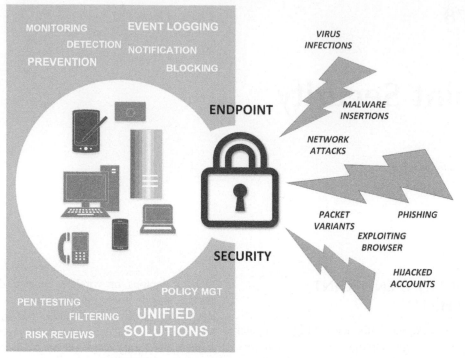

FIGURE 78.1 Endpoint security (EPS) unified solutions.

requirements and authorization settings. These requirement policy settings, like VPN, OS version, or antivirus software, fortifies your network threat prevention strategy from foreign, unsupported software or devices trying to access your private networking systems [4].

When considering to purchase and implement an Endpoint Unified Security Platform, Risk Assessment Evaluations should be conducted first to identify the vulnerabilities found in all levels of your infrastructure environment. Discussions with management and the security support teams should be conducted with careful planning in mind. Investing in security has good business justifications, but not when the expense is so large in platform purchasing and resource allocation that impacts a company's budget to the limits. Having a third-party subject matter expert and audit assessor specializing in security design (see Fig. 78.2) should be strongly considered as your business takes on this initiative.

4. ENDPOINT ARCHITECTURE: FUNCTIONAL CHALLENGES

Careful risk planning (see Fig. 78.2) is critical when it comes to designing and implementing your overall EPS defense strategy into your computer networking environments. It's important to anticipate the critical access points to protect as well as the first time implementation and ongoing costs involved to maintain the EPS solution. Some of the planning challenges that network engineers and technical support teams can run into are:

● Performance versus security quality
● Administrative "lifecycle" challenges
● Choke control

Performance Versus Security Quality

EPS solutions such as Symantec or Kaspersky End Protection suites can give outstanding protection from PC-to-server or leverage their Mobile Device Management (MDM) solution for wireless devices, such as mobile smartphones or tablets. However, there is such a thing as "too much of a good thing." Many of these solutions can tend to overwhelm your existing device system resources as they attempt to do fully or passive scanning, encryption processing, or traffic monitoring at the network card, file system, or browser level for your computer devices. When EPS solutions are installed, it's mostly up to the customer working with the vendor to identify what correct amount of enabled security features is right for their unique environments. Thresholds must be planned for and set up correctly. Applications or web-based interfaces may be accidently disabled due to network protection detections from the Endpoint solution detecting "false positives" and will require application whitelist configurations or security group zoning administration before full implementation is initiated. Symantec Endpoint Protection Suite has implemented a "resource leveling" feature to their toolset [5].

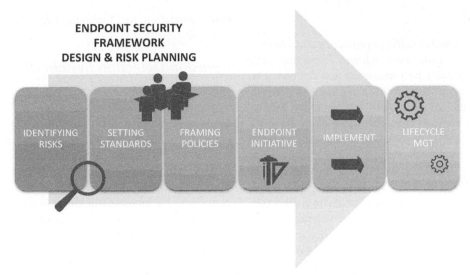

**ENDPOINT SECURITY
FRAMEWORK
DESIGN & RISK PLANNING**

IDENTIFYING RISKS | SETTING STANDARDS | FRAMING POLICIES | ENDPOINT INITIATIIVE | IMPLEMENT | LIFECYCLE MGT

FIGURE 78.2   Endpoint security framework design and risk planning.

This helps to scan the system's resources randomly to ensure resource utilization spikes are not being caused due to active access scanning by the toolset.

Administrative "Lifecycle" Challenges

Security systems are some of the most dynamic, continuously changing environments in your infrastructure. Choosing an Endpoint centralized suite does not solve all the problems or concerns in how these systems are managed and updated on a daily basis. Virus signature delivery system updates, application layer updates, network audit penetration scanning, event log monitoring, new virus outbreak mitigation support are just a few of the challenges network support engineers, and companies must manage on a regular basis. Your Endpoint solutions provider must also ensure they keep up the latest security technologies that may not have the latest compatible functionality. An example can be integrated solid-state disk (SSD) hard drives coming out with new mobile device solutions. Some of these newer technologies may not work due to the mobile device BIOS communication uniquely managing the I/O and storage symmetry functionality compared to regular hard drives, making encryption to these storage devices difficult or not available on some platforms. The Endpoint service provider must ensure they stay current with all the popular latest technology devices on the market today to help provide the previous protection levels they initially agreed to support when your company first purchased their solution suites.

With bots, phishing attacks, spam, bogus redirect malicious website links, and the continuous daily variation recreations of these hacking techniques, the Endpoint administration system must constantly be kept updated. The network engineering security support teams must be kept educated on making sure protection and vigilance are as optimal as possible for your company or organization's quality assurance in running your EPS framework.

Mobile device smartphones and tablets, or working from your home PC that uses VPN to access your protected business network, brings new lifecycle challenges to the Endpoint management models. For mobile devices, it should be a required policy to have company-owned mobile device assets be managed by installed MDM client configurations to safeguard these types of devices. If an employee wants to use a personal device to access his company's email account or file storage system, he or she must sign and agree to a Bring Your Own Device (BYOD) access agreement policy giving your network or computer support administrative teams the right to install protection software on their BYOD equipment. If, for example, an employee saved highly private company financial information on his smartphone device like his Apple iPhone or Google Android device, and the phone is lost with this data on it. The company's technical support administrators have permission to initiate a "device-wipe" command immediately and erase them remotely through the MDM administration systems to ensure the company asset and data information is fully protected from wrongful access or use by cyber criminals. The employee should not have access to the company's systems on his or her personal mobile device without this protection in place. Another challenge is the growing need for employees to Bring Your Own Application (BYOA) into their company computer environments. This opens up the company to exposure from nonsecurity-tested applications that may be freeware or open source tools with hidden malware or backdoor capabilities programmed directly in the software. EPS application audit management features leveraging the company's existing operating system security policies must work together with updated rulesets to manage these types of end user device management challenges.

Choke Control

Designing, setting up, and installing a protocol traffic choking standard solution for your users without impacting their remote access needs must be preplanned and defined. The word "choking" is an old engineering slang used by network engineers attempting to force port and protocol routing defaults to specific network areas through routers, Network Address Translation (NAT) systems, and switches that ensure a stronger level of security beyond application security layer. This means routing, blocking, or limiting protocol packet traffic such as TCP, UDP, SSH, HTTPS, SSL, TLS, FTP, POP, SMTP, or PPTP must be setup correctly to do this (see Fig. 78.3). Using the EPS application suites with the network equipment that is interfacing with routers, security appliances, or NAT systems on the company's network, these types of changes are possible. Port range allocations must also be considered should a company use different SSL ranges instead of the default ones like port 443 [2].

5. ENDPOINT INTRUSION SECURITY: MANAGEMENT SYSTEMS

Endpoint intrusion security isn't solely conducted from devices. Typical endpoint intrusion security solutions provide a two-pronged approach: with security software installed on a central server or management systems console, along with software installed on individual devices.

Intrusion Detection and Prevention

Implementing and designing Intrusion setups with ruleset policies and risk mitigation tools must meet all the company's risk accepted service level agreements for an EPS plan. Intrusion Detection (IDS), Intrusion Prevention (IPS) Systems, or the culmination of the two (IDPS) is a core foundation for Endpoint preventative infrastructure designs.

Intrusion Detection System (IDS)

When it comes to "monitoring" your EPS perimeter, an IDS that can come as either equipment or software-based solution is a required must to ensure real-time attacks are being detected and sending administrative alerts to the network security support teams responsible for managing those systems. The majority of functionality these systems provide are normally internal network-based, but can be configured for inbound/outbound monitoring depending on the needs of your security frameworks, as well. There are different types of IDS systems:

- NIDS: Network-based IDS
- HIDS: Host-based IDS
- IDPS: Intrusion Detection and Prevention Systems
- PIDS: Protocol-based IDS
- APIDS: Application-based IDS

Intrusion Prevention System (IPS)

These systems do the monitoring or work in tandem with IDS monitoring systems. They initiate preventive measures once a qualified, serious intrusion data breach attempt or suspicious network activity is detected. Most of these types of the system come in the form of server or appliance equipment-based solutions that sit on the perimeter or outside of the perimeter of your network. It will immediately initiate the appropriate prevention response based on the type of attack currently being detected in real time. Different from antivirus protection, IPS will monitor, interrogate, and react to the "network packet traffic streaming" levels of your network. This provides a strong protection layer that API-layered or software-layered protection solutions cannot provide. It will log the event,

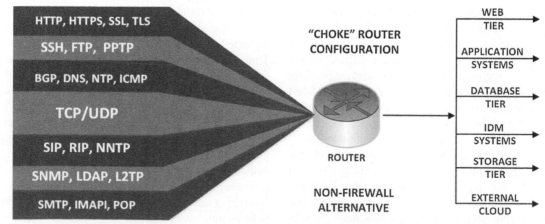

FIGURE 78.3 Choke router configuration and nonfirewall alternative.

notify security support personnel designated in the alert notification system residing on the IPS (see checklist: "An Agenda for Action for Prevention Measures Activated by the Event-Type").

An Agenda for Action for Prevention Measures Activated by the Event-Type

Prevention measures activated by the event-type includes the following key activities (check all tasks completed):

_____**1.** Dropping malicious network traffic.

_____**2.** Blocking detected offending IP address packet traffic.

_____**3.** Identifying and limiting unnecessary network traffic.

_____**4.** Inbound and outbound traffic detection enabled.

_____**5.** TCP/UDP port matching.

_____**6.** Detecting and correcting Cyclic Redundancy Check (CRC) generated errors.

_____**7.** Ransomware attack signature detection.

Network threats can also be identified and mitigated by IPSs. There are different types of IPS systems:

● NBA: Network behavior analysis systems
● WIPS: Wireless IPS
● NIPS: Network-based IPS
● HIPS: Host-based IPS

6. INTRUSION PREVENTION SYSTEM (IPS) NETWORK LOGGING TOOLS: SEEK AND TARGET (THE OFFENDER)

IPS EPS tools for network logging and event alert notification is an important feature to use. The IPS system will proactively or on a predefined scheduled basis set by the administrator, make a discovery on all network-detected devices currently residing on your topology and scan them for attacks or vulnerabilities. The most effective ones will already have the Endpoint client software on them. However, IPS discovery systems can also log existing IP address systems that may not have a security client installed. Imagine going through your network log list and you see hundreds of computers with Endpoint clients noting a protection event due to an OS attack: Microsoft Remote Procedure Call (MSRPC) Server Service event. The client will acknowledge hundreds of blocked and safe devices thanks to its security prevention system from the client software; however, it's not showing where this attack is coming from. The Endpoint discovery tools can list all the servers or workstations in its log files detected on the network, and identify the ones "without" the protection software installed. The network security support team just

needs to install those systems until finally eliminating the nonprotected system generating these attacks on your internal network. This is one example of how the EPS network event monitoring log activities are so important as an actively used security toolset for your network security engineering teams.

7. ENDPOINT UNIFICATION: NETWORK ACCESS CONTROL (NAC) DESIGN APPROACH (FROM THE GROUND-UP)

Network Access Control (NAC) design concepts to help have a unified EPS infrastructure framework is essential to consider when first purchasing or implementing an EPS solution suite that needs to work with your existing network and computer equipment. Unified Endpoint designs can greatly help reduce technical and resource complexity that normally comes with these types of security solutions. When leveraging NAC methodologies, security architects can use these as the "ground-up" way of setting security policies from the network node level. This can work all the way up through the seven (7) layers of the Open Systems Interconnection (OSI) model to help create and implement effective end-to-end security points from the physical to the application layer. With the use of multimedia and social media applications continuing to enter business environments with tools such as Microsoft Lync, Google Hangouts, WebRTC, or Slack, security attention toward anticipating these multiple environments into a company's private network is becoming more important. These systems, including Session Initiated Protocol (SIP) telephony based tools, are adding to the ever-growing pile of digital requirements an innovative company must use to stay ahead of their industry while introducing growing security support complexity to the IT environments they reside or communicate on. Unified EPS designs take all these technical points into consideration, and it is a requirement when bringing in or updating your company or organization's existing security framework environments.

8. SOFTWARE-AS-A-SERVICE (SAAS) ENDPOINT SECURITY

Software-as-a-Service (SaaS) cloud security solutions are becoming more important as businesses continue to leverage the benefits of cloud technology solutions. SaaS platform structures for EPS starts with the host, and client model structured with your office location being the "client" and the SaaS provider being the "host" in the cloud with the same EPS attention to regular company security requirements met, as needed. Some of the industry leaders in SaaS EPS suites are McAfee, Sophos, Cylance, and Symantec. SaaS provides client—local based solutions on your computer devices, but their host security platforms manage them in the cloud that is off-premise (off-prem) from your company's network.

9. SUMMARY

Finally, an organization should design an EPS policy to enforce access control. The policy is mainly driven by a prelogin sequence executed by an SSL VPN appliance before a user logs in. This sequence runs host integrity checks that require the host to download and run active content controls. These controls or applets ensure that the host complies with the organizations EPS policy.

The EPS policy is based on the access control policy. With that in mind, an organization-managed host is identified by a registry key, indicating that the host is managed by the organization. The host integrity check only needs to find this key to verify the host's identity.

Organization-managed hosts use a network extension to gain full access to the internal network. A packet filter is configured on the SSL VPN to prevent these hosts from accessing the restricted set of applications. If a user is permitted to use the restricted set of applications, a packet filter is configured on the SSL VPN to prevent the user from accessing any resource outside the applications. Users are permitted to keep all cookies, web browser cache entries, and downloaded files and attachments.

A host that is not organization-managed or is personally owned can only access web applications via proxy. The SSL VPN session is established in a virtual storage space and all data stored or downloaded during the session is erased after logout.

All hosts must run one or more specific versions of Windows, with each specific version using the most current set of updates. Critical security updates are also required to be installed. The host must run an antivirus software program certified by the organization that is active and uses a virus signature database that has been updated in the past month. The host must also run a firewall program.

Now, let's move on to the real interactive part of this Chapter: review questions/exercises, hands-on projects, case projects, and optional team case project. The answers and/or solutions by chapter can be found in Appendix K.

CHAPTER REVIEW QUESTIONS/ EXERCISES

True/False

1. True or False? Using Endpoint Security solutions as the digital "watchdog, shield, and doctor" role for your computer devices will not help secure and safeguard your systems.

2. True or False? Computer network infrastructures must have organized and secured framework methodologies when remote computers such as laptops or wireless disabled devices connect to them.

3. True or False? EPS does not require equipment and software standards and the permission structures surrounding them, before giving someone access to connect to your corporate environment.

4. True or False? Careful risk planning is not critical when it comes to designing and implementing your overall Endpoint Security defense strategy into your computer networking environments.

5. True or False? Endpoint Security solutions such as Symantec or Kaspersky End Protection suites, cannot give outstanding protection from PC-to-Server or leverage their Mobile Device Management solution for wireless devices, such as mobile smartphones or tablets.

Multiple Choice

1. What are some of the most dynamic, continuously changing environments in your infrastructure, today?
   A. Username
   B. Password
   C. Validations
   D. Security systems
   E. All of the above

2. The word "_____" is an old engineering slang used by network engineers attempting to force port and protocol routing defaults to specific network areas through routers, NAT systems, and switches that ensure a stronger level of security beyond application security layer.
   A. Attack
   B. Choking
   C. Token
   D. Security
   E. Questionnaire

3. Endpoint intrusion security isn't solely conducted from:
   A. Devices
   B. Solutions
   C. Data
   D. Backups
   E. All of the above

4. Implementing and designing Intrusion setups with ruleset policies and risk mitigation tools must meet all the company's risk accepted service level agreements for an:
   A. EPS plan
   B. Private plan
   C. Secure plan
   D. Virtual plan
   E. All of the above

5. When it comes to "_____" your EPS perimeter, an Intrusion Detection system that can come as either equipment or software-based solution is a requirement

to ensure real-time attacks are being detected and sending administrative alerts to the network security support teams responsible for managing those systems.

A. Monitoring
B. Securing
C. Governing
D. Complying
E. All of the above

EXERCISE

Problem

When location roaming is enabled (on an updating policy for roaming laptops), roaming laptops attempt to locate and update from the nearest update server location by querying other (fixed) endpoints on the local network they are connected to, minimizing update delays and bandwidth costs. So, which endpoints can use location roaming in a secure manner?

Hands-On Projects

Project

Will a fixed secure endpoint respond with its primary, secondary, or last successful location? What if the primary location was not available at the time of the last check?

Case Projects

Problem

Will secure endpoints be deployed from the console (or third-party tools) with a port listening?

Optional Team Case Project

Problem

Can location roaming be turned on/off from the secure endpoint client (override the console policy)?

REFERENCES

[1] S. McClure, J. Scambray, Hacking Exposed 7: Network Security Secrets & Solutions, seventh ed., McGraw-Hill Company, 2012.
[2] TrendMicro, 2016. <http://www.trendmicro.com/us/enterprise/product-security/>.
[3] NIST Guide to Intrusion Prevention Systems, 2007. <http://csrc.nist.gov/publications/nistpubs/800-94/SP800-94.pdf>.
[4] S. Donaldson, S. Siegel, C. Williams, A. Aslam, Enterprise Cybersecurity: How to Build a Successful Cyberdefense Program against Advanced Threats, first ed., Apress Publication, 2015.
[5] Symantec, 2016. https://www.symantec.com/content/dam/symantec/docs/data-sheets/endpoint-protection-en.pdf.

Chapter 79

Assessments and Audits

Lauren Collins

Winning Edge Communications, New Lennox, IL, United States

Note: This chapter is available in its entirety online at store.elsevier.com/product.jsp?isbn= 9780128038437 (click the Resources tab at the bottom of the page).

1. ABSTRACT

Risk management is a discipline that exists in every professional environment. Having the ability to gauge and measure exposure within an environment effectively prepares the organization to implement work flows and assessments proactively. Defining security holes in an organization is the delineation of risk that may exist. It is necessary to architect a framework to analyze exclusive incidents, potential outcomes that may arise from such incidents, and the impending consequences. Managing vulnerability in which a team can identify, classify, remediate, and mitigate potential situations is critical to keeping a business up and running. In addition, tools can be used to identify and classify possible vulnerabilities. Information security needs to be in line with the business objectives, and decisions must be made based on metrics and indicators of vulnerabilities. Regularly combining assessments and audits offers executives a clear, prioritized, and comprehensive view of risks and vulnerabilities while integrating information technology assets, resources, environment and processes into a single platform. Just as Internet Protocol addresses had to advance from IPv4 to IPv6, password lengths will have to increase, as will their complexity. Standardization and open collaboration benefit vendors and consumers and advance the industry as a whole. Security professionals benefit from the portability and ease of customization of assessing content, as well as assessing the impact of the latest vulnerability.

2. CONTENTS

Chapter 80

Fundamentals of Cryptography

Scott R. Ellis

kCura Corporation, Chicago, IL, United States

1. ASSURING PRIVACY WITH ENCRYPTION

Encryption provides a secure layer, at the storage byte level, under which information can be secured from prying eyes (see checklist: An Agenda for Action for Implementing Encryption and Other Information Security Functions). Data, or "plaintext" as it is called in cryptography, is rendered into cipher text through a ciphering process. Most importantly, encryption protects stored data. Files such as database data files, spreadsheets, documents, and reports can contain critical information—information which, if lost, could cause damage to:

- Sales generation
- Operations

- Reputation
- Competitive advantage
- Individuals
- Market capabilities
- Finances

Ultimately, the loss of enough data, especially if it were due to incompetence, could be a business-ending event. Inadvertent disclosure of data, especially personally identifiable data, can mean financial liabilities and the need for restitution to injured parties.

Ensuring that files are encrypted in storage, everywhere, allows the files to be protected in the event of a breach of physical security. Should a hacker gain access to a system, database encryption will prevent her from accessing the

---

An Agenda for Action for Implementing Encryption and Other Information Security Functions

Encryption implementation recommendations presented in this chapter enable organizations to ask the following questions (check all tasks completed):

_____**1.** Does your product perform "cryptography," or otherwise contain any parts or components that are capable of performing any of the following "information security" functions?

    _____**a.** encryption

    _____**b.** decryption only (no encryption)

    _____**c.** key management/public key infrastructure (PKI)

    _____**d.** authentication (password protection, digital signatures)

    _____**e.** copy protection

    _____**f.** antivirus protection

    _____**g.** other (please explain): _____

    _____**h.** NONE/NOT APPLICABLE

_____**2.** For items with encryption, decryption, and/or key management functions (1.a, 1.b, 1.c):

    _____**a.** What symmetric algorithms and key lengths (56-bit DES, 112/168-bit Triple-DES, 128/256-bit AES/Rijndael) are implemented or supported?

    _____**b.** What asymmetric algorithms and key lengths (512-bit RSA/Diffie-Hellman, 1024/2048-bit RSA/Diffie-Hellman) are implemented or supported?

    _____**c.** What encryption protocols (SSL, SSH, IPSEC, or PKCS standards) are implemented or supported?

    _____**d.** What type of data is encrypted?

_____**3.** For products that contain an "encryption component," can this encryption component be easily used by another product, or else accessed/retransferred by the end user for cryptographic use?

---

database files. Whole-disk encryption will prevent her from accessing drive shares and pulling Excel spreadsheets.

The early 21st century has seen additional liabilities and exposures of sensitive data in the form of lost backup tapes, lost laptops, and recycled computers that were not destroyed, encrypted, or wiped. After a third-party courier service lost a box of backup tapes, Bank of New York Mellon Corp. officials implemented a policy to encrypt data on all storage devices. Furthermore, they said they would limit the type and amount of confidential client data stored on tape backups. It took two losses of unencrypted data before the policy was launched.

Unfortunately, far too many companies wait for disaster to strike before they begin to think about all of the things they really need to do to ensure, or at least substantially mitigate, their risk of data loss. There are three primary reasons why industry executives are reticent to implement encryption:

1. The cost of doing it—the complexity of setting it up
2. Their feeling that it can't happen to them
3. The fear of data loss due to key loss—an inability to decrypt the data

The cost of implementing an encryption policy pales in comparison to the cost of a data loss due to a breach, or due to release of data simply because Joe Smith left his laptop on the train. In an interesting, real-life situation, the author of this chapter did, in fact, once find a small box of hard drives in a bag on a train. The drives were labeled backup01, backup02, and backup03. Fortunately, the box had a CDW Computer Centers, Inc. shipping label that identified a client number. After reaching out to a friend at the computer company on the label, who contacted the owner (a large university library), a reunion was arranged. The kindness and responsibility of strangers cannot serve, however, as a failsafe. If anything, the loss of ALL the backup data was narrowly averted. According to the library executive, the backup drives held everything. She also promised that the policy would be changing immediately.

Encryption also introduces an additional level of difficulty in the event of corruption. Certain segments of the drive, if they become corrupted, can make retrieval of the data more challenging. This necessitates the storage, offsite, of secure, unencrypted backups. This may seem contrary to the purpose of this chapter, but consider that:

a. The data must be delivered to the unencrypted disaster recovery (DR) site *encrypted*.
b. Access to the unencrypted backup site should be manned "access only" with biometric access controls and no Internet or network connectivity.
c. As physical security and controls *increase*, the need for encryption *decreases*.

Such a high level of security allows the data to be under a much higher degree of control than the data in production data centers. A regular program of data movement, refreshing, and redundancy checks should be in place to ensure against data corruption. Placing data on a disk is no guarantee that 2 years later (if the disk has sat idle) the data will be coherent. Data can become corrupt just sitting on a disk.

Organizations should consider and design a program that understands and includes recipient and sender environments, and ensures that data encryption and decryption are as seamless and unintrusive as possible. In Fig. 80.1, a clock-face approach to security balances the need for physical security against the need for encryption. Observe how, as the network segment approaches the 12th hour, everything is encrypted.

This model only inserts five categories of devices and activities. Each "hour" could conceivably have its own protocols. The analogy of "hour" is used by this author simply to explain and set forth this model as one plausible way of making it easier to think about security, and thus categorize applications based on the activity or on the type of encryption required.

Physical Versus Logical Security

In this clock-face model, the level of physical security decreases the need for encryption security. Physical and data security are applicable to each of the items shown in this diagram. For some items, such as digital cameras, security can get complicated. GPS locators and remote wiping are available for many personal devices, but digital cameras, for example, do not have any sort of a mechanism for encrypting their memory cards.

Consider ranking things in order of "Needs no encryption" to "Must be encrypted." As mentioned previously, the security requirement for encryption decreases as physical security increases. For example, a computer, sealed in cement and sunk to the bottom of the Mariana trench, needs not be encrypted. Cell phones and laptops, on the other hand, should be. Create a panel of advisors to assist with the ranking. Depending on the workplace and the industry, the threat level of various areas could vary. *Moving items from one position on the clock face to a lower number effectively diminishes the immediate need for encryption. This can be accomplished by increasing physical security.* For example, whether a PC in an office is more deserving of encryption than a data center that is hooked into the Internet and has lots of virtual traffic through it may be dependent on other factors. Increasing the security in the office may effectively reduce the need for encryption to a level beneath that of the data center.

Deciding which area is *more likely to be attacked first* requires some decision making—decisions that may, down the road, turn out to be wrong. Planning the implementation requires a *healthy* imagination, not a paranoid one. Too much paranoia can bog down the project, but a healthy dose of possible, real-life scenarios and a little imagination can

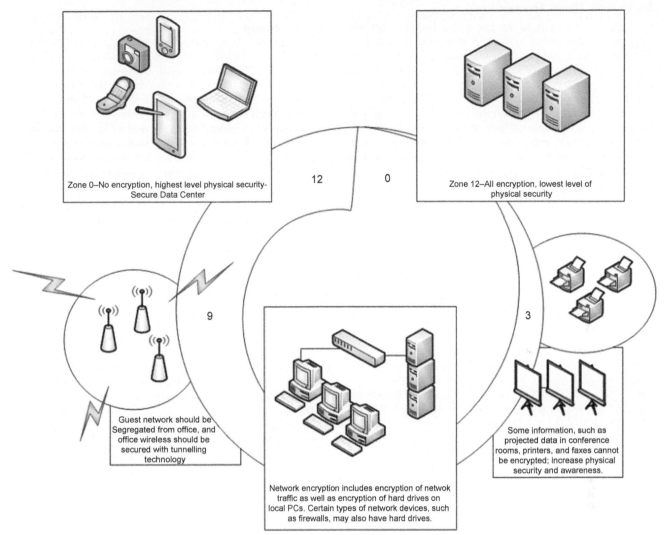

FIGURE 80.1 In a clock-face model, the most physically secure enterprise segments are at the zero hour, with the possibility of imminent attack or loss increasing up to the 12th hour. Note that the crescent line indicates increasing risk of loss, as well as a decrease in physical security.

make planning both enjoyable and effective. See the sidebar, Using Imagination to Effectively Plan, for an example scenario cooked up by the author with one of his coauthors.

As shown in Fig. 80.1, devices can (generally) be ordered by Highest Concern for Encryption and least physical security to Least Concern for Encryption and highest physical security:

- Cell phones, personal digital assitants (PDAs), memory sticks, universal serial bus (USB) drives, tablets
- Data center web farm (financial data)
- Office PCs
- Back office data center
- Printers and fax

- DR site (of course, in a failover, encryption protocols should be activated)
- Data vault

Most organizations will need to take into account their own strategy. This allows for deployment of a planned implementation of encryption in an orderly and risk-biased way.

The Confidentiality, Integrity, and Availability (CIA) Model and Beyond

CIA, or confidentiality, integrity, and availability, is a model for establishing security and risk. It dovetails into the clock-face model presented herein in that CIA provides the litmus tests needed for assessing into which zone things must be placed.

Imagination Allows Accurate Ranking

One way of ranking is to imagine that a hacker is actually employed (unbeknownst to you) in your organization. One afternoon, after a particularly strange day of slowness in the network that you finally have been able to trace, you've narrowed it down to a group of three people: Justin Smirks, Nate Doomer, and Scotty Potomac.[1,2] You mention it to HR, who immediately panics, and later in the afternoon you learn (from an email) that Justin, Nate, and Scott were all fired, simultaneously, and they are really angry about it, and uttered some threats on their way out. "I'll get you, my pretty!" they hear Justin shouting as they drag Justin out kicking and screaming. Scott escapes security, grabs his backpack, crashes through the 23rd floor plate glass window with fist shaking in the air, and base jumps out to safety. Nate snarls, laughs, and vanishes in a puff of smoke, with an evil, lingering laugh, echoing through the corridors.

What are you going to do first (besides change your pants because you assume that Scott is "in" and did his damage on the way down, before his parachute finished opening)? In order of importance, would you say (very generally speaking) that it is more important to have disk encryption on the back-office systems or on the PCs? What is the highest priority?

It takes a special kind of mind to examine an organization and architect a solution that will decrease the vulnerable surface area of a system. Such a plan includes intrusion detection, prevention, firewall policy, and encryption, holistically. Unfortunately, the challenges of creating a comprehensive encryption strategy are daunting. To achieve affective encryption, it must be both seamless and the default action. There are three types of encryption that are well known:

1. Secret Key Cryptography (SKC): A single key decrypts and encrypts data.
2. Public Key Cryptography (PKC): A user's public key is used to encrypt data, and a private key is used to decrypt.
3. Hash Functions: A mathematical formula transforms the data to a set length of characters. For example, an MD5 hash reduces large blocks of information to a single, 128 bit, hexadecimal string.

Fig. 80.2 demonstrates one example of how they are used and implemented in industry. Type 3 encryption is generally an augmentation of 1 and 2, used to send keys, to verify identity, and to ensure losslessness of information. By hashing a file before and after it is received, sender and recipient are then able to agree that they have the same file.

Users should be aware of the zones, what data lies within them, and the required encryption protocols. Auditors should check new processes, place them within the zones, and ensure compliance. If a new application happens to fail one of the tests, but passes another, move the application into a different zone until it can be made compliant. Zone 4 is "zone exceptions."

Step 1: Identify Areas of Risk:

1. The location of any personally identifiable information. This information takes priority.
2. Laptops, PDAs, any portable computers or systems, and remote workers that work with the data in item 1.
3. Email and other information transport communications.
4. Instant messages might be plaintext sent across the network and may be stored locally as well.
5. Vulnerable server drives and application communications.
6. Backups.

Step 2: Organize

Many organizations have very disparate legacy applications. Get organized—knowing the location, method of transport, and types of applications is critical. Understand where data is housed, how it gets transferred to other organizations, how employees generate and store data and where. Mapping out the ins and outs of how data gets generated and how it flows will both assist in understanding the overall security topology of the network and identify areas that should be encrypted. The end state may be that ALL information should be encrypted, and it may be that only some small amount of data should be encrypted. Ultimately, the following steps will assist in implementing an enterprise encryption strategy.

Step 3: Choose Cryptography Applications—Develop an Implementation Plan

All aspects of encryption that are planned for deployment should be fully understood. For example, using PKI encryption gives users of the Internet the ability to exchange private data, securely, through the use of a public and private key pair that both recipient and sender share through a mutually agreed upon, trusted authority. Without this man-in-the middle trust factor, the process will not work. Essentially, the authority provides assignment and revocation of digital certificates that identify individuals and organizations. See the sidebar, "How Public Key Infrastructure (PKI) Encryption Works," for more details on asymmetric key operations. The vendor selection team should have a great understanding.

Developing a strategy of encryption should be treated as a major project. From the outset, things like planning and compliance teams should be established. IT should be involved as well, and all access controls should be audited. Creating an encryption program makes sense, but only if the access controls system is tight. What good is an encrypted disk if the intruder can simply log in and see the unencrypted data right there? Additionally, the National Institute for Science and Technology (NIST) cryptographic toolkit provides standards and guidance over a wide range of the technology used in cryptography. Any vendors should be familiar with these standards and ensure compliance with them.

The final plan should be endorsed by management, and should be communicated to staff. It should include consequences for noncompliance. This plan should also mesh well with data destruction and retention policies.

Step 4: Implement Encryption Protocols

Sadly, no single "enterprise encryption" solution exists. Many vendors offer products A–Z that can be deployed and integrated together in a piecemeal solution, but this sort of hodgepodge approach can also be defined and planned by an experienced project manager. Such a plan will consider possible regulatory compliance requirements as well.

Step 5: Periodic Audits

Periodic audits will help ensure compliance. Conduct them as needed or as things change in significant ways. Maintenance of zone plans and software security measures should be frequent. All documentation should be kept up to date.

---

1. All persons listed in this sidebar are fictional. Any resemblance to any persons, living or dead, is purely noncoincidentally intentional.
2. The diagram in Fig. 80.2 represents the author's viewpoint of how encryption *might* be deployed across a network that he just imagined in his head. The purpose of this is to create a model, a framework of sorts, that can be copied and adjusted as needed. It is meant to start a conversation, not end one.

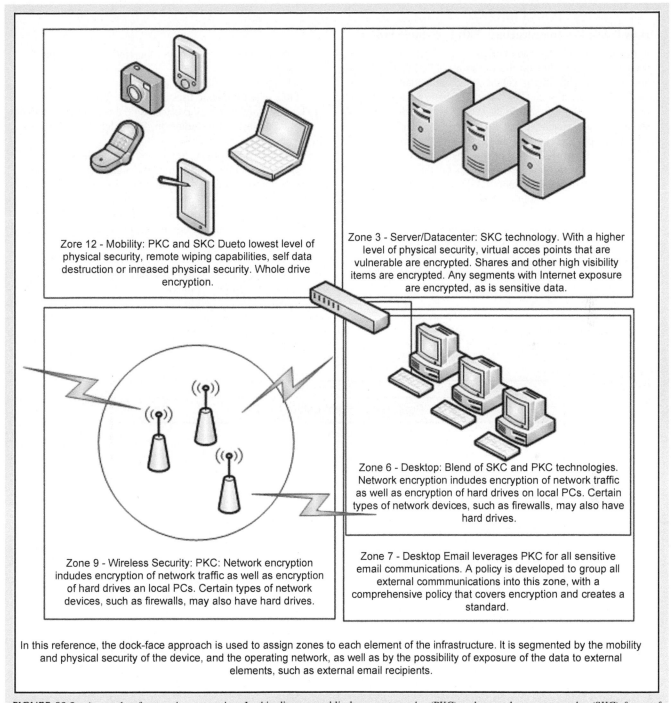

FIGURE 80.2 A sample of enterprise encryption. In this diagram, public key cryptography (PKC) and secret key cryptography (SKC) forms of encryption are layered across the network in a zoned model of encryption.

Confidentiality

To the degree that some information must be made available only to a certain group of people, this determines the level of restriction needed. Unauthorized access to information

must be prevented. In areas of the network where information transmissions are uncontrolled and breach the perimeter, encryption of confidential data must occur.

This is especially true of wireless networks. Frequently, wireless networks are set up with weak, flawed, or no security.

How Public Key Infrastructure (PKI) Encryption Works

In this scenario of message encryption, as shown in Fig. 80.3, the infrastructure relies on the use of a public key to encrypt any message sent. This is called PKC. Traditionally, cryptography relies on a secret key used for both encryption and decryption. The most serious flaw of this method is that the secret key can be uncovered, discovered, or stolen.

A PKC approach has a higher level of trust because, on the Internet, the transmission of a private key could be intercepted. So, the PKI is the preferred approach on the Internet. (The private key system is sometimes known as symmetric cryptography and the public key system as asymmetric cryptography.)

A PKI requires the following components:

- The certificate authority (CA) that performs the following functions:
  - Issues and verifies digital certificate that includes the public key
- A registration authority (RA):
  - Provides verification for the certificate authority
  - Issues the digital certificate to a requestor

- Storage directories to house the certificates and public keys
- A system of certificate management

In PKC, when someone uses the service, a public and private key are simultaneously created using the same algorithm, such as the Rivest-Shamir-Adleman (RSA) algorithm. The certificate authority creates the key.

Subsequently, the private key is sent only to the requesting party. Then, the public key is made available in a common storage location as defined above. The private key remains private.

The private key is then used to decrypt information that has been encrypted by someone else using your public key. People using the public key system can find another user's public key in a central repository and use it to encrypt information that they are sending to them. Users then decrypt the message using their private key. In fact, a message encrypted using a public key can only be decrypted in this fashion.

A number of services, such as RSA, Verisign, and Pretty Good Privacy (PGP), are all examples of companies in this vertical. Each of them provides PKI services.

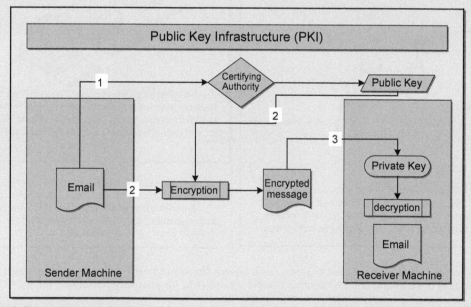

FIGURE 80.3 Step 1: The email requests the public key for the targeted recipient. Step 2: The email message is encrypted using the public key. Step 3: The email is unencrypted using the private key.

Integrity

Information should never be transmitted in ways that may disturb the integrity of the files or data. Unauthorized personnel should not be able to destroy or alter data. Hash values for files should be stored and transmitted with the file and accessed programmatically for validation.

Availability

Information that is so locked down that it is nearly inaccessible reduces the efficiency of operations. Information should be readily accessible to those who are authorized to view it.

Cryptographic Standards and Protocols: Block Ciphers—Approved Algorithms

Block ciphers utilize mathematical formulas that, when operated in cryptography, are called algorithms, and different flavors of algorithms are called ciphers. Block ciphers are a type of algorithm that converts plaintext into cypher text. They are called "block" ciphers because they work by enciphering a preset size of text at a time. Three well-known block ciphers are Advanced Encryption Standard (AES), Triple data encryption standard (DES), and Skipjack.

Advanced Encryption Standard (AES)

AES, published in Federal Information Processing Standard (FIPS) 197 in February 2001, replaced DES. The government reviewed several different algorithms, but ultimately chose the Rijndael encryption algorithm to serve as a FIPS-approved symmetric encryption algorithm. The primary consideration here is that, by virtue of publishing under FIPS, the government created a standard whereby the US government organizations (and others) may protect sensitive information.

Federal agencies also review the Office of Management and Budget (OMB) guidance, which suggests that AES is a standard that will be secure for 20—30 years. Furthermore, the OMB guidance warns agencies that the loss of cryptographic keys presents a risk to the availability of information needed to accomplish critical mission tasks and objectives.[3]

In today's world of extremely complex communication systems, the need for a full understanding of security, which includes a detailed understanding of the business itself first, has never been more apparent. The ability to protect and secure information depends entirely on the ability of those doing the protecting to understand the business. It cannot be solely dependent on the mathematical strengths of the encryption algorithm or the ability of someone to classify certain information. Likewise, you cannot count on the classification of the material to always be an accurate predictor of which encryption algorithm to use. Flexibility must be built into the system. There must be a way for the governing organization to stop, look, and listen. Many factors must be considered in choosing an algorithm and process for encryption, and these factors may, of course, change over time. An inflexible policy risks failure. The following factors are most relevant:

- How well the implementation of the algorithm will perform in specific software, firmware, or hardware configurations;
- The ability to develop a functional key management system, or of the algorithm to mesh with an existing solution;

- The fragility of the of the information to be protected; and/or
- Any requirements to interoperate, globally, where encryption algorithm restrictions may exist.

Considered in total, these requirements demand a flexible implementation and policy that mixes the best of breed software with best practices derived from the individual business requirements.[4]

2. SUMMARY

Ultimately, the best encryption protocol would be completely seamless, effective, and transparent. A seamless encryption utility would provide, across the enterprise, a single-console approach to management. Phones, PDAs, hard drives, servers, network communications, and the like all could be added to the encryption layer with the drag of a mouse. An effective algorithm is one that is not just unbreakable in the near foreseeable future, but rather is simply unbreakable. A transparent system would provide encryption services without any observation by the user. They would not know, nor would they have reason to know, that their emails are encrypted using PKC technology. Unfortunately, modern information technology has not been able to provide any sort of all-encompassing program for managing secure communications. In the meantime, it is up to information technologists to cobble together a best of breed solution that protects and secures information simultaneously.

Finally, let's move on to the real interactive part of this chapter: review questions/exercises, hands-on projects, case projects, and optional team case project. The answers and/or solutions by chapter can be found in the Online Instructor's Solutions Manual.

CHAPTER REVIEW QUESTIONS/EXERCISES

True/False

1. True or False? Encryption provides an insecure layer, at the storage byte level, under which information can be secured from prying eyes.
2. True or False? Ultimately, the gain of enough data, especially were it due to incompetence, could be a business-ending event.
3. True or False? Ensuring that files are encrypted in storage everywhere allows the files to be protected in the event of a breach of physical security.

---

3. http://csrc.nist.gov/drivers/documents/ombencryption-guidance.pdf.

4. Additional information regarding the use of AES can be found in CNSS Policy No. 15, Fact Sheet No. 1 National Policy on the Use of the AES to Protect National Security Systems and National Security Information, June 2003.

4. True or False? The cost of implementing an encryption policy pales in comparison to the cost of a data loss due to a breach or to release of data simply because Joe Smith left his laptop on the train. In an interesting, real-life situation, the author of this chapter did, in fact, once find a small box of hard drives in a bag on a train.
5. True or False? Encryption also introduces additional levels of difficulty in the event of corruption.

Multiple Choice

1. The data must be delivered to the following unencrypted DR site:
   A. Qualitative analysis
   B. Vulnerabilities
   C. Log
   D. Encrypted
   E. DHS
2. Which unencrypted backup site should be manned accessed with only biometric access controls and no Internet or network connectivity?
   A. Firewall
   B. Risk assessment
   C. Scale
   D. Access
   E. Active monitoring
3. As physical security and controls *increase*, the need for encryption does which one of the following:
   A. Organizations
   B. Fabric
   C. Decreases
   D. Logs
   E. Security
4. Who or what should consider and design a program that understands and includes recipient and sender environments, and ensures that data encryption and decryption are as seamless and unintrusive as possible?
   A. Organizations
   B. Denial-of-service attack
   C. WPA2-Personal
   D. Small networks
   E. Taps

5. Deciding which area is *more likely to be attacked first* requires some _____ decisions that may, down the road, turn out to be wrong.
   A. Systems security plan
   B. Consumer privacy protection
   C. Administrators
   D. Decision making
   E. Challenge-Handshake Authentication Protocol (CHAP)

EXERCISE
Problem

What are the cryptographic module specification types?

Hands-on Projects
Project

What is cryptographic key management?

Case Projects
Problem

What types of self-tests must the cryptographic module perform?

Optional Team Case Project
Problem

What is the minimum information required in a cryptographic module security policy?

Part XIII

Critical Infrastructure Security

Chapter 81

Securing the Infrastructure

Lauren Collins

Winning Edge Communications, New Lennox, IL, United States

1. COMMUNICATION SECURITY GOALS

Since the inception of technology, data security has revolved around cryptography. Because cryptography is only as good as the ability of a person or a program, new methods are constantly implemented as technology becomes more sophisticated.

Network Design and Components

Cipher text and secret keys are transported over the network and can be harvested for analysis; furthermore, they can impersonate a source, or worse, cause a service denial. Thus, to aid encryption and complex distribution methods, a network needs to be secure and elegant. That is, the network should have applicable appliances that monitor and detect attacks, intelligence that discriminates between degradations/failures and attacks, and a convention for vigorous countermeasure strategies to outmaneuver the attacker. Consequently, network security is a completely separate topic from data security; however, the devices chosen must complement your infrastructure.

The accumulation of advances in key technologies has enabled companies to envision the implementation of an infrastructure with no limitations. Among these advances are those in materials that underlie electronic components and optical technologies, including optical fibers. Improvements in electronic integrated circuits include both the speed at which these circuits can perform their functions and achievable complexity that allows a single chip to perform complex tasks. Advances in signal-processing techniques that use electronic circuits and software to convert information and information-carrying signals into forms suitable for transport over short or long distances arrange for data to be stored, processed, and transmitted lightning fast. Such advantages have even allowed engineers and scientists to work harder and think farther out to develop new technologies to follow suit for hardware and software transformations. Significant progress is required to realize and appreciate the vision of affordable media.

New algorithms and approaches complement the speed of transport networks, coupled with complex connection and session establishment and management. Total network approaches are required to resolve effective management of a cutting-edge infrastructure solution. Large costs are associated with installation and building out of fiber networks needed to provide an objective, robust network. Networks must be scalable and support multiple types of media, including coax, fiber, copper, and wireless, using both the shared media and switched approaches. Premise access must support the multiplexing of video, voice, and data sources requiring varied quality of service (QoS) levels and various bandwidths.

Several backbone options and avenues are available, mostly owing to the era of electronic trading. These can be comprehensively separated into time division techniques and wavelength division techniques. Determining the potential of each technology would significantly contribute to a company's success, depending completely on the type of business involved. Time domain limits are determined by the speed of the electro-optic transducers, the required buffer and memory, and the switching and control logic required to manage the system. In addition, high-speed regeneration technologies have a pivotal role in delivering benefits of time-division techniques to the system. Take long distances into consideration: Fiber properties such as loss and dispersion in the fiber limit the capabilities of the fiber span. Optical amplification, attenuators, and dispersion compensator devices can restore impairments induced by the fiber properties and allow the media to match the heat and light of the equipment chosen. Wavelength converters, wavelength filters, and wavelength division multipliers enable use of a greater capacity of the fiber. Optical regeneration techniques permit clock recovery and lead to full regeneration capabilities in the optical domain, avoiding unnecessary optical to electrical conversions.

Switching and Routing

Backbone networks require switches with tremendous capacity. Switches of this scale are not commercially available and much research, configuration, and testing must be done to make them perform a specific job. Total system throughputs of 15 terabits per second are possible with the latest and greatest equipment, and more is to come. A challenge for switching systems is to achieve systems that the access network can scale to either the amount of users or the amount of traffic being pumped through the network. Signaling systems for switch control must support a richer communication model than prior generations of switches. User channels can operate at any rate from a couple of bits per second to a gig per second and beyond. Multipoint communication channels (one-to-many and many-to-many) are necessary for applications such as video and voice. This requires a signaling and control system that supports a multipoint call model, in which a call may include multiple virtual circuits, each with its own individual characteristics. Certain applications place extreme demands on signaling systems.

Layer-specific functionality is an important role of a switch. When ordering a switch, you have to determine whether you only want Layer 2 or whether Layer 3 will be needed. Many switches have the capacity to install software to allow Layer 3 capabilities; however, some Layer 3 capabilities are tied to the hardware. The author's favorite Layer 3 function is Internet Protocol (IP) multicast through Internet Group Multicast Protocol (IGMP) snooping. IGMP snooping with proxy reporting actively sifts IGMP packets in an effort to reduce the amount of load the router is carrying that provides the multicast. When a join leaves and heads to the next routers, routes are filtered so that the smallest number of information is transported. A switch warrants that the router has one point to contend with, no matter how many listeners are out there in the network. The router is only aware of the most recent member who joined the group. Because a switch creates the Layer 1 connection both virtually and physically, it is no longer required to have systems interconnected to the same hardware or at the same physical location.

Several switches will meet an organization's needs, and several designs are available to fit in any data center or server room. Some switches, usually just in the home or small office setting, are not rackable and can be located on a desktop or server. Rack-mounted switches are intended to be used in racked environments and can range anywhere from 1 u to an entire cabinet of 42 u (u is the measurement relating to units). A chassis switch, as seen in Fig. 81.1, is one that has either vertical or horizontal blades that allow

FIGURE 81.1 Chassis switch.

for hot swapping and many different, custom options. There are many switch management features:

- bandwidth and duplex settings for circuits
- priority settings for ports
- Simple Network Management Protocol (SNMP) configuration to monitor devices and perform health checks
- message authentication code (MAC) filtering and port security
- link aggregation for versions < Elastic Sky X interface (ESXi) 5, trunking for versions of ESXi > 5
- Layer 2 and Layer 3 virtual local area network (VLAN)

Switching over to routers (no pun intended), we find that when choosing a router it is important to understand the job the router should perform. Just as there are many protocols, there are many types of routing platforms to accomplish services at the edge, the distribution layer, or the core. An edge router operates at the edge of a multiprotocol switching network. In an MPLS domain, IP datagrams are forwarded and routing information is used to determine which labels should accompany the datagram. The packets are then labeled accordingly and the labeled packets are forwarded into the MPLS domain.

Similarly, an edge router can strip the label and forward the resulting packet over using standard IP forwarding logic. Distribution routers can aggregate traffic from multiple-access routers and do not depend on site location or geographical region. Often, distribution routers are responsible for enforcing QoS across a wide area network (WAN), so they may have considerable amounts of memory installed, multiple WAN interfaces, and extensive on-board data processing routines. These types of routers are also capable of providing connectivity to large groups of servers, whether file servers or additional external networks. Core routers operate on the Internet backbone at an organization to transmit lightning-fast speeds and to forward IP packets just as quickly. Routing also needs to be done at the core level in some instances, and differs because edge routers have different features and sit at the edge of a network. Conversely, core routers can sit at the edge of a network if the engineer desires to build the infrastructure this way.

Ports and Protocols

Between the User Datagram Protocol (UDP) and the Transmission Control Protocol (TCP), 65,535 ports are available for communication between devices. Among this impressive number are three classes of ports:

1. well-known ports: range from 0 to 1023
2. registered ports: range from 1024 to 49,151
3. dynamic/private ports: range from 49,152 to 65,535

Understandably, not all ports listed in these three categories are secure. As a result, reference Table 81.1, which enumerates the most commonly used ports and the service/protocol that uses the port.

Ideally, when architecting a system, one should plan the intent for the environment and should configure only the services necessary for the network to pass traffic and servers to perform their intended functions.

Table 81.1 reflects protocols that may be open by default, as well as some that are necessary for the intended purpose of the environment. When installing equipment, it is imperative that the engineer be aware of the ports that need to be open for each device or piece of software and, if needed, can be referenced in the device white paper. It is also essential to recognize variations among the numerous types of attacks and the respective ports on which such attacks would be executed. It is necessary to monitor ports that are open, in an effort to detect protocols that may leave the network vulnerable. Running netstat on a workstation will allow one to view ports that are running and open. In addition, running a local port scan will portray which ports are exposed.

During an installation, many protocols may still be used of which system administrators and users are not aware, and those may leave the network vulnerable. SNMP and Domain Naming Service (DNS) were deployed years ago but still present security risks. SNMP can be employed to monitor the health of network equipment, servers, and other peripheral equipment. However, susceptibilities associated with the SNMP derive from use of SNMP v1. Although such vulnerabilities were raised years ago, exposures are still reported while using the current version of SNMP. Liabilities allow for authentication evasion and execution of proprietary code when using SNMP. The SNMP infrastructure has three components:

1. SNMP managed connections
2. SNMP instruments
3. SNMP network management servers

Where the devices are concerned, they load the agent, which in turn assembles information and forwards it to the management servers. Network management servers collect a substantial amount of significant network information and are possibly targets of attacks owing to their use of SNMP v1, which is not secure. A community name is a point of security; however, it may be similar to a password. Usually, the community name is public and is not secure, nor is it changed, which permits information to leak out to invasions. Conversely, SNMP v2 uses Message Digest Version 5 for authentication. The transmission can also be encrypted. SNMP v3 is used across firms as the criteria; however, a number of devices are not compatible and still need to use SNMP v1 or SNMP v2.

SNMP assists spiteful users in learning too much about a system, making password speculations easier. SNMP is often disregarded when checking for vulnerabilities owing to the UDP ports 161 and 162. Ensure network management servers are physically secured and secured on the network layer. Consider using a segregate management subnet, protecting it by using a router with an access list. Unless the service is required, it should be shut off by default. To defend a network infrastructure from incidents aimed at obsolete or unfamiliar ports and/or protocols, remove unnecessary protocols while creating access control lists to allow traffic on defined ports. This eliminates the possibility of obscure protocols being used while minimizing the danger of an incident.

Threats

Hijacking occurs when an intruder takes control of a session between a server and the client. The communication starts when a middle-man attack adds a request to the client, resulting in the client getting kicked off the session. Meanwhile, the rogue workstation talks with the server, and the attacker intercepts the source-side packets, replacing them with fresh packets that are sent to the destination. This type of hijacking, referred to as TCP/IP hijacking, most commonly occurs during telnet and Web sessions when security is nonexistent or lacking, and when session timeouts are improperly configured.

TABLE 81.1 Well-known Port Numbers and Their Respective Service Description and Protocol

Port	Service/Protocol
7	Echo/TCP and UDP
9	Systat/TCP and UDP
15	Netstat/TCP and UDP
20	FTP data transfer/TCP
21	FTP control/TCP
22	SSH/TCP
23	Telnet/TCP
24	Private mail/TCP and UDP
25	SMT/TCP
39	RLP/TCP and UDP
42	ARPA/TCP and UDP
42	Windows Internet Name Service/TCP and UCP
43	WHOIS/TCP
49	TACACS/TCP and UDP
53	DNS/TCP and UDP
69	TFTP/UDP
80	HTTP/TCP
88	Kerbos/TCP and UDP
101	NIC hostname/TCP
110	POP3/TCP
115	SFTP/TCP
119	Network News Transfer Protocol/TCP
123	NTP/UDP
143	IMAP/TCP
152	Background File Transfer Protocol/TCP and UDP
156	SQL Service/TCP and UDP
161	SNMP/UDP
162	SNMPTRAP/TCP and UDP
175	VMNET/TCP
179	BGP/TCP
220	IMAP/TCP and UDP
264	Border Gateway Multicast Protocol/TCP and UDP
280	http-mgmt/TCP and UDP
389	LDAP/TCP and UDP
443	HTTPS/TCP
500	Internet Security Association and Key Management Protocol/UDP

ARPA, Advanced Research Projects Agency; *BGP*, border gateway protocol; *DNS*, domain naming service; *FTP*, file transfer protocol; *HTTP*, hypertext transfer protocol; *IMAP*, internet message access protocol; *LDAP*, lightweight directory access protocol; *NIC*, network interface controller; *POP3*, post office protocol 3; *RLP*, radio link protocol; *SFTP*, secure shell file transfer protocol; *SMT*, soft machines transfer protocol; *SNMP*, simple network management protocol; *SNMPTRAP*, simple network management protocol trap; *SQL*, structured query language; *SSH*, secure shell protocol; *TACACS*, terminal access controller access control system; *TCP*, transmission control protocol; *TFTP*, trivial file transfer protocol; *UDP*, user datagram protocol.

During the course of a Web session, cookies are commonly used to authenticate and track users. While the authentic session is in session, an attacker may attempt to hijack a session by loading a modified cookie in the session page. Session hijacking may also ensue when a session timeout is set to be an extended period of time; this gives an attacker a chance to hijack a session. Telnet-type plaintext connections create the ideal situation for TCP hijacking. In an instance such as this, when an attacker surveys the data passing in the TCP session, he can take control of the user's session; this is yet another reason why it is called session hijacking. When a user is forced to authenticate before allowing transactions to occur, it prevents hijacking attacks. Protection mechanisms include the use of unique sequence numbers and Web session cookies. The more unique the cookies are, the harder it is to crack and hijack. Additional preventative measures for this type of attack include the use of encrypted session keys and Secure Socket Layer encryption.

Spoofing

Spoofing is a method of providing false identity information to gain unauthorized access. This can be achieved by modifying the source address of traffic or source of information. Spoofing seeks to bypass IP address filters by setting up a connection from a client and sourcing the packets with an IP address that is allowed through the filter. Blind spoofing occurs when the attacker sends only data and only makes assumptions of responses. Informed spoofing is when the attacker can participate in a session and can monitor bidirectional communications. Services that can be spoofed are:

1. email
2. Web
3. file transfers
4. caller ID

Web spoofing occurs when an attacker creates a convincing, fabricated copy of an entire website. The fabricated website will appear just as a real website would, and it has all of the pages and links. The attacker controls the fabricated website so that all network traffic between the user's browser and the site goes through the attacker. In the situation for email spoofing, a spammer or virus can forge the email packet information in an email so that it appears as if the email is coming from a trusted host, a friend, or even your own email. When you leave your email address at an Internet site, or exchange email with others, a spoofer may be able to use your email address as the sender address to blast spam. File transfer spoofing involves the File Transfer Protocol (FTP) service, and FTP is sent in clear, plain text. The data can be intercepted by an attacker. The data then can be viewed and altered before sending it over to the receiver. These types of attacks are intended to pull information from a network of users to accomplish a more comprehensive attack. By setting up a filter to deny traffic originating from the Internet that shows an internal network address, using the signing capabilities of certificates on servers and clients will allow Web and email services to be more secure. Using an Internet Protocol Security (IPSEC) tunnel adds more security between critical servers and their clients by preventing these types of attacks from transpiring.

Intercepting Traffic

The man-in-the-middle attack occurs when an attacker intercepts traffic and deceives the parties at both ends into believing they are communicating with one another. An attack such as this is possible because of the nature of the three-way TCP handshake process using SYNchronize (SYN) and ACKnowledge (ACK) packets. Because TCP is a connection-oriented protocol, a three-way handshake takes place when establishing a connection and when closing the session. When a session is established, the client sends a SYN request; then the server sends an ACK (sometimes referred to as SYN-ACK-ACK), completing the connection. During this process, the attacker initiates the man-in-the-middle attack by using a program that appears to be a server to the client and appears to be a client to the server. In telnet and wireless communications, this attack is common. This is a difficult attack to perform because of physical routing matters, the TCP sequencing number, and speed. Because the hacker must sniff both sides of the connection simultaneously, programs have been developed to aid the attacker to make man-in-the-middle easier.

If an attack is performed on an internal network, physical access to that network is mandatory. By ensuring that access to wiring closets and switches are restricted and that they are behind locked doors, physical access becomes difficult. Once the physical segment of the network has been secured, services and resources may allow a system to be inserted into a session, so those will need to be protected. DNS can be compromised and used to redirect the initial request for service, providing an opportunity to execute the man-in-the-middle attack. DNS access needs to be restricted, allowing read-only access for anyone but administrators. By using encryption and security controls and protocols, organizations can prevent these types of attacks on their infrastructure.

Packet Capturing

Packets are captured by sniffing devices in a replay attack. Once the relevant information is extracted, packets are put back on the network. An attack such as this can be used to replay a bank transaction or other comparable types of data transfers in the hope of replicating or changing activities such as transfers or deposits. Protecting oneself against a replay attack will involve some type of timestamp associated with the packets, or time-valued nonrepeating serial numbers. In addition, integrating secure protocols such as IPSEC prevents replays of data traffic while providing authentication and data encryption.

Denial of Service

When resources have been disrupted or services to which a user would expect to have access are compromised, they have experienced a denial of service (DoS) attack. These types of attacks are executed by manipulating protocols and can occur without the need to be validated by the network. An attack will usually involve flooding the listening port on a machine with packets. The purpose is to make that workstation so busy processing the new connections that it cannot process legitimate service requests. Several tools are available on the Internet that will produce a DoS attack. Information technology (IT) administrators use them daily to test connectivity and troubleshoot issues on their networks, whereas malicious users will use the tool to cause connectivity issues. Some examples of DoS attacks are:

- SYN flood: This attack takes advantage of the TCP three-way handshake. A source system will send a flood of SYN requests and will never send the final ACK, creating partially open TCP sessions. Because the TCP stack waits before resetting the port, the attack overflows the destination workstation connection buffer, making it impossible to service requests from valid users.
- Ping flood: This attack attempts to block service or reduce activity on a host by sending ping requests directly to the target. Variations of these attacks include the ping of death, in which the packet size is too large and the system is unable to handle the number of packets.
- Ping/smurfing: This attack is based on the Internet Control Message Protocol (ICMP) echo reply function. The common name is ping, the command line tool used to invoke the function. The attacker sends ping packets to the broadcast address of a network, replacing the original source address in the ping packets with the source address of the target, causing a flood of traffic to be sent to the unsuspecting network device.
- Fraggle: This attack is similar to smurfing. The difference is that fraggle uses UDP rather than ICMP. The attacker sends spoofed UDP packets to broadcast addresses, just as the smurf attack does. These UDP packets are directed to port 7, echo, or port 19, Chargen.

When connected to port 19, a character generator attack can be run. Refer to Table 81.1 for commonly exploited ports.
- Land: This attack exploits a behavior in the operating systems of several versions of Windows, UNIX, Mac, and Cisco IOS with respect to their TCP/IP stacks. The attacker spoofs a TCP/IP SYN packet to the victim system with the same source and destination IP address and the same source and destination ports. This confuses the system as it attempts to respond to the packet.
- Teardrop: This form of attack targets a known behavior of UDP in the TCP/IP stack of some operating systems. The teardrop attack will send fragmented UDP packets to the target with odd offset values in subsequent packets. When the operating system attempts to rebuild the original packets from the fragments, the fragments overwrite each other, causing confusion. Because some operating systems cannot handle the error elegantly, the system will either crash or restart.

DoS attacks come in many flavors, shapes, and sizes. Take the first step to protect the firm from an attack: Understand the types of attacks and the nature in which they operate.

Distributed Denial of Service

A modest expansion of denial of service can be referred to as distributed DoS attacks. Masters are computers that run the client software, where zombies will run the software. The attacker will create a master, which in turn creates a large number of zombies, or recruits. The software that runs on the zombies can launch multiple types of attacks, such as UDP or SYN flooding on a particular target. Fig. 81.2 depicts a distributed DoS attack.

Although distributed DoS attacks usually come from the outside the network to deny services, the impact of the attacks displayed inside the network should also be cogitated. Internal distributed DoS attacks allow disgruntled employees or malicious users to disrupt services with no outside influence or interaction. To help protect your network, set up filters on external routers to drop packets involved in these types of attacks. Also, set up an additional filter that denies traffic originating from the Internet but showing an internal IP address. By doing this, ping and some services are lost to test network connectivity, but this is where administrators should be on a network segment separate from users and would be on a segment where the filtering did not occur. If the operating system supports it, one can reduce the amount of time before the reset of an unfinished TCP connection. Doing so makes it harder to keep resources unavailable for extended periods of time.

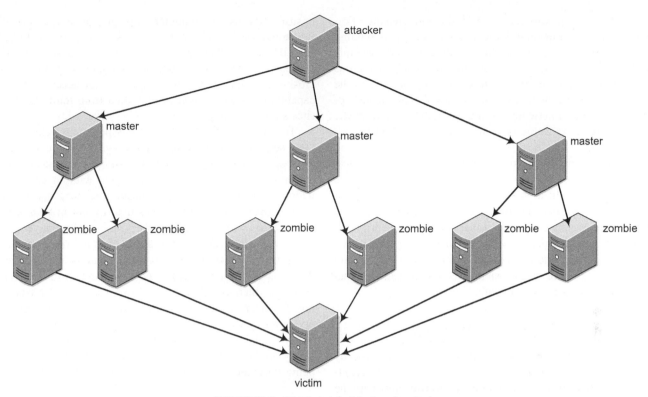

FIGURE 81.2   Distributed denial of service attack.

Tip: In case of a distributed DoS attack, it is best to get in touch with your service provider so it can divert traffic or block traffic at a higher level.

Address Resolution Protocol Poisoning

Every network card has a 48-bit address that is unique and hard-coded into the card. For network communications to occur, this hardware address must be associated with an IP address. Address resolution protocol (ARP), which operates at Layer 2 (data link layer) of the Open System Interconnection (OSI) model, associates MAC addresses to IP addresses. ARP is a lower-layer protocol that is straightforward and consists of requests and replies without validation. However, this simplicity leads to a lack of security.

When using a protocol analyzer to look at traffic, you will see an ARP request and an ARP reply, which are the two fundamental parts of ARP communication. There are also reverse ARP (RARP) requests and RARP replies. Devices maintain an ARP table that contains a cache of the IP addresses and MAC addresses that the device has already correlated. The host device searches its ARP table to see whether there is a MAC address corresponding to the destination host IP address. When there is no matching entry, it broadcasts an ARP request to the entire network. The broadcast is seen by all systems, but only the device that has the corresponding information replies. However,

devices can accept ARP replies even before requesting them. This type of entry is known as an unsolicited entry because the information was not explicitly requested.

Because ARP does not require a type of validation, as ARP requests are sent, the requesting devices believe that the incoming ARP replies are from the correct devices. This can allow a perpetrator to trick a device into thinking any IP is related to any MAC address. In addition, they can broadcast fake or spoofed ARP replies to an entire network and attack all computers. This is known as ARP poisoning. Simply worded, the attacker deceives a device on your network, poisoning its table associations of other devices.

ARP poisoning can lead to attacks such as DoS, man-in-the-middle, and MAC flooding. DoS and man-in-the-middle were discussed earlier in this chapter. MAC flooding is an attack directed at network switches. This type of attack is successful because of the way all switches and bridges work. The amount of space allocated to store source addresses of packets is limited. When the table becomes full, the device can no longer learn new information and becomes flooded. As a result, the switch can be forced into a hub-like state that will broadcast all network traffic to every device in the network. Macof is a tool that floods the network with random MAC addresses. Switches may get stuck in open repeating mode, leaving the network traffic susceptible to sniffing. Nonintelligent switches do not check the sender's identity, which allows this condition to happen.

A lesser vulnerability of ARP is port stealing. Port stealing is a man-in-the-middle attack that exploits binding between the port and the MAC address. The principle behind port stealing is that an attacker sends numerous packets with the source IP address of the victim and the destination MAC address of the attacker. This attack applies to broadcast networks built from switches. ARP traffic operates at Layer 2, the data link layer of the OSI model, and is broadcast on local subnets. ARP poisoning is limited to attacks that are local, so an intruder needs either physical access or control of a device on your network. To mitigate ARP poisoning on a small network, you can use static or script-based mapping for IP addresses and ARP tables. For larger networks, use equipment that offers port security. By doing so, you can permit only one MAC address for each physical port on the switch. In addition, you can deploy monitoring tools or an intrusion detection system to signal when suspicious activity occurs.

Domain Naming Service Poisoning

DNS poisoning enables a perpetrator to redirect traffic by changing the IP record for a specific domain, thus permitting the attacker to send legitimate traffic anywhere he chooses. This not only sends a requestor to a different website; it also caches this information for a short period and distributes the attack's effect to the server's users. DNS poisoning may also be referred to as DNS cache poisoning because it affects the information that is cached.

Because all Internet requests begin with a DNS query, if the IP address is not known locally, the request is sent to a DNS server. There are two types of DNS servers: authoritative and recursive. DNS servers share information, but recursive servers maintain information in their cache. This means caching or recursive servers can answer queries for resource records even if they cannot resolve the request directly. A flaw in the resolution algorithm allows the poisoning of DNS records on a server. All an attacker has to do is delegate a false name to the domain server along with providing a false address for the server. For example, an attacker creates a hostname hackattack.gov. Next, the attacker queries your DNS server to resolve the host hackattack.gov. The DNS server resolves the name and stores the information in its cache. Until the zone expiration, further requests for hackattack.gov do not result in lookups but are answered by the server from its cache. It is thus possible for the attacker to set your DNS server as the authoritative server for the zone with the domain registrar. If the attacker conducts malicious activity, the attacker can make it appear that your DNS server is being used for those malicious activities.

DNS poisoning can result in many different implications. Domain name servers can be used for distributed DoS attacks. Malicious software can be downloaded to an unsuspecting user's computer from the rogue site, and all future requests by that computer will be redirected to the fake IP address. This could be used to build an effective botnet. This method of poisoning could also allow for cross-site scripting exploits, especially because Web 2.0 capabilities allow content to be pulled from multiple websites simultaneously.

To minimize the effects of DNS poisoning, check the DNS setup if you are hosting your own DNS. Be sure the DNS server is not open-recursive. An open-recursive DNS server responds to any lookup request without checking where the request originated. Disable recursive access for other networks to resolve names that are not in your zone files. Also, use different servers for authoritative and recursive lookups and require that cached information to be discarded except from the com servers and the root servers. As far as users are concerned, educate them. However, it is becoming increasingly difficult to spot an issue by watching the address bar on an Internet browser. Therefore, operating system vendors are adding more protection by notifying the user that a program is attempting to change the system's settings, thus preventing the DNS cache from being poisoned.

2. ATTACKS AND COUNTERMEASURES

To secure a network, a firewall can be successfully implemented and used whether it is software or hardware based. The purpose of a firewall is to control incoming and outgoing traffic by analyzing packets and determining whether a rule set will allow the traffic in or not.

Network Firewall

In Fig. 81.3, the firewall is protecting the network rather than leaving it directly exposed to the Internet. The firewall will sit in conjunction with a network device and will serve as a gateway between two networks.

Firewalls inspect all traffic routed between two networks to determine whether that traffic meets predetermined criteria. If it does, the traffic is allowed through and routed to the appropriate destination. Otherwise, the traffic is blocked. Firewalls can also manage public access to private network resources, such as host applications. Hard drive space on firewalls is becoming increasingly important because log entries can grow to be terabytes of data, depending on the amount of traffic on your network. Consider your logging setup to log every attempt to enter into and exit the network. When half the company is surfing the Internet during its lunchtime, one can fathom how large the log files can grow to be. Firewalls can also filter packets specific to network types and is known as protocol filtering. Because the decision to forward or reject traffic depends on the protocol used, a user attempting to access a server via

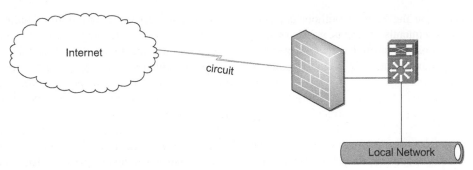

FIGURE 81.3 A firewall is placed between the outside world and the internal local network components.

Hypertext Transfer Protocol (HTTP), FTP, or telnet will be either allowed or denied based not only on access to the server but also on whether the firewall allows specific protocol access to that target server.

Firewalls use two approaches: allow all traffic unless said traffic meets a certain criterion or deny all traffic unless it meets a certain criterion. In addition, firewalls can fit into four categories: packet filters, circuit-level gateways, application-level gateways, and stateful multilayer inspection firewalls. Packet filtering firewalls sit at the network layer, or the IP layer of the TCP/IP layer. Depending on the packet criteria, the firewall can drop the packet, forward it, or send a message to the initiator. Rules can include source and destination IP address, source and destination port number, and protocol used. The advantage of packet filtering firewalls is that they are affordable and have no impact on network performance. If a higher-level firewall is used, packet filtering rules will not add overhead to the network traffic. A lower-level firewall will not support many other features that an organization may desire, such as network address translation (NAT). NAT is used in many different types of companies, whether it is a trading or law firm. Understanding private and public IP addressing is the first step in translating network addresses. Your internal network will communicate with internal IPs; however, if you have a client that needs to access a server on your network, giving them the internal IP on your network will not allow them access unless they are on your virtual private network. So, translating that IP to a public IP will allow the user to access that internal server, but the firewall is the tool that gives the user outside access by translating the IP. In addition, the firewall needs to know that 66.55.44.123 is a public IP that belongs to internal IP 10.10.10.100. How will the user access the server? If a user wants Remote DesktopProtocol (RDP) access to 10.10.10.100, the firewall must give RDP access to that server. Specific ports and protocols are allowed at the firewall level, too. When implementing a firewall, one must consider the following measures:

- Determine the access denial methodology: Most recommend denying all access by default right at the start.

That would have a gateway that routes no traffic and is a brick wall with no doors in it. If you prefer a solid, secure environment, this is the first step, and then you can allow access from here.

- Determine inbound access: If all of your Internet traffic originates on the local area network (LAN), an NAT router will block all inbound traffic that is not in response to requests originating from within the LAN. As mentioned in the preceding example, only the external IP address is given to a client. The internal IP addresses of hosts behind the firewall are never revealed to the outside world, which makes intrusion difficult. Most hosts are nonpublic IPs, so it would make it difficult unless the attacker was on the internal network; however, it is the best practice. Packets coming in from the Internet in response to requests from local hosts are addressed to allocate port numbers dynamically on the public side of the NAT router. These numbers change rapidly, making it nearly impossible for an intruder to make assumptions about which port number they could use. You may also want to determine which criteria can be used when a packet originates from the Internet and whether to allow it into the LAN. The more rigorous the rules, the more secure your network will be. Ideally, you will know which public IP addresses on the Internet originate inbound traffic, and by limiting inbound traffic to packets originating from specific hosts, you decrease the likelihood of hostile intrusion. Going further, earlier protocols were mentioned, and limiting communication-based off-protocol sets such as HTTP or FTP adds greater security.

- Determine outbound access: When users need only access to the Internet, a proxy server may provide enough security, with access granted based on user rights. This type of firewall can be a great deal to manage because it requires manual configuration of each Web browser on every machine. Outbound protocol filtering can also be transparently achieved with packet filtering and no sacrifice on security. If you are using NAT without inbound mapping or traffic originating from the Internet, it is possible to allow users access to all services on the Internet without compromising security. Consequently, there is a risk of employees acting irresponsibly through email or external hosts, but that is a management or human resources issue and not IT.

Proxies

Proxy servers are capable of functioning on dedicated hardware or as software on a utility server. They act as a transitional point of communication between two clients attempting to reach out to other servers. For example, if a client connects to a proxy server, requesting some file or connection, the proxy server will assess the request in an effort to simplify and regulate the intricacy of the communication, as shown in Fig. 81.4.

Proxies can perform just as a firewall would by handling connection requests for packets coming into an application and by blocking any other packets. A proxy server can be thought of as a gateway from Network A to a certain network application, while acting as a proxy for the user on the network. When an administrator properly designs the function of a proxy, it is much more difficult for an outside attacker to access the internal network. However, an attacker may employ a highly available system and use it as a proxy for his selfish means. This allows the proxy to deceive other machines, forcing them to think the proxy is safe and on their network, or their proxy. Using internal, private IP addresses add another layer for security; conversely, hackers could spoof the IP's attempt to gain access and transmit packets to a network.

Proxy servers have become prevalent in the gaming community since real-time Internet gaming surfaced. Considering how many kids and adults are into gaming, the network for real-time streaming multiplayer gaming requires a low-latency proxy server-network topology. Client-server or peer-to-peer topologies provide a variety of positive aspects and can be applied intricately, leading to

their high acquiescence for computer gaming. Both models also have many disadvantages, which results in weak QoS and constrains robust gaming architectures in which there is a high amount of users. As soon as the player numbers increase, client-server and peer-to-peer topologies do not scale well. In addition, the server in a client–server framework forms a single point of failure for the entire session. Although the peer-to-peer method eradicates the problem of a single point of failure, a hacked client can cheat, because acquiesced game updates are not filtered by a server instance and concealed information becomes readily available to the player.

Architecting a proxy server setup, stemming from a peer-to-peer server-network, is shown in Fig. 81.5. Using several interconnected proxy servers for a one-user gaming session shows each proxy server with a full view of the comprehensive game architecture. Each client communicates with a single proxy, sending user selections and obtaining updates of the game status.

Proxy servers process user actions and forward them to other proxies, manipulating multicast at the IP or application level to synchronize the disseminated game state. With regard to low-latency, Internet-centered sessions, proxy servers need to be disbursed among different Internet service providers (ISPs), such that each client will connect to a proxy at its local ISP. Through testing, the author has set up the servers manually; however, testing proves that a dynamic setup of proxies falls in line with user demand and quick response times. Rather than replicating a gaming world, one could partition the approach across servers, compelling clients to exchange servers depending on their region. This approach may work well to accommodate a slower flow of traffic, but it cannot be applied to the low-latency, graphic-intensive world. Pauses are annoying for users, as are noticeable server changes. Because the proxy has a wide spectrum to view the game state, best practices avoid a proxy server-network to attempt multiple reconnects during one session.

To manage replication using proxy servers in a gaming infrastructure, ensure that the architecture is scalable, responsive, and consistent, simulating large amounts of data. Although trade-offs may be involved, implementing strong consistency patterns will increase the amount of interproxy communication. For example, proxies would order changes of the game state using timestamps or a physical clock mechanism. This would delay the transmission of acknowledgments of user actions to clients, thus reducing the responsiveness of the game. Talk about detrimental: especially when you have stood in line for 18 h outside the store, and now you are competing with 500,000 other users during the first hour of the game! A scalable, distributed model with real-time performance can be achieved only if all the servers do not talk to each other simultaneously; nonetheless, servers must be able to share

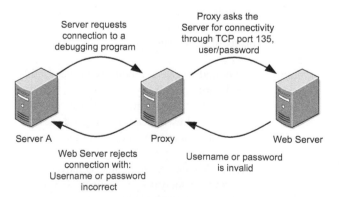

FIGURE 81.4 Communication between two servers connecting through a proxy, the third server. *TCP*, Transmission Control Protocol.

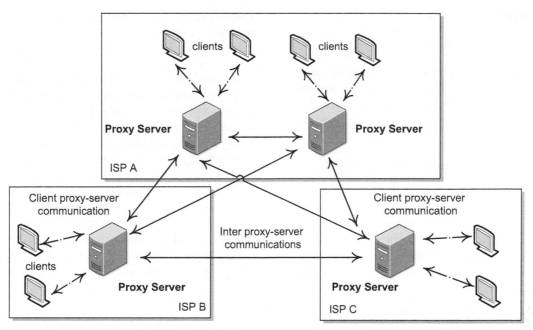

FIGURE 81.5   One session using the proxy server model. *ISP*, Internet service provider.

the same data at all times. To implement this architecture, allow only one process to alter specific parts of replicated data (Fig. 81.6). Changes must be propagated to other processes, certifying the reliability of the replicated state immediately as the message arrives. The process in Fig. 81.6 can be described by following these steps: (1) user actions are transferred from clients; (2) the server checks to see whether the input is authorized to block cheating before changing the state; (3) consistency for the altered part of the game state is guaranteed, and the clients receive acknowledgments for movement commands in a short amount of time; (4) informs proxies about updating position values; (5) update local copies consequently; (6) in the case of interactions, notified proxies also check whether local clients are affected, and if local clients are affected, the proxy updates the game state about its local client and informs other servers; and (7) for all state updates received from other proxy servers, each proxy evaluates which local clients are affected and informs them. The architecture presented allows for management of a distributed state, with efficient synchronization of the game state in conjunction with fast acknowledgment of user actions.

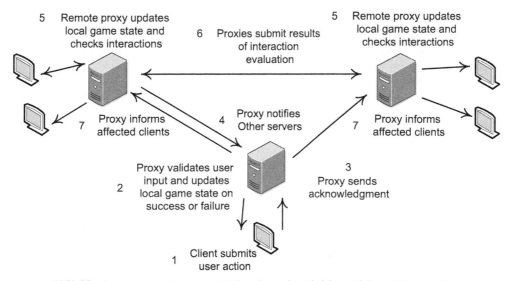

FIGURE 81.6   A user performing a single action: acknowledging and forwarding an action.

3. SUMMARY

This chapter focused on how security is presented to protect the infrastructure. Smart grid cybersecurity must address not only deliberate attacks, such as from disgruntled employees, industrial espionage, and terrorists, but also inadvertent compromises of the information infrastructure resulting from user error, equipment failure, and natural disasters.

Infrastructure Security Tasks Checklist

The primary intent of this chapter is to increase your awareness of specific technologies that secure the foundation of your infrastructure. Although this part of the chapter is called a checklist, each task in the checklist ("An Agenda for Action for Implementing Infrastructure Security Tasks") requires so much elaboration that it is easy to lose the thread

of organization. The guiding structure is first to summarize the major types of security vulnerabilities and mitigation techniques in general, and then to traverse the OSI communication reference model layers (previously discussed) while discussing specific security considerations.

This chapter also addressed critical cybersecurity needs in the areas of encryption key management, security requirements, testing criteria for remote upgrades, and privacy recommendations for third-party data use. The chapter also provided foundational cybersecurity guidance, outreach, and foster collaborations in the cross-cutting issue of cybersecurity in the smart grid. Remember that a system is only as secure as its most vulnerable path, and it is difficult (if not impossible) to build a secure voice solution if the infrastructure foundation is insecure.

Finally, let us move on to the real interactive part of this chapter: review questions/exercises, hands-on projects, case

---

An Agenda for Action for Implementing Infrastructure Security Tasks

Please see the following infrastructure security tasks (check all tasks completed):

Infrastructure security tasks are designed to thwart several types of threats:

_____ 1. Unauthorized traffic types going where they should not go (unauthorized access and DoS)

_____ 2. Authorized traffic types using more bandwidth or other resources than they should (DoS)

_____ 3. Unauthorized devices mimicking authorized devices (violating integrity)

_____ 4. Unauthorized devices intercepting communications intended for other devices (violating privacy).

At the infrastructure level, these threats are thwarted by:

_____ 5. Securing the routers and switches themselves so that they continue to perform their packet/frame forwarding and filtering functions

_____ 6. Keeping unauthorized devices from being in the communication path by using filters and security mitigation features at different layers of the protocol stack and protecting against frame forgery and spoofing attempts to bypass the filters.
Filters that operate at most layers of the protocol stack under various feature names are appropriate at the following points in the network:

_____ 7. Ingress directly on hosts, servers, or end-point devices (considered separately under host hardening, as opposed to infrastructure security features) (*Note*: This is distinct from filters that you can apply on Ethernet switches or other networking gear.)

_____ 8. Ingress Ethernet ports in wiring closet switches, where traffic first enters a network

_____ 9. IP subnet boundaries where traffic crosses between VLANs

_____ 10. Boundaries between network segments that are in different administrative domains.
The following protocols that form the core of IP network functionality are critical components to consider as candidates for spoofing attacks:

_____ 11. Ethernet frame headers that contain source/destination link layer addresses

_____ 12. IP packet headers that contain source/destination network layer addresses

_____ 13. ARP, which binds permanent Ethernet hardware addresses to configuration-specific IP logical addresses

_____ 14. Dynamic Host Configuration Protocol, which automatically assigns IP addresses to devices

_____ 15. Domain Name Service (DNS), which maps human-readable names to IP addresses

_____ 16. Hot Standby Router Protocol, which provides a single virtual Ethernet hardware address and IP address for a group of routers that provide redundant default gateway services

_____ 17. Institute of Electrical and Electronics Engineers (IEEE) 802.1d Spanning Tree Protocol, which controls the Layer 2 Ethernet frame forwarding behavior in a switched Ethernet LAN or metropolitan area network

_____ 18. IEEE 802.1q Ethernet trunk interfaces, which let a single physical Ethernet port share multiple VLANs

_____ 19. Virtual Trunking Protocol and other control protocols, which switch use to exchange VLAN configuration information

_____ 20. Routing protocols that control the Layer 3 packet forwarding behavior in a network projects, and the optional team case project. The answers and/or solutions by chapter can be found in the Online Instructor's Solutions Manual.

CHAPTER REVIEW QUESTIONS/ EXERCISES

True/False

1. True or False? Since the inception of technology, data security revolves around cryptography.
2. True or False? Cipher text and secret keys are transported over the network and can be harvested for analysis, and furthermore to impersonate a source or, worse, cause a service acceptance.
3. True or False? Backbone networks require switches with tremendous capacity.
4. True or False? Between the UDP and TCP protocols, 5535 ports are available for communication between devices.
5. True or False? Hijacking occurs when an intruder takes control of a session between a server and the port.

Multiple Choice

1. What is a method of providing false identity information to gain unauthorized access?
   A. Qualitative analysis
   B. Vulnerabilities
   C. Spoofing
   D. Misconfiguration
   E. Department of Homeland Security
2. What attack occurs when an attacker intercepts traffic and deceives the parties at both ends into believing they are communicating with one another?
   A. Firewall
   B. Risk assessment
   C. Scale
   D. Man-in-the-middle
   E. Bait
3. What are captured by sniffing devices in a replay attack?
   A. Organizations

B. Fabric
C. Packets
D. Web application firewall
E. Security

4. When resources have been disrupted or services are compromised to which a user would expect to have access, they have experienced a:
   A. Cabinet-level state office
   B. Denial of service attack
   C. Hardening
   D. Storage Area Network protocol
   E. Taps
5. A modest expansion of denial of service can be referred to as:
   A. Systems security plan
   B. Consumer privacy protection
   C. IP storage access
   D. Vulnerability
   E. Distributed denial of service attacks

EXERCISE

Problem

Which Ethernet ports require 802.1x authentication?

Hands-on Projects

Project

What 802.1x authentication mechanism should one use?

Case Projects

Problem

Do all clients support 802.1x?

Optional Team Case Project

Problem

Does 802.1x have security vulnerabilities?

Chapter 82

Homeland Security

Rahul Bhaskar and Bhushan Kapoor

California State University, Fullerton, CA, United States

Note: This chapter is available in its entirety online at store.elsevier.com/product.jsp?isbn= 9780128038437 (click the Resources tab at the bottom of the page).

1. ABSTRACT

The September 11, 2001, terrorist attacks, permanently changed the way the United States and the world's other most developed countries perceived the threat from terrorism. Massive amounts of resources were mobilized in a very short time to counter the perceived and actual threats from terrorists and terrorist organizations. In the United States, this refocus was pushed as a necessity for what was called *homeland security*. The homeland security threats were anticipated for the IT infrastructure as well. It was expected that not only the IT at the federal level was vulnerable to disruptions due to terrorism-related attacks but, due to the ubiquity of the availability of IT, any organization was vulnerable. Soon after the terrorist attacks, the US Congress passed various new laws and enhanced some existing ones that introduced sweeping changes to homeland security provisions and to the existing security organizations. The executive branch of the government also issued a series of Homeland Security Presidential Directives to maintain domestic security. These laws and directives are comprehensive and contain detailed provisions to make the United States secure from its vulnerabilities. Later in the chapter, we describe some principle provisions of these homeland security-related laws and presidential directives. Next, we discuss the organizational changes that were initiated to support homeland security in the United States. Then we highlight the 9-11 Commission that Congress charted to provide a full account of the circumstances surrounding the attacks and to develop recommendations for corrective measures that could be taken to prevent future acts of terrorism. We also detail the Intelligence Reform and Terrorism Prevention Act of 2004 and the Implementing the 9-11 Commission Recommendations Act of 2007. Finally, we summarize the chapter's discussion.

2. CONTENTS

Computer and Information Security Handbook. http://dx.doi.org/10.1016/B978-0-12-803843-7.00082-X

Chapter 83

Cyber Warfare

Anna Granova[1] and Marco Slaviero[2]

[1]*University of Pretoria, Johannesburg, Republic of South Africa;* [2]*SensePost Pty Ltd., University of Pretoria, Pretoria, South Africa*

October 20, 1969, marked the first message sent on the Internet,[1,2] and more 40 years later, we cannot imagine our lives without it. Internet banking, online gaming, and online shopping and social media have become as important to some as food and sleep. As the world has become more dependent on automated environments, interconnectivity, networks, and the Internet, instances of abuse and misuse of information technology (IT) infrastructures have increased proportionately.[3] Unfortunately, such abuse has not been limited to business information systems and websites; over time it has also penetrated the military domain of state security. This penetration of governmental IT infrastructures, including the military domain among others, is commonly referred to as *cyber warfare* (CW). However, these concepts are not yet clearly defined and understood. Furthermore, this type of warfare is a multi-disciplinary field requiring expertise from technical, legal, offensive, and defensive perspectives. Information security professionals are challenged to respond to this type of warfare issues in a professional and knowledgeable way.

The purpose of this chapter is to define the concept of cyber warfare (CW); discuss its most common tactics, weapons, and tools; compare CW terrorism with conventional warfare; and address the issues of liability and the available legal remedies under international law. To have this discussion, a proper model and definition of CW first needs to be established.

---

1. Egypt: AP Confirms Government has Disrupted Internet Service, 2011. http://pomed.org/blog/2011/01/egypt-ap-confirms-government-has-disrupted-internet-service.html/.

2. An Internet History, 2008. www.services.ex.ac.uk/cmit/modules/the_internet/webct/ch-history.html.

3. Symantec Global Internet Security Threat Report Trends for July—December 07, 2008, vol. 13, April 2008. Available at: http://eval.symantec.com/mktginfo/enterprise/white_papers/b-whitepaper_internet_security_threat_report_xiii_04-2008.en-us.pdf.

1. CYBER WARFARE MODEL

The authors propose a model for CW by mapping important concepts and regarding them on a single diagrammatic representation (Fig. 83.1). This aids in simplifying a complex concept and provides a holistic view of the phenomenon. To this end, this chapter addresses the four axes of CW: technical, legal, offensive, and defensive, as depicted in Fig. 83.1.

The technical side of CW deals with technical exploits on the one side and defensive measures on the other. As is apparent from Fig. 83.1, these range from the most destructive offensive strategies, such as a distributed denial of service (DDoS) attack or Stuxnet, to various workstation emergency response teams, such as US Computer Emergency Response Teams (US-CERT).

Considered from a legal perspective, CW can range from criminal prosecutions in international courts to the use of force in retaliation. Therefore, the four axes of CW continuously interact and influence each other, as will become clearer from the discussion that follows.

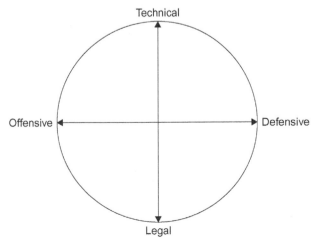

FIGURE 83.1 A perspective on cyber warfare.

Computer and Information Security Handbook. http://dx.doi.org/10.1016/B978-0-12-803843-7.00083-1

2. CYBER WARFARE DEFINED

The manner in which war is being conducted has evolved enormously,[4] and CW has not only been accepted as a new direction in military operations[5] but has also been incorporated into some of the top military forces in the world. China implemented a CW policy as early as 1995,[6] the US Cyber Command (USCYBERCOM) was established in 2009,[7] followed by China in July 2010,[8] the US Cyber Warfare Intelligence Center[9] was unveiled in November 2010, and the Cyber Warfare Administration in Israel breathed into life in 2012.[10] A number of definitions are relevant for the purposes of this chapter. Some authors[11] maintain that CW covers "the full range of competitive information operations from destroying IT equipment to subtle perception management, and from industrial espionage to marketing." If one regards the more "military" definition of CW, one could say that CW is "a subset of information operations": in other words "actions taken to adversely affect information and information systems while defending one's own information and information systems."[12]

The United Nations (UN) Secretary-General's report on *Development in the Field on Information and Telecommunications in the Context of International Security* describes CW as "actions aimed at achieving information superiority by executing measures to exploit, corrupt, destroy, destabilize, or damage the enemy's information and its functions."[13] This definition is similar to one of the more accepted definitions found in the literature that states that CW is "actions taken in support of objectives that influence decision-makers by affecting the information and/or information systems of others while protecting your own information and/or information systems."[14] However, if one

looks at CW in a purely military light, the following technical definition seems to be the most appropriate: "The broad class of activities aimed at leveraging data, information and knowledge in support of military goals."[15]

In light of the preceding, it is clear that CW is all about information superiority, because "the fundamental weapon and target of CW is information."[11] This being so, some authors[11] outline the basic strategies of CW as:

1. deny access to information
2. disrupt/destroy data
3. steal data
4. manipulate data to change its context or its perception

A slightly different perspective of the aims of CW is perhaps to see it as "an attack on information systems for military advantage using tactics of destruction, denial, exploitation or deception."[15] Since about 2008, however, CW started to cross over into the physical realm through one of its forms, cyber warfare, which can be defined as *"politically motivated hacking to conduct sabotage and espionage."*[16] With these definitions in mind, it is appropriate to consider whether CW is a concept that has been created by enthusiasts such as individual hackers to impress the rest of the world's population or is in fact part of daily military operations.

3. CYBER WARFARE: MYTH OR REALITY?

Groves once said: "... Nowhere it is safe ... no one knows of the scale of the threat, the silent deadly menace that stalks the network."[17] With the growing risk of terrorists and other hostile entities engaging in missions of sabotaging important public infrastructures through cyber attacks, either temporarily or permanently, the number of articles[18] on the topic has grown significantly. To understand the gravity of CW and its consequences, the following real-life examples need to be considered. At the outset, however, it is important to mention that the reason there is so little regulation (see checklist: " An Agenda for Action for Regulating High-Level Cyber Warfare Strategies") of computer-related activities with specific reference to CW on both national and international planes is that lawyers are reluctant to venture into the unknown. The following examples, however, demonstrate that CW has taken place consistently since at least 1991. One of the first CW incidents was recorded in 1991 during the first Gulf War, when CW was used by the United States against Iraq.[19]

4. Schmitt, Wired warfare-workstation network attack and jus in bello, International Review of the Red Cross (2002) 365.

5. Rogers, Protecting America against cyber terrorism, United States Foreign Policy Agenda (2001) 15.

6. Ball, Security Challenges 7 (2) (Winter 2011) 81−103. http://www.securitychallenges.org.au/ArticlePDFs/vol7no2Ball.pdf.

7. Cyber Command Achieves Full Operational Capability, 2010. http://www.defense.gov/releases/release.aspx?releaseid=14030.

8. Branigan, Chinese Army to Target Cyber War Threat, 2010. http://www.guardian.co.uk/world/2010/jul/22/chinese-army-cyber-war-department.

9. Construction Begins on First Cyber Warfare Intelligence Center, 2010. http://www.af.mil/news/story.asp?id=123204543.

10. Israel to Establish Cyber Warfare Administration, 2012. http://www.israelnationalnews.com/News/News.aspx/151713.

11. Hutchinson, Warren, CW—Corporate Attack and Defence in a Digital World, 2001, p. XVIII.

12. Schmitt, Wired Warfare-Workstation Network Attack and jus in bello, International Review of the Red Cross (2002) 365. See also the definition by Goldberg available online at: http://psycom.net/CWar.2.html.

13. UNG.A.Res A/56/164 dated July 3, 2001.

14. R. Thornton, Asymmetric Warfare—Threat and Response in the 21st Century 2007.

15. J.R. Vacca, Computer Forensics: Computer Crime Scene Investigation, second ed., Charles River Media, 2005.

16. Cyber warfare, 2012. http://en.wikipedia.org/wiki/Cyberwarfare.

17. I.J. Lloyd, Information Technology Law, fifth ed., Oxford University Press, 2008, p. 181.

18. Groves, The war on terrorism: cyberterrorist be ware, Informational Management Journal (January−Febrary 2002).

19. Goodwin, Don't Techno for an Answer: The False Promise of CW.

An Agenda for Action for Regulating High-Level Cyber Warfare Strategies

Please see the following recommendations for regulating high-level cyber warfare strategies (check all tasks completed):

_____**1.** The President of the United States should task the National Office for Cyberspace (NOC) to work with appropriate regulatory agencies to develop and issue standards and guidance for securing critical cyber infrastructure, which those agencies would then apply in their own regulations.

_____**2.** The NOC should work with the appropriate regulatory agencies and with the National Institute of Standards and Technology (NIST) to develop regulations for industrial control systems.

_____**3.** The government should reinforce regulations by making the development of secure control systems an element of any economic stimulus package.

_____**4.** The NOC should immediately determine the extent to which government-owned critical infrastructures are secure from cyber attack.

_____**5.** The president should direct the NOC and the federal Chief Information Officers Council, working with industry, to develop and implement security guidelines for the procurement of IT products (with software as the first priority).

_____**6.** The president should task the National Security Agency (NSA) and NIST, working with international partners, to reform the National Information Assurance Partnership.

_____**7.** The president should take steps to increase the use of secure Internet protocols.

_____**8.** The president should direct the Office of Management Office of Management and Budget and the NOC to develop mandatory requirements for agencies to contract only with telecommunications carriers that use secure Internet protocols.

In 1998 an Israeli national hacked into the government workstations of the United States.[20] In 1999, a number of cyber attacks took place in Kosovo. During the attacks the Serbian and North Atlantic Treaty Organization (NATO) websites were taken down with the aim of interfering with and indirectly influencing the public's perception and opinion of the conflict.[11]

These cyber attacks were executed for different reasons: Russians hacked US and Canadian websites "in protest" against NATO deployment,[21] Chinese joined the online war because their embassy in Belgrade was bombed by NATO,[22] and US nationals were paralyzing the White House[23] and NATO[24] websites "for fun." In 2000, classified information was distributed on the Internet,[25] and attacks were launched on the National Aeronautics and Space Administration's (NASA's) laboratories,[26] the US Postal Service, and the Canadian Defense Department.[27] As early

as 2001, detected intrusions into the US Defense Department's website numbered 23,662.[28] Furthermore, there were 1300 pending investigations into activities "ranging from criminal activity to national security intrusions."[29] Hackers also attempted to abuse the US Federal Court's database[30] to compromise the peace process in the Middle East.[31]

In 2002, incidents of cyber terrorism in Morocco, Spain, Moldova, and Georgia[32] proved once again that a "hacker influenced by politics is a terrorist," illustrated by more than 140,000 attacks in less than 48 h allegedly executed by the "G-Force" (Pakistan).[33] During this period, a series of convictions on charges of conspiracy, the destruction of energy facilities,[34] the destruction of telecommunications facilities, and the disabling of air navigation facilities,[35] as well as cases of successful international luring and subsequent prosecutions, were recorded.[36]

---

20. Israeli citizen arrested in Israel for hacking United States and Israeli Government Workstations (1998). http://www.usdoj.gov/criminal/cybercrime/ehudpr.hgm.

21. Skoric, 1999. http://amsterdam.nettime.org/Lists-Archives/net-time-1-9906/msg00152.html.

22. Messmer, 1999. http://www.cnn.com/TECH/computing/9905/12/cyberwar.idg/.

23. "Web Bandit" Hacker Sentenced to 15 months Imprisonment, 3 years of Supervised Release, for Hacking USIA, NATO, Web Sites, 1999. www.usdoj.gov/criminal/cybercrime/burns.htm.

24. Access to NATO's Website Disrupted, 1999. www.cnn.com/WORLD/europe/9903/31/nato.hack/.

25. Lusher, 2000. www.balkanpeace.org/hed/archive/april00/hed30.

26. Hacker Pleads Guilty in New York City to Hacking into Two NASA Jet Propulsion Lab Workstations Located in Pasadena, California (2000). www.usdoj.gov/criminal/cybercrime/rolex.htm.

27. (2000) www.usdoj.gov/criminal/cybercrime/VAhacker2.htm.

28. www.coe.int/T/E/Legal_affairs/Legal_co-operation/Combating_economic_crime/Cybercrime/International_conference/ConfCY(2001)5E-1.pdf.

29. Rogers, Protecting America against Cyber terrorism US Foreign Policy Agenda (2001).

30. Hacker into United States Courts' Information System Pleads Guilty, 2001. www.usdoj.gov/criminal/cybercrime/MamichPlea.htm.

31. Computer Hacker Intentionally Damages Protected Computer, 2001. www.usdoj.gov/criminal/cybercrime/khanindict.htm.

32. Hacker Influenced by Politics is also a Terrorist, 2002. www.utro.ru/articles/2002/07/24/91321.shtml.

33. www.echocct.org/main.html.

34. Hackers Hit Power Companies, 2002. www.cbsnews.com/stories/2002/07/08/tech/main514426.shtml.

35. U.S. v. Konopka (E.D.Wis.), www.usdoj.gov/criminal/cybercrime/konopkaIndict.htm.

36. U.S. v. Gorshkov (W.D.Wash), www.usdoj.gov/criminal/cybercrime/gorshkovSent.htm.

In the second half of 2007, 499,811 new malicious code threats were detected, which represented a 571% increase from the same period in 2006.[3] With two-thirds of more than 1 million identified viruses created in 2007,[3] the continued increase in malicious code threats has been linked to the sharp rise in the development of new Trojan viruses and the apparent existence of institutions that employ "professionals" dedicated to creation of new threats.[37] In 2008 it was reported in the media that "over the past year to 18 months, there has been "a huge increase in focused attacks on our [United States] national infrastructure networks ... and they have been coming from outside the United States."[38]

It is common knowledge that the United States has tried to save both manpower and costs by establishing a system to control and monitor electric utilities, pipelines, railroads, and oil companies remotely across the United States.[38] The reality of the threat of CW has been officially confirmed by the US Federal Energy Regulatory Commission, which approved eight cybersecurity standards for electric utilities, including "identity controls, training, security 'parameters' physical security of critical cyber equipment, incident reporting and recovery."[38] In January 2008, a CIA analyst warned the public that cyber attackers hacked into the workstation systems of utility companies outside the United States and made demands, which led to at least one instance in which, as a direct result, a power outage took place that affected multiple cities.[38]

Furthermore, since 2007, there have been a number of high-profile events that can be categorized as cyber attacks. Estonia was first in line to experience this debilitating form of aggression: a wave of DDoS attacks in which websites were swamped by tens of thousands of requests, which in turn disabled them by overcrowding the bandwidths for the servers running the websites of the Estonian government, political parties, half of media organizations, and the top two banks.[39]

Russia was blamed for the Estonian cyber conflict, which was caused by the removal of a statue of significant importance to Russian people. The repeat of the showdown, but with Georgia on the receiving end, was witnessed in 2008 when Georgia was blown offline during its military conflict with Russia.[40]

China also appeared to be waging a persistent low-profile campaign against many foreign nations, such as Japan,[41] the United States,[42] and the United Kingdom.[43] The United States itself is not above suspicion: some experts hint that that country[44] might have unleashed a powerful "cyber weapon" such as Stuxnet, which affected Iran's ability to conduct nuclear research.

With the Duqu worm, which was discovered on September 1, 2011, and show capabilities similar to Stuxnet,[45] it is only a matter of time before one is able to find the country behind the worm by analyzing the motives behind the facility that will experience its onslaught. Appropriate questions that arise are thus: How can CW be brought about and how can one ward against it?

4. PARTICIPANTS, ROLES, ATTRIBUTION, AND ASYMMETRY

In a field as nascent as CW in which doctrine, concepts, strategies, tactics, and techniques are currently being developed, writing about the state of the art is akin to chasing rainbows. As soon as a CW idea is postulated, those whom it will negatively affect will immediately begin planning its counteraction.[46] Work that focuses solely on the technicalities of CW are destined to be outdated in the very near future. Therefore our discussion will first define

37. Symantec Global Internet Security Threat Report Trends for July—December 07, 2008, vol. 13, April 2008. p. 46. Available at: http://eval.symantec.com/mktginfo/enterprise/white_papers/b-whitepaper_internet_security_threat_report_xiii_04-2008.en-us.pdf.

38. E. Nakashima, S. Mufson, Hackers have attacked foreign utilities, CIA Analysts Says, January 19, 2008. Available at: www.washingtonpost.com/wp/dyn/conmttent/atricle/2008/01/18/AR2008011803277bf.html.

39. Traynor, Russia Accused of Unleashing Cyberwar to Disable Estonia, 2007. http://www.guardian.co.uk/world/2007/may/17/topstories3.russia.

40. Danchev, Coordinated Russia versus Georgia Cyber Attack in Progress, 2008. http://www.zdnet.com/blog/security/coordinated-russia-vs-georgia-cyber-attack-in-progress/1670. Tikk, Cyber Attacks Against Georgia: Legal Lessons Identified, 2008. http://www.carlisle.army.mil/DIME/documents/Georgia%201%200.pdf.

41. Japan Parliament Hit by China-Based Cyber Attack, 2011. http://www.telegraph.co.uk/news/worldnews/asia/japan/8848100/Japan-parliament-hit-by-China-based-cyber-attack.html.

42. Identified Massive Global Cyber attack Targeting U.S., U.N. Discovered; Experts Blame China, 2011. http://www.foxnews.com/scitech/2011/08/03/massive-global-cyberattack-targeting-us-un-discovered-experts-blame-china/. Finkle, Cyber Attack from China Targets Chemical Firms: Symantec, 2011. http://www.msnbc.msn.com/id/45105397/ns/technology_and_science-security/t/cyber-attack-china-targets-chemical-firms-symantec/. Gorman, U.S. Report to Warn on Cyber attack Threat From China, 2012. http://online.wsj.com/article/SB10001424052970203961204577267923890777392.html.

43. Foster, China Chief Suspect in Major Cyber Attack, 2012. http://www.telegraph.co.uk/technology/news/8679658/China-chief-suspect-in-major-cyber-attack.html.

44. Langner, Cracking Stuxnet, a 21st-Century Cyber Weapon, 2011 http://www.ted.com/talks/ralph_langner_cracking_stuxnet_a_21st_century_cyberweapon.html. Waug, How the world's first cyber super weapon 'designed by the CIA' attacked Iran — and now threatens the world, (2011). http://www.dailymail.co.uk/sciencetech/article-2070690/How-worlds-cyber-super-weapon-attacked-Iran—threatens-world.html.

45. Naraine, Duqu FAQ. http://www.securelist.com/en/blog/208193178/Duqu_FAQ.

46. The commercial information security industry has seen this play out for decades now. When new hardening measures are implemented against memory corruption attacks, for example, exploit writers continue to find new ways to bypass the defensive measures. Similarly, defenders respond to new types of attacks. This adversarial nature where parties are diametrically opposed to each other makes security a particularly interesting field of research.

the combatants in CW and identify the roles and functions they perform. Thereafter we will cover the topic of attribution before moving on to how CW is waged.

Participants and Their Roles

Fighting a successful overt war is premised on knowing who the adversary actually is. In past years that was easy; the adversary was whoever was hurling threats, rocks, missiles, and other nasty things in your general direction (It says something about our progress that this basic test has held up for millennia.). However in the CW realm things are decidedly murkier. CW operations that are carried out over public networks (such as the Internet) are not easily attributable by purely technical means, and for a nation defending against a virtual onslaught it is not obvious who the adversary is. Although the political climate might provide clues, technical evidence is generally of poor quality, as we shall soon find out. The low cost of waging virtual attacks means that when tensions escalate between nations, overly patriotic citizens can insert themselves into situations by launching attacks against the enemy. Determining whether the attacks are state-sanctioned borders on the impossible.

The Tallinn Manual is an academic study of cyber war written at the request of NATO, and posits that no one is barred from participating in cyber operations, but that their legal consequences depend on the status of the individual. Armed forces and or citizens involved in a mass uprising enjoy combatant immunity and prisoner of war status in the event of capture, whereas mercenaries and civilians acting on their own do not.[47] These categories serve as a basis for potential participants in a cyber operation.

Armed Forces

Armed forces around the globe have embraced cyber as part of their military doctrine. USCYBERCOM is composed of units from different service branches, China has a range of military units dedicated to cyber operations, Iran is particularly active in cyberspace, and Russia's involvement in cyber attacks on former Soviet states is frequently asserted.

The line between armed forces and intelligence services blurs when it comes to CW. There is significant overlap between the two branches at both the operational and tactical levels; the difference between data theft and data destruction is a single command invocation. Although espionage activities might not count as acts of CW in a legal sense, they will share almost all aspects of their technical operations with an explicit act of CW.

In addition to the role of attacker, armed forces also have a useful defensive role. The resources and clout of armed forces means that when critical assets are under attack, cyber units are able to counter and theoretically repel attacks. By way of example, well-resourced armed forces will have experts on multiple platforms in their units along with strong IR skills. If an attack targets a previously unknown vulnerability, a well-resourced military would be able to quarantine the exploit, analyze it and uncover the underlying vulnerability.

Civilians

Cyber operations are not limited to members of the armed forces. Civilians acting alone or as part of a mass uprising can leverage widely available hacking tools and techniques to conduct cyber operations. They are not limited to publicly available tools or techniques; significant research and development skills are present in nonmilitary populations. The evidence for this is strong. Every year hundreds of security conferences take place at which nonmilitary individuals present new ideas and tools for attack. Breaches at major organizations continue unabated in the private sector by attackers looking to profit from their attacks. Privately funded research continues to generate a consistent stream of vulnerabilities found in widely used software.[48]

The ability for civilians to be involved in CW is established, but their effectiveness is not. Civilians can slot into the attacking role easily but will struggle to pick targets, and the targets they choose will likely be visible but largely irrelevant.[49] Furthermore, picking targets is not simply a case of choosing Internet Protocol (IP) addresses geolocated in the adversary's territory. Targeting requires preparation in the form of mapping out the adversary's networks far in advance, and is one of the hallmarks of CW professionals.

It may seem that civilians are not able to assist in defensive roles because the assets are not under their control; this is largely the case. A well-resourced defense has no need for external personnel. However for resource-constrained defenses where skills are weak, knowledgeable civilians would be able to offer services in the event of an attack.

Mercenaries

Separate from civilians are mercenaries. Mercenaries have a specific definition under the Geneva Conventions and in essence are those who are recruited to fight in a conflict

---

47. Schmitt, N. Michael (Eds.), Tallinn Manual on the International Law Applicable to Cyber Warfare, first ed., Cambridge University Press, Cambridge, 2013.

48. As of February 2016, Google's Project Zero had uncovered 600 vulnerabilities in the course of 18 months with fewer than two dozen team members. https://www.usenix.org/sites/default/files/conference/protected-files/enigma_slides_hawkes.pdf.

49. For example, flooding the CIA's http://cia.gov website and rendering it inaccessible will have no impact on the CIA's operational capability. The CIA example is not picked at random; it is regularly the target of DDoS attacks launched by a range of groups online.

primarily for private gain, and are not members of the armed forces or nationals of the parties involved in the conflict.[50]

The full impact of mercenaries on CW is yet to be seen. Whereas well-resourced militaries will have plenty of skills within their ranks and have no need to look externally, nations that have not yet built CW capabilities but find themselves approaching a conflict can purchase services of foreign attackers quickly. Hired hackers can operate over the Internet and anonymous payments make attributing cyber operations to the employer nation extremely difficult.

Turning to the defender role, the Tallinn Manual does not differentiate between mercenaries acting as either attacker or defender. Militaries could bring in mercenaries to help monitor, patch, and configure services, but the more likely reason for hiring mercenaries is incident response (IR). IR is an extremely specialized field that requires deep knowledge and skilled analysis. Incident responders aim to take compromised systems and extract a record of what happened and how it happened.[51] If a foreign IR firm is employed to investigate and repair an incident, does that meet the definition of mercenary participation? If it actively participates in defending the target by ejecting infections when found, then it appears to meet that bar, potentially bringing with it dramatic consequences.

Intelligence Services

Although the Tallinn Manual is silent on intelligence agencies and their role in CW, experience shows that the intelligence community is highly invested in CW knowledge. In 2013 Edward Snowden leaked a trove of NSA documents and in the process revealed attack and surveillance capabilities previously unknown, such as redirecting Cisco devices during transport so that modified firmware could be loaded before delivery to the paying customer.[52] Although modifying the firmware may not cause the customer harm at that point, in the event of a conflict, access to the device would be immensely powerful. By virtue of its skills, experience, and activities, the NSA and other intelligence agencies are involved in CW in both attacker and defender roles. With the participants and their capability for the roles explored, we return to the question of identifying the source of a cyber operation, the delicate art of attribution.

Attribution

Responding to a cyber operation without knowing who was responsible means that decisions are made in the dark; attribution is vital in understanding an attack. If a cyber operation can be definitively traced to a nation state, this could be the basis for kinetic response, but if an attack can be attributed to bored foreign teenagers, surely a kinetic response would be unlawful.

Basic Attribution

Asserting attribution's importance unfortunately does not make it easier. The problem faced by targets is that technical evidence is unreliable. For example, merely using an IP address to attribute an attack is incredibly dangerous; attackers route traffic through third-party nations with weak antihacking laws all the time (even in run-of-the-mill scams and hacking campaigns). When it comes to traffic sources, appearances *are* deceiving. In February 2013, computer IR firm Mandiant published a report stating that a hacking group called "APT1" was in fact a Chinese military unit engaged in long-term espionage, and claimed they had the evidence to prove it.[53] A significant support to their claim was based on IP addresses; they traced activity back to the Pudong New Area in Shanghai (using WHOIS data[54]) and drew the conclusion that a military unit stationed in Pudong was most likely responsible. However, Pudong New Area is $1210 \, \text{km}^2$ in size (virtually identical to Los Angeles, United States) and was where the main China–United States undersea cable landed. Attributing an attack to one military unit when 7 million people live in that area required unhealthy levels of credulity and showed the limits of technical evidence.

Moving away from IP addresses, attribution is also conducted on the basis of markers left behind by attackers. Captured malicious software (malware) samples could include the default language of the computer on which it was compiled; symbol names in the binaries might reveal variable names, and with those the programmer's preferred language; file paths in the binaries could provide hints as to who compiled the code; timestamps indicate when the malware was created. When monitoring live attackers, it is sometimes possible to extract information about the attackers' environment, such as their keyboard layout (which might indicate a particular country if the layout is not used elsewhere in the world.)

Behavioral patterns are also used in attribution. Investigators will attempt to correlate attacks with time zones,

50. International Committee of the Red Cross (ICRC), Protocol Additional to the Geneva Conventions of August 12, 1949, and relating to the Protection of Victims of International Armed Conflicts (Protocol I), June 8, 1977, 1125 UNTS three.

51. Kaspersky, Symantec and CrySys Lab have been instrumental in discovering and publishing details on sophisticated malware.

52. Gallagher, Photos of an NSA "upgrade" factory show Cisco router getting implant. http://arstechnica.com/tech-policy/2014/05/photos-of-an-nsa-upgrade-factory-show-cisco-router-getting-implant/.

53. Mandiant, APT1 — Exposing One of China's Cyber Espionage Units http://intelreport.mandiant.com/Mandiant_APT1_Report.pdf.

54. The WHOIS database is a distributed database of domain and IP address ownership records, and has wildly varying quality depending on the registrar responsible. It is not a reliable forensic tool.

under the assumption that attackers tend to follow regular hours. They will also try to correlate attack patterns with calendars around the globe; testing whether the attacks tend to decrease in number around major holidays in different countries.

A careful consideration of these technical and behavioral attribution components reveals that they all share a major flaw: they can be trivially faked. Artifacts in compiled programs are subject to modification, and any half-decent attacker will obscure the attack code so that it does not implicate the authors. They can go a step further and insert markers that point to rivals or even the nation being attacked. The point is that technical evidence extracted by the attack victim is unreliable.

Broader Attribution

So, can attribution be performed? There are factors that are harder to fake, which increase the confidence of an attribution decision. Tool chains, private vulnerabilities and exploits, chosen targets, and operational decisions are all aspects that give clues as to the identity of the attacker, because they are not trivial to mimic. In other words, a particular entity may be known to reuse a custom malware sample or command infrastructure; seeing those samples in other attacks provides an attribution clue. Similarly, if stolen information reappears in an adversary's possession, it is easy to point fingers.

As our knowledge of the terrain expands, some authors believe we are at the point where a nuanced view of attribution yields useful results. Rid and Buchanan argue that attribution occurs across tactical, operational, and strategic levels, and minimizing uncertainty is the goal. Technical attribution "is an art as much as a science," operational attribution is "a nuanced process, not a simple problem," and strategic attribution is "a function of what is at stake politically." Attribution is not a simple "yes-or-no," but has intervals.[55]

The same authors make the point that bringing to bear additional noncyber resources such as signals intelligence, human intelligence, and other forms of corroboration can enrich cyber attribution. An informant in a foreign military might be able to confirm that a cyber attack was launched, thereby negating the need for complex attribution. Even more directly, a powerful CW actor could have compromised the adversary's networks far in advance of hostilities, and be in a position to observe the adversary as it launches attacks. In these cases the attribution is not only based on easily faked technical information, but is backed up with additional observations that are more reliable.

Ultimately attribution is the confidence placed in the presentation and dissection of evidence, although the evidence may not be revealed when the attribution is publicly communicated, if it all. Although it may sound strange that an attacked nation keeps quiet or does not release evidence, there is a rational reason for this, called the "disclosure dilemma."

The Disclosure Dilemma

Consider Nation A, which has good visibility into its own networks and resources and is currently tracking Nation B as it probes and attacks Nation A's public infrastructure. On occasion Nation B is successful and breaches systems, where it pokes around, exfiltrates data if it finds them, then leaves behind malware to maintain access. Nation A's response could vary from merely cleaning up behind the attackers to repelling intrusions in real time and publicly accusing Nation B of the attacks along with full details to persuade the public of the accusations.

The latter approach, in which accusations and full details are released, may score moral points and solidify support inside Nation A for a strong response. But the very evidence that supports the accusations provides Nation B with vital insight into Nation A's operational capabilities. The attacking nation will look in its archives for attacks that were not reflected in the published evidence, and change its approach to be less visible.

On the other hand, if Nation A simply cleans up after the attacks occurred, with no public response, Nation B has little incentive to halt its actions unless pressure is brought to bear through other means.

This, in a nutshell, is the disclosure dilemma.[56] Attributing attacks (with or without evidence) reveals defensive capabilities; not attributing attacks signals to attackers that they remain undetected or are not posing a serious threat, and in either case they can continue to run wild.

When Sony Pictures Entertainment was breached in 2014, it first became aware of the hack after its internal systems were altered.[57] Over the next 2 weeks, stolen data including films and internal emails were released. A hacking group claimed initial responsibility, but just 5 days later sources close to the investigation indicated that North Korea was suspected to have had a role.[58] This accusation gained traction and was adopted as the official position of

55. Thomas Rid, Ben Buchanan, Attributing cyber attacks, Journal of Strategic Studies 38 (1–2) (2015) 4–37, http://dx.doi.org/10.1080/01402390.2014.977382.

56. M. Cavelty, Breaking the cyber-security dilemma: aligning security needs and removing vulnerabilities, Science and Engineering Ethics 20 (3) (2014) 701–715.

57. Williams, Sony Pictures hacked, entire computer system reportedly unusable. http://thenextweb.com/insider/2014/11/24/sony-pictures-hacked-employee-computers-offline/.

58. Hesseldahl, Sony Pictures Investigates North Korea Link in Hack Attack. http://recode.net/2014/11/28/sony-pictures-investigates-north-korea-link-in-hack-attack/.

the US government, leading to sanctions being levied against North Korea by the United States.[59] Evidence released to back up the North Korea claim was weak; a disclosure dilemma is one explanation for not wanting to provide too many. The danger of the approach is it requests trust without verification, and if later evidence emerges to show the attribution was weak, future claims without proof will be treated with more suspicion.

In covering attribution we have shown the mismatch between what attackers and defenders perceive is large; this is not the only asymmetry present. Let us explore a few more imbalances between attackers and defenders.

Asymmetry in Cyber Warfare

Mismatches between attacking and defending forces in combat can be found throughout recorded history. Differences in the number of combatants, number of weapons, type of weapons, supplies, terrain, and information are just some ways in which opponents may differ, and smart commanders will try to maximize these differences to their advantage. Information war is no different in that asymmetries exist, although they take different forms.

A prominent idea is that attacks cost less than defending against the attacks. The argument goes that attackers incur very low costs when launching an attack; if the attack works, they continue with postexploitation steps, but even if the attack is rebuffed, attackers can choose another target. Defenders, on the other hand, need to be constantly vigilant. This model of attack works for individual attackers, but it does not scale well to explain the costs of large attack teams. Although the costs for launching an individual attack might be low, the skills, research and development time, and infrastructure to support the attack add up.

Monte goes so far as to call cost a "false asymmetry."[60] He argues that building and maintaining serious attack capabilities incur significant costs, far more than what is commonly acknowledged. He notes that global defense spending is on the order of 50–70 billion dollars a year. However, the US Department of Defense (DoD) planned to spend $6.7 billion for cyber funding,[61] including allocations for defense and nonattack line items. There is little evidence to support the notion that attackers spend anywhere close to the amount spent by defenders. Monte explains this by asserting, "The supposed asymmetry of cost is actually just lack of defensive coordination." In other words, defenders do not learn from other defenders,

and so are doomed to repeat mistakes and duplicate costs. This may be so, but the reality is that combined defenders spend more than attackers.[62]

For commercial-grade attacks, professional attack tools intended for security consultants sell in the range of a few thousand dollars (depending on the number of licenses).[63] These regularly defeat multimillion dollar security defenses in corporations around the world; the cost asymmetry is present in the private sector as well.

Cost is not the only imbalance present when parties square off across cyber terrain. Monte highlights that attackers tend to have the advantage when it comes to motivation, initiative, focus, effects of failure, knowledge of technology, analysis of opponent, tailored software, and rate of change. Effects of failure are worth highlighting: If an attack fails, the impact to an attacker is typically low. They choose another target and carry on. For defenders the effects of failure could be catastrophic. Even a successful defensive action is still to the defender's disadvantage, because it has revealed part of the defender's capability.

The asymmetries do not completely favor the attacker; there are some advantages to the defender. Monte is in agreement that controlling the network provides a defender with major benefits. Monitoring and logging can reveal attackers, and the defender has full control over the logging configuration. The defender *should* have greater knowledge of the network layout and be aware of where sensitive data lie; an attacker with no preexisting knowledge must scour the network where each dead end is a detection opportunity for the defender.[64]

The second advantage the defender has is full configuration control of software and hardware. With automated configuration management becoming the norm, and software-defined networking centralizing network configuration, it is possible that future defenses will include completely reorganizing and rearranging network topology on a regular basis, so that any previous reconnaissance work by an attacker is rendered useless. Participants, roles, attribution, and asymmetries complete, it is time to examine the waging of CW.

5. MAKING CYBER WARFARE POSSIBLE

Wars require an arsenal of weapons combined with an array of defensive technologies as well as laboratories and

59. BBC, Sony cyber-attack: North Korea faces new US sanctions. http://www.bbc.com/news/world-us-canada-30661973.
60. M. Monte, Network Attacks & Exploitation, 2015. John Wiley & Sons, Inc.
61. Lyngaas, Pentagon looks to mature Cyber Command with FY17 budget. https://fcw.com/articles/2016/02/09/dod-it-budget-cyber.aspx.

62. The asymmetry is not an unbreakable rule, of course, and local exceptions occur all the time. Should a small technology company find themselves targeted by an intelligence service, the cost imbalance would tilt heavily toward the attacking agency, whose costs would exceed what the small company would spend on its security defenses.
63. We cover three examples later in this chapter.
64. We say "should" because attackers sometimes perform better network reconnaissance than defenders and have a more accurate understanding of installed software and network layout than the network owners.

factories for researching and producing both. This is true in kinetic war and holds true in CW as well. As far as CW is concerned, three general strategies need to be considered in building capabilities and executing operations: production strategies, offensive strategies, and defensive strategies.

Production

Without arms, wars cannot be fought. Weapons take time to develop and good preparation means having stockpiles of weapons ready to be deployed; CW is no different. Production will have a major role in CW because the actual hostile acts occur in seconds or minutes, but the acts themselves are the culmination of many human-years' worth of work to get an exploit working, in the right network location.

In addition to training new personnel and producing cyber weapons, production consists of a wide range of information-gathering activities. Effective warfare is premised on knowledge of the opponent's weaknesses; having extensive knowledge of an adversary's technology and networks before hostilities is important for planning.

Production thus broadly consists of training, research, reconnaissance, and vulnerability enumeration. It never reaches a conclusion. Ongoing research produces new tools, vulnerabilities and exploits; reconnaissance must continually discover new targets while removing stale targets; and vulnerability enumeration must keep track of new and old targets while testing for recent vulnerabilities.

Research

CW does not require the infrastructure investment that physical arms do,[65] however it depends heavily on highly trained personnel to develop cyber weapons, and the process of training to the required skill levels occupies a significant portion of activities before hostilities break out. Once personnel have the necessary skills, they need time to discover vulnerabilities and turn those into usable exploits or weapons. These are separate jobs; as the continued fragmentation of applications and hardware forces extreme specialization, vulnerability research as a discipline separate from exploit writing is well established. In the commercial information security market, vulnerability research and exploit writing are often separate tasks handed to different individuals, especially where memory corruption bugs are concerned. In the military sector specialization has the additional benefit that new recruits can be trained faster than if they were learning wider skills. The downside to highly specialized teams is that more coordination is required to achieve a broader goal.

The bug finders' skills tend toward rapidly understanding how an application or system is built, how they often fail employing common usage patterns, and the ability to reverse engineer protocols quickly. Good bug finders are adept at automating this process. Their task, for example, is to find input that will cause a memory corruption to occur, after which the test case is handed to an exploit writer. Vulnerabilities are found at all layers and are introduced at all stages of development, and vulnerability research strives to understand each component.

Exploit writers have extreme specialist knowledge of the inner working of the operating system on which the exploit runs, and are able to craft exploits that bypass operating system protections. With a working exploit in hand, the exploit writer then ensures it runs without crashing across a wide range of possible versions of the target software and operating system. The exploit will also often be obfuscated to avoid detection. For the moment it serves to simplify cyber arms by thinking of them as exploits, but as we shall see, cyber weapons consist of further components.

The combined process of finding a bug and writing an exploit for it can take months. Although not all vulnerabilities require that level of input, it is by no means extreme. Software bugs are not the only targets; flaws in algorithms are highly valued and common misconfigurations often yield trivial exploits.[66]

Reconnaissance

This activity of production focuses on identifying government organs, industries, infrastructure, companies, individuals, and organizations that are potential targets. This is fed by intelligence services and overlaps with targets for physical warfare. Targeting occurs as information is gathered about the purpose of the potential targets, data that they store, technologies in use, network presence (on public or private networks), and channels by which the target could be engaged. A discovery exercise is conducted on targets to determine which network services, if any, are accessible.

Vulnerability Enumeration

Following from reconnaissance is vulnerability enumeration or scanning. Vulnerability scanning is a common activity in the commercial security industry, and numerous scanners exist. A typical scanner has a database of tens of thousands of security vulnerabilities, and is able to test for the presence of those issues. The types of tests vary; in some instances a test consists of simply checking a

---

65. Of the $582.7 billion requested for the US DoD 2017 budget, just $6.7 billion was earmarked for all cyber activities.

66. The Flame malware discovered in 2012, included a legitimate-looking fake certificate that was created with a novel cryptographic attack.

software version number extracted from a service banner. Other tests may require running an actual exploit to confirm exploitability. By unleashing the scanner on a wide range of targets, a database of vulnerable machines can be saved before a CW.

Vulnerable systems are not the only benefit of wide-scale scanning. Even a database of version numbers or technology types will improve targeting: for example, when vulnerabilities for a system are discovered in the future.

The problem with scanners is that they are not subtle. They often test for issues unrelated to the technology on which the service runs, and protection mechanisms such as intrusion detection systems are tuned to detect vulnerability scans. One improvement is scanning for specific issues across the target's networks, which reduces the likelihood of detection and masks tests to evade signature-based detection methods. Passive vulnerability enumeration is also possible although the results are not as rich as active vulnerability scanning.

Offensive Strategies

Determining the scale of a CW capability is a crucial decision in deciding on a CW strategy. To extend the analogy of physical warfare, the strategic focus in CW could be on small but highly experienced and trained tactical teams who are able to compromise targets at will, or to deploy an overwhelming number of moderately skilled operators, each of whom tackles a small portion of the operation. The analogy has flaws: whereas adding an extra operator in the physical realm increases the capabilities of that unit, adding extra CW operators past some point starts to see diminishing returns. The reason for this is that many CW operations can be automated and parallelized; additional *infrastructure* is often more valuable than additional personnel. Smaller teams decrease personnel and training costs, although they are more vulnerable to physical attacks against the teams.

For well-resourced militaries, large numbers of moderately skilled operators make sense. The overall performance of the unit is not affected by losses, because no operator is so important that he cannot be replaced, and replacements can be trained quickly. One author with experience in the US intelligence community has written that "[I]n my experience, you are doing things right if, when needed, you can find or create a field expert in less than 2 months." [69]

A second consideration is the type of hostilities that CW covers. CW employed as a support to a kinetic war in the same way that ground troops value air cover is to be expected. A second set of tactics is *covert*, which is akin to espionage. Regardless of whether the strategy is overt or covert, we refer to it as a hostility.

The arsenal of CW includes weapons of a psychological and technical nature. Both are significant and a combination of the two can bring about astounding and highly disruptive results.

Psychological Arsenal

Psychological weapons include social engineering techniques and psychological operations (*psyops*, now termed *military information support operations* by the US military). Psyops include deceptive strategies, which have been part of warfare in general for hundreds of years.

Sun Tzu, in his fundamental work on warfare, says "All warfare is based on deception."[67] Deception has been described as "a contrast and rational effort … to mislead an opponent."[68] In December 2005, it became known that the Pentagon was planning to launch a US $300 million operation to place pro-US messages "in foreign media and on items such as T-shirts and bumper stickers without disclosing the US government as the source."[69] Online, the US government has paid to have favorable messages spread across social media.[70]

Trust is a central concept and a prerequisite for any psyops to succeed. Traditionally, trust was vested in institutions and roles. For some time, computer networks have been attacked by so-called "social engineers" who excel in gaining and exploiting trust, and cybercrime activities such as phishing rely on victims associating mere pictures on a website with the trust they invest in their bank.

However, this does not represent an exhaustive list of psyops. Psyops can also target the general population by substituting information on trusted news agencies' websites as well as public government sites with information favorable to the attackers. A good example is when the information disseminated online is misleading and does not reflect the actual situation on the ground. In 2014 we found evidence that the comments of news stories on popular sites such as CNN were overrun with fake identities.[71]

Social networks are highly efficient tools for spreading information. The instantaneous broadcast nature of micro-blogging sites such as Twitter mean that consumers rely more on social tools for obtaining information about current events than traditional media. In the heat of the moment, fact-checking quality decreases and the probability increases of inserting false information into social platforms. Social networks are also useful in guiding public conversations; Russia's legislative elections of 2011 saw

67. Sun Tzu, Art of War.
68. R. Thornton, Asymmetric Warfare — Threat and Response in the 21st Century, 2007.
69. http://usatoday30.usatoday.com/news/washington/2005-12-14-pentagon-pr_x.htm.
70. Waterman, U.S. Central Command 'friending' the enemy in psychological war. http://www.washingtontimes.com/news/2011/mar/1/us-central-command-friending-the-enemy-in-psycholo/?page=1.
71. Meer, et al., Weapons of Mass Distraction. http://conference.hitb.org/hitbsecconf2014kul/materials/D2T1%20-%20Haroon%20Meer%20Azhar%20Desai%20and%20Marco%20Slaviero%20-%20Weapons%20of%20Mass%20Distraction.pdf.

automated software posting thousands of messages on Twitter to drown out opposition Tweets.[72]

The problem with psyops is that it cannot be used in isolation, because once the enemy stops trusting the information it receives and disregards the bogus messages posted for its attention, psyops become useless, at least for some time. Therefore, technical measures of CW should also be employed to achieve the desired effect, such as denial of service (DoS) and botnet attacks. That way, the enemy might not only be deceived, the information the enemy holds can be destroyed, denied, or even exploited.

Technical Arsenal

There are unsubtle differences between weapons that exist in the physical realm and those that exist within the cyber realm, and the differences are useful to highlight. Bluntly put, there is no patch for an intercontinental ballistic missile. To refine this further, a significant challenge facing a cyber military is that, whereas their attacks can occur virtually instantly, the target is able to respond as rapidly. The response may be to roll out patches for known issues, develop new patches for new vulnerabilities, employ perimeter defenses to filter out the attack traffic, or simply disconnect the targeted system or network (perhaps, in the worst-case scenario, even disconnect a country).

A further challenge is the carrying of CW traffic. In the physical world, air and water provide the channels by which weapons are deployed, but in the cyber realm the path between two points is governed by a different geography. It is a truism that to attack a network, an access channel extending from the attacker to the target is required. It could be a disconnected channel using universal serial bus (USB) flash drives or a highly technical and difficult operation such as the conquest of military satellites with ground-based resources or breaking into submarine cables, but the attacker must have a viable means for delivering the attack. Although these complex or unreliable channels are possible, a more common carrier for CW traffic is commercial Internet infrastructure supplied and maintained by global Internet service providers (ISPs), because they provide publicly accessible network links among countries around the world. In relying on commercial ISPs, attackers have the benefit of plausible deniability on the one hand, and on the other the ability to extend their reach into the commercial space of the target country, before attacking government and military targets.

CW attacks have the advantage that their implementation can be deployed long before any declaration of war. Whereas it is difficult to deploy physical armaments in

preparation for detonation near a target before a declaration of war, cyber attacks do not have the same limitation. Preparing attack launch pads either by compromising systems or by renting data center space can be performed months if not years in advance of attacks. When CW commences, the attacker is already well placed to wreak damage. A particularly effective force will compromise the target's supply chain, infusing equipment with backdoors years before they are used.

Rules of engagement present a further challenge. Traditional weapons are deployed at predetermined points in a conflict: artillery is seldom deployed when friendly troops are in the vicinity of the target, nuclear weapons may be a disproportionate response to a minor border skirmish, and attacking schools or hospital without authorization may lie outside a force's rules of engagement. Each armament has known side effects and its impact can be predicted; a commander in a physical war will understand which weapons are appropriate in each circumstance and deploy those that achieve the objectives while remaining within the constraints that are the policies and procedures. However, these norms have not been established publicly for CW, for which *appropriate response* has yet to be defined. The dynamic nature of CW also means that regardless of tools and techniques developed in the preparation phase, tools will be rapidly written during hostilities in reaction to new information or circumstances, and these could be trialed in the field while a conflict is active. Without perfect knowledge of exactly what a system controls or influences, unexpected consequences will be common in CW because the effects of an attack cannot be completely predicted.

The final significant difference between CW weapons and physical armaments is that their deterrence value is markedly different. Physical weapons demonstrate capability, which a cautious enemy will note. Developing defenses and counterattacks against new weapons takes time in the real world, and so publicly exposing weapons capabilities can serve to avoid conflict. In the digital realm, however, revealing one's weapons to an opponent simply highlights the areas they need to monitor, patch, or upgrade. If an opponent provides evidence of working exploits against SoftwareX, then as a first line of defense, all of the target's machines running SoftwareX are moved behind additional defensive layers and a plan is formulated to migrate away from SoftwareX. The defense can also perform its own investigation into SoftwareX to determine the possible bug. By the time a conflict occurs, the revealed weapons are no longer useful. It has been shown in the commercial software exploit market that merely publishing seemingly innocuous descriptions of bugs can lead to experienced bug finders rapidly repeating the discovery without additional help. Demonstrating cyber capabilities is a confidence game in which a little skin is shown to imply the strength of weapons that remain hidden. This is

72. http://www.guardian.co.uk/world/2011/dec/09/russia-putin-twitter-facebook-battles.

susceptible to bluffing and subterfuge. That said, there is at least one benefit to "burning" a vulnerability: it signals capability and intent to potential adversaries.

Phases of Attack

Indiscriminate use of weapons is the hallmark of poor training, poor tactics, and poor leadership. Attack methodologies will improve the odds of successful attacks in the initial compromise but also in remaining present and hidden on targeted networks. Monte divides an attack into six stages: [60]

1. Targeting, in which networks, tactics, and strategies required for the attack are identified;
2. Initial access, where the first breach occurs and attacker code runs on the target;
3. Persistence, securing the initial beachhead and establishing reliable access that allows the attacker to return at a later time;
4. Expansion, whereby the attacker branches out from the initial access point, looking for additional systems and data;
5. Exfiltration, in which discovered data are transmitted from target to attacker;
6. Detection, where the defender discovers the breach.

This attack model is useful for both military and commercial attacks. In commercial security testing a single analyst may be required to conduct each stage of the attack, but in military operations each stage can be handed to specialist teams. With all of this in mind, what do cyber weapons look like?

Cyber Weapons

Previous editions of this book defined cyber weapons as individual tools such as viruses, Trojans, and so on. However, CW is fought on a larger scale than individual attacks, exploits, and vulnerabilities. A commander on a CW battlefield is concerned with achieving objectives such as disabling power grids to support a kinetic attack on a facility or knocking out antiaircraft defenses before an airborne attack. These operational goals are handed down by military strategists who combine CW with other military actions to form strategies.

The cyber campaign commander first requires a team and infrastructure that is able to communicate and act in a distributed fashion; channeling attacks across lone routes or network links exposes a single point of failure, and attacks should be launched from a platform that is close in network terms to the target. This platform may be some distance from the command post. The weapons should be capable of working across multiple locations, and the payloads, too, must run in parallel and from multiple points in the network. Second, the commander must remain in control of attacks. For example, a worm that is unleashed against a target cannot indiscriminately attack targets on the public Internet because this would not achieve the goal, and possibly would result in collateral damage of systems unrelated to the opponent. Attacks could be directly controlled by the commander through a command channel, use a intermittent control channel where reliable communications are scarce, or could be self-limiting in terms of time or through built-in target detection. [73] Finally, a feedback loop that keeps the commander updated about whether the attack has succeeded is important. If the attack has a physical effect (for example, knocking out a power grid), the feedback loop might include forces on the ground to provide real-time feedback about power status. However, when the impact is virtual, detecting attack success is not clear-cut. Consider the objective of disabling an opponent's logistics capability by preventing access to its logistics application through a deluge of traffic. If the application became unresponsive from an attacker's perspective, it would not be immediately apparent if the cause of the outage was a successful attack or because of the attack being detected and the attacker's traffic blocked. Telemetry is vitally important.

Remember that CW is an "attack on information systems for military advantage using tactics of destruction, denial, exploitation or deception." The tactics by which the advantage is gained are determined by the weaknesses in the opponent's systems, not the weapons in one's arsenal. This is important because it suggests that CW is not defined simply in terms of a set of tools or tactics; rather, the purpose or intent behind the deployment of an operation is what defines it to be part of a CW action. So-called cyber weapons, in many circumstances, are called viruses, Trojans, and the like when deployed by criminals or fraudsters. In that sense, the actual malicious components are less interesting because they are seldom unique to the field of CW and have already been covered in this book. The broader set of CW tools includes vulnerability databases, deployment tools, payloads, and control consoles.

Vulnerability Databases

The vulnerability database is the result of an effort to collect information about all known security flaws in software. From the outset, it is obvious this is a massive challenge because vulnerability information is generated by thousands of sources including software vendors, vulnerability researchers, and

---

73. Examples of target detection are hardcoded IP addresses or a set of heuristics for determining at runtime whether a potential target should be attacked. This was seen in the Stuxnet attack, in which the malicious code contained numerous heuristics to determine when it had finally migrated to the target SCADA installation. Until those heuristics were triggered, the program did nothing except attempt to migrate further.

users of the software. Public efforts exist to provide identifiers for security weaknesses in software applications, such as the MITRE Corporations' Common Vulnerabilities and Exposures (CVE) project, which defines itself as a "dictionary of common names (i.e., CVE Identifiers) for publicly known cybersecurity vulnerabilities."[74] The CVE contains information about a particular vulnerability in a software product, but for CW this is only part of the required information. A truly useful CW vulnerability database will center on adversary systems and the vulnerabilities detected in them. The weaknesses are not only software vulnerabilities; in many cases misconfigurations lead to compromise, and these are not problems with the code but snags resulting from the manner in which the system was configured.

Deployment Tools

Commonly seen in commercial malware where they are known as "droppers," deployment techniques are a separate beast from the payload that executes after compromise. These are used to obtain initial access and work by exploiting a vulnerability, attacking a misconfiguration, spreading misinformation, spoofing communications, and causing collusion or coercion. Stuxnet, for example, was deployed via four previously unknown vulnerabilities in Microsoft Windows, as well as through known network-based attacks. What made Stuxnet particularly interesting is that one infection mechanism was via USB flash disks, because the target was presumed not to have public Internet connectivity.

Development of droppers is ongoing as discovered vulnerabilities, their exploits' written form (the basis for deploying malicious code), and patches that defeat older droppers are released. A stockpile of these tools aids a CW action, especially where tools take advantage of unknown flaws in software (termed "zero day," "0 day," "0-day," and "oh-day"). There are well-established markets that sell 0 day to government and private customers. Individual researchers who discover 0 day can sell directly or via intermediaries.[75] Pricing of the exploits varies depending on the difficulty of exploitation, the reliability of the exploit, whether the exploit can be used remotely, the popularity of the targeted platform, and whether the buyer has exclusivity. Exploit markets are a fascinating topic all on their own.

Payloads

Merely loading malicious code onto a target does not constitute a full attack; an attacker must still achieve persistence and lateral movement. Compromise is rarely the sole CW goal;

rather, postcompromise is where the CW goals are executed. Payloads consist of the postcompromise logic and can be swapped out depending on the intended tactic. In this way, deployment and payload are separate tools but combined to form a single attack. Modularization is critical.

Payloads cover the full gamut of malicious actions, from silently observing keystrokes to causing centrifuges to tear themselves apart. We touch on a selection here.

A DoS attack is an overt example of CW in that its effects will be plainly visible to the target; an important system will no longer be accessible or usable. DoS attacks were among the first malicious tactics to be labeled as actual CW maneuvers in state-on-state disputes. In 2007, Estonia experienced a massive DoS attack that lasted 3 weeks and interrupted financial and governmental functions while in a dispute with Russia.[76] Whether the attack was conducted by organs of the Russian state has not been established; however, CW does not necessitate that actions be conducted only by nation states. Standards for attribution are not clearly defined, as discussed previously.

The adoption of Supervisory Control and Data Acquisition (SCADA) network-connected systems for critical US infrastructure such as power, water, and utilities[77] has made DoS attacks a lethal weapon of choice. Offline SCADA systems could have spectacular kinetic results. The 2010 Stuxnet attack succeeded in causing widespread damage by replacing control code on SCADA systems, and aimed to remain covert by feeding the operators false instrument information while the attack was under way.

Control Consoles

In the commercial information security business, attack consoles are a known quantity. Software such as CORE IMPACT,[78] CANVAS,[79] and Metasploit[80] provide interfaces that help the operator find vulnerabilities in target systems and launch exploits against those targets. The consoles ship with knowledge of hundreds of vulnerabilities and include exploits for each one. The consoles also contain a multitude of payloads that can be attached to any exploit, which perform tasks such as account creation, command shell access, or attacks against machines further in the network. A CW control console would contain the same elements as a commercial attack console but include

74. http://cve.mitre.org/about/index.html.
75. One example is Zerodium (https://www.zerodium.com/), who purchases vulnerabilities from private researchers and resells them.

76. K. Geers, Cyberspace and the Changing Nature of Warfare, BlackHat Asia, 2008.
77. S. McClure, J. Scambray, G. Kurtz, Hacking Exposed: Network Security Secrets & Solutions, fourth ed., McGraw-Hill, Osborne, 2003, p. 505.
78. https://www.coresecurity.com/core-impact-pro.
79. https://www.immunityinc.com/products/canvas/.
80. https://www.metasploit.com/.

the previously prepared vulnerability database as well as sport advanced telemetry to determine attack success.

Physical Weapons

At the end of 2013 an internal NSA technology catalog was leaked that included a host of previously unknown attack hardware and software.[81] On the software side, the catalog is full of attacks against basic input–output systems and firmware to create persistent infections that survive both reboots and reinstallations. Its hardware offerings include tiny wireless local area network controllers for remote access, peripheral component interconnect bus hardware implants to maintain persistence, a USB cable that hid a full wireless network stack for remote access inside the USB connector, and equipment to attack global system for mobile communication networks. Most of the items in the catalog date to 2008, and we can deduce that the physical side of CW has received loads of attention behind closed doors.

From all of this, it is clear that attackers have a wide array of tools, tactics, and strategies at their disposal. Where does this leave defenders?

Defensive Strategies

As far as prevention is concerned, experts agree that "there is no silver bullet against CW attacks."[82] In the United States, defense against CW is split between two entities: the Department of Defense (DoD) is responsible for defending military resources and the Department of Homeland Security (DHS) is responsible for protecting critical infrastructure. Purely in terms of military spending, the DoD requested $6.7 billion for cybersecurity in 2017, which includes $505 million in appropriations for USCY-BERCOM, a military command whose mission is to be the organization that "plans, coordinates, integrates, synchronizes, and conducts activities to: direct the operations and defense of specified Department of Defense information networks and; prepare to, and when directed, conduct full-spectrum military cyberspace operations in order to enable actions in all domains, ensure US/Allied freedom of action in cyberspace and deny the same to our adversaries."[83] This mission statement indicates that an offensive capability will be maintained. The importance of USCYBERCOM is growing as the number of US government breaches rises,

and moves are afoot to elevate it from a subcommand to a full military command.[84]

The defender's job is harder than that of the attackers in the current environment (although the asymmetry does not run solely against the defender, as we saw earlier). This is not to say it is a truism; it is certainly possible to envision a world in which uniform security is applied throughout all connected networks; however that world does not exist today. The defender's dilemma from a CW perspective has multiple facets. Apart from the oft-cited statement that a defender needs to cover all avenues of attack whereas the attacker needs only find a single vulnerability, CW also introduces the additional difficulty of defending networks that one potentially does not control. Would a CW defense commander have full access to all critical infrastructure networks such as power stations and airports? This is unlikely; rather, individual actions would have to be delegated to administrators of those networks, who best know the ins and outs of their own networks.

For the most part, the attacks listed here are preventable and detectable. The problem facing a large target such as a sovereign nation is to coordinate its defense of many possible individual targets. Policies and procedures must be consistent and thoroughly followed. This is a mammoth task, given the heterogeneous nature of large computing systems. CW defense calls for rapid communication among all points worthy of defense and the central defense command.

Current solutions are of an organizational nature. Many developed countries have response teams such as the CERT, but these deal only with technicalities of attacks. Higher-level involvement from governments is required to act as a line of defense for CW. The US DHS has forged a link with the private and public sector in the form of the US-CERT, with the blessing of a national strategy for cyberdefense, and DHS coordinates with USCYBERCOM to ensure protection across military, government, and critical infrastructure networks. In the United Kingdom, a similar role is played by the National Infrastructure Security Coordination Center.

South Africa, as an example country of the developing world, does not yet have a high-level commitment to digital defense; however, there are initiatives in the pipeline to address CW issues. A number of international efforts that aim to secure the Internet and prevent attacks such as the ones mentioned here have been implemented. One such initiative is adoption of the European Convention of Cybercrime 2001, which deals with the commercial aspects of Internet transactions. As far as the military aspects of CW are concerned, there have been calls from a number of

---

81. https://www.eff.org/files/2014/01/06/20131230-appelbaum-nsa_ant_catalog.pdf.

82. D.J. Lonsdale, The Nature of War and Information Age: Clausewitzian Future at 140.

83. U.S. Cyber Command Fact Sheet, https://www.stratcom.mil/factsheets/2/Cyber_Command/.

84. In 2015 the US Office of Personnel Management, a government agency that processed security-clearance documentation, experienced a data breach that led to the loss of personal details, security clearance information, and fingerprints for millions of US government employees and contractors.

countries, notably Russia, that important portions of the Internet be placed under control of the UN.

A common theme among defenders is that keeping attackers from breaching networks may not be attainable. One author proposes that "the purpose of cyberdefense is to preserve [the ability to exert military power] in the face of attack"[85] by concentrating on desirable qualities such as robustness, system integrity, and confidentiality. This is achieved by architecture decisions (e.g., air-gapped networks), policy positions (centralized planning including forensic abilities and decentralized execution), strategic analysis (determining the purpose of distributed attacks), and effective operations.

6. LEGAL ASPECTS OF CYBER WARFARE

The fact that the Internet is, by definition, international implies that any criminal activity that occurs within its domain is almost always of an international nature.[86] The question that raises concern, however, is the degree of severity of the cyber attacks. This concern merits the following discussion.

Terrorism and Sovereignty

More than 110 different definitions of terrorism exist and are in use. There is consensus regarding only one part of the definition: that the act of terrorism must "create a state of terror" in the minds of the people.[87]

The following definition of "workstation terrorism" as a variation of CW is suitable: "Computer terrorism is the act of destroying or of corrupting workstation systems with an aim of destabilizing a country or of applying pressure on a government,"[88] because the cyber attack's objective, inter alia, is to draw immediate attention by way of causing shock in the minds of a specific populace and thus diminishing that populace's faith in government.

Incidents such as hacking into energy plants, telecommunications facilities, and government websites cause a sense of instability in the minds of a nation's people, thereby applying pressure on the government of a particular country; therefore, these acts qualify as terrorism and should be treated as such. Factual manifestations of war, that is, use of force and overpowering the enemy, ceased to be part of the classical definition of "war" after World War I,[89] and international writers began to pay more attention to

the factual circumstances of each case to determine the status of an armed conflict. This is significant for current purposes because it means that depending on the scale and consequences of a cyber attack, the latter may be seen as a fully fledged war,[90] and the same restrictions (for example, prohibition of an attack on hospitals and churches) will apply.[91]

CW may seem to be a stranger to the concepts of public international law. However, this is not the case, because there are many similarities between CW and the notions of terrorism and war as embodied in international criminal law.

The impact of this discussion on sovereignty is enormous. Admittedly a cornerstone of the international law, the idea of sovereignty, was officially entrenched in 1945 in Article 2(1) of the UN Charter.[92] This being so, any CW attack, whatever form or shape it may take, will no doubt undermine the affected state's political independence, because without order there is no governance.

Furthermore, the prohibition of use of force[93] places an obligation on a state to ensure that all disputes are solved at a negotiation table and not by way of crashing the other state's websites or paralyzing its telecommunications facilities, thereby obtaining a favorable outcome of a dispute under duress. Finally, these rights of nonuse of force and sovereignty are of international character, and therefore "international responsibility"[94] for all cyber attacks may undermine regional or even international security.

Liability Under International Law

There are two possible routes that one could pursue to bring CW wrongdoers to justice: using the concept of "state responsibility," whereby the establishment of a material link between the state and the individual executing the attack is imperative, or acting directly against the person, who might incur individual criminal responsibility.

State Responsibility

Originally, states were the only possible actors on the international plane, and therefore a substantial amount of jurisprudence has developed concerning state responsibility. Two important aspects of state responsibility are important for our purposes: presence of a right on the part of the state claiming to have suffered from the cyber attack and imputation of the acts of individuals to a state.

85. M.C. Libicki, Cyberdeterrence and Cyberwar, RAND Corporation, Santa Monica, CA, 2009. http://www.rand.org/pubs/monographs/MG877.
86. Corell, 2002. www.un.org/law/counsel/english/remarks.pdf.
87. J. Dugard, International Law: A South African Perspective, second ed., vol. 149, 2000.
88. Galley, 1996. http://homer.span.ch/~spaw1165/infosec/sts_en/.
89. P. Macalister-Smith, Encyclopedia of Public International Law, 2000, p. 1135.

90. Barkham, Informational Warfare and International Law, 34 Journal of International Law and Politics, Fall 2001, at 65.
91. P. Macalister-Smith, Encyclopedia of Public International Law 1400 (2000).
92. www.unhchr.ch/pdf/UNcharter.pdf.
93. www.unhchr.ch/pdf/UNcharter.pdf.
94. Spanish Zone of Morocco claims two RIAA, 615 (1923) at 641.

Usually one would doubt that such acts as cyber attacks, which are so closely connected to an individual, could be attributable to a state, for no state is liable for acts of individuals unless the latter acts on its behalf.[95] The situation, however, would depend on the concrete facts of each case, because even an ex post facto approval of students' conduct by the head of the government[96] may give rise to state responsibility. Thus, this norm of international law has not become obsolete in the technology age and can still serve states and their protection on the international level.

Attribution in the context of CW, without somebody coming forward to claim responsibility for the attack, may prove to be a difficult task, if not impossible, because to hold a state liable one would have to show that the government had effective control over the attacker but, through its conduct, failed to curtail the latter's actions directed at another state and threatens international peace and security.[97]

As a result, even though many attacks emanate from China, for example, the Chinese government will be responsible only if it supported or at least was aware of the attacker and went along with that attacker's plans. Solid forensic investigation would therefore be required before there could be a hope of attributing responsibility.[98]

Individual Liability

With the advent of a human rights culture after the Second World War, there is no doubt that individuals have become participants in international law.[99] There are, however, two qualifications to the statement: First, such participation was considered indirect in that nationals of a state are involved in international law only if they act on the particular state's behalf. Second, individuals were regarded only as beneficiaries of the protection offered by the international law, specifically through international human rights instruments.[100]

Individual criminal responsibility, however, has been a much more debated issue, because introduction of such a concept would make natural persons equal players in international law. However, this was done in the cases of Nuremberg, the former Yugoslavia, and the Rwanda tribunals, and therefore[101] cyber attacks committed during the

time of war, such as attacks on NATO websites in the Kosovo war, should not be difficult to accommodate.

What made it easier is that in 2010, the Review Conference for the International Criminal Court (ICC) introduced Article *8bis* to the Rome Statute of the ICC, which finally defined the crime of "aggression" as "the planning, preparation, initiation or execution, by a person in a position effectively to exercise control over or to direct the political or military action of a State, of an act of aggression which, by its character, gravity and scale, constitutes a manifest violation of the Charter of the United Nations."[102]

There is no doubt that use of unilateral force that threatens universal peace is prohibited under international law.[103] The difficulty in holding an individual responsible is twofold: confirming jurisdiction of the ICC over the accused and proving the intention to commit the crime covered by the Rome Statute the ICC administers.

First, only persons who are found within the territory of the state that is a signatory to the Rome Statute or such state's nationals may be tried before the ICC.

Second, there may be difficulties with justifying use of the same terms and applying similar concepts to acts of CW, where the latter occurs independently from a conventional war. Conventionally, CW as an act of war sounds wrong, and to consider it as such requires a conventional classification. The definition of "international crimes" serves as a useful tool that saves the situation: Arguably, being part of jus cogens,[104] crimes described by terms such as "aggression," "torture," and "against humanity," provides us with ample space to fit all the possible variations of CW without disturbing the very foundation of international law. Thus, once again there is support for the notions of individual criminal responsibility for cyber attacks in general public international law, which stand as an alternative to state responsibility.

International criminal law offers two options to an agreed state, and it is up to the latter to decide which way to go. That there are no clear pronouncements on the subject by an international forum does not give a blank amnesty to actors on an international plane to abuse the apparent *lacuna,* ignore the general principles, and employ unlawful measures in retaliation.

Remedies Under International Law

In every discussion, the most interesting part is the one that answers the question: What are we going to do about it? In our case there are two main solutions or steps that a state can take in terms of international criminal law in the face of CW: employ self-defense or seek justice by bringing the

95. M.N. Shaw, International Law, second ed., 414, 1986.
96. For example, in Tehran Hostages Case (v.) I.C.J. Reports, 1980 at 3, 34–35.
97. Huntley, 2010. Controlling the use of force in cyber space: the application of the law of armed conflict during a time of fundamental change in the nature of warfare, 60 Naval L. Rev. 1 2010.
98. Friesen, Resolving tomorrow's conflicts today: How new developments within the U.N. Security Council can be used to combat cyber warfare, 58 Naval L. Rev. 89 2009.
99. J. Dugard, International Law: A South African Perspective, second ed., 2000, p. 1.
100. J. Dugard, International Law: A South African Perspective, second ed., 1, 2000, p. 234.
101. M.C. Bassiouni, International Criminal Law, second ed., 1999, p. 26.

102. Resolution RC/Res.6. http://www.icc-cpi.int/iccdocs/asp_docs/Resolutions/RC-Res.6-ENG.pdf.
103. Green, Questioning the peremptory status of the prohibition of the use of force, 32 Mich. J. Int'l L. 215 (2011) 2010–2011.
104. M.C. Bassiouni, International Criminal Law, second ed., 1999, p. 98.

responsible individual before an international forum. Both solutions, however, are premised on the assumption that the identity of the perpetrator is established.[105]

Self-Defense

States may engage in self-defense only in cases of an armed attack,[106] which in itself has become a hotly debated issue.[107] This is owing to recognition of obligation of nonuse of force in terms of Article 2(4) of the UN Charter as being not only customary international law but also jus cogens.[108]

Armed attack, however, can be explained away by reference to the time when the UN Charter was written, therefore accepting that other attacks may require the exercise of the right to self-defense.[109] What cannot be discarded is the requirement that this inherent right may be exercised only if it aims to extinguish the armed attack to avoid the conclusion of it constituting a unilateral use of force.[110] Finally, a state may invoke "collective self-defense" in the cases of CW. Although possible, this type of self-defense requires an unequivocal statement by a third state that it has been a victim of the attack; then, such a state must make a request for action on its behalf.[111]

Therefore, invoking self-defense in cases of CW, although possible,[112] might not be a plausible option, because it requires solid proof of an attack, obtained promptly and before the conclusion of such an attack,[113] which at this stage of technological advancement is difficult. The requirement that the attack should not be completed by the time the victim state retaliates hinges on the fact that once damage is done and the attack is finished, states are encouraged to turn to international courts and through legal debate resolve their grievances without causing more loss of life and damage to

infrastructure. Because most states would deny support of or acquiescence to the actions of its citizens in executing an attack, the more realistic court to which one would turn to in pursuit of justice is the ICC.

International Criminal Court

The ICC established by the Rome Statute of 1998 is not explicitly vested with a jurisdiction to try an individual who committed an act of terrorism. Therefore, in a narrow sense, cyber terrorism would also fall outside the competence of the ICC.

In the wide sense, however, terrorism, including cyber terrorism, could be and is seen by some authors as torture.[114] That being so, because torture is a crime against humanity, the ICC will in fact have a jurisdiction over cyber attacks, too.[115]

Cyber terrorism could also be seen as crime against peace, if it takes a form of fully fledged "war on the Internet," for an "aggressive war" has been proclaimed an international crime on a number of occasions.[116] Although not clearly pronounced on by the Nuremberg Trials,[117] the term "crime of aggression" is contained in the ICC Statute and therefore falls under its jurisdiction.[118]

Cyber crimes can also fall under crimes against nations, because in terms of customary international law, states are obliged to punish individuals who commit crimes against third states.[119] Furthermore, workstation-related attacks evolved into crimes that are universally recognized to be criminal and therefore against nations.[120] Therefore, thanks to the absence of *travaux préparatoires* of the Rome Statute, the ICC will be able to interpret provisions of the statute to the advantage of the international community, allow prosecutions of cyber terrorists, and ensure international peace and security.

In practical terms, this will mean that a cyber attack will most probably be interpreted as part of "any weapon"[121] within the scope of the definition of "aggression" of the Rome Statute and the attacker will face the full might of the

105. Murphy, Mission Impossible? International law and the changing character of war, 87 Int'l L. Stud. Ser. US Naval War Col. 13 2011, (2011). Lewis, Cyber warfare and its impact on international security. http://www.un.org/disarmament/HomePage/ODAPublications/OccasionalPapers/PDF/OP19.pdf.
106. UN Charter Art. 51.
107. Cammack, The Stuxnet worm and potential prosecution by the international criminal court under the newly defined crime of aggression, 20 Tul. J. Int'l & Comp. L. 303 (2011) 2011.
108. M. Dixon, Cases and Materials on International Law, third ed., 570, 2000.
109. P. Macalister-Smith, Encyclopedia of Public International Law, 362, 2000.
110. Military and Paramilitary Activities in and against Nicaragua (Nic. v. U.S.A.). www.icj-cij.org/icjwww/Icases/iNus/inus_ijudgment/inus_ijudgment_19860627.pdf.
111. M. Dixon, Cases and Materials on International Law, third ed., 575, 2000.
112. Barkham, Informational Warfare and International Law, Journal of International Law and Politics (2001) 80.
113. Otherwise a reaction of a state would amount to reprisals, which are unlawful; see also Nic. v. U.S.A. case in this regard. www.icj-cij.org/icjwww/Icases/iNus/inus_ijudgment/inus_ijudgment_19860627.pdf.

114. J. Rehman, International Human Rights Law: A Practical Approach, 2002, 464–465.
115. Rome Statute of the International Criminal Court of 1998 Art. 7. www.un.org/law/icc/statute/english/rome_statute(e).pdf.
116. League of Nations Draft Treaty of Mutual Assistance of 1923. www.mazal.org/archive/imt/03/IMT03-T096.htm. Geneva Protocol for the Pacific Settlement of International Disputes 1924. www.worldcourts.com/pcij/eng/laws/law07.htm.
117. P. Macalister-Smith, Encyclopedia of Public International Law, 1992, 873–874.
118. Art. 5(1)(d) of the Rome Statute of the International Criminal Court 1998. www.un.org/law/icc/statute/english/rome_statute(e).pdf.
119. P. Macalister-Smith, Encyclopedia of Public International Law, 876, 1992.
120. P. Macalister-Smith, Encyclopedia of Public International Law, 876, 1992.
121. Article 8 *bis* 2(b) of the Rome Statute. http://www.icc-cpi.int/iccdocs/asp_docs/Resolutions/RC-Res.6-ENG.pdf.

law as long as he or she is the national of the member state or finds himself or herself within the physical territorial boundaries of the state that is party to the Rome Statute even though the attacker's conduct may not be enough to make the country of its nationality liable for what he or she did.[122]

Other Remedies

Probably the most effective method of dealing with CW is by way of treaties. At the time of this writing, there has been only one such convention on a truly international level, the European Convention on Cybercrime 2001.

The effectiveness of the Convention can be easily seen from the list of states that joined and ratified it. By involving such technologically advanced countries as the United States, Japan, the United Kingdom, Canada, and Germany, the Convention can be said to have gained the status of instant customary international law,[123] because it adds *opinio juris* links to already existing practice of the states.

Furthermore, the Convention urges the member states to adopt uniform national legislation to deal with the ever-growing problem of this century[124] as well as provide a platform for solution of disputes on the international level.[125] Finally, taking the very nature of CW into consideration, "hard" international law may be the solution to possible large-scale threats in future.

The fact that remedies bring legitimacy of a rule cannot be overemphasized, because remedies available to parties at the time of a conflict have a decisive role in escalating the conflict to possible loss of life. By discussing the most pertinent remedies under international criminal law, the authors have shown that its old principles are still workable solutions, even for such a new development as the Internet.

Developing Countries Response

The attractiveness of looking into developing countries' response to a CW attack lies in the fact that usually these are the countries that appeal to transnational criminals owing to the lack of criminal sanctions for crimes they want to commit. For purposes of this chapter, the South African legal system will be used to answer the question of how a developing country would respond to such an instance of CW.

In a 1989 "end conscription" case, South African courts defined war as a "hostile contest between nations, states or different groups within a state, carried out by force of arms

against the foreign power or against an armed and organised group within the state."[126] In the 1996 *Azapo* case, the Constitutional Court, the highest court of the land, held that it had to consider international law when dealing with matters such as these.[127] In the 2005 *Basson* case, the Constitutional Court further held that South African courts have jurisdiction to hear cases involving international crimes, such as war crimes and crimes against humanity.[128]

A number of legislative provisions in South Africa prohibit South African citizens from engaging, directly or indirectly, in CW activities. These Acts include the Internal Security Intimidation Act 13 of 1991 and the Regulation of Foreign Military Assistance Act 15 of 1998. The main question here is whether the South African courts would have jurisdiction to hear matters in connection with them. A number of factors will have a role. First, if the incident takes place within the air, water, or terra firma space of South Africa, the court would have jurisdiction over the matter.[129]

The implementation of the Rome Statute Act will further assist the South African courts to deal with the matter because it confers jurisdiction over citizens who commit international crimes. It is well known that interference with the navigation of a civil aircraft, for example, is contrary to international law and is clearly prohibited in terms of the Montreal Convention.[130]

A further reason for jurisdiction is found in the 2004 Witwatersrand Local Division High Court decision of *Tsichlas* v *Touch Line Media*,[131] in which Acting Judge Kuny held that publication on a website takes place where it is accessed. In our case, if the sites in question are accessed in South Africa, the South African courts would have jurisdiction to hear the matter, provided that the courts can enforce its judgment effectively against the members of the group.

Finally, in terms of the new Electronic Communications and Transactions Act,[132] any act or preparation taken toward the offense taking place in South Africa would confer jurisdiction over such a crime, including interference with the Internet. This means that South African courts can be approached if preparation for the crime takes place in South Africa. Needless to say, imprisonment of up to 5 years would be a competent sentence for each and every participant of CW, including coconspirators.[133]

122. Schmitt, Cyber Operations and the *Jus in Bello*: Key Issues, 87 Int'l L. Stud. Ser. US Naval War Col. 89 (2011) 2011.
123. http://conventions.coe.int/Treaty/en/Treaties/Html/185.htm.
124. European Convention on Cybercrime of 2001 Art. 23. http://conventions.coe.int/Treaty/en/Treaties/Html/185.htm.
125. European Convention on Cybercrime of 2001 Art. 45. http://conventions.coe.int/Treaty/en/Treaties/Html/185.htm.
126. Transcription Campaign and Another v Minister of Defence and Another 1989 (2) SA 180 (C).
127. Azanian People's Organisation (AZAPO) v Truth and Reconciliation Commission 1996 (4) SA 671 (CC).
128. State v Basson, 2005. Available at: www.constitutionalcourt.org.za.
129. Supreme Court Act 59 of 1959 (South Africa).
130. Montreal Convention of 1971.
131. Tsichlas v Touch Media 2004 (2) SA 211 (W).
132. Electronic Communications and Transactions Act 25 of 2002.
133. Electronic Communications and Transactions Act 25 of 2002.

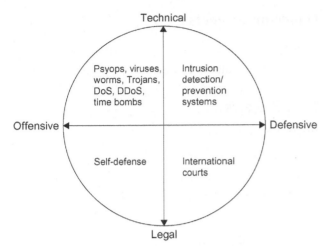

FIGURE 83.2 Holistic view of cyber warfare.

7. HOLISTIC VIEW OF CYBER WARFARE

This chapter has addressed the four axes of the CW model[134] presented at the beginning of this discussion: technical, legal, offensive, and defensive. Furthermore, the specific subgroups of the axes have also been discussed. For the complete picture of CW as relevant to the discussion at hand, however, Fig. 83.2 places each subgroup into its own field.[135]

8. SUMMARY

This discussion clearly demonstrated that CW is not only possible; it has already taken place and is growing internationally as a preferred way of warfare. It is clearly demonstrated that successful strategies, offensive or defensive, depend on taking a holistic view of the matter. Information security professionals should refrain from focusing only on the technical aspects of this area, because it is shown that legal frameworks, national as well as international, also have to be considered. The prevailing challenge for countries around the globe is to foster collaboration among lawyers, information security professionals, and IT professionals. They should continue striving at least to keep the registry of CW arsenal and remedies updated, which may in turn incite adversaries to provide us with more material for research.

Finally, let us move on to the real interactive part of this chapter: review questions/exercises, hands-on projects, case projects, and the optional team case project. The answers and/or solutions by chapter can be found in Appendix K.

CHAPTER REVIEW QUESTIONS/ EXERCISES

True/False

1. True or False? The technical side of CW deals with technical exploits on the one side and offensive measures on the other.
2. True or False? It is clear that CW is all about information superiority because "the fundamental weapon and target of CW is information."
3. True or False? In addition to training personnel and producing cyber weapons, the preparation stage consists of a wide range of information-gathering activities.
4. True or False? CW does not require the infrastructure investment that physical arms do[136]; however, it requires highly trained personnel to develop cyber weapons, and the process of training to the required skill levels occupies a significant portion of activities before hostilities break out.
5. True or False? The reconnaissance phase of preparation focuses on identifying government organs, industries, infrastructure, companies, individuals, and organizations that are not potential targets.

Multiple Choice

1. What type of scanning is a common activity in the commercial security industry, where numerous scanners exist?
   A. Qualitative analysis
   B. Vulnerabilities
   C. Data storage
   D. Vulnerability
   E. Department of Homeland Security
2. What is an important decision in deciding on a CW strategy?
   A. Network attached storage (NAS)
   B. Risk assessment
   C. Scale
   D. Subcomponents
   E. Bait
3. What type of weapons includes social engineering techniques and psychological operations (*psyops*)?
   A. Organizations
   B. Fabric
   C. Psychological
   D. Risk communication
   E. Security
4. There are _____ differences between weapons that exist in the physical realm and those

---

134. Supreme Court Act 59 of 1959 (South Africa).

135. Implementation of the Rome Statute of the International Criminal Court Act 27 of 2002 (South Africa).

136. Of the $707.5 billion requested for the US DoD 2012 budget, $159 million was earmarked for the Cyber Command.

that exist within the cyber realm, and the differences are useful to highlight.
A. Cabinet-level state office
B. Unsubtle
C. Infrastructure failure
D. Storage area network protocol
E. Taps

5. What type of database is the result of an effort to collect information about all known security flaws in software?
A. Irrelevant
B. Consumer privacy protection
C. IP storage access
D. Vulnerability
E. Unusable

EXERCISE

Problem

How can organizations address advanced persistent cyber threats?

Hands-on Projects

Project

How are cyber attacks carried out?

Case Projects

Problem

What targets can be attacked?

Optional Team Case Project

Problem

What are the implications of a cyber attack?

Chapter 84

Cyber-Attack Process

Nailah Mims
Bright Horizons

1. WHAT IS A CYBER-ATTACK?

With increasing reliance on computer-based electronic technology, cyberspace has become a critical component of the 21st century's private and public communications, business operations, relationships, commercial, industrial, and military systems. The spread of the devices which facilitate these capabilities has greatly expanded the cyberspace footprint from a relatively few stationary computer systems, to millions of mobile devices with which users can access cyberspace from anywhere in the world. The data that resides on these devices, and the networks and infrastructure through which they communicate contain all kinds of information, much of it personal and sensitive.

The 2003 National Strategy to Secure Cyberspace notes: "Our Nation's critical infrastructures consist of the physical and cyber assets of public and private institutions in several sectors: agriculture, food, water, public health, emergency services, government, defense industrial base, information and telecommunications, energy, transportation, banking and finance, chemicals and hazardous materials, and postal and shipping...Cyberspace comprises hundreds of thousands of interconnected computers, servers, routers, switches, and fiber optic cables that make our critical infrastructures work" [1]. This includes the software programs, applications, and data, as well as the people and processes which act within and guide the use of cyberspace.

Cyberspace's underlying infrastructure are "the electronic information and communications systems and services and the information contained therein; the information and communications systems and services composed of all hardware and software that process, store, and communicate information, or any combination of all of these elements" [2]. Indeed, cyberspace has become a centralized information repository which can essentially be accessed by anyone or thing with the appropriate tools connectivity. Furthermore, it includes the "interconnected information infrastructure of interactions among persons, processes, data, and information and communications technologies, along with the environment and conditions that influence those interactions" [2].

Given the extensive information available in cyberspace, much of it confidential or otherwise sensitive and accessible from anywhere there's a connection, there are significant security implications for such a high level of reliance on cyberspace. The confidentiality, integrity, availability, and nonrepudiation of information held in and processed through cyberspace are the established aims of information and data security. Activities which act to undermine these core attributes constitute a cyber-attack and any of the aforementioned components of cyberspace may be a target.

The National Institute of Standards and Technology (NIST) defines a cyber-attack as: "An attack, via cyberspace, targeting an enterprise's use of cyberspace for the purpose of disrupting, disabling, destroying, or maliciously controlling a computing environment/infrastructure; or destroying the integrity of the data or stealing controlled information" [3]. Thus, a cyber-attack could involve any of the following: attempting to gain unauthorized access to a cyberspace component; compromising the integrity of the data stored and processed, circumventing an organizations security controls; exploiting technical and human vulnerabilities; installing and/or executing specially designed malicious code or else manipulating systems to do functions not originally intended; or otherwise causing direct or indirect damage to an organization, entity, or person, or their assets by using cyber components.

Cyber-attacks are initiated by actors who may have a variety of motives with respect to their exploitation of cyberspace and depending on the sophistication, technical expertise, number of attackers, and their associations there are several classifications for the attackers. It should also be

Computer and Information Security Handbook. http://dx.doi.org/10.1016/B978-0-12-803843-7.00084-3

noted that a certain degree of anonymity cyberspace affords makes executing cyber-attacks low risk to the attacker and, as we will see in the next sections, the varied adversaries in a cyber-attack use a variety of tools and tactics to accomplish their goals. The application of these will play key roles in what constitutes the cyber-attack process as attackers will tend to follow common patterns in their approach to exploit cyberspace and target its users.

2. CYBER-ATTACK ADVERSARIES

Cyber-attackers are typically classified by their level of expertise, sophistication, and the end goals of their attacks. Furthermore, they may act alone or in groups. At one end, they may be "script kiddies" with limited technical knowledge or representatives of well-organized nation-states with highly refined cyber offensive and defensive capabilities. The former group tends to primarily make use of the many prebuilt tools found on the Internet which require little understanding of the underlying protocols and functions but with a few strokes can be used to facilitate a cyber-attack. Nation-state adversaries act on behalf of governments and militaries with significant resources and expertise. They often have dedicated units whose mission is to achieve economic, political, industrial, or military objective by engaging rivals in cyberspace.

Other categories of attacker include hacktivists who seek to further a political or social cause, and criminals primarily seek to gain financially through the exploitation of cyberspace and its users. Hacktivists may vary in sophistication and often strive to embarrass or punish a target by defacing websites, gaining access to and then releasing internal documents to the public, and disrupting an organization's computer and information systems. Criminals may use cyberspace to facilitate traditional crimes or launch an attack against cyberspace assets and the information stored on them themselves. Cyber security and computer crime laws outline what constitutes criminal cyber activity though the cyber-attack goal is usually some type of financial fraud or the theft of personal information.

A final category of attackers are those known as "trusted insiders," those who are validated members of the organizations which are targeted. Trusted insiders are a group that has been increasingly recognized as one of the largest threats to an organization as they include those embedded within an organization as a legitimate user. Many steps of the cyber-attack process that will be covered later, other than perhaps covering their tracks, will be unnecessary since this group already has access.

3. CYBER-ATTACK TARGETS

Recent estimates indicate 43% of the world's 7.3 billion people are now connected to cyberspace [4]. Cisco

Systems estimates that by the year 2020, 50 billion devices will be connected to the Internet [5]. These devices include computers, mobile devices, refrigerators, microwaves, doorbells, industrial systems, televisions, alarm systems, and much more in an Internet of Things (IoT). While they and the data they hold are potential targets for a cyber-attack it is the individual citizens, corporations, governments, schools, financial institutions, schools, law enforcement agencies, and retail stores who use these devices that are ultimately impacted.

Cyberspace entities store and transmit large amounts of personally identifiable information (PII), customer information, credit card or banking details, confidential information, intellectual property, and other sensitive data. Most of this information is processed through web or applications servers and stored in databases and storage or backup servers, all of which tend to be protected at least to some degree by various defensive mechanisms. Firewalls, intrusion detection prevention systems, log monitoring solutions, and other internal layers of defense present barriers for cyber-attackers. Thus, attackers find they must apply a process to maximize the likelihood of the success of their attacks while escaping detection and physical capture. The following sections break down the cyber-attack process and is then followed by real-world cases which demonstrate the process and its customized variations.

4. CYBER-ATTACK PROCESS

The cyber-attack process is generally divided into preattack activity, the actual attack, and postattack activities. There are a variety of tools, techniques, and tactics employed throughout the process, each of which target some aspect of cyberspace. Moreover, an attack will consist of a variety of technical and nontechnical approaches and a selection of the tools that are most likely to achieve the goal of the cyber-attack.

Preattack

Preattack activities include research and surveillance of potential targets with particular attention to their attributes and weaknesses. This assessment will yield valuable information and clues that will be later used by an attacker to actually conduct the cyber-attack. Once a target is selected, identifying the people, processes, and technologies associated with the target will yield information on opportunities for an attacker to launch their exploits.

An attacker will develop a profile of their target, initially through information available via open source methods. It helps that many prospective targets have websites and profiles on social media that identify key personnel, their positions (and in some cases email addresses and phone numbers), and insight into the specific technologies an organization uses. These sources can further provide information on the version of operating system and applications from which an attacker can use network and host scanners to discover open ports and services running on an organization's network. With that information, an attacker can determine if any of what they have discovered has known vulnerabilities. The National Vulnerability Database (NVD) by NIST at https://nvd.nist.gov is one of several available compilations of technical vulnerabilities.

After isolating a target's particular weaknesses, an attacker can move to the next part of the cyber-attack process, the actual attack itself.

The Attack

During the actual attack, the weaknesses that were discovered in the earlier opening stages are now exploited for the purposes of the attacker. Generally speaking, this phase consists of an attacker engaging resources at the targeted entity to gain access, running the exploits that accomplish their goals, exfiltration of data, and moving around the target's internal network looking for more targets of opportunity.

The attack is the actual successful breach of a target's defenses. An attacker has positioned themselves, often inside a target's internal networks and devices, and is free to move around the organization's network, steal data, spread malware, and disrupt operations at will.

Depending on the goal of the attacker, the attack may consist of a single action such as a website defacement. Alternatively, it may involve a complex multistep process that begins with a fake email tricking a target into clicking on a bad link which then uploads malware to a host within a targeted entity and from there, escalating privileges to gain access to sensitive hosts, stealing information, and sending it back to an attacker's machine.

Some other common types of attacks include those that intercept cyberspace communications called man-in-the-middle attacks. Compromise may also be achieved through the installation of malware such as bots, viruses, and worms; flooding a network or device with too much information in a denial of service attacks; and creating or sending legitimate looking emails or webpages from reputable organizations that actually contain malicious code in phishing and other forms of technical and nontechnical social engineering confidence tricks. SQL injection and cross-site scripting (XSS) attacks target databases and websites respectively. These will be discussed in greater detail in the next section along with some of the other specific tools and tactic that an attacker would use to accomplish these attacks.

Postattack

The end-game of an attack occurs whenever the aims of the attacker are met, or until the cyber-attack is detected or disrupted. Depending on the goals of the attacker, this will involve maintaining access into a targeted system for ongoing and future theft of information or covering their tracks to prevent detection. By covering their tracks, the attacker makes attribution and investigation difficult for target organizations and law enforcement.

It is important to note, while there are distinctive steps through which an attacker will advance their attack, the process proceeds based on the purposes of the attacker. In some cases, that means completing the activities required for their attack in serial fashion and in others an iterative approach is applied. For instance, once an attacker has gained access to a system, they may conduct further reconnaissance on their target, this time from the inside. Additionally, rather than gaining access and then leaving, the attacker may seek to establish a persistent presence in the organization's network and surreptitiously siphon sensitive data over an extended period of time. This type of attack, known as an Advanced Persistent Threat (APT), will be discussed later on. For now, we move on to the various tools and tactics an attacker will use in their execution of a cyber-attack.

5. TOOLS AND TACTICS OF A CYBER-ATTACK

We discussed earlier some of the common types of cyber-attacks. The tools and tactics used to perpetrate a cyber-attack include technical and nontechnical methods of targeting the various areas of cyberspace in order to overcome a target's security measures. We have discussed how the Internet, in particular a target's webpages, social media, presents an extremely large compilation of readily available information. Additionally, the webservers, applications, and databases, which support these public facing cyberspace elements, contain much of the personal and sensitive data, which an attacker seeks and thus are susceptible to the many tools and tactics of an attacker. Furthermore, much of this data is increasingly stored on mobile devices, making it more difficult to protect.

Passwords are the most common way users authenticate into their cyberspace assets, to include web-based portals, email, and devices. While not the most secure method of authentication, they are often the single gateway between an attacker and its targeted information system. With so many passwords, a user may make them overly simple, short, and reuse them for many accounts. The user that uses the same password for their personal email account, bank account, and social media account is an ideal target for an attacker. Password cracking tools are designed to try many combinations of letters, words, and in some cases symbols for more complex passwords in order to guess a system's password. These come in handy when attempting to gain access to a web portal, or any other account protected (user name/password) cyberspace object.

Another popular way of initiating a cyber-attack is by a type of attack called phishing. Phishing baits targets into installing the malicious code or into accessing malicious sites/links via an innocuous or legitimate looking email (see Fig. 84.1) which disguises the true intent of an attacker. The email could be sent to a large number of random email addresses, hoping to get an unsuspecting user to click on a link or open an attachment. Alternatively, the attacker could use information from an organization's website to target a specific individual, such as the CEO, or CFO.

The 2015 Verizon Data Report notes "The first 'phishing' campaigns typically involved an e-mail that appeared to be coming from a bank convincing users they needed to change their passwords or provide some piece of information, like, NOW. A fake web page and users' willingness to fix the nonexistent problem led to account takeovers and fraudulent transactions. Phishing campaigns have evolved in recent years to incorporate installation of malware as the second stage of the attack" (see Fig. 84.2). Furthermore: "phishing a favorite tactic of state-sponsored threat actors and criminal organizations, all with the intent to gain an initial foothold into a network" [6].

Phishing is actually an electronic version of another tactic known as social engineering. Social engineering, which typically occurs early in the cyber-attack process, relies on manipulating human nature, communication, and social behavior to gain information about a target or access their systems. Feelings of sympathy, trust, stress, confusion, and fear are all elicited and exploited by an attacker in what is essentially a confidence trick to gain information on how to access a target's cyberspace systems, or in more daring cases to be allowed physical access to a target's facilities [7]. The latter situation constitutes higher personal risk to an attacker, hence the preference for the safety and anonymity of launching an attack via computer, however, there is a very high reward for the attacker who is able to physically enter a target's facility and successfully gain direct, hands-on access to their computer and information systems.

Attackers aiming primarily for destruction may achieve their ends by flooding a target's network or device with too much traffic. These types of denial of service (DoS) attacks can take down websites, servers, and other devices critical to a target's operations. The deployment of bots and subsequent establishment of botnets are a common method of launching distributed denial of service (DDoS) attacks (see Fig. 84.3) which are particularly disruptive as they can potentially recruit hundreds or even thousands of unsuspecting host or zombie machines that have been infected by bots in order to launch the attack. Variants of this type of attack exploit communications protocols and built in network services in order to flood a target with traffic.

Bots are a type of malware, or malicious software. The installation of malware is another common method of exploiting a target. By directly gaining access to deploy malware or tricking a user into installing and executing malicious software within a target's cyberspace ecosystem, an attacker can accomplish a variety of things. Malware

FIGURE 84.1 Phishing email example.

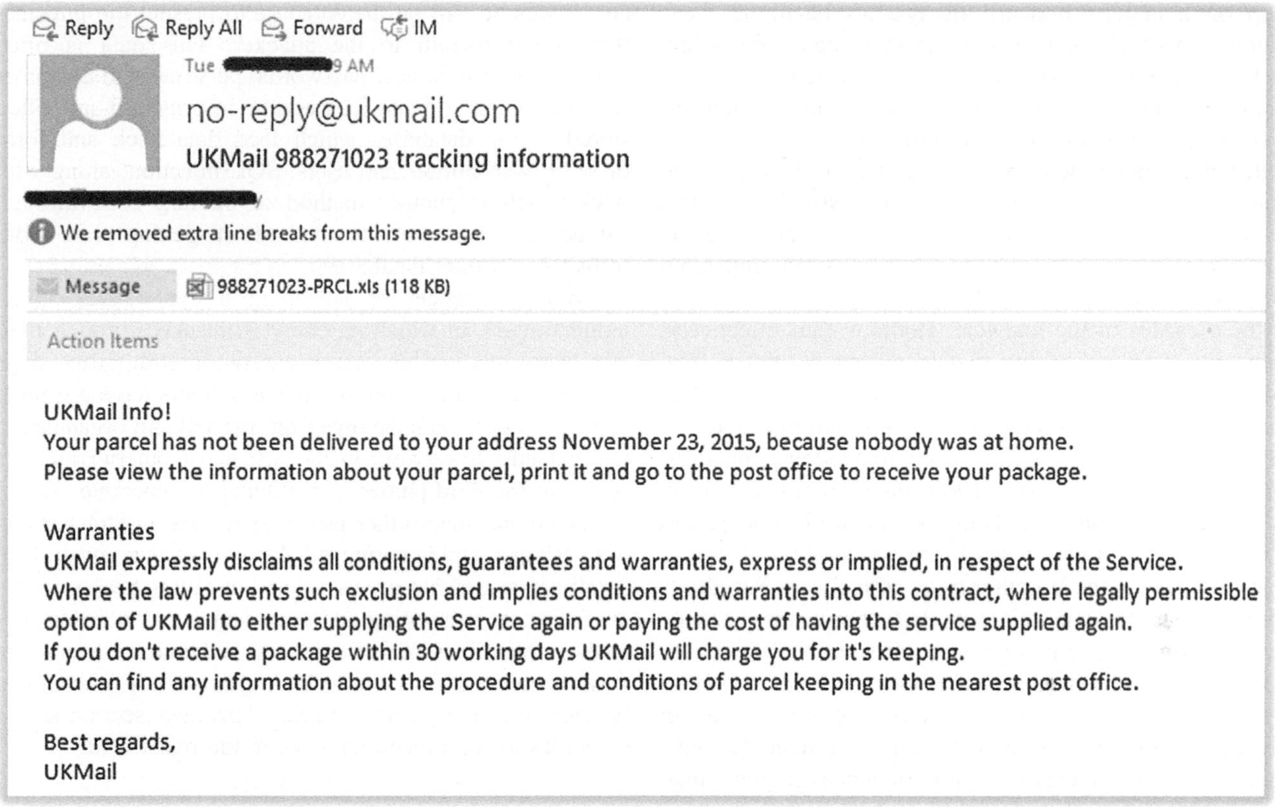

Reply Reply All Forward IM

Tue ⬛⬛⬛⬛⬛9 AM

no-reply@ukmail.com

UKMail 988271023 tracking information

⬛⬛⬛⬛⬛⬛⬛

ℹ️ We removed extra line breaks from this message.

✉️ Message 📊 988271023-PRCL.xls (118 KB)

Action Items

UKMail Info!
Your parcel has not been delivered to your address November 23, 2015, because nobody was at home.
Please view the information about your parcel, print it and go to the post office to receive your package.

Warranties
UKMail expressly disclaims all conditions, guarantees and warranties, express or implied, in respect of the Service.
Where the law prevents such exclusion and implies conditions and warranties into this contract, where legally permissible
option of UKMail to either supplying the Service again or paying the cost of having the service supplied again.
If you don't receive a package within 30 working days UKMail will charge you for it's keeping.
You can find any information about the procedure and conditions of parcel keeping in the nearest post office.

Best regards,
UKMail

FIGURE 84.2 Phishing email example #2.

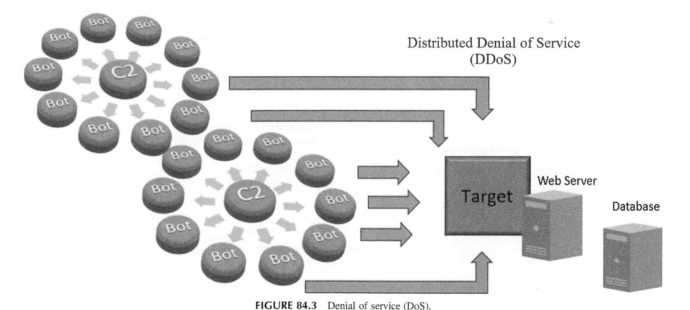

FIGURE 84.3 Denial of service (DoS).

may be a blend of many types of attacks and include software that has either been programmed to do harmful activity (i.e., stealing credentials to gain unauthorized access to a system, steal information from a system and send it via an outbound connection to an unauthorized machine) programmed to masquerade as legitimate programming, interrupt normal functionality, or establish backdoors, leaving the system open for ongoing access. Also, malware may be designed to take advantage of zero-day vulnerabilities if they are able to identify and exploit them on a target's network or systems based on their information-gathering efforts. Since software programs are likely to have many flaws and not all of which have been discovered, undiscovered flaws may result in a variety of zero-day openings for an attacker to exploit.

Rootkits are a type of malware that once installed on a system grants an attacker root access to a system and may be designed to systematically erase logs and registry evidence of its presence, manipulate host-based protection programs by turning them off or overwriting data alerting on the presence of the malware. Rootkits can "effectively over-write the functionality that may already exist within your environment in order to hide their activities. On Linux, this may consist of uploading a rootkit that mods ls, ps, w, who, netstat, login, and top. On Windows, this may consist of over-writing files within the system32 directory or hooking API calls" [8]. Thus rootkits are hard to detect and hard to get rid of.

Virus and worms are other types of malware that infect machines. The National Initiative for Cybersecurity Careers and Studies (NICCS) defines a virus as "a computer program that can replicate itself, infect a computer without permission or knowledge of the user, and then spread or propagate to another computer" and a worm as "a self-replicating, self-propagating, self-contained program that uses networking mechanisms to spread itself" [2]. Both of these will consume cyberspace resources, corrupt data, or delete information all together.

SQL injection targets an organization's databases, often through the external facing front-end website or ports, and is a method of passing commands, in many cases flawed commands, to call on the database to present the information stored therein to the attacker. This data is often sensitive as usernames, passwords, personal and customer information, and financial/banking information are often stored in the databases which feed data back and forth between web portals and users. SQL injection, along with XSS which is another method of passing code through webpages, are commons method of getting data from websites and their databases.

Another avenue for launching a cyber-attack is an indirect attack in which an entity is attacked through their third-party relationships. An organization with partnerships may be successfully attacked if the partners have a weaker level of security than the organization itself. An organization that extends its network to its partners or otherwise grants access to the third parties, is particularly vulnerable.

There are many other tactics and tools an attacker can use such as opening command shells to issue commands to list directory and file structures, and installing keyloggers to allow for eavesdropping and capturing a user's keystrokes as they create files, access websites, and otherwise navigate various object in cyberspace. The cyber-attack process can be summed in Fig. 84.4 below. The next section offers examples of the process at work in the real world.

6. CYBER-ATTACK CASE STUDIES

A challenge with examining real-world case studies is validating the details as an outsider. While laws have been passed requiring organizations meeting certain criteria to notify authorities in the event of a breach, gathering

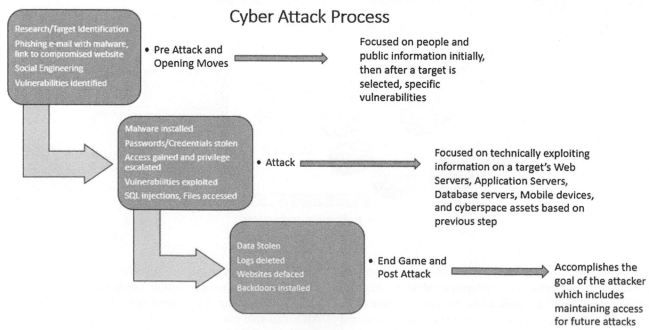

FIGURE 84.4 High-level cyber-attack process.

completely accurate information on suspected or confirmed cyber-attacks can be difficult particularly with respect to understanding the full scope of the attack, specific vulnerabilities successfully exploited and the impact to the target. Additionally, there are conflicting positions within industry regarding the tradeoff between disclosure of the details of an attack, information which if shared (see checklist: "An Agenda for Action for an Information-Sharing Process") can help others prevent similar attacks, and that same information being used by malicious users to exploit additional targets. With these stipulations, enough information is available to convey how attackers have used the previously discussed tactics to launch a cyber-attack.

An Agenda for Action for an Information-Sharing Process

Cyber-attack information-sharing process requirements include the following key activities (check all tasks completed):

_____**1.** Establish and actively participate in information-sharing relationships as part of a proactive, ongoing cyber-attack incident response capability.

_____**2.** Exchange threat information, tools, and techniques with sharing partners.

_____**3.** Increase the organization's cyber security posture and maturity by enhancing or augmenting local data collection, analysis, and management functions.

_____**4.** Share information about both attempted and successful intrusions.

_____**5.** Carefully evaluate potential sharing communities/ partners and select an information sharing model and community that is best suited for an organization or industry sector.

_____**6.** An organization should perform a self-assessment to determine if they have the capabilities to effectively engage in an information-sharing community.

_____**7.** Ensure that a basic, foundational computer network defensive capability is in place before engaging in information sharing and coordination activities.

_____**8.** As a new entrant in an information sharing community, use information from external sources to enhance existing internal incident response capabilities.

_____**9.** Mature organizations should expand internal data-collection operations, perform analysis, and begin to develop and publish indicators and actionable threat intelligence.

_____**10.** An organization may need to consider outsourcing incident response functions in cases where the personnel and skills necessary to perform a task are not readily available within the organization, or in cases where developing or maintaining a specific security capability in-house is not financially advantageous.

_____**11.** Before implementing an information-sharing program, define its overall goals, objectives, and scope; obtain formal approval from the management, privacy, and legal teams; and acquire the support of key organizational stakeholders.

_____**12.** Document the circumstances and rules under which information sharing is permitted by evaluating the risks of disclosure; the urgency of sharing; the trustworthiness of the information sharing community; and the methods used by the community to safeguard shared information.

_____**13.** Identify peers and other organizations with whom coordination and information-sharing relationships would be beneficial.

_____**14.** Ensure that the resources required for ongoing participation in a sharing community are available (personnel, training, hardware, software, and other infrastructure needed to support ongoing data collection, storage, analysis, and dissemination).

_____**15.** Establish points of contact and engage in on-going participation with the sharing community through established communication channels.

_____**16.** Protect sensitive information through the implementation of security controls, access control measures, and through the enforcement of the organization's information sharing rules.

_____**17.** Store and protect evidence that may be needed in the future; to help diagnose a future attack, or perhaps to support legal proceedings or disciplinary actions external sources to enhance existing internal incident response capabilities.

_____**18.** Implement the organizational processes, procedures, and infrastructure necessary to consume, protect, analyze, and respond to indicators, alerts, and incident reports received from external sources.

_____**19.** Produce and maintain written records throughout the incident response lifecycle, allowing the organization to later reconstruct the timeline and narrative of the response activity.

_____**20.** Produce and publish indicators based on local data collection and analysis activities, or through maturation or enrichment of indicators received from sharing community partners.

_____**21.** Produce and publish incident reports to provide initial notification of an incident, interim progress reporting during an incident, and a final report after the incident has been resolved.

_____**22.**]Enumerate risks of sharing incident and threat-intelligence data and identify appropriate mitigation strategies for each phase of the information life cycle.

_____**23.** To the extent possible, prepare for incident and threat-intelligence sharing activities in advance of an actual incident.

_____**24.** Develop a list of data types and content that can be shared quickly with minimal review.

Continued

An Agenda for Action for an Information-Sharing Process—cont'd

_____25. Develop a process for reviewing and protecting data types and content that is likely to contain sensitive information.

_____26. Employ standard data formats and transport protocols to facilitate the efficient and effective exchange of information.

_____27. Mark, store, and track information regarding the sensitivity of data to be shared.

_____28. Provide role-specific training to personnel so they understand how to handle incident and threat intelligence data appropriately.

Stuxnet Virus/Worm Against Nuclear Facilities

Stuxnet is a name given to a malware pairing that apparently included a worm stored on a USB drive designed to map out the workings of a nuclear power plant and a virus that slowly destroyed the nuclear centrifuges by surreptitiously manipulating the rate of spin, while ensuring feedback to operators monitoring the centrifuges reflected nothing amiss. It is reported to have been created as a part of a joint US and Israel project with the aim of disrupting Iran's ability to develop their nuclear capability [9].

The Stuxnet attack is an example of a nation-state attack that highlights the risks to industrial control systems which may be connected to a computer, much less the Internet itself. In some cases, those computers are connected to the Internet themselves, and as the next example demonstrates, makes this type of attack on the industrial or civilian infrastructure an ominous complement to the accomplishment of military objectives.

Nation-State Power Grid Targeted With Cyberwarfare

As of this writing, details are still emerging regarding the cyber-attacks which took down a significant portion of the power grid in the nation-state of Ukraine. The suspected attack occurred during an ongoing campaign of hostilities between Ukraine and Russia.

Reported in early 2016, the attack targeted Ukrainian power stations, and indications are the networks to which the power grid was connected were accessed by a platform which planted a piece of malware onto the systems. The malware deleted and overwrote data files causing a nationwide power outage [10].

The suspected attackers have been attributed to nation-state actors in Russia, and given the timing and the targeting of industrial control systems on which a nation's critical infrastructures and utilities rely, this particular cyber-attack demonstrates significant implications in the tactics of 21st century warfare. As of this writing, the conflict is ongoing and cyber researchers continue to learn about the malware and its impact [11].

Sony Hack

We've discussed how hacktivists launch cyber-attacks to further a cause. Their desired effects include disruption and embarrassment. In 2014, Sony was targeted in retaliation for a film whose characters plotted to kill the leader of North Korea. Reports indicate a group of hacktivists and/or disgruntled company insiders are the likely suspects instead of nation-state agents, despite the subject matter to which the attackers appeared to take offense. Regardless, there is some agreement that malware was installed on Sony's network that was designed to exfiltrate and possibly delete data from internal systems. The data that was lost included network architecture details, employee login info, and extensive PII (including salaries, social security numbers, and birthdates). Unfortunately, after this information was stolen it was posted in public forums. It is unclear how much time passed between the introduction of the malware and the loss of data but reports estimate it could have been upwards of a year [12].

This latter point will be noted in several of the other cases below as well. This gap in time also leads to the emerging classification of these types of attacks, as APTs, which will be discussed in a later section.

Dell Reported in Early January 2016

Not all cyber-attacks are limited to activities in cyberspace. As we discussed earlier, social engineering, fraud, extortion, impersonation, and other cons are often an "opening gambit" to the actual technical portion of a cyber-attack. In this case, there was no confirmed malware or intrusion, however, what occurred was a scam in which the attackers called customers masquerading as Dell support and informed them that their machines were infected with malware or were affected by some other issue. In order to remove the malware, customers were either directed to a malicious site to download software to "fix" a problem, asked to grant the "technician" remote access to their personal machine, and in some cases money was requested in order to fix the issue. It is unknown how the fake callers had access to accurate personal details about the customers and their accounts to include computer info, model number, and previous issue history and as of this writing there was no additional information released. It has been speculated that somehow customer data was breached or perhaps the attackers were insider(s) [13].

Target and Home Depot Reported in 2014

In Target's case, a type of malware was installed that functioned by siphoning data from payment cards when they were swiped at point-of-sale systems during the 2013 holiday shopping season [14]. It is estimated to have been on Target's network for 3 weeks before it was discovered, and in that amount of time, information on least 40 million credit and debit cards and personal information on many more customers had been stolen in a case of massive identity theft and credit card fraud. Since the attack, the impact on Target has been significant. The company closed all of its Canadian stores and laid off 17,000 workers. Financially, they settled a data breach lawsuit for $10 million [15].

Unfortunately, other organizations were targeted in similar fashion and it is suspected that the same malware used in Target breach hit another large retailer, Home Depot. That same year, Home Depot was targeted with a variant of the same software which was installed on payment card systems at self-checkout lanes. Identity theft and credit card fraud were again the aims of the attackers who were suspected of originating from groups in Russia and the Ukraine. The stolen information was ultimately discovered to have been on the underground cyber black market. This attack was reportedly discovered in September of that year, and it is estimated that the malware was installed in April/May 2014, making it 5 months from the initial breach to discovery [14].

Jeep Hack/Sprint Experiment

The cyber-attack on Jeep Chrysler vehicles, via their Sprint carrier that connects the vehicles to the Internet was more of a proof of concept by cyber security experts than the result of malicious agents. We mention it here, however, as a demonstration of the risks posed by the many devices now attached to the Internet. Cyber security experts were able to gain wireless access and remotely take control of a Jeep from 10 miles away. They accessed the vehicle through the vehicle's radio and navigation (GPS) system and then were able to pivot to the internal computers that controlled the vehicle's braking and steering systems.

Ultimately, 1.4 million cars were recalled to have this vulnerability fixed. Interestingly, the software upgrade with the remediation to the remote access vulnerability was provided by USB for users to install via a dashboard port; alternatively, according to Wired, users could download the patch on their home computer, save it to a USB and install it themselves. We have seen how an attacker could use also use either scenario in a cyber-attack [16,17].

Ransomware: CryptoWall

According to US-CERT, ransomware has been around for several years and "attempts to extort money from victims by displaying an onscreen alert … the ransom is in the range of $100–300 dollars" [18]. The years 2015 and 2016 have seen a significant increase in cyber-attacks in which malware is delivered to a target system and encrypts the files, or indeed the entire hard drive. A popup will inform the user that in order to decrypt or regain access to their information, they will need to pay a certain amount. The two main delivery mechanisms for this malware is email phishing, with an infected attachment, and by a user visiting an infected website where the malware is downloaded. Several police departments, hospitals, and schools have been recent targets of these attacks which, unfortunately, unless data has been backed up, often nets the attackers significant funds [19,20].

Rivest, Shamir, and Adelman Advanced Persistent Threat Reported in 2011

The last case we will look at was reported in 2011 and is significant because it is identified as one of the earliest examples of a category of cyber-attack called an APT. In this case, attackers sent phishing email to a group of employees with a legitimate subject line and an attached spreadsheet which contained a zero-day exploit that installed a backdoor via an Adobe Flash vulnerability. Once a user opened the infected spreadsheet, malicious code ran that connected from inside of the company's well-protected network to an outside computer. Once in place, it began to steal information and send it back to the attackers who were suspected of being nation-state actors. What is of note is the length of time from when the malware was originally installed to when it was discovered [21].

7. ADVANCED PERSISTENT THREAT

In recent years, there are attacks that have been characterized as APT. An APT (see Fig. 84.5) takes the cyber-attack process, particularly the middle and later stages and draws them out over an extended period of time (months, even years) undetected. NIST defines the advanced persistent threat as:

An adversary that possesses sophisticated levels of expertise and significant resources that allow it to create opportunities to achieve its objectives by using multiple attack vectors (e.g., cyber, physical, and deception). These objectives typically include establishing and extending footholds within the information technology infrastructure of the targeted organizations for purposes of exfiltrating information, undermining or impeding critical aspects of a mission, program, or organization; or positioning itself to carry out

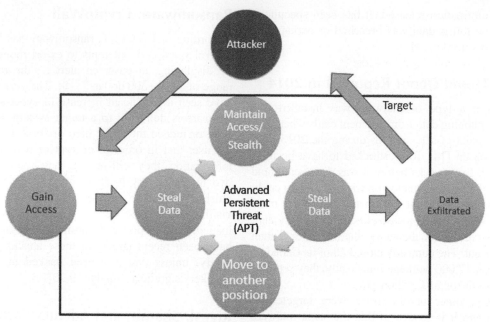

FIGURE 84.5 Advanced persistent threat (APT).

these objectives in the future. The advanced persistent threat: (i) pursues its objectives repeatedly over an extended period of time; (ii) adapts to defenders' efforts to resist it; and (iii) is determined to maintain the level of interaction needed to execute its objectives [22].

The nature of an APT is such that once an attacker has access to a system, they are able to stay inside undetected, combining all of the previous tools and tactics into a coordinated, long-term effort. The persistence aspect is accomplished through stealthy intrusion mechanisms and low key behaviors that don't trigger the usual security detection systems. As with several of the previously discussed cases, the attackers were inside the targeted networks for months and even years before the organization discovered they had been hacked.

"In the 2013 DBIR, phishing was associated with over 95% of incidents attributed to statesponsored actors, and for two years running, more than two-thirds of incidents that comprise the Cyber-Espionage pattern have featured phishing. The user interaction is not about eliciting information, but for attackers to establish persistence on user devices, set up camp, and continue their stealthy march inside the network" [6]. Accordingly, APTs consist of more than a single strike with the aim of getting in and then getting out or achieving a destructive effect. This category of cyber-attack is conducted with an increased level of sophistication and iterative implementation of the cyber-attack process. When APTs are discovered, it's likely been months or even years after the initial intrusion with a significant loss of valuable information.

8. ADDITIONAL CONSIDERATIONS

As technology and cyberspace expands there are additional implications of the cyber-attack process particularly where social media, cloud infrastructure, and mobile devices are concerned. The mobility and accessibility of data from a variety of devices and cloud locations has in many ways made information more vulnerable to cyber-attacks and under less control by those who own it. With mobile devices, the devices may be cloned, the devices themselves stolen, and are susceptible to the same attacks as mentioned above [23]. Furthermore, the spread of mobile devices adds to IoT, posing additional attractive targets for cyber-attacks, as many of the case studies have demonstrated. Everything from cars, refrigerators, Industrial (SCADA) systems, home security systems accessible either directly or indirectly by the Internet.

Lastly, the proliferation of the use of social media is a goldmine in the information-gathering and reconnaissance stages of an attack. As users post information about their families, pets, hobbies, travel plans, jobs, and other personal details, and reuse at least portions of this information for passwords, social media is an ideal target for mining information that could be further used by an attacker.

9. SUMMARY

As the perimeters of cyberspace have expanded, any area of an enterprise or organization may be targeted by a cyber-attack. The perpetrators of a cyber-attack may have a range of motives and technical expertise and there are a variety of tools and tactics at their disposal. While the cyber-attack process lends itself to discrete steps, the process is often customized to fit the attacker's aims.

Finally, let's move on to the real interactive part of this Chapter: review questions/exercises, hands-on projects, case projects and optional team case project. The answers and/or solutions by chapter can be found in Appendix K.

CHAPTER REVIEW QUESTIONS/ EXERCISES

True/False

1. True or False? Cyberspace comprises hundreds of inter-connected computers, servers, routers, switches, and fiber optic cables that make our critical infrastructures work.
2. True or False? Cyber-attackers are typically classified by their level of expertise, sophistication, and the end goals of their attacks.
3. True or False? Cyberspace entities store and transmit large amounts of personally identifiable information (PII), customer information, credit card or banking details, confidential information, intellectual property, and other sensitive data.
4. True or False? The cyber-attack process is generally divided into preattack activity, the actual attack, and postattack activities.
5. True or False? During the actual attack, the weaknesses that were discovered in the later closing stages are now exploited for the purposes of the attacker.

Multiple Choice

1. The _____ of an attack occurs whenever the aims of the attacker are met, or until the cyber-attack is detected or disrupted.
   A. End-game
   B. Targeted system
   C. Coverage of tracks
   D. Distinctive steps
   E. Persistent presence
2. The tools and tactics used to perpetrate a cyber-attack include technical and nontechnical methods of targeting the various areas of cyberspace in order to overcome a target's:
   A. Available information
   B. Webserver
   C. Sensitive data
   D. Mobile devices
   E. Security measures
3. In recent years, there are attacks that have been charac-terized as:
   A. Adversary
   B. Advanced persistent threats

   C. Cyber-attack process
   D. Undetected
   E. Significant resources
4. As technology and cyberspace expands there are addi-tional implications of the:
   A. Social media
   B. Cyber-attack process
   C. Cloud infrastructure
   D. Mobile devices
   E. Perimeters
5. As the _____ have expanded, any area of an enterprise or organization may be targeted by a cyber-attack.
   A. Perpetrators
   B. Motives
   C. Perimeters of cyberspace
   D. Technical expertise
   E. Cyber-attack processes

EXERCISE

Problem

A nation-state regularly targets companies in a certain industry sector for several months. The attacks come in the form of targeted emails that carry weaponized attachments containing a software exploit that, upon opening, launches malware on the victims system. Once compromised, these systems contact servers controlled by the adversary to receive further instructions and to exfiltrate data. What should the targeted companies do immediately?

Hands-On Projects

Project

Cybersecurity analysts from companies in a business sector have been sharing indicators and malware samples in an online forum over the past few years. Each company performs independent analysis of the attacks and observes consistent patterns over time, with groups of events often having a number of commonalities, such as the type of malware used, the domains of command and control channels, and other technical indicators. These observations lead the analysts to suspect that the attacks are not fully random. What should the online forum members do?

Case Projects

Problem

A hacktivist group targets a select set of companies for a large-scale distributed denial of service (DDoS) attack. The group employs a distributed botnet, loosely coordinated and controlled by members of the group. By analyzing the traffic generated by the botnet, one company is able to determine that the attackers are using a variant of a popular DDoS tool. What should the targeted companies do?

Optional Team Case Project

Problem

A cybercrime group made use of a popular business practices conferences attendee list to select targets for a wave of phishing emails. The group was able to identify multiple members of the business offices and, in some circumstances, compromise those machines and authorize electronic payments to overseas businesses. What should the targeted companies do to offset these phishing attacks?

REFERENCES

[1] US-Cert Publications, n.d. Retrieved from: https://www.us-cert.gov/security-publications.

[2] Cyber Glossary | National Initiative for Cybersecurity Careers and Studies (NICCS), n.d. Retrieved from: https://niccs.us-cert.gov/glossary.

[3] National Institute of Standards and Technology (NIST) Special Publication 800-53 Revision 4, Security and Privacy Controls for Federal Information Systems and Organizations, Joint Task Force Transformation Initiative, 2013, 2015. http://nvlpubs.nist.gov/nistpubs/SpecialPublications/NIST.SP.800-53r4.pdf.

[4] Number of Internet users 2005–2015 | Statistic, n.d. Retrieved from: http://www.statista.com/statistics/273018/number-of-Internet-users-worldwide/.

[5] Internet of Things (IoT), n.d. Retrieved from: http://www.cisco.com/web/solutions/trends/iot/overview.html.

[6] Verizon, 2015 Data Breach Investigations Report, 2015. Retrieved from: http://news.verizonenterprise.com/2015/04/2015-data-breach-report-info/.

[7] Social Engineer, Inc., The Social Engineering Framework, The Attack Cycle, 2016. Retrieved from: http://www.social-engineer.org/framework/general-discussion/attack-cycle/.

[8] Advanced Security Defenses, Control: File Integrity Monitoring, 2011. Retrieved from: http://www.advancedsecuritydefenses.com/controls/.

[9] M.B. Kelley, The Stuxnet Attack on Iran's Nuclear Plant Was 'Far More Dangerous' Than Previously Thought, 2013. Retrieved from: http://www.businessinsider.com/stuxnet-was-far-more-dangerous-than-previous-thought-2013-11.

[10] Fortune, Ukraine Utility Cyber-attack Wider than First Reported, 2016. Retrieved from: http://fortune.com/2016/01/05/cyber-attackukraine/.

[11] Motherboard, Malware Found inside Downed Ukrainian Grid Management Points to Cyberattack, 2016. Retrieved from: http://motherboard.vice.com/read/malware-found-inside-downed-ukrainian-power-plant-points-to-cyberattack.

[12] K. Zetter, Sony Got Hacked Hard: What We Know and Don't Know So Far, Wired, 2014. Retrieved from: http://www.wired.com/2014/12/sony-hack-what-we-know/.

[13] D. Goodin, Latest Tech Support Scam Stokes Concerns Dell Customer Data Was Breached, Arstechnica, 2016. Retrieved from: http://arstechnica.com/security/2016/01/latest-tech-support-scam-stokes-concerns-dell-customer-data-was-breached/.

[14] B. Krebs, In Home Depot Breach, Investigation Focuses on Self-checkout Lanes, 2014. Retrieved from: http://krebsonsecurity.com/tag/target-data-breach/ and Banks: Credit Card Breach at Home Depot. Retrieved from: http://krebsonsecurity.com/2014/09/banks-credit-card-breach-at-home-depot/.

[15] M. Parks, Target Offers $10 Million Settlement in Data Breach Lawsuit, 2015. Retrieved from: http://www.npr.org/sections/thetwo-way/2015/03/19/394039055/target-offers-10-million-settlement-in-data-breach-lawsuit.

[16] M. Casey, Fiat Chrysler Recalls 1.4M Cars after Hack Revelations, CBS News, 2015. Retrieved from: http://www.cbsnews.com/news/fiat-chrysler-recall-after-jeep-hack/.

[17] A. Greenberg, After Jeep Hack, Chrysler Recalls 1.4M Vehicles for Bug Fix, Wired, 2015. Retrieved from: http://www.wired.com/2015/07/jeep-hack-chrysler-recalls-1-4m-vehicles-bug-fix/.

[18] US-Cert Alert, Crypto Ransomware, 2014. Retrieved from: https://www.us-cert.gov/ncas/alerts/TA14–295A.

[19] FBI, Ransomware on the Rise, 2015. Retrieved from: https://www.fbi.gov/news/stories/2015/january/ransomware-on-the-rise/ransomware-on-the-rise.

[20] Symantec Security Response, CryptoDefense, the CryptoLocker Imitator, Makes Over $34,000 in One Month, 2014. Retrieved from: http://www.symantec.com/connect/blogs/cryptodefense-cryptolocker-imitator-makes-over-34000-one-month.

[21] RSA FraudAction Research Labs, Anatomy of an Attack, 2011. Retrieved from: https://blogs.rsa.com/anatomy-of-an-attack/.

[22] National Institute of Standards and Technology (NIST) Special Publication 800-39, Managing Information Security Risk Organization, Mission, and Information System View, Joint Task Force Transformation Initiative (2011). Retrieved from: http://nvlpubs.nist.gov/nistpubs/Legacy/SP/nistspecialpublication800-39.pdf.

[23] J. Adams, Latest Cybercrime Threat: Device Cloning, 2012. Retrieved from: http://www.americanbanker.com/issues/177_202/latest-cybercrime-threat-device-cloning-1053627-1.html.

Part XIV

Advanced Security

Chapter 85

Security Through Diversity

Kevin Noble

Terremark Worldwide Inc., Miami, FL, United States

The Internet and all the interconnected nodes reflect an aggregate of disparate technology, a new spectrum of human interaction, and the most competitive domain for nation-states, industry, and enterprise. The Internet is the mirror reflecting all things important or not. Revolutions are sparked, small grievances cascade into protest, and aspects of wars are waged in the digital medium that is the Internet. The interconnected scale assures that threats can succeed with a high probability of success while avoiding attribution. The characteristics of successful digital threats are creative with a high impact, requiring victims to adapt and pay attention. Most Internet-related threats are opportunistic, such as malware designed to steal access to bank accounts and computer virus infections primarily concerned with the theft of information. Yet none of these threats come close to the most successful attacks, which are excessive in magnitude of impact, causing economies to fail or governments to initiate a response other than to suppress social media.

Ubiquity and compatibility are the driving forces of the computer revolution, which are driving down costs, while the application of "security through diversity" is still emerging as a strategic decision. In most cases, geography and distribution of content achieve diversity. For the largest sites providing search capabilities, banking, and social media, connective computing becomes critical and relevant as the scale and risk increases; protecting any single host with the application of diversity typically fails. Internet services provided through distribution and replication achieve geographical diversity and perhaps some security, intended or otherwise. Distribution and replication is resistant to denial of service (DoS) and is an ideal response to cataclysmic events. Immense cataclysmic

events require strategic contingency planning by nation-states. In general, a decimated region such as the earthquake that hit Haiti in January 2010 required a rebuild of a telecommunications infrastructure. Mobile communication towers were deployed allowing mobile phones to communicate voice and SMS messages fairly quickly. As with many disasters, the distribution and volume of devices supported quickly provided a means to support the emergency needs and can be viewed as a principal of "security through diversity" and an aspect of "resilience." Emergency management can shorten the duration of recovery and intercede in cascading events and coordinate efforts.

An example of an unnatural threat that probably caused permanent physical damage and destruction would be the stuxnet worm in June of 2010. The stuxnet worm may exemplify threats to come as it targeted programmable logic controllers for a specific set number of centrifuges. Generally, centrifuges operate at high speed at a steady pace. The stuxnet worm disrupted and delayed the uranium enrichment process by changing centrifuge speeds in such a way as to damage the equipment while falsely reporting nominal speeds through the programmable logic controllers. The stuxnet worm had a direct impact on an Iranian program that, according to public information, delayed and disrupted the program successfully. The most successful targeted threats will achieve permanent physical damage and disruption.

To be successful, stuxnet had to contain enough exploits to vulnerabilities to ensure spreading and infecting enough host to achieve success. A defender that threat models may impose policies to forbid sharing of USB devices or an aggressive patch cycle. Direct Internet access was not a

1119

Computer and Information Security Handbook. http://dx.doi.org/10.1016/B978-0-12-803843-7.00085-5
Copyright © 2013 Elsevier Inc. All rights reserved.

factor in the successful exploit of the device; many organizations incorrectly consider devices and nodes safe based on "direct Internet access."

By volume, Internet-related attacks that seek targets of opportunity for financial gain and financial loss can be insured to a point. Also significant in volume are "targeted threats" where after an intrusion, sensitive data is targeted as part of a larger espionage effort. Information security practitioners focused on espionage-related intrusions joke, "How many of the fortune 500 companies have been exploited?" The answer given is "500."

Not as pervasive today, but in 2001–2005 worms were effective and opportunistic. Aggressive targeted attacks are rare but tend to exceed in magnitude of other threats and usually have an effective duration to achieve specific goals such as DoS (long duration) or the exfiltration of information (usually short). Exfiltration as an act itself usually only takes the time to find the location and compress and send the data out.

Specific distributed denial-of-service (DDoS) attacks require enough magnitude and duration to achieve goals set by the attacker(s). In general, DDoS must exceed the target's ability to resist for the intended duration or achieve short-term goals such as extortion. Response to DDoS threats generally require a balance of efforts to assure legitimate traffic remains while selectively banishing malicious traffic that can be dynamic, excessive, and requires logically adjusting content delivery, avoiding single-point failures in location, services, and peering. The diversification in points of presence, scalable services, and working with service providers has proven successful.

Diversity as an aspect of resilience and part of a larger information security (see checklist: "An Agenda for Action for Implementing Information Technology Security") effort is costly and difficult. Decisions to hosting divergent technologies that provide the same service redundantly might keep you operational, but it comes with a necessary investment in effort and skill. Intentionally going against top trends appears to be happening naturally as technology refreshes and proliferates. Implementing diversity as doctrine may not be necessary, diversity of product selection has introduced risk to individuals while proliferation may protect all devices as a larger digital biosphere. For technology, mass manufacturing and commoditized hardware reduces cost, and competition naturally introduces diversity. Software, for the most part, seeks to ensure uniformity across platforms and hardware; diversity in delivery comes at a price.

An Agenda for Action for Implementing Information Technology Security

This checklist is a high-level guide to assess the overall security and privacy status associated with a contracted IT service or outsourced business process. The objective of this checklist is to assist program managers, security officers, system owners, and contracting-officer representatives to identify areas of increased security risk and areas not in compliance with national and agency policy and standards. The key areas examined in this checklist include (check all tasks completed):

_____**1.** IT, physical, and personnel security policy
_____**2.** Organization/contract general provisions
_____**3.** System, data, and device inventory
_____**4.** System certification and accreditation
_____**5.** Contingency planning
_____**6.** Continuous monitoring/risk management
_____**7.** Weakness management
_____**8.** Incident handling and response
_____**9.** Security configuration management
_____**10.** Security training

The most common diversity strategy is in use today by most large-scale businesses that choose to store data far enough away from the original site as to be unaffected by natural disasters and phenomena such as power outages. But is this enough? Natural disasters cover only one threat vector to sustainability and operational readiness. The information age must balance uniformity and ubiquity in the face of threats though adaptation and vigilance.

1. UBIQUITY

Most modern attacks take advantage of the fact that the majority of personal computers on the Internet are quite nearly in the same state. The way an attack goes against a single host works identically on millions. At the global scale of interconnected systems, diversity is the best response to threats against ubiquity; it is the closest to a digital autoimmune system possible with the inclusion of patch remediation and defense-in-depth. Patch remediation only safeguards against known threats and assumes emerging threats pose little risk; the risk is worth absorbing or at least tolerated. Defense-in-depth as a strategy requires threat modeling that includes methods to detect and suppress attacks. Business continuity planning rarely includes cyber threats or considers intrusions that can impact the core business.

At the smallest level of individual hosts, delayed patching of applications or with the operating system (OS) itself can be viewed as the single cell microorganism prone to automated compromise. Home users pay little attention to software updates unless prompted by self-updating software. Users rely on notification and antivirus software to protect and inoculate against common threats to the Internet as a whole more than providing individual protection. The modicum of protection from automatic updates and an antivirus solution is sufficient to individuals. Working with this knowledge, an attacker will seek to automate attacks by taking advantage of the ubiquity of systems, targets of opportunity. Consider the nation-state threat, utilizing an exploit that works against a majority of home systems. The investment in developing an exploit provides a nation-state with capability to disable and disrupt.

You don't have to be a nation-state with an agenda to develop an offensive cyber capability. Imagine for a moment that you're an attacker or small collective of attackers. In general, the consideration is opportunistic and the effort is to develop exploits that within the collective skill-set of the group select popular OSs with the most common software packages, and select the most ideal target within that subset. An economist might see the concept as a "probability density function," or what is simply referred to as "getting the most bang for the buck." Targets of opportunity are proportional to the ubiquity of the vulnerability itself. It is certain that as a given computer system moves away from the densest pool of common systems, an attacker needs to work harder to accommodate the difference, which thus can reduce the likelihood of compromise.

Ubiquity at scale introduces complexity in engineering updates, distribution considerations, and can act as a safeguard. Large-scale solutions lead to naturally diverse properties. Still, engineering to requirements with anticipated tolerances might still be the best approach for any design; according to Bruce Schneier, "All security involves trade-offs."[1] To that end, diversity is not a security strategy in itself but is an aspect of defense-in-depth, part of a holistic approach to security and possibly an insurance policy against unenforceable odds.

2. EXAMPLE ATTACKS AGAINST UNIFORMITY

Ubiquitous systems are good, cheap, replaceable, and reliable—until mass failure occurs. It certainly pays to know that ubiquity and uniformity are the absolute right choices in the absence of threats. That is not the world we

occupy, even if not acknowledged. What would it take to survive an attack that had the potential to effectively disrupt a business or even destroy it?

If you operate in a service industry that is Internet based, this question is perhaps what keeps you up at night—an attack against all your systems and services, from which you might not recover. DoS is a simple and straightforward attack that involves an attacker making enough requests to saturate your network or service to the point at which legitimate business and communications fails. The distributed denial-of-service (DDoS) attack is the same type of attack against a uniform presence in the Internet space but with many attacking hosts operating in unison against a site or service.

Businesses with real bricks-and-mortar locations in addition to selling goods and services over the Internet can survive a sustainable DDoS attack against the Internet-based business because the bricks-and-mortar transactions can carry the company's survival. Inversely, businesses with the ubiquitous use of credit cards that require the merchant authorization process can suffer when the point-of-sale system can't process credit cards. That business will simply and routinely have to turn away customers who can only pay by credit card. Yet a business with both a strong Internet and a solid bricks-and-mortar presence can survive an outage through diversity.

For years, DDoS was used as a form of extortion. Internet-based gambling businesses were frequent targets of this type of attack and frequently made payouts to criminal attackers. It is common for Internet-based businesses to utilize DDoS mitigation services to absorb or offload the undesired traffic. The various means that an attacker can use in combination to conduct DDoS have escalated into a shifting asymmetrical warfare, with each side adapting to new techniques deployed by the other side.

Companies have failed to counter the straightforward attack and have gone out of business or ceased operations. A company called Blue Security Inc. that specialized in combating unsolicited email messages (spam) by automating a reply message to the senders had its subscribers attacked. Blue Security's antispam model failed in 2006 when spammers attacked its very customers, causing the company to shut down the service in the interest of protecting the customers.[2]

Successfully mitigating and combating an attack is achieved by either having enough resources to absorb the attack or offloading the attack at some point prior to reaching a site or service. The DDoS attack is partially successful where the target is uniformly presented and responsive and does not react fast enough to the attacks. A common means to protect against DDoS or Internet-based outages is to have a diverse

---

1. B. Schneier, *Beyond Fear*, Springer-Verlag, 2003.

2. "Blue Security, spam victim or just a really bad idea," *InfoWorld/Tech Watch* article, May 19, 2006.

business model that does not rely only on the Internet as a means to conduct business. Diverse business models may hold considerable cost and bring in differential revenue, but they ensure that one model may in fact support the other through sustained attacks, disasters, or even tough times. Employing the concept of security through diversity gives decision-makers more immediate options.

Though the DDoS attack represents the most simplistic and basic attack against an Internet-based institution, it does require an attacker to use enough resources against a given target to achieve bottlenecking or saturation. This represents the immediate and intentional attack, with one or more attackers making a concentrated effort against a target.

3. ATTACKING UBIQUITY WITH ANTIVIRUS TOOLS

Attackers use obfuscation, encryption, and compression to install malicious code such as viruses, worms, and Trojans. These techniques are tactical responses to bypass common antivirus solutions deployed by just about everyone. The number of permutations possible on a single executable file while retaining functionality is on the order of tens of thousands, and these changes create just enough diversity in each iteration to achieve a successful infection. An attacker needs to mutate an executable only enough to bypass detection from signature-based antivirus tools, the most common antivirus solutions deployed.[3]

It is possible for anyone to test a given piece of malicious code against a litany of antivirus solutions. It is common practice for attackers and defenders both to submit code to sites such as www.virustotal.com for inspection and detection against 26 or more common antivirus solutions. Attackers use the information to verify whether a specific antivirus product will fail to detect code while defenders inspect suspected binaries.

At the root of the problem is the signature-based method used to inspect malicious code. Not all antivirus solutions use signature-based detection exclusively, but in essence, it is the fast, cheap, and, until recently, most effective method. If malware sample A looks like signature X, it is most likely X. A harder and less-reliable way to detect malicious code is through a technique known as heuristics. Each antivirus will perform heuristics in a different manner, but it makes a guess or best-effort determination and will classify samples ranging from safe to highly suspect. Some antivirus solutions may declare a sample malicious, increasing the chances of finding a false positive.

Another factor in analysis is entropy, or how random the code looks upon inspection. Here again you can have

false positives when following the trend to pack, distort, encrypt, and otherwise obfuscate malicious code. The measurement of entropy is a good key indicator that something has attempted to hide itself from inspection. Keep in mind that because commercial software uses these techniques as well, you have a chance of false positives.

At the 2008 annual DEFCON conference in Las Vegas, a new challenge was presented: Teams were provided with existing malicious code and modified the code without changing functionality, to bypass all the antivirus solutions. The team that could best defeat detection won. The contest was called "race to zero." The organizers hoped to raise awareness about the decreased reliability on signature-based antivirus engines. It is very important to say again that the code is essentially the same except that it can avoid detection (or immediate detection).

Given that it is possible and relatively easy for attackers to modify existing malicious code enough to bypass all signature-based solutions yet retain functionality, it can be considered a threat against any enterprise that has a ubiquitous antivirus solution deployment. Infections are possible and likely and increasing; the risk is not a doomed enterprise, but usually information disclosure could lead to other things.

Those who choose Apple's OS X over PC OSs enjoy what might be coined in some circles as immunity or resistance in the arena of malicious code. An attacker would have to invest time and effort into attack strategies against the Apple platform over and above the efforts of attacking Windows, for example. Without getting caught up in market share percentages, Apple is not as attractive for attackers (at the time of this writing) from the OS perspective.

One might think the application of diversity can be applied simply by hosting differential OSs. This is true but rarely works if derived from a strict security perspective. It could be beneficial to switch entirely to a less attacked platform or host a differential OS in a single environment. On the sliding scales of diversity and complexity, you might have immune hosts to one attack type against a given OS. This also means that internal information technology and support teams would have to maintain support skills that can support each different platform hosted. Usually business decisions make better drivers for using and supporting diverse OSs than a strategy of diversity alone. In my observations, routine support will be applied where individuals have stronger skills and abilities while other platforms are neglected.

4. THE THREAT OF WORMS

In 2003 and 2004, the fast-spreading worm's probability represented the bigger threat for the Internet community at large because patching was not as commonplace and interconnectivity was largely ignored compared to today. A

3. G. Ollmann, "X-morphic exploitation," IBM Global Technology Services, May 2007.

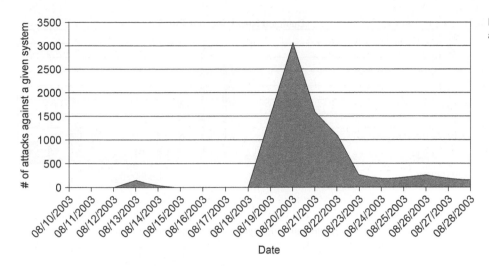

FIGURE 85.1 Tracking infected hosts as part of the Nachi outbreak.

number of self-replicating viruses propagating to new hosts autonomously are known as worms. A worm-infected host would seek to send the worm to other hosts, using methods that would allow for extremely aggressive and rapid spread. Infected hosts did not experience much in the way of damage or intentional data loss but simply were not able to communicate with other hosts on heavily infected networks. Essentially, the worms became an uncontrolled DDoS tool, causing outages and performance issues in networks in which the worm gained enough hosts to saturate the networks by seeking yet more hosts.

While responding to the outbreaks of both the Nachi and MSBlas worms in 2003 for a large business, there was enough statistical information about both worms from the various logs, host-based protection, and packet captures to reconstruct the infection process (see Fig. 85.1). The Nachi worm in particular appeared to have an optimized IP address-generating algorithm allowing nodes closer on the network to become infected faster. When you consider that the worm could only infect Windows-based systems against the total variety of hosts, you end up with a maximum threshold of targets. The network-accessible Windows hosts at the time of the worm attack were about 79.8% of the total network; other platforms and systems were based on Unix, printers, and routers. Certainly some of the hosts were patched against this particular vulnerability. Microsoft had released a patch prior to the outbreak. But at the time of the Nachi worm outbreak, patching was deployed at set intervals in excess of 60 days, and the particular vulnerability exploited by Nachi was not patched. The theoretical estimated number of systems that could succumb to infection was right at the total number of Windows systems on the network—just under 80%, as shown in Fig. 85.2—meaning that the network was fairly uniform.[4]

Given this scenario, it would stand to reason that the infection would achieve 100% and only depend on each newly infected system coming up with the appropriate IP address to infect new hosts. Yet the data reveals that the total infection was only 36% of the total Windows systems and took 17 days to really become effective, as shown in Fig. 85.3. It seemed that enough vulnerable Windows hosts had to be infected to seed the next wave of infected hosts.

The worm's pseudorandom IP address selection was a factor in the success of its spread; you had to have a vulnerable system online with a specific IP that was targeted at that time. Once enough seed systems became infected, even a poor pseudorandom IP generator would have been successful in allowing the worm to spread at speeds similar to a chemical chain reaction. Systems would become infected within seconds rather than minutes or hours of connecting to a network. Over the years the probability of a mass windows infection was reduced considerably by addressing vulnerabilities. Microsoft immunity response to reduce vulnerabilities is addressed by the "Secure Development Lifecycle," a process that has proven effective to worm behavior of exploiting vulnerabilities automatically. It has been argued that massive worm outbreaks have declined because the diverse number of systems has increased, the cost to develop an effective exploit has increased to a point where it would not be used carelessly, and DDoS can provide control while a worm may not.

Other factors for a successful defense against the worm included a deployment of host-based firewalls that blocked port traffic. The Nachi worm traffic was mostly from nonlocal untrusted networks making port filtering an easy block for the attack. Other factors that reduced the spread included the fact that a number of systems, such as mobile laptop computers, did not remain connected after business hours (users taking the laptops home, for example).

FIGURE 85.2 Nachi finding new hosts to infect.

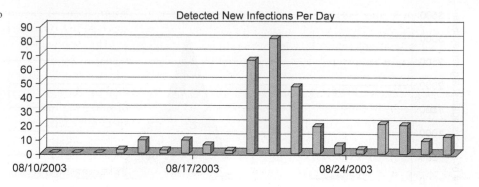

FIGURE 85.3 The Nachi worm requires continual infection to achieve network saturation.

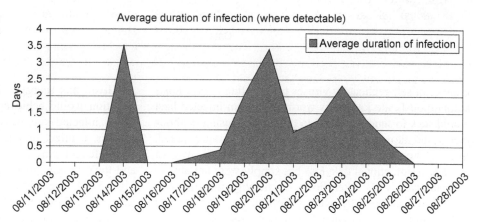

Emergency patching and efforts to contain the spread by various groups was also a big factor in reducing the number of vulnerable systems. The Nachi worm itself also prevented infection to some systems by simply generating too much traffic, causing a DoS within the network. Network engineers immediately began blocking traffic as generated by the Nachi worm and blocking entire subnets altogether. The speed of the infection caused a dramatic increase in traffic on infected networks and induced a reaction by many network engineers looking for the root cause and attacking the problem by blocking specific traffic.

Additional resistance to infection from the Nachi worm in this case was achieved through unintended diversity in time, location, and events surrounding the vulnerable systems. Perhaps we can call this being lucky; vulnerable hosts were protected by not being connected or not needing to connect during the potential infection window. The last interesting thing about worms that achieved mass infection during 2003 is that those worms still generate traffic on the Internet today—perhaps an indication of a sustained infection, reinfection, or intentional attack.

Though unintentional diversity and rapid response to the outbreak were success factors, an emerging response to automated attacks was intrusion detection systems (IDSs) being deployed in greater numbers. Though prevention is ideal, detection is the absolute first and necessary step in the process of defense. A natural transition to automating defense was the mass implementation of intrusion protection systems (IPSs), which detect and block based on predefined understandings of past attacks and in some cases block based on attack behavior.

Making a choice to be diverse as a means to improve security alone might not be beneficial. If you choose two different backup methodologies or split offices between two different OSs just for the sake of security and not business as the driver, then cost in theory nearly doubles without gaining much. Ideally, diversity is coupled with other concepts, such as security.

5. AUTOMATED NETWORK DEFENSE

Computer systems that transact information at great speed have similar properties to chemical reactions: once started, quite difficult or impossible to stop. The defense of the network can't happen in real time where humans alone provide security. Alternatively, machines may not make the best decision about traffic and thresholds. A balanced approached that blends human decision with machine response is ideal. Network security defense from the perspective of the security provided is to leverage automation simply because it is cheap, trying to keep out most of the bad things while allowing everything else to traverse without interference, reflecting customer demand.

If a security service provider took time to inspect every anomaly to the point where overall traffic performance were degraded, it would be advantageous for an attacker to exploit the heavy inspection process to create a performance issue up to the point of denying service. This very consideration causes both the default policies on IPS and IPS customers to acquiesce and to allow a percentage of bad traffic as a trade for performance or connectivity in general.

At first you might be surprised at the position taken by IPS vendors and customers. Denying all anomalous and malicious traffic might be the sales pitch from IPS vendors, but the dichotomy of having a device designed for automated protection being used for automated DoS by an attacker against the very business it was supposed to protect would scare off anyone. IDS as an industry does nothing more than strike a balance between common attack prevention while allowing everything else—perhaps a worthy goal on some fronts.

6. DIVERSITY AND THE BROWSER

An evolutionary adaptation to security has driven attackers to exploit the web browser. Because everyone has one, the web browser represents the most promising avenue for information exploitation. Straightforward attacks involving simply spraying an attack across the Internet are not how one exploits browsers. Attacks usually take advantage of vulnerabilities only after a browser retrieves code from a malicious website. The remote attack is not a sustainable attack. Most popular browsers that host the means for automatic patching allow the browsers to be secured against known vulnerabilities. Still, not everyone takes advantage of new browser releases that include patches for remote exploits and serious issues. Attacking the user behind the browser along with attacking the browser seems to be a winning combination yielding a higher percentage of compromised hosts for attackers.

Conceptually, could the browser be the weapon of choice that collapses an entire enterprise? It is possible but highly unlikely. The two most common browsers are Microsoft's Internet Explorer and Mozilla's Firefox, making them the most targeted. Most browsers are not monolithic; adding code to view pages and perform animation are common practices. Browser extensibility allows anyone to integrate software components. Serious vulnerabilities and poor implementation in some of these extensions has led to exploitable code but usually demands a visit from a vulnerable browser. Since many of us don't use the same software package added to our browsers, this sort of threat, though risky to any enterprise from the standpoint of

information disclosure, does not represent the sort of survivability issues security diversity seeks to remedy.

The application of diversity to browsers could be remedied by the selection of an uncommon browser or by choosing extensibility options offered by vendors other than the most common ones. The tradeoff is gaining a host of compatibility issues for the ability to thwart browser-specific attacks.

OSs are the Holy Grail of attacked platforms simply because the OS has all the control. Most attacks in some form or fashion seek to gain partial authority within the OS or to dominate and persist within the OS altogether. Rootkits seek to hide the behavior of code and allow code (usually malicious) to operate with impunity on a given system. Even when the browser or other services are attacked, it would probably be more advantageous for the attacker to seek a way into the OS without detection. Targeted threats are customized to evade detection and to leverage vulnerabilities discovered over time to infiltrate; these threats are difficult to detect and diversity at any layer is but an obstacle. Being a target means you have a specific value, either monetary or in information. Many Fortune 500 companies have been targeted for trade secrets, industrial espionage, pending patents, and have lost data, credibility, and information, but few went out of business as a result of an intrusion or series of intrusions. These types of threats do not appear to have a short-term effect on the institutions except in the case where the company H.B. Gary was targeted and had nearly all the internal emails of the organization released publicly. As a security firm, H.B. Gary lost considerable business unlike the institutions H.B. Gary sought to assist.

Opportunistic threats from generic malware and phishing affect individuals and the accounts and information they possess. Many individuals utilize a single account and password or a very short list of account and password pairs. Once accounts and passwords are exposed, attackers automate the use of those accounts against banking sites, social networking sites, and others. A unique and diverse set of accounts and passwords that are well protected offer the best defense against wholesale identity theft.

It is fairly safe to say that all systems host vulnerabilities, some are difficult to uncover, and establishing a defense against future unknown vulnerabilities makes sense. Many well-developed OSs can randomize memory layouts, and as a means to reduce the predictability, create specific offsets for code execution. Attackers craft exploits to take advantage of vulnerabilities found in code, and in some cases, well-crafted exploits allow remote command execution. The Windows OS, with the lion's share of systems, is the ubiquitous platform of choice for attackers. Microsoft has made considerable efforts in the past few years to combat the threats and has introduced technologies such as stack cookies, safe handler and chain validation, heap protection, data execution prevention (DEP), and address space layout randomization (ASLR). Each is designed to thwart or deter automated attacks and protect code execution from exploitation through any vulnerability. ASLR can be defeated and many examples exist in the public, but ASLR affords protection at scale from generic automated attacks and the diversity of memory layouts from hosts with the same vulnerability are afforded protection.

Of each of these low-level defenses implemented in code, ASLR seeks to increase security through diversity in the Vista OS. Theoretically, on a given system on which an attack is possible, it will not be possible again on another system or even the same system after a layout change that occurs after a reboot. Certainly altering the behavior between systems reduces risk.

The current implementation of ASLR on Vista requires complete randomized process address spacing to offer complete security from the next wave of attacks.[5] Certainly the balance of security falters and favors the attacker when promiscuous code meets any static state or even limited entropy of sorts.

7. SANDBOXING AND VIRTUALIZATION

The technique of sandboxing is sometimes used to contain code or fault isolation. Java, Flash, and other languages rely heavily on containing code as a security measure. Though sandboxing can be effective, it has the same issues as anything else that is ubiquitous—one flaw that can be exploited for a single sandbox can be exploited for all sandboxes.

Expanding the concept in a different way is the virtual hosting of many systems on a single system through the use of a hypervisor. Each instance of an OS connects to the physical host through the hypervisor, which acts as the hardware gateway and as a kernel of sorts. Frequently the concept of virtualization is coupled to security as the layer of abstraction and offers quite a bit of protection between environments in the absence of vulnerabilities.

The concept of virtualization has considerable long-term benefits by offering diversity within a single host but requires the same diligence as any physical system compounded by the number of virtual systems hosted. It is fair to say that each host that contains vulnerabilities may therefore put other hosts or the entire core of the hosting physical system at risk. The risk is no different than an entire room full of interconnected systems that have emergent properties. Frequently, security professionals and

attackers alike use virtualization as a platform for testing code and the ability to suspend and record activity, similar to a VCR.

In many cases, the push to virtualized system or service is a business decision with operational cost being a key driver. Systems that share resources can leverage unused resources. However, with increased frequency, security is considered a benefit of virtualization. This is true only in the context of virtual environments achieving isolation between guests or host and guest. This is a clear goal of all the hypervisors on the market, from the VMware product line to Windows virtualization products.

For quite some time it was possible for security researchers to work with malicious samples in a virtualized state. This allowed researchers to essentially use the context of a computer running on a computer with features similar to a digital video recorder, where time (for the malicious sample) can be recorded and played back at a speed of their choosing. That was true until the advent of malicious code with the ability to test whether it was hosted in a virtualized environment or not. Recent research has shown that it is possible for malicious code to escape the context of the virtual world and attack the host system or at least glean information from it.

Two competing factors nullify using virtualized environments as a means of archiving simple security through diversity. It will continue to be possible to detect hosting in a virtual environment, and it is possible to find the means to exploit virtual environments, even if the difficulty increases. However, this just means that you can't rely on the hypervisor alone. Vulnerabilities are at the heart of all software, and the evolutionary state of attacking the virtualized environments and the hypervisor will continue to progress.

The decline of virtualized environments as a security tool was natural as so many in the security field became dependent on hypervisors. In response, the security field will essentially adapt new features and functions to offset vulnerabilities and detect attacks. Examples include improved forensics and hosting virtualized environments in ways to avoid detection.

In nature, colorful insects represent a warning to others of toxicity or poison if eaten. Similarly, some in the security field have taken to setting virtualization flags on real, physical machines simply to foil malicious code. The more hostile malicious code will shut itself down and delete itself when it determines it is in a virtual host, thus preventing some infections.

8. DOMAIN NAME SERVER EXAMPLE OF DIVERSITY THROUGH SECURITY

It is fair to say that the Internet requires a means to resolve IP addresses to names and names back to IP addresses. The resolving capabilities are solved by the Domain Name

5. M. Dowd, A. Sotirov, 2008 Black Hat paper, "Bypassing browser memory protections," Black Hat USA 2008 Briefings and Training, Caesars Palace, Las Vegas August 2–7, 2008. https://www.blackhat.com/presentations/bh-usa-08/Sotirov_Dowd/bh08-sotirov-dowd.pdf.

Server (DNS) with a well-defined explanation on how any DNS is supposed to function being published and publicly available. In most cases you may choose to use a provider's implementation of DNS as a resolver or deploy your own to manage internal names and perform a lookup from other domains.

If prior to 2008 you had selected the less popular DJBDNS[6] over the more popular BIND, you would have been inoculated (for the most part[7]) against the DNS cache-poisoning attack made famous by Dan Kaminski. Depending on your understanding of the attack against what you are trying to protect, theoretically all information transacted over the Internet was at the complete mercy of an attacker. Nothing could be trusted. This is actually not the limit of the capabilities, but it is the most fundamental. The threat to survivability was real and caused many to consider secure DNS alternatives after the attack was made public.

Rapid and automated response is the most common defense technique. Making the decision to act late is still beneficial but risky because the number of attackers capable of performing the attack increases with time. Reaction is both a good procedural defense and offers immunity and lessons learned. As part of the reaction, you could assume that the DNS is not trusted and continue to operate with the idea that some information might not be from the intended sources. You could also make a decision to disconnect from the Internet until the threat is mitigated to a satisfactory level. Neither would seem reasonable, but it is important to know what threat would constitute such a reaction.

9. RECOVERY FROM DISASTER IS SURVIVAL

Disaster recovery is often thought of as being able to recover from partial data loss or complete data loss by restoring data from tape. With the considerably lower cost of dense media, it is now possible to continuously stream a copy of the data and recover at any point in time rather than the scheduled time associated with evening backup events. In many cases the backup procedure is tested frequently, whereas the recovery procedure is not.

Unfortunately, many assume that simply having backups means that recovery is inevitable or a foregone conclusion. For others, the risk associated with recovery has led to many organizations never testing the backups for fear of disruption or failure. Perhaps in the interest of diversity from the norm it is beneficial to frequently and procedurally test restore operations. Though security

diversity is a survival technique, recovery is the paramount survival tool in everyone's arsenal.

When does diversity work against you? It might not be possible to quantify the advantage of selecting diversity over ubiquity other than the cost in procurement, training, and interoperability. It is quite possible that an investment in "bucking the system" and using uncommon systems and services won't just cause issues, it would drive your competitive advantage into oblivion. This is the single biggest reason to avoid security through diversity, and it will be pointed out repeatedly. Security through diversity starts early and is embraced as a matter of survival. Military and financial institutions abide by the diversity principals in investments and decision-making. Though a threat is not always understood, the institutionalizing lessons learned tend to live on, forcing change and adaptation that require diversity as a fundamental principal of survival.

10. SUMMARY

In the digital domain, geodispersal or resources and disaster recovery concepts seems the ideal area in which to institute a separate and diverse architecture from that of a production environment. Segregation of resources and environments offers a tangible boundary that may increase resilience to threats. Software updates, early threat detection, and suppression is but only part of a solution. As Dan Geer indicated in his essay on the evolution of security,[8] we already have an evolutionary approach to systems by centralizing enterprises into safe, climate-controlled environments. We protect systems with IDS all while making copies of critical data and systems, just in case. Making changes to systems as we acquire them is rarely undertaken to the level necessary to ensure survival; most systems have very few changes from the "out-of-box" state or factory default because we fear that the changes will make the system unstable or ineffective.

"Diversity ad absurdum" is cost prohibitive and not ill advised. Making a leap to complete diversity will inevitably fail for businesses and institutions. Competition in products and solutions is naturally coupled to diversity in much the same way as DNA differs in iterations of generations. At some point, security through diversity is an action to be considered through threat modeling, where it can be applied on as many fronts as possible and at the lowest levels as feasible. At the higher levels, consideration for a process to apply hygiene to processes, code snippets, and each protocol adds cost but acts to protect. A changed state might be more desirable than the original state as an assurance against "native attack code." Forced change adds complexity and resilience at a cost yet might be required where untrusted computing takes place.

6. D.J. Bernstein, author and developer of DJBDNS.
7. Though DNS queries might be verified where DJBDNS was deployed, the upstream DNS server could still be vulnerable, making it important to know from where you get your DNS names.

8. D. Geer, "The evolution of security," *ACM Queue*, April 2007.

In selecting diversity and all the investment and issues that go along with it, an instant beneficial byproduct is a rich set of choices in many areas, not just security. Decision makers have options not available to monoculture networks and systems. For example, if you have deployed in production at least two different manufacturers, routers, or firewalls, you will have people trained specifically for each or both. Instead of a competitive nature of driving out competition, you have the ability to match the appropriate models to various parts of a given network and not depend on the product catalog of a single vendor. In the immediate situation of threats to an entire product line, a diverse decision process such as exchanging routers is available. Someone with a single affected vendor has a limited choice bracket of solutions. Additionally, anyone trained or certified in more than one company's equipment portfolio can more easily adapt to any additional needs increasing choices and options.

Of all the security diversity solutions available, perhaps having a skilled and adaptable workforce trained in all the fundamental aspects of computer security offers the best solution. The simplistic statement of "the best defense is a good offense," in this case, means that security professionals should be able to defend from attacks, understand attacks, and be prepared to perform the forensic analysis and reverse-engineering needed to understand attacks. Adaptation and resiliency are key traits to diversity.

Security through diversity starts early and is embraced as a matter of survival. Military and financial institutions abide by the diversity principals in investments and decision-making. Though a threat is not always understood, the lessons learned during an attack tend to live on, forcing change and adaptation that require diversity as a fundamental principal of survival of a diverse skill-set during a given threat to survival makes all the difference in the world.

Finally, let's move on to the real interactive part of this Chapter: review questions/exercises, hands-on projects, case projects, and optional team case project. The answers and/or solutions by chapter can be found in the Online Instructor's Solutions Manual.

CHAPTER REVIEW QUESTIONS/ EXERCISES

True/False

1. True or False? Ubiquity and compatibility are driving forces of the computer revolution driving down cost while the application of "security through diversity" is not emerging as a strategic decision.
2. True or False? By volume, Internet-related attacks that seek targets of opportunity for financial gain and financial loss cannot be insured to a point.

3. True or False? Specific DDoS attacks require enough magnitude and duration to achieve goals set by the attacker(s).
4. True or False? The most common diversity strategy is in use today by most large-scale businesses that choose to store data far enough away from the original site as to be affected by natural disasters and phenomena such as power outages.
5. True or False? Most modern attacks take advantage of the fact that the majority of personal computers on the Internet are quite nearly in the same state.

Multiple Choice

1. What systems are good, cheap, replaceable, and reliable—until mass failure occurs?
   A. Ubiquitous
   B. Vulnerabilities
   C. Log
   D. Encrypted
   E. DHS
2. Who uses obfuscation, encryption, and compression to install malicious code such as viruses, worms, and Trojans?
   A. Attackers
   B. Risk assessment
   C. Scale
   D. Access
   E. Active monitoring
3. A number of self-replicating viruses propagating to new hosts autonomously are known as:
   A. Organizations
   B. Fabric
   C. Worms
   D. Logs
   E. Security
4. Other factors for a successful defense against a worm include a deployment of host-based firewalls that block:
   A. Organizations
   B. Denial of service attack
   C. WPA2-Personal
   D. Port traffic
   E. Taps
5. If a security service provider took time to inspect every anomaly to the point where overall traffic performance were degraded, it would be advantageous for an attacker to exploit the heavy inspection process to create a performance issue up to the point of:
   A. Systems security plan
   B. Consumer privacy protection
   C. Denying service
   D. Decision making
   E. Challenge-Handshake Authentication Protocol (CHAP)

EXERCISE

Problem

The most common diversity strategy is in use today by most large-scale businesses that choose to store data far enough away from the original site as to be unaffected by natural disasters and phenomena such as power outages. But is this enough?

Hands-on Projects

Project

Ubiquitous systems are good, cheap, replaceable, and reliable—until mass failure occurs. It certainly pays to know that ubiquity and uniformity are the absolute right choices in the absence of threats. That is not the world we occupy, even if not acknowledged. What would it take to survive an attack that had the potential to effectively disrupt a business or even destroy it?

Case Projects

Problem

Conceptually, could the browser be the weapon of choice that collapses an entire enterprise?

Optional Team Case Project

Problem

When does diversity work against you?

Chapter 86

e-Reputation and Online Reputation Management Survey

Jean-Marc Seigneur

University of Geneva, Carouge, Switzerland

1. INTRODUCTION

Over the past 3 decades, the computing environment has changed from centralized stationary computers to distributed and mobile computing. This evolution has profound implications for the security models, policies, and mechanisms needed to protect users' information and resources in an increasingly globally interconnected open computing infrastructure. In centralized stationary computer systems, security is typically based on the authenticated identity of other parties. Strong authentication mechanisms such as public key infrastructures (PKIs) [1,2], have allowed this model to be extended to distributed systems within a single administrative domain or a few closely collaborating domains. However, small mobile devices are increasingly being equipped with wireless network capabilities that allow ubiquitous access to corporate resources and allow users with similar devices to collaborate while on the move. Traditional identity-based security mechanism cannot authorize an operation without authenticating the claiming entity. This means that no interaction can take place unless both parties are known to each other's authentication framework. Spontaneous interactions would therefore require a single or a few trusted Certificate Authorities (CAs) to emerge, which, based on the inability of a PKI to emerge over the past decade, seems highly unlikely in the foreseeable future. In the current environment, a user who wishes to partake in spontaneous collaboration with another party has the choice of enabling security and thereby disabling spontaneous collaboration or disabling security and thereby enabling spontaneous collaboration.

The state of the art is clearly unsatisfactory; instead, mobile users and devices need the ability to authenticate and authorize other parties that they encounter on their way autonomously, without relying on a common authentication infrastructure. The user's mobility implies that resources left in the home environment must be accessed via interconnected third parties. When the user moves to a foreign place for the first time, it is highly probable that the third parties of this place are a priori strangers. However, to interact with these strangers is necessary, for example, to access the remote home environment. It is a reality that users can move to potentially harmful places. For example, because of a lack of information or as a result of uncertainty, there is a probability that previously unknown computing third parties used to provide mobile computing in foreign places are malicious. The assumption of a known and closed computing environment held for fixed, centralized, and distributed computers until the advent of the Internet and, more recently, mobile computing. Legacy security models and mechanisms rely on the assumption of closed computing environments, in which it is possible to identify and fortify a security perimeter, which protects against potentially malicious entities. However, in these models, there is no room for anytime–anywhere mobility. Moreover, it is supposed that inside the security perimeter there is a common security infrastructure, a common security policy, or a common jurisdiction in which the notion of identity is globally meaningful. It does not work in the absence of this assumption.

A fundamental requirement for Internet and mobile computing environments is to allow for potential interaction and collaboration with unknown entities. Because of the potentially large number of previously unknown entities and for simple economic reasons, it makes no sense to assume the presence of a human administrator who

Computer and Information Security Handbook. http://dx.doi.org/10.1016/B978-0-12-803843-7.00086-7

configures and maintains the security framework for all users in the Internet: for example, in an online auction situation, or even in proximity, for example, when a user moves in a city from home to a workplace. This means that either the individuals or their computing devices must decide about each of these potential interactions themselves. It applies to security decisions as well: for example, concerning the enrollment of a large number of unknown entities. There is an inherent element of risk whenever a computing entity ventures into collaboration with a previously unknown party. One way to manage that risk is to develop models, policies, and mechanisms that allow the local entity to assess the risk of the proposed collaboration and explicitly reason about the trustworthiness of the other party to determine whether the other party is trustworthy enough to mitigate the risk of collaboration. Formation of trust may be based on previous experience, recommendations from reachable peers, or the perceived reputation of the other party. Reputation, for example, could be obtained through a reputation system such as the one used on eBay [3]. This chapter focuses on this new approach to computer security: namely, reputation management. Almost all communication and marketing agencies have online reputation monitoring and analysis as part of the services they propose to their customers. Although these services are the most well known, this chapter covers all types of services that compose a complete reputation management solution stack.

The next section of this chapter discusses a general understanding of the human notion of reputation. Section 3 explains how this concept of reputation fits into computer security. The fourth section presents the state of the art of attack-resistant reputation computation. Section 5 gives an overview of the current market of online reputation and e-reputation services. We conclude by underlining the need to standardize online reputation for increased adoption and robustness.

2. THE HUMAN NOTION OF REPUTATION

Reputation is an old human notion: Romans named it *reputatio*: *reputatio est vulgaris opinio ubi non est veritas* [4]. Reputation may be considered a social control mechanism [5] in which it is better to tell the truth than to have the reputation of being a liar. That social control mechanism may have been challenged in the past by the fact that people could change their region to clear their reputation. However, as we move toward an information society, changing region should have increasingly less impact in this regard because reputation information is no longer bound to a specific location, which is also good news for reputable people who have to move to other regions for other reasons, such as job relocation. For example,

someone might want to know the reputation of a person whom she or he does not know, especially when this person is considered to be chosen to carry out a risky task among a set of potential new collaborators. Another case may be that the reputation of a person is simply gossiped about. The information about reputation may be based on real, biased, or faked facts: for example, faked by a malicious recommender who wants to harm the target person or biased by a recommender who is a close friend of the person to be recommended. The above Latin quotation translates as "Reputation is a vulgar opinion where there is no truth" [4]. The target of the reputation may also be an organization, a product, a brand, a location, etc. The source of the information about reputation may not be clear; for example, it may come from gossip or rumors whose source is not known, or it may come from a known group of people. When the source is known, the term "recommendation" can be used. Reputation is different from a recommendation that is made by a specific known entity. Fig. 86.1 gives an overview of the reputation primitives.

As La Rochefoucauld wrote[1] a long time ago, recommending is also a trusting behavior. It has not only an impact on the recommender's overall trustworthiness (meaning it goes beyond recommending trustworthiness) but also on the overall level of trust in the network of the involved parties. La Rochefoucauld highlighted that when one recommends another, they should be aware that the outcome of their recommendation will reflect upon their trustworthiness and reputation since they are partly responsible for this outcome. Benjamin Franklin noted about recommendations that each time he made a recommendation, his recommending trustworthiness was impacted: "in consequence of my crediting such recommendations, my own are out of credit" [6]. However, his letter underlines that still he had to make recommendations about not very well-known parties because they made the request and not making recommendations could have upset them. This is in line with Covey's "Emotional Bank Account" [7,8], where any interaction modifies the amount of trust between the interacting parties and can be seen as favor or disfavor—deposit or withdrawal. As Romano underlined in her thesis, there are many definitions of trust in a wide range of domains [9], for example, psychology, economics, or sociology. In this chapter, we use Romano's definition of trust, which is supposed to

---

1. Original quotation in French: "La confiance ne nous laisse pas tant de liberté, ses règles sont plus étroites, elle demande plus de prudence et de retenue, et nous ne sommes pas toujours libres d'en disposer: il ne s'agit pas de nous uniquement, et nos intérêts sont mêlés d'ordinaire avec les intérêts des autres. Elle a besoin d'une grande justesse pour ne livrer pas nos amis en nous livrant nous-mêmes, et pour ne faire pas des présents de leur bien dans la vue d'augmenter le prix de ce que nous donnons."

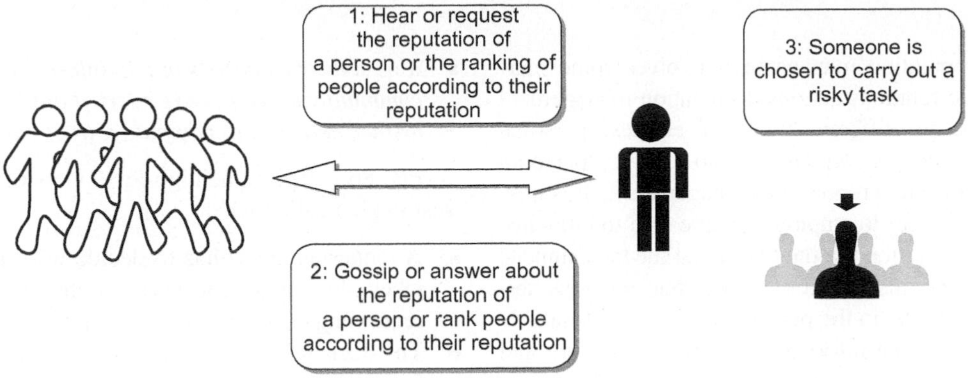

FIGURE 86.1 High-level reputation primitives.

integrate many aspects of previous work on trust research:

> *Trust is a subjective assessment of another's influence in terms of the extent of one's perceptions about the quality and significance of another's impact over one's outcomes in a given situation, such that one's expectation of, openness to, and inclination toward such influence provide a sense of control over the potential outcomes of the situation [9].*

In social research, there are three main types of trust: interpersonal trust, based on the outcomes of past interactions with the trustee; dispositional trust, provided by the trustor's general disposition toward trust, independent of the trustee; and system trust, provided by external means such as insurance or laws [10]. Depending on the situation, a high level of trust in one of these types can become sufficient for the trustor to make the decision to trust. When there is insurance against a negative outcome, or when the legal system acts as a credible deterrent against undesirable behavior, it means that the level of system trust is high and the level of risk is negligible—therefore the levels of interpersonal and dispositional trust are less important. It is usually assumed that by knowing the link to the real-world identity, there is insurance against harm that may be done by this entity: in essence, this is security based on authenticated identity and legal recourse. In this case, the level of system trust seems to be high, but one may argue that in practice, the legal system does not provide a credible deterrent against undesirable behavior (it makes no sense to sue someone for a single spam email, as the effort expended to gain redress outweighs the benefit).

The information on the outcomes of the past interactions with the trustee that are used for trust can come from different sources. First, the information on the outcomes may be based on direct observations: when the trustor has directly interacted with the requesting trustee and personally experienced the observation. Another type of observation is when a third-party observes itself an interaction between two parties and infers itself the type of outcome. Another source of information may be specific recommenders who report to the trustor the outcomes of interactions that have not been

directly observed by the trustor but by themselves or other recommenders. In this case, care must be taken not to count twice or many more times the same outcomes reported by different recommenders. Finally, reputation is another source of trust information but more difficult to analyze because generally it is not exactly known who the recommenders are and the chance to count many times the same outcomes of interactions is higher. As said in the introduction, reputation may be biased by faked evidence or other controversial influencing means. Reputation evidence is the riskiest type of evidence to process. When the evidence recommender is known, it is possible to take into account the recommender trustworthiness. Since some recommenders are more or less likely to produce good recommendations, even malicious ones, the notion of recommending trustworthiness mitigates the risk of bad or malicious recommendations. Intuitively, recommendations must only be accepted from senders that the local entity trusts to make judgments close to those that it would have made about others. We call the trust in a given situation, the trust context. For example, recommending trustworthiness happens in the context of trusting the recommendation of a recommender. Intuitively, recommendations must only be accepted from senders that the local entity trusts to make judgments close to those that it would have made about others. In the remainder of this chapter, we define reputation as follows:

> *Reputation is the subjective aggregated value, as perceived by the requester, of the assessments by other people, who are not exactly identified, of some quality, character, characteristic or ability of a specific entity with whom the requester has never interacted with previously.*

To be able to perceive the reputation of an entity is only one aspect of reputation management. The other aspects of reputation management for an entity consist of:

- Monitoring the entity reputation as broadly as possible in a proactive way;
- Analyzing the sources spreading the entity reputation;
- Influencing the number and content of these sources to spread an improved reputation.

Therefore, reputation management involves some marketing and public relations actions. Reputation management may be applied to different types of entities: personal reputation management, which is also called "personal branding" [11], business reputation management... It is now common for businesses to employ full time staff to influence the company's reputation via the traditional media channels. Politicians and stars also make use of public relations services. For mass people, in the past few media were available to easily retrieve people information, however as more and more people use the Web and leave digital traces, it now becomes possible to find information about any Web user via Google. For example, in a recent survey of 100 executive recruiters [12], 77% of these executive recruiters declared to use search engines to learn more about candidates.

3. REPUTATION APPLIED TO THE COMPUTING WORLD

Trust engines, based on computational models of the human notion of trust, have been proposed to make security decisions on behalf of their owner. For example, the EU-funded SECURE project [13] has built a generic and reusable trust engine that each computing entity would run. These trust engines allow the entities to compute levels of trust based on sources of trust evidence, that is, knowledge about the interacting entities: local observations of interaction outcomes or recommendations. Based on the computed trust value and given a trust policy, the trust engine can decide to grant or deny access to a requesting entity. Then, if access is given to an entity, the actions of the granted entity are monitored and the outcomes, positive or negative, are used to refine the trust value. The computed trust value represents the interpersonal trust part and is generally defined as follows:

- *A trust value is a non-enforceable estimate of the entity's future behavior in a given context based on past evidence.*

- *A trust metric consists of the different computations and communications that are carried out by the trustor (and his/her network) to compute a trust value in the trustee.*

Fig. 86.2 depicts the high-level view of a computational trust engine called when:

- A requested entity has to decide what action should be taken due to a request made by another entity, the requesting entity;
- The decision has been decided by the requested entity;
- Evidence about the actions and the outcomes is reported;
- The trustor has to select a trustee among several potential trustees.

A number of sub-components are used for the preceding cases:

- A component that is able to recognize the context, especially to recognize the involved entities. Depending on the confidence level in recognition of the involved entities, for example, the face has only been recognized with 82% of confidence, this may impact the overall trust decision. Context information may also consist of the time, the location and the activity of the user [14];
- Another component that can dynamically compute the trust value, that is, the trustworthiness of the requesting entity based on pieces of evidence (for example, direct observations, recommendations or reputation);
- A risk module that can dynamically evaluate the risk involved in the interaction based on the recognized context; risk evidence is also needed.

The chosen decision should maintain the appropriate cost–benefit ratio. In the background, another component is in charge of gathering and tracking evidence: recommendations, comparisons between expected outcomes of the chosen actions and real outcomes, and so on. This evidence is used to update risk and trust information. Thus, trust and risk follow a managed life cycle.

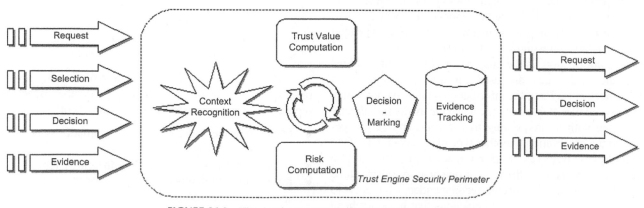

FIGURE 86.2 High-level components of a computational trust engine.

Depending on dispositional trust and system trust, the weight of the trust value in the final decision may be small. The level of dispositional trust may be set according to two main facts. First, the user manually sets a general level of trust, which is used in the application to obtain the level of trust in entities independently of the entities. Second, the current balance of gains and losses is positive and the risk policy allows new interactions as long as the balance is kept positive. Marsh uses the term "basic trust" [15] for dispositional trust; it may also be called self-trust.

Generally, as introduced by Rahman and Hailes [16], there are two main contexts for the trust values: "direct," which is about the properties of the trustee, and "recommend," which is the equivalent of recommending trustworthiness. In their case, recommending trustworthiness is based on consistency of the "semantic distance" between the real outcomes and the recommendations that have been made. The default metric for consistency is the standard deviation based on the frequency of specific semantic distance values: the higher the consistency, the smaller the standard deviation and the higher the trust value in recommending trustworthiness. A computational trust engine including an advanced risk computation module is the MUSES open source risk and trust analysis engine (RT2AE) [40]. The RT2AE is based on a novel approach to risk, called Opportunity-Enabled Risk Management (OPPRIM), in which not only threats are taken into account but also opportunities. An example of an opportunity may be that a consultant requests to access remote corporate data even if from an airport public Wi-Fi that is less secure than a corporate Wi-Fi. The consultant has to access those data to be able to finish a bid with a deadline for an important contract before the plane arrives. If the consultant cannot access the corporate data while waiting for the plane, the contract will be lost because the deadline will have passed. Then, despite some risk of using a public Wi-Fi, there is more gain for the consultant to access the corporate data. In this case the gain of winning the important bid is more valuable than the corporate data that may be compromised if the Wi-Fi is untrustworthy. Therefore access to the necessary corporate data should be granted even if it is outside the company buildings. An OPPRIM simulator able to test different trust and risk metrics is available on Github as open source software.[2]

As said in the previous section, another source for trust in human networks consists of real-world recourse mechanisms such as insurance or legal actions. Traditionally, it is assumed that if the actions made by a computing entity are bound to a real-world identity, the owner of the faulty computing entity can be brought to court, and reparations are possible. In an open environment with no unique authority,

the feasibility of this approach is questionable. An example in which prosecution is ineffective occurs when email spammers do not mind moving operations abroad where antispam laws are less developed, to escape the risk of prosecution. There are multiple different jurisdictions worldwide. Therefore, security based on the authenticated identity may be superfluous. Furthermore, in the first place, there is the question of which authority is in charge of certifying binding with the real-world identity, because there are no unique global authorities. "Who, after all, can authenticate US citizens abroad? The [United Nations]? Or thousands of pair wise national cross-certifications?" [17].

More important, is authentication of the real-world identity necessary to be able to use the human notion of trust? Indeed, a critical element for the use of trust is to retrieve trust evidence on the interacting entities, but trust evidence does not necessarily consist of information about the real-world identity of the owner: trust evidence may simply be the count of positive interactions with a pseudonym, as defended in Seigneur [13]. As long as the interacting computing entities can be recognized, direct observations and recommendations can be exchanged to build trust, interaction after interaction. This level of trust can be used for trusting decisions. Thus, trust engines can provide dynamic protection without the assumption that real-world recourse mechanisms such as legal recourse are available in case of harm.

The terms "trust/trusted/trustworthy," which appear in the traditional computer science literature, are not grounded on social science and often correspond to an implicit element of trust. For example, we have mentioned the use of trusted third parties, called CAs, which are common in PKI infrastructures. Another example is Trusted Computing [18], whose goal is to create enhanced hardware by using cost-effective security hardware (more or less comparable to a smart card chip) that acts as the "root of trust." *They are trusted* means that they are assumed to make use of some (strong) security protection mechanisms. Therefore, they can/must implicitly be blindly trusted and cannot fail. This cannot address security when it is not known who or whether to trust blindly. The term "trust management" was introduced in computer security by Blaze et al. [19], but others argued that their model relies on an implicit notion of trust because it only describes "a way of exploiting established trust relationships for distributed security policy management without determining how these relationships are formed" [20]. There is a need for trust formation mechanisms from scratch between two strangers. Trust engines build trust explicitly based on evidence that is personal, reported by known recommenders, or through reputation mechanisms.

As discussed in the previous section, reputation is different from a recommendation that is made by a known specific entity. However, in the digital world, it is still less easy to certify the identity of the recommender exactly, and

---

2. https://github.com/jmseigneur/opprim-sim.

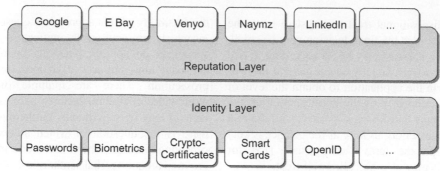

FIGURE 86.3 Identity management and reputation management layers.

in many cases the recommender can be recognized only to some extent. The entity recognition occurs with the help of the context recognition module and the level of confidence in recognition may be taken into account in the final trust computation: for example, as is done in advanced computational trust engines [13]. For simplicity's sake, in the remainder of this chapter, because the chapter focuses on reputation rather than trust, we assume that each entity can be recognized with a perfect confidence level in recognition. Thus, we obtain the following two layers depicted in Fig. 86.3: the identity management layer and the reputation management layer. In these layers, although we mention the world identity, we do not mean that the real-world identity behind each entity is supposed to be certified; we assume that it is sufficient to recognize the entity at a perfect level of confidence in recognition. For example, if a recommendation is received from an eBay account, it is sure that it comes from this account and that it is not spoofed. There are different rounded rectangles at the top of the reputation layer that represent a few of the different reputation services detailed in Section 5. There are also a number of rounded rectangles below the identity layer that represent the different types of authentication schemes that can be used to recognize an entity. Although password-based or OpenID[3]-based [21] authentication may be less secure than multimodal authentication combining biometrics, smart cards and crypto-certificates [13], because we assume that the level of confidence in recognition is perfect, as mentioned, the different identity management technologies are abstracted to a unique identity management layer for the remainder of the chapter.

As presented in the previous section, reputation management goes beyond mere reputation assessment and encompasses the monitoring, analysis, and influence of reputation sources. It is why we introduce the following categories, depicted in Fig. 86.4, for online reputation services:

- Reputation calculation: Based on evidence gathered by the service, the service either computes a value

representing the reputation of a specific entity or simply presents the reputation information without ranking.
- Reputation monitoring, analysis and warnings: The service monitors Web-based media (websites, blogs, social networks, digitalized archives of paper-based press and trademarks, etc.) to detect information affecting the entity reputation and warns the user in case of important changes.
- Reputation influencing, promotion and rewards: The service takes actions to influence the perceived reputation of the entity. The service actively promotes the entity reputation, for example, by publishing Web pages carefully designed to reach a high rank in major search engines or paid online advertisements, such as, Google AdWords. Users reaching a higher reputation may gain rewards other than promotion, such as discounts. Based on the monitoring services analysis, the service may be able to list the most important reputation sources and allow users to influence these sources. For example, in a 2006 blog bribe case, it was reported that free laptops preloaded with a new commercial operating system were shipped for free to the most important bloggers in the field of consumer-oriented software to improve the reputation of the new operating software; the bloggers did not mention that they had received the gifts.

FIGURE 86.4 Online reputation management services categories.

---

3. Please refer to Chapter 71 on Online Identity and User Management to learn more about OpenID.

- Interaction facilitation and follow-up: The service provides an environment to facilitate the interaction and its outcome between the trustor and the trustee. For example, eBay provides the online auction system to sellers and buyers, and monitors the follow-up of the commercial transaction between the buyer and the seller.
- Reputation certification and assurance: That type of service is closer to the notion of system trust than the human notion of reputation because it relies on external means to avoid ending up in a harmful situation. For example, insurance is paid as part of a commercial transaction. These services might need the certification of the link between the entity and its real-world identity in case of prosecution. Our assumption does not hold for services that require that kind of link, but that category of services had to be covered because a few services surveyed subsequently use them.
- Fraud protection, mediation, cleaning, and recovery: These promotion services aim to improve the ranking of reputation information provided by the user rather than external information provided by third parties. However, even if external information is hidden behind more controlled information, it can still be found. It is why some services try to force the owners of external sites hosting the damaging reputation information to delete the damaging information. Depending on where the server is located, it is more or less difficult to achieve. It may be as simple as filling in an online form on the site hosting the defaming information to contact the technical support employee who will check whether the information is really problematic. In the case of a reluctant administrator, lawyers or mediators specialized in online defamation laws have to be commissioned, and it is more or less easy depending on the legislation in the country hosting the server. Generally, in countries with clear defamation laws, administrators prefer to delete the information rather than go into a lengthy and costly legal process. Depending on the mediation and the degree of defamation, the host may have to add an apology in place of the defaming information, pay a fine, or more. Fraud protection is also needed against reputation calculation attacks. Different types of attacks can be carried out for flaw reputation calculation results [13]. Section 4 presents the state of the art of attack-resistant reputation computation.

4. STATE OF THE ART OF ATTACK-RESISTANT REPUTATION COMPUTATION

In most commercial reputation services surveyed in Section 5, the reputation calculation does not take into account the attack resistance of their algorithm. It is a pity because many different types of attacks can be carried out, especially at the identity level. In addition, most of these reputation algorithms correspond to a trust metric algorithm rather than reputation as we have defined it in Section 2, because they aggregate ratings submitted by recommenders or the rater itself rather than rely on evidence whose recommenders are unknown. Based on ratings that we can consider to be either direct observations or recommendations, the services compute a reputation score that we can consider to be a trust value, generally represented on a scale from 0% to 100%, or from zero to five stars. The exact reputation computation algorithm is not publicly disclosed by all services providers, and it is difficult to estimate the attack resistance of each of these algorithms without their full specification. However, it is clear that many of these algorithms do not provide a high level of attack resistance for the following reasons:

- Besides eBay, in which each transaction corresponds to a clear trust context with well-authenticated users and a real transaction that is confirmed by real money transfers, most services occur in a decentralized environment and allow for the rating of unconfirmed transactions (with no real evidence that the transaction really happened, and even worse by anonymous users).
- Still, eBay experiences difficulties with its reputation calculation algorithm. In fact, eBay has changed its reputation calculation algorithm: Sellers on eBay are no longer allowed to leave unfavorable or neutral messages about buyers, to diminish the risk that buyers fear to leave negative feedback owing to retaliatory negative feedback from the sellers. Finally, accounts on eBay, which are protected by passwords, may be usurped. According to Twigg and Dimmock [22], a trust metric is γ-resistant if more than γ nodes must be compromised for the attacker to drive the trust value successfully. For example, Rahman and Hailes' [16] trust metric is not γ-resistant for $\gamma > 1$ (a successful attack needs only one victim).

In contrast to the centralized environment of eBay, in decentralized settings there are a number of specific attacks. First, real-world identities may form an alliance and use their recommendation to undermine the reputation of entities. On the one hand, this may be seen as collusion. On the other hand, one may argue that real-world identities are free to vote as they wish. However, the impact is greater online. Even if more and more transactions and interactions are traced online, most transactions and interactions that happen in the real world are not reported online. Owing to the limited number of traced transactions and interactions, a few faked transactions and interactions can have a high impact on the computed reputation, and it is not fair.

Second, we focus next on attacks based on vulnerabilities in the identity approach and the subsequent use of these vulnerabilities (see checklist: "An Agenda for Action for Implementing a Network Vulnerability Assessment"). The vulnerabilities may have different origins: for example, technical weaknesses in the authentication mechanism. These attacks commonly rely on the possibility of identity multiplicity, meaning that a real-world identity uses many digital pseudonyms. A well-known identity multiplicity attack in the field of computational trust is Douceur's Sybil attack [23]. Douceur argues that in large-scale networks in which a centralized identity authority cannot be used to control the creation of pseudonyms, a powerful real-world entity may create as many digital pseudonyms as it wishes and recommend one of these pseudonyms to fool the reputation calculation algorithm. This is especially important in scenarios where the possibility of using many pseudonyms is facilitated: for example, in scenarios where pseudonym creation is provided for better privacy protection.

An Agenda for Action for Implementing a Network Vulnerability Assessment

Key areas examined in this checklist include (check all tasks completed):

_____ 1. Unique user ID and confidential password required

_____ 2. Additional identification required for remote access

_____ 3. Help screen access available only to logged-on users

_____ 4. Last session date and time message back to user at sign-on time

_____ 5. Exception reports for disruptions in either input or output

_____ 6. Session numbers for users/processors that are not constantly logged in

_____ 7. Notification to users of possible duplicate messages

_____ 8. Threshold of errors and consequential retransmission on the network related to management via automatic alarms

_____ 9. Encryption requirements

_____ 10. Encryption key management controls

_____ 11. Message authentication code requirements for unencrypted sensitive data transmission

_____ 12. System authentication at session start-up (wiretap controls)

_____ 13. Confirmation of host log-off to prevent line grabbing

_____ 14. Downloading controls for connected intelligent workstations

_____ 15. User priority designation process

_____ 16. Transaction handling for classified communications

_____ 17. Trace and snapshot facilities requirements

_____ 18. Log requirements for sensitive messages

_____ 19. Alternate path requirements between nodes

_____ 20. Contingency plans for hardware as well as all usual system requirements

_____ 21. Storage of critical messages in redundant locations

_____ 22. Packet recovery requirements

_____ 23. Physical access for workstations when units are not in use

_____ 24. Control units, hubs, routers, and cabinets secured

_____ 25. Environmental control critical requirements

_____ 26. Segregation for sections of the network that are deemed "untrustworthy"

_____ 27. Gateway identification for authorized nodes

_____ 28. Automatic disable of a user/account, line, or port if evidence an attack is under way

_____ 29. Naming convention to distinguish test messages from production

_____ 30. User switching application controls

_____ 31. Timeout reauthorization requirements

_____ 32. Password change (time/length/history) requirements

_____ 33. Encryption requirements for passwords, security parameters, encryption keys, tables, etc.

_____ 34. Shielding requirements for fiber-optic lines

_____ 35. Controls to prevent wiretapping

_____ 36. Reporting procedures for all interrupted telecommunication sessions

_____ 37. Identification requirements for station/terminal access connection to network

_____ 38. Printer control requirements for classified information

_____ 39. Appropriate "welcome" connection screens

_____ 40. Dial-up access control procedures

_____ 41. Antidaemon dialer controls

_____ 42. Standards for equipment, applications, protocols, and operating environment

_____ 43. Help desk procedures and telephone numbers

_____ 44. Protocol converters and access method converters dynamic change control requirements

_____ 45. Local area network (LAN) administrator responsibilities

_____ 46. Control requirements to add nodes to the network

_____ 47. Telephone number change requirements

_____ 48. Automatic sign-on controls

_____ 49. Telephone trace requirements

_____ 50. FTP access controlled

_____ 51. Are patches tested and applied?

_____ 52. Software distribution current

_____ 53. Employee policy awareness

_____ 54. Emergency incident response plan/procedure

_____ 55. Internal applications control

_____ 56. Proper control of the development environment

_____ 57. Software licensing compliance review

_____ 58. Portable device (laptop/notebook/personal digital assistant) handling procedures

_____ 59. Storage and disposal of sensitive data/information

_____ 60. Default password controls and settings

An Agenda for Action for Implementing a Network Vulnerability Assessment—cont'd

_____**61.** Review of off-site storage for disaster recovery resources	_____**80.** Monitoring website from attack (internal and external)
_____**62.** Unnecessary services disabled	_____**81.** Domain Name Server monitoring
_____**63.** Client server data transfer analyzed and secured	_____**82.** Hardware maintenance requirements
_____**64.** Restrict telnet and r-commands (rlogin, remote shell, etc.)	_____**83.** Hard drive repair, maintenance, and disposal procedures
_____**65.** Configuration management procedures	_____**84.** Basic input—output system boot order
_____**66.** Tracking port scans	_____**85.** Email content policy and monitoring
_____**67.** Review monitoring responsibilities	_____**86.** Email forwarding policy (hopping)
_____**68.** Separation between test and production environment	_____**87.** Spamming controls and testing procedures
_____**69.** Strong dial-in authentication	_____**88.** Employee termination and credential disablement
_____**70.** System administrator training	_____**89.** After-hours sign-in logs
_____**71.** Voice system protection procedures	_____**90.** Network sniffer policy, procedures, and monitoring
_____**72.** Tunneling for all remote access (inbound or outbound)	_____**91.** Validity of email accounts
_____**73.** Encryption of laptops	_____**92.** Background checks before hiring
_____**74.** Management awareness	_____**93.** Administrator accounts and password controls
_____**75.** Program and system change control procedures	_____**94.** Time synchronization procedures
_____**76.** Open "inbound" modem access for vendor support	_____**95.** Establishment of a security committee
_____**77.** Modem use policy	_____**96.** Testing process for LAN applications
_____**78.** Incident event coordination (procedures)	_____**97.** Business unit security person designated
_____**79.** Intrusion detection system implementation and monitoring	_____**98.** Log and review of all administrator changes
	_____**99.** Review and resolution of past audit comments
	_____**100.** Audit logs secured

In his doctoral thesis, Levien [24] says that a trust metric is attack resistant if the number of faked pseudonyms owned by the same real-world identity and that can be introduced is bounded. Levien argues that to mitigate the problem of Sybil-like attacks it is required to compute, "a trust value for all the nodes in the graph at once, rather than calculating independently the trust value independently for each node." Another approach proposed to protect against the Sybil attack is the use of mandatory "entry fees" [25] associated with the creation of each pseudonym. This approach raises some issues about its feasibility in a fully decentralized way and the choice of the minimal fee that guarantees protection. Also, "more generally, the optimal fee will often exclude some players yet still be insufficient to deter the wealthiest players from defecting" [25]. An alternative to entry fees may be the use of once in a lifetime (1L) [25] pseudonyms, in which an elected party per "arena" of application is responsible to certify only 1L to any real-world entity, and which possesses a key pair bound to this entity's real-world identity. The technique of a blind signature [26] is used to keep the link between the real-world identity and its chosen pseudonym in the arena unknown to the elected party. However, there are still two unresolved questions about this approach: how the elected party is chosen and how much the users would agree to pay for this approach. More important, a Sybil attack is possible during the voting phase, so the concept of electing a trusted

entity to stop Sybil attacks does not seem practical. However, relying on real money turns the trust mechanism into a type of system trust in which the use of reputation becomes almost superfluous. In the real world, tax authorities are likely to require traceability of money transfers, which would completely break privacy. Thus, when using pseudonyms, another means must be present to prevent users from taking advantage of the fact that they can create as many pseudonyms as they wish.

"Trust transfer" [13] has been introduced to encourage self-recommendations without attacks based on the creation and use of a large number of pseudonyms owned by the same real-world identity. In a system where there are pseudonyms that can potentially belong to the same real-world entity, a transitive trust process is open to abuse. Even if there is a high recommendation discounting factor owing to recommending trustworthiness, the real-world entity can diminish the impact of this discounting factor by sending a huge number of recommendations from his or her army of pseudonyms in a Sybil attack. When someone recommends another person, he or she has influence over the potential outcome of interaction between this person and the trustor. The inclination of the trustor with regard to this influence "provides a goal-oriented sense of control to attain desirable outcomes" [9]. Thus, the trustor should also be able to increase or decrease the influence of the recommenders according to his or her goals. Moreover, according to Romano, trust is not multiple constructs that vary in meaning across contexts but a single construct that varies in level across contexts. The overall trustworthiness depends on the complete set of different domains of trustworthiness. This overall trustworthiness must be put in context: It is not sufficient to limit the domain of trustworthiness strictly to the current trust context and the trustee; if recommenders are involved, the decision and the outcome should affect their overall trustworthiness according to the influence they had. Kinateder et al. [27] also take the position that there is dependence between different trust contexts. For example, a chef known to have both won cooking awards and murdered people may not be a trustworthy chef after all. Trust transfer introduces the possibility of dependence between trustworthiness and recommending trustworthiness. Trust transfer relies on the following assumptions:

- The trust value is based on direct observations or recommendations of the count of event outcomes from recognized entities (for example, the outcome of an eBay auction transaction with a specific seller from a specific buyer recognized by his eBay account pseudonyms);
- A pseudonym can be neither compromised nor spoofed; an attacker can neither take control of a pseudonym nor send spoofed recommendations; however, everyone is free to introduce as many pseudonyms as they wish;
- All messages are assumed to be signed and timestamped.

Trust transfer implies that recommendations cause trust on the trustor (T) side to be transferred from the recommender (R) to the subject (S) of the recommendation. A second effect is that the trust on the recommender side for the subject is reduced by the amount of transferred trustworthiness. If it is a self-recommendation, that is, recommendations from pseudonyms belonging to the same real-world identity, the second effect is moot because it does not make sense for a real-world entity to reduce trust in his or her own pseudonyms. Even if there are different trust contexts (such as trustworthiness in delivering on time or recommending trustworthiness), each trust context has its impact on the single construct trust value: they cannot be taken separately for the calculation of the single construct trust value. A transfer of trust is carried out if the exchange of communications depicted in Fig. 86.5 is successful. A local entity's Recommender Search Policy (RSP) dictates which contacts can be used as potential recommenders. Its

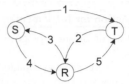

FIGURE 86.5 Trust transfer process.[4] R, recommender; S, subject; T, trustor.

Recommendation Policy (RP) decides which of its contacts it is willing to recommend to other entities, and how much trust it is willing to transfer to an entity.

Trust transfer (in its simplest form) can be decomposed into five steps:

1. The subject requests an action, requiring a total amount of trustworthiness TA in the subject, for the request to be accepted by the trustor; the actual value of TA is contingent upon the risk acceptable to the user, as well as dispositional trust and the context of the request; so the risk module of the trust engine has a role in the calculation of TA;
2. The trustor queries its contacts, which pass the RSP, to find recommenders willing to transfer some of their positive event outcomes count to the subject. Recall that trustworthiness is based on event outcomes count in trust transfer;
3. If the contact has directly interacted with the subject and the contact's RP allows it to permit the trustor to transfer an amount ($A \leq TA$) of the recommender's trustworthiness to the subject, the contact agrees to recommend the subject. It queries the subject whether it agrees to lose A of trustworthiness on the recommender side;
4. The subject returns a signed statement, indicating whether it agrees;
5. The recommender sends back a signed recommendation to the trustor, indicating the trust value it is prepared to transfer to the subject. This message includes the signed agreement of the subject.

Both the RSP and RP can be as simple or complex as the application environment demands. The trust transfer process is illustrated in Fig. 86.6, in which the subject requests an action, which requires 10 positive outcomes. We represent the trust value as a tree of (s,i,c)-triples, corresponding to a mathematical event structure [28]: an event outcome count is represented as an (s,i,c)-triple, where s is the number of events that supports the outcome, i is the number of events that have no information or are inconclusive about the outcome, and c is the number of events that contradict the expected outcome. This format takes into account the element of uncertainty via i.

The RSP of the trustor is to query a contact to propose transferring trust if the *balance* ($s - i - c$) is strictly greater than $2 TA$. This is because it is sensible to require the

---

4. In this type of figure, the circles represent the different entities that are involved: S corresponds to the sender, which is the subject of the recommendation and the requester; T is the trustor, which is also the target; and R is the recommender. The directed black arrows indicate a message sent from one entity to another. The arrows are ordered chronologically by their number.

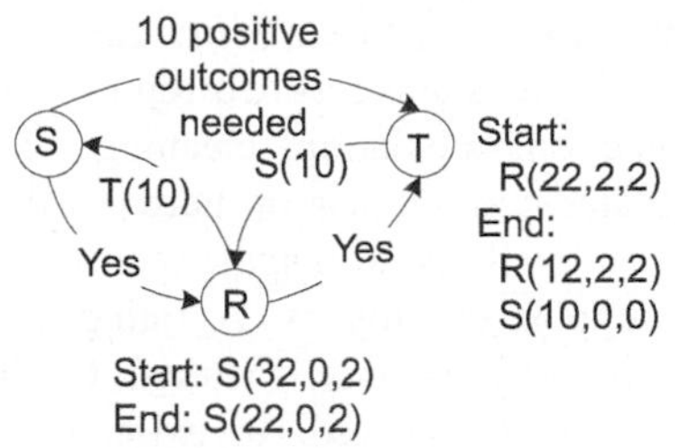

FIGURE 86.6 Trust transfer process example.[5] *R*, recommender; *S*, subject; *T*, trustor.

recommender to remain more trustworthy than the subject after the recommendation. The contact, having a balance passing the *RSP* ($s - i - c = 32 - 0 - 2 = 30$), is asked by the trustor whether he or she wants to recommend 10 good outcomes. The contact's *RP* is to agree to the transfer if the subject has a trust value greater than *TA*. The balance of the subject on the recommender's side is greater than 10 ($s - i - c = 22 - 2 - 2 = 18$). The subject is asked by the recommender whether he or she agrees that 10 good outcomes are to be transferred. Trustor *T* reduces its trust in recommender *R* by 10 and increases its trust in subject *S* by 10. Finally, the recommender reduces her or his trust in the subject by 10.

The recommender could make requests to a number of recommenders until the total amount of trust value is reached (the search requests to find the recommenders are not represented in the figures). For instance, in the previous example, two different recommenders could be contacted, with one recommending 3 good outcomes and the other one 7.

A recommender chain in trust transfer is not explicitly known to the trustor. The trustor only needs to know his or her contacts who agree to transfer some of their trustworthiness. This is useful from a privacy point of view because the full chain of recommenders is not disclosed. This is in contrast to other recommender chains such as public keys web of trust [29]. Because we assume that the entities cannot be compromised, we leave the issue surrounding the independence of recommender chains to increase the attack resistance of the trust metric for future work. The reason for searching more than one path is that it decreases the chance of a faulty path (caused by malicious intermediaries or unreliable ones). If the full list of recommenders must be detailed to be able to check the independence of recommender chains, the privacy protection is lost. This can be an application-specific design decision.

Thanks to trust transfer, although a real-world identity has many pseudonyms, the Sybil attack cannot happen because the number of direct observations (and hence, total amount of trust) remains the same on the trustor side. One

may argue that it is unfair for the recommender to lose the same amount of trustworthiness as specified in his or her recommendation or if the outcome is ultimately good. It is envisaged that a more complex sequence of messages can be put in place to revise the decrease of trustworthiness after a successful outcome. This has been left for future work, because it can lead to vulnerabilities (for example, based on Sybil attacks with careful cost–benefit analysis). The current trust transfer approach is still limited to scenarios in which there are many interactions among the recommenders and where the overall trustworthiness in the network (that is, the global number of good outcomes) is large enough that there is no major impact to entities when they agree to transfer some of their trust (such as in the email application domain [13]). Ultimately, without sacrificing the flexibility and privacy enhancing potential of limitless pseudonym creation, Sybil attacks are guaranteed to be avoided.

5. OVERVIEW OF PAST AND CURRENT ONLINE REPUTATION SERVICES

As explained in the previous section, most current online reputation services surveyed in this section do not really compute reputation as we have defined it in Section 2. Their reputation algorithms correspond more to a trust metric because they aggregate direct observations and recommendations of different users rather than base their assessment on evidence from a group of an unknown number of unknown users. However, one may consider that these services present reputations to their users if we assume that their users do not take the time to understand how it was computed and who made the recommendations.

First Generation of Online Reputation Management Services

The remainder of this section starts by comparing the first generation of online reputation services and then discusses the second generation including Klout, the winning e-reputation ranking service among the second-generation e-reputation ranking services. This section ends by presenting e-reputation monitoring services that have been created since 2012, e-reputation insurance services and e-reputation management tools for the travel industry, which is the major application domain of online reputation so far.

eBay

Founded in 1995, eBay has been a successful online auction marketplace where buyers can search for products offered by sellers and buy them either directly or after an auction. After each transaction, the buyers can rate the transaction with the seller as "positive," "negative," or

---

5. In this figure, an entity *E* associated with a triple (s,i,c) is indicated by $E(s,i,c)$.

"neutral." Since May 2008, the sellers have only the choice to rate the buyer experience as "positive." Short comments of a maximum of 80 characters can be left with the rating. Their reputation is based on the number of positive and negative ratings that are aggregated in the Feedback Score as well as the comments if the user reads them. Buyers or sellers can affect each other's Feedback Score by only one point per week. Each positive rating counts for one point and each negative counts for −1 point. The balance of points is calculated at the end of the week, and the Feedback Score is increased by 1 if the balance is positive or decreased by 1 if the balance is negative. Buyers can also leave anonymous "Detailed Seller Ratings" composed of different criteria such as "Item as described," "Communication," and "Shipping time" displayed as the number of stars from zero to five. Different image icons are also displayed to estimate the reputation of the user quickly: for example, a star whose color depends on the Feedback Score. After 90 days, detailed item information is removed. From a privacy point of view, on the one hand, it is possible to use a pseudonym; on the other hand, an exhaustive list of what has been bought is available, which is a privacy concern. There are different "Insertion" and "Final Value" fees, depending on the item type. eBay addresses the different reputation service categories as follows:

- Reputation calculation: As detailed previously, reputation is computed based on transactions that are well tracked, which is important to avoid faked evidence. However, eBay's reputation calculation still has problems. For example: as explained earlier, the algorithm had to be changed; the value of the transaction is not taken into account at time of the Feedback Score update (a good transaction of €10 should count less than a good transaction of €10,000); it is limited to the electronic commerce application domain.
- Monitoring, analysis and warnings: eBay does not monitor the reputation of its users outside its service.
- Influencing, promotion and rewards: eBay rewards its users through their public Feedback Score and their associated icon images. However, eBay does not promote the user reputation outside its system and does not facilitate this promotion owing to strict access to its full evidence pool, although some Feedback Score data can be accessed through the eBay software developer application programming interface.
- Interaction facilitation and follow-up: eBay provides a comprehensive Web-based site to facilitate online auctions between buyers and sellers, including a dedicated messaging service and advanced tools to manage the auction. Follow-up based on the Feedback Score is detailed.
- Reputation certification and assurance: eBay does not certify user reputation per se, but given its leading

position, the eBay Feedback Score can be considered, to some extent, as some certified reputation evidence.
- Fraud protection, mediation, cleaning, and recovery: eBay facilitates communication between the buyer and the seller as well as a dispute console with eBay customer support employees. A rating and comment cannot be deleted because "Mutual Feedback Withdrawal" has been removed. In extreme cases, if the buyer had paid through PayPal, which is now part of eBay, the item might be refunded after some time if the item is covered, and depending on the item price. Finally, eBay works with a number of escrow services that act as a third party, and which do not deliver the product until the payment is made. Again, if such third-party services are used, the use of reputation is less useful because these third-party services decrease a lot of the risk of a negative outcome. eBay does not offer to clean the reputation outside its own website.

Opinity

Founded in 2004 and existing until 2008, Opinity [30] was one of the first commercial efforts to build a decentralized online reputation for users in all contexts beyond eBay's limited e-commerce context. After creating an account, users had the possibility of specifying their login and passwords from other websites, especially eBay, to retrieve and consolidate all evidence in the user's Opinity account. Of course, asking users to provide their passwords was risky and seemed not to be a good security practice. Another, safer option was for users to put hidden text in the Hyper Text Markup Language pages of their external services, such as, eBay. Opinity was advanced at the identity layer because it supported OpenID and Microsoft Cardspace. In addition, Opinity could retrieve professional or education background and verify it to some extent using public listings or for a fee. Opinity users could rate other users in different contexts ("plumbing" or "humor"). Opinity addressed different reputation service categories as follows:

- Reputation calculation: Reputation was calculated based on all of the evidence sources and could be accessed by other Opinity partner sites. Reputation could be focused to a specific context called a reputation category.
- Monitoring, analysis, and warnings: Opinity did not really cover this category of services because most evidence was pointed out by users as they were adding external accounts that they owned.
- Influencing, promotion, and rewards: Opinity had the base "Opinity Reputation Score" and it was possible to include a Web badge representation that showed reputation on external websites.

- Interaction facilitation and follow-up: Opinity did not really cover this category of services besides the fact that users could mutually decide to disclose more detail about their profile via the "Exchange Profile" feature.
- Reputation certification and assurance: As mentioned, Opinity certified educational, personal, or professional information to some extent via public listings or for a fee to check information provided by users.
- Fraud protection, mediation, cleaning, and recovery: One Opinity relevant feature in this category is its reputation algorithm. However, it is not known how strongly resistant this algorithm was to attacks: for example, against a user who created many Opinity accounts and used them to rate a main account positively. Another relevant feature was that users could appeal bad reviews via a formal dispute process. Opinity did not offer to clean the reputation outside its own website.

Rapleaf

Founded in 2006, in its first version Rapleaf [31] computed reputation of email addresses. Any Rapleaf user was able to rate any other email address, which may have left the user open to defamation or other privacy issues because users behind the email addresses may not have given their consent. If the email address to be rated had never been rated before, Rapleaf informed the potential rater that it had started crawling the Web to search for information about that email address, and that once the crawling finished, it would invite the rater to add a rating. Different contexts were possible "Buyers, Sellers, Swappers and Friends." Once a rating was entered, it could not be removed. However, new comments were possible and users could rate an email address several times. We use the past tense because by this second edition of this book, Rapleaf changed its service. It no longer computes or provides a public reputation score. It provides marketing data about an email addresses to paying customers willing to carry out emails marketing campaigns, maybe owing to the issues depicted in the subsequent discussion.

Rapleaf was also crawling online social networks and any external profile linked to the searched email address was added to the Rapleaf profile. Email address owners could also add other email addresses that they owned to their profile to provide a unified view of their reputation. Unfortunately, Rapleaf's investors were also involved in two other related services: Upscoop.com, which allows users to import their list of social network friends after disclosing their online social networks passwords (which is a risky practice, as mentioned) and seeing to which other social networks their friends are subscribed; and Trustfuse.com, which is a third business that retrieves profile information for marketing businesses that submit lists of email addresses to TrustFuse. Officially, Rapleaf was not selling

its base of email addresses. However, according to their August 2007 policy, "information captured via Rapleaf could be used to assist TrustFuse services. Additionally, information collected by TrustFuse during the course of its business could also be displayed on Rapleaf for given profiles searched by e-mail address," which was worrisome from a privacy point of view and created a scandal at the time. In its first version, Rapleaf addressed the different reputation service categories thus:

- Reputation calculation: The "Rapleaf Score" takes into account ratings evidence in all contexts as well as how users have rated others and their social network connections. Unfortunately the algorithm is not public, and thus its attack resistance is unknown. In contrast to eBay, commercial transactions reported in Rapleaf are not substantiated by facts other than the rating information. Thus, the chance of faked transactions is higher. Apparently, a user rating may rate an email address several times. However, a user rating only counts for once in the overall reputation of the target email address.
- Monitoring, analysis, and warnings: Rapleaf warns the target email address when a new rating is added.
- Influencing, promotion, and rewards: The "Rapleaf Score" can be embedded in a Web badge and displayed on external Web pages.
- Interaction facilitation and follow-up: At least, it is possible for the target email address to be warned of a rating and to rate the rater.
- Reputation certification and assurance: There is no real feature in this category.
- Fraud protection, mediation, cleaning, and recovery: A form allows the owner of a particular email address to remove that email address from Rapleaf. For more important issues such as defamation, a support email address is provided. Rapleaf does not offer to clean the reputation outside its own website.

Venyo

Founded in 2006, Venyo [32] provided a worldwide people reputation index, called the Vindex, based on either direct ratings through the user profile on the Venyo website or indirect ratings through contributions or profiles on partner websites. Venyo was privacy friendly because it did not ask users for external passwords and did not crawl the Web to present user reputations without their initial consent. Unfortunately Venyo got fewer profiles than the other services that were more aggressive and less privacy friendly and was terminated in 2009. Venyo addressed the different reputation service categories as follows:

- Reputation calculation: Venyo's reputation algorithm is not public and therefore its attack resistance is unknown. At the time of rating, the rater specifies a value

FIGURE 86.7 Venyo e-reputation user interface.

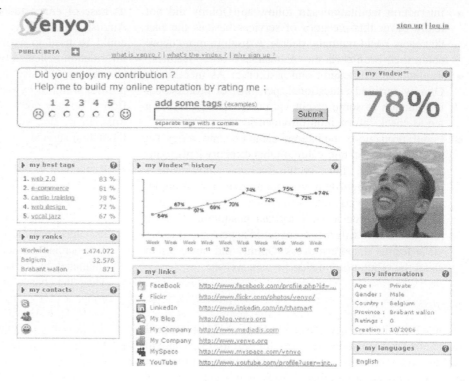

between 1 and 5 as well as keywords corresponding to tags contextualizing the rating, as depicted in Fig. 86.7. The rating is also contextualized according to where the rating has been done. For example, if the rating is done from a GaultMillau restaurant blog article, the tag "restaurant recommendation" is automatically added to the list of tags.

- Monitoring, analysis, and warnings: Venyo provides a reputation history chart to help users monitor the evolution of their reputation on Venyo's and its partners' websites. Venyo does not monitor external Web pages or information.
- Influencing, promotion, and rewards: The Vindex allows users to search for the most reputable users in different domains specified by tags; it can be tailored to specific locations. In addition, the Venyo Web badge can be embedded in external websites. There is also a Facebook plug-in to port Venyo reputation into a Facebook profile.
- Interaction facilitation and follow-up: The Vindex facilitates finding the most reputable user for the request context.
- Reputation certification and assurance: There is not yet a Venyo feature in this category.
- Fraud protection, mediation, cleaning, and recovery: As mentioned, Venyo's e-reputation algorithm attack resistance cannot be assessed because Venyo's algorithm is not public. The cleaning feature is less relevant because the users do not know who rated them. An account may

be closed if the user requests it. As discussed earlier, Venyo is more privacy friendly than other services that request passwords or display reputation without their consent.

TrustPlus + Xing + ZoomInfo + SageFire

TrustPlus is another decentralized e-reputation calculation service that existed when the first version of this chapter was written. Unfortunately TrustPlus closed in April 2012 before the second version of this book chapter was completed because its business model did not work. The company left a final message on its blog website that clearly stated that its business model did not work well enough to be able to continue its service.

Founded in 1999, ZoomInfo is more a people (and company) search directory than a reputation service. However, with its 42 million plus users, 3,8 million companies, and partnership with Xing.com (a business social network similar to LinkedIn.com) ZoomInfo had formed an alliance with TrustPlus [33], which was an online reputation service founded in 2006. The main initial feature of TrustPlus was a Web browser plug-in that allowed the user to see the TrustPlus reputation of an online profile appearing on Web pages on different sites such as Craigslist.org. At the identity layer, TrustPlus asked users to type their external account passwords (for example, eBay's or Facebook's) to validate that they owned these external accounts as well as create their list of contacts. This list of contacts could be used to specify who among the contacts could see the details of transactions or ratings.

The TrustPlus rating user interface and score were complex. There were different contexts: a commercial transaction, a relationship, and an interaction such as a chat or a date.

Thanks to its partnership with SageFire, which is a trusted eBay Certified Solution Provider that has access to historical archives of eBay reputation data, TrustPlus was able to display and use eBay's reputation evidence when users agreed to link their TrustPlus account with their eBay account. TrustPlus addressed the different reputation service categories as follows:

- Reputation calculation: TrustPlus reputation algorithm combines the different sources of reputation evidence reported to TrustPlus by its users and partner sites. However, TrustPlus reputation algorithm is not public and thus again it is difficult to assess its attack-resistance. At the time of rating a commercial transaction, it is possible to specify the amount involved in the transaction, which is interesting from a computational trust point of view. Unfortunately, the risk that this transaction is faked is higher than in eBay because there is no other real facts, such as the cost of the real banking transaction, that corroborate the information given by the rating user.
- Monitoring, analysis, and warnings: TrustPlus warns the user when a new rating has been entered or a new request for rating has been added. However, there is no broader monitoring of the global reputation of the user.
- Influencing, promotion, and rewards: TrustPlus provides different tools to propagate the user reputation: a Web badge that may include eBay's reputation, visibility once the TrustPlus Web browser plug-in viewer has been installed, and a link with the ZoomInfo directory.
- Interaction facilitation and follow-up: TrustPlus provides an internal messaging service that increases the tracking quality of interactions between the rated users and the raters.
- Reputation certification and assurance: There is no reputation certification done by TrustPlus per se but the certification is more formal when users have chosen the option to link their eBay reputation evidence.
- Fraud protection, mediation, cleaning, and recovery: As mentioned, the attack resistance of the TrustPlus reputation algorithm is unknown. In case of defamation or rating disputes, a "Dispute Rating" button is available in the "Explore Reputation" section of the TrustPlus site. When a dispute is initiated, users have to provide substantiating evidence to TrustPlus support employees via email. TrustPlus does not offer to clean the reputation outside its own website.

Naymz + Trufina: Visible.Me

Founded in 2006, Naymz [34] formed an alliance with Trufina.com, which is in charge of certifying identity and background user information. Premium features cost $9.95 per month at time this book chapter was first written. Users are asked for their passwords on external sites such as LinkedIn to invite their list of contacts on these external sites, which is a bad security practice, as mentioned several times. Unfortunately it seems that Naymz has been too aggressive concerning its email, policy and a number of users have complained about receiving unsolicited emails from Naymz: for example, "I have been spammed several times over the past several weeks by a service called Naymz."[6] In 2011, Naymz revised its business model and changed its name to visible.me. Naymz addressed the different reputation service categories as follows:

- Reputation calculation: The Naymz RepScore combines a surprising set of information: not only ratings given by other users but also points for user profile completeness and identity verifications from Trufina. Each rating is qualitative and is focused on the professional contexts of the target user ("Would you like to work on a team with the user?"). Answers can be changed at any time. Only users who are part of the target user list of contacts are allowed to rate the user. There is no specific transaction-based rating, for example, for an e-commerce transaction.
- Monitoring, analysis, and warnings: Naymz has many monitoring features for both inside and outside Naymz reputation evidence. A free list of Web sources (websites, forum, blogs, etc.) mentions the user's name. A premium monitoring tool allows the user to see on a worldwide map who has accessed the user Naymz profile, including the visitor's Internet Protocol address. It is possible to subscribe to other profiles' recent Web activities if they are part of the user's confirmed contacts.
- Influencing, promotion, and rewards: In addition to the RepScore and Web badges, users can achieve ranking in Web search engines for a fee or for free if they maintain a RepScore higher than 9. Users can also get other features for free if they maintain a certain level of RepScore: for example, free detailed monitoring above 10. For a fee of $1995, the company also proposes shooting and producing high-quality professional videos to improve the user's "personal brand."
- Interaction facilitation and follow-up: It is possible to search for users based on keywords, but the search options and index are not advanced at the time of this writing.

---

6. http://www.igotspam.com/50226711/naymz_sending_spamas_you.php, accessed on July 16, 2008.

- Reputation certification and assurance: As mentioned, Trufina is in charge of certifying identity and background user information.
- Fraud protection, mediation, cleaning, and recovery: There are links to report offensive or defaming information to support employees. The attack resistance of the RepScore cannot be assessed because the algorithm detail is not public. They also launched a service called "Naymz Reputation Repair," in which a user can indicate the location of external Web pages that contain embarrassing information as well as some information regarding the issues; after an analysis, Naymz may offer to take actions to remove the embarrassing information for a fee.

The GORB

Founded in 2006, The GORB [35] allowed anybody to rate any email address anonymously. At the time the second edition of this book chapter was written in 2012, this service was closed, apparently also because of a failing business model. Users could create an account to be allowed to display their GORB score with a Web badge and be notified of their and others' reputation evolution. The GORB was strict regarding their rule of anonymity: Users were not allowed to know who had rated them. The GORB addressed different reputation service categories as follows:

- Reputation calculation: They argued that, although they only used anonymous ratings, their reputation algorithm was attack resistant but it is impossible to assess because it was not public. Apparently, they allowed a user to rate another email address several times, but they warned that multiple ratings may decrease the GORB score of the rater. The rating had two contexts on a scale of 0–10: personal and professional. Keywords called tags could be added to the rating as well as a textual comment.
- Monitoring, analysis, and warnings: Users could be notified by email when their reputation evolved or when the reputation of user-defined email addresses evolved. However, it did not monitor evidence outside the GORB.
- Influencing, promotion, and rewards: A Web browser plug-in could be installed to visualize the reputation of email addresses appearing on Web pages in the Web browser. There was a ranking of users based on the GORB score.
- Interaction facilitation and follow-up: There was no follow-up because the ratings were anonymous.
- Reputation certification and assurance: There was no feature in this category.
- Fraud protection, mediation, cleaning, and recovery: The GORB did not allow users to remove their email

address from their list of emails. The GORB asked for users' passwords to import email addresses from the list of contacts of other websites. Thus, one may argue that even if the ratings were anonymous, the GORB was not privacy friendly.

ReputationDefender: Reputation.com

Founded in 2006, ReputationDefender [36] had the following products at the time the first version of this book chapter was written:

- MyReputation and MyPrivacy, which crawl the Web to find reputation information about users for $9.95 per month and allow them to ask for embarrassing information to be deleted for $29.95 per item;
- MyChild, which does the same as the first two, but for $9.95 per month and per child;
- MyEdge, which starts from $99 to $499 and allows the user, with the help of automated and professional copywriters, to improve his online presence: for example, in search engines such as Google and with third-person biographies written by professional copywriters.

At the time second version of the book chapter was written in 2012, ReputationDefender still had roughly the same set of reputation services as listed here. It is still aggressive regarding its marketing claims. Users who create an account have few free services. The service sends them many "alarming" emails about new reputation threats that have been discovered. However, they can see those threats only if they subscribe to an upgraded account, which is not free. Between the first and second editions of this book chapter, ReputationDefender was able to acquire the reputation.com URL, which the company did not previously own. ReputationDefender has addressed the different reputation service categories as follows:

- Reputation calculation: There is no feature in this category.
- Monitoring, analysis, and warnings: As mentioned, the whole Web is crawled and synthetic online reports are provided.
- Influencing, promotion, and rewards: The user reputation may be improved based on expert advice and be better positioned in Web search engines.
- Interaction facilitation and follow-up: There is no feature in this category.
- Reputation certification and assurance: There is no feature in this category.
- Fraud protection, mediation, cleaning, and recovery: There is no reputation algorithm. Cleaning may involve automated software or real people specialized in legal reputation issues.

	eBay	Opinity	Rapleaf	Trustplus	Venyo	The GORB	Naymz	Reputation Defender
Founding Year	1995	2004	2006	2006	2006	2006	2006	2006
Fee	%		N	P	N	N	P	Y
Reputation calculation	★★	★	★	★	★	★	★	
Monitoring, analysis and warnings			★	★	★	★	★★	★★
Influencing, promotion, and rewards	★★	★	★	★★	★★	★★	★★★	★★
Interaction facilitation and follow-up	★★★	★	★	★	★★			
Reputation certification and assurance	★	★★					★	
Fraud protection, mediation, cleaning, and recovery	★★	★	★	★	★★		★★	★★★

%, transaction percentage fee; *N*, no fee; *P*, premium services fee; *Y*, paid service.

Second Generation of Online Reputation Management Services

We first start this subsection by explaining Klout. Then we present e-reputation monitoring services, e-reputation insurance, and e-reputation management tools for the travel industry.

Klout, Winner of the Second Generation of Online Reputation Ranking Services

We have seen different e-reputation calculation services that existed at the time the first version of this chapter was written, and which disappeared before the second version of this chapter was finalized. Klout [39] was created in 2008 by Joé Fernandez in San Francisco, when he was injured and could not speak. Instead of computing the reputation of a person mainly based on recommendations from other users, as we have seen in previous reputation calculation services, Klout first analyzed the Twitter account of that person. The Klout score was initially based on three main criteria:

- True Reach: the number of followers of the user's Twitter account and following the user's tweets

- Amplification: the number of people who share a post (who distribute it to other users)
- Network: the influence of users composing the True Reach themselves

Klout integrates other evidence such as posts on other social networks (such as Facebook) or other users who recommend the user by adding a +K to the user on specific topics, meaning that they click on a link provided by Klout saying that the user has influenced them regarding that topic. Similar metrics have been created since Klout: for example, Twitalizer (which is a detailed one focusing on Twitter information), Peerindex, Kred, Identified, PROSkore, Jitterater (acquired at the time of this writing by Meltwater [10]), and so on. Unfortunately most of those metrics are not open (it is not clear how the results have been computed, and based on which evidence). Klout's initial business model is based on the fact that users with a high Klout score in some topic are rewarded by brands willing to influence that topic. For example, Virgin Airlines gave free airline tickets to users with a high Klout score. At the time the second version of this book chapter was written, it still was not possible to reward users outside the

United States, and its business model still had to prove its viability. Anyway, Klout has gained a decent level of visibility compared with earlier e-reputation calculation services, maybe because many more users use social networks than before and e-reputation has become a hot product in traditional marketing companies. In 2014, Klout was acquired by Lithium Technologies, a provider of social customer experience solutions for the enterprise, in a deal valued at nearly $200 million. Klout has addressed the different reputation service categories as follows:

- Reputation calculation: Klout calculates a score for the user, mainly based on Twitter's performance, but information from other social networks is also taken into account.
- Monitoring, analysis, and warnings: Once the Klout account is linked to a user's social network, it can detect automatically when the user sends a new post and check how much buzz it has generated. If another user gives the user a +K, she is informed by email or a notification on her social networks.
- Influencing, promotion, and rewards: Klout users with higher scores may be rewarded by brands willing to influence its network through those users. Klout rewards are called "perks."
- Interaction facilitation and follow-up: Although Klout provides a Web interface and widgets showing the user's Klout score, there is no secure check of information provided by another user concerning an interaction besides the fact that she can specify that she has been influenced by giving a +K in a specific topic.
- Reputation certification and assurance: There is no feature in this category.
- Fraud protection, mediation, cleaning, and recovery: There is no feature in this category, especially because Klout focuses on positive interactions, meaning that it is possible to say that another user has influenced the current user but not that she has been betrayed by this other user.

e-Reputation Monitoring Services

Since the first version of this book chapter, several online reputation monitoring services were created. Those services do not focus on computing the reputation score of a specific entity based on transactions but continuously analyze online posts about the entity and warn this entity if some posts may decrease its reputation. To facilitate reacting in case of a potentially harmful post by commenting a post on Facebook, most of these services provide an engagement Web-based interface in which posts' authors, content, and comments can be easily managed (stored, retrieved, commented, monitored, etc.). A few of these services allow many entities to be monitored based on archived content. However, the more

entities and post that can be retrieved, the more expensive the service is; at the time of writing, it is around several thousands of dollars per month. For example, Sysomos [37] products continuously crawl many sources (public websites, social networks, blogs, and such) and its MAP product allows the user to search for posts about an entity up to 2 years previously. Sysomos also has a cheaper service that focuses on only entity and provides engagement interfaces for this entity. The cheaper services do not give access to archives before the account is created for a specific search entity (the name of the company to be monitored). A few services argue for making automatic sentiment analysis of posts in different languages, and it works more or less well depending on the language; of course, English is the language that is the best processed. A few of these services existed before the term "online reputation" gained popularity: for example, Digimind [38], which is originally a business intelligence service that added e-reputation services such as engagement in 2012. Another, older service that specializes in newspapers monitoring, called Meltwater, added a social network influence score to its Meltwater Buzz product in 2012. Since 2012, the well-known Radian6 e-reputation monitoring tool was bought by Salesforce and integrated into its suite, and Microsoft bought and integrated the Swiss Netbreeze e-reputation monitoring tool. Thus, the market of e-reputation monitoring is being consolidated. Hundreds of providers claim that they achieve complete e-reputation monitoring with good quality, but actually their completeness and quality vary greatly from one provider to another. Forrester [44] regularly benchmarks those e-reputation monitoring providers. At time of this writing, Synthesio [41] leads the pack of e-reputation monitoring providers.

e-Reputation Insurance

Although e-reputation insurance did not exist at the time the first version of this book chapter was written, traditional insurance companies started selling online reputation insurance in June 2011. SwissLife was the first insurance company to propose insurance to protect a person against e-reputation damage. Axa also proposed such insurance. However, this type of insurance is limited with regard to the e-reputation damage it covers. The maximum amount it guarantees against online reputation damage is limited, up to around €10,000. It costs around €20 per month. The company guarantees to put in place the means to mitigate online reputation damage up to this maximum amount, but it do not guarantee full recovery from the online reputation damage. For example, it will cover the price of using an online reputation protection third-party service, which will try basic means to recover (creating positive well-referenced Web pages that appear first in Google search results before the Web pages with the reputation issues). Unfortunately they will stop covering the fees of an external specialized online reputation lawyer as soon as the fees reach the maximum amount of money guaranteed by the insurance.

e-Reputation Management Tools for the Travel Industry

One of the main e-reputation services that users check on the Web concern hotel ratings such as those on TripAdvisor [42] and Booking [43]. Attacks on Booking are harder to commit because Booking asks for ratings only after accommodations are paid for, which is not the case for TripAdvisor. Started in 2000, TripAdvisor became the most well-known e-reputation service in the travel industry. Unfortunately TripAdvisor experienced both issues (owing to successful attacks from users who wanted to increase or decrease the ranking of the hotel or from a competitor) owing to its own practices. For example, it was sued in the United Kingdom in 2009 and changed its slogan, "Reviews you can trust" to "Reviews from our community," and it was sued in France in 2011 because it was displaying nonpartner hotels as fully booked even when it was not the case. For example, during summer 2015, a journalist from an Italian gastronomic magazine succeeded in naming a fake restaurant as the best-ranked restaurant of the tourist city of Lombardy. Anyway, although those ratings are not perfect, they correspond to more than 80% of hotel and restaurant ratings found online in a study on French tourist territory [45].

To help the hotel owners and other owners of local businesses in the travel industry to manage those ratings and thus their e-reputation, different services have been created. TrustYou [46] is an advanced service that can monitor the e-reputation of competitors as well as other business information including pricing. In addition to ratings monitoring and alerting, TrustYou includes the monitoring of keywords on social networks with sentiment analysis and computes a so-called TrustScore based not only on the reviews score but also the response rate, especially for negative reviews. In fact, several rating services allows the hotel to respond to reviews left by their customers, and they should try to answer them in an appropriate way as quickly as possible to avoid a crisis from building up. TrustYou, which started as an aggregator and analyzer of ratings, such as Revinate [47] or ReviewPro [48], and then included functionalities from other competitors that started with on-site rating collection tools, such as GuestApp [49], Vinivi [50], and Customer Alliance [51], focuses on pricing intelligence or satisfaction surveys, such as Olakala [52], Medallia [53], and Qualitelis [54]. At the time of writing, the best of these competitors are able to improve collection on site and on different ratings services, and aggregate, analyze, monitor, alert, and automatically push new collected ratings to external ratings services as well as on the website of the hotel to increase its ranking on Google, because Google takes into account whether a website includes ratings, and display it in the search results.

6. SUMMARY

Online reputation management is an emerging complementary field of computer security whose traditional security mechanisms are challenged by the openness of the World Wide Web, where there is no a priori information of who is allowed to do what. Technical issues remain to be overcome: the attack resistance of the reputation algorithm is yet not mature; and it is difficult to represent in a consistent way a reputation that was built from different contexts (e-commerce and friendship).

Sustainable business models still have not been found. Opinity seems to have run out of business; Rapleaf had to move from a reputation service to a privacy-risky business of email address marketing profiling; TrustPlus had to form an alliance with ZoomInfo, Xing, and SageFire, but eventually had to close its service in April 2012; the GORB also had to close; Naymz decreased its own reputation by spamming its base of users in the hope of increasing its traffic and has changed its name to visibleme.com; and new services based on another type of calculation such as Klout emerged but their business model still needs to be confirmed over the next couple of years, although Klout was successfully sold. We expect that a number of these services will have merged or disappeared in a few years' time, and likewise for the new e-reputation services targeting the travel industry, especially if Google develops its service to manage local businesses including hotels and restaurants. Concerning e-reputation insurance services, traditional insurance companies created them, and therefore they are less prone to disappear than online reputation services launched by startup companies with unproven business models. However, their protection value is questionable.

It seems that both current technical and commercial issues may be improved by a standardization effort of online reputation management. The attack resistance of reputation algorithms cannot be certified to the degree it deserves if reputation algorithms remain private. It has been proven in other security domains that security through obscurity gives lower results: for example, concerning cryptographic algorithms that are open to review by the whole security research community. Open reputation algorithms will also improve the credibility of the reputation results because it will be possible to explain clearly to users how the reputation has been calculated. Standardization of the representation of reputation will also diminish confusion in the eyes of users. A clearer understanding of which reputation evidence is taken into account in reputation calculation will improve the situation regarding privacy and will open the door for stronger regulation regarding how reputation information flows. Fortunately, the International Telecommunication

Union (ITU) standardization body has started a Correspondence Group (CG) on Trust [55] as part of Study Group 13 on future networks including cloud computing, mobile, and next-generation networks. The author of this chapter contributes to this ITU CG Trust group and is the chief executive officer of a new service called Réputaction [56], which specializes in commercial attack-resistant trust metrics.

Finally, let us move on to the real interactive part of this chapter: review questions/exercises, hands-on projects, case projects, and the optional team case project. The answers and/or solutions by chapter can be found in Appendix K.

CHAPTER REVIEW QUESTIONS/ EXERCISES

True/False

1. True or False? The state of the art is clearly satisfactory; instead, mobile users and devices need the ability to authenticate and authorize other parties autonomously that they encounter on their way without relying on a common authentication infrastructure.
2. True or False? Information on the outcomes of current interactions with the trustee that are used for trust can come from different sources.
3. True or False? Trust engines, based on computational models of the human notion of trust, have been proposed to make security decisions on behalf of their owner.
4. True or False? In most commercial reputation services surveyed, the reputation calculation takes into account the attack resistance of their algorithm.
5. True or False? Most current online reputation services surveyed actually compute reputation.

Multiple Choice

1. What is computed based on transactions that are well tracked, which is important to avoid faked evidence?
   A. Reputation
   B. Vulnerabilities
   C. Log
   D. Encrypted
   E. Department of Homeland Security
2. What was one of the first commercial efforts to build decentralized online reputation for users in all contexts beyond eBay's limited e-commerce context?
   A. Opinity
   B. Risk assessment
   C. Scale
   D. Access
   E. Active monitoring
3. What is the first built reputation about email addresses?
   A. Organizations
   B. Rapleaf

   C. Worms
   D. Logs
   E. Security
4. What provided a worldwide people reputation index, called the Vindex, based on either direct ratings through the user profile on the Venyo website or indirect ratings through contributions or profiles on partners' websites?
   A. Organizations
   B. Denial of service attack
   C. Venyo
   D. Port traffic
   E. Taps
5. What is another decentralized e-reputation calculation service?
   A. Systems security plan
   B. TrustPlus
   C. Denying service
   D. Decision making
   E. Challenge-Handshake Authentication Protocol (CHAP)

EXERCISE
Problem

Can online e-reputation management services solve problems overnight?

Hands-on Projects
Project

Can online e-reputation management services make negative results disappear forever?

Case Projects
Problem

What is a Web e-reputation service?

Optional Team Case Project
Problem

What are the levels that determine whether access to a URL will be blocked or allowed?

REFERENCES

[1] C. Ellison, B. Schneier, Ten risks of PKI: what you're not being told about Public Key Infrastructure, Computer Security Journal 16 (Winter issue) (2000).
[2] R. Housley, T. Polk, Planning for PKI: Best Practices Guide for Deploying Public Key Infrastructure, 2001.

[3] P. Resnick, R. Zeckhauser, J. Swanson, K. Lockwood, The value of reputation on eBay: a controlled Experiment, Experimental Economics (2003).

[4] M. Bouvier, Maxims of Law, Law Dictionary, 1856.

[5] K. Kuwabara, Reputation: signals or incentives?, in: The Annual Meeting of the American Sociological Association, 2003.

[6] The Life and Letters of Benjamin Franklin.

[7] S.R. Covey, The 7 Habits of Highly Effective People, 1989.

[8] J. Seigneur, J. Abendroth, C.D. Jensen, Bank accounting and ubiquitous Brokering of Trustos, in: 7th Cabernet Radicals Workshop, 2002.

[9] D.M. Romano, The Nature of Trust: Conceptual and Operational Clarification, 2003.

[10] D.H. McKnight, N.L. Chervany, What is trust? A conceptual analysis and an interdisciplinary model, in: The Americas Conference on Information Systems, 2000.

[11] T. Peters, The Brand Called You, Fast Company, Mansueto Ventures LLC, 1997.

[12] Execunet. http://www.execunet.com.

[13] J.M. Seigneur, Trust, Security and Privacy in Global Computing, 2005.

[14] A.K. Dey, Understanding and using context, Personal and Ubiquitous Computing Journal 5 (2001).

[15] S. Marsh, Formalising Trust as a Computational Concept, 1994.

[16] A. Rahman, S. Hailes, Using recommendations for managing trust in distributed systems, CiteSeerX, in: Proceedings of IEEE Malaysia International Conference on Communication'97 (MICC'97), Kuala Lumpur, Malaysia (1997).

[17] R. Khare, What's in a name? Trust. (1999).

[18] Trusted Computing Group. https://www.trustedcomputinggroup.org/.

[19] M. Blaze, J. Feigenbaum, J. Lacy, Decentralized trust management, in: The 17th IEEE Symposium on Security and Privacy, 1996.

[20] S. Terzis, W. Wagealla, C. English, A. McGettrick, P. Nixon, The SECURE Collaboration Model, 2004.

[21] OpenID. http://openid.net/.

[22] A. Twigg, N. Dimmock, Attack-resistance of computational trust models, in: Proceedings of the Twelfth International Workshop on Enabling Technologies: Infrastructure for Collaborative Enterprises, 2003.

[23] J.R. Douceur, The Sybil attack, in: Proceedings of the 1st International Workshop on Peer-to-peer Systems, 2002.

[24] R. Levien, Attack Resistant Trust Metrics, 2004.

[25] E. Friedman, P. Resnick, The social cost of cheap pseudonyms, Journal of Economics & Management Strategy (2001) 173–199.

[26] D. Chaum, Achieving electronic privacy, Scientific American (1992) 96–100.

[27] M. Kinateder, K. Rothermel, Architecture and algorithms for a distributed reputation system, in: Proceedings of the First Conference on Trust Management, 2003.

[28] M. Nielsen, G. Plotkin, G. Winskel, Petri nets, event structures and domains, Theoritical Computer Science (1981) 85–108.

[29] P.R. Zimmerman, The Official PGP User's Guide, 1995.

[30] Opinity. http://www.opinity.com.

[31] Rapleaf. http://www.rapleaf.com.

[32] Venyo. http://www.venyo.org.

[33] Trustplus. http://www.trustplus.com.

[34] Naymz. http://www.naymz.com.

[35] The GORB. http://www.thegorb.com.

[36] ReputationDefender. http://www.reputationdefender.com.

[37] Sysomos, http://www.sysomos.com.

[38] Digimind, http://www.digimind.com.

[39] Klout, http://www.klout.com.

[40] A. Aldini, J.-M. Seigneur, C. Ballester Lafuente, X. Titi, J. Guislain, Formal modeling and verification of opportunity-enabled risk management, in: The Proceedings of IEEE Trustcom International Symposium on Recent Advances of Trust, Security and Privacy in Computing and Communications, 2015.

[41] Synthesio, http://www.synthesio.com.

[42] Tripadvisor, http://www.tripadvisor.com.

[43] Booking, http://www.booking.com.

[44] Forrester, The Forrester Wave™: Asia Pacific Enterprise Social Listening Platforms, Q1 2016 and the Forrester Wave™: Enterprise Social Listening Platforms, Q1 2016, 2016.

[45] TCI Research, Etude de l'impact du label Tourisme Sud de France sur la e-réputation des établissements adhérents, 2015.

[46] TrustYou, http://www.trustyou.com.

[47] Revinate, http://www.revinate.com.

[48] ReviewPro, http://www.reviewpro.com.

[49] GuestApp, http://www.guestapp.com.

[50] Vinivi, http://www.vinivi.com.

[51] CustomerAlliance, http://www.customer-alliance.com.

[52] Olakala, http://www.olakal.com.

[53] Medallia, http://www.medallia.com.

[54] Qualitelis, http://www.qualitelis.com.

[55] ITU, https://www.itu.int/ml/lists/arc/cg-trust.

[56] Réputaction, http://www.reputaction.com.

Chapter 87

Content Filtering

Pete F. Nicoletti

Virtustream, Inc., Tavernier, FL, United states

Note: This chapter is available in its entirety online at store.elsevier.com/product.jsp?isbn= 9780128038437 (click the Resources tab at the bottom of the page).

1. ABSTRACT

Content filtering is a powerful tool that, if properly deployed, can offer parents, companies, and local, state, and federal governments protection by classifying Internet-based content. It is disparaged as Orwellian and simultaneously embraced as a positive ROI project, depending on who you are and how it affects your online behavior. In this chapter we examine the many benefits and justifications of Web-based content filtering, such as legal liability, risk reduction, productivity gains, and bandwidth usage. We will explore the downside and unintended consequences and risks that improperly deployed or misconfigured systems create. We will also look into methods to subvert and bypass these systems and the reasons behind them. It is important for people who are considering content filtering to be aware of all the legal implications, and we will also review these. Content filtering is straightforward to deploy, and license costs are so reasonable they can offer extremely fast return on investment while providing a very effective risk reduction strategy. We will make sure that your project turns out successfully, since we'll look at all the angles: Executives will be happy with the project results and employees would not key your car in the parking lot!

2. CONTENTS

Computer and Information Security Handbook. http://dx.doi.org/10.1016/B978-0-12-803843-7.00087-9

Chapter 88

Data Loss Protection

Ken Perkins

Blazent, Inc., Denver, CO, United States

IT professionals are tasked with the some of the most complex and daunting tasks in any organization. Some of the roles and responsibilities are paramount to the company's livelihood and profitability and maybe even be the ultimate survival of the organization. Some of the most challenging issues facing IT professionals today are securing communications and complying with the vast number of data privacy regulations. Secure communications must protect the organization against spam, viruses, and worms; securing outbound traffic; guaranteeing the availability and continuity of the core business systems (such as corporate email, Internet connectivity, and phone systems), all while facing an increasing workload with the same workforce. In addition, many organizations face

challenges in meeting compliance goals, contingency plans for disasters, detecting and/or preventing data misappropriation, and dealing with hacking, both internally and externally.

Almost every week, IT professionals can open the newspaper or browse online news sites and read stories that would keep most people up at night (see sidebar, "Stealing Trade Secrets From E. I. du Pont de Nemours and Company"). The dollar amounts lost are staggering and growing each year (see sidebar, "Stored Secure Information Intrusions"). Pressures of compliance regulations, brand protection, and corporate intellectual property are all driving organizations to evaluate and/or adopt data loss protection (DLP) solutions.

Stealing Trade Secrets from E. I. du Pont de Nemours and Company

WILMINGTON, DE—Colm F. Connolly, United States Attorney for the District of Delaware; William D. Chase, Special Agent in Charge of the Baltimore Federal Bureau of Investigation (FBI) Field Office; and Darryl W. Jackson, Assistant Secretary of Commerce for Export Enforcement, announced today the unsealing of a one-count Criminal Information charging Gary Min, a.k.a. Yonggang Min, with stealing trade secrets from E. I. du Pont de Nemours and Company ("DuPont"). Min pleaded guilty to the charge on November 13, 2006. The offense carries a maximum prison sentence of 10 years, a fine of up to $250,000, and restitution.

Pursuant to the terms of the plea agreement, Min admitted that he misappropriated DuPont's proprietary trade secrets without the company's consent and agreed to cooperate with the government.

According to facts recited by the government and acknowledged by Min at Min's guilty plea hearing, Min began working for DuPont as a research chemist in November 1995. Throughout his tenure at DuPont, Min's research focused generally on polyimides, a category of heat and chemical

resistant polymers, and more specifically on high-performance films. Beginning in July 2005, Min began discussions with Victrex PLC about possible employment opportunities in Asia. Victrex manufactures PEEK, a polymer compound that is a functional competitor with two DuPont products, Vespel and Kapton. On October 18, 2005, Min signed an employment agreement with Victrex, with his employment set to begin in January 2006. Min did not tell DuPont that he had accepted a job with Victrex, however, until December 12, 2005.

Between August 2005 and December 12, 2005, Min accessed an unusually high volume of abstracts and full-text.pdf documents off of DuPont's Electronic Data Library (EDL). The EDL server, which is located at DuPont's experimental station in Wilmington, is one of DuPont's primary databases for storing confidential and proprietary information. Min downloaded approximately 22,000 abstracts from the EDL and accessed approximately 16,706 documents—fifteen times the number of abstracts and reports accessed by the next highest user of the EDL for that period. The vast majority of Min's EDL searches were unrelated to his research

Continued

Computer and Information Security Handbook. http://dx.doi.org/10.1016/B978-0-12-803843-7.00088-0

Stealing Trade Secrets from E. I. du Pont de Nemours and Company—cont'd

responsibilities and his work on high-performance films. Rather, Min's EDL searches covered most of DuPont's major technologies and product lines, as well as new and emerging technologies in the research and development stage. The fair market value of the technology accessed by Min exceeded $400 million.

After Min gave DuPont notice that he was resigning to take a position at Victrex, DuPont uncovered Min's unusually high EDL usage. DuPont immediately contacted the FBI in Wilmington, which launched a joint investigation with the United States Attorney's Office and the United States Department of Commerce. Min began working at Victrex on January 1, 2006. On or about February 2, 2006, Min uploaded approximately 180 DuPont documents—including documents containing confidential, trade secret information—to his Victrex-assigned laptop computer. On February 3, 2006, DuPont officials told Victrex officials in London about Min's EDL activities and explained that Min had accessed confidential and proprietary action. Victrex officials seized Min's laptop computer from him on February 8, 2006, and subsequently turned it over to the FBI."[1]

Stored Secure Information Intrusions

Retailer TJX suffered an unauthorized intrusion or intrusions into portions of its computer system that processes and stores information related to credit and debit card, check and unreceipted merchandise return transactions (the intrusion or intrusions, collectively, the "Computer Intrusion"), which was discovered during the fourth quarter of fiscal 2007. The theft of customer data primarily related to portions of the transactions at its stores (other than Bob's Stores) during the periods 2003 through June 2004 and mid-May 2006 through mid-December 2006.

During the first 6 months of fiscal 2007, TJX incurred pretax costs of $38 million for costs related to the Computer Intrusion. In addition, in the second quarter ended July 28, 2007, TJX established a pretax reserve for its estimated exposure to

potential losses related to the Computer Intrusion and recorded a pretax charge of $178 million. As of January 26, 2008, TJX reduced the reserve by $19 million, primarily due to insurance proceeds with respect to the Computer Intrusion, which had not previously been reflected in the reserve, as well as a reduction in estimated legal and other fees as the Company has continued to resolve outstanding disputes, litigation, and investigations. This reserve reflects the Company's current estimation of probable losses in accordance with generally accepted accounting principles with respect to the Computer Intrusion and includes a current estimation of total potential cash liabilities from pending litigation, proceedings, investigations, and other claims, as well as legal and other costs and expenses, arising from the Computer Intrusion. This reduction in the reserve results in a credit to the Provision for Computer Intrusion related costs of $19 million in the fiscal 2007 fourth quarter and a pretax charge of $197 million for the fiscal year ended January 26, 2008.

The Provision for Computer Intrusion related costs increased fiscal 2008 fourth quarter net income by $11 million, or $0.02 per share, and reduced net income from continuing operations for the full fiscal 2008 year by $119 million, or $0.25 per share.[2]

Note: In the June 2007 General Accounting Office article, "GAO-07-737 Personal Information: Data Breaches Are Frequent, But Evidence of Resulting Identity Theft Is Limited; However, the Full Extent Is Unknown," 31 companies that responded to a 2006 survey said they incurred an average of $1.4 million per data breach.[3]

1. "Guilty plea in trade secrets case," Department of Justice Press Release, February 15, 2007.
2. "SEC EDGAR filing information form 8-K," TJX Companies, Inc., February 20, 2008.
3. "GAO-07-737 personal information: Data breaches are frequent, but evidence of resulting identity theft is limited; however, the full extent is unknown," General Accounting Office, June 2007.

1. PRECURSORS OF DLP

Even before the Internet and its wonderful benefits, organizations' data were exposed to the outside world. Modems, telex, and fax machines were some of the first enablers of electronic communications. Electronic methods of communications, by default, increase the speed and ease of communication, but they also create inherent security risks. Once Information Technology (IT) organizations noticed they were at risk, they immediately started focusing on creating impenetrable moats to surround the "IT castle." As communication protocols standardized and with the mainstream adoption of the Internet, Transmission Control Protocol/Internet Protocol (TCP/IP) became the generally accepted default language of the Internet. This phenomenon

brought to light external-facing security technologies and consequently their quick adoption. Some common technologies that protect TCP/IP networks from external threats are:

- *Firewalls*: Inspect network traffic passing through it, and denies or permits passage based on a set of rules.
- *Intrusion detection systems (IDSs)*: Sensors log potential suspicious activity and allow for the remediation of the issue.
- *Intrusion prevention systems (IPSs)*: React to suspicious activity by automatically performing a reset to the connection or by adjusting the firewall to block network traffic from the suspected malicious source.
- *Antivirus protection*: Attempts to identify, neutralize, or eliminate malicious software.
- *Antispam technology*: Attempts to let in "good" emails and keep out "bad" emails.

The common thread in these technologies: Keep the "bad guys" out while letting normal, efficient business processes to occur. These technologies initially offered some very high-level, nongranular features such as blocking a TCP/IP port, allowing communications to and from a certain range of IP addresses, identifying keywords (without context or much flexibility), signatures of viruses, and blocking spam that used common techniques used by spammers.

Once IT organizations had a good handle on external-facing services, the next logical thought comes to mind: What happens if the "bad guy," undertrained, or undereducated users, already have access to the information contained in an organization? In some circles of IT, this animal is simply known as an employee. Employees, by their default, "inside" nature, have permission to access the company's most sensitive information to accomplish their jobs. Even though the behavior of nonmalicious employees might cause as much damage as an intentional act, the disgruntled employee or insider is a unique threat that needs to be addressed.

The disgruntled insider, working from within an organization, is a principal source of computer crimes. Insiders may not need a great deal of knowledge about computer hacking because their knowledge of a victim's system often allows them to gain unrestricted access to cause damage to the system or to steal system data. With the advent of technology outsourcing, even nonemployees have the rights to view/create/delete some of the most sensitive data assets within an organization. The insider threat could also include contractor personnel and even vendors working onsite. To make matters worse, the ease of finding information to help with hacking systems is no harder than typing a search string into popular search engines. The following is an example of how easy it is for non-"black hats" to perform complicated hacks without much technical knowledge:

1. Open a browser that is connected to the Internet.
2. Go to any popular Internet search engine site.
3. Search for the string "cracking WEP How to."

Note: Observe the number of articles, most with step-by-step instructions, on how to find the Wired Equivalent Privacy (WEP) encryption key to "hijack" a Wi-Fi access point.

So, what happens if an inside worker puts the organization at risk through his activity on the network or corporate assets? The next wave of technologies that IT organizations started to address dealt with the "inside man" issue. Some examples of these types of technologies include:

- *Web filtering*: Can allow/deny content to a user, especially when it is used to restrict material delivered over the web.

- *Proxy servers*: Services the requests of its clients by forwarding requests to other servers and may block entire functionality such as Internet messaging (IM)/chat, web email, and peer-to-peer file sharing programs.
- *Audit systems (both manual and automated)*: Technology that records every packet of data that enters/leave the organization's network. Can be thought of as a network "VCR." Automated appliances feature postevent investigative reports. Manual systems might just use open-source packet-capture technologies writing to a disk for a record of network events.
- *Computer forensic systems*: Is a branch of forensic science pertaining to legal evidence found in computers and digital storage media. Computer forensics adheres to standards of evidence admissible in a court of law. Computer forensics experts investigate data storage devices (such as hard drives, USB drives, CD-ROMs, floppy disks, tape drives, etc.), identifying, preserving, and then analyzing sources of documentary or other digital evidence.
- *Data stores* for email governance.
- *IM- and chat-monitoring services*: The adoption of IM across corporate networks outside the control of IT organizations creates risks and liabilities for companies who do not effectively manage and support IM use. Companies implement specialized IM archiving and security products and services to mitigate these risks and provide safe, secure, productive instant-messaging capabilities to their employees.
- *Document management systems*: A computer system (or set of computer programs) used to track and store electronic documents and/or images of paper documents.

Each of these technologies are necessary security measures implemented in (or "by") IT organizations to address point or niche areas of vulnerabilities in corporate networks and computer assets.

Even before DLP became a concept, IT organizations have been practicing the tenets of DLP for years. Firewalls at the edge of corporate networks can block access to IP addresses, subnets, and Internet sites. One could say this is the first attempt to keep data where it should reside, within the organization. DLP should be looked at nothing more than the natural progression of the IT security life cycle.

2. WHAT IS DATA LOSS PROTECTION (DLP)?

DLP is a term that has percolated up from the alphabet soup of computer security concepts in the past few years. Known in the past as information leak detection and prevention (ILDP), used by IDC; information protection and control (IPC); information leak prevention (ILP), coined by

Forrester; content monitoring and filtering (CMF), suggested by Gartner; or extrusion prevention system (EPS), the opposite of intrusion prevention system (IPS), the acronym DLP seems to have won out. No matter what acronym of the day is used, DLP is an automated system to identify anything that leaves the organization that could harm the organization.

DLP applications try to move away from the point or niche application and give a more holistic approach to coverage, remediation and reporting of data issues. One way of evaluating an organization's level of risk is to look around in an unbiased fashion. The most benign communication technologies could be used against the organization and cause harm.

Before embarking on a DLP project, understanding some example types of harm and/or the corresponding regulations can help with the evaluation. The following sidebar, "Current Data Privacy Legislation and Standards," addresses only a fraction of current data privacy legislation and standards but should give the reader a good understanding of the complexities involved in protecting data.

Current Data Privacy Legislation and Standards

Examples of Harm

Scenario
An administrative assistant confirms a hotel reservation for an upcoming conference by emailing a spreadsheet with employee's credit card numbers with expiration dates; sometimes if they want to make it really easy for the "bad guys," an admin will include the credit card's "secret" PIN, also known as card verification number (CVN).

Problem
Possible violation of Gramm-Leach-Bliley Act (GLBA) and puts the organization's employees at risk for identity theft and credit card fraud.

Legislation
Gramm-Leach-Bliley Act
GLBA compliance is mandatory; whether a financial institution discloses nonpublic information or not, there must be a policy in place to protect the information from foreseeable threats in security and data integrity.

Major components put into place to govern the collection, disclosure, and protection of consumers' nonpublic personal information; or personally identifiable information:

- Financial Privacy Rule
- Safeguards Rule
- Pretexting Protection

Financial Privacy Rule
(Subtitle A: Disclosure of Nonpublic Personal Information, codified at 15 U.S.C. § 6801—6809)

The Financial Privacy Rule requires financial institutions to provide each consumer with a privacy notice at the time the consumer relationship is established and annually thereafter. The privacy notice must explain the information collected about the consumer, where that information is shared, how that information is used, and how that information is protected. The notice must also identify the consumer's right to opt out of the information being shared with unaffiliated parties per the Fair Credit Reporting Act. Should the privacy policy change at any point in time, the consumer must be notified again for acceptance. Each time the privacy notice is reestablished, the consumer has the right to opt-out again. The unaffiliated parties receiving the nonpublic information are held to the acceptance terms of the consumer under the original relationship agreement. In summary, the Financial Privacy Rule provides for a privacy policy agreement between the company and the consumer pertaining to the protection of the consumer's personal nonpublic information.

Safeguards Rule
(Subtitle A: Disclosure of Nonpublic Personal Information, codified at 15 U.S.C. § 6801—6809)

The Safeguards Rule requires financial institutions to develop a written information security plan that describes how the company is prepared for and plans to continue to protect clients' nonpublic personal information. (The Safeguards Rule also applies to information of those no longer consumers of the financial institution.) This plan must include:

- Denoting at least one employee to manage the safeguards
- Constructing a thorough risk management on each department handling the nonpublic information
- Developing, monitoring, and testing a program to secure the information
- Changing the safeguards as needed with the changes in how information is collected, stored, and used

This rule is intended to do what most businesses should already be doing: protect their clients. The Safeguards Rule forces financial institutions to take a closer look at how they manage private data and to do a risk analysis on their current processes. No process is perfect, so this has meant that every financial institution has had to make some effort to comply with the GLBA.

Pretexting Protection
(Subtitle B: Fraudulent Access to Financial Information, codified at 15 U.S.C. § 6821—6827)

Pretexting (sometimes referred to as social engineering) occurs when someone tries to gain access to personal nonpublic information without proper authority to do so. This may entail requesting private information while impersonating the account holder, by phone, by mail, by email, or even by phishing (i.e., using a phony website or email to collect data). The GLBA encourages the organizations covered by the GLBA to implement Pretexting Protection, or safeguards against pretexting. For example, a well-written plan to meet GLBA's Safeguards Rule ("develop, monitor, and test a program to secure the information") ought to include a section on training employees to recognize and deflect inquiries made under pretext. In the United States, pretexting by individuals is punishable as a common law crime of False Pretenses.

Current Data Privacy Legislation and Standards—cont'd

Scenario

A human resources (HR) employee, whose main job function is to process claims, forwards via email an employee's Explanation of Benefits that contains a variety of Protected Health Information. The email is sent in the clear and unencrypted, to the organization's healthcare provider.

Problem

Could violate the Health Insurance Portability and Accountability Act (HIPAA), depending on the type of organization.

Legislation

The Privacy Rule

The Privacy Rule took effect on April 14, 2003, with a one-year extension for certain "small plans." It establishes regulations for the use and disclosure of Protected Health Information (PHI). PHI is any information about health status, provision of health care, or payment for health care that can be linked to an individual. This is interpreted rather broadly and includes any part of a patient's medical record or payment history.

Covered entities must disclose PHI to the individual within 30 days upon request. They also must disclose PHI when required to do so by law, such as reporting suspected child abuse to state child welfare agencies.

A covered entity may disclose PHI to facilitate treatment, payment, or healthcare operations or if the covered entity has obtained authorization from the individual. However, when a covered entity discloses any PHI, it must make a reasonable effort to disclose only the minimum necessary information required to achieve its purpose.

The Privacy Rule gives individuals the right to request that a covered entity correct any inaccurate PHI. It also requires covered entities to take reasonable steps to ensure the confidentiality of communications with individuals. For example, an individual can ask to be called at his or her work number, instead of home or cell phone number.

The Privacy Rule requires covered entities to notify individuals of uses of their PHI. Covered entities must also keep track of disclosures of PHI and document privacy policies and procedures. They must appoint a Privacy Official and a contact person responsible for receiving complaints and train all members of their workforce in procedures regarding PHI.

An individual who believes that the Privacy Rule is not being upheld can file a complaint with the Department of Health and Human Services Office for Civil Rights (OCR).

Scenario

An employee opens an email whose subject is "25 Reasons Why Beer is Better than Women." The employee finds this joke amusing and forwards the email to other coworkers using the corporate email system.

Problem

Puts the organization in an exposed position for claims of sexual harassment and a hostile workplace environment.

Legislation

In the United States, the Civil Rights Act of 1964 Title VII prohibits employment discrimination based on race, sex, color, national origin, or religion. The prohibition of sex discrimination covers both females and males. This discrimination occurs when the sex of the worker is made a condition of employment (i.e., all female waitpersons or male carpenters) or where this is a job requirement that does not mention sex but ends up barring many more persons of one sex than the other from the job (such as height and weight limits).

In 1998, Chevron settled, out of court, a lawsuit brought by several female employees after the "25 Reasons" email was widely circulated throughout the organization. Ultimately, Chevron settled out of court for $2.2 million.

Scenario

A retail store server electronically transmits daily point-of-sale (POS) transactions to the main corporate billing server. The POS system records the time, date, register number, employee number, part number, quantity, and if paid for by credit card, the card number. This transaction occurs nightly as part of a batch job and is transmitted over the store's Wi-Fi network.

Problem

The Payment Card Industry Data Security Standard (PCI DSS) was developed by the major credit card companies as a guideline to help organizations that process card payments prevent credit card fraud, cracking, and various other security vulnerabilities and threats. A company processing, storing, or transmitting payment card data must be PCI DSS compliant or risk losing its ability to process credit card payments and being audited and/or fined. Merchants and payment card service providers must validate their compliance periodically. This validation gets conducted by auditors (that is persons who are the PCI DSS Qualified Security Assessors, or QSAs). Although individuals receive QSA status, reports on compliance can only be signed off by an individual QSA on behalf of a PCI council-approved consultancy. Smaller companies, processing fewer than about 80,000 transactions a year, are allowed to perform a self-assessment questionnaire. Penalties are often accessed and fines of $25,000 per month are possible for large merchants for noncompliance.

PCI DSS requires 12 requirements to be in compliance:

Requirement 1: Install and maintain a firewall configuration to protect cardholder data

Firewalls are computer devices that control computer traffic allowed into and out of a company's network, as well as traffic into more sensitive areas within a company's internal network. A firewall examines all network traffic and blocks those transmissions that do not meet the specified security criteria.

Requirement 2: Do not use vendor-supplied defaults for system passwords and other security parameters

Hackers (external and internal to a company) often use vendor default passwords and other vendor default settings to compromise systems. These passwords and settings are well known in hacker communities and easily determined via public information.

Requirement 3: Protect stored cardholder data

Encryption is a critical component of cardholder data protection. If an intruder circumvents other network security controls and gains access to encrypted data, without the proper cryptographic keys, the data is unreadable and unusable to that person. Other effective methods of protecting stored data should be considered as potential risk mitigation opportunities. For example, methods for minimizing risk include not storing cardholder data unless absolutely necessary, truncating

Continued

Current Data Privacy Legislation and Standards—cont'd

cardholder data if full personal area network (PAN) is not needed and not sending PAN in unencrypted emails.

Requirement 4: Encrypt transmission of cardholder data across open, public networks

Sensitive information must be encrypted during transmission over networks that are easy and common for a hacker to intercept, modify, and divert data while in transit.

Requirement 5: Use and regularly update antivirus software or programs

Many vulnerabilities and malicious viruses enter the network via employees' email activities. Antivirus software must be used on all systems commonly affected by viruses to protect systems from malicious software.

Requirement 6: Develop and maintain secure systems and applications

Unscrupulous individuals use security vulnerabilities to gain privileged access to systems. Many of these vulnerabilities are fixed by vendor-provided security patches. All systems must have the most recently released, appropriate software patches to protect against exploitation by employees, external hackers, and viruses. Note: Appropriate software patches are those patches that have been evaluated and tested sufficiently to determine that the patches do not conflict with existing security configurations. For in-house developed applications, numerous vulnerabilities can be avoided by using standard system development processes and secure coding techniques.

Requirement 7: Restrict access to cardholder data by business need-to-know

This requirement ensures critical data can only be accessed by authorized personnel.

Requirement 8: Assign a unique ID to each person with computer access

Assigning a unique identification (ID) to each person with access ensures that actions taken on critical data and systems are performed by, and can be traced to, known and authorized users.

Requirement 9: Restrict physical access to cardholder data

Any physical access to data or systems that house cardholder data provides the opportunity for individuals to access devices or data and to remove systems or hard copies, and should be appropriately restricted.

Requirement 10: Track and monitor all access to network resources and cardholder data

Logging mechanisms and the ability to track user activities are critical. The presence of logs in all environments allows thorough tracking and analysis if something does go wrong. Determining the cause of a compromise is very difficult without system activity logs.

Requirement 11: Regularly test security systems and processes

Vulnerabilities are being discovered continually by hackers and researchers, and being introduced by new software. Systems, processes, and custom software should be tested frequently to ensure security is maintained over time and with any changes in software.

Requirement 12: Maintain a policy that addresses information security for employees and contractors

A strong security policy sets the security tone for the whole company and informs employees what is expected of them. All employees should be aware of the sensitivity of data and their responsibilities for protecting it.[1,2]

Organizations are facing pressure to become Sarbanes-Oxley (SOX) compliant.

SOX Section 404: Assessment of internal control

The most contentious aspect of SOX is Section 404, which requires management and the external auditor to report on the adequacy of the company's internal control over financial reporting (ICFR). This is the most costly aspect of the legislation for companies to implement, as documenting and testing important financial manual and automated controls requires enormous effort.

Under Section 404 of the Act, management is required to produce an "internal control report" as part of each annual Exchange Act report. The report must affirm "the responsibility of management for establishing and maintaining an adequate internal control structure and procedures for financial reporting." The report must also "contain an assessment, as of the end of the most recent fiscal year of the Company, of the effectiveness of the internal control structure and procedures of the issuer for financial reporting." To do this, managers are generally adopting an internal control framework such as that described in Committee of Sponsoring Organization of the Treadway Commission (COSO).

Both management and the external auditor are responsible for performing their assessment in the context of a top-down risk assessment, which requires management to base both the scope of its assessment and evidence gathered on risk. Both the Public Company Accounting Oversight Board (PCAOB) and SEC recently issued guidance on this topic to help alleviate the significant costs of compliance and better focus the assessment on the most critical risk areas.

The recently released Auditing Standard No. 5 of the PCAOB, which superseded Auditing Standard No 2. has the following key requirements for the external auditor:

- Assess both the design and operating effectiveness of selected internal controls related to significant accounts and relevant assertions, in the context of material misstatement risks.
- Understand the flow of transactions, including IT aspects, sufficiently to identify points at which a misstatement could arise.
- Evaluate company-level (entity-level) controls, which correspond to the components of the COSO framework.
- Perform a fraud risk assessment.
- Evaluate controls designed to prevent or detect fraud, including management override of controls.
- Evaluate controls over the period-end financial reporting process.
- Scale the assessment based on the size and complexity of the company.
- Rely on management's work based on factors such as competency, objectivity, and risk.
- Evaluate controls over the safeguarding of assets.
- Conclude on the adequacy of internal control over financial reporting.

Current Data Privacy Legislation and Standards—cont'd

The recently released SEC guidance is generally consistent with the PCAOB's guidance above, only intended for management.

After the release of this guidance, the SEC required smaller public companies to comply with SOX Section 404, companies with year ends after December 15, 2007. Smaller public companies performing their first management assessment under SOX Section 404 may find their first year of compliance after December 15, 2007 particularly challenging. To help unravel the maze of uncertainty, Lord & Benoit, a SOX compliance company, issued "10 Threats to Compliance for Smaller Companies" (www.section404.org/pdf/sox_404_10_threats_to_compliance_for_smaller_public_companies.pdf), which gathered historical evidence of material weaknesses from companies with revenues under $100 million. The research was compiled aggregating the results of 148 first-time companies with material weaknesses and revenues under $100 million. The following were the 10 leading material weaknesses in Lord & Benoit's study: accounting and disclosure controls, treasury, competency and training of accounting personnel, control environment, design of controls/lack of effective compensating controls, revenue recognition, financial closing process, inadequate account reconciliations, information technology and consolidations, mergers, and intercompany accounts.

Scenario
A guidance counselor at a high school gets a request from a student's prospective college. The college asked for the student's transcripts. The guidance counselor sends the transcript over the schools email system unencrypted.

Problem
FERPA privacy concerns, depending on the age of the student.

Legislation
The Family Educational Rights and Privacy Act (FERPA) (20 U.S.C. § 1232g; 34 CFR Part 99) is a federal law that protects the privacy of student education records. The law applies to all schools that receive funds under an applicable program of the US Department of Education.

FERPA gives parents certain rights with respect to their children's education records. These rights transfer to the student when he or she reaches the age of 18 or attends a school beyond the high school level. Students to whom the rights have transferred are "eligible students."

Parents or eligible students have the right to inspect and review the student's education records maintained by the school. Schools are not required to provide copies of records unless, for reasons such as great distance, it is impossible for parents or eligible students to review the records. Schools may charge a fee for copies.

Parents or eligible students have the right to request that a school correct records that they believe to be inaccurate or misleading. If the school decides not to amend the record, the parent or eligible student then has the right to a formal hearing. After the hearing, if the school still decides not to amend the record, the parent or eligible student has the right to place a statement with the record setting forth his or her view about the contested information.

Generally, schools must have written permission from the parent or eligible student in order to release any information from a student's education record. However, FERPA allows schools to disclose those records, without consent, to the following parties or under the following conditions (34 CFR § 99.31):

- School officials with legitimate educational interest
- Other schools to which a student is transferring
- Specified officials for audit or evaluation purposes
- Appropriate parties in connection with financial aid to a student
- Organizations conducting certain studies for or on behalf of the school
- Accrediting organizations
- To comply with a judicial order or lawfully issued subpoena
- Appropriate officials in cases of health and safety emergencies
- State and local authorities, within a juvenile justice system, pursuant to specific State law

Schools may disclose, without consent, "directory" information such as a student's name, address, telephone number, date and place of birth, honors and awards, and dates of attendance. However, schools must tell parents and eligible students about directory information and allow parents and eligible students a reasonable amount of time to request that the school not disclose directory information about them. Schools must notify parents and eligible students annually of their rights under FERPA. The actual means of notification (special letter, inclusion in a parent teacher association bulletin, student handbook, or newspaper article) is left to the discretion of each school.

Scenario
Employee job hunting, posting resumes, and trying to find another job while working. See Fig. 88.1 for an example of a DLP system capturing the full content of a user going through the resignation process.

Problem
Loss of productivity for that employee.

Warning sign for a possible disgruntled employee.

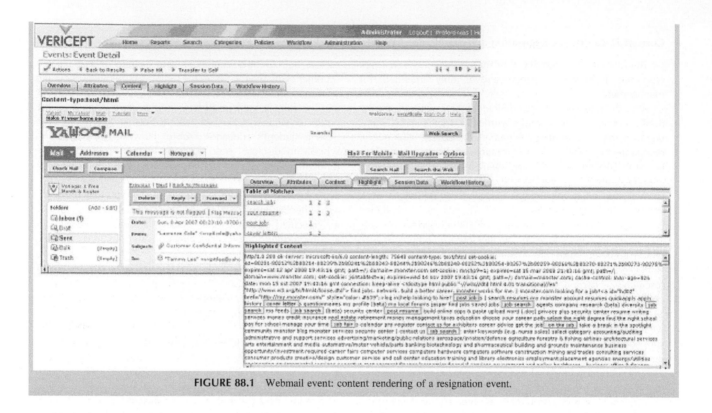

FIGURE 88.1 Webmail event: content rendering of a resignation event.

3. WHERE TO BEGIN?

A reasonable place to begin talking about DLP is with the department of the organization that handles corporate policy and/or governance (see sidebar, "An Example of an Acceptable Use Policy"). Monitoring employees is at best an interesting proposition. Corporate culture can drive whether monitoring of any kind is even allowed. A good litmus test would be the types of notice that appear in the employee handbook.

Another good indicator that the organization would be a good fit for a DLP application is the sign-on screen that appears before or after a computer user logs on to her workstation (see sidebar, "Accessing a Company's Information System").

Some organizations are more apt to take advantage of the laws and rights that companies have to defend themselves. Simply asking around and performing informal interviews with Human Resources, Security, and Legal can save days and weeks of time down the line.

In summary, implementing a DLP application without the proper Human Resources, Security, and Legal policies could be a waste of time because IT professionals will catch employees violating security standard. The events in a DLP system must be actionable and have "teeth" for changes to take place.

4. DATA IS LIKE WATER

As most anyone who has had a water leak in a home knows, water will find a way out of where it is supposed to go. Pipes are meant to direct the proper flow of water both in and out. If a leak happens, the occupant will eventually find a damp spot, a watermark, or a real drip. It might take minutes or days to notice the leak and might take just as long to find the source of the leak.

Much like the water analogy, employees are given data "pipes" to do their jobs with enabling technology provided by the IT organization. Instead of water flowing through, data can ingress/egress the organization in multiple methods.

Corporate email is a powerful, efficient time-saving tool that speeds communication. A user can attach a 10 megabyte file, personal pictures, a recipe for chili, and next quarter's marketing plan or an acquisition target. Chat and IM is the quickest growing form of electronic communication and a great enabler of efficient workflow. Files can be sent as well over these protocols or "pipes." Webmail is usually the "weapon of choice" by users who like to conduct personal business at work. Webmail allows users to attach files of any type.

An Example of an Acceptable Use Policy

Use of Email and Computer Systems

All information created, accessed, or stored using company applications, systems, or resources, including email, is the property of the company. Users do not have a right to privacy regarding any activity conducted using the company's system. The company can review, read, access, or otherwise monitor email and all activities on the company system or any other system accessed by use of the company system. In addition, the Company could be required to allow others to read email or other documents on the company's system in the context of a lawsuit or other legal action.

All users must abide by the rules of network etiquette, which include being polite and using the network and the Internet in a safe and legal manner. The company or authorized company officials will make a good-faith judgment as to which materials, files, information, software, communications, and other content and activity are permitted and prohibited based on the following guidelines and under the particular circumstances.

Among the uses that are considered unacceptable and constitute a violation of this policy are the following:

- Using, transmitting, receiving, or seeking inappropriate, offensive, swearing, vulgar, profane, suggestive, obscene, abusive, harassing, belligerent, threatening, defamatory (harming another's reputation by lies), or misleading language or materials; revealing personal information such as another's home address, home telephone number, or Social Security number; making ethnic, sexual-preference, age or gender-related slurs or jokes.

- Users may never harass, intimidate, threaten others, or engage in other illegal activity (including pornography, terrorism, espionage, theft, or drugs) by email or other posting. All such instances should be reported to management for appropriate action. In addition to violating this policy, such behavior may also violate other company policies or civil or criminal laws.

- Among the uses that are considered unacceptable and constitute a violation of this policy are downloading or

transmitting copyrighted materials without permission from the owner of the copyright on those materials. Even if materials on the network or the Internet are not marked with the copyright symbol, you should assume that they are protected under copyright laws unless there is explicit permission from the copyright holder on the materials to use them.

- Users must not use email or other communications methods, including but not limited to news group postings, blogs, forums, instant messaging, and chat servers, to send company proprietary or confidential information to any unauthorized party. Such information may be disclosed to authorized persons in encrypted files if sent over publicly accessible media such as the Internet or other broadcast media such as wireless communication. Such information may be sent in unencrypted files only within the company system. Users are responsible for properly labeling such information.

Certain specific policies extend the Company's acceptable use policy by placing further restrictions on that activity. Examples include, but are not limited to: software usage, network usage, shell policy, remote access policy, wireless policy, and the mobile email access policy. These and any additional policies are available from the IT website on the intranet.

Your use of the network and the Internet is a privilege, not a right. If you violate this policy, at a minimum you will be subject to having your access to the network and the Internet terminated. You breach this policy not only by affirmatively violating the above provisions but also by failing to report any violations of this policy by other users which come to your attention. Further, you violate this policy if you permit another to use your account or password to access the network or the Internet, including but not limited to someone whose access has been denied or terminated. Sharing your account with anyone is a violation of this policy. It is your responsibility to keep your account secure by choosing a sufficiently complex password and changing it on a regular basis.

Thus, the IT network "plumbing" needs to be monitored, maintained, and evaluated on an ongoing basis. The US government has published a complete and well-rounded standard that organizations can use as a good first step to compare where they are strong and where they can use improvement.

The US Government Federal Information Security Management Act of 2002 (FISMA) offers reasonable guidelines that most organizations could benefit by adopting. Even though FISMA is mandated for government agencies and contractors, it can be applied to the corporate world as well.

FISMA sets forth a comprehensive framework for ensuring the effectiveness of security controls over information resources that support federal operations and

assets. FISMA's framework creates a cycle of risk management activities necessary for an effective security program, and these activities are similar to the principles noted in our study of the risk management activities of leading private sector organizations—assessing risk, establishing a central management focal point, implementing appropriate policies and procedures, promoting awareness, and monitoring and evaluating policy and control effectiveness. More specifically, FISMA requires the head of each agency to provide information security protections commensurate with the risk and magnitude of harm resulting from the unauthorized access, use, disclosure, disruption, modification, or destruction of information and information systems used or operated by the agency or on behalf of the agency. In this regard, FISMA requires that agencies implement information security programs that, among other things, include:

- Periodic assessments of the risk
- Risk-based policies and procedures
- Subordinate plans for providing adequate information security for networks, facilities, and systems or groups of information systems, as appropriate
- Security awareness training for agency personnel, including contractors and other users of information systems that support the operations and assets of the agency
- Periodic testing and evaluation of the effectiveness of information security policies, procedures, and practices, performed with a frequency depending on risk, but no less than annually
- A process for planning, implementing, evaluating, and documenting remedial action to address any deficiencies
- Procedures for detecting, reporting, and responding to security incidents
- Plans and procedures to ensure continuity of operations

In addition, agencies must develop and maintain an inventory of major information systems that is updated at least annually and report annually to the Director of OMB (Office of Management and Budget) and several Congres-

sional Committees on the adequacy and effectiveness of their information security policies, procedures, and practices and compliance with the requirements of the act. An internal risk assessment of what types of "communication," both manual and electronic, that are allowed within the organization can give the DLP evaluator a baseline of the type of transmission that are probably taking place (see checklist: "An Agenda for Action for Evaluating Other Types of Manual and Electronic Communications").

Accessing a Company's Information System

You are accessing a Company's information system (IS) that is provided for Company-authorized use only. By using this IS, you consent to the following conditions:

- The Company routinely monitors communications occurring on this IS, and any device attached to this IS, for purposes including but not limited to penetration testing, monitoring, network defense, quality control, and employee misconduct, law enforcement, and counterintelligence investigations.
- At any time the Company may inspect and/or seize data stored on this IS and any device attached to this IS.
- Communications occurring on or data stored on this IS, or any device attached to this IS, are not private. They are subject to routine monitoring and search.
- Any communications occurring on or data stored on this IS, or any device attached to this IS, may be disclosed or used for any Company-authorized purpose.
- Security protections may be utilized on this IS to protect certain interests that are important to the Company. For example, password, access cards, encryption, or biometric access controls provide security for the benefit of the Company. These protections are not provided for your benefit or privacy and may be modified or eliminated at the Company's discretion.

An Agenda for Action for Evaluating Other Types of Manual and Electronic Communications

Some types of communications that should be evaluated are not always obvious but could be just as damaging as electronic methods. The following list encompasses some of those obvious and not so obvious methods (Check All Tasks Completed):

_____**1.** Pencil and paper
_____**2.** Photocopier
_____**3.** Fax
_____**4.** Voicemail
_____**5.** Digital camera
_____**6.** Jump drive
_____**7.** MP3/iPod
_____**8.** DVD/CD-ROM/3½ in. floppy
_____**9.** Magnetic tape
_____**10.** SATA drives
_____**11.** IM/chat
_____**12.** FTP/FTPS
_____**13.** SMTP/POP3/IMAP
_____**14.** HTTP post/response
_____**15.** HTTPS
_____**16.** Telnet
_____**17.** SCP
_____**18.** P2P
_____**19.** Rogue ports
_____**20.** GoToMyPC
_____**21.** Web conferencing systems

---

5. YOU DON'T KNOW WHAT YOU DON'T KNOW

Embarking on a DLP evaluation or implementation can be a straightforward exercise. The IT professional usually has a mandate in mind and a few problems that the DLP application will address. Invariably, many other issues will arise as DLP applications do a very good job at finding most potential security and privacy issues.

Reports that say that something hasn't happened are always interesting to me, because as we know, there are "known knowns"; there are things we know we know. We also know there are "known unknowns"; that is to say we know there are some things we do not know. But there are also "unknown unknowns"—the ones we don't know we don't know.

—Donald Rumsfeld, US Department of Defense, February 12, 2002

Once the corporate culture has established that DLP is worth investigating or worth implementing, the next logical step would be performing a risk/exposure assessment. Several DLP vendors offer free pilots or proof of concepts and should be leveraged to jumpstart the data risk assessment for a very low monetary cost.

A risk/exposure assessment usually involves placing a server on the edge of the corporate network and sampling/recording the network traffic that is egressing the organization. In addition, the assessment might involve look for high-risk files at rest and the activity of what is happening on the workstation environment. Most if not all DLP applications have predefined risk categories that cover a wide range of risk profiles. Some examples are:

- Regulations: GLBA, HIPAA, PCI DSS, SOX, FERPA, PHI
- Acceptable use: Violence, gangs, profanity, adult themes, weapons, harassment, racism, pornography
- Productivity: Streaming media, resignation, shopping, webmail
- Insider hacker activity: Root activity, nmap, stack, smashing code, keyloggers

Deciding what risk categories are most important to your organization can streamline the DLP evaluation. If data categories are turned on but will not likely impact what is truly important to the organization, the test/pilot result will contain a lot of "noise." Focus on the "low-hanging fruit." For example, if the organization's life blood is customer data, focus on the categories that address those types of leaks.

Precision Versus Recall

Before the precision versus recall discussion can take place, definitions are necessary:

- *False positive*: A false positive occurs when the DLP application-monitoring or DLP application-blocking techniques wrongly classify a legitimate transmission or event as "uninteresting" and, as a result, the event must be remediated anyway. Remediating an event is a time-consuming process which could involve one to many administrators dispositioning the event. A high number of false positives is normal during an initial implementation, but the number should fall after the DLP application is tuned.
- *False negative*: A false negative occurs when a transmission is not detected as interesting. The problem with false negatives is usually the DLP administrator does not know these transmissions are happening in the first place. An analogy would be a bank employee who embezzles thousands of dollars and the bank does not notice the theft until it is too late.
- *True positive*: Condition present and the DLP application records the event for remediation.

- *True negative*: Condition not present and the DLP application does not record it. DLP application testing and tuning can involve a trade-off:
- The acceptable level of false positives (in which a non-match is declared to be a match).
- The acceptable level of false negatives (in which an actual match is not detected).

An evaluator can think of this process as a slider bar concept, with false negatives on the left side and false positives on the right. A properly tuned DLP application minimizes false positives and diminishes the chances of false negatives.

This iterative process of tuning is called thresholding. Creating the proper threshold eventually leads to the minimization of acceptable amounts of false positives with no or minimal false negatives.

An easy way to achieve thresholding is to make the test more restrictive or more sensitive. The more restrictive the test is, the higher the risk of rejecting true positives; and, the less sensitive the test is, the higher the risk of accepting false positives.

6. HOW DO DATA LOSS PROTECTION (DLP) APPLICATIONS WORK?

The way that most DLP applications capture interesting events is through different kinds of analysis engines. Most support simple keyword matching. For example, any time you see the phrase "project phoenix" in a data transmission, the network event is stored for later review. Keywords can be grouped and joined. Regular expression (RegEx) support is featured in most of today's DLP applications. RegExs provide a concise and flexible means for identifying strings of text of interest, such as particular characters, words, or patterns of characters. RegExs are written in a formal language that can be interpreted by a regular expression processor, a program that either serves as a parser generator or examines text and identifies parts that match the provided specification. A real-world example would be the expression:

$$(r|b)?\text{ed}$$

Any transmission that contained the word red, bed, or even ed would be captured for later investigation. Regular expressions can also do pattern matching on credit card number and US Social Security numbers:

$$\wedge \backslash d\{3\} - ?\backslash d\{2\} - ?\backslash d\{4\}$$

which can be read: Any three numbers followed by an optional dash followed by any two numbers followed by an optional dash and then followed by any four numbers. Regular expressions offer a certain level of efficiencies but cannot address all DLP concerns. Weighting of either keyword(s) and/or RegExs can help. A real-world example might be the word red is worth three points and the SSN is worth five points, but for an event to hit the transmission, it must contain 22 points. In this example, four SSNs and the word *red* would trigger an event (4 times 5 plus 3 equals 23, which would trigger the event score rule). Scoring can help address the thresholding issue. To address some of the limitation of simple keyword and RegExs, DLP applications can also look for data "signatures" or hashes of data. Hashing creates a mathematical representation of the sensitive data and looks for that signature. Sensitive data or representative types of data can be bulk loaded from databases and example files.

7. EAT YOUR VEGETABLES

DLP is like the layers of an onion. Once the first layer of protection is implemented, the next layer should/could be addressed. There are many different forms of DLP applications, depending on the velocity and location of the sensitive data.

Data in Motion

Data in motion is an easy place to start implementing a DLP application because most can function in "passive" mode, meaning it looks at only a copy of the actual data egressing/ingressing the network. One way to look at data-in-motion monitoring is like a very intelligent VCR. Instead of recording every packet of information that passes in and out of an organization, DLP applications only capture, flag, and record the transmissions that fall within the categories/policies that are turned on (see sidebar, "Case Study: Data Loss Protection (DLP) Applications"). There are two main types of data-in-motion analysis:

- *Passive monitoring*: Using a Switched Port Analyzer (SPAN) on a router, port mirror on a switch, or a network tap(s) that feeds the outbound network traffic to the DLP application for analysis.
- Active (inline) enforcement: Using an active egress port or through a proxy server, some DLP applications can stop the transmission from happening. The port itself can be reset or the proxy server can show a failure of transmission. The event that keyed off the reset or failure is still recorded.

Data at Rest

Static computer files on drives, removable media, or even tape can grow to the millions in large multinational organizations. Unless tight controls are implemented, data can spawn out of control. Even though email transmissions account for more than 80% of DLP violations, data-at-rest

---

Case Study: Data Loss Protection (DLP) Applications

Background

A Fortune 500 Company has tens of thousands of employees with access to the Internet through an authenticated method. The Company has recently retired a version of laptops with the associated docking station, monitors, and mice. New laptops were purchased and given to the employees. The old assets were retired to a storage closet. One manager noticed some docking stations had gone missing. That in and of itself was not concerning as this company had a liberal policy of donating old computer assets to charity. After looking in the company's Asset Management System and talking to the organization's charity manager, the manager found this was not the case. An investigation was launched both electronically and through traditional investigative means.

Action

The organization had a DLP application in use with data-in-motion implemented. This particular DLP application had a strong acceptable use set of categories/policies. One of them was "Shopping," which covered both traditional shopping outlets but also popular online auction sites. The DLP investigator selected the report that returns all transmissions that violated the "Shopping" category and contained the keyword of the model number of the docking station. Within seconds, a user from within their network was found auctioning the exact same model docking stations as the ones the company had just retired.

Result

The Fortune 500 Company was able to remediate a situation quickly that not only stopped the loss of physical assets, but get rid of an employee that was stealing while at work. The real value of this exercise could have been, if an employee is "okay" with stealing assets to make a few extra dollars on the company's dime, one might ask, What else might an employee that thinks it is okay to steal do?

---

files that are resting where they are not supposed to be can be a major concern (see sidebar, "Case Study: Data-at-Rest Files").

Data-at-rest risk can occur in other places besides the personal computer's file system. One of the benefits of networked computer systems is the ability to share files. File shares can also pose a risk because the original owner of the file now has no idea what happened to the file after they share it.

The same can be said of many web-based collaboration and document management platforms that are available in the market today. Collaboration tools can be used to host websites that can be used to access shared workspaces and documents, as well as specialized applications such as wikis, blogs, and many other forms of applications, from within a browser. Once again, the wonderful world of shared computing can also put an organization's data at risk.

DLP application can help with databases as well and half the battle is knowing where the organizations most sensitive data resides. The data-at-rest function of DLP applications can definitely help.

Data in Use

DLP applications can also help keep data where it is supposed to stay (see sidebar, "Case Study: Data-in-Use Files"). Agent-based technologies that run resident on the guest operating system can track, monitor, block, report, quarantine, or notify the usage of particular kinds of data files and/or the contents of the file itself. Policies can be centrally administered and "pushed" out of the organization's computer assets. Since the agent is resident on the computer, it can also create an inventory of every file on the hard drives, removable media, and even music players. Since the agent knows of the file systems down to the operating system level, it can allow or disallow certain types of removable media. For example, an organization might allow a USB storage device if and only if the device supports encryption. The agent will disallow any other types of USB devices such as music players, cameras, removable hard drives, and so on.

Case Study: Data-at-Rest Files

Background

A Fortune 500 Company has multiple customer service centers located throughout the United States. Each customer server representative has a personal computer with a hard drive and Internet access. The representative's job entails taking inbound phone calls to help their customers with account management including auto-pay features. Auto-pay setup information could include taking a credit card number and expiration date and/or setting up an electronic fund transfer payment which includes an ABA routing number and account number. This sensitive information is supposed to be entered directly into the corporate enterprise resource planning (ERP) system application. Invariably, customer service representatives run into issues during this process (connectivity to the ERP system is interrupted, power goes down, computer needs to be rebooted, etc.) and sensitive data finds its way into unapproved places on the personal computer—a note text file, a word-processing document, an electronic spreadsheet, or in an email system. Even though employees went through training for their job that included handling of sensitive data, the management suspected that data was finding a way out of the ERP system. Another issue that the management faced was a very high turnover ratio and that employee training was falling behind.

Action

A DLP data-at-rest pilot was performed and over 1000 files that contained credit card numbers and other customer personal identifiable information were found.

Continued

Case Study: Data-at-Rest Files—cont'd

Result

The Fortune 500 Company was able to cleanse the hard drives of files that contained sensitive data by using the legend the DLP application provided. More important, the systemic cause of the problem had to be readdressed with training and tightening down the security of the representative, personal computers.

Case Study: Data-in-Use Files

Background

An electronics manufacturer has created a revolutionary new design for a cell phone and wants to keep the design and photographs of the prototype under wraps. They have had problems in the past with pictures ending up on blog sites, competitors "borrowing" design ideas, and even other countries creating similar products and launching an imitator within weeks of the initial product launch.

Action

Each document, whether a spreadsheet, document, diagram, or photograph, was secretly watermarked with a special secret code. At the same time, the main security group created an organizational unit within their main LDAP application. This was the only group that had permission to access the watermarked files. A DLP application agent was rolled out to the computer assets within the organization. If anyone "found" a marked file and tried to do something with it, unless they were in the privileged group, access was denied and an alert (see Fig. 88.2C) went back to the main DLP reporting server.

Result

The electronics manufacturer was able to deliver its revolutionary product to market in a secure manner and on time.

Much like the different flavors of DLP that are available (data in motion, data at rest, and data in use), conditions of the severity of action that DLP applications take on the event can vary. A good place to diagnose the problems organizations are currently facing would be to start with Monitoring (see sidebar, "Case Study in Monitoring"). Monitoring is only capturing the actual event that took place to review at a later time. Most DLP applications offer real-time or near-real-time monitoring of events that violated a policy. Monitoring coupled with escalation can help most organizations immediately. Escalation works well with monitoring as when an event happens, rules can be put into place on who should be notified and/or how the notification should take place. Email is the most common form of escalation.

FIGURE 88.2 (A) Email with user notification on the fly; (B) PC user tries to access a protected document; and (C) policy prompts a justification alert.

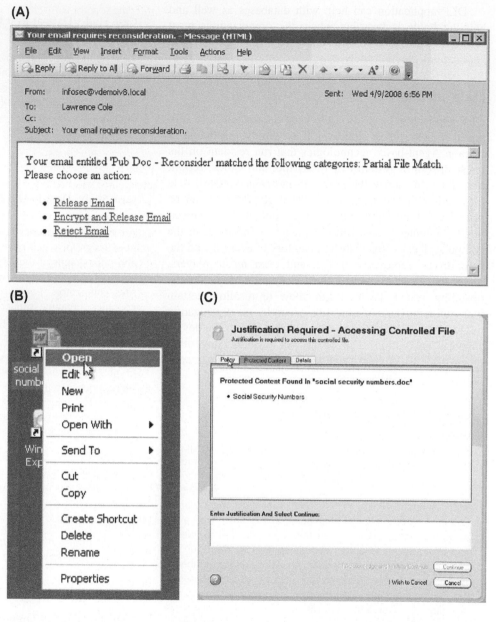

Another action that DLP application supports is notification. Notification can temporarily interrupt that transmission of an event and could require user interaction. See Fig. 88.2A for an example of the kind of "bounce" email a user could receive if she sends an email containing sensitive information. See Fig. 88.2B for an example of the type of notification a user could see if he tries to open a sensitive data document. The DLP application could make the user justify why access is needed, deny access, or simply log the attempt back to the main reporting console.

Notification can enhance the current user education program in place and serve as a gentle reminder. The onus of action lies solely on the end user and does not take resources from the already thinly stretched IT organization.

The next level of severity of implementing DLP could be quarantining and then outright blocking. Quarantining events places the transmission in "stasis" for review from a DLP administrator. The quarantine administrator can release, release with encryption, block, or send the event back to the offending user for remediation. Blocking is an action that stops the transmission in its entirety based upon the contents.

Both quarantining and blocking should be used sparingly and only after the organization feels comfortable with the policies and procedures. The first time an executive tries to send a transmission and cannot because of the action set forth in the DLP application, the IT professional can potentially lose his job.

8. IT'S A FAMILY AFFAIR, NOT JUST IT SECURITY'S PROBLEM

The IT organization most likely maintains the corporate email system; almost everyone across all departments within an organization uses email. The same can be said for the DLP application. Even though IT will implement and maintain the DLP application, the events will most likely come from all different types of users across the entire organization. When concerning events are captured, and there will be many captured by the DLP application, most management will turn to IT to resolve the problem. The IT organization should not become the "police and judge." Each business unit should have published standards on how events should be handled and escalated.

Most DLP applications can segregate duties to allow non-IT personnel to review the disposition of the event captured. One way to address DLP would be to assign certain types of events to administrators in the appropriate department. If a racial email is captured, the most appropriate department might be an HR employee. If a personal

information transmission is captured, a compliance officer should be assigned. IT might be tasked if the nature of the event is hacking related.

Users can also have a level of privilege within the DLP application. Reviewers can be assigned to initial investigations of only certain types or all events. If necessary, an event can be escalated to a reviewer's superior. Users can have administrative or reports-only rights.

Each of these functions relates to the concept of workflow within the DLP application. Events need to be prioritized, escalated, reviewed, annotated, ignored, and eventually closed. The workflow should be easy to use across the DLP community and reports should be easily assessable and created/tuned. See Fig. 88.3A for an example of an Executive Dashboard that allows the user to quickly assess the state of risk and allows for a quick-click drill down for more granular information. Fig. 88.3B is the result of a click from the Executive Dashboard to the full content capture of the event.

9. VENDORS, VENDORS EVERYWHERE! WHO DO YOU BELIEVE?

At the end of the day the DLP market and applications are maturing at an incredible pace. Vendors are releasing new features and functions almost every calendar quarter. In the past, when monitoring seemed sufficient to diagnose the central issue of data security, the marketplace was demanding more control, more granularity, easier user interfaces, and more actionable reports, as well as moving the DLP application off the main network egress point and parlaying the same functionality to the desktops/laptops, servers, and their respective endpoints to document storage repositories and databases.

In evaluating DLP applications, it is important to focus on the type of underlying engine that analyzes the data and then work up from that base. Next, rate the ease of configuring the data categories and the ability to preload certain documents and document types. Look for a mature product with plenty of industry-specific references. Company stability and financial health should also come into play. Roadmaps of future offerings can give an idea of the features and functions coming in the next release. The relationship with the vendor is an important requirement to make sure that the purchase and subsequent implementation goes smoothly. The vendor should offer training that empowers the IT organization to be somewhat self-sustaining instead of having to go back to the vendor every time a configuration needs to be implemented. The vendor should offer best practices that other customers have used to help with quick adoption of policies. This allows for an effective system that will improve and lower the overall risk profile of the organization. Analyst briefings

FIGURE **88.3** (A) Dashboard; (B) email event overview.

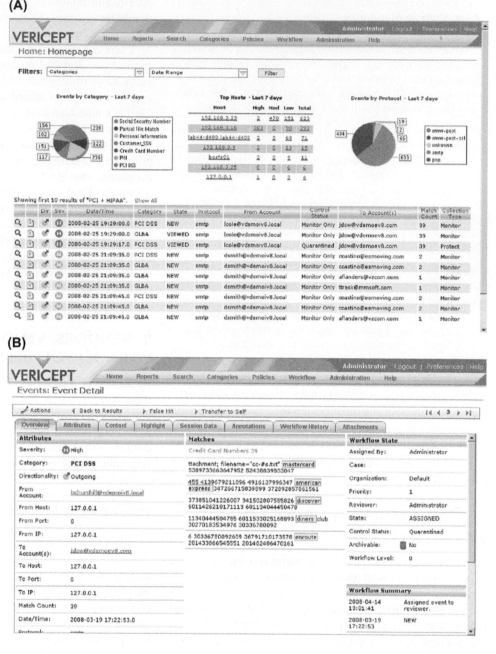

about the DLP space can be found on the Internet for free and can provide an unbiased view from a third party of things that should be evaluated during the selection process.

10. SUMMARY

DLP is an important tool that should at least be evaluated by organizations that are looking to protect their employees, customers, and stakeholders. An effectively implemented DLP application can augment current security

safeguards. A well-thought-out strategy for a DLP application and implementation should be designed first before a purchase. All parts of the organization are likely to be impacted by DLP, and IT should not be the only organization to evaluate and create policies. A holistic approach will help foster a successful implementation that is supported by the DLP vendor and other departments, and ultimately the employees should improve the data risk profile of an organization. The main goal is to keep the brand name and reputation of the organization safe and to continue to operate with minimal data security interruptions. Many types of DLP approaches are available in the market today; picking the right vendor and product with the right features and functions can foster best practices, augment already implemented employee training and policies, and ultimately safeguard the most critical data assets of the organization.

Finally, let's move on to the real interactive part of this Chapter: review questions/exercises, hands-on projects, case projects, and optional team case project. The answers and/or solutions by chapter can be found in the Online Instructor's Solutions Manual.

CHAPTER REVIEW QUESTIONS/ EXERCISES

True/False

1. True or False? The disgruntled insider, working from within an organization, is a principal source of computer crimes.
2. True or False? Even before DLP became a concept, IT organizations have not been practicing the tenets of DLP for years.
3. True or False? Data loss protection is a term that has percolated up from the alphabet soup of computer security concepts in the past few years.
4. True or False? A unreasonable place to begin talking about DLP is with the department of the organization that handles corporate policy and/or governance.
5. True or False? Employees are given data "pipes" to not do their jobs with enabling technology provided by the IT organization.

Multiple Choice

1. Embarking on a _____ evaluation or implementation can be a straightforward exercise.
   A. Reputation
   B. Internet filters
   C. DLP
   D. Encrypted
   E. Content-control software
2. What occurs when the DLP application-monitoring or DLP application-blocking techniques wrongly classify a legitimate transmission or event as "uninteresting" and, as a result, the event must be remediated anyway?
   A. Opinity
   B. Web content filtering
   C. Scale
   D. False positive
   E. Active monitoring
3. The way that most DLP applications capture interesting events is through different kinds of:
   A. Organizations
   B. Rapleaf

C. Analysis engines
D. Content
E. Security

4. There are many different forms of DLP applications, depending on the velocity and location of the:
   A. Keyword lists
   B. Denial of service attack
   C. Sensitive data
   D. Port traffic
   E. Taps
5. What is an easy place to start implementing a DLP application because most can function in "passive" mode, meaning it looks at only a copy of the actual data egressing/ingressing the network?
   A. Systems security plan
   B. TrustPlus
   C. Denying service
   D. Decision making
   E. Data in motion

EXERCISE

Problem

Data loss protection should be designed to help you improve endpoint security. With implementation, managed security services, and software, you should be able to protect sensitive data that is accessed, stored and transmitted on your endpoint devices. In other words, you should be able to do what else to protect your data?

Hands-on Projects

Project

You need to prevent sensitive data loss across your network without introducing complexity to the IT environment. You should also be able to provide a comprehensive solution that helps prevent data loss through enhanced visibility and control of all network ports and internal traffic. In other words, you should be able to do what else to protect your data?

Case Projects

Problem

You need to protect business data at rest, in motion, and in use, even beyond the enterprise network-without increasing complexity in your IT environment. You should also be able to use PGP encryption to provide a comprehensive solution that helps protect sensitive data across endpoints, removable storage media, and e-mail, against loss or unauthorized access. In other words, you should also be able to do what else to protect your data?

Optional Team Case Project

Problem

You need visibility into your information and how it is handled in order to protect sensitive data on endpoints against loss and unauthorized access. You should also be able to provide a comprehensive solution designed to automatically discover and classify sensitive data on desktops and servers, and monitor the data as it is used and exchanged. The solution helps enforce corporate security policies in real time and reduces the risk of data loss or misuse. In other words, you should also be able to do what else to protect your data?

Chapter 89

Satellite Cyber Attack Search and Destroy

Jeffrey Bardin

Treadstone, Barre, MA, Unites States

In the movie *Enemy of the State*, satellites have a vital role in making the viewer believe in the ultimate power of the National Security Agency (NSA). Satellites are repurposed and moved around the sky in moments. They peer down from the heavens, tracking the hero's movements, able to determine tiepin logos and license plate expiration dates. Viewers are made to believe that satellites are godlike, roving the atmosphere, seeing everything we do. The NSA does employ satellites for signals and other intelligence; however, it is the National Reconnaissance Office that normally owns and operates US spy satellites. The closest Hollywood has come to reality in spy satellites was during the movie *Patriot Games*, when Harrison Ford had to look at images through a microscope, trying to ascertain the identity, much less the gender, of people in the photographs. Grainy images with shadows that look like other images are more in line with reality.

When thinking of satellites, thoughts often drift to Hollywood's images and the surveillance aspects of their capabilities. However, satellites have many roles in society. They provide methods for communication and remote sensing of critical infrastructures, deliver global positioning systems (GPSs) for navigation, keep us occupied with broadband for entertainment, and support mechanisms for videoconferencing and telemedicine. We never see them, but they are essential components in daily human activity. According to the Satellite Industry Association, nearly 37% of all operational satellites are used for business communications. Civil communications accounts for 11%; military communications for 9%; military and surveillance, 9%; navigation, 8%; remote sensing, 9%; and meteorological, 4%. The Satellite Industry Association also maintains information about world satellite industry revenue. Satellite growth increased significantly between 2005 and 2011

at an average of 11% per year in growth. The Satellite Industry Association states that satellite services continue to represent the single largest industry sector driven by satellite-TV growth at around 10% [1]. Space launch industry and satellite manufacturing revenues reflect a history of aggregate growth by yearly fluctuation, whereas ground equipment revenue growth reflects slight but relatively consistent year-on-year consumer and network equipment sales. It is safe to say that satellites have a prominent role in everyday life.

Very small aperture terminals (VSATs) are prevalent in everyday lives. They consist of a parabolic dish and associated hardware and software. The purpose is to send and receive (uplink and downlink) signals via a satellite. They dot the landscape on homes, recreational vehicles, and boats. Human reliance on satellites is growing at an exponential rate. As with any growing commercial opportunity, security is less than the primary concern. Economics drives the opportunity.

1. HACKS, INTERFERENCE, AND JAMMING

April 2007 started a series of issues with satellites. Tamil rebels in Sri Lanka were accused of hacking the Intelsat satellite positioned over the Indian Ocean for communicating propaganda [2]. Intelsat responded, indicating this to be a case of signal piracy (not hacking) that would not be tolerated. In a response to the Intelsat press release, the Tamil Tiger rebels indicated that they were not accessing the satellite illegally, and therefore no signal piracy had occurred. The rebels intimated a relationship with the service provider for the satellite but would provide no further explanation [3].

Computer and Information Security Handbook. http://dx.doi.org/10.1016/B978-0-12-803843-7.00089-2

In 2007, the media reported that National Aeronautics and Space Administration (NASA) satellite Landsat-7 used for ground mapping was hacked, experiencing 12 min of interference [4]. The same article goes on to state that in 2008 another NASA satellite, Terra AM-1, was hacked for 2 min in June and for 9 min in October. The problem with the articles and subsequent follow-on by the media as well as the NASA Office of Inspector General is the depiction that the satellites were hacked. These two events were not cyber-related events but events characterized by the interference and jamming of radio signals to disrupt satellite send and receive transmissions. The point is that this had nothing to do with cybersecurity but rather with traditional satellite communication protocols using radio transmissions.

There have been writings on the Internet regarding the potential for hacking NASA satellites to access the *Curiosity* land rover on Mars. Although this is pure speculation, much discussion has occurred as a result of the subject. The initial topic focused on the pushing of updates to change *Curiosity's* payload. The idea would be to intercept or to play man-in-the-middle attack against communications between satellites and the rover. Although highly unlikely, the impact would be significant if such an activity occurred. It highlights a renewed focus on satellites as objects for disruption of command, control, communications, and computers. The Jet Propulsion Laboratory (JPL) in Pasadena, California, houses the scientists, engineers, specialists, and mission control center for *Curiosity*. NASA missions employ a highly compartmentalized framework for computer systems tied to the mission. They are self-contained systems located in self-contained buildings running variations of operating systems or operating systems created specifically for the mission at hand, operated by personnel vetted on several levels. Once a configuration of the operating system, firmware, or other related software is proven to work per the specifications of the designers and engineers, the configuration is locked down as a module ready for execution. It is highly unlikely that a hack or intercept of the encoded transmission between JPL mission control in Pasadena and the *Curiosity* rover on Mars could occur. Such an unlikely occurrence would have an enormous impact on the mission. However, the mission of discovering life on another planet is hardly a target for exploitation that a foreign intelligence service would undertake. It is more likely that a foreign intelligence service would target earth-born operations.

In October 2011, Creech Air Force Base (AFB) was the subject of a malicious software (malware) attack on the Predator and Reaper drones. It was reported that a keystroke logger infected the ground control stations for drones operating in the Afghanistan theater. The malware proved to be a resilient strain that continued to reoccur after multiple system cleanings. The malware was most likely

created by a foreign nation-state intent on learning as much information as possible about the United States' drone activities. What was not stated in the press is that the 30th Reconnaissance Squadron of the US Air Force operates out of Creech AFB. This is significant because this squadron operates the RQ-170 Sentinel unmanned aerial vehicle (UAV): the same UAV captured by Iran a mere 2 months after the keystroke logger event at Creech AFB. In what could be termed a coincidence, Iran stated that its army's electronic warfare unity had downed an RQ-170 violating Iranian airspace by overriding the UAV's controls. An Iranian engineer later stated that Iran used GPS coordinate spoofing, fooling the UAV into thinking it was landing at an air base in Afghanistan. The Iranian engineer further claimed that it was easy to exploit the navigational weakness in the drone system. It is possible that signal jamming of the encrypted channels used by the military forced the UAV to revert to a communications failover process that used unencrypted methods to communicate [5]. Once the failover took place, Iranian engineers were able to manipulate the drone GPS. If the Iranian claim of control override is true, the keystroke logging event at Creech AFB takes on new meaning for cybersecurity surrounding ground control stations for satellite-based weapons systems. Unsubstantiated claims of Russian or Chinese intelligence services actually executing the keystroke logger and subsequently downing of the RQ-170 become a potential premise that should be explored further. It demonstrates the need for improved cybersecurity measures for each component of the satellite command and control ecosystem. It also demonstrates that traditional cybersecurity countermeasures are not sufficient to prevent penetration, malware infection, or both. In most cases, ground control stations are air-gapped from other networks. Air gapping is a method of security control that delivers network compartmentalization, keeping all networks and devices not required to operate, manage, monitor, and/or control a sensitive system entirely separate. This is usually accompanied by stringent rules related to the use of removable media. It has been intimated that infected, nonauthorized hardware was attached to the air-gapped system, providing for the infection of the target ground control stations. Malware of this type with a keystroke logger payload is used for cyber intelligence collection for later disposition and cyber countermeasures to be deployed by the initiating entity. The ability for the malware to communicate data collection efforts back to a collection hub also requires additional review because the methods of cybersecurity detection are often devised to keep perpetrators out, not to prevent them from leaving as an additional level of security. It is interesting that a 2002 Government Accountability Office (GAO) report specifically warned of spoofing as a content-oriented threat for commercial satellites and the unauthorized modification or deliberate corruption of network information, services, and databases, including malware implanted into computer systems referencing ground control stations as a target [6]. Not much later, we have experienced exactly what the GAO warned against.

In June 2012, a group of researchers at the University of Texas at Austin used the spoofing method described by the Iranians to hack the GPS system of a drone. This demonstrates the viability of the claim and presents another issue for concern: Adversaries have the ability to both commandeer and use the drones as flying missiles, armed or not. The cost to spoof the drone was reported to be in the range of £700 or about $1100. This ratio of cost to the potential impact is a cornerstone of asymmetric warfare exhibited by Al-Qa'eda on 9/11. Questions regarding what security controls were or were not in place continue because US military authorities maintain a tight lid on the exact problems and remediation methods employed since the downing of the RQ-170. Additional rumors surfaced that Iran overrode the RQ-170 self-destruct capabilities, whereas others have claimed that no such capabilities exist on the drone.

A few years ago, a $29 program called SkyGrabber (Fig. 89.1) made the news. SkyGrabber allowed interception of packet radio service from a laptop connected to a small satellite. Insurgents in Iraq (Fig. 89.2) were using and training others to use SkyGrabber software to intercept satellite and small drones communications used to scout positions of enemies before special forces or military activities in that particular area. Insurgents were able to intercept these communications with the $29 program largely because of the lack of security regarding communications between satellite and drone. This flaw was

FIGURE 89.1 Jihadist use of SkyGrabber.

actually well known by the designers of the system. They did not apply the appropriate security controls because applying encryption to the process slowed communications down to the point where they thought it was ineffective. Regardless of their decision, insurgents intercepted this information for some time before being discovered. SkyGrabber uses what is called general packet radio service or GPRS. GPRS is a nonvoice service that is added to networks over 2.5- to 3-gigabit wireless communications. Consumers know this as 3G or 4G speeds [7]. The service uses Internet Protocol (IP) transmissions to its advantage. Because IP traffic is made of packets, the network does not need to have continuous data transmission. Each channel is divided eight time slots, with a maximum data transmission of 13.4 kb per second. One of these time slots is used for control, and normal allocation reserves two slots for voice traffic as well. Asymmetric traffic (more downloads and uploads) dictates the distribution of the remaining time slots.

Requests are sent via the local area network connection whereas responses are received from the satellite; because requests are usually small and responses are large, a narrowband connection is enough for requests. At the same time, responses were received at a high rate of 4 megabits per second, which makes working with the Internet comfortable. If there is no encryption, it is open for interception. When the activity of the insurgents using SkyGrabber was made public, many pundits and even cybersecurity professionals called this interception hacking. What needs to be understood is that this was not a hack because there was in fact nothing to hack. Without encryption, the communication mechanism is open for interception. Hacking refers to the reconfiguring or reprogramming of the system to function in ways not facilitated by the owner, administrator, or designer. The term has several related meanings in the information technology (IT) industry. A hack may refer to a clever quick fix to a computer program problem or to what may be perceived to be a clumsy solution to a problem. The terms *hack* and *hacking* are also used to refer to a modification of the programmer device to give the user access to features that were otherwise unavailable, such as do-it-yourself circuit bending [8]. It is from this usage that the term *hacking* is often employed incorrectly to refer to more nefarious criminal uses such as identity theft, credit card fraud, or other actions categorized as computer crime. Because there is a distinction between security breaking and hacking, a better term for security breaking would be *cracking* [8]. As we already know, responses are received from the satellite. However, the satellite cannot send data specifically to a particular user and so instead sends data to all dishes that receive a signal from it. Therefore, if you have the proper equipment, the signal is just waiting in the airwaves to be had.

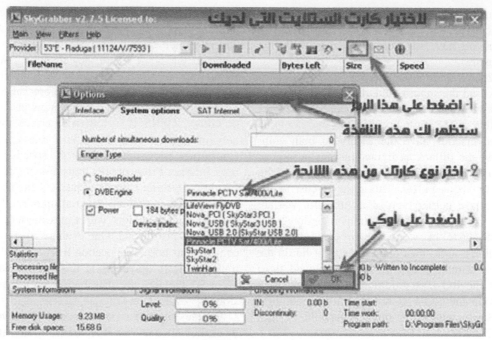

FIGURE 89.2 SkyGrabber.

As already surmised, it is not enough to position a small satellite dish; that dish will also receive a signal with the same data that other satellites receive. The satellite dish may get the signal, but the question remains as to how to extract data from the intercepted signal. That is the purpose of the SkyGrabber program. The program captures what other satellite dishes download and saves the captured information to a laptop. Internet access is not required for this interception. The satellite dish needs to be rotated toward the provider, and the SkyGrabber program will perform the data extraction, with some configuration. If the transmission is encrypted or encoded, data extraction is prevented.

As with any IT, information security and information assurance need to be built in from the beginning. Cybersecurity professionals have been stating this for years. Regardless, it seems that in the satellite industry as in many others, information security controls will not be built in until such time as a painful breach has occurred. This has been the standard mode of operation for designers, developers, and engineers for years.

Identifying Threats

In 1998 when Presidential Decision Directive 63 was originally issued, satellites were not included in the nation's critical infrastructures. This was seen as a significant oversight in the satellite industry. The GAO report in 2002 referenced issues concerning security regarding satellites and covered several different areas concerning security.

The GAO report covered secure data links and communication ground stations. The report also discussed issues referencing the use of satellites that have certain security controls especially established to enhance the availability of the satellite. Since the release of that report in 2002, much has been done to bolster the security of satellites. Satellites consist of ground station tracking and control links, which are referred to as a tracking telemetry and control links, and data links and satellites. The GAO report examined unintentional threats to commercial satellite systems and divided the threats into three different areas:

1. Ground-based threats
2. Space-based threats
3. Interference-oriented threats [6].

Examples of a ground-based threat could be naturally occurring ones such as acts of God, earthquakes, hurricanes, tornadoes, and floods. Space-based threats could be related to solar activity, different temperature variations, and different types of space debris as more countries launch satellites. Interference-oriented threats to commercial satellite systems focus more on IT. This deals with unintentional or intentional human interference caused by terrestrial and space-based wireless systems or computer systems intended to cause harm. Interference- and content-oriented threats that are intentional threaten commercial satellite systems with malware, denial of service attacks, distributed denial of service attacks, service moving data interception, and potential man-in-the-middle attack methods. This includes the jamming communications between ground stations and satellite systems. Over the years, the US government has worked to ensure the confidentiality, integrity, and availability of satellite systems, although the focus on security is limited based on risk. The likelihood of such an attack has not been high, although attacks are increasing each year as more attention is given to satellites. Because the attacks have not been of paramount concern, satellites related to cybersecurity controls have been limited in scope and function. It is probable that security controls will increase directly with the increase in threats and validated exploitation.

Communicating With Satellites

There are several methods for communicating with satellites. Many commercial satellites use baseband signals, a method that allows for only one car on the road at a time, so to speak. Only one transmission can occur at a time, either from the ground station to the satellite or from the satellite to the ground station. Direct broadcast satellites (DBSs) are common to consumers. DBS is used by vendors such as DISH and DirecTV. DBS transmissions use various methods to secure data transfer:

- Basic Interoperable Scrambling System (BISS) is a satellite signal scrambling system developed by the European Broadcasting Union and a consortium of hardware manufacturers. Before its development, ad hoc or "occasional use" satellite news feeds were transmitted either using proprietary encryption methods (PowerVu) or with no encryption. Unencrypted satellite feeds allowed anyone with the correct equipment to view the program material.
- PowerVu is a conditional access system for digital television developed by Scientific Atlanta [1]. It is used for professional broadcasting, notably by Retevision, Bloomberg Television, Discovery Channel, AFRTS, and American Forces Network. PowerVu is also used by cable companies to prevent viewing by unauthorized viewers. PowerVu has decoders that decode signals from certain satellites for cable distribution services. These decoders can also be used just like the Free-to-Air satellite receivers if properly configured. PowerVu is considered highly secure because it uses a complicated system to authorize each PowerVu receiver and trace its history of ownership and use. Most PowerVu users are professional cable or satellite companies, using the service and equipment for signal redistribution, because regular users cannot afford it. On March 10, 2010, a hacker called Colibri published a cryptanalysis of a PowerVU system implementation, after previous work done in 2005. The hacker described a flawed design that can be used to gain access to the encryption keys and ultimately decrypt the transmitted content.

- DigiCipher 2 (DCII) is a proprietary standard format of digital signal transmission and encryption with Moving Picture Experts Group (MPEG)-2 signal video compression used on many communications satellite television and audio signals. The DCII standard was originally developed in 1997 by General Instrument, which is now the Home and Network Mobility division of Motorola [9]. The original attempt for a North American digital signal encryption and compression standard was DigiCipher 1, which was used most notably in the now-defunct PrimeStar medium-power DBS system during the early 1990s. The DCII standard predates wide acceptance of digital video broadcasting (DVB)-based digital terrestrial television compression (although not cable or satellite DVB) and therefore is incompatible with the DVB standard [9]. The primary difference between DigiCipher 2 and DVB lies in how each standard handles System Information. DigiCipher 2 also relies on the fact that its signals must be understood in terms of a virtual channel number in addition to the DCII signal's downlink frequency, whereas DVB signals have no virtual channel number [9]. Approximately 70% of newer first-generation digital cable networks in North America use the 4DTV/DigiCipher 2 format. The use of DCII is most prevalent in North American digital cable television set top boxes. DCII is also used on Motorola's 4DTV digital satellite television tuner and Shaw Direct's DBS receiver [9].

Scrambling and descrambling equipment for cable and satellite televisions has been the norm for over 30 years. The solutions have evolved over the years to more advanced solutions for DBS.

There are other encryption methods for DBS, such as the use of smart cards allowing a single user to access television shows based on the smart card, receiver hardware, and associated software that securely and accurately identifies users and their individual subscriptions. This is truly commonplace in the commercial market. Advances have been made to incorporate the Advanced Encryption Standard in satellite transport networks, providing much greater security using encryption keys. Regardless of the security solution in use, the intent is to protect pay-TV signals enforcing subscription-based access to available programs.

Improving Cybersecurity

According to a 2009 report from IGI Global, as written by Marlyn Kemper Littman, entitled "Satellite Network Security," satellite transmissions are subject to lengthy delays, low bandwidth, and high bit-error rates that adversely affect real-time, interactive applications such as videoconferences and lead to data corruption, performance degradation, and cyber incursions [10]. Littman goes on to say that multiple layers of security covering all aspects of the satellite's ecosystem are needed to protect satellite networks adequately. This includes policies and legislation requiring minimum necessary security protocols and standards. The Defense Information Systems Network Satellite Transmission Services Global (DSTS-G) Performance Work Statement states that:

DODD 8581.1 E requires that commercial satellites used by the Department of Defense employ NSA-approved cryptography to encrypt and authenticate commands to the satellite if supporting Mission Assurance Category (MAC) I or II missions as defined in DoD Directive 8500.1. While NSA approved cryptography is preferred for satellites supporting MAC III missions, cryptography commensurate with commercial best practices is acceptable for encrypting and authenticating commands to satellites that only support MAC III missions.

The change in cryptography requirements is for commercial interoperability with Department of Defense (DoD) satellite systems. These changes went into effect in 2005 and represent a shift to encrypt using the latest technologies transmitted over higher bandwidth, using mission-specific data networks. The change also calls for continued modifications to the security environment as new threats appear and new solutions are available. The cryptography requirements directly align to the Satellite Internet Protocol Security (SatIPSec) initiative from 2004. This protocol provides for encrypted transmissions using a standard symmetric method that clearly identifies the sender and receiver. SatIPSec used in conjunction with the Satellite-Reliable Multicast Transport Protocol, which provides secure transmission methods for audio and video files, enhances the satellite ecosystem security posture.

There are several areas for improvement in satellite cybersecurity. As with many commercial ventures, the sharing of information is limited owing to the potential for leaking intellectual property or proprietary processes, procedures, and methods. The information and cybersecurity industry is rife with examples of limited information sharing. Most companies are remiss to share information on breaches because of the potential embarrassment public awareness could bring. What is missed is the opportunity to share remediation strategies and information about the attacker. This actionable intelligence could prevent other organizations from experiencing the same fate. Methods of remediation that are successful should be shared across the satellite industry and within federal and state governments. The opportunity to share effective security practices could vastly improve satellite cyber defenses. Information sharing coupled with the appropriate education and awareness-raising efforts for the satellite industry is an effective method of propagating actionable intelligence.

Until recently, organizations did not agree on what represented an attack. The underlying issue is the use of a common taxonomy relative to satellite security. Incorporating already defined words, phrases, and concepts from the information security community can and will speed up the adoption and integration of a common book of knowledge regarding satellite cybersecurity. Just as websites and applications on the Internet are subject to continuous probes, scans, denial of service, and distributed denial of service activity, the satellite industry faces continuous intentional interference and jamming. The satellite industry could learn how to adopt methods of interference and jamming prevention by incorporating proven principles and methods achieved over years of parallel activity on the Internet. In addition, organizations managing satellites need to distinguish between advertent and inadvertent events and events that are intentional and unintentional. The data points gathered by the scores of government and commercial satellite organizations worldwide could be organized into information that is analyzed for links, tendencies, and trends to help devices' ever-changing defenses to transmission penetration and jamming. The underlying premise is information sharing for the benefit of nonhostile entities to improve their defensive, preventive, and even predictive countermeasures through intelligence analysis of satellite-specific data points using proven methods in cybersecurity. An organization such as the National Council of Information Sharing and Analysis Centers (ISAC) could sponsor or propose an ISAC specific to the satellite industry adopting proven methods across member ISACs to assist in information-sharing activities. The Communications ISAC could further expand into the satellite industry with specific goals, emphasizing sharing information used to mitigate and prevent typical satellite-related impacts on confidentiality, integrity, and availability.

Many members of the cybersecurity industry may overlook the physical security aspects of satellite security. As any centralized management function, satellite monitoring and maintenance are performed from a ground location. Data centers require hardened perimeters and multiple layers of redundancy. Satellite ground controls stations require the same level of attention to security detail. These facilities should have standardized closed-circuit television and access control methods. Security guards performing 24×7 monitoring and response and employee training and awareness programs must be in place. Many ground control stations are not equipped to withstand electromagnetic plus radiological fallout, or instances of force majeure. They lack what many in the IT industry would term standard requirements for availability. Furthermore, many ground control stations are within proximity of public areas, providing potentially easy access for those with malicious intent. Standards for the continuity of operations for ground control stations should include conditioned and generated power, as well as backup locations in varied geographic locations with an inventory of equipment available in case of an incident. Ground control centers should also practice disaster recovery and business continuity through regularly scheduled exercises. The points mentioned here are standard functions of an IT data center that can and should be applied to the satellite industry. All ground control stations should have centralized and backup network operations, security operations, and satellite operations centers integrated into a cohesive monitoring and data-sharing environment.

Several "anti" solutions should be tested and embedded in each satellite's ecosystem based on risk. Sensitive or military satellites should be required to provide antijamming, antispoofing, and antitampering capabilities consistently and continually that can be monitored by the ground control station. Ground control stations need to be outfitted with prevention-based cybersecurity solutions that prevent or detect penetrations, prevent malware and data exfiltration, and monitor, record, and analyze malware characteristics.

Another concept for all US-based satellites is the use of all appropriate satellites to act as a sensor while in orbit. The idea is for each satellite to share information on surveilled targets after agreeing to install a government payload or sensor that provides a space-based surveillance and warning network. This concept borrows from cybersecurity technologies using sensors to monitor network activity across government or commercial entities. The government could offer some type of concession or support to the commercial organization in exchange for carrying the nonintrusive payload.

Although many of the recommendations are already a regular occurrence in military satellite systems, commercial systems do not necessarily require the same level of security or scrutiny. Regardless, interference and jamming of satellite-controlled devices under the military's purview and the penetration of malware of ground control stations indicate a need for increased attention to security, whether cyber or of a more traditional need. A call for all satellite ecosystems to undergo assessment and authorization procedures as defined in the Federal Information Security Management Act and as detailed on the DoD Information Assurance Certification and Accreditation Process (DIACAP) may be warranted based on the role satellites have in critical infrastructures. The use of DIACAP and DSTS-G can arrive at cybersecurity framework standardization for satellites (see checklist: An Agenda for Action for Implementing Cybersecurity Framework Standardization Methods for Satellites). They can help drive mitigation measures using onboard satellite radio-frequency encryption systems.

An Agenda for Action for Implementing Cybersecurity Framework Standardization Methods for Satellites

Standardization can introduce methods such as carrier lockup, uniqueness, autonomy, diversity, and out-of-band commanding (check all tasks completed):

_____**1.** Carrier lockup is a method used to maintain steady and continuous communication between satellite and the ground control stations, ensuring no other transmissions can be inserted from unauthorized ground control stations [11].

_____**2.** Uniqueness provides each satellite with a unique address much like a personal computer's media access control address [11].

_____**3.** Autonomy is a predefined protocol of self-operation, giving the satellite the capability to operate autonomously for certain periods in case there is some type of interference or jamming [11].

_____**4.** Diversity provides diverse and redundant routes for transmitting data, much like the use of multiple Internet connections from different providers in a data center [11].

_____**5.** Out-of-band commanding provides unique frequencies not shared by any other traffic or ground control stations [11].

When it comes to ground-based network operations centers and security operations centers, traditional cybersecurity standards and controls apply for both physical and virtual measures. Much the same applies to interference. Interference in the satellite ecosystem comes from several sources such as human error, other satellite interference, terrestrial interference, equipment failure, and intentional interference and jamming [11].

The satellite industry continues to take steps to mitigate and deliver countermeasures to various types of interference. Use of various types of shielding, filters, and regular training and awareness can help reduce most types of interference. Intentional or purposeful interference is not remediated through these measures. The satellite industry has created an IT mirror process and procedure called the Purposeful Interference Response Team (PIRT). Many of the same methods, processes, and procedures used in a computer emergency response team program have been adopted for use in the PIRT. Root cause analysis of PIRT incidents is shared back into the process and out to satellite owners to ensure that effective security practices and countermeasures are shared across the industry. Communications and transmission security measures are employed using standards such as those defined by the National Institutes of Standards and Technology and its Federal Information Process Standard 140−2.

As the satellite industry continues to move toward traditional IT-type hybrid networks, satellites will be subjected to the same types of IT vulnerabilities that ground-based systems experience today. Issues associated with this migration are apparent but so, too, are the solutions. Cybersecurity standards, processes, procedures, and methods are available without the need for creating them anew. Regardless, their application is required in the design phase of the satellite ecosystem to be fully effective. On-board IT systems provide greater features and real-time modifications, but they also introduce traditional IT vulnerabilities and exploits if not managed properly.

2. SUMMARY

Contrary to what is portrayed in Hollywood, satellites cannot be immediately retasked, nor can they see and hear everything humans do. Satellites have progressed substantially over the years, providing society with cell phone services; pay-TV solutions; hand-held global position systems; GPS for automobiles, motorcycles, and boats; telemedicine; and law enforcement. Satellites have roles in society that are commonplace. The ubiquitous nature of satellites combined with advances in computing power and capabilities is a double-edged sword for satellite ecosystems. The past several years have seen a parallel increase in satellite deployments and efforts to interfere purposefully with satellites, jam satellite transmissions, and penetrate components of the satellite ecosystem with malicious code. In many cases, radio-frequency interference and jamming have been confused with hacking. This may change in time as satellites increase the use of onboard computer capabilities with remote updating needs and patching requirements, much like land-based IT systems. Foreign intelligence services continue to target US satellite ecosystems in particular, with ground control stations as the path of least resistance method of penetration for traditional computer hacking and malware distribution. Once penetrated, the malware can perform various tasks based on its payload. To date, the payload has been intelligence gathering. Future penetrations could result in cyber sabotage or terrorist activities, resulting in the loss of life and disruptions to critical infrastructures.

The need to build cybersecurity into satellite ecosystems can remediate risk at inception. The risk-based approach, heavily reported to be the best method of cybersecurity posture management, could in fact be nothing more than a step toward developing a cybersecurity life cycle, one that could mature appreciably by transparently embedding cybersecurity into every facet of every process, procedure, method, and component of the satellite ecosystem.

Finally, let us move on to the real interactive part of this chapter: review questions/exercises, hands-on projects, case

projects, and the optional team case project. The answers and/or solutions by chapter can be found in the Online Instructor's Solutions Manual.

CHAPTER REVIEW QUESTIONS/ EXERCISES

True/False

1. True or False? Very small aperture terminals (VSATs) are prevalent in everyday lives.
2. True or False? There have been writings on the Internet of the potential for hacking NASA satellites to access the *Curiosity* land rover on Venus.
3. True or False? In October 2011, Wright Patterson Air Force Base was the subject of a malware attack on the Predator and Reaper drones.
4. True or False? In June 2012, a group of researchers at the University of Texas at Austin used the spoofing method described by the Iranians to hack the stealth system of a drone.
5. True or False? A few years ago, a $29 program called SkyGrabber made the news. The program allowed interception of packet radio service from a laptop connected to a large satellite.

Multiple Choice

1. Examples of the _____ could be those that are naturally occurring, such as acts of God, earthquakes, hurricanes, tornadoes, and floods.
   A. Reputation
   B. Internet filters
   C. Ground-based threat
   D. Encrypted
   E. Content-control software
2. There are several methods for communicating with satellites. Many commercial satellites use _____, a method that allows for only one car on the road at a time, so to speak.
   A. Opinity
   B. Web content filtering
   C. Scale
   D. Baseband signals
   E. Active monitoring
3. What is a satellite signal scrambling system developed by the European Broadcasting Union and a consortium of hardware manufacturers?
   A. Basic Interoperable Scrambling System (BISS)
   B. Rapleaf
   C. Worms
   D. Content
   E. Security

4. What is a conditional access system for digital television developed by Scientific Atlanta?
   A. PowerVu
   B. Denial of service attack
   C. Venyo
   D. Port traffic
   E. Taps
5. What is a proprietary standard format of digital signal transmission and encryption with MPEG-2 signal video compression used on many communications satellite television and audio signals?
   A. Systems security plan
   B. DigiCipher 2 (DCII)
   C. Denying service
   D. Decision making
   E. URL lists

EXERCISE
Problem

A GAO report examined unintentional threats to commercial satellite systems. The report broke the threats into three different areas. What were those areas?

Hands-on Projects
Project

Please explain in explicit detail the Basic Interoperable Scrambling System.

Case Projects
Problem

Please explain PowerVu in explicit detail.

Optional Team Case Project
Problem

Please explain DigiCipher 2 in explicit detail.

REFERENCES

[1] C. David, State of the Satellite Industry, Washington, DC, November 13, 2006.
[2] D. Morrill, Hack a Satellite while it Is in Orbit, April 13, 2007. http://it.toolbox.com/blogs/managing-infosec/hack-a-satellite-while-it-is-in-orbit-15690.
[3] Sri Lankan Rebels Deny Illegal Use of US Satellite, April 2007. http://www.radioaustralia.net.au/international/2007-04-13/sri-lankan-rebels-deny-illegal-use-of-us-satellite/721866.
[4] C. Franzen, Report: Chinese Military Suspected in Hacks of U.S. Government Satellites, October 27, 2011. http://idealab.talkingpointsmemo.com/2011/10/report-chinese-military-suspected-in-hacks-of-us-government-satellites.php.
[5] N. Owano, RQ-170 Drone's Ambush Facts Spilled by Iranian Engineer, December 17, 2011. http://phys.org/news/2011-12-rq-drone-ambush-facts-iranian.html.
[6] Office, United States General Accounting, Critical Infrastructure Protection Commercial Satellite Security Should Be More Fully Addressed, United States GAO, Washington, 2002.
[7] What Is Meant by Gprs Connection?, 9 1, 2006. http://answers.yahoo.com/question/index?qid=20060828085726AAKiqNr.
[8] Free Engineering Seminar PPT Slides DOC, February 10, 2012. http://www.urslides.com/.
[9] DigiCipher 2, January 1, 2012. http://mp3umax.org/?p=DigiCipher_2.
[10] M.K. Littman, Satellite Network Security, Nova Southeastern University, USA, Fort Lauderdale, 2009.
[11] Committee, President's National Security Telecommunications Advisory, NSTAC Report to the President on Commercial Satellite Communications Mission Assurance, NSTAC, Washington, DC, 2009.

Chapter 90

Verifiable Voting Systems

Thea Peacock[1], Peter Y.A. Ryan[1], Steve Schneider[2] and Zhe Xia[2]

[1]University of Luxemburg, Coudenhove-Kalergi, Luxembourg; [2]University of Surrey, Guildford, Surrey, United Kingdom

Note: This chapter is available in its entirety online at store.elsevier.com/product.jsp?isbn= 9780128038437 (click the Resources tab at the bottom of the page).

1. ABSTRACT

The introduction of technology into voting systems can bring a number of benefits, such as improving accessibility, remote voting, and efficient, accurate processing of votes. A voting system that uses electronic technology in any part of processing the votes, from vote capture and transfer through to vote tallying, is known as an e-voting system. In addition to the undoubted benefits, the introduction of such technology introduces particular security challenges, some of which are unique to voting systems because of their specific nature and requirements. The key role that voting systems play in democratic elections means that such systems must not only be secure and trustworthy, but must be seen by the electorate to be secure and trustworthy. This chapter emphasizes the challenge to reconcile the secrecy of the ballot, with demonstrable correctness of the result.

2. CONTENTS

Chapter 91

Advanced Data Encryption

Pramod Pandya

California State University, Fullerton, Avante, CA, United States

1. MATHEMATICAL CONCEPTS REVIEWED

In this section we introduce the necessary mathematics of cryptography: Integer and Modular Arithmetic, Fermat's Theorem [1]:

Euler's Phi-Function $\phi(n)$

Euler's totient function finds the number of integers that are both smaller than n and coprime to n:

1. $\phi(1) = 0$
2. $\phi(p) = p-1$ if p is a prime
3. $\phi(m \times n) = \phi(n) \times \phi(m)$ if m and n are coprime
4. $\phi(p^e) = p^e - p^{e-1}$ if p is a prime

Examples:

$$\phi(2) = 1; \phi(3) = 2; \phi(4) = 2; \phi(5) = 4; \phi(6)$$
$$= 2; \phi(7) = 6; \phi(8) = 4$$

Fermat's Little Theorem

In the 1970s, the creators of digital signatures and public-key cryptography realized that the framework for their research was already laid out in the body of work by Fermat and Euler. Generation of a key in public-key cryptography, involves an exponentiation modulo in a given modulus:

$a \equiv b \pmod{m}$ then $a^e \equiv b^e \pmod{m}$ for any positive integer e

$a^{e+d} \equiv a^e \cdot a^d \pmod{m}$

$(ab)^e \equiv a^e \cdot b^e \pmod{m}$

$(a^d)^e \equiv a^{de} \pmod{m}$

Theorem: Let p be a prime number:

1. If a is coprime to p, then $a^{p-1} \equiv 1 \pmod{p}$
2. $a^p \equiv a \pmod{p}$ for any integer a

Theorem: Let p and q be distinct primes:

1. If a is coprime to pq, then

$$a^{k(p-1)(q-1)} \equiv 1 \pmod{pq}, \text{k is any integer}$$

2. For any integer a,

$$a^{k(p-1)(q-1)+1} \equiv a \pmod{pq}, \text{k is any positive integer}$$

Discrete Logarithm

In this section we will deal with multiplicative group $G = <Z_{n*}, x>$. The order of a finite group is the number of elements in the group G. Let us take an example of a group,

$$G = <Z_{21*}, x>$$

$\phi(21) = \phi(3) \times \phi(7) = 2 \times 6 = 12$, that is, 12 elements in the group, and each is coprime to 21.

$$\{1, 2, 4, 5, 8, 10, 11, 13, 16, 17, 19, 20\}$$

The order of an element, ord(a), is the smallest integer i such that

$$a^i \equiv e \pmod{n}, \text{where } e = 1.$$

Find the order of all elements in $G = <Z_{10*}, x>$

$$\phi(10) = \phi(2) \times \phi(5) = 1 \times 4 = 4$$

$$\{1, 3, 7, 9\}$$

Primitive Roots

In the multiplicative group $G = <Z_{n*}, x>$, when the order of an element is the same as $\phi(n)$, then that element is called the primitive root of the group.

$G = <Z_{8*}, x>$ has no primitive roots. The order of this group is, $\phi(8) = 4$

Computer and Information Security Handbook. http://dx.doi.org/10.1016/B978-0-12-803843-7.00091-0

$$Z_{8*} = \{1, 3, 5, 7\}$$

1, 2, 4 each divide the order of the group which is 4:

$1^1 \equiv 1 \pmod 8$ $\rightarrow \mathrm{ord}(1) = 1$

$3^1 \equiv 3 \pmod 8; 3^2 \equiv 1 \pmod 8$ $\rightarrow \mathrm{ord}(3) = 2$

$5^1 \equiv 5 \pmod 8; 5^2 \equiv 1 \pmod 8$ $\rightarrow \mathrm{ord}(5) = 2$

$7^1 \equiv 7 \pmod 8; 7^2 \equiv 1 \pmod 8$ $\rightarrow \mathrm{ord}(7) = 2$

In the example above, none of the elements have an order of 4; hence this group has no primitive roots. The group $G = <Z_{n*}, x>$ has primitive roots only if n is 2, 4, p^t, or $2p^t$, where p is an odd prime not including 2 and t is an integer.

If the group $G = <Z_{n*}, x>$ has any primitive roots, the number of primitive roots is $\phi(\phi(n))$. If a group, $G = <Z_{n*}, x>$ has primitive roots, then it is cyclic, and each of its primitive root is a generator of the whole group.

Group $G = <Z_{10*}, x>$ has two primitive roots because $\phi(10) = 4$, and $\phi(\phi(10)) = 2$. These two primitive roots are {3, 7}:

$3^1 \bmod 10 = 3 \ \ 3^2 \bmod 10 = 9 \ \ 3^3 \bmod 10 = 7 \ \ 3^4 \bmod 10 = 1$

$7^1 \bmod 10 = 7 \ \ 7^2 \bmod 10 = 9 \ \ 7^3 \bmod 10 = 3 \ \ 7^4 \bmod 10 = 1$

Group, $G = <Z_{p*}, x>$ is always cyclic.
The group $G = <Z_{p*}, x>$ has the following properties:

1. Its elements are from 1 to (p−1) inclusive.
2. It always has primitive roots.
3. It is cyclic, and its elements can be generated using g where x is an integer from 1 to $\phi(n) = p-1$.
4. The primitive roots can be used as the base of logarithm—discrete logarithm.

Modern encryption algorithms such as DES, AES, RSA (Rivest, Shamir, and Adelman), and ElGammal, to name a few, are based on algebraic structures such as Group Theory and Field Theory as well as Number Theory. We will begin with a set S, with finite number of elements, and a binary operation (*) defined between any two elements of the set:

$$*: S \times S \rightarrow S$$

that is, if a and b∈ S, then a*b∈ S. This is important, for it implies that the set is closed under the binary operation. We have seen that the message space is finite, and we want to make sure that any algebraic operation on the message space satisfies the closure property. Hence, we want to treat the message space as a finite set of elements. We will remind the reader that messages that get encrypted must be finally decrypted by the received party; thus encryption algorithm must run in polynomial time. Furthermore, the algorithm must have the property that it be reversible to recover the original message. The goal of encryption is to confuse and diffuse the hacker such that it would make it almost impossible for the hacker to break the encrypted message. Therefore, encryption must consist of finite number substitutions and transpositions. The algebraic structure, Classical Group, facilitates the coding of the encryption algorithm. Next we give some relevant definitions and examples before we proceed to introduce the essential concept of a Galois Field, which is central to formulation of the Rijndael algorithm used in the Advanced Encryption Standard (AES).

Definition Group

A group (G, •) is a finite set G together with an operation • satisfying the following conditions:

1. Closure: $\forall$ a, b∈ G, then (a • b)∈ G
2. Associatively: $\forall$ a, b, c∈ G, then a •(b • c) = (a • b) • c
3. Existence of Identity: $\exists$ a unique element e∈ G such that $\forall$ a∈ G: a • e = e • a
4. $\forall$ a∈ G: $\exists$ a^{-1}∈ G: $a^{-1}a = a^{-1} • a = e$

Definition of Finite and Infinite Groups (Order of a Group)

A group G is said to be finite if the number of elements in the set G is finite. Otherwise, the group is infinite.

Definition of Abelian Group

A group G is abelian if for all a, b∈ G, a • b = b • a.

The reader should note that in a group, the elements in the set do not have to be a number or objects: They can be mappings, functions, or rules.

Examples of a Group

The set of integers Z is a group under addition (+); that is, (Z, +) is a group with identity e = 0, and the inverse of an element a is (−a). This is an additive abelian group, but infinite.

Nonzero elements of Q (rationals), R (reals), and C (complex) form a group under multiplication, with the identity element e = 1, and a^{-1} being the multiplicative inverse. For any n ≥ 1, the set of integers modulo n forms a finite additive group of n elements:

$$G = <Z_n, +> \text{ is an abelian group.}$$

The set of Z_{n*} with multiplication operator, $G = <Z_{n*}, x>$ is also an abelian group. The set Z_{n*}, is a subset of Z_n and includes only integers in Z_n that have a unique multiplicative inverse:

$$Z_{13} = \{0, 1, 2, 3, 4, 5, 6, 7, 8, 9, 10, 11, 12\}$$

$$Z_{13*} = \{1, 2, 3, 4, 5, 6, 7, 8, 9, 10, 11, 12\}$$

Definition Subgroup

A subgroup of a group G is a nonempty subset H of G, which itself is a group under the same operations as that of G. We denote that H is a subgroup of G as H⊆G, and H⊂G is a proper subgroup of G if the set H ≠ G. Examples of Subgroups:

Under addition, Z⊆Q⊆R⊆C.
H = <Z_{10}, +> is a proper subgroup of G = <Z_{12}, +>

Definition of Cyclic Group

A group G is said to be cyclic if there exists an element a∈ G such that for any b∈ G, and i ≥ 0, b = a^i. Element a is called a generator of G. The group G = <Z_{10*}, x>is a cyclic group with generators g = 3 and g = 7:

$$Z_{10*} = \{1,3,7,9\}$$

The group G = <Z_6, +> is a cyclic group with generators g = 1 and g = 5:

$$Z_6 = \{0,1,2,3,4,5\}$$

Rings

Let R be a nonempty set with two binary operations: addition (+) and multiplication (*).

Then R is called a ring if the following axioms are met:

1. Under addition, R is an abelian group with zero as the additive identity.
2. Under multiplication, R satisfies the closure, associative, and identity axiom; 1 is the multiplicative identity, and that 1 ≠ 0.
3. For every a, and b that belongs to R, a • b = b • a.
4. For every a, b, and c that belongs to R, then a • (b + c) = a • b+a • c

Examples

Z, Q, R, and C are all rings under addition and multiplication. For any n > 0, Z_n is a ring under addition and multiplication modulo n with 0 as identity under addition, 1 under multiplication.

Definition Field

If the nonzero elements of a ring form a group under multiplication, then the ring is called a field.

Examples

Q, R, and C are all fields under addition and multiplication, with 0 and 1 as identity under addition and multiplication.

(Note that Z under integer addition and multiplication is not a field because any nonzero element does not have a multiplicative inverse in Z.)

Finite Fields GF(2^n)

Construction of finite fields and computations in finite fields are based on polynomial computations. Finite fields play a significant role in cryptography and cryptographic protocols such as the Diffie and Hellman key exchange protocol, ElGamal cryptosystems, and AES:

For a prime number p, the quotient Z/p (or F_p) is a finite field with p number of elements. For any positive integer q, GF(q) = F_q

We define A to be algebraic structure such as a ring or a group or a field.

Definition

A polynomial over A is an expression of the form:

$$f(x) = \sum_{i=0}^{n} a_i x^n$$

where n is a nonnegative integer, the coefficient $a_i \in A$, $0 \le i \le n$, and $x \notin A$.

Definition

A polynomial f∈ A[x] is said to be irreducible in A[x] if f has a positive degree and f = gh for some g, h∈ A[x] implies that either g or h is a constant polynomial. The reader should be aware that a given polynomial can be reducible over one structure, but irreducible over another.

Definition

Let f, g, q, and r∈ A[x] with g≠0. Then we say that r is remainder of f divided by g:

$$r \equiv f(\bmod g)$$

The set of remainders of all the polynomials in A[x] (mod g) denoted as A[x]$_g$.

Theorem

Let F be a field and f be a nonzero polynomial in F[x]. Then F[x]$_f$ is a ring, and is a field if f is irreducible over F.

Theorem

Let F be field of p elements and f be irreducible polynomial over F. Then the number of elements in the field F[x]$_f$ is p^n.

For every prime p and every positive integer n there exist a finite field of p^n number of elements. For any prime number p, Z_p is a finite field under addition and multiplication modulo p, with 0 and 1 as the identity under addition and multiplication.

Z_p is an additive ring and nonzero elements of Z_p, denoted by Z_{p*} form a multiplicative group. Galois Field, $GF(p^n)$ is a finite field with number of elements p^n, where p is a prime number and n is a positive integer.

Example

Integer representation of Finite Field (Rijnadel) element. Polynomial $f(x) = x^8 + x^4 + x^3 + x + 1$ is irreducible over F_2.

The set of all polynomials (mod f) over F_2 forms a field of 2^8 elements; they are all polynomials over F_2 of degree less than 8. So any element in the field $F_2[x]_f$

$$b_7 x^7 + b_6 x^6 + b_5 x^5 + b_4 x^4 + b_3 x^3 + b_2 x^2 + b_1 x^1 + b_0$$

where $b_7, b_6, b_5, b_4, b_3, b_2, b_1, b_0 \in F_2$. Thus, any element in this field can represent a 8-bit binary number.

Data inside a computer is organized in bytes (8 bits) and is processed using Boolean logic; that is, bits are manipulated using binary operation addition and multiplication. These binary operations are implemented using the logical operator XOR, or in the language of finite fields, GF(2). Since the extended ASCII defines 8-bit per byte, an 8-bit byte has a natural representation using a polynomial of degree 8. Polynomial addition would be mod 2, and multiplication would be mod polynomial degree 8. Of course this polynomial degree 8 would have to be irreducible. Hence the Galois Field $GF(2^8)$ would be the most natural tool to implement the encryption algorithm. Furthermore, this would provide a close algebraic formulation. Consider polynomials over GF(2) with p = 2 and n = 1:

$$1, x, x+1, x^2+x+1, x^2+1, x^3+1$$

Polynomials with negative coefficients, −1 is the same as +1 in GF(2). Obviously, the number of such polynomials is infinite. In algebraic operations of addition and multiplication, the coefficients are added and multiplied according to the rules that apply to GF(2). The set of such polynomials forms a ring.

Modular Polynomial Arithmetic Over GF(2)

The Galois Field $GF(2^3)$: Construct this field with eight elements that can be represented by polynomials of the form:

$$ax^2 + bx + c \text{ where } a, b, c \in GF(2) = \{0, 1\}$$

Two choices for a, b, c gives $2 \times 2 \times 2 = 8$ polynomials of the form:

$$ax^2 + bx + c \in GF_2[x]$$

What is our choice of the irreducible polynomials for this field?

$$(x^3 + x^2 + x + 1), (x^3 + x^2 + 1), (x^3 + x^2 + x),$$
$$(x^3 + x + 1), (x^3 + x^2)$$

These two polynomials have no factors: (x^3+x^2+1), (x^3+x+1). So we choose polynomial (x^3+x+1). Hence all polynomial arithmetic multiplication and division is carried out with respect to (x^3+x+1). The eight polynomials that belong to $GF(2^3)$:

$$\{0, 1, x, x^2, 1+x, 1+x^2, x+x^2, 1+x+x^2\}$$

You will observe that GF(8) = {0,1,2,3,4,5,6,7} is not a field, since every element (excluding zero) does not have a multiplicative inverse such as {2, 4, 6} (mod 8).

Using a Generator to Represent the Elements of $GF(2^n)$

It is particularly convenient to represent the elements of a Galois Field with the help of a generator element. If α is a generator element, then every element of $GF(2^n)$, except for the 0 element, can be written down as some power of α. A generator is obtained from the irreducible polynomial that was used to construct a finite field. If $f(\alpha)$ is the irreducible polynomial used, then α is that element that satisfies the equation $f(\alpha) = 0$. You do not actually solve this equation for its roots since an irreducible polynomial cannot have actual roots in the field GF(2). Consider the case of $GF(2^3)$ defined with the irreducible polynomial x^3+x+1. The generator α is that element which satisfies $\alpha^3+\alpha+1 = 0$:

Suppose α is a root in $GF(2^3)$ of the polynomial $p(x) = 1 + x + x^3$

that is, $p(\alpha) = 0$, then $\alpha^3 = -\alpha-1 \pmod 2 = \alpha+1$
$\alpha^4 = \alpha(\alpha+1) = \alpha^2+\alpha$
$\alpha^5 = \alpha^4 \cdot \alpha = (\alpha^2+\alpha)\alpha = \alpha^3+\alpha^2 = (\alpha^2+\alpha+1)$
$\alpha^6 = \alpha^5 \cdot \alpha = \alpha \cdot (\alpha^2+\alpha+1) = (\alpha^2+1)$
$\alpha^7 = (\alpha^2+1) \cdot \alpha = (2\alpha+1) = 1$

All powers of α generate nonzero elements of GF_8.

We will now consider all polynomials defined over GF(2), modulo the irreducible polynomial x^3+x+1. When an algebraic operation (polynomial multiplication) results in a polynomial whose degree equals or exceeds that of the irreducible polynomial, we will take for our result the remainder modulo the irreducible polynomial. For example,

$$(x^2 + x + 1) * (x^2 + 1) \bmod (x^3 + x + 1)$$
$$= (x^4 + x^3 + x^2) + (x^2 + x + 1) \bmod (x^3 + x + 1)$$
$$= (x^4 + x^3 + x + 1) \bmod (x^3 + x + 1)$$
$$= -x^2 + x$$
$$= x^2 + x$$

Recall that $1 + 1 = 0$ in GF(2). With multiplications modulo (x^3+x+1), we have only the following eight polynomials in the set of polynomials over GF(2):

$$\{0, 1, x, x+1, x^2, x^2+1, x^2+x, x^2+x+1\}$$

We will refer to this set as $GF(2^3)$ where the power of 2 is the degree of the modulus polynomial. The eight elements of Z_8 are to be integers modulo 8. Similarly, $GF(2^3)$ maps all of the polynomials over GF(2) to the eight polynomials shown above. But you will note that the crucial difference between $GF(2^3)$ and 2^3: $GF(2^3)$ is a field, whereas Z_8 is NOT.

$GF(2^3)$ is a Finite Field

We know that $GF(2^3)$ is an Abelian group because the operation of polynomial addition satisfies all of the requirements on a group operator and because polynomial addition is commutative. $GF(2^3)$ is also a commutative ring because polynomial multiplication is a distributive over polynomial addition. $GF(2^3)$ is a finite field because it is a finite set and because it contains a unique multiplicative inverse for every nonzero element.

$GF(2^n)$ is a finite field for every n. To find all the polynomials in $GF(2^n)$, we need an irreducible polynomial of degree n. In general, $GF(p^n)$ is a finite field for any prime p. The elements of $GF(p^n)$ are polynomials over GF(p) (which is the same as the set of residues Z_p). Next we show how the multiplicative inverse of a polynomial is calculated using the Extended Euclidean Algorithm:

Multiplicative inverse of (x^2+x+1) in $F_2[x]/(x^4+x+1)$ is (x^2+x)
(x^2+x) $(x^2+x+1) = 1 \bmod (x^4+x+1)$
Multiplicative inverse of (x^6+x+1) in $F_2[x]/(x^8+x^4+x^3+x+1)$ is $(x^6+x^5+x^2+x+1)$
(x^6+x+1) $(x^6+x^5+x^2+x+1) = 1 \bmod (x^8+x^4+x^3+x+1)$ [1,2].

2. THE RIVEST, SHAMIR, AND ADELMAN CRYPTOSYSTEM

Now that we have reviewed the necessary mathematical preliminaries, we will focus on the subject matter of Asymmetric Cryptography, which uses a public and a private key to encrypt and decrypt the plaintext. If Alice wants to send plaintext to Bob, then she will use Bob's public key, which is advertised by Bob, to encrypt the plaintext, and then send it to Bob via an insecured channel. Bob would decrypt the data using his private key, which is known to him only. Of course, this would appear to be an ideal replacement for Symmetric-key cipher, but it is much slower since it has to encrypt each byte; hence it is useful in message authentication and communicating the secret key. See the following Key Generation Algorithm:

1. Select two prime numbers p and q such that $p \neq q$.
2. Construct $m = p \times q$.
3. Set up a commutative ring $R = <Z_m, +, x>$ which is public since m is made public.
4. Set up a multiplicative group $G = < Z^*_{\phi(m)}, x >$ which is used to generate public and private keys. This group is hidden from the public since $\phi(m)$ is kept hidden.
5. $\phi(m) = (p-1)(q-1)$.
6. Choose an integer e such that $1 < e < \phi(m)$ and e is coprime to $\phi(m)$.
7. Compute the secret exponent d such that, $1 < d < \phi(m)$ and that $ed \equiv 1 \pmod{\phi(m)}$.
8. The public key is "e" and the private key is "d".
9. The value of p, q, and $\phi(m)$ are kept private.

Encryption:

1. Alice obtains Bob's public key (m, e).
2. The plaintext x is treated as a number to lie in the range $1 < x < m-1$.
3. The ciphertext corresponding to x is $y = x^e \pmod m$.
4. Send the ciphertext y to Bob.

Decryption:

1. Bob uses his private key (m, d).
2. Computes the $x = y^d \pmod m$.

Why RSA works:

$$y^d \equiv (x^e \bmod m)^d$$

$$\equiv (x^{ed}) \bmod m$$

$$d \cdot e = 1 + km = 1 + k(p-1)(q-1)$$

$$y^d \equiv x^{ed} \equiv x^{1+k(p-1)(q-1)} \equiv x \pmod m$$

Example:
Choose $p = 7$ and $q = 11$, then $m = p \times q = 7 \times 11 = 77$.
$R = <Z_{77}, +, x>$ and $\phi(77) = \phi(7)$ $\phi(11) = 6 \times 10 = 60$.
The corresponding multiplicative group $G = < Z^*_{60}, x >$.
Choose $e = 13$ and $d = 37$ from Z^*_{60} such that $e \times d \equiv 1 \pmod{60}$.
Plaintext $= 5$ $y = x^e \pmod m = 5^{13} \pmod{77} = 26$.
$x = y^d \pmod m = 26^{37} \pmod{77} = 5$.
Note: 384-bit primes or larger are deemed sufficient to use RSA securely. The prime number $e = 2^{16} + 1$ is often used in modern RSA implementations.

Factorization Attack

The RSA algorithm relies on the fact that p and q are the distinct prime numbers and must be kept secret, even though $m = p \times q$ is made public. So if n is an extremely large number, then the problem reduces to finding the factors that make up the number n, which is known as the factorization attack. If the middle man, Eve, can factor n correctly, then she guesses correctly p, q, and $\phi(m)$.

Remind yourselves that if the public key e is public, then Eve has to compute the multiplicative inverse of e:

$$d \equiv e^{-1} (\text{mod } m)$$

So if the modulus m is chosen to be 1024 bits long, then it would take considerable time to break the RSA system unless an efficient factorization algorithm could be found [1,2].

Chosen-Ciphertext Attack

Z_n is a set of all positive integers from 0 to $(n-1)$.

Z_{n*} is a set all integers such that $\gcd(n, a) = 1$, where $a \in Z_{n*}$.

$$Z_{n*} \subset Z_n$$

$\Phi(n)$ calculates the number of elements in Z_{n*} that are smaller than n and coprime to n.

$$\Phi(21) = \Phi(3) \times \Phi(7) = 2 \times 6 = 12$$

Therefore the number of integers in $\in Z_{21*}$ is 12.
$Z_{21*} = \{1, 2, 4, 5, 8, 10, 11, 13, 16, 17, 19, 20\}$, each of which is coprime to 21.

$Z_{14*} = \{1, 3, 5, 9, 11, 13\}$, each of which is coprime to 14.
$\Phi(14) = \Phi(2) \times \Phi(7) = 1 \times 6 = 6$ number of integers in Z_{14*}.

Example:
Choose $p = 3$ and $q = 7$, then $m = 3 \times 7 = 21$.
Encryption and decryption take place in the ring, $R = <Z_{21}, +, \times>$.

$$\Phi(21) = \Phi(2)\Phi(6) = 12$$

Key-Generation Group, $G = < Z_{12*}, \times >$

$$\Phi(12) = \Phi(4)\Phi(3) = 2 \times 2 = 4 \text{ number in } Z_{12*}$$

$$Z_{12*} = \{1, 5, 7, 11\}$$

Alice encrypts the message P using the public key e of Bob and sends the encrypted message C to Bob:

$$C = P^e \text{ mod } m$$

Eve, the middle man, intercepts the message and manipulates the message before forwarding to Bob:

1. Eve chooses a random integer $X \in Z_{m*}$ (since m is public).
2. Eve calculates $Y = C \times X^e \pmod{m}$.
3. Bob receives Y from Eve, and he decrypts Y using his private key d.
4. $Z = Y^d \pmod{m}$.
5. Eve can easily discover the plaintext P as follows:

$$Z = Y^d (\text{mod } m) = [C \times X^e]^d (\text{mod } m)$$

$$= [C^d \times X^{ed}](\text{mod } m) = [C^d \times X] \ (\text{mod } m)$$

Hence, $Z = [P \times X] (\text{mod } m)$.

Eve, using the Extended Euclidean Algorithm, can then compute the multiplicative inverse of X and thus obtain P:

$$P = Z \times X^{-1} (\text{mod } m)$$

The ETH Roots Problem

Given:

1. A composite number n, the product of two prime numbers p and q.
2. An integer $e \geq 3$.
3. $\gcd(e, \Phi(n)) = 1$.
4. An integer $c \in Z_{12*}$.
5. Find an integer m such that $m^e \equiv c$ mod n [1,2].

Discrete Logarithm Problem

Discrete logarithms are perhaps simplest to understand in the group Z_{p*}, where p is the prime number. Let g be the generator of Z_{p*}; then the discrete logarithm problem reduces to computing a, given $(g, p, g^a \text{ mod } p)$ for a randomly chosen $a < (p-1)$.

If we want to find the kth power of one of the numbers in this group, we can do so by finding its kth power as an integer and then finding the remainder after division by p. This process is called *discrete exponentiation*. For example, consider Z_{23*}.

To compute 3^4 in this group, we first compute $3^4 = 81$, and then we divide 81 by 23, obtaining a remainder of 12. Thus $3^4 = 12$ in the group Z_{23*}.

Discrete logarithm is just the inverse operation. For example, take the equation $3^k \equiv 12 \pmod{23}$ for k. As shown above, $k = 4$ is a solution, but it is not the only solution. Since $3^{22} \equiv 1 \pmod{23}$, it also follows that if n is an integer then $3^{4+22n} \equiv 12 \times 1^n \equiv 12 \pmod{23}$. Hence the equation has infinitely many solutions of the form $4 + 22n$. Since 22 is the smallest positive integer m satisfying $3^m \equiv 1 \pmod{23}$, that is, 22 is the order of 3 in Z_{23*}, these are all solutions. Equivalently, the solution can be expressed as $k \equiv 4 \pmod{22}$ [1].

In designing public-key cryptosystems, two problems dominate the designs: the integer factorization problem and the discrete logarithm problem. Large instances of these problems are still intractable today.

Discrete logarithms have a natural extension into the realm of elliptic curves and hyperelliptic curves. And Elliptic ElGamal has proved to be a strong cryptosystem using elliptic curves and discrete logarithms. In the next part of the chapter, we will take a look at the discrete logarithm problem and discuss its application to cryptography.

Discrete Logarithm Problem (DLP)

The discrete logarithm problem in group G, given some generator α of a cyclic subgroup G^* of G and an element

$\beta \in G^*$, is to find the element x, $0 \leq x \leq (p-2)$, such that $\alpha^x = \beta$. The most frequently used cryptosystem utilizing the DLP is ElGamal; we give an elliptic curve variant of ElGamal below [1–3]. For example:

ElGamal Cryptosystem:
Alice wants to talk secretly with Bob.
Setting up: Sometime in the past, Bob has created his keys in the following way:

1. Bob chooses a random large prime p and a generator α of the multiplicative group Z_{p^*}.
2. Bob chooses a random integer a where $1 \leq a \leq (p-2)$.
3. Bob computes α^a mod p.
4. The triple $e_B = (p, \alpha, \alpha^a)$ is the public key, and d_B (p, α, a) is the private key. Alice obtains Bob's public key from some public key server.

Encryption: Alice wants to encrypt a plaintext M with the cipher $e_B = (e, d, n)$. She starts by choosing a random integer k where $1 \leq k \leq (p-2)$ and then encrypting the plaintext M into the cipher-text C:

$$E_{K_B}(M) = C = (\gamma, \delta) = \left(\alpha^k, M * (\alpha^a)^k \bmod p\right)$$

Alice then sends Bob the encrypted message C.
Decryption: Bob then decrypts the cipher-text $C = (\gamma, \delta)$ with the cipher.
$d_B = (e, d, n)$ in the following manner:

$$D_{K_B}(C) = M = (\gamma^{-\alpha}) * \delta \bmod p$$

Lattice-Based Cryptography: NTRU

An n-dimensional lattice (see Fig. 91.1) is generated using n-linearly independent vectors:

$v_1, \ldots, v_n \, \varepsilon \, R^n$; these vectors are known as the basis of the lattice. There are infinite numbers of such bases that can generate the same lattice.

$$L(v_1, \ldots, v_n) = \left\{ \sum_{i=1}^{n} \alpha_i v_i \middle| \alpha_i \varepsilon \, Z \right\}$$

What is a Lattice?

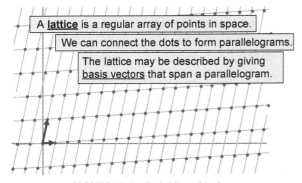

A **lattice** is a regular array of points in space.
We can connect the dots to form parallelograms.
The lattice may be described by giving basis vectors that span a parallelogram.

FIGURE 91.1 Definition of lattice.

What is the Closest Vector Problem?

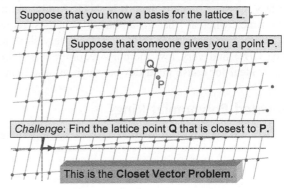

Suppose that you know a basis for the lattice **L**.
Suppose that someone gives you a point **P**.
Challenge: Find the lattice point **Q** that is closest to **P**.
This is the **Closet Vector Problem**.

FIGURE 91.2 Closest vector problem (CVP).

Why Is That A Hard Problem?
For lattices in the plane, you're right, it's very easy.
It's not even very hard in dimension 3, or 4, or 5.
However, the Closest Vector Problem is **very hard** in high dimension, say in dimension 500.

FIGURE 91.3 The hard closest vector problem.

In group theory, a lattice in R^n is a discrete subgroup of R^n which spans the real vector space R^n. A lattice is the symmetry group of discrete translational symmetry in n directions. Two NP-hard problems related to lattices are the shortest vector problem (SVP) and the closest vector problem (CVP; see Fig. 91.2). Given an arbitrary basis for a lattice, find the SVP in the lattice or find the CVP to an arbitrary nonlattice vector. In both the quantum and classical computational problems, these problems are hard to solve for high-dimensional lattices (see Fig. 91.3). There are a number of lattice-based cryptographic schemes, but the NTRU-based cryptographic algorithm appears to be most practical [4,5].

NTRU Cryptosystem

NTRU is not based on factorization or discrete logarithmic problems. Rather, it is a lattice-based alternative to RSA and ECC and is based on the shortest vector problem in a lattice. NTRU was founded in 1996 by three mathematicians: Jeffrey Hoffstein, Joseph H. Silverman, and Jill Pipher. Later on with the addition of yet another member, Daniel Lieman, to the team, NTRU Cryptosystems was incorporated in Boston. NTRU Cryptosystems was acquired by Security Innovation in 2009.

The NTRU cryptosystem was introduced at the rump session of Crypto'96 and was later published in the proceedings of the ANTS-III conference. NTRU is a ring-based public-key cryptosystem and is therefore quite different from the group-based cryptosystems whose security relies on the integer factorization problem or the discrete logarithm problem. This extra structure can be exploited to obtain a very fast cryptosystem: To encrypt/decrypt a message block of length N, NTRU only requires $O(N^2)$ time, whereas the group-based schemes require $O(N^3)$ time. Furthermore, NTRU also has a very short key size of $O(N)$ and very low memory requirements, which makes it ideal for constrained devices such as smart cards.

Truncated Polynomial Rings

Consider a polynomial of degree (N−1) having integer coefficients:

$$a = a_0 + a_1X + a_2X^2 + a_3X^3 + a_4X^4 \ldots\ldots\ldots\ldots$$
$$+ a_{(N-1)}X^{(N-1)}$$

The set of all such polynomials is denoted by R. The arithmetic on the polynomials in R is as follows. Consider two polynomials a and b:

$$a + b = (a_0 + b_0) + (a_1 + b_1)X + \ldots\ldots + (a_{(N-1)}$$
$$+ b_{(N-1)}X^{(N-1)})$$

Suppose N = 3 and $a = 2 - X + 3X^2$, $b = 1 + 2X - X^2$

$$a + b = 3 + X + 2X^2$$

$$a * b = (2 - X + 3X^2) * (1 + 2X = X^2)$$

$$= 2 + 4X - 2X^2 - X - 2X^2 + X^3 + 3X^2 + 6X^3 - 3X^4$$

N = 3; hence the polynomial cannot have powers of X more than 2, so we have to truncate powers of X higher than 2 with the following rules:

$$X^4 \text{ by } X$$

$$X^3 \text{ by } X^0 = 1$$

Hence,

$$a * b = 2 + 4X - 2X^2 - X - 2X^2 + 1 + 3X^2 + 6 - 3X$$
$$= (9 - X^2)$$

The distributive law also holds for the polynomials

$$a * (b + c) = a * b + a * c$$

The inclusion of the above law makes the algebraic structure of polynomials into a ring, the Ring of Truncated Polynomials. This ring R is isomorphic to the quotient ring, $Z[X]/(X^{(N-1)})$.

Inverses in Truncated Polynomial Ring

The inverse modulo q of a polynomial a is a polynomial a^{-1} with the property:

$$a * a^{-1} = 1 \pmod{q}$$

Example:

$$N = 7, \quad \text{and} \quad q = 11$$

$$a = 3 + 2X^2 - 3X^4 + X^6$$

then,

$$a^{-1} = 2 + 4X + 2X^2 + 4X^3 - 4X^4 + 2X^5 - 2X^6$$

$$= (3 + 2X^2 - 3X^4 + X^6)*$$

$$(2 + 4X + 2X^2 + 4X^3 - 4X^4 + 2X^5 - 2X^6)$$

$$= -10 + 22X - 22X^3 + 22X^6 = 1 \pmod{11}$$

NTRU Parameters and Keys

N—a polynomial in the ring R with degree N−1, with N being a prime number:

Q—a large modulus to which the coefficient is reduced.
P—a small modulus to which each coefficient is reduced.
q and p are coprime.
f—a polynomial that is a private key.
g—a polynomial that is used to generate the public key h from f.
   Note: g (secret) is discarded later on.
H—a polynomial that is a public key.
r—a random binding polynomial (discarded later on, but kept secret).
D—coefficient.

Key Generation

Consider a truncated polynomial ring with a degree at most N−1:

$$a_0 + a_1X + a_2X^2\ldots\ldots\ldots a_{N-1}X^{(N-1)}$$

1. Choose two small polynomials f and g in the ring R; polynomial f must have an inverse.
2. The inverse of f modulo q and the inverse of f modulo p are computed.
3. $F_q = f^{-1} \pmod{q}$ and $F_p = f^{-1} \pmod{p}$.
4. $f * F_q = 1 \pmod{q}$ and $f * F_p = 1 \pmod{p}$.
5. Compute $h = p * (F_q * g) \bmod q$.
6. Alice's private key: a pair of polynomials f and F_p.
7. Alice's public key: the polynomial h.
   Public parameters (N, p, q, d)=(7, 3, 41, 2).
   Alice chooses: $f(x) = X^6 - X^4 + X^3 + X^2 - 1$

$$g(x) = X^6 + X^4 - X^2 - X$$

$$F_q(x) = f^{-1}(X) - 1 (\mathrm{mod}\, q)$$
$$= 8X^6 + 26X^5 + 31X^4 + 21X^3 + 40X^2 + 2X$$
$$+ 37 (\mathrm{mod}\, 41)$$

Private Key
$$F_p(x) = f^{-1}(X) - 1 (\mathrm{mod}\, q)$$
$$= X^6 + 2X^5 + X^3 + X^2 + X + 1 (\mathrm{mod}\, 3)$$

Public Key
$$h(x) = p * (F_q) * g (\mathrm{mod}\, q)$$
$$= 20X^6 + 40X^5 + 2X^4 + 38X^3 + 8X^2$$
$$+ 26X + 30 (\mathrm{mod}\, 41)$$

NTRU Encryption

Alice has a message to transmit:

1. Puts the message in the form of polynomial m whose coefficient is chosen modulo p between $-p/2$ and $p/2$ (centered lift).
2. Randomly chooses another small polynomial r (to obscure the message).
3. Computes the encrypted message:

$$e = r * h + m (\mathrm{mod}\, q)$$

Example of NTRU Encryption

Alice decides to send Bob the message:
$$m(X) = -X^5 + X^3 + X^2 - X^1 + 1$$
using the random key $r(x) = X^6 - X^5 + X^1 - 1$
$$e = r * h + m (\mathrm{mod}\, q)$$
$$e(x) \equiv 31X^6 + 19X^5 + 4X^4 + 2X^3 + 40X^2 + 3X$$
$$+ 25 (\mathrm{mod}\, 41)$$
$$(N, p, q, d) = (7, 3, 41, 2)$$

NTRU Decryption

Bob receives a message e from Alice and would like to decrypt it.

Using his private polynomial f, he computes a polynomial
$$A = f * e (\mathrm{mod}\, q).$$

Bob needs to choose coefficients that lie in an interval of length q. He computes the polynomial $b = a (\mathrm{mod}\, p)$.

Bob reduces each of the coefficients of a modulo p. Bob uses the other private polynomial F_p to compute $c = F_p * b (\mathrm{mod}\, p)$, which is the original message of Alice.

Example of NTRU Decryption
$$a = f * e (\mathrm{mod}\, q)$$

Bob computes $a \equiv X^6 + 10X^5 + 33X^4 + 40X^3 + 40X^2 + X + 40 (\mathrm{mod}\, 41)$

Bob then center lifts modulo q to obtain
$$b = a (\mathrm{mod}\, p)$$
$$= X^6 + 10X^5 - 8X^4 - X^3 - X^2 + X - 1 (\mathrm{mod}\, 3)$$

Bob reduces a(x) modulo p and computes
$$c = F_p(x) * b(x) \equiv 2X^5 + X^3 + X^2 + 2X + 1 (\mathrm{mod}\, 3)$$

Center lifting modulo p retrieves Alice's plaintext
$$m(x) = -X^5 + X^3 + X^2 - X^1 + 1$$
$$(N, p, q, d) = (7, 3, 41, 2)$$

Why Does NTRU Work?
$$a = f * e (\mathrm{mod}\, q) = f * (r * h + m) (\mathrm{mod}\, q)$$
$$= f * (r * pF_q * g + m) (\mathrm{mod}\, q) = pr * g + f * m (\mathrm{mod}\, q)$$
$$b = a = f * m (\mathrm{mod}\, p)$$
$$c = F_p * b = F_p * f * m = m (\mathrm{mod}\, p)$$
$$NTRU167 \equiv ECC112 \equiv RSA512$$
$$NTRU263 \equiv ECC168 \equiv RSA1024$$
$$NTRU503 \equiv ECC196 \equiv RSA2048$$

Underlying every public-key cryptosystem lurks an extremely difficult mathematical problem waiting to be solved. There is no direct proof that breaking a cryptosystem is equivalent to solving the mathematical problem. Below we list the public-key cryptosystem and the corresponding mathematical problem (Table 91.1).

TABLE 91.1 NTRU Parameters

Security Level	N	q	p
Moderate	167	128	3
Standard	251	128	3
High	347	128	3
Highest	503	256	3

From www.ntru.com

RSA Integer Factorization Problem
Diffe-Hellman Discrete Logarithm Problem in F_{q*}
Elliptic Curve Discrete Logarithm Problem on an Cryptography Elliptic Curve
Lattices SVP and CVP

3. SUMMARY

In this chapter, we reviewed aspects of advanced data encryption security: number theory, group theory, and finite fields relevant to public-key cryptography, as well as ADE

An Agenda for Action for Implementing Advanced Data Encryption (ADE) Security Features

Please see the following advanced data encryption security features checklist that needs to be implemented in your organization (check all tasks completed):

Core Advanced Data Encryption (ADE) Security Functionality

_____1. Hard Drive Encryption.
_____2. Saved Files.
_____3. Temporary Files.
_____4. Page Files.
_____5. Deleted Files.
_____6. Secure File Deletion.
_____7. Registry or Operating System Boot Files.
_____8. Unused Sectors.
_____9. Hidden Partitions.
_____10. Hibernation Mode.
_____11. Logout/Lockout.
_____12. Nonmagnetic Drives.
_____13. Removable Drives.
_____14. Data Recovery by Administrator.

Conformance to Protocol Standards

_____15. Password Management/Recovery (Admin).
_____16. PKI Authentication.
_____17. Multifactor Authentication.
_____18. Revocation of Access.

PKI Standards

_____19. X.509 Certificates.
_____20. LDAP Repository.
_____21. Certificate Revocation.
_____22. Cryptographic Algorithms.

Cryptographic Standards
Encryption Algorithms
_____23. Advanced Encryption Standard (AES).
_____24. Triple-Data Encryption Standard (3DES).

Key Establishment Algorithms

_____25. Rivest, Shamir, Adleman (RSA).
_____26. Other algorithms based on exponentiation of finite fields.
_____27. Key Exchange Algorithm (KEA).
_____28. Elliptic Curve algorithms.

Digital Signature Algorithms

_____29. RSA.
_____30. Digital Signature Algorithm (DSA).

_____31. Other algorithms based on exponentiation of finite fields.
_____32. Elliptic Curve Digital Signature Algorithm (ECDSA).

Hashing Algorithms

_____33. SHA-1.
_____34. SHA-224.
_____35. SHA-256.
_____36. SHA-384.
_____37. SHA-512.

Assurance Standards

_____38. FIPS 140-1.
_____39. FIPS 140-2.

Cryptographic Algorithm Validation Program

_____40. Cryptographic Module Validated.

Configurability

_____41. Changeable default values.
_____42. Multiple users.
_____43. Different user access rights.
_____44. Transaction logging.
_____45. Log integrity.
_____46. Log centralization.
_____47. Security alerts.

Usability

_____48. Configuration by users.
_____49. Authentication by users.
_____50. Interruptions during initial encryption process.
_____51. Computer use during initial encryption process.
_____52. Software/hardware compatibility.
_____53. Maintenance by administrators.
_____54. Administrator recovery.
_____55. Third party recovery.

Manageability

_____56. Central management.
_____57. Remote management.
_____58. Unattended reboot.
_____59. Authentication of management traffic.
_____60. Encryption of management traffic.

Scalability

_____61. Degree of scalability.

security features (see checklist: An Agenda for Action for Implementing Advanced Data Encryption (ADE) Security Features). The security of public-key cryptography is determined by what is known as the DLP, and we gave an example of DLP based on the elliptic curve. In the final section of this chapter, we presented public-key cryptography based on lattice theory—known as the NTRU cryptosystem.

Finally, let's move on to the real interactive part of this chapter: review questions/exercises, hands-on projects, case projects, and optional team case project. The answers and/or solutions by chapter can be found in the Online Instructor's Solutions Manual.

CHAPTER REVIEW QUESTIONS/ EXERCISES

True/False

1. True or False? Generation of a key in public-key cryptography involves exponentiation modulo a given modulus.
2. True or False? The order of a finite group is the number of elements in the group H.
3. True or False? In the multiplicative group, $H=<Z_{n*}$, x>; when the order of an element is the same as $\phi(n)$, then that element is called the primitive root of the group.
4. True or False? A group H is said to be finite if the number of elements in the set H is finite.
5. True or False? The set of integers Z is a group under addition (+); that is (Z, +) is a group with identity e = 0, and inverse of an element a is (−a).

Multiple Choice

1. A subgroup of a group G is a nonempty subset H of G, which itself is a group under the same operations as that of:
   A. R
   B. I
   C. N
   D. E
   E. G
2. What group is said to be cyclic if there exists an element a∈ G such that for any b∈ G, and i ≥ 0, b = a^i?
   A. O
   B. W
   C. S
   D. G
   E. A
3. Let _____ be a nonempty set with two binary operations addition (+), and multiplication (*).
   A. R
   B. I

C. W
D. C
E. S
4. If the nonzero elements of a ring form a group under multiplication, then the ring is called a:
   A. field
   B. denial-of-service attack
   C. venyo
   D. port traffic
   E. taps
5. Construction of finite fields and computations in finite fields are based on:
   A. systems security plan
   B. polynomial computations
   C. denying service
   D. decision making
   E. URL lists

EXERCISE

Problem

How does advanced data encryption work?

Hands-On Projects

Project

What is a key?

Case Projects

Problem

What is the difference between public and private keys?

Optional Team Case Project

Problem

Which types of data can be encrypted.

REFERENCES

[1] W. Mao, Modern Cryptography, Theory & Practice, Prentice Hall, 2004.
[2] B.A. Forouzan, Cryptography and Network Security, McGraw-Hill, 2008.
[3] P.L. Jensen, Hyperelliptic Curves and Their Application to Cryptography, University of Copenhagen, 2004.
[4] J. Hoffstein, D. Lieman, J. Pipher, J. Silverman, "NTRU": A Public Key Cyrptosystem, NTRU Cryptosystems, Inc., 2006. www.ntru.com.
[5] J. Hoffstein, J. Pipher, J. Silverman, NTRU—A Ring Based Public Key Cryptosystem, 1998.

Index

'*Note:* Page numbers followed by "f" indicate figures, "t" indicate tables, and "b" indicates boxes.'